American Cars,
1960–1972

# American Cars, 1960–1972

*Every Model, Year by Year*

J. "KELLY" FLORY, JR.

McFarland & Company, Inc., Publishers
*Jefferson, North Carolina, and London*

**Acknowledgments:** Compiling a book of this scope required the help and input of several people whom I would like to publicly thank. First off, I want to thank my parents, John and Mary Jean Flory, and my friend, Dan Reinheimer, for encouraging me to write this book. Without their positive attitudes and helpful ideas, this project would not have happened. A special thanks is owed to my mom who spent many hours toiling over the pictures within this book, making sure each was ready for publishing. I also want to thank my friends Tom Millard and Brian Atwell. They provided many pieces of sales literature to help complete the pictures within this book. Space does not permit me to acknowledge individually the many other people whose input, ideas, and encouragement made this book a reality, but they know who they are, and I want them to know that their help was appreciated. Thank you to all.

Advertising slogans and pictures of original sales literature come from the following sources: American Motors Corporation, Chrysler Corporation, Ford Motor Company, General Motors Corporation, and Studebaker-Packard Corporation.

Other resources include the National Automobile Dealers (N.A.D.A.) *Used Car Guides*, published by National Automobile Dealers Association, 2000 K, N.W., Washington, DC 20006; *Motor* magazine, published by The Hearst Corporation, 250 West 55th St., New York, NY 10019; and the *NATB Motor Vehicle Identification Manual*, published by Palmer Publications Company, Downers Grove, IL 60515.

LIBRARY OF CONGRESS CATALOGUING-IN-PUBLICATION DATA

Flory, J. "Kelly" Jr.
American cars, 1960–1972 : every model, year by year / J. "Kelly" Flory, Jr.
p.    cm.
Includes bibliographical references and index.

ISBN-13: 978-0-7864-1273-0
illustrated case binding : 50# alkaline paper ∞

1. Automobiles — United States — History.   2. Automobile industry and trade — United States — History.   I. Title.
TL23.F59   2004          629.222'0973 — dc22          2003022481

British Library cataloguing data are available

Cover image: 1966 Dodge Coronet convertible.

Manufactured in the United States of America

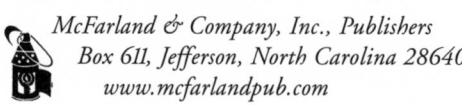

*McFarland & Company, Inc., Publishers*
*Box 611, Jefferson, North Carolina 28640*
*www.mcfarlandpub.com*

# Contents

# Abbreviations

## Auto body terminology

| | |
|---|---|
| **Bus. Cpe.** | Business Coupe |
| **Conv.** | Convertible or Convertible Coupe |
| **Cpe.** | Coupe |
| **Dr.** | Door |
| **FBK** | Fastback or Fastback Coupe |
| **HBK** | Hatchback or Hatchback Coupe |
| **HT** | Hardtop or Hardtop Coupe |
| **Hdtp.** | Hardtop or Hardtop Coupe |
| **NBK** | Notchback |
| **Sdn.** | Sedan |
| **Wgn.** | Wagon or Station Wagon |
| **# - p.** | Number of passengers vehicle is designed to carry (e.g., 6-p.) |
| **# - S.** | Number of seats in vehicle (usually refers to wagons) |

## Engine terminology

| | |
|---|---|
| **bbl.** | Barrels (ports or venturi) on a carburetor |
| **CID** | Cubic inch displacement |
| **DOHC** | Dual overhead cam |
| **Dual exhaust** | Two separate exhaust outlet systems (typically each carries half of engine exhaust) |
| **Dual-outlet exhaust** | Exhaust in single pipe off engine, but split into two outlets at back of car |
| **EFI** | Electronic fuel injection |
| **FI** | Fuel injection |
| **Hemi** | Hemispherical head |
| **HO** or **H.O.** | High output |
| **I#** | Inline engine block design (e.g. I6) |
| **MFI** or **MPFI** | Multi-port fuel injection |

| | |
|---|---|
| **OHC** | Overhead cam |
| **OHV** | Overhead valve |
| **SFI** | Sequential fuel injection |
| **TPI** | Throttle port injection |
| **VIH** | Valve in head |
| **V#** | V-shape engine block design (e.g., V8) |

## Measurements

| | |
|---|---|
| **Cap.** | Capacity |
| **Cu.** | Cubic |
| **F** | Front |
| **Ft.** | Feet |
| **G** or **gal.** | Gallon |
| **I** or **L** | Liter |
| **lbs.** | Pounds |
| **R** | Rear |
| **WB** | Wheelbase |

## Miscellaneous

| | |
|---|---|
| **AC** or **A/C** | Air conditioning |
| **CC** | Cruise control or clear coat paint |
| **EC** or **E/C** | Extra cost |
| **Met.** | Metallic paint |
| **MSRP** | Manufacturer's Suggested Retail Price |
| **NA** or **N/A** | Not available or not applicable |
| **NC** or **N/C** | No cost option |
| **PB** | Power brakes |
| **PS** | Power steering |
| **S** | Standard equipment |
| **$** | Available at extra cost, but price not known |

# Preface

The 1960s are defined in the automotive world by muscle cars, almost to the exclusion of any other type of vehicle. The decade and the vehicle type have become synonymous in the popular memory, much as fins shape today's notions of the fifties. Therefore, although this book includes all categories of cars, its period of coverage is the muscle car era, which continued into the early seventies.

Arranged year by year, this book includes all cars offered for sale in the United States by major American manufacturers from model years 1960 through 1972. For each of these model years, the reader will find an overview of developments in or affecting the automobile industry, followed by an annual status report of each nameplate and extensive data about every model sold that year: production numbers, pricing, specifications and dimensions, standard equipment and major options, paint color choices, running changes from the previous model year, and other information. A detailed description of the make and model listings appears below.

Trucks are not included, but each year's commentary includes brief remarks on events surrounding truck production by the major car manufacturers. Likewise, limited production models and the products of small, independent makes are not covered in full, but are noted briefly within the text. The Checker, for example, though an interesting car in its own right, did not have an established dealer network to sell to the general public; most of its vehicles instead were sold for fleet service. The Checker therefore is not covered in full herein. (It is worth noting that Checker vehicles changed little during this time period, beyond engine choices and the addition of federally mandated safety equipment.) Also, during the early sixties, Imperial offered a Crown Limousine model that was actually built by a coachbuilder outside Chrysler. Since production generally numbered between seven and fifteen cars a year, that model is not included.

Another notable exclusion is the category of "captive imports," or foreign-built automobiles that were imported, sometimes rebadged, and sold by each major Detroit manufacturer under one of its nameplates—such cars as the Dodge Colt, the Plymouth Cricket, the Ford Cortina and Anglia, the Mercury Capri and the Opels sold by Buick. Not until the fuel crisis that began in 1973 would these small imported cars become a truly significant part of auto sales in the United States. In the years 1960–1972, these cars sold in small numbers, and thus are not included in this book.

## Make and Model Listings

### LISTING BY MAKE

**Introduction.** Each make is listed alphabetically within a yearly grouping. Following the make's name is its main advertising slogan for the year, taken directly from factory sales literature. Next is a short overview of what was new for the year, including styling, powertrain and model lineup changes.

**Sales, pricing and production information.** This section includes sales totals for the model year (unless otherwise noted), percentage share of the make's production as compared to the entire industry, and the make's ranking amongst its competitors. Following the sales information is pricing information that includes the industry average base price for the year, the make's average base price, and its pricing range. Also listed is the make's date of model year introduction if available, or if not, the month of introduction. Listed next are the various assembly plants in which the cars were manufactured and their appropriate coding, if available, for decoding the Vehicle Identification Number.

**Data plate identification.** This section breaks down the various parts of the individual cars' Vehicle Identification Number (VIN). The meaning of each digit or letter of the VIN is identified and an example of a complete VIN is given. For many of the older cars (particularly prior to 1965), the body style cannot be determined from the VIN, but can be found on the body plate located somewhere upon the body of the car. Since body style is generally self-evident on this vintage of car, an identification chart for body plates is not given.

**Powertrains.** The chart presented in this section lists all known engine and transmission combinations that were offered at the time of the model introduction. In a few instances, there were engines offered (generally for racing purposes) on special order, and these may not be included within the chart. Also, some manufacturers offered overdrive transmissions as an optional feature, but did not list them with their powertrain accessories, but as a convenience feature. If that is the case, then an available overdrive transmission may not be listed, even though it was offered. Pricing information is given whenever an accurate price could be determined. The prices listed are for the engine and transmission together. For example, if a V-8 engine with automatic transmission is listed as an option for a car that had a 6-cylinder engine with 3-speed manual transmission as standard equipment, and the chart says the V-8 and automatic is a $350 option, that price is for the two options combined. This amount would be added to the base price of the car. If accurate pricing is not available, that will be stated within the text.

**Major options.** This is a chart listing the most popular or most heavily promoted options available across the full line of cars. Generally this would include air conditioning, power steering, power brakes, radio, wheel covers, whitewall tires, and certain power accessories. Certain options are included when they were at a peak in popularity. For the most part, option packages are not listed, as they often varied in price and content depending upon model or body style that they were applied to and could not be listed for space reasons. Option packages that are included are those that would become, or had been, part of a model line, such as the Pontiac GTO option, or the Olds 4-4-2.

**Paint colors.** This is a listing of all colors offered during the model year. Some colors were offered only on certain models; such cases are noted whenever possible. Some manufacturers offered certain colors only on special order, and that may not be designated in the listings. In general, this listing includes colors offered throughout the year as well as spring color introductions if any were made.

## MODEL LISTINGS

**Introduction.** Each model is listed, starting at the lowest priced or smallest model and continuing through the highest priced or largest model offered by the manufacturer. Usually manufacturers promoted their models in such a manner. This is only a general guideline, and there are exceptions, such as with Chevrolet: the Corvette is listed last because it is the prestige model in the line, and the manufacturer always promoted it as such. Following each model name is its main advertising slogan for the year, again taken directly from factory sales literature.

**Historical overview of the model.** Following the introduction is a section containing a few facts on the model, including the year the model first appeared, other models built from the same or similar platform, length of time the same basic body was used and models that preceded and followed the current one. Also listed is the percentage of the manufacturer's total sales recorded by this model, and then a general description of changes for the model year in question. The phrase "totally redesigned" indicates basically a new car from the ground up, whereas "totally restyled" indicates a car new in appearance, but still utilizing a similar chassis or powertrains within the new body. "Corporate siblings" are any cars manufactured by the parent company sharing most major components, including chassis and body. "Competitive makes" are any direct competitors, and on occasion some models that are indirect competition. For example, the AMC Ambassador was a car with no real competitors throughout most of the sixties. However, it was viewed as a luxury type car, and could be considered competition for the higher end Ford, Chevrolet and Plymouth full-size cars, even though the Ambassador itself was not a full-size car. It was actually more of a mid-size car, and was classified as a luxury compact by American Motors.

**Standard equipment.** This is a listing of the basic standard features for the model. Certain equipment is considered to be standard on all models during given time periods, and is not listed to conserve space. This list is based upon equipment deemed as standard by the manufacturer according to factory literature. Certain safety equipment became standard on all cars during 1966 and 1968, and will not be included in this listing.

**Models available.** This is a chart listing all models available under a model nameplate throughout the season. On many cars, particularly in the late sixties, cars were offered in a 6-cylinder and a V-8 line. An example would be the Chevrolet Chevelle or the Studebaker Lark. Where this is the case they generally had different body style numbers, but the listings will show the lowest priced offering, with the larger engine listed as optional, even though they were technically an individual model listing. This is done to keep the listings uniform between makes. Also, certain makes did not keep records by individual body style and trim level (particularly Chevrolet and Dodge), so production is listed as it was available, with footnotes explaining how the production is listed. Some manufacturers gave their two- and three-seat station wagons different model numbers, but kept production as one total, and this will be noted if known. Base Manufacturer's Suggested Retail Price (MSRP) is listed as of the beginning of the model year, unless otherwise noted. During the late sixties and early seventies, manufacturers were known to change pricing numerous times throughout the season, sometimes higher and sometimes lower, so pricing figures may differ from other sources. The columns for change from LY (last year) on pricing and the production show the increase or decrease in each and how they affected one another. Finally, the column for weight is most often the shipping weight, which does not include such things as fuel and oil. Curb weight (not used here) would be slightly higher and includes fuel, oil and other items in its total weight.

**Measurements.** In general, most of the measurements are for 4-Door Sedan models, when that model is available in a line. If a 4-Door model is not offered then measurements are for the lowest priced model in the line, or a note explains which model is represented. For the most part, measurements such as wheelbase, length, width, luggage capacity, and fuel tank capacity are the same amongst all variants of a model. Where there are significant differences, they are listed if available. Two measurements that may vary among models are headroom and legroom. Some manufacturers and sources publish the minimum headroom and some publish the maximum headroom. Often they do not identify which measurement they are using. In general, it is common for measurements on vehicles prior to 1963 to use the minimum headroom, and after 1966 to use the maximum headroom. Between 1963 and 1966, measurements were reported both ways, and then finally a standard was

agreed upon by an outside institution that eliminated the significant differences being reported by manufacturers. A clue applicable to many cars is that if the headroom is around the 33 to 34 inch range, it is probably the minimum figure. If it is around 38 to 39 inches, it is most likely the maximum figure. The difference comes into play because of the seat being placed fully forward (minimum) or fully to the rear (maximum). Similar differences can be found in the cargo capacity segment, where some manufacturers reported "usable cargo capacity," which accounts for the spare tire or other consumers of space. Other manufacturers would report "total cargo capacity."

## Further Reading

The author would recommend that anyone interested in learning more about the industry look into books on or by the many notable men and women that characterized the automotive world during this time period. Names of importance during the sixties include Virgil Exner, Lee Iacocca, George Romney, and John Z. Delorean, among many others. Books of this type can often give a contrasting view of how the corporations worked, as many of these people came from the engineering or finance sides of the company as opposed to the sales and marketing side. Various marque-specific histories and reference books are also available, and automotive magazines from the era can still be found fairly readily.

# Introduction

In the course of automotive history, arguably no time period has produced cars more enjoyed or better remembered than the 1960s. Every generation has its noteworthy achievements and outstanding automobiles that cement its place in memory, and the sixties are remembered for one thing above all else: speed. But it wasn't all about speed. It was a time of much change and turmoil, both in the automotive world and beyond. A growing civil rights movement, unrest with U.S. involvement in the Vietnam War, rapid advances in space exploration, and heightened tensions with the Soviet Union in space age and war technologies all affected American life. Turmoil during this period within the automotive industry can be found in several arenas: the continuing trend toward market consolidation; the proliferation of sizes and nameplates and categories of automobiles, unprecedented in the automotive scene; and finally, the "need for speed" that had started with the proliferation of the V-8 engine in the mid-fifties, and would not end until the gas shortages and OPEC oil embargoes of the 1970s.

## Consolidation of Manufacturers

Since World War II, nearly all "independent" manufacturers had disappeared. The only "independents" left were AMC and Studebaker, both of which had been through their own consolidations already. In 1954, Hudson and Nash had merged to form AMC, and Studebaker and Packard had merged to form Studebaker-Packard Corporation. The merged companies proved only as strong as their strongest part prior to the merger. American Motors was doing quite well by the beginning of the sixties, having totally abandoned products that the previous Hudson Motors had been selling, and concentrated on the economical vehicles that Nash had offered. The timing could not have been better. With the recession of 1958 and the resulting market shift toward smaller cars, the mid-price market was shrinking and crowded, and Hudson would likely not have survived on its own. American Motors had revived the compact Rambler just in time to help the company climb to an unprecedented number three position on the sales charts at the beginning of the sixties.

Studebaker and Packard were another story. The luxury-line Packard had been floundering since World War II, as it tried to sell mid-priced cars to make up for its lack of luxury-market sales. This strategy had worked in the thirties during the Depression, but with America's new-found wealth, people weren't buying the lower-priced Packard. By the early fifties, Packard had wised up to this and was actually making some money on its revived luxury car lines of the mid-fifties. Meanwhile, Studebaker was struggling with rising costs of materials and labor, yet trying to compete with the Big Three at the low end of the market. It had become a challenge that was costing Studebaker money on every car it sold. The time had come to try to spread out the company's fixed costs, and one way to do that was to add models to its existing line. Packard felt that it could benefit in much the same way, by spreading out fixed costs over more vehicles, thus allowing higher profit margins. So, in mid–1954, a decision to combine the two companies was made. Unfortunately for Packard, Studebaker quickly made some decisions that would spell its demise. The 1955 model Packards were set in their design, so they came to market as the "true" Packards that they were and continued as such for 1956. However, as the company sought to quickly consolidate overhead expenses, the restyled 1957 Packards became nothing more than Studebakers with more trim clumsily tacked on. In this same one-year time span, Packard was reduced from a true luxury car to a middle-price car. Needless to say, the public saw through this, and sales plummeted. By 1958 the recession spelled the end for Packard. The name was carried on in the corporation for about another five years, but then it became the Studebaker Corporation. Meanwhile Studebaker's products had not been very successful in the market for some time, the late forties Starlight coupes and the "Loewy" coupes introduced for 1953 being notable exceptions. Fortunately, someone had the foresight to see that smaller cars were selling at American Motors and with the numerous new imported cars coming ashore, Studebaker responded with the compact Lark line of cars. While sharing some componentry of the earlier Studebakers, they were the right cars at the right time. Through the early sixties, the Lark sold well, but it too was becoming a financial burden as Studebaker was forced to compete on cost with the larger companies. The somewhat successful introduction of the sporty Avanti did nothing for the bottom line but did boost Studebaker image, at least temporarily. By the end of 1964, Studebaker had consolidated all of its production to a single plant in Canada, and by 1966, the last car rolled off the line. It was an unfortunate ending for a company with the colorful history of Studebaker.

Some other marques also bowed out during the sixties. Of course, the story of the Edsel is well known. Technically it did not live to see the sixties, with its production ending in December 1959, but a few 1960 models were built. They were nothing more than 1960 Fords with a different grille and taillight treatment and a few minor trim changes. Chrysler Corporation's mid-range DeSoto was another casualty of the recession of the late fifties, having been essentially done in by its sister divisions. Dodge and Plymouth had both slowly crept up-market with the likes of the Fury and D-500 models, while Chrysler had been slowly moving down the price scale to make room for the luxury Imperial line, which had become its own marketing division in 1955. By 1960, Chrysler had four makes of cars, selling models that were priced within a few hundred dollars of each other. Something had to give, and after the 1961 model year, the DeSoto nameplate was laid to rest, although the car itself continued in the guise of the Dodge Custom 880 line through 1964.

Although trucks are outside the scope of this book, it is also worth noting the changes occurring in that segment of the automotive industry, and indeed brief notes on developments in the truck lines are provided in the introduction for each model year. One event from the 1960s stands out as especially important: the 1969 acquisition of Jeep by American Motors. Willys Corporation had been bought in 1955 by the Kaiser Corporation, mostly to gain access to the highly profitable and successful Jeep vehicles. In fact, anytime Jeep has changed manufacturers, it has been because of the name recognition, profitability and overall success that the Jeep name brings with it. Kaiser had continued marketing the Willys-Jeep products through the early sixties, when it made a series of successful additions to the product line. Among these were the Jeep pickup

and the Jeep Wagoneer. The Wagoneer is considered by many to be the modern day forerunner of the SUV (sport-utility vehicle) market. Of course, the Wagoneer itself was an offshoot of the Willys Jeepster Wagons of the late forties, but the Wagoneer was the first to offer many car-like conveniences in a formerly truck-type vehicle. The Wagoneer, along with the Jeep "CJ," would be the two mainstay products for Jeep for the next 20 or more years. But during the late sixties, Kaiser Corporation decided to get out of the constantly changing automotive market, and American Motors bought Jeep in 1969. This would give AMC the shot in the arm it needed to survive the seventies.

A final thought on consolidation during this period is the decline of the convertible and hardtop body styles. The convertible had been around since the mid-thirties. As an alternative to earlier open-air models, the convertible came with a weatherproof roof, and side windows that could allow the passengers to stay dry in inclement weather. Its popularity was slow to rise at first (Chevrolet didn't even offer a convertible in 1939), but after the war, its advantages as a sporty model in any model line made it one of the faster growing styles (along with the station wagon). All through the fifties and into the sixties, nearly every model of car on the road could be had in a convertible model. The zenith was reached in 1965, the year when the largest number of convertible models were available and the most were sold. From there it was a fast downhill ride. In 1968, AMC dropped all of its convertible models. By 1971, Chrysler would build the last of its convertibles, and in 1973, Ford would sell its last. General Motors' infamous "last convertible" came in 1976, with the Cadillac Eldorado "Special Editions." The convertible would return in the 1980s, but with a new purpose and new style.

Although rarely noted, the hardtop body style, an offshoot of the soft-top convertible models, also was dwindling in numbers during this period — not because the public was not buying them, but rather because of safety concerns from the insurance industry and government, and cost issues. From about 1970 on, nearly every new car design came only in pillared coupe and sedan formats. Exceptions were most full-size models and the mid-size Ford and Mopar models of 1971 and 1972, which continued into the mid-seventies, being available in at least four-door hardtop models and occasionally a true two-door hardtop.

## Proliferation of Models

The sixties brought about some fundamental changes in the marketing of the automobile. As history is proving, this proliferation will be as costly to the longevity of certain American nameplates as the consolidation process had been. Prior to 1960, most companies marketed their cars in two (occasionally three or in extreme cases four) trim levels of the same basic car. Sometimes, as in the case of Buick, two different sizes of cars were offered in two different trim levels, making for four variations of basically the same car, but covering the entire mid-price range for automobiles, sometimes edging into the luxury or high-end market. Occasional exceptions such as the Corvette or Thunderbird were introduced to cash in on a growing market niche created by imported cars. Such would be the case at the beginning of the sixties, but as the decade wore on, Detroit found itself drowning in a sea of models from all manufacturers, as all makes tried to cover all of the varying markets. This is best illustrated by a comparison of the number of manufacturers and nameplates on the market in 1960 as compared to 1970. In 1960, there were 16 major makes, producing 271 different models, or an average of about 17 per brand. In 1970, there were 13 major makes, producing 382 different models, or about 29 models per brand.

As mentioned earlier, the wave of import cars that hit the United States during the late fifties, and the renewed interest in the AMC Rambler of that time, had caused the powers that be to sit up and take notice. So for the 1960 model year, four new compact cars arrived on the market, at least one from each of the Big Three, and each with a different viewpoint on what a small car should be. This story is covered in more detail in the 1960 chapter, but essentially, Ford and Chrysler went the conventional route with front engined, rear wheel drive cars; Ford went after the bare bones economy market, while Chrysler offered a slightly more upscale car. Chevrolet, on the other hand, went right to the heart of the matter, copying the formula of the highest selling import, the VW "Beetle," and the result was the rear engined, rear-drive Chevrolet Corvair.

After the runaway success of the Ford Falcon, GM decided that it needed a more traditional compact, in case the Corvair turned out to be a novelty. So, in 1962 the Chevy II was introduced, and instantly gave the Falcon a run for its money.

Soon, what had started as basic, economy car entrants in the market gave way to upscale cousins, so that everyone could cash in on the compact car market. Mercury introduced its Comet alongside the Falcon in 1960. Nineteen sixty-one brought the Valiant's running mate, the Dodge Lancer, and a trio of larger compacts from Buick, Olds and Pontiac. After that came the personal/sporty/luxury car market explosion. General Motors had unknowingly started this market with its exclusive line of two-door hardtops, way back in 1949 and 1950. Generally a top of the line model, these hardtops were given "exotic" names such as BelAir, Catalina, Holiday and Riviera. They had become mainstays of the entire line by the mid-fifties. Then several exclusive convertibles were introduced, the Buick Skylark, Olds Fiesta and Cadillac Eldorado, all luxury cars with a sporty yet personal image.

Chrysler had introduced the ultimate in luxury with brute force, in its 1955 introduction of the Chrysler 300 series. Powered by a massive Hemi engine, these full-size luxury cars offered the best of sportiness and luxury, although sometimes sacrificing handling, as that technology had not been much improved upon since the forties. The 300 was a success in its own right, but was still at the upper end of the pricing scale.

Ford had successfully sold the Continental even earlier, and the personal-luxury 1956–57 Continental Mark II, but their price and market stature kept them from the masses. The right combination was finally hit upon with the introduction of the four-seat Thunderbird in 1958. While

| Make | Models, by Year | | | | | | | | | | |
|---|---|---|---|---|---|---|---|---|---|---|---|
| | *1960* | *1961* | *1962* | *1963* | *1964* | *1965* | *1966* | *1967* | *1968* | *1969* | *1970* |
| AMC | | | | | | | 26 | 26 | 24 | 22 | 24 |
| Buick | 19 | 22 | 25 | 26 | 30 | 39 | 41 | 39 | 35 | 37 | 36 |
| Cadillac | 13 | 12 | 13 | 12 | 11 | 11 | 12 | 12 | 11 | 11 | 11 |
| Chevrolet | 24 | 29 | 34 | 32 | 43 | 43 | 47 | 48 | 41 | 41 | 35 |
| Chrysler | 17 | 17 | 15 | 17 | 16 | 17 | 13 | 15 | 15 | 15 | 15 |
| DeSoto | 6 | 2 | | | | | | | | | |
| Dodge | 23 | 25 | 32 | 35 | 31 | 35 | 37 | 38 | 40 | 43 | 48 |
| Edsel | 7 | | | | | | | | | | |
| Ford | 23 | 23 | 36 | 42 | 43 | 41 | 46 | 44 | 48 | 53 | 54 |
| Imperial | 9 | 6 | 6 | 6 | 4 | 4 | 4 | 5 | 5 | 5 | 4 |
| Lincoln | 12 | 2 | 2 | 2 | 2 | 2 | 3 | 3 | 2 | 3 | 3 |
| Mercury | 17 | 19 | 29 | 39 | 31 | 26 | 30 | 31 | 27 | 32 | 38 |
| Oldsmobile | 17 | 27 | 27 | 26 | 34 | 32 | 35 | 36 | 31 | 30 | 29 |
| Plymouth | 23 | 23 | 25 | 28 | 27 | 35 | 35 | 38 | 42 | 45 | 49 |
| Pontiac | 16 | 19 | 19 | 21 | 24 | 26 | 33 | 37 | 35 | 34 | 36 |
| Rambler | 36 | 33 | 33 | 35 | 25 | 30 | | | | | |
| Studebaker | 9 | 10 | 11 | 14 | 14 | 6 | 5 | | | | |
| **Total** | 271 | 269 | 307 | 335 | 335 | 347 | 367 | 372 | 356 | 371 | 382 |

its two-seater predecessor was a success in its own market, this new four-seat version offered more room and comfort than before. While more expensive than a run of the mill Ford or Chevy, it was priced within the mid-range of the market, and that was what sparked its success.

Seeing this combination, other makers soon offered optional equipment to turn their cars into a Thunderbird knock-off. Bucket seats, consoles, floor shifters, wire wheel covers, hood bulges or scoops, and sporty lines with just enough chrome to accent the body were becoming a trend. The first to make it to market with actual Thunderbird-like cars, however, would be the 1961 Oldsmobile Starfire and 1962 Buick Wildcat and Pontiac Grand Prix models. These were still traditional full-size GM cars, but marketed with enough Thunderbird-style equipment for the public to want them. After the runaway success of the 1963 version of the Grand Prix, suddenly the marketing types saw that a lower priced car could capitalize on this market, and eventually the Dodge Monaco, Oldsmobile Jetstar, and Mercury S-55 entered the fray.

The car that would really set the personal luxury market on its ear was the 1963 Buick Riviera. Designed from the outset as a stand-alone model, the Riviera would bring back the uniqueness and luxury that the original 1958 Thunderbird had brought to market. The Riviera used elegant, understated styling cues and minimal chrome trim to highlight the outside, while interiors were designed with comfort for four adults in mind. The Riviera won many awards and is considered by many to be the true beginning of the personal-luxury car market, as the Thunderbird was originally more in the sporting vein. For all its success, though, the Riviera inspired few imitators at first. Within GM, the 1966 Oldsmobile Toronado and 1967 Cadillac Eldorado targeted essentially the same market. Then, in 1968, Lincoln introduced the Continental Mark III, a modern interpretation of its 1956–1957 Mark II personal-luxury car. By 1972, the toll on the Thunderbird was sufficiently taken that Ford opted for a true personal-luxury car in its restyling, thus succumbing to the Riviera's market-leading trend.

The next big market proliferation came with the advent of the new intermediate class of cars. While all makers had toyed with slightly smaller full-size cars early in the decade, none were truly successful. In fact the smaller Dodge and Plymouth models of 1962 were so poorly received that the Dodge was immediately enlarged for 1963 to recover lost sales. Ford was the first to market with a true mid-size car, although with somewhat limited success. That car was the 1962 Ford Fairlane and stable-mate Mercury Meteor. A solid yet very conventional car, the Fairlane was deemed by many in the public to be too close to the Falcon in performance and size, yet too close to the full-size Ford in price. American Motors had been offering a "mid-

size" choice for several years now in its Rambler Classic line. What would really set the market on fire would be the 1964 introduction of General Motors' line of mid-size cars. Since the introduction of the senior-compacts in 1961, these cars as well as the full-size cars had gradually gotten larger with each passing year. By 1965, in fact, the mid-size line had roughly matched the size and price of its full-size predecessor in 1955. Obviously, they were no longer compact cars, so GM marketing types took advantage of this and marketed the new cars as a whole new class of car, the intermediate or "mid-size" class.

To make sure these new cars were noticed on the street, Pontiac engineers decided to go under the hood and make some adjustments. The important adjustment that they had secretly made was to put the big 389 CID V-8 engine into the engine bay as optional equipment in the GTO package. This high-horsepower engine in a relatively lightweight car made for a legal street-racer, the likes of which America had never seen. Others to join the bandwagon were the Olds 4-4-2, Buick Gran Sport, Ford Torino/Cobra, Mercury Cyclone, Plymouth Road Runner/GTX and Dodge Coronet R/T and Super Bee. These muscle cars, as they came to be known, defined the era that this book covers.

Almost simultaneously, manufacturers were looking at their smaller, compact cars as vehicles that could use some more power and style. Studebaker had offered a V-8 engine in its compact Lark for several years, and even had super-charged versions available on certain models. By 1964, several other manufacturers were offering versions of their compact cars with more performance, including the Ford Falcon Sprint, Chevrolet Chevy II Nova SS and the AMC Rambler Classic Typhoon. But Ford would change everything in April 1964, with the introduction of the Mustang. Plymouth had given a preview of what could be done when it introduced a fastback variation of its Valiant compact, called the Barracuda. Nice looking, and definitely sporty in appearance, the Barracuda lacked the refinement, simplicity and visual styling to set it apart from the crowd. The Mustang, though, looked the part of a sports car. And buyers could equip the car however they liked, with powertrain options ranging from a 6-cylinder automatic, to a high-performance V-8 with 4-speed manual transmission, and a host of luxury features and trim options available. The Mustang was the success story of the decade. Most people, however, did not realize that many parts of the Mustang had originated from the Falcon, much as the Barracuda sprang from the Valiant. Later on, the same could be said for the Chevy Camaro and Pontiac Firebird, which were derived from the Chevy II.

In the late sixties and early seventies, manufacturers refocused attention on another vehicle class, the renewed "mid-size" personal-luxury/sporty coupe category. Much like the first time around, the initial offerings were based on existing cars, but by the time the idea really took off, there were totally fresh designs in the offing. The first cars of this type date back to the 1965 AMC Marlin and 1966 Dodge Charger. The Marlin was essentially a two-door Classic with a fastback roof grafted on. The Charger filled a more specific purpose, but was essentially a Coronet with a fastback roof grafted onto the top. However, the Charger was also meant to be a muscle car, at least originally, so it bridged the gap between muscle car and mid-sized personal car. Several years later, in 1969, the personal luxury car finally came into its own, with the introduction of the newly downsized Pontiac Grand Prix. Though it was based on the mid-sized LeMans platform, there was very little to relate the two cars in terms of style or purpose. Classic styling combined with luxury interior features and sporty intent under the hood were the key ingredients for this new type of car. Soon to follow were the 1970 Chevy Monte Carlo, 1971 Dodge Charger and Plymouth Sebring Plus models, as well as a repositioned 1971 Mercury Cougar. It was the 1974 Ford Elite and Mercury Cougar XR-7 that truly put Ford into this market category, though several years behind the competition.

As noted earlier, the market proliferation of the 1960s would prove fatal for some nameplates, though only much later. The two recent examples are Plymouth and Oldsmobile.

Plymouth's real problems began with the 1960 models, though it took another 40 years for the axe to drop on the brand. Since its introduction in 1928, Plymouth had always been tied to another Chrysler marque for sales support. The original idea was that the low cost Plymouth would help dealers sell cars in hard times, such as the Great Depression of the 1930s. Dodge-Plymouth, DeSoto-Plymouth and Chrysler-Plymouth dealerships were the rule, with a rare stand-alone Plymouth dealership. This pairing of cars helped Chrysler survive many difficult times. With the strong sales of Plymouth through the fifties, however, dealers wanted Chrysler to make Plymouth a stand-alone line, to allow better competition with Ford and Chevrolet. Chrysler marketing people had other plans, though, and ultimately made a fateful decision that would forever haunt and doom Plymouth.

At the introduction of the Valiant in 1960, it was decided the new compact would be marketed as its own division, much as Ford had done with the Edsel, or more recently GM with the Saturn. Thus, Chrysler would have four sales divisions: Dodge, Chrysler-DeSoto-Plymouth, Imperial and Valiant. At the same time, Dodge dealers had requested and were granted a slightly smaller car of their own in the full-size market, designed to help them compete better with Ford and Chevrolet. At the time this process was occurring, with the mid-price market retract-

ing in the 1958 recession, this may have sounded like a good idea (à la the 1928 Plymouth marketing idea) to keep sales within the corporation. But, unlike 1928, sales and the economy immediately improved after the 1958 recession, and the mid-range market came back to life, as seen in the astounding success of Pontiac all through the sixties. So by the time all of these changes were actually implemented it was 1960, the economy was healthy, and Plymouth and Dodge were competing for the same customers with Ford and Chevrolet. To make matters worse, Dodge landed its own version of the Valiant, known as the Lancer.

With the decision in late 1960 to drop the DeSoto line, Chrysler again reorganized and opted to pull the Valiant under the Plymouth nameplate, so that now there were three divisions: Dodge, Chrysler-Plymouth and Imperial. With the dropping of the DeSoto, Dodge rolled out a new 1962 Custom 880 line that was essentially a Chrysler Newport with a Dodge front end, and suddenly Dodge and Chrysler were competing for the same market also. So what did all of this mean for Plymouth? Historically Dodge had always carried more prestige than the Plymouth nameplate, so when Dodge and Plymouth offered similar cars at similar prices, the Dodge would almost always sell better. Plymouth desperately needed some brand differentiation. That would begin arriving in 1964 with the Barracuda, and a true full-size Fury in 1965. Sales would rebound, and on the strength of the Mopar racing program and successful publicity with NASCAR legend Richard Petty, the mid-size line of the late sixties would enjoy a fair amount of success. But this brief respite would soon fade, and by 1970, the same problems recurred. Dodge duplicated nearly every Plymouth model offered, and content and pricing were nearly identical on many of these cars. In fact, the 1970 Barracuda and Valiant Duster coupe were the last unique American-made offerings Plymouth sold until the 1997 Prowler.

After 1973, it was downhill for Plymouth, with a few exceptions in the early K-cars and the first generation minivans of the 1980s. Even those were duplicated in the Dodge line. The entire problem came down to identical products within the corporation, and thus sales were not taken away from another company, but instead cannibalized from within. Without a more distinct product line, the writing was on the wall for Plymouth by 1980, and it probably should have been dealt with at that time.

A similar problem accounts for the latest discontinuance, the dropping of the oldest line of cars made in America — Oldsmobile. The problems at Olds also began in the sixties, but did not manifest themselves upon Oldsmobile until the early nineties. In fact, all signs actually pointed to Pontiac getting the axe, until Pontiac was able to pull off a miracle at the last minute and establish an identity of its own. The roots of the Olds death sentence can be traced to 1961 and the introduction of the "senior" compact trio:

Buick Special, Oldsmobile F-85 and Pontiac Tempest. The problem was definitely not these cars or what they stood for, as each would become highly successful in its own right. The problem, as with Plymouth, was in the marketing choices made at the corporate level. As each car grew and became more successful, it became clear that Chevrolet should have a piece of the action, so the 1964 Chevelle was introduced. Of course, at the same time Pontiac had given the world the hot GTO, and each division wanted a piece of that action. By 1968, all four divisions marketed a full range of cars, from basic, to slightly luxurious, to all out sport car, all priced within dollars of each other. In fact, a 1968 Chevelle SS396 Convertible listed at $3,102 and a 1968 Buick Grand Sport 400 Convertible at $3,271—a difference of only $169, and the Buick was the better equipped car.

At about the same time, or so the story goes, General Motors had issued an order that executives from each division should drive cars made by that division. So Chevrolet executives were now being told to drive Chevrolets instead of Buicks and Cadillacs. Not wanting to do without their accustomed luxury, these executives went to the design departments and had the 1965 Caprice created—a car with much of the looks and comfort of a Cadillac at (almost) a Chevrolet price.

Therein lay another problem, the overlapping of car models. Early in GM history, Harley Earl had declared that each of the five divisions would be in its own market. Consumers could move up from one make to the next, and thus in theory GM catered to the market from the time they started driving until they died. So, following this theory, in the thirties a young buyer started with the 6-cylinder Chevrolet, moved up to the more well-appointed 6-cylinder or small 8-cylinder Pontiac, then to an 8-cylinder Oldsmobile, then to a semi-luxury 8-cylinder Buick, and finally into a luxury Cadillac model. Now with the introduction of a luxury model in the Chevrolet line (actually Pontiac had done the same with the 1964 Bonneville Brougham) and the proliferation of available accessories, a Chevrolet could be equipped very much like a Cadillac and be a near equal in driving comfort at a far lower price. An example is the 1972 Chevrolet Caprice four-door hardtop as compared to the 1972 Cadillac Calais four-door hardtop. Pricing is $4,076 versus $5,938, a difference of almost $1,900. If the buyer added about $300 for a larger engine and $100 here and there for such luxuries as power windows, courtesy lighting systems, vinyl top, and the like, the price difference was still over $1,000, or nearly 20 percent, for a similarly equipped car with minimal differences in comfort or luxury in look or ride. The marketing types no longer followed the edict that Chevrolet represented value, and Cadillac represented luxury. If Chevrolet buyers would buy luxury, that is what they would sell them. And if

Oldsmobile could make that same formula work, why not get a piece of the pie.

By the early seventies, Oldsmobile had successfully positioned itself as the cushy, vinyl top wearing, boulevard riding, middle-of-the-road, All-American car. With the energy crisis of 1973–74, Olds gained its own versions of the Chevy Nova (Omega) and Vega/Monza (Starfire), and was selling everything it could build with its hot Cutlass line. In fact, the Cutlass took the number one sales position from the big Chevy in the mid-seventies and gave it back only a few times over the next ten years. But Oldsmobile's image would become its downfall. Everyone was copying the successful Oldsmobile — not just within GM, but at Mercury, Ford, Dodge and Chrysler.

Pontiac had followed Oldsmobile's lead early in the seventies, marketing heavily to the vinyl top, velour upholstery crowd, on the theory that what worked for Oldsmobile would work elsewhere. Thus we were given Grand Ville Broughams, Luxury LeMans, and Bonneville Broughams to fill that market. Sales suffered all through the seventies with the exception of the 1977–79 period when most sales strength could be credited to the revived Firebird/Trans Am models and the successful Grand Prix downpricing and downsizing. Fortunately Pontiac realized, just in time, that it needed a direction, and that direction came in the form of a marketing slogan that led to new, exciting products: "Pontiac … We Build Excitement." The solution for Pontiac all came down to returning to its prior success as a marketer of sporty, fun to drive cars (Firebird, GTO, etc.), and by 1984 the turnaround for this division was well on its way.

Of course, Buick was the real maker of these cars that Oldsmobile and Pontiac had been copying, so it goes without saying that Buick was in little danger of losing much in the way of sales. For the most part, Buick buyers remained traditionalists, and this division was spared any big changes. Chevrolet was able to go back to its roots of economy and value to survive the eighties. Cadillac had its problems, but was virtually on its own in the luxury market for most of this time period.

Oldsmobile's problem was that it did not change with its consumers and had no distinct direction to follow. Who were Oldsmobile customers? Were they Pontiac buyers wanting to move up? Were they Buick buyers wanting a sportier car? Oldsmobile didn't know, and at the time probably didn't care, because any car bearing the Cutlass nameplate seemed to sell. In truth, what typical Oldsmobile buyers wanted, they increasingly found in an imported car, such as a BMW, Audi or even Honda or Toyota. Buyers wanted quality and value with their touch of luxury, and American manufacturers weren't up to speed on providing that. In fact, in the end, those were the very people Oldsmobile specifically tried to target, but it was too little, too late. Sales plummeted from over a million cars a year in 1985 to under 300,000 per year by the late nineties. Even with unique products in its line, Oldsmobile could not muster the sales to save itself. Perhaps a return to the company's earlier engineering leadership could have stemmed the slide. After all, Oldsmobile gave the world its first modern, fully automatic transmission and the first successful, high-volume OHV V-8 engine among others. If Olds had introduced the Aurora V-8 five or ten years sooner, it might have had a brighter fate. Or perhaps, if Oldsmobile had spent more time taking on the imports ten years earlier, and less time taking on Buick and Pontiac, they would be with us well into the future, selling those merry Oldsmobiles!

## Speed and the Horsepower Race

Since the inception of the motorcar, there were always drivers who wanted to go faster. In fact, the very notion of the automobile stemmed in part from a need to move faster. After all, a carriage can only be pulled so fast, no matter how many horses are hitched. But an automobile was more flexible: the car itself could be built smaller or larger, the engine could be larger, its fuel systems could be improved. Over time, all of these changes came about. Just prior to World War II, a flurry of technological change had begun, but most of it was put on hold until after the war. By 1949, the Overhead Valve V-8 engine had won the hearts of racing fans across the country, most famously in those Rocket Oldsmobiles of early stock car racing legend. At the time, the new type of engine seemed the most cost efficient and fuel efficient way to achieve higher levels of horsepower from the smallest amount of space. So the OHV V-8 became the powerplant of choice for everyone, and by 1955 every manufacturer offered one. Once the design had been perfected, the manufacturers were now out to see who could get the most power out of their engine. The "ideal" standard for optimum performance had been set at one horsepower per cubic inch of engine size. While not such a fantastic feat today, in the mid-fifties it seemed impossible; nonetheless engineers quickly set out to prove that they could do it. And if they couldn't, then they were going to increase the cubic inch displacement until the horsepower rose to the level they wanted. Thus began a long cycle of increasingly larger and more powerful engines, culminating with the likes of the 500 CID Cadillac V-8 of 1972, and the 425 horsepower, 426 CID Hemi V-8 built by Chrysler.

Along the way, various techniques were employed to boost the power, some more successful than others, but all pointing the way to the powerful yet fuel-efficient engines that we have today. The first forms of increased power came in increased fuel intake — or in other words, more carburetor inlets, bringing in more fuel and air to the engine. First there were four-barrel carburetors, replacing the nearly universal two-barrel models of old. Then came "Tri-Power" or three two-barrel carbs, lined up and connected to bring on more power as needed. Then came dual four-barrel carburetors, which would cover the top of virtually any engine in carburetor equipment. More enterprising engineers developed the first popular use of fuel injection in the late fifties for General Motors and Chrysler Corporation usage. These units did their intended job of increasing power, but they were expensive and troublesome and therefore did not achieve great popularity. With breakthroughs in computer technology some 15 years later, fuel injection would return in a much more successful bid to replace the carburetor as the fuel system of choice.

In the meantime, manufacturers worked with two other means to boost power, the different yet related techniques of turbocharging and supercharging. Supercharging had been used with limited success as early as the thirties. The biggest problems had been its bulk and expense. Supercharging generally used a belt driven by the crankshaft to drive a secondary prop that would increase the air intake speed and thus the output of the engine. By the early sixties, Studebaker was successfully using this method of increasing horsepower. Supercharging would go away temporarily, only to resurface in the late eighties as a way to get more power out of 6-cylinder and smaller engines. Chrysler also had a form of supercharging in its Ram-induction V-8's of the early sixties. While not using actual belt-driven components to boost power, the length of the intake rams could determine the amount of horsepower generated by controlling the airflow into the engine. Ram intakes typically were 10 to 30 inches in length. Turbocharging worked on a similar principle, but used exhaust gases to power the prop for added energy. Although this setup was more reliable in principle, it created huge amounts of heat that had to be dealt with. Therefore, turbocharging was not widely available until the late seventies, where it would mainly be employed on 4-cylinder and some 6-cylinder engines. The lone exception was the Oldsmobile Jetfire of 1962 and 1963.

# 1960

Nineteen-sixty was an important year for new products. This was the year of the compact car for American manufacturers. Studebaker and American Motors, of course, were already into this market, going head to head with the popular Volkswagen 1200 (Beetle) and other European and Japanese nameplates that were beginning to trickle into the United States. But 1960 marked the Big Three's first all out assault on the compact market.

Each went about the task in a different way. Ford took the most traditional route with its Ford Falcon and Mercury Comet lines. These cars shared basic structure, with the Comet being a slightly larger and better trimmed car than the base line Falcon. Power came from a new line of smaller 6-cylinder engines for obvious reasons, mainly improved fuel economy as compared to traditional Ford models.

Chrysler took a less traditional approach, in attempting to make its compact Valiant look like a larger car, complete with tailfins and a fake spare tire contour on the trunk lid, mimicking the Imperial. The result looked nice, if a little bulky for a compact car. Chrysler seemed unsure about the compact market, and wanted to take as few risks as possible. Of course, a new 6-cylinder powerplant was designed for the new car, but marketing was a little more guarded. The Valiant was marketed as a freestanding nameplate, sold through Plymouth dealerships. Officially, the Valiant was not a Plymouth until mid–1961. There is no reference to the Plymouth name in advertising until that time, other than statements that the car was "available at your local Plymouth dealer" or the like. That strategy may explain the car's resemblance to a Chrysler or Imperial.

Surprisingly, General Motors took the biggest gamble with its new compact, the Chevrolet Corvair. In retrospect, however, perhaps it was not as big a gamble as it first appears. General Motors was always considered the market leader, especially in sales and styling, but it also knew when it needed to take action to keep its market share. At the time, the goal was to stop the growing tide of import cars

from taking away market share. The biggest importer at the time was Volkswagen, whose most popular car was the rear engined, air cooled Model 1200 "Beetle." So in effect, GM went right for the source and tried to outdo the biggest competitor. Ford and Chrysler, on the other hand, opted to build more traditional compact cars and competed directly with a number of Japanese and European nameplates, as well as the Studebaker Lark and AMC Rambler American. Therefore, Ford and Chrysler had to entice new customers who might have purchased their larger cars anyway. General Motors' approach was not as likely to siphon off sales of its own larger cars, but would instead woo what would otherwise be an import car buyer into a GM showroom. If only it had continued this approach, General Motors might not have suffered dramatic losses of market share in later years. The Chevrolet Corvair took many honors for its engineering and style, among them the now coveted *Motor Trend* magazine Car of the Year award.

There was also a downside to the new model year. Sales of the 1960 Edsel had barely gotten under way when, in December 1959, Ford announced it was dropping the ill-fated car. After a reasonably good start in 1958, Ford was afraid that the recession of that year had hurt the mid-price market too much to continue marketing the Edsel in that range. So for 1959, the Edsel had moved to the upper-end of the low-price market. Unfortunately for Ford, the recession was short lived, but sales of mid-market cars had shriveled up in that timeframe and sales of smaller cars had improved, especially for American Motors and Studebaker. This left the Edsel with no real market to work with. It had already suffered somewhat from unpopular styling and a reputation for poor quality. In addition, Mercury had traditionally covered the market that was being taken by the Edsel. This meant Mercury had to move up the price scale. When the Edsel did not meet sales expectations for 1958, Ford immediately moved the Mercury back a notch for 1959. Therefore, since Mercury and Edsel marketing had

## 1960 Model Year Production by Make

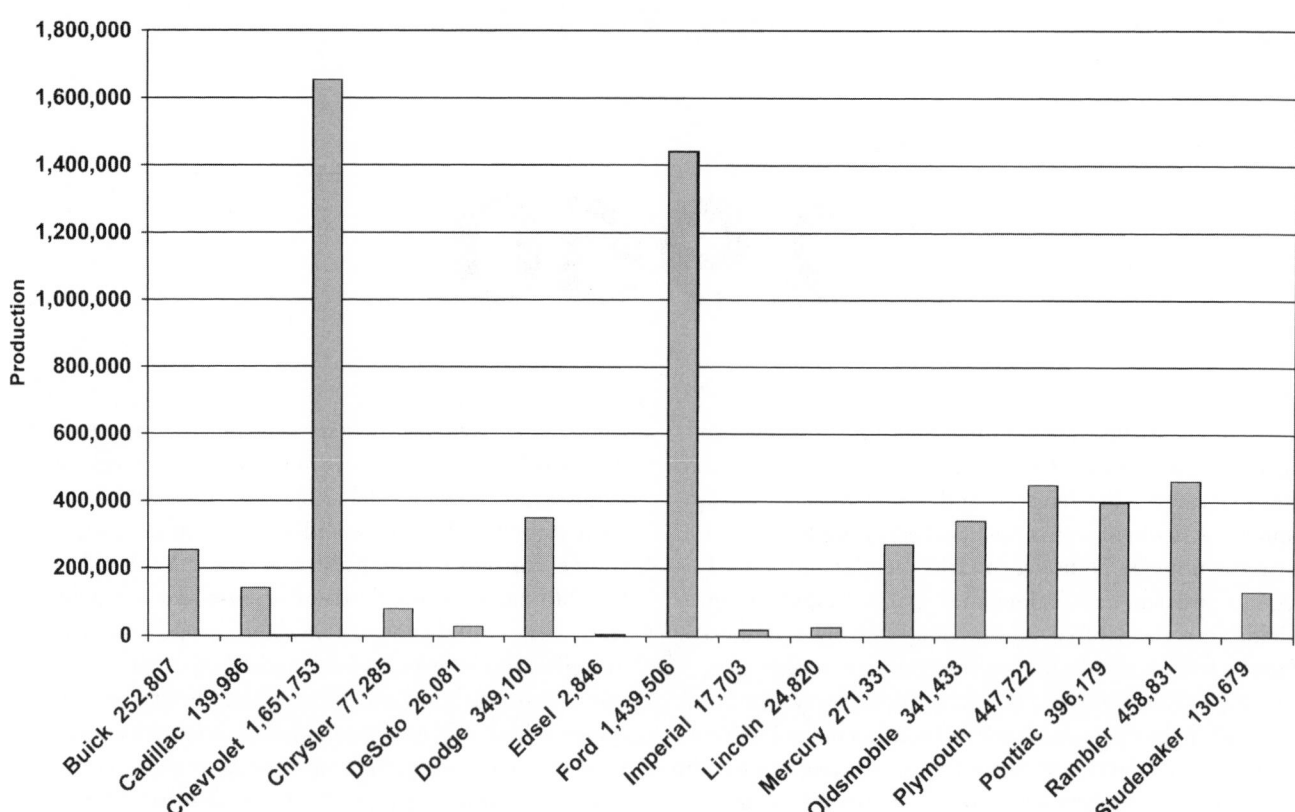

Buick 252,807 · Cadillac 139,986 · Chevrolet 1,651,753 · Chrysler 77,285 · DeSoto 26,081 · Dodge 349,100 · Edsel 2,846 · Ford 1,439,506 · Imperial 17,703 · Lincoln 24,820 · Mercury 271,331 · Oldsmobile 341,433 · Plymouth 447,722 · Pontiac 396,179 · Rambler 458,831 · Studebaker 130,679

been combined during 1958, sales were not necessarily lost, but just went to Mercury. By 1960, the Edsel was only a glorified Ford product, and wisely the plug was pulled.

Over at Chrysler, another soon-to-be casualty was the DeSoto. After a brief revival of sales in the mid-fifties, the problem-plagued 1957 models turned customers away from Mopar products. This shift, combined with the recession and a lack of identity for DeSoto models, was spelling the end for the relatively young nameplate. Several models were dropped for 1960 because of duplication with Chrysler or Dodge models, and by 1961 only two models remained.

Other changes were what could be expected from most manufacturers. The entire GM line had been totally re-designed and restyled for 1959, so 1960 brought only the usual annual styling revisions. Oldsmobile's successful Rocket V8 engines garnered the marque the opportunity to provide the Official Pace Car for the Indianapolis 500 race this year, an Oldsmobile 98 convertible. Ford was developing a habit of major redesigns of its cars every year, a practice that would continue through 1965. As previously mentioned, Ford-based Edsel models were similarly re-designed. Lincoln and Mercury, however, were mostly carry-over designs. Lincoln would introduce a new car for 1961, when a similarly new Thunderbird would also be introduced. Mercury received major styling revisions, but they were still based upon the 1959 models.

Chrysler models for 1960 were all-new and of unit-body design, something highly uncommon for the time. Even the large Imperial was given the new body design. However, being styled by some of the same designers that did the 1957–1959 models, the new cars turned out to look quite similar to the prior models. While other manufacturers were shedding their tailfins, Chryslers still wore them proudly. In fact, Plymouths of 1960 had some of the biggest fins seen to date. Engineering was still Chrysler's domain, as evidenced by the shift to unit-body construction, but styling would flounder for several more years. American Motors and Studebaker products continued relatively unchanged stylewise, but improvements were made to their drivetrains as detailed in the following sections.

In other segments of the auto industry, Checker Motors cars continued with relatively few changes to styling, but did make the important move into the retail consumer market this season. Chevrolet and GMC trucks were totally redesigned this year, with broad, flat hoods that covered the fender tops, and finally eliminated the old-style fendered look on trucks, bringing them into the modern era. The Chevrolet El Camino took on the updated styling of the regular 1960 Chevrolet line. Ford trucks were carried over into the new year with relatively few changes as were Dodge, Kaiser-Willys and International trucks.

# BUICK

*"The Turbine Drive Buick. When better automobiles are built, Buick will build them."*

After the dramatic "winged" styling of the 1959 model Buicks, no time was wasted in making the 1960 Buicks' appearance more conservative and traditional. The controversial angled front fenders and angled fins at the rear were flattened out somewhat, and rounded. Fender portholes, the traditional fifties Buick trademark, returned as Ventiports, a squarish version of the porthole. The greenhouse area was unchanged, as it was shared among all five GM divisions. The overall styling seemed to be cluttered, though, and sales fell once again. Under the hood powerplants remained little changed. The main contributor to the drop in sales appears to be the 4-Door Hardtop "Flat-top" body style, as sales fell off in every model line approximately 20 percent to 25 percent.

All-new interiors were designed for 1960, although they failed to be more conservative in style. The new dash-

board featured a "Mirrormatic" adjustable speedometer that could be adjusted up and down for different driver heights. A pod centrally located on the instrument panel held the optional electric clock, and at the far end, the dashboard just went away. There was a small, flat horizontal area that accommodated the glove compartment, but this design left the heater and optional air conditioning equipment within eyesight, although covered by a small "kick panel." The effect was definitely unique, but not one of the better dashboard designs. Floorpans were redesigned this year on all GM cars, to increase floor space by approximately 20 percent. Specifically, the size of the center floor hump was reduced, and the floor pans were lowered. Elsewhere inside the car, most models had their names spelled out on the lower door panels in the upholstery, a unique feature.

LeSabre 4-Door Sedan

LeSabre 4-Door Estate Wagon

Invicta 2-Door Hardtop

Invicta 2-Door Convertible

Electra 225 4-Door Hardtop

**Model year production:** 252,807, down 11.06% from 1959.
**Domestic market share:** 4.2% (9th place)
**Base price range:** $2,756 to $4,300.
**Industry average base price:** $3,391.
**Buick average base price:** $3,564.
**Introduction date:** October 8, 1959.
**Assembly plants:** Flint, MI (1); Southgate, CA (2); Linden, NJ (3); Fairfax, KS (4); Wilmington, DE (5); Atlanta, GA (6); and Arlington, TX (8).

**Data plate identification:** Nine digit code read as follows: 1st digit indicating series trim level and engine (see coding below); 2nd digit G for 1960; 3rd digit is assembly plant code; followed by sequential number 100001 and up for serial number. (Coding: 4 = LeSabre, 6 = Invicta, 7 = Electra, 8 = Electra 225.) *Example:* 4G4001001 is a 1960 Buick LeSabre, serial number 001001, built in Fairfax, KS. Check model number on body identification plate.

## Powertrains

| Engine | Gross HP | Transmission Availability | LeSabre | Invicta | Electra & Electra 225 |
|---|---|---|---|---|---|
| 364 CID Wildcat 375E, 2-bbl., V8 | 235 | 3-speed manual | $52 | - | - |
| | | Turbine-Drive Automatic | $272 | - | - |
| 364 CID Wildcat 384, 2-bbl., V8 | 250 | 3-speed manual | S | - | - |
| | | Turbine-Drive Automatic | $220 | - | - |
| 364 CID Wildcat 405, 4-bbl., V8 | 300 | 3-speed manual | $220 | - | - |
| | | Turbine-Drive Automatic | $440 | - | - |
| 401 CID Wildcat 445, 4-bbl., V8 | 325 | Turbine-Drive Automatic | - | S | S |

## Major Options

| | LeSabre | Invicta | Electra | Electra 225 |
|---|---|---|---|---|
| Air conditioning | $430 | $430 | $430 | $430 |
| Heater and defroster | $99 | $99 | $99 | $99 |
| Soft Ray tinted glass | $40 | $40 | $40 | $40 |
| Power steering | $108 | $108 | S | S |
| Power brakes | $43 | $43 | S | S |
| Power driver's seat/ Bench seat, 6-way | $97 | $97 | $69–$97 | $69–$97 |
| Power windows | $108 | $108 | $108 | $108* |
| Sonomatic AM radio | $99 | $99 | $99 | $99 |
| Deluxe wheel covers | $19 | S | S | S |

Options common to most models. (S = Standard equipment.) Items may be standard equipment, optional at different pricing, or unavailable on certain models. This chart is only a guide.

*Standard on convertible.

## Paint Colors

| | Code |
|---|---|
| Sable Black | AA |
| Gull Gray Metallic | BB |
| Arctic White | CC |
| Silver Mist Metallic | DD |
| Chalet Blue Metallic | HH |
| Lucerne Green Metallic | KK |
| Titian Red Metallic | LL |
| Casino Cream | MM |
| Cordovan Metallic | NN |
| Pearl Fawn Metallic | PP |
| Tahiti Beige | RR |
| Turquoise Metallic | TT |
| Tampico Red | VV |
| Midnight Blue Metallic | WW |
| Verde Green Metallic | XX |

# LeSabre

*"The lowest-priced Turbine Drive Buick."*

**Nameplate year of origin:** 1959.
**Current bodystyle lifespan:** 1959 through 1960.
**Predecessor to this model:** Special (1957 to 1958).
**Replacement for this model:** LeSabre (1961 to 1964).
**Percentage of division's sales volume:** 60.16%.
**Corporate siblings:** Chevrolet Biscayne/BelAir/Impala, Pontiac Catalina/Star Chief/Bonneville, Oldsmobile 88.
**Primary competition:** Chrysler Newport, DeSoto Adventurer, and Mercury Monterey.
**Notable changes:** Major restyling of sheetmetal.
**Major standard equipment:** Balfor cloth and vinyl bench seat, front door operated interior lighting, glove box light, full carpeting, front and rear armrests, padded instrument panel, heater and defroster, and 7.60 × 15 BSW tires.

## Measurements

| | |
|---|---|
| Wheelbase | 123.0" |
| Length | 217.9" |
| Width | 80.0" |
| Height | 57.2" |
| Legroom — front | 44.2" |
| Legroom — rear | 42.2" |
| Headroom — front | 34.7" |
| Headroom — rear | 33.9" |
| Luggage capacity (cu. ft.) | NA |
| Fuel capacity (gals.) | 20.0 |

## Models Available

|  | Style Number | Base MSRP | Change from LY | Shipping Wt. (lbs.) | Production | Change from LY |
|---|---|---|---|---|---|---|
| LeSabre 2-Door Sedan | 4411 | $2,756 | +0.58% | 4033 | 14,388 | +6.64% |
| LeSabre 2-Door Hardtop | 4437 | $2,915 | +2.32% | 4163 | 26,521 | -24.63% |
| LeSabre 2-Door Convertible | 4467 | $3,145 | +0.51% | 4233 | 13,588 | +29.55% |
| LeSabre 4-Door Sedan | 4419 | $2,870 | +2.35% | 4219 | 54,033 | +5.17% |
| LeSabre 4-Door Hardtop | 4439 | $2,991 | +2.26% | 4269 | 35,999 | -21.86% |
| LeSabre 4-Dr., 2-S. Estate Wgn. | 4435 | $3,386 | +1.99% | 4568 | 5,331 | -35.66% |
| LeSabre 4-Dr., 3-S. Estate Wgn. | 4445 | $3,493 | NEW | NA | 2,222 | NEW |
| TOTALS | Avg. price | $3,079 | +4.00% | Production | 152,082 | -7.78% |

# Invicta

*"The spirited Buick."*

**Nameplate year of origin:** 1959.
**Current bodystyle lifespan:** 1959 through 1960.
**Predecessor to this model:** Century (1957 to 1958).
**Replacement for this model:** Invicta (1961 to 1963) and Wildcat (1962 to 1964).
**Percentage of division's sales volume:** 17.96%.
**Corporate siblings:** Chevrolet Biscayne/BelAir/Impala, Pontiac Catalina/Star Chief/Bonneville, Oldsmobile 88.
**Primary competition:** Chrysler Windsor, DeSoto Adventurer, and Mercury Montclair.
**Notable changes:** Major restyling of sheetmetal.
**Major standard equipment:** Berkshire cloth or all-vinyl deluxe bench seat, full carpeting, front and rear armrests, deluxe steering wheel, padded instrument panel, electric clock, heater and defroster, Turbine Drive transmission, automatic trunk light, deluxe wheel covers and 7.60 × 15 BSW tires.

## Measurements

| | |
|---|---|
| Wheelbase | 123.0" |
| Length | 217.9" |
| Width | 80.0" |
| Height | 57.2" |
| Legroom — front | 44.0" |
| Legroom — rear | 42.0" |
| Headroom — front | 34.7" |
| Headroom — rear | 33.9" |
| Luggage capacity (cu. ft.) | NA |
| Fuel capacity (gals.) | 20.0 |

## Models Available

|  | Style Number | Base MSRP | Change from LY | Shipping Wt. (lbs.) | Production | Change from LY* |
|---|---|---|---|---|---|---|
| Invicta 2-Door HT | 4637 | $3,447 | 0.00% | 4255 | 8,960 | -21.75% |
| Invicta 2-Door Convertible | 4667 | $3,620 | 0.00% | 4347 | 5,236 | -3.87% |
| Invicta 4-Door Sedan | 4619 | $3,357 | 0.00% | 4324 | 10,839 | +2.58% |
| Invicta 4-Door HT | 4639 | $3,515 | 0.00% | 4365 | 15,300 | -24.09% |
| Invicta 4-Dr., 2-S. Estate Wgn. | 4635 | $3,841 | 0.00% | 4644 | 3,471 | -33.65% |
| Invicta 4-Dr., 3-S. Estate Wgn. | 4645 | $3,948 | NEW | NA | 1,605 | NEW |
| TOTALS | Avg. price | $3,621 | +1.83% | Production | 5,411 | -14.07% |

# Electra

*"The most luxurious Buick."*

**Nameplate year of origin:** 1959.
**Current bodystyle lifespan:** 1959 through 1960.
**Predecessor to this model:** Roadmaster (1957 to 1958).
**Replacement for this model:** Electra (1961 to 1964).
**Percentage of division's sales volume:** 14.12%.
**Corporate siblings:** Cadillac Series 62/de Ville, Oldsmobile Ninety-Eight.
**Primary competition:** Chrysler New Yorker and Mercury Park Lane.
**Notable changes:** Major restyling of sheetmetal.
**Major standard equipment:** Power steering, power brakes, Beaumont cloth bench seat, front door operated interior lighting, glove box light, padded instrument panel, deluxe steering wheel, deep-pile, carpeting, front and rear center armrests, electric clock, heater and defroster, deluxe wheel covers and 8.00 × 15 BSW tires.

## Measurements

| | |
|---|---|
| Wheelbase | 126.3" |
| Length | 221.2" |
| Width | 80.0" |
| Height | 57.3" |
| Legroom — front | 43.8" |
| Legroom — rear | 45.4" |
| Headroom — front | 34.2" |
| Headroom — rear | 33.4" |
| Luggage capacity (cu. ft.) | NA |
| Fuel capacity (gals.) | 20.0 |

## Models Available

| | Style Number | Base MSRP | Change from LY | Shipping Wt. (lbs.) | Production | Change from LY |
|---|---|---|---|---|---|---|
| Electra 2-Door Hardtop | 4737 | $3,818 | 0.00% | 4453 | 7,416 | -33.88% |
| Electra 4-Door Sedan | 4719 | $3,856 | 0.00% | 4544 | 13,794 | 11.63% |
| Electra 4-Door Hardtop | 4739 | $3,963 | 0.00% | 4554 | 14,488 | -29.71% |
| TOTALS | | Avg. price $3,879 | 0.00% | | Production 35,698 | -19.15% |

# Electra 225

*"The finest Buick of all."*

**Nameplate year of origin:** 1959.
**Current bodystyle lifespan:** 1959 through 1960.
**Predecessor to this model:** Limited (1958).
**Replacement for this model:** Electra 225 (1961 to 1964).
**Percentage of division's sales volume:** 7.76%.
**Corporate siblings:** Cadillac Series 62/de Ville, Oldsmobile Ninety-Eight.
**Primary competition:** Chrysler New Yorker and Mercury Park Lane.
**Notable changes:** Major restyling of sheetmetal.
**Major standard equipment:** Power steering, power brakes, Brisbane cloth bench seat (except convertible), genuine leather upholstery with 2-way power seat (convertible), safety and lighting package, padded instrument panel, deluxe steering wheel, deep-pile, carpeting, front and rear center armrests, electric clock, heater and defroster, super deluxe wheel covers and 8.00 × 15 BSW tires.

## Measurements

| | |
|---|---|
| Wheelbase | 126.3" |
| Length | 225.9" |
| Width | 80.0" |
| Height | 55.5" |
| Legroom — front | 43.8" |
| Legroom — rear | 45.0" |
| Headroom — front | 34.2" |
| Headroom — rear | 33.6" |
| Luggage capacity (cu. ft.) | NA |
| Fuel capacity (gals.) | 20.0 |

## Models Available

| | Style Number | Base MSRP | Change from LY | Shipping Wt. (lbs.) | Production | Change from LY |
|---|---|---|---|---|---|---|
| Electra 225 2-Door Convertible | 4867 | $4,192 | 0.00% | 4571 | 6,746 | 22.81% |
| Elec. 225 6-w., Riviera 4-Dr. HT | 4829 | $4,300 | 0.00% | 4653 | 8,029 | 26.96% |
| Electra 225 4-Door Hardtop | 4839 | $4,300 | 0.00% | 4650 | 4,841 | -53.86% |
| TOTALS | | *Avg. price* $4,264 | 0.00% | | *Production* 19,616 | -12.16% |

# CADILLAC

*"The Standard of the World … Cadillac for 1960."*

After the infamous 1959 Cadillac tail fins, someone at GM finally decided that bigger wasn't necessarily better. The 1960 Cadillac was given a slightly less dramatic fin, with a single tail lamp built into the trailing edge of the fin, as compared to the tacked on twin pod lamps used in 1959. Also, as was starting to become an industry standard, less chrome trim was used, and where it was used, the chrome was placed sparingly, and used as a highlight of the body design, not a decoration on the body. Powertrains were the same as the previous year, although this would be the last time a 2-barrel or a 3 × 2-barrel "Tri-Power" carburetor setup was offered. All through the sixties, fuel and air intake would be by way of a single 4-barrel carburetor. This was also the last year for the wrap-around windshield styling (except on Fleetwood 75 models). The model line itself was the same as in 1959.

The 1960 model Fleetwood Eldorado Brougham made for quite an interesting styling statement. The Brougham had always been a trend-setting model, but the 1959 and 1960 versions of this limited production car previewed the new styling for the entire 1961 line. While the front clip was mostly of 1960 styling from the main line, styling from the cowl back was nearly pure 1961 Cadillac. The look began with the new full-width windshield, no longer of a wrap-around design, but on the Brougham it was larger than other models would be and appeared very flat from certain angles. With the wrap-around windshield gone, so were the dogleg door vent windows. In place of the slab-sided 1959–60 era sheetmetal on the sides, there was a sculpted and very angular lower body crease running from the front door to the rear bumper. Taillamps were carried in the rear bumper pod areas. Fins on the rear quarter panel were slightly lower than other 1960 Cadillacs, and the entire rear bumper and decklid area was of the newer 1961 design, which actually varied little from 1959–1960 Broughams'.

**Series 62 4-Door Hardtop**

**Coupe de Ville 2-Door Hardtop**

**Eldorado Biarritz 2-Door Convertible**

**Brougham 4-Door Hardtop**

| | |
|---|---|
| **Model year production:** 139,986, down 0.10% from 1959. **Domestic market share:** 2.32% (10th place) **Base price range:** $4,892 to $13,075. **Industry average base price:** $3,391. **Cadillac average base price:** $6,934. **Introduction date:** October, 1959. | **Assembly plants:** Detroit, MI. **Data plate identification:** Nine digit code read as follows: 1st and 2nd digits identify year (60 for 1960); 3rd digit is style symbol (see list); followed by 000001 and up for serial number. *Example:* 60J000001 is a 1960 Cadillac de Ville 2-Door Hardtop, serial number 000001. |

## Powertrains

| Engine | Gross HP | Transmission Availability | S. 62, de Ville & Fleetwood | Eldorado |
|---|---|---|---|---|
| 390 CID, 2-bbl., V8 | 325 | Hydra-matic Automatic | S | - |
| 390 CID, 3 × 2-bbl., V8 | 345 | Hydra-matic Automatic | $134 | S |

## Major Options

| | Series 62 | de Ville | Eldorado | Sixty Special | Seventy-Five |
|---|---|---|---|---|---|
| Air conditioning | $474 | $474 | $474*** | $474 | $624* |
| Tinted glass | $52 | $52 | $52*** | $52 | $52 |
| Power windows | $118 | S | S | S | S |
| 6-way power seat | $113 | $85 | S | $85 | - |
| Power door locks | $46–$70 | $46–$70 | S | $70 | S |
| AM radio w/rear speaker | $165 | $165 | $165 | $165 | $247** |
| Autronic-Eye headlamp dimmers | $46 | $46 | $46*** | $46 | $46 |
| Cruise control | $97 | $97 | $97*** | $97 | $97 |
| Air suspension | $215 | $215 | S | $215 | $215 |
| Remote control trunk release/lock | $59 | $59 | $59 | $59 | - |
| White sidewall tires — std. size | $57 | $57 | $57 | $57 | $57 |

Options common to most models. (- = Not Available, S = Standard equipment) Items may be standard equipment, optional at different pricing, or unavailable on certain models. This chart is only a guide.

*Includes rear unit and controls.     **Signal seeking.     ***Standard on Brougham.

## Paint Colors

| | Code |
|---|---|
| Ebony Black | 10 |
| Olympic White | 12 |
| Platinum Gray Metallic | 14 |
| Aluetian Gray Metallic | 16 |
| Hampton Blue Metallic | 22 |
| Pelham Blue Metallic | 24 |
| York Blue Metallic | 26 |
| Arroyo Turquoise Metallic | 29 |
| Inverness Green Metallic | 32 |
| Glencoe Green Metallic | 36 |
| Beaumont Beige | 44 |
| Palomino | 45 |
| Fawn Metallic | 46 |
| Persian Sand Metallic | 48 |
| Pompeian Red Metallic | 50 |
| Lucerne Blue Metallic | 94 |
| Carrara Green Metallic | 96 |
| Champagne Metallic | 97 |
| Siena Rose Metallic | 98 |
| Heather Metallic | 99 |

**Cadillac Style Symbols: A**— 62 4-window Sedan or Calais 4-Dr. HT Sedan; **B**— Sedan de Ville 4-window; **C**— 62 Short Deck Sedan; **D**— Sedan de Ville Park Avenue; **E**— Eldorado Biarritz or Eldorado Convertible; **F**— 62 Convertible; **G**— 62 2-Door Hardtop or Calais 2-Door HT; **H**— Eldorado Seville HT or Eldorado Coupe; **J**— Coupe de Ville; **K**— 62 6-window Sedan; **L**— Sedan de Ville 6-window; **M**— Fleetwood 60 Special Sedan; **N**— 62 4-window Sedan (1963) or Calais Sedan; **P**— Fleetwood Brougham or Eldorado Brougham; **R**— Fleetwood 75 Sedan; **S**— Fleetwood 75 Limousine; **Z**— Commerical Chassis

# Sixty-Two

*"Its brilliant new styling and its beautiful appointments and equipment are luxurious and complete in every regard."*

**Nameplate year of origin:** 1940.
**Current bodystyle lifespan:** 1959 through 1960.
**Predecessor to this model:** Series 62 (1957 to 1958).
**Replacement for this model:** Series 62 (1961 to 1964).
**Percentage of division's sales volume:** 50.57%.
**Corporate siblings:** Buick Electra and Oldsmobile Ninety-Eight.
**Primary competition:** Imperial Custom and Lincoln.
**Notable changes:** Revised rear styling, minor trim and detail changes.

## Measurements

| | |
|---|---|
| Wheelbase | 130.0" |
| Length | 225.0" |
| Width | 79.9" |
| Height | 54.3" |
| Legroom — front | 45.8" |
| Legroom — rear | 45.6" |
| Headroom — front | 34.7" |
| Headroom — rear | 33.4" |

**Major standard equipment:** Caspian cloth or Cortina cord and vinyl upholstery (Florentine leather in convertible), two-way power seat (convertible only), 2-speed electric windshield wipers with washers, power windows (convertible only), power steering, power brakes, Hydra-matic automatic transmission, and 8.00 × 15 BSW tires.

## Measurements (cont.)

| | |
|---|---|
| Luggage capacity (cu. ft.) | NA |
| Fuel capacity (gals.) | 21.0 |

## Models Available

| | Style Number | Base MSRP | Change from LY | Shipping Wt. (lbs.) | Production | Change from LY |
|---|---|---|---|---|---|---|
| Sixty-Two 2-Door Hardtop | 6237 | $4,892 | 0.00% | 4670 | 19,978 | -8.97% |
| Sixty-Two 2-Door Convertible | 6267 | $5,455 | 0.00% | 4850 | 14,000 | 25.79% |
| Sixty-Two 4-Door, 4-w. HT | 6239 | $5,080 | 0.00% | 4775 | 9,984 | -29.38% |
| Sixty-Two 4-Door, 6-w. HT | 6229 | $5,080 | 0.00% | 4805 | 26,824 | 14.33% |
| TOTALS | Avg. price | $5,127 | +0.00% | Production | 70,786 | +0.15% |

# de Ville

*"A superb example of the craftsmanship and attention to detail that you will find in all 1960 Cadillacs."*

**Nameplate year of origin:** 1949 (as Hardtop designation), 1959 (as model name).
**Current bodystyle lifespan:** 1959 through 1960.
**Predecessor to this model:** de Ville (1957 to 1958).
**Replacement for this model:** de Ville (1961 to 1964).
**Percentage of division's sales volume:** 38.14%.
**Corporate siblings:** Buick Electra and Oldsmobile Ninety-Eight.
**Primary competition:** Imperial Crown, and Lincoln Premiere.
**Notable changes:** Revised rear styling, minor trim and detail changes.
**Major standard equipment:** Chadwick cloth or Cambray cloth and leather upholstery, two-way power seat, 2-speed electric windshield wipers with washers, power windows, power steering, power brakes, Hydra-matic automatic transmission, and 8.00 × 15 BSW tires.

## Measurements

| | |
|---|---|
| Wheelbase | 130.0" |
| Length | 225.0" |
| Width | 79.9" |
| Height | 54.3" |
| Legroom — front | 45.8" |
| Legroom — rear | 45.6" |
| Headroom — front | 34.7" |
| Headroom — rear | 33.4" |
| Luggage capacity (cu. ft.) | NA |
| Fuel capacity (gals.) | 21.0 |

## Models Available

| | Style Number | Base MSRP | Change from LY | Shipping Wt. (lbs.) | Production | Change from LY |
|---|---|---|---|---|---|---|
| Coupe de Ville 2-Door Hardtop | 6337 | $5,252 | 0.00% | 4705 | 21,585 | -1.55% |
| Sedan de Ville 4-Door, 4-w. HT | 6339 | $5,498 | 0.00% | 4815 | 9,225 | -25.05% |
| Sedan de Ville 4-Door, 6-w. HT | 6329 | $5,498 | 0.00% | 4835 | 22,579 | 17.86% |
| TOTALS | Avg. price | $5,416 | +0.00% | Production | 53,389 | +0.00% |

# Eldorado

*"The finest expression of the new era of automotive elegance created this year by Cadillac."*

**Nameplate year of origin:** 1953.
**Current bodystyle lifespan:** 1959 through 1960.
**Predecessor to this model:** Eldorado (1957 to 1958).
**Replacement for this model:** Eldorado (1961 to 1964).
**Percentage of division's sales volume:** 1.76%.
**Corporate siblings:** Buick Electra and Oldsmobile Ninety-Eight.
**Primary competition:** Lincoln Continental Mark V.
**Notable changes:** Revised rear styling, minor trim and detail changes. Brougham had revised grille.
**Major standard equipment:** Leather or cloth and leather upholstery, six-way power seat, 2-speed electric windshield wipers with washers, AM radio with antenna, Cadillac heating system, fog lamps, remote-control trunk release, power windows and vent windows, power door locks, power steering, power brakes, Hydra-matic automatic transmission, air suspension, and 8.00 × 15 WSW tires. Brougham adds: Custom coachwork body styling, cruise control, Guide-Matic headlamp dimmers, tinted glass and air conditioning.

## Measurements

| | |
|---|---|
| Wheelbase | 130.0" |
| Length | 225.0" |
| Width | 79.9" |
| Height | 54.3" |
| Legroom — front | 45.8" |
| Legroom — rear | 45.6" |
| Headroom — front | 34.7" |
| Headroom — rear | 33.4" |
| Luggage capacity (cu. ft.) | NA |
| Fuel capacity (gals.) | 21.0 |

## Models Available

| | Style Number | Base MSRP | Change from LY | Shipping Wt. (lbs.) | Production | Change from LY |
|---|---|---|---|---|---|---|
| Eldorado Seville 2-Door Hardtop | 6437 | $7,401 | 0.00% | 4855 | 1,075 | 10.26% |
| Eldorado Biarritz 2-Door Convertible | 6467 | $7,401 | 0.00% | 5060 | 1,285 | -2.65% |
| Brougham 4-Door Hardtop Sedan | 6929 | $13,075 | 0.00% | NA | 101 | 2.02% |
| TOTALS | | Avg. price $9,292 | +0.00% | Production 2,461 | | +2.79% |

# Fleetwood Sixty-Special

*"Recognized as a motor car of custom design and coachwork."*

**Nameplate year of origin:** 1938.
**Current bodystyle lifespan:** 1959 through 1960.
**Predecessor to this model:** Fleetwood Sixty-Special (1957 to 1958).
**Replacement for this model:** Fleetwood Sixty-Special (1961 to 1964).
**Percentage of division's sales volume:** 8.43%.
**Corporate siblings:** Buick Electra and Oldsmobile Ninety-Eight.
**Primary competition:** Imperial LeBaron and Lincoln Continental Mark V.
**Notable changes:** Revised rear styling, minor trim and detail changes.
**Major standard equipment:** Cardinal cloth or Clarion cloth and Florentine leather upholstery, two-way power seat, 2-speed electric windshield wipers with washers, power windows, power steering, power brakes, Hydra-matic automatic transmission, and 8.00 × 15 BSW tires.

## Measurements

| | |
|---|---|
| Wheelbase | 130.0" |
| Length | 225.0" |
| Width | 79.9" |
| Height | 56.2" |
| Legroom — front | 45.8" |
| Legroom — rear | 44.6" |
| Headroom — front | 33.9" |
| Headroom — rear | 33.1" |
| Luggage capacity (cu. ft.) | NA |
| Fuel capacity (gals.) | 21.0 |

## Models Available

| | Style Number | Base MSRP | Change from LY | Shipping Wt. (lbs.) | Production | Change from LY |
|---|---|---|---|---|---|---|
| Fl. Sixty-Special 4-Dr. Sedan | 6029 | $6,233 | 0.00% | 4880 | 11,800 | -3.67% |
| TOTALS | | Avg. price $6,233 | +0.00% | Production 11,800 | | -3.67% |

# Fleetwood Seventy-Five

*"Perhaps the most distinguished presentation
of Cadillac's new styling and craftsmanship."*

**Nameplate year of origin:** 1927 (Fleetwood bodies), 1936 (75 series).
**Current bodystyle lifespan:** 1959 through 1965.
**Predecessor to this model:** Fleetwood 75 (1957 to 1958).
**Replacement for this model:** Fleetwood 75 (1966).
**Percentage of division's sales volume:** 1.11%.
**Corporate siblings:** None.
**Primary competition:** Crown Imperial Limousine and Lincoln Continental
     Mark V Executive Sedan.
**Notable changes:** Revised rear styling, minor trim and detail changes.
**Major standard equipment:** Bedford cord or broadcloth upholstery with leather
     chauffeur compartment trim, two-way power seat, 2-speed electric windshield
     wipers with washers, power windows, power steering, power brakes, Hydra-
     matic automatic transmission, and 8.20 × 15 BSW tires.

## Measurements

| | |
|---|---|
| Wheelbase | 149.8" |
| Length | 244.8" |
| Width | 80.6" |
| Height | 59.3" |
| Legroom — front | 44.2" |
| Legroom — rear | 37.8"* |
| Headroom — front | 36.3" |
| Headroom — rear | 34.8" |
| Luggage capacity (cu. ft.) | NA |
| Fuel capacity (gals.) | 21.0 |

*With jump seats.*

## Models Available

| | Style Number | Base MSRP | Change from LY | Shipping Wt. (lbs.) | Production | Change from LY |
|---|---|---|---|---|---|---|
| Fl. Seventy-Five 4-Door Sedan | 6723 | $9,533 | 0.00% | 5475 | 718 | 1.13% |
| Fl. Seventy-Five 4-Dr. Limousine | 6733 | $9,748 | 0.00% | 5560 | 832 | 20.58% |
| TOTALS | | Avg. price $9,641 | +0.00% | Production | 1,550 | +10.7% |

# CHEVROLET

*"Space. Spirit. Splendor. '60 Chevrolet!"*

For 1960, Chevrolet entered the compact car market, as did its key competitors. However, the marketing strategy resulted in a different car from the others. While Ford and Chrysler went very much the conventional route, with a front engine (inline six-cylinder), rear wheel drive automobile, Chevrolet chose to combat the main competitive threat, Volkswagen, head-on. An all-aluminum, air-cooled, horizontally-opposed six-cylinder engine was chosen to power the small, rear wheel drive car that featured full "Quadri-Flex" independent suspension. Interiors were generally sparse, but did offer sporty features like bucket seats, gauges, and vinyl upholstery.

While styling was more conventional than the VW, the sporting connotation implied by the Corvair style was appealing to buyers. Initially, 4-Door Sedans were the only offerings, with 2-Doors coming on board at mid-year. However, a 4-Door was something that VW didn't offer, and as a result nearly three-quarters of all Corvairs sold were 4-Door models. The chosen strategy worked, as first year sales of over 250,000 were recorded. The best news for GM was that unlike its competition, the Corvair did not take away very many sales from the maker's traditional line of cars. With the Valiant and Falcon being essentially smaller versions of their manufacturers' big cars, they cannibalized sales of those full-size models. The Corvair was distinctive enough to generally pull sales away from those who would have bought imported cars or smaller domestic models like the Rambler. In that respect General Motors and Chevrolet had a success.

Full-size and Corvette models received the period-typical annual styling changes needed to differentiate model years. The Corvette received mostly trim and detail changes. Full-size models sported a toned-down version of their gull-wing tail fins. At the front end, they lost the vents above the headlights that somehow seemed to visually lighten the front end, and give it a cleaner look. As for model changes, a 2-Door Hardtop returned to the BelAir line, after a one-year absence. Finally, a new Fleetmaster sub-series was added to the base Biscayne models. Essentially this line was intended for fleet buyers, and it lacked amenities such as dual sun visors, electric windshield wipers, a cigarette lighter, and front arm rests.

Corvair, *Motor Trend* Car of the Year

Biscayne 4-Door Sedan

BelAir 4-Door Hardtop

Kingswood 4-Door Wagon

Impala 2-Door Hardtop

Corvette 2-Door Convertible

**Model year production:** 1,651,753, up 14.18% from 1959.
**Domestic market share:** 27.45% (1st place).
**Base price range:** $1,984 to $3,872.
**Industry average base price:** $3,391.
**Chevrolet average base price:** $2,493.
**Introduction date:** October 2, 1959. Corvair 500 and 700 coupes added January 1960, and Monza introduced May 1960.
**Assembly plants:** Atlanta, GA (A); Baltimore, MD (B); Flint, MI (F); Framingham, MA (G); Janesville, WI (J); Kansas City, MO (K); Los Angeles, CA (L); Norwood, OH (N); Oakland, CA (O); St. Louis, MO (S); Tarrytown, NY (T); and Willow Run, MI (W).
**Data plate identification:** Twelve digit code read as follows: 1st digit 0 for 1960; four digit style number (see listings below; 2nd and 3rd digits identify series and engine; 4th and 5th indicate body style); 6th digit is assembly plant code; 100001 and up for serial number. *Example:* 01511S100001 is a 1960 Chevrolet BelAir 2-Door Sedan, 6-cylinder, serial number 100001, built in St. Louis, MO.

## Powertrains

| Engine | Gross HP | Transmission Availability | Corvair | Biscayne/ BelAir/Impala | Corvette |
|---|---|---|---|---|---|
| 145 CID Turbo-Air, 2 × 1-bbl., Flat 6 | 80 | 3-speed manual | S | - | - |
| | | 4-speed manual | $65 | - | - |
| | | 2-sp. Powerglide Automatic | $146 | - | - |
| 145 CID Super Turbo-Air, 2 × 1-bbl., Flat 6 | 95 | 3-speed manual | $27 | - | - |
| | | 4-speed manual | $92 | - | - |
| | | 2-sp. Powerglide Automatic | $173 | - | - |
| 235.5 CID Hi-Thrift, 1-bbl., 6-cyl. | 135 | 3-speed manual | - | S | - |
| | | Overdrive | - | $108 | - |
| | | 2-sp. Powerglide Automatic | - | $188 | - |
| 283 CID Economy Turbo-Fire, 2-bbl., V8 | 170 | 3-speed manual | - | $107 | - |
| | | Overdrive | - | $215 | - |
| | | 2- sp. Powerglide Automatic | - | $306 | - |
| | | Turboglide Automatic | - | $317 | - |

| Engine | Gross HP | Transmission Availability | Corvair | Biscayne/ BelAir/Impala | Corvette |
|---|---|---|---|---|---|
| 283 CID Super Turbo-Fire, 4-bbl., V8 | 230 | 3-speed manual | - | $136 | S |
| | | 4-speed manual | - | - | $188 |
| | | Overdrive | - | $244 | - |
| | | 2- sp. Powerglide Automatic | - | $335 | $199 |
| | | Turboglide Automatic | - | $346 | - |
| 283 CID Corvette, 2 × 4-bbl., V8 | 245 | 3-speed manual | - | - | $151 |
| | | 4-speed manual | - | - | $334 |
| | | 2- sp. Powerglide Automatic | - | - | $345 |
| 283 CID Corvette, 2 × 4-bbl., V8 | 270 | 3-speed manual | - | - | $183 |
| | | 4-speed manual | - | - | $366 |
| | | 2- sp. Powerglide Automatic | - | - | $377 |
| 283 CID Ramjet, Fuel-Injected V8 | 275 | 3-speed manual | - | - | $484 |
| | | 4-speed manual | - | - | $672 |
| 348 CID Turbo-Thrust, 4-bbl., V8 | 250 | 3-speed manual | - | $188 | - |
| | | 4-speed manual | - | $376 | - |
| | | Turboglide Automatic | - | $398 | - |
| 348 CID Super Turbo-Thrust, 3 × 2-bbl., V8 | 280 | 3-speed manual | - | $268 | - |
| | | 4-speed manual | - | $456 | - |
| | | Turboglide Automatic | - | $478 | - |
| 348 CID Special Turbo-Thrust, 4-bbl., V8 | 305 | 2- sp. Powerglide Automatic — HD | - | $565 | - |
| 348 CID Turbo-Thrust, 4-bbl., V8 | 320 | 3-speed manual | - | $418 | - |
| | | 4-speed manual | - | $606 | - |
| 348 CID Special Turbo-Thrust, 3 × 2-bbl., V8 | 335 | 3-speed manual | - | $440 | - |
| | | 4-speed manual | - | $628 | - |

## Major Options

| | Corvair | Full-size | Corvette |
|---|---|---|---|
| Air conditioning (NA 4-cyl.) | - | $364 | - |
| Soft Ray tinted glass | $27 | $38 | $16 |
| Power steering (NA 4-cyl.) | - | $75 | - |
| Power brakes | - | $43 | - |
| Power windows (N/A on all) | - | $102 | $59 |
| Electric clock | $16 | $16 | S |
| Pushbutton AM radio | $57 | $57 | $138 |
| Whitewall tires — Std. size | $21 | $32–$40 | $32 |

Options common to most models. (- = Not Available; S = Standard.) Items may be standard equipment, optional at different pricing, or unavailable on certain models. This chart is only a guide.

## Paint Colors

| | Code |
|---|---|
| Tuxedo Black | 900* |
| Seafoam Green | 903 |
| Arbor Green Met. | 905 |
| Jewel Blue Met. | 912* |
| Midnight Blue Metallic | 914 |
| Twilight Turquoise Met. | 915 |
| Seamist Turquoise | 917 |
| Fawn Beige Metallic | 920* |
| Roman Red | 923* |
| Coronna Cream | 925 |
| Ermine White | 936* |
| Almond Beige | 938 |
| Sateen Silver Metallic | 940* |
| Shadow Gray Metallic | 941 |
| Honduras Maroon Met. | 948* |

*Available on Corvette also.

# Corvair

*"Specifically designed the way a compact car should be."*

**Nameplate year of origin:** 1960.
**Current bodystyle lifespan:** 1960 through 1964.
**Predecessor to this model:** None.

## Measurements

| | |
|---|---|
| Wheelbase | 108.0" |
| Length | 180.0" |

Replacement for this model: Corvair (1965 to 1969).
Percentage of division's sales volume: 15.14%.
Corporate siblings: None.
Primary competition: Rambler American, Ford Falcon, Plymouth Valiant and
   Studebaker Lark.
Notable changes: All-new model for 1960.
Major standard equipment: Fabric and vinyl front bench seat, left-hand sun
   visor, turn signals, center dome light, electric windshield wipers, and 6.50 ×
   13 BSW tires. 700 adds: Luggage compartment trim, color-keyed floor mats,
   dual horns, and automatic dome lamp switch. Monza adds: All-vinyl bucket
   seats, folding rear seat, dual sun visors, glove box light, and additional exterior chrome trim.

## Measurements (cont.)

| | |
|---|---|
| Width | 66.9" |
| Height | 51.3" |
| Legroom — front | 42.8" |
| Legroom — rear | 36.5" |
| Headroom — front | 38.9" |
| Headroom — rear | 38.0" |
| Cargo capacity (cu. ft.) | 15.6 |
| Fuel capacity (gals.) | 11.0 |

## Models Available

| | Style Number | Base MSRP | Change from LY | Shipping Wt. (lbs.) | Production | Change from LY |
|---|---|---|---|---|---|---|
| Corvair 500 2-Door Club Coupe | 0527 | $1,984 | NEW | 2270 | 14,628 | NEW |
| Corvair 500 4-Door Sedan | 0569 | $2,038 | NEW | 2305 | 47,683 | NEW |
| Corvair Deluxe 700 2-Door Coupe | 0727 | $2,049 | NEW | 2290 | 36,562 | NEW |
| Corvair Deluxe 700 4-Door Sedan | 0769 | $2,103 | NEW | 2315 | 139,208 | NEW |
| Corvair Monza 900 2-Dr. Club Cpe. | 0927 | $2,238 | NEW | 2280 | 11,926 | NEW |
| TOTALS | Avg. price | $2,082 | NEW | Production | 250,007 | NEW |

# Biscayne

*"Lowest priced of all full-sized Chevrolets."*

Nameplate year of origin: 1958.
Current bodystyle lifespan: 1959 through 1960.
Predecessor to this model: Biscayne (1958).
Replacement for this model: Biscayne (1961 to 1964).
Percentage of division's sales volume: 84.24% (all full-size Chevrolets com-
   bined).
Corporate siblings: Buick LeSabre/Invicta, Olds 88, Pontiac Catalina/Star
   Chief/Bonneville.
Primary competition: Rambler Ambassador, Dodge Polara, Ford
   Custom/Galaxie, and Plymouth Fury.
Notable changes: New grille and revised rear end and trim.
Major standard equipment: Nylon pattern cloth seat upholstery, foam cushion
   front seats, front door armrests, dual sun visors, electric windshield wipers,
   cigar lighter, glove compartment lock and 7.50 × 14 BSW tires. Brookwood
   adds: Simulated-weave vinyl upholstery and 8.00 × 14 BSW tires.

## Measurements

| | Cars | Wagons |
|---|---|---|
| Wheelbase | 119.0" | 119.0" |
| Length | 210.8" | 210.8" |
| Width | 80.8" | 80.8" |
| Height (Sedan only) | 56.0" | 56.0" |
| Legroom — front | 44.5" | 44.5" |
| Legroom — rear | 42.5" | 42.5" |
| Headroom — front | 36.1" | 36.1" |
| Headroom — rear | 34.3" | 34.3" |
| Cargo capacity (cu. ft.) | 30** | 90.0 |
| Fuel capacity (gals.) | 20.0 | 17.0* |

*18.0 on 9-passenger wagons.   **61 cu. ft. on Utility
Sedan.

## Models Available

| | Style Number | Base MSRP | Change from LY | Shipping Wt. (lbs.) | Production | Change from LY |
|---|---|---|---|---|---|---|
| Biscayne Fleetmaster 2-Dr. Sedan | 1311 | $2,230 | NEW | 3480 | | NEW |
| Biscayne Fleetmaster 4-Dr. Sedan | 1319 | $2,284 | NEW | 3545 | | NEW |
| Biscayne 2-Dr., 3-p. Utility Sedan | 1121 | $2,175 | 0.69% | 3455 | | - |
| Biscayne 2-Door Sedan | 1111 | $2,262 | 0.67% | 3485 | | - |
| Biscayne 4-Door Sedan | 1119 | $2,316 | 0.65% | 3555 | | - |
| Brookwood 2-Door Wagon | 1115 | $2,586 | 0.58% | 3845 | 14,663 | -29.37% |
| Brookwood 4-Dr., 2-S. Wagon | 1135 | $2,653 | 0.57% | 3935 | | - |
| TOTALS | Avg. price | $2,358 | -1.1% | | Production | NA |

# BelAir

*"A beautiful blend of elegance and economy."*

**Nameplate year of origin:** 1950.
**Current bodystyle lifespan:** 1959 through 1960.
**Predecessor to this model:** BelAir (1958).
**Replacement for this model:** BelAir (1961 to 1964).
**Percentage of division's sales volume:** 84.24% (all full-size Chevrolets combined).
**Corporate siblings:** Buick LeSabre/Invicta, Olds 88, Pontiac Catalina/Star Chief/Bonneville.
**Primary competition:** Rambler Ambassador, Dodge Polara, Ford Custom/Galaxie, and Plymouth Fury.
**Notable changes:** New grille and revised rear end and trim.
**Major standard equipment:** Nylon pattern cloth seat upholstery, cloth headliner, foam cushion front and rear seats, front and rear door armrests, combination carpet and vinyl coated rubber floor mats, electric windshield wipers, interior lighting, and 7.50 × 14 BSW tires. Parkwood and Kingswood add: Vinyl upholstery, vinyl headliner, power operated rear window (Kingswood only) and 8.00 × 14 BSW tires.

## Measurements

|  | Cars | Wagons |
|---|---|---|
| Wheelbase | 119.0" | 119.0" |
| Length | 210.8" | 210.8" |
| Width | 80.8" | 80.8" |
| Height (Sedan only) | 56.0" | 56.0" |
| Legroom — front | 44.5" | 44.5" |
| Legroom — rear | 42.5" | 42.5" |
| Headroom — front | 36.1" | 36.1" |
| Headroom — rear | 34.3" | 34.3" |
| Cargo capacity (cu. ft.) | 30.0 | 90.0 |
| Fuel capacity (gals.) | 20.0 | 17.0* |

*18.0 on 9-passenger wagons.

## Models Available

|  | Style Number | Base MSRP | Change from LY | Shipping Wt. (lbs.) | Production | Change from LY |
|---|---|---|---|---|---|---|
| Bel Air 2-Door Sedan | 1511 | $2,384 | -0.08% | 3490 | 228,322 | -19.01% |
| Bel Air 2-Door Hardtop | 1537 | $2,489 | NEW | 3515 |  | NEW |
| Bel Air 4-Door Sedan | 1519 | $2,438 | -0.08% | 3565 |  | - |
| Bel Air 4-Door Hardtop | 1539 | $2,554 | -0.08% | 3605 |  | - |
| Parkwood 4-Dr., 2-S. Wagon | 1535 | $2,747 | -0.07% | 3945 |  | - |
| Kingswood 4-Dr., 3-S. Wagon | 1545 | $2,850 | -0.07% | 3990 |  | - |
| TOTALS | | *Avg. price* $2,577 | -0.07% | | *Production* NA | |

# Impala

*"Here is the luxury leader of the low-price field."*

**Nameplate year of origin:** 1958.
**Current bodystyle lifespan:** 1959 through 1960.
**Predecessor to this model:** Impala (1958).
**Replacement for this model:** Impala (1961 to 1964).
**Percentage of division's sales volume:** 84.24% (all full-size Chevrolets combined).
**Corporate siblings:** Buick LeSabre/Invicta, Olds 88, Pontiac Catalina/Star Chief/Bonneville.
**Primary competition:** Rambler Ambassador, Dodge Polara, Ford Custom/Galaxie, and Plymouth Fury.
**Notable changes:** New grille and revised rear end and trim.
**Major standard equipment:** BelAir equipment plus: Nylon pattern cloth seat upholstery (Vinyl in convertible), vinyl headliner (Cloth in 4-Door Sedan), full carpeting (combination carpet and vinyl coated rubber floor mats in convertible), and dual backup lamps.

## Measurements

|  | Cars | Wagons |
|---|---|---|
| Wheelbase | 119.0" | 119.0" |
| Length | 210.8" | 210.8" |
| Width | 80.8" | 80.8" |
| Height (Sedan only) | 56.0" | 56.0" |
| Legroom — front | 44.5" | 44.5" |
| Legroom — rear | 42.5" | 42.5" |
| Headroom — front | 36.1" | 36.1" |
| Headroom — rear | 34.3" | 34.3" |
| Cargo capacity (cu. ft.) | 30.0 | 90.0 |
| Fuel capacity (gals.) | 20.0 | 17.0* |

*18.0 on 9-passenger wagons.

## Models Available

| | Style Number | Base MSRP | Change from LY | Shipping Wt. (lbs.) | Production | Change from LY |
|---|---|---|---|---|---|---|
| Impala 2-Door Sport Coupe | 1737 | $2,597 | -0.08% | 3530 | 204,467 | 23.99% |
| Impala 2-Door Convertible | 1767 | $2,847 | -0.07% | 3625 | 79,903 | 9.81% |
| Impala 4-Door Sedan | 1719 | $2,590 | -0.08% | 3575 | 497,048 | -5.41% |
| Impala 4-Door Hardtop | 1739 | $2,662 | -0.08% | 3625 | 169,016 | -7.40% |
| Nomad 4-Dr., 2-S. Wagon | 1735 | $2,889 | -0.07% | 3955 | 198,066 | 5.01% |
| TOTALS | | *Avg. price* $2,717 | -0.07% | | *Production* 1,148,500 | |

# Corvette

*"America's Sports Car."*

**Nameplate year of origin:** 1953 (also used on show car of same year).
**Current bodystyle lifespan:** 1956 through 1962.
**Predecessor to this model:** Corvette (1953 to 1955).
**Replacement for this model:** Corvette (1963 to 1967).
**Percentage of division's sales volume:** 0.62%.
**Corporate siblings:** None.
**Primary competition:** None.
**Notable changes:** Revised trim and detail changes.
**Major standard equipment:** Deep-contoured bucket seats, deep-pile carpeting, complete instrumentation, manually operated folding top or removable hardtop, and 6.70 × 15 BSW tires.

## Measurements

| | |
|---|---|
| Wheelbase | 102.0" |
| Length | 177.2" |
| Width | 72.8" |
| Height | 51.6" |
| Legroom — front | 45.1" |
| Legroom — rear | NA |
| Headroom — front | 35.3" |
| Headroom — rear | NA |
| Cargo capacity (cu. ft.) | NA |
| Fuel capacity (gals.) | 16.4 |

## Models Available

| | Style Number | Base MSRP | Change from LY | Shipping Wt. (lbs.) | Production | Change from LY |
|---|---|---|---|---|---|---|
| Corvette 2-Door Convertible | 0867 | $3,872 | -0.08% | 2840 | 10,261 | +6.11% |
| TOTALS | | *Avg. price* $3,872 | -0.08% | | *Production* 10,261 | +6.11% |

# CHRYSLER

*"The car of your life for the time of your life!"*

All new 1960 Chrysler models were built with unitbody construction. This meant that all major body components were welded to the frame instead of bolted, with the ensuing effect to be more rigidity and less noise. While it was an excellent attempt at modernization, and it did have the desired effect upon improving the cars and their quality, sales gains were made with a massive advertising effort. Unfortunately, the debacle over the 1957–1958 quality issues far overshadowed any good product that was coming out of Chrysler during this period. Styling for the new bodies featured the mighty Chrysler 300's grille on all models, albeit with some modifications.

The Windsor and Saratoga featured a crosshatch style grille, while the New Yorker had a horizontal bar grille.

Out back, a more slender tailfin seemingly aimed higher than ever towards the sky. On the Windsor, a full-length body molding ran from the trailing edge of the front wheel opening, back above the rear wheel opening, and ending at a point at the top edge of the rear bumper. On the Saratoga, this molding was available slightly larger with a paint accent. This piece of trim was not on the New Yorker, but the top line car did sport a full-length rocker panel molding that included wheel opening trim. Interiors featured a Chrysler-exclusive, three-dimensional instrument cluster coined "electro-luminescent Astra-Dome" instrumentation. This new ball-type cluster housed all gauges on three planes, and all were backlit, to give one of the most unusual instrument layouts of this period. It was surprisingly easy to read, even at night.

Windsor 2-Door Hardtop

Windsor 4-Door Sedan

New Yorker 2-Door Convertible

New Yorker 4-Door Hardtop
Town & Country Wagon

**Model year production:** 77,285, up 10.46% over 1959.
**Domestic market share:** 1.28% (12th place)
**Base price range:** $3194 to $5841.
**Industry average base price:** $3,391.
**Chrysler average base price:** $4,273.
**Introduction date:** October 1959.
**Assembly plants:** Detroit (Jefferson Ave.), MI (3); and Los Angeles, CA (5).

**Data plate identification:** Ten digit code read as follows: 1st digit is a make identity letter (C = Chrysler), 2nd number identifies series (1–7; Windsor is 1), 3rd digit indicates year (0 for 1960); 4th digit is assembly plant code; followed by 100001 and up for serial number. Body style identification found on separate plate *Example:* C103100001 is a 1960 Chrysler Windsor, serial number 100001, built in Detroit, MI.

## Powertrains

| Engine | Gross HP | Transmission Availability | Windsor | Saratoga | New Yorker | 300-F |
|---|---|---|---|---|---|---|
| 383 CID Golden Lion, 2-bbl., V8 | 305 | 3-speed manual | S | - | - | - |
|  |  | Torqueflite automatic | $227 | - | - | - |
| 383 CID Golden Lion, 4-bbl., V8 | 325 | Torqueflite automatic | - | S | - | - |
| 413 CID Golden Lion, 4-bbl., V8 | 350 | Torqueflite automatic | - | - | S | - |
| 413 CID Long Ram, 2 × 4-bbl., V8 | 375 | Torqueflite automatic* | - | - | - | S |
| 413 CID Short Ram, 2 × 4-bbl., V8 | 400 | Torqueflite automatic* | - | - | - | $ |

*A Pont-A-Mousson 4-speed manual transmission was installed in fewer than 15 300-F models at unknown cost.

## Major Options

|  | Windsor | Saratoga | New Yorker | 300-F |
|---|---|---|---|---|
| Heater and defroster | $102 | $102 | $102 | $102 |
| Airtemp air conditioning | $510 | $510 | $510 | $510 |
| Solex tinted glass | $43 | $43 | $43 | $43 |
| Power steering | $108 | S | S | S |
| Power brakes | $44 | S | S | S |
| Power seat (swivel on 300-F) | $102 | $102 | $102 | S |
| Power windows | $108 | $108 | S | S |
| Golden Tune AM radio | $100 | $100 | $100 | $100 |
| White sidewall tires — std. sizes | $42 | $46 | $51 | S |

Options common to most models. (S = Standard equipment.) Items may be standard equipment, optional at different pricing, or unavailable on certain models. This chart is only a guide.

## Paint Colors

|  | Code |
|---|---|
| Sunburst | AA-1 |
| Formal Black | BB-1 |
| Starlight Blue | CC-1 |
| Polar Blue Metallic | DD-1 |
| Spruce Green | FF-1 |
| Ivy Green Metallic | GG-1 |
| Silverpine Metallic | HH-1 |
| Seaspray | JJ-1 |
| Bluegrass Metallic | KK-1 |
| Sheffield Silver Metallic | LL-1 |
| Executive Gray Metallic | NN-1 |
| Regent Ruby | OO-1 |
| Toreador Red Metallic | PP-1 |
| Lilac | RR-1 |
| Daytona Sand | TT-1 |
| Autumn Haze Metallic | UU-1 |
| Alaskan White | WW-1 |
| Petal Pink | YY-1 |
| Terra Cotta Metallic | ZZ-1 |

# Windsor

*"Fresh, fiery beauty at a surprisingly modest price."*

**Nameplate year of origin:** 1939.
**Current bodystyle lifespan:** 1960 (Windsor); 1961 through 1964 (Newport — major restyle in 1963).
**Predecessor to this model:** Windsor (1957 to 1959).
**Replacement for this model:** Newport (1965 to 1966).
**Percentage of division's sales volume:** 53.25%.
**Corporate siblings:** Dodge Polara, and DeSoto Fireflite.
**Primary competition:** Buick Invicta, Mercury Monterey and Oldsmobile Super 88.
**Notable changes:** Completely restyled.
**Major standard equipment:** Cloth and vinyl front bench seat, full-floor coverings, sun visors, exterior bright side moldings and 8.00 × 14 BSW tires. Town & Country adds: 8.50 × 14 BSW tires.

## Measurements

|  | Cars | Wagons |
|---|---|---|
| Wheelbase | 122.0" | 122.0" |
| Length | 215.4" | 216.0" |
| Width | 79.4" | 79.4" |
| Height | 54.9" | 55.2" |
| Legroom — front | 46.2" | 46.2" |
| Legroom — rear | 44.1" | 44.0" |
| Headroom — front | 34.4" | 34.4" |
| Headroom — rear | 34.5" | 34.6" |
| Cargo capacity (cu. ft.) | NA | NA |
| Fuel capacity (gals.) | 23.0 | 22.0 |

## Models Available

|  | Style Number | Base MSRP | Change from LY | Shipping Wt. (lbs.) | Production | Change from LY |
|---|---|---|---|---|---|---|
| Windsor 2-Door Hardtop | PC-1 23 | $3,279 | -0.30% | 3855 | 6,496 | -4.12% |
| Windsor 2-Door Convertible | PC-1 27 | $3,623 | 0.08% | 3855 | 1,467 | 52.65% |
| Windsor 4-Door Sedan | PC-1 41 | $3,194 | -0.31% | 3815 | 25,152 | 26.33% |
| Windsor 4-Door Hardtop | PC-1 43 | $3,343 | -0.30% | 3850 | 5,897 | -3.07% |
| W. Town & Country 4-Dr., 2-S. Wgn. | PC-1 46 | $3,733 | 1.14% | 4235 | 1,120 | 12.90% |
| W. Town & Country 4-Dr., 3-S. Wgn. | PC-1 46 | $3,814 | -1.65% | 4390 | 1,026 | 36.62% |
| TOTALS |  | Avg. price $3,498 | -0.2%* | Production | 41,158 | +16.03% |

# Saratoga

*"Talented performer with a ready-to-go look."*

**Nameplate year of origin:** 1939.
**Current bodystyle lifespan:** 1960 (Saratoga); 1961 (Windsor); 1962 through 1964 (300 — major restyle in 1963).
**Predecessor to this model:** Saratoga (1957 to 1959).
**Replacement for this model:** 300 (1965 to 1966).
**Percentage of division's sales volume:** 20.09%.
**Corporate siblings:** Chrysler New Yorker, and 300-F and DeSoto Adventurer.
**Primary competition:** Buick Invicta, Mercury Park Lane and Oldsmobile Super 88.
**Notable changes:** Completely restyled.
**Major standard equipment:** Cloth and vinyl front bench seat, pile carpeting, padded dash, map lights, electric clock, sun visors, windshield washers, exterior bright side moldings, power steering, power brakes, automatic transmission, full wheel covers, and 8.50 × 14 BSW tires.

## Measurements

Wheelbase
126.0"
Length
219.4"
Width
79.4"
Height
55.1"
Legroom — front
46.2"
Legroom — rear

## Models Available

| | Style Number | Base MSRP | Change from LY | Shipping Wt. (lbs.) | Production | Change from LY |
|---|---|---|---|---|---|---|
| Saratoga 2-Door Hardtop | PC-2 23 | $3,989 | -0.92% | 4030 | 2,963 | -21.05% |
| Saratoga 4-Door Sedan | PC-2 41 | $3,929 | -0.93% | 4010 | 8,463 | -3.64% |
| Saratoga 4-Door Hardtop | PC-2 43 | $4,067 | -0.90% | 4035 | 4,099 | -17.07% |
| TOTALS | Avg. price | $3,995 | -0.91% | Production | 15,525 | -11.17% |

# New Yorker

*"The finest Chrysler ever built."*

**Nameplate year of origin:** 1939 (altered from 1938 New York Special model).
**Current bodystyle lifespan:** 1960 through 1964 (major restyle in 1963).
**Predecessor to this model:** New Yorker (1957 to 1959).
**Replacement for this model:** New Yorker (1965 to 1966).
**Percentage of division's sales volume:** 19.24%.
**Corporate siblings:** Chrysler Saratoga, and 300-F, and DeSoto Adventurer.
**Primary competition:** Buick Electra, Lincoln and Oldsmobile 98.
**Notable changes:** Completely restyled.
**Major standard equipment:** Cloth and vinyl front bench seat, pile carpeting, padded dash, map lights, power windows, electric clock, sun visors, remote-control LH outside rearview mirror, windshield washers, exterior protection package, exclusive exterior bright trim, power steering, power brakes, automatic transmission, full wheel covers, and 9.00 × 14 BSW tires.

## Measurements

| | Cars | Wagons |
|---|---|---|
| Wheelbase | 126.0" | 126.0" |
| Length | 219.6" | 220.0" |
| Width | 79.4" | 79.4" |
| Height | 55.6" | 55.2" |
| Legroom — front | 46.2" | 46.2" |
| Legroom — rear | 44.1" | 44.0" |
| Headroom — front | 34.4" | 34.4" |
| Headroom — rear | 34.5" | 34.6" |
| Cargo capacity (cu. ft.) | NA | NA |
| Fuel capacity (gals.) | 23.0 | 22.0 |

## Models Available

| | Style Number | Base MSRP | Change from LY | Shipping Wt. (lbs.) | Production | Change from LY |
|---|---|---|---|---|---|---|
| New Yorker 2-Door Hardtop | PC-3 23 | $4,461 | -0.34% | 4175 | 2,835 | 16.43% |
| New Yorker 2-Door Convertible | PC-3 27 | $4,875 | -0.31% | 4185 | 556 | 94.41% |

| | Style Number | Base MSRP | Change from LY | Shipping Wt. (lbs.) | Production | Change from LY |
|---|---|---|---|---|---|---|
| New Yorker 4-Door Sedan | PC-3 41 | $4,409 | -0.34% | 4145 | 9,079 | 16.52% |
| New Yorker 4-Door Hardtop | PC-3 43 | $4,518 | -0.33% | 4175 | 5,625 | 17.07% |
| N. Y. Town & Country 4-Dr., 2-S. W. | PC-3 46 | $5,022 | 0.50% | 4515 | 624 | 40.54% |
| N. Y. Town & Country 4-Dr., 3-S. W. | PC-3 46 | $5,131 | -1.55% | 4535 | 671 | 18.97% |
| TOTALS | | Avg. price $4,736 | -0.39% | Production | 19,390 | +18.77% |

# 300-F

*"The lion-hearted Chrysler sport car."*

**Nameplate year of origin:** 1955.
**Current bodystyle lifespan:** 1960 through 1964 (Letter series — major restyle in 1963).
**Predecessor to this model:** 300 (Letter series; 1957 to 1959).
**Replacement for this model:** 300-L (1965).
**Percentage of division's sales volume:** 19.24%.
**Corporate siblings:** Chrysler Saratoga, New Yorker and DeSoto Adventurer.
**Primary competition:** Ford Thunderbird.
**Notable changes:** Completely restyled.
**Major standard equipment:** Leather power-swivel bucket front seats, pile carpeting, padded dash, map lights, power windows, electric clock, sun visors, exclusive exterior bright trim, power steering, power brakes, automatic transmission, full wheel covers, and 9.00 × 14 WSW tires.

### Measurements

| | |
|---|---|
| Wheelbase | 126.0" |
| Length | 219.6" |
| Width | 79.4" |
| Height | 55.1" |
| Legroom — front | 45.6" |
| Legroom — rear | 35.5" |
| Headroom — front | 34.1" |
| Headroom — rear | 34.2" |
| Cargo capacity (cu. ft.) | NA |
| Fuel capacity (gals.) | 23.0 |

### Models Available

| | Style Number | Base MSRP | Change from LY | Shipping Wt. (lbs.) | Production | Change from LY |
|---|---|---|---|---|---|---|
| 300-F 2-Door Hardtop | PC-3 23 | $5,411 | 1.73% | 4270 | 964 | 75.27% |
| 300-F 2-Door Convertible | PC-3 27 | $5,841 | 1.60% | 4310 | 248 | 77.14% |
| TOTALS | | Avg. price $5,626 | +1.66% | Production | 1,212 | +75.65% |

# DESOTO

*"Nothing says Quality like the 1960 DeSoto."*

DeSoto entered the 1960 model year with all-new styling and unit-body construction, sharing nearly everything with the new Chryslers. The front styling was very similar to the new Chryslers, except that at the bottom of the grille, a thin strip extended to the outer edges, under the headlights, and ended where the bumper kicked up at the ends. From the side or rear, it was next to impossible to tell a DeSoto from a Chrysler Windsor as only minor trim variations distinguished them. A uniquely DeSoto instrument panel was designed, being far more traditional in execution than the three-dimensional affair adopted by Chrysler. It too featured a three-level instrument cluster, however. A lower level of push and pull knobs was topped by a mid-level row of push buttons for airflow control and transmission selection. The top line of sight held the gauges.

In 1959, there had been four separate and distinct model lines. For the new model year, the model line and powertrain options were scaled back considerably. All sta-

tion wagon models were discontinued, as were the convertibles. Only the Fireflite and Adventurer series were left, and they were distinguished by the powerplant under the hood. Obviously, Chrysler was preparing for the demise of the DeSoto.

Adventurer 2-Door Hardtop

Adventurer 2-Door Hardtop

**Model year production:** 26,081, down 43.95% from 1959.
**Domestic market share:** 0.43% (13th place).
**Base price range:** $3,017 to $3,727.
**Industry average base price:** $3,391.
**DeSoto average base price:** $3,376.
**Introduction date:** October 1959.
**Assembly plants:** Detroit (Jefferson Ave.) MI (3).

**Data plate identification:** Ten digit code read as follows: 1st and 2nd numbers identify series (Fireflite is 71, Adventurer is 72); 3rd digit 0 for 1960; 4th digit is assembly plant code; followed by 100001 and up for serial number. Body style identification found on separate plate. *Example:* 7103100001 is a 1960 DeSoto Fireflite, serial number 100001, built in Detroit, MI.

## Powertrains

| Engine | Gross HP | Transmission Availability | Fireflite | Adventurer |
|---|---|---|---|---|
| 361 CID Turbo Flash, 2-bbl., V8 | 295 | 3-speed manual | S | – |
| | | Powerflite automatic | $189 | – |
| | | Torqueflite automatic | $227 | – |
| 383 CID Adventurer, 2-bbl., V8 | 305 | 3-speed manual | $31 | – |
| | | Powerflite automatic | $220 | |
| | | Torqueflite automatic | $258 | S |
| 383 CID Adventurer Mark I, 4-bbl., V8 | 325 | Torqueflite automatic | $312 | $54 |
| 383 CID Ram Charge, 2 × 4-bbl., V8 | 330 | Torqueflite automatic | – | $283 |

## Major Options

| | Fireflite | Adventurer |
|---|---|---|
| Heater and defroster | $98 | $98 |
| Airtemp air conditioning | $501 | $501 |
| Solex tinted glass | $43 | $43 |
| Variable speed windshield wipers | $7 | S |
| Power steering (with automatic) | $106 | $106 |
| Power brakes (with automatic) | $43 | $43 |
| Power seat — six-way | $101 | $101 |
| Power windows | $106 | $106 |
| AM radio | $89 | $89 |
| Full wheel covers | $19 | S |
| White sidewall tires — std. sizes | $42 | $42 |

Options common to most models. (S = Standard equipment.) Items may be standard equipment, optional at different pricing, or unavailable on certain models. This chart is only a guide.

## Paint Colors

| | Code |
|---|---|
| Yuma Yellow | AA-1 |
| Black | BB-1 |
| Jamaica Blue | CC-1 |
| Arctic Blue Metallic | DD-1 |
| Willow Green | FF-1 |
| Cypress Green Metallic | GG-1 |
| Marine Aqua | JJ-1 |
| Marine Turquoise Metallic | KK-1 |
| Silverglow Metallic | LL-1 |
| Smoke Pearl Metallic | NN-1 |
| Calcutta Ivory | TT-1 |
| Gabardine Metallic | UU-1 |
| Shell White | WW-1 |
| Adobe Rust Metallic | YY-1 |
| Russett Red Metallic | ZZ-1 |
| Bradenton Blue | QQQ |

# Fireflite

*"The quality speaks for itself."*

**Nameplate year of origin:** 1955.
**Current bodystyle lifespan:** 1960 through 1961.
**Predecessor to this model:** Fireflite (1957 to 1959).
**Replacement for this model:** Dodge Custom 880 (1962 through 1964).
**Percentage of division's sales volume:** 55.53%.
**Corporate siblings:** Chrysler Windsor, Dodge Polara and DeSoto Adventurer.
**Primary competition:** Buick LeSabre, Mercury Monterey and Oldsmobile 88.
**Notable changes:** Completely restyled. Former DeSoto line leader, now designated as entry level model.
**Major standard equipment:** Cloth and vinyl front bench 6-way manual seat, full-floor carpeting, electric windshield wipers, exterior bright side moldings and 8.00 × 14 BSW tires.

### Measurements

| | |
|---|---|
| Wheelbase | 122.0" |
| Length | 215.4" |
| Width | 79.4" |
| Height | 55.0" |
| Legroom — front | 46.1" |
| Legroom — rear | 44.1" |
| Headroom — front | 34.6" |
| Headroom — rear | 34.5" |
| Cargo capacity (cu. ft.) | NA |
| Fuel capacity (gals.) | 23.0 |

### Models Available

| | Style Number | Base MSRP | Change from LY | Shipping Wt. (lbs.) | Production | Change from LY |
|---|---|---|---|---|---|---|
| Fireflite 2-Door Hardtop | PS1-L23 | $3,102 | -19.02% | 3885 | 3,494 | +150.83% |
| Fireflite 4-Door Sedan | PS1-L41 | $3,017 | -19.82% | 3865 | 9,032 | +101.61% |
| Fireflite 4-Door Hardtop | PS1-L43 | $3,167 | -18.02% | 3865 | 1,958 | -17.17% |
| TOTALS | Avg. price | $3,095 | -23.30% | Production | 14,484 | +58.69% |

# Adventurer

*"The car you will either own or envy."*

**Nameplate year of origin:** 1956.
**Current bodystyle lifespan:** 1960 through 1961.
**Predecessor to this model:** Adventurer (1957 to 1959).
**Replacement for this model:** Dodge Custom 880 (1962 through 1964).
**Percentage of division's sales volume:** 44.47%.
**Corporate siblings:** Chrysler Windsor, Dodge Polara and DeSoto Fireflite.
**Primary competition:** Buick Invicta, Mercury Monterey and Oldsmobile Super 88.
**Notable changes:** Completely restyled. Former sport model nameplate, now designated as top line model.
**Major standard equipment:** Cloth and vinyl front bench 6-way manual seat, full-floor carpeting, padded instrument panel, Easy-Grip steering wheel, variable-speed, electric windshield wipers, backup lights, exterior bright side moldings, stainless steel wheel covers, Torqueflite automatic transmission, and 8.00 × 14 BSW tires.

### Measurements

| | |
|---|---|
| Wheelbase | 122.0" |
| Length | 217.0" |
| Width | 79.4" |
| Height | 55.0" |
| Legroom — front | 46.1" |
| Legroom — rear | 44.1" |
| Headroom — front | 34.6" |
| Headroom — rear | 33.1" |
| Cargo capacity (cu. ft.) | NA |
| Fuel capacity (gals.) | 23.0 |

### Models Available

| | Style Number | Base MSRP | Change from LY | Shipping Wt. (lbs.) | Production | Change from LY |
|---|---|---|---|---|---|---|
| Adventurer 2-Door Hardtop | PS3-M23 | $3,663 | -17.25% | 3945 | 3,092 | +424.07% |
| Adventurer 4-Door Sedan | PS3-M41 | $3,579 | NEW | 3895 | 5,746 | NEW |
| Adventurer 4-Door Hardtop | PS3-M43 | $3,727 | NEW | 3940 | 2,759 | NEW |
| TOTALS | Avg. price | $3,656 | -20.31% | Production | 11,597 | +1588.1% |

# DODGE

*"Presenting the 1960 Dodge ... in two new lines!"*

As were all other 1960 Chrysler Corporation products (except Imperial), new Dodge models were built with unit-body construction. This meant that all major body components were welded to the frame instead of bolted, making them more rigid and quieter. While it was an excellent attempt at modernization, and it did have the desired effect upon improving the cars and their quality, it did not do much to help sales, despite massive advertising of the new feature. Unfortunately, the notorious 1957–1958 quality issues far overshadowed any good coming out of Chrysler during this period. Styling was similar among all models but still carried the look of a Dodge, which was first set out with the 1955 Forward-Look cars. New for Dodge this year, and perhaps a first warning sign that Chrysler was intending to do away with the DeSoto, was a two-wheelbase carline. The smaller cars, considered economy competition for Ford and Chevrolet, rode on a 118" wheelbase shared with Plymouth. This new line was called the Dart series, and came in three trim levels: Seneca, Pioneer and Phoenix. The larger cars rode on a 122" wheelbase that was shared with DeSoto and the smaller Chryslers, as well as all Mopar station wagons. This was the conventional Dodge line and came in two models, the Matador and Polara. Dodge would use this type of split, full-size lineup through 1964. The

Dart series had taken over the position formerly occupied by the Coronet, and the larger Dodge line took the place of the Royal and Custom Royal.

Two new engines were offered in conjunction with the introduction of the smaller line of full-size cars, and both would prove very important. The first was the famous 225 CID OHV 6-cylinder "Slant 6," as it became known. This new engine put out 10 more horsepower with 5 cubic inches less displacement than the six it replaced, and had a slightly higher compression ratio. The engine was initially offered in aluminum and steel block versions, but the aluminum block was not very popular with buyers and was soon dropped. The engine was known as the "Slant 6" for its unique positioning, angled over 30 degrees in the engine compartment. The second new powerplant was the equally well known 318 CID V8, which replaced the 326 CID V8 of 1959. This new V8, specifically designed for the new, smaller full-size cars of Plymouth and Dodge, quickly proved to be a reliable engine that delivered good fuel economy. The V8 also spawned several other bored-out variants. As history has shown, both of these engines turned out to be so dependable and popular that they would survive in car applications through the early 1980s, and in truck applications through the late 1990s.

Matador 4-Door Hardtop

Polara 2-Door Convertible

Polara 4-Door Hardtop

Polara 4-Door Hardtop

**Model year production:** 565,919, up 2.6% over 1959.
**Domestic market share:** 6.1% (6th place).
**Base price range:** $2,316 to $4,756.
**Industry average base price:** $3,391.
**Dodge average base price:** $2,906.
**Introduction date:** October 1959.
**Assembly plants:** Detroit (Lynch Road), MI (2); Detroit (Jefferson Ave.) MI (3); Los Angeles, CA (5); Newark, DE (6); and St. Louis, MO (7).

**Data plate identification:** Ten digit code read as follows: 1st digit is a series letter (e.g., 6 = Polara V8 series); 2nd number identifies trim grade (1–7; Polara is 7); 3rd digit 0 for 1960; 4th digit is assembly plant code; followed by 100001 and up for serial number. Body style identification found on separate plate. *Example:* 6702100001 is a 1960 Dodge Polara with a 318 CID V8 engine, serial number 100001, built in Detroit, MI.

## Powertrains

| Engine | Gross HP | Transmission Availability | Dart | Matador | Polara |
|---|---|---|---|---|---|
| 225 CID Aluminum or Cast Iron Block, 1-bbl., 6-cyl. | 145 | 3-speed manual | S | - | - |
| | | Powerflite automatic | $189 | - | - |
| | | Torqueflite automatic | $211 | - | - |
| 318 CID Dart, 2-bbl., V8 | 230 | 3-speed manual | $119 | - | - |
| | | Powerflite automatic | $308 | - | - |
| | | Torqueflite automatic | $340 | - | - |
| 361 CID Super Red Ram, 2-bbl., V8 | 295 | 3-speed manual | $158 | S | - |
| | | Powerflite automatic | $347 | $189 | - |
| | | Torqueflite automatic | $369 | $211 | - |
| 383 CID Ram Fire, 4-bbl., V8 | 325 | 3-speed manual | $178 | $20 | S |
| | | Torqueflite automatic | $389 | $231 | $211 |
| 383 CID D-500 Ram Induction, 2 × 4-bbl., V8 | 330 | 3-speed manual | $537 | $379 | $359 |
| | | Torqueflite automatic | $748 | $590 | $570 |

## Major Options

| | Dart | Polara |
|---|---|---|
| Heater and defroster | $74 | $74 |
| Airtemp air conditioning | $445 | $445 |
| Tinted glass | $30 | $30 |
| Power steering | $77 | $77 |
| Power brakes | $43 | $43 |
| Power seat | $96 | $96 |
| Power windows | $102 | $102 |
| Electric clock | $16 | $16 |
| Music Master AM radio | $58 | $58 |
| White sidewall tires — std. sizes | $34 | $58 |

Options common to most models. Items may be standard equipment, optional at different pricing, or unavailable on certain models. This chart is only a guide.

## Paint Colors

| | Code |
|---|---|
| Raw Sienna | AA-1 |
| Raven | BB-1 |
| Azure | CC-1 |
| Mediterranean Metallic | DD-1 |
| Spray | FF-1 |
| Spruce Metallic | GG-1 |
| Cactus Metallic | HH-1 |
| Frost Turquoise | JJ-1 |
| Teal Metallic | KK-1 |
| Cloud | LL-1 |
| Pewter Metallic | MM-1 |
| Charcoal Metallic | NN-1 |
| Deep Burgundy Metallic | OO-1 |
| Vermilion | PP-1 |
| Fawn | TT-1 |
| Cocoa Metallic | UU-1 |
| Satin | WW-1 |

# Dart

*"The first fine economy car!"*

**Nameplate year of origin:** 1960.
**Current bodystyle lifespan:** 1960 through 1961.
**Predecessor to this model:** Coronet (1957 to 1959).
**Replacement for this model:** Dart (1962) and 330/440 (1963 to 1964).
**Percentage of division's sales volume:** 75.14%.
**Corporate siblings:** Plymouth Fury.
**Primary competition:** Chevrolet Biscayne/BelAir/Impala and Ford Galaxie.
**Notable changes:** Completely restyled. New smaller wheelbase, entry-level model.
**Major standard equipment:** Cloth and vinyl front bench seat, full-floor coverings, sun visors, exterior bright side moldings and 8.00 × 14 BSW tires.

## Measurements

|  | Cars | Wagons |
|---|---|---|
| Wheelbase | 118.0" | 122.0" |
| Length | 208.6" | 214.8" |
| Width | 78.0" | 78.0" |
| Height | 54.8" | NA |
| Legroom — front | 46.3" | 46.3" |
| Legroom — rear | 43.1" | NA |
| Headroom — front | 34.6" | NA |
| Headroom — rear | 34.5" | NA |
| Cargo capacity (cu. ft.) | NA | NA |
| Fuel capacity (gals.) | 20.0 | 22.0 |

## Models Available

|  | Style Number | Change from Base MSRP | Shipping LY | Wt. (lbs.) | Change from Production | LY |
|---|---|---|---|---|---|---|
| Dart Seneca 2-Door Sedan | 3L-21 | $2,278 | NEW | 3385 | 111,600 | NEW |
| Dart Seneca 4-Door Sedan | 3L-41 | $2,330 | NEW | 3420 | * | NEW |
| Dart Seneca 4-Dr., 2-S. Wagon | 3L-45 | $2,695 | NEW | 3805 | * | NEW |
| Dart Pioneer 2-Door Sedan | 3M-21 | $2,410 | NEW | 3375 | 80,000 | NEW |
| Dart Pioneer 2-Door Hardtop | 3M-23 | $2,488 | NEW | 3410 | * | NEW |
| Dart Pioneer 4-Door Sedan | 3M-41 | $2,459 | NEW | 3430 | * | NEW |
| Dart Pioneer 4-Door, 2-Seat Wagon | 3M-45 | $2,787 | NEW | 3820 | * | NEW |
| Dart Pioneer 4-Door, 3-Seat Wagon | 3M-45 | $2,892 | NEW | 3875 | * | NEW |
| Dart Phoenix 2-Door Hardtop | 3H-23 | $2,618 | -0.98% | 3410 | 70,700 | - |
| Dart Phoenix 2-Door Convertible | 3H-27 | $2,868 | -7.15% | 3460 | * | - |
| Dart Phoenix 4-Door Sedan | 3H-41 | $2,595 | +0.31% | 3420 | * | - |
| Dart Phoenix 4-Door Hardtop | 3H-43 | $2,677 | -5.81% | 3460 | * | - |
| TOTALS |  | Avg. price $2,591 | -5.31% |  | Production available only by trim level. | |

*\*Production estimates by trim level—e.g., 111,600 Seneca models built.*

# Matador

*"A remarkable achievement in fine-car luxury at a very moderate cost."*

**Nameplate year of origin:** 1960.
**Current bodystyle lifespan:** 1960 through 1961 (Matador/Polara).
**Predecessor to this model:** Royal (1957 to 1959).
**Replacement for this model:** Polara (1962 to 1965).
**Percentage of division's sales volume:** 21.54%.
**Corporate siblings:** Chrysler Windsor and DeSoto Fireflite/Adventurer.
**Primary competition:** Chevrolet BelAir/Impala and Ford Galaxie.
**Notable changes:** Completely restyled.
**Major standard equipment:** Cloth and vinyl front bench seat, full floor coverings, sun visors, exterior bright side moldings and 8.00 × 14 BSW tires.

## Measurements

|  | Cars | Wagons |
|---|---|---|
| Wheelbase | 122.0" | 122.0" |
| Length | 214.5" | 216.5" |
| Width | 78.0" | 78.0" |
| Height | 54.9" | 55.1" |
| Legroom — front | 46.6" | NA |
| Legroom — rear | 44.1" | NA |
| Headroom — front | 34.6" | NA |
| Headroom — rear | 34.5" | NA |
| Cargo capacity (cu. ft.) | NA | NA |
| Fuel capacity (gals.) | 20.0 | 22.0 |

## Models Available

| | Style Number | Base MSRP | Change from LY | Shipping Wt. (lbs.) | Production | Change from LY |
|---|---|---|---|---|---|---|
| Matador 2-Door Hardtop | 1L-23 | $2,996 | +0.20% | 3705 | 23,600 | - |
| Matador 4-Door Sedan | 1L-41 | $2,930 | -0.14% | 3725 | - | - |
| Matador 4-Door Hardtop | 1L-43 | $3,075 | +0.20% | 3820 | - | - |
| Matador 4-Door, 2-Seat Wagon | 1L-45 | $3,239 | +4.38% | 4045 | 51,600 | - |
| Matador 4-Door, 3-Seat Wagon | 1L-45 | $3,354 | +4.03% | 4120 | (Incl. w/2-Seat Wagon) | - |
| TOTALS | Avg. price | $3,119 | +1.80% | | Production available only by series. | |

# Polara

## "Solid luxury without compromise!"

**Nameplate year of origin:** 1960.
**Current bodystyle lifespan:** 1960 through 1961.
**Predecessor to this model:** Custom Royal (1957 to 1959).
**Replacement for this model:** Polara (1962 to 1965).
**Percentage of division's sales volume:** 3.33%.
**Corporate siblings:** Chrysler Windsor, and DeSoto Fireflite/Adventurer.
**Primary competition:** Chevrolet BelAir/Impala and Ford Galaxie.
**Notable changes:** Completely restyled.
**Major standard equipment:** Cloth and vinyl front bench seat, deep-pile carpeting, deluxe interior appointments, sun visors, additional exterior bright side moldings (over Matador), dual exhausts and 8.00 × 14 BSW tires.

## Measurements

| | Cars | Wagons |
|---|---|---|
| Wheelbase | 122.0" | 122.0" |
| Length | 214.5" | 216.5" |
| Width | 78.0" | 78.0" |
| Height | 54.9" | 55.1" |
| Legroom — front | 46.6" | NA |
| Legroom — rear | 44.1" | NA |
| Headroom — front | 34.6" | NA |
| Headroom — rear | 34.5" | NA |
| Cargo capacity (cu. ft.) | NA | NA |
| Fuel capacity (gals.) | 20.0 | 22.0 |

## Models Available

| | Style Number | Base MSRP | Change from LY | Shipping Wt. (lbs.) | Production | Change from LY |
|---|---|---|---|---|---|---|
| Polara 2-Door Hardtop | 2H-23 | $3,196 | -0.16% | 3740 | 11,600 | - |
| Polara 2-Door Convertible | 2H-27 | $3,416 | -0.18% | 3765 | - | - |
| Polara 4-Door Sedan | 2H-41 | $3,141 | -0.13% | 3735 | - | - |
| Polara 4-Door Hardtop | 2H-43 | $3,275 | -0.12% | 3815 | - | - |
| Polara 4-Door, 2-Seat Wagon | 2H-46 | $3,506 | +5.67% | 4085 | - | - |
| Polara 4-Door, 3-Seat Wagon | 2H-46 | $3,621 | +5.29% | 4220 | - | - |
| TOTALS | Avg. price | $3,359 | +1.76% | | Production available only by series. | |

# EDSEL

## "New — Nifty — Thrifty!"

From the beginning, the Edsel was marked to be a marketing person's dream come true or else a nightmare.

Numerous public relations appearances were made, cars were shown, customers were questioned — it should have turned out to be the perfect car. In some respects it was, or might have been if introduced in 1955, when the research took place. But, as so often happens, buying habits changed more quickly than production plans, and by late 1957, when the Edsel finally appeared, it was in the wrong market.

Ford's plans for the Edsel were related to how Mercury fit into the Ford family of cars. Originally Mercury was the "senior" Ford model. It looked like a Ford, was usually powered by a variation of a Ford engine, and was generally trimmed similarly to the upper-priced Ford models. It was successful, but only moderately so, as compared to GM's Buick-Oldsmobile-Pontiac lineup. To correct that situation, during the fifties, as Americans became more affluent, the Mercury moved upscale with them, and for the first time became more of a "junior" Lincoln, rather than a "senior" Ford. When Ford looked at adding a fourth line, the "E-Car" or Edsel, to the line, Ford executives felt that they could position the Edsel into the market held by Mercury, and move Mercury further upmarket into territory that twenty years earlier would have been held by the Lincoln Zephyr. This would give Ford a Mercury-Edsel combo to compete with the GM B-O-P models and the Chrysler-Dodge-DeSoto trio. What happened, as history has shown, was that the Edsel came to market too late, and in the middle of a nationwide recession. Typically, during a recession the mid-price range of cars are the first to be affected by slowing sales; thus the Edsel failed as much because of circumstance as because of its own faults. To quickly repair damage, Ford shifted the Edsel downmarket, overlapping many Ford models in the process, and brought the Mercury back into its former market position.

Unfortunately, despite the repositioning, or maybe because of it, the Edsel did not gain consumer acceptance. By 1960, the Edsel was left with a single line of Ranger models that were not as well-equipped as the best Ford (Galaxie) had to offer. Ford obviously had recognized this, as the car itself was a thinly disguised Ford. The major differences were the 1959 Pontiac-style split grille at the front and the slender-oval, upright taillamps at the rear end. Powertrains, accessories and trim options followed those offered by Ford. Barely two months into production, Ford decided to drop the Edsel and focus on its latest success, the Falcon and Comet.

Ranger 2-Door Hardtop

Ranger 2-Door Convertible

**Model year production:** 2,846, down 93.7% from 1959.
**Base price range:** $2,643 to $3,072.
**Domestic market share:** 0.01% (16th place).
**Industry average base price:** $3,391.
**Edsel average base price:** $2,839.
**Introduction date:** October 1959.
**Assembly plants:** Louisville, KY (U).

**Data plate identification:** Eleven digit code read as follows: 0 for 1960; 2nd digit is assembly plant code; 3rd digit is series (e.g., 1 is Ranger); 4th digit is body style; 5th digit is engine code; followed by 700001 and up for serial number. *Example:* 0U13W700001 is a 1960 Edsel Ranger 2-Door Hardtop with a 292 CID V8 engine, serial number 700001, built in Louisville, KY.

## Powertrains

| Engine | Gross HP | Engine Code | Transmission Availability | Ranger |
|---|---|---|---|---|
| 223 CID Economy Six, 1-bbl., 6-cyl. | 145 | V | 3-speed manual<br>Mile-O-Matic Auto. | S<br>$190 |
| 292 CID Ranger, 2-bbl., V8 | 185 | W | 3-speed manual<br>Mile-O-Matic Auto. | $84<br>$274 |
| 352 CID Super Express, 4-bbl., V8 | 300 | Y | Mile-O-Matic Auto.<br>Dual-Power Drive 3-speed Automatic | $332<br>$373 |

## Major Options

| | |
|---|---|
| Lever-Temp heater and defroster | $74 |
| Lever-Temp air conditioning | $404 |
| Tinted glass | $38 |
| Power steering | $82 |
| Power brakes | $43 |
| Power windows | $102 |
| 4-way power seat adjustment | $70 |
| Electric clock | $15 |
| Pushbutton AM radio | $65 |
| White sidewall tires | $36 |
| Full wheel covers | $17 |

Options common to most models. Items may be standard equipment, optional at different pricing, or unavailable on certain models. This chart is only a guide.

## Paint Colors

| | Code |
|---|---|
| Black Velvet | A |
| Turquoise | C |
| Cadet Blue Metallic | E |
| Hawaiian Blue | F |
| Alaskan Gold Metallic | H |
| Regal Red | J |
| Turquoise Metallic | K |
| Polar White | M |
| Sahara Beige | N |
| Lilac Metallic | Q |
| Buttercup Yellow | R |
| Sherwood Green Metallic | T |
| Bronze Rose Metallic | U |
| Sea Foam Green | W |
| Cloud Silver Metallic | Z |

# Ranger

*"For people who want fresh, good looks."*

**Nameplate year of origin:** 1958.
**Current bodystyle lifespan:** 1960.
**Predecessor to this model:** Ranger (1959).
**Replacement for this model:** None.
**Percentage of division's sales volume:** 90.34%.
**Corporate siblings:** Ford Fairlane and Galaxie.
**Primary competition:** AMC Ambassador, Chevrolet Biscayne/BelAir/Impala, Plymouth Belvedere, and Dodge Dart.
**Notable changes:** Completely restyled.
**Major standard equipment:** Cloth and vinyl front bench seat, wall-to-wall carpeting, electric clock, front and rear arm rests, power-booster windshield wipers and 7.50 × 14 BSW tires.

## Measurements

| | |
|---|---|
| Wheelbase | 120.0" |
| Length | 216.0" |
| Width | 81.5" |
| Height | 55.0" |
| Legroom — front | 43.3" |
| Legroom — rear | 41.6" |
| Headroom — front | 34.0" |
| Headroom — rear | 33.9" |
| Cargo capacity (cu. ft.) | 33.0 |
| Fuel capacity (gals.) | 20.0 |

## Models Available

| | Style Number | Base MSRP | Change from LY | Shipping Wt. (lbs.) | Production | Change from LY |
|---|---|---|---|---|---|---|
| Ranger 2-Door Sedan | 64A | $2,643 | +0.53% | 3601 | 777 | -90.01% |
| Ranger 2-Door Hardtop | 63A | $2,705 | +0.52% | 3641 | 295 | -94.61% |
| Ranger 2-Door Convertible | 76B | $3,000 | NEW | 3836 | 76 | NEW |
| Ranger 4-Door Sedan | 58A | $2,697 | +0.48% | 3700 | 1,288 | -89.94% |
| Ranger 4-Door Hardtop | 57A | $2,770 | +0.51% | 3718 | 135 | -94.26% |
| TOTALS | | *Avg. price* $2,763 | +2.71% | | *Production* 2,571 | -90.86% |

# Villager

*"For thrifty-minded people on the go."*

**Nameplate year of origin:** 1958.
**Current bodystyle lifespan:** 1960.
**Predecessor to this model:** Ranger (1959).

## Measurements

| | |
|---|---|
| Wheelbase | 120.0" |
| Length | 214.8" |

**Replacement for this model:** None.
**Percentage of division's sales volume:** 9.65%.
**Corporate siblings:** Ford Fairlane and Galaxie.
**Primary competition:** AMC Ambassador, Chevrolet Biscayne/BelAir/Impala, Plymouth Belvedere, and Dodge Dart.
**Notable changes:** Completely restyled.
**Major standard equipment:** All-vinyl front bench seat, electric clock, front and rear arm rests, power-booster windshield wipers and 7.50 × 14 BSW tires.

## Measurements (cont.)

| | |
|---|---|
| Width | 81.5" |
| Height | 55.0" |
| Legroom — front | 43.3" |
| Legroom — rear | 41.6" |
| Headroom — front | 34.0" |
| Headroom — rear | 33.9" |
| Cargo capacity (cu. ft.) | 100.5 |
| Fuel capacity (gals.) | 20.0 |

## Models Available

| | Style Number | Base MSRP | Change from LY | Shipping Wt. (lbs.) | Production | Change from LY |
|---|---|---|---|---|---|---|
| Villager 4-Door, 6-pass. Wgn. | 71F | $2,989 | +0.61% | 3840 | 216 | -96.20% |
| Villager 4-Door, 9-pass. Wgn. | 71E | $3,072 | +0.56% | 3930 | 59 | -97.23% |
| TOTALS | | *Avg. price* $3,031 | +0.59% | | *Production* 275 | -96.49% |

# FORD

*"A wonderful new world of Fords! From any Point of View …
from every Point of Value … these are the finest Fords of a lifetime!"*

For 1960, Ford was betting the farm on a totally revamped line of full-size cars as well as the totally new compact Falcon. The full-size Fords, which shared their bodies, mechanicals and nearly everything else with the nearly deceased Edsel, represented a departure from the boxy, upright cars of 1959. In contrast, the 1960 models looked lighter and more appealing, partly because of their new thinner rooflines and window treatments. Up front, for the first time on Ford models, was a full-width grille with headlamps inset at each end. Fords would use this type of grille treatment through the 1964 models. Bodysides were not highly sculpted, but featured a chrome trim molding that ran up the front fender line from the bumper, back along the fender ridge across the doors, and then along the edge of the small, flat tail fin that remained on Fords. At the rear, there was a half-circle taillamp, mounted below the fin, but above the rear bumper. In all, the exterior styling was probably among the nicest of the year. Interiors were also modernized, and a typically sparse Ford dashboard was seen once again. The 332 CID V8 was no longer offered. The sporty Thunderbird continued with a new grille and trim changes, and added as optional equipment a sliding sunroof and the Lincoln-Mercury 430 CID V8 engine. The sliding sunroof was the first commercially successful sunroof offering since the "Sunshine Turret-top" offered in a variety of 1939–40 GM cars.

The newest addition to the family was the compact Falcon. Purposefully styled to look very much like a smaller Ford, the Falcon was one of Ford Motor Company's biggest successes ever. While all of the major players in the marketplace would have a compact-sized car by 1961, the battle of the Big Three (Ford, Chevrolet and Plymouth) was definitely won by Ford. The Falcon offered the most traditional styling, the most traditional powertrain and the most traditional (if spartan) interior styling, and all of this at the lowest price of its three major competitors. Americans were definitely more comfortable with tradition, and Ford definitely knew how to build traditional cars, as historically their cars were often lagging behind the competition in innovative features. The Falcon was the only compact model of the Big Three to be offered in a 2-Door Coupe or 4-Door Sedan from the start. The Corvair was only available in a 4-Door Sedan at introduction, and the Valiant came as a 4-Door Sedan or Wagon from the beginning. By mid-year, a 2-Door and 4-Door Wagon were added to the line.

Falcon 2-Door Sedan

Falcon 4-Door Sedan

Fairlane 2-Door Sedan

Galaxie 4-Door Victoria Hardtop

Country Squire 4-Door Wagon

Thunderbird 2-Door Convertible

**Model year production:** 1,439,506, down 0.79% from 1959.
**Domestic market share:** 23.93% (2nd place).
**Base price range:** $1,912 to $4,222.
**Industry average base price:** $3,391.
**Ford average base price:** $2,584.
**Introduction date:** October 8, 1959; Falcon wagons March 1960.
**Assembly plants:** Atlanta, GA (A); Dallas, TX (D); Chicago, IL (G); Dearborn, MI (F); Kansas City, MO (K); Lorain, OH (H); Los Angeles, CA (J); Louisville, KY (U); Mahwah, NJ (E); Metuchen, NJ (T); Norfolk, VA (N); San Jose, CA (R); Twin Cities, MN (P); Wayne, MI (W); Wixom, MI (Y); St. Thomas, Ontario, Can. (X); Oakville, Ontario, Can. (B).

**Data plate identification:** Eleven digit code read as follows: 0 for 1960; 2nd digit is assembly plant code; 3rd digit is series (e.g., 1 is Falcon, 3 is Fairlane, 7 is Thunderbird, etc.); 4th digit is body style; 5th digit is engine code; followed by 100001 and up for serial number. *Example:* 0Y73J100001 is a 1960 Ford Thunderbird 2-Door Hardtop with a 430 CID V8 engine, serial number 100001, built in Wixom, MI.

## Powertrains

| Engine | Gross HP | Engine Code | Transmission Availability | Falcon | Full-size Ford | Thunderbird |
|---|---|---|---|---|---|---|
| 144.3 CID, 1-bbl., 6-cyl. | 90 | S | 3-speed manual | S | - | - |
| | | | Fordomatic | $159 | - | - |
| 223 CID Mileage Maker Six, 1-bbl., 6-cyl. | 145 | V | 3-speed manual | - | S | - |
| | | | Overdrive | - | $108 | - |
| | | | Fordomatic | - | $180 | - |
| 292 CID Thunderbird, 2-bbl., V8 | 185 | W | 3-speed manual | - | $107 | - |
| | | | Overdrive | - | $215 | - |
| | | | Fordomatic | - | $297 | - |
| | | | Cruise-O-Matic | - | $318 | - |
| 352 CID Thunderbird, 2-bbl., V8 | 235 | X | 3-speed manual | - | $148 | - |
| | | | Overdrive | - | $256 | - |
| | | | Fordomatic | - | $338 | - |
| | | | Cruise-O-Matic | - | $359 | - |
| 352 CID Thunderbird Special, 4-bbl., V8 | 300 | Y | 3-speed manual | - | $177 | S |
| | | | Overdrive | - | $285 | $145 |
| | | | Cruise-O-Matic | - | $388 | $242 |
| 352 CID Interceptor Special, 4-bbl., V8 | 360 | R | 3-speed manual | - | $* | - |
| | | | Overdrive | - | $* | - |
| | | | Cruise-O-Matic | - | $* | - |
| 430 CID Thunderbird Special, 4-bbl., V8 | 350 | J | 3-speed manual | - | - | $177 |
| | | | Overdrive | - | - | $322 |
| | | | Cruise-O-Matic | - | - | $419 |

*Pricing not currently available.*

## Major Options

|                          | Falcon | Full-size Ford | Thunderbird |
|--------------------------|--------|----------------|-------------|
| Recirculation heater and defroster | $68 | $75 | $83 |
| SelectAire air conditioning | - | $404 | $466 |
| I-Rest tinted glass | - | $43 | $43 |
| Power steering | - | $77 | $75 |
| Power brakes | - | $43 | $43 |
| Power windows | - | $102 | $102 |
| Electric windshield wipers w/washers | $23 | $24 | $14 |
| Electric clock | $15 | $15 | S |
| Pushbutton AM radio (Falcon Man.) | $54 | $59 | S |
| White sidewall tires | $34 | $34 | $42 |
| Full wheel covers | $16 | $17 | S |

Options common to most models. (- = Not Available; S = Standard equipment.) Items may be standard equipment, optional at different pricing, or unavailable on certain models. This chart is only a guide.

## Paint Colors

|                          | Code | Falcon | Ford | Thunderbird |
|--------------------------|------|--------|------|-------------|
| Raven Black | A | X | X | X |
| Kingston Blue Metallic | B |  |  | X |
| Aquamarine | C |  | X | X |
| Acapulco Blue/Belmont Blue | E | X | X | X |
| Surf Foam Blue | F | X | X | X |
| Yosemite Yellow | G |  | X |  |
| Beechwood Brown Metallic | H |  | X | X |
| Monte Carlo Red | J | X | X | X |
| Sultana Turquoise Metallic | K | X | X | X |
| Corinthian White | M |  | X | X |
| Diamond Blue | N |  |  | X |
| Orchid Gray Metallic | Q |  | X |  |
| Moroccan Ivory | R |  |  | X |
| Briar Cliff Green Metallic | S |  |  | X |
| Meadowvale Green Metallic | T | X | X | X |
| Springdale Rose Metallic | U |  |  | X |
| Palm Springs Rose | V |  |  | X |
| Adriatic Green | W | X | X | X |
| Royal Burgundy Metallic | X |  |  | X |
| Gunpowder Gray Metallic | Y |  |  | X |
| Platinum Metallic | Z | X | X | X |

# Falcon

*"The new-size Ford. The world's most experienced new car, and the easiest car in the world to own."*

**Nameplate year of origin:** 1960.
**Current bodystyle lifespan:** 1960 through 1963.
**Predecessor to this model:** None.
**Replacement for this model:** Falcon (1964 to 1965).
**Percentage of division's sales volume:** 30.27%.
**Corporate siblings:** Mercury Comet.
**Primary competition:** Rambler American, Chevrolet Corvair, Plymouth Valiant and Studebaker Lark.
**Notable changes:** All-new model for 1960.
**Major standard equipment:** Nylon and vinyl front bench seat with foam cushions, black carpet textured rubber floor covering, 17" Lifeguard steering wheel, dual front armrests and dual sun visors, dome light, glove compartment, bright metal front and rear window trim, and 6.00 × 13 BSW tires.

## Measurements

|                          | Cars | Wagons |
|--------------------------|------|--------|
| Wheelbase | 109.5" | 109.5" |
| Length | 181.2" | 189.0" |
| Width | 70.6" | 70.6" |
| Height | 54.5" | 55.1" |
| Legroom — front | 44.6" | 44.6" |
| Legroom — rear | 40.1" | 40.1" |
| Headroom — front | 38.9" | 38.9" |
| Headroom — rear | 37.3" | 37.2" |
| Cargo capacity (cu. ft.) | 23.7 | 76.2 |
| Fuel capacity (gals.) | 14.0 | 14.0 |

## Models Available

|                      | Style Number | Base MSRP | Change from LY | Shipping Wt. (lbs.) | Production | Change from LY |
|----------------------|--------------|-----------|----------------|---------------------|------------|----------------|
| Falcon 2-Door Sedan | 64A | $1,912 | NEW | 2259 | 193,470 | NEW |
| Falcon 4-Door Sedan | 58A | $1,974 | NEW | 2288 | 167,896 | NEW |
| Falcon 2-Door Wagon | 59A | $2,225 | NEW | 2540 | 27,552 | NEW |
| Falcon 4-Door Wagon | 71A | $2,287 | NEW | 2575 | 46,758 | NEW |
| TOTALS | | Avg. price $2,100 | NEW | | Production 435,676 | NEW |

# Custom & Fairlane

*"A wonderful new world of Fords!"*

**Nameplate year of origin:** 1957 (Custom) and 1955 (Fairlane).
**Current bodystyle lifespan:** 1960 through 1962.
**Predecessor to this model:** Custom & Fairlane (1959).
**Replacement for this model:** Custom (1963 to 1964).
**Percentage of division's sales volume:** 36.19%.
**Corporate siblings:** None.
**Primary competition:** Chevrolet Biscayne/BelAir, Plymouth Belvedere, and Dodge Dart.
**Notable changes:** Completely restyled.
**Major standard equipment:** Nylon and vinyl front bench seats, rubber floor mats, chrome front and rear window trim, and 7.50 × 14 BSW tires. Fairlane adds: dual sun visors, and arm rests on all doors. Fairlane 500 adds: upgraded interior trim, and additional exterior trim. Wagons add: 8.00 × 14 BSW tires.

## Measurements

| | |
|---|---|
| Wheelbase | 119.0" |
| Length | 213.7" |
| Width | 81.5" |
| Height | 55.0" |
| Legroom — front | 43.3" |
| Legroom — rear | 41.6" |
| Headroom — front | 34.0" |
| Headroom — rear | 33.9" |
| Cargo capacity (cu. ft.) | NA |
| Fuel capacity (gals.) | 20.0 |

## Models Available

| | Style Number | Base MSRP | Change from LY | Shipping Wt. (lbs.) | Production | Change from LY |
|---|---|---|---|---|---|---|
| Custom 300 2-Door Club Sedan | 64H | $2,230 | +0.50% | NA | 300 | -99.87% |
| Custom 300 4-Door Town Sedan | 58F | $2,284 | +0.48% | NA | 572 | -99.77% |
| Fairlane 2-Door Business Sedan | 64G | $2,170 | NEW | 3505 | 1,733 | NEW |
| Fairlane 2-Door Club Sedan | 64F | $2,257 | -4.24% | 3532 | 93,261 | 165.50% |
| Fairlane 4-Door Town Sedan | 58E | $2,311 | -4.15% | 3606 | 109,799 | 69.80% |
| Fairlane 500 2-Door Club Sedan | 64A | $2,334 | -5.74% | 3536 | 91,041 | 797.75% |
| Fairlane 500 4-Door Town Sedan | 58A | $2,388 | -5.61% | 3610 | 153,234 | 329.59% |
| Ranch Wagon 2-Dr., 6-pass. Wgn. | 59C | $2,586 | 0.74% | 3831 | 27,136 | -40.44% |
| Ranch Wagon 4-Dr., 6-pass. Wgn. | 71H | $2,656 | 0.84% | 3948 | 43,872 | -34.85% |
| TOTALS | *Avg. Custom & Fairlane price* | $2,282 | -4.04% | | *Custom & Fairlane production* 520,948 | -29.27% |

# Galaxie

*"Meet the aristocrats of the low-priced field."*

**Nameplate year of origin:** 1959.
**Current bodystyle lifespan:** 1960 through 1962.
**Predecessor to this model:** Galaxie (1959).
**Replacement for this model:** Galaxie (1963 to 1964).
**Percentage of division's sales volume:** 27.10%.
**Corporate siblings:** None.
**Primary competition:** Chevrolet Biscayne/BelAir/Impala, Plymouth Belvedere/Fury, and Dodge Dart.
**Notable changes:** Completely restyled.
**Major standard equipment:** Fairlane 500 equipment plus Cloth and vinyl front bench seat, chrome exterior trim on all windows, body side chrome trim and aluminum rear quarter protection shield, and Galaxie identification. Starliner and Sunliner add: All-vinyl, high-level interior trim, and special identification script. Country Squire adds: Wood-grained exterior side trim.

## Measurements

| | |
|---|---|
| Wheelbase | 119.0" |
| Length | 213.7" |
| Width | 81.5" |
| Height | 55.0" |
| Legroom — front | 43.3" |
| Legroom — rear | 41.6" |
| Headroom — front | 34.0" |
| Headroom — rear | 33.9" |
| Cargo capacity (cu. ft.) | NA |
| Fuel capacity (gals.) | 20.0 |

## Models Available

| | Style Number | Base MSRP | Change from LY | Shipping Wt. (lbs.) | Production | Change from LY |
|---|---|---|---|---|---|---|
| Galaxie 2-Door Club Sedan | 62A | $2,549 | +0.83% | 3553 | 31,866 | -39.70% |
| Galaxie 2-Door Starliner Hardtop | 63A | $2,610 | +0.81% | 3567 | 68,641 | -43.68% |
| Galaxie 2-Door Sunliner Conv. | 76B | $2,860 | +0.74% | 3741 | 44,762 | -2.41% |
| Galaxie 4-Door Town Sedan | 54A | $2,603 | +0.81% | 3634 | 103,784 | -43.32% |
| Galaxie 4-Door Victoria HT | 75A | $2,675 | +0.79% | 3642 | 40,215 | -15.74% |
| Country Sedan 4-Dr., 6-p. Wgn. | 71F | $2,752 | +0.26% | 3962 | 59,302 | -37.31% |
| Country Sedan 4-Door, 9-p. Wgn. | 71E | $2,837 | +0.28% | 4008 | 19,277 | -33.25% |
| Country Squire 4-Dr., 9-p. Wgn. | 71G | $2,967 | +0.30% | 4022 | 22,237 | -8.63% |
| TOTALS | Avg. Galaxie price | $2,732 | +0.59% | Galaxie production | 390,084 | -34.90% |

# Thunderbird

### "The World's Most Wanted Car!"

**Nameplate year of origin:** 1955.
**Current bodystyle lifespan:** 1958 through 1960.
**Predecessor to this model:** Thunderbird (1955 to 1957).
**Replacement for this model:** Thunderbird (1961 to 1963).
**Percentage of division's sales volume:** 6.45%.
**Corporate siblings:** None.
**Primary competition:** None.
**Notable changes:** Revised grille, taillights and side trim, and minor detail changes.
**Major standard equipment:** Nylon and vinyl (or leather in convertible) bucket seats, full-carpeting, Lifeguard cushioned sun visors and instrument panel, electric clock, automatic dome light, courtesy light, glove box light, trunk light, Cruise-O-Matic automatic transmission, power steering, power brakes, full wheel covers and 8.00 × 14 BSW tires.

## Measurements

| | |
|---|---|
| Wheelbase | 113.0" |
| Length | 205.3" |
| Width | 77.9" |
| Height | 53.1" |
| Legroom — front | 43.6" |
| Legroom — rear | 38.1" |
| Headroom — front | 35.3" |
| Headroom — rear | 33.6" |
| Cargo capacity (cu. ft.) | NA |
| Fuel capacity (gals.) | 20.0 |

## Models Available

| | Style Number | Base MSRP | Change from LY | Shipping Wt. (lbs.) | Production | Change from LY |
|---|---|---|---|---|---|---|
| Thunderbird 2-Door Hardtop | 63A | $3,755 | +1.60% | 3799 | 80,938 | +41.51% |
| Thunderbird 2-Door Conv. | 76A | $4,222 | +6.11% | 3897 | 11,860 | +15.58% |
| TOTALS | Avg. price | $3,989 | +3.93% | Production | 92,798 | +37.57% |

# IMPERIAL

### "America's most carefully built car."

For 1960, Imperial styling was new, as was every other Chrysler Corporation offering. However, these cars were not given the all-new construction used on other Mopar offerings. All other Chrysler products utilized unit-body construction, while Imperial featured a revision to the 1957–1959 body-on-frame construction. Chrysler gave the Imperial an all-new look by incorporating many detail and trim changes and heavily revising the interior. Once again,

the Crown Imperial Limousine Sedan model was available as a custom-built model. It is not included herein as its production usually totaled ten or fewer per season and Chrysler considered it a custom-built model.

Custom Imperial 4-Door Sedan

Interior

LeBaron 4-Door Sedan

**Model year production:** 17,703, up 2.51% over 1959.
**Domestic market share:** 0.29% (15th place).
**Base price range:** $4,923 to $6,318.
**Industry average base price:** $3,391.
**Imperial average base price:** $5,565.
**Introduction date:** September 1959.
**Assembly plants:** Detroit, MI (3).

**Data plate identification:** Ten digit code read as follows: 1st digit 9 = Imperial; 2nd number identifies series (e.g., 2 is for Crown); 0 for 1960; 4th digit is assembly plant code; and 100001 and up for serial number. Body style numbers found on body plate. *Example:* 9203100001 is a 1960 Imperial Crown, serial number 100001, built in Detroit, MI.

## Powertrains

| Engine | Gross HP | Transmission Availability | Imperial |
|---|---|---|---|
| 413 CID, 4-bbl., V8 | 350 | Torqueflite Automatic | S |

## Major Options

| | Custom | Crown | LeBaron |
|---|---|---|---|
| Heater and defroster | $136 | $136 | $136 |
| Air conditioning | $590 | $590 | $590 |
| Auto Pilot automatic speed control | $97 | $97 | $97 |
| Solex tinted glass | $54 | $54 | $54 |
| Rear window defogger | $21 | $21 | $21 |
| Power door locks | $47 (2-Dr)/ $72 (4-Dr) | $47 (2-Dr)/ $72 (4-Dr) | $72 |
| Power driver's seat/Bench seat | $125 | S | S |
| Power windows | $125 | S | S |
| Electric Touch-Tuner radio w/pwr. antenna | $169 | $169 | $169 |
| Stainless steel roof (4-Doors only) | $62 | $62 | S |
| Whitewall tires—standard size | $55 | $55 | S |

Options common to most models. (S = Standard equipment.) Items may be standard equipment, optional at different pricing, or unavailable on certain models. This chart is only a guide.

## Paint Colors

| | Code |
|---|---|
| Sunburst | AA-1 |
| Formal Black | BB-1 |
| Glacier Blue | CC-1 |
| Moonstone Blue Metallic | DD-1 |
| Midnight Blue Metallic | EE-1 |
| Light Mint | FF-1 |
| Cedar Green Metallic | GG-1 |
| Silverpine Metallic | HH-1 |
| Sheffield Silver Metallic | LL-1 |
| Dove Gray | MM-1 |
| Executive Gray Metallic | NN-1 |
| Regent Ruby | OO-1 |
| Regal Red | PP-1 |
| Dawn Mauve | RR-1 |
| Dusk Mauve | SS-1 |
| Beach Beige | TT-1 |
| Powdered Bronze Metallic | UU-1 |
| Alaskan White | WW-1 |

# Custom

*"So smoothly, so carefully assembled that it looks as if it were fashioned from a single sheet of steel ... the new Imperial of 1960."*

**Nameplate year of origin:** 1959 (Name was used on Chrysler Imperial models prior to 1955 also).
**Current bodystyle lifespan:** 1960 through 1963.
**Predecessor to this model:** Imperial (1957 to 1958) and Custom (1959).
**Replacement for this model:** Crown (1964 to 1966).
**Percentage of division's sales volume:** 43.98%.
**Corporate siblings:** Crown and LeBaron.
**Primary competition:** Cadillac Sixty-Two, and Lincoln.
**Notable changes:** Completely restyled.
**Major standard equipment:** Torqueflite automatic transmission, power steering, power brakes, front and rear armrests (hardtops), pile carpeting, interior courtesy lamps, variable-speed electric windshield wipers with washers, wheel covers and 8.20 × 15 BSW tires.

## Measurements

| | |
|---|---|
| Wheelbase | 129.0" |
| Length | 226.3" |
| Width | 80.1" |
| Height | 56.7" |
| Legroom — front | 46.3" |
| Legroom — rear | 42.3" |
| Headroom — front | 34.5" |
| Headroom — rear | 33.8" |
| Cargo capacity (cu. ft.) | NA |
| Fuel capacity (gals.) | 23.0 |

## Models Available

| | Style Number | Base MSRP | Change from LY | Shipping Wt. (lbs.) | Production | Change from LY |
|---|---|---|---|---|---|---|
| Custom Imp. Southampton 2-Dr. HT | 912 | $4,923 | +0.26% | 4655 | 1,498 | -14.06% |
| Custom Imperial 4-Door Sedan | 913 | $5,029 | +0.26% | 4700 | 2,335 | 12.75% |
| Custom Imp. Southampton 4-Dr. HT | 914 | $5,029 | +0.26% | 4670 | 3,953 | -0.78% |
| TOTALS | | Avg. price $4,994 | +0.26% | | Production 7,786 | -0.16% |

# Crown

*"A liveliness you'd never expect of a car this size."*

**Nameplate year of origin:** 1957 (Not the same as Crown Imperial series).
**Current bodystyle lifespan:** 1960 through 1963.
**Predecessor to this model:** Crown (1957 to 1959).
**Replacement for this model:** Crown (1964 to 1966).
**Percentage of division's sales volume:** 46.47%.
**Corporate siblings:** Custom and LeBaron.
**Primary competition:** Cadillac Sixty-Two, and Lincoln Premiere.
**Notable changes:** Completely restyled.
**Major standard equipment:** Torqueflite automatic transmission, power steering, power brakes, front and rear armrests (hardtops), pile carpeting, power windows, interior dome and map lights, variable-speed electric windshield wipers with washers, trunk carpeting, wheel covers and 8.20 × 15 BSW tires.

## Measurements

| | |
|---|---|
| Wheelbase | 129.0" |
| Length | 226.3" |
| Width | 80.1" |
| Height | 56.7" |
| Legroom — front | 46.3" |
| Legroom — rear | 42.3" |
| Headroom — front | 34.5" |
| Headroom — rear | 33.8" |
| Cargo capacity (cu. ft.) | NA |
| Fuel capacity (gals.) | 23.0 |

## Models Available

| | Style Number | Base MSRP | Change from LY | Shipping Wt. (lbs.) | Production | Change from LY |
|---|---|---|---|---|---|---|
| Crown Southampton 2-Door HT | 922 | $5,403 | 0.00% | 4720 | 1,504 | -12.96% |
| Crown 2-Door Convertible | 925 | $5,774 | 0.00% | 4820 | 618 | +11.35% |
| Crown 4-Door Sedan | 923 | $5,647 | 0.00% | 4770 | 1,594 | +19.40% |
| Crown Southampton 4-Door HT | 924 | $5,647 | 0.00% | 4765 | 4,510 | -4.33% |
| TOTALS | | Avg. price $5,618 | 0.00% | | Production 8,226 | -1.27% |

# LeBaron

*"Meet excellence face to face."*

**Nameplate year of origin:** 1924 (as Chrysler Sedan model designation); 1926 (as series).
**Current bodystyle lifespan:** 1960 through 1963.
**Predecessor to this model:** LeBaron (1957 to 1959).
**Replacement for this model:** LeBaron (1964 to 1966).
**Percentage of division's sales volume:** 9.55%.
**Corporate siblings:** Custom and Crown.
**Primary competition:** Cadillac de Ville, and Lincoln Continental Mark V.
**Notable changes:** Completely restyled.
**Major standard equipment:** Torqueflite automatic transmission, power steering, power brakes, pile carpeting, 6-way power seat, power windows and vent windows, electric clock, interior dome and reading lamps, variable-speed electric windshield wipers with washers, carpeted trunk floor, wheel covers and 8.20 × 15 WSW tires.

## Measurements

| | |
|---|---|
| Wheelbase | 129.0" |
| Length | 226.3" |
| Width | 80.1" |
| Height | 56.7" |
| Legroom — front | 46.3" |
| Legroom — rear | 42.3" |
| Headroom — front | 34.5" |
| Headroom — rear | 33.8" |
| Cargo capacity (cu. ft.) | NA |
| Fuel capacity (gals.) | 23.0 |

## Models Available

| | Style Number | Base MSRP | Change from LY | Shipping Wt. (lbs.) | Production | Change from LY |
|---|---|---|---|---|---|---|
| LeBaron 4-Door Sedan | 933 | $6,318 | +3.52% | 4860 | 692 | +35.69% |
| LeBaron Southampton 4-Door HT | 934 | $6,318 | +3.52% | 4835 | 999 | +60.61% |
| TOTALS | | *Avg. price* $6,318 | +3.52% | *Production* 1,691 | | +49.38% |

# LINCOLN

*"The finest Lincolns in forty years."*

The newest Lincolns may have been advertised as the finest in forty years, but finest in what respect could be debated. They were definitely the largest, heaviest and most cumbersome of just about any new vehicle on the road in 1960. They were also probably the most luxurious, most powerful and most fully equipped of any Lincoln up to their time. These Lincolns were also most likely the roomiest and most comfortable to ride in of any to that time. So to a point the advertising is true. For 1960, the large and boxy styling of the 1958–59 models was continued. Up front, all Lincoln models still carried dual headlamps, canted at about a 45-degree angle from the massive front bumper. The grill was of a fine mesh made up of small horizontal bars on the Lincoln and Premiere. The Continental Mark V used a slightly finer looking grille. The rear end styling, while massive, was a rather simple affair, with grille work that mimicked the front end right above the rear bumper. Taillamps were small horizontal lenses within the bumper area. Body sides continued as long, flat slab sides, with a horizontal crease running body length, and dropping slightly at the rear. The body feature line that exaggerated the front wheel opening styling continued. Also carried over was the unitized body and frame construction, which the Lincoln shared with the Ford Thunderbird.

Standard power continued to be the 430 CID V8 engine, which was also found optionally this year in the Ford Thunderbird. All Lincolns were treated to a newly designed rear suspension system for this season also. The only change to the model line was the renaming of the Capri, to simply Lincoln.

**2-Door Hardtop**

**Premiere 4-Door Landau Hardtop**

**Continental Mark V 4-Door Landau Hardtop**

**Continental Mark V 4-Door Town Car Sedan**

**Model year production:** 24,820, down 7.75% from 1959.
**Base price range:** $5,253 to $10,230.
**Domestic market share:** 0.41% (14th place).
**Industry average base price:** $3,391.
**Lincoln average base price:** $6,709.
**Introduction date:** September 1959.
**Assembly plants:** Wixom, MI (Y).

**Data plate identification:** Eleven digit code read as follows: 0 for 1960; 2nd digit is assembly plant code; 2-digit model number (see listings below); 5th digit is engine code; 400001 and up for serial number. *Example:* 0Y82H400001 is a 1960 Lincoln Continental Mark V 4-Door Sedan with a 430 CID V8 engine, serial number 400001, built in Wixom, MI.

## Powertrains

| Engine | Gross HP | Engine Code | Transmission Availability | All models |
|---|---|---|---|---|
| 430 CID, 4-bbl., V8 | 315 | H | Turbo-Drive Automatic | S |

## Major Options

| | Lincoln | Premiere | Continental |
|---|---|---|---|
| Air conditioning (manual) | $475 | $475 | $475 |
| Automatic headlight dimmers | $46 | $46 | $46 |
| Tinted glass | $54 | $54 | S |
| Power door locks | $39–$64 | $39–$64 | $39–$64 |
| Power windows | $95 | S | S |
| 6-way power seat | $119 | $50 | S |
| AM radio | S | S | S |
| Leather upholstery | $100 | $100 | $100 |
| Speed control | $97 | $97 | $97 |
| Remote control trunk release (sedans) | $53 | $53 | $53 |

Options common to most models. (S = Standard equipment.) Items may be standard equipment, optional at different pricing, or unavailable on certain models. This chart is only a guide.

## Paint Colors

| | Code |
|---|---|
| Presidential Black | A |
| Royal Red Metallic | B |
| Turquoise Mist Metallic | C |
| Blue Haze | D |
| Saxon Green Metallic | E |
| Sunburst Yellow | F |
| Empress Blue Metallic | H |
| Green Velvet Metallic | I |
| Crystal Green Metallic | K |
| Sultana White | M |
| Platinum | N |
| Executive Gray Metallic | P |
| Sheffield Gray Metallic | Q |
| Columbia Blue Haze Metallic | R |
| Honey Beige | T |
| Rose Glow Metallic | U |
| Summer Rose | V |
| Regency Turquoise Metallic | W |
| Black Cherry Metallic | X |
| Briar Brown Metallic | Y |
| Desert Frost Metallic | Z |

# Lincoln

*"New achievement in classic design: Lincoln 'town car' elegance."*

**Nameplate year of origin:** 1920 (used most years for base level models — with few exceptions).

**Current bodystyle lifespan:** 1958 through 1960 (Capri nameplate in 1958 and 1959).

**Predecessor to this model:** Capri (1956 to 1957).

**Replacement for this model:** Continental (1961 to 1969).

**Percentage of division's sales volume:** 28.85%.

**Corporate siblings:** None.

**Primary competition:** Cadillac Sixty-Two and Imperial Crown.

**Notable changes:** New grille and minor revisions.

**Major standard equipment:** Nylon and vinyl bench seat, rear center armrest, padded instrument panel and sun visors, electric clock, heater and defroster, Travel-tuner AM radio, windshield washers, remote control outside mirror, power steering, power brakes, Twin-Range Turbo-Drive automatic transmission, full wheel covers and 9.50 × 14 WSW tires.

## Measurements

| | |
|---|---|
| Wheelbase | 131.0" |
| Length | 227.2" |
| Width | 80.3" |
| Height | 56.7" |
| Legroom — front | 44.1" |
| Legroom — rear | 46.1" |
| Headroom — front | 34.9" |
| Headroom — rear | 33.8" |
| Luggage capacity (cu. ft.) | NA |
| Fuel capacity (gals.) | 25.0 |

## Models Available

| | Style Number | Base MSRP | Change from LY | Shipping Wt. (lbs.) | Production | Change from LY |
|---|---|---|---|---|---|---|
| 2-Door Hardtop | 63A | $5,253 | +7.16% | 4917 | 1,670 | -24.09% |
| 4-Door Sedan | 53A | $5,441 | +6.90% | 5016 | 1,093 | -16.69% |
| 4-Door Landau Hardtop | 57A | $5,441 | +6.90% | 5012 | 4,397 | -0.45% |
| TOTALS | *Avg. price* | $5,378 | +6.98% | *Production* | 7,160 | -9.69% |

# Premiere

*"Luxurious new spaciousness awaits you in Lincoln for 1960."*

**Nameplate year of origin:** 1956.

**Current bodystyle lifespan:** 1958 through 1960.

**Predecessor to this model:** Premiere (1956 to 1957).

**Replacement for this model:** Continental (1961 to 1969).

**Percentage of division's sales volume:** 26.49%.

**Corporate siblings:** None.

**Primary competition:** Cadillac de Ville, Imperial Crown and LeBaron.

**Notable changes:** New grille and minor revisions.

**Major standard equipment:** Leather bench 4-way power seat, rear center armrest, padded instrument panel and sun visors, power windows, electric clock, rear compartment reading lamps, heater and defroster, Travel-tuner AM radio, windshield washers, remote control outside mirror, power steering, power brakes, Twin-Range Turbo-Drive automatic transmission, full wheel covers and 9.50 × 14 WSW tires.

## Measurements

| | |
|---|---|
| Wheelbase | 131.0" |
| Length | 227.2" |
| Width | 80.3" |
| Height | 56.7" |
| Legroom — front | 44.1" |
| Legroom — rear | 46.1" |
| Headroom — front | 34.9" |
| Headroom — rear | 33.8" |
| Luggage capacity (cu. ft.) | NA |
| Fuel capacity (gals.) | 25.0 |

## Models Available

| | Style Number | Base MSRP | Change from LY | Shipping Wt. (lbs.) | Production | Change from LY |
|---|---|---|---|---|---|---|
| Premiere 2-Door Hardtop | 63B | $5,698 | +6.56% | 4965 | 1,364 | -30.51% |

| | Style Number | Base MSRP | Change from LY | Shipping Wt. (lbs.) | Production | Change from LY |
|---|---|---|---|---|---|---|
| Premiere 4-Door Sedan | 53B | $5,945 | +6.27% | 5064 | 1,010 | -21.22% |
| Premiere 4-Door Landau HT | 57B | $5,945 | +6.27% | 5060 | 4,200 | -8.81% |
| TOTALS | | Avg. price $5,863 | +6.37% | Production | 6,574 | -16.27% |

# Continental Mark V

*"A new peak of perfection for America's finest motorcar."*

**Nameplate year of origin:** 1940.
**Current bodystyle lifespan:** 1958 through 1960.
**Predecessor to this model:** Continental Mark II (1956 to 1957).
**Replacement for this model:** Continental (1961 to 1969).
**Percentage of division's sales volume:** 44.67%.
**Corporate siblings:** None.
**Primary competition:** Cadillac de Ville and Imperial LeBaron.
**Notable changes:** New grille and minor revisions.
**Major standard equipment:** Premiere features plus: Leather bench 6-way power seat, rear compartment reading lamps, power vent windows, retractable rear window, rear compartment reading lamps, and remote control outside mirror. Town Car and Limousine add: 2-way power seats (Limo.), rear seat radio (Limo.), air conditioning (front in Town Car, front and rear in Limo.), delete retractable rear window.

## Measurements

| | |
|---|---|
| Wheelbase | 131.0" |
| Length | 227.2" |
| Width | 80.3" |
| Height | 56.7" |
| Legroom — front | 44.1" |
| Legroom — rear | 46.1" |
| Headroom — front | 34.9" |
| Headroom — rear | 33.8" |
| Luggage capacity (cu. ft.) | NA |
| Fuel capacity (gals.) | 25.0 |

## Models Available

| | Style Number | Base MSRP | Change from LY | Shipping Wt. (lbs.) | Production | Change from LY |
|---|---|---|---|---|---|---|
| Continental Mark V 2-Door HT | 65A | $6,598 | 0.00% | 5044 | 1,461 | -14.21% |
| Continental Mark V 2-Door Conv. | 68A | $7,056 | 0.00% | 5180 | 2,044 | -6.88% |
| Continental Mark V 4-Door Sedan | 54A | $6,845 | 0.00% | 5143 | 807 | -15.50% |
| Continental Mark V 4-Door HT | 75A | $6,845 | 0.00% | 5139 | 6,604 | +7.45% |
| Continental Mark V 4-Door Town Car | 23B | $9,208 | 0.00% | 5272 | 136 | +74.36% |
| Continental Mark V 4-Dr. Limousine | 23A | $10,230 | 0.00% | 5481 | 34 | -30.61% |
| TOTALS | | Avg. price $7,797 | 0.00% | Production | 11,086 | -0.36% |

# MERCURY

*"Don't Buy Any Car Until You've Driven the Road-Tuned 1960 Mercury. The Best-Built Car in America Today."*

Mercury has traditionally been the Ford division that flexes to meet market demands more than any other. The best reason that can be given is that the mid-price market sees the most frequent changes. Early on in life, Mercury was the "senior" Ford model. It looked like a Ford, was usually powered by a variation of a Ford engine, and was trimmed similarly to the upper-price Ford models. In the fifties, as Americans became more affluent, the Mercury moved upscale with them, and for the first time had become more of a "junior" Lincoln, rather than a "senior" Ford. When Ford looked at adding a fourth line, the "E-Car" or Edsel, to the line, Ford executives felt that they could position the Edsel into the market held by Mercury, and move Mercury farther upmarket into territory that, twenty years earlier, would have been held by the Lincoln Zephyr. When the Edsel failed to meet expectations, Ford shifted the Edsel downmarket, overlapping many Ford models in the process, and brought the Mercury back into its former market position. To demonstrate this shift, a price comparison of the top model convertibles available for each year gives insight into the marketing strategy.

| 1956 | 1957 | 1958 | 1959 | 1960 | 1961 |
|------|------|------|------|------|------|
| $2900 | $4103 | $4118 | $4206 | $4018 | $3126 |

Throughout this market shifting, the Monterey became the mainstay of the line, and the most popular of all the Mercury models. Engine choices were similar to prior years, and the only noteworthy model change for 1960 was the elimination of the 2-Door Station Wagon body style.

What made really big news for 1960 was the all-new Comet model. Technically not a Mercury until the 1962 model year, the Comet was a stand-alone model, marketed primarily by Mercury dealers. This would be the first six-cylinder powered Mercury ever. Based largely on the Ford Falcon, the Comet was slightly larger and better equipped, and was styled to look like the smaller Mercury that it was. Powertrain and model availability was similar to those on the Falcon. Introduction of the Comet was very successful, and created a nearly unheard of 85 percent increase in model year sales for the Mercury division (Comet sales were calculated with Mercury for 1960 and 1961), making up for many lost Edsel sales. It is now widely believed that originally the Comet was intended as an Edsel replacement as Ford fought against the public perception that the Edsel was a failure.

Comet 2-Door Wagon

Comet 4-Door Sedan

Monterey 4-Door Sedan

Commuter 4-Door Hardtop Wagon

Park Lane 4-Door Cruiser Hardtop

**Model year production:** 271,331, up 85.2% over 1959.
**Domestic market share:** 4.50% (8th place).
**Base price range:** $1,998 to $4,018.
**Industry average base price:** $3,391.
**Mercury average base price:** $3,025.
**Introduction date:** October, 1959.
**Assembly plants:** Lorain, OH (H); Los Angeles, CA (J); Kansas City, MO (K); San Jose, CA (R); Wixom, MI (S); Metuchen, NJ (T); Wayne, MI (W); St. Louis, MO (Z).

**Data plate identification:** Eleven digit code read as follows: 0 for 1960; 2nd digit is assembly plant code; 3rd digit is series (0 is Comet, 3 is Monterey, 4 is Montclair and 5 is Park Lane); 4th digit is body style; 5th digit is engine code; 500001 and up for serial number (800001 and up for Comet). *Example:* 0W33P100001 is a 1960 Mercury Monterey 2-Door Hardtop with a 312 CID V8 engine, serial number 500001, built in Wayne, MI.

## Powertrains

| Engine | Gross HP | Engine Code | Transmission Availability | Comet | Commuter & Monterey | Colony Park & Montclair | Park Lane |
|--------|----------|-------------|---------------------------|-------|---------------------|-------------------------|-----------|
| 144.3 CID Thrift-Power Six, 1-bbl., 6-cyl. | 85 | S | 3-speed manual | S | - | - | - |
| | | | Comet Drive 2-sp. Automatic | $172 | - | - | - |

| Engine | Gross HP | Engine Code | Transmission Availability | Comet | Commuter & Monterey | Colony Park & Montclair | Park Lane |
|---|---|---|---|---|---|---|---|
| 312 CID Economy, 2-bbl., V8 | 205 | P | 3-speed manual | - | S | - | - |
| | | | Merc-O-Matic Automatic | - | $173 | - | - |
| 383 CID Marauder, 4-bbl., V8 | 280 | N | 3-speed manual | - | $83 | - | - |
| | | | Merc-O-Matic Automatic | - | $256 | - | - |
| | | | Multi-Drive Auto. | - | $282 | - | - |
| 430 CID Marauder, 4-bbl., V8 | 310 | M | 3-speed manual | - | $177 | - | - |
| | | | Merc-O-Matic Automatic | - | $350 | S | - |
| | | | Multi-Drive Auto. | - | $376 | $26 | S |

## Major Options

| | Comet | Monterey | Montclair | Park Lane |
|---|---|---|---|---|
| Heater and defroster | $74 | $79 | $79 | $79 |
| SelectAire air conditioning | - | $472 | $472 | $472 |
| Tinted glass (windshield on Comet) | $10 | $43 | $43 | $43 |
| Power steering | - | $106 | $106 | S |
| Power brakes | - | $43 | $43 | S |
| Power windows | - | $106 | $106 | $106 |
| Electric windshield wipers w/washer | $23 | $25 | $25 | S |
| Electric clock | - | $15 | S | S |
| Pushbutton AM radio | $59 | $86 | $86 | $86 |
| White sidewall tires — std. Sizes | $43 | $43 | $43 | $43 |
| Full wheel covers | $16 | $19 | S | S |

Options common to most models. (- = Not Available, S = Standard equipment.) Items may be standard equipment, optional at different pricing, or unavailable on certain models. This chart is only a guide.

## Paint Colors

| | Code |
|---|---|
| Tuxedo Black | A |
| Marine Blue Metallic | B |
| Crystal Turquoise | C |
| Aztec Turquoise Metallic | D |
| Cote D'azur Blue Metallic | E |
| Inlet Blue | F |
| Javelin Bronze Metallic | H |
| Signal Red | J |
| Twilight Turquoise Metallic | K |
| Sultana White | M |
| Polynesian Beige | N |
| Royal Lilac Metallic | Q |
| Sun Haze Yellow | R |
| Valley Green Metallic | T |
| Mountain Rose Metallic | U |
| Summer Rose | V |
| Cameo Green | W |
| Tuscon Turquoise | X |
| Cloud Silver Metallic | Z |

# Comet

*"Fine car styling for the economy-wise."*

**Nameplate year of origin:** 1960.
**Current bodystyle lifespan:** 1960 through 1963.
**Predecessor to this model:** None.
**Replacement for this model:** Comet (1964 to 1965).
**Percentage of division's sales volume:** 42.87%.
**Corporate siblings:** Ford Falcon.
**Primary competition:** Plymouth Valiant and Studebaker Lark.
**Notable changes:** All-new model for 1960.
**Major standard equipment:** Nylon and vinyl front bench seat with foam cushions, black carpet textured rubber floor covering, dual front armrests and dual sun visors, dome light, glove compartment, bright metal front and rear window trim, and 6.00 × 13 BSW tires (6.50 × 13 BSW tires on station wagons).

## Measurements

| | Cars | Wagons |
|---|---|---|
| Wheelbase | 114.0" | 109.5" |
| Length | 194.9" | 191.8" |
| Width | 70.4" | 70.4" |
| Height | 54.5" | 55.1" |
| Legroom — front | 43.3" | 43.3" |
| Legroom — rear | 39.4" | 39.4" |
| Headroom — front | 33.9" | 33.9" |
| Headroom — rear | 32.8" | 33.2" |
| Cargo capacity (cu. ft.) | 28.5 | 76.2 |
| Fuel capacity (gals.) | 14.0 | 14.0 |

## Models Available

| | Style Number | Base MSRP | Change from LY | Shipping Wt. (lbs.) | Production | Change from LY |
|---|---|---|---|---|---|---|
| Comet 2-Door Sedan | 62A | $1,998 | NEW | 2399 | 45,374 | NEW |
| Comet 4-Door Sedan | 54A | $2,053 | NEW | 2432 | 47,416 | NEW |
| Comet 2-Door Wagon | 59A | $2,310 | NEW | 2548 | 5,115 | NEW |
| Comet 4-Door Wagon | 71A | $2,365 | NEW | 2581 | 18,426 | NEW |
| TOTALS | Avg. price | $2,182 | NEW | Production | 116,331 | NEW |

# Monterey

*"The Fashionable Monterey."*

**Nameplate year of origin:** 1952.
**Current bodystyle lifespan:** 1961 through 1962.
**Predecessor to this model:** Monterey and Montclair (1959 to 1960).
**Replacement for this model:** Monterey (1963 to 1964).
**Percentage of division's sales volume:** 37.79%.
**Corporate siblings:** Ford Fairlane and Galaxie.
**Primary competition:** Buick LeSabre, Dodge Polara, Oldsmobile 88 and Pontiac Catalina.
**Notable changes:** Completely restyled front and rear end treatments.
**Major standard equipment:** Cloth and vinyl front bench seat, foam front seat cushion, full carpeting, 3-speed electric windshield wipers, dual fender ornaments, bright exterior window trim and 8.00 × 14 BSW tires.

### Measurements

| | |
|---|---|
| Wheelbase | 126.0" |
| Length | 219.2" |
| Width | 81.5" |
| Height | 55.7" |
| Legroom — front | 46.2" |
| Legroom — rear | 43.0" |
| Headroom — front | 38.5" |
| Headroom — rear | 37.1" |
| Cargo capacity (cu. ft.) | 31.5 |
| Fuel capacity (gals.) | 20.0 |

## Models Available

| | Style Number | Base MSRP | Change from LY | Shipping Wt. (lbs.) | Production | Change from LY |
|---|---|---|---|---|---|---|
| Monterey 2-Door Sedan | 64A | $2,631 | -4.95% | 3901 | 21,557 | 69.82% |
| Monterey 2-Door Cruiser Hardtop | 63A | $2,781 | -2.56% | 3931 | 15,790 | -8.37% |
| Monterey 2-Door Convertible | 76A | $3,077 | -2.32% | 4131 | 6,062 | 36.96% |
| Monterey 4-Door Sedan | 58A | $2,730 | -3.60% | 3981 | 49,594 | 13.83% |
| Monterey 4-Door Cruiser Hardtop | 57A | $2,845 | -2.50% | 4011 | 9,536 | -16.02% |
| TOTALS | Avg. price | $2,813 | -3.13% | Production | 102,539 | +14.85% |

# Montclair

*"The Elegant Montclair."*

**Nameplate year of origin:** 1955.
**Current bodystyle lifespan:** 1959 through 1960.
**Predecessor to this model:** Montclair (1957 to 1958).
**Replacement for this model:** Monterey Custom (1962).
**Percentage of division's sales volume:** 7.31%.
**Corporate siblings:** Mercury Monterey and Park Lane.
**Primary competition:** Buick Invicta, DeSoto Fireflite, Oldsmobile 88 and Pontiac Star Chief/Bonneville.
**Notable changes:** Completely restyled front and rear end treatments.

### Measurements

| | |
|---|---|
| Wheelbase | 126.0" |
| Length | 219.2" |
| Width | 81.5" |
| Height | 55.7" |
| Legroom — front | 46.2" |
| Legroom — rear | 43.0" |
| Headroom — front | 38.5" |
| Headroom — rear | 37.1" |

**Major standard equipment:** Cloth and vinyl front bench seat, foam front seat cushion, full carpeting, padded instrument panel, 3-speed electric windshield wipers, dual fender ornaments, bright exterior window trim and 8.50 × 14 BSW tires.

### Measurements (cont.)

| | |
|---|---|
| Cargo capacity (cu. ft.) | 31.5 |
| Fuel capacity (gals.) | 20.0 |

## Models Available

| | Style Number | Base MSRP | Change from LY | Shipping Wt. (lbs.) | Production | Change from LY |
|---|---|---|---|---|---|---|
| Montclair 2-Door Cruiser Hardtop | 63B | $3,331 | -0.77% | 4205 | 5,756 | -21.95% |
| Montclair 4-Door Sedan | 58B | $3,280 | -0.85% | 4255 | 8,510 | -10.55% |
| Montclair 4-Door Cruiser Hardtop | 57B | $3,394 | -1.25% | 4285 | 5,548 | -17.35% |
| TOTALS | | *Avg. price* $3,335 | -0.86% | | *Production* 19,814 | -16.04% |

# Park Lane

*"The Distinguished Park Lane."*

**Nameplate year of origin:** 1958.
**Current bodystyle lifespan:** 1959 through 1960.
**Predecessor to this model:** Turnpike Cruiser (1957 to 1958).
**Replacement for this model:** None (Park Lane returned in 1964).
**Percentage of division's sales volume:** 3.79%.
**Corporate siblings:** Mercury Monterey and Montclair.
**Primary competition:** Buick Electra, Chrysler Saratoga, DeSoto Adventurer, and Oldsmobile 98.
**Notable changes:** Completely restyled front and rear end treatments.
**Major standard equipment:** Cloth and vinyl front bench seat, foam front seat cushion, full carpeting, padded instrument panel, 3-speed electric windshield wipers with washers, dual fender ornaments, bright exterior window trim, automatic transmission, power steering, power brakes, and 8.50 × 14 BSW tires.

### Measurements

| | |
|---|---|
| Wheelbase | 126.0" |
| Length | 219.2" |
| Width | 81.5" |
| Height | 55.7" |
| Legroom — front | 46.2" |
| Legroom — rear | 43.0" |
| Headroom — front | 38.5" |
| Headroom — rear | 37.1" |
| Cargo capacity (cu. ft.) | 31.5 |
| Fuel capacity (gals.) | 20.0 |

## Models Available

| | Style Number | Base MSRP | Change from LY | Shipping Wt. (lbs.) | Production | Change from LY |
|---|---|---|---|---|---|---|
| Park Lane 2-Door Cruiser Hardtop | 63F | $3,794 | -4.07% | 4300 | 2,974 | -26.75% |
| Park Lane 2-Door Convertible | 76D | $4,018 | -4.47% | 4500 | 1,525 | 21.32% |
| Park Lane 4-Door Cruiser Hardtop | 57F | $3,858 | -4.29% | 4380 | 5,788 | -19.68% |
| TOTALS | | *Avg. price* $3,890 | -4.28% | | *Production* 10,287 | -17.86% |

# Country Cruisers

*"Mercury's Spacious Country Cruisers."*

**Nameplate year of origin:** 1957 (Commuter and Colony Park).
**Current bodystyle lifespan:** 1959 through 1960.
**Predecessor to this model:** Station Wagons (1957 to 1958).
**Replacement for this model:** Station Wagons (1961 to 1962).

### Measurements

| | |
|---|---|
| Wheelbase | 126.0" |
| Length | 219.2" |
| Width | 81.5" |

**Percentage of division's sales volume:** 8.24%.
**Corporate siblings:** Mercury Monterey, Montclair and Park Lane.
**Primary competition:** Buick LeSabre/Invicta Estate Wagons, Chrysler Town & Country, and Oldsmobile 88 Fiesta Wagons.
**Notable changes:** Completely restyled front and rear end treatments.
**Major standard equipment:** Cloth and vinyl front bench seat, full carpeting, padded instrument panel, bright exterior window trim and 8.50 × 14 BSW tires. Colony Park adds: Exterior vinyl wood-grained trim, power rear tailgate window, automatic transmission, and padded instrument panel.

## Measurements (cont.)

| | |
|---|---|
| Height | 56.0" |
| Legroom — front | 44.2" |
| Legroom — rear | 43.6" |
| Headroom — front | 33.3" |
| Headroom — rear | 33.0" |
| Cargo capacity (cu. ft.) | NA |
| Fuel capacity (gals.) | 20.0 |

## Models Available

| | Style Number | Base MSRP | Change from LY | Shipping Wt. (lbs.) | Production | Change from LY |
|---|---|---|---|---|---|---|
| Commuter 4-Door HT Wagon | 77A | $3,127 | -2.74% | 4301 | 14,949 | -1.14% |
| Colony Park 4-Door HT Wagon | 77B | $3,837 | -2.42% | 4558 | 7,411 | +24.37% |
| TOTALS | | *Avg. price* $3,482 | -2.57% | | *Production* 22,360 | +6.07% |

# OLDSMOBILE

*"For 1960 … It's Mighty Satisfying to Own an Olds!"*

The 1960 Oldsmobile line underwent a major styling overhaul this year. While still based on the new, dramatically lower silhouette platform of the 1959 model, the front and back ends were so drastically altered that the cars appeared to be all-new. Up front, the headlights separated by parking lamps were discontinued as a styling feature, but would return again. The parking lights would move to the bumper for 1960 and 1961, but in the mid-sixties they would move back between the headlights, in what would become a styling trademark for the next twenty years. At the back end, Oldsmobiles were identifiable by a pair of small, horizontal taillights set into the upper tail fin section, and "Oldsmobile" spelled out across the back. Oldsmobile had never been known as a style leader, instead opting for the title of powertrain and driveline innovator within General Motors. In that department, there was nothing new for the start of the new decade, but given time, that would all change.

A 7-passenger Super 88 Fiesta wagon was added as an official model, as opposed to an option package. A 98 2-Door Convertible was selected to be this year's Official Pace Car for the Indianapolis 500 race. This was only the second time in Oldsmobile's long history that it had been selected to pace the race. However, in the next 40 years it would take the honors eight more times. Also noteworthy, this would be the last year for Olds to offer its traditional three-model lineup.

**98 2-Door Convertible,
Indianapolis 500 Pace Car**

**88 4-Door Fiesta Wagon**

**Super 88 2-Door SceniCoupe Hardtop**

**Super 88 4-Door Holiday Hardtop**

**Model year production:** 341,433, down 10.67% from 1959.
**Domestic market share:** 5.66% (7th place).
**Base price range:** $2,835 to $4,362.
**Industry average base price:** $3,391.
**Oldsmobile average base price:** $3,486.
**Introduction date:** October 1, 1959.
**Assembly Plants:** Atlanta, GA (A); Southgate, CA (C); Fairfax, KS (K); Linden, NJ (L); Lansing, MI (M); Arlington, TX (T); and Wilmington, DE (W).

**Data plate identification:** Nine digit code read as follows: 1st two digits 60 = 1960 year; 3rd digit designates trim level; 4th digit identifies assembly plant; 01001 and up for serial number. Check model number on body plate for body style. *Example* 609M01001 is a 1960 Oldsmobile Ninety-Eight, built in Lansing, MI, serial number 01001.

## Powertrains

| Engine | Gross HP | Transmission Availability | Dynamic 88 | Super 88 | 98 |
|---|---|---|---|---|---|
| 371 CID Rocket, 2-bbl., V8 | 240 | 3-speed manual | S | - | - |
| | | Hydra-Matic Automatic | $231 | - | - |
| 394 CID Rocket, 4-bbl., V8 | 315 | 3-speed manual | - | S | - |
| | | Hydra-Matic Automatic | - | $231 | S |

## Major Options

| | Dynamic 88 | Super 88 | Ninety-Eight |
|---|---|---|---|
| Heater/defroster | $97 | $97 | S |
| Air conditioning | $430 | $430 | $430 |
| Soft Ray tinted glass | $ | $ | $ |
| Courtesy lamps | $5 | S | S |
| Outside rear view mirror — LH | $4 | $4 | $4 |
| Power steering — variable-ratio | $107 | $107 | S |
| Power brakes | $43 | $43 | S |
| Power driver's seat/Bench seat | $68 | $68 | $68 |
| Power windows | $106 | $106 | S/$106-Sedan |
| AM radio | $88 | $88 | $88 |
| Electric clock | $19 | $19 | S |
| Windshield washers | $11 | $11 | S |

Options common to most models. (S = Standard equipment.) Items may be standard equipment, optional at different pricing, or unavailable on certain models. This chart is only a guide.

## Paint Colors

| | Code |
|---|---|
| Ebony Black | A |
| Charcoal Mist Metallic | B |
| Provincial White | C |
| Platinum Mist Metallic | D |
| Gulf Blue Metallic | F |
| Dresden Blue Metallic | H |
| Palmetto Mist Metallic | J |
| Fern Mist Metallic | K |
| Garnet Mist Metallic | L |
| Citron | M |
| Cordovan Metallic | N |
| Golden Mist Metallic | P |
| Shell Beige | R |
| Copper Mist Metallic | S |
| Turquoise Metallic | T |

# Dynamic 88

*"Rocket 'Go' on lower-cost, regular gas! Every dollar-saving Dynamic 88 puts glamor on the go … with special attention to the economy-minded!"*

**Nameplate year of origin:** 1949 (1958 for Dynamic nameplate).
**Current bodystyle lifespan:** 1959 through 1960.
**Predecessor to this model:** Dynamic/Golden Rocket 88 (1957 to 1958).
**Replacement for this model:** Dynamic 88 (1961 to 1964).
**Percentage of division's sales volume:** 53.94%.
**Corporate siblings:** Buick LeSabre, Chevrolet Impala, Pontiac Catalina.
**Primary competition:** AMC Ambassador, Dodge Polara, Mercury Monterey.
**Notable changes:** Restyled front and rear end.
**Major standard equipment:** Cloth-and-vinyl bench seat, nylon-blend carpet, full wheel covers, and 8.50 × 14 BSW tires.

## Measurements

| | |
|---|---|
| Wheelbase | 123.0" |
| Length | 217.6" |
| Width | 80.6" |
| Height | 54.2" |
| Legroom — front | 44.2" |
| Legroom — rear | 42.2" |
| Headroom — front | 34.7" |
| Headroom — rear | 33.9" |
| Luggage capacity (cu. ft.) | NA |
| Fuel capacity (gals.) | 20.0 |

## Models Available

| | Style Number | Base MSRP | Change from LY | Shipping Wt. (lbs.) | Production | Change from LY |
|---|---|---|---|---|---|---|
| 88 2-Door Sedan | 3211 | $2,835 | -0.07% | 4026 | 13,545 | -10.43% |
| 88 2-Door HT Sceni-Coupe | 3237 | $2,956 | -0.07% | 4049 | 29,368 | -23.70% |
| 88 2-Door Convertible | 3267 | $3,284 | -0.06% | 4101 | 12,271 | 44.52% |
| 88 4-Door Celebrity Sedan | 3219 | $2,900 | -0.07% | 4091 | 76,377 | 7.58% |
| 88 4-Door Holiday Hardtop | 3239 | $3,034 | -0.07% | 4139 | 43,761 | -10.15% |
| 88 4-Dr., 2-S. Fiesta Wagon | 3235 | $3,363 | -0.06% | 4449 | 8,834 | -21.81% |
| 88 4-Dr., 3-S. Fiesta Wagon | 3245 | $3,471 | NEW | 4470 | * | NEW |
| TOTALS | Avg. price | $3,120 | -0.06% | Production | 184,156 | -4.63% |

*3-Seat Wagon production included with 2-Seat Wagon.

# Super 88

*"Spirited, super action! Super sparkle of new interiors, radiantly styled for the Rocketing Sixties! Most satisfying ride you ever tried!"*

**Nameplate year of origin:** 1951 (88 series started 1949).
**Current bodystyle lifespan:** 1959 through 1960.
**Predecessor to this model:** Super 88 (1957 to 1958).
**Replacement for this model:** Super 88 (1961 to 1964).
**Percentage of division's sales volume:** 28.68%.
**Corporate siblings:** Buick Invicta, Chevrolet Impala, Pontiac Star Chief.
**Primary competition:** AMC Ambassador, DeSoto Adventurer, and Mercury Montclair.
**Notable changes:** Restyled front and rear end.
**Major standard equipment:** Nylon and vinyl bench seat, nylon-blend carpet, Deluxe steering wheel, glove box and courtesy lamps, full wheel covers, and 8.50 × 14 BSW tires.

## Measurements

| | |
|---|---|
| Wheelbase | 123.0" |
| Length | 217.6" |
| Width | 80.6" |
| Height | 54.2" |
| Legroom — front | 44.2" |
| Legroom — rear | 42.2" |
| Headroom — front | 34.7" |
| Headroom — rear | 33.9" |
| Luggage capacity (cu. ft.) | NA |
| Fuel capacity (gals.) | 20.0 |

## Models Available

| | Style No. | Base MSRP | Change from LY | Shipping Wt. (lbs.) | Production | Change from LY |
|---|---|---|---|---|---|---|
| Super 88 2-Dr. HT Sceni-Coupe | 3537 | $3,325 | -0.09% | 4086 | 16,464 | -18.73% |
| Super 88 2-Door Convertible | 3567 | $3,592 | -0.08% | 4134 | 5,830 | 19.10% |
| Super 88 4-Door Celebrity Sedan | 3519 | $3,176 | -0.06% | 4128 | 35,094 | -4.77% |
| Super 88 4-Door Holiday Hardtop | 3539 | $3,402 | -0.09% | 4182 | 33,285 | -13.47% |
| Super 88 4-Dr., 2-S. Fiesta Wgn. | 3535 | $3,665 | -0.11% | 4483 | 3,765 | -46.33% |
| Super 88 4-Dr., 3-S. Fiesta Wgn. | 3545 | $3,773 | NEW | 4506 | 3,475 | NEW |
| TOTALS | Avg. price | $3,489 | +1.57% | Production | 97,913 | -8.90% |

# Ninety-Eight

*"Who could ask for anything more! Here's the height of elegant satisfaction, the finest car the medium-price class can offer!"*

**Nameplate year of origin:** 1941.
**Current bodystyle lifespan:** 1959 through 1960.
**Predecessor to this model:** Ninety-Eight (1957 to 1958).
**Replacement for this model:** Ninety-Eight (1961 to 1964).
**Percentage of division's sales volume:** 17.38%.
**Corporate siblings:** Buick Electra and Cadillac de Ville.
**Primary competition:** Chrysler New Yorker and Mercury Park Lane.
**Notable changes:** Restyled front and rear end.
**Major standard equipment:** Leather, nylon and vinyl bench seat with fold-down center armrest, deep-pile carpeting, deluxe steering wheel, power windows (except sedan), electric clock, trunk lamp, trunk mat, power steering, power brakes, Jetaway Hydra-matic automatic transmission, full wheel covers, and 9.00 × 14 BSW tires.

### Measurements

| | |
|---|---|
| Wheelbase | 126.3" |
| Length | 220.9" |
| Width | 80.6" |
| Height | 54.2" |
| Legroom — front | 43.8" |
| Legroom — rear | 44.4" |
| Headroom — front | 32.3" |
| Headroom — rear | 33.8" |
| Luggage capacity (cu. ft.) | NA |
| Fuel capacity (gals.) | 20.0 |

## Models Available

| | Style No. | Base MSRP | Change from LY | Shipping Wt. (lbs.) | Production | Change from LY |
|---|---|---|---|---|---|---|
| Ninety-Eight 2-Dr HT Sceni-Cpe | 3837 | $4,083 | -0.07% | 4322 | 7,635 | -44.27% |
| Ninety-Eight 2-Door Convertible | 3867 | $4,362 | -0.09% | 4349 | 7,284 | -9.02% |
| Ninety-Eight 4-Dr. Celebrity Sdn | 3819 | $3,887 | -0.08% | 4360 | 17,188 | -25.61% |
| Ninety-Eight 4-Door Holiday HT | 3839 | $4,159 | -0.07% | 4431 | 27,257 | -25.96% |
| TOTALS | Avg. price | $4,123 | -0.08% | Production | 59,364 | -27.27% |

# PLYMOUTH

*"The Story of the Solid Plymouth for 1960."*

Plymouth sales had been riding high during the late fifties, and it was hoped that Plymouth would continue that success well into the new decade. There were numerous roadblocks to overcome, but one of those, the rising popularity of the American Motors line of smaller cars, was about to be addressed by Chrysler. Chrysler Corporation officially entered the 1960 compact car contest with the dressy looking Valiant. While listed here as a Plymouth, the make it would officially be identified with from 1961, its actual marketing position was as a stand-alone model (see below). The Valiant was a product of genuine American competition. Chrysler had a financial interest in a European company (Simca would eventually market the Plymouth Cricket in the early seventies) that could have easily provided a compact car to compete with the Corvair or Falcon. The problem was no one in the United States was certain how American built compact cars would be accepted by the buying public. Ford took the approach of strict conservatism with the Falcon. General Motors held the unusual position of reaching out on a limb for a head-to-head combatant for the VW in their Corvair. Chrysler had been working on a more or less conservative approach, but wanted its car to offer some of the styling and features that Americans were used to, not just a plain jane "econobox." The result was the Valiant, styled to look like a larger car, with big car equipment and ride. Therefore, like all other Mopar products for 1960, the Valiant featured "unit-body" construction with torsion bar suspension in the front for a solid ride and feel. Under the hood was the largest standard engine of any of the "Big 3" compacts for more power. Interior and exterior styling mimicked Chrysler products everywhere you looked, including tailfins at the rear, a fake spare tire cover on the decklid, dual headlamps up front, and a push-button automatic transmission selector.

Officially the Valiant was introduced as its own make within Chrysler Corporation. It was built by Dodge, but sold mostly through Plymouth dealerships. In retrospect, the reasoning for selling through Plymouth dealerships most likely has to do with the coming demise of the De-Soto, which was generally sold through dual Plymouth-DeSoto dealerships. Nearly all Plymouths were sold through some type of dual (or multiple) dealer setup. This type of marketing kept the dealers happy, as they still had sales coming in the door, even though they were about to lose an entire line of cars.

The full-size Plymouth line received the same makeover as the other Chrysler offerings for 1960. All were based on the new unit-body construction. Overall styling was evolutionary from the look of the 1957–1959 line, but came off a bit overdone and unusual. The front end featured a grille that looked like it belonged on a Chrysler or DeSoto, with small horizontal bars set within vertical groupings. Dual headlamps were fitted at each end of the grille, with square parking lamps and turn signals centered below each pair of headlamps. These were mounted atop a much thinner front bumper. The unique styling came with the lone bodyside style treatment. This styling cue actually started at the front outside edge of the hood, wrapped up across the headlamps, around the front corner of the fender, then came back across the top of the front wheel opening, where it followed the wheel opening down to the rocker panel with a slight forward "kick" to it. Otherwise body side panels were smooth and uncluttered, which was quite a departure from most other American products of the time. At the rear, Plymouth bucked the Detroit trend and featured tail fins that were as tall as any ever to be seen on a Plymouth. Rear styling was similar to prior years, with 2-door Hardtop models featuring a unique "Ski-Hi" rear window treatment that went forward, well over the rear seating area. Powertrains were similar to prior years with two notable exceptions. The first was the new 225 CID 6-cylinder, which replaced the aging L-Head Six used for so many years. This new engine was more powerful and dependable, and would serve Plymouth in millions of cars for the next thirty years. The other new engine was the 383 CID V8. This powerful new "SonoRamic Commando" engine was based on the proven Dodge engines of the day, and would prove to be quite a powerhouse in the lighter weight Plymouth.

Valiant V200 4-Door Sedan

Valiant V200 4-Door Wagon

Savoy 4-Door Sedan

Belvedere 2-Door Club Sedan

Fury 2-Door Convertible

Fury 4-Door Hardtop

Sport Suburban 4-Door Wagon

**Model year production:** 447,722, up 6.42% over 1959.
**Domestic market share:** 7.43% (3rd place).
**Base price range:** $2,053 to $2,990.
**Industry average base price:** $3,391.
**Plymouth average base price:** $2,650.
**Introduction date:** October, 1959.
**Assembly plants:** Lynch Road, MI (1); Hamtramck, MI (2); Detroit, MI (3); Los Angeles, CA (5); Newark DE (6); and St. Louis, MO (7).
**Data plate identification:** Ten digit code read as follows: First number designates type of powerplant (see engine code); second number is series designation (0 = Fleet, 1 = Valiant or Savoy, 2 = Belvedere, 3 = Valiant V200 or Fury, 5 = Valiant Wagon or Suburban, 7 = Valiant V200 Wagon); third digit 0 for 1960; fourth digit is assembly plant code; 100001 and up for serial number. *Example:* 2302100001 is a 1960 Plymouth Fury with a 225 CID 6-cyl., built at Hamtramck, MI, serial number 100001. Body style cannot be identified through the VIN.

## Powertrains

| Engine | Gross HP | Engine Code | Transmission Availability | Valiant | Savoy*/ Belvedere | Fury** |
|---|---|---|---|---|---|---|
| 170 CID, 1-bbl., 6-cyl. | 101 | 1 | 3-speed manual | S | - | - |
| | | | Torqueflite automatic | $172 | - | - |
| 170 CID, 4-bbl., 6-cyl. | 148 | 1 | 3-speed manual | $ | - | - |
| | | | Torqueflite automatic | $ | - | - |
| 225 CID 30-D Economy Six, 1-bbl., 6-cyl. | 145 | 2 | 3-speed manual | - | S | - |
| | | | Powerflite automatic | - | $189 | - |
| | | | Torqueflite automatic | - | $192 | - |
| 318 CID Fury V-800, 2-bbl., V8 | 230 | 3 | 3-speed manual | - | $119 | S |
| | | | PowerFlite automatic | - | $308 | $189 |
| | | | Torqueflite automatic | - | $318 | $199 |
| 318 CID Super Pack, 4-bbl., V8 | 260 | 3 | 3-speed manual | - | $158 | $39 |
| | | | PowerFlite automatic | - | $347 | $228 |
| | | | Torqueflite automatic | - | $357 | $238 |
| 361 CID Golden Commando, 4-bbl., V8 | 305 | 3 | 3-speed manual | - | $325 | $206 |
| | | | Torqueflite automatic | - | $524 | $405 |
| 383 CID SonoRamic Commando, 4-bbl., V8 | 310 | 3 | 3-speed manual | - | $508 | $389 |
| | | | Torqueflite automatic | - | $707 | $588 |
| 383 CID SonoRamic Commando, 2 × 4-bbl., V8 | 330 | 3 | 3-speed manual | - | $524 | $405 |
| | | | Torqueflite automatic | - | $723 | $604 |

*Fury 2- and 4-Door HT and 4-Door Sedan also included.   **Fury Convertible, Custom Suburban 9-passenger and Sport Suburban wagons only.*

## Major Options

| | Valiant | Savoy/Belvedere | Fury |
|---|---|---|---|
| Push-button heater and defroster | $74 | $74 | $74 |
| Air conditioning (V8 only) | - | $446 | $446 |
| Tinted glass | $37 | $43 | $43 |
| Power steering | $73 | $77 | $77 |
| Power brakes | $41 | $43 | $43 |
| Power windows | - | $102 | $102 |
| Electric clock | $16 | $16 | S |
| AM radio | $59 | $59 | $59 |
| White sidewall tires — std. sizes | $29 | $34 | $34 |
| Full wheel covers | $16 | $19 | $19 |

Options common to most models. (- = Not Available; S = Standard equipment.) Items may be standard equipment, optional at different pricing, or unavailable on certain models. This chart is only a guide.

## Paint Colors

| | Code |
|---|---|
| Buttercup Yellow | AA-1 |
| Jet Black | BB-1 |
| Sky Blue | CC-1 |
| Twilight Blue Metallic | DD-1 |
| Spring Green | FF-1 |
| Chrome Green Metallic | GG-1 |
| Aqua Mist | JJ-1 |
| Turquoise Metallic | KK-1 |
| Platinum Metallic | LL-1 |
| Silver Metallic | MM-1 |
| Plum Red M./Valiant Red | PP-1 |
| Desert Beige | TT-1 |
| Oyster White | WW-1 |
| Caramel Metallic | YY-1 |

# Valiant

*"Valiant is the car you'd want at any price."*

**Nameplate year of origin:** 1960.
**Current bodystyle lifespan:** 1960 through 1962.
**Predecessor to this model:** None.
**Replacement for this model:** Valiant (1963 to 1966).
**Percentage of division's sales volume:** 43.40%.
**Corporate siblings:** None.
**Primary competition:** AMC Rambler American, Chevrolet Corvair, Ford Falcon and Studebaker Lark.
**Notable changes:** All-new for 1960.
**Major standard equipment:** Fabric and vinyl bench seat, rubber floor mat, chrome exterior front and rear window trim, Torsion-Aire suspension and 6.50 × 13 BSW tires. V200 adds: Side window chrome trim and color-keyed floor mats.

## Measurements

|  | Cars | Wagons |
|---|---|---|
| Wheelbase | 106.5" | 106.5" |
| Length | 183.7" | 183.7" |
| Width | 70.4" | 70.4" |
| Height | 53.3" | 53.5" |
| Legroom — front | 44.4" | 44.4" |
| Legroom — rear | 38.9" | 38.1" |
| Headroom — front | 33.6" | 33.6" |
| Headroom — rear | 33.4" | 33.5" |
| Cargo capacity (cu. ft.) | 24.9 | 72.3 |
| Fuel capacity (gals.) | 13.0 | 13.0 |

## Models Available

|  | Style Number | Base MSRP | Change from LY | Shipping Wt. (lbs.) | Production | Change from LY |
|---|---|---|---|---|---|---|
| Valiant V100 4-Door Sedan | 110 | $2,053 | NEW | 2635 | 52,788 | NEW |
| Valiant V100 4-Door, 2-S. Wagon | 150 | $2,365 | NEW | 2815 | 12,018 | NEW |
| Valiant V100 4-Door, 3-S. Wagon | 150 | $2,488 | NEW | 2845 | 1,928 | NEW |
| Valiant V200 4-Door Sedan | 130 | $2,130 | NEW | 2655 | 106,515 | NEW |
| Valiant V200 4-Door, 2-S. Wagon | 170 | $2,443 | NEW | 2855 | 16,368 | NEW |
| Valiant V200 4-Door, 3-S. Wagon | 170 | $2,566 | NEW | 2860 | 4,675 | NEW |
| TOTALS | | Avg. price $2,341 | NEW | | Production 194,292 | NEW |

# Savoy

*"No other full-size car costs less to operate than the Savoy."*

**Nameplate year of origin:** 1951 (Concord 2-Door Suburban designation), 1954 (as series).
**Current bodystyle lifespan:** 1960 through 1961.
**Predecessor to this model:** Plaza and Savoy (1957 to 1959).
**Replacement for this model:** Savoy (1962 to 1964).
**Percentage of division's sales volume:** 17.47%.
**Corporate siblings:** Dodge Dart.
**Primary competition:** AMC Rambler, Chevrolet Biscayne/BelAir/Impala, and Ford Fairlane/Galaxie.
**Notable changes:** Completely redesigned.
**Major standard equipment:** Cloth and vinyl bench seat, Color-keyed rubber floor covering, and 7.50 × 14 BSW tires.

## Measurements

| | |
|---|---|
| Wheelbase | 118.0" |
| Length | 209.5" |
| Width | 78.6" |
| Height | 54.6" |
| Legroom — front | 45.1" |
| Legroom — rear | 42.1" |
| Headroom — front | 37.8" |
| Headroom — rear | 38.0" |
| Cargo capacity (cu. ft.) | NA |
| Fuel capacity (gals.) | 21.0 |

## Models Available

|  | Style Number | Base MSRP | Change from LY | Shipping Wt. (lbs.) | Production | Change from LY |
|---|---|---|---|---|---|---|
| Fleet Special 2-Door Sedan | - | $2,227 | NEW | NA | * | NEW |
| Fleet Special 4-Door Sedan | - | $2,277 | NEW | NA | * | NEW |

| | Style Number | Base MSRP | Change from LY | Shipping Wt. (lbs.) | Production | Change from LY |
|---|---|---|---|---|---|---|
| Savoy 2-Door Club Sedan | 21 | $2,260 | +1.25% | 3330 | 26,820 | -42.91% |
| Savoy 4-Door Sedan | 41 | $2,310 | +1.18% | 3365 | 51,384 | -39.03% |
| TOTALS | | Avg. price $2,269 | +0.49% | | Production 78,204 | -40.41% |

*Fleet Special production included with Savoy models.

# Belvedere

*"You will be proud of your Belvedere."*

**Nameplate year of origin:** 1951 (HT model); 1954 (series).
**Current bodystyle lifespan:** 1960 through 1961.
**Predecessor to this model:** Belvedere (1957 to 1959).
**Replacement for this model:** Belvedere (1962 to 1964).
**Percentage of division's sales volume:** 14.01%.
**Corporate siblings:** Dodge Dart.
**Primary competition:** AMC Ambassador, Chevrolet Biscayne/BelAir/Impala, and Ford Fairlane/Galaxie.
**Notable changes:** Completely redesigned.
**Major standard equipment:** Cloth and vinyl bench seat, trunk mat, color-keyed carpeting, dome light, and 7.50 × 14 BSW tires.

## Measurements

| | |
|---|---|
| Wheelbase | 118.0" |
| Length | 209.5" |
| Width | 78.6" |
| Height | 54.6" |
| Legroom — front | 45.1" |
| Legroom — rear | 42.1" |
| Headroom — front | 37.8" |
| Headroom — rear | 38.0" |
| Cargo capacity (cu. ft.) | NA |
| Fuel capacity (gals.) | 21.0 |

## Models Available

| | Style Number | Base MSRP | Change from LY | Shipping Wt. (lbs.) | Production | Change from LY |
|---|---|---|---|---|---|---|
| Belvedere 2-Door Club Sedan | 21 | $2,389 | 0.00% | 3340 | 6,529 | -52.74% |
| Belvedere 2-Door Hardtop | 23 | $2,461 | 0.00% | 3370 | 14,085 | -39.98% |
| Belvedere 4-Door Sedan | 41 | $2,439 | -0.04% | 3375 | 42,130 | -38.03% |
| TOTALS | | Avg. price $2,430 | -0.01% | | Production 62,744 | -40.39% |

# Fury

*"This is Plymouth's luxury line for 1960."*

**Nameplate year of origin:** 1956.
**Current bodystyle lifespan:** 1960 through 1961.
**Predecessor to this model:** Fury (1957 to 1959).
**Replacement for this model:** Fury (1962 to 1964).
**Percentage of division's sales volume:** 12.39%.
**Corporate siblings:** Dodge Polara and Matador.
**Primary competition:** AMC Ambassador, Chevrolet Biscayne/BelAir/Impala, and Ford Galaxie.
**Notable changes:** Completely redesigned.
**Major standard equipment:** All-vinyl or cloth and vinyl front bench seat, deep-pile carpeting, dual sun visors, front and rear armrests, 2-speed windshield wipers with washers, wheel covers, and 7.50 × 14 BSW tires.

## Measurements

| | |
|---|---|
| Wheelbase | 118.0" |
| Length | 209.5" |
| Width | 78.6" |
| Height | 54.6" |
| Legroom — front | 45.1" |
| Legroom — rear | 42.1" |
| Headroom — front | 37.8" |
| Headroom — rear | 38.0" |
| Cargo capacity (cu. ft.) | NA |
| Fuel capacity (gals.) | 21.0 |

## Models Available

| | Style Number | Base MSRP | Change from LY | Shipping Wt. (lbs.) | Production | Change from LY |
|---|---|---|---|---|---|---|
| Fury 2-Door Hardtop | 23 | $2,599 | -4.24% | 3395 | 18,079 | -15.89% |
| Fury 2-Door Convertible | 27 | $2,967 | NEW | 3630 | 7,080 | NEW |
| Fury 4-Door Sedan | 41 | $2,575 | -4.31% | 3400 | 21,292 | -29.38% |
| Fury 4-Door Hardtop | 43 | $2,656 | -4.15% | 3445 | 9,036 | -33.63% |
| TOTALS | | Avg. price $2,699 | -4.51% | | Production 55,487 | -14.97% |

# Suburban

*"The best built wagon in the U.S.A.—Solid Pymouth 1960."*

**Nameplate year of origin:** 1950.
**Current bodystyle lifespan:** 1960 through 1961.
**Predecessor to this model:** Suburban (1957 to 1959).
**Replacement for this model:** Savoy, Belvedere and Fury Wagons (1962 to 1964).
**Percentage of division's sales volume:** 34.77%.
**Corporate siblings:** Dodge Polara.
**Primary competition:** AMC Ambassador, Chevrolet Biscayne/BelAir/Impala, and Ford Galaxie.
**Notable changes:** Completely redesigned.
**Major standard equipment:** Deluxe features similar to Savoy plus 8.00 × 14 BSW tires. Custom adds: features similar to Belvedere. Sport adds: features similar to Fury.

## Measurements

| | |
|---|---|
| Wheelbase | 122.0" |
| Length | 214.9" |
| Width | 78.6" |
| Height | 55.4" |
| Legroom — front | 45.5" |
| Legroom — rear | 42.5" |
| Headroom — front | 35.7" |
| Headroom — rear | 34.6" |
| Cargo capacity (cu. ft.) | 95.8 |
| Fuel capacity (gals.) | 21.0 |

## Models Available

| | Style Number | Base MSRP | Change from LY | Shipping Wt. (lbs.) | Production | Change from LY |
|---|---|---|---|---|---|---|
| Deluxe Sub. 2-Door, 2-Seat Wagon | 25 | $2,602 | +1.09% | 3680 | 5,503 | -63.49% |
| Deluxe Sub. 4-Door, 2-Seat Wagon | 45 | $2,668 | +1.02% | 3740 | 18,482 | -47.32% |
| Custom Sub. 4-Dr., 2-Seat Wagon | 45 | $2,761 | -0.04% | 3750 | 17,308 | -50.58% |
| Custom Sub. 4-Dr., 3-Seat Wagon | 45 | $2,990 | -0.03% | 4000 | 8,116 | -52.24% |
| Sport Sub. 4-Door, 2-Seat Wagon | 45 | $3,024 | +0.10% | 3895 | 3,333 | -53.86% |
| Sport Sub. 4-Door, 3-Seat Wagon | 45 | $3,134 | +0.10% | 4020 | 4,253 | -55.46% |
| TOTALS | | Avg. price $2,863 | +0.35% | | Production 56,995 | -52.09% |

# PONTIAC

*"Fresh point of view ... from Pontiac 1960. The only car with wide-track wheels."*

Pontiac entered the new decade on a roll. Ever since 1955, when a powerful new V8 engine with great potential came onto the scene, the old image of Pontiac had quickly been shed. For years, Pontiacs were known as the solid, dependable family car, a little more posh than Chevrolet at only slightly more cost. The new V8 engine for Pontiac was just the beginning of a transformation that would position Pontiac as the market leader on many fronts. For now, that position was an important combination of power and style. The redesigned 1959 Pontiacs set the world on its ear with the distinctive split-grille front styling and the GM-style hardtop models' ultra-thin roofline styling. Most would have expected the 1960 models to follow the hot 1959 formula, but at the time design work was underway, the 1959 models were not yet on sale, so the designers didn't know what they had on their hands.

The 1960 models were given totally clean, horizontal bar grille work resembling that used on California-style customs of the period. Dual, round taillamps in the rear capped off a "customized" looking rear quarter area, marked by twin barrels from the rear window line to the taillamps. The overall look was as well received as the 1959 models, yet looked totally different.

Continued for the 1960 model year was the "Wide-Track" marketing theme. While Wide-Track was an actual product improvement, providing a greater distance between wheels for greater stability on the road, in reality the difference was sometimes minuscule. But it gave the buying public something to compare to other products, and thus it helped Pontiac gain a competitive edge.

Few changes were made to the engine line this year. The success of Pontiacs in racing probably had much to do with the durability of the 389 V8 in production usage. Pontiac, by now, had earned a strong reputation for speed and endurance, and Pontiac drivers were winning numerous races on the relatively new NASCAR racing circuit. As a tip-off to the street car's relation to the race car, a 4-speed manual transmission became available during the year. However, this transmission was not a regular production option, as most were shipped to racing teams and owners. A few nonetheless found their way into street cars.

Catalina 2-Door Sport Sedan

Catalina 2-Door Convertible

Star Chief 4-Door Vista Hardtop

Bonneville 2-Door Sport Hardtop

Bonneville 4-Door Custom Safari Wagon

**Model year production:** 396,179, up 3.46% over 1959.
**Domestic market share:** 6.57% (5th place).
**Base price range:** $2,631 to $3,530.
**Industry average base price:** $3,391.
**Pontiac average base price:** $3,063.
**Introduction date:** October, 1959.
**Assembly plants:** Arlington, TX (A); Doraville, GA (D); Fairfax, KS (K); Linden, NJ (L); Pontiac, MI (P); Southgate, CA (S); Wilmington, DE (W).

**Data plate identification:** Eight to ten digit code read as follows: 1st digit identifies the series (the second digit of the body style number in the charts below); 2nd and 3rd digits 60 for 1960; 4th digit is assembly plant code; and 1001 and up for serial number. A separate plate contains body style number. *Example:* 160X1001 is a 1960 Pontiac Catalina, serial number 1001, built in Fairfax, KS.

## Powertrains*

| Engine | Gross HP | Transmission Availability | Catalina & Ventura | Star Chief | Bonneville |
|---|---|---|---|---|---|
| 389 CID Tempest — 425E, 2-bbl., V8 | 215 | 3-speed manual | S | S | - |
|  |  | Hydra-matic Automatic | $231 | $231 | No cost |
| 389 CID Tempest 425, 2-bbl., V8 | 283 | Hydra-matic Automatic | $231 | $231 | - |
| 389 CID Tempest 425, 4-bbl., V8 | 281 | 3-speed manual | $24 | $24 | S |
|  | 303 | Hydra-matic Automatic | $255 | $255 | $231 |

| Engine | Gross HP | Transmission Availability | Catalina & Ventura | Star Chief | Bonneville |
|---|---|---|---|---|---|
| 389 CID Tempest 425, 4-bbl., V8 | 333 | 3-speed manual | $293 | $293 | $280 |
|  |  | Hydra-matic Automatic | $524 | $524 | $511 |
| 389 CID Tri-Power 425, 3 × 2-bbl., V8 | 315 | 3-speed manual | $142 | $132 | $89 |
|  |  | Hydra-matic Automatic | $373 | $363 | $320 |
| 389 CID Tri-Power 425, 3 × 2-bbl., V8 | 348 | 3-speed manual | $369 | $359 | $316 |
|  |  | Hydra-matic Automatic | $600 | $590 | $547 |

*Horsepower ratings and prices may vary with model and transmission attachment. Other combinations possible due to dealer installations or factory limited-outputs.*

## Major Options

| | Catalina | Ventura | Star Chief | Bonneville |
|---|---|---|---|---|
| Circ-L-Aire heater and defroster | $94 | $94 | $94 | $94 |
| Circ-L-Aire air conditioning | $430 | $430 | $430 | $430 |
| E-Z-Eye tinted glass | $43 | $43 | $43 | $43 |
| Power steering | $108 | $108 | $108 | $108 |
| Power brakes | $43 | $43 | $43 | $43 |
| Power driver's seat/Bench seat | $97 | $97 | $97 | $97 |
| Power windows — 4 windows | $106 | $106 | $106 | $106 |
| AM radio — manual | $89 | $89 | $89 | $89 |
| White stripe tires (base size; average) | $40 | $40 | $40 | $40 |

Options common to most models. (Items may be standard equipment, optional at different pricing, or unavailable on certain models. This chart is only a guide.

## Paint Colors

| | Code |
|---|---|
| Regent Black | A |
| Black Pearl Metallic | B |
| Shelltone Ivory | C |
| Richmond Gray Metallic | D |
| Newport Blue Metallic | F |
| Skymist Blue Metallic | H |
| Fairway Green Metallic | J |
| Berkshire Green Metallic | K |
| Coronado Red Metallic | L |
| Stardust Yellow | M |
| Mahogany Metallic | N |
| Shoreline Gold Metallic | P |
| Palomino Beige | R |
| Sierra Copper Metallic | S |
| Caribe Turquoise Metallic | T |

# Catalina

*"The Luxurious Catalina."*

**Nameplate year of origin:** 1950 on hardtop models, 1959 as series.
**Current bodystyle lifespan:** 1959 through 1960.
**Predecessor to this model:** Chieftain (1958).
**Replacement for this model:** Catalina (1961 to 1964).
**Corporate siblings:** Chevrolet Biscayne/BelAir/Impala, Oldsmobile 88, Buick LeSabre/Invicta.
**Primary competition:** Mercury Montclair, and Dodge Dart.
**Percentage of division's sales volume:** 53.24%.
**Notable changes:** Major front and rear end restyling.
**Major standard equipment:** Nylon and vinyl bench seat, nylon-blend deep-pile carpet, dual sun visors, front and rear armrests, one front and two rear ashtrays, instrument panel snack bar, trunk mat, electric clock, front stabilizer bar, and 8.00 × 14 BSW tires (8.50 × 14 on wagons).

## Measurements

| | |
|---|---|
| Wheelbase | 122.0" |
| Length | 213.7" |
| Width | 80.0" |
| Height | 56.6" |
| Legroom — front | 45.3" |
| Legroom — rear | 41.9" |
| Headroom — front | 34.8" |
| Headroom — rear | 33.9" |
| Cargo capacity (cu. ft.) | NA |
| Fuel capacity (gals.) | 23.0 |

## Models Available

| | Style Number | Base MSRP | Change from LY | Shipping Wt. (lbs.) | Production | Change from LY |
|---|---|---|---|---|---|---|
| Catalina 2-Door Sport Sedan | 2111 | $2,631 | -0.08% | 3835 | 25,504 | -2.29% |
| Catalina 2-Door Sport Hardtop | 2137 | $2,766 | -0.07% | 3850 | 27,496 | -28.23% |

| | Style Number | Base MSRP | Change from LY | Shipping Wt. (lbs.) | Production | Change from LY |
|---|---|---|---|---|---|---|
| Catalina 2-Door Convertible | 2167 | $3,078 | -0.06% | 3940 | 17,172 | 18.31% |
| Catalina 4-Door Sedan | 2119 | $2,702 | -0.07% | 3935 | 72,650 | 0.38% |
| Catalina 4-Door Vista Hardtop | 2139 | $2,842 | -0.07% | 3990 | 32,710 | -27.33% |
| Catalina Safari 4-Dr., 2-S. Wagon | 2135 | $3,099 | -0.06% | 4310 | 21,253 | 0.43% |
| Catalina Safari 4-Dr., 3-S. Wagon | 2145 | $3,207 | -0.06% | 4365 | 14,149 | 0.46% |
| TOTALS | | Avg. price $2,904 | -0.06% | | Production 210,934 | -8.09% |

# Ventura

*"The Custom-Styled Ventura."*

**Nameplate year of origin:** 1960.
**Current bodystyle lifespan:** 1959 through 1960.
**Predecessor to this model:** Super Chief (1958).
**Replacement for this model:** Ventura (1961; option package only 1962 to 1964).
**Corporate siblings:** Chevrolet Biscayne/BelAir/Impala, Oldsmobile 88, Buick LeSabre/Invicta.
**Primary competition:** Mercury Montclair, and Dodge Dart.
**Percentage of division's sales volume:** 14.20%.
**Notable changes:** Major front and rear end restyling.
**Major standard equipment:** Three-tone Morrokide vinyl bench seat, deep-pile carpet, dual sun visors, front and rear armrests, one front and two rear ashtrays, custom steering wheel, trunk mat, electric clock, front stabilizer bar, deluxe wheel covers, and 8.00 × 14 BSW tires.

## Measurements

| | |
|---|---|
| Wheelbase | 122.0" |
| Length | 213.7" |
| Width | 80.0" |
| Height | 56.6" |
| Legroom — front | 45.3" |
| Legroom — rear | 41.9" |
| Headroom — front | 34.8" |
| Headroom — rear | 33.9" |
| Cargo capacity (cu. ft.) | NA |
| Fuel capacity (gals.) | 23.0 |

## Models Available

| | Style Number | Base MSRP | Change from LY | Shipping Wt. (lbs.) | Production | Change from LY |
|---|---|---|---|---|---|---|
| Ventura 2-Door Sport HT | 2337 | $2,971 | NEW | 3865 | 27,577 | NEW |
| Ventura 4-Door Vista Hardtop | 2339 | $3,047 | NEW | 3990 | 28,700 | NEW |
| TOTALS | | Avg. price $3,009 | NEW | | Production 56,277 | NEW |

# Star Chief

*"The Sparkling Star Chief."*

**Nameplate year of origin:** 1954.
**Current bodystyle lifespan:** 1959 through 1960.
**Predecessor to this model:** Star Chief (1958).
**Replacement for this model:** Star Chief (1961 to 1964).
**Corporate siblings:** Chevrolet Biscayne/BelAir/Impala, Oldsmobile 88, Buick LeSabre/Invicta.
**Primary competition:** Mercury Park Lane, and DeSoto.
**Percentage of division's sales volume:** 11.03%.
**Notable changes:** Major front and rear end restyling.
**Major standard equipment:** Nylon and vinyl bench seat, deep-pile carpet, dual sun visors, front and rear armrests, two front and two rear ashtrays, custom steering wheel, trunk mat, electric clock, front stabilizer bar, deluxe wheel covers, and 8.00 × 14 BSW tires.

## Measurements

| | |
|---|---|
| Wheelbase | 124.0" |
| Length | 220.7" |
| Width | 80.0" |
| Height | 56.6" |
| Legroom — front | 45.3" |
| Legroom — rear | 41.4" |
| Headroom — front | 34.8" |
| Headroom — rear | 33.9" |
| Cargo capacity (cu. ft.) | NA |
| Fuel capacity (gals.) | 23.0 |

## Models Available

| | Style Number | Base MSRP | Change from LY | Shipping Wt. (lbs.) | Production | Change from LY |
|---|---|---|---|---|---|---|
| Star Chief 2-Door Sport Sedan | 2411 | $2,932 | -0.07% | 3910 | 5,797 | -43.47% |
| Star Chief 4-Door Sedan | 2419 | $3,003 | -0.07% | 3995 | 23,038 | -17.34% |
| Star Chief 4-Door Hardtop | 2439 | $3,136 | -0.06% | 4040 | 14,856 | -51.59% |
| TOTALS | | Avg. price $3,024 | -0.07% | | Production 43,691 | -36.51% |

# Bonneville

*"The Elegant Bonneville."*

**Nameplate year of origin:** 1957.
**Current bodystyle lifespan:** 1959 through 1960.
**Predecessor to this model:** Bonneville (1958).
**Replacement for this model:** Bonneville (1961 to 1964).
**Corporate siblings:** Chevrolet Biscayne/BelAir/Impala, Oldsmobile 88, Buick LeSabre/Invicta.
**Primary competition:** Mercury Park Lane, Dodge Polara and DeSoto.
**Percentage of division's sales volume:** 21.52%.
**Notable changes:** Major front and rear end restyling.
**Major standard equipment:** Three-tone striped wool broadcloth and nylon with vinyl bench seat (except convertible), genuine leather tri-tone upholstery (convertible only), deep-pile carpet extended onto door panels, dual sun visors, rear seat center armrests, two front and two rear ashtrays, cushioned handrail assist on instrument panel, custom steering wheel, trunk mat, electric clock, front stabilizer bar, deluxe wheel covers, and 8.00 × 14 BSW tires.

### Measurements

| | |
|---|---|
| Wheelbase | 124.0" |
| Length | 220.7" |
| Width | 80.0" |
| Height | 54.8" |
| Legroom — front | 45.2" |
| Legroom — rear | 40.3" |
| Headroom — front | 32.9" |
| Headroom — rear | 34.2" |
| Cargo capacity (cu. ft.) | NA |
| Fuel capacity (gals.) | 23.0 |

## Models Available

| | Style Number | Base MSRP | Change from LY | Shipping Wt. (lbs.) | Production | Change from LY |
|---|---|---|---|---|---|---|
| Bonneville 2-Door Hardtop | 2837 | $3,255 | -0.06% | 3965 | 24,015 | -13.52% |
| Bonneville 2-Door Convertible | 2867 | $3,476 | -0.06% | 4030 | 17,062 | 49.33% |
| Bonneville 4-Door Vista Hardtop | 2839 | $3,331 | -0.06% | 4065 | 39,037 | 0.88% |
| Bonn. Cust. Safari 4-Dr., 2-S. Wgn. | 2735 | $3,530 | -0.06% | 4360 | 5,163 | 10.49% |
| TOTALS | | Avg. price $3,398 | -0.06% | | Production 85,277 | +3.29% |

# RAMBLER

*"The New Standard of Basic Excellence, from the World's Largest Builder of Compact Cars."*

For 1960, Rambler did not mess with the success of prior years. As a newly formed corporation, American Motors had spent a lot of resources repositioning its cars in the marketplace and reorganizing the corporate workings. Now with the dawn of a new decade, Rambler was working to update its cars, but had not spent sufficient time yet for major restylings. A new greenhouse area did distinguish the 1960 Rebel and Ambassador lines, however. A new compound curved, wraparound windshield gave the cars a more modern appearance. Also, revised tail-sections, more conservative side trim, and new grilles were seen on these cars this year. Powertrains for these models continued to be the same as those offered from several prior years. The Rambler American line received trim changes, to distinguish it from prior years. Also, a new top of the line Custom model was added to the Deluxe and Super models previously offered. The biggest news though, was the newly available 4-Door Sedan models, offered in all three trim levels. This new model was offered with this year's styling for only the one model year, but it would prove to be a highly popular model, selling over 50,000 units.

American Custom 2-Door Sedan

American Super 2-Door Wagon

Custom 4-Door Sedan

Deluxe 4-Door Sedan

Ambassador Super 4-Door Wagon

**Model year production:** 458,831,* up 22.61% over 1959.
**Domestic market share:** 7.61%* (4th place).
**Base price range:** $1,781 to $3,151.
**Industry average base price:** $3,391.
**Rambler average base price:** $2,477.
**Introduction date:** October 14, 1959.
**Assembly plants:** Kenosha, Wisconsin.
**Data plate identification:** VIN code read as follows: 60 for 1960; serial number (American, B100001 and up; Rambler Six, C100001 and up; Rambler Rebel, A100001 and up; and Ambassador V8, H100001 and up). Export cars added a K after the letter, and also had a slightly revised serial number order. Body style is determined by body plate. *Example:* 60C100001 is a 1960 Rambler Six built in Kenosha, WI, serial number 100001.

*Estimated from calendar year figures

## Powertrains

| Engine | Gross HP | Transmission Availability | Rambler American | Rambler | Rambler Rebel | Ambassador |
|---|---|---|---|---|---|---|
| 195.6 CID, 1-bbl., L-Head 6-cyl. | 90 | 3-speed manual, col. | S | - | - | - |
| | | 3-speed w/Overdrive | $102 | - | - | - |
| | | Flash-O-Matic Automatic | $179 | - | - | - |
| 195.6 CID, 1-bbl., OHV 6-cyl. | 125 (127 on Rambler) | 3-speed manual, col. | $80 (Custom) | S | - | - |
| | | 3-speed w/Overdrive | $182 (Custom) | $113 | - | - |
| | | Flash-O-Matic Automatic | $259 (Custom) | $200 | - | - |
| 195.6 CID, 2-bbl., OHV 6-cyl. | 138 | 3-speed manual, col. | - | $20 | - | - |
| | | 3-speed w/Overdrive | - | $133 | - | - |
| | | Flash-O-Matic Automatic | - | $220 | - | - |
| 250 CID, 2-bbl., OHV V8 | 200 | 3-speed manual | - | - | $119 | - |
| | | 3-speed w/Overdrive | - | - | $232 | - |
| | | Flash-O-Matic Automatic | - | - | $339 | - |

| Engine | Gross HP | Transmission Availability | Rambler American | Rambler | Rambler Rebel | Ambassador |
|---|---|---|---|---|---|---|
| 250 CID, 4-bbl., OHV V8 | 215 | 3-speed manual | - | - | $199 | - |
| | | 3-speed w/Overdrive | - | - | $312 | - |
| | | Flash-O-Matic Automatic | - | - | $419 | - |
| 327 CID, 2-bbl., OHV V8 | 250 | 3-speed manual | - | - | - | S |
| | | 3-speed w/Overdrive | - | - | - | $115 |
| | | Flash-O-Matic Automatic | - | - | - | $230 |
| 327 CID, 4-bbl., OHV V8 | 270 | 3-speed manual | - | - | - | $90 |
| | | 3-speed w/Overdrive | - | - | - | $205 |
| | | Flash-O-Matic Automatic | - | - | - | $320 |

## Major Options

| | American | Rambler | Ambassador |
|---|---|---|---|
| Weather-Eye heater | $72 | $76 | $38 |
| Air conditioning (requires tinted glass) | - | - | $398 |
| Tinted glass — full | $27 | $33 | $34 |
| Power steering | $70 | $70–$80 | $90 |
| Power brakes | - | $42 | $44 |
| Electric clock | $15 | $16 | $17 |
| Outside rear view mirror — left | $4 | $5 | $5 |
| AM radio (manual) w/antenna | $58 | $65 | $65 |
| White sidewall tires — Standard size | $28 | $30 | $35 |
| Two-tone paint | $16–$18 | $20–$22 | $20–$22 |
| Backup lights | $10 | $10 | $10 |
| Wheel covers | $15 | $15 | $17 |
| Side hinge tailgate (6-pass. Wagons) | - | $40 | $40 |

Options common to most models. (- = Not Available.) Items may be standard equipment, optional at different pricing, or unavailable on certain models. This chart is only a guide.

## Paint Colors

| | Code |
|---|---|
| Classic Black | P1 |
| Alamo Beige | P4 |
| Autumn Yellow | P5 |
| Chatsworth Green Light | P8 |
| Placid Blue Light | P10 |
| Oriental Red | P13 |
| Aqua Mist Metallic | P15 |
| Westchester Green Met. | P18 |
| Sovereign Blue Met. Med. | P19 |
| Darsmouth Gray Light | P20 |
| Harvard Gray Met. Med. | P21 |
| Echo Green Metallic | P23 |
| Auburn Red Metallic | P24 |
| Festival Rose | P25 |
| Frost White | P72 |
| Cinnamon Bronze Met. | P94 |

Two-tones: first number is body color, second number is roof/accent color.

# Rambler American

*"The most imitated car in America."*

**Nameplate year of origin:** 1950 (Nash).
**Current bodystyle lifespan:** 1958 through 1960.
**Predecessor to this model:** Nash Rambler (1953 to 1955).
**Replacement for this model:** American (1961 to 1963).
**Corporate siblings:** None.
**Percentage of division's sales volume:** 26.28%.
**Primary competition:** Chevrolet Corvair, Ford Falcon, Plymouth Valiant, and Studebaker Lark.
**Notable changes:** Revised trim and detail changes. New 4-Door Sedan models added, and a top line Custom was introduced.
**Major standard equipment:** All-vinyl upholstery, black rubber floor mats, black rubber trunk mat or cargo mat on wagons, manual dome light, one horn, hub caps, and 5.90 × 15 BSW tires (6.40 × 15 on wagons). Super adds: front foam cushion, automatic dome light, deluxe steering wheel, front arm rests and ash trays, two-tone interiors, roof top rack on wagons, and exterior bright trim.

## Measurements

| | |
|---|---|
| Wheelbase | 100.0" |
| Length | 178.3" |
| Width | 73.0" |
| Height | 57.3" |
| Legroom — front | 44.0" |
| Legroom — rear | 37.5" |
| Headroom — front | 35.3" |
| Headroom — rear | 34.0" |
| Luggage Cap. (cu. ft.) | * |
| Fuel capacity (gals.) | 22 |

*Not available for cars. Wagons — 52 cubic feet.

## Models Available

| | Style Number | Base MSRP | Change from LY | Shipping Wt. (lbs.) | Production | Change from LY |
|---|---|---|---|---|---|---|
| American Deluxe 2-Dr. Bus. Sdn. | 6002 | $1,833 | 0.66% | 2454 | 630 | 42.21% |
| American Deluxe 2-Door Sedan | 6006 | $1,847 | 0.65% | 2480 | 23,960 | -20.01% |
| American Deluxe 4-Door Sedan | 6005 | $1,896 | NEW | 2500 | 22,593 | NEW |
| American Deluxe 2-Door Wagon | 6004 | $2,082 | 1.07% | 2555 | 12,290 | -19.44% |
| American Super 2-Door Sedan | 6006-1 | $1,932 | 0.63% | 2492 | 17,233 | -39.42% |
| American Super 4-Door Sedan | 6005-1 | $1,981 | NEW | 2512 | 21,108 | NEW |
| American Super 2-Door Wagon | 6004-1 | $2,167 | 1.03% | 2565 | 15,093 | -13.17% |
| American Custom 2-Door Sedan | 6006-2 | $2,062 | NEW | 2492 | 2,994 | NEW |
| American Custom 4-Door Sedan | 6005-2 | $2,111 | NEW | 2512 | 3,272 | NEW |
| American Custom 2-Door Wagon | 6004-2 | $2,297 | NEW | 2565 | 1,430 | NEW |
| TOTALS | Avg. price | $2,021 | +3.32% | Production | 120,603 | +31.83% |

# Rambler & Rambler Rebel

*"Your Rambler Dollar Is a Bigger Dollar!"*

**Nameplate year of origin:** 1957.
**Current bodystyle lifespan:** 1958 through 1962 (restyled in 1960).
**Predecessor to this model:** Hudson and Nash Rambler (1956 to 1957).
**Replacement for this model:** Rambler Classic (1963 to 1966).
**Corporate siblings:** Ambassador (shared components from cowl back).
**Percentage of division's sales volume:** 68.53%.
**Primary competition:** Ford Falcon, Plymouth Valiant, and Studebaker Lark.
**Notable changes:** Revised rear end treatment and new front grille styling. Wagons added an 8-passenger model. The 4-Door Hardtop model moved from the Super to the Custom line.
**Major standard equipment:** Front arm rests and ash trays, front foam cushion seat, black rubber cargo mat (wagons), and 6.40 × 15 BSW tires (7.50 × 14 on Rebel V8 models). Super adds: Dual horns, door-activated dome lights, twin sun visors, full hubcaps, and dual headlights. Custom adds: Electric clock, custom trim level.

### Measurements*

| | |
|---|---|
| Wheelbase | 108.0" |
| Length | 189.5" |
| Width | 72.4" |
| Height | 57.5" |
| Legroom — front | 43.0" |
| Legroom — rear | 40.0" |
| Headroom — front | 35.0" |
| Headroom — rear | 34.0" |
| Luggage Cap. (cu. ft.) | 80.0 (Wagon) |
| Fuel capacity (gals.) | 20.0 |

*Dimensions given are for 4-Door Sedan.*

## Models Available

| | Style Number | Base MSRP | Change from LY | Shipping Wt. (lbs.) | Production | Change from LY |
|---|---|---|---|---|---|---|
| Deluxe 4-Door Sedan | 6015 | $2,098 | 0.00% | 2912 | 37,666 | 44.00% |
| Deluxe 4-Dr., 6-pass. Wgn. | 6018 | $2,427 | 0.00% | 3051 | 24,001 | 5587.44% |
| Super 4-Door Sedan | 6015-1 | $2,268 | 0.00% | 2930 | 88,004 | 21.26% |
| Super 4-Dr., 6-pass. Wgn. | 6018-1 | $2,562 | 0.00% | 3054 | 59,491 | -10.86% |
| Super 4-Dr., 8-pass. Wgn. | 6018-3 | $2,687 | NEW | 3117 | 8,456 | NEW |
| Custom 4-Door Sedan | 6015-2 | $2,383 | 0.00% | 2929 | 38,003 | 7.83% |
| Custom 4-Door Hardtop | 6019-2 | $2,458 | NEW | 2981 | 3,937 | NEW |
| Custom 4-Dr., 6-pass. Wgn. | 6018-2 | $2,677 | 0.00% | 3057 | 32,092 | -17.21% |
| Custom 4-Dr., 8-pass. Wgn. | 6018-4 | $2,802 | NEW | 3137 | 5,718 | NEW |
| Rebel Deluxe 4-Door Sedan | 6025 | $2,217 | -0.49% | 2912 | 143 | 26.55% |
| Rebel Super 4-Door Sedan | 6025-1 | $2,387 | -0.46% | 2930 | 3,826 | 9.69% |
| Rebel Super 4-Dr., 6-pass. Wgn. | 6028-1 | $2,681 | -0.41% | 3054 | 3,328 | -8.42% |
| Rebel Super 4-Dr., 8-pass. Wgn. | 6028-3 | $2,806 | NEW | 3117 | 718 | NEW |
| Rebel Custom 4-Door Sedan | 6025-2 | $2,502 | -0.44% | 2929 | 3,969 | -1.90% |
| Rebel Custom 4-Door Hardtop | 6029-2 | $2,577 | -0.43% | 2981 | 579 | -16.21% |
| Rebel Custom 4-Dr., 6-pass. Wgn. | 6028-2 | $2,796 | -0.39% | 3057 | 3,613 | -18.39% |

| | Style Number | Base MSRP | Change from LY | Shipping Wt. (lbs.) | Production | Change from LY |
|---|---|---|---|---|---|---|
| Rebel Custom 4-Dr., 8-pass. Wgn. | 6028-4 | $2,921 | NEW | 3137 | 886 | NEW |
| TOTALS | | Avg. price $2,544 | +3.42% | | Production 314,430 | +21.41% |

*Rebel V8 models have style number starting with 602.   **Not available as a Rebel V8 model.*

# Ambassador

### *"America's Compact Luxury Car."*

**Nameplate year of origin:** 1933 (From top-of-the-line Nash).

**Current bodystyle lifespan:** 1958 through 1962 (Shared basic structure with Rambler).

**Predecessor to this model:** Ambassador (1952 to 1957; major restyle in 1955).

**Corporate siblings:** Rambler (shared components from cowl back).

**Replacement for this model:** None.

**Percentage of division's sales volume:** 5.18%.

**Primary competition:** Chevrolet BelAir/Impala, Dodge Dart, Ford Fairlane/Galaxie, and Plymouth Belvedere.

**Notable changes:** Revised rear end treatment and new front grille styling.

**Major standard equipment:** Front arm rests and ash trays, front foam cushion seat, dual sunvisors, dual horns, hood insulation, rear seat speaker, and 8.00 × 14 BSW tires. Custom adds: Fender ornaments, and Handi-Pak net carrier.

## Measurements

| | |
|---|---|
| Wheelbase | 117.0" |
| Length | 198.5" |
| Width | 72.2" |
| Height | 56.9" |
| Legroom — front | 43.0" |
| Legroom — rear | 40.0" |
| Headroom — front | 35.0" |
| Headroom — rear | 34.0" |
| Luggage Cap. (cu. ft.) | 80.0 (Wagon) |
| Fuel capacity (gals.) | 20.0 |

## Models Available

| | Style Number | Base MSRP | Change from LY | Shipping Wt. (lbs.) | Production | Change from LY |
|---|---|---|---|---|---|---|
| Ambassador Deluxe 4-Dr. Sedan | 6085 | $2,395 | 0.00% | 3384 | 302 | 94.84% |
| Ambassador Super 4-Dr. Sedan | 6085-1 | $2,587 | 0.00% | 3395 | 3,990 | -14.65% |
| Ambassador Super 4-Dr., 6-p. Wgn. | 6088-1 | $2,881 | 0.00% | 3531 | 1,342 | -24.69% |
| Ambassador Super 4-Dr., 8-p. Wgn. | 6088-3 | $3,006 | NEW | 3581 | 637 | NEW |
| Ambassador Custom 4-Dr. Sedan | 6085-2 | $2,732 | 0.00% | 3408 | 10,949 | 1.46% |
| Ambassador Custom 4-Dr. Hardtop | 6089-2 | $2,822 | 0.00% | 3465 | 1,141 | -21.15% |
| Ambassador Custom 4-Dr., 6-p. Wgn. | 6088-2 | $3,026 | 0.00% | 3538 | 3,849 | -11.33% |
| Ambassador Custom 4-Dr., 8-p. Wgn. | 6088-4 | $3,151 | NEW | 3592 | 1,153 | NEW |
| Ambassador Custom 4-Dr. HT Wgn. | 6083-2 | $3,116 | NEW | 3583 | 435 | NEW |
| TOTALS | | Avg. price $2,857 | +2.25% | | Production 23,798 | +0.12% |

# STUDEBAKER

### *"Studebaker-Packard Corporation for 1960."*

After five tumultuous years and a successful introductory year for the Lark compact car line, Studebaker had lit-tle cash with which to develop new models or revise cars that were only a year old. Surprisingly, they did manage to put together a new Lark convertible and 4-Door station wagon for 1960, benefiting from high parts interchangeability and the fact that the basics for each model were already at hand. Although its origins were little recognized, the Lark was in essence a very well done remake of the 1953 through 1958 Studebaker models and only appeared to be an all-new model. Another reason for the new models was the onslaught of compact cars from the Big Three manufacturers, of which none would be available as a convertible in the initial year. Only Ford would offer its compact as a 4-Door Wagon right from introduction.

The Hawk Sport Coupe was a new model designation resulting from dropping "Silver" from the name. In 1958, there had been Silver and Golden Hawks, but with only one trim level, it was useless to designate a model as such. Studebaker was trying to reposition the aging Raymond Loewy designed coupe just below the spot occupied by the successful 4-passenger Thunderbird. By 1962, the price and content of the Hawk would be increased significantly enough that it was renamed the Gran Turismo Hawk (or GT Hawk), and its mission would be fulfilled. For the time being, the car was based on the 2-Door Coupe body, but by 1962 it would return to the Hardtop configuration.

Lark Regal 2-Door Convertible

Lark Deluxe 4-Door Wagon

Lark Instrument Panel

Hawk 2-Door Sport Coupe

---

**Model year production:** 130,679, down 5.13% from 1959.
**Domestic market share:** 2.17% (11th place).
**Base price range:** $1,976 to $2,650.
**Industry average base price:** $3,391.
**Studebaker average base price:** $2,354.
**Introduction date:** October, 1959.
**Assembly plants:** South Bend, IN (No coding) and Canada (C).

**Data plate identification (VIN):** Up to ten digit code read as follows: 60 for 1960; S for 6-cylinder or V for V8 engine; C if built in Canada; followed by Serial Number 1001 and up. Body style numbers are found on a separate plate on the vehicle. *Example:* 60S100001 is a 1960 Studebaker Lark Six built in South Bend, IN, serial number 1001.

---

## Powertrains

| Engine | Gross HP | Transmission Availability | Lark | Hawk |
|---|---|---|---|---|
| 169.6 CID, 1-bbl., L-Head 6-cyl. | 90 | 3-speed manual | S | – |
| | | 3-speed w/Overdrive | $110 | – |
| | | Flightomatic Automatic | $179 | – |
| 259.2 CID, 2-bbl., OHV V8 | 180 | 3-speed manual | $135 | – |
| | | 3-speed w/Overdrive | $245 | – |
| | | Flash-O-Matic Automatic | $335 | – |
| 259.2 CID, 4-bbl., OHV V8 | 195 | 3-speed manual | $170 | – |

| Engine | Gross HP | Transmission Availability | Lark | Hawk |
|--------|----------|--------------------------|------|------|
| | | 3-speed w/Overdrive | $290 | - |
| | | Flash-O-Matic Automatic | $380 | - |
| 289 CID, 2-bbl., OHV V8 | 210 | 3-speed manual | - | S |
| | | 3-speed w/Overdrive | - | $110 |
| | | Flash-O-Matic Automatic | - | $200 |
| 289 CID, 4-bbl., OHV V8 | 225 | 3-speed manual | - | $45 |
| | | 3-speed w/Overdrive | - | $155 |
| | | Flash-O-Matic Automatic | - | $245 |

## Major Options

| | Lark | Hawk |
|--|------|------|
| Heater and defroster | $71 | $71 |
| Air conditioning | $325 | $325 |
| Tinted glass — full | $32 | $32 |
| Power steering (V8 only) | $75 | $75 |
| Power brakes | $38 | $38 |
| Electric clock | $15 | $15 |
| Windshield washers | $11 | $11 |
| AM radio — manual | $57 | $57 |
| White sidewall tires — standard size | $28–$48 | $28–$48 |
| Wheel covers | $16 | $16 |

Options common to most models. Items may be standard equipment, optional at different pricing, or unavailable on certain models. This chart is only a guide.

## Paint Colors

| | Code |
|--|------|
| Velvet Black | P6010 |
| White Sand | P6011 |
| Gulfstream Blue | P6012 |
| Oasis Green | P6013 |
| Williamsburg Green | P6014 |
| Sandalwood Beige | P6015 |
| Colonial Red | P6016 |
| Jonquil Yellow | P6017 |
| Pacific Blue | P6023 |
| Sudan Beige | P6024 |

# Lark

*"Look … and you'll love that Lark!"*

**Nameplate year of origin:** 1959.
**Current bodystyle lifespan:** 1959 through 1961.
**Predecessor to this model:** Champion (1953 to 1958).
**Replacement for this model:** Lark (1962 to 1966).
**Corporate siblings:** None.
**Percentage of division's sales volume:** 96.72%.
**Primary competition:** AMC Rambler American, Chevrolet Corvair, Ford Falcon, Mercury Comet and Plymouth Valiant.
**Notable changes:** Revised trim and detail changes.
**Major standard equipment:** All-vinyl or cloth and vinyl front bench seats, armrests, rubber floor mats, and 5.90 × 15 BSW tires (6.40 × 15 BSW on convertible).

## Measurements

| | Cars | Econ-O-Miler | Wagons |
|--|------|--------------|--------|
| Wheelbase | 108.5" | 113.0" | 113.0" |
| Length | 175.0" | 179.0" | 184.5" |
| Width | 71.4" | 71.4" | 71.4" |
| Height | 57.5" | 57.5" | 58.8" |
| Legroom — front | 44.0" | 44.0" | 44.0" |
| Legroom — rear | 39.0" | 42.0" | 42.0" |
| Headroom — front | 36.0" | 36.0" | 36.0" |
| Headroom — rear | 35.0" | 35.0" | 35.3" |
| Luggage Cap. (cu. ft.) | NA | NA | 93.0 |
| Fuel capacity (gals.) | 18.0 | 18.0 | 18.0 |

## Models Available

| | Style Number | Base MSRP | Change from LY | Shipping Wt. (lbs.) | Production | Change from LY |
|--|--------------|-----------|----------------|---------------------|------------|----------------|
| Lark Deluxe 2-Door Sedan | F4 | $1,976 | 2.65% | 2588 | 32,707 | -3.26% |
| Lark Deluxe 4-Door Sedan | W4 | $2,046 | 2.56% | 2592 | 36,765 | 31.62% |
| Lark Deluxe 2-Door, 2-Seat Wagon | D4 | $2,366 | 3.09% | 2763 | 5,231 | -61.55% |

| | Style Number | Base MSRP | Change from LY | Shipping Wt. (lbs.) | Production | Change from LY |
|---|---|---|---|---|---|---|
| Lark Deluxe 4-Door, 2-Seat Wagon | P4 | $2,441 | NEW | 2792 | 11,131 | NEW |
| Lark Regal 2-Door Hardtop | J6 | $2,296 | 0.92% | 2697 | 7,394 | -50.94% |
| Lark Regal 2-Door Convertible | L6 | $2,621 | NEW | 2961 | 8,571 | NEW |
| Lark Regal 4-Door Sedan | W6 | $2,196 | 0.97% | 2619 | 16,934 | -35.92% |
| Lark Regal 4-Door, 2-Seat Wagon | P6 | $2,591 | NEW | 2836 | 7,666 | NEW |
| TOTALS | Avg. price | $2,316 | +5.90% | | Production 126,399 | -2.74% |

# Hawk

*"The most distinctive car in America! Styled for lovers of sporting design and powered for people who enjoy performance."*

**Nameplate year of origin:** 1956.
**Current bodystyle lifespan:** 1953 through 1964 (1960 to 1961 as Hawk model).
**Predecessor to this model:** Silver Hawk (1956 to 1959).
**Replacement for this model:** GT Hawk (1962 to 1964).
**Corporate siblings:** None.
**Percentage of division's sales volume:** 3.28%.
**Primary competition:** None.
**Notable changes:** Minor trim and detail changes. Silver Hawk name shortened to Hawk for 1960.
**Major standard equipment:** All-vinyl front seat covering, full carpeting, and 6.40 × 15 BSW tires.

## Measurements

| | |
|---|---|
| Wheelbase | 120.5" |
| Length | 204.0" |
| Width | 71.3" |
| Height | 55.5" |
| Legroom — front | 44.0" |
| Legroom — rear | 42.0" |
| Headroom — front | 36.0" |
| Headroom — rear | 35.3" |
| Luggage Cap. (cu. ft.) | NA |
| Fuel capacity (gals.) | 18.0 |

## Models Available

| | Style Number | Base MSRP | Change from LY | Shipping Wt. (lbs.) | Production | Change from LY |
|---|---|---|---|---|---|---|
| Hawk 2-Door Coupe | C6 | $2,650 | +6.21% | 3207 | 4,280 | -45.04% |
| TOTALS | Avg. price | $2,650 | +6.21% | | Production 4,280 | -45.04% |

# 1961

"Bigger is better" seemed to characterize the attitude of Detroit from the fifties to the early seventies. But there was one year that, across nearly all makes, took exception to that unwritten rule. Nineteen-sixty-one is that year. The 1961 models were being designed as far back as 1957-58, when the country was in a recession and the import invasion was beginning. Even sales of so-called "captive imports" like the Metropolitan, Opel and Vauxhall did quite well during this period. The manufacturers all took note and by 1960 had introduced their first wave of compact car lines. This year, the second wave of compacts hit, consisting of higher priced models such as the Pontiac Tempest, Oldsmobile F-85, Buick Special, and Dodge Lancer.

Even the full-sized models from GM and Ford were somewhat trimmer in 1961 than in previous years, and Chrysler would follow in 1962. Though only slightly smaller in most cases, some models appeared much smaller as trim and body lines gave a leaner look. Apparently the public did not really want smaller full-size cars, as sales did not jump significantly; part of the reason was surely the aforementioned new compact cars. All told, the year was a good one, but far better ones were to come shortly, especially for Chrysler which was in the depths of an automobile styling depression. Certainly outstanding among manufacturers, the '61 Dodge and Plymouth lines are among the most unusually styled cars of the sixties.

The stylists at Chrysler took a different approach to "style" in each division. The Plymouth went the totally finless route and eliminated the use of some rather strangely shaped wheel openings that had been used in 1960. Chrome trim ran entirely around the car on upper series models at the beltline, and was the only highlight to the body sides. Chrome trim was also used to surround the quad headlights at the front, setting them apart from the grille, and making them seem to float in the front end. At the rear, small round taillamps occupied pods that extended from each side of the rear fenders. Rooflines continued as on the 1960 models, with the 2-Door Hardtops continuing their unique forward dogleg at the back window. Full-size Dodge models, on the other hand, while receiving a pleasant appearance at the front end, featured a novel forward-canting rear fin design that most people did not like. The body line from the sides flowed back under the round bullet-style taillamps, then went up and over them into a fin that continued forward to a point near where the roof met the car body, then went sharply downward to meet the bodyside. This created a disjointed look, as the fairly clean front end styling did not seem to fit with the rear of the car. Chrysler and the two remaining DeSoto models continued with a look similar to that of their 1960 counterparts. The DeSoto did gain a unique oval bar, located above the grille, that housed the name DeSoto. The DeSoto line would be produced for only about two months before the plug was pulled. The writing was on the wall early in the model year when Chrysler announced the new Newport, which was priced at about $3000, right in the middle of DeSoto territory. After the announcement was made, someone felt that Dodge should have a product in the former DeSoto price range, and the 1962 Dodge Custom 880 was the resulting car — essentially the 1962 Chrysler body with a 1961 Dodge front clip. The need for both the Dodge Custom 880 and the Chrysler Newport is not clear. The luxury Imperial received a new front-end treatment that sported stand-alone headlamps, reminiscent of the classic thirties Chryslers, and a smaller, more formal grille treatment. Out back, the 1960 fins returned, and would not start their retreat until 1962. The compact Valiant returned with minimal changes, but did add an upscale stablemate in the Dodge Lancer. Slightly larger than the Valiant, the Lancer was aimed at families who needed more space than the traditional compact offered, while giving them more luxurious style and accessories. It was quite popular in its first year on the market, holding its own against the new trio from GM.

General Motors' new line of compact cars — more often termed "senior" compacts because of their larger-than-compact size — were introduced to rave reviews by most automotive editors of the time. All three cars shared basic body components, and some undercarriage components, but they differed significantly in frontal styling and engineering. Each of the trio of cars offered something unique to the consumer. Pontiac offered the most uniqueness in its Tempest. Stylewise, the front end was a throwback to the highly popular split grille of the 1959 Pontiac. The big news in this car, though, was its engineering. Standard power for the Tempest was a 194.5 CID 4-cylinder. This was the first 4-cylinder engine to be offered by one of the Big Three manufacturers since the early 1930s. Its design was quite conventional, however, as it was essentially patterned from one half of a 389 CID V8, allowing for parts and accessory interchangeability between the two motors, and also a service staff that was familiar with the engine. Behind the engine, it got even more interesting. The Tempest used a variation of the Chevy Corvair's rear-mounted transmission, and the engine's power passed to this transmission through the use of a flexible drive shaft, often termed the "rope shaft," eliminating the need for numerous U-joints to accommodate the rear suspension travel. With the transmission mounted in the rear, an independent rear suspension was used, which improved ride, but not the handling. Another benefit of the rear transmission was near perfect weight distribution which helped compensate for other handling drawbacks. For those who wanted something a little more traditional, there was the option of a Buick V8 engine for power, although it was made with a new and unproven aluminum block. Very few Tempest buyers opted for the V8, as the 4-cylinder nearly equaled the V8 in all critical areas except operating smoothness. Because of the significance of the aforementioned design and engineering qualities, *Motor Trend* magazine named the Pontiac Tempest as "Car of the Year" for 1961. The Buick Special and Oldsmobile's F-85 variant were somewhat more traditional than the Tempest. All Buick and Oldsmobile compact models came with the aluminum V8 powerplant and carried contemporary Buick and Oldsmobile styling.

All of GM's full-size models were totally redesigned this year. Once again, all five divisions shared two common platforms for all models. This cost-saving strategy was implemented with the 1959 model year, and would basically be used by GM on its full-size line through 1985. (Of course, GM and all other manufacturers use platform sharing as a common cost-saving measure today.) The basic styling of most models was simple, fairly straightforward bodyside sculpting, with a strong frontal identity for each make, and a new rear appearance that lacked tailfin styling — except for Cadillac. The originator of the tailfin would be the last to shed them. As for the frontal appearance, the strongest statement was made by Pontiac, which successfully revised its highly popular split grille from 1959 to fit the 1961 styling. A reverse canting grille, separated by the body color panel that came down from the hood, and the Pontiac logo on the divider, made for an unmistakable styling statement. As in the past, the 2-Door Hardtop models featured slender, sporty lines, except Cadillac models, which featured more formal rooflines this year. The Chevrolet Corvair and Corvette models continued into 1961 with few changes.

At Ford, with the unsuccessful Edsel line gone, it was time for a revamping of the product line again. Unfortunately, as in the past, this meant that Mercury would be most affected, and usually at the expense of its sales numbers. The new-for-1960 Mercury Comet and Ford Falcon entered the new year with few changes. The full-size Ford and Mercury lines were restyled, but were based upon the 1960 Ford and Edsel platform. For Ford, this meant all-new front and rear styling. The front grille was a slightly convex affair that was full-width with headlamps at each end. At the rear, Ford returned to its trademark round taillamps, mounted under a tiny appendage that passed for a tailfin. Mercury adopted a cross between the Ford and the new Lincoln look for the front end — a full-width grille, slightly convex in appearance, but carrying on a link to the 1960 models at the same time. At the rear was a pleasing, full-width panel that housed triple taillamps on most models. Like Ford, Mercury retained a small tailfin for one more season. Mercury added the Meteor, which effectively took the place of the Edsel in the corporate lineup. This addition helped to lower Mercury's entry level pricing, but also took some of the premium ambiance away from the mid-class car line as a whole. That risk always exists when a mid-price or luxury line adds a car at the lower end of the pricing scale.

Two totally redesigned models appeared from Ford for the new year. The all-new Lincoln Continental and the Ford Thunderbird were restyled and redesigned, and both proved to be very popular with the buying public. The Lincoln Continental came in two models, a 4-Door Sedan and a 4-Door Convertible. This was the first 4-Door Convertible (phaeton) since prior to World War II. These two models sold as many cars as the entire 10-model lineup had in 1960. The new Lincolns were smaller, cleanly styled and very luxurious on the inside. Exterior styling included a thin blade fender edge highlighted with chrome trim. Chrome trim also adorned the window and front and rear grilles and bumpers, but the rest of the car was devoid of chrome. This new trimmer Lincoln also drove and handled better as there was less bulk to be thrown into a corner, and the unit-body construction kept body stiffness intact. The Thunderbird was also completely restyled and featured unit-body construction. The Thunderbird profile was that of a missile, long, low, and sleek. The leading edge of the

## 1961 Model Year Production by Make

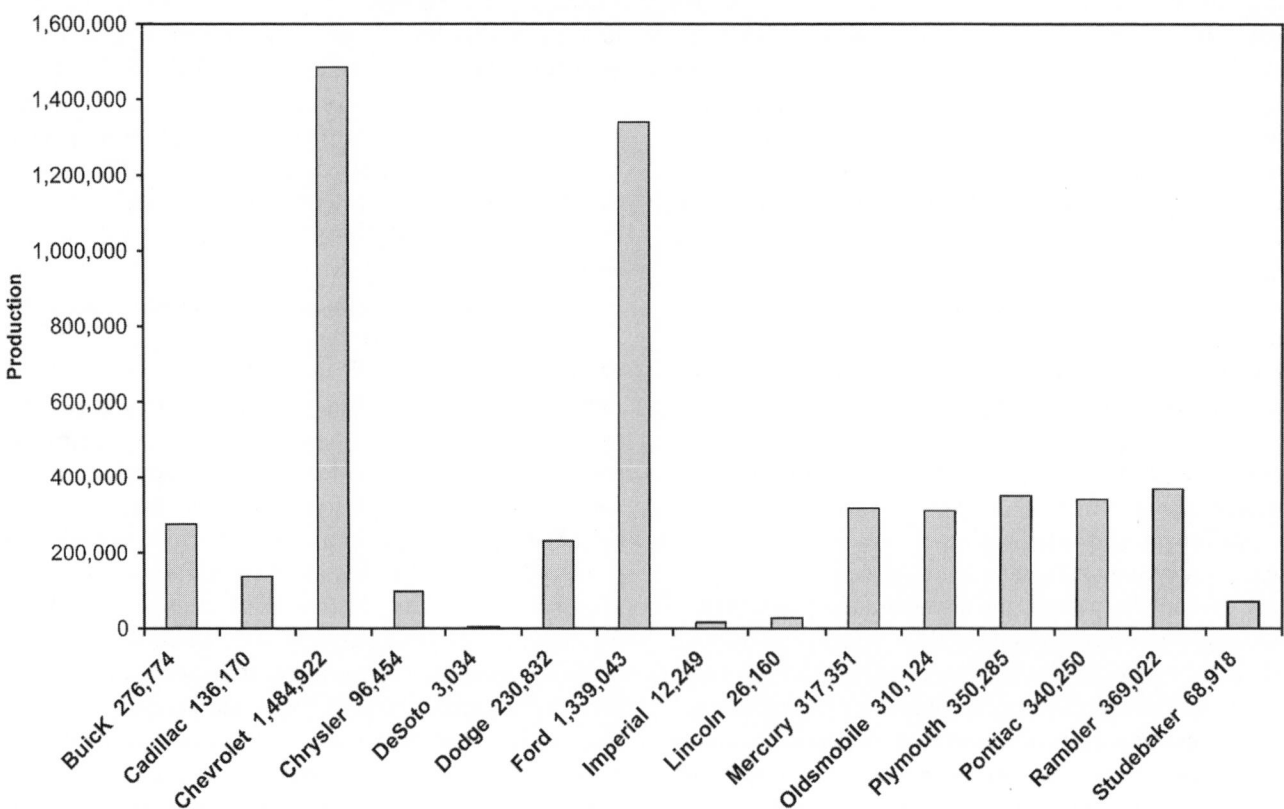

front fenders came to a point, and this shape was copied across the width of the car, with the grille, which was integrated into the bumper, below the point, and the hood arching down to the point from the top. In the center of the hood was the traditional hood scoop air inlet. Down the sides, the T-Bird had fender tops trimmed in chrome like the Lincoln, but the T-Bird had its door handles integrated into this trim, for a very smooth side panel appearance. At the rear were the round Ford taillamps, topped off with a small tailfin.

American Motors revamped the aging Rambler American line for 1961. Last restyled in 1955, the American was really showing its age as compared to the new round of compacts. Though still based upon some of the same structure, the new American came off as modern and somewhat cute in its role as one of the smaller compact cars offered in the U.S. A full range of body styles were offered, except for a convertible, which would be added in 1962. Other AMC products received their annual facelifts, with the Ambassador gaining the "chubby cheek" look, with a rounded lower front fender edge that made the front ends of the Ambassador look very heavy. The Rambler Classic and Rebel were more conservatively styled, and continued among the most popular of new cars.

Studebaker offered little in the way of new product or changes for the year. As was typical, the Checker Motors line was not changed. Truck offerings from GM and Kaiser-Jeep were carryovers from 1960, having some minor trim changes, with a few exceptions. Ford fielded all-new styling for its F-series truck line, and the same was true for Dodge and International light-duty trucks.

Modern interiors with car-like features were one of several attractive claims for the new Ford. Exterior styling featured the curved windshield and non-dogleg vent window. Simply styled grille bars at the front, a full-length body side crease at the belt line, and another crease a foot or so above the rocker gave the trucks a little style. One other bit of noteworthy truck news was the discontinuance of the Chevrolet El Camino and Sedan Delivery models. Citing slow sales, Chevrolet decided to leave this market in favor of the up and coming Corvair Greenbrier van and truck models. Wisely, GM saw the potential in van-based delivery and utility vehicles. Of course, the El Camino would return as the popularity of the Ford Ranchero grew again, but the next time around it would be based on the mid-sized Chevelle platform.

# BUICK

*"As new, as fine as you can go. Full-size Turbine Drive Buicks, and the Special Size Buick Special."*

The all-new compact Special models were among the smallest Buicks built since the twenties. In line with the corporate and industry-wide swing to compact cars, the new Buick Special fit into the category known as the "senior compact" car. These vehicles were slightly larger than the typical small car and offered many features that one would expect to find only in a large luxury car. The Special also offered a V8 engine as standard equipment, an alternative not even thought of in other compact cars. This definitely gave Buick the edge in power and driveability amongst all the new competition. The most interesting feature of the V8 engine was not its power capabilities or design, but the material chosen for construction: aluminum. By utilizing aluminum for the block, Buick engineers were able to create a V8 powerplant that was as dependable as their cast iron V8's, yet weighed only about 320 pounds. These weight savings and the smaller platform boosted fuel economy greatly. A mid-year Special Deluxe Sport Coupe, dubbed "Skylark," was introduced as an alternative to other sporty coupes being offered.

The full-size Buick line was totally redesigned this year, following General Motors' company-wide restyling of the B- and C-body full-size cars. Gone were wrap-around windshields with their accompanying knee-knocker posts, as were tail fins, and non-traditional styling touches. The 1961 Buicks were a very conservative, very fine-tuned car, right from the start. The front styling was a simple grille, with a floating Buick emblem in the center and quad headlights at each end. The grille ends were capped by the curvaceous leading edge of the front fenders that flowed back into two horizontal body lines—one just below the beltline, and one just above the top line of the rear wheel opening. The two were parallel to each other for the length of the car. At the back, the lower rear bumper area mimicked the front fenders in shape, and single hooded, oval tail lamps were inset into each end of the bumper just below the deck lid line. Overall styling of the Special was similar with one major exception being that the lower body side line on the Special dropped off as it neared the back of the car, resulting in a rear-slanting top arch on the rear wheel opening, similar to its sister cars, the Tempest and F-85. As for model changes, the Invicta and Electra 225 lines lost their 4-Door Sedan variations, and the Invicta also lost its wagon models, but they would return for 1963.

Electra 225 Dash

Electra 225 2-Door Convertible

LeSabre 4-Door Hardtop

Special Deluxe 4-Door Sedan

Special Deluxe 4-Door Wagon

Model year production: 276,774, up 9.48% from 1960.
Base price range: $2,330 to $4,350.
Domestic market share: 5.16% (8th place).
Industry average base price: $3,048.
Buick average base price: $3,274.
Introduction date: September 1960; Skylark introduced January 1961.
Assembly plants: Flint, MI (1); Southgate, CA (2); Linden, NJ (3); Fairfax, KS (4); Wilmington, DE (5); Atlanta, GA (6); Framingham, MA (7); and Arlington, TX (8).

Data plate identification: Nine digit code read as follows: 1st digit indicates series trim level and engine (see coding below); 2nd digit H for 1961 year; 3rd digit is assembly plant code; followed by sequential number 001001 and up for serial number. (Coding: 0 = V8 Special, 1 = V8 Special Deluxe, 4 = LeSabre, 6 = Invicta, 7 = Electra, 8 — Electra 225.) *Example:* 4H4001001 is a 1961 Buick LeSabre, serial number 001001, built in Fairfax, KS. Check model number on body identification plate.

## Powertrains

| Engine | Gross HP | Transmission Availability | Special | LeSabre | Invicta | Electra |
|---|---|---|---|---|---|---|
| 215 CID Aluminum Fireball, 2-bbl., V8 | 155 | 3-speed manual | S | - | - | - |
| | | Dual-Path Turbine Drive Automatic | $189 | - | - | - |
| 364 CID Wildcat 375E, 2-bbl., V8 | 235 | Turbine Drive Automatic | - | No cost | - | - |
| 364 CID Wildcat 384, 2-bbl., V8 | 250 | Turbine Drive Automatic | - | S | - | - |
| 364 CID Wildcat 405, 4-bbl., V8 | 300 | Turbine Drive Automatic | - | $22 | - | - |
| 401 CID Wildcat 445, 4-bbl., V8 | 325 | Turbine Drive Automatic | - | - | S | S |

*Special only.    **Skylark only.*

## Major Options

| | Special/Skylark | LeSabre | Invicta | Electra |
|---|---|---|---|---|
| Air conditioning | $378 | $430 | $430 | $430 |
| Heater and defroster | $74 | $99 | $99 | $99 |
| Soft Ray tinted glass | $41 | $43 | $43 | $43 |
| Power steering | $86 | $108 | $108 | S |
| Power brakes | - | $43 | $43 | S |
| Power door locks | - | $70 | $70 | $70 |
| Power driver's seat/ Bench seat, 6-way | - | $97 | $97 | $69–$97 |
| Power windows | - | $108 | $108 | $108* |
| Sonomatic AM radio | $66 | $90 | $90 | $90 |

Options common to most models. (- = Not Available, S = Standard equipment.) Items may be standard equipment, optional at different pricing, or unavailable on certain models. This chart is only a guide.

*Standard on Electra 225.

## Paint Colors

| | Code |
|---|---|
| Sable Black | A |
| Arctic White | C |
| Newport Silver Metallic | D |
| Venice Blue Metallic | E |
| Laguna Blue Metallic | F |
| Bimini Blue | H |
| Dublin Green Metallic | J |
| Kerry Green | K |
| Rio Red Metallic | L |
| Sun Valley Cream | M |
| Cordovan Metallic | N |
| Turquoise Metallic | P |
| Phoenix Beige | R |
| Desert Fawn Metallic | T |
| Tampico Red | V |

# Special

*"The Best of Both Worlds ... The Special Size 1961 Buick Special."*

Nameplate year of origin: Special—1935.
Current bodystyle lifespan: 1961 through 1963.
Predecessor to this model: None.
Replacement for this model: Special/Skylark (1964 to 1965).
Percentage of division's sales volume: 31.39%.

## Measurements

| | | |
|---|---|---|
| Wheelbase | 112.0" | 112.0" |
| Length | 188.4" | 188.4" |
| Width | 71.3" | 71.3" |
| Height | 52.8" | 52.8" |

**1961**

**Corporate siblings:** Olds F-85 and Pontiac Tempest.
**Primary competition:** Dodge Lancer, and Mercury Comet.
**Notable changes:** All-new model.
**Major standard equipment:** Bolera cloth seats with foam cushions, dual armrests, dual sun visors, cigar lighter, air-cooled brakes, electric windshield wipers, and 6.50 × 13 BSW tires. Special Deluxe adds: Custom padded cushions, full carpeting, deluxe interior trim, rear seat armrests, deluxe steering wheel, and custom exterior moldings. Skylark adds: Skylark interior and exterior trim, and all-vinyl interior.

## Measurements (cont.)

| | | |
|---|---|---|
| Legroom — front | 44.6" | 44.6" |
| Legroom — rear | 37.8" | 37.8" |
| Headroom — front | 33.9" | 33.9" |
| Headroom — rear | 33.7" | 33.7" |
| Luggage capacity (cu. ft.) | 25.5 | 73.3 Wagon |
| Fuel capacity (gals.) | 14.0 | 14.0 |

## Models Available

| | Style Number | Base MSRP | Change from LY | Shipping Wt. (lbs.) | Production | Change from LY |
|---|---|---|---|---|---|---|
| Special 2-Door Coupe | 4027 | $2,330 | NEW | 2638 | 4,232 | NEW |
| Special 4-Door Sedan | 4019 | $2,384 | NEW | 2666 | 18,339 | NEW |
| Special 4-Door, 2-Seat Wagon | 4035 | $2,681 | NEW | 2876 | 6,101 | NEW |
| Special 4-Door, 3-Seat Wagon | 4045 | $2,762 | NEW | 2896 | 798 | NEW |
| Special Deluxe 4-Door Sedan | 4119 | $2,519 | NEW | 2648 | 32,986 | NEW |
| Special Deluxe 4-Dr., 2-Seat Wgn. | 4135 | $2,816 | NEW | 2845 | 11,729 | NEW |
| Skylark 2-Door Sport Coupe | 4317 | $2,621 | NEW | 2687 | 12,683 | NEW |
| TOTALS | Avg. price | $2,588 | NEW | Production | 86,868 | NEW |

# LeSabre

*"A value at any price, a sensation at Buick's price."*

**Nameplate year of origin:** 1959.
**Current bodystyle lifespan:** 1961 through 1964.
**Predecessor to this model:** LeSabre (1959 to 1960).
**Replacement for this model:** LeSabre (1965 to 1966).
**Percentage of division's sales volume:** 40.92%.
**Corporate siblings:** Chevrolet Biscayne/Bel-Air/Impala, Pontiac Catalina/Star Chief/Bonneville, Oldsmobile 88.
**Primary competition:** Chrysler Newport, DeSoto, and Mercury Meteor 800 & Monterey.
**Notable changes:** Completely restyled.
**Major standard equipment:** Vinyl and cloth interior, Mirro-magic instrument panel, electric windshield wipers, glove compartment light, trip mileage indicator, cigarette lighter, dual sunshades, Turbine-Drive automatic transmission, power rear window on three-seat wagon, and 7.60 × 15 BSW tires.

## Measurements

| | |
|---|---|
| Wheelbase | 123.0" |
| Length | 213.2" |
| Width | 78.0" |
| Height | 56.3" |
| Legroom — front | 44.5" |
| Legroom — rear | 41.4" |
| Headroom — front | 34.5" |
| Headroom — rear | 34.2" |
| Luggage capacity (cu. ft.) | NA |
| Fuel capacity (gals.) | 20.0 |

## Models Available

| | Style Number | Base MSRP | Change from LY | Shipping Wt. (lbs.) | Production | Change from LY |
|---|---|---|---|---|---|---|
| LeSabre 2-Door Sedan | 4411 | $2,993 | +8.60% | 4033 | 5,959 | -58.58% |
| LeSabre 2-Door Hardtop | 4437 | $3,152 | +8.13% | 4054 | 14,474 | -45.42% |
| LeSabre 2-Door Convertible | 4467 | $3,382 | +7.54% | 4186 | 11,971 | -11.90% |
| LeSabre 4-Door Sedan | 4469 | $3,107 | +8.26% | 4102 | 35,005 | -35.22% |
| LeSabre 4-Door Hardtop | 4439 | $3,228 | +7.92% | 4129 | 37,790 | +4.98% |
| LeSabre 4-Dr., 2-S. Estate Wagon | 4435 | $3,623 | +7.00% | 4450 | 5,628 | +5.57% |
| LeSabre 4-Dr., 3-S. Estate Wagon | 4445 | $3,730 | +6.78% | 4483 | 2,423 | +9.05% |
| TOTALS | Avg. price | $3,316 | +7.70% | Production | 113,250 | -25.53% |

# Invicta

*"More than ever, an automobile man's kind of automobile."*

**Nameplate year of origin:** 1959.
**Current bodystyle lifespan:** 1961 through 1963.
**Predecessor to this model:** Invicta (1959 to 1960).
**Replacement for this model:** Wildcat (1963 to 1964).
**Percentage of division's sales volume:** 10.38%.
**Corporate siblings:** Chevrolet Biscayne/Bel Air/Impala, Pontiac Catalina/Star Chief/Bonneville, Oldsmobile 88.
**Primary competition:** Chrysler Windsor, DeSoto, and Mercury Monterey.
**Notable changes:** Completely restyled.
**Major standard equipment:** Vinyl and cloth interior, two-way power driver's seat (2-Door Hardtop only), front and rear seat center armrests, Mirro-magic instrument panel, electric clock, electric windshield wipers, glove compartment light, trip mileage indicator, cigarette lighter, dual sunshades, automatic trunk light, deluxe steering wheel, deluxe wheel covers, Turbine-Drive automatic transmission, and 7.60 × 15 BSW tires.

## Measurements

| | |
|---|---|
| Wheelbase | 123.0" |
| Length | 213.2" |
| Width | 78.0" |
| Height | 56.3" |
| Legroom — front | 44.5" |
| Legroom — rear | 41.4" |
| Headroom — front | 34.5" |
| Headroom — rear | 34.2" |
| Luggage capacity (cu. ft.) | NA |
| Fuel capacity (gals.) | 20.0 |

## Models Available

| | Style Number | Base MSRP | Change from LY | Shipping Wt. (lbs.) | Production | Change from LY |
|---|---|---|---|---|---|---|
| Invicta 2-Door HT | 4637 | $3,447 | 0.00% | 4090 | 6,382 | -28.77% |
| Invicta 2-Door Convertible | 4667 | $3,620 | 0.00% | 4206 | 3,953 | -24.50% |
| Invicta 4-Door HT | 4639 | $3,515 | 0.00% | 4179 | 18,398 | 20.25% |
| TOTALS | | Avg. price $3,527 | -2.60%* | | Production 28,733 | -36.73%* |

*Due to discontinuation of wagon models.*

# Electra

*"The ultimate in Buick luxury."*

**Nameplate year of origin:** 1959.
**Current bodystyle lifespan:** 1961 through 1964.
**Predecessor to this model:** Electra & Electra 225 (1959 to 1960).
**Replacement for this model:** Electra 225 (1965 to 1966).
**Percentage of division's sales volume:** 17.31%.
**Corporate siblings:** Cadillac Series 62/de Ville, Oldsmobile Ninety-Eight.
**Primary competition:** Chrysler New Yorker.
**Notable changes:** Completely restyled.
**Major standard equipment:** Vinyl and cloth interior, front and rear seat center armrests, Mirro-magic instrument panel, electric clock, dual-speed electric windshield wipers with washers, Glove compartment light, trip mileage indicator, cigarette lighter, dual sunshades, automatic trunk light, deluxe steering wheel, deluxe wheel covers, power steering, power brakes, Turbine-Drive automatic transmission, and 8.00 × 15 BSW tires. Electra 225 adds: 2-way power driver's seat (Convertible), backup lights, and power windows.

## Measurements

| | |
|---|---|
| Wheelbase | 126.0" |
| Length | 219.2" |
| Width | 78.0" |
| Height | 57.1" |
| Legroom — front | 44.5" |
| Legroom — rear | 44.0" |
| Headroom — front | 34.6" |
| Headroom — rear | 34.5" |
| Luggage capacity (cu. ft.) | NA |
| Fuel capacity (gals.) | 20.0 |

## Models Available

| | Style Number | Base MSRP | Change from LY | Shipping Wt. (lbs.) | Production | Change from LY |
|---|---|---|---|---|---|---|
| Electra 2-Door Hardtop | 4737 | $3,818 | +0.00% | 4260 | 4,250 | -42.69% |
| Electra 4-Door Sedan | 4719 | $3,825 | -0.80% | 4298 | 13,818 | +0.17% |
| Electra 4-Door Hardtop | 4739 | $3,932 | -0.78% | 4333 | 8,978 | -38.03% |
| Electra 225 2-Door Convertible | 4867 | $4,192 | +0.00% | 4441 | 7,158 | +6.11% |
| Electra 225 6-w., Riviera 4-Dr. HT | 4829 | $4,350 | +1.16% | 4417 | 13,719 | +70.87% |
| TOTALS | *Avg. price* | $4,023 | +3.71% | *Production* | 47,923 | +34.25% |

**1961**

# CADILLAC

*"For 1961, Cadillac has truly created a new inspiration for all motordom … it could have come from no other source but the builder of the accepted Standard of the World."*

The 1961 model Cadillacs were a total departure from the chrome-laden, high-finned behemoths of the 1959–60 model years. The 1961, while still resembling its predecessors in some respects, was visually a slightly smaller and lighter car. The styling itself made the car look lighter. The front end featured a new grille which angled in a V back towards the hoodline and bumper. The bumper itself was not as big and heavy looking as previous years. The grille was a finer egg-crate affair, as opposed to the block-style makeup of the 1958–60 models. Body sides were sculpted with vertical lines top and bottom that gradually tapered to the rear where they met the round taillights/backup lamps mounted in oval pods at each end of the bumper. The rear bumper had small fins pointing downward that mimicked the smaller fins atop the rear fenders, which each housed a blade style taillamp. Rooflines were of the formal type, with thicker, more upright C-pillars than previously

used. Gone, except on the Fleetwood 75, was the annoying dogleg created by the reverse slanting front door vent windows. All models were powered by the same engine for the first time in many years. Only in the late sixties would an additional powertrain be introduced into the line. A better chassis design, along with improved spring and stabilizer designs and reduced weight, added up to a Cadillac that drove better than any prior model. Ride and driveability would become a battleground for luxury makes throughout the sixties. Lincoln would win on ride, and Cadillac on handling. Missing from the line this year were the Eldorado Seville 2-Door Hardtop and the Eldorado Brougham 4-Door Hardtop. A new addition mid-year was the de Ville Town Sedan, which was essentially a 6-window de Ville 4-Door Hardtop with a 10-inch section removed from the trunk area, allowing the car to fit into smaller garages.

**Series 62 2-Door Convertible**

**Series 62 4-Door, 6-Window Hardtop**

**Sedan de Ville 4-Door, 6-Window Hardtop**

**Eldorado Biarritz 2-Door Convertible**

**Model year production:** 136,170, down 2.68% from 1960.
**Domestic market share:** 2.54% (10th place).
**Base price range:** $4,892 to $9,748.
**Industry average base price:** $3,048.
**Cadillac average base price:** $6,187.
**Introduction date:** October 1960.

**Assembly plants:** Detroit, MI.
**Data plate identification:** Nine digit code read as follows: 1st and 2nd digits identify year (61 for 1961); 3rd digit is style symbol (see list); followed by 000001 and up for serial number. *Example:* 61J000001 is a 1961 Cadillac de Ville 2-Door Hardtop, serial number 000001.

## Powertrains

| Engine | Intake/Cylinder Arrangement | Gross HP | Transmission Availability | All models |
|---|---|---|---|---|
| 390 CID, 4-bbl., V8 | | 325 | Hydra-matic Automatic | S |

## Major Options

| | Sixty-Two | de Ville | Eldorado | Sixty Special | Seventy-Five |
|---|---|---|---|---|---|
| Air conditioning | $474 | $474 | $474 | $474 | $624* |
| Power Windows | $118 | S | S | S | S |
| 6-way power seat | $113 | $85 | S | $85 | – |
| Power door locks | $46–$70 | $46–$70 | $46 | $70 | S |
| AM radio w/rear speaker | $165 | $165 | $165 | $165 | $247** |
| Guide-Matic headlamp dimmers | $45 | $45 | $45 | $45 | – |
| Cruise control | $97 | $97 | $97 | $97 | $97 |
| Remote control trunk release/lock | $59 | $59 | $59 | $59 | – |

Options common to most models. (– = Not Available, S = Standard equipment.) Items may be standard equipment, optional at different pricing, or unavailable on certain models. This chart is only a guide.

**Cadillac Style Symbols: A**— 62 4-window Sedan or Calais 4-Dr. HT Sedan; **B**— Sedan de Ville 4-window; **C**— 62 Short Deck Sedan; **D**— Sedan de Ville Park Avenue; **E**— Eldorado Biarritz or Eldorado Convertible; **F**— 62 Convertible; **G**— 62 2-Door Hardtop or Calais 2-Door HT; **H**— Eldorado Seville HT or Eldorado Coupe; **J**— Coupe de Ville; **K**— 62 6-window Sedan; **L**— Sedan de Ville 6-window; **M**— Fleetwood 60 Special Sedan; **N**— 62 4-window Sedan (1963) or Calais Sedan; **P**— Fleetwood Brougham or Eldorado Brougham; **R**— Fleetwood 75 Sedan; **S**— Fleetwood 75 Limousine; **Z**— Commerical Chassis

## Paint Colors

| | Code |
|---|---|
| Ebony Black | 10 |
| Olympic White | 12 |
| Platinum Metallic | 14 |
| Aleutian Gray Metallic | 16 |
| Bristol Blue Metallic | 22 |
| Dresden Blue Metallic | 24 |
| York Blue Metallic | 26 |
| San Remo Turquoise Metallic | 29 |
| Concord Green Metallic | 32 |
| Lexington Green Metallic | 34 |
| Granada Green Metallic | 36 |
| Laredo Tan | 44 |
| Tunis Beige Metallic | 46 |
| Fontana Rose Metallic | 48 |
| Pompeian Red Metallic | 50 |
| Nautilus Blue Metallic | 94 |
| Jade Metallic | 96 |
| Aspen Gold Metallic | 97 |
| Topaz Metallic | 98 |
| Shell Pearl Metallic | 99 |

# Sixty-Two

*"The crisp new Cadillac silhouette makes this an automobile of surpassing beauty."*

**Nameplate year of origin:** 1940.
**Current bodystyle lifespan:** 1961 through 1964.
**Predecessor to this model:** Series Sixty-Two (1959 to 1960).
**Replacement for this model:** Calais (1965 to 1966).
**Percentage of division's sales volume:** 45.84%.
**Corporate siblings:** Buick Electra and Oldsmobile Ninety-Eight.
**Primary competition:** Imperial Custom.
**Notable changes:** Completely restyled.
**Major standard equipment:** Cloth or cloth and vinyl seat upholstery, rear seat center armrests, interior courtesy and map lights, left-hand outside remote control mirror, windshield wipers and washers, electric clock, right side visor vanity mirrors, rear fender skirts, front cornering lamps, power steering, power brakes, Hydra-matic transmission, and 8.00 × 15 BSW tires.

## Measurements

| | |
|---|---|
| Wheelbase | 129.5" |
| Length | 222.0" |
| Width | 79.8" |
| Height | 56.3" |
| Legroom — front | 46.0" |
| Legroom — rear | 44.5" |
| Headroom — front | 34.4" |
| Headroom — rear | 34.1" |
| Luggage capacity (cu. ft.) | NA |
| Fuel capacity (gals.) | 21.0 |

## Models Available

| | Style Number | Base MSRP | Change from LY | Shipping Wt. (lbs.) | Production | Change from LY |
|---|---|---|---|---|---|---|
| Sixty-Two 2-Door Hardtop | 6237 | $4,892 | 0.00% | 4560 | 16,005 | -19.89% |
| Sixty-Two 2-Door Convertible | 6267 | $5,455 | 0.00% | 4720 | 15,500 | +10.71% |
| Sixty-Two 4-Door, 4-w. Hardtop | 6239 | $5,080 | 0.00% | 4660 | 4,700 | -52.92% |
| Sixty-Two 4-Door, 6-w. Hardtop | 6229 | $5,080 | 0.00% | 4680 | 26,216 | -2.27% |
| TOTALS | Avg. price | $5,127 | 0.00% | Production | 62,421 | -11.81% |

# de Ville

*"Seeking new horizons in design for motion."*

**Nameplate year of origin:** 1949 (as Hardtop designation), 1959 (series).
**Current bodystyle lifespan:** 1961 through 1964.
**Predecessor to this model:** de Ville (1959 to 1960).
**Replacement for this model:** de Ville (1965 to 1966).
**Percentage of division's sales volume:** 40.52%.
**Corporate siblings:** Buick Electra and Oldsmobile Ninety-Eight.
**Primary competition:** Imperial Crown and Lincoln Continental.
**Notable changes:** Completely restyled.
**Major standard equipment:** Cloth or cloth and leather seat upholstery, front and rear seat center armrests, power operated front seat adjustment, power windows, interior courtesy and map lights, left-hand outside remote control mirror, windshield wipers and washers, electric clock, right side visor vanity mirrors, rear fender skirts, front cornering lamps, power steering, power brakes, Hydra-matic transmission, and 8.00 × 15 BSW tires.

### Measurements

| | |
|---|---|
| Wheelbase | 129.5" |
| Length | 222.0"/ |
| | Town Sedan 215.0" |
| Width | 79.8" |
| Height | 56.3" |
| Legroom — front | 46.0" |
| Legroom — rear | 44.5" |
| Headroom — front | 34.4" |
| Headroom — rear | 34.1" |
| Luggage capacity (cu. ft.) | NA |
| Fuel capacity (gals.) | 21.0 |

## Models Available

| | Style Number | Base MSRP | Change from LY | Shipping Wt. (lbs.) | Production | Change from LY |
|---|---|---|---|---|---|---|
| Coupe de Ville 2-Door Hardtop | 6337 | $5,252 | 0.00% | 4595 | 20,156 | -6.6% |
| Sedan de Ville 4-Dr. Town Sedan | 6399 | $5,498 | NEW | 4705 | 3,756 | NEW |
| Sedan de Ville 4-Dr., 4-Wind. HT | 6339 | $5,498 | 0.00% | 4715 | 4,847 | -47.5% |
| Sedan de Ville 4-Dr., 6-Wind. HT | 6329 | $5,498 | 0.00% | 4710 | 26,415 | +17.0% |
| TOTALS | Avg. price | $5,437 | +0.39% | Production | 55,174 | +3.3% |

# Eldorado

*"Rarely, and only to a supremely fortunate few, there comes an automobile the very sight of which summons forth visions of distant mountains, pounding surf and soft Southern skies."*

**Nameplate year of origin:** 1953.
**Current bodystyle lifespan:** 1961 through 1964.
**Predecessor to this model:** Eldorado (1959 to 1960).
**Replacement for this model:** Eldorado (1965 to 1966).
**Percentage of division's sales volume:** 1.06%.

### Measurements

| | |
|---|---|
| Wheelbase | 129.5" |
| Length | 222.0" |
| Width | 79.9" |

**Corporate siblings:** Buick Electra and Oldsmobile Ninety-Eight.

**Primary competition:** Imperial Crown and Lincoln Continental.

**Notable changes:** Completely restyled. Seville Hardtop and Brougham Sedan models dropped.

**Major standard equipment:** Leather seat upholstery, front and rear seat center armrests, power operated front seat adjustment, power windows and vent windows, interior courtesy and map lights, left-hand outside remote control mirror, windshield wipers and washers, electric clock, right side visor vanity mirrors, rear fender skirts, front cornering lamps, power steering, power brakes, Turbo Hydra-matic transmission, and 8.20 × 15 WSW tires.

## Measurements (cont.)

| | |
|---|---|
| Height | 56.3" |
| Legroom — front | 46.0" |
| Legroom — rear | 44.5" |
| Headroom — front | 34.4" |
| Headroom — rear | 34.1" |
| Luggage capacity (cu. ft.) | NA |
| Fuel capacity (gals.) | 21.0 |

## Models Available

| | Style Number | Base MSRP | Change from LY | Shipping Wt. (lbs.) | Production | Change from LY |
|---|---|---|---|---|---|---|
| Fl. Eldorado Biarritz 2-Dr. Conv. | 6367 | $6,477 | -12.5% | 4620 | 1,450 | +12.8% |
| TOTALS | | Avg. price $6,477 | -12.5% | | Production 1,450 | -41.1% |

# Fleetwood Sixty-Special

*"Cadillac designers have achieved new luxury, spaciousness and good taste, combined in a supreme expression of the stylist's craft."*

**Nameplate year of origin:** 1938.

**Current bodystyle lifespan:** 1961 through 1964.

**Predecessor to this model:** Fleetwood Sixty-Special (1959 to 1960).

**Replacement for this model:** Fleetwood Sixty-Special (1965 to 1966).

**Percentage of division's sales volume:** 11.38%.

**Corporate siblings:** Buick Electra and Oldsmobile Ninety-Eight.

**Primary competition:** Imperial LeBaron.

**Notable changes:** Completely restyled.

**Major standard equipment:** Fabric and leather or wool broadcloth seat upholstery, front and rear seat center armrests, power operated front seat adjustment, power windows, interior courtesy and map lights, left-hand outside remote control mirror, windshield wipers and washers, electric clock, right side visor vanity mirrors, rear fender skirts, front cornering lamps, power steering, power brakes, Hydra-matic transmission, and 8.00 × 15 BSW tires.

## Measurements

| | |
|---|---|
| Wheelbase | 129.5" |
| Length | 222.0" |
| Width | 79.8" |
| Height | 56.6" |
| Legroom — front | 46.0" |
| Legroom — rear | 44.5" |
| Headroom — front | 34.6" |
| Headroom — rear | 34.5" |
| Luggage capacity (cu. ft.) | NA |
| Fuel capacity (gals.) | 21.0 |

## Models Available

| | Style Number | Base MSRP | Change from LY | Shipping Wt. (lbs.) | Production | Change from LY |
|---|---|---|---|---|---|---|
| Fl. Sixty-Special 4-Door Sedan | 6039 | $6,233 | 0.00% | 4770 | 15,500 | +31.4% |
| TOTALS | | Avg. price $6,233 | 0.00% | | Production 15,500 | +31.4% |

# Fleetwood Seventy-Five

*"Justly famed as the most distinguished automobile on the American scene."*

**Nameplate year of origin:** 1927 (Fleetwood bodies), 1936 (75 series).

**Current bodystyle lifespan:** 1959 through 1965.

**Predecessor to this model:** Fleetwood 75 (1957 to 1958).

**Replacement for this model:** Fleetwood 75 (1966).

**Percentage of division's sales volume:** 1.19%.

**Corporate siblings:** None.

**Primary competition:** None.

**Notable changes:** Completely restyled, but still carried the 1959-60 model basic body shell, chassis and roofline.

**Major standard equipment:** Wool broadcloth or cord cloth seat upholstery with front compartment in harmonizing leather upholstery, rear seat center armrests, power operated front seat adjustment, power windows, interior courtesy and map lights, left-hand outside remote control mirror, windshield wipers and washers, electric clock, right side visor vanity mirrors, rear fender skirts, front cornering lamps, power steering, power brakes, Hydra-matic transmission, and 8.00 × 15 BSW tires.

## Measurements

| | |
|---|---|
| Wheelbase | 149.8" |
| Length | 242.3" |
| Width | 80.6" |
| Height | 59.1" |
| Legroom — front | 44.2" |
| Legroom — rear | Not calculated |
| Headroom — front | 36.6" |
| Headroom — rear | 34.8" |
| Luggage capacity (cu. ft.) | NA |
| Fuel capacity (gals.) | 21.0 |

## Models Available

| | Style Number | Base MSRP | Change from LY | Shipping Wt. (lbs.) | Production | Change from LY |
|---|---|---|---|---|---|---|
| Fl. Seventy-Five 4-Door Sdn., 9-p. | 6723 | $9,533 | 0.00% | 5390 | 699 | -2.6% |
| Fl. Seventy-Five 4-Door Limo., 9-p. | 6733 | $9,748 | 0.00% | 5420 | 926 | +11.3% |
| TOTALS | | *Avg. price* $9,641 | 0.00% | | *Production* 1,625 | +4.80% |

# CHEVROLET

*"See the U.S.A. ... Go Chevrolet!"*

In five short years, the number one selling automaker had become even more popular with its renowned line of V8 engines. To add to that line, the fabled 409 CID V8 engine was introduced in mid-year 1961. Through this time period, most GM divisions that were active in racing would provide street versions of their racing engines. The 409 was one of those that would become legendary. Offering as much as 360 horsepower in its initial year, it would be developed to put out as much as 409 horsepower within a year. Accompanying the 409 V8 introduction was the Impala Super Sport option package. Available on any Impala model for 1961, the Super Sport was initially offered as a

dealer installed option. It would become a staple in the Chevy high-performance line throughout the muscle car era. For 1961, the SS, as it was known, featured emblems on interior and exterior areas, power steering and brakes, heavy duty suspension, and SS wheel covers.

The 1961 full-size Chevrolet line was totally revamped for the new year. As with all other full-size GM lines, the new cars finally did away with the knee-banger, wraparound windshields and tailfins and shed some of the length and width that had been gained in the prior three years. The new look for Chevy was very clean and pleasing to look at. The front end sported a full-width grille with dual headlamps mounted at each end. Turn signals and parking lamps were mounted above the headlamps. Body sides were cleaned up greatly, with a single body side line running from the headlamp area and gradually sloping downward until just before the rear of the car, where there was a slight kick up, that brought the line up to the top of the rear fender and deck lid line. Across the rear the line continued with a "V" dip in the center. The model line continued as in 1960, with two additions: an Impala 2-Door Sedan (a one-year-only model), and a 9-passenger Nomad wagon.

With the ensuing model proliferation that would mark most of the sixties, full-size Chevrolets were now being marketed more as a unit, so all are listed together within this book from 1962 forward.

Elsewhere in the Chevrolet line, the popular Corvair added a Lakewood station wagon model to the 500 and 700 lines, and a 4-Door Sedan was added to the Monza line. While not covered here in detail, the Corvair 95

Greenbrier Wagon (or Van as they would become known) was introduced this year. This model provided a 6-passenger vehicle with enormous cargo capacity, or could be equipped to take the place of earlier Sedan Delivery wagons, which were no longer offered by Chevrolet. This would eventually become the Greenbrier's larger market, and would lead to the eventual development of the modern Chevy van, which was introduced in 1965.

The Corvette featured a new grille and some trim and option changes, but was otherwise unchanged. The new grille greatly simplified the front-end look, and was probably the best of this period. Of course, as powertrain upgrades came along, the Corvette was benefiting from these also, but the 409 CID V8 would not see use in the Corvette because of limited space under the hood and available quantities of the new engine. They were built in small numbers, and most went to racing teams rather than production vehicles.

BelAir 2-Door Hardtop

Biscayne 4-Door Sedan

Corvair 500 4-Door Sedan

Corvair 700 Lakewood 4-Door Wagon

Impala 2-Door Convertible

Parkwood 4-Door, 6-passenger wagon

**Model year production:** 1,484,922 (based on estimates), down 10.11% from 1960.
**Domestic market share:** 27.70% (1st place; based on estimates).
**Base price range:** $1,920 to $3,934.
**Industry average base price:** $3,048.
**Chevrolet average base price:** $2,486.
**Introduction date:** October 1960.
**Assembly plants:** Atlanta, GA (A); Baltimore, MD (B); Flint, MI (F); Framingham, MA (G); Janesville, WI (J); Kansas City, MO (K), Los Angeles, CA (L), Norwood, OH (N); Oakland, CA (O); St. Louis, MO (S); Tarrytown, NY (T); and Willow Run, MI (W).
**Data plate identification:** Twelve digit code read as follows: 1st digit 1 for 1961; four digit style number (see listings below: 2nd and 3rd numbers identify series and engine, 4th and 5th indicate body style); 6th digit is assembly plant code; 100001 and up for serial number. *Example:* 11511S100001 is a 1961 Chevrolet BelAir 2-Door Sedan, 6-cylinder, serial number 100001, built in St. Louis, MO.

## Powertrains

| Engine | Gross HP | Transmission Availability | Corvair | Biscayne/ BelAir/Impala | Corvette |
|---|---|---|---|---|---|
| 145 CID Turbo-Air, 2 × 1-bbl., Flat 6 | 80 | 3-speed manual | S | - | - |
| | | 4-speed manual | $65 | - | - |
| | | 2-sp. Powerglide Automatic | $157 | - | - |
| 145 CID Super Turbo-Air, 2 × 1-bbl., Flat 6 | 98 | 3-speed manual | $27 | - | - |
| | | 4-speed manual | $92 | - | - |
| | | 2-sp. Powerglide Automatic | $184 | - | - |
| 235.5 CID Hi-Thrift, 1-bbl., 6-cyl. | 135 | 3-speed manual | - | S | - |
| | | Overdrive | - | $108 | - |
| | | 2-sp. Powerglide Automatic | - | $188 | - |
| 283 CID Economy Turbo-Fire, 2-bbl., V8 | 170 | 3-speed manual | - | $107 | - |
| | | Overdrive | - | $215 | |
| | | 2- sp. Powerglide Automatic | - | $306 | - |
| | | Turboglide Automatic | - | $317 | |
| 283 CID Super Turbo-Fire, 4-bbl., V8 | 230 | 3-speed manual | - | $136 | S |
| | | 4-speed manual | - | - | $188 |
| | | Overdrive | - | $244 | |
| | | 2- sp. Powerglide Automatic | - | $335 | $199 |
| | | Turboglide Automatic | - | $346 | - |
| 283 CID Corvette, 2 × 4-bbl., V8 | 245 | 3-speed manual | - | - | $151 |
| | | 4-speed manual | - | - | $334 |
| | | 2- sp. Powerglide Automatic | - | - | |
| | $345 | | | | |
| 283 CID Ramjet, Fuel-Injected V8 | 275 | 3-speed manual | - | - | $484 |
| | | 4-speed manual | - | - | $672 |
| 348 CID Turbo-Thrust, 4-bbl., V8 | 250 | 3-speed manual | - | $201 | - |
| | | 4-speed manual | - | $389 | - |
| | | Turboglide Automatic | - | $411 | - |
| 348 CID Super Turbo-Thrust, 3 × 2-bbl., V8 | 280 | 3-speed manual | - | $271 | - |
| | | 4-speed manual | - | $459 | - |
| | | Turboglide Automatic | - | $481 | - |
| 348 CID Special Turbo-Thrust, 4-bbl., V8 | 305 | 3-speed manual | - | $424 | - |
| | | 4-speed manual | - | $612 | - |
| 348 CID Special Turbo-Thrust, 4-bbl., V8 | 340 | 3-speed manual | - | $451 | - |
| | | 4-speed manual | - | $639 | - |
| 348 CID Special Turbo-Thrust, 3 × 2-bbl., V8 | 350 | 3-speed manual | - | $472 | - |
| | | 4-speed manual | - | $658 | - |
| 409 CID Turbo-Fire, 2 × 4-bbl., V8 | 360 | 3-speed manual | - | NA | - |
| | | 4-speed manual | - | NA | - |

## Major Options

| | Corvair | Full-size | Corvette |
|---|---|---|---|
| Air conditioning (NA 4-cyl.) | $350 | $364 | - |
| Soft Ray tinted glass | $27 | $38 | $16 |
| Power steering (NA 4-cyl.) | - | $75 | - |
| Power brakes | - | $43 | - |
| Power windows | - | $102 | $59 |
| Electric clock | $16 | $16 | S |
| Pushbutton AM Radio | $57 | $57 | $137 |
| Whitewall tires — Std. size | $29 | $32–$40 | $32 |

Options common to most models. (– = Not Available, S = Standard equipment.) Items may be standard equipment, optional at different pricing, or unavailable on certain models. This chart is only a guide.

## Paint Colors

| | Code |
|---|---|
| Tuxedo Black | 900* |
| Seafoam Green | 903 |
| Arbor Green Met. | 905 |
| Jewel Blue Met. | 912* |
| Midnight Blue Metallic | 914 |
| Twillight Turquoise Met. | 915 |
| Seamist Turquoise | 917 |
| Fawn Beige Metallic | 920* |
| Roman Red | 923* |
| Coronna Cream | 925 |

**Paint Colors** (cont.)

| | |
|---|---|
| Ermine White | 936* |
| Almond Beige | 938 |
| Sateen Silver Metallic | 940* |
| Shadow Gray Metallic | 941 |
| Honduras Maroon Met. | 948* |

*Available on Corvette also.*

# Corvair

*"Now—A complete line of complete thrift cars."*

**Nameplate year of origin:** 1960.
**Current bodystyle lifespan:** 1960 through 1964.
**Predecessor to this model:** None.
**Replacement for this model:** Corvair (1965 to 1969).
**Percentage of division's sales volume:** 19.00%.
**Corporate siblings:** None.
**Primary competition:** Rambler American, Ford Falcon, Plymouth Valiant and Studebaker Lark.
**Notable changes:** Minor trim and detail changes.
**Major standard equipment:** Cloth and vinyl front bench seat, left-hand sun visor, turn signals, center dome light, electric windshield wipers, and 6.50 × 13 BSW tires. 700 adds: Luggage compartment trim, color-keyed floor mats, dual horns, and automatic dome lamp switch. Monza adds: All-vinyl bucket seats, folding rear seat, dual sun visors, glove box light, and additional exterior chrome trim.

## Measurements

| | Cars | Wagons |
|---|---|---|
| Wheelbase | 108.0" | 108.0" |
| Length | 180.0" | 180.0" |
| Width | 67.0" | 67.0" |
| Height | 51.5" | 51.8" |
| Legroom — front | 44.0" | 44.0" |
| Legroom — rear | 36.5" | 36.5" |
| Headroom — front | 33.5" | 33.5" |
| Headroom — rear | 33.5" | 33.8" |
| Cargo capacity (cu. ft.) | 13.0 | 58.0 |
| Fuel capacity (gals.) | 14.0 | 14.0 |

## Models Available

| | Style Number | Base MSRP | Change from LY | Shipping Wt. (lbs.) | Production | Change from LY |
|---|---|---|---|---|---|---|
| Corvair 500 2-Door Club Coupe | 0527 | $1,920 | -3.23% | 2320 | 16,857 | 15.24% |
| Corvair 500 4-Door Sedan | 0569 | $1,974 | -3.14% | 2355 | 18,752 | -60.67% |
| Corvair 500 Lakewood 4-Dr. Wagon | 0535 | $2,266 | NEW | 2530 | 5,591 | NEW |
| Corvair 700 2-Door Club Coupe | 0727 | $1,985 | -3.12% | 2350 | 24,786 | -32.21% |
| Corvair 700 4-Door Sedan | 0769 | $2,039 | -3.04% | 2380 | 51,948 | -62.68% |
| Corvair 700 Lakewood 4-Dr. Wagon | 0735 | $2,331 | NEW | 2555 | 20,451 | NEW |
| Corvair Monza 900 2-Dr. Club Cpe. | 0927 | $2,201 | -3.63% | 2395 | 109,945 | 821.89% |
| Corvair Monza 900 4-Door Sedan | 0969 | $2,201 | NEW | 2420 | 33,745 | NEW |
| TOTALS | | Avg. price $2,115 | +1.59% | | Production 282,075 | +12.83% |

# Biscayne

*"For the budget-minded who need big car room at small car prices—Go Biscayne."*

**Nameplate year of origin:** 1958.
**Current bodystyle lifespan:** 1959 through 1960.
**Predecessor to this model:** Biscayne (1958).
**Replacement for this model:** Biscayne (1961 to 1964).

## Measurements

| | Cars | Wagons |
|---|---|---|
| Wheelbase | 119.0" | 119.0" |

**Percentage of division's sales volume:** See Impala for combined full-size data.
**Corporate siblings:** Buick LeSabre/Invicta, Olds 88, Pontiac Catalina/Star Chief/Bonneville.
**Primary competition:** Rambler Ambassador, Dodge Polara, Ford Custom/Galaxie, and Plymouth Fury.
**Notable changes:** New grille and revised rear end and trim.
**Major standard equipment:** Nylon pattern cloth seat upholstery, foam cushion front seats, front door armrests, dual sun visors, electric windshield wipers, cigar lighter, glove compartment lock and 7.50 × 14 BSW tires. Brookwood adds: Simulated-weave vinyl upholstery and 8.00 × 14 BSW tires.

| | Cars | Wagons |
|---|---|---|
| Length | 209.3" | 209.3" |
| Width | 78.4" | 78.4" |
| Height (Sedan) | 55.5" | 55.8" |
| Legroom — front | 45.0" | 45.0" |
| Legroom — rear | 42.0" | 41.8" |
| Headroom — front | 34.5" | 34.5" |
| Headroom — rear | 34.0" | 34.2" |
| Cargo capacity (cu. ft.) | NA | 97.5 |
| Fuel capacity (gals.) | 20.0 | 19.0 |

**1961**

## Models Available

| | Style Number | Base MSRP | Change from LY | Shipping Wt. (lbs.) | Production | Change from LY |
|---|---|---|---|---|---|---|
| Biscayne Fleetmaster 2-Dr. Sedan | 1311 | $2,230 | 0.00% | 3410 | * | - |
| Biscayne Fleetmaster 4-Dr. Sedan | 1369 | $2,284 | 0.00% | 3495 | * | - |
| Biscayne 2-Dr., 3-p. Utility Sedan | 1121 | $2,175 | 0.00% | 3390 | * | - |
| Biscayne 2-Door Sedan | 1111 | $2,262 | 0.00% | 3415 | * | - |
| Biscayne 4-Door Sedan | 1169 | $2,316 | 0.00% | 3500 | * | - |
| Brookwood 4-Dr., 2-S. Wagon | 1135 | $2,653 | +2.59% | 3850 | * | - |
| Brookwood 4-Dr., 3-S. Wagon | 1145 | $2,756 | +3.88% | 3900 | * | - |
| TOTALS | Avg. price | $2,382 | +1.02% | | See Impala for total full-size production | |

# BelAir

*"Planned for modern tastes in comfort and convenience."*

**Nameplate year of origin:** 1950.
**Current bodystyle lifespan:** 1959 through 1960.
**Predecessor to this model:** BelAir (1958).
**Replacement for this model:** BelAir (1962 to 1964).
**Percentage of division's sales volume:** See Impala for combined full-size data.
**Corporate siblings:** Buick LeSabre/Invicta, Olds 88, Pontiac Catalina/Star Chief/Bonneville.
**Primary competition:** Rambler Ambassador, Dodge Polara, Ford Custom/Galaxie, and Plymouth Fury.
**Notable changes:** New grille and revised rear end and trim.
**Major standard equipment:** Nylon pattern cloth seat upholstery, cloth headliner, foam cushion front and rear seats, front and rear door armrests, combination carpet and vinyl coated rubber floor mats, electric windshield wipers, interior lighting, and 7.50 × 14 BSW tires. Parkwood adds: Vinyl upholstery, vinyl headliner, and 8.00 × 14 BSW tires.

## Measurements

| | Cars | Wagons |
|---|---|---|
| Wheelbase | 119.0" | 119.0" |
| Length | 209.3" | 209.3" |
| Width | 78.4" | 78.4" |
| Height | 55.5" | 55.8" |
| Legroom — front | 45.0" | 45.0" |
| Legroom — rear | 42.0" | 41.8" |
| Headroom — front | 34.5" | 34.5" |
| Headroom — rear | 34.0" | 34.2" |
| Cargo capacity (cu. ft.) | NA | 97.5 |
| Fuel capacity (gals.) | 20.0 | 19.0 |

## Models Available

| | Style Number | Base MSRP | Change from LY | Shipping Wt. (lbs.) | Production | Change from LY |
|---|---|---|---|---|---|---|
| Bel Air 2-Door Sedan | 1511 | $2,384 | 0.00% | 3430 | * | - |
| Bel Air 2-Door Hardtop | 1537 | $2,489 | 0.00% | 3475 | * | - |
| Bel Air 4-Door Sedan | 1569 | $2,438 | 0.00% | 3515 | * | - |
| Bel Air 4-Door Hardtop | 1539 | $2,554 | 0.00% | 3550 | * | - |

| | Style Number | Base MSRP | Change from LY | Shipping Wt. (lbs.) | Production | Change from LY |
|---|---|---|---|---|---|---|
| Parkwood 4-Dr., 2-S. Wagon | 1535 | $2,747 | 0.00% | 3865 | * | - |
| Parkwood 4-Dr., 3-S. Wagon | 1545 | $2,850 | 0.00% | 3910 | * | - |
| TOTALS | | Avg. price $2,577 | 0.00% | See Impala for total full-size production | | |

# Impala

*"America's most popular cars, now trimmer in size."*

**Nameplate year of origin:** 1958.
**Current bodystyle lifespan:** 1959 through 1960.
**Predecessor to this model:** Impala (1958).
**Replacement for this model:** Impala (1962 to 1964).
**Percentage of division's sales volume:** 80.27% (includes Biscayne and BelAir).
**Corporate siblings:** Buick LeSabre/Invicta, Olds 88, Pontiac Catalina/Star Chief/Bonneville.
**Primary competition:** Rambler Ambassador, Dodge Polara, Ford Custom/Galaxie, and Plymouth Fury.
**Notable changes:** New grille and revised rear end and trim.
**Major standard equipment:** BelAir equipment plus: Nylon pattern cloth seat upholstery (vinyl in convertible), vinyl headliner (cloth in 4-Door Sedan), electric clock, full carpeting (combination carpet and vinyl coated rubber floor mats in convertible), and dual backup lamps.
Nomad adds: 8.00 × 14 BSW tires.

## Measurements

| | Cars | Wagons |
|---|---|---|
| Wheelbase | 119.0" | 119.0" |
| Length | 209.3" | 209.3" |
| Width | 78.4" | 78.4" |
| Height | 55.5" | 55.8" |
| Legroom — front | 45.0" | 45.0" |
| Legroom — rear | 42.0" | 41.8" |
| Headroom — front | 34.5" | 34.5" |
| Headroom — rear | 34.0" | 34.2" |
| Cargo capacity (cu. ft.) | NA | 97.5 |
| Fuel capacity (gals.) | 20.0 | 19.0 |

## Models Available

| | Style Number | Base MSRP | Change from LY | Shipping Wt. (lbs.) | Production* | Change from LY |
|---|---|---|---|---|---|---|
| Impala 2-Door Sedan | 1711 | $2,536 | NEW | 3445 | 153,988 | NA |
| Impala 2-Door Sport Coupe | 1737 | $2,597 | 0.00% | 3485 | 177,969 | -12.96% |
| Impala 2-Door Convertible | 1767 | $2,847 | 0.00% | 3605 | 64,624 | -19.12% |
| Impala 4-Door Sedan | 1769 | $2,590 | 0.00% | 3530 | 452,251 | -9.01% |
| Impala 4-Door Hardtop | 1739 | $2,662 | 0.00% | 3575 | 174,141 | 3.03% |
| Nomad 4-Dr., 2-S. Wagon | 1735 | $2,889 | 0.00% | 3885 | 168,935 | -14.71% |
| Nomad 4-Dr., 3-S. Wagon | 1745 | $2,992 | NEW | 3835 | NA | NEW |
| TOTALS | | Avg. price $2,730 | +0.48% | Production 1,191,908* | | -14.35% |

# Corvette

*"America's true sports car!"*

**Nameplate year of origin:** 1953 (Also used on show car of same year).
**Current bodystyle lifespan:** 1956 through 1962.
**Predecessor to this model:** Corvette (1953 to 1955).
**Replacement for this model:** Corvette (1963 to 1967).
**Percentage of division's sales volume:** 0.74%.
**Corporate siblings:** None.
**Primary competition:** None.

## Measurements

| | |
|---|---|
| Wheelbase | 102.0" |
| Length | 177.7" |
| Width | 70.4" |
| Height | 52.2" |
| Legroom — front | 46.4" |
| Legroom — rear | NA |

**Notable changes:** Revised trim and detail changes.

**Major standard equipment:** Deep-contoured bucket seats, deep-pile carpeting, complete instrumentation, manually operated folding top or removable hard-top, and 6.70 × 15 BSW tires.

## Measurements (cont.)

| | |
|---|---|
| Headroom — front | 37.1" |
| Headroom — rear | NA |
| Cargo capacity (cu. ft.) | NA |
| Fuel capacity (gals.) | 16.4 |

## Models Available

| | Style Number | Base MSRP | Change from LY | Shipping Wt. (lbs.) | Production | Change from LY |
|---|---|---|---|---|---|---|
| Corvette 2-Door Convertible | 0867 | $3,934 | +1.60% | 2905 | 10,939 | +6.61% |
| TOTALS | *Avg. price* | $3,934 | +1.60% | *Production* | 10,939 | +6.61% |

# CHRYSLER

*"Every Chrysler is a full-size, grown up car with real six-people room."*

All Chrysler Corporation big cars received a facelift this year, and Chrysler got the best deal of the group. While Dodge and Plymouth models were overdone to put it mildly, Chrysler came off with a unique look that still was pleasing. Copying the 1959 Buick slanted headlamp theme, Chrysler built these around a 300-letter-series style grille, turned upside down. Basic body design continued the pleasing 1960 theme, including the large tail fins at the rear. This would be the last year for tall fins on any make of American car. While DeSoto copied the same styling, the DeSoto featured its taillamps where the Chrysler had its backup lamps in the fins, and the DeSoto had its backup lamps just above the bumper, where the Chrysler had its taillamps. Smaller fins would continue on for many years, particularly on Cadillac models. But Chrysler would leave them behind for good.

Under the hood, things remained largely the same.

After all, why mess with success? Chrysler had developed some of the most dependable and powerful engines of any manufacturer. The Dodge and DeSoto derived 361 CID V8 was implemented as the base powerplant for the newly named Newport line. Changes to the model line were not major, except for name changes. A revived Newport nameplate replaced the Windsor at the bottom of the Chrysler line. Essentially it was equivalent to the soon to be defunct DeSoto, with the prestige of the Chrysler nameplate. The middle line model, the Saratoga, was renamed Windsor, but still rode on the former Windsor's 122-inch wheelbase. The luxury hot-rod 300 advanced its suffix to the letter G. The luxurious New Yorker line returned unchanged. The luxury wagon line continued to be offered in 4-Door Hardtop configuration, while other manufacturers had abandoned the stylish models.

Newport 4-Door Hardtop

Newport Town & Country 4-Door Wagon

New Yorker 2-Door Convertible

Windsor 4-Door Sedan

**Model year production:** 96,454, up 24.80% over 1960.
**Base price range:** $2,964 to $5,843.
**Domestic market share:** 1.80% (11th place).
**Industry average base price:** $3,048.
**Chrysler average base price:** $3,980.
**Introduction date:** October 1959.
**Assembly plants:** Detroit (Jefferson Ave.) MI (3); Los Angeles, CA (5).

**Data plate identification:** Ten digit code read as follows: 1st digit is make identitiy letter (8 = Chrysler); 2nd number identifies series (Newport is 1); 3rd digit indicates year (1 for 1961); 4th digit is assembly plant code; followed by 100001 and up for serial number. Body style identification found on separate plate. *Example:* 8113100001 is a 1961 Chrysler Newport, serial number 100001, built in Detroit, MI.

## Powertrains

| Engine | Gross HP | Transmission Availability | Newport | Windsor | New Yorker | 300-G |
|---|---|---|---|---|---|---|
| 361 CID Firebolt, 2-bbl., V8 | 265 | 3-speed manual | S | - | - | - |
| | | Torqueflite automatic | $227 | - | - | - |
| 383 CID Golden Lion, 2-bbl., V8 | 305 | 3-speed manual | - | S | - | - |
| | | Torqueflite automatic | - | $227 | - | - |
| 413 CID Golden Lion, 4-bbl., V8 | 350 | Torqueflite automatic | - | - | S | - |
| 413 CID Long Ram, 2 × 4-bbl., V8 | 375 | Torqueflite automatic* | - | - | - | S |
| 413 CID Short Ram, 2 × 4-bbl., V8 | 400 | Torqueflite automatic* | - | - | - | $ |

*A 3-speed manual transmission was installed in a few 300-G models at unknown cost and in unknown quantities.*

## Major Options

| | Newport | Windsor | New Yorker | 300-G |
|---|---|---|---|---|
| Heater and defroster | $102 | $102 | $102 | $102 |
| Airtemp air conditioning | $510 | $510 | $510 | $510 |
| Solex tinted glass | $43 | $43 | $43 | $43 |
| Power steering | $108 | $108 | S | S |
| Power brakes | $44 | $44 | S | S |
| Power seat (swivel on 300-G) | $102 | $102 | $102 | S |
| Power windows | $108 | $108 | S | S |
| Golden Tune AM radio | $100 | $100 | $100 | $100 |
| White sidewall tires — std. sizes | $42 | $46 | $51 | S |

Options common to most models. (S = Standard equipment.) Items may be standard equipment, optional at different pricing, or unavailable on certain models. This chart is only a guide.

## Paint Colors

| | Code |
|---|---|
| Formal Black | BB-1 |
| Parisian Blue | CC-1 |
| Capri Blue Metallic | DD-1 |
| Pinehurst Green Metallic | GG-1 |
| Tahitian Turquoise | JJ-1 |
| Sheffield Silver Metallic | LL-1 |
| Dove Gray | MM-1 |
| Dubonnet Metallic | OO-1 |
| Mardi Gras Red | PP-1 |
| Cinnamon Metallic | RR-1 |
| Alaskan White | WW-1 |
| Sahara Sand | YY-1 |
| Tuscan Bronze Metallic | ZZ-1 |

# Newport

*"A full-size Chrysler in a new, lower price range."*

**Nameplate year of origin:** 1961 (as series); 1950 (as Hardtop model designation).

**Current bodystyle lifespan:** Windsor (1960); Newport (1961 through 1964 with major restyle in 1963).

**Predecessor to this model:** Windsor (1957 to 1959).

**Replacement for this model:** Newport (1965 to 1966).

**Percentage of division's sales volume:** 59.20%.

**Corporate siblings:** Dodge Polara, and DeSoto.

**Primary competition:** Buick Invicta, Mercury Monterey and Oldsmobile Super 88.

**Notable changes:** Front end restyled and minor trim and detail changes.

**Major standard equipment:** Cloth and vinyl front bench seat, full-floor carpeting, sun visors, exterior bright side moldings and 8.00 × 14 BSW tires. Town & Country adds: 9.00 × 14 BSW tires.

## Measurements

|  | Cars | Wagons |
|---|---|---|
| Wheelbase | 122.0" | 122.0" |
| Length | 215.6" | 216.1" |
| Width | 79.4" | 79.4" |
| Height | 55.0" | 55.2" |
| Legroom — front | 45.1" | 45.1" |
| Legroom — rear | 44.2" | 44.0" |
| Headroom — front | 37.8" | 37.8" |
| Headroom — rear | 38.1" | 38.1" |
| Cargo capacity (cu. ft.) | 33.0 | 95.0 |
| Fuel capacity (gals.) | 23.0 | 22.0 |

## Models Available

|  | Style Number | Base MSRP | Change from LY | Shipping Wt. (lbs.) | Production | Change from LY |
|---|---|---|---|---|---|---|
| Newport 2-Door Hardtop | 812 | $3,027 | -7.69% | 3690 | 9,405 | +44.78% |
| Newport 2-Door Convertible | 815 | $3,444 | -4.94% | 3760 | 2,135 | +45.54% |
| Newport 4-Door Sedan | 813 | $2,964 | -7.20% | 3710 | 34,370 | +36.65% |
| Newport 4-Door Hardtop | 814 | $3,106 | -7.09% | 3730 | 7,789 | +32.08% |
| N. Town & Country 4-Dr., 2-S. Wgn. | 858 | $3,543 | -5.09% | 4070 | 1,832 | +63.57% |
| N. Town & Country 4-Dr., 3-S. Wgn. | 859 | $3,624 | -4.98% | 4155 | 1,571 | +53.12% |
| TOTALS | | *Avg. price* $3,285 | -6.09% | | *Production* 57,102 | +38.74% |

# Windsor

*"Who says a high-performance car can't be comfortable?*
*Let the Windsor prove it can!"*

**Nameplate year of origin:** 1961 (as series); 1950 (as Hardtop model designation).

**Current bodystyle lifespan:** Windsor (1960); Newport (1961 through 1964 with major restyle in 1963).

**Predecessor to this model:** Windsor (1957 to 1959).

**Replacement for this model:** Newport (1965 to 1966).

**Percentage of division's sales volume:** 59.20%.

**Corporate siblings:** Dodge Polara, and DeSoto.

**Primary competition:** Buick Invicta, Mercury Monterey and Oldsmobile Super 88.

**Notable changes:** Front end restyled and minor trim and detail changes.

**Major standard equipment:** Cloth and vinyl front bench seat, full-floor carpeting, sun visors, exterior bright side moldings and 8.00 × 14 BSW tires. Town & Country adds: 9.00 × 14 BSW tires.

## Measurements

|  | Cars | Wagons |
|---|---|---|
| Wheelbase | 122.0" | 122.0" |
| Length | 215.6" | 216.1" |
| Width | 79.4" | 79.4" |
| Height | 55.0" | 55.2" |
| Legroom — front | 45.1" | 45.1" |
| Legroom — rear | 44.2" | 44.0" |
| Headroom — front | 37.8" | 37.8" |
| Headroom — rear | 38.1" | 38.1" |
| Cargo capacity (cu. ft.) | 33.0 | 95.0 |
| Fuel capacity (gals.) | 23.0 | 22.0 |

## Models Available

| | Style Number | Base MSRP | Change from LY | Shipping Wt. (lbs.) | Production | Change from LY |
|---|---|---|---|---|---|---|
| Newport 2-Door Hardtop | 812 | $3,027 | -7.69% | 3690 | 9,405 | +44.78% |
| Newport 2-Door Convertible | 815 | $3,444 | -4.94% | 3760 | 2,135 | +45.54% |
| Newport 4-Door Sedan | 813 | $2,964 | -7.20% | 3710 | 34,370 | +36.65% |
| Newport 4-Door Hardtop | 814 | $3,106 | -7.09% | 3730 | 7,789 | +32.08% |
| N. Town & Country 4-Dr., 2-S. Wgn. | 858 | $3,543 | -5.09% | 4070 | 1,832 | +63.57% |
| N. Town & Country 4-Dr., 3-S. Wgn. | 859 | $3,624 | -4.98% | 4155 | 1,571 | +53.12% |
| TOTALS | | Avg. price $3,285 | -6.09% | | Production 57,102 | +38.74% |

# New Yorker

*"Weigh it against any car you've known before. It's Chrysler's finest."*

**Nameplate year of origin:** 1939 (altered from 1938 New York Special model).

**Current bodystyle lifespan:** New Yorker (1960 through 1964 with major restyle in 1963).

**Predecessor to this model:** New Yorker (1957 to 1959).

**Replacement for this model:** New Yorker (1965 to 1966).

**Percentage of division's sales volume:** 21.15%.

**Corporate siblings:** Chrysler 300-G.

**Primary competition:** Buick Electra, and Oldsmobile 98.

**Notable changes:** Front end restyled and minor trim and detail changes.

**Major standard equipment:** Nylon and vinyl front bench seat (vinyl on convertible), pile carpeting, padded dash, map lights, power windows, electric clock, sun visors, exclusive exterior bright trim, power steering, power brakes, automatic transmission, full wheel covers, and 8.50 × 14 BSW tires. Town & Country adds: 9.00 × 14 BSW tires.

## Measurements

| | Cars | Wagons |
|---|---|---|
| Wheelbase | 126.0" | 126.0" |
| Length | 219.8" | 220.1" |
| Width | 79.4" | 79.4" |
| Height | 55.1" | 55.2" |
| Legroom — front | 45.6" | 46.2" |
| Legroom — rear | 42.4" | 44.0" |
| Headroom — front | 37.8" | 37.8" |
| Headroom — rear | 38.1" | 38.0" |
| Cargo capacity (cu. ft.) | NA | 95.0 |
| Fuel capacity (gals.) | 23.0 | 22.0 |

## Models Available

| | Style Number | Base MSRP | Change from LY | Shipping Wt. (lbs.) | Production | Change from LY |
|---|---|---|---|---|---|---|
| New Yorker 2-Door Hardtop | 832 | $4,177 | -6.37% | 4065 | 2,541 | -10.37% |
| New Yorker 2-Door Convertible | 835 | $4,594 | -5.76% | 4070 | 576 | +3.60% |
| New Yorker 4-Door Sedan | 833 | $4,125 | -6.44% | 4055 | 9,984 | +9.97% |
| New Yorker 4-Door Hardtop | 834 | $4,263 | -5.64% | 4100 | 5,862 | +4.21% |
| N. Y. Town & Country 4-Dr., 2-S. W. | 878 | $4,766 | -5.10% | 4766 | 676 | +8.33% |
| N. Y. Town & Country 4-Dr., 3-S. W. | 879 | $4,873 | -5.03% | 4873 | 760 | +13.26% |
| TOTALS | | Avg. price $4,466 | -5.71% | | Production 20,399 | +5.20% |

# 300-G

*"Chrysler's luxury sports car."*

**Nameplate year of origin:** 1955.

**Current bodystyle lifespan:** 1960 through 1964 with major restyle in 1963.

**Predecessor to this model:** 300 letter series (1957 to 1959).

## Measurements

| | |
|---|---|
| Wheelbase | 126.0" |
| Length | 219.8" |

**Replacement for this model:** 300-L (1965).
**Percentage of division's sales volume:** 1.67%.
**Corporate siblings:** Chrysler New Yorker.
**Primary competition:** Ford Thunderbird.
**Notable changes:** Front end restyled and minor trim and detail changes.
**Major standard equipment:** Leather power-swivel bucket front seats, pile carpeting, padded dash, map lights, power windows, electric clock, sun visors, exclusive exterior bright trim, power steering, power brakes, automatic transmission, full wheel covers, and 8.00 × 15 WSW tires.

## Measurements (cont.)

| | |
|---|---|
| Width | 79.4" |
| Height | 55.6" |
| Legroom — front | 45.6" |
| Legroom — rear | 35.4" |
| Headroom — front | 33.4" |
| Headroom — rear | 33.5" |
| Cargo capacity (cu. ft.) | NA |
| Fuel capacity (gals.) | 23.0 |

**1961**

## Models Available

| | Style Number | Base MSRP | Change from LY | Shipping Wt. (lbs.) | Production | Change from LY |
|---|---|---|---|---|---|---|
| 300-G 2-Door Hardtop | 842 | $5,413 | 0.04% | 4260 | 1,280 | 32.78% |
| 300-G 2-Door Convertible | 845 | $5,843 | 0.03% | 4315 | 337 | 35.89% |
| TOTALS | | Avg. price $5,628 | +0.03% | | Production 1,617 | +33.42% |

# DESOTO

*"Its quality sets it apart, its price keeps it within your reach."*

By the time the 1961 models were introduced, the writing was on the wall. Seemingly the only reason for the 1961 DeSoto to exist was to fill production capacity while plans were completed to design a Dodge replacement for the DeSoto. There were two models of DeSoto left for the new year, a 2-Door and a 4-Door Hardtop, and they were in a nameless series. Officially, they were sold only through authorized Plymouth-DeSoto dealers. Essentially, the new cars were equivalent to the 1960 Fireflite. They also received a facelift that was similar to the new 1961 Chrysler makeover. The major difference was in the grille, which on DeSoto featured a two-tier design with the top portion carrying the DeSoto name in it. Headlights were slanted outward from the bottom up, while the remainder of the styling was carried over from 1960. Interiors were essentially equivalent to Chrysler Windsor models. On November 30, 1960, after just over 3,000 DeSoto models had been built, they were officially discontinued. Only a little over 2 million DeSoto's had been built since their introduction in 1928. Considering that most mid-price range marquees build that many cars every 6 to 8 years, it is not a terribly impressive figure. But in that time, DeSoto had gained many loyal owners for Chrysler.

2-Door Hardtop

4-Door Hardtop

| Model year production: 3,034, down 88.37% from 1960. | Data plate identification: Ten digit code read as follows: 1st |
|---|---|

**Model year production:** 3,034, down 88.37% from 1960.
**Base price range:** $3102 to $3166.
**Domestic market share:** 0.01% (15th place).
**Industry average base price:** $3,048.
**DeSoto average base price:** $3,134.
**Introduction date:** October 14, 1960.
**Assembly plants:** Detroit (Jefferson Ave.) MI (3).

**Data plate identification:** Ten digit code read as follows: 1st and 2nd numbers identify series (i.e., DeSoto is number 61), 3rd digit indicates year (1 for 1961); 4th digit is assembly plant code; followed by 100001 and up for serial number. Body style identification found on separate plate. *Example:* 6113100001 is a 1961 DeSoto, serial number 100001, built in Detroit, MI.

## Powertrains

| Engine | Gross HP | Transmission Availability | DeSoto |
|---|---|---|---|
| 361 CID Turbo Flash, 2-bbl., V8 | 265 | 3-speed manual | -$227 credit |
| | | Torqueflite automatic | S |

## Major Options

| | DeSoto |
|---|---|
| Heater and defroster | $98 |
| Airtemp air conditioning | $501 |
| Solex tinted glass | $43 |
| Variable speed windshield wipers | $7 |
| Power steering (with automatic) | $106 |
| Power brakes (with automatic) | $43 |
| Power seat — Six-way | $101 |
| Power windows | $106 |
| AM radio | $89 |
| Full wheel covers | $19 |
| White sidewall tires — std. sizes | $42 |

Options common to most models. Items may be standard equipment, optional at different pricing, or unavailable on certain models. This chart is only a guide.

## Paint Colors

| | Code |
|---|---|
| Golden Rod Yellow | AA-1 |
| Black | BB-1 |
| Morning Blue | CC-1 |
| Mediterranean Blue Met. | DD-1 |
| Spring Green | FF-1 |
| Jade Green Metallic | GG-1 |
| Tangier Aqua | JJ-1 |
| Surf Turquoise Metallic | KK-1 |
| Platinum Gray Metallic | LL-1 |
| Regal Red | PP-1 |
| Glacier White | WW-1 |
| Tahiti Tan | YY-1 |
| Bahama Bronze Metallic | ZZ-1 |

# DeSoto

*"A new car rich in traditional DeSoto quality, fresh in the way it looks and performs."*

**Nameplate year of origin:** 1928.
**Current bodystyle lifespan:** Fireflite/DeSoto (1960 through 1961).
**Predecessor to this model:** Fireflite (1957 to 1959).
**Replacement for this model:** Dodge Custom 880 (1962 through 1964).
**Percentage of division's sales volume:** 100%.
**Corporate siblings:** Chrysler Newport and Dodge Polara.
**Primary competition:** Buick LeSabre, Mercury Monterey and Oldsmobile 88.
**Notable changes:** New front end styling and minor trim and detail changes.
**Major standard equipment:** Cloth and vinyl front bench seat, full-floor carpeting, sun visors, exterior bright side moldings and 8.00 × 14 BSW tires.

## Measurements

| | |
|---|---|
| Wheelbase | 122.0" |
| Length | 215.8" |
| Width | 79.4" |
| Height | 55.0" |
| Legroom — front | 45.1" |
| Legroom — rear | 42.4" |
| Headroom — front | 37.6" |
| Headroom — rear | 38.1" |
| Cargo capacity (cu. ft.) | 32.8 |
| Fuel capacity (gals.) | 23.0 |

## Models Available

| | Style Number | Base MSRP | Change from LY | Shipping Wt. (lbs.) | Production | Change from LY* |
|---|---|---|---|---|---|---|
| DeSoto 2-Door Hardtop | RS1-L23 | $3,102 | 0.00% | 3760 | 911 | -73.93% |
| DeSoto 4-Door Hardtop | RS1-L43 | $3,166 | 4.94% | 3820 | 2,123 | -76.49% |
| TOTALS | Avg. price | $3,134 | +5.8%* | Production | 3,034 | -88.37% |

*Based on comparison with Fireflite series. Total based on entire model line.*

# DODGE

*"Again in 1961, Dodge upsets the apple cart."*

Dodge really did upset the apple cart for 1961— not someone else's, but its own family's. Chrysler had introduced the Valiant as a stand-alone model, to be sold in Chrysler-Plymouth and DeSoto-Plymouth dealerships. Dodge had seen the success of moving to a lower price bracket with the Dart and now wanted a piece of the compact car market. So the Lancer was introduced, as a sportier, more upscale alternative to the Valiant. Both the Lancer and the Valiant looked like larger cars, but the Lancer benefitted from a simpler, full-width grille design as compared to the Valiant's trapezoidal affair. Sales were good for the first few seasons, but it would take a full redesign in 1963 to bring true success.

After the successful introduction of the Dart series in 1960, Dodge was taking many sales away from Plymouth, but not having much success at tackling Ford or Chevy. Apparently, Plymouth owners really liked the idea of moving "up" to a Dodge at about the same price level. Unfortunately, Chrysler Corporation in general was misfiring badly in the styling department. No matter what it did, it seemed to be wrong for the public. As a result, sales of the new smaller Dodge Dart series dropped off more than 45 percent. The new styling was certainly not as underwhelming as the new Plymouth with which it shared basic body design, but certain elements made the design not seem fluid. The front design was generally pleasing, with a full-width concave grille underscored by a full-width bumper containing a round parking lamp at each end. Front fenders had a prominent peak at the leading edge that flowed back into the windshield area. A side feature line that started a few inches back from the front fender edge paralleled the edge upward, angling forward and then making a sharp turn straight back over the wheel opening, and ending just before the front door. This was basically the same frontal styling used for the big Dodge Polara. The back portion of the car featured reverse-style fins that began at the rear window area with a sharp kick-up, then faded downward to a point just above trunk lid level. At this point, the body side feature line curved down and sharply back to the front, with a horizontal line ending at a point on the front door. On the Dart series, this point was level with the front fender line but ended about four inches behind it. On the Polara series, the styling was similar, but the line coming to the front ran onto the lower front fender about 6 inches below the front fender feature line. The Polara (and Wagons) housed a bullet-style tail lamp within the curve at the rear. The Dart used a small, horizontal tail lamp that appeared to be mounted on top of the rear bumper. The front and rear of these cars appeared to have been styled by separate departments, then put together. They were not terrible looking cars, but there would be better ones to come.

Dart Phoenix 2-Door Hardtop

Dart Seneca 4-Door Wagon

Lancer 2-Door Hardtop and 4-Door Sedan

Lancer 770 4-Door Wagon

Polara 4-Door Hardtop

Dodge Polara Dashboard

**Model year production:** 230,832, down 33.87% from 1960.
**Domestic market share:** 4.31% (9th place).
**Base price range:** $1,981 to $3,411.
**Industry average base price:** $3,048.
**Industry average base price:** $2,621.
**Introduction date:** September 1960.
**Assembly plants:** Lynch Road, MI (A); Hamtramck, MI (B); Detroit( Jefferson Ave.) MI (C); Belvidere, IL (D); Los Angeles, CA (E); Newark, DE (F); St. Louis, MO (G); Windsor, Ontario, Canada (R).

**Data plate identification:** Ten digit code read as follows: Four digit style number (see listings below) in which 1st digit is series letter (e.g., 5 = Polara V8 series), 2nd number identifies trim grade (e.g., L is for base trim, M for Mid-level, etc.), 3rd digit indicates year (1 for 1961), and 4th digit is assembly plant code; followed by 100001 and up for serial number. Body style identification found on separate plate. *Example:* 541C100001 is a 1961 Dodge Polara with a 361 CID V8 engine, serial number 100001, built in Detroit, MI.

## Powertrains

| Engine | Gross HP | Transmission Availability | Lancer | Dart | Polara |
|---|---|---|---|---|---|
| 170 CID, 1-bbl., 6-cyl. | 101 | 3-speed manual | S | - | - |
| | | Torqueflite automatic | $172 | - | - |
| 225 CID (Aluminum), 1-bbl., 6-cyl. | 145 | 3-speed manual | $47 | S[1] | - |
| | | Torqueflite automatic | $219 | $192[1] | - |
| 225 CID Hyper-Pak, 4-bbl., 6-cyl. | 195 | 3-speed manual | $** | - | - |
| | | Torqueflite automatic | $** | - | - |
| 318 CID Dart, 2-bbl., V8 $107[1] | 230 - | 3-speed manual | - | S[2]/ | |
| | | Powerflite automatic | - | $** | - |
| $318[1] | - | Torqueflite automatic | - | $211[2]/ | |
| 318 CID Dart Power Package, 4-bbl., V8 | 250 | 3-speed manual | - | $** | - |
| | | Powerflite automatic | - | $** | - |
| | | Torqueflite automatic | - | $** | - |
| 361 CID Polara, 2-bbl., V8 | 265 | 3-speed manual | - | $** | S |
| | | Powerflite automatic | - | $** | $** |
| | | Torqueflite automatic | - | $** | $** |
| 361 CID Dart D-500, 4-bbl., V8 | 305 | 3-speed manual | - | $** | - |
| | | Torqueflite automatic | - | $** | - |
| 383 CID Polara D-500, 4-bbl., V8 | 325 | 3-speed manual | - | - | $** |
| | | Torqueflite automatic | - | - | $** |

| Engine | Gross HP | Transmission Availability | Lancer | Dart | Polara |
|---|---|---|---|---|---|
| 383 CID Polara D-500 Ram Induction, 2 × 4-bbl., V8 | 330 | 3-speed manual | - | $** | $** |
|  |  | Torqueflite automatic | - | $** | $** |
| 413 CID Ramcharger, 4-bbl., V8 | 410 |  | - | - | $** |
| 413 CID Ramcharger, 2 × 4-bbl., V8 | 415 |  | - | - | $** |

¹All except Phoenix Convertible.   ²Phoenix Convertible.   **Pricing information unavailable.

## Major Options

| | Lancer | Dart | Polara |
|---|---|---|---|
| Heater and defroster | $74 | $74 | $74 |
| Airtemp air conditioning | $425 | $445 | $445 |
| Tinted glass | $24 | $30 | $30 |
| Power steering | $73 | $77 | $77 |
| Power brakes | $43 | $43 | $43 |
| Power seat | - | $96 | $96 |
| Power windows | - | $102 | $102 |
| Electric clock | $16 | $16 | $16 |
| Music Master AM Radio | $169 | $58 | $58 |
| White sidewall tires — std. sizes | $29 | $33–$48 | $33–$48 |

Options common to most models. (- = Not Available) Items may be standard equipment, optional at different pricing, or unavailable on certain models. This chart is only a guide.

## Paint Colors

| | Code |
|---|---|
| Bamboo | AA-1 |
| Midnight | BB-1 |
| Glacier Blue | CC-1 |
| Marlin Blue Metallic | DD-1 |
| Spring Green | FF-1 |
| Frosted Mint Metallic | GG-1 |
| Cactus Metallic | HH-1 |
| Turquoise | JJ-1 |
| Nassau Green Metallic | KK-1 |
| Silver Gray Metallic | LL-1 |
| Vermilion | PP-1 |
| Rose Mist Metallic | SS-1 |
| Aztec Gold Metallic | UU-1 |
| Snow | WW-1 |
| Buckskin | YY-1 |
| Roman Bronze Metallic | ZZ-1 |

# Lancer

*"Look what Dodge has done for compacts!"*

**Nameplate year of origin:** 1961.
**Current bodystyle lifespan:** 1961 through 1962.
**Predecessor to this model:** None.
**Replacement for this model:** Dart (1963 to 1966).
**Percentage of division's sales volume:** 32.40%.
**Corporate siblings:** Plymouth Valiant.
**Primary competition:** Buick Special, Mercury Comet, Oldsmobile F-85, Pontiac Tempest and Studebaker Lark.
**Notable changes:** All-new model for 1961.
**Major standard equipment:** Cloth and vinyl front bench seats, rubber floor mats, chrome windshield trim and 6.50 × 13 BSW tires. 770 adds: color-keyed floor covering, full-vinyl door coverings, additional interior and exterior bright trim.

## Measurements

| | Cars | Wagons |
|---|---|---|
| Wheelbase | 106.5" | 106.5" |
| Length | 188.8" | 188.8" |
| Width | 72.3" | 72.3" |
| Height | 53.3" | 53.8" |
| Legroom — front | 42.8" | 42.8" |
| Legroom — rear | 39.8" | 39.8" |
| Headroom — front | 33.3" | 33.3" |
| Headroom — rear | 33.5" | NA |
| Cargo capacity (cu. ft.) | 24.8 | 72.0 |
| Fuel capacity (gals.) | 13.0 | 13.0 |

## Models Available

| | Style Number | Base MSRP | Change from LY | Shipping Wt. (lbs.) | Production | Change from LY |
|---|---|---|---|---|---|---|
| Lancer 170 2-Door Sedan | 711 | $1,981 | NEW | 2585 | 20,800 | NEW |
| Lancer 170 4-Door Sedan | 713 | $2,043 | NEW | 2595 | * | NEW |

| | Style Number | Base MSRP | Change from LY | Shipping Wt. (lbs.) | Production | Change from LY |
|---|---|---|---|---|---|---|
| Lancer 170 4-Door, 2-Seat Wagon | 756 | $2,356 | NEW | 2760 | * | NEW |
| Lancer 770 2-Door Sedan | 731 | $2,077 | NEW | 2595 | 36,748 | NEW |
| Lancer 770 2-Door Hardtop | 732 | $2,166 | NEW | 2595 | 7,552 | NEW |
| Lancer 770 4-Door Sedan | 733 | $2,139 | NEW | 2605 | * | NEW |
| Lancer 770 4-Door, 2-Seat Wagon | 776 | $2,451 | NEW | 2775 | 9,700 | NEW |
| TOTALS | Avg. price | $2,173 | NEW | Production | 74,800* | NEW |

*Production estimates available only by body style.*

# Dart

*"A full-sized Dodge priced model for model with Ford and Chevrolet."*

**Nameplate year of origin:** 1960.
**Current bodystyle lifespan:** 1960 through 1961.
**Predecessor to this model:** Coronet (1957 to 1959).
**Replacement for this model:** Dart (1962) and 330/440 (1963 to 1964).
**Percentage of division's sales volume:** 61.51%.
**Corporate siblings:** Plymouth Fury.
**Primary competition:** Chevrolet Biscayne/BelAir and Ford Galaxie.
**Notable changes:** Completely restyled.
**Major standard equipment:** Cloth-and-vinyl bench seat, full rubber floor mats, electric windshield wipers, dual sun visors, exterior bright trim around windshield and back window, and 7.00 × 14 BSW tires (8.00 × 14 BSW tires on wagons). Pioneer adds: Full-carpeting, exterior bright trim around side windows and body sides. Phoenix adds: additional exterior brightwork, deluxe interior trim, Towerback front seat design, and 8.00 × 14 BSW tires for convertible.

## Measurements

| | Cars | Wagons |
|---|---|---|
| Wheelbase | 118.0" | 122.0" |
| Length | 213.1" | 217.6" |
| Width | 78.7" | 78.7" |
| Height | 54.8" | NA |
| Legroom — front | 45.1" | 45.1" |
| Legroom — rear | 42.1" | 42.4" |
| Headroom — front | 33.3" | 33.3" |
| Headroom — rear | 33.5" | 33.6" |
| Cargo capacity (cu. ft.) | NA | NA |
| Fuel capacity (gals.) | 20.0 | 22.0 |

## Models Available

| | Style Number | Base MSRP | Change from LY | Shipping Wt. (lbs.) | Production | Change from LY |
|---|---|---|---|---|---|---|
| Dart Seneca 2-Door Sedan | 411 | $2,280 | +0.09% | 3290 | 66,100 | -40.77% |
| Dart Seneca 4-Door Sedan | 413 | $2,332 | +0.09% | 3335 | | - |
| Dart Seneca 4-Dr., 2-S. Wagon | 456 | $2,697 | +0.07% | 3740 | | - |
| Dart Pioneer 2-Door Sedan | 421 | $2,412 | +0.08% | 3290 | 38,600 | -51.75% |
| Dart Pioneer 2-Door Hardtop | 422 | $2,490 | +0.08% | 3335 | | - |
| Dart Pioneer 4-Door Sedan | 423 | $2,461 | +0.08% | 3335 | | - |
| Dart Pioneer 4-Door, 2-Seat Wagon | 466 | $2,789 | +0.07% | 3740 | | - |
| Dart Pioneer 4-Door, 3-Seat Wagon | 467 | $2,894 | +0.07% | 3825 | | - |
| Dart Phoenix 2-Door Hardtop | 432 | $2,620 | +0.08% | 3325 | 37,300 | -47.24% |
| Dart Phoenix 2-Door Convertible | 535 | $2,990 | +4.25% | 3580 | | - |
| Dart Phoenix 4-Door Sedan | 433 | $2,597 | +0.08% | 3350 | | - |
| Dart Phoenix 4-Door Hardtop | 434 | $2,679 | +0.07% | 3385 | | - |
| TOTALS | Avg. price | $2,603 | +0.46% | Production | 142,000 | -45.87% |

# Polara

*"The best of Dodge at very modest cost."*

**Nameplate year of origin:** 1960.
**Current bodystyle lifespan:** Polara (1960 through 1961).
**Predecessor to this model:** Custom Royal (1957 to 1959).
**Replacement for this model:** Polara (1962 to 1965); Coronet (1965).
**Percentage of division's sales volume:** 6.08%.
**Corporate siblings:** Plymouth Fury.
**Primary competition:** Chevrolet BelAir/Impala, and Ford Galaxie.
**Notable changes:** Completely restyled.
**Major standard equipment:** All-vinyl (Hardtops and Convertible) or cloth-and-vinyl (Sedan) bench seat with foam front cushion, deep-pile carpeting, electric windshield wipers, dual sun visors, exterior bright trim around all glass and body sides, hood louvers and 8.00 × 14 BSW tires.

## Measurements

|                        | Cars   | Wagons |
|------------------------|--------|--------|
| Wheelbase              | 122.0" | 122.0" |
| Length                 | 217.1" | 217.6" |
| Width                  | 78.7"  | 78.7"  |
| Height                 | 54.9"  | NA     |
| Legroom — front        | 45.1"  | 45.1"  |
| Legroom — rear         | 42.4"  | 42.4"  |
| Headroom — front       | 33.3"  | 33.3"  |
| Headroom — rear        | 33.6"  | 33.6"  |
| Cargo capacity (cu. ft.) | NA   | NA     |
| Fuel capacity (gals.)  | 20.0   | 22.0   |

## Models Available

|                              | Style Number | Base MSRP | Change from LY | Shipping Wt. (lbs.) | Production | Change from LY |
|------------------------------|--------------|-----------|----------------|---------------------|------------|----------------|
| Polara 2-Door Hardtop        | 542          | $3,034    | -5.07%         | 3690                | 14,032     | +20.97%        |
| Polara 2-Door Convertible    | 545          | $3,254    | -4.74%         | 3765                | *          | *              |
| Polara 4-Door Sedan          | 543          | $2,968    | -5.51%         | 3700                | *          | *              |
| Polara 4-Door Hardtop        | 544          | $3,112    | -4.98%         | 3740                | *          | *              |
| Polara 4-Door, 2-Seat Wagon  | 578          | $3,296    | -5.99%         | 4115                | *          | *              |
| Polara 4-Door, 3-Seat Wagon  | 579          | $3,411    | -5.80%         | 4125                | *          | *              |
| TOTALS                       | Avg. price   | $3,179    | -5.36%         | Production          | 14,032     | +20.97%        |

*Production by body style unavailable.*

# FORD

*"The beautifully built '61 Fords!"*

Ford made yet another major styling change to its full-size Ford line and introduced a brand-new Thunderbird for the new year. The Fairlane and Galaxie line, while still based upon the 1960 body shell, featured what Ford called "the classic Ford look." A full-width grille with a center horizontal bar started out the look, followed by rather clean side styling, and a slight contour of the rear quarter that led to "traditional" round Ford taillights at the rear. A very small tailfin remained atop the rear fender. As a whole package the styling was much cleaner and more modern than what most of the competition had to offer. A family resemblance was gained among all lines this year by particular styling cues, among them the "Big Circle" Thunderbird taillamps, the formal Thunderbird roofline on certain coupe and sedan models, and the large, flat decklid. The big Ford model line lost the Custom 300 and the Fairlane Business Coupe, but added a 6-passenger version of the Country Squire wagon. Powertrains and model choices continued as in prior years with the addition of an optional 390 CID Thunderbird V8 for top end performance.

The all-new Thunderbird added more of a luxury flair with its new style. Side trim and sculpting was kept to a minimum (except for the hash marks on the side), and the rear end treatment was similar to other Fords as described previously. The front end styling utilized a grille which swept under the front of the car to meet the massive bumper, a design that would continue through the 1966 season. A new 390 CID Thunderbird V8 engine was offered as standard equipment, eliminating the need for the optional Lincoln 430 CID V8. The highly popular Falcon continued into the new year with a new convex grille design and a new Futura Sport Coupe model.

Country Sedan 4-Door Wagon

Fairlane 500 2-Door Sedan

Fairlane 4-Door Sedan

Falcon 2-Door Sedan

Falcon 2-Door Wagon

Galaxie 2-Door Convertible

Thunderbird 2-Door Convertible,
Indianapolis 500 Pace Car

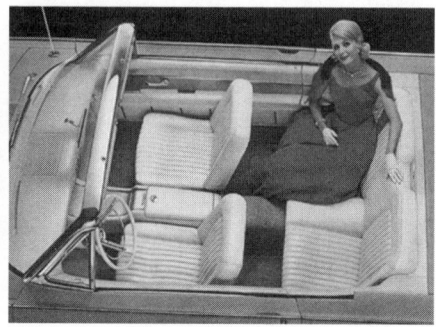

Thunderbird Convertible Interior

**Model year production:** 1,339,043, down 6.98% from 1960.
**Domestic market share:** 24.98% (2nd place, based on estimated Chevrolet production).
**Base price range:** $1,914 to $4,639.
**Industry average base price:** $3,048.
**Ford average base price:** $2,670.
**Introduction date:** October 1960.
**Assembly plants:** Atlanta, GA (A); Dallas, TX (D); Chicago, IL (G); Dearborn, MI (F); Kansas City, MO (K); Lorain, OH (H); Los Angeles, CA (J); Louisville, KY (U); Mahwah, NJ (E); Metuchen, NJ (T); Norfolk, VA (N); San Jose, CA (R); Twin Cities, MN (P); Wayne, MI (W); Wixom, MI (Y); St. Thomas, Ontario, Can. (X); Oakville, Ontario, Can. (B).
**Data plate identification:** Eleven digit code read as follows: 1 for 1961; 2nd digit is assembly plant code; 3rd digit is series (1 is Falcon, 3 is Fairlane, 7 is Thunderbird, etc.); 4th digit is body style (5th digit is engine code; 100001 and up for serial number. *Example:* 1Y73Z100001 is a 1961 Ford Thunderbird 2-Door Hardtop with a 390 CID V8 engine, serial number 100001, built in Wixom, MI.

## Powertrains

| Engine | Gross HP | Engine Code | Transmission Availability | Falcon | Full-size Ford | Thunderbird |
|---|---|---|---|---|---|---|
| 144.3 CID Falcon Six, 1-bbl., 6-cyl. | 85 | S | 3-speed manual | S | - | - |
| | | | Fordomatic | $163 | - | - |

| Engine | Gross HP | Engine Code | Transmission Availability | Falcon | Full-size Ford | Thunderbird |
|---|---|---|---|---|---|---|
| 170 CID Falcon Special Six, 1-bbl., 6-cyl. | 101 | S | 3-speed manual | $37 | - | - |
| | | | Fordomatic | $200 | - | - |
| 223 CID Mileage Maker Six, 1-bbl., 6-cyl. | 135 | V | 3-speed manual | - | S | - |
| | | | Overdrive | - | $108 | - |
| | | | Fordomatic | - | $180 | - |
| 292 CID Thunderbird, 2-bbl., V8 | 175 | W | 3-speed manual | - | $116 | - |
| | | | Overdrive | - | $224 | - |
| | | | Fordomatic | - | $306 | - |
| | | | Cruise-O-Matic | - | $328 | - |
| 352 CID Interceptor, 2-bbl., V8 | 220 | X | 3-speed manual | - | $148 | - |
| | | | Overdrive | - | $256 | - |
| | | | Fordomatic | - | $338 | - |
| | | | Cruise-O-Matic | - | $360 | - |
| 390 CID Thunderbird, 4-bbl., V8 | 300 | Z | 3-speed manual | - | $197 | - |
| | | | Cruise-O-Matic | - | $409 | S |
| 390 CID Thunderbird Super, 4-bbl., V8 | 375 | R | Cruise-O-Matic | - | Special order w/3-speed only | $81 |
| 390 CID Thunderbird Special, 3 × 2-bbl., V8 | 401 | R | Cruise-O-Matic | - | - | $242 |

## Major Options

| | Falcon | Fairlane | Galaxie | Thunderbird |
|---|---|---|---|---|
| MagicAire heater and defroster | $73 | $75 | $75 | S |
| SelectAire air conditioning | - | $436 | $436 | $463 |
| I-Rest tinted glass | - | $43 | $43 | $43 |
| Master-Guide power steering | - | $82 | $82 | S |
| Swift Sure power brakes | - | $43 | $43 | S |
| Power windows | - | $102 | $102 | $106 |
| Electric clock | $15 | $15 | $15 | S |
| Pushbutton AM radio (Falcon man) | $54 | $59 | $59 | S |
| White Sidewall tires | $34 | $34 | $34 | $42 |
| Full wheel covers | $16 | $19 | S | S |

Options common to most models. (- = Not Available, S = Standard equipment.) Items may be standard equipment, optional at different pricing, or unavailable on certain models. This chart is only a guide.

## Paint Colors

| | Code | Falcon | Ford | Thunderbird |
|---|---|---|---|---|
| Raven Black | A | X | X | X |
| Aquamarine | C | X | X | X |
| Starlight Blue | D | X | X | X |
| Laurel Green Metallic | E | X | X | X |
| Desert Gold | F | | X | X |
| Chesapeake Blue Metallic | H | X | X | X |
| Monte Carlo Red | J | X | X | X |
| Algiers Bronze Metallic | K | X | X | |
| Corinthian White | M | X | X | X |
| Diamond Blue | N | | | X |
| Nautilus Gray Metallic | P | | | X |
| Silver Gray Metallic | Q | X | X | X |
| Cambridge Blue Metallic | R | X | X | X |
| Mint Green Metallic | S | X | X | X |
| Honey Beige | T | | | X |
| Palm Springs Rose | V | | | X |
| Garden Turquoise Metallic | W | X | X | X |
| Heritage Burgundy Metallic | X | | | X |
| Mahogany Metallic | Y | | | X |
| Fieldstone Tan Metallic | Z | | | X |

# Falcon

*"The world's most successful new car."*

**Nameplate year of origin:** 1960.
**Current bodystyle lifespan:** 1960 through 1963.
**Predecessor to this model:** None.
**Replacement for this model:** Falcon (1964 to 1965).
**Percentage of division's sales volume:** 35.41%.
**Corporate siblings:** Mercury Comet.
**Primary competition:** Rambler American, Chevrolet Corvair, Plymouth Valiant and Studebaker Lark.
**Notable changes:** Revised grille and minor trim and detail changes.
**Major standard equipment:** Nylon and vinyl front bench seat with foam cushions, black carpet textured rubber floor covering, 17" Lifeguard steering wheel, dual front armrests and dual sun visors, dome light, glove compartment, bright metal front and rear window trim, and 6.00 × 13 BSW tires.

## Measurements

| | Cars | Wagons |
|---|---|---|
| Wheelbase | 109.5" | 109.5" |
| Length | 181.2" | 189.0" |
| Width | 70.6" | 70.6" |
| Height | 54.5" | 55.1" |
| Legroom — front | 44.6" | 44.6" |
| Legroom — rear | 40.1" | 40.1" |
| Headroom — front | 38.9" | 38.9" |
| Headroom — rear | 37.3" | 37.2" |
| Cargo capacity (cu. ft.) | 23.7 | 76.2 |
| Fuel capacity (gals.) | 14.0 | 14.0 |

## Models Available

| | Style Number | Base MSRP | Change from LY | Shipping Wt. (lbs.) | Production | Change from LY |
|---|---|---|---|---|---|---|
| Falcon 2-Door Sedan | 64A | $1,914 | 0.10% | 2254 | 149,982 | -22.48% |
| Falcon 4-Door Sedan | 58A | $1,976 | 0.10% | 2289 | 159,761 | -4.85% |
| Falcon 2-Door Wagon | 59A | $2,227 | 0.09% | 2525 | 32,045 | 16.31% |
| Falcon 4-Door Wagon | 71A | $2,270 | -0.74% | 2558 | 87,933 | 88.06% |
| Falc. Futura 2-Door Sport Cpe. | 62A | $2,162 | NEW | 2322 | 44,470 | NEW |
| TOTALS | | Avg. price $2,110 | +0.48% | | Production 474,191 | +8.84% |

# Fairlane

*"Budgetwise Fairlanes ... and value leader Fairlane 500's!"*

**Nameplate year of origin:** 1955.
**Current bodystyle lifespan:** 1960 through 1962.
**Predecessor to this model:** Fairlane (1959).
**Replacement for this model:** Custom (1963 to 1964).
**Percentage of division's sales volume:** 28.12%.
**Corporate siblings:** Mercury Meteor.
**Primary competition:** AMC Ambassador, Chevrolet Biscayne/BelAir, Plymouth Belvedere, and Dodge Dart.
**Notable changes:** Completely restyled from the beltline down.
**Major standard equipment:** Nylon and vinyl front bench seats, rubber floor mats, dual sun visors, arm rests on all doors, chrome front and rear window trim, and 7.50 × 14 BSW tires. Fairlane 500 adds: upgraded interior trim and additional exterior trim. Wagons add: 8.00 × 14 BSW tires.

## Measurements

| | Cars | Wagons |
|---|---|---|
| Wheelbase | 119.0" | 119.0" |
| Length | 209.9" | 209.9" |
| Width | 79.9" | 79.9" |
| Height | 55.0" | 55.4" |
| Legroom — front | 43.3" | 43.3" |
| Legroom — rear | 41.6" | 41.5" |
| Headroom — front | 33.5" | 33.5" |
| Headroom — rear | 33.9" | NA |
| Cargo capacity (cu. ft.) | 30.5 | 93.5 |
| Fuel capacity (gals.) | 20.0 | 20.0 |

## Models Available

| | Style Number | Base MSRP | Change from LY | Shipping Wt. (lbs.) | Production | Change from LY |
|---|---|---|---|---|---|---|
| Fairlane 2-Door Club Sedan | 64F | $2,263 | +0.27% | 3487 | 97,208 | 4.23% |
| Fairlane 4-Door Town Sedan | 58E | $2,317 | +0.26% | 3585 | 66,924 | -39.05% |
| Fairlane 500 2-Door Club Sedan | 64A | $2,378 | +1.89% | 3502 | 42,468 | -53.35% |
| Fairlane 500 4-Door Town Sedan | 58A | $2,432 | +1.84% | 3593 | 98,917 | -35.45% |
| Ranch Wagon 2-Dr., 6-pass. Wgn. | 59C | $2,588 | 0.08% | 3816 | 12,042 | -55.62% |
| Ranch Wagon 4-Dr., 6-pass. Wgn. | 71H | $2,658 | 0.08% | 3911 | 30,292 | -30.95% |
| TOTALS | | Avg. price $2,439 | +1.07% | | Production 376,525 | -27.61% |

# Galaxie

*"Beautifully proportioned to the classic Ford look …*
*beautifully built to take care of itself."*

**Nameplate year of origin:** 1959.
**Current bodystyle lifespan:** 1960 through 1962.
**Predecessor to this model:** Galaxie (1959).
**Replacement for this model:** Galaxie (1963 to 1964).
**Percentage of division's sales volume:** 33.15%.
**Corporate siblings:** Mercury Monterey.
**Primary competition:** AMC Ambassador, Chevrolet Impala, Plymouth Belvedere, and Dodge Dart.
**Notable changes:** Completely restyled from the beltline down.
**Major standard equipment:** Fairlane 500 equipment plus cloth and vinyl front bench seat, chrome exterior trim on all windows, body side chrome trim and aluminum rear quarter protection shield, and Galaxie identification. Starliner and Sunliner add: All-vinyl, high-level interior trim, and special identification script. Country Squire adds: Wood-grained exterior side trim.

## Measurements

| | Cars | Wagons |
|---|---|---|
| Wheelbase | 119.0" | 119.0" |
| Length | 209.9" | 209.9" |
| Width | 79.9" | 79.9" |
| Height | 55.0" | 55.4" |
| Legroom — front | 43.3" | 43.3" |
| Legroom — rear | 41.6" | 41.5" |
| Headroom — front | 33.5" | 33.5" |
| Headroom — rear | 33.9" | NA |
| Cargo capacity (cu. ft.) | 30.5 | 93.5 |
| Fuel capacity (gals.) | 20.0 | 20.0 |

## Models Available

| | Style Number | Base MSRP | Change from LY | Shipping Wt. (lbs.) | Production | Change from LY |
|---|---|---|---|---|---|---|
| Galaxie 2-Door Club Sedan | 62A | $2,538 | -0.43% | 3488 | 27,780 | -12.82% |
| Galaxie 2-Door Victoria Hardtop | 65A | $2,599 | NEW | 3545 | 75,437 | NEW |
| Galaxie 2-Door Starliner Hardtop | 63A | $2,599 | -0.42% | 3517 | 29,669 | -56.78% |
| Galaxie 2-Door Sunliner Conv. | 76B | $2,849 | -0.38% | 3694 | 44,614 | -0.33% |
| Galaxie 4-Door Town Sedan | 54A | $2,592 | -0.42% | 3570 | 141,823 | +36.65% |
| Galaxie 4-Door Victoria HT | 75A | $2,664 | -0.41% | 3588 | 30,342 | -24.55% |
| Country Sedan 4-Dr., 6-pass. Wgn. | 71F | $2,754 | +0.07% | 3934 | 46,311 | -21.91% |
| Country Sedan 4-Door, 9-pass. Wgn. | 71E | $2,858 | +0.74% | 3962 | 16,356 | -15.15% |
| Country Squire 4-Dr., 6-pass. Wgn. | 71J | $2,943 | NEW | 3938 | 16,961 | NEW |
| Country Squire 4-Dr., 9-pass. Wgn. | 71G | $3,013 | +1.55% | 3966 | 14,657 | -34.09% |
| TOTALS | | Avg. price $2,741 | +0.33% | | Production 443,950 | +13.81% |

# Thunderbird

*"Unique in all the World!"*

**Nameplate year of origin:** 1955.
**Current bodystyle lifespan:** 1961 through 1963.
**Predecessor to this model:** Thunderbird (1958 to 1960).
**Replacement for this model:** Thunderbird (1964 to 1966).
**Percentage of division's sales volume:** 5.46%.
**Corporate siblings:** None.
**Primary competition:** None.
**Notable changes:** Completely restyled.
**Major standard equipment:** Nylon and vinyl or leather (convertible) bucket seats, full-carpeting, Lifeguard cushioned sun visors and instrument panel, electric clock, automatic dome light, courtesy light, glove box light, trunk light, Cruise-O-Matic automatic transmission, power steering, power brakes, full wheel covers and 8.00 × 14 BSW tires.

## Measurements

| | |
|---|---|
| Wheelbase | 113.0" |
| Length | 205.0" |
| Width | 75.9" |
| Height | 52.5" |
| Legroom — front | 44.4" |
| Legroom — rear | 37.7" |
| Headroom — front | 34.2" |
| Headroom — rear | 33.1" |
| Cargo capacity (cu. ft.) | 20.1* |
| Fuel capacity (gals.) | 20.0 |

*Excludes convertible.*

## Models Available

| | Style Number | Base MSRP | Change from LY | Shipping Wt. (lbs.) | Production | Change from LY |
|---|---|---|---|---|---|---|
| Thunderbird 2-Door Hardtop | 63A | $4,172 | +11.11% | 3958 | 62,535 | -22.74% |
| Thunderbird 2-Door Convertible | 76A | $4,639 | +9.88% | 4130 | 10,516 | -11.33% |
| TOTALS | | *Avg. price* $4,406 | +10.45% | | *Production* 73,051 | -21.28% |

# IMPERIAL

*"America's most carefully built car."*

After receiving the all-new unit-body construction and accompanying restyle in 1960, the Imperial might have been expected not to receive a major restyle for 1961. However, Chrysler did not always do what was expected, especially in this four or five year period. As for the Imperial in particular, styling was generally of a conservative nature, but the restyle was not always seen as a conservative move. Controversial free-standing headlamps were introduced on the 1961 Imperial. Each headlamp was built into its own pod set at the end of a finely styled, horizontal bar grille.

The fenders cleanly swept behind the headlights, and carried a parking lamp in the upper portion above the free-standing lights. The rear end treatment was only slightly revised from the 1960 models.

Once again the Crown Imperial Limousine Sedan model was available as a custom-built model. These are not included herein as their production usually totaled ten or fewer per season, and they were considered custom-built by Chrysler.

Crown 4-Door Hardtop

LeBaron 4-Door Hardtop

*Right:* LeBaron Interior

**Model year production:** 12,249, down 30.81% from 1960.
**Base price range:** $4,925 to $6,428.
**Domestic market share:** 0.23% (14th place).
**Industry average base price:** $3,048.
**Imperial average base price:** $5,549.
**Introduction date:** September 24, 1960.
**Assembly plants:** Detroit, MI (3).

**Data plate identification:** Ten digit code read as follows: 1st digit 9 for Imperial; 2nd number identifies series (e.g., 2 is for Crown); 1 for 1961; 4th digit is assembly plant code; 100001 and up for serial number. Body style numbers found on body plate. *Example:* 9213100001 is a 1961 Imperial Crown, serial number 100001, built in Detroit, MI.

## Powertrains

| Engine | Intake/Cylinder Arrangement | Gross HP | Transmission Availability | Imperial |
|---|---|---|---|---|
| 413 CID, 4-bbl., V8 | | 350 | Torqueflite Automatic | S |

## Major Options

| | Custom | Crown | LeBaron |
|---|---|---|---|
| Air conditioning | $590 | $590 | $590 |
| Auto Pilot automatic speed control | $97 | $97 | $97 |
| Solex tinted glass | $54 | $54 | $54 |
| Rear window defogger | $21 | $21 | $21 |
| Power steering — variable-ratio | S | S | S |
| Power brakes | S | S | S |
| Power door locks | $47 (2-Dr)/ $72 (4-Dr) | $47 (2-Dr)/ $72 (4-Dr) | $72 |
| Power driver's seat/ Bench seat | $125 | S | S |
| Power windows | $125 | S | S |
| Electric Touch-Tuner radio w/pwr. antenna | $169 | $169 | $169 |
| Whitewall tires — standard size | $55 | $55 | S |

Options common to most models. (S = Standard equipment.) Items may be standard equipment, optional at different pricing, or unavailable on certain models. This chart is only a guide.

## Paint Colors

| | Code |
|---|---|
| Coronado Cream | AA-1 |
| Formal Black | BB-1 |
| Ice Blue | CC-1 |
| Capri Blue Metallic | DD-1 |
| Moonlight Blue Metallic | EE-1 |
| Pinehurst Green Metallic | GG-1 |
| Teal Blue Metallic | KK-1 |
| Sheffield Silver Metallic | LL-1 |
| Dove Gray | MM-1 |
| Executive Gray Metallic | NN-1 |
| Coronation Red | PP-1 |
| Alaskan White | WW-1 |
| Malibu Tan | YY-1 |
| Autumn Russet Metallic | ZZ-1 |

1961

# Custom

*"The Imperial Custom is a thoroughly luxurious automobile ... yet it doesn't demand that you accept luxury as the only measure of its competence."*

**Nameplate year of origin:** 1959 (Name was used on Chrysler Imperial models prior to 1955 also).
**Current bodystyle lifespan:** 1960 through 1963.
**Predecessor to this model:** Imperial (1957 to 1958) and Custom (1959).
**Replacement for this model:** Crown (1964 to 1966).
**Percentage of division's sales volume:** 40.97%.
**Corporate siblings:** Crown and LeBaron.
**Primary competition:** Cadillac Sixty-Two and Lincoln Continental.
**Notable changes:** All-new front and rear styling.
**Major standard equipment:** Nylon and leather padded bench seat, rear armrests, pile carpeting, remote-control left-hand outside mirror, interior courtesy lamps, variable-speed electric windshield wipers with washers, Torqueflite automatic transmission, Constant-control power steering, Total-contact power brakes, wheel covers and 8.20 × 15 BSW tires.

## Measurements

| | |
|---|---|
| Wheelbase | 129.0" |
| Length | 227.3" |
| Width | 81.7" |
| Height | 56.7" |
| Legroom — front | 46.9" |
| Legroom — rear | 42.9" |
| Headroom — front | 34.4" |
| Headroom — rear | 38.3" |
| Cargo capacity (cu. ft.) | NA |
| Fuel capacity (gals.) | 23.0 |

## Models Available

| | Style Number | Base MSRP | Change from LY | Shipping Wt. (lbs.) | Production | Change from LY |
|---|---|---|---|---|---|---|
| Custom Imp. Southampton 2-Dr. HT | 912 | $4,925 | +0.04% | 4715 | 889 | -40.65% |
| Custom Imp. Southampton 4-Dr. HT | 914 | $5,111 | +1.63% | 4740 | 4,129 | +4.45% |
| TOTALS | | *Avg. price* $5,018 | +0.48% | | *Production* 5,018 | -35.56% |

# Crown

*"The Imperial Crown gives you even more luxuries and conveniences than are available in the Custom."*

**Nameplate year of origin:** 1957 (Not the same as Crown Imperial series).
**Current bodystyle lifespan:** 1960 through 1963.
**Predecessor to this model:** Crown (1957 to 1959).
**Replacement for this model:** Crown (1964 to 1966).
**Percentage of division's sales volume:** 50.66%.
**Corporate siblings:** Custom and LeBaron.
**Primary competition:** Cadillac Sixty-Two and Lincoln Continental.
**Notable changes:** All-new front and rear styling.
**Major standard equipment:** Nylon and leather (all leather in convertible) 6-way power bench seat, front and rear armrests (4-Door HT), pile carpeting, remote-control left-hand outside mirror, power windows, interior dome and map lights, variable-speed electric windshield wipers with washers, trunk carpeting, Torqueflite automatic transmission, Constant-control power steering, Total-contact power brakes, wheel covers and 8.20 × 15 BSW tires.

## Measurements

| | |
|---|---|
| Wheelbase | 129.0" |
| Length | 227.3" |
| Width | 82.7" |
| Height | 56.7" |
| Legroom — front | 46.9" |
| Legroom — rear | 42.9" |
| Headroom — front | 34.4" |
| Headroom — rear | 38.3" |
| Cargo capacity (cu. ft.) | NA |
| Fuel capacity (gals.) | 23.0 |

## Models Available

| | Style Number | Base MSRP | Change from LY | Shipping Wt. (lbs.) | Production | Change from LY |
|---|---|---|---|---|---|---|
| Crown Southampton 2-Door HT | 922 | $5,405 | +0.04% | 4790 | 1,007 | -33.05% |
| Crown 2-Door Convertible | 925 | $5,776 | +0.03% | 4865 | 429 | -30.58% |
| Crown Southampton 4-Door HT | 924 | $5,649 | +0.04% | 4855 | 4,769 | +5.74% |
| TOTALS | *Avg. price* $5,610 | | +0.04% | *Production* 6,205 | | -24.57% |

# LeBaron

*"This is, by all measures, the most exclusive car now being made in America."*

**Nameplate year of origin:** 1924 (as Chrysler Sedan model designation); 1926 (as series).
**Current bodystyle lifespan:** 1960 through 1963.
**Predecessor to this model:** LeBaron (1957 to 1959).
**Replacement for this model:** LeBaron (1964 to 1966).
**Percentage of division's sales volume:** 8.38%.
**Corporate siblings:** Custom and Crown.
**Primary competition:** Cadillac de Ville and Lincoln Continental.
**Notable changes:** All-new front and rear styling.
**Major standard equipment:** Broadcloth or leather 6-way power bench seat, front and rear armrests, pile carpeting, remote-control left-hand outside mirror, power windows and vent windows, interior dome and map lights, variable-speed electric windshield wipers with washers, trunk carpeting, Torqueflite automatic transmission, Constant-control power steering, Total-contact power brakes, wheel covers and 8.20 × 15 BSW tires.

## Measurements

| | |
|---|---|
| Wheelbase | 129.0" |
| Length | 227.3" |
| Width | 81.7" |
| Height | 56.7" |
| Legroom — front | 46.9" |
| Legroom — rear | 42.9" |
| Headroom — front | 34.4" |
| Headroom — rear | 38.3" |
| Cargo capacity (cu. ft.) | NA |
| Fuel capacity (gals.) | 23.0 |

## Models Available

| | Style Number | Base MSRP | Change from LY | Shipping Wt. (lbs.) | Production | Change from LY |
|---|---|---|---|---|---|---|
| LeBaron Southampton 4-Door HT | 934 | $6,428 | 1.74% | 4875 | 1,026 | +2.70% |
| TOTALS | *Avg. price* $6,428 | | +1.74% | *Production* 1,026 | | +2.70% |

# LINCOLN

*"America's first ideally-sized fine car."*

Ford Motor Company and Lincoln-Mercury Division in particular had much to be proud of with the introduction of the 1961 Lincoln automobiles. For probably the first time in history, Lincoln beat its competition to market with a modern, stylish automobile for the new decade, one that would set trends for other luxury cars to follow. The new design was highlighted by a near total lack of chrome, very slab-sided bodies, and a very formal roofline. The front end was somewhat Ford-like in appearance, featuring a full-width grille with a horizontal bar between the headlamps.

The bumper ends capped off the lower portion of the razor-edge fenders. The back end mimicked the front with blade-like taillamps mounted in small fins at the rear quarter trailing edges, and a grillework between the two fins. Overall, the new Lincolns were more than a foot shorter than their predecessors. Who said Lincolns weren't downsized until 1980?

Another leg up on the competition came in the form of the new 4-Door Convertible model. No two-door Lincolns were available at all, as they had never been big sellers in this market. So when a convertible was developed, it was designed around the 4-Door Sedan. This unique 4-Door convertible was the first factory produced model available from the Big Three since prior to World War II. Convertible top operation was similar to that pioneered on the Ford Thunderbird with electric and hydraulic motors operating the deck lid, and storing the top below the car's body lines. This had the unfortunate effect of limiting luggage space, but that is not usually a major concern of convertible buyers. Power continued to come from the 430 CID V8. Interiors were of a new design and were very formal in appearance also, with an instrument cluster that was years ahead of the competition in layout and design.

With the introduction of the 1961, Lincoln simplified its lineup to a single nameplate: Continental.

Continental 4-Door Convertible

Continental 4-Door Sedan

**Model year production:** 25,160, up 1.37% over 1960.
**Domestic market share:** 0.47% (13th place) ranking.
**Base price range:** $6,069 to $6,715.
**Industry average base price:** $3,048.
**Lincoln average base price:** $6,392.
**Introduction date:** September, 1961.
**Assembly plants:** Wixom, MI (Y).

**Data plate identification:** Eleven digit code read as follows: 2 for 1962; 2nd digit is assembly plant code; 2-digit model number (see listings below); 5th digit is engine code; 400001 and up for serial number. *Example:* 1Y82H800001 is a 1961 Lincoln Continental 4-Door Sedan with a 430 CID V8 engine, serial number 400001, built in Wixom, MI.

## Powertrains

| Engine | Gross HP | Engine Code | Transmission Availability | Continental |
|---|---|---|---|---|
| 430 CID, 4-bbl., V8 | 300 | H | Select-Shift Automatic | S |

## Major Options

| | Continental |
|---|---|
| Air condtioning — manual | $506 |
| Automatic headlight dimmers | $46 |
| Tinted glass | $54 |
| 6-way power seat | $119 |
| AM radio | S |
| Leather upholstery | $100 |
| Speed control | $97 |
| Remote control trunk release — sedans | $53 |

Options common to most models. (S = Standard equipment.) Items may be standard equipment, optional at different pricing, or unavailable on certain models. This chart is only a guide.

## Paint Colors

| | Code |
|---|---|
| Presidential Black | A |
| Royal Red Metallic | B |
| Turquoise Mist Metallic | C |
| Blue Haze | D |
| Saxon Green Metallic | E |
| Sunburst Yellow | F |
| Empress Blue Metallic | H |
| Green Velvet Metallic | I |
| Crystal Green Metallic | K |
| Sultana White | M |
| Platinum | N |

| | Code |
|---|---|
| Executive Gray Metallic | P |
| Sheffield Gray Metallic | Q |
| Columbia Blue Haze Metallic | R |
| Honey Beige | T |
| Rose Glow Metallic | U |
| Summer Rose | V |
| Regency Turquoise Metallic | W |
| Black Cherry Metallic | X |
| Briar Brown Metallic | Y |
| Desert Frost Metallic | Z |

# Continental

*"Classic beauty in a smart new size."*

**Nameplate year of origin:** 1940 (1961 as a standard sedan nameplate).
**Current bodystyle lifespan:** 1961 through 1969 (major restyles in 1964 and 1966).
**Predecessor to this model:** Premiere (1958 to 1960).
**Replacement for this model:** Continental (1970 to 1979).
**Percentage of division's sales volume:** 100%.
**Corporate siblings:** None.
**Primary competition:** Cadillac de Ville and Imperial Crown and LeBaron.
**Notable changes:** Completely redesigned.
**Major standard equipment:** Nylon and leather (sedan) or leather (convertible) front bench seat upholstery with folding center armrests front and rear, vanity mirror, looped-pile carpeting, AM transistor radio, power operated door latching system, padded instrument panel, hydraulic windshield wipers with electric washers, power steering, power brakes, automatic transmission and 9.00 × 14 WSW tires (9.50 × 14 WSW on convertible).

## Measurements

| | |
|---|---|
| Wheelbase | 123.0" |
| Length | 212.4" |
| Width | 78.6" |
| Height | 53.5" |
| Legroom — front | 44.2" |
| Legroom — rear | 40.6" |
| Headroom — front | 33.5" |
| Headroom — rear | 33.4" |
| Luggage capacity (cu. ft.) | NA |
| Fuel capacity (gals.) | 21.0 |

## Models Available

| | Style Number | Base MSRP | Change from LY | Shipping Wt. (lbs.) | Production | Change from LY |
|---|---|---|---|---|---|---|
| Continental 4-Door Sedan | 53A | $6,069 | -11.34% | 4927 | 22,303 | +2663.69%* |
| Continental 4-Door Convertible | 74A | $6,715 | NEW | 5215 | 2,857 | NEW |
| TOTALS | *Avg. price* $6,392 | | -4.73% | | *Production* 25,160 | +1.37%* |

*Sedan production compared to 1960 Continental Mark V; overall production compared to total 1960 Lincoln.*

# MERCURY

*"Truly, from every standpoint of value — Mercury is the better low-price car."*

Ford took a big gamble that paid off with the 1961 Mercury line. With the Edsel gone and a wide array of new compact models flooding the market, the buying public seemed to want smaller, less expensive cars. Dodge had first taken the smaller, lower price approach to full-size cars in 1960, so this year, it was Ford's turn with Mercury. The 1961 Mercury line shared most major body panels, drivetrains and many accessories with their Ford counterparts. Styling was differentiated through a concave grille, triple taillamp styling, and different trim. The designations of old were gone, save the Monterey, which was Mercury's most popular nameplate of the era. The new lower-price line was known as the Meteor 600 and Meteor 800, with the Mon-

terey the luxury line for 1961. The payoff for Mercury was one of its best sales years in history, and one of its highest market shares ever.

An entirely new line of engines was offered for full-size Mercurys, and a new powerplant was offered for the compact Comet. All of these powerplants came from the Ford line. This year's full-size wagon line was marketed separately for a final season. However, since it was down to two models, they have been broken down and included below with their corresponding line of passenger cars. Finally, the Comet received a new grille and added an S-22 sport model to the line.

Colony Park 4-Door Wagon

Comet 2-Door Sedan

Comet 4-Door Wagon

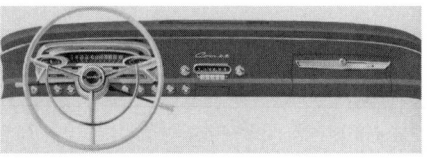

Comet Dashboard

Monterey 2-Door Hardtop

Meteor 800 4-Door Sedan

Meteor 800 2-Door Hardtop

**Model year production:** 317,351, up 14.51% over 1960.
**Domestic market share:** 5.92% (6th place).
**Base price range:** $2,000 to $3,191.
**Industry average base price:** $3,048.
**Mercury average base price:** $2,699.
**Introduction date:** October, 1960.
**Assembly plants:** Mahwah, NJ (E); Lorain, OH (H); Los Angeles, CA (J); Kansas City, MO (K); San Jose, CA (R); Wixom, MI (S); Wayne, MI (W); St. Louis, MO (Z).

**Data plate identification:** Eleven digit code read as follows: 1 for 1961; 2nd digit is assembly plant code; 3rd digit is series (1 or 2 is Comet, 3 or 4 is Meteor, 6 is Monterey); 4th digit is body style; 5th digit is engine code; 500001 and up for serial number (800001 and up for Comet). *Example:* 1W63Z100001 is a 1961 Mercury Monterey 2-Door Hardtop with a 390 CID V8 engine, serial number 500001, built in Wayne, MI.

**1961**

## Powertrains

| Engine | Gross HP | Engine Code | Transmission Availability | Comet | Meteor | Monterey |
|---|---|---|---|---|---|---|
| 144.3 CID Thrift-Power Six, 1-bbl., 6-cyl. | 85 | S | 3-speed manual | S | - | - |
| | | | 2-sp. Automatic | $163 | - | - |
| 170 CID Thrift-Power Six, 1-bbl., 6-cyl. | 101 | U | 3-speed manual | $37 | - | - |
| | | | 2-sp. Automatic | $200 | - | - |
| 223 CID Six, 1-bbl., 6-cyl. | 135 | V | 3-speed manual | - | S | - |
| | | | Overdrive | - | $108 | - |
| | | | Merc-O-Matic Automatic | - | $180 | - |
| 292 CID, 2-bbl., V8 | 175 | W | 3-speed manual | - | $116 | S |
| | | | Overdrive | - | $224 | $108 |
| | | | Merc-O-Matic Automatic | - | $306 | $180 |
| | | | Multi-Drive Automatic | - | $332 | $206 |
| 352 CID Marauder, 2-bbl., V8 | 220 | X | 3-speed manual | - | $148 | $32 |
| | | | Overdrive | - | $256 | $140 |
| | | | Merc-O-Matic Automatic | - | $338 | $212 |
| | | | Multi-Drive Automatic | - | $364 | $238 |
| 390 CID Marauder, 4-bbl., V8 | 300 | Z | 3-speed manual | - | $199 | $83 |
| | | | Multi-Drive Automatic | - | $405 | $289 |
| 390 CID Marauder, 4-bbl., V8 | 330 | R | Multi-Drive Automatic | - | * | * |

*Limited availability; pricing not available.*

## Major Options

| | Comet | Meteor | Monterey |
|---|---|---|---|
| Comet-Aire or heater and defroster | $74 | $75 | $75 |
| SelectAire air conditioning | - | $436 | $436 |
| Tinted glass (windshield only on Comet) | $10 | $43 | $43 |
| Power steering | - | $82 | $82 |
| Power brakes | - | $43 | $43 |
| Power windows | - | $102 | $102 |
| Electric windshield wipers w/washer | $23 | $26 | $26 |
| Electric clock | - | $15 | $15 |
| Pushbutton AM radio | $59 | $59 | $59 |
| White sidewall tires — std. Sizes | $43 | $34 | $34 |
| Full wheel covers | $16 | $19 | S |

Options common to most models. (- = Not Available, S = Standard equipment.) Items may be standard equipment, optional at different pricing, or unavailable on certain models. This chart is only a guide.

## Paint Colors

| | Code |
|---|---|
| Presidential Black | A |
| Turquoise Mist | C |
| Blue Haze | D |
| Saxon Green Metallic | E |
| Sunburst Yellow | F |
| Tawny Beige | G |
| Empress Blue Metallic | H |
| Signal Red | J |
| Golden Bronze Metallic | K |
| Gold Dust Metallic | L |
| Sultana White | M |
| Sheffield Gray Metallic | Q |
| Columbia Blue Haze Met. | R |
| Green Frost | S |
| Summer Rose | V |
| Regency Turquoise Metallic | W |

# Comet

*"The Better compact car. Fine-car styling ... big-car ride ... small-car handling."*

**Nameplate year of origin:** 1960.
**Current bodystyle lifespan:** 1960 through 1963.
**Predecessor to this model:** None.
**Replacement for this model:** Comet (1964 to 1965).
**Percentage of division's sales volume:** 62.16%.
**Corporate siblings:** Ford Falcon.
**Primary competition:** Buick Special, Dodge Lancer, Oldsmobile F-85, Pontiac Tempest and Studebaker.
**Notable changes:** Revised grille and minor trim and detail changes. New S-22 model added mid-year.
**Major standard equipment:** Nylon and vinyl front bench seat with foam cushions, black carpet textured rubber floor covering, dual front armrests and sun visors, dome light, bright metal front and rear window trim, and 6.50 × 13 BSW tires. S-22 adds: Front bucket seats, vinyl-covered center floor console, deep-pile carpeting, rear armrests, Deluxe steering wheel, S-22 exterior trim and additional sound deadening.

## Measurements

|  | Cars | Wagons |
|---|---|---|
| Wheelbase | 114.0" | 109.5" |
| Length | 194.8" | 191.8" |
| Width | 70.4" | 70.4" |
| Height | 54.5" | 55.1" |
| Legroom — front | 43.3" | 43.3" |
| Legroom — rear | 39.4" | 39.4" |
| Headroom — front | 33.8" | 33.8" |
| Headroom — rear | 32.7" | 32.6" |
| Cargo capacity (cu. ft.) | 28.5 | 76.2 |
| Fuel capacity (gals.) | 14.0 | 14.0 |

## Models Available

|  | Style Number | Base MSRP | Change from LY | Shipping Wt. (lbs.) | Production | Change from LY |
|---|---|---|---|---|---|---|
| Comet 2-Door Sedan | 62A | $2,000 | +0.10% | 2376 | 71,563 | +57.72% |
| Comet 4-Door Sedan | 54A | $2,055 | +0.10% | 2411 | 85,332 | +79.96% |
| Comet 2-Door Wagon | 59A | $2,312 | +0.09% | 2548 | 4,199 | -17.91% |
| Comet 4-Door Wagon | 71A | $2,355 | -0.42% | 2581 | 22,165 | +20.29% |
| Comet S-22 2-Door Sedan | 62C | $2,284 | NEW | 2441 | 14,004 | NEW |
| TOTALS | | Avg. price $2,201 | +0.87% | | Production 197,263 | +69.57% |

# Meteor

*"For 1961, Mercury introduces a line of new and better low-price cars ... featuring the new Meteor 600 and 800 series priced right in the heart of the low-price field!"*

**Nameplate year of origin:** 1961.
**Current bodystyle lifespan:** 1961 through 1962.
**Predecessor to this model:** Edsel (1960).
**Replacement for this model:** Meteor (1962 to 1963).
**Percentage of division's sales volume:** 16.74%.
**Corporate siblings:** Ford Fairlane and Galaxie.
**Primary competition:** Dodge Dart, Oldsmobile 88 and Plymouth Fury.
**Notable changes:** All-new model for 1961. Lower-priced running mate to the Monterey.
**Major standard equipment:** Cloth and vinyl front bench seat, full carpeting, bright exterior window trim and 7.50 × 14 BSW tires. 800 adds: additional interior and exterior trim, deep-pile carpeting. Commuter wagons add: 8.00 × 14 BSW tires.

## Measurements

|  | Cars | Wagons |
|---|---|---|
| Wheelbase | 120.0" | 120.0" |
| Length | 214.6" | 214.4" |
| Width | 79.9" | 79.9" |
| Height | 55.0" | 55.3" |
| Legroom — front | 43.4" | 43.4" |
| Legroom — rear | 41.6" | 41.6" |
| Headroom — front | 33.5" | NA |
| Headroom — rear | 33.9" | NA |
| Cargo capacity (cu. ft.) | 30.5 | 93.5 |
| Fuel capacity (gals.) | 20.0 | 20.0 |

## Models Available

| | Style Number | Base MSRP | Change from LY | Shipping Wt. (lbs.) | Production | Change from LY |
|---|---|---|---|---|---|---|
| Meteor 600 2-Door Sedan | 64A | $2,535 | -3.65% | 3647 | * | * |
| Meteor 600 4-Door Sedan | 58A | $2,589 | -5.16% | 3714 | * | * |
| Meteor 800 2-Door Sedan | 62A | $2,713 | NEW | 3680 | * | NEW |
| Meteor 800 2-Door Hardtop | 65A | $2,774 | -16.72% | 3694 | * | * |
| Meteor 800 4-Door Sedan | 54A | $2,767 | -15.64% | 3762 | * | * |
| Meteor 800 4-Door Hardtop | 75A | $2,839 | -16.35% | 3780 | * | * |
| Commuter 4-Door, 2-Seat Wgn. | 71A | $2,924 | -6.49% | 4115 | * | * |
| Commuter 4-Door, 3-Seat Wgn. | 71C | $2,994 | NEW | NA | | NEW |
| TOTALS | Avg. price | $2,703 | -5.66%* | Production | 53,122* | +2.21%* |

*Comparisons to 1960 Monterey line. Production not available by body style.*

# Monterey

*"The luxury full-size car priced with the low-price field."*

**Nameplate year of origin:** 1952.
**Current bodystyle lifespan:** 1961 through 1962.
**Predecessor to this model:** Monterey and Montclair (1959 to 1960).
**Replacement for this model:** Monterey (1963 to 1964).
**Percentage of division's sales volume:** 21.10%.
**Corporate siblings:** Ford Fairlane and Galaxie.
**Primary competition:** Buick Invicta, Dodge Polara, Oldsmobile 88 and Pontiac Star Chief/Bonneville.
**Notable changes:** Completely restyled.
**Major standard equipment:** Cloth and vinyl front bench seat, full carpeting, padded instrument panel, bright exterior window trim and 7.50 × 14 BSW tires. Colony Park wagon adds: exterior wood-grain vinyl trim, power tailgate window, and 8.00 × 14 BSW tires.

## Measurements

| | Cars | Wagons |
|---|---|---|
| Wheelbase | 120.0" | 120.0" |
| Length | 214.6" | 214.4" |
| Width | 79.9" | 79.9" |
| Height | 55.0" | 55.3" |
| Legroom — front | 43.4" | 43.4" |
| Legroom — rear | 41.6" | 41.6" |
| Headroom — front | 33.5" | NA |
| Headroom — rear | 33.9" | NA |
| Cargo capacity (cu. ft.) | 30.5 | 93.5 |
| Fuel capacity (gals.) | 20.0 | 20.0 |

## Models Available

| | Style Number | Base MSRP | Change from LY | Shipping Wt. (lbs.) | Production | Change from LY |
|---|---|---|---|---|---|---|
| Monterey 2-Door Hardtop | 65B | $2,878 | -24.14% | 3709 | 10,942 | +267.92% |
| Monterey 2-Door Convertible | 76A | $3,128 | -22.15% | 3872 | 7,053 | +362.49% |
| Monterey 4-Door Sedan | 54B | $2,871 | NEW | 3777 | 22,881 | NEW |
| Monterey 4-Door Hardtop | 75B | $2,943 | -23.72% | 3795 | 9,252 | +59.85% |
| Colony Park 4-Door, 2-Seat Wagon | 71B | $3,120 | -18.69% | 4131 | 7,887 | +6.42% |
| Colony Park 4-Door, 3-Seat Wagon | 71D | $3,191 | NEW | NA | * | NEW |
| TOTALS | Avg. price | $3,006 | -13.15%* | Production | 66,966 | +145.97%* |

*Included with 2-Seat Wagon production. Comparisons to 1960 Montclair production.*

# OLDSMOBILE

*"The action line in performance … The fashion line in design!"*

The biggest Oldsmobile news for 1961 was the new compact F-85, introduced to compete with the Ford Falcon, Chrysler's Valiant, the Rambler American, and the growing tide of small imported cars. One of the smallest Olds models since the early years of the century, the F-85 was more nicely trimmed than many of its counterparts, and offered something almost none of the others did: strictly V8 power. The obvious advantage was more power, better acceleration, albeit with a slightly higher price tag. The disadvantage for marketing purposes was that the new Buick-designed V8 was an aluminum block, a technology not widely explored at this point in time, causing many potential customers to be wary of the car. After all, for less money, there were any number of six-cylinder compacts available, though with slightly less power. On the road though, the F-85 was probably the best of the new crop of compacts from GM, boasting the best balance of ride, handling and performance characteristics. Inside, the new F-85 was much larger than many other compacts. In fact, from the driver's seat it was often hard to tell you were driving a small car, until you went to turn a corner or park the car, and then its smaller dimensions were fully realized.

Just as important, but often overlooked, was a newly redesigned and restyled line of full-size Oldsmobiles. The surprising feature of these and the other big GM cars this year was that they were actually smaller than their immediate predecessors. The new models were between one and five inches shorter overall, on fractionally smaller wheelbases. This physically shorter size, coupled with styling that had a light and airy feel, made the new cars look lighter and sportier than previous Oldsmobiles. Powerplants remained the same, although the 371 CID V8 offered in the Dynamic 88 line was discontinued, and all models now offered a variation of the 394 CID V8. For unknown reasons, Oldsmobile officially decided to name the Ninety-Eight series the Classic Ninety-Eight, but for this year only. No reference as to the reason for this change has been found, but most factory literature refers to the line as the Ninety-Eight. To simplify matters, all references to this line herein will call it the Ninety-Eight.

Dynamic 88 4-Door Wagon

Super 88 4-Door Hardtop

F-85 Deluxe 4-Door Sedan

F-85 Deluxe 4-Door Wagon

Ninety-Eight 2-Door Hardtop

**Model year production:** 310,124, down 9.17% from 1960.
**Domestic market share:** 5.79% (7th place).
**Base price range:** $2,330 to $4,362.
**Industry average base price:** $3,048.
**Oldsmobile average base price:** $3,294.
**Introduction date:** October 6, 1960. Starfire introduced January 1, 1961.
**Assembly plants:** Atlanta, GA (A); Southgate, CA (C); Fairfax, KS (K); Linden, NJ (L); Lansing, MI (M); Arlington, TX (T); and Wilmington, DE (W).

**Data plate identification:** Nine digit code read as follows: 1st two digits 61 for 1961 year; 3rd digit designates trim level; 4th digit identifies assembly plant; 01001 and up for serial number. Check model number on body plate for body style. *Example:* 618M01001 is a 1961 Oldsmobile Ninety-Eight 2-Door Convertible, built in Lansing, MI, serial number 01001.

## Powertrains

| Engine | Gross HP | Transmission Availability | F-85 | Dynamic 88 | Super 88 | Starfire & Ninety-Eight |
|---|---|---|---|---|---|---|
| 215 CID Rockette, 2-bbl., V8 | 155 | 3-speed manual | S | - | - | - |
| | | Hydra-Matic Automatic | $189 | - | - | - |
| 215 CID Power Pack, 4-bbl., V8 | 185 | 3-speed manual | $ | - | - | - |
| | | Hydra-Matic Automatic | $ | - | - | - |
| 394 CID Rocket, 2-bbl., V8 | 250 | 3-speed manual | - | S | - | - |
| | | Hydra-Matic Automatic | - | $231 | - | - |
| 394 CID Skyrocket, 4-bbl., V8 | 325 | 3-speed manual | - | - | S | - |
| | | Hydra-Matic Automatic | - | - | $231 | S (98) |
| 394 CID Starfire Rocket, 4-bbl., V8 | 330 | 3-speed manual | - | - | - | S (Starfire) |
| | | Hydra-Matic Automatic | - | - | - | $231 (Starfire) |

## Major Options

| | F-85 | Dynamic 88 | Super 88 | Starfire | Ninety-Eight |
|---|---|---|---|---|---|
| Air conditioning | $378 | $430 | $430 | $430 | $430 |
| Soft Ray tinted glass | $ | $ | $ | $ | $ |
| Courtesy lamps | $5 | $5 | $5 | S | S |
| Outside rear view mirror — LH | $4 | $5 | $5 | $5 | $5 |
| Power steering — variable-ratio | $86 | $108 | $108 | S | S |
| Power brakes | - | $43 | $43 | S | S |
| Power driver's seat/ Bench seat | - | $97 | $97 | S | S |
| Power windows | - | $106 | $106 | S | S |
| Electric clock | $16 | $19 | $19 | S | S |
| Windshield washers | $11 | $12 | $12 | $12 | $12 |
| AM radio | $66 | $89 | $89 | $89 | $89 |

Options common to most models. (- = Not Available, S = Standard equipment.) Items may be standard equipment, optional at different pricing, or unavailable on certain models. This chart is only a guide.

## Paint Colors

| | Code |
|---|---|
| Ebony Black | A |
| Twilight Mist Metallic | B |
| Provincial White | C |
| Platinum Mist Metallic | D |
| Azure Mist Metallic | F |
| Glacier Blue | H |
| Tropic Mist Metallic | J |
| Alpine Green | K |
| Garnet Mist Metallic | L |
| Cordovan Mist Metallic | N |
| Turquoise Mist Metallic | P |
| Aqua | Q |
| Sandalwood | R |
| Autumn Mist Metallic | S |
| Fawn Mist Metallic | T |

# F-85

*"The New-Size, Low-Priced Car ... with OLDS style and spirit!"*

**Nameplate year of origin:** 1961— F-85.
**Current bodystyle lifespan:** 1961 through 1963.
**Predecessor to this model:** None.
**Replacement for this model:** F-85/Cutlass (1964 to 1965).
**Percentage of division's sales volume:** 24.63%.
**Corporate siblings:** Buick Special, Pontiac Tempest.
**Primary competition:** AMC Classic, Mercury Comet, Plymouth Valiant and Studebaker Lark.
**Notable changes:** All-new model.
**Major standard equipment:** Cloth and vinyl upholstery, foam cushion front seats, and 6.50 × 13 BSW tires. Deluxe adds: full carpeting, Deluxe steering wheel, and interior and exterior chrome trim moldings.

## Measurements

| | |
|---|---|
| Wheelbase | 112.0" |
| Length | 188.2" |
| Width | 71.5" |
| Height | 52.6" |
| Legroom — front | 44.0" |
| Legroom — rear | 37.5" |
| Headroom — front | 35.3" |
| Headroom — rear | 33.6" |
| Luggage capacity (cu. ft.) | 25.5/Wagon 73.3 |
| Fuel capacity (gals.) | 16.0 |

## Models Available

| | Style Number | Base MSRP | Change from LY | Shipping Wt. (lbs.) | Production | Change from LY |
|---|---|---|---|---|---|---|
| F-85 2-Door Club Coupe | 3027 | $2,330 | NEW | 2587 | 2,336 | NEW |
| F-85 4-Door Sedan | 3019 | $2,384 | NEW | 2541 | 19,765 | NEW |
| F-85 4-Door, 2-Seat Wagon | 3035 | $2,681 | NEW | 2716 | 6,677 | NEW |
| F-85 4-Door, 3-Seat Wagon | 3045 | $2,762 | NEW | 2800 | 10,087 | NEW |
| F-85 Deluxe Cutlass 2-Dr. Sp. Cpe. | 3117 | $2,621 | NEW | 2612 | 9,935 | NEW |
| F-85 Deluxe 4-Door Sedan | 3119 | $2,519 | NEW | 2547 | 26,311 | NEW |
| F-85 Deluxe 4-Door, 2-Seat Wagon | 3135 | $2,816 | NEW | 2731 | 526 | NEW |
| F-85 Deluxe 4-Door, 3-Seat Wagon | 3145 | $2,897 | NEW | 2822 | 757 | NEW |
| TOTALS | | *Avg. price* $2,626 | NEW | *Production* 76,394 | | NEW |

# Dynamic 88

*"Dynamic performer! Dollar saver!"*

**Nameplate year of origin:** 1949 —(1958 for Dynamic nameplate).
**Current bodystyle lifespan:** 1961 through 1964.
**Predecessor to this model:** 88 (1959 to 1960).
**Replacement for this model:** Jetstar 88 (1964).
**Percentage of division's sales volume:** 44.30%.
**Corporate siblings:** Buick LeSabre, Chevrolet Impala, Pontiac Catalina.
**Primary competition:** AMC Ambassador, Dodge Polara, Mercury Monterey.
**Notable changes:** Completely restyled.
**Major standard equipment:** Cloth-and-vinyl bench seat, nylon-blend carpet, padded dash, safety spectrum speedometer, heater and defroster, full wheel covers, and 8.00 × 14 BSW tires.

## Measurements
## (4-Door models)

| | |
|---|---|
| Wheelbase | 123.0" |
| Length | 212.0" |
| Width | 77.2" |
| Height | 55.8" |
| Legroom — front | 44.4" |
| Legroom — rear | 41.4" |
| Headroom — front | 34.5" |
| Headroom — rear | 34.4" |
| Luggage capacity (cu. ft.) | NA |
| Fuel capacity (gals.) | 20.0 |

## Models Available

| | Style Number | Base MSRP | Change from LY | Shipping Wt. (lbs.) | Production | Change from LY |
|---|---|---|---|---|---|---|
| 88 2-Door Sedan | 3211 | $2,835 | 0.00% | 3966 | 4,920 | -63.68% |
| 88 2-Door Holiday Hardtop | 3237 | $2,956 | 0.00% | 3981 | 19,872 | -32.33% |
| 88 2-Door Convertible | 3267 | $3,284 | 0.00% | 4068 | 9,049 | -26.26% |
| 88 4-Door Celebrity Sedan | 3269 | $2,900 | 0.00% | 4031 | 42,584 | -44.24% |
| 88 4-Door Holiday Hardtop | 3239 | $3,034 | 0.00% | 4074 | 51,562 | +17.83% |
| 88 4-Dr., 2-S. Wagon | 3235 | $3,363 | 0.00% | 4354 | 5,374 | -39.17% |
| 88 4-Dr., 3-S. Wagon | 3245 | $3,471 | 0.00% | 4428 | 4,013 | Incl. w/2-Seat Wagon |
| TOTALS | Avg. price | $3,120 | 0.00% | Production | 137,374 | -25.41% |

# Super 88

*"The look of luxury ... the feel of flight!"*

**Nameplate year of origin:** 1951 (88 series started 1949).
**Current bodystyle lifespan:** 1961 through 1964.
**Predecessor to this model:** Super 88 (1959 to 1960).
**Replacement for this model:** Delta 88 (1965 to 1966).
**Percentage of division's sales volume:** 17.14%.
**Corporate siblings:** Buick Invicta, Chevrolet Impala, Pontiac Star Chief.
**Primary competition:** AMC Ambassador, DeSoto, Ford Galaxie 500, and Mercury Montclair.
**Notable changes:** Completely restyled.
**Major standard equipment:** Cloth-and-vinyl bench seat, nylon-blend carpet, padded dash, safety spectrum speedometer, courtesy lamps, deluxe steering wheel, heater and defroster, two-speed electric wipers, full wheel covers, and 8.00 × 14 BSW tires.

## Measurements (4-Door models)

| | |
|---|---|
| Wheelbase | 123.0" |
| Length | 212.0" |
| Width | 77.2" |
| Height | 55.8" |
| Legroom — front | 44.4" |
| Legroom — rear | 41.4" |
| Headroom — front | 34.5" |
| Headroom — rear | 34.4" |
| Luggage capacity (cu. ft.) | NA |
| Fuel capacity (gals.) | 20.0 |

## Models Available

| | Style Number | Base MSRP | Change from LY | Shipping Wt. (lbs.) | Production | Change from LY |
|---|---|---|---|---|---|---|
| Super 88 2-Door Holiday Hardtop | 3537 | $3,325 | 0.00% | 4024 | 7,009 | -57.43% |
| Super 88 2-Door Convertible | 3567 | $3,592 | 0.00% | 4099 | 2,624 | -54.99% |
| Super 88 4-Door Celebrity Sedan | 3569 | $3,176 | 0.00% | 4065 | 15,328 | -56.32% |
| Super 88 4-Door Holiday Hardtop | 3539 | $3,402 | 0.00% | 4099 | 23,272 | -30.08% |
| Super 88 4-Dr., 2-S. Fiesta Wagon | 3535 | $3,665 | 0.00% | 4382 | 2,761 | -26.67% |
| Super 88 4-Dr., 3-S. Fiesta Wagon | 3545 | $3,773 | 0.00% | 4445 | 2,170 | -37.55% |
| TOTALS | Avg. price | $3,489 | 0.00% | Production | 53,164 | -45.71% |

# Starfire

*"Leader in high-compression performance ... pioneer in automatic driving."*

**Nameplate year of origin:** 1954 (as designation for 98 Convertible); 1961 (as series).
**Current bodystyle lifespan:** 1961 through 1964.
**Predecessor to this model:** None.
**Replacement for this model:** Starfire (1965 to 1966).

## Measurements

| | |
|---|---|
| Wheelbase | 123.0" |
| Length | 212.0" |
| Width | 77.2" |
| Height | 55.1" |

Percentage of division's sales volume: 2.52%.
Corporate siblings: None.
Primary competition: Chrysler 300-G and Ford Thunderbird.
Notable changes: All-new model.
Major standard equipment: Power front bucket seats, nylon-blend carpet, padded dash, console, tachometer, courtesy lamps, deluxe steering wheel, heater and defroster, two-speed electric wipers, full wheel covers, brushed aluminum exterior side trim, dual exhausts, and 8.00 × 14 BSW tires.

## Measurements (cont.)

| | |
|---|---|
| Legroom — front | 44.4" |
| Legroom — rear | 41.4" |
| Headroom — front | 34.5" |
| Headroom — rear | 34.4" |
| Luggage capacity (cu. ft.) | NA |
| Fuel capacity (gals.) | 20.0 |

## Models Available

| | Style Number | Base MSRP | Change from LY | Shipping Wt. (lbs.) | Production | Change from LY |
|---|---|---|---|---|---|---|
| Starfire 2-Door Convertible | 3667 | $4,647 | NEW | 4330 | 7,800 | NEW |
| TOTALS | Avg. price | $4,647 | NEW | Production | 7,800 | NEW |

# Ninety-Eight

*"Distinguished … Distinctive … Decidedly New!"*

Nameplate year of origin: 1941.
Current bodystyle lifespan: 1961 through 1964.
Predecessor to this model: Ninety-Eight (1959 to 1960).
Replacement for this model: Ninety-Eight (1965 to 1966).
Percentage of division's sales volume: 11.41%.
Corporate siblings: Buick Electra and Cadillac Series 62/de Ville.
Primary competition: Chrysler New Yorker and Mercury Park Lane.
Notable changes: Completely restyled.
Major standard equipment: Luxury cloth bench seat, nylon-blend carpet, padded dash, safety spectrum speedometer, courtesy lamps, electric clock, deluxe steering wheel, heater and defroster, two-speed electric wipers with washers, power steering, power brakes, automatic transmission, full wheel covers, and 8.50 × 14 BSW tires.

## Measurements

| | |
|---|---|
| Wheelbase | 126.0" |
| Length | 218.0" |
| Width | 77.2" |
| Height | 55.8" |
| Legroom — front | 44.5" |
| Legroom — rear | 44.6" |
| Headroom — front | 35.2" |
| Headroom — rear | 34.4" |
| Luggage capacity (cu. ft.) | NA |
| Fuel capacity (gals.) | 20.0 |

## Models Available

| | Style Number | Base MSRP | Change from LY | Shipping Wt. (lbs.) | Production | Change from LY |
|---|---|---|---|---|---|---|
| Ninety-Eight 2-Door Holiday HT | 3837 | $4,083 | 0.00% | 4187 | 4,005 | -47.54% |
| Ninety-Eight 2-Door Convertible | 3867 | $4,362 | 0.00% | 4225 | 3,804 | -47.78% |
| Ninety-Eight 4-Door Town Sedan | 3819 | $3,887 | 0.00% | 4231 | 9,807 | -42.94% |
| Ninety-Eight 4-Door Sports Sedan | 3839 | $4,159 | NEW | 4319 | 4,445 | NEW |
| Ninety-Eight 4-Door Holiday HT | 3829 | $4,021 | -3.32% | 4269 | 13,331 | -51.09% |
| TOTALS | Avg. price | $4,102 | -0.51% | Production | 35,392 | -40.39% |

# PLYMOUTH

*"Introducing new Solid Beauty … 1961 Plymouth!"*

Of all the words in Plymouth's advertising slogan for 1961, "beauty" is easily the most questionable. Most beholders would agree the 1961 Plymouth was hit with the ugly stick. While certain elements of the 1960 styling can be seen in the new model, for the most part they were a totally different looking car. Rooflines were carried over from 1960, but there were two distinguishing features to set the Plymouth apart from other cars. The first was the straight beltline that ran entirely around the car from one front fender tip to the opposite front fender tip. At the front the feature line angled downward over the headlamps; then, at a point just inside the headlamps, it did a near 180 degree turn back towards the middle of the inside headlamp where it ended. In between the headlights was an aluminum egg-crate grille that sloped back as it went down, and met the bumper. The second notable styling feature was the use of varying modes of sheetmetal sculpting, sometimes right next to each other. For the most part, hood, roof, deck lid, and doors were generally flat or smooth sheet metal. However, the front fenders, rear panel, and rear quarters were a mixture. The rear panel was a concave affair with bullet-shaped taillamps set onto each end of the panel. Backup

lamps, when ordered, were set in closer to the center license plate mount. This concave rear panel wrapped around to the quarter where it sat between a convex lower rear quarter and the upper convex belt line shape. All panels flattened out by the time they reached the door areas. The front fenders had a convex area that came back from the round edge of the headlights, with a feature line that dropped off behind the front wheel openings. Model and powertrain choices were relatively unchanged, with the exception of the introduction of the 413 CID V8 engine. This powerplant, installed in few cars, earned a reputation as the hottest engine around on the racetrack, where it would become a legend.

The compact Valiant added the 225 CID "Slant 6" to its option list during 1961, and soon it became the engine of choice for most buyers. A new addition to the line was the 2-Door model, offered as a sedan in the V100 series and a hardtop in the V200 line. This new model was an immediate hit, selling 40,000 copies in its first season. Overall Valiant sales were down, however, mostly as a result of new competition from GM and of course, its new sister car, the Dodge Lancer.

Belvedere 2-Door Sedan

Deluxe Suburban 2-Door Wagon

Fury 2-Door Hardtop

Valiant V200 4-Door Sedan

Valiant V200 4-Door Wagon

Valiant Wagon with 3rd Seat

**Model year production:** 350,285, down 21.77% from 1960.
**Domestic market share:** 6.53% (4th place).
**Base price range:** $1,953 to $3,134.
**Industry average base price:** $3,048.
**Plymouth average base price:** $2,493.
**Introduction date:** September, 1960.
**Assembly plants:** Lynch Road, MI (1): Hamtramck, MI (2); Detroit, MI (3); Los Angeles, CA (5); Newark DE (6); and St. Louis, MO (7).

**Data plate identification:** Ten digit code read as follows: First and second digits are series designation (first two numbers of model number in charts below); third digit 1 for 1961; fourth digit is assembly plant code; 100001 and up for serial number. *Example:* 2322100001 is a 1961 Plymouth Fury, with a 225 CID 6-cyl., built at Hamtramck, MI, serial number 100001. Body style cannot be identified through the VIN.

## Powertrains

| Engine | Gross HP | Transmission Availability | Valiant | Savoy/ Belvedere | Fury |
|---|---|---|---|---|---|
| 170 CID, 1-bbl., 6-cyl. | 101 | 3-speed manual | S | - | - |
| | | Torqueflite automatic | $172 | - | - |
| 225 CID Slant Six, 1-bbl., 6-cyl. | 145 | 3-speed manual | $49 | S | S[2] |
| | | Torqueflite automatic | $221 | $192 | $192[2] |
| 318 CID Fury V-800, 2-bbl., V8 | 230 | 3-speed manual | - | $119 | S[1]/$119[2] |
| | | PowerFlite automatic | - | $308 | $189[1]/$308[2] |
| | | Torqueflite automatic | - | $330 | $211[1]/ $330[2] |
| 318 CID Super Fury V-800, 4-bbl., V8 | 260 | 3-speed manual | - | $158 | $39[1]/$158[2] |
| | | PowerFlite automatic | - | $347 | $228[1]/$347[2] |
| | | Torqueflite automatic | - | $369 | $250[1]/ $369[2] |
| 361 CID Golden Commando, 4-bbl., V8 | 305 | 3-speed manual | - | $206 | $87[1]/$206[2] |
| | | Torqueflite automatic | - | $417 | $298[1]/$417[2] |
| 383 CID SonoRamic Commando, 2 × 4-bbl., V8 | 330 | 3-speed manual | - | $405 | $286[1]/$405[2] |
| | | Torqueflite automatic | - | $616 | $497[1]/$616[2] |
| 413 CID Commando, 2 × 4-bbl., V8 | 375 | | - | $ | $ |

[1]*Fury Convertible, Sport Suburbans, and 9-passenger Custom Suburban only.*  [2]*All models but Convertible, Sport Suburban and 9-passenger Custom Suburban.*

## Major Options

| | Valiant | Savoy/Belvedere | Fury |
|---|---|---|---|
| Push-button heater and defroster | $74 | $74 | $74 |
| Air conditioning (V8 only) | - | $446 | $446 |
| Solex tinted glass | $37 | $43 | $43 |
| Power steering | $73 | $77 | $77 |
| Power brakes | $43 | $43 | $43 |
| Electric clock | $15 | $15 | S |
| AM radio | $59 | $59 | $59 |
| White sidewall tires — std. sizes | $29 | $35 | $35 |

Options common to most models. (- = Not Available, S = Standard equipment.) Items may be standard equipment, optional at different pricing, or unavailable on certain models. This chart is only a guide.

*See individual model sections for details.*

## Paint Colors

| | Code |
|---|---|
| Hawaiian Blue | 22-1 |
| Buffed Silver Metallic | AA-1 |
| Black | BB-1 |
| Medium Blue Metallic | CC-1 |
| Mist Blue Metallic | DD-1 |
| Midnight Blue Metallic | EE-1 |
| Mist Green Metallic | FF-1 |
| Forest Green Metallic | GG-1 |
| Yellow Gold | HH-1 |
| Ember Gold Metallic | JJ-1 |
| Mist Turquoise Metallic | KK-1 |
| Surf Turquoise Met. | LL-1 |
| Turbine Bronze Metallic | MM-1 |
| Matador Red | PP-1 |
| Electric Blue Metallic | QQ-1 |
| Burgundy Metallic | RR-1 |
| Sunfire Yellow | SS-1 |
| Avacado Green Metallic | TT-1 |
| Frost Blue Metallic | UU-1 |

|  | Code |
|---|---|
| Sable White | WW-1 |
| Satin Beige | XX-1 |
| Sierra Tan Metallic | YY-1 |

# Valiant

*"Looks and drives like twice the price.*
*Chrysler Corporation's low-priced compact car for 1961."*

**Nameplate year of origin:** 1960.
**Current bodystyle lifespan:** 1960 through 1962.
**Predecessor to this model:** None.
**Replacement for this model:** Valiant (1963 to 1966).
**Percentage of division's sales volume:** 40.85%.
**Corporate siblings:** Dodge Lancer.
**Primary competition:** Rambler American, Chevrolet Corvair, Ford Falcon and Studebaker Lark.
**Notable changes:** Minor trim and detail changes.
**Major standard equipment:** Fabric and vinyl bench seat, rubber floor mat, chrome exterior front and rear window trim, Torsion-Aire suspension and 6.50 × 13 BSW tires. V200 adds: Side window chrome trim and color-keyed floor mats.

## Measurements

|  | Cars | Wagons |
|---|---|---|
| Wheelbase | 106.5" | 106.5" |
| Length | 183.7" | 183.7" |
| Width | 70.4" | 70.4" |
| Height | 53.3" | 53.5" |
| Legroom — front | 42.8" | 42.8" |
| Legroom — rear | 39.8" | 38.4" |
| Headroom — front | 37.9" | 37.9" |
| Headroom — rear | 37.4" | 37.5" |
| Cargo capacity (cu. ft.) | 24.9 | 72.3 |
| Fuel capacity (gals.) | 13.0 | 13.0 |

## Models Available

|  | Style Number | Base MSRP | Change from LY | Shipping Wt. (lbs.) | Production | Change from LY |
|---|---|---|---|---|---|---|
| Valiant V100 2-Door Sedan | 111 | $1,955 | NEW | 2565 | 22,230 | NEW |
| Valiant V100 4-Door Sedan | 113 | $2,016 | -1.80% | 2590 | 25,695 | -51.32% |
| Valiant V100 4-Door Wagon | 156 | $2,329 | -1.52% | 2745 | 6,717 | -44.11% |
| Valiant V200 2-Door Hardtop | 132 | $2,139 | NEW | 2605 | 18,586 | NEW |
| Valiant V200 4-Door Sedan | 133 | $2,112 | -0.85% | 2600 | 59,056 | -44.56% |
| Valiant V200 4-Door Wagon | 176 | $2,425 | -0.74% | 2770 | 10,794 | -34.05% |
| TOTALS | | *Avg. price* $2,163 | -7.61% | | *Production* 143,078 | -26.36% |

# Savoy

*"The popular, low-price line for 1961."*

**Nameplate year of origin:** 1951 (Concord 2-Door Suburban designation); 1954 (as series).
**Current bodystyle lifespan:** 1960 through 1961.
**Predecessor to this model:** Plaza and Savoy (1957 to 1959).
**Replacement for this model:** Savoy (1962 to 1964).
**Percentage of division's sales volume:** 18.17%.
**Corporate siblings:** Dodge Dart.
**Primary competition:** AMC Ambassador, Chevrolet Biscayne/BelAir, and Ford Fairlane.
**Notable changes:** Completely restyled with same basic chassis.
**Major standard equipment:** Cloth and vinyl bench seat, color-keyed rubber floor covering, and 7.00 × 14 BSW tires.

## Measurements

|  |  |
|---|---|
| Wheelbase | 118.0" |
| Length | 209.5" |
| Width | 80.0" |
| Height | 54.6" |
| Legroom — front | 45.1" |
| Legroom — rear | 42.1" |
| Headroom — front | 37.8" |
| Headroom — rear | 38.0" |
| Cargo capacity (cu. ft.) | NA |
| Fuel capacity (gals.) | 21.0 |

## Models Available

| | Style Number | Base MSRP | Change from LY | Shipping Wt. (lbs.) | Production | Change from LY |
|---|---|---|---|---|---|---|
| Fleet Special 2-Door Sedan | 201 | $2,227 | 0.00% | 3295 | * | * |
| Fleet Special 4-Door Sedan | 203 | $2,277 | 0.00% | 3305 | * | * |
| Savoy 2-Door Sedan | 211 | $2,262 | +0.09% | 3300 | 18,729 | -30.17% |
| Savoy 4-Door Sedan | 213 | $2,312 | +0.09% | 3310 | 44,913 | -12.59% |
| TOTALS | | Avg. price $2,270 | +0.01% | | Production 63,642 | -18.62% |

*Production of Fleet Specials included with Savoy models.*

# Belvedere

*"Plymouth's most popular, low-price line for 1961."*

**Nameplate year of origin:** 1951 (HT model); 1954 (series).
**Current bodystyle lifespan:** 1960 through 1961.
**Predecessor to this model:** Belvedere (1957 to 1959).
**Replacement for this model:** Belvedere (1962 to 1964).
**Percentage of division's sales volume:** 15.54%.
**Corporate siblings:** Dodge Coronet.
**Primary competition:** AMC Ambassador, Chevrolet Biscayne/BelAir, and Ford Fairlane.
**Notable changes:** Completely restyled with same basic chassis.
**Major standard equipment:** Cloth and vinyl bench seat, trunk mat, color-keyed carpeting, dome light, and 7.00 × 14 BSW tires.

### Measurements

| | |
|---|---|
| Wheelbase | 118.0" |
| Length | 209.5" |
| Width | 80.0" |
| Height | 54.6" |
| Legroom — front | 45.1" |
| Legroom — rear | 42.1" |
| Headroom — front | 37.8" |
| Headroom — rear | 38.0" |
| Cargo capacity (cu. ft.) | NA |
| Fuel capacity (gals.) | 21.0 |

## Models Available

| | Style Number | Base MSRP | Change from LY | Shipping Wt. (lbs.) | Production | Change from LY |
|---|---|---|---|---|---|---|
| Belvedere 2-Door Club Sedan | 221 | $2,391 | +0.08% | 3300 | 4,740 | -27.40% |
| Belvedere 2-Door Hardtop | 222 | $2,463 | +0.08% | 3320 | 9,591 | -31.91% |
| Belvedere 4-Door Sedan | 223 | $2,441 | +0.08% | 3315 | 40,090 | -4.84% |
| TOTALS | | Avg. price $2,432 | +0.08% | | Production 54,421 | -13.27% |

# Fury

*"The luxury line for 1961."*

**Nameplate year of origin:** 1956.
**Current bodystyle lifespan:** 1960 through 1961.
**Predecessor to this model:** Fury (1957 to 1959).
**Replacement for this model:** Fury (1962 to 1964).
**Percentage of division's sales volume:** 15.48%.
**Corporate siblings:** Dodge Polara and Monaco.
**Primary competition:** AMC Ambassador, Chevrolet Biscayne/BelAir/Impala, and Ford Galaxie.
**Notable changes:** Completely restyled with same basic chassis.
**Major standard equipment:** All-vinyl or cloth and vinyl front bench seat, deep-pile carpeting, dual sun visors, front and rear armrests, 2-speed windshield wipers with washers, wheel covers, and 7.00 × 14 BSW tires. Convertible adds: 7.50 × 14 BSW tires.

### Measurements

| | |
|---|---|
| Wheelbase | 118.0" |
| Length | 209.5" |
| Width | 80.0" |
| Height | 54.6" |
| Legroom — front | 45.1" |
| Legroom — rear | 42.1" |
| Headroom — front | 37.8" |
| Headroom — rear | 38.0" |
| Cargo capacity (cu. ft.) | NA |
| Fuel capacity (gals.) | 21.0 |

## Models Available

| | Style Number | Base MSRP | Change from LY | Shipping Wt. (lbs.) | Production | Change from LY |
|---|---|---|---|---|---|---|
| Fury 2-Door Hardtop | 232 | $2,601 | +0.08% | 3330 | 16,141 | -10.72% |
| Fury 2-Door Convertible | 335 | $2,969 | +0.07% | 3535 | 6,948 | -1.86% |
| Fury 4-Door Sedan | 233 | $2,577 | +0.08% | 3350 | 22,619 | 6.23% |
| Fury 4-Door Hardtop | 234 | $2,658 | +0.08% | 3390 | 8,507 | -5.85% |
| TOTALS | Avg. price | $2,701 | +0.08% | | Production 54,215 | -2.29% |

# Suburban

*"Wagons with Solid Beauty for 1961."*

**Nameplate year of origin:** 1950.
**Current bodystyle lifespan:** 1960 through 1961.
**Predecessor to this model:** Suburban (1957 to 1959).
**Replacement for this model:** Savoy, Belvedere and Fury Wagons (1962 to 1964).
**Percentage of division's sales volume:** 9.97%.
**Corporate siblings:** Dodge Polara.
**Primary competition:** AMC Ambassador, Chevrolet Biscayne/BelAir/Impala, and Ford Galaxie.
**Notable changes:** Completely restyled.
**Major standard equipment:** Deluxe features similar to Savoy plus 7.50 × 14 BSW tires. Custom adds: features similar to Belvedere plus 8.00 × 14 BSW tires on 9-passenger models. Sport adds: features similar to Fury.

## Measurements

| | |
|---|---|
| Wheelbase | 122.0" |
| Length | 215.0" |
| Width | 80.0" |
| Height | 55.4" |
| Legroom — front | 45.5" |
| Legroom — rear | 42.5" |
| Headroom — front | 35.7" |
| Headroom — rear | 34.6" |
| Cargo capacity (cu. ft.) | 95.8 |
| Fuel capacity (gals.) | 21.0 |

## Models Available

| | Style Number | Base MSRP | Change from LY | Shipping Wt. (lbs.) | Production | Change from LY |
|---|---|---|---|---|---|---|
| Deluxe Sub. 2-Door, 2-Seat Wagon | 255 | $2,604 | +0.08% | 3675 | 2,464 | -55.22% |
| Deluxe Sub. 4-Door, 2-Seat Wagon | 256 | $2,670 | +0.07% | 3715 | 12,980 | -29.77% |
| Custom Sub. 4-Dr., 2-Seat Wagon | 266 | $2,763 | +0.07% | 3730 | 13,553 | -21.70% |
| Custom Sub. 4-Dr., 3-Seat Wagon | 367 | $2,992 | +0.07% | 3985 | * | * |
| Sport Sub. 4-Door, 2-Seat Wagon | 376 | $3,026 | +0.07% | 3890 | 2,844 | -14.67% |
| Sport Sub. 4-Door, 3-Seat Wagon | 377 | $3,136 | +0.06% | 3995 | 3,088 | -27.39% |
| TOTALS | Avg. price | $2,865 | +0.07% | | Production 34,929 | -38.71% |

*Production included with the 6-passenger Suburban.

# PONTIAC

*"It's all Pontiac! On a new Wide-Track!"*

In a year when nearly all General Motors cars were totally new for 1961, the biggest newsmaker for Pontiac was the Tempest. "The Balanced Car," so called because of its near perfect weight distribution, was the most ambitiously engineered of the three GM compact models introduced this year. Wanting a car that handled well on the road, Pontiac put much effort into balancing the weight of the car. At the front, power came in two forms. First was the all-new 194.5 CID 4-cylinder Trophy 4 (or Indy 4 as it is sometimes called) engine. This large displacement 4-cylinder engine was unique in that it was essentially one half of a 389 CID V8 engine. This design was already known to be reliable, mechanics knew how to service it, and there were numerous part interchange possibilities. The second choice was the all-new aluminum block V8 engine developed by Buick for its new compact Special. This engine, while good in design, put out no more power than the 4-barrel version of the 4-cylinder yet cost significantly more, and customers worried about durability issues presented by the aluminum blocks. As a result very few Tempests were sold with the V8 engine. The next part of the balancing act came from the rear-mounted transmission. By placing the transmission at the rear of the car, a significant portion of weight was moved to the back axle, thereby balancing the car. Since Chevrolet had already developed transmissions for its rear-engined Corvair, Pontiac adapted the existing units to suit its own needs. This left the problem of transmitting the engine's power to the transmission. For that job, engineers developed a "rope" style driveshaft. Flexible in all directions, it eliminated the need for U-joints and also allowed a smaller floor hump down the middle of the car. Without a typical rear axle, independent rear suspension (IRS) was adopted. Unfortunately, what should have made the car handle and ride better ended up causing many problems, as drivers were not experienced in handling a car with IRS. Handling issues would become the downfall of the Corvair, but the Tempest weighed enough to lessen its problems and did not suffer from the Corvair's tail-heaviness.

The big Pontiacs were redesigned along the lines of other GM cars. Slightly smaller than previous years, the new cars used thin rooflines, sculpted body sides, and an aggressive twin grille design up front. The 1959 grille design had proven so popular that it was imitated by none other than the Edsel for 1960, but Pontiac had returned to a full-width grille, not knowing at the time that the split grille theme would be so well received. When the 1961 Pontiacs returned to that styling, it was once again a very popular look. This time it was retained for good; the basic design still characterizes new Pontiacs some 40 years later. Sales of big Pontiacs, as well as many other larger cars, dropped about 40 percent due to the introduction of the new compact models, but they would soon recover. All prior body styles and nameplates were retained, except for the Star Chief 2-Door Sedan, which had been a two-year-only style. With the rise in popularity of the 2-Door Hardtop, it seems odd in retrospect that a Sedan was ever made part of the line, when a Hardtop would certainly have been a better seller.

**Bonneville 2-Door Convertible**

**Catalina 2-Door Sedan**

**Catalina 4-Door, 9 passenger Safari Wagon**

**Star Chief 4-Door Hardtop**

**Tempest,** *Motor Trend* **Car of the Year**

**Model year production:** 340,250, down 14.12% from 1960.
**Domestic market share:** 6.35% (5th place).
**Base price range:** $2,167 to $3,530.
**Industry average base price:** $3,048.
**Pontiac average base price:** $2,899.
**Introduction date:** October, 1960.
**Assembly plants:** Baltimore, MD (B); Southgate, CA (C); Doraville, GA (D); Linden, NJ (E); Framingham, MA (G); Fairfax, KS (K); Pontiac, MI (P); Arlington, TX (R); Fremont, CA (Z).

**Data plate identification:** Eight to ten digit code read as follows: 1st digit identifies the series (the second digit of the body style number in the charts below); 2nd and 3rd digits 61 for 1961; 4th digit is assembly plant code; and 1001 and up for serial number. A separate plate contains body style number. *Example:* 361X1001 is a 1961 Pontiac Catalina, serial number 1001, built in Fairfax, KS.

1961

## Powertrains

| Engine | Gross HP* | Transmission Availability | Tempest | Catalina & Ventura | Star Chief | Bonneville |
|---|---|---|---|---|---|---|
| 194.5 CID Trophy 4, 1-bbl., 4-cyl. | 110/130 | 3-speed manual | S | – | – | – |
| | | TempesTorque 2-sp. Auto. | $173 | – | – | – |
| 194.5 CID Trophy 4, 1-bbl., 4-cyl. | 120/140 | 3-speed manual | No cost | – | – | – |
| | | TempesTorque 2-sp. Auto. | $173 | – | – | – |
| 194.5 CID Trophy 4, 4-bbl., 4-cyl. | 155 | 3-speed manual | $26 | – | – | – |
| | | TempesTorque 2-sp. Auto. | $199 | – | – | – |
| 215 CID Tempest, 2-bbl., V8 | 155 | 3-speed manual | $216 | – | – | – |
| | | TempesTorque 2-sp. Auto. | $389 | – | – | – |
| 389 CID Trophy E, 2-bbl., V8 | 215 | 3-speed manual | – | S | S | – |
| | 230 | Hydra-matic Automatic | – | $231 | $231 | – |
| 389 CID Trophy, 2-bbl., V8 | 267/283 SC | Hydra-matic Automatic | – | $231 | $231 | – |
| 389 CID Trophy, 4-bbl., V8 | 235 | 3-speed manual | – | $24 | $24 | S |
| | | 4-speed manual | – | $205 | $205 | $188 |
| | 287/303 | Hydra-matic Automatic | – | $255 | $255 | $231 |
| 389 CID Trophy, 4-bbl., V8 | 333 | 3-speed manual | – | $293 | $293 | $280 |
| | | 4-speed manual | – | $481 | $481 | $468 |
| | | Hydra-matic Automatic | – | $524 | $524 | $511 |
| 389 CID Tri-Power, 3 × 2-bbl., V8 | 318 | 3-speed manual | – | $120 | $120 | $110 |
| | | 4-speed manual | – | $308 | $308 | $298 |
| | | Hydra-matic Automatic | – | $351 | $351 | $341 |
| 389 CID Tri-Power, 3 × 2-bbl., V8 | 348 | 3-speed manual | – | $396 | $396 | $386 |
| | | 4-speed manual | – | $584 | $584 | $574 |
| | | Hydra-matic Automatic | – | $627 | $627 | $617 |

*Ratings vary with model and transmission attachment. Many other combinations possible due to dealer installations or factory limited-outputs.*

## Major Options

| | Tempest | Catalina | Ventura | Star Chief | Bonneville |
|---|---|---|---|---|---|
| Deluxe heater and defroster | $74 | $94 | $94 | $94 | $94 |
| Air conditioning | $319 | $430 | $430 | $430 | $430 |
| Soft Ray tinted glass | $37 | $43 | $43 | $43 | $43 |
| Power steering — variable-ratio | $75 | $108 | $108 | $108 | $108 |
| Power brakes | – | $43 | $43 | $43 | $43 |
| Power driver's seat/ Bench seat | – | $97 | $97 | $97 | $97 |
| Power windows | – | $q06 | $106 | $106 | $106 |
| AM radio — manual | $62 | $89 | $89 | $89 | $89 |
| White stripe tires (base size) | $35 | $40 | $40 | $40 | $40 |

## Paint Colors

| | Code |
|---|---|
| Regent Black | A |
| Shelltone Ivory | C |
| Richmond Gray Metallic | D |
| Bristol Blue Metallic | E |
| Richelieu Blue Metallic | F |
| Tradewind Blue | H |
| Jadestone Green Metallic | J |
| Seacrest Green | K |
| Coronado Red Metallic | L |
| Bamboo Cream | M |
| Cherrywood Bronze Metallic | N |
| Ranier Turquoise Metallic | P |

| | Tempest | Catalina | Ventura | Star Chief | Bonneville | | Code |
|---|---|---|---|---|---|---|---|
| Aluminum (8-lug) | | | | | | Fernando Beige | R |
| hubs and drums | - | $107 | $107 | $107 | $107 | Dawnfire Mist Metallic | S |
| | | | | | | Mayan Gold Metallic | T |

Options common to most models (- = Not Available.) Items may be standard equipment, optional at different pricing, or unavailable on certain models. This chart is only a guide.

# Tempest

*"The Quality New Comer from Pontiac!"*

**Nameplate year of origin:** 1961.
**Current bodystyle lifespan:** 1961 through 1963.
**Predecessor to this model:** None.
**Replacement for this model:** Tempest/LeMans (1964 to 1965).
**Percentage of division's sales volume:** 29.62%.
**Corporate siblings:** Oldsmobile F-85 and Buick Special.
**Primary competition:** Dodge Lancer, Mercury Comet, and Studebaker Lark.
**Notable changes:** All-new model.
**Major standard equipment:** Cloth and vinyl bench seat, dual sun visors, electric windshield wipers, and 6.00 × 15 BSW tires (6.50 × 15 BSW tires on wagons).

## Measurements

| | Cars | Wagons |
|---|---|---|
| Wheelbase | 112.0" | 112.0" |
| Length | 194.3" | 194.3" |
| Width | 74.2" | 74.2" |
| Height | 53.5" | 53.6" |
| Legroom — front | 44.1" | 44.1" |
| Legroom — rear | 37.8" | 37.8" |
| Headroom — front | 34.0" | 34.0" |
| Headroom — rear | 33.7" | 33.7" |
| Cargo capacity (cu. ft.) | NA | NA |
| Fuel capacity (gals.) | 15.5 | 15.5 |

## Models Available

| | Style Number | Base MSRP | Change from LY | Shipping Wt. (lbs.) | Production | Change from LY |
|---|---|---|---|---|---|---|
| Tempest 2-Door Coupe | 2127 | $2,113 | NEW | 2785 | 7,432 | NEW |
| Tempest 2-Door Custom Coupe | 2117 | $2,297 | NEW | 2795 | 7,455 | NEW |
| Tempest 4-Door Sedan | 2119 | $2,167 | NEW | 2800 | 62,639 | NEW |
| Tempest 4-Door, 2-Seat Wagon | 2135 | $2,438 | NEW | 2980 | 23,257 | NEW |
| TOTALS | | *Avg. price* $2,254 | NEW | | *Production* 100,783 | NEW |

# Catalina

*"Look anywhere — you won't find a car even close to the Catalina in price that provides the pleasure of the wonderful move to Pontiac ... the only Wide-Track car."*

**Nameplate year of origin:** 1950 on hardtop models, 1959 as series.
**Current bodystyle lifespan:** 1961 through 1964.
**Predecessor to this model:** Catalina (1959 to 1960).
**Replacement for this model:** Catalina (1965 to 1966).
**Corporate siblings:** Chevrolet Biscayne/BelAir/Impala, Oldsmobile 88, Buick LeSabre/Invicta.
**Primary competition:** Mercury Monterey and Dodge Polara.
**Percentage of division's sales volume:** 33.31%.
**Notable changes:** Completely restyled.
**Major standard equipment:** Cloth and vinyl bench seat, deep loop pile carpeting, cigarette lighter, dual sun visors, automatic dome lamp, dual front and rear arm rests and ash trays, trunk trim, electric windshield wipers, and 8.00 × 14 BSW tires (Wagons: 8.50 × 14 BSW tires).

## Measurements

| | Cars | Wagon |
|---|---|---|
| Wheelbase | 119.0" | 119.0" |
| Length | 210.0" | 209.7" |
| Width | 78.2" | 78.2" |
| Height | 55.7" | 55.8" |
| Legroom — front | 45.3" | 45.3" |
| Legroom — rear | 40.8" | 40.7" |
| Headroom — front | 34.2" | 34.2" |
| Headroom — rear | 34.4" | 34.5" |
| Cargo capacity (cu. ft.) | NA | NA |
| Fuel capacity (gals.) | 25.0 | 19.0 |

## Models Available

| | Style Number | Base MSRP | Change from LY | Shipping Wt. (lbs.) | Production | Change from LY |
|---|---|---|---|---|---|---|
| Catalina 2-Door Sport Sedan | 2311 | $2,631 | 0.00% | 3650 | 9,846 | -61.39% |
| Catalina 2-Door Sport Hardtop | 2337 | $2,766 | 0.00% | 3680 | 14,524 | -47.18% |
| Catalina 2-Door Convertible | 2367 | $3,078 | 0.00% | 3805 | 12,379 | -27.91% |
| Catalina 4-Door Sedan | 2369 | $2,702 | 0.00% | 3725 | 38,638 | -46.82% |
| Catalina 4-Door Vista Hardtop | 2339 | $2,842 | 0.00% | 3785 | 17,589 | -46.23% |
| Catalina Safari 4-Dr., 2-S. Wagon | 2335 | $3,099 | 0.00% | 4135 | 12,595 | -40.74% |
| Catalina Safari 4-Dr., 3-S. Wagon | 2345 | $3,207 | 0.00% | 4175 | 7,783 | -44.99% |
| TOTALS | Avg. price | $2,904 | 0.00% | Production | 113,354 | -46.27% |

# Ventura

*"This is the step up only the Wide-Track Pontiac makes possible."*

**Nameplate year of origin:** 1960.
**Current bodystyle lifespan:** 1961 through 1964.
**Predecessor to this model:** Ventura (1960).
**Replacement for this model:** None (offered as an option package for 1961 to 1964).
**Corporate siblings:** Chevrolet Biscayne/BelAir/Impala, Oldsmobile 88, Buick LeSabre/Invicta.
**Primary competition:** Mercury Monterey and Dodge Polara.
**Percentage of division's sales volume:** 8.00%.
**Notable changes:** Completely restyled.
**Major standard equipment:** Jeweltone Morrokide vinyl bench seat, deep loop pile carpeting, cigarette lighter, dual sun visors, automatic dome lamp, dual front and rear arm rests and ash trays, trunk trim, electric windshield wipers, exterior chrome trim, and 8.00 × 14 BSW tires.

## Measurements

| | |
|---|---|
| Wheelbase | 119.0" |
| Length | 210.0" |
| Width | 78.2" |
| Height | 55.7" |
| Legroom — front | 45.3" |
| Legroom — rear | 40.8" |
| Headroom — front | 34.2" |
| Headroom — rear | 34.4" |
| Cargo capacity (cu. ft.) | NA |
| Fuel capacity (gals.) | 25.0 |

## Models Available

| | Style Number | Base MSRP | Change from LY | Shipping Wt. (lbs.) | Production | Change from LY |
|---|---|---|---|---|---|---|
| Ventura 2-Door Sport Hardtop | 2537 | $2,971 | 0.00% | 3685 | 13,297 | -51.78% |
| Ventura 4-Door Vista Hardtop | 2539 | $3,047 | 0.00% | 3795 | 13,912 | -51.53% |
| TOTALS | Avg. price | $3,009 | 0.00% | Production | 27,209 | -51.66% |

# Star Chief

*"Here's a superb, proud car that shares its quality with no other car."*

**Nameplate year of origin:** 1954.
**Current bodystyle lifespan:** 1961 through 1964.
**Predecessor to this model:** Star Chief (1959 to 1960).
**Replacement for this model:** Executive (1965 to 1966).
**Corporate siblings:** Chevrolet Biscayne/BelAir/Impala, Oldsmobile 88, Buick LeSabre/Invicta.
**Primary competition:** Mercury Montclair and Dodge Custom 880.
**Percentage of division's sales volume:** 8.69%.
**Notable changes:** Completely restyled.

## Measurements

| | |
|---|---|
| Wheelbase | 123.0" |
| Length | 217.0" |
| Width | 78.2" |
| Height | 55.7" |
| Legroom — front | 45.1" |
| Legroom — rear | 40.9" |
| Headroom — front | 34.2" |
| Headroom — rear | 34.0" |

**Major standard equipment:** Cloth and vinyl bench seat, deep loop pile carpeting, cigarette lighter, dual sun visors, automatic dome lamp, custom steering wheel, dual instrument panel ash trays, trunk trim, electric windshield wipers, and 8.00 × 14 BSW tires.

### Measurements (cont.)

| | |
|---|---|
| Cargo capacity (cu. ft.) | NA |
| Fuel capacity (gals.) | 25.0 |

## Models Available

| | Style Number | Base MSRP | Change from LY | Shipping Wt. (lbs.) | Production | Change from LY |
|---|---|---|---|---|---|---|
| Star Chief 4-Door Sedan | 2669 | $3,003 | 0.00% | 3840 | 16,024 | -30.45% |
| Star Chief 4-Door Hardtop | 2639 | $3,136 | 0.00% | 3870 | 13,557 | -8.74% |
| TOTALS | | Avg. price $3,070 | +1.52% | | Production 29,581 | -32.29% |

# Bonneville

*"Motoring doesn't come any finer than in the elegant Bonneville by Pontiac ... the only Wide-Track car!"*

**Nameplate year of origin:** 1957.
**Current bodystyle lifespan:** 1961 through 1964.
**Predecessor to this model:** Bonneville (1959 to 1960).
**Replacement for this model:** Bonneville (1965 to 1966).
**Corporate siblings:** Chevrolet Biscayne/BelAir/Impala, Oldsmobile 88, Buick LeSabre/Invicta.
**Primary competition:** Mercury Park Lane, Dodge Polara and DeSoto.
**Percentage of division's sales volume:** 20.37%.
**Notable changes:** Completely restyled.
**Major standard equipment:** Cloth and vinyl bench seat (leather in convertible), deep loop pile carpeting, padded hand rail assist and instrument panel, aluminum seat ends and side panels, custom steering wheel, dual sun visors, automatic dome lamp, dual front and rear arm rests and ash trays, trunk trim, electric windshield wipers, unique exterior trim, and 8.00 × 14 BSW tires (Wagons: 8.50 × 14 BSW tires).

### Measurements

| | Cars | Wagon |
|---|---|---|
| Wheelbase | 123.0" | 119.0" |
| Length | 217.0" | 209.7" |
| Width | 78.2" | 78.2" |
| Height | 55.7" | 55.8" |
| Legroom — front | 44.9" | 44.9" |
| Legroom — rear | 40.9" | 40.9" |
| Headroom — front | 34.1" | 34.1" |
| Headroom — rear | 33.8" | 33.8" |
| Cargo capacity (cu. ft.) | NA | NA |
| Fuel capacity (gals.) | 25.0 | 19.0 |

## Models Available

| | Style Number | Base MSRP | Change from LY | Shipping Wt. (lbs.) | Production | Change from LY |
|---|---|---|---|---|---|---|
| Bonneville 2-Door Hardtop | 2837 | $3,255 | 0.00% | 3810 | 16,906 | -29.60% |
| Bonneville 2-Door Convertible | 2867 | $3,476 | 0.00% | 3905 | 18,264 | 7.04% |
| Bonneville 4-Door Vista Hardtop | 2839 | $3,331 | 0.00% | 3895 | 30,830 | -21.02% |
| Bonn. Cust. Safari 4-Dr., 2-S. Wgn. | 2735 | $3,530 | 0.00% | 4185 | 3,323 | -35.64% |
| TOTALS | | Avg. price $3,398 | 0.00% | | Production 69,323 | -18.71% |

# RAMBLER

*"World's Widest Choice of Compact Cars.
The New World Standard of Basic Excellence."*

Competition is something that American Motors did not have a lot of through the late 1950s. Small cars were the mainstay of Rambler, and they were dominating the market. At the turn of the decade, the Big Three unveiled their highly successful trio of import fighters — Corvair, Falcon and Valiant. Then came 1961, and everybody who was anybody in the car business suddenly had a "compact" car. Fortunately, Rambler knew small cars, and none of the new matched up directly in value, size and price. The impact to Rambler's model year sales total was minimal, thanks to American Motors' having done a good job marketing its cars. In fact, other manufacturers' sales were down so much that AMC actually moved up in market position from fourth to third place in the industry. This would be its best performance in history.

Sales of Rambler's biggest car, the Ambassador, suffered most. While it had been nothing more than a stretched Rambler Rebel for several years, the Ambassador was given a facelift that many people found to be ungainly, especially compared to the Classic. An effort to offer what was probably thought to be "modern" styling, the pointed, rocket shape front fenders of the 1961 model turned out to be an unwelcome styling touch. Meanwhile, the newly named Classic (formerly Rambler and Rebel) line received a more up-to-date headlight-in-grille theme that was much cleaner looking, and would be carried into the 1962 model year.

By far the biggest news for the year was the totally redesigned American line. Built on the same wheelbase as before, the new American was five inches shorter than the 1960 model yet just as roomy inside, and offered better visibility and driving ease. New models added included a 4-Door Wagon and a 2-Door Convertible. The public loved the looks of the new Rambler, and sales rose respectably despite all of the new compact car competition.

Ambassador Custom 4-Door Wagon

Ambassador Super 4-Door Sedan

American Super 4-Door Sedan

Classic Custom 4-Door Wagon

American Super 4-Door Wagon

Classic Deluxe 4-Door Sedan

**Model year production:** 369,022, down 19.61% from 1960.
**Domestic market share:** 6.88% (3rd place).
**Base price range:** $1,833 to $3,113.
**Industry average base price:** $3,048.
**Rambler average base price:** $2,391.
**Introduction date:** October 5, 1960.
**Assembly plants:** Kenosha, Wisconsin.

**Data plate identification (VIN):** code read as follows: 61 for 1961 followed by serial number (American, B375001 and up; Classic Six, C625001 and up; and Ambassador V8, H160001 and up). Export cars added a K after the letter, and also had a slightly revised serial number order. *Example:* 61C625001 is a 1961 Rambler Classic Six built in Kenosha, WI, serial number 625001.

## Powertrains

| Engine | Gross HP | Transmission Availability | American | Classic* | Ambassador |
|---|---|---|---|---|---|
| 195.6 CID Super Flying Scot, 1-bbl., L-Head 6-cyl. | 90 | 3-speed manual, col. | S (ex. 400) | - | - |
| | | 3-speed w/Overdrive | $102 (ex. 400) | - | - |
| | | Flash-O-Matic Automatic | $165 (ex. 400) | - | - |
| 195.6 CID Cust. Flying Scot, 1-bbl., OHV 6-cyl. | 125 127 — Classic | 3-speed manual, col. | $60/S (400) | S | - |
| | | 3-speed w/Overdrive | $162/ $102 (400) | $109 | - |
| | | Flash-O-Matic Automatic | $225/ $165 (400) | $187 | - |
| 195.6 CID, 2-bbl., OHV 6-cyl. | 138 | 3-speed manual, col. | - | $12 | - |
| | | 3-speed w/Overdrive | - | $121 | - |
| | | Flash-O-Matic Automatic | - | $199 | - |
| 327 CID, 2-bbl., OHV V8 | 250 | 3-speed manual | - | - | S |
| | | 3-speed w/Overdrive | - | - | $115 |
| | | Flash-O-Matic Automatic | - | - | $220 |
| 327 CID, 4-bbl., OHV V8 | 270 | 3-speed manual | - | - | $48 |
| | | 3-speed w/Overdrive | - | - | $163 |
| | | Flash-O-Matic Automatic | - | - | $268 |

*Aluminum engine block available for the Classic DeLuxe and Custom, standard on Classic 400 models.*

## Major Options

| | American | Classic | Ambassador |
|---|---|---|---|
| Weather-Eye heater | $74 | $76 | $76 |
| Air conditioning (requires tinted glass) | $360 | $370 | $399 |
| Tinted glass — full | $27 | $32 | $32 |
| Power steering | $72 | $74 | $81 |
| Power brakes | $40 | $42 | $44 |
| Electric clock | $15 | $16 | S |
| Outside rear view mirror — Left | $8 | $5 | $5 |
| AM radio — pushbutton w/Antenna | $59 | $65 | $65 |
| Light package | $10 | $10 | $10 |
| White sidewall tires — Standard size | $28 | $30 | $30 |
| Two-tone paint | - | $20–22 | $20–22 |
| Wheel covers | $15 | $15 | $15 |
| Side hinge tailgate — 6-pass. wagons | - | $40 | $40 |
| E-Stick Auto-Clutch transmission (w/3-speed manual or Overdrive only) | $60 | - | - |

Options common to most models. (- = Not Available, S = Standard equipment.) Items may be standard equipment, optional at different pricing, or unavailable on certain models. This chart is only a guide.

## Paint Colors

| | Code |
|---|---|
| Classic Black | P1 |
| Alamo Beige | P4 |
| Chatsworth Green | P8 |
| Aqua Mist Metallic | P15 |
| Echo Green Metallic | P23 |
| Valley Green Metallic | P26 |
| Sonata Blue | P27 |
| Berkeley Blue Metallic | P28 |
| Whirlwind Tan Metallic | P29 |
| Briarcliff Red | P30 |
| Inca Silver Metallic | P31 |
| Waikiki Gold | P32 |
| Jasmine Rose | P33 |
| Fireglow Red Metallic | P34 |
| Frost White | P72 |

*Two-tones: first number is body color, second number is roof/accent color.*

# American

*"America's Leading Economy Compact."*

**Nameplate year of origin:** 1950 (Nash).
**Current bodystyle lifespan:** 1961 through 1963.
**Predecessor to this model:** Rambler American (1958 to 1960).
**Corporate siblings:** None.
**Replacement for this model:** American (1964 to 1969).
**Percentage of division's sales volume:** 36.85%.

## Measurements

| | |
|---|---|
| Wheelbase | 100.0" |
| Length | 173.1" |
| Width | 70.0" |
| Height | 56.1" |
| Legroom — front | 44.0" |

**Primary competition:** Chevrolet Corvair, Ford Falcon, Plymouth Valiant, and Studebaker Lark.

**Notable changes:** Completely redesigned. New 4-Door Wagon models.

**Major standard equipment:** Front arm rests and ash trays, front foam cushion seat, dual sunvisors, black rubber floor mats, air cleaner, oil filter, black rubber cargo mat on wagons, and 6.00 × 15 BSW tires. Super adds: Rear door (side) armrests, door-activated dome lights, chrome horn ring, color-keyed carpeting (wagons), and chrome luggage rack (wagons). Custom adds: Dual-note horn, deluxe steering wheel, vinyl-pleated upholstery with deluxe trim level, padded instrument panel, glove box lock, and wheel covers.

### Measurements (cont.)

| | |
|---|---|
| Legroom — rear | 37.8" |
| Headroom — front | 35.0" |
| Headroom — rear | 33.0" |
| Luggage cap. (cu. ft.) | NA (wagons 64.0) |
| Fuel capacity (gals.) | 20 |

**1961**

## Models Available

| | Style Number | Base MSRP | Change from LY | Shipping Wt. (lbs.) | Production | Change from LY |
|---|---|---|---|---|---|---|
| Am. DeL. 2-Dr. Business Sdn. | 6102-0 | $1,833 | 0.00% | 2454 | 355 | -43.65% |
| American DeLuxe 2-Dr. Sdn. | 6106-0 | $1,847 | 0.00% | 2480 | 28,555 | +19.18% |
| American DeLuxe 4-Dr. Sdn. | 6105-0 | $1,896 | 0.00% | 2500 | 17,811 | -21.17% |
| American DeLuxe 2-Dr. Wgn | 6104-0 | $2,082 | 0.00% | 2555 | 5,666 | -53.90% |
| American DeLuxe 4-Dr. Wgn | 6108-0 | $2,131 | NEW | 2573 | 7,260 | NEW |
| American Super 2-Dr. Sdn. | 6106-1 | $1,932 | 0.00% | 2492 | 14,349 | -16.74% |
| American Super 4-Dr. Sdn. | 6105-1 | $1,981 | 0.00% | 2512 | 15,741 | -25.43% |
| American Super 2-Dr. Wgn | 6104-1 | $2,167 | 0.00% | 2565 | 5,749 | -61.91% |
| American Super 4-Dr. Wgn | 6108-1 | $2,216 | NEW | 2600 | 10,071 | NEW |
| American Custom 2-Dr. Sdn. | 6106-2 | $2,062 | 0.00% | 2492 | 4,883 | +63.09% |
| American Custom 2-Dr. Conv. | 6106-2 | $2,371 | NEW | 2712 | 10,855 | NEW |
| American Custom 4-Dr. Sdn. | 6105-2 | $2,111 | 0.00% | 2512 | 5,920 | +80.93% |
| American Custom 2-Dr. Wgn | 6104-2 | $2,297 | 0.00% | 2565 | 1,417 | -0.91% |
| American Custom 4-Dr. Wgn | 6108-2 | $2,346 | NEW | 2600 | 3,679 | NEW |
| Am. Custom 400 2-Dr. Conv. | 6107-5 | $2,461 | NEW | 2745 | 2,063 | NEW |
| Am. Custom 400 4-Door Sedan | 6105-5 | $2,201 | NEW | 2606 | 1,629 | NEW |
| TOTALS | Avg. price | $2,121 | +4.95% | Production | 136,003 | +12.77% |

# Classic

*"The All-Purpose Compact Car."*

**Nameplate year of origin:** 1961.

**Current bodystyle lifespan:** 1958 through 1962 (restyled in 1960).

**Predecessor to this model:** Hudson and Nash Rambler (1956 to 1957).

**Corporate siblings:** Ambassador (shared components from cowl back).

**Replacement for this model:** Rambler Classic (1963 to 1966).

**Percentage of division's sales volume:** 58.04%.

**Primary competition:** Dodge Lancer, Ford Falcon, Plymouth Valiant, and Studebaker Lark.

**Notable changes:** Restyled front end.

**Major standard equipment:** Front arm rests and ash trays, front foam cushion seat, dual sunvisors, air cleaner, oil filter, black rubber cargo mat (wagons), chrome luggage rack (wagons) and 6.50 × 15 BSW tires. Super adds: Rear door (side) armrests and ash trays, door-activated dome lights, and electric clock. Custom adds: Dual-note horn, deluxe two-tone steering wheel, deluxe trim level, padded instrument panel, rear side vent windows, robe rail (wagons), and aluminum engine block (cast iron available at no charge).

### Measurements*

| | |
|---|---|
| Wheelbase | 108.0" |
| Length | 190.0" |
| Width | 72.4" |
| Height | 57.5" |
| Legroom — front | 43.5" |
| Legroom — rear | 40.3" |
| Headroom — front | 36.0" |
| Headroom — rear | 34.5" |
| Luggage cap. (cu. ft.) | NA (wagon 80.0) |
| Fuel capacity (gals.) | 20.0 |

*Dimensions given are for 4-Door Sedan

## Models Available

| | Style Number | Base MSRP | Change from LY | Shipping Wt. (lbs.) | Production | Change from LY |
|---|---|---|---|---|---|---|
| Classic DeLuxe 4-Door Sedan | 6115-0 | $2,100 | +0.10% | 2905 | 40,398 | +7.25% |
| Classic DeL. 4-Dr., 2-S. Wgn. | 6118-0 | $2,439 | +0.49% | 3037 | 19,848 | -17.30% |
| Classic Super 4-Door Sedan | 6115-1 | $2,270 | +0.09% | 2923 | 62,563 | -28.91% |
| Classic Spr. 4-Dr., 2-S. Wagon | 6118-1 | $2,574 | +0.47% | 3046 | 38,370 | -35.50% |
| Classic Spr. 5-Dr., 3-S. Wagon | 6118-3 | $2,699 | +0.45% | 3087 | 4,465 | -47.20% |
| Classic Custom 4-Door Sedan | 6115-2 | $2,415 | +1.34% | 2863 | 26,497 | -30.28% |
| Classic Cst. 4-Dr., 2-S. Wagon | 6118-2 | $2,719 | +1.57% | 2984 | 16,394 | -48.92% |
| Classic Cst. 5-Dr., 3-S. Wagon | 6118-4 | $2,844 | +1.50% | 3023 | 2,741 | -52.06% |
| Classic Custom 400 4-Dr. Sdn. | 6115-5 | $2,565 | NEW | 2873 | 2,901 | NEW |
| TOTALS | | Avg. price $2,514 | -1.18% | | Production 214,177 | -31.89% |

# Ambassador

## "America's First Compact Luxury Car."

**Nameplate year of origin:** 1933 (From top-of-the-line Nash).

**Current bodystyle lifespan:** 1958 through 1962 (Shared basic structure with Classic).

**Predecessor to this model:** Ambassador (1952 to 1957; major restyle in 1955).

**Corporate siblings:** Classic (shared components from cowl back).

**Replacement for this model:** None.

**Percentage of division's sales volume:** 5.11%.

**Primary competition:** Chevrolet BelAir/Impala, Dodge Dart, Ford Fairlane/Galaxie, and Plymouth Belvedere.

**Notable changes:** Completely restyled front and rear end.

**Major standard equipment:** Front arm rests and ash trays, front foam cushion seat, dual sunvisors, dual horns, air cleaner, oil filter, black rubber cargo mat on wagons, and 8.00 × 14 BSW tires. Super adds: Rear door (side) armrests, rear side vent windows, door-activated dome lights, electric clock, color-keyed carpeting, underhood insulation, and chrome luggage rack (wagons). Custom adds: deluxe steering wheel, deluxe trim level, padded instrument panel, rear seat foam cushions, robe rail (wagons), and wheel covers.

### Measurements*

| | |
|---|---|
| Wheelbase | 117.0" |
| Length | 199.0" |
| Width | 72.4" |
| Height | 57.5" |
| Legroom — front | 43.5" |
| Legroom — rear | 40.3" |
| Headroom — front | 36.0" |
| Headroom — rear | 34.5" |
| Luggage cap. (cu. ft.) | NA (wagon 80.0) |
| Fuel capacity (gals.) | 20.0 |

*Dimensions given are for 4-Door Sedan*

## Models Available

| | Style Number | Base MSRP | Change from LY | Shipping Wt. (lbs.) | Production | Change from LY |
|---|---|---|---|---|---|---|
| Ambassador DeLuxe 4-Door Sedan | 6185-0 | $2,397 | 0.08% | 3343 | 273 | -9.60% |
| Ambassador Super 4-Door Sedan | 6185-1 | $2,539 | -1.86% | 3361 | 3,299 | -17.32% |
| Ambassador Super 4-Dr., 2-S. Wgn. | 6188-1 | $2,843 | -1.32% | 3493 | 1,099 | -18.11% |
| Ambassador Super 5-Dr., 3-S. Wgn. | 6188-3 | $2,968 | -1.26% | 3560 | 277 | -56.51% |
| Ambassador Custom 4-Door Sedan | 6185-2 | $2,684 | -1.76% | 3380 | 9,269 | -15.34% |
| Ambassador Cst. 4-Dr., 2-S. Wagon | 6188-2 | $2,988 | -1.26% | 3495 | 3,010 | -21.80% |
| Ambassador Cst. 5-Dr., 3-S. Wagon | 6186-4 | $3,113 | -1.21% | 3566 | 784 | -32.00% |
| Ambassador Custom 400 4-Door Sdn. | 6185-5 | $2,814 | NEW | 3387 | 831 | NEW |
| TOTALS | | Avg. price $2,793 | -2.25% | | Production 18,842 | -20.83% |

*Built primarily for fleet use.

# STUDEBAKER

*"Studebaker announces a new kind of performance."*

Nineteen-sixty-one was a year of little change for Studebaker. After the successful launch of the Lark line, there was little cash left to fund restyling or new lines. That which remained was being funneled into the upcoming Avanti sports car. For this year, the only new offering was the Lark Cruiser 4-Door Sedan, which actually replaced the mid-season Econ-O-Miler sedan of 1960. Based upon the station wagon platform (and wheelbase), the longer Cruiser gave more room and some added style to the typical Lark Sedan. All Cruisers were available with a V8 engine only. The minimal styling changes given to all Lark models this year included replacement of the small side grilles between the headlamp and grille area with a round parking/turn signal lamp. The old familiar L-Head 6-cylinder powerplant was also given a boost with an increase in its com-

pression ratio and a new overhead valve design, increasing horsepower from 90 @ 4000 rpm to 112 @ 4500 rpm.

Some interesting but little known special-order models were offered this year. These included the Marshal package for most sedan or wagon models, adding special amenities (or lack thereof) for use as police cars. There was the 6-cylinder City Marshal, 259 V8 Patrol Marshal, and 289 V8 Pursuit Marshal. There was also a Heavy Duty 4-Door Sedan, based on the stretched Cruiser body, that was offered for taxicab use. A Lark Deluxe 2-Door Sedan could be ordered without the rear seat under Utility Sedanette. Finally, a conversion kit was offered for about $35 to allow 2-Door Wagon owners to convert their car to a Sedan Delivery.

**Hawk 2-Door Coupe**

**Lark Cruiser 4-Door Sedan**

**Lark Deluxe 4-Door Wagon**

**Lark Regal 2-Door Hardtop**

**Model year production:** 68,918, down 47.26% from 1960.
**Base price range:** $1,935 to $2,650.
**Domestic market share:** 1.29% (12th place).
**Industry average base price:** $3,048.
**Studebaker average base price:** $2,318.
**Introduction date:** October 1960.
**Assembly plants:** South Bend, IN (No coding) and Canada (C).

**Data plate identification (VIN):** Up to ten digit code read as follows: 61 for 1961; S for 6-cylinder or V for V8 engine; C only if built in Canada; Serial Number 1001 and up. Body style numbers are found on a separate plate on the vehicle. *Example:* 61S100001 is a 1961 Studebaker Lark Six built in South Bend, IN, serial number 1001.

## Powertrains

| Engine | Gross HP | Transmission Availability | Lark | Hawk |
|---|---|---|---|---|
| 169.6 CID Skybolt, 1-bbl., OHV 6-cyl. | 112 | 3-speed manual | S | - |
| | | 3-speed w/Overdrive | $110 | - |
| | | Flightomatic Automatic | $165 | - |
| 259.2 CID, 2-bbl., OHV V8 | 180 | 3-speed manual | $135 | - |
| | | 3-speed w/Overdrive | $245 | - |
| | | Flightomatic Automatic | $335 | - |
| 259.2 CID, 4-bbl., OHV V8 | 195 | 3-speed manual | $157 | - |
| | | 3-speed w/Overdrive | $267 | - |
| | | Flightomatic Automatic | $357 | - |
| 289 CID, 2-bbl., OHV V8 | 210 | 3-speed manual | - | S |
| | | 3-speed w/Overdrive | - | $110 |
| | | 4-speed manual | - | $188 |
| | | Flightomatic Automatic | - | $200 |
| 289 CID, 4-bbl., OHV V8 | 225 | 3-speed manual | - | $22 |
| | | 3-speed w/Overdrive | - | $132 |
| | | 4-speed manual | - | $210 |
| | | Flightomatic Automatic | - | $222 |

## Major Options

| | Lark | Hawk |
|---|---|---|
| Heater and defroster | $71 | $71 |
| Air conditioning | $278 | $325 |
| Tinted glass — full | $32 | $32 |
| Power steering (V8 only) | $75 | $75 |
| Power brakes | $38 | $38 |
| Electric clock | $16 | $16 |
| Windshield washers | $12 | $12 |
| AM radio — manual | $59 | $59 |
| White sidewall tires — Standard size | $28–$48 | $28–$48 |
| Wheel covers | $16 | $16 |
| Rear facing third seat (wagon only) | $124 | - |

Options common to most models. (- = Not Available.) Items may be standard equipment, optional at different pricing, or unavailable on certain models. This chart is only a guide.

## Paint Colors

| | Code |
|---|---|
| Black Velvet | P6110 |
| Ermine | P6111 |
| Riviera Blue | P6112 |
| Green Jade | P6113 |
| Flamingo | P6114 |
| Desert Sand | P6115 |
| Blaze | P6116 |
| Suntone | P6117 |
| Autumn Haze | P6118 |
| Pearl Beige (Insert only) | 1149 |

# Lark

*"New Performability! New Luxury! New Safety!*
*You have to drive the Lark to believe it!"*

**Nameplate year of origin:** 1959.
**Current bodystyle lifespan:** 1959 through 1961.
**Predecessor to this model:** Champion (1953 to 1958).
**Replacement for this model:** Lark (1962 to 1966).
**Corporate siblings:** None.
**Percentage of division's sales volume:** 94.68%.
**Primary competition:** AMC Rambler American, Chevrolet Corvair, Ford Falcon, Mercury Comet and Plymouth Valiant.
**Notable changes:** Revised trim and detail changes.

## Measurements

| | Cars | Cruiser | Wagons |
|---|---|---|---|
| Wheelbase | 108.5" | 113.0" | 113.0" |
| Length | 175.0" | 179.0" | 184.5" |
| Width | 71.4" | 71.4" | 71.4" |
| Height | 56.5" | 57.5" | 58.8" |
| Legroom — front | 43.5" | 44.0" | 44.0" |
| Legroom — rear | 40.0" | 42.0" | 42.0" |

**Major standard equipment:** All-vinyl or cloth and vinyl front bench seats, armrests, rubber floor mats, and 6.00 × 15 BSW tires (6.70 × 15 BSW on Lark Cruiser and convertible).

|  | Cars | Cruiser | Wagons |
|---|---|---|---|
| Headroom — front | 35.3" | 35.3" | 35.3" |
| Headroom — rear | 34.8" | 34.8" | 35.0" |
| Luggage cap. (cu. ft.) | NA | NA | 93.0 |
| Fuel capacity (gals.) | 18.0 | 18.0 | 18.0 |

## Models Available

| | Style Number | Base MSRP | Change from LY | Shipping Wt. (lbs.) | Production | Change from LY |
|---|---|---|---|---|---|---|
| Lark Deluxe 2-Door Sedan | F4 | $1,935 | -2.07% | 2661 | 14,574 | -55.44% |
| Lark Deluxe 4-Door Sedan | W4 | $2,005 | -2.00% | 2665 | 23,234 | -36.80% |
| Lark Deluxe 2-Door, 2-Seat Wagon | D4 | $2,290 | -3.21% | 2836 | 2,387 | -54.37% |
| Lark Deluxe 4-Door, 2-Seat Wagon | P4 | $2,370 | -2.91% | 2865 | 4,739 | -57.43% |
| Lark Regal 2-Door Hardtop | J6 | $2,243 | -2.31% | 2770 | 3,536 | -52.18% |
| Lark Regal 2-Door Convertible | L6 | $2,554 | -2.56% | 3034 | 1,981 | -76.89% |
| Lark Regal 4-Door Sedan | W6 | $2,155 | -1.87% | 2692 | 7,004 | -58.64% |
| Lark Regal 4-Door, 2-Seat Wagon | P6 | $2,520 | -2.74% | 2836 | 2,544 | -66.81% |
| Lark Cruiser 4-Door Sedan | Y8 | $2,458 | NEW | 3001 | 5,256 | NEW |
| TOTALS | Avg. price | $2,281 | -1.55% | Production | 65,255 | -40.38% |

# Hawk

*"The sophisticated Hawk Sports Coupe. The car for sports-minded families."*

**Nameplate year of origin:** 1956.
**Current bodystyle lifespan:** 1953 through 1964.
**Predecessor to this model:** None.
**Replacement for this model:** None.
**Corporate siblings:** None.
**Percentage of division's sales volume:** 5.32%.
**Primary competition:** None.
**Notable changes:** Minor trim and detail changes.
**Major standard equipment:** All-vinyl front seat covering, full carpeting, and 6.70 × 15 BSW tires.

## Measurements

| | |
|---|---|
| Wheelbase | 120.5" |
| Length | 204.0" |
| Width | 71.3" |
| Height | 55.5" |
| Legroom — front | 44.0" |
| Legroom — rear | 37.0" |
| Headroom — front | 34.5" |
| Headroom — rear | 33.8" |
| Luggage cap. (cu. ft.) | NA |
| Fuel capacity (gals.) | 18.0 |

## Models Available

| | Style Number | Base MSRP | Change from LY | Shipping Wt. (lbs.) | Production | Change from LY |
|---|---|---|---|---|---|---|
| Hawk 2-Door Coupe | C6 | $2,650 | 0.00% | 3205 | 3,663 | -14.42% |
| TOTALS | Avg. price | $2,650 | 0.00% | Production | 3,663 | -14.42% |

# 1962

Nineteen-sixty-two brought a second wave of model lineup expansion, with most of the growth coming from Ford and Chrysler. After the success of the compacts in 1960, and then the very successful introductions of the senior compacts by GM in 1961, the marketing types were apparently feeling that the time was right for a smaller full-size car, or as we would soon know them, an "intermediate" line. Full-size cars had grown by leaps and bounds in the prior five years, with a small downsizing effort seen for 1961. What was once considered a full-size car, in terms of power and size, no longer existed, except for the Rambler Ambassador line, which had proven itself quite popular in the past several seasons.

Ford, as when entering the compact market two years earlier, took the most conservative approach. A car sized directly between the Falcon/Comet and the full-size models was introduced as the Ford Fairlane and Mercury Meteor. These intermediate models were very similar in size to, for example, the 1955 Fords, and were powered by engines of similar capacity. As could be expected in a time of little inflation, pricing was similar also. The marketers were correct in a certain amount of the population was ready for this size of car, but their conservative design approach did not satisfy buyers looking for style and pizzazz in a new car purchase. In fact, the Mercury Meteor would only last two years, as the Comet, which was already larger than the Falcon it was based upon, became a hot seller in the category. The Fairlane would not realize its full potential until the 1966 redesign, which placed it in the forefront with the newer GM mid-size cars.

Chrysler chose a much different formula for its new smaller, full-size cars. The company was in the midst of a realignment of all of its products now that the DeSoto was gone and the compact Valiant was being brought under the Plymouth nameplate. A multi-layered strategy focused mostly on rebuilding the Plymouth and Dodge product lines. With the compact Valiant under the Plymouth brand,

and in view of Plymouth's economy reputation, a decision was made to have Plymouth's full-size models use only the new platform. This new body utilized a wheelbase six inches shorter than previous models yet had nearly as much interior room as its predecessors in all critical areas. A shorter wheelbase meant a shorter overall length for easier maneuverability in traffic and parking situations than a traditional full-size car. It also meant slightly less luggage space and less room under the hood for bigger powerplants (which weren't necessary), but somehow that situation was remedied for those who were racing minded! Overall, the cars were a very nice package. Although the styling was a little unorthodox, it was much better than the previous year's garish looks. But there were still a lot of traditional, full-size car buyers out there who didn't necessarily want a smaller Plymouth, even if the ads said it was "full-size" on the inside. Sales totals would reflect this lack of interest, as Pontiac would surpass Plymouth, and Oldsmobile, Buick and even Dodge made sizeable gains on the marque.

Dodge fared much better. Having picked up its own version of the Valiant, called the Lancer, in 1961, Dodge was already in the compact market. With the demise of the DeSoto, Chrysler grafted a 1961 Dodge full-sized front clip onto a 1962 Chrysler body and created the 1962 Dodge Custom 880, which gave Dodge its traditional full-size model to offer consumers. Dodge also got its own intermediate model, which was much nicer in appearance than the Plymouth, giving Dodge the upper hand all the way around. In fact, for 1963 Dodge would even gain a slight wheelbase extension, to make its cars larger than the Plymouths, and their sales showed the effects of this improvement. By 1963, Chrysler was seeing the light, so to speak, and began a program to categorize its cars into a platform lineup similar to what GM was using. Therefore, when new full-size models were introduced in 1965, Plymouth finally got its true big car back. But for three painful years, Plymouth was stuck with a mid-sized car for which little demand existed.

## 1962 Model Year Production by Make

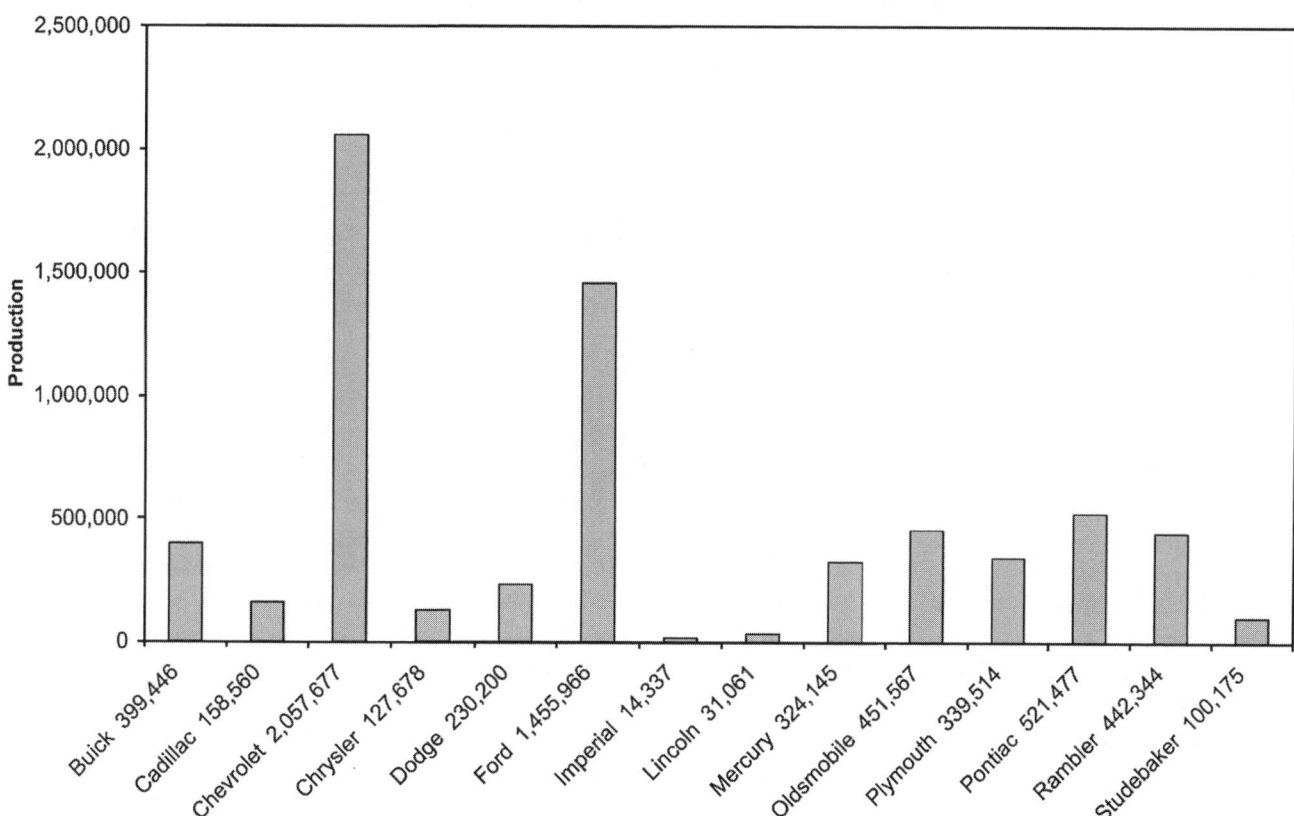

General Motors was not quite ready to jump into the emerging intermediate market. The one-year-old trio of "senior compacts" were meant to fill the gap between compact and full-size, only they were approaching that size class from the opposite end, being slightly smaller than cars such as the Fairlane and new Plymouths. These new cars were highly successful in the minds of automotive editors across the country, who admired their engineering. This meant that they would keep the names and images of these cars in front of the public. In an unusual move, the 1962 Buick Special was chosen as *Motor Trend* magazine's "Car of the Year" for its highly successful new V6 engine design. This was unusual in that the Special was a new model in 1961, the year its stablemate, the Pontiac Tempest, won the award for its engineering distinctiveness, with its front engine, rear transmission design. The all-new V6 garnered the award for Buick because of its high power output and high economy rankings, and the Special's overall pleasing ride and handling qualities.

General Motors was concentrating on other segments of the market at the time. For starters, since day one, the conservative, traditional Ford Falcon had been outselling the Chevrolet Corvair by quite a margin, and Chevrolet in its competitive quest to remain the number one seller couldn't allow that to continue. So for 1962, the new Chevy II, just as conservative as the Falcon, was introduced. As if

to one-up Ford, the Chevy offered a choice of four- or six-cylinder powerplants and an array of body styles, including a 2-Door Convertible, something Ford would not have until 1963. The Chevy II was an instant hit and had little if any effect on sales of the Corvair, as the two were really competing for different buyers. The Corvair was in a sporty, import-type market, whereas the Chevy II was strictly conventional and traditional. At the other end of the spectrum, GM was beginning to introduce its second round of sporting personal luxury cars, the descendants of the 1953 Buick Skylark, Cadillac Eldorado, Chevrolet Corvette, and Oldsmobile Fiesta. This second wave included the mid–1961 Oldsmobile Starfire, based on the Olds 98, and the 1962 Buick Wildcat coupe, based on the LeSabre 2-Door Hardtop, and Pontiac Grand Prix, based on the Catalina 2-Door Hardtop. These models, while not as exclusive or expensive as their predecessors, brought some extra attention to the showrooms of their respective nameplates. Each was generally equipped with bucket seats, floor shifter, console, sporty styled wheels, and a powerful engine. This combination was generally reserved for the wealthier buyers of Chrysler 300's, Ford Thunderbirds or imports such as Mercedes. But GM put such features into the common buyer's price range. Special design touches and exclusive advertising campaigns put these cars into the forefront of buyers' minds this year.

The independent manufacturers this season had a mixed bag of news. This year American Motors introduced its revamped Rambler American line. While still based loosely on the previous car, the new model was slightly longer, wider and much more comfortable. As a bonus, the overall styling was much more modern and pleasing to look at. The newly named Classic and Ambassador lines received a frontal face-lift that was also much more appealing. Sales of all Rambler models continued to be strong, but were falling off from their record 1960 and 1961 levels. Studebaker continued to struggle, both financially and from falling sales. The much anticipated Avanti had been set to hit showrooms at mid-year and was to have paced the Indianapolis 500 race this year. But, with numerous engineering and financial setbacks, the car did not arrive in time. Race officials were left with a Lark convertible to do the honors as the official pace car. It would be the final time that the Indiana-based car company would get to pace the prestigious home-state racing classic. As for the rest of the Studebaker line, the Hawk completed its metamorphosis to become the GT Hawk, a timely introduction given the new Grand Prix and Wildcat coming from General Motors. Unfortunately the GT Hawk was still based on the 1953 Studebaker design, as were all other Studebakers of the period.

Most other news for the year was limited to the usual model year changes of grilles, taillamps, trim, and the like. Chrysler opted to replace its mid-range Windsor line with the "300" moniker, not to be confused with the 300 letter series cars (presumably Chrysler was hoping for a little confusion, though). Dodge, International and Ford trucks were all-new for 1961 and continued with few changes for 1962. Chevrolet and GMC pickups, last redesigned in 1960, continued with slightly revised frontal styling this year. Kaiser-Jeep models continued relatively unchanged, as did the Studebaker truck line. The new for '61 Ford Falcon Club Wagon and Chevrolet Corvair Greenbrier Wagon were little changed, but finding a loyal following of buyers. People found these "small vans" to be easier to drive and able to carry a larger load than the sedan delivery models they were replacing in the market. The Falcon still offered a Sedan Delivery and the Ranchero pickup in the utility field, but all other car makers had abandoned the utility and delivery vehicles to move towards the upcoming van market.

# BUICK

*"When better automobiles are built, Buick will build them."*

The Buick Special, introduced a year earlier, earned the distinction of winning the *Motor Trend* magazine Car of the Year award for 1962. Typically, the award is given to an all-new car, but the new V6 engine warranted the honor. The new V6 engine for the base Special line was the first volume production V6 in modern U.S. built automobiles. Also offered for the first time in a Buick was a 4-speed manual transmission for the Special and Skylark models. The V6 engine was lighter than typical in-line 6-cylinder engines, yet offered better power, torque, acceleration and fuel economy than its counterparts. New convertible models were added in regular and new Skylark trim variants. The Skylark was a new top-level trim package that included the convertible and the 2-Door Coupe from 1961. Other changes to the Special line included restyling touches to the front and rear end of the car.

The big Buicks received new styling from the beltline down. The LeSabre Convertible was dropped for this season only, and the Estate Wagons moved from the LeSabre to the Invicta line. The Electra and Electra 225 models were combined into a single Electra 225 line. A new model was introduced after the start of the model year to compete with the Ford Thunderbird and other upcoming personal/sports/luxury cars. This model was the Wildcat, part of the Invicta line, and was offered in a 2-Door Hardtop body style only. All full-sized Buicks for 1962 were powered by the 401 CID V8. This was unusual for Buick, as for decades the smaller series cars (i.e. LeSabre) had always used a smaller displacement engine, while the mid-range used the smaller series' bodies with the top model's engine. Now, all cars were powered by the same engine, but with varying power output levels. Heater and defroster were made standard equipment this year on all models, but could still be deleted by request.

Electra 225 4-Door Hardtop

Invicta 4-Door Hardtop

Invicta 2-Door Convertible and
LeSabre 2-Door Hardtop

1962

Special, *Motor Trend* Car of the Year

Special Deluxe 4-Door Sedan and
Skylark 2-Door Hardtop

**Model year production:** 399,446, up 44.32% from 1961.
**Base price range:** $2,304 to $4,448.
**Domestic market share:** 6.00% (6th place).
**Industry average base price:** $3,025.
**Buick average base price:** $3,344.
**Introduction date:** September 1961.
**Assembly plants:** Flint, MI (1); Southgate, CA (2); Linden, NJ (3); Fairfax, KS (4); Wilmington, DE (5); Atlanta, GA (6); Framingham, MA (7); and Arlington, TX (8).

**Data plate identification:** Nine digit code read as follows: 1st digit indicates series trim level and engine (see coding below); 2nd digit 1 for 1962; 3rd digit is assembly plant code, followed by sequential number 100001 and up for serial number. (Coding: A = V6 Special, 0 = V8 Special, 1 = V8 Special Deluxe, 3 = V8 Skylark, 4 = LeSabre, 6 = Invicta/Wildcat, 8 = Electra). *Example:* 4I4001001 is a 1962 Buick LeSabre, serial number 001001, built in Fairfax, KS. Check model number on body identification plate.

## Powertrains

| Engine | Gross HP | Transmission Availability | Special/ Skylark | LeSabre | Invicta | Electra |
|---|---|---|---|---|---|---|
| 198 CID Fireball, 2-bbl., V6 | 135 | 3-speed manual | S* | - | - | - |
| | | 4-speed manual | $200* | - | - | - |
| | | Turbine Drive Automatic | $189* | - | - | - |
| 215 CID Fireball Aluminum, 2-bbl., V8 | 155 | 3-speed manual | $118*/S—Deluxe | - | - | - |
| | | 4-speed manual | $318*/$200—Del. | - | - | - |
| | | Turbine Drive Automatic | $307*/$189—Del. | - | - | - |
| 215 CID Skylark Aluminum, 4-bbl., V8 | 190 | 3-speed manual | S**/$167*/ $50—Del. | - | - | - |
| | | 4-speed manual | $200**/$367*/ $250—Del. | - | - | - |
| | | Turbine Drive Automatic | $189**/$356*/ $239—Del. | - | - | - |
| 401 CID Wildcat 375, 2-bbl., V8 | 265 | Turbine Drive Automatic | - | No cost | - | - |
| 401 CID Wildcat 410, 2-bbl., V8 | 280 | Turbine Drive Automatic | - | S | - | - |
| 401 CID Wildcat 445, 4-bbl., V8 | 325 | Turbine Drive Automatic | - | $22 | S | S |

*Special only.   **Skylark only.*

## Major Options

| | Special/Skylark | LeSabre | Invicta | Electra |
|---|---|---|---|---|
| Air conditioning | $351 | $430 | $430 | $430 |
| Soft Ray tinted glass | $41 | $43 | $43 | $43 |
| Deck lid remote release | - | $10 | $10 | $10 |
| Power steering | $86 | $108 | $108 | S |
| Power brakes | $43 | $43 | $43 | S |
| Power door locks | - | $70 | $70 | $70 |
| Power driver's seat/Bench seat, 6-way | - | $97 | $97 | $69–$97 |
| Power windows | $102** | $108 | $108 | $108* |
| Sonomatic AM radio | $66 | $90 | $90 | $90 |

Options common to most models. (- = Not Available, S = Standard equipment.) Items may be standard equipment, optional at different pricing, or unavailable on certain models. This chart is only a guide.

*Standard on Convertible.*    **Skylark and Deluxe Convertible only.*

## Paint Colors

| | Code |
|---|---|
| Regal Black | A |
| Arctic White | C |
| Silver Cloud Metallic | D |
| Cadet Blue Metallic | E |
| Marlin Blue Metallic | F |
| Glacier Blue | H |
| Willow Mist Metallic | J |
| Cameo Cream | M |
| Burgundy Metallic | N |
| Teal Mist Metallic | P |
| Aquamarine | Q |
| Desert Sand | R |
| Fawn Mist Metallic | T |
| Cardinal Red | V |
| Camelot Rose Metallic | X |

# Special and Skylark

*"Acclaimed for its performance, ride and handling."*

**Nameplate year of origin:** Special 1935, Skylark 1953.
**Current bodystyle lifespan:** 1961 through 1963.
**Predecessor to this model:** None.
**Replacement for this model:** Special/Skylark (1964 to 1965).
**Percentage of division's sales volume:** 38.49%.
**Corporate siblings:** Olds F-85 and Pontiac Tempest.
**Primary competition:** Dodge Lancer, and Mercury Comet.
**Notable changes:** New grille, trim and detail changes.
**Major standard equipment:** Calais cloth and vinyl bench seat, dual sun visors, electric windshield wipers, and 6.50 × 13 BSW tires. Deluxe adds: Full carpeting, deluxe interior and exterior trim, power top on convertible, and V8 engine. Skylark adds: Skylark interior and exterior trim, and all-vinyl interior.

## Measurements

| | |
|---|---|
| Wheelbase | 112.0" |
| Length | 188.4" |
| Width | 71.3" |
| Height | 52.8" |
| Legroom — front | 44.6" |
| Legroom — rear | 38.7" |
| Headroom — front | 33.9" |
| Headroom — rear | 33.7" |
| Luggage capacity (cu. ft.) | 25.5/Wagons 73.3 |
| Fuel capacity (gals.) | 16.0 |

## Models Available

| | Style Number | Base MSRP | Change from LY | Shipping Wt. (lbs.) | Production | Change from LY |
|---|---|---|---|---|---|---|
| Special 2-Door Coupe | 4027 | $2,304 | -1.12% | 2638 | 19,135 | 295.27% |
| Special 2-Door Convertible | 4067 | $2,587 | NEW | 2858 | 7,918 | NEW |
| Special 4-Door Sedan | 4019 | $2,358 | -1.09% | 2666 | 23,249 | 26.77% |
| Special 4-Door, 2-Seat Wagon | 4035 | $2,655 | -0.97% | 2876 | 7,382 | 21.00% |
| Special 4-Door, 3-Seat Wagon | 4045 | $2,736 | -0.94% | 2896 | 2,814 | 252.63% |
| Special Deluxe 2-Door Convertible | 4167 | $2,879 | NEW | 2820 | 8,332 | NEW |
| Special Deluxe 4-Door Sedan | 4119 | $2,593 | +2.94% | 2648 | 31,660 | 169.93% |
| Special Deluxe 4-Dr., 2-Seat Wgn. | 4135 | $2,890 | +2.63% | 2845 | 10,300 | -18.79% |
| Skylark 2-Door Hardtop | 4347 | $2,787 | +6.33% | 2707 | 34,060 | 471.57% |
| Skylark 2-Door Convertible | 4367 | $3,012 | NEW | NA | 8,913 | NEW |
| TOTALS | | Avg. price $2,680 | +3.55% | | Production 153,763 | +77.00% |

# LeSabre

*"Majestic performance, luxurious ride and smart interior décor combined with an attractive price."*

**Nameplate year of origin:** 1959.
**Current bodystyle lifespan:** 1961 through 1964.
**Predecessor to this model:** LeSabre (1959 to 1960).
**Replacement for this model:** LeSabre (1965 to 1966).
**Percentage of division's sales volume:** 31.84%.
**Corporate siblings:** Chevrolet Biscayne/Bel Air/Impala, Pontiac Catalina/Star Chief/Bonneville, Oldsmobile 88.
**Primary competition:** Chrysler Newport, Dodge Polara, and Mercury Monterey.
**Notable changes:** New front end, revised rear end, and trim and detail changes.
**Major standard equipment:** Vinyl and cloth interior, electric windshield wipers, glove compartment light, trip mileage indicator, cigarette lighter, dual sunshades, Turbine-Drive automatic transmission, and 7.60 × 15 BSW tires.

### Measurements*

| | |
|---|---|
| Wheelbase | 123.0" |
| Length | 214.1" |
| Width | 78.0" |
| Height | 52.4" |
| Legroom — front | 44.8" |
| Legroom — rear | 41.4" |
| Headroom — front | 34.4" |
| Headroom — rear | 34.2" |
| Luggage capacity (cu. ft.) | NA |
| Fuel capacity (gals.) | 20.0 |

*Dimensions given for 4-Door Hardtop models*

**1962**

## Models Available

| | Style Number | Base MSRP | Change from LY | Shipping Wt. (lbs.) | Production | Change from LY |
|---|---|---|---|---|---|---|
| LeSabre 2-Door Sedan | 4411 | $3,091 | +3.27% | 4041 | 7,418 | +24.48% |
| LeSabre 2-Door Hardtop | 4447 | $3,293 | +4.47% | 4054 | 25,479 | +76.03% |
| LeSabre 4-Door Sedan | 4469 | $3,227 | -4.58% | 4104 | 56,783 | +62.21% |
| LeSabre 4-Door Hardtop | 4439 | $3,369 | +8.43% | 4156 | 37,518 | -0.72% |
| TOTALS | *Avg. price* | $3,245 | -2.14% | *Production* | 127,198 | +12.32% |

# Invicta

*"The spirited, richly appointed performance leader among full-size Buicks."*

**Nameplate year of origin:** 1959.
**Current bodystyle lifespan:** 1961 through 1963.
**Predecessor to this model:** Invicta (1959 to 1960).
**Replacement for this model:** Wildcat (1963 to 1964).
**Percentage of division's sales volume:** 14.02%.
**Corporate siblings:** Chevrolet Biscayne/Bel Air/Impala, Pontiac Catalina/Star Chief/Bonneville, Oldsmobile 88.
**Primary competition:** Chrysler 300, Dodge Custom 880, and Mercury Monterey Custom.
**Notable changes:** New front end, revised rear end, and trim and detail changes. New Wildcat coupe.
**Major standard equipment:** Vinyl and cloth interior (all-vinyl on convertible), front and rear seat center armrests, electric clock, electric windshield wipers, glove compartment light, trip mileage indicator, deluxe wheel covers, Turbine-Drive automatic transmission, and 7.60 × 15 BSW tires. Wildcat adds: Bucket seats, floor console, deluxe steering wheel, tachometer, special exterior trim and rocker panel moldings.

### Measurements

| | |
|---|---|
| Wheelbase | 123.0" |
| Length | 214.1" |
| Width | 78.0" |
| Height | 52.4" |
| Legroom — front | 44.8" |
| Legroom — rear | 41.4" |
| Headroom — front | 34.5" |
| Headroom — rear | 34.1" |
| Luggage capacity (cu. ft.) | NA |
| Fuel capacity (gals.) | 20.0 |

## Models Available

| | Style Number | Base MSRP | Change from LY | Shipping Wt. (lbs.) | Production | Change from LY |
|---|---|---|---|---|---|---|
| Invicta 2-Door HT | 4647 | $3,733 | +15.64% | 4077 | 12,355 | -67.31% |
| Invicta 2-Door Convertible | 4667 | $3,617 | -0.17% | 4217 | 13,471 | +139.36% |
| Invicta 4-Door HT | 4639 | $3,667 | -1.69% | 4159 | 16,443 | +578.62% |
| Invicta 4-Dr., 2-S. Estate Wagon | 4635 | $3,836 | +5.88% | 4471 | 9,131 | +62.24% |
| Invicta 4-Dr., 3-S. Estate Wagon | 4645 | $3,917 | +5.01% | 4505 | 4,617 | +90.55% |
| Wildcat 2-Door HT | 4647 | $3,927 | NEW | 4150 | * | NEW |
| TOTALS | | Avg. price $3,783 | +7.26% | | Production 56,017 | +52.29% |

*Included in the total Invicta 2-Door Hardtop production figures.

# Electra 225

*"Quality and good taste are immediately evident in the Buick Electra 225."*

**Nameplate year of origin:** 1959.
**Current bodystyle lifespan:** 1961 through 1964.
**Predecessor to this model:** Electra (1959 to 1960).
**Replacement for this model:** Electra 225 (1965 to 1966).
**Percentage of division's sales volume:** 15.64%.
**Corporate siblings:** Cadillac Series 62/de Ville, Oldsmobile Ninety-Eight.
**Primary competition:** Chrysler New Yorker.
**Notable changes:** New grille, revised rear end, and trim and detail changes.
**Major standard equipment:** Vinyl and cloth interior, 2-way power driver's seat (on Hardtops and Convertible), front and rear seat center armrests, power windows, electric clock, dual-speed electric windshield wipers with washers, glove compartment light, trip mileage indicator, cigarette lighter, automatic trunk light, deluxe steering wheel, deluxe wheel covers, backup lights, power steering, power brakes, Turbine-Drive automatic transmission, and 8.00 × 15 BSW tires.

## Measurements*

| | |
|---|---|
| Wheelbase | 126.0" |
| Length | 220.1" |
| Width | 78.0" |
| Height | 52.4" |
| Legroom — front | 44.8" |
| Legroom — rear | 44.0" |
| Headroom — front | 34.3" |
| Headroom — rear | 34.5" |
| Luggage capacity (cu. ft.) | NA |
| Fuel capacity (gals.) | 20.0 |

*Dimensions given for 4-Door Hardtop models.

## Models Available

| | Style Number | Base MSRP | Change from LY | Shipping Wt. (lbs.) | Production | Change from LY |
|---|---|---|---|---|---|---|
| Electra 225 2-Door Hardtop | 4847 | $4,062 | +6.39% | 4235 | 8,922 | +109.93% |
| Electra 225 2-Door Convertible | 4867 | $4,366 | +4.15% | 4396 | 7,894 | +10.28% |
| Electra 225 4-Door Sedan | 4819 | $4,051 | +5.91% | 4304 | 13,523 | -2.13% |
| Electra 225 6-w., Riviera 4-Dr. HT | 4829 | $4,448 | +2.25% | 4390 | 15,395 | +12.22% |
| Electra 225 4-Door Hardtop | 4839 | $4,186 | +6.46% | 4309 | 16,734 | +86.39% |
| TOTALS | | Avg. price $4,223 | +4.97% | | Production 62,468 | +30.35% |

# CADILLAC

*"Cadillac presents the Masterwork of the Motoring Age.*
*For sixty years the Standard of the World."*

Improvements for the 1962 Cadillacs centered on a quieter ride and attention to detail. The powerful Cadillac engine was made smoother and quieter, and additional insulation was added under the floors and within the firewall area. Interiors were given new trim and details. Exterior styling changes were minimal and consisted of revised grille design and trim. The only change to the model line was the one-year only addition of a short-deck Hardtop Town Sedan to the Series Sixty-Two that complemented the newly named Sedan de Ville Park Avenue short deck sedan.

Series 62 2-Door Convertible

Sedan de Ville 4-Door, 6-window Hardtop

Eldorado Biarritz 2-Door Convertible

Brochure Cover with Logo

**Model year production:** 158,560, up 16.44% from 1961.
**Base price range:** $5,025 to $9,937.
**Domestic market share:** 2.38% (10th place).
**Industry average base price:** $3,025.
**Cadillac average base price:** $6,243.
**Introduction date:** September 1961.

**Assembly plants:** Detroit, MI.
**Data plate identification:** Nine digit code read as follows: 1st and 2nd digits identify year (62 for 1962); 3rd digit is style symbol (see list); 000001 and up for serial number. *Example:* 62J000001 is a 1962 Cadillac de Ville 2-Door Hardtop, serial number 000001.

## Powertrains

| Engine | Gross HP | Transmission Availability | All models |
|---|---|---|---|
| 390 CID, 4-bbl., V8 | 325 | Hydra-matic Automatic | S |

## Major Options

| | Sixty-Two | de Ville | Eldorado | Sixty Special | Seventy-Five |
|---|---|---|---|---|---|
| Air conditioning | $474 | $474 | $474 | $474 | $624* |
| Power windows | $118 | S | S | S | S |
| 6-way power seat | $113 | $85 | S | $85 | – |
| Power door locks | $46–$70 | $46–$70 | $46 | $70 | S |
| AM radio w/rear speaker | $165 | $165 | $165 | $165 | $247** |
| Guide-Matic headlamp dimmers | $45 | $45 | $45 | $45 | – |

## Paint Colors

| | Code |
|---|---|
| Ebony Black | 10 |
| Olympic White | 12 |
| Nevada Silver Metallic | 14 |
| Aleutian Gray Metallic | 16 |
| Newport Blue Metallic | 22 |
| Avalon Blue Metallic | 24 |
| York Blue Metallic | 26 |

| | Sixty-Two | de Ville | Eldorado | Sixty Special | Seventy-Five | | | Code |
|---|---|---|---|---|---|---|---|---|
| Cruise control | $97 | $97 | $97 | $97 | $97 | | Turquoise Metallic | 29 |
| Remote control trunk | | | | | | | Sage Metallic | 32 |
| release/lock | $59 | $59 | $59 | $59 | – | | Granada Green Metallic | 36 |
| | | | | | | | Sandalwood | 44 |
| | | | | | | | Maize | 45 |
| | | | | | | | Driftwood Beige Metallic | 46 |
| | | | | | | | Laurel Metallic | 48 |
| | | | | | | | Pompeian Red Metallic | 50 |
| | | | | | | | Burgundy Metallic | 52 |
| | | | | | | | Neptune Blue Metallic | 94 |
| | | | | | | | Pinehurst Green Metallic | 96 |
| | | | | | | | Victorian Gold Metallic | 97 |
| | | | | | | | Bronze Metallic | 98 |
| | | | | | | | Heather Metallic | 99 |

Options common to most models. (– = Not Available, S = Standard equipment.) Items may be standard equipment, optional at different pricing, or unavailable on certain models. This chart is only a guide.   *Includes rear unit and controls.   **Signal seeking.

**Cadillac Style Symbols: A**— 62 4-window Sedan or Calais 4-Dr. HT Sedan; **B**— Sedan de Ville 4-window; **C**— 62 Short Deck Sedan; **D**— Sedan de Ville Park Avenue; **E**— Eldorado Biarritz or Eldorado Convertible; **F**— 62 Convertible; **G**— 62 2-Door Hardtop or Calais 2-Door HT; **H**— Eldorado Seville HT or Eldorado Coupe; **J**— Coupe de Ville; **K**— 62 6-window Sedan; **L**— Sedan de Ville 6-window; **M**— Fleetwood 60 Special Sedan; **N**— 62 4-window Sedan (1963) or Calais Sedan; **P**— Fleetwood Brougham or Eldorado Brougham; **R**— Fleetwood 75 Sedan; **S**— Fleetwood 75 Limousine; **Z**— Commerical Chassis

# Sixty-Two

*"Beauty that inspires— Value that endures."*

**Nameplate year of origin:** 1940.
**Current bodystyle lifespan:** 1961 through 1964.
**Predecessor to this model:** Series Sixty-Two (1959 to 1960).
**Replacement for this model:** Calais (1965 to 1966).
**Percentage of division's sales volume:** 44.32%.
**Corporate siblings:** Buick Electra and Oldsmobile Ninety-Eight.
**Primary competition:** Imperial Custom and Lincoln Continental.
**Notable changes:** New grille, minor trim and detail changes.
**Major standard equipment:** Cloth or cloth and vinyl seat upholstery, rear seat center armrests, interior courtesy and map lights, left-hand outside remote control mirror, windshield wipers and washers, electric clock, right side visor vanity mirrors, rear fender skirts, front cornering lamps, power steering, power brakes, Hydra-matic transmission, and 8.00 × 15 BSW tires.

## Measurements

| | |
|---|---|
| Wheelbase | 129.5" |
| Length | 222.0" |
| | (Town Sedan Short-deck sedan 215.0") |
| Width | 79.9" |
| Height | 56.3" |
| Legroom — front | 45.6" |
| Legroom — rear | 44.3" |
| Headroom — front | 34.3" |
| Headroom — rear | 34.1" |
| Luggage capacity (cu. ft.) | NA |
| Fuel capacity (gals.) | 26.0 |
| | (Town Sedan 21.0) |

## Models Available

| | Style Number | Base MSRP | Change from LY | Shipping Wt. (lbs.) | Production | Change from LY |
|---|---|---|---|---|---|---|
| Sixty-Two 2-Door Hardtop | 6247 | $5,025 | +2.7% | 4530 | 16,833 | +5.2% |
| Sixty-Two 2-Door Convertible | 6267 | $5,588 | +2.4% | 4630 | 16,800 | +8.4% |
| Sixty-Two 4-Door Town Sedan | 6389 | $5,213 | NEW | 4590 | 2,600 | NEW |
| Sixty-Two 4-Door, 4-Wind. HT | 6239 | $5,213 | +2.6% | 4645 | 17,314 | +268.4% |
| Sixty-Two 4-Door, 6-Wind. HT | 6229 | $5,213 | +2.6% | 4640 | 16,730 | -36.2% |
| TOTALS | | *Avg. price* $5,250 | +2.4% | | *Production* 70,277 | +12.6% |

# de Ville

*"Luxury and comfort the whole world admires."*

**Nameplate year of origin:** 1949 (as Hardtop designation), 1959 (series).
**Current bodystyle lifespan:** 1961 through 1964.
**Predecessor to this model:** de Ville (1959 to 1960).
**Replacement for this model:** de Ville (1965 to 1966).
**Percentage of division's sales volume:** 45.33%.
**Corporate siblings:** Buick Electra and Oldsmobile Ninety-Eight.
**Primary competition:** Imperial Crown and Lincoln Continental.
**Notable changes:** New grille, minor trim and detail changes.
**Major standard equipment:** Cloth or cloth and leather seat upholstery, front and rear seat center armrests, power operated front seat adjustment, power windows, interior courtesy and map lights, left-hand outside remote control mirror, windshield wipers and washers, electric clock, right side visor vanity mirrors, rear fender skirts, front cornering lamps, power steering, power brakes, Hydra-matic transmission, and 8.00 × 15 BSW tires.

## Measurements

| | |
|---|---|
| Wheelbase | 129.5" |
| Length | 222.0" |
| | (Park Avenue 215.0") |
| Width | 79.9" |
| Height | 56.3" |
| Legroom — front | 45.6" |
| Legroom — rear | 44.3" |
| Headroom — front | 34.3" |
| Headroom — rear | 34.1" |
| Luggage capacity (cu. ft.) | NA |
| Fuel capacity (gals.) | 26.0 |

## Models Available

| | Style Number | Base MSRP | Change from LY | Shipping Wt. (lbs.) | Production | Change from LY |
|---|---|---|---|---|---|---|
| Coupe de Ville 2-Door Hardtop | 6347 | $5,385 | +2.5% | 4595 | 25,675 | +27.4% |
| Sedan de Ville 4-Dr. Park Avenue | 6389 | $5,631 | +2.4% | 4655 | 2,600 | -30.7% |
| Sedan de Ville 4-Door, 4-Wind. HT | 6339 | $5,631 | +2.4% | 4675 | 27,378 | +464.8% |
| Sedan de Ville 4-Door, 6-Wind. HT | 6329 | $5,631 | +2.4% | 4660 | 16,230 | -38.6% |
| TOTALS | Avg. price | $5,570 | +2.4% | Production | 71,883 | +30.3% |

# Eldorado

*"Unanimous approval wherever highways lead."*

**Nameplate year of origin:** 1953.
**Current bodystyle lifespan:** 1961 through 1964.
**Predecessor to this model:** Eldorado (1959 to 1960).
**Replacement for this model:** Eldorado (1965 to 1966).
**Percentage of division's sales volume:** 0.91%.
**Corporate siblings:** Buick Electra and Oldsmobile Ninety-Eight.
**Primary competition:** None.
**Notable changes:** New grille, minor trim and detail changes.
**Major standard equipment:** Cannes leather seat upholstery, front and rear seat center armrests, power operated front seat adjustment, power windows and vent windows, interior courtesy and map lights, left-hand outside remote control mirror, windshield wipers and washers, electric clock, right side visor vanity mirrors, rear fender skirts, front cornering lamps, power steering, power brakes, Turbo Hydra-matic transmission, and 8.20 × 15 WSW tires.

## Measurements

| | |
|---|---|
| Wheelbase | 129.5" |
| Length | 222.0" |
| Width | 79.9" |
| Height | 56.3" |
| Legroom — front | 45.6" |
| Legroom — rear | 44.3" |
| Headroom — front | 34.3" |
| Headroom — rear | 34.1" |
| Luggage capacity (cu. ft.) | NA |
| Fuel capacity (gals.) | 26.0 |

## Models Available

| | Style Number | Base MSRP | Change from LY | Shipping Wt. (lbs.) | Production | Change from LY |
|---|---|---|---|---|---|---|
| Fl. Eldorado Biarritz 2-Dr. Convertible | 6367 | $6,610 | +2.1% | 4620 | 1,450 | EVEN |
| TOTALS | Avg. price | $6,610 | +2.1% | Production | 1,450 | EVEN |

# Fleetwood Sixty-Special

*"Almost writes its Owner's Biography."*

**Nameplate year of origin:** 1938.
**Current bodystyle lifespan:** 1961 through 1964.
**Predecessor to this model:** Fleetwood Sixty-Special (1959 to 1960).
**Replacement for this model:** Fleetwood Sixty-Special (1965 to 1966).
**Percentage of division's sales volume:** 8.42%.
**Corporate siblings:** Buick Electra and Oldsmobile Ninety-Eight.
**Primary competition:** Imperial LeBaron.
**Notable changes:** New grille, minor trim and detail changes.
**Major standard equipment:** Fabric and leather or wool broadcloth seat upholstery, front and rear seat center armrests, power operated front seat adjustment, power windows, interior courtesy and map lights, left-hand outside remote control mirror, windshield wipers and washers, electric clock, right side visor vanity mirrors, rear fender skirts, front cornering lamps, power steering, power brakes, Hydra-matic transmission, and 8.00 × 15 BSW tires.

## Measurements

| | |
|---|---|
| Wheelbase | 129.5" |
| Length | 222.0" |
| Width | 79.9" |
| Height | 56.6" |
| Legroom — front | 45.6" |
| Legroom — rear | 44.2" |
| Headroom — front | 34.2" |
| Headroom — rear | 34.5" |
| Luggage capacity (cu. ft.) | NA |
| Fuel capacity (gals.) | 26.0 |

## Models Available

| | Style Number | Base MSRP | Change from LY | Shipping Wt. (lbs.) | Production | Change from LY |
|---|---|---|---|---|---|---|
| Fleetwood Sixty-Special 4-Door Sdn. | 6039 | $6,366 | +2.1% | 4710 | 13,350 | -13.9% |
| TOTALS | | Avg. price $6,366 | +2.1% | Production | 13,350 | -13.9% |

# Fleetwood Seventy-Five

*"Wherever you see people of prominence gather,*
*the uniquely splendid Fleetwood Seventy-Five is part of the scene."*

**Nameplate year of origin:** 1927 (Fleetwood bodies), 1936 (75 series).
**Current bodystyle lifespan:** 1959 through 1965.
**Predecessor to this model:** Fleetwood 75 (1957 to 1958).
**Replacement for this model:** Fleetwood 75 (1966).
**Percentage of division's sales volume:** 1.01%.
**Corporate siblings:** None.
**Primary competition:** None.
**Notable changes:** Minor trim and detail changes.
**Major standard equipment:** Wool broadcloth or cord cloth seat upholstery with front compartment in harmonizing leather upholstery, rear seat center armrests, power operated front seat adjustment, power windows, interior courtesy and map lights, left-hand outside remote control mirror, windshield wipers and washers, electric clock, right side visor vanity mirrors, rear fender skirts, front cornering lamps, power steering, power brakes, Hydra-matic transmission, and 8.00 × 15 BSW tires.

## Measurements

| | |
|---|---|
| Wheelbase | 149.8" |
| Length | 242.3" |
| Width | 80.6" |
| Height | 59.1" |
| Legroom — front | 44.3" |
| Legroom — rear | Not calculated |
| Headroom — front | 35.9" |
| Headroom — rear | 34.4" |
| Luggage capacity (cu. ft.) | NA |
| Fuel capacity (gals.) | 26.0 |

## Models Available

| | Style Number | Base MSRP | Change from LY | Shipping Wt. (lbs.) | Production | Change from LY |
|---|---|---|---|---|---|---|
| Fleetwood Seventy-Five 4-Door Sdn., 9-pass. | 6723 | $9,722 | +2.0% | 5325 | 696 | -0.43% |
| Fleetwood Seventy-Five 4-Door Limo., 9-pass. | 6733 | $9,937 | +1.9% | 5390 | 904 | -2.4% |
| TOTALS | | Avg. price $9,830 | +2.0% | Production | 1,600 | -0.92% |

# CHEVROLET

*"A new world of worth from Chevrolet."*

Chevrolet made a very important introduction for 1962. Sales of the compact Corvair had been very good since its introduction, but Chevy was always behind Ford in sales of compacts. The main reason for this seemed to be that the Ford Falcon was a totally traditional design, meaning front engine, rear drive, with traditional styling such as a grille up front and few sporty pretensions to its manner. To counter this, Chevrolet developed the Chevy II. Styled after the big Chevy line, the new compact Chevy II matched the Falcon for traditional style, handling and price. And to top it all off, Chevrolet was able to do this without taking any sales away from either its own Corvair, or other GM compacts. Falcon lost about 100,000 in sales this year and was the main loser during the Chevy II's initial season. The Chevy II introduced a 4-cylinder engine to the Chevrolet line for the first time since the twenties. This rugged little 4-cylinder put out nearly as much horsepower as some competitors' 6-cylinder engines. While never a big seller, it would continue through to the third generation Nova models.

Full-size Chevrolet models received a restyling from the beltline down. The lines were generally smoother than the '61 models and continued the now traditional full-width grille and triple lens (dual on Biscayne and BelAir) taillamp designs. Model changes included the discontinuation of the Fleetmaster line, the BelAir 4-Door Hardtop and the Impala 2-Door Sedan. Station wagon model names were dropped and each trim level was sold under its corresponding car nameplate. The sporty Corvette and compact Corvair continued with few styling changes. However, there was a big change under the hood for the Corvette and full-size Chevy models. A new 250-horsepower, 327 CID V8 engine was now standard on Corvette, and available on full-size Chevys. This new engine, developed from the durable 283 CID block, was more powerful yet weighed no more than its predecessor. This engine was so well executed, that it would eventually be tuned to develop 375 horsepower with the help of fuel injection.

BelAir 4-Door Wagon

Chevy II 300 4-Door Sedan

Corvair 500 2-Door Coupe

Corvette 2-Door Convertible

Impala 2-Door Hardtop

Corvair 700 Lakewood 4-Door Wagon

Chevy II Nova 400 4-Door Wagon

Model year production: 2,057,677, up 38.57% from 1961.
Domestic market share: 30.92% (1st place).
Base price range: $1,992 to $4,038.
Industry average base price: $3,025.
Chevrolet average base price: $2,492.
Introduction date: September 1961.
Assembly plants: Atlanta, GA (A); Baltimore, MD (B); Flint, MI (F); Framingham, MA (G); Janesville, WI (J); Kansas City, MO (K), Los Angeles, CA (L), Norwood, OH (N);

Oakland, CA (O); St. Louis, MO (S); Tarrytown, NY (T); and Willow Run, MI (W).

Data plate identification: Twelve digit code read as follows: 1st digit 2 for 1962; four digit style number (see listings below) with 2nd and 3rd number identifying series and engine, 4th and 5th indicating body style; 6th digit is assembly plant code; 100001 and up for serial number. *Example:* 21511S100001 is a 1962 Chevrolet BelAir 2-Door Sedan, 6-cylinder, serial number 100001, built in St. Louis, MO.

## Powertrains

| Engine | Gross HP | Transmission Availability | Corvair | Chevy II | Biscayne/ BelAir/Impala | Corvette |
|---|---|---|---|---|---|---|
| 153 CID Super-Thrift, 1-bbl., 4-cyl. | 90 | 3-speed manual | - | S* | - | - |
| | | 2-sp. Powerglide Automatic | - | $167* | - | - |
| 145 CID Turbo-Air, 2 × 1-bbl., Flat 6 | 80 | | | | | |
| | 84 | 3-speed manual | S | - | - | - |
| | | 4-speed manual | $65 | - | - | - |
| | | 2-sp. Powerglide Automatic | $157 | - | - | - |
| 145 CID Turbo-Air, 2 × 1-bbl., Flat 6 | 102 | 3-speed manual | $27 | - | - | - |
| | | 4-speed manual | $92 | - | - | - |
| | | 2-sp. Powerglide Automatic | $184 | - | - | - |
| 194 CID Hi-Thrift, 1-bbl., 6-cyl. | 120 | 3-speed manual | - | S (Nova)/$60* | - | - |
| | | 2-sp. Powerglide Automatic | - | $167 (Nova)/$227* | - | - |
| 235 CID Turbo-Thrift, 1-bbl., 6-cyl. | 135 | 3-speed manual | - | - | S | - |
| | | Overdrive | - | - | $108 | - |
| | | 2-sp. Powerglide Automatic | - | - | $188 | - |
| 283 CID Turbo-Fire, 2-bbl., V8 | 170 | 3-speed manual | - | - | $107 | - |
| | | Overdrive | - | - | $215 | - |
| | | 2-sp. Powerglide Automatic | - | - | $306 | - |
| 327 CID Turbo-Fire, 4-bbl., V8 | 250 | 3-speed manual | - | - | $191 | S |
| | | 4-speed manual | - | - | $428 | $188 |
| | | 2-sp. Powerglide Automatic | - | - | $390 | $199 |
| 327 CID Turbo-Fire, 2 × 4-bbl., V8 | 300 | 3-speed manual | - | - | $244 | $54 |
| | | 4-speed manual | - | - | $482 | $242 |
| | | 2-sp. Powerglide Automatic | - | - | $444 | $253 |
| 327 CID Corvette, 4-bbl., V8 | 340 | 3-speed manual | - | - | - | $108 |
| | | 4-speed manual | - | - | - | $296 |
| | | 2-sp. Powerglide Automatic | - | - | - | $307 |
| 327 CID Ramjet, Fuel-Injected V8 | 360 | 3-speed manual | - | - | - | $484 |
| | | 4-speed manual | - | - | - | $672 |
| 409 CID Turbo-Fire, 4-bbl., V8 | 380 | 3-speed manual | - | - | $428 | - |
| | | 4-speed manual | - | - | $616 | - |

| Engine | Gross HP | Transmission Availability | Corvair | Chevy II | Biscayne/ BelAir/Impala | Corvette |
|---|---|---|---|---|---|---|
| 409 CID Turbo-Fire, 2 × 4-bbl., V8 | 425 | 3-speed manual | - | - | $484 | - |
| | | 4-speed manual | - | - | $672 | - |

*Chevy II 100 only.

**1962**

## Major Options

| | Corvair | Chevy II | Full-size | Corvette |
|---|---|---|---|---|
| Air conditioning (NA 4-cyl.) | $350 | $317 | $364 | - |
| Soft Ray tinted glass | $27 | $31 | $38 | $16 |
| Power steering (NA 4-cyl.) | - | $75 | $75 | - |
| Power brakes | - | $43 | $43 | - |
| Power windows | - | - | $102 | $59 |
| Electric clock | $16 | $16 | $16 | S |
| Pushbutton AM radio | $57 | $57 | $57 | $137 |
| Whitewall tires — std. size | $29 | $31 | $32–$40 | $32 |

Options common to most models. (- = Not Available, S = Standard equipment.) Items may be standard equipment, optional at different pricing, or unavailable on certain models. This chart is only a guide.

## Paint Colors

| | Code |
|---|---|
| Tuxedo Black | 900* |
| Seafoam Green | 903 |
| Arbor Green Met. | 905 |
| Jewel Blue Met. | 912* |
| Midnight Blue Metallic | 914 |
| Twilight Turquoise Met. | 915 |
| Seamist Turquoise | 917 |
| Fawn Beige Metallic | 920* |
| Roman Red | 923* |
| Coronna Cream | 925 |
| Ermine White | 936* |
| Almond Beige | 938 |
| Sateen Silver Metallic | 940* |
| Shadow Gray Metallic | 941 |
| Honduras Maroon Met. | 948* |

*Available on Corvette also.

# Corvair

*"The sporty side of Chevrolet's new world of worth!"*

**Nameplate year of origin:** 1960.
**Current bodystyle lifespan:** 1960 through 1964.
**Predecessor to this model:** None.
**Replacement for this model:** Corvair (1965 to 1969).
**Percentage of division's sales volume:** 14.22%.
**Corporate siblings:** None.
**Primary competition:** Rambler American, Ford Falcon, Plymouth Valiant and Studebaker Lark.
**Notable changes:** Revised trim and detail changes.
**Major standard equipment:** Cloth and vinyl front bench seat, left-hand sun visor, turn signals, center dome light, electric windshield wipers, and 6.50 × 13 BSW tires. 700 adds: Luggage compartment trim, color-keyed floor mats, dual horns, and automatic dome lamp switch. Monza adds: All-vinyl bucket seats, folding rear seat, dual sun visors, glove box light, and additional exterior chrome trim.

## Measurements

| | Cars | Wagons |
|---|---|---|
| Wheelbase | 108.0" | 108.0" |
| Length | 180.0" | 180.0" |
| Width | 67.0" | 67.0" |
| Height | 51.5" | 51.8" |
| Legroom — front | 44.0" | 44.0" |
| Legroom — rear | 36.5" | 36.5" |
| Headroom — front | 33.5" | 33.5" |
| Headroom — rear | 33.5" | 33.8" |
| Cargo capacity (cu. ft.) | 13.0 | 58.0 |
| Fuel capacity (gals.) | 14.0 | 14.0 |

## Models Available

| | Style Number | Base MSRP | Change from LY | Shipping Wt. (lbs.) | Production | Change from LY |
|---|---|---|---|---|---|---|
| Corvair 500 2-Door Club Coupe | 0527 | $1,992 | +3.75% | 2350 | 16,245 | -3.63% |
| Corvair 700 2-Door Club Coupe | 0727 | $2,057 | +3.63% | 2390 | 18,474 | -25.47% |
| Corvair 700 4-Door Sedan | 0769 | $2,111 | +3.53% | 2410 | 35,368 | -31.92% |

| | Style Number | Base MSRP | Change from LY | Shipping Wt. (lbs.) | Production | Change from LY |
|---|---|---|---|---|---|---|
| Corvair 700 Lakewood 4-Dr. Wagon | 0735 | $2,407 | +3.26% | 2590 | 3,716 | -81.83% |
| Corvair Monza 2-Door Club Coupe | 0927 | $2,273 | +3.27% | 2440 | 151,738 | +38.01% |
| Corvair Monza 2-Door Convertible | 0967 | $2,483 | NEW | 2625 | 16,569 | NEW |
| Corvair Monza 4-Door Sedan | 0969 | $2,273 | +3.27% | 2455 | 48,059 | +42.42% |
| Corvair Monza Lakewood 4-Dr. Wgn. | 0935 | $2,569 | NEW | 2590 | 2,362 | NEW |
| TOTALS | | Avg. price $2,271 | +7.38% | | Production 292,531 | +3.71% |

# Chevy II

*"Modern basic transportation in a totally new line of cars!"*

**Nameplate year of origin:** 1962.
**Current bodystyle lifespan:** 1962 through 1965.
**Predecessor to this model:** None.
**Replacement for this model:** Chevy II (1966 through 1967).
**Percentage of division's sales volume:** 15.87%.
**Corporate siblings:** None.
**Primary competition:** Rambler American, Ford Falcon, Plymouth Valiant, and Studebaker Lark.
**Notable changes:** All-new model for 1962.
**Major standard equipment:** Cloth and vinyl front bench seat, left-hand sun visor, turn signals, center dome light, electric windshield wipers, and 6.00 × 13 BSW tires (6.50 × 13 BSW tires on wagons). 300 adds: Luggage compartment trim, color-keyed floor mats, dual horns, and automatic dome lamp switch. Nova adds: Dual sun visors, glove box light, additional exterior chrome trim, and 6.50 × 13 BSW tires.

## Measurements

| | Cars | Wagons |
|---|---|---|
| Wheelbase | 110.0" | 110.0" |
| Length | 183.0" | 187.4" |
| Width | 70.8" | 70.8" |
| Height (Sedan) | 55.0" | 55.1" |
| Legroom — front | 43.5" | 43.5" |
| Legroom — rear | 38.5" | 38.3" |
| Headroom — front | 39.0" | 39.0" |
| Headroom — rear | 38.0" | 38.2" |
| Cargo capacity (cu. ft.) | 25.5 | 76.2 |
| Fuel capacity (gals.) | 16.0 | 16.0 |

## Models Available

| | Style Number | Base MSRP | Change from LY | Shipping Wt. (lbs.) | Production | Change from LY |
|---|---|---|---|---|---|---|
| Chevy II 100 2-Door Coupe | 0111 | $2,003 | NEW | 2410 | * | NEW |
| Chevy II 100 4-Door Sedan | 0169 | $2,041 | NEW | 2445 | * | NEW |
| Chevy II 100 4-Door Wagon | 0235 | $2,399 | NEW | 2755 | * | NEW |
| Chevy II 300 2-Door Coupe | 0311 | $2,084 | NEW | 2425 | * | NEW |
| Chevy II 300 4-Door Sedan | 0369 | $2,122 | NEW | 2460 | * | NEW |
| Chevy II 300 4-Door Wagon | 0345 | $2,517 | NEW | 2765 | * | NEW |
| Chevy II Nova 400 2-Door Sedan | 0441 | $2,198 | NEW | 2540 | 44,390 | NEW |
| Chevy II Nova 400 2-Door HT | 0437 | $2,264 | NEW | 2550 | 59,586 | NEW |
| Chevy II Nova 400 2-Door Conv. | 0467 | $2,475 | NEW | 2745 | 23,741 | NEW |
| Chevy II Nova 400 4-Door Sedan | 0449 | $2,236 | NEW | 2575 | 139,004 | NEW |
| Chevy II Nova 400 4-Door Wagon | 0435 | $2,497 | NEW | 2775 | 59,886 | NEW |
| TOTALS | | Avg. price $2,258 | NEW | | Production 326,607 | NEW |

*Production by series not available. Figures given are by body style totals for all series.

# Chevrolet Full-Size

*"Rich new styling with a jet-smooth ride!"*

**1962**

**Nameplate year of origin:** Impala 1958; BelAir 1950; Biscayne 1958.
**Current bodystyle lifespan:** 1961 through 1964.
**Predecessor to this model:** Biscayne/BelAir/Impala (1959 to 1960).
**Replacement for this model:** Biscayne/BelAir/Impala/Caprice (1965 to 1966).
**Percentage of division's sales volume:** 69.20%.
**Corporate siblings:** Buick LeSabre/Wildcat, Olds 88, Pontiac Catalina/Star Chief/Bonneville.
**Primary competition:** Rambler Ambassador, Dodge Polara, Ford Custom/Galaxie, and Plymouth Fury.
**Notable changes:** Revised front and rear end styling.
**Major standard equipment:** Biscayne: Nylon pattern cloth seat upholstery, foam cushion front seats, front door armrests, dual sun visors, electric windshield wipers, cigar lighter, glove compartment lock and 7.00 × 14 BSW tires (8.00 × 14 BSW tires on wagons). BelAir adds: Cloth headliner, foam cushion front and rear seats, front and rear door armrests, combination carpet and vinyl coated rubber floor mats, interior lighting, and 7.50 × 14 BSW tires. Impala adds: Vinyl upholstery in convertible, vinyl headliner (cloth in 4-Door Sedan), electric clock, full-carpeting, and dual backup lamps.

## Measurements

|  | Cars | Wagons |
|---|---|---|
| Wheelbase | 119.0" | 119.0" |
| Length | 209.6" | 209.6" |
| Width | 79.0" | 79.0" |
| Height | 55.5" | 55.8" |
| Legroom — front | 45.0" | 45.0" |
| Legroom — rear | 42.0" | 41.8" |
| Headroom — front | 34.5" | 34.5" |
| Headroom — rear | 34.0" | 34.2" |
| Cargo capacity (cu. ft.) | NA | 97.5 |
| Fuel capacity (gals.) | 20.0 | 19.0 |

## Models Available

|  | Style Number | Base MSRP | Change from LY | Shipping Wt. (lbs.) | Production | Change from LY |
|---|---|---|---|---|---|---|
| Biscayne 2-Door Sedan | 1111 | $2,324 | +2.74% | 3405 | * | * |
| Biscayne 4-Door Sedan | 1169 | $2,378 | +2.68% | 3480 | * | * |
| Biscayne 4-Dr., 2-S. Wagon | 1135 | $2,725 | +2.71% | 3845 | * | * |
| Bel Air 2-Door Sedan | 1511 | $2,456 | +3.02% | 3410 | 127,870 | * |
| Bel Air 2-Door Hardtop | 1537 | $2,561 | +2.89% | 3445 | * | * |
| Bel Air 4-Door Sedan | 1569 | $2,510 | +2.95% | 3480 | * | * |
| BelAir 4-Dr., 2-S. Wagon | 1535 | $2,819 | +2.62% | 3845 | * | * |
| BelAir 4-Dr., 3-S. Wagon | 1545 | $2,922 | +2.53% | 3895 | * | * |
| Impala 2-Door Sport Coupe | 1747 | $2,669 | +2.77% | 3455 | 323,427 | 81.73% |
| Impala 2-Door Convertible | 1767 | $2,919 | +2.53% | 3565 | 75,719 | 17.17% |
| Impala 4-Door Sedan | 1769 | $2,662 | +2.78% | 3510 | 533,349 | 17.93% |
| Impala 4-Door Hardtop | 1739 | $2,734 | +2.70% | 3540 | 176,077 | 1.11% |
| Impala 4-Dr., 2-S. Wagon | 1735 | $2,961 | +2.49% | 3870 | 187,566 | 11.03% |
| Impala 4-Dr., 3-S. Wagon | 1745 | $3,064 | +2.41% | 3925 | * | * |
| TOTALS | | *Avg. price* $2,693 | +5.07% | | *Production* 1,424,008 | +19.47% |

*Production by series not available. Figures given are by body style totals for all series.*

# Corvette

*"New power, New profile for America's sports car!"*

**Nameplate year of origin:** 1953 (Also used on show car of same year).
**Current bodystyle lifespan:** 1956 through 1962.
**Predecessor to this model:** Corvette (1953 to 1955).
**Replacement for this model:** Corvette (1963 to 1967).

## Measurements

| | |
|---|---|
| Wheelbase | 102.0" |
| Length | 176.7" |
| Width | 70.4" |

**Percentage of division's sales volume:** 0.71%.
**Corporate siblings:** None.
**Primary competition:** None.
**Notable changes:** New grille, revised trim and detail changes.
**Major standard equipment:** Deep-contoured bucket seats, deep-pile carpeting, complete instrumentation, Manually-operated folding top or removable hard-top, and 6.70 × 15 BSW tires.

## Measurements (cont.)

| | |
|---|---|
| Height | 52.2" |
| Legroom — front | 46.4" |
| Legroom — rear | NA |
| Headroom — front | 33.5" |
| Headroom — rear | NA |
| Cargo capacity (cu. ft.) | NA |
| Fuel capacity (gals.) | 16.4 |

## Models Available

| | Style Number | Base MSRP | Change from LY | Shipping Wt. (lbs.) | Production | Change from LY |
|---|---|---|---|---|---|---|
| Corvette 2-Door Convertible | 0867 | $4,038 | +2.64% | 2925 | 14,531 | +32.84% |
| TOTALS | | *Avg. price* $4,038 | +2.64% | *Production* | 14,531 | +32.84% |

# CHRYSLER

*"Each series is a Chrysler's worth of big full-size comfort. No jr. editions to compromise your investments!"*

The car that took the tailfin idea and ran with it, creating the beautifully finned line of 1957 cars, suddenly had no fins — not so much as a trace. The new 1962 models looked the same as the 1961 models from the front, but one look at the rear identified these as new models. The rear fenders were shaved off smooth with the rear deck lid level, which was raised slightly. Taillamps were placed in the fender ends starting on top of the fender and wrapping down the edge to a vertical stem on the back of the fender. Wagons carried a variation of the 1961 models' lower wrap-around lights. The remainder of the body styling continued to be based on the 1960 line, including the wagons' 4-Door Hardtop styling. This would also be the last year for two different wheelbases, as next year would see all models go to the 122" wheelbase.

Two fateful mistakes were made in regards to the 300 line this year. First, the 300-H letter series was moved to the smaller Newport platform, presumably because all 2-Doors in the New Yorker line, which had previously shared the 300 letter cars' bodies, were eliminated. This was the first time the 2-Door New Yorker models were pulled from the line, although they would return by 1965. Secondly, taking advantage of the well-known performance nameplate "300," Chrysler made a soon-to-be tragic error by watering the 300 nameplate down and placing it on a mid-range line. Essentially, the new non–letter series 300 replaced the 1961 Windsor line. The thinking was that the public would perceive these cars as having the prestige and performance of the 300 letter series, but the public should have been given more credit. Sales initially improved, but after several years they began to fall again, and eventually the mid-range Chrysler would be replaced by a higher trim level Newport line. For the time being, the new 300 line had the appearance of a "real" 300, with the exception of the 4-Door model, which wasn't fooling anyone. A 2-Door convertible replaced the 4-Door Sedan in the model lineup, and at least the 4-Door 300 was a hardtop, so it could pretend to be sporty!

300 2-Door Hardtop

Newport 4-Door Hardtop

Newport 2-Door Convertible

New Yorker Town & Country 9-passenger,
4-Door Wagon

**Model year production:** 127,678, up 32.37% over 1961.
**Domestic market share:** 1.92% (11th place).
**Base price range:** $2,964 to $5,461.
**Industry average base price:** $3,025.
**Chrysler average base price:** $3,916.
**Introduction date:** September 1961.
**Assembly plants:** Detroit (Jefferson Ave.) MI (3).

**Data plate identification:** Ten digit code read as follows: 1st digit is make identity letter (8 = Chrysler); 2nd number identifies series (1 through 7; Newport is 1); 3rd digit 2 for 1962; 4th digit is assembly plant code; followed by 100001 and up for serial number. Body style identification found on separate plate. *Example:* 8123100001 is a 1962 Chrysler Newport, serial number 100001, built in Detroit, MI.

## Powertrains

| Engine | Gross HP | Transmission Availability | Newport | 300 | New Yorker | 300-H |
|---|---|---|---|---|---|---|
| 361 CID, 2-bbl., V8 | 265 | 3-speed manual | S | - | - | - |
| | | Torqueflite automatic | $227 | - | - | - |
| 383 CID, 2-bbl., V8 | 305 | 3-speed manual | - | S | - | - |
| | | Torqueflite automatic | - | $227 | - | - |
| 413 CID, 4-bbl., V8 | 340 | Torqueflite automatic | - | $389 | S | - |
| 413 CID Long Ram, 2 × 4-bbl., V8 | 380 | Torqueflite automatic | - | $713 | $486 | S |
| 413 CID Short Ram, 2 × 4-bbl., V8 | 405 | Torqueflite automatic | - | - | - | $ |

## Major Options

| | Newport | 300 | New Yorker | 300-H |
|---|---|---|---|---|
| Heater and defroster | $102 | $102 | $102 | $102 |
| Airtemp air conditioning | $510 | $510 | $510 | $510 |
| Solex tinted glass | $43 | $43 | $43 | $43 |

## Paint Colors

| | Code |
|---|---|
| Formal Black | BB-1 |
| Dawn Blue | CC-1 |
| Sapphire Blue Metallic | DD-1 |

| | Newport | 300 | New Yorker | 300-H | | | Code |
|---|---|---|---|---|---|---|---|
| Auto Pilot cruise control | $86 | $86 | $86 | $86 | Willow Green | | FF-1 |
| Power steering | $108 | $108 | S | S | Sage Green Metallic | | GG-1 |
| Power brakes | $48 | $48 | S | S | Bermuda Turquoise | | JJ-1 |
| Power seat | $102 | $102 | $102 | S | Limelight | | LL-1 |
| Power windows | $108 | $108 | S | S | Dove Gray | | MM-1 |
| Golden Touch Tone AM radio | $93 | $93 | $93 | $93 | Festival Red | | PP-1 |
| White sidewall tires — std. sizes | $42 | $46 | $51 | S | Coral Gray | | TT-1 |
| | | | | | Seascape | | VV-1 |
| | | | | | Oyster White | | WW-1 |
| | | | | | Rosewood Metallic | | YY-1 |
| | | | | | Caramel | | ZZ-1 |

Options common to most models. (S = Standard equipment.) Items may be standard equipment, optional at different pricing, or unavailable on certain models. This chart is only a guide.

# Newport

*"Still the easiest-to-own Chrysler, with a low price that's again surprising everybody."*

**Nameplate year of origin:** 1961 (as series), 1950 (as Hardtop model designation).

**Current bodystyle lifespan:** Windsor 1960; Newport 1961 through 1964, with major restyle in 1963.

**Predecessor to this model:** Windsor (1957 to 1959).

**Replacement for this model:** Newport (1965 to 1966).

**Percentage of division's sales volume:** 65.10%.

**Corporate siblings:** Dodge Custom 880, Chrysler 300 and 300-H.

**Primary competition:** Buick Invicta, Mercury Monterey and Oldsmobile Super 88.

**Notable changes:** Rear end restyled and minor trim and detail changes.

**Major standard equipment:** Cloth and vinyl front bench seat, full-floor coverings, sun visors, exterior bright side moldings and 8.00 × 14 BSW tires. Town & Country adds: 8.50 × 14 BSW tires.

## Measurements

| | Cars | Wagons |
|---|---|---|
| Wheelbase | 122.0" | 122.0" |
| Length | 214.9" | 216.4" |
| Width | 79.4" | 80.0" |
| Height | 55.2" | 55.2" |
| Legroom — front | 45.8" | 45.8" |
| Legroom — rear | 40.6" | 40.5" |
| Headroom — front | 37.8" | 37.8" |
| Headroom — rear | 33.6" | 34.0" |
| Cargo capacity (cu. ft.) | 33.0 | 95.0 |
| Fuel capacity (gals.) | 23.0 | 21.0 |

## Models Available

| | Style Number | Base MSRP | Change from LY | Shipping Wt. (lbs.) | Production | Change from LY |
|---|---|---|---|---|---|---|
| Newport 2-Door Hardtop | 812 | $3,027 | 0.00% | 3650 | 11,910 | +26.63% |
| Newport 2-Door Convertible | 815 | $3,399 | -1.31% | 3740 | 2,051 | -3.93% |
| Newport 4-Door Sedan | 813 | $2,964 | 0.00% | 3690 | 54,813 | +59.48% |
| Newport 4-Door Hardtop | 814 | $3,106 | 0.00% | 3715 | 8,712 | +11.85% |
| N. Town & Country 4-Dr., 2-S. Wgn. | 858 | $3,478 | -1.83% | 4060 | 3,271 | +78.55% |
| N. Town & Country 4-Dr., 3-S. Wgn. | 859 | $3,586 | -1.05% | 4090 | 2,363 | +50.41% |
| TOTALS | | *Avg. price* $3,260 | -0.77% | *Production* 83,120 | | +45.56% |

# 300

*"A high-performance sports series in a new popular price range, direct descendant of the fabulous cars with an unequalled seven-year performance record."*

**Nameplate year of origin:** 1955 (1962 as non-letter series).

**Current bodystyle lifespan:** Saratoga 1960; Windsor 1961; 300 1962 through 1964, with major restyle in 1963.

## Measurements

| | |
|---|---|
| Wheelbase | 122.0" |
| Length | 214.9" |

**Predecessor to this model:** Saratoga (1957 to 1959).
**Replacement for this model:** 300 (1965 to 1966).
**Percentage of division's sales volume:** 18.62%.
**Corporate siblings:** Dodge Custom 880, Chrysler Newport and 300-H.
**Primary competition:** Buick Invicta, Mercury Monterey S-55 and Oldsmobile Super 88.
**Notable changes:** Rear end restyled and minor trim and detail changes.
**Major standard equipment:** Cloth and vinyl front bench seat, pile carpeting, padded dash, map lights, electric clock, sun visors, exterior bright side moldings, power steering, power brakes, automatic transmission, full wheel covers, and 8.00 × 14 BSW tires.

### Measurements (cont.)

| | |
|---|---|
| Width | 79.4" |
| Height | 55.2" |
| Legroom — front | 45.8" |
| Legroom — rear | 40.6" |
| Headroom — front | 37.8" |
| Headroom — rear | 33.6" |
| Cargo capacity (cu. ft.) | 33.0 |
| Fuel capacity (gals.) | 23.0 |

**1962**

## Models Available

| | Style Number | Base MSRP | Change from LY | Shipping Wt. (lbs.) | Production | Change from LY |
|---|---|---|---|---|---|---|
| 300 2-Door Hardtop | 822 | $3,323 | 0.54% | 3750 | 11,776 | 300.41% |
| 300 2-Door Convertible | 825 | $3,883 | NEW | 3815 | 1,971 | NEW |
| 300 4-Door Hardtop | 824 | $3,400 | 0.92% | 3760 | 10,030 | 141.34% |
| TOTALS | | Avg. price $3,535 | +7.19% | | Production 23,777 | +37.15% |

# New Yorker

*"The great New Yorker, the most luxurious Chrysler."*

**Nameplate year of origin:** 1939 (altered from 1938 New York Special model).
**Current bodystyle lifespan:** New Yorker (1960 through 1964 — major restyle in 1963).
**Predecessor to this model:** New Yorker (1957 to 1959).
**Replacement for this model:** New Yorker (1965 to 1966).
**Percentage of division's sales volume:** 15.84%.
**Corporate siblings:** Chrysler Newport and 300 (shorter wheelbase models).
**Primary competition:** Buick Electra, and Oldsmobile 98.
**Notable changes:** Rear end restyled and minor trim and detail changes.
**Major standard equipment:** Cloth and vinyl front bench seat, pile carpeting, padded dash, map lights, power windows, electric clock, sun visors, exclusive exterior bright trim, power steering, power brakes, automatic transmission, full wheel covers, and 8.50 × 14 BSW tires. Town & Country adds: 9.00 × 14 BSW tires.

### Measurements

| | Cars | Wagons |
|---|---|---|
| Wheelbase | 126.0" | 126.0" |
| Length | 219.3" | 220.4" |
| Width | 79.4" | 80.0" |
| Height | 55.4" | 55.4" |
| Legroom — front | 45.8" | 46.2" |
| Legroom — rear | 40.6" | 40.6" |
| Headroom — front | 37.2" | 37.2" |
| Headroom — rear | 33.6" | 33.8" |
| Cargo capacity (cu. ft.) | NA | 95.0 |
| Fuel capacity (gals.) | 23.0 | 21.0 |

## Models Available

| | Style Number | Base MSRP | Change from LY | Shipping Wt. (lbs.) | Production | Change from LY |
|---|---|---|---|---|---|---|
| New Yorker 4-Door Sedan | 833 | $4,125 | 0.00% | 3925 | 12,056 | +20.75% |
| New Yorker 4-Door Hardtop | 834 | $4,263 | 0.00% | 4005 | 6,646 | +13.37% |
| N. Y. Town & Country 4-Dr., 2-S. W. | 878 | $4,766 | 0.00% | 4425 | 728 | +7.69% |
| N. Y. Town & Country 4-Dr., 3-S. W. | 879 | $4,873 | 0.00% | 4445 | 793 | +4.34% |
| TOTALS | | Avg. price $4,507 | +0.92% | | Production 20,223 | -0.87% |

# 300-H

*"The high-performance luxury Chrysler."*

**Nameplate year of origin:** 1955.
**Current bodystyle lifespan:** 1960 through 1964, with major restyle in 1963.
**Predecessor to this model:** 300 letter series (1957 to 1959).
**Replacement for this model:** 300-L (1965).
**Percentage of division's sales volume:** 0.44%.
**Corporate siblings:** Dodge Custom 880, Chrysler Newport and 300.
**Primary competition:** Ford Thunderbird.
**Notable changes:** Rear end restyled and minor trim and detail changes, now based on Newport platform.
**Major standard equipment:** Leather power bucket front seats, pile carpeting, padded dash, map lights, power windows, electric clock, sun visors, exclusive exterior bright trim, power steering, power brakes, automatic transmission, full wheel covers, and 7.60 × 15 WSW tires.

## Measurements

| | |
|---|---|
| Wheelbase | 122.0" |
| Length | 214.9" |
| Width | 79.4" |
| Height | 55.5" |
| Legroom — front | 45.6" |
| Legroom — rear | 35.2" |
| Headroom — front | 37.4" |
| Headroom — rear | 34.3" |
| Cargo capacity (cu. ft.) | 33.0 |
| Fuel capacity (gals.) | 23.0 |

## Models Available

| | Style Number | Base MSRP | Change from LY | Shipping Wt. (lbs.) | Production | Change from LY |
|---|---|---|---|---|---|---|
| 300-H 2-Door Hardtop | 842 | $5,090 | -5.97% | 4010 | 435 | -66.02% |
| 300-H 2-Door Convertible | 845 | $5,461 | -6.54% | 4080 | 123 | -63.50% |
| TOTALS | | *Avg. price* $5,276 | -6.26% | | *Production* 558 | -65.50% |

# DODGE

*"The New Lean Breed!"*

Dodge for 1962 was out to give its sister division Plymouth a run for its money. This situation came about through some tactful lobbying by certain people with Dodge division, including many dealers. The problem, as seen by those at Dodge, was that Plymouth was traditionally the low-price make, and Chrysler the upper- medium-price brand. With DeSoto gone as the medium-price make, Chrysler had moved down to fill the gap with the Newport. This put the Newport in competition with the upper trim-level Dodge models. Therefore, Dodge reasoned that they should be allowed to move down in price range to allow for higher volume for its dealers, and hopefully in return, higher profits.

The first phase of this strategy was the 1961 Lancer. A twin to the Plymouth Valiant, the Lancer was slightly larger and more nicely trimmed, for just a few dollars more than the Valiant. The second part was the introduction of a new smaller Plymouth and Dodge "full-size" car. This new full-size model was actually more of an intermediate or mid-size car, in comparison with other full-size models of the day. Riding on a 116-inch wheelbase, these new cars were lighter, more economical, and better handling than any other full-size model. Unfortunately for both Dodge and Plymouth, sales of these new "down-sized" models went nowhere. Perhaps the styling was as much to blame as the smaller size, because the restyled models for 1963 were much more successful. For Dodge, the 1962 front end consisted of a trapezoid shaped grille, with one set of headlights set within the grille area, and the second set placed at a lower level outside of the grille area on the leading edge of the front fender.

A feature line ran from the top of the grille, horizontally along the front fender edge and ended just short of the back end of the front door. A rear quarter feature line started at the rocker panel in front of the rear wheel, went up and over the top curve of the wheel opening, then straight back to meet the round backup light housing at the rear end. Below each backup lamp was a single taillamp. Overall, the body styling was an enlarged copy of the Valiant. The engine choices were much the same as previous years, with the exception of the temporary dropping of the 383 CID V8 engine. The model line was much the same also, with a few name changes and one new line. The Dart Seneca became the Dart, the Dart Pioneer was known as the Dart 330, and the Dart Phoenix line was now the Dart 440. The Polara 500 was a new top line designation for a three-model series of hardtops and a convertible.

New for the model year was the Custom 880, which essentially was a 1961 Polara front clip placed onto the Chrysler Newport body. This clever body sharing trick actually made a nicer looking car than the 1961 Polara. The Custom 880 was priced the same as the Chrysler Newport and served a dual purpose: it provided a replacement for the DeSoto line, and it gave Dodge dealers a traditional full-size model to sell beside their new downsized models. Changes to the compact Lancer were limited to a few trim changes and rebadging the 770 Hardtop as a Lancer GT model.

**1962**

Custom 880 4-Door Wagon

Dart 440 2-Door Hardtop

Dart 440 4-Door Sedan

Dart 2-Door Sedan

Dart 440 4-Door Wagon

Lancer 770 4-Door Wagon

**Model year production:** 230,200, down 0.28% from 1961.
**Domestic market share:** 3.46% (9th place).
**Base price range:** $1,951 to $3,407.
**Industry average base price:** $3,025.
**Dodge average base price:** $2,653.
**Introduction date:** September 1961.
**Assembly plants:** Lynch Road, MI (A); Hamtramck, MI (B); Detroit (Jefferson Ave.) MI (C); Belvidere, IL (D); Los Angeles, CA (E); Newark, DE (F); St. Louis, MO (G); Windsor, Ontario, Canada (R).

**Data plate identification:** Ten digit code read as follows: Four digit style number (see listings below) in which 1st digit is series letter (e.g., 5 = Polara V8 series), 2nd number identifies trim grade (L is for base trim, M for Mid-level, etc.), 3rd digit 2 for 1962, and 4th digit is assembly plant code; followed by 100001 and up for serial number. Body style identification found on separate plate. *Example:* 532C100001 is a 1962 Dodge Polara with a 361 CID V8 engine, serial number 100001, built in Detroit, MI.

## Powertrains

| Engine | Gross HP | Transmission Availability | Lancer | Dart | Polara | Custom 880 |
|---|---|---|---|---|---|---|
| 170 CID, 1-bbl., 6-cyl. | 101 | 3-speed manual | S | - | - | - |
| | | Torqueflite automatic | $172 | - | - | - |
| 225 CID Aluminum, 1-bbl., 6-cyl | 145 | 3-speed manual | $47** | S[2] | - | - |
| | | Torqueflite automatic | $219 | $192[2] | - | - |
| 225 CID Hyper-Pak, 4-bbl., 6-cyl. | 195 | 3-speed manual | $ | - | - | - |
| | | Torqueflite automatic | $ | - | - | - |

| Engine | Gross HP | Transmission Availability | Lancer | Dart | Polara | Custom 880 |
|---|---|---|---|---|---|---|
| 318 CID Dart, 2-bbl., V8 | 230 | 3-speed manual | - | S[1]/$107[2] | - | - |
|  |  | 4-speed manual | - | $146[1]/$253[2] | - | - |
|  |  | Torqueflite automatic | - | $211[1]/$318[2] | - | - |
| 361 CID Polara, 4-bbl., V8 | 305 | 3-speed manual | - | $59[1]/$166[2] | S | S |
|  |  | 4-speed manual | - | $205[1]/$312[2] | $146 | $146 |
|  |  | Torqueflite automatic | - | $270[1]/$377[2] | $211 | $211 |
| 413 CID Ramcharger, 4-bbl., V8 | 410 |  | - | * | * | - |
| 413 CID Ramcharger, 2 × 4-bbl., V8 | 415 |  | - | * | * | - |

[1]330 9-passenger wagon, 440 Wagon models, and 440 4-Door Hardtop and Convertible only.  [2]All models but 330 9-passenger Wagon, 440 Wagon models, and 440 4-door Hardtop and Convertible.  *Accurate pricing information unavailable.  **Standard on GT Coupe.

## Major Options

| | Lancer | Dart | Polara | Custom 880 |
|---|---|---|---|---|
| Heater and defroster | $74 | $74 | $74 | S |
| Airtemp air conditioning | $425 | $445 | $445 | $445 |
| Tinted glass | $24 | $30 | $30 | $24 |
| Power steering | $73 | $77 | $77 | $77 |
| Power brakes | $43 | $43 | $43 | $43 |
| Power seat | - | $96 | $96 | $96 |
| Power windows | - | $102 | $102 | $102 |
| Electric clock | $16 | $16 | $16 | $16 |
| Music Master AM radio | $169 | $58 | $58 | $58 |
| White sidewall tires — std. sizes | $29 | $33–$48 | $33–$48 | $33–$48 |

Options common to most models. (- = Not Available, S = Standard equipment.) Item may be standard equipment, optional at different pricing, or unavailable on certain models. This chart is only a guide.

## Paint Colors

| | Code |
|---|---|
| Flax | AA-1 |
| Onyx | BB-1 |
| Powder Blue | CC-1 |
| Medium Blue Metallic | DD-1 |
| Cobalt Blue Metallic | EE-1 |
| Light Green | FF-1 |
| Glade Green Metallic | GG-1 |
| Metallic Emerald Metallic | HH-1 |
| Pearl Gray | MM-1 |
| Vermilion | PP-1 |
| Dusty Rose Metallic | RR-1 |
| Deep Cordovan Metallic | SS-1 |
| Buff | TT-1 |
| Shell Beige | UU-1 |
| Polar White | WW-1 |
| Nutmeg Brown Metallic | YY-1 |

# Lancer

*"This compact Dodge packs a wallop."*

**Nameplate year of origin:** 1961.
**Current bodystyle lifespan:** 1961 through 1962.
**Predecessor to this model:** None.
**Replacement for this model:** Dart (1963 to 1966).
**Percentage of division's sales volume:** 27.93%.
**Corporate siblings:** Plymouth Valiant.
**Primary competition:** Buick Special, Mercury Comet, Oldsmobile F-85, Pontiac Tempest and Studebaker Lark.
**Notable changes:** Minor trim and detail changes.
**Major standard equipment:** Cloth and vinyl front bench seats, rubber floor mats, chrome windshield trim and 6.50 × 13 BSW tires. 770 adds: Color-keyed floor covering, full-vinyl door coverings, additional interior and exterior bright trim.

## Measurements

| | Cars | Wagons |
|---|---|---|
| Wheelbase | 106.5" | 106.5" |
| Length | 188.8" | 188.8" |
| Width | 72.3" | 72.3" |
| Height | 53.3" | 53.8" |
| Legroom — front | 42.8" | 42.8" |
| Legroom — rear | 39.8" | 39.8" |
| Headroom — front | 33.3" | 33.3" |
| Headroom — rear | 33.5" | NA |
| Cargo capacity (cu. ft.) | 24.8 | 72.0 |
| Fuel capacity (gals.) | 13.0 | 13.0 |

## Models Available

| | Style Number | Base MSRP | Change from LY | Shipping Wt. (lbs.) | Production | Change from LY |
|---|---|---|---|---|---|---|
| Lancer 170 2-Door Sedan | 711 | $1,951 | -1.51% | 2495 | 17,100 | -17.79% |
| Lancer 170 4-Door Sedan | 713 | $2,011 | -1.57% | 2525 | * | * |
| Lancer 170 4-Door, 2-Seat Wagon | 756 | $2,306 | -2.12% | 2685 | * | * |
| Lancer 770 2-Door Sedan | 731 | $2,052 | -1.20% | 2520 | 26,100 | -28.98% |
| Lancer 770 4-Door Sedan | 733 | $2,114 | -1.17% | 2540 | * | * |
| Lancer 770 4-Door, 2-Seat Wagon | 776 | $2,408 | -1.75% | 2705 | 7,000 | -27.84% |
| Lancer GT 2-Door Hardtop | 742 | $2,257 | +4.20% | 2560 | 14,100 | +86.71% |
| TOTALS | Avg. price | $2,157 | -0.74% | Production | 64,300* | -14.04% |

*Production figure estimates available only by body style.*

# Dart

*"A new lean breed of Dodge."*

**Nameplate year of origin:** 1960.

**Current bodystyle lifespan:** 1962 through 1965 (330 and 440 from 1963 to 1964; Coronet in 1965).

**Predecessor to this model:** Dart Seneca and Pioneer (1960 to 1961).

**Replacement for this model:** Coronet (1966 to 1967).

**Percentage of division's sales volume:** 59.04%.

**Corporate siblings:** Plymouth Fury.

**Primary competition:** AMC Classic, Chevrolet Biscayne/BelAir and Ford Galaxie.

**Notable changes:** Completely redesigned.

**Major standard equipment:** Cloth-and-vinyl bench seat, full rubber floor mats, electric windshield wipers, dual sun visors, exterior bright trim around windshield and back window, and 6.50 × 14 BSW tires. 440 adds: Full-carpeting, exterior bright trim around side windows and body sides. Polara adds: additional exterior brightwork, deluxe interior trim, and 7.00 × 14 BSW tires.

## Measurements

| | Cars | Wagons |
|---|---|---|
| Wheelbase | 116.0" | 116.0" |
| Length | 202.2" | 210.7" |
| Width | 76.5" | 76.5" |
| Height | 53.7" | 54.0" |
| Legroom — front | 46.0" | 46.0" |
| Legroom — rear | 39.1" | 39.0" |
| Headroom — front | 33.5" | 33.5" |
| Headroom — rear | 33.5" | 33.5" |
| Cargo capacity (cu. ft.) | NA | 84.4 |
| Fuel capacity (gals.) | 20.0 | 20.0 |

## Models Available

| | Style Number | Base MSRP | Change from LY | Shipping Wt. (lbs.) | Production | Change from LY |
|---|---|---|---|---|---|---|
| Fleet Special 2-Door Sedan | 401 | $2,158 | NEW | NA | * | NEW |
| Fleet Special 4-Door Sedan | 403 | $2,214 | NEW | NA | * | NEW |
| Dart 2-Door Sedan | 411 | $2,241 | -1.71% | 2970 | 48,200 | -27.08% |
| Dart 4-Door Sedan | 413 | $2,297 | -1.50% | 3000 | * | * |
| Dart 4-Dr., 2-S. Wagon | 456 | $2,644 | -1.97% | 3270 | * | * |
| Dart 330 2-Door Sedan | 421 | $2,375 | -1.53% | 2965 | 25,500 | -33.94% |
| Dart 330 2-Door Hardtop | 422 | $2,463 | -1.08% | 2985 | * | * |
| Dart 330 4-Door Sedan | 423 | $2,432 | -1.18% | 3000 | * | * |
| Dart 330 4-Door, 2-Seat Wagon | 466 | $2,739 | -1.79% | 3275 | * | * |
| Dart 330 4-Door, 3-Seat Wagon | 567 | $2,949 | +1.90% | 3500 | * | * |
| Dart 440 2-Door Hardtop | 432 | $2,606 | -0.53% | 3025 | 37,800 | +1.34% |
| Dart 440 2-Door Convertible | 535 | $2,945 | -1.51% | 3285 | * | * |
| Dart 440 4-Door Sedan | 433 | $2,584 | -0.50% | 3045 | * | * |
| Dart 440 4-Door Hardtop | 534 | $2,763 | +3.14% | 3260 | * | * |
| Dart 440 4-Door, 2-Seat Wagon | 576 | $2,989 | NEW | 3460 | 24,400 | NEW |
| Dart 440 4-Door, 3-Seat Wagon | 577 | $3,092 | NEW | 3530 | * | NEW |
| TOTALS | Avg. price | $2,593 | -0.39% | Production | 135,900 | -4.29% |

# Polara 500

*"You'll like what's happened to Dodge."*

**Nameplate year of origin:** 1960.
**Current bodystyle lifespan:** 1962 through 1965 (Coronet in 1965).
**Predecessor to this model:** Dart Phoenix (1960 to 1961).
**Replacement for this model:** Polara (1965 to 1966).
**Percentage of division's sales volume:** 5.43%.
**Corporate siblings:** Plymouth Fury.
**Primary competition:** AMC Ambassador, Chevrolet BelAir/Impala, and Ford Galaxie.
**Notable changes:** Completely redesigned.
**Major standard equipment:** Cloth-and-vinyl bench seat, deluxe interior trim, full-carpeting, exterior bright trim around side windows and body sides, and 7.00 × 14 BSW tires.

## Measurements

| | |
|---|---|
| Wheelbase | 116.0" |
| Length | 202.2" |
| Width | 76.5" |
| Height | 54.0" |
| Legroom — front | 45.9" |
| Legroom — rear | 39.6" |
| Headroom — front | 34.3" |
| Headroom — rear | 33.5" |
| Cargo capacity (cu. ft.) | NA |
| Fuel capacity (gals.) | 20.0 |

## Models Available

| | Style Number | Base MSRP | Change from LY | Shipping Wt. (lbs.) | Production | Change from LY |
|---|---|---|---|---|---|---|
| Polara 500 2-Door Hardtop | 542 | $3,019 | NEW | 3315 | 12,500 | NEW |
| Polara 500 2-Door Convertible | 545 | $3,268 | NEW | 3430 | * | NEW |
| Polara 500 4-Door Hardtop | 544 | $2,960 | NEW | 3360 | * | NEW |
| TOTALS | | Avg. price $3,082 | NEW* | | Production 12,500 | NEW* |

*Polara 500 series is upgraded replacement for former Polara series. Production by body style not available.

# Custom 880

*"Big room. Big ride. Big power."*

**Nameplate year of origin:** 1962.
**Current bodystyle lifespan:** 1962 through 1964.
**Predecessor to this model:** DeSoto (1960 to 1961).
**Replacement for this model:** Custom 880 (1965) and Monaco (1965 to 1966).
**Percentage of division's sales volume:** 7.60%.
**Corporate siblings:** Chrysler Newport and 300.
**Primary competition:** Buick LeSabre, Mercury Montclair, Oldsmobile 88, and Pontiac Catalina/Star Chief/Bonneville.
**Notable changes:** All-new model based on the 1961 DeSoto body with a 1961 Dodge front clip.
**Major standard equipment:** Cloth and vinyl upholstery, full carpeting, glove box lock, dual sunvisors, dome lamp, front and rear armrests, electric windshield wipers and 8.00 × 14 BSW tires.

## Measurements

| | Cars | Wagons |
|---|---|---|
| Wheelbase | 122.0" | 122.0" |
| Length | 214.8" | 216.3" |
| Width | 79.0" | 80.0" |
| Height | 55.2" | 55.9" |
| Legroom — front | 45.8" | 45.8" |
| Legroom — rear | 40.6" | 40.6" |
| Headroom — front | 37.8" | 37.8" |
| Headroom — rear | 33.6" | 34.0" |
| Cargo capacity (cu. ft.) | NA | 91.5 |
| Fuel capacity (gals.) | 23 | 21 |

## Models Available

| | Style Number | Base MSRP | Change from LY | Shipping Wt. (lbs.) | Production | Change from LY |
|---|---|---|---|---|---|---|
| Custom 880 2-Door Hardtop | 612 | $3,030 | -0.13%* | 3615 | 15,400 | +9.75%* |
| Custom 880 2-Door Convertible | 615 | $3,251 | -0.09%* | 3705 | * | * |

| | Style Number | Base MSRP | Change from LY | Shipping Wt. (lbs.) | Production | Change from LY |
|---|---|---|---|---|---|---|
| Custom 880 4-Door Sedan | 613 | $2,964 | -0.13%* | 3655 | * | * |
| Custom 880 4-Door Hardtop | 614 | $3,109 | -0.10%* | 3680 | * | * |
| Custom 880 4-Dr., 2-S. HT Wgn. | 658 | $3,292 | -0.12%* | 4025 | 2,100 | * |
| Custom 880 4-Dr., 3-S. HT Wgn. | 659 | $3,407 | -0.12%* | 4055 | * | * |
| TOTALS | Avg. price | $3,176 | -0.12%* | Production | 17,500 | +9.75%* |

*As compared to 1961 Polara which the Custom 880 replaced. Production by body style not available.

**1962**

---

# FORD

### "Features of the future … now!"

---

Of all the manufacturers marketing a smaller full-size car to a public that proved reluctant for the first few years, Ford had the most success. Plymouth and Dodge had missed the mark by discontinuing (at least temporarily) their regular full-size lines. General Motors had not even bothered with the smaller cars since its senior compacts approached the size of these newcomers. Ford made the smartest choice by introducing its new Fairlane. Styled to look much like the full-size Galaxie line, the new Fairlane came in a basic array of sedan body styles and enjoyed a strong sales year. Power came from a choice of standard six cylinder or small displacement V8 engines. The Fairlane would sell reasonably well until GM took advantage of this new mid-size arena in 1964; thereafter the GM cars would dominate the market for several decades.

Ford's full-size Galaxie was totally restyled again, from the beltline down. A more flatly styled, full-width grille once again dominated the front, while a new, slightly sloping rear treatment still housed a single, large, round taillamp at each side. In between, bodysides were relatively smooth, with Galaxie 500 models featuring large, chrome sweepspears on the sides. Powertrain offerings continued as in previous years. The Galaxie 500 Starliner Hardtop was discontinued this year. The former Fairlane and Fairlane 500 were renamed the Galaxie Mainliner and Galaxie respectively. Galaxie 500 replaced Galaxie as the top line, and a new Galaxie 500 XL was introduced as the sporty alternative to the Chevrolet Impala Super Sport. The new-for-1961 Thunderbird received new trim treatments and gained two new model offerings. A new Landau Hardtop with vinyl roof and a new Sport Roadster Convertible with a tonneau cover over the rear seats were introduced. The popular Falcon featured a new line of Deluxe and Futura models with revised grilles and trim.

Falcon Futura 2-Door Coupe

Falcon Squire 4-Door Wagon

Fairlane 500 4-Door Sedan

Galaxie 500 Sunliner 2-Door Convertible

Thunderbird 2-Door Hardtop

Galaxie 500 4-Door Hardtop

**Model year production:** 1,455,966, up 8.73% over 1961.
**Domestic market share:** 21.88% (2nd place).
**Base price range:** $1,985 to $5,439.
**Industry average base price:** $3,025.
**Ford average base price:** $2,771.
**Introduction date:** September 29, 1961. Thunderbird introduced October 12, 1961. Fairlane introduced November 16, 1961.
**Assembly plants:** Atlanta, GA (A); Chicago, IL (G); Dallas, TX (D); Dearborn, MI (F); Kansas City, MO (K); Lorain, OH (H); Los Angeles, CA (J); Louisville, KY (U); Mahwah, NJ (E); Metuchen, NJ (T); Norfolk, VA (N); San Jose, CA (R); Twin Cities, MN (P); Wayne, MI (W); Wixom, MI (Y); Oakville, Ontario, Can. (B).
**Data plate identification:** Eleven digit code read as follows: 3 for 1963; 2nd digit is assembly plant code; 2-digit model number (see listings below); 5th digit is engine code; 100001 and up for serial number. *Example:* 3Y83Z100001 is a 1963 Ford Thunderbird 2-Door Hardtop with a 390 CID V8 engine, serial number 100001, built in Wixom, MI.

## Powertrains

| Engine | Gross HP | Engine Code | Transmission Availability | Falcon | Fairlane | Full-size | Thunderbird |
|---|---|---|---|---|---|---|---|
| 144 CID, 1-bbl., 6-cyl. | 85 | S | 3-speed manual | S | - | - | - |
|  |  |  | Ford-O-Matic | $163 | - | - | - |
| 170 CID, 1-bbl., 6-cyl. | 101 | U | 3-speed manual | $38 | S | - | - |
|  |  |  | Ford-O-Matic | $201 | $180 | - | - |
| 221 CID, 2-bbl., V8 | 145 | L | 3-speed manual | - | $103 | - | - |
|  |  |  | Overdrive | - | $211 | - | - |
|  |  |  | Ford-O-Matic | - | $283 | - | - |
| 223 CID Mileage Mkr., 1-bbl., 6-cyl. | 138 | V | 3-speed manual | - | - | S* | - |
|  |  |  | Overdrive | - | - | $108* | - |
|  |  |  | Ford-O-Matic | - | - | $190* | - |
| 260 CID, 2-bbl., V8 | 164 | F | 3-speed manual | - | $155 | - | - |
|  |  |  | Overdrive | - | $263 | - | - |
|  |  |  | Ford-O-Matic | - | $335 | - | - |
| 292 CID, 4-bbl., V8 | 170 | W | 3-speed manual | - | - | S (XL)/$116* | - |
|  |  |  | Overdrive | - | - | $108 (XL)/$224* | - |
|  |  |  | Ford-O-Matic | - | - | $190 (XL)/$306* | - |
|  |  |  | Cruise-O-Matic | - | - | $212 (XL)/$328* | - |
| 352 CID Interceptor, 4-bbl., V8 | 220 | X | 3-speed manual | - | - | $52 (XL)/$168* | - |
|  |  |  | Overdrive | - | - | $160 (XL)/$276* | - |
|  |  |  | Ford-O-Matic | - | - | $242 (XL)/$358* | - |
|  |  |  | Cruise-O-Matic | - | - | $264 (XL)/$380* | - |
| 390 CID Interceptor, 2-bbl., V8 | 300 | Z | 3-speed manual | - | - | $138 (XL)/$254* | - |
|  |  |  | Overdrive | - | - | $246 (XL)/$362* | - |
|  |  |  | Cruise-O-Matic | - | - | $350 (XL)/$466* | S |
| 390 CID Thunderbird, 3 × 2-bbl., V8 | 340 | M | Cruise-O-Matic | - | - | - | $242 |
| 390 CID Thunderbird, 4-bbl., V8 | 375 | B | 4-speed manual | - | - | $478 (XL)/$594* | - |
| 390 CID Thunderbird, 3 × 2-bbl., V8 | 401 | G | 4-speed manual | - | - | $544 (XL)/$660* | - |

| Engine | Gross HP | Engine Code | Transmission Availability | Falcon | Fairlane | Full-size | Thunderbird |
|---|---|---|---|---|---|---|---|
| 406 CID Thunderbird, 4-bbl., V8 | 385 | ** | 4-speed manual | - | - | $** | - |
| 406 CID T-Bird Special, 3 × 2-bbl., V8 | 405 | ** | 4-speed manual | - | - | $** | - |

*Except XL.    **Available mid-year. Accurate pricing information not available at this time.*

## Major Options

| | Falcon | Fairlane | Galaxie | Thunderbird |
|---|---|---|---|---|
| Air Conditioning (w/V8) | - | $361 | $361 | $415 |
| Tinted glass | $27 | $40 | $40 | $43 |
| Power steering | - | $82 | $82 | S |
| Power brakes | - | $43 | $43 | S |
| Power driver's seat/Bench seat | - | - | $64 | $184 |
| Power windows | - | - | $102 | $106 |
| AM radio with antenna | $59 | $59 | $59 | S |
| Front bucket seats w/console | $120 | $ | $ | S |
| Swing-Away steering wheel | - | - | - | S |
| Vinyl roof (on select models) | - | $75 | $75 | $ |
| White sidewall tires | $30 | $33 | $33 | $42 |
| Deluxe wheel covers | $16 | $18 | $19 | S |

Options common to most models. (- = Not Available, S = Standard equipment.) Items may be standard equipment, optional at different pricing, or unavailable on certain models. This chart is only a guide.

## Paint Colors

| | Code |
|---|---|
| Raven Black | A |
| Patrician Green Metallic | D |
| Acapulco/Viking Blue Met. | E |
| Baffin/Skymist Blue | F |
| Silver Mink Metallic | G |
| Caspian/Oxford Blue Met. | H |
| Castillian Gold Met. | I |
| Rangoon Red | J |
| Chalfonte Blue | K |
| Sahara Rose | L |
| Corinthian White | M |
| Diamond Blue | N |
| Silver Moss Metallic | P |
| Silver Gray Metallic | Q |
| Tucson Yellow | R |
| Cascade Green Metallic | S |
| Sandshell Beige | T |
| Deep Sea Blue Metallic | U |
| Chestnut Metallic | V |
| Heritage Burgundy Metallic | X |
| Fieldstone Tan Metallic | Z |

# Falcon

*"Falcon offers savings that start with a low, low price tag."*

**Nameplate year of origin:** 1960.
**Current bodystyle lifespan:** 1960 through 1963.
**Predecessor to this model:** None.
**Replacement for this model:** Falcon (1964 to 1965).
**Corporate siblings:** Mercury Comet.
**Percentage of division's sales volume:** 25.81%.
**Primary competition:** Rambler American, Chevrolet Chevy II, Dodge Lancer, Plymouth Valiant, and Studebaker Lark.
**Notable changes:** New grille and revised trim.
**Major standard equipment:** Cloth and vinyl interior trim, front-door armrests, dual horns, chrome windshield and rear window moldings, small hubcaps, and 6.00 × 13 BSW tires (6.50 × 13 on Wagons). Deluxe adds: Deluxe interior trim, rear armrests with ashtrays, side window moldings, full-length side trim molding, and full-wheel covers. Futura adds: Bucket seats, front console, full carpeting, and deluxe trim. Squire adds: Wood-grain exterior trim and power tailgate window.

## Measurements

| | Cars | Wagons |
|---|---|---|
| Wheelbase | 109.5" | 109.5" |
| Length | 181.1" | 189.0" |
| Width | 70.6" | 70.6" |
| Height | 54.5" | 54.5" |
| Legroom — front | 43.5" | 43.5" |
| Legroom — rear | 39.3" | 39.1" |
| Headroom — front | 34.0" | 34.0" |
| Headroom — rear | 33.0" | 33.0" |
| Cargo capacity (cu. ft.) | 23.7 | 76.2 |
| Fuel capacity (gals.) | 14.0 | 14.0 |

**1962**

## Models Available

| | Style Number | Base MSRP | Change from LY | Shipping Wt. (lbs.) | Production | Change from LY |
|---|---|---|---|---|---|---|
| Falcon 2-Door Sedan | 64A | $1,985 | +3.71% | 2243 | 143,650 | -4.22% |
| Falcon 4-Door Sedan | 58A | $2,047 | +3.59% | 2279 | 126,041 | -21.11% |
| Falcon 2-Door Wagon | 59A | $2,298 | +3.19% | 2539 | * | * |
| Falcon 4-Door Wagon | 71A | $2,341 | +3.13% | 2575 | 66,819 | -24.01% |
| Falcon Deluxe 2-Door Sedan | 64B | $2,071 | NEW | 2249 | * | NEW |
| Falcon Deluxe 4-Door Sedan | 58B | $2,133 | NEW | 2285 | * | NEW |
| Falcon Deluxe 2-Door Wagon | 59B | $2,384 | NEW | 2545 | * | NEW |
| Falcon Deluxe 4-Door Wagon | 71B | $2,427 | NEW | 2581 | * | NEW |
| Falcon Futura 2-Door Coupe | 64C | $2,232 | +3.24% | 2328 | 17,011 | -61.75% |
| Falc. Futura 2-Door Sport Cpe. | 62C | $2,273 | NEW | 2343 | * | NEW |
| Falcon Squire 4-Door Wagon | 71C | $2,603 | NEW | 2591 | 22,583 | NEW |
| TOTALS | | Avg. price $2,254 | +6.82% | | Production 376,104* | -20.69%* |

*Production not available by trim level, or distinguished by 2- and 4-Door Wagon models.*

# Fairlane

*"Combines fine car luxury with compact car price."*

**Nameplate year of origin:** 1955.
**Current bodystyle lifespan:** 1962 through 1965.
**Predecessor to this model:** None.
**Replacement for this model:** Fairlane (1966 to 1967).
**Corporate siblings:** Mercury Meteor.
**Percentage of division's sales volume:** 20.41%.
**Primary competition:** Rambler Classic, Dodge Dart, and Plymouth Savoy/Belvedere.
**Notable changes:** All-new model for 1962.
**Major standard equipment:** Cloth and vinyl bench seat, rubber floor mats, front and rear armrests, chrome windshield and rear window moldings, and 6.50 × 13 BSW tires. Fairlane 500 adds: Full carpeting, deluxe interior trim, chrome side window moldings, and full-length chrome side trim.

## Measurements

### Cars

| | |
|---|---|
| Wheelbase | 115.5" |
| Length | 197.0" |
| Width | 71.3" |
| Height | 54.9" |
| Legroom — front | 44.8" |
| Legroom — rear | 38.4" |
| Headroom — front | 34.0" |
| Headroom — rear | 33.5" |
| Cargo capacity (cu. ft.) | 29.0 |
| Fuel capacity (gals.) | 20.0 |

## Models Available

| | Style Number | Base MSRP | Change from LY | Shipping Wt. (lbs.) | Production | Change from LY |
|---|---|---|---|---|---|---|
| Fairlane 2-Door Club Sedan | 62A | $2,154 | NEW | 2736 | 34,264 | NEW |
| Fairlane 4-Door Town Sedan | 54A | $2,216 | NEW | 2769 | 45,342 | NEW |
| Fairlane 500 2-Door Club Sedan | 62B | $2,242 | NEW | 2753 | 68,624 | NEW |
| Fairlane 500 2-Door Sport Coupe | 62C | $2,403 | NEW | 2849 | 19,628 | NEW |
| Fairlane 500 4-Door Town Sedan | 54B | $2,304 | NEW | 2786 | 129,258 | NEW |
| TOTALS | | Avg. price $2,264 | NEW | | Production 297,116 | NEW |

# Galaxie

*"Built-for-people room and comfort, with Thunderbird spirit and sparkle."*

**Nameplate year of origin:** 1959.
**Current bodystyle lifespan:** 1960 through 1962.
**Predecessor to this model:** Fairlane and Galaxie (1959).
**Replacement for this model:** Custom, and Galaxie (1963 to 1964).
**Corporate siblings:** Mercury Monterey and S-55.
**Percentage of division's sales volume:** 48.41%.
**Primary competition:** AMC Ambassador, Chevrolet
  BelAir/Impala/Caprice, Dodge Polara/Custom 880/Monaco, Plymouth
  Fury, and Pontiac Catalina.
**Notable changes:** Completely restyled, yet still based on 1961 chassis.
**Major standard equipment:** Silent-Flo ventilation system, curved side
  glass, suspended accelerator pedal, rubber mats, dual sunvisors, arm
  rests on all doors, rear window trim molding, and 7.50 × 14 BSW tires.
  Galaxie adds: Nylon carpeting, windshield molding, short exterior
  trim side molding. Galaxie 500 adds: Two-tone interior trim, chrome
  hood ornament, chrome side window trim, and backup lights. XL
  adds: Bucket seats with floor-mounted transmission selector, lower
  door carpet trim and polished trim, courtesy and reading lamps, and
  special badging.

## Measurements

|  | Cars | Wagons |
|---|---|---|
| Wheelbase | 119.0" | 119.0" |
| Length | 209.3" | 209.3" |
| Width | 79.2" | 79.2" |
| Height | 54.9" | 55.0" |
| Legroom — front | 44.3" | 44.3" |
| Legroom — rear | 40.5" | 40.5" |
| Headroom — front | 33.5" | 33.5" |
| Headroom — rear | 34.0" | 34.0" |
| Cargo capacity (cu. ft.) | 28.0 | 93.5 |
| Fuel capacity (gals.) | 20.0 | 20.0 |

**1962**

## Models Available

| | Style Number | Base MSRP | Change from LY | Shipping Wt. (lbs.) | Production | Change from LY |
|---|---|---|---|---|---|---|
| Galaxie Mainliner 2-Door Sedan | 62E | $2,335 | +3.18% | NA | * | * |
| Galaxie Mainliner 4-Door Sedan | 54E | $2,389 | +3.11% | NA | * | * |
| Galaxie 2-Door Club Sedan | 62B | $2,453 | +3.15% | 3499 | 54,930 | 29.34% |
| Galaxie 4-Door Town Sedan | 54B | $2,507 | +3.08% | 3581 | 115,594 | 16.86% |
| Galaxie 500 2-Door Club Sedan | 62A | $2,613 | +2.96% | 3512 | 27,824 | 0.16% |
| Galaxie 500 2-Door Victoria HT | 65A | $2,674 | +2.89% | 3513 | 87,562 | 16.07% |
| Galaxie 500 2-Door Sunliner Conv. | 76A | $2,924 | +2.63% | 3675 | 42,646 | -4.41% |
| Galaxie 500 4-Door Town Sedan | 54A | $2,667 | +2.89% | 3594 | 174,195 | 22.83% |
| Galaxie 500 4-Door Victoria HT | 75A | $2,739 | +2.82% | 3585 | 30,778 | 1.44% |
| Galaxie 500 XL 2-Door Victoria HT | 65B | $3,268 | NEW | 3672 | 28,412 | NEW |
| Gal. 500 XL 2-Dr. Sunliner Conv. | 76B | $3,518 | NEW | 3831 | 13,183 | NEW |
| Ranch Wagon 4-Dr., 6-pass. Wgn. | 71D | $2,733 | +2.82% | 3913 | 33,674 | 11.16% |
| Country Sedan 4-Dr., 6-pass. Wgn. | 71B | $2,829 | +2.72% | 3936 | 47,635 | 2.86% |
| Country Sedan 4-Door, 9-p. Wgn. | 71C | $2,933 | +2.62% | 3954 | 16,562 | 1.26% |
| Country Squire 4-Dr., 6-pass. Wgn. | 71E | $3,018 | +2.55% | 3950 | 16,114 | -4.99% |
| Country Squire 4-Dr., 9-pass. Wgn. | 71A | $3,088 | +2.49% | 3967 | 15,666 | 6.88% |
| TOTALS | *Avg. price* | $2,793 | +6.28% | *Production* | 704,775 | -9.3% |

*Mainliner production included with Galaxie base series.*

# Thunderbird

*"Unique in all the world."*

**Nameplate year of origin:** 1955.
**Current bodystyle lifespan:** 1961 through 1963.
**Predecessor to this model:** Thunderbird (1958 to 1960).

## Measurements

| | |
|---|---|
| Wheelbase | 113.0" |
| Length | 205.0" |

**Replacement for this model:** Thunderbird (1964 to 1966).
**Corporate siblings:** None.
**Percentage of division's sales volume:** 5.36%.
**Primary competition:** Oldsmobile Starfire, and Chrysler 300.
**Notable changes:** Revised trim and detail changes.
**Major standard equipment:** Bucket seats, full carpeting, heater and defroster, seat belts, full instrumentation, Swing-away steering wheel, AM radio, reversible entry keys, sequential turn signals, power steering, power brakes, and 8.00 × 14 BSW tires. Convertible adds: Unique trunk-stored power convertible top. Landau adds: Special interior and vinyl top.

### Measurements (cont.)

| | |
|---|---|
| Width | 76.0" |
| Height | 52.5" |
| Legroom — front | 44.9" |
| Legroom — rear | 37.4" |
| Headroom — front | 34.3" |
| Headroom — rear | 33.2" |
| Cargo capacity (cu. ft.) | NA |
| Fuel capacity (gals.) | 20.0 |

## Models Available

| | Style Number | Base MSRP | Change from LY | Shipping Wt. (lbs.) | Production | Change from LY |
|---|---|---|---|---|---|---|
| Thunderbird 2-Door Hardtop | 63A | $4,321 | +3.57% | 4132 | 68,127 | +8.94% |
| Thunderbird 2-Door Landau HT | 63B | $4,398 | NEW | 4144 | * | NEW |
| Thunderbird 2-Door Convertible | 76A | $4,788 | +3.21% | 4370 | 8,417 | -19.96% |
| T-Bird 2-Dr. Conv. Sports Rdstr. | 76B | $5,439 | NEW | 4471 | 1,427 | NEW |
| TOTALS | | *Avg. price* $4,737 | +7.51% | | *Production* 77,971 | +6.74% |

# IMPERIAL

*"America's most carefully built car."*

The controversial free-standing headlamps introduced on the 1961 Imperial were continued for the new year. Joining them in a move that was just as controversial were free-standing, bullet-style taillamps that were mounted atop lowered rear fender fins. At some point during the model year, the gross horsepower rating of the engine was detuned from 350 to 340 horsepower. Many books list this year's gross horsepower at 340, but the original issue sales brochures and other Chrysler information state the horsepower as 350.

Once again the Crown Imperial Limousine Sedan model was available as a custom-built model. These are not detailed within this book as their production usually totaled ten or fewer per season, and they are considered custom-built by Chrysler.

Crown 2-Door Hardtop

Crown 2-Door Convertible

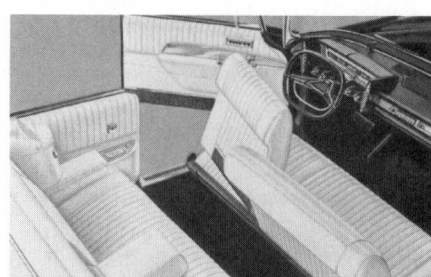

Crown Interior

**Model year production:** 14,337, up 17.05% over 1961.
**Domestic market share:** 0.22% (14th place).
**Base price range:** $4,920 to $6,428.
**Industry average base price:** $3,025.
**Imperial average base price:** $5,544.
**Introduction date:** September 26, 1961.
**Assembly plants:** Detroit, MI (3).

**Data plate identification:** Ten digit code read as follows: 1st digit 9 = Imperial; 2nd number identifies series (e.g., 2 is for Crown); 2 for 1962; 4th digit is assembly plant code; 100001 and up for serial number. Body style numbers found on body plate. *Example:* 9223100001 is a 1962 Imperial Crown, serial number 100001, built in Detroit, MI.

## Powertrains

| Engine | Gross HP | Transmission Availability | Imperial |
|--------|----------|---------------------------|----------|
| 413 CID, 4-bbl., V8 | 350 | Torqueflite Automatic | S |

## Major Options

| | Custom | Crown | LeBaron |
|---|--------|-------|---------|
| Air conditioning | $590 | $590 | $590 |
| Auto Pilot automatic speed control | $99 | $99 | $99 |
| Tinted glass | $54 | $54 | $54 |
| Rear window defogger | $21 | $21 | $21 |
| Power steering — variable-ratio | S | S | S |
| Power brakes | S | S | S |
| Power door locks | $47 (2-Dr)/ $72 (4-Dr) | $47 (2-Dr)/ $72 (4-Dr) | $72 |
| Power driver's seat/Bench seat | $125 | S | S |
| Power windows | $125 | S | S |
| Electric Touch-Tuner radio w/pwr. antenna | $169 | $169 | $169 |
| Whitewall tires — standard size | $55 | $55 | S |

Options common to most models. (S = Standard equipment.) Items may be standard equipment, optional at different pricing, or unavailable on certain models. This chart is only a guide.

## Paint Colors

| | Code |
|---|------|
| Formal Black | BB-1 |
| Dawn Blue | CC-1 |
| Sapphire Blue Metallic | DD-1 |
| Moonlight Blue Metallic | EE-1 |
| Willow Green | FF-1 |
| Sage Green Metallic | GG-1 |
| Bermuda Turquoise | JJ-1 |
| Limelight | LL-1 |
| Dove Gray | MM-1 |
| Alabaster | NN-1 |
| Embassy Red | OO-1 |
| Festival Red | PP-1 |
| Silver Lilac Metallic | RR-1 |
| Cordovan Metallic | SS-1 |
| Coral Gray | TT-1 |
| Seascape | VV-1 |
| Oyster White | WW-1 |
| Rosewood Metallic | YY-1 |
| Caramel | ZZ-1 |

# Custom

*"The most conservatively priced of the three Imperial series."*

**Nameplate year of origin:** 1959 (Name was used on Chrysler Imperial models prior to 1955 also).
**Current bodystyle lifespan:** 1960 through 1963.
**Predecessor to this model:** Imperial (1957 to 1958) and Custom (1959).
**Replacement for this model:** Crown (1964 to 1966).
**Percentage of division's sales volume:** 30.78%.
**Corporate siblings:** Crown and LeBaron.
**Primary competition:** Cadillac Sixty-Two and Lincoln Continental.
**Notable changes:** New grille, taillamps atop fender edge, and minor trim and detail changes.
**Major standard equipment:** Torqueflite automatic transmission, power steering, power brakes, front and rear armrests (hardtops), pile carpeting, remote-control left-hand outside mirror, interior courtesy lamps, variable-speed electric windshield wipers with washers, wheel covers and 8.20 × 15 BSW tires.

## Measurements

| | |
|---|---|
| Wheelbase | 129.0" |
| Length | 227.1" |
| Width | 81.7" |
| Height | 56.8" |
| Legroom — front | 47.0" |
| Legroom — rear | 42.8" |
| Headroom — front | 34.4" |
| Headroom — rear | 33.8" |
| Cargo capacity (cu. ft.) | NA |
| Fuel capacity (gals.) | 23.0 |

## Models Available

| | Style Number | Base MSRP | Change from LY | Shipping Wt. (lbs.) | Production | Change from LY |
|---|---|---|---|---|---|---|
| Custom Imp. Southampton 2-Dr. HT | 912 | $4,920 | -0.10% | 4540 | 826 | -7.09% |
| Custom Imp. Southampton 4-Dr. HT | 914 | $5,106 | -0.10% | 4620 | 3,587 | -13.13% |
| TOTALS | | Avg. price $5,013 | -0.10% | | Production 4,413 | -12.06% |

# Crown

*"Imperial Crowns are more completely equipped than Customs."*

**Nameplate year of origin:** 1957 (Not the same as Crown Imperial series).
**Current bodystyle lifespan:** 1960 through 1963.
**Predecessor to this model:** Crown (1957 to 1959).
**Replacement for this model:** Crown (1964 to 1966).
**Percentage of division's sales volume:** 59.11%.
**Corporate siblings:** Custom and LeBaron.
**Primary competition:** Cadillac Sixty-Two and Lincoln Continental.
**Notable changes:** New grille, taillamps atop fender edge, and minor trim and detail changes.
**Major standard equipment:** Torqueflite automatic transmission, power steering, power brakes, front and rear armrests (hardtops), pile carpeting, remote-control left-hand outside mirror, power windows, interior dome and map lights, variable-speed electric windshield wipers with washers, trunk carpeting, Wheel covers and 8.20 × 15 BSW tires.

### Measurements

| | |
|---|---|
| Wheelbase | 129.0" |
| Length | 227.1" |
| Width | 81.7" |
| Height | 56.8" |
| Legroom — front | 47.0" |
| Legroom — rear | 42.8" |
| Headroom — front | 34.4" |
| Headroom — rear | 33.8" |
| Cargo capacity (cu. ft.) | NA |
| Fuel capacity (gals.) | 23.0 |

## Models Available

| | Style Number | Base MSRP | Change from LY | Shipping Wt. (lbs.) | Production | Change from LY |
|---|---|---|---|---|---|---|
| Crown Southampton 2-Door HT | 922 | $5,400 | -0.09% | 4650 | 1,010 | +0.30% |
| Crown 2-Door Convertible | 925 | $5,770 | -0.10% | 4765 | 554 | +29.14% |
| Crown Southampton 4-Door HT | 924 | $5,644 | -0.09% | 4680 | 6,911 | +44.92% |
| TOTALS | | Avg. price $5,605 | -0.09% | | Production 8,475 | +36.58% |

# LeBaron

*"The crisp roofline and the smaller rear window mark LeBaron.
It offers nearly every driving convenience, its interiors are more luxurious."*

**Nameplate year of origin:** 1924 (as Chrysler Sedan model designation); 1926 (as series).
**Current bodystyle lifespan:** 1960 through 1963.
**Predecessor to this model:** LeBaron (1957 to 1959).
**Replacement for this model:** LeBaron (1964 to 1966).
**Percentage of division's sales volume:** 10.11%.
**Corporate siblings:** Custom and Crown.
**Primary competition:** Cadillac de Ville and Lincoln Continental.
**Notable changes:** New grille, taillamps atop fender edge, and minor trim and detail changes.
**Major standard equipment:** Torqueflite automatic transmission, power steering,

### Measurements

| | |
|---|---|
| Wheelbase | 129.0" |
| Length | 227.1" |
| Width | 81.7" |
| Height | 56.8" |
| Legroom — front | 47.0" |
| Legroom — rear | 42.8" |
| Headroom — front | 34.4" |
| Headroom — rear | 33.8" |
| Cargo capacity (cu. ft.) | NA |
| Fuel capacity (gals.) | 23.0 |

power brakes, pile carpeting, 6-way power seat, power windows and vent windows, electric clock, interior dome and reading lamps, variable-speed electric windshield wipers with washers, carpeted trunk floor, wheel covers and 8.20 × 15 WSW tires.

## Models Available

| | Style Number | Base MSRP | Change from LY | Shipping Wt. (lbs.) | Production | Change from LY |
|---|---|---|---|---|---|---|
| LeBaron Southampton 4-Door HT | 934 | $6,422 | -0.09% | 4725 | 1,449 | +41.23% |
| TOTALS | | *Avg. price* $6,422 | -0.09% | *Production* | 1,449 | +41.23% |

# LINCOLN

*"An unmatched investment in motoring value and satisfaction ... an automobile designed, in every way, to endure.*

Lincoln models for 1962 continued the success begun with the 1961 models. Very little was changed visually, and underneath the story was much the same. The most obvious change was a redesigned grille and front bumper. Sales of all luxury makes improved this year, although Lincoln's gains were minimal in terms of quantity of cars built. However, the percentage gain was impressive.

Continental 4-Door Convertible

Instrument Panel

Continental 4-Door Sedan

**Model year production:** 31,061, up 23.45% over 1961.
**Domestic market share:** 0.47% (13th place).
**Base price range:** $6,074 to $6,720.
**Industry average base price:** $3,025.
**Lincoln average base price:** $6,397.
**Introduction date:** September 1961.
**Assembly Plants:** Allen Park, MI (S); and Wixom, MI (Y).

**Data plate identification:** Eleven digit code read as follows: 2 for 1962; 2nd digit is assembly plant code; 2-digit model number (see listings below); 5th digit is engine code; 400001 and up for serial number. *Example:* 2Y82H400001 is a 1962 Lincoln Continental 4-Door Sedan with a 430 CID V8 engine, serial number 400001, built in Wixom, MI.

## Powertrains

| Engine | Intake/Cylinder Arrangement | Gross HP | Engine Code | Transmission Availability | Continental |
|---|---|---|---|---|---|
| 430 CID, 4-bbl., V8 | | 300 | H | Turbo Drive Automatic | S |

## Major Options

| | Continental |
|---|---|
| Air conditioning — manual | $506 |
| Automatic headlight dimmers | $46 |
| Tinted glass | $54 |
| 6-way power seat | $119 |
| AM radio | S |
| Leather upholstery | $100 |
| Speed control | $97 |
| Remote control trunk release (sedans) | $53 |

Options common to most models. (S = Standard equipment.) Items may be standard equipment, optional at different pricing, or unavailable on certain models. This chart is only a guide.

## Paint Colors

| | Code |
|---|---|
| Presidential Black | A |
| Royal Red Metallic | B |
| Oxford Gray Metallic | C |
| Riviera Turquoise Metallic | D |
| Bermuda Blue Metallic | E |
| Powder Blue | F |
| Silver Mink Metallic | G |
| Nocturne Blue Metallic | H |
| Castillian Gold Metallic | I |
| Teaberry | L |
| Sultana White | M |
| Platinum | N |
| Scotch Green Metallic | P |
| Jamaica Yellow | R |
| Highlander Green Metallic | S |
| Champagne | T |
| Velvet Turquoise Metallic | U |
| Chestnut Metallic | V |
| Black Cherry Metallic | X |
| Desert Frost Metallic | Z |

# Continental

*"The car that cannot be outdated by the calendar."*

**Nameplate year of origin:** 1940 (1961 as a standard sedan nameplate).
**Current bodystyle lifespan:** 1961 through 1969 (major restyles in 1964 and 1966).
**Predecessor to this model:** Premiere (1958 to 1960).
**Replacement for this model:** Continental (1970 to 1979).
**Percentage of division's sales volume:** 100%.
**Corporate siblings:** None.
**Primary competition:** Cadillac de Ville and Imperial Crown and LeBaron.
**Notable changes:** New grille and minor revisions.
**Major standard equipment:** Nylon and leather (sedan) or leather (convertible) front bench seat upholstery with folding center armrests front and rear, vanity mirror, looped-pile carpeting, AM transistor radio, power operated door latching system, padded instrument panel, electric windshield wipers with electric washers, power steering, power brakes, automatic transmission and 9.00 × 14 WSW tires (9.50 × 14 WSW on convertible).

### Measurements

| Wheelbase | 123.0" |
|---|---|
| Length | 213.0" |
| Width | 78.6" |
| Height | 53.7" |
| Legroom — front | 44.2" |
| Legroom — rear | 46.3" |
| Headroom — front | 33.5" |
| Headroom — rear | 33.4" |
| Luggage capacity (cu. ft.) | NA |
| Fuel capacity (gals.) | 21.0 |

## Models Available

| | Style Number | Base MSRP | Change from LY | Shipping Wt. (lbs.) | Production | Change from LY |
|---|---|---|---|---|---|---|
| Continental 4-Door Sedan | 53A | $6,074 | +0.08% | 4966 | 27,849 | +24.87% |
| Continental 4-Door Convertible | 74A | $6,720 | +0.07% | 5370 | 3,212 | +12.43% |
| TOTALS | | Avg. price $6,397 | +0.08% | | Production 31,061 | +23.45% |

# MERCURY

*"1962 Mercury … best-looking buys … now in each size."*

This year brought the introduction of an all-new size of Mercury. The Meteor was a mid-size or intermediate car, offered before most of the buying public was ready for such a car. In fact, considering the fiasco developing with the smaller 1962 Plymouths, it is amazing that Mercury continued to offer cars so close in the market with Ford. The new Meteor was a stablemate of the Ford Fairlane. Both of these new models were loosely based upon some Falcon components; however, they were larger cars and better equipped than the Falcon or Comet. The Meteor and Fairlane were about the same size cars as the new Plymouth and Dodge Dart lines. Unfortunately, the public saw all of these cars as smaller full-size models (particularly since both nameplates had actually been full-sized cars in prior years), and they were reluctant to buy what they perceived to be a watered down Mercury. Mercury even promoted the Meteor as the new standard size Mercury. The Meteor was also too close in size and price to its own Comet, and by 1964,

the Meteor would be replaced totally by the Comet line. A model line limited to 2-Door and 4-Door Sedans probably contributed to lack of public interest in the new-size Mercury.

The traditional but smaller full-size Mercury Montereys were once again based on the full-size Ford platform. Styling was freshened, but in a manner that actually looked more like a Ford than in prior years. With the Meteor nameplate on a new mid-size car, the Monterey became the base line, with a new Monterey Custom replacing the prior Monterey. A new S-55 model was introduced to compete with the new Pontiac Grand Prix and Buick Wildcat from GM. This sporty 2-door line could be optioned out with bucket seats, floor consoles, floor shifting and all the other Mercury luxury items. For the compact Comet, a new upgraded Custom line was introduced, along with a new grille and side trim.

Comet 4-Door Sedan

Comet Custom 2-Door Wagon

Meteor Custom 3-Door Sedan

Meteor Interior

Monterey Custom 2-Door Convertible

Monterey Custom 4-Door Sedan

**Model year production:** 324,145, up 2.14% over 1961.
**Domestic market share:** 4.87% (8th place).
**Base price range:** $2,084 to $3,738.
**Industry average base price:** $3,025.
**Mercury average base price:** $2,698.
**Introduction date:** October 1961.
**Assembly plants:** Mahwah, NJ (E); Dearborn, MI (F); Lorain, OH (H); Los Angeles, CA ( J); Kansas City, MO (K); San Jose, CA (R); Wixom, MI (S); Metuchen, NJ (T); Wayne, MI (W); and St. Louis, MO (Z).

**Data plate identification:** Eleven digit code read as follows: 2 for 1962; 2nd digit is assembly plant code; 3rd digit is series (1 or 2 is Comet, 3 or 4 is Meteor, 6 is Monterey); 4th digit is body style; 5th digit is engine code; 500001 and up for serial number (800001 and up for Comet). *Example:* 2W63Z100001 is a 1962 Mercury Monterey 2-Door Hardtop with a 390 CID V8 engine, serial number 500001, built in Wayne, MI.

## Powertrains

| Engine | Gross HP | Engine Code | Transmission Availability | Comet | Meteor | Monterey & S-55 | Monterey Custom |
|---|---|---|---|---|---|---|---|
| 144.3 CID Thrift-Power Six, 1-bbl., 6-cyl. | 85 | S | 3-speed manual | S | – | – | – |
| | | | 2-sp. Automatic | $172 | – | – | – |
| 170 CID Thrift-Power Six, 1-bbl., 6-cyl. | 101 | U | 3-speed manual | $45 | S | – | – |
| | | | 2-sp. Automatic | $217 | $172 | – | – |
| 221 CID, 2-bbl., V8 | 145 | L | 3-speed manual | – | $103 | – | – |
| | | | Overdrive | – | $211 | – | – |
| | | | Merc-O-Matic Automatic | – | $275 | – | – |
| 223 CID Six, 1-bbl., 6-cyl. | 138 | V | 3-speed manual | – | $45 | S[2] | – |
| | | | Overdrive | – | $153 | – | – |
| | | | Merc-O-Matic Automatic | – | $217 | $217[2] | – |
| 260 CID, 2-bbl., V8 | 164 | F | 3-speed manual | – | $155 | – | – |
| | | | Overdrive | – | $263 | – | – |
| | | | Merc-O-Matic Automatic | – | $327 | – | – |
| 292 CID, 2-bbl., V8 | 170 | W | 3-speed manual | – | – | $109[2] | S |
| | | | 4-speed manual | – | – | $297[2] | $188 |
| | | | Multi-Drive Automatic | – | – | $326[2] | $217 |
| 352 CID Marauder, 2-bbl., V8 | 220 | X | 3-speed manual | – | – | $161[2] | $52 |
| | | | 4-speed manual | – | – | $349[2] | $240 |
| | | | Multi-Drive Automatic | – | – | $378[2] | $269 |
| 390 CID Marauder, 4-bbl., V8 | 300 | Z | 3-speed manual | – | – | $247[2] | $138 |
| | | | 4-speed manual | – | – | S[1]/$435[2] | $326 |
| | | | Multi-Drive Automatic | – | – | S[1]/$464[2] | $355 |
| 406 CID Marauder, 4-bbl., V8 | 385 | B | 4-speed manual | – | – | $333[1]/$630[2] | $521 |
| | | | Multi-Drive Automatic | – | – | $333[1]/$559[2] | $550 |
| 406 CID Marauder, 3 × 2-bbl., V8 | 405 | B | 4-speed manual | – | – | $391[1]/$688[2] | $579 |
| | | | Multi-Drive Automatic | – | – | $391[1]/$717[2] | $608 |

[1]*S-55 models.*    [2]*All but S-55.*

## Major Options

| | Comet | Meteor | Monterey |
|---|---|---|---|
| SelectAire air conditioning | $271 | $271 | $361 |
| Tinted glass | $31 | $40 | $43 |
| Power steering | – | $82 | $82 |
| Power brakes | – | $43 | $43 |
| Power windows | – | – | $102 |
| Electric windshield wipers w/washer | $23 | $21 | $21 |
| Electric clock | – | $15 | $15 |
| Pushbutton AM radio | $59 | $59 | $59 |
| White sidewall tires — std. sizes | $30–$33 | $37 | $37–$53 |
| Full wheel covers | $16 | $19 | S |

## Paint Colors

| | Code |
|---|---|
| Presidential Black | A |
| Peacock | B |
| Ocean Turquoise Metallic | D |
| Pacific Blue Metallic | E |
| Sea Blue | F |
| Blue Satin Metallic | H |
| Castilian Gold Metallic | I |
| Carnival Red | J |
| Light Aqua | K |
| Teaberry* | L |

Options common to most models. (- = Not Available, S = Standard equipment.) Items may be standard equipment, optional at different pricing, or unavailable on certain models. This chart is only a guide.

|  | Code |
|---|---|
| Sultana White | M |
| Scotch Green Metallic | P |
| Sheffield Gray Metallic | Q |
| Jamaica Yellow | R |
| Champagne | T |
| Velvet Turquoise Metallic* | U |
| Black Cherry Metallic | X |
| Desert Frost Metallic | Z |

*Monterey only.

**1962**

# Comet

*"The compact Mercury—smartly ahead of the compact crowd!!"*

**Nameplate year of origin:** 1960.

**Current bodystyle lifespan:** 1960 through 1963.

**Predecessor to this model:** None.

**Replacement for this model:** Comet (1964 to 1965).

**Percentage of division's sales volume:** 50.97%.

**Corporate siblings:** Ford Falcon.

**Primary competition:** Buick Special, Dodge Lancer, Oldsmobile F-85, Pontiac Tempest and Studebaker.

**Notable changes:** Revised grille and minor trim and detail changes.

**Major standard equipment:** Nylon and vinyl front bench seat with foam cushions, black carpet textured rubber floor covering, 17" Lifeguard steering wheel, dual front armrests and dual sun visors, dome light, glove compartment, bright metal front and rear window trim, and 6.50 × 13 BSW tires. Custom adds: deep-pile carpeting, front and rear armrests, deluxe steering wheel, and additional sound deadening materials. S-22 adds: All-vinyl front bucket seats, vinyl-covered center floor console, S-22 exterior trim.

## Measurements

|  | Cars | Wagons |
|---|---|---|
| Wheelbase | 114.0" | 109.5" |
| Length | 194.8" | 191.8" |
| Width | 70.4" | 70.4" |
| Height | 54.5" | 55.1" |
| Legroom — front | 43.4" | 43.5" |
| Legroom — rear | 39.3" | 39.1" |
| Headroom — front | 34.2" | 34.0" |
| Headroom — rear | 32.7" | 33.0" |
| Cargo capacity (cu. ft.) | 29.1 | 76.2 |
| Fuel capacity (gals.) | 14.0 | 14.0 |

## Models Available

|  | Style Number | Base MSRP | Change from LY | Shipping Wt. (lbs.) | Production | Change from LY |
|---|---|---|---|---|---|---|
| Comet 2-Door Sedan | 62A | $2,084 | +4.20% | 2420 | 73,800 | +3.13% |
| Comet 4-Door Sedan | 54A | $2,139 | +4.09% | 2457 | 70,227 | -17.70% |
| Comet 2-Door Wagon | 59A | $2,396 | +3.63% | 2626 | 2,121 | -49.49% |
| Comet 4-Door Wagon | 71A | $2,439 | +3.57% | 2662 | 16,758 | -24.39% |
| Comet Custom 2-Door Sedan | 62B | $2,171 | NEW | 2431 | * | NEW |
| Comet Custom 4-Door Sedan | 54B | $2,226 | NEW | 2468 | * | NEW |
| Comet Custom 2-Door Wagon | 59B | $2,483 | NEW | 2642 | * | NEW |
| Comet Custom 4-Door Wagon | 71B | $2,526 | NEW | 2679 | * | NEW |
| Comet Villager 4-Door Wagon | 71C | $2,710 | NEW | 2712 | 2,318 | NEW |
| Comet S-22 2-Door Sedan | 62C | $2,368 | +3.68% | 2458 | * | * |
| TOTALS | | Avg. price $2,354 | +6.95% | | Production 165,224 | -16.25% |

*Production not available by trim level, only by body style.

# Meteor

*"The beautiful balance between big cars and compacts.*
*The new standard-size Meteor."*

**Nameplate year of origin:** 1961.
**Current bodystyle lifespan:** 1962 through 1963.
**Predecessor to this model:** None.
**Replacement for this model:** Comet (1966 to 1967).
**Percentage of division's sales volume:** 16.02%.
**Corporate siblings:** Ford Fairlane.
**Primary competition:** Dodge Dart, and Plymouth Fury.
**Notable changes:** All-new model for 1962.
**Major standard equipment:** Cloth and vinyl front bench seat, bright exterior window trim and 6.50 × 14 BSW tires. Custom adds: All-vinyl upholstery (no cost option), additional interior and exterior trim, twist-pile carpeting. S-33 adds: All-vinyl bucket seats, center floor console and S-33 badging.

## Measurements

| | |
|---|---|
| Wheelbase | 116.5" |
| Length | 203.8" |
| Width | 71.3" |
| Height | 55.8" |
| Legroom — front | 45.8" |
| Legroom — rear | 38.4" |
| Headroom — front | 34.0" |
| Headroom — rear | 33.5" |
| Cargo capacity (cu. ft.) | 31.5 |
| Fuel capacity (gals.) | 16.0 |

## Models Available

| | Style Number | Base MSRP | Change from LY | Shipping Wt. (lbs.) | Production | Change from LY |
|---|---|---|---|---|---|---|
| Meteor 2-Door Sedan | 62A | $2,278 | NEW | 2843 | 3,935 | NEW |
| Meteor 4-Door Sedan | 54A | $2,340 | NEW | 2877 | 9,183 | NEW |
| Meteor Custom 2-Door Sedan | 62B | $2,366 | NEW | 2851 | 9,410 | NEW |
| Meteor Custom 4-Door Sedan | 54B | $2,428 | NEW | 2885 | 23,484 | NEW |
| Meteor S-33 2-Door Sport Coupe | 62C | $2,509 | NEW | NA | 5,900 | NEW |
| TOTALS | | *Avg. price* $2,384 | NEW | | *Production* 51,912 | NEW |

# Monterey

*"Raises your standard of driving, yet is well within the popular-price range!"*

**Nameplate year of origin:** 1952.
**Current bodystyle lifespan:** 1961 through 1962.
**Predecessor to this model:** Monterey and Montclair (1959 to 1960).
**Replacement for this model:** Monterey (1963 to 1964).
**Percentage of division's sales volume:** 31.75%.
**Corporate siblings:** Ford Galaxie.
**Primary competition:** Buick Invicta, Dodge Custom 880, Oldsmobile 88 and Pontiac Star Chief/Bonneville.
**Notable changes:** Restyled front and rear ends.
**Major standard equipment:** Cloth and vinyl front bench seat, full carpeting, padded instrument panel, bright exterior window trim and 7.50 × 14 BSW tires (8.00 × 14 BSW tires on convertible). Commuter adds: 8.00 × 14 BSW tires. Custom adds: V8 engine, electric clock, courtesy lights, and electric windshield wipers. Colony Park wagons adds: exterior wood-grain vinyl trim, and power tailgate window.

## Measurements

| | Cars | Wagons |
|---|---|---|
| Wheelbase | 120.0" | 120.0" |
| Length | 215.5" | 215.4" |
| Width | 79.5" | 79.5" |
| Height | 54.9" | 55.0" |
| Legroom — front | 43.4" | 43.4" |
| Legroom — rear | 41.6" | 41.6" |
| Headroom — front | 33.5" | 33.5" |
| Headroom — rear | 33.9" | 33.9" |
| Cargo capacity (cu. ft.) | 30.7 | 93.5 |
| Fuel capacity (gals.) | 20.0 | 20.0 |

## Models Available

| | Style Number | Base MSRP | Change from LY | Shipping Wt. (lbs.) | Production | Change from LY |
|---|---|---|---|---|---|---|
| Monterey 2-Door Sedan | 62A | $2,672 | -1.51% | 3644 | 5,117 | * |
| Monterey 2-Door Hardtop | 65A | $2,733 | -1.48% | 3661 | 5,328 | * |
| Monterey 4-Door Sedan | 54A | $2,726 | -1.48% | 3721 | 18,975 | -45.79% |
| Monterey 4-Door Hardtop | 75A | $2,798 | -1.44% | 3737 | 2,691 | * |
| Commuter 4-Door, 2-Seat Wagon | 71A | $2,920 | -0.14% | 4069 | 8,389 | -6.28% |
| Commuter 4-Door, 3-Seat Wagon | 71C | $2,990 | -0.13% | 4081 | * | * |
| Monterey Custom 2-Door Hardtop | 65B | $2,972 | +3.27% | 3772 | 10,814 | -1.17% |
| Monterey Custom 2-Door Conv. | 76A | $3,222 | +3.01% | 3938 | 5,489 | -22.17% |
| Monterey Custom 4-Door Sedan | 54B | $2,965 | +3.27% | 3836 | 27,591 | +20.58% |
| Monterey Custom 4-Door Hardtop | 75B | $3,037 | +3.19% | 3851 | 8,932 | -3.46% |
| Colony Park 4-Door, 2-Seat Wagon | 71B | $3,219 | +3.17% | 4186 | 9,596 | +21.67% |
| Colony Park 4-Door, 3-Seat Wagon | 71D | $3,289 | +3.07% | 4198 | * | * |
| TOTALS | | Avg. price $2,962 | -1.47% | | Production 102,922 | +53.69% |

*Production from previous year not available for comparison.*

# S-55

## *"The new Mercury that's big in performance!"*

**Nameplate year of origin:** 1962.
**Current bodystyle lifespan:** 1961 through 1962.
**Predecessor to this model:** None.
**Replacement for this model:** S-55 (1963).
**Percentage of division's sales volume:** 1.11%.
**Corporate siblings:** Ford Galaxie 500 XL.
**Primary competition:** Buick Wildcat, Dodge Polara, Oldsmobile Starfire and Pontiac Grand Prix.
**Notable changes:** All-new model for 1962.
**Major standard equipment:** All-vinyl front bucket seats, front floor console, full carpeting, padded instrument panel, specific bright exterior trim and 7.50 × 14 BSW tires (8.00 × 14 BSW tires on convertible).

## Measurements

| | |
|---|---|
| Wheelbase | 120.0" |
| Length | 215.5" |
| Width | 79.5" |
| Height | 54.9" |
| Legroom — front | 43.4" |
| Legroom — rear | 41.6" |
| Headroom — front | 33.5" |
| Headroom — rear | 33.9" |
| Cargo capacity (cu. ft.) | 30.7 |
| Fuel capacity (gals.) | 20.0 |

## Models Available

| | Style Number | Base MSRP | Change from LY | Shipping Wt. (lbs.) | Production | Change from LY |
|---|---|---|---|---|---|---|
| S-55 2-Door Hardtop | 65C | $3,488 | NEW | NA | 2,772 | NEW |
| S-55 2-Door Convertible | 76B | $3,738 | NEW | NA | 1,315 | NEW |
| TOTALS | | Avg. price $3,613 | NEW | | Production 3,613 | NEW |

# OLDSMOBILE

*"There's 'Something Extra' about owning an OLDS!"*

Oldsmobile refined its cars for 1962. Full-size Oldsmobiles were given a more massive looking front end, after last year's downsizing maneuver. Starfire models were put into reverse style-wise by adding larger brushed aluminum side panels after several years of "de-chroming" by most of Detroit. This nearly foot-wide panel was not garish, and did easily distinguish a Starfire from any other car on the road, but looked a little outdated, especially next to the all-new Pontiac Grand Prix or Buick Wildcat models which used minimal chrome trim.

The compact F-85 line retained the look of its popular first year models, but did make several important additions to the line. The F-85 Deluxe added a 4-Door Sedan model and two Cutlass-trimmed models: a 2-Door Coupe and a Convertible. A convertible model was also added to the standard F-85 line. The two Cutlass models added nicer interior trim and a sporty image. It was this image the Oldsmobile would turn into a marketing wonder, and eventually make the Cutlass nameplate one of the most recognized on the road. Just as important, but not as popular, was the mid-year introduction of the Jetfire Turbocharged V8. This high-powered, all-aluminum V8 engine was the earliest forerunner of the "muscle" car or "pony" car market. It offered the magical "one horsepower per cubic inch" equation that so many manufacturers strove for as the maximum potential of an engine.

Ninety-Eight 4-Door Town Sedan

F-85 Cutlass 2-Door Convertible

Dynamic 88 4-Door Hardtop

F-85 Deluxe 4-Door Wagon

Starfire 2-Door Convertible

**Model year production:** 451,567, up 45.61% over 1961.
**Domestic market share:** 6.79% (4th place).
**Base price range:** $2,403 to $4,744.
**Industry average base price:** $3,025.
**Oldsmobile average base price:** $3,367.
**Introduction date:** September 22, 1961.
**Assembly plants:** Atlanta, GA (A); Southgate, CA (C); Fairfax, KS (K); Linden, NJ (L); Lansing, MI (M); Arlington, TX (T); and Wilmington, DE (W).

**Data plate identification:** Nine digit code read as follows: 1st two digits 62 for 1962; 3rd designates trim level; 4th identifies assembly plant; 01001 and up for serial number. Check model number on body plate for body style. *Example:* 628M01001 is a 1962 Oldsmobile Ninety-Eight, built in Lansing, MI, serial number 01001.

## Powertrains

| Engine | Gross HP | Transmission Availability | F-85/Cutlass & Jetfire | Dynamic 88 | Super 88 | Starfire & 98 |
|---|---|---|---|---|---|---|
| 215 CID Rockette, 2-bbl., V8 | 155 | 3-speed manual | S (F-85) | - | - | - |
| | | Hydra-Matic Automatic | $189 (F-85) | - | - | - |
| 215 CID Cutlass, 4-bbl., V8 | 185 | 3-speed manual | S (Cutlass) | - | - | - |
| | | Hydra-Matic Automatic | $189 (Cutlass) | - | - | - |
| 215 CID Turbo-Rocket, Turbocharged 4-bbl., V8 | 215 | 3-speed manual | S (Jetfire) | - | - | - |
| | | Hydra-Matic Automatic | $189 (Jetfire) | - | - | - |
| 394 CID Rocket, 2-bbl., V8 | 280 | 3-speed manual | - | S | - | - |
| | | Hydra-Matic Automatic | - | $231 | - | - |
| 394 CID Rocket, 4-bbl., V8 | 330 | 3-speed manual | - | - | S | - |
| | | Hydra-Matic Automatic | - | - | $231 | S (98) |
| 394 CID Starfire Rocket, 4-bbl., V8 | 345 | Hydra-Matic Automatic | - | - | - | S (Starfire) |

## Major Options

| | F-85 | Dynamic 88 | Super 88 | Starfire | Ninety-Eight |
|---|---|---|---|---|---|
| Air conditioning | $378 | $430 | $430 | $430 | $430 |
| Soft Ray tinted glass | $ | $ | $ | $ | $ |
| Courtesy lamps | $5 | $5 | $5 | S | S |
| Outside rear view mirror — LH | $5 | $5 | $5 | $5 | $5 |
| Power steering — variable-ratio | $86 | $108 | $108 | S | S |
| Power brakes | - | $48 | $48 | S | S |
| Power driver's seat/Bench seat | - | $97 | $97 | S | S |
| Power windows | $102 | $106 | $106 | S | S |
| Electric clock | $15 | $20 | $20 | S | S |
| Windshield washers | $12 | $13 | $13 | $13 | $13 |
| AM radio | $66 | $89 | $89 | $89 | $89 |

Options common to most models (- = Not Available, S = Standard equipment.) Items may be standard equipment, optional at different pricing, or unavailable on certain models. This chart is only a guide.

## Paint Colors

| | Code |
|---|---|
| Ebony Black | A |
| Heather Mist Metallic | B |
| Provincial White | C |
| Sheffield Mist Metallic | D |
| Wedgewood Mist Metallic | F |
| Cirrus Blue | H |
| Willow Mist Metallic | J |
| Surf Green | K |
| Garnet Mist Metallic | L |
| Cameo Cream | M |
| Royal Mist Metallic | N |
| Pacific Mist Metallic | P |
| Sand Beige | R |
| Sahara Mist Metallic | T |
| Chariot Red | V |
| Sunset Mist Metallic | X |

# F-85 and Cutlass

*"In a class by itself ... in the low-price field!"*

**Nameplate year of origin:** 1961 (F-85); 1962 (Cutlass, as F-85 model designation); 1955 (show car).

**Current bodystyle lifespan:** 1961 through 1963.

**Predecessor to this model:** None.

**Replacement for this model:** F-85/Cutlass (1964 to 1965).

**Percentage of division's sales volume:** 21.06%.

**Corporate siblings:** Buick Special/Skylark, Pontiac Tempest/LeMans.

**Primary competition:** AMC Classic, Dodge Lancer, Ford Falcon, Mercury Comet, and Studebaker Lark.

**Notable changes:** New grille and minor trim and detail changes. Cutlass and Jetfire models added during the year.

**Major standard equipment:** Cloth and vinyl upholstery, foam cushion front seats, heater and defroster, and 6.50 × 13 BSW tires. Deluxe adds: full car-

## Measurements

| | |
|---|---|
| Wheelbase | 112.0" |
| Length | 188.2" |
| Width | 71.6" |
| Height | 52.7" |
| Legroom — front | 43.9" |
| Legroom — rear | 40.5" |
| Headroom — front | 33.9" |
| Headroom — rear | 33.2" |
| Luggage capacity (cu. ft.) | 25.5 (Wagon 73.3) |
| Fuel capacity (gals.) | 16.0 |

peting, deluxe steering wheel, and interior and exterior chrome trim moldings. Jetfire adds: turbocharged engine.

## Models Available

| | Style Number | Base MSRP | Change from LY | Shipping Wt. (lbs.) | Production | Change from LY |
|---|---|---|---|---|---|---|
| F-85 2-Door Club Coupe | 3027 | $2,403 | +3.13% | 2607 | 7,909 | +238.57% |
| F-85 2-Door Convertible | 3067 | $2,760 | NEW | 2790 | 3,660 | NEW |
| F-85 4-Door Sedan | 3019 | $2,457 | +3.06% | 2599 | 8,074 | -59.15% |
| F-85 4-Door, 2-Seat Wagon | 3035 | $2,754 | +2.72% | 2780 | 3,204 | -52.01% |
| F-85 4-Door, 3-Seat Wagon | 3045 | $2,835 | +2.64% | 2852 | 1,887 | -81.29% |
| F-85 Deluxe Cutlass 2-Dr. Club Cpe. | 3117 | $2,694 | +2.79% | 2651 | 33,018 | +232.34% |
| F-85 Deluxe Cutlass 2-Dr. Conv. | 3167 | $2,971 | NEW | 2830 | 9,868 | NEW |
| F-85 Deluxe 4-Door Sedan | 3119 | $2,592 | +2.90% | 2634 | 18,736 | -28.79% |
| F-85 Deluxe 4-Door, 2-Seat Wagon | 3135 | $2,889 | +2.59% | 2812 | 4,974 | +845.63% |
| Jetfire 2-Door Hardtop | 3147 | $3,049 | NEW | 2739 | 3,765 | NEW |
| TOTALS | | Avg. price $2,740 | +4.34% | | Production 95,095 | +24.48% |

# Dynamic 88

*"Popular performer ... with economy to match!"*

**Nameplate year of origin:** 1949 (1958 for Dynamic nameplate).
**Current bodystyle lifespan:** 1961 through 1964.
**Predecessor to this model:** 88 (1959 to 1960).
**Replacement for this model:** Jetstar 88 (1964).
**Percentage of division's sales volume:** 41.79%.
**Corporate siblings:** Buick LeSabre, Chevrolet Impala, Pontiac Catalina.
**Primary competition:** AMC Ambassador, Dodge Polara, Mercury Monterey.
**Notable changes:** Restyle of front, rear and bodysides.
**Major standard equipment:** Cloth-and-vinyl bench seat, nylon-blend carpet, heater and defroster, full wheel covers, and 8.00 × 14 BSW tires.

## Measurements*

| | |
|---|---|
| Wheelbase | 123.0" |
| Length | 213.9" |
| Width | 77.9" |
| Height | 55.8" |
| Legroom — front | 44.4" |
| Legroom — rear | 41.4" |
| Headroom — front | 34.6" |
| Headroom — rear | 34.1" |
| Luggage capacity (cu. ft.) | 85.1 (wagon) |
| Fuel capacity (gals.) | 20.0 |

*4-Door models.

## Models Available

| | Style Number | Base MSRP | Change from LY | Shipping Wt. (lbs.) | Production | Change from LY |
|---|---|---|---|---|---|---|
| 88 2-Door Holiday Hardtop | 3247 | $3,054 | +3.32% | 3992 | 39,676 | +99.66% |
| 88 2-Door Convertible | 3267 | $3,381 | +2.95% | 4104 | 12,212 | +34.95% |
| 88 4-Door Celebrity Sedan | 3269 | $2,997 | +3.34% | 4038 | 68,467 | +60.78% |
| 88 4-Door Holiday Hardtop | 3239 | $3,131 | +3.20% | 4080 | 53,428 | +3.62% |
| 88 4-Dr., 2-S. Wagon | 3235 | $3,460 | +2.88% | 4392 | 8,527 | +58.67% |
| 88 4-Dr., 3-S. Wagon | 3245 | $3,568 | +2.79% | 4428 | 6,417 | +59.91% |
| TOTALS | | Avg. price $3,265 | +4.65% | | Production 188,727 | +37.38% |

# Super 88

*"Out ahead in style … out front in action!"*

**Nameplate year of origin:** 1951 (88 series started 1949).
**Current bodystyle lifespan:** 1961 through 1964.
**Predecessor to this model:** Super 88 (1959 to 1960).
**Replacement for this model:** Delta 88 (1965 to 1966).
**Percentage of division's sales volume:** 12.88%.
**Corporate siblings:** Buick Wildcat, Chevrolet Impala, Pontiac Star Chief.
**Primary competition:** Chrysler Newport, Dodge Custom 880, Ford Galaxie, and Mercury Monterey.
**Notable changes:** Restyle of front, rear and bodysides.
**Major standard equipment:** All-vinyl bench seat with fold-down center armrest (except Celebrity Sedan), nylon-blend carpet, deluxe steering wheel, heater and defroster, glove box and courtesy lamps, full wheel covers, and 8.00 × 14 BSW tires.

### Measurements*

| | |
|---|---|
| Wheelbase | 123.0" |
| Length | 213.9" |
| Width | 77.9" |
| Height | 55.8" |
| Legroom — front | 44.4" |
| Legroom — rear | 41.4" |
| Headroom — front | 34.6" |
| Headroom — rear | 34.1" |
| Luggage capacity (cu. ft.) | 85.1 (wagon) |
| Fuel capacity (gals.) | 20.0 |

*4-Door models.*

## Models Available

| | Style Number | Base MSRP | Change from LY | Shipping Wt. (lbs.) | Production | Change from LY |
|---|---|---|---|---|---|---|
| Super 88 2-Door Holiday Hardtop | 3547 | $3,422 | +2.92% | 4022 | 9,010 | +28.55% |
| Super 88 4-Door Celebrity Sedan | 3569 | $3,273 | +3.05% | 4069 | 24,125 | +57.39% |
| Super 88 4-Door Holiday Hardtop | 3539 | $3,499 | +2.85% | 4117 | 21,175 | -9.01% |
| Super 88 4-Dr., 2-S. Fiesta Wagon | 3535 | $3,762 | +2.65% | 4412 | 3,837 | +38.97% |
| TOTALS | *Avg. price* | $3,489 | 0.00 | *Production* | 58,147 | +9.37% |

# Starfire

*"There is only one Starfire—the original, made by Oldsmobile!"*

**Nameplate year of origin:** 1954 (as designation for 98 Convertible); 1961 (as series).
**Current bodystyle lifespan:** 1961 through 1964.
**Predecessor to this model:** None.
**Replacement for this model:** Starfire (1965 to 1966).
**Percentage of division's sales volume:** 9.30%.
**Corporate siblings:** Buick Wildcat, and Pontiac Grand Prix.
**Primary competition:** Chrysler 300, Ford Thunderbird, and Mercury S-55.
**Notable changes:** Restyle of front, rear and bodysides, and new 2-Door Hardtop added.
**Major standard equipment:** Leather bucket seats with center console, nylon-blend carpet, deluxe steering wheel, power windows, heater and defroster, glove box and courtesy lamps, color-keyed full wheel covers, and 8.50 × 14 BSW tires.

### Measurements

| | |
|---|---|
| Wheelbase | 123.0" |
| Length | 213.9" |
| Width | 77.9" |
| Height | 54.7" |
| Legroom — front | 44.4" |
| Legroom — rear | 41.4" |
| Headroom — front | 34.6" |
| Headroom — rear | 34.1" |
| Luggage capacity (cu. ft.) | NA |
| Fuel capacity (gals.) | 20.0 |

## Models Available

| | Style Number | Base MSRP | Change from LY | Shipping Wt. (lbs.) | Production | Change from LY |
|---|---|---|---|---|---|---|
| Starfire 2-Door Hardtop | 3647 | $4,131 | NEW | 4213 | 34,839 | NEW |
| Starfire 2-Door Convertible | 3667 | $4,744 | +2.09% | 4334 | 7,149 | -8.35% |
| TOTALS | *Avg. price* | $4,438 | -4.50% | *Production* | 41,988 | +438.31% |

# Ninety-Eight

*"Long on looks ... great on 'go'!"*

**Nameplate year of origin:** 1941.
**Current bodystyle lifespan:** 1961 through 1964.
**Predecessor to this model:** Ninety-Eight (1959 to 1960).
**Replacement for this model:** Ninety-Eight (1965 to 1966).
**Percentage of division's sales volume:** 14.97%.
**Corporate siblings:** Buick Electra, and Cadillac Series 62/de Ville.
**Primary competition:** Chrysler New Yorker.
**Notable changes:** Restyle of front, rear and bodysides.
**Major standard equipment:** Cloth and vinyl bench seat with fold-down center armrest, deep-pile carpeting floor and kick panels, deluxe steering wheel, electric clock, trunk lamp, trunk mat, full wheel covers, power steering and brakes, 8.50 × 14 BSW tires. Luxury Sedan adds: special design interior.

### Measurements*

| | |
|---|---|
| Wheelbase | 126.0" |
| Length | 220.0" |
| Width | 77.9" |
| Height | 56.6" |
| Legroom — front | 44.2" |
| Legroom — rear | 44.7" |
| Headroom — front | 34.8" |
| Headroom — rear | 34.2" |
| Luggage capacity (cu. ft.) | NA |
| Fuel capacity (gals.) | 20.0 |

*Dimensions given for 4-Door Hardtop models.*

## Models Available

| | Style Number | Base MSRP | Change from LY | Shipping Wt. (lbs.) | Production | Change from LY |
|---|---|---|---|---|---|---|
| Ninety-Eight 2-Door Sports Coupe | 3847 | $4,180 | +2.38% | 4231 | 7,546 | +88.41% |
| Ninety-Eight 2-Door Convertible | 3867 | $4,459 | +2.22% | 4298 | 7,149 | +87.93% |
| Ninety-Eight 4-Door Town Sedan | 3819 | $3,984 | +2.50% | 4258 | 12,167 | +24.06% |
| Ninety-Eight 4-Door Sports Sedan | 3839 | $4,256 | +2.33% | 4337 | 33,095 | +644.54% |
| Ninety-Eight Luxury 4-Door Sedan | 3829 | $4,118 | +2.41% | 4306 | 7,653 | -42.59% |
| TOTALS | *Avg. price* | $4,199 | +2.36% | *Production* | 67,610 | +91.03% |

# PLYMOUTH

*"Look at Plymouth now!"*

The 1962 model year saddled Plymouth with another in a series of miscues by Chrysler, following the highly controversial styling of the 1960 and 1961 Plymouths. Chrysler designers had already taken steps to move toward smaller full-size cars, beginning as far back as 1958, when the country was in an economic recession and sales of smaller cars such as AMC Rambler models, Studebaker's Lark and imported small cars, particularly the Volkswagen, had risen sharply. Chrysler's first response to these cars was the 1960 introduction of the Valiant. While Ford and GM designers had made their 1961 models slightly smaller, Chrysler would not be ready until 1962. Unfortunately for Chrysler, the public was only temporarily enamored with the smaller

cars, and quickly sales of larger cars began to rise. Of course, one could look at the 1962 Plymouth as a matter of Chrysler being ahead of its time. The physical size of the new Plymouth was the same as the new intermediate size cars that GM would successfully introduce in 1964. In fact, the 1962 Plymouth body would become the basis for Chrysler's own "mid-size" cars when the 1965 Dodge Coronet and Plymouth Belvedere line arrived. But for the time being Plymouth was stuck with a nice car that few buyers wanted. Chrysler quickly corrected the situation for Dodge in 1963, giving the Dodge line a slightly stretched wheelbase and longer body, but Plymouth had to make do with the smaller body for a few years.

The general styling was nice, especially compared to the finned 1960s and wildly styled 1961 models. The front end was highlighted by dual headlamps — one set into a large chrome pod at the far end of the electric razor–like grille and the other inset a foot or so into the grille. At the rear were tiny round taillamps set in from the fender edge. A prominent body line ran from the front door on one side forward along the side of the fender, across the leading edge of the hood, and back down the opposite side, ending at the front door. A similar body line ran from just behind the rear side window, across the trunk lid, and back up the rear fender on the opposite side. The thin rooflines and awkward fender arches of prior years were gone. Plymouth dubbed the new style "Forward Flair Design" and touted it as a new concept in Plymouth's field" giving the cars a "poised look of power and purpose."

Significant model changes included the mid-year return of the Sport Fury line after a two-year absence. Also, Suburban wagon models were returned to their respective model lines, instead of being marketed as a separate line. In the process the entry-level 9-passenger model was dropped.

A new grille marked the biggest change visually for the popular Valiant compact line. A new Signet 2-Door Hardtop, effectively replaced the 1961 V200 Hardtop and a 2-Door Sedan model took its place in the V200 line. Powertrain choices remained the same for the model year.

Valiant V200 2-Door Sedan

Belvedere 2-Door Sedan

Fury 2-Door Convertible

Savoy 4-Door Wagon

Valiant Signet 2-Door Hardtop

**Model year production:** 339,514, down 3.08% from 1961.
**Domestic market share:** 5.10% (7th place).
**Base price range:** $1,930 to $3,082.
**Industry average base price:** $3,025.
**Plymouth average base price:** $2,477.
**Introduction date:** September 1961.
**Assembly plants:** Lynch Road, MI (1): Hamtramck, MI (2); Detroit, MI (3); Los Angeles, CA (5); Newark DE (6); and St. Louis, MO (7).

**Data plate identification:** Ten digit code read as follows: First and second digits are series designation (first two numbers of model number in charts below); third digit 2 for 1962; fourth digit is assembly plant code; 100001 and up for serial number. *Example:* 2322100001 is a 1962 Plymouth Fury, with a 225 CID 6-cyl., built at Hamtramck, MI, serial number 100001. Body style cannot be identified through the VIN.

## Powertrains

| Engine | Gross HP | Engine Code | Transmission Availability | Valiant | Savoy/ Belvedere | Fury | Sport Fury |
|---|---|---|---|---|---|---|---|
| 170 CID, 1-bbl., 6-cyl. | 101 | A | 3-speed manual | S | - | - | - |
| | | | Torqueflite automatic | $172 | - | - | - |
| 225 CID 30-D Economy Six, 2-bbl., 6-cyl. | 145 | B | 3-speed manual | $47 | S | S[1] | - |
| | | | Torqueflite automatic | $219 | $192 | $192[1] | - |

| Engine | Gross HP | Engine Code | Transmission Availability | Valiant | Savoy/ Belvedere | Fury | Sport Fury |
|---|---|---|---|---|---|---|---|
| 318 CID Fury V-800, 2-bbl., V8 | 230 | F | 3-speed manual | | $107 | S[2]/ $107[1] | - |
| | | | Torqueflite automatic | | $318 | $211[2]/$318[1] | - |
| 318 CID Super Fury V-800, 4-bbl., V8 | 260 | NA | 3-speed manual | | $126 | $19[2]/$126[1] | - |
| | | | Torqueflite automatic | | $337 | $230[2]/$337[1] | - |
| 361 CID Golden Commando, 4-bbl., V8 | 305 | NA | 3-speed manual | - | $146 | $39[2]/$146[1] | S |
| | | | Torqueflite automatic | - | $357 | $250[2]/$103[1] | $211 |
| 383 CID Golden Commando, 4-bbl., V8 | 330 | NA | 3-speed manual | - | $210 | $103[2]/$314[1] | $62 |
| | | | Torqueflite automatic | - | $421 | $314[2]/$421[1] | $273 |

[1]Fury 2-Dr. HT, 4-Dr. Sedan.    [2]All but Fury 2-Dr. HT, 4-Dr. Sedan.

## Major Options

| | Valiant | Savoy/Belvedere | Fury |
|---|---|---|---|
| Push-button heater and defroster | $74 | $74 | $74 |
| Air conditioning (V8 only) | - | $445 | $445 |
| Solex tinted glass | $30 | $42 | $42 |
| Power steering | $73 | $76 | $76 |
| Power brakes | $40 | $42 | $42 |
| Electric clock | $16 | $16 | S |
| AM radio | $58 | $58 | $58 |
| White sidewall tires — std. sizes | $35 | $38 | $38 |

## Paint Colors

| | Code |
|---|---|
| Hawaiian Blue | 22-1 |
| Buffed Silver Metallic | AA-1 |
| Black | BB-1 |
| Medium Blue Metallic | CC-1 |
| Mist Blue Metallic | DD-1 |
| Midnight Blue Metallic | EE-1 |
| Mist Green Metallic | FF-1 |
| Forest Green Metallic | GG-1 |
| Yellow Gold | HH-1 |
| Ember Gold Metallic | JJ-1 |
| Mist Turquoise Metallic | KK-1 |
| Surf Turquoise Met. | LL-1 |
| Turbine Bronze Metallic | MM-1 |
| Matador Red | PP-1 |
| Electric Blue Metallic | QQ-1 |
| Burgundy Metallic | RR-1 |
| Sunfire Yellow | SS-1 |
| Avacado Green Metallic | TT-1 |
| Frost Blue Metallic | UU-1 |
| Sable White | WW-1 |
| Satin Beige | XX-1 |
| Sierra Tan Metallic | YY-1 |

# Valiant

*"In 1962, nobody beats Valiant for value!"*

**Nameplate year of origin:** 1960.
**Current bodystyle lifespan:** 1960 through 1962.
**Predecessor to this model:** None.
**Replacement for this model:** Valiant (1963 to 1966).
**Percentage of division's sales volume:** 46.33%.
**Corporate siblings:** Dodge Lancer.
**Primary competition:** Rambler American, Chevrolet Chevy II, Ford Falcon and Studebaker Lark.
**Notable changes:** Minor trim and detail changes.
**Major standard equipment:** Fabric and vinyl bench seat, rubber floor mat, chrome exterior front and rear window trim, Torsion-Aire suspension and 6.50 × 13 BSW tires. V200 adds: Side window chrome trim and color-keyed floor mats. Signet adds: All-vinyl bucket seats, color-keyed carpeting, and special instrumentation.

## Measurements

| | Cars | Wagons |
|---|---|---|
| Wheelbase | 106.5" | 106.5" |
| Length | 183.7" | 183.7" |
| Width | 70.4" | 70.4" |
| Height | 53.3" | 53.5" |
| Legroom — front | 42.8" | 42.8" |
| Legroom — rear | 39.8" | 38.4" |
| Headroom — front | 37.9" | 37.9" |
| Headroom — rear | 37.4" | 37.5" |
| Cargo capacity (cu. ft.) | 24.9 | 72.3 |
| Fuel capacity (gals.) | 13.0 | 13.0 |

## Models Available

| | Style Number | Base MSRP | Change from LY | Shipping Wt. (lbs.) | Production | Change from LY |
|---|---|---|---|---|---|---|
| Valiant V100 2-Door Sedan | 111 | $1,930 | -1.28% | 2480 | 19,679 | -11.48% |
| Valiant V100 4-Door Sedan | 113 | $1,991 | -1.24% | 2500 | 33,769 | +31.42% |
| Valiant V100 4-Door Wagon | 156 | $2,285 | -1.89% | 2660 | 5,932 | -11.69% |
| Valiant V200 2-Door Sedan | 131 | $2,026 | -5.28% | 2500 | 8,484 | -54.35% |
| Valiant V200 4-Door Sedan | 133 | $2,087 | -1.18% | 2510 | 55,789 | -5.53% |
| Valiant V200 4-Door Wagon | 176 | $2,381 | -1.81% | 2690 | 8,055 | -25.38% |
| Valiant Signet 200 2-Door HT | 142 | $2,230 | NEW | 2515 | 25,586 | NEW |
| TOTALS | | Avg. price $2,133 | -1.39% | | Production 157,294 | +9.94% |

# Savoy

*"You would never guess this is the lowest-priced line
of any car, and neither will your neighbors."*

**Nameplate year of origin:** 1951 (Concord 2-Door Suburban designation); 1954 (as series).
**Current bodystyle lifespan:** 1962 through 1965.
**Predecessor to this model:** Savoy (1960 to 1961).
**Replacement for this model:** Fury I (1965 to 1966).
**Percentage of division's sales volume:** 23.95%.
**Corporate siblings:** Dodge Dart.
**Primary competition:** AMC Ambassador, Chevrolet Biscayne/BelAir, and Ford Galaxie.
**Notable changes:** Completely restyled.
**Major standard equipment:** Cloth and vinyl front bench seat, color-keyed rubber floor mats, front armrests, dual sunvisors, electric windshield wipers, exterior bright trim around front window, and 6.50 × 14 BSW tires (7.00 × 14 BSW on Wagons).

## Measurements

| | Cars | Wagons |
|---|---|---|
| Wheelbase | 116.0" | 116.0" |
| Length | 202.0" | 210.0" |
| Width | 75.6" | 75.6" |
| Height | 53.7" | 53.9" |
| Legroom — front | 46.0" | 46.0" |
| Legroom — rear | 40.9" | 39.2" |
| Headroom — front | 38.0" | 38.0" |
| Headroom — rear | 37.8" | 38.6" |
| Cargo capacity (cu. ft.) | NA | NA |
| Fuel capacity (gals.) | 20.0 | 21.5 |

## Models Available

| | Style Number | Base MSRP | Change from LY | Shipping Wt. (lbs.) | Production | Change from LY |
|---|---|---|---|---|---|---|
| Fleet Special 2-Door Sedan | 201 | $2,137 | -4.04% | 2930 | * | * |
| Fleet Special 4-Door Sedan | 203 | $2,193 | -3.69% | 2955 | * | * |
| Savoy 2-Door Sedan | 211 | $2,206 | -2.48% | 2930 | 18,825 | +0.51% |
| Savoy 4-Door Sedan | 213 | $2,262 | -2.16% | 2960 | 49,777 | +10.83% |
| Savoy 4-Door, 2-Seat Wagon | 256 | $2,609 | -2.28% | 3225 | 12,710 | -2.08% |
| TOTALS | | Avg. price $2,281 | -4.65% | | Production 81,312 | +2.81% |

*Production of Fleet Special models included with Savoy.*

# Belvedere

*"This is the choice for the person who wants luxury combined with an easy-on-the-checkbook price tag."*

**Nameplate year of origin:** 1951 (HT model); 1954 (as series).
**Current bodystyle lifespan:** 1962 through 1965.
**Predecessor to this model:** Belvedere (1960 to 1961).
**Replacement for this model:** Belvedere (1966 to 1967 — as new mid-size car) and Fury II (1965 to 1966 — conceptual replacement).
**Percentage of division's sales volume:** 15.73%.
**Corporate siblings:** Dodge Dart.
**Primary competition:** AMC Ambassador, Chevrolet Biscayne/BelAir, and Ford Galaxie.
**Notable changes:** Completely restyled.
**Major standard equipment:** Cloth and vinyl front bench seat, full carpeting, front armrests, dual sunvisors, electric windshield wipers, exterior bright trim around windows, and front fender line, and 6.50 × 14 BSW tires (7.00 × 14 BSW on Wagons).

## Measurements

|  | Cars | Wagons |
|---|---|---|
| Wheelbase | 116.0" | 116.0" |
| Length | 202.0" | 210.0" |
| Width | 75.6" | 75.6" |
| Height | 53.7" | 53.9" |
| Legroom — front | 46.0" | 46.0" |
| Legroom — rear | 40.9" | 39.2" |
| Headroom — front | 38.0" | 38.0" |
| Headroom — rear | 37.8" | 38.6" |
| Cargo capacity (cu. ft.) | NA | NA |
| Fuel capacity (gals.) | 20.0 | 21.5 |

## Models Available

|  | Style Number | Base MSRP | Change from LY | Shipping Wt. (lbs.) | Production | Change from LY |
|---|---|---|---|---|---|---|
| Belvedere 2-Door Sedan | 221 | $2,342 | -2.05% | 2930 | 3,128 | -34.01% |
| Belvedere 2-Door Hardtop | 222 | $2,431 | -1.30% | 2945 | 5,086 | -46.97% |
| Belvedere 4-Door Sedan | 223 | $2,399 | -1.72% | 2960 | 31,263 | -22.02% |
| Belvedere 4-Dr., 2-Seat Wagon | 266 | $2,708 | -1.99% | 3245 | 9,781 | -27.83% |
| Belvedere 4-Dr., 3-Seat Wagon | 367 | $2,917 | -2.51% | 3440 | 4,168 | * |
| TOTALS | | Avg. price $2,559 | -1.96% | | Production 53,426 | -21.41% |

*Production of 1961 model for comparison is not available.

# Fury

*"Furys are the most glamorous of all Plymouths."*

**Nameplate year of origin:** 1956.
**Current bodystyle lifespan:** 1962 through 1965.
**Predecessor to this model:** Fury (1960 to 1961).
**Replacement for this model:** Fury III and Sport Fury (1965 to 1966).
**Percentage of division's sales volume:** 13.86%.
**Corporate siblings:** Dodge Dart.
**Primary competition:** AMC Ambassador, Chevrolet Biscayne/BelAir/Impala, and Ford Galaxie 500.
**Notable changes:** Minor trim and detail changes.
**Major standard equipment:** Cloth and vinyl front bench seat, deep-pile carpeting, tower-back front seat, front armrests, dual sunvisors, electric windshield wipers, electric clock, exterior bright trim around windows, front fender line, and wheel openings, backup lights, and 6.50 × 14 BSW tires (7.00 × 14 BSW on Wagons). Sport Fury adds: V8 engine, all-vinyl interior, and special trim.

## Measurements

|  | Cars | Wagons |
|---|---|---|
| Wheelbase | 116.0" | 116.0" |
| Length | 202.0" | 210.0" |
| Width | 75.6" | 75.6" |
| Height | 53.7" | 53.9" |
| Legroom — front | 46.0" | 46.0" |
| Legroom — rear | 40.9" | 39.2" |
| Headroom — front | 38.0" | 38.0" |
| Headroom — rear | 37.8" | 38.6" |
| Cargo capacity (cu. ft.) | NA | NA |
| Fuel capacity (gals.) | 20.0 | 21.5 |

## Models Available

| | Style Number | Base MSRP | Change from LY | Shipping Wt. (lbs.) | Production | Change from LY |
|---|---|---|---|---|---|---|
| Fury 2-Door Hardtop | 232 | $2,585 | -0.62% | 2960 | 9,589 | -40.59% |
| Fury 2-Door Convertible | 335 | $2,924 | -1.52% | 3210 | 4,349 | -37.41% |
| Fury 4-Door Sedan | 233 | $2,563 | -0.54% | 2990 | 17,231 | -23.82% |
| Fury 4-Door Hardtop | 334 | $2,742 | +3.16% | 3190 | 5,995 | -29.53% |
| Fury 4-Door, 2-Seat Wagon | 376 | $2,968 | -1.92% | 3395 | 2,352 | -17.30% |
| Fury 4-Door, 3-Seat Wagon | 377 | $3,071 | -2.07% | 3455 | 2,411 | -21.92% |
| Sport Fury 2-Door Hardtop | 342 | $2,851 | NEW | 3195 | 4,039 | NEW |
| Sport Fury 2-Door Convertible | 345 | $3,082 | NEW | 3295 | 1,516 | NEW |
| TOTALS | *Avg. price* $2,848 | | +0.71% | | *Production* 47,482 | -21.06% |

1962

# PONTIAC

*"Wide-Track Pontiac for '62!"*

Revised frontal styling highlighted the major changes for the 1962 Pontiacs. Both Tempest and the big car lines received all-new grille styling and revised trim and rear end treatments. Under the hood of the big cars, there was not much change, though there was a big announcement for racing enthusiasts. The 405-horsepower, 421 CID V8 engine, which had been basically experimental in 1961, was offered as a regular production option for 1962. Priced at $2,250, the 421 offered performance that was unbeatable anywhere else. It didn't take long for the new 421 to supplant the 389 V8 as king of the track. Nineteen sixty-two was also a sales success, the first of many years of third place finishes for Pontiac.

The other important new offering for the year was the Grand Prix, a luxury/sports car. The formula of combining performance and luxury features had been used successfully for years by Buick, even as early as the 1930s. Take a small bodied car (the Special in Buick's case), put your high performance engine under the hood (Roadmaster in this case), and you've created a little sport to go with the luxury (as in the Buick Century). Pontiac started experimenting with this formula in 1960 with the Ventura series, a Catalina body with Bonneville trim. While somewhat successful, Pontiac marketers were seeing great success in the Ford Thunderbird, Olds Starfire and Chrysler 300 series, as these "personal" luxury/sport coupes were selling well. Not wanting to be left out, Pontiac created its own coupe from available hardware, while adding special touches to create the "personal" type car. The result was the Grand Prix, a bucket seated, floor-shifted luxury coupe. While the Ventura concept would remain as a Catalina option package for many years to come, the Grand Prix was what the buyers wanted. The 1962 model was a definite success, but the 1963, offering some unique styling features, would be the car that hit the home run.

Other changes to the model line included the addition of a 2-Door Sport Coupe and a 2-Door Convertible to the Tempest line. The Ventura line was discontinued, but the Ventura Custom trim package was still available for Catalina hardtop models at $118. Finally, this was the last year that the Bonneville Custom Safari wagon was considered a separate series. This Series 27 Bonneville used a Catalina wagon body for its basis; hence the differing series identification, which was a remnant of Pontiac's 1950s body style numbering system. The issue was resolved for 1963, as the car continued to be based on a Catalina wagon, but was thereafter considered a Bonneville model.

Bonneville 2-Door Convertible

Grand Prix 2-Door Hardtop

Star Chief 4-Door Sedan

Tempest 2-Door Convertible

Tempest 4-Door Safari Wagon

**Model year production:** 521,477, up 53.26% over 1961.
**Domestic market share:** 7.84% (3rd place).
**Base price range:** $2,186 to $3,624.
**Industry average base price:** $3,025.
**Pontiac average base price:** $2,977.
**Introduction date:** September, 1961.
**Assembly plants:** Baltimore, MD (B); Southgate, CA (C); Doraville, GA (D); Linden, NJ (E); Framingham, MA (G); Fairfax, KS (K); Pontiac, MI (P); Arlington, TX (R); Fremont, CA (Z).

**Data plate identification:** Eight to ten digit code read as follows: 1st digit identifies the series (the second digit of the body style number in the charts below); 2nd and 3rd digits 62 for 1962; 4th digit is assembly plant code; 1001 and up for serial number. A separate plate contains body style number. *Example:* 362X1001 is a 1962 Pontiac Catalina, serial number 1001, built in Fairfax, KS.

## Powertrains

| Engine | Gross HP* | Transmission Availability | Tempest | Catalina & Star Chief | Grand Prix | Bonneville |
|---|---|---|---|---|---|---|
| 194.5 CID Indy 4, 1-bbl., 4-cyl. | 110/115 | 3-speed manual | S | - | - | - |
| | | 4-speed manual TempesTorque | $173 | - | - | - |
| | | 2-sp. Automatic | $173 | - | - | - |
| 194.5 CID Indy 4, 1-bbl., 4-cyl. | 120/140 | 3-speed manual | No cost | - | - | - |
| | | 4-speed manual TempesTorque | $173 | - | - | - |
| | | 2-sp. Automatic | $173 | - | - | - |
| 194.5 CID Indy 4, 4-bbl., 4-cyl. | 166 | 3-speed manual | $39 | - | - | - |
| | | 4-speed manual TempesTorque | $212 | - | - | - |
| | | 2-sp. Automatic | $212 | - | - | - |
| 215 CID, 2-bbl., V8 | 190 | 3-speed manual TempesTorque | $261 | - | - | - |
| | | 2-sp. Automatic | $438 | - | - | - |

| Engine | Gross HP* | Transmission Availability | Tempest | Catalina & Star Chief | Grand Prix | Bonneville |
|---|---|---|---|---|---|---|
| 389 CID Trophy, 2-bbl., V8 | 215 | 3-speed manual | - | S | - | - |
| | | 4-speed manual | - | $231 | - | - |
| | 267/283 SC | Hydra-matic Automatic | - | $231 | - | - |
| 389 CID Trophy — E, 4-bbl., V8 | 235 | 3-speed manual | - | $35 | - | S |
| | | 4-speed manual | - | $266 | - | $231 |
| 389 CID Trophy, 4-bbl., V8 | 303 | 3-speed manual | - | $35 | S | S |
| | | 4-speed manual | - | $266 | $231 | $231 |
| | | Hydra-matic Automatic | - | $266 | $231 | $231 |
| 389 CID Trophy, 4-bbl., V8 | 333 | 3-speed manual | - | $294 | $194 | $194 |
| | | 4-speed manual | - | $525 | $425 | $425 |
| | | Hydra-matic Automatic | - | $525 | $425 | $425 |
| 389 CID Tri-Power, 3 × 2-bbl., V8 | 313 | 3-speed manual | - | $174 | $116 | $116 |
| | | 4-speed manual | - | $405 | $347 | $347 |
| | | Hydra-matic Automatic | - | $405 | $347 | $347 |
| 389 CID Tri-Power, 3 × 2-bbl., V8 | 348 | 3-speed manual | - | $401 | $312 | $312 |
| | | 4-speed manual | - | $632 | $543 | $543 |
| | | Hydra-matic Automatic | - | $632 | $543 | $543 |
| 421 CID Trophy SD, 2 × 4-bbl., V8 | 405 | 3-speed manual | - | $2250 | $2250 | $2250 |
| | | 4-speed HD manual | - | $ | $ | $ |

*Ratings vary with model and transmission attachment. Many other combinations possible due to dealer installations or factory limited-outputs.*

## Major Options

| | Tempest | Catalina | Star Chief | Bonneville | Grand Prix |
|---|---|---|---|---|---|
| Air conditioning | $319 | $430 | $430 | $430 | $430 |
| Soft Ray tinted glass | $35 | $40 | $40 | $40 | $40 |
| Power steering — variable-ratio | $75 | $108 | $108 | $108 | $108 |
| Power brakes | - | $43 | $43 | $43 | $43 |
| Power driver's seat/ bench seat | - | $97 | $97 | $97 | $97 |
| Power windows | - | $106 | $106 | $106 | $106 |
| AM radio — manual | $62 | $89 | $89 | $89 | $89 |
| White stripe tires | $35 | $40 | $40 | $40 | $40 |
| Aluminum (8-lug) hubs and drums | - | $122 | $122 | $108 | $108 |

Options common to most models (- = Not Available.) Items may be standard equipment, optional at different pricing, or unavailable on certain models. This chart is only a guide.

## Paint Colors

| | Code |
|---|---|
| Starlight Black | A |
| Cameo Ivory | C |
| Silvermist Gray Metallic | D |
| Ensign Blue Metallic | E |
| Yorktown Blue Metallic | F |
| Kimberley Blue | H |
| Silverleaf Green Metallic | J |
| Belmar Red Metallic | L |
| Bamboo Cream | M |
| Burgundy Metallic | N |
| Aquamarine Metallic | P |
| Seafoam Aqua | Q |
| Yuma Beige | R |
| Caravan Gold Metallic | T |
| Mandalay Red | V |

# Tempest

*"The gas-saving '4' with Pontiac punch!"*

**Nameplate year of origin:** 1961.
**Current bodystyle lifespan:** 1961 through 1963.
**Predecessor to this model:** None.
**Replacement for this model:** Tempest/LeMans (1964 to 1965).
**Percentage of division's sales volume:** 27.47%.
**Corporate siblings:** Oldsmobile F-85 and Buick Special.
**Primary competition:** Dodge Lancer, Mercury Comet, and Studebaker Lark.

## Measurements

| | Cars | Wagons |
|---|---|---|
| Wheelbase | 112.0" | 112.0" |
| Length | 189.3" | 189.3" |
| Width | 72.2" | 72.2" |
| Height | 53.6" | 54.8" |
| Legroom — front | 44.1" | 44.1" |

1962

**Notable changes:** Revised front-end styling and trim and detail changes.

**Major standard equipment:** Cloth and vinyl bench seat, dual sun visors, electric windshield wipers, and 6.00 × 15 BSW tires (6.50 × 15 BSW tires on wagons).

| | Cars | Wagons |
|---|---|---|
| Legroom — rear | 37.8" | 37.8" |
| Headroom — front | 34.0" | 34.0" |
| Headroom — rear | 33.7" | 33.7" |
| Cargo capacity (cu. ft.) | 27.5 | 72.6 |
| Fuel capacity (gals.) | 15.5 | 15.5 |

## Models Available

| | Style Number | Base MSRP | Change from LY | Shipping Wt. (lbs.) | Production | Change from LY |
|---|---|---|---|---|---|---|
| Tempest 2-Door Coupe | 2127 | $2,186 | +3.45% | 2785 | 15,473 | +108.19% |
| Tempest 2-Door Sports Coupe | 2117 | $2,294 | -0.13% | 2800 | 51,981 | +597.26% |
| Tempest 2-Door Convertible | 2167 | $2,564 | NEW | 2955 | 20,675 | NEW |
| Tempest 4-Door Sedan | 2119 | $2,240 | +3.37% | 2815 | 37,430 | -40.24% |
| Tempest 4-Door, 2-Seat Wagon | 2135 | $2,511 | +2.99% | 2995 | 17,674 | -24.01% |
| TOTALS | Avg. price | $2,359 | +4.66% | Production | 143,233 | +42.12% |

# Catalina

*"Pontiac with a pace and price that's easy to live with!"*

**Nameplate year of origin:** 1950 on hardtop models, 1959 as series.

**Current bodystyle lifespan:** 1961 through 1964.

**Predecessor to this model:** Catalina (1959 to 1960).

**Replacement for this model:** Catalina (1965 to 1966).

**Corporate siblings:** Chevrolet Biscayne/BelAir/Impala, Oldsmobile 88, Buick LeSabre/Invicta.

**Primary competition:** Mercury Monterey, and Dodge Polara.

**Percentage of division's sales volume:** 39.25%.

**Notable changes:** Revised front and rear styling, and minor trim and detail changes.

**Major standard equipment:** Cloth and vinyl or all-vinyl bench seat, nylon-blend carpet, cushioned instrument panel, automatic interior lighting, electric windshield wipers, chrome exterior trim and 8.00 × 14 BSW tires (8.50 × 14 BSW tires on Safari wagons).

## Measurements

| | Cars | Wagon |
|---|---|---|
| Wheelbase | 120.0" | 119.0" |
| Length | 211.6" | 212.3" |
| Width | 78.6" | 78.6" |
| Height | 55.9" | 55.9" |
| Legroom — front | 45.3" | 45.3" |
| Legroom — rear | 41.6" | 41.6" |
| Headroom — front | 34.5" | 34.5" |
| Headroom — rear | 34.6" | 34.6" |
| Cargo capacity (cu. ft.) | NA | NA |
| Fuel capacity (gals.) | 25.0 | 19.0 |

## Models Available

| | Style Number | Base MSRP | Change from LY | Shipping Wt. (lbs.) | Production | Change from LY |
|---|---|---|---|---|---|---|
| Catalina 2-Door Sport Sedan | 2311 | $2,725 | +3.57% | 3705 | 14,263 | +44.86% |
| Catalina 2-Door Sport Hardtop | 2347 | $2,860 | +3.40% | 3730 | 46,024 | +216.88% |
| Catalina 2-Door Convertible | 2367 | $3,172 | +3.05% | 3855 | 16,877 | +36.34% |
| Catalina 4-Door Sedan | 2369 | $2,796 | +3.48% | 3765 | 68,124 | +76.31% |
| Catalina 4-Door Vista Hardtop | 2339 | $2,936 | +3.31% | 3825 | 29,251 | +66.30% |
| Catalina Safari 4-Dr., 2-S. Wagon | 2335 | $3,193 | +3.03% | 4180 | 19,399 | +54.02% |
| Catalina Safari 4-Dr., 3-S. Wagon | 2345 | $3,301 | +2.93% | 4220 | 10,716 | +37.68% |
| TOTALS | Avg. price | $2,998 | +3.24% | Production | 204,654 | +80.54% |

# Star Chief

*"Distinctive in size, excitement and road-leveling comfort!"*

**Nameplate year of origin:** 1954.
**Current bodystyle lifespan:** 1961 through 1964.
**Predecessor to this model:** Star Chief (1959 to 1960).
**Replacement for this model:** Executive (1965 to 1966).
**Corporate siblings:** Chevrolet Biscayne/BelAir/Impala, Oldsmobile 88, Buick LeSabre/Invicta.
**Primary competition:** Mercury Montclair, and Dodge Custom 880.
**Percentage of division's sales volume:** 7.99%.
**Notable changes:** Revised front and rear styling, and minor trim and detail changes.
**Major standard equipment:** Cloth and vinyl or all-vinyl bench seat, nylon-blend carpet, cushioned instrument panel, automatic interior lighting, electric windshield wipers, chrome exterior trim and 8.00 × 14 BSW tires.

## Measurements

| | |
|---|---|
| Wheelbase | 123.0" |
| Length | 218.6" |
| Width | 78.6" |
| Height | 55.9" |
| Legroom — front | 45.3" |
| Legroom — rear | 41.6" |
| Headroom — front | 34.5" |
| Headroom — rear | 34.4" |
| Cargo capacity (cu. ft.) | NA |
| Fuel capacity (gals.) | 25.0 |

## Models Available

| | Style Number | Base MSRP | Change from LY | Shipping Wt. (lbs.) | Production | Change from LY |
|---|---|---|---|---|---|---|
| Star Chief 4-Door Sedan | 2669 | $3,097 | +3.13% | 3875 | 27,760 | +73.24% |
| Star Chief 4-Door Hardtop | 2639 | $3,230 | +3.00% | 3925 | 13,882 | +2.40% |
| TOTALS | | *Avg. price* $3,164 | +3.06% | *Production* 41,642 | | +40.77% |

# Grand Prix

*"A potent new kind of car by Pontiac.*
*The personally styled car with the power personality!"*

**Nameplate year of origin:** 1962.
**Current bodystyle lifespan:** 1962 through 1964.
**Predecessor to this model:** None.
**Replacement for this model:** Grand Prix (1965 to 1966).
**Corporate siblings:** Buick Wildcat and Oldsmobile Starfire.
**Primary competition:** Chrysler 300 and Mercury S-55.
**Percentage of division's sales volume:** 5.79%.
**Notable changes:** All-new model based on Catalina body with Bonneville level trim.
**Major standard equipment:** Front bucket seats with all-vinyl trim, center console with tachometer, loop-pile carpeting, electric clock, lamp package, deluxe wheel covers, and 8.00 × 14 BSW tires.

## Measurements

| | |
|---|---|
| Wheelbase | 120.0" |
| Length | 211.6" |
| Width | 78.6" |
| Height | 54.4" |
| Legroom — front | 44.5" |
| Legroom — rear | 40.4" |
| Headroom — front | 33.8" |
| Headroom — rear | 33.8" |
| Cargo capacity (cu. ft.) | NA |
| Fuel capacity (gals.) | 25.0 |

## Models Available

| | Style Number | Base MSRP | Change from LY | Shipping Wt. (lbs.) | Production | Change from LY |
|---|---|---|---|---|---|---|
| Grand Prix 2-Door Hardtop | 2947 | $3,490 | NEW | 3835 | 30,195 | NEW |
| TOTALS | | *Avg. price* $3,490 | NEW | *Production* 30,195 | | NEW |

# Bonneville

*"Famous for its own brand of fashion and fire!"*

**Nameplate year of origin:** 1957.
**Current bodystyle lifespan:** 1961 through 1964.
**Predecessor to this model:** Bonneville (1959 to 1960).
**Replacement for this model:** Bonneville (1965 to 1966).
**Corporate siblings:** Chevrolet Biscayne/BelAir/Impala, Oldsmobile 88, Buick LeSabre/Invicta.
**Primary competition:** Mercury Park Lane, and Dodge Custom 880.
**Percentage of division's sales volume:** 19.51%.
**Notable changes:** Revised front and rear styling, and minor trim and detail changes.
**Major standard equipment:** Cloth and vinyl or all-vinyl bench seat (leather bucket seats on convertible), full carpeting including lower door panels, cushioned instrument panel, automatic interior lighting, electric windshield wipers, chrome exterior trim, deluxe wheel covers and 8.00 × 14 BSW tires (8.50 × 14 BSW tires on Safari wagon).

## Measurements

|  | Cars | Wagon |
|---|---|---|
| Wheelbase | 123.0" | 119.0" |
| Length | 218.6" | 212.3" |
| Width | 78.6" | 78.6" |
| Height | 55.9" | 55.9" |
| Legroom — front | 45.3" | 45.3" |
| Legroom — rear | 41.6" | 41.6" |
| Headroom — front | 34.5" | 34.5" |
| Headroom — rear | 34.1" | 34.4" |
| Cargo capacity (cu. ft.) | NA | NA |
| Fuel capacity (gals.) | 25.0 | 19.0 |

## Models Available

| | Style Number | Base MSRP | Change from LY | Shipping Wt. (lbs.) | Production | Change from LY |
|---|---|---|---|---|---|---|
| Bonneville 2-Door Hardtop | 2847 | $3,349 | +2.89% | 3900 | 31,629 | +87.09% |
| Bonneville 2-Door Convertible | 2867 | $3,570 | +2.70% | 4005 | 21,582 | +18.17% |
| Bonneville 4-Door Vista Hardtop | 2839 | $3,425 | +2.82% | 4005 | 44,015 | +42.77% |
| Bonn. Cust. Safari 4-Dr., 2-S. Wgn. | 2735 | $3,624 | +2.66% | 4255 | 4,527 | +36.23% |
| TOTALS | *Avg. price* | $3,492 | +2.77% | *Production* | 101,753 | +46.78% |

# RAMBLER

*"Rambler—World Standard of Compact Car Excellence.*
*New Style! New Savings! New Safety!"*

After several fantastic years for upstart American Motors, the fire had started to cool in the sales arena. One reason was pure economics. Rambler built small cars, and when the economy went down in 1958, the buying public went for the smaller, more economical cars offered by AMC and Studebaker. However, this economic downturn was short-lived, and by late 1959, things were rolling upward once again. Fortunately for AMC, they had a good product that was a good value for the consumer, so sales kept pace with a growing economy. A new American line had been introduced for 1961, rejuvenating sales for that model.

By the time the 1962 Ramblers made it to market, though, the Classic and Ambassador were beginning to look dated compared to the smooth, finless lines of the competition. The basic design had been in use since the 1956 Rambler, and some components were even older in design. This was at a time when the Big Three automakers were making major design changes every three years or less. The 1961 Classic and Ambassador had both been given a facelift, but unfortunately for the Ambassador, the Classic looked and sold much better. Also, during this time frame, GM, Ford and Chrysler had all turned to slightly downsized full-size models during 1961. With Ambassador sales sluggish, AMC decided to follow, and the 1962 model was essentially an "upmarket" Classic, sharing all sheetmetal but with slightly revised trim. This downsized Ambassador would stay in the lineup until the full-size Ambassador returned in 1965.

Since the Ambassador, with V8 power, was essentially identical to a Classic, the Classic was now offered only as a 6-cylinder model. The 250 CID V8 powerplant was no longer available. Also, a new 2-Door Sedan model was offered in both Classic and Ambassador lines. Series designations and trim levels within each model were once again juggled. This time the Super was dropped across the board, and any non-duplicating models were integrated under the Deluxe trim level. In the American line, the Custom series was designated the 400 and lost the 2-Door Wagon variant, and the Custom 400 line was dropped.

Ambassador 400 4-Door Sedan

American 400 2-Door Convertible

American 400 4-Door Wagon

Classic 400 4-Door Wagon

Classic Custom 2-Door Sedan

**Model year production:** 442,344, up 19.87% over 1961.
**Domestic market share:** 6.65% (5th place).
**Base price range:** $1,832 to $3,023.
**Industry average base price:** $3,025.
**Rambler average base price:** $2,298.
**Introduction date:** October 6, 1961.
**Assembly plants:** Kenosha, Wisconsin, and Brampton, Ontario, Canada (T designation added to serial number).

**Data plate identification (VIN):** Code read as follows: 62 for 1962 followed by serial number (American, B375001 and up; Classic Six, C625001 and up; and Ambassador V8, H160001 and up). Export cars added a K after the letter, and cars built in Canada (American and Classic only) added a T after the letter, and also had a slightly revised serial number order. *Example:* 62C625001 is a 1962 Rambler Classic Six built in Kenosha, WI, serial number 625001.

## Powertrains

| Engine | Gross HP | Transmission Availability | American | Classic* | Ambassador |
|---|---|---|---|---|---|
| 195.6 CID, 1-bbl., L-Head 6-cyl. | 90 | 3-speed manual, col. | S (ex. 400) | – | – |
| | | 3-speed w/Overdrive | $102 (ex. 400) | – | – |
| | | Flash-O-Matic Automatic | $165 (ex. 400) | – | – |
| 195.6 CID, 1-bbl., OHV 6-cyl. | 125 (127 on Classic) | 3-speed manual, col. | $60, S (400) | S | – |
| | | 3-speed w/Overdrive | $162, $102 (400) | $109 | – |
| | | Flash-O-Matic Automatic | $225, $165 (400) | $187 | – |
| 195.6 CID, 2-bbl., OHV 6-cyl. | 138 | 3-speed manual, col. | – | $12 | – |
| | | 3-speed w/Overdrive | – | $121 | – |
| | | Flash-O-Matic Automatic | – | $199 | – |

| Engine | Gross HP | Transmission Availability | American | Classic* | Ambassador |
|---|---|---|---|---|---|
| 327 CID, 2-bbl., OHV V8 | 250 | 3-speed manual | - | - | S |
|  |  | 3-speed w/Overdrive |  | - | $115 |
|  |  | Flash-O-Matic Automatic | - | - | $220 |
| 327 CID, 4-bbl., OHV V8 | 270 | 3-speed manual | - | - | $48 |
|  |  | 3-speed w/Overdrive |  | - | $163 |
|  |  | Flash-O-Matic Automatic | - | - | $268 |

*Aluminum engine block available for the Classic DeLuxe and Custom; standard on Classic 400 models.*

## Major Options

|  | American | Classic | Ambassador |
|---|---|---|---|
| Weather-Eye heater | $74 | $76 | $76 |
| Air conditioning (requires tinted glass) | $360 | $370 | $399 |
| Tinted glass — full | $27 | $32 | $32 |
| Power steering | $72 | $74 | $81 |
| Power brakes | $40 | $42 | $44 |
| Electric clock | $15 | $16 | S |
| Outside rear view mirror — left | $8 | $5 | $5 |
| AM radio — pushbutton w/antenna | $59 | $65 | $65 |
| Light package | $10 | $10 | $10 |
| White sidewall tires — standard size | $28 | $30 | $30 |
| Two-tone paint | - | $20-22 | $20-22 |
| Wheel covers | $15 | $15 | $15 |
| Side hinge tailgate — 6-pass. wagons | - | $40 | $40 |
| E-Stick Auto-Clutch transmission (w/3-speed manual or Overdrive only) | $60 | - | - |

Options common to most models (- = Not Available, S = Standard equipment.) Items may be standard equipment, optional at different pricing, or unavailable on certain models. This chart is only a guide.

## Paint Colors

|  | Code |
|---|---|
| Classic Black | P1 |
| Aqua Mist Metallic | P15 |
| Sonata Blue | P27 |
| Briarcliff Red | P30 |
| Inca Silver Metallic | P31 |
| Jasmine Rose | P33 |
| Baron Blue Metallic | P35 |
| Glen Cove Green | P36 |
| Elmhurst Green Metallic | P37 |
| Algiers Rose Copper Met. | P38 |
| Villa Red Metallic | P39 |
| Majestic Blue Metallic | P40 |
| Corsican Gold Metallic | P41 |
| Sirocco Beige | P42 |
| Frost White | P72 |

*Two-tones: first number is body color, second number is roof/accent color.*

# American

*"Quality-Built, Family-Sized, Lowest-Priced."*

**Nameplate year of origin:** 1950 (Nash).
**Current bodystyle lifespan:** 1961 through 1963.
**Predecessor to this model:** Rambler American (1958 to 1960).
**Corporate siblings:** None.
**Replacement for this model:** American (1964 to 1969).
**Percentage of division's sales volume:** 28.41%.
**Primary competition:** Chevrolet Chevy II, Ford Falcon, Plymouth Valiant, and Studebaker Lark.
**Notable changes:** Revised trim and detail changes. Super models dropped.
**Major standard equipment:** Front arm rests and ash trays, front foam cushion seat, dual sunvisors, black rubber floor mats, air cleaner, oil filter, black rubber cargo mat on wagons, and 6.00 × 15 BSW tires. Custom adds: Rear door (side) armrests, door-activated dome lights, chrome horn ring, color-keyed carpeting (wagons), and chrome luggage rack (wagons). 400 adds: Dual-note horn, deluxe steering wheel, vinyl-pleated upholstery with deluxe trim level, padded instrument panel, glove box lock, and wheel covers.

## Measurements

| Wheelbase | 100.0" |
|---|---|
| Length | 173.1" |
| Width | 70.0" |
| Height | 56.1" |
| Legroom — front | 44.0" |
| Legroom — rear | 37.8" |
| Headroom — front | 35.0" |
| Headroom — rear | 33.0" |
| Luggage cap. (cu. ft.) | NA |
| Fuel capacity (gals.) | 20 |

## Models Available

| | Style Number | Base MSRP | Change from LY | Shipping Wt. (lbs.) | Production | Change from LY |
|---|---|---|---|---|---|---|
| Amcn. DeL., 2-Dr Business Sdn. | 6202-0 | $1,832 | NEW | 2454 | 281 | NEW |
| American DeLuxe 2-Dr. Sdn. | 6206-0 | $1,846 | -0.05% | 2480 | 29,665 | +3.89% |
| American DeLuxe 4-Dr. Sdn. | 6205-0 | $1,895 | -0.05% | 2500 | 17,758 | -0.30% |
| American DeLuxe 2-Dr. Wgn. | 6204-0 | $2,081 | -0.05% | 2555 | 4,434 | -21.74% |
| American DeLuxe 4-Dr. Wgn. | 6208-0 | $2,130 | -0.05% | 2573 | 6,304 | -13.17% |
| American Custom 2-Dr. Sdn. | 6206-2 | $1,909 | -1.19% | 2492 | 12,710 | -11.42% |
| American Custom 4-Dr. Sdn. | 6205-2 | $1,958 | -1.16% | 2512 | 13,884 | -11.80% |
| American Custom 2-Dr. Wgn. | 6204-2 | $2,141 | -1.20% | 2565 | 4,398 | -23.50% |
| American Custom 4-Dr. Wgn. | 6208-2 | $2,190 | -1.17% | 2600 | 8,998 | -10.65% |
| American 400 2-Door Sedan | 6206-5 | $2,040 | -1.07% | 2558 | 4,840 | -0.88% |
| American 400 2-Dr. Convertible | 6207-5 | $2,344 | -1.14% | 2735 | 13,497 | +24.34% |
| American 400 4-Door Sedan | 6205-5 | $2,089 | -1.04% | 2585 | 5,773 | -2.48% |
| American 400 4-Door Wagon | 6208-5 | $2,320 | -1.11% | 2692 | 3,134 | -14.81% |
| TOTALS | Avg. price | $2,060 | -2.88% | Production | 125,676 | -7.60% |

# Classic

*"The All-Purpose Compact."*

**Nameplate year of origin:** 1961.
**Current bodystyle lifespan:** 1958 through 1962 (restyled in 1960).
**Predecessor to this model:** Hudson and Nash Rambler (1956 to 1957).
**Corporate siblings:** Ambassador.
**Replacement for this model:** Rambler Classic (1963 to 1966).
**Percentage of division's sales volume:** 63.41%.
**Primary competition:** Chevrolet Chevy II, Ford Falcon, Plymouth Valiant, and Studebaker Lark.
**Notable changes:** Revised trim and detail changes. Super line dropped, and Custom 400 renamed 400.
**Major standard equipment:** Front arm rests and ash trays, front foam cushion seat, dual sunvisors, air cleaner, oil filter, black rubber cargo mat (wagons), chrome luggage rack (wagons) and 6.50 × 15 BSW tires. Custom adds: Rear door (side) armrests and ash trays, door-activated dome lights, and electric clock. 400 adds: Dual-note horn, deluxe two-tone steering wheel, deluxe trim level, padded instrument panel, rear side vent windows, robe rail (wagons), and aluminum engine block (cast-iron available at no charge).

## Measurements

| | |
|---|---|
| Wheelbase | 108.0" |
| Length | 190.0" |
| Width | 72.4" |
| Height | 57.5" |
| Legroom — front | 43.5" |
| Legroom — rear | 40.3" |
| Headroom — front | 36.0" |
| Headroom — rear | 34.5" |
| Luggage cap. (cu. ft.) | NA |
| Fuel capacity (gals.) | 20.0 |

## Models Available

| | Style Number | Base MSRP | Change from LY | Shipping Wt. (lbs.) | Production | Change from LY |
|---|---|---|---|---|---|---|
| Classic DeLuxe 2-Door Sedan | 6216-0 | $2,000 | NEW | 2866 | 14,811 | NEW |
| Classic DeLuxe 4-Door Sedan | 6215-0 | $2,050 | -2.38% | 2888 | 38,082 | -5.73% |
| Classic DeL. 4-Dr., 2-S. Wgn. | 6218-0 | $2,380 | -2.42% | 3014 | 28,203 | +42.09% |
| Classic Custom 2-Door Sedan | 6216-2 | $2,150 | NEW | 2876 | 12,652 | NEW |
| Classic Custom 4-Door Sedan | 6215-2 | $2,200 | -8.90% | 2898 | 68,699 | +159.27% |
| Classic Cst. 4-Dr., 2-S. Wagon | 6218-2 | $2,492 | -8.35% | 3024 | 53,671 | +227.38% |
| Classic Cst. 5-Dr., 3-S. Wagon | 6218-4 | $2,614 | -8.09% | 3094 | 6,322 | +130.65% |
| Classic 400 2-Door Sedan | 6216-5 | $2,299 | NEW | 2841 | 5,521 | NEW |
| Classic 400 4-Door Sedan | 6215-5 | $2,349 | -8.42% | 2853 | 31,255 | +977.39% |
| Classic 400 4-Dr., 2-S. Wagon | 6218-5 | $2,640 | NEW | 2985 | 21,281 | NEW |
| TOTALS | Avg. price | $2,317 | -7.84% | Production | 280,497 | +30.97% |

# Ambassador

*"The Action-Packed Compact."*

**Nameplate year of origin:** 1933 (from top-of-the-line Nash).

**Current bodystyle lifespan:** 1958 through 1962 (shared basic structure with Classic).

**Predecessor to this model:** Ambassador (1957 to 1961).

**Corporate siblings:** Classic.

**Replacement for this model:** None.

**Percentage of division's sales volume:** 8.17%.

**Primary competition:** Buick Special, Dodge Lancer, Mercury Comet, Oldsmobile F-85, Pontiac Tempest, and Studebaker Lark.

**Notable changes:** Minor restyling of 1961 Classic, with Ambassador trim level appointments. Now based on smaller Classic chassis. Super line dropped, and Custom 400 renamed 400.

**Major standard equipment:** Front arm rests and ash trays, front foam cushion seat, dual sunvisors, dual horns, air cleaner, oil filter, black rubber cargo mat on wagons, and 7.50 × 14 BSW tires. Custom adds: Rear door (side) armrests, rear side vent windows, door-activated dome lights, electric clock, color-keyed carpeting, underhood insulation, and chrome luggage rack (wagons). 400 adds: deluxe steering wheel, deluxe trim level, padded instrument panel, rear seat foam cushions, robe rail (wagons), and wheel covers.

## Measurements*

| | |
|---|---|
| Wheelbase | 108.0" |
| Length | 190.0" |
| Width | 72.4" |
| Height | 57.5" |
| Legroom — front | 43.5" |
| Legroom — rear | 40.3" |
| Headroom — front | 36.0" |
| Headroom — rear | 34.5" |
| Luggage cap. (cu. ft.) | NA |
| Fuel capacity (gals.) | 20.0 |

*Dimensions are for 4-Door Sedan.*

## Models Available

| | Style Number | Base MSRP | Change from LY | Shipping Wt. (lbs.) | Production | Change from LY |
|---|---|---|---|---|---|---|
| Ambassador DeLuxe 2-Door Sedan | 6286-0 | $2,282 | NEW | 3227 | 45* | NEW |
| Ambassador DeLuxe 4-Door Sedan | 6285-0 | $2,336 | -2.54% | 3249 | 421* | +54.21% |
| Ambassador DeLuxe 4-Dr., 2-S. Wgn. | 6288-0 | $2,648 | NEW | 3375 | 77* | NEW |
| Ambassador Custom 2-Door Sedan | 6286-2 | $2,410 | NEW | 3237 | 659 | NEW |
| Ambassador Custom 4-Door Sedan | 6285-2 | $2,464 | -2.95% | 3259 | 7,398 | +124.25% |
| Ambassador Cst. 4-Dr., 2-S. Wagon | 6288-2 | $2,760 | -2.92% | 3385 | 4,302 | +291.45% |
| Ambassador 400 2-Door Sedan | 6286-5 | $2,551 | NEW | 3261 | 459 | NEW |
| Ambassador 400 4-Door Sedan | 6285-5 | $2,605 | -2.94% | 3283 | 15,120 | +63.12% |
| Ambassador 400 4-Dr., 2-S. Wagon | 6288-5 | $2,901 | -2.91% | 3408 | 6,401 | +112.66% |
| Ambassador 400 5-Dr., 3-S. Wagon | 6288-6 | $3,023 | -2.89% | 3471 | 1,289 | +64.41% |
| TOTALS | | Avg. price $2,598 | -6.98% | | Production 36,171 | +91.97% |

*Built primarily for fleet use.*

# STUDEBAKER

*"Endurance-built by Studebaker."*

This model year was supposed to be the turning point for Studebaker. If all had gone according to plan, the all-new 4-seat sports car, the Avanti, would have arrived in time to garner the national spotlight as the Official Pace Car for the Indianapolis 500 race in May 1962. This would have brought added attention to the remainder of the line, which was given a major facelift, and in turn brought more sales to the dealers. The added sales would boost morale, as well as the company coffers, which were now drained. As luck would have it, numerous problems crept up in the development and production of the Avanti. The resulting delay caused a Lark Convertible to be pressed into duty as the official pace car. The Avanti would finally appear as a 1963 model.

The restyled Studebakers were pleasing in appearance, but still showed signs of their forebears, especially inside.

Outside, the effects of a several year long marketing program with Mercedes-Benz were showing. Particular evidence of this appears in the grille style and textures when compared to a Mercedes of the period. Probably the nicest looking car was the newly named Gran Turismo Hawk 2-Door Hardtop, introduced after the start of the model year. Based upon the original 1953 Raymond Loewy coupe, this car had classic good looks and outstanding performance for a car of its size. Newly available was a 4-speed manual, adding performance and showing some of the German influence on Studebaker. Finally, the 2-Door Wagon was no longer offered in the Lark line.

**1962**

Lark Deluxe 2-Door Sedan

Lark Daytona 2-Door Convertible

Indianapolis 500 Pace Car

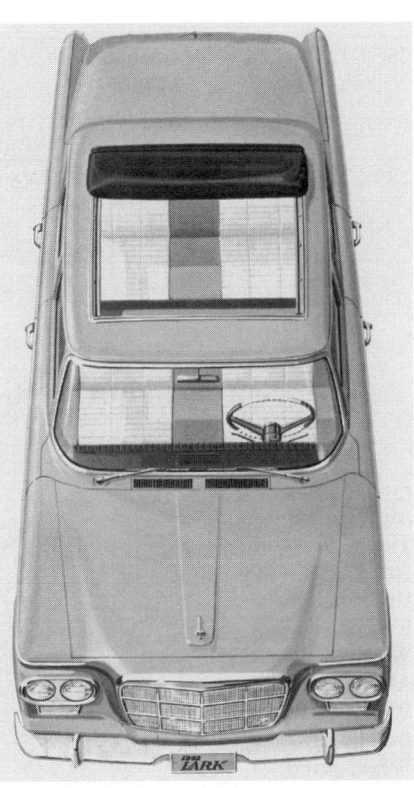

Lark Cruiser 4-Door Sedan w/optional sunroof

GT Hawk 2-Door Hardtop

---

**Model year production:** 100,175, up 45.35% over 1961.
**Domestic market share:** 1.51% (12th place).
**Base price range:** $1,935 to $3,095.
**Industry average base price:** $3,025.
**Studebaker average base price:** $2,410.
**Introduction date:** October, 1961.
**Assembly plants:** South Bend, IN (no coding) and Canada (C).

**Data plate identification (VIN):** Up to ten digit code read as follows: 62 for 1962; S for 6-cylinder or V for V8 engine; C (only if built in Canada); followed by Serial Number 1001 and up. Body style numbers are found on a separate plate on the vehicle. *Example:* 62S1001 is a 1962 Studebaker Lark Six built in South Bend, IN, serial number 1001.

## Powertrains

| Engine | Gross HP | Transmission Availability | Lark | Cruiser | GT Hawk |
|---|---|---|---|---|---|
| 169.6 CID Skybolt, 1-bbl., OHV 6-cyl. | 112 | 3-speed manual | S | - | - |
| | | 3-speed w/Overdrive | $110 | - | - |
| | | Flightomatic Automatic | $179 | - | - |
| 259.2 CID, 2-bbl., OHV V8 | 180 | 3-speed manual | $135 | S | - |
| | | 3-speed w/Overdrive | $245 | $110 | - |
| | | 4-speed manual* | $188 | - | - |
| | | Flightomatic Automatic | $335 | $200 | - |
| 259.2 CID, 4-bbl., OHV V8 | 195 | 3-speed manual | $170 | $35 | - |
| | | 3-speed w/Overdrive | $290 | $145 | - |
| | | 4-speed manual* | $358 | - | - |
| | | Flightomatic Automatic | $380 | $235 | - |
| 289 CID Thunderbolt, 2-bbl., OHV V8 | 210 | 3-speed manual | - | $73 | S |
| | | 3-speed w/Overdrive | - | $183 | $110 |
| | | 4-speed manual | - | - | $188 |
| | | Flightomatic Automatic | - | $273 | $200 |
| 289 CID Thunderbolt, 4-bbl., OHV V8 | 225 | 3-speed manual | - | $118 | $45 |
| | | 3-speed w/Overdrive | - | $228 | $155 |
| | | 4-speed manual | - | - | $233 |
| | | Flightomatic Automatic | - | $318 | $245 |

*Daytona only.

## Major Options

| | Lark | GT Hawk |
|---|---|---|
| Heater and defroster | $71 | $71 |
| Air conditioning | $325 | $325 |
| Tinted glass—full | $32 | $32 |
| Power steering (V8 only) | $75 | $75 |
| Power brakes | $38 | $38 |
| Electric clock | $15 | $15 |
| Windshield washers | $11 | $11 |
| AM radio—manual | $57 | $57 |
| White sidewall tires—standard size | $28–$48 | $28–$48 |
| Backup lights | $10 | $10 |
| Wheel covers | $16 | $16 |

Options common to most models. Items may be standard equipment, optional at different pricing, or unavailable on certain models. This chart is only a guide.

## Paint Colors

| | Code |
|---|---|
| Velvet Black | P6210 |
| Ermine White | P6211 |
| Riviera Blue | P6212 |
| Metallic Green | P6213 |
| Metallic Silver | P6214 |
| Desert Tan | P6215 |
| Blaze Red | P6216 |
| Metallic Brown | P6217 |

# Lark

*"The most beautiful automobile value on the road today."*

**Nameplate year of origin:** 1959.
**Current bodystyle lifespan:** 1962 through 1966.
**Predecessor to this model:** Lark (1959 to 1961).
**Replacement for this model:** None.
**Corporate siblings:** None.
**Percentage of division's sales volume:** 90.68%.
**Primary competition:** Rambler American, Chevrolet Chevy II, Ford Falcon, and Plymouth Valiant.

## Measurements

| | Cars | 4-Dr. & Cruiser | Wagons |
|---|---|---|---|
| Wheelbase | 109.0" | 113.0" | 113.0" |
| Length | 184.0" | 188.0" | 187.0" |
| Width | 71.3" | 71.3" | 71.3" |
| Height | 55.8" | 55.8" | 57.0" |
| Legroom—front | 44.3" | 44.3" | 44.3" |

**Notable changes:** Restyled front and rear end.
**Major standard equipment:** Cloth and vinyl front bench seats, armrests, beauty vanity, rubber floor mats, and 6.00 × 15 BSW tires. Regal adds: Chrome trim around windows and body side trim, and 6.50 × 15 BSW tires on convertible. Cruiser adds: Full-carpeting, and all-vinyl interior.

| | Cars | 4-Dr. & Cruiser | Wagons |
|---|---|---|---|
| Legroom — rear | 39.0" | 43.0" | 40.3" |
| Headroom — front | 36.0" | 36.0" | 37.0" |
| Headroom — rear | 35.0" | 35.0" | 36.0" |
| Luggage cap. (cu. ft.) | NA | NA | 72.0 |
| Fuel capacity (gals.) | 18.0 | 18.0 | 18.0 |

## Models Available

| | Style Number | Base MSRP | Change from LY | Shipping Wt. (lbs.) | Production | Change from LY |
|---|---|---|---|---|---|---|
| Lark Deluxe 2-Door Sedan | F4 | $1,935 | +0.00% | 2655 | 19,196 | 31.71% |
| Lark Deluxe 4-Door Sedan | Y4 | $2,040 | +1.75% | 2760 | 49,961 | 115.03% |
| Lark Deluxe 4-Door, 2-Seat Wagon | P4 | $2,405 | +1.48% | 2845 | 10,522 | 122.03% |
| Lark Regal 2-Door Hardtop | J6 | $2,218 | -1.11% | 2765 | * | * |
| Lark Regal 2-Door Convertible | L6 | $2,589 | +1.37% | 3075 | * | * |
| Lark Regal 4-Door Sedan | Y6 | $2,190 | +1.62% | 2770 | * | * |
| Lark Regal 4-Door, 2-Seat Wagon | P6 | $2,555 | +1.39% | 2875 | * | * |
| Daytona 2-Door Hardtop | J8 | $2,308 | NEW | 2765 | 8,480 | NEW |
| Daytona 2-Door Convertible | L8 | $2,679 | NEW | 3075 | 2,681 | NEW |
| Cruiser 4-Door Sedan | Y8 | $2,493 | +1.42% | 3030 | * | * |
| TOTALS | Avg. price | $2,341 | +2.63% | Production | 90,840 | +39.21% |

*Production not available by series.*

# Gran Turismo Hawk

*"A distinctive new sports classic."*

**Nameplate year of origin:** 1962.
**Current bodystyle lifespan:** 1953 through 1964.
**Predecessor to this model:** None.
**Replacement for this model:** None.
**Corporate siblings:** None.
**Percentage of division's sales volume:** 9.32%.
**Primary competition:** Mercury Monterey S-55, Oldsmobile Starfire and Pontiac Grand Prix.
**Notable changes:** All-new front and rear styling and new roof line. GT Hawk replaces prior year's Hawk models.
**Major standard equipment:** All-vinyl front bucket seats, full deep-pile carpeting, padded instrument panel, rear seat center armrest, exterior bright trim including windows and rocker panel moldings and 6.70 × 15 BSW tires.

## Measurements

| | |
|---|---|
| Wheelbase | 120.5" |
| Length | 204.0" |
| Width | 71.0" |
| Height | 54.6" |
| Legroom — front | 45.9" |
| Legroom — rear | 36.7" |
| Headroom — front | 34.5" |
| Headroom — rear | 33.8" |
| Luggage cap. (cu. ft.) | NA |
| Fuel capacity (gals.) | 18.0 |

## Models Available

| | Style Number | Base MSRP | Change from LY | Shipping Wt. (lbs.) | Production | Change from LY |
|---|---|---|---|---|---|---|
| Gran Turismo Hawk 2-Door HT | K6 | $3,095 | +16.79% | 3230 | 9,335 | +154.85% |
| TOTALS | Avg. price | $3,095 | +16.79% | Production | 9,335 | +154.85% |

# 1963

The 1963 model year brought with it a host of new and newly restyled models. In fact, it was rather difficult to find cars that weren't changed. A few compacts went relatively unchanged, such as the Corvair, Chevy II, Falcon, American and Lark. Also little changed were the luxurious Thunderbird, Lincoln and Imperial and a few models such as the Fairlane that were too new to be greatly changed. Several of 1963's all-new or heavily restyled models are still looked upon as great styling successes: the Buick Riviera, Studebaker Avanti, Pontiac Grand Prix, and Chevrolet Corvette. Beyond these cars, nearly every full-size car on the market was restyled or redesigned, and many of the compact models were restyled. There had not been a year with this much new styling activity since 1959.

Under the hood was a different story. The new year brought few new engines. Most manufacturers had invested heavily in powertrains for their new compacts during 1960 and 1961, and also had invested in new high performance engines during 1961 and 1962. By 1963, there just was not money left to develop new engines. Among those that were new include the Ford 406 CID V8, developed through their racing program, the Ford 260 CID V8 and 289 CID V8 developed for smaller cars, and the Pontiac 326 CID V8 for the Tempest compact.

Ford spent most of its energy in styling new full-size models this year. The Ford Galaxie and Mercury full-size models continued to share basic body structures. Their new styling was boxier, with the formal Thunderbird-style rooflines continuing. Mercury reintroduced the retracting rear window on closed cars that had been used in 1957 on the Turnpike Cruiser line. This time around all closed models offered it, and it was known as the Breezeway. At midyear, Ford introduced the semi-fastback version of the Galaxie 500 2-Door Hardtop and Mercury offered the same under the Marauder name, and had an immediate hit. This introduction was joined by the new Comet and Falcon Sprint Hardtops that were also a semi-fastback design.

American Motors introduced its first entirely new Classic and Ambassador models since 1955. The new cars, which took full advantage of AMC's unit-body construction techniques, were among the first mass-produced cars to utilize curved side door glass. Up until this time, most cars had used flat glass, but new techniques were discovered to give side glass the required strength to be curved. This allowed cars to be designed so that they were wider in the middle where more interior space was needed. In terms of styling, this would enable designers to depart from the prevailing "three box" school of styling and introduce more flowing shapes and designs. The new Classic and Ambassador earned *Motor Trend* magazine's Car of the Year award.

In terms of model offerings, the Classic and the Ambassador offered more 2-door models and fewer wagon models this year. While the Ambassador had always been built on a Classic (Rambler) platform, the new Ambassador was nothing more than a V8 version of the Classic. By 1965, however, the Ambassador would once again become a larger car built on the Classic platform.

Chrysler Corporation revamped its entire line except for the Imperial. The Imperial received more traditional headlamp and taillamps, but the basic design remained the same. This would be the last year for the body style first seen in 1960. Other full-size products, including the smaller Dodge and Plymouth models, received major facelifts based upon last year's bodies. The Chrysler line itself appeared totally new sporting horizontally placed headlights and finless rear quarters with taillights inset to the trailing ends. A regular line Chrysler 300 Convertible was selected as the Official Indianapolis 500 Pace Car for 1963. In an effort to promote the car, Chrysler offered two versions of repli-cars called the 300 Pacesetter. This model came in 2-Door Hardtop and 2-Door Convertible versions. Sales of the two cars totaled 306 and 1,861 respectively. The Dodge Custom 880 received a new front end treatment that brought it more in line with other Dodge products. The standard

## 1963 Model Year Production by Make

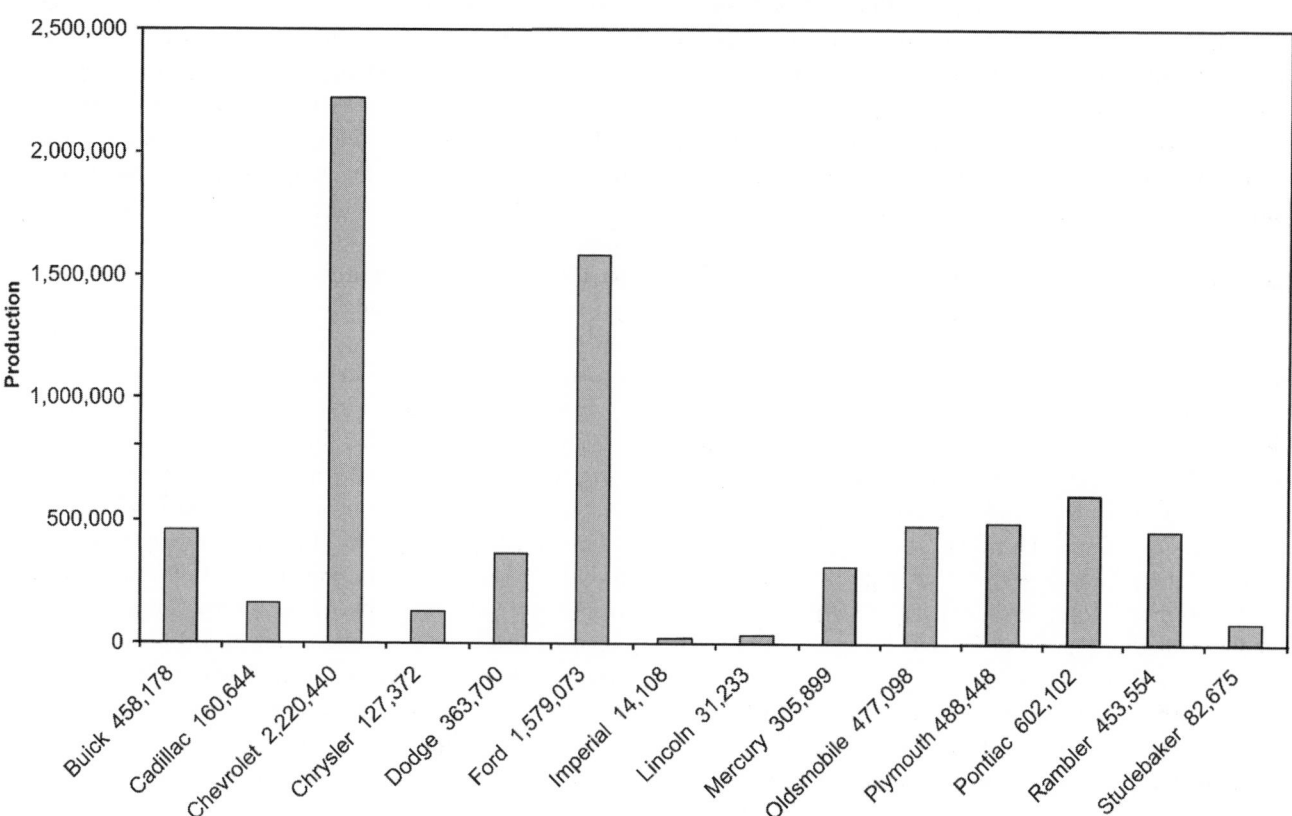

Dodge line was restyled and renamed, with the exception of the Polara. The Dart name moved to the restyled compact line where it replaced the Lancer, so the large cars were now labeled the 330 and 440. The Dodge was also lengthened to distance it somewhat from the smaller Plymouth. The new smaller Dodges and Plymouths introduced in 1962 had not been successful, and some quick restyling helped. Also, an effort to promote the Chrysler racing triumphs helped to improve sales of these vehicles. The full-size Plymouth line remained on its 116" wheelbase, but was heavily revamped. The compact Valiant and newly named Dart lines were also totally restyled with a more sporting appearance. The new cars looked less bulky than their predecessors though they were much the same in size. The model lines were expanded with more emphasis placed upon the sportier models, the Valiant Signet and the Dart GT.

After several years of ho-hum styling, GM again took center stage. Three models in particular set the tone for automobile styling for years to come: the Buick Riviera, Chevrolet Corvette and Pontiac Grand Prix. The Riviera was an all-new model, originally intended to be a Cadillac model. When Cadillac decided not to take the car, Buick jumped in and saw it as an able competitor for the Ford Thunderbird. Loaded with luxury features, Buick's most powerful engine, and clean, formal styling, the Riviera sold

40,000 copies in its initial year. This was quite a feat for a car in this price range. The Corvette was new from the ground up. Styling was a major breakthrough, descended from show cars of the early sixties. The new car rode on a smaller wheelbase, which provided better handling, and ride improvements were accomplished through new suspension components. Powertrains were mostly carry-over, but more power would be on the way soon. A big change was the introduction of a closed coupe model. The new 1963 coupe would be known as the "split-window" coupe for its large wraparound rear glass, divided by a body panel in the center. Because the divider restricted rear visibility, Chevy changed to a one-piece window for 1964. The coupe was initially less popular than the convertible, but that would soon change. Finally, the Pontiac Grand Prix was heavily revised a year after its introduction as a 1962 model, using the formula many manufacturers were offering of a large engine in a smaller bodied full-size car, and offering luxury and sporting features. The 1962 Grand Prix was successful, but the styling department had ideas to make it even better. The entire Pontiac full-size line received a facelift that included vertically stacked headlamps and of course the trademark split grille theme. Body side styling featured what is known as the "Coke bottle" form, in which the body widens slightly at the center and towards the rear of the car. To that, the Grand Prix added grille mounted parking lamps, which gave the front a sporty appearance. A unique roofline was shared with the Oldsmobile Starfire. The rear end styling included taillamps hidden behind a full-width grille work. Finally, the body carried no unnecessary chrome. The only chrome to be found (besides bumpers and grille work) was a rocker molding and trim around the greenhouse area. The result was a spectacular looking automobile that other makers scrambled to copy.

Other GM full-size models were restyled. Still based upon the 1961–62 framework, they were given lines that were more square and modern in appearance. Many models were dropping chrome trim to keep up with the latest trends. An arguable exception was Oldsmobile, whose Starfire still carried a large body side aluminum trim piece. The car was attractive but seemed overdone. Buick Electra, Olds 98 and Cadillac 4-Door Hardtop models received more formal rooflines that created rather large blind spots to the rear for drivers. The GM "senior compact" trio of Tempest, Special and F-85 were all slightly enlarged and restyled to move closer to the styling of GM's larger cars. The Chevrolet Chevy II and Corvair compacts were given minor trim and detail changes.

Studebaker came off a remarkably good year in 1962 with high hopes for its newest car, the Avanti. Designed by Raymond Loewy, who had styled the pretty 1953 Studebaker coupes, the Avanti was a styling masterpiece, though the stricture that the Avanti be built upon the Lark platform resulted in a slightly awkward appearance from some angles. But the Avanti did not bring the traffic to dealerships that Studebaker hoped it would, partly because lengthy delays in production caused the public to grow weary of hearing about the car and being unable to see it or drive it. Studebaker's fragile finances could not bear the disappointing reception, and by the end of 1964, the company would move all production to Canada, terminating the Avanti's brief run. It would reappear the next year under the name Avanti II, built by two Studebaker dealers in the old factory buildings. The design was so modern that it would last another 30 years under different manufacturing guises, and its styling would be copied in the early 21st century for a Pontiac Firebird–based Avanti revival. With better marketing and a slightly lower price, the Avanti could have been the savior Studebaker was looking for. The Lark and GT Hawk models continued with little change this season.

As usual, Checker models saw little change this year. The near-twin GM truck lines were slightly restyled this year, with new grilles and trim on most models. The Corvair vans were also similar to last year. At Ford there were no major changes to the truck lines, although the Ranchero did receive a new grille to match that of the Falcon. Dodge trucks were also little changed. International Trucks revised its truck line, and the Scout pickup continued with relatively few changes. Jeep made few changes but did introduce what could be described as the first modern day SUV (sport utility vehicle). The Jeep Wagoneer made its debut in 1963 and was an immediate success. The truck-based wagon offered off-road capabilities combined with a car-like interior layout, features and comfort. Earlier Jeepster models were similar in concept, but often spartan on the interior styling and comfort. The Wagoneer set out to change that, and it would be several years before the competition took notice.

# BUICK

*"When better automobiles are built, Buick will build them."*

Buick's big introduction of the year was the luxurious and sporty Riviera. Taking its name from the former hardtop designator, the Riviera was patterned after the successful Thunderbird formula, with a typically Buick touch. Originally designed to be a Cadillac model, the Riviera came in only the 2-Door hardtop body style. Styling was crisp and clean, with no unwanted chrome to clutter the look. Up front was a full width grille with headlamps at each end, flanked by forward canting fenders. Simple character lines down the side led to a cleanly styled rear treatment. The top was of a formal design, which led to the unfortunate blind spot so typical of cars of this type. Powering the Riviera was the 325-horsepower, 401 CID V8 engine, Buick's top performance motor. Interiors were of typical Buick luxury quality, with a full complement of power accessories offered.

After several years of all full-size Buicks being powered by the Turbine Drive Automatic transmission, a 3-

speed synchromesh manual transmission once again became standard equipment on the entry-level LeSabre. As if to emphasize that Buick owners liked to shift for themselves, a new 4-speed manual was offered on certain full-size models. Most manufacturers except the luxury makes offered 4-speed transmissions at some point during the period, only to drop them, then revive them a few years later in the mid-size and pony car models, where they were much better suited for sporty shifting.

All models were facelifted this year at Buick, with full-size models receiving the revised greenhouse of all full-size GM models, and body lines that were more squared and slab-sided. The look came off particularly nicely on the

Electra 225 models, whose long flat quarter panels, unadorned in chrome, looked huge yet added to the cars' luxury status. The Invicta name continued as the nameplate for the Estate Wagon, while the Wildcat expanded into 4-door models this year that had formerly been Invicta models. The Special and Skylark senior compacts received a facelift that paralleled the look given their big brothers, complete with full-width grille and quad headlamps mounted at the outer edges of the grille. Rear styling followed that of the larger cars also. With the restyling came a slight increase in size. This new size was just one of two steps that would take the car into the intermediate size class.

1963

Buick Electra 225 4-Door Hardtop

LeSabre 2-Door Sedan

Riviera 2-Door Hardtop

Special 2-Door Convertible

Special 4-Door Sedan

Wildcat 2-Door Hardtop

**Model year production:** 458,178, up 14.70% from 1962.
**Domestic market share:** 6.22% (6th place).
**Base price range:** $2,309 to $4,365.
**Industry average base price:** $3,028.
**Buick average base price:** $3,357.
**Introduction date:** September 1962.
**Assembly plants:** Flint, MI (1); Southgate, CA (2); Linden, NJ (3); Fairfax, KS (4); Wilmington, DE (5); Atlanta, GA (6); Framingham, MA (7); and Arlington, TX (8).
**Data plate identification:** Nine digit code read as follows: 1st

digit indicates series trim level and engine (see coding below); 2nd digit J for 1963 year; 3rd digit is assembly plant code; followed by sequential number 100001 and up for serial number. (Coding: A = V6 Special, B = V6 Special Deluxe, C = V6 Skylark, 0 = V8 Special, 1 = V8 Special Deluxe, 2 = V8 Skylark, 4 = LeSabre, 6 = Wildcat, 7 = Riviera, 8 = Electra.) *Example:* 4J4001001 is a 1963 Buick LeSabre, serial number 001001, built in Fairfax, KS. Check model number on body identification plate.

## Powertrains

| Engine | Gross HP | Transmission Availability | Special/ Skylark | LeSabre | Invicta/ Wildcat | Electra/ Riviera |
|---|---|---|---|---|---|---|
| 198 CID Fireball, 2-bbl., V6 | 135 | 3-speed manual | S* | - | - | - |
| | | 4-speed manual | $200* | - | - | - |
| | | Turbine Drive Automatic | $189* | - | - | - |
| 215 CID Fireball Aluminum, 2-bbl., V8 | 155 | 3-speed manual | $118*/S (Deluxe) | - | - | - |
| | | 4-speed manual | $318*/$200 (Del.) | - | - | - |
| | | Turbine Drive Automatic | $307*/$189 (Del.) | - | - | - |
| 215 CID Skylark Aluminum, 4-bbl., V8 | 200 | 3-speed manual | S**/$167*/$50 (Del.) | - | - | - |

| Engine | Gross HP | Transmission Availability | Special/ Skylark | LeSabre | Invicta/ Wildcat | Electra/ Riviera |
|---|---|---|---|---|---|---|
| | | 4-speed manual | $200**/$367*/ $250 (Del.) | - | - | - |
| | | Turbine Drive Automatic | $189**/$356*/ $239 (Del.) | - | - | - |
| 401 CID Wildcat 410, 2-bbl., V8 | 280*** | 3-speed manual | - | S | - | - |
| | | 4-speed manual | - | $263 | - | - |
| | | Turbine Drive Automatic | - | $231 | - | - |
| 401 CID Wildcat 445, 4-bbl., V8 | 325 | 4-speed manual | - | $285 | $32 | - |
| | | Turbine Drive Automatic | - | $253 | S | S |

*Special only. V6 available for credit on Special Deluxe models.   **Skylark only.   ***Also available in 265-hp, 410 CID Wildcat 375 version at no cost.

## Major Options

| | Special/Skylark | LeSabre | Invicta/Wildcat | Electra | Riviera |
|---|---|---|---|---|---|
| Air conditioning | $351 | $430 | $430 | $430 | $430 |
| Soft Ray tinted glass | $41 | $43 | $43 | $43 | $43 |
| Deck lid remote release | - | $10 | $10 | $10 | $10 |
| Power steering | $86 | $108 | $108 | S | S |
| Power brakes | $43 | $43 | $43 | S | S |
| Power door locks | - | $71 | $71 | $71 | $71 |
| Power driver's seat/ Bench seat, 6-way | - | $97 | $97 | $69–$97 | $97 |
| Power windows | $102** | $108 | $108 | $108* | $108 |
| AM radio | $66 | $90 | $90 | $90 | $90 |

Options common to most models. (- = Not Available; S = Standard equipment.) Items may be standard equipment, optional at different pricing, or unavailable on certain models. This chart is only a guide.

*Standard on Convertible.   **Skylark only.

## Paint Colors

| | Code |
|---|---|
| Regal Black | A |
| Arctic White | C |
| Silver Cloud Metallic | D |
| Spruce Green Metallic | E |
| Marlin Blue Metallic | F |
| Glacier Blue | H |
| Willow Mist Metallic | J |
| Burgundy Metallic | N |
| Teal Mist Metallic | P |
| Twilight Aqua Metallic | Q |
| Desert Sand | R |
| Bronze Mist Metallic | S |
| Fawn Mist Metallic | T |
| Granada Red | V |
| Diplomat Blue Metallic | W |
| Rose Mist Metallic | X |

# Special and Skylark

*"Many cars are economical, but only the Buick Special has the faculty of making economy so pleasant."*

**Nameplate year of origin:** 1935 (Special); 1953 (Skylark).
**Current bodystyle lifespan:** 1961 through 1963.
**Predecessor to this model:** None.
**Replacement for this model:** Special/Skylark (1964 to 1967).
**Percentage of division's sales volume:** 32.47%.
**Corporate siblings:** Olds F-85 and Pontiac Tempest.
**Primary competition:** Dodge Dart and Mercury Comet.
**Notable changes:** Restyled front and rear ends.
**Major standard equipment:** Cloth and vinyl bench seat, dual sun visors, electric windshield wipers, and 6.50 × 13 BSW tires. Deluxe adds: Full carpeting, deluxe trim, and V8 engine. Skylark adds: Skylark interior and exterior trim, and all-vinyl interior in convertibles.

## Measurements

| | |
|---|---|
| Wheelbase | 112.0" |
| Length | 192.1" |
| Width | 70.2" |
| Height | 54.0" |
| Legroom — front | 40.8" |
| Legroom — rear | 36.2" |
| Headroom — front | 37.7" |
| Headroom — rear | 36.2" |
| Luggage capacity (cu. ft.) | 73.8 (Wgn.) |
| Fuel capacity (gals.) | 16.0 |

## Models Available

| | Style Number | Base MSRP | Change from LY | Shipping Wt. (lbs.) | Production | Change from LY |
|---|---|---|---|---|---|---|
| Special 2-Door Coupe | 4027 | $2,309 | +0.22% | 2661 | 21,866 | +14.27% |
| Special 2-Door Convertible | 4067 | $2,591 | +0.15% | 2768 | 8,082 | +2.07% |
| Special 4-Door Sedan | 4019 | $2,363 | +0.21% | 2696 | 21,733 | -6.52% |
| Special 4-Door, 2-Seat Wagon | 4035 | $2,659 | +0.15% | 2866 | 5,867 | -20.52% |
| Special 4-Door, 3-Seat Wagon | 4045 | $2,740 | +0.15% | 2903 | 2,415 | -14.18% |
| Special Deluxe 4-Door Sedan | 4119 | $2,521 | -2.78% | 2735 | 37,695 | +19.06% |
| Special Deluxe 4-Dr., 2-Seat Wgn. | 4135 | $2,818 | -2.49% | 2909 | 8,771 | -14.84% |
| Skylark 2-Door Hardtop | 4347 | $2,857 | +2.51% | 2757 | 32,109 | -5.73% |
| Skylark 2-Door Convertible | 4367 | $3,011 | -0.03% | 2810 | 10,212 | +14.57% |
| TOTALS | Avg. price | $2,652 | -1.05% | Production | 148,750 | -3.26% |

1963

# LeSabre

*"Buick's smartest. No car gives you quite so much for your money as the Buick LeSabre."*

**Nameplate year of origin:** 1959.
**Current bodystyle lifespan:** 1961 through 1964.
**Predecessor to this model:** LeSabre (1959 to 1960).
**Replacement for this model:** LeSabre (1965 to 1966).
**Percentage of division's sales volume:** 37.36%.
**Corporate siblings:** Chevrolet Biscayne/BelAir/Impala, Pontiac Catalina/Star Chief/Bonneville, Oldsmobile 88.
**Primary competition:** Chrysler Newport, Dodge Polara, and Mercury Monterey.
**Notable changes:** New grille, revised front and rear end, and trim and detail changes.
**Major standard equipment:** Vinyl and cloth interior, electric windshield wipers, glove compartment light, trip mileage indicator, cigarette lighter, dual sunshades, and 7.60 × 15 BSW tires.

## Measurements*

| | |
|---|---|
| Wheelbase | 123.0" |
| Length | 215.7" |
| Width | 78.0" |
| Height | 56.7" |
| Legroom — front | 40.5" |
| Legroom — rear | 38.2" |
| Headroom — front | 38.2" |
| Headroom — rear | 37.6" |
| Luggage capacity (cu. ft.) | 86.7 (Wgn.) |
| Fuel capacity (gals.) | 20.0 |

*Dimensions given for 4-Door Hardtop models.*

## Models Available

| | Style Number | Base MSRP | Change from LY | Shipping Wt. (lbs.) | Production | Change from LY |
|---|---|---|---|---|---|---|
| LeSabre 2-Door Sedan | 4411 | $2,869 | -7.18% | 3905 | 8,328 | +12.27% |
| LeSabre 2-Door Hardtop | 4447 | $3,070 | -6.77% | 3924 | 27,977 | +9.80% |
| LeSabre 2-Door Convertible | 4467 | $3,339 | NEW | 4052 | 9,975 | NEW |
| LeSabre 4-Door Sedan | 4469 | $3,004 | -6.91% | 3970 | 64,995 | +14.46% |
| LeSabre 4-Door Hardtop | 4439 | $3,146 | -6.62% | 4007 | 50,420 | +34.39% |
| LeSabre 4-Dr., 2-S. Estate Wagon | 4435 | $3,526 | NEW | 4320 | 5,566 | NEW |
| LeSabre 4-Dr., 3-S. Estate Wagon | 4445 | $3,606 | NEW | 4340 | 3,922 | NEW |
| TOTALS | Avg. price | $3,223 | -0.68% | Production | 171,183 | +34.58% |

# Invicta

*"Buick's brawniest."*

**Nameplate year of origin:** 1959.
**Current bodystyle lifespan:** 1961 through 1963.
**Predecessor to this model:** Invicta (1959 to 1960).
**Replacement for this model:** Wildcat (1963 to 1964).
**Percentage of division's sales volume:** 0.76%.
**Corporate siblings:** Chevrolet Biscayne/Bel Air/Impala, Pontiac Catalina/Bonneville, Oldsmobile 88.
**Primary competition:** Chrysler Town & Country, Dodge Custom 880, and Mercury Colony Park.
**Notable changes:** New front end, revised rear end, and trim and detail changes.
**Major standard equipment:** Vinyl and cloth interior, electric clock, electric windshield wipers, glove compartment light, trip mileage indicator, power rear window, deluxe wheel covers, Turbine-Drive automatic transmission, and 7.60 × 15 BSW tires.

### Measurements

| | |
|---|---|
| Wheelbase | 123.0" |
| Length | 215.7" |
| Width | 78.0" |
| Height | 56.7" |
| Legroom — front | 40.5" |
| Legroom — rear | 38.0" |
| Headroom — front | 38.8" |
| Headroom — rear | 37.6" |
| Luggage capacity (cu. ft.) | 86.7 |
| Fuel capacity (gals.) | 20.0 |

### Models Available

| | Style Number | Base MSRP | Change from LY | Shipping Wt. (lbs.) | Production | Change from LY |
|---|---|---|---|---|---|---|
| Invicta 4-Dr., 2-S. Estate Wagon | 4635 | $3,969 | +3.47% | 4397 | 3,495 | -61.72% |
| TOTALS | | Avg. price $3,969 | +5.72% | | Production 3,495 | -93.77% |

# Wildcat

*"Buick's liveliest. As its name suggests, the Wildcat is the star among Buick performers."*

**Nameplate year of origin:** 1962.
**Current bodystyle lifespan:** 1962 through 1964.
**Predecessor to this model:** Invicta (1961 to 1962).
**Replacement for this model:** Wildcat (1965 to 1966).
**Percentage of division's sales volume:** 7.79%.
**Corporate siblings:** Chevrolet Biscayne/Bel Air/Impala, Pontiac Catalina/Star Chief/Bonneville, Oldsmobile 88.
**Primary competition:** Chrysler 300, Dodge Custom 880, and Mercury S-55.
**Notable changes:** New grille, revised front and rear end, and trim and detail changes.
**Major standard equipment:** Vinyl and cloth interior (all-vinyl on convertible), bucket seats on 2-Doors, bench seat on 4-Door, front and rear seat center armrests, electric clock, electric windshield wipers, glove compartment light, trip mileage indicator, trunk light, tachometer, dual exhausts, deluxe wheel covers, Turbine-Drive automatic transmission, and 7.60 × 15 BSW tires.

### Measurements

| | |
|---|---|
| Wheelbase | 123.0" |
| Length | 215.7" |
| Width | 78.0" |
| Height | 55.6" |
| Legroom — front | 40.5" |
| Legroom — rear | 37.5" |
| Headroom — front | 37.8" |
| Headroom — rear | 37.6" |
| Luggage capacity (cu. ft.) | NA |
| Fuel capacity (gals.) | 20.0 |

### Models Available

| | Style Number | Base MSRP | Change from LY* | Shipping Wt. (lbs.) | Production | Change from LY* |
|---|---|---|---|---|---|---|
| Wildcat 2-Door HT | 4647 | $3,849 | -1.99% | 4123 | 12,185 | -1.38% |
| Wildcat 2-Door Convertible | 4667 | $3,961 | +9.51% | 4228 | 6,021 | -55.30% |

| | Style Number | Base MSRP | Change from LY* | Shipping Wt. (lbs.) | Production | Change from LY* |
|---|---|---|---|---|---|---|
| Wildcat 4-Door HT | 4639 | $3,871 | +5.56% | 4222 | 17,519 | +6.54% |
| TOTALS | | Avg. price $3,894 | -0.85% | | Production 35,725 | -15.49% |

*Comparisons made to 1962 Invicta models.*

# Electra 225

*"Buick's finest. The Electra 225 is designed to be impressive, and we feel it succeeds admirably."*

**Nameplate year of origin:** 1959.
**Current bodystyle lifespan:** 1961 through 1964.
**Predecessor to this model:** Electra (1959 to 1960).
**Replacement for this model:** Electra 225 (1965 to 1966).
**Percentage of division's sales volume:** 12.88%.
**Corporate siblings:** Cadillac Series 62/de Ville, Oldsmobile Ninety-Eight.
**Primary competition:** Chrysler New Yorker.
**Notable changes:** New grille, revised front and rear end, and trim and detail changes.
**Major standard equipment:** Vinyl and cloth interior, 2-way power driver's seat (convertible), front and rear seat center armrests, power windows (convertible), electric clock, dual-speed electric windshield wipers with washers, glove compartment light, trip mileage indicator, cigarette lighter, automatic trunk light, deluxe steering wheel, deluxe wheel covers, backup lights, power steering, power brakes, Turbine-Drive automatic transmission, and 8.00 × 15 BSW tires.

### Measurements*

| | |
|---|---|
| Wheelbase | 126.0" |
| Length | 221.7" |
| Width | 78.0" |
| Height | 57.5" |
| Legroom — front | 40.7" |
| Legroom — rear | 41.2" |
| Headroom — front | 39.5" |
| Headroom — rear | 38.6" |
| Luggage capacity (cu. ft.) | NA |
| Fuel capacity (gals.) | 20.0 |

*Dimensions given for 4-Door Hardtop models.*

## Models Available

| | Style Number | Base MSRP | Change from LY | Shipping Wt. (lbs.) | Production | Change from LY |
|---|---|---|---|---|---|---|
| Electra 225 2-Door Hardtop | 4847 | $4,062 | 0.00% | 4153 | 6,848 | -23.25% |
| Electra 225 2-Door Convertible | 4867 | $4,365 | -0.02% | 4297 | 6,367 | -19.34% |
| Electra 225 4-Door Sedan | 4819 | $4,015 | -0.89% | 4241 | 14,628 | +8.17% |
| Electra 225 6-window, 4-Door HT | 4829 | $4,254 | -4.36% | 4284 | 11,468 | -25.51% |
| Electra 225 4-Door Hardtop | 4839 | $4,186 | 0.00% | 4272 | 19,714 | +17.81% |
| TOTALS | | Avg. price $4,176 | -1.12% | | Production 59,025 | -5.52% |

# Riviera

*"Buick's newest. An exciting combination of classic styling and sports car performance."*

**Nameplate year of origin:** 1949 (for 2-Dr. HT); 1963 (series).
**Current bodystyle lifespan:** 1963 through 1965.
**Predecessor to this model:** None.
**Replacement for this model:** Riviera (1966 to 1970).
**Percentage of division's sales volume:** 8.73%.
**Corporate siblings:** None.
**Primary competition:** Chrysler 300-K, Ford Thunderbird and Studebaker Avanti.
**Notable changes:** All-new for 1963.
**Major standard equipment:** Bucket seats, center console, rear seat center armrests,

### Measurements

| | |
|---|---|
| Wheelbase | 117.0" |
| Length | 208.0" |
| Width | 76.6" |
| Height | 53.3" |
| Legroom — front | 40.2" |
| Legroom — rear | 35.4" |
| Headroom — front | 37.4" |
| Headroom — rear | 37.5" |

1963

electric clock, dual-speed electric windshield wipers with washers, glove compartment light, trip mileage indicator, cigarette lighter, automatic trunk light, deluxe steering wheel, deluxe wheel covers, backup lights, power steering, power brakes, Turbine-Drive automatic transmission, and 8.00 × 15 BSW tires.

## Measurements (cont.)

| | |
|---|---|
| Luggage capacity (cu. ft.) | NA |
| Fuel capacity (gals.) | 20.0 |

## Models Available

| | Style Number | Base MSRP | Change from LY | Shipping Wt. (lbs.) | Production | Change from LY |
|---|---|---|---|---|---|---|
| Riviera 2-Door Hardtop | 4747 | $4,333 | NEW | 3998 | 40,000 | NEW |
| TOTALS | | *Avg. price* $4,333 | NEW | *Production* 40,000 | | NEW |

# CADILLAC

*"Cadillac for 1963 has surpassed its own great reputation."*

New styling for the 1963 model Cadillacs brought a return to a slightly bulkier looking car. However, less sculpted body sides imparted cleaner overall styling, and therefore the 1963 Cadillac actually looked more elegant, particularly in the sparsely chrome trimmed Eldorado model. Headlamps were raised to the top of the fender edges, with parking lamps mounted underneath in the full-width grille. At the rear, the fins were shrunk once again, barely noticeable at the trailing edges of the fenders. Tail-

lamps were redesigned into the tip of the fin, with backup lamps mounted in the vertical portions of the rear bumper. The rear end looked very much like the exhaust area of a jet engine mounted at the end of each rear quarter panel. The short-deck Series 62 4-Door was dropped for the new year, leaving the de Ville Park Avenue as the sole short-decklid offering. With all of the new styling touches, there were minor changes made to the powertrain and several handling and ride quality improvements.

Sixty Special 4-Door Sedan

Series 62 6-window, 4-Door Hardtop

Fleetwood 75 9-passenger, 4-Door Sedan

Fleetwood Eldorado 2-Door Convertible

**Model year production:** 160,644, up 1.31% from 1962.
**Domestic market share:** 2.18% (10th place).
**Base price range:** $5,026 to $9,939.
**Industry average base price:** $3,028.
**Cadillac average base price:** $6,331.
**Introduction date:** October 1962.

**Assembly plants:** Detroit, MI, and Linden, NJ.
**Data plate identification:** Nine digit code read as follows: 1st and 2nd digit identify year ("63" for 1963); 3rd digit is style symbol (see list); followed by 000001 and up for serial number. *Example:* 63J000001 is a 1963 Cadillac de Ville 2-Door Hardtop, serial number 000001.

## Powertrains

| Engine | Gross HP | Transmission Availability | All models |
|---|---|---|---|
| 390 CID, 4-bbl., V8 | 325 | Hydra-matic Automatic | S |

## Major Options

| | Sixty-Two | de Ville | Eldorado | Sixty Special | Seventy-Five |
|---|---|---|---|---|---|
| Air conditioning | $474 | $474 | $474 | $474 | $624* |
| Power windows | $118 | S | S | S | S |
| 6-way power seat | $113 | $85 | S | $85 | - |
| Power door locks | $46–$70 | $46–$70 | $46 | $70 | S |
| AM radio w/rear speaker | $165 | $165 | $165 | $165 | $247** |
| Guide-Matic headlamp dimmers | $45 | $45 | $45 | $45 | - |
| Tilt steering wheel | $48 | $48 | $48 | $48 | $48 |
| Cruise control | $97 | $97 | $97 | $97 | $97 |
| Remote control trunk release/lock | $53 | $53 | $53 | $53 | - |

Options common to most models. (- = Not Available, S = standard equipment.) Items may be standard equipment, optional at different pricing, or unavailable on certain models. This chart is only a guide.

*Includes rear unit and controls.    **Signal seeking.*

**Cadillac Style Symbols: A**— 62 4-window Sedan or Calais 4-Dr. HT Sedan; **B**— Sedan de Ville 4-window; **C**— 62 Short Deck Sedan; **D**— Sedan de Ville Park Avenue; **E**— Eldorado Biarritz or Eldorado Convertible; **F**— 62 Convertible; **G**— 62 2-Door Hardtop or Calais 2-Door HT; **H**— Eldorado Seville HT or Eldorado Coupe; **J**— Coupe de Ville; **K**— 62 6-window Sedan; **L**— Sedan de Ville 6-window; **M**— Fleetwood 60 Special Sedan; **N**— 62 4-window Sedan (1963) or Calais Sedan; **P**— Fleetwood Brougham or Eldorado Brougham; **R**— Fleetwood 75 Sedan; **S**— Fleetwood 75 Limousine; **Z**— Commerical Chassis

## Paint Colors

| | Code |
|---|---|
| Ebony Black | 10 |
| Aspen White | 12 |
| Nevada Silver Metallic | 14 |
| Cardiff Gray Metallic | 16 |
| Benton Blue Metallic | 22 |
| Basque Blue Metallic | 24 |
| Somerset Blue Metallic | 26 |
| Turino Turquoise Metallic | 29 |
| Basildon Green Metallic | 32 |
| Brewster Green Metallic | 36 |
| Bahama Sand | 44 |
| Fawn Metallic | 46 |
| Palomino Metallic | 47 |
| Briar Rose Metallic | 48 |
| Matador Red Metallic | 50 |
| Royal Maroon Metallic | 52 |
| Firemist Blue Metallic* | 92 |
| Firemist Aquamarine Metallic* | 94 |
| Firemist Green Metallic* | 96 |
| Firemist Gold Metallic* | 97 |
| Firemist Red Metallic* | 98 |

*Firemist colors available only on Eldorado.*

# Sixty-Two

*"A new spirit of vitality and youth."*

**Nameplate year of origin:** 1940.
**Current bodystyle lifespan:** 1961 through 1964.
**Predecessor to this model:** Series Sixty-Two (1959 to 1960).
**Replacement for this model:** Calais (1965 to 1966).
**Percentage of division's sales volume:** 40.00%.
**Corporate siblings:** Buick Electra and Oldsmobile Ninety-Eight.
**Primary competition:** Imperial Custom and Lincoln Continental.
**Notable changes:** Revised front and rear styling and new greenhouse area.
**Major standard equipment:** Carleton, Claridge and Caravelle cloth seat upholstery, rear seat center armrests, interior courtesy and map lights, left-hand outside remote control mirror, windshield wipers and washers, electric clock, right side visor vanity mirrors, rear fender skirts, front cornering lamps, power steering, power brakes, Hydra-matic transmission, and 8.00 × 15 BSW tires.

## Measurements

| | |
|---|---|
| Wheelbase | 129.5" |
| Length | 223.0" |
| Width | 79.7" |
| Height | 56.4" |
| Legroom — front | 40.8" |
| Legroom — rear | 38.8" |
| Headroom — front | 40.0" |
| Headroom — rear | 38.8" |
| Luggage capacity (cu. ft.) | NA |
| Fuel capacity (gals.) | 26.0 |

## Models Available

| | Style Number | Base MSRP | Change from LY | Shipping Wt. (lbs.) | Production | Change from LY |
|---|---|---|---|---|---|---|
| Sixty-Two 2-Door Hardtop | 6247 | $5,025 | +2.72% | 4530 | 16,833 | +5.17% |
| Sixty-Two 2-Door Convertible | 6267 | $5,588 | +2.44% | 4630 | 16,800 | +8.39% |
| Sixty-Two 4-Dr. Town Sedan | 6289 | $5,213 | NEW | 4590 | 2,600 | NEW |
| Sixty-Two 4-Door, 4-w. Hardtop | 6239 | $5,213 | +2.62% | 4645 | 17,314 | +268.38% |
| Sixty-Two 4-Door, 6-w. Hardtop | 6229 | $5,213 | +2.62% | 4640 | 16,730 | -36.18% |
| TOTALS | | Avg. price $5,261 | +0.01% | | Production 64,295 | -8.52% |

# de Ville

*"A man finds new excitement in driving when he steps into the 1963 de Ville."*

**Nameplate year of origin:** 1949 (as Hardtop designation); 1959 (series).
**Current bodystyle lifespan:** 1961 through 1964.
**Predecessor to this model:** de Ville (1959 to 1960).
**Replacement for this model:** de Ville (1965 to 1966).
**Percentage of division's sales volume:** 49.21%.
**Corporate siblings:** Buick Electra and Oldsmobile Ninety-Eight.
**Primary competition:** Imperial Crown and Lincoln Continental.
**Notable changes:** Revised front and rear styling and new greenhouse area.
**Major standard equipment:** Cambria, Clarendon or Cameo cloth and leather seat upholstery, front and rear seat center armrests, power operated front seat adjustment, power windows, interior courtesy and map lights, left-hand outside remote control mirror, windshield wipers and washers, electric clock, right side visor vanity mirrors, rear fender skirts, front cornering lamps, power steering, power brakes, Hydra-matic transmission, and 8.00 × 15 BSW tires.

## Measurements

| | |
|---|---|
| Wheelbase | 129.5" |
| Length | 223.0"* |
| Width | 79.7" |
| Height | 56.4" |
| Legroom — front | 40.8" |
| Legroom — rear | 38.8" |
| Headroom — front | 40.0" |
| Headroom — rear | 38.8" |
| Luggage capacity (cu. ft.) | NA |
| Fuel capacity (gals.) | 26.0** |

*Park Avenue Short-deck sedan ... 215.0"
**21.0 gallons on Park Avenue.

## Models Available

| | Style Number | Base MSRP | Change from LY | Shipping Wt. (lbs.) | Production | Change from LY |
|---|---|---|---|---|---|---|
| Coupe de Ville 2-Door Hardtop | 6357 | $5,386 | +0.01% | 4520 | 31,749 | +23.7% |
| Sedan de Ville 4-Dr. Park Avenue | 6389 | $5,633 | +0.01% | 4590 | 1,575 | -39.4% |
| Sedan de Ville 4-Door, 4-Wind. HT | 6339 | $5,633 | +0.01% | 4605 | 30,579 | +11.7% |
| Sedan de Ville 4-Door, 6-Wind. HT | 6329 | $5,633 | +0.01% | 4650 | 15,146 | -6.7% |
| TOTALS | | Avg. price $5,571 | +0.01% | | Production 79,049 | +9.9% |

# Eldorado

*"The most glamorous wonders of Cadillac's greatness are yours in the Eldorado Biarritz."*

**Nameplate year of origin:** 1953.
**Current bodystyle lifespan:** 1961 through 1964.
**Predecessor to this model:** Eldorado (1959 to 1960).
**Replacement for this model:** Eldorado (1965 to 1966).
**Percentage of division's sales volume:** 1.14%.
**Corporate siblings:** Buick Electra and Oldsmobile Ninety-Eight.

## Measurements

| | |
|---|---|
| Wheelbase | 129.5" |
| Length | 223.0" |
| Width | 79.7" |
| Height | 56.4" |
| Legroom — front | 40.8" |

**Primary competition:** None.
**Notable changes:** Revised front and rear styling and new greenhouse area.
**Major standard equipment:** Leather seat upholstery, front and rear seat center armrests, power operated front seat adjustment, power windows and vent windows, interior courtesy and map lights, left-hand outside remote control mirror, windshield wipers and washers, electric clock, right side visor vanity mirrors, rear fender skirts, front cornering lamps, power steering, power brakes, Turbo Hydra-matic transmission, and 8.20 × 15 WSW tires.

## Measurements (cont.)

| | |
|---|---|
| Legroom — rear | 38.8" |
| Headroom — front | 40.0" |
| Headroom — rear | 38.8" |
| Luggage capacity (cu. ft.) | NA |
| Fuel capacity (gals.) | 26.0 |

## Models Available

| | Style Number | Base MSRP | Change from LY | Shipping Wt. (lbs.) | Production | Change from LY |
|---|---|---|---|---|---|---|
| Fl. Eldorado Biarritz 2-Dr. Convertible | 6367 | $6,608 | -0.01% | 4640 | 1,825 | +25.9% |
| TOTALS | Avg. price | $6,608 | -0.01% | Production | 1,825 | +25.9% |

# Fleetwood Sixty-Special

*"The Cadillac that stands out among other Cadillacs is the Fleetwood Sixty Special Sedan."*

**Nameplate year of origin:** 1938.
**Current bodystyle lifespan:** 1961 through 1964.
**Predecessor to this model:** Fleetwood Sixty-Special (1959 to 1960).
**Replacement for this model:** Fleetwood Sixty-Special (1965 to 1966).
**Percentage of division's sales volume:** 8.71%.
**Corporate siblings:** Buick Electra and Oldsmobile Ninety-Eight.
**Primary competition:** Imperial LeBaron.
**Notable changes:** Revised front and rear styling and new greenhouse area.
**Major standard equipment:** Leather, fabric and leather or broadcloth seat upholstery, front and rear seat center armrests, power operated front seat adjustment, power windows, interior courtesy and map lights, left-hand outside remote control mirror, windshield wipers and washers, electric clock, right side visor vanity mirrors, rear fender skirts, front cornering lamps, power steering, power brakes, Hydra-matic transmission, and 8.00 × 15 BSW tires.

## Measurements

| | |
|---|---|
| Wheelbase | 129.5" |
| Length | 223.0" |
| Width | 79.7" |
| Height | 56.7" |
| Legroom — front | 40.7" |
| Legroom — rear | 40.2" |
| Headroom — front | 40.1" |
| Headroom — rear | 39.5" |
| Luggage capacity (cu. ft.) | NA |
| Fuel capacity (gals.) | 26.0 |

## Models Available

| | Style Number | Base MSRP | Change from LY | Shipping Wt. (lbs.) | Production | Change from LY |
|---|---|---|---|---|---|---|
| Fleetwood Sixty-Special 4-Door Sedan | 6039 | $6,366 | No change | 4690 | 14,000 | +4.9% |
| TOTALS | Avg. price | $6,366 | No change | Production | 14,000 | +4.9% |

# Fleetwood Seventy-Five

*"Never has the Cadillac emblem adorned more impressive cars than the 1963 Fleetwood Seventy-Fives."*

**Nameplate year of origin:** 1927 (Fleetwood bodies), 1936 (75 series).
**Current bodystyle lifespan:** 1959 through 1965.
**Predecessor to this model:** Fleetwood 75 (1957 to 1958).
**Replacement for this model:** Fleetwood 75 (1966).
**Percentage of division's sales volume:** 0.92%.
**Corporate siblings:** None.
**Primary competition:** None.
**Notable changes:** Revised front and rear styling.
**Major standard equipment:** Wool broadcloth, cord cloth or leather seat upholstery with front compartment in harmonizing leather upholstery, rear seat center armrests, power operated front seat adjustment, power windows, interior courtesy and map lights, left-hand outside remote control mirror, windshield wipers and washers, electric clock, right side visor vanity mirrors, rear fender skirts, front cornering lamps, power steering, power brakes, Hydramatic transmission, and 8.00 × 15 BSW tires.

### Measurements

| | |
|---|---|
| Wheelbase | 149.8" |
| Length | 243.3" |
| Width | 79.9" |
| Height | 59.2" |
| Legroom — front | 39.8" |
| Legroom — rear | 41.3" |
| Headroom — front | 40.2" |
| Headroom — rear | 39.1" |
| Luggage capacity (cu. ft.) | NA |
| Fuel capacity (gals.) | 26.0 |

## Models Available

| | Style Number | Base MSRP | Change from LY | Shipping Wt. (lbs.) | Production | Change from LY |
|---|---|---|---|---|---|---|
| Fleetwood Seventy-Five 4-Door Sdn., 9-p. | 7523 | $9,724 | +0.01% | 5240 | 680 | -2.3% |
| Fleetwood Seventy-Five 4-Door Limo., 9-p. | 7533 | $9,939 | +0.01% | 5300 | 795 | -12.1% |
| TOTALS | *Avg. price* $9,832 | | +0.01% | *Production* 1,475 | | -7.8% |

# CHEVROLET

*"Chevrolet for '63 gives you four different kinds of new cars. GO Chevrolet for '63 — it's exciting!"*

Chevrolet had seen its sales rise remarkably in the past year and wanted to continue that success going forward. With some outstanding new product, they were able to accomplish that goal. Part of that success lay in the fact that Chevrolet was able to introduce a new model, or a totally redesigned existing model, every year throughout the sixties. This year it was the Corvette's turn. The all-new, aerodynamic looking Corvette came in a new coupe body style to accompany the convertible model. The fiberglass sports car rode on a four inch shorter wheelbase, although the overall length was nearly the same. This provided better sports car handling capabilities, while new suspension geometry improved the ride. Power under the hood came from the same engines offered in prior years. The never before offered Sting Ray Sport Coupe model featured a center body crease that ran lengthwise through the louvered hood, through the fastback style roof, down the one-year-only split back window, and down the rear deck (there was no trunk lid) to meet the rear body panel. This new Corvette was definitely a big improvement over previous Corvettes.

Full-size Chevrolet models received the same overhaul

other big GM cars were given. This included the new rooflines and greenhouse areas for certain 2-door and 4-door models. Frontal design was highlighted by a v-shaped front fender line that complemented the full width grille of similar shape. Two full-length body side character lines were featured: One began at the point of the "V" of the front fender and continued the entire vehicle length to a complementary "V" at the rear quarter. The second line ran from the mid-point of the trailing front wheel opening edge, across the top of the rear wheel opening, to the top of the rear bumper. Rear styling continued the two or three taillamp configurations (depending upon model) started in 1958, dropped in 1959, then resumed for 1960. The only model change was the dropping of the BelAir 2-Door

Hardtop, as this line continued to become a more spartan offering following the success of the more upscale Impala. The 6-cylinder engine standard in most models was given an overhaul this year. It now displaced 230 cubic inches and developed more horsepower at 140. Also the popular Powerglide automatic transmission was redesigned for better performance. The compact Chevys, the Corvair and Chevy II, received new grilles, or in the Corvair's case, a new front panel trim piece. Otherwise these lines were little changed. The Corvair Lakewood wagon was discontinued after a short two-year lifespan, but the Chevy II wagon proved far more popular with buyers. Also, the Chevy II Nova 400 2-Door Sedan was discontinued as most Nova 2-Door buyers were opting for the Hardtop version.

**1963**

Biscayne 2-Door Sedan and
Biscayne 4-Door Sedan

Chevy II Nova 400 2-Door Hardtop

Corvair 900 Monza 2-Door Convertible

Corvette 2-Door Coupe

Impala Interior

Impala SS 2-Door Hardtop

**Model year production:** 2,220,440, up 7.91% from 1962.
**Domestic market share:** 30.15% (1st place).
**Base price range:** $1,992 to $4,252.
**Industry average base price:** $3,028.
**Chevrolet average base price:** $2,544.
**Introduction date:** October 1962.
**Assembly plants:** Atlanta, GA (A); Baltimore, MD (B); Flint, MI (F); Framingham, MA (G); Janesville, WI (J); Kansas City, MO (K), Los Angeles, CA (L), Norwood, OH (N);

Oakland, CA (O); Arlington, TX (R); St. Louis, MO (S); Tarrytown, NY (T); and Willow Run, MI (W).
**Data plate identification:** Twelve digit code read as follows: 1st digit 3 for 1963; Four digit style number (see listings below) in which 2nd and 3rd digits identify series and engine, 4th and 5th indicate body style; 6th digit is assembly plant code; 100001 and up for serial number. *Example:* 31511S100001 is a 1963 Chevrolet BelAir 2-Door Sedan, 6-cylinder, serial number 100001, built in St. Louis, MO.

## Powertrains

| Engine | Gross HP | Transmission Availability | Corvair | Chevy II | Biscayne/ BelAir/Impala | Corvette |
|---|---|---|---|---|---|---|
| 153 CID Super-Thrift, 1-bbl., 4-cyl. | 90 | 3-speed manual | - | S* | - | - |
| | | 2-sp. Powerglide Automatic | - | $167* | - | - |
| 164 CID Turbo-Air, 2 × 1-bbl., Flat 6 | 80 | 3-speed manual | S | - | - | - |
| | | 4-speed manual | $92 | - | - | - |
| | | 2-sp. Powerglide Automatic | $157 | - | - | - |
| 164 CID Turbo-Air, 2 × 1-bbl., Flat 6 | 102 | 3-speed manual | $27 | - | - | - |
| | | 4-speed manual | $119 | - | - | - |
| | | 2-sp. Powerglide Automatic | $184 | - | - | - |
| 164 CID Turbo-Air, Turbo-charged, Flat 6 | 150 | 3-speed manual | S** | - | - | - |
| | | 4-speed manual | $92** | - | - | - |
| 194 CID Hi-Thrift, 1-bbl., 6-cyl. | 120 | 3-speed manual | - | S (Nova) $60* | - | - |
| | | 2-sp. Powerglide Automatic | - | $167 (Nova)/ $227* | - | - |
| 230 CID Turbo-Thrift, 1-bbl., 6-cyl. | 140 | 3-speed manual | - | - | S | - |
| | | Overdrive | - | - | $108 | - |
| | | 2-sp. Powerglide Automatic | - | - | $188 | - |
| 283 CID Turbo-Fire, 2-bbl., V8 | 195 | 3-speed manual | - | - | $107 | - |
| | | Overdrive | - | - | $215 | - |
| | | 2-sp. Powerglide Automatic | - | - | $306 | - |
| 327 CID Turbo-Fire, 4-bbl., V8 | 250 | 3-speed manual | - | - | $191 | S |
| | | 4-speed manual | - | - | $428 | $188 |
| | | 2-sp. Powerglide Automatic | - | - | $390 | $199 |
| 327 CID Turbo-Fire, 2 × 4-bbl., V8 | 300 | 3-speed manual | - | - | $242 | $54 |
| | | 4-speed manual | - | - | $479 | $242 |
| | | 2-sp. Powerglide Automatic | - | - | $441 | $253 |
| 327 CID Corvette, 4-bbl., V8 | 340 | 3-speed manual | - | - | - | $108 |
| | | 4-speed manual | - | - | - | $296 |
| | | 2-sp. Powerglide Automatic | - | - | - | $307 |
| 327 CID Ramjet, Fuel-Injected V8 | 360 | 3-speed manual | - | - | - | $430 |
| | | 4-speed manual | - | - | - | $618 |
| 409 CID Turbo-Fire, 4-bbl., V8 | 340 | 3-speed manual | - | - | $349 | - |
| | | 4-speed manual | - | - | $586 | - |
| | | 2-sp. Powerglide Automatic | - | - | $548 | - |
| 409 CID Turbo-Fire, 4-bbl., V8 | 400 | 3-speed manual | - | - | $428 | - |
| | | 4-speed manual | - | - | $665 | - |
| | | 2-sp. Powerglide Automatic | - | - | $627 | - |
| 409 CID Turbo-Fire, 4-bbl., V8 | 425 | 3-speed manual | - | - | $484 | - |
| | | 4-speed manual | - | - | $720 | - |
| | | 2-sp. Powerglide Automatic | - | - | $682 | - |

*Chevy II 100 only.    ** Monza only.

## Major Options

| | Corvair | Chevy II | Full-size | Corvette |
|---|---|---|---|---|
| Air conditioning (NA 4-cyl.) | $350 | $317 | $364 | $422 |
| Soft Ray tinted glass | $27 | $31 | $38 | $16 |
| ComforTilt steering wheel | - | - | $43 | - |
| Power steering (NA 4-cyl.) | - | $86 | $86 | $86 |
| Power brakes | - | $43 | $43 | $43 |
| Power windows | - | - | $102 | $59 |
| Electric clock | $16 | $16 | $16 | S |
| Pushbutton AM radio | $59 | $59 | $59 | - |
| AM/FM radio | - | - | $137 | $177 |
| Whitewall Tires — std. size | $29 | $31 | $32–$40 | $32 |
| Super Sport package | - | $161 | $161 | - |

Options common to most models (- = Not Available; S = standard equipment.) Items may be standard equipment, optional at different pricing, or unavailable on certain models. This chart is only a guide.

## Paint Colors

| | Code |
|---|---|
| Tuxedo Black | 900 |
| Laurel Green Met. | 905 |
| Ivy Green Metallic | 908 |
| Silver Blue Met. | 912 |
| Monaco Blue Metallic | 914 |
| Daytona Blue Metallic | 916 |
| Azure Aqua Met. | 918 |
| Marine Aqua Met. | 919 |
| Autumn Gold Metallic | 920 |
| Ember Red | 922 |
| Riverside Red | 923 |
| Anniversary Gold Met. | 927 |
| Saddle Tan Met. | 932 |
| Cordovan Brown Met. | 934 |
| Ermine White | 936 |
| Adobe Beige | 938 |
| Satin Silver Metallic | 940 |
| Sebring Silver Metallic | 941 |
| Palomar Red Met. | 948 |

**1963**

# Corvair

*"Corvair keeps the zest in driving."*

**Nameplate year of origin:** 1960.
**Current bodystyle lifespan:** 1960 through 1964.
**Predecessor to this model:** None.
**Replacement for this model:** Corvair (1965 to 1969).
**Percentage of division's sales volume:** 11.46%.
**Corporate siblings:** None.
**Primary competition:** Rambler American, Ford Falcon, Plymouth Valiant and Studebaker Lark.
**Notable changes:** Revised trim and detail changes.
**Major standard equipment:** Cloth and vinyl front bench seat, left-hand sun visor, turn signals, center dome light, electric windshield wipers, and 6.50 × 13 BSW tires. 700 adds: Luggage compartment trim, color-keyed floor mats, dual horns, and automatic dome lamp switch. Monza adds: All-vinyl bucket seats, folding rear seat, dual sun visors, glove box light, and additional exterior chrome trim.

## Measurements

| | |
|---|---|
| Wheelbase | 108.0" |
| Length | 180.0" |
| Width | 67.0" |
| Height | 51.5" |
| Legroom — front | 41.5" |
| Legroom — rear | 32.5" |
| Headroom — front | 37.5" |
| Headroom — rear | 36.5" |
| Cargo capacity (cu. ft.) | 12.6 |
| Fuel capacity (gals.) | 14.0 |

## Models Available

| | Style Number | Base MSRP | Change from LY | Shipping Wt. (lbs.) | Production | Change from LY |
|---|---|---|---|---|---|---|
| Corvair 500 2-Door Club Coupe | 0527 | $1,992 | 0.00% | 2330 | 16,680 | +2.68% |
| Corvair 700 2-Door Club Coupe | 0727 | $2,056 | -0.05% | 2355 | 12,378 | -33.00% |
| Corvair 700 4-Door Sedan | 0769 | $2,110 | -0.05% | 2385 | 20,684 | -41.52% |
| Corvair Monza 2-Door Club Coupe | 0927 | $2,272 | -0.04% | 2415 | 129,544 | -14.63% |
| Corvair Monza 2-Door Convertible | 0967 | $2,481 | -0.08% | 2525 | 44,165 | +166.55% |
| Corvair Monza 4-Door Sedan | 0969 | $2,326 | +2.33% | 2450 | 31,120 | -35.25% |
| TOTALS | | Avg. price $2,206 | -2.87% | | Production 254,571 | -12.98% |

# Chevy II

*"Fresh, fashionable ... carefree, too!"*

**Nameplate year of origin:** 1962.
**Current bodystyle lifespan:** 1962 through 1965.
**Predecessor to this model:** None.
**Replacement for this model:** Chevy II (1966 through 1967).
**Percentage of division's sales volume:** 16.78%.
**Corporate siblings:** None.
**Primary competition:** Rambler American, Ford Falcon, Plymouth Valiant, and Studebaker Lark.
**Notable changes:** Revised trim and detail changes.
**Major standard equipment:** Cloth and vinyl front bench seat, left-hand sun visor, turn signals, center dome light, electric windshield wipers, and 6.00 × 13 BSW tires (6.50 × 13 BSW tires on wagons). 300 adds: Luggage compartment trim, color-keyed floor mats, dual horns, and automatic dome lamp switch. Nova adds: Dual sun visors, glove box light, additional exterior chrome trim, and 6.50 × 13 BSW tires.

## Measurements

|  | Cars | Wagons |
|---|---|---|
| Wheelbase | 110.0" | 110.0" |
| Length | 183.0" | 187.4" |
| Width | 70.8" | 70.8" |
| Height | 55.0" | 55.0" |
| Legroom — front | 40.5" | 40.5" |
| Legroom — rear | 36.5" | 36.3" |
| Headroom — front | 39.0" | 39.0" |
| Headroom — rear | 38.0" | 37.8" |
| Cargo capacity (cu. ft.) | 25.5 | 76.2 |
| Fuel capacity (gals.) | 16.0 | 16.0 |

## Models Available

|  | Style Number | Base MSRP | Change from LY | Shipping Wt. (lbs.) | Production | Change from LY |
|---|---|---|---|---|---|---|
| Chevy II 100 2-Door Coupe | 0111 | $2,003 | 0.00% | 2430 | * | * |
| Chevy II 100 4-Door Sedan | 0169 | $2,040 | -0.05% | 2455 | * | * |
| Chevy II 100 4-Door Wagon | 0235 | $2,397 | -0.08% | 2810 | * | * |
| Chevy II 300 2-Door Coupe | 0311 | $2,084 | 0.00% | 2440 | * | * |
| Chevy II 300 4-Door Sedan | 0369 | $2,121 | -0.05% | 2470 | * | * |
| Chevy II 300 4-Door Wagon | 0345 | $2,516 | -0.04% | 2810 | * | * |
| Chevy II Nova 400 2-Door Sedan | 0411 | $2,143 | -2.50% | 2530 | 42,017 | -5.35% |
| Chevy II Nova 400 2-Door Hardtop | 0437 | $2,262 | -0.09% | 2590 | 87,415 | +46.70% |
| Chevy II Nova 400 2-Door Conv. | 0467 | $2,472 | -0.12% | 2760 | 24,823 | +4.56% |
| Chevy II Nova 400 4-Door Sedan | 0449 | $2,235 | -0.04% | 2590 | 146,097 | +5.10% |
| Chevy II Nova 400 4-Door Wagon | 0435 | $2,494 | -0.12% | 2835 | 72,274 | +20.69% |
| TOTALS | | Avg. price $2,252 | -0.27% | | Production 372,626 | +14.09% |

*Production figures not available by series.

# Chevrolet Full-size

*"Clean-cut as a jewel, smooth-riding as a jet."*

**Nameplate year of origin:** 1950 (BelAir); 1958 (Biscayne); 1958 (Impala).
**Current bodystyle lifespan:** 1961 through 1964.
**Predecessor to this model:** Biscayne/BelAir/Impala (1959 to 1960).
**Replacement for this model:** Biscayne/BelAir/Impala/Caprice (1965 to 1966).
**Percentage of division's sales volume:** 70.78%.
**Corporate siblings:** Buick LeSabre/Wildcat, Olds 88, Pontiac Catalina/Star Chief/Bonneville.
**Primary competition:** Rambler Ambassador, Dodge 330/440, Ford Custom/Galaxie, and Plymouth Full-size.
**Notable changes:** Revised front and rear end styling.
**Major standard equipment:** Biscayne: Nylon pattern cloth seat upholstery,

## Measurements

|  | Cars | Wagons |
|---|---|---|
| Wheelbase | 119.0" | 119.0" |
| Length | 210.4" | 210.4" |
| Width | 79.0" | 79.0" |
| Height (Sedan only) | 55.5" | 55.8" |
| Legroom — front | 41.0" | 41.0" |
| Legroom — rear | 38.0" | 38.0" |
| Headroom — front | 39.0" | 39.0" |
| Headroom — rear | 38.0" | 38.0" |

foam cushion front seats, front door armrests, dual sun visors, electric windshield wipers, cigar lighter, glove compartment lock and 7.00 × 14 BSW tires (8.00 × 14 BSW tires on wagons). BelAir adds: Cloth headliner, foam cushion front and rear seats, front and rear door armrests, combination carpet and vinyl coated rubber floor mats, and interior lighting. Impala adds: Vinyl upholstery in convertible, vinyl headliner (cloth in 4-Door Sedan), electric clock, full carpeting, dual backup lamps and 7.50 × 14 BSW tires on convertible.

|  | Cars | Wagons |
|---|---|---|
| Cargo capacity (cu. ft.) | NA | 97.5 |
| Fuel capacity (gals.) | 20.0 | 19.0 |

## Models Available

| | Style Number | Base MSRP | Change from LY | Shipping Wt. (lbs.) | Production | Change from LY |
|---|---|---|---|---|---|---|
| Biscayne 2-Door Sedan | 1111 | $2,322 | -0.09% | 3205 | * | * |
| Biscayne 4-Door Sedan | 1169 | $2,376 | -0.08% | 3280 | * | * |
| Biscayne 4-Dr., 2-S. Wagon | 1135 | $2,723 | -0.07% | 3685 | * | * |
| Bel Air 2-Door Sedan | 1511 | $2,454 | -0.08% | 3215 | 135,636 | +6.07% |
| Bel Air 4-Door Sedan | 1569 | $2,508 | -0.08% | 3280 | * | * |
| BelAir 4-Dr., 2-S. Wagon | 1535 | $2,818 | -0.04% | 3685 | * | * |
| BelAir 4-Dr., 3-S. Wagon | 1545 | $2,921 | -0.03% | 3720 | * | * |
| Impala 2-Door Sport Coupe | 1747 | $2,667 | -0.07% | 3265 | 399,224 | +23.44% |
| Impala 2-Door Convertible | 1767 | $2,917 | -0.07% | 3400 | 82,659 | +9.17% |
| Impala 4-Door Sedan | 1769 | $2,661 | -0.04% | 3310 | 561,511 | +5.28% |
| Impala 4-Door Hardtop | 1739 | $2,732 | -0.07% | 3350 | 194,158 | +10.27% |
| Impala 4-Dr., 2-S. Wagon | 1735 | $2,960 | -0.03% | 3705 | 198,542 | +5.85% |
| Impala 4-Dr., 3-S. Wagon | 1745 | $3,063 | -0.03% | 3745 | * | * |
| TOTALS | | Avg. price $2,702 | +0.03% | | Production 1,571,730 | +10.37% |

*Production not available by series.

# Corvette

*"Two new classic looks for America's sports car."*

**Nameplate year of origin:** 1953 (Also used on show car of same year).
**Current bodystyle lifespan:** 1963 through 1967.
**Predecessor to this model:** Corvette (1956 to 1962).
**Replacement for this model:** Corvette (1968 to 1982).
**Percentage of division's sales volume:** 0.97%.
**Corporate siblings:** None.
**Primary competition:** None.
**Notable changes:** Completely redesigned.
**Major standard equipment:** Bucket seats, cockpit-cluster console, deep-twist carpeting, complete instrumentation, Manually-operated folding top (convertible), and 6.70 × 15 BSW tires.

## Measurements

| Wheelbase | 98.0" |
|---|---|
| Length | 175.4" |
| Width | 69.3" |
| Height | 49.8" |
| Legroom — front | 43.7" |
| Legroom — rear | NA |
| Headroom — front | 37.0" |
| Headroom — rear | NA |
| Cargo capacity (cu. ft.) | NA |
| Fuel capacity (gals.) | 20.0 |

## Models Available

| | Style Number | Base MSRP | Change from LY | Shipping Wt. (lbs.) | Production | Change from LY |
|---|---|---|---|---|---|---|
| Corvette 2-Door Coupe | 0837 | $4,252 | NEW | 2859 | 10,594 | NEW |
| Corvette 2-Door Convertible | 0867 | $4,037 | -0.02% | 2881 | 10,919 | -24.86% |
| TOTALS | | Avg. price $4,145 | +2.65% | | Production 21,513 | +48.05% |

1963

# CHRYSLER

*"The crisp, new custom look of Chrysler '63."*

All new 1963 Chryslers rode on the 122-inch wheelbase of the Newport and 300 line this year. With this move, the 1960 unit-body was given a completely new outer skin and roofline. Without looking under the hood, or under the car, it was difficult to find traces of the old car around, but they were there. The new outer sheetmetal eliminated most connections to the beleaguered 1960–1962 period. Up front the now traditional, trapezoidal grille shape was retained, flanked by horizontally placed quad headlamps. A detail line went up from the outer edges of the grille, and wrapped up the top of the hood, and continued to a point just short of the bottom windshield corners. Bodysides were now of a slab-sided design that followed back to a simple, attractive rear design that consisted of mostly horizontal lines, and single, round taillamps. The most noticeable change was the loss of the light, thin rooflines. They were now of a more formal, upright and heavy design. Powertrain choices were given a big boost of horsepower this year. The famous 426 CID V8 engine made its debut this year. Available in short or long ram intake versions, the new engines developed 373 to 425 horsepower, depending upon which version was chosen. This engine would be developed and refined sufficiently to make it one of the most memorable powerplants on the street or the racetrack. However, it earned its fame in Dodge and Plymouth products, as it was not offered in Chrysler models after this year. Another

development of major importance this year was the implementation of a first-ever long-term warranty program. On all major driveline components, Chrysler warranted for 5 years or 50,000 miles (whichever occurred first) that with recorded, regular maintenance, any defective components would be repaired or replaced. This was major news in a period when some manufacturers would only offer 6 months or 6,000 miles. Probably more than any other single factor, this helped to revive Chrysler sales and improve their image of engineering excellence.

The year brought no major new model introductions, but a few unique limited editions were available during this year. The regular series 300 2-Door Convertible was selected to be the Indianapolis 500 Pace Car for this season, and in response, Chrysler celebrated by offering two 300 Pacesetter special editions, a Convertible and a 2-Door Hardtop. The Pacesetter models, while not letter series cars, featured special blue paint, unique interiors, and a checkered flag emblem under the 300 logo on the front fender. Another new offering was the New Yorker Salon 4-Door Hardtop. The Salon was a near fully equipped luxury car filling the void to be left by the impending cancellation of the Imperial Custom line. Visual cues to set apart the Salon included a vinyl top, unique side moldings, Salon nameplates and a more luxurious interior. Further information on these cars is included below in the model breakouts.

Newport Town & Country 4-Door,
6 passenger Wagon

Newport 2-Door Hardtop

New Yorker 4-Door Sedan

300 Convertible, Indianapolis 500 Pace Car

Model year production: 127,372, down 0.24% from 1962.
Domestic market share: 1.73% (11th place).
Base price range: $2,964 to $5,860.
Industry average base price: $3,028.
Chrysler average base price: $3,926.
Introduction date: October 1962.
Assembly plants: Detroit (Jefferson Ave.) MI (3).

Data plate identification: Ten digit code read as follows: 1st digit 8 for Chrysler; 2nd number identifies series (1–7; Newport is 1); 3rd digit 3 for 1963; 4th digit is assembly plant code; followed by 100001 and up for serial number. Body style identification found on separate plate. *Example:* 8133100001 is a 1963 Chrysler Newport, serial number 100001, built in Detroit, MI.

## Powertrains

| Engine | Gross HP | Transmission Availability | Newport | 300 | New Yorker | 300-J |
|---|---|---|---|---|---|---|
| 361 CID Firebolt, 2-bbl., V8 | 265 | 3-speed manual | S | - | - | - |
| | | Torqueflite automatic | $227 | - | - | - |
| 383 CID FirePower, 2-bbl., V8 | 305 | 3-speed manual | - | S | - | - |
| | | Torqueflite automatic | - | $227 | - | - |
| 413 CID FirePower, 4-bbl., V8 | 340 | Torqueflite automatic | - | $389 | S | - |
| 413 CID Long Ram, 2 × 4-bbl., V8 | 360 | Torqueflite automatic | - | $551 | $162 | - |
| 413 CID Short Ram, 2 × 4-bbl., V8 | 365 | Torqueflite automatic | - | $* | $* | - |
| 413 CID Short Ram, 2 × 4-bbl., V8 | 390 | Torqueflite automatic | - | - | - | S |
| 426 CID Long Ram, 2 × 4-bbl., V8 | 373 | Torqueflite automatic | - | - | - | $* |
| 426 CID Short Ram, 2 × 4-bbl., V8 | 415 | Torqueflite automatic | - | - | - | $* |
| 426 CID Short Ram, 2 × 4-bbl., V8 | 425 | Torqueflite automatic | - | - | - | $* |

*Accurate pricing information not currently available.*

## Major Options

| | Newport | 300 | New Yorker | 300-J |
|---|---|---|---|---|
| Heater and defroster | $102 | $102 | $102 | $102 |
| Airtemp air conditioning | $510 | $510 | $510 | $510 |
| Solex tinted glass | $43 | $43 | $43 | $43 |
| Rear window defogger | $21 | $21 | $21 | $21 |
| Auto Pilot cruise control | $86 | $86 | $86 | $86 |
| Power steering | $108 | $108 | S | S |
| Power brakes | $48 | $48 | S | S |
| Power seat — bench | $101 | $101 | $101 | - |
| Power seat — LH bucket seat | - | $93–$201 | $179 | S |
| Power windows | $108 | $108 | S | S |
| Golden Touch Tone AM radio | $93 | $93 | $93 | $93 |
| White sidewall tires — std. sizes | $42 | $46 | $51 | S |

Options common to most models. (- = Not Available, S = Standard equipment.) Items may be standard equipment, optional at different pricing, or unavailable on certain models. This chart is only a guide.

## Paint Colors

| | Code |
|---|---|
| Formal Black | BB-1 |
| Glacier Blue | CC-1 |
| Cord Blue Metallic | DD-1 |
| Navy Blue Metallic | EE-1 |
| Surf Green Metallic | GG-1 |
| Forest Green Metallic | HH-1 |
| Bermuda Turquoise | JJ-1 |
| Holiday Turquoise Met. | KK-1 |
| Teal Metallic | LL-1 |
| Alabaster | MM-1 |
| Madison Gray Metallic | NN-1 |
| Festival Red | PP-1 |
| Claret Metallic | TT-1 |
| Embassy Gold Metallic | UU-1 |
| Pace Car Blue Metallic | VV-1 |
| Oyster White | WW-1 |
| Fawn | XX-1 |
| Cypress Tan Metallic | YY-1 |

# Newport

*"Full-size price surprise. Hundreds of dollars less than you'd expect."*

**Nameplate year of origin:** 1961 (as series); 1950 (as Hardtop model designation).
**Current bodystyle lifespan:** Windsor 1960; Newport 1961 through 1964 (major restyle in 1963).
**Predecessor to this model:** Windsor (1957 to 1959).
**Replacement for this model:** Newport (1965 to 1966).
**Percentage of division's sales volume:** 59.65%.
**Corporate siblings:** Dodge Custom 880, Chrysler 300, New Yorker and 300-J.
**Primary competition:** Buick Wildcat/Invicta, Mercury Monterey and Oldsmobile Super 88.
**Notable changes:** Completely restyled sheetmetal.
**Major standard equipment:** Cloth and vinyl front bench seat, full-floor coverings, sun visors, exterior bright side moldings and 8.00 × 14 BSW tires. Town & Country adds: 8.50 × 14 BSW tires.

## Measurements

| | Cars | Wagons |
|---|---|---|
| Wheelbase | 122.0" | 122.0" |
| Length | 215.3" | 219.4" |
| Width | 79.0" | 80.0" |
| Height | 55.0" | 55.3" |
| Legroom — front | 41.8" | 41.8" |
| Legroom — rear | 39.3" | 39.3" |
| Headroom — front | 38.0" | 38.0" |
| Headroom — rear | 37.8" | 37.8" |
| Cargo capacity (cu. ft.) | NA | 91.9 |
| Fuel capacity (gals.) | 23.0 | 22.0 |

## Models Available

| | Style Number | Base MSRP | Change from LY | Shipping Wt. (lbs.) | Production | Change from LY |
|---|---|---|---|---|---|---|
| Newport 2-Door Hardtop | 812 | $3,027 | 0.00% | 3760 | 9,809 | -17.64% |
| Newport 2-Door Convertible | 815 | $3,399 | 0.00% | 3825 | 2,093 | +2.05% |
| Newport 4-Door Sedan | 813 | $2,964 | 0.00% | 3770 | 49,067 | -10.48% |
| Newport 4-Door Hardtop | 814 | $3,106 | 0.00% | 3800 | 8,437 | -3.16% |
| N. Town & Country 4-Dr., 2-S. Wgn. | 858 | $3,478 | 0.00% | 4200 | 3,618 | +10.61% |
| N. Town & Country 4-Dr., 3-S. Wgn. | 859 | $3,586 | 0.00% | 4215 | 2,948 | +24.76% |
| TOTALS | | Avg. price $3,260 | 0.00% | | Production 75,972 | -8.60% |

# 300

*"Sports car excitement. Deep-seated comfort— side by side.*
*A crisp, new custom beauty eager to go anywhere— in style."*

**Nameplate year of origin:** 1955; 1962 (as non-letter series).
**Current bodystyle lifespan:** Saratoga 1960; Windsor 1961; 300 1962 through 1964 (major restyle in 1963).
**Predecessor to this model:** Saratoga (1957 to 1959).
**Replacement for this model:** 300 (1965 to 1966).
**Percentage of division's sales volume:** 18.08%.
**Corporate siblings:** Dodge Custom 880, Chrysler Newport, New Yorker and 300-J.
**Primary competition:** Buick Wildcat, Mercury S-55 and Oldsmobile Starfire.
**Notable changes:** Completely restyled sheetmetal.
**Major standard equipment:** Cloth and vinyl front bench seat, pile carpeting, padded dash, map lights, electric clock, sun visors, exterior bright side moldings, power steering, power brakes, automatic transmission, full wheel covers, and 8.00 × 14 BSW tires.

## Measurements

| | |
|---|---|
| Wheelbase | 122.0" |
| Length | 215.3" |
| Width | 79.0" |
| Height | 55.0" |
| Legroom — front | 41.8" |
| Legroom — rear | 39.3" |
| Headroom — front | 38.0" |
| Headroom — rear | 37.8" |
| Cargo capacity (cu. ft.) | NA |
| Fuel capacity (gals.) | 23.0 |

## Models Available

| | Style Number | Base MSRP | Change from LY | Shipping Wt. (lbs.) | Production | Change from LY |
|---|---|---|---|---|---|---|
| 300 2-Door Hardtop | 822 | $3,430 | +3.22% | 3790 | 9,423 | -19.98% |
| 300 2-Door Convertible | 825 | $3,790 | -2.40% | 3845 | 1,535 | -22.12% |
| 300 4-Door Hardtop | 824 | $3,400 | 0.00% | 3815 | 9,915 | -1.15% |
| 300 Pace Setter 2-Door Hardtop | 802 | $3,769 | NEW | 3790 | 306 | NEW |
| 300 Pace Setter 2-Door Conv. | 805 | $4,129 | NEW | 3840 | 1,861 | NEW |
| TOTALS | | Avg. price $3,704 | +4.78% | | Production 23,040 | -3.10% |

# New Yorker

*"Named after the most exciting city in the world.
It lives up to the name. It's the finest of all Chryslers."*

**1963**

**Nameplate year of origin:** 1939 (altered from 1938 New York Special model).

**Current bodystyle lifespan:** 1960 through 1964 (major restyle in 1963).

**Predecessor to this model:** New Yorker (1957 to 1959).

**Replacement for this model:** New Yorker (1965 to 1966).

**Percentage of division's sales volume:** 21.95%.

**Corporate siblings:** Dodge Custom 880, Chrysler Newport, 300 and 300-J.

**Primary competition:** Buick Electra, and Oldsmobile 98.

**Notable changes:** Completely restyled sheetmetal.

**Major standard equipment:** Cloth and vinyl front bench seat, pile carpeting, padded dash, map lights, electric clock, exclusive exterior bright trim, power steering & brakes, automatic transmission, wheel covers, and 8.50 × 14 BSW tires. Town & Country adds: 9.00 × 14 BSW tires. Salon adds: Leather interior trim, air conditioning, AM/FM radio w/dual speakers, Auto-Pilot, 6-way power seat, power windows, reclining passenger seat, rear window defogger, power door locks, tinted glass vanity mirror, and twin body-side paint stripes.

## Measurements

| | Cars | Wagons |
|---|---|---|
| Wheelbase | 122.0" | 122.0" |
| Length | 215.5" | 219.7" |
| Width | 79.0" | 80.0" |
| Height | 55.3" | 55.3" |
| Legroom — front | 41.8" | 41.8" |
| Legroom — rear | 39.3" | 39.3" |
| Headroom — front | 38.0" | 38.0" |
| Headroom — rear | 37.8" | 37.8" |
| Cargo capacity (cu. ft.) | NA | 91.9 |
| Fuel capacity (gals.) | 23.0 | 22.0 |

## Models Available

| | Style Number | Base MSRP | Change from LY | Shipping Wt. (lbs.) | Production | Change from LY |
|---|---|---|---|---|---|---|
| New Yorker 4-Door Sedan | 833 | $3,981 | -3.49% | 3910 | 14,884 | +23.46% |
| New Yorker 4-Door Hardtop | 834 | $4,118 | -3.40% | 3950 | 10,289 | +54.81% |
| New Yorker Salon 4-Door Hardtop | 884 | $5,860 | NEW | 4290 | 593 | NEW |
| N. Y. Town & Country 4-Dr., 2-S. W. | 878 | $4,708 | -1.22% | 4350 | 950 | +30.49% |
| N. Y. Town & Country 4-Dr., 3-S. W. | 879 | $4,815 | -1.19% | 4370 | 1,244 | +56.87% |
| TOTALS | | Avg. price $4,696 | +4.19% | | Production 27,960 | +38.26% |

# 300-J

*"Close cousin to the most powerful of racing machines,
with unmatched interior luxury."*

**Nameplate year of origin:** 1955.
**Current bodystyle lifespan:** 1960 through 1964 (major restyle in 1963).
**Predecessor to this model:** 300 Letter series (1957 to 1959).
**Replacement for this model:** 300-L (1965).
**Percentage of division's sales volume:** 0.31%.
**Corporate siblings:** Dodge Custom 880, Chrysler Newport, New Yorker and 300.
**Primary competition:** Buick Riviera and Ford Thunderbird.
**Notable changes:** Completely restyled sheetmetal.
**Major standard equipment:** Leather power bucket front seats, pile carpeting, padded dash, map lights, power windows, electric clock, sun visors, exclusive exterior bright trim, power steering, power brakes, automatic transmission, full wheel covers, and 7.60 × 15 WSW tires.

## Measurements

| | |
|---|---|
| Wheelbase | 122.0" |
| Length | 215.5" |
| Width | 79.0" |
| Height | 55.6" |
| Legroom — front | 41.2" |
| Legroom — rear | 39.8" |
| Headroom — front | 37.8" |
| Headroom — rear | 37.8" |
| Cargo capacity (cu. ft.) | NA |
| Fuel capacity (gals.) | 23.0 |

## Models Available

| | Style Number | Base MSRP | Change from LY | Shipping Wt. (lbs.) | Production | Change from LY |
|---|---|---|---|---|---|---|
| 300-J 2-Door Hardtop | 842 | $5,184 | +1.85% | 4000 | 400 | -8.05% |
| TOTALS | Avg. price | $5,184 | -1.75% | Production | 400 | -28.32% |

# DODGE

*"These are the 1963 Dependables from Dodge.
Pick a size! Pick a price! Pick a Dodge!"*

All Dodge models received new styling this year, and the compact Lancer took on the Dart label, along with new styling. Similar in concept to the Lancer, the Dart was a slightly larger car, riding on a wheelbase that had grown to 111 inches from 106.5 inches (wagons, however, rode on a smaller 106 inch wheelbase shared with the Plymouth Valiant). The new Dart model line closely followed that of the Lancer, with two new convertible models added to the mid-range Dart 270 and sporty Dart GT lines. The changes must have been what the public wanted as sales more than doubled. Powertrains were the same with one exception. The aluminum block version of the 225 Slant Six was discontinued during the year, because of a lack of consumer interest in the engine. However, the regular cast iron block version was very popular and continued into the new year with few revisions.

Poor sales of the Plymouth-sized 1962 Dodge Dart line, gave Dodge reason to take note and enlarge the renamed Dodge 330, 440 and Polara lines. Styling was greatly improved over the 1962 version, although the odd headlamp arrangement was continued, only with the inboard lights now mounted lower than the outboard lamps. Rear styling was very clean and simple compared to 1962, and bodyside lines were cleaned up and simplified. As a result of the changes, sales were greatly improved, mostly in the top line Polara series, which expanded to include a 4-Door Sedan and a sporty Polara 500 line. The biggest Dodge, the 880 series, received a face lift that brought its appearance more in line with other Dodge models, and as a result its sales were also improved. Under the hood, the biggest news was the addition of the 413 CID V8 and 426 CID V8 to the option list. These high power engines were first developed for Chrysler and then introduced for racing use only, but soon became tuned for the road.

330 4-Door, 9 passenger Wagon and
Dodge 440 4-Door, 9 passenger Wagon

440 2-Door Hardtop

Custom 880 4-Door Hardtop

Custom 880 4-Door Hardtop Wagon

Dart 170 4-Door Sedan

Dart GT 2-Door Convertible

Polara 500 2-Door Hardtop and Interior

**Model year production:** 363,700, up 57.99% over 1962.
**Domestic market share:** 4.93% (8th place).
**Base price range:** $1,983 to $3,407.
**Industry average base price:** $3,028.
**Dodge average base price:** $2,659.
**Introduction date:** October 1962.
**Assembly plants:** Lynch Road, MI (A); Hamtramck, MI (B); Detroit (Jefferson Ave.) MI (C); Belvidere, IL (D); Los Angeles, CA (E); Newark, DE (F); St. Louis, MO (G); Windsor, Ontario, Canada (R).

**Data plate identification:** Ten digit code read as follows: Four digit style number (see listings below) in which 1st digit indicates series (e.g., 6 = Polara V8 series), 2nd number identifies trim grade (L is for base trim, M for Midlevel, etc.), 3rd digit 3 for 1963; 4th digit is assembly plant code; followed by 100001 and up for serial number. Body style identification found on separate plate. *Example:* 633C100001 is a 1963 Dodge Polara with a 318 CID V8 engine, serial number 100001, built in Detroit, MI.

## Powertrains

| Engine | Gross HP | Transmission Availability | Dart | 330 & 440 | Polara | 880 |
|---|---|---|---|---|---|---|
| 170 CID, 1-bbl., 6-cyl. | 101 | 3-speed manual | S | - | - | - |
| | | Torqueflite automatic | $172 | - | - | - |
| 225 CID, 1-bbl., 6-cyl. | 145 | 3-speed manual | $47 | S[2] | S[4] | - |
| | | Torqueflite automatic | $219 | $192[2] | $192[4] | - |
| 225 CID Aluminum, 1-bbl., 6-cyl. | 145 | 3-speed manual | $47 | S[2] | S[4] | - |
| | | Torqueflite automatic | $219 | $192[2] | $192[4] | - |
| 318 CID, 2-bbl., V8 | 230 | 3-speed manual | - | S[1]/$107[2] | S[3]/$107[4] | - |
| | | 4-speed manual | - | $146[1]/$253[2] | $146[3]/$253[4] | - |
| | | Torqueflite automatic | - | $211[1]/$318[2] | $211[3]/$318[4] | - |
| 361 CID Polara, 2-bbl., V8 | 265 | 3-speed manual | - | $59[1]/$166[2] | $59[3]/$166[4] | S |
| | | Torqueflite automatic | - | $270[1]/$377[2] | $270[3]/$377[4] | $211 |
| 383 CID Polara, 2-bbl., V8 | 305 | 3-speed manual | - | $72[1]/$179[2] | $72[3]/$179[4] | $13 |
| | | 4-speed manual | - | $218[1]/$325[2] | $218[3]/$325[4] | $159 |
| | | Torqueflite automatic | - | $283[1]/$390[2] | $283[3]/$390[4] | $224 |
| 383 CID Polara, 4-bbl., V8 | 330 | 3-speed manual | - | $123[1]/$230[2] | $123[3]/$230[4] | - |
| | | 4-speed manual | - | $269[1]/$376[2] | $269[3]/$376[4] | - |
| | | Torqueflite automatic | - | $334[1]/$441[2] | $334[3]/$441[4] | - |
| 413 CID, 4-bbl., V8 | 360 | Torqueflite automatic | - | - | - | $* |
| 426 CID Ramcharger, 4-bbl., V8 | 415 | | - | ** | ** | - |
| 426 CID Ramcharger, 2 × 4-bbl., V8 | 425 | | - | ** | ** | - |

*Accurate pricing information unavailable.  [1]440 Wagon models only.  [2]All but 440 Wagon.  [3]Polara 4-Door Hardtop and Convertible only.  [4]All but Polara 4-Door Hardtop and Convertible.

## Major Options

| | Dart | 330 & 440 | Polara | 880 |
|---|---|---|---|---|
| Heater and defroster | $74 | $74 | $74 | S |
| Airtemp air conditioning | $425 | $445 | $445 | $445 |
| Tinted glass | $24 | $30 | $30 | $24 |
| Power steering | $73 | $77 | $77 | $77 |
| Power brakes | $43 | $43 | $43 | $43 |
| Power seat | - | $96 | $96 | $96 |
| Power windows | - | $102 | $102 | $102 |
| Electric clock | $16 | $16 | $16 | $16 |
| Music Master AM radio | $169 | $58 | $58 | $58 |
| White sidewall tires — std. sizes | $29 | $33–$48 | $33–$48 | $33–$48 |

Options common to most models. (- = Not Available, S = Standard equipment.) Items may be standard equipment, optional at different pricing, or unavailable on certain models. This chart is only a guide.

## Paint Colors

| | Code |
|---|---|
| Turquoise Metallic | AA-1 |
| Onyx | BB-1 |
| Light Blue Metallic | CC-1 |
| Medium Blue Metallic | DD-1 |
| Dark Blue Metallic | EE-1 |
| Light Green Metallic | GG-1 |
| Forest Green Metallic | HH-1 |
| Aqua Metallic | JJ-1 |
| Slate Turquoise Met. | KK-1 |
| Dark Turquoise Metallic | LL-1 |
| Ivory | MM-1 |
| Steel Gray Metallic | NN-1 |
| Vermilion | PP-1 |
| Polar White | WW-1 |
| Beige | XX-1 |
| Sandalwood Metallic | YY-1 |
| Cordovan Metallic | ZZ-1 |

# Dart

*"A new idea. A smart idea. Now a compact in a neat,*
*easy-going, saving size — with room and comfort for a family."*

**Nameplate year of origin:** 1960 (on low-end full-size models).
**Current bodystyle lifespan:** 1963 through 1966.
**Predecessor to this model:** Lancer (1961 to 1962).
**Replacement for this model:** Dart (1967 to 1976).
**Percentage of division's sales volume:** 42.32%.
**Corporate siblings:** Plymouth Valiant.
**Primary competition:** Buick Special, Mercury Comet, Oldsmobile F-85, and
  Pontiac Tempest.
**Notable changes:** Completely restyled.
**Major standard equipment:** Nylon and vinyl front bench seats, rubber floor
  mats, chrome windshield trim and 6.50 × 13 BSW tires. 270 adds: All-
  vinyl upholstery on convertible, color-keyed carpeting, additional interior
  and exterior bright trim. GT adds: All-vinyl bucket seats, padded instru-
  ment panel and specific GT trim.

## Measurements

|  | Cars | Wagons |
|---|---|---|
| Wheelbase | 111.0" | 106.0" |
| Length | 195.9" | 190.2" |
| Width | 69.8" | 69.8" |
| Height | 54.0" | 54.0" |
| Legroom — front | 40.0" | 40.0" |
| Legroom — rear | 37.2" | 35.5" |
| Headroom — front | 38.0" | 38.1" |
| Headroom — rear | 37.2" | 37.2" |
| Cargo capacity (cu. ft.) | 30.2 | 68.9 |
| Fuel capacity (gals.) | 18.0 | 18.0 |

**1963**

## Models Available

| | Style Number | Base MSRP | Change from LY | Shipping Wt. (lbs.) | Production | Change from LY |
|---|---|---|---|---|---|---|
| Dart 170 2-Door Sedan | 711 | $1,983 | +1.64% | 2605 | 51,300 | 200.00% |
| Dart 170 4-Door Sedan | 713 | $2,041 | +1.49% | 2625 | * | * |
| Dart 170 4-Door, 2-Seat Wagon | 756 | $2,309 | +0.13% | 2710 | * | * |
| Dart 270 2-Door Sedan | 731 | $2,079 | +1.32% | 2610 | 55,300 | 111.88% |
| Dart 270 2-Door Convertible | 735 | $2,385 | NEW | 2740 | * | NEW |
| Dart 270 4-Door Sedan | 733 | $2,135 | +0.99% | 2635 | * | * |
| Dart 270 4-Door, 2-Seat Wagon | 776 | $2,433 | +1.04% | 2735 | 13,000 | 85.71% |
| Dart GT 2-Door Hardtop | 742 | $2,289 | +1.42% | 2690 | 34,300 | 143.26% |
| Dart GT 2-Door Convertible | 745 | $2,512 | NEW | 2765 | * | NEW |
| TOTALS | *Avg. price* | $2,241 | +3.89% | *Production* | 153,900 | +139.35% |

*Production not available by series. Comparisons are to 1962 Lancer models.*

# 330 & 440

*"The beautiful way to go in the low-price field."*

**Nameplate year of origin:** 1962.
**Current bodystyle lifespan:** 1962 through 1965.
**Predecessor to this model:** Dart Seneca and Pioneer (1960 to 1961).
**Replacement for this model:** Coronet (1966 to 1967).
**Percentage of division's sales volume:** 36.98%.
**Corporate siblings:** Plymouth Savoy/Belvedere/Fury.
**Primary competition:** AMC Classic, Chevrolet Biscayne/BelAir and Ford Galaxie.
**Notable changes:** Completely restyled front and rear end, revised side styling,
  wheelbase stretched at front to differentiate from Plymouth models.
**Major standard equipment:** Cloth-and-vinyl bench seat with foam front cushion,
  full rubber floor mats, electric windshield wipers, dual sun visors, exterior bright
  trim around windshield and back window, and 7.00 × 14 BSW tires (7.50 × 14
  BSW tires on wagons). 440 adds: Full carpeting, exterior bright trim around side
  windows and body sides.

## Measurements

|  | Cars | Wagons |
|---|---|---|
| Wheelbase | 119.0" | 116.0" |
| Length | 208.2" | 210.7" |
| Width | 76.5" | 76.5" |
| Height | 53.8" | 54.5" |
| Legroom — front | 41.8" | 41.8" |
| Legroom — rear | 37.8" | 36.4" |
| Headroom — front | 38.2" | 38.2" |
| Headroom — rear | 37.5" | 37.5" |
| Cargo capacity (cu. ft.) | NA | 84.4 |
| Fuel capacity (gals.) | 20.0 | 21.5 |

## Models Available

| | Style Number | Base MSRP | Change from LY | Shipping Wt. (lbs.) | Production | Change from LY |
|---|---|---|---|---|---|---|
| Fleet Special 2-Door Sedan | 401 | $2,205 | +2.18% | 3040 | * | * |
| Fleet Special 4-Door Sedan | 403 | $2,261 | +2.12% | 3065 | * | * |
| 330 2-Door Sedan | 411 | $2,245 | -5.47% | 3050 | 64,100 | * |
| 330 4-Door Sedan | 413 | $2,301 | -5.39% | 3070 | * | * |
| 330 4-Dr., 2-S. Wagon | 456 | $2,648 | -3.32% | 3320 | * | * |
| 330 4-Dr., 3-S. Wagon | 457 | $2,749 | -6.78% | 3380 | * | * |
| 440 2-Door Sedan | 421 | $2,381 | NEW | 3050 | * | NEW |
| 440 2-Door Hardtop | 422 | $2,470 | -5.22% | 3050 | 44,300 | * |
| 440 4-Door Sedan | 423 | $2,438 | -5.65% | 3075 | * | * |
| 440 4-Door, 2-Seat Wagon | 666 | $2,854 | -4.52% | 3495 | 26,100 | * |
| 440 4-Door, 3-Seat Wagon | 667 | $2,956 | -4.40% | 3555 | * | * |
| TOTALS | | Avg. price $2,501 | -3.55% | | Production 134,500 | -30.0% |

*Production not available by series. Production listed is by body styles.

# Polara

*"Luxury never came in such a low-price package!!!!!!!"*

**Nameplate year of origin:** 1960.
**Current bodystyle lifespan:** 1962 through 1965.
**Predecessor to this model:** Dart Phoenix (1960 to 1961).
**Replacement for this model:** Polara (1965 to 1966).
**Percentage of division's sales volume:** 12.95%.
**Corporate siblings:** Plymouth Fury.
**Primary competition:** AMC Ambassador, Chevrolet BelAir/Impala, and Ford Galaxie.
**Notable changes:** Completely restyled front and rear end, revised side styling, wheelbase stretched at front to differentiate from Plymouth models.
**Major standard equipment:** All-vinyl (hardtops and convertible) or cloth-and-vinyl (sedan) bench seat with foam front cushion, deep-pile carpeting, electric windshield wipers, dual sun visors, exterior bright trim around all glass and body sides, and 7.00 × 14 BSW tires. 500 adds: Bucket seats, special interior and exterior trim.

## Measurements

| | Cars | Wagons |
|---|---|---|
| Wheelbase | 119.0" | 116.0" |
| Length | 208.2" | 210.7" |
| Width | 76.5" | 76.5" |
| Height | 53.8" | 54.5" |
| Legroom — front | 41.8" | 41.8" |
| Legroom — rear | 37.8" | 36.4" |
| Headroom — front | 38.2" | 38.2" |
| Headroom — rear | 37.5" | 37.5" |
| Cargo capacity (cu. ft.) | NA | 84.4 |
| Fuel capacity (gals.) | 20.0 | 21.5 |

## Models Available

| | Style Number | Base MSRP | Change from LY | Shipping Wt. (lbs.) | Production | Change from LY |
|---|---|---|---|---|---|---|
| Polara 2-Door Hardtop | 432 | $2,624 | -13.08% | 3105 | 39,800 | +218.40% |
| Polara 2-Door Convertible | 635 | $2,963 | -9.33% | 3340 | | * |
| Polara 4-Door Sedan | 433 | $2,602 | NEW | 3105 | | NEW |
| Polara 4-Door Hardtop | 634 | $2,781 | -6.05% | 3275 | | * |
| Polara 500 2-Door Hardtop | 642 | $2,965 | NEW | 3375 | 7,300 | NEW |
| Polara 500 2-Door Convertible | 645 | $3,196 | NEW | 3455 | | NEW |
| TOTALS | | Avg. price $2,855 | -7.37% | | Production 47,100 | +276.80% |

*Production not available by series.

# 880

*"This is the 1963 luxury automobile with a strong sense of value."*

**Nameplate year of origin:** 1962.
**Current bodystyle lifespan:** 1962 through 1964.
**Predecessor to this model:** DeSoto (1960 to 1961).
**Replacement for this model:** Custom 880 (1965) and Monaco (1965 to 1966).
**Percentage of division's sales volume:** 7.75%.
**Corporate siblings:** Chrysler Newport, New Yorker and 300.
**Primary competition:** Buick LeSabre, Mercury Montclair, Oldsmobile 88, and Pontiac Catalina.
**Notable changes:** All-new front end styling, revised trim and detail changes.
**Major standard equipment:** Cloth and vinyl upholstery, full carpeting, glove box lock, dual sunvisors, dome lamp, front and rear armrests, rear tinted window, electric windshield wipers and 8.00 × 14 BSW tires. Custom adds: Vinyl or vinyl and nylon upholstery (depending on model), additional bright metal exterior and interior trim, and full horn ring.

## Measurements

|  | Cars | Wagons |
|---|---|---|
| Wheelbase | 122.0" | 122.0" |
| Length | 214.8" | 216.3" |
| Width | 79.0" | 80.0" |
| Height | 55.2" | 55.9" |
| Legroom — front | 41.9" | 41.9" |
| Legroom — rear | 39.3" | 39.1" |
| Headroom — front | 38.0" | 38.0" |
| Headroom — rear | 37.9" | 38.0" |
| Cargo capacity (cu. ft.) | NA | 91.5 |
| Fuel capacity (gals.) | 23 | 21 |

**1963**

## Models Available

|  | Style Number | Base MSRP | Change from LY | Shipping Wt. (lbs.) | Production | Change from LY |
|---|---|---|---|---|---|---|
| 880 4-Door Sedan | 503 | $2,813 | NEW | 3800 | 7,200 | NEW |
| 880 4-Door, 2-Seat Wagon | 556 | $3,142 | NEW | 4145 | * | NEW |
| 880 4-Door, 3-Seat Wagon | 557 | $3,257 | NEW | 4175 | * | NEW |
| Custom 880 2-Door Hardtop | 512 | $3,030 | 0.00% | 3825 | 15,400 | 0.00% |
| Custom 880 2-Door Convertible | 515 | $3,251 | 0.00% | 3845 | * | * |
| Custom 880 4-Door Sedan | 513 | $2,964 | 0.00% | 3815 | * | * |
| Custom 880 4-Door Hardtop | 514 | $3,109 | 0.00% | 3840 | * | * |
| Custom 880 4-Dr., 2-S. HT Wgn. | 558 | $3,292 | 0.00% | 4160 | 5,600 | +166.67% |
| Custom 880 4-Dr., 3-S. HT Wgn. | 559 | $3,407 | 0.00% | 4186 | * | * |
| TOTALS | Avg. price | $3,141 | -1.11% | Production | 28,200 | +61.14% |

*Production not available by series.*

# FORD

*"America's liveliest, most care-free cars … '63 Fords."*

The full-size Ford line saw all-new styling for 1963. Traditional Ford styling cues were still seen, but the lines were squared off more than in the previous years. All Ford models still retained a family look. The bigger news was under the hood where the new 406 CID V8 engine was now available in full-size Ford models. This engine, a response to Chevy's 409 CID V8, was a proven performer on the race track. At mid-year a new semi-fastback style 2-Door Hardtop was introduced, along with a Fairlane Sports Coupe and a new Falcon Futura 2-Door Hardtop model. These new mid-year entries were given a lot of publicity, and sales soon began to improve for the entire Ford line. Sales had been lagging behind Chevrolet, and this was just the boost needed for Ford. Model names on full-size Fords were shuffled slightly, with the Mainliner being renamed the 300. The full-size Ranch Wagon was temporarily missing from the lineup, with the moniker being moved to the new Fairlane Station Wagon.

Very few new features were to be found on the Fairlane line. Styling remained similar to 1962. There was, however, a new powerplant under the hood. This was the 289 CID V8, a bored out version of the popular 260 CID V8. This new engine would become one of Ford's most popular choices over the years and would become the basis for many more powerful engines. The compact Falcon line was also very similar to 1962. A new grille and new brightwork were the most noticeable changes. The sport-luxury Thunderbird line also received only minor revisions. The most distinguishing feature was the three "hash marks" that were moved from the rear quarters to the doors. This is one of the easiest ways to identify a 1963 T-Bird.

Country Squire 4-Door Wagon

Falcon Deluxe 2-Door Wagon

Falcon Futura 4-Door Sedan

Fairlane 2-Door Sedan

Fairlane 500 2-Door Hardtop

Galaxie 2-Door Sedan

Galaxie XL 2-Door Convertible

Thunderbird Landau 2-Door Hardtop

Thunderbird 2-Door Sports Roadster

**Model year production:** 1,579,073, up 8.46% over 1962.
**Domestic market share:** 21.44% (2nd place).
**Base price range:** $1,985 to $5,563.

**Industry average base price:** $3,028.
**Ford average base price:** $2,795.
**Introduction date:** September 1962.

**Assembly plants:** Atlanta, GA (A); Chicago, IL (G); Dallas, TX (D); Dearborn, MI (F); Kansas City, MO (K); Lorain, OH (H); Los Angeles, CA (J); Louisville, KY (U); Mahwah, NJ (E); Metuchen, NJ (T); Norfolk, VA (N); San Jose, CA (R); Twin Cities, MN (P); Wayne, MI (W); Wixom, MI (Y); Oakville, Ontario, Can. (B).

**Data plate identification:** Eleven digit code read as follows: 3 for 1963; 2nd digit is assembly plant code; 2-digit model number (see listings below); 5th digit is engine code; 100001 and up for serial number. *Example:* 3Y83Z100001 is a 1963 Ford Thunderbird 2-Door Hardtop with a 390 CID V8 engine, serial number 100001, built in Wixom, MI.

## Powertrains

| Engine | Gross HP | Engine Code | Transmission Availability | Falcon | Fairlane | Full-size | Thunderbird |
|---|---|---|---|---|---|---|---|
| 144 CID, 1-bbl., 6-cyl. | 85 | S | 3-speed manual | S | - | - | - |
| | | | 4-speed manual | - | - | - | - |
| | | | Ford-O-Matic | $177 | - | - | - |
| 170 CID, 1-bbl., 6-cyl. | 101 | U | 3-speed manual | $17 | S | - | - |
| | | | 4-speed manual | - | - | - | - |
| | | | Ford-O-Matic | $194 | $189 | - | - |
| | | | Cruise-O-Matic | - | $189 | - | - |
| 221 CID, 2-bbl., V8 | 145 | L | 3-speed manual | - | - | - | - |
| | | | 4-speed manual | - | - | - | - |
| | | | Cruise-O-Matic | - | - | - | - |
| 223 CID Big Six, 1-bbl., 6-cyl. | 138 | E | 3-speed manual | - | - | S (ex. XL) | - |
| | | | Overdrive | - | - | $108 (ex. XL) | - |
| | | | Cruise-O-Matic | - | - | $189 (ex. XL) | - |
| 260 CID Challenger, 2-bbl., V8 | 164 | F | 3-speed manual | $170 | $100 | NA (XL)/$108 (others) | - |
| | | | Overdrive | $278 | $208 | NA (XL)/$216 (others) | - |
| | | | 4-speed manual* | $358 | $288 | $35 (XL)/$296 (others) | - |
| | | | Ford-O-Matic | $347 | $289 | NA (XL)/$298 (others) | - |
| | | | Cruise-O-Matic | - | $289 | S (XL)/$320 (others) | - |
| 289 CID Challenger High-Perf., 4-bbl., V8 | 271 | K | 4-speed manual* | - | $*** | - | - |
| | | | Cruise-O-Matic | - | $*** | - | - |
| 352 CID Interceptor, 2-bbl., V8 | 220 | X | 3-speed manual | - | - | NA (XL)/$160 (others) | - |
| | | | Overdrive | - | - | NA (XL)/$354 (others) | - |
| | | | 4-speed manual | - | - | $17 (XL)/$348 (others) | - |
| | | | Cruise-O-Matic | - | - | $52 (XL)/$372 (others) | - |
| 390 CID Thunderbird, 2-bbl., V8 | 300 | Z | 3-speed manual | - | - | NA (XL)/$246 (others) | - |
| | | | Overdrive | - | - | NA (XL)/$354 (others) | - |
| | | | 4-speed manual* | - | - | $103 (XL)/$434 (others) | - |
| | | | Cruise-O-Matic | - | - | $138 (XL)/$458 (others) | S |
| 390 CID Thunderbird Special, 4-bbl., V8 | 330 | P | 3-speed manual | - | - | $** (XL)/$*** (others) | - |
| | | | 4-speed manual* | - | - | $*** (XL)/$*** (others) | - |
| | | | Cruise-O-Matic | - | - | $*** (XL)/$*** (others) | $*** |
| 390 CID Thunderbird Special, 3 × 2-bbl., V8 | 340 | G | 3-speed manual | - | - | $***—XL/$***—others | - |
| | | | 4-speed manual* | - | - | $*** (XL)/$*** (others) | - |
| | | | Cruise-O-Matic | - | - | $*** (XL)/$*** (others) | $*** |
| 406 CID Thunderbird High-Perf., 4-bbl., V8 | 385 | Q | Overdrive | - | - | NA (XL)/$550 (others) | - |
| | | | 4-speed manual* | - | - | $298 (XL)/$630 (others) | 0 |
| 406 CID T-Bird High-Perf., 2 × 4-bbl., V8 | 405 | R | Overdrive | - | - | NA (XL)/$608 (others) | - |
| | | | 4-speed manual* | - | - | $356 (XL)/$688 (others) | - |

*4-speed manual shift not available on wagon models.    **Limited availability.    ***Pricing information unavailable.*

## Major Options

|  | Falcon | Mustang | Fairlane | Full-size | Thunderbird |
|---|---|---|---|---|---|
| Air conditioning | - | $283 | $283 | $364 | $415 |
| Tinted glass | - | $31 | $40 | $40 | $43 |
| Power steering | - | $86 | $86 | $86 | S |
| Power brakes | - | $43 | $43 | $43 | S |
| Power driver's seat/bench seat | - | - | - | - | $184 |
| Power windows | - | - | - | $102 | $106 |
| AM radio | $58 | $59 | $58 | $58 | S |
| AM/FM radio | - | - | - | $142 | $83 |
| Front console | - | $32–$52 | $ | $ | S |
| Front bucket seats | $ | S | $ | $ | S |
| Swing-Away steering wheel | - | - | - | - | S |
| Vinyl roof (only on select models) | - | $76 | $75 | $75 | $ |
| White sidewall tires | $30 | $30 | $33 | $33 | $44 |
| Deluxe wheel covers | - | $18 | $18 | $45 | $16 |

Options common to most models. (- = Not Available; S = standard equipment.) Items may be standard equipment, optional at different pricing, or unavailable on certain models. This chart is only a guide.

## Paint Colors

|  | Code | Thunderbird | Other models |
|---|---|---|---|
| Black | A | X | X |
| Pagoda Green | B | X | X |
| Gunmetal Gray Metallic | C | X |  |
| Dynasty Green Metallic | D |  | X |
| Silver Blue Metallic | E | X |  |
| Powder Blue | F | X |  |
| Guardsman Blue Metallic | F |  | X |
| Prairie Tan | G | X | X |
| Caspian Blue Metallic | H | X | X |
| Champagne Beige Met. | I |  | X |
| Rangoon Red | J | X | X |
| Silver Smoke Gray Metallic | K |  | X |
| Wimbledon White | M | X | X |
| Diamond Blue | N | X |  |
| Tropical Turquoise | O |  |  |
| Prairie Bronze Metallic | P | X | X |
| Huron Blue Metallic | Q | X |  |
| Phoenician Yellow/Encino | R | X | X |
| Cascade Green Metallic | S | X | X |
| Navajo Beige | T | X | X |
| Regal Turquoise Metallic | U | X |  |
| Sunlight Yellow | V | X | X |
| Rose Beige Metallic | W | X |  |
| Vintage Burgundy Metallic | X | X | X |
| Skylight Blue | Y |  | X |
| Chantilly Beige Metallic | Z | X | X |
| Poppy Red | 3 |  | X |

# Falcon

*"America's favorite compact."*

**Nameplate year of origin:** 1960.
**Current bodystyle lifespan:** 1960 through 1963.
**Predecessor to this model:** None.
**Replacement for this model:** Falcon (1964 to 1965).
**Corporate siblings:** Mercury Comet.
**Percentage of division's sales volume:** 20.79%.
**Primary competition:** Rambler American, Chevrolet Chevy II, Plymouth Valiant, and Studebaker Lark.
**Notable changes:** New grille and minor trim and detail changes.
**Major standard equipment:** Cloth and vinyl interior trim, Front-door armrests, Dual horns, Chrome windshield and rear window moldings, small hubcaps, and 6.50 × 13 BSW tires (7.00 × 13 on Wagons). Futura adds: Deluxe interior trim, rear armrests with ashtrays, side window moldings, hood ornament, full-length side trim molding, and full-wheel covers. Squire adds: Wood-grain exterior trim.

## Measurements

|  | Cars | Wagons |
| --- | --- | --- |
| Wheelbase | 109.5" | 109.5" |
| Length | 181.1" | 190.0" |
| Width | 70.6" | 70.6" |
| Height | 54.5" | 54.5" |
| Legroom — front | 41.5" | 41.5" |
| Legroom — rear | 34.7" | 34.6" |
| Headroom — front | 38.0" | 38.0" |
| Headroom — rear | 37.4" | 37.3" |
| Cargo capacity (cu. ft.) | NA | 77.9 |
| Fuel capacity (gals.) | 14.0 | 14.0 |

## Models Available

|  | Style Number | Base MSRP | Change from LY | Shipping Wt. (lbs.) | Production | Change from LY |
| --- | --- | --- | --- | --- | --- | --- |
| Falcon 2-Door Sedan | 62A | $1,985 | 0.00% | 2300 | 70,630 | -50.83% |
| Falcon 4-Door Sedan | 54A | $2,047 | 0.00% | 2337 | 62,365 | -50.52% |
| Falcon 2-Door Wagon | 59A | $2,298 | 0.00% | 2580 | 7,322 | * |
| Falcon 4-Door Wagon | 71A | $2,341 | 0.00% | 2617 | 18,484 | -72.34% |
| Falcon Futura 2-Door Sedan | 62B | $2,116 | +2.17% | 2308 | 27,018 | * |
| Falcon Futura 2-Door HT | 63B | $2,198 | -3.30% | 2438 | 38,975 | * |
| Falcon Futura 2-Door Conv. | 76A | $2,470 | NEW | 2645 | 35,794 | NEW |
| Falcon Futura 4-Door Sedan | 54B | $2,165 | +1.50% | 2345 | 31,736 | * |
| Falcon Deluxe 2-Door Wagon | 59B | $2,384 | 0.00% | 2586 | 4,269 | * |
| Falcon Deluxe 4-Door Wagon | 71B | $2,427 | 0.00% | 2623 | 23,477 | * |
| Falcon Squire 4-Door Wagon | 71C | $2,603 | 0.00% | 2639 | 8,269 | -63.38% |
| TOTALS | Avg. price | $2,276 | -0.98% | Production | 328,339 | -12.70% |

*Production comparisons with 1962 models cannot be calculated.*

# Fairlane

*"The car that gives you the best of two worlds—the luxury and comfort of a big car and the economy and parking ease of a compact."*

**Nameplate year of origin:** 1955.
**Current bodystyle lifespan:** 1962 through 1965.
**Predecessor to this model:** None.
**Replacement for this model:** Fairlane (1966 to 1967).
**Corporate siblings:** Mercury Meteor.
**Percentage of division's sales volume:** 21.71%.
**Primary competition:** Rambler Classic, Dodge Dart, and Pontiac Tempest.
**Notable changes:** New grille and minor trim and detail changes.
**Major standard equipment:** Cloth and vinyl bench seat, rubber floor mats, front and rear armrests, chrome windshield and rear window moldings, and 6.50 × 13 BSW tires (7.00 × 14 BSW on Wagons). 500 adds: Full carpet-

## Measurements

|  | Cars | Wagons |
| --- | --- | --- |
| Wheelbase | 115.5" | 115.5" |
| Length | 197.6" | 197.6" |
| Width | 71.3" | 71.3" |
| Height | 55.4" | 55.5" |
| Legroom — front | 42.0" | 42.0" |
| Legroom — rear | 37.0" | 37.0" |
| Headroom — front | 38.7" | 38.7" |
| Headroom — rear | 37.0" | 37.0" |

ing, deluxe interior trim, chrome side window moldings, chrome hood ornament, full-length side trim and Ford crests on C pillar and rear panel.

| | Cars | Wagons |
|---|---|---|
| Cargo capacity (cu. ft.) | 29.0 | NA |
| Fuel capacity (gals.) | 16.0 | 16.0 |

## Models Available

| | Style Number | Base MSRP | Change from LY | Shipping Wt. (lbs.) | Production | Change from LY |
|---|---|---|---|---|---|---|
| Fairlane 2-Door Sedan | 62A | $2,154 | 0.00% | 2824 | 28,984 | -15.41% |
| Fairlane 4-Door Sedan | 54A | $2,216 | 0.00% | 2864 | 44,454 | -1.96% |
| Fairlane 4-Door Ranch Wagon | 71D | $2,525 | NEW | 3215 | 24,006 | NEW |
| Fairlane 500 2-Door Sedan | 62B | $2,242 | 0.00% | 2839 | 34,764 | -49.34% |
| Fairlane 500 2-Door Hardtop | 65A | $2,324 | NEW | 2857 | 41,641 | NEW |
| Fairlane 500 2-Door Sport HT | 65B | $2,504 | NEW | 2857 | 28,268 | NEW |
| Fairlane 500 4-Door Sedan | 54B | $2,304 | 0.00% | 2879 | 103,175 | -20.18% |
| Fairlane 4-Dr. Custom Ranch Wgn. | 71B | $2,613 | NEW | 3232 | 29,612 | NEW |
| Fairlane 4-Door Squire Wagon | 71E | $2,781 | NEW | 3229 | 7,983 | NEW |
| TOTALS | Avg. price | $2,407 | +6.32% | Production | 342,887 | +15.41% |

# Galaxie and 300

*"The car that matches Thunderbird's beauty and power, now captures the velvet smoothness of Thunderbird's ride."*

**Nameplate year of origin:** 1957 (300) and 1959 (Galaxie).
**Current bodystyle lifespan:** 1963 through 1964.
**Predecessor to this model:** Fairlane and Galaxie (1961 to 1962).
**Replacement for this model:** Custom, Galaxie and LTD (1965 to 1966).
**Corporate siblings:** Mercury Monterey.
**Percentage of division's sales volume:** 53.48%.
**Primary competition:** Chevrolet BelAir/Impala, Dodge 330/440, and Plymouth Full-size.
**Notable changes:** Completely restyled.
**Major standard equipment:** Rubber mats, dual sunvisors, arm rests on all doors, rear window trim molding, and 7.50 × 14 BSW tires. Galaxie adds: Nylon carpeting, windshield molding, short exterior trim side molding and 8.00 × 14 BSW tires on wagons. Galaxie 500 adds: Two-tone interior trim, chrome hood ornament, chrome side window trim, and backup lights. XL adds: Bucket seats with floor-mounted transmission selector, lower door carpet trim and polished trim, courtesy and reading lamps, and special badging.

## Measurements

| | Cars | Wagons |
|---|---|---|
| Wheelbase | 119.0" | 119.0" |
| Length | 209.9" | 209.9" |
| Width | 79.9" | 79.9" |
| Height | 55.5" | 55.6" |
| Legroom — front | 41.7" | 41.7" |
| Legroom — rear | 38.8" | 38.8" |
| Headroom — front | 38.7" | 38.7" |
| Headroom — rear | 38.4" | 38.3" |
| Cargo capacity (cu. ft.) | NA | NA |
| Fuel capacity (gals.) | 20.0 | 20.0 |

## Models Available

| | Style Number | Base MSRP | Change from LY | Shipping Wt. (lbs.) | Production | Change from LY |
|---|---|---|---|---|---|---|
| 300 2-Door Sedan | 62E | $2,324 | -0.47% | 3550 | 26,010 | * |
| 300 4-Door Sedan | 54E | $2,378 | -0.46% | 3630 | 44,142 | * |
| Galaxie 2-Door Sedan | 62B | $2,453 | 0.00% | 3570 | 30,335 | -44.78% |
| Galaxie 4-Door Sedan | 54B | $2,507 | 0.00% | 3650 | 82,419 | -28.70% |
| Galaxie 500 2-Door Sedan | 62A | $2,613 | 0.00% | 3590 | 21,137 | -24.03% |
| Galaxie 500 2-Door Hardtop | 65A | $2,674 | 0.00% | 3602 | 49,733 | -43.20% |
| Galaxie 500 2-Door Fastback HT | 63B | $2,674 | NEW | 3775 | 100,500 | NEW |
| Galaxie 500 2-Door Sunliner Conv. | 76A | $2,924 | 0.00% | 3760 | 36,876 | -13.53% |

| | Style Number | Base MSRP | Change from LY | Shipping Wt. (lbs.) | Production | Change from LY |
|---|---|---|---|---|---|---|
| Galaxie 500 4-Door Sedan | 54A | $2,667 | 0.00% | 3670 | 205,722 | 18.10% |
| Galaxie 500 4-Door Hardtop | 75A | $2,739 | 0.00% | 3682 | 26,558 | -13.71% |
| Galaxie 500 XL 2-Door Hardtop | 65B | $3,268 | 0.00% | 3611 | 29,713 | 4.58% |
| Galaxie 500 XL 2-Dr. Fastback HT | 63C | $3,268 | NEW | 3825 | 33,870 | NEW |
| Galaxie 500 XL 2-Door Convertible | 76B | $3,518 | 0.00% | 3762 | 18,551 | 40.72% |
| Galaxie 500 XL 4-Door Hardtop | 75C | $3,333 | NEW | 3691 | 12,596 | NEW |
| Country Sedan 4-Dr., 6-pass. Wgn. | 71B | $2,829 | 0.00% | 3980 | 64,954 | 36.36% |
| Country Sedan 4-Dr., 9-pass. Wgn. | 71C | $2,933 | 0.00% | 3992 | 22,250 | 34.34% |
| Country Squire 4-Dr., 6-pass. Wgn. | 71E | $3,018 | 0.00% | 3994 | 19,922 | 23.63% |
| Country Squire 4-Dr., 9-pass. Wgn. | 71A | $3,088 | 0.00% | 4006 | 19,246 | 22.85% |
| TOTALS | | Avg. price $2,845 | +1.86% | | Production 844,534 | +19.83% |

*Specific 1962 production not available for comparison.*

**1963** *(vertical side tab)*

# Thunderbird

## "Unique in all the world."

**Nameplate year of origin:** 1955.
**Current bodystyle lifespan:** 1961 through 1963.
**Predecessor to this model:** Thunderbird (1958 to 1960).
**Replacement for this model:** Thunderbird (1964 to 1966).
**Corporate siblings:** None.
**Percentage of division's sales volume:** 4.01%.
**Primary competition:** Buick Riviera, Oldsmobile Starfire, Chrysler 300, and Studebaker Avanti.
**Notable changes:** New grille and minor trim and detail changes.
**Major standard equipment:** Bucket seats, full carpeting, heater and defroster, full instrumentation, Swing-Away steering wheel, power steering, power brakes, and 8.00 × 14 BSW tires. Convertible adds: Unique trunk-stored power convertible top. Landau adds: Special interior and vinyl top. Sports Roadster adds: Tonneau cover for rear seats.

## Measurements

| | |
|---|---|
| Wheelbase | 113.2" |
| Length | 205.0" |
| Width | 76.5" |
| Height | 52.5" |
| Legroom — front | 40.9" |
| Legroom — rear | 32.2" |
| Headroom — front | 37.8" |
| Headroom — rear | 37.5" |
| Cargo capacity (cu. ft.) | NA |
| Fuel capacity (gals.) | 20.0 |

## Models Available

| | Style Number | Base MSRP | Change from LY | Shipping Wt. (lbs.) | Production | Change from LY |
|---|---|---|---|---|---|---|
| Thunderbird 2-Door Hardtop | 63A | $4,445 | +2.87% | 4195 | 42,806 | -37.17% |
| Thunderbird 2-Door Landau HT | 63B | $4,548 | +3.41% | 4203 | 14,139 | * |
| Thunderbird 2-Door Convertible | 76A | $4,912 | +2.59% | 4322 | 5,913 | -29.75% |
| T-Bird 2-Dr. Conv. Sports Roadster | 76B | $5,563 | +2.28% | 4396 | 455 | -68.11% |
| TOTALS | | Avg. price $4,867 | +2.74% | | Production 63,313 | -18.80% |

*Specific 1962 production not available for comparison.*

# IMPERIAL

*"America's most carefully built car."*

Styling was similar to prior years, with a new, less-pronounced split grille appearing at the front end. At the rear the free-standing taillamps were done away with, and in their place were thin, blade-like taillamps running vertically in the trailing edge of the rear fin. This made for a much cleaner line that was arguably the best looking of this body style's four year run. Rooflines were slightly redesigned on some models to provide a more formal appearance.

Once again the Crown Imperial Limousine Sedan model was available as a custom-built model. These are not included herein as their production usually totaled ten or fewer per season, and they are considered custom-built by Chrysler.

Crown 4-Door Hardtop

Custom 2-Door Hardtop

**Model year production:** 14,108, down 1.60% from 1962.
**Domestic market share:** 0.19% (14th place).
**Base price range:** $5,058 to $6,434.
**Industry average base price:** $3,028.
**Imperial average base price:** $5,598.
**Introduction date:** September 26, 1962.
**Assembly plants:** Detroit, MI (3).

**Data plate identification:** Ten digit code read as follows: 1st digit 9 = Imperial; 2nd number identifies series (e.g., 2 is for Crown); 3 for 1963; 4th digit is assembly plant code; 100001 and up for serial number. Body style numbers found on body plate. *Example:* 9233100001 is a 1963 Imperial Crown, serial number 100001, built in Detroit, MI.

## Powertrains

| Engine | Gross HP | Transmission Availability | Imperial |
|---|---|---|---|
| 413 CID, 4-bbl., V8 | 340 | Torqueflite Automatic | S |

## Major Options

| | Custom | Crown | LeBaron |
|---|---|---|---|
| Air conditioning | $590 | $590 | $590 |
| Auto Pilot automatic speed control | $99 | $99 | $99 |
| Tinted glass | $54 | $54 | $54 |
| Rear window defogger | $21 | $21 | $21 |
| Deck lid remote release | $53 | $53 | $53 |
| Power steering (variable-ratio) | S | S | S |
| Power brakes | S | S | S |
| Power door locks | $47 (2-Dr)/ $72 (4-Dr) | $47 (2-Dr)/ $72 (4-Dr) | $72 |

## Paint Colors

| | Code |
|---|---|
| Formal Black | BB-1 |
| Glacier Blue | CC-1 |
| Cord Blue Metallic | DD-1 |
| Navy Blue Metallic | EE-1 |
| Surf Green Metallic | GG-1 |
| Forest Green Metallic | HH-1 |
| Holiday Turquoise Metallic | KK-1 |
| Teal Metallic | LL-1 |
| Alabaster | MM-1 |

|                                  | Custom | Crown | LeBaron |
|----------------------------------|--------|-------|---------|
| Power driver's seat/Bench seat   | $125   | S     | S       |
| Power windows                    | S      | S     | S       |
| AM radio w/power antenna         | $169   | $169  | $169    |
| AM/FM radio w/power antenna      | $196   | $196  | $196    |
| Whitewall tires — standard size  | $55    | $55   | S       |

| | Code |
|---|---|
| Madison Gray Metallic | NN-1 |
| Charcoal Metallic | OO-1 |
| Festival Red | PP-1 |
| Mayan Gold Metallic | RR-1 |
| Ivory | SS-1 |
| Claret Metallic | TT-1 |
| Embassy Gold metallic | UU-1 |
| Oyster White | WW-1 |
| Fawn | XX-1 |
| Cypress Tan Metallic | YY-1 |
| Mahogany Metallic | ZZ-1 |

Options common to most models. (S = Standard equipment.) Items may be standard equipment, optional at different pricing, or unavailable on certain models. This chart is only a guide.

**1963**

# Custom

*"Its price is surprisingly little more than that
of comparably equipped medium priced cars."*

**Nameplate year of origin:** 1959 (Name was used on Chrysler Imperial models prior to 1955 also).
**Current bodystyle lifespan:** 1960 through 1963.
**Predecessor to this model:** Imperial (1957 to 1958) and Custom (1959).
**Replacement for this model:** Crown (1964 to 1966).
**Percentage of division's sales volume:** 28.44%.
**Corporate siblings:** Crown and LeBaron.
**Primary competition:** Cadillac Sixty-Two, and Lincoln Continental.
**Notable changes:** New grille, taillamps inset into trailing fender edge, and minor trim and detail changes.
**Major standard equipment:** Torqueflite automatic transmission, power steering, power brakes, front and rear armrests (hardtops), pile carpeting, remote-control left-hand outside mirror, power windows, interior courtesy lamps, variable-speed electric windshield wipers with washers, wheel covers and 8.20 × 15 BSW tires.

## Measurements

| | |
|---|---|
| Wheelbase | 129.0" |
| Length | 227.8" |
| Width | 81.7" |
| Height | 56.7" |
| Legroom — front | 42.3" |
| Legroom — rear | 41.1" |
| Headroom — front | 39.3" |
| Headroom — rear | 38.5" |
| Cargo capacity (cu. ft.) | NA |
| Fuel capacity (gals.) | 23.0 |

## Models Available

| | Style Number | Base MSRP | Change from LY | Shipping Wt. (lbs.) | Production | Change from LY |
|---|---|---|---|---|---|---|
| Custom Imp. Southampton 2-Dr. HT | 912 | $5,058 | +2.80% | 4640 | 749 | -9.32% |
| Custom Imp. Southampton 4-Dr. HT | 914 | $5,243 | +2.68% | 4690 | 3,264 | -9.00% |
| TOTALS | | *Avg. price* $5,151 | +2.75% | | *Production* 4,013 | -9.07% |

# Crown

*"An Imperial that balances its spirited performance with its spirited personality."*

**Nameplate year of origin:** 1957 (Not the same as Crown Imperial series).
**Current bodystyle lifespan:** 1960 through 1963.
**Predecessor to this model:** Crown (1957 to 1959).
**Replacement for this model:** Crown (1964 to 1966).
**Percentage of division's sales volume:** 60.66%.

## Measurements

| | |
|---|---|
| Wheelbase | 129.0" |
| Length | 227.8" |
| Width | 81.7" |
| Height | 56.7" |

Corporate siblings: Custom and LeBaron.
Primary competition: Cadillac Sixty-Two and Lincoln Continental.
Notable changes: New grille, taillamps inset into trailing fender edge, and minor trim and detail changes.
Major standard equipment: Torqueflite automatic transmission, power steering, power brakes, front and rear armrests (hardtops), pile carpeting, remote-control left-hand outside mirror, power windows, interior dome and map lights, variable-speed electric windshield wipers with washers, trunk carpeting, wheel covers and 8.20 × 15 BSW tires.

## Measurements (cont.)

| | |
|---|---|
| Legroom — front | 42.3" |
| Legroom — rear | 41.1" |
| Headroom — front | 39.3" |
| Headroom — rear | 38.5" |
| Cargo capacity (cu. ft.) | NA |
| Fuel capacity (gals.) | 23.0 |

## Models Available

| | Style Number | Base MSRP | Change from LY | Shipping Wt. (lbs.) | Production | Change from LY |
|---|---|---|---|---|---|---|
| Crown Southampton 2-Door HT | 922 | $5,412 | +0.22% | 4720 | 1,067 | 5.64% |
| Crown 2-Door Convertible | 925 | $5,782 | +0.21% | 4795 | 531 | -4.15% |
| Crown Southampton 4-Door HT | 924 | $5,656 | +0.21% | 4740 | 6,960 | 0.71% |
| TOTALS | Avg. price | $5,617 | +0.21% | Production | 8,558 | +0.98% |

# LeBaron

*"Its classic town-car roof and formal rear window heighten the elegance of Imperial design."*

Nameplate year of origin: 1924 (as Chrysler Sedan model designation); 1926 (as series).
Current bodystyle lifespan: 1960 through 1963.
Predecessor to this model: LeBaron (1957 to 1959).
Replacement for this model: LeBaron (1964 to 1966).
Percentage of division's sales volume: 10.89%.
Corporate siblings: Custom and Crown.
Primary competition: Cadillac de Ville and Lincoln Continental.
Notable changes: New grille, taillamps inset into trailing fender edge, and minor trim and detail changes.
Major standard equipment: Torqueflite automatic transmission, power steering, power brakes, pile carpeting, 6-way power seat, power windows and vent windows, electric clock, interior dome and reading lamps, variable-speed electric windshield wipers with washers, carpeted trunk floor, wheel covers and 8.20 × 15 WSW tires.

## Measurements

| | |
|---|---|
| Wheelbase | 129.0" |
| Length | 227.8" |
| Width | 81.7" |
| Height | 56.7" |
| Legroom — front | 42.3" |
| Legroom — rear | 41.1" |
| Headroom — front | 39.3" |
| Headroom — rear | 38.5" |
| Cargo capacity (cu. ft.) | NA |
| Fuel capacity (gals.) | 23.0 |

## Models Available

| | Style Number | Base MSRP | Change from LY | Shipping Wt. (lbs.) | Production | Change from LY |
|---|---|---|---|---|---|---|
| LeBaron Southampton 4-Door HT | 934 | $6,434 | 0.19% | 4830 | 1,537 | +6.07% |
| TOTALS | Avg. price | $6,434 | -1.2% | Production | 1,537 | +6.07% |

# LINCOLN

*"With pride we present for your considered evaluation,
Lincoln Continental for '63."*

The 1963 Lincoln continued the styling and engineering introduced in 1961, with some important improvements. New carburetion and pistons improved responsiveness of the engine and fuel economy. A redesign of the luggage area and trunk lid increased luggage capacity. And a redesigning of the interior provided more passenger space. Otherwise, minor trim changes and a new grille distinguished the 1963 Lincoln from its predecessors.

Continental 4-Door Convertible

Continental Leather Interior

**Model year production:** 31,233, up 0.55% over 1962.
**Domestic market share:** 0.42% (13th place).
**Base price range:** $6,270 to $6,916.
**Industry average base price:** $3,028.
**Lincoln average base price:** $6,592.
**Introduction date:** October 1962.
**Assembly plants:** Allen Park, MI (S); and Wixom, MI (Y).

**Data plate identification:** Eleven digit code read as follows: 3 for 1963; 2nd digit is assembly plant code; 2-digit model number (see listings below); 5th digit is engine code; 400001 and up for serial number. *Example:* 3Y82H400001 is a 1963 Lincoln Continental 4-Door Sedan with a 430 CID V8 engine, serial number 400001, built in Wixom, MI.

## Powertrains

| Engine | Gross HP | Engine Code | Transmission Availability | Continental |
|---|---|---|---|---|
| 430 CID, 4-bbl., V8 | 320 | H | Turbo Drive Automatic | S |

## Major Options

| | Continental |
|---|---|
| Air conditioning—manual | $505 |
| Automatic headlight dimmers | $46 |
| Tinted glass | $54 |
| 6-way power seat | S |
| AM/FM radio | $85 |
| Leather upholstery | $100 |

## Paint Colors

| | Code |
|---|---|
| Black Satin | A |
| Oxford Gray Metallic | C |
| Riviera Turquoise Metallic | D |
| Bermuda Blue Metallic | E |
| Silver Mink Metallic | G |
| Nocturne Blue Metallic | H |

|  | *Continental* |  |  | *Code* |
|---|---|---|---|---|
| Speed control | $97 | Polynesian Gold Metallic | | I |
| Remote control trunk release/lock | $53 | Teaberry | | L |
| | | Ermine White | | M |

Options common to most models. (- = Not Available; S = Standard equipment.) Items may be standard equipment, optional at different pricing, or unavailable on certain models. This chart is only a guide.

| Color | Code |
|---|---|
| Platinum | N |
| Inverness Green Metallic | O |
| Spanish Red Metallic | Q |
| Premiere Yellow | R |
| Highlander Green Metallic | S |
| Nassau Beige | T |
| Rose Metallic | W |
| Burgundy Frost Metallic | X |
| Autumn Frost Metallic | Z |

# Continental

*"Classic grace ... commanding action."*

**Nameplate year of origin:** 1940 (1961 as a standard sedan nameplate).
**Current bodystyle lifespan:** 1961 through 1969 (major restyles in 1964 and 1966).
**Predecessor to this model:** Premiere (1958 to 1960).
**Replacement for this model:** Continental (1970 to 1979).
**Percentage of division's sales volume:** 100%.
**Corporate siblings:** None.
**Primary competition:** Cadillac de Ville, and Imperial Crown and LeBaron.
**Notable changes:** New grille and minor revisions.
**Major standard equipment:** Cloth and leather (sedan) or leather (convertible) front bench seat upholstery with folding center armrests front and rear, vanity mirror, looped-pile carpeting, AM transistor radio, Power operated door latching system, padded instrument panel, hydraulic windshield wipers with electric washers, power steering, power brakes, automatic transmission and 9.00 × 14 WSW tires (9.50 × 14 WSW on convertible).

## Measurements

| | |
|---|---|
| Wheelbase | 123.0" |
| Length | 213.0" |
| Width | 78.6" |
| Height | 53.7" |
| Legroom — front | 41.4" |
| Legroom — rear | 37.8" |
| Headroom — front | 37.7" |
| Headroom — rear | 38.2" |
| Luggage capacity (cu. ft.) | NA |
| Fuel capacity (gals.) | 21.0 |

## Models Available

| | Style Number | Base MSRP | Change from LY | Shipping Wt. (lbs.) | Production | Change from LY |
|---|---|---|---|---|---|---|
| Continental 4-Door Sedan | 53A | $6,270 | +3.23% | 4936 | 28,095 | 0.88% |
| Continental 4-Door Convertible | 74A | $6,913 | +2.87% | 5340 | 3,138 | -2.30% |
| TOTALS | | *Avg. price* $6,592 | +3.05% | *Production* 31,233 | | +0.55% |

# MERCURY

*"Available in three sizes … whichever
'63 Mercury you choose, you choose value!"*

For 1963, full-size Mercury models were given a facelift that was in line with the styling given the full-size Ford models. Mercury had suffered somewhat from being a dressed up Ford, and the revised styling tried to separate the two lines by giving the Mercury a more "Lincoln-like" grille. This coupled with a distinctive rear end treatment, helped to distance the two lines. It would be 1965 before the big Merc would become a more distinctive line. Mercury did, however, return to offering up some styling uniqueness in their line, with the introduction of the Breezeway window treatment. The Breezeway sported a power operated roll-down rear window that was canted inward at the bottom and provided ventilation and increased headroom. This was similar to the 1957 Turnpike Cruiser rear window treatment. Mid-year offerings included a 2-Door semi-fastback body style, known as the Marauder, to complement the same style at Ford. The Marauder was available in all full-size lines. Also added was a 4-Door Hardtop S-55 model, complete with all regular S-55 equipment including bucket seats and floor console.

The mid-range Meteor line was given the same changes as the Ford Fairlane, adding 2-Door Hardtop and 4-Door Station Wagon body styles to the line. Other changes to the line were minimal, but included a revised grille and trim. A new 260 CID V8 engine was available for the first time in the Comet line and also offered in the Meteor. This engine would be the basis for the soon to be released, more powerful and popular 289 CID V8 engine. The Comet line's sales were hurt slightly by the Meteor. Since the Meteor was only slightly larger than the Comet, the two lines seemed to be competing for the same market, a situation that would be corrected for 1964. New models in the Comet range included a 2-Door Hardtop and 2-Door Convertible for the S-22 and Custom lines. The 2-Door Hardtops were mid-year offerings introduced at the same time as the Falcon 2-Door Hardtops. Other changes to the Comet included a new grille and frontal styling, and revised rear end treatment.

Comet 4-Door Wagon

Comet S-22 2-Door Convertible

Meteor 2-Door Sedan

Meteor Country Cruiser 4-Door Wagon

Monterey 4-Door Sedan

S-55 2-Door Convertible

**Model year production:** 305,899, down 5.63% from 1962.
**Domestic market share:** 4.15% (9th place).
**Base price range:** $2,084 to $3,900.

**Industry average base price:** $3,028.
**Mercury average base price:** $2,778.
**Introduction date:** October 1962.

**Assembly plants:** Mahwah, NJ (E); Lorain, OH (H); Los Angeles, CA (J); Kansas City, MO (K); San Jose, CA (R); Wixom, MI (S); Metuchan, NJ (T); Wayne, MI (W); and St. Louis, MO (Z).

**Data plate identification:** Eleven digit code read as follows: 3 for 1963; 2nd digit is assembly plant code; 3rd digit is series

(1 or 2 is Comet, 3 or 4 is Meteor, 6 is Monterey); 4th digit is body style; 5th digit is engine code; 500001 and up for serial number (800001 and up for Comet). *Example:* 3W53Z100001 is a 1963 Mercury Monterey 2-Door Hardtop with a 390 CID V8 engine, serial number 500001, built in Wayne, MI.

## Powertrains

| Engine | Gross HP | Engine Code | Transmission Availability | Comet | Meteor | Monterey |
|---|---|---|---|---|---|---|
| 144.3 CID Comet, 1-bbl., 6-cyl. | 85 | S | 3-speed manual | S[2] | - | - |
| | | | 2-sp. Automatic | $172[2] | - | - |
| 170 CID Comet 170, 1-bbl., 6-cyl. | 101 | U | 3-speed manual | S[1]/$45[2] | S | - |
| | | | 2-sp. Automatic | $172[1]/$217[2] | $172 | - |
| 221 CID Meteor, 2-bbl., V8 | 145 | L | 3-speed manual | - | $103 | - |
| | | | Overdrive | - | $211 | - |
| | | | Merc-O-Matic Automatic | - | $275 | - |
| 223 CID Six, 1-bbl., 6-cyl. | 138 | V | 3-speed manual | - | $45 | - |
| | | | Overdrive | - | $153 | - |
| | | | Merc-O-Matic Automatic | - | $217 | - |
| 260 CID Meteor Lightning, 2-bbl., V8 | 164 | F | 3-speed manual | $76[1]/$121[2] | $155 | - |
| | | | 4-speed manual[5] | 264[1]/$309[2] | $263 | - |
| | | | Merc-O-Matic Automatic | $248[1]/$293[2] | $327 | - |
| 390 CID Marauder, 2-bbl., V8 | 250 | Y | 3-speed manual | - | - | S[4] |
| | | | 4-speed manual[5] | - | - | $221[4] |
| | | | Multi-Drive Automatic | - | - | $221[4] |
| 390 CID Marauder Super, 4-bbl., V8 | 300 | Z | 3-speed manual | - | - | $52[4] |
| | | | 4-speed manual[5] | - | - | No cost[3]/$276[4] |
| | | | Multi-Drive Automatic | - | - | S[3]/$276[4] |
| 427 CID Marauder, 4-bbl., V8 | 410 | B | 4-speed manual[5] | - | - | $406[3]/$665[4] |
| | | | Multi-Drive Automatic | - | - | $406[3]/$665[4] |
| 427 CID Marauder Super*, 3 × 2-bbl., V8 | 425 | B | 4-speed manual[5] | - | - | $488[3]/$708[4] |
| | | | Multi-Drive Automatic | - | - | $488[3]/$708[4] |

*Special order only. [1]Wagons and S-22. [2]All but Wagons and S-22. [3]S-55. [4]All but S-55. [5]Not available on wagons.

## Major Options

| | Comet | Meteor | Monterey |
|---|---|---|---|
| SelectAire air conditioning | $271 | $271 | $361 |
| Tinted glass | $31 | $40 | $43 |
| Power steering | - | $82 | $82 |
| Power brakes | - | $43 | $43 |
| Power windows | - | - | $102 |
| Electric windshield wipers w/washer | $23 | $21 | $21 |
| Electric clock | - | $15 | $15 |
| Pushbutton AM radio | $59 | $59 | $59 |
| White sidewall tires — std. sizes | $30–$33 | $37 | $37–$53 |
| Full wheel covers | $16 | $19 | S |

Options common to most models. (- = Not Available; S = Standard equipment.) Items may be standard equipment, optional at different pricing, or unavailable on certain models. This chart is only a guide.

## Paint Colors

| | Code |
|---|---|
| Presidential Black | A |
| Peacock Turquoise | B |
| Ocean Turquoise Metallic | D |
| Pacific Blue Metallic | E |
| Pink Lustre | F |
| Blue Satin Metallic | H |
| Castilian Gold Metallic | I |
| Carnival Red | J |
| Sultana White | M |
| Scotch Green Metallic | P |
| Jamaica Yellow | R |
| Champagne | T |
| Pink Frost Metallic | W |
| Black Cherry Metallic | X |
| Cascade Blue | Y |
| Desert Frost Metallic | Z |

# Comet

*"Step out ahead … and stay there!"*

**Nameplate year of origin:** 1960.
**Current bodystyle lifespan:** 1960 through 1963.
**Predecessor to this model:** None.
**Replacement for this model:** Comet (1964 to 1965).
**Percentage of division's sales volume:** 44.01%.
**Corporate siblings:** Ford Falcon.
**Primary competition:** Buick Special, Dodge Dart, Oldsmobile F-85, Pontiac Tempest and Studebaker.
**Notable changes:** Revised grille and minor trim and detail changes.
**Major standard equipment:** Nylon and vinyl front bench seat with foam cushions, carpet textured rubber floor covering, dual front armrests and dual sun visors, dome light, glove compartment, bright metal front and rear window trim, and 6.00 × 13 BSW tires (6.50 × 13 BSW tires on wagons). Custom adds: Distinctive trim, loop-pile carpeting, deluxe steering wheel, front and rear door armrests, power-operated top on convertible, and 6.50 × 13 BSW tires on convertible. S-22 adds: Front bucket seats, vinyl-covered center floor console, S-22 exterior trim and additional sound deadening materials.

## Measurements

|  | Cars | Wagons |
| --- | --- | --- |
| Wheelbase | 114.0" | 109.5" |
| Length | 194.8" | 191.8" |
| Width | 70.4" | 70.4" |
| Height | 54.5" | 55.0" |
| Legroom — front | 41.5" | 41.5" |
| Legroom — rear | 34.7" | 34.7" |
| Headroom — front | 38.0" | 38.0" |
| Headroom — rear | 37.5" | 37.5" |
| Cargo capacity (cu. ft.) | 29.8 | 76.2 |
| Fuel capacity (gals.) | 14.0 | 14.0 |

**1963**

## Models Available

|  | Style Number | Base MSRP | Change from LY | Shipping Wt. (lbs.) | Production | Change from LY |
| --- | --- | --- | --- | --- | --- | --- |
| Comet 2-Door Sedan | 62A | $2,084 | 0.00% | 2462 | 24,351 | -67.00% |
| Comet 4-Door Sedan | 54A | $2,139 | 0.00% | 2499 | 24,230 | -65.50% |
| Comet 2-Door Wagon | 59A | $2,440 | +1.84% | 2644 | 623 | -70.63% |
| Comet 4-Door Wagon | 71A | $2,483 | +1.80% | 2681 | 4,419 | -73.63% |
| Comet Custom 2-Door Sedan | 62B | $2,171 | 0.00% | 2471 | 11,897 | * |
| Comet Custom 2-Door Hardtop | 63B | $2,300 | NEW | 2572 | 9,432 | NEW |
| Comet Custom 2-Door Conv. | 76A | $2,557 | NEW | 2784 | 7,354 | NEW |
| Comet Custom 4-Door Sedan | 54B | $2,226 | 0.00% | 2508 | 27,498 | * |
| Comet Custom 2-Door Wagon | 59B | $2,527 | +1.77% | 2659 | 272 | * |
| Comet Custom 4-Door Wagon | 71B | $2,570 | +1.74% | 2696 | 5,151 | * |
| Comet Villager 4-Door Wagon | 71C | $2,754 | +1.62% | 2736 | 1,529 | -34.04% |
| Comet S-22 2-Door Sedan | 62C | $2,368 | 0.00% | 2512 | 6,303 | * |
| Comet S-22 2-Door Hardtop | 63C | $2,400 | NEW | 2613 | 5,807 | NEW |
| Comet S-22 2-Door Convertible | 76B | $2,710 | NEW | 2825 | 5,757 | NEW |
| TOTALS | *Avg. price* | $2,409 | +2.34% | *Production* | 134,623 | -18.53% |

*Production figures for 1962 not available for comparisons.*

# Meteor

*"Spirit, sparkle and brawn … bright words that mean Mercury Meteor for 1963."*

**Nameplate year of origin:** 1961.
**Current bodystyle lifespan:** 1962 through 1963.
**Predecessor to this model:** Meteor (1961).
**Replacement for this model:** Comet (1966 to 1967).
**Percentage of division's sales volume:** 16.42%.

## Measurements

|  | Cars | Wagons |
| --- | --- | --- |
| Wheelbase | 116.5" | 115.5" |
| Length | 203.8" | 202.3" |

**Corporate siblings:** Ford Fairlane.
**Primary competition:** Dodge 330/440 and Plymouth Fury.
**Notable changes:** Revised grille and taillamp treatment. Minor trim and detail changes.
**Major standard equipment:** Cloth and vinyl front bench seat, bright exterior window trim and 6.50 × 14 BSW tires. Custom adds: All-vinyl upholstery (no cost option), additional interior and exterior trim, twist-pile carpeting. S-33 adds: All-vinyl bucket seats, center floor console and S-33 badging.

|  | Cars | Wagons |
|---|---|---|
| Width | 71.3" | 71.3" |
| Height | 55.8" | 56.6" |
| Legroom — front | 42.4" | 42.4" |
| Legroom — rear | 36.7" | 36.1" |
| Headroom — front | 38.2" | 38.2" |
| Headroom — rear | 38.0" | 38.1" |
| Cargo capacity (cu. ft.) | 31.5 | 86.2 |
| Fuel capacity (gals.) | 16.0 | 16.0 |

## Models Available

|  | Style Number | Base MSRP | Change from LY | Shipping Wt. (lbs.) | Production | Change from LY |
|---|---|---|---|---|---|---|
| Meteor 2-Door Sedan | 62A | $2,278 | 0.00% | 2920 | 3,935 | 0.00% |
| Meteor 4-Door Sedan | 54A | $2,340 | 0.00% | 2959 | 9,183 | 0.00% |
| Meteor 4-Door Wagon | 71B | $2,631 | NEW | 3237 | 2,359 | NEW |
| Meteor Custom 2-Door Sedan | 62B | $2,366 | 0.00% | 2926 | 2,704 | -71.26% |
| Meteor Custom 2-Door Hardtop | 65A | $2,448 | NEW | 2944 | 7,565 | NEW |
| Meteor Custom 4-Door Sedan | 54B | $2,428 | 0.00% | 2965 | 14,498 | -38.26% |
| Meteor Custom 4-Door Wagon | 71E | $2,719 | NEW | 3245 | 3,636 | NEW |
| Meteor S-33 2-Door Hardtop | 65B | $2,628 | NEW | 2964 | 4,865 | NEW |
| Meteor Country Cruiser 4-Dr. Wgn. | 71D | $2,886 | NEW | 3253 | 1,485 | NEW |
| TOTALS | | Avg. price $2,525 | +5.91% | | Production 50,230 | -3.24% |

# Monterey

*"So much luxury and style … so little maintenance.*
*Only one new car looks like this."*

**Nameplate year of origin:** 1952.
**Current bodystyle lifespan:** 1963 through 1964.
**Predecessor to this model:** Monterey (1961 to 1962).
**Replacement for this model:** Monterey (1965 to 1966).
**Percentage of division's sales volume:** 39.57%.
**Corporate siblings:** Ford Galaxie.
**Primary competition:** Buick Wildcat, Dodge Polara, Oldsmobile 88 and Pontiac Star Chief/Bonneville.
**Notable changes:** Completely restyled. New Breezeway 4-Door with roll-down rear window, and mid-year Marauder Fastback 2-Door body styles introduced this year.
**Major standard equipment:** Cloth and vinyl front bench seat, full carpeting, padded instrument panel, electric windshield wipers, bright exterior window trim and 7.50 × 14 BSW tires. Custom adds: Electric clock, courtesy lights, and back up lights. Colony Park wagons adds: exterior wood-grain vinyl trim, and power tailgate window. S-55 adds: Bucket seats, floor console, special interior trim, and dual exhausts.

## Measurements

|  | Cars | Wagons |
|---|---|---|
| Wheelbase | 120.0" | 120.0" |
| Length | 215.0" | 209.9" |
| Width | 80.0" | 79.9" |
| Height | 55.5" | 56.9" |
| Legroom — front | 41.6" | 41.6" |
| Legroom — rear | 38.6" | 38.5" |
| Headroom — front | 38.7" | 38.8" |
| Headroom — rear | 38.2" | 38.4" |
| Cargo capacity (cu. ft.) | NA | 91.5 |
| Fuel capacity (gals.) | 20.0 | 20.0 |

## Models Available

|  | Style Number | Base MSRP | Change from LY | Shipping Wt. (lbs.) | Production | Change from LY |
|---|---|---|---|---|---|---|
| Monterey 2-Door Sedan | 62A | $2,834 | +6.06% | 3854 | 4,640 | -9.32% |
| Monterey 2-Door Hardtop | 65A | $2,930 | +7.21% | 3869 | 2,879 | -45.96% |

| | Style Number | Base MSRP | Change from LY | Shipping Wt. (lbs.) | Production | Change from LY |
|---|---|---|---|---|---|---|
| Monterey 2-Door Fastback | 63A | $2,930 | NEW | 3875 | 1,000 | NEW |
| Monterey 4-Door Breezeway Sdn. | 54A | $2,887 | +5.91% | 3944 | 18,177 | -4.21% |
| Monterey 4-Door Hardtop | 75A | $2,995 | +7.04% | 3959 | 1,692 | -37.12% |
| Monterey Custom 2-Door Hardtop | 65B | $3,083 | +3.73% | 3881 | 10,693 | -1.12% |
| Monterey Custom 2-Dr. Fastback | 63B | $3,083 | NEW | 3887 | 7,298 | NEW |
| Monterey Custom 2-Door Conv. | 76A | $3,333 | +3.45% | 4043 | 3,783 | -31.08% |
| Monterey Custom 4-Door Sedan | 54B | $3,075 | +3.71% | 3956 | 39,542 | +43.31% |
| Monterey Custom 4-Door Hardtop | 75B | $3,148 | +3.65% | 3971 | 8,604 | -3.67% |
| S-55 2-Door Hardtop | 65C | $3,650 | +4.64% | 3894 | 3,863 | 39.36% |
| S-55 2-Door Fastback | 63C | $3,650 | NEW | 3900 | 2,317 | NEW |
| S-55 2-Door Convertible | 76B | $3,900 | +4.33% | 4049 | 1,379 | 4.87% |
| S-55 4-Door Hardtop | 75C | $3,715 | NEW | 3984 | 1,203 | NEW |
| Colony Park 4-Door, 2-Seat Wagon | 71B | $3,295 | +2.36% | 4306 | 6,447 | -32.82% |
| Colony Park 4-Door, 3-Seat Wagon | 71D | $3,365 | +2.31% | 4318 | 7,529 | * |
| TOTALS | | Avg. price $3,242 | +6.12% | | Production 121,046 | +13.12% |

*Wagon production combined in 1962.

1963

# OLDSMOBILE

*"There's 'Something Extra' about owning an OLDSMOBILE!"*

Major styling revisions were seen across the line on the 1963 Oldsmobiles. Full-size models wore revised greenhouses and windshields, and new sheetmetal all the way around. Similarly, the compact F-85 line was given an all-new look with new sheetmetal that lengthened the cars by several inches. All models were styled to look like each other in certain ways: the full-width, cross-hatch grilles, the rear fenders ending in vestigial tail fins atop a squarish taillight, and flat-topped rear wheel openings that were cut significantly lower than the front openings. The Starfire Coupe gained a concave rear window treatment that it shared with the newly styled Pontiac Grand Prix. This window treatment would become a styling feature of Grand Prix models for the next ten years, but would only last at Oldsmobile through 1966.

There was minimal news on other fronts for 1963. Powertrains were carried over, but it is interesting to note that over 99 percent of full-size Oldsmobiles were built with an automatic transmission. Newly available on the option list this year was a 4-speed manual transmission for F-85 Cutlass and Jetfire models. Also, as on other GM models, a tilt steering column was now offered, and AM/FM radios began their rise in popularity this year as an automotive accessory.

98 4-Door Hardtop

98 Custom 2-Door Sport Coupe

Dynamic 88 4-Door Sedan

Super 88 4-Door Sedan

Starfire 2-Door Convertible

F-85 Deluxe 4-Door Sedan and 4-Door Wagon

**Model year production:** 477,098, up 5.65% over 1962.
**Domestic market share:** 6.48% (5th place).
**Base price range:** $2,403 to $4,742.
**Industry average base price:** $3,028.
**Oldsmobile average base price:** $3,451.
**Introduction date:** October 4, 1962.
**Assembly plants:** Atlanta, GA (A); Southgate, CA (C); Kansas City, MO (K); Fairfax, KS (K); Linden, NJ (L); Lansing, MI (M); Arlington, TX (T); and Wilmington, DE (W).

**Data plate identification:** Nine digit code read as follows: 1st two digits 63 for year; 3rd designates trim level; 4th identifies assembly plant; 01001 and up for serial number. Check model number on body plate for body style. *Example:* 638M01001 is a 1963 Oldsmobile Ninety-Eight, built in Lansing, MI, serial number 01001.

## Powertrains

| Engine | Gross HP | Transmission Availability | F-85 | Cutlass & Jetfire | Dynamic 88 | Super 88 | Starfire & 98 |
|---|---|---|---|---|---|---|---|
| 215 CID Rockette, 2-bbl., V8 | 155 | 3-speed manual | S | - | - | - | - |
| | | 4-speed manual | $200 | - | - | - | |
| | | Jetaway Automatic | $189 | - | - | - | - |
| 215 CID Cutlass, 4-bbl., V8 | 185 | 3-speed manual | - | S (Cut.) | - | - | - |
| | | 4-speed manual | - | $200 (Cut.) | - | - | |
| | | Jetaway Automatic | - | $189 (Cut.) | - | - | |
| 215 CID Turbo-Rocket, Turbocharged V8 | 215 | 3-speed manual | - | S (Jet.) | - | - | - |
| | | 4-speed manual | - | $200 (Jet.) | - | - | |
| | | Jetaway Automatic | - | $189 (Jet.) | - | - | |
| 394 CID Rocket, 2-bbl., V8 | 280 | 3-speed manual | - | - | S | - | - |
| | | Jetaway Automatic | - | - | $231 | - | - |
| 394 CID Rocket, 4-bbl., V8 | 330 | 3-speed manual | - | - | - | S | - |
| | | Jetaway Automatic | - | - | - | $231 | S (98)* |
| 394 CID Starfire Rocket, 4-bbl., V8 | 345 | Jetaway Automatic | - | - | - | - | S (St. & 98 Cst. Sp.) |

*345-hp/394 CID V8 with Automatic, standard on 98 Custom Sports Coupe.

## Major Options

| | F-85 | Dynamic 88 | Super 88 | Starfire | Ninety-Eight |
|---|---|---|---|---|---|
| Air conditioning | $378 | $430 | $430 | $430 | $430 |
| Soft Ray tinted glass | $31 | $43 | $43 | $43 | $43 |
| Deck lid remote release | - | $10 | $10 | $10 | $10 |
| Tilt-Away steering wheel | - | $43 | $43 | $43 | $43 |
| Power steering— variable-ratio | $86 | $108 | $108 | S | S |
| Power brakes | $43 | $43 | $43 | S | S |
| Power driver's seat/Bench seat | - | $97 | $97 | S*/$28 | S*/$97 |
| Power windows | $102 | $106 | $106 | S/$106 | S/$106 |

## Paint Colors

| | Code |
|---|---|
| Ebony Black | A |
| Provincial White | C |
| Sheffield Mist Metallic | D |
| Wedgewood Mist Metallic | F |
| Cirrus Blue | H |
| Willow Mist Metallic | J |
| Barktone Mist Metallic | K |
| Regal Mist Metallic | L |
| Pacific Mist Metallic | P |

| | F-85 | Dynamic 88 | Super 88 | Starfire | Ninety-Eight | | Code |
|---|---|---|---|---|---|---|---|
| Electric clock | $16 | $16 | S | S | S | Sand Beige | R |
| AM radio | $66 | $89 | $89 | $89 | $89 | Saddle Mist Metallic | S |
| | | | | | | Sahara Mist Metallic | T |
| | | | | | | Holiday Red | V |
| | | | | | | Midnight Mist Metallic | W |
| | | | | | | Antique Rose Metallic | X |

Options common to most models. (– = Not Available; S = Standard equipment.) Items may be standard equipment, optional at different pricing, or unavailable on certain models. This chart is only a guide.

*See individual model sections for details.*

# F-85 and Cutlass

*"Exciting new blend of beauty and action ... in the low-price field!"*

**Nameplate year of origin:** 1961 (F-85); 1962 (Cutlass, as F-85 designation); 1955 (show car).
**Current bodystyle lifespan:** 1961 through 1963.
**Predecessor to this model:** None.
**Replacement for this model:** F-85/Cutlass (1964 to 1965).
**Percentage of division's sales volume:** 24.90%.
**Corporate siblings:** Buick Special/Skylark, Pontiac Tempest/LeMans.
**Primary competition:** Rambler Classic, Mercury Meteor, Dodge Dart, and Studebaker Lark.
**Notable changes:** Restyled exterior.
**Major standard equipment:** Cloth and vinyl upholstery, foam cushion front seats, heater and defroster, and 6.50 × 13 BSW tires. Deluxe adds: full carpeting, deluxe steering wheel, and interior and exterior chrome trim moldings. Jetfire adds: fluid-injected turbo-charged engine.

## Measurements

| | |
|---|---|
| Wheelbase | 112.0" |
| Length | 192.2" |
| Width | 73.7" |
| Height | 52.7" |
| Legroom — front | 40.4" |
| Legroom — rear | 36.5" |
| Headroom — front | 38.0" |
| Headroom — rear | 36.8" |
| Luggage capacity (cu. ft.) | 25.5/ Wagon 73.3 |
| Fuel capacity (gals.) | 16.0 |

## Models Available

| | Style Number | Base MSRP | Change from LY | Shipping Wt. (lbs.) | Production | Change from LY |
|---|---|---|---|---|---|---|
| F-85 2-Door Club Coupe | 3027 | $2,403 | 0.00% | 2599 | 11,276 | +42.57% |
| F-85 4-Door Sedan | 3019 | $2,457 | 0.00% | 2629 | 8,937 | +10.69% |
| F-85 4-Door, 2-Seat Wagon | 3035 | $2,754 | 0.00% | 2812 | 3,348 | +4.49% |
| F-85 Deluxe Cutlass 2-Dr. Club Cpe. | 3117 | $2,694 | 0.00% | 2679 | 41,343 | +25.21% |
| F-85 Deluxe Cutlass 2-Dr. Conv. | 3167 | $2,971 | 0.00% | 2858 | 12,149 | +23.12% |
| F-85 Deluxe 4-Door Sedan | 3119 | $2,592 | 0.00% | 2659 | 29,269 | +56.22% |
| F-85 Deluxe 4-Door, 2-Seat Wagon | 3135 | $2,889 | 0.00% | 2833 | 6,647 | +33.63% |
| Jetfire 2-Door Hardtop | 3147 | $3,048 | -0.03% | 2774 | 5,842 | +55.17% |
| TOTALS | *Avg. price* | $2,726 | -0.52% | *Production* | 118,811 | +24.94% |

# Dynamic 88

*"Big and beautiful ... value leader of the medium-price field!"*

**Nameplate year of origin:** 1949 (1958 for Dynamic nameplate).
**Current bodystyle lifespan:** 1961 through 1964.
**Predecessor to this model:** 88 (1959 to 1960).
**Replacement for this model:** Jetstar 88 (1964).
**Percentage of division's sales volume:** 41.78%.
**Corporate siblings:** Buick LeSabre, Chevrolet Impala, Pontiac Catalina.

## Measurements*

| | |
|---|---|
| Wheelbase | 123.0" |
| Length | 214.4" |
| Width | 77.9" |
| Height | 56.3" |
| Legroom — front | 44.4" |

**Primary competition:** Chrysler Newport, Dodge Custom 880, Mercury Monterey.
**Notable changes:** Major restyle of front, rear and greenhouse areas.
**Major standard equipment:** Cloth-and-vinyl bench seat, nylon-blend carpet, heater and defroster, full wheel covers, and 8.00 × 14 BSW tires.

## Measurements* (cont.)

| | |
|---|---|
| Legroom — rear | 41.4" |
| Headroom — front | 38.4" |
| Headroom — rear | 38.1" |
| Luggage capacity (cu. ft.) | 85.1 (wagon) |
| Fuel capacity (gals.) | 21.0 |

*Door models

## Models Available

| | Style Number | Base MSRP | Change from LY | Shipping Wt. (lbs.) | Production | Change from LY |
|---|---|---|---|---|---|---|
| Dynamic 88 2-Door Holiday Hardtop | 3247 | $3,052 | -0.07% | 3939 | 39,071 | -1.52% |
| Dynamic 88 2-Door Convertible | 3267 | $3,379 | -0.06% | 4039 | 12,551 | +2.78% |
| Dynamic 88 4-Door Celebrity Sedan | 3269 | $2,995 | -0.07% | 3998 | 68,611 | +0.21% |
| Dynamic 88 4-Door Holiday Hardtop | 3239 | $3,130 | -0.03% | 4059 | 62,355 | +16.71% |
| Dynamic 88 4-Dr., 2-S. Wagon | 3235 | $3,459 | -0.03% | 4322 | 9,615 | +12.76% |
| Dynamic 88 4-Dr., 3-S. Wagon | 3245 | $3,566 | -0.06% | 4354 | 7,116 | +10.89% |
| TOTALS | | Avg. price $3,264 | -0.01% | | Production 199,319 | +5.61% |

# Super 88

*"Puts the accent on action!"*

**Nameplate year of origin:** 1951 (88 series started 1949).
**Current bodystyle lifespan:** 1961 through 1964.
**Predecessor to this model:** Super 88 (1959 to 1960).
**Replacement for this model:** Delta 88 (1965 to 1966).
**Percentage of division's sales volume:** 13.16%.
**Corporate siblings:** Buick Wildcat, Chevrolet Impala, Pontiac Star Chief.
**Primary competition:** Chrysler Newport, Dodge Custom 880, and Mercury Monterey Custom.
**Notable changes:** Major restyle of front, rear and greenhouse areas.
**Major standard equipment:** All-vinyl bench seat with fold-down center armrest (except Celebrity Sedan), nylon-blend carpet, Deluxe steering wheel, heater and defroster, glove box and courtesy lamps, full wheel covers, and 8.00 × 14 BSW tires.

## Measurements*

| | |
|---|---|
| Wheelbase | 123.0" |
| Length | 214.4" |
| Width | 77.9" |
| Height | 56.3" |
| Legroom — front | 44.4" |
| Legroom — rear | 41.4" |
| Headroom — front | 38.4" |
| Headroom — rear | 38.1" |
| Luggage capacity (cu. ft.) | 85.1 (wagon) |
| Fuel capacity (gals.) | 21.0 |

*4-Door models.

## Models Available

| | Style Number | Base MSRP | Change from LY | Shipping Wt. (lbs.) | Production | Change from LY |
|---|---|---|---|---|---|---|
| Super 88 2-Door Holiday Hardtop | 3547 | $3,408 | -0.41% | 3966 | 8,930 | -0.89% |
| Super 88 4-Door Celebrity Sedan | 3569 | $3,246 | -0.82% | 4027 | 24,575 | +1.87% |
| Super 88 4-Door Holiday Hardtop | 3539 | $3,473 | -0.74% | 4083 | 25,387 | +19.89% |
| Super 88 4-Dr., 2-S. Fiesta Wagon | 3535 | $3,748 | -0.37% | 4347 | 3,878 | +1.07% |
| TOTALS | | Avg. price $3,469 | -0.58% | | Production 62,770 | +7.95% |

# Starfire

*"An Oldsmobile original ... pure glamor with a touch of adventure!"*

**Nameplate year of origin:** 1954 (as designation for 98 Convertible); 1961 (as series).
**Current bodystyle lifespan:** 1961 through 1964.
**Predecessor to this model:** None.
**Replacement for this model:** Starfire (1965 to 1966).
**Percentage of division's sales volume:** 5.43%.
**Corporate siblings:** Buick Wildcat, and Pontiac Grand Prix.
**Primary competition:** Chrysler 300, Ford Thunderbird, and Mercury S-55.
**Notable changes:** Major restyle of front, rear and greenhouse areas.
**Major standard equipment:** Leather bucket seats with center console, nylon-blend carpet, deluxe steering wheel, power windows, heater and defroster, glove box and courtesy lamps, color-keyed full wheel covers, tachometer, unique exterior aluminum trim and 8.00 × 14 BSW tires.

## Measurements

| | |
|---|---|
| Wheelbase | 123.0" |
| Length | 214.4" |
| Width | 77.9" |
| Height | 54.7" |
| Legroom — front | 44.4" |
| Legroom — rear | 41.4" |
| Headroom — front | 38.4" |
| Headroom — rear | 38.1" |
| Luggage capacity (cu. ft.) | NA |
| Fuel capacity (gals.) | 21.0 |

**1963**

## Models Available

| | Style Number | Base MSRP | Change from LY | Shipping Wt. (lbs.) | Production | Change from LY |
|---|---|---|---|---|---|---|
| Starfire 2-Door Hardtop | 3657 | $4,129 | -0.05% | 4172 | 21,489 | -38.32% |
| Starfire 2-Door Convertible | 3667 | $4,742 | -0.04% | 4293 | 4,401 | -38.44% |
| TOTALS | | Avg. price $4,436 | -0.01% | | Production 25,890 | -38.34% |

# Ninety-Eight

*"The long look of luxury!"*

**Nameplate year of origin:** 1941.
**Current bodystyle lifespan:** 1961 through 1964.
**Predecessor to this model:** Ninety-Eight (1959 to 1960).
**Replacement for this model:** Ninety-Eight (1965 to 1966).
**Percentage of division's sales volume:** 14.74%.
**Corporate siblings:** Buick Electra 225, and Cadillac Series 62/de Ville.
**Primary competition:** Chrysler New Yorker, and 300-J.
**Notable changes:** Major restyle of front, rear and greenhouse areas.
**Major standard equipment:** Cloth and vinyl bench seat with fold-down center armrest, deep-pile carpeting floor and kick panels, deluxe steering wheel, electric clock, trunk lamp, trunk mat, full wheel covers, power steering and brakes, 8.50 × 14 BSW tires. Luxury Sedan adds: special design interior.

## Measurements*

| | |
|---|---|
| Wheelbase | 126.0" |
| Length | 221.5" |
| Width | 77.9" |
| Height | 57.1" |
| Legroom — front | 44.2" |
| Legroom — rear | 44.8" |
| Headroom — front | 38.4" |
| Headroom — rear | 38.1" |
| Luggage capacity (cu. ft.) | NA |
| Fuel capacity (gals.) | 21.0 |

*4-Door Hardtop models.*

## Models Available

| | Style Number | Base MSRP | Change from LY | Shipping Wt. (lbs.) | Production | Change from LY |
|---|---|---|---|---|---|---|
| Ninety-Eight 2-Door Sports Coupe | 3847 | $4,178 | -0.05% | 4215 | 4,984 | -33.95% |
| Ninety-Eight 2-Door Convertible | 3867 | $4,457 | -0.04% | 4272 | 4,267 | -40.31% |
| Ninety-Eight 4-Door Town Sedan | 3819 | $3,982 | -0.05% | 4240 | 11,053 | -9.16% |
| Ninety-Eight 4-Door Sports Sedan | 3839 | $4,254 | -0.05% | 4347 | 23,330 | -29.51% |
| Ninety-Eight Luxury 4-Door Sedan | 3829 | $4,332 | +5.20% | 4362 | 19,252 | +151.56% |
| Ninety-Eight Custom 2-Dr. Sp. Cpe. | 3947 | $4,381 | NEW | 4285 | 7,422 | NEW |
| TOTALS | | Avg. price $4,264 | +1.55% | | Production 70,308 | +3.99% |

# PLYMOUTH

*"Plymouth 63! Plymouth's on the move."*

Totally new sheetmetal adorned every new 1963 Plymouth. And for the first time in several years, the full-size Plymouth line looked subdued. Gone were the big fins, the overly flared wheel openings, and the peculiar grille and headlamp designs of prior years. This one was the most conservative Plymouth since the mid-fifties. It showed in the improved sales, too, as customers were used to their low-priced cars being conservative not conspicuous. Un-

fortunately, Plymouth was still lacking the true full-size model it needed to go head to head with Ford and Chevy, but the new look brought it a great leap forward.

An oddity of Plymouth's marketing techniques for 1963 was that every photograph of any importance in sales literature for the year showed either a red car or a black car with a red interior.

Fury 4-Door Hardtop

Fury 2-Door Convertible and Interior

Valiant Signet 2-Door Hardtop

Valiant V200 4-Door Wagon

**Model year production:** 488,448, up 43.87% over 1962.
**Domestic market share:** 6.63% (4th place).
**Base price range:** $1,910 to $3,082.
**Industry average base price:** $3,028.
**Industry average base price:** $2,482.
**Introduction date:** October 1962.
**Assembly plants:** Lynch Road, MI (1): Hamtramck, MI (2); Detroit, MI (3); Los Angeles, CA (5); Newark DE (6); and St. Louis, MO (7).

**Data plate identification:** Ten digit code read as follows: First and second digits are series designation (first two numbers of model number in charts below); third digit 3 for 1963; fourth digit is assembly plant code; 100001 and up for serial number. *Example:* 2323100001 is a 1963 Plymouth Fury with a 225 CID 6-cyl., built at Hamtramck, MI, serial number 100001. Body style cannot be identified through the VIN.

## Powertrains

| Engine[1] | Gross HP | Engine Code | Transmission Availability[2] | Valiant | Savoy/ Belvedere | Fury |
|---|---|---|---|---|---|---|
| 170 CID, 1-bbl., 6-cyl. | 101 | A | 3-speed manual | S | - | - |
| | | | Torqueflite automatic | $172 | - | - |
| 225 CID 30-D Economy Six, 2-bbl., 6-cyl. | 145 | B | 3-speed manual | $47 | S | S[3] |
| | | | Torqueflite automatic | $219 | $192 | $192[3] |
| 318 CID Fury V-800, 2-bbl., V8 | 230 | F | 3-speed manual | | $107 | S[4]/$107[3] |
| | | | Torqueflite automatic | | $318 | $211[4]/$318[3] |
| 361 CID Golden Commando, 2-bbl., V8 | 265 | NA | 3-speed manual | - | $167 | $60[4]/$167[3] |
| | | | Torqueflite automatic | - | $378 | $271[4]/$378[3] |
| 383 CID Golden Commando, 4-bbl., V8 | 330 | NA | 3-speed manual | - | $218 | $111[4]/$218[3] |
| | | | Torqueflite automatic | | $439 | $322[4]/$439[3] |

[1]Super Stock II 426 CID V8 "Wedge" engine options available after start of the year on V8 full-size cars.  [2]4-speed manual transmission available mid-year on V8 Full-size models.  [3]Fury 2-Dr. HT, 4-Dr. Sedan.  [4]All but Fury 2-Dr. HT, 4-Dr. Sedan.

## Major Options

| | Valiant | Savoy/Belvedere | Fury |
|---|---|---|---|
| Push-button heater and defroster | | | |
| Air conditioning (V8 only) | $335 | $355 | $355 |
| Solex tinted glass | $30 | $42 | $42 |
| Power steering | $84 | $94 | $94 |
| Power brakes | $44 | $44 | $44 |
| Front disc brakes | $73 | $73 | $73 |
| Power windows | | | |
| Electric clock | $16 | $16 | S/$16 — Fury I |
| AM radio | $60 | $60 | $60 |
| White sidewall tires — std. sizes | $79 | $79 | $106 |
| Full wheel covers | - | $102 | $61–$102 |

Options common to most models. (– = Not Available; S = Standard equipment.) Items may be standard equipment, optional at different pricing, or unavailable on certain models. This chart is only a guide.

## Paint Colors

| | Code |
|---|---|
| Hawaiian Blue | 22-1 |
| Buffed Silver Metallic | AA-1 |
| Black | BB-1 |
| Medium Blue Metallic | CC-1 |
| Mist Blue Metallic | DD-1 |
| Midnight Blue Metallic | EE-1 |
| Mist Green Metallic | FF-1 |
| Forest Green Metallic | GG-1 |
| Yellow Gold | HH-1 |
| Ember Gold Metallic | JJ-1 |
| Mist Turquoise Metallic | KK-1 |
| Surf Turquoise Met. | LL-1 |
| Turbine Bronze Metallic | MM-1 |
| Matador Red | PP-1 |
| Electric Blue Metallic | QQ-1 |
| Burgundy Metallic | RR-1 |
| Sunfire Yellow | SS-1 |
| Avacado Green Metallic | TT-1 |
| Frost Blue Metallic | UU-1 |
| Sable White | WW-1 |
| Satin Beige | XX-1 |
| Sierra Tan Metallic | YY-1 |

# Valiant

*"The New Valiant. Best all-around compact anybody has come up with yet..."*

**Nameplate year of origin:** 1960.
**Current bodystyle lifespan:** 1963 through 1966.
**Predecessor to this model:** Valiant (1960 to 1962).
**Replacement for this model:** Valiant (1967 to 1976).
**Percentage of division's sales volume:** 46.10%.

## Measurements

| | Cars | Wagons |
|---|---|---|
| Wheelbase | 106.0" | 106.0" |
| Length | 186.2" | 186.8" |

**Corporate siblings:** Dodge Dart.
**Primary competition:** Rambler American, Chevrolet Chevy II, Ford Falcon and Studebaker Lark.
**Notable changes:** Completely redesigned.
**Major standard equipment:** Fabric and vinyl bench seat, rubber floor mat, chrome exterior front and rear window trim, Torsion-Aire suspension and 6.50 × 13 BSW tires. V200 adds: Side window chrome trim and color-keyed floor mats. Signet adds: All-vinyl bucket seats, color-keyed carpeting, and special instrumentation.

| | Cars | Wagons |
|---|---|---|
| Width | 68.8" | 68.8" |
| Height | 53.4" | 53.1" |
| Legroom — front | 40.9" | 40.9" |
| Legroom — rear | 34.4" | 34.4" |
| Headroom — front | 38.1" | 38.4" |
| Headroom — rear | 37.2" | 37.9" |
| Cargo capacity (cu. ft.) | 23.6 | NA |
| Fuel capacity (gals.) | 18.0 | 18.0 |

## Models Available

| | Style Number | Base MSRP | Change from LY | Shipping Wt. (lbs.) | Production | Change from LY |
|---|---|---|---|---|---|---|
| Valiant V100 2-Door Sedan | 111 | $1,910 | -1.04% | 2515 | 32,761 | +66.48% |
| Valiant V100 4-Door Sedan | 113 | $1,973 | -0.90% | 2535 | 54,617 | +61.74% |
| Valiant V100 4-Door Wagon | 156 | $2,268 | -0.74% | 2700 | 11,864 | +100.00% |
| Valiant V200 2-Door Sedan | 131 | $2,035 | +0.44% | 2515 | 10,605 | +25.00% |
| Valiant V200 2-Door Convertible | 135 | $2,340 | NEW | 2640 | 7,122 | NEW |
| Valiant V200 4-Door Sedan | 133 | $2,097 | +0.48% | 2555 | 57,029 | +2.22% |
| Valiant V200 4-Door Wagon | 176 | $2,392 | +0.46% | 2715 | 11,147 | +38.39% |
| Valiant Signet 200 2-Door HT | 142 | $2,230 | 0.00% | 2570 | 30,857 | +20.60% |
| Valiant Signet 200 2-Door Conv. | 145 | $2,454 | NEW | 2675 | 9,164 | NEW |
| TOTALS | Avg. price | $2,189 | +2.63% | | Production 225,166 | +43.15% |

# Savoy

*"A Gold Mine of Standard Equipment— offered on every Plymouth 63."*

**Nameplate year of origin:** 1951 (Concord 2-Door Suburban designation); 1954 (as series).
**Current bodystyle lifespan:** 1962 through 1965.
**Predecessor to this model:** Savoy (1960 to 1961).
**Replacement for this model:** Fury I (1965 to 1966).
**Percentage of division's sales volume:** 19.21%.
**Corporate siblings:** Dodge 330.
**Primary competition:** AMC Ambassador, Chevrolet Biscayne/BelAir, and Ford Galaxie.
**Notable changes:** All-new exterior styling.
**Major standard equipment:** Cloth and vinyl front bench seat, color-keyed rubber floor mats, front armrests, dual sunvisors, electric windshield wipers, exterior bright trim around front window, and 6.50 × 14 BSW tires (7.00 × 14 BSW on Wagons).

## Measurements

| | Cars | Wagons |
|---|---|---|
| Wheelbase | 116.0" | 116.0" |
| Length | 205.0" | 210.1" |
| Width | 75.6" | 75.1" |
| Height | 54.1" | 53.9" |
| Legroom — front | 41.9" | 41.9" |
| Legroom — rear | 36.4" | 36.4" |
| Headroom — front | 38.1" | 38.4" |
| Headroom — rear | 37.5" | 38.5" |
| Cargo capacity (cu. ft.) | NA | NA |
| Fuel capacity (gals.) | 20.0 | 21.5 |

## Models Available

| | Style Number | Base MSRP | Change from LY | Shipping Wt. (lbs.) | Production | Change from LY |
|---|---|---|---|---|---|---|
| Fleet Special 2-Door Sedan | 201 | $2,137 | 0.00% | 2975 | * | * |
| Fleet Special 4-Door Sedan | 203 | $2,193 | 0.00% | 3015 | * | * |
| Savoy 2-Door Sedan | 211 | $2,206 | 0.00% | 2980 | 20,281 | +7.73% |
| Savoy 4-Door Sedan | 213 | $2,262 | 0.00% | 3020 | 56,313 | +13.13% |
| Savoy 4-Door, 2-Seat Wagon | 256 | $2,609 | 0.00% | 3325 | 12,874 | +1.29% |

| | Style Number | Base MSRP | Change from LY | Shipping Wt. (lbs.) | Production | Change from LY |
|---|---|---|---|---|---|---|
| Savoy 4-Door, 3-Seat Wagon | 257 | $2,710 | NEW | 3375 | 4,342 | NEW |
| TOTALS | | Avg. price $2,353 | +3.16% | | Production 93,810 | +15.37% |

*Production included with regular Savoy line.

# Belvedere

### "Put together with exacting care and quality."

**Nameplate year of origin:** 1951 (HT model); 1954 (as series).
**Current bodystyle lifespan:** 1962 through 1965.
**Predecessor to this model:** Belvedere (1960 to 1961).
**Replacement for this model:** Belvedere (1966 to 1967, as new mid-size car) and Fury II (1965 to 1966, as conceptual replacement).
**Percentage of division's sales volume:** 17.33%.
**Corporate siblings:** Dodge 440.
**Primary competition:** AMC Ambassador, Chevrolet Biscayne/BelAir, and Ford Galaxie.
**Notable changes:** All-new exterior styling.
**Major standard equipment:** Cloth and vinyl front bench seat, full carpeting, front armrests, dual sunvisors, electric windshield wipers, Exterior bright trim around windows, and front fender line, and 6.50 × 14 BSW tires (7.00 × 14 BSW on Wagons).

## Measurements

| | Cars | Wagons |
|---|---|---|
| Wheelbase | 116.0" | 116.0" |
| Length | 202.0" | 210.0" |
| Width | 75.6" | 75.6" |
| Height | 53.7" | 53.9" |
| Legroom — front | 46.0" | 46.0" |
| Legroom — rear | 40.9" | 39.2" |
| Headroom — front | 38.0" | 38.0" |
| Headroom — rear | 37.8" | 38.6" |
| Cargo capacity (cu. ft.) | NA | NA |
| Fuel capacity (gals.) | 20.0 | 21.5 |

## Models Available

| | Style Number | Base MSRP | Change from LY | Shipping Wt. (lbs.) | Production | Change from LY |
|---|---|---|---|---|---|---|
| Belvedere 2-Door Sedan | 221 | $2,342 | 0.00% | 3000 | 6,218 | 98.79% |
| Belvedere 2-Door Hardtop | 222 | $2,431 | 0.00% | 3025 | 9,204 | 80.97% |
| Belvedere 4-Door Sedan | 223 | $2,399 | 0.00% | 3020 | 54,929 | 75.70% |
| Belvedere 4-Dr., 2-Seat Wagon | 366 | $2,815 | +3.95% | 3490 | 10,297 | 5.28% |
| Belvedere 4-Dr., 3-Seat Wagon | 367 | $2,917 | 0.00% | 3585 | 4,012 | -3.74% |
| TOTALS | | Avg. price $2,581 | +0.86% | | Production 84,660 | +58.46% |

# Fury

### "A shape for road or wind or eye — Plymouth 63 is meant to thrill you on sight."

**Nameplate year of origin:** 1956.
**Current bodystyle lifespan:** 1962 through 1965.
**Predecessor to this model:** Fury (1960 to 1961).
**Replacement for this model:** Fury III and Sport Fury (1965 to 1966).
**Percentage of division's sales volume:** 17.36%.
**Corporate siblings:** Dodge Polara.
**Primary competition:** AMC Ambassador, Chevrolet BelAir/Impala, and Ford Galaxie.
**Notable changes:** All-new exterior styling.
**Major standard equipment:** Cloth and vinyl front bench seat, deep-pile car-

## Measurements

| | Cars | Wagons |
|---|---|---|
| Wheelbase | 116.0" | 116.0" |
| Length | 202.0" | 210.0" |
| Width | 75.6" | 75.6" |
| Height | 53.7" | 53.9" |
| Legroom — front | 46.0" | 46.0" |
| Legroom — rear | 40.9" | 39.2" |
| Headroom — front | 38.0" | 38.0" |

1963

peting, tower-back front seat, front armrests, dual sunvisors, electric windshield wipers, electric clock, Exterior bright trim around windows and wheel openings, backup lights, and 6.50 × 14 BSW tires (7.00 × 14 BSW on Wagons).

|  | Cars | Wagons |
|---|---|---|
| Headroom — rear | 37.8" | 38.6" |
| Cargo capacity (cu. ft.) | NA | NA |
| Fuel capacity (gals.) | 20.0 | 21.5 |

## Models Available

|  | Style Number | Base MSRP | Change from LY | Shipping Wt. (lbs.) | Production | Change from LY |
|---|---|---|---|---|---|---|
| Fury 2-Door Hardtop | 232 | $2,585 | 0.00% | 3030 | 13,832 | +44.25% |
| Fury 2-Door Convertible | 335 | $2,924 | 0.00% | 3340 | 5,221 | +20.05% |
| Fury 4-Door Sedan | 233 | $2,563 | 0.00% | 3075 | 31,891 | +85.08% |
| Fury 4-Door Hardtop | 334 | $2,742 | 0.00% | 3295 | 11,877 | +98.12% |
| Fury 4-Door, 2-Seat Wagon | 376 | $2,968 | 0.00% | 3545 | 3,304 | +40.48% |
| Fury 4-Door, 3-Seat Wagon | 377 | $3,071 | 0.00% | 3590 | 3,368 | +39.69% |
| Sport Fury 2-Door Hardtop | 342 | $2,851 | 0.00% | 3235 | 11,483 | +184.30% |
| Sport Fury 2-Door Convertible | 345 | $3,082 | 0.00% | 3385 | 3,836 | +153.03% |
| TOTALS | | *Avg. price* $2,848 | 0.00% | | *Production* 84,812 | +78.62% |

# PONTIAC

*"Come see our '63 Pontiacs."*

The 1963 model year brought all-new, trend setting style to the full-size Pontiacs, and heavily restyling to the compact Tempest models. Once again, the full-size Pontiac received a facelift, but this time the stylist broke with tradition and executed what proved a highly popular styling feature: vertically stacked headlamps. Buick and Chrysler had tried angled or "slanted" headlamps in recent years, and Nash had used vertical headlamps without much success, but Pontiac would make the first popular use of vertical lamps. That feature coupled with the powerful split-grille theme made quite a statement. Plus, nearly all body panels were new for 1963, so the big Pontiacs had a totally new look, even though many parts under the skin were carried over. The styling came together best on the Grand Prix, which featured a new concave rear window treatment that was shared only with the Oldsmobile Starfire. The Grand Prix made use of chrome trim only to highlight body features, continuing a trend that started several years prior and greatly cleaned up automotive styling. No changes were made to the model lineup, although the Bonneville Custom Safari, which was previously considered its own series, officially became part of the Series 28 Bonneville line.

Tempest models were also given a major redesign this year. Still based on their original bodies, and still carrying their unique 4-cylinder engines and rear transmissions, the cars now looked more modern. The front end appearance was brought in line with the big Pontiacs (albeit with horizontally placed headlights), and the rear wheel openings were opened more fully this year. The Tempest was a physically bigger car this year, as were the other "senior compacts," though they remained smaller than the intermediates that would replace them. Probably the most important change this year was the all-new 326 CID V8 engine. Based on the larger 389, but with smaller pistons, the new 326 replaced the slow selling Aluminum V8 as an optional powerplant. The 326 V8, very conventional in design, sold over 10 times better than the previous V8. It was also a peek at what was to come for the Tempest. Here was V8 power in a compact car that was 100 pounds lighter and 10 inches shorter than the GTO to come that would get the 389 CID V8. No, the Tempest 326 was not a GTO, but it is easy to see in retrospect that some engineers at Pontiac already saw the possibilities. After all, if a 326 and a 389 were the same block, a 389 would fit under the hood of a Tempest. You can bet that combination was tested many times!

Catalina 4-Door Sedan

Catalina 4-Door, 9-passenger Wagon

Bonneville 2-Door Convertible and
Star Chief 4-Door Hardtop

Grand Prix 2-Door Hardtop

Tempest LeMans 2-Door Convertible

Tempest Safari 4-Door Wagon

**1963**

---

**Model year production:** 602,102, up 15.46% over 1962.
**Domestic market share:** 8.18% (3rd place).
**Base price range:** $2,188 to $3,623.
**Industry average base price:** $3,028.
**Pontiac average base price:** $2,939.
**Introduction date:** October 1962.
**Assembly plants:** Baltimore, MD (B); Southgate, CA (C); Doraville, GA (D); Linden, NJ (E); Framingham, MA (G); Kansas City, MO (K); Pontiac, MI (P); Arlington, TX (R);

Lordstown, OH (U); Fairfax, KS (X); Fremont, CA (Z).
**Data plate identification:** Eight to ten digit code read as follows: 1st digit identifies the series (the second digit of the body style number in the charts below); 2nd and 3rd digits 63 for 1963; 4th digit is assembly plant code; and 1001 and up for serial number. A separate plate contains body style number. *Example:* 363X1001 is a 1963 Pontiac Catalina, serial number 1001, built in Fairfax, KS.

---

## Powertrains

| Engine | Gross HP* | Transmission Availability | Tempest | Catalina & Star Chief | Grand Prix | Bonneville |
|---|---|---|---|---|---|---|
| 194.5 CID Indy 4, 1-bbl., 4-cyl. | 115 | 3-speed manual | S | – | – | – |
| | | 4-speed manual | $173 | – | – | – |
| | | TempesTorque 2-sp. Automatic | $189 | – | – | – |
| 194.5 CID Indy 4, 1-bbl., 4-cyl. | 120/140 | 3-speed manual | No cost | – | – | – |
| | | 4-speed manual | $173 | – | – | – |
| | | TempesTorque 2-sp. Automatic | $189 | – | – | – |
| 194.5 CID Indy 4, 4-bbl., 4-cyl. | 166 | 3-speed manual | $39 | – | – | – |
| | | 4-speed manual | $212 | – | – | – |
| | | TempesTorque 2-sp. Automatic | $228 | – | – | – |
| 326 CID, 2-bbl., V8 | 260 | 3-speed manual | $167 | – | – | – |
| | | TempesTorque 2-sp. Automatic | $356 | – | – | – |
| 389 CID Trophy, 2-bbl., V8 | 215 | 3-speed manual | – | S | – | – |
| | | 4-speed manual | – | $231 | – | – |
| | 267/283 SC | Hydra-matic Automatic | – | $231 | – | – |
| 389 CID Trophy E, 4-bbl., V8 | 235 | 3-speed manual | – | $35 | – | S |
| | | 4-speed manual | – | $266 | – | $231 |
| 389 CID Trophy, 4-bbl., V8 | 303 | 3-speed manual | – | $35 | S | S |
| | | 4-speed manual | – | $266 | $231 | $231 |
| | | Hydra-matic Automatic | – | $266 | $231 | $231 |
| 389 CID Tri-Power, 3 × 2-bbl., V8 | 313 | 3-speed manual | – | $126 | $116 | $116 |
| | | 4-speed manual | – | $357 | $347 | $347 |

| Engine | Gross HP* | Transmission Availability | Tempest | Catalina & Star Chief | Grand Prix | Bonneville |
|---|---|---|---|---|---|---|
| | | Hydra-matic Automatic | - | $357 | $347 | $347 |
| 421 CID Trophy H.O., 4-bbl., V8 | 320 | 3-speed manual | - | $343 | $291 | $291 |
| | | 4-speed manual | - | $605 | $524 | $524 |
| | | Hydra-matic Automatic | - | $605 | $524 | $524 |
| 421 CID Tri-Power H.O., 3 × 2-bbl., V8 | 350 | 3-speed HD man. | - | $445 | $404 | $404 |
| | | 4-speed manual | - | $676 | $635 | $635 |
| | | Hydra-matic Automatic | - | $676 | $635 | $635 |

*Ratings vary with model and transmission attachment.*

## Major Options

| | Tempest | Catalina | Star Chief | Bonneville | Grand Prix |
|---|---|---|---|---|---|
| Air conditioning | $319 | $430 | $430 | $430 | $430 |
| Soft Ray tinted glass | $35 | $40 | $43 | $43 | $43 |
| Power steering — variable-ratio | $75 | $108 | $108 | $108 | $108 |
| Power brakes | - | $43 | $43 | $43 | $43 |
| Power driver's seat/Bench seat | - | $97 | $97 | $97 | $97 |
| Power windows | - | $106 | $106 | $106 | $106 |
| AM radio — manual | $62 | $89 | $89 | $89 | $89 |
| Front seat console | - | $161 | - | $161 | S |
| Front bucket seats | $134 | $116 | - | $116 | S |
| White stripe tires (base size — average) | $35 | $40 | $40 | $40 | $40 |
| Aluminum (8-lug) hubs and drums | - | $138 | $138 | $122 | $122 |

Options common to most models. (- = Not Available; S = Standard equipment.) Items may be standard equipment, optional at different pricing, or unavailable on certain models. This chart is only a guide.

## Paint Colors

| | Code |
|---|---|
| Starlight Black | A |
| Cameo Ivory | C |
| Silvermist Gray Metallic | D |
| Yorktown Blue Metallic | F |
| Kimberley Blue | H |
| Silverleaf Green Metallic | J |
| Cordovan Metallic | K |
| Marimba Red Metallic | L |
| Aquamarine Metallic | P |
| Marlin Aqua Metallic | Q |
| Yuma Beige | R |
| Saddle Bronze Metallic | S |
| Caravan Gold Metallic | T |
| Grenadier Red | V |
| Nocturne Blue Metallic | W |

# Tempest

*"You demand beauty? Expect luxury? You're hard to impress? This is your year!"*

**Nameplate year of origin:** 1961.
**Current bodystyle lifespan:** 1961 through 1963.
**Predecessor to this model:** None.
**Replacement for this model:** Tempest/LeMans (1964 to 1965).
**Percentage of division's sales volume:** 23.97%.
**Corporate siblings:** Oldsmobile F-85, and Buick Special.
**Primary competition:** Dodge Dart, Mercury Comet and Studebaker Lark.
**Notable changes:** Revised front and rear end styling.
**Major standard equipment:** Cloth and vinyl bench seat, dual sun visors, electric windshield wipers, and 6.00 × 15 BSW tires (6.50 × 15 BSW tires on wagons). LeMans adds: Bucket seats, power top on convertible, and specific LeMans trim.

## Measurements

| | Cars | Wagons |
|---|---|---|
| Wheelbase | 112.0" | 112.0" |
| Length | 194.3" | 194.3" |
| Width | 74.2" | 74.2" |
| Height | 54.0" | 55.3" |
| Legroom — front | 40.6" | 40.6" |
| Legroom — rear | 34.1" | 35.8" |
| Headroom — front | 38.1" | 38.6" |
| Headroom — rear | 37.2" | 37.8" |
| Cargo capacity (cu. ft.) | 14.1 | 72.2 |
| Fuel capacity (gals.) | 20.0 | 20.0 |

## Models Available

| | Style Number | Base MSRP | Change from LY | Shipping Wt. (lbs.) | Production | Change from LY |
|---|---|---|---|---|---|---|
| Tempest 2-Door Coupe | 2127 | $2,188 | 0.09% | 2810 | 26,464 | +71.03% |
| Tempest 2-Door Sports Coupe | 2117 | $2,294 | 0.00% | 2820 | 12,808 | -75.36% |
| Tempest 2-Door Convertible | 2167 | $2,564 | 0.00% | 2980 | 5,012 | -75.76% |
| Tempest 4-Door Sedan | 2119 | $2,241 | 0.04% | 2835 | 28,221 | -24.60% |
| Tempest 4-Door, 2-Seat Wagon | 2135 | $2,512 | 0.04% | 2995 | 10,135 | -42.66% |
| Tempest LeMans 2-Door Sp. Cpe. | 2217 | $2,418 | NEW | 2865 | 45,701 | NEW |
| Tempest LeMans 2-Door Conv. | 2267 | $2,742 | NEW | 3035 | 15,957 | NEW |
| TOTALS | Avg. price | $2,423 | +2.71% | Production | 144,298 | +0.74% |

**1963**

# Catalina

*"We don't budge an inch on the craftsmanship and quality of these lowest priced Pontiacs."*

**Nameplate year of origin:** 1950 on hardtop models, 1959 as series.
**Current bodystyle lifespan:** 1961 through 1964.
**Predecessor to this model:** Catalina (1959 to 1960).
**Replacement for this model:** Catalina (1965 to 1966).
**Corporate siblings:** Chevrolet Biscayne/BelAir/Impala, Oldsmobile 88, Buick LeSabre/Wildcat.
**Primary competition:** Mercury Monterey, and Dodge Polara.
**Percentage of division's sales volume:** 38.96%.
**Notable changes:** Completely restyled.
**Major standard equipment:** Cloth and vinyl (all-vinyl in convertible) bench seat, nylon-blend carpet, cushioned instrument panel, automatic interior lighting, heater and defroster, electric windshield wipers, chrome exterior trim and 8.00 × 14 BSW tires (8.50 × 14 BSW tires on Safari wagons).

## Measurements

| | Cars | Wagon |
|---|---|---|
| Wheelbase | 120.0" | 119.0" |
| Length | 211.9" | 212.8" |
| Width | 78.7" | 78.7" |
| Height | 55.2" | 56.5" |
| Legroom — front | 40.9" | 41.0" |
| Legroom — rear | 38.0" | 37.3" |
| Headroom — front | 38.6" | 38.6" |
| Headroom — rear | 37.6" | 39.2" |
| Cargo capacity (cu. ft.) | NA | 92.1 |
| Fuel capacity (gals.) | 25.0 | 19.0 |

## Models Available

| | Style Number | Base MSRP | Change from LY | Shipping Wt. (lbs.) | Production | Change from LY |
|---|---|---|---|---|---|---|
| Catalina 2-Door Sport Sedan | 2311 | $2,725 | 0.00% | 3685 | 14,091 | -1.21% |
| Catalina 2-Door Sport Hardtop | 2347 | $2,859 | -0.03% | 3725 | 60,795 | +32.09% |
| Catalina 2-Door Convertible | 2367 | $3,171 | -0.03% | 3835 | 18,249 | +8.13% |
| Catalina 4-Door Sedan | 2369 | $2,795 | -0.04% | 3755 | 79,961 | +17.38% |
| Catalina 4-Door Vista Hardtop | 2339 | $2,935 | -0.03% | 3815 | 31,256 | +6.85% |
| Catalina Safari 4-Dr., 2-S. Wagon | 2335 | $3,193 | 0.00% | 4175 | 18,446 | -4.91% |
| Catalina Safari 4-Dr., 3-S. Wagon | 2345 | $3,300 | -0.03% | 4230 | 11,751 | +9.66% |
| TOTALS | Avg. price | $2,997 | -0.01% | Production | 234,549 | +14.61% |

# Star Chief

*"For some very special people, we blend spaciousness, luxury, and simply stated styling."*

**Nameplate year of origin:** 1954.
**Current bodystyle lifespan:** 1961 through 1964.
**Predecessor to this model:** Star Chief (1959 to 1960).
**Replacement for this model:** Executive (1965 to 1966).
**Corporate siblings:** Chevrolet Biscayne/BelAir/Impala, Oldsmobile 88, Buick LeSabre/Wildcat.
**Primary competition:** Mercury Montclair, and Dodge Custom 880.
**Percentage of division's sales volume:** 6.77%.
**Notable changes:** Completely restyled.
**Major standard equipment:** Cloth and vinyl or all-vinyl bench seat, nylon-blend carpet, custom steering wheel, cushioned instrument panel, automatic interior lighting, 2-speed electric windshield wipers, luggage compartment trim, chrome exterior trim, wheel covers, and 8.00 × 14 BSW tires.

## Measurements

| | |
|---|---|
| Wheelbase | 123.0" |
| Length | 218.9" |
| Width | 78.7" |
| Height | 55.2" |
| Legroom — front | 40.9" |
| Legroom — rear | 38.0" |
| Headroom — front | 38.6" |
| Headroom — rear | 37.6" |
| Cargo capacity (cu. ft.) | NA |
| Fuel capacity (gals.) | 25.0 |

## Models Available

| | Style Number | Base MSRP | Change from LY | Shipping Wt. (lbs.) | Production | Change from LY |
|---|---|---|---|---|---|---|
| Star Chief 4-Door Sedan | 2669 | $3,096 | -0.03% | 3885 | 28,309 | 1.98% |
| Star Chief 4-Door Hardtop | 2639 | $3,229 | -0.03% | 3915 | 12,448 | -10.33% |
| TOTALS | | Avg. price $3,163 | -0.03% | Production | 40,757 | -2.13% |

# Grand Prix

*"This is a Pontiac? This is a Pontiac Grand Prix!"*

**Nameplate year of origin:** 1962.
**Current bodystyle lifespan:** 1962 through 1964.
**Predecessor to this model:** None.
**Replacement for this model:** Grand Prix (1965 to 1966).
**Corporate siblings:** Buick Wildcat and Oldsmobile Starfire.
**Primary competition:** Chrysler 300 and Mercury S-55.
**Percentage of division's sales volume:** 12.12%.
**Notable changes:** Completely restyled.
**Major standard equipment:** Front bucket seats with all-vinyl trim, center console with vacuum gauge, loop-pile carpeting, electric clock, lamp package, deluxe wheel covers, and 8.00 × 14 BSW tires.

## Measurements

| | |
|---|---|
| Wheelbase | 120.0" |
| Length | 211.9" |
| Width | 78.7" |
| Height | 54.1" |
| Legroom — front | 40.9" |
| Legroom — rear | 36.1" |
| Headroom — front | 37.9" |
| Headroom — rear | 37.6" |
| Cargo capacity (cu. ft.) | NA |
| Fuel capacity (gals.) | 25.0 |

## Models Available

| | Style Number | Base MSRP | Change from LY | Shipping Wt. (lbs.) | Production | Change from LY |
|---|---|---|---|---|---|---|
| Grand Prix 2-Door Hardtop | 2957 | $3,489 | -0.03% | 3915 | 72,959 | +141.63% |
| TOTALS | | Avg. price $3,489 | -0.03% | Production | 72,959 | +141.63% |

# Bonneville

*"For those who want the finest we build."*

**Nameplate year of origin:** 1957.
**Current bodystyle lifespan:** 1961 through 1964.
**Predecessor to this model:** Bonneville (1959 to 1960).
**Replacement for this model:** Bonneville (1965 to 1966).
**Corporate siblings:** Chevrolet Biscayne/BelAir/Impala, Oldsmobile 88, Buick LeSabre/Wildcat.
**Primary competition:** Mercury Monterey Custom, and Dodge Custom 880.
**Percentage of division's sales volume:** 18.19%.
**Notable changes:** Completely restyled.
**Major standard equipment:** Cloth and vinyl or all-vinyl bench seat (leather bucket seats on convertible), full carpeting including lower door panels, cushioned instrument panel, automatic interior lighting, electric windshield wipers, chrome exterior trim, deluxe wheel covers and 8.00 × 14 BSW tires (8.50 × 14 BSW tires on Safari wagon).

## Measurements

|                        | Cars    | Wagon   |
|------------------------|---------|---------|
| Wheelbase              | 123.0"  | 119.0"  |
| Length                 | 218.9"  | 212.8"  |
| Width                  | 78.7"   | 78.7"   |
| Height                 | 54.4"   | 56.5"   |
| Legroom — front        | 40.8"   | 41.0"   |
| Legroom — rear         | 37.1"   | 37.3"   |
| Headroom — front       | 38.1"   | 38.8"   |
| Headroom — rear        | 37.3"   | 39.2"   |
| Cargo capacity (cu. ft.) | NA    | 92.1    |
| Fuel capacity (gals.)  | 25.0    | 19.0    |

**1963**

## Models Available

|                                  | Style Number | Base MSRP | Change from LY | Shipping Wt. (lbs.) | Production | Change from LY |
|----------------------------------|--------------|-----------|----------------|---------------------|------------|----------------|
| Bonneville 2-Door Hardtop        | 2847         | $3,348    | -0.03%         | 3895                | 30,995     | -2.00%         |
| Bonneville 2-Door Convertible    | 2867         | $3,568    | -0.06%         | 3970                | 23,459     | +8.70%         |
| Bonneville 4-Door Vista Hardtop  | 2839         | $3,423    | -0.06%         | 3985                | 49,929     | +13.44%        |
| Bonneville Safari 4-Dr., 2-S. Wgn. | 2835       | $3,623    | -0.03%         | 4245                | 5,156      | +13.89%        |
| TOTALS                           | *Avg. price* | $3,491    | -0.03%         | *Production*        | 109,539    | +7.65%         |

# RAMBLER

*"All New ... All Beautiful ... All Rambler!"*

Nineteen-sixty-three brought about big changes for the larger Rambler models. The first total redesign of the Classic and Ambassador since the mid-fifties, these new cars were lower, longer, and much more modern in appearance than any models prior to these. They also incorporated many new styling and design features. Well-known for its use of unitized body construction, AMC now used this as an advantageous marketing tool. Advertising would show a bare unitized body and point out the various benefits, as compared to the standard body-on-frame construction, such as fewer rattles, structural integrity and weight savings. As one of the first cars in the industry to make wide-spread use of curved side glass windows, the new Ramblers could boast of greater hip and shoulder room allowed by designing the car to be wider through the middle section. The physical appearance of the '63 models was more angular, and very smooth and clean-lined. Both models also sported new, longer wheelbases, for better overall ride, as well as styling. The front-end design featured a full-width grille, slightly V-shaped from top to bottom, with inset dual headlights at each end. Rear styling mimicked the front with a V shape from top to bottom, and had small taillights placed at the outer edges of the car. Interior styling was almost as dramatic a leap forward as the exterior styling. In fact, the cars were good enough to be named the *Motor Trend* magazine Car of the Year.

As good as these cars looked (especially as compared to previous models), they were unfortunately on the trailing edge as far as industry styling trends (with the exception of the curved side glass). If AMC could have afforded the resources to have this design ready for 1961 or 1962 models, they probably would have been even more successful. Still, these models were a sales success. Generally, AMC would run a given body style for a minimum of five to six years (instead of the then traditional three years), to allow time to recoup tooling costs and make a profit. Since the basic body shell was used for longer than the industry norm, it would be face-lifted more frequently (which was a less costly proposition), thus giving the appearance of more frequent styling changes. This new body design ran for two years before AMC had to play catch-up with Pontiac (the early '60s industry styling leader), so the '65 Ramblers, while using the same body, underwent a major restyle.

By 1966, the larger Ramblers were good-looking cars, but they were being quickly outdated by their competition. So, in 1967 a more modern looking restyle would occur on the Rebel (Classic) and Ambassador, a body design that would last until these cars made their final appearance in 1977 (1974 for the Ambassador).

Finally, the mainstay American line made its final appearance in its present form, with a redesigned grille, and an important look into the future of its model lineup. A new 2-Door hardtop body style was added to the top trim level line, which now carried a new 440-H designation. As with the entire line, series designators were numeric, starting with the 220 at the bottom of the American line. Each step up added to the previous trim level, from 330 to 440, then the bottom line Classic started at 550, and so on to the Ambassador 990. This numeric series designation would be continued by AMC throughout the sixties.

Ambassador 990 4-Door, 3-Seat Wagon

Ambassador 990 4-Door Sedan

American 440 4-Door Wagon

American 440 2-Door Convertible

Classic, *Motor Trend* Car of the Year

Classic 770 4-Door Wagon

**Model year production:** 453,554, up 2.53% over 1962 (total is estimated).
**Domestic market share:** 6.16% (7th place).
**Base price range:** $1,832 to $3,018.
**Industry average base price:** $3,028.
**Industry average base price:** $2,318.
**Introduction date:** October 5, 1962.
**Assembly plants:** Kenosha, Wisconsin, and Brampton, Ontario, Canada (T designation added to serial number).

**Data plate identification (VIN):** Code read as follows: 63 for 1963 followed by serial number starting as follows: American, B515001 and up; Classic Six, G100001 and up; Classic V8, Z100001 and up; and Ambassador V8, H210001 and up. Export cars added a "K" after the letter, and cars built in Canada (Americans and Classic Six only) added a "T" after the letter. *Example:* 63G100001 is a 1963 Rambler Classic Six built in Kenosha, WI, serial number 100001.

## Powertrains

| Engine | Gross HP | Transmission Availability | American | Classic | Ambassador |
|---|---|---|---|---|---|
| 195.6 CID, 1-bbl., 6-cyl. L-Head, (OHV —$60 extra) | 90 | 3-speed manual, col. | S (ex. 440) | - | - |
|  |  | 3-speed w/Overdrive | $102 | - | - |
|  |  | Flash-O-Matic Automatic | $165 | - | - |

| Engine | Gross HP | Transmission Availability | American | Classic | Ambassador |
|---|---|---|---|---|---|
| 195.6 CID, 1-bbl., 6-cyl. | 125 | 3-speed manual, col. | $38/S (440) | S | - |
| | 127 Classic | 3-speed w/Overdrive | $147 | $109 | - |
| | | Flash-O-Matic Automatic | $225 | - | - |
| 195.6 CID, 2-bbl., 6-cyl. | 138 | 3-speed manual, col. | S (440H) | $12 | - |
| | | 3-speed w/Overdrive | $* | $109 | - |
| | | Flash-O-Matic Automatic | $* | $187 | - |
| 287 CID, 2-bbl., V8 | 198 | 3-speed manual | - | $122 (550) | - |
| | | 3-speed w/Overdrive | - | $* | - |
| | | Flash-O-Matic Automatic | - | $293 (550) | - |
| 327 CID, 2-bbl., V8** | 250 | 3-speed manual | - | - | S |
| | | 3-speed w/Overdrive | - | - | $* |
| | | Flash-O-Matic Automatic | - | - | $* |

*Accurate pricing information not currently available.   **327 CID, 4-bbl. "Power Pak," V8, w/270-hp introduced mid-year as a $24 option.

**1963**

## Major Options

| | American | Classic | Ambassador |
|---|---|---|---|
| Weather-Eye heater | $74 | $78 | $78 |
| Air conditioning | $360 | $380 | $399 |
| Tinted glass | $27 | $40–46 | $40–46 |
| Power steering | $72 | $81 | $81 |
| Power brakes | $40 | $43 | $44 |
| Outside rearview mirror (left) | $4 | $6 | $6 |
| Power windows | - | $102 | $102 |
| AM radio | $59 | $65 | $65 |
| Electric clock | $15 | $16 | $16 |
| Bucket seats | $100 | $100 | $100 |
| Light group | $20 | $20 | $20 |
| Wheel covers | $15 | $15 | $15 |
| Two-tone paint | $16–38 | $20–22 | $20–22 |

Options common to most models. (- = Not Available.) Items may be standard equipment, optional at different pricing, or unavailable on certain models. This chart is only a guide.

## Paint Colors

| | Code |
|---|---|
| Classic Black | P1 |
| Briarcliff Red | P30 |
| Majestic Blue Metallic | P40 |
| Corsican Gold Metallic | P41 |
| Sceptre Silver Metallic | P43 |
| Bahama Blue | P44 |
| Cape Cod Blue Metallic | P45 |
| Palisade Green | P46 |
| Aegean Aqua Metallic | P47 |
| Calais Coral Metallic | P48 |
| Valencia Ivory | P49 |
| Concord Maroon Metallic | P50 |
| Frost White | P72 |

Two-tones: first number is body color, second number is roof/accent color.

# American

*"The 1963 Rambler American is family-size, with a flair for fun!"*

**Nameplate year of origin:** 1958.
**Current bodystyle lifespan:** 1961 through 1963.
**Predecessor to this model:** Rambler American (1958 to 1960).
**Corporate siblings:** None.
**Replacement for this model:** Rambler American (1964 to 1969).
**Percentage of division's sales volume:** 21.11%.
**Primary competition:** Chevrolet Chevy II, Dodge Dart, Ford Falcon, and Plymouth Valiant.
**Notable changes:** Trim and detail changes.
**Major standard equipment:** Front arm rests and ash trays, front foam cushion seat, dual sunvisors, black rubber floor mats, air cleaner, oil filter, black rubber cargo mat on wagons, and 6.00 × 15 BSW tires. 330 adds: Rear door (side) armrests, door-activated dome lights, chrome horn ring, color-keyed carpeting (wagons), and chrome luggage rack (wagons). 440 adds: OHV engine, dual-note horn, deluxe steering wheel, vinyl-pleated upholstery with deluxe trim level, padded instrument panel, glove box lock, and wheel covers.

## Measurements

| | |
|---|---|
| Wheelbase | 100.0" |
| Length | 173.1" |
| Width | 70.0" |
| Height | 56.2" |
| Legroom — front | 41.8" |
| Legroom — rear | 35.6" |
| Headroom — front | 37.8" |
| Headroom — rear | 35.5" |
| Luggage cap. (cu. ft.) | NA |
| Fuel capacity (gals.) | 20 |

## Models Available

| | Style Number | Base MSRP | Change from LY | Shipping Wt. (lbs.) | Production | Change from LY |
|---|---|---|---|---|---|---|
| R. Am. 220 2-Dr. Business Sdn. | 6302-0 | $1,832 | 0.00% | 2446 | 162 | -42.4% |
| Rmblr. American 220 2-Dr. Sdn. | 6306-0 | $1,846 | 0.00% | 2472 | 27,780 | -6.3% |
| Rmblr. American 220 4-Dr. Sdn. | 6305-0 | $1,895 | 0.00% | 2485 | 14,419 | -18.8% |
| Rmblr. American 220 2-Dr. Wgn | 6304-0 | $2,081 | 0.00% | 2528 | 3,312 | -25.3% |
| Rmblr. American 220 4-Dr. Wgn | 6308-0 | $2,130 | 0.00% | 2549 | 4,436 | -29.6% |
| Rmblr. American 330 2-Dr. Sdn. | 6306-2 | $1.909 | 0.00% | 2484 | 7,000* | -44.9%* |
| Rmblr. American 330 4-Dr. Sdn. | 6305-2 | $1,958 | 0.00% | 2500 | 9,666 | -30.3% |
| Rmblr. American 330 2-Dr. Wgn | 6304-2 | $2,141 | 0.00% | 2539 | 3,204 | -27.1% |
| Rmblr. American 330 4-Dr. Wgn | 6308-2 | $2,190 | 0.00% | 2561 | 6,848 | -23.9% |
| Rmblr. American 440 2-Dr. Sdn. | 6306-5 | $2,040 | 0.00% | 2556 | 1,486 | -69.3% |
| Rmblr. American 440 2-Dr. HT | 6309-5 | $2,136 | NEW | 2550 | 5,101 | NEW |
| Rblr. American 440 2-Dr. Conv. | 6307-5 | $2,344 | 0.00% | 2743 | 4,750 | -64.8% |
| Rmblr. American 440 4-Dr. Sdn. | 6305-5 | $2,089 | 0.00% | 2575 | 2,937 | -49.1% |
| Rmblr. American 440 4-Dr. Wgn | 6308-5 | $2,320 | 0.00% | 2638 | 1,874 | -40.2% |
| Rblr. American 440-H 2-Dr. HT | 6309-7 | $2,281 | NEW | 2567 | 9,749 | NEW |
| TOTALS | Avg. price | $2,079 | +0.91% | Production | 102,724 | -19.2% |

*Total is estimated as accurate information is not available at this time.*

# Classic

*"The only car with the best of both: Big-car room and comfort ... small-car economy and handling ease ... plus All-New Beauty!"*

**Nameplate year of origin:** 1957 (Nash Rambler model).
**Current bodystyle lifespan:** 1963 through 1966 (restyled in 1965).
**Predecessor to this model:** Rambler Classic (1957 to 1962).
**Corporate siblings:** Ambassador.
**Replacement for this model:** Rebel (1967 to 1970).
**Percentage of division's sales volume:** 69.48%.
**Primary competition:** Ford Fairlane, Plymouth Savoy/Belvedere, Pontiac Tempest, and Studebaker Daytona.
**Notable changes:** Completely redesigned.
**Major standard equipment:** Front arm rests and ash trays, front foam cushion seat, dual sunvisors, air cleaner, oil filter, black rubber cargo mat (wagons), chrome luggage rack (wagons) and 6.50 × 14 BSW tires (7.00 × 14 BSW tires on wagons). 660 adds: Rear door armrests and ash trays, door-activated dome lights, and electric clock. 770 adds: Additional chrome exterior trim and deluxe interior trim level.

## Measurements*

| | |
|---|---|
| Wheelbase | 112.0" |
| Length | 188.8" |
| Width | 71.3" |
| Height | 55.3" |
| Legroom — front | 41.0" |
| Legroom — rear | 36.4" |
| Headroom — front | 39.3" |
| Headroom — rear | 37.5" |
| Luggage cap. (cu. ft.) | NA |
| Fuel capacity (gals.) | 19.0 |

*4-Door Sedan.*

## Models Available

| | Style Number | Base MSRP | Change from LY | Shipping Wt. (lbs.) | Production | Change from LY |
|---|---|---|---|---|---|---|
| Classic 550 2-Door Sedan | 6316-0 | $2,055 | +2.75% | 2720 | 15,410 | +4.04% |
| Classic 550 4-Door Sedan | 6315-0 | $2,105 | +2.68% | 2729 | 46,759 | +22.79% |
| Classic 550 4-Door Wagon | 6318-0 | $2,435 | +2.31% | 2893 | 28,579 | +1.33% |
| Classic 660 2-Door Sedan | 6316-2 | $2,195 | +2.09% | 2725 | 12,433 | -1.73% |
| Classic 660 4-Door Sedan | 6315-2 | $2,245 | +2.05% | 2740 | 82,713 | +20.40% |
| Classic 660 4-Dr, 6-pass. Wgn. | 6318-2 | $2,537 | +1.81% | 2890 | 53,519 | -0.28% |
| Classic 660 5-Dr, 8-pass. Wgn. | 6318-4 | $2,609 | -0.19% | 2885 | 6,902 | +9.17% |
| Classic 770 2-Door Sedan | 6316-5 | $2,299 | 0.00% | 2663 | 6,837 | +23.84% |
| Classic 770 4-Door Sedan | 6315-5 | $2,349 | 0.00% | 2686 | 43,050 | +38.06% |

| | Style Number | Base MSRP | Change from LY | Shipping Wt. (lbs.) | Production | Change from LY |
|---|---|---|---|---|---|---|
| Classic 770 4-Door Wagon | 6318-5 | $2,640 | 0.00% | 2828 | 23,718 | +11.45% |
| TOTALS | Avg. price | $2,347 | +1.30% | Production | 319,920 | +14.10% |

# Ambassador

*"With more style, more luxury, more performance,
Rambler Ambassador V-8 for 1963 is the new action-packed beauty!"*

**1963**

**Nameplate year of origin:** 1933 (From top-of-the-line Nash).
**Current bodystyle lifespan:** 1963 through 1966 (shared basic structure with Classic).
**Predecessor to this model:** Ambassador (1957 to 1962).
**Corporate siblings:** Classic.
**Replacement for this model:** None.
**Percentage of division's sales volume:** 8.21%.
**Primary competition:** Buick Special, Dodge 330/440, Oldsmobile F-85, and Studebaker Daytona.
**Notable changes:** Completely restyled.
**Major standard equipment:** Front arm rests and ashtrays, front foam cushion seat, black rubber cargo mat on wagons, and 7.50 × 14 BSW tires. 880 adds: Rear door armrests, door-activated dome lights, electric clock, color-keyed carpeting, underhood insulation, and chrome luggage rack (wagons). 990 adds: deluxe steering wheel, deluxe trim level, padded instrument panel, rear seat foam cushions, and full wheel covers.

## Measurements*

| | |
|---|---|
| Wheelbase | 112.0" |
| Length | 188.8" |
| Width | 71.3" |
| Height | 55.3" |
| Legroom — front | 41.0" |
| Legroom — rear | 36.4" |
| Headroom — front | 39.3" |
| Headroom — rear | 37.5" |
| Luggage cap. (cu. ft.) | NA |
| Fuel capacity (gals.) | 19.0 |

*4-Door Sedan.

## Models Available

| | Style Number | Base MSRP | Change from LY | Shipping Wt. (lbs.) | Production | Change from LY |
|---|---|---|---|---|---|---|
| Ambassador 800 2-Door Sedan | 6386-0 | $2,337 | +2.41% | 3110 | 41 | -8.89% |
| Ambassador 800 4-Door Sedan | 6385-0 | $2,391 | +2.35% | 3140 | 437 | +3.80% |
| Ambassador 800 4-Door Wagon | 6388-0 | $2,703 | +6.08% | 3270 | 113 | +46.75% |
| Ambassador 880 2-Door Sedan | 6386-2 | $2,465 | +2.28% | 3116 | 1,042 | +58.12% |
| Ambassador 880 4-Door Sedan | 6385-2 | $2,519 | +2.23% | 3145 | 7,667 | +3.64% |
| Ambassador 880 4-Door Wagon | 6388-2 | $2,815 | +1.99% | 3275 | 4,929 | +14.57% |
| Ambassador 990 2-Door Sedan | 6386-5 | $2,606 | +2.16% | 3132 | 1,764 | +284.31% |
| Ambassador 990 4-Door Sedan | 6385-5 | $2,660 | +2.11% | 3158 | 14,019 | -7.28% |
| Ambassador 990 4-Dr., 6-pass. Wgn. | 6388-5 | $2,956 | +1.90% | 3298 | 6,112 | -4.51% |
| Ambassador 990 5-Dr., 8-pass. Wgn. | 6388-6 | $3,018 | -0.17% | 3305 | 1,687 | +30.88% |
| TOTALS | Avg. price | $2,647 | +1.90% | Production | 37,811 | +4.50% |

# STUDEBAKER

*"From the advanced thinking of Studebaker Corporation ...
the exciting world of tomorrow from Studebaker today!"*

The Avanti finally arrived. After delay upon delay, the highly anticipated 4-seat sports car had arrived and Studebaker and its dealer network proudly rolled out the first totally new Studebaker in ten years. The hope was that all of the media attention would divert enough public attention to their cars and away from their finances, and that Studebaker would start increasing its car sales to become profitable. Alas, it was not to be.

The Avanti itself proved to be everything promised and more. Built from a modified Lark chassis, the Avanti wore an all fiberglass body designed by Raymond Loewy (hence the inspiration for the "Coke bottle" styling theme). The front end of the car was simple, with the grille hidden under a thin, blade-like bumper. Sharply creased fender edges led down the beltline and wrapped around the simply styled back end, and up the opposite side. Taillights were set between the thin rear bumper and upper belt crease that crossed the upper trunk edge. The thin lined roof led to a sweeping, fastback style rear window, and rear quarter side windows were distinguished by their rear upsweep. It was a fantastic alternative to more ordinary personal/sports/luxury cars on the market such as the Ford Thunderbird and Chrysler 300. The Avanti was as powerful and

roomy as these, but in a much more sporty package. It offered something a Corvette couldn't at any price — room for four, and luggage space to boot! The supercharged versions added even more sport to the equation, but were limited in availability. By the end of the model year, though, it was clear that the Avanti was not going to meet its sales goals, no matter how brilliant the execution may have been.

Other Studebaker models were given a flatter, non-wraparound windshield this year that greatly improved upon the looks of the cars. A few model changes were made, and the Lark name was de-emphasized on the cars, as each trim level was beginning to be marketed as its own line. A mid-year Standard line was introduced as a bare bones price leader for Studebaker. The Cruiser dropped its Lark prefix to become a stand alone model. Lark Deluxe and Regal names were replaced with Lark Regal and Custom — that meant the Regal dropped down a notch on the price scale. The previous Regal wagon became part of the Daytona line. For ease of comparison, the Lark line is listed as a model, and continues to include the Daytona and Cruiser as part of this line. With the shift of production to Canada in 1964, these actually are listed as separate models, and will be done so here as well.

Avanti 2-Door Coupe

Cruiser 4-Door Sedan

GT Hawk 2-Door Hardtop

Lark Daytona 2-Door Hardtop

Lark Daytona 4-Door Wagonaire

**Model year production:** 82,675, down 17.47% from 1962.
**Domestic market share:** 1.12% (12th place).
**Base price range:** $1,935 to $4,445.
**Industry average base price:** $3,028.
**Industry average base price:** $2,533.
**Introduction date:** October 1962.
**Assembly plants:** South Bend, IN (No coding) and Canada (C).

**Data plate identification (VIN):** Up to ten digit code read as follows: 63 for 1963; S for 6-cylinder or V for V8 engine; C (included only if built in Canada); followed by serial number 1001 and up. Body style numbers are found on a separate plate on the vehicle. *Example: 63S1001 is a 1963 Studebaker Lark Six built in South Bend, IN, serial number 1001.*

## Powertrains

| Engine | Gross HP | Transmission Availability | Lark | Cruiser & GT Hawk | Avanti |
|---|---|---|---|---|---|
| 169.6 CID, 1-bbl., OHV 6-cyl. Skybolt Six | 90 | 3-speed manual | S | - | - |
| | | 3-speed w/Overdrive | $110 | - | - |
| | | Flightomatic Automatic | $180 | - | - |
| 259.2 CID, 2-bbl., OHV V8 | 180 | 3-speed manual | $135 | - | - |
| | | 3-speed w/Overdrive | $245 | - | - |
| | | 4-speed manual | $223 | - | - |
| | | Flightomatic Automatic | $345 | - | - |
| 259.2 CID, 4-bbl., OHV V8 | 195 | 3-speed manual | $157 | - | - |
| | | 3-speed w/Overdrive | $267 | - | - |
| | | 4-speed manual | $345 | - | - |
| | | Flightomatic Automatic | $367 | - | - |
| 289 CID, 2-bbl., OHV V8 Thunderbolt | 210 | 3-speed manual | $208 | S | - |
| | | 3-speed w/Overdrive | $318 | $110 | - |
| | | 4-speed manual | $296 | $188 | - |
| | | Flightomatic Automatic | $418 | $210 | - |
| 289 CID, 4-bbl., OHV V8 Thunderbolt | 225 | 3-speed manual | $253 | $45 | - |
| | | 3-speed w/Overdrive | $363 | $155 | - |
| | | 4-speed manual | $341 | $233 | - |
| | | Flightomatic Automatic | $453 | $255 | - |
| 289 CID R1, 4-bbl., OHV V8 Jet-Thrust | 240 | 3-speed manual | $343 | $157 | S |
| | | 4-speed manual | $531 | $345 | $188 |
| | | Flightomatic Automatic | $553 | $367 | $210 |
| 289 CID R2 Supercharged, 4-bbl., OHV V8 Jet-Thrust | 289 | 3-speed manual | $553 | $367 | $210 |
| | | 4-speed manual | $741 | $555 | $398 |
| | | Flightomatic Automatic | $763 | $577 | $420 |

## Major Options

| | Lark | GT Hawk | Avanti |
|---|---|---|---|
| Heater and defroster | $80 | $80 | $80 |
| Air conditioning | $278–$325 | $325 | $325 |
| Tinted glass — full | $32 | $32 | $32 |
| Power steering (V8 only) | $77 | $77 | $77 |
| Power brakes | $45 | $45 | S |
| Electric clock | $15 | $15 | $15 |
| Windshield washers | $12 | $12 | $14 |
| AM pushbutton radio | $57 | $57 | $65 |
| White sidewall tires — standard size | $28–$48 | $28–$48 | $32–$49 |
| Wheel covers | $16 | $16 | S |

Options common to most models. (S = Standard equipment.) Items may be standard equipment, optional at different pricing, or unavailable on certain models. This chart is only a guide.

## Paint Colors

| | Code |
|---|---|
| Velvet Black | P6310 |
| Ermine White | P6311 |
| Blue Mist Metallic | P6312 |
| Green Mist Metallic | P6313 |
| Silver Mist Metallic | P6314 |
| Champagne Gold Metallic | P6315 |
| Regal Red | P6316 |
| Rose Mist Metallic | P6317 |
| Super Red Metallic | P6325 |
| Seaspray Green | P6326 |
| Seabeach Sand | P6327 |
| Avanti Black* | P6330 |
| Avanti White* | P6331 |
| Avanti Turquoise* | P6332 |
| Avanti Gold* | P6333 |

**1963**

| | Code |
|---|---|
| Avanti Red* | P6334 |
| Avanti Gray Metallic* | P6335 |

*Colors for Avanti only.*

# Lark

*"The budget-priced Lark and luxurious Cruiser."*

**Nameplate year of origin:** 1959.
**Current bodystyle lifespan:** 1962 through 1966.
**Predecessor to this model:** Lark (1959 to 1961).
**Replacement for this model:** None.
**Corporate siblings:** None.
**Percentage of division's sales volume:** 89.76%.
**Primary competition:** Rambler American, Chevrolet Chevy II, Dodge Dart, Ford Falcon, Mercury Comet, and Plymouth Valiant.
**Notable changes:** New grille and minor trim and detail changes.
**Major standard equipment:** Cloth and vinyl front bench seats, armrests, beauty vanity, rubber floor mats, and 6.00 × 15 BSW tires. Custom adds: Chrome trim around windows and body side trim. Daytona and Cruiser add: Full-carpeting, all-vinyl interiors and 6.50 × 15 BSW on convertible.

## Measurements

| | Cars | Cruiser | Wagons |
|---|---|---|---|
| Wheelbase | 109.0" | 113.0" | 113.0" |
| Length | 184.0" | 188.0" | 190.2" |
| Width | 71.3" | 71.3" | 71.3" |
| Height | 55.7" | 55.7" | 57.0" |
| Legroom — front | 39.3" | 39.3" | 39.3" |
| Legroom — rear | 27.5" | 27.5" | 26.1" |
| Headroom — front | 43.7" | 43.7" | 43.7" |
| Headroom — rear | 41.9" | 41.9" | 39.8" |
| Luggage cap. (cu. ft.) | NA | NA | 93.0 |
| Fuel capacity (gals.) | 18 | 18 | 18 |

## Models Available

| | Style Number | Base MSRP | Change from LY | Shipping Wt. (lbs.) | Production | Change from LY |
|---|---|---|---|---|---|---|
| Lark 2-Door Sedan | F2 | $1,935 | 0.00% | 2650 | 17,401 | -9.35% |
| Lark 4-Door Sedan | Y2 | $2,040 | 0.00% | 2775 | 40,113 | -19.71% |
| Lark 4-Door, 2-Seat Wagon | P2 | $2,430 | +1.04% | 3285 | 11,915 | +13.24% |
| Lark Regal 2-Door Sedan | F4 | $2,055 | -7.35% | 2665 | * | * |
| Lark Regal 4-Door Sedan | Y4 | $2,160 | -1.37% | 2790 | * | * |
| Lark Regal 4-Door, 2-Seat Wagon | P4 | $2,550 | -0.20% | 3200 | * | * |
| Lark Custom 2-Door Sedan | F6 | $2,180 | NEW | 2680 | * | NEW |
| Lark Custom 4-Door Sedan | Y6 | $2,285 | NEW | 2800 | * | NEW |
| Daytona 2-Door Hardtop | J8 | $2,308 | 0.00% | 2795 | 3,763 | -55.63% |
| Daytona 2-Door Convertible | L8 | $2,679 | 0.00% | 3045 | 1,015 | -62.14% |
| Daytona 4-Door, 2-Seat Wagon | P8 | $2,700 | NEW | 3245 | * | NEW |
| Cruiser 4-Door Sedan | Y8 | $2,595 | +4.09% | 3065 | * | * |
| TOTALS | | *Avg. price* $2,326 | -0.64% | | *Production* 74,207 | -18.31% |

*Production not available by series.*

# Gran Turismo Hawk

*"Classic styling ... timeless elegance ... enhanced for '63 in keeping with its traditional lasting beauty and bold new approach to luxury and power!"*

**Nameplate year of origin:** 1956.
**Current bodystyle lifespan:** 1953 through 1964.
**Predecessor to this model:** None.

## Measurements

| | |
|---|---|
| Wheelbase | 120.5" |
| Length | 204.0" |

**Replacement for this model:** None.
**Corporate siblings:** None.
**Percentage of division's sales volume:** 5.61%.
**Primary competition:** Mercury Monterey S-55, Oldsmobile Starfire and Pontiac Grand Prix.
**Notable changes:** Minor trim and detail changes.
**Major standard equipment:** All-vinyl front bucket seats, full deep-pile carpeting, padded instrument panel, rear seat center armrest, exterior bright trim including windows and rocker panel moldings and 6.70 × 15 BSW tires.

## Measurements (cont.)

| | |
|---|---|
| Width | 71.0" |
| Height | 54.6" |
| Legroom — front | 42.6" |
| Legroom — rear | 22.1" |
| Headroom — front | 41.5" |
| Headroom — rear | 41.3" |
| Luggage cap. (cu. ft.) | NA |
| Fuel capacity (gals.) | 18.0 |

## Models Available

| | Style Number | Base MSRP | Change from LY | Shipping Wt. (lbs.) | Production | Change from LY |
|---|---|---|---|---|---|---|
| Gran Turismo Hawk 2-Door HT | VK6 | $3,095 | 0.00% | 3280 | 4,634 | -50.36% |
| TOTALS | | *Avg. price* $3,095 | 0.00% | | *Production* 4,634 | -50.36% |

# Avanti

*"The Avanti is a car with a unique dual personality ...
that of an elegant prestige car and a car of high performance."*

**Nameplate year of origin:** 1963.
**Current bodystyle lifespan:** 1963 through 1964.
**Predecessor to this model:** None.
**Replacement for this model:** None.
**Corporate siblings:** None.
**Percentage of division's sales volume:** 4.64%.
**Primary competition:** Chevrolet Corvette.
**Notable changes:** All-new model for 1963.
**Major standard equipment:** All-vinyl front bucket seats, full deep-pile carpeting, padded instrument panel, rear seat center armrest, exterior bright trim including windows and rocker panel moldings and 6.70 × 15 BSW tires.

## Measurements

| | |
|---|---|
| Wheelbase | 109.0" |
| Length | 192.5" |
| Width | 70.4" |
| Height | 53.8" |
| Legroom — front | 42.1" |
| Legroom — rear | 26.0" |
| Headroom — front | 41.9" |
| Headroom — rear | 39.3" |
| Luggage cap. (cu. ft.) | NA |
| Fuel capacity (gals.) | 21.0 |

## Models Available

| | Style Number | Base MSRP | Change from LY | Shipping Wt. (lbs.) | Production | Change from LY |
|---|---|---|---|---|---|---|
| Avanti 2-Door Hardtop | R-Q | $4,445 | NEW | 3140 | 3,834 | NEW |
| TOTALS | | *Avg. price* $4,445 | NEW | | *Production* 3,834 | NEW |

# 1964

In the automotive world, some years are more memorable than others, generally because of the introduction or discontinuation of certain significant cars. Unquestionably 1964 was a landmark year in this respect. Not only were the Ford Mustang and Pontiac GTO introduced during the year, but also the Plymouth Barracuda, the Olds 4-4-2, and the Chevrolet Chevelle and Malibu. These new models would be among the best selling in the soon-to-be-hot muscle car market. However, ten years later only the Mustang, Malibu and 4-4-2 names would survive: the Mustang as an economy/sporty car (more true to its original purpose than the car it had become in the late sixties and early seventies), the Malibu as the run-of-the-mill mid-size Chevrolet (not much sportiness left), and the 4-4-2 still offering the same formula minus the horsepower. It is true that 1965 would be more memorable for its fantastic sales numbers and the many restyled cars introduced, but the groundwork was laid in 1964 at the introduction of these new models. During the next year or two, each of these cars would be at the top of its respective portion of the market. There were other new cars on the market, such as the lower-priced personal-luxury Oldsmobile Jetstar I and the totally redesigned Rambler American. But the muscle cars will always be what 1964 is remembered for.

American Motors' newly designed American for 1964 was a sorely needed replacement for its cute but aging predecessor. The new American took its best shot at upstaging the compact cars from the Big Three and did a very good job indeed. By adopting styling that updated the successful 1963 Classic and Ambassador look, the new American looked far more modern than any of its competition. In fact, it would be 1966 before Ford or GM came up with more appealing compacts. In the Classic and Ambassador lines, there were detail changes outside, but the big news was under the hood, where an all-new Typhoon 6 was offered. This new engine would prove to be so strong and dependable that it would still be offered as standard equip-

ment on some Jeep models more than 35 years later, as the 4.0L Six.

At Chrysler, 1964 was a chance to regroup and rethink its products after seven years of ups and downs — mostly downs. Chrysler had been riding high in 1956 and 1957 with its entirely new line of "Forward Thinking" cars. Any 1957 Mopar product could be considered the best looking car in its class, and of course Chrysler engineering was highly regarded in most circles, so they were destined to be a hit. The cars did sell well, until the public discovered their many quality problems. Unfortunately, this was not the first time quality had been an issue with Chrysler, but it was the most well-known. Among the most notable concerns were fit and finish issues, premature rust-through (as quickly as 12 months in some extreme cases) and torsion bars that would break without warning. Chrysler quickly addressed most of these issues, but public confidence in its products had fallen badly. These issues, coupled with the recession of 1958, put a brake on Chrysler's rising sales. Then some highly unorthodox styling ventures on certain 1960 and 1961 models led to even lower sales. With a change to Uni-Body construction on most models, the quality issues were generally gone. When most of the 1962 line was redesigned, Chrysler had unwisely gambled that the buying public would want smaller full-size cars, much as they had gone for slightly smaller Ford and GM versions in 1961. Chrysler made the mistake of doing too much downsizing, too late. The new Dodge and Plymouth models looked pleasing (even better for 1963), but were not what the public wanted. Dodge was able to make a quick fix, by mating a Dodge front end to a Chrysler body for the new 880 model, effectively taking DeSoto's place in the market. But volume and price leader Plymouth was left out to dry.

After the compact car lines were revised for 1963, the new 1964 model year would be a year for employing some marketing strategy as Chrysler laid the groundwork for sev-

## 1964 Model Year Production by Make

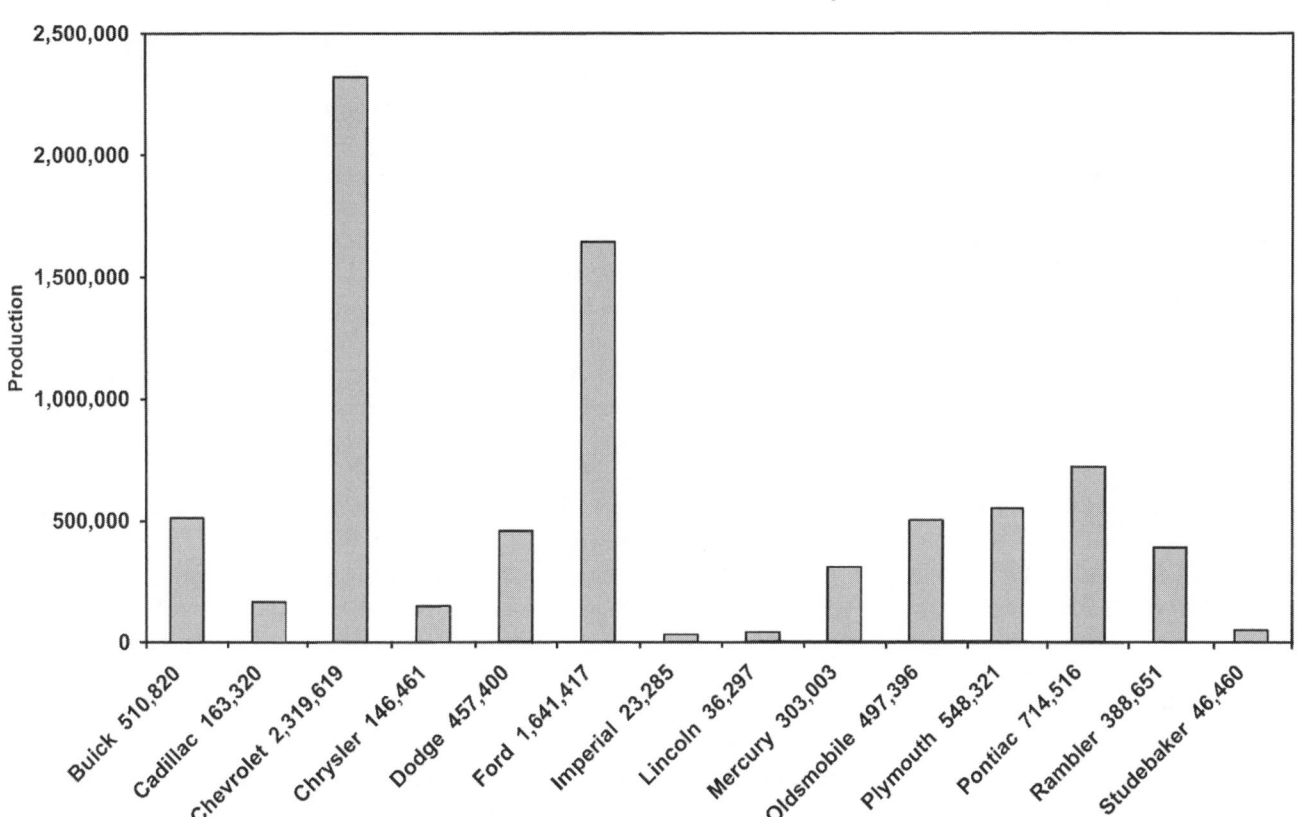

1964

eral redesigned lines to be introduced in 1965. The only noteworthy introduction of the 1964 season was really not a new car at all. The Barracuda was a sporty fastback variation of the compact Valiant, much as the Mustang was based on the Falcon—but whereas Ford spent the money to do a whole new body for the Mustang, Plymouth was forced to make do with the Valiant body and graft on a glass fastback window. The concept was a good one, though, as the Barracuda was a success. As time went on, the Barracuda would gain its own identity, separate from the Valiant. In the Dodge truck line, only minor revisions were seen this season.

Ford entered the 1964 model year with facelifts for nearly all of its models. Important upgrades to engines and transmissions were also made this year. The 289 CID V8 engine made its debut midway through the season and quickly became the engine of choice not only in the Mustang, but also in mid-size cars and truck models throughout the Ford line. In fact, enough was new at Ford for *Motor Trend* magazine to give the entire Ford line the "Car of the Year" award. The compact Falcon and Comet lines were more angular and modern in appearance, while still utilizing many of their original components underneath the skin. The mid-size Fairlane was one of the few carry-over products, but it's probably just as well given all the new competition from General Motors this year. All full-size

models were given major redesigns. While not totally new, they were different enough to appear all new. This was the eighth straight year that Ford had redesigned its full-size offerings. Not even General Motors kept up with that pace. Under the hood, no significant changes took place. Lines on the new models were generally softer than the squarish 1963 lines. The luxurious Lincoln Continental was all-new this year, but looked very much like the car it replaced. It was decided that the clean looks of the 1961–63 models should be kept, but the car needed to be larger and updated on the interior, so those were the main changes. Similarly, the Thunderbird was given a styling update, with square lines replacing the curves and roundness of the 1961–63 models. The big news at Ford came in April 1964, when the all-new "pony car," the Mustang, was launched. Introduced at the World's Fair in New York, the Mustang was an instant hit. Taking the basic inner workings of the Falcon, Ford built a sporty and appealing four-passenger car that had the sex appeal of the original Thunderbird, the sensibility of the Falcon, and its own sporty flair added to the mix. Helping to promote the sporty car image was the selection of a Mustang convertible to pace the 1964 Indianapolis 500 race. Ford wisely chose to keep the base-level Mustang spartan and allow the customer to "build" his or her own car by adding options from an extensive list. So a customer could have a "plain Jane" economy car, a luxurious sportster, or an all-out performance car. The Mustang became the most successful new car introduction to date, selling 500,000 in its first full year of production. Although many call the original Mustang a 1965 model, Ford titled the very first cars as 1964 models (or 1964½ if you will). Therefore, the Mustang will be covered in this section, with more coverage in the 1965 section. In the Ford truck line, Ranchero lines followed changes made to the Falcon. The Club Wagon was a virtual carry-over, as were the F-series trucks. One noteworthy item on the F-series was that 1964 would be the last year for a solid front axle, as the 1965 models would get the Twin I-Beam suspension.

General Motors' big news was the introduction of an all-new intermediate line of cars. When introduced in 1961, the Buick Special, Oldsmobile F-85 and Pontiac Tempest line were considered senior compact cars, slightly larger and better equipped than the regular compacts, such as the Rambler American, Ford Falcon, Chevy Corvair or Plymouth Valiant. For the 1962 model year, Plymouth and Dodge fielded smaller full-size cars that sold fairly well, even if the market wasn't ready for downsizing yet. That same year Ford introduced its "family size" Fairlane, to counter the smaller Mopar offerings and to compete with GM's senior compacts by offering more interior space. Of course, GM was the market leader and had to have a car in response that would set the market on its ear. As had seemingly become tradition in Detroit during the late fifties and early sixties, whenever a car underwent a major restyling, it became a larger car. So it was with the senior compacts for the 1964 model year. Gaining three to four inches in wheelbase and upwards of a foot in length, the new cars were no longer compact, and thus the intermediate, or mid-size car, was born. Obviously, cars of this size had existed for many years, but the key to their success was in the marketing. Styling, pricing, and content were all geared toward a slightly younger crowd than those who bought traditional family cars. And, just to make sure all the bases were covered, GM offered its new intermediates in nearly every body style available on the full-size cars. Sticking to GM tradition, the lower-priced Chevrolet Chevelle was slightly smaller, while at the top end the Buick Special was a little bigger, with a more powerful standard engine and a higher price tag. The real marketing success came from the Pontiac Division. John Z. DeLorean and his team at

Pontiac managed to go against corporate policy and fit an engine larger than the 330 cubic inches that GM allowed in the smaller cars at that time. The limit was set due to internal politics and the corporate ban on racing sponsorship begun in 1963. To do this, Pontiac stuffed its 389 CID V8 into the Tempest by way of an option package called the GTO. Putting the engine in as an option package dodged the red tape associated with getting a new model approved. By the time the car hit the streets, it was a success, and GM leaders soon realized that they would be foolish to stop it now. Soon, other GM divisions followed with their own versions, and the muscle car was born.

Other models at GM were given their traditional annual updates. The Corvette, which was all new for 1963, was given some powertrain upgrades. Full-size GM cars would be all-new for 1965, so they were in a holding pattern. The compact Chevrolet Corvair and Chevy II were little changed as well. In the Chevrolet and GMC truck lines, there was some freshening of the trim and grilles, but the biggest news was the return of the Chevrolet El Camino. This time around, though, it was based on the new intermediate Chevelle platform. This allowed for slightly larger dimensions in all areas as compared to the Ford Ranchero. An instant success, the El Camino would go on to surpass sales of the Ranchero. Most pertinent powertrain and option information for the El Camino is similar to that for the Chevelle, but the El Camino is not further detailed herein, as it was marketed as a truck.

The end of the line was near for Studebaker, as production was halted at the South Bend, Indiana, plant and all car production moved to Canada during the year. The model lineup was similar to previous years, but there was not much interest in cars based on an eleven-year-old design. The oldest competitive design in Studebaker's market was the Chevrolet Chevy II which was introduced in 1962. Everything else had been restyled or redesigned since then. The unique Avanti would be let go at the end of the model year, only to have its design rights bought and return as a product of a privately held company as the Avanti II. Independent light-duty truck makers International and Kaiser-Jeep made a few upgrades, but their products remained essentially as in prior years. On a final note, the Checker returned with minimal changes.

# BUICK

*"When better automobiles are built, Buick will build them."*

The popular Buick Special and Skylark were officially upgraded to mid-size status with their completely new design and size. As with all other GM senior compacts, 1964 brought a redesign that saw the cars get bigger in most areas, and with that upsizing, they officially left the compact market for greener pastures. Joined by a new Chevrolet Chevelle model, the new mid-size cars were much more traditional in design than their predecessors, with the single exception that the Buick line continued the use of the V6 engine. The unique V6 powerplant was enlarged to 225 cubic inches. With the greater size came more horsepower, now rated at 155. As for the new styling, the new Special and Skylark models could easily be mistaken for a LeSabre or Wildcat model. The full-size Buick design influence was very much evident. The Skylark 2-Door Hardtop could be outfitted with a unique vinyl top of a "halo" design, being placed only on the flat surface of the roof top, but encircling the rear window on the back. A mid-year addition was the Sport Wagon. This wagon shared its "Vista-dome" type roof and longer wheelbase with the Oldsmobile Vista-Cruiser. The Sport Wagon was not marketed as a Special or Skylark model per se, but it did use the front clip of a Skylark as well as similar trim inside and out. By 1965, it would serve as a replacement for the full-size Buick Estate Wagons, until 1970 when the Estate Wagon would return. Other model changes for the new size cars included the additions of a Special Deluxe Coupe, Skylark 4-Door Sedan, and Skylark Wagons.

Full-size Buicks wore a new face and rear design this year. LeSabre and Wildcat models used new horizontal style taillamps, while the Electra 225 went to vertical lamps. Also new was a 300 CID aluminum block V8 engine and a larger displacement 425 CID "Nailhead" V8 engine. Model changes to the big Buicks were limited to the dropping of the slow selling LeSabre 2-Door Sedan and the addition of an equally slow selling Wildcat 4-Door Sedan. The new-for-'63 Riviera saw only minor changes for the new season, except for a larger new standard engine, the new 340-horsepower, 425 CID V8.

Riviera 2-Door Hardtop

LeSabre 4-Door Sedan and
LeSabre 2-Door Convertible

Electra 225 4-Door Hardtop

Skylark 2-Door Hardtop

Special 4-Door Wagon

Special Deluxe 2-Door Coupe

Wildcat 2-Door Hardtop

**Model year production:** 510,820, up 11.49% from 1963.
**Domestic market share:** 6.55% (5th place).
**Base price range:** $2,343 to $4,385.
**Industry average base price:** $3,024.
**Buick average base price:** $3,224.
**Introduction date:** October 1963.
**Assembly plants:** Flint, MI (1); Southgate, CA (2); Linden, NJ (3); Fairfax, KS (4); Wilmington, DE (5); Atlanta, GA (6); Framingham, MA (7); and Arlington, TX (8).
**Data plate identification:** Nine digit code read as follows: 1st digit indicates series trim level and engine (see coding below); 2nd digit K for 1964; 3rd digit is assembly plant code; followed by sequential number 100001 and up for serial number. (Coding: A-V6 Special, B-V6 Special Deluxe, C-V6 Skylark, 0-V8 Special, 1-V8 Special Deluxe, 2-V8 Skylark, 4-LeSabre, 6-Wildcat, 7-Riviera, 8-Electra). *Example:* 4K4001001 is a 1964 Buick LeSabre, serial number 001001, built in Fairfax, KS. Check model number on body identification plate.

# Powertrains

| Engine | Gross HP | Transmission Availability | Special/ Skylark | LeSabre (ex. Wgn.) | Estate Wagons/ Wildcat/Electra | Riviera |
|---|---|---|---|---|---|---|
| 225 CID Fireball, 2-bbl., V6 | 155 | 3-speed manual | S | - | - | - |
| | | 4-speed manual | $199 | - | - | - |
| | | Super Turbine 300 Automatic | $198 | - | - | - |
| 300 CID Wildcat 310, 2-bbl., V8 | 210 | 3-speed manual | S[1]/$71[2] | S | - | - |
| | | 4-speed manual | $199[1]/$270[2] | - | - | - |
| | | Super Turbine 300 Automatic | $210[1]/$281[2] | $210 | - | - |
| | | Super Turbine 400 Automatic | - | $231 | - | - |
| 300 CID Wildcat 355, 4-bbl., V8 | 250 | 3-speed manual | $22[1]/$93[2] | $22 | - | - |
| | | 4-speed manual | $221[1]/$292[2] | - | - | - |
| | | Super Turbine 300 Automatic | $232[1]/$303[2] | $232 | - | - |
| | | Super Turbine 400 Automatic | - | $253 | - | - |
| 401 CID Wildcat 445, 4-bbl., V8 | 325 | 3-speed manual | - | - | S[3] | - |
| | | 4-speed manual | - | - | $231[3] | - |
| | | Super Turbine 400 Automatic | - | - | S (Electra)/$231[3] | - |
| 425 CID Wildcat 465, 4-bbl., V8 | 340 | 3-speed manual | - | - | $48[3] | - |
| | | 4-speed manual | - | - | $279[3] | - |
| | | Super Turbine 400 Automatic | - | - | $48 (Electra)/$279[3] | S |
| 425 CID Super Wildcat, 2 × 4-bbl., V8 | 360 | 3-speed manual | - | - | $188[3] | - |
| | | 4-speed manual | - | - | $419[3] | - |
| | | Super Turbine 400 Automatic | - | - | $188 (Electra)/$419[3] | $140 |

[1]*Sport Wagon only.* [2]*All but Sport Wagon.* [3]*Wildcat and LeSabre Estate Wagons only.*

## Major Options

| | Special/Skylark | LeSabre | Wildcat | Electra 225 | Riviera |
|---|---|---|---|---|---|
| Air conditioning | $351 | $430 | $430 | $430 | $430 |
| Soft Ray tinted glass | $41 | $43 | $43 | $43 | $43 |
| Deck lid remote release | - | $10 | $10 | $10 | $10 |
| Tilt steering wheel | $43 | $43 | $43 | $43 | $43 |
| Power steering | $97 | $97 | $108 | S | S |
| Power brakes | $43 | $43 | $43 | S | S |
| Power door locks | - | $71 | $71 | $71 | $71 |
| Power driver's seat/ bench seat, 4-way | $67 | $71 | $71 | $43–$71 | $71 |
| Power windows (except on 6-cylinder) | $102 | $108 | $108 | $108* | $108 |
| AM radio | $66 | $90 | $90 | $90 | $90 |
| AM/FM radio | - | $179 | $179 | $179 | $179 |

Options common to most models. (- = Not Available, S = Standard equipment.) Items may be standard equipment, optional at different pricing, or unavailable on certain models. This chart is only a guide.

*Standard on Convertible.*

## Paint Colors

| | Code |
|---|---|
| Regal Black | A |
| Arctic White | C |
| Silver Cloud Metallic | D |
| Marlin Blue Metallic | F |
| Wedgewood Blue | H |
| Surf Green Metallic | J |
| Sunburst Yellow | K |
| Claret Mist Metallic | L |
| Coral Mist Metallic | N |
| Teal Mist Metallic | P |
| Desert Beige | R |
| Bronze Mist Metallic | S |
| Tawny Mist Metallic | T |
| Granada Red | V |
| Diplomat Blue Metallic | W |

**1964**

# Special and Skylark

*"It's bigger, sleeker and smoother in '64, yet it's light on its feet as a kitten."*

**Nameplate year of origin:** 1935 (Special); 1953 (Skylark).
**Current bodystyle lifespan:** 1964 through 1967.
**Predecessor to this model:** Special/Skylark (1961 to 1963).
**Replacement for this model:** Special/Skylark (1968 to 1972).
**Percentage of division's sales volume:** 33.48%.
**Corporate siblings:** Chevrolet Chevelle, Olds F-85/Cutlass, and Pontiac Tempest/LeMans.
**Primary competition:** Dodge Dart, and Mercury Comet.
**Notable changes:** Completely restyled.
**Major standard equipment:** Brigade cloth and vinyl front bench seat, heater and defroster, electric windshield wipers, front armrests, and 6.50 × 14 BSW tires (7.50 × 14 BSW tires on wagons). Special Deluxe adds: Belgrave cloth and vinyl foam padded seat cushions, deluxe steering wheel, rear arm rests, full carpeting, padded instrument panel, and front-door operated dome lights. Skylark adds: Cloth and vinyl or all-vinyl seats, Skylark steering wheel, exterior trim and hubcaps, and additional interior lighting.

## Measurements

| | Cars | Wagon |
|---|---|---|
| Wheelbase | 115.0" | 115.0" |
| Length | 203.5" | 203.5" |
| Width | 73.6" | 73.6" |
| Height | 54.4" | 54.8" |
| Legroom — front | 42.0" | 42.1" |
| Legroom — rear | 36.5" | 36.2" |
| Headroom — front | 38.2" | 38.4" |
| Headroom — rear | 37.2" | 38.4" |
| Luggage capacity (cu. ft.) | NA | 86.4 |
| Fuel capacity (gals.) | 20.0 | 20.0 |

## Models Available

| | Style Number | Base MSRP | Change from LY | Shipping Wt. (lbs.) | Production | Change from LY |
|---|---|---|---|---|---|---|
| Special 2-Door Coupe | 4027 | $2,343 | +1.47% | 2983 | 15,030 | -31.26% |
| Special 2-Door Convertible | 4067 | $2,605 | +0.54% | 3099 | 6,308 | -21.95% |
| Special 4-Door Sedan | 4069 | $2,397 | +1.44% | 3000 | 17,983 | -17.25% |
| Special 4-Door, 2-Seat Wagon | 4035 | $2,689 | +1.13% | 3258 | 6,270 | +6.87% |
| Special Deluxe 2-Door Coupe | 4127 | $2,457 | NEW | 2998 | 11,962 | NEW |
| Special Deluxe 4-Door Sedan | 4169 | $2,490 | -1.23% | 3018 | 31,742 | -15.79% |
| Special Deluxe 4-Dr., 2-Seat Wgn. | 4135 | $2,787 | -1.10% | 3277 | 9,467 | +7.94% |
| Skylark 2-Door Hardtop | 4337 | $2,680 | -6.20% | 3049 | 42,356 | +31.91% |
| Skylark 2-Door Convertible | 4367 | $2,834 | -5.88% | 3169 | 10,255 | +0.42% |
| Skylark 4-Door Sedan | 4369 | $2,669 | NEW | 3062 | 19,635 | NEW |
| TOTALS | *Avg. price* | $2,595 | -2.15% | *Production* | 171,008 | +14.96% |

# Sport Wagon

*"This wagon rides like a dream and looks sharp, too!"*

**Nameplate year of origin:** 1964.
**Current bodystyle lifespan:** 1964 through 1967.
**Predecessor to this model:** None.
**Replacement for this model:** Sportwagon (1968 to 1969).
**Percentage of division's sales volume:** 2.67%.
**Corporate siblings:** Oldsmobile Vista-Cruiser.
**Primary competition:** Dodge 330/440, and Mercury Comet.
**Notable changes:** All-new model for 1964.
**Major standard equipment:** Cloth and vinyl foam padded seat cushions, deluxe steering wheel, rear arm rests, full carpeting, padded instrument panel, front-door operated dome lights, roof mounted sight-seeing glass, and 7.50 × 14 BSW tires.

## Measurements

| | |
|---|---|
| Wheelbase | 120.0" |
| Length | 208.5" |
| Width | 73.6" |
| Height | NA |
| Legroom — front | 42.1" |
| Legroom — rear | 38.5" |
| Headroom — front | 38.4" |
| Headroom — rear | 39.0" |
| Luggage capacity (cu. ft.) | NA |
| Fuel capacity (gals.) | 20.0 |

## Models Available

| | Style Number | Base MSRP | Change from LY | Shipping Wt. (lbs.) | Production | Change from LY |
|---|---|---|---|---|---|---|
| Sport Wagon 4-Dr., 2-St. Wgn. | 4255 | $2,989 | NEW | 3557 | 2,709 | NEW |
| Sport Wagon 4-Dr., 3-St. Wgn. | 4265 | $3,124 | NEW | 3689 | 2,586 | NEW |
| Sport Wagon Cust. 4-Dr., 2-S. Wgn. | 4355 | $3,161 | NEW | 3595 | 3,913 | NEW |
| Sport Wagon Cust. 4-Dr., 3-S. Wgn. | 4365 | $3,286 | NEW | 3727 | 4,446 | NEW |
| TOTALS | | Avg. price $3,140 | NEW | | Production 13,654 | NEW |

# LeSabre

*"It looks very expensive but it's not."*

**Nameplate year of origin:** 1959.
**Current bodystyle lifespan:** 1961 through 1964.
**Predecessor to this model:** LeSabre (1959 to 1960).
**Replacement for this model:** LeSabre (1965 to 1966).
**Percentage of division's sales volume:** 26.46%.
**Corporate siblings:** Chevrolet Biscayne/Bel/Air/Impala, Pontiac Catalina/Star Chief/Bonneville, Oldsmobile 88.
**Primary competition:** Chrysler Newport, Dodge Polara, and Mercury Monterey.
**Notable changes:** New grille, revised rear end, and trim and detail changes.
**Major standard equipment:** Cloth and vinyl front bench seat, padded instrument panel, glove compartment light, smoking set, dual arm rests, front-door operated courtesy light, and 7.10 × 15 BSW tires.

## Measurements

| | Cars | Wagon |
|---|---|---|
| Wheelbase | 123.0" | 123.0" |
| Length | 218.9" | 216.8" |
| Width | 78.0" | 78.0" |
| Height | 55.7" | 57.9" |
| Legroom — front | 40.9" | 44.5" |
| Legroom — rear | 38.7" | 38.1" |
| Headroom — front | 39.3" | 38.3" |
| Headroom — rear | 38.8" | 39.7" |
| Luggage capacity (cu. ft.) | NA | 86.6 |
| Fuel capacity (gals.) | 20.0 | 20.0 |

## Models Available

| | Style Number | Base MSRP | Change from LY | Shipping Wt. (lbs.) | Production | Change from LY |
|---|---|---|---|---|---|---|
| LeSabre 2-Door Hardtop | 4447 | $3,061 | -0.29% | 3629 | 24,177 | -13.58% |
| LeSabre 2-Door Convertible | 4467 | $3,314 | -0.75% | 3787 | 6,685 | -32.98% |
| LeSabre 4-Door Sedan | 4469 | $2,980 | -0.80% | 3693 | 56,729 | -12.72% |

| | Style Number | Base MSRP | Change from LY | Shipping Wt. (lbs.) | Production | Change from LY |
|---|---|---|---|---|---|---|
| LeSabre 4-Door Hardtop | 4439 | $3,122 | -0.76% | 3730 | 37,052 | -26.51% |
| LeSabre 4-Dr., 2-S. Estate Wagon | 4635 | $3,554 | +0.79% | 4352 | 6,517 | +17.09% |
| LeSabre 4-Dr., 3-S. Estate Wagon | 4645 | $3,635 | +0.80% | 4362 | 4,003 | +2.07% |
| TOTALS | Avg. price | $3,278 | +1.71% | Production | 135,163 | -21.04% |

# Wildcat

*"The regular engine is 325 horsepower with options up to 360. This should suggest something to you about Wildcat performance."*

**Nameplate year of origin:** 1962.
**Current bodystyle lifespan:** 1962 through 1964.
**Predecessor to this model:** Invicta (1961 to 1962).
**Replacement for this model:** Wildcat (1965 to 1966).
**Percentage of division's sales volume:** 16.49%.
**Corporate siblings:** Chevrolet Biscayne/Bel Air/Impala, Pontiac Catalina/Star Chief/Bonneville, Oldsmobile 88.
**Primary competition:** Chrysler 300, Dodge Custom 880, and Mercury Montclair.
**Notable changes:** New grille, revised rear end, and trim and detail changes.
**Major standard equipment:** All vinyl front bench seat, padded instrument panel, full carpeting, glove compartment light, smoking set, dual arm rests, front-door operated courtesy light, Wildcat wheel covers and specific exterior trim, and 7.60 × 15 BSW tires.

## Measurements

| | |
|---|---|
| Wheelbase | 123.0" |
| Length | 218.9" |
| Width | 78.0" |
| Height | 55.7" |
| Legroom — front | 40.9" |
| Legroom — rear | 38.7" |
| Headroom — front | 39.3" |
| Headroom — rear | 38.5" |
| Luggage capacity (cu. ft.) | NA |
| Fuel capacity (gals.) | 20.0 |

## Models Available

| | Style Number | Base MSRP | Change from LY | Shipping Wt. (lbs.) | Production | Change from LY |
|---|---|---|---|---|---|---|
| Wildcat 2-Door HT | 4647 | $3,267 | -15.12% | 4003 | 22,893 | +87.88% |
| Wildcat 2-Door Convertible | 4667 | $3,455 | -12.77% | 4076 | 7,850 | +30.38% |
| Wildcat 4-Door Sedan | 4669 | $3,164 | NEW | 4021 | 20,144 | NEW |
| Wildcat 4-Door HT | 4639 | $3,327 | -14.05% | 4058 | 33,358 | +90.41% |
| TOTALS | Avg. price | $3,303 | -15.18% | Production | 84,245 | +135.82% |

# Electra 225

*"This is a nice way to do the simple things ... splendidly."*

**Nameplate year of origin:** 1959.
**Current bodystyle lifespan:** 1961 through 1964.
**Predecessor to this model:** Electra (1959 to 1960).
**Replacement for this model:** Electra 225 (1965 to 1966).
**Percentage of division's sales volume:** 13.47%.
**Corporate siblings:** Cadillac Series 62/de Ville, Oldsmobile Ninety-Eight.
**Primary competition:** Chrysler New Yorker, Dodge Custom 880 and Mercury Park Lane.
**Notable changes:** New grille, revised rear end, and trim and detail changes.
**Major standard equipment:** Cloth and vinyl front bench seat, padded instrument panel, deep-pile carpeting (also on lower door panels), map, glove com-

## Measurements

| | |
|---|---|
| Wheelbase | 126.0" |
| Length | 222.8" |
| Width | 78.0" |
| Height | 57.5" |
| Legroom — front | 40.9" |
| Legroom — rear | 40.5" |
| Headroom — front | 40.1" |
| Headroom — rear | 38.6" |
| Luggage capacity (cu. ft.) | NA |
| Fuel capacity (gals.) | 20.0 |

partment and trunk lights, smoking set, dual arm rests, front-door operated courtesy light, power steering, power brakes, 2-speed electric windshield wipers, Super Deluxe wheel covers, and 8.00 × 15 BSW tires. Convertible adds: power windows and 2-way power seat.

## Models Available

| | Style Number | Base MSRP | Change from LY | Shipping Wt. (lbs.) | Production | Change from LY |
|---|---|---|---|---|---|---|
| Electra 225 2-Door Hardtop | 4847 | $4,070 | +0.20% | 4149 | 9,045 | +32.08% |
| Electra 225 2-Door Convertible | 4867 | $4,374 | +0.21% | 4280 | 7,181 | +12.78% |
| Electra 225 4-Door Sedan | 4819 | $4,059 | +1.10% | 4212 | 15,968 | +9.16% |
| Electra 225 6-window, 4-Door HT | 4829 | $4,261 | +0.16% | 4238 | 11,663 | +1.70% |
| Electra 225 4-Door Hardtop | 4839 | $4,194 | +0.19% | 4229 | 24,935 | +26.48% |
| TOTALS | | Avg. price $4,192 | +0.38% | Production | 68,792 | +16.55% |

# Riviera

*"Take a good look at yourself. This may be just the car you need."*

**Nameplate year of origin:** 1949 (for 2-Dr. HTs); 1963 (series).
**Current bodystyle lifespan:** 1963 through 1965.
**Predecessor to this model:** None.
**Replacement for this model:** Riviera (1966 to 1970).
**Percentage of division's sales volume:** 7.43%.
**Corporate siblings:** None.
**Primary competition:** Chrysler 300-K, Ford Thunderbird and Studebaker Avanti.
**Notable changes:** Revised grille and minor trim and detail changes.
**Major standard equipment:** Vinyl bucket seats with floor console, deep-pile carpeting, electric clock, map and trunk lights, power steering, power brakes, dual exhaust system, 2-speed electric windshield wipers with washers, and 7.10 × 15 BSW tires.

## Measurements

| | |
|---|---|
| Wheelbase | 117.0" |
| Length | 208.1" |
| Width | 76.6" |
| Height | 53.2" |
| Legroom — front | 40.1" |
| Legroom — rear | 35.1" |
| Headroom — front | 37.6" |
| Headroom — rear | 37.3" |
| Luggage capacity (cu. ft.) | NA |
| Fuel capacity (gals.) | 20.0 |

## Models Available

| | Style Number | Base MSRP | Change from LY | Shipping Wt. (lbs.) | Production | Change from LY |
|---|---|---|---|---|---|---|
| Riviera 2-Door Hardtop | 4747 | $4,385 | +1.20% | 3951 | 37,958 | -5.11% |
| TOTALS | | Avg. price $4,385 | +1.20% | Production | 37,958 | -5.11% |

# CADILLAC

*"More Tempting Than Ever! Just wait till you drive it!"*

For the most part, the new 1964 Cadillacs appeared quite similar to their predecessors. It was not until you sat behind the wheel and fired the ignition that you experienced as Cadillac put it, "an exciting adventure the instant you touch your toe to the accelerator pedal." Power transfer was improved this year through the use of GM's new Turbo Hydra-matic automatic transmission. The already dependable Hydra-matic was given a thorough rethinking, and the result was a more reliable, smoother shifting transmission. Even today, the Turbo Hydra-matic in this form, is considered one of the best automatics ever produced. For its introductory year, the new transmission was available in the de Ville, Sixty-Special and Fleetwood Eldorado lines. Putting the power through this new transmission was a new 429 CID, 340-hp V8 engine. In a game where numbers mattered, Cadillac had finally arrived. These numbers matched Lincoln's displacement (430 CID, 320-hp V8) and Imperial's horsepower (413 CID, 340-hp V8), and Cadillac's engine delivered a phenomenal 480 foot-pounds of torque. By mating this engine to the smooth-shifting Turbo Hydra-matic, Cadillac had a combination that couldn't be beat under the hood. On the road was another story though. Ford and Chrysler had been steadily working to improve the ride and driveability of their Lincoln and Imperial models, which were both unit-body construction. The resulting efforts gave better ride control and better handling than the Cadillacs could offer. The only model changes of significance were the Model 6267 Series Sixty-Two Convertible moving to the de Ville series, and the dropping of the slow-selling short-deck de Ville Park Avenue Sedan.

Series 62 2-Door Hardtop

Fleetwood models

De Ville Interior

Sedan de Ville 4-window, 4-Door Hardtop

**Model year production:** 163,320, up 1.7% from 1963.
**Domestic market share:** 2.09% (10th place).
**Base price range:** $5,048 to $9,960.

**Industry average base price:** $3,024.
**Cadillac average base price:** $6,416.
**Introduction date:** October 1963.

**Assembly plants:** Detroit, MI, and Linden, NJ.
**Data plate identification:** Nine digit code read as follows: 1st and 2nd digit 64 for 1964; 3rd digit is style symbol (last letter from the model number charts below), followed by 000001 and up for serial number. *Example:* 64J000001 is a 1964 Cadillac de Ville 2-Door Hardtop, serial number 000001.

## Powertrains

| Engine | Gross HP | Transmission Availability | Models |
|---|---|---|---|
| 429 CID, 4-bbl., V8 | 340 | Hydra-matic | 62 & Fleetwood 75 series |
| 429 CID, 4-bbl., V8 | 340 | Turbo Hydra-matic | S (except 62 & Fleetwood 75) |

## Major Options

| | Sixty-Two | de Ville | Eldorado | Sixty Special | Seventy-Five |
|---|---|---|---|---|---|
| Automatic climate control | $495 | $495 | $495 | $495 | $624 |
| Power windows | $118 | S | S | S | S |
| 6-way power seat | $113 | $85 | S | $85 | – |
| Power door locks | $46–$70 | $46–$70 | $46 | $70 | S |
| AM radio w/rear speaker | $165 | $165 | $165 | $165 | $165 |
| AM-FM radio | $191 | $191 | $191 | $191 | $191 |
| Guide-Matic headlamp dimmers | $45 | $45 | $45 | $45 | – |
| Tilt steering wheel | $48 | $48 | $48 | $48 | $48 |
| Cruise control | $97 | $97 | $97 | $97 | $97 |
| Remote control trunk release/lock | $53 | $53 | $53 | $53 | – |

Options common to most models. (– = Not Available, S or STD. = Standard equipment.) Items may be standard equipment, optional at different pricing, or unavailable on certain models. This chart is only a guide.

**Cadillac Style Symbols: A**— 62 4-window Sedan or Calais 4-Dr. HT Sedan; **B**— Sedan de Ville 4-window; **C**— 62 Short Deck Sedan; **D**— Sedan de Ville Park Avenue; **E**— Eldorado Biarritz or Eldorado Convertible; **F**— 62 Convertible; **G**— 62 2-Door Hardtop or Calais 2-Door HT; **H**— Eldorado Seville HT or Eldorado Coupe; **J**— Coupe de Ville; **K**— 62 6-window Sedan; **L**— Sedan de Ville 6-window; **M**— Fleetwood 60 Special Sedan; **N**— 62 4-window Sedan (1963) or Calais Sedan; **P**— Fleetwood Brougham or Eldorado Brougham; **R**— Fleetwood 75 Sedan; **S**— Fleetwood 75 Limousine; **Z**— Commerical Chassis

## Paint Colors

| | Code |
|---|---|
| Ebony Black | 10 |
| Aspen White | 12 |
| Nevada Silver Metallic | 14 |
| Cardiff Gray Metallic | 16 |
| Beacon Blue Metallic | 22 |
| Spruce Blue Metallic | 24 |
| Somerset Blue Metallic | 26 |
| Turino Turquoise Metallic | 29 |
| Seacrest Green Metallic | 32 |
| Lime Green | 34 |
| Nile Green Metallic | 36 |
| Bahama Sand | 44 |
| Sierra Gold Metallic | 46 |
| Palomino Metallic | 47 |
| Matador Red Metallic | 50 |
| Royal Maroon Metallic | 52 |
| Firemist Blue Metallic* | 92 |
| Firemist Aquamarine Metallic* | 94 |
| Firemist Green Metallic* | 96 |
| Firemist Saddle Metallic* | 97 |
| Firemist Red Metallic* | 98 |

*Firemist colors available only on Eldorado.*

# Sixty-Two

*"The Youthful Sixty-Two Series."*

**Nameplate year of origin:** 1940.
**Current bodystyle lifespan:** 1961 through 1964.
**Predecessor to this model:** Series Sixty-Two (1959 to 1960).
**Replacement for this model:** Calais (1965 to 1966).
**Percentage of division's sales volume:** 21.48%.
**Corporate siblings:** Buick Electra 225 and Oldsmobile Ninety-Eight.
**Primary competition:** Chrysler New Yorker and Lincoln Continental.
**Notable changes:** Minor trim and detail changes.
**Major standard equipment:** Dunsmuir or Doncaster cloth seat upholstery, rear seat center armrests, interior courtesy and map lights, left-hand outside remote control mirror, windshield wipers and washers, electric clock, right side visor vanity mirrors, rear fender skirts, front cornering lamps, power steering, power brakes, Hydra-matic transmission, and 8.00 × 15 BSW tires.

## Measurements

| | |
|---|---|
| Wheelbase | 129.5" |
| Length | 223.5" |
| Width | 79.7" |
| Height | 56.4" |
| Legroom — front | 40.8" |
| Legroom — rear | 38.8" |
| Headroom — front | 40.0" |
| Headroom — rear | 38.8" |
| Luggage capacity (cu. ft.) | NA |
| Fuel capacity (gals.) | 26.0 |

## Models Available

| | Style Number | Base MSRP | Change from LY | Shipping Wt. (lbs.) | Production | Change from LY |
|---|---|---|---|---|---|---|
| Sixty-Two 2-Door Hardtop | 6257 | $5,048 | +0.44% | 4475 | 12,166 | -27.52% |
| Sixty-Two 4-Door, 4-w. Hardtop | 6239 | $5,236 | +0.42% | 4550 | 13,670 | -19.49% |
| Sixty-Two 4-Door, 6-w. Hardtop | 6229 | $5,236 | +0.42% | 4575 | 9,243 | -28.51% |
| TOTALS | Avg. price | $5,173 | -1.70% | Production* | 35,079 | -45.4% |

*Production figure totals and average price affected by shift of Model 6267 Convertible from Series 62 to de Ville line this year.

# de Ville

*"The Brilliant de Ville Series."*

**Nameplate year of origin:** 1949 (as Hardtop designation), 1959 (series).
**Current bodystyle lifespan:** 1961 through 1964.
**Predecessor to this model:** de Ville (1959 to 1960).
**Replacement for this model:** de Ville (1965 to 1966).
**Percentage of divisions' sales volume:** 67.59%.
**Corporate siblings:** Buick Electra 225 and Oldsmobile Ninety-Eight.
**Primary competition:** Imperial Crown and Lincoln Continental.
**Notable changes:** Minor trim and detail changes.
**Major standard equipment:** Dover or Dorchester cloth and leather seat upholstery, front and rear seat center armrests, power operated front seat adjustment, power windows, interior courtesy and map lights, left-hand outside remote control mirror, windshield wipers and washers, electric clock, right side visor vanity mirrors, rear fender skirts, front cornering lamps, power steering, power brakes, Turbo Hydra-matic transmission, and 8.00 × 15 BSW tires.

### Measurements

| | |
|---|---|
| Wheelbase | 129.5" |
| Length | 223.5" |
| Width | 79.7" |
| Height | 56.4" |
| Legroom — front | 40.8" |
| Legroom — rear | 38.8" |
| Headroom — front | 40.0" |
| Headroom — rear | 38.8" |
| Luggage capacity (cu. ft.) | NA |
| Fuel capacity (gals.) | 26.0 |

## Models Available

| | Style Number | Base MSRP | Change from LY | Shipping Wt. (lbs.) | Production | Change from LY |
|---|---|---|---|---|---|---|
| Coupe de Ville 2-Door Hardtop | 6357 | $5,408 | +0.41% | 4495 | 38,195 | +20.30% |
| de Ville 2-Door Convertible* | 6267 | $5,612 | +0.39% | 4545 | 17,900 | +1.70% |
| Sedan de Ville 4-Door, 4-Wind. HT | 6339 | $5,655 | +0.39% | 4575 | 39,674 | +29.74% |
| Sedan de Ville 4-Door, 6-Wind. HT | 6329 | $5,655 | +0.39% | 4600 | 14,627 | -3.43% |
| TOTALS | Avg. price | $5,582 | +0.19% | Production* | 110,396 | +39.7% |

*Production figure totals and average price affected by shift of Model 6267 Convertible from Series 62 to de Ville line this year.

# Eldorado

*"The Impeccable Fleetwood series featuring the Eldorado Convertible."*

**Nameplate year of origin:** 1953.
**Current bodystyle lifespan:** 1961 through 1964.
**Predecessor to this model:** Eldorado (1959 to 1960).
**Replacement for this model:** Eldorado (1965 to 1966).
**Percentage of divisions' sales volume:** 1.15%.
**Corporate siblings:** Buick Electra 225 and Oldsmobile Ninety-Eight.
**Primary competition:** None.

### Measurements

| | |
|---|---|
| Wheelbase | 129.5" |
| Length | 223.5" |
| Width | 79.7" |
| Height | 56.4" |
| Legroom — front | 40.8" |
| Legroom — rear | 38.8" |

**Notable changes:** Minor trim and detail changes.

**Major standard equipment:** Leather seat upholstery, front and rear seat center armrests, power operated front seat adjustment, power windows and vent windows, interior courtesy and map lights, left-hand outside remote control mirror, windshield wipers and washers, electric clock, right side visor vanity mirrors, rear fender skirts, front cornering lamps, power steering, power brakes, Turbo Hydramatic transmission, and 8.20 × 15 WSW tires.

### Measurements (cont.)

| | |
|---|---|
| Headroom — front | 40.0" |
| Headroom — rear | 38.8" |
| Luggage capacity (cu. ft.) | NA |
| Fuel capacity (gals.) | 26.0 |

## Models Available

| | Style Number | Base MSRP | Change from LY | Shipping Wt. (lbs.) | Production | Change from LY |
|---|---|---|---|---|---|---|
| Fl. Eldorado Biarritz 2-Dr. Convertible | 6367 | $6,630 | +0.33% | 4605 | 1,870 | +2.5% |
| TOTALS | | Avg. price $6,630 | +0.33% | Production 1,870 | | +2.5% |

# Fleetwood Sixty-Special

*"The Impeccable Fleetwood Series Sixty Special Sedan."*

**Nameplate year of origin:** 1938.
**Current bodystyle lifespan:** 1961 through 1964.
**Predecessor to this model:** Fleetwood Sixty-Special (1959 to 1960).
**Replacement for this model:** Fleetwood Sixty-Special (1965 to 1966).
**Percentage of division's sales volume:** 8.91%.
**Corporate siblings:** Buick Electra 225 and Oldsmobile Ninety-Eight.
**Primary competition:** Imperial LeBaron.
**Notable changes:** Minor trim and detail changes.
**Major standard equipment:** Cloth and leather seat upholstery, front and rear seat center armrests, power operated front seat adjustment, power windows, interior courtesy and map lights, left-hand outside remote control mirror, windshield wipers and washers, electric clock, right side visor vanity mirrors, rear fender skirts, front cornering lamps, power steering, power brakes, Turbo Hydra-matic transmission, and 8.00 × 15 BSW tires.

### Measurements

| | |
|---|---|
| Wheelbase | 129.5" |
| Length | 223.5" |
| Width | 79.7" |
| Height | 56.7" |
| Legroom — front | 40.7" |
| Legroom — rear | 40.2" |
| Headroom — front | 40.1" |
| Headroom — rear | 39.5" |
| Luggage capacity (cu. ft.) | NA |
| Fuel capacity (gals.) | 26.0 |

## Models Available

| | Style Number | Base MSRP | Change from LY | Shipping Wt. (lbs.) | Production | Change from LY |
|---|---|---|---|---|---|---|
| Fleetwood Sixty-Special 4-Door Sedan | 6039 | $6,388 | +0.35% | 4680 | 14,550 | +3.9% |
| TOTALS | | Avg. price $6,388 | +0.35% | Production 14,550 | | +3.9% |

# Fleetwood Seventy-Five

*"Universally acknowledged as the most aristocratic motor cars in the world."*

**Nameplate year of origin:** 1927 (Fleetwood bodies), 1936 (75 series).
**Current bodystyle lifespan:** 1959 through 1965.
**Predecessor to this model:** Fleetwood 75 (1957 to 1958).
**Replacement for this model:** Fleetwood 75 (1966).
**Percentage of division's sales volume:** 0.87%.
**Corporate siblings:** None.

### Measurements

| | |
|---|---|
| Wheelbase | 149.75" |
| Length | 243.8" |
| Width | 79.9" |
| Height | 59.0" |
| Legroom — front | 39.8" |

**Primary competition:** None.
**Notable changes:** Minor trim and detail changes.
**Major standard equipment:** Wool broadcloth, cord cloth or leather seat upholstery with front compartment in harmonizing leather upholstery, rear seat center armrests, power operated front seat adjustment, power windows, interior courtesy and map lights, left-hand outside remote control mirror, windshield wipers and washers, electric clock, right side visor vanity mirrors, Rear fender skirts, front cornering lamps, power steering, power brakes, Hydra-matic transmission, and 8.00 × 15 BSW tires.

## Measurements (cont.)

| | |
|---|---|
| Legroom — rear | 41.3" |
| Headroom — front | 40.2" |
| Headroom — rear | 39.1" |
| Luggage capacity (cu. ft.) | NA |
| Fuel capacity (gals.) | 26.0 |

## Models Available

| | Style Number | Base MSRP | Change from LY | Shipping Wt. (lbs.) | Production | Change from LY |
|---|---|---|---|---|---|---|
| Fleetwood Seventy-Five 4-Door Sdn., 9-p. | 7523 | $9,746 | +0.23% | 5215 | 617 | -9.3% |
| Fleetwood Seventy-Five 4-Door Limo., 9-p. | 7533 | $9,960 | +0.21% | 5300 | 808 | +1.6% |
| TOTALS | | *Avg. price* $9,853 | +0.22% | | *Production* 1,425 | -3.4% |

**1964**

# CHEVROLET

*"Count on Chevrolet to build the one you want. There's 5 in '64."*

Chevrolet introduced its third new model line in five years. The Chevelle mid-size line filled a size gap between the Chevy II and the big Chevy. Joined by its GM stablemates, the Tempest, F-85 and Special, the Chevelle would help create a highly popular category of car that to this day is the largest selling category of cars. The Chevelle came in a full array of body styles, including a revived El Camino car/pickup style that would literally walk away with that market from Ford. The most celebrated line to come from the Chevelle, though, would be the Super Sport line. Though the Pontiac GTO really ignited the muscle car movement, the Chevelle Malibu SS made the muscle car an affordable reality for many buyers. The initial SS models could be had with 6 cylinders or V8 power, with a wide variety of equipment from plain Jane to fully equipped. The attention garnered by these models brought buyers by the thousands to dealer showrooms to buy other Chevelle models. Chevrolet and GM had a marketer's dream with cars such as the SS. Styling of the new line was typical of the period and closely resembled that of the full-size Chevrolet.

The full-size Chevys received a new grille treatment that was flatter this year, and a redesigned rear panel. The compact Chevy II Nova line offered a V8 powerplant as optional equipment for the first time this year. Of course, V8 engines were also being offered by the competition in the Falcon and Valiant lines as well as the slightly larger Mercury Comet and Studebaker Lark. Sales of the Chevy II dropped sharply with the introduction of the mid-size Chevelle, but would rebound in a few years. The sporty compact Corvair gained a more powerful powerplant, with an increase of 19 cubic inches and 15 horsepower to its base flat six engine. Both compact car lines received only minor styling and trim changes. The Corvette, which had been totally new last year, lost its split window styling on the coupe in favor of a one-piece rear glass. The 327 CID V8 engine was still the largest powerplant offered for the Corvette.

BelAir 4-Door Sedan

Chevy II Nova 4-Door Sedan

Chevelle Malibu SS 2-Door Hardtop

Chevelle 300 2-Door Wagon

Corvette 2-Door Coupe

Corvair Monza Spyder 2-Door Convertible

Impala SS 2-Door Hardtop

**Model year production:** 2,319,619, up 4.47% from 1963.
**Domestic market share:** 29.75% (1st place).
**Base price range:** $2,000 to $4,252.
**Industry average base price:** $3,024.
**Chevrolet average base price:** $2,602.
**Introduction date:** October 1963.
**Assembly plants:** Atlanta, GA (A); Baltimore, MD (B); Doraville, GA (C); Flint, MI (F); Framingham, MA (G); Fremont, CA (H); Janesville, WI (J); Kansas City, MO (K), Los Angeles, CA (L), Norwood, OH (N); Arlington, TX (R); St. Louis, MO (S); Tarrytown, NY (T); Southgate, CA (U); Willow Run, MI (W) and Wilmington, DE (Y).

**Data plate identification:** Twelve digit code read as follows: 1st digit 4 for 1964; four digit style number (see listings below) in which 2nd and 3rd numbers identify series and engine, 4th and 5th indicate body styles; 6th digit is assembly plant code; 100001 and up for serial number. *Example:* 41511S100001 is a 1964 Chevrolet BelAir 2-Door Sedan, 6-cylinder, serial number 100001, built in St. Louis, MO.

## Powertrains

| Engine | Gross HP | Transmission Availability | Corvair | Chevy II | Chevelle | Full-size Chevrolet | Corvette |
|---|---|---|---|---|---|---|---|
| 153 CID Super-Thrift, 1-bbl., 4-cyl. | 90 | 3-speed manual | - | S* | - | - | - |
| | | 2-sp. Powerglide Automatic | - | $167* | - | - | - |
| 164 CID Turbo-Air, 2 × 1-bbl., Flat 6 | 95 | 3-speed manual | S | - | - | - | - |
| | | 4-speed manual | $92 | - | - | - | - |
| | | 2-sp. Powerglide Automatic | $157 | - | - | - | - |
| 164 CID Turbo-Air, 2 × 1-bbl., Flat 6 | 110 | 3-speed manual | $27 | - | - | - | - |
| | | 4-speed manual | $119 | - | - | - | - |
| | | 2-sp. Powerglide Automatic | $184 | - | - | - | - |
| 164 CID Turbo-Air, Turbo-charged, Flat 6 | 150 | 3-speed manual | S** | - | - | - | - |
| | | 4-speed manual | $92** | - | - | - | - |
| 194 CID Hi-Thrift, 1-bbl., 6-cyl. | 120 | 3-speed manual | - | S (Nova)/$60* | S | - | - |
| | | Overdrive | - | - | $108 | - | - |
| | | 2-sp. Powerglide Automatic | - | $167 (Nova)/$227* | $188 | - | - |
| 230 CID Turbo-Thrift, 1-bbl., 6-cyl. | 140 | 3-speed manual | - | - | - | S | - |
| | | Overdrive | - | - | - | $108 | - |
| | | 2-sp. Powerglide Automatic | - | - | - | $188 | - |

| Engine | Gross HP | Transmission Availability | Corvair | Chevy II | Chevelle | Full-size Chevrolet | Corvette |
|---|---|---|---|---|---|---|---|
| 230 CID Turbo-Thrift, 1-bbl., 6-cyl. | 155 | 3-speed manual | - | $43 (Nova)/$103* | $43 | - | - |
| | | 2-sp. Powerglide Automatic | - | $210 (Nova)/$270* | $231 | - | - |
| 283 CID Turbo-Fire, 2-bbl., V8 | 195 | 3-speed manual | - | $108 (Nova)/$168* | $108 | $108 | - |
| | | Overdrive | - | - | $216 | $216 | - |
| | | 4-speed manual | - | $296 (Nova)/$356* | $296 | - | - |
| | | 2- sp. Powerglide Automatic | - | $286 (Nova)/$346* | $307 | $307 | - |
| 283 CID Turbo-Fire, 4-bbl., V8 | 220 | 3-speed manual | - | - | $162 | - | - |
| | | 4-speed manual | - | - | $350 | - | - |
| | | 2- sp. Powerglide Automatic | - | - | $361 | - | - |
| 327 CID Turbo-Fire, 4-bbl., V8 | 250 | 3-speed manual | - | - | - | $203 | S |
| | | 4-speed manual | - | - | - | $440 | $188 |
| | | 2- sp. Powerglide Automatic | - | - | - | $402 | $199 |
| 327 CID Turbo-Fire, 2 × 4-bbl., V8 | 300 | 3-speed manual | - | - | - | $246 | $54 |
| | | 4-speed manual | - | - | - | $483 | $242 |
| | | 2- sp. Powerglide Automatic | - | - | - | $445 | $253 |
| 327 CID Turbo-Fire, 4-bbl., V8 | 365 | 3-speed manual | - | - | - | - | $108 |
| | | 4-speed manual | - | - | - | - | $296 |
| | | 2- sp. Powerglide Automatic | - | - | - | - | $307 |
| 327 CID Ramjet, Fuel-Injected V8 | 375 | 3-speed manual | - | - | - | - | $538 |
| | | 4-speed manual | - | - | - | - | $726 |
| | | 2- sp. Powerglide Automatic | - | - | - | - | $737 |
| 409 CID Turbo-Jet, 4-bbl., V8 | 340 | 3-speed manual | - | - | - | $350 | - |
| | | 4-speed manual | - | - | - | $587 | - |
| | | 2- sp. Powerglide Automatic | - | - | - | $549 | - |
| 409 CID Turbo-Jet, 4-bbl., V8 | 400 | 3-speed manual | - | - | - | $429 | - |
| | | 4-speed manual | - | - | - | $666 | - |
| | | 2- sp. Powerglide Automatic | - | - | - | $628 | - |
| 409 CID Turbo-Jet, 4-bbl., V8 | 425 | 3-speed manual | - | - | - | $485 | - |
| | | 4-speed manual | - | - | - | $722 | - |
| | | 2- sp. Powerglide Automatic | - | - | - | $684 | - |

*Chevy II 100 only.   ** Monza only.

## Major Options

| | Corvair | Chevy II | Chevelle | Full-size | Corvette |
|---|---|---|---|---|---|
| Air conditioning (NA 4-cyl.) | $350 | $317 | $364 | $364 | $422 |
| Soft Ray tinted glass | $27 | $31 | $31 | $38 | $16 |
| ComforTilt steering wheel | - | - | $43 | $43 | - |
| Power steering (NA 4-cyl.) | - | $86 | $86 | $86 | $86 |
| Power brakes | - | $43 | $43 | $43 | $43 |
| Power windows | - | - | $102 | $102 | $59 |
| Electric clock | $16 | $16 | $16 | $16 | S |
| Pushbutton AM radio | $59 | $59 | $59 | $59 | - |
| AM/FM radio | - | - | - | $137 | $177 |
| Whitewall tires — std. size | $29 | $31 | $32 | $32–$40 | $32 |

Options common to most models. (- = Not Available; S = Standard equipment.) Items may be standard equipment, optional at different pricing, or unavailable on certain models. This chart is only a guide.

## Paint Colors

| | Code |
|---|---|
| Tuxedo Black | 900 |
| Meadow Green Met. | 905 |
| Bahama Green Metallic | 908 |
| Silver Blue Met. | 912 |
| Daytona Blue Metallic | 916 |
| Azure Aqua Met. | 918 |
| Lagoon Aqua Met. | 919 |
| Almond Fawn Metallic | 920 |
| Ember Red | 922 |
| Riverside Red | 923 |
| Saddle Tan Met. | 932 |
| Ermine White | 936 |
| Desert Beige | 938 |
| Satin Silver Metallic | 940 |
| Goldwood Yellow | 943 |
| Palomar Red Met. | 948 |

1964

# Corvair

*"Corvair for '64 puts new driving fun within everyone's reach."*

**Nameplate year of origin:** 1960.
**Current bodystyle lifespan:** 1960 through 1964.
**Predecessor to this model:** None.
**Replacement for this model:** Corvair (1965 to 1969).
**Percentage of division's sales volume:** 8.27%.
**Corporate siblings:** None.
**Primary competition:** Rambler American, Ford Falcon, Plymouth Valiant and Studebaker Lark.
**Notable changes:** Revised trim and detail changes.
**Major standard equipment:** Cloth and vinyl front bench seat, dual sun visors, turn signals, center dome light, electric windshield wipers, and 6.50 × 13 BSW tires. 700 adds: Luggage compartment trim, color-keyed floor mats, dual horns, and automatic dome lamp switch. Monza adds: All-vinyl bucket seats, folding rear seat, glove box light, front door map pockets, and additional exterior chrome trim. Spyder adds: instrument panel gauges, special identifying trim, and turbo-charged engine.

## Measurements

| | |
|---|---|
| Wheelbase | 108.0" |
| Length | 180.0" |
| Width | 67.0" |
| Height | 51.5" |
| Legroom — front | 41.1" |
| Legroom — rear | 33.7" |
| Headroom — front | 37.8" |
| Headroom — rear | 36.7" |
| Cargo capacity (cu. ft.) | 12.6 |
| Fuel capacity (gals.) | 14.0 |

## Models Available

| | Style Number | Base MSRP | Change from LY | Shipping Wt. (lbs.) | Production | Change from LY |
|---|---|---|---|---|---|---|
| Corvair 500 2-Door Club Coupe | 0527 | $2,000 | +0.40% | 2365 | 22,968 | 37.70% |
| Corvair 700 4-Door Sedan | 0769 | $2,119 | +0.43% | 2415 | 16,295 | -21.22% |
| Corvair Monza 2-Door Club Coupe | 0927 | $2,281 | +0.40% | 2445 | 88,440 | -31.73% |
| Corvair Monza 2-Door Convertible | 0967 | $2,492 | +0.44% | 2555 | 31,045 | -29.71% |
| Corvair Monza 4-Door Sedan | 0969 | $2,335 | +0.39% | 2470 | 21,926 | -29.54% |
| Corvair Monza Spyder 2-Dr. Coupe | 0627 | $2,599 | NEW | 2470 | 6,480 | NEW |
| Corvair Monza Spyder 2-Dr. Conv. | 0667 | $2,811 | NEW | 2580 | 4,761 | NEW |
| TOTALS | *Avg. price* | $2,377 | +7.75% | *Production* | 191,915 | -24.61% |

# Chevy II

*"New V8 power perks up its pleasing, practical style."*

**Nameplate year of origin:** 1962.
**Current bodystyle lifespan:** 1962 through 1965.
**Predecessor to this model:** None.
**Replacement for this model:** Chevy II (1966 through 1967).
**Percentage of division's sales volume:** 8.26%.
**Corporate siblings:** None.
**Primary competition:** Rambler American, Ford Falcon, Plymouth Valiant, and Studebaker Lark.
**Notable changes:** Revised trim and detail changes.
**Major standard equipment:** Cloth and vinyl front bench seat, center dome light, electric windshield wipers, and 6.00 × 13 BSW tires (6.50 × 13 BSW tires on wagons). Nova adds: Full carpeting, deluxe steering wheel, glove box light, additional exterior chrome trim, and 6.50 × 13 BSW tires. SS adds: All vinyl seats and special SS trim.

## Measurements

| | Cars | Wagons |
|---|---|---|
| Wheelbase | 110.0" | 110.0" |
| Length | 182.9" | 187.6" |
| Width | 70.8" | 70.8" |
| Height | 55.0" | 55.1" |
| Legroom — front | 40.1" | 40.1" |
| Legroom — rear | 36.1" | 36.1" |
| Headroom — front | 39.0" | 39.0" |
| Headroom — rear | 37.6" | 37.4" |
| Cargo capacity (cu. ft.) | 25.5 | 76.0 |
| Fuel capacity (gals.) | 16.0 | 16.0 |

## Models Available

| | Style Number | Base MSRP | Change from LY | Shipping Wt. (lbs.) | Production | Change from LY |
|---|---|---|---|---|---|---|
| Chevy II 100 2-Door Coupe | 0111 | $2,011 | +0.40% | 2455 | * | * |
| Chevy II 100 4-Door Sedan | 0169 | $2,048 | +0.39% | 2495 | * | * |
| Chevy II 100 4-Door Wagon | 0235 | $2,406 | +0.38% | 2840 | * | * |
| Chevy II Nova 400 2-Door Sedan | 0411 | $2,206 | +2.94% | 2560 | 40,348 | -3.97% |
| Chevy II Nova 400 2-Door Hardtop | 0437 | $2,271 | +0.40% | 2660 | 30,827 | -64.73% |
| Chevy II Nova 400 4-Door Sedan | 0469 | $2,243 | +0.36% | 2595 | 84,846 | -41.92% |
| Chevy II Nova 400 4-Door Wagon | 0435 | $2,503 | +0.36% | 2860 | 35,670 | -50.65% |
| Chevy II Nova SS 2-Door HT | 0447 | $2,433 | NEW | 2675 | * | NEW |
| TOTALS | Avg. price | $2,265 | +0.58% | | Production 191,691 | -48.56% |

*Production not available by trim level, only by body style.*

# Chevelle

*"Youthful looks and Chevy spirit in a completely new car!"*

**Nameplate year of origin:** 1964.
**Current bodystyle lifespan:** 1964 through 1965.
**Predecessor to this model:** None.
**Replacement for this model:** Chevelle (1966 to 1967).
**Corporate siblings:** Buick Special, Oldsmobile F-85, and Pontiac Tempest.
**Percentage of division's sales volume:** 14.58%.
**Primary competition:** Rambler Classic, Dodge 330/440, Ford Fairlane, and Plymouth Belvedere.
**Notable changes:** All-new model for 1964.
**Major standard equipment:** Cloth and vinyl front bench seat, color-keyed vinyl-coated rubber floor mats, hubcaps, and 6.50 × 14 BSW tires (7.00 × 14 BSW tires on wagons). Malibu adds: Color-keyed deep-twist carpeting, full wheel covers, electric clock and dual sun visors. SS adds: All vinyl bucket seats, special instrumentation, deluxe steering wheel and distinctive SS trim and wheel covers.

## Measurements

| | Cars | Wagons |
|---|---|---|
| Wheelbase | 115.0" | 115.0" |
| Length | 193.9" | 198.8" |
| Width | 74.6" | 74.6" |
| Height | 54.5" | 54.9" |
| Legroom — front | 42.0" | 42.0" |
| Legroom — rear | 35.9" | 35.8" |
| Headroom — front | 38.7" | 38.7" |
| Headroom — rear | 37.3" | 37.4" |
| Cargo capacity (cu. ft.) | NA | 86.0 |
| Fuel capacity (gals.) | 20.0 | 20.0 |

## Models Available

| | Style Number | Base MSRP | Change from LY | Shipping Wt. (lbs.) | Production | Change from LY |
|---|---|---|---|---|---|---|
| Chevelle 300 2-Door Coupe | 5311 | $2,231 | NEW | 2825 | 22,588 | NEW |
| Chevelle 300 4-Door Sedan | 5369 | $2,268 | NEW | 2850 | * | NEW |
| Chevelle 300 2-Door Wagon | 5315 | $2,528 | NEW | 3050 | 2,710 | NEW |
| Chevelle 300 4-Door Wagon | 5335 | $2,566 | NEW | 3130 | * | NEW |
| Chevelle Malibu 2-Door Hardtop | 5537 | $2,376 | NEW | 2850 | 134,670 | NEW |
| Chevelle Malibu 2-Dr. Convertible | 5567 | $2,587 | NEW | 2995 | 23,158 | NEW |
| Chevelle Malibu 4-Door Sedan | 5569 | $2,349 | NEW | 2870 | 113,816 | NEW |
| Chevelle Malibu 4-Dr., 6 pass. Wgn. | 5535 | $2,647 | NEW | 3140 | 41,374 | NEW |
| Chevelle Malibu 4-Dr., 9 pass. Wgn. | 5545 | $2,744 | NEW | 3240 | * | NEW |
| Chevelle SS 2-Door Hardtop | 5737 | $2,538 | NEW | 2875 | * | NEW |
| Chevelle SS 2-Dr. Convertible | 5767 | $2,749 | NEW | 3020 | * | NEW |
| TOTALS | Avg. price | $2,508 | NEW | | Production 338,316 | NEW |

*Production not available by trim level, only by body style.*

# Chevrolet Full-size

*"New looks in a great new Jet-smooth luxury lineup."*

**Nameplate year of origin:** 1958 (Impala, Biscayne); 1950 (BelAir).
**Current bodystyle lifespan:** 1961 through 1964.
**Predecessor to this model:** Biscayne/BelAir/Impala (1959 to 1960).
**Replacement for this model:** Biscayne/BelAir/Impala/Caprice (1965 to 1966).
**Percentage of division's sales volume:** 67.88%.
**Corporate siblings:** Buick LeSabre/Wildcat, Olds 88, Pontiac Catalina/Star Chief/Bonneville.
**Primary competition:** Rambler Ambassador, Dodge Polara, Ford Custom/Galaxie, and Plymouth Fury.
**Notable changes:** Revised front and rear end styling.
**Major standard equipment:** Biscayne: Cloth and vinyl bench seat, foam cushion front and rear seats, front and rear door armrests, electric windshield wipers, glove compartment lock and 7.00 × 14 BSW tires (8.00 × 14 BSW tires on wagons). BelAir adds: Vinyl headliner, full carpeting, and automatic interior lighting. Impala adds: Vinyl upholstery in convertible, extra-long armrests, electric clock, dual backup lamps and 7.50 × 14 BSW tires on convertible. SS adds: All vinyl bucket seats, center floor console, and special SS wheel covers, body trim and interior trim.

## Measurements

|  | Cars | Wagons |
|---|---|---|
| Wheelbase | 119.0" | 119.0" |
| Length | 209.9" | 210.8" |
| Width | 78.1" | 78.1" |
| Height (Sedan only) | 56.2" | 56.7" |
| Legroom — front | 41.8" | 41.8" |
| Legroom — rear | 38.3" | 38.0" |
| Headroom — front | 39.2" | 39.3" |
| Headroom — rear | 38.0" | 38.2" |
| Cargo capacity (cu. ft.) | NA | 97.5 |
| Fuel capacity (gals.) | 20.0 | 19.0 |

## Models Available

| | Style Number | Base MSRP | Change from LY | Shipping Wt. (lbs.) | Production | Change from LY |
|---|---|---|---|---|---|---|
| Biscayne 2-Door Sedan | 1111 | $2,363 | +1.77% | 3230 | * | * |
| Biscayne 4-Door Sedan | 1169 | $2,417 | +1.73% | 3300 | * | * |
| Biscayne 4-Dr., 2-S. Wagon | 1135 | $2,763 | +1.47% | 3700 | * | * |
| Bel Air 2-Door Sedan | 1511 | $2,465 | +0.45% | 3235 | 120,951 | -10.83% |
| Bel Air 4-Door Sedan | 1569 | $2,519 | +0.44% | 3305 | * | * |
| BelAir 4-Dr., 2-S. Wagon | 1535 | $2,828 | +0.35% | 3745 | * | * |
| BelAir 4-Dr., 3-S. Wagon | 1545 | $2,931 | +0.34% | 3705 | * | * |
| Impala 2-Door Sport Coupe | 1747 | $2,678 | +0.41% | 3295 | 442,292 | +10.79% |
| Impala 2-Door Convertible | 1767 | $2,927 | +0.34% | 3400 | 81,897 | -0.92% |
| Impala 4-Door Sedan | 1769 | $2,671 | +0.38% | 3340 | 536,329 | -4.48% |
| Impala 4-Door Hardtop | 1739 | $2,742 | +0.37% | 3370 | 200,172 | +3.10% |
| Impala 4-Dr., 2-S. Wagon | 1735 | $2,970 | +0.34% | 3725 | 192,827 | -2.88% |
| Impala 4-Dr., 3-S. Wagon | 1745 | $3,073 | +0.33% | 3770 | * | * |
| Impala SS 2-Door Sport Coupe | 1347 | $2,839 | NEW | 3325 | * | NEW |
| Impala SS 2-Door Convertible | 1367 | $3,088 | NEW | 3435 | * | NEW |
| TOTALS | | Avg. price $2,752 | +1.85% | | Production 1,574,468 | +1.74% |

*Production not available by trim level, only by body style.*

# Corvette

*"New smooth ride, improved performance for America's sports car."*

**Nameplate year of origin:** 1953 (Also used on show car of same year).
**Current bodystyle lifespan:** 1963 through 1967.
**Predecessor to this model:** Corvette (1956 to 1962).
**Replacement for this model:** Corvette (1968 to 1982).

## Measurements

| | |
|---|---|
| Wheelbase | 98.0" |
| Length | 173.3" |
| Width | 69.6" |

Percentage of division's sales volume: 1.00%.
Corporate siblings: None.
Primary competition: None.
Notable changes: Minor trim and detail changes.
Major standard equipment: Bucket seats, cockpit-cluster console, simu-
    lated walnut steering wheel, full carpeting, complete instrumentation,
    manually operated folding convertible top, and 6.70 × 15 BSW tires.

## Measurements (cont.)

| | |
|---|---|
| Height | 49.8" |
| Legroom — front | 43.1" |
| Legroom — rear | NA |
| Headroom — front | 36.3" |
| Headroom — rear | NA |
| Cargo capacity (cu. ft.) | NA |
| Fuel capacity (gals.) | 20.0 |

## Models Available

| | Style Number | Base MSRP | Change from LY | Shipping Wt. (lbs.) | Production | Change from LY |
|---|---|---|---|---|---|---|
| Corvette 2-Door Coupe | 0837 | $4,252 | 0.00% | 2960 | 8,304 | -21.62% |
| Corvette 2-Door Convertible | 0867 | $4,037 | 0.00% | 2945 | 14,925 | +36.69% |
| TOTALS | | *Avg. price* $4,145 | 0.00% | | *Production* 23,229 | +7.98% |

**1964**

# CHRYSLER

*"Move up to Chrysler '64."*

The 1964 Chrysler models were very similar to their 1963 predecessors. Grilles were altered, and interior and exterior trim items were revised, but the basic lines remained the same. Powertrain choices were juggled around, with the 426 CID V8 no longer being offered, as it was chosen to be used by Dodge and Plymouth for racing purposes. Three model lineup changes were made, as the base 300 4-Door Sedan was dropped due to poor sales. Returning after brief absences were the 300 letter-series 2-Door Convertible, and the New Yorker 2-Door Hardtop. The New Yorker 2-Door hardtop was never a high volume seller, and in fact, only sold 300 cars this season. But with its new body for 1965, it would become one of the best looking and most popular of the luxury 2-Door Hardtops on the market, much as it had been in the 1955–1959 period.

The most memorable cars of this year, however, are probably those that were not offered for sale at all, namely the fifty experimental Turbine Cars that were released for public use by Chrysler, to test their roadworthiness and the public's acceptance of such a car. The cars, most of which were painted Turbine Bronze with black vinyl tops, were styled with very sporting lines, very much in the contemporary Ford Thunderbird idiom. The public seemed to like the cars, although there were still concerns of excessive heat created by the cars, and their energy efficiency was not on a par with ordinary cars of the time. Chrysler would continue working with turbine power through the mid-eighties, but it would never be able to bring one to market. Although the experiment could be considered successful, most of these 50 cars wound up being destroyed due to strict taxes imposed by the government if they were kept by Chrysler, since their bodies were imported from Italy. Several cars do remain in museums throughout the country.

The 1964 model year marked the final offering (to date) of a hardtop station wagon on the market; in the form of Chrysler's and Dodge's full-size wagons.

300 4-Door Hardtop

300-K 2-Door Convertible

Newport Town & Country 4-Door Wagon

New Yorker Salon 4-Door Sedan

**Model year production:** 146,461, up 14.99% over 1963.
**Domestic market share:** 1.88% (11th place).
**Base price range:** $2,901 to $5,860.
**Industry average base price:** $3,024.
**Chrysler average base price:** $3,878.
**Introduction date:** September 20, 1963.
**Assembly plants:** Detroit (Jefferson Ave.), MI (3).

**Data plate identification:** Ten digit code read as follows: 1st digit is make identity letter (8 = Chrysler), 2nd number identifies series (1–7; Newport is 1); 3rd digit 4 for 1964; 4th digit is assembly plant code; followed by 100001 and up for serial number. Body style identification found on separate plate. *Example:* 8143100001 is a 1964 Chrysler Newport, serial number 100001, built in Detroit, MI.

## Powertrains

| Engine | Gross HP | Transmission Availability | Newport | 300 | New Yorker | 300-K |
|---|---|---|---|---|---|---|
| 361 CID, 2-bbl., V8 | 265 | 3-speed manual | S | - | - | - |
| | | 4-speed manual | $227 | - | - | - |
| | | Torqueflite automatic | $227 | - | - | - |
| 383 CID, 2-bbl., V8 | 305 | 3-speed manual | - | S | - | - |
| | | 4-speed manual | - | $227 | - | - |
| | | Torqueflite automatic | - | $227 | - | - |
| 413 CID, 4-bbl., V8 | 340 | Torqueflite automatic | - | - | S | - |
| 413 CID Long Ram, 4-bbl., V8 | 360 | Torqueflite automatic | - | $270 | $162 | S |
| 413 CID Short Ram, 2 × 4-bbl., V8 | 390 | Torqueflite automatic | - | $375 | $267 | $105 |

## Major Options

| | Newport | 300 | New Yorker | 300-K |
|---|---|---|---|---|
| Heater and defroster | $102 | $102 | $102 | $102 |
| Airtemp air conditioning | $510 | $510 | $510 | $510 |
| Solex tinted glass | $43 | $43 | $43 | $43 |
| Rear window defogger | $21 | $21 | $21 | $21 |
| Tilt steering wheel | $47 | $47 | $47 | $47 |
| Auto Pilot cruise control | $86 | $86 | $86 | $86 |
| Power steering | $108 | $108 | S | S |
| Power brakes | $48 | $48 | S | S |
| Power seat — bench | $102 | $102 | $102 | - |
| Power windows | $108 | $108 | S | S |
| Golden Touch Tone AM radio | $93 | $93 | $93 | $93 |
| AM/FM radio | $157 | $157 | $157 | $157 |
| White sidewall tires — std. sizes | $42 | $46 | $51 | S |

## Paint Colors

| | Code |
|---|---|
| Formal Black | BB-1 |
| Wedgewood | CC-1 |
| Nassau Blue Metallic | DD-1 |
| Monarch Blue Metallic | EE-1 |
| Pine Mist Metallic | FF-1 |
| Sequoia Green Metallic | GG-1 |
| Silver Turquoise Metallic | KK-1 |
| Royal Turquoise Metallic | LL-1 |
| Madison Gray Metallic | MM-1 |
| Rosewood Metallic | OO-1 |
| Royal Ruby Metallic | RR-1 |
| Roman Red Metallic | TT-1 |
| Embassy Gold Metallic | UU-1 |

## Major Options (cont.)

Options common to most models. (- = Not Available, S = Standard equipment.) Items may be standard equipment, optional at different pricing, or unavailable on certain models. This chart is only a guide.

|  | Code |
|---|---|
| Persian White | WW-1 |
| Dune Beige | XX-1 |
| Sable Tan Metallic | YY-1 |
| Silver Mist Metallic | 22-1 |

**1964**

# Newport

*"The easy-to-own Chrysler series."*

**Nameplate year of origin:** 1961 (as series); 1950 (as Hardtop model designation).
**Current bodystyle lifespan:** 1960 (as Windsor); 1961 through 1964 with major restyle in 1963.
**Predecessor to this model:** Windsor (1957 to 1959).
**Replacement for this model:** Newport (1965 to 1966).
**Percentage of division's sales volume:** 58.16%.
**Corporate siblings:** Dodge Custom 880, Chrysler New Yorker, 300 and 300-K.
**Primary competition:** Buick Wildcat, Mercury Monterey and Oldsmobile 88.
**Notable changes:** Revised grille, and minor trim and detail changes.
**Major standard equipment:** Cloth and vinyl front bench seat, deep-pile carpeting, padded instrument panel, passenger assist handles, exterior bright side moldings and 8.00 × 14 BSW tires. Town & Country adds: Power tailgate window, 8.50 × 14 BSW tires.

### Measurements

|  | Cars | Wagons |
|---|---|---|
| Wheelbase | 122.0" | 122.0" |
| Length | 215.3" | 219.4" |
| Width | 80.0" | 80.0" |
| Height | 55.1" | 55.4" |
| Legroom — front | 41.9" | 41.9" |
| Legroom — rear | 39.3" | 39.3" |
| Headroom — front | 38.0" | 38.0" |
| Headroom — rear | 37.9" | 37.9" |
| Cargo capacity (cu. ft.) | NA | 91.2 |
| Fuel capacity (gals.) | 23.0 | 21.0 |

### Models Available

|  | Style Number | Base MSRP | Change from LY | Shipping Wt. (lbs.) | Production | Change from LY |
|---|---|---|---|---|---|---|
| Newport 2-Door Hardtop | 812 | $2,962 | -2.15% | 3760 | 10,579 | +7.85% |
| Newport 2-Door Convertible | 815 | $3,334 | -1.91% | 3810 | 2,176 | +3.97% |
| Newport 4-Door Sedan | 813 | $2,901 | -2.13% | 3805 | 55,957 | +14.04% |
| Newport 4-Door Hardtop | 814 | $3,042 | -2.06% | 3795 | 9,710 | +15.09% |
| N. Town & Country 4-Dr. HT, 2-S. Wgn. | 858 | $3,414 | -1.84% | 4175 | 3,720 | +2.82% |
| N. Town & Country 4-Dr. HT, 3-S. Wgn. | 859 | $3,521 | -1.81% | 4200 | 3,041 | +3.15% |
| TOTALS | *Avg. price* | $3,196 | -1.97% | *Production* | 85,183 | +12.12% |

# 300

*"The sports-bred Chrysler series."*

**Nameplate year of origin:** 1955; 1962 (as non-letter series).
**Current bodystyle lifespan:** 1960 (as Saratoga); 1961 (as Windsor); 1962 through 1964 with major restyle in 1963.
**Predecessor to this model:** Saratoga (1957 to 1959).
**Replacement for this model:** 300 (1965 to 1966).
**Percentage of division's sales volume:** 18.36%.
**Corporate siblings:** Dodge Custom 880, Chrysler Newport, New Yorker and 300-K.
**Primary competition:** Buick Wildcat, Mercury Monterey S-55 and Oldsmobile 88.
**Notable changes:** Revised grille, and minor trim and detail changes.
**Major standard equipment:** All-vinyl bucket seats, deep-pile carpeting, padded dash, deluxe interior appointments, map lights, variable-speed electric windshield wipers, special 300 trim and identification, wheel covers, and 8.00 × 14 BSW tires.

### Measurements

|  |  |
|---|---|
| Wheelbase | 122.0" |
| Length | 215.3" |
| Width | 80.0" |
| Height | 55.1" |
| Legroom — front | 41.2" |
| Legroom — rear | 39.3" |
| Headroom — front | 37.9" |
| Headroom — rear | 37.9" |
| Cargo capacity (cu. ft.) | NA |
| Fuel capacity (gals.) | 23.0 |

## Models Available

| | Style Number | Base MSRP | Change from LY | Shipping Wt. (lbs.) | Production | Change from LY |
|---|---|---|---|---|---|---|
| 300 2-Door Hardtop | 822 | $3,443 | +0.38% | 3850 | 13,401 | +42.22% |
| 300 2-Door Convertible | 825 | $3,803 | +0.34% | 4120 | 2,026 | +31.99% |
| 300 4-Door Hardtop | 824 | $3,521 | +3.56% | 3865 | 11,460 | +15.58% |
| TOTALS | Avg. price | $3,589 | -3.11% | | Production 26,887 | +16.70% |

# New Yorker

*"The luxurious Chrysler series."*

**Nameplate year of origin:** 1939 (altered from 1938 New York Special model).

**Current bodystyle lifespan:** 1960 through 1964 with major restyle in 1963.

**Predecessor to this model:** New Yorker (1957 to 1959).

**Replacement for this model:** New Yorker (1965 to 1966).

**Percentage of division's sales volume:** 20.99%.

**Corporate siblings:** Chrysler Newport, 300-K and 300.

**Primary competition:** Buick Electra, Mercury Park Lane and Oldsmobile 98.

**Notable changes:** Revised grille, and minor trim and detail changes.

**Major standard equipment:** Cloth and vinyl front bench seat with front and rear center armrests, deep-pile carpeting, padded dash, map and trunk lights, electric clock, remote-control outside LH rear view mirror, exclusive exterior bright trim, power steering, power brakes, automatic transmission, color-keyed wheel covers, and 8.50 × 14 BSW tires. Salon adds: Leather interior trim, air conditioning, AM/FM radio w/dual speakers, Auto-Pilot, 6-way power seat, power windows, reclining passenger seat, rear window defogger, power door locks, tinted glass vanity mirror, twin body-side paint stripes and 9.00 × 14 WSW tires.

## Measurements

| | Cars | Wagons |
|---|---|---|
| Wheelbase | 122.0" | 122.0" |
| Length | 215.3" | 219.4" |
| Width | 80.0" | 80.0" |
| Height | 55.5" | 55.4" |
| Legroom — front | 41.9" | 41.9" |
| Legroom — rear | 39.3" | 39.3" |
| Headroom — front | 38.0" | 38.0" |
| Headroom — rear | 37.9" | 37.9" |
| Cargo capacity (cu. ft.) | NA | 91.2 |
| Fuel capacity (gals.) | 23.0 | 21.0 |

## Models Available

| | Style Number | Base MSRP | Change from LY | Shipping Wt. (lbs.) | Production | Change from LY |
|---|---|---|---|---|---|---|
| New Yorker 4-Door Sedan | 833 | $3,994 | +0.33% | 4015 | 15,443 | +3.76% |
| New Yorker 4-Door Hardtop | 834 | $4,131 | +0.32% | 4035 | 10,887 | +5.81% |
| New Yorker Salon 4-Door Hardtop | 884 | $5,860 | +0.00% | 4280 | 1,621 | +173.36% |
| N.Y. Town & Country 4-Dr. HT, 2-S. W | 878 | $4,721 | +0.28% | 4385 | 1,190 | +25.26% |
| N.Y. Town & Country 4-Dr. HT, 3-S. W | 879 | $4,828 | +0.27% | 4395 | 1,603 | +28.86% |
| TOTALS | Avg. price | $4,707 | +0.23% | | Production 30,744 | +9.96% |

# 300-K

*"Chrysler's fiery-spirited full-size sports car."*

**Nameplate year of origin:** 1955.

**Current bodystyle lifespan:** 1960 through 1964 with major restyle in 1963.

**Predecessor to this model:** 300 letter series (1957 to 1959).

**Replacement for this model:** 300-L (1965).

**Percentage of division's sales volume:** 2.49%.

## Measurements

| | |
|---|---|
| Wheelbase | 122.0" |
| Length | 215.3" |
| Width | 80.0" |
| Height | 55.7" |

**Corporate siblings:** Chrysler Newport, New Yorker and 300.
**Primary competition:** Buick Riviera and Ford Thunderbird.
**Notable changes:** Revised grille, and minor trim and detail changes.
**Major standard equipment:** Leather power bucket front seats, floor console, deep-pile carpeting, padded dash, map lights, electric clock, exclusive exterior bright trim, power steering, power brakes, automatic transmission, full wheel covers, and 7.60 × 15 WSW tires.

| | | | | | | |
|---|---|---|---|---|---|---|
| Legroom — front | 41.2" |
| Legroom — rear | 39.9" |
| Headroom — front | 37.9" |
| Headroom — rear | 37.9" |
| Cargo capacity (cu. ft.) | NA |
| Fuel capacity (gals.) | 23.0 |

## Models Available

| | Style Number | Base MSRP | Change from LY | Shipping Wt. (lbs.) | Production | Change from LY |
|---|---|---|---|---|---|---|
| 300-K 2-Door Hardtop | 842 | $4,056 | -21.76% | 3965 | 3,022 | +655.50% |
| 300-K 2-Door Convertible | 845 | $4,522 | NEW | 3995 | 625 | NEW |
| TOTALS | *Avg. price* $4,289 | | -17.26% | *Production* 3,647 | | +811.75% |

# DODGE

*"Fifty Years of Dependability — Dodge: 1914–1964."*

Dodge entered its fiftieth anniversary year with mostly carry-over models, but a couple of new powerplants. A new V8 engine option was introduced for the compact Dart line. The new engine, derived from the popular 318 CID V8 engine would prove to be a worthy performer in the Dart. The Dart received a new grille and trim, but there were few other changes. The big 880 and Custom 880 series were also little changed and made no model changes. The latter in station wagon form, along with its Chrysler counterparts, was the last hardtop wagon sold.

For standard-size Dodge models, the 330, 440 and Polara, a hemispherical head version of the 426 V8 would become available mid-year. This engine would tear up the drag strips and win many, many NASCAR and stock car racing awards and championships. It had first appeared in Chrysler models, but quickly became a favorite in the lighter weight Dodges and Plymouths. Styling was cleaned up a little more this season: headlights were now placed on a horizontal plane, a full-width grille was utilized and body side trim was changed. The Fleet Special models were dropped, as was the Polara 500 series. There was, however, a Polara 500 Sport package available for Polara models.

440 2-Door Hardtop

Custom 880 2-Door Hardtop and
4-Door Hardtop

Custom 880 2-Door Convertible

Dart 270 4-Door Sedan

Dart GT 2-Door Hardtop

**Model year production:** 457,400, up 25.76% over 1963.
**Domestic market share:** 5.87% (7th place).
**Base price range:** $1,988 to $3,420.
**Industry average base price:** $3,024.
**Dodge average base price:** $2,672.
**Introduction date:** September 1963.
**Assembly plants:** Lynch Road, MI (A); Hamtramck, MI (B); Detroit (Jefferson Ave.), MI (C); Belvidere, IL (D); Los Angeles, CA (E); Newark, DE (F); St. Louis, MO (G); Windsor, Ontario, Canada (R).

**Data plate identification:** Ten digit code read as follows: Four digit style number (see listings below) in which 1st digit is series letter (e.g., 6 = Polara V8 series), 2nd number identifies trim grade (L is for base trim, M for Mid-level, etc.), 3rd digit indicates year (4 for 1964), 4th digit is assembly plant code; followed by 100001 and up for serial number. Body style identification found on separate plate. *Example:* 634C100001 is a 1964 Dodge Polara with a 318 CID V8 engine, serial number 100001, built in Detroit, MI.

## Powertrains

| Engine | Gross HP | Transmission Availability | Dart | 330 & 440 | Polara | 880 |
|---|---|---|---|---|---|---|
| 170 CID, 1-bbl., 6-cyl. | 101 | 3-speed manual | S | – | – | – |
| | | Torqueflite automatic | $172 | – | – | – |
| 225 CID, 1-bbl., 6-cyl. | 145 | 3-speed manual | $47 | S[2] | S[4] | – |
| | | Torqueflite automatic | $219 | $192[2] | $192[4] | – |
| 273 CID, 2-bbl., V8 | 180 | 3-speed manual | $131 | – | – | – |
| | | Torqueflite automatic | $350 | – | – | – |
| 318 CID, 2-bbl., V8 | 230 | 3-speed manual | – | S[1]/$107[2] | S[3]/$107[4] | – |
| | | 4-speed manual | – | $146[1]/$253[2] | $146[3]/$253[4] | – |
| | | Torqueflite automatic | – | $211[1]/$318[2] | $211[3]/$318[4] | – |
| 361 CID, 2-bbl., V8 | 265 | 3-speed manual | – | $59[1]/$166[2] | $59[3]/$166[4] | S |
| | | Torqueflite automatic | – | $270[1]/$377[2] | $270[3]/$377[4] | $211 |
| 383 CID, 2-bbl., V8 | 305 | 3-speed manual | – | $72[1]/$179[2] | $72[3]/$179[4] | $13 |
| | | 4-speed manual | – | $218[1]/$325[2] | $218[3]/$325[4] | $159 |
| | | Torqueflite automatic | – | $283[1]/$390[2] | $283[3]/$390[4] | $224 |
| 383 CID, 4-bbl., V8 | 330 | 3-speed manual | – | $123[1]/$230[2] | $123[3]/$230[4] | $64 |
| | | 4-speed manual | – | $269[1]/$376[2] | $269[3]/$376[4] | $210 |
| | | Torqueflite automatic | – | $334[1]/$441[2] | $334[3]/$441[4] | $275 |
| 426 CID Ramcharger, 4-bbl., V8 | 365/415 | | – | ** | ** | – |
| 426 CID Ramcharger, 2 × 4-bbl., V8 | 425 | | – | ** | ** | – |
| 426 CID Hemi-Charger, 4-bbl., V8 | 415 | | – | ** | ** | – |
| 426 CID Hemi-Charger, 2 × 4-bbl., V8 | 425 | | – | ** | ** | – |

[1]*440 Wagon models only.* [2]*All but 440 Wagon.* [3]*4-Door Hardtop and Convertible only.* [4]*All but 4-Door Hardtop and Convertible.* **Accurate pricing information unavailable.*

## Major Options

| | Dart | 330 & 440 | Polara | 880 |
|---|---|---|---|---|
| Heater and defroster | $74 | $74 | $74 | S |
| Airtemp air conditioning | $425 | $445 | $445 | $445 |
| Tinted glass | $24 | $30 | $30 | $24 |
| Power steering | $73 | $77 | $77 | $77 |
| Power brakes | $43 | $43 | $43 | $43 |
| Power seat | - | $96 | $96 | $96 |
| Power windows | - | $102 | $102 | $102 |
| Electric clock | $16 | $16 | $16 | $16 |
| Music Master AM radio | $169 | $58 | $58 | $58 |
| White sidewall tires — std. sizes | $29 | $33–$48 | $33–$48 | $33–$48 |

Options common to most models. (- = Not Available; S or STD. = Standard equipment.) Items may be standard equipment, optional at different pricing, or unavailable on certain models. This chart is only a guide.

## Paint Colors

| | Code |
|---|---|
| Black | BB-1 |
| Light Blue Metallic | CC-1 |
| Medium Blue Metallic | DD-1 |
| Dark Blue Metallic | EE-1 |
| Aqua Metallic | JJ-1 |
| Medium Turquoise Met. | KK-1 |
| Dark Green Metallic | LL-1 |
| Gray Metallic | MM-1 |
| Red | PP-1 |
| Ivory | SS-1 |
| Signet Royal Red Metallic | TT-1 |
| White | WW-1 |
| Beige | XX-1 |
| Tan Metallic | YY-1 |
| Anniversary Gold Metallic | ZZ-1 |

**1964**

# Dart

*"The family-sized, family-priced compact."*

**Nameplate year of origin:** 1960 (On low-end full-size models).
**Current bodystyle lifespan:** 1963 through 1966.
**Predecessor to this model:** Lancer (1961 to 1962).
**Replacement for this model:** Dart (1967 to 1976).
**Percentage of division's sales volume:** 42.70%.
**Corporate siblings:** Plymouth Valiant.
**Primary competition:** Buick Special, Mercury Comet, Oldsmobile F-85, Pontiac Tempest and Studebaker Lark.
**Notable changes:** Minor trim and detail changes.
**Major standard equipment:** Nylon and vinyl front bench seats, rubber floor mats, chrome windshield trim and 6.50 × 13 BSW tires. 270 adds: All-vinyl upholstery on convertible, color-keyed carpeting, additional interior and exterior bright trim. GT adds: All-vinyl bucket seats, padded instrument panel and specific GT trim.

## Measurements

| | Cars | Wagons |
|---|---|---|
| Wheelbase | 111.0" | 106.0" |
| Length | 196.3" | 190.2" |
| Width | 69.8" | 69.8" |
| Height | 53.5" | NA |
| Legroom — front | 40.0" | 40.0" |
| Legroom — rear | 36.6" | NA |
| Headroom — front | 38.1" | 38.1" |
| Headroom — rear | 37.2" | 37.0" |
| Cargo capacity (cu. ft.) | NA | NA |
| Fuel capacity (gals.) | 18.0 | 18.0 |

## Models Available

| | Style Number | Base MSRP | Change from LY | Shipping Wt. (lbs.) | Production | Change from LY |
|---|---|---|---|---|---|---|
| Dart 170 2-Door Sedan | 711 | $1,988 | +0.25% | 2615 | 70,200 | +36.84% |
| Dart 170 4-Door Sedan | 713 | $2,053 | +0.59% | 2640 | * | * |
| Dart 170 4-Door, 2-Seat Wagon | 756 | $2,315 | +0.26% | 2740 | * | * |
| Dart 270 2-Door Sedan | 731 | $2,094 | +0.72% | 2625 | 60,400 | +9.22% |
| Dart 270 2-Door Convertible | 735 | $2,389 | +0.17% | 2735 | * | * |
| Dart 270 4-Door Sedan | 733 | $2,160 | +1.17% | 2645 | * | * |
| Dart 270 4-Door, 2-Seat Wagon | 776 | $2,414 | -0.78% | 2745 | 14,000 | +7.69% |
| Dart GT 2-Door Hardtop | 742 | $2,318 | +1.27% | 2670 | 50,700 | +47.81% |
| Dart GT 2-Door Convertible | 745 | $2,536 | +0.96% | 2770 | * | * |
| TOTALS | | *Avg. price* $2,252 | +0.49% | | *Production* 195,300 | +26.90% |

*Production is estimated and not available by trim level.

# 330 & 440

*"The full-sized Dodge priced with the low-price models."*

**Nameplate year of origin:** 1962.
**Current bodystyle lifespan:** 1962 through 1965.
**Predecessor to this model:** Dart Seneca and Pioneer (1960 to 1961).
**Replacement for this model:** Coronet (1966 to 1967).
**Percentage of division's sales volume:** 36.16%.
**Corporate siblings:** Dodge Polara and Plymouth Savoy/Belvedere/Fury.
**Primary competition:** AMC Classic, Chevrolet Chevelle, Ford Fairlane, and Pontiac Tempest.
**Notable changes:** Completely restyled front and rear end.
**Major standard equipment:** Cloth-and-vinyl bench seat with foam front cushion, full rubber floor mats, electric windshield wipers, dual sun visors, exterior bright trim around windshield and back window, and 7.00 × 14 BSW tires (7.50 × 14 BSW tires on wagons). 440 adds: Full carpeting, exterior bright trim around side windows and body sides.

## Measurements

|  | Cars | Wagons |
|---|---|---|
| Wheelbase | 119.0" | 116.0" |
| Length | 209.8" | 212.3" |
| Width | 75.0" | 75.0" |
| Height | 55.1" | 55.4" |
| Legroom — front | 41.9" | 41.9" |
| Legroom — rear | 36.5" | 36.5" |
| Headroom — front | 39.2" | 39.2" |
| Headroom — rear | 39.2" | 39.2" |
| Cargo capacity (cu. ft.) | NA | NA |
| Fuel capacity (gals.) | 19.0 | 19.0 |

## Models Available

|  | Style Number | Base MSRP | Change from LY | Shipping Wt. (lbs.) | Production | Change from LY |
|---|---|---|---|---|---|---|
| 330 2-Door Sedan | 411 | $2,264 | +0.85% | 3115 | 76,400 | 19.19% |
| 330 4-Door Sedan | 413 | $2,317 | +0.70% | 3145 | * | * |
| 330 4-Dr., 2-S. Wagon | 456 | $2,654 | +0.23% | 3400 | * | * |
| 330 4-Dr., 3-S. Wagon | 457 | $2,755 | +0.22% | 3475 | * | * |
| 440 2-Door Sedan | 421 | $2,401 | +0.84% | 3110 | * | * |
| 440 2-Door Hardtop | 422 | $2,483 | +0.53% | 3120 | 58,700 | 32.51% |
| 440 4-Door Sedan | 423 | $2,454 | +0.66% | 3145 | * | * |
| 440 4-Door, 2-S. Wagon | 666 | $2,861 | +0.25% | 3585 | 30,300 | 16.09% |
| 440 4-Door, 3-S. Wagon | 667 | $2,962 | +0.20% | 3640 | * | * |
| TOTALS | *Avg. price* | $2,572 | +2.84% | *Production* | 165,400 | +22.97% |

*Production is estimated and not available by trim level.*

# Polara

*"Luxury priced so low!"*

**Nameplate year of origin:** 1959.
**Current bodystyle lifespan:** 1962 through 1965.
**Predecessor to this model:** Dart Phoenix (1960 to 1961).
**Replacement for this model:** Polara (1965 to 1966).
**Percentage of division's sales volume:** 14.19%.
**Corporate siblings:** Dodge 330/440 and Plymouth Savoy/Belvedere/Fury.
**Primary competition:** AMC Ambassador, Chevrolet BelAir/Impala, and Ford Galaxie.
**Notable changes:** Completely restyled front and rear end.
**Major standard equipment:** All-vinyl (Hardtops and Convertible) or Cloth-and-vinyl (Sedan) bench seat with foam front cushion, deep-pile carpeting, electric windshield wipers, dual sun visors, exterior bright trim around all glass and body sides, and 7.00 × 14 BSW tires.

## Measurements

| | |
|---|---|
| Wheelbase | 119.0" |
| Length | 209.8" |
| Width | 75.0" |
| Legroom — front | 55.1" |
| Height | 41.9" |
| Legroom — rear | 36.5" |
| Headroom — front | 39.2" |
| Headroom — rear | 39.2" |
| Cargo capacity (cu. ft.) | NA |
| Fuel capacity (gals.) | 19.0 |

## Models Available

| | Style Number | Base MSRP | Change from LY | Shipping Wt. (lbs.) | Production | Change from LY |
|---|---|---|---|---|---|---|
| Polara 2-Door Hardtop | 432 | $2,637 | +0.50% | 3135 | 64,900 | +37.79% |
| Polara 2-Door Convertible | 635 | $2,994 | +1.05% | 3435 | * | * |
| Polara 4-Door Sedan | 433 | $2,615 | +0.50% | 3170 | * | * |
| Polara 4-Door Hardtop | 634 | $2,794 | +0.47% | 3395 | * | * |
| TOTALS | Avg. price | $2,760 | -3.33%* | Production | 64,900 | +37.79%* |

*Production is estimated and not available by trim level. Comparison totals include 1962 Polara 500 series.*

# 880

*"Simply said: The 1964 Dodge 880 is the most elegant automobile ever fashioned by Dodge."*

**Nameplate year of origin:** 1962.

**Current bodystyle lifespan:** 1962 through 1964.

**Predecessor to this model:** DeSoto (1960 to 1961).

**Replacement for this model:** Custom 880 (1965) and Monaco (1965 to 1966).

**Percentage of division's sales volume:** 6.95%.

**Corporate siblings:** Chrysler Newport, New Yorker, 300-K and 300.

**Primary competition:** Buick LeSabre, Mercury Montclair, Olds 88, and Pontiac Star Chief.

**Notable changes:** Revised rear styling, and minor trim and detail changes.

**Major standard equipment:** Cloth and vinyl upholstery, full carpeting, glove box lock, dual sunvisors, dome lamp, front and rear armrests, rear tinted window, electric windshield wipers and 8.00 × 14 BSW tires. Custom adds: Vinyl or vinyl and nylon upholstery (depending on model), additional bright metal exterior and interior trim, and full horn ring.

## Measurements

| | Cars | Wagons |
|---|---|---|
| Wheelbase | 122.0" | 122.0" |
| Length | 214.8" | 216.3" |
| Width | 79.0" | 80.0" |
| Height | 55.2" | 55.8" |
| Legroom — front | 41.9" | 41.9" |
| Legroom — rear | 39.3" | 39.1" |
| Headroom — front | 38.0" | 38.0" |
| Headroom — rear | 37.9" | 38.0" |
| Cargo capacity (cu. ft.) | NA | 91.9 |
| Fuel capacity (gals.) | 23 | 22 |

## Models Available

| | Style Number | Base MSRP | Change from LY | Shipping Wt. (lbs.) | Production | Change from LY |
|---|---|---|---|---|---|---|
| 880 4-Door Sedan | 513 | $2,826 | +0.46% | 3795 | 7,500 | +4.17% |
| 880 4-Door, 2-Seat Wagon | 556 | $3,155 | +0.41% | 4165 | * | * |
| 880 4-Door, 3-Seat Wagon | 557 | $3,270 | +0.40% | 4185 | * | * |
| Custom 880 2-Door Hardtop | 522 | $3,043 | +0.43% | 3765 | 17,800 | +15.58% |
| Custom 880 2-Door Convertible | 525 | $3,264 | +0.40% | 3850 | * | * |
| Custom 880 4-Door Sedan | 523 | $2,977 | +0.44% | 3825 | * | * |
| Custom 880 4-Door Hardtop | 524 | $3,122 | +0.42% | 3860 | * | * |
| Custom 880 4-Dr., 2-S. HT Wgn. | 568 | $3,305 | +0.39% | 4155 | 6,500 | +16.07% |
| Custom 880 4-Dr., 3-S. HT Wgn. | 569 | $3,420 | +0.38% | 4185 | * | * |
| TOTALS | Avg. price | $3,154 | +0.41% | Production | 31,800 | +12.77% |

*Production is estimated and not available by trim level.*

# FORD

*"The TOTAL PERFORMANCE Cars for 1964."*

For the eighth year running, the full-size Fords were a totally new looking car. But it was not just the full-size models that were new. The Falcon, Fairlane and Thunderbird were all given major restyles, and to top it all off at mid-year the sensational new Mustang would hit the dealers' showrooms. All of this excitement led *Motor Trend* magazine to award the entire Ford line its Car of the Year award. Here's a run-down on the entire line from the bottom up. The Falcon received its first restyling since introduction. The new, more angular and modern looking themes brought the Falcon up to a styling par with the Rambler American and put it ahead of the Chevy II and Valiant. The larger Fairlane's 200 CID 6-cylinder was now offered in the Falcon also. The Sprint package was now a regular model offering, and the 2-Door Station Wagons were dropped in the restyling.

At the World's Fair in New York, on April 17, 1964, Ford created a major sensation with the introduction of the sporty Mustang. The Mustang offered something the up and coming muscle cars couldn't. A relatively simple, straightforward car, easy to drive and easy to work on, it was very stylish, available with just about any option the customer wanted to put on the car, and most importantly very affordable. The Mustang was based upon the Falcon, which helped to keep costs down and provided for the car's simplicity. Powerplants were picked from those already in the Ford line, and initially included the 170 CID 6-cylinder and the 260 CID V8. Initial model offerings included the 2-Door Hardtop and Convertible in base models only. A Mustang 2-Door Convertible was picked to be the Official

Pace Car for the 1964 Indianapolis 500 race. For purposes of comparison, the early "1964½" Mustang models are listed here with the 1964 models, because Ford kept production and sales records in this manner.

The restyled Fairlane shed its small tail fins and gained a sportier flair in its bodyside styling with a fake louvered vent. Cruise-O-Matic was now available for the mid-sized Ford. The only model change was the discontinuance of the Squire "wood-grained" Station Wagon model.

As mentioned previously, the full-size Ford line was given a major overhaul once again. The styling was typical Ford, with more rounded lines as compared to the 1963 models. All hardtop models gained a semi-fastback roofline appearance. Emphasis was placed on quality and ride, giving Ford a slight edge on its competition. To keep up in the horsepower race, a new 427 CID V8 engine was introduced. As with other companies, the engine was developed on the race track before being offered to the public. Changes to the model line included renaming the 300 and Galaxie base models to Custom and Custom 500. Also, the Galaxie 500 and 500 XL lines dropped their regular 2-Door Hardtop models in favor of the new fastback styling.

Finally, the Thunderbird was restyled and given sharper lines that brought it more into line with other Ford models, while still retaining a Thunderbird identity. One departure from past T-Birds was the switch from round taillights to a rectangular shape separated by a backup light in the center. The Sports Roadster model was officially dropped, although the Tonneau cover was listed as an option at $269.

Falcon Futura 2-Door Hardtop

Fairlane 4-Door Custom Ranch Wagon

Fairlane 500 2-Door Sport Coupe Interior

Galaxie 500 4-Door Hardtop

Galaxie 500 XL 2-Door Hardtop

Mustang 2-Door Hardtop (1965 model shown)

Thunderbird 2-Door Hardtop

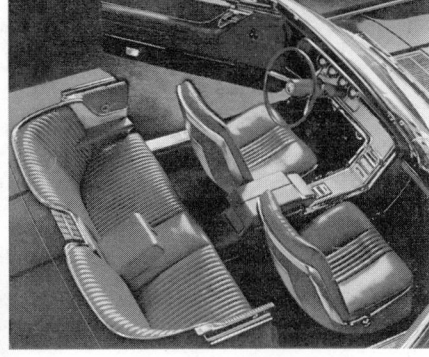

Thunderbird Interior

Full-line, *Motor Trend* Car of the Year

Mustang 2-Door Convertible,
Indianapolis 500 Pace Car

**1964**

**Model year production:** 1,641,417, up 3.95% over 1963.
**Domestic market share:** 21.05% (2nd place).
**Base price range:** $1,996 to $4,953.
**Industry average base price:** $3,024.
**Ford average base price:** $2,703.
**Introduction date:** September 27, 1963; Mustang introduced April 17, 1964.
**Assembly plants:** Atlanta, GA (A); Chicago, IL (G); Dallas, TX (D); Dearborn, MI (F); Kansas City, MO (K); Lorain, OH (H); Los Angeles, CA (J); Louisville, KY (U); Mah-wah, NJ (E); Metuchen, NJ (T); Norfolk, VA (N); San Jose, CA (R); Twin Cities, MN (P); Wayne, MI (W); Wixom, MI (Y); Oakville, Ontario, Can. (B).
**Data plate identification:** Eleven digit code read as follows: 4 for 1964; 2nd digit is assembly plant code; 2-digit model number (see listings below); 5th digit is engine code; 100001 and up for serial number. *Example:* 4Y83Z100001 is a 1964 Ford Thunderbird 2-Door Hardtop with a 390 CID V8 engine, serial number 100001, built in Wixom, MI.

## Powertrains

| Engine | Gross HP | Engine Code | Transmission Availability | Falcon | Mustang | Fairlane | Full-size | T-Bird |
|---|---|---|---|---|---|---|---|---|
| 144 CID, 1-bbl., 6-cyl. | 85 | S | 3-speed manual | S | - | - | - | - |
| | | | Ford-O-Matic | $177 | - | - | - | - |
| 170 CID, 1-bbl., 6-cyl. | 1011 | U | 3-speed manual | $17 | S | S | - | - |
| | | | 4-speed manual | - | $116 | - | - | - |
| | | | Ford-O-Matic | $194 | - | $189 | - | - |
| | | | Cruise-O-Matic | - | $180 | $189 | - | - |

| Engine | Gross HP | Engine Code | Transmission Availability | Falcon | Mustang | Fairlane | Full-size | T-Bird |
|---|---|---|---|---|---|---|---|---|
| 200 CID**, 1-bbl., 6-cyl. | 120 | T | 3-speed manual | - | S** | - | - | - |
| | | | 4-speed manual | - | $116** | - | | - |
| | | | Cruise-O-Matic | - | $180** | - | - | - |
| 223 CID Big Six, 1-bbl., 6-cyl. | 138 | E | 3-speed manual | - | - | - | S (except XL) | - |
| | | | Overdrive | - | - | - | $108 (except XL) | - |
| | | | Cruise-O-Matic | - | - | - | $189 (except XL) | - |
| 260 CID, 2-bbl., V8 | 164 | F | 3-speed manual | $170 | $75 | $100 | | - |
| | | | Overdrive | $278 | - | $208 | - | - |
| | | | 4-speed man.* | $358 | $251 | $288 | - | - |
| | | | Ford-O-Matic | $347 | - | $289 | - | - |
| | | | Cruise-O-Matic | - | $265 | $289 | - | - |
| 289 CID Challenger, 2-bbl., V8 | 195 | C | 3-speed manual | - | $108 | $145 | NA (XL)/$109 (others) | - |
| | | | Overdrive | - | - | $253 | NA (XL)/$217 (others) | - |
| | | | 4-speed manual* | - | $284 | $333 | –$11 (XL)/$297 (others) | - |
| | | | Cruise-O-Matic | - | $298 | $334 | S (XL)/$288 (others) | - |
| 289 CID Challenger Special, 4-bbl., V8 | 220 | D | 3-speed manual | - | $162 | - | - | - |
| | | | 4-speed man.* | - | $338 | - | - | - |
| | | | Cruise-O-Matic | - | $352 | - | - | - |
| 289 CID Challenger High-Perf., 4-bbl., V8 | 271 | K | 4-speed manual* | - | $619 | - | - | - |
| | | | Cruise-O-Matic | - | $633 | - | - | - |
| 352 CID Interceptor, 4-bbl., V8 | 250 | X | 3-speed manual | - | - | - | NA (XL)/$180 (others) | - |
| | | | Cruise-O-Matic | - | - | - | $94 (XL)/$392 (others) | - |
| 390 CID Thunderbird, 4-bbl., V8 | 300 | Z | 3-speed manual | - | - | - | NA (XL)/$247 (others) | - |
| | | | 4-speed manual* | - | - | - | $117 (XL)/$435 (others) | - |
| | | | Cruise-O-Matic | - | - | - | $161 (XL)/$439(others) | S |
| 427 CID Thunderbird High-Perf., Dual 4-bbl., V8*** | 410 | Q | 4-speed manual* | - | - | - | $384 (XL)/$593 | $406 |
| 427 CID T-Bird Super High-Perf., Dual 4-bbl., V8*** | 425 | R | 4-speed manual* | - | - | - | $440 (XL)/$649 | $462 |

*4-speed manual shift not available on wagon models.    **Offered late in the year for Mustang only.    ***Limited availability.

## Major Options

| | Falcon | Mustang | Fairlane | Full-size | Thunderbird |
|---|---|---|---|---|---|
| Air conditioning | - | $283 | $283 | $364 | $415 |
| Tinted glass | - | $31 | $40 | $40 | $43 |
| Power steering | - | $86 | $86 | $86 | S |
| Power brakes | - | $43 | $43 | $43 | S |
| Power driver's seat/bench seat | - | - | - | - | $184 |
| Power windows | - | - | - | $102 | $106 |
| AM radio | $58 | $59 | $58 | $58 | S |
| AM/FM radio | - | - | - | $142 | $83 |
| Swing-Away steering wheel | - | - | - | - | S |
| Vinyl roof (only on select models) | - | $76 | $75 | $75 | $ |
| White sidewall tires | $30 | $30 | $33 | $33 | $44 |
| Deluxe wheel covers | - | $18 | $18 | $45 | $16 |

Options common to most models. (- = Not Available, S = Standard equipment.) Items may be standard equipment, optional at different pricing, or unavailable on certain models. This chart is only a guide.

## Paint Colors

| | Code | Thunderbird | Other models |
|---|---|---|---|
| Black | A | X | X |
| Pagoda Green | B | X | X |
| Gunmetal Gray Metallic | C | X | |
| Dynasty Green Metallic | D | | X |
| Silver Blue Metallic | E | X | |
| Powder Blue | F | X | |
| Guardsman Blue Metallic | F | | X |
| Prairie Tan | G | X | X |
| Caspian Blue Metallic | H | X | X |
| Champagne Beige Met. | I | | X |
| Rangoon Red | J | X | X |
| Silver Smoke Gray Metallic | K | | X |
| Wimbledon White | M | X | X |
| Diamond Blue | N | X | |
| Tropical Turquoise | O | | |
| Prairie Bronze Metallic | P | X | X |
| Huron Blue Metallic | Q | X | |
| Phoenician Yellow/Encino | R | X | X |
| Cascade Green Metallic | S | X | X |
| Navajo Beige | T | X | X |
| Regal Turquoise Metallic | U | X | |
| Sunlight Yellow | V | X | X |
| Rose Beige Metallic | W | X | |
| Vintage Burgundy Metallic | X | X | X |
| Skylight Blue | Y | | X |
| Chantilly Beige Metallic | Z | X | X |
| Poppy Red | 3 | | X |

# Falcon

*"Falcon's kept its famous economy, but everything else is changed."*

**Nameplate year of origin:** 1960.
**Current bodystyle lifespan:** 1964 through 1965.
**Predecessor to this model:** Falcon (1960 to 1963).
**Replacement for this model:** Falcon (1966 to 1970).
**Corporate siblings:** Mercury Comet.
**Percentage of division's sales volume:** 14.05%.
**Primary competition:** Rambler American, Chevrolet Chevy II, Plymouth Valiant, and Studebaker Lark.
**Notable changes:** Completely restyled.
**Major standard equipment:** Cloth and vinyl interior trim, front-door armrests, dual horns, chrome windshield and rear window moldings, small hubcaps, and 6.00 × 13 BSW tires (6.50 × 13 on Wagons). Futura adds: Deluxe interior trim, side window moldings, hood ornament, full-length side trim molding, and full-wheel covers. Futura models 11 and 12 add: Bucket seats and deluxe interior trim. Squire adds: Wood-grain exterior trim, power tailgate window and carpeted floors. Sprint adds: Bucket seats, console, sports steering wheel, tachometer and wire wheel covers.

## Measurements

| | Cars | Wagons |
|---|---|---|
| Wheelbase | 109.5" | 109.5" |
| Length | 181.6" | 190.0" |
| Width | 71.6" | 71.0" |
| Height | 54.5" | 54.9" |
| Legroom — front | 41.5" | 41.5" |
| Legroom — rear | 34.7" | 34.4" |
| Headroom — front | 38.9" | 38.9" |
| Headroom — rear | 36.9" | 37.7" |
| Cargo capacity (cu. ft.) | NA | 78.5 |
| Fuel capacity (gals.) | 14.0 | 14.0 |

## Models Available

| | Style Number | Base MSRP | Change from LY | Shipping Wt. (lbs.) | Production | Change from LY |
|---|---|---|---|---|---|---|
| Falcon 2-Door Sedan | 01 | $1,996 | +0.55% | 2365 | 36,441 | -48.41% |
| Falcon 4-Door Sedan | 02 | $2,058 | +0.54% | 2400 | 28,411 | -54.44% |
| Falcon 2-Door Wagon | 21 | $2,326 | +1.22% | 2660 | 6,034 | -17.59% |
| Falcon 4-Door Wagon | 22 | $2,360 | +0.81% | 2695 | 1,779 | -90.38% |
| Falcon Futura 2-Door Sedan | 19 | $2,127 | +0.52% | 2375 | 16,883 | -37.51% |
| Falcon Futura 2-Door Hardtop | 17 | $2,209 | +0.50% | 2515 | 32,608 | -16.34% |
| Falcon Futura 2-Door HT w/Buckets | 11 | $2,325 | NEW | 2545 | 8,607 | NEW |
| Falcon Futura 2-Door Convertible | 15 | $2,481 | +0.45% | 2710 | 13,220 | -63.07% |
| F. Futura 2-Door Conv. w/Buckets | 12 | $2,597 | NEW | 2735 | 2,980 | NEW |
| Falcon Futura 4-Door Sedan | 16 | $2,176 | +0.51% | 2410 | 38,032 | +19.84% |
| Falcon Deluxe 4-Door Wagon | 24 | $2,446 | +0.78% | 2715 | 20,697 | -11.84% |
| Falcon Squire 4-Door Wagon | 26 | $2,622 | +0.73% | 2720 | 6,766 | -18.18% |
| Falcon Sprint 2-Door Hardtop | 13 | $2,436 | NEW | 2813 | 13,830 | NEW |
| Falcon Sprint 2-Door Convertible | 14 | $2,671 | NEW | 3008 | 4,278 | NEW |
| TOTALS | Avg. price | $2,345 | +3.03% | Production | 230,566 | -29.78% |

# Mustang

*"New addition to the Total Performance Ford line."*

**Nameplate year of origin:** 1964½ (also on a 1963 show car).
**Current bodystyle lifespan:** 1964½ through 1968.
**Predecessor to this model:** None.
**Replacement for this model:** Mustang (1969 to 1970).
**Corporate siblings:** None.
**Percentage of division's sales volume:** 5.48%.
**Primary competition:** Chevrolet Corvair and Plymouth Barracuda.
**Notable changes:** All-new as a 1964½ model.
**Major standard equipment:** Bucket front seats with vinyl upholstery, dual sun visors, seat belts, padded instrument panel, courtesy lights, full carpeting, sports steering wheel, chrome window moldings, heater and defroster, self-adjusting front brakes, alternator, and 6.50 × 13 BSW tires (6.95 × 14 with V8 engine).

## Measurements

| | |
|---|---|
| Wheelbase | 108.0" |
| Length | 181.6" |
| Width | 68.5" |
| Height | 51.1" |
| Legroom — front | 41.8" |
| Legroom — rear | 28.8" |
| Headroom — front | 29.2" |
| Headroom — rear | NA |
| Cargo capacity (cu. ft.) | 9.0 (Cvt. 7.7) |
| Fuel capacity (gals.) | 16.0 |

## Models Available

| | Style Number | Base MSRP | Change from LY | Shipping Wt. (lbs.) | Production | Change from LY |
|---|---|---|---|---|---|---|
| Mustang 2-Door Hardtop | 07 | $2,372 | NEW | 2436 | 97,705 | NEW |
| Mustang 2-Door Convertible | 08 | $2,614 | NEW | 2621 | 28,833 | NEW |
| TOTALS | Avg. price | $2,493 | NEW | Production | 126,538 | NEW |

# Fairlane

*"A combination of family-size room and sports-car feel that will change your mind about how much you can get at so low a price."*

**Nameplate year of origin:** 1955.
**Current bodystyle lifespan:** 1962 through 1965.
**Predecessor to this model:** None.
**Replacement for this model:** Fairlane (1966 to 1967).
**Corporate siblings:** None.
**Percentage of division's sales volume:** 16.36%.
**Primary competition:** Rambler Classic, Chevrolet Chevelle, Dodge Dart, and Pontiac Tempest.
**Notable changes:** New styling for all sheet metal, based on same body shell as before.
**Major standard equipment:** Cloth and vinyl bench seat, rubber floor mats, front and rear armrests, chrome windshield and rear window moldings, and 6.50 × 13 BSW tires (7.00 × 14 BSW on Wagons). 500 adds: Full carpeting, deluxe interior trim, chrome side window moldings, full-length side trim and Ford crests on C pillar and rear panel.

## Measurements

|  | Cars | Wagons |
|---|---|---|
| Wheelbase | 115.5" | 115.5" |
| Length | 197.6" | 197.0" |
| Width | 72.2" | 72.2" |
| Height | 55.4" | 55.9" |
| Legroom — front | 42.1" | 42.1" |
| Legroom — rear | 36.9" | 36.6" |
| Headroom — front | 38.7" | 38.7" |
| Headroom — rear | 37.9" | 38.0" |
| Cargo capacity (cu. ft.) | 15.0 | 98.6 |
| Fuel capacity (gals.) | 16.0 | 16.0 |

**1964**

## Models Available

|  | Style Number | Base MSRP | Change from LY | Shipping Wt. (lbs.) | Production | Change from LY |
|---|---|---|---|---|---|---|
| Fairlane 2-Door Sedan | 31 | $2,194 | +1.86% | 2788 | 20,421 | -29.54% |
| Fairlane 4-Door Sedan | 32 | $2,235 | +0.86% | 2828 | 36,693 | -17.46% |
| Fairlane 4-Door Ranch Wagon | 38 | $2,531 | +0.24% | 3223 | 20,980 | -12.61% |
| Fairlane 500 2-Door Sedan | 41 | $2,276 | +1.52% | 2813 | 23,477 | -32.47% |
| Fairlane 500 2-Door Hardtop | 43 | $2,341 | +0.73% | 2858 | 42,733 | +2.62% |
| Fairlane 500 2-Door Sport Hardtop | 47 | $2,502 | -0.08% | 2878 | 12,431 | -56.02% |
| Fairlane 500 4-Door Sedan | 42 | $2,317 | +0.56% | 2843 | 86,919 | -15.76% |
| Fairlane 4-Door Custom Ranch Wgn. | 48 | $2,612 | -0.04% | 3243 | 24,962 | -15.70% |
| TOTALS | Avg. price | $2,376 | -1.29% | Production | 268,616 | -21.67% |

# Custom & Galaxie

*"The '64 Super Torque Fords ... measurably stronger, steadier, smoother than any other cars in their class."*

**Nameplate year of origin:** 1957 (Custom) and 1959 (Galaxie).
**Current bodystyle lifespan:** 1963 through 1964.
**Predecessor to this model:** Fairlane and Galaxie (1961 to 1962).
**Replacement for this model:** Custom, Galaxie and LTD (1965 to 1966).
**Corporate siblings:** Mercury Monterey, Montclair and Park Lane.
**Percentage of division's sales volume:** 56.25%.
**Primary competition:** Chevrolet Biscayne/BelAir/Impala, Dodge 330/440/Polara, and Plymouth Savoy/Belvedere/Fury.
**Notable changes:** Completely restyled, yet still based on 1963 chassis.
**Major standard equipment:** Rubber mats, dual sunvisors, armrests on all doors, rear window trim molding, and 7.50 × 14 BSW tires. Custom 500 adds: Nylon carpeting, windshield molding, short exterior trim side molding and 8.00 × 14 BSW tires on wagons. Galaxie 500 adds: Two-

## Measurements

|  | Cars | Wagons |
|---|---|---|
| Wheelbase | 119.0" | 119.0" |
| Length | 209.8" | 209.8" |
| Width | 80.0" | 80.0" |
| Height | 56.5" | 56.8" |
| Legroom — front | 41.9" | 41.9" |
| Legroom — rear | 36.7" | 36.7" |
| Headroom — front | 39.1" | 39.1" |
| Headroom — rear | 38.4" | 38.4" |
| Cargo capacity (cu. ft.) | 28.9 | 99.2 |
| Fuel capacity (gals.) | 20.0 | 20.0 |

tone interior trim, chrome hood ornament, chrome side window trim, and backup lights. XL adds: Bucket seats with floor-mounted transmission selector, lower door carpet trim and polished trim, courtesy and reading lamps, and special badging. Squire wagon adds: Wood-grain exterior trim.

## Models Available

| | Style Number | Base MSRP | Change from LY | Shipping Wt. (lbs.) | Production | Change from LY |
|---|---|---|---|---|---|---|
| Custom 2-Door Sedan | 53 | $2,361 | +1.59% | 3531 | 41,359 | +59.01% |
| Custom 4-Door Sedan | 54 | $2,415 | +1.56% | 3621 | 57,964 | +31.31% |
| Custom 500 2-Door Sedan | 51 | $2,464 | +0.45% | 3561 | 20,619 | -32.03% |
| Custom 500 4-Door Sedan | 52 | $2,518 | +0.44% | 3661 | 68,828 | -16.49% |
| Galaxie 500 2-Door Sedan | 61 | $2,624 | +0.42% | 3576 | 13,041 | -38.30% |
| Galaxie 500 2-Door Hardtop | 66 | $2,685 | +0.41% | 3586 | 206,998 | +316.22% |
| Galaxie 500 2-Door Sunliner Conv. | 65 | $2,947 | +0.79% | 3761 | 37,311 | +1.18% |
| Galaxie 500 4-Door Sedan | 62 | $2,678 | +0.41% | 3676 | 198,805 | -3.36% |
| Galaxie 500 4-Door Hardtop | 64 | $2,750 | +0.40% | 3691 | 49,242 | +85.41% |
| Galaxie 500 XL 2-Door Hardtop | 68 | $3,233 | -1.07% | 3622 | 58,306 | +96.23% |
| Galaxie 500 XL 2-Door Convertible | 69 | $3,495 | -0.65% | 3787 | 15,169 | -18.23% |
| Galaxie 500 XL 4-Door Hardtop | 60 | $3,298 | -1.05% | 3722 | 14,661 | +16.39% |
| Country Sedan 4-Dr., 6-pass. Wgn. | 72 | $2,840 | +0.39% | 3975 | 68,578 | +5.58% |
| Country Sedan 4-Door, 9-pass. Wgn. | 74 | $2,944 | +0.38% | 3985 | 25,661 | +15.33% |
| Country Squire 4-Dr., 6-pass. Wgn. | 76 | $3,029 | +0.36% | 3990 | 23,570 | +18.31% |
| Country Squire 4-Dr., 9-pass. Wgn. | 78 | $3,099 | +0.36% | 4000 | 23,120 | +20.13% |
| TOTALS | | Avg. price $2,836 | -0.32% | | Production 923,232 | +9.32% |

# Thunderbird

*"The look is new — yet so typically Thunderbird. Unique in all the world."*

**Nameplate year of origin:** 1955.
**Current bodystyle lifespan:** 1964 through 1966.
**Predecessor to this model:** Thunderbird (1961 to 1963).
**Replacement for this model:** Thunderbird (1967 to 1971).
**Corporate siblings:** None.
**Percentage of division's sales volume:** 5.63%.
**Primary competition:** Buick Riviera, Oldsmobile Starfire, Chrysler 300, and Studebaker Avanti.
**Notable changes:** Completely restyled, yet still based on 1961–1963 chassis.
**Major standard equipment:** Bucket seats, full carpeting, heater and defroster, seat belts, full instrumentation, Swing-Away steering wheel, AM radio, reversible entry keys, sequential turn signals, power steering, power brakes, and 8.15 × 15 BSW tires. Convertible adds: Unique trunk-stored power convertible top. Landau adds: Special interior and vinyl top.

## Measurements

| | |
|---|---|
| Wheelbase | 113.2" |
| Length | 205.4" |
| Width | 77.1" |
| Height | 52.6" |
| Legroom — front | 39.7" |
| Legroom — rear | 33.2" |
| Headroom — front | 37.4" |
| Headroom — rear | 37.5" |
| Cargo capacity (cu. ft.) | 24.5 |
| Fuel capacity (gals.) | 22.0 |

## Models Available

| | Style Number | Base MSRP | Change from LY | Shipping Wt. (lbs.) | Production | Change from LY |
|---|---|---|---|---|---|---|
| Thunderbird 2-Door Hardtop | 83 | $4,486 | +0.92% | 4431 | 60,552 | +41.46% |
| Thunderbird 2-Door Landau HT | 87 | $4,589 | +0.90% | 4441 | 22,715 | +60.65% |
| Thunderbird 2-Door Convertible | 85 | $4,953 | +0.83% | 4586 | 9,198 | +55.56% |
| TOTALS | | Avg. price $4,676 | -3.92% | | Production 92,465 | +46.04% |

# IMPERIAL

*"The Incomparable Imperial for 1964."*

Sales for the Imperial finally improved thanks to a total restyling. The new design was done by a former Ford stylist who had worked on the 1961 Thunderbird and Lincoln Continental, and the influence is easily recognized. The 1964 Imperial, while retaining certain Imperial characteristics like a divided grille, had slab-sided body panels, and a very formal trunk and roofline that were very much of Lincoln influence. All Imperial models were still based upon the same basic platform introduced in 1960, with some major changes. The similarities are most evident in the roof and glass areas. Power continued to come from the Chrysler 413 CID V8 engine. The price-leader Custom Imperial line was dropped, as sales had steadily declined to only 4,000 per year. All other models continued as in previous years. Once again the Crown Imperial Limousine Sedan model was available as a custom-built model. These are not detailed herein as their production usually totalled ten or fewer per season, and they are considered custom-built by Chrysler.

Crown 2-Door Convertible

LeBaron Interior

**Model year production:** 23,285, up 65.05% over 1963.
**Domestic market share:** 0.30% (14th place).
**Base price range:** $5,581 to $6,455.
**Industry average base price:** $3,024.
**Imperial average base price:** $5,945.
**Introduction date:** September 25, 1963.
**Assembly plants:** Detroit, MI (3).

**Data plate identification:** Ten digit code read as follows: 1st digit 9 = Imperial; 2nd number identifies series (e.g., 2 is for Crown); 4 for 1964; 4th digit is assembly plant code; 100001 and up for serial number. Body style numbers found on body plate. *Example:* 9243100001 is a 1964 Imperial Crown, serial number 100001, built in Detroit, MI.

## Powertrains

| Engine | Gross HP | Transmission Availability | Imperial |
|---|---|---|---|
| 413 CID, 4-bbl., V8 | 340 | Torqueflite Automatic | S |

## Major Options

| | Crown | LeBaron |
|---|---|---|
| Air conditioning | $462 | $462 |
| Auto Pilot automatic speed control | $97 | $97 |
| Tinted glass | $54 | $54 |

## Paint Colors

| | Code |
|---|---|
| Silver Mist Metallic | 22-1 |
| Formal Black | BB-1 |
| Wedgewood | CC-1 |

| | Crown | LeBaron | | | Code |
|---|---|---|---|---|---|
| Rear window defogger | $21 | $21 | | Nassau Blue Metallic | DD-1 |
| Deck lid remote release | $29 | $29 | | Monarch Blue Metallic | EE-1 |
| Power steering — variable-ratio | S | S | | Pine Mist Metallic | FF-1 |
| Power brakes | S | S | | Sequoia Green Metallic | GG-1 |
| Power door locks | $47 (2-Dr)/$72 (4-Dr) | $72 | | Silver Turquoise Metallic | KK-1 |
| Power driver's seat/bench seat | $125 | S | | Royal Turquoise Metallic | LL-1 |
| Power windows | S | S | | Madison Gray Metallic | MM-1 |
| AM radio w/power antenna | $169 | $169 | | Charcoal Gray Metallic | NN-1 |
| AM/FM radio w/power antenna | $196 | $196 | | Rosewood Metallic | OO-1 |
| Adjustable steering wheel | $51 | $51 | | Royal Ruby Metallic | RR-1 |
| Vinyl roof | $91–$111 | $111 | | Ivory | SS-1 |
| Whitewall tires — standard size | $55 | S | | Roman Red Metallic | TT-1 |
| | | | | Embassy Gold metallic | UU-1 |
| | | | | Persian White | WW-1 |
| | | | | Dune Beige | XX-1 |
| | | | | Sable Tan Metallic | YY-1 |

Options common to most models. (S = Standard equipment.) Items may be standard equipment, optional at different pricing, or unavailable on certain models. This chart is only a guide.

# Crown

*"This is the new look of Imperial. Beautifully proportioned. Quietly elegant."*

**Nameplate year of origin:** 1957 (Not the same as Crown Imperial series).
**Current bodystyle lifespan:** 1964 through 1966.
**Predecessor to this model:** Crown (1960 to 1963).
**Replacement for this model:** Crown (1967 to 1968).
**Percentage of division's sales volume:** 87.34%.
**Corporate siblings:** LeBaron.
**Primary competition:** Cadillac Sixty-Two and Lincoln Continental.
**Notable changes:** Completely restyled.
**Major standard equipment:** Torqueflite automatic transmission, power steering, power brakes, front and rear armrests (hardtops), pile carpeting, remote-control left-hand outside mirror, power windows, electric clock, trip odometer, 3-speed electric windshield wipers with washers, wheel covers and 8.20 × 15 BSW tires.

## Measurements

| | |
|---|---|
| Wheelbase | 129.0" |
| Length | 227.8" |
| Width | 80.0" |
| Height | 56.8" |
| Legroom — front | 41.5" |
| Legroom — rear | 41.5" |
| Headroom — front | 39.3" |
| Headroom — rear | 38.7" |
| Cargo capacity (cu. ft.) | NA |
| Fuel capacity (gals.) | 23.0 |

## Models Available

| | Style Number | Base MSRP | Change from LY | Shipping Wt. (lbs.) | Production | Change from LY |
|---|---|---|---|---|---|---|
| Crown 2-Door Hardtop | 922 | $5,739 | +6.04% | 4950 | 5,233 | +390.44% |
| Crown 2-Door Convertible | 925 | $6,003 | +3.82% | 5185 | 922 | +73.63% |
| Crown 4-Door Hardtop | 924 | $5,581 | -1.33% | 4970 | 14,181 | +103.75% |
| TOTALS | | Avg. price $5,774 | +2.80% | | Production 20,336 | +137.63% |

# LeBaron

*"This is the ultimate in America's largest ... finest ...
quietest ... and most distinguished luxury car."*

**Nameplate year of origin:** 1924 (as Chrysler Sedan model designation); 1926 (as series).
**Current bodystyle lifespan:** 1964 through 1966.
**Predecessor to this model:** LeBaron (1960 to 1963).
**Replacement for this model:** LeBaron (1967 to 1968).
**Percentage of division's sales volume:** 12.66%.
**Corporate siblings:** Crown.
**Primary competition:** Cadillac de Ville and Lincoln Continental.
**Notable changes:** Completely restyled.
**Major standard equipment:** Torqueflite automatic transmission, power steering, power brakes, pile carpeting, 6-way power seat, power windows and vent windows, electric clock, trip odometer, 3-speed electric windshield wipers with washers, wheel covers and 8.20 × 15 WSW tires.

## Measurements

| | |
|---|---|
| Wheelbase | 129.0" |
| Length | 227.8" |
| Width | 80.0" |
| Height | 56.8" |
| Legroom — front | 41.5" |
| Legroom — rear | 41.5" |
| Headroom — front | 39.3" |
| Headroom — rear | 38.7" |
| Cargo capacity (cu. ft.) | NA |
| Fuel capacity (gals.) | 23.0 |

**1964**

## Models Available

| | Style Number | Base MSRP | Change from LY | Shipping Wt. (lbs.) | Production | Change from LY |
|---|---|---|---|---|---|---|
| LeBaron 4-Door Hardtop | 934 | $6,455 | +0.33% | 5005 | 2,949 | +91.87% |
| TOTALS | *Avg. price* | $6,455 | +0.33% | *Production* | 2,949 | +91.87% |

# LINCOLN

*"Discover the significant changes in the
timeless Lincoln Continental for 1964."*

The 1964 Lincoln looked the same as its predecessors, but in fact it was vastly improved. The main improvement was to lengthen the wheelbase by three inches, which greatly expanded luggage and interior space and allowed for larger door openings. Ride quality also improved because of the extra length in the wheelbase. Buyers responded well to the greater length and the continuation of the classic styling. Another factor in the Lincoln Continental's continued success was the quality checks performed on each vehicle. As compared to Cadillac, the perception of better quality was worth the extra money to purchase a Lincoln. In reality, quality probably did exceed either Cadillac or Imperial, but Cadillac had a firm grip on the luxury market and had no intentions of letting go of that lead.

Continental 4-Door Sedan

Continental 4-Door Convertible

**Model year production:** 36,297, up 16.21% over 1963.
**Domestic market share:** 0.47% (13th place).
**Base price range:** $6,292 to $6,938.
**Industry average base price:** $3,024.
**Lincoln average base price:** $6,615.
**Introduction date:** September 1963.
**Assembly plants:** Allen Park, MI (S); and Wixom, MI (Y).

**Data plate identification:** Eleven digit code read as follows: 4 for 1964; 2nd digit is assembly plant code; 2-digit model number (see listings below); 5th digit is engine code; 400001 and up for serial number. *Example:* 4Y82H400001 is a 1964 Lincoln Continental 4-Door Sedan with a 430 CID V8 engine, serial number 400001, built in Wixom, MI.

## Powertrains

| Engine | Gross HP | Engine Code | Transmission Availability | Continental |
|---|---|---|---|---|
| 430 CID, 4-bbl., V8 | 320 | H | Turbo Drive Automatic | S |

## Major Options

| | Continental |
|---|---|
| Air conditioning — manual | $505 |
| Automatic headlight dimmers | $46 |
| Tinted glass | $54 |
| 6-way power seat | S |
| AM/FM radio | $85 |
| Leather upholstery | $100 |
| Speed control | $97 |
| Remote control trunk release (sedans) | $53 |

Options common to most models. (S = Standard equipment.) Items may be standard equipment, optional at different pricing, or unavailable on certain models. This chart is only a guide.

## Paint Colors

| | Code |
|---|---|
| Black Satin | A |
| Princeton Gray Metallic | C |
| Silver Mink Metallic | E |
| Arcadian Blue | F |
| Buckskin Tan | G |
| Caspian Blue Metallic | H |
| Rangoon Red | J |
| Wimbledon White | M |
| Platinum Blue | N |
| Silver Green Metallic | O |
| Burnished Bronze Metallic | P |
| Huron Blue Metallic | Q |
| Phoenician Yellow | R |
| Cascade Green Metallic | S |
| Desert Sand | T |
| Patrician Green Metallic | U |
| Rose Beige Metallic | W |
| Vintage Burgundy Metallic | X |
| Silver Sand Metallic | Z |

# Continental

*"New size, new styling, but unmistakably Continental: the classic profile has been lengthened to provide you with greater interior space and comfort."*

**Nameplate year of origin:** 1940 (1961 as a standard sedan nameplate).
**Current bodystyle lifespan:** 1961 through 1969 (major restyles in 1964 and 1966).
**Predecessor to this model:** Premiere (1958 to 1960).
**Replacement for this model:** Continental (1970 to 1979).
**Percentage of division's sales volume:** 100%.
**Corporate siblings:** None.
**Primary competition:** Cadillac de Ville and Imperial Crown/LeBaron.
**Notable changes:** Restyled, lengthened and interior space increased.
**Major standard equipment:** Nylon and leather (sedan) or leather (convertible) front bench seat upholstery w/folding center armrests front & rear, vanity mirror, looped-pile carpeting, power windows, AM transistor radio w/power antenna, power operated door latching system, padded instrument panel, electric windshield wipers w/washers, power steering, power brakes, automatic transmission and 9.15 × 15 WSW tires.

## Measurements

| | |
|---|---|
| Wheelbase | 126.0" |
| Length | 216.3" |
| Width | 78.6" |
| Height | 54.2" |
| Legroom — front | 41.1" |
| Legroom — rear | 40.5" |
| Headroom — front | 39.0" |
| Headroom — rear | 38.4" |
| Luggage capacity (cu. ft.) | 15.5 |
| Fuel capacity (gals.) | 21.0 |

**1964**

## Models Available

| | Style Number | Base MSRP | Change from LY | Shipping Wt. (lbs.) | Production | Change from LY |
|---|---|---|---|---|---|---|
| Continental 4-Door Sedan | 82 | $6,292 | +0.35% | 5055 | 32,969 | +17.35% |
| Continental 4-Door Conv. | 86 | $6,938 | +0.36% | 5393 | 3,328 | +6.05% |
| TOTALS | | *Avg. price* $6,615 | +0.35% | | *Production* 36,297 | +16.21% |

# MERCURY

*"The price is medium ... the choice maximum ... the car is Mercury."*

Mercury's 25th anniversary season was a somewhat happy one. Sales were down slightly—less than 3,000 units, which was not bad considering that the mid-sized Meteor was gone. After several years of floundering about with typical mid-market cars and experimenting with compact cars, Mercury finally hit the right combination for 1964. The slow selling mid-size Meteor line was dropped this season only to have its position more effectively covered by an all-new Comet. The Comet had more angular lines this season and a Lincoln style grille up front, giving it the appearance of an expensive car. Not only was styling more bold, but so was the power under the hood. The first "hot" Comets appeared this year with the appearance of the Caliente and Cyclone models. The Caliente essentially replaced the S-22 of last season as the sports models, but the Cyclone added to that with a standard V8 engine and other performance features, to make it one of the first pseudo-muscle cars on the market. With a 289 CID V8 under the hood, it couldn't yet be called a true muscle car, but that would happen in time. The base Comet and Comet Custom were replaced by the Comet 202 and Comet 404 nameplates.

Following a common family styling theme, the full-size Mercurys gained a Lincoln-style grille this year also. The remainder of the body styling was an update on the nice looking 1963 styling. Two-door and four-door models gained a semi-fastback styling theme this year. Returning after a three year absence were the mid-line Montclair and top-of-the-line Park Lane series.

Powertrains were upgraded this year also. The 289 CID V8, a bored-out version of the 260 CID V8, was one of those engines that offered the right amount of power and size for the price, and was a perfect fit in cars such as the Comet. Also new this year was the 427 CID V8 in large Mercury models. On Comets, the 170 CID 6-cylinder was made standard on all models.

Comet 404 2-Door Sedan

Comet Villager 4-Door Wagon

Comet Caliente 2-Door Convertible

Monterey 2-Door Marauder Hardtop

Montclair 4-Door Marauder Hardtop

Park Lane 2-Door Hardtop

**Model year production:** 303,003, down 0.95% from 1963.
**Domestic market share:** 3.87% (9th place).
**Base price range:** $2,126 to $3,549.
**Industry average base price:** $3,024.
**Mercury average base price:** $2,925.
**Introduction date:** October 1963.
**Assembly plants:** Mahwah, NJ (E); Lorain, OH (H); Los Angeles, CA (J); Kansas City, MO (K); San Jose, CA (R); Wixom, MI (S); Metuchen, NJ (T); Wayne, MI (W); and St. Louis, MO (Z).

**Data plate identification:** Eleven digit code read as follows: 4 for 1964; 2nd digit is assembly plant code; 3rd digit is series (1 or 2 is Comet, 4 is Monterey, etc.); 4th digit is body style; 5th digit is engine code; 500001 and up for serial number. *Example:* 4W43Z100001 is a 1964 Mercury Monterey 2-Door Hardtop with a 390 CID V8 engine, serial number 500001, built in Wayne, MI.

## Powertrains

| Engine | Gross HP | Engine Code | Transmission Availability | Comet | Monterey & Montclair | Park Lane |
|---|---|---|---|---|---|---|
| 170 CID Thrift-Power Six, 1-bbl., 6-cyl. | 101 | U | 3-speed manual | S[2] | – | – |
| | | | 2-sp. Automatic | $172[2] | – | – |
| 200 CID Six, 1-bbl., 6-cyl. | 116 | T | 3-speed manual | $45[2] | – | – |
| | | | 2-sp. Automatic | $217[2] | – | – |
| 260 CID, 2-bbl., V8 | 164 | F | 3-speed manual | $76[1]/$121[2] | – | – |
| | | | 4-speed manual | 264[1]/$309[2] | – | – |
| | | | Merc-O-Matic Automatic | $248[1]/$293[2] | – | – |
| 289 CID, 2-bbl., V8 | 210 | K | 3-speed manual | $76[1]/$121[2] | – | – |
| | | | 4-speed manual | 264[1]/$309[2] | – | – |
| | | | Merc-O-Matic Automatic | $248[1]/$293[2] | – | – |
| 390 CID, 2-bbl., V8 | 250 | Y | 3-speed manual | – | S | – |
| | | | 4-speed manual | – | $232* | – |
| | 266 | | Multi-Drive Automatic | – | $232 | – |
| 390 CID, 4-bbl., V8 | 300 | Z | 3-speed manual | – | $52 | S |

| Engine | Gross HP | Engine Code | Transmission Availability | Comet | Monterey & Montclair | Park Lane |
|--------|----------|-------------|---------------------------|-------|----------------------|-----------|
| | | | 4-speed manual | - | $284* | $232 |
| | | | Multi-Drive Automatic | - | $284 | $232 |
| 427 CID, 4-bbl., V8 | 410 | Q | 4-speed manual | - | $646* | $594 |
| | | | Multi-Drive Automatic | - | $675* | $623 |
| 427 CID, 2 × 4-bbl., V8 | 425 | R | 4-speed manual | - | $702* | $650 |
| | | | Multi-Drive Automatic | - | $731* | $679 |

¹Cyclone.   ²All but Cyclone.   *Not available on wagons.

## Major Options

| | Comet | Monterey/Montclair | Park Lane |
|--|-------|--------------------|-----------| 
| SelectAire air conditioning | $232 | $402 | $402 |
| Tinted glass | $27 | $43 | $43 |
| Speed control | - | $93 | $93 |
| Tilt steering wheel | - | $43 | $43 |
| Power steering | $86 | $106 | $106 |
| Power brakes | $43 | $43 | $43 |
| Power windows | - | $106 | $106 |
| Power seat — six-way | - | $92 | $92 |
| Electric windshield wipers w/washer | $22 | $14 | $14 |
| Electric clock | $15 | $16 — Monterey | S |
| Pushbutton AM radio | $59 | $59 | $59 |
| AM/FM radio | - | $149 | $149 |
| White sidewall tires — std. sizes | $30–$33 | $37 | $37–$53 |
| Full wheel covers | $19 | S | S |
| Sports package | - | $370 | $370 |

Options common to most models. (- = Not Available; S = Standard equipment.) Items may be standard equipment, optional at different pricing, or unavailable on certain models. This chart is only a guide.

## Paint Colors

| | Code |
|--|------|
| Onyx | A |
| Peacock | B |
| Silver Turquoise | D |
| Pacific Blue Metallic | F |
| Palomino | G |
| Aztec Gold Metallic* | I |
| Carnival Red | J |
| Anniversary Silver Metallic | K |
| Bittersweet* | L |
| Polar White | M |
| Pecan Frost Metallic | P |
| Yellow Mist | R |
| Cypress Green Metallic** | S |
| Fawn | T |
| Pink Frost Metallic* | W |
| Burgundy Metallic | X |
| Glacier Blue | Y |
| Platinum Beige Metallic | Z |

*Full-size only.   **Comet only.

**1964**

# Comet

*"A totally new kind of Comet— every bit as hot as it looks!"*

**Nameplate year of origin:** 1960.
**Current bodystyle lifespan:** 1964 through 1965.
**Predecessor to this model:** Comet (1960 to 1963).
**Replacement for this model:** Comet (1966 to 1967).
**Percentage of division's sales volume:** 62.68%.
**Corporate siblings:** Ford Falcon.
**Primary competition:** Buick Special, Dodge Dart, Oldsmobile F-85, Pontiac Tempest and Studebaker.
**Notable changes:** Completely restyled.
**Major standard equipment:** Nylon and vinyl front bench seat with foam cushions, front and rear armrests, carpet textured rubber floor covering, bright metal front and rear window trim, and 6.50 × 14 BSW tires. 404 adds: Deluxe interior appointments and additional bright exterior trim. Caliente adds: Deep-pile carpeting, deluxe steering wheel, padded instrument panel, simulated walnut interior trim and additional sound deadening materials.

## Measurements

| | Cars | Wagons |
|--|------|--------|
| Wheelbase | 114.0" | 109.5" |
| Length | 195.1" | 191.9" |
| Width | 71.6" | 71.6" |
| Height | 55.3" | 55.3" |
| Legroom — front | 42.0" | 42.0" |
| Legroom — rear | 35.5" | 35.5" |
| Headroom — front | 38.8" | 38.8" |
| Headroom — rear | 36.7" | 36.5" |
| Cargo capacity (cu. ft.) | NA | 78.5 |
| Fuel capacity (gals.) | 20.0 | 20.0 |

## Models Available

| | Style Number | Base MSRP | Change from LY | Shipping Wt. (lbs.) | Production | Change from LY |
|---|---|---|---|---|---|---|
| Comet 202 2-Door Sedan | 01 | $2,126 | +2.02% | 2539 | 33,824 | +38.90% |
| Comet 202 4-Door Sedan | 02 | $2,182 | +2.01% | 2580 | 29,147 | +20.29% |
| Comet 202 4-Door Wagon | 32 | $2,463 | -0.81% | 2727 | 5,504 | +24.55% |
| Comet 404 2-Door Sedan | 11 | $2,213 | +1.93% | 2551 | 12,512 | +5.17% |
| Comet 404 4-Door Sedan | 12 | $2,269 | +1.93% | 2588 | 25,136 | -8.59% |
| Comet 404 4-Door Wagon | 34 | $2,550 | -0.78% | 2741 | 6,918 | +34.30% |
| Comet Villager 4-Door Wagon | 36 | $2,734 | -0.73% | 2745 | 1,980 | +29.50% |
| Comet Caliente 2-Door Hardtop | 23 | $2,375 | -1.04% | 2688 | 31,204 | +437.35% |
| Comet Caliente 2-Door Conv. | 25 | $2,636 | -2.73% | 2861 | 9,039 | +57.01% |
| Comet Caliente 4-Door Sedan | 22 | $2,350 | NEW | 2668 | 27,218 | NEW |
| Comet Cyclone 2-Door Hardtop | 27 | $2,655 | NEW | NA | 7,454 | NEW |
| TOTALS | | *Avg. price* $2,414 | +0.21% | | *Production* 189,936 | +41.09% |

# Monterey

*"Montereys are packed with an elegance that
sets them apart from other medium-price cars."*

**Nameplate year of origin:** 1952.
**Current bodystyle lifespan:** 1963 through 1964.
**Predecessor to this model:** Monterey (1961 to 1962).
**Replacement for this model:** Monterey (1965 to 1966).
**Percentage of division's sales volume:** 15.81%.
**Corporate siblings:** Ford Galaxie.
**Primary competition:** Buick Wildcat, Dodge Polara, Oldsmobile 88 and Pontiac Star Chief/Bonneville.
**Notable changes:** Revised front and rear styling.
**Major standard equipment:** Cloth and vinyl front bench seat, full carpeting, padded instrument panel, bright exterior window trim and 8.00 × 14 BSW tires.

## Measurements

| | Cars | Commuter |
|---|---|---|
| Wheelbase | 120.0" | 120.0" |
| Length | 215.5" | 210.3" |
| Width | 80.0" | 80.0" |
| Height | 56.7" | 56.7" |
| Legroom — front | 41.9" | 41.9" |
| Legroom — rear | 38.7" | 38.7" |
| Headroom — front | 39.1" | 39.1" |
| Headroom — rear | 38.3" | 38.1" |
| Cargo capacity (cu. ft.) | 17.1 | 99.2 |
| Fuel capacity (gals.) | 20.0 | 20.0 |

## Models Available

| | Style Number | Base MSRP | Change from LY | Shipping Wt. (lbs.) | Production | Change from LY |
|---|---|---|---|---|---|---|
| Monterey 2-Door Sedan | 41 | $2,819 | -0.53% | 3895 | 3,932 | -15.26% |
| Monterey 2-Door Hardtop | 43 | $2,884 | -1.57% | 2910 | 2,926 | +1.63% |
| Monterey 2-Door Marauder Fstbk. | 47 | $2,884 | -1.57% | 2910 | 8,760 | +776.00% |
| Monterey 2-Door Convertible | 45 | $3,226 | NEW | 4027 | 2,592 | NEW |
| Monterey 4-Door Breezeway Sdn. | 42 | $2,892 | +0.17% | 3985 | 20,234 | +11.32% |
| Monterey 4-Door Marauder Hdtp. | 48 | $2,957 | -1.27% | 4000 | 4,143 | +144.86% |
| Commuter 4-Door, 2-Seat Wagon | 72 | $3,236 | NEW | 4259 | 3,484 | NEW |
| Commuter 4-Door, 3-Seat Wagon | 72 | $3,306 | NEW | 4271 | 1,839 | NEW |
| TOTALS | | *Avg. price* $3,026 | -1.76%* | | *Production* 47,910 | -57.29%* |

*Comparison made to entire 1962 Monterey line including Monterey Custom series.

# Montclair

*"More of what you buy a medium-price car for."*

**Nameplate year of origin:** 1955.
**Current bodystyle lifespan:** 1964.
**Predecessor to this model:** Monterey Custom (1961 to 1962).
**Replacement for this model:** Montclair (1965 to 1966).
**Percentage of division's sales volume:** 11.21%.
**Corporate siblings:** Ford Galaxie.
**Primary competition:** Buick Wildcat, Dodge Polara, Oldsmobile 88 and Pontiac Star Chief.
**Notable changes:** Revised front and rear styling.
**Major standard equipment:** Cloth and vinyl front bench seat, full carpeting, padded instrument panel, bright exterior window trim and 8.00 × 14 BSW tires.

## Measurements

| | |
|---|---|
| Wheelbase | 120.0" |
| Length | 215.5" |
| Width | 80.0" |
| Height | 56.7" |
| Legroom — front | 41.9" |
| Legroom — rear | 38.7" |
| Headroom — front | 39.1" |
| Headroom — rear | 38.3" |
| Cargo capacity (cu. ft.) | 17.1 |
| Fuel capacity (gals.) | 20.0 |

## Models Available

| | Style Number | Base MSRP | Change from LY | Shipping Wt. (lbs.) | Production | Change from LY |
|---|---|---|---|---|---|---|
| Montclair 2-Door Hardtop | 53 | $3,127 | NEW | 3921 | 2,329 | NEW |
| Montclair 2-Door Marauder Fbk. | 57 | $3,127 | NEW | 3927 | 6,459 | NEW |
| Montclair 4-Door Sedan | 52 | $3,116 | NEW | 3996 | 15,520 | NEW |
| Montclair 4-Door Marauder HT | 58 | $3,181 | NEW | 4017 | 9,655 | NEW |
| TOTALS | | Avg. price $3,138 | NEW | Production 33,963 | | NEW |

# Park Lane

*"This is '64's most elegant Mercury."*

**Nameplate year of origin:** 1958.
**Current bodystyle lifespan:** 1964.
**Predecessor to this model:** Park Lane (1959 to 1960).
**Replacement for this model:** Park Lane (1965 to 1966).
**Percentage of division's sales volume:** 10.29%.
**Corporate siblings:** Ford Galaxie.
**Primary competition:** Buick Wildcat, Dodge Custom 880, Oldsmobile 88 and Pontiac Bonneville.
**Notable changes:** Revised front and rear styling. Nameplate returning for 1964, replacing the S-55.
**Major standard equipment:** Cloth and vinyl front bench seat, full carpeting, padded panel, bright exterior window trim and 8.00 × 14 BSW tires. Colony Park adds: exterior simulated mahogany panel trim, and power tailgate window.

## Measurements

| | Cars | Colony Park |
|---|---|---|
| Wheelbase | 120.0" | 120.0" |
| Length | 215.5" | 210.3" |
| Width | 80.0" | 80.0" |
| Height | 56.7" | 56.7" |
| Legroom — front | 41.9" | 41.9" |
| Legroom — rear | 38.7" | 38.7" |
| Headroom — front | 39.1" | 39.1" |
| Headroom — rear | 38.3" | 38.1" |
| Cargo capacity (cu. ft.) | 17.1 | 99.2 |
| Fuel capacity (gals.) | 20.0 | 20.0 |

## Models Available

| | Style Number | Base MSRP | Change from LY | Shipping Wt. (lbs.) | Production | Change from LY |
|---|---|---|---|---|---|---|
| Park Lane 2-Door Hardtop | 63 | $3,359 | NEW | 3960 | 1,786 | NEW |
| Park Lane 2-Dr. Marauder HT | 67 | $3,359 | NEW | 3966 | 2,721 | NEW |
| Park Lane 2-Door Convertible | 65 | $3,549 | NEW | 4066 | 1,967 | NEW |

| | Style Number | Base MSRP | Change from LY | Shipping Wt. (lbs.) | Production | Change from LY |
|---|---|---|---|---|---|---|
| Park Lane 4-Door Sedan | 62 | $3,348 | NEW | 4035 | 6,230 | NEW |
| Park Lane 4-Door Hardtop | 64 | $3,413 | NEW | 4050 | 2,402 | NEW |
| Park Lane 4-Dr. Marauder HT | 68 | $3,413 | NEW | 4056 | 6,230 | NEW |
| Colony Park 4-Dr., 2-S. Wgn. | 76 | $3,434 | 4.22% | 4275 | 4,234 | -34.33% |
| Colony Park 4-Dr., 3-S. Wgn. | 76 | $3,504 | 4.13% | 4287 | 5,624 | -25.30% |
| TOTALS | | Avg. price $3,422 | * | | Production 31,194 | * |

*Comparisons of totals not made as Park Lane was a new model, although it technically replaced the S-55.

# OLDSMOBILE

*"Breeze along in an Action-packed 1964 Oldsmobile."*

Oldsmobile was trying to reinvent itself during the mid-sixties. The mid-price GM division was finding itself in the same predicament that Pontiac and Buick had gone through in the past ten years. The mid-market range was becoming very popular with buyers, but the more upscale buyers were demanding more value for their car-buying dollar. This year Oldsmobile responded in two ways. The most recognizable was the newly redesigned intermediate F-85 line. Larger and more powerful this year, the F-85 looked very much like the full-size 88 line. All major structural components were shared with the rest of the new GM mid-size line. Shared with Buick was a new V6 engine; also offered was an all-new 330 CID V8 based upon the larger 394 CID V8 Oldsmobile engine. The F-85 line was expanded by making the Cutlass a separate model (previously it had been part of the Deluxe line). The new Cutlass line added a 2-Door Coupe to its line, as did the Deluxe line. The turbocharged Jetfire was no longer around, having failed to meet sales expectations. A mid-year performance model was added under the name 4-4-2 (for 4-barrel carburetor, 4-speed manual transmission and dual exhausts). While relatively few were sold, especially when compared to the Pontiac GTO, the 4-4-2 would wind up winning the popularity contest, as versions of the car would be sold well into the 1980s. Another new addition, although not formally part of the F-85/Cutlass line, was a "vista-roof" Vista-Cruiser station wagon. This new wagon had a raised roof section above the rear seat and extending to the

back of the wagon. Incorporated within its raised roof were glass panels, allowing rear passengers to view the scenery more easily. Riding on a wheelbase five inches longer than regular F-85 wagons, the Vista-Cruiser did share most styling features with the mid-size line. All of the extra length was added in the rear passenger compartment area. The Vista-Cruiser was added to the line after the start of the model year, and it shared its new look with the Buick Sport Wagon.

The second step in the revamping process affected the 88 series model lineup. A new lower priced line was introduced to more effectively compete with Pontiac, Mercury, and upper-end Chevy, Ford, Plymouth and Dodge models. This new series, the Jetstar, came in two varieties. The Jetstar 88 was the entry level full-size Oldsmobile. Basically it was similar to a Dynamic 88, but standard equipment included a smaller engine and slightly lower level of trim. The other series was the Jetstar I, essentially a Starfire 2-Door Hardtop with less accessory and trim content. Other Oldsmobile series returned with the same models as in previous years, except for the Super 88, which offered only a 4-Door Sedan and 4-Door Hardtop this year. Styling for all full-size Oldsmobiles was an update on the 1963 styling, meaning new grilles, taillamp treatments, and trim changes. This would also be the last year for the full-size Oldsmobile Fiesta wagon until 1971 when it would return as the Custom Cruiser. Declining sales and the popularity of the Vista-Cruiser would seal the big wagon's fate.

98 4-Door Hardtop

Dynamic 88 4-Door Fiesta Wagon

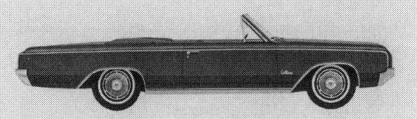
F-85 Cutlass 2-Door Convertible

F-85 Cutlass 2-Door Hardtop

Jetstar 88 2-Door Hardtop

Jetstar I 2-Door Hardtop

**1964**

**Model year production:** 497,396, up 4.25% over 1963.
**Domestic market share:** 6.38% (6th place).
**Base price range:** $2,343 to $4,753.
**Industry average base price:** $3,024.
**Oldsmobile average base price:** $3,322.
**Introduction date:** October 1963.
**Assembly plants:** Southgate, CA (C); Atlanta, GA (D); Framingham, MA (G); Fremont, CA (Z); Lansing, MI (M); Fairfax, KS (X); and Linden, NJ (E).

**Data plate identification:** Ten digit code read as follows: 1st digit 6 or 8 for number of engine cylinders; 2nd digit identifies trim level; 4 for 1964 year; 4th digit is assembly plant; 001001 and up for serial number. Check model number on body plate for body style. *Example:* 884M001001 is a 1964 Oldsmobile 98 with a V8 engine, built in Lansing, MI, serial number 001001.

## Powertrains

| Engine | Gross HP | Transmission Availability | F-85** | Vista-Cruiser & Jetstar 88 | Dyn. 88 | Jetstar I & Starfire | Spr. 88 98 |
|---|---|---|---|---|---|---|---|
| 225 CID Econ-O-Way, 1-bbl., V6 | 155 | 3-speed manual | S | - | - | - | - |
| | | 4-speed manual | $188 | - | - | - | - |
| | | Jetaway Automatic | $199 | - | - | - | - |
| 330 CID Jetfire Rocket, 2-bbl., V8 | 230 (245 — Prem.) | 3-speed manual | $72 | S | - | - | - |
| | | 4-speed manual | $260 | $188 | - | - | - |
| | | Jetaway Automatic | $282 | $210 | - | - | - |
| 330 CID Cutlass, 4-bbl., V8 | 290 | 3-speed manual | S (Cutlass)/ $106 (F-85) | $34 | - | - | - |
| | | 4-speed manual | $188 (Cut.)/ $294 (F-85) | $222 | - | - | - |
| | | Jetaway Automatic | $210 (Cut.)/ $316 (F-85) | $244 | - | - | - |
| 394 CID Rocket, 2-bbl., V8 | 280 | 3-speed manual | - | - | S | - | - |
| | | Jetaway Automatic | - | - | $231 | - | - |
| 394 CID Rocket, 4-bbl., V8 | 330 | 3-speed manual | - | - | $38 | - | S (S.88) |
| | | Jetaway Automatic | - | - | $269 | - | $231 (S.88)/ S (98*) |
| 394 CID Starfire Rocket, 4-bbl., V8 | 345 | 3-speed manual | - | - | - | S (Jetstar I) | $65 (Super 88) |
| | | Jetaway Automatic | - | - | - | $231 (Jet. I)/ S (Starfire) | $296 (S.88)/ $65 (98*) |

*345-hp/394 CID V8 with automatic, standard on 98 Custom Sports Coupe.   **V8 required for 4-4-2 option package.*

## Major Options

| | F-85 | Vista-Cruiser | Jetstar 88 | Jetstar I | Dynamic 88 | Super 88 | Starfire | 98 |
|---|---|---|---|---|---|---|---|---|
| Air conditioning | $351 | $351 | $430 | $430 | $430 | $430 | $430 | $430 |
| Soft Ray tinted glass | $38 | $38 | $43 | $43 | $43 | $43 | $43 | $43 |
| Deck lid remote release | - | - | $10 | $10 | $10 | $10 | $10 | $10 |
| Tilt-Away steering wheel | $43 | $43 | $43 | $43 | $43 | $43 | $43 | $43 |
| Power steering | $97 | $97 | $97 | $108 | $108 | $108 | S | S |
| Power brakes | $43 | $43 | $43 | $43 | $43 | $43 | S | S |
| Power driver's seat | $67 | $67 | $71 | $71 | $71 | $71 | $71 | $43–$71 |
| Power windows | $102 | $102 | $106 | $106 | $106 | $106 | S* | S* |
| Electric clock | $16 | $16 | $16 | S | $16 | S | S | S |
| AM radio | $66 | $66 | $89 | $89 | $89 | $89 | $89 | $89 |
| AM/FM radio | - | - | $151 | $151 | $151 | $151 | $151 | $151 |
| Front seat console | $ | - | $ | S | $ | $ | S | $ |
| Front bucket seats | $ | - | $ | S | $ | $ | S | $ |
| 4-4-2 Option package | $136 | - | - | - | - | - | - | - |

Options common to most models. (- = Not Available; S = Standard equipment.) Items may be standard equipment, optional at different pricing, or unavailable on certain models. This chart is only a guide.

*Optional at $106 on certain models. See individual model sections for details.*

## Paint Colors

| | Code | | Code |
|---|---|---|---|
| Ebony Black | A | Regal Mist Metallic | L |
| Provincial White | C | Pacific Mist Metallic | P |
| Sheffield Mist Metallic | D | Aqua Mist Metallic | Q |
| Jade Mist Metallic | E | Cashmere Beige | R |
| Wedgewood Mist Metallic | F | Saddle Mist Metallic | S |
| Bermuda Blue | H | Holiday Red | V |
| Fern Mist Metallic | J | Midnight Mist Metallic | W |
| Tahitian Yellow | K | | |

# F-85 and Cutlass

*"The trim, eye-catching F-85 for '64."*

**Nameplate year of origin:** 1961 (F-85); 1962 (Cutlass; as F-85 model designation); 1955 (show car).

**Current bodystyle lifespan:** 1964 through 1965.

**Predecessor to this model:** F-85 (1961 to 1963).

**Replacement for this model:** F-85/Cutlass (1966 to 1967).

**Percentage of division's sales volume:** 26.99%.

**Corporate siblings:** Buick Special/Skylark, Chevrolet Chevelle, Pontiac Tempest/LeMans.

**Primary competition:** Rambler Classic, Dodge Coronet, Ford Fairlane 500, and Mercury Comet.

**Notable changes:** Completely restyled, larger model.

**Major standard equipment:** Cloth and vinyl front bench seat, floor mats, and 6.50 × 14 BSW tires. Deluxe adds: Deluxe interior trim, bucket seats on Sport Coupe, and additional exterior bright trim. Cutlass adds: bucket seats, full carpeting, deluxe steering wheel, and 7.00 × 14 BSW tires. 4-4-2 option-package adds: Floor-mounted heavy-duty shifter, heavy-duty wheels, heavy-duty motor mounts, and dual exhausts.

## Measurements

| | Cars | Wagon |
|---|---|---|
| Wheelbase | 115.0" | 115.0" |
| Length | 203.0" | 203.0" |
| Width | 73.8" | 74.3" |
| Height | 54.0" | 54.5" |
| Legroom — front | 42.0" | 42.0" |
| Legroom — rear | 35.5" | 35.5" |
| Headroom — front | 38.8" | 38.8" |
| Headroom — rear | 36.7" | 36.7" |
| Luggage capacity (cu. ft.) | NA | NA |
| Fuel capacity (gals.) | 20.0 | 20.0 |

## Models Available

|  | Style Number | Base MSRP | Change from LY | Shipping Wt. (lbs.) | Production | Change from LY |
|---|---|---|---|---|---|---|
| F-85 2-Door Club Coupe | 3027 | $2,343 | -2.50% | 2894 | 8,314 | -26.27% |
| F-85 4-Door Sedan | 3069 | $2,397 | -2.44% | 2940 | 6,331 | -29.16% |
| F-85 4-Door, 2-Seat Wagon | 3035 | $2,689 | -2.36% | 3186 | 4,047 | 20.88% |
| F-85 Deluxe 2-Door Sports Coupe | 3127 | $2,537 | -5.83% | 3006 | 7,984 | -80.69% |
| F-85 Deluxe 4-Door Sedan | 3169 | $2,505 | -3.36% | 3121 | 42,237 | 44.31% |
| F-85 Deluxe 4-Door, 2-Seat Wagon | 3135 | $2,797 | -3.18% | 3271 | 909 | -86.32% |
| Cutlass 2-Door Sport Coupe | 3227 | $2,644 | NEW | 3141 | 15,440 | NEW |
| Cutlass 2-Door Holiday Hardtop | 3237 | $2,784 | NEW | 3180 | 36,153 | NEW |
| Cutlass 2-Door Convertible | 3267 | $2,984 | NEW | 3263 | 12,822 | NEW |
| TOTALS | Avg. price | $2,631 | -3.48% | Production | 134,237 | +12.98% |

# Vista-Cruiser

*"A new way to view the road, with giant-size cargo capacity."*

**Nameplate year of origin:** 1964.
**Current bodystyle lifespan:** 1964 through 1965.
**Predecessor to this model:** None.
**Replacement for this model:** Vista-Cruiser (1966 to 1967).
**Percentage of division's sales volume:** 2.13%.
**Corporate siblings:** Buick Sport Wagon.
**Primary competition:** AMC Ambassador and Dodge 330/440/Polara.
**Notable changes:** All-new model.
**Major standard equipment:** All-vinyl front bench seat, full carpeting, vista-roof windows, padded second seat sun visors, and 7.50 × 14 BSW tires.
  Custom adds: Deluxe interior trim.

## Measurements

|  |  |
|---|---|
| Wheelbase | 120.0" |
| Length | 208.0" |
| Width | 74.3" |
| Height | 58.2" |
| Legroom — front | 42.0" |
| Legroom — rear | 38.5" |
| Headroom — front | 38.8" |
| Headroom — rear | 40.5" |
| Luggage capacity (cu. ft.) | NA |
| Fuel capacity (gals.) | 20.0 |

## Models Available

|  | Style Number | Base MSRP | Change from LY | Shipping Wt. (lbs.) | Production | Change from LY |
|---|---|---|---|---|---|---|
| Vista-Cruiser 4-Dr., 2-S. Wagon | 3055 | $2,938 | NEW | 3652 | 3,320 | NEW |
| Vista-Cruiser 4-Dr., 3-S. Wagon | 3065 | $3,072 | NEW | 3729 | 7,286 | NEW |
| Vista-Cruiser Cust. 4-Dr., 2-S. Wgn. | 3255 | $3,146 | NEW | 3714 | * | NEW |
| Vista-Cruiser Cust. 4-Dr., 3-S. Wgn. | 3265 | $3,270 | NEW | 3781 | * | NEW |
| TOTALS | Avg. price | $3,107 | NEW | Production | 10,606* | NEW* |

*Production totals not separated by trim level.

# Jetstar 88

*"A new series of lower-priced 88's,*
*boasting a new Jetfire Rocket V8 engine."*

**Nameplate year of origin:** 1964 (88 series started 1949).
**Current bodystyle lifespan:** 1961 through 1964.
**Predecessor to this model:** 88 (1961 to 1963).
**Replacement for this model:** Jetstar 88 (1965 to 1966).
**Percentage of division's sales volume:** 12.97%.
**Corporate siblings:** Buick LeSabre, Chevrolet Impala, Pontiac Catalina.
**Primary competition:** AMC Ambassador, Dodge Polara, Ford Galaxie 500, Mercury Monterey, Plymouth Fury.
**Notable changes:** All-new model replacing the base 88 model.
**Major standard equipment:** Cloth-and-vinyl bench seat, nylon-blend carpet, heater and defroster, full wheel covers, and 7.50 × 14 BSW tires.

## Measurements

| | |
|---|---|
| Wheelbase | 123.0" |
| Length | 215.3" |
| Width | 78.0" |
| Height | 55.8" |
| Legroom — front | 42.0" |
| Legroom — rear | 36.8" |
| Headroom — front | 39.4" |
| Headroom — rear | 37.7" |
| Luggage capacity (cu. ft.) | 17.1 |
| Fuel capacity (gals.) | 21.0 |

## Models Available

| | Style Number | Base MSRP | Change from LY | Shipping Wt. (lbs.) | Production | Change from LY |
|---|---|---|---|---|---|---|
| Jetstar 88 2-Door Holiday Hardtop | 3347 | $2,992 | NEW | 3701 | 16,663 | NEW |
| Jetstar 88 2-Door Convertible | 3367 | $3,318 | NEW | 3754 | 3,903 | NEW |
| Jetstar 88 4-Door Celebrity Sedan | 3369 | $2,935 | NEW | 3729 | 24,614 | NEW |
| Jetstar 88 4-Door Holiday Hardtop | 3339 | $3,069 | NEW | 3783 | 19,324 | NEW |
| TOTALS | | *Avg. price* $3,079 | NEW | *Production* 64,504 | | NEW |

# Jetstar I

*"The brand new Sport Coupe with exceptional performance."*

**Nameplate year of origin:** 1964.
**Current bodystyle lifespan:** 1964.
**Predecessor to this model:** None.
**Replacement for this model:** Jetstar I (1965 to 1966).
**Percentage of division's sales volume:** 3.23%.
**Corporate siblings:** Buick Wildcat, Chevrolet Impala SS, and Pontiac 2+2/Grand Prix.
**Primary competition:** Ford Galaxie 500 XL, and Mercury Park Lane with Sports Package.
**Notable changes:** All-new model.
**Major standard equipment:** All-vinyl bucket seats with center console, nylon-blend carpet, Deluxe steering wheel, heater and defroster, glove box and courtesy lamps, full wheel covers, and 8.25 × 14 BSW tires.

## Measurements

| | |
|---|---|
| Wheelbase | 123.0" |
| Length | 215.3" |
| Width | 78.0" |
| Height | 54.2" |
| Legroom — front | 41.4" |
| Legroom — rear | 36.7" |
| Headroom — front | 37.8" |
| Headroom — rear | 37.9" |
| Luggage capacity (cu. ft.) | 17.1 |
| Fuel capacity (gals.) | 21.0 |

## Models Available

| | Style Number | Base MSRP | Change from LY | Shipping Wt. (lbs.) | Production | Change from LY |
|---|---|---|---|---|---|---|
| Jetstar I 2-Door Sport Coupe | 3457 | $3,603 | NEW | 4019 | 16,084 | NEW |
| TOTALS | | *Avg. price* $3,603 | NEW | *Production* 16,084 | | NEW |

# Dynamic 88

*"The ever popular Dynamic 88 is again loaded with value in '64."*

**Nameplate year of origin:** 1964 (88 series started 1949).
**Current bodystyle lifespan:** 1961 through 1964.
**Predecessor to this model:** 88 (1959 to 1960).
**Replacement for this model:** Dynamic 88 (1965 to 1966).
**Percentage of division's sales volume:** 33.71%.
**Corporate siblings:** Buick LeSabre, Chevrolet Biscayne/BelAir/Impala, Pontiac Catalina/Star Chief/Bonneville.
**Primary competition:** AMC Ambassador, Dodge Polara, Ford Galaxie 500, Mercury Montclair, Plymouth Fury.
**Notable changes:** Restyled front end and minor trim and detail changes.
**Major standard equipment:** Cloth-and-vinyl bench seat, nylon-blend carpet, heater and defroster, full wheel covers, and 8.00 × 14 BSW tires.

## Measurements

| | |
|---|---|
| Wheelbase | 123.0" |
| Length | 215.3" |
| Width | 78.0" |
| Height | 55.8" |
| Legroom — front | 42.0" |
| Legroom — rear | 36.8" |
| Headroom — front | 39.4" |
| Headroom — rear | 37.7" |
| Luggage capacity (cu. ft.) | 17.1 |
| Fuel capacity (gals.) | 21.0 |

**1964**

## Models Available

| | Style Number | Base MSRP | Change from LY | Shipping Wt. (lbs.) | Production | Change from LY |
|---|---|---|---|---|---|---|
| Dynamic 88 2-Door Holiday Hardtop | 3447 | $3,062 | +0.33% | 3924 | 32,369 | -17.15% |
| Dynamic 88 2-Door Convertible | 3467 | $3,389 | +0.30% | 3996 | 10,042 | -19.99% |
| Dynamic 88 4-Door Celebrity Sedan | 3469 | $3,005 | +0.33% | 3966 | 57,590 | -16.06% |
| Dynamic 88 4-Door Holiday Hardtop | 3439 | $3,139 | +0.29% | 4012 | 50,327 | -19.29% |
| Dynamic 88 4-Dr., 2-S. Wagon | 3435 | $3,468 | +0.26% | 4286 | 10,747 | +11.77% |
| Dynamic 88 4-Dr., 3-S. Wagon | 3445 | $3,576 | +0.28% | 4324 | 6,599 | -7.27% |
| TOTALS | | Avg. price $3,273 | +0.28% | | Production 167,674 | -15.88% |

# Super 88

*"Radiant good looks of a sleek new profile make the Super 88 a dashing entry for '64."*

**Nameplate year of origin:** 1951 (88 series started 1949).
**Current bodystyle lifespan:** 1961 through 1964.
**Predecessor to this model:** Super 88 (1959 to 1960).
**Replacement for this model:** Delta 88 (1965 to 1966).
**Percentage of division's sales volume:** 3.92%.
**Corporate siblings:** Buick Wildcat, Chevrolet Impala, Pontiac Star Chief/Bonneville.
**Primary competition:** AMC Ambassador, Dodge Polara, Ford Galaxie 500, and Mercury Montclair.
**Notable changes:** Restyled front end and minor trim and detail changes.
**Major standard equipment:** Vinyl and cloth bench seat, deluxe interior trim, deep-pile carpeting, deluxe steering wheel, glove box and courtesy lamps, full wheel covers, and 8.00 × 14 BSW tires.

## Measurements

| | |
|---|---|
| Wheelbase | 123.0" |
| Length | 215.3" |
| Width | 78.0" |
| Height | 55.8" |
| Legroom — front | 42.0" |
| Legroom — rear | 36.8" |
| Headroom — front | 39.4" |
| Headroom — rear | 37.7" |
| Luggage capacity (cu. ft.) | 17.1 |
| Fuel capacity (gals.) | 21.0 |

## Models Available

| | Style Number | Base MSRP | Change from LY | Shipping Wt. (lbs.) | Production | Change from LY |
|---|---|---|---|---|---|---|
| Super 88 4-Door Celebrity Sedan | 3569 | $3,256 | +0.31% | 4009 | 1,736 | -92.94% |
| Super 88 4-Door Holiday Hardtop | 3539 | $3,486 | +0.37% | 4069 | 17,778 | -29.97% |
| TOTALS | | Avg. price $3,371 | -2.83% | | Production 19,514 | -68.92% |

# Starfire

*"Excitement plus is the keystone of Starfire."*

**Nameplate year of origin:** 1954 as designation for 98 Convertible; 1961 as a series.
**Current bodystyle lifespan:** 1961 through 1964.
**Predecessor to this model:** None.
**Replacement for this model:** Starfire (1965 to 1966).
**Percentage of division's sales volume:** 3.25%.
**Corporate siblings:** Buick Wildcat, Pontiac Grand Prix.
**Primary competition:** Chrysler 300, Ford Galaxie 500 XL, and Mercury Park Lane with Sports Pkg.
**Notable changes:** Restyled front end and minor trim and detail changes.
**Major standard equipment:** Leather bucket seats with center console, nylon-blend carpet, deluxe steering wheel, power steering, power brakes, glove box and courtesy lamps, Starfire wheel covers, and 8.00 × 14 BSW tires.

### Measurements

| | |
|---|---|
| Wheelbase | 123.0" |
| Length | 215.3" |
| Width | 78.0" |
| Height | 54.2" |
| Legroom — front | 41.4" |
| Legroom — rear | 36.7" |
| Headroom — front | 37.8" |
| Headroom — rear | 37.9" |
| Luggage capacity (cu. ft.) | 17.1 |
| Fuel capacity (gals.) | 21.0 |

## Models Available

| | Style Number | Base MSRP | Change from LY | Shipping Wt. (lbs.) | Production | Change from LY |
|---|---|---|---|---|---|---|
| Starfire 2-Door Hardtop | 3657 | $4,138 | +0.22% | 4167 | 13,753 | -36.00% |
| Starfire 2-Door Convertible | 3667 | $4,753 | +0.23% | 4253 | 2,410 | -45.24% |
| TOTALS | | Avg. price $4,446 | +0.23% | | Production 16,163 | -37.58% |

# Ninety-Eight

*"Limousine luxury is the best way to describe the beautiful Oldsmobile Ninety-Eight."*

**Nameplate year of origin:** 1941.
**Current bodystyle lifespan:** 1961 through 1964.
**Predecessor to this model:** Ninety-Eight (1959 to 1960).
**Replacement for this model:** Ninety-Eight (1965 to 1966).
**Percentage of division's sales volume:** 13.79%.
**Corporate siblings:** Buick Electra and Cadillac Series 62/de Ville.
**Primary competition:** Chrysler New Yorker and Mercury Park Lane.
**Notable changes:** Restyled front end and minor trim and detail changes.
**Major standard equipment:** Cloth and vinyl bench seat with fold-down center armrest, deep-pile carpeting floor and kick panels, deluxe steering wheel, electric clock, power windows and two-way power seat (except Town Sedan), trunk lamp, trunk mat, full wheel covers, rear wheel opening covers, and 8.50 × 14

### Measurements

| | |
|---|---|
| Wheelbase | 126.0" |
| Length | 222.3" |
| Width | 78.0" |
| Height | 56.5" |
| Legroom — front | 42.1" |
| Legroom — rear | 40.2" |
| Headroom — front | 40.0" |
| Headroom — rear | 38.7" |
| Luggage capacity (cu. ft.) | NA |
| Fuel capacity (gals.) | 21.0 |

BSW tires. Luxury Sedan adds: special interior trim, special front and rear door pulls, and rear folding center armrests. Custom adds: Bucket seats and floor console.

## Models Available

| | Style Number | Base MSRP | Change from LY | Shipping Wt. (lbs.) | Production | Change from LY |
|---|---|---|---|---|---|---|
| Ninety-Eight 2-Door Sports Coupe | 3847 | $4,188 | +0.24% | 4205 | 6,139 | +23.17% |
| Ninety-Eight 2-Door Convertible | 3867 | $4,468 | +0.25% | 4255 | 4,004 | -6.16% |
| Ninety-Eight 4-Door Town Sedan | 3819 | $3,993 | +0.28% | 4234 | 11,380 | +2.96% |
| Ninety-Eight 4-Door Sports Sedan | 3839 | $4,265 | +0.26% | 4323 | 24,791 | +6.26% |
| Ninety-Eight Luxury 4-Door Sedan | 3829 | $4,342 | +0.23% | 4337 | 17,346 | -9.90% |
| Ninety-Eight Custom 2-Dr. Sp. Cpe. | 3947 | $4,391 | +0.23% | 4271 | 4,954 | -33.25% |
| TOTALS | *Avg. price* | $4,275 | +0.26% | *Production* | 68,614 | -2.41% |

1964

# PLYMOUTH

*"If this is the year you picked to buy a new car,*
*you picked a beautiful year to Get up and Go Plymouth."*

Even without totally new product to shout about, the Plymouth division had been somewhat successful in reviving itself with a limited array of styling changes and marketing techniques, not the least of which was a highly successful racing program with the future "King" himself, Richard Petty, at its heart. The Petty family had already seen the successes of father Lee Petty, and Richard had just begun to make a name for himself. Chrysler wisely chose to tie in with Richard Petty for marketing purposes, and for the next 10 years, Plymouth and Richard Petty seemed inseparable. Of course, this winning on the track translated into winning in the showroom. The powerplants were selling the cars, as the styling had been lackluster for several years. However, to their credit, the 1964 model Plymouth line was a very handsome restyle of what had been one of the poorest styled Plymouths. The front end styling was much more traditional this year, with quad headlamps set into a relatively simple "electric razor" grille affair. A traditional full-width bumper with inset parking lamps was below the grille opening. Bodysides were slightly cleaned up and led to a simple, rear end treatment that featured square taillamps at the far outside edges. This was the best styling yet on this body. Of course, the expansion of 426 CID V8 offerings was the big draw for Plymouth buyers

this year, although very few cars were actually sold with this engine. Perception is everything.

Two things boosted the Valiant line this year. First, after being totally redesigned in 1963, the Valiant received a facelift for 1964 and gained a full-width grille in place of the prior Chrysler-style grille opening. Then, in a move intended to upstage Ford, Plymouth introduced the second pony car, the Barracuda, during May 1964. Unfortunately the Barracuda was as similar to the Valiant as the Mustang was different from the Falcon, and its introduction was barely noticed by most buyers. Essentially a Valiant from the cowl forward, the Barracuda differed in its rear roofline and interior accommodations. A full-width, wraparound rear window covered loads of cargo space that was accessible through a decent sized trunk opening, or from inside by way of fold-down rear seats, a novel idea at the time. This gave Barracuda a big space advantage over the Mustang. However, with convenience and economy to tout, the Barracuda came off as more of an economy car, whereas the Mustang seemed to lead the sporty car image. In time, Plymouth would address this issue, but in the meantime, the Mustang was off to a lead that no one would soon overcome.

Belvedere 2-Door Sedan

Fury 2-Door Hardtop

Fury 4-Door Wagon

Valiant Signet 2-Door Hardtop

Valiant V100 4-Door Sedan

**Model year production:** 548,321, up 12.26% over 1963.
**Domestic market share:** 7.03% (4th place).
**Base price range:** $1,921 to $3,095.
**Industry average base price:** $3,024.
**Plymouth average base price:** $2,514.
**Introduction date:** September 1963.
**Assembly plants:** Lynch Road, MI (1): Hamtramck, MI (2); Detroit, MI (3); Los Angeles, CA (5); Newark DE (6); and St. Louis, MO (7).

**Data plate identification:** Ten digit code read as follows: First and second are series designation (first two numbers of model number in charts below); third digit 4 for 1964; fourth digit is assembly plant code; 100001 and up for serial number. *Example:* 2324100001 is a 1964 Plymouth Fury with a 225 CID 6-cyl., built at Hamtramck, MI, serial number 100001. Body style cannot be identified through the VIN.

## Powertrains

| Engine | Gross HP | Transmission Availability | Valiant | Barracuda | Savoy/ Belvedere | Fury |
|---|---|---|---|---|---|---|
| 170 CID, 1-bbl., 6-cyl. | 101 | 3-speed manual | S | S | – | – |
| | | Torqueflite automatic | $172 | $172 | – | – |
| 225 CID, 1-bbl., 6-cyl. | 145 | 3-speed manual | $46 | $46 | S[2] | S[3] |
| | | 4-speed manual | $215 | $215 | $188[2] | $188[3] |
| | | Torqueflite automatic | $218 | $218 | $191[2] | $191[3] |
| 273 CID, 2-bbl., V8 | 180 | 3-speed manual | $131 | $131 | – | – |
| | | 4-speed manual | $310 | $310 | – | – |
| | | Torqueflite automatic | $312 | $312 | – | – |
| 318 CID, 2-bbl., V8 | 230 | 3-speed manual | – | – | S[1]/$108[2] | S[4]/$108[3] |
| | | 4-speed manual | – | – | $188[1]/$296[2] | $188[4]/$296[3] |
| | | Torqueflite automatic | – | – | $191[1]/$299[2] | $191[4]/$299[3] |
| 361 CID Commando, 2-bbl., V8 | 265 | 3-speed manual | – | – | $59[1]/$167[2] | $59[4]/$167[3] |
| | | 4-speed manual | – | – | $247[1]/$354[2] | $247[4]/$354[3] |
| | | Torqueflite automatic | – | – | $269[1]/$377[2] | $269[4]/$377[3] |
| 383 CID Commando, 2-bbl., V8 | 305 | 3-speed manual | – | – | $71[1]/$179[2] | $71[4]/$179[3] |
| | | 4-speed manual | – | – | $259[1]/$366[2] | $259[4]/$366[3] |
| | | Torqueflite automatic | – | – | $271[1]/$389[2] | $271[4]/$389[3] |

| Engine | Gross HP | Transmission Availability | Valiant | Barracuda | Savoy/ Belvedere | Fury |
|---|---|---|---|---|---|---|
| 383 CID Commando, 4-bbl., V8 | 330 | 3-speed manual | – | – | $122[1]/$230[2] | $122[4]/$230[3] |
| | | 4-speed manual | – | – | $310[1]/$417[2] | $310[4]/$417[3] |
| | | Torqueflite automatic | – | – | $323[1]/$440[2] | $323[4]/$440[3] |
| 426 CID Commando, 4-bbl., V8 | 365 | 4-speed manual | – | – | $671[1]/$778[2] | $671[4]/$778[3] |
| | | Torqueflite automatic | – | – | $684[1]/$801[2] | $684[4]/$801[3] |
| 426 CID Commando, 4-bbl., V8 | 415–425 | 4-speed manual | – | – | *** | *** |
| | | Torqueflite automatic | – | – | *** | *** |
| 426 CID Hemi V8, 4-bbl., V8 | 415–425 | 4-speed manual | – | – | *** | *** |
| | | Torqueflite automatic | – | – | *** | *** |

[1]Belvedere Wagons only. [2]All but Belvedere Wagon. [3]Fury 2-Door HT and 4-Door Sedan only. [4]All but Fury 2-Dr. HT and 4-Dr. Sedan. ***Available at varying prices and installation rate. Accurate pricing is unavailable at this time.

## Major Options

| | Valiant | Barracuda | Savoy/Belvedere | Fury |
|---|---|---|---|---|
| Air conditioning (V8 only) | $364 | $364 | $417 | $417 |
| Solex tinted glass | $29 | $14 | $40 | $40 |
| Power steering | $82 | $82 | $86 | $86 |
| Power brakes | $43 | $43 | $43 | $43 |
| Power windows | – | – | $102 | $102 |
| Power front seat — 4-way bucket | – | – | $78 | $78 |
| Electric clock | $16 | $16 | $16 | $16 |
| Transaudio AM radio | $60 | $60 | $60 | $60 |
| Variable speed wipers and washer | $17 | $17 | $17 | $17 |
| Full wheel covers | $16 | $16 | $102 | $61–$102 |

Options common to most models. (– = Not Available.) Items may be standard equipment, optional at different pricing, or unavailable on certain models. This chart is only a guide.

## Paint Colors

| | Code |
|---|---|
| Barracuda Gold Metallic | AA-1 |
| Ebony Black | BB-1 |
| Light Blue Metallic | CC-1 |
| Medium Blue Metallic | DD-1 |
| Dark Blue Metallic | EE-1 |
| Sandalwood Metallic | HH-1 |
| Valiant Light Turquoise Met. | JJ-1 |
| Turquoise Metallic | KK-1 |
| Dark Turquoise Met. | LL-1 |
| Silver Gray Metallic | MM-1 |
| Ruby | PP-1 |
| Signet Royal Red Metallic | TT-1 |
| Chestnut Metallic | VV-1 |
| White | WW-1 |
| Light Beige | XX-1 |
| Medium Beige Metallic | YY-1 |

# Valiant

## "Best all-around compact."

**Nameplate year of origin:** 1960.
**Current bodystyle lifespan:** 1963 through 1966.
**Predecessor to this model:** Valiant (1960 to 1962).
**Replacement for this model:** Valiant (1967 to 1976).
**Percentage of division's sales volume:** 41.51%.
**Corporate siblings:** Dodge Dart.
**Primary competition:** Rambler American, Chevrolet Chevy II, Ford Falcon and Studebaker Lark.
**Notable changes:** New grille, and trim and detail changes.
**Major standard equipment:** Cloth and vinyl bench seat, rubber floor mat, vinyl headlining, chrome exterior front and rear window trim, Torsion-Aire suspension and 6.50 × 13 BSW tires. V200 adds: Side window chrome trim, color-keyed carpeting, front and rear armrests, courtesy or map lights, and deluxe wheel covers. Signet adds: All-vinyl bucket seats, color-keyed deep-pile carpeting, backup lights, rear deck trim and 6-way adjustable front seats.

## Measurement

| | Cars | Wagons |
|---|---|---|
| Wheelbase | 106.0" | 106.0" |
| Length | 188.2" | 188.8" |
| Width | 70.1" | 70.1" |
| Height | 53.4" | 53.1" |
| Legroom — front | 40.0" | 40.0" |
| Legroom — rear | 35.5" | 35.5" |
| Headroom — front | 38.2" | 38.2" |
| Headroom — rear | 37.2" | 37.6" |
| Cargo capacity (cu. ft.) | 23.6 | NA |
| Fuel capacity (gals.) | 18.0 | 18.0 |

## Models Available

| | Style Number | Base MSRP | Change from LY | Shipping Wt. (lbs.) | Production | Change from LY |
|---|---|---|---|---|---|---|
| Valiant 100 2-Door Sedan | 111 | $1,921 | +0.58% | 2540 | 35,403 | +8.06% |
| Valiant 100 4-Door Sedan | 113 | $1,992 | +0.96% | 2575 | 44,208 | -19.06% |
| Valiant 100 4-Door Wagon | 156 | $2,273 | +0.22% | 2725 | 10,759 | -9.31% |
| Valiant 200 2-Door Sedan | 131 | $2,044 | +0.44% | 2545 | 11,013 | +3.85% |
| Valiant 200 2-Door Convertible | 135 | $2,349 | +0.38% | 2670 | 5,856 | -17.78% |
| Valiant 200 4-Door Sedan | 133 | $2,112 | +0.72% | 2570 | 63,828 | +11.92% |
| Valiant 200 4-Door Wagon | 176 | $2,388 | -0.17% | 2730 | 11,146 | -0.01% |
| Valiant Signet 2-Door Hardtop | 142 | $2,256 | +1.17% | 2600 | 37,736 | +22.29% |
| Valiant Signet 2-Door Convertible | 145 | $2,473 | +0.77% | 2690 | 7,636 | -16.67% |
| TOTALS | | Avg. price $2,201 | +0.55% | | Production 227,585 | +1.07% |

# Barracuda

*"Utility and economy with fastback flair."*

**Nameplate year of origin:** 1964.
**Current bodystyle lifespan:** 1964 through 1966.
**Predecessor to this model:** None.
**Replacement for this model:** Barracuda (1967 to 1969).
**Percentage of division's sales volume:** 4.28%.
**Corporate siblings:** Dodge Dart.
**Primary competition:** Ford Mustang.
**Notable changes:** All-new model for 1964, based upon Valiant platform.
**Major standard equipment:** All-vinyl front bucket seats, full carpeting, chrome exterior front and rear window trim, specific Barracuda trim, Torsion-Aire suspension and 6.50 × 13 BSW tires.

## Measurements

| | |
|---|---|
| Wheelbase | 106.0" |
| Length | 188.2" |
| Width | 70.1" |
| Height | 53.4" |
| Legroom — front | 40.0" |
| Legroom — rear | 35.5" |
| Headroom — front | 38.2" |
| Headroom — rear | 37.2" |
| Cargo capacity (cu. ft.) | 23.6 |
| Fuel capacity (gals.) | 18.0 |

## Models Available

| | Style Number | Base MSRP | Change from LY | Shipping Wt. (lbs.) | Production | Change from LY |
|---|---|---|---|---|---|---|
| Barracuda 2-Door Fastback HT | 149 | $2,365 | NEW | 2740 | 23,443 | NEW |
| TOTALS | | Avg. price $2,365 | NEW | | Production 23,443 | NEW |

# Savoy

*"For all its top-notch economy, its rich styling will turn many heads in any waiting line."*

**Nameplate year of origin:** 1951 (Concord 2-Door Suburban designation), 1954 (as series).
**Current bodystyle lifespan:** 1962 through 1965.
**Predecessor to this model:** Savoy (1960 to 1961).
**Replacement for this model:** Fury I (1965 to 1966).
**Percentage of division's sales volume:** 16.05%.
**Corporate siblings:** Dodge 330.
**Primary competition:** AMC Ambassador, Chevrolet Biscayne/BelAir, and Ford Galaxie.

## Measurements

| | Cars | Wagons |
|---|---|---|
| Wheelbase | 116.0" | 116.0" |
| Length | 206.5" | 211.5" |
| Width | 75.6" | 75.1" |
| Height | 55.1" | 54.8" |
| Legroom — front | 41.9" | 41.9" |
| Legroom — rear | 36.6" | 36.5" |

**Notable changes:** All-new exterior styling.

**Major standard equipment:** Cloth and vinyl front bench seat, color-keyed rubber floor mats, front armrests, dual sunvisors, electric windshield wipers, exterior bright trim around front window, and 7.00 × 14 BSW tires.

|  | Cars | Wagons |
|---|---|---|
| Headroom — front | 39.1" | 39.5" |
| Headroom — rear | 38.4" | 39.5" |
| Cargo capacity (cu. ft.) | 25.3 | NA |
| Fuel capacity (gals.) | 20.0 | 21.5 |

## Models Available

|  | Style Number | Base MSRP | Change from LY | Shipping Wt. (lbs.) | Production | Change from LY |
|---|---|---|---|---|---|---|
| Savoy 2-Door Sedan | 211 | $2,224 | +0.82% | 2990 | 21,326 | +5.15% |
| Savoy 4-Door Sedan | 213 | $2,280 | +0.80% | 3040 | 51,024 | -9.39% |
| Savoy 4-Door, 2-Seat Wagon | 256 | $2,620 | +0.42% | 3345 | 12,401 | -3.67% |
| Savoy 4-Door, 3-Seat Wagon | 259 | $2,721 | +0.41% | 3400 | 3,242 | -25.33% |
| TOTALS | Avg. price | $2,461 | +4.59% | Production | 87,993 | -6.21% |

# Belvedere

*"Seats six adults in style. And the more you look at how little it costs, the more you realize how much style for the money."*

**Nameplate year of origin:** 1951 (HT model), 1954 (as series).
**Current bodystyle lifespan:** 1962 through 1965.
**Predecessor to this model:** Belvedere (1960 to 1961).
**Replacement for this model:** Belvedere (1966 to 1967).
**Percentage of division's sales volume:** 10.47%.
**Corporate siblings:** Dodge 440.
**Primary competition:** AMC Ambassador, Chevrolet Biscayne/BelAir, and Ford Galaxie.
**Notable changes:** All-new exterior styling.
**Major standard equipment:** Cloth and vinyl front bench seat with Super foam cushions, color-keyed deep-pile carpeting, front and rear armrests, dual sunvisors, electric windshield wipers, exterior bright trim around windows and front fender line, and 7.00 × 14 BSW tires.

## Measurements

|  | Cars | Wagons |
|---|---|---|
| Wheelbase | 116.0" | 116.0" |
| Length | 206.5" | 211.5" |
| Width | 75.6" | 75.1" |
| Height | 55.1" | 54.8" |
| Legroom — front | 41.9" | 41.9" |
| Legroom — rear | 36.6" | 36.5" |
| Headroom — front | 39.1" | 39.5" |
| Headroom — rear | 38.4" | 39.5" |
| Cargo capacity (cu. ft.) | 25.3 | NA |
| Fuel capacity (gals.) | 20.0 | 21.5 |

## Models Available

|  | Style Number | Base MSRP | Change from LY | Shipping Wt. (lbs.) | Production | Change from LY |
|---|---|---|---|---|---|---|
| Belvedere 2-Door Sedan | 221 | $2,359 | +0.73% | 3000 | 5,364 | -13.73% |
| Belvedere 2-Door Hardtop | 222 | $2,444 | +0.53% | 3010 | 16,334 | +77.47% |
| Belvedere 4-Door Sedan | 223 | $2,417 | +0.75% | 3065 | 57,307 | +4.33% |
| Belvedere 4-Dr., 2-Seat Wagon | 366 | $2,826 | +0.39% | 3510 | 10,317 | +0.19% |
| Belvedere 4-Dr., 3-Seat Wagon | 367 | $2,928 | +0.38% | 3605 | 4,207 | +4.86% |
| TOTALS | Avg. price | $2,595 | +0.54% | Production | 93,529 | +10.48% |

1964

# Fury

*"Finest example in the low price field, of combining luxury, size, performance and economy in one car."*

**Nameplate year of origin:** 1956.
**Current bodystyle lifespan:** 1962 through 1965.
**Predecessor to this model:** Fury (1960 to 1961).
**Replacement for this model:** Fury III and Sport Fury (1965 to 1966).
**Percentage of division's sales volume:** 21.11%.
**Corporate siblings:** Dodge Polara.
**Primary competition:** AMC Ambassador, Chevrolet Biscayne/BelAir/Impala, Ford Galaxie/LTD, and Pontiac Catalina.
**Notable changes:** All-new exterior styling.
**Major standard equipment:** Cloth and vinyl front bench seat (all-vinyl on convertible and wagons) with Super foam cushions, color-keyed deep-pile carpeting, tower-back front seat, front and rear armrests, dual sunvisors, electric windshield wipers, electric clock, exterior bright trim around windows, electrically operated convertible top, backup lights, and 7.00 × 14 BSW tires. Sport Fury adds: Padded instrument panel, all-vinyl bucket seats, floor-mounted shifter and console with compartment, and deluxe steering wheel.

## Measurements

|  | Cars | Wagons |
|---|---|---|
| Wheelbase | 116.0" | 116.0" |
| Length | 206.5" | 211.5" |
| Width | 75.6" | 75.1" |
| Height | 55.1" | 54.8" |
| Legroom — front | 41.9" | 41.9" |
| Legroom — rear | 36.6" | 36.5" |
| Headroom — front | 39.1" | 39.5" |
| Headroom — rear | 38.4" | 39.5" |
| Cargo capacity (cu. ft.) | 25.3 | NA |
| Fuel capacity (gals.) | 20.0 | 21.5 |

## Models Available

| | Style Number | Base MSRP | Change from LY | Shipping Wt. (lbs.) | Production | Change from LY |
|---|---|---|---|---|---|---|
| Fury 2-Door Hardtop | 232 | $2,598 | +0.50% | 3040 | 26,303 | +90.16% |
| Fury 2-Door Convertible | 335 | $2,937 | +0.44% | 3345 | 5,173 | -0.92% |
| Fury 4-Door Sedan | 233 | $2,573 | +0.39% | 3045 | 34,901 | +9.44% |
| Fury 4-Door Hardtop | 334 | $2,752 | +0.36% | 3300 | 13,713 | +15.46% |
| Fury 4-Door, 2-Seat Wagon | 376 | $2,981 | +0.44% | 3530 | 3,646 | +10.35% |
| Fury 4-Door, 3-Seat Wagon | 377 | $3,084 | +0.42% | 3630 | 4,482 | +33.08% |
| Sport Fury 2-Door Hardtop | 342 | $2,864 | +0.46% | 3270 | 23,695 | +106.35% |
| Sport Fury 2-Door Convertible | 345 | $3,095 | +0.42% | 3405 | 3,858 | +0.57% |
| TOTALS | *Avg. price* | $2,861 | +0.46% | | *Production* 115,771 | +36.50% |

# PONTIAC

*"Success Story ... '64 Edition."*

The 1964 Pontiac line was a continuation of the successful 1963 models, with an all-new, much more conventional Tempest line adding to the success. Sharing its dimensions with the other three new GM mid-size models, the new Tempest lost its unique 4-cylinder engine, rear transmission and rope driveshaft in the makeover. What was lost in engineering uniqueness was replaced by a conventional 6-cylinder engine of Chevrolet design and a conventional drivetrain. Available power included the new for '63 326 CID V8, and after the start of the year, Pontiac's own 389 CID V8 was available in an important new option package, the GTO — the package that started the muscle car revolution. For only $296, a buyer of any Tempest LeMans model could get the power of a 325-horsepower V8 under the hood, plus an all-vinyl bucket seat interior, 3-speed transmission with Hurst shifter and 7.50 × 14 Redline tires. This power came at a total price starting as low as $2,787 and quickly became known as one of the best bargains in horsepower. The '64 Tempest line looked very much like a slightly more aggressive version of the '63 models. As for the model lineup, the top line LeMans added a 2-Door Hardtop, and the base Tempest models became the new Tempest Custom and dropped the 2-Door Coupe offering. A new "low-content" base Tempest line offered a 2-Door Coupe, 4-Door Sedan and a 4-Door Wagon.

Full-size Pontiacs continued relatively unchanged for 1964. Styling changes featured revised front fenders and new grilles, with the vertical leading edge of the front fenders now being totally flat. Rear styling sported new boomerang-shaped taillamps that ran vertically from the top of the rear quarter to the bottom of the rear bumper. There were no model changes for the big Pontiac this season, but there were two interesting option packages. The 2+2 was a Catalina 2-Door Hardtop or Convertible option that added bucket seats, special trim and a bit more power under the hood. It was the equivalent of a full-size GTO. The second option was the Bonneville Brougham for 4-Door Hardtops, which added a padded vinyl top, luxurious interior trim and special model identification trim.

**1964**

Bonneville 2-Door Convertible

Catalina 4-Door Hardtop

Grand Prix 2-Door Hardtop

Tempest Custom 4-Door Sedan

Tempest LeMans 2-Door Coupe

Tempest GTO 2-Door Convertible

**Model year production:** 714,516, up 18.67% over 1963.
**Domestic market share:** 9.16% (3rd place).
**Base price range:** $2,259 to $3,633.
**Industry average base price:** $3,024.
**Pontiac average base price:** $2,916.
**Introduction date:** September 1963.
**Assembly plants:** Baltimore, MD (B); Southgate, CA (C); Doraville, GA (D); Linden, NJ (E); Framingham, MA (G); Kansas City, MO (K); Pontiac, MI (P); Arlington, TX (R); Lordstown, OH (U); Fairfax, KS (X); Fremont, CA (Z).

**Data plate identification:** Eight to ten digit code read as follows: 1st digit 6 for 6-cylinder or 8 for V8; 2nd identifies series (second digit of the body style number in the charts below); 3rd digit 4 for 1964; 4th digit is assembly plant code; and 1001 and up for serial number. A separate plate contains body style number. *Example:* 834X1001 is a 1964 Pontiac Catalina, serial number 1001, built in Fairfax, KS.

## Powertrains

| Engine | Gross HP* | Transmission Availability | Tempest/ LeMans | Catalina & Star Chief | Bonneville & Grand Prix |
|---|---|---|---|---|---|
| 215 CID Trophy, 1-bbl., 6-cyl. | 140 | 3-speed manual | S (ex. GTO) | - | - |
| | | 4-speed manual | $188 (ex. GTO) | - | - |
| | | 2-sp. Automatic | $188 (ex. GTO) | - | - |

| Engine | Gross HP* | Transmission Availability | Tempest/ LeMans | Catalina & Star Chief | Bonneville & Grand Prix |
|---|---|---|---|---|---|
| 326 CID Trophy, 2-bbl., V8 | 250 | 3-speed manual | $108 (ex. GTO) | - | - |
| | | 4-speed manual | $296 (ex. GTO) | - | - |
| | | 2-sp. Automatic | $307 (ex. GTO) | - | - |
| 326 CID Trophy, 4-bbl., V8 | 280 | 3-speed manual | $173 (ex. GTO) | - | - |
| | | 4-speed manual | $361 (ex. GTO) | - | - |
| | | 2-sp. Automatic | $372 (ex. GTO) | - | - |
| 389 CID Trophy E, 2-bbl., V8 | 230 | Jetaway Automatic | - | $231 | - |
| 389 CID Trophy, 2-bbl., V8 | 235 | 3-speed manual | - | S | - |
| | 283 | 4-speed manual | - | $231 | |
| | 267 | Jetaway Automatic | - | $231 | - |
| 389 CID Trophy, 4-bbl., V8 | 306/325 | 3-speed manual | S (GTO) | $35 | S |
| | 306/325 | 4-speed manual | $188 (GTO) | $266 | $231 |
| | 303/325 | Jetaway Automatic | $199 (GTO) | $266 | $231 |
| 389 CID Tri-Power, 3 × 2-bbl., V8 | 330 | 3-speed HD man. | - | $168 | $133 |
| | | 4-speed manual | - | $399 | $364 |
| | | Jetaway Automatic | - | $399 | $364 |
| 389 CID Tri-Power, 3 × 2-bbl., V8 | 348 | 3-speed HD man. | $116 (GTO) | $ | $ |
| | | 4-speed manual | $304 (GTO) | $ | $ |
| | | Jetaway Automatic | $315 (GTO) | $ | $ |
| 421 CID Trophy, 4-bbl., V8 | 320 | 3-speed HD man. | - | $143 | $108 |
| | | 4-speed manual | - | $374 | $339 |
| | | Jetaway Automatic | - | $374 | $339 |
| 421 CID Tri-Power, 3 × 2-bbl., V8 | 350 | 3-speed HD man. | - | $276 | $241 |
| | | 4-speed manual | - | $507 | $472 |
| | | Jetaway Automatic | - | $507 | $472 |
| 421 CID Tri-Power, 3 × 2-bbl., V8 | 370 | 3-speed HD man. | - | $439 | $404 |
| | | 4-speed manual | - | $670 | $635 |
| | | Jetaway Automatic | - | $670 | $635 |

*Ratings vary with model and transmission attachment.*

## Major Options

| | Tempest/LeMans | Catalina | Star Chief | Bonneville | Grand Prix |
|---|---|---|---|---|---|
| Air conditioning (V8 only) | $346 | $430 | $430 | $430 | $430 |
| Soft Ray tinted glass | $37 | $43 | $43 | $43 | $43 |
| Tilt steering wheel | $43 | $43 | $43 | $43 | $43 |
| Power steering — variable-ratio | $97 | $97 | $108 | $108 | $108 |
| Power brakes | $43 | $43 | $43 | $43 | $43 |
| Power driver's seat/Bench seat | $71 | $97 | $97 | $97 | $97 |
| Power windows | $102 | $106 | $106 | $106 | $106 |
| AM radio — manual | $62 | $88 | $88 | $88 | $88 |
| AM/FM radio — manual | - | $151 | $151 | $151 | $151 |
| Front seat console | $ | $161 | - | $161 | S |
| Front bucket seats | $134 | $ | - | $ | S |
| White stripe tires | $35 | $40 | $40 | $40 | $40 |
| Aluminum (8-lug) hubs and drums | - | $138 | $138 | $122 | $122 |
| GTO package (LeMans only) | $296 | - | - | - | - |
| 2 + 2 package (2-Door HT/Conv. only) | - | $291 | - | - | - |
| Brougham packagem (4-Dr. HT only) | - | - | - | $247 | - |

Options common to most models (- = Not Available; S = Standard equipment.) Items may be standard equipment, optional at different pricing, or unavailable on certain models. This chart is only a guide.

## Paint Colors

| | Code | | Code |
|---|---|---|---|
| Starlight Black | A | Aquamarine Metallic | P |
| Cameo Ivory | C | Gulfstream Aqua Metallic | Q |
| Silvermist Gray Metallic | D | Alamo Beige | R |
| Yorktown Blue Metallic | F | Saddle Bronze Metallic | S |
| Skyline Blue | H | Singapore Gold Metallic | T |
| Pinehurst Green Metallic | J | Grenadier Red | V |
| Marimba Red Metallic | L | Nocturne Blue Metallic | W |
| Sunfire Red Metallic | N | | |

# Tempest

*"The Pontiac Tempest. Longer, roomier, and a new smooth ride."*

**1964**

**Nameplate year of origin:** 1961.
**Current bodystyle lifespan:** 1964 through 1965.
**Predecessor to this model:** Tempest/LeMans (1961 to 1963).
**Replacement for this model:** Tempest/LeMans/GTO (1966 to 1967).
**Percentage of division's sales volume:** 32.89%.
**Corporate siblings:** Chevrolet Chevelle, Oldsmobile F-85/Cutlass, and Buick Special/Skylark.
**Primary competition:** Ford Fairlane, Mercury Comet, and Dodge Coronet.
**Notable changes:** Completely redesigned.
**Major standard equipment:** Cloth and vinyl bench seat, dual sun visors, electric windshield wipers, and 6.50 × 14 BSW tires. Custom adds: Deluxe interior trim, and additional exterior bright work. LeMans adds: All-vinyl bucket seats, deep-pile carpeting, power top on convertible, and specific LeMans trim.

## Measurements

| | Cars | Wagons |
|---|---|---|
| Wheelbase | 115.0" | 115.0" |
| Length | 203.0" | 203.0" |
| Width | 73.3" | 73.3" |
| Height | 53.5" | 53.5" |
| Legroom — front | 42.3" | 42.3" |
| Legroom — rear | 35.1" | 35.1" |
| Headroom — front | 38.1" | 38.1" |
| Headroom — rear | 36.8" | 36.6" |
| Cargo capacity (cu. ft.) | 32.1 | 86.4 |
| Fuel capacity (gals.) | 21.5 | 21.5 |

## Models Available

| | Style Number | Base MSRP | Change from LY | Shipping Wt. (lbs.) | Production | Change from LY |
|---|---|---|---|---|---|---|
| Tempest 2-Door Sports Coupe | 2027 | $2,259 | -1.53% | 2930 | 21,765 | +69.93% |
| Tempest 4-Door Sedan | 2069 | $2,313 | +3.21% | 2970 | 19,427 | -31.16% |
| Tempest Safari 4-Dr., 2-S. Wagon | 2035 | $2,605 | +3.70% | 3245 | 6,834 | -32.57% |
| Tempest Custom 2-Dr. Sports Cpe. | 2127 | $2,345 | NEW | 2955 | 25,833 | NEW |
| Tempest Custom 2-Door Conv. | 2167 | $2,641 | NEW | 3075 | 7,987 | NEW |
| Tempest Custom 4-Door Sedan | 2169 | $2,399 | NEW | 2990 | 29,948 | NEW |
| Tempest Custom Safari 4-Dr. Wgn. | 2135 | $2,691 | NEW | 3260 | 10,696 | NEW |
| Tempest LeMans 2-Door Sp. Cpe. | 2227 | $2,491 | +3.02% | 2975 | 38,701 | -15.32% |
| Tempest LeMans 2-Door HT | 2237 | $2,556 | NEW | 2995 | 49,732 | NEW |
| Tempest LeMans 2-Door Conv. | 2267 | $2,796 | +1.97% | 3125 | 24,103 | +51.05% |
| TOTALS | | *Avg. price* $2,510 | +3.59% | | *Production* 235,026 | +62.88% |

# Catalina

*"Impressive quality, styling and performance
in our lowest-priced full-size car."*

**Nameplate year of origin:** 1950 (hardtop models), 1959 (as series).
**Current bodystyle lifespan:** 1961 through 1964.
**Predecessor to this model:** Catalina (1959 to 1960).
**Replacement for this model:** Catalina (1965 to 1966).
**Corporate siblings:** Chevrolet Biscayne/BelAir/Impala, Oldsmobile 88, Buick LeSabre/Wildcat.
**Primary competition:** Mercury Monterey, and Dodge Polara.
**Percentage of division's sales volume:** 36.08%.
**Notable changes:** Revised front and rear styling.
**Major standard equipment:** Cloth and vinyl (all-vinyl in convertible) bench seat, nylon-blend carpet, cushioned instrument panel, automatic interior lighting, heater and defroster, electric windshield wipers, chrome exterior trim and 8.00 × 14 BSW tires (8.50 × 14 BSW tires on Safari wagons).

## Measurements

|  | Cars | Wagon |
| --- | --- | --- |
| Wheelbase | 120.0" | 119.0" |
| Length | 213.0" | 213.8" |
| Width | 79.2" | 79.2" |
| Height | 55.8" | 56.0" |
| Legroom — front | 42.0" | 42.0" |
| Legroom — rear | 38.1" | 38.1" |
| Headroom — front | 39.0" | 39.0" |
| Headroom — rear | 37.8" | 37.8" |
| Cargo capacity (cu. ft.) | NA | NA |
| Fuel capacity (gals.) | 25.0 | 25.0 |

## Models Available

|  | Style Number | Base MSRP | Change from LY | Shipping Wt. (lbs.) | Production | Change from LY |
| --- | --- | --- | --- | --- | --- | --- |
| Catalina 2-Door Sedan | 2311 | $2,735 | +0.37% | 3695 | 12,480 | -11.43% |
| Catalina 2-Door Hardtop | 2347 | $2,869 | +0.35% | 3750 | 74,793 | +23.02% |
| Catalina 2-Door Convertible | 2367 | $3,181 | +0.32% | 3825 | 18,693 | +2.43% |
| Catalina 4-Door Sedan | 2369 | $2,806 | +0.39% | 3770 | 84,457 | +5.62% |
| Catalina 4-Door Vista Hardtop | 2339 | $2,945 | +0.34% | 3835 | 33,849 | +8.30% |
| Catalina Safari 4-Dr., 2-S. Wagon | 2335 | $3,203 | +0.31% | 4190 | 20,356 | +10.35% |
| Catalina Safari 4-Dr., 3-S. Wagon | 2345 | $3,311 | +0.33% | 4235 | 13,140 | +11.82% |
| TOTALS | *Avg. price* | $3,007 | +0.33% | *Production* | 257,768 | +9.90% |

# Star Chief

*"A comfortable and luxurious traveling companion."*

**Nameplate year of origin:** 1954.
**Current bodystyle lifespan:** 1961 through 1964.
**Predecessor to this model:** Star Chief (1959 to 1960).
**Replacement for this model:** Executive (1965 to 1966).
**Corporate siblings:** Chevrolet Biscayne/BelAir/Impala, Oldsmobile 88, Buick LeSabre/Wildcat.
**Primary competition:** Mercury Montclair, and Dodge Custom 880.
**Percentage of division's sales volume:** 5.27%.
**Notable changes:** Revised front and rear styling.
**Major standard equipment:** Cloth and vinyl or all-vinyl bench seat, nylon-blend carpet, custom steering wheel, cushioned instrument panel, automatic interior lighting, 2-speed electric windshield wipers, luggage compartment trim, chrome exterior trim, wheel covers, and 8.00 × 14 BSW tires.

## Measurements

| Wheelbase | 123.0" |
| --- | --- |
| Length | 220.0" |
| Width | 79.2" |
| Height | 55.8" |
| Legroom — front | 41.9" |
| Legroom — rear | 38.3" |
| Headroom — front | 39.0" |
| Headroom — rear | 37.3" |
| Cargo capacity (cu. ft.) | NA |
| Fuel capacity (gals.) | 25.0 |

## Models Available

| | Style Number | Base MSRP | Change from LY | Shipping Wt. (lbs.) | Production | Change from LY |
|---|---|---|---|---|---|---|
| Star Chief 4-Door Sedan | 2669 | $3,107 | +0.36% | 3885 | 26,453 | -6.56% |
| Star Chief 4-Door Hardtop | 2639 | $3,239 | +0.31% | 3945 | 11,200 | -10.03% |
| TOTALS | | *Avg. price* $3,173 | +0.33% | | *Production* 37,653 | -7.62% |

# Grand Prix

*"The distinctive Grand Prix."*

**Nameplate year of origin:** 1962.
**Current bodystyle lifespan:** 1962 through 1964.
**Predecessor to this model:** None.
**Replacement for this model:** Grand Prix (1965 to 1966).
**Corporate siblings:** Buick Wildcat and Oldsmobile Starfire.
**Primary competition:** Chrysler 300 and Mercury S-55.
**Percentage of division's sales volume:** 8.93%.
**Notable changes:** Revised front and rear styling.
**Major standard equipment:** Front bucket seats with all-vinyl trim, center console with vacuum gauge, loop-pile carpeting, electric clock, lamp package, deluxe wheel covers, and 8.00 × 14 BSW tires.

### Measurements

| | |
|---|---|
| Wheelbase | 120.0" |
| Length | 213.0" |
| Width | 79.2" |
| Height | 54.6" |
| Legroom — front | 41.2" |
| Legroom — rear | 37.0" |
| Headroom — front | 38.2" |
| Headroom — rear | 38.0" |
| Cargo capacity (cu. ft.) | NA |
| Fuel capacity (gals.) | 25.0 |

## Models Available

| | Style Number | Base MSRP | Change from LY | Shipping Wt. (lbs.) | Production | Change from LY |
|---|---|---|---|---|---|---|
| Grand Prix 2-Door Hardtop | 2957 | $3,499 | +0.29% | 3930 | 63,810 | -12.54% |
| TOTALS | | *Avg. price* $3,499 | +0.29% | | *Production* 63,810 | -12.54% |

# Bonneville

*"Sculptured beauty, traditional craftsmanship ... Bonneville delivers high performance and smooth responsiveness."*

**Nameplate year of origin:** 1957.
**Current bodystyle lifespan:** 1961 through 1964.
**Predecessor to this model:** Bonneville (1959 to 1960).
**Replacement for this model:** Bonneville (1965 to 1966).
**Corporate siblings:** Chevrolet Biscayne/BelAir/Impala, Oldsmobile 88, Buick LeSabre/Wildcat.
**Primary competition:** Mercury Park Lane, and Dodge Custom 880.
**Percentage of division's sales volume:** 16.83%.
**Notable changes:** Revised front and rear styling.
**Major standard equipment:** Cloth and vinyl or all-vinyl bench seat, full carpeting including lower door panels, cushioned instrument panel, automatic interior lighting, electric windshield wipers, chrome exterior trim, deluxe wheel covers and 8.00 × 14 BSW tires (8.50 × 14 BSW tires on Safari wagon).

### Measurements

| | Cars | Wagon |
|---|---|---|
| Wheelbase | 123.0" | 119.0" |
| Length | 220.0" | 213.8" |
| Width | 79.2" | 79.2" |
| Height | 54.7" | 56.0" |
| Legroom — front | 41.6" | 42.0" |
| Legroom — rear | 39.0" | 38.1" |
| Headroom — front | 39.8" | 39.0" |
| Headroom — rear | 39.6" | 37.8" |
| Cargo capacity (cu. ft.) | NA | NA |
| Fuel capacity (gals.) | 25.0 | 25.0 |

1964

## Models Available

| | Style Number | Base MSRP | Change from LY | Shipping Wt. (lbs.) | Production | Change from LY |
|---|---|---|---|---|---|---|
| Bonneville 2-Door Hardtop | 2847 | $3,358 | 0.30% | 3920 | 34,769 | 12.18% |
| Bonneville 2-Door Convertible | 2867 | $3,578 | 0.28% | 3985 | 22,016 | -6.15% |
| Bonneville 4-Door Hardtop | 2839 | $3,433 | 0.29% | 3995 | 57,630 | 15.42% |
| Bonneville Safari 4-Dr., 2-S. Wgn. | 2835 | $3,633 | 0.28% | 4275 | 5,844 | 13.34% |
| TOTALS | *Avg. price* $3,501 | | +0.29% | *Production* 120,259 | | +9.79% |

# RAMBLER

*"More of what you ask for in style, stamina, economy and comfort."*

Last year, the Classic and Ambassador were totally re-designed, so this year was the opportunity for the American to bask in the spotlight. A completely redesigned American with cleaner, more rounded lines appeared, and was a success from the start. In fact, with its new styling, the compact American seemed to appeal especially to consumers in the market for something more than basic transportation, as sales of the mid-level and top-line 330 and 440 models increased at a more dramatic rate than those of the low-line 220. Also contributing to increased sales were the increased dimensions of the newly styled car. Wheelbase increased from 100 to 106 inches, providing a better ride and better driver control. Prior Rambler Americans were based on a basic platform design that dated back to the original Rambler of the 1950s. To most observers of the time, the new American was seen as a more modern product as compared to the Chevrolet Chevy II, Ford Falcon, and the Plymouth Valiant. It certainly had good looks going for it, if nothing else.

The Classic and Ambassador gained new 2-Door Hardtop body styles, but styling changes were limited to a new grille and revised trim. The biggest news for the year came in the form of powerplants and sports models. In the Classic line, a Typhoon 2-Door Hardtop was introduced in April of 1964. Outside, all of these special cars were painted Solar Yellow with Black roof and carried special Typhoon badging. Under the hood was a 145-horsepower, 232 cubic-inch 6-cylinder engine. This engine was also offered on a limited number of other Classic models for the remainder of the 1964 model season. For the top-of-the-line Ambassador, a new 990-H 2-Door Hardtop was offered, featuring more luxurious appointments and a sportier 4-barrel version of the 327 CID V8 with higher compression 9.7:1 heads. Each of these models was an indicator of things to come at American Motors — from the upcoming 390 cubic-inch V8s, to the sporty Marlin and Javelin. Unfortunately, these performance options did not save these two lines from taking a major hit in model year sales, dropping a combined total of nearly 40 percent from 1963 levels. Many of these sales were lost to the newly revamped line of "intermediate" GM cars. No longer classified senior-compacts, the new GM offerings were more direct competition for the two mid-size Rambler models.

Ambassador 990-H 2-Door Hardtop

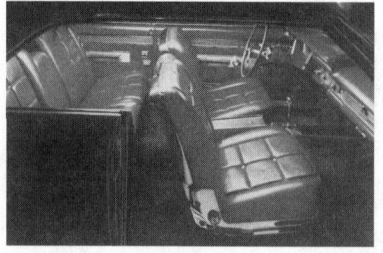

Ambassador 990-H Interior

Classic 770 4-Door Sedan

American 440 2-Door Convertible

American 330 4-Door Wagon

**Model year production:** 388,651, down 15.6% from 1963.
**Domestic market share:** 4.98% (8th place).
**Base price range:** $1,907 to $2,985.
**Industry average base price:** $3,024.
**Rambler average base price:** $2,343.
**Introduction date:** October 5, 1963.
**Assembly plants:** Kenosha, Wisconsin, and Brampton, Ontario, Canada.
**Data plate identification:** Code read as follows: 64 = 1964,

followed by serial number starting as follows: American, B-650001 and up; Classic Six, G-500001 and up; Classic V8, Z155001 and up; Ambassador, H-255001 and up. Export cars added a "K" after the letter, and cars built in Canada added a "T" after the letter. Export and Canadian cars also started at differing serial numbers. *Example:* 64G500001 is a 1964 Rambler Classic Six built in Kenosha, WI, serial number 500001.

**1964**

## Powertrains

| Engine | Gross HP | Engine Code | Transmission Availability | Trans Code | American | Classic | Ambassador |
|---|---|---|---|---|---|---|---|
| 195.6 CID, 1-bbl., 6-cyl. | 90 | A | 3-speed manual, col. | S | S (ex. 440) | – | – |
| | | | 3-speed w/Overdrive | O | $109 | – | – |
| | | | Shift-Command Automatic — col./flr. | A/C | $187 | – | – |
| 195.6 CID, 1-bbl., 6-cyl. | 125 | A | 3-speed manual, col. | S | $38 | – | – |
| | | | 3-speed w/Overdrive | O | $147 | – | – |
| | | | Shift-Command Automatic — col./flr. | A/C | $225 | – | – |
| 199 CID, 1-bbl., 6-cyl. | 128 | A | 3-speed manual, col. | S | – | S (550) | – |
| | | | 3-speed w/Overdrive | O | – | $109 | – |
| | | | Shift-Command Automatic — col./flr. | A/C | – | $187 | – |
| 232 CID*, 1-bbl., 6-cyl. | 145 | E/F/V | 3-speed manual | S | S (440) | S (660/770) | S |
| | | | 3-speed w/Overdrive | O | – | $109 | $109 |
| | | | Shift-Command Automatic — col./flr. | A/C | – | $187 | $187 |
| 232 CID*, 2-bbl., 6-cyl. | 155 | B/G/S/M | 3-speed manual | S | $49 (440)/ $83 (220/330) | $12 | $12 |
| | | | Shift-Command Automatic — col./flr. | A/C | $238 | $199 | $199 |
| 287 CID, 2-bbl., V8 | 198 | H/T/N | 3-speed manual | S | – | $122 (550) | – |
| | | | Shift-Command Automatic — col./flr. | A/C | – | $293 (550) | – |
| 327 CID, 2-bbl., V8 | 250 | J/W/P | 3-speed manual | S | – | $138 (660/770) | – |
| | | | Shift-Command Automatic — col./flr. | A/C | – | $325 (660/770) | – |
| 327 CID, 4-bbl., V8 | 270 | K/U/Q | 3-speed manual | S | – | $241 (660/770) | $171 |
| | | | Shift-Command Automatic — col./flr. | A/C | – | $428 (660/770) | $358 |

*Introduced late in the model year.

## Major Options

| | American | Classic | Ambassador |
|---|---|---|---|
| Weather-Eye heater | $74 | $78 | $78 |
| Air conditioning | $360 | $380 | $399 |
| Tinted glass | $34 | $42 | $42 |
| Power steering | $86 | $86 | $86 |
| Power brakes | $43 | $43 | $43 |
| AM radio | $59 | $65 | $65 |
| Electric clock | $16 | $16 | $16 |
| Bucket seats | $100 | $100 | $100 |
| Station Wagon third seat | - | $85 | $85 |

Options common to most models (- = Not Available). Items may be standard equipment, optional at different pricing, or unavailable on certain models. This chart is only a guide.

## Paint Colors*

| | Code |
|---|---|
| Classic Black | P1 |
| Solar Yellow | P13A |
| Sceptre Silver Metallic | P43 |
| Sceptre Siver Metallic | P43A |
| Rampart Red | P51 |
| Sentry Light Blue Met. | P52A |
| Forum Dark Blue | P53 |
| Woodwide Dark Grn. Met. | P54A |
| Westminster Dark Green | P55 |
| Aurora Light Turquoise | P56 |
| Lancelot Med. Turquoise | P57 |
| Bengal Ivory | P58 |
| Emperor Light Gold Met. | P59 |
| Contessa Rose Metallic | P60A |
| Vintage Maroon Metallic | P61 |
| Frost White | P72 |

*"A" indicates acrylic enamel paints. Two-tones: first number is body color, second number is roof/accent color.

# American

*"All-new line of heart-teasing compact hardtops, sedans, wagons and convertibles."*

**Nameplate year of origin:** 1958.
**Current bodystyle lifespan:** 1964 through 1969.
**Predecessor to this model:** Rambler American (1961 to 1963).
**Corporate siblings:** None.
**Replacement for this model:** Hornet (1970 to 1977).
**Percentage of division's sales volume:** 42.11%.
**Primary competition:** Chevrolet Chevy II, Dodge Dart, Ford Falcon, and Plymouth Valiant.
**Notable changes:** Completely restyled.
**Major standard equipment:** Front arm rests and ash trays, front foam cushion seat, dual sunvisors, black rubber floor mats, air cleaner, oil filter, black rubber cargo mat on wagons, and 6.00 × 15 BSW tires. 330 adds: Rear door (side) armrests, door-activated dome lights, chrome horn ring, color-keyed carpeting (wagons), and chrome luggage rack (wagons). 440 adds: OHV engine, Dual-note horn, deluxe steering wheel, vinyl-pleated upholstery with deluxe trim level, padded instrument panel, glove box lock, and wheel covers. 440-H adds: Bucket seats, floor console, floor shift, special trim and identification.

## Measurements

| | |
|---|---|
| Wheelbase | 106.0" |
| Length | 181.0" |
| Width | 70.9" |
| Height | 54.2" |
| Legroom — front | 42.0" |
| Legroom — rear | 35.0" |
| Headroom — front | 39.0" |
| Headroom — rear | 39.0" |
| Luggage capacity (cu. ft.) | 75.0 (wagon) |
| Fuel capacity (gals.) | 16 |

## Models Available

| | Style Number | Base MSRP | Change from LY | Shipping Wt. (lbs.) | Production | Change from LY |
|---|---|---|---|---|---|---|
| American 220 2-Door Sedan | 6406 | $1,907 | +3.30% | 2506 | 32,716 | +17.77% |
| American 220 4-Door Sedan | 6405 | $1,964 | +3.64% | 2527 | 18,225 | +26.40% |
| American 220 4-Door Wagon | 6408 | $2,240 | +5.16% | 2661 | 8,062 | +81.74% |
| American 330 2-Door Sedan | 6406-2 | $2,000 | +4.77% | 2504 | 15,171 | * |
| American 330 4-Door Sedan | 6405-2 | $2,057 | +5.06% | 2526 | 19,379 | +100.49% |

| | Style Number | Base MSRP | Change from LY | Shipping Wt. (lbs.) | Production | Change from LY |
|---|---|---|---|---|---|---|
| American 330 4-Door Wagon | 6408-2 | $2,324 | +6.12% | 2675 | 20,587 | +200.63% |
| American 440 2-Door Hardtop | 6409-5 | $2,133 | -0.14% | 2596 | 19,495 | +282.18% |
| American 440 2-Door Convertible | 6407-5 | $2,346 | +0.09% | 2752 | 8,907 | +87.52% |
| American 440 4-Door Sedan | 6405-5 | $2,150 | +2.92% | 2572 | 6,590 | +124.38% |
| American 440-H 2-Door Hardtop | 6409-7 | $2,292 | +0.48% | 2617 | 14,527 | +49.01% |
| TOTALS | Avg. price | $2,141 | +2.90% | Production | 163,659 | +59.30% |

*Comparison to 1963 model unavailable.

# Classic

*"Big inside where a car should be big—
trim outside where a car should be trim."*

**Nameplate year of origin:** 1957 (Nash Rambler model).
**Current bodystyle lifespan:** 1963 through 1966 (restyled in 1965).
**Predecessor to this model:** Rambler Classic (1957 to 1962).
**Corporate siblings:** Ambassador (Shared components from the cowl back).
**Replacement for this model:** Rebel (1967 to 1970).
**Percentage of division's sales volume:** 53.08%.
**Primary competition:** Chevrolet Chevelle, Dodge Coronet, Ford Fairlane, Plymouth Belvedere, and Studebaker Daytona.
**Notable changes:** Completely restyled.
**Major standard equipment:** Front arm rests and ash trays, front foam cushion seat, dual sunvisors, air cleaner, oil filter, black rubber cargo mat (wagons), chrome luggage rack (wagons) and 6.50 × 14 BSW tires (7.00 × 14 BSW tires on wagons). 660 adds: Rear door armrests and ash trays, door-activated dome lights, and electric clock. 770 adds: Additional chrome exterior trim and deluxe interior trim level. Typhoon adds: Bucket seats, floor shift, Solar Yellow paint with black roof, and special trim and identification.

## Measurements

| | |
|---|---|
| Wheelbase | 112.0" |
| Length | 190.0"/Wagon 190.5" |
| Width | 73.8" |
| Height | 54.6" |
| Legroom — front | 41.1" |
| Legroom — rear | 36.3" |
| Headroom — front | 39.3" |
| Headroom — rear | 37.8" |
| Luggage cap. (cu. ft.) | NA** |
| Fuel capacity (gals.) | 19.0 |

## Models Available

| | Style Number | Base MSRP | Change from LY | Shipping Wt. (lbs.) | Production | Change from LY |
|---|---|---|---|---|---|---|
| Classic 550 2-Door Sedan | 6416-0 | $2,066 | +0.54% | 2732 | 6,999 | -54.6% |
| Classic 550 4-Door Sedan | 6415-0 | $2,116 | +0.52% | 2755 | 24,070 | -48.6% |
| Classic 550 4-Door Wagon | 6418-0 | $2,446 | +0.45% | 2915 | 15,363 | -46.2% |
| Classic 660 2-Door Sedan | 6416-2 | $2,206 | +0.5% | 2736 | 4,849 | -61.0% |
| Classic 660 4-Door Sedan | 6415-2 | $2,256 | +0.49% | 2758 | 48,958 | -40.8% |
| Classic 660 4-Door Wagon | 6418-2 | $2,548 | +0.43% | 2916 | 37,579 | -29.8% |
| Classic 770 2-Door Sedan | 6416-5 | $2,310 | +0.48% | 2740 | 1,947 | -71.5% |
| Classic 770 2-Door Hardtop | 6419-5 | $2,397 | NEW | 2789 | 20,868 | NEW |
| Classic 770 4-Door Sedan | 6415-5 | $2,360 | +0.47% | 2763 | 23,788 | -44.7% |
| Classic 770 4-Door Wagon | 6418-5 | $2,651 | +0.42% | 2921 | 19,358 | -18.3% |
| Classic Typhoon 2-Door HT | 6419-7 | $2,509 | NEW | 2818 | 2,520 | NEW |
| TOTALS | Avg. price | $2,351 | +0.17% | Production | 206,299 | -35.5% |

# Ambassador

*"A superb, limited-edition series with luxury
features as standard equipment."*

**Nameplate year of origin:** 1933 (from top-of-the-line Nash).
**Current bodystyle lifespan:** 1963 through 1966.
**Predecessor to this model:** Ambassador (1957 to 1962).
**Corporate siblings:** Classic (shared components from the cowl back).
**Replacement for this model:** None.
**Percentage of division's sales volume:** 4.81%.
**Primary competition:** Buick Skylark, Dodge Coronet, Mercury Comet, and
  Oldsmobile F-85.
**Notable changes:** Completely restyled.
**Major standard equipment:** Front arm rests and ashtrays, front and rear foam
  cushion seats, door-activated dome lights, electric clock, color-keyed carpet-
  ing, underhood insulation, chrome luggage rack (wagons), deluxe steering
  wheel, padded instrument panel, full wheel covers, and 7.50 × 14 BSW tires.
  990-H adds: All-vinyl bucket seats, floor console and floor shift.

## Measurements

| | |
|---|---|
| Wheelbase | 112.0" |
| Length | 190.0"/ |
| | Wagon 190.5" |
| Width | 73.8" |
| Height | 55.3" |
| Legroom — front | 41.1" |
| Legroom — rear | 36.3" |
| Headroom — front | 39.3" |
| Headroom — rear | 37.8" |
| Luggage cap. (cu. ft.) | 80.0 (Wagon) |
| Fuel capacity (gals.) | 19.0 |

## Models Available

| | Style Number | Base MSRP | Change from LY | Shipping Wt. (lbs.) | Production | Change from LY |
|---|---|---|---|---|---|---|
| Ambassador 990 2-Door Hardtop | 6489-5 | $2,736 | NEW | 3213 | 4,407 | NEW |
| Ambassador 990 4-Door Sedan | 6485-5 | $2,671 | +0.42% | 3204 | 9,827 | -29.9% |
| Ambassador 990 4-Door Wagon | 6488-5 | $2,985 | +1.0% | 3350 | 2,995 | -51.0% |
| Ambassador 990-H 2-Door HT | 6489-7 | $2,917 | NEW | 3255 | 1,464 | NEW |
| TOTALS | | *Avg. price* $2,827 | +6.8% | | *Production* 18,693 | -50.6% |

# STUDEBAKER

*"Different ... by Design."*

A facelift was given to all of the cars in the former Lark line. With the new styling came new nameplates for most of the models. The standard Lark became the Challenger. The Regal took on a name from Studebaker's past, Commander. The Lark Custom was discontinued, but the Daytona continued as an expanded model line. The Cruiser, GT Hawk and Avanti were all returning, at least for the beginning of the model year. Sales continued to fall and the financial situation for the company continued to worsen. A decision was made that was intended to help the ailing company, but in the end sealed its fate. All Studebaker production was moved to Canada effective January 2, 1964. With this move production of the Gran Turismo Hawk, Avanti, certain Lark models, and Champ pickups was discontinued. To the buying public, this signal meant trouble was looming, and no one wanted to buy a car that would soon disappear. This made the situation even worse. By the end of the season, sales totaled nearly half what they had been in 1963, which itself was far from a robust year. At least the cars were still 100 percent Studebaker products. Attempts to restyle the now 12 year old basic structure were not helping, and even loyal Studebaker customers were turning to the much more modern designs from the Big Three manufacturers, and the newly designed AMC Rambler Classic.

Unfortunately, the timing was not good for the newly introduced Avanti, or for the GT Hawk, which was now entering its third season in this form. The GT Hawk had finally become a respectable competitor in power and content when the plug was pulled. Its demise is sad because it was one of the better looking modern day products to come from South Bend. The same fate would befall the futuristic looking Avanti, but it would have a savior in the form of two Studebaker dealers who would buy the tooling and the rights to continue production as the Avanti II.

Avanti 2-Door Hardtop

Challenger 4-Door Sedan

Commander 4-Door Wagonaire

**1964**

**Model year production:** 46,460, down 44.81% from 1963.
**Domestic market share:** 0.60% (12th place).
**Base price range:** $1,943 to $4,445.
**Industry average base price:** $3,024.
**Studebaker average base price:** $2,541.
**Introduction date:** September 1963.
**Assembly plants:** South Bend, IN (No coding) and Canada (C).

**Data plate identification (VIN):** Up to ten digit code read as follows: 64 for 1964; S for 6-cylinder or V for V8 engine; C only if built in Canada; followed by Serial Number 1001 and up. Body style numbers are found on a separate plate on the vehicle. *Example:* 64S1001 is a 1964 Studebaker Six built in South Bend, IN, serial number 1001.

## Powertrains

| Engine | Gross HP | Transmission Availability | Challenger/ Cammander/Daytona | Cruiser & GT Hawk | Avanti |
|---|---|---|---|---|---|
| 169.6 CID, 1-bbl., OHV 6-cyl. | 90 | 3-speed manual | S | - | - |
| | | 3-speed w/Overdrive | $110 | - | - |
| | | Flightomatic Automatic | $180 | - | - |
| 259.2 CID, 2-bbl., OHV V8 | 180 | 3-speed manual | $135 | - | - |
| | | 3-speed w/Overdrive | $245 | - | - |
| | | 4-speed manual | $223 | - | - |
| | | Flightomatic Automatic | $345 | - | - |
| 259.2 CID, 4-bbl., OHV V8 | 195 | 3-speed manual | $157 | - | - |
| | | 3-speed w/Overdrive | $267 | - | - |
| | | 4-speed manual | $345 | - | - |
| | | Flightomatic Automatic | $367 | - | - |
| 289 CID, 2-bbl., OHV V8 | 210 | 3-speed manual | $208 | S | - |
| | | 3-speed w/Overdrive | $318 | $110 | - |
| | | 4-speed manual | $296 | $188 | - |
| | | Flightomatic Automatic | $418 | $210 | - |
| 289 CID, 4-bbl., OHV V8 | 225 | 3-speed manual | $253 | $45 | - |
| | | 3-speed w/Overdrive | $363 | $155 | - |
| | | 4-speed manual | $341 | $233 | - |
| | | Flightomatic Automatic | $453 | $255 | - |
| 289 CID R1, 4-bbl., OHV V8 | 240 | 3-speed manual | $343 | $157 | S |
| | | 4-speed manual | $531 | $345 | $188 |
| | | Flightomatic Automatic | $553 | $367 | $210 |

| Engine | Gross HP | Transmission Availability | Challenger/Cammander/Daytona | Cruiser & GT Hawk | Avanti |
|---|---|---|---|---|---|
| 289 CID R2 Supercharged, 4-bbl., OHV V8 | 289 | 3-speed manual | $553 | $367 | $210 |
| | | 4-speed manual | $741 | $555 | $398 |
| | | Flightomatic Automatic | $763 | $577 | $420 |

## Major Options

| | Challenger/ Commander | Daytona/Cruiser | GT Hawk | Avanti |
|---|---|---|---|---|
| Heater and defroster | $80 | $80 | $80 | $80 |
| Air conditioning | $278–$325 | $278–$325 | $325 | $325 |
| Tinted glass — full | $32 | $32 | $32 | $32 |
| Power Steering (V8 only) | $77 | $77 | $77 | $77 |
| Power brakes | $45 | $45 | $45 | S |
| Electric clock | $15 | $15 | $15 | $15 |
| Windshield washers | $12 | $12 | $12 | $14 |
| AM pushbutton radio | $57 | $57 | $57 | $65 |
| White sidewall tires — standard size | $28–$48 | $28–$48 | $28–$48 | $32–$49 |
| Wheel covers | $16 | $16 | $16 | S |

Options common to most models (S or STD. = Standard equipment.) Items may be standard equipment, optional at different pricing, or unavailable on certain models. This chart is only a guide.

## Paint Colors

| | Code |
|---|---|
| Midnight Black | P6410 |
| Astra White | P6411 |
| Laguna Blue Metallic | P6412 |
| Strato Blue Metallic | P6413 |
| Horizon Green Metallic | P6414 |
| Jet Green Metallic | P6415 |
| Moonlight Silver Metallic | P6416 |
| Golden Sand Metallic | P6417 |
| Bordeaux Red | P6418 |
| Bermuda Brown Metallic | P6419 |
| Avanti Black* | P6330 |
| Avanti White* | P6331 |
| Avanti Turquoise* | P6332 |
| Avanti Gold* | P6333 |
| Avanti Red* | P6334 |
| Avanti Gray Metallic* | P6335 |
| Avanti Maroon Metallic* | P6336 |
| Avanti Gold Metallic* | P6337 |

*Avanti only.

# Challenger & Commander

## "Handsome New Leaders of the Low-Price Field."

**Nameplate year of origin:** 1964 (Challenger); 1927 (Commander).
**Current bodystyle lifespan:** 1962 through 1966.
**Predecessor to this model:** Standard line (1963) and Lark (1962 to 1963).
**Replacement for this model:** None.
**Corporate siblings:** Cruiser and Daytona.
**Percentage of division's sales volume:** 87.75%.
**Primary competition:** AMC Rambler American, Chevrolet Chevy II, Dodge Dart, Ford Falcon, Mercury Comet, and Plymouth Valiant.
**Notable changes:** Restyled front and rear end.
**Major standard equipment:** All-vinyl or cloth and vinyl front bench seats, armrests, rubber floor mats, and 6.00 × 15 BSW tires (6.50 × 15 BSW on Wagonnaire).

## Measurements

| | 2-Doors | 4-Doors | Wagons |
|---|---|---|---|
| Wheelbase | 109.0" | 113.0" | 113.0" |
| Length | 190.0" | 194.0" | 193.0" |
| Width | 71.5" | 71.5" | 71.5" |
| Height | 54.7" | 54.7" | 57.0" |
| Legroom — front | 39.7" | 39.7" | 39.7" |
| Legroom — rear | 31.8" | 35.8" | 36.2" |
| Headroom — front | 39.0" | 39.0" | 40.0" |
| Headroom — rear | 38.0" | 38.0" | 36.7" |
| Luggage cap. (cu. ft.) | NA | NA | NA |
| Fuel capacity (gals.) | 18.0 | 18.0 | 18.0 |

## Models Available

| | Style Number | Base MSRP | Change from LY | Shipping Wt. (lbs.) | Production | Change from LY |
|---|---|---|---|---|---|---|
| Challenger 2-Door Sedan | F2 | $1,943 | 0.41% | 2660 | 8,315 | -52.22% |
| Challenger 4-Door Sedan | Y2 | $2,048 | 0.39% | 2780 | 27,289 | -31.97% |
| Challenger 4-Door, 2-Seat Wagon | P2 | $2,438 | 0.33% | 3230 | 5,163 | -56.67% |

| | Style Number | Base MSRP | Change from LY | Shipping Wt. (lbs.) | Production | Change from LY |
|---|---|---|---|---|---|---|
| Commander 2-Door Sedan | F4 | $2,063 | 0.39% | 2695 | * | * |
| Commander Special 2-Door Sedan | F4 | $2,193 | NEW | NA | * | NEW |
| Commander 4-Door Sedan | Y4 | $2,168 | 0.37% | 2815 | * | * |
| Commander 4-Door, 2-Seat Wagon | P4 | $2,558 | 0.31% | 3265 | * | * |
| TOTALS | | Avg. price $2,202 | * | | Production 40,767 | * |

*Production not available by series. Comparisons not available due to model line changes.

# Cruiser & Daytona

*"Studebaker's spirited fun cars and luxurious family cars."*

**Nameplate year of origin:** 1961 (Cruiser); 1962 (Daytona).
**Current bodystyle lifespan:** 1962 through 1966.
**Predecessor to this model:** Cruiser (1961).
**Replacement for this model:** None.
**Corporate siblings:** Commander and Challenger.
**Percentage of division's sales volume:** 6.71%.
**Primary competition:** AMC Rambler American, Chevrolet Chevy II, Dodge Dart, Ford Falcon, Mercury Comet, and Plymouth Valiant.
**Notable changes:** Restyled front and rear end.
**Major standard equipment:** All-vinyl or cloth and vinyl front bench seats, armrests, rubber floor mats, and 6.00 × 15 BSW tires (6.50 × 15 BSW on Cruiser and Wagonnaire).

## Measurements

| | 2-Doors | 4-Doors | Wagons |
|---|---|---|---|
| Wheelbase | 109.0" | 113.0" | 113.0" |
| Length | 190.0" | 194.0" | 193.0" |
| Width | 71.5" | 71.5" | 71.5" |
| Height | 54.7" | 54.7" | 57.0" |
| Legroom — front | 40.3" | 39.7" | 39.7" |
| Legroom — rear | 31.8" | 35.8" | 36.2" |
| Headroom — front | 40.3" | 39.0" | 40.0" |
| Headroom — rear | 38.0" | 38.0" | 36.7" |
| Luggage cap. (cu. ft.) | NA | NA | NA |
| Fuel capacity (gals.) | 18.0 | 18.0 | 18.0 |

## Models Available

| | Style Number | Base MSRP | Change from LY | Shipping Wt. (lbs.) | Production | Change from LY |
|---|---|---|---|---|---|---|
| Daytona 2-Door Hardtop | J8 | $2,451 | +6.20% | 3060 | 2,414 | -35.85% |
| Daytona 2-Door Convertible | L8 | $2,670 | -0.34% | NA | 703 | -30.74% |
| Daytona 4-Door Sedan | Y8 | $2,318 | NEW | NA | * | NEW |
| Daytona 4-Door, 2-Seat Wagon | P8 | $2,708 | +0.30% | NA | * | * |
| Cruiser 4-Door Sedan | Y9 | $2,603 | +0.31% | 3120 | * | * |
| TOTALS | | Avg. price $2,550 | * | | Production 3,117 | * |

*Production not available by series. Comparisons not available due to model line changes.

# Gran Turismo Hawk

*"Classic performer ... full family style."*

**Nameplate year of origin:** 1956.
**Current bodystyle lifespan:** 1953 through 1964.
**Predecessor to this model:** None.
**Replacement for this model:** None.
**Corporate siblings:** None.
**Percentage of division's sales volume:** 3.80%.
**Primary competition:** Mercury Monterey S-55, Oldsmobile Starfire and Pontiac Grand Prix.

## Measurements

| | |
|---|---|
| Wheelbase | 120.5" |
| Length | 204.0" |
| Width | 71.4" |
| Height | 54.6" |
| Legroom — front | 41.8" |
| Legroom — rear | 33.2" |
| Headroom — front | 38.6" |

**Notable changes:** New grille and minor trim and detail changes.
**Major standard equipment:** All-vinyl front bucket seats, full deep-pile carpeting, padded instrument panel, rear seat center armrest, exterior bright trim including windows and rocker panel moldings and 6.70 × 15 BSW tires.

## Measurements (cont.)

| | |
|---|---|
| Headroom — rear | 36.6" |
| Luggage cap. (cu. ft.) | NA |
| Fuel capacity (gals.) | 18.0 |

## Models Available

| | Style Number | Base MSRP | Change from LY | Shipping Wt. (lbs.) | Production | Change from LY |
|---|---|---|---|---|---|---|
| Gran Turismo Hawk 2-Door HT | K6 | $2,966 | -4.17% | 3280 | 1,767 | -61.87% |
| TOTALS | | Avg. price $2,966 | -4.17% | Production | 1,767 | -61.87% |

# Avanti

*"America's only 4 passenger high performance car!"*

**Nameplate year of origin:** 1963.
**Current bodystyle lifespan:** 1963 through 1964.
**Predecessor to this model:** None.
**Replacement for this model:** None.
**Corporate siblings:** None.
**Percentage of division's sales volume:** 1.74%.
**Primary competition:** Chevrolet Corvette.
**Notable changes:** Minor trim and detail changes. Most 1964 Avantis have a square headlamp housing.
**Major standard equipment:** All-vinyl front bucket seats, full deep-pile carpeting, padded instrument panel, rear seat center armrest, exterior bright trim including windows and rocker panel moldings and 6.70 × 15 BSW tires.

## Measurements

| | |
|---|---|
| Wheelbase | 109.0" |
| Length | 192.5" |
| Width | 70.4" |
| Height | 53.8" |
| Legroom — front | 42.3" |
| Legroom — rear | 26.3" |
| Headroom — front | 37.5" |
| Headroom — rear | 34.8" |
| Luggage cap. (cu. ft.) | NA |
| Fuel capacity (gals.) | 21.0 |

## Models Available

| | Style Number | Base MSRP | Change from LY | Shipping Wt. (lbs.) | Production | Change from LY |
|---|---|---|---|---|---|---|
| Avanti 2-Door Hardtop | R-Q | $4,445 | 0.00% | 3195 | 809 | -78.90% |
| TOTALS | | Avg. price $4,445 | 0.00% | Production | 809 | -78.90% |

# 1965

In many ways, 1965 was comparable to the 1955 selling season. Advertising for both years reflected a trend toward greater performance. Nearly all of Detroit's full-size models wore all-new sheetmetal and were longer, lower and wider than the previous year. Many manufacturers exceeded production records (some of which were set in 1955) or reached heights that they would not reach again for many years. It was an exciting year that produced some remarkable cars.

American Motors entered 1965 with several notable changes. Foremost was the new Marlin, introduced in February 1965. This 6-passenger 2-Door featured a unique fastback roof treatment on a Rambler Classic body. The Classic's new front-end styling was shared with the Marlin. The Classic line also featured new rear styling and a new 770 Convertible. A convertible also joined the Ambassador 990 series, marking the first time for a Rambler Classic or Ambassador of this body style. The Ambassador line received new front and rear styling, plus a 4 inch longer wheelbase than previous years. Also, a new lower-priced 880 series was added to the Ambassador line to broaden its appeal. The Rambler American would have to make do with minor refinements. This would be the last year for the Rambler name to be used except for the Rambler American, which would retain the name through 1969.

Chrysler Corporation restyled nearly the entire line, save the Plymouth Valiant and Imperial, which received only minor refinements. The new intermediate-size line featured the Dodge Coronet and the Plymouth Belvedere. These cars utilized the 1964 standard-size Plymouth and Dodge bodies, but with more modern sheetmetal wrapped around them. A sporty addition to the Belvedere line was known as the Satellite, which offered bucket seats, console and other trim additions. The Coronet line offered a new muscle-car variant known as the Hemi-Charger. This car was a Coronet 2-Door Sedan with the 426 CID Hemi V8, produced for street use and sold "as is," without the usual new car warranty.

The standard-size Chrysler Corporation offerings were all-new for 1965. Larger, more stylish and more luxurious, the cars were just what Chrysler needed to boost sales. Plymouth offered a new Fury line in four series, Fury I, II, III and Sport Fury. A Sport Fury Convertible was selected as official Pace Car for the 1965 Indianapolis 500 race. The Dodge Polara series replaced the 1964 880 line. The Polara series also included a top-line Custom 880, and a new specialty offering, the Monaco. The Monaco was a 2-door Hardtop designed to compete with the Pontiac Grand Prix, offering bucket seats, console, 383 CID V8, and other luxury/sport equipment. Appearing for the first time this year also, was a Polara 500 Sport Package offered on the Polara 2-door Hardtop and Convertible models.

The Chrysler line received as dramatic a restyling as did the Fury and Polara. This year's Chryslers featured a sculptured body side highlighted with a strip of stainless steel at the top belt line edge and lower rocker panel area. The dramatic new styling, crisper and more modern, boosted Chrysler's sales more than 50 percent over 1964. Two new models, a Newport 6-window 4-door Sedan and a 300 6-window 4-door Sedan, were added to the lineup, but neither was very successful. The 1965 300L would prove to be the last year for the 300 letter series, basically being replaced by the lower-priced 300 series which offered all of the 300-letter series equipment and looks.

In other lines, the Dodge Dart received new front and rear styling, following the new Coronet and Polara. As previously mentioned the Imperial line was further refined from its 1964 restyle. Finally, the Valiant line received refinements, and the Barracuda got a small but significant change. Technically, it was still a Valiant Barracuda, but the Valiant name was removed from the car, indicating future distinction of the Barracuda as a separate (and soon to be sportier) model.

After a year of thorough restyling at Ford Motor Company, many Ford and Mercury models were once again re-

## 1965 Model Year Production by Make

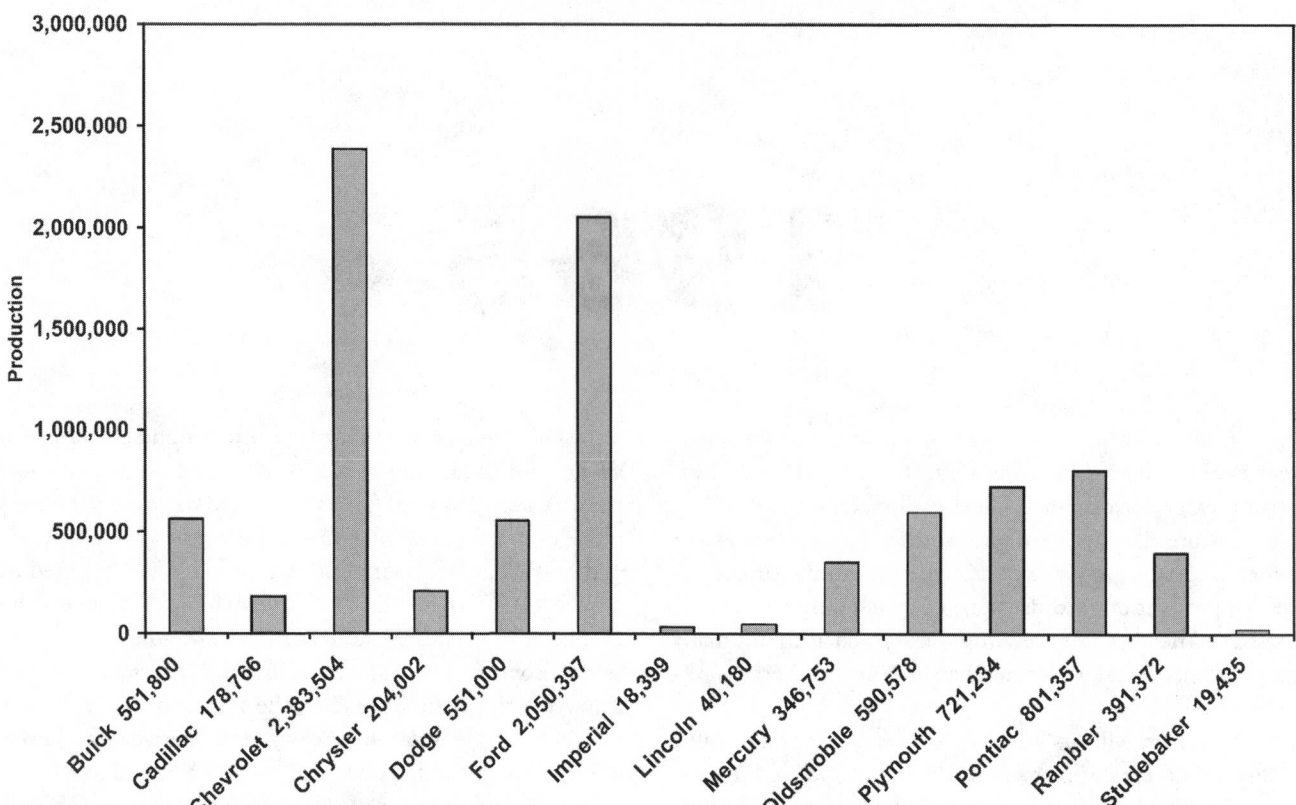

designed. The full-size Fords and Mercurys featured clean, crisp, square lines and looked much more luxurious and Lincoln-like than previous models. As proof of being more luxurious, Ford added a new Galaxie 500 LTD in 2 and 4 door hardtop models as its top trim levels. At the other end of the price scale, the Ranch Wagon returned as the price-leading full-size wagon. This year Ford dropped the descriptive names it had used for the various body styles offered including Club Victoria (2-Door Hardtop), Club Sedan (2-Door Sedan), Town Victoria (4-Door Hardtop), Town Sedan (4-Door Sedan), and the Sunliner (Convertible).

Intermediate-sized Ford products received new lower body sheet metal giving them an all-new appearance. The compact Falcon received only trim changes, as did the luxurious Thunderbird, which now had a simulated chrome scoop on the front fenders. The Lincoln Sedan and Convertible received new grille and hood styling after a major 1964 redesign.

Of course the biggest news from Ford was the April 17, 1964, introduction of the Mustang. These first "'64½" models were essentially the same as the official '65 models introduced on October 1, 1964. A new model, the 2 + 2 fastback, was introduced this day, as was a GT package. As for powerplant changes in the 1965 Mustangs, a 200 CID 6-cylinder replaced the 170 CID 6-cylinder engine, and a 289 CID V8 replaced the 260 CID V8.

Not to be left out, General Motors also redesigned its entire full-size lineup and restyled many of its other models. The full-size B- and C- bodied cars featured smoother, more curvaceous and flowing lines. The two-door hardtops had what was called by some a "semi-fastback" roofline that made the car look longer and lower than any previous models. Changes within each division include:

- Buick — New trim levels added.
- LeSabre Custom, Wildcat Deluxe, Wildcat Custom and Electra 225 Custom, all featuring upgraded interiors compared to base models. Also, the full-size LeSabre Wagon was dropped.
- Cadillac — All Cadillacs featured crisp new styling, except the Fleetwood 75 series which still had the basic body used since 1959, with an updated front clip. The new styling was clean and smooth, with more square edges than other C-bodied cars, following Cadillac's more conservative nature. This new styling saw the last traces of tailfins disappear. A new option, the tilt and telescope steering column, was introduced for 1965. As for specific nameplates, the new Calais replaced the Series 62 and the Series 63 Eldorado became the Fleetwood Eldorado. The 60 Special Fleetwood became the Fleetwood 60 Special and regained its longer, 133 inch wheelbase last seen in 1958.
- Chevrolet — A now familiar name, Caprice, was in-

troduced as the Caprice Custom Sedan option on the Impala 4-door Hardtop.

• Oldsmobile—Another familiar name, Delta 88 (officially Dynamic 88 Delta for the 1965 season only), replaced the Super 88 series, which had been around since 1951. Oldsmobile joined Buick in dropping its standard-size wagon, the Dynamic 88.

• Pontiac—The newly restyled full-size Pontiac joined the rest of the Pontiac lineup in accepting *Motor Trend* magazine's Car of the Year award for "styling and engineering leadership in the development of personalized passenger cars."

All of the intermediate size GM cars—Special, Chevelle, F-85 and Tempest—received new front and rear styling updates. Other changes at GM included a new grille on the Chevy II and cancellation of the 400 designation on the Nova. The Chevrolet Corvair received new Italian—inspired styling that saw all closed models receive pillarless hardtop styling. The engines in Corvairs received healthy boosts in horse power. Also, the Monza Spyder series became known as the Corsa series. Changes for the Corvette included the addition of three functional vertical louvers to the front fenders and a new L78 396 CID V8 option that would propel the Corvette 0–60 in 5.7 seconds. The Buick

division officially got into the muscle car market with a mid-year Skylark Gran Sport option package that included a 325-hp, 401 CID V8. Finally, the Buick Riviera received a distinctive new hidden-headlamp front end treatment and offered a Gran Sport model boasting a 360-hp, dual 4-bbl., 401 CID V8.

Making up a small percentage of the 1965 auto market were three independent manufacturers, all utilizing GM powerplants. First there was Studebaker, now producing all of its vehicles in Canada. Studebaker did not change the styling of its cars, but did switch to engines designed by GM of Canada. This year the Daytona 4-door Wagonaire had no fixed roof option available, only the sliding roof, though a fixed roof option was offered in 1964 and 1966. Second, there was Checker, which once again (surprise!) made no styling changes, but did switch from Continental Motor Company's 6-cylinder engine to Chevrolet power plants—a 230 CID 6-cylinder or 283 CID V8. Finally, there was the Avanti II. After it was discontinued by Studebaker in 1964, Studebaker-Packard dealers Leo Newman and Nathaniel Altman bought all dies, parts and rights to the Avanti and built it themselves in a portion of the vacated Studebaker South Bend factory. They chose a Corvette 327 CID 4-bbl. V8 as the engine for the Avanti II, but otherwise the car was little changed.

# BUICK

*"Wouldn't you really rather have a Buick?"*

All of the full-size Buick line—LeSabre, Wildcat and Electra—were completely redesigned and restyled, in line with GM's other full-size cars. As with the other cars, the results were an unqualified success. Much as they had done in 1955, GM took the automotive world to the next level in styling. The cars were clean, uncluttered, with a minimum of chrome. Rooflines, particularly on 2-Door Hardtop models, were graceful and sweeping. The LeSabre and Wildcat models were close to a fastback design. Traditional Venti-ports were still used on the LeSabre and Electra, while the Wildcat used a modified form of the trademark with a three-fingered chrome piece on the lower portion of the front fender. Up front, the grille styling was the usual, modern Buick look. Wildcat models now rode on the longer Electra wheelbase, but still used the LeSabre body styling.

The full-size wagon was temporarily gone from the lineup. In its place was the new-for-1964 Sport Wagon based on the Special. Other model changes were minimal, although the actual number of models increased dramatically due to the addition of various trim levels now made into model designations as opposed to the prior interior trim options. The Electra 225 and LeSabre added "Custom" levels, while the Wildcat added "Deluxe" and "Custom" to its line. Powertrains continued as in prior seasons.

The mid-size Special and Skylark line returned with new grilles that closely followed those on the new full-size cars. The Skylark line added a 2-Door "Thin-Pillared" Coupe that had been dropped from the Special Deluxe line. "Thin-Pillared" Coupe was Buick's euphemistic name for a 2-Door Sedan, which they used diligently for the next eight years. At mid-year a powerful new option package was introduced. The Gran Sport (or GS) package was available for the Skylark 2-Door Coupe, Hardtop or Convertible. It was an attempt by Buick to test the muscle car waters. The GS featured a 325-horsepower, 401 CID V8 engine. Interior and exterior GS badging identified what lay under the hood. The GS was so popular that in 1966 it became a regular model offering.

The top-of-the-line Riviera continued for a final season in its original sheetmetal. However, it was wearing an all-new front end for 1965. The headlights were moved from the grille area to a stacked position in the leading edge of the front fenders, hidden behind motorized doors. The result was a more muscular look, particular in the new Gran Sport version. The Riviera GS was powered by the Super Wildcat, dual 4-barrel, 425 cubic inch V8 that was rated at 360 horsepower. Other features included dual exhausts, performance gearing and GS wheel covers.

Electra 225 4-Door Hardtop

LeSabre 2-Door Hardtop

LeSabre Custom 2-Door Convertible

Riviera 2-Door Hardtop

Wildcat 4-Door Sedan

Skylark 2-Door Convertible

Special Deluxe 4-Door Wagon

**Model year production:** 561,800, up 9.98% from 1964.
**Domestic market share:** 6.34% (6th place).
**Base price range:** $2,343 to $4,440.
**Industry average base price:** $3,017.
**Buick average base price:** $3,226.
**Introduction date:** September 1964.
**Assembly plants:** Southgate, CA (C); Atlanta, GA (D); Flint, MI (H); Kansas City, MO (K); Fairfax, KS (X); Wilming-ton, DE (Y); Fremont, CA (Z); and Oshawa, Ontario (1).
**Data plate identification:** Thirteen digit code read as follows: Five digit style number which 4 = Buick, 2nd number identifies series (3 is Skylark, 8 is Electra, etc.), 3rd through 5th digits indicate model number; 5 for 1965 year; assembly plant code; 100001 and up for serial number. *Example:* 452375X100001 is a 1965 Buick LeSabre 2-Door Hardtop, serial number 100001, built in Fairfax, KS.

## Powertrains

| Engine | Gross HP | Transmission Availability | Special/ Skylark | Sport Wagon | LeSabre | Wildcat, Elec. & Riv. |
|---|---|---|---|---|---|---|
| 225 CID Fireball, 2-bbl., V6 | 155 | 3-speed manual | S | - | - | - |
| | | 4-speed manual | $199 | - | - | - |
| | | Super Turbine 300 Automatic | $198 | - | - | - |
| 300 CID, 2-bbl., V8 | 210 | 3-speed manual | $71 | S | S | - |
| | | 4-speed manual | $270 | $199 | $199 | - |
| | | Super Turbine 300 Automatic | $302 | $231 | $231 | - |
| 300 CID, 4-bbl., V8 | 250 | 3-speed manual | $93 | $22 | $22 | - |
| | | 4-speed manual | $292 | $221 | - | - |
| | | Super Turbine 300 Automatic | $324 | $253 | $253 | - |
| 401 CID, 4-bbl., V8 | 325 | 3-speed manual | - | - | - | S (Wildcat) |
| | | 4-speed manual | - | - | - | $199 (Wildcat) |

| Engine | Gross HP | Transmission Availability | Special/ Skylark | Sport Wagon | LeSabre | Wildcat, Elec. & Riv. |
|---|---|---|---|---|---|---|
| | | Super Turbine Automatic | - | - | - | S (Elec. & Riv.)/$232 (Wildcat) |
| 425 CID, 4-bbl., V8 | 340 | 4-speed manual | - | - | - | $247 (Wildcat) |
| | | Super Turbine Automatic | - | - | - | $48 (Elec. & Riv.)/$280 (Wildcat) |
| 425 CID, 2 × 4-bbl., V8 | 360 | 4-speed manual | - | - | - | $418 (Wildcat) |
| | | Super Turbine Automatic | - | - | - | $188 (Elec. & Riv.)/$450 (Wild.) |

## Major Options

| | Skylark | LeSabre | Wildcat | Electra 225 | Riviera |
|---|---|---|---|---|---|
| Air conditioning — manual | $376 | $421 | $421 | $421 | $421 |
| Air conditioning — automatic | - | $500 | $500 | $500 | $500 |
| Cruise Master speed control | $58 | $63 | $63 | $63 | $63 |
| Soft Ray tinted glass | $39 | $44 | $44 | $44 | $47 |
| Deck lid remote release | $14 | $14 | $14 | $14 | $14 |
| Tilt steering wheel | $45 | $45 | $45 | $45 | S |
| Power steering — variable-ratio | $100 | $111 | $111 | S | S |
| Power brakes | $42 | $42 | $42 | S | S |
| Power driver's seat/Bench seat, 4-way | $74 (ex. 6-cyl.) | $74 | $74 | $47–$74 | $74 |
| Power windows (except on 6-cylinder) | $105 | $110 | $110 | $110* | $110 |
| AM radio | $70 | $88 | $88 | $88 | $88 |
| AM/FM stereo (not stereo in Skylark) | $134 | $268 | $268 | $268 | $268 |
| Front bucket Seats | $ | - | - | - | $ |
| Vinyl roof | $102 | $123 | S | $139 | $128 |
| White sidewall tires — standard size | $31–$36 | $42 | $42 | $47 | $42 |
| Wheel trim covers (Deluxe on Electra) | $21 | $21-base | S | S | S |

Options common to most models. (- = Not Available; S = Standard equipment.) Items may be standard equipment, optional at different pricing, or unavailable on certain models. This chart is only a guide.

*Standard on Convertible.

## Paint Colors

| | Code |
|---|---|
| Regal Black | A |
| Arctic White | C |
| Astro Blue Metallic | D |
| Midnight Blue Metallic | E |
| Seafoam Green Metallic | H |
| Verde Green Metallic | J |
| Turquoise Mist Metallic | K |
| Midnight Aqua Metallic | L |
| Burgundy Mist Metallic | N |
| Flame Red | R |
| Sahara Mist Metallic | S |
| Champagne Mist Metallic | T |
| Shell Beige | V |
| Bamboo Cream | Y |
| Silver Cloud Metallic | Z |

**1965**

# Special, Skylark and GS

*"Here's the answer to people who demand the luxury of a big car in a slightly smaller size."*

**Nameplate year of origin:** Special 1935; Skylark 1953.
**Current bodystyle lifespan:** 1964 through 1967.
**Predecessor to this model:** Special/Skylark (1961 to 1963).
**Replacement for this model:** Special/Skylark (1968 to 1972).
**Percentage of division's sales volume:** 36.57%.
**Corporate siblings:** Chevrolet Chevelle, Olds F-85/Cutlass, and Pontiac Tempest/LeMans.
**Primary competition:** Dodge Coronet, and Mercury Comet.
**Notable changes:** Revised front and rear styling.
**Major standard equipment:** Balmere cloth and vinyl front bench seat, rubber floor mats (carpet in convertible), electric windshield wipers, front door operated courtesy lights, and 6.95 × 14 BSW tires (7.35 × 14 BSW tires on wagon). Deluxe adds: Instrument panel safety pad, full carpeting, and dual horns. Skylark adds: Paddle-type door arm rests, glove compartment and rear compartment courtesy lights (2-doors), and full wheel covers.

## Measurements

| | Cars | Wagon |
|---|---|---|
| Wheelbase | 115.0" | 115.0" |
| Length | 203.4" | 203.2" |
| Width | 73.6" | 73.6" |
| Height | 54.4" | 55.2" |
| Legroom — front | 41.1" | 41.2" |
| Legroom — rear | 35.8" | 35.9" |
| Headroom — front | 38.2" | 37.8" |
| Headroom — rear | 37.2" | 38.4" |
| Luggage capacity (cu. ft.) | NA | 86.6 |
| Fuel capacity (gals.) | 20.0 | 20.0 |

## Models Available

| | Style Number | Base MSRP | Change from LY | Shipping Wt. (lbs.) | Production | Change from LY |
|---|---|---|---|---|---|---|
| Special 2-Door Coupe | 43327 | $2,292 | -2.18% | 2977 | 21,949 | +46.03% |
| Special 2-Door Convertible | 43367 | $2,549 | -2.15% | 3087 | 6,722 | +6.56% |
| Special 4-Door Sedan | 43369 | $2,345 | -2.17% | 3010 | 18,254 | +1.51% |
| Special 4-Door, 2-Seat Wagon | 43335 | $2,630 | -2.19% | 3258 | 6,544 | +4.37% |
| Special Deluxe 4-Door Sedan | 43569 | $2,436 | -2.17% | 3016 | 36,636 | +15.42% |
| Special Deluxe 4-Dr., 2-Seat Wgn. | 43535 | $2,727 | -2.15% | 3242 | 10,800 | +14.08% |
| Skylark 2-Door Coupe | 44327 | $2,482 | NEW | 3035 | 16,072 | NEW |
| Skylark 2-Door Hardtop | 44337 | $2,622 | -2.16% | 3057 | 51,199 | +20.88% |
| Skylark 2-Door Convertible | 44367 | $2,773 | -2.15% | 3149 | 11,637 | +13.48% |
| Skylark 4-Door Sedan | 44369 | $2,611 | -2.17% | 3086 | 25,624 | +30.50% |
| TOTALS | Avg. price | $2,547 | -1.85% | Production | 205,437 | +20.13% |

# Sportwagon

*"The beauty of the Buick Sport Wagon is just that— it's beautiful."*

**Nameplate year of origin:** 1964.
**Current bodystyle lifespan:** 1964 through 1967.
**Predecessor to this model:** None.
**Replacement for this model:** Sport Wagon (1968 to 1969).
**Percentage of division's sales volume:** 5.05%.
**Corporate siblings:** Oldsmobile Vista Cruiser.
**Primary competition:** Dodge Coronet, and Mercury Comet.
**Notable changes:** Revised front and rear styling.
**Major standard equipment:** Cloth and vinyl front bench seat, rubber floor mats, electric windshield wipers, front door operated dome light, dual arm rests, tinted glass observation-style roof, full wheel covers and 7.35 × 14 BSW tires. Custom adds: All-vinyl front bench seat, dual front and rear sunshades, instrument panel safety pad, paddle-type door arm rests, and full carpeting on passenger, door and cowl areas.

## Measurements

| | |
|---|---|
| Wheelbase | 120.0" |
| Length | 208.2" |
| Width | 73.9" |
| Height | 57.5" |
| Legroom — front | 41.3" |
| Legroom — rear | 39.0" |
| Headroom — front | 37.7" |
| Headroom — rear | 40.2" |
| Luggage capacity (cu. ft.) | 96.5 |
| Fuel capacity (gals.) | 20.0 |

## Models Available

| | Style Number | Base MSRP | Change from LY | Shipping Wt. (lbs.) | Production | Change from LY |
|---|---|---|---|---|---|---|
| Sport Wagon 4-Door, 2-St. Wagon | 44255 | $2,925 | -2.14% | 3642 | 4,226 | +56.00% |
| Sport Wagon 4-Door, 3-St. Wagon | 44265 | $3,056 | -2.18% | 3750 | 4,664 | +80.36% |
| Sport Wagon Custom 4-Dr., 2-St. Wgn. | 44455 | $3,092 | -2.18% | 3690 | 8,300 | +112.11% |
| Sport Wagon Custom 4-Dr., 3-St. Wgn. | 44465 | $3,214 | -2.19% | 3802 | 11,166 | +151.15% |
| TOTALS | Avg. price | $3,072 | -2.17% | Production | 28,356 | +107.68% |

# LeSabre

*"The single, most-compelling reason for owning a LeSabre is that it's a Buick."*

**Nameplate year of origin:** 1959.
**Current bodystyle lifespan:** 1965 through 1966.
**Predecessor to this model:** LeSabre (1961 to 1964) and Invicta Wagons (1962 to 1963).
**Replacement for this model:** LeSabre (1967 to 1968).
**Percentage of division's sales volume:** 25.45%.
**Corporate siblings:** Chevrolet Biscayne/BelAir/Impala, Pontiac Catalina/Star Chief/Bonneville, Olds 88.
**Primary competition:** Chrysler Newport, Dodge Polara, and Mercury Monterey.
**Notable changes:** Completely restyled.
**Major standard equipment:** Bartine cloth and vinyl front bench seat, front door operated interior lighting, glove box light, full carpeting, front and rear armrests, map light, and 8.15 × 15 BSW tires. Custom adds: Bimini cloth and vinyl upholstery (all vinyl on Convertible), deluxe steering wheel, "Custom" nameplates, and additional exterior trim moldings.

## Measurements

| | |
|---|---|
| Wheelbase | 123.0" |
| Length | 216.8" |
| Width | 80.0" |
| Height | 55.5" |
| Legroom — front | 42.2" |
| Legroom — rear | 39.0" |
| Headroom — front | 38.9" |
| Headroom — rear | 37.7" |
| Luggage capacity (cu. ft.) | NA |
| Fuel capacity (gals.) | 25.0 |

## Models Available

| | Style Number | Base MSRP | Change from LY | Shipping Wt. (lbs.) | Production | Change from LY |
|---|---|---|---|---|---|---|
| LeSabre 2-Door Hardtop | 45237 | $2,968 | -3.04% | 3753 | 15,786 | -34.71% |
| LeSabre 4-Door Sedan | 45269 | $2,888 | -3.09% | 3788 | 37,788 | -33.39% |
| LeSabre 4-Door Hardtop | 45239 | $3,027 | -3.04% | 3809 | 18,384 | -50.38% |
| LeSabre Custom 2-Door Hardtop | 45437 | $3,037 | NEW | 3724 | 21,049 | NEW |
| LeSabre Custom 2-Door Convertible | 45467 | $3,257 | NEW | 3812 | 6,543 | NEW |
| LeSabre Custom 4-Door Sedan | 45469 | $2,962 | NEW | 3777 | 20,052 | NEW |
| LeSabre Custom 4-Door Hardtop | 45439 | $3,101 | NEW | 3811 | 23,394 | NEW |
| TOTALS | *Avg. price* $3,034 | -7.44% | | *Production* 142,996 | +5.79% |

# Wildcat

*"Style and flair won't make a car go any faster, run any smoother or ride any softer, but it certainly does a lot for the man behind the wheel."*

**Nameplate year of origin:** 1962.
**Current bodystyle lifespan:** 1965 through 1966.
**Predecessor to this model:** Wildcat (1962 to 1964) and Invicta (1961 to 1962).
**Replacement for this model:** Wildcat (1967 to 1968).
**Percentage of division's sales volume:** 11.32%.
**Corporate siblings:** Chevrolet Biscayne/Bel/Air/Impala, Pontiac Catalina/Star Chief/Bonneville, Olds 88.
**Primary competition:** Chrysler 300, Dodge Custom 880, and Mercury Montclair.
**Notable changes:** Completely restyled.
**Major standard equipment:** All vinyl front bench seat, front door operated interior lighting, glove box light, full carpeting, front and rear armrests, instrument panel safety pad, and 8.45 × 15 BSW tires. Deluxe adds: Deluxe steering wheel, deluxe interior trim and additional interior lighting. Custom adds: Bucket seats and console (2-Door models), "Custom" nameplates, and additional exterior trim moldings.

## Measurements

| | |
|---|---|
| Wheelbase | 126.0" |
| Length | 219.8" |
| Width | 80.0" |
| Height | 55.5" |
| Legroom — front | 42.2" |
| Legroom — rear | 39.0" |
| Headroom — front | 38.9" |
| Headroom — rear | 37.7" |
| Luggage capacity (cu. ft.) | NA |
| Fuel capacity (gals.) | 25.0 |

**1965**

## Models Available

| | Style Number | Base MSRP | Change from LY | Shipping Wt. (lbs.) | Production | Change from LY |
|---|---|---|---|---|---|---|
| Wildcat 2-Door HT | 46237 | $3,219 | -1.47% | 3988 | 6,031 | -73.66% |
| Wildcat 4-Door Sedan | 46269 | $3,117 | -1.49% | 4058 | 10,184 | -49.44% |
| Wildcat 4-Door HT | 46239 | $3,278 | -1.47% | 4089 | 7,499 | -77.52% |
| Wildcat Deluxe 2-Door HT | 46437 | $3,272 | NEW | 4014 | 11,617 | NEW |
| Wildcat Deluxe 2-Door Convertible | 46467 | $3,431 | NEW | 4069 | 4,616 | NEW |
| Wildcat Deluxe 4-Door Sedan | 46469 | $3,218 | NEW | 4046 | 9,765 | NEW |
| Wildcat Deluxe 4-Door HT | 46439 | $3,338 | NEW | 4075 | 13,903 | NEW |
| Wildcat Custom 2-Door Hardtop | 46637 | $3,493 | NEW | 4047 | * | NEW |
| Wildcat Custom 2-Door Convertible | 46667 | $3,651 | NEW | 4087 | * | NEW |
| Wildcat Custom 4-Door Hardtop | 46639 | $3,552 | NEW | 4160 | * | NEW |
| TOTALS | Avg. price | $3,357 | +1.64% | | Production 63,615 | -24.49% |

*Production included with Deluxe models.

# Electra 225

*"When you've arrived, there's no harm in letting other people know it."*

**Nameplate year of origin:** 1959.
**Current bodystyle lifespan:** 1965 through 1966.
**Predecessor to this model:** Electra 225 (1961 to 1964).
**Replacement for this model:** Electra 225 (1967 to 1968).
**Percentage of division's sales volume:** 15.45%.
**Corporate siblings:** Cadillac Calais/de Ville, Oldsmobile Ninety-Eight.
**Primary competition:** Chrysler New Yorker and Mercury Park Lane.
**Notable changes:** Completely restyled.
**Major standard equipment:** Beaucrest cloth and vinyl bench seats, full floor and lower door carpeting, instrument panel safety pad, trunk light, rocker panel and wheel opening moldings, rear fender skirts, deluxe wheel covers and 8.75 × 15 BSW tires. Custom adds: Custom trim, front & rear center arm rests, power windows (convertible), 2-way power seat (convertible), and outside rear view mirror (convertible).

## Measurements

| | |
|---|---|
| Wheelbase | 126.0" |
| Length | 224.1" |
| Width | 80.0" |
| Height | 56.0" |
| Legroom — front | 42.2" |
| Legroom — rear | 40.3" |
| Headroom — front | 39.6" |
| Headroom — rear | 38.2" |
| Luggage capacity (cu. ft.) | NA |
| Fuel capacity (gals.) | 25.0 |

## Models Available

| | Style Number | Base MSRP | Change from LY | Shipping Wt. (lbs.) | Production | Change from LY |
|---|---|---|---|---|---|---|
| Electra 225 2-Door Hardtop | 48237 | $3,999 | -1.74% | 4208 | 6,302 | -30.33% |
| Electra 225 4-Door Sedan | 48269 | $3,989 | -1.72% | 4261 | 12,459 | -21.98% |
| Electra 225 4-Door Hardtop | 48239 | $4,121 | -1.74% | 4284 | 12,842 | -48.50% |
| Electra 225 Custom 2-Door HT | 48437 | $3,999 | NEW | 4208 | 9,570 | NEW |
| Electra 225 Custom 2-Door Conv. | 48467 | $4,350 | NEW | 4325 | 8,508 | NEW |
| Electra 225 Custom 4-Door Sedan | 48469 | $4,168 | NEW | 4292 | 7,197 | NEW |
| Electra 225 Custom 4-Door HT | 48439 | $4,300 | NEW | 4344 | 29,932 | NEW |
| TOTALS | Avg. price | $4,132 | -1.44% | | Production 86,810 | +26.19% |

# Riviera

*"Think of a car that's loaded with action, classic in line, agile as a cat, and luxurious beyond belief. The car you're thinking about is the Riviera by Buick."*

**Nameplate year of origin:** 1949 (for 2-Dr. HT); 1963 (series).
**Current bodystyle lifespan:** 1963 through 1965.
**Predecessor to this model:** None.
**Replacement for this model:** Riviera (1966 to 1970).
**Percentage of division's sales volume:** 4.96%.
**Corporate siblings:** None.
**Primary competition:** Ford Thunderbird.
**Notable changes:** Revised front and rear styling.
**Major standard equipment:** All-vinyl bucket seats with center console, instrument panel safety pad, walnut interior trim, full interior lighting, double door release handles, electric clock, 2-speed electric windshield wipers with washers, tilt steering wheel, trunk light, power steering, power brakes, dual exhaust system, Super Turbine automatic transmission, and 8.45 × 15 BSW tires.

## Measurements

| | |
|---|---|
| Wheelbase | 117.0" |
| Length | 209.0" |
| Width | 76.6" |
| Height | 53.0" |
| Legroom — front | 40.1" |
| Legroom — rear | 34.7" |
| Headroom — front | 38.0" |
| Headroom — rear | 37.4" |
| Luggage capacity (cu. ft.) | NA |
| Fuel capacity (gals.) | 20.0 |

## Models Available

| | Style Number | Base MSRP | Change from LY | Shipping Wt. (lbs.) | Production | Change from LY |
|---|---|---|---|---|---|---|
| Riviera 2-Door Hardtop | 49447 | $4,318 | -1.53% | 4036 | 34,586 | -8.88% |
| TOTALS | | Avg. price $4,318 | -1.53% | Production | 34,586 | -8.88% |

# CADILLAC

*"So new ... so right ... so obviously Cadillac! Standard of the World."*

The majority of the Cadillac line was completely redesigned and restyled for 1965. The lone exception was the Fleetwood 75 Sedan series, which would not gain full benefit of this year's redesign until 1966. As for the other models, styling was updated in line with other GM cars. The lines were more flowing and graceful, and the cars were physically longer and lower than in previous years. This appearance was enhanced by vertical headlights up front and vertical taillights mounted in chrome-encased, dwindling tailfins. Inside the new cars, upholstery materials were given upgrades, and the Cadillac was once again the styling leader in its class. Ride comfort and handling were also greatly improved, thanks to careful engineering attention to the chassis and suspension components.

The new for 1964 Turbo Hydra-matic transmission was available in the new Calais line, but still not in the Fleetwood 75 line. The Calais, essentially a rebadged Series 62, was introduced in hopes of giving new life to the entry-level Cadillac, but despite repeated efforts, it never really took off. In retrospect, it seems Cadillac was a little slow on the learning curve, as the Calais lingered until 1976.

Calais 4-Door Sedan

Coupe de Ville 2-Door Hardtop

Fleetwood 60 Special 4-Door Sedan

Fleetwood Eldorado 2-Door Convertible

**Model year production:** 178,766; up 9.46% from 1964.
**Domestic market share:** 2.02% (11th place).
**Base price range:** $5,059 to $9,960.
**Industry average base price:** $3,017.
**Cadillac average base price:** $6,315.
**Introduction date:** September 1964.

**Assembly plants:** Detroit, MI, and Linden, NJ.
**Data plate identification:** Eight digit code read as follows: 1st digit is style symbol (see list); 2nd digit 5 for 1965; followed by 100001 and up for serial number. *Example:* J5100001 is a 1965 Cadillac de Ville 2-Door Hardtop, serial number 100001.

## Powertrains

| Engine | Gross HP | Transmission Availability | All models |
|---|---|---|---|
| 429 CID, 4-bbl., V8 | 340 | Hydra-matic | Fl. 75 series |
| 429 CID, 4-bbl., V8 | 340 | Turbo Hydra-matic | S — ex. Fl. 75 |

## Major Options

| | Calais | de Ville | Fl. Eldorado | 60 Special | Seventy-Five |
|---|---|---|---|---|---|
| Automatic Climate Control | $495 | $495 | $495 | $495 | $624 |
| Power windows | $119 | S | S | S | S |
| 6-way power seat | $113 | $85 | S | $85/S (Brougham) | $85 |
| Power door locks | $46–$70 | $46–$70 | $46 | $70 | S |
| AM radio w/rear speaker | $165 | $165 | $165 | $165 | $165 |
| AM-FM radio | $191 | $191 | $191 | $191 | $191 |
| Padded vinyl roof | - | $124–$140 | - | S (Brougham) | - |
| Twilight Sentinel (auto. dimmers) | $57 | $57 | S | $57 | - |
| Tilt and telescope steering wheel | $91 | $91 | $91 | $91 | - |
| Leather upholstery | - | $141 | $141 | S | - |
| Cruise control | $97 | $97 | $97 | $97 | $97 |
| Tinted glass | $52 | $52 | $52 | $52 | $52 |
| Rear window defogger | $27 | $27 (NA convertible) | - | $27 | S |
| Automatic level control | $79 | $79 | S | S | - |
| Remote control trunk release/lock | $53 | $53 | $53 | $53 | - |
| Brougham package | - | - | - | $199 | - |

Options common to most models. (- = Not Available; S = Standard equipment.) Items may be standard equipment, optional at different pricing, or unavailable on certain models. This chart is only a guide.

## Paint Colors

| | Code |
|---|---|
| Sable Black | 10 |
| Aspen White | 12 |
| Starlight Silver Metallic | 16 |

**Cadillac Style Symbols: A**— 62 4-window Sedan or Calais 4-Dr. HT Sedan; **B**— Sedan de Ville 4-window; **C**— 62 Short Deck Sedan; **D**— Sedan de Ville Park Avenue; **E**— Eldorado Biarritz or Eldorado Convertible; **F**— 62 Convertible; **G**— 62 2-Door Hardtop or Calais 2-Door HT; **H**— Eldorado Seville HT or Eldorado Coupe; **J**— Coupe de Ville; **K**— 62 6-window Sedan; **L**— Sedan de Ville 6-window; **M**— Fleetwood 60 Special Sedan; **N**— 62 4-window Sedan (1963) or Calais Sedan; **P**— Fleetwood Brougham or Eldorado Brougham; **R**— Fleetwood 75 Sedan; **S**— Fleetwood 75 Limousine; **Z**— Commerical Chassis

|                              | Code |
| ---------------------------- | ---- |
| Ascot Gray Metallic          | 18   |
| Hampton Blue Metallic        | 20   |
| Tahoe Blue Metallic          | 24   |
| Ensign Blue                  | 26   |
| Alpine Turquoise Metallic    | 28   |
| Cascade Green Metallic       | 30   |
| Inverness Green Metallic     | 36   |
| Cape Ivory                   | 40   |
| Sandalwood                   | 42   |
| Sierra Gold Metallic         | 44   |
| Samoan Bronze Metallic       | 46   |
| Matador Red Metallic         | 48   |
| Claret Maroon Metallic       | 49   |
| Peacock Firemist Metallic*   | 90   |
| Sheffield Firemist Metallic* | 92   |
| Jade Firemist Metallic*      | 96   |
| Saddle Firemist Metallic*    | 97   |
| Crimson Firemist Metallic*   | 98   |

*Firemist colors available only on Eldorado.*

**1965**

# Calais

*"Elegant newcomer to the fine car world."*

**Nameplate year of origin:** 1965.
**Current bodystyle lifespan:** 1965 through 1966.
**Predecessor to this model:** Series Sixty-Two (1961 to 1964).
**Replacement for this model:** Calais (1967 to 1968).
**Percentage of division's sales volume:** 19.14%.
**Corporate siblings:** Buick Electra 225 and Oldsmobile Ninety-Eight.
**Primary competition:** Chrysler New Yorker and Lincoln Continental.
**Notable changes:** Completely restyled, and newly named model.
**Major standard equipment:** Delhi or Delmar cloth and vinyl seat upholstery, front (Coupe) or rear (Sedan) center armrests, rear fender skirts, interior courtesy lights, electric clock, windshield wipers and washers, right side visor vanity mirrors, front cornering lamps, power steering, power brakes, Turbo Hydra-matic transmission, and 8.00 × 15 BSW tires.

## Measurements

| Wheelbase                | 129.5" |
| ------------------------ | ------ |
| Length                   | 224.0" |
| Width                    | 79.9"  |
| Height                   | 56.4"  |
| Legroom — front          | 40.8"  |
| Legroom — rear           | 38.8"  |
| Headroom — front         | 40.0"  |
| Headroom — rear          | 38.8"  |
| Luggage capacity (cu. ft.) | NA   |
| Fuel capacity (gals.)    | 26.0   |

## Models Available

|                      | Style Number | Base MSRP | Change from LY | Shipping Wt. (lbs.) | Production | Change from LY |
| -------------------- | ------------ | --------- | -------------- | ------------------- | ---------- | -------------- |
| Calais 2-Door Hardtop | 68257        | $4,959    | -1.76%         | 4435                | 12,515     | +2.87%         |
| Calais 4-Door Sedan   | 68269        | $5,144    | NEW            | 4490                | 7,721      | NEW            |
| Calais 4-Door Hardtop | 68239        | $5,144    | -1.76%         | 4500                | 13,975     | +2.23%         |
| TOTALS               | Avg. price   | $5,082    | -1.76%         | Production          | 34,211     | -2.48%         |

# de Ville

*"A new dimension in motoring excellence."*

**Nameplate year of origin:** 1949 (as Hardtop designation); 1959 (series).
**Current bodystyle lifespan:** 1965 through 1966.
**Predecessor to this model:** de Ville (1961 to 1964).
**Replacement for this model:** de Ville (1967 to 1968).
**Percentage of division's sales volume:** 68.85%.
**Corporate siblings:** Buick Electra 225 and Oldsmobile Ninety-Eight.
**Primary competition:** Imperial Crown and Lincoln Continental.
**Notable changes:** Completely restyled.
**Major standard equipment:** Drummond or Delta cloth and leather seat upholstery (all leather in convertible), front and rear center armrests, power front seat, power windows, rear fender skirts, interior courtesy lights, electric clock, windshield wipers and washers, right side visor vanity mirrors, front cornering lamps, power steering, power brakes, Turbo Hydra-matic transmission, and 8.00 × 15 BSW tires.

## Measurements

| | |
|---|---|
| Wheelbase | 129.5" |
| Length | 224.0" |
| Width | 79.9" |
| Height | 56.4" |
| Legroom — front | 40.8" |
| Legroom — rear | 38.8" |
| Headroom — front | 40.0" |
| Headroom — rear | 38.8" |
| Luggage capacity (cu. ft.) | NA |
| Fuel capacity (gals.) | 26.0 |

## Models Available

| | Style Number | Base MSRP | Change from LY | Shipping Wt. (lbs.) | Production | Change from LY |
|---|---|---|---|---|---|---|
| Coupe de Ville 2-Door Hardtop | 68357 | $5,312 | -1.78% | 4480 | 43,345 | +13.48% |
| de Ville 2-Door Convertible | 68367 | $5,528 | -1.50% | 4690 | 19,200 | +7.26% |
| Sedan de Ville 4-Door Sedan | 68369 | $5,554 | NEW | 4555 | 15,000 | NEW |
| Sedan de Ville 4-Door Hardtop | 68339 | $5,554 | -1.79% | 4560 | 45,535 | +14.77% |
| TOTALS | | *Avg. price* $5,487 | -1.72% | | *Production* 123,080 | +11.49% |

# Fleetwood Eldorado

*"The exciting Eldorado convertible is impressive in its styling and elegance."*

**Nameplate year of origin:** 1953.
**Current bodystyle lifespan:** 1965 through 1966.
**Predecessor to this model:** Fleetwood Eldorado (1961 to 1964).
**Replacement for this model:** Eldorado (1967 to 1970).
**Percentage of division's sales volume:** 1.19%.
**Corporate siblings:** Buick Electra 225 and Oldsmobile Ninety-Eight.
**Primary competition:** None.
**Notable changes:** Completely restyled.
**Major standard equipment:** Perforated leather bench or bucket-style seat, power front seat, power windows, power vent windows, rear fender skirts, interior courtesy lights, electric clock, windshield wipers and washers, visor vanity mirror, 3-way inside rear view mirror, front cornering lamps, power steering, power brakes, Turbo Hydra-matic transmission, and 9.00 × 15 WSW tires.

## Measurements

| | |
|---|---|
| Wheelbase | 129.0" |
| Length | 224.0" |
| Width | 79.9" |
| Height | 56.4" |
| Legroom — front | 40.8" |
| Legroom — rear | 38.8" |
| Headroom — front | 40.0" |
| Headroom — rear | 38.8" |
| Luggage capacity (cu. ft.) | NA |
| Fuel capacity (gals.) | 26.0 |

## Models Available

| | Style Number | Base MSRP | Change from LY | Shipping Wt. (lbs.) | Production | Change from LY |
|---|---|---|---|---|---|---|
| Eldorado 2-Door Convertible | 68467 | $6,604 | -0.39% | 4660 | 2,125 | +13.64% |
| TOTALS | | *Avg. price* $6,604 | -0.39% | | *Production* 2,125 | +13.64% |

# Fleetwood Sixty-Special

*"Created for those who can be satisfied with nothing but the finest."*

**Nameplate year of origin:** 1938.
**Current bodystyle lifespan:** 1965 through 1966.
**Predecessor to this model:** Fleetwood Sixty-Special (1961 to 1964).
**Replacement for this model:** Fleetwood Sixty-Special (1967 to 1968).
**Percentage of division's sales volume:** 10.12%.
**Corporate siblings:** None.
**Primary competition:** Imperial LeBaron.
**Notable changes:** Completely restyled.
**Major standard equipment:** Danforth cloth upholstery, front and rear center armrests, power front seat, power windows, power vent windows, rear fender skirts, interior courtesy lights, electric clock, windshield wipers and washers, visor vanity mirror, 3-way inside rear view mirror, front cornering lamps, power steering, power brakes, Turbo Hydra-matic transmission, and 8.00 × 15 BSW tires.

## Measurements

| | |
|---|---|
| Wheelbase | 133.0" |
| Length | 227.5" |
| Width | 79.9" |
| Height | 56.6" |
| Legroom — front | 40.7" |
| Legroom — rear | 40.2" |
| Headroom — front | 40.1" |
| Headroom — rear | 39.5" |
| Luggage capacity (cu. ft.) | NA |
| Fuel capacity (gals.) | 26.0 |

## Models Available

| | Style Number | Base MSRP | Change from LY | Shipping Wt. (lbs.) | Production | Change from LY |
|---|---|---|---|---|---|---|
| Fl. Sixty Special 4-Dr. Sedan | 68069 | $6,351 | -0.58% | 4670 | 18,100 | +24.40% |
| TOTALS | | *Avg. price* $6,351 | -0.58% | *Production* | 18,100 | +24.40% |

# Fleetwood Seventy-Five

*"A masterpiece even among Cadillacs!"*

**Nameplate year of origin:** 1927 (Fleetwood bodies), 1936 (75 series).
**Current bodystyle lifespan:** 1959 through 1965.
**Predecessor to this model:** Fleetwood 75 (1957 to 1958).
**Replacement for this model:** Fleetwood 75 (1966).
**Percentage of division's sales volume:** 0.70%.
**Corporate siblings:** None.
**Primary competition:** None.
**Notable changes:** Minor trim and detail changes.
**Major standard equipment:** Cloth upholstery, power front seat, power windows, power vent windows, rear fender skirts, interior courtesy lights, electric clock, windshield wipers and washers, visor vanity mirror, 3-way inside rear view mirror, front cornering lamps, power steering, power brakes, Hydra-matic transmission, and 8.00 × 15 BSW tires.

## Measurements

| | |
|---|---|
| Wheelbase | 149.8" |
| Length | 243.8" |
| Width | 79.9" |
| Height | 59.0" |
| Legroom — front | 39.9" |
| Legroom — rear | 41.3" |
| Headroom — front | 40.3" |
| Headroom — rear | 39.1" |
| Luggage capacity (cu. ft.) | NA |
| Fuel capacity (gals.) | 26.0 |

## Models Available

| | Style Number | Base MSRP | Change from LY | Shipping Wt. (lbs.) | Production | Change from LY |
|---|---|---|---|---|---|---|
| Fl. Seventy-Five 4-Door Sedan | 69723 | $9,553 | -1.98% | 5190 | 455 | -26.26% |
| Fl. Seventy-Five 4-Dr. Limousine | 69733 | $9,762 | -1.99% | 5260 | 795 | -1.61% |
| TOTALS | | *Avg. price* $9,658 | -1.98% | *Production* | 1,250 | -12.28% |

1965

# CHEVROLET

*"Look to Chevrolet for what you like!"*

Nineteen-sixty-five was a stellar year for Chevrolet, as sales topped the golden year of 1955. The full-size Chevrolet line was totally revamped, as was the sporty compact Corvair. Other models received trim changes, and the one-year-old Chevelle received a front-end restyle. Under the hood of all this new sheetmetal, the choices of powertrains had been proliferating at an amazing rate. Eight different engines, in a wide variety of outputs and tuning, gave an astounding array of choices. Just five years earlier, many makes offered no more than one choice in a car, and now it seemed every manufacturer wanted to let customers build their new cars the way they wanted them. Apparently that is what the customer wanted, as sales for all makes soared to new heights.

The full-size Chevy line was one of the best looking since the mid-fifties. As with other GM big cars, the lines were smooth and flowing, devoid of excess chrome trim, and they were luxurious on the interior. They were also the largest Chevrolet models to date. However, the sporty and modern lines made them appear to be trimmer cars than their predecessors. All traditional Chevrolet styling cues, such as the round taillights, were in evidence. At mid-year a Caprice Custom option package was offered for the Impala 4-Door Hardtop. This was essentially a luxurious interior trim package designed to compete with the new Ford Galaxie 500 LTD. For 1966, the Caprice would become a regular model line. Otherwise, the model line was the same

as in 1964, as were the powertrain offerings. Mid-size Chevelle models received a new grille and rear end treatment. The 300 line added a new 300 Deluxe that included a 2- and 4-Door Sedan, plus the 4-Door Wagon from the prior year's 300 line. The Malibu and Malibu SS lines were the same as last season.

The sporty Corvair received its only major styling change of its lifespan for the 1965 model year. The squarish lines of the original Corvair were now rounded, and all body styles were of a hardtop design. This was a sure sign that Chevrolet intended for the Corvair image to be sporty and not economical. Overall styling was very pleasing, even in the 4-Door Hardtop design. A new sports model was the Corsa, which was offered in 2-Door Hardtop or Convertible versions, powered by a 140-horsepower engine.

The rear-engined Corvair 95 wagon (i.e. van) was around for one final year. Sales of the newly introduced Chevy Van were eating away at the Corvair vans' market, and there was no need for Chevy to continue with two competing designs.

The Chevy II and Corvette were both carry over designs, with only minor trim changes. The Chevy II Nova line dropped the 2-Door Sedan variant. Up front, the grille was cleaned up a bit to look more like its Chevrolet stablemates. Corvette models saw refinements in a new hood design, new grille and new sill moldings. Also redesigned were the instrument cluster and interior door trim.

**Biscayne 4-Door Sedan**

**Chevy II Nova SS 2-Door Hardtop**

**Chevelle 300 Deluxe 4-Door Sedan**

**Chevelle Malibu 2-Door Convertible**

**Corvair 500 4-Door Hardtop Sport Sedan**

**Monza 2-Door Hardtop**

Impala SS 2-Door Hardtop

Corvette 2-Door Coupe and
Corvette 2-Door Convertible

Impala 4-Door Hardtop

**1965**

**Model year production:** 2,383,504, up 2.75% from 1964.
**Domestic market share:** 26.91% (1st place).
**Base price range:** $2,011 to $4,321.
**Industry average base price:** $3,017.
**Chevrolet average base price:** $2,535.
**Introduction date:** September 1964.
**Assembly plants:** Atlanta, GA (A); Baltimore, MD (B); Southgate, CA (C); Flint, MI (F); Framingham, MA (G); Janesville, WI (J); Kansas City, MO (K), Los Angeles, CA (L), Norwood, OH (N); Pontiac, MI (P); Arlington, TX (R); St. Louis, MO (S); Tarrytown, NY (T); Lordstown,

OH (U); Willow Run, MI (W); Wilmington, DE (Y); Fremont, CA (Z), Oshawa, Ontario, Canada (1); and St. Therese, Quebec, Canada (2).
**Data plate identification:** Thirteen digit code read as follows: 1st digit 1 for Chevrolet; four digit style number (see listings below) in which 2nd and 3rd numbers identify series, 4th and 5th indicate body style; 5 for 1965; 7th digit is assembly plant code; 100001 and up for serial number. Actual beginning serial numbers depend upon series. *Example:* 155115T100001 is a 1965 Chevrolet BelAir 2-Door Sedan, 6-cylinder, serial number 100001, built in Arlington, TX.

## Powertrains

| Engine | Gross HP | Transmission Availability | Corvair | Chevy II | Chevelle | Biscayne/ BelAir/Impala | Corvette |
|---|---|---|---|---|---|---|---|
| 153 CID, 1-bbl., 4-cyl. | 90 | 3-speed manual | - | S* | - | - | - |
|  |  | Powerglide Automatic | - | $167* | - | - | - |
| 164 CID — OHV, 2 × 1-bbl., Flat 6 | 95 | 3-speed manual | S | - | - | - | - |
|  |  | 4-speed manual | $92 | - | - | - | - |
|  |  | Powerglide Automatic | $157 | - | - | - | - |
| 164 CID Turbo-Air, 2 × 1-bbl., Flat 6 | 110 | 3-speed manual | $27 | - | - | - | - |
|  |  | 4-speed manual | $119 | - | - | - | - |
|  |  | Powerglide Automatic | $184 | - | - | - | - |
| 164 CID Turbo-Air, 4 × 1-bbl., Flat 6 | 140 | 3-speed manual | $81 | - | - | - | - |
|  |  | 4-speed manual | $172 | - | - | - | - |
|  |  | Powerglide Automatic | $238 | - | - | - | - |
| 164 CID Turbo-Charged, 4 × 1-bbl., Flat 6 | 180 | 3-speed manual | S* | - | - | - | - |
|  |  | 4-speed manual | $92* | - | - | - | - |
| 194 CID Turbo-Thrift, 1-bbl., 6-cyl. | 120 | 3-speed manual | - | S (Nova)/$100[1] | S[3] | - | - |
|  |  | Overdrive | - | - | $108 | - | - |
|  |  | Powerglide Automatic | - | $167 (Nova)/$267[1] | $188[3] | - | - |
| 230 CID Turbo-Thrift, 1-bbl., 6-cyl. | 140 | 3-speed manual | - | $37 (Nova)/$137[1] | $37[3] | - | - |
|  |  | Overdrive | - | - | - | $108 | - |
|  |  | Powerglide Automatic | - | $204 (Nova)/$304[1] | $225[3] | $188 | - |
| 283 CID Turbo-Fire, 2-bbl., V8 | 195 | 3-speed manual | - | $105 (Nova)/$204[1] | $58[3] | $107 | - |
|  |  | Overdrive | - | - | $166[3] | $215 | - |
|  |  | 4-speed manual | - | $289 (Nova)/$393[1] | $246[3] | - | - |
|  |  | Powerglide Automatic | - | $279 (Nova)/$378[1] | $257[3] | $295 | - |
| 283 CID Turbo-Fire, | 220 | 3-speed manual | - | $150 (Nova)/$249[1] | $103[3] | $152 | - |

| Engine | Gross HP | Transmission Availability | Corvair | Chevy II | Chevelle | Biscayne/ BelAir/Impala | Corvette |
|---|---|---|---|---|---|---|---|
| 4-bbl., V8 | | 4-speed manual | - | $334 (Nova)/$438[1] | $291[3] | - | - |
| | | Powerglide Automatic | - | $324 (Nova)/$423[1] | $302[3] | $340 | - |
| 327 CID Turbo-Fire, 4-bbl., V8 | 250 | 3-speed manual | - | $198 (SS or Nova) | $153[3] | $202 | S |
| | | 4-speed manual | - | $382 (SS or Nova) | $341[3] | $390 | $188 |
| | | Powerglide Automatic | - | $372 (SS or Nova) | $352[3] | $401 | $199 |
| 327 CID Turbo-Fire, 2 × 4-bbl., V8 | 300 | 3-speed manual | - | - | $196[3] | $245 | - |
| | | 4-speed manual | - | - | $384[3] | $482 | $242 |
| | | Powerglide Automatic | - | - | $395[3] | $444 | $253 |
| 327 CID Turbo-Fire, 2 × 4-bbl., V8 | 350 | 3-speed manual | - | - | $260[3] | - | - |
| | | 4-speed manual | - | - | $459[3] | - | $296 |
| 327 CID Turbo-Fire, 4-bbl., V8 | 365 | 4-speed manual | - | - | - | - | $317 |
| 327 CID Turbo-Fire, Fuel-Injected V8 | 375 | 4-speed manual | - | - | - | - | $726 |
| 396 CID Turbo-Jet, 4-bbl., V8 | 325 | 3-speed manual | - | - | - | $ | - |
| | | 4-speed manual | - | - | - | $ | - |
| | | Powerglide Automatic | - | - | - | $ | - |
| | | Turbo Hydra-Matic | - | - | - | $ | - |
| 396 CID Ramjet F.I., 4-bbl., V8 | 375 | 4-speed manual | - | - | S[2] | - | - |
| 396 CID Turbo-Jet, 4-bbl., V8 | 425 | 3-speed manual | - | - | - | $ | - |
| | | 4-speed manual | - | - | - | $ | $481 |
| 409 CID Turbo-Jet, 4-bbl., V8 | 340 | 4-speed manual | - | - | - | $587 | - |
| | | Powerglide Automatic | - | - | - | $548 | - |
| 409 CID Turbo-Jet, 4-bbl., V8 | 400 | 4-speed manual | - | - | - | $665 | - |
| | | Powerglide Automatic | - | - | - | $627 | - |

[1]Chevy II 100 only.   [2]Mid-year Z16 package SS 396 only.   [3]All but Z16 package SS 396.   *Corsa only.

## Major Options

| | Corvair | Chevy II | Chevelle | Full-size | Corvette |
|---|---|---|---|---|---|
| Air conditioning (NA 4-cyl.) | $350 | $317 | $364 | $363 | $422 |
| Soft Ray tinted glass | $27 | $31 | $31 | $38 | $16 |
| ComforTilt steering wheel | $43 | | | | |
| (Telescopic) | - | $43 | $43 | $43 | |
| (Telescopic) | | | | | |
| Power steering (NA 4-cyl.) | - | $86 | $86 | $96 | $97 |
| Power brakes | - | $43 | $43 | $43 | $43 |
| Power windows | - | - | $102 | $102 | $59 |
| Electric clock | $16 | $16 | $16 | $16 | S |
| Pushbutton AM radio | $59 | $59 | $59 | $59 | - |
| AM/FM radio | $137 | $137 | $137 | $137 | $203 |
| Whitewall tires — Std. size | $29 | $31 | $32 | $32–$40 | $32 |
| Z16 SS 396 package | - | - | $1501 | - | - |
| Caprice custom package[1] | - | - | - | $200 | - |

Options common to most models. (- = Not Available, S = Standard equipment.) Items may be standard equipment, optional at different pricing, or unavailable on certain models. This chart is only a guide.

[1]Only available on Impala 4-Door Hardtop.

## Paint Colors

| | Code |
|---|---|
| Tuxedo Black | AA |
| Ermine White | CC |
| Mist Blue Metallic | DD |
| Danube Blue Met. | EE |
| Nassau Blue Met. | FF |
| Glen Green Metallic | GG |
| Willow Green Met. | HH |
| Cypress Green Metallic | JJ |
| Artesian Turquoise Met. | KK |
| Tahitian Turquoise Met. | LL |
| Milano Maroon Metallic | MM |
| Madeira Maroon Met. | NN |
| Evening Orchid Metallic | PP |
| Silver Pearl Metallic | QQ |
| Regal Red | RR |
| Sierra Tan Met. | TT |
| Cameo Beige | VV |
| Glacier Gray Metallic | WW |
| Goldwood Yellow | XX |
| Crocus Yellow | YY |

# Corvair

*"A new stunner in style and spirit. New hardtop looks, sportier-than-ever go."*

**Nameplate year of origin:** 1960.
**Current bodystyle lifespan:** 1965 through 1969.
**Predecessor to this model:** Corvair (1960 to 1964).
**Replacement for this model:** Vega (1971 to 1977).
**Percentage of division's sales volume:** 9.88%.
**Corporate siblings:** None.
**Primary competition:** Rambler American, Ford Falcon, Plymouth Valiant and Studebaker Lark.
**Notable changes:** Completely restyled.
**Major standard equipment:** Cloth and vinyl front bench seat, dual sun visors, center dome light, and 6.50 × 13 BSW tires. Monza adds: All-vinyl bucket seats, full carpeting, folding rear seat, glove box light, front door map pockets, and additional exterior chrome trim. Corsa adds: instrument panel gauges, electric clock, and special identifying trim.

## Measurements

| | |
|---|---|
| Wheelbase | 108.0" |
| Length | 183.3" |
| Width | 69.7" |
| Height | 51.2" |
| Legroom — front | 41.0" |
| Legroom — rear | 35.4" |
| Headroom — front | 30.1" |
| Headroom — rear | 30.0" |
| Cargo capacity (cu. ft.) | 6.9 |
| Fuel capacity (gals.) | 14.0 |

**1965**

## Models Available

| | Style Number | Base MSRP | Change from LY | Shipping Wt. (lbs.) | Production | Change from LY |
|---|---|---|---|---|---|---|
| Corvair 500 2-Door HT Sport Coupe | 10137 | $2,022 | +1.10% | 2385 | 36,747 | +59.99% |
| Corvair 500 4-Door HT Sport Sedan | 10139 | $2,096 | NEW | 2405 | 17,560 | NEW |
| Corvair Monza 2-Door HT Sport Cpe, | 10537 | $2,297 | +0.70% | 2440 | 88,954 | +0.58% |
| Corvair Monza 2-Door Convertible | 10567 | $2,440 | -2.09% | 2675 | 26,466 | -14.75% |
| Corvair Monza 4-Door HT Sport Sdn. | 10539 | $2,370 | +1.50% | 2465 | 37,157 | +69.47% |
| Corvair Corsa 2-Door HT Sport Cpe, | 10737 | $2,465 | -5.16% | 2475 | 20,291 | +213.13% |
| Corvair Corsa 2-Door Convertible | 10767 | $2,608 | -7.22% | 2710 | 8,353 | +75.45% |
| TOTALS | | *Avg. price* $2,328 | -2.06% | | *Production* 235,528 | +22.73% |

# Chevy II

*"Smart-looking, smart-stepping saver."*

**Nameplate year of origin:** 1962.
**Current bodystyle lifespan:** 1962 through 1965.
**Predecessor to this model:** None.
**Replacement for this model:** Chevy II (1966 through 1967).
**Percentage of division's sales volume:** 4.95%.
**Corporate siblings:** None.
**Primary competition:** Rambler American, Ford Falcon, Plymouth Valiant, and Studebaker Lark.
**Notable changes:** Revised trim and detail changes.
**Major standard equipment:** Cloth and vinyl front bench seat (all vinyl in wagons), center dome light, and 6.00 × 13 BSW tires (7.00 × 13 BSW tires on wagons). Nova adds: Deluxe steering wheel, courtesy and glove box lights, additional exterior chrome trim, and 6.50 × 13 BSW tires. SS adds: All vinyl seats, full carpeting, electric clock, SS trim and 6.95 × 14 BSW tires.

## Measurements

| | Cars | Wagons |
|---|---|---|
| Wheelbase | 110.0" | 110.0" |
| Length | 182.9" | 187.6" |
| Width | 69.9" | 69.9" |
| Height | 55.0" | 55.1" |
| Legroom — front | 40.1" | 40.1" |
| Legroom — rear | 36.1" | 36.1" |
| Headroom — front | 31.0" | 31.0" |
| Headroom — rear | 29.9" | 29.9" |
| Cargo capacity (cu. ft.) | NA | 76.2 |
| Fuel capacity (gals.) | 16.0 | 16.0 |

## Models Available

|  | Style Number | Base MSRP | Change from LY | Shipping Wt. (lbs.) | Production | Change from LY |
|---|---|---|---|---|---|---|
| Chevy II 100 2-Door Coupe | 11111 | $1,968 | -2.14% | 2505 | 40,500 | * |
| Chevy II 100 4-Door Sedan | 11169 | $2,005 | -2.10% | 2520 | * | * |
| Chevy II 100 4-Door Wagon | 11335 | $2,362 | -1.83% | 2875 | 21,500 | * |
| Chevy II Nova 2-Door Hardtop | 11537 | $2,222 | -2.16% | 2645 | 51,700 | 67.71% |
| Chevy II Nova 4-Door Sedan | 11569 | $2,195 | -2.14% | 2645 | * | * |
| Chevy II Nova 4-Door Wagon | 11535 | $2,456 | -1.88% | 2880 | * | * |
| Chevy II Nova SS 2-Door HT | 11737 | $2,381 | -2.14% | 2690 | 4,300 | * |
| TOTALS | | *Avg. price* $2,227 | -1.68% | | *Production* 118,000 | -38.44% |

*Production is estimated, and not available by series.*

# Chevelle

### "The beautiful in-betweener. Popular-size highway performer."

**Nameplate year of origin:** 1964.
**Current bodystyle lifespan:** 1964 through 1965.
**Predecessor to this model:** None.
**Replacement for this model:** Chevelle (1966 to 1967).
**Percentage of division's sales volume:** 15.05%.
**Corporate siblings:** Buick Special, Oldsmobile F-85, Pontiac Tempest.
**Primary competition:** AMC Classic, Dodge Coronet, Ford Fairlane, and Plymouth Belvedere.
**Notable changes:** Restyled front end, and trim and detail changes.
**Major standard equipment:** Cloth and vinyl front bench seat, black rubber floor mats, hubcaps, and 6.95 × 14 BSW tires (7.35 × 14 BSW tires on wagons). 300 Deluxe adds: Color-keyed floor mats and additional exterior trim. Malibu adds: Color-keyed deep-twist carpeting, full wheel covers, electric clock and dual sun visors. SS adds: All vinyl bucket seats, console, special instrumentation, and SS trim and wheel covers.

## Measurements

|  | Cars | Wagons |
|---|---|---|
| Wheelbase | 115.0" | 115.0" |
| Length | 196.6" | 201.4" |
| Width | 74.6" | 74.6" |
| Height | 53.2" | 55.1" |
| Legroom — front | 42.0" | 42.0" |
| Legroom — rear | 36.3" | 36.3" |
| Headroom — front | 29.9" | 29.9" |
| Headroom — rear | 29.4" | 29.4" |
| Cargo capacity (cu. ft.) | 27.3 | 86.0 |
| Fuel capacity (gals.) | 20.0 | 20.0 |

## Models Available

|  | Style Number | Base MSRP | Change from LY | Shipping Wt. (lbs.) | Production | Change from LY |
|---|---|---|---|---|---|---|
| Chevelle 300 2-Door Coupe | 13111 | $2,033 | -8.87% | 2605 | 31,600 | +39.90% |
| Chevelle 300 4-Door Sedan | 13169 | $2,146 | -5.38% | 2900 | * | * |
| Chevelle 300 2-Door Wagon | 13115 | $2,400 | -5.06% | 3140 | * | * |
| Chevelle 300 Deluxe 2-Door Coupe | 13311 | $2,183 | NEW | 2870 | 41,600 | NEW |
| Chevelle 300 Deluxe 4-Door Sedan | 13369 | $2,220 | NEW | 2910 | * | NEW |
| Chevelle 300 Deluxe 4-Dr. Wagon | 13335 | $2,511 | NEW | 3185 | * | NEW |
| Chevelle Malibu 2-Door Hardtop | 13537 | $2,326 | -2.10% | 2930 | 147,135 | +9.26% |
| Chevelle Malibu 2-Dr. Convertible | 13567 | $2,532 | -2.13% | 3025 | 19,765 | -14.65% |
| Chevelle Malibu 4-Door Sedan | 13569 | $2,299 | -2.13% | 2945 | * | * |
| Chevelle Malibu 4-Door Wagon | 13535 | $2,590 | -2.15% | 3225 | 37,600 | -9.12% |
| Chevelle SS 2-Door Hardtop | 13737 | $2,484 | -2.13% | 2980 | 81,100 | * |
| Chevelle SS 2-Dr. Convertible | 13767 | $2,690 | -2.15% | 3075 | * | * |
| TOTALS | | *Avg. price* $2,368 | -5.59% | | *Production* 358,800 | +6.05% |

*Production is estimated, and not available by series. SS production is for both body styles.*

# Chevrolet Full-size

*"Exciting new look of elegance."*

**Nameplate year of origin:** BelAir 1950; Biscayne 1958; Impala 1958
**Current bodystyle lifespan:** 1965 through 1966.
**Predecessor to this model:** Biscayne/BelAir/Impala (1961 to 1964).
**Replacement for this model:** Biscayne/BelAir/Impala/Caprice (1967 to 1968).
**Percentage of division's sales volume:** 69.13%.
**Corporate siblings:** Buick LeSabre/Wildcat, Olds 88, Pontiac Catalina/Star Chief/Bonneville.
**Primary competition:** Rambler Ambassador, Dodge Polara, Ford Custom/Galaxie/LTD, and Plymouth Fury.
**Notable changes:** Completely restyled.
**Major standard equipment:** Biscayne: Cloth and vinyl bench seat, foam cushion front and rear seats, front and rear door armrests, electric windshield wipers, glove compartment lock and 7.35 × 14 BSW tires (8.25 × 14 BSW tires on wagons). BelAir adds: Full carpeting, and automatic interior lighting. Impala adds: Vinyl upholstery in convertible, extra-long armrests, walnut trim on instrument panel, electric clock, trunk lamp and 7.75 × 14 BSW tires on convertible. SS adds: All vinyl bucket seats, center floor console, and special SS wheel covers, body trim and interior trim.

## Measurements

|  | Cars | Wagons |
|---|---|---|
| Wheelbase | 119.0" | 119.0" |
| Length | 213.1" | 213.3" |
| Width | 79.6" | 79.6" |
| Height | 55.4" | 55.4" |
| Legroom — front | 42.2" | 42.2" |
| Legroom — rear | 39.5" | 39.5" |
| Headroom — front | 30.4" | 30.4" |
| Headroom — rear | 30.0" | 30.0" |
| Cargo capacity (cu. ft.) | NA | 106.1 |
| Fuel capacity (gals.) | 20.0 | 20.0 |

**1965**

## Models Available

| | Style Number | Base MSRP | Change from LY | Shipping Wt. (lbs.) | Production | Change from LY |
|---|---|---|---|---|---|---|
| Biscayne 2-Door Sedan | 15311 | $2,314 | -2.07% | 3305 | 145,300 | * |
| Biscayne 4-Door Sedan | 15369 | $2,367 | -2.07% | 3365 | * | * |
| Biscayne 4-Dr., 2-S. Wagon | 15335 | $2,707 | -2.03% | 3765 | * | * |
| Bel Air 2-Door Sedan | 15511 | $2,414 | -2.07% | 3310 | 271,400 | +124.39% |
| Bel Air 4-Door Sedan | 15569 | $2,467 | -2.06% | 3380 | * | * |
| BelAir 4-Dr., 2-S. Wagon | 15535 | $2,770 | -2.05% | 3765 | * | * |
| BelAir 4-Dr., 3-S. Wagon | 15545 | $2,871 | -2.05% | 3810 | * | * |
| Impala 2-Door Sport Coupe | 16337 | $2,623 | -2.05% | 3385 | 803,400 | +81.64% |
| Impala 2-Door Convertible | 16367 | $2,882 | -1.54% | 3470 | * | * |
| Impala 4-Door Sedan | 16369 | $2,617 | -2.02% | 3460 | * | * |
| Impala 4-Door Hardtop | 16339 | $2,685 | -2.08% | 3490 | * | * |
| Impala 4-Dr., 2-S. Wagon | 16335 | $2,909 | -2.05% | 3825 | 184,400 | -4.37% |
| Impala 4-Dr., 3-S. Wagon | 16345 | $3,010 | -2.05% | 3865 | * | * |
| Impala SS 2-Door Sport Coupe | 16537 | $2,780 | -2.08% | 3435 | 216,114 | * |
| Impala SS 2-Door Convertible | 16567 | $3,040 | -1.55% | 3505 | 27,000 | * |
| TOTALS | | Avg. price $2,697 | -1.99% | | Production 1,647,614 | +4.64% |

*Production is estimated, and not available by series.*

# Corvette

*"From rubber to roof, still America's true sports car."*

**Nameplate year of origin:** 1953 (also used on showcar of same year).
**Current bodystyle lifespan:** 1963 through 1967.
**Predecessor to this model:** Corvette (1956 to 1962).
**Replacement for this model:** Corvette (1968 to 1982).
**Percentage of division's sales volume:** 0.99%.

## Measurements

| | |
|---|---|
| Wheelbase | 98.0" |
| Length | 175.1" |
| Width | 69.2" |

**Corporate siblings:** None.
**Primary competition:** None.
**Notable changes:** Minor trim and detail changes.
**Major standard equipment:** Bucket seats, cockpit-cluster console, simulated walnut steering wheel, full carpeting, complete instrumentation, manually operated folding convertible top, and 6.70 × 15 BSW tires.

## Measurements (cont.)

| | |
|---|---|
| Height | 49.8" |
| Legroom — front | 42.7" |
| Legroom — rear | NA |
| Headroom — front | 30.2 |
| Headroom — rear | NA |
| Cargo capacity (cu. ft.) | NA |
| Fuel capacity (gals.) | 20.0 |

## Models Available

| | Style Number | Base MSRP | Change from LY | Shipping Wt. (lbs.) | Production | Change from LY |
|---|---|---|---|---|---|---|
| Corvette 2-Door Coupe | 19437 | $4,233 | -0.45% | 2975 | 8,186 | -1.42% |
| Corvette 2-Door Convertible | 19467 | $4,022 | -0.37% | 2985 | 15,376 | +3.02% |
| TOTALS | | Avg. price $4,128 | -0.42% | | Production 23,562 | +1.43% |

# CHRYSLER

*"The most beautiful Chrysler ever built. Make your move up to Chrysler."*

A totally new line of 1965 Chrysler models were the most stylish, best looking models to hit their showroom floors since the 1957 season. Truth in advertising for a change! The new angular styling, right in step with similar models from Ford and GM, brought Chrysler back into the mainstream of styling and marketability. No major changes were made to the actual model lineup, other than the addition of a poorly timed, slow-selling, 6-window Town Sedan in the Newport line, and the dropping of the New Yorker Salon 4-Door Hardtop. This was the final season for the traditional 300 letter series line. The increasingly popular mid-size models, such as the Pontiac GTO and Oldsmobile 4-4-2, were taking their bite out of sales of the larger performance models. There would be a one-year-only model in 1970 based on a Hurst performance upgrade, and then the 1999 return of the 300M sport sedan line, but neither of these was in the strictly big-brute, high-horsepower, all-out luxury tradition of the original. This was also the last year the 413 CID V8 engine would be available. It would be replaced by a modern 440 CID V8 for 1966.

300 4-Door Hardtop

Newport 2-Door Hardtop

Newport 4-Door Hardtop

**Model year production:** 204,002, up 39.29% over 1964.
**Domestic market share:** 2.30% (10th place)
**Base price range:** $2,968 to $4,856.
**Industry average base price:** $3,017.
**Chrysler average base price:** $3,829.
**Introduction date:** September 1964.
**Assembly plants:** Detroit (Jefferson Ave.), MI (3); and Newark, DE (6).

**Data plate identification:** Ten digit code read as follows: 1st digit C for Chrysler; 2nd number identifies series (1–7; Newport is 1); 3rd digit 5 for 1965; 4th digit is assembly plant code; followed by 100001 and up for serial number. Body style identification found on separate plate. *Example:* C143100001 is a 1965 Chrysler Newport, serial number 100001, built in Detroit, MI.

## Powertrains

| Engine | Gross HP | Transmission Availability | Newport | 300 | New Yorker | 300-L |
|---|---|---|---|---|---|---|
| 383 CID, 2-bbl., V8 | 270 | 3-speed manual | S | - | - | - |
| | | 4-speed manual | $227 | - | - | - |
| | | Torqueflite automatic | $227 | - | - | - |
| 383 CID, 4-bbl., V8 | 315 | 3-speed manual | $* | S | - | - |
| | | 4-speed manual | $* | $227 | - | - |
| | | Torqueflite automatic | $* | $227 | - | - |
| 413 CID, 4-bbl., V8 | 340 | Torqueflite automatic | - | - | S | - |
| 413 CID, 4-bbl., V8 | 360 | 4-speed manual | - | $* | - | S |
| | | Torqueflite automatic | - | $* | $* | S |

*Accurate pricing information not available.*

## Major Options

| | Newport | 300 | New Yorker | 300-L |
|---|---|---|---|---|
| Heater and defroster | $102 | $102 | $102 | $102 |
| Airtemp air conditioning | $510 | $510 | $510 | $510 |
| Solex tinted glass | $43 | $43 | $43 | $43 |
| Rear window defogger | $21 | $21 | $21 | $21 |
| Tilt steering wheel | $47 | $47 | $47 | $47 |
| Auto Pilot cruise control | $86 | $86 | $86 | $86 |
| Power steering | $107 | $107 | S | S |
| Power brakes | $47 | $47 | S | S |
| Power seat (Bench) | $102 | $102 | $102 | - |
| Power windows | $108 | $108 | S | S |
| Golden Touch Tone AM radio | $93 | $93 | $93 | $93 |
| AM/FM radio | $157 | $157 | $157 | $157 |
| White sidewall tires — std. sizes | $42 | $46 | $51 | S |

Options common to most models. (- = Not Available; S = Standard equipment.) Items may be standard equipment, optional at different pricing, or unavailable on certain models. This chart is only a guide.

## Paint Colors

| | Code |
|---|---|
| Regal Gold Metallic | AA-1 |
| Formal Black | BB-1 |
| Ice Blue | CC-1 |
| Nassau Blue Metallic | DD-1 |
| Navy Blue Metallic | EE-1 |
| Mist Blue Metallic | FF-1 |
| Sequoia Green Metallic | GG-1 |
| Peacock Turquoise Met. | KK-1 |
| Royal Turquoise Metallic | LL-1 |
| Granite Gray Metallic | MM-1 |
| Silver Mist Metallic | NN-1 |
| Sierra Sand | RR-1 |
| French Ivory | SS-1 |
| Spanish Red Metallic | TT-1 |
| Cordovan Metallic | VV-1 |
| Persian White | WW-1 |
| Sand Dune Beige | XX-1 |
| Sable Tan Metallic | YY-1 |
| Frost Turquoise Metallic | ZZ-1 |
| Silver Mist Metallic | 22-1 |
| Pink Silver Metallic | 33-1 |
| Moss Gold Metallic | 44-1 |
| Black Plum Metallic | 55-1 |
| Mauve Metallic | 66-1 |
| Patrician Gold Metallic | 77-1 |

**1965**

# Newport

*"Believe it or not, this is our easy-to-own Chrysler Newport.
You can't buy this much car anywhere for less."*

**Nameplate year of origin:** 1961 (as series); 1950 (as Hardtop model designation).
**Current bodystyle lifespan:** Windsor 1960; Newport 1961 through 1964 (major restyle in 1963).
**Predecessor to this model:** Windsor (1960), Newport (1961 to 1964).
**Replacement for this model:** Newport (1967 to 1968).
**Percentage of division's sales volume:** 61.66%.
**Corporate siblings:** Chrysler New Yorker, 300 and 300-L.
**Primary competition:** Buick Wildcat, Mercury Monterey and Oldsmobile 88.
**Notable changes:** Completely restyled.
**Major standard equipment:** Cloth and vinyl front bench seat, full-floor coverings, sun visors, exterior bright side moldings and 8.25 × 14 BSW tires. Town & Country adds: 8.55 × 14 BSW tires.

## Measurements

| | Cars | Wagons |
|---|---|---|
| Wheelbase | 124.0" | 121.0" |
| Length | 218.2" | 218.4" |
| Width | 79.5" | 79.5" |
| Height | 56.9" | 57.5" |
| Legroom — front | 42.0" | 42.0" |
| Legroom — rear | 40.9" | 40.9" |
| Headroom — front | 39.3" | 39.3" |
| Headroom — rear | 38.5" | 38.5" |
| Cargo capacity (cu. ft.) | NA | NA |
| Fuel capacity (gals.) | 25.0 | 25.0 |

## Models Available

| | Style Number | Base MSRP | Change from LY | Shipping Wt. (lbs.) | Production | Change from LY |
|---|---|---|---|---|---|---|
| Newport 2-Door Hardtop | C12 | $3,070 | +3.65% | 3935 | 23,655 | +123.60% |
| Newport 2-Door Convertible | C15 | $3,442 | +3.24% | 4020 | 3,192 | +46.69% |
| Newport 4-Door Sedan | C13 | $3,009 | +3.72% | 3975 | 61,054 | +9.11% |
| Newport 4-Dr., 6-w. Town Sedan | C18 | $3,143 | NEW | 3990 | 12,411 | NEW |
| Newport 4-Door Hardtop | C14 | $3,149 | +3.52% | 3990 | 17,062 | +75.72% |
| N. Town & Country 4-Dr., 2-S. Wgn. | C56 | $3,521 | +3.13% | 4350 | 4,683 | +25.89% |
| N. Town & Country 4-Dr., 3-S. Wgn. | C57 | $3,629 | +3.07% | 4415 | 3,738 | +22.92% |
| TOTALS | | Avg. price $3,280 | +2.63% | | Production 125,795 | +47.68% |

# 300

*"The sports-bred Chrysler."*

**Nameplate year of origin:** 1955; 1962 (as non-letter series).
**Current bodystyle lifespan:** 300 (1965 through 1966).
**Predecessor to this model:** Saratoga (1960); Windsor (1961); 300 (1962 through 1964 with major restyle in 1963).
**Replacement for this model:** 300 (1967 to 1968).
**Percentage of division's sales volume:** 12.50%.
**Corporate siblings:** Chrysler Newport, New Yorker and 300-L.
**Primary competition:** Buick Wildcat, Mercury Monterey S-55 and Oldsmobile 88.
**Notable changes:** Completely restyled.
**Major standard equipment:** Front bucket seats, pile carpeting, padded dash, map lights, electric clock, sun visors, exterior bright side moldings, full wheel covers, and 8.55 × 14 BSW tires.

## Measurements

| | |
|---|---|
| Wheelbase | 124.0" |
| Length | 218.2" |
| Width | 79.5" |
| Height | 56.7" |
| Legroom — front | 41.3" |
| Legroom — rear | 40.0" |
| Headroom — front | 38.7" |
| Headroom — rear | 37.9" |
| Cargo capacity (cu. ft.) | NA |
| Fuel capacity (gals.) | 25.0 |

## Models Available

| | Style Number | Base MSRP | Change from LY | Shipping Wt. (lbs.) | Production | Change from LY |
|---|---|---|---|---|---|---|
| 300 2-Door Hardtop | C22 | $3,551 | +3.14% | 4105 | 11,621 | -13.28% |
| 300 2-Door Convertible | C25 | $3,911 | +2.84% | 4135 | 1,418 | -30.01% |
| 300 4-Door Hardtop | C24 | $3,628 | +3.04% | 4160 | 12,452 | +8.66% |
| TOTALS | | *Avg. price* $3,697 | +3.01% | | *Production* 25,491 | -5.19% |

# New Yorker

*"Here's to sheer, unadulterated elegance."*

**Nameplate year of origin:** 1939 (Altered from 1938 New York Special model).

**Current bodystyle lifespan:** New Yorker (1965 through 1966).

**Predecessor to this model:** New Yorker (1960 to 1964).

**Replacement for this model:** New Yorker (1967 to 1968).

**Percentage of division's sales volume:** 24.45%.

**Corporate siblings:** Chrysler Newport, 300-L and 300.

**Primary competition:** Buick Electra, Mercury Park Lane and Oldsmobile 98.

**Notable changes:** Completely restyled.

**Major standard equipment:** Cloth and vinyl front bench seat, pile carpeting, padded dash, map lights, power windows, electric clock, sun visors, exclusive exterior bright trim, power steering, power brakes, automatic transmission, full wheel covers, and 8.50 × 14 BSW tires.
Town & Country adds: 9.00 × 14 BSW tires.

## Measurements

| | Cars | Wagons |
|---|---|---|
| Wheelbase | 124.0" | 121.0" |
| Length | 218.2" | 219.0" |
| Width | 79.5" | 79.5" |
| Height | 55.8" | 57.5" |
| Legroom — front | 42.0" | 42.0" |
| Legroom — rear | 39.9" | 40.9" |
| Headroom — front | 38.5" | 39.3" |
| Headroom — rear | 37.9" | 38.5" |
| Cargo capacity (cu. ft.) | NA | NA |
| Fuel capacity (gals.) | 25.0 | 25.0 |

**1965**

## Models Available

| | Style Number | Base MSRP | Change from LY | Shipping Wt. (lbs.) | Production | Change from LY |
|---|---|---|---|---|---|---|
| New Yorker 2-Door Hardtop | C32 | $4,161 | NEW | 4190 | 9,357 | NEW |
| New Yorker 4-Door Town Sedan | C38 | $4,104 | +2.75% | 4245 | 16,339 | +5.80% |
| New Yorker 4-Door Hardtop | C34 | $4,238 | +2.59% | 4245 | 21,110 | +93.90% |
| N. Y. Town & Country 4-Dr., 2-S. W. | C76 | $4,827 | +2.25% | 4645 | 1,368 | +14.96% |
| N. Y. Town & Country 4-Dr., 3-S. W. | C77 | $4,935 | +2.22% | 4710 | 1,697 | +5.86% |
| TOTALS | | *Avg. price* $4,453 | -5.39% | | *Production* 49,871 | +62.21% |

# 300-L

*"A brawling, hustling brute of a car with a heritage 10 years deep."*

**Nameplate year of origin:** 1955.

**Current bodystyle lifespan:** 1965.

**Predecessor to this model:** 300 letter series (1960 to 1964).

**Replacement for this model:** None.

**Percentage of division's sales volume:** 1.39%.

**Corporate siblings:** Chrysler Newport, New Yorker and 300.

**Primary competition:** Buick Riviera and Ford Thunderbird.

## Measurements

| | |
|---|---|
| Wheelbase | 124.0" |
| Length | 218.2" |
| Width | 79.5" |
| Height | 55.3" |
| Legroom — front | 41.3" |
| Legroom — rear | 40.0" |

**Notable changes:** Completely restyled.
**Major standard equipment:** Leather power bucket front seats, pile carpeting, padded dash, map lights, power windows, electric clock, sun visors, exclusive exterior bright trim, power steering, power brakes, automatic transmission, full wheel covers, and 7.60 × 15 WSW tires.

## Measurements (cont.)

| | |
|---|---|
| Headroom — front | 38.7" |
| Headroom — rear | 37.9" |
| Cargo capacity (cu. ft.) | NA |
| Fuel capacity (gals.) | 25.0 |

## Models Available

| | Style Number | Base MSRP | Change from LY | Shipping Wt. (lbs.) | Production | Change from LY |
|---|---|---|---|---|---|---|
| 300-L 2-Door Hardtop | C42 | $4,153 | +2.39% | 4225 | 2,405 | -20.42% |
| 300-L 2-Door Convertible | C45 | $4,618 | +2.12% | 4155 | 440 | -29.60% |
| TOTALS | | *Avg. price* $4,386 | +2.26% | | *Production* 2,845 | -21.99% |

# DODGE

*"Dodge comes on big for 1965."*

Nineteen sixty-five was a breakthrough year for Dodge and all of Chrysler Corporation. After years of floundering in the full-size market, Dodge introduced a totally new line of full-size 121-inch wheelbase cars that finally took the division back away from the low-price field that had once been Plymouth's domain. This helped Dodge, because of the mid-sixties popularity of mid-range cars such as Pontiac and Oldsmobile, and also helped Plymouth by eliminating some of the intra-family rivalry. At the same time, a major restyling effort on the former full-size (now intermediate) platform provided the basis for a popular new line of Coronet models. While riding a slightly shortened 117-inch wheelbase, the basic body structure of the 1962–1964 era was retained (very evident in the wagon models), and a very pleasant, one-year-only look was created that set the Mopar mid-size cars on their way to success. The new look of both the full-size and mid-size cars was part of a styling period characterized by very boxy dimensions, with minimal character lines (at least at first), simply designed grilles, and taillamp treatments that took on a "delta" shaped theme (on full-sized models). As was typical of the period, GM took the styling lead with more curvaceous lines, and Ford was somewhere between Chrysler and GM on the "sexy" styling scale. Powertrain choices remained similar to 1964.

As previously mentioned, a revived Coronet was the new name for the former Dodge 330 and 440 series, and it was marketed in the mid-size level. A new 500 was added as a sporty top-line model, and a Convertible replaced the 440 2-Door Sedan in the Coronet 440 line. The newly designed Polara moved upmarket to take the place of the prior 880 line, and expanded to include 2-door Hardtop and Convertible models. The Custom 880 line continued as the upper trim level Polara model. Finally, a new Monaco 2-Door Hardtop rounded out the line as a competitor to the successful Pontiac Grand Prix. The "compact" Dart line returned with new frontal styling and revised rear treatments including oval taillamps, but no other major changes.

Coronet 500 2-Door Convertible

Custom 880 4-Door Sedan

Dart GT 2-Door Hardtop

Monaco 2-Door Hardtop

Polara 2-Door Hardtop

**Model year production:** 551,000, up 20.46% over 1964.
**Domestic market share:** 6.22% (7th place).
**Base price range:** $2,074 to $3,527.
**Industry average base price:** $3,017.
**Dodge average base:** $2,709.
**Introduction date:** September 25, 1964.
**Assembly plants:** Lynch Road, MI (1); Hamtramck, MI (2); Detroit (Jefferson Ave.), MI (3); Los Angeles, CA (5); Newark, DE (6); and St. Louis, MO (7).

**Data plate identification:** Ten digit code read as follows: Four digit style number (see listings below) in which 1st digit series letter (e.g., D = Polara series), 2nd number identifies car model (1 is for base Polara, 3 for Custom 880, 4 for Monaco), 3rd digit 5 for 1965; 4th digit is assembly plant code; followed by 100001 (500001 for Dart) and up for serial number. Body style identification found on separate plate. *Example:* D153100001 is a 1965 Dodge Polara, serial number 100001, built in Detroit, MI.

**1965**

# Powertrains

| Engine | Gross HP | Transmission Availability | Dart | Coronet | Polara 318 & Polara | C. 880 & Monaco |
|---|---|---|---|---|---|---|
| 170 CID, 1-bbl., 6-cyl. | 101 | 3-speed manual | S | - | - | - |
| | | Torqueflite automatic | $140 | - | - | - |
| 225 CID, 1-bbl., 6-cyl. | 145 | 3-speed manual | $39 | S (ex. 500) | - | - |
| | | 4-speed manual | $191 | $146 (ex. 500) | - | - |
| | | Torqueflite automatic | $187 | $165 (ex. 500) | - | - |
| 273 CID, 2-bbl., V8 | 180 | 3-speed manual | $96 | S (500)/$94 (Others) | - | - |
| | | 4-speed manual | $242 | $180 (500)/$274 (Others) | - | - |
| | | Torqueflite automatic | $244 | $181 (500)/$275 (Others) | - | - |
| 318 CID, 2-bbl., V8 | 230 | 3-speed manual | - | $25 (500)/$119 (Others) | S[1] | - |
| | | 4-speed manual | - | $205 (500)/$299 (Others) | $180[1] | - |
| | | Torqueflite automatic | - | $206 (500)/$300 (Others) | $181[1] | - |
| 383 CID, 2-bbl., V8 | 270 | 3-speed manual | - | $73 (500)/$167 (Others) | $73[1]/S[2] | S[4] |
| | | 4-speed manual | - | $253 (500)/$347 (Others) | $253[1]/$180[2] | $180[4] |
| | | Torqueflite automatic | - | $254 (500)/$348 (Others) | $254[1]/$181[2] | $181[4] |
| 383 CID, 4-bbl., V8 | 315/330 | 3-speed manual | - | $86 (500)/$180 (Others) | $86[1]/$13[2] | S[3]/$13[4] |
| | | 4-speed manual | - | $266 (500)/$360 (Others) | $266[1]/$193[2] | $180[3]/$193[4] |
| | | Torqueflite automatic | - | $267 (500)/$361 (Others) | $267[1]/$194[2] | $181[3]/$194[4] |
| 413 CID, 4-bbl., V8 | 340 | | - | * | * | * |

| Engine | Gross HP | Transmission Availability | Dart | Coronet | Polara 318 & Polara | C. 880 & Monaco |
|--------|----------|--------------------------|------|---------|---------------------|------------------|
| 426 CID, 4-bbl., V8 | 365 | | - | * | * | * |
| 426 CID Hemi-Charger, 4-bbl., V8 | 415 | | - | * | * | * |
| 426 CID Hemi-Charger, 2 × 4-bbl., V8 | 425 | | - | * | * | * |

¹Polara 318 only.  ²All but Polara 318.  ³Monaco only.  ⁴Custom 880 only.  *Accurate pricing information currently unavailable.*

## Major Options

| | Dart | Coronet | Polara/880 | Monaco |
|--|------|---------|-----------|--------|
| Heater and defroster | S | S | S | S |
| Airtemp air conditioning | $285 | $315 | $315 | $315 |
| Tinted glass | $22 | $31 | $31 | $31 |
| Auto Pilot cruise control | - | $66 | $66 | $66 |
| Power steering | $67 | $67 | $74 | $74 |
| Power brakes | $33 | $33 | $33 | $33 |
| Power seat | - | $74 | $74 | $61 |
| Power windows | - | $102 | $102 | $102 |
| Electric clock | $12 | $12 | $12 | S |
| Music Master AM radio | $79 | $45 | $45 | $45 |
| White sidewall tires — std. sizes | $23–$25 | $25–$40 | $25–$40 | $40 |

Options common to most models. (- = Not Available, S = Standard equipment.) Items may be standard equipment, optional at different pricing, or unavailable on certain models. This chart is only a guide.

## Paint Colors

| | Code |
|--|------|
| Gold Metallic | AA-1 |
| Black | BB-1 |
| Light Blue Metallic | CC-1 |
| Medium Blue Metallic | DD-1 |
| Dark Blue Metallic | EE-1 |
| Pale Blue Metallic | FF-1 |
| Dark Green Metallic | GG-1 |
| Light Turquoise | JJ-1 |
| Medium Turquoise Met. | KK-1 |
| Dark Turquoise Metallic | LL-1 |
| Pale Silver Metallic | NN-1 |
| Bright Red | PP-1 |
| Beige | RR-1 |
| Ivory | SS-1 |
| Ruby Red Metallic | TT-1 |
| Cordovan Metallic | VV-1 |
| White | WW-1 |
| Light Tan | XX-1 |
| Medium Tan Metallic | YY-1 |
| Pale Turquoise Metallic | ZZ-1 |
| Medium Green Metallic | 22-1 |
| Pink Gold Metallic | 33-1 |
| Pale Gold Metallic | 77-1 |
| Yellow | 88-1 |

# Dart

*"The Dodge-size Compact."*

**Nameplate year of origin:** 1960 (on low-end full-size models).
**Current bodystyle lifespan:** 1963 through 1966.
**Predecessor to this model:** Lancer (1961 to 1962).
**Replacement for this model:** Dart (1967 to 1976).
**Percentage of division's sales volume:** 37.51%.
**Corporate siblings:** Plymouth Valiant.
**Primary competition:** Rambler American, Chevrolet Chevy II, Ford Falcon, and Studebaker Lark.
**Notable changes:** Revised front and rear styling.
**Major standard equipment:** Nylon and vinyl front bench seats, rubber floor mats, chrome windshield trim and 6.50 × 13 BSW tires. 270 adds: All-vinyl upholstery on convertible, color-keyed carpeting, additional interior and exterior bright trim. GT adds: All-vinyl bucket seats, padded instrument panel, full wheel covers and specific GT trim.

## Measurements

| | Cars | Wagons |
|--|------|--------|
| Wheelbase | 111.0" | 106.0" |
| Length | 196.4" | 190.2" |
| Width | 69.9" | 69.0" |
| Height | 54.4" | 54.5" |
| Legroom — front | 40.7" | 40.7" |
| Legroom — rear | 35.6" | 34.2" |
| Headroom — front | 38.2" | 38.2" |
| Headroom — rear | 37.2" | 37.2" |
| Cargo capacity (cu. ft.) | NA | NA |
| Fuel capacity (gals.) | 18.0 | 18.0 |

## Models Available

| | Style Number | Base MSRP | Change from LY | Shipping Wt. (lbs.) | Production | Change from LY |
|---|---|---|---|---|---|---|
| Dart 170 2-Door Sedan | L11 | $2,074 | +4.33% | 2645 | 73,800 | +5.13% |
| Dart 170 4-Door Sedan | L13 | $2,139 | +4.19% | 2660 | * | * |
| Dart 170 4-Door, 2-Seat Wagon | L56 | $2,407 | +3.97% | 2770 | * | * |
| Dart 270 2-Door Sedan | L31 | $2,180 | +4.11% | 2650 | 62,800 | +3.97% |
| Dart 270 2-Door Hardtop | L32 | $2,274 | NEW | 2675 | * | NEW |
| Dart 270 2-Door Convertible | L35 | $2,481 | +3.85% | 2765 | * | * |
| Dart 270 4-Door Sedan | L33 | $2,247 | +4.03% | 2670 | * | * |
| Dart 270 4-Door, 2-Seat Wagon | L76 | $2,506 | +3.81% | 2770 | 29,400 | +110.00% |
| Dart GT 2-Door Hardtop | L42 | $2,404 | +3.71% | 2715 | 40,700 | -19.72% |
| Dart GT 2-Door Convertible | L45 | $2,628 | +3.63% | 2795 | * | * |
| TOTALS | Avg. price | $2,334 | +3.64% | | Production 206,700 | +5.84% |

*Production by series not available. Totals are estimated.

# Coronet

## "The hot new Dodge at a new lower price."

**Nameplate year of origin:** 1949.
**Current bodystyle lifespan:** 1962 through 1965 (including Dart and 330/440).
**Predecessor to this model:** Dart Seneca and Pioneer (1960 to 1961).
**Replacement for this model:** Coronet (1966 to 1967).
**Percentage of division's sales volume:** 38.02%.
**Corporate siblings:** Plymouth Belvedere.
**Primary competition:** AMC Classic, Chevrolet Chevelle, Ford Fairlane, and Pontiac Tempest.
**Notable changes:** Completely restyled front and rear end. Renamed from prior 330/440 series.
**Major standard equipment:** Cloth-and-vinyl bench seat with foam front cushion, full rubber floor mats, electric windshield wipers, dual sun visors, exterior bright trim around windshield and back window, and 7.35 × 14 BSW tires (7.75 × 14 BSW tires on wagons). 440 adds: Full carpeting, exterior bright trim around side windows and body sides. 500 adds: All-vinyl front bucket seats, center floor console, deluxe door armrests, padded instrument panel, and deluxe spinner wheel covers. Hemi-Charger adds over base: 426 CID V8 engine, special suspension and dual exhausts.

## Measurements

| | Cars | Wagons |
|---|---|---|
| Wheelbase | 117.0" | 116.0" |
| Length | 204.3" | 209.3" |
| Width | 75.6" | 75.1" |
| Height | 55.8" | 55.9" |
| Legroom — front | 41.9" | 41.9" |
| Legroom — rear | 36.6" | 36.6" |
| Headroom — front | 39.1" | 39.1" |
| Headroom — rear | 38.4" | 38.4" |
| Cargo capacity (cu. ft.) | NA | NA |
| Fuel capacity (gals.) | 19.0 | 19.0 |

## Models Available

| | Style Number | Base MSRP | Change from LY | Shipping Wt. (lbs.) | Production | Change from LY |
|---|---|---|---|---|---|---|
| Coronet 2-Door Coupe | W11 | $2,257 | -0.31% | 3090 | 63,100 | * |
| Coronet 4-Door Sedan | W13 | $2,296 | -0.91% | 3140 | * | * |
| Coronet 4-Dr., 2-S. Wagon | W56 | $2,592 | -2.34% | 3390 | 25,600 | * |
| Coronet 440 2-Door Hardtop | W32 | $2,403 | -8.87% | 3100 | 87,500 | * |
| Coronet 440 2-Door Convertible | W35 | $2,622 | -12.42% | 3230 | * | * |
| Coronet 440 4-Door Sedan | W33 | $2,377 | -9.10% | 3125 | * | * |
| Coronet 440 4-Dr., 2-S. Wagon | W76 | $2,674 | NEW | 3395 | * | NEW |
| Coronet 440 4-Dr., 3-S. Wagon | W77 | $2,868 | NEW | 3560 | * | NEW |
| Coronet 500 2-Door Hardtop | W42 | $2,674 | NEW | 3255 | 33,300 | NEW |
| Coronet 500 2-Door Convertible | W45 | $2,894 | NEW | 3340 | * | NEW |
| Coronet Hemi-Charger 2-Door Sdn. | W01 | NA | NEW | NA | * | NEW |
| TOTALS | Avg. price | $2,566 | -0.24% | | Production 209,500 | +26.66% |

*Production by series not available. Totals are estimated. Comparisons made to 1964 Dodge 330/440 line.

# Polara

*"Beautiful way to leave the low-price field."*

**Nameplate year of origin:** 1959.
**Current bodystyle lifespan:** 1965 through 1966.
**Predecessor to this model:** Custom 880 (1962 to 1964).
**Replacement for this model:** Polara (1967 to 1968).
**Percentage of division's sales volume:** 13.63%.
**Corporate siblings:** Plymouth Fury.
**Primary competition:** AMC Ambassador, Chevrolet BelAir/Impala, and Ford Galaxie/LTD.
**Notable changes:** Completely redesigned. Now based on full-size Chrysler platform.
**Major standard equipment:** Cloth-and-vinyl bench seat, full carpeting, electric windshield wipers, dual circular instrument cluster, dual sun visors, exterior bright trim on windows and body sides, power tailgate window (3-Seat wagon), and 8.25 × 14 BSW tires (8.55 × 14 BSW tires on wagons).

## Measurements

|  | Cars | Wagons |
| --- | --- | --- |
| Wheelbase | 121.0" | 121.0" |
| Length | 212.3" | 217.1" |
| Width | 79.0" | 79.0" |
| Height | 57.2" | 57.5" |
| Legroom — front | 41.9" | 41.9" |
| Legroom — rear | 40.8" | 40.8" |
| Headroom — front | 39.3" | 39.3" |
| Headroom — rear | 38.5" | 38.5" |
| Cargo capacity (cu. ft.) | NA | NA |
| Fuel capacity (gals.) | 19.0 | 19.0 |

## Models Available

|  | Style Number | Base MSRP | Change from LY | Shipping Wt. (lbs.) | Production | Change from LY |
| --- | --- | --- | --- | --- | --- | --- |
| Polara 318 4-Door Sedan | D23 | $2,695 | NEW | 3847 | * | NEW |
| Polara 2-Door Hardtop | D12 | $2,800 | NEW | 3850 | * | NEW |
| Polara 2-Door Convertible | D15 | $3,088 | NEW | 3940 | * | NEW |
| Polara 4-Door Sedan | D13 | $2,770 | -1.98% | 3905 | * | * |
| Polara 4-Door Hardtop | D14 | $2,874 | NEW | 3965 | * | NEW |
| Polara 4-Door, 2-S. Wagon | D56 | $3,110 | -1.43% | 4220 | * | * |
| Polara 4-Door, 3-S. Wagon | D57 | $3,214 | -1.71% | 4255 | * | * |
| TOTALS | | Avg. price $2,936 | +6.38% | | Production 75,100 | +15.72% |

*Production by model not available. Totals are estimated.*

# Custom 880

*"If elegance were spelled in numbers, this would be it."*

**Nameplate year of origin:** 1962.
**Current bodystyle lifespan:** 1965 through 1966.
**Predecessor to this model:** Custom 880 (1962 to 1964).
**Replacement for this model:** Monaco (1967 to 1968).
**Percentage of division's sales volume:** 8.44%.
**Corporate siblings:** Plymouth Fury.
**Primary competition:** AMC Ambassador, Chevrolet BelAir/Impala, and Ford Galaxie/LTD.
**Notable changes:** Completely redesigned.
**Major standard equipment:** Cloth-and-vinyl bench seat, deep-pile carpeting, electric windshield wipers, dual circular instrument cluster, dual sun visors, exterior bright trim around all glass and body sides, walnut-grain exterior trim and power tailgate window on wagons, and 8.25 × 14 BSW tires (8.55 × 14 BSW tires on wagon).

## Measurements

|  | Cars | Wagons |
| --- | --- | --- |
| Wheelbase | 122.0" | 122.0" |
| Length | 220.4" | 223.8" |
| Width | 79.2" | 79.2" |
| Legroom — front | 41.8" | 41.8" |
| Height | 55.7" | 57.1" |
| Legroom — rear | 39.1" | 39.1" |
| Headroom — front | 38.8" | 39.6" |
| Headroom — rear | 38.4" | 39.2" |
| Cargo capacity (cu. ft.) | 22.4 | 104.2 |
| Fuel capacity (gals.) | 24 | 23 |

## Models Available

| | Style Number | Base MSRP | Change from LY | Shipping Wt. (lbs.) | Production | Change from LY |
|---|---|---|---|---|---|---|
| Custom 880 2-Door Hardtop | D32 | $3,043 | 0.00% | 3945 | * | * |
| Custom 880 2-Door Convertible | D35 | $3,288 | 0.74% | 3965 | * | * |
| Custom 880 4-Door Sedan | D38 | $2,970 | -0.24% | 3915 | * | * |
| Custom 880 4-Door Hardtop | D34 | $3,107 | -0.48% | 4155 | * | * |
| Custom 880 4-Dr., 2-S. Wgn. | D76 | $3,373 | 2.06% | 4270 | * | * |
| Custom 880 4-Dr., 3-S. Wgn. | D77 | $3,476 | 1.64% | 4355 | * | * |
| TOTALS | Avg. price | $3,210 | +5.8% | Production | 46,500 | +46.23% |

*Production by model not available. Totals are estimated.*

# Monaco

*"The limited-edition Dodge for the man with unlimited taste."*

**Nameplate year of origin:** 1965.
**Current bodystyle lifespan:** 1965 through 1966.
**Predecessor to this model:** None.
**Replacement for this model:** Monaco 500 (1967 to 1968).
**Percentage of division's sales volume:** 2.40%.
**Corporate siblings:** Plymouth Fury.
**Primary competition:** Buick Wildcat, Mercury S-55, Oldsmobile Starfire, and Pontiac Grand Prix.
**Notable changes:** All-new model based on new Polara platform.
**Major standard equipment:** All-vinyl or cloth and vinyl bucket seats, deep-pile carpeting, full-length center floor console, padded dash, electric windshield wipers, electric clock, light package, dual circular instrument cluster, dual sun visors, remote-control LH outside rear view mirror, fender-mounted turn signal indicators, exterior bright trim around all glass and body sides, deluxe wheel covers, spare tire cover, and 8.25 × 14 BSW tires.

### Measurements

| | |
|---|---|
| Wheelbase | 121.0" |
| Length | 212.3" |
| Width | 79.0" |
| Height | 56.3" |
| Legroom — front | 41.8" |
| Legroom — rear | 40.8" |
| Headroom — front | 39.1" |
| Headroom — rear | 38.4" |
| Cargo capacity (cu. ft.) | NA |
| Fuel capacity (gals.) | 19.0 |

## Models Available

| | Style Number | Base MSRP | Change from LY | Shipping Wt. (lbs.) | Production | Change from LY |
|---|---|---|---|---|---|---|
| Monaco 2-Door Hardtop | D42 | $3,308 | NEW | 4000 | 13,200 | NEW |
| TOTALS | Avg. price | $3,308 | NEW | Production | 13,200 | NEW |

# FORD

*"The Five Different Total Performance Cars! Best Year Yet To Go Ford!"*

Ford entered the 1965 model year with the most popular car in the country selling as fast as they could produce it. The Mustang, which went on sale as a 1964½ model on April 17, 1964, sold over 100,000 units in its first three months in production and set a record of over 418,000 sold in its first year on the market. Based on the successful Falcon platform, the Mustang was virtually without competition at its introduction, having only the rear-engined, six-cylinder Corvair from Chevrolet, and the new Valiant-based Barracuda from Plymouth as counterparts. The Mustang's success lay in its remarkably simple, yet sporty and elegant styling, its low base price, and the capability of the consumer to "build" the car however he liked from the long optional equipment list. A new body style was added at the beginning of the model year also — the 2+2 Fastback Coupe. This sporty looking model would turn out to be one of the slower-selling Mustang models, but at the time, fastback models were the "in" thing, and every new sporty car line seemed to have a fastback or semi fastback model. Other changes at the beginning of the model year included a change in standard engine from the 170 CID Six to the 200 CID Six, and the 260 CID V8 was dropped as the base V8 engine. A new GT option package included such dress-up items as driving lights, wood-grained interior trim and additional gauges with the 289 CID V8 engine.

There was other news from Ford for 1965, but it was overshadowed by the Mustang success story. The biggest news was the total redesign of the volume-leading full-size Fords. The 1965 model year would prove very similar to the 1955 season, in that each of the three low-priced full-size lines (Chevrolet, Ford and Plymouth) fielded all-new models. Over the next few years this led to some intense competition that would benefit everyone in the form of increased features and continually updated styling, at a relatively steady price. For Ford, the 1965 Custom and Galaxie were the best looking cars that had come out of Dearborn yet. However, it was a case of follow the leader, as Ford (and Plymouth) adopted the popular Pontiac "stacked headlight" treatment. This design feature would be used for three model years on Ford full-size cars. Other styling traits of the new Fords included more slab-sided styling, with chrome highlights, and more squared-off front and rear treatments. Rooflines were also more angular, with the continuation of the successful Fastback theme on 2-Door Hardtops. Mid-sized Fairlane models, while still based on the 1964 body, were restyled to mimic the new full-size Ford. Falcon and Thunderbird received mostly trim and detail changes to differentiate them from the previous year.

Country Squire 4-Door Wagon

Fairlane 2-Door Sedan

Galaxie 500 XL 2-Door Convertible

Falcon Futura 2-Door Convertible

Mustang 2+2 2-Door Fastback

Falcon Futura 4-Door Sedan

Galaxie 500 LTD 2-Door Hardtop

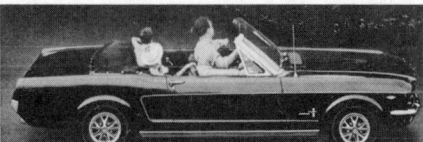

Mustang 2-Door Convertible

Thunderbird Landau 2-Door Hardtop

**Model year production:** 2,050,397, up 24.92% over 1964.
**Domestic market share:** 23.15% (2nd place).
**Base price range:** $1960 to $5293.
**Industry average base price:** $3,017.
**Ford average base price:** $2,753.
**Introduction date:** September 24, 1964.
**Assembly plants:** Atlanta, GA (A); Chicago, IL (G); Dallas, TX (D); Dearborn, MI (F); Kansas City, MO (K); Lorain, OH (H); Los Angeles, CA (J); Louisville, KY (U); Mah-wah, NJ (E); Metuchen, NJ (T); Norfolk, VA (N); San Jose, CA (R); Twin Cities, MN (P); Wayne, MI (W); Wixom, MI (Y); Oakville, Ontario, Can. (B).

**Data plate identification:** Eleven digit code read as follows: 5 for 1965; 2nd digit is assembly plant code; 2-digit model number (see listings below); 5th digit is engine code; 100001 and up for serial number. *Example:* 5Y83Z100001 is a 1965 Ford Thunderbird 2-Door Hardtop with a 390 CID V8 engine, serial number 100001, built in Wixom, MI.

## Powertrains

| Engine | Gross HP | Engine Code | Transmission Availability | Falcon | Mustang | Fairlane | Full-size | T-Bird |
|---|---|---|---|---|---|---|---|---|
| 170 CID, 1-bbl., 6-cyl. | 105 | U | 3-speed manual | S | - | - | - | - |
| | | | Cruise-O-Matic | $172 | - | - | - | - |
| 200 CID, 1-bbl., 6-cyl. | 120 | T | 3-speed manual | S — Fut.& Wgn/ $45 — Others | S | S | - | - |
| | | | 4-speed manual | - | $116 | - | - | - |
| | | | Cruise-O-Matic | $217 | $180 | $190 | - | - |
| 240 CID Big Six, 1-bbl., 6-cyl. | 150 | E | 3-speed manual | - | - | - | S (ex. XL & LTD) | - |
| | | | Overdrive | - | - | - | $108 (ex. XL & LTD) | - |
| | | | Cruise-O-Matic | - | - | - | $189 (ex. XL & LTD) | - |
| 289 CID Challenger, 2-bbl., V8 | 200 | C | Synchro-Smooth Drive, 3-speed man. | $153 | $108 | $108 | $109 (ex. XL & LTD) | - |
| | | | Overdrive | - | - | $216 | $217 (ex. XL & LTD) | - |
| | | | 4-speed manual* | $341 | $296 | - | - | - |
| | | | Cruise-O-Matic | $335 | $298 | $298 | S (XL & LTD), $298 (others) | - |
| 289 CID Challenger Special, 4-bbl., V8 | 225 | A | Synchro-Smooth Drive, 3-speed man. | - | $162 | $162 | - | - |
| | | | 4-speed manual* | - | $350 | $350 | - | - |
| | | | Cruise-O-Matic | - | $352 | $352 | - | - |
| 289 CID Challenger High-Perf., 4-bbl., V8 | 271 | K | 4-speed manual* | - | $631 | $618 (ex. Wagons) | - | - |
| | | | Cruise-O-Matic | - | - | $620 (ex. Wagons) | - | - |
| 352 CID Thunderbird 4-bbl., V8 | 250 | X | Synchro-Smooth Drive, 3-speed man. | - | - | - | $180 (ex. XL & LTD) | - |
| | | | Cruise-O-Matic | - | - | - | $71 (XL & LTD)/ $392 (others) | - |
| 390 CID Thunderbird Special, 2-bbl., V8 | 300 | Z | Synchro-Smooth Drive, 3-speed man. | - | - | - | $246 (ex. XL & LTD) | - |
| | | | Overdrive | - | - | - | $354 (ex. XL & LTD) | - |
| | | | 4-speed manual* | - | - | - | $137 (XL, $434 — others) | - |
| | | | Cruise-O-Matic | - | - | - | $137 (XL & LTD), $436 (others) | S |
| 427 CID Thunderbird | 425 | R | 4-speed manual* | - | - | - | $462 (XL & LTD), | |

| Engine | Gross HP | Engine Code | Transmission Availability | Falcon | Mustang | Fairlane | Full-size | T-Bird |
|--------|----------|-------------|---------------------------|--------|---------|----------|-----------|--------|
| High-Perf., 2 × 4-bbl., V8 | | | | | | | $759 (others, ex. Wgns.) | - |

*4-speed manual shift not available on wagon models.*

## Major Options

|  | Falcon | Mustang | Fairlane | Full-size | Thunderbird |
|--|--------|---------|----------|-----------|-------------|
| Air conditioning | - | $283 | $364 | $364 | $425 |
| Vacuum trunk release | - | - | - | - | $13 |
| Tinted glass | - | $31 | $40 | $40 | $43 |
| Power steering | - | $86 | $86 | $97 | S |
| Power brakes — discs (certain models) | - | $43 | $43 | $43 | S |
| Power driver's seat/ bench seat | - | - | - | - | $184 |
| Power windows | - | - | - | $102 | $106 |
| AM radio | $58 | $59 | $58 | $72 | S |
| AM/FM radio | - | - | - | $142 | $84 |
| Front console | - | $32–$52 | $ | $ | S |
| Front bucket seats | $69 | S | $ | $ | S |
| Swing-Away steering wheel | - | - | - | - | S |
| Vinyl roof (only on select models) | $ | $76 | $76 | $76 | $ |
| White sidewall tires | $30 | $30 | $34 | $34 | $44 |
| Deluxe wheel covers | - | $18 | $22 | $25 | $16 |

Options common to most models. (- = Not Available; S = Standard equipment.) Items may be standard equipment, optional at different pricing, or unavailable on certain models. This chart is only a guide.

## Paint Colors

|  | Code | Thunderbird | Other models |
|--|------|-------------|--------------|
| Black | A | X | X |
| Midnight Turquoise Metallic | B | X | |
| Honey Gold Metallic | C | X | X |
| Dynasty Green Metallic | D | | X |
| Silver Mink Metallic | E | X | |
| Arcadian Blue | F | | X |
| Pastel Yellow | G | X | X |
| Caspian Blue Metallic | H | X | |
| Champagne Beige Met. | I | | X |
| Rangoon Red | J | X | X |
| Silver Smoke Gray Metallic | K | | X |
| Wimbledon White | M | X | X |
| Diamond Blue | N | X | |
| Tropical Turquoise | O | | X |
| Prairie Bronze Metallic | P | X | X |
| Ivy Green Metallic | R | X | X |
| Charcoal Gray Metallic | S | X | |
| Navajo Beige | T | X | |
| Patrician Green Metallic | U | X | |
| Emberglo Metallic | V | X | |
| Rose Beige Metallic | W | X | |
| Vintage Burgundy Metallic | X | X | X |
| Silver Blue Metallic | Y | | X |

| | Code | Thunderbird | Other models |
|---|---|---|---|
| Chantilly Beige Metallic | Z | X | |
| Poppy Red | 3 | X | X |
| Frost Turquoise | 4 | X | |
| Twilight Turquoise Metallic | 5 | X | X |
| Phoenician Yellow | 7 | | X |
| Springtime Yellow | 8 | X | X |

# Falcon

*"Up to 15% Greater Fuel Economy!"*

**Nameplate year of origin:** 1960.
**Current bodystyle lifespan:** 1964 through 1965.
**Predecessor to this model:** Falcon (1960 to 1963).
**Corporate siblings:** Mercury Comet.
**Replacement for this model:** Falcon (1966 to 1970).
**Percentage of division's sales volume:** 10.41%.
**Primary competition:** Rambler American, Chevrolet Chevy II, Dodge Dart, and Plymouth Valiant.
**Notable changes:** Minor trim and detail changes.
**Major standard equipment:** Cloth and vinyl interior trim, front-door armrests, chrome windshield and rear window moldings, hubcaps, and 6.00 × 13 BSW tires (6.45 × 14 on Wagons). Futura adds: Deluxe interior, rear armrest w/ashtrays, hood ornament, body side and window moldings, full-wheel covers and 6.50 × 13 BSW tires on Conv/HT. Squire adds: Wood-grain exterior trim.

## Measurements

| | Cars | Wagons |
|---|---|---|
| Wheelbase | 109.5" | 109.5" |
| Length | 181.6" | 190.0" |
| Width | 71.6" | 71.0" |
| Height | 54.5" | NA |
| Legroom — front | 41.9" | 41.9" |
| Legroom — rear | 34.2" | 34.2" |
| Headroom — front | 38.8" | 38.8" |
| Headroom — rear | 37.2" | 37.2" |
| Cargo capacity (cu. ft.) | 12.2 | 77.9 |
| Fuel capacity (gals.) | 14.0 | 14.0 |

**1965**

## Models Available

| | Style Number | Base MSRP | Change from LY | Shipping Wt. (lbs.) | Production | Change from LY |
|---|---|---|---|---|---|---|
| Falcon 2-Door Club Coupe | 01 | $2,020 | +1.20% | 2381 | 49,682 | +36.34% |
| Falcon 4-Door Sedan | 02 | $2,082 | +1.17% | 2416 | 44,036 | +55.00% |
| Falcon 2-Door Wagon | 21 | $2,333 | +0.30% | 2676 | 4,891 | -18.94% |
| Falcon 4-Door Wagon | 22 | $2,367 | +0.30% | 2711 | 14,911 | +738.17% |
| Falcon Futura 2-Door Sedan | 19 | $2,144 | +0.80% | 2391 | 11,670 | -30.88% |
| Falcon Futura 2-Door Hardtop | 17 | $2,226 | +0.77% | 2531 | 28,560 | -12.41% |
| Falcon Futura 2-Door Convertible | 15 | $2,481 | +0.00% | 2726 | 6,515 | -50.72% |
| Falcon Futura 4-Door Sedan | 16 | $2,192 | +0.74% | 2426 | 33,985 | -10.64% |
| Falcon Futura 4-Door Wagon | 24 | $2,506 | +2.45% | 2731 | 12,548 | -39.37% |
| Falcon Futura Squire 4-Door Wgn. | 26 | $2,665 | +1.64% | 2736 | 6,703 | -0.93% |
| TOTALS | | *Avg. price* $2,302 | -1.84% | | *Production* 213,501 | -7.40% |

# Mustang

*"Total Performance Trio!"*

**Nameplate year of origin:** 1964½ (also on a 1963 show car).
**Current bodystyle lifespan:** 1964½ through 1968.
**Predecessor to this model:** None.
**Corporate siblings:** None

## Measurements

| | |
|---|---|
| Wheelbase | 108.0" |
| Length | 181.6" |
| Width | 68.2" |

**Replacement for this model:** Mustang (1969 to 1970).
**Percentage of division's sales volume:** 27.29%.
**Primary competition:** Chevrolet Corvair and Plymouth Barracuda.
**Notable changes:** All-new as a 1964½ model. New 2 + 2 Fastback model added at the beginning of the 1965 model year. 260 CID V8 dropped as base V8, and 170 CID 6-cylinder dropped as base Six. Changes for 1965 models limited to minor trim and detail changes.
**Major standard equipment:** Bucket front seats with vinyl upholstery, dual sun visors, seat belts, padded instrument panel, courtesy lights, full carpeting, sports steering wheel, chrome window moldings, self-adjusting brakes, alternator, and 6.50 × 13 BSW tires (6.95 × 14 with V8 engine).

## Measurements (cont.)

| | |
|---|---|
| Height | 51.1" |
| Legroom — front | 41.8" |
| Legroom — rear | 28.8" |
| Headroom — front | 37.0" |
| Headroom — rear | 35.6" |
| Cargo capacity (cu. ft.) | 9.0 (Cvt. 7.7, Fb. 5.0) |
| Fuel capacity (gals.) | 16.0 |

## Models Available

| | Style Number | Base MSRP | Change from LY | Shipping Wt. (lbs.) | Production | Change from LY |
|---|---|---|---|---|---|---|
| Mustang 2-Door Hardtop | 07 | $2,372 | 0.00% | 2436 | 409,260 | +318.87% |
| Mustang 2-Door Fastback | 09 | $2,589 | NEW | 2486 | 77,079 | NEW |
| Mustang 2-Door Convertible | 08 | $2,614 | 0.00% | 2621 | 73,112 | +153.57% |
| TOTALS | | Avg. price $2,525 | +1.28% | | Production 559,451 | +342.12% |

# Fairlane

*"Bigger, Bolder, More Beauty, More Value."*

**Nameplate year of origin:** 1955.
**Current bodystyle lifespan:** 1962 through 1965.
**Predecessor to this model:** None.
**Corporate siblings:** None.
**Replacement for this model:** Fairlane (1966 to 1967).
**Percentage of division's sales volume:** 10.92%.
**Primary competition:** Rambler Classic and Marlin, Chevrolet Chevelle, and Plymouth Belvedere.
**Notable changes:** New styling for all sheet metal, based on same body shell as before.
**Major standard equipment:** Cloth and vinyl bench seat, rubber floor mats, front and rear armrests, chrome windshield and rear window moldings, and 6.95 × 14 BSW tires (7.35 × 14 BSW on Wagons). 500 adds: Full carpeting, deluxe interior trim, chrome side window moldings, chrome hood ornament, full-length side trim and Ford crests on C pillar and rear panel.

## Measurements

| | Cars | Wagons |
|---|---|---|
| Wheelbase | 116.0" | 116.0" |
| Length | 198.4" | 203.0" |
| Width | 73.8" | 73.8" |
| Height | 55.7" | 55.8" |
| Legroom — front | 42.2" | 42.2" |
| Legroom — rear | 37.5" | 37.5" |
| Headroom — front | 38.7" | 38.7" |
| Headroom — rear | 37.8" | 38.0" |
| Cargo capacity (cu. ft.) | 15.0 | 98.6 |
| Fuel capacity (gals.) | 16.0 | 16.0 |

## Models Available

| | Style No. | Base MSRP | Change from LY | Shipping Wt. (lbs.) | Production | Change from LY |
|---|---|---|---|---|---|---|
| Fairlane 2-Door Sedan | 31 | $2,230 | +1.64% | 2806 | 13,685 | -32.99% |
| Fairlane 4-Door Sedan | 32 | $2,271 | +1.61% | 2858 | 25,378 | -30.84% |
| Fairlane 4-Door, 2-Seat Wagon | 38 | $2,567 | +1.42% | 3183 | 13,911 | -33.69% |
| Fairlane 500 2-Door Sedan | 41 | $2,312 | +1.58% | 2805 | 16,092 | -31.46% |
| Fairlane 500 2-Door Hardtop | 43 | $2,377 | +1.54% | 2877 | 41,405 | -3.11% |
| Fairlane 500 2-Door Sport HT | 47 | $2,538 | +1.44% | 2888 | 15,141 | 21.80% |
| Fairlane 500 4-Door Sedan | 42 | $2,353 | +1.55% | 2863 | 77,836 | -10.45% |
| Fairlane 500 4-Dr., 2-Seat Wgn. | 48 | $2,648 | +1.38% | 3220 | 20,506 | -17.85% |
| TOTALS | | Avg. price $2,412 | +1.52% | | Production 223,954 | -16.63% |

# Custom & Galaxie

*"Solid, Silent, Elegant."*

**Nameplate year of origin:** 1957 (Custom), 1959 (Galaxie) and 1965 (LTD).
**Current bodystyle lifespan:** 1965 through 1966.
**Predecessor to this model:** Full-size Ford (1963 to 1964).
**Corporate siblings:** Mercury Monterey and Park Lane.
**Replacement for this model:** Custom, Galaxie and LTD (1967 to 1968).
**Percentage of division's sales volume:** 47.72%.
**Primary competition:** AMC Ambassador, Chevrolet BelAir/Impala/Caprice, Dodge Polara/Custom 880/Monaco, Plymouth Fury, and Pontiac Catalina.
**Notable changes:** Completely restyled.
**Major standard equipment:** Rubber mats, dual sunvisors, arm rests on all doors, rear window trim molding, and 7.35 × 15 BSW tires. Custom 500 adds: Nylon carpeting, windshield molding, short exterior trim side molding and 8.15 × 15 BSW tires on wagons. Galaxie 500 adds: Two-tone interior trim, chrome hood ornament, chrome side window trim, and backup lights. XL adds: bucket seats with floor-mounted transmission selector, lower door carpet trim and polished trim, courtesy and reading lamps, and special badging. Squire wagon adds: Wood-grain exterior trim. LTD adds: Luxury cloth bench seats with Scotchguard® treatment, wood-grained interior trim vinyl top, and additional acoustical insulation.

## Measurements

|                       | Cars         | Wagons  |
|-----------------------|--------------|---------|
| Wheelbase             | 119.0"       | 119.0"  |
| Length                | 210.0"       | 210.0"  |
| Width                 | 77.3"        | 77.3"   |
| Height                | 55.6"        | 55.8"   |
| Legroom — front       | 41.4"        | 41.4"   |
| Legroom — rear        | 37.8"        | 37.6"   |
| Headroom — front      | 38.9"        | 38.9"   |
| Headroom — rear       | 37.7"        | 37.8"   |
| Cargo capacity (cu. ft.) | 19.1      |         |
|                       | (Cvt. 18.0)  | 103*    |
| Fuel capacity (gals.) | 20.0         | 20.0    |

*98.9 with dual folding rear seats, 9-pass.*

**1965**

## Models Available

|                                   | Style No. | Base MSRP | Change from LY | Shipping Wt. (lbs.) | Production | Change from LY |
|-----------------------------------|-----------|-----------|----------------|---------------------|------------|----------------|
| Custom 2-Door Sedan               | 53        | $2,361    | 0.00%          | 3253                | 49,034     | +18.56%        |
| Custom 4-Door Sedan               | 54        | $2,415    | 0.00%          | 3333                | 96,393     | +66.30%        |
| Custom 500 2-Door Sedan           | 51        | $2,464    | 0.00%          | 3283                | 19,603     | -4.93%         |
| Custom 500 4-Door Sedan           | 52        | $2,518    | 0.00%          | 3363                | 71,727     | +4.21%         |
| Galaxie 500 2-Door Hardtop        | 66        | $2,685    | 0.00%          | 3331                | 157,284    | -24.02%        |
| Galaxie 500 2-Door Convertible    | 65        | $2,950    | +0.10%         | 3486                | 31,930     | -14.42%        |
| Galaxie 500 4-Door Sedan          | 62        | $2,678    | 0.00%          | 3391                | 181,183    | -8.86%         |
| Galaxie 500 4-Door Hardtop        | 64        | $2,765    | +0.55%         | 3407                | 49,982     | +1.50%         |
| Galaxie 500 XL 2-Door Hardtop     | 68        | $3,233    | +0.00%         | 3450                | 28,141     | -51.74%        |
| Galaxie 500 XL 2-Door Convertible | 69        | $3,498    | +0.09%         | 3605                | 9,849      | -35.07%        |
| Galaxie 500 LTD 2-Door Hardtop    | 67        | $3,233    | NEW            | 3442                | 37,691     | NEW            |
| Galaxie 500 LTD 4-Door Hardtop    | 60        | $3,313    | NEW            | 3518                | 68,038     | NEW            |
| Ranch Wagon 4-Door, 2-Seat        | 71        | $2,763    | NEW            | 3711                | 30,817     | NEW            |
| Country Sedan 4-Dr., 6-pass. Wgn. | 72        | $2,855    | +0.53%         | 3721                | 59,693     | -12.96%        |
| Country Sedan 4-Dr., 9-pass. Wgn. | 74        | $2,959    | +0.51%         | 3735                | 32,344     | +26.04%        |
| Country Squire 4-Dr., 6-pass. Wgn.| 76        | $3,104    | +2.48%         | 3745                | 24,308     | +3.13%         |
| Country Squire 4-Dr., 9-pass. Wgn.| 78        | $3,174    | +2.42%         | 3759                | 30,502     | +31.93%        |
| TOTALS                            | Avg. price| $2,880    | +1.56%         | Production          | 978,519    | +5.99%         |

# Thunderbird

*"The Private World of Thunderbird for 1965."*

**Nameplate year of origin:** 1955.
**Current bodystyle lifespan:** 1964 through 1966.
**Predecessor to this model:** Thunderbird (1961 to 1963).

## Measurements

|            |         |
|------------|---------|
| Wheelbase  | 120.4"  |
| Length     | 214.0"  |

**Corporate siblings:** None.
**Replacement for this model:** Thunderbird (1967 to 1971).
**Percentage of division's sales volume:** 3.66%.
**Primary competition:** Buick Riviera and Cadillac Eldorado.
**Notable changes:** Trim and detail changes.
**Major standard equipment:** Bucket seats, full carpeting, heater and defroster, seat belts, full instrumentation, Swing-Away steering wheel, AM radio, reversible entry keys, sequential turn signals, power steering, power front disc brakes, and 8.15 × 15 BSW tires. Convertible adds: Unique trunk-stored power convertible top. Landau adds: Special interior and vinyl top.

## Measurements (cont.)

| | |
|---|---|
| Width | 77.3" |
| Height | 52.5" |
| Legroom — front | 39.7" |
| Legroom — rear | 33.2" |
| Headroom — front | NA |
| Headroom — rear | NA |
| Cargo capacity (cu. ft.) | 11.5 (Cvt. 6.1) |
| Fuel capacity (gals.) | 22.0 |

## Models Available

| | Style No. | Base MSRP | Change from LY | Shipping Wt. (lbs.) | Production | Change from LY |
|---|---|---|---|---|---|---|
| Thunderbird 2-Door Hardtop | 83 | $4,486 | 0.00% | 4470 | 42,652 | -29.56% |
| Thunderbird 2-Door Landau HT | 87 | $4,589 | 0.00% | 4478 | 25,474 | +12.15% |
| Thunderbird 2-Door Convertible | 85 | $4,953 | 0.00% | 4588 | 6,846 | -25.57% |
| TOTALS | | *Avg. price* $4,676 | 0.00% | | *Production* 74,972 | -18.92% |

# IMPERIAL

*"The Incomparable Imperial — Vintage 1965."*

Imperial models continued this year with the successful styling introduced in 1964. Despite the pleasant styling and Lincoln-like appearance, sales could not be saved from their continuing downward trend. Except for minor increases that accompanied a styling change in 1960 and 1962, the 1964 model year had been the only one in the last nine years that created a significant sales increase. Unfortunately, as in years past, timing was everything, and Cadillac this season had introduced some of its finest looking cars. With

Cadillac already dominating the luxury market, Imperial was not in much of a position for improvement. This was the last year for the 413 CID V8 engine, but the new powerplant for '66 would not do anything to help sales. For a final season, the Crown Imperial Limousine Sedan model was available as a custom-built model. These are not shown below as their production usually totaled ten or fewer per season, and they are considered custom-built by Chrysler.

**Crown 4-Door Hardtop**

**Crown 2-Door Convertible**

**Model year production:** 18,399, down 20.98% from 1964.
**Base price range:** $5,772 to $6,596.
**Domestic market share:** 0.21% (14th place).
**Industry average base price:** $3,017.
**Imperial average base price:** $6,035.
**Introduction date:** September 30,1964.
**Assembly plants:** Detroit, MI (3).

**Data plate identification:** Ten digit code read as follows: 1st digit Y = Imperial; 2nd number identifies series (e.g., 2 is for Crown); 5 for 1965; 4th digit is assembly plant code; 100001 and up for serial number. Body style numbers found on body plate. *Example:* Y253100001 is a 1965 Imperial Crown, serial number 100001, built in Detroit, MI.

## Powertrains

| Engine | Gross HP | Transmission Availability | Imperial |
|--------|----------|---------------------------|----------|
| 413 CID, 4-bbl., V8 | 340 | Torqueflite Automatic | S |

## Major Options

|  | Crown | LeBaron |
|--|-------|---------|
| Air conditioning | $462 | $462 |
| Auto Pilot automatic speed control | $97 | $97 |
| Tinted glass | $54 | $54 |
| Rear window defogger | $21 | $21 |
| Deck lid remote release | $29 | $29 |
| Power steering — variable-ratio | S | S |
| Power brakes | S | S |
| Power door locks | $47 (2-Dr)/$72 (4-Dr) | $72 |
| Power driver's seat/bench seat | $125 | S |
| Power windows | S | S |
| AM radio w/power antenna | $169 | $169 |
| AM/FM radio w/power antenna | $196 | $196 |
| Adjustable steering wheel | $51 | $51 |
| Vinyl roof | $91–$111 | $111 |
| Whitewall tires — standard size | $55 | S |

Options common to most models. (- = Not Available; S = Standard equipment.) Items may be standard equipment, optional at different pricing, or unavailable on certain models. This chart is only a guide.

## Paint Colors

| | Code |
|--|------|
| Sage Green Metallic | 22-1 |
| Pink Silver Metallic | 33-1 |
| Moss Gold Metallic | 44-1 |
| Black Plum Metallic | 55-1 |
| Mauve Metallic | 66-1 |
| Patrician Gold Metallic | 77-1 |
| Regal Gold Metallic | AA-1 |
| Formal Black | BB-1 |
| Ice Blue | CC-1 |
| Nassau Blue Metallic | DD-1 |
| Navy Blue Metallic | EE-1 |
| Mist Blue Metallic | FF-1 |
| Sequoia Green Metallic | GG-1 |
| Peacock Turquoise Metallic | KK-1 |
| Royal Turquoise Metallic | LL-1 |
| Granite Gray Metallic | MM-1 |
| Silver Mist Metallic | NN-1 |
| Sierra Sand | RR-1 |
| French Ivory | SS-1 |
| Spanish Red Metallic | TT-1 |
| Persian White | WW-1 |
| Sand Dune Beige | XX-1 |
| Sable Tan Metallic | YY-1 |
| Frost Turquoise Metallic | ZZ-1 |

**1965**

# Crown

*"There are many qualifications for Imperial ownership. Age is not one."*

**Nameplate year of origin:** 1957 (Not the same as Crown Imperial series).
**Current bodystyle lifespan:** 1964 through 1966.
**Predecessor to this model:** Crown (1960 to 1963).
**Replacement for this model:** Crown (1967 to 1968).
**Percentage of division's sales volume:** 88.24%.
**Corporate siblings:** LeBaron.
**Primary competition:** Cadillac Calais and Lincoln Continental.
**Notable changes:** New grille, minor trim and detail changes.

## Measurements

| | |
|--|--|
| Wheelbase | 129.0" |
| Length | 227.8" |
| Width | 80.0" |
| Height | 57.2" |
| Legroom — front | 41.6" |
| Legroom — rear | 41.5" |
| Headroom — front | 39.3" |

**Major standard equipment:** Torqueflite automatic transmission, power steering, power brakes, front and rear armrests (hardtops), pile carpeting, remote-control left-hand outside mirror, power windows, electric clock, trip odometer, 3-speed electric windshield wipers with washers, wheel covers and 9.15 × 15 BSW tires.

## Measurements (cont.)

| | |
|---|---|
| Headroom — rear | 38.7" |
| Cargo capacity (cu. ft.) | NA |
| Fuel capacity (gals.) | 23.0 |

## Models Available

| | Style No. | Base MSRP | Change from LY | Shipping Wt. (lbs.) | Production | Change from LY |
|---|---|---|---|---|---|---|
| Crown 2-Door Hardtop | Y22 | $5,846 | +1.86% | 5075 | 3,974 | -24.06% |
| Crown 2-Door Convertible | Y25 | $6,105 | +1.70% | 5345 | 633 | -31.34% |
| Crown 4-Door Hardtop | Y24 | $5,691 | +1.97% | 5015 | 11,628 | -18.00% |
| TOTALS | Avg. price | $5,881 | +1.85% | Production | 16,235 | -20.16% |

# LeBaron

*"In the quiet expression of good taste, Imperial has no equal."*

**Nameplate year of origin:** 1924 (as Chrysler Sedan model designation); 1926 (as series).
**Current bodystyle lifespan:** 1964 through 1966.
**Predecessor to this model:** LeBaron (1960 to 1963).
**Replacement for this model:** LeBaron (1967 to 1968).
**Percentage of division's sales volume:** 11.76%.
**Corporate siblings:** Crown.
**Primary competition:** Cadillac de Ville and Lincoln Continental.
**Notable changes:** New grille, minor trim and detail changes.
**Major standard equipment:** Torqueflite automatic transmission, power steering, power brakes, pile carpeting, 6-way power seat, power windows and vent windows, electric clock, trip odometer, 3-speed electric windshield wipers with washers, wheel covers and 9.15 × 15 WSW tires.

## Measurements

| | |
|---|---|
| Wheelbase | 129.0" |
| Length | 227.8" |
| Width | 80.0" |
| Height | 57.2" |
| Legroom — front | 41.6" |
| Legroom — rear | 41.5" |
| Headroom — front | 39.3" |
| Headroom — rear | 38.7" |
| Cargo capacity (cu. ft.) | NA |
| Fuel capacity (gals.) | 23.0 |

## Models Available

| | Style No. | Base MSRP | Change from LY | Shipping Wt. (lbs.) | Production | Change from LY |
|---|---|---|---|---|---|---|
| LeBaron 4-Door Hardtop | Y34 | $6,499 | +0.68% | 5080 | 2,164 | -26.62% |
| TOTALS | Avg. price | $6,499 | +0.68% | Production | 2,164 | -26.62% |

# LINCOLN

*"America's most distinguished motorcar."*

After a restyling that increased the size of the Lincoln, 1965 would bring its first major change in frontal appearance. A new full-width, horizontal bar grille was used, with turn signal and parking lamps mounted as one unit at the leading edge of the front fenders. The rear end appearance was changed by doing away with the rear grille area and putting horizontal bars into the bumper area. New fabrics and colors highlighted changes to the interiors of the '65 Lincoln. Under the hood remained the 430 CID V8 engine linked to a Twin-range Turbo-drive automatic transmission.

Continental 4-Door Convertible

Continental 4-Door Sedan

**1965**

**Model year production:** 40,180, up 10.70% over 1964.
**Domestic market share:** 0.45% (12th place).
**Base price range:** $6,292 to $6,938.
**Industry average base price:** $3,017.
**Lincoln average base price:** $6,615.
**Introduction date:** September 1964.
**Assembly plants:** Allen Park, MI (S); and Wixom, MI (Y).

**Data plate identification:** Eleven digit code read as follows: 5 for 1965; 2nd digit is assembly plant code; 2-digit model number (see listings below); 5th digit is engine code; 400001 and up for serial number. *Example:* 5Y82H400001 is a 1965 Lincoln Continental 4-Door Sedan with a 430 CID V8 engine, serial number 400001, built in Wixom, MI.

## Powertrains

| Engine | Gross HP | Engine Code | Transmission Availability | Continental |
|---|---|---|---|---|
| 430 CID, 4-bbl., V8 | 320 | H | Turbo Drive Automatic | S |

## Major Options

| | Continental |
|---|---|
| Air condtioning — manual | $505 |
| Automatic headlight dimmers | $46 |
| Tinted glass | $54 |
| Tilt steering wheel | $60 |
| 6-way power seat | S |
| AM/FM radio | $85 |
| Leather upholstery | $100 |
| Speed control | $97 |
| Remote control trunk release (sedans) | $53 |

## Paint Colors

| | Code |
|---|---|
| Black Satin | A |
| Turino Turquoise Metallic | B |
| Persian Gold Metallic | C |
| Silver Mink Metallic | E |
| Arcadian Blue | F |
| Willow Gold | G |
| Nocturne Blue Metallic | H |
| Fiesta Red | J |
| Heather Metallic | L |

Options common to most models. (S = Standard equipment.) Items may be standard equipment, optional at different pricing, or unavailable on certain models. This chart is only a guide.

| Color | Code |
|---|---|
| Arctic White | M |
| Platinum | N |
| Burnished Bronze Metallic | P |
| Huron Blue Metallic | Q |
| Spanish Moss Metallic | R |
| Charcoal Frost Metallic | S |
| Desert Sand | T |
| Teal Metallic | U |
| Russet Metallic | V |
| Royal Maroon Metallic | X |
| Silver Sand Metallic | Z |
| Neptune Blue | 4 |

# Continental

*"This is the luxury motorcar that stands apart from all other cars.
This is the Lincoln Continental for 1965."*

**Nameplate year of origin:** 1940 (1961 as a standard sedan nameplate).
**Current bodystyle lifespan:** 1961 through 1969 (major restyles in 1964 and 1966).
**Predecessor to this model:** Premiere (1958 to 1960).
**Replacement for this model:** Continental (1970 to 1979).
**Percentage of division's sales volume:** 100%.
**Corporate siblings:** None.
**Primary competition:** Cadillac de Ville and Imperial Crown and LeBaron.
**Notable changes:** Restyled grille and rear end treatment.
**Major standard equipment:** Nylon and leather (sedan) or leather (convertible) front bench seat upholstery with folding center armrests front and rear, vanity mirror, looped-pile carpeting, AM transistor radio with power antenna, power operated door latching system, padded instrument panel, variable speed windshield wipers with washers, power side and vent windows, power steering, power brakes, automatic transmission and 9.15 × 15 WSW tires.

## Measurements

| | |
|---|---|
| Wheelbase | 126.0" |
| Length | 216.3" |
| Width | 78.6" |
| Height | 54.2" |
| Legroom — front | 41.1" |
| Legroom — rear | 40.5" |
| Headroom — front | 39.0" |
| Headroom — rear | 38.4" |
| Luggage capacity (cu. ft.) | 14.4 |
| Fuel capacity (gals.) | 21.0 |

## Models Available

| | Style No. | Base MSRP | Change from LY | Shipping Wt. (lbs.) | Production | Change from LY |
|---|---|---|---|---|---|---|
| Continental 4-Door Sedan | 82 | $6,292 | 0.00% | 5075 | 36,824 | +11.69% |
| Continental 4-Door Convertible | 86 | $6,938 | 0.00% | 5475 | 3,356 | +0.84% |
| TOTALS | | Avg. price $6,615 | 0.00% | | Production 40,180 | +10.70% |

# MERCURY

*"...now in the Lincoln Continental tradition."*

As for most other manufacturers, the 1965 season was an important one for Mercury. The full-size Mercury line was given a major overhaul, as was every other full-size American car line. The importance to Mercury was twofold however. First, the Mercury was being redesigned to move slightly upscale in its market, to compete more directly with cars like Buick and Chrysler, rather than with Dodge and Pontiac. This meant giving the Mercury styling that leaned more toward the Lincoln than toward the Ford it had copied for the past five years. As stated in the introduction of the sales brochure for this year, "Mercury assumes a new posture in the medium-priced field ... one inspired by the Lincoln Continental heritage for elegance, interior appointments and road-handling characteristics." This was the second time Mercury had taken this chance, the first time having been the 1949 to 1956 models which were designed as junior Lincolns, prior to having their own unique styling from 1957 through 1960. It was more costly to Ford to design totally different models for Mercury, but it was just as costly to lose sales because of the cars' looking like over-chromed Fords. Secondly, the only real sales success the Mercury line had seen since 1956 had been the Comet line. If Mercury was to continue as a full-line division of Ford, it had to gain sales and market share, and the way to do that was to take the sales from the heart of GM, specifically from the Oldsmobile and Buick full-size models. That's where the profitable models were, and Mercury needed them. Overall, the Mercury was a very nice if somewhat boxy design that was not as appealing as the GM cars it sought to overtake, though it was definitely as modern and stylish as the new Chrysler offerings. As the advertising suggested, it was very much "in the Lincoln Continental tradition." The full-size wagon lines were technically marketed as their own lines once again. However, since the Commuter was based upon the Monterey and the Colony Park upon the Montclair, they are listed with those models below.

The compact Comet line was given its second facelift in as many years. While technically too big to be considered a compact any longer, the Comet had not officially made that jump to the 115-inch wheelbase that tended to define a mid-size car. This would have to wait one more year. For most marketing types, mid-size or intermediate tended to be defined by a wheelbase of 115 to 118 inches, a fairly narrow definition that in time expanded to 112–118 inches. In the mean time, the new styling previewed its new intermediate styling, with stacked headlights up front flanking a full-width grille, and somewhat boxy and conservative side styling. Powertrain choices remained similar to prior years.

Colony Park 4-Door Wagon

Comet 404 4-Door Sedan

Comet Caliente 2-Door Hardtop

Park Lane 2-Door Convertible

Monterey 2-Door Sedan and Monterey 4-Door Sedan

Park Lane 2-Door Hardtop

**Model year production:** 346,753, up 14.44% over 1964.
**Domestic market share:** 3.91% (8th place).
**Base price range:** $2,154 to $3,599.
**Industry average base price:** $3,017.
**Mercury average base price:** $2,862.
**Introduction date:** October 1964.
**Assembly plants:** Mahwah, NJ (E); Lorain, OH (H); Los Angeles, CA (J); Wixom, MI (S); Metuchen, NJ (T); Wayne, MI (W); and St. Louis, MO (Z).

**Data plate identification:** Eleven digit code read as follows: 5 for 1965; 2nd digit is assembly plant code; 3rd digit is series (1 or 2 is Comet, 4 is Monterey, etc.); 4th digit is body style; 5th digit is engine code; 500001 and up for serial number. *Example:* 5W43Z100001 is a 1965 Mercury Monterey 2-Door Hardtop with a 390 CID V8 engine, serial number 500001, built in Wayne, MI.

## Powertrains

| Engine | Gross HP | Engine Code | Transmission Availability | Comet | Monterey & Montclair | Park Lane |
|---|---|---|---|---|---|---|
| 200 CID Six, 1-bbl., 6-cyl. | 120 | T | 3-speed manual | S[2] | - | - |
| | | | 2-sp. Automatic | $188[2] | - | - |
| 289 CID, 2-bbl., V8 | 200 | C | 3-speed manual | $76[1]/$121[2] | - | - |
| | | | 4-speed manual | 264[1]/$309[2] | - | - |
| | | | Merc-O-Matic Automatic | $248[1]/$293[2] | - | - |
| Super 289 CID, 4-bbl., V8 | 225 | A | 3-speed manual | $106[1]/$151[2] | - | - |
| | | | 4-speed manual | 294[1]/$339[2] | - | - |
| | | | Merc-O-Matic Automatic | $278[1]/$323[2] | - | - |
| 390 CID, 2-bbl., V8 | 250 | Y | 3-speed manual | - | S | - |
| | | | 4-speed manual | - | $232* | - |
| | 266 | | Multi-Drive Automatic | - | $232 | - |
| Super 390 CID, 4-bbl., V8 | 300 | Z | 3-speed manual | - | $52 | S |
| | | | 4-speed manual | - | $284* | $232 |
| | | | Multi-Drive Automatic | - | $284 | $232 |
| Interceptor 390 CID, 4-bbl., V8 | 330 | - | 4-speed manual | - | $* | $ |
| | | | Multi-Drive Automatic | - | $ | $ |
| Super 427 CID, 2 × 4-bbl., V8 | 425 | R | 4-speed manual | - | $* | $ |
| | | | Multi-Drive Automatic | - | $* | $ |

[1]*Cyclone.*   [2]*All but Cyclone.*   **Not available on wagons.*

## Major Options

| | Comet | Monterey/Montclair | Park Lane |
|---|---|---|---|
| SelectAire air conditioning | $258 | $430 | $430 |
| Tinted glass | $28 | $43 | $43 |
| Speed control | - | $93 | $93 |
| Tilt steering wheel | - | $43 | $43 |
| Power steering | $86 | $106 | $106 |
| Power brakes | $43 | $43 | $43 |
| Power windows | - | $106 | $106 |
| Power seat — six-way | - | $97 | $97 |
| Bucket seats | $80 | $161 | S |
| Electric windshield wipers w/washer | $22 | $14 | $14 |
| Electric clock | $15 | $16 (Monterey) | S |
| Pushbutton AM radio | $59 | $61 | $61 |
| AM/FM radio | - | $149 | $149 |
| White sidewall tires — std. sizes | $30–$33 | $37 | $37–$53 |
| Full wheel covers | $19 | S | S |

Options common to most models. (- = Not Available; S = Standard equipment.) Items may be standard equipment, optional at different pricing, or unavailable on certain models. This chart is only a guide.

## Paint Colors

| | Code |
|---|---|
| Onyx | A |
| Ivy Gold Metallic | B |
| Silver Turquoise | D |
| Tiffany Blue Metallic | F |
| Midnight Blue Metallic | H |
| Sandrift Metallic | I |
| Carnival Red | J |
| Pearl Gray Metallic | K |
| Polar White | M |
| Aquamarine | O |
| Pecan Frost Metallic | P |
| Olive Mist Metallic | R |
| Fawn | T |
| Burgundy Metallic | X |
| Blue Ice Metallic | Y |
| Ocean Turquoise Metallic | 5 |
| Yellow Mist | 7 |
| Jamaican Yellow | 8 |

# Comet

*"The world's 100,000-mile durability champion."*

**Nameplate year of origin:** 1960.
**Current bodystyle lifespan:** 1964 through 1965.
**Predecessor to this model:** Comet (1960 to 1963).
**Replacement for this model:** Comet (1966 to 1967).
**Percentage of division's sales volume:** 47.60%.
**Corporate siblings:** Ford Falcon.
**Primary competition:** Buick Special, Dodge Dart, Oldsmobile F-85, Pontiac Tempest and Studebaker.
**Notable changes:** Completely restyled.
**Major standard equipment:** Milieu fabric and vinyl front bench seat with foam cushions, front and rear armrests, carpet textured rubber floor covering, bright metal front and rear window trim, and 6.95 × 14 BSW tires. 404 adds: Tivoli cloth and vinyl interior trim, full carpeting and additional bright exterior trim. Caliente adds: Deluxe steering wheel, padded instrument panel, simulated walnut interior trim power top on convertible, and additional sound deadening materials. Villager adds: Exterior wood-grain trim. Cyclone adds: All vinyl bucket seats with floor console, specific Cyclone exterior trim and engine dress-up kit.

## Measurements

|  | Cars | Wagons |
|---|---|---|
| Wheelbase | 114.0" | 109.5" |
| Length | 195.3" | 192.0" |
| Width | 72.9" | 71.6" |
| Height | 55.1" | 55.1" |
| Legroom — front | 41.8" | 41.9" |
| Legroom — rear | 35.5" | 34.2" |
| Headroom — front | 38.1" | 38.8" |
| Headroom — rear | 37.4" | 37.2" |
| Cargo capacity (cu. ft.) | 13.5 | 77.9 |
| Fuel capacity (gals.) | 20.0 | 20.0 |

**1965**

## Models Available

|  | Style No. | Base MSRP | Change from LY | Shipping Wt. (lbs.) | Production | Change from LY |
|---|---|---|---|---|---|---|
| Comet 202 2-Door Sedan | 01 | $2,154 | +1.32% | 2584 | 32,425 | -4.14% |
| Comet 202 4-Door Sedan | 02 | $2,210 | +1.28% | 2624 | 23,501 | -19.37% |
| Comet 202 4-Door Wagon | 32 | $2,491 | +1.14% | 2784 | 4,814 | -12.54% |
| Comet 404 2-Door Sedan | 11 | $2,241 | +1.27% | 2594 | 10,900 | -12.88% |
| Comet 404 4-Door Sedan | 12 | $2,297 | +1.23% | 2629 | 18,628 | -25.89% |
| Comet 404 4-Door Wagon | 34 | $2,578 | +1.10% | 2789 | 5,226 | -24.46% |
| Comet Villager 4-Door Wagon | 36 | $2,762 | +1.02% | 2789 | 1,592 | -19.60% |
| Comet Caliente 2-Door Hardtop | 23 | $2,403 | +1.18% | 2684 | 29,247 | -6.27% |
| Comet Caliente 2-Door Convertible | 25 | $2,664 | +1.06% | 2869 | 6,035 | -33.23% |
| Comet Caliente 4-Door Sedan | 22 | $2,378 | +1.19% | 2659 | 20,337 | -25.28% |
| Comet Cyclone 2-Door Hardtop | 27 | $2,683 | +1.05% | 2994 | 12,347 | +65.64% |
| TOTALS | | *Avg. price* $2,442 | +1.16% | *Production* | 165,052 | -13.10% |

# Monterey

*"The Monterey series brings you six ways to indulge your taste for exceptional space and luxury without straining the budget. Plus, the Commuter wagon is a styling standout in the wagon field."*

**Nameplate year of origin:** 1952.
**Current bodystyle lifespan:** 1965 through 1966.
**Predecessor to this model:** Monterey (1963 to 1964).
**Replacement for this model:** Monterey (1967 to 1968).
**Percentage of division's sales volume:** 25.51%.
**Corporate siblings:** Ford Galaxie.
**Primary competition:** Buick LeSabre, Dodge Polara, Oldsmobile 88 and Pontiac Catalina.

## Measurements

|  | Cars | Commuter |
|---|---|---|
| Wheelbase | 123.0" | 119.0" |
| Length | 218.4" | 214.5" |
| Width | 79.6" | 79.6" |
| Height | 56.0" | 56.1" |
| Legroom — front | 41.9" | 41.6" |

**Notable changes:** Completely redesigned.
**Major standard equipment:** Seville fabric and vinyl front bench seat (all-vinyl on convertible), full carpeting, padded instrument panel, and 8.15 × 15 BSW tires. Commuter adds: power tailgate window.

|  | Cars | Commuter |
|---|---|---|
| Legroom — rear | 38.6" | 37.8" |
| Headroom — front | 39.1" | 38.9" |
| Headroom — rear | 38.3" | 38.1" |
| Cargo capacity (cu. ft.) | 18.6 | 91.3 |
| Fuel capacity (gals.) | 21.0 | 21.0 |

## Models Available

|  | Style No. | Base MSRP | Change from LY | Shipping Wt. (lbs.) | Production | Change from LY |
|---|---|---|---|---|---|---|
| Monterey 2-Door Sedan | 43 | $2,767 | -1.84% | 3788 | 5,775 | +46.87% |
| Monterey 2-Door Hardtop | 47 | $2,902 | +0.62% | 3823 | 16,857 | +476.11% |
| Monterey 2-Door Convertible | 45 | $3,230 | +0.12% | 3928 | 4,762 | +83.72% |
| Monterey 4-Door Sedan | 44 | $2,839 | NEW | 3853 | 23,363 | NEW |
| Monterey 4-Door Breezeway Sdn. | 42 | $2,904 | +0.41% | 3898 | 19,569 | -3.29% |
| Monterey 4-Door Hardtop | 48 | $2,978 | +0.71% | 3893 | 10,047 | +142.51% |
| Commuter 4-Door, 2-Seat Wagon | 72 | $3,235 | -0.03% | 4178 | 8,081 | +131.95% |
| TOTALS | | *Avg. price* $2,979 | -1.55% | | *Production* 88,454 | +84.63% |

# Montclair

*"The Montclair proudly takes its position in the popular middle segment of the medium-price class. And, the Colony Park shows how beauty can be built into a wagon."*

**Nameplate year of origin:** 1955.
**Current bodystyle lifespan:** 1965 through 1966.
**Predecessor to this model:** Monterey Custom (1964).
**Replacement for this model:** Montclair (1967 to 1968).
**Percentage of division's sales volume:** 17.55%.
**Corporate siblings:** Ford Galaxie/LTD.
**Primary competition:** Buick Wildcat, Dodge Polara, Oldsmobile 88 and Pontiac Star Chief.
**Notable changes:** Completely restyled.
**Major standard equipment:** Lamay fabric and vinyl front bench seat, full carpeting, padded instrument panel, interval selector windshield wipers, electric clock, bright exterior trim, deluxe wheel covers, and 8.15 × 15 BSW tires. Colony Park wagons adds: exterior wood-grain vinyl trim, and power tailgate window.

## Measurements

|  | Cars | Colony Park |
|---|---|---|
| Wheelbase | 123.0" | 119.0" |
| Length | 218.4" | 214.5" |
| Width | 79.6" | 79.6" |
| Height | 56.0" | 56.1" |
| Legroom — front | 41.9" | 41.6" |
| Legroom — rear | 38.6" | 37.8" |
| Headroom — front | 39.1" | 38.9" |
| Headroom — rear | 38.3" | 38.1" |
| Cargo capacity (cu. ft.) | 18.6 | 91.3 |
| Fuel capacity (gals.) | 21.0 | 21.0 |

## Models Available

|  | Style No. | Base MSRP | Change from LY | Shipping Wt. (lbs.) | Production | Change from LY |
|---|---|---|---|---|---|---|
| Montclair 2-Door Hardtop | 57 | $3,135 | +0.26% | 3848 | 9,645 | +314.13% |
| Montclair 4-Door Breezeway Sdn. | 52 | $3,137 | +0.67% | 3933 | 18,924 | +21.93% |
| Montclair 4-Door Hardtop | 58 | $3,210 | +0.91% | 3928 | 16,977 | +75.84% |
| Colony Park 4-Door, 2-Seat Wgn. | 76 | $3,434 | 0.00% | 4228 | 15,294 | +261.22% |
| TOTALS | | *Avg. price* $3,229 | +1.00% | | *Production* 60,840 | +38.84% |

# Park Lane

*"Mercury's most elegant series is presented as
the luxury leader of the medium-price class."*

**Nameplate year of origin:** 1958.
**Current bodystyle lifespan:** 1965 through 1966.
**Predecessor to this model:** Park Lane or S-55 (1963 to 1964).
**Replacement for this model:** Park Lane (1967 to 1968).
**Percentage of division's sales volume:** 9.35%.
**Corporate siblings:** Ford Galaxie/LTD.
**Primary competition:** Buick Wildcat, Chrysler Newport, Oldsmobile 88 and
   Pontiac Bonneville.
**Notable changes:** Completely restyled.
**Major standard equipment:** Moselle fabric and crinkle vinyl front bench seat
   (all-vinyl for convertible), full carpeting, padded instrument panel, trip
   odometer, automatic parking brake release, courtesy lights, interval selector
   windshield wipers, electric clock, custom grip door handles, bright exterior
   window trim, full wheel covers and 8.15 × 15 BSW tires.

## Measurements

| | |
|---|---|
| Wheelbase | 123.0" |
| Length | 218.4" |
| Width | 79.6" |
| Height | 56.0" |
| Legroom — front | 41.9" |
| Legroom — rear | 38.6" |
| Headroom — front | 39.1" |
| Headroom — rear | 38.3" |
| Cargo capacity (cu. ft.) | 18.6 |
| Fuel capacity (gals.) | 21.0 |

**1965**

## Models Available

| | Style No. | Base MSRP | Change from LY | Shipping Wt. (lbs.) | Production | Change from LY |
|---|---|---|---|---|---|---|
| Park Lane 2-Door Hardtop | 67 | $3,367 | +0.24% | 3908 | 6,853 | +283.71% |
| Park Lane 2-Door Convertible | 65 | $3,599 | +1.41% | 4013 | 3,008 | +52.92% |
| Park Lane 4-Door Breezeway Sdn. | 62 | $3,369 | +0.63% | 3988 | 8,335 | +33.79% |
| Park Lane 4-Door Hardtop | 68 | $3,442 | +0.85% | 3983 | 14,211 | +491.63% |
| TOTALS | *Avg. price* | $3,444 | +1.09% | *Production* | 32,407 | +51.89% |

# OLDSMOBILE

*"The Rocket Action Car. Styled to go … where the action is!"*

All of General Motors' divisions brought all-new full-size cars to the market in 1956 — the best looking big cars on the market by far. Long, low-slung, sculpted lines with minimal trim replaced the heavily chromed, boxy look of 1963 and 1964. The body side feature line on Oldsmobiles ran low to the ground, making them look longer and lower than other full-size offerings. Up front the new cars sported a traditional full-width grille, with headlamps set at the far ends and parking lights in the bumper. At the back end, taillights were blended into the rear sculpting, making them a part of the styling, rather than tacked on.

Oldsmobile took the opportunity of a new car to introduce a new engine also. Manufacturers rarely introduce a new car and a new engine in the same year, but the new 425 CID V8 was based on the proven 394 CID V8 it replaced. The larger displacement engine put out about 5 percent greater horsepower. New behind the engine was GM's new Turbo Hydra-matic transmission. Oldsmobile had developed and first introduced Hydra-matic back in 1940, and the new Turbo was a much-improved offspring of that popular and dependable transmission. Turbo Hydra-matic offered smoother shifting and held up better when mated to the newer, more powerful engines.

There were several casualties related to the restyling of

the full-size Oldsmobiles'. The full-size wagon was gone from the lineup this year, as the larger-than-mid-size Vista-Cruiser had proven to be a very successful station wagon. The next full-size Olds wagon would not appear in showrooms until the 1971 Custom Cruiser wagon was introduced. The long-running Super 88 line was gone this year, its place taken by a new, and soon to be very popular, Delta 88. The Delta 88 came in 2-Door Hardtop, 4-Door Sedan, and 4-Door Hardtop varieties. The Delta name would be used for all 88 models by 1969. In the similarly restyled Ninety-Eight line, the 2-Door "Sport" Coupe was no

longer offered, as 4-Door luxury models would gradually become the mainstay.

In the intermediate size F-85 line, the front and rear styling was updated to bear a stronger family likeness to the new 88 line. The only model line changes were the addition of a Custom trim level on the Vista-Cruiser wagon. This year's sales of Vista-Cruiser station wagons would triple the 1964 sales total. It seems that Oldsmobile retained all sales lost from dropping the full-size Jetstar 88 and Dynamic 88 wagons in additional Vista-Cruiser sales.

98 Holiday 4-Door Hardtop

Dynamic 88 Delta 2-Door Hardtop

F-85 Cutlass 2-Door Hardtop

Jetstar 88 4-Door Hardtop

Jetstar I 2-Door Hardtop

Starfire 2-Door Hardtop

Vista-Cruiser Custom 9-passenger, 4-Door Wagon

**Model year production:** 590,578, up 18.73% over 1964.
**Domestic market share:** 6.67% (5th place).
**Base price range:** $2,344 to $4,778.
**Industry average base price:** $3,017.
**Oldsmobile average base price:** $3,271.
**Introduction date:** September 1964.
**Assembly plants:** Southgate, CA (C); Atlanta, GA (D); Framingham, MA (G); Fremont, CA (Z); Lansing, MI (M); Fairfax, KS (X); and Linden, NJ (E).

**Data plate identification:** Thirteen digit code read as follows: 1st digit 3 = Oldsmobile; 2nd through 5th identify series/body style number; 5 = 1965 year; 7th digit is assembly plant code; 100001 and up for serial number (except Toronado is 500001). *Example:* 358395X100001 is a 1965 Oldsmobile Delta 88 4-Door Hardtop, serial number 100001, built in Fairfax, KS.

## Powertrains

| Engine | Gross HP | Transmission Availability | F-85 & Cutlass** | Vista-Cruiser | Jetstar 88 | Jetstar II/Star. Dynamic 88 | 98 |
|---|---|---|---|---|---|---|---|
| 225 CID Econ-O-Way, 1-bbl., V6 | 155 | 3-speed manual | S* | - | - | - | - |
| | | Jetaway Automatic | $195* | - | - | - | - |
| 330 CID Jetfire Rocket, 2-bbl., V8 | 250 (260— Prem.) | 3-speed manual | S (Cutlass)/$70* | S | S | - | - |
| | | 4-speed manual | $205 (Cut.)/$275* | $205 | - | - | - |

| Engine | Gross HP | Transmission Availability | F-85 & Cutlass** | Vista-Cruiser | Jetstar 88 | Jetstar I/Star. Dynamic 88 | 98 |
|---|---|---|---|---|---|---|---|
| | | Jetaway Automatic | $205 (Cut.)/$275* | $205 | $205 | - | - |
| | | Turbo Hydra-matic | - | - | $245 | - | - |
| 330 CID Jetfire Rocket, 4-bbl., V8 | 315 | 3-speed manual | $55 (Cut.)/$125* | $55 | $55 | - | - |
| | | 4-speed manual* | $260 (Cut.)/$330* | $260 | - | - | - |
| | | Jetaway Automatic | $260 (Cut.)/$330* | $260 | $260 | - | - |
| 400 CID 4-4-2**, 4-bbl., V8 | 345 | 4-speed manual | $** | - | - | - | - |
| | | Jetaway Automatic | $** | - | - | - | - |
| 425 CID Super Rocket, 2-bbl., V8 | 300 (310—Auto.) | 3-speed manual | - | - | - | S (Dynamic 88) | - |
| | | Turbo Hydra-matic | - | - | - | $245 (Dynamic 88) | - |
| 425 CID Super Rocket, 4-bbl., V8 | 360 | 3-speed manual | - | - | - | $60 (Dynamic 88) | - |
| | | Turbo Hydra-matic | - | - | - | $305 (Dynamic 88) | S |
| 425 CID Starfire Rocket, 4-bbl., V8 | 370 | 3-speed manual | - | - | - | S (Jetstar I) | - |
| | | Turbo Hydra-matic | - | - | - | S (Starfire)/ $245 (Jetst. I) | $78 |

*F-85 only.   **V8 required for 4-4-2 option package available on any F-85 coupe or convertible.

## Major Options

| | F-85 | Vista-Cr. | Jetstar 88 | Jetstar I | Dynamic 88 | Starfire | 98 |
|---|---|---|---|---|---|---|---|
| Air conditioning | $343 | $343 | $421 | $421 | $421 | $421 | $421 |
| Cruise control (V8 only) | - | - | $91 | $91 | $91 | $91 | $91 |
| Soft Ray tinted glass | $39 | $39 | $44 | $47 | $47 | $47 | $44 |
| Deck lid remote release | $12 | - | $12 | $12 | $12 | $12 | $12 |
| Tilt-Away steering wheel | $44 | $44 | $44 | $44 | $44 | $44 | $44 |
| Power steering—variable-ratio | $95 | $95 | $109 | $109 | $109 | S | S |
| Power brakes | $45 | $45 | $45 | $45 | $45 | S | S |
| Power driver's seat/bench seat | - | - | $71 | $71 | $71 | S | S |
| Power windows | $104 | $104 | $110 | $110 | $110 | S | S |
| Electric clock | $16 | $16 | $16 | S | $16 | S | S |
| AM radio | $64 | $64 | $64 | $64 | $64 | $64 | $64 |
| AM/FM radio | $133 | $133 | $133 | $133 | $133 | $133 | $133 |
| Front seat console | $ | - | $ | S | $ | S | $ |
| Front bucket seats | $ | - | $ | S | $ | S | $ |
| White sidewall tires (base size) | $30–$40 | $40 | $40 | $45 | $45 | $45 | $45 |
| 4-4-2 performance and handling package | $156 | - | - | - | - | - | - |

Options common to most models. (- = Not Available; S = Standard equipment.) Items may be standard equipment, optional at different pricing, or unavailable on certain models. This chart is only a guide.

## Paint Colors

| | Code | | Code |
|---|---|---|---|
| Ebony Black | A | Turquoise Metallic | L |
| Nocturne Mist Metallic | B | Burgundy Mist Metallic | N |
| Provincial White | C | Target Red | R |
| Lucerne Mist Metallic | D | Champagne Mist Metallic | S |
| Royal Mist Metallic | E | Mojave Mist Metallic | T |
| Laurel Mist Metallic | H | Almond Beige | V |
| Forest Mist Metallic | J | Sterling Mist Metallic | W |
| Ocean Mist Metallic | K | Saffron Yellow | Y |

1965

# F-85 and Cutlass

*"Action leader of the low-price field!"*

**Nameplate year of origin:** 1961 (F-85); 1962 (Cutlass, as F-85 model); 1955 (show car).

**Current bodystyle lifespan:** 1964 through 1965.

**Predecessor to this model:** F-85 (1961 to 1963).

**Replacement for this model:** F-85/Cutlass (1966 to 1967).

**Percentage of division's sales volume:** 30.38%.

**Corporate siblings:** Buick Special/Skylark, Chevrolet Chevelle, Pontiac Tempest/LeMans.

**Primary competition:** Rambler Classic, Dodge Coronet, Mercury Comet, and Plymouth Belvedere.

**Notable changes:** Revised front-end styling, minor trim and detail changes.

**Major standard equipment:** Cloth and vinyl front bench seat, heavy-duty floor covering, electric windshield wipers, and 6.95 × 14 BSW tires. Deluxe adds: Full carpeting, deluxe steering wheel, and padded instrument panel. Cutlass adds: All-vinyl bucket seats. 4-4-2 option-package adds: 400 CID V8 engine, dual exhausts, heavy duty suspension, and F70 × 14 redline tires.

## Measurements

|  | Cars | Wagon |
|---|---|---|
| Wheelbase | 115.0" | 115.0" |
| Length | 204.3" | 204.3" |
| Width | 73.8" | 73.8" |
| Height | 54.5" | 54.8" |
| Legroom — front | 41.7" | 41.7" |
| Legroom — rear | 36.0" | 35.9" |
| Headroom — front | 38.2" | 38.2" |
| Headroom — rear | 37.2" | 37.3" |
| Luggage capacity (cu. ft.) | NA | 85.2 |
| Fuel capacity (gals.) | 20 | 20 |

## Models Available

|  | Style No. | Base MSRP | Change from LY | Shipping Wt. (lbs.) | Production | Change from LY |
|---|---|---|---|---|---|---|
| F-85 2-Door Club Coupe | 3327 | $2,344 | +0.04% | 2940 | 13,009 | +56.47% |
| F-85 2-Door Sports Coupe | 3527 | $2,538 | NEW | 2980 | 6,141 | NEW |
| F-85 4-Door Sedan | 3369 | $2,398 | +0.04% | 2991 | 8,078 | +27.59% |
| F-85 4-Door, 2-Seat Wagon | 3335 | $2,689 | 0.00% | 3236 | 3,210 | -20.68% |
| F-85 Deluxe 4-Door Sedan | 3569 | $2,505 | 0.00% | 3016 | 52,756 | +24.90% |
| F-85 Deluxe 4-Door, 2-Seat Wagon | 3535 | $2,797 | 0.00% | 3258 | 11,024 | +1112.76% |
| Cutlass 2-Door Sport Coupe | 3807 | $2,643 | -0.04% | 3221 | 26,441 | +71.25% |
| Cutlass 2-Door Holiday Hardtop | 3817 | $2,784 | 0.00% | 3245 | 46,138 | +27.62% |
| Cutlass 2-Door Convertible | 3867 | $2,983 | -0.03% | 3338 | 12,628 | -1.51% |
| TOTALS | | Avg. price $2,631 | 0.00% | | Production 179,425 | +33.66% |

# Vista-Cruiser

*"Pack up your cares and go ... where the family action is!"*

**Nameplate year of origin:** 1964.

**Current bodystyle lifespan:** 1964 through 1965.

**Predecessor to this model:** None.

**Replacement for this model:** Vista-Cruiser (1966 to 1967).

**Percentage of division's sales volume:** 5.42%.

**Corporate siblings:** Buick Sport Wagon.

**Primary competition:** AMC Ambassador and Dodge Coronet.

**Notable changes:** Completely restyled.

**Major standard equipment:** All-vinyl front bench seat, full carpeting, heater and defroster, Deluxe steering wheel, Vista-roof windows, padded second seat sun visors, and 7.75 × 14 BSW tires.

## Measurements

| Wheelbase | 120.0" |
|---|---|
| Length | 207.7" |
| Width | 73.8" |
| Height | 58.3" |
| Legroom — front | 41.7" |
| Legroom — rear | 38.9" |
| Headroom — front | 38.8" |
| Headroom — rear | 40.3" |
| Luggage capacity (cu. ft.) | 101.1 |
| Fuel capacity (gals.) | 20.0 |

## Models Available

| | Style No. | Base MSRP | Change from LY | Shipping Wt. (lbs.) | Production | Change from LY |
|---|---|---|---|---|---|---|
| Vista-Cruiser 4-Dr., 2-S. Wagon | 3455 | $2,937 | -0.03% | 3684 | 2,110 | * |
| Vista-Cruiser 4-Dr., 3-S. Wagon | 3465 | $3,072 | 0.00% | 3809 | 3,335 | * |
| Vista-Cruiser Cust. 4-Dr., 2-S. Wgn. | 3855 | $3,146 | 0.00% | 3762 | 9,355 | * |
| Vista-Cruiser Cust. 4-Dr., 3-S. Wgn. | 3865 | $3,270 | 0.00% | 3864 | 17,205 | * |
| TOTALS | | *Avg. price* $3,106 | -0.02% | | *Production* 32,005 | +201.76% |

*Production by trim level not available from 1964 for comparison.*

# Jetstar 88

*"A dollar never went farther ... or more beautifully!"*

**Nameplate year of origin:** 1964 (88 series started 1949).
**Current bodystyle lifespan:** 1965 through 1966.
**Predecessor to this model:** 88/Jetstar 88 (1961 to 1964).
**Replacement for this model:** Delmont 88 (1967 to 1968).
**Percentage of division's sales volume:** 8.97%.
**Corporate siblings:** Buick LeSabre/Wildcat, Chevrolet
   Biscayne/BelAir/Impala/Caprice, Pontiac Catalina/Executive/Bonneville.
**Primary competition:** AMC Ambassador, Dodge Polara, and Mercury Monterey.
**Notable changes:** Completely redesigned.
**Major standard equipment:** Cloth-and-vinyl front bench seat, full carpeting,
   electric windshield wipers, padded instrument panel, rocker panel moldings,
   wheel covers, and 7.75 × 14 BSW tires.

### Measurements

| | |
|---|---|
| Wheelbase | 123.0" |
| Length | 216.9" |
| Width | 80.0" |
| Height | 55.5" |
| Legroom — front | 41.7" |
| Legroom — rear | 39.2" |
| Headroom — front | 38.7" |
| Headroom — rear | 37.8" |
| Luggage capacity (cu. ft.) | NA |
| Fuel capacity (gals.) | 25.0 |

**1965**

## Models Available

| | Style No. | Base MSRP | Change from LY | Shipping Wt. (lbs.) | Production | Change from LY |
|---|---|---|---|---|---|---|
| Jetstar 88 2-Door Holiday Hardtop | 5237 | $2,995 | +0.10% | 3688 | 13,911 | -16.52% |
| Jetstar 88 2-Door Convertible | 5267 | $3,337 | +0.57% | 3853 | 2,980 | -23.65% |
| Jetstar 88 4-Door Celebrity Sedan | 5269 | $2,938 | +0.10% | 3726 | 20,143 | -18.16% |
| Jetstar 88 4-Door Holiday Hardtop | 5239 | $3,072 | +0.10% | 3775 | 15,922 | -17.61% |
| TOTALS | | *Avg. price* $3,086 | +0.22% | | *Production* 52,956 | -17.91% |

# Jetstar I

*"Has everything going for you ... including an easy-going price!"*

**Nameplate year of origin:** 1964.
**Current bodystyle lifespan:** 1965 through 1966.
**Predecessor to this model:** Jetstar I (1964).
**Replacement for this model:** None.
**Percentage of division's sales volume:** 1.11%.
**Corporate siblings:** Buick Wildcat, Chevrolet Impala SS, Pontiac Grand Prix.
**Primary competition:** Dodge Monaco, Ford Galaxie 500 XL, and Mercury S-55.
**Notable changes:** Completely redesigned.
**Major standard equipment:** All-vinyl bucket seats with center console, full carpet-

### Measurements

| | |
|---|---|
| Wheelbase | 123.0" |
| Length | 216.9" |
| Width | 80.0" |
| Height | 54.1" |
| Legroom — front | 41.5" |
| Legroom — rear | 35.3" |
| Headroom — front | 37.3" |
| Headroom — rear | 37.3" |

ing, padded instrument panel, electric clock, glove box and courtesy lamps, electric windshield wipers with washers, full wheel covers, and 8.25 × 14 BSW tires.

| | |
|---|---|
| Luggage capacity (cu. ft.) | NA |
| Fuel capacity (gals.) | 25.0 |

## Models Available

| | Style No. | Base MSRP | Change from LY | Shipping Wt. (lbs.) | Production | Change from LY |
|---|---|---|---|---|---|---|
| Jetstar I 2-Door Sport Coupe | 5457 | $3,602 | -0.03% | 3982 | 6,552 | -59.26% |
| TOTALS | Avg. price | $3,602 | -0.03% | Production | 6,552 | -59.26% |

# Dynamic 88

*"Super new way to go Olds with a Super Rocket flourish!"*

**Nameplate year of origin:** 1964 (88 series started 1949).
**Current bodystyle lifespan:** 1965 through 1966.
**Predecessor to this model:** Dynamic 88/Super 88 (1961 to 1964).
**Replacement for this model:** Delmont 88/Delta 88 (1967 to 1968).
**Percentage of division's sales volume:** 35.55%.
**Corporate siblings:** Buick LeSabre/Wildcat, Chevrolet Full-size, and Pontiac Full-size.
**Primary competition:** Chrysler Newport, Dodge Custom 880, and Mercury Montclair.
**Notable changes:** Completely redesigned.
**Major standard equipment:** Cloth-and-vinyl front bench seat, full carpeting, padded instrument panel, electric windshield wipers, full wheel covers, and 8.25 × 14 BSW tires. Delta adds: All-vinyl Custom Sport seat w/folding center armrests, courtesy lamps, and Delta interior and exterior trim.

### Measurements

| | |
|---|---|
| Wheelbase | 123.0" |
| Length | 216.9" |
| Width | 80.0" |
| Height | 55.5" |
| Legroom — front | 41.7" |
| Legroom — rear | 39.2" |
| Headroom — front | 38.7" |
| Headroom — rear | 37.8" |
| Luggage capacity (cu. ft.) | NA |
| Fuel capacity (gals.) | 25 |

## Models Available

| | Style No. | Base MSRP | Change from LY | Shipping Wt. (lbs.) | Production | Change from LY |
|---|---|---|---|---|---|---|
| Dynamic 88 2-Door Holiday Hardtop | 5637 | $3,065 | +0.10% | 3873 | 24,756 | -23.52% |
| Dynamic 88 2-Door Convertible | 5667 | $3,408 | +0.56% | 3946 | 8,832 | -12.05% |
| Dynamic 88 4-Door Celebrity Sedan | 5669 | $3,008 | +0.10% | 3908 | 47,030 | -18.34% |
| Dynamic 88 4-Door Holiday Hardtop | 5639 | $3,143 | +0.13% | 3961 | 38,889 | -22.73% |
| Dyn. 88 Delta 2-Door Hardtop | 5837 | $3,253 | NEW | 3924 | 23,194 | NEW |
| Dyn. 88 Delta 4-Door Celebrity Sdn. | 5869 | $3,158 | -3.01%* | 3940 | 29,915 | +1623.21%* |
| Dyn. 88 Delta 4-Door Hardtop | 5839 | $3,330 | -4.48%* | 4010 | 37,358 | +110.14%* |
| TOTALS | Avg. price | $3,195 | -3.12% | Production | 209,974 | +25.23% |

*Comparisons made to 1964 Super 88 models.*

# Starfire

*"The car that makes luxury a sporting proposition!"*

**Nameplate year of origin:** 1954 (as designation for 98 Convertible); 1961 (as series).
**Current bodystyle lifespan:** 1965 through 1966.
**Predecessor to this model:** Starfire (1961 to 1964).
**Replacement for this model:** None.
**Percentage of division's sales volume:** 2.58%.
**Corporate siblings:** Buick Wildcat, Chevrolet Impala SS, Pontiac Grand Prix.
**Primary competition:** Chrysler 300, Dodge Monaco, Ford Galaxie 500 XL, and Mercury S-55.
**Notable changes:** Completely redesigned.
**Major standard equipment:** All-vinyl bucket seats with center console, full carpeting, padded instrument panel, tachometer, electric clock, deluxe steering wheel, glove box and courtesy lamps, power steering, power brakes, automatic transmission, full wheel covers, and 8.25 × 14 BSW tires. Convertible adds: Power windows, power drivers seat, power top and 8.25 × 14 WSW tires.

## Measurements

| | |
|---|---|
| Wheelbase | 123.0" |
| Length | 216.9" |
| Width | 80.0" |
| Height | 54.1" |
| Legroom — front | 41.5" |
| Legroom — rear | 35.3" |
| Headroom — front | 37.3" |
| Headroom — rear | 37.3" |
| Luggage capacity (cu. ft.) | NA |
| Fuel capacity (gals.) | 25 |

## Models Available

| | Style No. | Base MSRP | Change from LY | Shipping Wt. (lbs.) | Production | Change from LY |
|---|---|---|---|---|---|---|
| Starfire 2-Door Hardtop | 6657 | $4,148 | +0.24% | 4152 | 13,024 | -5.30% |
| Starfire 2-Door Convertible | 6667 | $4,778 | +0.53% | 4247 | 2,236 | -7.22% |
| TOTALS | | *Avg. price* $4,463 | +0.38% | | *Production* 15,260 | -5.59% |

# Ninety-Eight

*"The most beautiful compliment you can pay yourself!"*

**Nameplate year of origin:** 1941.
**Current bodystyle lifespan:** 1965 through 1966.
**Predecessor to this model:** Ninety-Eight (1961 to 1964).
**Replacement for this model:** Ninety-Eight (1967 to 1968).
**Percentage of division's sales volume:** 15.99%.
**Corporate siblings:** Buick Electra and Cadillac Calais/de Ville.
**Primary competition:** Chrysler New Yorker and Mercury Park Lane.
**Notable changes:** Completely redesigned.
**Major standard equipment:** Cloth and vinyl bench seat with fold-down center armrest (all-vinyl Custom Sport seat on Hardtop and Convertible models), deep-pile carpeting on floor and kick panels, deluxe steering wheel, electric clock, power windows and two-way power seat (except Town Sedan), full wheel covers, rear wheel opening covers, power steering, power front disc brakes, 8.55 × 14 BSW tires. Luxury Sedan adds: Special design interior trim and vinyl top.

## Measurements

| | |
|---|---|
| Wheelbase | 126.0" |
| Length | 222.9" |
| Width | 80.0" |
| Height | 55.8" |
| Legroom — front | 41.4" |
| Legroom — rear | 40.9" |
| Headroom — front | 39.5" |
| Headroom — rear | 38.2" |
| Luggage capacity (cu. ft.) | NA |
| Fuel capacity (gals.) | 25.0 |

## Models Available

| | Style No. | Base MSRP | Change from LY | Shipping Wt. (lbs.) | Production | Change from LY |
|---|---|---|---|---|---|---|
| Ninety-Eight 2-Door Sports Coupe | 8437 | $4,197 | +0.21% | 4178 | 12,166 | +98.18% |
| Ninety-Eight 2-Door Convertible | 8467 | $4,493 | +0.56% | 4250 | 4,903 | +22.45% |

| | Style No. | Base MSRP | Change from LY | Shipping Wt. (lbs.) | Production | Change from LY |
|---|---|---|---|---|---|---|
| Ninety-Eight 4-Door Town Sedan | 8469 | $4,001 | +0.20% | 4186 | 13,266 | +16.57% |
| Ninety-Eight 4-Door Sports Sedan | 8439 | $4,273 | +0.19% | 4286 | 28,480 | +14.88% |
| Ninety-Eight Luxury 4-Door Sedan | 8669 | $4,351 | +0.21% | 4285 | 35,591 | +105.18% |
| TOTALS | | *Avg. price* $4,263 | -0.29% | | *Production* 94,406 | +37.59% |

# PLYMOUTH

*"If this is the year you picked to buy a new car, you picked a beautiful year to Get up and Go Plymouth. The Roaring '65's!"*

Nineteen sixty-five was Plymouth's last chance comeback year. Following its long-time success through the mid-fifties as a conservative, somewhat staid, low-priced make, the flashy and stylish 1957 models had thrown caution to the wind and put Plymouth squarely into the same class as Ford and Chevrolet from powertrain to body styling to accessories and features. Then as if overreacting to the success, Chrysler had its failures in the design department, followed by a terribly timed marketing move that put Dodge into direct competition with Plymouth and nearly killed it off. Now with one totally new full-size line and a heavily redesigned mid-size line of cars, Plymouth finally had the chance to show what it had. While there would be later years with greater sales success, none was more important than this one to the longer-term viability of Plymouth. As history has shown, this time it was a success, but the next time Chrysler would not be so fortunate. The all-new full-size Fury line finally came back to Plymouth, after a three-year absence. The new models pulled out all the stops, successfully mimicking the popular Pontiac vertical headlight theme. Body sides were conservative but nicely done, with

a full-length mid-body feature line, followed by square tail-lamps at the back end. Rooflines also were cautious, upright affairs, with the 2-Door Hardtops gaining a nice convertible profile. The Fury line was greatly expanded to cover the lower-priced end of the market, a move that brought back a lot of fleet business to Plymouth from Dodge and Ford. New models were the Fury I and II Sedan and Wagon models, with a Fury III moniker replacing the former Fury nameplate. As a special honor, a Sport Fury Convertible was chosen to be the Official Pace Car for the Indianapolis 500 race this year.

The mid-sized line was really the former "full-size" Plymouth with a new facelift that followed the Fury family lines sans the vertical headlamp treatment. New name-plates Belvedere I, Belvedere II and Satellite replaced Savoy, Fury and Sport Fury model for model at a cost of $50–$250 less than 1964, with similar features. The wise marketing paid off handsomely in increased sales volume. At the compact end of the line, the Valiant and accompanying Barracuda were fresh off a facelift in 1964, so this season saw few visual changes.

Barracuda 2-Door Hardtop

Belvedere II 4-Door Sedan

Fury I 2-Door Sedan

Fury III 9-passenger, 4-Door Wagon

Satellite 2-Door Hardtop

Sport Fury 2-Door Convertible,
Indianapolis 500 Pace Car

Valiant 200 4-Door Sedan

**1965**

**Model year production:** 721,234, up 31.53% over 1964.
**Domestic market share:** 8.14% (4th place).
**Base price range:** $2,004 to $3,209.
**Industry average base price:** $3,017.
**Plymouth average base price:** $2,591.
**Introduction date:** September 25, 1964.
**Assembly plants:** Lynch Road, MI (1): Hamtramck, MI (2); Los Angeles, CA (5); Newark DE (6); and St. Louis, MO (7).

**Data plate identification:** Ten digit code read as follows: First digit is car line (e.g., P for Fury V8); second number identifies body type (e.g., 3 is a Fury III — see model number in charts below); third digit 5 for 1965; fourth digit is assembly plant code; 100001 and up for serial number (500001 and up for Valiant). *Example:* P352100001 is a 1965 Plymouth Fury III, built at Hamtramck, MI, serial number 100001. Body style cannot be identified through the VIN except on station wagons.

## Powertrains

| Engine | Gross HP | Transmission Availability | Valiant | Barracuda | Belvedere | Fury |
|---|---|---|---|---|---|---|
| 170 CID, 1-bbl., 6-cyl. | 101 | 3-speed manual | S | - | - | - |
| | | Torqueflite automatic | $172 | - | - | - |
| 225 CID, 1-bbl., 6-cyl. | 145 | 3-speed manual | $46 | S | S[2] | S[3] |
| | | 4-speed manual | $215 | $186 | - | - |
| | | Torqueflite automatic | $218 | $172 | $192[2] | $192[3] |
| 273 CID, 2-bbl., V8 | 180 | 3-speed manual | $131 | $82 | S[1]/$94[2] | - |
| | | 4-speed manual | $310 | $261 | - | - |
| | | Torqueflite automatic | $312 | $263 | $203[1]/$297[2] | - |
| 273 CID Formula S, 4-bbl., V8 | 235 | 3-speed manual | - | $230 | - | - |
| | | 4-speed manual | - | $309 | - | - |
| | | Torqueflite automatic | - | $311 | - | - |
| 318 CID, 2-bbl., V8 | 230 | 3-speed manual | - | - | $31[1]/$125[2] | S[4]/ $104[3] |
| | | Torqueflite automatic | - | - | $242[1]/$336[2] | $211[4]/$315[3] |
| 361 CID Commando, 2-bbl., V8 | 265 | 3-speed manual | - | - | $88[1]/$182[2] | $59[4]$163[3] |
| | | 4-speed manual | - | - | $276[1]/$370[2] | $247[4]/$351[3] |
| | | Torqueflite automatic | - | - | $299[1]/$393[2] | $270[4]/$374[3] |
| 383 CID Commando, 2-bbl., V8 | 305 | 3-speed manual | - | - | - | $71[4]$185[3] |
| | | 4-speed manual | - | - | - | $259[4]/$373[3] |

| Engine | Gross HP | Transmission Availability | Valiant | Barracuda | Belvedere | Fury |
|---|---|---|---|---|---|---|
| | | Torqueflite automatic | - | - | - | $282[4]/$396[3] |
| 383 CID Commando, 4-bbl., V8 | 330 | 3-speed manual | - | - | $153[1]/$247[2] | $122[4]/$226[2] |
| | | 4-speed manual | - | - | $341[1]/$435[2] | $310[4]/$414[3] |
| | | Torqueflite automatic | - | - | $364[1]/$458[2] | $333[4]/$437[3] |
| 426 CID Commando, 4-bbl., V8 | 365 | 4-speed manual | - | - | $514[1]/$608[2] | $483[4]/$597[3] |
| | | Torqueflite automatic | - | - | $537[1]/$631[2] | $515[4]/$619[3] |
| 426 CID Commando, 4-bbl., V8 | 415–425 | 4-speed manual | - | - | * | * |
| | | Torqueflite automatic | - | - | * | * |
| 426 CID Hemi V8, 4-bbl., V8 | 415–425 | 4-speed manual | - | - | * | * |
| | | Torqueflite automatic | - | - | * | * |

[1]Satellite models only. [2]All but Satellite. [3]Fury I (All), Fury II Sedans, Fury III 2-Door HT and 4-Door Sedan only. [4]All but Fury I, Fury II Sedans, Fury III 2-Dr. HT and Fury III 4-Dr. Sedan. *Available at varying prices and installation rate. Accurate pricing is unavailable at this time.

## Major Options

| | Valiant | Barracuda | Savoy/Belvedere | Fury |
|---|---|---|---|---|
| Air Conditioning (V8 only) | $319 | $319 | $338 | $338 |
| Solex tinted glass | $29 | $14 | $40 | $40 |
| Power steering | $84 | $84 | $84 | $84 |
| Power brakes | $43 | $43 | $43 | $43 |
| Power windows | - | - | $102 | $102 |
| Power front seat — 4-way bucket | - | - | $78 | $78 |
| Electric clock | $16 | $16 | $16 | $16 |
| Transaudio AM radio | $59 | $59 | $59 | $59 |
| Variable speed wipers and washer | $17 | $17 | $17 | $17 |
| Full wheel covers | $16 | - | $102 | $61–$102 |

Options common to most models. (– = Not Available.) Items may be standard equipment, optional at different pricing, or unavailable on certain models. This chart is only a guide.

## Paint Colors

| | Code |
|---|---|
| Gold Metallic | AA-1 |
| Black | BB-1 |
| Light Blue Metallic | CC-1 |
| Medium Blue Metallic | DD-1 |
| Dark Blue Metallic | EE-1 |
| Copper Metallic | HH-1 |
| Light Turquoise Met. | JJ-1 |
| Medium Turquoise Metallic | KK-1 |
| Dark Turquoise Met. | LL-1 |
| Barracuda Silver Metallic | NN-1 |
| Ruby | PP-1 |
| Ivory | SS-1 |
| Medium Red Metallic | TT-1 |
| White | WW-1 |
| Light Tan | XX-1 |
| Medium Tan Metallic | YY-1 |

# Valiant

*"The compact that hasn't forgotten why you buy a compact."*

**Nameplate year of origin:** 1960.
**Current bodystyle lifespan:** 1963 through 1966.
**Predecessor to this model:** Valiant (1960 to 1962).
**Replacement for this model:** Valiant (1967 to 1976).
**Percentage of division's sales volume:** 23.18%.
**Corporate siblings:** Dodge Dart.
**Primary competition:** Rambler American, Chevrolet Chevy II, Ford Falcon and Studebaker Lark.
**Notable changes:** Revised grille, and trim and detail changes.
**Major standard equipment:** Cloth and vinyl bench seat, rubber floor mat, vinyl headlining, chrome exterior front and rear window trim, Torsion-Aire suspension and 6.50 × 13 BSW tires. 200 adds: Side window chrome trim, color-keyed carpeting, front and rear armrests, courtesy or map lights, and deluxe wheel covers. Signet adds: All-vinyl bucket seats, color-keyed deep-pile carpeting, backup lights, rear deck trim and 6-way adjustable front seats.

## Measurements

| | Cars | Wagons |
|---|---|---|
| Wheelbase | 106.0" | 106.0" |
| Length | 188.2" | 188.8" |
| Width | 70.1" | 70.1" |
| Height | 54.4" | 53.1" |
| Legroom — front | 40.1" | 40.0" |
| Legroom — rear | 35.0" | 35.5" |
| Headroom — front | 38.2" | 38.2" |
| Headroom — rear | 37.2" | 37.6" |
| Cargo capacity (cu. ft.) | 23.6 | NA |
| Fuel capacity (gals.) | 18.0 | 18.0 |

## Models Available

| | Style No. | Base MSRP | Change from LY | Shipping Wt. (lbs.) | Production | Change from LY |
|---|---|---|---|---|---|---|
| Valiant 100 2-Door Sedan | V11 | $2,004 | +4.32% | 2557 | 40,434 | +14.21% |
| Valiant 100 4-Door Sedan | V13 | $2,075 | +4.17% | 2582 | 42,857 | -3.06% |
| Valiant 100 4-Door Wagon | V56 | $2,361 | +3.87% | 2757 | 10,822 | +0.59% |
| Valiant 200 2-Door Sedan | V31 | $2,127 | +4.06% | 2577 | 8,919 | -19.01% |
| Valiant 200 2-Door Convertible | V35 | $2,437 | +3.75% | 2647 | 2,769 | -52.72% |
| Valiant 200 4-Door Sedan | V33 | $2,195 | +3.93% | 2602 | 41,642 | -34.76% |
| Valiant 200 4-Door Wagon | V76 | $2,476 | +3.69% | 2757 | 6,133 | -44.98% |
| Valiant Signet 2-Door Hardtop | V42 | $2,340 | +3.72% | 2617 | 10,999 | -70.85% |
| Valiant Signet 2-Door Convertible | V45 | $2,561 | +3.56% | 2717 | 2,578 | -66.24% |
| TOTALS | | *Avg. price* $2,286 | +3.86% | | *Production* 167,153 | -26.55% |

# Barracuda

*"This is the one that has them all talking."*

**Nameplate year of origin:** 1964.
**Current bodystyle lifespan:** 1964 through 1966.
**Predecessor to this model:** None.
**Replacement for this model:** Barracuda (1967 to 1969).
**Percentage of division's sales volume:** 8.96%.
**Corporate siblings:** Dodge Dart.
**Primary competition:** Ford Mustang.
**Notable changes:** Revised grille.
**Major standard equipment:** All-vinyl front bucket seats, full carpeting (including cargo compartment), chrome exterior front and rear window trim, specific Barracuda trim, Torsion-Aire suspension and 6.50 × 13 BSW tires.

### Measurements

| | |
|---|---|
| Wheelbase | 106.0" |
| Length | 188.2" |
| Width | 70.1" |
| Height | 54.4" |
| Legroom — front | 40.6" |
| Legroom — rear | 31.1" |
| Headroom — front | 38.5" |
| Headroom — rear | 36.8" |
| Cargo capacity (cu. ft.) | NA |
| Fuel capacity (gals.) | 18.0 |

## Models Available

| | Style No. | Base MSRP | Change from LY | Shipping Wt. (lbs.) | Production | Change from LY |
|---|---|---|---|---|---|---|
| Barracuda 2-Door Fastback HT | V89 | $2,487 | +5.16% | 2747 | 64,596 | +175.54% |
| TOTALS | | *Avg. price* $2,487 | +5.16% | | *Production* 64,596 | +175.54% |

# Belvedere

*"The Belvedere offers a wider range of style-and-performance choices than any other car of comparable price today. It's a new way to swing without going out on a limb."*

**Nameplate year of origin:** 1951 (HT model), 1954 (as series).
**Current bodystyle lifespan:** 1962 through 1965.
**Predecessor to this model:** Belvedere (1960 to 1961).
**Replacement for this model:** Belvedere (1966 to 1967).
**Percentage of division's sales volume:** 22.12%.
**Corporate siblings:** Dodge Coronet.

### Measurements

| | Cars | Wagons |
|---|---|---|
| Wheelbase | 116.0" | 116.0" |
| Length | 203.4" | 208.5" |
| Width | 75.6" | 75.1" |

**Primary competition:** Rambler Classic, Chevrolet Chevelle, and Ford Fairlane.
**Notable changes:** All-new exterior sheetmetal below the greenhouse area.
**Major standard equipment:** Cloth and vinyl front bench seat, color-keyed floor coverings, front and rear armrests, dual sunvisors, electric windshield wipers, bright trim around front and rear windows, and rear fender line, and 7.35 × 14 BSW tires (Station wagon adds 7.75 × 14 BSW tires). Belvedere II adds: Full carpeting, specific interior trim and full-length body side moldings. Satellite adds: All-vinyl bucket seats, padded instrument panel and specific ornamentation.

| | Cars | Wagons |
|---|---|---|
| Height | 55.0" | 55.1" |
| Legroom — front | 41.9" | 41.9" |
| Legroom — rear | 36.6" | 36.5" |
| Headroom — front | 39.1" | 39.5" |
| Headroom — rear | 38.4" | 39.5" |
| Cargo capacity (cu. ft.) | 25.3 | NA |
| Fuel capacity (gals.) | 20.0 | 21.5 |

## Models Available

| | Style No. | Base MSRP | Change from LY | Shipping Wt. (lbs.) | Production | Change from LY |
|---|---|---|---|---|---|---|
| Belvedere I 2-Door Sedan | R11 | $2,226 | +0.09% | 3076 | 12,536 | -41.22% |
| Belvedere I 4-Door Sedan | R13 | $2,265 | -0.66% | 3106 | 35,968 | -29.51% |
| Belvedere I 4-Door, 2-Seat Wagon | R56 | $2,562 | -2.21% | 3411 | 8,338 | -32.76% |
| Belvedere II 2-Door Hardtop | R32 | $2,378 | -2.70% | 3086 | 24,924 | +52.59% |
| Belvedere II 2-Door Convertible | R35 | $2,597 | NEW | 3186 | 1,921 | NEW |
| Belvedere II 4-Door Sedan | R33 | $2,352 | -2.69% | 3121 | 41,445 | -27.68% |
| Belvedere II 4-Dr., 2-Seat Wagon | R76 | $2,649 | -6.26% | 3421 | 5,908 | -42.74% |
| Belvedere II 4-Dr., 3-Seat Wagon | R77 | $2,747 | -6.18% | 3491 | 3,294 | -21.70% |
| Satellite 2-Door Hardtop | R42 | $2,649 | NEW | 3251 | 23,341 | NEW |
| Satellite 2-Door Convertible | R45 | $2,869 | NEW | 3356 | 1,860 | NEW |
| TOTALS | | Avg. price $2,529 | -2.54% | | Production 159,535 | -12.11% |

*Comparisons made to 1964 Savoy and Belvedere lines.*

# Fury

*"It's the biggest, plushest Plymouth ever."*

**Nameplate year of origin:** 1956.
**Current bodystyle lifespan:** 1965 through 1966.
**Predecessor to this model:** Fury and Sport Fury (1962 to 1964).
**Replacement for this model:** Fury (1967 to 1968).
**Percentage of division's sales volume:** 45.75%.
**Corporate siblings:** Dodge Polara.
**Primary competition:** AMC Ambassador, Chevrolet Biscayne/BelAir/Impala, and Ford Galaxie/LTD.
**Notable changes:** Completely redesigned. Returned to "full-size" status.
**Major standard equipment:** Cloth and vinyl front bench seat, color-keyed floor covering, front and rear armrests, dual sunvisors, electric windshield wipers, bright trim around front and rear windows, and 7.35 × 14 BSW tires (8.25 × 14 BSW tire on wagon). Fury II adds: Full carpeting and full-length body side molding and 8.55 × 14 BSW tires on wagon. Fury III adds: all-vinyl upholstery on hardtop and convertible, backup lights, distinctive exterior trim and 7.75 × 14 BSW tires on Convertible and 4-Door Hardtop. Sport Fury adds: Padded instrument panel, All-vinyl bucket seats, floor-mounted shifter and console with compartment, deluxe steering wheel and 7.75 × 14 BSW tires.

## Measurements

| | Cars | Wagons |
|---|---|---|
| Wheelbase | 119.0" | 121.0" |
| Length | 209.4" | 216.1" |
| Width | 78.0" | 78.1" |
| Height | 56.0" | 56.2" |
| Legroom — front | 42.0" | 42.0" |
| Legroom — rear | 38.6" | 39.4" |
| Headroom — front | 39.0" | 39.0" |
| Headroom — rear | 38.2" | 38.3" |
| Cargo capacity (cu. ft.) | NA | NA |
| Fuel capacity (gals.) | 25.0 | 25.0 |

## Models Available

| | Style No. | Base MSRP | Change from LY | Shipping Wt. (lbs.) | Production | Change from LY |
|---|---|---|---|---|---|---|
| Fury I 2-Door Sedan | P11 | $2,376 | NEW | 3430 | 17,294 | NEW |
| Fury I 4-Door Sedan | P13 | $2,430 | NEW | 3485 | 48,575 | NEW |
| Fury I 4-Door, 2-Seat Wagon | P56 | $2,776 | NEW | 3970 | 13,360 | NEW |
| Fury II 2-Door Sedan | P21 | $2,478 | NEW | 3430 | 4,109 | NEW |
| Fury II 4-Door Sedan | P23 | $2,532 | NEW | 3485 | 43,350 | NEW |
| Fury II 4-Door, 2-Seat Wagon | P66 | $2,948 | NEW | 4140 | 12,853 | NEW |
| Fury II 4-Door, 3-Seat Wagon | P67 | $3,051 | NEW | 4205 | 6,445 | NEW |
| Fury III 2-Door Hardtop | P32 | $2,691 | +3.58% | 3465 | 43,251 | +64.43% |
| Fury III 2-Door Convertible | P35 | $3,048 | +3.78% | 3725 | 5,524 | +6.79% |
| Fury III 4-Door Sedan | P33 | $2,684 | +4.31% | 3510 | 50,725 | +45.34% |
| Fury III 4-Door Hardtop | P34 | $2,863 | +4.03% | 3720 | 21,367 | +55.82% |
| Fury III 4-Door, 2-Seat Wagon | P76 | $3,090 | +3.66% | 4165 | 8,931 | +144.95% |
| Fury III 4-Door, 3-Seat Wagon | P77 | $3,193 | +3.53% | 4230 | 9,546 | +112.99% |
| Sport Fury 2-Door Hardtop | P42 | $2,960 | +3.35% | 3700 | 38,348 | +61.84% |
| Sport Fury 2-Door Convertible | P45 | $3,209 | +3.68% | 3760 | 6,272 | +62.57% |
| TOTALS | | Avg. price $2,822 | -1.36% | | Production 329,950 | +185.00% |

# PONTIAC

*"The Year of the Quick Wide-Tracks."*

Nineteen sixty-five was a standout year for Pontiac. Coming off the success of its 1964 introduction of the GTO, and the styling success of its 1963–64 full-size cars, everyone's attention was on Pontiac to see what it would do next. Even Ford, with the runaway success of its Mustang, had bowed to the status quo and given its full-size 1965 models a new face that included the trend-setting vertical headlamps of the 1963 Pontiac models. The new 1965 Pontiac line would have a lot to live up to, but aided by the newly designed GM A- and B-body, Pontiac turned out some of its best looking models ever. The new GM rooflines blended beautifully with the Pontiac "coke-bottle" design theme which was taken to extremes this year with a sharply creased line following the lower body contours. Of course, vertical headlamps and the pointed nose, split grille theme continued up front. At the back, on certain models, full-width trim moldings concealing the taillamps completed a very sleek package. The new styling looked best on those models that carried only enough chrome trim to highlight the new bodylines — generally speaking the Grand Prix and Catalina (especially 2 + 2 models). The Bonneville, with its wide, grooved lower rocker moldings, also looked quite nice, as its added length accentuated the flowing lines.

Also new for the year was revised styling for the intermediate line. All Tempest and LeMans models were given a facelift that brought their styling more in line with that of the big Pontiacs. Stacked headlamps were a first for the Tempest, and soon other mid-size cars would follow. Sales of the GTO gained over 100% this year, as more people discovered its highly desired power-to-cost ratio. A 2-Door Hardtop model was added to the Tempest Custom line, and a 4-Door Sedan was introduced in the LeMans line, an addition which would take the LeMans into the mainstream, and make way for the GTO as the sporty, top-line model. The combination of styling, handling and performance offered by the new Pontiacs was enough to have *Motor Trend* magazine award their Car of the Year award to the entire line.

Bonneville 4-Door Hardtop

Grand Prix 2-Door Hardtop

Catalina 2 + 2 2-Door Convertible

Catalina 6-passenger, 4-Door Safari Wagon

Star Chief 4-Door Hardtop

GTO 2-Door Coupe and GTO 2-Door Convertible, Full-line, *Motor Trend* Car of the Year

Tempest 4-Door Sedan

Tempest Custom 4-Door Safari Wagon

**Model year production:** 801,357, up 12.15% over 1964.
**Domestic market share:** 9.05% (3rd place).
**Base price range:** $2,260 to $3,632.
**Industry average base price:** $3,017.
**Pontiac average base price:** $2,884.
**Introduction date:** September 1964.
**Assembly plants:** Baltimore, MD (B); Southgate, CA (C); Doraville, GA (D); Linden, NJ (E); Framingham, MA (G); Kansas City, MO (K); Pontiac, MI (P); Arlington, TX (R); Lordstown, OH (U); Fairfax, KS (X); Fremont, CA (Z); and Oshawa, Ontario, Canada (1).
**Data plate identification:** Thirteen digit code read as follows: 1st digit 2 = Pontiac; 2nd through 5th digits identify series/body style number (see style number in listings); 5 = 1965 year; 7th digit is assembly plant code; 100001 and up (600001 and up on 6-cylinders) for serial number. *Example:* 252395X100001 is a 1965 Pontiac Catalina 4-Door Hardtop, serial number 100001, built in Fairfax, KS.

## Powertrains

| Engine | Gross HP | Transmission Availability | Tempest/ LeMans/GTO | Catalina & Star Chief | 2 + 2 | Bonneville & Grand Prix |
|---|---|---|---|---|---|---|
| 215 CID, 1-bbl., 6-cyl. | 140 | 3-speed manual | S — ex. GTO | - | - | - |
|  |  | 4-speed manual | $188 (ex. GTO) | - | - | - |
|  |  | 2-sp. Automatic | $188 (ex. GTO) | - | - | - |
| 326 CID, 2-bbl., V8 | 250 | 3-speed manual | $108 (ex. GTO) | - | - | - |
|  |  | 4-speed manual | $296 (ex. GTO) | - | - | - |
|  |  | 2-sp. Automatic | $307 (ex. GTO) | - | - | - |

| Engine | Gross HP | Transmission Availability | Tempest/ LeMans/GTO | Catalina & Star Chief | 2 + 2 | Bonneville & Grand Prix |
|---|---|---|---|---|---|---|
| 326 CID, 4-bbl., V8 | 285 | 3-speed manual | $173 (ex. GTO) | - | - | - |
| | | 4-speed manual | $361 (ex. GTO) | - | - | - |
| | | 2-sp. Automatic | $372 (ex. GTO) | - | - | - |
| 389 CID, 2-bbl., V8 | 256 | 3-speed manual | - | S | - | - |
| | 290 | Automatic | - | $231 | - | - |
| 389 CID, 4-bbl., V8 | 335 | 3-speed manual | S (GTO) | $44 | - | S |
| | | 4-speed manual | $188 (GTO) | $275 | - | $231 |
| | 325 | Automatic | $199 (GTO) | $275 | - | $231 |
| 389 CID Tri-Power, 3 × 2-bbl., V8 | 338/360 | 3-speed HD man. | $116 (GTO) | $174 | - | $134 |
| | | 4-speed manual | $304 (GTO) | $405 | - | $365 |
| | | Automatic | $315 (GTO) | $405 | - | $365 |
| 421 CID, 4-bbl., V8 | 338 | 3-speed HD man. | - | $174 | S | $108 |
| | | 4-speed manual | - | $405 | $231 | $339 |
| | | Turbo Hydra-matic | - | $405 | $231 | $339 |
| 421 CID Tri-Power, 3 × 2-bbl., V8 | 356 | 3-speed HD man. | - | $307 | $133 | $241 |
| | | 4-speed manual | - | $538 | $364 | $472 |
| | | Turbo Hydra-matic | - | $538 | $364 | $472 |
| 421 CID Tri-Power H.O., 8 3 × 2-bbl., V | 376 | 3-speed HD man. | - | $410 | $236 | $344 |
| | | 4-speed manual | - | $641 | $467 | $575 |
| | | Turbo Hydra-matic | - | $641 | $467 | $575 |

*Ratings vary with model and transmission attachment.*

**1965**

## Major Options

| | Tempest/ LeMans | Catalina | Star Chief | Bonneville | Grand Prix |
|---|---|---|---|---|---|
| Air conditioning (V8 only) | $343 | $430 | $430 | $430 | $430 |
| Soft Ray tinted glass | $37 | $43 | $43 | $43 | $43 |
| Tilt steering wheel | $42 | $45 | $45 | $45 | $45 |
| Power steering— variable-ratio | $95 | $97 | $97 | $97 | $97 |
| Power brakes | $43 | $43 | $43 | $43 | $43 |
| Power drivers seat/ bench seat | $71 | $97 | $97 | $97 | $97 |
| Power windows | $102 | $106 | $106 | $106 | $106 |
| AM radio — manual | $61 | $89 | $89 | $89 | $89 |
| AM/FM radio — manual | $137 | $151 | $151 | $151 | $151 |
| Front seat console | $ | $108 | - | $108 | S |
| Front bucket seats | $ | $105 | - | $105 | S |
| White stripe tires (base size — average) | $35 | $40 | $40 | $40 | $40 |
| Aluminum (8-lug) hubs and drums | - | $138 | $138 | $120 | $120 |
| GTO performance package | $355 | - | - | - | - |
| Ventura Custom interior package | - | $118 | - | - | - |
| Brougham package | - | - | - | $161 | - |
| 2 + 2 performance package | - | $397–$419 | - | - | - |

Options common to most models. (- = Not Available, S = Standard equipment.) Items may be standard equipment, optional at different pricing, or unavailable on certain models. This chart is only a guide.

## Paint Colors

| | Code |
|---|---|
| Starlight Black | A |
| Blue Charcoal Metallic | B |
| Cameo Ivory | C |
| Fontaine Blue Metallic | D |
| Nightwatch Blue Metallic | E |
| Palmetto Green Metallic | H |
| Reef Turquoise Metallic | K |
| Teal Turquoise Metallic | L |
| Burgundy Red Metallic | N |
| Iris Mist Metallic | P |
| Montero Red | R |
| Capri Gold Metallic | T |
| Mission Beige | V |
| Bluemist Slate Metallic | W |
| Mayfair Maize | Y |
| Tiger Gold Metallic | No code |

# Tempest & LeMans

*"If ever a car made the low-priced cars look to their laurels, this is it."*

**Nameplate year of origin:** 1961 (Tempest); 1961 (LeMans, as a Tempest sub-series).

**Current bodystyle lifespan:** 1964 through 1965.

**Predecessor to this model:** Tempest/LeMans (1961 to 1963).

**Replacement for this model:** Tempest/LeMans/GTO (1966 to 1967).

**Percentage of division's sales volume:** 38.32%.

**Corporate siblings:** Chevrolet Chevelle, Oldsmobile F-85/Cutlass, and Buick Special/Skylark.

**Primary competition:** Ford Fairlane, Mercury Comet, and Dodge Coronet.

**Notable changes:** Major front and rear end restyling.

**Major standard equipment:** Cloth and vinyl front bench seat, front door armrests, dual sun visors and 6.95 × 14 BSW tires. Custom adds: All-vinyl front bench seats, full carpeting, rear armrests and rocker panel moldings. LeMans adds: Cloth and vinyl or all-vinyl LeMans interior trim, padded assist bar on dash, carpet on lower door panels and front fender louvers. GTO option adds: All-vinyl bucket seats, floor shifter, dual exhausts, custom pinstriping, 389 CID V8 with engine dress-up kit, heavy duty suspension and 7.75 × 14 red-line tires.

## Measurements

|  | Cars | Wagons |
|---|---|---|
| Wheelbase | 115.0" | 115.0" |
| Length | 206.1" | 204.4" |
| Width | 73.1" | 73.1" |
| Height | 54.0" | 55.2" |
| Legroom — front | 41.8" | 41.7" |
| Legroom — rear | 35.8" | 35.8" |
| Headroom — front | 38.1" | 37.7" |
| Headroom — rear | 37.2" | 38.3" |
| Cargo capacity (cu. ft.) | 30.1 | 86.4 |
| Fuel capacity (gals.) | 21.5 | 21.5 |

## Models Available

| | Style No. | Base MSRP | Change from LY | Shipping Wt. (lbs.) | Production | Change from LY |
|---|---|---|---|---|---|---|
| Tempest 2-Door Sports Coupe | 23327 | $2,260 | +0.04% | 2930 | 18,198 | -16.39% |
| Tempest 4-Door Sedan | 23369 | $2,313 | 0.00% | 2975 | 15,705 | -19.16% |
| Tempest 4-Door, 2-Seat Wagon | 23335 | $2,605 | 0.00% | 3220 | 5,622 | -17.73% |
| Tempest Custom 2-Dr. Sports Cpe. | 23527 | $2,346 | +0.04% | 2975 | 18,367 | -28.90% |
| Tempest Custom 2-Door Hardtop | 23537 | $2,411 | NEW | 2975 | 21,906 | NEW |
| Tempest Custom 2-Door Conv. | 23567 | $2,641 | 0.00% | 3080 | 8,346 | +4.49% |
| Tempest Custom 4-Door Sedan | 23569 | $2,400 | +0.04% | 2980 | 25,242 | -15.71% |
| Tempest Custom Safari 4-Dr. Wgn. | 23535 | $2,691 | 0.00% | 3215 | 10,792 | +0.90% |
| Tempest LeMans 2-Door Sp. Cpe. | 23727 | $2,491 | 0.00% | 3020 | 27,200 | -29.72% |
| Tempest LeMans 2-Door HT | 23737 | $2,556 | 0.00% | 3030 | 116,270 | +133.79% |
| Tempest LeMans 2-Door Conv. | 23767 | $2,797 | +0.04% | 3115 | 25,208 | +4.58% |
| Tempest LeMans 4-Door Sdn. | 23769 | $2,551 | NEW | 3020 | 14,227 | NEW |
| TOTALS | *Avg. price* | $2,505 | -0.19% | *Production* | 307,083 | +30.66% |

# Catalina

*"You say you want a quick and agile car? Handsome. But practical. You must mean a Catalina."*

**Nameplate year of origin:** 1950 on hardtop models, 1959 as series.

**Current bodystyle lifespan:** 1965 through 1966.

**Predecessor to this model:** Catalina (1961 to 1964).

**Replacement for this model:** Catalina (1967 to 1968).

**Percentage of division's sales volume:** 33.82%.

**Corporate siblings:** Chevrolet Biscayne/BelAir/Impala/Caprice, Oldsmobile 88, Buick LeSabre/Wildcat.

**Primary competition:** Mercury Monterey and Dodge Polara.

## Measurements

|  | Cars | Wagons |
|---|---|---|
| Wheelbase | 121.0" | 121.0" |
| Length | 214.6" | 217.9" |
| Width | 79.6" | 79.6" |
| Height | 55.2" | 56.0" |
| Legroom — front | 42.7" | 42.8" |

| | Cars | Wagons |
|---|---|---|
| Legroom — rear | 38.3" | 37.2" |
| Headroom — front | 38.4" | 38.6" |
| Headroom — rear | 37.7" | 39.0" |
| Cargo capacity (cu. ft.) | 31.3 | 101.2 |
| Fuel capacity (gals.) | 26.5 | 24.0 |

**Notable changes:** Completely redesigned.
**Major standard equipment:** Cloth and vinyl front bench seat (all-vinyl on convertible and wagons), full carpeting, electric windshield wipers, and 8.25 × 14 BSW tires (8.55 × 14 BSW tires on Safari). Ventura Custom option adds: All-vinyl upholstery with specific trim. 2 + 2 option adds: 421 CID V8 engine w/dress-up kit, all-vinyl bucket seats, vertical front fender louvers, heavy duty handling package, and Hurst Shifter.

## Models Available

| | Style No. | Base MSRP | Change from LY | Shipping Wt. (lbs.) | Production | Change from LY |
|---|---|---|---|---|---|---|
| Catalina 2-Door Sedan | 25211 | $2,734 | -0.04% | 3695 | 9,526 | -23.67% |
| Catalina 2-Door Hardtop | 25237 | $2,868 | -0.03% | 3750 | 92,009 | +23.02% |
| Catalina 2-Door Convertible | 25267 | $3,196 | +0.47% | 3815 | 18,347 | -1.85% |
| Catalina 4-Door Sedan | 25269 | $2,805 | -0.04% | 3750 | 78,853 | -6.64% |
| Catalina 4-Door Vista Hardtop | 25239 | $2,945 | 0.00% | 3855 | 34,814 | +2.85% |
| Catalina Safari 4-Dr., 2-S. Wagon | 25235 | $3,202 | -0.03% | 4165 | 22,399 | +10.04% |
| Catalina Safari 4-Dr., 3-S. Wagon | 25245 | $3,309 | -0.06% | 4210 | 15,110 | +14.99% |
| TOTALS | Avg. price | $3,008 | +0.03% | Production | 271,058 | +5.16% |

# Star Chief

*"Though it's altogether new this year,
Star Chief doesn't forget its Pontiac tradition."*

**Nameplate year of origin:** 1954.
**Current bodystyle lifespan:** 1965 through 1966.
**Predecessor to this model:** Star Chief (1961 to 1964).
**Replacement for this model:** Executive (1967 to 1968).
**Percentage of division's sales volume:** 3.91%.
**Corporate siblings:** Chevrolet Biscayne/BelAir/Impala/Caprice, Oldsmobile 88, Buick LeSabre/Wildcat.
**Primary competition:** Mercury Montclair and Dodge Custom 880.
**Notable changes:** Completely redesigned.
**Major standard equipment:** Cloth and vinyl bench seat, full carpeting, perforated vinyl headliner, electric clock, full length lower body molding, full wheel covers and 8.25 × 14 BSW tires.

## Measurements

| | |
|---|---|
| Wheelbase | 124.0" |
| Length | 221.7" |
| Width | 79.6" |
| Height | 55.2" |
| Legroom — front | 42.8" |
| Legroom — rear | 38.1" |
| Headroom — front | 38.4" |
| Headroom — rear | 37.7" |
| Cargo capacity (cu. ft.) | 34.5 |
| Fuel capacity (gals.) | 26.5 |

## Models Available

| | Style No. | Base MSRP | Change from LY | Shipping Wt. (lbs.) | Production | Change from LY |
|---|---|---|---|---|---|---|
| Star Chief 4-Door Sedan | 25669 | $3,106 | -0.03% | 3860 | 22,183 | -16.14% |
| Star Chief 4-Door Hardtop | 25639 | $3,238 | -0.03% | 3925 | 9,132 | -18.46% |
| TOTALS | Avg. price | $3,172 | -0.03% | Production | 31,315 | -16.83% |

1965

# Bonneville

*"Maybe the year of the Quick Wide-Tracks is your
year for moving up to Bonneville."*

**Nameplate year of origin:** 1957.
**Current bodystyle lifespan:** 1965 through 1966.
**Predecessor to this model:** Bonneville (1961 to 1964).
**Replacement for this model:** Bonneville (1967 to 1968).
**Percentage of division's sales volume:** 16.72%.
**Corporate siblings:** Chevrolet Biscayne/BelAir/Impala/Caprice, Oldsmobile
    88, Buick LeSabre/Wildcat.
**Primary competition:** Mercury Park Lane and Dodge Custom 880.
**Notable changes:** Completely restyled.
**Major standard equipment:** Vinyl or cloth and vinyl front bench seat
    (leather and vinyl in convertible), full carpeting, walnut instrument panel
    trim, electric clock, courtesy lights, padded assist grip, dual-speed electric
    windshield wipers, deluxe wheel covers and 8.25 × 14 BSW tires. Safari
    adds: 8.55 × 14 BSW tires. Brougham option adds: Pontchartrain pattern
    cloth and Plaza gabardine upholstery, special interior trim with fold down
    center armrests, padded Cordova top and exterior name badges.

## Measurements

|                        | Cars    | Wagon   |
| ---------------------- | ------- | ------- |
| Wheelbase              | 124.0"  | 121.0"  |
| Length                 | 221.7"  | 217.9"  |
| Width                  | 79.6"   | 79.6"   |
| Height                 | 54.3"   | 56.0"   |
| Legroom — front        | 42.4"   | 42.4"   |
| Legroom — rear         | 37.6"   | 36.9"   |
| Headroom — front       | 37.8"   | 38.5"   |
| Headroom — rear        | 37.2"   | 39.0"   |
| Cargo capacity (cu. ft.) | 34.5  | 100.3   |
| Fuel capacity (gals.)  | 26.5    | 24.0    |

## Models Available

|                                    | Style No. | Base MSRP | Change from LY | Shipping Wt. (lbs.) | Production | Change from LY |
| ---------------------------------- | --------- | --------- | -------------- | ------------------- | ---------- | -------------- |
| Bonneville 2-Door Hardtop          | 26237     | $3,357    | -0.03%         | 3890                | 44,030     | +26.64%        |
| Bonneville 2-Door Convertible      | 26267     | $3,594    | +0.45%         | 3950                | 21,050     | -4.39%         |
| Bonneville 4-Door Hardtop          | 26239     | $3,433    | 0.00%          | 3990                | 62,480     | +8.42%         |
| Bonneville Safari 4-Dr., 2-S. Wgn. | 26235     | $3,632    | -0.03%         | 4310                | 6,460      | +10.54%        |
| TOTALS                             | Avg. price | $3,504   | +0.09%         | Production          | 134,020    | +11.44%        |

# Grand Prix

*"Where do we start to tell you what's new
on the beautifully all-new Grand Prix for '65?"*

**Nameplate year of origin:** 1962.
**Current bodystyle lifespan:** 1965 through 1966.
**Predecessor to this model:** Grand Prix (1962 to 1964).
**Replacement for this model:** Grand Prix (1967 to 1968).
**Percentage of division's sales volume:** 7.22%.
**Corporate siblings:** Oldsmobile Starfire.
**Primary competition:** Chrysler 300, Dodge Monaco, and Mercury S-55.
**Notable changes:** Completely restyled.
**Major standard equipment:** All-vinyl or cloth and vinyl bucket seat or bench
    seat, full carpeting, padded instrument panel, padded assist bar, additional ac-
    coustical insulation, deluxe wheel covers and 8.25 × 14 BSW tires.

## Measurements

|                          |         |
| ------------------------ | ------- |
| Wheelbase                | 121.0"  |
| Length                   | 214.6"  |
| Width                    | 79.6"   |
| Height                   | 53.9"   |
| Legroom — front          | 42.6"   |
| Legroom — rear           | 34.9"   |
| Headroom — front         | 38.0"   |
| Headroom — rear          | 37.2"   |
| Cargo capacity (cu. ft.) | 33.8    |
| Fuel capacity (gals.)    | 26.5    |

## Models Available

| | Style No. | Base MSRP | Change from LY | Shipping Wt. (lbs.) | Production | Change from LY |
|---|---|---|---|---|---|---|
| Grand Prix 2-Door Hardtop | 26657 | $3,498 | -0.03% | 3940 | 57,881 | -9.29% |
| TOTALS | | *Avg. price* $3,498 | -0.03% | | *Production* 57,881 | -9.29% |

# RAMBLER

*"The SENSIBLE SPECTACULARS by Rambler! Dedicated to Excellence."*

For 1965, newly restyled Classic and Ambassador lines were introduced. Still offering unit-body construction and the same basic powertrains, the exterior sheetmetal was totally new. There were enough visual differences that these cars did appear to be all-new. With Detroit automobiles, appearance will sell cars—and AMC did just that. Also this year, a move was made to further distinguish the Classic and Ambassador lines from each other, by moving the Ambassador up to the full-size market. This was accomplished by stretching the wheelbase of the new Ambassador by 4 inches and giving it a totally unique front-end design. The new front end featured dual stacked headlights, bowing to the trend popularized by Pontiac in 1963. In successive years, the Ambassador would add many standard features to its equipment list, until it ultimately was competing in a market well above Ford and Chevrolet.

Following the introduction of the new Classic and Ambassador, a sporty fastback model, the Marlin, was introduced. Based on the Classic platform, the Marlin was given a roofline similar to the 1964 Tarpoon American based show car. Although it was bigger than the new Mustang and Barracuda fastbacks, they were obviously the originally intended competitive targets. What AMC hoped to capitalize on was the larger Marlin's spaciousness and possible 6-passenger seating. Unfortunately, they failed to realize that people buying a sporty car like the Marlin were not concerned with roominess as much as performance. AMC would eventually correct that problem with the 1968 Javelin, but by then it was too little, too late.

Ambassador 990 2-Door Convertible

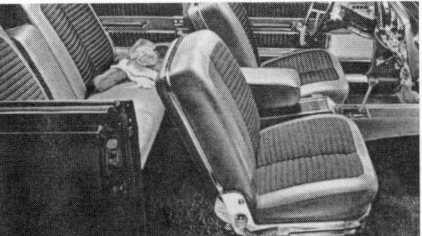

Ambassador 990-H Interior

American 440-H 2-Door Hardtop

Marlin 2-Door Hardtop

Classic 770 4-Door Sedan

**Model year production:** 391,372, up 0.70% over 1964.
**Domestic market share:** 4.42% (9th place).
**Base price range:** $1,979 to $3,063.
**Industry average base price:** $3,017.
**Rambler average base price:** $2,421.
**Introduction date:** October 7, 1964. The Marlin followed later in the model year.
**Assembly plants:** Kenosha, Wisconsin (K), and Brampton, Ontario, Canada (B).
**Data plate identification:** Seven or eight digit code read as follows: First digit designates series as follows: American with 196 CID 6-cyl. = P; American with 232 CID 6-cyl. = W; Classic with 199 CID 6-cyl. = J; Classic with 232 CID 6-cyl. = L; Classic with 287 CID V8 = Z; Classic with 327 CID V8 = U; Marlin with 232 CID 6-cyl. = 2; Marlin with 287 CID V8 = 3; Marlin with 327 CID V8 = 4; Ambassador with 232 CID 6-cyl. = S; Ambassador with 287 CID V8 = E; Ambassador with 327 CID V8 = H. Export cars added a "K" after the letter. Letters followed by serial numbers starting at 100001 (except Classic 232 Six start at 1500001, and Classic V8's which started at 275001). Example: J-100001 is a 1965 Rambler Classic 199 Six built in Kenosha, WI, serial number 100001.

## Powertrains

| Engine | Gross HP | Engine Code | Transmission Availability | Tran. Code | Rambler American | Rambler Classic | Marlin | Ambsdr. |
|---|---|---|---|---|---|---|---|---|
| 195.6 CID, 1-bbl., 6-cyl. | 90 | A | 3-speed manual, col. | S | S (ex. 440) | - | - | - |
| | | | 3-speed w/Overdrive | O | $109 | - | - | - |
| | | | Shift-Command Automatic — col./flr. | A/C | $187 | - | - | - |
| 195.6 CID, 1-bbl., 6-cyl. | 125 | A | 3-speed manual, col. | S | $38 | - | - | - |
| | | | 3-speed w/Overdrive | O | $147 | - | - | - |
| | | | Shift-Command Automatic — col./flr. | A/C | $225 | - | - | - |
| 199 CID, 1-bbl., 6-cyl. | 128 | A | 3-speed manual, col. | S | - | S (550) | - | - |
| | | | 3-speed w/Overdrive | O | - | $109 | - | - |
| | | | Shift-Command Automatic — col./flr. | A/C | - | $187 | - | - |
| 232 CID, 1-bbl., 6-cyl. | 145 | E/F/V | 3-speed manual | S | S (440) | S (660/770) | S | S |
| | | | 3-speed w/Overdrive | O | - | $109 | $109 | $109 |
| | | | Shift-Command Automatic — col./flr. | A/C | - | $187 | $187 | $187 |
| 232 CID, 2-bbl., 6-cyl. | 155 | B/G/S/M | 3-speed manual | S | $49 (440)/ $83 (220/330) | $12 | $12 | $12 |
| | | | Shift-Command Automatic — col./flr. | A/C | $238 | $199 | $199 | $199 |
| 287 CID, 2-bbl., V8 | 198 | H/T/N | 3-speed manual Shift-Command | S | - | $122 (550) | - | - |
| | | | Automatic — col./flr. | A/C | - | $293 (550) | - | - |
| 327 CID, 2-bbl., V8 | 250 | J/W/P | 3-speed manual Shift-Command | S | - | $138 (660/770) | $138 | - |
| | | | Automatic — col./flr. | A/C | - | $325 (660/770) | $325 | - |
| 327 CID, 4-bbl., V8 | 270 | K/U/Q | 3-speed manual Shift-Command | S | - | $241 (660/770) | $241 | $171 |
| | | | Automatic — col./flr. | A/C | - | $428 (660/770) | $428 | $358 |

## Major Options

| | American | Classic | Marlin | Ambassador |
|---|---|---|---|---|
| Air conditioning | $296 | $312 | $312 | $321 |
| Tinted glass | $34 | $42 | $37 | $42 |
| Power steering | $86 | $86 | $86 | $86 |
| Power brakes | $42 | $42 | S | $42 |
| AM radio | $49 | $58 | $58 | $58 |

## Paint Colors

| | Code |
|---|---|
| Classic Black | P1A |
| Antigua Red | P3A |
| Mystic Gold Metallic | P4A |
| Legion Light Blue | P5A |
| Viscount Med. Blue Met. | P6A |

| | American | Classic | Marlin | Ambassador |
|---|---|---|---|---|
| AM/FM radio | - | $ | $ | $ |
| Bucket seats | $ | $ | $ | $ |
| Custom wheel covers | $ | $ | $ | $ |
| Station Wagon third seat | - | $85 | - | $85 |

Options common to most models. (- = Not Available; S = Standard equipment.) Items may be standard equipment, optional at different pricing, or unavailable on certain models. This chart is only a guide.

| | Code |
|---|---|
| Seaside Light Aqua | P7A |
| Marina Medium Aqua Met. | P8A |
| Atlantis Dark Aqua Met. | P9A |
| Montego Light Rose | P10A |
| Barcelona Med. Taupe Met. | P11A |
| Corral Cordovan Metallic | P12A |
| Solar Yellow | P13A |
| Marlin Silver Metallic | P14A |
| Woodwide Light Green Met. | P54A |
| Frost White | P72A |

*Two-tones: first number is body color, second number is roof/accent color.*

# American

## *"The compact economy king."*

**Nameplate year of origin:** 1958.
**Current bodystyle lifespan:** 1964 through 1969.
**Predecessor to this model:** Rambler American (1961 to 1963).
**Replacement for this model:** Hornet (1970 to 1977).
**Percentage of division's sales volume:** 28.84%.
**Corporate siblings:** None.
**Primary competition:** Chevrolet Chevy II, Dodge Dart, Ford Falcon, and Plymouth Valiant.
**Notable changes:** Trim and detail changes.
**Major standard equipment:** Cloth and vinyl foam cushion front bench seat, front arm rests and ash trays, dual sun visors, black rubber floor mats, black rubber cargo mat on wagons, and 6.45 × 14 BSW tires. 330 adds: Rear door armrests, door-activated dome lights, chrome horn ring, color-keyed carpeting, and chrome luggage rack (wagons). 440 adds: Dual-note horn, deluxe steering wheel, vinyl-pleated upholstery with deluxe trim level, padded instrument panel, glove box lock, and wheel covers. 440-H adds: All-vinyl bucket seats, floor console, floor shift, special trim and identification.

## Measurements

| | |
|---|---|
| Wheelbase | 106.0" |
| Length | 177.2" |
| Width | 68.6" |
| Height | 53.4" |
| Legroom — front | 41.0" |
| Legroom — rear | 36.5" |
| Headroom — front | 38.8" |
| Headroom — rear | 37.0" |
| Luggage cap. (cu. ft.) | NA |
| Fuel capacity (gals.) | 16.0 |

**1965**

## Models Available

| | Style No. | Base MSRP | Change from LY | Shipping Wt. (lbs.) | Production | Change from LY |
|---|---|---|---|---|---|---|
| American 220 2-Door Sedan | 6506 | $1,942 | +1.84% | 2492 | 26,409 | -19.28% |
| American 220 4-Door Sedan | 6505 | $1,997 | +1.68% | 2518 | 13,700 | -24.83% |
| American 220 4-Door Wagon | 6508 | $2,268 | +1.25% | 2684 | 5,224 | -35.20% |
| American 330 2-Door Sedan | 6506-2 | $2,033 | +1.65% | 2490 | 9,065 | -40.25% |
| American 330 4-Door Sedan | 6505-2 | $2,088 | +1.51% | 2522 | 15,148 | -21.83% |
| American 330 4-Door Wagon | 6508-2 | $2,350 | +1.12% | 2682 | 12,313 | -40.19% |
| American 440 2-Door Hardtop | 6509-5 | $2,163 | +1.41% | 2596 | 13,785 | -29.29% |
| American 440 2-Door Convertible | 6507-5 | $2,371 | +1.07% | 2747 | 3,882 | -56.42% |
| American 440 4-Door Sedan | 6505-5 | $2,179 | +1.35% | 2580 | 5,194 | -21.18% |
| American 440-H 2-Door Hardtop | 6509-7 | $2,282 | -0.44% | 2622 | 8,164 | -43.80% |
| TOTALS | *Avg. price* | $2,167 | +1.30% | | *Production* 112,883 | -31.10% |

# Classic

*"New intermediate-size Rambler."*

**Nameplate year of origin:** 1957 (Nash Rambler model).
**Current bodystyle lifespan:** 1963 through 1966 (restyled in 1965).
**Predecessor to this model:** Rambler Classic (1957 to 1962).
**Replacement for this model:** Rebel (1967 to 1970).
**Percentage of division's sales volume:** 52.13%.
**Corporate siblings:** Ambassador (shared components from the cowl back) and Marlin (shared body components).
**Primary competition:** Chevrolet Chevelle, Dodge Coronet, Ford Fairlane, Plymouth Belvedere, and Studebaker Daytona.
**Notable changes:** Completely restyled.
**Major standard equipment:** Cloth and vinyl front foam cushion bench seat, front arm rests and ash trays, dual sun visors, black rubber cargo mat (wagons), chrome luggage rack (wagons) and 6.95 × 14 BSW tires. 660 adds: Rear door armrests and ash trays, door-activated dome lights, and electric clock. 770 adds: Additional chrome exterior trim and deluxe interior trim level. 770-H adds: All-vinyl bucket seats, floor shift, and special trim and identification.

## Measurements

| | Cars | Wagons |
|---|---|---|
| Wheelbase | 112.0" | 112.0" |
| Length | 195.0" | 193.0" |
| Width | 74.5" | 74.5" |
| Height | 54.4" | 54.8" |
| Legroom — front | 41.0" | 41.0" |
| Legroom — rear | 37.6" | 37.6" |
| Headroom — front | 38.8" | 38.8" |
| Headroom — rear | 37.0" | 37.0" |
| Luggage cap. (cu. ft.) | NA | NA |
| Fuel capacity (gals.) | 19.0 | 19.0 |

## Models Available

| | Style No. | Base MSRP | Change from LY | Shipping Wt. (lbs.) | Production | Change from LY |
|---|---|---|---|---|---|---|
| Classic 550 2-Door Sedan | 6516-0 | $2,101 | +1.69% | 2803 | 7,082 | +1.19% |
| Classic 550 4-Door Sedan | 6515-0 | $2,150 | +1.61% | 2827 | 30,869 | +28.25% |
| Classic 550 4-Door Wagon | 6518-0 | $2,473 | +1.10% | 2974 | 13,759 | -10.44% |
| Classic 660 2-Door Sedan | 6516-2 | $2,289 | +3.76% | 2858 | 4,561 | -5.94% |
| Classic 660 4-Door Sedan | 6515-2 | $2,287 | +1.37% | 2882 | 50,638 | +3.43% |
| Classic 660 4-Door Wagon | 6518-2 | $2,573 | +0.98% | 3031 | 32,444 | -13.66% |
| Classic 770 2-Door Hardtop | 6519-5 | $2,389 | -0.33% | 2929 | 14,778 | -29.18% |
| Classic 770 2-Door Convertible | 6517-5 | $2,644 | NEW | 3035 | 4,953 | NEW |
| Classic 770 4-Door Sedan | 6515-5 | $2,389 | +1.23% | 2895 | 23,603 | -0.78% |
| Classic 770 4-Door Wagon | 6518-5 | $2,674 | +0.87% | 3046 | 15,623 | -19.29% |
| Classic 770-H 2-Door Hardtop | 6519-7 | $2,499 | -0.40% | 2955 | 5,706 | +126.43% |
| TOTALS | | Avg. price $2,406 | +2.34% | | Production 204,016 | -1.10% |

# Marlin

*"The swinging new man-size sports-fastback by Rambler."*

**Nameplate year of origin:** 1965.
**Current bodystyle lifespan:** 1965 through 1967.
**Predecessor to this model:** None.
**Replacement for this model:** Javelin (1968 to 1970).
**Percentage of division's sales volume:** 2.64%.
**Corporate siblings:** Classic and Ambassador (Shared body components with unique roofline).
**Primary competition:** Plymouth Barracuda and Ford Mustang (although these were smaller cars).
**Notable changes:** New model for 1965.
**Major standard equipment:** Cloth and vinyl with front bench seat individually adjustable reclining backs, full carpeting, front and rear arm rests and ash trays, padded instrument panel, courtesy lights, power front disc brakes, full wheel covers and 7.35 × 14 BSW tires.

## Measurements

| | |
|---|---|
| Wheelbase | 112.0" |
| Length | 195.0" |
| Width | 74.5" |
| Height | 54.2" |
| Legroom — front | 41.0" |
| Legroom — rear | 37.6" |
| Headroom — front | 38.8" |
| Headroom — rear | 36.0" |
| Luggage cap. (cu. ft.) | 11.7 |
| Fuel capacity (gals.) | 19.0 |

## Models Available

| | Style No. | Base MSRP | Change from LY | Shipping Wt. (lbs.) | Production | Change from LY |
|---|---|---|---|---|---|---|
| Marlin 2-Door Hardtop | 6559-7 | $2,841 | NEW | 3100 | 10,327 | NEW |
| TOTALS | Avg. price | $2,841 | NEW | Production | 10,327 | NEW |

# Ambassador

*"Largest, finest new Rambler."*

**Nameplate year of origin:** 1933 (from top-of-the-line Nash).
**Current bodystyle lifespan:** 1963 through 1966 (shared basic structure with Classic).
**Predecessor to this model:** Ambassador (1957 to 1962).
**Replacement for this model:** Ambassador (1967 to 1974).
**Percentage of division's sales volume:** 16.39%.
**Corporate siblings:** Classic (shared components from the cowl back).
**Primary competition:** Chevrolet BelAir/Impala/Caprice, Ford Custom/Galaxie, and Plymouth Fury.
**Notable changes:** Completely restyled.
**Major standard equipment:** Cloth and vinyl front bench seat, courtesy lights, electric clock, full carpeting, chrome luggage rack (wagons), padded instrument panel, full wheel covers, and 7.35 × 14 BSW tires. 990 adds: Additional interior and exterior trim. 990-H adds: All-vinyl bucket seats and floor console.

## Measurements

| | Cars | Wagons |
|---|---|---|
| Wheelbase | 116.0" | 116.0" |
| Length | 200.0" | 197.0" |
| Width | 74.5" | 74.5" |
| Height | 55.0" | 55.4" |
| Legroom — front | 41.0" | 41.0" |
| Legroom — rear | 37.6" | 37.6" |
| Headroom — front | 38.8" | 38.8" |
| Headroom — rear | 37.0" | 37.0" |
| Luggage cap. (cu. ft.) | NA | NA |
| Fuel capacity (gals.) | 19.0 | 19.0 |

## Models Available

| | Style No. | Base MSRP | Change from LY | Shipping Wt. (lbs.) | Production | Change from LY |
|---|---|---|---|---|---|---|
| Ambassador 880 2-Door Sedan | 6586-2 | $2,467 | NEW | 2967 | 1,301 | NEW |
| Ambassador 880 4-Door Sedan | 6585-2 | $2,519 | NEW | 3000 | 10,564 | NEW |
| Ambassador 880 4-Door Wagon | 6588-2 | $2,826 | NEW | 3122 | 3,812 | NEW |
| Ambassador 990 2-Door Hardtop | 6589-5 | $2,621 | -4.20% | 3048 | 5,034 | +14.23% |
| Ambassador 990 2-Door Convertible | 6587-5 | $2,901 | NEW | 3145 | 3,499 | NEW |
| Ambassador 990 4-Door Sedan | 6585-5 | $2,608 | -2.36% | 3031 | 24,852 | +152.90% |
| Ambassador 990 4-Door Wagon | 6588-5 | $2,916 | -2.31% | 3148 | 8,701 | +190.52% |
| Ambassador 990-H 2-Door HT | 6589-7 | $2,785 | -4.53% | 3078 | 6,382 | +335.93% |
| TOTALS | Avg. price | $2,705 | -4.32% | Production | 64,145 | +243.15% |

# STUDEBAKER

*"The common-sense car."*

As the end neared for Studebaker, the model line was considerably pared down this season. After moving car production moved to Canada during 1964, the GT Hawk and Avanti were dropped. Of the remaining Lark based models, the one-year-only Challenger line was dropped. Also discontinued were the convertible models, which had slowed to a mere trickle out of the factory. Styling changes were limited to new grilles and trim. The engine assembly plant in South Bend was closed, and all engines were sourced from General Motors of Canada this season. These new engines were based on Chevrolet designs, and were basically the same engines offered as the base 6-cylinder and V8 powerplants for the Chevy II.

Commander 2-Door Sedan and
Commander 4-Door Sedan

Cruiser 4-Door Sedan

Daytona 2-Door Sport Sedan

**Model year production:** 19,435, down 58.17% from 1964.
**Domestic market share:** 0.22% (13th place).
**Base price range:** $2,125 to $2,890.
**Industry average base price:** $3,017.
**Studebaker average base price:** $2,483.
**Introduction date:** October 1964.
**Assembly plants:** Hamilton, Ontario, Canada (C).

**Data plate identification (VIN):** Seven digit code read as follows: 1st digit C for Canadian plant; 1 for 6-cylinder or 5 for V8 engine; followed by Serial Number 10001 and up. Body style numbers are found on a separate plate on the vehicle. *Example:* C110001 is a 1965 Studebaker Six built in Hamilton, Canada, serial number 10001.

## Powertrains

| Engine | Gross HP | Transmission Availability | Cruiser & Commander | Daytona |
|---|---|---|---|---|
| 194 CID, 1-bbl., OHV 6-cyl. | 120 | 3-speed manual | S | - |
| | | 3-speed w/Overdrive | $110 | - |
| | | Flightomatic Automatic | $172 | - |
| 283 CID, 2-bbl., OHV V8 | 180 | 3-speed manual | $140 | S |
| | | 3-speed w/Overdrive | $250 | $110 |
| | | Flightomatic Automatic | $340 | $200 |

## Major Options

| | |
|---|---|
| Heater and defroster | $80 |
| Air conditioning | $278–$325 |
| Tinted glass — full | $32 |
| Power Steering (V8 only) | $77 |
| Power brakes | $45 |
| Electric clock | $15 |
| Windshield washers | $12 |
| AM pushbutton radio | $57 |
| White sidewall tires — standard size | $28–$48 |
| Wheel Covers | $16 |

Options common to most models. Items may be standard equipment, optional at different pricing, or unavailable on certain models. This chart is only a guide.

## Paint Colors

| | Code |
|---|---|
| Astra White | 0040 |
| Bermuda Brown Metallic | 0087 |
| Bordeaux Red | 0120 |
| Executive Blue Metallic | 0124 |
| Horizon Green Metallic | 0451 |
| Laguna Blue Metallic | 0463 |
| Sienna Red | 0715 |
| Turquoise | 0826 |
| Midnight Black | 0841 |
| Yukon Gold | 0899 |

# Commander

*"The Get-About, Gad-About World of the Commander ...
Hustle, Muscle ... common-sense price."*

**Nameplate year of origin:** 1927.
**Current bodystyle lifespan:** 1962 through 1966.
**Predecessor to this model:** Standard line (1963) and Lark (1962 to 1963).
**Replacement for this model:** None.
**Corporate siblings:** Cruiser and Daytona.
**Percentage of division's sales volume:** Unknown.
**Primary competition:** Rambler American, Chevrolet Chevy II, Dodge Dart, Ford Falcon, Plymouth Valiant.
**Notable changes:** Minor trim and detail changes.
**Major standard equipment:** Cloth and vinyl front bench seats, armrests, padded instrument panel, rubber floor mats, and 7.35 × 15 BSW tires. Wagonaire adds: All-vinyl front bench seat and sliding rear roof section.

## Measurements

| | 2-Door | 4-Door | Wagonaire |
|---|---|---|---|
| Wheelbase | 109.0" | 113.0" | 113.0" |
| Length | 190.0" | 194.0" | 193.0" |
| Width | 71.5" | 71.5" | 71.5" |
| Height | 57.5" | 57.5" | 58.8" |
| Legroom — front | 39.9" | 39.9" | 39.9" |
| Legroom — rear | 31.8" | 35.7" | 36.1" |
| Headroom — front | 39.0" | 39.0" | 40.0" |
| Headroom — rear | 38.0" | 38.0" | 36.9" |
| Luggage cap. (cu. ft.) | NA | NA | 93.0 |
| Fuel capacity (gals.) | 18.0 | 18.0 | 18.0 |

## Models Available

| | Style No. | Base MSRP | Change from LY | Shipping Wt. (lbs.) | Production | Change from LY |
|---|---|---|---|---|---|---|
| Commander 2-Door Sedan | SF4 | $2,125 | +3.01% | 2695 | 7,372 | -11.34% |
| Commander 4-Door Sedan | SY4 | $2,230 | +2.86% | 2815 | 10,239 | -62.48% |
| Commander 4-Door, 2-Seat Wagon | SP4 | $2,620 | +2.42% | 3265 | 1,824 | -64.67% |
| TOTALS | | Avg. price $2,325 | +2.76% | | Production 19,435 | -58.17% |

*Production is by body style and therefore includes Cruiser and Daytona models.

1965

# Cruiser & Daytona

*"The elegant world of the Cruiser and the lively world of the Daytona Sport Sedan."*

**Nameplate year of origin:** 1961 (Cruiser); 1962 (Daytona).
**Current bodystyle lifespan:** 1962 through 1966.
**Predecessor to this model:** Cruiser (1961).
**Replacement for this model:** None.
**Corporate siblings:** Commander and Challenger.
**Percentage of division's sales volume:** Unknown.
**Primary competition:** Rambler American, Chevrolet Chevy II, Dodge Dart, Ford Falcon, Plymouth Valiant.
**Notable changes:** Minor trim and detail changes.
**Major standard equipment:** All-vinyl front bucket seats with floor console, armrests, full carpeting, padded instrument panel, vinyl top, deluxe chrome trim, wheel covers, and 7.35 × 15 BSW tires. Wagonaire add : All-vinyl front bench seat, sliding rear roof section and fold-down tailgate step. Cruiser adds: Cloth and vinyl front bench seat with center armrests front and rear, electric clock, deluxe horn ring, ventilated rear side windows and electric windshield wipers with washers.

## Measurements

|  | Daytona | Cruiser | Wagonaire |
|---|---|---|---|
| Wheelbase | 109.0" | 113.0" | 113.0" |
| Length | 190.0" | 194.0" | 193.0" |
| Width | 71.5" | 71.5" | 71.5" |
| Height | 57.5" | 57.5" | 58.8" |
| Legroom — front | 39.9" | 39.9" | 39.9" |
| Legroom — rear | 31.8" | 35.7" | 36.1" |
| Headroom — front | 39.0" | 39.0" | 40.0" |
| Headroom — rear | 38.0" | 38.0" | 36.9" |
| Luggage cap. (cu. ft.) | NA | NA | 93.0 |
| Fuel capacity (gals.) | 18.0 | 18.0 | 18.0 |

## Models Available

|  | Style No. | Base MSRP | Change from LY | Shipping Wt. (lbs.) | Production | Change from LY |
|---|---|---|---|---|---|---|
| Daytona 2-Door Hardtop | VF8 | $2,565 | +4.65% | 2970 | * | * |
| Daytona 4-Door, 2-Seat Wagon | VP8 | $2,890 | +6.72% | 3505 | * | * |
| Cruiser 4-Door Sedan | SY9 | $2,470 | -5.11% | 2820 | * | * |
| TOTALS | | Avg. price $2,642 | +2.09% | | Production * | * |

*Production is by body style and therefore included with Commander models.*

# 1966

In 1966, you could choose to drive "The Tuned Car" (Buick), "America's Total Performance Cars" (Ford), "America's Most Distinguished Motorcars" (Lincoln), or you could "Let Yourself Go … Plymouth." Then again, you might have preferred to "Move ahead with Mercury in the Lincoln Continental tradition" or "Make your move up to Chrysler." However, as in many previous years, most people would go "The Chevrolet Way." These certainly were not the most memorable advertising slogans ever to come out of Detroit, but fortunately the cars were more memorable.

One of the most noteworthy events of 1966 was the passing of the Studebaker name from the automotive scene. The Studebaker Corporation had its beginnings in South Bend, Indiana, in 1852, as a horsedrawn vehicle producer. It would go on to become a major player in the new automotive industry after the turn of the century, but fell on hard times in the mid–1950s and by late 1963 would see its South Bend factory closed. Automobile production continued in Hamilton, Ontario, Canada, until the board of directors decided to close the plant in March 1966. The final Studebakers were distinguished from the 1965 models by their new grille with single headlights up front, and other minor trim changes.

With Studebaker fading away, American Motors would be the last surviving "independent" car manufacturer. For 1966, the Rambler American would receive the most changes. The American had new styling with a more "modern," squared look, compared to previous models. Also new were a 290 CID V8 engine and 4-speed manual transmission. The American 330 series was dropped for 1966. The next model up the size scale was the Rambler Classic, which featured revised grille and taillight styling. In this model line, the Classic 660 series was dropped. In a move intended to spur sales, the Marlin entered 1966 with a revised grille, had its base price cut $500 (accomplished by making some previously standard features optional for

'66), and no longer bore the Rambler name. These changes, however, did not help, and sales fell nearly 60 percent. The Ambassador line received only minor trim changes. Three new models were added to the AMC lineup, all with an eye towards the luxury/sport market. They were the Rambler American Rogue 2-door HT, the Rambler Classic Rebel 2-door HT, and the Ambassador DPL 2-door HT.

The General Motors passenger car divisions featured a restyling of many models. Among the most visible models were the relatively new mid-size lineup. All featured more rounded contours, new 4-door hardtop models in the top-line series, and distinctive rear window treatments on 2-door models. Buick's Skylark Gran Sport package was upgraded to series status (formerly an option package) with a 2-door coupe, 2-door sport coupe, and convertible models, all powered by a 325-hp, 401 CID 4-bbl. V8 engine. The Chevrolet Chevelle 300 2-door wagon was dropped. Oldsmobile's F-85 series offered the first in-line 6-cylinder engine in an Oldsmobile since 1950. The Pontiac Tempest line offered an all-new overhead cam 6-cylinder (230 CID) engine in all models except the GTO.

The popular Buick Sport Wagon and Oldsmobile Vista-Cruiser featured styling changes along the lines of the restyled intermediates. All of the full-size GM cars received minor styling revisions, fresh on the heels of 1965's complete redesign. At Buick Motor Division, the Wildcat Deluxe series was dropped and a convertible model was added to the Wildcat Custom series. New at Cadillac was the Fleetwood 60 Special Brougham model. New Cadillac standard features included variable-ratio steering, head rests and reclining seats. New optional features included carbon cloth heat pads in the front seat cushions and an AM/FM stereo system. Also at Cadillac, the Fleetwood 75 series received a major restyle to bring it up to date with the other Cadillac models. Full-size Chevrolets gained a new Caprice series. Formerly offered as the Caprice Custom option package on the Impala series, the new Caprice included a

## 1966 Model Year Production by Make

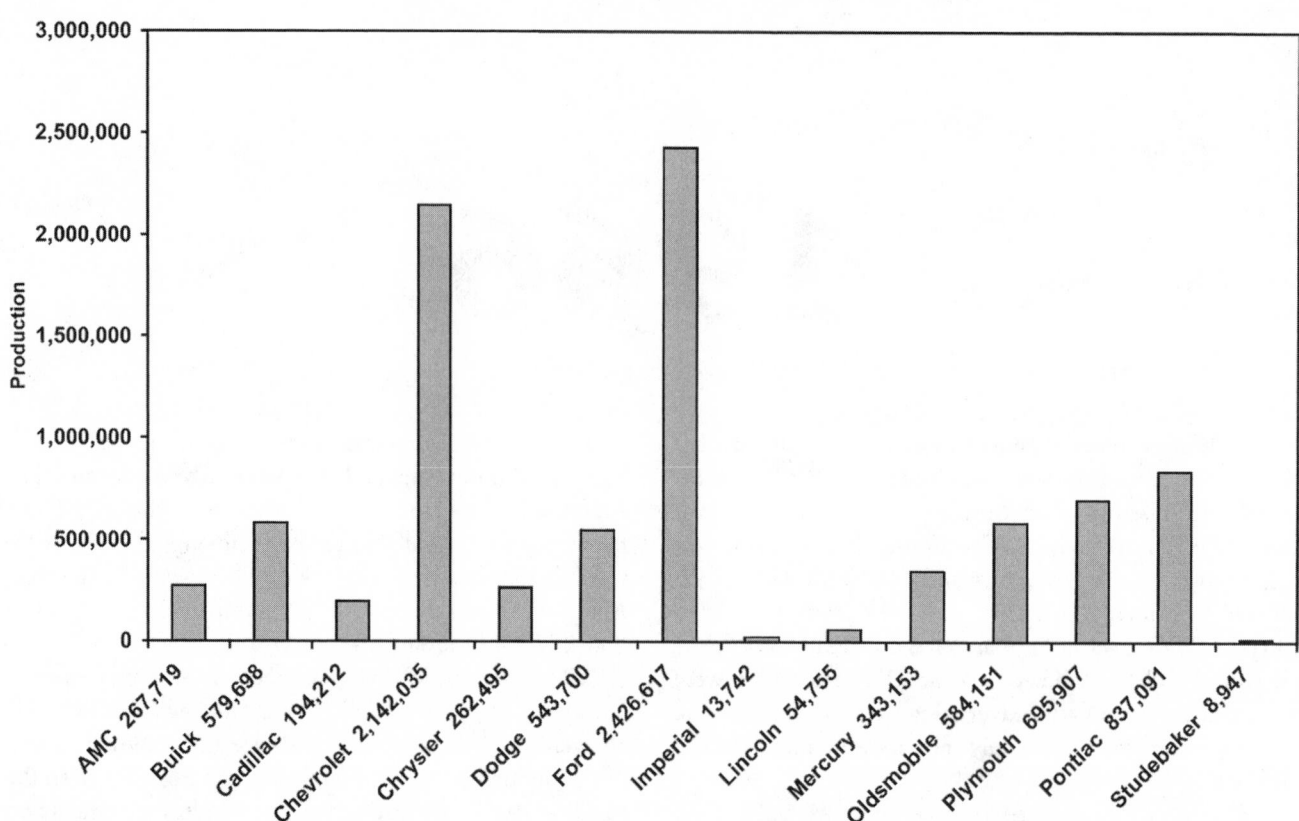

2-door Hardtop, 4-door Hardtop, and 6- and 9-passenger 4-door wagons. Also, the traditional round Chevy taillights were replaced by rectangular units. Changes at Oldsmobile included the dropping of the Jetstar 88 convertible, Starfire convertible and the Jetstar I series. The Delta 88 became a full-fledged series this year and gained a convertible model. At Pontiac the Catalina 2 + 2 became a separate series, and the Star Chief was christened the Star Chief Executive and added a 2-door HT model.

Other changes at GM abounded. The Buick Riviera was completely restyled with sleek new looks and featured GM's first use of ventless side windows in a modern car. Ventless side windows were also seen on the new Olds Toronado. The Toronado was an all-new front-wheel drive, personal/luxury 2-door. It was the first domestic front-wheel drive car in 30 years, and featured a long list of standard equipment and features. The combination of new engineering features and unique styling helped the Toronado win *Motor Trend* magazine's Car of the Year Award. Over 40,000 were sold in its first year. The Chevrolet Chevy II received new, clean, smooth styling and was much more modern in appearance than its predecessors. The Chevy Corvair featured a revised rear grille and taillights. Last and certainly not least, the Chevrolet Corvette sported a new eggcrate grille replacing the previous horizontal grille, and the side roof vents on coupe models were eliminated. Under

the hood, a new 427 CID V8 was offered in 390-hp (L39) or 425-hp (172) versions. All 427-equipped Corvettes featured a "Power Bulge" hood.

The General's light-duty truck lines, consisting of Chevrolet and GMC trucks, entered 1966 with relatively few changes. The Chevrolet El Camino, which featured styling changes seen in the mid-size Chevelle passenger cars, offered a Super Sport package with a 396 CID V8 engine. Otherwise only trim changes were seen on Chevrolet light-duty trucks, although the Chevy van did offer a new "pop-up" camper option. As could be expected, the GMC line closely resembled Chevrolet's. GMC models included the Handi-Van, Handi-Bus and a full-line of ½-, ¼-, and 1-ton pickups, panel delivery and Carryall Suburban models.

Like General Motors, the Chrysler Corporation's intermediate car line was completely restyled. However, instead of the smooth, rounded lines of GM's cars, the Dodge Coronet and Plymouth Belvedere had very squared-off lines in both the front and rear-end styling with sculpted lines down the side. The Coronet line added Deluxe 2- and 4-door sedans, Deluxe 4-door wagon and a 500 4-door sedan. Both the Coronet and Belvedere lines offered a street version of the 426 CID "Hemi" V8 with 425 horsepower. The real excitement at Chrysler came in the form of the new Dodge Charger. Based on the Coronet chassis, the Charger featured a slick-looking fastback roofline and a unique, full-length, front-to-rear floor console. Several V8 engines were available, from the 273 CID up to the 426 "Hemi." Smaller Chrysler Corporation offerings received new grilles for 1966, but were otherwise similar to previous models. The Valiant V200 2-door and convertible models were dropped. Also, as of 1966, the Barracuda was marketed as a separate series, even though it still had Valiant styling and running gear.

The large Chrysler lines were essentially carryover models with new grille and taillight treatments. The regular Chrysler line dropped the New Yorker Town & Country, leaving only the Newport Town & Country wagon. The Crown Imperial limousine did not appear for 1966. Dodge's full-size line saw the Monaco nameplate replace the Custom 880 series, and a new Monaco 500 badge replaced the 1965 Monaco series. Plymouth's Fury line offered a luxurious new VIP series in 2-door and 4-door hardtop models to counter the Chevrolet Caprice and Ford Galaxie 500 LTD.

The Dodge truck division of Chrysler Corporation offered the same models it had for 1965. There was no new styling and prices remained the same. Model offerings included the A-100 compact pickup, van and wagon models, and a full-line of D100, D200, D300 2-wheel-drive pickups and W100, W200, and W300 4 × 4 trucks.

Not to be outdone by General Motors or Chrysler, Ford Motor Company also fielded a newly restyled line of mid-size cars. The Ford Fairlane was quite sporty looking and backed up those looks with new Fairlane 500 XL and Fairlane 500 GT series, plus the first ever convertible models in the Fairlane 500, 500 XL, and 500 GT designations. Mercury's Comet line moved up-market, from compact to intermediate-sized, and shared styling features with the Fairlane. Nameplate changes in the Comet line involved the Comet Capri replacing the Comet 404, and a totally new Comet Cyclone GT series available in 2-door hardtop and convertible models. A Comet Cyclone GT convertible was selected as the official pace car for the 1966 Indianapolis 500 race.

The phenomenal success of the Ford Mustang continued for 1966 with the only changes being a new grille, redesigned side emblems and other assorted trim changes. Why change a good thing? An interesting variation of the Mustang was the Shelby-Mustang GT-350 built by Carroll Shelby. First offered in 1965, these specially modified Mustangs featured a 306-horsepower, 289 CID 4-bbl. V8 engine and 4-speed transmission and were offered in one body style, a 2-door fastback. However, for 1966, there were 936 built for Hertz Rental Car Company, designated GT-350H. Also, six convertibles were assembled for Carroll Shelby's friends and certain employees.

Ford's Falcon line was completely restyled for 1966. With the new look, the line returned to a more economy-minded approach to driving, and as a result all 2-door hardtop and convertible models were discontinued and the Sprint series was dropped. Also receiving a complete restyle, but marketed at the opposite extreme of the price scale, was the Lincoln Continental. It maintained the traditional Continental look, but it was 4 inches longer, and offered a new 2-door hardtop model. Along with the new looks came a new 340-horsepower, 462 CID V8 powerplant. Ford Motor Company's other luxury car offering, the Thunderbird, received minor styling changes giving it a new look, with a separate grille and bumper up front and full-width taillights at the rear. The Thunderbird was also available in a new 2-door Hardtop town coupe.

The full-size Ford and Mercury models looked similar to their 1965 counterparts, but actually had many styling updates. Ford offered a new Galaxie 500 7-Litre series in 2-door fastback and convertible models. They featured a 345-horsepower, 428 CID VS, automatic transmission, bucket seats, floor shift, dual exhaust and power disc brakes. Mercury returned the S-55 2-door hardtop and convertible to its model lineup after a two-year absence. Finally, the Montclair Breezeway sedan was replaced by a traditional 4-door sedan, although a Breezeway sedan was still available in Monterey and Park Lane trim levels.

The Ford truck division for 1966 fielded a brand new Bronco off-road vehicle. This vehicle offered a 170 CID 6-cylinder or 289 CID VS to power the boxy-looking, 152 inch long 4 × 4, that was available in roadster, sport utility, or wagon models. The Ranchero received some styling updates this year, in what was a transitional period for the formerly Falcon-based pickup. For 1966, the front end styling was similar to that of the new Falcons, but many of its other components were shared with the Fairlane. The Econoline series and the Falcon Club Wagon (passenger van) returned for the new year basically unchanged. Ford F-series pickups were also quite similar to preceding models, but did receive a new grille and trim changes.

Kaiser-Jeep Corporation offerings for 1966 included CJ-3, CJ-5, CJ-6 (DJ- for 2WD models), FC-150 and FC-170 (forward control), Wagoneer (J-100), and J-series pickups. A new 225 CID V6 powerplant was offered for CJ models. Styling for all models was similar to that of previous years.

At the low end of the production scale, the Avanti II continued with minimal changes. Although the Checker line saw no styling changes, the Chevrolet 327 CID VS engine appeared as a new option for 1966.

Nineteen sixty-six would mark the beginning of the end for convertible production in the United States. Actually, 1965 was a peak year and numerous models were offered during 1966, but they would quickly fade to a handful of choices by 1972. The chart below ranks the models from the most popular to the rarest offered in 1966.

## 1966 U.S. Convertible Production

| | | | | |
|---|---|---|---|---|
| Ford Mustang (3,190 w/Bench Seat) | 72,119 | | Buick LeSabre Custom | 4,994 |
| Chevrolet Impala | 38,000 | | Oldsmobile 98 | 4,568 |
| Ford Galaxie 500 | 27,454 | | Ford Fairlane 500 XL | 4,560 |
| Chevrolet Chevelle Malibu and SS | 27,000 | | Ford Fairlane 500 XL GT | 4,327 |
| Cadillac de Ville | 19,200 | | Plymouth Fury III | 2,690 |
| Chevrolet Corvette | 17,762 | | Mercury Park Lane (602 w/Buckets) | 2,546 |
| Pontiac Bonneville | 16,229 | | Plymouth Valiant Signet | 2,507 |
| Chevy Impala SS | 15,872 | | Plymouth Belvedere 11 | 2,502 |
| Pontiac Catalina | 14,837 | | Chrysler 300 | 2,500 |
| Pontiac Tempest LeMans | 13,080 | | Ford Galaxie 500 7-Litre | 2,368 |
| Pontiac Tempest LeMans GTO | 12,798 | | Cadillac Fleetwood Eldorado | 2,250 |
| Oldsmobile F85 Cutlass | 12,154 | | Mercury Comet Cyclone GT | 2,158 |
| Chevrolet Corvair Monza | 10,345 | | AMC Rambler American 440 | 2,092 |
| Ford Fairlane 500 | 9,299 | | Buick Skylark GS | 2,047 |
| Buick Electra 225 Custom | 7,175 | | AMC Rambler Classic 770 | 1,806 |
| Buick Skylark (6,129 w/V8 engine) | 6,737 | | AMC Ambassador 990 | 1,798 |
| Ford Galaxie 500 XL | 6,360 | | Mercury Comet Cyclone | 1,305 |
| Pontiac Tempest Custom | 5,557 | | Mercury S55 | 669 |
| Olds Dynamic 88 | 5,540 | | Imperial Crown | 514 |
| Ford Thunderbird | 5,049 | | Shelby-Mustang GT-350 | 6 |

*Dodge Dart 270, Dodge Dart GT, Dodge Coronet 440, Dodge Coronet 500, Dodge Polara, and Pontiac Catalina 2 + 2 convertible production figures are not available, but are estimated to be between 2,000 and 6,000 units each.*

# AMERICAN MOTORS

*"Where quality is built in, not added on."*

Nineteen sixty-six was a year of little styling change for American Motors. The only changes of note were made to the Rambler American line, which had been totally new in 1964. This year the front end received a more square leading edge on the hood and fender lines and slightly less "busy" side trim. Gone were the round headlight trim housings, replaced by a square housing. Following the successful restyle in 1965 of the Rambler Classic and Ambassador lines, there was no need to make an immediate styling change to any of the models. Most efforts were concentrated on the upcoming 1967 Rebel and Ambassador models. The mid-range Classic 660 line was discontinued for the new year. As was typical industry practice in the mid-sixties, most models were given new grilles and or exterior trim changes. Also, where needed interior trim would be upgraded or revised, just enough to distinguish a new model year. Changes to the Marlin fastback were similar to those seen on the Classic line. One exception was the removal of the name Rambler from the exterior of the Marlin. Rambler suggested "economy" more than "sporty," so

the name was dropped, much as it had been earlier from the "luxury" Ambassador line.

Powertrains for 1966 were not greatly changed, with one exception. The 290 CID V8 was introduced mid-year on the compact Rambler American line. The eventual replacement for the 287 CID V8, was a slightly more powerful, yet fuel-efficient design that would become a popular choice for many AMC buyers. The new 290 would be available across the line for 1967.

Other changes were not so readily seen, but would indicate the future for American Motors. As the reader may have noticed, up through 1965, this line of cars was listed under the Rambler make. A change began with the 1966 model year that would conclude with the 1970 models. That change was the phasing out of the Rambler nameplate and its replacement by the AMC name. Up until this time, American Motors marketed its cars as Ramblers "by American Motors." Beginning with 1966, the Ambassador and Marlin were marketed as AMC products, available from an "American Motors/Rambler" dealer. In 1968, the Rambler

Rebel would become the AMC Rebel. Finally, in 1969 the last Rambler American (which for 1969 lost its "American" suffix) would be sold. By 1970, all products would be designated AMC products.

Ambassador 990 2-Door Convertible

Ambassador 990 4-Door Sedan

Marlin 2-Door Hardtop

Rambler American Rogue 2-Door Hardtop

Rambler American 440 4-Door Wagon

Rambler Classic Rebel 2-Door Hardtop

Rambler Classic 770 4-Door Wagon

**1966**

**Model year production:** 267,719, down 31.59% from 1965.
**Domestic market share:** 2.99% (9th place) ranking.
**Base price range:** $2,017 to $2,968.
**Industry average base price:** $3,070.
**AMC average base price:** $2,454.
**Introduction date:** October 7, 1965.
**Assembly plants:** Kenosha, Wisconsin (K), and Brampton, Ontario, Canada (B).

**Data plate identification:** Thirteen digit code read as follows: A = American Motors; 6 = 1966; assembly plant code; transmission code (see chart); body style-series number (see last two digits of style number); engine code (see chart); 100001 and up for serial number. *Example:* A6KA97H100001 is a 1966, built in Kenosha, Shift-Command Automatic (column-shift), Rambler Classic Rebel 2-Door, 287 CID V8 2-bbl., serial number 100001.

## Powertrains

| Engine | Gross HP | Engine Code | Transmission Availability | Tran. Code | Rambler American | Rambler Classic | Marlin | Ambsdr. |
|---|---|---|---|---|---|---|---|---|
| 199 CID, 1-bbl., 6-cyl. | 128 | A | 3-speed manual, col. | S | S (base) | - | - | - |
| | | | 3-speed w/Overdrive | O | $109 | - | - | - |
| | | | Shift-Command Automatic — col./flr. | A/C | $187 | - | - | - |
| 232 CID, 1-bbl., 6-cyl. | 145 | E/F/V | 3-speed manual | S | $39 | S | S | - |
| | | | 3-speed w/Overdrive | O | $148 | $115 | $115 | - |
| | | | Shift-Command Automatic — col./flr. | A/C | $226 | $187 | $187 | - |
| 232 CID, 2-bbl., 6-cyl. | 155 | B/G/S/M | 3-speed manual | S | $51 | $12 | $12 | S |
| | | | Shift-Command Automatic — col./flr. | A/C | $238 | $199 | $199 | $187 |
| 287 CID, 2-bbl., V8 | 198 | H/T/N | 3-speed manual | S | - | $106 | $106 | $106 |
| | | | 4-speed manual | F | - | $290 | $290 | $290 |
| | | | Shift-Command Automatic — col./flr. | A/C | - | $293 | $293 | $293 |
| 290 CID*, | 200 | C | 3-speed manual | S | $298 | - | - | - |

| Engine | Gross HP | Engine Code | Transmission Availability | Tran. Code | Rambler American | Rambler Classic | Marlin | Ambsdr. |
|--------|----------|-------------|---------------------------|------------|------------------|-----------------|--------|---------|
| 2-bbl., V8 | | | Shift-Command Automatic — col./flr. | A/C | $495 | - | - | - |
| 290 CID*, 4-bbl., V8 | 210 | D | 3-speed manual | S | $331 | - | - | - |
| | | | Shift-Command Automatic — col./flr. | A/C | $528 | - | - | - |
| 327 CID, 2-bbl., V8 | 250 | J/W/P | 3-speed manual | S | - | $138 | $138 | $138 |
| | | | 4-speed manual | F | - | $322 | $322 | $322 |
| | | | Shift-Command Automatic — col./flr. | A/C | - | $325 | $325 | $325 |
| 327 CID, 4-bbl., V8 | 270 | K/U/Q | 3-speed manual | S | - | $171 | $171 | $171 |
| | | | 4-speed manual | F | - | $355 | $355 | $355 |
| | | | Shift-Command Automatic — col./flr. | A/C | - | $358 | $358 | $358 |

*Introduced late in the model year.*

## Major Options

| | Rambler American | Classic | Marlin | Ambassador |
|--|------------------|---------|--------|------------|
| Air conditioning | $303 | $319 | $319 | $328 |
| Speed control | - | - | $60 | $60 |
| Soft Ray tinted glass | $34 | $42 | $37 | $42 |
| Power steering | $84 | $84 | $84 | $84 |
| Power brakes | $42 | $42 | $42 | $42 |
| AM radio | $49 | $49 | $49 | $49 |
| AM/FM radio | - | $130 | $130 | $130 |
| Bucket seats | $98 | $98 | $95 | $98 |
| Custom Trim Package (770/990 only) | - | $124 | - | $98 |
| Custom wheel covers | $20 | $20 | $20 | $20 |
| Turbo Cast wheel covers | $60 | $60 | $60 | $60 |
| Station Wagon third seat | - | $85 | - | $85 |

Options common to most models. (- = Not Available.) Items may be standard equipment, optional at different pricing, or unavailable on certain models. This chart is only a guide.

## Paint Colors

| | Code |
|--|------|
| Classic Black | P1A |
| Antigua Red | P3A |
| Brisbane Light Blue Met. | P15A |
| Britannia Dark Blue Met. | P16A |
| Crescent Light Green | P17A |
| Granada Med. Green Met. | P18A |
| Balboa Light Aqua | P19A |
| Cortez Med. Aqua Met. | P20A |
| Marquessa Light Mauve | P21A |
| Samoa Light Gold Met. | P23A |
| Caballero Medium Tan | P24A |
| Apollo Yellow | P25A |
| Sungold Amber Metallic | P37A |
| Frost White | P72A |

*Two-tones: first number is body color, second number is roof/accent color.*

# Rambler American

*"The new Rambler American, packing its standard engine, can outperform any comparably equipped car in its class."*

**Nameplate year of origin:** 1950 (Nash).
**Current bodystyle lifespan:** 1964 through 1969.
**Predecessor to this model:** Rambler American (1958 to 1963).
**Replacement for this model:** Hornet (1970 to 1977).
**Percentage of division's sales volume:** 38.45%.
**Corporate siblings:** None.
**Primary competition:** Chevrolet Chevy II, Dodge Dart, Ford Falcon, and Plymouth Valiant.
**Notable changes:** Redesigned front end styling and trim and detail changes.
**Major standard equipment:** Cloth and vinyl front bench seat, front arm rests and ash trays, variable speed windshield wipers, rubber floor mats, cargo mat, and 6.45 × 14 BSW tires. 440 adds: Full carpeting, rear armrests, roof-top travel rack on wagon, vinyl-pleated upholstery and power top on convertible, and wheel covers. Rogue adds: All-vinyl bucket seats, floor console, floor shift, special trim and identification.

## Measurements

| | Cars | Wagons |
|--|------|--------|
| Wheelbase | 106.0" | 106.0" |
| Length | 181.0" | 181.0" |
| Width | 69.5" | 69.5" |
| Height | 54.5" | 54.5" |
| Legroom — front | 41.0" | 41.0" |
| Legroom — rear | 36.5" | 36.5" |
| Headroom — front | 39.3" | 39.3" |
| Headroom — rear | 37.0" | 37.1" |
| Luggage cap. (cu. ft.) | 12.0 | 75.4 |
| Fuel capacity (gals.) | 16.0 | 16.0 |

## Models Available

| | Style Number | Base MSRP | Change from LY | Shipping Wt. (lbs.) | Production | Change from LY |
|---|---|---|---|---|---|---|
| Rmblr. American 220 2-Dr. Sdn. | 6606-0 | $2,017 | +3.86% | 2554 | 24,440 | -7.46% |
| Rmblr. American 220 4-Dr. Sdn. | 6605-0 | $2,086 | +4.46% | 2574 | 15,940 | +16.35% |
| Rmblr. American 220 4-Dr. Wgn | 6608-0 | $2,369 | +4.45% | 2740 | 5,809 | +11.20% |
| Rmblr. American 440 2-Dr. Sdn. | 6606-5 | $2,134 | NEW | 2562 | 14,543 | NEW |
| Rmblr. American 440 2-Dr. HT | 6609-5 | $2,227 | +2.96% | 2610 | 10,255 | -25.61% |
| Rblr. American 440 2-Dr. Conv. | 6607-7 | $2,486 | +4.85% | 2782 | 2,092 | -46.11% |
| Rmblr. American 440 4-Dr. Sdn. | 6605-5 | $2,203 | +1.10% | 2582 | 14,543 | +180.00% |
| Rmblr. American 440 4-Dr.Wgn. | 6608-5 | $2,477 | NEW | 2745 | 6,603 | NEW |
| Rblr. American Rogue 2-Dr. HT | 6609-7 | $2,370 | +3.86% | 2630 | 8,718 | +6.79% |
| TOTALS | | *Avg. price* $2,263 | +4.40% | | *Production* 102,943 | -8.81% |

# Rambler Classic

*"The '66 Rambler Classic won't cramp your style.*
*Or your legs. Or your garage. Or your bank account."*

**Nameplate year of origin:** 1957 (Nash Rambler model).
**Current bodystyle lifespan:** 1963 through 1966 (restyled in 1965).
**Predecessor to this model:** Rambler Classic (1957 to 1962).
**Replacement for this model:** Rebel (1967 to 1970).
**Percentage of division's sales volume:** 47.07%.
**Corporate siblings:** Ambassador (shared components from the cowl back) and Marlin (shared body components).
**Primary competition:** Chevrolet Chevelle, Dodge Coronet, Ford Fairlane, and Plymouth Belvedere.
**Notable changes:** New grille and trim and detail changes.
**Major standard equipment:** Cloth and vinyl front foam cushion bench seat, front arm rests and ash trays, rubber floor mat, cargo mat, variable speed windshield wipers, chrome luggage rack (wagons) and 6.95 × 14 BSW tires (7.35 × 14 BSW tires on wagon). 770 adds: Full carpeting, rear armrests, power-operated convertible top, additional chrome exterior trim and deluxe interior trim level. Rebel adds: All-vinyl bucket seats, center armrest, electric clock, and special trim and identification.

## Measurements

| | Cars | Wagons |
|---|---|---|
| Wheelbase | 112.0" | 112.0" |
| Length | 195.0" | 195.0" |
| Width | 74.5" | 74.5" |
| Height | 54.3" | 54.6" |
| Legroom — front | 41.0" | 41.0" |
| Legroom — rear | 37.6" | 37.5" |
| Headroom — front | 39.3" | 39.3" |
| Headroom — rear | 37.0" | 37.1" |
| Luggage cap. (cu. ft.) | 15.2 | 83.0 |
| Fuel capacity (gals.) | 19.0 | 19.0 |

**1966**

## Models Available

| | Style Number | Base MSRP | Change from LY | Shipping Wt. (lbs.) | Production | Change from LY |
|---|---|---|---|---|---|---|
| Classic 550 2-Door Sedan | 6616-0 | $2,189 | +4.19% | 2860 | 5,505 | -22.27% |
| Classic 550 4-Door Sedan | 6615-0 | $2,238 | +4.09% | 2885 | 22,485 | -27.16% |
| Classic 550 4-Door Wagon | 6618-0 | $2,542 | +2.79% | 3071 | 9,390 | -31.75% |
| Classic 770 2-Door Hardtop | 6619-5 | $2,363 | -1.09% | 2935 | 8,736 | -40.89% |
| Classic 770 2-Door Convertible | 6617-5 | $2,616 | -1.06% | 3070 | 1,806 | -63.54% |
| Classic 770 4-Door Sedan | 6615-5 | $2,337 | -2.18% | 2905 | 46,044 | +95.08% |
| Classic 770 4-Door Wagon | 6618-5 | $2,629 | -1.68% | 3070 | 24,528 | +57.00% |
| Classic Rebel 2-Door Hardtop | 6619-7 | $2,523 | +0.96% | 2950 | 7,512 | +31.65% |
| TOTALS | | *Avg. price* $2,430 | +1.00% | | *Production* 126,006 | -38.24% |

*\*Production by body style is not available.*   *\*\*Differences in percentages due to discontinuance of certain models.*

# Marlin

*"There's one sure way to tell a '66 Marlin from other sports fastbacks. Put your family in it."*

**Nameplate year of origin:** 1965.
**Current bodystyle lifespan:** 1965 through 1967.
**Predecessor to this model:** None.
**Replacement for this model:** Javelin (1968 to 1970).
**Percentage of division's sales volume:** 1.70%.
**Corporate siblings:** Classic and Ambassador (shared body components with unique roofline).
**Primary competition:** Dodge Charger.
**Notable changes:** Minor trim and detail changes.
**Major standard equipment:** Cloth and vinyl front bench seat with individually adjustable reclining backs, full carpeting, tinted glass rear window, courtesy lights, variable speed windshield wipers, full wheel covers and 7.35 × 14 BSW tires.

## Measurements

| | |
|---|---|
| Wheelbase | 112.0" |
| Length | 195.0" |
| Width | 74.5" |
| Height | 54.2" |
| Legroom — front | 41.0" |
| Legroom — rear | 36.0" |
| Headroom — front | 38.8" |
| Headroom — rear | 36.5" |
| Luggage cap. (cu. ft.) | 11.7 |
| Fuel capacity (gals.) | 19.0 |

## Models Available

| | Style Number | Base MSRP | Change from LY | Shipping Wt. (lbs.) | Production | Change from LY |
|---|---|---|---|---|---|---|
| Marlin 2-Door Hardtop | 6659-7 | $2,601 | -8.45% | 3050 | 4,547 | -55.97% |
| TOTALS | | Avg. price $2,601 | -8.45% | | Production 4,547 | -55.97% |

# Ambassador

*"It's the one luxury car that isn't oversize, overweight, and overpriced."*

**Nameplate year of origin:** 1933 (from top-of-the-line Nash).
**Current bodystyle lifespan:** 1963 through 1966 (shares basic structure with Classic).
**Predecessor to this model:** Ambassador (1957 to 1962).
**Replacement for this model:** Ambassador (1967 to 1974).
**Percentage of division's sales volume:** 12.78%.
**Corporate siblings:** Classic (shared components from the cowl back).
**Primary competition:** Chevrolet BelAir/Impala/Caprice, Ford Galaxie/LTD, and Plymouth Fury/VIP.
**Notable changes:** Revised rear styling, new grille, and trim and detail changes.
**Major standard equipment:** Cloth and vinyl front foam cushion bench seat, full carpeting, cargo mat, variable speed windshield wipers, chrome luggage rack (wagon) and 7.35 × 14 BSW tires. 990 adds: Power-operated convertible top, additional chrome exterior trim and deluxe interior trim level. DPL adds: All-vinyl reclining bucket seats, center armrest, walnut interior trim, electric clock, and special trim.

## Measurements

| | Cars | Wagons |
|---|---|---|
| Wheelbase | 116.0" | 116.0" |
| Length | 200.0" | 199.0" |
| Width | 74.5" | 74.5" |
| Height | 55.0" | 54.9" |
| Legroom — front | 41.0" | 41.0" |
| Legroom — rear | 37.6" | 37.5" |
| Headroom — front | 39.3" | 39.3" |
| Headroom — rear | 37.0" | 37.1" |
| Luggage cap. (cu. ft.) | 15.2 | 83.0 |
| Fuel capacity (gals.) | 19.0 | 19.0 |

## Models Available

| | Style Number | Base MSRP | Change from LY | Shipping Wt. (lbs.) | Production | Change from LY |
|---|---|---|---|---|---|---|
| Ambassador 880 2-Door Sedan | 6686-2 | $2,404 | -2.55% | 2970 | 800* | -38.51% |
| Ambassador 880 4-Door Sedan | 6685-2 | $2,455 | -2.54% | 3006 | 6200* | -41.31% |

|  | Style Number | Base MSRP | Change from LY | Shipping Wt. (lbs.) | Production | Change from LY |
|---|---|---|---|---|---|---|
| Ambassador 880 4-Door Wagon | 6688-2 | $2,759 | -2.37% | 3160 | 2200* | -42.29% |
| Ambassador 990 2-Door Hardtop | 6689-5 | $2,600 | -0.80% | 3056 | 2800* | -44.38% |
| Ambassador 990 2-Door Convertible | 6687-7 | $2,968 | +2.31% | 3432 | 1798 | -48.61% |
| Ambassador 990 4-Door Sedan | 6685-5 | $2,574 | -1.30% | 3034 | 13000* | -47.69% |
| Ambassador 990 4-Door Wagon | 6688-5 | $2,880 | -1.23% | 3180 | 4925* | -43.40% |
| Ambassador DPL 2-Door HT | 6689-7 | $2,756 | -1.04% | 3090 | 2500* | -60.83% |
| TOTALS | Avg. price | $2,675 | -1.10% | Production* | 34,223 | -46.64% |

*Estimated model year production shown. No breakout by body style is available, except for the convertible.*

# BUICK

*"Introducing the tuned car. 1966 Buick. Wouldn't you really rather have a Buick?"*

Buick set out to make 1966 their sixth straight year of sales increases. By the end of the season they had succeeded — It was close, but with the help of the newly restyled Special/Skylark and Riviera models the goal was met. The mid-size line took its turn at being re-created this season. Based upon the same basic underpinnings as in 1964 and 1965, the Special and Skylark models wore completely different outer skins. Interiors were also totally re-vamped. Power continued to come from the same engine sources, with two exceptions. A new 340 CID V8 was added to the line as a high-end powerhouse. Also a version of the 401 CID V8 used in full-size Buicks was issued for the mid-size line, but here it was measured as a 400 CID V8. This 325-horsepower pavement-eater was used in the high-performance, luxury hot rod known as the Gran Sport (GS). The GS was a more luxurious alternative to cars such as the GTO that tended to be strictly get-up-and-go cars, and came in a full range of 2-Door models. Styling for the entire mid-size line continued to closely follow that of the big Buick, including the famed venti-ports. A 2-Door Coupe and 2-Door Hardtop were added to the mid-range

Special Deluxe line, and the Skylark 4-Door Sedan was replaced by a new 4-Door Hardtop body style.

The totally restyled Riviera shared some components with its new sister, the Oldsmobile Toronado. Granted, there was little to be shared as the Toronado utilized a front-wheel-drive configuration and the Riviera was rear-wheel-drive. Body styling also differed greatly between the two, but some structural components were shared. Styling on the new Riviera was bulkier than the first generation car, but still carried a sporty theme, with fully-rounded wheel openings and enclosed headlamps mounted behind the horizontal bar grille. Rear styling featured full-width taillamps and interior ventilation exiting below the rear window.

Full-size Buick Electra, Wildcat and LeSabre models continued into the new year with few changes. New grilles and revised trim were the bulk of the changes seen. The 300 CID V8 engine used in the LeSabre was replaced by the new 340 CID V8. The only model change was the dropping of the base Wildcat trim level and the renaming of the Wildcat Deluxe as Wildcat.

**Electra 225 Custom 2-Door Hardtop**

**Riviera 2-Door Hardtop**

Skylark GS 2-Door Hardtop

Wildcat GS Package Interior

**Model year production:** 579,698, up 3.19% from 1965.
**Domestic market share:** 6.47% (6th place).
**Base price range:** $2,348 to $4,424.
**Industry average base price:** $3,070.
**Buick average base price:** $3,238.
**Introduction date:** October 1965.
**Assembly plants:** Southgate, CA (C); Atlanta, GA (D); Flint, MI (H); Kansas City, MO (K); Fairfax, KS (X); Wilmington, DE (Y); Fremont, CA (Z); and Oshawa, Ontario, (1).

**Data plate identification:** Thirteen digit code read as follows: five digit style number in which 4 = Buick, 2nd number identifies series (3 is Skylark, 8 is Electra, etc.), and 3rd through 5th digits indicate model number; 6 = 1966 year; assembly plant code; 100001 and up for serial number. *Example:* 452376X100001 is a 1966 Buick LeSabre 2-Door Hardtop, serial number 100001, built in Fairfax, KS

## Powertrains

| Engine | Gross HP | Transmission Availability | Special/ Skylark | Sport Wagon | GS | LeSabre | Wildcat/Elec. & Riviera |
|---|---|---|---|---|---|---|---|
| 225 CID Fireball, 2-bbl., V6 | 160 | 3-speed manual | S | - | - | - | - |
| | | Super Turbine Automatic | $199 | - | - | - | - |
| 300 CID, 2-bbl., V8 | 210 | 3-speed manual | $70 | - | - | - | - |
| | | Super Turbine Automatic | $269 | - | - | - | - |
| 340 CID, 2-bbl., V8 | 220 | 3-speed manual | $96 | S | - | S | - |
| | | Super Turbine Automatic | $301 | $231 | - | $231 | |
| 340 CID, 4-bbl., V8 | 260 | Super Turbine Automatic | $333 | $263 | - | $263* | - |
| 401 CID, 4-bbl., V8 | 325 | 3-speed manual | - | - | S | - | S (Wildcat) |
| | | 4-speed manual | - | - | $184 | - | - |
| | | Super Turbine Automatic | - | - | $205 | - | S (Electra)/$231 (Wildcat) |
| 425 CID, 4-bbl., V8 | 340 | 3-speed manual | - | - | - | - | $ (Wildcat) |
| | | Turbo Hydra-matic | - | - | - | - | S (Riviera)/$ (Wildcat)/ $ (Electra) |

*As part of the LeSabre 400 option package.

## Major Options

| | Skylark | LeSabre | Wildcat | Electra 225 | Riviera |
|---|---|---|---|---|---|
| Air Conditioning — manual | $376 | $421 | $421 | $421 | $421 |
| Air Conditioning — automatic | - | $500 | $500 | $500 | $500 |
| Cruise Master speed control | $58 | $63 | $63 | $63 | $63 |

| | Skylark | LeSabre | Wildcat | Electra 225 | Riviera |
|---|---|---|---|---|---|
| Soft Ray tinted glass | $39 | $44 | $44 | $44 | $47 |
| Deck lid remote release | $14 | $14 | $14 | $14 | $14 |
| Tilt steering wheel | $45 | $45 | $45 | $45 | S |
| Power steering—variable-ratio | $100 | $111 | $111 | S | S |
| Power brakes | $42 | $42 | $42 | S | S |
| Power driver's seat/bench seat, 4-way | $74 (ex. 6-cyl.) | $74 | $74 | $47–$74 | $74 |
| Power windows (except on 6-cylinder) | $105 | $110 | $110 | $110* | $110 |
| AM radio | $70 | $88 | $88 | $88 | $88 |
| AM/FM stereo (mono in Skylark) | $134 | $268 | $268 | $268 | $268 |
| Vinyl roof | $102 | $123 | S | $139 | $128 |
| White sidewall tires—standard size | $31–$36 | $42 | $42 | $47 | $42 |
| Wheel trim covers—Deluxe on Electra | $21 | $21 (base) | S | S | S |

Options common to most models. (- = Not Available; S = Standard equipment.) Items may be standard equipment, optional at different pricing, or unavailable on certain models. This chart is only a guide.

*Standard on Convertible.*

## Paint Colors

| | Code | | Code |
|---|---|---|---|
| Regal Black | A | Riviera Red Metallic | M |
| Riviera Gunmetal Metallic | B | Burgundy Mist Metallic | N |
| Arctic White | C | Flame Red | R |
| Astro Blue Metallic | D | Riviera Champagne Metallic | S |
| Midnight Blue Metallic | E | Saddle Mist Metallic | T |
| Blue Mist Metallic | F | Riviera Plum | U |
| Riviera Gold Metallic | G | Shell Beige | V |
| Seafoam Green Metallic | H | Silver Mist Metallic | W |
| Verde Green Metallic | J | Riviera White | X |
| Turquoise Mist Metallic | K | Cream | Y |
| Shadow Turquoise Metallic | L | Riviera Silver Green Metallic | Z |

1966

# Special, Skylark and GS

*"It's the most car for the least money. Fair enough?"*

**Nameplate year of origin:** 1935 (Special); 1953 (Skylark).
**Current bodystyle lifespan:** 1964 through 1967.
**Predecessor to this model:** Special/Skylark (1961 to 1963).
**Replacement for this model:** Special/Skylark (1968 to 1972).
**Percentage of division's sales volume:** 35.98%.
**Corporate siblings:** Chevrolet Chevelle, Olds F-85/Cutlass, and Pontiac Tempest/LeMans.
**Primary competition:** Dodge Coronet, and Mercury Comet/Montego.
**Notable changes:** Major redesign of exterior bodywork.
**Major standard equipment:** Cloth and vinyl front bench seat, rubber floor mats (carpet in convertible), electric windshield wipers, front door operated courtesy lights, and 6.95 × 14 BSW tires (7.35 × 14 BSW tires on convertible, 7.75 × 14 BSW tires on wagon). Deluxe adds: Instrument panel safety pad, full carpeting, and dual horns. Skylark adds: Paddle-type door arm rests, glove compartment and rear compartment courtesy lights (2-Doors), and full wheel covers. Gran Sport adds: All-vinyl notchback bench seat, heavy-duty suspension, floor shift and 7.75 × 14 BSW tires.

## Measurements

| | Cars | Wagon |
|---|---|---|
| Wheelbase | 115.0" | 115.0" |
| Length | 204.0" | 204.0" |
| Width | 75.0" | 75.0" |
| Height | 55.3" | 55.4" |
| Legroom — front | 41.1" | 41.1" |
| Legroom — rear | 36.0" | 35.7" |
| Headroom — front | 37.8" | 37.8" |
| Headroom — rear | 38.3" | 37.2" |
| Luggage capacity (cu. ft.) | 18.8 | 85.6 |
| Fuel capacity (gals.) | 20.0 | 20.0 |

## Models Available

| | Style Number | Base MSRP | Change from LY | Shipping Wt. (lbs.) | Production | Change from LY |
|---|---|---|---|---|---|---|
| Special 2-Door Coupe | 43307 | $2,348 | +2.44% | 3009 | 15,041 | -31.47% |
| Special 2-Door Convertible | 43367 | $2,604 | +2.16% | 3092 | 3,393 | -49.52% |
| Special 4-Door Sedan | 43369 | $2,401 | +2.39% | 3046 | 18,152 | -0.56% |
| Special 4-Door, 2-Seat Wagon | 43335 | $2,695 | +2.47% | 3296 | 4,489 | -31.40% |
| Special Deluxe 2-Door Coupe | 43507 | $2,432 | NEW | 3009 | 7,267 | NEW |
| Special Deluxe 2-Door Hardtop | 43517 | $2,504 | NEW | 3038 | 35,421 | NEW |
| Special Deluxe 4-Door Sedan | 43569 | $2,485 | +2.01% | 3045 | 32,274 | -11.91% |
| Special Deluxe 4-Dr., 2-Seat Wgn. | 43535 | $2,783 | +2.05% | 3290 | 8,416 | -22.07% |
| Skylark 2-Door Coupe | 44307 | $2,624 | +5.72% | 3034 | 7,881 | -50.96% |
| Skylark 2-Door Hardtop | 44317 | $2,687 | +2.48% | 3069 | 35,542 | -30.58% |
| Skylark 2-Door Convertible | 44367 | $2,837 | +2.31% | 3158 | 6,737 | -42.11% |
| Skylark 4-Door Hardtop | 44339 | $2,846 | NEW | 3172 | 20,151 | NEW |
| Gran Sport 2-Door Coupe | 44607 | $2,956 | NEW | 3479 | 1,835 | NEW |
| Gran Sport 2-Door Hardtop | 44617 | $3,019 | NEW | 3428 | 9,934 | NEW |
| Gran Sport 2-Door Convertible | 44667 | $3,167 | NEW | 3532 | 2,047 | NEW |
| TOTALS | | Avg. price $2,693 | +5.73% | | Production 208,580 | +1.53% |

# Sport Wagon

*"Pack up the gang; see the world. See it better;*
*see more of it. (See us first, of course.)"*

**Nameplate year of origin:** 1964.
**Current bodystyle lifespan:** 1964 through 1967.
**Predecessor to this model:** None.
**Replacement for this model:** Sportwagon (1968 to 1969).
**Percentage of division's sales volume:** 3.73%.
**Corporate siblings:** Oldsmobile Vista-Cruiser.
**Primary competition:** Dodge Coronet, and Mercury Comet.
**Notable changes:** Major redesign of exterior bodywork.
**Major standard equipment:** Cloth and vinyl front bench seat, rubber floor mats, electric windshield wipers, front door operated dome light, dual arm rests, tinted glass observation-style roof, full wheel covers and 8.25 × 14 BSW tires. Custom adds: All-vinyl front bench seat, dual front and rear sunshades, instrument panel safety pad, paddle-type door arm rests, and full carpeting on passenger, door and cowl areas.

## Measurements

| | |
|---|---|
| Wheelbase | 120.0" |
| Length | 210.0" |
| Width | 75.0" |
| Height | 57.5" |
| Legroom — front | 41.3" |
| Legroom — rear | 39.0" |
| Headroom — front | 37.7" |
| Headroom — rear | 40.2" |
| Luggage capacity (cu. ft.) | 97.9 |
| Fuel capacity (gals.) | 20.0 |

## Models Available

| | Style Number | Base MSRP | Change from LY | Shipping Wt. (lbs.) | Production | Change from LY |
|---|---|---|---|---|---|---|
| Sport Wagon 4-Door, 2-St. Wagon | 44255 | $3,025 | +3.42% | 3713 | 2,469 | -41.58% |
| Sport Wagon 4-Door, 3-St. Wagon | 44265 | $3,173 | +3.83% | 3811 | 2,667 | -42.82% |
| Sport Wagon Cust. 4-Dr., 2-St. Wgn. | 44455 | $3,155 | +2.04% | 3720 | 6,964 | -16.10% |
| Sport Wagon Cust. 4-Dr., 3-St. Wgn. | 44465 | $3,293 | +2.46% | 3844 | 9,510 | -14.83% |
| TOTALS | | Avg. price $3,162 | +2.93% | | Production 21,610 | -23.79% |

# LeSabre

*"Our sly fox—a miser disguised as big-spending royalty."*

**Nameplate year of origin:** 1959.
**Current bodystyle lifespan:** 1965 through 1966.
**Predecessor to this model:** LeSabre (1961 to 1964) and Invicta Wagon (1962 to 1963).
**Replacement for this model:** LeSabre (1967 to 1968).
**Percentage of division's sales volume:** 25.43%.
**Corporate siblings:** Chevrolet Biscayne/BelAir/Impala/Caprice, Pontiac Catalina/Executive/Bonneville, Oldsmobile Delta 88.
**Primary competition:** Chrysler Newport, Dodge Polara, and Mercury Monterey.
**Notable changes:** New grille and minor trim and detail changes.
**Major standard equipment:** Cloth and vinyl front bench seat, front door operated interior lighting, glove box light, full carpeting, front and rear armrests, and 8.55 × 15 BSW tires. Custom adds: Custom interior trim (all vinyl on Convertible), deluxe steering wheel, wheel opening moldings, "Custom" nameplates, and additional exterior trim moldings.

## Measurements

| | |
|---|---|
| Wheelbase | 123.0" |
| Length | 217.0" |
| Width | 80.0" |
| Height | 55.2" |
| Legroom — front | 42.2" |
| Legroom — rear | 39.0" |
| Headroom — front | 38.9" |
| Headroom — rear | 37.7" |
| Luggage capacity (cu. ft.) | NA |
| Fuel capacity (gals.) | 25.0 |

## Models Available

| | Style Number | Base MSRP | Change from LY | Shipping Wt. (lbs.) | Production | Change from LY |
|---|---|---|---|---|---|---|
| LeSabre 2-Door Hardtop | 45237 | $3,022 | +1.82% | 3751 | 13,843 | -12.31% |
| LeSabre 4-Door Sedan | 45269 | $2,942 | +1.87% | 3796 | 39,146 | +3.59% |
| LeSabre 4-Door Hardtop | 45239 | $3,081 | +1.78% | 3828 | 17,740 | -3.50% |
| LeSabre Custom 2-Door Hardtop | 45437 | $3,109 | +2.37% | 3746 | 18,830 | -10.54% |
| LeSabre Custom 2-Door Convertible | 45467 | $3,326 | +2.12% | 3833 | 4,994 | -23.67% |
| LeSabre Custom 4-Door Sedan | 45469 | $3,035 | +2.46% | 3788 | 25,932 | +29.32% |
| LeSabre Custom 4-Door Hardtop | 45439 | $3,174 | +2.35% | 3824 | 26,914 | +15.05% |
| TOTALS | *Avg. price* | $3,098 | +2.11% | *Production* | 147,399 | +3.08% |

# Wildcat

*"It's the full-size family car that purrs quietly.*
*(A wonderful pet to have around.)"*

**Nameplate year of origin:** 1962.
**Current bodystyle lifespan:** 1965 through 1966.
**Predecessor to this model:** Wildcat (1962 to 1964) and Invicta (1961 to 1962).
**Replacement for this model:** Wildcat (1967 to 1968).
**Percentage of division's sales volume:** 11.83%.
**Corporate siblings:** Chevrolet Full-size, Pontiac Full-size, and Oldsmobile Delta 88.
**Primary competition:** Chrysler 300, Dodge Monaco, and Mercury Montclair.
**Notable changes:** New grille and minor trim and detail changes.
**Major standard equipment:** Cloth and vinyl bench seat, front door operated interior lighting, full carpeting, front and rear armrests, deluxe steering wheel, rocker panel and wheel opening moldings, and 8.45 × 15 BSW tires. Custom adds: Custom interior trim, and custom headlining.

## Measurements

| | |
|---|---|
| Wheelbase | 126.0" |
| Length | 220.1" |
| Width | 80.0" |
| Height | 55.2" |
| Legroom — front | 42.2" |
| Legroom — rear | 39.0" |
| Headroom — front | 38.9" |
| Headroom — rear | 37.7" |
| Luggage capacity (cu. ft.) | NA |
| Fuel capacity (gals.) | 25.0 |

1966

## Models Available

| | Style Number | Base MSRP | Change from LY | Shipping Wt. (lbs.) | Production | Change from LY |
|---|---|---|---|---|---|---|
| Wildcat 2-Door HT | 46437 | $3,326 | +1.65% | 4003 | 9,774 | -15.86% |
| Wildcat 2-Door Convertible | 46467 | $3,480 | +1.43% | 4065 | 2,690 | -41.72% |
| Wildcat 4-Door Sedan | 46469 | $3,233 | +0.47% | 4070 | 14,389 | 47.35% |
| Wildcat 4-Door HT | 46439 | $3,391 | +1.59% | 4108 | 15,081 | 8.47% |
| Wildcat Custom 2-Door Hardtop | 46637 | $3,547 | +1.55% | 4018 | 10,800 | * |
| Wildcat Custom 2-Door Convertible | 46667 | $3,701 | +1.37% | 4079 | 2,790 | * |
| Wildcat Custom 4-Door Hardtop | 46639 | $3,606 | +1.52% | 4176 | 13,060 | * |
| TOTALS | Avg. price | $3,469 | +3.34% | Production | 68,584 | +7.81% |

*Production of Wildcat Custom from 1965 model year unavailable for comparison.*

# Electra 225

*"It's the car to arrive in when you've arrived."*

**Nameplate year of origin:** 1959.
**Current bodystyle lifespan:** 1965 through 1966.
**Predecessor to this model:** Electra 225 (1961 to 1964).
**Replacement for this model:** Electra 225 (1967 to 1968).
**Percentage of division's sales volume:** 15.21%.
**Corporate siblings:** Cadillac Calais/de Ville, Oldsmobile Ninety-Eight.
**Primary competition:** Chrysler New Yorker, Dodge Custom 880 and Mercury Park Lane.
**Notable changes:** New grille and minor trim and detail changes.
**Major standard equipment:** Cloth and vinyl bench seat, full carpeting and lower door carpeting, deluxe steering wheel, power steering, power brakes, trunk light, bright rocker panel molding and wheel opening moldings, rear fender skirts, deluxe wheel covers and 8.85 × 15 BSW tires. Custom adds: custom interior trim.

### Measurements

| | |
|---|---|
| Wheelbase | 126.0" |
| Length | 223.5" |
| Width | 80.0" |
| Height | 55.8" |
| Legroom — front | 42.2" |
| Legroom — rear | 39.0" |
| Headroom — front | 39.7" |
| Headroom — rear | 38.2" |
| Luggage capacity (cu. ft.) | NA |
| Fuel capacity (gals.) | 25.0 |

## Models Available

| | Style Number | Base MSRP | Change from LY | Shipping Wt. (lbs.) | Production | Change from LY |
|---|---|---|---|---|---|---|
| Electra 225 2-Door Hardtop | 48237 | $4,032 | +0.83% | 4176 | 4,882 | -22.53% |
| Electra 225 4-Door Sedan | 48269 | $4,022 | +0.83% | 4255 | 11,692 | -6.16% |
| Electra 225 4-Door Hardtop | 48239 | $4,153 | +0.78% | 4271 | 10,792 | -15.96% |
| Electra 225 Custom 2-Door HT | 48437 | $4,211 | +5.30% | 4230 | 10,119 | +5.74% |
| Electra 225 Custom 2-Door Conv. | 48467 | $4,378 | +0.64% | 4298 | 7,175 | -15.67% |
| Electra 225 Custom 4-Door Sedan | 48469 | $4,201 | +0.79% | 4292 | 9,368 | +30.17% |
| Electra 225 Custom 4-Door HT | 48439 | $4,332 | +0.74% | 4323 | 34,149 | +14.09% |
| TOTALS | Avg. price | $4,190 | +1.40% | Production | 88,177 | +1.57% |

# Riviera

*"This is it— the new silhouette, the new international classic. The new Riviera."*

**Nameplate year of origin:** 1949 (for 2-Dr. HTs); 1963 (series).
**Current bodystyle lifespan:** 1966 through 1970.
**Predecessor to this model:** Riviera (1963 to 1965).
**Replacement for this model:** Riviera (1971 to 1976).
**Percentage of division's sales volume:** 7.82%.
**Corporate siblings:** Oldsmobile Toronado.
**Primary competition:** Ford Thunderbird.
**Notable changes:** Completely redesigned.
**Major standard equipment:** All-vinyl bench or bucket front seats, electric clock, trunk light, bright exterior window and rocker moldings, ventless front door windows, power steering, power brakes, dual exhaust system, and 8.55 × 15 BSW tires.

## Measurements

| | |
|---|---|
| Wheelbase | 119.0" |
| Length | 211.2" |
| Width | 78.8" |
| Height | 53.4" |
| Legroom — front | 41.3" |
| Legroom — rear | 35.2" |
| Headroom — front | 38.0" |
| Headroom — rear | 37.5" |
| Luggage capacity (cu. ft.) | NA |
| Fuel capacity (gals.) | 21.0 |

## Models Available

| | Style Number | Base MSRP | Change from LY | Shipping Wt. (lbs.) | Production | Change from LY |
|---|---|---|---|---|---|---|
| Riviera 2-Door Hardtop | 49487 | $4,424 | +2.45% | 4180 | 45,348 | +31.12% |
| TOTALS | | Avg. price $4,424 | +2.45% | | Production 45,348 | +31.12% |

**1966**

# CADILLAC

*"New elegance ... new excellence ... new excitement.
Cadillac remains Standard of the World."*

After a highly successful 1965 season, there were few changes to the Cadillac line for 1966 except for the Fleetwood 75 line, which received a styling facelift to bring it up to date with the rest of the Cadillac line in terms of style and engineering. Up through 1965, this line consisting of the 9-passenger Sedan and Limousine was still based on the 1959 Cadillac platform, with slightly newer body styling (i.e., 1963-64 vintage). This also meant that the prestige line did not have the newly redesigned Turbo Hydra-matic transmission until this year, nor the Automatic Level Control system. All of this modernization meant an increase of over 60 percent in sales.

Cadillac Motor Division as a whole had an excellent sales year; in fact it managed to finish with its best year ever for 1966. Sales were just shy of the magical 200,000 unit mark. Minor styling revisions were made to the rest of the line, but most of the other changes for the new year were technical in nature. Variable-ratio power steering was introduced, as was a front seat heating system. Also new were reclining front seat backs, head rests and an AM/FM Stereo system.

Calais 4-Door Hardtop

Coupe de Ville 2-Door Hardtop

Fleetwood 60 Special 4-Door Sedan

Fleetwood 75 9-passenger Limousine

Fleetwood Eldorado 2-Door Convertible

**Model year production:** 194,212, up 8.64% from 1965.
**Domestic market share:** 2.17% (11th place).
**Base price range:** $4,986 to $10,521.
**Industry average base price:** $3,070.
**Cadillac average base price:** $6,502.
**Introduction date:** October 14, 1965.

**Assembly plants:** Detroit, MI, and Linden, NJ.
**Data plate identification:** Eight digit code read as follows: 1st digit is style symbol (see list); 2nd digit 6 for 1966; followed by 100001 and up for serial number. *Example:* J6100001 is a 1966 Cadillac de Ville 2-Door Hardtop, serial number 100001.

## Powertrains

| Engine | Gross HP | Transmission Availability | All models |
|--------|----------|---------------------------|------------|
| 429 CID, 4-bbl., V8 | 340 | Turbo Hydra-matic | S |

## Major Options

|  | *Calais* | *de Ville* | *Eldorado* | *60 Special* | *75* |
|--|----------|------------|------------|--------------|------|
| Automatic climate control | $495 | $495 | $495 | $495 | $624 |
| Power windows | $119 | S | S | S | S |
| 6-way power seat | $113 | $85 | S | $85/S (Brougham) | $85 |
| Power door locks | $46–$70 | $46–$70 | $46 | $70 | S |
| AM radio w/rear speaker | $165 | $165 | $165 | $165 | $165 |
| AM-FM radio | $191 | $191 | $191 | $191 | $191 |
| Padded vinyl roof | - | $124–$140 | - | S (Brougham) | NA |
| Twilight Sentinel (auto. dimmers) | $57 | $57 | S | $57 | - |
| Tilt & telescope steering wheel | $91 | $91 | $91 | $91 | $91 |
| Leather upholstery | - | $141 | $141 | S | - |
| Cruise control | $97 | $97 | $97 | $97 | $97 |
| Tinted glass | $52 | $52 | $52 | $52 | $52 |
| Rear window defogger | $27 | $27 (NA conv.) | - | $27 | S |
| Automatic Level Control | $79 | $79 | S | S | S |
| Remote trunk release/lock | $53 | $53 | $53 | $53 | - |

Options common to most models. (- = Not Available; S = Standard equipment.) Items may be standard equipment, optional at different pricing, or unavailable on certain models. This chart is only a guide.

**Cadillac Style Symbols: A**— 62 4-window Sedan or Calais 4-Dr. HT Sedan; **B**— Sedan de Ville 4-window; **C**— 62 Short Deck Sedan; **D**— Sedan de Ville Park Avenue; **E**— Eldorado Biarritz or Eldorado Convertible; **F**— 62 Convertible; **G**— 62 2-Door Hardtop or Calais 2-Door HT; **H**— Eldorado Seville HT or Eldorado Coupe; **J**— Coupe de Ville; **K**— 62 6-window Sedan; **L**— Sedan de Ville 6-window; **M**— Fleetwood 60 Special Sedan; **N**— 62 4-window Sedan (1963) or Calais Sedan; **P**— Fleetwood Brougham or Eldorado Brougham; **R**— Fleetwood 75 Sedan; **S**— Fleetwood 75 Limousine; **Z**— Commerical Chassis

## Paint Colors

| | Code | | Code |
|---|---|---|---|
| Sable Black | 10 | Sandalwood | 42 |
| Strathmore White | 12 | Antique Gold Metallic | 44 |
| Starlight Silver Metallic | 16 | Autumn Rust Metallic | 46 |
| Summit Gray Metallic | 18 | Flamenco Red | 48 |
| Mist Blue | 20 | Claret Maroon Metallic | 49 |
| Marlin Blue Metallic | 24 | Cobalt Firemist Metallic* | 90 |
| Nocturne Blue Metallic | 26 | Crystal Firemist Metallic* | 92 |
| Caribbean Aqua Metallic | 28 | Tropic Green Firemist Metallic* | 96 |
| Cascade Green Metallic | 30 | Florentine Bronze Firemist Metallic* | 97 |
| Inverness Green Metallic | 36 | Ember Firemist Metallic* | 98 |
| Cape Ivory | 40 | | |

*Firemist colors available only on Eldorado.*

# Calais

*"Standard of the world in luxury and practicality."*

**Nameplate year of origin:** 1965.
**Current bodystyle lifespan:** 1965 through 1966.
**Predecessor to this model:** Series Sixty-Two (1961 to 1964).
**Replacement for this model:** Calais (1967 to 1968).
**Percentage of division's sales volume:** 14.77%.
**Corporate siblings:** Buick Electra 225 and Oldsmobile Ninety-Eight.
**Primary competition:** Chrysler New Yorker and Lincoln Continental.
**Notable changes:** Minor trim and detail changes.
**Major standard equipment:** Danbury cloth and vinyl seat upholstery, front center armrests, rear fender skirts, left side remote control outside rear view mirror, interior courtesy and warning lights, three-speed windshield wipers and washers, right side visor vanity mirrors, front cornering lamps, variable ratio power steering, power front disc brakes, Turbo Hydra-matic transmission, and 9.00 × 15 BSW tires.

## Measurements

| | |
|---|---|
| Wheelbase | 129.5" |
| Length | 224.0" |
| Width | 79.9" |
| Height | 54.5" |
| Legroom — front | 41.0" |
| Legroom — rear | 40.1" |
| Headroom — front | 38.5" |
| Headroom — rear | 38.4" |
| Luggage capacity (cu. ft.) | 17.1 |
| Fuel capacity (gals.) | 26.0 |

## Models Available

| | Style Number | Base MSRP | Change from LY | Shipping Wt. (lbs.) | Production | Change from LY |
|---|---|---|---|---|---|---|
| Calais 2-Door Hardtop | 68257 | $4,986 | +0.54% | 4390 | 11,080 | -11.47% |
| Calais 4-Door Sedan | 68269 | $5,171 | +0.52% | 4460 | 4,575 | -40.75% |
| Calais 4-Door Hardtop | 68239 | $5,171 | +0.52% | 4465 | 13,025 | -6.80% |
| TOTALS | | Avg. price $5,109 | +0.53% | Production | 28,680 | -16.17% |

# de Ville

*"Standard of the world in glamor and excitement."*

**Nameplate year of origin:** 1949 (as Hardtop designation); 1959 (series).
**Current bodystyle lifespan:** 1965 through 1966.
**Predecessor to this model:** de Ville (1961 to 1964).
**Replacement for this model:** de Ville (1967 to 1968).

## Measurements

| | |
|---|---|
| Wheelbase | 129.5" |
| Length | 224.0" |
| Width | 79.9" |

**Percentage of division's sales volume:** 73.21%.
**Corporate siblings:** Buick Electra 225 and Oldsmobile Ninety-Eight.
**Primary competition:** Imperial Crown and Lincoln Continental.
**Notable changes:** Minor trim and detail changes.
**Major standard equipment:** Cloth and vinyl seat upholstery (leather in convertible), two-way power seat adjustment, front and rear center armrests (front only on convertible), rear fender skirts, left side remote control outside rear view mirror, power windows, interior courtesy and warning lights, three-speed windshield wipers and washers, right side visor vanity mirrors, front cornering lamps, variable ratio power steering, power front disc brakes, Turbo Hydra-matic transmission, and 9.00 × 15 BSW tires.

### Measurements (cont.)

| | |
|---|---|
| Height | 54.5" |
| Legroom — front | 41.0" |
| Legroom — rear | 40.1" |
| Headroom — front | 38.5" |
| Headroom — rear | 38.4" |
| Luggage capacity (cu. ft.) | 17.1 |
| Fuel capacity (gals.) | 26.0 |

## Models Available

| | Style Number | Base MSRP | Change from LY | Shipping Wt. (lbs.) | Production | Change from LY |
|---|---|---|---|---|---|---|
| Coupe de Ville 2-Door Hardtop | 68357 | $5,339 | +0.51% | 4460 | 50,580 | +16.69% |
| de Ville 2-Door Convertible | 68367 | $5,555 | +0.49% | 4445 | 19,200 | 0.00% |
| Sedan de Ville 4-Door Sedan | 68369 | $5,581 | +0.49% | 4535 | 11,860 | -20.93% |
| Sedan de Ville 4-Door Hardtop | 68339 | $5,581 | +0.49% | 4515 | 60,550 | +32.97% |
| TOTALS | Avg. price | $5,514 | +0.49% | Production | 142,190 | +15.53% |

# Fleetwood Eldorado

*"Standard of the world in motoring pleasure."*

**Nameplate year of origin:** 1953.
**Current bodystyle lifespan:** 1965 through 1966.
**Predecessor to this model:** Fleetwood Eldorado (1961 to 1964).
**Replacement for this model:** Eldorado (1967 to 1970).
**Percentage of division's sales volume:** 1.16%.
**Corporate siblings:** Buick Electra 225 and Oldsmobile Ninety-Eight.
**Primary competition:** None.
**Notable changes:** Minor trim and detail changes.
**Major standard equipment:** Leather front bucket or split bench seat, two-way power seat adjustment, front center armrests, left side remote control outside rear view mirror, power windows, interior door, courtesy and warning lights, three-speed windshield wipers and washers, right side visor vanity mirrors, rear fender skirts, front cornering lamps, variable ratio power steering, power front disc brakes, Turbo Hydra-matic transmission, and 9.00 × 15 WSW tires.

### Measurements

| | |
|---|---|
| Wheelbase | 129.5" |
| Length | 224.0" |
| Width | 79.9" |
| Height | 54.5" |
| Legroom — front | 41.0" |
| Legroom — rear | 40.1" |
| Headroom — front | 38.5" |
| Headroom — rear | 38.4" |
| Luggage capacity (cu. ft.) | 17.1 |
| Fuel capacity (gals.) | 26.0 |

## Models Available

| | Style Number | Base MSRP | Change from LY | Shipping Wt. (lbs.) | Production | Change from LY |
|---|---|---|---|---|---|---|
| Eldorado 2-Door Convertible | 68467 | $6,631 | +0.41% | 4500 | 2,250 | +5.88% |
| TOTALS | Avg. price | $6,631 | +0.41% | Production | 2,250 | +5.88% |

# Fleetwood Brougham & Sixty-Special

*"Standard of the world in magnificence and dignity."*

**Nameplate year of origin:** 1938.
**Current bodystyle lifespan:** 1965 through 1966.
**Predecessor to this model:** Fleetwood Sixty-Special (1961 to 1964).
**Replacement for this model:** Fleetwood Sixty-Special (1967 to 1968).
**Percentage of division's sales volume:** 9.82%.
**Corporate siblings:** None.
**Primary competition:** Imperial LeBaron.
**Notable changes:** Minor trim and detail changes.
**Major standard equipment:** Cloth seat upholstery, two-way power seat adjustment, front and rear center armrests, rear fender skirts, left side remote control outside rear view mirror, power windows, interior door, courtesy and warning lights, three-speed windshield wipers and washers, right side visor vanity mirrors, front cornering lamps, variable ratio power steering, power front disc brakes, Turbo Hydra-matic transmission, and 9.00 × 15 BSW tires. Brougham adds: Driver's side only seat adjustment, reading lights and padded vinyl top.

## Measurements

| | |
|---|---|
| Wheelbase | 133.0" |
| Length | 227.5" |
| Width | 79.9" |
| Height | 56.7" |
| Legroom — front | 41.0" |
| Legroom — rear | 39.6" |
| Headroom — front | 39.5" |
| Headroom — rear | 38.2" |
| Luggage capacity (cu. ft.) | 17.1 |
| Fuel capacity (gals.) | 26.0 |

## Models Available

| | Style Number | Base MSRP | Change from LY | Shipping Wt. (lbs.) | Production | Change from LY |
|---|---|---|---|---|---|---|
| Fl. Sixty Special 4-Dr. Sedan | 68069 | $6,378 | +0.43% | 4615 | 5,445 | -69.92% |
| Fl. Brougham 4-Dr. Sedan | 68169 | $6,695 | NEW | 4665 | 13,630 | NEW |
| TOTALS | | *Avg. price* $6,537 | +2.93% | | *Production* 19,075 | +5.39% |

**1966**

# Fleetwood Seventy-Five

*"The most distinguished Cadillac."*

**Nameplate year of origin:** 1927 (Fleetwood bodies); 1936 (75 series).
**Current bodystyle lifespan:** 1966.
**Predecessor to this model:** Fleetwood 75 (1959 to 1965).
**Replacement for this model:** Fleetwood 75 (1967 to 1968).
**Percentage of division's sales volume:** 1.04%.
**Corporate siblings:** None.
**Primary competition:** Custom Imperial Limousine.
**Notable changes:** Completely redesigned in line with current regular Cadillac models.
**Major standard equipment:** Divan cloth seat upholstery, two-way power seat adjustment, rear center armrests, automatic climate control, rear window defogger, rear fender skirts, left side remote control outside rear view mirror, power windows, interior door, courtesy and warning lights, three-speed windshield wipers and washers, right side visor vanity mirrors, front cornering lamps, fixed ratio power steering, power front disc brakes, Turbo Hydra-matic transmission, and 9.00 × 15 BSW tires.

## Measurements

| | |
|---|---|
| Wheelbase | 149.8" |
| Length | 244.5" |
| Width | 79.9" |
| Height | 57.4" |
| Legroom — front | 41.3" |
| Legroom — rear | 41.3" |
| Headroom — front | 39.8" |
| Headroom — rear | 38.0" |
| Luggage capacity (cu. ft.) | 16.2 |
| Fuel capacity (gals.) | 26.0 |

## Models Available

| | Style Number | Base MSRP | Change from LY | Shipping Wt. (lbs.) | Production | Change from LY |
|---|---|---|---|---|---|---|
| Fl. Seventy-Five 4-Door Sedan | 69723 | $10,360 | +8.45% | 5335 | 980 | +115.38% |
| Fl. Seventy-Five 4-Dr. Limousine | 69733 | $10,571 | +8.29% | 5450 | 1,037 | +30.44% |
| TOTALS | | Avg. price $10,466 | +8.37% | Production | 2,017 | +61.36% |

# CHEVROLET

*"The Chevrolet way—1966."*

"Chevrolet USA-1" did not hold true this year. The top manufacturer in the country took a beating from several sides this season, and in the end, Ford with its successful Mustang and newly redesigned full-size and Fairlane lines ended up winning the sales race. For Chevy, the biggest hurt was not having direct competition for the Mustang.

Chevrolet marketers had what they thought could be competition, if only temporarily, in the Corvair, but it took a direct hit from outside sources that would destroy its value in the marketplace. Realistically, a rear-engined economy car could not compete with the Mustang in most arenas. Chevrolet's only front-engine, rear-wheel drive offering that could come close to the Mustang was the Chevy II with a V8 engine, but in reality, it was not a sporty car and wound up being the traditional Falcon competitor. The second factor in the loss of Corvair sales was the recently published book *Unsafe at Any Speed* by attorney Ralph Nader. This book was highly critical of the safety record of the auto industry, and in particular the Corvair, mainly due to some handling characteristics of early models. As with the modern day SUV roll-over problems, a lot of the blame can be shared by consumers driving their vehicles as they would a normal large, front-engine, rear-wheel-drive car. Consideration must be given to the differing handling characteristics of a rear-engined vehicle, or in the modern case, a high-center-of-gravity, off-road vehicle. Obviously, the manufacturer has a responsibility to make the cars safe, and GM did correct the problems, albeit a little too late in some respects. The major result of all of this attention was that Congress passed a bill in 1966 requiring more stringent auto safety standards beginning with the 1968 model year. By the time the 1966 model year was completed, the damage was done and Corvair sales dropped over 50 percent.

There would be no recovery, and the car would be quietly discontinued in 1969. As a side note, the Corvair 95 Greenbrier van was discontinued, as it had been replaced by a modern, front-engine Chevy Van.

On the brighter side, the popular mid-size Chevelle line received a totally new exterior and redesigned interior for 1966. Body lines were a little more curvaceous than previous models, and used the tunneled rear window design on 2-Door models that was shared with other GM intermediates. The front styling was highlighted by a full-width grille that swept back at the outer edges, giving a look of motion while standing still. Lack of side trim gave a clean, modern look. Model changes were limited to the dropping of the 2-Door Wagon, and the addition of a 4-Door Hardtop Sports Sedan in the Malibu line. Also receiving a major restyle was the Chevy II line. Like the Chevelle, the popular compact car was still based upon the same chassis components as in prior years, but the outer skin and interior styling were all-new. There were no model changes made to the Chevy II line. Under the hoods, both lines continued the same offerings as in previous years, but added new powerhouses to the top end of the line. The Chevy II added a 350-horsepower version of the famous 327 CID V8 engine. The Chevelle added a 396 CID V8 engine in several power choices to the Super Sport model line. This SS 396 model would put Chevy on the map in the muscle car wars.

Chevrolet's remaining two model lines, Corvette and full-size; each added a new engine to their powertrain line-ups also. It was the 427 CID V8 engine option. Replacing the 409 CID V8 of song and racing legend, the new 427 CID V8 was built to blow the doors off anything on the road. It was quite capable of doing so, especially in the Corvette. Corvettes equipped with this engine had a new "power bulge" hood. Other Corvette changes for the season included revised fender louvers and interior trim. Full-size models received new front and rear styling treatments. A new top-of-the-line Caprice model was added to the line this year. Introduced in 1965 as a mid-year luxury option for the Impala 4-Door Hardtop, the Caprice proved to be popular and a worthy competitor for the new Ford Galaxie 500 LTD and Plymouth VIP.

Caprice 4-Door, 3-Seat Custom Wagon

Chevelle 300 Deluxe 4-Door, 2-Seat Wagon

Chevy II 100 4-Door Wagon

Chevy II Nova SS 2-Door Hardtop

Chevelle SS 396 2-Door Hardtop

Corvair Corsa 2-Door Hardtop

Impala 2-Door Hardtop

Impala 4-Door Sedan

Corvette 2-Door Coupe

**Model year production:** 2,142,035, down 10.13% from 1965.
**Domestic market share:** 23.92% (2nd place).
**Base price range:** $2,028 to $4,295.
**Industry average base price:** $3,070.
**Chevrolet average base price:** $2,654.
**Introduction date:** October 7, 1965.
**Assembly plants:** Atlanta, GA (A); Baltimore, MD (B); Southgate, CA (C); Flint, MI (F); Framingham, MA (G); Janesville, WI (J); Kansas City, MO (K), Los Angeles, CA (L), Norwood, OH (N); Pontiac, MI (P); Arlington, TX (R); St. Louis, MO (S); Tarrytown, NY (T); Lordstown, OH (U); Willow Run, MI (W); Wilmington, DE (Y); Fremont, CA (Z), Oshawa, Ontario, Canada (1); and St. Therese, Quebec, Canada (2).

**Data plate identification:** Thirteen digit code read as follows: 1st digit 1 for Chevrolet; four digit style number (see listings below) in which 2nd and 3rd numbers identify series, 4th and 5th indicate body style; 6 for 1966; 7th digit is assembly plant code; 100001 and up for serial number. Actual beginning serial numbers depend upon series. *Example:* 155116T100001 is a 1966 Chevrolet BelAir 2-Door Sedan, 6-cylinder, serial number 100001, built in Arlington, TX.

## Powertrains

| Engine | Gross HP | Transmission Availability | Corvair | Chevy II | Chevelle | Biscayne/ BelAir/Imp | Caprice | Corvette |
|--------|----------|---------------------------|---------|----------|----------|---------------------|---------|----------|
| 153 CID, 1-bbl., 4-cyl. | 90 | 3-speed manual | - | S[1] | - | - | - | - |
| | | 2-sp. Powerglide Automatic | - | $164[1] | - | - | - | - |
| 164 CID OHV, 2 × 1-bbl., Flat 6 | 95 | 3-speed manual | S | - | - | - | - | - |
| | | 4-speed manual | $92 | - | - | - | - | - |
| | | 2-sp. Powerglide Automatic | $157 | - | - | - | - | - |

| Engine | Gross HP | Transmission Availability | Corvair | Chevy II | Chevelle | Biscayne/ BelAir/Imp | Caprice | Corvette |
|---|---|---|---|---|---|---|---|---|
| 164 CID Turbo-Air, 2 × 1-bbl., Flat 6 | 110 | 3-speed manual | $26 | - | - | - | - | - |
|  |  | 4-speed manual | $118 | - | - | - | - | - |
|  |  | 2-sp. Powerglide Automatic | $183 | - | - | - | - | - |
| 164 CID Turbo-Air, 4 × 1-bbl., Flat 6 | 140 | 3-speed manual | $79 | - | - | - | - | - |
|  |  | 4-speed manual | $171 | - | - | - | - | - |
|  |  | 2-sp. Powerglide Automatic | $236*** | - | - | - | - | - |
| 194 CID Turbo-Thrift, 1-bbl., 6-cyl. | 120 | 3-speed manual | - | S (Nova)/ $62[1] | S[4] | - | - | - |
|  |  | Overdrive | - | - | $116 | - | - | - |
|  |  | 2-sp. Powerglide Automatic | - | $164(Nova) /$226[1] | $184[4] | - | - | - |
| 230 CID Turbo-Thrift, 1-bbl., 6-cyl. | 140 | 3-speed manual | - | $37 (Nova)/ $99[1] | $37[4] | - | - | - |
|  |  | 2-sp. Powerglide Automatic | - | $201(Nova)/ $263[1] | $221[4] | - | - | - |
| 250 CID Turbo-Thrift, 1-bbl., 6-cyl. | 155 | 3-speed manual | - | - | - | S | - | - |
|  |  | Overdrive | - | - | - | $115 | - | - |
|  |  | 2-sp. Powerglide Automatic | - | - | - | $184 | - | - |
| 283 CID Turbo-Fire, 2-bbl., V8 | 195 | 3-speed manual | - | $105(Nova)/ $204[1] | $94[4] | $105 | S | - |
|  |  | Overdrive | - | - | $210[4] | $220 | $115 | |
|  |  | 4-speed manual | - | $289(Nova)/ $393[1] | $278[4] | $289 | $184 | - |
|  |  | 2-sp. Powerglide Automatic | - | $279(Nova)/ $378[1] | $278[4] | $300 | $195 | - |
| 283 CID Turbo-Fire, 4-bbl., V8 | 220 | 3-speed manual | - | $150(Nova)/ $249[1] | $139[4] | $150 | $45 | - |
|  |  | 4-speed manual | - | $334(Nova)/ $438[1] | $323[4] | $334 | $229 | - |
|  |  | 2-sp. Powerglide Automatic | - | $324(Nova)/ $423[1] | $323[4] | $345 | $240 | - |
| 327 CID Turbo-Fire, 4-bbl., V8 | 275 300— Corvette | 3-speed manual | - | $198 (SS or Nova) | $187[4] | $198 | $93 | S |
|  |  | 4-speed manual | - | $382 (SS or Nova) | $371[4] | $382 | $277 | $184 |
|  |  | 2- sp. Powerglide Automatic | - | $372 (SS or Nova) | $371[4] | $393 | $288 | $195 |
| 327 CID Turbo-Fire, 4-bbl., V8 | 350 | 3-speed manual | - | $291[2] | $291[4] | - | - | - |
|  |  | 4-speed manual | - | $475[2] | $475[4] | - | - | $289 |
|  |  | 2- sp. Powerglide Automatic | - | $489[2] | $476[4] | - | - | - |
| 396 CID Turbo-Jet, 4-bbl., V8 | 325 | 3-speed manual | - | - | S[3] | $263 | $158 | - |
|  |  | 4-speed manual | - | - | $105[3] | $447 | $342 | - |
|  |  | 2- sp. Powerglide Automatic | - | - | $147[3] | $489 | $384 | - |
|  |  | Turbo Hydra-Matic | - | - | - | $519 | $414 | - |
| 396 CID Turbo-Jet, | 360 | 3-speed manual | - | - | $105[3] | - | - | - |

| Engine | Gross HP | Transmission Availability | Corvair | Chevy II | Chevelle | Biscayne/ BelAir/Imp | Caprice | Corvette |
|---|---|---|---|---|---|---|---|---|
| 4-bbl., V8 | | 4-speed manual | - | - | $210[3] | - | - | - |
| | | 2-sp. Powerglide Automatic | - | - | $252[3] | - | - | - |
| 396 CID Turbo-Jet, 4-bbl., V8 | 375 | 3-speed manual | - | - | $[3] | - | - | - |
| | | 4-speed manual | - | - | $[3] | - | - | - |
| | | 2-sp. Powerglide Automatic | - | - | $[3] | - | - | - |
| 427 CID Turbo-Jet, 4-bbl., V8 | 390 | 3-speed manual | - | - | - | $421 | $316 | - |
| | | 4-speed manual | - | - | - | $605 | $500 | $365 |
| | | Turbo Hydra-Matic | - | - | - | $647 | $542 | |
| 427 CID Turbo-Jet, 4-bbl., V8 | 425 | 3-speed manual | - | - | - | $ | $ | - |
| | | 4-speed manual | - | - | - | $ | $ | $526 |

[1]*Chevy II 100 only.*   [2]*All but Chevy II 100.*   [3]*SS 396 only.*   [4]*All but SS 396.*   *Standard in Corsa.*

## Major Options

| | Corvair | Chevy II | Chevelle | Full-size | Corvette |
|---|---|---|---|---|---|
| Air conditioning (NA 4-cyl.) | $342 | $311 | $356 | $356 | $413 |
| Soft Ray tinted glass | $31 | $31 | $31 | $37 | $16 |
| ComforTilt steering wheel (Telescopic) | $42 | | | | |
| (Telescopic) | - | $45 | $42 | $42 | |
| Power steering (NA 4-cyl.) | - | $84 | $84 | $95 | $95 |
| Power brakes | - | $42 | $42 | $42 | $42 |
| Power windows (N/A on all) | - | - | - | $100 | $58 |
| Electric clock | $16 | $16 | $16 | $16 | S |
| Pushbutton AM radio | $57 | $57 | $57 | $57 | $ |
| AM/FM radio | $133 | $134 | $134 | $134 | $173 |
| Front seat console | - | $ | $ | (incl. w/buckets) | S |
| Front bucket seats | S | $ | $111 | $158 | S |
| Vinyl roof | - | - | $74 | $100 | - |
| Whitewall tires — Std. size | $28 | $31 | $33 | $32–$40 | $31 |

Options common to most models. (– = Not Available; S = Standard equipment.) Items may be standard equipment, optional at different pricing, or unavailable on certain models. This chart is only a guide.

## Paint Colors

| | Code | Corvette | Other Chevrolet models |
|---|---|---|---|
| Tuxedo Black | AA/900 | X | X |
| Ermine White | CC/972 | | X |
| Mist Blue Metallic | DD | | X |
| Danube Blue Met. | EE | | X |
| Marina Blue Met. | FF | | X |
| Willow Green Met. | HH | | X |
| Artesian Turquoise Met. | KK | | X |
| Tropic Turquoise Met. | LL | | X |
| Aztec Bronze Metallic | MM | | x |
| Madeira Maroon Met. | NN | | X |
| Regal Red | RR | | X |
| Sandalwood Tan Met. | TT | | X |
| Cameo Beige | VV | | X |
| Chateau Slate Metallic | WW | | X |
| Butternut Yellow | YY | | X |
| Rallye Red | 974 | X | |

1966

| | Code | Corvette | Other Chevrolet models |
|---|---|---|---|
| Nassau Blue Metallic | 976 | X | |
| Laguna Blue Metallic | 978 | X | |
| Trophy Blue Metallic | 980 | X | |
| Mosport Green Metallic | 982 | X | |
| Sunfire Yellow | 984 | X | |
| Silver Pearl Metallic | 986 | X | |
| Milano Maroon Met. | 988 | X | |

# Corvair

*"Chevrolet's rear-engined fun car."*

**Nameplate year of origin:** 1960.
**Current bodystyle lifespan:** 1965 through 1969.
**Predecessor to this model:** Corvair (1960 to 1964).
**Replacement for this model:** Vega (1971 to 1977).
**Percentage of division's sales volume:** 4.84%.
**Corporate siblings:** None.
**Primary competition:** AMC Rambler American, Ford Falcon and Plymouth Valiant.
**Notable changes:** Minor trim and detail changes.
**Major standard equipment:** Cloth and vinyl front bench seat, dual sun visors, center dome light, and 7.00 × 14 BSW tires. Monza adds: All-vinyl bucket seats, full carpeting, folding rear seat, glove box light, front door map pockets, and additional exterior chrome trim. Corsa adds: instrument panel gauges, electric clock, and special identifying trim.

## Measurements

| | |
|---|---|
| Wheelbase | 108.0" |
| Length | 183.3" |
| Width | 69.7" |
| Height | 51.2" |
| Legroom — front | 41.1" |
| Legroom — rear | 35.4" |
| Headroom — front | 37.6" |
| Headroom — rear | 36.4" |
| Cargo capacity (cu. ft.) | 7.0 |
| Fuel capacity (gals.) | 14.0 |

## Models Available

| | Style Number | Base MSRP | Change from LY | Shipping Wt. (lbs.) | Production | Change from LY |
|---|---|---|---|---|---|---|
| Corvair 500 2-Door HT Sport Coupe | 10137 | $2,083 | +3.02% | 2400 | 24,045 | -34.57% |
| Corvair 500 4-Door HT Sport Sedan | 10139 | $2,157 | +2.91% | 2445 | 8,779 | -50.01% |
| Corvair Monza 2-Door HT Sport Cpe, | 10537 | $2,350 | +2.31% | 2445 | 37,605 | -57.73% |
| Corvair Monza 2-Door Convertible | 10567 | $2,493 | +2.17% | 2675 | 10,345 | -60.91% |
| Corvair Monza 4-Door HT Sport Sdn. | 10539 | $2,424 | +2.28% | 2495 | 12,497 | -66.37% |
| Corvair Corsa 2-Door HT Sport Cpe, | 10737 | $2,519 | +2.19% | 2485 | 7,330 | -63.88% |
| Corvair Corsa 2-Door Convertible | 10767 | $2,662 | +2.07% | 2720 | 3,142 | -62.38% |
| TOTALS | *Avg. price* | $2,384 | +2.41% | *Production* | 103,743 | -55.95% |

# Chevy II

*"Step smartly ... sensibility's wrapped up in fresh sparkle!"*

**Nameplate year of origin:** 1962.
**Current bodystyle lifespan:** 1966 through 1967.
**Predecessor to this model:** Chevy II (1962 to 1965).
**Replacement for this model:** Chevy II/Nova (1968 through 1972).
**Percentage of division's sales volume:** 6.12%.
**Corporate siblings:** None.

## Measurements

| | Cars | Wagons |
|---|---|---|
| Wheelbase | 110.0" | 110.0" |
| Length | 183.0" | 187.4" |
| Width | 71.3" | 71.3" |

**Primary competition:** AMC Rambler American, Dodge Dart, Ford Falcon, and Plymouth Valiant.

**Notable changes:** Completely restyled.

**Major standard equipment:** Cloth and vinyl front bench seat (all vinyl in wagons), black rubber floor mats, 2-speed windshield wipers with washers, and 6.50 × 13 BSW tires (6.95 × 14 BSW tires on wagon). Nova adds: Deluxe steering wheel, full carpeting, courtesy and glove box lights, and additional exterior chrome trim. SS adds: All vinyl seats, electric clock, SS trim and 6.95 × 14 BSW tires.

|  | Cars | Wagons |
|---|---|---|
| Height | 55.1" | 55.7" |
| Legroom — front | 40.7" | 40.7" |
| Legroom — rear | 36.2" | 36.2" |
| Headroom — front | 38.8" | 38.8" |
| Headroom — rear | 37.3" | 37.3" |
| Cargo capacity (cu. ft.) | 13.0 | 76.2 |
| Fuel capacity (gals.) | 16.0 | 16.0 |

## Models Available

|  | Style Number | Base MSRP | Change from LY | Shipping Wt. (lbs.) | Production | Change from LY |
|---|---|---|---|---|---|---|
| Chevy II 100 2-Door Coupe | 11111 | $2,028 | +3.05% | 2520 | 47,000 | * |
| Chevy II 100 4-Door Sedan | 11169 | $2,065 | +2.99% | 2535 | * | * |
| Chevy II 100 4-Door Wagon | 11335 | $2,430 | +2.88% | 2855 | * | * |
| Chevy II Nova 2-Door Hardtop | 11537 | $2,271 | +2.21% | 2675 | 73,900 | * |
| Chevy II Nova 4-Door Sedan | 11569 | $2,245 | +2.28% | 2640 | * | * |
| Chevy II Nova 4-Door Wagon | 11535 | $2,518 | +2.52% | 2885 | * | * |
| Chevy II Nova SS 2-Door HT | 11737 | $2,430 | +2.06% | 2740 | 10,100 | +134.88% |
| TOTALS | | *Avg. price* $2,284 | +2.56% | | *Production* 131,000 | +11.02% |

*Production is estimated and not available by series, only body style totals.*

# Chevelle

*"The most popular value of its size."*

**Nameplate year of origin:** 1964.

**Current bodystyle lifespan:** 1966 through 1967.

**Predecessor to this model:** Chevelle (1964 to 1965).

**Replacement for this model:** Chevelle (1968 to 1972).

**Percentage of division's sales volume:** 17.73%.

**Corporate siblings:** Buick Special/Skylark, Oldsmobile F-85/Cutlass, Pontiac Tempest/LeMans.

**Primary competition:** AMC Classic, Dodge Coronet, Ford Fairlane, and Plymouth Belvedere/Satellite.

**Notable changes:** Completely restyled.

**Major standard equipment:** Cloth and vinyl front bench seat, black rubber floor mats, hubcaps, and 6.95 × 14 BSW tires (7.35 × 14 BSW tires on wagons). 300 Deluxe adds: All-vinyl interior trim for wagon, color-keyed floor mats and additional exterior trim. Malibu adds: Color-keyed deep-twist carpeting, full wheel covers, electric clock and dual sun visors. SS 396 adds: All-vinyl bucket seats, console, special instrumentation, 396 CID V8 engine, and SS trim and wheel covers.

## Measurements

|  | Cars | Wagons |
|---|---|---|
| Wheelbase | 115.0" | 115.0" |
| Length | 197.0" | 199.9" |
| Width | 75.0" | 75.0" |
| Height | 53.0" | 54.6" |
| Legroom — front | 41.9" | 41.9" |
| Legroom — rear | 36.0" | 36.0" |
| Headroom — front | 38.5" | 38.5" |
| Headroom — rear | 37.3" | 37.3" |
| Cargo capacity (cu. ft.) | NA | 86.0 |
| Fuel capacity (gals.) | 20.0 | 20.0 |

## Models Available

|  | Style Number | Base MSRP | Change from LY | Shipping Wt. (lbs.) | Production | Change from LY |
|---|---|---|---|---|---|---|
| Chevelle 300 2-Door Coupe | 13111 | $2,165 | +6.49% | 2895 | 28,600 | * |
| Chevelle 300 4-Door Sedan | 13169 | $2,202 | +2.61% | 2935 | * | * |
| Chevelle 300 Deluxe 2-Door Coupe | 13311 | $2,239 | +2.57% | 2910 | 37,500 | * |
| Chevelle 300 Deluxe 4-Door Sedan | 13369 | $2,276 | +2.52% | 2945 | * | * |

| | Style Number | Base MSRP | Change from LY | Shipping Wt. (lbs.) | Production | Change from LY |
|---|---|---|---|---|---|---|
| Chevelle 300 Deluxe 4-Dr. Wagon | 13335 | $2,575 | +2.55% | 3210 | * | * |
| Chevelle Malibu 2-Door Hardtop | 13517 | $2,378 | +2.24% | 2935 | 241,500 | * |
| Chevelle Malibu 2-Dr. Convertible | 13567 | $2,588 | +2.21% | 3030 | * | * |
| Chevelle Malibu 4-Door Sedan | 13569 | $2,352 | +2.31% | 2960 | * | * |
| Chevelle Malibu 4-Door Hardtop | 13539 | $2,458 | NEW | 3035 | * | NEW |
| Chevelle Malibu 4-Door Wagon | 13535 | $2,651 | +2.36% | 3235 | * | * |
| Chevelle SS396 2-Door Hardtop | 13817 | $2,776 | +11.76% | 3375 | 72,272 | -10.89% |
| Chevelle SS396 2-Dr. Convertible | 13867 | $2,984 | +10.93% | 3470 | * | * |
| TOTALS | | *Avg. price* $2,470 | +4.31% | | *Production* 379,872 | +5.87% |

*Production is estimated, and not available by series. SS 396 production is for both body styles.*

# Chevrolet Full-size

*"Choose any Jet-smooth 1966 Chevrolet. It'll be well built, comfortable, dependable and good looking."*

**Nameplate year of origin:** 1966 (Caprice); (1958) Impala; (1950) BelAir; (1958) Biscayne.

**Current bodystyle lifespan:** 1965 through 1966.

**Predecessor to this model:** Biscayne/BelAir/Impala (1961 to 1964).

**Replacement for this model:** Biscayne/BelAir/Impala/Caprice (1967 to 1968).

**Percentage of division's sales volume:** 70.01%.

**Corporate siblings:** Buick LeSabre/Wildcat, Olds 88, Pontiac Catalina/Bonneville.

**Primary competition:** AMC Ambassador, Dodge Polara, Ford Custom/Galaxie/LTD, and Plymouth Fury.

**Notable changes:** Revised front and rear styling. New Caprice series created from 1965 Impala 4-Door Hardtop Caprice option package.

**Major standard equipment:** Biscayne: Cloth and vinyl bench seat, full carpeting, front and rear door armrests, 2-speed electric windshield wipers with washers, and 7.35 × 14 BSW tires (8.55 × 14 BSW tires on wagons). BelAir adds: Automatic interior lighting, bright body side molding, and power tailgate window on 3-Seat wagon models. Impala adds: Vinyl upholstery in convertible, extra-long armrests, electric clock, trunk lamp and 7.75 × 14 BSW tires. SS adds: All vinyl bucket seats, center floor console, and special SS wheel covers, body trim and interior trim. Caprice adds: Tufted cloth and vinyl front bench seats (with center fold-down armrest on sedan), all-vinyl upholstery in wagons, simulated walnut interior trim, dual pinstriping, deluxe wheel covers, wide rocker panel moldings, simulated walnut exterior trim on wagons, and special ornamentation.

## Measurements

| | Cars | Wagons |
|---|---|---|
| Wheelbase | 119.0" | 119.0" |
| Length | 213.2" | 212.4" |
| Width | 79.6" | 79.6" |
| Height | 55.4" | 56.7" |
| Legroom — front | 42.2" | 42.2" |
| Legroom — rear | 39.5" | 39.5" |
| Headroom — front | 39.1" | 39.1" |
| Headroom — rear | 37.8" | 37.8" |
| Cargo capacity (cu. ft.) | 17.8 | 106.1 |
| Fuel capacity (gals.) | 20.0 | 20.0 |

## Models Available

| | Style Number | Base MSRP | Change from LY | Shipping Wt. (lbs.) | Production | Change from LY |
|---|---|---|---|---|---|---|
| Biscayne 2-Door Sedan | 15311 | $2,379 | +2.81% | 3310 | 122,400 | * |
| Biscayne 4-Door Sedan | 15369 | $2,431 | +2.70% | 3375 | * | * |
| Biscayne 4-Dr., 2-S. Wagon | 15335 | $2,772 | +2.40% | 3770 | * | * |
| Bel Air 2-Door Sedan | 15511 | $2,479 | +2.69% | 3315 | 236,600 | * |
| Bel Air 4-Door Sedan | 15569 | $2,531 | +2.59% | 3390 | * | * |
| BelAir 4-Dr., 2-S. Wagon | 15535 | $2,835 | +2.35% | 3770 | * | * |
| BelAir 4-Dr., 3-S. Wagon | 15545 | $2,948 | +2.68% | 3815 | * | * |
| Impala 2-Door Sport Coupe | 16337 | $2,684 | +2.33% | 3430 | 654,900 | * |

| | Style Number | Base MSRP | Change from LY | Shipping Wt. (lbs.) | Production | Change from LY |
|---|---|---|---|---|---|---|
| Impala 2-Door Convertible | 16367 | $2,935 | +1.84% | 3485 | * | * |
| Impala 4-Door Sedan | 16369 | $2,678 | +2.33% | 3435 | * | * |
| Impala 4-Door Hardtop | 16339 | $2,747 | +2.31% | 3525 | * | * |
| Impala 4-Dr., 2-S. Wagon | 16335 | $2,971 | +2.13% | 3805 | 185,500 | * |
| Impala 4-Dr., 3-S. Wagon | 16345 | $3,083 | +2.43% | 3860 | * | * |
| Impala SS 2-Door Sport Coupe | 16737 | $2,842 | +2.23% | 3460 | 119,300 | * |
| Impala SS 2-Door Convertible | 16767 | $3,093 | +1.74% | 3505 | * | * |
| Caprice 2-Door Custom Hardtop | 16647 | $3,000 | NEW | 3585 | 181,000 | NEW |
| Caprice 4-Door Custom Hardtop | 16639 | $3,063 | NEW | 3675 | * | NEW |
| Caprice 4-Dr., 2-S. Custom Wagon | 16635 | $3,234 | NEW | 3970 | * | NEW |
| Caprice 4-Dr., 3-S. Custom Wagon | 16645 | $3,347 | NEW | 4020 | * | NEW |
| TOTALS | Avg. price | $2,845 | +5.49% | | Production 1,499,700 | -8.98% |

*Production is estimated and not available by series, only body style totals.*

# Corvette

*"Two brand-new 427-cu.-in. Turbo-Jet V8s cap Corvette's quartet of engines."*

**Nameplate year of origin:** 1953 (also used on show car of same year).
**Current bodystyle lifespan:** 1963 through 1967.
**Predecessor to this model:** Corvette (1956 to 1962).
**Replacement for this model:** Corvette (1968 to 1982).
**Percentage of division's sales volume:** 1.29%.
**Corporate siblings:** None.
**Primary competition:** None.
**Notable changes:** Minor trim and detail changes.
**Major standard equipment:** Bucket seats, cockpit-cluster console, simulated walnut steering wheel, full carpeting, complete instrumentation, manually operated folding convertible top, and 6.70 × 15 BSW tires.

## Measurements

| | |
|---|---|
| Wheelbase | 98.0" |
| Length | 175.1" |
| Width | 69.2" |
| Height | 49.6" |
| Legroom — front | 42.7" |
| Legroom — rear | NA |
| Headroom — front | 37.0" |
| Headroom — rear | NA |
| Cargo capacity (cu. ft.) | 10.6 |
| Fuel capacity (gals.) | 20.0 |

**1966**

## Models Available

| | Style Number | Base MSRP | Change from LY | Shipping Wt. (lbs.) | Production | Change from LY |
|---|---|---|---|---|---|---|
| Corvette 2-Door Coupe | 19437 | $4,295 | +1.46% | 2985 | 9,958 | +21.65% |
| Corvette 2-Door Convertible | 19467 | $4,084 | +1.54% | 3005 | 17,762 | +15.52% |
| TOTALS | Avg. price | $4,190 | +1.50% | | Production 27,720 | +17.65% |

# CHRYSLER

*"Youth comes twice in life. When you're young and when you want to be.
The 1966 Chrysler is built for both. Move up to Chrysler."*

The very successful Chryslers that had been totally restyled for 1965 were left little changed for the new year. New grilles were designed that seemed more streamlined and fit the overall appearance of the big Chryslers better than the first round. Detail changes were made such as discontinuing the glass covers on the 300 and New Yorker headlamps, and the clear outer taillamp lenses of the New Yorker were changed to a red lens. The 300 letter series was no longer offered, but the regular 300 line was available with every accessory anyway, so a buyer could still build a letter-series look-alike. Chrysler repositioned the Town & Country wagon so that it was now offered only in the Newport trim level. This move had little effect on sales, as there had traditionally been little to distinguish the New Yorker and Newport trim levels on the wagons, other than their interior appointments. In fact, gradually rising sales of this popular body style in the mid-to-luxury price category

would facilitate the Town & Country becoming its own separate entity in the model line by 1969. The slow-selling New Yorker 6-window Town Sedan was dropped at the end of the model year.

More important than the styling changes this season was the introduction of the 440 CID V8 engine to the Chrysler line. This 4.326 bore × 3.75 stroke engine, with 10.1:1 compression ratio, put out 350 horsepower at 4400 rpm, with a 4-barrel carburetor. The powerful engine was by no means economical, but given its output potential, it was more economical than its many competitors. In fact, this engine would power many big Chryslers right up through their demise in 1978 — not so much because of its power (by 1975 it was only rated at 215 net hp), but the adaptability of the engine to the necessary emission and fuel economy standards made it a prudent choice for meeting the objectives of the government programs.

Newport 6-window, 4-Door Sedan

New Yorker 4-Door Hardtop

300 4-Door Hardtop

Town & Country 4-Door Wagon

**Model year production:** 262,495, up 28.67% over 1965.
**Domestic market share:** 2.93% (10th place).
**Base price range:** $3,052 to $4,233.
**Industry average base price:** $3,070.
**Chrysler average base price:** $3,689.
**Introduction date:** September 1965.
**Assembly plants:** Detroit (Jefferson Ave.), MI (3); and Newark, DE (6).
**Data plate identification:** thirteen digit code read as follows:

1st digit C = Chrysler; 2nd number identifies series (L is Newport, M is 300, H is New Yorker); 3rd and 4th digits indicate body style; 5th digit indicates engine code (see chart below); 6th digit 6 for 1966; 7th digit is assembly plant code; followed by 100001 and up for serial number. Body style identification found on separate plate. *Example:* CL23G63100001 is a 1966 Chrysler Newport 2-Door Hardtop with a 383 CID 2-bbl. V8 engine, serial number 100001, built in Detroit, MI.

## Powertrains

| Engine | Gross HP | Transmission Availability | Newport | 300 | New Yorker |
|---|---|---|---|---|---|
| FirePower 383 CID, 2-bbl., V8 | 270 | 3-speed manual | S | - | - |
| | | Torqueflite automatic | $222 | - | - |
| FirePower 383 CID XP, 4-bbl., V8 | 325 | 3-speed manual | $34 | S | - |
| | | Torqueflite automatic | $256 | $222 | - |
| FirePower 440 CID, 4-bbl., V8 | 350 | Torqueflite automatic | - | - | S |
| FirePower 440 CID TNT, 4-bbl., V8 | 365 | Torqueflite automatic | $335 | $301 | $79 |

## Major Options

| | Newport | 300 | New Yorker |
|---|---|---|---|
| Heater and defroster | $102 | $102 | $102 |
| Airtemp air conditioning | $510 | $510 | $510 |
| Solex tinted glass | $43 | $43 | $43 |
| Rear window defogger | $21 | $21 | $21 |
| Tilt-A-Scope steering wheel | $47 | $47 | $47 |
| Auto Pilot cruise control | $86 | $86 | $86 |
| Power steering | $108 | $108 | S |
| Power brakes | $48 | $48 | S |
| Power seat — Bench | $102 | $102 | $102 |
| Power windows | $108 | $108 | S |
| Golden Touch Tone AM radio | $93 | $93 | $93 |
| AM/FM radio | $157 | $157 | $157 |
| White sidewall tires — std. sizes | $42 | $46 | $51 |

Options common to most models. (S = Standard equipment.) Items may be standard equipment, optional at different pricing, or unavailable on certain models. This chart is only a guide.

## Paint Colors

| | Code |
|---|---|
| Silver Mist Metallic | AA-1 |
| Formal Black | BB-1 |
| Powder Blue | CC-1 |
| Crystal Blue Metallic | DD-1 |
| Regal Blue Metallic | EE-1 |
| Haze Green Metallic | FF-1 |
| Sequoia Green Metallic | GG-1 |
| Frost Turquoise Met. | KK-1 |
| Royal Turquoise Metallic | LL-1 |
| Scorch Red | PP-1 |
| Spanish Red Metallic | QQ-1 |
| Daffodil Yellow | RR-1 |
| Ivory | SS-1 |
| Persian White | WW-1 |
| Desert Beige | XX-1 |
| Saddle Bronze Metallic | YY-1 |
| Spice Gold Metallic | ZZ-1 |
| Dove Tan | 33-1 |
| Moss Gold Metallic | 44-1 |
| Dusty Gold Metallic | 55-1 |
| Lilac Metallic | 66-1 |
| Ruby Metallic | 77-1 |
| Deep Plum Metallic | 88-1 |

**1966**

# Newport

*"Priced to make young dreams come true."*

**Nameplate year of origin:** 1961 (as series); 1950 (as Hardtop model designation).
**Current bodystyle lifespan:** Windsor 1960; Newport 1961 through 1964 with major restyle in 1963.
**Predecessor to this model:** Windsor (1960), Newport (1961 to 1964).
**Replacement for this model:** Newport (1967 to 1968).
**Percentage of division's sales volume:** 63.88%.
**Corporate siblings:** Chrysler 300 and New Yorker.
**Primary competition:** Buick Wildcat, Mercury Monterey and Oldsmobile 88.
**Notable changes:** Revised grille, and minor trim and detail changes.
**Major standard equipment:** Cloth and vinyl front bench seat, deep-pile carpeting, exterior bright side moldings, variable-speed windshield wipers w/washers, trip odometer, rear wheel opening fender skirts, and 8.25 × 14 BSW tires.
Town & Country adds: Power rear window, map courtesy light, carpeted cargo

## Measurements

| | Cars | Wagons |
|---|---|---|
| Wheelbase | 124.0" | 121.0" |
| Length | 219.0" | 219.0" |
| Width | 79.5" | 79.4" |
| Height | 55.5" | 56.8" |
| Legroom — front | 42.0" | 42.0" |
| Legroom — rear | 36.2" | 36.0" |
| Headroom — front | 37.9" | 37.9" |
| Headroom — rear | 38.0" | 38.0" |
| Cargo capacity (cu. ft.) | 17.4 | 107.0 |
| Fuel capacity (gals.) | 25.0 | 22.0 |

area, deluxe wheel covers, power steering, power brakes, automatic transmission, exterior wood-grain trim, rear bumper guards w/step pads on 3-Seat, and 9.00 × 14 BSW tires.

## Models Available

| | Style Number | Base MSRP | Change from LY | Shipping Wt. (lbs.) | Production | Change from LY |
|---|---|---|---|---|---|---|
| Newport 2-Door Hardtop | CE23 | $3,112 | +1.37% | 3920 | 37,622 | +59.04% |
| Newport 2-Door Convertible | CE27 | $3,476 | +0.99% | 4020 | 3,085 | -3.35% |
| Newport 4-Door Sedan | CE41 | $3,052 | +1.43% | 3875 | 74,964 | +22.78% |
| Newport 4-Dr., 6-w. Town Sedan | CE42 | $3,183 | +1.27% | 3910 | 9,432 | -24.00% |
| Newport 4-Door Hardtop | CE43 | $3,190 | +1.30% | 4010 | 24,966 | +46.33% |
| Town & Country 4-Dr., 2-S. Wagon | CL45 | $4,086 | +16.05% | 4370 | 9,035 | +92.93% |
| Town & Country 4-Dr., 3-S. Wagon | CL46 | $4,192 | +15.51% | 4550 | 8,567 | +129.19% |
| TOTALS | | Avg. price $3,470 | +5.79% | | Production 167,671 | +33.29% |

# 300

*"The Chrysler 300 is going to be very hard to resist. Wouldn't you say?"*

**Nameplate year of origin:** 1955; 1962 (as non-letter series).
**Current bodystyle lifespan:** 1965 through 1966.
**Predecessor to this model:** Saratoga (1960); Windsor (1961); 300 (1962 through 1964 with major restyle in 1963).
**Replacement for this model:** 300 (1967 to 1968).
**Percentage of division's sales volume:** 18.00%.
**Corporate siblings:** Chrysler Newport and New Yorker.
**Primary competition:** Buick Wildcat, Mercury Monterey S-55 and Oldsmobile 88.
**Notable changes:** Revised grille, and minor trim and detail changes.
**Major standard equipment:** All-vinyl bucket seats, pile carpeting, padded dash, electric clock, exterior bright side moldings, full wheel covers, rear wheel opening fender skirts, and 8.55 × 14 BSW tires.

## Measurements

| | |
|---|---|
| Wheelbase | 124.0" |
| Length | 221.9" |
| Width | 79.5" |
| Height | 55.2" |
| Legroom — front | 42.0" |
| Legroom — rear | 34.8" |
| Headroom — front | 37.9" |
| Headroom — rear | 38.1" |
| Cargo capacity (cu. ft.) | 17.4 |
| Fuel capacity (gals.) | 25.0 |

## Models Available

| | Style Number | Base MSRP | Change from LY | Shipping Wt. (lbs.) | Production | Change from LY |
|---|---|---|---|---|---|---|
| 300 2-Door Hardtop | CM23 | $3,583 | +0.90% | 3940 | 24,103 | +107.41% |
| 300 2-Door Convertible | CM27 | $3,936 | +0.64% | 4015 | 2,500 | +76.30% |
| 300 4-Door Hardtop | CM43 | $3,659 | +0.85% | 4000 | 20,642 | +65.77% |
| TOTALS | | Avg. price $3,726 | +0.78% | | Production 47,245 | +85.34% |

# New Yorker

*"Remember this first impression. That's how people will see you in New Yorker."*

**Nameplate year of origin:** 1939 (altered from 1938 New York Special model).
**Current bodystyle lifespan:** New Yorker (1965 through 1966).
**Predecessor to this model:** New Yorker (1960 to 1964).
**Replacement for this model:** New Yorker (1967 to 1968).

## Measurements

| | |
|---|---|
| Wheelbase | 124.0" |
| Length | 219.0" |
| Width | 79.5" |

**Percentage of division's sales volume:** 18.19%.
**Corporate siblings:** Chrysler Newport and 300.
**Primary competition:** Buick Electra, Mercury Park Lane and Oldsmobile 98.
**Notable changes:** Revised grille, minor trim and detail changes.
**Major standard equipment:** Cloth and vinyl front bench seat, pile carpeting, padded dash, map lights, power windows, electric clock, exclusive exterior bright trim, power steering, power brakes, automatic transmission, full wheel covers, rear wheel opening fender skirts, and 8.55 × 14 BSW tires.

## Measurements (cont.)

| | |
|---|---|
| Height | 55.7" |
| Legroom — front | 42.0" |
| Legroom — rear | 40.8" |
| Headroom — front | 38.5" |
| Headroom — rear | 37.3" |
| Cargo capacity (cu. ft.) | 17.4 |
| Fuel capacity (gals.) | 25.0 |

## Models Available

| | Style Number | Base MSRP | Change from LY | Shipping Wt. (lbs.) | Production | Change from LY |
|---|---|---|---|---|---|---|
| New Yorker 2-Door Hardtop | CH23 | $4,157 | -0.10% | 4095 | 7,955 | -14.98% |
| New Yorker 4-Door Town Sedan | CH41 | $4,101 | -0.07% | 4110 | 13,025 | -20.28% |
| New Yorker 4-Door Hardtop | CH43 | $4,233 | -0.12% | 4140 | 26,599 | +26.00% |
| TOTALS | | *Avg. price* $4,164 | -5.49% | | *Production* 47,759 | -4.59% |

# DODGE

*"Join the Dodge rebellion!"*

**1966**

What a difference a few years make! After all the successes of the mid-fifties, then the failures of early sixties, Dodge was once again on a roll. Sales were down slightly this year, but styling and power choices were at the forefront of the automotive industry. At the top of the list were the all-new intermediate or mid-size models. They had already earned their respect in the power department through numerous racing wins around the country as the Dodge 330/440 line, and generally equipped with a 413 or 426 CID V8 engine. These cars were at the center of the muscle car revolution. Now it was time to wrap that muscle in some style. Derived from the "full-size" 1962–1964 Plymouth/Dodge platform and 1965 "mid-size" platform, these new cars were stylish, angular cars, with then popular Coke-bottle side styling treatments. The front end consisted of fairly basic split grille designs mounted flush with the front fenders and hood edges. By far the most talked about of the new cars was the fastback Charger, which was based on a Coronet Hardtop chassis. This new body style was just becoming popular, having previously been seen on the Plymouth Barracuda, AMC Rambler Marlin and the relatively new Ford Mustang. The Charger was the largest adaptation of the design yet, and it looked wonderful. The lines flowed cleanly from front to back, and despite the size of the car, it did not come off awkward looking, as some larger fastbacks did. The interior was a special sight also, featuring 4-place bucket seating with a full-length console. Trim inside and out was unique to the Charger, belying its meager Coronet basis. Powertrains ran the gamut from a standard 318 CID V8, all the way to the mighty new 440 CID V8 engine.

As for the other Dodge lines, the Dart was given revised styling for a final season, before being updated as an even larger "compact" model for 1967. A mid-year, high-performance version of the popular 273 CID V8 engine was introduced, giving the Dart a needed jolt under the hood. At the opposite end of the line, the full-size Dodge models shuffled nameplates to take advantage of the popularity of the new Monaco nameplate. The Monaco name replaced the Custom 880, and a new Monaco 500 replaced the former Monaco model. A Polara 318 model was once again offered, although basically intended for fleet purchase.

Charger 2-Door Hardtop (front)

Charger 2-Door Hardtop (rear)

Coronet 440 2-Door Convertible

Coronet 500 2-Door Hardtop

Dart 4-Door Wagon

Dart GT 2-Door Convertible

Monaco 500 2-Door Hardtop

Monaco 4-Door Hardtop

Polara 500 2-Door Convertible

**Model year production:** 543,700, down 1.32% from 1965.
**Domestic market share:** 6.07% (7th place).
**Base price range:** $2,094 to $3,604.
**Industry average base price:** $3,070.
**Dodge average base price:** $2,726.
**Introduction date:** September 29, 1965.
**Assembly plants:** Lynch Road, MI (1); Hamtramck, MI (2); Detroit (Jefferson Ave.), MI (3); Belvidere, IL (4); Los Angeles, CA (5); Newark, DE (6); St. Louis, MO (7) and Windsor, Ontario, Canada (9).
**Data plate identification:** Thirteen digit code read as follows:
four digit style number (see listings below) in which 1st digit is series letter (e.g., D = Polara/Monaco series), 2nd number identifies car model (L is for Low line base Polara, H for High-line Monaco, etc.), 3rd and 4th digits are body style (see charts below); 5th digit is engine code (see chart below); 6th digit 6 for 1966; 7th digit is the assembly plant code; followed by 100001 (500001 for Dart) and up for serial number. *Example:* DL23G63100001 is a 1966 Dodge Polara 2-Door Hardtop with a 383 CID V8, serial number 100001, built in Detroit, MI.

## Powertrains

| Engine | Gross HP | Engine Code | Transmission Availability | Dart | Coronet | Charger | Polara/ Monaco |
|---|---|---|---|---|---|---|---|
| 170 CID, 1-bbl., 6-cyl. | 101 | A | 3-speed manual | S | - | - | - |
| | | | Torqueflite automatic | $140 | - | - | - |
| 225 CID, 1-bbl., 6-cyl. | 145 | B | 3-speed manual | $39 | S (ex. 500) | - | - |
| | | | 4-speed manual | $191 | $146 (ex. 500 | - | - |
| | | | Torqueflite automatic | $187 | $165 (ex. 500 | - | - |
| 273 CID, | 180 | D | 3-speed manual | $96 | S (500)/$94 (Others) | - | - |

| Engine | Gross HP | Engine Code | Transmission Availability | Dart | Coronet | Charger | Polara/ Monaco |
|---|---|---|---|---|---|---|---|
| 2-bbl., V8 | | | 4-speed manual | $242 | $180 (500)/$274 (Others) | – | – |
| | | | Torqueflite automatic | $244 | $181 (500)/$275 (Others) | – | – |
| 273 CID High-Performance, 4-bbl., V8 | 235 | E | 3-speed manual | $193 | – | – | – |
| | | | 4-speed manual | $339 | – | – | – |
| | | | Torqueflite automatic | $341 | – | – | – |
| 318 CID, 2-bbl., V8 | 230 | E/F | 3-speed manual | – | $25 (500)/$119 (Others) | S | S[1] |
| | | | Torqueflite automatic | – | $236 (500)/$330 (Others) | $211 | $211[1] |
| 361 CID, 2-bbl., V8 | 265 | G | 3-speed manual | – | $ (500)/$ (Others)* | $* | – |
| | | | 4-speed manual | – | $ (500)/$ (Others)* | $* | – |
| | | | Torqueflite automatic | – | $ (500)/$ (Others)* | $* | – |
| 383 CID, 2-bbl., V8 | 270 | G | 3-speed manual | – | – | – | $[1]/S[2] |
| | | | 4-speed manual | – | – | – | $[1]/$[2] |
| | | | Torqueflite automatic | – | – | – | $[1]/$[2] |
| 383 CID, 4-bbl., V8 | 325 | G/H | 3-speed manual | – | $ (500)/$ (Others)* | $* | $[1]/$[2] |
| | | | 4-speed manual | – | $ (500)/$ (Others)* | $* | $[1]/$[2] |
| | | | Torqueflite automatic | – | $ (500)/$ (Others)* | $* | $[1]/$[2] |
| 426 CID Hemi-Charger, 2 × 4-bbl., V8 | 425 | K | 4-speed manual | – | $* | $* | – |
| | | | Torqueflite automatic | – | $* | $* | – |
| 440 CID, 4-bbl., V8 | 350/365 | J | 4-speed manual | – | – | – | $* |
| | | | Torqueflite automatic | – | – | – | $* |

[1]Polara 318 only.    [2]All but Polara 381.    *Accurate pricing information currently unavailable.

## Major Options

| | Dart | Coronet | Charger | Polara | Monaco |
|---|---|---|---|---|---|
| Airtemp air conditioning | $285 | $315 | $315 | $315 | $315 |
| Tinted glass | $22 | $31 | $31 | $31 | $31 |
| Auto Pilot cruise control | – | $66 | $66 | $66 | $66 |
| Power steering | $67 | $67 | $74 | $74 | $74 |
| Power brakes | $33 | $33 | $33 | $33 | $33 |
| Power seat | – | $74 | $74 | $61 | $61 |
| Power windows | – | $102 | $102 | $102 | $102 |
| Electric clock | $12 | $12 | S | $12 | S |
| Music Master AM radio | $79 | $45 | $45 | $45 | $45 |
| White sidewall tires— std. sizes | $23–$25 | $25–$40 | $25–$40 | $40 | $40 |
| Polara 500 Sport package | – | – | – | $199 | – |

Options common to most models. (– = Not Available; S = Standard equipment.) Items may be standard equipment, optional at different pricing, or unavailable on certain models. This chart is only a guide.

## Paint Colors

| | Code |
|---|---|
| Silver Metallic | AA-1 |
| Black | BB-1 |
| Light Blue Metallic | CC-1 |
| Medium Blue Metallic | DD-1 |
| Dark Blue Metallic | EE-1 |
| Light Green Metallic | FF-1 |
| Dark Green Metallic | GG-1 |
| Pale Med. Turquoise Met. | KK-1 |
| Dark Turquoise Metallic | LL-1 |
| Turbine Bronze Metallic | MM-1 |
| Bright Red | PP-1 |
| Yellow | RR-1 |
| Cream | SS-1 |
| White | WW-1 |
| Beige | XX-1 |
| Bronze Metallic | YY-1 |
| Gold Metallic | ZZ-1 |
| Sandstone Metallic | 44-1 |
| Mauve Metallic | 66-1 |
| Maroon Metallic | 77-1 |

1966

# Dart

*"Stamp out cramped compacts. Up with man-sized Dart."*

**Nameplate year of origin:** 1960 (On low-end full-size models).
**Current bodystyle lifespan:** 1963 through 1966.
**Predecessor to this model:** Lancer (1961 to 1962).
**Replacement for this model:** Dart (1967 to 1976).
**Percentage of division's sales volume:** 20.77%.
**Corporate siblings:** Plymouth Valiant.
**Primary competition:** AMC Rambler American, Chevrolet Chevy II, Mercury Comet, and Studebaker.
**Notable changes:** Revised front and rear styling.
**Major standard equipment:** Cloth and vinyl front bench seats (all-vinyl on wagon), color-keyed rubber floor mats, chrome windshield trim and 6.50 × 13 BSW tires. 270 adds: All-vinyl upholstery on convertible, full carpeting, additional interior and exterior bright trim. GT adds: All-vinyl bucket seats, deluxe wheel covers, sill moldings and specific GT trim.

## Measurements

| | Cars | Wagons |
|---|---|---|
| Wheelbase | 111.0" | 106.0" |
| Length | 196.3" | 190.2" |
| Width | 70.8" | 70.7" |
| Height | 52.7" | 53.0" |
| Legroom — front | 40.7" | 40.7" |
| Legroom — rear | 35.6" | 35.4" |
| Headroom — front | 38.2" | 38.2" |
| Headroom — rear | 37.3" | 37.2" |
| Cargo capacity (cu. ft.) | 17.3 | 68.3 |
| Fuel capacity (gals.) | 18.0 | 18.0 |

## Models Available

| | Style Number | Base MSRP | Change from LY | Shipping Wt. (lbs.) | Production | Change from LY |
|---|---|---|---|---|---|---|
| Dart 2-Door Sedan | LL21 | $2,094 | +0.96% | 2670 | 29,800 | -59.62% |
| Dart 4-Door Sedan | LL41 | $2,158 | +0.89% | 2695 | * | * |
| Dart 4-Door, 2-Seat Wagon | LL45 | $2,436 | +1.20% | 2780 | * | * |
| Dart 270 2-Door Sedan | LH21 | $2,214 | +1.56% | 2665 | 29,300 | -53.34% |
| Dart 270 2-Door Hardtop | LH23 | $2,307 | +1.45% | 2720 | * | * |
| Dart 270 2-Door Convertible | LH27 | $2,570 | +3.59% | 2805 | * | * |
| Dart 270 4-Door Sedan | LH41 | $2,280 | +1.47% | 2680 | * | * |
| Dart 270 4-Door, 2-Seat Wagon | LH45 | $2,533 | +1.08% | 2795 | 35,100 | +19.39% |
| Dart GT 2-Door Hardtop | LP23 | $2,417 | +0.54% | 2735 | 18,700 | -54.05% |
| Dart GT 2-Door Convertible | LP27 | $2,700 | +2.74% | 2845 | * | * |
| TOTALS | | Avg. price $2,371 | +1.59% | | Production 112,900 | -45.38% |

*Production by series not available. Totals are estimated.*

# Coronet

*"Announcing a beautiful rebellion on wheels: '66 Dodge Coronet!"*

**Nameplate year of origin:** 1949.
**Current bodystyle lifespan:** Dart and 330/440 (1962 through 1965).
**Predecessor to this model:** Dart Seneca and Pioneer (1960 to 1961).
**Replacement for this model:** Coronet (1966 to 1967).
**Percentage of division's sales volume:** 46.15%.
**Corporate siblings:** Plymouth Belvedere.
**Primary competition:** AMC Classic, Chevrolet Chevelle, Ford Fairlane, and Pontiac Tempest.
**Notable changes:** Completely restyled front and rear end. Renamed from prior 330/440 series.
**Major standard equipment:** Cloth and vinyl bench seat, black rubber floor mats, variable speed windshield wipers with washers, and 6.95 × 14 BSW tires. Deluxe adds: All-vinyl bench seats (wagons), color-keyed rubber

## Measurements

| | Cars | Wagons |
|---|---|---|
| Wheelbase | 117.0" | 117.0" |
| Length | 203.0" | 207.9" |
| Width | 75.3" | 75.3" |
| Height | 53.7" | 54.7" |
| Legroom — front | 42.0" | 42.0" |
| Legroom — rear | 36.5" | 36.5" |
| Headroom — front | 38.8" | 38.8" |
| Headroom — rear | 37.8" | 37.8" |
| Cargo capacity (cu. ft.) | 17.0 | 88.0 |
| Fuel capacity (gals.) | 19.0 | 19.0 |

floor mats, full horn ring and 8.25 × 14 BSW tires on wagon. 440 adds: All-vinyl seats (2-Doors), exterior bright trim package, full carpeting, and sill moldings. 500 adds: Full wheel covers and additional exterior and interior trim.

## Models Available

| | Style Number | Base MSRP | Change from LY | Shipping Wt. (lbs.) | Production | Change from LY |
|---|---|---|---|---|---|---|
| Coronet 2-Door Sedan | WE21 | $2,264 | NEW | 3055 | 10,700 | NEW |
| Coronet 4-Door Sedan | WE41 | $2,302 | NEW | 3077 | * | NEW |
| Coronet Deluxe 2-Door Coupe | WL21 | $2,303 | +2.04% | 3050 | 46,200 | -26.78% |
| Coronet Deluxe 4-Door Sedan | WL41 | $2,341 | +1.96% | 3075 | * | * |
| Coronet Deluxe 4-Dr., 2-S. Wagon | WL45 | $2,631 | +1.50% | 3480 | 27,700 | 8.20% |
| Coronet 440 2-Door Hardtop | WH23 | $2,457 | +2.25% | 3075 | 110,600 | 26.40% |
| Coronet 440 2-Door Convertible | WH27 | $2,672 | +1.91% | 3165 | * | * |
| Coronet 440 4-Door Sedan | WH41 | $2,432 | +2.31% | 3070 | * | * |
| Coronet 440 4-Dr., 2-S. Wagon | WH45 | $2,722 | +1.80% | 3515 | * | * |
| Coronet 440 4-Dr., 3-S. Wagon | WH46 | $2,926 | +2.02% | 3680 | * | * |
| Coronet 500 2-Door Hardtop | WP23 | $2,611 | -2.36% | NA | 55,700 | 67.27% |
| Coronet 500 2-Door Convertible | WP27 | $2,827 | -2.32% | NA | * | * |
| Coronet 500 4-Door Sedan | WP41 | $2,586 | NEW | 3115 | * | NEW |
| TOTALS | | Avg. price $2,544 | -0.86% | | Production 250,900 | +19.76% |

*Production by series not available. Totals are estimated.*

# Charger

*"This is no dream car. Plant one of these in your driveway."*

**Nameplate year of origin:** 1966.
**Current bodystyle lifespan:** 1966 through 1967.
**Predecessor to this model:** None.
**Replacement for this model:** Charger (1968 to 1970).
**Percentage of division's sales volume:** 6.86%.
**Corporate siblings:** None.
**Primary competition:** AMC Marlin and Mercury Comet Caliente.
**Notable changes:** All-new model for 1966.
**Major standard equipment:** All vinyl bucket seats (front and rear), full-length center console, full carpeting, variable speed windshield wipers with washers, interior courtesy lights, tinted rear window, tachometer, oil pressure gauge, and 7.35 × 14 BSW tires.

## Measurements

| | |
|---|---|
| Wheelbase | 117.0" |
| Length | 203.6" |
| Width | 75.3" |
| Height | 53.0" |
| Legroom — front | 41.6" |
| Legroom — rear | 34.0" |
| Headroom — front | 37.7" |
| Headroom — rear | 36.5" |
| Cargo capacity (cu. ft.) | NA |
| Fuel capacity (gals.) | 19.0 |

## Models Available

| | Style Number | Base MSRP | Change from LY | Shipping Wt. (lbs.) | Production | Change from LY |
|---|---|---|---|---|---|---|
| Charger 2-Door Hardtop | XP29 | $3,146 | NEW | 3499 | 37,300 | NEW |
| TOTALS | | Avg. price $3,146 | NEW | | Production 37,300 | NEW |

1966

# Polara

*"Demand more 'big' in your big car. Swing with Dodge Polara."*

**Nameplate year of origin:** 1959.
**Current bodystyle lifespan:** 1965 through 1966.
**Predecessor to this model:** Custom 880 (1962 to 1964).
**Replacement for this model:** Polara (1967 to 1968).
**Percentage of division's sales volume:** 13.87%.
**Corporate siblings:** Plymouth Fury.
**Primary competition:** AMC Ambassador, Chevrolet BelAir/Impala, and Ford Galaxie/LTD.
**Notable changes:** New grille and revised trim and detail changes.
**Major standard equipment:** Cloth-and-vinyl bench seat, full carpeting, variable speed windshield wipers with washers, power tailgate window (3-Seat wagon), and 8.25 × 14 BSW tires (8.55 × 14 BSW tires on wagons). Polara 500 package adds: Vinyl bucket seats, tachometer, center console and wheel covers.

## Measurements

| | Cars | Wagons |
|---|---|---|
| Wheelbase | 121.0" | 121.0" |
| Length | 213.3" | 217.1" |
| Width | 80.0" | 79.4" |
| Height | 54.7" | 56.0" |
| Legroom — front | 42.0" | 42.0" |
| Legroom — rear | 40.8" | 40.8" |
| Headroom — front | 39.3" | 39.3" |
| Headroom — rear | 38.5" | 38.5" |
| Cargo capacity (cu. ft.) | NA | 96.9 |
| Fuel capacity (gals.) | 19.0 | 19.0 |

## Models Available

| | Style Number | Base MSRP | Change from LY | Shipping Wt. (lbs.) | Production | Change from LY |
|---|---|---|---|---|---|---|
| Polara 318 4-Door Sedan | DE41 | $2,763 | +2.52% | 3765 | 12,400 | * |
| Polara 2-Door Hardtop | DL23 | $2,874 | +2.64% | 3800 | * | * |
| Polara 2-Door Convertible | DL27 | $3,161 | +2.36% | 3885 | * | * |
| Polara 4-Door Sedan | DL41 | $2,838 | +2.45% | 3820 | * | * |
| Polara 4-Door Hardtop | DL43 | $2,948 | +2.57% | 3860 | * | * |
| Polara 4-Door, 2-S. Wagon | DL45 | $3,183 | +2.35% | 4245 | * | * |
| Polara 4-Door, 3-S. Wagon | DL46 | $3,286 | +2.24% | 4295 | * | * |
| TOTALS | | Avg. price $3,008 | +2.45% | | Production 75,400 | +0.40% |

*Production by body style not available. Totals are estimated.*

# Monaco

*"The largest, most luxurious Dodge for '66!"*

**Nameplate year of origin:** 1965.
**Current bodystyle lifespan:** 1965 through 1966.
**Predecessor to this model:** Custom 880 (1962 to 1964).
**Replacement for this model:** Monaco and Monaco 500 (1967 to 1968).
**Percentage of division's sales volume:** 12.36%.
**Corporate siblings:** Plymouth Fury.
**Primary competition:** Buick Wildcat, Mercury Park Lane, Oldsmobile Starfire, and Pontiac Grand Prix.
**Notable changes:** New grille and revised trim and detail changes.
**Major standard equipment:** All vinyl bench seat (cloth and vinyl in sedan), full carpeting, variable speed windshield wipers with washers, power tailgate window on wagons, courtesy and trunk lights, power convertible top, simulated walnut exterior paneling on wagon, and 8.25 × 14 BSW tires (8.55 × 14 BSW tires on wagons). Monaco 500 adds: All-vinyl bucket seats, wicker door inserts, tach and center console.

## Measurements

| | Cars | Wagons |
|---|---|---|
| Wheelbase | 121.0" | 121.0" |
| Length | 213.3" | 217.1" |
| Width | 80.0" | 79.4" |
| Height | 54.7" | 56.0" |
| Legroom — front | 42.0" | 42.0" |
| Legroom — rear | 40.8" | 40.8" |
| Headroom — front | 39.3" | 39.3" |
| Headroom — rear | 38.5" | 38.5" |
| Cargo capacity (cu. ft.) | NA | 96.9 |
| Fuel capacity (gals.) | 19.0 | 19.0 |

## Models Available

| | Style Number | Base MSRP | Change from LY | Shipping Wt. (lbs.) | Production | Change from LY |
|---|---|---|---|---|---|---|
| Monaco 2-Door Hardtop | DH23 | $3,107 | +2.10% | 3855 | * | * |
| Monaco 4-Door Sedan | DH41 | $3,033 | +2.12% | 3890 | * | * |
| Monaco 4-Door Hardtop | DH43 | $3,170 | +2.03% | 3905 | * | * |
| Monaco 4-Dr., 2-S. Wgn. | DH45 | $3,436 | +1.87% | 4270 | * | * |
| Monaco 4-Dr., 3-S. Wgn. | DH46 | $3,539 | +1.81% | 4315 | * | * |
| Monaco 500 2-Door Hardtop | DP23 | $3,604 | +8.95% | 3895 | 7,300 | * |
| TOTALS | Avg. price | $3,315 | +0.21% | | Production 67,200 | +409.09% |

*Totals are estimated. Comparison made to 1965 Custom 880 & Monaco.*

# FORD

*"Take a second look at the '66's from Ford."*

This year Ford updated its smaller series of cars and managed to seize the top spot on the sales charts. The Falcon and Fairlane, which shared some components under the skin this year, were both totally redesigned. The compact Falcon took on more of an economy role this year, and in the process lost its Convertible and 2-Door Hardtop models. The Futura remained as the top line option, with a 2-Door Sports Coupe (Sedan) left as the remaining sporty link to the past. The new Falcons offered a choice of two 6-cylinder engines and one 289 CID V8 powerplant. Outside, the new Falcons adopted the more angular lines of other Ford products, featuring single headlamps in a full-width grille up front, and square taillamps at the rear. In what could be interpreted as a cost saving move, Fairlane and Falcon wagons shared the same body components from the cowl back, and were based on the same chassis platform. Sheetmetal would distinguish the two cars, and in particular the front clip which was shared with their regular car line namesakes. This new sharing of platforms also explains why the Ranchero pickup of this year is based on a Falcon, yet the 1967 model is based on the Fairlane. It is essentially because of the same type of platform component sharing that made this possible.

Fairlane models for this year took on the styling characteristics of the popular 1965 Ford full-size line. Up front was a vertical dual headlamp style, with full-width, horizontal grille in between. Body side lines took on a slight Coke-bottle effect, flaring out just ahead of the rear wheels. Out back were the now typical, for Ford, square taillamps. New Fairlane models included a Fairlane 500 XL and GT line. The GT line was powered exclusively by the mighty 390 CID V8 engine, producing 335 horsepower in stock form. When equipped with Cruise-O-Matic automatic transmission, the cars became known as the GT-A. Also new for the Fairlane this year was a 2-Door Convertible available in Fairlane 500, 500 XL or 500 XL GT trim. Changes to other lines were minimal for 1966. The new Mustang continued to sell as fast as it could be produced, so it underwent no major changes. The full-size Fords, which were restyled in 1965, received a makeover of the front and rear ends that clearly distinguished them from their predecessors. The Galaxie 500 XL 7-Litre was a new high-performance offering destined to compete more with Ford's own Thunderbird than other manufacturers' high-performance models, such as the Chevrolet Impala Super Sport, which leaned more towards power than luxury. Powered by a 428 CID V8 with Cruise-O-Matic automatic transmission, the 7-Litre was a short-lived attempt at a powerful yet luxurious "gentleman's Car." Probable competition would include the Pontiac Grand Prix, Buick Riviera, Chrysler 300 and Dodge Monaco. Overall, the 7-litre was a very nice package, with plenty of power, exceptional ride quality, good looks, and a healthy appetite for petrol. Finally, the Thunderbird models received a new frontal design that separated the bumper and grille, yet looked similar to previous years. At the rear, a full-width taillamp assembly gave the 1966 models a unique look. A new Town Hardtop style was introduced for 1966, which featured the Landau roofline, minus the Landau bars and some other trim pieces.

Country Squire 4-Door Wagon

Falcon Futura 4-Door Sedan

Fairlane 500 XL 2-Door Hardtop

Fairlane Squire 4-Door Wagon

Galaxie 500 7-Litre 2-Door Convertible

LTD 4-Door Hardtop

Mustang 2-Door Hardtop

Thunderbird 2-Door Town Hardtop
and Interior

**Model year production:** 2,426,617, up 18.35% over 1965.
**Domestic market share:** 27.10% (1st place).
**Base price range:** $2,060 to $4,879.
**Industry average base price:** $3.070.
**Ford average base price:** $2,872.
**Introduction date:** October 1, 1965.
**Assembly plants:** Atlanta, GA (A); Chicago, IL (G); Dallas, TX (D); Dearborn, MI (F); Kansas City, MO (K); Lorain, OH (H); Los Angeles, CA (J); Louisville, KY (U); Mah-wah, NJ (E); Metuchen, NJ (T); Norfolk, VA (N); San Jose, CA (R); Twin Cities, MN (P); Wayne, MI (W); Wixom, MI (Y); Oakville, Ontario, Can. (B).

**Data plate identification:** Eleven digit code read as follows: 6 for 1966; 2nd digit is assembly plant code; 2-digit model number (see listings below); 5th digit is engine code; 100001 and up for serial number. *Example:* 6Y83Z100001 is a 1966 Ford Thunderbird 2-Door Hardtop with a 390 CID V8 engine, serial number 100001, built in Wixom, MI.

## Powertrains

| Engine | Gross HP | Engine Code | Transmission Availability | Falcon | Mustang | Fairlane | Full-size | T-Bird |
|---|---|---|---|---|---|---|---|---|
| 170 CID, 1-bbl., 6-cyl. | 105 | U | 3-speed manual | S | - | - | - | - |
| | | | Cruise-O-Matic | $167 | - | - | - | - |
| 200 CID, 1-bbl., 6-cyl. | 120 | T | 3-speed manual | S*/$26 | S | S**** | - | - |
| | | | 4-speed manual | - | $113 | $183**** | - | - |
| | | | Cruise-O-Matic | $167*/$193 | $176 | $184**** | - | - |
| 240 CID Big Six, 1-bbl., 6-cyl. | 150 | V | 3-speed manual | - | - | - | S**** | - |
| | | | Overdrive | - | - | - | $108**** | - |
| | | | Cruise-O-Matic | - | - | - | $184**** | - |
| 289 CID Challenger, 2-bbl., V8 | 200 | C | Synchro-Smooth Drive, 3-speed man. | $105*/$131 | $106 | $105**** | $106**** | - |
| | | | Overdrive | - | - | - | $212**** | - |

| Engine | Gross HP | Engine Code | Transmission Availability | Falcon | Mustang | Fairlane | Full-size | T-Bird |
|---|---|---|---|---|---|---|---|---|
| | | | 4-speed manual** | - | $290 | $288**** | - | - |
| | | | Cruise-O-Matic | $281*/$307 | $291 | $289**** | S (XL/LTD), $290**** | - |
| 289 CID Challenger Special, 4-bbl., V8 | 225 | A | Synchro-Smooth Drive, 3-speed man. | - | $158 | - | - | - |
| | | | 4-speed manual** | - | $342 | - | - | - |
| | | | Cruise-O-Matic | - | $343 | - | - | - |
| 289 CID Challenger High-Perf., 4-bbl., V8 | 271 | K | 3-speed manual | - | $434 | - | - | - |
| | | | 4-speed manual** | - | $618 | - | - | - |
| | | | Cruise-O-Matic | - | $650 | - | - | - |
| 352 CID Interceptor, 4-bbl., V8 | 250 | X | Cruise-O-Matic | - | - | - | $58 (XL & LTD), $372**** | - |
| 390 CID Thunderbird Special, 2-bbl., V8 | 275 | H/Y | Cruise-O-Matic | - | - | - | $101 (XL/LTD)/ $391**** | No cost |
| 390 CID Thunderbird Special, 4-bbl., V8 | 315 | Z | Cruise-O-Matic | - | - | - | $153 (XL/ LTD)/ $443**** | S |
| 390 CID GT, 4-bbl., V8 | 335 | S | Synchro-Smooth Drive, 3-speed man. | - | - | S (GT)/ $206**** | - | - |
| | | | 4-speed manual** | - | - | $183 (GT) $389**** | - | - |
| | | | Cruise-O-Matic | - | - | $214 (GT) $420**** | - | - |
| 427 CID Thunderbird High-Perf., 4-bbl., V8 | 410 | W | 4-speed manual** | - | - | $*** | $*** | - |
| 427 CID Thunderbird High-Perf., 2 × 4-bbl., V8 | 425 | R | 4-speed manual** | - | - | $*** | $1027*** | - |
| 428 CID Thunderbird Special, 4-bbl., V8 | 345 | Q | 4-speed manual | - | - | - | No cost (7-Litre) | - |
| | | | Cruise-O-Matic | - | - | - | S (7-Litre) | $64 |
| 428 CID Police Interceptor, 4-bbl., V8 | 360 | P | Cruise-O-Matic | - | - | - | $ (limited availability) | - |

*Futura Sport Coupe only.   **4-speed manual shift not available on wagon models.   ***427 CID V8s mostly sold for racing applications; only 237 installed.
****Other than GT, XL or LTD models.

## Major Options

| | Falcon | Mustang | Fairlane | Full-size | Thunderbird |
|---|---|---|---|---|---|
| Air conditioning | - | $311 | $353 | $353 | $413 |
| Tinted glass | - | $30 | $40 | $40 | $40 |
| Power steering | $84 | $84 | $84 | $94 | S |
| Power brakes — discs (certain models) | - | $42 | $42 | $42 | S |
| Power driver's seat/six-way | - | - | - | - | $193 |
| Power windows | - | - | - | $99 | $103 |
| AM radio | $57 | $57 | $57 | $57 | S |
| AM/FM radio | - | - | - | $133 | $82 |
| Front console | - | $32–$50 | $ | $ | S |
| Front bucket seats | $ | S | $ | $ | S |
| Swing-Away steering wheel | - | - | - | - | S |
| Vinyl roof (only on select models) | $74 | $74 | $76 | $74 | $ |
| White sidewall tires — std. sizes | $32 | $33 | $33 | $33 | $43 |
| Deluxe wheel covers | $21 | $58 — Wire | $21 | $22 | - |

Options common to most models. (- = Not Available; S = Standard equipment.) Items may be standard equipment, optional at different pricing, or unavailable on certain models. This chart is only a guide.

## Paint Colors

|  | Code | Thunderbird | Other models |
|---|---|---|---|
| Black | A | X | X |
| Sundust Beige | B | X | |
| Silver Mink Metallic | E | X | |
| Arcadian Blue | F | X | X |
| Sapphire Blue Metallic | G | X | |
| Sahara Beige | H | X | |
| Nightmist Blue Metallic | K | X | X |
| Honeydew Yellow | L | X | |
| Wimbledon White | M | X | X |
| Diamond Blue | N | X | |
| Silver Rose Metallic | O | X | |
| Antique Bronze Metallic | P | X | X |
| Brittany Blue Metallic | Q | X | |
| Ivy Green Metallic | R | X | X |
| Candyapple Red | T | X | X |
| Tahoe Turquoise Metallic | U | X | X |
| Emberglo Metallic | V | X | X |
| Vintage Burgundy Metallic | X | X | X |
| Silver Blue Metallic | Y | | X |
| Sauterne Gold Metallic | Z | X | X |
| Mariner Turquoise Metallic | 2 | X | |
| Frost Turquoise | 4 | | X |
| Signal Flare Red | 5 | | X |
| Springtime Yellow | 8 | | X |

# Falcon

*"America's economy champ, now on its third
million with a sporty new look for '66!"*

**Nameplate year of origin:** 1960.
**Current bodystyle lifespan:** 1966 through 1970.
**Predecessor to this model:** Falcon (1964 to 1965).
**Replacement for this model:** Maverick (1969 to 1977).
**Percentage of division's sales volume:** 7.53%.
**Corporate siblings:** Ford Fairlane Wagon and Mercury Comet Wagon.
**Primary competition:** AMC Rambler American, Chevrolet Chevy II, Dodge
Dart, and Plymouth Valiant.
**Notable changes:** Completely restyled.
**Major standard equipment:** Cloth and vinyl interior trim, front-door armrests,
chrome windshield and rear window moldings, small hubcaps, and 6.50 × 13
BSW tires (7.75 × 14 on Wagons). Futura adds: Deluxe interior trim, rear
armrests with ashtrays, side window moldings, and full-wheel covers.

## Measurements

|  | Cars | Wagons |
|---|---|---|
| Wheelbase | 111.0" | 113.0" |
| Length | 184.3" | 199.0" |
| Width | 73.5" | 73.5" |
| Height | 54.6" | 55.0" |
| Legroom — front | 42.1" | 42.1" |
| Legroom — rear | 36.4" | 36.8" |
| Headroom — front | 38.3" | 38.3" |
| Headroom — rear | 37.7" | 37.8" |
| Cargo capacity (cu. ft.) | 12.3 | 98.6 |
| Fuel capacity (gals.) | 16.0 | 20.0 |

## Models Available

|  | Style Number | Base MSRP | Change from LY | Shipping Wt. (lbs.) | Production | Change from LY |
|---|---|---|---|---|---|---|
| Falcon 2-Door Club Coupe | 01 | $2,060 | +1.98% | 2519 | 41,432 | -16.61% |
| Falcon 4-Door Sedan | 02 | $2,114 | +1.54% | 2559 | 34,685 | -21.23% |
| Falcon 4-Door Wagon | 06 | $2,442 | +3.17% | 3037 | 16,653 | +11.68% |
| Falcon Futura 2-Door Club Coupe | 11 | $2,183 | +1.82% | 2527 | 21,997 | +88.49% |
| Falcon Futura 2-Door Sports Cpe. | 13 | $2,328 | NEW | 2597 | 20,289 | NEW |

| | Style Number | Base MSRP | Change from LY | Shipping Wt. (lbs.) | Production | Change from LY |
|---|---|---|---|---|---|---|
| Falcon Futura 4-Door Sedan | 12 | $2,237 | +2.05% | 2567 | 34,039 | +0.16% |
| Falcon Futura 4-Door Wagon | 16 | $2,553 | -4.20% | 3045 | 13,574 | +102.51% |
| TOTALS | | Avg. price $2,274 | -1.22% | | Production 182,669 | -14.44% |

# Mustang

*"If you thought we couldn't improve on a winner — try Mustang '66!"*

**Nameplate year of origin:** 1964½ (also on a 1963 show car).
**Current bodystyle lifespan:** 1964½ through 1968.
**Predecessor to this model:** None.
**Replacement for this model:** Mustang (1969 to 1970).
**Percentage of division's sales volume:** 25.04%.
**Corporate siblings:** None.
**Primary competition:** Chevrolet Corvair and Plymouth Barracuda.
**Notable changes:** Minor trim and detail changes.
**Major standard equipment:** Bucket front seats with vinyl upholstery, dual sun visors, Seat belts, padded instrument panel, courtesy lights, full carpeting, sports steering wheel, chrome window moldings, heater and defroster, self-adjusting front brakes, alternator, and 6.50 × 13 BSW tires (6.95 × 14 with V8 engine).

## Measurements

| | |
|---|---|
| Wheelbase | 108.0" |
| Length | 181.6" |
| Width | 68.2" |
| Height | 51.1" |
| Legroom — front | 41.8" |
| Legroom — rear | 28.8" |
| Headroom — front | 37.0" |
| Headroom — rear | 35.6" |
| Cargo capacity (cu. ft.) | 9.0 (Cvt. 7.7; Flo. 5.0) |
| Fuel capacity (gals.) | 16.0 |

## Models Available

| | Style Number | Base MSRP | Change from LY | Shipping Wt. (lbs.) | Production | Change from LY |
|---|---|---|---|---|---|---|
| Mustang 2-Door Hardtop | 07 | $2,416 | +1.85% | 2488 | 499,751 | +22.11% |
| Mustang 2-Door Fastback | 09 | $2,607 | +0.70% | 2519 | 35,698 | -53.69% |
| Mustang 2-Door Convertible | 08 | $2,653 | +1.49% | 2650 | 72,119 | -1.36% |
| TOTALS | | Avg. price $2,559 | +1.35% | | Production 607,568 | +8.60% |

# Fairlane

*"Fairlane re-invented: Still the rugged, reliable family car ... but with all new performance for '66! New GT's! New XL's! New Convertibles!"*

**Nameplate year of origin:** 1955.
**Current bodystyle lifespan:** 1966 through 1967.
**Predecessor to this model:** Fairlane (1962 to 1965).
**Replacement for this model:** Fairlane (1968 to 1969).
**Percentage of division's sales volume:** 21.69%.
**Corporate siblings:** Mercury Comet.
**Primary competition:** AMC Rambler Classic and Marlin, Chevrolet Chevelle, Dodge Coronet, Plymouth Belvedere, and Pontiac Tempest.
**Notable changes:** Completely restyled.
**Major standard equipment:** Cloth and vinyl bench seat, rubber floor mats, front and rear armrests, chrome windshield and rear window moldings, and 6.95 × 14 BSW tires (7.75 × 14 BSW on Wagons). 500 adds: Full carpeting, deluxe interior trim, and chrome side window

## Measurements

| | Cars | Wagons |
|---|---|---|
| Wheelbase | 116.0" | 113.0" |
| Length | 197.0" | 200.0" |
| Width | 74.7" | 73.5" |
| Height | 55.0" | 55.0" |
| Legroom — front | 42.2" | 42.1" |
| Legroom — rear | 38.6" | 36.8" |
| Headroom — front | 37.8" | 38.3" |
| Headroom — rear | 37.5" | 37.8" |
| Cargo capacity (cu. ft.) | 15.2 | 98.6 |
| Fuel capacity (gals.) | 20.0 | 20.0 |

**1966**

moldings. Squire adds: Exterior wood-grain trim. XL adds: All-vinyl bucket front seats, center console, and rocker panel moldings. GT adds: Special exterior striping and identification, clock, tachometer and 390 CID V8 engine.

## Models Available

| | Style | Base MSRP | Change from LY | Shipping Wt. (lbs.) | Production | Change from LY |
|---|---|---|---|---|---|---|
| Fairlane 2-Door Club Coupe | 31 | $2,240 | +0.45% | 2747 | 13,498 | -1.37% |
| Fairlane 4-Door Sedan | 32 | $2,280 | +0.40% | 2792 | 26,170 | +3.12% |
| Fairlane 4-Door, 2-Seat Wagon | 38 | $2,589 | +0.86% | 3182 | 12,379 | -11.01% |
| Fairlane 500 2-Door Club Coupe | 41 | $2,317 | +0.22% | 2754 | 14,118 | -12.27% |
| Fairlane 500 2-Door Hardtop | 43 | $2,378 | +0.04% | 2856 | 75,947 | +83.42% |
| Fairlane 500 2-Door Convertible | 45 | $2,603 | NEW | 3084 | 9,299 | NEW |
| Fairlane 500 4-Door Sedan | 42 | $2,357 | +0.17% | 2798 | 68,635 | -11.82% |
| Fairlane 500 4-Dr., 2-Seat Wagon | 48 | $2,665 | +0.64% | 3192 | 19,826 | -3.32% |
| Fairlane Squire 4-Dr., 2-Seat Wgn. | 49 | $2,796 | NEW | 3200 | 11,558 | NEW |
| Fairlane 500 XL 2-Door Hardtop | 47 | $2,543 | NEW | 2884 | 232,942 | NEW |
| Fairlane 500 XL 2-Door Convertible | 46 | $2,768 | NEW | 3099 | 4,560 | NEW |
| Fairlane GT 2-Door Hardtop | 40 | $2,843 | NEW | 3493 | 33,015 | NEW |
| Fairlane GT 2-Door Convertible | 44 | $3,068 | NEW | 3700 | 4,327 | NEW |
| TOTALS | Avg. price | $2,573 | +6.67% | Production | 526,274 | +134.99% |

# Custom, Galaxie & LTD

*"Quiet quality ... powered by Ford."*

**Nameplate year of origin:** 1957 (Custom), 1959 (Galaxie) and 1965 (LTD).
**Current bodystyle lifespan:** 1965 through 1966.
**Predecessor to this model:** Full-size Ford (1963 to 1964).
**Replacement for this model:** Custom, Galaxie and LTD (1967 to 1968).
**Percentage of division's sales volume:** 42.90%.
**Corporate siblings:** Mercury Monterey and Park Lane.
**Primary competition:** AMC Ambassador, Chevrolet BelAir/Impala/Caprice, Dodge Polara/Monaco, Plymouth Fury, and Pontiac Catalina.
**Notable changes:** Revised front and rear styling, and minor trim and detail changes.
**Major standard equipment:** Cloth and vinyl front bench seat, rubber floor mats, arm rests on all doors, rear window trim molding, and 7.35 × 15 BSW tires (8.45 × 15 BSW tires on Wagon). Custom 500 adds: Full carpeting, and chrome windshield molding. Galaxie 500 adds: Deluxe interior trim, chrome side window moldings, 7.75 × 15 BSW tires on Hardtop models and 8.15 × 15 BSW tires on Convertibles. XL adds: Bucket seats with floor-mounted transmission selector, lower door carpet trim and polished trim, courtesy and reading lamps, and special badging. Galaxie 500 7-Litre adds: power disc brakes and 428 CID V8 engine. LTD adds: Padded cloth upholstery with Scotchguard® treatment, simulated wood interior trim, additional courtesy lights, and self-regulating clock.

## Measurements

| | Cars | Wagons |
|---|---|---|
| Wheelbase | 119.0" | 119.0" |
| Length | 210.0" | 211.2" |
| Width | 79.0" | 79.0" |
| Height | 55.6" | 55.9" |
| Legroom — front | 41.4" | 41.4" |
| Legroom — rear | 40.6" | 40.4" |
| Headroom — front | 38.9" | 38.9" |
| Headroom — rear | 37.7" | 37.8" |
| Cargo capacity (cu. ft.) | 19.1 | 103.0 |
| Fuel capacity (gals.) | 25.0 | 25.0 |

## Models Available

| | Style | Base MSRP | Change from LY | Shipping Wt. (lbs.) | Production | Change from LY |
|---|---|---|---|---|---|---|
| Custom 2-Door Sedan | 53 | $2,380 | +0.80% | 3333 | 32,292 | -34.14% |
| Custom 4-Door Sedan | 54 | $2,432 | +0.70% | 3433 | 72,245 | -25.05% |
| Custom 500 2-Door Sedan | 51 | $2,481 | +0.69% | 3375 | 28,789 | +46.86% |
| Custom 500 4-Door Sedan | 52 | $2,533 | +0.60% | 3444 | 109,449 | +52.59% |
| Galaxie 500 2-Door Hardtop | 66 | $2,685 | +0.00% | 3437 | 198,532 | +26.23% |
| Galaxie 500 2-Door Convertible | 65 | $2,934 | -0.54% | 3633 | 27,454 | -14.02% |
| Galaxie 500 4-Door Sedan | 62 | $2,677 | -0.04% | 3456 | 171,886 | -5.13% |
| Galaxie 500 4-Door Hardtop | 64 | $2,762 | -0.11% | 3526 | 54,886 | +9.81% |
| Galaxie 500 XL 2-Door Hardtop | 68 | $3,231 | -0.06% | 3616 | 25,715 | -8.62% |
| Galaxie 500 XL 2-Door Conv. | 69 | $3,480 | -0.51% | 3761 | 6,360 | -35.42% |
| Galaxie 500 7-Litre 2-Door HT | 61 | $3,621 | NEW | 3914 | 8,705 | NEW |
| Galaxie 500 7-Litre 2-Door Conv. | 63 | $3,872 | NEW | 4059 | 2,368 | NEW |
| LTD 2-Door Hardtop | 67 | $3,201 | -0.99% | 3601 | 31,696 | -15.91% |
| LTD 4-Door Hardtop | 60 | $3,278 | -1.06% | 3649 | 69,400 | +2.00% |
| Ranch Wagon 4-Door, 2-Seat | 71 | $2,793 | +1.09% | 3919 | 33,306 | +8.08% |
| Country Sedan 4-Door Wagon | 72 | $2,882 | +0.95% | 3934 | 55,616 | -6.83% |
| Country Sedan 4-Door w/DFRS* | 74 | $2,999 | +1.35% | 3975 | 36,633 | +13.26% |
| Country Squire 4-Door Wagon | 76 | $3,182 | +2.51% | 4004 | 27,645 | +13.73% |
| Country Squire 4-Dr. Wgn. w/DFRS* | 78 | $3,265 | +2.87% | 4018 | 47,953 | +57.21% |
| TOTALS | Avg. price | $2,984 | +3.61% | Production | 1,040,930 | +6.38% |

*Dual facing near seats

# Thunderbird

*"America's personal luxury car."*

**Nameplate year of origin:** 1955.
**Current bodystyle lifespan:** 1964 through 1966.
**Predecessor to this model:** Thunderbird (1961 to 1963).
**Replacement for this model:** Thunderbird (1967 to 1971).
**Percentage of division's sales volume:** 2.85%.
**Corporate siblings:** None.
**Primary competition:** Buick Riviera, and Oldsmobile Toronado.
**Notable changes:** Revised taillamps, and trim and detail changes.
**Major standard equipment:** Bucket seats, full carpeting, full instrumentation, Swing-Away steering wheel, AM radio, reversible entry keys, sequential turn signals, power steering, power front disc brakes, and 8.15 × 15 BSW tires. Convertible adds: Unique trunk-stored power convertible top. Town Hardtop adds: Distinctive roofline with no rear quarter windows. Town Landau adds: Special interior and vinyl top.

## Measurements

| | |
|---|---|
| Wheelbase | 113.0" |
| Length | 205.4" |
| Width | 77.3" |
| Height | 52.5" |
| Legroom — front | 39.7" |
| Legroom — rear | 33.2" |
| Headroom — front | 37.4" |
| Headroom — rear | 37.6" |
| Cargo capacity (cu. ft.) | 11.5 |
| Fuel capacity (gals.) | 22.0 |

## Models Available

| | Style | Base MSRP | Change from LY | Shipping Wt. (lbs.) | Production | Change from LY |
|---|---|---|---|---|---|---|
| Thunderbird 2-Door Hardtop | 83 | $4,426 | -1.34% | 4386 | 13,389 | -68.61% |
| Thunderbird 2-Door Town Hardtop | 81 | $4,483 | NEW | 4359 | 15,633 | NEW |
| Thunderbird 2-Door Town Landau | 87 | $4,584 | -0.11% | 4367 | 35,105 | +37.81% |
| Thunderbird 2-Door Convertible | 85 | $4,879 | -1.49% | 4496 | 5,049 | -26.25% |
| TOTALS | Avg. price | $4,593 | -1.78% | Production | 69,176 | -7.73% |

# IMPERIAL

*"The Incomparable Imperial for 1966. Finest of the fine cars built by Chrysler Corporation."*

Imperial entered 1966 with its final year in the "Lincoln-style" body design. In its third season, the formal-looking Imperials failed to realize any significant gain in the sales charts, so the line would be restyled for 1967 and begin sharing more componentry with the Chrysler line. Just over 55,000 units of this body style Imperial were sold over their three year lifespan. The 1966 model was arguably the best because of its new engine. The all-new 440 CID V8 powerplant was the new standard engine for all Imperials this year. The 440 CID was the largest displacement engine Chrysler had ever built. It was not exclusively for Imperial, however, and would be used in all Mopar lines within a few years.

Crown 2-Door Convertible

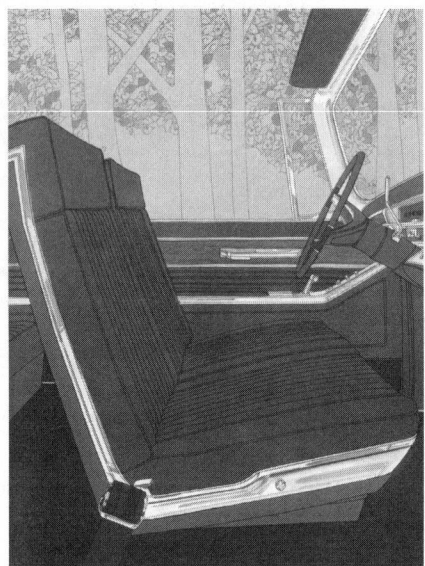

Crown Interior

**Model year production:** 13,742, down 25.31% from 1965.
**Domestic market share:** 0.15% (13th place).
**Base price range:** $5,733 to $6,540.
**Industry average base price:** $3,070.
**Imperial average base price:** $6,077.
**Introduction date:** September 1965.
**Assembly plants:** Detroit, MI (3).
**Data plate identification:** Thirteen digit code read as follows:

Four digit style number (see listings below) in which Y = Imperial, 2nd number identifies series (e.g., M is for Crown), 3rd and 4th digits indicate body style; 5th digit is engine code; 6 for 1966; assembly plant code; 100001 and up for serial number. *Example:* YM23T63100001 is a 1966 Imperial Crown 2-Door Hardtop with a 440 CID V8 engine, serial number 100001, built in Detroit, MI.

## Powertrains

| Engine | Engine Code | Gross HP | Transmission Availability | Imperial |
|--------|-------------|----------|---------------------------|----------|
| 440 CID, 4-bbl., V8 | T | 350 | Torqueflite Automatic | S |

## Major Options

|  | Crown | LeBaron |
|---|---|---|
| Air conditioning | $452 | $452 |
| Auto Pilot automatic speed control | $95 | $95 |
| Tinted glass | $53 | $53 |
| Rear window defogger | $26 | $26 |
| Deck lid remote release | $28 | $28 |
| Power steering — variable-ratio | S | S |
| Power brakes | S | S |
| Power door locks | $47 (2-Dr)/$71 (4-Dr) | $71 |
| Power driver's seat/Bench seat | $105 | S |
| Power windows | S | S |
| AM radio w/power antenna | $165 | $165 |
| AM/FM radio w/power antenna | $228 | $228 |
| Tilt-A-Scope steering wheel | $92 | $92 |
| Vinyl roof | $130 | S |
| Whitewall tires — std. size | $54 | S |

Options common to most models. (S = Standard equipment.) Items may be standard equipment, optional at different pricing, or unavailable on certain models. This chart is only a guide.

## Paint Colors

|  | Code |
|---|---|
| Dove Tan | 33-1 |
| Moss Gold Metallic | 44-1 |
| Dusty Gold Metallic | 55-1 |
| Lilac Metallic | 66-1 |
| Ruby Metallic | 77-1 |
| Deep Plum Metallic | 88-1 |
| Silver Mist Metallic | AA-1 |
| Formal Black | BB-1 |
| Powder Blue | CC-1 |
| Crystal Blue Metallic | DD-1 |
| Regal Blue Metallic | EE-1 |
| Haze Green Metallic | FF-1 |
| Sequoia Green Metallic | GG-1 |
| Frost Turquoise Metallic | KK-1 |
| Royal Turquoise Metallic | LL-1 |
| Scorch Red | PP-1 |
| Spanish Red Metallic | QQ-1 |
| Daffodil Yellow | RR-1 |
| Ivory | SS-1 |
| Persian White | WW-1 |
| Desert Beige | XX-1 |
| Saddle Bronze Metallic | YY-1 |
| Spice Gold Metallic | ZZ-1 |

**1966**

# Crown

*"The sportiest and thriftiest of all Imperials."*

**Nameplate year of origin:** 1957 (not the same as Crown Imperial series).
**Current bodystyle lifespan:** 1967 through 1968.
**Predecessor to this model:** Crown (1964 to 1966).
**Replacement for this model:** Crown (1969 to 1970).
**Percentage of division's sales volume:** 86.33%.
**Corporate siblings:** LeBaron.
**Primary competition:** Cadillac Calais, and Lincoln Continental.
**Notable changes:** New grille, and minor trim and detail changes.
**Major standard equipment:** Cloth and vinyl bench seat (leather on convertible), front and rear armrests (hardtops), pile carpeting, remote-control left-hand outside mirror, power windows, electric clock, trip odometer, 3-speed electric windshield wipers with washers, automatic transmission, power steering, power brakes, wheel covers and 9.15 × 15 BSW tires.

## Measurements

|  |  |
|---|---|
| Wheelbase | 129.0" |
| Length | 227.8" |
| Width | 80.0" |
| Height | 55.8" |
| Legroom — front | 41.5" |
| Legroom — rear | 40.5" |
| Headroom — front | 38.4" |
| Headroom — rear | 38.7" |
| Cargo capacity (cu. ft.) | NA |
| Fuel capacity (gals.) | 23.0 |

## Models Available

|  | Style | Base MSRP | Change from LY | Shipping Wt. (lbs.) | Production | Change from LY |
|---|---|---|---|---|---|---|
| Crown 2-Door Hardtop | YM23 | $5,887 | 0.70% | 5000 | 2,373 | -40.29% |
| Crown 2-Door Convertible | YM27 | $6,146 | 0.67% | 5315 | 514 | -18.80% |
| Crown 4-Door Hardtop | YM43 | $5,733 | 0.74% | 4990 | 8,977 | -22.80% |
| TOTALS | | Avg. price $5,922 | +0.70% | | Production 11,864 | +36.7% |

# LeBaron

*"The most luxurious automobile built by Chrysler Corporation."*

**Nameplate year of origin:** 1924 (as Chrysler Sedan model designation); 1926 (as series).
**Current bodystyle lifespan:** 1967 through 1968.
**Predecessor to this model:** LeBaron (1964 to 1966).
**Replacement for this model:** LeBaron (1969 to 1973).
**Percentage of division's sales volume:** 13.67%.
**Corporate siblings:** Crown.
**Primary competition:** Cadillac de Ville and Lincoln Continental.
**Notable changes:** New grille, and minor trim and detail changes.
**Major standard equipment:** Cloth or leather bench seat with center armrests, deep-pile carpeting, 6-way power seat, power windows and vent windows, electric clock, trip odometer, 3-speed electric windshield wipers with washers, automatic transmission, power steering, power brakes, wheel covers and 9.15 × 15 WSW tires.

## Measurements

| | |
|---|---|
| Wheelbase | 129.0" |
| Length | 227.8" |
| Width | 80.0" |
| Height | 55.8" |
| Legroom — front | 41.5" |
| Legroom — rear | 40.5" |
| Headroom — front | 38.4" |
| Headroom — rear | 38.7" |
| Cargo capacity (cu. ft.) | NA |
| Fuel capacity (gals.) | 23.0 |

## Models Available

| | Style | Base MSRP | Change from LY | Shipping Wt. (lbs.) | Production | Change from LY |
|---|---|---|---|---|---|---|
| LeBaron 4-Door Hardtop | YH43 | $6,540 | +0.63% | 5090 | 1,878 | -13.22% |
| TOTALS | *Avg. price* | $6,540 | +0.63% | *Production* | 1,878 | -13.22% |

# LINCOLN

*"America's most distinguished motorcar."*

Most important on the minds of Lincoln buyers this season was the large price cut that Ford made in the Lincoln line. After many years of average prices hovering near $6,500, this year's models were priced about $600 lower. Most of the standard equipment content was retained, but the intent of the lower pricing was to lure some Cadillac buyers to Lincoln. The strategy could be considered a success in light of the 36 percent increase in sales for the year. New features include a larger displacement engine that powered a larger Lincoln for 1966. The new 462 CID V8 engine was introduced at the same time as the new larger engine in the Imperial. Also new for 1966 was the exterior styling. While the cars were still based on a similar platform and still carried familiar Lincoln cues, there were numerous changes. Besides new styling, there was a 2-Door Hardtop model in the line for the first time since 1960. Also, curved side window glass made its appearance in the Lincoln line.

**Continental 2-Door Hardtop**

**Continental 4-Door Sedan**

**Model year production:** 54,755, up 36.27% over 1965.
**Domestic market share:** 0.61% (12th place).
**Base price range:** $5,485 to $6,383.
**Industry average base price:** $3,070.
**Lincoln average base price:** $5,873.
**Introduction date:** September 1965.
**Assembly plants:** Allen Park, MI (S); and Wixom, MI (Y).

**Data plate identification:** Eleven digit code read as follows: 6 for 1966; 2nd digit is assembly plant code; 2-digit model number (see listings below); 5th digit is engine code; 400001 and up for serial number. *Example:* 6Y82H400001 is a 1966 Lincoln Continental 4-Door Sedan with a 462 CID V8 engine, serial number 400001, built in Wixom, MI.

## Powertrains

| Engine | Gross HP | Engine Code | Transmission Availability | Continental |
|---|---|---|---|---|
| 462 CID, 4-bbl., V8 | 340 | H | Turbo Drive Automatic | S |

## Major Options

| | Continental |
|---|---|
| Air condtioning—manual | $505 |
| Automatic headlight dimmers | $46 |
| Tinted glass | $54 |
| Tilt steering wheel | $60 |
| 6-way power seat | S |
| AM/FM radio | $85 |
| Leather upholstery | $100 |
| Speed control | $97 |
| Remote control trunk release (sedans) | $53 |

Options common to most models (S = Standard equipment.) Items may be standard equipment, optional at different pricing, or unavailable on certain models. This chart is only a guide.

## Paint Colors

| | Code |
|---|---|
| Black Satin | A |
| Chesterfield Beige Metallic | B |
| Madison Gray Metallic | E |
| Arcadian Blue | F |
| Teakwood | H |
| Pitcairn Blue Metallic | K |
| Venetian Yellow | L |
| Wimbledon White | M |
| Platinum | N |
| Rose Mist Metallic | O |
| Sandalwood Metallic | P |
| Huron Blue Metallic | Q |
| Spanish Moss Metallic | R |
| Charcoal Frost Metallic | S |
| Cranberry | T |
| Teal Metallic | U |
| Russet Metallic | V |
| Royal Maroon Metallic | X |
| Florentine Gold Metallic | Z |
| Empress Turquoise Metallic | 2 |

1966

# Continental
*"Unmistakably new, yet unmistakably Continental."*

**Nameplate year of origin:** 1940 (1961 as a standard sedan nameplate).
**Current bodystyle lifespan:** 1961 through 1969 (major restyles in 1964 and 1966).
**Predecessor to this model:** Premiere (1958 to 1960).
**Replacement for this model:** Continental (1970 to 1979).
**Percentage of division's sales volume:** 100%.
**Corporate siblings:** None.
**Primary competition:** Cadillac de Ville and Imperial Crown and LeBaron.
**Notable changes:** Restyled and lengthened body. New 2-Door HT added.
**Major standard equipment:** Cloth, cloth and leather (coupe and sedan) or leather (convertible) 2-way power front bench seat with folding center armrests front and rear, vanity mirror, deep-pile carpeting, power windows, AM transistor radio, power operated door latching system, padded instrument panel, windshield wipers with electric washers, and 9.15 × 15 WSW tires.

## Measurements

| | |
|---|---|
| Wheelbase | 123.0" |
| Length | 213.0" |
| Width | 78.6" |
| Height | 55.0" |
| Legroom — front | 41.1" |
| Legroom — rear | 41.0" |
| Headroom — front | 39.0" |
| Headroom — rear | 38.6" |
| Luggage capacity (cu. ft.) | 18.0 |
| Fuel capacity (gals.) | 21.0 |

## Models Available

| | Style | Base MSRP | Change from LY | Shipping Wt. (lbs.) | Production | Change from LY |
|---|---|---|---|---|---|---|
| Continental 2-Door Hardtop | 89 | $5,485 | NEW | 4985 | 15,766 | NEW |
| Continental 4-Door Sedan | 82 | $5,750 | -8.61% | 5085 | 35,809 | -2.76% |
| Continental 4-Door Convertible | 86 | $6,383 | -8.00% | 5480 | 3,180 | -5.24% |
| TOTALS | | Avg. price $5,873 | -11.21% | | Production 54,755 | +36.27% |

# MERCURY
*"Move ahead with Mercury ... for 1966."*

The "compact" Mercury Comet officially made the jump to the mid-size category this year. After six years as a rather large compact model, based upon the Falcon, the Comet now shared its body and chassis components with the redesigned Ford Fairlane. All models sported stacked headlamps up front, with simple side styling and sweeping fastback rooflines on 2-Door Hardtops. Interiors were much more luxurious than in previous years, and offered many new luxury appointments as optional equipment. As with the Fairlane line, several new models were added, including the mid-line Capri (replacement for the 404), and sporty Cyclone GT and GTA. Cyclone GT and GTA models came with a standard 390 CID V8 engine, and the GTA featured and automatic transmission as standard equipment. A Cyclone GT Convertible was chosen as the Official Pace Car of the 1966 Indianapolis 500 race.

Full-size Mercury models wore new grilles and revised rear end styling, as well as revised interior treatments. The sporty S-55 line made a two-year return to the lineup, replacing the 1965 Park Lane Sports Package option. A new feature on all full-size and Comet station wagons, as well as Ford wagons, was the Dual-Action tailgate. This new tailgate opened as a conventional door or dropped down for loading long loads. This tailgate design would soon be adopted by all manufacturers, as the station wagon gained in popularity.

Comet Caliente 4-Door Sedan

Comet Cyclone 2-Door Convertible,
Indianapolis 500 Pace Car

Colony Park 4-Door Wagon

Monterey 2-Door Sedan

Park Lane 2-Door Convertible

S-55 2-Door Hardtop

**Model year production:** 343,153, down 1.13% from 1965.
**Domestic market share:** 3.83% (8th place).
**Base price range:** $2,206 to $3,614.
**Industry average base price:** $3,070.
**Mercury average base price:** $2,953.
**Introduction date:** October 1965.
**Assembly plants:** Mahwah, NJ (E); Lorain, OH (H); Los Angeles, CA ( J); Wixom, MI (S); Metuchen, NJ (T); Wayne, MI (W); and St. Louis, MO (Z).

**Data plate identification:** Eleven digit code read as follows: 6 for 1966; 2nd digit is assembly plant code; 3rd digit is series (1 or 2 is Comet, 4 is Monterey, etc.); 4th digit is body style; 5th digit is engine code; 500001 and up for serial number. *Example:* 6W43Z100001 is a 1966 Mercury Monterey 2-Door Hardtop with a 390 CID V8 engine, serial number 500001, built in Wayne, MI.

**1966**

## Powertrains

| Engine | Gross HP | Engine Code | Transmission Availability | Comet | Monterey & Montclair | S-55 | Park Lane |
|---|---|---|---|---|---|---|---|
| 200 CID Six, 1-bbl., 6-cyl. | 120 | T | 3-speed manual | S[2] | - | - | - |
| | | | Multi-Drive Merc-O-Matic | $172[2] | - | - | - |
| 289 CID Cyclone, 2-bbl., V8 | 200 | C | 3-speed manual | S[1]/$106[2] | - | - | - |
| | | | 4-speed manual | $188[1]/$294[2] | - | - | - |
| | | | Multi-Drive Merc-O-Matic | $186[1]/$292[2] | - | - | - |
| 289 CID Cyclone, 4-bbl., V8 | 225 | A | 3-speed manual | $45[1]/$151[2] | - | - | - |
| | | | 4-speed manual | $233[1]/$339[2] | - | - | - |
| | | | Multi-Drive Merc-O-Matic | $231[1]/$337[2] | - | - | - |
| 390 CID, 2-bbl., V8 | 265 275 | Y | 3-speed manual | $[2] | S | - | - |
| | | | 4-speed manual | $[2] | - | - | - |
| | | | Multi-Drive Merc-O-Matic | $[2] | $217 | - | - |
| 390 CID Cyclone GT, 4-bbl., V8 | 335 | Z | 3-speed manual | S (GT only) | - | - | - |
| | | | 4-speed manual | $188 (GT) | - | - | - |
| | | | Sport-Shift Merc-O-Matic | S (GTA) | - | - | - |
| 410 CID Marauder, 4-bbl., V8 | 330 | M | 3-speed manual | - | $79[3] | - | S[3] |
| | | | 4-speed manual | - | $306* | - | S |
| | | | Multi-Drive Merc-O-Matic | - | $306 | - | S |
| 428 CID Super Marauder, 4-bbl., V8 | 345 | Q | 4-speed manual | - | $406* | S | $98 |
| | | | Multi-Drive Merc-O-Matic | - | $406 | S | $98 |

[1]*Cyclone.*    [2]*All but Cyclone.*    [3]*Bench seat only.*    **Not available on wagons.*

## Major Options

| | Comet | Monterey/Montclair | Park Lane | S-55 |
|---|---|---|---|---|
| SelectAire air conditioning | $258 | $430 | $430 | $430 |
| Tinted glass | $27 | $43 | $43 | $43 |
| Remote-control trunk release | $11 | $11 | $11 | $11 |
| Speed control | - | $93 | $93 | $93 |
| Tilt steering wheel | - | $43 | $43 | $43 |
| Power steering | $86 | $106 | $106 | $106 |
| Power brakes | $43 | $43 | $43 | $43 |
| Power windows | - | $106 | $106 | $106 |
| Power seat — six-way | - | $97 | $97 | $97 |
| Bucket seats | $80 | $161 | S | S |
| Electric windshield wipers w/washer | $22 | $14 | $14 | $14 |
| Electric clock | $15 | $16 (Monterey) | S | S |
| Pushbutton AM radio | $59 | $61 | $61 | $61 |
| AM/FM radio | - | $149 | $149 | $149 |
| White sidewall tires — std. sizes | $33 | $41 | $41 | $41 |
| Full wheel covers | $19 | S | S | S |

Options common to most models. (- = Not Available; S = Standard equipment.) Items may be standard equipment, optional at different pricing, or unavailable on certain models. This chart is only a guide.

## Paint Colors

| | Code |
|---|---|
| Onyx | A |
| Coventry Gray Metallic | C |
| Tiffany Blue Metallic | F |
| Sandstone | H |
| Caspian Blue Metallic | K |
| Polar White | M |
| Bronze Metallic | P |
| Olive Mist Metallic | R |
| Cardinal Red | T |
| Turquoise Frost Metallic | U |
| Emberglo Metallic | V |
| Burgundy Metallic | X |
| Blue Ice Metallic | Y |
| Sage Gold Metallic | Z |
| Palisade Turquoise Metallic | 2 |
| Sheffield Silver Metallic | 4 |
| Jamaican Yellow | 8 |

# Comet

*"Introducing the big, new-generation Comet."*

**Nameplate year of origin:** 1960.
**Current bodystyle lifespan:** 1966 through 1967.
**Predecessor to this model:** Comet (1964 to 1965).
**Replacement for this model:** Comet/Montego (1968 to 1969).
**Percentage of division's sales volume:** 49.66%.
**Corporate siblings:** Ford Fairlane.
**Primary competition:** Buick Special, Dodge Coronet, Oldsmobile F-85, and Pontiac Tempest.
**Notable changes:** Completely restyled. Wagons share platform with the Falcon and Fairlane.
**Major standard equipment:** Nylon and vinyl front bench seat, rubber floor covering, dome light, bright metal front and rear window trim, and 6.95 × 14 BSW tires (7.75 × 14 BSW tires on wagon). Capri adds: Full carpeting, and additional interior and exterior trim. Villager adds: Dual-action tailgate and exterior wood-grain trim. Caliente adds: Deluxe steering wheel, simulated walnut interior trim, power top on convertible, and additional sound deadening materials. Villager adds: Exterior wood-grain trim. Cyclone adds: All vinyl bucket seats with floor console, specific Cyclone exterior trim and engine dress-up kit. Cyclone GT adds: 390 CID V8 engine, and GT identification. Cyclone GTA adds: Automatic transmission.

## Measurements

| | Comet 202 | Capri/Caliente/ Cyclone | Wagons |
|---|---|---|---|
| Wheelbase | 116.0" | 116.0" | 113.0" |
| Length | 195.9" | 203.0" | 200.0" |
| Width | 73.8" | 73.8" | 73.8" |
| Height | 55.0" | 55.0" | 55.2" |
| Legroom — front | 42.1" | 42.1" | 42.2" |
| Legroom — rear | 36.1" | 36.1" | 36.4" |
| Headroom — front | 38.1" | 38.1" | 38.3" |
| Headroom — rear | 37.3" | 37.3" | 37.5" |
| Cargo capacity (cu. ft.) | 15.5 | 17.0 | 85.2 |
| Fuel capacity (gals.) | 20.0 | 20.0 | 20.0 |

## Models Available

| | Style | Base MSRP | Change from LY | Shipping Wt. (lbs.) | Production | Change from LY |
|---|---|---|---|---|---|---|
| Comet 202 2-Door Sedan | 01 | $2,206 | +2.41% | 2779 | 35,964 | +10.91% |
| Comet 202 4-Door Sedan | 02 | $2,263 | +2.40% | 2823 | 20,440 | -13.02% |
| Comet Voyager 4-Door Wagon | 06 | $2,553 | +2.49% | 3201 | 7,595 | +57.77% |
| Comet Capri 2-Door Hardtop | 13 | $2,400 | NEW | 2876 | 15,031 | NEW |
| Comet Capri 4-Door Sedan | 12 | $2,378 | +3.53% | 2844 | 15,635 | -16.07% |
| Comet Villager 4-Door Wagon | 16 | $2,790 | +1.01% | 3244 | 3,880 | +143.72% |
| Comet Caliente 2-Door Hardtop | 23 | $2,475 | +3.00% | 2882 | 25,862 | -11.57% |
| Comet Caliente 2-Door Convertible | 25 | $2,735 | +2.67% | 3143 | 3,922 | -35.01% |
| Comet Caliente 4-Door Sedan | 22 | $2,453 | +3.15% | 2846 | 17,933 | -11.82% |
| Comet Cyclone 2-Door Hardtop | 27 | $2,700 | +0.63% | 3074 | 6,889 | -44.21% |
| Comet Cyclone 2-Door Convertible | 29 | $2,961 | NEW | 3321 | 1,305 | NEW |
| Comet Cyclone GT 2-Door Hardtop | 28 | $2,891 | NEW | 3315 | 13,812 | NEW |
| Comet Cyclone GT 2-Dr. Convertible | 26 | $3,152 | NEW | 3595 | 2,158 | NEW |
| TOTALS | | Avg. price $2,612 | +6.96% | | Production 170,426 | +3.26% |

# Monterey

*"Tasteful. Elegant."*

**Nameplate year of origin:** 1952.
**Current bodystyle lifespan:** 1965 through 1966.
**Predecessor to this model:** Monterey (1963 to 1964).
**Replacement for this model:** Monterey (1967 to 1968).
**Percentage of division's sales volume:** 21.14%.
**Corporate siblings:** Ford Galaxie/LTD.
**Primary competition:** Buick Wildcat, Dodge Polara, Oldsmobile 88 and Pontiac Star Chief/Bonneville.
**Notable changes:** Revised front and rear styling.
**Major standard equipment:** Cloth and vinyl front bench seat, full carpeting, bright exterior window trim and 8.15 × 15 BSW tires. Commuter wagon adds: power tailgate window, and 8.45 × 15 BSW tires.

## Measurements

| | Cars | Commuter |
|---|---|---|
| Wheelbase | 123.0" | 119.0" |
| Length | 220.4" | 216.4" |
| Width | 79.6" | 79.6" |
| Height | 56.0" | 56.2" |
| Legroom — front | 41.8" | 41.8" |
| Legroom — rear | 37.7" | 37.6" |
| Headroom — front | 38.9" | 38.9" |
| Headroom — rear | 37.7" | 37.8" |
| Cargo capacity (cu. ft.) | 18.6 | 91.3 |
| Fuel capacity (gals.) | 25.0 | 25.0 |

**1966**

## Models Available

| | Style | Base MSRP | Change from LY | Shipping Wt. (lbs.) | Production | Change from LY |
|---|---|---|---|---|---|---|
| Monterey 2-Door Sedan | 43 | $2,783 | +0.58% | 3835 | 2,487 | -56.94% |
| Monterey 2-Door Hardtop | 47 | $2,915 | +0.45% | 3885 | 19,103 | +13.32% |
| Monterey 2-Door Convertible | 45 | $3,237 | +0.22% | 4039 | 3,279 | -31.14% |
| Monterey 4-Door Sedan | 44 | $2,854 | +0.53% | 3903 | 18,998 | -18.68% |
| Monterey 4-Door Breezeway Sedan | 42 | $2,917 | +0.45% | 3966 | 14,174 | -27.57% |
| Monterey 4-Door Hardtop | 48 | $2,990 | +0.40% | 3928 | 7,647 | -23.89% |
| Commuter 4-Door, 2-Seat Wagon | 72 | $3,240 | +0.15% | 4280 | 6,847 | -15.27% |
| TOTALS | | Avg. price $2,991 | +0.40% | | Production 72,535 | -17.99% |

# Montclair

*"A great car becomes even greater."*

**Nameplate year of origin:** 1955.
**Current bodystyle lifespan:** 1965 through 1966.
**Predecessor to this model:** Monterey Custom (1964).
**Replacement for this model:** Montclair (1967 to 1968).
**Percentage of division's sales volume:** 16.85%.
**Corporate siblings:** Ford Galaxie/LTD.
**Primary competition:** Buick Wildcat, Dodge Polara, Oldsmobile 88 and Pontiac Star Chief.
**Notable changes:** Completely restyled.
**Major standard equipment:** Cloth and vinyl front bench seat, full carpeting, interval selector windshield wipers, electric clock, bright exterior trim, deluxe wheel covers, and 8.15 × 15 BSW tires. Colony Park wagon adds: exterior wood-grain vinyl trim, power tailgate window and 8.45 × 15 BSW tires.

## Measurements

|  | Cars | Colony Park |
|---|---|---|
| Wheelbase | 123.0" | 119.0" |
| Length | 220.4" | 216.4" |
| Width | 79.6" | 79.6" |
| Height | 56.0" | 56.2" |
| Legroom — front | 41.8" | 41.8" |
| Legroom — rear | 37.7" | 37.6" |
| Headroom — front | 38.9" | 38.9" |
| Headroom — rear | 37.7" | 37.8" |
| Cargo capacity (cu. ft.) | 18.6 | 91.3 |
| Fuel capacity (gals.) | 25.0 | 25.0 |

## Models Available

| | Style | Base MSRP | Change from LY | Shipping Wt. (lbs.) | Production | Change from LY |
|---|---|---|---|---|---|---|
| Montclair 2-Door Hardtop | 57 | $3,144 | +0.29% | 3887 | 11,290 | +17.06% |
| Montclair 4-Door Sedan | 54 | $3,087 | -1.59% | 3921 | 11,856 | -37.35% |
| Montclair 4-Door Hardtop | 58 | $3,217 | +0.22% | 3971 | 15,767 | -7.13% |
| Colony Park 4-Door, 2-Seat Wagon | 76 | $3,502 | +1.98% | 4332 | 18,894 | +23.54% |
| TOTALS | | *Avg. price* $3,238 | +0.28% | | *Production* 57,807 | -4.98% |

# S-55

*"The sports-minded Mercury."*

**Nameplate year of origin:** 1962.
**Current bodystyle lifespan:** 1965 through 1966.
**Predecessor to this model:** Park Lane with Sports Package (1965).
**Replacement for this model:** S-55 (1967).
**Percentage of division's sales volume:** 1.04%.
**Corporate siblings:** Ford Galaxie 500 XL.
**Primary competition:** Buick Wildcat, Dodge Monaco, Oldsmobile Starfire and Pontiac Grand Prix & 2 + 2.
**Notable changes:** New model for 1966.
**Major standard equipment:** All-vinyl front bucket seats, front console, full carpeting, interval selector windshield wipers, electric clock, bright exterior trim, deluxe wheel covers, and 8.15 × 15 BSW tires.

## Measurements

| | |
|---|---|
| Wheelbase | 123.0" |
| Length | 220.4" |
| Width | 79.6" |
| Height | 56.0" |
| Legroom — front | 41.8" |
| Legroom — rear | 37.7" |
| Headroom — front | 38.9" |
| Headroom — rear | 37.7" |
| Cargo capacity (cu. ft.) | 18.6 |
| Fuel capacity (gals.) | 25.0 |

## Models Available

| | Style | Base MSRP | Change from LY | Shipping Wt. (lbs.) | Production | Change from LY |
|---|---|---|---|---|---|---|
| S-55 2-Door Hardtop | 49 | $3,292 | NEW | 4031 | 2,916 | NEW |
| S-55 2-Door Convertible | 46 | $3,614 | NEW | 4148 | 669 | NEW |
| TOTALS | | *Avg. price* $3,453 | NEW | | *Production* 3,585 | NEW |

# Park Lane

*"Move ahead with new style ... spirit ... and luxury."*

**Nameplate year of origin:** 1958.
**Current bodystyle lifespan:** 1965 through 1966.
**Predecessor to this model:** Park Lane or S-55 (1963 to 1964).
**Replacement for this model:** Park Lane (1967 to 1968).
**Percentage of division's sales volume:** 11.31%.
**Corporate siblings:** Ford Galaxie/LTD.
**Primary competition:** Buick Wildcat, Chrysler Newport, Oldsmobile 88 and Pontiac Bonneville.
**Notable changes:** Completely restyled.
**Major standard equipment:** Cloth and vinyl front bench seat (all-vinyl for convertible), full carpeting, trip odometer, automatic parking brake release, courtesy lights, interval selector windshield wipers, electric clock, custom grip door handles, bright exterior window trim, full wheel covers and 8.15 × 15 BSW tires.

## Measurements

| | |
|---|---|
| Wheelbase | 123.0" |
| Length | 220.4" |
| Width | 79.6" |
| Height | 56.0" |
| Legroom — front | 41.8" |
| Legroom — rear | 37.7" |
| Headroom — front | 38.9" |
| Headroom — rear | 37.7" |
| Cargo capacity (cu. ft.) | 18.6 |
| Fuel capacity (gals.) | 25.0 |

## Models Available

| | Style | Base MSRP | Change from LY | Shipping Wt. (lbs.) | Production | Change from LY |
|---|---|---|---|---|---|---|
| Park Lane 2-Door Hardtop | 67 | $3,387 | +0.59% | 3971 | 8,354 | +21.90% |
| Park Lane 2-Door Convertible | 65 | $3,608 | +0.25% | 4148 | 2,546 | -15.36% |
| Park Lane 4-Door Breezeway Sedan | 62 | $3,389 | +0.59% | 4051 | 8,696 | +4.33% |
| Park Lane 4-Door Hardtop | 68 | $3,460 | +0.52% | 4070 | 19,204 | +35.13% |
| TOTALS | | *Avg. price* $3,461 | +0.49% | | *Production* 38,800 | +19.72% |

**1966**

# OLDSMOBILE

*"Step out front in '66 ... in a Rocket Action Olds!"*

Oldsmobile created the news of the year with the first front-wheel-drive car of the modern automotive era. The Toronado was a full-size luxury/sport car with a look unlike anything else on the road. A very large 2-Door Hardtop model, the Toronado was distinguished by large, rounded wheel cut-outs, a sloping fastback roofline, a full-width grille and hidden headlights mounted between the grille and hood line. By no means a sports car, the Toronado was meant to have the appearance of one, and had an engine that unleashed plenty of horsepower. The 425 CID Oldsmobile engine put out 385 horsepower in the Toronado. Space under the hood was not an issue, so the engine was mounted longitudinally, as opposed to a cross-mounted

engine as ordinarily used in more modern front-wheel-drive cars. The technology used in the Toronado, along with its ride and handling achievements, garnered the Toronado the 1966 *Motor Trend* magazine Car of the Year award.

The mid-size F-85 and Cutlass models received a major restyling this year. While still following a contemporary Olds look, the rooflines were sporty, with "tunneled" rear windows on 2-Door models. A new 4-Door Hardtop model joined the newly created Cutlass Supreme line, as well as the F-85 Deluxe. A new engine was offered for the mid-size Cutlass line, a 400 CID V8 available in Cutlass 2-Doors or any 4-4-2 equipped model. This new engine offered horsepower comparable to the larger displacement engines, but in a smaller, lighter package. Also new for '66 was an F-85 Deluxe 2-Door Hardtop, and a Cutlass 4-Door Sedan. The full-size Oldsmobile models received new grilles and trim. Also, model lines were shuffled around to accommodate the new Toronado. The Jetstar 88 lost its Convertible model, and the Jetstar I was discontinued. The Delta 88 became a full-fledged model line and added a Convertible, while the Starfire was pared down to a single 2-Door Hardtop model. The Ninety-Eight line made no model changes.

Dynamic 88 4-Door Hardtop

F-85 4-4-2-2 Hardtop

F-85 Deluxe 4-Door Sedan

F-85 Deluxe 4-Door Wagon

Jetstar 88 4-Door Hardtop

Starfire 2-Door Hardtop

Toronado 2-Door Hardtop

Toronado Custom 2-Door Hardtop,
*Motor Trend* Car of the Year

**Model year production:** 584,151, down 1.09% from 1965.
**Domestic market share:** 6.52% (5th place).
**Base price range:** $2,348 to $4,812.
**Industry average base price:** $3,070.
**Oldsmobile average base price:** $3,235.
**Introduction date:** September 1965.
**Assembly plants:** Southgate, CA (C); Framingham, MA (G); Fremont, CA (Z); Lansing, MI (M); Fairfax, KS (X); and Linden, NJ (E).

**Data plate identification:** Thirteen digit code read as follows: 1st digit 3 = Oldsmobile; 2nd through 5th digits identify series/body style; 6 = 1966; 7th digit is assembly plant code; 100001 and up for serial number (except Toronado is 500001). *Example:* 358396X100001 is a 1966 Oldsmobile Delta 88 4-Door Hardtop with a 425 CID V8, serial number 100001, built in Fairfax, KS.

## Powertrains

| Engine | Gross HP | Transmission Availability | F-85/ 4-4-2 | Supreme & Vista-Cruiser | Jet./ Dyn. 88 & Delta 88 | Starfire/ 98 | Toronado |
|---|---|---|---|---|---|---|---|
| 250 CID Action-Line, 1-bbl., 6-cyl. | 155 | 3-speed man. | S* | - | - | - | - |
| | | Jetaway Automatic | $236* | - | - | - | |
| 330 CID Jetfire Rocket, 2-bbl., V8 | 250 (260— Prem.) | 3-speed man. | $70* | S (V.Cr.) | S (Jetstar 88) | - | - |

| Engine | Gross HP | Transmission Availability | F-85/ 4-4-2 | Supreme & Vista-Cruiser | Jet./ Dyn. 88 & Delta 88 | Starfire/ 98 | Toronado |
|---|---|---|---|---|---|---|---|
| | | 4-speed man. | $254* | $184 (V.Cr.) | - | - | - |
| | | Jetaway Automatic | $306* | $236 (V.Cr.) | $236 (Jetstar 88) | - | - |
| 330 CID Cutlass, 4-bbl., V8 | 310 (320— Prem.) | 3-speed man. | $103* | S (Cutl.)/ $33 (V.Cr.) | - | - | - |
| | | 4-speed man.* | $287* | $184 (Cutl.)/ $217 (V.Cr.) | - | - | - |
| | | Jetaway Automatic | $339* | $236 (Cutl.)/ $269 (V.Cr.) | - | | |
| 400 CID 4-4-2, 4-bbl., V8 | 350 | 3-speed man. | S** | - | - | - | - |
| | | 4-speed man. | $184** | - | - | - | - |
| | | Turbo Hydra-matic | $236** | - | - | - | - |
| 425 CID Super Rocket, 2-bbl., V8 | 300 (310— Auto.) | 3-speed man. | - | - | S (Delta/Dyn.) | - | - |
| | | Turbo Hydra-matic | - | - | $236 (Delta/Dyn.) | - | - |
| 425 CID Super Rocket, 4-bbl., V8 | 365 | 3-speed man. | - | - | $36 (Delta/Dyn.) | - | - |
| | | Turbo Hydra-matic | - | - | $272 (Delta/Dyn.) | S — 98 | - |
| 425 CID Starfire, 4-bbl., V8 | 375 | 3-speed man. | - | - | $100 (Delta/Dyn.) | S (Strfr.) | - |
| | | Turbo Hydra-matic | - | - | $336 (Delta/Dyn.) | $236 (Strfr.)/ $64 (98) | - |
| 425 CID Toronado Rocket, 4-bbl., V8 | 385 | Turbo Hydra-matic | - | - | - | - | S |

*F-85 and Deluxe only.    **With 4-4-2 option only.    ***Available only on 2-Door models.

## Major Options

| | F-85 | Vista-Cr. | Jetstar 88 | Dynamic 88 | Delta 88/Stfr. | 98 | Toronado |
|---|---|---|---|---|---|---|---|
| Air conditioning | $343 | $343 | $390 | $390 | $390 | $390 | $390 |
| Electronic cruise control | $41 | $41 | $49 | $49 | $49 | $49 | $49 |
| Deck lid remote release | $12 | - | $12 | $12 | $12 | $12 | $12 |
| Tilt-Away steering wheel | $42 | $42 | $42 | $42 | $42 | $42 | $42 |
| Power steering | $94 | $94 | $104 | $104 | $104 | S | S |
| Power brakes | $41 | $41 | $41 | $41 | $41 | S | S |
| Power driver's seat | $69 | $69 | $69 | $69 | $69 | $69–$100* | $69 |
| Power windows | $104 | $104 | $110 | $110 | $110 | S/$110* | $110 |
| Electric clock | $15 | $15 | $15 | $15 | S-Strfr./$15 | S | S |
| AM radio | $64 | $64 | $64 | $64 | $64 | $64 | $64 |
| AM/FM radio | $147 | $147 | $147 | $147 | $147 | $147 | $147 |
| Vinyl roof | $74 | - | $74 | $74 | $74 | $74 | $74 |
| White sidewall tires | $30–40 | $40 | $40 | $45 | $45 | $45 | $45 |
| Wire wheel trim covers | $61 | $61 | $61 | $61 | $61 | $61 | - |
| 4-4-2 performance pkg. | $152 | - | - | - | - | - | - |

*4-Door Town Sedan only.

Options common to most models. (- = Not Available; S = Standard equipment.) Items may be standard equipment, optional at different pricing, or unavailable on certain models. This chart is only a guide.

1966

## Paint Colors

| | Code | | Code |
|---|---|---|---|
| Ebony Black | A | Autumn Bronze Metallic | M |
| Nocturne Mist Metallic | B | Burgundy Mist Metallic | N |
| Provincial White | C | Target Red | R |
| Lucerne Mist Metallic | D | Champagne Mist Metallic | S |
| Royal Mist Metallic | E | Sierra Mist Metallic | T |
| Trumpet Gold Metallic | G | Dubonnet | U |
| Laurel Mist Metallic | H | Almond Beige | V |
| Forest Mist Metallic | J | Silver Mist Metallic | W |
| Ocean Mist Metallic | K | Porcelain White | X |
| Tropic Turquoise Metallic | L | Frost Green Metallic | Z |

# F-85 and Cutlass

*"Big-car look. Big-car ride. Big-car interior comfort.*
*Big-car action. Big money? Nope."*

**Nameplate year of origin:** 1962 (as a F-85 model designation); 1955 (Show car).

**Current bodystyle lifespan:** 1966 through 1967.

**Predecessor to this model:** F-85/Cutlass (1964 to 1965).

**Replacement for this model:** Cutlass (1968 to 1972).

**Percentage of division's sales volume:** 34.59%.

**Corporate siblings:** Buick Special/Skylark, Chevrolet Chevelle, Pontiac Tempest/LeMans.

**Primary competition:** AMC Classic, Dodge Coronet, Ford Fairlane, Mercury Comet, Plymouth Belvedere.

**Notable changes:** Completely restyled.

**Major standard equipment:** Cloth and vinyl front bench seat, heavy-duty floor covering, electric windshield wipers, and 6.95 × 14 BSW tires. Deluxe adds: Full carpeting, padded instrument panel and 7.35 × 14 BSW tires. Cutlass adds: All-vinyl bucket seats. Cutlass Supreme adds: Fold-down center arm rests, deluxe steering wheel, and full-length body molding. 4-4-2 option-package adds: 400 CID V8 engine, dual exhausts, heavy duty suspension, and F70 × 14 redline tires.

## Measurements

| | Cars | Wagon |
|---|---|---|
| Wheelbase | 115.0" | 115.0" |
| Length | 204.2" | 204.2" |
| Width | 75.4" | 75.4" |
| Height | 54.5" | 55.3" |
| Legroom — front | 41.3" | 41.2" |
| Legroom — rear | 36.0" | 35.9" |
| Headroom — front | 38.1" | 38.0" |
| Headroom — rear | 37.2" | 37.5" |
| Luggage capacity (cu. ft.) | 20.1 | 85.2 |
| Fuel capacity (gals.) | 20.0 | 20.0 |

## Models Available

| | Style | Base MSRP | Change from LY | Shipping Wt. (lbs.) | Production | Change from LY |
|---|---|---|---|---|---|---|
| F-85 2-Door Club Coupe | 3307 | $2,348 | +0.17% | 2951 | 12,694 | -2.42% |
| F-85 4-Door Sedan | 3369 | $2,401 | +0.13% | 3001 | 6,616 | -18.10% |
| F-85 4-Door, 2-Seat Wagon | 3335 | $2,695 | +0.22% | 3246 | 2,160 | -32.71% |
| F-85 Deluxe 2-Door Hardtop | 3517 | $2,513 | NEW | 2990 | 19,942 | NEW |
| F-85 Deluxe 4-Door Sedan | 3569 | $2,497 | -0.32% | 3023 | 31,020 | -41.20% |
| F-85 Deluxe 4-Door Hardtop | 3539 | $2,629 | NEW | 3077 | 7,013 | NEW |
| F-85 Deluxe 4-Door, 2-Seat Wagon | 3535 | $2,793 | -0.14% | 3273 | 8,492 | -22.97% |
| Cutlass 2-Door Sport Coupe | 3807 | $2,633 | -0.38% | 3219 | 17,455 | -33.99% |
| Cutlass 2-Door Holiday Hardtop | 3817 | $2,770 | -0.50% | 3243 | 44,633 | -3.26% |
| Cutlass 2-Door Convertible | 3867 | $2,965 | -0.60% | 3349 | 12,154 | -3.75% |
| Cutlass 4-Door Sedan | 3869 | $2,673 | NEW | 3240 | 9,017 | NEW |
| Cutlass Supreme 4-Door Hardtop | 3839 | $2,846 | NEW | 3296 | 30,871 | NEW |
| TOTALS | *Avg. price* | $2,647 | +0.61% | *Production* | 202,067 | +12.62% |

# Vista-Cruiser

*"Whatever you want in a station wagon,*
*you've got it made in the new Olds Vista-Cruisers!"*

**Nameplate year of origin:** 1964.
**Current bodystyle lifespan:** 1966 through 1967.
**Predecessor to this model:** Vista-Cruiser (1964 to 1965).
**Replacement for this model:** Vista-Cruiser (1968 to 1972).
**Percentage of division's sales volume:** 4.54%.
**Corporate siblings:** Buick Sportwagon.
**Primary competition:** AMC Ambassador and Dodge Coronet.
**Notable changes:** Completely restyled.
**Major standard equipment:** All-vinyl front bench seat, full carpeting, heater and
 defroster, deluxe steering wheel, Vista-roof windows, padded second seat sun
 visors, and 8.25 × 14 BSW tires. Custom adds: Special interior appointments.

## Measurements

| | |
|---|---|
| Wheelbase | 120.0" |
| Length | 209.1" |
| Width | 75.4" |
| Height | 58.3" |
| Legroom — front | 41.3" |
| Legroom — rear | 38.9" |
| Headroom — front | 38.0" |
| Headroom — rear | 40.3" |
| Luggage capacity (cu. ft.) | 101.1 |
| Fuel capacity (gals.) | 20.0 |

## Models Available

| | Style | Base MSRP | Change from LY | Shipping Wt. (lbs.) | Production | Change from LY |
|---|---|---|---|---|---|---|
| Vista-Cruiser 4-Dr., 2-S. Wagon | 3455 | $2,935 | -0.07% | 3713 | 1,600 | -24.17% |
| Vista-Cruiser 4-Dr., 3-S. Wagon | 3465 | $3,087 | +0.49% | 3815 | 1,869 | -43.96% |
| Vista-Cruiser Cust. 4-Dr., 2-S. Wgn. | 3855 | $3,137 | -0.29% | 3765 | 8,910 | -4.76% |
| Vista-Cruiser Cust. 4-Dr., 3-S. Wgn. | 3865 | $3,278 | +0.24% | 3861 | 14,167 | -17.66% |
| TOTALS | | Avg. price $3,109 | +0.09% | | Production 26,546 | -17.06% |

**1966**

# Jetstar 88

*"Fresh new look. Fashionable interior. Rollicking Rocket action."*

**Nameplate year of origin:** 1964 (88 series started 1949).
**Current bodystyle lifespan:** 1965 through 1966.
**Predecessor to this model:** 88/Jetstar 88 (1961 to 1964).
**Replacement for this model:** Delmont 88 (1967 to 1968).
**Percentage of division's sales volume:** 5.01%.
**Corporate siblings:** Buick LeSabre, Chevrolet Impala, Pontiac Catalina.
**Primary competition:** AMC Ambassador, Dodge Polara, Mercury Monterey,
 and Plymouth VIP.
**Notable changes:** New grille, and minor trim and detail changes.
**Major standard equipment:** Cloth-and-vinyl front bench seat, full carpeting,
 electric windshield wipers, rocker panel moldings, wheel covers, and 7.75 ×
 14 BSW tires.

## Measurements

| | |
|---|---|
| Wheelbase | 123.0" |
| Length | 217.0" |
| Width | 80.0" |
| Height | 55.5" |
| Legroom — front | 41.1" |
| Legroom — rear | 39.0" |
| Headroom — front | 38.8" |
| Headroom — rear | 37.8" |
| Luggage capacity (cu. ft.) | 19.4 |
| Fuel capacity (gals.) | 25.0 |

## Models Available

| | Style | Base MSRP | Change from LY | Shipping Wt. (lbs.) | Production | Change from LY |
|---|---|---|---|---|---|---|
| Jetstar 88 2-Door Holiday Hardtop | 5237 | $2,983 | -0.40% | 3730 | 8,575 | -38.36% |
| Jetstar 88 4-Door Celebrity Sedan | 5269 | $2,927 | -0.37% | 3765 | 12,734 | -36.78% |
| Jetstar 88 4-Door Holiday Hardtop | 5239 | $3,059 | -0.42% | 3808 | 7,938 | -50.14% |
| TOTALS | | Avg. price $2,990 | -3.11% | | Production 29,247 | -44.78% |

# Dynamic 88

*"Leave it to Oldsmobile's Dynamic 88 to move you— more ways than one!"*

**Nameplate year of origin:** 1964 (88 series started 1949).
**Current bodystyle lifespan:** 1965 through 1966.
**Predecessor to this model:** Dynamic 88/Super 88 (1961 to 1964).
**Replacement for this model:** Delmont 88 (1967 to 1968).
**Percentage of division's sales volume:** 16.41%.
**Corporate siblings:** Buick LeSabre, Chevrolet Impala/Caprice, Pontiac Catalina/Executive.
**Primary competition:** AMC Ambassador, Dodge Polara, and Mercury Montclair.
**Notable changes:** New grille, and minor trim and detail changes.
**Major standard equipment:** Cloth-and-vinyl front bench seat, full carpeting, electric windshield wipers, full wheel covers, and 8.25 × 14 BSW tires.

## Measurements

| | |
|---|---|
| Wheelbase | 123.0" |
| Length | 217.0" |
| Width | 80.0" |
| Height | 55.5" |
| Legroom — front | 41.1" |
| Legroom — rear | 39.0" |
| Headroom — front | 38.8" |
| Headroom — rear | 37.8" |
| Luggage capacity (cu. ft.) | 19.4 |
| Fuel capacity (gals.) | 25.0 |

## Models Available

| | Style | Base MSRP | Change from LY | Shipping Wt. (lbs.) | Production | Change from LY |
|---|---|---|---|---|---|---|
| Dynamic 88 2-Door Holiday HT | 5637 | $3,069 | +0.13% | 3888 | 20,768 | -16.11% |
| Dynamic 88 2-Door Convertible | 5667 | $3,404 | -0.12% | 3967 | 5,540 | -37.27% |
| Dynamic 88 4-Door Celebrity Sedan | 5669 | $3,013 | +0.17% | 3920 | 38,742 | -17.62% |
| Dynamic 88 4-Door Holiday HT | 5639 | $3,144 | +0.03% | 3957 | 30,784 | -20.84% |
| TOTALS | *Avg. price* | $3,158 | +0.06% | *Production* | 95,834 | -19.81% |

# Delta 88

*"You're in for some of the most powerful convincing a car can muster."*

**Nameplate year of origin:** 1965 (88 series started 1949).
**Current bodystyle lifespan:** 1965 through 1966.
**Predecessor to this model:** Super 88 (1964).
**Replacement for this model:** Delta 88 (1967 to 1968).
**Percentage of division's sales volume:** 15.13%.
**Corporate siblings:** Buick Wildcat, Chevrolet Caprice, Pontiac Executive/Bonneville.
**Primary competition:** AMC Ambassador, Dodge Polara, and Mercury Montclair.
**Notable changes:** New grille and minor trim and detail changes.
**Major standard equipment:** All-vinyl Custom Sport seat w/folding center armrests, courtesy lamps, deluxe steering wheel and 8.25 × 14 BSW tires.

## Measurements

| | |
|---|---|
| Wheelbase | 123.0" |
| Length | 217.0" |
| Width | 80.0" |
| Height | 55.5" |
| Legroom — front | 41.1" |
| Legroom — rear | 39.0" |
| Headroom — front | 38.8" |
| Headroom — rear | 37.8" |
| Luggage capacity (cu. ft.) | 19.4 |
| Fuel capacity (gals.) | 25.0 |

## Models Available

| | Style | Base MSRP | Change from LY | Shipping Wt. (lbs.) | Production | Change from LY |
|---|---|---|---|---|---|---|
| Delta 88 2-Door Holiday Hardtop | 5837 | $3,253 | 0.00% | 3946 | 20,587 | -11.24% |
| Delta 88 2-Door Convertible | 5867 | $3,588 | NEW | 4012 | 4,303 | NEW |
| Delta 88 4-Door Celebrity Sdn. | 5869 | $3,160 | +0.06% | 3969 | 30,140 | 0.75% |
| Delta 88 4-Door Holiday Hardtop | 5839 | $3,328 | -0.06% | 4026 | 33,326 | -10.79% |
| TOTALS | *Avg. price* | $3,332 | +2.62% | *Production* | 88,356 | -2.33% |

# Starfire

*"This year Starfire sports a dashing new look all its own."*

**Nameplate year of origin:** 1954 (as designation for 98 Convertible); 1961 (as series).
**Current bodystyle lifespan:** 1965 through 1966.
**Predecessor to this model:** Starfire (1961 to 1964).
**Replacement for this model:** None.
**Percentage of division's sales volume:** 2.22%.
**Corporate siblings:** Buick Wildcat, Chevrolet Impala SS, and Pontiac Grand Prix.
**Primary competition:** Chrysler 300, Dodge Monaco, Ford Galaxie 500 XL, and Mercury S-55.
**Notable changes:** New grille, roofline, and minor trim and detail changes.
**Major standard equipment:** All-vinyl bucket seats with center console, full carpeting, tachometer, electric clock, deluxe steering wheel, glove box and courtesy lamps, full wheel covers, and 8.25 × 14 BSW tires.

## Measurements

| | |
|---|---|
| Wheelbase | 123.0" |
| Length | 217.0" |
| Width | 80.0" |
| Height | 54.1" |
| Legroom — front | 41.3" |
| Legroom — rear | 39.0" |
| Headroom — front | 37.7" |
| Headroom — rear | 37.2" |
| Luggage capacity (cu. ft.) | 19.4 |
| Fuel capacity (gals.) | 25.0 |

## Models Available

| | Style | Base MSRP | Change from LY | Shipping Wt. (lbs.) | Production | Change from LY |
|---|---|---|---|---|---|---|
| Starfire 2-Door Hardtop | 5457 | $3,564 | -14.08% | 3988 | 13,019 | -0.04% |
| TOTALS | | *Avg. price* $3,564 | -20.14% | *Production* | 13,019 | -14.69% |

# Ninety-Eight

*"Trust your instincts. Your first good impression of the new Oldsmobile Ninety-Eight is sure to last a long, long time!"*

**Nameplate year of origin:** 1941.
**Current bodystyle lifespan:** 1965 through 1966.
**Predecessor to this model:** Ninety-Eight (1961 to 1964).
**Replacement for this model:** Ninety-Eight (1967 to 1968).
**Percentage of division's sales volume:** 15.08%.
**Corporate siblings:** Buick Electra and Cadillac Calais/de Ville.
**Primary competition:** Chrysler New Yorker and Mercury Park Lane.
**Notable changes:** New grille and minor trim and detail changes.
**Major standard equipment:** Cloth and vinyl bench seat with fold-down center armrest (all-vinyl on Hardtop and Convertible), deep-pile carpeting, deluxe steering wheel, electric clock, power windows and two-way power seat (except Town Sedan), full wheel covers, rear wheel opening covers, power steering, power brakes, and 8.55 × 14 BSW tires. Luxury Sedan adds: Special interior trim and vinyl top.

## Measurements

| | |
|---|---|
| Wheelbase | 126.0" |
| Length | 223.0" |
| Width | 80.0" |
| Height | 55.8" |
| Legroom — front | 41.0" |
| Legroom — rear | 42.2" |
| Headroom — front | 39.5" |
| Headroom — rear | 38.2" |
| Luggage capacity (cu. ft.) | 23.4 |
| Fuel capacity (gals.) | 25.0 |

## Models Available

| | Style | Base MSRP | Change from LY | Shipping Wt. (lbs.) | Production | Change from LY |
|---|---|---|---|---|---|---|
| Ninety-Eight 2-Door Hardtop | 8457 | $4,158 | -0.93% | 4150 | 11,488 | -5.57% |
| Ninety-Eight 2-Door Convertible | 8467 | $4,443 | -1.11% | 4229 | 4,568 | -6.83% |
| Ninety-Eight 4-Door Town Sedan | 8469 | $3,966 | -0.87% | 4182 | 10,892 | -17.90% |

1966

| | Style | Base MSRP | Change from LY | Shipping Wt. (lbs.) | Production | Change from LY |
|---|---|---|---|---|---|---|
| Ninety-Eight 4-Door Hardtop | 8439 | $4,233 | -0.94% | 4254 | 23,048 | -19.07% |
| Ninety-Eight Luxury 4-Door Sedan | 8669 | $4,308 | -0.99% | 4268 | 38,123 | +7.11% |
| TOTALS | | Avg. price $4,222 | -0.96% | | Production 88,119 | -6.66% |

# Toronado

*"New one-of-a-kind car ... engineered by Oldsmobile!"*

**Nameplate year of origin:** 1966.
**Current bodystyle lifespan:** 1966 through 1970.
**Predecessor to this model:** None.
**Replacement for this model:** Toronado (1971 to 1978).
**Percentage of division's sales volume:** 7.01%.
**Corporate siblings:** Buick Riviera.
**Primary competition:** Imperial LeBaron Coupe and Ford Thunderbird.
**Notable changes:** All-new model.
**Major standard equipment:** All-vinyl bench seat, fold-down center armrest, deep-pile carpeting, electric clock, LH outside rearview mirror, front wheel drive, power brakes, and 8.85 × 15 BSW tires. Custom adds: Stratobench seat, dual interior door handle releases and wheel trim rings.

## Measurements

| | |
|---|---|
| Wheelbase | 119.0" |
| Length | 211.0" |
| Width | 78.5" |
| Height | 52.8" |
| Legroom — front | 41.8" |
| Legroom — rear | 35.5" |
| Headroom — front | 37.9" |
| Headroom — rear | 37.5" |
| Luggage capacity (cu. ft.) | 14.5 |
| Fuel capacity (gals.) | 24.0 |

## Models Available

| | Style | Base MSRP | Change from LY | Shipping Wt. (lbs.) | Production | Change from LY |
|---|---|---|---|---|---|---|
| Toronado 2-Door Hardtop | 9487 | $4,617 | NEW | 4312 | 6,333 | NEW |
| Toronado Custom 2-Door Hardtop | 9687 | $4,812 | NEW | 4386 | 34,630 | NEW |
| TOTALS | | Avg. price $4,715 | NEW | | Production 40,963 | NEW |

# PLYMOUTH

*"There are five ways to Let yourself go ... Plymouth in '66."*

Confidence had finally taken hold at Plymouth, and with the introduction of an all-new line of intermediate Belvedere and Satellite models, it seemed they could do no wrong. The new Belvedere line was very angular, but updated the Plymouth look created in 1965 quite nicely. The front end featured single headlamps, with parking lamps set a few inches inside the lights, all within a simple horizontal bar grille. Body sides generally looked to be slab sided, but actually had two body length feature lines, between which was a gently arched body panel. Front wheel openings were full-cut arches, while the rear wheel openings were low cut. These were some of the most attractive cars from Plymouth yet. The model line was left untouched this year.

Full-size Plymouth Fury models were facelifted lightly this season, now wearing a split-style grille. Other features were given cosmetic updates. There was an important addition to the line though. A new top-of-the line Fury, called simply VIP, was introduced. As noted elsewhere in this book, marketing maneuvers such as this would become a major reason for the demise of Plymouth and Oldsmobile. During 1965 Chevrolet had introduced the luxury-level Caprice option for its Impala line, which then became a regular model for 1966. Similarly, Ford had introduced the LTD to top off its Galaxie line, so Plymouth had to keep up, and thus the VIP was born. To briefly recap, these cars were seen as image builders, to promote the luxury offered in the lower-priced lines. It was only a matter of time before every luxury found on a Cadillac was available on Chevrolet (or Imperial and Plymouth). Thus, the lines became blurred between what was a luxury car and what was an entry-level car, and sales suffered because of the inter-corporate rivalries. Not only did an Imperial have to compete with Lincoln and Cadillac, but it had always had upper-level Buick, Oldsmobile, Mercury and Chrysler models to compete with, and now Ford, Chevrolet and Plymouth as well. Needless to say, eventually things had to change.

The Valiant and Barracuda lines also underwent minor facelifts for 1966. They too were given a split grille up front with parking lamps moving from the grille to the bumper. The slow-selling Valiant 200 2-Door Sedan and Convertible models were dropped this season.

Belvedere I 4-Door Wagon

Belvedere II 4-Door Sedan

Fury II 4-Door Sedan

Valiant 100 2-Door Sedan

Valiant 200 4-Door Sedan

VIP Interior

**Model year production:** 695,907, down 3.52% from 1965.
**Domestic market share:** 7.77% (4th place).
**Base price range:** $2,025 to $3,251.
**Industry average base price:** $3,070.
**Plymouth average base price:** $2,671.
**Introduction date:** September 29, 1965.
**Assembly plants:** Lynch Road, MI (1): Hamtramck, MI (2); Los Angeles, CA (5); Newark DE (6); St. Louis, MO (7); and Windsor, Ontario, Canada (9).
**Data plate identification:** Thirteen digit code read as follows:

First digit is car line (e.g., P for Fury); second number identifies series (L is low, M is mid, H is High, etc.); 3rd and 4th digits indicate body style (see model number in charts below); fifth digit is engine code (see chart below); sixth digit 6 for 1966; seventh digit is assembly plant code; 100001 and up for serial number. *Example:* PH23E62100001 is a 1966 Plymouth Fury III 2-Door Hardtop with a 318 CID V8 engine, built at Hamtramck, MI, serial number 100001.

## Powertrains

| Engine | Gross HP | Engine Code | Transmission Availability | Valiant | Barracuda | Belvedere | Fury |
|---|---|---|---|---|---|---|---|
| 170 CID, 1-bbl., 6-cyl. | 101 | A | 3-speed manual | S | - | - | - |
| | | | 4-speed manual | $179 | - | - | - |
| | | | Torqueflite automatic | $172 | - | - | - |
| 225 CID, 1-bbl., 6-cyl. | 145 | B | 3-speed manual | $46 | S | S[2] | S[3] |

| Engine | Gross HP | Engine Code | Transmission Availability | Valiant | Barracuda | Belvedere | Fury |
|---|---|---|---|---|---|---|---|
| | | | 4-speed manual | $232 | $186 | - | - |
| | | | Torqueflite automatic | $218 | $172 | $192[2] | $192[3] |
| 273 CID, 2-bbl., V8 | 180 | D | 3-speed manual | $131 | $82 | S[1]/$94[2] | - |
| | | | 4-speed manual | $310 | $261 | - | - |
| | | | Torqueflite automatic | $312 | $263 | $203[1]/$297[2] | - |
| 273 CID Formula S, 4-bbl., V8 | 235 | D | 3-speed manual | - | $165 | - | - |
| | | | 4-speed manual | - | $344 | - | - |
| | | | Torqueflite automatic | - | $346 | - | - |
| 318 CID, 2-bbl., V8 | 230 | E | 3-speed manual | - | - | $30[1]/$124[2] | S[4]/$104[3] |
| | | | Torqueflite automatic | - | - | $241[1]/$335[2] | $211[4]/$315[3] |
| 361 CID Commando, 2-bbl., V8 | 265 | F | 3-speed manual | - | - | $88[1]/$182[2] | - |
| | | | 4-speed manual | - | - | $276[1]/$370[2] | - |
| | | | Torqueflite automatic | - | - | $299[1]/$393[2] | - |
| 383 CID Commando, 2-bbl., V8 | 305 | G | 3-speed manual | - | - | - | $71[4]/$185[3] |
| | | | 4-speed manual | - | - | - | $259[4]/$373[3] |
| | | | Torqueflite automatic | - | - | - | $282[4]/$396[3] |
| 383 CID Commando, 4-bbl., V8 | 325 | G | 3-speed manual | - | - | $150[1]/$244[2] | $120[4]/$224[3] |
| | | | 4-speed manual | - | - | $338[1]/$432[2] | $308[4]/$412[3] |
| | | | Torqueflite automatic | - | - | $361[1]/$455[2] | $331[4]/$435[3] |
| 426 CID Commando, 4-bbl., V8 | 365 | H | 4-speed manual | - | - | * | * |
| | | | Torqueflite automatic | - | - | * | * |
| 426 CID Commando, 4-bbl., V8 | 415–425 | H | 4-speed manual | - | - | * | * |
| | | | Torqueflite automatic | - | - | * | * |
| 426 CID Hemi V8, 4-bbl., V8 | 415–425 | K | 4-speed manual | - | - | * | * |
| | | | Torqueflite automatic | - | - | * | * |
| 440 CID, 4-bbl., V8 | 375 | J | Torqueflite automatic | - | - | - | $445[4]/$549[3] |

[1]Satellite models only. [2]All but Satellite. [3]Fury I (All), Fury II Sedans, Fury III 2-Door HT and 4-Door Sedan only. [4]All but Fury I, Fury II Sedan and Fury III 2-Dr. HT and 4-Dr. Sedan. *Available at varying prices and installation rates. Accurate pricing is unavailable at this time.

## Major Options

| | Valiant | Barracuda | Savoy/Belvedere | Fury |
|---|---|---|---|---|
| Air conditioning (V8 only) | $319 | $319 | $338 | $338 |
| Solex tinted glass | $29 | $14 | $40 | $40 |
| Power steering | $80 | $80 | $84 | $95 |
| Power brakes | $42 | $42 | $42 | $42 |
| Power windows | - | - | $102 | $102 |
| Power front seat — 4-way bucket | - | - | $78 | $78 |
| Electric clock | $16 | $16 | $16 | $16 |
| AM radio | $59 | $59 | $59 | $59 |
| Variable speed wipers and washer | $17 | $17 | $17 | $17 |

Options common to most models. (- = Not Available.) Items may be standard equipment, optional at different pricing, or unavailable on certain models. This chart is only a guide.

## Paint Colors

| | Code |
|---|---|
| Silver Metallic | AA-1 |
| Black | BB-1 |
| Light Blue | CC-1 |
| Light Blue Metallic | DD-1 |
| Dark Blue Metallic | EE-1 |
| Dark Green Metallic | GG-1 |
| Light Turquoise Metallic | KK-1 |
| Dark Turquoise Met. | LL-1 |
| Turbine Bronze Metallic | MM-1 |
| Bright Red | PP-1 |
| Dark Red Metallic | QQ-1 |
| Yellow | RR-1 |
| Soft Yellow | SS-1 |
| White | WW-1 |
| Beige | XX-1 |
| Bronze Metallic | YY-1 |
| Citron Gold Metallic | ZZ-1 |
| Charcoal Metallic | 22-1 |
| Light Mauve Metallic | 66-1 |

# Valiant

*"The car that really lets you live … within your budget."*

**Nameplate year of origin:** 1960.
**Current bodystyle lifespan:** 1963 through 1966.
**Predecessor to this model:** Valiant (1960 to 1962).
**Replacement for this model:** Valiant (1967 to 1976).
**Percentage of division's sales volume:** 19.85%.
**Corporate siblings:** Dodge Dart.
**Primary competition:** AMC Rambler American, Chevrolet Chevy II, Ford Falcon and Studebaker.
**Notable changes:** Revised front end treatment, and trim and detail changes.
**Major standard equipment:** Cloth and vinyl bench seat, rubber floor mat, vinyl headlining, chrome exterior front and rear window trim, and 6.50 × 13 BSW tires. 200 adds: Side window chrome trim, color-keyed carpeting, front and rear armrests, courtesy or map lights, and wheel covers. Signet adds: All-vinyl bucket seats, color-keyed deep-pile carpeting, rear deck trim and 6-way adjustable front seats.

## Measurements

|  | Cars | Wagons |
|---|---|---|
| Wheelbase | 106.0" | 106.0" |
| Length | 188.3" | 188.8" |
| Width | 70.2" | 70.2" |
| Height | 53.1" | 53.1" |
| Legroom — front | 40.7" | 40.7" |
| Legroom — rear | 34.2" | 34.2" |
| Headroom — front | 38.6" | 38.6" |
| Headroom — rear | 37.8" | 37.6" |
| Cargo capacity (cu. ft.) | 14.1 | NA |
| Fuel capacity (gals.) | 18.0 | 18.0 |

## Models Available

|  | Style | Base MSRP | Change from LY | Shipping Wt. (lbs.) | Production | Change from LY |
|---|---|---|---|---|---|---|
| Valiant 100 2-Door Sedan | VL21 | $2,025 | +1.05% | 2600 | 35,787 | -11.49% |
| Valiant 100 4-Door Sedan | VL41 | $2,095 | +0.96% | 2630 | 36,031 | -15.93% |
| Valiant 100 4-Door Wagon | VL45 | $2,387 | +1.10% | 2780 | 6,838 | -36.81% |
| Valiant 200 4-Door Sedan | VH41 | $2,226 | +1.41% | 2635 | 39,392 | -5.40% |
| Valiant 200 4-Door Wagon | VH45 | $2,502 | +1.05% | 2780 | 4,537 | -26.02% |
| Valiant Signet 2-Door Hardtop | VH23 | $2,261 | -3.38% | 2635 | 13,045 | +18.60% |
| Valiant Signet 2-Door Convertible | VH27 | $2,527 | -1.33% | 2735 | 2,507 | -2.75% |
| TOTALS | | *Avg. price* $2,289 | +0.13% | | *Production* 138,137 | -17.36% |

# Barracuda

*"Swiftly and surely, selective sports-minded people are going Plymouth Barracuda — the fast new version of the car that started America thinking fastback."*

**Nameplate year of origin:** 1964.
**Current bodystyle lifespan:** 1964 through 1966.
**Predecessor to this model:** None.
**Replacement for this model:** Barracuda (1967 to 1969).
**Percentage of division's sales volume:** 5.46%.
**Corporate siblings:** Dodge Dart.
**Primary competition:** Ford Mustang.
**Notable changes:** Revised front-end treatment, and trim and detail changes.
**Major standard equipment:** All-vinyl front bucket seats, full carpeting (including cargo compartment), chrome exterior front and rear window trim, specific Barracuda trim, Torsion-Aire suspension and 6.50 × 13 BSW tires.

## Measurements

|  |  |
|---|---|
| Wheelbase | 106.0" |
| Length | 188.2" |
| Width | 70.1" |
| Height | 53.4" |
| Legroom — front | 40.0" |
| Legroom — rear | 35.5" |
| Headroom — front | 38.2" |
| Headroom — rear | 37.2" |
| Cargo capacity (cu. ft.) | 5.7 |
| Fuel capacity (gals.) | 18.0 |

## Models Available

| | Style | Base MSRP | Change from LY | Shipping Wt. (lbs.) | Production | Change from LY |
|---|---|---|---|---|---|---|
| Barracuda 2-Door Fastback HT | BP29 | $2,556 | +2.77% | 2800 | 38,029 | -41.13% |
| TOTALS | Avg. price | $2,556 | +2.77% | Production | 38,029 | -41.13% |

# Belvedere

*"New style and new performance in a large economy size."*

**Nameplate year of origin:** 1951 (HT model); 1954 (as series).
**Current bodystyle lifespan:** 1966 through 1967.
**Predecessor to this model:** Belvedere (1962 to 1965).
**Replacement for this model:** Belvedere (1968 to 1970).
**Percentage of division's sales volume:** 27.20%.
**Corporate siblings:** Dodge Coronet.
**Primary competition:** AMC Rambler Classic, Chevrolet Chevelle, and Ford Fairlane.
**Notable changes:** Completely restyled.
**Major standard equipment:** Cloth and vinyl front bench seat, color-keyed floor coverings, front and rear armrests, dual sunvisors, electric windshield wipers, bright trim around front and rear windows, and rear fender line, and 6.95 × 14 BSW tires (7.75 × 14 BSW tires on wagon). Belvedere II adds: Full carpeting, specific interior trim, full-length body side moldings, 8.25 × 14 BSW tires on 3-Seat Wagon and 7.35 × 14 BSW tires on convertible. Satellite adds: All-vinyl bucket seats, padded instrument panel, and specific ornamentation.

### Measurements

| | Cars | Wagons |
|---|---|---|
| Wheelbase | 116.0" | 117.0" |
| Length | 200.5" | 208.5" |
| Width | 75.5" | 75.5" |
| Height | 54.0" | 54.8" |
| Legroom — front | 42.0" | 42.0" |
| Legroom — rear | 36.5" | 36.5" |
| Headroom — front | 38.8" | 38.8" |
| Headroom — rear | 37.8" | 37.8" |
| Cargo capacity (cu. ft.) | 17.0 | NA |
| Fuel capacity (gals.) | 19.0 | 19.0 |

## Models Available

| | Style | Base MSRP | Change from LY | Shipping Wt. (lbs.) | Production | Change from LY |
|---|---|---|---|---|---|---|
| Belvedere I 2-Door Coupe | RL21 | $2,277 | +2.29% | 3015 | 9,381 | -25.17% |
| Belvedere I 4-Door Sedan | RL41 | $2,315 | +2.21% | 3040 | 31,063 | -13.64% |
| Belvedere I 4-Door, 2-Seat Wagon | RL45 | $2,605 | +1.68% | 3470 | 8,200 | -1.66% |
| Belvedere II 2-Door Hardtop | RH23 | $2,430 | +2.19% | 3040 | 36,644 | +47.02% |
| Belvedere II 2-Door Convertible | RH27 | $2,644 | +1.81% | 3115 | 2,502 | +30.24% |
| Belvedere II 4-Door Sedan | RH41 | $2,405 | +2.25% | 3035 | 49,911 | +20.43% |
| Belvedere II 4-Dr., 2-Seat Wagon | RH45 | $2,695 | +1.74% | 3465 | 4,726 | -20.01% |
| Belvedere II 4-Dr., 3-Seat Wagon | RH46 | $2,804 | +2.07% | 3565 | 8,667 | +163.11% |
| Satellite 2-Door Hardtop | RP23 | $2,695 | +1.74% | 3255 | 35,399 | +51.66% |
| Satellite 2-Door Convertible | RP27 | $2,910 | +1.43% | 3320 | 2,759 | +48.33% |
| TOTALS | Avg. price | $2,578 | +1.94% | Production | 189,252 | +18.63% |

# Fury & VIP

*"The big new beauty in a great big hurry."*

**Nameplate year of origin:** 1956 (Fury); 1966 (VIP).
**Current bodystyle lifespan:** 1965 through 1966.
**Predecessor to this model:** Fury and Sport Fury (1962 to 1964).
**Replacement for this model:** Fury (1967 to 1968).
**Percentage of division's sales volume:** 47.49%.
**Corporate siblings:** Dodge Polara and Monaco.
**Primary competition:** AMC Ambassador, Chevrolet Biscayne/BelAir/Impala, and Ford Galaxie/LTD.
**Notable changes:** New grille and minor trim and detail changes. New VIP line.
**Major standard equipment:** Cloth and vinyl front bench seat, color-keyed floor covering, front and rear armrests, variable speed electric windshield wipers, bright trim around front and rear windows, and 7.35 × 14 BSW tires (8.55 × 14 BSW tire on wagon). Fury II adds: Full carpeting and full-length body side molding. Fury III adds: All-vinyl upholstery on hardtop and convertible, backup lights, distinctive exterior trim and 7.75 × 14 BSW tires on Convertible and 4-Door Hardtop. Sport Fury adds: Padded instrument panel, all-vinyl bucket seats, floor-mounted shifter and console with compartment, and deluxe steering wheel. VIP adds: Cloth and vinyl bench seats with fold-down center armrests, reading lamps, vinyl top and specific VIP trim.

## Measurements

|  | Cars | Wagons |
|---|---|---|
| Wheelbase | 119.0" | 121.0" |
| Length | 209.8" | 217.4" |
| Width | 78.7" | 78.7" |
| Height | 55.3" | 55.6" |
| Legroom — front | 42.0" | 42.0" |
| Legroom — rear | 38.7" | 38.7" |
| Headroom — front | 39.0" | 39.0" |
| Headroom — rear | 37.7" | 37.7" |
| Cargo capacity (cu. ft.) | 17.0 | NA |
| Fuel capacity (gals.) | 20.0 | 21.5 |

**1966**

## Models Available

|  | Style | Base MSRP | Change from LY | Shipping Wt. (lbs.) | Production | Change from LY |
|---|---|---|---|---|---|---|
| Fury I 2-Door Sedan | PL21 | $2,426 | +2.10% | 3425 | 12,538 | -27.50% |
| Fury I 4-Door Sedan | PL41 | $2,479 | +2.02% | 3485 | 39,698 | -18.27% |
| Fury I 4-Door, 2-Seat Wagon | PL45 | $2,836 | +2.16% | 3965 | 9,690 | -27.47% |
| Fury II 2-Door Sedan | PM21 | $2,526 | +1.94% | 3430 | 2,503 | -39.08% |
| Fury II 4-Door Sedan | PM41 | $2,579 | +1.86% | 3480 | 55,016 | +26.91% |
| Fury II 4-Door, 2-Seat Wagon | PM45 | $2,986 | +1.29% | 4145 | 10,718 | -16.61% |
| Fury II 4-Door, 3-Seat Wagon | PM46 | $3,087 | +1.18% | 4175 | 5,580 | -13.42% |
| Fury III 2-Door Hardtop | PH23 | $2,724 | +1.23% | 3480 | 41,869 | -3.20% |
| Fury III 2-Door Convertible | PH27 | $3,074 | +0.85% | 3720 | 4,326 | -21.69% |
| Fury III 4-Door Sedan | PH41 | $2,718 | +1.27% | 3505 | 46,505 | -8.32% |
| Fury III 4-Door Hardtop | PH43 | $2,893 | +1.05% | 3730 | 33,922 | +58.76% |
| Fury III 4-Door, 2-Seat Wagon | PH45 | $3,115 | +0.81% | 4155 | 9,239 | +3.45% |
| Fury III 4-Door, 3-Seat Wagon | PH46 | $3,216 | +0.72% | 4165 | 10,886 | +14.04% |
| Sport Fury 2-Door Hardtop | PP23 | $3,006 | +1.55% | 3730 | 32,523 | -15.19% |
| Sport Fury 2-Door Convertible | PP27 | $3,251 | +1.31% | 3755 | 3,418 | -45.50% |
| VIP 2-Door Hardtop | PS23 | $3,069 | NEW | 3700 | *W/ Fury III | NEW |
| VIP 4-Door Hardtop | PS43 | $3,133 | NEW | 3780 | 12,058 | NEW |
| TOTALS | *Avg. price* | $2,889 | +2.37% | *Production* | 330,489 | +0.16% |

# PONTIAC

*"Wide-Track Pontiac for '66!"*

Completely restyled intermediate models and an all-new 6-cylinder engine topped the news from Pontiac for 1966. An exotic (for the times) new Overhead Cam 6-cylinder engine was implemented as the base powertrain in the Tempest and LeMans lines. This type of engine, normally found in for more exotic European models, had not been offered in a modern American car until now. The overhead cam design offered more horsepower from a smaller displacement engine. In fact, the power was equal to many smaller V8 engines, but it was more economical to operate. This engine also offered a 4-barrel, high-output variant that would be quite popular with budget-minded performance types. Elsewhere while still using many of the 1964–65 years parts underneath, the new Tempest, LeMans and GTO models now had styling that more closely resembled their big brothers. Body sides were smoothed and rounded, and the style-setting vertical headlamps were set into fenders that were now straight up and down at the leading edge, instead of canted forward. This year also marked a significant landmark in the GTO history. For 1966, the GTO became its own model, no longer just an option package. The line consisted of the 2-Door Sport Coupe, 2-Door Hardtop and a 2-Door Convertible. The new marketing ploy worked, and sales of the GTO increased about 30 percent over the previous year. Unfortu-

nately, this would be the best year the GTO would see for sales. In the other intermediate lines, a new 4-Door Hardtop model was added for the Tempest Custom and LeMans lines. In the LeMans line the Hardtop had replaced the 4-Door Sedan model.

In the full-size lines, styling changes included revised front ends and taillamp styling. Also the 2 + 2 was marketed as a separate model, but only for this year. The only other significant model change was made to the newly named Star Chief Executive line. In an attempt to revive sales in this mid-range model line, a 2-Door Hardtop was brought back, and the Executive name was added. This was done as a cross-over measure to give some continuity to the line, but it would be simply the Executive by 1967. The Star Chief name had run its course and was the final link remaining in the Pontiac line to its pre–1957 days of Silver Streaks and chrome "star" body decorations. This was also the final year of production for the famous 389 CID V8. Putting this engine into the intermediate size platform and creating the GTO had set into motion the whole muscle car movement, and it would be a sad passing for many Pontiac enthusiasts. However, in its place was a similar engine with slightly more cubic inches, the new 400 CID V8, and it would prove to be just as legendary in the years to come.

2 + 2 2-Door Convertible

Bonneville 2-Door Hardtop and
4-Door Hardtop

Catalina 2-Door Convertible with
Ventura package

Grand Prix 2-Door Hardtop

Tempest GTO 2-Door Convertible

Tempest 2-Door Coupe

Tempest Custom 4-Door Safari Wagon

**1966**

**Model year production:** 837,091, up 4.46% over 1965.
**Domestic market share:** 9.35% (3rd place).
**Base price range:** $2,278 to $3,747.
**Industry average base price:** $3,070.
**Pontiac average base price:** $2,936.
**Introduction date:** October 1965.
**Assembly plants:** Baltimore, MD (B); Southgate, CA (C); Doraville, GA (D); Linden, NJ (E); Framingham, MA (G); Kansas City, MO (K); Pontiac, MI (P); Arlington, TX (R); Lordstown, OH (U); Fairfax, KS (X); Fremont, CA (Z); and Oshawa, Ontario, Canada (1).
**Data plate identification:** Thirteen digit code read as follows: 1st digit 2 = Pontiac; 2nd through 5th digits identify series/body style number (see style number in listings); 6 = 1966 year; 7th digit is assembly plant code; 100001 and up (600001 and up on 6-cylinders) for serial number. *Example:* 252396X100001 is a 1966 Pontiac Catalina 4-Door Hardtop, serial number 100001, built in Fairfax, KS.

## Powertrains

| Engine | Gross HP | Transmission Availability | Tempest LeMans/GTO | Catalina & Star Chief | 2 + 2 | Bonneville/ Grand Prix |
|---|---|---|---|---|---|---|
| 230 CID OHC, 1-bbl., 6-cyl. | 165 | 3-speed manual | S (ex. GTO) | - | - | - |
| | | 4-speed manual | $188 (ex. GTO) | - | - | - |
| | | 2-sp. Automatic | $188 (ex. GTO) | - | - | - |
| 230 CID OHC, 4-bbl., 6-cyl. | 215 | 3-speed manual | $127** (ex. GTO) | - | - | - |
| | | 4-speed manual | $315** (ex. GTO) | - | - | - |
| | | 2-sp. Automatic | $315** (ex. GTO) | - | - | - |
| 326 CID, 2-bbl., V8 | 250 | 3-speed manual | $95 (ex. GTO) | - | - | - |
| | | 4-speed manual | $283 (ex. GTO) | - | - | - |
| | | 2-sp. Automatic | $294 (ex. GTO) | - | - | - |
| 326 CID H.O., 4-bbl., V8 | 285 | 3-speed manual | $160 (ex. GTO) | - | - | - |
| | | 4-speed manual | $348 (ex. GTO) | - | - | - |
| | | | $359 (ex. GTO) | - | - | - |
| 389 CID, 2-bbl., V8 | 256 | 3-speed manual | - | S | - | - |
| | 290 | Turbo Hydra-matic | - | $231 | - | - |
| 389 CID, 4-bbl., V8 | 335 | 3-speed manual | S (GTO) | $44 | - | S |
| | | 4-speed manual | $184 (GTO) | $275 | - | $231 |
| | 325 | Turbo Hydra-matic | $226 (GTO) | $275 | - | $231 |
| 389 CID Tri-Power, 3 × 2-bbl., V8 | 338/360 | 3-speed HD man. | $116 (GTO) | $174 | - | $134 |
| | | 4-speed manual | $304 (GTO) | $405 | - | $365 |
| | | Turbo Hydra-matic | $315 (GTO) | $405 | - | $365 |

| Engine | Gross HP | Transmission Availability | Tempest LeMans/GTO | Catalina & Star Chief | 2 + 2 | Bonneville/ Grand Prix |
|---|---|---|---|---|---|---|
| 421 CID, 4-bbl., V8 | 338 | 3-speed HD man. | - | $174 | S | $108 |
| | | 4-speed manual | - | $405 | $231 | $339 |
| | | Turbo Hydra-matic | - | $405 | $231 | $339 |
| 421 CID Tri-Power, 3 × 2-bbl., V8 | 356 | 3-speed HD man. | - | $307 | $133 | $241 |
| | | 4-speed manual | - | $538 | $364 | $472 |
| | | Turbo Hydra-matic | - | $538 | $364 | $472 |

*Ratings vary with model and transmission attachment.   **Includes Sprint option package.

## Major Options

| | Tempest/LeMans | Catalina | 2 + 2 | Executive | Bonneville | Grand Prix |
|---|---|---|---|---|---|---|
| Air conditioning (V8 only) | $343 | $430 | $430 | $430 | $430 | $430 |
| Soft Ray tinted glass | $37 | $43 | $43 | $43 | $43 | $43 |
| Tilt steering wheel | $42 | $45 | $45 | $45 | $45 | $45 |
| Power steering — variable-ratio | $95 | $97 | $97 | $97 | $97 | $97 |
| Power brakes | $43 | $43 | $43 | $43 | $43 | $43 |
| Power driver's seat/Bench seat | - | $97 | $97 | $97 | $97 | $97 |
| Power windows | $102 | $106 | $106 | $106 | $106 | $106 |
| AM radio — manual | $61 | $89 | $89 | $89 | $89 | $89 |
| AM/FM radio — manual | $137 | $151 | $151 | $151 | $151 | $151 |
| Front seat console | $68 | $108 | $108 | - | $108 | S |
| Front bucket seats | $ | $105 | S | - | $105 | S |
| White stripe tires (base size) | $35 | $40 | $40 | $40 | $40 | $40 |
| Aluminum (8-lug) hubs and drums | - | $138 | $120 | $138 | $120 | $120 |
| Sprint package | $127 | - | - | - | - | - |
| Ventura Custom package | - | $118 | - | - | - | - |
| Brougham package | - | - | - | - | $161 | - |

Options common to most models. (- = Not Available; S = Standard equipment.) Items may be standard equipment, optional at different pricing, or unavailable on certain models. This chart is only a guide.

## Paint Colors

| | Code | | Code |
|---|---|---|---|
| Starlight Black | A | Burgundy Metallic | N |
| Blue Charcoal Metallic | B | Barrier Blue Metallic | P |
| Cameo Ivory | C | Montero Red | R |
| Fontaine Blue Metallic | D | Martinique Bronze Metallic | T |
| Nightwatch Blue Metallic | E | Mission Beige | V |
| Palmetto Green Metallic | H | Platinum Metallic | W |
| Reef Turquoise Metallic | K | Candlelight Cream | Y |
| Marina Turquoise Metallic | L | | |

# Tempest, LeMans & GTO

*"The most beautiful car you can buy for the money."*

**Nameplate year of origin:** 1961 (Tempest); 1961 (LeMans, as Tempest sub-series); 1964 (GTO).
**Current bodystyle lifespan:** 1966 through 1967.
**Predecessor to this model:** Tempest/LeMans (1964 to 1965).
**Replacement for this model:** LeMans (1968 to 1972).
**Percentage of division's sales volume:** 42.90%.

## Measurements

| | Cars | Wagons |
|---|---|---|
| Wheelbase | 115.0" | 115.0" |
| Length | 206.4" | 203.6" |
| Width | 74.4" | 74.4" |

**Corporate siblings:** Chevrolet Chevelle, Oldsmobile F-85/Cutlass, and Buick Special/Skylark.

**Primary competition:** Mercury Comet, Dodge Coronet, and AMC Rambler Classic.

**Notable changes:** Completely restyled, and new OHC-6 base engine.

**Major standard equipment:** Cloth and vinyl front bench seat, front door armrests, dual sun visors and 6.95 × 14 BSW tires. Custom adds: All-vinyl front bench seats, full carpeting, rear armrests and rocker panel moldings. LeMans adds: Cloth and vinyl or all-vinyl LeMans interior trim, padded assist bar on dash, carpet on lower door panels and front fender louvers. GTO adds: All-vinyl bucket seats, floor shifter, dual exhausts, custom pinstriping, 389 CID V8 with engine dress-up kit, heavy duty suspension and 7.75 × 14 redline tires.

|                              | Cars   | Wagons |
|------------------------------|--------|--------|
| Height                       | 54.0"  | 55.4"  |
| Legroom — front              | 41.2"  | 40.9"  |
| Legroom — rear               | 35.7"  | 35.7"  |
| Headroom — front             | 38.1"  | 37.8"  |
| Headroom — rear              | 37.3"  | 38.3"  |
| Cargo capacity (cu. ft.)     | 29.1   | 85.3   |
| Fuel capacity (gals.)        | 21.5   | 21.5   |

## Models Available

|                                  | Style | Base MSRP | Change from LY | Shipping Wt. (lbs.) | Production | Change from LY |
|----------------------------------|-------|-----------|----------------|---------------------|------------|----------------|
| Tempest 2-Door Sports Coupe      | 23307 | $2,278    | +0.80%         | 3040                | 22,266     | +22.35%        |
| Tempest 4-Door Sedan             | 23369 | $2,331    | +0.78%         | 3075                | 17,392     | +10.74%        |
| Tempest 4-Door, 2-Seat Wagon     | 23335 | $2,624    | +0.73%         | 3340                | 4,095      | -27.16%        |
| Tempest Custom 2-Dr. Sports Cpe. | 23507 | $2,362    | +0.68%         | 3060                | 17,182     | -6.45%         |
| Tempest Custom 2-Door Hardtop    | 23517 | $2,426    | +0.62%         | 3075                | 31,322     | +42.98%        |
| Tempest Custom 2-Door Conv.      | 23567 | $2,655    | +0.53%         | 3170                | 5,557      | -33.42%        |
| Tempest Custom 4-Door Sedan      | 23569 | $2,415    | +0.63%         | 3100                | 23,988     | -4.97%         |
| Tempest Custom 4-Door Hardtop    | 23539 | $2,547    | NEW            | 3195                | 10,996     | NEW            |
| Tempest Custom 4-Dr., 2-S. Wgn.  | 23535 | $2,709    | +0.67%         | 3355                | 7,614      | -29.45%        |
| LeMans 2-Door Sports Coupe       | 23707 | $2,505    | +0.56%         | 3090                | 16,654     | -38.77%        |
| LeMans 2-Door Hardtop            | 23717 | $2,568    | +0.47%         | 3125                | 78,109     | -32.82%        |
| LeMans 2-Door Convertible        | 23767 | $2,806    | +0.32%         | 3220                | 13,080     | -48.11%        |
| LeMans 4-Door Hardtop            | 23739 | $2,701    | NEW            | 3195                | 13,897     | NEW            |
| GTO 2-Door Sports Coupe          | 24207 | $2,783    | NEW            | 3445                | 10,363     | NEW            |
| GTO 2-Door Hardtop               | 24217 | $2,847    | NEW            | 3465                | 73,785     | NEW            |
| GTO 2-Door Convertible           | 24267 | $3,082    | NEW            | 3555                | 12,798     | NEW            |
| TOTALS                           | *Avg. price* | $2,602 | +3.87%      | *Production*        | 359,098    | +16.94%        |

# Catalina

*"It's the big-selling, swinging Wide-Track tiger that combines luxury, looks, and performance at so low a price you'll have to look twice to believe it."*

**Nameplate year of origin:** 1950 (HT models); 1959 (as series).

**Current bodystyle lifespan:** 1965 through 1966.

**Predecessor to this model:** Catalina (1961 to 1964).

**Replacement for this model:** Catalina (1967 to 1968).

**Corporate siblings:** Chevrolet Biscayne/BelAir/Impala/Caprice, Oldsmobile 88, Buick LeSabre/Wildcat.

**Primary competition:** Mercury Monterey and Dodge Polara.

**Percentage of division's sales volume:** 30.38%.

**Notable changes:** Revised styling and minor trim and detail changes.

**Major standard equipment:** Cloth and vinyl front bench seat (all-vinyl on convertible and wagons), full carpeting, electric windshield wipers, and 8.25 × 14 BSW tires (8.55 × 14 BSW tires on Safari). Ventura Custom option adds: All-vinyl upholstery with specific trim.

## Measurements

|                              | Cars   | Wagons |
|------------------------------|--------|--------|
| Wheelbase                    | 121.0" | 121.0" |
| Length                       | 214.8" | 218.1" |
| Width                        | 79.7"  | 79.7"  |
| Height                       | 55.3"  | 56.0"  |
| Legroom — front              | 42.6"  | 41.6"  |
| Legroom — rear               | 38.3"  | 38.2"  |
| Headroom — front             | 38.4"  | 38.7"  |
| Headroom — rear              | 37.7"  | 39.0"  |
| Cargo capacity (cu. ft.)     | 31.2   | 91.7   |
| Fuel capacity (gals.)        | 26.5   | 24.0   |

1966

## Models Available

| | Style | Base MSRP | Change from LY | Shipping Wt. (lbs.) | Production | Change from LY |
|---|---|---|---|---|---|---|
| Catalina 2-Door Sedan | 25211 | $2,762 | +1.02% | 3715 | 7,925 | -16.81% |
| Catalina 2-Door Hardtop | 25237 | $2,893 | +0.87% | 3835 | 79,013 | -14.12% |
| Catalina 2-Door Convertible | 25267 | $3,219 | +0.72% | 3860 | 14,837 | -19.13% |
| Catalina 4-Door Sedan | 25269 | $2,831 | +0.93% | 3785 | 80,483 | +2.07% |
| Catalina 4-Door Hardtop | 25239 | $2,968 | +0.78% | 3910 | 38,005 | +9.17% |
| Catalina Safari 4-Dr., 2-S. Wagon | 25235 | $3,217 | +0.47% | 4250 | 21,082 | -5.88% |
| Catalina Safari 4-Dr., 3-S. Wagon | 25245 | $3,338 | +0.88% | 4315 | 12,965 | -14.20% |
| TOTALS | Avg. price | $3,033 | +0.83% | Production | 254,310 | -6.18% |

# 2 + 2

*"The wonderful Wide-Track way to go from place to place."*

**Nameplate year of origin:** 1964 (as an option package on Catalina models).
**Current bodystyle lifespan:** 1965 through 1966.
**Predecessor to this model:** Catalina 2 + 2 option package (1961 to 1964).
**Replacement for this model:** Catalina 2 + 2 option package (1967 to 1968).
**Percentage of division's sales volume:** 0.76%.
**Corporate siblings:** Chevrolet Impala Super Sport.
**Primary competition:** Ford Galaxie 500/XL, Mercury S-55 and Plymouth Sport Fury.
**Notable changes:** All-new model for 1966, having previously been an option package.
**Major standard equipment:** All-vinyl bucket or bench seats, vertical front fender louvers, pinstriping, heavy duty handling package, 421 CID V8 engine w/dress-up kit, Hurst Shifter, and 8.25 × 14 BSW tires.

### Measurements

| | |
|---|---|
| Wheelbase | 121.0" |
| Length | 214.8" |
| Width | 79.7" |
| Height | 54.4" |
| Legroom — front | 42.3" |
| Legroom — rear | 35.2" |
| Headroom — front | 38.2" |
| Headroom — rear | 37.1" |
| Cargo capacity (cu. ft.) | 33.7 |
| Fuel capacity (gals.) | 26.5 |

## Models Available

| | Style | Base MSRP | Change from LY | Shipping Wt. (lbs.) | Production | Change from LY |
|---|---|---|---|---|---|---|
| 2 + 2 2-Door Hardtop | 25437 | $3,298 | NEW | 4005 | 6,383 | NEW |
| 2 + 2 2-Door Convertible | 25467 | $3,602 | NEW | 4030 | *W/ HT | NEW |
| TOTALS | Avg. price | $3,450 | NEW | Production | 6,383 | NEW |

# Star Chief Executive

*"Proof that big, handsome, luxurious cars can still be economical as well as elegant."*

**Nameplate year of origin:** 1954 (Star Chief); 1966 (Executive).
**Current bodystyle lifespan:** 1965 through 1966.
**Predecessor to this model:** Star Chief (1961 to 1964).
**Replacement for this model:** Executive (1967 to 1968).
**Percentage of division's sales volume:** 5.40%.
**Corporate siblings:** Chevrolet Biscayne/BelAir/Impala/Caprice, Oldsmobile 88, Buick LeSabre/Wildcat.
**Primary competition:** Mercury Montclair, and Dodge Monaco.
**Notable changes:** Revised styling and minor trim and detail changes.

### Measurements

| | |
|---|---|
| Wheelbase | 124.0" |
| Length | 221.8" |
| Width | 79.7" |
| Height | 55.3" |
| Legroom — front | 42.7" |
| Legroom — rear | 38.1" |
| Headroom — front | 38.3" |
| Headroom — rear | 37.6" |

**Major standard equipment:** Cloth and vinyl bench seat, full carpeting, perforated vinyl headliner, electric clock, full length lower body molding, full wheel covers and 8.25 × 14 BSW tires.

### Measurements (cont.)

| | |
|---|---|
| Cargo capacity (cu. ft.) | 34.4 |
| Fuel capacity (gals.) | 26.5 |

## Models Available

| | Style | Base MSRP | Change from LY | Shipping Wt. (lbs.) | Production | Change from LY |
|---|---|---|---|---|---|---|
| Star Chief Executive 2-Door HT | 25637 | $3,170 | NEW | 3920 | 10,140 | NEW |
| Star Chief Executive 4-Door Sdn. | 25669 | $3,114 | +0.26% | 3920 | 24,489 | +10.40% |
| Star Chief Executive 4-Door HT | 25639 | $3,244 | +0.19% | 3980 | 10,583 | +15.89% |
| TOTALS | Avg. price | $3,176 | +0.13% | Production | 45,212 | +44.38% |

# Bonneville

*"Bonneville has a great reputation for beauty, performance, prestige and quality, but you know in your heart it hasn't rested on its laurels for 1966."*

**Nameplate year of origin:** 1957.
**Current bodystyle lifespan:** 1965 through 1966.
**Predecessor to this model:** Bonneville (1961 to 1964).
**Replacement for this model:** Bonneville (1967 to 1968).
**Percentage of division's sales volume:** 16.17%.
**Corporate siblings:** Chevrolet Biscayne/BelAir/Impala/Caprice, Oldsmobile 88, Buick LeSabre/Wildcat.
**Primary competition:** Ford LTD, Mercury Park Lane, and Dodge Monaco.
**Notable changes:** Revised styling and minor trim and detail changes.
**Major standard equipment:** Vinyl or cloth and vinyl front bench seat (Leather and vinyl in convertible), full carpeting, walnut instrument panel trim, electric clock, courtesy lights, padded assist grip, dual-speed electric windshield wipers, deluxe wheel covers and 8.25 × 14 BSW tires. Safari adds: 8.55 × 14 BSW tires. Brougham option adds: Special upholstery trim with fold down center armrests, and exterior badges.

### Measurements

| | Cars | Wagons |
|---|---|---|
| Wheelbase | 124.0" | 121.0" |
| Length | 221.8" | 218.1" |
| Width | 79.7" | 79.7" |
| Height | 54.3" | 56.0" |
| Legroom — front | 42.3" | 41.3" |
| Legroom — rear | 37.5" | 38.2" |
| Headroom — front | 37.8" | 38.7" |
| Headroom — rear | 37.2" | 39.0" |
| Cargo capacity (cu. ft.) | 34.4 | 90.8 |
| Fuel capacity (gals.) | 26.5 | 24.0 |

1966

## Models Available

| | Style | Base MSRP | Change from LY | Shipping Wt. (lbs.) | Production | Change from LY |
|---|---|---|---|---|---|---|
| Bonneville 2-Door Hardtop | 26237 | $3,354 | -0.09% | 4020 | 42,004 | -4.60% |
| Bonneville 2-Door Convertible | 26267 | $3,586 | -0.22% | 4015 | 16,229 | -22.90% |
| Bonneville 4-Door Hardtop | 26239 | $3,428 | -0.15% | 4070 | 68,646 | +9.87% |
| Bonneville Safari 4-Dr., 3-S. Wgn. | 26245 | $3,747 | +3.17% | 4390 | 8,452 | +30.84% |
| TOTALS | Avg. price | $3,529 | +0.71% | Production | 135,331 | +0.98% |

# Grand Prix

*"Grand Prix proved itself a classic the day it was introduced, four years ago.
And since then, many cars have tried to follow in its Wide-Track. Let them try."*

**Nameplate year of origin:** 1962.
**Current bodystyle lifespan:** 1965 through 1966.
**Predecessor to this model:** Grand Prix (1962 to 1964).
**Replacement for this model:** Grand Prix (1967 to 1968).
**Percentage of division's sales volume:** 4.39%.
**Corporate siblings:** Buick Wildcat and Oldsmobile Starfire.
**Primary competition:** Chrysler 300, Dodge Monaco 500, and Mercury S-55.
**Notable changes:** Revised styling and minor trim and detail changes.
**Major standard equipment:** All-vinyl or cloth and vinyl bucket seat or bench seat, full carpeting, padded instrument panel, padded assist bar, additional acoustical insulation, deluxe wheel covers and 8.25 × 14 BSW tires.

## Measurements

| | |
|---|---|
| Wheelbase | 121.0" |
| Length | 214.8" |
| Width | 79.7" |
| Height | 53.9" |
| Legroom — front | 42.3" |
| Legroom — rear | 35.2" |
| Headroom — front | 37.7" |
| Headroom — rear | 37.1" |
| Cargo capacity (cu. ft.) | 33.7 |
| Fuel capacity (gals.) | 26.5 |

## Models Available

| | Style | Base MSRP | Change from LY | Shipping Wt. (lbs.) | Production | Change from LY |
|---|---|---|---|---|---|---|
| Grand Prix 2-Door Hardtop | 26657 | $3,492 | -0.17% | 4015 | 36,757 | -36.50% |
| TOTALS | | *Avg. price* $3,492 | -0.17% | *Production* | 36,757 | -36.50% |

# STUDEBAKER

*"The smart new look."*

A new face greeted Studebaker customers this season in the showroom. Little did they know that it would be their last chance to own one of the oldest names in the automotive business. The model line was pared down again this season, with only five models left. The Daytona Wagonaire was the casualty this season. The front end received a facelift featuring single headlamps and a four port grille opening that looked very modern compared to the rest of the car. Rear styling continued as in prior years with few alterations. A new engine option was added with the 230 CID 6-cylinder Chevrolet powerplant available for all models. It was a sad ending for what had been a very successful motor car company. While the company's automotive business would disappear, the Studebaker name would continue in other ventures. The legacy would also continue in the Avanti. Already returned to production since the 1965 model year by enterprising Studebaker dealers, it would continue into the 1990s through various styling alterations and under several different owners. For the 2001 model year, the name returned but with nothing in common with the original car except its name. The 2001 Avanti was based upon a Pontiac Firebird with styling reminiscent of the original Raymond Loewy design.

Cruiser 4-Door Sedan

Daytona 2-Door Sport Sedan

Wagonaire 4-Door Wagon

**Model year production:** 8,947, down 53.96% from 1965.
**Domestic market share:** 0.01% (14th place).
**Base price range:** $2,215 to $2,665.
**Industry average base price:** $3,070.
**Studebaker average base price:** $2,438.
**Introduction date:** September 1965.
**Assembly plants:** Hamilton, Ontario, Canada (C).

**Data plate identification (VIN):** Seven digit code read as follows: 1st digit C for Canadian plant; 1 for 6-cylinder or 5 for V8 engine; followed by serial number 30001 and up. Body style numbers are found on a separate plate on the vehicle. *Example:* C130001 is a 1966 Studebaker Six built in Hamilton, Canada, serial number 30001.

## Powertrains

| Engine | Gross HP | Transmission Availability | All models |
|---|---|---|---|
| 194 CID, 1-bbl., OHV 6-cyl. | 120 | 3-speed manual | S |
| | | 3-speed w/Overdrive | $113 |
| | | Flightomatic Automatic | $192 |
| 230 CID, 1-bbl., OHV 6-cyl. | 120 | 3-speed manual | $45 |
| | | 3-speed w/Overdrive | $158 |
| | | Flightomatic Automatic | $237 |
| 283 CID, 2-bbl., OHV V8 | 195 | 3-speed manual | $176 |
| | | 3-speed w/Overdrive | $289 |
| | | Flightomatic Automatic | $401 |

## Major Options

| | All models |
|---|---|
| Heater and defroster | $80 |
| Air conditioning | $278–$325 |
| Tinted glass — full | $32 |
| Power steering | $77 |
| Power brakes | $45 |
| Electric clock | $15 |
| Windshield washers | $12 |
| AM pushbutton radio | $57 |
| White sidewall tires — std. size | $28–$48 |
| Wheel covers | $16 |

Options common to most models. Items may be standard equipment, optional at different pricing, or unavailable on certain models. This chart is only a guide.

## Paint Colors

| | Code |
|---|---|
| Niagra Blue Mist Metallic | 6481 |
| Timberline Turquoise Met. | 6482 |
| Yellowknife Gold Metallic | 6483 |
| Mount Royal Red Metallic | 6484 |
| Arctic White | 6485 |
| Midnight Black | 6486 |
| Richelieu Blue Metallic | 6487 |
| Algonquin Green Metallic | 6488 |

1966

# Commander

*"Spirited and lively, yet keeps a sharp eye on your fuel and maintenance budget."*

**Nameplate year of origin:** 1927.
**Current bodystyle lifespan:** 1962 through 1966.
**Predecessor to this model:** Standard line (1963) and Lark (1962 to 1963).
**Replacement for this model:** None.
**Corporate siblings:** Wagonaire, Cruiser and Daytona.
**Percentage of division's sales volume:** Unavailable.
**Primary competition:** AMC Rambler American, Chevrolet Chevy II, Ford Falcon, and Plymouth Valiant.
**Notable changes:** New grille and minor trim and detail changes.
**Major standard equipment:** All-vinyl or cloth and vinyl front bench seats, armrests, 2-speed electric windshield wipers with washers, rubber floor mats, and 7.35 × 15 BSW tires.

## Measurements

|  | 2-Door | 4-Door |
|---|---|---|
| Wheelbase | 109.0" | 113.0" |
| Length | 190.0" | 194.0" |
| Width | 71.5" | 71.5" |
| Height | 54.8" | 54.8" |
| Legroom — front | 39.9" | 39.9" |
| Legroom — rear | 31.8" | 35.7" |
| Headroom — front | 39.5" | 39.0" |
| Headroom — rear | 38.0" | 38.0" |
| Luggage cap. (cu. ft.) | 13.6 | 13.6 |
| Fuel capacity (gals.) | 18.0 | 18.0 |

## Models Available

|  | Style | Base MSRP | Change from LY | Shipping Wt. (lbs.) | Production | Change from LY |
|---|---|---|---|---|---|---|
| Commander 2-Door Sedan | SF4 | $2,215 | 4.24% | 2780 | 2,321* | -68.52% |
| Commander 4-Door Sedan | SY4 | $2,319 | 3.99% | 2880 | 5,686* | -44.47% |
| TOTALS |  | Avg. price $2,267 | +0.5% |  | Production 8,007* | -56.49% |

*Production totals include Cruiser and Daytona models.*

# Cruiser & Daytona

*"An exciting debonair new car-about-town that exhibits true sports car flair—the Daytona. And Studebaker's great performance, enduring quality, luxurious appointments, and classic styling reach highest attainment in the superb new Cruiser '66."*

**Nameplate year of origin:** 1961 (Cruiser); (1962) Daytona.
**Current bodystyle lifespan:** 1962 through 1966.
**Predecessor to this model:** Cruiser (1961).
**Replacement for this model:** None.
**Corporate siblings:** Commander and Wagonaire.
**Percentage of division's sales volume:** Unavailable.
**Primary competition:** AMC Rambler American, Chevrolet Chevy II, Ford Falcon, and Plymouth Valiant.
**Notable changes:** New grille and minor trim and detail changes.
**Major standard equipment:** Cloth and vinyl or all-vinyl front bench seats, armrests, full carpeting, wood-grain interior trim, 2-speed electric windshield wipers with washers, rubber floor mats, and 7.35 × 15 BSW tires. Daytona adds: All-vinyl upholstery and transistorized ignition.

## Measurements

|  | Daytona | Cruiser |
|---|---|---|
| Wheelbase | 109.0" | 113.0" |
| Length | 190.0" | 194.0" |
| Width | 71.5" | 71.5" |
| Height | 54.8" | 54.8" |
| Legroom — front | 39.9" | 39.9" |
| Legroom — rear | 31.8" | 35.7" |
| Headroom — front | 39.5" | 39.0" |
| Headroom — rear | 38.0" | 38.0" |
| Luggage cap. (cu. ft.) | 13.6 | 13.6 |
| Fuel capacity (gals.) | 18.0 | 18.0 |

## Models Available

| | Style | Base MSRP | Change from LY | Shipping Wt. (lbs.) | Production | Change from LY |
|---|---|---|---|---|---|---|
| Daytona 2-Door Sport Sedan | SF8 | $2,444 | -4.72% | 2800 | * | * |
| Cruiser 4-Door Sedan | SY9 | $2,545 | +3.04% | 2900 | * | * |
| TOTALS | | Avg. price $2,495 | -0.84% | | Production * | * |

*Production totals included with Commander models.*

# Wagonaire

*"Here are the real welcome wagons of the year!"*

**Nameplate year of origin:** 1966; 1965 (as body style designation)
**Current bodystyle lifespan:** 1962 through 1966.
**Predecessor to this model:** Lark wagons (1962 to 1965).
**Replacement for this model:** None.
**Corporate siblings:** Commander, Cruiser and Daytona.
**Percentage of division's sales volume:** 10.51%.
**Primary competition:** AMC Rambler American, Chevrolet Chevy II, Ford Falcon, and Plymouth Valiant.
**Notable changes:** New grille, and minor trim and detail changes.
**Major standard equipment:** All-vinyl or cloth and vinyl front bench seats, armrests, 2-speed electric windshield wipers with washers, rubber floor mats, and 7.35 × 15 BSW tires.

## Measurements

| | |
|---|---|
| Wheelbase | 113.0" |
| Length | 193.0" |
| Width | 71.5" |
| Height | 58.8" |
| Legroom — front | 39.9" |
| Legroom — rear | 36.1" |
| Headroom — front | 40.0" |
| Headroom — rear | 36.9" |
| Luggage cap. (cu. ft.) | 93.0 |
| Fuel capacity (gals.) | 18.0 |

## Models Available

| | Style | Base MSRP | Change from LY | Shipping Wt. (lbs.) | Production | Change from LY |
|---|---|---|---|---|---|---|
| Wagonaire 4-Door, 2-Seat Wagon | SP | $2,665 | -7.79% | 3077 | 940 | -48.46% |
| TOTALS | | Avg. price $2,665 | -7.79% | | Production 940 | -48.46% |

# 1967

Nineteen sixty-seven would bring a second wave of "pony cars" (most notably Camaro and Firebird) to compete with the highly successful Ford Mustang. There would also be major styling changes to most standard-size (or full-size) automobiles and completely new Ford and Chevrolet truck offerings. Meanwhile, Chrysler introduced new compact car lines, and Mercury also had a new pony car competitor ready for market.

At American Motors there were some new faces, a new name, and a familiar old friend. The latter was the Rambler American, which continued basically unchanged. The former 440 convertible moved upmarket into the Rogue series, but with this move sales slipped further to 921, and this would prove to be the last year for an American convertible. The Rambler Classic was gone, its place taken by the all-new Rebel. Some of the basic design features of this car would be used through 1978 under various nameplates. The new Rebel was available in 550, 770 and SST models. The top of the line SST was offered in 2-Door Hardtop and Convertible models, while the 550 and 770 lines offered the traditional assortment of Hardtops, Sedans and Wagons. AMC introduced three limited-production station wagons in February 1967: the Briarcliff (400 sold in the eastern U.S.), the Mariner (600 sold in coastal areas), and the Westerner (500 sold in the midwest). Powering the mid-size Rebel was a standard 145-horsepower, 232 CID 6-cylinder. Available powerplants included a 155-hp, 232 CID 6-cylinder, a 200-hp or a 225-hp, 290 CID V8, or the newly available 343 CID V8 in 235-hp and 280-hp versions.

The sporty, fastback Marlin was now riding on a longer wheelbase, thanks to a move up to the Ambassador chassis. The Marlin shared the new styling of the Ambassador's front end, which included stacked headlamps, as well as offering interior appointments that were similar to those found in the Ambassador. New powertrain offerings included the 290 CID V8 and the 343 CID V8. Unfortu-

nately, this would be the last year for the Marlin. A full-size Marlin seemed to be a move in the wrong direction for AMC, as the sales of standard-sized cars this year would drop below 50 percent of the total automotive market for the first time ever. The Ambassador, however, sold quite well, thanks in part to its all-new styling. Much of its basic design and mechanical componentry was shared with the mid-size Rebel, although the Ambassador (along with the Marlin) was 4 inches longer at the front and was therefore marketed as a full-size car to compete with the Impala, Galaxie and Fury. The only change to the Ambassador model lineup was the convertible moving from the 990 line to the DPL line. The Ambassador offered the same new engine options as the Marlin.

"When better automobiles are built, Buick will build them," claimed a famous slogan of the 64-year-old company, and this year would be no exception. There were completely restyled full-size Buicks and detail changes for the Riviera and Special/Skylark series. The 1967 Riviera was carried over essentially unchanged from its 1966 counterpart except for new grille and taillight styling. The Special and Skylark lines also sported new grilles as well as other minor trim changes. The Special Convertible and the Special Deluxe 2-Door Coupe were dropped from the lineup, and a Skylark 4-Door Sedan was added to it. The Gran Sport series was expanded this year offering a GS 340 2-Door Hardtop (basically a Skylark HT with a standard 340 CID V8 and GS trim), and the GS 400 in 2-Door Hardtop, 2-Door Coupe, and Convertible models (offering a standard 400 CID V8). This would be the last year for Buick's 225 CID V6 offered in many Special and Skylark models. The Sport Wagon featured the same styling changes as the Special/Skylark line, and its name was now spelled as one word, formerly being the Sport Wagon. Buick's full-size LeSabre, Wildcat and Electra 225 models were completely restyled and sported a full-length bodyside line reminiscent of the sweep spear seen on earlier

## 1967 Model Year Production by Make

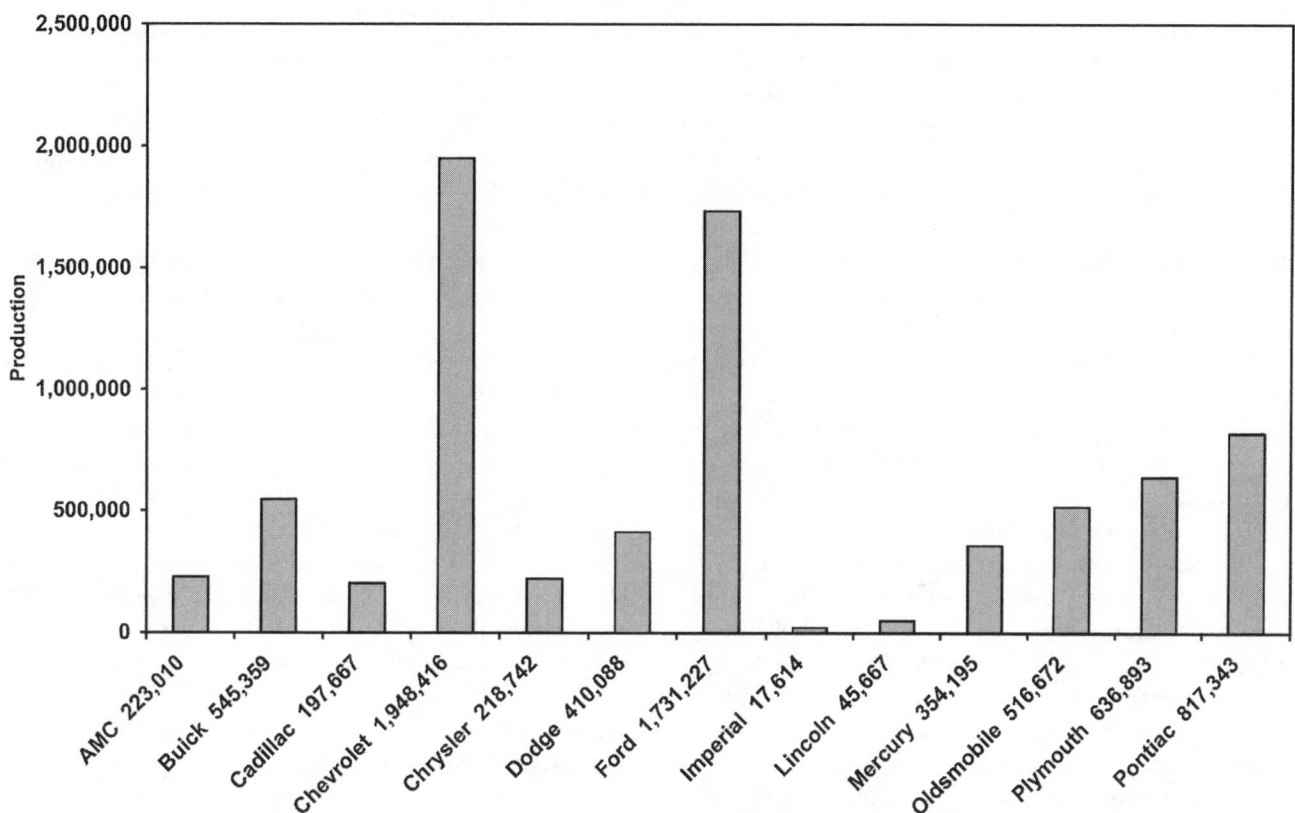

AMC 223,010 · Buick 545,359 · Cadillac 197,667 · Chevrolet 1,948,416 · Chrysler 218,742 · Dodge 410,088 · Ford 1,731,227 · Imperial 17,614 · Lincoln 45,667 · Mercury 354,195 · Oldsmobile 516,672 · Plymouth 636,893 · Pontiac 817,343

Buicks. Model offerings and powertrain options remained the same as in 1966.

Still the "Standard of the World," Cadillac unveiled its new Eldorado, as well as new styling for all other models. The new, front-wheel drive Eldorado 2-Door Hardtop shared only its nameplate with any previous Cadillac. This new luxury coupe, based on the Oldsmobile Toronado platform, featured ventless front side windows, concealed headlamps, variable ratio power steering, automatic level control, and a front disc brake option. The styling was very crisp and angular, and devoid of chrome. Power was provided by Cadillac's 429 CID V8, common to all Cadillac models. These other models — Calais, de Ville, Fleetwood Sixty-Special and Fleetwood 75 — offered all-new styling with forward-thrusting fenders, and side lines that accentuated the length of the car. More formal roof lines added that extra touch of luxury that was expected by Cadillac customers.

Chevrolet for 1967 was telling customers that they could "Get that sure feeling from a Chevrolet." And what better way to get that feeling than in the all-new Camaro, Chevrolet's "pony car," designed to compete effectively with the Ford Mustang. The sharply styled Camaro, available in 2-Door Coupe or Convertible form, offered numerous trim and drivetrain options to allow the customer to tailor the car to his taste. The base engine offering was a 230 CID,

140-hp 6-cylinder and the base V8 was the 327 CID developing 210 hp. Both powerplants were teamed with a 3-speed manual transmission. Other engines offered included a 250 CID 6-cylinder and various V8's displacing 327 CID (275 hp), 350 CID (295 hp), and 396 CID (in 325- or 375-hp variations). Gearboxes available included a heavy-duty 3-speed manual transmission (for 350 V8 and 396 V8 only), a 4-speed manual, Powerglide automatic (with the 230, 250, 327 or 350), and GM's Turbo-Hydramatic (offered only with the 325-hp, 396 CID V8). The exterior dimensions of the Camaro nearly matched those of the Mustang with a wheelbase of 108.1 inches (the Mustang's was 108.0) and an overall length of 184.6 inches (Mustang: 183.6). Trim packages included the Z22 Rally Sport Package, featuring a special grille with concealed headlamps, bright trim moldings, wide lower body moldings, and various RS emblems. The L48 SS350 Package, available in conjunction with the Z22 package, included a special hood, front hood stripes and "SS" emblems. The Z28 Package, ordered on 602 coupes, included a 290-hp, 302 CID V8 engine, 4-speed manual transmission, and front disc brakes, as well as other performance oriented features. One final choice was a Pace Car replica package, as the Camaro was chosen to be the official pace car for the 1967 Indianapolis 500 race; approximately 100 replica cars were sold.

Chevrolet's Chevy II and Corvair lines continued relatively unchanged. One noteworthy model missing, however, was the Corvair Corsa, which presumably was gone to make way for the more conventional new Camaro as the bargain-priced sports car. The mid-size Chevelle lineup featured revised frontal styling and one new model, a Concours Estate Wagon that sported wood-grain exterior trim and a black-accented grille. Full-size Chevys were completely restyled, with a continuation of the fastback styling theme found on 2-Door Hardtop models. The new look was not quite as sharp as the '65–'66 models, but was for the most part still a good-looking car, leaning more and more toward a luxury look to capitalize on the popularity of the Impala and Caprice lines. Model offerings continued as in 1966. The new standard engine was a 250 CID 6-cylinder. Finally, the 1967 Corvette was the last of the first generation Sting Rays and was identifiable by five functional louvers on each front fender. Most other features continued as in previous years.

Hoping to continue a strong sales rebound, Chrysler wanted their customers to "Take Charge … Move Up to Chrysler." Unfortunately, not as many people would, as sales slipped slightly. All 1967 Chryslers received a restyling, with new front and rear treatments as well as new rooflines. The six-window sedan was gone from the model lineup, but all other models continued. A new Newport Custom line was introduced in 2 and 4-Door Hardtop models, plus a 4-Door Sedan, all with trim slightly upgraded from the base Newport. This new model sold quite well in its first year, albeit mostly at the expense of the 300 series which was pushed upmarket in trim level and price.

"The Dodge Rebellion Wants You" to know that for 1967 it was offering newly styled Dart, Polara and Monaco lines, as well as revised Coronet and Charger models. The "compact" Dart was completely redesigned and restyled, looking much larger than previous years though it was actually ½ inch shorter than the 1966. These cars were quite nice looking and would continue through 1976 with relatively few changes. With the restyle the station wagon models were gone from the lineup. The lone remaining convertible model was offered in the GT series. A restyling in the Polara and Monaco lines gave these cars a longer, lower appearance. The Polara was joined by a sub-series Polara 500, consisting of 2-Door Hardtop and Convertible models. The mid-size Coronet entered the new model year with new grilles and revised rear-end treatments. The base Coro-

net series was gone, but a high-performance Coronet R/T, available in 2-Door Hardtop and Convertible body styles, joined the lineup. The R/T featured the 440 CID, 375-hp, 4-bbl. Magnum V8 engine, Torqueflite automatic transmission, dual exhaust, red-line tires and a special hood with intake scoops. The 361 CID V8 engine was not offered this year for Coronet models; nor was it available in the sporty Charger models. The Charger line received only minor trim changes for 1967.

"You're ahead in a Ford" was a slogan that was quite appropriate this year. Not only did Ford offer newly styled full-size models, but also a Thunderbird with four doors and loads of luxury-car features, plus mildly restyled Mustangs that were sportier than ever. The 1967 edition of the successful Mustang featured more pronounced side-scoop styling and revised grille and taillight designs, while still maintaining the original car's look. The 2 + 2 Fastback looked particularly nice with the new styling cues, and as a result, sales of this model increased, while sales of the Hardtop and Convertible declined. To make these cars more powerful, a 320-hp, 390 CID V8 engine was offered as optional equipment.

Checker made no changes to its Marathon line of sturdy sedan and wagon models. They still carried a 230 CID 6-cylinder as standard or an optional 283 CID V8 engine from Chevrolet. The Avanti II also continued with relatively few changes. Light-duty truck lines from General Motors and Ford were all-new for 1967. Ford offered a modern, angular styling, while GM went for a slightly more rounded look to its new Chevy and GMC trucks. Both were pleasing to look at, rode better than their predecessors, and offered more luxury type "car" accessories than ever before. Ford's Ranchero made a move to the mid-size Fairlane styling this season. It was an easy move to make as the Ranchero was based on station wagon components, and the wagons were shared between the Falcon and Fairlane lines. Chevrolet's Chevelle-based El Camino received updates similar to those on the Chevelle line. Dodge, International and Jeep made minor changes to their truck lines. One other new truck model came from Jeep. This was the modern Jeepster. Riding on a 101-inch wheelbase and powered by a 4-cylinder engine, the Jeepster Convertible and two Commando models were formidable competition for Ford's popular Bronco introduced in 1966.

# AMERICAN MOTORS

*"Quality built in—so the value stays in."*

For 1967, American Motors offered up all-new versions of its popular family cars, the Ambassador and newly named Rebel, as well as an entirely new line of V8 powerplants. The Rambler Rebel nameplate replaced the Rambler Classic line. The Rebel had been the top model in that line. These cars received a longer wheelbase for better ride, more angular sheetmetal, and racier-looking rooflines replacing the previous, boxy-looking greenhouses. Oddly, considering the declining sales of convertibles, a convertible version of the Rebel was designed, but built for only two years. Since the new Rebel shared major body structure with the Ambassador, there was also an Ambassador DPL convertible, but only for the 1967 model year. In the two-year, 1967-68 period, only 4,144 convertibles were built in both series. In another rather odd move, the Marlin fastback, entering what proved its last year, was moved from the mid-size line to the full-size Ambassador body. It was a rather easy move to make, since the Rebel and Ambassador shared major body components, but it was a puzzling marketing shift. Finally, two more unique models, the Rebel 550 2-Door Sports Sedan and Ambassador 880 2-Door Sports Sedan, were offered only for the 1967 model year. It seems that a lot of expense was made for models with relatively little payback.

Newly designed "Typhoon" V8 engines were introduced for 1967. These overhead valve V8 engines were dependable and economical, and were among the most modern designs on the market. The 290 CID V8 offered a horsepower range of 200 to 225, and the 343 CID V8 created 235 to 280 horsepower. These new engines could be mated to a full range of transmissions including 3- and 4-speed manuals, overdrive, Flash-O-Matic and Shift-Command automatics.

The Rambler American returned with minimal changes. The sporty convertible model was moved from the mid-range 440 to the Rogue line. Sales for the compact American were down drastically this year, partially due to the sales effects from the popular pony cars and intermediates, and partly from the popularity of the totally redesigned compact Mopar twins, the Dodge Dart and Plymouth Valiant.

**1967**

Ambassador 990 4-Door Sedan

Ambassador DPL 2-Door Convertible

Marlin 2-Door Hardtop

Rebel Cross Country 4-Door Wagon

Rebel SST 2-Door Hardtop

Rambler American Rogue 2-Door Convertible

**Model year production:** 223,010, down 16.7% from 1966.
**Domestic market share:** 2.91% (9th place).
**Base price range:** $1,839 to $3,143.
**Industry average base price:** $3,159.
**AMC average base price:** $2,485.
**Introduction date:** October 6, 1966.
**Assembly plants:** Kenosha, Wisconsin (K), and Brampton, Ontario, Canada (B).
**Data plate identification:** Thirteen digit code read as follows:

A for American Motors; 7 = 1967; assembly plant code (see above); transmission code (see chart); series/body style number (fourth and fifth digits from model charts); series engine code (see chart); 100001 and up for serial number (700001 and up for cars built in Ontario). *Example:* A7KA97U100001 is a 1967, built in Kenosha, column-shift Shift-Command Automatic, Marlin 2-Door, 304 CID V8, serial number 100001.

## Powertrains

| Engine | Gross HP | Engine Code | Transmission Availability** | Trans. Code* | Rambler American | Rambler Rebel | Marlin & Ambassador |
|---|---|---|---|---|---|---|---|
| 199 CID, 1-bbl., 6-cyl. | 128 | A | 3-speed manual | S | S | - | - |
| | | | 3-speed w/Overdrive | O | $109 | - | - |
| | | | Shift-Command Automatic (col./flr.) | A/C | $174 | - | - |
| 232 CID, 1-bbl., 6-cyl. | 145 | E/F/S/P | 3-speed manual | S | $39 | S | S*** |
| | | | 3-speed w/Overdrive | O | $148 | $115 | $115*** |
| | | | Shift-Command Automatic (col./flr.) | A/C | $213 | $186 | $217*** |
| 232 CID, 2-bbl., 6-cyl. | 155 | B/G/T/M | 3-speed manual | S | $51 | $12 | $12*** |
| | | | 3-speed w/Overdrive | O | $160 | $127 | $127*** |
| | | | Shift-Command Automatic (col./flr.) | A/C | $225 | $198 | $229*** |
| 290 CID, 2-bbl., V8 | 200 | C/H/U/N | 3-speed manual | S | $119 | $106 | S (Conv.)/$104*** |
| | | | 4-speed manual | M/F | $303 | $290 | $184 (Conv.)/$288*** |
| | | | Shift-Command Automatic (col./flr.) | A/C | $303 | $292 | $217 (Conv.)/$321*** |
| 290 CID, 4-bbl., V8 | 225 | D | 3-speed manual | S | $151 | - | - |
| | | | 4-speed manual | M/F | $335 | - | - |
| | | | Shift-Command Automatic (col./flr.) | A/C | $335 | - | - |
| 343 CID, 2-bbl., V8 | 235 | J/V/R | 3-speed manual | S | - | $164 | $58 (Conv.)/$162*** |
| | | | 4-speed manual | M/F | - | $348 | $242 (Conv.)/$346*** |
| | | | Shift-Command Automatic (col./flr.) | A/C | - | $351 | $275 (Conv.)/$379*** |
| 343 CID, 4-bbl., V8 | 280 | X/K/W/Q | 3-speed manual | S | - | $197 | $91 (Conv.)/$195*** |
| | | | 4-speed manual | M/F | - | $381 | $275 (Conv.)/$379*** |
| | | | Shift-Command Automatic— col./flr. | A/C | - | $383 | $308 (Conv.)/$412*** |

*M code is floor-mounted shifter; F code is for console-mounted shifter. **Add $19 for floor-shift Automatic in American Rogue and Rebel 770/SST models. Not available in other American models, Rebel 550, or wagons. ***Except Ambassador DPL Convertible.

## Major Options

| | Rambler American | Rebel | Marlin | Ambassador |
|---|---|---|---|---|
| Air conditioning | $311 | $350 | $350 | $350 |
| Adjust-O-Tilt steering wheel | - | $45 | $42 | $45 |
| Speed control | - | $60 | $44 | $60 |
| Soft Ray tinted glass | $34 | $37 | $34 | $42 |
| Electric windshield wipers w/washer | $18 | $18 | $18 | $18 |
| Power steering — variable-ratio | $84 | $84 | $84 | $95 |
| Power brakes — Disc (except American) | $42 | $43 | $91 | $43 |
| AM radio — pushbutton | $57 | $57 | $57 | $57 |
| 8-Track stereo system | - | $134 | $134 | $134 |

| | Rambler American | Rebel | Marlin | Ambassador |
|---|---|---|---|---|
| Reclining seats — Bench seat | $25 | $45 | $45 | $45 |
| Reclining seats — Bucket seat | $98 | $78 | $142 | $142 |
| Vinyl top (N/A on all body styles) | $75 | $75 | - | $75 |
| Full wheel covers (Std. top lines) | $21 | $21 | S | $21 |
| Turbo Cast wheel covers | $61 | $61 | $40 | $40–61 |
| Twin Grip differential | $37 | $37 | $37 | $37 |
| Station Wagon third seat | - | $112 | - | $112 |

Options common to most models. (- = Not Available; S = Standard equipment.) Items may be standard equipment, optional at different pricing, or unavailable on certain models. This chart is only a guide.

## Paint Colors

| | Code | | Code |
|---|---|---|---|
| Classic Black | P1A | Sungold Amber Metallic | P37A |
| Marina Aqua Metallic | P8A | Stallion Brown Metallic | P38A |
| Granada Green Met. | P18A | Matador Red | P39A |
| Apollo Yellow | P25A | Flamingo Burgundy Met. | P40A |
| Stratos Blue Met. | P31A | Rajah Burgundy Metallic | P41A |
| Barbados Blue Met. | P32A | Satin Chrome (2-tone) | P42A |
| Royal Blue Met. | P33A | Hialeah Yellow | P58A |
| Alameda Aqua | P34A | Polo Green Metallic | P59A |
| Yuma Tan Metallic | P36A | Frost White | P72A |

# Rambler

*"Now—Typhoon V-8 thunder comes to America's low-price economy champ."*

**1967**

**Nameplate year of origin:** 1950 (Nash).
**Current bodystyle lifespan:** 1964 through 1969.
**Predecessor to this model:** Rambler American (1958 to 1963).
**Replacement for this model:** Hornet (1970 to 1977).
**Percentage of division's sales volume:** 28.11%.
**Corporate siblings:** None.
**Primary competition:** Chevrolet Chevy II, Dodge Dart, Ford Falcon, and Plymouth Valiant.
**Notable changes:** Trim and detail changes.
**Major standard equipment:** Cloth and vinyl front bench seat, front arm rests and ash trays, variable speed windshield wipers, rubber floor mats, cargo mat, and 6.45 × 14 BSW tires (6.95 × 14 BSW tires on wagons). 440 adds: Full carpeting, rear armrests, roof-top travel rack on wagon, vinyl-pleated upholstery and power top on convertible. Rogue adds: All-vinyl bucket seats, wheel covers, special trim and ID.

## Measurements

| | Cars | Wagons |
|---|---|---|
| Wheelbase | 106.0" | 106.0" |
| Length | 181.0" | 181.0" |
| Width | 70.8" | 70.8" |
| Height | 54.5" | 54.5" |
| Legroom — front | 41.0" | 41.0" |
| Legroom — rear | 36.5" | 36.5" |
| Headroom — front | 39.3" | 39.3" |
| Headroom — rear | 37.0" | 37.0" |
| Luggage cap. (cu. ft.) | 12.0 | 75.4 |
| Fuel capacity (gals.) | 16 | 16 |

## Models Available

| | Style Number | Base MSRP | Change from LY | Shipping Wt. (lbs.) | Production | Change from LY |
|---|---|---|---|---|---|---|
| Rmblr. American 220 2-Dr. Sdn. | 6706-0 | $1,839 | -8.82% | 2591 | 24,834 | +1.61% |
| Rmblr. American 220 4-Dr. Sdn. | 6705-0 | $1,945 | -6.76% | 2621 | 10,362 | -34.99% |
| Rmblr. American 220 4-Dr. Wgn | 6708-0 | $2,231 | -5.83% | 2767 | 2,489 | -57.15% |
| Rmblr. American 440 2-Dr. Sdn. | 6706-5 | $1,997 | -6.42% | 2586 | 3,317 | -77.19% |
| Rmblr. American 440 2-Dr. HT | 6709-5 | $2,129 | -4.40% | 2643 | 4,970 | -51.54% |
| Rmblr. American 440 4-Dr. Sdn. | 6705-5 | $2,083 | -5.45% | 2613 | 7,523 | -48.27% |

| | Style Number | Base MSRP | Change from LY | Shipping Wt. (lbs.) | Production | Change from LY |
|---|---|---|---|---|---|---|
| Rmblr. American 440 4-Dr.Wgn. | 6708-5 | $2,368 | -4.40% | 2769 | 4,135 | -37.38% |
| Rblr. American Rogue 2-Dr. HT | 6709-7 | $2,266 | -4.39% | 2663 | 4,129 | -52.64% |
| Rblr. Am. Rogue 2-Dr. Conv. | 6707-7 | $2,442 | NEW | 2821 | 921 | NEW |
| TOTALS | | Avg. price $2,144 | +2.40% | | Production 62,680 | -33.10% |

# Rebel

*"The first Excitement Machine in the intermediate class!"*

**Nameplate year of origin:** 1957 (Nash Rambler model).
**Current bodystyle lifespan:** 1967 through 1978 (restyles in 1969, 1971, and 1974).
**Predecessor to this model:** Rambler Classic (1963 to 1966).
**Replacement for this model:** Matador (1971 to 1978).
**Percentage of division's sales volume:** 42.68%.
**Corporate siblings:** Ambassador (shared components cowl back) and Marlin (shared body components).
**Primary competition:** Chevrolet Chevelle, Dodge Coronet, Ford Fairlane, and Plymouth Belvedere.
**Notable changes:** Totally redesigned.
**Major standard equipment:** Cloth and vinyl front bench seat, front arm rests, dual horns, hidden compartment (Wagons), Weather-Eye heating & ventilation system, roof-top travel rack (wagons) and 7.35 × 14 BSW tires (7.75 × 14 BSW tires on Wagons). 770 adds: Full carpeting, rear arm rests, and lock for glove box and hidden compartment on wagons. SST adds: All-vinyl bench seat and 7.75 × 14 BSW tires on convertible.

## Measurements

| | Cars | Wagons |
|---|---|---|
| Wheelbase | 114.0" | 114.0" |
| Length | 197.0" | 198.0" |
| Width | 78.4" | 78.4" |
| Height | 54.6" | 54.6" |
| Legroom — front | 41.6" | 41.6" |
| Legroom — rear | 36.5" | 36.5" |
| Headroom — front | 39.8" | 39.8" |
| Headroom — rear | 37.8" | 37.8" |
| Luggage cap. (cu. ft.) | 18.2 | 91.0 |
| Fuel capacity (gals.) | 21.5 | 21.5 |

## Models Available

| | Style Number | Base MSRP | Change from LY | Shipping Wt. (lbs.) | Production | Change from LY |
|---|---|---|---|---|---|---|
| Rebel 550 2-Door Sedan | 6716-0 | $2,294 | +4.80% | 3089 | 9,121 | +65.69% |
| Rebel 550 4-Door Sedan | 6715-0 | $2,319 | +3.62% | 3055 | 10,249 | -54.42% |
| Rebel 550 4-Door Wagon | 6718-0 | $2,623 | +3.19% | 3287 | 6,845 | -27.10% |
| Rebel 770 2-Door Hardtop | 6719-5 | $2,443 | +3.39% | 3092 | 9,685 | +10.86% |
| Rebel 770 4-Door Sedan | 6715-5 | $2,418 | +3.47% | 3053 | 24,057 | -47.75% |
| Rebel 770 4-Door Wagon | 6718-5 | $2,710 | +3.08% | 3288 | 18,240 | -25.64% |
| Rebel SST 2-Door Hardtop | 6719-7 | $2,604 | +3.21% | 3109 | 15,287 | +103.50% |
| Rebel SST 2-Door Convertible | 6717-7 | $2,782 | NEW | 3180 | 1,686 | NEW |
| TOTALS | | Avg. price $2,524 | +3.87% | | Production 95,170 | -24.48% |

*\*Production by body style is not available. Differences in percentages due to discontinuance of certain models.*

# Marlin

*"The flair of a fastback, the luxury of Ambassador."*

**Nameplate year of origin:** 1965.
**Current bodystyle lifespan:** 1965 through 1967.
**Predecessor to this model:** None.
**Replacement for this model:** None.

## Measurements

| | |
|---|---|
| Wheelbase | 118.0" |
| Length | 201.5" |
| Width | 78.4" |

**Percentage of division's sales volume:** 1.14%.
**Corporate siblings:** Rebel and Ambassador (shared body components with unique roofline).
**Primary competition:** Dodge Charger.
**Notable changes:** New design for front, utilizing the Ambassador front end and platform.
**Major standard equipment:** Cloth and vinyl individually-adjustable reclining front bench seat, full carpeting, tinted glass rear window, courtesy lights, variable speed windshield wipers, grille mounted parking/turn signal lamps, full wheel covers and 7.35 × 14 BSW tires.

## Measurements (cont.)

| | |
|---|---|
| Height | 53.8" |
| Legroom — front | 41.6" |
| Legroom — rear | 36.5" |
| Headroom — front | 38.7" |
| Headroom — rear | 36.5" |
| Luggage cap. (cu. ft.) | 11.7 |
| Fuel capacity (gals.) | 21.5 |

## Models Available

| | Style Number | Base MSRP | Change from LY | Shipping Wt. (lbs.) | Production | Change from LY |
|---|---|---|---|---|---|---|
| Marlin 2-Door Hardtop | 6759-7 | $2,859 | +9.92% | 3174 | 2,545 | -44.03% |
| TOTALS | | Avg. price $2,859 | +9.92% | | Production 2,545 | -44.03% |

# Ambassador

*"A luxury car for today that lists with today's lowest-priced standard-size cars."*

**Nameplate year of origin:** 1933 (from top-of-the-line Nash).
**Current bodystyle lifespan:** 1967 through 1974 (shared basic structure with Matador through 1978).
**Predecessor to this model:** Ambassador (1963 to 1966).
**Replacement for this model:** None.
**Percentage of division's sales volume:** 28.08%.
**Corporate siblings:** Rebel and Marlin (Shared components from the cowl back).
**Primary competition:** Chevrolet BelAir/Impala/Caprice, Ford LTD, and Plymouth Fury.
**Notable changes:** Totally redesigned for 1967.
**Major standard equipment:** Cloth and vinyl front foam cushion bench seat, full carpeting, cargo mat, variable speed windshield wipers, roof-top travel rack (wagon) and 7.35 × 14 BSW tires (8.25 × 14 BSW tires on wagons). 990 adds: Additional chrome exterior trim and deluxe interior trim level. DPL adds: All-vinyl reclining bucket seats (bench on convertible), power-operated convertible top, center armrest, walnut-grain interior trim, light group, electric clock, special exterior trim, rallye lights in grille, full wheel covers, and 7.75 × 14 BSW tires on convertible.

## Measurements

| | Cars | Wagons |
|---|---|---|
| Wheelbase | 114.0" | 114.0" |
| Length | 202.5" | 203.0" |
| Width | 78.4" | 78.4" |
| Height | 54.6" | 55.0" |
| Legroom — front | 41.6" | 41.6" |
| Legroom — rear | 36.5" | 36.5" |
| Headroom — front | 39.8" | 39.8" |
| Headroom — rear | 37.8" | 37.8" |
| Luggage cap. (cu. ft.) | 18.2 | 91.0 |
| Fuel capacity (gals.) | 21.5 | 21.5 |

**1967**

## Models Available

| | Style Number | Base MSRP | Change from LY | Shipping Wt. (lbs.) | Production | Change from LY |
|---|---|---|---|---|---|---|
| Ambassador 880 2-Door Sedan | 6786-2 | $2,515 | +4.62% | 3142 | 3,623 | +352.88% |
| Ambassador 880 4-Door Sedan | 6785-2 | $2,553 | +3.99% | 3111 | 9,772 | +57.61% |
| Ambassador 880 4-Door Wagon | 6788-2 | $2,857 | +3.55% | 3318 | 3,540 | +60.91% |
| Ambassador 990 2-Door Hardtop | 6789-5 | $2,698 | +3.77% | 3208 | 6,140 | +119.29% |
| Ambassador 990 4-Door Sedan | 6785-5 | $2,671 | +3.77% | 3156 | 17,809 | +36.99% |
| Ambassador 990 4-Door Wagon | 6788-5 | $2,978 | +3.40% | 3377 | 7,919 | +60.79% |
| Ambassador DPL 2-Door HT | 6789-7 | $2,854 | +3.56% | 3226 | 12,552 | +402.08% |
| Ambassador DPL 2-Door Conv. | 6787-7 | $3,143 | NEW | 3434 | 1,260 | NEW |
| TOTALS | | Avg. price $2,784 | +4.07% | | Production* 62,615 | +82.96% |

*Estimated model year production shown. Breakout by body style not available from 1966 model year for comparisons.*

# BUICK

*"Buick for '67 ... Wouldn't you really rather have a Buick?"*

Buick full-size models for 1967 were totally restyled, while the mid-size Special and Skylark and luxury Riviera models featured minor styling alterations. The full-size LeSabre, Wildcat and Electra were given a facelift that featured a new divided grille styling up front, more angular body panels, and full-width taillamp styling at the rear. Rooflines were similar to the 1965 and 1966 models. A new 430 CID V8 engine replaced the old reliable 425 CID "Nailhead" V8 that was descended from the original 1953 Buick V8. The 430 CID V8 was an all-new modern V8 design that put out 360 horses in its original form. Interiors received upgrades to materials and styling as well as a more luxurious appearance. No model changes were made to any of the full-size lines, including the Riviera which received a new grille and trim updates.

The mid-size Special models wore a new grille similar to the Wildcat's. The SportWagon (now one word) wore a grille similar to Skylark models, but still shared its overall body design with the Oldsmobile Vista-Cruiser, and interior trim with the Skylark models. Numerous model changes included dropping the Special 2-Door Convertible, Special Deluxe 2-Door Coupe, and the base SportWagon trim level. A Skylark 4-Door Sedan and a Skylark Grand Sport 340 2-Door Hardtop joined the lineup. The 1966 Grand Sport line was renamed Grand Sport 400 to designate the difference in engine displacement between the two GS lines offered this season.

Electra 225 4-Door Hardtop

Le Sabre Custom 2-Door Convertible

Riviera 2-Door Hardtop

Skylark 2-Door Hardtop

Special 2-Door Coupe

Sportwagon Custom 4-Door Wagon

Wildcat 4-Door Hardtop

**Model year production:** 545,359, down 5.94% from 1966.
**Domestic market share:** 7.12% (5th place).
**Base price range:** $2,411 to $4,469.
**Industry average base price:** $3,159.
**Buick average base price:** $3,311.
**Introduction date:** September 1966.
**Assembly plants:** Southgate, CA (C); Atlanta, GA (D); Flint, MI (H); Kansas City, MO (K); Fairfax, KS (X); Wilmington, DE (Y); Fremont, CA (Z); and Oshawa, Ontario, (1).

**Data plate identification:** Thirteen digit code read as follows: Five digit style number in which 4 = Buick, 2nd number identifies series (3 is Skylark, 8 is Electra, etc.), 3rd through 5th indicate model number; 7 = 1967; assembly plant code; 100001 and up for serial number. *Example:* 452377X100001 is a 1967 Buick LeSabre 2-Door Hardtop, serial number 100001, built in Fairfax, KS

## Powertrains

| Engine | Gross HP | Transmission Availability | Special/ Skylark | Sky. 4-Dr. HT/ SportWagon | GS | LeSabre | Wild./Elec. /Riviera |
|---|---|---|---|---|---|---|---|
| 225 CID, 2-bbl., V6 | 160 | 3-speed manual | S | - | - | - | - |
|  |  | Super Turbine 300 Auto. | $199 | - | - | - | - |
| 300 CID, 2-bbl., V8 | 210 | 3-speed manual | S[1]/$70[2] | - | - | - | - |
|  |  | Super Turbine 300 Auto. | $199[1]/$269[2] | - | - | - | - |
| 340 CID, 2-bbl., V8 | 220 | 3-speed manual | $47[1]/$117[2] | S | S | S | - |
|  |  | 4-speed manual | | - | $184 (340) | - | - |
|  |  | Super Turbine 400 Auto. | $277[1]/$347[2] | $230 | $230 (340) | $230 | - |
| 340 CID, 4-bbl., V8 | 260 | 3-speed manual | $77[1]/$147[2] | $30 | $30 (340) | - | - |
|  |  | 4-speed manual | - | - | $214 (340) | - | - |
|  |  | Super Turbine 400 Auto. | $310[1]/$380[2] | $263 (SportWagon) | $263 (340) | $263 (400) | - |
| 400 CID, 4-bbl., V8 | 340 | 3-speed manual | - | S (400 pkg.) | S (400 pkg.) | - | - |
|  |  | 4-speed manual | - | - | $184 (400) | - | - |
|  |  | Super Turbine 400 Auto. | - | $230 (400) | $230 (400) | - | - |
| 430 CID, 4-bbl., V8 | 360 | Super Turbine 400 Auto. | - | - | - | - | S |

[1]Special Deluxe Wagon and Skylark (except 4-Door Hardtop) only. [2]All but Special Deluxe Wagon and Skylark (but including Skylark 4-Door Hardtop).

## Major Options

|  | Skylark | SportWagon | LeSabre | Wildcat | Electra 225 | Riviera |
|---|---|---|---|---|---|---|
| Air conditioning — manual | $343 | $343 | $421 | $421 | $421 | $421 |
| Air conditioning — automatic | - | - | $500 | $500 | $500 | $500 |
| Cruise Master speed control | $58 | $63 | $63 | $63 | $63 | $63 |
| Soft Ray tinted glass | $39 | $44 | $44 | $44 | $44 | $47 |
| Deck lid remote release | $14 | $14 | $14 | $14 | $14 | $14 |
| Tilt steering wheel | $45 | $45 | $45 | $45 | $45 | S |
| Power steering | $95 | $111 | $111 | $111 | S | S |
| Power brakes | $42 | $42 | $42 | $42 | S | S |
| Power driver's seat/Bench seat, 4-way | $74 | $74 | $74 | $74 | $47–$74 | $74 |
| Power windows | $105 | $110 | $110 | $110 | $110* | $110 |
| AM radio | $70 | $88 | $88 | $88 | $88 | $88 |
| AM/FM stereo (not stereo in Skylark) | $134 | $268 | $268 | $268 | $268 | $268 |
| Front bucket seats | $ | - | - | - | - | $ |
| Vinyl roof | $102 | $123 | $123 | S | $139 | $128 |
| White sidewall tires — standard size | $31–$36 | $42 | $42 | $42 | $47 | $42 |
| Wheel trim covers (Deluxe on Electra) | $21 | $21 (base) | $21 (base) | S | S | S |
| GS package | - | - | - | - | - | $138 |
| 400 Performance package | - | $269 | $263 | - | - | - |

Options common to most models. (- = Not Available; S = Standard equipment.) Items may be standard equipment, optional at different pricing, or unavailable on certain models. This chart is only a guide.

*Standard on Convertible.

## Paint Colors

| Color | Code | Color | Code |
|---|---|---|---|
| Regal Black | A | Burgundy Mist Metallic | N |
| Riviera Turquoise Metallic* | B | Platinum Mist Metallic | P |
| Arctic White | C | Apple Red | R |
| Sapphire Blue Metallic | D | Champagne Mist Metallic | S |
| Midnight Blue Metallic | E | Ivory | T |
| Blue Mist Metallic | F | Riviera Plum* | U |
| Gold Mist Metallic | G | Riviera Charcoal Metallic* | V |
| Green Mist Metallic | H | Riviera Fawn Metallic* | W |
| Verde Green Metallic | J | Riviera Red Metallic* | X |
| Aquamarine Metallic | K | Riviera Gold Metallic* | Z |
| Shadow Turquoise Metallic | L | | |

*Specific Riviera colors.

# Special, Skylark and GS

*"Stops the show again this year with its perennial ability to change the pace.
Now it's the family car ... then, presto—a quick change and
... now, it's a sporty personal car."*

**Nameplate year of origin:** 1935 (Special); and 1953 (Skylark).
**Current bodystyle lifespan:** 1964 through 1967.
**Predecessor to this model:** Special/Skylark (1961 to 1963).
**Replacement for this model:** Special/Skylark (1968 to 1972).
**Percentage of division's sales volume:** 31.08%.
**Corporate siblings:** Chevrolet Chevelle, Olds F-85/Cutlass, and Pontiac Tempest/LeMans.
**Primary competition:** Dodge Coronet, and Mercury Comet/Montego.
**Notable changes:** New grille and minor trim and detail changes.
**Major standard equipment:** Cloth and vinyl front bench seat, rubber floor mats (carpet in convertible), electric windshield wipers, front door operated courtesy lights, and 7.75 × 14 BSW tires. Deluxe adds: Instrument panel safety pad, full carpeting, and dual horns. Skylark adds: Paddle-type door arm rests, glove compartment and rear compartment courtesy lights (2-Doors), and full wheel covers. Gran Sport adds: 340 CID V8 or 400 CID V8 (depending on model), all-vinyl notchback bench seat, heavy-duty suspension, and floor shift.

## Measurements

| | Cars | Wagon |
|---|---|---|
| Wheelbase | 115.0" | 115.0" |
| Length | 205.0" | 209.3" |
| Width | 75.4" | 75.4" |
| Height | 54.0" | 55.7" |
| Legroom — front | 41.3" | 41.2" |
| Legroom — rear | 35.7" | 35.7" |
| Headroom — front | 38.1" | 37.8" |
| Headroom — rear | 37.2" | 38.3" |
| Luggage capacity (cu. ft.) | 18.8 | 85.6 |
| Fuel capacity (gals.) | 20.0 | 20.0 |

## Models Available

| | Style Number | Base MSRP | Change from LY | Shipping Wt. (lbs.) | Production | Change from LY |
|---|---|---|---|---|---|---|
| Special 2-Door Coupe | 43307 | $2,411 | +2.68% | 3071 | 15,926 | +5.88% |
| Special 4-Door Sedan | 43369 | $2,462 | +2.54% | 3077 | 10,504 | -42.13% |
| Special 4-Door, 2-Seat Wagon | 43335 | $2,742 | +1.74% | 3343 | 2,596 | -42.17% |
| Special Deluxe 2-Door Hardtop | 43517 | $2,566 | +2.48% | 3127 | 16,741 | -52.74% |
| Special Deluxe 4-Door Sedan | 43569 | $2,545 | +2.41% | 3142 | 28,963 | -10.26% |
| Special Deluxe 4-Dr., 2-Seat Wgn. | 43635 | $2,901 | +4.24% | 3317 | 6,851 | -18.60% |
| Skylark 2-Door Coupe | 44307 | $2,665 | +1.56% | 3137 | 4,059 | -48.50% |
| Skylark 2-Door Hardtop | 44417 | $2,798 | +4.13% | 3199 | 40,940 | +15.19% |
| Skylark 2-Door Convertible | 44467 | $2,945 | +3.81% | 3335 | 6,319 | -6.20% |
| Skylark 4-Door Sedan | 44469 | $2,767 | NEW | 3324 | 9,123 | NEW |
| Skylark 4-Door Hardtop | 44439 | $2,950 | +12.42% | 3373 | 13,673 | +73.49% |
| GS 340 2-Door Hardtop | 43417 | $2,845 | NEW | 3283 | * | NEW |
| GS 400 2-Door Coupe | 44607 | $2,956 | 0.00% | 3439 | 1,014 | -44.74% |
| GS 400 2-Door Hardtop | 44617 | $3,019 | 0.00% | 3500 | 10,659 | +7.30% |
| GS 400 2-Door Convertible | 44667 | $3,167 | 0.00% | 3505 | 2,140 | +4.54% |
| TOTALS | *Avg. price* | $2,783 | +3.34% | *Production* | 169,508 | -18.73% |

# SportWagon

*"The up-and-coming family cars that'll serve double-duty with extra loadspace."*

**Nameplate year of origin:** 1964.
**Current bodystyle lifespan:** 1964 through 1967.
**Predecessor to this model:** None.
**Replacement for this model:** SportWagon (1968 to 1969).

## Measurements

| | |
|---|---|
| Wheelbase | 120.0" |
| Length | 214.3" |
| Width | 75.4" |

**Percentage of division's sales volume:** 3.50%.
**Corporate siblings:** Oldsmobile Vista-Cruiser.
**Primary competition:** Dodge Coronet, and Mercury Montego.
**Notable changes:** New grille and minor trim and detail changes.
**Major standard equipment:** All-vinyl front bench seat, full carpeting, electric windshield wipers, front door operated dome light, dual arm rests, tinted glass observation-style roof, full wheel covers and 8.25 × 14 BSW tires.

## Measurements (cont.)

| | |
|---|---|
| Height | 58.8" |
| Legroom — front | 41.3" |
| Legroom — rear | 38.7" |
| Headroom — front | 37.9" |
| Headroom — rear | 40.5" |
| Luggage capacity (cu. ft.) | 97.9 |
| Fuel capacity (gals.) | 20.0 |

## Models Available

| | Style Number | Base MSRP | Change from LY | Shipping Wt. (lbs.) | Production | Change from LY |
|---|---|---|---|---|---|---|
| Sportwagon Custom 4-Dr., 2-St. Wgn. | 44455 | $3,202 | +1.49% | 3772 | 8,554 | +22.83% |
| Sportwagon Custom 4-Dr., 3-St. Wgn. | 44465 | $3,340 | +1.43% | 3876 | 10,529 | +10.72% |
| TOTALS | | Avg. price $3,271 | +3.45% | | Production 19,083 | -11.69% |

# LeSabre

*"Continuing to provide magnificent room and comfort at an unequaled price."*

**Nameplate year of origin:** 1959.
**Current bodystyle lifespan:** 1967 through 1968.
**Predecessor to this model:** LeSabre (1965 to 1966).
**Replacement for this model:** LeSabre (1969 to 1970).
**Percentage of division's sales volume:** 26.16%.
**Corporate siblings:** Chevrolet Biscayne/Bel Air/Impala/Caprice, Pontiac Catalina/Executive/Bonneville, Oldsmobile 88.
**Primary competition:** Chrysler Newport, Dodge Monaco, and Mercury Monterey.
**Notable changes:** Completely restyled.
**Major standard equipment:** Cloth and vinyl front bench seat, front door operated interior lighting, glove box light, full carpeting, front and rear armrests, and 8.55 × 15 BSW tires. Custom adds: Custom interior trim, "Custom" nameplates, and additional exterior trim moldings.

## Measurements

| | |
|---|---|
| Wheelbase | 123.2" |
| Length | 217.5" |
| Width | 80.0" |
| Height | 55.6" |
| Legroom — front | 42.2" |
| Legroom — rear | 39.0" |
| Headroom — front | 38.9" |
| Headroom — rear | 37.7" |
| Luggage capacity (cu. ft.) | 16.8 |
| Fuel capacity (gals.) | 25.0 |

1967

## Models Available

| | Style Number | Base MSRP | Change from LY | Shipping Wt. (lbs.) | Production | Change from LY |
|---|---|---|---|---|---|---|
| LeSabre 2-Door Hardtop | 45287 | $3,084 | +2.05% | 3819 | 13,760 | -0.60% |
| LeSabre 4-Door Sedan | 45269 | $3,002 | +2.04% | 3847 | 36,220 | -7.47% |
| LeSabre 4-Door Hardtop | 45239 | $3,142 | +1.98% | 3878 | 17,464 | -1.56% |
| LeSabre Custom 2-Door Hardtop | 45487 | $3,172 | +2.03% | 3853 | 11,871 | -36.96% |
| LeSabre Custom 2-Door Convertible | 45467 | $3,388 | +1.86% | 3890 | 2,913 | -41.67% |
| LeSabre Custom 4-Door Sedan | 45469 | $3,096 | +2.01% | 3855 | 27,930 | +7.70% |
| LeSabre Custom 4-Door Hardtop | 45439 | $3,236 | +1.95% | 3873 | 32,526 | +20.85% |
| TOTALS | | Avg. price $3,160 | +2.00% | | Production 142,684 | -3.19% |

# Wildcat

*"It's made for its role as a performer with fire and flair."*

**Nameplate year of origin:** 1962.
**Current bodystyle lifespan:** 1967 through 1968.
**Predecessor to this model:** Wildcat (1965 to 1966).
**Replacement for this model:** Wildcat (1969 to 1970).
**Percentage of division's sales volume:** 13.02%.
**Corporate siblings:** Chevrolet Biscayne/Bel/Air/Impala/Caprice, Pontiac Catalina/Executive/Bonneville, Oldsmobile 88.
**Primary competition:** Chrysler 300, Dodge Monaco, and Mercury Marquis.
**Notable changes:** Completely restyled.
**Major standard equipment:** Cloth and vinyl bench seat, front door operated interior lighting, full carpeting, front and rear armrests, deluxe steering wheel, rocker panel and wheel opening moldings, and 8.45 × 15 BSW tires. Custom adds: Custom interior trim, and custom headlining.

## Measurements

| | |
|---|---|
| Wheelbase | 126.0" |
| Length | 220.5" |
| Width | 80.0" |
| Height | 55.7" |
| Legroom — front | 42.2" |
| Legroom — rear | 39.0" |
| Headroom — front | 38.9" |
| Headroom — rear | 37.7" |
| Luggage capacity (cu. ft.) | 16.8 |
| Fuel capacity (gals.) | 25.0 |

## Models Available

| | Style Number | Base MSRP | Change from LY | Shipping Wt. (lbs.) | Production | Change from LY |
|---|---|---|---|---|---|---|
| Wildcat 2-Door HT | 46487 | $3,382 | +1.68% | 4021 | 10,585 | +8.30% |
| Wildcat 2-Door Convertible | 46467 | $3,536 | +1.61% | 4064 | 2,276 | -15.39% |
| Wildcat 4-Door Sedan | 46469 | $3,277 | +1.36% | 4008 | 14,579 | +1.32% |
| Wildcat 4-Door HT | 46439 | $3,437 | +1.36% | 4069 | 15,510 | +2.84% |
| Wildcat Custom 2-Door Hardtop | 46687 | $3,603 | +1.58% | 4055 | 11,571 | +7.14% |
| Wildcat Custom 2-Door Convertible | 46667 | $3,757 | +1.51% | 4046 | 2,913 | +4.41% |
| Wildcat Custom 4-Door Hardtop | 46639 | $3,652 | +1.28% | 4119 | 13,547 | +3.73% |
| TOTALS | | *Avg. price* $3,521 | +1.50% | | *Production* 70,981 | +3.49% |

# Electra 225

*"Stars in the luxury class that epitomizes all that's high in quality and pleasant to the senses."*

**Nameplate year of origin:** 1959.
**Current bodystyle lifespan:** 1967 through 1968.
**Predecessor to this model:** Electra 225 (1965 to 1966).
**Replacement for this model:** Electra 225 (1969 to 1970).
**Percentage of division's sales volume:** 18.39%.
**Corporate siblings:** Cadillac Calais/de Ville, Oldsmobile Ninety-Eight.
**Primary competition:** Chrysler New Yorker, and Mercury Park Lane.
**Notable changes:** Completely restyled.
**Major standard equipment:** Cloth and vinyl bench seat, full carpeting and lower door carpeting, deluxe steering wheel, power steering, power brakes, trunk light, bright rocker panel molding and wheel opening moldings, rear fender skirts, deluxe wheel covers and 8.85 × 15 BSW tires. Custom adds: Custom interior trim and exterior identification.

## Measurements

| | |
|---|---|
| Wheelbase | 126.0" |
| Length | 223.9" |
| Width | 80.0" |
| Height | 56.2" |
| Legroom — front | 42.2" |
| Legroom — rear | 42.1" |
| Headroom — front | 39.5" |
| Headroom — rear | 38.2" |
| Luggage capacity (cu. ft.) | 17.0 |
| Fuel capacity (gals.) | 25.0 |

## Models Available

| | Style Number | Base MSRP | Change from LY | Shipping Wt. (lbs.) | Production | Change from LY |
|---|---|---|---|---|---|---|
| Electra 225 2-Door Hardtop | 48257 | $4,075 | +1.07% | 4197 | 6,845 | +40.21% |
| Electra 225 4-Door Sedan | 48269 | $4,054 | +0.80% | 4246 | 10,787 | -7.74% |
| Electra 225 4-Door Hardtop | 48239 | $4,184 | +0.75% | 4293 | 12,491 | +15.74% |
| Electra 225 Custom 2-Door HT | 48457 | $4,254 | +1.02% | 4242 | 12,156 | +20.13% |
| Electra 225 Custom 2-Door Conv. | 48467 | $4,421 | +0.98% | 4304 | 6,941 | -3.26% |
| Electra 225 Custom 4-Door Sedan | 48469 | $4,270 | +1.64% | 4312 | 10,106 | +7.88% |
| Electra 225 Custom 4-Door HT | 48439 | $4,363 | +0.72% | 4336 | 40,978 | +20.00% |
| TOTALS | Avg. price | $4,232 | +1.00% | Production | 100,304 | +13.75% |

# Riviera

*"Unique in style and dramatic in action, the new
Riviera is all that's fine from Buick."*

**Nameplate year of origin:** 1949 (for 2-Dr. HT); 1963 (series).
**Current bodystyle lifespan:** 1966 through 1970.
**Predecessor to this model:** Riviera (1963 to 1965).
**Replacement for this model:** Riviera (1971 to 1976).
**Percentage of division's sales volume:** 7.85%.
**Corporate siblings:** Cadillac Eldorado, and Oldsmobile Toronado.
**Primary competition:** Ford Thunderbird.
**Notable changes:** Revised trim and detail changes.
**Major standard equipment:** All-vinyl bench or bucket front seats, electric clock, trunk light, bright exterior window and rocker moldings, ventless front door windows, power steering, power brakes, dual exhaust system, and 8.55 × 15 BSW tires.

## Measurements

| | |
|---|---|
| Wheelbase | 119.0" |
| Length | 211.3" |
| Width | 79.4" |
| Height | 53.2" |
| Legroom — front | 41.2" |
| Legroom — rear | 36.6" |
| Headroom — front | 41.2" |
| Headroom — rear | 37.4" |
| Luggage capacity (cu. ft.) | 10.3 |
| Fuel capacity (gals.) | 21.0 |

**1967**

## Models Available

| | Style Number | Base MSRP | Change from LY | Shipping Wt. (lbs.) | Production | Change from LY |
|---|---|---|---|---|---|---|
| Riviera 2-Door Hardtop | 49487 | $4,469 | +1.02% | 4189 | 42,799 | -5.62% |
| TOTALS | Avg. price | $4,469 | +1.02% | Production | 42,799 | -5.62% |

# CADILLAC

*"The 1967 Standard of the World."*

An all-new sports-type model, the Eldorado, debuted for 1967. Built on the Oldsmobile Toronado platform and sharing many of its technological advances, the Eldorado's distinguishing features were its styling and its Cadillac-level of trim and appointments. Where the Toronado was rounded and sleek looking, the Eldorado came off razor sharp. There were thin, blade-like front fender edges that followed a sharp beltline crease right through the doors. Then immediately following the doors a vertical line went up to the top of the rear fenders and ran back to thin, blade-like vertical taillights at the rear. Squared wheel openings and a formal roofline completed the look. It was quite a departure for Cadillac, yet it was identifiable as a Cadillac by its egg-crate grille (with hidden headlights), chrome outline moldings, and large Cadillac wreath emblems adorning the wheels, hood and trunk.

Other Cadillac models were restyled this year, with an obvious link to Cadillacs of the recent past. The popular vertical headlight arrangement was continued, were the vertical taillamps in the rear fin area. Bodyside sculpting was a simple full-length crease that dropped off ever so slightly towards the rear of the car. At the front end, the hood was vee'd slightly more and the headlamp opening slanted forward, making the cars appear longer than they already were. Powertrains continued as in prior years.

Calais 4-Door Hardtop

de Ville 2-Door Convertible

Eldorado 2-Door Hardtop

Fleetwood 75 9-passengr 4-Door Sedan

Fleetwood Sixty-Special 4-Door Sedan

**Model year production:** 197,667, up 1.78% over 1966.
**Domestic market share:** 2.58% (11th place).
**Base price range:** $5,040 to $10,571.
**Industry average base price:** $3,159.
**Cadillac average base price:** $6,508.
**Introduction date:** October 6, 1966.

**Assembly plants:** Detroit, MI, and Linden, NJ
**Data plate identification:** Eight digit code read as follows: 1st digit is style symbol (see list); 2nd digit 7 for 1967; followed by 100001 and up for serial number. *Example:* J7100001 is a 1967 Cadillac de Ville 2-Door Hardtop, serial number 100001.

## Powertrains

| Engine | Gross HP | Transmission Availability | All models |
|---|---|---|---|
| 429 CID, 4-bbl., V8 | 340 | Turbo Hydra-matic | S |

## Major Options

| | Eldorado | Calais | de Ville | 60 Special | Seventy-Five |
|---|---|---|---|---|---|
| Automatic climate control | $516 | $516 | $516 | $516 | S |
| Power windows | S | $116 | S | S | S |
| 6-way power seat | $83 | $111 | $83 | $83 | $83 — NA Limo |
| Power door locks | $47 | $47–$68 | $47–$68 | $68 | $116 |
| AM radio w/rear speaker | $162 | $162 | $162 | $162 | $162 |
| AM-FM radio | $188 | $188 | $188 | $188 | $188 |
| Vinyl roof | $132 | - | $132–$137 | S — Brougham | NA |
| Twilight Sentinel (auto. dimmers) | $37 | $50 | $50 | $50 | $50 |
| Tilt and Telescope steering wheel | $90 | $90 | $90 | $90 | $90 |
| Leather upholstery | $158 | - | $138 | $138 | - |
| Cruise control | $95 | $95 | $95 | $95 | $95 |
| Tinted glass | $51 | $51 | $51 | $51 | $51 |

| | Eldorado | Calais | de Ville | 60 Special | Seventy-Five |
|---|---|---|---|---|---|
| Rear window defogger | - | $27 | $27 (NA convertible) | $27 | S |
| Automatic level control | S | $79 | $79 | S | S |
| Remote control trunk release/lock | $52 | $52 | $52 | $52 | $52 |
| Firemist paint colors | $132 | $132 | $132 | $132 | $132 |

Options common to most models. (- = Not Available; S = Standard equipment.) Items may be standard equipment, optional at different pricing, or unavailable on certain models. This chart is only a guide.

**Cadillac Style Symbols: A**— 62 4-window Sedan or Calais 4-Dr. HT Sedan; **B**— Sedan de Ville 4-window; **C**— 62 Short Deck Sedan; **D**— Sedan de Ville Park Avenue; **E**— Eldorado Biarritz or Eldorado Convertible; **F**— 62 Convertible; **G**— 62 2-Door Hardtop or Calais 2-Door HT; **H**— Eldorado Seville HT or Eldorado Coupe; **J**— Coupe de Ville; **K**— 62 6-window Sedan; **L**— Sedan de Ville 6-window; **M**— Fleetwood 60 Special Sedan; **N**— 62 4-window Sedan (1963) or Calais Sedan; **P**— Fleetwood Brougham or Eldorado Brougham; **R**— Fleetwood 75 Sedan; **S**— Fleetwood 75 Limousine; **Z**— Comerical Chassis

## Paint Colors

| | Code |
|---|---|
| Sable Black | 10 |
| Grecian White | 12 |
| Regal Silver Metallic | 16 |
| Summit Gray Metallic | 18 |
| Venetian Blue | 20 |
| Marina Blue Metallic | 24 |
| Admiralty Blue Metallic | 26 |
| Capri Aqua Metallic | 28 |
| Pinecrest Green Metallic | 30 |
| Sherwood Green Metallic | 36 |
| Persian Ivory | 40 |
| Sudan Beige | 42 |
| Baroque Gold Metallic | 43 |
| Doeskin Metallic | 44 |
| Flamenco Red | 48 |
| Regent Maroon Metallic | 49 |
| Atlantis Blue Firemist Metallic* | 90 |
| Crystal Firemist Metallic* | 92 |
| Tropic Green Firemist Metallic* | 96 |
| Olympic Bronze Firemist Metallic* | 97 |
| Ember Firemist Metallic* | 98 |

*Firemist colors available at extra cost, only on Eldorado.

**1967**

# Calais

*"A practical investment in fine-car distinction."*

**Nameplate year of origin:** 1965.
**Current bodystyle lifespan:** 1967 through 1968.
**Predecessor to this model:** Calais (1965 to 1966).
**Replacement for this model:** Calais (1969 to 1970).
**Percentage of division's sales volume:** 11.04%.
**Corporate siblings:** Buick Electra 225 and Oldsmobile Ninety-Eight.
**Primary competition:** Chrysler New Yorker and Lincoln Continental.
**Notable changes:** Completely restyled.
**Major standard equipment:** Duet cloth and vinyl seat upholstery, front center armrests, rear fender skirts, left side remote control outside rear view mirror, interior courtesy and warning lights, three-speed windshield wipers and washers, right side visor vanity mirrors, front cornering lamps, variable ratio power steering, power front disc brakes, Turbo Hydra-matic transmission, and 9.00 × 15 BSW tires.

## Measurements

| | |
|---|---|
| Wheelbase | 129.5" |
| Length | 224.0" |
| Width | 80.0" |
| Height | 55.6" |
| Legroom — front | 41.0" |
| Legroom — rear | 41.9" |
| Headroom — front | 39.1" |
| Headroom — rear | 38.2" |
| Luggage capacity (cu. ft.) | 17.1 |
| Fuel capacity (gals.) | 26.0 |

## Models Available

| | Style Number | Base MSRP | Change from LY | Shipping Wt. (lbs.) | Production | Change from LY |
|---|---|---|---|---|---|---|
| Calais 2-Door Hardtop | 68247 | $5,040 | +1.08% | 4570 | 9,085 | -18.01% |
| Calais 4-Door Sedan | 68269 | $5,215 | +0.85% | 4520 | 2,865 | -37.38% |
| Calais 4-Door Hardtop | 68249 | $5,215 | +0.85% | 4640 | 9,880 | -24.15% |
| TOTALS | Avg. price | $5,157 | +0.94% | | Production 21,830 | -23.88% |

# de Ville

*"An elegant opportunity for individual expression."*

**Nameplate year of origin:** 1949 (as Hardtop designation); 1959 (series).
**Current bodystyle lifespan:** 1967 through 1968.
**Predecessor to this model:** de Ville (1965 to 1966).
**Replacement for this model:** de Ville (1969 to 1970).
**Percentage of division's sales volume:** 70.73%.
**Corporate siblings:** Buick Electra 225 and Oldsmobile Ninety-Eight.
**Primary competition:** Imperial Crown and Lincoln Continental.
**Notable changes:** Completely restyled.
**Major standard equipment:** Cloth and vinyl seat upholstery (leather in convertible), two-way power seat adjustment, front and rear center armrests (front only on convertible), rear fender skirts, left side remote control outside rear view mirror, power windows, interior courtesy and warning lights, three-speed windshield wipers and washers, right side visor vanity mirrors, front cornering lamps, variable ratio power steering, power front disc brakes, Turbo Hydramatic transmission, and 9.00 × 15 BSW tires.

### Measurements

| | |
|---|---|
| Wheelbase | 129.5" |
| Length | 224.0" |
| Width | 80.0" |
| Height | 55.6" |
| Legroom — front | 41.0" |
| Legroom — rear | 39.7" |
| Headroom — front | 39.0" |
| Headroom — rear | 38.2" |
| Luggage capacity (cu. ft.) | 17.1 |
| Fuel capacity (gals.) | 26.0 |

## Models Available

| | Style Number | Base MSRP | Change from LY | Shipping Wt. (lbs.) | Production | Change from LY |
|---|---|---|---|---|---|---|
| Coupe de Ville 2-Door Hardtop | 68347 | $5,392 | +0.99% | 4595 | 52,905 | +4.60% |
| de Ville 2-Door Convertible | 68367 | $5,608 | +0.95% | 4600 | 18,200 | -5.21% |
| Sedan de Ville 4-Door Sedan | 68369 | $5,625 | +0.79% | 4680 | 8,800 | -25.80% |
| Sedan de Ville 4-Door Hardtop | 68349 | $5,625 | +0.79% | 4675 | 59,902 | -1.07% |
| TOTALS | Avg. price | $5,563 | +0.89% | | Production 139,807 | -1.68% |

# Eldorado

*"World's finest personal car."*

**Nameplate year of origin:** 1953.
**Current bodystyle lifespan:** 1967 through 1970.
**Predecessor to this model:** Fleetwood Eldorado (1965 to 1966).
**Replacement for this model:** Eldorado (1971 to 1978).
**Percentage of division's sales volume:** 9.07%.
**Corporate siblings:** Buick Riviera and Oldsmobile Toronado.
**Primary competition:** Ford Thunderbird.
**Notable changes:** All-new model, based on Oldsmobile Toronado platform.

### Measurements

| | |
|---|---|
| Wheelbase | 120.0" |
| Length | 221.0" |
| Width | 79.9" |
| Height | 53.8" |
| Legroom — front | 41.2" |
| Legroom — rear | 36.2" |
| Headroom — front | 37.9" |

**Major standard equipment:** Darien cloth and vinyl front Strato bench seat, two-way power seat adjustment, front center armrests, left side remote control outside rear view mirror, power windows, interior door, courtesy and warning lights, three-speed windshield wipers and washers, right side visor vanity mirrors, front cornering lamps, variable ratio power steering, power brakes, Turbo Hydra-matic transmission, front wheel drive, and 9.00 × 15 BSW tires.

## Measurements (cont.)

| | |
|---|---|
| Headroom — rear | 37.7" |
| Luggage capacity (cu. ft.) | 13.4 |
| Fuel capacity (gals.) | 24.0 |

## Models Available

| | Style Number | Base MSRP | Change from LY | Shipping Wt. (lbs.) | Production | Change from LY |
|---|---|---|---|---|---|---|
| Fl. Eldorado 2-Door Hardtop | 69347 | $6,277 | NEW | 4580 | 17,930 | NEW |
| TOTALS | | *Avg. price* $6,277 | NEW | | *Production* 17,930 | NEW |

# Fleetwood Brougham & Sixty-Special

*"Unmatched comfort and spacious dignity."*

**Nameplate year of origin:** 1938.
**Current bodystyle lifespan:** 1967 through 1968.
**Predecessor to this model:** Fleetwood Sixty-Special (1965 to 1966).
**Replacement for this model:** Fleetwood Sixty-Special (1969 to 1970).
**Percentage of division's sales volume:** 8.25%.
**Corporate siblings:** None.
**Primary competition:** None.
**Notable changes:** Completely restyled.
**Major standard equipment:** Damascus cloth and leather seat upholstery, two-way power seat adjustment, front and rear center armrests, rear fender skirts, left side remote control outside rear view mirror, power windows, interior door, courtesy and warning lights, three-speed windshield wipers and washers, right side visor vanity mirrors, front cornering lamps, variable ratio power steering, power front disc brakes, Turbo Hydra-matic transmission, and 9.00 × 15 BSW tires. Brougham adds: Diplomat cloth and leather upholstery, driver's side only seat adjustment, reading lights and padded vinyl top.

## Measurements

| | |
|---|---|
| Wheelbase | 133.0" |
| Length | 227.5" |
| Width | 80.0" |
| Height | 56.7" |
| Legroom — front | 41.0" |
| Legroom — rear | 39.6" |
| Headroom — front | 39.5" |
| Headroom — rear | 38.2" |
| Luggage capacity (cu. ft.) | 17.1 |
| Fuel capacity (gals.) | 26.0 |

**1967**

## Models Available

| | Style Number | Base MSRP | Change from LY | Shipping Wt. (lbs.) | Production | Change from LY |
|---|---|---|---|---|---|---|
| Fl. Sixty Special 4-Dr. Sedan | 68069 | $6,423 | +0.71% | 4795 | 3,550 | -34.80% |
| Fl. Brougham 4-Dr. Sedan | 68169 | $6,739 | +0.66% | 4805 | 12,750 | -6.46% |
| TOTALS | | *Avg. price* $6,581 | +0.67% | | *Production* 16,300 | -14.55% |

# Fleetwood Seventy-Five

*"A motorcar completely worthy of the distinguished wreath
and crest that identify a 1967 Fleetwood by Cadillac."*

**Nameplate year of origin:** 1927 (Fleetwood bodies); 1936 (75 series).
**Current bodystyle lifespan:** 1967 through 1968.
**Predecessor to this model:** Fleetwood 75 (1966).
**Replacement for this model:** Fleetwood 75 (1969 to 1970).
**Percentage of division's sales volume:** 0.91%.
**Corporate siblings:** None.
**Primary competition:** None.
**Notable changes:** Completely restyled.
**Major standard equipment:** Devonshire cloth seat upholstery, rear center armrests, automatic climate control, rear fender skirts, left side remote control outside rear view mirror, power windows, interior door, courtesy and warning lights, three-speed windshield wipers and washers, right side visor vanity mirrors, front cornering lamps, automatic level control, fixed ratio power steering, power front disc brakes, Turbo Hydra-matic transmission, and 8.20 × 15 BSW tires.

## Measurements

| | |
|---|---|
| Wheelbase | 149.8" |
| Length | 244.5" |
| Width | 80.0" |
| Height | 57.4" |
| Legroom — front | 41.3" |
| Legroom — rear | 41.3" |
| Headroom — front | 39.8" |
| Headroom — rear | 38.0" |
| Luggage capacity (cu. ft.) | 16.2 |
| Fuel capacity (gals.) | 26.0 |

## Models Available

| | Style Number | Base MSRP | Change from LY | Shipping Wt. (lbs.) | Production | Change from LY |
|---|---|---|---|---|---|---|
| Fl. Seventy-Five 4-Door Sedan | 69723 | $10,360 | 0.00% | 5300 | 835 | -14.80% |
| Fl. Seventy-Five 4-Dr. Limousine | 69733 | $10,571 | 0.00% | 5385 | 965 | -6.94% |
| TOTALS | | *Avg. price* $10,466 | 0.00% | | *Production* 1,800 | -10.76% |

# CHEVROLET

*"Command performance Chevrolets for 1967."*

Chevrolet and General Motors finally caught up with Ford and Chrysler by fielding a pony car, with the new Chevrolet Camaro and sister car, Pontiac Firebird. Like the Mustang and Barracuda, the Camaro was based upon an existing compact car line. In the case of the Camaro that car was the newly redesigned Chevy II line. Introduced over two years after the successful Mustang launch, the Camaro benefited from more modern design techniques, but had a lot of ground to make up in the sales race. The Camaro looked more like a sports car than the Mustang and was offered right from the start with a full range of Chevrolet engines. A variety of powerplants from a 230 CID 6-cylinder, up through a 325-horsepower, 396 CID V8 engine were available from its introduction. As was typical, a full range of accessories was offered to make a Camaro any-

thing from "plain jane" to luxurious to all-out sports car. Unlike the Mustang and Barracuda, a fastback model was not offered. Although a certain group of buyers were going after fastback models, they were still a relatively small percentage of the overall market, so GM went for the more traditional 2-Door Hardtop and Convertible body styles. The Hardtop style had a sort of "semi-fastback" look to it, but was considered a Hardtop or Coupe.

The full-size Chevy line was restyled this season, in line with other big cars from GM. Continuing a traditional Chevy look, the new cars were slightly boxier in appearance but still very pleasing. Styles like the Impala 2-Door Hardtop were quite racy looking. Powertrain choices and the model line were unchanged from 1966. The mid-size Chevelle line received a new frontal treatment, with the grille design no longer wrapping around the front fender edge. The rear styling was cleaned up a bit, too. The only change to the model line was the addition of a top-end Concours 4-Door Station Wagon.

Styling changes for the Corvair, Chevy II and Corvette were limited to trim and detail changes. The Chevy II offered a 250 CID 6-cylinder engine in place of last year's 230 CID 6-cylinder. The Corvair line dropped the top end Corsa performance line and its 140-horsepower powerplant. Finally, the Corvette received minor alterations as it awaited its fresh new replacement for the 1968 model year.

Although Chevrolet's overall production fell 9 percent from 1966, Chevy regained the top sales position this year as Ford's sales dropped more sharply.

Bel Air 4-Door Wagon

Camaro RS/SS 2-Door Convertible,
Indianapolis 500 Pace Car

Camaro 2-Door Hardtop

Caprice 4-Door Hardtop

Chevelle 300 Deluxe 4-Door Sedan

Chevy II 100 4-Door Sedan

Chevelle SS396 2-Door Convertible

Corvair Monza 2-Door Hardtop

Impala SS 2-Door Hardtop

Corvette 2-Door Convertible

**1967**

**Model year production:** 1,948,416, down 9.04% from 1966.
**Domestic market share:** 25.43% (1st place).
**Base price range:** $2,090 to $4,353.
**Industry average base price:** $3,159.
**Chevrolet average base price:** $2,707.
**Introduction date:** September 1966.
**Assembly plants:** Atlanta, GA (A); Baltimore, MD (B); Southgate, CA (C); Flint, MI (F); Framingham, MA (G); Janesville, WI (J); Kansas City, MO (K), Los Angeles, CA (L), Norwood, OH (N); Pontiac, MI (P); Arlington, TX (R); St. Louis, MO (S); Tarrytown, NY (T); Lordstown, OH (U); Willow Run, MI (W); Wilmington, DE (Y); Fremont, CA (Z), Oshawa, Ontario, Canada (1); and St. Therese, Quebec, Canada (2).
**Data plate identification:** Thirteen digit code read as follows: 1st digit 1 for Chevrolet; four digit style number (see listings below) in which 2nd and 3rd digits identify series, 4th and 5th indicate body style; 7 for 1967; 7th digit is assembly plant code; 100001 and up for serial number. Actual beginning serial numbers depend upon series. *Example:* 155117T100001 is a 1967 Chevrolet BelAir 2-Door Sedan, 6-cylinder, serial number 100001, built in Arlington, TX.

## Powertrains

| Engine | Gross HP | Transmission Availability | Corvair/ Chevy II | Camaro | Chevelle | Biscayne/ Bel Air/ Imp. | Caprice | Cor-vette |
|---|---|---|---|---|---|---|---|---|
| 153 CID, 1-bbl., 4-cyl. | 90 | 3-speed manual | S[1] | - | - | - | - | - |
| | | 2-sp. Powerglide Automatic | $164[1] | - | - | - | - | - |
| 164 CID — OHV, 2-bbl., Flat 6 | 95 | 3-speed manual | S (Cor.) | - | - | - | - | - |
| | | 4-speed manual | $90 (Cor.) | - | - | - | - | - |
| | | 2-sp. Powerglide Automatic | $153 (Cor.) | - | - | - | - | - |
| 164 CID Turbo-Air, 2-bbl., Flat 6 | 110 | 3-speed manual | $26 (Cor.) | - | - | - | - | - |
| | | 4-speed manual | $116 (Cor.) | - | - | - | - | - |
| | | 2-sp. Powerglide Automatic | $179 (Cor.) | - | - | - | - | - |
| 164 CID Turbo-Air, 4-bbl., Flat 6 | 140 | 3-speed manual | $79 (Cor.) | - | - | - | - | - |
| | | 4-speed manual | $169 (Cor.) | - | - | - | - | - |
| | | 2-sp. Powerglide Automatic | $232 (Cor.) | - | - | - | - | - |
| 194 CID Turbo-Thrift, 1-bbl., 6-cyl | 120 | 3-speed manual | S (Nova)/$62[1] | - | S[3] | - | - | - |
| | | 2-sp. Powerglide Automatic | $164 (Nova)/$226[1] | - | $164[3] | - | - | - |
| 230 CID Turbo-Thrift, 1-bbl., 6-cyl. | 140 | 3-speed manual | - | S | - | - | - | - |
| | | 4-speed manual | - | $184 | - | - | - | - |
| | | 2-sp. Powerglide Automatic | - | $184 | - | - | - | - |
| 250 CID Turbo-Thrift, 1-bbl., 6-cyl. | 155 | 3-speed manual | $37 (Nova)/$99[1] | - | $26[3] | S | - | - |
| | | Overdrive | - | - | - | $16 | | |
| | | 2-sp. Powerglide Automatic | $201 (Nova)/$263[1] | - | $190[3] | $184 | - | - |
| 283 CID Turbo-Fire, 2-bbl., V8 | 195 | 3-speed manual | $105 (Nova)/$204[1] | - | $94[3] | $105 | S | - |
| | | 4-speed manual | $289 (Nova)/$393[1] | - | $278[3] | $289 | $184 | - |
| | | 2- sp. Powerglide Automatic | $279 (Nova)/$378[1] | - | $289[3] | $300 | $195 | - |
| 302 CID Z28 Opt., 4-bbl., V8 | 290 | 4-speed manual | - | S (Z28) | - | - | - | - |
| 327 CID Turbo-Fire, 2-bbl., V8 | 210 | 3-speed manual | - | $105 | - | - | - | - |
| | | 4-speed manual | - | $289 | - | - | - | - |
| | | 2- sp. Powerglide Automatic | - | $300 | - | - | - | - |
| 327 CID Turbo-Fire, 4-bbl., V8 | 275 300 (Corvette) | 3-speed manual | $198 (SS) | $198 | $198[3] | $198 | $93 | S |
| | | 4-speed manual | $382 (SS) | $382 | $382[3] | $382 | $277 | $184 |
| | | 2- sp. Powerglide Automatic | $372 (SS) | $393 | $396[3] | $393 | $288 | $195 |
| | | Turbo Hydra-matic | - | - | - | $424 | $319 | - |
| 327 CID Turbo-Fire, 4-bbl., V8 | 325 350 — Corvette | 3-speed manual | - | - | $291[3] | - | - | $105 |
| | | 4-speed manual | - | - | $475[3] | - | - | $289 |
| | | 2- sp. Powerglide Automatic | - | - | $489[3] | - | - | $300 |
| 350 CID Turbo-Fire, 4-bbl., V8 | 295 | 3-speed manual | - | $210 (SS) | - | - | - | - |
| | | 4-speed manual | - | $394 (SS) | - | - | - | - |
| | | Turbo Hydra-matic | - | $405 (SS) | - | - | - | - |
| 396 CID Turbo-Jet, 4-bbl., V8 | 325 | 3-speed manual | - | $359 (SS) | S[2] | $263 | $158 | - |
| | | 4-speed manual | - | $554 (SS) | $105[2] | $447 | $342 | - |

| Engine | Gross HP | Transmission Availability | Corvair/ Chevy II | Camaro | Chevelle | Biscayne/ Bel Air/ Imp. | Caprice | Cor- vette |
|---|---|---|---|---|---|---|---|---|
| | | 2- sp. Powerglide Automatic | – | – | – | $458 | $353 | |
| | | Turbo Hydra-matic | – | $581 (SS) | $147[2] | $489 | $384 | – |
| 396 CID Turbo-Jet, 4-bbl., V8 | 375 | 3-speed manual | – | $632 (SS) | $105[2] | – | – | – |
| | | 4-speed manual | – | $827 (SS) | $210[2] | – | – | – |
| | | Turbo Hydra-matic | – | $854 (SS) | $252[2] | – | – | – |
| 427 CID Turbo-Jet, 4-bbl., V8 | 385/ 390 (Corvette) | 3-speed manual | – | – | – | $421 | $316 | $200 |
| | | 4-speed manual | – | – | – | $605 | $500 | $384 |
| | | Turbo Hydra-matic | – | – | – | $647 | $542 | $395 |
| 427 CID Turbo-Jet, 3 × 2-bbl., V8 | 400 | 3-speed manual | – | – | – | – | – | $305 |
| | | 4-speed manual | – | – | – | – | – | $489 |
| | | Turbo Hydra-matic | – | – | – | – | – | $500 |
| 427 CID Turbo-Jet, 3 × 2-bbl., V8 (L89 Aluminum heads add $368) | 435 | 3-speed manual | – | – | – | – | – | $437 |
| | | 4-speed manual | – | – | – | – | – | $621 |
| | | Turbo Hydra-matic | – | – | – | – | – | $632 |

[1]Chevy II 100 only.   [2]SS 396 only.   [3]All but SS 396.

## Major Options

| | Corvair | Chevy II | Camaro | Chevelle | Full-size | Corvette |
|---|---|---|---|---|---|---|
| Air conditioning | $342 | $311 | $356 | $356 | $356 | $413 |
| Heater and defroster | S | S | S | S | S | $98 |
| Soft Ray tinted glass | $31 | $31 | $31 | $31 | $37 | $16 |
| ComforTilt steering wheel | $42 (Telescopic) | – | $42 | $45 | $42 | $42 (Telescopic) |
| Power steering | – | $84 | $84 | $84 | $95 | $95 |
| Power brakes | – | $42 | $42 | $42 | $42 | $42 |
| Power windows (N/A on all) | – | – | $100 | – | $100 | $58 |
| Electric clock | $16 | $16 | $16 | $16 | $16 | S |
| Pushbutton AM radio | $57 | $57 | $57 | $57 | $57 | $ |
| AM/FM radio | $133 | – | $133 | $134 | $134 | $173 |
| Front seat console | – | $ | $ | $ | (incl. w/buckets) | S |
| Front bucket seats | S | $ | S | $111 | $158 | S |
| Vinyl roof | – | – | $74 | $74 | $100 | – |
| Whitewall tires — Std. size | $28 | $31 | $32 | $33 | $32–$40 | $31 |
| SS 350 package | – | – | $105 | – | – | – |
| Rally Sport package | – | – | $105 | – | – | – |

Options common to most models. (– = Not Available; S = Standard equipment.) Items may be standard equipment, optional at different pricing, or unavailable on certain models. This chart is only a guide.

## Paint Colors

| | Code | Corvette | Other Chevrolet models |
|---|---|---|---|
| Tuxedo Black | AA/900 | X | X |
| Ermine White | CC/972 | | X |
| Nantucket Blue Metallic | DD | | X |
| Deepwater Blue Met. | EE | | X |
| Marina Blue Met. | FF | | X |
| Granada Gold Met. | GG | | X |
| Mountain Green Met. | HH | | X |
| Emerald Turquoise Met. | KK | | X |
| Tahoe Turquoise Met. | LL | | X |
| Royal Plum Metallic | MM | | X |

1967

| | Code | Corvette | Other Chevrolet models |
|---|---|---|---|
| Madeira Maroon Met. | NN | | X |
| Bolero Red | RR | | X |
| Sierra Fawn Metallic | SS | | X |
| Capri Cream | TT | | X |
| Butternut Yellow | YY | | X |
| Rallye Red | 974 | X | |
| Marina Blue Metallic | 976 | X | |
| Lynndale Blue Met. | 977 | X | |
| Goodwood Green Met. | 983 | X | |
| Sunfire Yellow | 984 | X | |
| Silver Pearl Metallic | 986 | X | |
| Marlboro Maroon Met. | 988 | X | |

# Corvair

*"The all-time popular Corvair … continues to put out
rear-engine driving fun by the buckets."*

**Nameplate year of origin:** 1960.
**Current bodystyle lifespan:** 1965 through 1969.
**Predecessor to this model:** Corvair (1960 to 1964).
**Replacement for this model:** Vega (1971 to 1977).
**Percentage of division's sales volume:** 1.40%.
**Corporate siblings:** None.
**Primary competition:** AMC Rambler American, Ford Falcon and Plymouth Valiant.
**Notable changes:** Minor trim and detail changes.
**Major standard equipment:** Cloth and vinyl front bench seat, dual sun visors, center dome light, and 7.00 × 13 BSW tires. Monza adds: All-vinyl bucket seats, full carpeting, folding rear seat, glove box light, front door map pockets, and additional exterior chrome trim.

## Measurements

| | |
|---|---|
| Wheelbase | 108.0" |
| Length | 183.3" |
| Width | 69.7" |
| Height | 51.2" |
| Legroom — front | 41.1" |
| Legroom — rear | 35.4" |
| Headroom — front | 37.6" |
| Headroom — rear | 36.4" |
| Cargo capacity (cu. ft.) | 7.0 |
| Fuel capacity (gals.) | 14.0 |

## Models Available

| | Style Number | Base MSRP | Change from LY | Shipping Wt. (lbs.) | Production | Change from LY |
|---|---|---|---|---|---|---|
| Corvair 500 2-Door HT Sport Coupe | 10137 | $2,128 | +2.16% | 2435 | 9,257 | -61.50% |
| Corvair 500 4-Door HT Sport Sedan | 10139 | $2,194 | +1.72% | 2470 | 2,959 | -66.29% |
| Corvair Monza 2-Door HT Sport Cpe, | 10537 | $2,398 | +2.04% | 2465 | 9,771 | -74.02% |
| Corvair Monza 2-Door Convertible | 10567 | $2,540 | +1.89% | 2695 | 2,109 | -79.61% |
| Corvair Monza 4-Door HT Sport Sdn. | 10539 | $2,464 | +1.65% | 2515 | 3,157 | -74.74% |
| TOTALS | | *Avg. price* $2,345 | -1.64% | | *Production* 27,253 | -73.73% |

# Chevy II

*"It's designed to keep upkeep down and make you look good at the same time."*

**Nameplate year of origin:** 1962.
**Current bodystyle lifespan:** 1966 through 1967.
**Predecessor to this model:** Chevy II (1962 to 1965).
**Replacement for this model:** Chevy II/Nova (1968 through 1972).

## Measurements

| | Cars | Wagons |
|---|---|---|
| Wheelbase | 110.0" | 110.0" |

|  | Cars | Wagons |
|---|---|---|
| Length | 183.0" | 187.4" |
| Width | 71.3" | 71.3" |
| Height | 55.3" | 55.7" |
| Legroom — front | 40.7" | 40.7" |
| Legroom — rear | 36.2" | 36.2" |
| Headroom — front | 38.8" | 38.8" |
| Headroom — rear | 37.3" | 37.3" |
| Cargo capacity (cu. ft.) | 13.0 | 76.2 |
| Fuel capacity (gals.) | 16.0 | 16.0 |

**Percentage of division's sales volume:** 5.47%.
**Corporate siblings:** None.
**Primary competition:** AMC Rambler American, Dodge Dart, Ford Falcon, and Plymouth Valiant.
**Notable changes:** Minor trim and detail changes.
**Major standard equipment:** Cloth and vinyl front bench seat (All vinyl in wagons), black rubber floor mats, 2-speed windshield wipers with washers, and 6.95 × 14 BSW tires. Nova adds: Deluxe steering wheel, full carpeting, courtesy and glove box lights, and additional exterior chrome trim. SS adds: All vinyl seats, electric clock, and SS trim.

## Models Available

| | Style Number | Base MSRP | Change from LY | Shipping Wt. (lbs.) | Production | Change from LY |
|---|---|---|---|---|---|---|
| Chevy II 100 2-Door Coupe | 11111 | $2,090 | +3.06% | 2555 | 48,800 | * |
| Chevy II 100 4-Door Sedan | 11169 | $2,120 | +2.66% | 2560 | * | * |
| Chevy II 100 4-Door Wagon | 11335 | $2,478 | +1.98% | 2865 | * | * |
| Chevy II Nova 2-Door Hardtop | 11537 | $2,330 | +2.60% | 2660 | 47,600 | * |
| Chevy II Nova 4-Door Sedan | 11569 | $2,298 | +2.36% | 2660 | * | * |
| Chevy II Nova 4-Door Wagon | 11535 | $2,566 | +1.91% | 2890 | * | * |
| Chevy II Nova SS 2-Door HT | 11737 | $2,487 | +2.35% | 2690 | 10,100 | * |
| TOTALS | Avg. price | $2,338 | +2.36% | Production | 106,500 | -18.71% |

*Production is estimated and not available by series, only body style totals.*

# Camaro

*"Wide stance stability and big-car power keynote this exciting new road machine from Chevrolet."*

**1967**

## Measurements

| | |
|---|---|
| Wheelbase | 108.0" |
| Length | 184.7" |
| Width | 72.5" |
| Height | 51.0" |
| Legroom — front | 42.5" |
| Legroom — rear | 29.9" |
| Headroom — front | 37.7" |
| Headroom — rear | 36.7" |
| Cargo capacity (cu. ft.) | 8.3 |
| Fuel capacity (gals.) | 18.5 |

**Nameplate year of origin:** 1967.
**Current bodystyle lifespan:** 1967 through 1969.
**Predecessor to this model:** None.
**Replacement for this model:** Camaro (1970 to 1981).
**Percentage of division's sales volume:** 11.34%.
**Corporate siblings:** Pontiac Firebird.
**Primary competition:** Ford Mustang and Plymouth Barracuda.
**Notable changes:** All-new model for 1967.
**Major standard equipment:** All-vinyl bucket seats, full carpeting, front arm rests, dome and courtesy lights, windshield molding, hubcaps, and 7.35 × 14 BSW tires. RS package adds: Style trim package, parking lamps below front bumper and back-up lamps below rear bumper, concealed headlamps, rocker molding trim, and specific RS trim. SS 350 package adds: 350 CID V8 engine, specific hood with simulated air intakes, hood stripes, SS emblems, and D70 × 14 redline or WSW tires.

## Models Available

| | Style Number | Base MSRP | Change from LY | Shipping Wt. (lbs.) | Production | Change from LY |
|---|---|---|---|---|---|---|
| Camaro 2-Door Sport Coupe | 12337 | $2,466 | NEW | 2770 | 195,776 | NEW |
| Camaro 2-Door Convertible | 12367 | $2,704 | NEW | 3025 | 25,141 | NEW |
| TOTALS | Avg. price | $2,585 | NEW | Production | 220,917 | NEW |

# Chevelle

*"The quick-size Chevelle. Maneuvers like magic."*

**Nameplate year of origin:** 1964.
**Current bodystyle lifespan:** 1966 through 1967.
**Predecessor to this model:** Chevelle (1964 to 1965).
**Replacement for this model:** Chevelle (1968 to 1972).
**Corporate siblings:** Buick Special/Skylark, Oldsmobile F-85/Cutlass, Pontiac Tempest/LeMans.
**Percentage of division's sales volume:** 18.94%.
**Primary competition:** AMC Rebel, Dodge Coronet, Ford Fairlane, and Plymouth Belvedere/Satellite.
**Notable changes:** Revised grille, trim and detail changes.
**Major standard equipment:** Cloth and vinyl front bench seat, black rubber floor mats, hubcaps, and 6.95 × 14 BSW tires (7.35 × 14 BSW tires on wagons). 300 Deluxe adds: All-vinyl interior trim for wagon, color-keyed floor mats and additional exterior trim. Malibu adds: Color-keyed deep-twist carpeting, full wheel covers, electric clock and dual sun visors. SS 396 adds: All-vinyl bucket seats, console, special instrumentation, 396 CID V8 engine, and SS trim and wheel covers.

## Measurements

|  | Cars | Wagons |
|---|---|---|
| Wheelbase | 115.0" | 115.0" |
| Length | 197.0" | 199.9" |
| Width | 75.0" | 75.0" |
| Height | 53.0" | 54.6" |
| Legroom — front | 41.9" | 41.9" |
| Legroom — rear | 36.0" | 36.0" |
| Headroom — front | 38.5" | 38.5" |
| Headroom — rear | 37.3" | 37.3" |
| Cargo capacity (cu. ft.) | 17.1 | 86.0 |
| Fuel capacity (gals.) | 20.0 | 20.0 |

## Models Available

|  | Style Number | Base MSRP | Change from LY | Shipping Wt. (lbs.) | Production | Change from LY |
|---|---|---|---|---|---|---|
| Chevelle 300 2-Door Coupe | 13111 | $2,221 | +2.59% | 2935 | 24,700 | * |
| Chevelle 300 4-Door Sedan | 13169 | $2,250 | +2.18% | 2955 | * | * |
| Chevelle 300 Deluxe 2-Door Coupe | 13311 | $2,295 | +2.50% | 2955 | 26,300 | * |
| Chevelle 300 Deluxe 4-Door Sedan | 13369 | $2,324 | +2.11% | 2980 | * | * |
| Chevelle 300 Deluxe 4-Dr. Wagon | 13335 | $2,619 | +1.71% | 3230 | * | * |
| Chevelle Malibu 2-Door Hardtop | 13517 | $2,434 | +2.35% | 2980 | 227,800 | * |
| Chevelle Malibu 2-Dr. Convertible | 13567 | $2,637 | +1.89% | 3050 | * | * |
| Chevelle Malibu 4-Door Sedan | 13569 | $2,400 | +2.04% | 3000 | * | * |
| Chevelle Malibu 4-Door Hardtop | 13539 | $2,506 | +1.95% | 3065 | * | * |
| Chevelle Malibu 4-Door Wagon | 13535 | $2,695 | +1.66% | 3260 | 27,300 | * |
| Chevelle SS396 2-Door Hardtop | 13817 | $2,825 | +1.77% | 3415 | 63,006 | * |
| Chevelle SS396 2-Dr. Convertible | 13867 | $3,033 | +1.64% | 3495 | * | * |
| Chevelle Concours 4-Door Wagon | 13735 | $2,827 | NEW | 3270 | * | NEW |
| TOTALS | | Avg. price $2,544 | +3.00% | | Production 369,106 | -2.84% |

*Production is estimated and not available by series, only body style totals.*

# Chevrolet Full-size

*"Step in and enjoy that sure feeling!"*

**Nameplate year of origin:** 1950 (BelAir); 1958 (Biscayne, Impala); 1699 (Caprice)
**Current bodystyle lifespan:** 1967 through 1968.
**Predecessor to this model:** Full-size Chevrolet (1965 to 1966).
**Replacement for this model:** Biscayne/BelAir/Impala/Caprice (1969 to 1970).
**Percentage of division's sales volume:** 61.68%.
**Corporate siblings:** Buick LeSabre/Wildcat, Olds 88, Pontiac Catalina/Bonneville.

## Measurements

|  | Cars | Wagons |
|---|---|---|
| Wheelbase | 119.0" | 119.0" |
| Length | 212.4" | 213.2" |
| Width | 79.9" | 79.9" |
| Height | 55.4" | 56.7" |
| Legroom — front | 42.2" | 42.2" |

**Primary competition:** AMC Ambassador, Dodge Polara, Ford
  Custom/Galaxie/LTD, and Plymouth Fury.
**Notable changes:** Completely redesigned.
**Major standard equipment:** Biscayne: Cloth and vinyl bench seat, full carpeting, front and rear door armrests, 2-speed electric windshield wipers with
  washers, and 8.25 × 14 BSW tires (8.55 × 14 BSW tires on wagons). BelAir
  adds: Automatic interior lighting, bright body side molding, and power tailgate window on 3-Seat wagon models. Impala adds: Vinyl upholstery in convertible, extra-long armrests, electric clock, and trunk lamp. SS adds: All
  vinyl bucket seats, center floor console, and special SS wheel covers, body
  and interior trim. Caprice adds: Specific cloth and vinyl front bench seats
  (with center fold-down armrest on sedan), all-vinyl upholstery in wagons,
  simulated walnut interior trim, dual pinstriping, deluxe wheel covers, rocker
  panel moldings, simulated walnut exterior trim on wagons, and special ornamentation.

|  | Cars | Wagons |
|---|---|---|
| Legroom — rear | 39.5" | 39.5" |
| Headroom — front | 39.1" | 39.1" |
| Headroom — rear | 37.7" | 37.7" |
| Cargo capacity (cu. ft.) | 18.3 | 106.1 |
| Fuel capacity (gals.) | 24.0 | 24.0 |

## Models Available

| | Style Number | Base MSRP | Change from LY | Shipping Wt. (lbs.) | Production | Change from LY |
|---|---|---|---|---|---|---|
| Biscayne 2-Door Sedan | 15311 | $2,442 | +2.65% | 3335 | 92,800 | * |
| Biscayne 4-Door Sedan | 15369 | $2,484 | +2.18% | 3395 | * | * |
| Biscayne 4-Dr., 2-S. Wagon | 15335 | $2,817 | +1.62% | 3765 | * | * |
| Bel Air 2-Door Sedan | 15511 | $2,542 | +2.54% | 3340 | 179,700 | * |
| Bel Air 4-Door Sedan | 15569 | $2,584 | +2.09% | 3410 | * | * |
| BelAir 4-Dr., 2-S. Wagon | 15535 | $2,881 | +1.62% | 3770 | * | * |
| BelAir 4-Dr., 3-S. Wagon | 15545 | $2,993 | +1.53% | 3825 | * | * |
| Impala 2-Door Sport Coupe | 16387 | $2,740 | +2.09% | 3475 | 575,600 | * |
| Impala 2-Door Convertible | 16367 | $2,991 | +1.91% | 3515 | * | * |
| Impala 4-Door Sedan | 16369 | $2,723 | +1.68% | 3455 | * | * |
| Impala 4-Door Hardtop | 16339 | $2,793 | +1.67% | 3540 | * | * |
| Impala 4-Dr., 2-S. Wagon | 16335 | $3,016 | +1.51% | 3805 | 155,100 | * |
| Impala 4-Dr., 3-S. Wagon | 16345 | $3,129 | +1.49% | 3860 | * | * |
| Impala SS 2-Door Sport Coupe | 16787 | $2,898 | +1.97% | 3500 | 74,000 | * |
| Impala SS 2-Door Convertible | 16767 | $3,149 | +1.81% | 3535 | * | * |
| Caprice 2-Door Hardtop | 16647 | $3,078 | +2.60% | 3605 | 124,500 | * |
| Caprice 4-Door Hardtop | 16639 | $3,130 | +2.19% | 3710 | * | * |
| Caprice 4-Dr., 2-S. Wagon | 16635 | $3,301 | +2.07% | 3935 | * | * |
| Caprice 4-Dr., 3-S. Wagon | 16645 | $3,413 | +1.97% | 3990 | * | * |
| TOTALS | | *Avg. price* $2,900 | +1.93% | | *Production* 1,201,700 | -19.87% |

*Production is estimated and not available by series, only body style totals.*

# Corvette

*"Individual. Personal. Luxurious. Energetic. Tenacious."*

**Nameplate year of origin:** 1953 (also used on showcar of same year).
**Current bodystyle lifespan:** 1963 through 1967.
**Predecessor to this model:** Corvette (1956 to 1962).
**Replacement for this model:** Corvette (1968 to 1982).
**Percentage of division's sales volume:** 1.18%.
**Corporate siblings:** None.
**Primary competition:** None.
**Notable changes:** Minor trim and detail changes.
**Major standard equipment:** Bucket seats, cockpit-cluster console, simulated
  walnut steering wheel, full carpeting, complete instrumentation, manually op-
  erated folding convertible top, and 7.75 × 14 BSW tires.

## Measurements

| | |
|---|---|
| Wheelbase | 98.0" |
| Length | 175.1" |
| Width | 69.6" |
| Height | 49.6" |
| Legroom — front | 42.7" |
| Legroom — rear | NA |
| Headroom — front | 37.0" |
| Headroom — rear | NA |
| Cargo capacity (cu. ft.) | 10.6 |
| Fuel capacity (gals.) | 20.0 |

1967

## Models Available

| | Style Number | Base MSRP | Change from LY | Shipping Wt. (lbs.) | Production | Change from LY |
|---|---|---|---|---|---|---|
| Corvette 2-Door Coupe | 19437 | $4,353 | +1.35% | 3000 | 8,504 | -14.60% |
| Corvette 2-Door Convertible | 19467 | $4,141 | +1.40% | 3020 | 14,436 | -18.73% |
| TOTALS | Avg. price | $4,247 | +1.36% | | Production 22,940 | -17.24% |

# CHRYSLER

*"Take charge ... Move up to Chrysler '67."*

The entire Chrysler line received a styling makeover for the '67 season. Fenders that swept forward past the grille and rear quarters that extended rearward beyond the trunk line were the first noticeable signs of the new styling. Body side panels were concave between the belt line and a lower body feature line. Two-Door Hardtop models used the sweeping "semi-fastback" styled roofline shared by Dodge and Plymouth. Powertrains continued as in 1966. The 6-window Town Sedan was discontinued in all lines. A new Newport Custom line was added as an intermediate step between the Newport and 300 lines. Essentially, the Custom added nicer interior trim as its big selling point.

The Town & Country wagon models were offered only in the Newport line once again, but the equipment varies significantly enough that they are listed separately under the powertrain and optional equipment categories below, as well as being listed as a separate model line. Most reference sources were listing the Town & Country as a separate line by 1966 because the Newport name was dropped from the car itself, but it was not officially taken out of the Newport line until 1969.

300 2-Door Convertible

Newport 4-Door Hardtop

Newport Custom 2-Door Hardtop

New Yorker 4-Door Hardtop

Town & Country 4-Door Wagon

**Model year production:** 218,742, down 16.67% from 1966.
**Domestic market share:** 2.85% (10th place).
**Base price range:** $3,159 to $4,339.
**Industry average base price:** $3,159.
**Chrysler average base price:** $3,803.

**Introduction date:** September 29, 1966.
**Assembly plants:** Newark, DE (6), and Detroit, MI (3).
**Data plate identification:** Thirteen digit code read as follows: Four digit style number (see listings below) in which C = Chrysler, 2nd number identifies series (e.g., H is for New

| Yorker), 3rd and 4th indicate body style; 5th digit is engine code; 7 for 1967; assembly plant code; 100001 and up for serial number. *Example:* CH23K73100001 is a 1967 | Chrysler New Yorker 2-Door Hardtop with a 440 CID V8 engine, serial number 100001, built in Detroit, MI. |
|---|---|

## Powertrains

| Engine | Engine Code | Gross HP | Transmission Availability | Newport | Town & Country | 300 | New Yorker |
|---|---|---|---|---|---|---|---|
| 383 CID, 2-bbl., V8 | G | 270 | 3-speed man. | S | - | - | - |
|  |  |  | TorqueFlite Automatic | $222 | S | - | - |
| 383 CID, 4-bbl., V8 | H | 325 | 3-speed man. | $35 | - | - | - |
|  |  |  | TorqueFlite Automatic | $257 | $35 | - | - |
| 440 CID, 4-bbl., V8 | K | 350 | TorqueFlite Automatic | - | - | S | S |
|  |  |  | 4-speed man. | - | - | $* | - |
| 440 CID TNT, 4-bbl., V8 | L | 375 | TorqueFlite Automatic | $420 | $164 | $79 | $79 |

*Offered only in hardtop models. Pricing not available.*

## Major Options

| | Newport | Town & Country | 300 | New Yorker |
|---|---|---|---|---|
| Air conditioning | $406 | $406 | $406 | $406 |
| Auto Pilot cruise control | $84 | $84 | $84 | $84 |
| Tinted glass | $42 | $42 | $42 | $42 |
| Deck lid remote release | $11 | - | $11 | $11 |
| Power steering | $107 | S | $107 | S |
| Power brakes | $47 | S | $47 | S |
| Power door locks | $37–$55 | $55 | $37–$55 | $37–$55 |
| Power 6-way bench seat/ |  |  |  |  |
| Bucket on 300 | $100 | $100 | $183 | $100 |
| Power windows | $106 | $106 | $106 | $106 |
| Electric clock | $19 | $19 | $19 | S |
| Golden Tone AM radio | $91 | $91 | $91 | $91 |
| Golden Tone AM/ |  |  |  |  |
| FM radio | $154 | $154 | $154 | $154 |

Options common to most models. (- = Not Available; S = Standard equipment.) Items may be standard equipment, optional at different pricing, or unavailable on certain models. This chart is only a guide.

## Paint Colors

| | Code |
|---|---|
| Charcoal Gray Metallic | 55-1 |
| Mauve Mist Metallic | 66-1 |
| Mediterranean Blue Metallic | 88-1 |
| Silver Mist Metallic | AA-1 |
| Formal Black | BB-1 |
| Arctic Blue Metallic | CC-1 |
| Crystal Blue Metallic | DD-1 |
| Regal Blue Metallic | EE-1 |
| Mint Green Metallic | FF-1 |
| Pine Green Metallic | GG-1 |
| Mahogany Metallic | JJ-1 |
| Mist Turquoise Metallic | KK-1 |
| Twilight Turquoise Metallic | LL-1 |
| Turbine Bronze Metallic | MM-1 |
| Scorch Red | PP-1 |
| Ruby Red Metallic | QQ-1 |
| Daffodil Yellow | RR-1 |
| Ivory | SS-1 |
| Persian White | WW-1 |
| Sandalwood | XX-1 |
| Desert Dune Metallic | YY-1 |
| Spice Gold Metallic | ZZ-1 |

1967

# Newport

*"The more-car-for-your-money car."*

**Nameplate year of origin:** 1950 (as HT model of the T & C); 1961 (as series).
**Current bodystyle lifespan:** 1965 through 1968 (restyled in 1967).
**Predecessor to this model:** Newport (1963 to 1964).
**Replacement for this model:** Newport (1969 to 1973).
**Percentage of division's sales volume:** 65.23%.
**Corporate siblings:** Chrysler 300 and New Yorker.

## Measurements

| | |
|---|---|
| Wheelbase | 124.0" |
| Length | 219.3" |
| Width | 78.7" |
| Height | 56.4" |
| Legroom — front | 42.0" |

**Primary competition:** Buick LeSabre, Mercury Monterey, and Oldsmobile Delta 88.
**Notable changes:** Major restyle to front, rear, body sides and roofline.
**Major standard equipment:** Cloth and vinyl front bench seat, deep-pile carpeting, exterior bright side moldings, 3-speed windshield wipers w/washers, trip odometer, remote-control outside LH rear view mirror, rear wheel opening fender skirts, and 8.25 × 14 BSW tires. Custom adds: Jacquard fabric and Cologne vinyl front bench seat with fold-down arm rest, vinyl-covered trunk lift handles, and specific exterior trim.

## Measurements (cont.)

| | |
|---|---|
| Legroom — rear | 36.2" |
| Headroom — front | 37.9" |
| Headroom — rear | 38.0" |
| Cargo capacity (cu. ft.) | 17.4 |
| Fuel capacity (gals.) | 25.0 |

## Models Available

| | Style Number | Base MSRP | Change from LY | Shipping Wt. (lbs.) | Production | Change from LY |
|---|---|---|---|---|---|---|
| Newport 2-Door Hardtop | CE23 | $3,219 | +3.44% | 3845 | 26,583 | -29.34% |
| Newport 2-Door Convertible | CE27 | $3,583 | +3.08% | 3915 | 2,891 | -6.29% |
| Newport 4-Door Sedan | CE41 | $3,159 | +3.51% | 3880 | 48,945 | -34.71% |
| Newport 4-Door Hardtop | CE43 | $3,296 | +3.32% | 3900 | 14,247 | -42.93% |
| Newport Custom 2-Door Hardtop | CL23 | $3,407 | NEW | 3875 | 14,193 | NEW |
| Newport Custom 4-Door Sedan | CL41 | $3,347 | NEW | 3915 | 23,101 | NEW |
| Newport Custom 4-Door Hardtop | CL43 | $3,485 | NEW | 3935 | 12,728 | NEW |
| TOTALS | | Avg. price $3,357 | +4.81% | | Production 142,688 | -4.92% |

# 300

*"If they built sports cars big, they'd look like this."*

**Nameplate year of origin:** 1955 (letter series cars); 1962 (standard line cars).
**Current bodystyle lifespan:** 1965 through 1968.
**Predecessor to this model:** 300 (1963 to 1964).
**Replacement for this model:** 300 (1969 to 1971).
**Percentage of division's sales volume:** 10.00%.
**Corporate siblings:** Chrysler Newport and New Yorker.
**Primary competition:** Buick Wildcat, Mercury Montclair and Pontiac Bonneville.
**Notable changes:** Major restyle to front, rear, body sides and roofline.
**Major standard equipment:** All-vinyl bucket seats, deep-pile carpeting, 3-speed windshield wipers with washers, electric clock, trip odometer, exterior side moldings, full wheel covers, rear wheel opening fender skirts, automatic transmission, deluxe wheel covers, and 8.55 × 14 BSW tires.

## Measurements

| | |
|---|---|
| Wheelbase | 124.0" |
| Length | 223.4" |
| Width | 78.7" |
| Height | 56.1" |
| Legroom — front | 42.0" |
| Legroom — rear | 34.8" |
| Headroom — front | 37.9" |
| Headroom — rear | 38.1" |
| Cargo capacity (cu. ft.) | 17.4 |
| Fuel capacity (gals.) | 25.0 |

## Models Available

| | Style Number | Base MSRP | Change from LY | Shipping Wt. (lbs.) | Production | Change from LY |
|---|---|---|---|---|---|---|
| 300 2-Door Hardtop | CM23 | $3,936 | +9.85% | 3980 | 11,556 | -52.06% |
| 300 2-Door Convertible | CM27 | $4,289 | +8.97% | 4045 | 1,594 | -36.24% |
| 300 4-Door Hardtop | CM43 | $4,012 | +9.65% | 4035 | 8,744 | -57.64% |
| TOTALS | | Avg. price $4,079 | +9.47% | | Production 21,894 | -53.66% |

# Town & Country

*"Unless you look back, you forget you're riding in a wagon."*

**Nameplate year of origin:** 1941.
**Current bodystyle lifespan:** 1965 through 1968 (restyled in 1967).
**Predecessor to this model:** Town & Country (1963 to 1964).
**Replacement for this model:** Town & Country (1969 to 1973).
**Percentage of division's sales volume:** 6.72%.
**Corporate siblings:** Dodge Monaco/Polara, and Plymouth Fury Suburban.
**Primary competition:** Mercury Colony Park.
**Notable changes:** Major restyle to front, rear, body sides and roofline.
**Major standard equipment:** All-vinyl front bench seat with folding center armrest, simulated walnut instrument panel trim, carpeted lower door trim and load floor, 3-speed windshield wipers with washers, map and courtesy lights, electric clock, remote-control LH outside rear view mirror and RH outside mirror, lockable luggage compartment, power operated tailgate window, Torqueflite Automatic transmission, power steering, power front disc brakes, full wheel covers, and 8.85 × 14 BSW tires.

## Measurements

| | |
|---|---|
| Wheelbase | 121.0" |
| Length | 219.5" |
| Width | 78.7" |
| Height | 57.5" |
| Legroom — front | 42.0" |
| Legroom — rear | 36.0" |
| Headroom — front | 37.9" |
| Headroom — rear | 38.0" |
| Cargo capacity (cu. ft.) | 107.0 |
| Fuel capacity (gals.) | 22.0 |

## Models Available

| | Style Number | Base MSRP | Change from LY | Shipping Wt. (lbs.) | Production | Change from LY |
|---|---|---|---|---|---|---|
| Town & Country 4-Dr., 2-S. Wagon | CE45 | $4,195 | +2.67% | 4495 | 7,183 | -20.50% |
| Town & Country 4-Dr., 3-S. Wagon | CE46 | $4,299 | +2.55% | 4550 | 7,520 | -12.22% |
| TOTALS | | *Avg. price* $4,247 | +2.61% | | *Production* 14,703 | -16.47% |

# New Yorker

*"This year — this is the one the others have to live up to."*

**Nameplate year of origin:** 1939.
**Current bodystyle lifespan:** 1965 through 1968 (restyled in 1967).
**Predecessor to this model:** New Yorker (1963 to 1964).
**Replacement for this model:** New Yorker (1969 to 1973).
**Percentage of division's sales volume:** 18.04%.
**Corporate siblings:** Chrysler Newport and 300.
**Primary competition:** Buick Electra 225, Cadillac Calais, and Oldsmobile Ninety-Eight.
**Notable changes:** Major restyle to front, rear, body sides and roofline.
**Major standard equipment:** Cloth and vinyl front bench seat with pull-down center arm rests front and rear, deep-pile carpeting, deluxe steering wheel, map lights, trip odometer, electric clock, carpeted trunk with trunk light, exclusive exterior bright trim, power steering, power brakes, automatic transmission, deluxe wheel covers, rear wheel opening fender skirts, and 8.55 × 14 BSW tires.

## Measurements

| | |
|---|---|
| Wheelbase | 124.0" |
| Length | 219.3" |
| Width | 78.7" |
| Height | 55.9" |
| Legroom — front | 42.0" |
| Legroom — rear | 40.8" |
| Headroom — front | 38.5" |
| Headroom — rear | 37.3" |
| Cargo capacity (cu. ft.) | 17.4 |
| Fuel capacity (gals.) | 25.0 |

## Models Available

| | Style Number | Base MSRP | Change from LY | Shipping Wt. (lbs.) | Production | Change from LY |
|---|---|---|---|---|---|---|
| New Yorker 2-Door Hardtop | CH23 | $4,264 | +2.57% | 4045 | 6,885 | -13.45% |

**1967**

| | Style Number | Base MSRP | Change from LY | Shipping Wt. (lbs.) | Production | Change from LY |
|---|---|---|---|---|---|---|
| New Yorker 4-Door Sedan | CH41 | $4,208 | +2.61% | 4080 | 10,907 | -16.26% |
| New Yorker 4-Door Hardtop | CH43 | $4,339 | +2.50% | 4105 | 21,665 | -18.55% |
| TOTALS | | *Avg. price* $4,270 | +2.55% | | *Production* 39,457 | -17.07% |

# DODGE

*"Dodge Rebellion—Operation '67—We want you!"*

The "Dodge Boys," as they were now known, caused another stir with the introduction of their all-new full-size line and the first totally new Dart since its introduction in 1963. The Dart and its slightly smaller sister car, the Plymouth Valiant, were restyled along the same lines as last year's mid-size line, meaning a more angular body with simple character lines and grille designs. The delta shaped taillamps that were becoming a Dodge trademark were present. Also part of the Dodge package were sportier models, and the Dart did not disappoint there either. New GT models were offered in 2-Door Hardtop and Convertible models. These new sport models were offered with powerplants up to the small-block V8's, but more power would arrive for 1968 in the form of the new 340 CID V8. The Dart wagons were no longer offered, as sales in the small wagon market had been slowly eroding over the past few years.

The new full-size line was given more definition and sculpting in the form of exaggerated "Coke-bottle" side styling, and the delta shaped taillamps were enlarged and then mimicked at the front end in the grille shape and outlining. The new cars were quite attractive, especially in Monaco trim. Among the model line changes was the addition of the Polara 500 sport package as a regular model, as opposed to a production option. Also, the base Polara 318 added 2- and 4-Door Hardtop variations.

The popular mid-size line underwent minor changes, mostly in the form of revised grilles, taillamps, and trim pieces. Two model line changes were made at each end of the price spectrum. The base Coronet line changed from a two model, 2-Door and 4-Door Sedan line to a strictly 4-Door station wagon line. At the top end, as a belated GTO competitor, a new R/T (Road and Track) 2-Door Hardtop and Convertible were welcome additions to the Coronet line. This was the first of a long line of R/T models to come, and each featured the requisite powerful V8 engine, good (for the time) handling, and comfortable, yet sporting accommodations.

Charger 2-Door Hardtop

Coronet 440 4-Door Wagon

Coronet R/T 2-Door Hardtop

Dart GT 2-Door Hardtop

Monaco 4-Door Wagon

Monaco 500 2-Door Hardtop

Polara 500 2-Door Hardtop

**Model year production:** 410,088, down 24.57% from 1966.
**Domestic market share:** 5.35% (7th place).
**Base price range:** $2,187 to $3,712.
**Industry average base price:** $3,159.
**Dodge average base price:** $2,908.
**Introduction date:** September 29, 1966.
**Assembly plants:** Lynch Road, MI (1); Hamtramck, MI (2); Detroit (Jefferson Ave.), MI (3); Belvidere, IL (4); Los Angeles, CA (5); Newark, DE (6); St. Louis, MO (7) and Windsor, Ontario, Canada (9).
**Data plate identification:** Thirteen digit code read as follows:

Four digit style number (see listings below) in which 1st digit is series letter (e.g., D = Polara/Monaco series), 2nd number identifies car model (e.g., L is for Low-line base Polara, H for High-line Monaco, etc.), 3rd and 4th digits are body style (see charts below); 5th digit is engine code (see chart below); 6th digit 7 for 1967; 7th digit is the assembly plant code; followed by 100001 (500001 for Dart) and up for serial number. *Example:* DL23G73100001 is a 1967 Dodge Polara 2-Door Hardtop with a 383 CID V8, serial number 100001, built in Detroit, MI.

**1967**

## Powertrains

| Engine | Gross HP | Engine Code | Transmission Availability | Dart | Coronet | Charger | Polara & Monaco* |
|---|---|---|---|---|---|---|---|
| 170 CID, 1-bbl., 6-cyl. | 101 | A | 3-speed manual | S | - | - | - |
| | | | Torqueflite automatic | $140 | - | - | - |
| 225 CID, 1-bbl., 6-cyl. | 145 | B | 3-speed manual | $38 | S (Ex. R/T) | - | - |
| | | | 4-speed manual | $183 | $145 (Ex. R/T) | - | - |
| | | | Torqueflite automatic | $177 | $153 (Ex. R/T) | - | - |
| 273 CID, 2-bbl., V8 | 180 | D | 3-speed manual | $79 | $94 (Ex. R/T) | - | - |
| | | | 4-speed manual | $224 | $269 (Ex. R/T) | - | - |
| | | | Torqueflite automatic | $226 | $257 (Ex. R/T) | - | - |
| 318 CID, 2-bbl., V8 | 230 | F | 3-speed manual | - | $119 (Ex. R/T) | S | S[1] |
| | | | Torqueflite automatic | - | $330 (Ex. R/T) | $176 | $176[1] |
| 383 CID, 2-bbl., V8 | 270 | G | 3-speed manual | - | $118 (Ex. R/T) | $56 | S[2] |
| | | | 4-speed manual | - | $293 (Ex. R/T) | $231 | $175[2] |
| | | | Torqueflite automatic | - | $294 (Ex. R/T) | $232 | $176[2] |
| 383 CID, 4-bbl., V8 | 325 | H | 3-speed manual | - | $175 (Ex. R/T) | $97 | $28[2] |
| | | | 4-speed manual | - | $350 (Ex. R/T) | $172 | $203[2] |
| | | | Torqueflite automatic | - | $351 (Ex. R/T) | $173 | $204[2] |
| 426 CID Hemi-Charger, 4-bbl., V8 | 415 | J | 4-sp. Man. Or Auto. | - | $457 (R/T) | $712 | * |

| Engine | Gross HP | Engine Code | Transmission Availability | Dart | Coronet | Charger | Polara & Monaco* |
|---|---|---|---|---|---|---|---|
| 426 CID Hemi-Charger, 2 × 4-bbl., V8 | 425 | M | 4-sp. Man. Or Auto. | - | * | * | * |
| 440 CID, 4-bbl., V8 | 365 | K | 4-speed manual | - | S (R/T) | - | $245–$273 |
| | | | Torqueflite automatic | - | S (R/T) | - | $245–$273 |
| 440 CID Magnum****, 4-bbl., V8 | 375 | L | Torqueflite automatic | - | $69 (R/T) | - | $309 |

*Polara 318 only.*   *²All but Polara 381.*   *Accurate pricing information currently unavailable.*   **Monaco 500 standard with 4-speed manual or Torqueflite automatic transmission; deduct $175 from optional powertrain pricing.*   ***NA on wagons.*

## Major Options

| | Dart | Coronet | Charger | Polara | Monaco |
|---|---|---|---|---|---|
| Airtemp air conditioning | $274 | $274 | $274 | $311 | $311 |
| Tinted glass | $22 | $30 | $30 | $31 | $31 |
| Auto Pilot cruise control | - | $64 | $64 | $64 | $64 |
| Power steering | $65 | $73 | $73 | $73 | $73 |
| Power brakes w/front discs | $54 | $54 | $54 | $54 | $54 |
| Power seat | - | $74 | $74 | $61 | $61 |
| Power windows | - | $102 | $102 | $102 | $102 |
| Electric clock | $11 | $11 | S | $11 | S |
| Music Master AM radio | $44 | $44 | $44 | $47 | $47 |
| Vinyl top (style varies by model) | $58 | $58–$70 | - | $58–$70 | $58–$70 |

Options common to most models. (- = Not Available, S = Standard equipment.) Items may be standard equipment, optional at different pricing, or unavailable on certain models. This chart is only a guide.

## Paint Colors

| | Code |
|---|---|
| Silver Metallic | AA-1 |
| Black | BB-1 |
| Light Blue Metallic | CC-1 |
| Medium Blue Metallic | DD-1 |
| Dark Blue Metallic | EE-1 |
| Light Green Metallic | FF-1 |
| Dark Green Metallic | GG-1 |
| Dark Copper Metallic | HH-1 |
| Chestnut Metallic | JJ-1 |
| Medium Turquoise Met. | KK-1 |
| Dark Turquoise Metallic | LL-1 |
| Turbine Bronze Metallic | MM-1 |
| Bright Red | PP-1 |
| Dark Red Metallic | QQ-1 |
| Yellow | RR-1 |
| Cream | SS-1 |
| Medium Copper Metallic | TT-1 |
| White | WW-1 |
| Light Tan | XX-1 |
| Medium Tan Metallic | YY-1 |
| Gold Metallic | ZZ-1 |
| Mauve Metallic | 66-1 |
| Bright Blue Metallic | 88-1 |

# Dart

*"Looking for an escape from cramped compacts?"*

**Nameplate year of origin:** 1960 (on low-end full-size models).
**Current bodystyle lifespan:** 1967 through 1976.
**Predecessor to this model:** Dart (1963 to 1966).
**Replacement for this model:** Aspen (1976 to 1980).
**Percentage of division's sales volume:** 37.60%.
**Corporate siblings:** Plymouth Valiant.
**Primary competition:** AMC Rambler American, Chevrolet Chevy II, and Ford Falcon.
**Notable changes:** Completely redesigned.
**Major standard equipment:** Cloth and vinyl front bench seat, dome light, black rubber floor mats, 2-speed windshield wipers, and 6.50 × 13 BSW tires. 270 adds: Full carpeting, drip rail molding, deluxe instrument panel décor, cigarette lighter and wheel covers. GT adds: Vinyl front bucket seats (Hardtop), map and courtesy light (Convertible), front fender-top turn signal indicators, and deluxe wheel covers.

## Measurements

| | |
|---|---|
| Wheelbase | 111.0" |
| Length | 195.4" |
| Width | 69.7" |
| Height | 53.6" |
| Legroom — front | 40.8" |
| Legroom — rear | 36.5" |
| Headroom — front | 38.3" |
| Headroom — rear | 37.3" |
| Cargo capacity (cu. ft.) | 14.3 |
| Fuel capacity (gals.) | 18.0 |

## Models Available

| | Style Number | Base MSRP | Change from LY | Shipping Wt. (lbs.) | Production | Change from LY |
|---|---|---|---|---|---|---|
| Dart 2-Door Sedan | LL21 | $2,187 | +4.44% | 2685 | 53,100 | * |
| Dart 4-Door Sedan | LL41 | $2,224 | +3.06% | 2715 | * | * |
| Dart 270 2-Door Hardtop | LH23 | $2,388 | +3.51% | 2705 | 63,200 | * |
| Dart 270 4-Door Sedan | LH41 | $2,362 | +3.60% | 2720 | * | * |
| Dart GT 2-Door Hardtop | LP23 | $2,499 | +3.39% | 2735 | 38,200 | * |
| Dart GT 2-Door Convertible | LP27 | $2,732 | +1.19% | 2815 | * | * |
| TOTALS | Avg. price | $2,399 | +1.18% | Production | 154,500 | +36.85% |

*Production by series not available. Totals are estimated.*

# Coronet

*"Prepare for action!"*

**Nameplate year of origin:** 1949.
**Current bodystyle lifespan:** Coronet (1966 to 1967).
**Predecessor to this model:** Coronet, Dart and 330/440 (1962 through 1965).
**Replacement for this model:** Coronet (1968 to 1970).
**Percentage of division's sales volume:** 44.92%.
**Corporate siblings:** Plymouth Belvedere.
**Primary competition:** AMC Rebel, Chevrolet Chevelle, Ford Fairlane, and Pontiac Tempest.
**Notable changes:** Minor trim and detail changes.
**Major standard equipment:** Cloth and vinyl bench seat, black rubber floor mats, variable speed windshield wipers with washers, hubcaps, and 7.35 × 14 BSW tires. Deluxe adds: All-vinyl bench seats (wagons), color-keyed rubber floor mats, full horn ring and 7.75 × 14 BSW tires on wagon. 440 adds: All-vinyl seats (2-Doors), exterior bright trim package, full carpeting, sill moldings and 8.25 × 14 BSW tires on 3-Seat wagon. 500 adds: Deluxe wheel covers and additional exterior and interior trim. R/T adds: Map and courtesy lamps, body side paint stripe, heavy duty suspension, special R/T hood with air intake, Torqueflite automatic transmission and 7.75 × 14 Redline tires.

## Measurements

| | Cars | Wagons |
|---|---|---|
| Wheelbase | 117.0" | 117.0" |
| Length | 203.0" | 207.9" |
| Width | 75.3" | 75.3" |
| Height | 55.0" | 55.6" |
| Legroom — front | 42.0" | 42.0" |
| Legroom — rear | 37.8" | 37.8" |
| Headroom — front | 38.8" | 38.8" |
| Headroom — rear | 37.8" | 37.8" |
| Cargo capacity (cu. ft.) | 17.0 | 88.0 |
| Fuel capacity (gals.) | 19.0 | 19.0 |

**1967**

## Models Available

| | Style Number | Base MSRP | Change from LY | Shipping Wt. (lbs.) | Production | Change from LY |
|---|---|---|---|---|---|---|
| Coronet 4-Door, 2-Seat Wagon | WE45 | $2,622 | NEW | 3465 | * | NEW |
| Coronet Deluxe 2-Door Coupe | WL21 | $2,359 | +2.43% | 3065 | 27,800 | * |
| Coronet Deluxe 4-Door Sedan | WL41 | $2,397 | +2.39% | 3080 | * | * |
| Coronet Deluxe 4-Dr., 2-S. Wagon | WL45 | $2,693 | +2.36% | 3480 | 24,200 | * |
| Coronet 440 2-Door Hardtop | WH23 | $2,500 | +1.75% | 3085 | 92,500 | * |
| Coronet 440 2-Door Convertible | WH27 | $2,740 | +2.54% | 3140 | * | * |
| Coronet 440 4-Door Sedan | WH41 | $2,475 | +1.77% | 3070 | * | * |
| Coronet 440 4-Dr., 2-S. Wagon | WH45 | $2,771 | +1.80% | 3465 | * | * |
| Coronet 440 4-Dr., 3-S. Wagon | WH46 | $2,975 | +1.67% | 3675 | * | * |
| Coronet 500 2-Door Hardtop | WP23 | $2,679 | +2.60% | 3110 | 29,300 | * |
| Coronet 500 2-Door Convertible | WP27 | $2,919 | +3.25% | 3190 | * | * |
| Coronet 500 SE 4-Door Sedan | WP41 | $2,654 | +2.63% | 3090 | * | * |
| Coronet R/T 2-Door Hardtop | WS23 | $3,199 | NEW | 3475 | 10,400 | NEW |
| Coronet R/T 2-Door Convertible | WS27 | $3,438 | NEW | 3640 | * | NEW |
| TOTALS | Avg. price | $2,744 | +7.86% | Production | 184,200 | -26.59% |

*Production by series not available. Totals are estimated.*

# Charger

*"Blast Behind-the-Wheel Boredom!"*

**Nameplate year of origin:** 1966.
**Current bodystyle lifespan:** 1966 through 1967.
**Predecessor to this model:** None.
**Replacement for this model:** Charger (1968 to 1970).
**Percentage of division's sales volume:** 3.85%.
**Corporate siblings:** None.
**Primary competition:** AMC Marlin and Mercury Comet Cyclone.
**Notable changes:** Revised grille and trim and detail changes.
**Major standard equipment:** All vinyl bucket seats (front and rear), full carpeting, 2-speed windshield wipers with washers, interior courtesy lights, tinted rear window, body side paint stripe, tachometer, oil pressure gauge, and 7.35 × 14 BSW tires.

## Measurements

| | |
|---|---|
| Wheelbase | 117.0" |
| Length | 203.6" |
| Width | 75.3" |
| Height | 53.8" |
| Legroom — front | 41.6" |
| Legroom — rear | 34.0" |
| Headroom — front | 37.7" |
| Headroom — rear | 36.5" |
| Cargo capacity (cu. ft.) | NA |
| Fuel capacity (gals.) | 19.0 |

## Models Available

| | Style Number | Base MSRP | Change from LY | Shipping Wt. (lbs.) | Production | Change from LY |
|---|---|---|---|---|---|---|
| Charger 2-Door Hardtop | XP29 | $3,128 | -0.57% | 3475 | 15,788 | -57.67% |
| TOTALS | *Avg. price* | $3,128 | -0.57% | *Production* | 15,788 | -57.67% |

# Polara

*"Break Away! Go Polara!"*

**Nameplate year of origin:** 1959.
**Current bodystyle lifespan:** 1967 through 1968.
**Predecessor to this model:** Polara (1965 to 1966).
**Replacement for this model:** Polara (1969 to 1973).
**Percentage of division's sales volume:** 8.00%.
**Corporate siblings:** Plymouth Fury.
**Primary competition:** AMC Ambassador, Chevrolet Impala/Caprice, and Ford Galaxie/LTD.
**Notable changes:** Completely redesigned.
**Major standard equipment:** Cloth-and-vinyl bench seat, full carpeting, 2-speed windshield wipers with washers, and 8.25 × 14 BSW tires (8.45 × 15 BSW tires on wagons). Polara 500 adds: Vinyl bucket seats, tachometer, center console and wheel covers.

## Measurements

| | Cars | Wagons |
|---|---|---|
| Wheelbase | 122.0" | 122.0" |
| Length | 219.6" | 219.6" |
| Width | 80.0" | 79.7" |
| Height | 56.4" | 57.1" |
| Legroom — front | 42.0" | 42.0" |
| Legroom — rear | 39.1" | 39.1" |
| Headroom — front | 39.3" | 39.3" |
| Headroom — rear | 38.5" | 38.5" |
| Cargo capacity (cu. ft.) | NA | 107.0 |
| Fuel capacity (gals.) | 25.0 | 21.0 |

## Models Available

| | Style Number | Base MSRP | Change from LY | Shipping Wt. (lbs.) | Production | Change from LY |
|---|---|---|---|---|---|---|
| Polara 318 2-Door Hardtop | DE23 | $2,878 | NEW | 3670 | * | NEW |
| Polara 318 4-Door Sedan | DE41 | $2,843 | +2.90% | 3700 | 5,600 | * |
| Polara 318 4-Door Hardtop | DE43 | $2,954 | NEW | 3730 | * | NEW |
| Polara 2-Door Hardtop | DL23 | $2,953 | +2.75% | 3785 | * | * |
| Polara 2-Door Convertible | DL27 | $3,241 | +2.53% | 3845 | * | * |
| Polara 4-Door Sedan | DL41 | $2,918 | +2.82% | 3815 | 24,000 | * |
| Polara 4-Door Hardtop | DL43 | $3,028 | +2.71% | 3845 | * | * |

| | Style Number | Base MSRP | Change from LY | Shipping Wt. (lbs.) | Production | Change from LY |
|---|---|---|---|---|---|---|
| Polara 4-Door, 2-S. Wagon | DL45 | $3,265 | +2.58% | 4225 | * | * |
| Polara 4-Door, 3-S. Wagon | DL46 | $3,368 | +2.50% | 4285 | * | * |
| Polara 500 2-Door Hardtop | DM23 | $3,155 | NEW | 3825 | 3,200 | NEW |
| Polara 500 2-Door Convertible | DM27 | $3,443 | NEW | 3860 | * | NEW |
| TOTALS | | Avg. price $3,095 | +2.89% | | Production 32,800 | -56.50% |

*Production by series not available. Totals are estimated.

# Monaco

*"Monaco speaks softly but carries a big kick!"*

**Nameplate year of origin:** 1965.
**Current bodystyle lifespan:** 1967 through 1968.
**Predecessor to this model:** Monaco (1965 to 1966).
**Replacement for this model:** Monaco (1969 to 1973).
**Percentage of division's sales volume:** 5.56%.
**Corporate siblings:** Plymouth Fury.
**Primary competition:** Buick Wildcat, Oldsmobile Delta 88, and Pontiac Bonneville/Grand Prix.
**Notable changes:** Completely redesigned.
**Major standard equipment:** Cloth-and-vinyl bench seat, full carpeting, ashtray, map and courtesy lights, 2-speed windshield wipers with washers, front fender top turn signal indicators, and 8.25 × 14 BSW tires (8.45 × 15 BSW tires on wagons). 500 adds: Vinyl bucket seats, door-mounted courtesy lights, electric clock, automatic transmission, and body side paint stripes.

## Measurements

| | Cars | Wagons |
|---|---|---|
| Wheelbase | 122.0" | 122.0" |
| Length | 219.6" | 219.6" |
| Width | 80.0" | 79.7" |
| Height | 56.4" | 57.1" |
| Legroom — front | 42.0" | 42.0" |
| Legroom — rear | 39.1" | 39.1" |
| Headroom — front | 39.3" | 39.3" |
| Headroom — rear | 38.5" | 38.5" |
| Cargo capacity (cu. ft.) | NA | 107.0 |
| Fuel capacity (gals.) | 25.0 | 21.0 |

**1967**

## Models Available

| | Style Number | Base MSRP | Change from LY | Shipping Wt. (lbs.) | Production | Change from LY |
|---|---|---|---|---|---|---|
| Monaco 2-Door Hardtop | DH23 | $3,213 | +3.41% | 3820 | 11,400 | * |
| Monaco 4-Door Sedan | DH41 | $3,138 | +3.46% | 3850 | * | * |
| Monaco 4-Door Hardtop | DH43 | $3,275 | +3.31% | 3885 | * | * |
| Monaco 4-Dr., 2-S. Wgn. | DH45 | $3,543 | +3.11% | 4260 | 8,900 | * |
| Monaco 4-Dr., 3-S. Wgn. | DH46 | $3,646 | +3.02% | 4325 | * | * |
| Monaco 500 2-Door Hardtop | DP23 | $3,712 | +3.00% | 3850 | 2,500 | * |
| TOTALS | | Avg. price $3,421 | +3.20% | | Production 22,800 | -66.07% |

*Production by series not available. Totals are estimated.

# FORD

*"You're ahead in a '67 Ford."*

Ford entered the 1967 model year with many newly restyled models, and one totally rethought car that took up a new position in the marketplace. That particular car would be the Thunderbird, which moved from the luxury/

sport/personal car arena to the more upmarket luxury/personal car category. What this meant in terms of styling was added bulk and weight, less crispness of line and more rounded edges. What it meant in terms of performance was the same power moving more car. What it meant for the model lineup was the addition of a 4-Door Sedan model, and the dropping of the Convertible. Ford's marketing research department seemed at first to be right on, as sales of the Thunderbird increased over the 1966 models. As time went on, though, sales would slide annually, until the new 2-Door model was introduced in 1972. No matter what the eventual outcome, for now Ford had what looked to be a successful marketing move with one of its more popular models.

The full-size Ford models were totally redesigned once again, this time with more rounded lines that looked sleeker and more elegant, while still carrying traditional Ford lines.

Most 2-Door models continued to carry a fastback roofline. One powertrain choice was added to the line: the 428 CID V8 engine, available in all models. The only model changes were the addition of an LTD 4-Door Sedan and the renaming of the Galaxie 500 XL line as just the XL series.

The highly successful Mustang pony car underwent its first styling update since its introduction in April of 1964. The restyling continued the successful Mustang look but appeared a bit more muscular, which it was with a new 390 CID V8 engine option available. The 390 CID V8 put out 320 horsepower and made the Mustang a top performer among its class of cars. The mid-size Fairlane and compact Falcon carried on in 1967 with relatively minor changes. The Fairlane 500 GT was now simply the Fairlane GT, and the Falcon Squire wagon was replaced by the Falcon Futura wagon.

Falcon 2-Door Coupe

Fairlane 500 4-Door Sedan

Fairlane 500 XL 2-Door Convertible

LTD 4-Door Hardtop

Mustang 2-Door Convertible

Mustang 2-Door Hardtop

Thunderbird 2-Door Landau Hardtop

XL 2-Door Convertible

**Model year production:** 1,731,227, down 28.66% from 1966.
**Domestic market share:** 22.59% (2nd place).
**Base price range:** $2,118 to $4,825.
**Industry average base price:** $3,159.
**Ford average base price:** $2,865.
**Introduction date:** September 30, 1966.
**Assembly plants:** Atlanta, GA (A); Dallas, TX (D); Chicago, IL (G); Dearborn, MI (F); Kansas City, MO (K); Lorain, OH (H); Los Angeles, CA (J); Louisville, KY (U); Mahwah, NJ (E); Metuchen, NJ (T); Norfolk, VA (N); San Jose, CA (R); Twin Cities, MN (P); Wayne, MI (W); Wixom, MI (Y); St. Thomas, Ontario, Can. (X); Oakville, Ontario, Can. (B).
**Data plate identification:** Eleven digit code read as follows: 7 for 1967; 2nd digit is assembly plant code; 2-digit model number (see listings below); 5th digit is engine code; 100001 and up for serial number. *Example:* 7Y81Z100001 is a 1967 Ford Thunderbird 2-Door Hardtop with a 390 CID V8 engine, serial number 100001, built in Wixom, MI.

## Powertrains

| Engine | Gross HP | Engine Code | Transmission Availability | Falcon | Mustang | Fairlane | Full-size | T-Bird |
|---|---|---|---|---|---|---|---|---|
| 170 CID, 1-bbl., 6-cyl. | 100 | U | 3-speed manual | S* | – | – | – | – |
| | | | Cruise-O-Matic | $187* | – | – | – | – |
| 200 CID, 1-bbl., 6-cyl. | 115 | T | 3-speed manual | $26* | S | S* | – | – |
| | | | 4-speed manual | $184* | $184 | $184* | – | – |
| | | | Cruise-O-Matic | $213* | $188 | $188* | – | – |
| 240 CID, 1-bbl., 6-cyl. | 150 | V | 3-speed manual | – | – | – | S*** | |
| | | | Overdrive | – | – | – | $117*** | |
| | | | Cruise-O-Matic | – | – | – | $188*** | – |
| 289 CID Challenger, 2-bbl., V8 | 200 | C | 3-speed manual | $132* | $106 | S (GT)/$105* | $107*** | – |
| | | | Overdrive | – | – | – | $224*** | |
| | | | 4-speed manual | $316* | $290 | $184 (GT)/$290* | No cost (XL, LTD)/$291*** | – |
| | | | Cruise-O-Matic | $319* | $304 | $188 (GT)/$304* | S (XL, LTD)/$295*** | |
| 289 CID Challenger, 4-bbl., V8 | 225 | A | 3-speed manual | $183* | $158 | $53 (GT)/$158* | – | – |
| | | | 4-speed manual | $367* | $342 | $236 (GT)/$342* | – | – |
| | | | Cruise-O-Matic | $370* | $356 | $250 (GT)/$356* | – | – |
| 289 CID High-Perf., 4-bbl., V8 | 271 | K | 3-speed manual | – | $434** | – | – | – |
| | | | 4-speed manual | – | $667** | – | – | – |
| | | | Cruise-O-Matic | – | $666** | – | – | – |
| 390 CID, 2-bbl., V8 | 275 | Y | 3-speed manual | – | – | $77 (GT)/$184* | $263*** | – |
| | | | 4-speed manual | – | – | $261 (GT)/$368* | $78 (XL, LTD)/$368*** | – |
| | | | Cruise-O-Matic | – | – | $278 (GT)/$385* | $78 (XL, LTD)/$404*** | – |
| 390 CID, 4-bbl., V8 | 315/325 | Z/S | 3-speed manual | – | $343 | $157 (GT)/$264* | $345*** | – |
| | | | 4-speed manual | – | $497 | $341 (GT)/$448* | $158 (XL, LTD)/$449*** | – |
| | | | Cruise-O-Matic | – | $496 | $377 (GT)/$484* | $158 (XL, LTD)/$485*** | S |
| 427 CID Thunderbird Hi-Perf., 4-bbl., V8 | 410 | W/L | 4-speed manual | – | – | $ | $975 (XL, LTD)/$1276*** | – |
| 427 CID Thunderbird Hi-Perf., 2 × 4-bbl., V8 | 425 | R/D | 4-speed manual | – | – | – | $975 (XL, LTD)/$1276*** | – |
| 428 CID, 4-bbl., V8 | 345 | Q | 4-speed manual | – | – | – | $179 (XL, LTD)/$498*** | |
| | | | Cruise-O-Matic | – | – | – | $179 (XL, LTD)/$498*** | $91 |

*Except GT or Falcon Sport Coupe models. Falcon Sport Coupe has standard 200 CID 6-cyl.; subtract $26 from optional pricing.  **Includes GT package.  ***Except XL and LTD.

## Major Options

| | Falcon | Mustang | Fairlane | Full-size | Thunderbird |
|---|---|---|---|---|---|
| Select Aire air conditioning | – | $356 | $356 | $356 | $421 |
| Tinted glass | $21 | $30 | $30 | $35 | S |
| Power steering | $84 | $84 | $84 | $95 | S |
| Power brakes | – | $54 | $54 | $42 | S |
| Power driver's seat/bench seat | – | – | $ | $ | $98 |
| Power windows | – | – | $ | $ | $104 |
| AM radio | $57 | $61 | $57 | $57 | S |
| AM/FM radio | – | $135 | $134 | $134 | $164 (Stereo) |
| Front seat console | – | $54 | $ | $ | $ |
| Front bucket seats | – | S | $ | $ | $ |
| Tilt steering wheel | – | $66 | – | $ | S |
| Vinyl roof | $74 | $74 | $74 | $74–$83 | S |
| White sidewall tires | $32 | $33 | $34 | $35 | $52 |

Options common to most models. (– = Not Available; S = Standard equipment.) Items may be standard equipment, optional at different pricing, or unavailable on certain models. This chart is only a guide.

## Paint Colors

| | Code | Others | Thunderbird | | Code | Others | Thunderbird |
|---|---|---|---|---|---|---|---|
| Silver Frost Metallic | 4 | X | X | Wimbledon White | M | X | X |
| Dark Gray Metallic | 5 | X | | Diamond Blue | N | | X |
| Pebble Beige | 6 | X | X | Pewter Mist Metallic | P | | X |
| Springtime Yellow | 8 | X | | Brittany Blue Metallic | Q | X | X |
| Raven Black | A | X | X | Ivy Green Metallic | R | | X |
| Frost Turquoise | B | X | X | Candyapple Red | T | X | X |
| Charcoal Gray Metallic | C | | X | Tahoe Turquoise Metallic | U | | X |
| Acapulco Blue Metallic | D | X | | Burnt Amber Metallic | V | X | X |
| Beige Mist Metallic | E | | X | Clearwater Aqua Metallic | W | X | |
| Arcadian Blue | F | X | X | Vintage Burgundy Metallic | X | X | X |
| Diamond Green Metallic | H | | X | Dark Moss Green Metallic | Y | X | |
| Lime Gold Metallic | I | X | X | Sauterne Gold Metallic | Z | X | X |
| Nightmist Blue Metallic | K | X | X | | | | |

# Falcon

*"Go pert, peppy and proud … in a Falcon."*

**Nameplate year of origin:** 1960.
**Current bodystyle lifespan:** 1966 through 1970.
**Predecessor to this model:** Falcon (1964 to 1965).
**Replacement for this model:** Maverick (1969 to 1977).
**Percentage of division's sales volume:** 3.72%.
**Corporate siblings:** None (wagon bodies shared with Fairlane).
**Primary competition:** AMC Rambler American, Chevrolet Chevy II, Dodge Dart, and Plymouth Valiant.
**Notable changes:** Minor trim and detail changes.
**Major standard equipment:** Cloth and vinyl interior trim, front-door armrests, chrome windshield and rear window moldings, small hubcaps, and 6.95 × 14 BSW tires (7.75 × 14 on Wagons). Futura adds: Deluxe interior trim, rear armrests with ashtrays, side window moldings, wheel covers. Sport Coupe adds: Vinyl bucket seats, deluxe wheel covers, and 7.35 × 14 BSW tires.

## Measurements

| | Cars | Wagons |
|---|---|---|
| Wheelbase | 111.0" | 113.0" |
| Length | 184.3" | 199.0" |
| Width | 73.5" | 73.5" |
| Height | 54.6" | 55.0" |
| Legroom — front | 42.1" | 42.1" |
| Legroom — rear | 36.4" | 36.8" |
| Headroom — front | 38.7" | 38.7" |
| Headroom — rear | 37.8" | 37.8" |
| Cargo capacity (cu. ft.) | 12.3 | 98.6 |
| Fuel capacity (gals.) | 16.0 | 20.0 |

## Models Available

| | Style Number | Base MSRP | Change from LY | Shipping Wt. (lbs.) | Production | Change from LY |
|---|---|---|---|---|---|---|
| Falcon 2-Door Sedan | 10 | $2,118 | +2.82% | 2564 | 16,082 | -61.18% |
| Falcon 4-Door Sedan | 11 | $2,167 | +2.51% | 2598 | 13,554 | -60.92% |
| Falcon 4-Door Wagon | 12 | $2,497 | +2.25% | 3056 | 5,553 | -66.65% |
| Falcon Futura 2-Door Sedan | 20 | $2,280 | +4.44% | 2597 | 6,287 | -71.42% |
| Falcon Futura 2-Door Sports Cpe. | 22 | $2,437 | +4.68% | 2614 | 7,053 | -65.24% |
| Falcon Futura 4-Door Sedan | 21 | $2,322 | +3.80% | 2631 | 11,254 | -66.94% |
| Falcon Futura Squire 4-Door Wgn. | 23 | $2,609 | +2.19% | 3074 | 4,552 | -66.47% |
| TOTALS | | *Avg. price* $2,347 | +3.21% | | *Production* 64,335 | -64.78% |

# Mustang

*"There are three new ways to answer the call of the Mustang for '67."*

**Nameplate year of origin:** 1964½ (also, on a 1963 show car).
**Current bodystyle lifespan:** 1964½ through 1968.
**Predecessor to this model:** None.
**Replacement for this model:** Mustang (1969 to 1970).
**Percentage of division's sales volume:** 27.27%.
**Corporate siblings:** Mercury Cougar.
**Primary competition:** Chevrolet Camaro, Plymouth Barracuda, and Pontiac Firebird.
**Notable changes:** Restyled sheet metal and interior trim changes.
**Major standard equipment:** All-vinyl bucket front seats, courtesy lights, full carpeting, sports steering wheel, chrome window moldings, and 6.95 × 14 BSW tires.

## Measurements

| | |
|---|---|
| Wheelbase | 108.0" |
| Length | 183.6" |
| Width | 70.9" |
| Height | 51.6" |
| Legroom — front | 41.8" |
| Legroom — rear | 28.8" |
| Headroom — front | 37.4" |
| Headroom — rear | 35.9" |
| Cargo capacity (cu. ft.) | 9.2 |
| Fuel capacity (gals.) | 17.0 |

## Models Available

| | Style Number | Base MSRP | Change from LY | Shipping Wt. (lbs.) | Production | Change from LY |
|---|---|---|---|---|---|---|
| Mustang 2-Door Hardtop | 1 | $2,461 | +1.86% | 2624 | 356,271 | -28.71% |
| Mustang 2-Door Fastback | 2 | $2,592 | -0.58% | 2651 | 71,042 | +99.01% |
| Mustang 2-Door Convertible | 3 | $2,698 | +1.70% | 2778 | 44,808 | -37.87% |
| TOTALS | | Avg. price $2,584 | +0.98% | | Production 472,121 | -22.29% |

# Fairlane

*"Join the Fairlaners ... people who have more fun in the car that has more to offer."*

**Nameplate year of origin:** 1955.
**Current bodystyle lifespan:** 1966 through 1967.
**Predecessor to this model:** Fairlane (1962 to 1965).
**Replacement for this model:** Fairlane/Torino (1968 to 1969).
**Percentage of division's sales volume:** 13.84%.
**Corporate siblings:** Mercury Comet.
**Primary competition:** AMC Rambler Rebel, Chevrolet Chevelle, and Plymouth Belvedere.
**Notable changes:** Minor trim and detail changes.
**Major standard equipment:** Cloth and vinyl bench seat, rubber floor mats, front and rear armrests, chrome windshield and rear window moldings, and 6.95 × 14 BSW tires (7.75 × 14 BSW on Wagons). 500 adds: Full carpeting, deluxe interior trim, and chrome side window moldings. Squire adds: Exterior wood-grain trim. XL adds: All-vinyl bucket front seats, center console, and rocker panel moldings. GT adds: Special exterior striping and identification, clock, tachometer and 289 CID V8 engine.

## Measurements

| | Cars | Wagons |
|---|---|---|
| Wheelbase | 116.0" | 113.0" |
| Length | 197.0" | 200.0" |
| Width | 74.7" | 73.5" |
| Height | 55.0" | 55.0" |
| Legroom — front | 42.1" | 42.1" |
| Legroom — rear | 38.6" | 36.8" |
| Headroom — front | 37.8" | 38.3" |
| Headroom — rear | 37.6" | 37.8" |
| Cargo capacity (cu. ft.) | 15.2 | 98.6 |
| Fuel capacity (gals.) | 20.0 | 20.0 |

**1967**

## Models Available

| | Style Number | Base MSRP | Change from LY | Shipping Wt. (lbs.) | Production | Change from LY |
|---|---|---|---|---|---|---|
| Fairlane 2-Door Club Coupe | 30 | $2,297 | +2.54% | 2775 | 10,628 | -21.26% |
| Fairlane 4-Door Sedan | 31 | $2,339 | +2.59% | 2813 | 19,740 | -24.57% |
| Fairlane 4-Door, 2-Seat Wagon | 32 | $2,643 | +2.09% | 3216 | 10,881 | -12.10% |
| Fairlane 500 2-Door Club Coupe | 33 | $2,377 | +2.59% | 2785 | 8,473 | -39.98% |
| Fairlane 500 2-Door Hardtop | 35 | $2,439 | +2.57% | 2863 | 70,135 | -7.65% |
| Fairlane 500 2-Door Convertible | 36 | $2,664 | +2.34% | 3186 | 5,428 | -41.63% |
| Fairlane 500 4-Door Sedan | 34 | $2,417 | +2.55% | 2833 | 52,552 | -23.43% |
| Fairlane 500 4-Dr., 2-Seat Wagon | 37 | $2,718 | +1.99% | 3228 | 15,902 | -19.79% |
| Fairlane Squire 4-Dr., 2-Seat Wgn. | 38 | $2,902 | +3.79% | 3237 | 8,348 | -27.77% |
| Fairlane 500 XL 2-Door Hardtop | 40 | $2,619 | +2.99% | 2890 | 14,871 | -93.62% |
| Fairlane 500 XL 2-Door Convertible | 41 | $2,843 | +2.71% | 3213 | 1,943 | -57.39% |
| Fairlane GT 2-Door Hardtop | 42 | $2,839 | -0.14% | 3004 | 18,670 | -43.45% |
| Fairlane GT 2-Door Convertible | 43 | $3,064 | -0.13% | 3327 | 2,117 | -51.07% |
| TOTALS | | Avg. price $2,628 | +2.14% | | Production 239,688 | -54.46% |

# Custom, Galaxie & LTD

*"Luxury leaders of the volume car field."*

**Nameplate year of origin:** 1957 (Custom); 1959 (Galaxie); 1965 (LTD).
**Current bodystyle lifespan:** 1967 through 1968.
**Predecessor to this model:** Full-size Ford (1965 to 1966).
**Replacement for this model:** Custom, Galaxie and LTD (1969 to 1970).
**Percentage of division's sales volume:** 50.67%.
**Corporate siblings:** Mercury Monterey, Montclair and Park Lane.
**Primary competition:** AMC Ambassador, Chevrolet Biscayne/BelAir/Impala/Caprice, and Plymouth Fury.
**Notable changes:** Completely restyled.
**Major standard equipment:** Cloth and vinyl front bench seat, rubber floor mats, arm rests on all doors, rear window trim molding, and 7.75 × 15 BSW tires (8.45 × 15 BSW tires on Wagon). Custom 500 adds: Full carpeting, and chrome windshield molding. Galaxie 500 adds: Deluxe interior trim, chrome side window moldings, and 8.15 × 15 BSW tires on Hardtop and Convertible. XL adds: Bucket seats with floor-mounted transmission selector, lower door carpet trim and polished trim, courtesy and reading lamps, and special badging. LTD adds: Padded cloth upholstery with Scotchguard® treatment, simulated wood interior trim, additional courtesy lights, self-regulating clock, and 8.15 × 15 BSW tires.

## Measurements

| | Cars | Wagons |
|---|---|---|
| Wheelbase | 119.0" | 119.0" |
| Length | 213.0" | 220.0" |
| Width | 79.0" | 79.0" |
| Height | 55.7" | 55.7" |
| Legroom — front | 41.8" | 41.8" |
| Legroom — rear | 37.7" | 37.7" |
| Headroom — front | 38.9" | 38.9" |
| Headroom — rear | 37.7" | 37.7" |
| Cargo capacity (cu. ft.) | 19.1 | 103.0 |
| Fuel capacity (gals.) | 25.0 | 25.0 |

## Models Available

| | Style Number | Base MSRP | Change from LY | Shipping Wt. (lbs.) | Production | Change from LY |
|---|---|---|---|---|---|---|
| Custom 2-Door Sedan | 50 | $2,441 | +2.56% | 3419 | 18,107 | -43.93% |
| Custom 4-Door Sedan | 51 | $2,496 | +2.63% | 3445 | 41,417 | -42.67% |
| Custom 500 2-Door Sedan | 52 | $2,553 | +2.90% | 3408 | 18,146 | -36.97% |
| Custom 500 4-Door Sedan | 53 | $2,595 | +2.45% | 3459 | 83,260 | -23.93% |
| Galaxie 500 2-Door Hardtop | 55 | $2,755 | +2.61% | 3482 | 197,388 | -0.58% |
| Galaxie 500 2-Door Convertible | 57 | $3,003 | +2.35% | 3627 | 19,068 | -30.55% |
| Galaxie 500 4-Door Sedan | 54 | $2,732 | +2.05% | 3464 | 130,063 | -24.33% |
| Galaxie 500 4-Door Hardtop | 56 | $2,808 | +1.67% | 3510 | 57,087 | +4.01% |
| XL 2-Door Hardtop | 60 | $3,243 | +0.37% | 3574 | 18,174 | -29.33% |

| | Style Number | Base MSRP | Change from LY | Shipping Wt. (lbs.) | Production | Change from LY |
|---|---|---|---|---|---|---|
| XL 2-Door Convertible | 61 | $3,493 | +0.37% | 3731 | 5,161 | -18.85% |
| LTD 2-Door Hardtop | 62 | $3,362 | +5.03% | 3645 | 46,036 | +45.24% |
| LTD 4-Door Sedan | 64 | $3,298 | NEW | 3562 | 12,491 | NEW |
| LTD 4-Door Hardtop | 66 | $3,363 | +2.59% | 3608 | 51,978 | -25.10% |
| Ranch Wagon 4-Door, 2-Seat | 70 | $2,836 | +1.54% | 3873 | 23,932 | -28.15% |
| Country Sedan 4-Door Wagon | 71 | $2,935 | +1.84% | 3884 | 50,818 | -8.63% |
| Country Sedan 4-Door Wgn. w/DFRS* | 72 | $3,061 | +2.07% | 3941 | 34,377 | -6.16% |
| Country Squire 4-Door Wagon | 73 | $3,234 | +1.63% | 3933 | 25,600 | -7.40% |
| Country Squire 4-Dr. Wgn. w/DFRS* | 74 | $3,359 | +2.88% | 3979 | 44,024 | -8.19% |
| TOTALS | *Avg. price* | $2,976 | -0.27% | *Production* | 877,127 | -15.74% |

*Dual facing rear seats

# Thunderbird

*"Completely changed, still completely Thunderbird …
offers driving luxury unique in all the world."*

**Nameplate year of origin:** 1955.
**Current bodystyle lifespan:** 1967 through 1971 (restyled in 1970).
**Predecessor to this model:** Thunderbird (1964 to 1966).
**Replacement for this model:** Thunderbird (1972 to 1976).
**Percentage of division's sales volume:** 4.50%.
**Corporate siblings:** None.
**Primary competition:** Buick Riviera and Oldsmobile Toronado.
**Notable changes:** Completely redesigned. New 4-Door model added.
**Major standard equipment:** Luxury all-cloth interior with cut-pile carpeting, bucket seats, console, tilt away steering wheel, AM radio, "rolling lock" power door locks, power steering, power front disc brakes, sequential turn signals, full wheel covers, and 8.15 × 15 BSW tires.

## Measurements

| | 2-Doors | 4-Doors |
|---|---|---|
| Wheelbase | 115.0" | 117.0" |
| Length | 206.9" | 209.4" |
| Width | 77.3" | 77.3" |
| Height | 52.8" | 53.8" |
| Legroom — front | 41.5" | 41.5" |
| Legroom — rear | 32.2" | 34.0" |
| Headroom — front | 37.4" | 38.1" |
| Headroom — rear | 36.9" | 37.2" |
| Cargo capacity (cu. ft.) | 12.3 | 12.3 |
| Fuel capacity (gals.) | 24.1 | 24.1 |

**1967**

## Models Available

| | Style Number | Base MSRP | Change from LY | Shipping Wt. (lbs.) | Production | Change from LY |
|---|---|---|---|---|---|---|
| Thunderbird 2-Door Hardtop | 81 | $4,603 | +4.00% | 4228 | 15,567 | +16.27% |
| Thunderbird 2-Dr. Landau Cpe | 82 | $4,704 | +2.62% | 4238 | 37,422 | +6.60% |
| Thunderbird 4-Dr. Landau Sdn. | 84 | $4,825 | NEW | 4318 | 24,967 | NEW |
| TOTALS | *Avg. price* | $4,711 | +2.57% | *Production* | 77,956 | +12.69% |

# IMPERIAL

*"Newest prestige car in a decade."*

The first totally new Imperial since the 1960 models appeared in showrooms this year. The new Imperial shared some of its basic structure with Chrysler models, but still appeared as a distinct car. Imperials also shared their 440 CID V8 engine with other Mopar models. Sales of the new body style, which lasted for only two model years, improved. However, it would take the new 1969 "fuselage bodied" Imperials to make a big sales gain. As always, interior trimmings of the Imperial were luxurious and loaded with features. A new 4-Door Sedan model joined the Convertible in a renamed "Imperial" line. While still carrying a model number within the Crown line, these two models did not bear the Crown insignia. For 1968, these two body styles would rejoin the Crown line.

Crown 2-Door Hardtop

Crown 2-Door Convertible

LeBaron 4-Door Hardtop

**Model year production:** 17,614, up 28.18% over 1966.
**Domestic market share:** 0.23% (13th place).
**Base price range:** $5,374 to $6,661.
**Industry average base price:** $3,159.
**Imperial average base price:** $6,025.
**Introduction date:** September 1966.
**Assembly plants:** Detroit, MI (3).
**Data plate identification:** Thirteen digit code read as follows:

Four digit style number (see listings below) in which Y = Imperial, 2nd number identifies series (e.g., M is for Crown), 3rd and 4th indicate body style; 5th digit is engine code; 7 for 1967; assembly plant code; 100001; and up for serial number. *Example:* YM23T73100001 is a 1967 Imperial Crown 2-Door Hardtop with a 440 CID V8 engine, serial number 100001, built in Detroit, MI.

## Powertrains

| Engine | Engine Code | Gross HP | Transmission Availability | All Imperial |
|---|---|---|---|---|
| 440 CID, 4-bbl., V8 | T | 350 | Torqueflite Automatic | S |

## Major Options

| | Imperial | Crown | LeBaron |
|---|---|---|---|
| Air conditioning | $452 | $452 | $452 |
| Auto Pilot automatic speed control | $95 | $95 | $95 |
| Tinted glass | $53 | $53 | $53 |
| Rear window defogger | $26 | $26 | $26 |
| Deck lid remote release | $30 | $30 | $30 |
| Power steering — variable-ratio | S | S | S |
| Power brakes | S | S | S |
| Power door locks | $71 | $47 (2-Dr)/$71 (4-Dr) | $71 |
| Power driver's seat/bench seat | $105 | $105 | S |

## Paint Colors

| | Code |
|---|---|
| Charcoal Gray Metallic | 55-1 |
| Dusty Pink Metallic | 66-1 |
| Ruby Metallic | 77-1 |
| Silver Mist Metallic | AA-1 |
| Formal Black | BB-1 |
| Aegean Blue Metallic | CC-1 |
| Wedgewood Blue Metallic | DD-1 |
| Regal Blue Metallic | EE-1 |
| Haze Green Metallic | FF-1 |

|  | Imperial | Crown | LeBaron |
|---|---|---|---|
| Power windows | S | S | S |
| AM radio w/power antenna | $165 | $165 | $165 |
| AM/FM radio w/power antenna | $228 | $228 | $228 |
| Tilt-A-Scope steering wheel | $92 | $92 | $92 |
| Vinyl roof | $130 | $130 | S |
| Whitewall tires — standard size | $45 | $45 | S |

Options common to most models. (– = Not Available; S = Standard equipment.) Items may be standard equipment, optional at different pricing, or unavailable on certain models. This chart is only a guide.

|  | Code |
|---|---|
| Forest Green Metallic | GG-1 |
| Sepia Metallic | JJ-1 |
| Aqua Turquoise Metallic | KK-1 |
| Twilight Turquoise Metallic | LL-1 |
| Turbine Bronze Metallic | MM-1 |
| Flame Red | PP-1 |
| Plum Red Metallic | QQ-1 |
| Daffodil Yellow | RR-1 |
| Ivory | SS-1 |
| Persian White | WW-1 |
| Imperial Navaho Beige | XX-1 |
| Imperial Fawn Metallic | YY-1 |
| Cinnamon Gold Metallic | ZZ-1 |

# Imperial

*"Specifically designed to extend the invitation of Imperial ownership to more fine-car buyers than ever before."*

**Nameplate year of origin:** 1955 (Used at various times under Chrysler nameplate prior to 1955).
**Current bodystyle lifespan:** 1967 through 1968.
**Predecessor to this model:** Crown (1964 to 1966).
**Replacement for this model:** Crown (1969 to 1970).
**Percentage of division's sales volume:** 15.73%.
**Corporate siblings:** Crown and LeBaron.
**Primary competition:** Cadillac Calais and Lincoln Continental.
**Notable changes:** Completely restyled. Imperial line was a one-year only attempt at a lower price offering.
**Major standard equipment:** Torqueflite automatic transmission, power steering, power brakes, full carpeting, remote-control left-hand outside mirror, power windows, electric clock, trip odometer, 3-speed electric windshield wipers with washers, wheel covers and 9.15 × 15 BSW tires.

## Measurements

| | |
|---|---|
| Wheelbase | 127.0" |
| Length | 224.7" |
| Width | 79.6" |
| Height | 56.2" |
| Legroom — front | 42.0" |
| Legroom — rear | 39.8" |
| Headroom — front | 39.4" |
| Headroom — rear | 38.6" |
| Cargo capacity (cu. ft.) | NA |
| Fuel capacity (gals.) | 25.0 |

**1967**

## Models Available

|  | Style Number | Base MSRP | Change from LY | Shipping Wt. (lbs.) | Production | Change from LY |
|---|---|---|---|---|---|---|
| Imperial 2-Door Convertible | YM27 | $6,244 | +1.59% | 4800 | 577 | +12.26% |
| Imperial 4-Door Sedan | YM41 | $5,374 | NEW | 4715 | 2,193 | NEW |
| TOTALS | | Avg. price $5,809 | -1.91% | | Production 2,770 | +438.91% |

# Crown

*"The new style of travel. A style you should discover yourself."*

**Nameplate year of origin:** 1957 (not the same as Crown Imperial series).
**Current bodystyle lifespan:** 1967 through 1968.
**Predecessor to this model:** Crown (1964 to 1966).
**Replacement for this model:** Crown (1969 to 1970).

## Measurements

| | |
|---|---|
| Wheelbase | 127.0" |
| Length | 224.7" |
| Width | 79.6" |

**Percentage of division's sales volume:** 71.82%.
**Corporate siblings:** Imperial and LeBaron.
**Primary competition:** Cadillac Calais and Lincoln Continental.
**Notable changes:** Completely restyled.
**Major standard equipment:** Torqueflite automatic transmission, power steering, power brakes, bucket seats with leather upholstery (convertible), front and rear armrests (hardtops), pile carpeting, remote-control left-hand outside mirror, power windows, electric clock, trip odometer, 3-speed electric windshield wipers with washers, wheel covers and 9.15 × 15 BSW tires.

## Measurements (cont.)

| | |
|---|---|
| Height | 56.2" |
| Legroom — front | 42.0" |
| Legroom — rear | 39.8" |
| Headroom — front | 39.4" |
| Headroom — rear | 38.6" |
| Cargo capacity (cu. ft.) | NA |
| Fuel capacity (gals.) | 25.0 |

## Models Available

| | Style Number | Base MSRP | Change from LY | Shipping Wt. (lbs.) | Production | Change from LY |
|---|---|---|---|---|---|---|
| Crown 2-Door Hardtop | YM23 | $6,011 | +2.11% | 4735 | 3,235 | +36.33% |
| Crown 4-Door Hardtop | YM43 | $5,836 | +1.80% | 4725 | 9,415 | +4.88% |
| TOTALS | | Avg. price $5,924 | +0.03% | | Production 12,650 | +11.45% |

# LeBaron

*"This is what a luxury car was always meant to be."*

**Nameplate year of origin:** 1924 (as Chrysler Sedan model designation); 1926 (as series).
**Current bodystyle lifespan:** 1967 through 1968.
**Predecessor to this model:** LeBaron (1964 to 1966).
**Replacement for this model:** LeBaron (1969 to 1973).
**Percentage of division's sales volume:** 12.46%.
**Corporate siblings:** Imperial and Crown.
**Primary competition:** Cadillac de Ville and Lincoln Continental.
**Notable changes:** Completely restyled.
**Major standard equipment:** Torqueflite automatic transmission, power steering, power brakes, pile carpeting, cloth and fabric-and-leather or broadcloth split-bench front seat, power seat, power windows and vent windows, electric clock, trip odometer, Seville-grain vinyl roof with formal carriage rear window, 3-speed electric windshield wipers with washers, wheel covers and 9.15 × 15 WSW tires.

## Measurements

| | |
|---|---|
| Wheelbase | 127.0" |
| Length | 224.7" |
| Width | 79.6" |
| Height | 56.2" |
| Legroom — front | 42.0" |
| Legroom — rear | 39.8" |
| Headroom — front | 39.4" |
| Headroom — rear | 38.6" |
| Cargo capacity (cu. ft.) | NA |
| Fuel capacity (gals.) | 25.0 |

## Models Available

| | Style Number | Base MSRP | Change from LY | Shipping Wt. (lbs.) | Production | Change from LY |
|---|---|---|---|---|---|---|
| LeBaron 4-Door Hardtop | YH43 | $6,661 | +1.85% | 4790 | 2,194 | +16.83% |
| TOTALS | | Avg. price $6,661 | +1.85% | | Production 2,194 | +16.83% |

# LINCOLN

*"America's most distinguished motorcar."*

There were no significant changes to the Ford Motor Company's luxury brand this year. In fact, advertising bragged about the classic Continental look, as a style that did not change every year. A new "Fresh-Flow" ventilation system was introduced along with a new shift quadrant pattern that standardized the shifting for all automobiles. Other minor detail changes included transposing the headlamp and windshield wiper switches, and adding a dual hydraulic brake system. This would be the last season for the 4-Door Convertible body style.

Continental 4-Door Convertible

Continental 4-Door Sedan

**Model year production:** 45,667, down 16.59% from 1966.
**Domestic market share:** 0.60% (12th place).
**Base price range:** $5,553 to $6,449.
**Industry average base price:** $3,159.
**Lincoln average base price:** $5,932.
**Introduction date:** September 1966.
**Assembly plants:** Allen Park, MI (S) and Wixom, MI (Y).

**Data plate identification:** Eleven digit code read as follows: 7 for 1967; 2nd digit is assembly plant code; 2-digit model number (see listings below); 5th digit is engine code; 400001 and up for serial number. *Example:* 7Y82H400001 is a 1967 Lincoln Continental 4-Door Sedan with a 430 CID V8 engine, serial number 400001, built in Wixom, MI.

## Powertrains

| Engine | Gross HP | Engine Code | Transmission Availability | Continental |
|---|---|---|---|---|
| 462 CID, 4-bbl., V8 | 340 | H | Turbo Drive Automatic | S |

## Major Options

| | Continental |
|---|---|
| Air condtioning — manual | $505 |
| Automatic headlight dimmers | $46 |
| Tinted glass | $54 |
| Tilt steering wheel | $60 |
| 6-way power seat | S |
| AM/FM radio | $85 |
| Leather upholstery | $100 |
| Speed control | $97 |
| Remote control trunk release (sedans) | $53 |

## Paint Colors

| | Code |
|---|---|
| Black Satin | A |
| Palomar Blue | B |
| Huntington Gray Metallic | C |
| Antique Beige Metallic | E |
| Powder Blue | F |
| Cameo Green | H |
| Pitcairn Blue Metallic | K |
| Arctic White | M |
| Platinum | N |

1967

Options common to most models. (- = Not Available; S = Standard equipment.) Items may be standard equipment, optional at different pricing, or unavailable on certain models. This chart is only a guide.

| | Code |
|---|---|
| Champagne Metallic | P |
| Huron Blue Metallic | Q |
| Spanish Moss Metallic | R |
| Cranberry | T |
| Teal Metallic | U |
| Aegean Bronze Metallic | V |
| Vintage Burgundy Metallic | X |
| Florentine Gold Metallic | Z |
| Granada Yellow | 2 |
| Silver Mist Metallic | 4 |
| Desert Sand | 6 |

# Continental

*"Come live the Continental life '67 style."*

**Nameplate year of origin:** 1940 (1961 as a standard sedan nameplate).
**Current bodystyle lifespan:** 1961 through 1969 (major restyles in 1964 and 1966).
**Predecessor to this model:** Premiere (1958 to 1960).
**Replacement for this model:** Continental (1970 to 1979).
**Percentage of division's sales volume:** 100%.
**Corporate siblings:** None.
**Primary competition:** Cadillac de Ville, Imperial Crown and LeBaron.
**Notable changes:** Revised grille, minor trim and detail changes.
**Major standard equipment:** Cloth and leather or leather and vinyl (convertible) front bench seat upholstery with folding center armrests front and rear, vanity mirror, cut-pile carpeting, power windows, remote control LH outside rear view mirror, variable-speed windshield wipers with washers, power steering, power brakes, automatic transmission and 9.15 × 15 BSW tires.

## Measurements

| | |
|---|---|
| Wheelbase | 126.0" |
| Length | 220.9" |
| Width | 79.7" |
| Height | 55.0" |
| Legroom — front | 41.0" |
| Legroom — rear | 40.5" |
| Headroom — front | 39.0" |
| Headroom — rear | 38.6" |
| Luggage capacity (cu. ft.) | 18.0 |
| Fuel capacity (gals.) | 25.5 |

## Models Available

| | Style Number | Base MSRP | Change from LY | Shipping Wt. (lbs.) | Production | Change from LY |
|---|---|---|---|---|---|---|
| Continental 2-Door Hardtop | 89 | $5,553 | +1.24% | 4940 | 11,060 | -29.85% |
| Continental 4-Door Sedan | 82 | $5,795 | +0.78% | 5049 | 32,331 | -9.71% |
| Continental 4-Door Convertible | 86 | $6,449 | +1.03% | 5505 | 2,276 | -28.43% |
| TOTALS | | *Avg. price* $5,932 | +1.00% | | *Production* 45,667 | -16.59% |

# MERCURY

*"The Man's Car."*

If Mercury had any female buyers, they lost them all this year. The sales brochure started with the following passage: "The relationship between a man and his car is a very special thing. For a car is many things to a man. A passport to adventure … an open road beckoning … and a well-traveled trip to work." However true this may have been, nowhere did the copy make mention of women drivers or buyers. Mercury was not the only automobile company to use this type of selling technique, as Chrysler's 1967 brochure gave Chrysler specifications with line, "At last—specifications your wife can understand." The women's movement was just gearing up, and this type of advertising was proof of the prejudice still aimed at women when it came to automobiles. Over the next ten years the industry would make a dramatic turnaround.

Mercury introduced a new breed of pony car to America this year. Sharing major components with the best selling Ford Mustang but stretched 3 inches in wheelbase, the Mercury Cougar was designed to be something of a luxury sports car. Hidden headlights, contoured body panels and a plush interior were all standard equipment. Motivation was by way of a full range of V8 engines, including a 390 CID V8 that was included as part of the Cougar GT package.

Full-size Mercurys were completely restyled this season, and once again shared major body components with Ford, although outside of the rooflines, they had totally different body panels and longer wheelbases. The grille had a now common "Lincoln" appearance, and at the back were vertical taillamps mounted in the trailing edges of the rear quarter panels. The 4-Door Breezeway Sedans this year operated differently than in the past. The entire back glass retracted, but only a few inches—just enough to provide ventilation. This allowed the glass to be mounted in the standard position (as opposed to being rear-slanting), and still keep moisture out of the car. Model changes included the discontinuance of the Monterey 2-Door Sedan and the addition of four new models: the Montclair 4-Door (non–Breezeway) Sedan, and three new top-of-the-line models. The Brougham 4-Door Hardtop and 4-Door Sedan and the Marquis 2-Door Hardtop were all new "near luxury" type cars that took Mercury to the top end of the mid-price market. This was territory that Mercury had been into in the late fifties when the Edsel was introduced. At the time, they had little success with models such as the Turnpike Cruiser, but this time around, the cars were very stylish and met consumer demands. The mid-sized Comet/Capri/Cyclone line returned with only minor trim and detail changes. Last year's Cyclone GTA models were classified as GT models with automatic transmissions this year.

Brougham 4-Door Sedan

Capri 2-Door Hardtop

Comet Villager 4-Door Wagon

Cougar 2-Door Hardtop,
*Motor Trend* Car of the Year

Cyclone 2-Door Hardtop

Montclair 2-Door Hardtop

Monterey 2-Door Hardtop

Park Lane 4-Door Hardtop

**Model year production:** 354,195, up 3.22% over 1966.
**Domestic market share:** 4.62% (8th place).
**Base price range:** $2,284 to $3,989.
**Industry average base price:** $3,159.
**Mercury average base price:** $3,121.
**Introduction date:** October 1966.
**Assembly plants:** Oakville, Ontario, Canada (B); Mahwah, NJ (E); Dearborn, MI (F); Lorain, OH (H); Los Angeles, CA (J); Wixom, MI (S); Wayne, MI (W); and St. Louis, MO (Z).

**Data plate identification:** Eleven digit code read as follows: 7 for 1967; 2nd digit is assembly plant code; 3rd digit is series (0 or 1 is Comet, 4 is Monterey, etc.); 4th digit is body style; 5th digit is engine code; 500001 and up for serial number. *Example:* 7W47Z100001 is a 1967 Mercury Monterey 2-Door Hardtop with a 390 CID V8 engine, serial number 500001, built in Wayne, MI.

## Powertrains

| Engine | Gross HP | Engine Code | Transmission Availability | Comet | Cougar | Monterey/ Montclair | Marquis/Br./ Park Lane |
|---|---|---|---|---|---|---|---|
| 200 CID Six, 1-bbl., 6-cyl. | 120 | T | 3-speed manual | S[2] | - | - | - |
| | | | Merc-O-Matic Automatic | $172[2] | - | - | - |
| 289 CID Cyclone/Cougar, 2-bbl., V8 | 200 | C | 3-speed manual | S[1]/$106[2] | S[4] | - | - |
| | | | 4-speed manual | $188[1]/$294[2] | S[3]/$188[4] | - | - |
| | | | Merc-O-Matic Automatic | $188[1]/$294[2] | NC[3]/$188[4] | - | - |
| 289 CID Super Cougar, 4-bbl., V8 | 225 | A | 3-speed manual | - | $45[3] | - | - |
| | | | 4-speed manual | - | $45[3]/$233[4] | - | - |
| | | | Merc-O-Matic Automatic | - | $45[3]/$233[4] | - | - |
| 390 CID Marauder, 2-bbl., V8 | 270 | Y | 3-speed manual | $[1]/$[2] | - | S | - |
| | | | 4-speed manual | $[1]/$[2] | - | $227* | - |
| | | | Merc-O-Matic Automatic | $[1]/$[2] | - | $227 | - |
| 390 CID Marauder GT, 4-bbl., V8 | 320 | Z | 3-speed manual | S (w/GT) | S (w/GT)/ $ (Others) | $ | - |
| | | | 4-speed manual | $188 (w/GT) | $188 (w/GT)/ $ (Others) | $* | - |
| | | | Merc-O-Matic Automatic | $226 (w/GT) | $226 (w/GT)/ $ (Others) | $ | - |
| 410 CID Marauder, 4-bbl., V8 | 330 | M | 4-speed manual | - | - | $289* | S |
| | | | Merc-O-Matic Automatic | - | - | $289 | S |
| 427 CID Cyclone, 4-bbl., V8 | 410 | W | 4-speed manual | $** | - | - | - |
| 427 CID Cyclone, 4-bbl., V8 | 425 | | 4-speed manual | $** | - | - | - |
| 428 CID Super Marauder, 4-bbl., V8 | 345 | Q | 4-speed manual | - | - | $376* | S (S-55)/$82 (Others) |
| | | | Merc-O-Matic Automatic | - | - | $376 | S (S-55)/$82 (Others) |

[1]*Cyclone.*   [2]*All but Cyclone.*   [3]*XR-7 only.*   [4]*All but XR-7.*   *\*Not available on wagons.*   *\*\*2-Door closed cars only.*

## Major Options

| | Comet | Cougar | Monterey/Montclair | Park Lane | Marquis/Br. |
|---|---|---|---|---|---|
| SelectAire air conditioning | $356 | $356 | $422 | $422 | $422 |
| Tinted glass | $27 | $30 | $42 | $42 | $42 |
| Remote-control trunk release | $13 | $13 | $13 | $13 | $13 |
| Speed control | - | $71 | $93 | $93 | $93 |

|                                        | Comet | Cougar | Monterey/Montclair | Park Lane | Marquis/Br. |
|----------------------------------------|-------|--------|--------------------|-----------|-------------|
| Tilt steering wheel                    | -     | $60    | $43                | $43       | $43         |
| Power steering                         | $95   | $95    | $104               | $104      | $104        |
| Power brakes                           | $42   | $42    | $42                | $42       | S           |
| Power windows                          | $100  | $100   | $104               | $104      | $104        |
| Power seat — six-way                   | $62   | $62    | $94                | $84       | $84         |
| Bucket seats                           | $80   | $80    | $168               | S         | -           |
| Electric windshield wipers w/washer    | $12   | $12    | $14                | $14       | $14         |
| Electric clock                         | $16   | $16    | $16 (Monterey)     | S         | S           |
| Pushbutton AM radio                    | $59   | $59    | $62                | $62       | $62         |
| AM/FM radio                            | -     | $134   | $151               | $151      | $151        |
| White sidewall tires — std. sizes      | $33   | $33    | $41                | $41       | $41         |
| Styled steel wheels                    | $115  | $115   | -                  | -         | -           |
| GT package                             | $190  | $324   | -                  | -         | -           |
| S-55 Sports package (Mntry. 2-Drs.)    | -     | -      | $526               | -         | -           |

Options common to most models. (- = Not Available; S = Standard equipment.) Items may be standard equipment, optional at different pricing, or unavailable on certain models. This chart is only a guide.

## Paint Colors

|                            | Code |                              | Code |
|----------------------------|------|------------------------------|------|
| Onyx                       | A    | Cardinal Red                 | T    |
| Turquoise                  | B    | Cinnamon Frost Metallic      | V    |
| Nordic Blue Metallic       | D    | Trafalgar Blue Metallic      | W    |
| Cumberland Beige Metallic  | E    | Burgundy Metallic            | X    |
| Tiffany Blue Metallic      | F    | Inverness Green Metallic     | Y    |
| Lime Frost Metallic        | I    | Sage Gold Metallic           | Z    |
| Caspian Blue Metallic      | K    | Sheffield Silver Metallic    | 4    |
| Polar White                | M    | Fawn                         | 6    |
| Sea Foam Green             | O    | Jamaican Yellow              | 8    |
| Glacier Blue Metallic      | Q    |                              |      |

# Cougar

*"Untamed elegance."*

**Nameplate year of origin:** 1967.
**Current bodystyle lifespan:** 1967 through 1968.
**Predecessor to this model:** None.
**Replacement for this model:** Cougar (1969 to 1970).
**Percentage of division's sales volume:** 42.60%.
**Corporate siblings:** Ford Mustang.
**Primary competition:** Chevrolet Camaro, Plymouth Barracuda and Pontiac Firebird.
**Notable changes:** All-new model for 1967.
**Major standard equipment:** Vinyl front bucket seats with foam cushions, full carpeting, dual front armrests and dual sun visors, dome light, glove compartment, bright metal front and rear window trim, and 7.35 × 14 BSW tires.

## Measurements

| Wheelbase              | 111.0" |
|------------------------|--------|
| Length                 | 190.3" |
| Width                  | 71.2"  |
| Height                 | 51.8"  |
| Legroom — front        | 41.8"  |
| Legroom — rear         | 31.7"  |
| Headroom — front       | 37.1"  |
| Headroom — rear        | 35.9"  |
| Cargo capacity (cu. ft.) | 9.1  |
| Fuel capacity (gals.)  | 17.0   |

## Models Available

|                            | Style Number | Base MSRP | Change from LY | Shipping Wt. (lbs.) | Production | Change from LY |
|----------------------------|--------------|-----------|----------------|---------------------|------------|----------------|
| Cougar 2-Door Hardtop      | 91           | $2,851    | NEW            | 3005                | 123,672    | NEW            |
| Cougar XR-7 2-Door Hardtop | 93           | $3,081    | NEW            | 3015                | 27,221     | NEW            |
| TOTALS                     |              | Avg. price $2,966 | NEW    |                     | Production 150,893 | NEW    |

1967

# Comet, Capri, Caliente and Cyclone

*"For modern styling, elegant interiors and all-around value."*

**Nameplate year of origin:** 1960.
**Current bodystyle lifespan:** 1966 through 1967.
**Predecessor to this model:** Comet (1964 to 1965).
**Replacement for this model:** Montego (1968 to 1969).
**Percentage of division's sales volume:** 22.91%.
**Corporate siblings:** Ford Fairlane.
**Primary competition:** Buick Special, Dodge Coronet, Oldsmobile F-85, and Pontiac Tempest.
**Notable changes:** New grille, minor trim and detail changes.
**Major standard equipment:** Nylon and vinyl front bench seat, rubber floor covering, dome light, bright metal front and rear window trim, and 7.35 × 14 BSW tires (7.75 × 14 BSW tires on wagon). Capri adds: Full carpeting and additional interior and exterior trim. Villager adds: Dual-action tailgate and exterior wood-grain trim. Caliente adds: Deluxe steering wheel, simulated walnut interior trim, power top on convertible, and additional sound deadening materials. Villager adds: Exterior wood-grain trim. Cyclone adds: All vinyl bucket seats with floor console, specific Cyclone exterior trim and engine dress-up kit. Cyclone GT adds: 390 CID V8 engine, GT identification, and 7.75 × 14 WSW tires.

## Measurements

| | Comet 202 | Capri/Caliente/Cyclone | Wagons |
|---|---|---|---|
| Wheelbase | 116.0" | 116.0" | 113.0" |
| Length | 196.4" | 203.5" | 199.9" |
| Width | 73.8" | 73.8" | 73.8" |
| Height | 55.0" | 55.0" | 56.2" |
| Legroom — front | 42.1" | 42.1" | 42.2" |
| Legroom — rear | 36.0" | 36.0" | 34.5" |
| Headroom — front | 38.8" | 38.8" | 38.6" |
| Headroom — rear | 37.6" | 37.6" | 39.1" |
| Cargo capacity (cu. ft.) | 13.5 | 17.1 | 85.2 |
| Fuel capacity (gals.) | 20.0 | 20.0 | 20.0 |

## Models Available

| | Style Number | Base MSRP | Change from LY | Shipping Wt. (lbs.) | Production | Change from LY |
|---|---|---|---|---|---|---|
| Comet 202 2-Door Sedan | 01 | $2,284 | +3.54% | 2787 | 14,251 | -60.37% |
| Comet 202 4-Door Sedan | 02 | $2,336 | +3.23% | 2825 | 10,281 | -49.70% |
| Comet Voyager 4-Door Wagon | 03 | $2,604 | +2.00% | 3230 | 4,930 | -35.09% |
| Comet Capri 2-Door Hardtop | 07 | $2,459 | +2.46% | 2889 | 11,671 | -22.35% |
| Comet Capri 4-Door Sedan | 06 | $2,436 | +2.44% | 2860 | 9,292 | -40.57% |
| Comet Villager 4-Door Wagon | 08 | $2,841 | +1.83% | 3252 | 3,140 | -19.07% |
| Comet Caliente 2-Door Hardtop | 11 | $2,558 | +3.35% | 2901 | 9,966 | -61.46% |
| Comet Caliente 2-Door Convertible | 12 | $2,818 | +3.03% | 3170 | 1,539 | -60.76% |
| Comet Caliente 4-Door Sedan | 10 | $2,535 | +3.34% | 2871 | 9,153 | -48.96% |
| Comet Cyclone 2-Door Hardtop | 15 | $2,737 | +1.37% | 3075 | 6,101 | -11.44% |
| Comet Cyclone 2-Door Convertible | 16 | $2,997 | +1.22% | 3339 | 809 | -38.01% |
| TOTALS | | Avg. price $2,600 | -0.46% | | Production 81,133 | -52.39% |

# Monterey

*"The Man's Car anyone can afford to own."*

**Nameplate year of origin:** 1952.
**Current bodystyle lifespan:** 1967 through 1968.
**Predecessor to this model:** Monterey (1965 to 1966).
**Replacement for this model:** Monterey (1969 to 1970).
**Percentage of division's sales volume:** 20.48%.
**Corporate siblings:** Ford Galaxie/LTD.

## Measurements

| | Cars | Commuter |
|---|---|---|
| Wheelbase | 123.0" | 119.0" |
| Length | 218.5" | 213.8" |
| Width | 78.2" | 78.2" |

**Primary competition:** Buick Wildcat, Dodge Monaco, Oldsmobile 88 and Pontiac Executive/Bonneville.
**Notable changes:** Completely restyled.
**Major standard equipment:** Cloth and vinyl front bench seat, full carpeting, bright exterior window trim and 8.15 × 15 BSW tires. Commuter wagons adds: power tailgate window, and 8.45 × 15 BSW tires.

|  | Cars | Commuter |
|---|---|---|
| Height | 56.1" | 56.9" |
| Legroom — front | 41.9" | 41.9" |
| Legroom — rear | 37.6" | 36.8" |
| Headroom — front | 38.9" | 39.1" |
| Headroom — rear | 37.7" | 40.0" |
| Cargo capacity (cu. ft.) | 19.1 | 91.3 |
| Fuel capacity (gals.) | 25.0 | 25.0 |

## Models Available

|  | Style Number | Base MSRP | Change from LY | Shipping Wt. (lbs.) | Production | Change from LY |
|---|---|---|---|---|---|---|
| Monterey 2-Door Hardtop | 47 | $2,985 | +2.40% | 3820 | 16,910 | -11.48% |
| Monterey 2-Door Convertible | 45 | $3,311 | +2.29% | 3943 | 2,673 | -18.48% |
| Monterey 4-Door Sedan | 44 | $2,904 | +1.75% | 3798 | 15,177 | -20.11% |
| Monterey 4-Door Breezeway Sedan | 44 | $2,904 | -0.45% | 3847 | 5,910 | -58.30% |
| Monterey 4-Door Hardtop | 48 | $3,059 | +2.31% | 3858 | 8,013 | +4.79% |
| Commuter 4-Door, 2-Seat Wagon | 72 | $3,289 | +1.51% | 4178 | 7,898 | +15.35% |
| TOTALS | | Avg. price $2,991 | +0.40% | | Production 72,535 | -18.00% |

# Montclair

*"Inside and outside, the big Montclair is value-packed."*

**Nameplate year of origin:** 1955.
**Current bodystyle lifespan:** 1967 through 1968.
**Predecessor to this model:** Montclair (1965 to 1966).
**Replacement for this model:** Monterey Custom (1969 to 1970).
**Percentage of division's sales volume:** 5.62%.
**Corporate siblings:** Ford Galaxie/LTD.
**Primary competition:** Buick Wildcat, Dodge Monaco, Oldsmobile 88 and Pontiac Bonneville.
**Notable changes:** Completely restyled.
**Major standard equipment:** Cloth and vinyl front bench seat, full carpeting, interval selector windshield wipers, electric clock, bright exterior trim, deluxe wheel covers, and 8.15 × 15 BSW tires.

## Measurements

| Wheelbase | 123.0" |
|---|---|
| Length | 218.5" |
| Width | 78.2" |
| Height | 56.1" |
| Legroom — front | 41.9" |
| Legroom — rear | 37.6" |
| Headroom — front | 38.9" |
| Headroom — rear | 37.7" |
| Cargo capacity (cu. ft.) | 19.1 |
| Fuel capacity (gals.) | 25.0 |

**1967**

## Models Available

|  | Style Number | Base MSRP | Change from LY | Shipping Wt. (lbs.) | Production | Change from LY |
|---|---|---|---|---|---|---|
| Montclair 2-Door Hardtop | 57 | $3,244 | +3.18% | 3848 | 4,118 | -63.53% |
| Montclair 4-Door Sedan | 54 | $3,187 | +3.24% | 863 | 5,783 | -51.22% |
| Montclair 4-Door Breezeway Sedan | 54 | $3,187 | NEW | 3881 | 4,151 | NEW |
| Montclair 4-Door Hardtop | 58 | $3,316 | +3.08% | 3943 | 5,870 | -62.77% |
| TOTALS | | Avg. price $3,234 | +2.70% | | Production 19,922 | -48.80% |

# Park Lane

*"Mercury stylists have given all-new grace and natural beauty to the Park Lane and Colony Park for 1967."*

**Nameplate year of origin:** 1958.
**Current bodystyle lifespan:** 1967 through 1968.
**Predecessor to this model:** Park Lane (1965 to 1966).
**Replacement for this model:** Marquis (1969 to 1970).
**Percentage of division's sales volume:** 8.93%.
**Corporate siblings:** Ford Galaxie/LTD.
**Primary competition:** Buick Wildcat, Chrysler Newport, Oldsmobile 88 and Pontiac Bonneville.
**Notable changes:** Completely restyled.
**Major standard equipment:** Cloth and vinyl front bench seat (all-vinyl for convertible), full carpeting, trip odometer, automatic parking brake release, courtesy lights, interval selector windshield wipers, electric clock, custom grip door handles, bright exterior window trim, full wheel covers and 8.15 × 15 BSW tires. Colony Park wagons adds: exterior wood-grain vinyl trim, power tailgate window and 8.45 × 15 BSW tires.

## Measurements

|  | Cars | Colony Park |
|---|---|---|
| Wheelbase | 123.0" | 119.0" |
| Length | 218.5" | 213.8" |
| Width | 78.2" | 78.2" |
| Height | 56.1" | 56.9" |
| Legroom — front | 41.9" | 41.9" |
| Legroom — rear | 37.6" | 36.8" |
| Headroom — front | 38.9" | 39.1" |
| Headroom — rear | 37.7" | 40.0" |
| Cargo capacity (cu. ft.) | 19.1 | 91.3 |
| Fuel capacity (gals.) | 25.0 | 25.0 |

## Models Available

|  | Style Number | Base MSRP | Change from LY | Shipping Wt. (lbs.) | Production | Change from LY |
|---|---|---|---|---|---|---|
| Park Lane 2-Door Hardtop | 67 | $3,752 | +10.78% | 3947 | 2,196 | -73.71% |
| Park Lane 2-Door Convertible | 65 | $3,984 | +10.42% | 4114 | 1,191 | -53.22% |
| Park Lane 4-Door Breezeway Sdn. | 64 | $3,736 | +10.24% | 4011 | 4,163 | -52.13% |
| Park Lane 4-Door Hardtop | 68 | $3,826 | +10.58% | 3992 | 5,412 | -71.82% |
| Colony Park 4-Door, 2-Seat Wagon | 76 | $3,657 | +4.43% | 4258 | 18,680 | -1.13% |
| TOTALS | | *Avg. price* $3,791 | +9.28% | *Production* | 31,642 | -45.16% |

# Brougham & Marquis

*"Elegant and handsome luxury motoring."*

**Nameplate year of origin:** 1967.
**Current bodystyle lifespan:** 1967 through 1968.
**Predecessor to this model:** Park Lane (1965 to 1966).
**Replacement for this model:** Marquis (1969 to 1970).
**Percentage of division's sales volume:** 3.96%.
**Corporate siblings:** Ford Galaxie/LTD.
**Primary competition:** Buick Wildcat, Chrysler Newport, Oldsmobile 88 and Pontiac Bonneville.
**Notable changes:** All-new models.
**Major standard equipment:** Cloth and vinyl Twin-Comfort lounge bench seat, full carpeting, trip odometer, wood-toned steering wheel (Marquis), wood-grain interior trim, automatic parking brake release, courtesy light group, interval selector windshield wipers, electric clock, bright exterior window trim, vinyl top, power brakes, 4-speed manual or automatic transmission, full wheel covers and 8.15 × 15 BSW tires.

## Measurements

| Wheelbase | 123.0" |
|---|---|
| Length | 218.5" |
| Width | 78.2" |
| Height | 56.1" |
| Legroom — front | 41.9" |
| Legroom — rear | 37.6" |
| Headroom — front | 38.9" |
| Headroom — rear | 37.7" |
| Cargo capacity (cu. ft.) | 19.1 |
| Fuel capacity (gals.) | 25.0 |

## Models Available

|  | Style Number | Base MSRP | Change from LY | Shipping Wt. (lbs.) | Production | Change from LY |
|---|---|---|---|---|---|---|
| Marquis 2-Door Hardtop | 69 | $3,989 | NEW | 3995 | 6,510 | NEW |
| Brougham 4-Door Breezeway Sdn. | 61 | $3,896 | NEW | 3980 | 3,325 | NEW |
| Brougham 4-Door Hardtop | 62 | $3,986 | NEW | 4000 | 4,189 | NEW |
| TOTALS | | Avg. price $3,957 | NEW | Production | 14,024 | NEW |

# OLDSMOBILE

*"The Rocket Action Cars Are Out Front Again!"*

After the whirlwind of success with the Toronado in 1966, and all the attention garnered from its introduction, Oldsmobile took full advantage of the Toronado for marketing its 1967 line. Nearly every Oldsmobile line was compared to the Toronado in some respect in the majority of its advertising. With the restyling of the full-size Ninety-Eight and 88 series, certain aspects of the Toronado styling were carried to these lines, such as round wheel arches, minimal chrome exterior trim, and egg-crate grille. Only minor changes were made to the Toronado itself for its second season on the market. The only major appearance change was to make the area around the headlight openings flush, as compared to the small indented area above the first year model's light opening.

Although the full-size models were totally restyled this year, their change was evolutionary. Customers would still recognize the Ninety-Eight and 88 as Oldsmobiles, but front end styling featured a now trademark appearance, consisting of wide-spaced headlights with the parking/turn signal lamps placed between them and a two-piece grille section in between. A newly christened Delmont 88 line replaced both the Jetstar 88 and Dynamic 88. An expanded Delta 88 line added a top-line Custom series.

The mid-sized F-85/Cutlass and Cutlass-based Vista-Cruiser were little changed style-wise from their '66 counterparts, except for a front end restyling that included the same frontal appearance as the full-size models. Also new for the year was the Cutlass Supreme line. For people who did a lot of highway driving, a new Turnpike Cruising option that included a 400 CID V8 and economy gearing was a popular choice. As consumers looked for more comfort and convenience features in their automobiles, luxury models became increasingly popular. All mid-size GM models had been gaining in popularity since their 1964 restyle that took them from the large-compact market to a true mid-size line. Part of this popularity is no doubt due to the fact that full-size models had grown so much in the past decade, so that a mid-size 1967 Cutlass model was similar in physical size and price to a 1957 Oldsmobile 88 model. This was definitely a size and price segment of the market that the buying public liked. As the mid-size cars gained more powertrains choices and comfort and convenience features, the popularity of these cars continued to grow. By the mid-seventies, the Cutlass would reach the pinnacle of its sales success.

**1967**

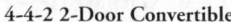

4-4-2 2-Door Convertible

Ninety-Eight LS 4-Door Hardtop

Cutlass Supreme 4-Door Hardtop

Delta 88 2-Door Hardtop

Delmont 88 4-Door Hardtop

Toronado 2-Door Hardtop

Vista-Cruiser 4-Door Wagon

**Model year production:** 516,672, down 11.55% from 1966.
**Domestic market share:** 6.74% (6th place).
**Base price range:** $2,410 to $4,869.
**Industry average base price:** $3,159.
**Oldsmobile average base price:** $3,294.
**Introduction date:** September 1966.
**Assembly plants:** Southgate, CA (C); Framingham, MA (G); Fremont, CA (Z); Lansing, MI (M); Fairfax, KS (X); and Linden, NJ (E).

**Data plate identification:** Thirteen digit code read as follows: 1st digit 3 = Oldsmobile; 2nd through 5th digits identify series/body style number; 7 = 1967; 7th digit is assembly plant code; 100001 and up for serial number (except Toronado is 600001). *Example:* 358397X100001 is a 1967 Oldsmobile Delta 88 4-Door Hardtop, serial number 100001, built in Fairfax, KS.

## Powertrains

| Engine | Gross HP | Transmission Availability | Cutlass/ 4-4-2 | Cut. Sup./ Vista-Cr. | Delm. 88/ Delta 88 | 98 | Toronado |
|---|---|---|---|---|---|---|---|
| 250 CID Action-Line, 1-bbl., 6-cyl. | 155 | 3-speed manual | S* | - | - | - | - |
| | | Jetaway Automatic | $236* | - | - | - | |
| 330 CID Jetfire Rocket, 2-bbl., V8 | 250 (260 Prem.) | 3-speed manual | $70* | S (V.Cr.) | S (Delmt.) | - | - |
| | | 4-speed manual | $254* | $184 (V.Cr.) | - | - | - |
| | | Jetaway Automatic | $306* | $236 (V.Cr.) | $236 (Delmt.) | | |
| | | Turbo Hydra-matic | - | $236 (V.Cr.) | $236 (Delmt.) | | |
| 330 CID Jetfire Rocket, 4-bbl., V8 | 320 | 3-speed manual | $103* | S (Supr.)/ $33 (V.Cr.) | - | - | - |
| | | 4-speed manual | $287* | $184 (Supr.)/ $217 (V.Cr.) | | | |
| | | Jetaway Automatic | $339* | $236 (Supr.)/ $269 (V.Cr.) | | | |
| | | Turbo Hydra-matic | - | $269 (V.Cr.) | - | - | - |
| 400 CID Rocket, 8 2-bbl., V | 300 | 3-speed manual | - | $98*** | - | - | - |
| | | Turbo Hydra-matic | - | $334*** | - | - | - |
| 400 CID 4-4-2, 4-bbl., V8 | 350 | 3-speed manual | S** | - | - | - | - |
| | | 4-speed manual | $184** | - | - | - | - |
| | | Turbo Hydra-matic | $236** | - | - | - | - |
| 425 CID Super Rocket, 2-bbl., V8 | 300 (310 w/Auto.) | 3-speed manual | - | - | S (Delta)/$89 (Delmt.) | - | - |
| | | Turbo Hydra-matic | - | - | $236 (Delta) $325 (Delmt.) | - | - |
| 425 CID Super Rocket, 4-bbl., V8 | 365 | 3-speed manual | - | - | $36 (Delta) $125 (Delmt.) | - | - |
| | | Turbo Hydra-matic | - | - | $272 (Delta) $451 (Delmt.) | S | - |
| 425 CID Starfire Rocket, 4-bbl., V8 | 375 | 3-speed manual | - | - | $100 (Delta) $189 (Delmt.) | - | - |
| | | Turbo Hydra-matic | - | - | $336 (Delta) $425 (Delmt.) | $64 | - |

| Engine | Gross HP | Transmission Availability | Cutlass/ 4-4-2 | Cut. Sup./ Vista-Cr. | Delm. 88/ Delta 88 | 98 | Toronado |
|---|---|---|---|---|---|---|---|
| 425 CID Toronado Rocket, 4-bbl., V8 | 385 | Turbo Hydra-matic | - | - | - | - | S |

*F-85 and Cutlass only.   **With 4-4-2 option only.   ***Available only on Supreme 2-Door with Turnpike Cruising Package.*

## Major Options

| | Cutlass | Vista-Cruiser | Delmont 88 | Delta 88 | Ninety-Eight | Toronado |
|---|---|---|---|---|---|---|
| Air conditioning | $343 | $343 | $390 | $390 | $390 | $390 |
| Electronic cruise control (V8 only) | $44 | $44 | $49 | $49 | $49 | $49 |
| Soft Ray tinted glass | $39 | $39 | $44 | $44 | $44 | $47 |
| Deck lid remote release | $12 | - | $12 | $12 | $12 | $12 |
| Tilt-Away steering wheel | $42 | $42 | $42 | $42 | $42 | $42 |
| Power steering — variable-ratio | $94 | $94 | $104 | $104 | S | S |
| Power brakes | $42 | $42 | $42 | $42 | S | S |
| Power driver's seat/bench seat | $94 | $94 | $100 | $100 | $74–$100* | $74 |
| Power windows | $104 | $104 | $110 | $110 | S/$110* | $110 |
| Electric clock | $35 | $35 | $35 | $35 | S | S |
| AM radio | $64 | $64 | $64 | $64 | $64 | $64 |
| AM/FM radio | $133 | $133 | $133 | $133 | $133 | $133 |
| Front seat console | $54 | - | $54 | $54 | - | $54 |
| Vinyl roof | $84 | - | $105 | $105 | $110 | $110 |
| White sidewall tires (base size) | $30–$40 | $40 | $40 | $40 | $45 | $45 |
| Wire wheel trim covers | $68 | $68 | $68 | $68 | $68 | - |

Options common to most models. (- = Not Available; S = Standard equipment.) Items may be standard equipment, optional at different pricing, or unavailable on certain models. This chart is only a guide.

*4-Door Town Sedan only.*

## Paint Colors

| | Code | | Code |
|---|---|---|---|
| Ebony Black | A | Burgundy Mist Metallic | N |
| Turquoise Frost Metallic* | B | Pewter Metallic | P |
| Provincial White | C | Spanish Red | R |
| Crystal Blue Metallic | D | Champagne Metallic | S |
| Midnight Blue Metallic | E | Cameo Ivory | T |
| Bimini Blue Metallic* | F | Dubonnet* | U |
| Gold Metallic | G | Antique Pewter Metallic | V |
| Aspen Green Metallic | H | Sauterne Metallic* | W |
| Emerald Green Metallic* | J | Garnet Red Metallic* | X |
| Aquamarine Metallic | K | Saffron | Y |
| Tahoe Turquoise Metallic | L | Florentine Gold Metallic* | Z |

*Available only on Toronado.*

# F-85 and Cutlass

*"What are you trying to do, Olds? Please everybody? You bet!"*

**Nameplate year of origin:** 1962 (as F-85 model designation)— 1955 Show car.
**Current bodystyle lifespan:** 1966 through 1967.
**Predecessor to this model:** F-85/Cutlass (1964 to 1965).
**Replacement for this model:** Cutlass (1968 to 1972).

## Measurements

| | 2-Doors | 4-Doors | Wagon |
|---|---|---|---|
| Wheelbase | 115.0" | 115.0" | 115.0" |
| Length | 204.2" | 204.2" | 204.2" |

**Percentage of division's sales volume:** 39.09%.

**Corporate siblings:** Buick Special/Skylark, Chevrolet Chevelle, Pontiac Tempest/LeMans.

**Primary competition:** AMC Rebel, Dodge Coronet, Ford Fairlane, Mercury Comet, Plymouth Belvedere/Satellite.

**Notable changes:** Minor trim and detail changes.

**Major standard equipment:** All vinyl front bench seat, dual master-cylinder brake system, and 7.75 × 14 BSW tires. Cutlass adds: full carpeting, deluxe steering wheel, heater and defroster, and exterior chrome trim moldings. Cutlass Supreme adds: Woodgrain interior trim, Strato-bucket seats (2-Doors), Custom Sport Seat (4-Door Hardtop), and full-length exterior rocker moldings. 4-4-2 package adds: Floor-mounted heavy-duty shifter, heavy-duty wheels, heavy-duty motor mounts, and F70 × 14 redline tires.

|  | 2-Doors | 4-Doors | Wagon |
|---|---|---|---|
| Width | 76.0" | 76.0" | 76.0" |
| Height | 53.6" | 54.4" | 55.3" |
| Legroom — front | 41.7" | 41.2" | 41.2" |
| Legroom — rear | 32.3" | 35.9" | 35.9" |
| Headroom — front | 37.7" | 38.1" | 38.0" |
| Headroom — rear | 36.2" | 37.3" | 37.5" |
| Luggage capacity (cu. ft.) | 20.1 | 20.1 | 85.5 |
| Fuel capacity (gals.) | 20.0 | 20.0 | 20.0 |

## Models Available

|  | Style Number | Base MSRP | Change from LY | Shipping Wt. (lbs.) | Production | Change from LY |
|---|---|---|---|---|---|---|
| F-85 2-Door Sport Coupe | 3307 | $2,410 | +2.64% | 3014 | 12,049 | -5.08% |
| F-85 4-Door Town Sedan | 3369 | $2,457 | +2.33% | 3031 | 7,584 | +14.63% |
| F-85 4-Door, 2-Seat Wagon | 3335 | $2,749 | +2.00% | 3295 | 4,376 | +102.59% |
| Cutlass 2-Door Hardtop | 3517 | $2,574 | +2.43% | 3033 | 12,049 | -39.58% |
| Cutlass 2-Door Convertible | 3567 | $2,770 | NEW | 3125 | 4,337 | NEW |
| Cutlass 4-Door Town Sedan | 3569 | $2,552 | +2.20% | 3055 | 31,281 | +0.84% |
| Cutlass 4-Door Hardtop | 3539 | $2,683 | +2.05% | 3125 | 7,988 | +13.90% |
| Cutlass 4-Door, 2-Seat Wagon | 3535 | $2,848 | +1.97% | 3308 | 4,376 | -48.47% |
| Cutlass Supreme 2-Door Club Cpe. | 3807 | $2,694 | +2.32% | 3238 | 18,256 | +4.59% |
| Cutlass Supreme 2-Door Hardtop | 3817 | $2,831 | +2.20% | 3262 | 57,858 | +29.63% |
| Cutlass Supreme 2-Door Conv. | 3867 | $3,026 | +2.06% | 3358 | 10,897 | -10.34% |
| Cutlass Supreme 4-Dr. Town Sdn. | 3869 | $2,726 | +1.98% | 3258 | 8,346 | -7.44% |
| Cutlass Supreme 4-Door Hardtop | 3839 | $2,900 | +1.90% | 3346 | 22,571 | -26.89% |
| TOTALS | Avg. price | $2,709 | +2.34% | Production | 201,968 | -0.49% |

# Vista-Cruiser

*"Lets you get away from it all—and take it all with you, too!"*

**Nameplate year of origin:** 1964.

**Current bodystyle lifespan:** 1966 through 1967.

**Predecessor to this model:** Vista-Cruiser (1964 to 1965).

**Replacement for this model:** Vista-Cruiser (1968 to 1972).

**Percentage of division's sales volume:** 5.33%.

**Corporate siblings:** Buick SportWagon.

**Primary competition:** AMC Ambassador and Dodge Coronet.

**Notable changes:** Minor trim and detail changes.

**Major standard equipment:** All-vinyl front bench seat, rear carpeting, Vista-roof windows, and 8.25 × 14 BSW tires. Custom adds: Front carpeting, below-deck storage compartment, deluxe steering wheel and padded second seat sun visors.

### Measurements

| Wheelbase | 120.0" |
|---|---|
| Length | 209.5" |
| Width | 76.0" |
| Height | 58.2" |
| Legroom — front | 41.6" |
| Legroom — rear | 38.9" |
| Headroom — front | 38.0" |
| Headroom — rear | 40.5" |
| Luggage capacity (cu. ft.) | 101.1 |
| Fuel capacity (gals.) | 20.0 |

## Models Available

| | Style Number | Base MSRP | Change from LY | Shipping Wt. (lbs.) | Production | Change from LY |
|---|---|---|---|---|---|---|
| Vista-Cruiser 4-Dr., 3-S. Wagon | 3465 | $3,136 | +1.59% | 3858 | 2,748 | +47.03% |
| Vista-Cruiser Cust. 4-Dr., 2-S. Wgn. | 3855 | $3,228 | +2.90% | 3796 | 9,513 | +6.77% |
| Vista-Cruiser Cust. 4-Dr., 3-S. Wgn. | 3865 | $3,369 | +2.78% | 3907 | 15,293 | +7.95% |
| TOTALS | Avg. price | $3,244 | +4.34% | Production | 27,554 | +3.80% |

# Delmont 88

*"Brand-new 88 series! Goes to show what Olds can do with a modest price tag … and a lot of Toronado inspiration."*

**Nameplate year of origin:** 1967 (88 series started 1949).
**Current bodystyle lifespan:** 1967 through 1968.
**Predecessor to this model:** Jetstar 88/Dynamic 88 (1965 to 1966).
**Replacement for this model:** Delta 88 (1969 to 1970).
**Percentage of division's sales volume:** 19.37%.
**Corporate siblings:** Buick LeSabre/Wildcat, Chevrolet Impala/Caprice, Pontiac Catalina/Bonneville.
**Primary competition:** AMC Ambassador, Dodge Polara, Ford LTD, and Mercury Monterey.
**Notable changes:** All-new for 1967, replacing the Jetstar 88.
**Major standard equipment:** Cloth-and-vinyl bench seat, nylon-blend carpet, heater and defroster, full wheel covers, and 8.55 × 14 BSW tires.

### Measurements

| | |
|---|---|
| Wheelbase | 123.0" |
| Length | 217.0" |
| Width | 80.0" |
| Height | 55.5" |
| Legroom — front | 41.1" |
| Legroom — rear | 39.0" |
| Headroom — front | 38.7" |
| Headroom — rear | 37.9" |
| Luggage capacity (cu. ft.) | 17.1 |
| Fuel capacity (gals.) | 25.0 |

## Models Available

| | Style Number | Base MSRP | Change from LY | Shipping Wt. (lbs.) | Production | Change from LY |
|---|---|---|---|---|---|---|
| Delmont 88 330 2-Door Hardtop | 5287 | $3,063 | +2.68% | 3819 | 10,786 | +25.78% |
| Delmont 88 330 4-Door Town Sedan | 5269 | $3,008 | +2.77% | 3867 | 15,076 | +18.39% |
| Delmont 88 330 4-Door Hardtop | 5239 | $3,139 | +2.62% | 3932 | 10,600 | +33.53% |
| Delmont 88 425 2-Door Hardtop | 5687 | $3,126 | +1.86% | 3914 | 16,669 | -19.74% |
| Delmont 88 425 2-Door Convertible | 5667 | $3,462 | +1.70% | 4010 | 3,525 | -36.37% |
| Delmont 88 425 4-Door Town Sedan | 5669 | $3,071 | +1.92% | 3968 | 21,511 | -44.48% |
| Delmont 88 425 4-Door Hardtop | 5639 | $3,202 | +1.84% | 4007 | 21,909 | -28.83% |
| TOTALS | Avg. price | $3,153 | -0.16% | Production | 100,076 | +4.43% |

*Comparisons made to 1966 Jetstar 88 and Dynamic 88 models*

# Delta 88

*"Some people may think your new Delta looks like a Toronado. So be it."*

**Nameplate year of origin:** 1965 (88 series started 1949).
**Current bodystyle lifespan:** 1967 through 1968.
**Predecessor to this model:** Dynamic/Delta 88 (1965 to 1966).
**Replacement for this model:** Delta 88 (1969 to 1970).
**Percentage of division's sales volume:** 17.24%.
**Corporate siblings:** Buick LeSabre/Wildcat, Chevrolet Impala/Caprice, Pontiac Catalina.

### Measurements

| | |
|---|---|
| Wheelbase | 123.0" |
| Length | 217.0" |
| Width | 80.0" |
| Height | 54.5" |
| Legroom — front | 41.1" |

**1967**

**Primary competition:** AMC Ambassador, Dodge Polara, Ford LTD, and Mercury Monterey.

**Notable changes:** Completely restyled.

**Major standard equipment:** All-vinyl bench seat with fold-down center armrest (except Town Sedan), nylon-blend carpet, deluxe steering wheel, heater and defroster, glove box and courtesy lamps, full wheel covers, and 8.55 × 14 BSW tires. Custom adds: Bucket seats and floor console (coupe) or Strato-Bench seat (Sedan), full-length bodyside molding, and unique rear treatment.

## Measurements (cont.)

| | |
|---|---|
| Legroom — rear | 39.0" |
| Headroom — front | 38.7" |
| Headroom — rear | 37.9" |
| Luggage capacity (cu. ft.) | 17.1 |
| Fuel capacity (gals.) | 25.0 |

## Models Available

| | Style Number | Base MSRP | Change from LY | Shipping Wt. (lbs.) | Production | Change from LY |
|---|---|---|---|---|---|---|
| Delta 88 2-Door Hardtop | 5887 | $3,310 | +1.75% | 3956 | 14,471 | -29.71% |
| Delta 88 2-Door Convertible | 5867 | $3,646 | +1.62% | 4039 | 3,447 | -19.89% |
| Delta 88 4-Door Town Sdn. | 5869 | $3,218 | +1.84% | 3986 | 22,770 | -24.45% |
| Delta 88 4-Door Hardtop | 5839 | $3,386 | +1.74% | 4053 | 21,909 | -34.26% |
| Delta 88 Custom 2-Door Hardtop | 5487 | $3,522 | NEW | 3994 | 12,192 | NEW |
| Delta 88 Custom 4-Door Hardtop | 5439 | $3,582 | NEW | 4081 | 14,306 | NEW |
| TOTALS | | Avg. price $3,444 | +3.36% | | Production 89,095 | +0.84% |

# Ninety-Eight

*"It's a very good year."*

**Nameplate year of origin:** 1941.

**Current bodystyle lifespan:** 1967 through 1968.

**Predecessor to this model:** Ninety-Eight (1965 to 1966).

**Replacement for this model:** Ninety-Eight (1969 to 1970).

**Percentage of division's sales volume:** 14.75%.

**Corporate siblings:** Buick Electra, and Cadillac Calais/de Ville.

**Primary competition:** Chrysler New Yorker and Mercury Marquis.

**Notable changes:** Completely restyled.

**Major standard equipment:** Cloth and vinyl bench seat with fold-down center armrest, deep-pile carpeting floor and kick panels, deluxe steering wheel, electric clock, power windows and two-way power seat (except Town Sedan), trunk lamp, trunk mat, full wheel covers, rear wheel opening covers, power steering, power front disc brakes, 8.85 × 14 BSW tires. Luxury Sedan adds: special design interior, recessed vanity and assist handles, special front and rear door pulls, and rear folding center armrests.

## Measurements

| | |
|---|---|
| Wheelbase | 126.0" |
| Length | 223.0" |
| Width | 80.0" |
| Height | 55.8" |
| Legroom — front | 41.0" |
| Legroom — rear | 42.2" |
| Headroom — front | 39.5" |
| Headroom — rear | 38.2" |
| Luggage capacity (cu. ft.) | 18.2 |
| Fuel capacity (gals.) | 25.0 |

## Models Available

| | Style Number | Base MSRP | Change from LY | Shipping Wt. (lbs.) | Production | Change from LY |
|---|---|---|---|---|---|---|
| Ninety-Eight 2-Door Hardtop | 8457 | $4,214 | +1.35% | 4221 | 10,476 | -8.81% |
| Ninety-Eight 2-Door Convertible | 8467 | $4,498 | +1.24% | 4271 | 3,769 | -17.49% |
| Ninety-Eight 4-Door Town Sedan | 8469 | $4,009 | +1.08% | 4242 | 8,900 | -18.29% |
| Ninety-Eight 4-Door Hardtop | 8439 | $4,276 | +1.02% | 4323 | 17,533 | -23.93% |
| Ninety-Eight Luxury 4-Door Sedan | 8669 | $4,351 | +1.00% | 4309 | 35,511 | -6.85% |
| TOTALS | | Avg. price $4,270 | +1.14% | | Production 76,189 | -13.54% |

# Toronado

*"Imitated. Emulated. Borrowed from. But nothing really tops the genuine article. Back with a flair. Better than ever."*

**Nameplate year of origin:** 1966.
**Current bodystyle lifespan:** 1966 through 1970.
**Predecessor to this model:** None.
**Replacement for this model:** Toronado (1971 to 1978).
**Percentage of division's sales volume:** 4.22%.
**Corporate siblings:** Buick Riviera and Cadillac Eldorado.
**Primary competition:** Imperial LeBaron Coupe and Ford Thunderbird.
**Notable changes:** Revised front styling, minor trim and detail changes.
**Major standard equipment:** All-vinyl bench seat, deep-pile carpeting, heater and defroster, electric clock, LH outside rearview mirror, front wheel drive, power brakes, and 8.85 × 15 BSW tires. Deluxe adds: Foam padded Strato bench seat with fold-down center armrest or bucket seats and deluxe wheel covers.

## Measurements

| | |
|---|---|
| Wheelbase | 119.0" |
| Length | 211.0" |
| Width | 78.5" |
| Height | 52.8" |
| Legroom — front | 41.2" |
| Legroom — rear | 35.5" |
| Headroom — front | 37.9" |
| Headroom — rear | 37.3" |
| Luggage capacity (cu. ft.) | 14.1 |
| Fuel capacity (gals.) | 24.0 |

## Models Available

| | Style Number | Base MSRP | Change from LY | Shipping Wt. (lbs.) | Production | Change from LY |
|---|---|---|---|---|---|---|
| Toronado 2-Door Hardtop | 9487 | $4,674 | +1.23% | 4310 | 1,770 | -72.05% |
| Toronado Deluxe 2-Door Hardtop | 9687 | $4,869 | +1.18% | 4362 | 20,020 | -42.19% |
| TOTALS | | Avg. price $4,772 | +1.21% | | Production 21,790 | -46.81% |

# PLYMOUTH

*"Plymouth is out to win you over."*

Nineteen-sixty-seven brought the introduction of a totally new line of Valiant, Barracuda and Fury models, with significant new model introductions to the revised Belvedere line. The compact, "entry-level" Valiant was redesigned based on styling similar to the squarish Belvedere from 1966. A more pronounced split grille styling theme up front and vertical taillamps at the rear were strong visual cues. Under the hood were the same powerplants as in previous model years. The Barracuda, based heavily upon Valiant components, was also totally redesigned for 1967. The Barracuda featured a split grille theme up front and small C-shaped taillamps. Most important were two new model choices, the Convertible and the Hardtop. These two models were a significant portion of the new Barracuda's sales, and essentially replaced those same styles in the Valiant line. The Barracuda became more of a sports car with the addition of an available 383 CID V8 to its option list. This allowed the "Cuda" to keep up with the Mustang and Camaro.

The mid-size Belvedere line was given a slight facelift, but the big news was the new models available. New for the season were the GTX 2-Door Hardtop and Convertible models. These top-line muscle cars were outfitted with the sportiest of Belvedere accessories. They were powered by the 440 CID V8 Super Commando engine, which was the largest engine offered in any muscle car to date. The optional 426 Hemi added even more power. Features included hood scoops, redline tires, and a luxurious bucket seat interior. Other changes to the Belvedere line included the addition of a base Belvedere Wagon.

The full-size Fury line also made news this year, with all-new styling and sporty fastback rooflines for some 2-Door Hardtop models. The front styling continued to feature vertically stacked headlamps, now flanking a new 4-port grille design. Rear styling was highlighted by horizontal taillamps. The only new model addition was a Sport Fury 2-Door FastTop with semi-fastback styling similar to other Mopar 2-Door Hardtops.

Belvedere I 4-Door Sedan

Barracuda 2-Door Fastback

Barracuda 2-Door Hardtop

Fury III 4-Door Sedan

GTX 2-Door Hardtop

Satellite 2-Door Convertible

Sport Fury 2-Door Convertible

Valiant 100 4-Door Sedan

VIP 2-Door Hardtop

**Model year production:** 636,893, down 8.48% from 1966.
**Domestic market share:** 8.31% (4th place).
**Base price range:** $2,117 to $3,418.
**Industry average base price:** $3,159.
**Plymouth average base price:** $2,761.
**Introduction date:** September 29, 1966. Barracuda introduced November 25, 1966.
**Assembly plants:** Lynch Road, MI (1): Hamtramck, MI (2); Belvidere, IL (4); Los Angeles, CA (5); Newark DE (6); St. Louis, MO (7); and Windsor, Ontario, Canada (9).

**Data plate identification:** Thirteen digit code read as follows: First digit is car line (e.g., P for Fury); second number identifies series (L is low, M is mid, H is High, etc.); 3rd and 4th digits indicate body style (see model number in charts below), fifth digit is engine code (see chart below); sixth digit 7 for 1967; seventh digit is assembly plant code; and 100001 and up for serial number. *Example:* PM23E72100001 is a 1967 Plymouth Fury III 2-Door Hardtop with a 318 CID V8 engine, built at Hamtramck, MI, serial number 100001.

## Powertrains

| Engine | Gross HP | Engine Code | Transmission Availability | Valiant | Barracuda | Belvedere | Fury |
|---|---|---|---|---|---|---|---|
| 170 CID, 1-bbl., 6-cyl. | 101 | A | 3-speed manual | S | - | - | - |
| | | | 4-speed manual | $179 | - | - | - |
| | | | Torqueflite automatic | $172 | - | - | - |
| 225 CID, 1-bbl., 6-cyl. | 145 | B | 3-speed manual | $46 | S | S[2] | S[3] |
| | | | 4-speed manual | $232 | $186 | - | - |
| | | | Torqueflite automatic | $218 | $172 | $192[2] | $192[3] |

| Engine | Gross HP | Engine Code | Transmission Availability | Valiant | Barracuda | Belvedere | Fury |
|---|---|---|---|---|---|---|---|
| 273 CID, 2-bbl., V8 | 180 | D | 3-speed manual | $131 | $82 | S[1]/$94[2] | - |
| | | | 4-speed manual | $310 | $261 | - | - |
| | | | Torqueflite automatic | $312 | $263 | $203[1]/$297[2] | - |
| 273 CID Formula S, 4-bbl., V8 | 235 | E | 3-speed manual | - | $165 | - | - |
| | | | 4-speed manual | - | $344 | - | - |
| | | | Torqueflite automatic | - | $346 | - | - |
| 318 CID, 2-bbl., V8 | 230 | F | 3-speed manual | - | - | $30[1]/$124[2] | S[4]/$104[3] |
| | | | Torqueflite automatic | - | - | $241[1]/$335[2] | $211[4]/$315[3] |
| 383 CID Commando, 2-bbl., V8 | 305 | G | 3-speed manual | - | - | - | $71[4]/$185[3] |
| | | | 4-speed manual | - | - | - | $259[4]/$373[3] |
| | | | Torqueflite automatic | - | - | - | $282[4]/$396[3] |
| 383 CID Commando, 4-bbl., V8 | 325 | H | 3-speed manual | - | - | $150[1]/$244[2] | $120[4]/$224[3] |
| | | | 4-speed manual | - | - | $338[1]/$432[2] | $308[4]/$412[3] |
| | | | Torqueflite automatic | - | - | $361[1]/$455[2] | $331[4]/$435[3] |
| 426 CID Commando, 4-bbl., V8 | 365 | J | 4-speed manual | - | - | * | * |
| | | | Torqueflite automatic | - | - | * | * |
| 426 CID Commando, 4-bbl., V8 | 415–425 | M | 4-speed manual | - | - | * | * |
| | | | Torqueflite automatic | - | - | * | * |
| 426 CID Hemi V8, 4-bbl., V8 | 415–425 | M | 4-speed manual | - | - | * | * |
| | | | Torqueflite automatic | - | - | * | * |
| 440 CID, 4-bbl., V8 | 350 | K | Torqueflite automatic | - | - | - | $4[4]/$3[3] |
| 440 CID, 4-bbl., V8 | 375 | L | Torqueflite automatic | - | - | S (GTX) | $445[4]/$549[3] |

[1]Satellite models only.   [2]All but Satellite.   [3]Fury I (All), Fury II Sedans, Fury III 2-Door HT and 4-Door Sedan only.   [4]All but Fury I, Fury II Sedan, and Fury III 2-Dr. HT and 4-Dr. Sedan.   *Available at varying prices and installation rate. Accurate pricing is unavailable at this time.

## Major Options

| | Valiant | Barracuda | Belvedere | Fury |
|---|---|---|---|---|
| Air conditioning | $319 | $319 | $338 | $338 |
| Tinted glass | $29 | $14 | $40 | $40 |
| Power steering | $80 | $80 | $84 | $95 |
| Power brakes | $42 | $42 | $42 | $42 |
| Power windows | - | - | $102 | $102 |
| Power front seat — 4-way bucket | - | - | $78 | $78 |
| Electric clock | $15 | $15 | $15 | $15 |
| AM radio | $57 | $57 | $57 | $57 |

Options common to most models (- = Not Available.) Items may be standard equipment, optional at different pricing, or unavailable on certain models. This chart is only a guide.

## Paint Colors

| | Code |
|---|---|
| Silver Metallic | AA-1 |
| Black | BB-1 |
| Medium Blue Metallic | CC-1 |
| Light Blue Metallic | DD-1 |
| Dark Blue Metallic | EE-1 |
| Light Green Metallic | FF-1 |
| Dark Green Metallic | GG-1 |
| Dark Copper Metallic | HH-1 |
| Light Turquoise Metallic | KK-1 |
| Dark Turquoise Met. | LL-1 |
| Turbine Bronze Metallic | MM-1 |
| Bright Red | PP-1 |
| Dark Red Metallic | QQ-1 |
| Yellow | RR-1 |
| Soft Yellow | SS-1 |
| Medium Copper Metallic | TT-1 |
| White | WW-1 |
| Beige | XX-1 |
| Light Tan Metallic | YY-1 |
| Gold Metallic | ZZ-1 |
| Mauve Metallic | 66-1 |
| Bright Blue Metallic | 88-1 |

1967

# Valiant

*"Who says a compact has to look like you saved a lot of money?"*

**Nameplate year of origin:** 1960.
**Current bodystyle lifespan:** 1967 through 1976.
**Predecessor to this model:** Valiant (1963 to 1966).
**Replacement for this model:** Volare (1976 to 1980).
**Percentage of division's sales volume:** 17.11%.
**Corporate siblings:** Dodge Dart.
**Primary competition:** AMC Rambler American, Chevrolet Chevy II, and Ford Falcon.
**Notable changes:** Completely redesigned.
**Major standard equipment:** Cloth and vinyl bench seat, rubber floor mat, 2-speed windshield wipers with washers, full length body side molding, and 6.50 × 13 BSW tires. Signet adds: Cologne grain vinyl bench seat, color-keyed carpeting, fender-top mounted turn signals, and interior courtesy lighting.

## Measurements

| | |
|---|---|
| Wheelbase | 108.0" |
| Length | 188.4" |
| Width | 71.1" |
| Height | 53.6" |
| Legroom — front | 40.8" |
| Legroom — rear | 35.4" |
| Headroom — front | 38.4" |
| Headroom — rear | 37.3" |
| Cargo capacity (cu. ft.) | NA |
| Fuel capacity (gals.) | 18.0 |

## Models Available

| | Style Number | Base MSRP | Change from LY | Shipping Wt. (lbs.) | Production | Change from LY |
|---|---|---|---|---|---|---|
| Valiant 100 2-Door Sedan | VL21 | $2,117 | +4.54% | 2655 | 29,093 | -18.71% |
| Valiant 100 4-Door Sedan | VL41 | $2,163 | +3.25% | 2675 | 46,638 | +29.44% |
| Valiant Signet 2-Door Sedan | VH21 | $2,262 | NEW | 2660 | 6,843 | NEW |
| Valiant Signet 4-Door Sedan | VH41 | $2,308 | NEW | 2680 | 26,395 | NEW |
| TOTALS | | *Avg. price* $2,213 | -3.32% | | *Production* 108,969 | -21.11% |

# Barracuda

*"So you've always wanted a European GT. On a small-car budget."*

**Nameplate year of origin:** 1964.
**Current bodystyle lifespan:** 1967 through 1969.
**Predecessor to this model:** Barracuda (1964 to 1966).
**Replacement for this model:** Barracuda (1970 to 1974).
**Percentage of division's sales volume:** 9.82%.
**Corporate siblings:** Dodge Dart.
**Primary competition:** Chevrolet Camaro, Ford Mustang, Mercury Cougar and Pontiac Firebird.
**Notable changes:** Completely redesigned.
**Major standard equipment:** All-vinyl bench seat with center arm rest (bucket seats on convertible), full carpeting, fold-down rear seat (Fastback), power top (Convertible), rallye lights, full instrumentation, trip odometer and 6.50 × 13 BSW tires.

## Measurements

| | |
|---|---|
| Wheelbase | 108.0" |
| Length | 192.8" |
| Width | 71.6" |
| Height | 53.7" |
| Legroom — front | 40.9" |
| Legroom — rear | 30.5" |
| Headroom — front | 37.4" |
| Headroom — rear | 36.5" |
| Cargo capacity (cu. ft.) | NA |
| Fuel capacity (gals.) | 18.0 |

## Models Available

| | Style Number | Base MSRP | Change from LY | Shipping Wt. (lbs.) | Production | Change from LY |
|---|---|---|---|---|---|---|
| Barracuda 2-Door Hardtop | BH23 | $2,449 | NEW | 2730 | 28,196 | NEW |

| | Style Number | Base MSRP | Change from LY | Shipping Wt. (lbs.) | Production | Change from LY |
|---|---|---|---|---|---|---|
| Barracuda 2-Door Fastback HT | BH29 | $2,639 | +3.25% | 2815 | 30,110 | -20.82% |
| Barracuda 2-Door Convertible | BH27 | $2,779 | NEW | 2840 | 4,228 | NEW |
| TOTALS | | Avg. price $2,622 | +2.58% | | Production 62,534 | +64.44% |

# Belvedere

*"If your present rig has you feeling powerless all of a sudden—surrender."*

**Nameplate year of origin:** 1951 (HT model); 1954 (series); 1965 Satellite (as a Belvedere trim level); 1967 (GTX).

**Current bodystyle lifespan:** 1966 through 1967.

**Predecessor to this model:** Belvedere (1962 to 1965).

**Replacement for this model:** Belvedere (1968 to 1970).

**Percentage of division's sales volume:** 23.25%.

**Corporate siblings:** Dodge Coronet.

**Primary competition:** AMC Rambler Classic, Chevrolet Chevelle, and Ford Fairlane.

**Notable changes:** New grille and minor trim and detail changes.

**Major standard equipment:** Cloth and vinyl front bench seat, rubber floor mats, front and rear armrests, 2-speed electric windshield wipers with washers, exterior bright trim around windows and rocker molding, hubcaps, and 7.35 × 14 BSW tires (7.75 × 14 BSW tires on wagons). Base Belvedere wagon deducts: rocker moldings, hubcaps and interior trim is lacking ornamentation. Belvedere II adds: Full carpeting, additional interior and exterior trim, and 8.25 × 14 BSW tires on 3-Seat wagon. Satellite adds: All vinyl bucket seats, center console or arm rest/seat insert, fender mounted turn signals, deluxe wheel covers, and additional interior lighting. GTX adds: Pit-stop gas cap, dual hood scoops, dual exhausts, 440 CID V8, 4-speed manual or automatic transmission, and 7.75 × 14 Redline tires.

## Measurements

| | Cars | Wagons |
|---|---|---|
| Wheelbase | 116.0" | 117.0" |
| Length | 200.5" | 208.5" |
| Width | 76.4" | 76.4" |
| Height | 55.0" | 55.8" |
| Legroom — front | 42.0" | 42.0" |
| Legroom — rear | 36.2" | 36.3" |
| Headroom — front | 38.8" | 38.8" |
| Headroom — rear | 37.8" | 37.9" |
| Cargo capacity (cu. ft.) | NA | NA |
| Fuel capacity (gals.) | 19.0 | 19.0 |

**1967**

## Models Available

| | Style Number | Base MSRP | Change from LY | Shipping Wt. (lbs.) | Production | Change from LY |
|---|---|---|---|---|---|---|
| Belvedere 4-Door, 2-Seat Wagon | RE45 | $2,579 | NEW | 3455 | 5,477 | NEW |
| Belvedere I 2-Door Coupe | RL21 | $2,318 | +1.80% | 3025 | 4,718 | -49.71% |
| Belvedere I 4-Door Sedan | RL41 | $2,356 | +1.77% | 3065 | 13,988 | -54.97% |
| Belvedere I 4-Door, 2-Seat Wagon | RL45 | $2,652 | +1.80% | 3470 | 3,172 | -61.32% |
| Belvedere II 2-Door Hardtop | RH23 | $2,457 | +1.11% | 3050 | 34,550 | -5.71% |
| Belvedere II 2-Door Convertible | RH27 | $2,695 | +1.93% | 3120 | 1,552 | -37.97% |
| Belvedere II 4-Door Sedan | RH41 | $2,434 | +1.21% | 3055 | 42,694 | -14.46% |
| Belvedere II 4-Dr., 2-Seat Wagon | RH45 | $2,729 | +1.26% | 3485 | 5,583 | +18.13% |
| Belvedere II 4-Dr., 3-Seat Wagon | RH46 | $2,836 | +1.14% | 3555 | 3,968 | -54.22% |
| Satellite 2-Door Hardtop | RP23 | $2,747 | +1.93% | 3245 | 30,328 | -14.33% |
| Satellite 2-Door Convertible | RP27 | $2,986 | +2.61% | 3335 | 2,050 | -25.70% |
| GTX 2-Door Hardtop | RS23 | $3,178 | NEW | 3535 | incl. w/Satellite | NEW |
| GTX 2-Door Convertible | RS27 | $3,418 | NEW | 3615 | incl. w/Satellite | NEW |
| TOTALS | | Avg. price $2,722 | +5.59% | | Production 148,080 | -21.76% |

# Fury

*"Whatever it takes to please you, it's here."*

**Nameplate year of origin:** 1956.
**Current bodystyle lifespan:** 1967 through 1968.
**Predecessor to this model:** Fury (1965 to 1966).
**Replacement for this model:** Fury (1969 to 1973).
**Percentage of division's sales volume:** 49.82%.
**Corporate siblings:** Dodge Polara.
**Primary competition:** AMC Ambassador, Chevrolet Biscayne/BelAir/Impala, and Ford Galaxie/LTD.
**Notable changes:** Completely restyled.
**Major standard equipment:** Cloth and vinyl front bench seat, color-keyed floor covering, front and rear armrests, variable speed electric windshield wipers, bright trim around front and rear windows, and 7.75 × 14 BSW tires (8.55 × 14 BSW tire on wagon). Fury II adds: Full carpeting and full-length body side molding. Fury III adds: All-vinyl upholstery on hardtop and convertible, backup lights, and distinctive exterior trim. Sport Fury adds: All-vinyl bucket seats, floor-mounted shifter and console with compartment, and deluxe steering wheel. VIP adds: Cloth and vinyl bench seats with fold-down center armrests, reading lamps, vinyl top and specific VIP trim.

## Measurements

|  | Cars | Wagons |
|---|---|---|
| Wheelbase | 119.0" | 121.0" |
| Length | 213.1" | 211.5" |
| Width | 77.7" | 77.7" |
| Height | 56.1" | 56.7" |
| Legroom — front | 41.8" | 41.8" |
| Legroom — rear | 37.0" | 37.4" |
| Headroom — front | 39.4" | 39.4" |
| Headroom — rear | 37.7" | 38.5" |
| Cargo capacity (cu. ft.) | NA | NA |
| Fuel capacity (gals.) | 25.0 | 25.0 |

## Models Available

| | Style Number | Base MSRP | Change from LY | Shipping Wt. (lbs.) | Production | Change from LY |
|---|---|---|---|---|---|---|
| Fury I 2-Door Sedan | PE21 | $2,473 | +1.94% | 3435 | 6,647 | -46.99% |
| Fury I 4-Door Sedan | PE41 | $2,517 | +1.53% | 3490 | 29,354 | -26.06% |
| Fury I 4-Door, 2-Seat Wagon | PL45 | $2,884 | +1.69% | 3945 | 6,067 | -37.39% |
| Fury II 2-Door Sedan | PL21 | $2,571 | +1.78% | 3435 | 2,783 | +11.19% |
| Fury II 4-Door Sedan | PL41 | $2,614 | +1.36% | 3470 | 45,673 | -16.98% |
| Fury II 4-Door, 2-Seat Wagon | PL45 | $3,021 | +1.17% | 4060 | 10,736 | +0.17% |
| Fury II 4-Door, 3-Seat Wagon | PL46 | $3,122 | +1.13% | 4100 | 5,649 | +1.24% |
| Fury III 2-Door Hardtop | PM23 | $2,767 | +1.58% | 3475 | 37,448 | -10.56% |
| Fury III 2-Door Convertible | PM27 | $3,118 | +1.43% | 3670 | 4,523 | +4.55% |
| Fury III 4-Door Sedan | PM41 | $2,746 | +1.03% | 3515 | 52,690 | +13.30% |
| Fury III 4-Door Hardtop | PM43 | $2,922 | +1.00% | 3665 | 43,614 | +28.57% |
| Fury III 4-Door, 2-Seat Wagon | PM45 | $3,144 | +0.93% | 4080 | 9,270 | +0.34% |
| Fury III 4-Door, 3-Seat Wagon | PM46 | $3,245 | +0.90% | 4125 | 12,533 | +15.13% |
| Sport Fury 2-Door Hardtop | PH23 | $3,033 | +0.90% | 3625 | 28,448 | -12.53% |
| Sport Fury 2-Door Fast Top HT | PS23 | $3,062 | NEW | 3630 | incl. w/Sp. Fury HT | NEW |
| Sport Fury 2-Door Convertible | PH27 | $3,279 | +0.86% | 3705 | 3,133 | -8.34% |
| VIP 2-Door Hardtop | PP23 | $3,117 | +1.56% | 3630 | 7,912 | * |
| VIP 4-Door Hardtop | PP43 | $3,182 | +1.56% | 3705 | 10,830 | -10.18% |
| TOTALS | *Avg. price* | $2,934 | +1.56% | | *Production* 317,310 | -3.99% |

# PONTIAC

*"1967 Pontiac Wide-Tracks."*

Pontiac sales were on a roll through the sixties, and 1967 brought more of the same. They were so busy selling cars that officially there was not even a sales slogan for the new year. Front and center for the new year was the Firebird, which actually didn't make its official debut until the middle of the season. Still, with the success of the Ford Mustang and the recently released Chevy Camaro, it was undoubtedly going to be a hit with buyers. Pontiac offered coupe and convertible variants as a beginning choice. Then buyers could chose from five different performance levels. They included the base series, the Sprint with a High-Output OHC Six engine, the 326 with a 326 CID V8 engine, the 326 H.O. with a higher-output variant of the same engine, and finally the 400 with the new 400 CID V8 engine as standard equipment. The 400 CID V8 turned out to be a catalyst for starting the horsepower race in the smaller "pony car" market. Up until this time, Ford had offered the 289 CID V8 as it largest offering in the Mustang, but with its restyling in 1967, Ford added a top line GT model that offered a 390 CID V8 engine rated at 315 horsepower. Of course, GM could not let that stand, and when the Firebird was introduced, the 400 model, with the 400 CID V8 engine rated at 325 horsepower was at the top of the line. Within a few years the Firebird would be up to a 455 CID V8 as its top offering, with competitors very nearly matching that size. For now, each Firebird model offered slightly different trim and features to announce what it was to the world — for example, dual hood scoops and chrome engine parts graced the Firebird 400. With all of these performance choices the customer could still choose upgrades as well as many comfort and convenience options that would have been unthinkable on a sporty car five years earlier.

Full-size Pontiacs were given a total redesign this year with a slightly bulkier appearance and more curvaceous lines. The stacked dual headlamps continued for one more year, with the top lamp set into the leading edge of the front fender, and the lower lamp set into the new integral grille and bumper design. A horizontal body crease ran midway down the body side for the length of the car. Also a body crease ran forward from the bottom of the rear bumper, through the rear wheel opening (if equipped with rear fender skirts), and then kicked up pointing towards the windshield area, but ending at a point just short of the horizontal beltline crease. Still attractive cars, the new Pontiacs were not a match for the beautiful 1965 models that had been such a hit. This year's Grand Prix received styling cues that set it further apart from the regular Pontiac line. Up front, headlamps were mounted side by side and hidden behind hide-away doors, while the parking lamps were hidden behind louvers in the leading edge of the front fender. Also hidden on the Grand Prix were the windshield wipers and taillamps (set into louvered slots in the tail panel). Missing on the coupe were the vent windows. A new model offering was the Convertible, but apparently not many people were interested in a GP Convertible, and the model was dropped at the end of the model year. Other reasons for the short life span of the convertible probably include the declining convertible market in general, and the fact that Pontiac had numerous full-size convertible models already, and most of them could be equipped much the same as the new Grand Prix version. Too bad, because it really made a nice looking car. The mid-size Pontiac models saw few changes, except for the addition of a new LeMans Safari wagon, complete with the wood-grain vinyl side applique then in vogue. Also, the new 400 CID V8 engine found its way under the hood of the GTO, as the legendary 389 CID V8 was relegated to the history books.

Bonneville 2-Door Hardtop

Bonneville 4-Door Wagon

Catalina 2-Door Convertible
with Ventura package

Catalina 2-Door Hardtop with 2 + 2 package

Executive 4-Door Sedan

Firebird 2-Door Convertible

Grand Prix 2-Door Convertible

GTO 2-Door Convertible

LeMans 4-Door Hardtop

**Model year production:** 817,343, down 2.36% from 1966.
**Domestic market share:** 10.66% (3rd place).
**Base price range:** $2,341 to $3,819.
**Industry average base price:** $3,159.
**Pontiac average base price:** $3,017.
**Introduction date:** September 1966. Firebird introduced February 23, 1967.
**Assembly plants:** Atlanta, GA (A); Baltimore, MD (B); Southgate, CA (C); Linden, NJ (E); Framingham, MA (G); Kansas City, MO (K); Van Nuys, CA (L); Norwood, OH (N); Pontiac, MI (P); Arlington, TX (R); Fairfax, KS (X); Fremont, CA (Z); and Oshawa, Ontario, Canada (1).

**Data plate identification:** Thirteen digit code read as follows: 1st digit 2 = Pontiac; 2nd through 5th digits identify series/body style (see style number in listings); 7 = 1967; 7th digit is assembly plant code; 100001 and up (600001 and up on 6-cylinders) for serial number. *Example:* 252397X100001 is a 1967 Pontiac Catalina 4-Door Hardtop, serial number 100001, built in Fairfax, KS.

## Powertrains

| Engine | Gross HP* | Transmission Availability | Firebird | Tempest/ LeMans/GTO | Catalina/ Executive | Bonne- ville | Grand Prix |
|---|---|---|---|---|---|---|---|
| 230 CID OHC, 1-bbl., 6-cyl. | 165 | 3-speed manual | S | S (ex. GTO) | - | - | - |
| | | 4-speed manual | $184 | $184 (ex. GTO) | - | - | - |
| | | 2-sp. Automatic | $226 | $226 (ex. GTO) | - | - | - |
| 230 CID OHC, 4-bbl., 6-cyl. | 215 | 3-speed manual | $116** | $116** (ex. GTO) | - | - | - |
| | | 4-speed manual | $300** | $300** (ex. GTO) | - | - | - |
| | | 2-sp. Automatic | $342** | $342** (ex. GTO) | - | - | - |
| 326 CID, 2-bbl., V8 | 250 | 3-speed manual | $95 | $95 (ex. GTO) | - | - | - |
| | | 3-speed HD man. | $179 | $179 (ex. GTO) | - | - | - |
| | | 4-speed manual | $279 | $279 (ex. GTO) | - | - | - |
| | | 2-sp. Automatic | $321 | $321 (ex. GTO) | - | - | - |
| 326 CID H.O., 4-bbl., V8 | 285 | 3-speed manual | $159 | $159 (ex. GTO) | - | - | - |
| | | 3-speed HD man. | $243 | $243 (ex. GTO) | - | - | - |

| Engine | Gross HP* | Transmission Availability | Firebird | Tempest/ LeMans/GTO | Catalina/ Executive | Bonne- ville | Grand Prix |
|---|---|---|---|---|---|---|---|
| | | 4-speed manual | $343 | $343 (ex. GTO) | - | - | - |
| | | Turbo Hydra-matic | $385 | $385 (ex. GTO) | - | - | - |
| 400 CID, 2-bbl., V8 | 255/265 | 3-speed manual | - | No cost (GTO) | S | - | - |
| | | Turbo Hydra-matic | - | $226 (GTO) | $226 | - | - |
| 400 CID, 2-bbl., V8 | 290 | Turbo Hydra-matic | - | - | $226 | - | - |
| 400 CID, 4-bbl., V8 | 325/335 | 3-speed HD man. | S–w/400*** | S (GTO) | $35 | S | - |
| | | 4-speed manual | $195*** | $184 (GTO) | $270 | $226 | - |
| | | Turbo Hydra-matic | $226*** | $226 (GTO) | $270 | $226 | - |
| 400 CID H.O. Ram Air, 4-bbl., V8 | 325/360 | 4-speed manual | $*** | $ (GTO) | - | - | - |
| | | Turbo Hydra-matic | $*** | $ (GTO) | - | - | - |
| 400 CID, 4-bbl., V8 | 350 | 3-speed manual | - | - | - | - | S |
| | | 4-speed manual | - | - | - | - | $226 |
| | | Turbo Hydra-matic | - | - | - | - | $226 |
| 428 CID Quadra-Power, 4-bbl., V8 | 360 | 3-speed HD man. | - | - | $114 | $79 | $79 |
| | | 4-speed manual | - | - | $340 | $305 | $305 |
| | | Turbo Hydra-matic | - | - | $340 | $305 | $305 |
| 428 CID H.O. Quadra-Power, 4-bbl., V8 | 376 | 3-speed HD man. | - | - | $263 | $119 | $119 |
| | | 4-speed manual | - | - | $489 | $345 | $345 |
| | | Turbo Hydra-matic | - | - | $489 | $345 | $345 |

*Ratings vary with model and transmission attachment.    **Includes Sprint option package.    ***Available with 400 Option package.

## Major Options

| | Firebird | Tempest/LeMans | Catalina | Executive | Bonneville | Grand Prix |
|---|---|---|---|---|---|---|
| Air conditioning (V8 only) | $343 | $343 | $421 | $421 | $421 | $421 |
| Electronic cruise control (V8 auto.) | - | $53 | $63 | $63 | $63 | $63 |
| Soft Ray tinted glass | $37 | $37 | $44 | $44 | $44 | $44 |
| Tilt steering wheel | $42 | $42 | $45 | $45 | $45 | $45 |
| Power steering — variable-ratio | $95 | $95 | $105 | $105 | $105 | $105 |
| Power brakes | $43 | $43 | $43 | $43 | $43 | $43 |
| Power driver's seat/bench seat | $74 | $74 | $74 | $74 | $74 | $74 |
| Power windows | $100 | $100 | $106 | $106 | $106 | $106 |
| AM radio | $61 | $61 | $87 | $87 | $87 | $87 |
| AM/FM stereo | $239 | $239 | $239 | $239 | $239 | $239 |
| Front seat console | $60 | $68 | $105 | - | $105 | S |
| Front bucket seats | S | $70 | $72–$114 | - | $114 | S |
| Vinyl roof | $ | $ | $105–132 | $105–132 | $105–132 | $105 |
| White stripe tires (base size) | $35 | $35 | $41 | $41 | $41 | $41 |
| Rally II wheels | $56 | $56–$72 | $65–$73 | $73 | $65 | $65 |
| Ventura package | - | - | $134* | - | - | - |
| 2+2 package | - | - | $389* | - | - | - |
| Brougham package | - | - | - | - | $273 | - |
| Sprint package | $106* | $106* | - | - | - | - |
| Firebird 326 package | $95* | - | - | - | - | - |
| Firebird H.O. package | $159* | - | - | - | - | - |
| Firebird 400 package | $274* | - | - | - | - | - |

Options common to most models. (- = Not Available; S = Standard equipment.) Items may be standard equipment, optional at different pricing, or unavailable on certain models. This chart is only a guide.

*Prices may vary between models on certain packages.

1967

## Paint Colors

| | Code | | Code |
|---|---|---|---|
| Starlight Black | A | Plum Mist Metallic | M |
| Cameo Ivory | C | Burgundy Metallic | N |
| Montreux Blue Metallic | D | Coronado Gold Metallic | O |
| Fathom Blue Metallic | E | Silverglaze Metallic | P |
| Tyrol Blue Metallic | F | Verdoro Green Metallic | Q |
| Signet Gold Metallic | G | Regimental Red | R |
| Linden Green Metallic | H | Champagne Metallic | S |
| Gulf Turquoise Metallic | K | Montego Cream | T |
| Mariner Turquoise Metallic | L | Mayfair Maize | Y |

# Firebird

*"The Magnificent Five are here / the Pontiac Firebirds."*

**Nameplate year of origin:** 1967 (used on Motorama show cars as early as 1954).

**Current bodystyle lifespan:** 1967 through 1969.

**Predecessor to this model:** None.

**Replacement for this model:** Firebird (1970 to 1981).

**Percentage of division's sales volume:** 10.10%.

**Corporate siblings:** Chevrolet Camaro.

**Primary competition:** Ford Mustang, Mercury Cougar, and Plymouth Barracuda.

**Notable changes:** All-new model for 1967.

**Major standard equipment:** All-vinyl front bucket seats, wood grain dash, full carpeting, 2-speed windshield wipers with washers, steering column shifter, and E70 × 14 Wide-Oval BSW tires. Sprint package adds: 4-bbl. OHC 6-cylinder, floor mounted shifter, and heavy-duty suspension. 326 adds: 326 CID V8 engine and column mounted shifter. H.O. adds: Exterior striping, 4-bbl. Carburetor and dual exhausts. 400 adds: 400 CID V8, floor mounted shifter, dual hood scoops, dual exhausts, heavy-duty suspension, and E70 × 14 Wide-Oval Redline or BSW tires.

## Measurements

| | |
|---|---|
| Wheelbase | 108.1" |
| Length | 188.8" |
| Width | 72.6" |
| Height | 51.5" |
| Legroom — front | 42.5" |
| Legroom — rear | 29.5" |
| Headroom — front | 37.0" |
| Headroom — rear | 36.7" |
| Cargo capacity (cu. ft.) | 9.9 |
| Fuel capacity (gals.) | 18.5 |

## Models Available

| | Style Number | Base MSRP | Change from LY | Shipping Wt. (lbs.) | Production | Change from LY |
|---|---|---|---|---|---|---|
| Firebird 2-Door Hardtop | 22337 | $2,666 | NEW | 2955 | 67,032 | NEW |
| Firebird 2-Door Convertible | 22367 | $2,903 | NEW | 3247 | 15,528 | NEW |
| TOTALS | | *Avg. price* $2,785 | NEW | *Production* 82,560 | | NEW |

# Tempest, LeMans & GTO

*"You say you could go for a sprightly Pontiac with its distinctive split grille, superb years ahead styling, and Wide-Track? Or maybe an idea on wheels— GTO— the idea that there's more to driving than moving from place to place in isolated indifference."*

**Nameplate year of origin:** 1961 (Tempest); 1961 (LeMans, as a Tempest sub-series); 1964 (GTO).

**Current bodystyle lifespan:** 1966 through 1967.

**Predecessor to this model:** Tempest/LeMans (1964 to 1965).

**Replacement for this model:** LeMans (1968 to 1972).

**Percentage of division's sales volume:** 36.84%.

**Corporate siblings:** Chevrolet Chevelle, Oldsmobile Cutlass, and Buick Skylark.

**Primary competition:** AMC Rebel, Mercury Montego, and Dodge Coronet.

**Notable changes:** New grille, and minor trim and detail changes.

**Major standard equipment:** Cloth and vinyl front bench seat, vinyl floor covering, courtesy lights, 2-speed windshield wipers with washers, and 7.75 × 14 BSW tires. Custom adds: All-vinyl front bench seats, full carpeting, and rocker panel moldings. LeMans adds: All-vinyl bucket seats or bench seat (2-Doors), cloth and vinyl bench seats (4-Doors), padded assist bar on dash, and rear quarter louvers. GTO adds: All-vinyl bucket seats, floor shifter, dual exhausts, custom pinstriping, 400 CID V8 with engine dress-up kit, heavy duty suspension and F70 × 14 Red-line tires.

## Measurements

| | Cars | Wagons |
|---|---|---|
| Wheelbase | 115.0" | 115.0" |
| Length | 206.6" | 203.4" |
| Width | 74.4" | 74.4" |
| Height | 55.0" | 55.4" |
| Legroom — front | 40.6" | 40.6" |
| Legroom — rear | 35.7" | 35.7" |
| Headroom — front | 38.1" | 37.8" |
| Headroom — rear | 37.2" | 38.3" |
| Cargo capacity (cu. ft.) | 29.1 | 84.5 |
| Fuel capacity (gals.) | 21.5 | 21.5 |

## Models Available

| | Style Number | Base MSRP | Change from LY | Shipping Wt. (lbs.) | Production | Change from LY |
|---|---|---|---|---|---|---|
| Tempest 2-Door Sports Coupe | 23307 | $2,341 | +2.77% | 3110 | 17,978 | -19.26% |
| Tempest 4-Door Sedan | 23369 | $2,388 | +2.45% | 3140 | 13,136 | -24.47% |
| Tempest 4-Door, 2-Seat Wagon | 23335 | $2,666 | +1.60% | 3370 | 3,495 | -14.65% |
| Tempest Custom 2-Dr. Sports Cpe. | 23507 | $2,434 | +3.05% | 3130 | 12,469 | -27.43% |
| Tempest Custom 2-Door Hardtop | 23517 | $2,494 | +2.80% | 3140 | 30,512 | -2.59% |
| Tempest Custom 2-Door Conv. | 23567 | $2,723 | +2.56% | 3240 | 4,082 | -26.54% |
| Tempest Custom 4-Door Sedan | 23569 | $2,482 | +2.77% | 3145 | 17,445 | -27.28% |
| Tempest Custom 4-Door Hardtop | 23539 | $2,608 | +2.39% | 3240 | 5,493 | -50.05% |
| Tempest Custom 4-Dr., 2-S. Wgn. | 23535 | $2,760 | +1.88% | 3370 | 5,324 | -30.08% |
| LeMans 2-Door Sports Coupe | 23707 | $2,586 | +3.23% | 3155 | 10,693 | -35.79% |
| LeMans 2-Door Hardtop | 23717 | $2,648 | +3.12% | 3155 | 75,965 | -2.74% |
| LeMans 2-Door Convertible | 23767 | $2,881 | +2.67% | 3250 | 9,820 | -24.92% |
| LeMans 4-Door Hardtop | 23739 | $2,771 | +2.59% | 3265 | 8,424 | -39.38% |
| LeMans Safari 4-Dr., 2-S. Wagon | 23935 | $2,936 | NEW | 3390 | 4,511 | NEW |
| GTO 2-Door Sports Coupe | 24207 | $2,871 | +3.16% | 3425 | 7,029 | -32.17% |
| GTO 2-Door Hardtop | 24217 | $2,935 | +3.09% | 3430 | 65,176 | -11.67% |
| GTO 2-Door Convertible | 24267 | $3,165 | +2.69% | 3515 | 9,517 | -25.64% |
| TOTALS | *Avg. price* | $2,688 | +3.31% | *Production* | 301,069 | -16.16% |

1967

# Catalina

*"Catalina is back with more of everything that has made it the envy of every car maker who has tried to match its looks, luxury and performance, at so low a price. And failed."*

**Nameplate year of origin:** 1950 on hardtop models, 1959 as series.
**Current bodystyle lifespan:** 1967 through 1968.
**Predecessor to this model:** Catalina (1965 to 1966).
**Replacement for this model:** Catalina (1969 to 1970).
**Corporate siblings:** Chevrolet Impala/Caprice, Olds Delta 88, Buick LeSabre.
**Primary competition:** Ford LTD, Mercury Monterey, Plymouth Fury, Dodge Polara, and AMC Ambassador.
**Percentage of division's sales volume:** 29.46%.
**Notable changes:** Completely restyled.
**Major standard equipment:** Cloth and vinyl front bench seat (all-vinyl on convertible and wagons), full carpeting, 2-speed windshield wipers with washers, and 8.55 × 14 BSW tires (8.25 × 14 BSW tires on Sedans). Ventura Custom option adds: All-vinyl upholstery with specific trim. 2 + 2 option adds: 428 CID V8 engine, floor mounted shifter, all-vinyl bucket seats, heavy-duty suspension, and front fender louvers.

## Measurements

|  | Cars | Wagons |
|---|---|---|
| Wheelbase | 121.0" | 121.0" |
| Length | 215.6" | 218.4" |
| Width | 79.7" | 79.7" |
| Height | 55.3" | 56.0" |
| Legroom — front | 42.7" | 41.6" |
| Legroom — rear | 38.1" | 38.2" |
| Headroom — front | 38.4" | 38.7" |
| Headroom — rear | 37.7" | 39.0" |
| Cargo capacity (cu. ft.) | 31.4 | 91.7 |
| Fuel capacity (gals.) | 26.5 | 24.0 |

## Models Available

| | Style Number | Base MSRP | Change from LY | Shipping Wt. (lbs.) | Production | Change from LY |
|---|---|---|---|---|---|---|
| Catalina 2-Door Sedan | 25211 | $2,807 | +1.63% | 3735 | 5,633 | -28.92% |
| Catalina 2-Door Hardtop | 25287 | $2,951 | +2.00% | 3860 | 77,932 | -1.37% |
| Catalina 2-Door Convertible | 25267 | $3,276 | +1.77% | 3910 | 10,033 | -32.38% |
| Catalina 4-Door Sedan | 25269 | $2,866 | +1.24% | 3825 | 80,551 | +0.08% |
| Catalina 4-Door Hardtop | 25239 | $3,020 | +1.75% | 3960 | 37,256 | -1.97% |
| Catalina Safari 4-Dr., 2-S. Wagon | 25235 | $3,252 | +1.09% | 4275 | 18,305 | -13.17% |
| Catalina Safari 4-Dr., 3-S. Wagon | 25245 | $3,374 | +1.08% | 4340 | 11,040 | -14.85% |
| TOTALS | Avg. price | $3,078 | +1.48% | Production | 240,750 | -5.33% |

# Executive

*"Here's where our stylist and engineers got together to prove that a big luxury car needn't come with a price tag to match."*

**Nameplate year of origin:** 1966.
**Current bodystyle lifespan:** 1967 through 1968.
**Predecessor to this model:** Star Chief/Executive (1965 to 1966).
**Replacement for this model:** Bonneville (1969 to 1970).
**Percentage of division's sales volume:** 5.75%.
**Corporate siblings:** Chevrolet Impala/Caprice, Oldsmobile Delta 88, Buick Wildcat.
**Primary competition:** Ford LTD, Mercury Marquis, Plymouth Fury, Dodge Monaco, and AMC Ambassador.
**Notable changes:** Completely restyled.
**Major standard equipment:** Cloth and vinyl bench seat, full carpeting, perforated vinyl headliner, walnut grain trim on dash, electric clock, full length lower body molding, exterior wood grain trim on station wagons, full wheel covers and 8.55 × 14 BSW tires.

## Measurements

|  | Cars | Wagon |
|---|---|---|
| Wheelbase | 124.0" | 121.0" |
| Length | 222.6" | 218.4" |
| Width | 79.7" | 79.7" |
| Height | 55.6" | 56.0" |
| Legroom — front | 42.7" | 41.3" |
| Legroom — rear | 38.1" | 38.2" |
| Headroom — front | 38.3" | 38.7" |
| Headroom — rear | 37.6" | 39.0" |
| Cargo capacity (cu. ft.) | 35.0 | 91.7 |
| Fuel capacity (gals.) | 26.5 | 24.0 |

## Models Available

| | Style Number | Base MSRP | Change from LY | Shipping Wt. (lbs.) | Production | Change from LY |
|---|---|---|---|---|---|---|
| Executive 2-Door Hardtop | 25687 | $3,227 | +1.80% | 3925 | 6,931 | -31.65% |
| Executive 4-Door Sedan | 25669 | $3,165 | +1.64% | 3955 | 19,861 | -18.90% |
| Executive 4-Door Hardtop | 25639 | $3,296 | +1.60% | 4020 | 8,699 | -17.80% |
| Executive Safari 4-Dr., 2-S. Wagon | 25635 | $3,600 | NEW | 4290 | 5,903 | NEW |
| Executive Safari 4-Dr., 3-S. Wagon | 25645 | $3,722 | NEW | 4370 | 5,593 | NEW |
| TOTALS | | Avg. price $3,402 | +7.12% | | Production 46,987 | +3.93% |

# Bonneville

*"The strikingly new Bonneville may be synonymous with luxury—
but let us not forget what, in fact, inspired its name."*

**Nameplate year of origin:** 1957.
**Current bodystyle lifespan:** 1967 through 1968.
**Predecessor to this model:** Bonneville (1965 to 1966).
**Replacement for this model:** Bonneville (1969 to 1970).
**Percentage of division's sales volume:** 12.61%.
**Corporate siblings:** Chevrolet Impala/Caprice, Oldsmobile Delta 88, Buick LeSabre/Wildcat.
**Primary competition:** Mercury Park Lane, Dodge Monaco and Plymouth Fury VIP.
**Notable changes:** Completely restyled.
**Major standard equipment:** All-vinyl or cloth and vinyl front bench seat, full carpeting, Carpathian elm grain dash trim, electric clock, courtesy lights, padded assist grip, dual-speed electric windshield wipers, rear fender skirts, deluxe wheel covers and 8.25 × 14 BSW tires. Brougham option adds: Special upholstery trim with fold down center armrests, and exterior badges.

## Measurements

| | Cars | Wagon |
|---|---|---|
| Wheelbase | 124.0" | 121.0" |
| Length | 222.6" | 218.4" |
| Width | 79.4" | 79.4" |
| Height | 54.6" | 56.0" |
| Legroom — front | 42.3" | 41.3" |
| Legroom — rear | 37.5" | 38.2" |
| Headroom — front | 37.9" | 38.7" |
| Headroom — rear | 37.1" | 39.0" |
| Cargo capacity (cu. ft.) | 35.0 | 90.8 |
| Fuel capacity (gals.) | 26.5 | 24.0 |

**1967**

## Models Available

| | Style Number | Base MSRP | Change from LY | Shipping Wt. (lbs.) | Production | Change from LY |
|---|---|---|---|---|---|---|
| Bonneville 2-Door Hardtop | 26287 | $3,448 | +2.80% | 3975 | 31,016 | -26.16% |
| Bonneville 2-Door Convertible | 26267 | $3,680 | +2.62% | 4010 | v8,902 | -45.15% |
| Bonneville 4-Door Hardtop | 26239 | $3,517 | +2.60% | 4110 | 56,307 | -17.97% |
| Bonneville Safari 4-Dr., 3-S. Wgn. | 26245 | $3,819 | +1.92% | 4415 | 6,771 | -19.89% |
| TOTALS | | Avg. price $3,616 | +2.47% | | Production 102,996 | -23.89% |

# Grand Prix

*"Next year someone might come up with a
reasonable facsimile of our 1967 Grand Prix."*

**Nameplate year of origin:** 1962.
**Current bodystyle lifespan:** 1967 through 1968.
**Predecessor to this model:** Grand Prix (1965 to 1966).

## Measurements

| | |
|---|---|
| Wheelbase | 121.0" |
| Length | 215.6" |

**Replacement for this model:** Grand Prix (1969 to 1972).
**Percentage of division's sales volume:** 5.26%.
**Corporate siblings:** Buick Wildcat.
**Primary competition:** Chrysler 300, Dodge Monaco 500, and Mercury Marquis.
**Notable changes:** Completely restyled. New convertible model added.
**Major standard equipment:** All-vinyl or cloth and vinyl bucket seat or bench seat, full carpeting, padded instrument panel, padded assist bar, additional acoustical insulation, concealed headlights, concealed windshield wipers, ventless door windows (Hardtop), deluxe wheel covers and 8.55 × 14 BSW tires.

## Measurements

| | |
|---|---|
| Width | 79.4" |
| Height | 54.2" |
| Legroom — front | 42.3" |
| Legroom — rear | 35.2" |
| Headroom — front | 37.7" |
| Headroom — rear | 37.1" |
| Cargo capacity (cu. ft.) | 33.9 |
| Fuel capacity (gals.) | 26.5 |

## Models Available

| | Style Number | Base MSRP | Change from LY | Shipping Wt. (lbs.) | Production | Change from LY |
|---|---|---|---|---|---|---|
| Grand Prix 2-Door Hardtop | 26657 | $3,549 | +1.63% | 4005 | 37,125 | +1.00% |
| Grand Prix 2-Door Convertible | 26667 | $3,813 | NEW | 4040 | 5,856 | NEW |
| TOTALS | | *Avg. price* $3,681 | +5.41% | | *Production* 42,981 | +16.93% |

# 1968

The 1968 model year is best known for the vast array of federally mandated safety equipment required for all automobiles sold after January 1, 1968. Among the features required were front seat head restraints, safety belts, and side marker lamps. Most manufacturers had these items installed by the beginning of the 1968 model year, but a few did wait until the last minute to install them.

Heated competition amongst the mid-size Ford, GM and Chrysler lines found these models totally restyled for 1968 with the GM models seeing the most significant changes. The Chevy Chevelle, Pontiac Tempest, Olds F-85, and Buick Special lines all received rounded, smooth-sided lines with a semi-fastback 2 door roofline that would become widely copied.

The quartet of cars that were leading the muscle car market were, of course, included in this restyling. The front runner, Pontiac GTO, led the way with an innovative "Endura" flexible front bumper system. This flexible material allowed for no damage to the vehicle during minor impacts. It also gave stylists more freedom in design. As an example, the GTO sported a full width, "loop-style" bumper that was body color and could be blended into the body lines. Powertrains continued as in previous years, with the base Pontiac OHC-6 adding 20 cubes and additional horsepower.

The new Ford Fairlane and Mercury Montego lines were essentially larger versions of their predecessors. As with all other Ford products during this period, styling became boxier and bulkier. Fastback rooflines were adopted for the sportiest 2-door models, and they became quite popular for high-speed stock car racing. Ford also began heavily promoting their 428 Cobra jet engine, particularly in this mid-size line. Torino, Cobra Jet, and Cyclone CJ's became very popular with the racing crowd. The compact Falcon continued to share its station wagon body with the mid-size Ford lines.

The mid-size Dodge Coronet and Plymouth Belvedere were restyled along with the Charger line. Styling was generally conservative with rooflines following conventional lines, except for the Dodge Charger which utilized a semi-fastback line with a tunneled rear window like that used on the '66–'67 GM intermediates. The sporty Charger was an immediate hit and ushered in a new era of mid-size sporty personal cars. Interest in full-size models such as the Grand Prix, Ford 500XL, and Chrysler 300 had waned and buyers increasingly turned to the better handling mid-size cars.

A totally new Corvette with styling based on the Mako Shark concept appeared. This new Corvette was extremely advanced compared with other automobiles on the market, and as such, it would continue basically unaltered into the 1980s. Styling was somewhat futuristic for the time, with highly arched wheel openings, and a rakish windshield and "tunneled" rear window being the most prominent features. Engine choices were either a 350 CID V8 or a 427 CID V8 in various horsepower outputs. Few changes were made to any of the compact lines, except the Chevy II Nova, which was all-new for '68. Based on a heavily updated '66–'67 Chevy II with a new unibody and front stub-frame suspension setup, the new Nova was one of the best handling compacts on the road to date. Styling followed conventional Chevrolet lines. The compact Ford Falcon, AMC Rambler American, Plymouth Valiant and Dodge Dart continued relatively unchanged from their recent overhauls.

Sporty pony cars were mostly carry-overs with one notable exception. The all new AMC Javelin was the latest interpretation of the pony car style. Utilizing compact car dimensions, powerful engines, fastback styling and sporty interiors, the Javelin was proof that AMC could build successful cars. New powerplants were pulled from the regular AMC line. Underpinnings were based on the compact American, much as Ford Mustang had used the Falcon and Chevy Camaro the Chevy II. A unique spin-off of the Javelin was the 2-seat AMX, a worthy competitor to the Corvette. With a 390 V8, an AMX could hold its own

## 1968 Model Year Production by Make

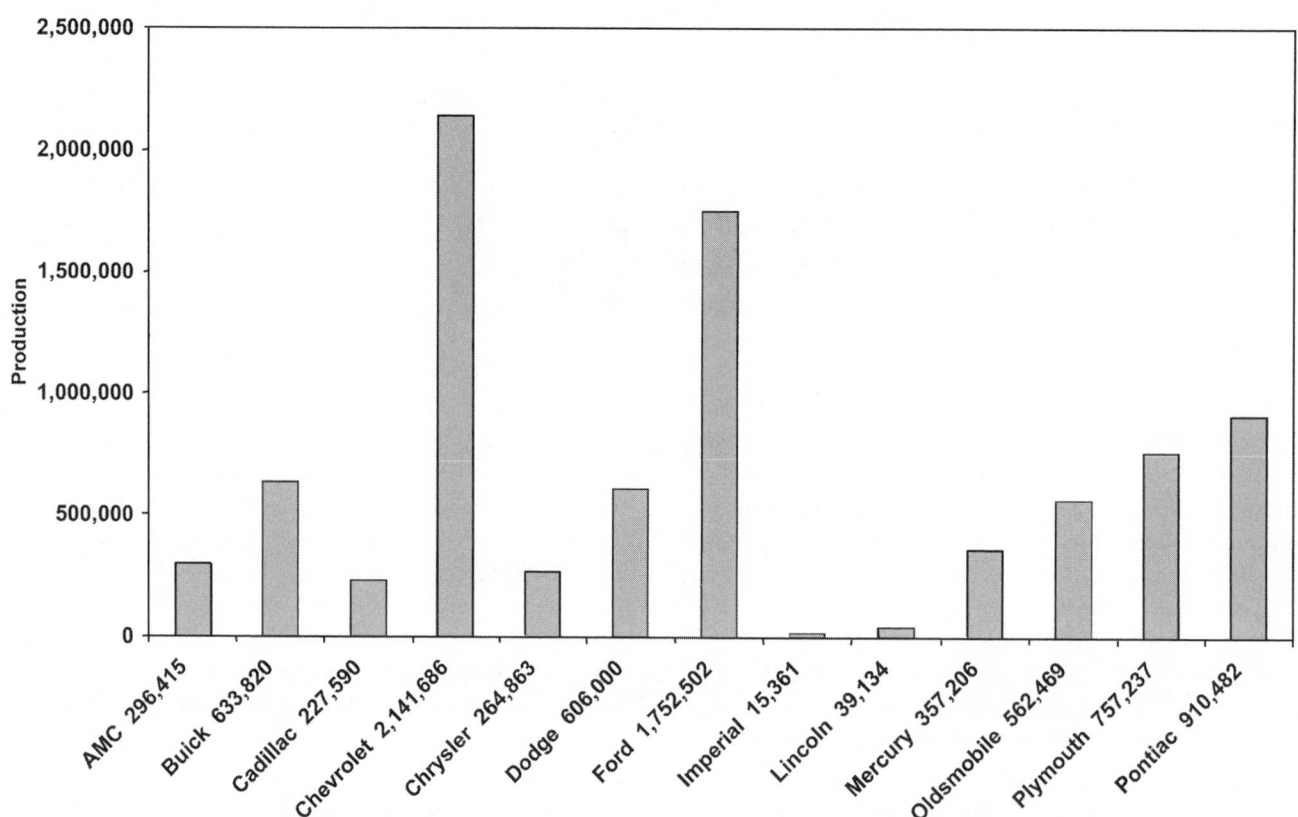

against most any pony car or sports car. The AMX was created by taking 12 inches out of the mid-section of a Javelin. The shortened Javelin sported all the good looks and power in a lighter package.

Full size models for Chrysler, GM and Ford were all given facelifts after heavy redesigns for '67. Chrysler continued to feature "Coke-bottle" side styling and fastback 2-door rooflines. Ford and GM went for slightly boxier styling based on their 1967 foundations. For the most part

Ford and GM full size cars came off looking a lot bulkier than their predecessors.

The Checker and Avanti II once again entered the new year with few changes, except for those required by federal law. Most truck lines were also carry-overs, with the obvious exceptions being the Ford Ranchero and Chevrolet El Camino. Both of these lines were based upon their respective mid-size car lines, the Fairlane and Chevelle, and received the full make-over for 1968.

# AMERICAN MOTORS

*"You get more for your American dollar."*

As with the rest of the automotive industry, spending for new styling on 1968 models was somewhat limited. The newly mandated safety regulations would affect the smaller American Motors much more than the larger companies. Therefore, the only major addition for the year was the all-

new Javelin and AMX pony cars. The Javelin was an all-new creation, design to compete with the wildly successful Mustang and Camaro. Unlike the Marlin which had preceded it, the Javelin showed no visible link to other AMC products. It was a fresh, new product, designed to pull customers from Ford and Chevy showrooms into the unknown floors of an AMC dealership. To a certain extent this worked, but it did not work quite as well as had been planned. Part of the problem was timing. By 1968, the pony car craze (Mustang/Camaro/Barracuda) was beginning to wane, and the muscle-car craze (GTO/4-4-2/Road Runner) was reaching its peak. Adding to the problem was the looming threat of higher insurance rates on muscle cars, or anything that looked like one. Of course another problem (from an enthusiast's perspective) was that the Javelin used some existing AMC components for drivetrains and suspension. This was a minor problem, at least at first, because to look at the Javelin, it was a car unlike any other — very modern looking and not another Mustang copy.

On the other hand, the AMX was a brilliant stroke of marketing and engineering from AMC. And the design of the AMX was already in place with the Javelin. By cleverly removing about a foot of length from the rear passenger compartment of a Javelin, AMC designers were able to create a car for a totally different market, the two-passenger sports car. The AMX was hyped as an all-out, two-seat sports car (though AMC did stop short of calling it a Corvette replacement) at an affordable price. Being a sports car, the AMX included an all-new, available 315-horsepower, 390 Cubic Inch 4-barrel, V8 engine. Of course, many features optional on a Javelin were offered as standard equipment on the AMX.

With plunging sales and fears of increasing insurance rates, American Motors decided to drop the American and Ambassador convertible models, leaving only the Rebel. However, a Rebel 550 Convertible was a new model that took the place (in price-level and content, at least) of the American Convertible. This would be the last year for any true American Motors convertible. The only subsequent Convertible model that would pass through AMC dealerships (not considering Jeep models) was the Renault Alliance from the mid-eighties. The Rebel received a slight freshening of its one-year-old styling, and some trim upgrades.

Ambassador and Rambler American models would receive new grille styling and other trim changes. Also, in an effort to move the Ambassador more up-market, a lot of additional standard equipment was being added each year, and this year was no exception. At the same time, the series designations were being dropped at the bottom end of the price scale, and new ones added at the top end. This year's change was to drop the 880 from the low-priced models, replace the 990 with the DPL designation, and add the SST to the top-line replacing the former top-line DPL model. AMC would make a similar change again in 1971 on Ambassador models.

Ambassador 4-Door Sedan

Ambassador SST Interior

Rambler American 2-Door Sedan

Rambler American Rogue 2-Door Hardtop

Javelin SST 2-Door Hardtop                    Rebel SST 2-Door Convertible

**Model year production:** 296,415, up 32.92% over 1967.
**Domestic market share:** 3.46% (9th place).
**Base price range:** $1,946 to $3,207.
**Industry average base price:** $3,292.
**American Motors average base price:** $2,678.
**Introduction date:** September 26, 1967. The AMX followed in March 1968.
**Assembly plants:** Kenosha, Wisconsin, and Brampton, Ontario, Canada.

**Data plate identification:** Thirteen digit code read as follows: A = American Motors; 8 = 1968; transmission code (see chart); car line/body type/series numbers (see last three digits of style number); engine code (see chart); 100001 and up for serial number (700001 and up for cars built in Ontario). *Example:* A8A797N100001 is a 1968 Shift-Command Automatic, Javelin SST 2-Door, 290 CID V8 4-bbl., serial number 100001, built in Kenosha.

## Powertrains

| Engine | Gross HP | Engine Code | Transmission Availability | Tran Code | Rmblr. Amcn. | AMX | Javelin | Rebel | Amb. |
|---|---|---|---|---|---|---|---|---|---|
| 199 CID, 1-bbl., 6-cyl. | 128 | A | 3-speed man., col./flr. | S/C | S (base) | - | - | - | - |
| | | | 3-sp. w/Overdr. | O | $110 | - | - | - | - |
| | | | Shift-Command Automatic | A | $174 | - | - | - | - |
| 232 CID, 1-bbl., 6-cyl. | 145 | B | 3-speed man., col./flr. | S/C | $45 | - | S | S | S (base & DPL) |
| | | | 3-sp. w/Overdr. | O | $155 | - | - | $110 | - |
| | | | Shift-Command Automatic | A | $219 | - | $220 | $220 | $220 (base & DPL) |
| 232 CID, 2-bbl., 6-cyl. | 155 | C | 3-speed man. | S/C | - | - | - | $ | - |
| | | | Shift-Command Automatic | A | - | - | - | $ | - |
| 290 CID, 2-bbl., V8 | 200 | M | 3-speed man., col./flr. | S/C | $119 | - | $106 | $106 | $106 (DPL)/S (SST) |
| | | | 4-speed man. | M | $303 | | | | |
| | | | Shift-Command Automatic, col./flr. | A | $301 | - | $326 | $326 | $326 (DPL)/ $220 (SST) |
| 290 CID, 4-bbl., V8 | 235 (225 — Am.) | N | 3-speed man., col./flr. | S/C | $163 | - | $150 | - | - |
| | | | 4-speed man. | M | $347 | S | $334 | - | - |
| | | | Shift-Command Automatic, col./flr. | A | $355 | $269 | $370 | - | - |
| 343 CID, 2-bbl., V8 | 235 | S | 3-speed man. | S | - | - | - | $151 | $164 (base & DPL)/ $58 (SST) |
| | | | Shift-Command Automatic, col./flr. | A | - | - | - | $371 | $364 (base & DPL)/ $278 (SST) |
| 343 CID, 4-bbl., V8 | 280 | T | 3-speed man., col./flr. | S/C | - | - | $182 | $182 | $197 (base & DPL)/ $91 (SST) |
| | | | 4-speed man. | M | - | $75 | $366 | - | - |
| | | | Shift-Command Automatic, col./flr. | A | - | $344 | $450 | $402 | $397 (base & DPL)/ $311 (SST) |
| 390 CID, 2-bbl., V8 | 280 | W | 3-speed man., col./flr. | S/C | - | - | $* | - | - |
| | | | 4-speed man. | M | - | $ | $* | - | - |
| | | | Shift-Command Automatic, col./flr. | A | - | $ | $* | - | - |
| 390 CID, 4-bbl., V8 | 315 | X | 3-speed man., col./flr. | S/C | - | - | $* | - | - |
| | | | 4-speed man. | M | - | $ | $* | - | - |
| | | | Shift-Command Automatic, col./flr. | A | - | $ | $* | - | - |

*Available Javelin 390 CID V8 in Javelin SST models only.*

## Major Options

|  | Rambler | AMX | Javelin | Rebel | Ambassador |
|---|---|---|---|---|---|
| Air conditioning | $380 | $380 | $380 | $380 | S |
| Tilt-O-Just steering wheel | - | - | - | $45 | $45 |
| Speed control | - | - | - | $60 | $60 |
| Soft Ray tinted glass | $34 | $34 | $34 | $37 | $42 |
| Vinyl top | - | - | $84 | $95 | $106 |
| Power steering — variable-ratio | $96 | $96 | $105 | $105 | $105 |
| Power brakes | $43 | $43 | $43 | $43 | $43 |
| Power windows | - | - | - | - | $105 |
| AM radio | $62 | $62 | $62 | $62 | $62 |
| AM/FM stereo | - | - | $224 | $224 | $224 |
| Custom wheel covers | $50 | $50 | $50 | $53 | $53 |
| Turbo Cast wheel covers | $75 | $75 | $75 | $78 | $78 |
| Station wagon third seat | - | - | - | $118 | $118 |

Options common to most models. (- = Not Available; S = Standard equipment.) Items may be standard equipment, optional at different pricing, or unavailable on certain models. This chart is only a guide.

## Paint Colors

|  | Code |
|---|---|
| Classic Black | P1A |
| Matador Red | P39A |
| Saturn Blue Met. | P43A |
| Caravelle Blue Met. | P44A |
| Blazer Blue Met. | P45A |
| Laurel Green Met. | P46A |
| Rally Green Met. | P47A |
| Tahiti Turquoise Met. | P48A |
| Laredo Tan | P49A |
| Calcutta Russet Met. | P50A |
| Scarab Gold Met. | P52A |
| Turbo Silver Metallic | P54A |
| Hialeah Yellow | P58A |
| Frost White | P72A |

# Rambler American

*"The only compact car made in America that's not overpriced."*

**Nameplate year of origin:** 1950 (Nash).
**Current bodystyle lifespan:** 1964 through 1969.
**Predecessor to this model:** Rambler American (1958 to 1963).
**Replacement for this model:** Hornet (1970 to 1977).
**Percentage of division's sales volume:** 31.84%.
**Corporate siblings:** None.
**Primary competition:** Chevrolet Chevy II, Ford Falcon, and Plymouth Valiant.
**Notable changes:** Trim and detail changes.
**Major standard equipment:** Cloth and vinyl front bench seat, front arm rests and ash trays, variable speed windshield wipers, rubber floor mats, cargo mat, and 6.45 × 14 BSW tires (6.95 × 14 BSW tires on wagons). 440 adds: Full carpeting, rear armrests, and custom steering wheel. Rogue adds: All-vinyl front bench seat, wheel covers, special trim and identification.

## Measurements

|  | Cars | Wagons |
|---|---|---|
| Wheelbase | 106.0" | 106.0" |
| Length | 181.0" | 181.0" |
| Width | 70.8" | 70.8" |
| Height | 54.2" | 54.5" |
| Legroom — front | 42.0" | 41.0" |
| Legroom — rear | 35.0" | 36.5" |
| Headroom — front | 39.0" | 39.3" |
| Headroom — rear | 39.0" | 37.0" |
| Luggage cap. (cu. ft.) | 12.0 | 66.0 |
| Fuel capacity (gals.) | 13.3 | 13.3 |

**1968**

## Models Available

|  | Style Number | Base MSRP | Change from LY | Shipping Wt. (lbs.) | Production | Change from LY |
|---|---|---|---|---|---|---|
| Rambler American 2-Door Sdn. | 6806-0 | $1,946 | +5.82% | 2604 | 53,824 | +116.74% |
| Rambler American 4-Door Sdn. | 6805-0 | $2,024 | +4.06% | 2638 | 16,595 | +60.15% |
| Rambler Am. 440 4-Dr. Sdn. | 6805-5 | $2,166 | +3.98% | 2643 | 11,116 | +47.76% |
| Rambler Am. 440 4-Dr. Wgn. | 6808-5 | $2,426 | +2.45% | 2800 | 8,285 | +100.36% |
| Rambler Am. Rogue 2-Dr. HT | 6809-7 | $2,244 | -0.97% | 2678 | 4,549 | +10.17% |
| TOTALS | | *Avg. price* $2,161 | +0.79% | | *Production* 94,369 | +50.56% |

# AMX

*"Sexy. Racy. It really moves you."*

**Nameplate year of origin:** 1968.
**Current bodystyle lifespan:** 1968 through 1970.
**Predecessor to this model:** None.
**Replacement for this model:** None.
**Percentage of division's sales volume:** 2.27%.
**Corporate siblings:** Javelin (AMX created from shortened Javelin body).
**Primary competition:** Chevrolet Corvette, Chevrolet Camaro, Dodge Challenger, Ford Mustang, Plymouth Barracuda, and Pontiac Firebird.
**Notable changes:** All-new for 1968.
**Major standard equipment:** All-vinyl front bucket seats, front armrests, full carpeting, interior courtesy lights, Weather-Eye heating & ventilation system, custom steering wheel, and E70 × 14 Wide-Oval BSW tires.

## Measurements

| | |
|---|---|
| Wheelbase | 97.0" |
| Length | 178.0" |
| Width | 72.0" |
| Height | NA |
| Legroom — front | 42.0" |
| Legroom — rear | NA |
| Headroom — front | 39.0" |
| Headroom — rear | NA |
| Luggage cap. (cu. ft.) | NA |
| Fuel capacity (gals.) | 16 |

## Models Available

| | Style Number | Base MSRP | Change from LY | Shipping Wt. (lbs.) | Production | Change from LY |
|---|---|---|---|---|---|---|
| AMX 2-Door Hardtop | 6839-7 | $3,245 | NEW | 3094 | 6,725 | NEW |
| TOTALS | | Avg. price $3,245 | NEW | | Production 6,725 | NEW |

# Javelin

*"Its price is much less than the Mustang's, yet you get much more."*

**Nameplate year of origin:** 1968.
**Current bodystyle lifespan:** 1968 through 1970.
**Predecessor to this model:** Marlin (1965 to 1967).
**Replacement for this model:** Javelin (1971 to 1974).
**Percentage of division's sales volume:** 18.60%.
**Corporate siblings:** AMX (created through a shortened Javelin body).
**Primary competition:** Chevrolet Camaro, Dodge Challenger, Ford Mustang, Plymouth Barracuda, and Pontiac Firebird.
**Notable changes:** All-new for 1968.
**Major standard equipment:** All-vinyl front bucket seats, front armrests, full carpeting, interior courtesy lights, Weather-Eye heating & ventilation system, and 6.95 × 14 BSW tires. SST adds: Reclining bucket seats, wood-grain sports steering wheel and door panel trim, rocker panel moldings, wheel covers and hood-scoop moldings.

## Measurements

| | |
|---|---|
| Wheelbase | 109.0" |
| Length | 190.0" |
| Width | 72.0" |
| Height | 54.0" |
| Legroom — front | 42.0" |
| Legroom — rear | 35.0" |
| Headroom — front | 39.0" |
| Headroom — rear | 36.6" |
| Luggage cap. (cu. ft.) | 10.2 |
| Fuel capacity (gals.) | 15.8 |

## Models Available

| | Style Number | Base MSRP | Change from LY | Shipping Wt. (lbs.) | Production | Change from LY |
|---|---|---|---|---|---|---|
| Javelin 2-Door Hardtop | 6879-5 | $2,482 | NEW | 2826 | 29,097 | NEW |
| Javelin SST 2-Door Hardtop | 6879-7 | $2,587 | NEW | 2836 | 26,027 | NEW |
| TOTALS | | Avg. price $2,535 | NEW | | Production 55,124 | NEW |

# Rebel

*"It's the best dollar value in the automobile business."*

**Nameplate year of origin:** 1957 (Nash Rambler model).
**Current bodystyle lifespan:** 1967 through 1978 (restyles in 1969, 1971, and 1974).
**Predecessor to this model:** Rambler Classic (1963 to 1966).
**Replacement for this model:** Matador (1971 to 1978).
**Percentage of division's sales volume:** 26.76%.
**Corporate siblings:** Ambassador (Shared components from the cowl back).
**Primary competition:** Chevrolet Chevelle, Ford Fairlane, and Plymouth Belvedere/Satellite.
**Notable changes:** New grille, trim and detail changes.
**Major standard equipment:** Cloth and vinyl front bench seat, front arm rests, rubber floor mats, hidden compartment (Wagons), Weather-Eye heating & ventilation system, roof-top travel rack (wagons) and 7.35 × 14 BSW tires (7.75 × 14 BSW tires on Wagons). 770 adds: Full carpeting, rear arm rests, custom steering wheel, dual horns, and lock for glove box and hidden compartment on wagons. SST adds: All-vinyl reclining front bench seat, underhood insulation, and full wheel covers.

## Measurements

|  | Cars | Wagons |
|---|---|---|
| Wheelbase | 114.0" | 114.0" |
| Length | 197.0" | 198.0" |
| Width | 77.0" | 77.0" |
| Height | 55.0" | 55.0" |
| Legroom — front | 42.6" | 42.6" |
| Legroom — rear | 38.6" | 38.6" |
| Headroom — front | 39.8" | 39.8" |
| Headroom — rear | 38.0" | 38.0" |
| Luggage cap. (cu. ft.) | 18.2 | 91.0 |
| Fuel capacity (gals.) | 17.9 | 17.9 |

## Models Available

| | Style Number | Base MSRP | Change from LY | Shipping Wt. (lbs.) | Production | Change from LY |
|---|---|---|---|---|---|---|
| Rebel 550 2-Door Hardtop | 6819-0 | $2,454 | NEW | 3117 | 7,377 | NEW |
| Rebel 550 2-Door Convertible | 6817-0 | $2,736 | NEW | 3195 | 377 | NEW |
| Rebel 550 4-Door Sedan | 6815-0 | $2,443 | +5.35% | 3062 | 14,712 | +43.55% |
| Rebel 550 4-Door Wagon | 6818-0 | $2,729 | +4.04% | 3301 | 7,427 | +8.50% |
| Rebel 770 2-Door Hardtop | 6819-5 | $2,556 | +4.63% | 3116 | 4,420 | -54.36% |
| Rebel 770 4-Door Sedan | 6815-5 | $2,542 | +5.13% | 3074 | 22,938 | -4.65% |
| Rebel 770 4-Door Wagon | 6818-5 | $2,854 | +5.31% | 3306 | 11,375 | -37.64% |
| Rebel SST 2-Door Hardtop | 6819-7 | $2,775 | +6.57% | 3348 | 9,876 | -35.40% |
| Rebel SST 2-Door Convertible | 6817-7 | $2,999 | +7.80% | 3427 | 823 | -51.19% |
| TOTALS | *Avg. price* | $2,676 | +6.02% | *Production* | 79,325 | -16.65% |

# Ambassador

*"The only American built car with air conditioning standard."*

**Nameplate year of origin:** 1933 (from top-of-the-line Nash).
**Current bodystyle lifespan:** 1967 through 1978 (shared basic structure with Matador).
**Predecessor to this model:** Ambassador (1963 to 1966).
**Replacement for this model:** None.
**Percentage of division's sales volume:** 20.54%.
**Corporate siblings:** Rebel (shared components from the cowl back).
**Primary competition:** Chevrolet BelAir/Impala/Caprice, Ford LTD, and Plymouth Fury.
**Notable changes:** New grille and trim and detail changes.
**Major standard equipment:** Cloth and vinyl front bench seat, full carpeting, all-season air conditioning, cargo mat, roof-top travel rack (wagon) and 7.35 × 14 BSW tires (8.25 × 14 BSW tires on wagons). DPL adds: Addi-

## Measurements

|  | Cars | Wagons |
|---|---|---|
| Wheelbase | 118.0" | 118.0" |
| Length | 202.5" | 203.0" |
| Width | 77.2" | 77.2" |
| Height | 55.0" | 55.0" |
| Legroom — front | 42.6" | 42.6" |
| Legroom — rear | 38.6" | 38.6" |
| Headroom — front | 39.8" | 39.8" |
| Headroom — rear | 38.0" | 38.0" |
| Luggage cap. (cu. ft.) | 18.2 | 91.0 |
| Fuel capacity (gals.) | 21.5 | 20.0 |

**1968**

tional chrome exterior trim, full wheel covers, and deluxe interior trim level. SST adds: All-vinyl reclining seats, center armrest, walnut-grain interior trim, light group, electric clock, exterior paint striping, rallye lights in grille, and 7.75 × 14 BSW tires.

## Models Available

| | Style Number | Base MSRP | Change from LY | Shipping Wt. (lbs.) | Production | Change from LY |
|---|---|---|---|---|---|---|
| Ambassador 2-Door Hardtop | 6889-2 | $2,842 | NEW | 3252 | 3,360 | NEW |
| Ambassador 4-Door Sedan | 6885-2 | $2,820 | +10.46% | 3193 | 8,788 | -10.07% |
| Ambassador DPL 2-Door Hardtop | 6889-5 | $2,941 | +9.01% | 3321 | 3,696 | -39.80% |
| Ambassador DPL 4-Door Sedan | 6885-5 | $2,920 | +9.32% | 3265 | 13,265 | -25.52% |
| Ambassador DPL 4-Door Wagon | 6888-5 | $3,207 | +7.69% | 3475 | 10,690 | 34.99% |
| Ambassador SST 2-Door HT | 6889-7 | $3,172 | +11.14% | 3520 | 7,686 | -38.77% |
| Ambassador SST 4-Door Sdn. | 6885-7 | $3,151 | NEW | 3476 | 13,387 | NEW |
| TOTALS | | Avg. price $3,008 | +8.05% | | Production 60,873 | -2.79% |

# BUICK

### "Now wouldn't you really rather have a 1968 Buick?"

The 1968 Buick model line saw the second major restyling of the Special and Skylark lines since their introduction in 1961 as a compact car line. Now a full-fledged intermediate line, complete with "muscle-bound" Gran Sport models, the Special and Skylark were very much a pseudo-luxury car. Their new styling was marked with a throwback to the fifties era Buick "sweep spear" motif and "portholes." Top line models included rear fender skirts, and the complete look was one geared towards the luxury market, and less towards the sporty market. As usual the SportWagon followed typical Skylark styling cues. With the new body styling several model changes were made. The base Special was discontinued, leaving only the Special Deluxe. The Skylark line became a two model midrange line, and a new Skylark Custom took the place of last

year's Skylark, with the 2-Door Coupe no longer in the line. The GS 340 became a GS 350 with the new large displacement 350 CID V8 engine as standard equipment. The GS 400 line also lost its 2-Door Coupe. As a side note, the remaining 2-Door Coupe models were known as Thin-pillared Coupes, but were still essentially 2-Door Sedans.

Full-size Buick models received new grilles and minor detail changes. All models continued with the split grille theme. The Riviera wore completely new front "grille in bumper" styling that would soon be in vogue with many manufacturers. Overall, though, Riviera styling was a continuation of the 1966-67 look. As in the Skylark and Special lines, a new 350 CID V8 engine replaced the former 340 CID V8 engine under the hood of LeSabre models.

Electra 225 Custom 2-Door Hardtop

GS350 2-Door Convertible

LeSabre 4-Door Sedan

Riviera 2-Door Hardtop

Skylark 2-Door Hardtop

Skylark 4-Door Sedan

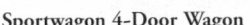

Sportwagon 4-Door Wagon

Wildcat 4-Door Hardtop

**Model year production:** 633,820, up 16.22% over 1967.
**Domestic market share:** 7.40% (5th place).
**Base price range:** $2,513 to $4,615.
**Industry average base price:** $3,292.
**Buick average base price:** $3,489.
**Introduction date:** September 1967.
**Assembly plants:** Southgate, CA (C); Atlanta, GA (D); Flint, MI (H); Kansas City, MO (K); Fairfax, KS (X); Wilmington, DE (Y); Fremont, CA (Z); and Oshawa, Ontario, (1).

**Data plate identification:** Thirteen digit code read as follows: Five digit style number in which 4 = Buick, 2nd number identifies series (3 is Skylark, 8 is Electra, etc.), 3rd through 5th indicate model number; 8 = 1968; assembly plant code; 100001 and up for serial number. *Example:* 452378X100001 is a 1968 Buick LeSabre 2-Door Hardtop, serial number 100001, built in Fairfax, KS

## Powertrains

| Engine | Gross HP | Transmission Availability | Special/ Skylark | GS | Sport Wagon | LeSabre | Wildcat/Elec. & Riviera |
|---|---|---|---|---|---|---|---|
| 250 CID, 2-bbl., 6-cyl. | 155 | 3-speed manual | S | - | - | - | - |
| | | Super Turbine 300 Automatic | $174 | - | - | - | - |
| 350 CID, 2-bbl., V8 | 230 | 3-speed manual | S[1]/$111[2] | - | S | S | - |
| | | Super Turbine 300 Automatic | $185[1]/$296[2] | - | - | $185 | - |
| | | Turbo Hydra-matic | $206[1] | - | $206 | - | - |
| 350 CID, 4-bbl., V8 | 280 | 3-speed manual | $47[1]/$158[2] | S —* | $47 | - | - |
| | | 4-speed manual | - | $185 —* | - | - | - |
| | | Super Turbine 300 Automatic | $343[2] | - | - | $232 | - |
| | | Turbo Hydra-matic | $253[1] | $206 —* | $253 | $275 (400) | - |
| 400 CID, 4-bbl., V8 | 340 | 3-speed manual | - | S (400) | - | - | - |
| | | 4-speed manual | - | $185 (400) | - | - | - |
| | | Turbo Hydra-matic | - | $227 (400) | $348 | - | - |
| 430 CID, 4-bbl., V8 | 360 | 3-speed manual | - | - | - | - | S (Wildcat) |
| | | Turbo Hydra-matic | - | - | - | - | S (Electra & Riviera)/ $227 (Wildcat) |

[1]*Skylark Custom only.*    [2]*All but Skylark Custom.*    **California GS and GS 350 models.*

## Major Options

| | Skylark | LeSabre | Wildcat | Electra 225 | Riviera |
|---|---|---|---|---|---|
| Air conditioning — manual | $376 | $421 | $421 | $421 | $421 |
| Air conditioning — automatic | - | $500 | $500 | $500 | $500 |
| Cruise Master speed control | $58 | $63 | $63 | $63 | $63 |
| Soft Ray tinted glass | $39 | $44 | $44 | $44 | $47 |
| Deck lid remote release | $14 | $14 | $14 | $14 | $14 |
| Tilt steering wheel | $45 | $45 | $45 | $45 | S |

1968

| | Skylark | LeSabre | Wildcat | Electra 225 | Riviera |
|---|---|---|---|---|---|
| Power steering — variable-ratio | $100 | $111 | $111 | S | S |
| Power brakes | $42 | $42 | $42 | S | S |
| Power driver's seat/bench seat, 4-way | $74 (ex. 6-cyl.) | $74 | $74 | $47–$74 | $74 |
| Power windows (except on 6-cylinder) | $105 | $110 | $110 | $110* | $110 |
| AM radio | $70 | $88 | $88 | $88 | $88 |
| AM/FM stereo (not stereo in Skylark) | $134 | $268 | $268 | $268 | $268 |
| Vinyl roof | $102 | $123 | S | $139 | $128 |
| White sidewall tires — standard size | $31–$36 | $42 | $42 | $47 | $42 |
| Wheel trim covers — Deluxe on Electra | $21 | $21 (base) | S | S | S |

Options common to most models. (- = Not Available; S = Standard equipment.) Items may be standard equipment, optional at different pricing, or unavailable on certain models. This chart is only a guide.

*Standard on Convertible.*

## Paint Colors

| | Code | | Code |
|---|---|---|---|
| Regal Black | A | Maroon Metallic | N |
| Midnight Teal Metallic | B | Tarpon Green Mist Metallic | P |
| Arctic White | C | Scarlet Red | R |
| Blue Mist Metallic | D | Olive Gold Metallic* | S |
| Deep Blue Metallic | E | Desert Beige | T |
| Teal Blue Mist Metallic | F | Charcoal Metallic | V |
| Ivory Gold Mist Metallic | G | Silver Beige Mist Metallic* | W |
| Aqua Mist Metallic | K | Buckskin* | X |
| Medium Teal Blue Mist Met. | L | Cameo Cream | Y |
| Burnished Saddle Metallic | M | Inca Silver Mist* | |

*Specific Riviera colors.*

# Special, Skylark and GS

*"Here's something we've done to beautify our highways."*

**Nameplate year of origin:** (1935) Special; 1953 (Skylark)
**Current bodystyle lifespan:** 1968 through 1972.
**Predecessor to this model:** Special/Skylark (1964 to 1967).
**Replacement for this model:** Century (1973 to 1977).
**Percentage of division's sales volume:** 32.27%.
**Corporate siblings:** Chevrolet Chevelle, Olds Cutlass, and Pontiac Tempest and LeMans.
**Primary competition:** Dodge Coronet, and Mercury Comet and Montego.
**Notable changes:** Completely redesigned.
**Major standard equipment:** Front door operated interior light, heater and defroster, cigarette lighter, front ash trays and arm rests, crank-operated vent windows, Magic-Mirror finish paint, self adjusting brakes, vinyl bench seat, and 7.75 × 14 BSW tires. Skylark adds: Deluxe steering wheel, rear arm rests and ash trays, full carpeting, ventless front door windows (2-Doors). Custom adds: Custom padded seat cushions, lower body rocker moldings. California GS adds: Vinyl top, Super Sport wheels, special exterior moldings. GS adds: All-vinyl seats, dual exhausts, finned aluminum brake drums (400), heavy duty springs, shocks, stabilizer bar and F70 × 14 Wide-Oval WSW tires.

## Measurements

| | 2-Doors | 4-Doors | Wagon |
|---|---|---|---|
| Wheelbase | 112.0" | 116.0" | 116.0" |
| Length | 200.6" | 204.6" | 209.0" |
| Width | 75.6" | 75.6" | 75.6" |
| Height | 52.8" | 53.6" | 53.6" |
| Legroom — front | 42.8" | 42.8" | 42.8" |
| Legroom — rear | 32.7" | 35.1" | 35.1" |
| Headroom — front | 37.8" | 38.6" | 38.6" |
| Headroom — rear | 36.4" | 37.3" | 38.9" |
| Luggage capacity (cu. ft.) | NA | NA | NA |
| Fuel capacity (gals.) | 20.0 | 20.0 | 20.0 |

## Models Available

| | Style Number | Base MSRP | Change from LY | Shipping Wt. (lbs.) | Production | Change from LY |
|---|---|---|---|---|---|---|
| Special Deluxe 2-Door Coupe | 43327 | $2,513 | +4.23% | 3125 | 21,988 | +38.06% |
| Special Deluxe 4-Door Sedan | 43369 | $2,564 | +4.14% | 3217 | 16,571 | +57.76% |
| Special Deluxe 4-Dr., 2-Seat Wgn. | 43435 | $3,001 | +9.45% | 3670 | 10,916 | +320.49% |
| Skylark 2-Door Hardtop | 43527 | $2,793 | +8.85% | 3347 | 32,795 | +95.90% |
| Skylark 4-Door Sedan | 43569 | $2,771 | +8.88% | 3435 | 27,384 | -5.45% |
| Skylark Custom 2-Door Hardtop | 44437 | $2,956 | +5.65% | 3344 | 44,143 | +7.82% |
| Skylark Custom 2-Door Convertible | 44467 | $3,098 | +5.20% | 3394 | 8,188 | +29.58% |
| Skylark Custom 4-Door Sedan | 44469 | $2,924 | +5.67% | 3377 | 8,066 | -11.59% |
| Skylark Custom 4-Door Hardtop | 44439 | $3,108 | +5.36% | 3481 | 12,984 | -5.04% |
| GS 350 2-Door Hardtop | 43437 | $2,926 | +2.85% | 3375 | 8,317 | * |
| GS 400 2-Door Hardtop | 44637 | $3,127 | +3.58% | 3514 | 10,743 | +0.79% |
| GS 400 2-Door Convertible | 44667 | $3,271 | +3.28% | 3547 | 2,454 | +14.67% |
| TOTALS | Avg. price | $2,921 | +4.96% | Production | 204,549 | +20.67% |

*Production figures for 1967 GS 340 not available for comparison.

# SportWagon

*"The name SportWagon might give you the idea
that this Buick is something pretty sporty. That's the idea."*

**Nameplate year of origin:** 1964.
**Current bodystyle lifespan:** 1968 through 1969.
**Predecessor to this model:** SportWagon (1966 to 1967).
**Replacement for this model:** None.
**Percentage of division's sales volume:** 3.61%.
**Corporate siblings:** Oldsmobile Vista-Cruiser.
**Primary competition:** Dodge Coronet and Mercury Montego.
**Notable changes:** Completely redesigned.
**Major standard equipment:** All-vinyl bench seat, front door operated interior light, front and rear arm rests and ash trays, full carpeting, custom padded seat cushions, deluxe steering wheel, crank-operated vent windows, Magic-Mirror finish paint, self adjusting brakes, tinted glass observation-style roof, dual-action tailgate, 8.25 × 14 BSW tires on 2-Seat wagon and 8.55 × 14 BSW tires on 3-Seat Wagon.

## Measurements

| | |
|---|---|
| Wheelbase | 121.0" |
| Length | 214.1" |
| Width | 75.6" |
| Height | 58.8" |
| Legroom — front | 41.6" |
| Legroom — rear | 37.8" |
| Headroom — front | 38.0" |
| Headroom — rear | 39.9" |
| Luggage capacity (cu. ft.) | 100.0 |
| Fuel capacity (gals.) | 20.0 |

**1968**

## Models Available

| | Style Number | Base MSRP | Change from LY | Shipping Wt. (lbs.) | Production | Change from LY |
|---|---|---|---|---|---|---|
| Sportwagon 4-Door, 2-Seat Wagon | 44455 | $3,341 | +4.34% | 3975 | 10,530 | +23.10% |
| Sportwagon 4-Door, 3-Seat Wagon | 44465 | $3,499 | +4.76% | 4118 | 12,358 | +17.37% |
| TOTALS | Avg. price | $3,420 | +4.55% | Production | 22,888 | +19.94% |

# LeSabre

*"A Buick like this can make anyone enjoy driving."*

**Nameplate year of origin:** 1959.
**Current bodystyle lifespan:** 1967 through 1968.
**Predecessor to this model:** LeSabre (1965 to 1966).
**Replacement for this model:** LeSabre (1969 to 1970).
**Percentage of division's sales volume:** 27.10%.
**Corporate siblings:** Chevrolet Full-size, Pontiac Full-size, Oldsmobile Delta 88.
**Primary competition:** Chrysler Newport, Dodge Monaco, and Mercury Monterey.
**Notable changes:** Revised grille and minor trim and detail changes.
**Major standard equipment:** Cloth and vinyl bench seat, front door operated interior lighting, glove box light, full carpeting, Magic-Mirror finish, and 8.45 × 15 BSW tires. Custom adds: Custom interior trim (all vinyl on Convertible), deluxe steering wheel, wheel opening moldings, "Custom" nameplates, and additional exterior trim moldings.

## Measurements

| | |
|---|---|
| Wheelbase | 123.0" |
| Length | 217.5" |
| Width | 80.0" |
| Height | 55.3" |
| Legroom — front | 42.2" |
| Legroom — rear | 39.0" |
| Headroom — front | 39.6" |
| Headroom — rear | 38.3" |
| Luggage capacity (cu. ft.) | NA |
| Fuel capacity (gals.) | 25.0 |

## Models Available

| | Style Number | Base MSRP | Change from LY | Shipping Wt. (lbs.) | Production | Change from LY |
|---|---|---|---|---|---|---|
| LeSabre 2-Door Hardtop | 45287 | $3,223 | +4.51% | 3923 | 14,922 | +8.44% |
| LeSabre 4-Door Sedan | 45269 | $3,141 | +4.63% | 3946 | 37,433 | +3.35% |
| LeSabre 4-Door Hardtop | 45239 | $3,281 | +4.42% | 3980 | 10,058 | -42.41% |
| LeSabre Custom 2-Door Hardtop | 45487 | $3,311 | +4.38% | 3932 | 29,596 | +149.31% |
| LeSabre Custom 2-Door Convertible | 45467 | $3,504 | +3.42% | 3966 | 5,257 | +80.47% |
| LeSabre Custom 4-Door Sedan | 45469 | $3,235 | +4.49% | 3950 | 34,112 | +22.13% |
| LeSabre Custom 4-Door Hardtop | 45439 | $3,375 | +4.30% | 4007 | 40,370 | +24.12% |
| TOTALS | *Avg. price* | $3,296 | +4.30% | *Production* | 171,748 | +20.37% |

# Wildcat

*"We can think of just one thing greater than the Wildcat you're driving today: the Wildcat you'll be driving tomorrow."*

**Nameplate year of origin:** 1962.
**Current bodystyle lifespan:** 1967 through 1968.
**Predecessor to this model:** Wildcat (1965 to 1966).
**Replacement for this model:** Wildcat (1969 to 1970).
**Percentage of division's sales volume:** 11.04%.
**Corporate siblings:** Chevrolet Full-size, Pontiac Full-size, Oldsmobile Delta 88.
**Primary competition:** Chrysler 300, Dodge Monaco, and Mercury Marquis.
**Notable changes:** Revised grille and minor trim and detail changes.
**Major standard equipment:** All-vinyl front bench seat (2-Doors), cloth and vinyl front bench seat (4-Doors), glove box light, full carpeting, deluxe steering wheel, Magic-Mirror finish, rocker panel moldings, rear fender skirts, and 8.45 × 15 BSW tires. Custom adds: Custom interior trim and custom headlining.

## Measurements

| | |
|---|---|
| Wheelbase | 126.0" |
| Length | 220.5" |
| Width | 80.0" |
| Height | 55.3" |
| Legroom — front | 42.2" |
| Legroom — rear | 39.0" |
| Headroom — front | 39.6" |
| Headroom — rear | 38.3" |
| Luggage capacity (cu. ft.) | NA |
| Fuel capacity (gals.) | 25.0 |

## Models Available

|  | Style Number | Base MSRP | Change from LY | Shipping Wt. (lbs.) | Production | Change from LY |
|---|---|---|---|---|---|---|
| Wildcat 2-Door HT | 46487 | $3,521 | +4.11% | 4065 | 10,708 | +1.16% |
| Wildcat 4-Door Sedan | 46469 | $3,416 | +4.24% | 4076 | 15,201 | +4.27% |
| Wildcat 4-Door HT | 46439 | $3,576 | +4.04% | 4133 | 15,173 | -2.17% |
| Wildcat Custom 2-Door Hardtop | 46687 | $3,742 | +3.86% | 4082 | 11,276 | -2.55% |
| Wildcat Custom 2-Door Convertible | 46667 | $3,873 | +3.09% | 4118 | 3,572 | +22.62% |
| Wildcat Custom 4-Door Hardtop | 46639 | $3,791 | +3.81% | 4162 | 14,059 | +3.78% |
| TOTALS | Avg. price | $3,653 | +3.75% | Production | 69,989 | -1.39% |

# Electra 225

*"You didn't think it was possible to make an*
*Electra more beautiful than last year's, did you?"*

**Nameplate year of origin:** 1959.
**Current bodystyle lifespan:** 1967 through 1968.
**Predecessor to this model:** Electra 225 (1965 to 1966).
**Replacement for this model:** Electra 225 (1969 to 1970).
**Percentage of division's sales volume:** 18.20%.
**Corporate siblings:** Cadillac Calais/de Ville, Oldsmobile Ninety-Eight.
**Primary competition:** Chrysler New Yorker and Mercury Park Lane.
**Notable changes:** Revised grille and minor trim and detail changes.
**Major standard equipment:** Cloth and vinyl bench seat, full carpeting and lower door carpeting, deluxe steering wheel, trunk light, bright rocker panel molding and wheel opening moldings, rear fender skirts, variable ratio power steering, power front brakes, Turbo Hydra-matic 400 transmission, deluxe wheel covers and 8.85 × 15 BSW tires. Custom adds: Custom interior trim (all-vinyl on coupe and convertible).

## Measurements

| | |
|---|---|
| Wheelbase | 126.0" |
| Length | 224.9" |
| Width | 80.0" |
| Height | 56.2" |
| Legroom — front | 42.1" |
| Legroom — rear | 42.1" |
| Headroom — front | 39.5" |
| Headroom — rear | 38.2" |
| Luggage capacity (cu. ft.) | NA |
| Fuel capacity (gals.) | 25.0 |

**1968**

## Models Available

|  | Style Number | Base MSRP | Change from LY | Shipping Wt. (lbs.) | Production | Change from LY |
|---|---|---|---|---|---|---|
| Electra 225 2-Door Hardtop | 48257 | $4,221 | +3.58% | 4180 | 10,705 | +56.39% |
| Electra 225 4-Door Sedan | 48269 | $4,200 | +3.60% | 4253 | 12,723 | +17.95% |
| Electra 225 4-Door Hardtop | 48239 | $4,330 | +3.49% | 4270 | 15,376 | +23.10% |
| Electra 225 Custom 2-Door HT | 48457 | $4,400 | +3.43% | 4223 | 6,826 | -43.85% |
| Electra 225 Custom 2-Door Conv. | 48467 | $4,541 | +2.71% | 4285 | 7,976 | +14.91% |
| Electra 225 Custom 4-Door Sedan | 48469 | $4,415 | +3.40% | 4304 | 10,910 | +7.96% |
| Electra 225 Custom 4-Door HT | 48439 | $4,509 | +3.35% | 4314 | 50,846 | +24.08% |
| TOTALS | Avg. price | $4,374 | +3.36% | Production | 115,362 | +15.01% |

# Riviera

*"All the beautiful things that can be said about the
Riviera have been said beautifully already. By the Riviera."*

**Nameplate year of origin:** 1949 (for 2-Dr. HTs); 1963 (series).
**Current bodystyle lifespan:** 1966 through 1970.
**Predecessor to this model:** Riviera (1963 to 1965).
**Replacement for this model:** Riviera (1971 to 1976).
**Percentage of division's sales volume:** 7.78%.
**Corporate siblings:** Cadillac Eldorado and Oldsmobile Toronado.
**Primary competition:** Ford Thunderbird.
**Notable changes:** Revised trim and detail changes.
**Major standard equipment:** All-vinyl bench or bucket seats with custom padding, electric clock, trunk light, bright exterior moldings, variable ratio power steering, power brakes, dual exhaust system, Turbo Hydra-matic 400 transmission, and 8.45 × 15 BSW tires.

## Measurements

| | |
|---|---|
| Wheelbase | 119.0" |
| Length | 215.2" |
| Width | 78.5" |
| Height | 53.4" |
| Legroom — front | 41.1" |
| Legroom — rear | 36.5" |
| Headroom — front | 38.0" |
| Headroom — rear | 37.4" |
| Luggage capacity (cu. ft.) | NA |
| Fuel capacity (gals.) | 21.0 |

## Models Available

| | Style Number | Base MSRP | Change from LY | Shipping Wt. (lbs.) | Production | Change from LY |
|---|---|---|---|---|---|---|
| Riviera 2-Door Hardtop | 49487 | $4,615 | +3.27% | 4222 | 49,284 | +15.15% |
| TOTALS | | *Avg. price* $4,615 | +3.27% | *Production* | 49,284 | +15.15% |

# CADILLAC

*"Cadillac elegance in action. Standard of the World."*

Cadillacs for 1968 featured an all-new 472 CID V8, giving Cadillac the largest displacement engine available at the time. It also offered one of the highest torque output ratings of any domestic car engine. Also this season, Cadillac would finally break the 200,000 mark in production for the model year. The prior two years were very close to that mark, and in truth the number was only meaningful to the personal satisfaction of General Motors management.

Lincoln was the closest competitor for Cadillac at this time, and its production was about one-fifth that of the GM luxury division. Styling changes for 1968 were minimal, but as with every other American car, there were plenty of updates to accommodate the newly mandated safety regulations. The only model change was the cancellation of the Calais 4-Door Sedan.

Calais 4-Door Hardtop

de Ville 2-Door Convertible

Fleetwood Sixty-Special 4-Door Sedan

Fleetwood Brougham 4-Door Sedan

Fleetwood Eldorado 2-Door Hardtop

**Model year production:** 227,590, up 15.14% over 1967.
**Domestic market share:** 2.66% (11th place).
**Base price range:** $5,315 to $10,768.
**Industry average base price:** $3,292.
**Cadillac average base price:** $6,832.
**Introduction date:** September 1967.
**Assembly plants:** Detroit, MI (Q), and Linden, NJ (E).
**Data plate identification:** Thirteen digit code read as follows:

Five digit style number in which 6 = Cadillac, 2nd and 3rd digits identify series (e.g., 82 is Calais), 4th and 5th digits indicate body style number (2nd through 5th digit of VIN make up 2nd through 5th digit of body style number in listings); 8 for 1968; 7th digit is assembly plant code; 100001 and up for serial number. *Example:* 683478Q100001 is a 1968 Cadillac de Ville 2-Door Hardtop, serial number 100001, built in Detroit, MI.

## Powertrains

| Engine | Gross HP | Transmission Availability | All models |
|---|---|---|---|
| 472 CID, 4-bbl., V8 | 375 | Turbo Hydra-matic | S |

## Major Options

| | Eldorado | de Ville/Calais | 60 Special | Seventy-Five |
|---|---|---|---|---|
| Automatic climate control | $516 | $516 | $516 | S |
| 6-way power seat | $90 | $90 (deV.)/$116 (Cal.) | $90 | $90 (NA Limo) |
| Power door locks | $68 | $68 | $68 | $116 |
| AM-FM radio | $188 | $188 | $188 | $188 |
| Vinyl roof | $158 | $153 (de Ville only) | S (Brougham) | NA |
| Twilight Sentinel (auto. dimmers) | $37 | $37 | $37 | $37 |
| Tilt and Telescope steering wheel | $95 | $95 | $95 | $95 |
| Leather upholstery | $184 | $158 (de Ville only) | $158 | – |
| Cruise control | $95 | $95 | $95 | $95 |
| Tinted glass | $53 | $53 | $53 | $53 |
| Rear window defogger | $26 | $26 ($36 convertible) | $26 | S |
| Automatic level control | S | $79 | S | S |
| Remote control trunk release | $53 | $53 | $53 | $53 |
| Firemist paint colors | $132 | $132 | $132 | $132 |

Options common to most models. (- = Not Available; S = Standard equipment.) Items may be standard equipment, optional at different pricing, or unavailable on certain models. This chart is only a guide.

## Paint Colors

| | Code |
|---|---|
| Sable Black | 10 |
| Grecian White | 12 |
| Regal Silver Metallic | 16 |
| Summit Gray Metallic | 18 |
| Arctic Blue | 20 |
| Normandy Blue Metallic | 24 |
| Emperor Blue Metallic | 26 |
| Caribe Aqua Metallic | 28 |
| Silverpine Green Metallic | 30 |
| Ivanhoe Green Metallic | 36 |
| Kashmir Ivory | 40 |
| Sudan Beige | 42 |
| Baroque Gold Metallic | 43 |
| Chestnut Brown Metallic | 44 |
| San Mateo Red Metallic | 48 |
| Regent Maroon Metallic | 49 |
| Spectre Blue Firemist Metallic* | 90 |
| Topaz Gold Firemist Metallic* | 94 |
| Monterey Green Firemist Metallic* | 96 |
| Rosewood Firemist Metallic* | 97 |
| Madeira Plum Firemist Metallic* | 98 |

*Firemist colors available at extra cost.*

**1968**

**Cadillac Style Symbols:** **A**— 62 4-window Sedan or Calais 4-Dr. HT Sedan; **B**— Sedan de Ville 4-window; **C**— 62 Short Deck Sedan; **D**— Sedan de Ville Park Avenue; **E**— Eldorado Biarritz or Eldorado Convertible; **F**— 62 Convertible; **G**— 62 2-Door Hardtop or Calais 2-Door HT; **H**— Eldorado Seville HT or Eldorado Coupe; **J**— Coupe de Ville; **K**— 62 6-window Sedan; **L**— Sedan de Ville 6-window; **M**— Fleetwood 60 Special Sedan; **N**— 62 4-window Sedan (1963) or Calais Sedan; **P**— Fleetwood Brougham or Eldorado Brougham; **R**— Fleetwood 75 Sedan; **S**— Fleetwood 75 Limousine; **Z**— Commerical Chassis

# Calais

*"The Calais series represents your easiest investment in
Cadillac distinction, luxury, performance and long-lasting value."*

**Nameplate year of origin:** 1965.
**Current bodystyle lifespan:** 1967 through 1968.
**Predecessor to this model:** Calais (1965 to 1966).
**Replacement for this model:** Calais (1969 to 1970).
**Percentage of division's sales volume:** 7.99%.
**Corporate siblings:** Buick Electra 225 and Oldsmobile Ninety-Eight.
**Primary competition:** Chrysler New Yorker and Lincoln Continental.
**Notable changes:** Revised grille and detail changes.
**Major standard equipment:** Dakarta cloth and vinyl seat upholstery (Sedan) or all-vinyl front bench seat (Coupe), front center armrests, rear fender skirts, left side remote control outside rear view mirror, power windows, interior courtesy and warning lights, three-speed windshield wipers and washers, right side visor vanity mirrors, front cornering lamps, variable ratio power steering, power front disc brakes, Turbo Hydra-matic transmission, and 9.00 × 15 BSW tires.

### Measurements

| | |
|---|---|
| Wheelbase | 129.5" |
| Length | 224.7" |
| Width | 79.9" |
| Height | 54.5" |
| Legroom — front | 41.0" |
| Legroom — rear | 39.7" |
| Headroom — front | 37.8" |
| Headroom — rear | 37.2" |
| Luggage capacity (cu. ft.) | NA |
| Fuel capacity (gals.) | 26.0 |

### Models Available

| | Style Number | Base MSRP | Change from LY | Shipping Wt. (lbs.) | Production | Change from LY |
|---|---|---|---|---|---|---|
| Calais 2-Door Hardtop | 68247 | $5,315 | +5.46% | 4570 | 8,165 | -10.13% |
| Calais 4-Door Hardtop | 68249 | $5,491 | +5.29% | 4640 | 10,025 | +1.47% |
| TOTALS | | Avg. price $5,403 | +4.77% | | Production 18,190 | -16.67% |

# de Ville

*"The popularity of the De Ville Series among luxury car buyers can be attributed in
great measure to its distinctive beauty and to its wide selection of body styles."*

**Nameplate year of origin:** 1949 (as Hardtop designation); 1959 (series).
**Current bodystyle lifespan:** 1967 through 1968.
**Predecessor to this model:** de Ville (1965 to 1966).
**Replacement for this model:** de Ville (1969 to 1970).
**Percentage of division's sales volume:** 72.27%.
**Corporate siblings:** Buick Electra 225 and Oldsmobile Ninety-Eight.
**Primary competition:** Imperial LeBaron and Lincoln Continental.
**Notable changes:** Revised grille and detail changes.
**Major standard equipment:** Domino pattern cloth and vinyl front bench seat (leather on convertible), two-way power seat adjustment, front and rear center armrests, rear fender skirts, left side remote control outside rear view mirror, power windows, interior door, courtesy and warning lights, three-speed windshield wipers and washers, right side visor vanity mirrors, front cornering lamps, variable ratio power steering, power front disc brakes, Turbo Hydra-matic transmission, and 9.00 × 15 BSW tires.

### Measurements

| | |
|---|---|
| Wheelbase | 129.5" |
| Length | 224.7" |
| Width | 79.9" |
| Height | 54.5" |
| Legroom — front | 41.0" |
| Legroom — rear | 39.7" |
| Headroom — front | 37.8" |
| Headroom — rear | 37.2" |
| Luggage capacity (cu. ft.) | NA |
| Fuel capacity (gals.) | 26.0 |

## Models Available

| | Style Number | Base MSRP | Change from LY | Shipping Wt. (lbs.) | Production | Change from LY |
|---|---|---|---|---|---|---|
| Coupe de Ville 2-Door Hardtop | 68347 | $5,552 | +2.97% | 4595 | 63,935 | +20.85% |
| de Ville 2-Door Convertible | 68367 | $5,736 | +2.28% | 4600 | 18,025 | -0.96% |
| Sedan de Ville 4-Door Sedan | 68369 | $5,785 | +2.84% | 4680 | 9,850 | +11.93% |
| Sedan de Ville 4-Door Hardtop | 68349 | $5,785 | +2.84% | 4675 | 72,662 | +21.30% |
| TOTALS | | *Avg. price* $5,715 | +2.73% | | *Production* 164,472 | +17.64% |

# Eldorado

*"The world's finest personal car."*

**Nameplate year of origin:** 1953.
**Current bodystyle lifespan:** 1967 through 1970.
**Predecessor to this model:** Fleetwood Eldorado (1965 to 1966).
**Replacement for this model:** Eldorado (1971 to 1978).
**Percentage of division's sales volume:** 10.78%.
**Corporate siblings:** Buick Riviera and Oldsmobile Toronado.
**Primary competition:** None.
**Notable changes:** Revised grille and detail changes.
**Major standard equipment:** Deauville cloth and vinyl seat upholstery, two-way power seat adjustment, front center armrests, left side remote control outside rear view mirror, power windows, interior door, courtesy and warning lights, three-speed windshield wipers and washers, right side visor vanity mirrors, front cornering lamps, variable ratio power steering, power front disc brakes, Turbo Hydra-matic transmission, front wheel drive, and 9.00 × 15 BSW tires.

## Measurements

| | |
|---|---|
| Wheelbase | 120.0" |
| Length | 221.0" |
| Width | 80.0" |
| Height | 53.3" |
| Legroom — front | 41.1" |
| Legroom — rear | 36.2" |
| Headroom — front | 37.7" |
| Headroom — rear | 37.6" |
| Luggage capacity (cu. ft.) | NA |
| Fuel capacity (gals.) | 24.0 |

## Models Available

| | Style Number | Base MSRP | Change from LY | Shipping Wt. (lbs.) | Production | Change from LY |
|---|---|---|---|---|---|---|
| Fl. Eldorado 2-Door Hardtop | 69347 | $6,605 | +5.23% | 4580 | 24,528 | +36.80% |
| TOTALS | | *Avg. price* $6,605 | +5.23% | | *Production* 24,528 | +36.80% |

# Fleetwood Brougham & Sixty-Special

*"Truly majestic motor cars."*

**Nameplate year of origin:** 1938.
**Current bodystyle lifespan:** 1967 through 1968.
**Predecessor to this model:** Fleetwood Sixty-Special (1965 to 1966).
**Replacement for this model:** Fleetwood Sixty-Special (1969 to 1970).
**Percentage of division's sales volume:** 8.17%.
**Corporate siblings:** None.
**Primary competition:** None.
**Notable changes:** Revised grille and detail changes.
**Major standard equipment:** Damsel cloth seat upholstery, two-way power seat adjust-ment, front and rear center armrests, rear fender skirts, left side remote control out-side rear view mirror, power windows, interior door, courtesy and warning lights,

## Measurements

| | |
|---|---|
| Wheelbase | 133.0" |
| Length | 228.2" |
| Width | 79.9" |
| Height | 56.7" |
| Legroom — front | 42.0" |
| Legroom — rear | 44.4" |
| Headroom — front | 39.1" |
| Headroom — rear | 38.0" |
| Luggage capacity (cu. ft.) | NA |
| Fuel capacity (gals.) | 26.0 |

**1968**

three-speed windshield wipers and washers, right side visor vanity mirrors, front cornering lamps, variable ratio power steering, power front disc brakes, Turbo Hydramatic transmission, and 9.00 × 15 BSW tires. Brougham adds: Driver's side only seat adjustment, reading lights and padded vinyl top.

## Models Available

| | Style Number | Base MSRP | Change from LY | Shipping Wt. (lbs.) | Production | Change from LY |
|---|---|---|---|---|---|---|
| Fl. Sixty Special 4-Dr. Sedan | 68069 | $6,583 | +2.49% | 4795 | 3,300 | -7.04% |
| Fl. Brougham 4-Dr. Sedan | 68169 | $6,899 | +2.37% | 4805 | 15,300 | +20.00% |
| TOTALS | Avg. price | $6,741 | +2.43% | | Production 18,600 | +14.11% |

# Fleetwood Seventy-Five

*"The most impressive of the world's fine automobiles."*

**Nameplate year of origin:** 1927 (Fleetwood bodies), 1936 (75 series).
**Current bodystyle lifespan:** 1967 through 1968.
**Predecessor to this model:** Fleetwood 75 (1966).
**Replacement for this model:** Fleetwood 75 (1969 to 1970).
**Percentage of division's sales volume:** 0.79%.
**Corporate siblings:** None.
**Primary competition:** None.
**Notable changes:** Revised grille and detail changes.
**Major standard equipment:** Dunstan cloth upholstery (Sedan) or DuBarry cloth and leather seat upholstery (Limousine), two-way power seat adjustment, rear center armrests, automatic climate control, rear window defogger, rear fender skirts, left side remote control outside rear view mirror, power windows, interior door, courtesy and warning lights, three-speed windshield wipers and washers, right side visor vanity mirrors, front cornering lamps, fixed ratio power steering, power front disc brakes, Turbo Hydra-matic transmission, and 8.20 × 15 BSW tires.

## Measurements

| | |
|---|---|
| Wheelbase | 149.8" |
| Length | 245.2" |
| Width | 79.8" |
| Height | 57.0" |
| Legroom — front | 42.0" |
| Legroom — rear | NA |
| Headroom — front | 39.1" |
| Headroom — rear | NA |
| Luggage capacity (cu. ft.) | NA |
| Fuel capacity (gals.) | 26.0 |

## Models Available

| | Style Number | Base MSRP | Change from LY | Shipping Wt. (lbs.) | Production | Change from LY |
|---|---|---|---|---|---|---|
| Fl. Seventy-Five 4-Door Sedan | 69723 | $10,629 | +2.60% | 5300 | 805 | -3.59% |
| Fl. Seventy-Five 4-Dr. Limousine | 69733 | $10,768 | +1.86% | 5385 | 995 | +3.11% |
| TOTALS | Avg. price | $10,699 | +2.23% | | Production 1,800 | 0.00% |

# CHEVROLET

*"Be smart. Be sure. Buy Chevrolet!"*

The 1968 Chevrolet line saw the introduction of three completely redesigned models that would be important to Chevy and General Motors in the next few years. The most important to GM was the new Chevy II Nova line. Mostly new from the ground up, this Nova would become the basis for a full line of GM compact cars in the early seventies when concerns over fuel availability would send consumers after more fuel efficient cars. Its adaptability allowed GM to create new cars from its basic platform. The basic platform would continue in production through the 1979 model year, as the Chevy Nova/Concours, Pontiac Ventura/Phoenix, Oldsmobile Omega, Buick Apollo/Skylark, and Cadillac Seville. This new Nova, while still sharing some chassis components with the Camaro, proved to be highly reliable and roomy for an American compact car. Although it would carry the Chevy II prefix for another year, most people began referring to the car as simply the Nova. Interiors were brought up to date, and powerplant options were revised. The 230 CID 6-cylinder introduced in the Camaro last season replaced the 194 CID 6-cylinder in the Nova this year. Also, there was a new 307 CID V8 that replaced the popular 283 CID V8 engine. Finally, there was a new top-end 350 CID V8 engine, that turned the compact economy car into a real performance car. It was the offering of this engine that forever changed the Nova's stodgy compact car image.

The second important introduction for enthusiasts was the all-new Corvette. Heavily based upon the most recent Mako Shark show car, particularly its styling, the new Corvette clearly brought the sports car into the modern era. High arched fender edges, sleek styling, modern cockpit style interior and the most powerful of GM engines were the shining features of the Corvette. A new tunneled rear window coupe style replaced the fastback coupe. Also first seen on the 1968 model were removable roof panels on coupes, later to be known as T-tops, that would soon replace the convertible model completely. This new Corvette was so modern in design that it would continue in its basic form through the 1982 model year.

The third important introduction was the redesigned mid-size Chevelle line. Continuing to share its basic structure with the other GM mid-size lines, the new Chevelle was more powerful on the street, and less angular in design. New engine offerings included the larger standard equipment 230 CID 6-cylinder and the new base level 307 CID V8 engine. This iteration of the body would be the design that produced such famous muscle cars as the "Heavy Chevy" and the 1970–72 Chevelle SS 454 models. For 1968, there was the SS 396, which in itself was a fast car. Model changes included the elimination of the Chevelle 300 4-Door Sedan and the addition of a Chevelle 300 Nomad 4-Door Wagon and Chevelle 300 Deluxe 2-Door Hardtop.

The full-size Chevy line received a facelift for 1968, donning a grille that extended down through the front bumper area (much like the 1965 models). On Caprice models, concealed headlights were available. At the rear, round taillamps were built into the back bumper. A new formal roofline was seen on the Caprice Coupe and the new Impala Custom Coupe. Finally, the Camaro and Corvair saw minimal changes. The Camaro received a revised grille design and switched to ventless door glass. The Corvair was virtually unchanged other than the required safety features and the elimination of the 4-Door Sport Sedan models.

**1968**

Bel Air 4-Door Wagon

Camaro 2-Door Convertible with RS package

Camaro 2-Door Hardtop

Caprice 4-Door Hardtop

Concours 4-Door Estate Wagon

Chevy II Nova 2-Door Coupe

Chevelle Malibu 2-Door Convertible

Chevelle SS396 2-Door Hardtop

Corvair Monza 2-Door Convertible

Impala 2-Door Convertible

Corvette 2-Door Coupe

**Model year production:** 2,141,686, up 9.92% over 1967.
**Domestic market share:** 25.00% (1st place).
**Base price range:** $2,222 to $4,663.
**Industry average base price:** $3,292.
**Chevrolet average base price:** $2,886.
**Introduction date:** September 26, 1967.
**Assembly plants:** Lakewood, GA (A), Atlanta, GA (D), Kansas City, MO (K), Fremont, CA (Z), Van Nuys, CA (L), Norwood, OH (N), Tarrytown, NY (T), Oshawa, Ontario, Canada (1), Baltimore, MD (B); Framingham, MA (G); Flint, MI (F); Southgate, CA (C); Arlington, TX (R); Janesville, WI (J); Wilmington, DE (Y), and St. Louis, MO (S).

**Data plate identification:** Thirteen digit code read as follows: 1st digit 1 for Chevrolet; four digit style number (see listings below) in which 2nd and 3rd digits identify series, 4th and 5th indicate body style; 8 for 1968; 7th digit is assembly plant code; 100001 and up for serial number. *Example:* 155118T100001 is a 1968 Chevrolet BelAir 2-Door Sedan, serial number 100001, built in Arlington, TX.

## Powertrains

| Engine | Gross HP | Transmission Availability | Corvair Chevy II | Camaro | Chevelle | †Bisc./ BelAir/Imp.* | Imp./ †Capr | Cor- vette |
|---|---|---|---|---|---|---|---|---|
| 153 CID, 1-bbl., 4-cyl. | 90 | 3-speed manual | S | - | - | - | - | - |
| | | Torque-Drive | $69 | - | - | - | - | - |
| | | 2-sp. Powerglide Automatic | $148 | - | - | - | - | - |
| 164 CID, 2-bbl., Flat 6 | 95 | 3-speed manual | S* | - | - | - | - | - |
| | | 4-speed manual | $90* | - | - | - | - | - |
| | | 2-sp. Powerglide Automatic | $148* | - | - | - | - | - |
| 164 CID Turbo-Air, 2-bbl., Flat 6 | 110 | 3-speed manual | $26* | - | - | - | - | - |
| | | 4-speed manual | $116* | - | - | - | - | - |

| Engine | Gross HP | Transmission Availability | Corvair Chevy II | Camaro | Chevelle | †Bisc./BelAir/Imp.* | Imp./†Capr | Cor-vette |
|---|---|---|---|---|---|---|---|---|
| | | 2-sp. Powerglide Automatic | $174* | - | - | - | - | - |
| 164 CID Turbo-Air, 4-bbl., Flat 6 | 140 | 3-speed manual | $79* | - | - | - | - | - |
| | | 4-speed manual | $169* | - | - | - | - | - |
| | | 2-sp. Powerglide Automatic | $227* | - | - | - | - | - |
| 230 CID Turbo-Thrift, 1-bbl., 6-cyl. | 140 | 3-speed manual | $78 | S | S[2] | - | - | - |
| | | 4-speed manual | - | $195 | - | - | - | - |
| | | Torque-Drive | $147 | $69 | - | - | - | - |
| | | 2-sp. Powerglide Automatic | $226 | $164 | $164 | - | - | - |
| 250 CID Turbo-Thrift, 1-bbl., 6-cyl. | 155 | 3-speed manual | $104 | $26 | $26[2] | S | - | - |
| | | 4-speed manual | - | $221 | - | - | - | - |
| | | Torque-Drive | $273 | $95 | - | - | - | - |
| | | 2-sp. Powerglide Automatic | $252 | $190 | $190[2] | $180 | - | - |
| | | Turbo Hydra-matic | $278 | $216 | $216[2] | $190 | - | - |
| 302 CID, 4-bbl., V8 Plus cost of Z/28 package | 350 | 4-speed manual | - | S — Z28 | - | - | - | - |
| | | Turbo Hydra-matic | - | $222 — Z28 | - | - | - | - |
| 307 CID Turbo-Fire, 2-bbl., V8 | 200 | 3-speed manual | $167 | - | S[1]/$90 (Others) | - | - | - |
| | | 2-sp. Powerglide Automatic | $325 | - | $174[1]/$264 (Others) | - | - | - |
| | | Turbo Hydra-matic | $357 | - | $222[1]/$312 (Others) | - | - | - |
| 327 CID Turbo-Fire, 2-bbl., V8 | 210/235 | 3-speed manual | - | $89 | - | $95 | S | - |
| | | 4-speed manual | - | $284 | - | - | - | |
| | | 2-sp. Powerglide Automatic | - | $263 | - | $269 | $174 | - |
| | | Turbo Hydra-matic | - | $311 | - | $317 | $222 | - |
| 350 CID Turbo-Fire, 2-bbl., V8 | 255 | 3-speed manual | $220 | $142 | $26[1]/$116 (Others) | $148 | $53 | - |
| | | 4-speed manual | $405 | $337 | $211[1]/$301 (Others) | $333 | $238 | - |
| | | 2-sp. Powerglide Automatic | $394 | $316 | $200[1]/$290 (Others) | $322 | $227 | - |
| | | Turbo Hydra-matic | $421 | $364 | $243[1]/$338 (Others) | $370 | $275 | - |
| 350 CID Turbo-Fire, 4-bbl., V8 | 300 | 3-speed manual | $281 (SS) | $385 (SS)** | $69[1]/$159 (Others) | $201 | $106 | S |
| | | 4-speed manual | $466 (SS) | $580 (SS)** | $254[1]/$348 (Others) | $386 | $291 | $184 |
| | | Turbo Hydra-matic | $471 (SS) | $585 (SS)** | $291[1]/$381 (Others) | $423 | $328 | $222 |
| 350 CID Turbo-Fire, 4-bbl., V8 | 350 | 4-speed manual | - | - | - | - | - | $316 |
| | | Turbo Hydra-matic | - | - | - | - | - | $354 |
| 396 CID Turbo-Fire, 2-bbl., V8 | 265 | 3-speed manual | - | - | - | $164 | $69 | - |
| | | 4-speed manual | | | | $349 | $254 | |
| | | Turbo Hydra-matic | | | | $386 | $295 | |

| Engine | Gross HP | Transmission Availability | Corvair Chevy II | Camaro | Chevelle | †Bisc./ BelAir/Imp.* | Imp./ †Capr | Cor-vette |
|---|---|---|---|---|---|---|---|---|
| 396 CID Turbo-Jet, 4-bbl., V8 | 325 | 3-speed manual | - | $359 (SS) | S (SS)/$348[1]/ $438 (Others) | - | - | - |
| | | 4-speed manual | - | $554 (SS) | $185 (SS)/$533[1]/ $623 (Others) | - | - | - |
| | | 4-speed manual-heavy-duty | - | $681 (SS) | $322 (SS)/$670[1]/ $760 (Others) | - | - | - |
| | | Turbo Hydra-matic | - | $581 (SS) | $222 (SS)/$570[1]/ $660 (Others) | - | - | - |
| 396 CID Turbo-Jet, 4-bbl., V8 | 350** | 3-speed manual | $184 (SS) | $632 (SS) | $121 (SS)/$469[1]/ $559 (Others) | - | - | - |
| | | 4-speed manual | $379 (SS) | $827 (SS) | $306 (SS)/$654[1]/ $744 (Others) | - | - | - |
| | | 4-speed manual-heavy-duty | $497 (SS) | $854 (SS) | $443 (SS)/$791[1]/ $881 (Others) | - | - | - |
| | | Turbo Hydra-matic | $406 (SS) | $854 (SS) | $343 (SS)/$691[1]/ $781 (Others) | - | - | - |
| 427 CID Turbo-Jet, 4-bbl., V8 | 335 375 (Corvette) | 3-speed manual | - | $675 (SS) | - | $258 | $163 | $221 |
| | | 4-speed manual | - | $870 (SS) | - | $443 | $348 | $405 |
| | | Turbo Hydra-matic | - | $907 (SS) | - | $480 | $385 | $443 |
| 427 CID Turbo-Jet, 4-bbl., V8 | 390 | 3-speed manual | - | - | - | $332 | S (SS)/ $237 $221 | |
| | | 4-speed manual | - | - | - | $517 | $313(SS)/ $422 | $405 |
| | | Turbo Hydra-matic | - | - | - | $554 | $290(SS)/ $459 | $443 |
| 427 CID Turbo-Jet, 3 × 2-bbl., V8 | 400/425 | 3-speed manual | - | - | - | $543 | $184(SS)/ $448 $327 | |
| | | 4-speed manual | - | - | - | $856 | $497(SS)/ $761 | $510 |
| | | Turbo Hydra-matic | - | - | - | $840 | $474(SS)/ $745 | $548 |
| 427 CID Turbo-Jet 3 × 2-bbl., V8 (L89 Aluminum heads add $395) | 435 | 3-speed manual | - | - | - | - | - | $437 |
| | | 4-speed manual | - | $1070 (SS) | - | - | - | $621 |
| | | Turbo Hydra-matic | - | $1361 (SS) | - | - | - | $732 |

[1]Greenbrier 9-passenger and Concours wagons only.   [2]All but Greenbrier 9-passenger and Concours wagons.   *2- & 4-Dr. HT and 4-Dr. Sedan only.   **Aluminum head version also available, 375-hp.   †See text for corresponding wagon models.

## Major Options

| | Corvair | Chevy II | Camaro | Chevelle | Full-size | Corvette |
|---|---|---|---|---|---|---|
| Air conditioning | $ | $363 | $376 | $376 | $384 | $429 |
| Soft Ray tinted glass | $33 | $33 | $33 | $37 | $42 | $17 |
| Electronic speed control | - | - | - | - | $58 | - |

|                                      | Corvair | Chevy II | Camaro | Chevelle | Full-size | Corvette |
|--------------------------------------|---------|----------|--------|----------|-----------|----------|
| Tilt steering wheel (telescoping on Corvette) | $42 (Telescopic) | – | $45 | $45 | $45 | $84 |
| Power steering                       | –       | $90      | $95    | $100–$105 | $100–$105 | $105 |
| Power brakes                         | –       | $42      | $42    | $42      | $42       | $42      |
| Front disc brakes (req. PB)          | –       | $22      | $22    | $22      | $22       | S        |
| Power door locks                     | –       | –        | –      | –        | $45–$69   | –        |
| Power windows (N/A on all)           | –       | –        | $105   | $105     | $105      | $63      |
| AM radio                             | $61     | $61      | $61    | $61      | $61       | S        |
| AM/FM radio                          | $134    | $134     | $134   | $134     | $134      | $173     |
| Front seat console                   | –       | $        | $      | $        | $         | S        |
| Front bucket seats                   | S       | $        | S      | $        | $         | S        |
| Vinyl roof                           | –       | $79      | $84    | $90      | $100      | –        |
| Wheel trim covers                    | $21 (500)/S (Monza) | $21 | $21 | $21 | $21/S (Capr.) | S |
| Whitewall Tires — Std. size          | $28     | $31      | $32    | $33      | $36–$41   | $31      |
| Rally Sport package                  | –       | –        | $105   | –        | –         | –        |
| Concours Sedan package               | –       | –        | –      | $132     | –         | –        |
| Super Sport equipment package        | $280    |          | $312–350/ $348–396 | $ | $422 | – |

Options common to most models. (– = Not Available; S = Standard equipment.) Items may be standard equipment, optional at different pricing, or unavailable on certain models. This chart is only a guide.

*Not available with 6-cylinder engine.

## Paint Colors*

|                          | Code   | Camaro | Corvette | Other Chevrolet models |
|--------------------------|--------|--------|----------|------------------------|
| Tuxedo Black             | AA/900 | X      | X        | X                      |
| Ermine White             | CC     | X      |          | X                      |
| Grotto Blue Metallic     | DD     | X      |          | X                      |
| Fathom Blue Metallic     | EE     | X      |          | X                      |
| Island Teal Met.         | FF     | X      |          | X                      |
| Ash Gold Met.            | GG     | X      |          | X                      |
| Grecian Green Met.       | HH     | X      |          | X                      |
| Rallye Green Metallic    | JJ     | X      |          |                        |
| Tripoli Turqoise Met.    | KK     | X      |          | X                      |
| Teal Blue Metallic       | LL     | X      |          | X                      |
| Cordovan Maroon Met.     | NN     | X      |          | X                      |
| Corvette Bronze Met.     | OO/992 | X      | X        |                        |
| Seafrost Green Met.      | PP     | X      |          | X                      |
| Matador Red              | RR     | X      |          | X                      |
| Palomino Ivory           | TT     | X      |          | X                      |
| LeMans Blue Metallic     | UU/976 | X      | X        |                        |
| Sequoia Green Met.       | VV     | X      |          | X                      |
| Butternut Yellow         | YY     | X      |          | X                      |
| British Green Metallic   | ZZ/983 | X      | X        |                        |
| Polar White              | 972    |        | X        |                        |
| Rallye Red               | 974    |        | X        |                        |
| International Blue Met.   | 978    |        | X        |                        |
| Safari Yellow            | 984    |        | X        |                        |
| Silverstone Silver Met.  | 986    |        | X        |                        |
| Corvette Maroon Met.     | 988    |        | X        |                        |

*Corvette color codes may be different on some colors.

**1968**

# Corvair

*"America's rear-engine sportster from Chevrolet."*

**Nameplate year of origin:** 1960.
**Current bodystyle lifespan:** 1965 through 1969.
**Predecessor to this model:** Corvair (1960 to 1964).
**Replacement for this model:** Vega (1971 to 1977).
**Percentage of division's sales volume:** 0.72%.
**Corporate siblings:** None.
**Primary competition:** AMC Rambler American, Ford Falcon and Plymouth Valiant.
**Notable changes:** Minor trim and detail changes.
**Major standard equipment:** Cloth and vinyl front bench seat, dual sun visors, center dome light, and 7.00 × 13 BSW tires. Monza adds: All-vinyl bucket seats, full carpeting, folding rear seat, glove box light, front door map pockets, and additional exterior chrome trim.

## Measurements

| | |
|---|---|
| Wheelbase | 108.0" |
| Length | 183.3" |
| Width | 69.7" |
| Height | 51.3" |
| Legroom — front | 40.9" |
| Legroom — rear | 30.7" |
| Headroom — front | 37.9" |
| Headroom — rear | 36.4" |
| Cargo capacity (cu. ft.) | 7.0 |
| Fuel capacity (gals.) | 14.0 |

## Models Available

| | Style Number | Base MSRP | Change from LY | Shipping Wt. (lbs.) | Production | Change from LY |
|---|---|---|---|---|---|---|
| Corvair 500 2-Door Sport Coupe | 10137 | $2,243 | +5.40% | 2477 | 7,206 | -22.16% |
| Corvair Monza 2-Door Sport Coupe | 10537 | $2,507 | +4.55% | 2506 | 6,807 | -30.33% |
| Corvair Monza 2-Door Convertible | 10567 | $2,626 | +3.39% | 2730 | 1,386 | -34.28% |
| TOTALS | Avg. price | $2,459 | +4.86% | Production | 15,399 | -44.50% |

# Camaro

*"The 'hugger' from Chevrolet."*

**Nameplate year of origin:** 1967.
**Current bodystyle lifespan:** 1967 through 1969.
**Predecessor to this model:** None.
**Replacement for this model:** Camaro (1970 to 1981).
**Percentage of division's sales volume:** 10.98%.
**Corporate siblings:** Pontiac Firebird.
**Primary competition:** AMC Javelin, Ford Mustang, and Plymouth Barracuda.
**Notable changes:** Revised grille and minor trim and detail changes.
**Major standard equipment:** All-vinyl front bucket seats, cockpit-style instrumentation, full color-keyed carpeting, hubcaps, three-spoke steering wheel, and 7.35 × 14 BSW tires. RS package adds: Style trim package, parking lamps below front bumper and back-up lamps below rear bumper, concealed headlamps, rocker molding trim, and specific RS trim. SS 350 package adds: 350 CID V8 engine, specific hood with simulated air intakes, hood stripes, SS emblems, and D70 × 14 redline or WSW tires.

## Measurements

| | |
|---|---|
| Wheelbase | 108.0" |
| Length | 184.7" |
| Width | 72.6" |
| Height | 51.5" |
| Legroom — front | 42.5" |
| Legroom — rear | 29.2" |
| Headroom — front | 37.0" |
| Headroom — rear | 36.7" |
| Cargo capacity (cu. ft.) | 8.3 |
| Fuel capacity (gals.) | 18.0 |

## Models Available

| | Style Number | Base MSRP | Change from LY | Shipping Wt. (lbs.) | Production | Change from LY |
|---|---|---|---|---|---|---|
| Camaro 2-Door Sport Coupe | 12337 | $2,588 | +4.95% | 2855 | 214,711 | +9.67% |
| Camaro 2-Door Convertible | 12367 | $2,802 | +3.62% | 3108 | 20,440 | -18.70% |
| TOTALS | Avg. price | $2,695 | +4.26% | Production | 235,151 | +6.44% |

# Chevy II

*"Value never looked so good before."*

**Nameplate year of origin:** 1962.
**Current bodystyle lifespan:** 1968 through 1972.
**Predecessor to this model:** Chevy II (1966 to 1967).
**Replacement for this model:** Nova (1973 through 1979, with restyle in 1975).
**Percentage of division's sales volume:** 9.39%.
**Corporate siblings:** None.
**Primary competition:** AMC Rambler American, Ford Falcon, and Plymouth Valiant.
**Notable changes:** Completely redesigned.
**Major standard equipment:** Cloth and vinyl bench seat, vinyl-coated rubber floor coverings, hubcaps, front-door vent windows, bright moldings on windshield and rear window, and 7.35 × 14 BSW tires.

## Measurements

| | |
|---|---|
| Wheelbase | 111.0" |
| Length | 189.3" |
| Width | 72.4" |
| Height | 53.9" |
| Legroom — front | 41.6" |
| Legroom — rear | 35.3" |
| Headroom — front | 37.6" |
| Headroom — rear | 32.6" |
| Cargo capacity (cu. ft.) | 12.4 |
| Fuel capacity (gals.) | 18.0 |

## Models Available

| | Style Number | Base MSRP | Change from LY | Shipping Wt. (lbs.) | Production | Change from LY |
|---|---|---|---|---|---|---|
| Chevy II Nova 2-Door Coupe | 11127 | $2,222 | -4.64% | 2749 | 200,970 | * |
| Chevy II Nova 4-Door Sedan | 11169 | $2,252 | -2.00% | 2773 | * | * |
| TOTALS | | *Avg. price* $2,237 | -4.32% | | *Production* 200,970 | +88.70% |

*Production is estimated and not available by body style totals.*

# Chevelle

*"The quick-size performer from Chevrolet."*

**Nameplate year of origin:** 1964.
**Current bodystyle lifespan:** 1968 through 1972.
**Predecessor to this model:** Chevelle (1966 to 1967).
**Replacement for this model:** Chevelle (1973 to 1977).
**Percentage of division's sales volume:** 19.86%.
**Corporate siblings:** Pontiac LeMans, Oldsmobile Cutlass, Buick Skylark.
**Primary competition:** AMC Rebel, Dodge Coronet, Ford Fairlane, and Plymouth Belvedere/Satellite.
**Notable changes:** Completely redesigned.
**Major standard equipment:** Cloth and vinyl front bench seat, black rubber floor mats, hubcaps, and 7.35 × 14 BSW tires (7.75 × 14 BSW tires on wagons). 300 Deluxe adds: All-vinyl interior trim for wagon, color-keyed floor mats and rocker panel moldings. Malibu adds: Full carpeting, full wheel covers, electric clock, and hide-away windshield wipers. Concours Estate Wagon adds: Wood-grain exterior trim, and power tailgate window and courtesy lights for optional 3-Seat Wagon model. SS 396 adds: All-vinyl bucket seats, console, special instrumentation, 396 CID V8 engine, SS trim and wheel covers and F70 × 14 Redline or WSW tires.

## Measurements

| | 2-Doors | 4-Doors | Wagons |
|---|---|---|---|
| Wheelbase | 112.0" | 116.0" | 116.0" |
| Length | 197.1" | 201.1" | 207.1" |
| Width | 75.7" | 75.7" | 75.7" |
| Height | 52.7" | 53.3" | 55.2" |
| Legroom — front | 42.6" | 42.7" | 42.7" |
| Legroom — rear | 32.2" | 34.7" | 34.7" |
| Headroom — front | 37.9" | 38.2" | 38.2" |
| Headroom — rear | 36.3" | 37.1" | 37.4" |
| Cargo capacity (cu. ft.) | NA | NA | 94.0 |
| Fuel capacity (gals.) | 20.0 | 20.0 | 20.0 |

**1968**

## Models Available

| | Style Number | Base MSRP | Change from LY | Shipping Wt. (lbs.) | Production | Change from LY |
|---|---|---|---|---|---|---|
| Chevelle 300 2-Door Coupe | 13127 | $2,341 | +5.40% | 2968 | 12,600 | * |
| Ch. 300 Nomad 4-Door Wagon | 13135 | $2,625 | NEW | 3350 | * | NEW |
| Chevelle 300 Deluxe 2-Door Coupe | 13327 | $2,415 | +5.23% | 3005 | 43,200 | * |
| Chevelle 300 Deluxe 2-Door HT | 13337 | $2,479 | NEW | 3036 | * | NEW |
| Chevelle 300 Deluxe 4-Door Sedan | 13369 | $2,445 | +5.21% | 3071 | * | * |
| Ch. 300 Nomad Custom 4-Dr. Wgn. | 13335 | $2,736 | +4.47% | 3409 | * | * |
| Chevelle Malibu 2-Door Hardtop | 13537 | $2,558 | +5.09% | 3037 | 266,400 | * |
| Chevelle Malibu 2-Dr. Convertible | 13567 | $2,757 | +4.55% | 3115 | * | * |
| Chevelle Malibu 4-Door Sedan | 13569 | $2,524 | +5.17% | 3090 | * | * |
| Chevelle Malibu 4-Door Hardtop | 13539 | $2,629 | +4.91% | 3165 | * | * |
| Chevelle Malibu 4-Door Wagon | 13535 | $2,846 | +5.60% | 3421 | 45,500 | * |
| Chevelle SS396 2-Door Hardtop | 13837 | $2,899 | +2.62% | 3475 | 57,600 | * |
| Chevelle SS396 2-Dr. Convertible | 13867 | $3,102 | +2.27% | 3551 | * | * |
| Ch. Concours Estate 4-Door Wagon | 13835 | $2,978 | +5.34% | 3561 | * | * |
| TOTALS | | Avg. price $2,667 | +4.83% | | Production 425,300 | +15.22% |

*Production is estimated and not available by series, only body style totals.*

# Chevrolet Full-size

*"The best yet from America's first name in cars."*

**Nameplate year of origin:** 1950 (BelAir); 1958 (Biscayne, Impala); 1966 (Caprice)

**Current bodystyle lifespan:** 1967 through 1968.

**Predecessor to this model:** Full-size Chevrolet (1965 to 1966).

**Replacement for this model:** Biscayne/BelAir/Impala/Caprice (1969 to 1970).

**Percentage of division's sales volume:** 57.73%.

**Corporate siblings:** Buick LeSabre/Wildcat, Olds 88, Pontiac Catalina/Bonneville.

**Primary competition:** AMC Ambassador, Dodge Polara, Ford Custom/Galaxie/LTD, and Plymouth Fury.

**Notable changes:** Restyled exterior and interior.

**Major standard equipment:** Biscayne: Cloth and vinyl bench seat, full carpeting, front and rear door armrests, 2-speed electric windshield wipers with washers, and 8.25 × 14 BSW tires (8.55 × 14 BSW tires on wagons). BelAir adds: Automatic interior lighting, bright body side molding, and power tailgate window on 3-Seat wagon models. Impala adds: Vinyl upholstery in convertible, extra-long armrests, electric clock, and trunk lamp. SS package adds: All vinyl bucket seats, center floor console, and special SS wheel covers, body and interior trim. Caprice adds: Specific cloth and vinyl front bench seats (with center fold-down armrest on sedan), all-vinyl upholstery in wagons, simulated walnut interior trim, dual pinstriping, deluxe wheel covers, rocker panel moldings, simulated walnut exterior trim on wagons, and special ornamentation.

## Measurements

| | Cars | Wagons |
|---|---|---|
| Wheelbase | 119.0" | 119.0" |
| Length | 214.7" | 213.9" |
| Width | 79.6" | 79.6" |
| Height | 55.8" | 56.7" |
| Legroom — front | 41.7" | 41.7" |
| Legroom — rear | 39.5" | 39.5" |
| Headroom — front | 38.9" | 38.9" |
| Headroom — rear | 37.9" | 37.9" |
| Cargo capacity (cu. ft.) | 17.0 | 106.1 |
| Fuel capacity (gals.) | 24.0 | 24.0 |

## Models Available

| | Style Number | Base MSRP | Change from LY | Shipping Wt. (lbs.) | Production | Change from LY |
|---|---|---|---|---|---|---|
| Biscayne 2-Door Sedan | 15311 | $2,581 | +5.69% | 3399 | 82,100 | * |
| Biscayne 4-Door Sedan | 15369 | $2,623 | +5.60% | 3464 | * | * |
| Biscayne 4-Dr., 2-S. Wagon | 15335 | $2,957 | +4.97% | 3819 | * | * |
| Bel Air 2-Door Sedan | 15511 | $2,681 | +5.47% | 3404 | 152,200 | * |

| | Style Number | Base MSRP | Change from LY | Shipping Wt. (lbs.) | Production | Change from LY |
|---|---|---|---|---|---|---|
| Bel Air 4-Door Sedan | 15569 | $2,723 | +5.38% | 3466 | * | * |
| Bel Air 4-Dr., 2-S. Wagon | 15535 | $3,020 | +4.82% | 3823 | * | * |
| Bel Air 4-Dr., 3-S. Wagon | 15545 | $3,133 | +4.68% | 3878 | * | * |
| Impala 2-Door Sport Coupe | 16387 | $2,863 | +4.49% | 3517 | 710,900 | * |
| Impala 2-Door Custom Coupe | 16447 | $3,021 | NEW | 3628 | * | NEW |
| Impala 2-Door Convertible | 16467 | $3,197 | +6.89% | 3677 | * | * |
| Impala 4-Door Sedan | 16369 | $2,846 | +4.52% | 3513 | * | * |
| Impala 4-Door Hardtop | 16339 | $2,917 | +4.44% | 3601 | * | * |
| Impala 4-Dr., 2-S. Wagon | 16435 | $3,245 | +7.59% | 3984 | 175,600 | * |
| Impala 4-Dr., 3-S. Wagon | 16445 | $3,358 | +7.32% | 4042 | * | * |
| Caprice 2-Door Hardtop | 16647 | $3,219 | +4.58% | 3648 | 115,500 | * |
| Caprice 4-Door Hardtop | 16639 | $3,271 | +4.50% | 3754 | * | * |
| Caprice Estate 4-Dr., 2-S. Wgn. | 16635 | $3,458 | +4.76% | 4003 | * | * |
| Caprice Estate 4-Dr., 3-S. Wgn. | 16645 | $3,570 | +4.60% | 4062 | * | * |
| TOTALS | | Avg. price $3,038 | +4.76% | | Production 1,236,300 | +2.88% |

*Production is estimated and not available by series, only body style totals.*

# Corvette

*"The true sports car from Chevrolet."*

**Nameplate year of origin:** 1953 (also used on showcar of same year).
**Current bodystyle lifespan:** 1968 through 1982.
**Predecessor to this model:** Corvette (1963 to 1967).
**Replacement for this model:** Corvette (1984 to 1996).
**Percentage of division's sales volume:** 1.33%.
**Corporate siblings:** None.
**Primary competition:** None.
**Notable changes:** Completely redesigned.
**Major standard equipment:** All-vinyl bucket seats with full-length center floor console, complete instrumentation, Astro ventilation, removable roof panels (Coupe), manually operated folding top (Convertible), wheels with bright trim ring and ribbed center hub, Soft-Ray tinted glass, 4-wheel disc brakes, and F70 × 15 BSW tires.

## Measurements

| | |
|---|---|
| Wheelbase | 98.0" |
| Length | 182.1" |
| Width | 69.2" |
| Height | 47.8" |
| Legroom — front | 43.0" |
| Legroom — rear | NA |
| Headroom — front | 36.2" |
| Headroom — rear | NA |
| Cargo capacity (cu. ft.) | NA |
| Fuel capacity (gals.) | 20.0 |

**1968**

## Models Available

| | Style Number | Base MSRP | Change from LY | Shipping Wt. (lbs.) | Production | Change from LY |
|---|---|---|---|---|---|---|
| Corvette 2-Door Coupe | 19437 | $4,663 | +7.12% | 3055 | 9,936 | +16.84% |
| Corvette 2-Door Convertible | 19467 | $4,320 | +4.32% | 3068 | 18,630 | +29.05% |
| TOTALS | | Avg. price $4,492 | +5.77% | | Production 28,556 | +24.48% |

# CHRYSLER

*"Make your move. Move up to Chrysler '68."*

The 1968 Chrysler line continued with the popular 1967 styling themes and the same powertrain choices. However, engines for the Newport line were given a slight boost in horsepower for 1968. This was the final year that the Town & Country Wagon would be listed as part of the individual model lines. Beginning in 1969, it would be marketed as its own line, as sales of luxury station wagons would begin to rise during the seventies. The Town & Country wagon models were offered only in the Newport line, but the equipment varies significantly enough that they are listed separately under the powertrain and optional equipment categories below, as well as given a separate model listing.

300 2-Door Hardtop

Newport 2-Door Convertible

Newport Custom 4-Door Sedan

New Yorker 2-Door Hardtop

Town & Country 4-Door, 3-Seat Wagon

**Model year production:** 264,863, up 21.08% over 1967.
**Domestic market share:** 3.09% (10th place).
**Base price range:** $3,306 to $4,523.
**Industry average base price:** $3,292.
**Chrysler average base price:** $3,944.
**Introduction date:** September 1967.
**Assembly plants:** Newark, DE (F) and Detroit, MI (C).
**Data plate identification:** Thirteen digit code read as follows:

Four digit style number (see listings below) in which C = Chrysler, 2nd number identifies series (e.g., H is for New Yorker), 3rd and 4th indicate body style; 5th digit is engine code; 8 for 1968; assembly plant code; 100001 and up for serial number. *Example:* CH23K8C100001 is a 1968 Chrysler New Yorker 2-Door Hardtop with a 440 CID V8 engine, serial number 100001, built in Detroit, MI.

## Powertrains

| Engine | Engine Code | Gross HP | Transmission Availability | Newport | Town & Country | 300 & N. Yorker |
|---|---|---|---|---|---|---|
| 383 CID, 2-bbl., V8 | G | 290 | 3-speed man. | S | - | - |

| Engine | Engine Code | Gross HP | Transmission Availability | Newport | Town & Country | 300 & N.Yorker |
|--------|-------------|----------|---------------------------|---------|----------------|----------------|
| | | | TorqueFlite Automatic | $222 | S | - |
| 383 CID, 4-bbl., V8 | H | 330 | TorqueFlite Automatic | $295 | $68 | - |
| 440 CID, 4-bbl., V8 | K | 350 | TorqueFlite Automatic | - | $164 | S |
| 440 CID TNT, 4-bbl., V8 | L | 375 | TorqueFlite Automatic | $420 | $198 | $79 |

## Major Options

| | Newport | Town & Country | 300 | New Yorker |
|--|---------|----------------|-----|------------|
| Air conditioning | $406 | $406 | $406 | $406 |
| Electronic cruise control | $67 | $67 | $67 | $67 |
| Soft Ray tinted glass | $45 | $45 | $45 | $45 |
| Deck lid remote release | $15 | - | $15 | $15 |
| Power steering — variable-ratio | $117 | S | $117 | S |
| Power brakes | $47 | S | $47 | S |
| Power door locks | $46–$70 | $70 | $46–$70 | $46–$70 |
| Power 6-way bench seat (bucket on 300) | $103 | $103 | $188 | $103 |
| Power windows | $112 | $112 | $112 | $112 |
| AM radio | $92 | $92 | $92 | $92 |
| AM/FM stereo | $187 | $187 | $187 | $187 |
| Tilt & telescoping steering wheel | $91 | $91 | $91 | $91 |
| Vinyl roof | $125 | $125 | $125 | $125 |
| Chrome Road Wheels | $99 | - | $99 | $99 |

Options common to most models. (- = Not Available; S = Standard equipment.) Items may be standard equipment, optional at different pricing, or unavailable on certain models. This chart is only a guide.

## Paint Colors

| | Code |
|--|------|
| Bright Turquoise | 44-1 |
| Silver Haze | AA-1 |
| Formal Black | BB-1 |
| Consort Blue Metallic | CC-1 |
| Sky Blue Metallic | DD-1 |
| Military Blue Metallic | EE-1 |
| Frost Green Metallic | FF-1 |
| Forest Green Metallic | GG-1 |
| Antique Ivory | HH-1 |
| Sovereign Gold Metallic | JJ-1 |
| Mist Turquoise Metallic | KK-1 |
| Turbine Bronze Metallic | MM-1 |
| Scorch Red | PP-1 |
| Burgundy Metallic | RR-1 |
| Meadow Green Metallic | TT-1 |
| Polar White | WW-1 |
| Sandalwood | XX-1 |
| Beige Mist Metallic | YY-1 |

# Newport

*"The lowest-priced Chrysler. Positive proof that we've something full-sized—and luxurious—for everyone."*

**1968**

**Nameplate year of origin:** 1950 (as HT model of T & C); 1961 (as series).
**Current bodystyle lifespan:** 1965 through 1968 (restyled in 1967).
**Predecessor to this model:** Newport (1963 to 1964).
**Replacement for this model:** Newport (1969 to 1973).
**Percentage of division's sales volume:** 60.39%.
**Corporate siblings:** Chrysler 300 and New Yorker.
**Primary competition:** Buick LeSabre, Mercury Monterey, and Oldsmobile Delta 88.
**Notable changes:** Revised front and rear styling.
**Major standard equipment:** Cloth and vinyl front bench seat (all-vinyl on convertible), deep-pile carpeting, exterior bright side moldings, 3-speed windshield wipers w/washers, trip odometer, rear wheel opening fender skirts, and 8.55 × 14 BSW tires. Custom adds: Cloth and vinyl front bench seat with fold-down arm rest, and specific exterior trim.

## Measurements

| | |
|--|--|
| Wheelbase | 124.0" |
| Length | 219.2" |
| Width | 78.6" |
| Height | 56.8" |
| Legroom — front | 41.8" |
| Legroom — rear | 38.9" |
| Headroom — front | 39.8" |
| Headroom — rear | 38.5" |
| Cargo capacity (cu. ft.) | 17.4 |
| Fuel capacity (gals.) | 24.0 |

## Models Available

| | Style Number | Base MSRP | Change from LY | Shipping Wt. (lbs.) | Production | Change from LY |
|---|---|---|---|---|---|---|
| Newport 2-Door Hardtop | CE23 | $3,366 | +4.57% | 3840 | 36,768 | +38.31% |
| Newport 2-Door Convertible | CE27 | $3,704 | +3.38% | 3910 | 2,847 | -1.52% |
| Newport 4-Door Sedan | CE41 | $3,306 | +4.65% | 3850 | 61,436 | +25.52% |
| Newport 4-Door Hardtop | CE43 | $3,444 | +4.49% | 3865 | 20,191 | +41.72% |
| Newport Custom 2-Door Hardtop | CL23 | $3,552 | +4.26% | 3860 | 10,341 | -27.14% |
| Newport Custom 4-Door Sedan | CL41 | $3,493 | +4.36% | 3855 | 16,915 | -26.78% |
| Newport Custom 4-Door Hardtop | CL43 | $3,631 | +4.19% | 3890 | 11,460 | -9.96% |
| TOTALS | | Avg. price $3,499 | +4.23% | | Production 159,958 | +12.10% |

# 300

*"The sports-bred Chrysler. The genuine article."*

**Nameplate year of origin:** 1955 (letter series cars); 1962 (standard line cars).
**Current bodystyle lifespan:** 1965 through 1968.
**Predecessor to this model:** 300 (1963 to 1964).
**Replacement for this model:** 300 (1969 to 1971).
**Percentage of division's sales volume:** 13.07%.
**Corporate siblings:** Chrysler Newport and New Yorker.
**Primary competition:** Buick Wildcat, Mercury Montclair and Pontiac Bonneville.
**Notable changes:** Revised front and rear styling.
**Major standard equipment:** All-vinyl bucket seats, deep-pile carpeting, 3-speed windshield wipers with washers, electric clock, trip odometer, exterior side moldings, full wheel covers, rear wheel opening fender skirts, automatic transmission, deluxe wheel covers, and 8.55 × 14 BSW tires.

### Measurements

| | |
|---|---|
| Wheelbase | 124.0" |
| Length | 221.7" |
| Width | 78.7" |
| Height | 55.6" |
| Legroom — front | 41.8" |
| Legroom — rear | 35.9" |
| Headroom — front | 38.6" |
| Headroom — rear | 37.4" |
| Cargo capacity (cu. ft.) | 17.4 |
| Fuel capacity (gals.) | 24.0 |

## Models Available

| | Style Number | Base MSRP | Change from LY | Shipping Wt. (lbs.) | Production | Change from LY |
|---|---|---|---|---|---|---|
| 300 2-Door Hardtop | CM23 | $4,010 | +1.88% | 3985 | 16,953 | +46.70% |
| 300 2-Door Convertible | CM27 | $4,337 | +1.12% | 4050 | 2,161 | +35.57% |
| 300 4-Door Hardtop | CM43 | $4,086 | +1.84% | 4015 | 15,507 | +77.34% |
| TOTALS | | Avg. price $4,144 | +1.59% | | Production 34,621 | +58.13% |

# Town & Country

*"This one musters up the kind of luxuries most other wagons can only dream of. Which is why it's simply the most elegant wagon about town. Or country."*

**Nameplate year of origin:** 1939.
**Current bodystyle lifespan:** 1965 through 1968 (restyled in 1967).
**Predecessor to this model:** New Yorker (1963 to 1964).
**Replacement for this model:** New Yorker (1969 to 1973).
**Percentage of division's sales volume:** 8.36%.
**Corporate siblings:** Dodge Polara and Plymouth Fury.
**Primary competition:** Mercury Colony Park.

### Measurements

| | |
|---|---|
| Wheelbase | 122.0" |
| Length | 219.5" |
| Width | 78.6" |
| Height | 57.6" |
| Legroom — front | 41.8" |
| Legroom — rear | 37.9" |

**Notable changes:** Revised front and rear styling.
**Major standard equipment:** All-vinyl front bench seat with folding center armrest, simulated walnut instrument panel trim, carpeted lower door trim and load floor, 3-speed windshield wipers with washers, map and courtesy lights, electric clock, remote-control LH outside rear view mirror and RH outside mirror, lockable luggage compartment, power operated tailgate window, Torqueflite automatic transmission, power steering, power front disc brakes, full wheel covers, and 8.85 × 14 BSW tires.

## Measurements (cont.)

| | |
|---|---|
| Headroom — front | 40.1" |
| Headroom — rear | 39.6" |
| Cargo capacity (cu. ft.) | 97.0 |
| Fuel capacity (gals.) | 22.0 |

## Models Available

| | Style Number | Base MSRP | Change from LY | Shipping Wt. (lbs.) | Production | Change from LY |
|---|---|---|---|---|---|---|
| Town & Country 4-Dr., 2-S. Wagon | CE45 | $4,418 | +5.32% | 4340 | 9,908 | +37.94% |
| Town & Country 4-Dr., 3-S. Wagon | CE46 | $4,523 | +5.21% | 4410 | 12,233 | +62.67% |
| TOTALS | | Avg. price $4,471 | +5.27% | | Production 22,141 | +50.59% |

# New Yorker

*"This is the ultimate Chrysler. In detail, and by design."*

**Nameplate year of origin:** 1939.
**Current bodystyle lifespan:** 1965 through 1968 (restyled in 1967).
**Predecessor to this model:** New Yorker (1963 to 1964).
**Replacement for this model:** New Yorker (1969 to 1973).
**Percentage of division's sales volume:** 18.18%.
**Corporate siblings:** Chrysler Newport and 300.
**Primary competition:** Buick Electra 225, Cadillac Calais, and Oldsmobile Ninety-Eight.
**Notable changes:** Revised front and rear styling.
**Major standard equipment:** Cloth and vinyl front bench seat with pull-down center arm rests front and rear, deep-pile carpeting, deluxe steering wheel, map lights, trip odometer, electric clock, carpeted trunk with trunk light, exclusive exterior bright trim, power steering, power brakes, automatic transmission, deluxe wheel covers, rear wheel opening fender skirts, and 8.55 × 14 BSW tires.

## Measurements

| | |
|---|---|
| Wheelbase | 124.0" |
| Length | 219.2" |
| Width | 78.6" |
| Height | 55.9" |
| Legroom — front | 41.8" |
| Legroom — rear | 38.9" |
| Headroom — front | 39.0" |
| Headroom — rear | 37.3" |
| Cargo capacity (cu. ft.) | 17.4 |
| Fuel capacity (gals.) | 24.0 |

**1968**

## Models Available

| | Style Number | Base MSRP | Change from LY | Shipping Wt. (lbs.) | Production | Change from LY |
|---|---|---|---|---|---|---|
| New Yorker 2-Door Hardtop | CH23 | $4,424 | +3.75% | 4060 | 8,060 | +17.07% |
| New Yorker 4-Door Sedan | CH41 | $4,367 | +3.78% | 4055 | 13,092 | +20.03% |
| New Yorker 4-Door Hardtop | CH43 | $4,500 | +3.71% | 4090 | 26,991 | +24.58% |
| TOTALS | | Avg. price $4,430 | +3.75% | | Production 48,143 | +22.01% |

# DODGE

*"Announcing Dodge fever — one look, and you've got it."*

Two totally redesigned lines shared the spotlight at Dodge dealers this season: the all-new mid-size Coronets and Chargers. While still sporting boxy front and rear end treatments, everything in between was a little more rounded. Side lines of both models featured the Coke-bottle styling that GM had been using for several years now. The Charger was no longer a real fastback, instead using what was termed a "semi-fastback" roofline. This was a handsome look for the Charger and the 1968-1970 models were probably the best looking Chargers ever offered. For that matter, so were the Coronets, especially in Hardtop or Convertible models. Judging from the sales charts, most of the buying public must have agreed. The new Mopar intermediates had to compete with equally new and good-looking mid-size models from General Motors, and the loser in the battle would be Ford. In fact, Ford would never be a really big factor in the mid-size market again until the Taurus in the mid-eighties. Unfortunately for Dodge (and Plymouth), this would be their last success in the mid-size market until the mid-eighties also, as General Motors would own the mid-size market for the next 15 years. Under the hood, both Coronet and Charger offered a full array of powertrains from the famous Slant Sixes (Coronet only) up to the powerful Magnum 440s and Hemi 426s. Interior

trim was also updated and upgraded in these Dodge models to better compete in the mid-price range. A new budget-priced muscle car was also introduced this year. Known as the Super Bee, it was initially offered in only a 2-Door Coupe variation. The lightweight coupe, combined with minimal accessories and a powerful engine, made it a return to the original muscle car concept at an affordable price.

Compact Dart and full-size Dodge models received new grille treatments and other trim revisions, both having been new designs for 1967. A new high-powered 275-horsepower, 340 cubic inch V8 was added to the lineup for the Dart models. This new engine was standard equipment in the new top line GTS 2-Door Hardtop and Convertible models. Lacking a pony car model to compete with the Mustang and Camaro, the idea was to create a small muscle car from an existing line. The Dart GTS certainly looked the part, with bumblebee stripes at the back, hood louvers, and special Rallye wheels. And there was no denying it could act the part, with the 340 CID V8 under that hood. Full-size model offerings remained relatively unchanged, although the Polara 500 was officially a separate model this year, versus the option package status of 1967.

Charger 2-Door Hardtop

"Scat Pack" — Charger R/T 2-Door Hardtop, Coronet R/T 2-Door Hardtop and Dart GTS 2-Door Hardtop

Coronet 500 2-Door Hardtop

Coronet R/T 2-Door Hardtop

Dart GT 2-Door Hardtop

Monaco 4-Door Hardtop

Polara 4-Door Hardtop

**Model year production:** 606,000, up 47.77% over 1967.
**Domestic market share:** 7.08% (6th place).
**Base price range:** $2,323 to $3,869.
**Industry average base price:** $3,292.
**Dodge average base price:** $3,072.
**Introduction date:** September 1967.
**Assembly plants:** Lynch Road, MI (A); Hamtramck, MI (B); Detroit (Jefferson Ave.), MI (C); Belvidere, IL (D); Los Angeles, CA (E); Newark, DE (F); St. Louis, MO (G); Windsor, Ontario, Canada (R).

**Data plate identification:** Thirteen digit code read as follows: Four digit style number (see listings below) in which 1st digit is series letter (e.g., D = Polara series), 2nd number identifies trim grade (e.g., L is for base trim), 3rd and 4th digits indicate body style; 5th digit is engine code; 8 for 1968; assembly plant code; 100001 and up for serial number. *Example:* DL23F8C100001 is a 1968 Dodge Polara 2-Door Hardtop with a 318 CID V8 engine, serial number 100001, built in Detroit, MI.

## Powertrains

| Engine | Engine Code | Gross HP | Transmission Availability | Dart | Coronet | Charger | Polara | Monaco |
|---|---|---|---|---|---|---|---|---|
| 170 CID, 1-bbl., 6-cyl. | A | 125 | 3-speed man. | S | - | - | - | - |
| | | | Torqueflite automatic | $172 | - | - | - | - |
| 225 CID, 1-bbl., 6-cyl. | B | 145 | 3-speed man. | $38 | S* | - | - | - |
| | | | Torqueflite automatic | $209 | $153* | - | - | - |
| 273 CID, 2-bbl., V8 | D | 190 | 3-speed man. | $128 | S (Wgns.)/$94* | - | - | - |
| | | | 4-speed man. | $307 | - | - | - | - |
| | | | Torqueflite automatic | $309 | $163 (Wgns.)/$257* | - | - | - |
| 318 CID, 2-bbl., V8 | F | 230 | 3-speed man. | $128 | S (500)/$118*/ $24 (Wgns.) | S* | S | - |
| | | | 4-speed man. | $307 | $145 (500)/ $263* | $145* | - | - |
| | | | Torqueflite automatic | $309 | $163 (500)/$281*/ $187 (Wgns.) | $163* | $163 | - |
| 340 CID, 4-bbl., V8 | P | 275 | 4-speed man. | S (GTS) | - | - | - | - |
| | | | Torqueflite automatic | S (GTS) | - | - | - | - |
| 383 CID, 2-bbl., V8 | G | 290 | 3-speed man. | - | $81 (500)/$105 (Wgns.)/$199* | $81* | $56 | S |
| | | | 4-speed man. | - | $256 (500) | $256* | - | - |
| | | | Torqueflite automatic | - | $257 (500)/$281 (Wgns.)/$366* | $257* | $232 | S (500)/ $176 (ex.500) |
| 383 CID, 4-bbl., V8 | H | 330 | 3-speed man. | - | S (S.B.)/$121 (500)/$320* | $121* | $84 | $28 (ex. 500) |
| | | | 4-speed man. | - | $175 (S.B.)/ $296 | | | |

| Engine | Engine Code | Gross HP | Transmission Availability | Dart | Coronet | Charger | Polara | Monaco |
|---|---|---|---|---|---|---|---|---|
| | | | | | (500)/$495* | $296* | - | - |
| | | | Torqueflite automatic | - | $176 (S.B.)/$297 (500)/$496* | $297* | $260 | $28 (500)/$204 (Others) |
| 426 CID Street Hemi, 2 × 4-bbl., V8 | J | 425 | 4-speed man. | - | $457 (R/T)/$712 (S.B.) | $457 (R/T) | - | - |
| | | | Torqueflite automatic | - | $457 (R/T)/$712 (S.B.) | $457 (R/T) | - | - |
| 440 CID Magnum, 4-bbl., V8 | K/L | 350/375** | 4-speed man. | - | No cost (R/T) $278 (S.B.) | No cost (R/T) | - | - |
| | | | Torqueflite automatic | | S (R/T) $280 (S.B.) | S (R/T) | $309 | $68 (500)/$244 (Others) |

*Except Coronet 500, R/T & Wagons, Super Bee, and Charger R/T.    **Additional cost for 375 horsepower engine.

## Major Options

| | Dart | Coronet | Charger | Polara | Monaco |
|---|---|---|---|---|---|
| Air conditioning | $335 | $274 | $274 | $311 | $311 |
| Auto Pilot cruise control | - | $64 | $64 | $64 | $64 |
| Tinted glass | $24 | $30 | $30 | $30 | $30 |
| Power steering | $80 | $73 | $73 | $73 | $73 |
| Power brakes | $16 | $16 | $16 | $16 | $16 |
| Power brakes — front disc | - | $54 | $54 | $54 | $54 |
| Power door locks | - | $42 | $42 | $42 | $42 |
| Power windows | - | $ | $ | $ | $ |
| Electric clock | $11 | $11 | S | $11 | $11 |
| Music Master AM radio | $44 | $44 | $44 | $47 | $47 |
| Tilt steering wheel | - | $67 | $67 | $67 | $67 |
| Road Wheels | - | $75 | $59 | $75 | $75 |
| Vinyl roof | $58 | $58–$75 | $75 | $58–$75 | $58–$75 |

Options common to most models. (- = Not Available; S = Standard equipment.) Items may be standard equipment, optional at different pricing, or unavailable on certain models. This chart is only a guide.

## Paint Colors

| | Code |
|---|---|
| Charger Red | 33-1 |
| Dark Green Metallic | 66-1 |
| Silver Metallic | AA-1 |
| Black | BB-1 |
| Medium Blue Metallic | CC-1 |
| Pale Blue Metallic | DD-1 |
| Dark Blue Metallic | EE-1 |
| Light Green Metallic | FF-1 |
| Racing Green Metallic | GG-1 |
| Light Gold | HH-1 |
| Medium Gold Metallic | JJ-1 |
| Light Turquoise Met. | KK-1 |
| Medium Dark Turquoise Met. | LL-1 |
| Bronze Metallic | MM-1 |
| Red | PP-1 |
| Bright Blue Metallic | QQ-1 |
| Burgundy Metallic | RR-1 |
| Yellow | SS-1 |
| Medium Green Metallic | TT-1 |
| Light Blue Metallic | UU-1 |
| White | WW-1 |
| Beige | XX-1 |
| Medium Tan Metallic | YY-1 |

# Dart

*"Best looking reason in the world to save money."*

**Nameplate year of origin:** 1960 (on low-end full-size models).
**Current bodystyle lifespan:** 1967 through 1976.
**Predecessor to this model:** Dart (1963 to 1966).
**Replacement for this model:** Aspen (1976 to 1980).

## Measurements

| | |
|---|---|
| Wheelbase | 111.0" |
| Length | 194.5" |
| Width | 69.7" |

**Percentage of division's sales volume:** 28.35%.

**Corporate siblings:** Plymouth Valiant.

**Primary competition:** AMC Rambler American, Chevrolet Chevy II, and Ford Falcon.

**Notable changes:** Minor trim and detail changes.

**Major standard equipment:** Cloth and vinyl front bench seat, dome light, black rubber floor mats, 2-speed windshield wipers, and 6.50 × 13 BSW tires. 270 adds: All-vinyl front bench seat (Hardtops), full carpeting, drip rail molding, deluxe instrument panel décor, cigarette lighter and wheel covers. GT adds: Vinyl front bucket seats (Hardtop), map and courtesy light (Convertible), front fender-top turn signal indicators, deluxe wheel covers and 7.00 × 13 BSW tires on convertibles. GTS adds: Bumblebee exterior striping on rear quarters, 340 CID V8 engine with dress-up kit, 4-speed manual or automatic transmission, heavy-duty suspension and handling, and E70 × 14 Wide-Oval Redline tires.

## Measurements (cont.)

| | |
|---|---|
| Height | 53.6" |
| Legroom — front | 41.7" |
| Legroom — rear | 35.7" |
| Headroom — front | 38.3" |
| Headroom — rear | 37.3" |
| Cargo capacity (cu. ft.) | 14.3 |
| Fuel capacity (gals.) | 18.0 |

## Models Available

| | Style Number | Base MSRP | Change from LY | Shipping Wt. (lbs.) | Production | Change from LY |
|---|---|---|---|---|---|---|
| Dart 2-Door Sedan | LL21 | $2,323 | +6.22% | 2705 | 60,300 | * |
| Dart 4-Door Sedan | LL41 | $2,360 | +6.12% | 2725 | * | * |
| Dart 270 2-Door Hardtop | LH23 | $2,525 | +5.74% | 2710 | 76,500 | * |
| Dart 270 4-Door Sedan | LH41 | $2,499 | +5.80% | 2725 | * | * |
| Dart GT 2-Door Hardtop | LP23 | $2,637 | +5.52% | 2715 | 35,000 | * |
| Dart GT 2-Door Convertible | LP27 | $2,831 | +3.62% | 2790 | * | * |
| Dart GTS 2-Door Hardtop | LS23 | $3,189 | NEW | 3065 | * | NEW |
| Dart GTS 2-Door Convertible | LS27 | $3,383 | NEW | 3150 | * | NEW |
| TOTALS | Avg. price | $2,718 | +13.30% | | Production 171,800 | +11.20% |

*Production by series not available. Totals are estimated.*

# Coronet

*"Your kind of beauty at your kind of price."*

**Nameplate year of origin:** 1950 (hardtop models); 1953 (series).

**Current bodystyle lifespan:** 1968 through 1970.

**Predecessor to this model:** Coronet (1966 to 1967).

**Replacement for this model:** Coronet/Monaco (1971 to 1978).

**Percentage of division's sales volume:** 36.73%.

**Corporate siblings:** Plymouth Belvedere/Satellite.

**Primary competition:** AMC Rebel, Chevrolet Chevelle, Ford Fairlane, and Pontiac Tempest/LeMans.

**Notable changes:** Completely restyled.

**Major standard equipment:** All-vinyl bench seat, glove box lock, trunk mat, color-keyed rubber floor mats, cigarette lighter, front and rear armrests, windshield wipers with washers, and 7.35 × 14 BSW tires (8.25 × 14 BSW on wagons). 440 adds: Cloth and vinyl bench seat (4-Door only), deep-pile carpeting and 3-spoke steering wheel. 500 adds: All-vinyl bucket seats (2-Doors), exterior bright trim package, and power tailgate window on 3-Seat wagon. Super Bee adds to base Coronet: All-vinyl bench seat, bumblebee striping, Rallye suspension, and floor shift transmission. R/T adds: All-vinyl bucket seats, choice of body side or bumblebee stripes, 4-speed manual or Torqueflite transmission and F70 × 14 Wide-Oval Redline tires.

## Measurements

| | Cars | Wagons |
|---|---|---|
| Wheelbase | 117.0" | 117.0" |
| Length | 206.6" | 211.5" |
| Width | 76.7" | 76.7" |
| Height | 54.7" | 55.3" |
| Legroom — front | 41.9" | 41.9" |
| Legroom — rear | 41.4" | 41.4" |
| Headroom — front | 34.6" | 34.6" |
| Headroom — rear | 37.4" | 37.4" |
| Cargo capacity (cu. ft.) | NA | NA |
| Fuel capacity (gals.) | 19.0 | 19.0 |

## Models Available

| | Style Number | Base MSRP | Change from LY | Shipping Wt. (lbs.) | Production | Change from LY |
|---|---|---|---|---|---|---|
| Coronet Deluxe 2-Door Coupe | WL21 | $2,487 | +5.43% | 3015 | 45,000 | * |
| Coronet Deluxe 4-Door Sedan | WL41 | $2,525 | +5.34% | 3035 | * | * |
| Coronet Deluxe 4-Dr., 2-S. Wagon | WL45 | $2,816 | +4.57% | 3455 | 33,100 | * |
| Coronet 440 2-Door Coupe | WH21 | $2,565 | NEW | 3015 | 103,500 | * |
| Coronet 440 2-Door Hardtop | WH23 | $2,627 | +5.08% | 3040 | * | * |
| Coronet 440 4-Door Sedan | WH41 | $2,603 | +5.17% | 3035 | * | * |
| Coronet 440 4-Dr., 2-S. Wagon | WH45 | $2,924 | +5.52% | 3450 | * | * |
| Coronet 440 4-Dr., 3-S. Wagon | WH46 | $3,140 | +5.55% | 3680 | * | * |
| Coronet 500 2-Door Hardtop | WP23 | $2,879 | +7.47% | 3260 | 30,100 | * |
| Coronet 500 2-Door Convertible | WP27 | $3,036 | +4.01% | 3360 | * | * |
| Coronet 500 4-Door Sedan | WP41 | $2,912 | +9.72% | 3240 | * | * |
| Coronet 500 4-Dr., 2-S. Wgn. | WP45 | $3,212 | NEW | 3610 | * | NEW |
| Coronet 500 4-Dr., 3-S. Wgn. | WP46 | $3,322 | NEW | 3700 | * | NEW |
| Coronet Super Bee 2-Door Coupe | WM21 | $3,027 | NEW | 3395 | * | NEW |
| Coronet R/T 2-Door Hardtop | WS23 | $3,379 | +5.63% | 3530 | 10,900 | * |
| Coronet R/T 2-Door Convertible | WS27 | $3,613 | +5.09% | 3630 | * | * |
| TOTALS | Avg. price | $2,942 | +7.22% | Production | 222,600 | +20.85% |

*Production by series not available. Totals are estimated.*

# Charger

*"What a great shape to be in!"*

**Nameplate year of origin:** 1966.
**Current bodystyle lifespan:** 1968 through 1970.
**Predecessor to this model:** Charger (1966 to 1967).
**Replacement for this model:** Charger (1971 to 1974).
**Percentage of division's sales volume:** 15.86%.
**Corporate siblings:** None.
**Primary competition:** Ford Torino SportsRoof models and Mercury Cyclone.
**Notable changes:** Completely restyled.
**Major standard equipment:** All-vinyl front bucket seats, full carpeting, 3-spoke steering wheel, electric clock, concealed headlamps, and 7.35 × 14 BSW tires. R/T adds: Bumblebee stripes, Magnum 440 engine, automatic transmission, dual exhausts, handling package, and F70 × 14 Wide-Oval Redline tires.

## Measurements

| | |
|---|---|
| Wheelbase | 117.0" |
| Length | 208.0" |
| Width | 76.6" |
| Height | 53.2" |
| Legroom — front | 39.3" |
| Legroom — rear | 39.1" |
| Headroom — front | 38.6" |
| Headroom — rear | 36.4" |
| Cargo capacity (cu. ft.) | NA |
| Fuel capacity (gals.) | 19.0 |

## Models Available

| | Style Number | Base MSRP | Change from LY | Shipping Wt. (lbs.) | Production | Change from LY |
|---|---|---|---|---|---|---|
| Charger 2-Door Hardtop | XP29 | $3,040 | -2.81% | 3305 | 96,100 | * |
| Charger R/T 2-Door Hardtop | XS29 | $3,506 | NEW | 3575 | * | NEW |
| TOTALS | Avg. price | $3,273 | +4.64% | Production | 96,100 | +508.69% |

*Production by series not available. Totals are estimated.*

# Polara

*"Have you seen the low price it's running around with?"*

**Nameplate year of origin:** 1959.
**Current bodystyle lifespan:** 1967 through 1968.
**Predecessor to this model:** Polara (1965 to 1966).
**Replacement for this model:** Polara (1969 to 1973).
**Percentage of division's sales volume:** 12.23%.
**Corporate siblings:** Dodge Monaco and Plymouth Fury.
**Primary competition:** AMC Ambassador, Chevrolet Caprice, Ford LTD, and Pontiac Catalina.
**Notable changes:** Minor trim and detail changes.
**Major standard equipment:** Cloth-and-vinyl bench seat, full carpeting, 2-speed windshield wipers with washers, and 8.25 × 14 BSW tires (8.55 × 14 tires on wagons). Polara 500 adds: All-vinyl bucket seats with folding center arm rests or center floor console, wheel lip and window moldings, and wheel covers.

## Measurements

|  | Cars | Wagons |
|---|---|---|
| Wheelbase | 122.0" | 122.0" |
| Length | 219.0" | 220.0" |
| Width | 80.0" | 80.0" |
| Height | 54.5" | 57.1" |
| Legroom — front | 41.8" | 41.8" |
| Legroom — rear | 39.0" | 39.1" |
| Headroom — front | 39.8" | 39.6" |
| Headroom — rear | 38.5" | 39.2" |
| Cargo capacity (cu. ft.) | NA | 107.0 |
| Fuel capacity (gals.) | 24.0 | 22.0 |

## Models Available

|  | Style Number | Base MSRP | Change from LY | Shipping Wt. (lbs.) | Production | Change from LY |
|---|---|---|---|---|---|---|
| Polara 2-Door Hardtop | DL23 | $3,027 | +2.51% | 3700 | * | * |
| Polara 2-Door Convertible | DL27 | $3,288 | +1.45% | 3755 | * | * |
| Polara 4-Door Sedan | DL41 | $3,005 | +2.98% | 3735 | 70,100 | * |
| Polara 4-Door Hardtop | DL43 | $3,100 | +2.38% | 3755 | * | * |
| Polara 4-Door, 2-S. Wagon | DL45 | $3,388 | +3.77% | 4155 | * | * |
| Polara 4-Door, 3-S. Wagon | DL46 | $3,454 | +2.55% | 4210 | * | * |
| Polara 500 2-Door Hardtop | DM23 | $3,226 | +2.25% | 3740 | 4,000 | * |
| Polara 500 2-Door Convertible | DM27 | $3,487 | +1.28% | 3780 | * | * |
| TOTALS | *Avg. price* | $3,247 | +4.91% | | *Production* 74,100 | +125.91% |

# Monaco

*"The luxury you long for at a price you can live with."*

**Nameplate year of origin:** 1965.
**Current bodystyle lifespan:** 1967 through 1968.
**Predecessor to this model:** Custom 880 (1965) and Monaco (1965 to 1966).
**Replacement for this model:** Monaco (1969 to 1973).
**Percentage of division's sales volume:** 6.83%.
**Corporate siblings:** Dodge Polara and Plymouth Fury.
**Primary competition:** Buick LeSabre, Mercury Monterey, Oldsmobile 88, and Pontiac Bonneville.
**Notable changes:** Minor trim and detail changes.
**Major standard equipment:** Cloth-and-vinyl bench seat, full carpeting, ashtray, map and courtesy lights, 2-speed windshield wipers with washers, front fender top turn signal indicators, and 8.25 × 14 BSW tires (8.55 × 14 BSW tires on wagons). 500 adds: Vinyl bucket seats with center arm rests or center floor console, door-mounted courtesy lights, electric clock, automatic transmission, and bodyside paint stripes.

## Measurements

|  | Cars | Wagons |
|---|---|---|
| Wheelbase | 122.0" | 122.0" |
| Length | 219.0" | 220.0" |
| Width | 80.0" | 80.0" |
| Height | 54.5" | 57.1" |
| Legroom — front | 41.8" | 41.8" |
| Legroom — rear | 39.0" | 39.1" |
| Headroom — front | 39.8" | 39.6" |
| Headroom — rear | 38.5" | 39.2" |
| Cargo capacity (cu. ft.) | NA | 107.0 |
| Fuel capacity (gals.) | 24.0 | 22.0 |

1968

## Models Available

| | Style Number | Base MSRP | Change from LY | Shipping Wt. (lbs.) | Production | Change from LY |
|---|---|---|---|---|---|---|
| Monaco 2-Door Hardtop | DH23 | $3,396 | +5.70% | 3845 | 21,100 | * |
| Monaco 4-Door Sedan | DH41 | $3,294 | +4.97% | 3885 | * | * |
| Monaco 4-Door Hardtop | DH43 | $3,432 | +4.79% | 3910 | * | * |
| Monaco 4-Dr., 2-S. Wgn. | DH45 | $3,702 | +4.49% | 4295 | 16,900 | * |
| Monaco 4-Dr., 3-S. Wgn. | DH46 | $3,835 | +5.18% | 4360 | * | * |
| Monaco 500 2-Door Hardtop | DP23 | $3,869 | +4.23% | 3885 | 3,400 | +36.00% |
| TOTALS | | *Avg. price* $3,588 | +4.88% | | *Production* 41,400 | +81.58% |

# FORD

*"For '68 Ford ... has a better idea."*

The introduction of the 1968 Ford line was a little quieter than what it had been through much of the sixties. The only completely new car this year was the restyled Fairlane lineup. The new Fairlane gained the look of its bigger brethren Galaxie and LTD models. Slightly pointed front fender caps that contained parking lamps/turn signals in their lower half flanked full-width grilles with dual stacked headlamps set at each end. Bodylines were relatively straight and simple affairs, while the rear end had rectangular taillamps that were now somewhat traditional for Ford. The biggest news in body styles was the new 2-Door Fastback models, which featured side windows that curved up to meet the top window line at the rear, and a radically sloped rear window. This new body style came in Fairlane 500 and Fairlane GT versions. A 1968 Fairlane GT Convertible with special Torino trim was chosen as the official Pace Car for the 52nd annual Indianapolis 500 race. Fairlane station wagon models continued to share all major components from the cowl back with the Falcon wagon. New under the hood of many Ford models was the 302 CID V8 engine offering more horsepower and torque than the popular 289 CID V8 it would replace. Also, during this year the 427 CID V8 would be dropped in favor of the 428 CID V8 and the new 429 CID Thunderbird V8 engine.

Most other cars in the Ford line received only minor styling revisions and the previously mentioned engine lineup adjustments. The full-size Ford line looked totally new thanks to very clever restyling of the existing body. The biggest change was to the front fenders and grille area, which now accommodated horizontally placed headlamps as opposed to the previous vertical units. At the back end, taillamps were enlarged and the rear quarter panel was squared up, making the car look larger. Falcon, Mustang and Thunderbird lines were little changed. Mustang and Thunderbird received new grilles and taillamps, and the Mustang's familiar side scoop was toned down to a thin chrome strip this year. A new larger displacement 250 CID 6-cylinder was available for Mustang models this year. Former race car driver Carroll Shelby had been selling modified "Shelby-Mustangs" since the 1965 Mustangs were introduced. The initial cars were all fastbacks, but convertibles were added in 1966. Nineteen-sixty-eight was the peak year for Shelby-Mustang sales and a variety of models featuring the GT 350, GT500 and GT500 KR. The only noteworthy model line changes were the addition of a traditional 2-Door Hardtop model to the Galaxie 500 line, the aforementioned new Fastback Fairlane models, elimination of the Fairlane 500 XL, and renaming the Fairlane 500 XL GT to Fairlane GT.

Custom 500 4-Door Sedan

Country Squire 4-Door Wagon, Torino Squire
4-Door Wagon, Falcon Futura 4-Door Wagon
and Bronco 2-Door Wagon

Falcon Futura 2-Door Sports Coupe

Torino 2-Door Convertible,
Indianapolis 500 Pace Car

Torino 2-Door Hardtop

Torino GT 2-Door Fastback

Galaxie 500 2-Door Convertible

Mustang 2-Door Fastback

Mustang/Shelby Cobra GT500
2-Door Convertible

Thunderbird 2-Door Hardtop

**1968**

**Model year production:** 1,752,502, up 1.23% over 1967.
**Domestic market share:** 20.46% (2nd place).
**Base price range:** $1960 to $5293.
**Industry average base price:** $3,292.
**Ford average base price:** $2,956.
**Introduction date:** September 1967.
**Assembly plants:** Atlanta, GA (A); Dallas, TX (D); Chicago, IL (G); Dearborn, MI (F); Kansas City, MO (K); Lorain, OH (H); Los Angeles, CA (J); Louisville, KY (U); Mahwah, NJ (E); Metuchen, NJ (T); Norfolk, VA (N); San Jose, CA (R); Twin Cities, MN (P); Wayne, MI (W); Wixom, MI (Y); St. Thomas, Ontario, Can. (X); Oakville, Ontario, Can. (B).
**Data plate identification:** Eleven digit code read as follows: 8 for 1968; 2nd digit is assembly plant code; 2-digit model number (see listings below); 5th digit is engine code; 100001 and up for serial number. *Example:* 8Y83Z100001 is a 1968 Ford Thunderbird 2-Door Hardtop with a 390 CID V8 engine, serial number 100001, built in Wixom, MI.

# Powertrains

| Engine | Gross HP | Engine Code | Transmission Availability | Falcon | Mustang | Fairlane | Full-size | T-Bird |
|---|---|---|---|---|---|---|---|---|
| 170 CID, 1-bbl., 6-cyl. | 100 | U | 3-speed manual | S | – | – | – | – |
| | | | Cruise-O-Matic | $187 | – | – | – | – |
| 200 CID, 1-bbl., 6-cyl. | 115 | T | 3-speed manual | $26 | S | S* | – | – |
| | | | Cruise-O-Matic | $213 | $199 | $187* | – | – |
| 240 CID, 1-bbl., 6-cyl. | 150 | V | 3-speed manual | – | – | – | S** | – |
| | | | Cruise-O-Matic | – | – | – | $188** | – |
| 250 CID, 1-bbl., 6-cyl. | 155 | L | 3-speed manual | – | $26 | – | – | – |
| | | | Cruise-O-Matic | – | $225 | – | – | – |
| 289 CID Challenger, 2-bbl., V8 | 195 | C | 3-speed manual | $132 | $106 | $87* | S (Ctry Sq.)/$107** | – |
| | | | 4-speed manual | $316 | $290 | $271* | – | |
| | | | Cruise-O-Matic | $319 | $307 | $275* | $188 (Ctry. Sq.)/ $295** | |
| 302 CID, 2-bbl., V8 | 210/220 | F | 3-speed manual | $183 | $157 | S (GT)/$107* | S (XL/LTD)/$110 (Ctry. Sq.)/ $217** | |
| | | | 4-speed manual | $367 | $341 | $184 (GT)/$291* | – | – |
| | | | Cruise-O-Matic | $370 | $358 | $201 (GT)/$308* | $188 (XL/LTD)/ $298 (Ctry. Sq.)/ $405** | – |
| 302 CID, 4-bbl., V8 | 230 | J | 3-speed manual | – | $172 | – | – | – |
| | | | 4-speed manual | – | $356 | – | – | – |
| | | | Cruise-O-Matic | – | $373 | – | – | – |
| 390 CID Thunderbird, 2-bbl., V8 | 265 | Y | 3-speed manual | – | – | $77 (GT)/$184* | $78 (XL/LTD)/ $184 (Ctry. Sq.)/ $291** | |
| | | | 4-speed manual | – | – | $261 (GT)/$368* | – | |
| | | | Cruise-O-Matic | – | – | $278 (GT)/$385* | $298 (XL/LTD)/ $404 (Ctry. Sq.)/ $511** | – |
| 390 CID Thunderbird, 4-bbl., V8 | 280 | H | Cruise-O-Matic | – | – | – | $ (XL/LTD)/ $ (Ctry. Sq.)/$** | – |
| 390 CID Thunderbird, 4-bbl., V8 | 315 | Z | Cruise-O-Matic | – | – | – | $378 (XL/LTD)/ $484 (Ctry. Sq.)/ $591** | S |
| 390 CID GT, 4-bbl., V8 | 325 | S | 3-speed manual | – | $264 | $157 (GT)/$264* | – | – |
| | | | 4-speed manual | – | $497 | $341 (GT)/$448* | – | – |
| | | | Cruise-O-Matic | – | $497 | $377 (GT)/$484* | – | – |
| 427 CID Thunderbird Hi-Perf., 4-bbl., V8 | 390 | W | 4-speed manual | – | $ | – | – | – |
| | | | Cruise-O-Matic | – | $ | – | – | – |
| 428 CID Cobra Jet, 4-bbl., V8 | 335 | Q | 4-speed manual | – | $ | – | – | – |
| | | | Cruise-O-Matic | – | $ | – | – | – |
| 428 CID Police Interceptor, 4-bbl., V8 | 340 | Q | Cruise-O-Matic | – | – | – | $ (XL/LTD)/ $ (Ctry. Sq.)/$** | – |
| 428 CID Super Cobra Jet, 4-bbl., V8 | 360 | R | Cruise-O-Matic | – | $ | – | – | – |
| 429 CID Thunder Jet, 4-bbl., V8 | 360 | N | Cruise-O-Matic | – | – | – | – | $ |

*All except GT.    **Except XL, LTD and Country Squire.    ***Available on a limited basis on specific models only.

## Major Options

|  | Falcon | Mustang | Fairlane | Full-size | Thunderbird |
|---|---|---|---|---|---|
| Select Aire air conditioning | - | $360 | $356 | $356 | $421 |
| Tinted glass | $30 | $30 | $30 | $35 | S |
| Power steering | $84 | $84 | $84 | $95 | S |
| Power brakes | - | $54 | $54 | $42 | S |
| Power driver's seat/ |  |  |  |  |  |
|   Bench seat | - | - | $ | $ | $98 |
| Power windows | - | - | $ | $ | $104 |
| AM radio | $57 | $61 | $57 | $57 | S |
| AM/FM radio | - | $135 | $134 | $134 | $164–Stereo |
| Front seat console | - | $54 | $ | $ | $ |
| Front bucket Seats | - | S | $ | $ | $ |
| Tilt steering wheel | - | $66 | - | $ | S |
| Vinyl roof | $74 | $74 | $74 | $74–$83 | S |
| White sidewall tires | $32 | $33 | $34 | $35 | $52 |

Options common to most models. (- = Not Available; S = Standard equipment.) Items may be standard equipment, optional at different pricing, or unavailable on certain models. This chart is only a guide.

## Paint Colors

|  | Code | Others | Thunderbird |
|---|---|---|---|
| Pebble Beige | 6 | X | X |
| Raven Black | A | X | X |
| Royal Maroon | B | X | X |
| Acapulco Blue Metallic | D | X |  |
| Beige Mist Metallic | E |  | X |
| Gulfstream Aqua Metallic | F | X |  |
| Belmont Green Metallic | G |  | X |
| Diamond Green Metallic | H |  | X |
| Lime Gold Metallic | I | X | X |
| Midnight Aqua Metallic | J |  | X |
| Silver Pearl Metallic | L |  | X |
| Wimbledon White | M | X | X |
| Diamond Blue | N |  | X |
| Seafoam Green | O | X |  |
| Pewter Mist Metallic | P |  | X |
| Brittany Blue Metallic | Q |  | X |
| Highland Green Metallic | R | X | X |
| Candy Apple Red | T | X | X |
| Tahoe Turquoise Metallic | U | X | X |
| Alaska Blue | V |  | X |
| Meadowlark Yellow | W | X | X |
| Presidential Blue Metallic | X | X | X |
| Sunlit Gold Metallic | Y | X | X |
| Oxford Gray Metallic | Z |  | X |

1968

# Falcon

*"The compact car for a big, fast country."*

**Nameplate year of origin:** 1960.
**Current bodystyle lifespan:** 1966 through 1970.
**Predecessor to this model:** Falcon (1964 to 1965).
**Replacement for this model:** Maverick (1969 to 1977).

## Measurements

|  | Cars | Wagons |
|---|---|---|
| Wheelbase | 111.0" | 113.0" |

**Percentage of division's sales volume:** 7.50%.
**Corporate siblings:** None (Wagon bodies shared with Fairlane).
**Primary competition:** AMC Rambler American, Chevrolet Chevy II, Dodge Dart, and Plymouth Valiant.
**Notable changes:** Minor trim and detail changes.
**Major standard equipment:** Cloth and vinyl interior trim, front-door armrests, chrome windshield and rear window moldings, small hubcaps, and 6.95 × 14 BSW tires (7.75 × 14 on Wagons). Futura adds: Deluxe interior trim, rear armrests with ashtrays, side window moldings, wheel covers. Sport Coupe adds: Vinyl bucket seats, deluxe wheel covers, and 7.35 × 14 BSW tires.

| | Cars | Wagons |
|---|---|---|
| Length | 184.3" | 199.0" |
| Width | 73.2" | 73.2" |
| Height | 55.0" | 55.5" |
| Legroom — front | 42.4" | 42.1" |
| Legroom — rear | 33.9" | 36.8" |
| Headroom — front | 38.6" | 38.7" |
| Headroom — rear | 38.8" | 37.8" |
| Cargo capacity (cu. ft.) | 16.2 | 85.0 |
| Fuel capacity (gals.) | 16.0 | 20.0 |

## Models Available

| | Style Number | Base MSRP | Change from LY | Shipping Wt. (lbs.) | Production | Change from LY |
|---|---|---|---|---|---|---|
| Falcon 2-Door Sedan | 10 | $2,252 | +6.33% | 2702 | 36,443 | +126.61% |
| Falcon 4-Door Sedan | 11 | $2,301 | +6.18% | 2436 | 29,166 | +115.18% |
| Falcon 4-Door Wagon | 12 | $2,617 | +4.81% | 3116 | 15,576 | +180.50% |
| Falcon Futura 2-Door Sedan | 20 | $2,415 | +5.92% | 2715 | 10,633 | +69.13% |
| Falcon Futura 2-Door Sports Cpe. | 22 | $2,541 | +4.27% | 2739 | 10,077 | +42.88% |
| Falcon Futura 4-Door Sedan | 21 | $2,457 | +5.81% | 2749 | 18,733 | +66.46% |
| Falcon Futura 4-Door Wagon | 23 | $2,728 | +4.56% | 3124 | 10,761 | +136.40% |
| TOTALS | | Avg. price $2,473 | +5.37% | | Production 131,389 | +104.23% |

# Mustang

*"Only Mustang makes it happen!"*

**Nameplate year of origin:** 1964½ (also on a 1963 show car).
**Current bodystyle lifespan:** 1964½ through 1968.
**Predecessor to this model:** None.
**Replacement for this model:** Mustang (1969 to 1970).
**Percentage of division's sales volume:** 18.10%.
**Corporate siblings:** Mercury Cougar.
**Primary competition:** AMC Javelin, Chevrolet Camaro, Plymouth Barracuda, and Pontiac Firebird.
**Notable changes:** New grille and trim and detail changes.
**Major standard equipment:** All-vinyl bucket front seats, courtesy lights, full carpeting, sports steering wheel, chrome window moldings, and 6.95 × 14 BSW tires.

### Measurements

| | |
|---|---|
| Wheelbase | 108.0" |
| Length | 183.6" |
| Width | 70.9" |
| Height | 51.6" |
| Legroom — front | 42.0" |
| Legroom — rear | 27.0" |
| Headroom — front | 37.4" |
| Headroom — rear | 35.8" |
| Cargo capacity (cu. ft.) | 9.3 |
| Fuel capacity (gals.) | 16.0 |

## Models Available

| | Style Number | Base MSRP | Change from LY | Shipping Wt. (lbs.) | Production | Change from LY |
|---|---|---|---|---|---|---|
| Mustang 2-Door Hardtop | 1 | $2,602 | +5.73% | 2666 | 249,447 | -29.98% |
| Mustang 2-Door Fastback | 2 | $2,712 | +4.63% | 2690 | 42,325 | -40.42% |
| Mustang 2-Door Convertible | 3 | $2,814 | +4.30% | 2776 | 25,376 | -43.37% |
| TOTALS | | Avg. price $2,709 | +4.84% | | Production 317,148 | -32.82% |

# Fairlane and Torino

*"Ford's newest bright idea!"*

**Nameplate year of origin:** 1955 (Fairlane); 1968 (Torino).
**Current bodystyle lifespan:** 1968 through 1969.
**Predecessor to this model:** Fairlane (1966 to 1967).
**Replacement for this model:** Fairlane/Torino (1970 to 1971).
**Percentage of division's sales volume:** 21.21%.
**Corporate siblings:** Mercury Comet.
**Primary competition:** AMC Rebel, Chevrolet Chevelle, Plymouth Belvedere, and Dodge Coronet.
**Notable changes:** Completely restyled.
**Major standard equipment:** Cloth and vinyl bench seat, rubber floor mats, front and rear armrests, chrome windshield and rear window moldings, and 7.35 × 14 BSW tires (7.75 × 14 BSW on Wagons). 500 adds: Full carpeting, deluxe interior trim, and chrome side window moldings. Torino adds: Luxury interior trim, and exterior body moldings. Torino Squire adds: Exterior wood-grain trim. Torino GT adds: All-vinyl bucket front seats, center console, special exterior striping and identification, electric clock, tachometer and 302 CID V8 engine, and F70 × 14 Wide-Oval tires.

## Measurements

|  | Cars | Wagons |
| --- | --- | --- |
| Wheelbase | 116.0" | 113.0" |
| Length | 201.0" | 204.0" |
| Width | 74.6" | 74.6" |
| Height | 55.0" | 55.5" |
| Legroom — front | 42.4" | 42.4" |
| Legroom — rear | 36.0" | 36.0" |
| Headroom — front | 38.6" | 38.6" |
| Headroom — rear | 37.4" | 37.4" |
| Cargo capacity (cu. ft.) | 16.2 | 85.0 |
| Fuel capacity (gals.) | 20.0 | 20.0 |

## Models Available

|  | Style Number | Base MSRP | Change from LY | Shipping Wt. (lbs.) | Production | Change from LY |
| --- | --- | --- | --- | --- | --- | --- |
| Fairlane 2-Door Hardtop | 30 | $2,456 | +6.92% | 2994 | 44,683 | +320.43% |
| Fairlane 4-Door Sedan | 31 | $2,464 | +5.34% | 2946 | 18,146 | -8.07% |
| Fairlane 4-Door, 2-Seat Wagon | 32 | $2,770 | +4.81% | 3310 | 14,800 | +36.02% |
| Fairlane 500 2-Door Formal Hardtop | 33 | $2,591 | +6.23% | 3005 | 33,282 | -52.55% |
| Fairlane 500 2-Dr. Fastback HT | 35 | $2,566 | NEW | 3017 | 32,452 | NEW |
| Fairlane 500 2-Door Convertible | 36 | $2,822 | +5.93% | 3164 | 3,761 | -30.71% |
| Fairlane 500 4-Door Sedan | 34 | $2,543 | +5.21% | 2955 | 42,390 | -19.34% |
| Fairlane 500 4-Dr., 2-Seat Wagon | 37 | $2,881 | +6.00% | 3315 | 10,190 | -35.92% |
| Fairlane Torino 2-Door Hardtop | 40 | $2,710 | NEW | 3059 | 35,964 | NEW |
| Fairlane Torino 4-Door Sedan | 41 | $2,688 | NEW | 3009 | 17,962 | NEW |
| F. Torino Squire 4-Dr., 2-Seat Wgn. | 38 | $3,032 | +4.48% | 3360 | 14,773 | +76.96% |
| Fairlane Torino GT 2-Door Hardtop | 44 | $2,772 | -2.36% | 3197 | 23,939 | +28.22% |
| Fairlane Torino GT 2-Door Fastback | 42 | $2,747 | NEW | 3220 | 74,135 | NEW |
| Fairlane Torino GT 2-Door Conv. | 43 | $3,001 | -2.06% | 3343 | 5,310 | +150.83% |
| TOTALS | *Avg. price* | $2,717 | +3.39% | *Production* | 371,787 | +55.11% |

1968

# Custom, Galaxie & LTD

*"Quiet. Strong. Beautiful. A great road car."*

**Nameplate year of origin:** 1957 (Custom); 1959 (Galaxie); 1965 (LTD).
**Current bodystyle lifespan:** 1967 through 1968.
**Predecessor to this model:** Full-size Ford (1965 to 1966).
**Replacement for this model:** Custom, Galaxie and LTD (1969 to 1970).
**Percentage of division's sales volume:** 49.49%.
**Corporate siblings:** Mercury Monterey, Montclair and Marquis.
**Primary competition:** AMC Ambassador, Chevrolet Biscayne/BelAir/Im-

## Measurements

|  | Cars | Wagons |
| --- | --- | --- |
| Wheelbase | 119.0" | 119.0" |
| Length | 213.3" | 220.2" |
| Width | 78.0" | 78.0" |
| Height | 55.8" | 55.8" |

pala/Caprice, Dodge Polara/Monaco, Plymouth Fury, and Pontiac Catalina.

**Notable changes:** Major front end restyling, revised trim and detail changes.

**Major standard equipment:** Cloth and vinyl front bench seat, rubber floor mats, arm rests on all doors, rear window trim molding, and 7.75 × 15 BSW tires (8.45 × 15 BSW tires on Wagon). Custom 500 adds: Full carpeting, and chrome windshield molding. Galaxie 500 adds: Deluxe interior trim, chrome side window moldings, and 8.15 × 15 BSW tires on Hardtop and Convertibles. XL adds: Bucket seats with floor-mounted transmission selector, lower door carpet trim and polished trim, courtesy and reading lamps, and special badging. LTD adds: Padded cloth upholstery with Scotchguard® treatment, simulated wood interior trim, additional courtesy lights, self-regulating clock, and 8.15 × 15 BSW tires.

| | Cars | Wagons |
|---|---|---|
| Legroom — front | 41.9" | 41.9" |
| Legroom — rear | 37.6" | 37.6" |
| Headroom — front | 38.9" | 38.9" |
| Headroom — rear | 37.8" | 37.8" |
| Cargo capacity (cu. ft.) | 19.1 | 103.0 |
| Fuel capacity (gals.) | 25.0 | 25.0 |

## Models Available

| | Style Number | Base MSRP | Change from LY | Shipping Wt. (lbs.) | Production | Change from LY |
|---|---|---|---|---|---|---|
| Custom 2-Door Sedan | 50 | $2,584 | +5.86% | 3490 | 18,485 | +2.09% |
| Custom 4-Door Sedan | 51 | $2,642 | +5.85% | 3516 | 45,980 | +11.02% |
| Custom 500 2-Door Sedan | 52 | $2,699 | +5.72% | 3479 | 8,938 | -50.74% |
| Custom 500 4-Door Sedan | 53 | $2,741 | +5.63% | 3530 | 49,398 | -40.67% |
| Galaxie 500 2-Door Hardtop | 58 | $2,916 | +5.84% | 3563 | 84,332 | -57.28% |
| Galaxie 500 2-Door Fastback HT | 55 | $2,881 | NEW | 3567 | 69,760 | NEW |
| Galaxie 500 2-Door Convertible | 57 | $3,109 | +3.53% | 3713 | 11,832 | -37.95% |
| Galaxie 500 4-Door Sedan | 54 | $2,864 | +4.83% | 3547 | 117,877 | -9.37% |
| Galaxie 500 4-Door Hardtop | 56 | $2,936 | +4.56% | 3589 | 55,461 | -2.85% |
| XL 2-Door Hardtop | 60 | $2,985 | -7.96% | 3607 | 50,048 | +175.38% |
| XL 2-Door Convertible | 61 | $3,214 | -7.99% | 3764 | 6,066 | +17.54% |
| LTD 2-Door Hardtop | 62 | $3,153 | -6.22% | 3644 | 54,163 | +17.65% |
| LTD 4-Door Sedan | 64 | $3,135 | -4.94% | 3614 | 22,834 | +82.80% |
| LTD 4-Door Hardtop | 66 | $3,206 | -4.67% | 3652 | 61,755 | +18.81% |
| Ranch Wagon 4-Door, 2-Seat | 70 | $3,000 | +5.78% | 3955 | 18,237 | -23.80% |
| Ranch Wagon 500 4-Door, 2-Seat | 71 | $3,063 | NEW | 3965 | 18,181 | NEW |
| Ranch Wagon 500 4-Dr., w/DFRS* | 72 | $3,176 | NEW | 4011 | 13,421 | NEW |
| Country Sedan 4-Door Wagon | 73 | $3,181 | +8.38% | 3974 | 39,335 | -22.60% |
| Country Sedan 4-Door w/DFRS* | 74 | $3,295 | +7.64% | 4031 | 29,374 | -14.55% |
| Country Squire 4-Door Wagon | 75 | $3,539 | +9.43% | 4020 | 33,994 | +32.79% |
| Country Squire 4-Dr. Wgn. w/DFRS* | 76 | $3,619 | +7.74% | 4066 | 57,776 | +31.24% |
| TOTALS | Avg. price | $3,045 | +2.32% | Production | 867,247 | -1.13% |

*Dual facing rear seats

# Thunderbird

*"New Thunder from the 'Bird!"*

**Nameplate year of origin:** 1955.

**Current bodystyle lifespan:** 1967 through 1971 (restyled in 1970).

**Predecessor to this model:** Thunderbird (1964 to 1966).

**Replacement for this model:** Thunderbird (1972 to 1976).

**Percentage of division's sales volume:** 3.71%.

**Corporate siblings:** Lincoln Continental Mark III.

**Primary competition:** Buick Riviera and Oldsmobile Toronado.

**Notable changes:** Revised grille and taillights, minor trim and detail changes.

**Major standard equipment:** Luxury all-cloth interior with cut-pile carpeting, front bench seat, tilt away steering wheel, AM radio, "rolling

## Measurements

| | 2-Doors | 4-Doors |
|---|---|---|
| Wheelbase | 114.7" | 117.2" |
| Length | 206.9" | 209.4" |
| Width | 77.3" | 77.3" |
| Height | 53.4" | 54.0" |
| Legroom — front | 42.1" | 42.1" |
| Legroom — rear | 32.2" | 34.0" |
| Headroom — front | 37.4" | 38.1" |
| Headroom — rear | 36.9" | 37.2" |

lock" power door locks, power steering, power front disc brakes, sequential turn signals, full wheel covers, and 8.15 × 15 BSW tires (8.45 × 15 BSW tires on 4-Door).

|  | 2-Doors | 4-Doors |
|---|---|---|
| Cargo capacity (cu. ft.) | 12.3 | 12.3 |
| Fuel capacity (gals.) | 24.1 | 24.1 |

## Models Available

| | Style Number | Base MSRP | Change from LY | Shipping Wt. (lbs.) | Production | Change from LY |
|---|---|---|---|---|---|---|
| Thunderbird 2-Door Hardtop | 83 | $4,716 | +2.45% | 4327 | 9,977 | -35.91% |
| Thunderbird 2-Dr. Landau Coupe | 84 | $4,845 | +3.00% | 4337 | 33,029 | -11.74% |
| Thunderbird 4-Door Landau Sedan | 87 | $4,924 | +2.05% | 4427 | 21,925 | -12.18% |
| TOTALS | *Avg. price* | $4,828 | +2.48% | | *Production* 64,931 | -16.71% |

# IMPERIAL

*"Imperial '68 ... If you want more than luxury in your luxury car."*

Imperials received a new grille and front bumper design for 1968. Body side moldings and interior trim were also new for the year, but it was hard to find anything else changed about the '68 Imperials. This would be the final season for an Imperial convertible. The base Imperial and the Crown lines were combined into a single Crown line for 1968. This really had no effect on anything, except to expand the Crown line and drop the number of series back to only the Crown and LeBaron.

Crown 2-Door Hardtop

Crown 4-Door Hardtop

**Model year production:** 15,361, down 12.79% from 1967
**Domestic market share:** 0.18% (13th place).
**Base price range:** $5,654 to $6,940.
**Industry average base price:** $3,292.
**Imperial average base price:** $6,186.
**Introduction date:** September 1967.
**Assembly plants:** Detroit, MI (C).
**Data plate identification:** Thirteen digit code read as follows:

four digit style number (see listings below) in which Y = Imperial, 2nd number identifies series (e.g., M is for Crown), 3rd and 4th digits indicate body style; 5th digit is engine code; 8 for 1968; assembly plant code; 100001 and up for serial number. *Example:* YM23T8C100001 is a 1968 Imperial Crown 2-Door Hardtop with a 440 CID V8 engine, serial number 100001, built in Detroit, MI.

## Powertrains

| Engine | Engine Code | Gross HP | Transmission Availability | Imperial |
|---|---|---|---|---|
| 440 CID, 4-bbl., V8 | T | 350 | Torqueflite Automatic | S |

## Major Options

| | Crown | LeBaron |
|---|---|---|
| Air conditioning | $494 | $494 |
| Auto Pilot automatic speed control | $95 | $95 |
| Tinted glass | $53 | $53 |
| Rear window defogger | $26 | $26 |
| Deck lid remote release | $30 | $30 |
| Power steering — variable-ratio | S | S |
| Power brakes | S | S |
| Power door locks | $47 (2-Dr)/$71 (4-Dr) | $71 |
| Power driver's seat/Bench seat | $105 | S |
| Power windows | S | S |
| AM radio w/power antenna | $165 | $165 |
| AM/FM radio w/power antenna | $228 | $228 |
| Tilt-A-Scope steering wheel | $92 | $92 |
| Vinyl roof | $103–$136 | S |
| Whitewall tires — standard size | $45 | S |

Options common to most models. (S = Standard equipment.) Items may be standard equipment, optional at different pricing, or unavailable on certain models. This chart is only a guide.

## Paint Colors

| | Code |
|---|---|
| Charcoal Gray Metallic | 55-1 |
| Silver Haze | AA-1 |
| Formal Black | BB-1 |
| Consort Blue Metallic | CC-1 |
| Sky Blue Metallic | DD-1 |
| Military Blue Metallic | EE-1 |
| Frost Green Metallic | FF-1 |
| Forest Green Metallic | GG-1 |
| Champagne | HH-1 |
| Sovereign Gold Metallic | JJ-1 |
| Mist Turquoise Metallic | KK-1 |
| Turbine Bronze Metallic | MM-1 |
| Flame Red | PP-1 |
| Burgundy Metallic | RR-1 |
| Meadow Green Metallic | TT-1 |
| Polar White | WW-1 |
| Imperial Navaho Beige | XX-1 |
| Beige Mist Metallic | YY-1 |

# Crown

*"Built to make Imperial ownership an easy, logical decision."*

**Nameplate year of origin:** 1957 (not the same as Crown Imperial series).
**Current bodystyle lifespan:** 1967 through 1968.
**Predecessor to this model:** Crown (1964 to 1966).
**Replacement for this model:** Crown (1969 to 1970).
**Percentage of division's sales volume:** 87.94%.
**Corporate siblings:** LeBaron.
**Primary competition:** Cadillac Calais and Lincoln Continental.
**Notable changes:** New grille, minor trim and detail changes.
**Major standard equipment:** Cloth and vinyl front bench seat (Sedan), cloth and leather (Hardtops) and bucket seats with leather upholstery (convertible), Torqueflite automatic transmission, power steering, power brakes, front and rear armrests (hardtops), pile carpeting, remote-control left-hand outside mirror, power windows, electric clock, trip odometer, 3-speed electric windshield wipers with washers, wheel covers and 9.15 × 15 BSW tires.

## Measurements

| | |
|---|---|
| Wheelbase | 127.0" |
| Length | 224.5" |
| Width | 79.6" |
| Height | 57.0" |
| Legroom — front | 41.9" |
| Legroom — rear | 39.1" |
| Headroom — front | 39.4" |
| Headroom — rear | 38.0" |
| Cargo capacity (cu. ft.) | NA |
| Fuel capacity (gals.) | 25.0 |

## Models Available

| | Style Number | Base MSRP | Change from LY | Shipping Wt. (lbs.) | Production | Change from LY |
|---|---|---|---|---|---|---|
| Crown 2-Door Hardtop | YM23 | $5,722 | -4.81% | 4660 | 2,656 | -17.90% |
| Crown 2-Door Convertible | YM27 | $6,497 | +4.05% | 4795 | 474 | -17.85% |
| Crown 4-Door Sedan | YM41 | $5,654 | +5.21% | 4685 | 1,887 | -13.95% |

| | Style Number | Base MSRP | Change from LY | Shipping Wt. (lbs.) | Production | Change from LY |
|---|---|---|---|---|---|---|
| Crown 4-Door Hardtop | YM43 | $6,115 | +4.78% | 4715 | 8,492 | -9.80% |
| TOTALS | | Avg. price $5,997 | +2.23% | | Production 13,509 | -12.39% |

# LeBaron

*"As distinguished among luxury cars as its owner is among men."*

**Nameplate year of origin:** 1924 (as Chrysler Sedan model designation); 1926 (as series).

**Current bodystyle lifespan:** 1967 through 1968.

**Predecessor to this model:** LeBaron (1964 to 1966).

**Replacement for this model:** LeBaron (1969 to 1973).

**Percentage of division's sales volume:** 12.06%.

**Corporate siblings:** Crown.

**Primary competition:** Cadillac de Ville and Lincoln Continental.

**Notable changes:** New grille, minor trim and detail changes.

**Major standard equipment:** Cloth and fabric-and-leather or broadcloth split-bench front seat, Torqueflite automatic transmission, power steering, power brakes, pile carpeting, power seat, power windows and vent windows, electric clock, trip odometer, Seville-grain vinyl roof with formal carriage rear window, 3-speed electric windshield wipers with washers, wheel covers and 9.15 × 15 WSW tires.

## Measurements

| | |
|---|---|
| Wheelbase | 127.0" |
| Length | 224.5" |
| Width | 79.6" |
| Height | 57.0" |
| Legroom — front | 41.9" |
| Legroom — rear | 39.1" |
| Headroom — front | 39.4" |
| Headroom — rear | 38.0" |
| Cargo capacity (cu. ft.) | NA |
| Fuel capacity (gals.) | 25.0 |

## Models Available

| | Style Number | Base MSRP | Change from LY | Shipping Wt. (lbs.) | Production | Change from LY |
|---|---|---|---|---|---|---|
| LeBaron 4-Door Hardtop | YH43 | $6,940 | +4.19% | 4815 | 1,852 | -15.59% |
| TOTALS | | Avg. price $6,940 | +4.19% | | Production 1,852 | -15.59% |

**1968**

# LINCOLN

*"America's most distinguished motorcar."*

The luxury line of Ford Motor Company was pared down to two models once again. Now the 2-Door Coupe and the 4-Door Sedan were the sole bearers of the Lincoln nameplate. Outward physical appearance was changed minimally: There was the typical new grille and interior trim, and the 2-Door Coupe sported a revised roofline, which rounded forward at the bottom trailing edge of the rear quarter windows. Also, the Continental offered a revised instrument panel for 1968. Under the hood, the Lincoln 462 CID V8 engine powered Lincolns for the last time. Next year they would have a version of the new corporate 460 CID V8 engine. Gone this year was the unique 4-Door Convertible. During April of 1968 the first totally new Lincoln in nearly ten years would arrive, the Lincoln Continental Mark III. Officially sold as a 1969 model, the Mark III will not be covered in the 1968 section.

Continental 4-Door Sedan

Continental 2-Door Coupe new roofline and interior

**Model year production:** 39,134, down 14.31% from 1967.
**Domestic market share:** 0.46% (12th place).
**Base price range:** $5,736 to $5,970.
**Industry average base price:** $3,292.
**Lincoln average base price:** $5,853.
**Introduction date:** September 1967.
**Assembly plants:** Allen Park, MI (S); and Wixom, MI (Y).

**Data plate identification:** Eleven digit code read as follows: 8 for 1968; 2nd digit is assembly plant code; 2-digit model number (see listings); 5th digit is engine code; 400001 and up for serial number. *Example:* 8Y82H400001 is a 1968 Lincoln Continental 4-Door Sedan with a 462 CID V8 engine, serial number 400001, built in Wixom, MI.

## Powertrains

| Engine | Gross HP | Engine Code | Transmission Availability | Continental |
|---|---|---|---|---|
| 462 CID, 4-bbl., V8 | 340 | H | Turbo-Drive Automatic | S |

## Major Options

| | Continental |
|---|---|
| Air conditioning — manual | $505 |
| Automatic headlight dimmers | $46 |
| Tinted glass | $54 |
| Tilt steering wheel | $60 |
| 6-way power seat | S |
| AM/FM radio | $85 |
| Leather upholstery | $100 |
| Speed control | $97 |
| Remote control trunk release (sedans) | $53 |

Options common to most models. (S = Standard equipment.) Items may be standard equipment, optional at different pricing, or unavailable on certain models. This chart is only a guide.

## Paint Colors

| | Code |
|---|---|
| Black Satin | A |
| Royal Burgundy | B |
| Antique Beige Metallic | E |
| Belmont Green | G |
| Cameo Green | H |
| Aspen Green Metallic | I |
| Mediterranean Metallic | J |
| Foxcroft Silver Metallic | L |
| Arctic White | M |
| Platinum | N |
| Champagne Metallic | P |
| Huron Blue Metallic | Q |
| Grenoble Green Metallic | R |
| Ascot Gray Metallic | S |
| Cranberry | T |
| Teal Metallic | U |
| Daulton Blue | V |
| Mikado Yellow | W |
| Admiralty Blue Metallic | X |
| Chancery Gold Metallic | Y |
| Eton Gray Metallic | Z |
| Desert Sand | 6 |

# Continental

*"Only a Continental owner knows the complete assurance that comes with owning America's most distinguished motorcar."*

**Nameplate year of origin:** 1940 (1961 as a standard sedan nameplate).
**Current bodystyle lifespan:** 1961 through 1969 (major restyles in 1964 and 1966).
**Predecessor to this model:** Premiere (1958 to 1960).
**Replacement for this model:** Continental (1970 to 1979).
**Percentage of division's sales volume:** 100%.
**Corporate siblings:** None.
**Primary competition:** Cadillac de Ville and Imperial.
**Notable changes:** Revised hood and grille, minor trim and detail changes.
**Major standard equipment:** Cloth and leather front bench seat upholstery with folding center armrests front and rear, two-way power seat, trip odometer, walnut-tone instrument panel and door appliques, vanity mirror, looped-pile carpeting, variable-speed windshield wipers with washers, lined luggage compartment, power steering, power brakes, automatic transmission and 9.15 × 15 BSW tires.

## Measurements

| | |
|---|---|
| Wheelbase | 126.0" |
| Length | 221.0" |
| Width | 79.7" |
| Height | 54.9" |
| Legroom — front | 41.0" |
| Legroom — rear | 40.5" |
| Headroom — front | 39.4" |
| Headroom — rear | 38.6" |
| Luggage capacity (cu. ft.) | 18.0 |
| Fuel capacity (gals.) | 25.0 |

## Models Available

| | Style Number | Base MSRP | Change from LY | Shipping Wt. (lbs.) | Production | Change from LY |
|---|---|---|---|---|---|---|
| Continental 2-Door Hardtop | 81 | $5,736 | +3.30% | 4842 | 9,415 | -14.87% |
| Continental 4-Door Sedan | 82 | $5,970 | +3.02% | 4937 | 29,719 | -8.08% |
| TOTALS | | *Avg. price* $5,853 | -1.34% | | *Production* 39,134 | -14.31% |

# MERCURY

*"Thirty-three models with the fine car touch ... by the makers of Lincoln Continental."*

The 1968 Mercury line featured a totally new, and re-named, mid-size Montego line. There was a single Comet model left as an entry-level car. The new Montego was based upon the Ford Fairlane line, and as such it included the sporty new fastback models. Essentially, the new Montego MX replaced a combined Capri and Caliente line, the Montego replaced the base Comet line, and this year's Comet was a single model entry level 2-Door Hardtop. At the top end, the new fastback Cyclone replaced the 1967 vintage convertible in the lineup. A new engine powered the new mid-size line with the 302 CID V8 replacing the 289 CID V8 in the Montego and Cougar lines. The 302 V8 was a powerful and efficient engine that would live well into the 1990s. Styling for the new mid-size cars very closely resembled the full-size Mercury models.

The Cougar pony car received minor styling changes but added some important option packages. The GT and GT-E packages were available on any standard Cougar model. These high-performance cats featured Marauder 390 GT engines, special suspensions, power front disc brakes, dual exhausts and F70 × 14 Wide-Oval tires. The GT-E added special exterior trim with 7.0 litre badging, modified grille and taillamp design, beefier suspensions twin-scoop hood, automatic transmission, power steering, quad exhaust pipes and styled steel wheels.

Full-size Mercury models wore revised front and rear styling touches. The model line was not significantly changed, although the Breezeway Sedan models were discontinued this year. Also, the Brougham Sedan was demoted to an option package on the Park Lane 4-Door

Hardtop. The long-lived 410 CID V8 engine was dropped this season. A final note: the Mercury slogan refers to 33 models, but this includes some offered as option packages, such as the Brougham and the Cougar GT.

Cougar XR-7 2-Door Hardtop

Commuter 4-Door Wagon

Montego 4-Door Sedan

Montego MX 2-Door Convertible

Monterey 2-Door Convertible

Monterey 4-Door Sedan

Park Lane Brougham Interior

**Model year production:** 357,208, up 0.85% over 1967.
**Domestic market share:** 4.17% (8th place).
**Base price range:** $2,583 to $3,888.
**Industry average base price:** $3,292.
**Mercury average base price:** $3,224.
**Introduction date:** October 1967.
**Assembly plants:** Oakville, Ontario, Canada (B); Mahwah, NJ (E); Dearborn, MI (F); Lorain, OH (H); Los Angeles, CA (J); Wixom, MI (S); Wayne, MI (W); and St. Louis, MO (Z).

**Data plate identification:** Eleven digit code read as follows: 8 for 1968; 2nd digit is assembly plant code; 3rd digit is series (1 or 2 is Comet, 4 is Monterey, etc.); 4th digit is body style; 5th digit is engine code; 500001 and up for serial number. *Example:* 8W47Z100001 is a 1968 Mercury Monterey 2-Door Hardtop with a 390 CID V8 engine, serial number 500001, built in Wayne, MI.

## Powertrains

| Engine | Gross HP | Engine Code | Transmission Availability | Comet & Montego | Cougar | Monterey & Montclair | Marquis/ Park Lane |
|---|---|---|---|---|---|---|---|
| 200 CID Six, 1-bbl., 6-cyl. | 115 | T | 3-speed manual | S[2] | - | - | - |
| | | | Merc-O-Matic Automatic | $200[2] | - | - | - |
| 302 CID, 2-bbl., V8 | 210 | F | 3-speed manual | S[1]/$106[2] | S | - | - |
| | | | 4-speed manual | $184[1]/$300[2] | $184 | - | - |
| | | | Merc-O-Matic Automatic | $207[1]/$313[2] | $207 | - | - |
| Super 302 CID, 4-bbl., V8 | 230 | J | 3-speed manual | $[1]/$[2] | $ | - | - |
| | | | 4-speed manual | $[1]/$[2] | $ | - | - |
| | | | Merc-O-Matic Automatic | $[1]/$[2] | $ | - | - |
| 390 CID Marauder, 2-bbl., V8 | 265/280 | Y | 3-speed manual | $[1]/$[2] | - | S | - |
| | | | 4-speed manual | $[1]/$[2] | - | - | - |
| | | | Merc-O-Matic Automatic | $[1]/$[2] | - | $226 | - |
| 390 CID Marauder, 4-bbl., V8 | 315 | S | 3-speed manual | - | - | $ | S |
| | | | Merc-O-Matic Automatic | - | - | $ | $ |
| 390 CID GT, 4-bbl., V8 | 325 | Z | 3-speed manual | S (w/GT) | $ | - | - |
| | | | 3-sp. HD man. | - | $ | - | - |
| | | | 4-speed manual | $188 (w/GT) | $ | - | - |
| | | | Merc-O-Matic Automatic | $226 (w/GT) | $ | - | - |
| 427 CID, 4-bbl., V8 | 390 | W | Merc-O-Matic Automatic | - | - | $ | $ |
| 428 CID, 4-bbl., V8 | 340 | Q | Merc-O-Matic Automatic | - | - | $ | $ |

[1]Cyclone. [2]All but Cyclone.

## Major Options

| | Comet | Cougar | Monterey/ Montclair | Park Lane | Marquis |
|---|---|---|---|---|---|
| SelectAire air conditioning | $361 | $361 | $422 | $422 | $422 |
| Tinted glass | $35 | $30 | $43 | $43 | $43 |
| Remote-control trunk release | $13 | $13 | $11 | $11 | $11 |
| Speed control | - | $71 | $91 | $91 | $91 |
| Tilt steering wheel | - | $66 | $43 | $43 | $43 |
| Power steering | $95 | $95 | $116 | $116 | $116 |
| Power brakes | $42 | $42 | $43 | $43 | $43 |
| Power windows | $100 | $100 | $104 | $104 | $104 |
| Power seat — six-way | $62 | $62 | $97 | $97 | $97 |
| Bucket seats | $110 | S | $161 | S | S |
| Electric windshield wipers w/washer | $12 | $12 | $14 | $14 | $14 |
| Electric clock | $16 | $16 | $16— Monterey | S | S |
| Pushbutton AM radio | $59 | $59 | $61 | $61 | $61 |
| AM/FM stereo | $185 | $211 | $189 | $189 | $189 |
| White sidewall tires — std. sizes | $33 | $33 | $41 | $41 | $41 |

Options common to most models. (- = Not Available; S = Standard equipment.) Items may be standard equipment, optional at different pricing, or unavailable on certain models. This chart is only a guide.

## Paint Colors

| | Code |
|---|---|
| Onyx | A |
| Black Cherry | B |
| Nordic Blue Metallic | D |
| Madras Blue Metallic | F |
| Lime Frost Metallic | I |
| Polar White | M |
| Sea Foam Green | O |
| Pewter Beige Metallic | P |
| Glacier Blue Metallic | Q |
| Augusta Green Metallic | R |
| Cardinal Red | T |
| Caribbean Blue Metallic | U |
| Saxony | W |
| Wellington Blue Metallic | X |
| Grecian Gold Metallic | Y |
| Tahitian Rose Metallic | 2 |
| Calypso Coral | 3 |
| Fawn | 6 |

1968

# Cougar

*"No cat leads two lives so beautifully!"*

**Nameplate year of origin:** 1967.
**Current bodystyle lifespan:** 1967 through 1968.
**Predecessor to this model:** None.
**Replacement for this model:** Cougar (1969 to 1970).
**Percentage of division's sales volume:** 31.84%.
**Corporate siblings:** Ford Mustang.
**Primary competition:** AMC Javelin, Chevrolet Camaro, Plymouth Barracuda and Pontiac Firebird.
**Notable changes:** All-new model for 1967.
**Major standard equipment:** All-vinyl front bucket seats, full carpeting, hidden headlights, rocker panel moldings, and E70 × 14 BSW tires.

## Measurements

| | |
|---|---|
| Wheelbase | 111.0" |
| Length | 190.3" |
| Width | 71.3" |
| Height | 51.7" |
| Legroom — front | 42.7" |
| Legroom — rear | 29.8" |
| Headroom — front | 37.3" |
| Headroom — rear | 35.8" |
| Cargo capacity (cu. ft.) | 9.2 |
| Fuel capacity (gals.) | 17.0 |

## Models Available

| | Style Number | Base MSRP | Change from LY | Shipping Wt. (lbs.) | Production | Change from LY |
|---|---|---|---|---|---|---|
| Cougar 2-Door Hardtop | 91 | $2,933 | +2.88% | 3117 | 81,014 | -34.49% |
| Cougar XR-7 2-Door Hardtop | 93 | $3,232 | +4.90% | 3157 | 32,712 | +20.17% |
| TOTALS | | *Avg. price* $3,083 | +3.95% | | *Production* 113,726 | -24.64% |

# Comet & Montego

*"Beautifully on target for style and economy."*

**Nameplate year of origin:** 1960.
**Current bodystyle lifespan:** 1968 through 1969.
**Predecessor to this model:** Comet (1966 to 1967).
**Replacement for this model:** Montego (1970 to 1971).
**Percentage of division's sales volume:** 32.89%.
**Corporate siblings:** Ford Fairlane.
**Primary competition:** Buick Special, Dodge Coronet, Oldsmobile F-85, and Pontiac Tempest.
**Notable changes:** Completely restyled. New Montego nameplates replacing Capri and Caliente.
**Major standard equipment:** Nylon and vinyl front bench seat, rubber floor covering, dome light, bright metal front, rear and side window trim, and 7.35 × 14 BSW tires. Montego adds: Full carpeting, deluxe interior trim, rocker moldings, and 7.75 × 14 BSW tires. Montego MX adds: Cloth and vinyl luxury interior trim (all-vinyl on convertible), deluxe steering wheel, simulated walnut interior trim, power top on convertible, and additional sound deadening materials. Cyclone adds: All vinyl bench seat, power front disc brakes, tinted rear window (fastback), specific Cyclone exterior trim, heavy duty suspension, and engine dress-up kit.

## Measurements

| | Cars | Wagons |
|---|---|---|
| Wheelbase | 116.0" | 113.0" |
| Length | 206.1" | 203.9" |
| Width | 76.0" | 76.0" |
| Height | 55.0" | 56.0" |
| Legroom — front | 42.5" | 42.0" |
| Legroom — rear | 36.0" | 34.5" |
| Headroom — front | 38.5" | 38.5" |
| Headroom — rear | 37.5" | 39.0" |
| Cargo capacity (cu. ft.) | 18.0 | 85.0 |
| Fuel capacity (gals.) | 20.0 | 20.0 |

## Models Available

| | Style Number | Base MSRP | Change from LY | Shipping Wt. (lbs.) | Production | Change from LY |
|---|---|---|---|---|---|---|
| Comet 2-Door Hardtop | 01 | $2,583 | NEW | 3272 | 16,693 | NEW |
| Montego 2-Door Hardtop | 07 | $2,658 | +8.09% | 3251 | 15,002 | +28.54% |
| Montego 4-Door Sedan | 06 | $2,609 | +7.10% | 3176 | 18,492 | +99.01% |
| Montego MX 2-Door Hardtop | 11 | $2,781 | +8.72% | 3275 | 25,827 | +159.15% |
| Montego MX 2-Door Convertible | 12 | $3,040 | +7.88% | 3429 | 3,248 | +111.05% |
| Montego MX 4-Door Sedan | 10 | $2,763 | +8.99% | 3201 | 15,264 | +66.76% |
| Montego MX 4-Door Wagon | 08 | $2,981 | +4.93% | 3549 | 9,328 | +197.07% |
| Cyclone 2-Door Hardtop | 17 | $2,768 | +1.13% | 3208 | 1,368 | -77.58% |
| Cyclone 2-Door Fastback | 15 | $2,768 | NEW | 3254 | 12,260 | NEW |
| TOTALS | Avg. price | $2,772 | +6.62% | Production | 117,482 | +44.80% |

# Monterey

*"Fine car touches in every detail."*

**Nameplate year of origin:** 1952.
**Current bodystyle lifespan:** 1967 through 1968.
**Predecessor to this model:** Monterey (1965 to 1966).
**Replacement for this model:** Monterey (1969 to 1970).
**Percentage of division's sales volume:** 18.20%.
**Corporate siblings:** Ford Galaxie/LTD.
**Primary competition:** Buick Wildcat, Dodge Monaco, Oldsmobile 88 and Pontiac Executive/Bonneville.
**Notable changes:** New grille and rear styling.
**Major standard equipment:** Cloth and vinyl front bench seat, full carpeting, wood-grain trim on instrument panel, courtesy light group, rocker panel moldings, bright exterior front and rear window trim and 8.15 × 15 BSW tires.

## Measurements

| | Cars | Commuter |
|---|---|---|
| Wheelbase | 123.0" | 119.0" |
| Length | 220.1" | 215.4" |
| Width | 77.9" | 77.9" |
| Height | 56.0" | 56.8" |
| Legroom — front | 41.9" | 41.9" |
| Legroom — rear | 37.6" | 36.8" |
| Headroom — front | 38.9" | 39.0" |
| Headroom — rear | 37.7" | 40.0" |
| Cargo capacity (cu. ft.) | 19.1 | 91.3 |
| Fuel capacity (gals.) | 24.0 | 24.0 |

**1968**

## Models Available

| | Style Number | Base MSRP | Change from LY | Shipping Wt. (lbs.) | Production | Change from LY |
|---|---|---|---|---|---|---|
| Monterey 2-Door Fastback | 47 | $3,133 | +4.96% | 3854 | 15,145 | -10.44% |
| Monterey 2-Door Convertible | 45 | $3,436 | +3.78% | 3977 | 1,515 | -43.32% |
| Monterey 4-Door Sedan | 44 | $3,052 | +5.10% | 3895 | 30,727 | +102.46% |
| Monterey 4-Door Hardtop | 48 | $3,207 | +4.84% | 3892 | 8,927 | +11.41% |
| Commuter 4-Door, 2-Seat Wagon | 72 | $3,441 | +4.62% | 4212 | 3,497 | -55.72% |
| Commuter 4-Door, 3-Seat Wagon | 72 | $3,569 | NEW | 4331 | 5,191 | NEW |
| TOTALS | Avg. price | $3,306 | +7.51% | Production | 65,002 | +14.88% |

# Montclair

*"Make beautiful tracks anywhere."*

**Nameplate year of origin:** 1955.
**Current bodystyle lifespan:** 1967 through 1968.
**Predecessor to this model:** Montclair (1965 to 1966).
**Replacement for this model:** Monterey Custom (1969 to 1970).
**Percentage of division's sales volume:** 4.13%.
**Corporate siblings:** Ford Galaxie/LTD.
**Primary competition:** Buick Wildcat, Dodge Monaco, Oldsmobile 88 and Pontiac Bonneville.
**Notable changes:** New grille and rear styling.
**Major standard equipment:** Cloth and vinyl front bench seat, full carpeting, wood-grain trim on instrument panel, electric clock, courtesy light group, body side moldings, bright exterior front, rear and side window trim, deluxe wheel covers, and 8.15 × 15 BSW tires.

## Measurements

| | |
|---|---|
| Wheelbase | 123.0" |
| Length | 220.1" |
| Width | 77.9" |
| Height | 56.0" |
| Legroom — front | 41.9" |
| Legroom — rear | 37.6" |
| Headroom — front | 38.9" |
| Headroom — rear | 37.7" |
| Cargo capacity (cu. ft.) | 19.1 |
| Fuel capacity (gals.) | 24.0 |

## Models Available

| | Style Number | Base MSRP | Change from LY | Shipping Wt. (lbs.) | Production | Change from LY |
|---|---|---|---|---|---|---|
| Montclair 2-Door Fastback | 57 | $3,387 | +4.41% | 3882 | 3,497 | -15.08% |
| Montclair 4-Door Sedan | 54 | $3,331 | +4.52% | 3897 | 7,255 | +25.45% |
| Montclair 4-Door Hardtop | 58 | $3,459 | +4.31% | 3907 | 4,008 | -31.72% |
| TOTALS | | Avg. price $3,392 | +4.89% | | Production 14,760 | -25.92% |

# Park Lane

*"Modern styling and luxurious appointments with a quiet ride ... that's a better idea!"*

**Nameplate year of origin:** 1958.
**Current bodystyle lifespan:** 1967 through 1968.
**Predecessor to this model:** Park Lane (1965 to 1966).
**Replacement for this model:** Marquis (1969 to 1970).
**Percentage of division's sales volume:** 11.83%.
**Corporate siblings:** Ford Galaxie/LTD.
**Primary competition:** Buick Wildcat, Chrysler Newport, Oldsmobile 88 and Pontiac Bonneville.
**Notable changes:** New grille and rear styling.
**Major standard equipment:** Cloth and vinyl front bench seat, full carpeting, wood-grain trim on instrument panel, electric clock, courtesy light group, body side moldings, bright exterior front, rear and side window trim, deluxe wheel covers, and 8.15 × 15 BSW tires. Colony Park wagons adds: exterior wood-grain vinyl trim, and power tailgate window.

## Measurements

| | Cars | Colony Park |
|---|---|---|
| Wheelbase | 123.0" | 119.0" |
| Length | 220.1" | 215.4" |
| Width | 77.9" | 77.9" |
| Height | 56.0" | 56.8" |
| Legroom — front | 41.9" | 41.9" |
| Legroom — rear | 37.6" | 36.8" |
| Headroom — front | 38.9" | 39.0" |
| Headroom — rear | 37.7" | 40.0" |
| Cargo capacity (cu. ft.) | 19.1 | 91.3 |
| Fuel capacity (gals.) | 24.0 | 24.0 |

## Models Available

| | Style Number | Base MSRP | Change from LY | Shipping Wt. (lbs.) | Production | Change from LY |
|---|---|---|---|---|---|---|
| Park Lane 2-Door Fastback | 67 | $3,575 | -4.72% | 3955 | 2,584 | +17.67% |

| | Style Number | Base MSRP | Change from LY | Shipping Wt. (lbs.) | Production | Change from LY |
|---|---|---|---|---|---|---|
| Park Lane 2-Door Convertible | 65 | $3,822 | -4.07% | 4122 | 1,112 | -6.63% |
| Park Lane 4-Door Sedan | 64 | $3,552 | -4.93% | 4019 | 7,008 | +68.34% |
| Park Lane 4-Door Hardtop | 68 | $3,647 | -4.68% | 4000 | 10,390 | +91.98% |
| Colony Park 4-Door, 2-Seat Wagon | 76 | $3,760 | +2.82% | 4259 | 5,674 | -69.63% |
| Colony Park 4-Door, DFRS* Wagon | 76 | $3,888 | NEW | 4295 | 15,505 | NEW |
| TOTALS | Avg. price | $3,707 | -2.22% | Production | 42,273 | +33.60% |

*Dual facing rear seats

# Marquis

*"A uniquely luxurious 2-door hardtop."*

**Nameplate year of origin:** 1967.
**Current bodystyle lifespan:** 1967 through 1968.
**Predecessor to this model:** Park Lane (1965 to 1966).
**Replacement for this model:** Marquis (1969 to 1970).
**Percentage of division's sales volume:** 1.11%.
**Corporate siblings:** Ford Galaxie/LTD.
**Primary competition:** Buick Wildcat, Chrysler Newport, Oldsmobile 88 and Pontiac Bonneville.
**Notable changes:** New grille and rear styling.
**Major standard equipment:** Unique Marquis upholstered front bench seat, full carpeting, wood-grain trim on instrument panel, electric clock, courtesy light group, vinyl top, special exterior trim with five lower body tape stripes, deluxe wheel covers, spare tire cover, and 8.15 × 15 BSW tires.

## Measurements

| | |
|---|---|
| Wheelbase | 123.0" |
| Length | 220.1" |
| Width | 77.9" |
| Height | 54.9" |
| Legroom — front | 41.9" |
| Legroom — rear | 33.3" |
| Headroom — front | 37.9" |
| Headroom — rear | 37.4" |
| Cargo capacity (cu. ft.) | 18.9 |
| Fuel capacity (gals.) | 25.0 |

## Models Available

| | Style Number | Base MSRP | Change from LY | Shipping Wt. (lbs.) | Production | Change from LY |
|---|---|---|---|---|---|---|
| Marquis 2-Door Hardtop | 69 | $3,685 | -7.62% | 3987 | 3,965 | -39.09% |
| TOTALS | Avg. price | $3,685 | -7.62% | Production | 3,965 | -39.09% |

**1968**

# OLDSMOBILE

*"'68 Youngmobiles from Oldsmobile."*

New mid-size models were the feature attraction at Oldsmobile when the new models were released. As with its sister GM divisions, the F-85, Cutlass, 4-4-2 and Vista-Cruiser all sported more rounded contours and, in Oldsmobile's case, three different wheelbases, depending upon the model. The new styling continued placement of the park-ing lamp between the headlamps and the narrow grille opening between the headlamps. At the back, narrow horizontal taillamps were placed onto the top edge of the rear bumper. Two-door models were given a fastback look, while four-door models had a slightly more formal design. Numerous model changes were made for the new year. The base F-85 wagon was dropped, as were the Cutlass Supreme 2-Door Club Coupe and Convertible. Mid-range Cutlass models were split into two monikers, the two-doors being called Cutlass S, while the four-doors went by Cutlass. After four years, the 4-4-2 officially became its own model. Content was much the same as when it had been an option package. Under the hood of the restyled line, the 350 CID V8 replaced the 330 CID engine as the base V8 powerplant.

Toronado and the full-size Oldsmobile line under-went some face lifting. The Toronado wore an all-new "grille within bumper" style that was starting to become commonplace among many cars. Other full-size models had a slightly more refined frontal style. Model changes included the discontinuance of the Delmont 330 line and the Delta 88 Convertible. The Delmont 425 was renamed the Delmont 88. All models that previously used the 330 V8, now had the new 350 V8 and the 425 V8 engine was replaced by a new 455 Rocket V8.

4-4-2 2-Door Hardtop

Ninety-Eight 4-Door Luxury Sedan

Cutlass Supreme 4-Door Hardtop

Delmont 88 4-Door Hardtop

Delta 88 Custom 2-Door Hardtop

Toronado 2-Door Hardtop

Vista-Cruiser 4-Door Wagon

**Model year production:** 562,469, up 8.86% over 1967.
**Domestic market share:** 6.57% (7th place).
**Base price range:** $2957 to $5340.
**Industry average base price:** $3,292.
**Oldsmobile average base price:** $3,382.
**Introduction date:** September, 1967.
**Assembly plants:** Atlanta, GA (G); Fremont, CA (Z); Lansing, MI (M); Arlington, TX (R); Fairfax, KS (X); and Linden, NJ (F).

**Data plate identification:** Thirteen digit code read as follows: 1st digit 3 = Oldsmobile; 2nd through 5th digits identify series/body style number; 8 = 1968 year; 7th digit is assembly plant code; 100001 and up for serial number (except Toronado is 600001). 364398X100001 is a 1968 Oldsmobile Delta 88 4-Door Hardtop with a 455 CID V8, serial number 100001, built in Fairfax, KS. *Example:* 364398X100001 is a 1968 Oldsmobile Delta 88 4-Door Hardtop with a 455 CID V8, serial number 100001, built in Fairfax, KS.

## Powertrains

| Engine | Gross HP | Engine Code | Transmission Availability | Cutlass & 4-4-2 | Supreme & Vista-Cruiser | Delmont 88 & Delta 88 | Toro. & 98 |
|---|---|---|---|---|---|---|---|
| 250 CID, 1-bbl., 6-cyl. | 155 | V | 3-speed manual | S* | - | - | - |
| | | | Jetaway Automatic | $174* | - | - | - |
| 350 CID, 2-bbl., V8 | 250 | Q/S | 3-speed manual | $111* | S (V.Cr.) | S (base) | - |
| | | | 4-speed manual | $296* | $185 (V.Cr.) | - | - |
| | | | Jetaway Automatic | $296* | - | $185 (base) | |
| | | | Turbo Hydra-matic 350 | - | $227 (V.Cr.) | $227 (base) | |
| 350 CID, 4-bbl., V8 | 310 | Q/S | 3-speed manual | $158* | S (Supr.)/ $47 (V.Cr.) | - | - |
| | | | 4-speed manual* | $344* | $185 (Supr.)/ $232 (V.Cr.) | - | |
| | | | Jetaway Automatic | $344* | - | - | |
| | | | Turbo Hydra-matic 350 | $365* | $206 (Supr.)/ $274 (V.Cr.) | - | - |
| 400 CID, 4-bbl., V8 | 350 (325 w/Auto.) | Q/O | 3-speed manual | S** | - | - | - |
| | | | 4-speed manual | $185** | - | - | - |
| | | | Turbo Hydra-matic 400 | $227** | $348 (V.Cr.) | - | - |
| 400 CID — W30/W31, 4-bbl., V8 | 360 | Q/O | 3-speed manual | $310*/$264** | - | - | - |
| | | | 4-speed manual | $495*/$449** | - | - | - |
| | | | Turbo Hydra-matic 400 | $537*/$491** | - | - | - |
| 455 CID Rocket, 2-bbl., V8 | 310 | U | 3-speed manual | - | - | S (ex. Base)/ $63 (base) | - |
| | | | Turbo Hydra-matic 400 | - | - | $227 (ex. base)/ $290 (base) | |
| 455 CID Rocket, 4-bbl., V8 | 365/375*** | U | 3-speed manual | - | - | $47 (ex. base)/ $111 (base) | - |
| | | | Turbo Hydra-matic 400 | - | - | $274 (ex. base)/ $338 (base) | S |
| 455 CID Hi-Po Rocket, 4-bbl., V8 | 390/400*** | U | 3-speed manual | - | - | $78 (ex. base)/ $141 (base) | - |
| | | | Turbo Hydra-matic 400 | - | - | $305 (ex. base)/ $368 (base) | $47*** |

*F-85 and Cutlass only.    **4-4-2 only.    ***Toronado only.

## Major Options

| | Cutlass | Vista-Cruiser | Delta 88 | Ninety-Eight | Toronado |
|---|---|---|---|---|---|
| Air conditioning | $376 | $376 | $422 | $422 | $422 |
| Electronic cruise control (V8 only) | $58 | $58 | $63 | $63 | $63 |
| Soft Ray tinted glass | $39 | $39 | $44 | $44 | $47 |
| Deck lid remote release | $14 | - | $14 | $14 | $14 |
| Tilt-Away steering wheel | $45 | $45 | $45 | $45 | $45 |

## Paint Colors

| | Code |
|---|---|
| Ebony Black | A |
| Twilight Teal Metallic* | B |
| Provincial White | C |
| Sapphire Blue Metallic | D |
| Nocturne Blue Metallic | E |
| Teal Frost Metallic | F |

| | Cutlass | Vista-Cruiser | Delta 88 | Ninety-Eight | Toronado |
|---|---|---|---|---|---|
| Power steering— variable-ratio | $105 | $105 | $116 | S | S |
| Power brakes | $42 | $42 | $42 | S | S |
| Power driver's seat/ Bench seat | $74 | $74 | $100 | $74–$100* | $74 |
| Power windows | $105 | $105 | $111 | S/$111* | $111 |
| AM radio | $70 | $70 | $87 | $87 | $87 |
| AM/FM stereo | $238 | $238 | $238 | $238 | $238 |
| Front seat console | $61 | – | $62 | – | $62 |
| Front bucket seats | $ | – | $ | – | $ |
| Vinyl roof | $100 | – | $121** | $137 | $126 |
| White sidewall tires (base size) | $32–40 | $44 | $44 | $49 | $49 |
| Wheel trim covers | $21 | $21 | S | S | S |

| Color | Code |
|---|---|
| Willow Gold Metallic | G |
| Ocean Turquoise Metallic | K |
| Teal Blue Metallic | L |
| Cinnamon Bronze Metallic | M |
| Burgundy Metallic | N |
| Silver Green Metallic | P |
| Scarlet | R |
| Jade Gold Metallic | S |
| Ivory | T |
| Juneau Gray Metallic | V |
| Silver Beige Metallic* | W |
| Buckskin* | X |
| Saffron | Y |
| Peruvian Silver Metallic* | Z |

Options common to most models. (– = Not Available; S = Standard equipment.) Items may be standard equipment, optional at different pricing, or unavailable on certain models. This chart is only a guide.

*4-Door Town Sedan only.    **Standard on Royale.

*Available only on Toronado.

# Cutlass, F-85 and 4-4-2

*"For doing the things you do, and going the places you go."*

**Nameplate year of origin:** 1961 (F85); 1962 (Cutlass as F-85 model designation); 1955 (Cutlass Show car).

**Current bodystyle lifespan:** 1968 through 1972.

**Predecessor to this model:** F-85/Cutlass (1966 to 1967).

**Replacement for this model:** Cutlass (1973 to 1977).

**Percentage of division's sales volume:** 42.49%.

**Corporate siblings:** Buick Special/Skylark, Chevrolet Chevelle, Pontiac Tempest/LeMans.

**Primary competition:** AMC Rebel, Dodge Coronet and Mercury Comet/Montego.

**Notable changes:** Completely redesigned.

**Major standard equipment:** Cloth and vinyl front bench seat, aluminized exhaust system, and 7.75 × 14 BSW tires. Cutlass adds: Front and rear armrests, full carpeting, deluxe steering wheel, and exterior chrome trim moldings. Cutlass S adds: Deluxe bench seat (bucket seats on convertible) and simulated chrome hood louvers. Cutlass Supreme adds: Woodgrain interior trim, all-vinyl bench seats, and unique grille. 4-4-2 adds: All-vinyl bucket seats, floor shifter, 400 CID V8 engine, dual exhausts, heavy duty suspension, and F70 × 14 Wide-Oval Redline tires.

## Measurements

| | 2-Doors | 4-Doors | Wagon |
|---|---|---|---|
| Wheelbase | 112.0" | 116.0" | 116.0" |
| Length | 201.6" | 205.6" | 213.3" |
| Width | 76.8" | 76.8" | 76.8" |
| Height | 53.5" | 53.5" | 54.8" |
| Legroom — front | 42.7" | 42.8" | 42.8" |
| Legroom — rear | 32.7" | 35.1" | 34.6" |
| Headroom — front | 37.6" | 38.9" | 38.4" |
| Headroom — rear | 36.3" | 37.1" | 38.3" |
| Luggage capacity (cu. ft.) | 17.5 | 17.5 | 87.5 |
| Fuel capacity (gals.) | 20.0 | 20.0 | 20.0 |

## Models Available

| | Style Number | Base MSRP | Change from LY | Shipping Wt. (lbs.) | Production | Change from LY |
|---|---|---|---|---|---|---|
| F-85 2-Door Sport Coupe | 3177 | $2,512 | +4.23% | 3062 | 9,478 | -21.34% |
| F-85 4-Door Town Sedan | 3169 | $2,560 | +4.19% | 3108 | 5,831 | -23.11% |
| Cutlass 4-Door Town Sedan | 3569 | $2,674 | +4.78% | 3143 | 27,299 | -12.73% |
| Cutlass 4-Door Hardtop | 3539 | $2,804 | +4.51% | 3193 | 8,104 | +1.45% |
| Cutlass 4-Door, 2-Seat Wagon | 3535 | $2,969 | +4.25% | 3473 | 9,645 | +120.41% |
| Cutlass S 2-Door Sports Coupe | 3577 | $2,632 | NEW | 3064 | 15,767 | NEW |
| Cutlass S 2-Door Hardtop | 3587 | $2,696 | +4.74% | 3108 | 61,069 | +406.84% |

| | Style Number | Base MSRP | Change from LY | Shipping Wt. (lbs.) | Production | Change from LY |
|---|---|---|---|---|---|---|
| Cutlass S 2-Door Convertible | 3567 | $2,949 | +6.46% | 3161 | 14,087 | +224.81% |
| Cutlass Supreme 2-Door Hardtop | 4287 | $2,982 | +5.33% | 3312 | 33,518 | -42.07% |
| Cutlass Supreme 4-Dr. Town Sdn. | 4269 | $2,884 | +5.80% | 3335 | 5,524 | -33.81% |
| Cutlass Supreme 4-Door Hardtop | 4239 | $3,057 | +5.41% | 3421 | 15,067 | -33.25% |
| 4-4-2 2-Door Sport Coupe | 4477 | $3,087 | NEW | 3502 | 4,282 | NEW |
| 4-4-2 2-Door Hardtop | 4487 | $3,150 | NEW | 3512 | 24,183 | NEW |
| 4-4-2 2-Door Convertible | 4467 | $3,341 | NEW | 3580 | 5,142 | NEW |
| TOTALS | Avg. price | $2,878 | +6.24% | Production | 238,996 | +18.33% |

# Vista-Cruiser

*"Whopping new Youngmobile wagon."*

**Nameplate year of origin:** 1964.
**Current bodystyle lifespan:** 1968 through 1972.
**Predecessor to this model:** None.
**Replacement for this model:** Vista-Cruiser (1973 to 1977).
**Percentage of division's sales volume:** 6.43%.
**Corporate siblings:** Buick SportWagon.
**Primary competition:** AMC Ambassador, Dodge Coronet, and Mercury Montego.
**Notable changes:** Completely redesigned.
**Major standard equipment:** All-vinyl front bench seats, full carpeting, Deluxe steering wheel, wood-grain exterior trim, Vista-roof windows, and H78 × 14 BSW tires.

## Measurements

| | |
|---|---|
| Wheelbase | 121.0" |
| Length | 217.5" |
| Width | 76.7" |
| Height | 56.8" |
| Legroom — front | 42.7" |
| Legroom — rear | 37.7" |
| Headroom — front | 38.5" |
| Headroom — rear | 39.4" |
| Luggage capacity (cu. ft.) | 100.5 |
| Fuel capacity (gals.) | 20.0 |

## Models Available

| | Style Number | Base MSRP | Change from LY | Shipping Wt. (lbs.) | Production | Change from LY |
|---|---|---|---|---|---|---|
| Vista-Cruiser Cust. 4-Dr., 2-S. Wgn. | 4855 | $3,367 | +4.31% | 3917 | 13,375 | +40.60% |
| Vista-Cruiser Cust. 4-Dr., 3-S. Wgn. | 4865 | $3,508 | +4.13% | 4027 | 22,768 | +48.88% |
| TOTALS | Avg. price | $3,438 | +5.98% | Production | 36,143 | +31.17% |

# Delmont 88

*"Lowest-priced of all the full-size '68 Youngmobiles."*

**Nameplate year of origin:** 1967 (88 series started 1949).
**Current bodystyle lifespan:** 1967 through 1968.
**Predecessor to this model:** Jetstar 88/Dynamic 88 (1965 to 1966).
**Replacement for this model:** Delta 88 (1969 to 1970).
**Percentage of division's sales volume:** 11.84%.
**Corporate siblings:** Buick LeSabre/Wildcat, Chevrolet Impala/Caprice, Pontiac Catalina/Bonneville.
**Primary competition:** Dodge Polara, Ford LTD, and Mercury Monterey.
**Notable changes:** Revised grille and trim and detail changes.
**Major standard equipment:** Cloth-and-vinyl bench seat, full carpeting, full wheel covers, and 8.55 × 14 BSW tires.

## Measurements

| | |
|---|---|
| Wheelbase | 123.0" |
| Length | 217.8" |
| Width | 80.0" |
| Height | 55.5" |
| Legroom — front | 42.7" |
| Legroom — rear | 39.0" |
| Headroom — front | 38.9" |
| Headroom — rear | 37.7" |
| Luggage capacity (cu. ft.) | 19.0 |
| Fuel capacity (gals.) | 25.0 |

## Models Available

| | Style Number | Base MSRP | Change from LY | Shipping Wt. (lbs.) | Production | Change from LY |
|---|---|---|---|---|---|---|
| Delmont 88 2-Door Hardtop | 5487 | $3,202 | +2.43% | 3844 | 18,391 | +10.33% |
| Delmont 88 2-Door Convertible | 5467 | $3,515 | +1.53% | 3916 | 2,812 | -20.23% |
| Delmont 88 4-Door Town Sedan | 5469 | $3,146 | +2.44% | 3873 | 24,365 | +13.27% |
| Delmont 88 4-Door Hardtop | 5439 | $3,278 | +2.37% | 3928 | 21,056 | -3.89% |
| TOTALS | | Avg. price $3,285 | +4.19% | | Production 66,624 | -33.43% |

# Delta 88

*"For the family that likes its action king-size and its car to match."*

**Nameplate year of origin:** 1965 (88 series started 1949).
**Current bodystyle lifespan:** 1967 through 1968.
**Predecessor to this model:** Dynamic/Delta 88 (1965 to 1966).
**Replacement for this model:** Delta 88 (1969 to 1970).
**Percentage of division's sales volume:** 18.22%.
**Corporate siblings:** Buick LeSabre/Wildcat, Chevrolet Impala/Caprice, Pontiac Catalina/Bonneville.
**Primary competition:** Dodge Monaco and Mercury Montclair/Park Lane.
**Notable changes:** Revised grille and trim and detail changes.
**Major standard equipment:** All-vinyl bench seat with fold-down center armrest (except Town Sedan), full carpeting, deluxe steering wheel, glove box and courtesy lamps, full wheel covers, and 8.55 × 14 BSW tires. Custom adds: Strato-Bench seat and full-length bodyside molding.

### Measurements

| | |
|---|---|
| Wheelbase | 123.0" |
| Length | 217.8" |
| Width | 80.0" |
| Height | 55.5" |
| Legroom — front | 42.7" |
| Legroom — rear | 39.0" |
| Headroom — front | 38.9" |
| Headroom — rear | 37.7" |
| Luggage capacity (cu. ft.) | 19.0 |
| Fuel capacity (gals.) | 25.0 |

## Models Available

| | Style Number | Base MSRP | Change from LY | Shipping Wt. (lbs.) | Production | Change from LY |
|---|---|---|---|---|---|---|
| Delta 88 2-Door Hardtop | 6487 | $3,449 | +4.20% | 3950 | 18,501 | +27.85% |
| Delta 88 4-Door Town Sdn. | 6469 | $3,357 | +4.32% | 3979 | 33,689 | +47.95% |
| Delta 88 4-Door Hardtop | 6439 | $3,525 | +4.11% | 4038 | 30,048 | +37.15% |
| Delta 88 Custom 2-Door Hardtop | 6687 | $3,661 | +3.95% | 3982 | 9,540 | -21.75% |
| Delta 88 Custom 4-Door Hardtop | 6639 | $3,721 | +3.88% | 4059 | 10,727 | -25.02% |
| TOTALS | | Avg. price $3,543 | +2.87% | | Production 102,505 | +15.05% |

# Ninety-Eight

*"With impressive looks and impeccable appointments to substantiate its claim as Oldsmobile's finest."*

**Nameplate year of origin:** 1941.
**Current bodystyle lifespan:** 1967 through 1968.
**Predecessor to this model:** Ninety-Eight (1965 to 1966).
**Replacement for this model:** Ninety-Eight (1969 to 1970).
**Percentage of division's sales volume:** 16.31%.
**Corporate siblings:** Buick Electra and Cadillac Calais/de Ville.
**Primary competition:** Chrysler New Yorker and Mercury Marquis.

### Measurements

| | |
|---|---|
| Wheelbase | 126.0" |
| Length | 223.7" |
| Width | 80.0" |
| Height | 55.8" |
| Legroom — front | 42.2" |
| Legroom — rear | 40.5" |

**Notable changes:** Revised grille and trim and detail changes.

**Major standard equipment:** Cloth and vinyl bench seat with fold-down center armrest, full carpeting on floor and kick panels, electric clock, power windows and two-way power seat (except Town Sedan), trunk lamp, trunk mat, full wheel covers, rear fender skirts, power steering, power front disc brakes, 8.85 × 14 BSW tires. Luxury Sedan adds: special design interior, special door pulls, and rear center arm rests.

## Measurements (cont.)

| | |
|---|---|
| Headroom — front | 39.6" |
| Headroom — rear | 38.2" |
| Luggage capacity (cu. ft.) | 20.1 |
| Fuel capacity (gals.) | 25.0 |

## Models Available

| | Style Number | Base MSRP | Change from LY | Shipping Wt. (lbs.) | Production | Change from LY |
|---|---|---|---|---|---|---|
| Ninety-Eight 2-Door Hardtop | 8457 | $4,360 | +3.46% | 4185 | 15,319 | +46.23% |
| Ninety-Eight 2-Door Convertible | 8467 | $4,618 | +2.67% | 4264 | 3,942 | +4.59% |
| Ninety-Eight 4-Door Town Sedan | 8469 | $4,155 | +3.64% | 4197 | 10,584 | +18.92% |
| Ninety-Eight 4-Door Hardtop | 8439 | $4,422 | +3.41% | 4278 | 21,147 | +20.61% |
| Ninety-Eight Luxury 4-Door Sedan | 8669 | $4,497 | +3.36% | 4273 | 40,755 | +14.77% |
| TOTALS | | Avg. price $4,410 | +3.28% | | Production 91,747 | +20.42% |

# Toronado

*"The front-wheel-drive Youngmobile. With an exciting new look outside. Acres of new luxury inside. Smooth new ride below. And up front, the added performance of a 455-cubic-inch Rocket V8 engine."*

**Nameplate year of origin:** 1966.
**Current bodystyle lifespan:** 1966 through 1970.
**Predecessor to this model:** None.
**Replacement for this model:** Toronado (1971 to 1978).
**Percentage of division's sales volume:** 4.70%.
**Corporate siblings:** Buick Riviera and Cadillac Eldorado.
**Primary competition:** Imperial LeBaron Coupe and Ford Thunderbird.
**Notable changes:** Major restyling.
**Major standard equipment:** All-vinyl bench seat, deep-pile carpeting, electric clock, LH outside rearview mirror, front wheel drive, power brakes, power steering and 8.85 × 15 BSW tires.

## Measurements

| | |
|---|---|
| Wheelbase | 119.0" |
| Length | 211.4" |
| Width | 78.5" |
| Height | 52.8" |
| Legroom — front | 41.3" |
| Legroom — rear | 36.6" |
| Headroom — front | 37.9" |
| Headroom — rear | 37.3" |
| Luggage capacity (cu. ft.) | 14.5 |
| Fuel capacity (gals.) | 24.0 |

**1968**

## Models Available

| | Style Number | Base MSRP | Change from LY | Shipping Wt. (lbs.) | Production | Change from LY |
|---|---|---|---|---|---|---|
| Toronado 2-Door Hardtop | 9487 | $4,750 | +1.63% | 4322 | 26,454 | +1394.58% |
| TOTALS | | Avg. price $4,750 | -0.47% | | Production 26,454 | +21.40% |

# PLYMOUTH

*"The Plymouth Win-You-Over Beat Goes On."*

For 1968, Plymouth introduced an all-new mid-size line. The "mid-size five," as they were known, consisted of the Belvedere, Satellite, Sport Satellite, Road Runner and GTX. Exterior styling was evolutionary, featuring more curves and fewer straight lines. Underneath, 2-Door and 4-Door models rode on differing wheelbases, as GM mid-size cars did this year. Numerous model changes accompanied the introduction of the new styling. At the top of the list was an all-new, more affordable performance model, the Road Runner. It was equipped similarly (with a few additions) to the base Belvedere, but under the hood lurked a 383 CID V8 engine. Offered only in 2-Door Coupe or Hardtop form, the Road Runner was more affordable than the highly equipped GTX. Other model changes included

the renaming of the Belvedere I series to Belvedere and the elimination of the former base Belvedere wagon. The old Belvedere II line became the Satellite, and the former Satellite line was now known as the Sport Satellite. A top of the line Satellite Sport Wagon, with the requisite wood grain exterior trim, was new for 1968.

Changes to other lines were limited to the usual grille and trim changes. Both the compact Valiant and Barracuda models had been completely restyled in 1967, so the bulk of the changes to these two models were made to meet new federal safety standards that took effect on January 1, 1968. The full-size Fury had also been all-new for 1967, so changes to this line were also minimal.

Barracuda 2-Door Convertible

Barracuda 2-Door Fastback with
Formula S package

Fury I 2-Door Sedan

Fury III 2-Door Convertible

GTX 2-Door Convertible

Road Runner 2-Door Coupe

Satellite Sport 4-Door, 2-Seat Wagon

Sport Fury 2-Door FastTop and
Sport Fury 2-Door Hardtop

Valiant Signet 2-Door Sedan and
Valiant Signet 4-Door Sedan

**Model year production:** 757,237, up 18.90% over 1967.
**Domestic market share:** 8.84% (4th place).
**Base price range:** $2,254 to $3,590.
**Industry average base price:** $3,292.
**Plymouth average base price:** $2,934.
**Introduction date:** September 14, 1967.
**Assembly plants:** Lynch Road, MI (A): Hamtramck, MI (B); Belvidere, IL (D); Los Angeles, CA (E); Newark DE (F); St. Louis, MO (G); and Windsor, Ontario, Canada (R).

**Data plate identification:** Thirteen digit code read as follows: four digit style number code in which first letter is series, second letter is trim level, third and fourth digits are body style; engine code (see chart); sixth digit 8 for 1968; seventh digit is assembly plant code; 100001 and up for serial number. *Example:* PM23C8B100001 is a 1968 Plymouth Fury III 2-Door Hardtop, with a 225 CID 6-cyl., built at Hamtramck, MI, serial number 100001.

## Powertrains

| Engine | Gross HP | Engine Code | Transmission Availability | Valiant | Barra. | Belv./ Sat. | Sp.Sat./ RR/GTX | Fury |
|---|---|---|---|---|---|---|---|---|
| 170 CID, 1-bbl., 6-cyl. | 115 | A | 3-speed manual | S | – | – | – | – |
| | | | Torqueflite automatic | $180 | – | – | – | – |
| 225 CID, 1-bbl., 6-cyl. | 145 | B | 3-speed manual | $49 | S | S | – | S[2] |
| | | | Torqueflite automatic | $229 | $199 | $199 | – | $199[2] |
| 273 CID, 2-bbl., V8 | 190 | D | 3-speed manual | $181 | – | $94 | – | – |
| | | | 4-speed manual | $369 | – | – | – | – |
| | | | Torqueflite automatic | $371 | – | $311 | – | – |
| 318 CID, 2-bbl., V8 | 230 | F | 3-speed manual | $213 | $106 | $126 | S[1] | S[3]/$105[2] |
| | | | 4-speed manual | $401 | $294 | – | – | – |
| | | | Torqueflite automatic | $407 | $318 | $353 | $227[1] | $227[3]/$332[2] |
| 340 CID Commando, 4-bbl., V8 | 275 | P | 3-speed manual | – | $318 | – | – | – |
| | | | 4-speed manual | – | $516 | – | – | – |
| | | | Torqueflite automatic | – | $530 | – | – | – |
| 383 CID Commando, 2-bbl., V8 | 290 | G | 3-speed manual | – | – | $199 | $73[1] | $73[3]/$178[2] |
| | | | 4-speed manual | – | – | $397 | $271[1] | $271[3]/$376[2] |
| | | | Torqueflite automatic | – | – | $426 | $300[1] | $297[3]/$402[2] |
| 383 CID Super Commando, 4-bbl., V8 | 330, 335-R.R., 300-Barracuda | H | 3-speed manual | – | $357 | $270 | $144[1] | $144[3]/$249[2] |
| | | | 4-speed manual | – | $555 | $468 | S (RR/$342)[1] | $342[3]/$447[2] |
| | | | Torqueflite automatic | – | $569 | $497 | $39 (RR)/ $371[1] | $371[3]/$476[2] |
| 426 CID Street-Hemi, 4-bbl., V8 | 425 | J | 4-speed manual | – | – | – | $714 (RR)/ $605 (GTX) | – |
| 440 CID, 4-bbl., V8 | 350 | K | Torqueflite automatic | – | – | – | No cost (GTX) | $472 (Wgn) |
| 440 CID Super Commando, 4-bbl., V8 | 375 | L | 4-speed manual | – | – | – | No cost (GTX) | – |
| | | | Torqueflite automatic | – | – | – | S (GTX) | $508[3] |

[1]*Except Road Runner and GTX.* [2]*Fury I, II, and III (2-Dr. HT and 4-Dr. Sedan) only. 4-speed N/A on Wagons.* [3]*All but Fury I, II and III (2-Dr. HT and 4-Dr. Sedan).*

## Major Options

| | Valiant | Barracuda | Belvedere/Satellite | Fury |
|---|---|---|---|---|
| Air conditioning | $335 | $335 | $355 | $355 |
| Tinted glass | $30 | $33 | $42 | $42 |
| Power steering | $84 | $84 | $94 | $94 |
| Power brakes | $44 | $44 | $44 | $44 |
| Front disc brakes | $73 | $73 | $73 | $73 |
| AM radio | $60 | $60 | $60 | $60 |
| AM/FM Solid-State radio | – | $140 | $140 | $140 |
| Electric clock | $16 | $16 | $16 | S/$16 (Fury I) |

## Paint Colors

| | Code |
|---|---|
| Hawaiian Blue | 22-1 |
| Buffed Silver Metallic | AA-1 |
| Black | BB-1 |
| Medium Blue Metallic | CC-1 |
| Mist Blue Metallic | DD-1 |
| Midnight Blue Metallic | EE-1 |
| Mist Green Metallic | FF-1 |
| Forest Green Metallic | GG-1 |

**1968**

|  | Valiant | Barracuda | Belvedere/Satellite | Fury |
|---|---|---|---|---|
| Bucket seats — |  |  |  |  |
| vinyl (leather opt.) | - | S | S (GTX/Conv)/$100 | $102 |
| Center console | - | $51 | $54 | NC (Sp. Fury) |
| Vinyl roof | $79 | $79 | $79 | $106 |
| Chrome Road Wheels | - | - | $102 | $61–$102 |

Options common to most models. (- = Not Available; S = Standard equipment.) Items may be standard equipment, optional at different pricing, or unavailable on certain models. This chart is only a guide.

| Color | Code |
|---|---|
| Yellow Gold | HH-1 |
| Ember Gold Metallic | JJ-1 |
| Mist Turquoise Metallic | KK-1 |
| Surf Turquoise Met. | LL-1 |
| Turbine Bronze Metallic | MM-1 |
| Matador Red | PP-1 |
| Electric Blue Metallic | QQ-1 |
| Burgundy Metallic | RR-1 |
| Sunfire Yellow | SS-1 |
| Avocado Green Metallic | TT-1 |
| Frost Blue Metallic | UU-1 |
| Sable White | WW-1 |
| Satin Beige | XX-1 |
| Sierra Tan Metallic | YY-1 |

# Valiant

*"Valiant sticks to the original compact car idea, skip the doodads and concentrate on more car for less money."*

**Nameplate year of origin:** 1960.
**Current bodystyle lifespan:** 1967 through 1976.
**Predecessor to this model:** Valiant (1963 to 1966).
**Replacement for this model:** Volare (1976 to 1980).
**Percentage of division's sales volume:** 14.63%.
**Corporate siblings:** Dodge Dart.
**Primary competition:** AMC Rambler American, Chevrolet Nova, and Ford Falcon.
**Notable changes:** Minor trim and detail changes.
**Major standard equipment:** Cloth and vinyl bench seat, rubber floor mat, 2-speed windshield wipers with washers, full length body side molding, and 6.50 × 13 BSW tires. Signet adds: All-vinyl bench seat, color-keyed carpeting, fender-top mounted turn signals, and interior courtesy lighting.

## Measurements

| | |
|---|---|
| Wheelbase | 108.0" |
| Length | 188.4" |
| Width | 71.0" |
| Height | 53.7" |
| Legroom — front | 41.7" |
| Legroom — rear | 34.5" |
| Headroom — front | 38.4" |
| Headroom — rear | 37.3" |
| Cargo capacity (cu. ft.) | 14.5 |
| Fuel capacity (gals.) | 18.0 |

## Models Available

| | Style Number | Base MSRP | Change from LY | Shipping Wt. (lbs.) | Production | Change from LY |
|---|---|---|---|---|---|---|
| Valiant 100 2-Door Sedan | VL21 | $2,254 | +6.47% | 2655 | 31,178 | +7.17% |
| Valiant 100 4-Door Sedan | VL41 | $2,301 | +6.38% | 2675 | 49,446 | +6.02% |
| Valiant Signet 2-Door Sedan | VH21 | $2,400 | +6.10% | 2660 | 6,265 | -8.45% |
| Valiant Signet 4-Door Sedan | VH41 | $2,447 | +6.02% | 2680 | 23,906 | -9.43% |
| TOTALS | Avg. price | $2,351 | +6.24% | Production | 110,795 | +1.68% |

# Barracuda

*"Call them unique. They are. The one-of-a-kind sports-cars with a zest for the fun life."*

**Nameplate year of origin:** 1964.
**Current bodystyle lifespan:** 1967 through 1969.
**Predecessor to this model:** Barracuda (1964 to 1966).

## Measurements

| | |
|---|---|
| Wheelbase | 108.0" |
| Length | 192.8" |

**Replacement for this model:** Barracuda (1970 to 1974).
**Percentage of division's sales volume:** 6.00%.
**Corporate siblings:** None.
**Primary competition:** AMC Javelin, Chevrolet Camaro, Ford Mustang, Mercury Cougar and Pontiac Firebird.
**Notable changes:** Minor trim and detail changes.
**Major standard equipment:** All-vinyl bench seat with center arm rest (bucket seats on convertible), full carpeting, fold-down rear seat (fastback), power top (convertible), Rallye lights, full instrumentation, trip odometer and 6.95 × 14 BSW tires.

## Measurements (cont.)

| | |
|---|---|
| Width | 71.6" |
| Height | 52.6" |
| Legroom — front | 41.7" |
| Legroom — rear | 30.2" |
| Headroom — front | 37.4" |
| Headroom — rear | 35.8" |
| Cargo capacity (cu. ft.) | NA |
| Fuel capacity (gals.) | 18 |

## Models Available

| | Style Number | Base MSRP | Change from LY | Shipping Wt. (lbs.) | Production | Change from LY |
|---|---|---|---|---|---|---|
| Barracuda 2-Door Hardtop | BH23 | $2,605 | +6.37% | 2725 | 19,997 | -29.08% |
| Barracuda 2-Door Fastback HT | BH29 | $2,762 | +4.66% | 2810 | 22,575 | -25.02% |
| Barracuda 2-Door Convertible | BH27 | $2,907 | +4.61% | 2835 | 2,840 | -32.83% |
| TOTALS | | Avg. price $2,758 | +5.19% | | Production 45,412 | -17.38% |

# Belvedere, Satellite and GTX

*"If you're looking for 'plain-vanilla' transportation, you'd best look elsewhere."*

**Nameplate year of origin:** Belvedere: 1951 (HT model); 1954 (series). Satellite: 1965 (as a Belvedere trim level). GTX: 1967.
**Current bodystyle lifespan:** 1968 through 1970.
**Predecessor to this model:** Belvedere (1966 to 1967).
**Replacement for this model:** Satellite (1971 to 1974).
**Percentage of division's sales volume:** 33.22%.
**Corporate siblings:** Dodge Coronet.
**Primary competition:** AMC Rebel, Chevrolet Chevelle, Ford Fairlane/Torino, and Pontiac Tempest/LeMans.
**Notable changes:** Completely restyled.
**Major standard equipment:** Cloth and vinyl front bench seat, rubber floor mats, front and rear armrests, 2-speed electric windshield wipers with washers, exterior bright trim around windows and rocker molding, hubcaps, and 7.35 × 14 BSW tires (8.25 × 14 BSW tires on wagons). Satellite adds: Full carpeting and additional interior and exterior trim. Sport Satellite adds: All vinyl bucket seats, fender mounted turn signals, deluxe wheel covers, and additional interior lighting. Road Runner adds to Belvedere: 383 CID V8, Road Runner horn and logos, and F70 × 14 Wide-Oval tires. GTX adds to Sport Satellite: Dual hood scoops, dual exhausts, 440 CID V8, and automatic transmission.

## Measurements

| | Cars | Wagons |
|---|---|---|
| Wheelbase | 116.0" | 117.0" |
| Length | 202.7" | 207.6" |
| Width | 76.4" | 76.4" |
| Height | 54.7" | 55.4" |
| Legroom — front | 41.9" | 41.9" |
| Legroom — rear | 36.3" | 36.7" |
| Headroom — front | 38.6" | 38.7" |
| Headroom — rear | 37.4" | 38.1" |
| Cargo capacity (cu. ft.) | NA | 88.0 |
| Fuel capacity (gals.) | 19.5 | 21.0 |

**1968**

## Models Available

| | Style Number | Base MSRP | Change from LY | Shipping Wt. (lbs.) | Production | Change from LY |
|---|---|---|---|---|---|---|
| Belvedere 2-Door Coupe | RL21 | $2,444 | +5.44% | 2970 | 15,702 | +232.81% |
| Belvedere 4-Door Sedan | RL41 | $2,483 | +5.39% | 2995 | 17,214 | +23.06% |
| Belvedere 4-Door, 2-Seat Wagon | RL45 | $2,773 | +4.56% | 3500 | 8,982 | +183.17% |
| Road Runner 2-Door Coupe | RM21 | $2,896 | NEW | 3390 | 29,240 | NEW |
| Road Runner 2-Door Hardtop | RM23 | $3,034 | NEW | 3400 | 15,359 | NEW |

| | Style Number | Base MSRP | Change from LY | Shipping Wt. (lbs.) | Production | Change from LY |
|---|---|---|---|---|---|---|
| Satellite 2-Door Hardtop | RH23 | $2,594 | +5.58% | 2995 | 46,539 | +34.70% |
| Satellite 2-Door Convertible | RH27 | $2,824 | +4.79% | 3105 | 1,771 | +14.11% |
| Satellite 4-Door Sedan | RH41 | $2,572 | +5.67% | 3000 | 42,309 | -0.90% |
| Satellite 4-Dr., 2-Seat Wagon | RH45 | $2,891 | +5.94% | 3500 | 12,097 | +116.68% |
| Satellite 4-Dr., 3-Seat Wagon | RH46 | $2,998 | +5.71% | 3575 | 10,883 | +174.27% |
| Sport Satellite 2-Door Hardtop | RP23 | $2,822 | +2.73% | 3155 | 31,014 | +2.26% |
| Sport Satellite 2-Door Convertible | RP27 | $3,036 | +1.67% | 3285 | 1,523 | -25.71% |
| Satellite Sport 4-Dr., 2-S. Wagon | RP45 | $3,131 | NEW | 3610 | *W/Satellite Wagons | NEW |
| Satellite Sport 4-Dr., 3-S. Wagon | RP46 | $3,239 | NEW | 3685 | *W/Satellite Wagons | NEW |
| GTX 2-Door Hardtop | RS23 | $3,355 | +5.57% | 3470 | 17,914 | * |
| GTX 2-Door Convertible | RS27 | $3,590 | +5.03% | 3595 | 1,026 | * |
| TOTALS | Avg. price | $2,918 | +7.20% | | Production 251,573 | +69.89% |

*Comparison figures to 1967 models unavailable.*

# Fury

*"Our stylists went out of their way to make last year's best selling Fury a trend setter again in '68."*

**Nameplate year of origin:** 1956.
**Current bodystyle lifespan:** 1967 through 1968.
**Predecessor to this model:** Fury (1965 to 1966).
**Replacement for this model:** Fury (1969 to 1973).
**Percentage of division's sales volume:** 46.15%.
**Corporate siblings:** Dodge Polara and Monaco.
**Primary competition:** AMC Ambassador, Chevrolet Biscayne/BelAir/Impala, Ford Galaxie/LTD, and Pontiac Catalina.
**Notable changes:** Minor trim and detail changes.
**Major standard equipment:** Cloth and vinyl front bench seat, color-keyed floor covering, front and rear armrests, variable speed electric windshield wipers, bright trim around front and rear windows, and 8.25 × 14 BSW tires (8.55 × 14 BSW tire on wagon). Fury II adds: Full carpeting and full-length body side molding. Fury III adds: All-vinyl upholstery on hardtop and convertible, backup lights, and distinctive exterior trim. Sport Fury adds: All-vinyl bucket seats, floor-mounted shifter and console with compartment, and deluxe steering wheel. VIP adds: Cloth and vinyl bench seats with fold-down center armrests, reading lamps, vinyl top and specific VIP trim.

## Measurements

| | Cars | Wagons |
|---|---|---|
| Wheelbase | 119.0" | 122.0" |
| Length | 213.1" | 216.1" |
| Width | 77.7" | 77.7" |
| Height | 56.3" | 56.7" |
| Legroom — front | 41.8" | 41.8" |
| Legroom — rear | 37.0" | 37.4" |
| Headroom — front | 39.5" | 39.5" |
| Headroom — rear | 37.7" | 37.9" |
| Cargo capacity (cu. ft.) | NA | 96.9 |
| Fuel capacity (gals.) | 19.0 | 24.0 |

## Models Available

| | Style Number | Base MSRP | Change from LY | Shipping Wt. (lbs.) | Production | Change from LY |
|---|---|---|---|---|---|---|
| Fury I 2-Door Sedan | PE21 | $2,617 | +5.82% | 3420 | 5,788 | -12.92% |
| Fury I 4-Door Sedan | PE41 | $2,660 | +5.68% | 3455 | 23,208 | -20.94% |
| Fury I 4-Dr., 2-S. Suburban Wagon | PL45 | $3,048 | +5.69% | 3950 | 6,749 | +11.24% |
| Fury II 2-Door Sedan | PL21 | $2,715 | +5.60% | 3430 | 3,112 | +11.82% |
| Fury II 4-Door Sedan | PL41 | $2,757 | +5.47% | 3470 | 49,423 | +8.21% |
| Fury II 4-Dr., 2-S. Cust. Sub. Wgn. | PL45 | $3,252 | +7.65% | 4045 | 17,078 | +59.07% |
| Fury II 4-Dr., 3-S. Cust. Sub. Wgn. | PL46 | $3,353 | +7.40% | 4090 | 9,954 | +76.21% |
| Fury III 2-Door Hardtop | PM23 | $2,912 | +5.24% | 3480 | 60,472 | +61.48% |
| Fury III 2-Door Fast Top HT | PX23 | $2,932 | NEW | 3480 | * | NEW |
| Fury III 2-Door Convertible | PM27 | $3,236 | +3.78% | 3680 | 4,483 | -0.88% |

| | Style Number | Base MSRP | Change from LY | Shipping Wt. (lbs.) | Production | Change from LY |
|---|---|---|---|---|---|---|
| Fury III 4-Door Sedan | PM41 | $2,890 | +5.24% | 3485 | 57,899 | +9.89% |
| Fury III 4-Door Hardtop | PM43 | $3,067 | +4.96% | 3635 | 45,147 | +3.51% |
| Fury III 4-Dr., 2-S. Sport Sub. Wgn. | PM45 | $3,442 | +9.48% | 4055 | 9,203 | -0.72% |
| Fury III 4-Dr., 3-S. Sport Sub. Wgn. | PM46 | $3,543 | +9.18% | 4100 | 13,224 | +5.51% |
| Sport Fury 2-Door Hardtop | PH23 | $3,206 | +5.70% | 3620 | 6,642 | -76.65% |
| Sport Fury 2-Door Fast Top HT | PS23 | $3,225 | +5.32% | 3615 | 17,073 | * |
| Sport Fury 2-Door Convertible | PH27 | $3,425 | +4.45% | 3710 | 2,489 | -20.56% |
| VIP 2-Door Fast Top Hardtop | PP23 | $3,260 | +4.59% | 3615 | 6,768 | -14.46% |
| VIP 4-Door Hardtop | PP43 | $3,326 | +4.53% | 3655 | 10,745 | -0.78% |
| TOTALS | *Avg. price* | $3,098 | +5.59% | *Production* | 349,457 | +10.13% |

*Comparison figures to 1967 models unavailable.*

# PONTIAC

*"Pontiac Wide-Track 1968."*

Sleek styling and Pontiac's powerful engine line highlighted the new mid-size Tempest, LeMans and GTO line for 1968. For the base models, as well as the Firebird, a larger displacement overhead cam 6-cylinder engine was introduced. At 250 cubic inches, this was one of the most powerful 6-cylinder engines in production. The next step up in engines offered a new 350 CID V8 engine, in place of last year's 326 CID V8. The 400 CID V8 engine continued to be the top engine in the mid-size and Firebird lines.

The most important styling feature for the year turned out to be the Endura bumper system on the GTO models. The Endura bumper was made of a highly impact absorbent rubber material that stylists could shape pleasingly while providing dent resistance. The Endura bumper could be body color and blend with the car instead of looking tacked onto the car. The basic design of this bumper was the same as the chrome bumper with inset grille that was used on the Tempest and LeMans lines. This new technology combined with the beautiful styling prompted *Motor Trend* magazine to name the new GTO its Car of the Year. Model changes within the mid-size line included the dropping of the base Tempest wagon and the GTO 2-Door Coupe.

The full-size line received a restyling that saw the end of the trend-setting stacked headlamp design that Pontiac had started in 1963. This year's front end featured side-by-side lamps within a loop-style grille — the next big styling trend that Pontiac helped to popularize. Of course, the familiar Pontiac split grille was retained. The Grand Prix, in its last season as a full-size car, used a hidden headlamp motif. The Ventura trim package continued to be available on certain Catalina models, as was the Brougham package on the Bonneville. A Bonneville 4-Door Sedan was added to the line, and the one-year-only Grand Prix convertible was, of course, discontinued. The sporty Firebird, which debuted in 1967, saw only minor styling changes, with ventless door glass and wrap-around parking lamps among the few new items.

1968

Bonneville 2-Door Convertible with
Brougham package

Catalina 2-Door Convertible

Executive 4-Door Safari Wagon

Firebird 400 2-Door Convertible

Grand Prix 2-Door Hardtop

GTO 2-Door Convertible and
GTO 2-Door Hardtop,
*Motor Trend* Car of the Year

GTO Interior

Tempest Custom 4-Door Hardtop

**Model year production:** 910,482, up 11.40% over 1967.
**Domestic market share:** 10.63% (3rd place).
**Base price range:** $2,461 to $3,987.
**Industry average base price:** $3,292.
**Pontiac average base price:** $3,157.
**Introduction date:** September, 1967.
**Assembly plants:** Atlanta, GA (A); Baltimore, MD (B); Southgate, CA (C); Linden, NJ (E); Framingham, MA (G); Kansas City, MO (K); Van Nuys, CA (L); Norwood, OH (N); Pontiac, MI (P); Arlington, TX (R); Fairfax, KS (X); Fremont, CA (Z); and Oshawa, Ontario, Canada (1).
**Data plate identification:** Thirteen digit code read as follows: 1st digit 2 = Pontiac; 2nd through 5th digits identify series/body style number (see style number in listings); 8 = 1968; 7th digit is assembly plant code; 100001 and up (600001 and up on 6-cylinders) for serial number. *Example:* 252398X100001 is a 1968 Pontiac Catalina 4-Door Hardtop, serial number 100001, built in Fairfax, KS.

## Powertrains

| Engine | Gross HP | Transmission Availability | Firebird | Tempest/ LeMans/GTO | Catalina/ Executive | Bonneville | Grand Prix |
|---|---|---|---|---|---|---|---|
| 250 CID OHC, 1-bbl., 6-cyl. | 175 | 3-speed manual | S | S (ex. GTO) | - | - | - |
| | | 4-speed manual | $195 | - | - | - | - |
| | | 2-sp. Automatic | $174 | $174 (ex. GTO) | - | - | - |
| | | Turbo Hydra-matic | $195 | $195 (ex. GTO) | - | - | - |
| 250 CID OHC, 4-bbl., 6-cyl. | 230 | 3-speed manual | $130* | $125* (ex. GTO) | - | - | - |
| | | 4-speed manual | $325* | $310* (ex. GTO) | - | - | - |
| | | Turbo Hydra-matic | 325* | $320* (ex. GTO) | - | - | - |
| 350 CID, 2-bbl., V8 | 255 | 3-speed manual | $111 | $111 (ex. GTO) | - | - | - |
| | | 3-speed HD man. | $195 | $195 (ex. GTO) | - | - | - |
| | | 4-speed manual | $306 | $306 (ex. GTO) | - | - | - |
| | | 2-sp. Automatic | $296 (w/o A/C) | $296 (w/o A/C) | - | - | - |
| | | Turbo Hydra-matic | $317 (w/o A/C) $338 (w/ A/C) | $317 (w/o A/C) $338 (w/A/C) | - | - | - |
| 350 CID, 4-bbl., V8 | 325/330 | 3-speed manual | $199 | $189 (ex. GTO) | - | - | - |
| | | 3-speed HD man. | $283 | $274 (ex. GTO) | - | - | - |
| | | 4-speed manual | $394 | $384 (ex. GTO) | - | - | - |
| | | Turbo Hydra-matic | $426 | $416 (ex. GTO) | - | - | - |
| 400 CID, 2-bbl., V8 | 265 | Turbo Hydra-matic | - | No cost (GTO) | No cost | - | - |
| 400 CID, 2-bbl., V8 | 290 | 3-speed manual | - | - | S | - | - |
| | | Turbo Hydra-matic | - | - | $227 | - | - |
| 400 CID, 4-bbl., V8 | 330 (FB,LeM)/ 340 (Full-size) 350 (GP/GTO) | 3-speed HD man. | S (w/400)** | S (GTO) | - | - | S |
| | | 4-speed manual | $195** | $185 (GTO) | - | - | $227 |
| | | Turbo Hydra-matic | $227** | $227 (GTO) | $274 | - | $227 |
| 400 CID H.O. Ram Air, 4-bbl., V8 | 335 | 4-speed manual | S (Trans Am)/ $ (400) | | - | - | |
| | | Turbo Hydra-matic | $ (Trans Am)/ $ (400) | | - | - | - |
| 400 CID Ram Air SD, 4-bbl., V8 | 345 | 4-speed manual | $ (Trans Am) | - | - | - | - |
| | | Turbo Hydra-matic | $ (Trans Am) | - | - | - | - |
| 428 CID, 4-bbl., V8 | 360 | 3-speed HD man. | - | - | - | S | $58 |
| | | 4-speed manual | - | - | - | - | $285 |
| | | Turbo Hydra-matic | - | - | $332 | $227 | $285 |
| 428 CID H.O., 4-bbl., V8 | 390 | 3-speed HD man. | - | - | - | - | $177 |
| | | 4-speed manual | - | - | - | - | $404 |
| | | Turbo Hydra-matic | - | - | $482 (ex. Wagon) | $386 (ex. Wagon) | $404 |

*Includes Sprint option package.   **Included with 400 Option package.*

## Major Options

| | Firebird | Tempest/LeMans | Catalina | Executive | Bonneville | Grand Prix |
|---|---|---|---|---|---|---|
| Air conditioning | $376 | $376 | $421 | $421 | $421 | $421 |
| Electronic cruise control | - | $58 | $63 | $63 | $63 | $63 |
| Soft Ray tinted glass | $37 | $37 | $44 | $44 | $44 | $44 |
| Tilt steering wheel | $45 | $45 | $45 | $45 | $45 | $45 |
| Power steering — variable-ratio | $105 | $105 | $116 | $116 | $116 | $116 |

| | Firebird | Tempest/LeMans | Catalina | Executive | Bonneville | Grand Prix |
|---|---|---|---|---|---|---|
| Power brakes | $64 | $64 | $72 | $72 | $72 | S |
| Power driver's seat/Bench seat | $74 | $74 | $100 | $100 | $100 | $74 |
| Power windows | $105 | $105 | $111 | $111 | $111 | $111 |
| AM radio | $61 | $61 | $87 | $87 | $87 | $87 |
| AM/FM stereo | $239 | $239 | $239 | $239 | $239 | $239 |
| Vinyl roof | $ | $100 | $116–142 | $116–142 | $116–142 | $142 |
| White stripe tires (base size) | $32 | $32 | $44–$48 | $44–$48 | $44 | $40 |
| Rally II wheels | $56 | $87 | $87 | $87 | $87 | $87 |
| Ventura package | - | - | $105 | - | - | - |
| Brougham package | - | - | - | - | $273–$316 | - |
| Sprint package | $116 | $106–$126 | - | - | - | - |
| Firebird 350 package | $106 | - | - | - | - | - |
| Firebird H.O. package | $181 | - | - | - | - | - |
| Firebird 400 package | $351 | - | - | - | - | - |

Options common to most models. (- = Not Available; S = Standard equipment.) Items may be standard equipment, optional at different pricing, or unavailable on certain models. This chart is only a guide.

## Paint Colors

| | Code | | Code |
|---|---|---|---|
| Starlight Black | A | Aleutian Blue Metallic | L |
| Cameo Ivory | C | Flambeau Burgundy Metallic | N |
| Alplne Blue Metallic | D | Spring Mist Green Metallic | P |
| Aegena Blue Metallic | E | Verdoro Green Metallic | Q |
| Nordic Blue Metallic | F | Solar Red | R |
| April Gold Metallic | G | Primavera Beige | T |
| Autumn Bronze Metallic | I | Nightshade Green Metallic | V |
| Meridian Turquoise Metallic | K | Mayfair Maize | Y |

# Firebird

*"The magnificent five ... the Pontiac Firebirds."*

**Nameplate year of origin:** 1967 (used on Motorama show cars as early as 1954).
**Current bodystyle lifespan:** 1967 through 1969.
**Predecessor to this model:** None.
**Replacement for this model:** Firebird (1970 to 1981).
**Percentage of division's sales volume:** 11.76%.
**Corporate siblings:** Chevrolet Camaro.
**Primary competition:** Ford Mustang, Plymouth Barracuda, and AMC Javelin.
**Notable changes:** Major restyle and interior revisions.
**Major standard equipment:** All-vinyl front bucket seats, wood grain dash, full carpeting, 2-speed windshield wipers with washers, steering column shifter, and E70 × 14 Wide-Oval BSW tires. Sprint package adds: 4-bbl. OHC 6-cylinder, floor mounted shifter, and heavy-duty suspension. 350 adds: 350 CID V8 engine and column mounted shifter. H.O. adds: Exterior striping, 4-bbl. carburetor and dual exhausts. 400 adds: 400 CID V8, floor mounted shifter, dual hood scoops, dual exhausts, heavy-duty suspension, and E70 × 14 Wide-Oval Redline or BSW tires.

## Measurements

| | |
|---|---|
| Wheelbase | 108.0" |
| Length | 188.8" |
| Width | 72.8" |
| Height | 50.0" |
| Legroom — front | 42.5" |
| Legroom — rear | 29.5" |
| Headroom — front | 37.0" |
| Headroom — rear | 36.7" |
| Cargo capacity (cu. ft.) | 9.9 |
| Fuel capacity (gals.) | 18.5 |

## Models Available

| | Style Number | Base MSRP | Change from LY | Shipping Wt. (lbs.) | Production | Change from LY |
|---|---|---|---|---|---|---|
| Firebird 2-Door Hardtop | 22337 | $2,781 | +4.31% | 3061 | 90,152 | +34.49% |

| | Style Number | Base MSRP | Change from LY | Shipping Wt. (lbs.) | Production | Change from LY |
|---|---|---|---|---|---|---|
| Firebird 2-Door Convertible | 22367 | $2,996 | +3.20% | 3346 | 16,960 | +9.22% |
| TOTALS | | Avg. price $2,889 | +3.73% | | Production 107,112 | +29.74% |

# Tempest, LeMans & GTO

*"The best way to describe it is to let you sit back and just look."*

**Nameplate year of origin:** 1961 (Tempest); 1961 (LeMans, as Tempest sub-series); 1964 (GTO).

**Current bodystyle lifespan:** 1968 through 1972.

**Predecessor to this model:** Tempest/LeMans (1966 to 1967).

**Replacement for this model:** LeMans (1973 to 1977).

**Percentage of division's sales volume:** 27.06%.

**Corporate siblings:** Chevrolet Chevelle, Oldsmobile Cutlass, and Buick Skylark.

**Primary competition:** AMC Rebel, Ford Fairlane, Mercury Montego, Plymouth Belvedere/Satellite, and Dodge Coronet.

**Notable changes:** Completely redesigned.

**Major standard equipment:** Cloth and vinyl front bench seat, vinyl floor covering, courtesy lights, 2-speed windshield wipers with washers, and 7.75 × 14 BSW tires. Custom adds: All-vinyl front bench seats, full carpeting, and rocker panel moldings. LeMans adds: All-vinyl bucket seats or bench seat (2-Doors), cloth and vinyl bench seats (4-Doors), and simulated walnut trim on dash. GTO adds: All-vinyl bucket seats, floor shifter, dual exhausts, 400 CID V8 with engine dress-up kit, heavy duty suspension and G70 × 14 Redline tires.

## Measurements

| | 2-Doors | 4-Doors | Wagons |
|---|---|---|---|
| Wheelbase | 112.0" | 116.0" | 116.0" |
| Length | 200.7" | 204.7" | 211.0" |
| Width | 74.8" | 74.8" | 74.8" |
| Height | 51.8" | 52.5" | 54.4" |
| Legroom — front | 41.2" | 41.2" | 42.6" |
| Legroom — rear | 32.2" | 33.8" | 34.8" |
| Headroom — front | 37.8" | 38.5" | 38.4" |
| Headroom — rear | 36.3" | 37.1" | 38.3" |
| Cargo capacity (cu. ft.) | 13.1 | 13.1 | 94.0 |
| Fuel capacity (gals.) | 21.5 | 21.5 | 21.5 |

**1968**

## Models Available

| | Style Number | Base MSRP | Change from LY | Shipping Wt. (lbs.) | Production | Change from LY |
|---|---|---|---|---|---|---|
| Tempest 2-Door Sports Coupe | 23327 | $2,461 | +5.13% | 3242 | 19,991 | +11.20% |
| Tempest 4-Door Sedan | 23369 | $2,509 | +5.07% | 3307 | 11,590 | -11.77% |
| Tempest Custom 2-Dr. Sports Cpe. | 23527 | $2,554 | +4.93% | 3252 | 10,634 | -14.72% |
| Tempest Custom 2-Door Hardtop | 23537 | $2,614 | +4.81% | 3277 | 40,574 | +32.98% |
| Tempest Custom 2-Door Conv. | 23567 | $2,839 | +4.26% | 3337 | 3,518 | -13.82% |
| Tempest Custom 4-Door Sedan | 23569 | $2,602 | +4.83% | 3297 | 17,304 | -0.81% |
| Tempest Custom 4-Door Hardtop | 23539 | $2,728 | +4.60% | 3382 | 6,147 | +11.91% |
| Tempest Custom 4-Dr., 2-S. Wgn. | 23535 | $2,906 | +5.29% | 3667 | 8,253 | +55.02% |
| LeMans 2-Door Sports Coupe | 23727 | $2,724 | +5.34% | 3287 | 8,439 | -21.08% |
| LeMans 2-Door Hardtop | 23737 | $2,786 | +5.21% | 3302 | 110,036 | +44.85% |
| LeMans 2-Door Convertible | 23767 | $3,015 | +4.65% | 3377 | 8,820 | -10.18% |
| LeMans 4-Door Hardtop | 23739 | $2,916 | +5.23% | 3407 | 9,002 | +6.86% |
| LeMans Safari 4-Dr., 2-S. Wagon | 23935 | $3,107 | +5.82% | 3677 | 4,414 | -2.15% |
| GTO 2-Door Hardtop | 24237 | $3,101 | +5.66% | 3506 | 77,704 | +19.22% |
| GTO 2-Door Convertible | 24267 | $3,327 | +5.12% | 3590 | 9,980 | +4.86% |
| TOTALS | | Avg. price $2,813 | +4.65% | | Production 346,406 | +15.06% |

# Catalina

*"Every year, people try to build a better Catalina than Pontiac does. We do.*

**Nameplate year of origin:** 1950 (hardtop models), 1959 (series).
**Current bodystyle lifespan:** 1967 through 1968.
**Predecessor to this model:** Catalina (1965 to 1966).
**Replacement for this model:** Catalina (1969 to 1970).
**Corporate siblings:** Chevrolet Impala/Caprice, Olds Delta 88, Buick LeSabre.
**Primary competition:** Ford LTD, Mercury Monterey, Plymouth Fury, Dodge Polara, and AMC Ambassador.
**Percentage of division's sales volume:** 30.33%.
**Notable changes:** Restyled front and rear ends.
**Major standard equipment:** Cloth and vinyl front bench seat (all-vinyl on convertible and wagons), full carpeting, 2-speed windshield wipers with washers, and 8.55 × 14 BSW tires (8.25 × 14 BSW tires on Sedans and 8.85 × 14 BSW tires on 3-Seat Wagon). Ventura Custom option adds: All-vinyl upholstery with specific trim.

## Measurements

|  | Cars | Wagons |
|---|---|---|
| Wheelbase | 121.0" | 121.0" |
| Length | 216.5" | 217.8" |
| Width | 79.8" | 79.8" |
| Height | 54.8" | 55.9" |
| Legroom — front | 42.4" | 41.5" |
| Legroom — rear | 38.1" | 38.2" |
| Headroom — front | 39.1" | 39.2" |
| Headroom — rear | 37.7" | 39.0" |
| Cargo capacity (cu. ft.) | NA | 99.9 |
| Fuel capacity (gals.) | 26.5 | 24.0 |

## Models Available

|  | Style Number | Base MSRP | Change from LY | Shipping Wt. (lbs.) | Production | Change from LY |
|---|---|---|---|---|---|---|
| Catalina 2-Door Sedan | 25211 | $2,945 | +4.92% | 3839 | 5,247 | -6.85% |
| Catalina 2-Door Hardtop | 25287 | $3,089 | +4.68% | 3943 | 92,217 | +18.33% |
| Catalina 2-Door Convertible | 25267 | $3,391 | +3.51% | 3980 | 7,339 | -26.85% |
| Catalina 4-Door Sedan | 25269 | $3,004 | +4.82% | 3888 | 94,441 | +17.24% |
| Catalina 4-Door Hardtop | 25239 | $3,158 | +4.57% | 4012 | 41,727 | +12.00% |
| Catalina 4-Dr., 2-S. Wagon | 25235 | $3,390 | +4.24% | 4327 | 21,848 | +19.36% |
| Catalina 4-Dr., 3-S. Wagon | 25245 | $3,537 | +4.83% | 4408 | 13,363 | +21.04% |
| TOTALS | | Avg. price $3,216 | +4.48% | | Production 276,182 | +14.72% |

# Executive

*"Our 1968 Executive. Luxury continued. More affordable."*

**Nameplate year of origin:** 1966.
**Current bodystyle lifespan:** 1967 through 1968.
**Predecessor to this model:** Star Chief/Executive (1965 to 1966).
**Replacement for this model:** Bonneville (1969 to 1970).
**Corporate siblings:** Chevrolet Impala/Caprice, Oldsmobile Delta 88, Buick Wildcat.
**Primary competition:** Ford LTD, Mercury Marquis, Plymouth Fury, Dodge Monaco, and AMC Ambassador.
**Percentage of division's sales volume:** 4.90%.
**Notable changes:** Restyled front and rear ends.
**Major standard equipment:** Cloth and vinyl bench seat, full carpeting, perforated vinyl headliner, walnut grain trim on dash, electric clock, full length lower body molding, exterior wood grain trim on station wagons, full wheel covers and 8.55 × 14 BSW tires (8.85 × 14 BSW tires on 3-Seat Wagon).

## Measurements

|  | Cars | Wagons |
|---|---|---|
| Wheelbase | 124.0" | 121.0" |
| Length | 223.5" | 217.8" |
| Width | 79.8" | 79.8" |
| Height | 54.8" | 55.9" |
| Legroom — front | 42.4" | 41.5" |
| Legroom — rear | 38.1" | 38.2" |
| Headroom — front | 39.0" | 39.2" |
| Headroom — rear | 37.6" | 39.0" |
| Cargo capacity (cu. ft.) | NA | 99.9 |
| Fuel capacity (gals.) | 26.5 | 24.0 |

## Models Available

| | Style Number | Base MSRP | Change from LY | Shipping Wt. (lbs.) | Production | Change from LY |
|---|---|---|---|---|---|---|
| Executive 2-Door Hardtop | 25687 | $3,371 | +4.46% | 3975 | 5,880 | -15.16% |
| Executive 4-Door Sedan | 25669 | $3,309 | +4.55% | 4022 | 18,869 | -4.99% |
| Executive 4-Door Hardtop | 25639 | $3,439 | +4.34% | 4077 | 7,848 | -9.78% |
| Executive Safari 4-Dr., 2-S. Wagon | 25635 | $3,744 | +4.00% | 4378 | 6,195 | +4.95% |
| Executive Safari 4-Dr., 3-S. Wagon | 25645 | $3,890 | +4.51% | 4453 | 5,843 | +4.47% |
| TOTALS | | Avg. price $3,551 | +4.38% | | Production 44,635 | -5.01% |

# Bonneville

*"Remember where we got the name."*

**Nameplate year of origin:** 1957.
**Current bodystyle lifespan:** 1967 through 1968.
**Predecessor to this model:** Bonneville (1965 to 1966).
**Replacement for this model:** Bonneville (1969 to 1970).
**Corporate siblings:** Chevrolet Impala/Caprice, Oldsmobile Delta 88, Buick LeSabre/Wildcat.
**Primary competition:** Ford LTD, Mercury Park Lane, Dodge Monaco and Plymouth Fury VIP.
**Percentage of division's sales volume:** 11.47%.
**Notable changes:** Restyled front and rear end.
**Major standard equipment:** All-vinyl or cloth and vinyl front bench seat, full carpeting, Carpathian burled elm grain dash trim, electric clock, courtesy lights, dual-speed electric windshield wipers, rear fender skirts, deluxe wheel covers and 8.25 × 14 BSW tires (8.85 × 14 BSW tires Wagon). Brougham option adds: Special upholstery trim with fold down center armrests, and exterior badges.

## Measurements

| | Cars | Wagons |
|---|---|---|
| Wheelbase | 124.0" | 121.0" |
| Length | 223.5" | 217.8" |
| Width | 79.8" | 79.8" |
| Height | 53.8" | 55.9" |
| Legroom — front | 42.4" | 41.5" |
| Legroom — rear | 37.7" | 38.2" |
| Headroom — front | 38.2" | 39.2" |
| Headroom — rear | 37.1" | 39.0" |
| Cargo capacity (cu. ft.) | NA | 99.9 |
| Fuel capacity (gals.) | 26.5 | 24.0 |

**1968**

## Models Available

| | Style Number | Base MSRP | Change from LY | Shipping Wt. (lbs.) | Production | Change from LY |
|---|---|---|---|---|---|---|
| Bonneville 2-Door Hardtop | 26287 | $3,592 | +4.18% | 4054 | 29,598 | -4.57% |
| Bonneville 2-Door Convertible | 26267 | $3,800 | +3.26% | 4090 | 7,358 | -17.34% |
| Bonneville 4-Door Sedan | 26269 | $3,530 | NEW | 4122 | 3,499 | NEW |
| Bonneville 4-Door Hardtop | 26239 | $3,660 | +4.07% | 4171 | 57,055 | +1.33% |
| Bonneville Safari 4-Dr., 3-S. Wgn. | 26245 | $3,987 | +4.40% | 4485 | 6,926 | +2.29% |
| TOTALS | | Avg. price $3,714 | +2.71% | | Production 104,436 | +1.40% |

# Grand Prix

*"The exuberant luxury that's made Grand Prix America's premier personal luxury car is back. Abundantly."*

**Nameplate year of origin:** 1962.
**Current bodystyle lifespan:** 1967 through 1968.
**Predecessor to this model:** Grand Prix (1965 to 1966).
**Replacement for this model:** Grand Prix (1969 to 1972).
**Percentage of division's sales volume:** 3.48%.
**Corporate siblings:** Buick Wildcat.
**Primary competition:** Chrysler 300, Dodge Monaco, and Mercury Marquis.
**Notable changes:** Restyled front and rear ends.
**Major standard equipment:** All-vinyl or cloth and vinyl bucket seat with console or bench seat, full carpeting, Carpathian burled elm trim on dash and door panels, additional acoustical insulation, concealed headlights, concealed windshield wipers, ventless door windows, rear fender skirts, deluxe wheel covers and 8.55 × 14 BSW tires.

## Measurements

| | |
|---|---|
| Wheelbase | 121.0" |
| Length | 216.3" |
| Width | 79.8" |
| Height | 53.0" |
| Legroom — front | 42.3" |
| Legroom — rear | 35.2" |
| Headroom — front | 37.9" |
| Headroom — rear | 37.2" |
| Cargo capacity (cu. ft.) | NA |
| Fuel capacity (gals.) | 26.5 |

## Models Available

| | Style Number | Base MSRP | Change from LY | Shipping Wt. (lbs.) | Production | Change from LY |
|---|---|---|---|---|---|---|
| Grand Prix 2-Door Hardtop | 26657 | $3,697 | +4.17% | 4075 | 31,711 | -14.58% |
| TOTALS | | *Avg. price* $3,697 | +0.43% | | *Production* 31,711 | -26.22% |

# 1969

The 1969 season brought relatively few all-new cars of note, principally the Ford Maverick, the downsized Pontiac Grand Prix, heavily restyled Ford Mustang and Mercury Cougar models, and the all new "fuselage" design Chrysler Corporation full size models. Ford and General Motors redesigned their full-size cars to compete with the new Chrysler introductions, but it would be two more years before they had their all-new models ready. All of the intermediate lines, save AMC's, had been redesigned in 1968, so for 1969 changes were limited to powertrains and grille or trim changes. Most of the compacts had been redesigned within the past two years, so there was limited news on that front also. The period from 1970 to 1971 would bring a new round of sub-compact models, so changes to the compacts were generally minor. For the pony car category, as mentioned previously, the Mustang and Cougar were completely restyled, while GM's Camaro and Firebird wore new sheetmetal on the same body structure, and the Plymouth Barracuda and AMC Javelin and AMX continued into 1969 with only minor changes.

Chrysler's fuselage styling was derived from the same concept as that used in airplanes. The "fuselage" styling featured rounded body sides that would accommodate wider seating areas with more aerodynamic exterior styling. By 1971, all Mopar products except the compact Plymouth Valiant and Dodge Dart would feature that styling theme. As with most new designs, the first year efforts came off looking better than any succeeding years. The main model change that came with the new design was the elimination of the Fast Top fastback body style, although the remaining 2-Door Hardtop was of a less formal roofline design than its predecessors. Mid-size and compact Chrysler products were essentially carried over with the requisite grille and trim changes.

At Ford, the popular Mustang and Cougar were heavily reworked. This was the second of three restylings that would take both cars to much larger proportions. The Mustang and Cougar received evolutionary changes on the exterior, with beefier suspensions underneath, and more luxury features inside. The Cougar added two Convertible models to its line and moved toward the personal/luxury category, away from the pony car market where it originated. Option packages made the CJ (Cobra-Jet) engine a hot combination with performance types. The Mustang added a new Mach 1 with potent engine options of a 351 CID V8 or 429 CID V8. Interiors expanded on the "cockpit" styling theme with luxury type bucket seats and full-length center floor console available in both the Mustang and Cougar. A new compact named Maverick was launched in the spring of 1969 and sold alongside of the Falcon, initially. Ford was not sure a smaller, sportier coupe could successfully fill the Falcon role, but it did from day one. The Maverick rode on a wheelbase about 8 inches shorter than the Falcon; however when Ford introduced the 4-Door Maverick in 1971, to replace the Falcon, its wheelbase was only two inches shorter than that of the Falcon.

The mid-sized Ford Fairlane and Mercury Comet/Montego, the compact Falcon, and luxury Thunderbird all received minor annual styling changes. Full size Fords and Mercurys were restyled with new side body panels and revised interior trim. New for Mercury was a 2-Door Fastback Marauder line with styling copied from the Ford 500XL Fastback. The Marauder rode on a shorter 121-wheelbase that it shared with Ford, while all other big Mercurys rode on a 124-inch wheelbase. The top-of-the-line Marauder X-100 featured a unique tunneled rear window, with matte-black paint surrounding the window and covering the decklid.

At GM, Pontiac reintroduced the Grand Prix as an all new mid-size personal luxury car. The full size Grand Prix had been a hit at introduction, but had gradually faded and needed to be re-energized. The new Grand Prix was built upon a stretched A-body, mid-size 4-Door platform and shared powertrains and suspensions with the mid-size Tem-

## 1969 Model Year Production by Make

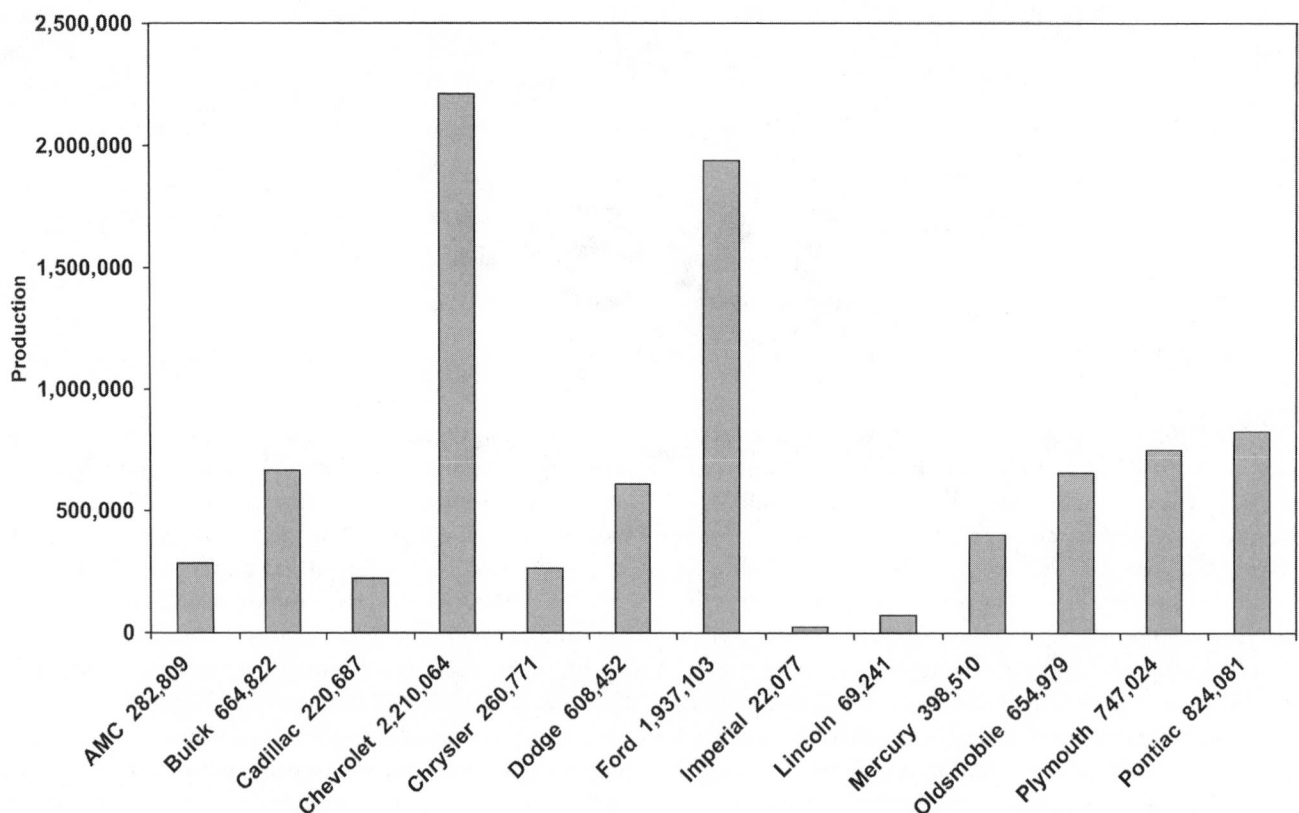

AMC 282,809 | Buick 664,822 | Cadillac 220,687 | Chevrolet 2,210,064 | Chrysler 260,771 | Dodge 608,452 | Ford 1,937,103 | Imperial 22,077 | Lincoln 69,241 | Mercury 398,510 | Oldsmobile 654,979 | Plymouth 747,024 | Pontiac 824,081

pest/LeMans. Proportions followed the long hood, short deck theme that was popularized by pony cars such as the Firebird. Body panels were totally unique to the GP, and the hood was the longest ever used on a Pontiac. The revitalized Grand Prix was once again a success and had no real competition for its first year. The Dodge Charger was its closest competitor, but the Charger leaned more to the muscle car lines. GM's other mid-size lines were updated with the typical annual changes. A new "Judge" option for the Pontiac GTO offered GTO power in a lower content package. It was the same concept introduced successfully in 1968 by Plymouth with the Road Runner.

The Chevy compacts saw few changes, and the Corvair finished its life in midyear 1969 with little fanfare. A brochure was not even printed for the cars as they vanished into the sunset. The last several years had seen sales fall drastically. Chevrolet had originally planned to keep the car in the line until the Vega arrived in 1971, but sales had fallen from over 100,000 units as recently as 1966 to a mere 6,000 units during the 1969 run, and the plug was pulled.

Full size GM cars received a major restyling, while still utilizing a majority of their 1967–1968 parts under the skin. Chevrolets moved ever closer to being a Cadillac look-alike with new cross-hatch grilles, plus concealed headlamps offered on several models. Full-sized Pontiacs gained a center bumper section made of Endura, the material that was first seen on the GTO bumpers. Oldsmobile retained its split grille styling up front, while Buick went for the new "loop-style" bumper encasing the grille. Cadillac abandoned the stacked headlamp styling in favor of traditional side-by-side units set within the grille.

AMC's line served up only a few changes, the most significant being updates to the Rebel and Ambassador styling. These changes set the course for the designs of these two models for the next five years. Checker and Avanti II received very few changes.

Ford and Chevy truck lines had been redesigned in 1967, so only minor styling updates were seen this year. Dodge, Jeep and International were all relatively unchanged. Ford introduced a new Econoline van that was larger and more powerful than the Falcon based van it replaced. Styling updates for the Ford Ranchero and Chevy El Camino followed those of the Ford Fairlane and Chevy Chevelle.

# AMERICAN MOTORS

*"American Motors 1969."*

For 1969, American Motors offered improvements to what seemed to be a solid, sales-performing line of automobiles. The new-for-1968 Javelin and AMX had been quite popular in their initial year, so little was done to them for 1969. The Rambler, which was entering its last model year, was little changed also, except for its name. Apparently the name "American" was over-used (American Motors Rambler American is a bit of a mouthful!). Through the car's lifespan, it had been known as the Nash (and Hudson) Rambler (1950 to 1955), then the Rambler American (1958 to 1968), and now, for its final year, it was back to the Rambler. Despite nameplate changes, there was little else to differentiate the 1969 Rambler from the 1968 Rambler American. One bright note was the offering of the high performance Hurst SC/Rambler model. Marketing such a high profile performance model in a car's last model run seems rather odd, but AMC marketers were ingenious people who managed to turn this car into the showroom attention-getter that the company was always searching for, but rarely found. This one was a winner! Initial plans had called for about 500 of these V8 equipped "Scramblers" to be produced, but they were so successful that two more

runs were built. The first run of cars was finished in white paint with red bodysides and a blue stripe over the hood, roof and decklid. The second and third runs (totalling about 500 cars each), were also white cars but had more modest, narrow red and blue stripes. Power for the SC/Rambler came from the AMX 390 CID, 4-barrel, V8 linked to a 4-speed, close-ratio transmission with Hurst shifter. Other features included a Sun tachometer, dual exhaust, Twin-Grip differential, cold air induction hood scoop, and special suspension and cooling components.

The larger AMC models, Rebel and Ambassador, received styling revisions. The mid-sized Rebel featured a new grille design and new taillight and decklid styling. The full-sized Ambassador was given a more extensive facelift. The fad of vertically stacked headlights had apparently run its course by this time, and AMC chose to revert to the more traditional horizontal positioning on the restyled Ambassador. Hood, fenders, grille and front bumper were all affected by this styling update. The new look was quite pleasant and would serve the Ambassador in this basic form through 1973.

**1969**

Ambassador DPL 2-Door Hardtop

AMX 2-Door Hardtop

Javelin SST 2-Door Hardtop

Rambler 440 4-Door Wagon

Rambler Rogue 2-Door Hardtop

Rebel SST 2-Door Hardtop

**Model year production:** 282,809, down 4.59% from 1968.
**Domestic market share:** 3.18% (9th place)
**Base price range:** $1,998 to $3,998.
**Industry average base price:** $3,386.
**American Motors average base price:** $2,837.
**Introduction date:** October 1, 1968.
**Assembly plants:** Kenosha, Wisconsin, and Brampton, Ontario, Canada.

**Data plate identification:** Thirteen digit code read as follows: A = American Motors; 9 = 1969; transmission code (see chart); car line–body type-series numbers (see last three digits of style number); engine code (see chart); 100001 and up for serial number (700001 and up for cars built in Ontario). *Example:* A9A797I100001 is a 1969 Torque-Command Automatic, Javelin SST 2-Door, 304 CID V8, serial number 100001 built in Kenosha.

## Powertrains

| Engine | Gross HP | Engine Code | Transmission Availability | Trans. Code | Rambler | AMX | Javelin | Rebel | Amb. |
|---|---|---|---|---|---|---|---|---|---|
| 199 CID, 1-bbl., 6-cyl. | 128 | A | 3-speed manual, col./flr. | S/C | S (base) | - | - | - | - |
| | | | 3-speed w/Overdrive | O | $116 | - | - | - | - |
| | | | Shift-Command Automatic | A | $171 | - | - | - | - |
| 232 CID, 1-bbl., 6-cyl. | 145 | B | 3-speed manual | S/C | S (Rogue)/$45 | - | S | S | - |
| | | | 3-speed w/Overdrive | O | - | - | - | $116 | |
| | | | Shift-Command Automatic | A | $171 (R.)/$216 | - | $223 | $223 | - |
| 232 CID, 2-bbl., 6-cyl. | 155 | C | 3-speed manual | S/C | $16 (R.)/$61 | - | - | $16 | S — DPL |
| | | | Shift-Command Automatic | A | $187 (R.)/$232 | - | - | $187 | $223 (DPL) |
| 290 CID, 2-bbl., V8 | 200 | M | 3-speed manual | S/C | - | - | $45 | $45 | $45 (DPL)/ (SST) |
| | | | Shift-Command Automatic (col./flr.) | A | $224 (R.)/$277 | - | $268 | $268 | $268 (DPL)/ $223 (SST) |
| 290 CID, 4-bbl., V8 | 225 | N | 3-speed manual | S/C | - | - | $80 | - | - |
| | | | 4-speed manual | M | $193 (R.) | S | $313 | - | - |
| | | | Shift-Command Automatic (col./flr.) | A | - | $21 | - | - | - |
| 343 CID, 2-bbl., V8 | 230 | S | 3-speed manual | S | - | - | - | $52 | $52 |
| | | | Shift-Command Automatic (col./flr.) | A | - | - | - | $275 | $275 |
| 343 CID, 4-bbl., V8 | 280 | T | 3-speed manual | S/C | - | - | $91 | $91 | $91 |
| | | | 4-speed manual | M | - | $45 | $296 | - | - |
| | | | Shift-Command Automatic (col./flr.) | A | - | $66 | $315 | $315 | $315 |
| 390 CID, 4-bbl., V8 | 315 | X | 3-speed manual | S/C | - | - | $168* | - | $168 (SST) |
| | | | 4-speed manual | M | - | $123 | $373* | - | - |
| | | | Shift-Command Automatic (col./flr.) | A | - | $141 | $391* | - | $391 (SST) |

*Available Javelin 390 CID V8 in Javelin SST models only.

## Major Options

| | Rambler | AMX | Javelin | Rebel | Ambassador |
|---|---|---|---|---|---|
| Air conditioning | $387 | $376 | $376 | $376 | S |
| Adjust-O-Tilt steering wheel | - | - | - | $45 | $45 |
| Speed control | - | - | - | $52 | $52 |
| Soft Ray tinted glass | $32 | $32 | $32 | $36 | $39 |
| Vinyl top (excluding Wagon models) | - | - | $100 | $90 | $100 |
| Power steering — variable-ratio | $90 | $95 | $95 | $100 | $100 |
| Power brakes | $42 | $42 | $42 | $42 | $42 |
| Power windows | - | - | - | - | $105 |
| AM radio | $62 | $62 | $62 | $62 | $62 |
| AM/FM radio | - | $134 | $134 | $134 | $134 |

| | Rambler | AMX | Javelin | Rebel | Ambassador |
|---|---|---|---|---|---|
| Custom wheel covers | $21 | - | $21 | $21 | S-SST/$21 |
| Turbo Cast wheel covers | - | $46 | $67 | $76 | $46–$76 |
| Station Wagon third seat | - | - | - | $118 | $118 |

Options common to most models. (- = Not Available; S = Standard equipment.) Items may be standard equipment, optional at different pricing, or unavailable on certain models. This chart is only a guide.

## Paint Colors

| | Code | | Code |
|---|---|---|---|
| Big Bad Blue* | P2 | Alamosa Aqua Met. | P68 |
| Big Bad Orange* | P3 | Surf Green Metallic | P70 |
| Big Bad Green* | P4 | Hunter Green Met. | P71 |
| Flat Black** | P7 | Frost White | P72 |
| Bright Red** | P9 | Willow Green Metallic | P75 |
| Bright Blue** | P10 | Pompeii Yellow | P76 |
| Matador Red | P39 | Butternut Beige Met. | P77 |
| Ascot Gray | P62 | Cordoba Brown Met. | P78 |
| Castillian Gray Met. | P63 | Bittersweet Orange Met. | P79 |
| Beal Street Blue Met. | P64 | Black Mink Metallic | P80 |
| Regatta Blue Met. | P65 | White** | P88 |

*Spring colors available only on select models. **Special SC/Rambler colors.

# Rambler

*"One American car against the world."*

**Nameplate year of origin:** 1950 (Nash).
**Current bodystyle lifespan:** 1964 through 1969.
**Predecessor to this model:** Rambler American (1958 to 1963).
**Replacement for this model:** Hornet (1970 to 1977).
**Percentage of division's sales volume:** 34.49%.
**Corporate siblings:** None.
**Primary competition:** Chevrolet Nova, Dodge Dart, Ford Falcon, and Plymouth Valiant.
**Notable changes:** Trim and detail changes.
**Major standard equipment:** Cloth and vinyl front bench seat, front arm rests and ash trays, variable speed windshield wipers, rubber floor mats, cargo mat, and 6.45 × 14 BSW tires (6.95 × 14 BSW tires on wagons). 440 adds: Full carpeting, rear armrests, and custom steering wheel. Rogue adds: All-vinyl front bench seat, wheel covers, special trim and identification.

## Measurements

| | Cars | Wagons |
|---|---|---|
| Wheelbase | 106.0" | 106.0" |
| Length | 181.0" | 181.0" |
| Width | 70.8" | 70.8" |
| Height | 54.2" | 54.5" |
| Legroom — front | 42.0" | 41.0" |
| Legroom — rear | 35.0" | 36.5" |
| Headroom — front | 39.0" | 39.3" |
| Headroom — rear | 39.0" | 37.0" |
| Luggage cap. (cu. ft.) | 12.0 | 66.0 |
| Fuel capacity (gals.) | 16.0 | 16.0 |

**1969**

## Models Available

| | Style Number | Base MSRP | Change from LY | Shipping Wt. (lbs.) | Production | Change from LY |
|---|---|---|---|---|---|---|
| Rambler 2-Door Sedan | 6906 | $1,998 | +2.67% | 2636 | 51,062 | -5.13% |
| Rambler 4-Door Sedan | 6905 | $2,076 | +2.57% | 2667 | 16,234 | -2.18% |
| Rambler 440 4-Door Sedan | 6905-5 | $2,218 | +2.40% | 2679 | 11,957 | +7.57% |
| Rambler 440 40Door Wagon | 6908-5 | $2,478 | +2.14% | 2815 | 13,233 | +59.72% |
| Rambler Rogue 2-Door Hardtop | 6909-7 | $2,296 | +2.32% | 2717 | 3,543 | -22.11% |
| Rambler SC/Rambler-Hurst 2-Dr. HT | 6909-7 | $2,998 | NEW | 3160 | 1,512 | NEW |
| TOTALS | Avg. price | $2,213 | +8.47% | Production | 97,541 | +3.36% |

# AMX

*"The performer."*

**Nameplate year of origin:** 1968.
**Current bodystyle lifespan:** 1968 through 1970.
**Predecessor to this model:** None.
**Replacement for this model:** None.
**Percentage of division's sales volume:** 2.93%.
**Corporate siblings:** Javelin (AMX created from shortened Javelin body).
**Primary competition:** Chevrolet Corvette, Chevrolet Camaro, Dodge Challenger, Ford Mustang, Plymouth Barracuda, and Pontiac Firebird.
**Notable changes:** Minor trim and detail changes.
**Major standard equipment:** All-vinyl front bucket seats, front armrests, full carpeting, interior courtesy lights, Weather-Eye heating & ventilation system, custom steering wheel, and E70 × 14 Wide-Oval BSW tires.

### Measurements

| | |
|---|---|
| Wheelbase | 97.0" |
| Length | 177.2" |
| Width | 71.6" |
| Height | NA |
| Legroom — front | 42.0" |
| Legroom — rear | NA |
| Headroom — front | 39.0" |
| Headroom — rear | NA |
| Luggage cap. (cu. ft.) | 9.6 |
| Fuel capacity (gals.) | 19.0 |

### Models Available

| | Style Number | Base MSRP | Change from LY | Shipping Wt. (lbs.) | Production | Change from LY |
|---|---|---|---|---|---|---|
| AMX 2-Door Hardtop | 6939-7 | $3,297 | +1.60% | 3094 | 8,293 | +23.32% |
| TOTALS | | Avg. price $3,297 | +1.60% | | Production 8,293 | +23.32% |

# Javelin

*"You can see why we call it the Javelin."*

**Nameplate year of origin:** 1968.
**Current bodystyle lifespan:** 1968 through 1970.
**Predecessor to this model:** Marlin (1965 to 1967).
**Replacement for this model:** Javelin (1971 to 1974).
**Percentage of division's sales volume:** 14.38%.
**Corporate siblings:** AMX (created through a shortened Javelin body).
**Primary competition:** Chevrolet Camaro, Dodge Challenger, Ford Mustang, Plymouth Barracuda, and Pontiac Firebird.
**Notable changes:** Minor trim and detail changes.
**Major standard equipment:** All-vinyl front bucket seats, front armrests, full carpeting, interior courtesy lights, Weather-Eye heating & ventilation system, and 6.95 × 14 BSW tires. SST adds: Reclining bucket seats, wood-grain sports steering wheel and door panel trim, rocker panel moldings, wheel covers and hood-scoop moldings.

### Measurements

| | |
|---|---|
| Wheelbase | 109.0" |
| Length | 189.2" |
| Width | 71.9" |
| Height | NA |
| Legroom — front | 42.0" |
| Legroom — rear | 29.8" |
| Headroom — front | 39.0" |
| Headroom — rear | 36.7" |
| Luggage cap. (cu. ft.) | 10.2 |
| Fuel capacity (gals.) | 19.0 |

### Models Available

| | Style Number | Base MSRP | Change from LY | Shipping Wt. (lbs.) | Production | Change from LY |
|---|---|---|---|---|---|---|
| Javelin 2-Door Hardtop | 6979-5 | $2,512 | +1.21% | 2810 | 17,389 | -40.24% |
| Javelin SST 2-Door Hardtop | 6979-7 | $2,633 | +1.78% | 2827 | 23,286 | -10.53% |
| TOTALS | | Avg. price $2,573 | +1.50% | | Production 40,675 | -26.24% |

# Rebel

*"The car for people."*

**Nameplate year of origin:** 1957 (Nash Rambler model).
**Current bodystyle lifespan:** 1967 through 1978 (restyles in 1969, 1971, and 1974).
**Predecessor to this model:** Rambler Classic (1963 to 1966).
**Replacement for this model:** Matador (1971 to 1978).
**Percentage of division's sales volume:** 21.25%.
**Corporate siblings:** Ambassador (shared components from the cowl back).
**Primary competition:** Chevrolet Chevelle, Dodge Coronet, Ford Fairlane, and Plymouth Belvedere/Satellite.
**Notable changes:** Revised front end styling and trim and detail changes.
**Major standard equipment:** Cloth and vinyl front bench seat, front arm rests, rubber floor mats, hidden compartment (Wagons), Weather-Eye heating & ventilation system, roof-top travel rack (wagons) and 7.35 × 14 BSW tires (7.75 × 14 BSW tires on Wagons). SST adds: Full carpeting, rear arm rests, custom steering wheel, dual horns, lock for glove box and hidden compartment on wagons and full wheel covers.

## Measurements

|  | Cars | Wagons |
|---|---|---|
| Wheelbase | 114.0" | 114.0" |
| Length | 197.0" | 198.0" |
| Width | 77.2" | 77.2" |
| Height | 55.0" | 55.4" |
| Legroom — front | 42.6" | 42.6" |
| Legroom — rear | 38.6" | 38.6" |
| Headroom — front | 39.8" | 39.8" |
| Headroom — rear | 38.0" | 38.0" |
| Luggage cap. (cu. ft.) | 18.2 | 94.6 |
| Fuel capacity (gals.) | 21.5 | 21.5 |

## Models Available

|  | Style Number | Base MSRP | Change from LY | Shipping Wt. (lbs.) | Production | Change from LY |
|---|---|---|---|---|---|---|
| Rebel 2-Door Hardtop | 6919-0 | $2,496 | +1.71% | 3153 | 5,396 | -26.85% |
| Rebel 4-Door Sedan | 6915-0 | $2,484 | +1.68% | 3089 | 10,885 | -26.01% |
| Rebel 4-Door Wagon | 6918-0 | $2,817 | +3.22% | 3357 | 8,569 | +15.38% |
| Rebel SST 2-Door Hardtop | 6919-7 | $2,598 | -6.38% | 3136 | 5,405 | -45.27% |
| Rebel SST 4-Door Sedan | 6915-7 | $2,584 | NEW | 3074 | 20,595 | NEW |
| Rebel SST 4-Door Wagon | 6918-7 | $2,947 | NEW | 3349 | 9,256 | NEW |
| TOTALS | *Avg. price* | $2,654 | -0.83% | *Production* | 60,106 | -24.23% |

*\*Production by body style is not available.*  *\*\*Differences in percentages due to discontinuance of certain models.*

# Ambassador

*"It will remind you of the days when money really bought something."*

**Nameplate year of origin:** 1933 (From top-of-the-line Nash).
**Current bodystyle lifespan:** 1967 through 1978 (Shared basic structure with Matador).
**Predecessor to this model:** Ambassador (1963 to 1966).
**Replacement for this model:** None.
**Percentage of division's sales volume:** 27.65%.
**Corporate siblings:** Rebel (Shared components from the cowl back).
**Primary competition:** Chevrolet BelAir/Impala/Caprice, Ford LTD, and Plymouth Fury.
**Notable changes:** Revised front end styling, and trim and detail changes.
**Major standard equipment:** Cloth and vinyl front bench seat, full carpeting, all-season air conditioning, cargo mat, and 7.75 × 14 BSW tires. DPL adds: Additional exterior trim, full wheel covers, roof-top travel rack (wagon), deluxe interior trim level, and 8.25 × 14 BSW tires on wagons. SST adds: All-vinyl reclining seats, center armrest, walnut-grain interior trim, light group, electric clock, and exterior wood grain trim.

## Measurements

|  | Cars | Wagons |
|---|---|---|
| Wheelbase | 114.0" | 114.0" |
| Length | 197.0" | 198.0" |
| Width | 77.2" | 77.2" |
| Height | 55.0" | 55.4" |
| Legroom — front | 42.6" | 42.6" |
| Legroom — rear | 38.6" | 38.6" |
| Headroom — front | 39.8" | 39.8" |
| Headroom — rear | 38.0" | 38.0" |
| Luggage cap. (cu. ft.) | 18.2 | 94.6 |
| Fuel capacity (gals.) | 21.5 | 21.5 |

**1969**

## Models Available

| | Style Number | Base MSRP | Change from LY | Shipping Wt. (lbs.) | Production | Change from LY |
|---|---|---|---|---|---|---|
| Ambassador 4-Door Sedan | 6985-2 | $2,914 | +3.33% | 3276 | 14,617 | +66.33% |
| Ambassador DPL 2-Door Hardtop | 6989-5 | $3,182 | +8.19% | 3371 | 4,504 | +21.86% |
| Ambassador DPL 4-Door Sedan | 6985-5 | $3,165 | +8.39% | 3320 | 12,665 | -4.52% |
| Ambassador DPL 4-Door Wagon | 6988-5 | $3,504 | +9.26% | 3560 | 8,866 | -17.06% |
| Ambassador SST 2-Door HT | 6989-7 | $3,622 | +14.19% | 3554 | 8,998 | +17.07% |
| Ambassador SST 4-Door Sdn. | 6985-7 | $3,605 | +14.41% | 3516 | 18,719 | +39.83% |
| Ambassador SST 4-Door Wgn. | 6988-7 | $3,998 | NEW | 3753 | 7,825 | NEW |
| TOTALS | | *Avg. price* $3,427 | +13.93% | | *Production* 76,194 | +25.17% |

# BUICK

*"Now, wouldn't you really rather have a 1969 Buick?"*

The full-size Buick models took their turn at a major facelift this year. LeSabre, Wildcat and Electra models all had slightly more formal rooflines and more squared off fender lines. The familiar "sweepspear" body side lines of the LeSabre and Wildcat returned, with an arch over each front wheel opening that ran to the front of the rear wheel opening, and from the rear opening to the top of the rear bumper. On the Electra, the bodyline ran straight from the front fender to the bottom edge of the rear bumper. Wildcat models now shared the LeSabre chassis, instead of the longer Electra chassis. Other exterior styling features included a "loop-style" grille with the grille encased by the bumper, and taillights set into the rear bumper. Interiors were also upgraded, and the 400 CID and 430 CID V8 engines were into their last year of production.

Special, Skylark and Sportwagon models sported new grilles and updated interiors, but were otherwise little changed. A new model offering was the one-year-only California GS 2-Door Coupe. Based on a Special Deluxe Coupe, the California GS offered a 350 CID V8 engine, vinyl top, and other dress-up items. This new California GS model put a Gran Sport Buick into a lower price range and was intended to boost sales. Unfortunately, everyone else had the same idea, and sales of these lower content, lower price pseudo-muscle cars never reached their expected levels. The Riviera carried on through 1969 with revised interior and exterior trim.

California GS 2-Door Coupe

Electra 225 Custom 2-Door Hardtop

GS 400 2 Door Convertible and
GS 350 2-Door Hardtop

LeSabre Custom 4-Door Hardtop and
LeSabre 4-Door Sedan

Riviera 2-Door Hardtop

Skylark Custom 4-Door Hardtop and
Skylark 4-Door Sedan

Sportwagon 4-Door Wagon

Wildcat Custom 4-Door Hardtop and
2-Door Convertible

**Model year production:** 664,822, up 4.89% over 1968.
**Domestic market share:** 7.47% (5th place).
**Base price range:** $2,562 to $4,701.
**Industry average base price:** $3,386.
**Buick average base price:** $3,547.
**Introduction date:** September 1968.
**Assembly plants:** Southgate, CA (C); Atlanta, GA (D); Flint, MI (H); Kansas City, MO (K); Fairfax, KS (X); Wilmington, DE (Y); Fremont, CA (Z); and Oshawa, Ontario, (1).

**Data plate identification:** Thirteen digit code read as follows: five digit style number in which 4 = Buick, 2nd number identifies series (3 is Skylark, 8 is Electra, etc.), 3rd through 5th digits indicate model number; 9 = 1969 year; assembly plant code; 100001 and up for serial number. *Example:* 452379X100001 is a 1969 Buick LeSabre 2-Door Hardtop, serial number 100001, built in Fairfax, KS.

## Powertrains

| Engine | Gross HP | Transmission Availability | Special/ Skylark | GS | Sport-wagon | LeSabre | Wild./Elec./ Riviera |
|---|---|---|---|---|---|---|---|
| 250 CID, 2-bbl., 6-cyl. | 155 | 3-speed manual | S | - | - | - | - |
|  |  | Super Turbine 300 Automatic | $174 | - | - | - | - |
| 350 CID, 2-bbl., V8 | 230 | 3-speed manual | S[1]/$111[2] | - | S | S | - |
|  |  | Super Turbine 300 Automatic | $185[1]/$296[2] | - | - | $185 | - |
|  |  | Turbo Hydra-matic | $206[1] | - | $206 | - | - |
| 350 CID, 4-bbl., V8 | 280 | 3-speed manual | $47[1]/$158[2] | S —* | $47 | - | - |
|  |  | 4-speed manual | - | $185 —* | - | - | - |
|  |  | Super Turbine 300 Automatic | $343[2] | - | - | $232 | - |
|  |  | Turbo Hydra-matic | $253[1] | $206 —* | $253 | $275–400 | - |
| 400 CID, 4-bbl., V8 | 340 | 3-speed manual | - | S (400) | - | - | - |
|  |  | 4-speed manual | - | $185 (400) | - | - | - |
|  |  | Turbo Hydra-matic | - | $227 (400) | $348 | - | - |
| 430 CID, 4-bbl., V8 | 360 | 3-speed manual | - | - | - | - | S (Wildcat) |
|  |  | Turbo Hydra-matic | - | - | - | - | S (Elec. & Riv.)/ $227 (Wildcat) |

[1]*Skylark Custom only.*   [2]*All but Skylark Custom.*   **California GS and GS 350 models.*

**1969**

## Major Options

| | Skylark | LeSabre | Wildcat | Electra 225 | Riviera |
|---|---|---|---|---|---|
| Air conditioning — Manual | $376 | $421 | $421 | $421 | $421 |
| Air conditioning — Automatic | - | $500 | $500 | $500 | $500 |
| Cruise Master speed control | $58 | $63 | $63 | $63 | $63 |
| Soft Ray tinted glass | $39 | $44 | $44 | $44 | $47 |
| Deck lid remote release | $14 | $14 | $14 | $14 | $14 |
| Tilt steering wheel | $45 | $45 | $45 | $45 | S |
| Power steering — variable-ratio | $100 | $111 | $111 | S | S |
| Power brakes | $42 | $42 | $42 | S | S |
| Power door locks | - | $68[1] | $68[1] | $68[1] | $47 |
| Power driver's seat/Bench seat, 4-way | $74 (ex. 6-cyl.) | $74 | $74 | $47–$74 | $74 |
| Power windows (except on 6-cylinder) | $105 | $110 | $110 | $110* | $110 |
| AM radio | $70 | $88 | $88 | $88 | $88 |
| AM/FM stereo (not stereo in Skylark) | $134 | $268 | $268 | $268 | $268 |
| Front bucket seats | $ | - | - | - | $ |
| Vinyl roof | $102 | $123 | S | $139 | $128 |
| White sidewall tires — standard size | $31–$36 | $42 | $42 | $47 | $42 |
| Wheel trim covers (Deluxe on Electra) | $21 | $21 (base) | S | S | S |

*Standard on Convertible. Options common to most models. (- = Not Available; S = Standard equipment.) Items may be standard equipment, optional at different pricing, or unavailable on certain models. This chart is only a guide.  [1]Two-Door models $47.

## Paint Colors

| | Code | Skylark | LeSabre/Wildcat/Electra | Riviera |
|---|---|---|---|---|
| Arctic White | 11 | x | x | x |
| Platinum Mist | 13 | x | x | x |
| Tealmist Gray Met. | 16 | x | x | x |
| Regal Black | 19 | | x | |
| Cascade Blue Met. | 24 | x | x | |
| Stratomist Blue Met. | 26 | x | x | x |
| Nocturne Blue Met. | 29 | | x | x |
| Twilight Turquoise Met. | 39 | x | x | |
| Silver Fern Met. | 41 | x | x | |
| Willowmist Green | 42 | x | x | |
| Lime Mist Met. | 43 | x | x | |
| Verdemist Green Met. | 49 | | | x |
| Bamboo Cream | 50 | | x | x |
| Cortez Gold Met. | 53 | x | | |
| Cornet Gold Met. | 55 | | x | x |
| Sandpiper Beige | 61 | x | x | x |
| Bittersweet Mist Met. | 62 | x | x | x |
| Copper Mist Met. | 65 | | | x |
| Burnished Cinnamon Met. | 67 | x | x | |
| Deep Chestnut Met. | 68 | | | x |
| Pearl Beige Met. | 70 | | | x |
| Sunset Mist Met. | 73 | | | x |
| Vintage Red Met. | 74 | | | x |
| Fire Red | 75 | x | x | |
| Rosewood Met. | 78 | | x | x |

# Special, Skylark and GS

*"Welcome additions to your most wanted list."*

**Nameplate year of origin:** 1935 (Special; 1953 (Skylark).
**Current bodystyle lifespan:** 1968 through 1972.
**Predecessor to this model:** Special/Skylark (1964 to 1967).
**Replacement for this model:** Century (1973 to 1977).
**Percentage of division's sales volume:** 25.17%.
**Corporate siblings:** Chevrolet Chevelle, Olds Cutlass, and Pontiac Tempest and LeMans.
**Primary competition:** Dodge Coronet and Mercury Comet and Montego.
**Notable changes:** Revised grille, minor trim and detail changes.
**Major standard equipment:** Cloth and vinyl front bench seat (all-vinyl on wagon), cigarette lighter, front ash trays and arm rests, crank-operated vent windows, Magic-Mirror finish paint, self adjusting brakes, 7.75 × 14 BSW tires. Skylark adds: All-vinyl upholstery on coupes and convertible, deluxe steering wheel, rear arm rests and ash trays, full carpeting, ventless front door windows (2-Doors). Custom adds: Custom padded seat cushions, lower body rocker moldings. California GS adds: Cloth and vinyl bench seat, vinyl top, Super Sport wheels, special exterior moldings and functional hood scoops. GS adds: All-vinyl seats, dual exhausts, finned aluminum brake drums (400), heavy duty springs, shocks and stabilizer bar.

## Measurements

|  | 2-Doors | 4-Doors | Wagon |
|---|---|---|---|
| Wheelbase | 112.0" | 116.0" | 116.0" |
| Length | 200.7" | 204.7" | 209.1" |
| Width | 75.6" | 75.6" | 75.6" |
| Height | 53.4" | 54.1" | 54.5" |
| Legroom — front | 41.3" | 41.3" | 41.5" |
| Legroom — rear | 32.4" | 35.0" | 34.8" |
| Headroom — front | 37.9" | 38.6" | 38.4" |
| Headroom — rear | 36.3" | 37.3" | 38.3" |
| Luggage capacity (cu. ft.) | NA | NA | NA |
| Fuel capacity (gals.) | 20.0 | 20.0 | 20.0 |

## Models Available

|  | Style Number | Base MSRP | Change from LY | Shipping Wt. (lbs.) | Production | Change from LY |
|---|---|---|---|---|---|---|
| Special Deluxe 2-Door Coupe | 43327 | $2,562 | +1.95% | 3126 | 15,268 | -30.56% |
| Special Deluxe 4-Door Sedan | 43369 | $2,613 | +1.91% | 3182 | 11,113 | -32.94% |
| Special Deluxe 4-Dr., 2-Seat Wgn. | 43435 | $3,092 | +3.03% | 3736 | 2,590 | -76.27% |
| Special Deluxe 4-Dr., 3-Seat Wgn. | 43436 | $3,124 | NEW | 3783 | 6,677 | NEW |
| Skylark 2-Door Hardtop | 43537 | $2,736 | -2.04% | 3179 | 38,658 | +17.88% |
| Skylark 4-Door Sedan | 43569 | $2,715 | -2.02% | 3209 | 22,349 | -18.39% |
| Skylark Custom 2-Door Hardtop | 44437 | $3,009 | +1.79% | 3341 | 35,639 | -19.26% |
| Skylark Custom 2-Door Convertible | 44467 | $3,152 | +1.74% | 3398 | 6,552 | -19.98% |
| Skylark Custom 4-Door Sedan | 44469 | $2,978 | +1.85% | 3397 | 6,423 | -20.37% |
| Skylark Custom 4-Door Hardtop | 44439 | $3,151 | +1.38% | 3477 | 9,609 | -25.99% |
| California GS 2-Door Sport Coupe | 43327 | NA | NEW | NA | * | NEW |
| GS 350 2-Door Hardtop | 43437 | $2,980 | +1.85% | 3406 | 4,933 | -40.69% |
| GS 400 2-Door Hardtop | 44637 | $3,181 | +1.73% | 3549 | 6,356 | -40.84% |
| GS 400 2-Door Convertible | 44667 | $3,325 | +1.65% | 3594 | 1,176 | -52.08% |
| TOTALS | | Avg. price $2,971 | +1.71% | | Production 167,343 | -18.19% |

# Sportwagon

*"Buick's sporty wagon for the family."*

**Nameplate year of origin:** 1964.
**Current bodystyle lifespan:** 1968 through 1969.
**Predecessor to this model:** Sportwagon (1966 to 1967).
**Replacement for this model:** None.
**Percentage of division's sales volume:** 3.11%.
**Corporate siblings:** Oldsmobile Vista-Cruiser.
**Primary competition:** Dodge Coronet, and Mercury Montego.
**Notable changes:** Revised grille. Minor trim and detail changes.
**Major standard equipment:** All-vinyl bench seat, front door operated interior light, front and rear arm rests and ash trays, full carpeting, custom padded seat cushions, deluxe steering wheel, crank-operated vent windows, Magic-Mirror finish paint, self adjusting brakes, tinted glass-observation style roof, dual-action tailgate, and 8.55 × 14 BSW tires.

## Measurements

| | |
|---|---|
| Wheelbase | 121.0" |
| Length | 214.1" |
| Width | 75.6" |
| Height | 58.9" |
| Legroom — front | 41.6" |
| Legroom — rear | 37.8" |
| Headroom — front | 38.0" |
| Headroom — rear | 39.9" |
| Luggage capacity (cu. ft.) | 100.0 |
| Fuel capacity (gals.) | 20.0 |

## Models Available

| | Style Number | Base MSRP | Change from LY | Shipping Wt. (lbs.) | Production | Change from LY |
|---|---|---|---|---|---|---|
| Sportwagon 4-Door, 2-Seat Wagon | 44456 | $3,465 | +3.71% | 4106 | 9,157 | -13.04% |
| Sportwagon 4-Door, 3-Seat Wagon | 44466 | $3,621 | +3.49% | 4231 | 11,513 | -6.84% |
| TOTALS | | *Avg. price* $3,543 | +3.60% | | *Production* 20,670 | -9.69% |

# LeSabre

*"The 1969 Buick LeSabre."*

**Nameplate year of origin:** 1959.
**Current bodystyle lifespan:** 1969 through 1970.
**Predecessor to this model:** LeSabre (1967 to 1968).
**Replacement for this model:** LeSabre (1971 to 1976).
**Percentage of division's sales volume:** 29.76%.
**Corporate siblings:** Chevrolet Full-size, Pontiac Full-size, Oldsmobile Delta 88.
**Primary competition:** Chrysler Newport, Dodge Monaco, and Mercury Monterey.
**Notable changes:** Major restyling.
**Major standard equipment:** Cloth and vinyl front bench seat, glove box light, full carpeting, front and rear armrests, Magic-Mirror finish, and 8.55 × 15 BSW tires. Custom adds: Custom interior trim (all vinyl on Convertible), deluxe steering wheel, wheel opening moldings, "Custom" nameplates, and additional exterior trim moldings.

## Measurements

| | |
|---|---|
| Wheelbase | 123.2" |
| Length | 218.2" |
| Width | 79.5" |
| Height | 55.3" |
| Legroom — front | 42.3" |
| Legroom — rear | 37.9" |
| Headroom — front | 39.1" |
| Headroom — rear | 37.7" |
| Luggage capacity (cu. ft.) | NA |
| Fuel capacity (gals.) | 25.0 |

## Models Available

| | Style Number | Base MSRP | Change from LY | Shipping Wt. (lbs.) | Production | Change from LY |
|---|---|---|---|---|---|---|
| LeSabre 2-Door Hardtop | 45237 | $3,298 | +2.33% | 3936 | 16,201 | +8.57% |
| LeSabre 4-Door Sedan | 45269 | $3,216 | +2.39% | 3966 | 36,664 | -2.05% |
| LeSabre 4-Door Hardtop | 45239 | $3,356 | +2.29% | 3983 | 17,235 | +71.36% |
| LeSabre Custom 2-Door Hardtop | 45437 | $3,386 | +2.27% | 4018 | 38,887 | +31.39% |

| | Style Number | Base MSRP | Change from LY | Shipping Wt. (lbs.) | Production | Change from LY |
|---|---|---|---|---|---|---|
| LeSabre Custom 2-Door Convertible | 45467 | $3,579 | +2.14% | 3958 | 3,620 | -31.14% |
| LeSabre Custom 4-Door Sedan | 45469 | $3,310 | +2.32% | 3941 | 37,136 | +8.86% |
| LeSabre Custom 4-Door Hardtop | 45439 | $3,450 | +2.22% | 4073 | 48,123 | +19.20% |
| TOTALS | | Avg. price $3,371 | +2.28% | | Production 197,866 | +15.21% |

# Wildcat

*"No wonder Buick owners keep selling Buicks for us."*

**Nameplate year of origin:** 1962.
**Current bodystyle lifespan:** 1969 through 1970.
**Predecessor to this model:** Wildcat (1967 to 1968).
**Replacement for this model:** Centurion (1971 to 1973).
**Percentage of division's sales volume:** 10.15%.
**Corporate siblings:** Chevrolet Full-size, Pontiac Full-size, Oldsmobile Delta 88.
**Primary competition:** Chrysler 300, Dodge Monaco, and Mercury Marauder.
**Notable changes:** Major restyling.
**Major standard equipment:** Cloth and vinyl front bench seat, glove box light, full carpeting, front and rear armrests, deluxe steering wheel, Magic-Mirror finish, rocker panel and wheel opening moldings, heater and defroster, self adjusting brakes and 8.55 × 15 BSW tires. Custom adds: All-vinyl Notchback front bench seat for Coupe and Convertible, custom interior trim, and custom headlining.

## Measurements

| | |
|---|---|
| Wheelbase | 123.2" |
| Length | 218.2" |
| Width | 80.0" |
| Height | 55.3" |
| Legroom — front | 42.2" |
| Legroom — rear | 37.9" |
| Headroom — front | 38.9" |
| Headroom — rear | 37.7" |
| Luggage capacity (cu. ft.) | NA |
| Fuel capacity (gals.) | 25.0 |

## Models Available

| | Style Number | Base MSRP | Change from LY | Shipping Wt. (lbs.) | Production | Change from LY |
|---|---|---|---|---|---|---|
| Wildcat 2-Door HT | 46437 | $3,596 | +2.13% | 3926 | 12,416 | +15.95% |
| Wildcat 4-Door Sedan | 46469 | $3,491 | +2.20% | 4102 | 13,126 | -13.65% |
| Wildcat 4-Door HT | 46439 | $3,651 | +2.10% | 4204 | 13,805 | -9.02% |
| Wildcat Custom 2-Door Hardtop | 46637 | $3,817 | +2.00% | 4134 | 12,136 | +7.63% |
| Wildcat Custom 2-Door Convertible | 46667 | $3,948 | +1.94% | 4152 | 2,374 | -33.54% |
| Wildcat Custom 4-Door Hardtop | 46639 | $3,866 | +1.98% | 4220 | 13,596 | -3.29% |
| TOTALS | | Avg. price $3,728 | +2.05% | | Production 67,453 | -3.62% |

**1969**

# Electra 225

*"The most luxurious Buick."*

**Nameplate year of origin:** 1959.
**Current bodystyle lifespan:** 1969 through 1970.
**Predecessor to this model:** Electra 225 (1967 to 1968).
**Replacement for this model:** Electra (1971 to 1976).
**Percentage of division's sales volume:** 23.86%.
**Corporate siblings:** Cadillac Calais/de Ville, Oldsmobile Ninety-Eight.
**Primary competition:** Chrysler New Yorker, and Mercury Marquis.
**Notable changes:** Major restyling.
**Major standard equipment:** Cloth and vinyl bench seat, full carpeting and lower door carpeting, deluxe steering wheel, trunk light, bright rocker panel molding and wheel opening moldings, rear fender skirts, variable ratio power steering, power

## Measurements

| | |
|---|---|
| Wheelbase | 126.2" |
| Length | 224.8" |
| Width | 80.0" |
| Height | 55.8" |
| Legroom — front | 42.2" |
| Legroom — rear | 40.9" |
| Headroom — front | 39.4" |
| Headroom — rear | 38.3" |
| Luggage capacity (cu. ft.) | NA |
| Fuel capacity (gals.) | 25.0 |

front brakes, Turbo Hydra-matic 400 transmission, deluxe wheel covers and 8.85 × 15 BSW tires. Custom adds: Custom interior trim.

## Models Available

| | Style Number | Base MSRP | Change from LY | Shipping Wt. (lbs.) | Production | Change from LY |
|---|---|---|---|---|---|---|
| Electra 225 2-Door Hardtop | 48257 | $4,323 | +2.42% | 4203 | 13,128 | +22.63% |
| Electra 225 4-Door Sedan | 48269 | $4,302 | +2.43% | 4238 | 14,521 | +14.13% |
| Electra 225 4-Door Hardtop | 48239 | $4,432 | +2.36% | 4294 | 15,983 | +3.95% |
| Electra 225 Custom 2-Door HT | 48457 | $4,502 | +2.32% | 4222 | 27,018 | +295.81% |
| Electra 225 Custom 2-Door Conv. | 48467 | $4,643 | +2.25% | 4309 | 8,294 | +3.99% |
| Electra 225 Custom 4-Door Sedan | 48469 | $4,517 | +2.31% | 4281 | 14,434 | +32.30% |
| Electra 225 Custom 4-Door HT | 48439 | $4,611 | +2.26% | 4328 | 65,240 | +28.31% |
| TOTALS | Avg. price | $4,476 | +2.33% | Production | 158,618 | +37.50% |

# Riviera

*"The beautiful 1969 Riviera."*

**Nameplate year of origin:** 1949 (2-Dr. HT); 1963 (series).
**Current bodystyle lifespan:** 1966 through 1970.
**Predecessor to this model:** Riviera (1963 to 1965).
**Replacement for this model:** Riviera (1971 to 1976).
**Percentage of division's sales volume:** 7.95%.
**Corporate siblings:** Cadillac Eldorado and Oldsmobile Toronado.
**Primary competition:** Ford Thunderbird and Lincoln Continental Mark III.
**Notable changes:** Revised trim and detail changes.
**Major standard equipment:** Electric clock, trunk light, vinyl bench or bucket seats with custom padding, bright exterior moldings, variable ratio power steering, power brakes, Dual exhaust system, Turbo Hydra-matic 400 transmission, and 8.55 × 15 BSW tires.

## Measurements

| | |
|---|---|
| Wheelbase | 119.0" |
| Length | 215.2" |
| Width | 79.2" |
| Height | 53.2" |
| Legroom — front | 41.1" |
| Legroom — rear | 36.6" |
| Headroom — front | 37.8" |
| Headroom — rear | 37.5" |
| Luggage capacity (cu. ft.) | NA |
| Fuel capacity (gals.) | 21.0 |

## Models Available

| | Style Number | Base MSRP | Change from LY | Shipping Wt. (lbs.) | Production | Change from LY |
|---|---|---|---|---|---|---|
| Riviera 2-Door Hardtop | 49487 | $4,701 | +1.86% | 4199 | 52,872 | +7.28% |
| TOTALS | Avg. price | $4,701 | +1.86% | Production | 52,872 | +7.28% |

# CADILLAC

*"A masterpiece from the master craftsmen."*

The majority of Cadillac lines were restyled this year, the lone exception being the personal luxury Eldorado. All full-size General Motors cars were given a more massive look, and Cadillac bulked up along with the rest of the line. The vertically stacked headlights were dropped in favor of side by side lamps, set into a full-width grille. Fender edges came out to a point and held the parking lights. A full-length body crease, reminiscent of the earlier models, ran in a straight line from the top of the front fender edge, down the entire side to a point about midway down the body at the back bumper. Taillamps were of a typical Cadillac fashion, narrow vertical units inset into the trailing edge of the rear quarters. The model line and powertrains continued as in previous years.

The Eldorado entered 1969 with a new face to set it apart from the '67 and '68 models. Hidden headlights were gone, and new dual headlights were set at the ends of a full-width grille that had a smaller, more refined eggcrate pattern. At the back, the razor thin taillights were replaced by larger lenses. Other changes to the Eldorado were minor in nature.

Calais 4-Door Hardtop

de Ville 2-Door Convertible

Eldorado 2-Door Hardtop

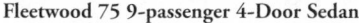

Fleetwood 75 9-passenger 4-Door Sedan

Fleetwood Brougham 4-Door Sedan

**Model year production:** 220,687, down 3.03% from 1968.
**Domestic market share:** 2.48% (11th place).
**Base price range:** $5,484 to $10,979.
**Industry average base price:** $3,386.
**Cadillac average base price:** $7,009.
**Introduction date:** September 1968.
**Assembly plants:** Detroit, MI (Q) and Linden, NJ (E).
**Data plate identification:** Thirteen digit code read as follows:

Five digit style number in which 6 = Cadillac, 2nd and 3rd digits identify series (e.g., 82 is Calais), 4th and 5th digits indicate body style number (2nd through 5th digit of VIN make up 2nd through 5th digit of body style number in listings); 9 for 1969; 7th digit is assembly plant code; 100001 and up for serial number. *Example:* 683479Q100001 is a 1969 Cadillac de Ville 2-Door Hardtop, serial number 100001, built in Detroit, MI.

**1969**

## Powertrains

| Engine | Gross HP | Transmission Availability | All models |
|---|---|---|---|
| 472 CID, 4-bbl., V8 | 375 | Turbo Hydra-matic | S |

## Major Options

| | Eldorado | de Ville/Calais | Brougham/60 Special | Seventy-Five |
|---|---|---|---|---|
| Automatic climate control | $516 | $516 | $516 | S |
| 6-way power seat | $90 | $90 (de V.)/$116 (Cal.) | $90 | $90 — NA Limo |
| Power door locks | $68 | $68 | $68 | $116 |
| AM-FM radio | $188 | $188 | $188 | $188 |
| Vinyl roof | $158 | $153 (de Ville only) | S — Brougham | NA |
| Twilight Sentinel (auto. dimmers) | $37 | $37 | $37 | $37 |
| Tilt and telescope steering wheel | $95 | $95 | $95 | $95 |

| | Eldorado | de Ville/Calais | Brougham/60 Special | Seventy-Five |
|---|---|---|---|---|
| Leather upholstery | $184 | $158 (de Ville only) | $158 | - |
| Cruise control | $95 | $95 | $95 | $95 |
| Tinted glass | $53 | $53 | $53 | $53 |
| Rear window defogger | $26 | $26 ($36 — convertible) | $26 | S |
| Automatic level control | S | $79 | S | S |
| Remote control trunk release | $53 | $53 | $53 | $53 |
| Firemist paint colors | $132 | $132 | $132 | $132 |

Options common to most models. (– = Not Available; S = Standard equipment.) Items may be standard equipment, optional at different pricing, or unavailable on certain models. This chart is only a guide.

## Paint Colors

| | Code |
|---|---|
| Sable Black | 10 |
| Cotillion White | 12 |
| Patina Silver Metallic | 16 |
| Phantom Gray Metallic | 18 |
| Astral Blue Metallic | 24 |
| Athenian Blue Metallic | 26 |
| Persian Aqua Metallic | 28 |
| Palmetto Green Metallic | 30 |
| Rampur Green Metallic | 36 |
| Colonial Yellow | 40 |
| Cameo Beige Metallic | 42 |
| Shalimar Gold Metallic | 44 |
| Cordovan Metallic | 46 |
| Wisteria Metallic | 47 |
| San Mateo Red Metallic | 48 |
| Empire Maroon Metallic | 49 |
| Sapphire Blue Firemist Metallic* | 90 |
| Chalice Gold Firemist Metallic* | 94 |
| Biscay Aqua Firemist Metallic* | 96 |
| Nutmeg Brown Firemist Metallic* | 97 |
| Chateau Mauve Firemist Metallic* | 99 |

*Firemist colors available at extra cost.

# Calais

*"The Calais is your easiest step to the pleasures of Cadillac ownership."*

**Nameplate year of origin:** 1965.
**Current bodystyle lifespan:** 1969 through 1970.
**Predecessor to this model:** Calais (1967 to 1968).
**Replacement for this model:** Calais (1971 to 1976).
**Percentage of division's sales volume:** 5.63%.
**Corporate siblings:** Buick Electra 225 and Oldsmobile Ninety-Eight.
**Primary competition:** Chrysler New Yorker and Lincoln Continental.
**Notable changes:** Completely restyled.
**Major standard equipment:** Cloth and vinyl seat upholstery, front center armrests, rear fender skirts, left side remote control outside rear view mirror, power windows, interior courtesy and warning lights, three-speed windshield wipers and washers, right side visor vanity mirrors, front cornering lamps, variable ratio power steering, power front disc brakes, Turbo Hydra-matic transmission, and 9.00 × 15 BSW tires.

## Measurements

| | |
|---|---|
| Wheelbase | 129.5" |
| Length | 225.0" |
| Width | 79.8" |
| Height | 54.5" |
| Legroom — front | 41.0" |
| Legroom — rear | 39.7" |
| Headroom — front | 37.8" |
| Headroom — rear | 37.2" |
| Luggage capacity (cu. ft.) | NA |
| Fuel capacity (gals.) | 26.0 |

## Models Available

| | Style Number | Base MSRP | Change from LY | Shipping Wt. (lbs.) | Production | Change from LY |
|---|---|---|---|---|---|---|
| Calais 2-Door Hardtop | 68247 | $5,484 | +3.18% | 4555 | 5,600 | -31.41% |
| Calais 4-Door Hardtop | 68249 | $5,660 | +3.08% | 4630 | 6,825 | -31.92% |
| TOTALS | | Avg. price $5,572 | +3.13% | | Production 12,425 | -31.69% |

# De Ville

*"The spirited performance so unique to Cadillac in the luxury field is yours, with spacious six-passenger roominess, in the de Ville."*

**Nameplate year of origin:** 1949 (as Hardtop designation); 1959 (series).
**Current bodystyle lifespan:** 1969 through 1970.
**Predecessor to this model:** de Ville (1967 to 1968).
**Replacement for this model:** de Ville (1971 to 1976).
**Percentage of division's sales volume:** 73.88%.
**Corporate siblings:** Buick Electra 225 and Oldsmobile Ninety-Eight.
**Primary competition:** Imperial, and Lincoln Continental.
**Notable changes:** Completely restyled.
**Major standard equipment:** Cloth and vinyl seat upholstery (leather on convertible), Two-way power seat adjustment, front and rear center armrests, rear fender skirts, left side remote control outside rear view mirror, power windows, interior door, courtesy and warning lights, three-speed windshield wipers and washers, right side visor vanity mirrors, front cornering lamps, variable ratio power steering, power front disc brakes, Turbo Hydra-matic transmission, and 9.00 × 15 BSW tires.

### Measurements

| | |
|---|---|
| Wheelbase | 129.5" |
| Length | 225.0" |
| Width | 79.8" |
| Height | 54.5" |
| Legroom — front | 41.0" |
| Legroom — rear | 39.7" |
| Headroom — front | 37.8" |
| Headroom — rear | 37.2" |
| Luggage capacity (cu. ft.) | NA |
| Fuel capacity (gals.) | 26.0 |

## Models Available

| | Style Number | Base MSRP | Change from LY | Shipping Wt. (lbs.) | Production | Change from LY |
|---|---|---|---|---|---|---|
| Coupe de Ville 2-Door Hardtop | 68347 | $5,721 | +3.04% | 4595 | 65,755 | +2.85% |
| de Ville 2-Door Convertible | 68367 | $5,905 | +2.95% | 4590 | 16,445 | -8.77% |
| Sedan de Ville 4-Door Sedan | 68369 | $5,954 | +2.92% | 4640 | 7,890 | -19.90% |
| Sedan de Ville 4-Door Hardtop | 68349 | $5,954 | +2.92% | 4660 | 72,958 | +0.41% |
| TOTALS | | Avg. price $5,884 | +2.96% | | Production 163,048 | -0.87% |

# Eldorado

*"The third edition of a motor car already a classic in its time."*

**Nameplate year of origin:** 1953.
**Current bodystyle lifespan:** 1967 through 1970.
**Predecessor to this model:** Fleetwood Eldorado (1965 to 1966).
**Replacement for this model:** Eldorado (1971 to 1978).
**Percentage of division's sales volume:** 10.57%.
**Corporate siblings:** Buick Riviera and Oldsmobile Toronado.
**Primary competition:** Lincoln Continental Mark III.
**Notable changes:** New front and rear styling and revised roofline.

### Measurements

| | |
|---|---|
| Wheelbase | 120.0" |
| Length | 221.0" |
| Width | 79.9" |
| Height | 53.3" |
| Legroom — front | 41.1" |
| Legroom — rear | 36.2" |
| Headroom — front | 37.7" |

**1969**

**Major standard equipment:** Cloth and vinyl seat upholstery, two-way power seat adjustment, front center armrests, left side remote control outside rear view mirror, power windows, interior door, courtesy and warning lights, three-speed windshield wipers and washers, right side visor vanity mirrors, front cornering lamps, variable ratio power steering, power front disc brakes, Turbo Hydra-matic transmission, front wheel drive, and 9.00 × 15 BSW tires.

### Measurements (cont.)

| | |
|---|---|
| Headroom — rear | 37.6" |
| Luggage capacity (cu. ft.) | NA |
| Fuel capacity (gals.) | 24.0 |

## Models Available

| | Style Number | Base MSRP | Change from LY | Shipping Wt. (lbs.) | Production | Change from LY |
|---|---|---|---|---|---|---|
| Fleetwood Eldorado 2-Door HT | 69347 | $6,711 | +1.60% | 4550 | 23,333 | -4.87% |
| TOTALS | Avg. price | $6,711 | +1.60% | Production | 23,333 | -4.87% |

# Fleetwood Brougham & Sixty-Special

*"No automobile in years has so captured the admiration of luxury car buyers as the magnificent Fleetwood Brougham & Sixty Special."*

**Nameplate year of origin:** 1938.
**Current bodystyle lifespan:** 1969 through 1970.
**Predecessor to this model:** Fleetwood Sixty-Special (1967 to 1968).
**Replacement for this model:** Fleetwood Sixty-Special (1971 to 1976).
**Percentage of division's sales volume:** 8.99%.
**Corporate siblings:** None.
**Primary competition:** None.
**Notable changes:** Completely restyled.
**Major standard equipment:** Cloth seat upholstery, two-way power seat adjustment, front and rear center armrests, rear fender skirts, left side remote control outside rear view mirror, power windows, interior courtesy lights, three-speed windshield wipers and washers, right side visor vanity mirrors, front cornering lamps, variable ratio power steering, power front disc brakes, Turbo Hydra-matic transmission, and 9.00 × 15 BSW tires. Brougham adds: Driver's side only seat adjustment, reading lights and padded vinyl top.

### Measurements

| | |
|---|---|
| Wheelbase | 133.0" |
| Length | 228.5" |
| Width | 79.8" |
| Height | 56.7" |
| Legroom — front | 42.0" |
| Legroom — rear | 44.4" |
| Headroom — front | 39.1" |
| Headroom — rear | 38.0" |
| Luggage capacity (cu. ft.) | NA |
| Fuel capacity (gals.) | 26.0 |

## Models Available

| | Style Number | Base MSRP | Change from LY | Shipping Wt. (lbs.) | Production | Change from LY |
|---|---|---|---|---|---|---|
| Fleetwood Sixty Special 4-Door Sdn. | 68069 | $6,779 | +2.98% | 4765 | 2,545 | -22.88% |
| Fleetwood Brougham 4-Door Sedan | 68169 | $7,110 | +3.06% | 4770 | 17,300 | +13.07% |
| TOTALS | Avg. price | $6,945 | +3.03% | Production | 19,845 | +6.69% |

# Fleetwood Seventy-Five

*"Among the world's fine cars, none are more respected than the Cadillac
Fleetwood Seventy-Five Limousine and 9-passenger Sedan."*

**Nameplate year of origin:** 1927 (Fleetwood bodies), 1936 (75 series).
**Current bodystyle lifespan:** 1969 through 1970.
**Predecessor to this model:** Fleetwood 75 (1967 to 1968).
**Replacement for this model:** Fleetwood 75 (1971 to 1976).
**Percentage of division's sales volume:** 0.92%.
**Corporate siblings:** None.
**Primary competition:** None.
**Notable changes:** Completely restyled.
**Major standard equipment:** Cloth seat upholstery, two-way power seat adjustment, rear center armrests, Automatic climate control, rear window defogger, rear fender skirts, left side remote control outside rear view mirror, power windows, interior door, courtesy and warning lights, three-speed windshield wipers and washers, right side visor vanity mirrors, front cornering lamps, fixed ratio power steering, power front disc brakes, Turbo Hydra-matic transmission, and 9.00 × 15 BSW tires.

## Measurements

| | |
|---|---|
| Wheelbase | 149.8" |
| Length | 245.3" |
| Width | 79.8" |
| Height | 57.0" |
| Legroom — front | 42.0" |
| Legroom — rear | NA |
| Headroom — front | 39.1" |
| Headroom — rear | NA |
| Luggage capacity (cu. ft.) | NA |
| Fuel capacity (gals.) | 26.0 |

## Models Available

| | Style Number | Base MSRP | Change from LY | Shipping Wt. (lbs.) | Production | Change from LY |
|---|---|---|---|---|---|---|
| Fleetwood Seventy-Five 4-Door Sdn. | 69723 | $10,841 | +1.99% | 5430 | 880 | +9.32% |
| Fleetwood Seventy-Five Limousine | 69733 | $10,979 | +1.96% | 5555 | 1,156 | +16.18% |
| TOTALS | | *Avg. price* $10,910 | +1.98% | | *Production* 2,036 | +13.11% |

# CHEVROLET

*"Putting you first, keeps us first."*

The 1969 model year was a quiet one for Chevy, closing a decade in which an extraordinary number of cars, engines and styling features were introduced — not to mention the recognition (good and bad) that some of them attained. Four legendary powertrains would be gone after this model year: the 230 CID 6-cylinder, the 327, 396 and the 427 CID V8s, to be replaced by the 250, 350, 400 and 454 cube engines. Also gone after this year were the horizontally opposed flat six from the Corvair, and the 4-cylinder Nova engine.

The most notable styling news was the restyling of the full-size line. All of the big Chevys sported a loop-style bumper, surrounding a very "Cadillac-like" eggcrate grille.

Body sides had a unique bubbled-out area around each wheel well that gave the cars a very masculine, sporty look. The wheel wells themselves were arched beyond the traditional semi-circle, creating an interesting effect. While still retaining a familiar Chevrolet look, the new cars looked even more like a luxury car, which was exactly Chevrolet's intent. The model lineup did not change, but the marketing of it did change. All wagon models carried their own nameplates and were marketed separately from their respective car nameplates. For example, the former Impala wagon was now the Kingswood wagon. Naming the wagon models separately from the rest of the passenger car line was not something new, but to actually market them as a separate line was a new twist for Chevrolet. Station wagons would remain as a separate line for marketing purposes until the late seventies, but putting different nameplates on the wagons would last only until 1972.

Another Chevrolet line making big changes was the Camaro. Still based on the '67 to '68 body and underpinnings, the 1969 model was more "macho" looking with broader looking fenders, larger wheel openings, and a more aggressive grille. A body side crease started at the front lip of each wheel opening, then trailed off from the top most edge of the opening for several feet. This styling was not as similar to the Pontiac Firebird as the first two models were. Unique as a one-year-only style, the '69 Camaro would be sold well into the 1970 season, as an all-new replacement would be available by February 1970. All information pertaining to any 1969 Camaro models built or sold as early 1970 models will be included in this section. A very rare car offered this year was the ZL1 option, which featured a 425-horsepower, 427 CID V8 engine. And for the second time in its short three-year history, a Camaro SS/RS 396 Convertible was selected as the official pace car for the Indianapolis 500 race.

Other models saw little change. The mid-size Chevelle received a new grille and rear trim. Also, the base level Chevelle 300 was dropped, and the Super Sport was once again an optional equipment package (instead of a separate model offering). The Corvette received new side louvers and detail improvements to an already exceptional package. This would be the last year for the Chevy II nameplate, as it would now become known as the Nova. The Chevy II name was not used on the car, but only in internal GM reference. That change was bound to happen, as there had not been any other trim levels offered since the 1968 restyling. Finally, the always controversial Corvair reached its final year of production virtually unchanged from 1968. There were a few interior trim changes, but Chevy wisely chose to let it go away quietly and gracefully. In fact, Chevrolet did not even print a sales brochure for the 1969 Corvair. Its replacement, the Vega, would not be ready until 1971, but there weren't enough sales left to justify carrying the Corvair on for one more year.

Camaro 2-Door Hardtop

Caprice 2-Door Hardtop

Malibu 2-Door Hardtop

Camaro Z/28 2-Door Hardtop

Corvair Monza 2-Door Convertible

Camaro SS 2-Door Convertible,
Indianapolis 500 Pace Car

Chevelle 300 Deluxe 4-Door Sedan

Corvette 2-Door Coupe

Impala 2-Door Convertible

Kingswood Estate 4-Door Wagon

Nova 4-Door Sedan

**Model year production:** 2,210,064, up 3.19% over 1968.
**Domestic market share:** 24.83% (1st place).
**Base price range:** $2,237 to $4,781.
**Industry average base price:** $3.386.
**Industry average base price:** $2,974.
**Introduction date:** September 26, 1968.
**Assembly plants:** Lakewood, GA (A), Atlanta, GA (D), Kansas City, MO (K), Fremont, CA (Z), Van Nuys, CA (L), Norwood, OH (N), Tarrytown, NY (T), Oshawa, Ontario, Canada (1), Baltimore, MD (B); Framingham, MA (G);

Flint, MI (F); Southgate, CA (C); Arlington, TX (R); Janesville, WI (J); Wilmington, DE (Y), and St. Louis, MO (S).
**Data plate identification:** Thirteen digit code read as follows: 1st digit 1 for Chevrolet; four digit style number (see listings below) in which 2nd and 3rd numbers identify series, 4th and 5th indicate body style; 9 for 1969; 7th digit is assembly plant code; 100001 and up for serial number. *Example:* 155119T100001 is a 1969 Chevrolet BelAir 2-Door Sedan, serial number 100001, built in Arlington, TX.

## Powertrains

| Engine | Gross HP | Transmission Availability | Corvair & Nova | Camaro | Chevelle | †Bisc./ BelA./Imp.* | Impala/ †Capr. | Cor-vette |
|---|---|---|---|---|---|---|---|---|
| 153 CID, 1-bbl., 4-cyl. | 90 | 3-speed manual | S | - | - | - | - | - |
| | | Torque-Drive | $69 | - | - | - | - | - |
| | | Powerglide Automatic | $148 | - | - | - | - | - |
| 164 CID — OHV, 2-bbl., Flat 6 | 95 | 3-speed manual | S (Corv.) | - | - | - | - | - |
| | | 4-speed manual | $90 (Corv.) | - | - | - | - | - |
| | | Powerglide Automatic | $148 (Corv.) | - | - | - | - | - |
| 164 CID Turbo-Air, 2-bbl., Flat 6 | 110 | 3-speed manual | $26 (Corv.) | - | - | - | - | - |
| | | 4-speed manual | $116 (Corv.) | - | - | - | - | - |
| | | Powerglide Automatic | $174 (Corv.) | - | - | - | - | - |
| 164 CID Turbo-Air, 4-bbl., Flat 6 | 140 | 3-speed manual | $79 (Corv.) | - | - | - | - | - |
| | | 4-speed manual | $169 (Corv.) | - | - | - | - | - |
| | | Powerglide Automatic | $227 (Corv.) | - | - | - | - | - |
| 230 CID Turbo-Thrift, 1-bbl., 6-cyl. | 140 | 3-speed manual | $78 | S | S[2] | - | - | - |
| | | 4-speed manual | - | $195 | - | - | - | - |
| | | Torque-Drive | $147 | $69 | - | - | - | - |
| | | Powerglide Automatic | $226 | $164 | $164 | - | - | - |
| 250 CID Turbo-Thrift, 1-bbl., 6-cyl. | 155 | 3-speed manual | $104 | $26 | $26[2] | S | - | - |
| | | 4-speed manual | - | $221 | - | - | - | - |
| | | Torque-Drive | $273 | $95 | - | - | - | - |
| | | Powerglide Automatic | $252 | $190 | $190[2] | $180 | - | - |
| | | Turbo Hydra-matic | $278 | $216 | $216[2] | $190 | - | - |
| 302 CID, 4-bbl., V8 Plus cost of Z28 package | 350 | 4-speed manual | - | S (Z28) | - | - | - | - |
| | | Turbo Hydra-matic | - | $222 (Z28) | - | - | - | - |
| 307 CID Turbo-Fire, 2-bbl., V8 | 200 | 3-speed manual | $167 | - | S[1]/$90 (Others) | - | - | - |
| | | Powerglide Automatic | $325 | - | $174[1]/$264 | - | - | - |

1969

| Engine | Gross HP | Transmission Availability | Corvair & Nova | Camaro | Chevelle | †Bisc./ BelA./Imp.* | Impala/ †Capr. | Cor-vette |
|---|---|---|---|---|---|---|---|---|
| | | | | | (Others) | - | - | - |
| | | Turbo Hydra-matic | $357 | - | $222¹/$312 | | | |
| | | | | | (Others) | - | - | - |
| 327 CID Turbo-Fire, 2-bbl., V8 | 210/235 | 3-speed manual | - | $89 | - | $95 | S | - |
| | | 4-speed manual | - | $284 | - | - | - | |
| | | Powerglide Automatic | - | $263 | - | $269 | $174 | - |
| | | Turbo Hydra-matic | - | $311 | - | $317 | $222 | - |
| 350 CID Turbo-Fire, 2-bbl., V8 | 255 | 3-speed manual | $220 | $142 | $26¹/$116 (Others) | $148 | $53 | - |
| | | 4-speed manual | $405 | $337 | $211¹/$301 (Others) | $333 | $238 | - |
| | | Powerglide Automatic | $394 | $316 | $200¹/$290 (Others) | $322 | $227 | - |
| | | Turbo Hydra-matic | $421 | $364 | $243¹/$338 (Others) | $370 | $275 | - |
| 350 CID Turbo-Fire, 4-bbl., V8 | 300 | 3-speed manual | $281 (SS) | $385 (SS)** | $69¹/$159 (Others) | $201 | $106 | S |
| | | 4-speed manual | $466 (SS) | $580 (SS)** | $254¹/$348 (Others) | $386 | $291 | $184 |
| | | Turbo Hydra-matic | $471 (SS) | $585 (SS)** | $291¹/$381 (Others) | $423 | $328 | $222 |
| 350 CID Turbo-Fire, 4-bbl., V8 | 350 | 4-speed manual | - | - | - | - | - | $316 |
| | | Turbo Hydra-matic | - | - | - | - | - | $354 |
| 396 CID Turbo-Fire, 2-bbl., V8 | 265 | 3-speed manual | - | - | - | $164 | $69 | - |
| | | 4-speed manual | | | | $349 | $254 | |
| | | Turbo Hydra-matic | | | | $386 | $295 | |
| 396 CID Turbo-Jet, 4-bbl., V8 | 325 | 3-speed manual | - | $359 (SS) | S (SS)/ $348¹/$438 (Others) | - | - | - |
| | | 4-speed manual | - | $554 (SS) | $185 (SS)/ $533¹/$623 (Others) | - | - | - |
| | | 4-speed manual heavy-duty | - | $681 (SS) | $322 (SS)/ $670¹/$760 (Others) | - | - | - |
| | | Turbo Hydra-matic | - | $581 (SS) | $222 (SS)/ $570¹/$660 (Others) | - | - | - |
| 396 CID Turbo-Jet, 4-bbl., V8, 350** | | 3-speed manual | $184 (SS) | $632 (SS) | $121 (SS)/ $469¹/$559 (Others) | - | - | - |
| | | 4-speed manual | $379 (SS) | $827 (SS) | $306 (SS)/ $654¹/$744 (Others) | - | - | - |
| | | 4-speed manual-heavy-duty | $497 (SS) | $854 (SS) | $443 (SS)/ $791¹/$881 (Others) | - | - | - |
| | | Turbo Hydra-matic | $406 (SS) | $854 (SS) | $343 (SS)/ $691¹/$781 (Others) | - | - | - |
| 427 CID Turbo-Jet, 4-bbl., V8 | 335 375 (Corvette) | 3-speed manual | - | $675 (SS) | - | $258 | $163 | $221 |
| | | 4-speed manual | - | $870 (SS) | - | $443 | $348 | $405 |
| | | Turbo Hydra-matic | - | $907 (SS) | - | $480 | $385 | $443 |
| 427 CID Turbo-Jet, 4-bbl., V8 | 390 | 3-speed manual | - | - | - | $332 | S (SS)/ $237 | $221 |

| Engine | Gross HP | Transmission Availability | Corvair & Nova | Camaro | Chevelle | †Bisc./ BelA./Imp.* | Impala/ †Capr. | Corvette |
|---|---|---|---|---|---|---|---|---|
| | | 4-speed manual | - | - | - | $517 | $313 (SS)/ $422 | $405 |
| | | Turbo Hydra-matic | - | - | - | $554 | $290 (SS)/ $459 | $443 |
| 427 CID Turbo-Jet, 3 × 2-bbl., V8 | 400/425 | 3-speed manual | - | - | - | $543 $448 | $184 (SS)/ $327 | |
| | | 4-speed manual | - | - | - | $856 $761 | $497 (SS)/ $510 | |
| | | Turbo Hydra-matic | - | - | - | $840 $745 | $474 (SS)/ $548 | |
| 427 CID Turbo-Jet, 3 × 2-bbl., V8 (L89 Aluminum heads add $395) | 435 | 3-speed manual | - | - | - | - | - | $437 |
| | | 4-speed manual | - | $1070 (SS) | - | - | - | $621 |
| | | Turbo Hydra-matic | - | $1361 (SS) | - | - | - | $732 |

*Biscayne, BelAir, and Impala 2- & 4-Dr. HT and 4-Door Sedan only.   **Aluminum head version also available, 375-hp.   ¹Greenbrier 9-passenger and Concours wagons only.   ²All but Greenbrier 9-passenger and Concours wagons.   †See text for corresponding wagon models.

## Major Options

| | Corvair | Nova | Camaro | Chevelle | Full-size | Corvette |
|---|---|---|---|---|---|---|
| Air conditioning | $ | $363 | $376 | $376 | $384 | $429 |
| Soft Ray tinted glass | $33 | $33 | $33 | $37 | $42 | $17 |
| Electronic speed control | - | - | - | - | $58 | - |
| Tilt steering wheel (with Telescopic on Corvette) | $42 | | | | | |
| (Telescopic) | - | $45 | $45 | $45 | $84 | |
| Power steering | - | $90 | $95 | $100–$105 | $100–$105 | $105 |
| Power brakes | - | $42 | $42 | $42 | $42 | $42 |
| Front disc brakes (req. PB) | - | $22 | $22 | $22 | $22 | S |
| Power door locks | - | - | $45–$69 | $45–$69 | $45–69 | - |
| Power windows (N/A on all) | - | - | $105 | $105 | $105 | $63 |
| AM radio | $61 | $61 | $61 | $61 | $61 | S |
| AM/FM radio | $134 | $134 | $134 | $134 | $134 | $173 |
| Front seat console | - | $ | $54 | $54 | $47 | S |
| Front bucket seats | S | $ | S | $122 | $122 | S |
| Vinyl roof | - | $79 | $84 | $90 | $100 | - |
| Wheel trim covers | $21 (500)/S (M.) | $21 | $21 | $21 | $21/S (Capr.) | S |
| Whitewall tires — Std. size | $28 | $31 | $32 | $33 | $36–$41 | $31 |
| Concours Sedan package | - | - | $132 | - | - | |
| Super Sport equipment package | $280 | $312 (350)/ | | | | |
| | | | $348 (396) | $348 (396) | $422 | - |
| Z/28 package | - | - | $507 | - | - | - |

Options common to most models. (- = Not Available; S = Standard equipment.) Items may be standard equipment, optional at different pricing, or unavailable on certain models. This chart is only a guide.   *Not available with 6-cylinder engine.

## Paint Colors

| | Code* | Camaro | Corvette | Other Chevrolet models |
|---|---|---|---|---|
| Tuxedo Black | 10 | x | x | x |
| Butternut Yellow | 40 | | | x |
| Dover White | 50 | | | x |
| Dusk Blue Metallic | 51 | | | x |
| Garnet Red | 52 | | | x |
| Glacier Blue Metallic | 53 | | | x |
| Azure Turquoise Met. | 55 | | | x |
| Fathom Green Met. | 57 | x | x | x |
| Frost Green Metallic | 59 | | | x |

1969

| | Code* | Camaro | Corvette | Other Chevrolet models |
|---|---|---|---|---|
| Burnished Brown Met. | 61 | | | x |
| Champagne Metallic | 63 | | | x |
| Olympic Gold Met. | 65 | | | x |
| Burgundy Metallic | 67 | x | x | x |
| Cortez Silver Metallic | 69 | x | x | x |
| LeMans Blue Metallic | 71 | x | x | x |
| Hugger Orange | 72 | x | | x |
| Daytona Yellow | 76 | x | | x |
| Rallye Green Metallic | 79 | x | | x |
| Can-Am White | 972 | | x | |
| Monza Red | 974 | | x | |
| Riverside Gold Met. | 980 | | x | |
| Monaco Orange | 990 | | x | |

*Corvette color codes may be different on some colors.*

# Corvair

*"Putting the engine behind is what puts
Corvair well ahead of its counterparts."*

**Nameplate year of origin:** 1960.
**Current bodystyle lifespan:** 1965 through 1969.
**Predecessor to this model:** Corvair (1960 to 1964).
**Replacement for this model:** Vega (1971 to 1977).
**Percentage of division's sales volume:** 0.27%.
**Corporate siblings:** None.
**Primary competition:** AMC Rambler, Ford Falcon and Plymouth Valiant.
**Notable changes:** Minor trim and detail changes.
**Major standard equipment:** Cloth and vinyl front bench seat, dual sun visors, center dome light, and 7.00 × 13 BSW tires. Monza adds: All-vinyl bucket seats, full carpeting, folding rear seat, glove box light, front door map pockets, and additional exterior chrome trim.

## Measurements

| | |
|---|---|
| Wheelbase | 108.0" |
| Length | 183.3" |
| Width | 69.7" |
| Height | 51.3" |
| Legroom — front | 40.9" |
| Legroom — rear | 30.7" |
| Headroom — front | 37.9" |
| Headroom — rear | 36.4" |
| Cargo capacity (cu. ft.) | 7.0 |
| Fuel capacity (gals.) | 14.0 |

## Models Available

| | Style Number | Base MSRP | Change from LY | Shipping Wt. (lbs.) | Production | Change from LY |
|---|---|---|---|---|---|---|
| Corvair 500 2-Door Sport Coupe | 10137 | $2,258 | +0.67% | 2515 | 2,762 | -61.67% |
| Corvair Monza 2-Door Sport Coupe | 10537 | $2,522 | +0.60% | 2545 | 2,717 | -60.09% |
| Corvair Monza 2-Door Convertible | 10567 | $2,641 | +0.57% | 2770 | 521 | -62.41% |
| TOTALS | | *Avg. price* $2,474 | +0.61% | | *Production* 6,000 | -61.04% |

# Camaro

*"Chevrolet's incomparable Hugger."*

**Nameplate year of origin:** 1967.
**Current bodystyle lifespan:** 1967 through 1969.
**Predecessor to this model:** None.
**Replacement for this model:** Camaro (1970 to 1981).

## Measurements

| | |
|---|---|
| Wheelbase | 108.0" |
| Length | 186.0" |
| Width | 74.0" |

Percentage of division's sales volume: 10.44%.
Corporate siblings: Pontiac Firebird.
Primary competition: AMC Javelin, Ford Mustang, and Plymouth Barracuda.
Notable changes: Restyled exterior and revised powertrain offerings.
Major standard equipment: All-vinyl front bucket seats, cockpit-style instru-
    mentation, full color-keyed carpeting, hubcaps, three-spoke steering wheel,
    and, 7.35 × 14 BSW tires. RS package adds: Style trim package, parking lamps
    below front bumper and back-up lamps below rear bumper, concealed head-
    lamps, rocker molding trim, and specific RS trim. SS package adds: 350 CID
    V8 engine, specific hood with simulated air intakes, hood stripes, SS emblems,
    and D70 × 14 redline or WSW tires.

## Measurements (cont.)

| | |
|---|---|
| Height | 49.1" |
| Legroom — front | 43.8" |
| Legroom — rear | 30.7" |
| Headroom — front | 37.4" |
| Headroom — rear | 36.1" |
| Cargo capacity (cu. ft.) | 6.4 |
| Fuel capacity (gals.) | 18.0 |

## Models Available

| | Style Number | Base MSRP | Change from LY | Shipping Wt. (lbs.) | Production | Change from LY |
|---|---|---|---|---|---|---|
| Camaro 2-Door Sport Coupe | 12337 | $2,638 | +1.93% | 3040 | 214,280 | -0.20% |
| Camaro 2-Door Convertible | 12367 | $2,852 | +1.78% | 3160 | 16,519 | -19.18% |
| TOTALS | | Avg. price $2,745 | +1.86% | | Production 230,799 | -1.85% |

# Nova

*"Don't be fooled by expensive imitations."*

Nameplate year of origin: 1962.
Current bodystyle lifespan: 1968 through 1972.
Predecessor to this model: Chevy II (1966 to 1967).
Replacement for this model: Nova (1973 through 1979, with restyle in 1975).
Percentage of division's sales volume: 11.40%.
Corporate siblings: None.
Primary competition: AMC Rambler American, Dodge Dart, Ford Falcon, and
    Plymouth Valiant.
Notable changes: Refinements.
Major standard equipment: Cloth and vinyl bench seat, vinyl-coated rubber
    floor coverings, hubcaps, front-door vent windows, bright moldings on wind-
    shield and rear window, and 7.35 × 14 BSW tires.

## Measurements

| | |
|---|---|
| Wheelbase | 111.0" |
| Length | 189.4" |
| Width | 72.4" |
| Height | 53.9" |
| Legroom — front | 41.6" |
| Legroom — rear | 35.3" |
| Headroom — front | 37.6" |
| Headroom — rear | 32.6" |
| Cargo capacity (cu. ft.) | 12.4 |
| Fuel capacity (gals.) | 18.0 |

**1969**

## Models Available

| | Style Number | Base MSRP | Change from LY | Shipping Wt. (lbs.) | Production | Change from LY |
|---|---|---|---|---|---|---|
| Chevy II Nova 2-Door Coupe | 11127 | $2,237 | +0.68% | 2785 | 251,903 | * |
| Chevy II Nova 4-Door Sedan | 11169 | $2,267 | +0.67% | 2810 | * | * |
| TOTALS | | Avg. price $2,252 | +0.67% | | Production 251,903 | +25.34% |

*Production is estimated and not available by body style totals.*

# Chevelle

*"If competition had one like this, we'd have a lot more competition."*

**Nameplate year of origin:** 1964.

**Current bodystyle lifespan:** 1968 through 1972.

**Predecessor to this model:** Chevelle (1966 to 1967).

**Replacement for this model:** Chevelle (1973 to 1977).

**Percentage of division's sales volume:** 20.59%.

**Corporate siblings:** Pontiac LeMans, Oldsmobile Cutlass, Buick Skylark.

**Primary competition:** AMC Rebel, Dodge Coronet, Ford Fairlane/Torino, and Plymouth Satellite.

**Notable changes:** Revised trim and detail changes.

**Major standard equipment:** Cloth and vinyl front bench seat, color-keyed floor mats, hubcaps, and 7.35 × 14 BSW tires (7.75 × 14 BSW tires on wagons). Malibu adds: Full carpeting, full wheel covers, electric clock, and hide-away windshield wipers. Concours Estate Wagon adds: Wood-grain exterior trim, and power tailgate window and courtesy lights for optional 3-Seat Wagon model. SS 396 package adds: All-vinyl bucket seats, console, special instrumentation, 396 CID V8 engine, SS trim and wheel covers and F70 × 14 Redline or WSW tires.

## Measurements

|  | 2-Doors | 4-Doors | Wagons |
|---|---|---|---|
| Wheelbase | 112.0" | 116.0" | 116.0" |
| Length | 196.9" | 200.9" | 207.9" |
| Width | 76.0" | 76.0" | 76.0" |
| Height | 52.0" | 52.6" | 52.6" |
| Legroom — front | 42.4" | 42.4" | 42.4" |
| Legroom — rear | 32.2" | 34.8" | 34.8" |
| Headroom — front | 37.9" | 38.5" | 38.5" |
| Headroom — rear | 36.3" | 37.1" | 37.4" |
| Cargo capacity (cu. ft.) | NA | NA | 83.6 |
| Fuel capacity (gals.) | 20.0 | 20.0 | 20.0 |

## Models Available

| | Style Number | Base MSRP | Change from LY | Shipping Wt. (lbs.) | Production | Change from LY |
|---|---|---|---|---|---|---|
| Chevelle 300 Deluxe 2-Door Coupe | 13327 | $2,458 | +1.78% | 3035 | 42,000 | * |
| Chevelle 300 Deluxe 2-Door HT | 13337 | $2,521 | +1.69% | 3075 | * | * |
| Chevelle 300 Deluxe 4-Door Sedan | 13369 | $2,488 | +1.76% | 3100 | * | * |
| Chevelle Malibu 2-Door Hardtop | 13537 | $2,601 | +1.68% | 3095 | 367,100 | * |
| Chevelle Malibu 2-Dr. Convertible | 13567 | $2,800 | +1.56% | 3175 | * | * |
| Chevelle Malibu 4-Door Sedan | 13569 | $2,567 | +1.70% | 3130 | * | * |
| Chevelle Malibu 4-Door Hardtop | 13539 | $2,672 | +1.64% | 3205 | * | * |
| Nomad 4-Door, 2-Seat Wagon | 13135 | $2,668 | +1.64% | 3390 | * | * |
| Greenbrier 4-Door, 2-Seat Wagon | 13335 | $2,779 | +1.57% | 3445 | * | * |
| Greenbrier 4-Door, 3-Seat Wagon | 13346 | $2,892 | NEW | 3615 | * | NEW |
| Concours 4-Door, 2-Seat Wagon | 13536 | $2,931 | +2.99% | 3545 | 45,900 | * |
| Concours 4-Door, 3-Seat Wagon | 13546 | $3,044 | NEW | 3625 | * | NEW |
| Concours Estate 4-Dr., 2-S. Wagon | 13836 | $3,153 | +2.27% | 3680 | * | * |
| Concours Estate 4-Dr., 3-S. Wagon | 13846 | $3,266 | NEW | 3730 | * | NEW |
| TOTALS | | Avg. price $2,774 | +3.74% | | Production 455,000 | +6.98% |

*Production is estimated and not available by series, only body style totals.*

# Chevrolet Full-size

*"Never has so little money bought so much happiness."*

**Nameplate year of origin:** 1950 (BelAir); 1958 (Biscayne, Impala); 1966 (Caprice).

**Current bodystyle lifespan:** 1969 through 1970.

**Predecessor to this model:** Full-size Chevrolet (1967 to 1968).

**Replacement for this model:** Biscayne/BelAir/Impala/Caprice (1971 to 1976).

## Measurements

|  | Cars | Wagons |
|---|---|---|
| Wheelbase | 119.0" | 119.0" |
| Length | 215.9" | 216.7" |

**Percentage of division's sales volume:** 55.55%.

**Corporate siblings:** Buick LeSabre/Wildcat, Olds 88, Pontiac Catalina/Bonneville.

**Primary competition:** AMC Ambassador, Dodge Polara, Ford Custom/Galaxie/LTD, and Plymouth Fury.

**Notable changes:** Restyled exterior and interior.

**Major standard equipment:** Biscayne: Cloth and vinyl bench seat, full carpeting, front and rear door armrests, 2-speed electric windshield wipers with washers, and 8.25 × 14 BSW tires (8.55 × 14 BSW tires on wagons). BelAir adds: Automatic interior lighting, bright body side molding, and power tailgate window on 3-Seat wagon models. Impala adds: Vinyl upholstery in convertible, extra-long armrests, electric clock, and trunk lamp. SS package adds: All vinyl bucket seats, center floor console, and special SS wheel covers, body and interior trim. Caprice adds: Specific cloth and vinyl front bench seats (with center fold-down armrest on sedan), all-vinyl upholstery in wagons, simulated walnut interior trim, deluxe wheel covers, rocker panel moldings, simulated walnut exterior trim on wagons, and special ornamentation.

| | Cars | Wagons |
|---|---|---|
| Width | 79.8" | 79.8" |
| Height (Sedan only) | 53.4" | 57.1" |
| Legroom — front | 42.6" | 42.6" |
| Legroom — rear | 38.5" | 38.5" |
| Headroom — front | 38.9" | 38.9" |
| Headroom — rear | 38.0" | 38.5" |
| Cargo capacity (cu. ft.) | 18.1 | 93.3 |
| Fuel capacity (gals.) | 24.0 | 24.0 |

## Models Available

| | Style Number | Base MSRP | Change from LY | Shipping Wt. (lbs.) | Production | Change from LY |
|---|---|---|---|---|---|---|
| Biscayne 2-Door Sedan | 15311 | $2,645 | +2.48% | 3530 | 68,700 | * |
| Biscayne 4-Door Sedan | 15369 | $2,687 | +2.44% | 3590 | * | * |
| Bel Air 2-Door Sedan | 15511 | $2,745 | +2.39% | 3540 | 155,700 | * |
| Bel Air 4-Door Sedan | 15569 | $2,787 | +2.35% | 3590 | * | * |
| Impala 2-Door Sport Coupe | 16337 | $2,927 | +2.24% | 3650 | 777,000 | * |
| Impala 2-Door Custom Coupe | 16447 | $3,085 | +2.12% | 3800 | * | * |
| Impala 2-Door Convertible | 16467 | $3,261 | +2.00% | 3835 | * | * |
| Impala 4-Door Sedan | 16369 | $2,911 | +2.28% | 3640 | * | * |
| Impala 4-Door Hardtop | 16439 | $3,086 | +5.79% | 3855 | * | * |
| Caprice 2-Door Hardtop | 16647 | $3,294 | +2.33% | 3815 | 166,900 | * |
| Caprice 4-Door Hardtop | 16639 | $3,346 | +2.29% | 3895 | * | * |
| Brookwood 4-Dr., 2-S. Wagon | 15336 | $3,064 | +3.62% | 4045 | * | * |
| Townsman 4-Dr., 2-S. Wagon | 15636 | $3,232 | +7.02% | 4175 | * | * |
| Townsman 4-Dr., 3-S. Wagon | 15646 | $3,345 | +6.77% | 4230 | * | * |
| Kingswood 4-Dr., 2-S. Wagon | 16436 | $3,352 | +3.30% | 4225 | 59,300 | * |
| Kingswood 4-Dr., 3-S. Wagon | 16446 | $3,465 | +3.19% | 4300 | * | * |
| Kingswood Estate 4-Dr., 2-S. Wgn. | 16636 | $3,565 | +3.09% | 4245 | * | * |
| Kingswood Estate 4-Dr., 3-S. Wgn. | 16646 | $3,678 | +3.03% | 4300 | * | * |
| TOTALS | *Avg. price* | $3,138 | +3.29% | *Production* | 1,010,125 | +32.1% |

*Production is estimated and not available by series, only body style totals.*

# Corvette

*"No need to beware of substitutes. There aren't any."*

**Nameplate year of origin:** 1953 (Also used on showcar of same year).

**Current bodystyle lifespan:** 1968 through 1982.

**Predecessor to this model:** Corvette (1963 to 1967).

**Replacement for this model:** Corvette (1984 to 1996).

**Percentage of division's sales volume:** 1.75%.

**Corporate siblings:** None.

**Primary competition:** None.

**Notable changes:** Trim and detail changes.

## Measurements

| | |
|---|---|
| Wheelbase | 98.0" |
| Length | 182.5" |
| Width | 69.2" |
| Height | 47.8" |
| Legroom — front | 43.0" |
| Legroom — rear | NA |
| Headroom — front | 36.2" |

**Major standard equipment:** All-vinyl bucket seats with full-length center floor console, complete instrumentation, Astro ventilation, removable roof panels (Coupe), manually operated folding top (Convertible), wheels with bright trim ring and ribbed center hub, 4-wheel disc brakes, and F70 × 15 BSW tires.

## Measurements

| | |
|---|---|
| Headroom — rear | NA |
| Cargo capacity (cu. ft.) | NA |
| Fuel capacity (gals.) | 20.0 |

## Models Available

| | Style Number | Base MSRP | Change from LY | Shipping Wt. (lbs.) | Production | Change from LY |
|---|---|---|---|---|---|---|
| Corvette 2-Door Coupe | 19437 | $4,781 | +2.53% | 3140 | 22,154 | +122.97% |
| Corvette 2-Door Convertible | 19467 | $4,438 | +2.73% | 3145 | 16,608 | -10.85% |
| TOTALS | | *Avg. price* $4,610 | +2.63% | | *Production* 38,762 | +35.69% |

# CHRYSLER

*"Your next car: The great new Chrysler."*

Chrysler styling had come a long way in five short years. Always known more for its engineering qualities than its styling leadership, Chrysler introduced new full-size models across the board that were far ahead of the competition — it was 1957 all over again! Only this time the cars actually had the quality to go with the modern design. They also had the engineering advances to go with the new bodies. While some basic styling cues were retained from prior years, it was only enough to identify the cars as Chrysler products. The basic design was called the "fuselage" look. It began with a "loop-style" bumper which surrounded the grille and headlights. This led into a large, flat hood and smooth, slightly rounded body sides. The expansive glass and roof area flowed neatly into the rear quarter with no distinguishing lines where one stopped and the other started. All of this flowed into simply styled rear bumper and taillight arrangements. The look was very modern and beat GM's similarly styled full-size cars to market by two years. Ford would not go for this styling look, instead opting for a more traditional "three box" styling effect. Un-

derneath, Chryslers still carried their famous torsion bar suspension system. Interior styling also made a significant advancement, as upholstery materials became more luxurious. Layout of the entire driver cockpit area was carefully planned for both safety and convenience. Chrysler was heavily into non-protruding dashboard switches, so any switch that could be a flat pushbutton was changed to this style.

New to the model breakout, but not a new offering, was the Town & Country. Previously part of the Newport line, the luxury wagon was given its own spot in the model lineup. Powertrain options remained similar to previous years. As was common Detroit practice, it was considered risky to change styling and engineering in the same year. Similarly, no changes were made to the model offerings. An interesting option listed in the years's sales brochure was simulated teakwood-grain planking for Newport 2-Door Hardtops and Convertibles. It is not known if any were actually built with that option. Chrysler and Mercury both unsuccessfully offered the same option in 1968.

300 2-Door Convertible

Newport 4-Door Sedan

New Yorker 4-Door Sedan

Newport 2-Door Convertible with
simulated teakwood-grain applique

300 2-Door Hardtop

**Model year production:** 260,771, down 1.54% from 1968.
**Domestic market share:** 2.93% (10th place).
**Base price range:** $3,414 to $4,669.
**Industry average base price:** $3,386.
**Chrysler average base price:** $4,058.
**Introduction date:** September 1969.
**Assembly plants:** Newark, DE (F), and Detroit, MI (C).
**Data plate identification:** Thirteen digit code read as follows:

four digit style number (see listings below) in which C = Chrysler, 2nd number identifies series (e.g., H is for New Yorker), 3rd and 4th indicate body style; 5th digit is engine code; 9 for 1969; assembly plant code; 100001 and up for serial number. *Example:* CH23T9C100001 is a 1969 Chrysler New Yorker 2-Door Hardtop with a 440 CID V8 engine, serial number 100001, built in Detroit, MI.

## Powertrains

| Engine | Engine Code | Gross HP | Transmission Availability | Newport | 300 | Town & Country | N.Y. |
|---|---|---|---|---|---|---|---|
| 383 CID, 2-bbl., V8 | L | 290 | 3-speed man. | S | - | - | - |
| | | | TorqueFlite Automatic | $228 | - | S | - |
| 383 CID, 4-bbl., V8 | N | 335 | 3-speed man. | $68 | - | - | - |
| | | | TorqueFlite Automatic | $301 | - | $68 | - |
| 440 CID, 4-bbl., V8 | T | 350 | TorqueFlite Automatic | - | S | $164 | S |
| 440 CID TNT, 4-bbl., V8 | U | 375 | TorqueFlite Automatic | $433 | $79 | $198 | $79 |

## Major Options

| | Newport | 300 | Town & Country | New Yorker |
|---|---|---|---|---|
| Air conditioning | $406 | $406 | $406 | $406 |
| Electronic cruise control | $67 | $67 | $67 | $67 |
| Soft Ray tinted glass | $45 | $45 | $45 | $45 |
| Deck lid remote release | $15 | $15 | - | $15 |
| Power steering — variable-ratio | $117 | $117 | S | S |
| Power brakes | $47 | $47 | S | S |

## Paint Colors

| | Code |
|---|---|
| Platinum Metallic | A4 |
| Dark Gray Metallic | A9 |
| Bahama Blue | B3 |
| Jubilee Blue Metallic | B7 |
| Dark Briar Metallic | E7 |
| Surf Green Metallic | F3 |
| Avocado Metallic | F5 |

**1969**

|  | Newport | 300 | Town & Country | New Yorker |
|---|---|---|---|---|
| Power door locks | $46–$70 | $46–$70 | $70 | $46–$70 |
| Power 6-way Bench seat (bucket on 300) | $103 | $188 | $103 | $103 |
| Power windows | $112 | $112 | $112 | $112 |
| AM radio | $92 | $92 | $92 | $92 |
| AM/FM stereo | $187 | $187 | $187 | $187 |
| Tilt & telescoping steering wheel | $91 | $91 | $91 | $91 |
| Vinyl roof | $125 | $125 | $125 | $125 |
| Chrome Road Wheels | $99 | $99 | - | $99 |

Options common to most models. (- = Not Available; S = Standard equipment.) Items may be standard equipment, optional at different pricing, or unavailable on certain models. This chart is only a guide.

| Color | Code |
|---|---|
| Jade Green Metallic | F8 |
| Sandalwood | L1 |
| Aquamarine Metallic | Q4 |
| Crimson | R6 |
| Bronze Mist Metallic | T3 |
| Burnished Bronze Metallic | T5 |
| Tuscan Bronze Metallic | T7 |
| Spinnaker White | W1 |
| Formal Black | X9 |
| Antique Ivory | Y3 |
| Classic Gold Metallic | Y4 |
| Mystic Gold Metallic | Y5 |

# Newport

*"Your next car: The only resemblance to smaller cars should be in its price sticker."*

**Nameplate year of origin:** 1950 (as a HT model of the T & C); 1961 (as series).
**Current bodystyle lifespan:** 1969 through 1973.
**Predecessor to this model:** Newport (1965 to 1968).
**Replacement for this model:** Newport (1974 to 1978).
**Percentage of division's sales volume:** 60.14%.
**Corporate siblings:** Chrysler 300 and New Yorker.
**Primary competition:** Buick LeSabre, Mercury Monterey, and Oldsmobile Delta 88.
**Notable changes:** Completely redesigned.
**Major standard equipment:** Cloth and vinyl front bench seat (all-vinyl with center armrest on convertible), deep-pile carpeting, exterior bright side moldings, 2-speed windshield wipers w/washers, tripometer, and 8.55 × 14 BSW tires. Custom adds: Cloth and vinyl front bench seat with fold-down arm rest, and specific exterior trim.

## Measurements

| | |
|---|---|
| Wheelbase | 124.0" |
| Length | 224.7" |
| Width | 79.1" |
| Height | 56.3" |
| Legroom — front | 41.8" |
| Legroom — rear | 42.2" |
| Headroom — front | 38.7" |
| Headroom — rear | 37.9" |
| Cargo capacity (cu. ft.) | NA |
| Fuel capacity (gals.) | 23.0 |

## Models Available

| | Style Number | Base MSRP | Change from LY | Shipping Wt. (lbs.) | Production | Change from LY |
|---|---|---|---|---|---|---|
| Newport 2-Door Hardtop | CE23 | $3,485 | +3.54% | 3891 | 33,639 | -8.51% |
| Newport 2-Door Convertible | CE27 | $3,823 | +3.21% | 4026 | 2,169 | -23.81% |
| Newport 4-Door Sedan | CE41 | $3,414 | +3.27% | 3941 | 55,083 | -10.34% |
| Newport 4-Door Hardtop | CE43 | $3,549 | +3.05% | 4156 | 20,608 | +2.07% |
| Newport Custom 2-Door Hardtop | CL23 | $3,652 | +2.82% | 3891 | 10,955 | +5.94% |
| Newport Custom 4-Door Sedan | CL41 | $3,580 | +2.49% | 3951 | 18,401 | +8.79% |
| Newport Custom 4-Door Hardtop | CL43 | $3,730 | +2.73% | 3971 | 15,981 | +39.45% |
| TOTALS | | *Avg. price* $3,605 | +3.03% | | *Production* 156,836 | -1.95% |

# 300

*"Your next car: It can take on a feeling of soaring freedom."*

**Nameplate year of origin:** 1955 (letter series cars); 1962 (standard line cars).
**Current bodystyle lifespan:** 1969 through 1971.
**Predecessor to this model:** 300 (1965 to 1968).
**Replacement for this model:** None.
**Percentage of division's sales volume:** 12.45%.
**Corporate siblings:** Chrysler Newport and New Yorker.
**Primary competition:** Buick Wildcat, Mercury Marauder and Pontiac Bonneville.
**Notable changes:** Completely redesigned.
**Major standard equipment:** Cloth and vinyl bench seat (all-vinyl bucket seats on convertible), deep-pile carpeting, 3-speed windshield wipers with washers, electric clock, tripometer, power concealed headlamps, exterior side moldings, full wheel covers, automatic transmission, deluxe wheel covers, and 8.55 × 14 BSW tires.

## Measurements

| | |
|---|---|
| Wheelbase | 124.0" |
| Length | 224.7" |
| Width | 79.1" |
| Height | 56.3" |
| Legroom — front | 41.8" |
| Legroom — rear | 42.2" |
| Headroom — front | 38.7" |
| Headroom — rear | 37.2" |
| Cargo capacity (cu. ft.) | NA |
| Fuel capacity (gals.) | 23.0 |

## Models Available

| | Style Number | Base MSRP | Change from LY | Shipping Wt. (lbs.) | Production | Change from LY |
|---|---|---|---|---|---|---|
| 300 2-Door Hardtop | CM23 | $4,104 | +2.34% | 3965 | 16,075 | -5.18% |
| 300 2-Door Convertible | CM27 | $4,450 | +2.61% | 4095 | 1,933 | -10.55% |
| 300 4-Door Hardtop | CM43 | $4,183 | +2.37% | 4045 | 14,464 | -6.73% |
| TOTALS | | *Avg. price* $4,246 | +2.46% | | *Production* 32,472 | -6.21% |

# Town & Country

*"Your next car: It can be the world's best equipped station wagon."*

**Nameplate year of origin:** 1941.
**Current bodystyle lifespan:** 1969 through 1973.
**Predecessor to this model:** Newport Town & Country (1965 to 1968).
**Replacement for this model:** Town & Country (1974 to 1978).
**Percentage of division's sales volume:** 9.40%.
**Corporate siblings:** Dodge Monaco/Polara, and Plymouth Fury Suburban.
**Primary competition:** Mercury Colony Park.
**Notable changes:** Completely redesigned.
**Major standard equipment:** All-vinyl front bench seat with folding center armrest, simulated walnut instrument panel trim, carpeted lower door trim and load floor, Torqueflite automatic transmission, power steering, power front disc brakes, electric clock, lockable luggage compartment, power operated tailgate window, bodyside and rear tailgate Brazilian rosewood woodgrain applique, and 8.85 × 15 BSW tires.

## Measurements

| | |
|---|---|
| Wheelbase | 122.0" |
| Length | 224.8" |
| Width | 79.1" |
| Height | 57.9" |
| Legroom — front | 41.8" |
| Legroom — rear | 39.4" |
| Headroom — front | 39.6" |
| Headroom — rear | 40.2" |
| Cargo capacity (cu. ft.) | 102.1 |
| Fuel capacity (gals.) | 24.0 |

1969

## Models Available

| | Style Number | Base MSRP | Change from LY | Shipping Wt. (lbs.) | Production | Change from LY |
|---|---|---|---|---|---|---|
| Town & Country 4-Dr., 2-S. Wagon | CP45 | $4,583 | +3.73% | 4435 | 10,108 | +2.02% |
| Town & Country 4-Dr., 3-S. Wagon | CP46 | $4,669 | +3.23% | 4485 | 14,408 | +17.78% |
| TOTALS | | *Avg. price* $4,626 | +3.47% | | *Production* 24,516 | +10.73% |

# New Yorker

*"Your next car can be a member of the most elegant Chrysler series."*

**Nameplate year of origin:** 1939.
**Current bodystyle lifespan:** 1969 through 1973.
**Predecessor to this model:** New Yorker (1965 to 1968).
**Replacement for this model:** New Yorker (1974 to 1978).
**Percentage of division's sales volume:** 18.00%.
**Corporate siblings:** Chrysler Newport and 300.
**Primary competition:** Buick Electra 225, Cadillac Calais, Mercury Marquis, and Oldsmobile Ninety-Eight.
**Notable changes:** Completely redesigned.
**Major standard equipment:** Cloth and vinyl seats with folding center armrests front and rear — front only on 2-Door, simulated walnut instrument panel trim, Torqueflite automatic transmission, power front disc brakes, power steering, electric clock, 3-speed windshield wipers, fender-top turn signal indicator, LH remote outside rear view mirror, trunk carpeting and 8.55 × 15 BSW tires.

## Measurements

| | |
|---|---|
| Wheelbase | 124.0" |
| Length | 224.7" |
| Width | 79.1" |
| Height | 56.3" |
| Legroom — front | 41.8" |
| Legroom — rear | 42.2" |
| Headroom — front | 38.6" |
| Headroom — rear | 37.9" |
| Cargo capacity (cu. ft.) | NA |
| Fuel capacity (gals.) | 23.0 |

## Models Available

| | Style Number | Base MSRP | Change from LY | Shipping Wt. (lbs.) | Production | Change from LY |
|---|---|---|---|---|---|---|
| New Yorker 2-Door Hardtop | CH23 | $4,539 | +2.60% | 4070 | 7,537 | -6.49% |
| New Yorker 4-Door Sedan | CH41 | $4,487 | +2.75% | 4135 | 12,253 | -6.41% |
| New Yorker 4-Door Hardtop | CH43 | $4,615 | +2.56% | 4165 | 27,157 | +0.62% |
| TOTALS | | *Avg. price* $4,547 | +2.64% | | *Production* 46,947 | -2.48% |

# DODGE

*"Dodge fever 1969 style."*

For 1969 along with other Mopar lines, the full-size Dodges were completely redesigned. They offered the same fuselage body design as the other cars but were given a slightly different front-end treatment from the more expensive Chrysler and Imperial models. The difference was that they used a separate grille and bumper assembly (as did Plymouth) instead of the "loop-style" grille (which Dodge and Plymouth would take on for '70). Bodysides lost all of their sculpting and racy lines, in favor of the aerodynamic, smooth look of the future. Powertrain offerings in full-size models were similar to previous years with one exception. Available on various Dodge models, the Six-Pack 440 CID V8 was introduced in 1969. Creating nearly 400 horsepower, this engine would become the street racer's engine

of choice, right after the Hemi 426. The only change to the model lineup was the discontinuance of the Monaco 500 Hardtop.

Changes for all other Dodge lines consisted of new grilles and taillight treatments. One model making big news, however, was the Charger Daytona. Built specifically for NASCAR racing requirements, the Daytona was the first of two winged warriors created by Chrysler Corporation. The most distinguishing visual features of the Daytona were its long, sloping hood and fender styling and the roof-high, trunk mounted rear spoiler wing. While the Daytona and 1970 Plymouth Superbird looked similar, they were very different style-wise, other than sharing the midsize platform and powertrains. The Daytona was obviously based on the Charger body, which was slightly larger than the 1970 Plymouth Superbird's Satellite body shell. Such things as rooflines, glass, and front fenders were among the most obvious differences. But the essential purpose of these cars was to go racing! And race they did, winning many events and creating a huge amount of publicity for Dodge. Another, less famous new Charger was the 500, which was also designed with winning races in mind. The main fea-

ture distinguishing this Charger from others was the flush mounted grille and headlight design for the front end. Either a Magnum 440 or Hemi 426 V8 engine powered both the Charger 500 and Daytona. Other model changes for Dodge this year included the addition of a Super Bee 2-Door Hardtop, the Dart Swinger (replacing the Dart 2-Door Sedan) and Swinger 340 2-Door Hardtops, and the renaming of the Dart 270 line to Dart Custom.

Charger 2-Door Hardtop

Coronet R/T 2-Door Hardtop

Dart GTS 2-Door Hardtop

Monaco 4-Door Hardtop and
Polara 4-Door Wagon

**1969**

**Model year production:** 608,452, up 0.40% over 1968.
**Domestic market share:** 6.84% (7th place).
**Base price range:** $2,400 to $4,046.
**Industry average base price:** $3,386.
**Dodge average base price:** $3,148.
**Introduction date:** September 1968.
**Assembly plants:** Lynch Road, MI (A); Hamtramck, MI (B); Detroit (Jefferson Ave.), MI (C); Belvidere, IL (D); Los Angeles, CA (E); Newark, DE (F); St. Louis, MO (G); Windsor, Ontario, Canada (R).

**Data plate identification:** Thirteen digit code read as follows: four digit style number (see listings below) of which 1st digit is series letter (e.g., D = Polara series), 2nd number identifies trim grade (e.g., L is for base trim), 3rd and 4th indicate body style; 5th digit is engine code; 9 for 1969; assembly plant code; 100001 and up for serial number. *Example:* DL23F9C100001 is a 1969 Dodge Polara 2-Door Hardtop with a 318 CID V8 engine, serial number 100001, built in Detroit, MI.

## Powertrains

| Engine | Engine Code | Gross HP | Transmission Availability | Dart* | Coronet | Charger | Polara | Monaco |
|--------|-------------|----------|---------------------------|-------|---------|---------|--------|--------|
| 170 CID, 1-bbl., 6-cyl. | A | 125 | 3-speed manual | S | – | – | – | – |
| | | | Torqueflite automatic | $175 | – | – | – | – |
| 225 CID, 1-bbl., 6-cyl. | B | 145 | 3-speed manual | $46 | S** | S** | – | – |
| | | | Torqueflite automatic | $221 | $199** | $199** | – | – |
| 273 CID, | D | 190 | 3-speed manual | $79 | – | – | – | – |

| Engine | Engine Code | Gross HP | Transmission Availability | Dart* | Coronet | Charger | Polara | Monaco |
|---|---|---|---|---|---|---|---|---|
| 2-bbl., V8 | | | 4-speed manual | $267 | - | - | - | - |
| | | | Torqueflite automatic | $270 | - | - | - | - |
| 318 CID, 2-bbl., V8 | F | 230 | 3-speed manual | $111 | S (500)/$107** | S (SE)/$106** | S | - |
| | | | 4-speed manual | $299 | - | $197 (SE)/$303** | $197 | - |
| | | | Torqueflite automatic | $302 | $199 (500)/$306** | $206 (SE)/$312** | $206 | - |
| 340 CID, 4-bbl., V8 | P | 275 | 3-speed manual | S* | - | - | - | - |
| | | | 4-speed manual | $188* | - | - | - | - |
| | | | Torqueflite automatic | $191* | - | - | - | - |
| 383 CID, 2-bbl., V8 | G | 290 | 3-speed manual | - | $70 (500)/$176** | $70 (SE)/$176** | $70 | S |
| | | | 4-speed manual | - | $267 (500)/$373** | $267 (SE)/$373** | $267 | $197 |
| | | | Torqueflite automatic | - | $276 (500)/$382** | $276 (SE)/$382** | $276 | $206 |
| 383 CID, 4-bbl., V8 | H | 330/335 | 3-speed manual | - | S (Super Bee)/$245** | $245** | $138 | $68 |
| | | | 4-speed manual | - | $188 (Super Bee)/$453** | $453** | $335 | $265 |
| | | | Torqueflite automatic | - | $199 (Super Bee)/$444** | $444** | $344 | $274 |
| 383 CID Magnum, 4-bbl., V8 | H | 350 | 4-speed manual | - | $290 (Super Bee)/$438** | - | - | - |
| | | | Torqueflite automatic | - | $301 (Super Bee)/$449** | - | - | - |
| 426 CID Street Hemi, 2 × 4-bbl., V8 | J | 425 | 4-speed manual | | $718 (R/T)/$848 (S.B.) | $648 (R/T) $ (Others)- | - | - |
| | | | Torqueflite automatic | - | $718 (R/T)/$848 (S.B.) | $648 (R/T) $ (Others) | - | - |
| 440 CID, 4-bbl., V8 | K | 350 | Torqueflite automatic | - | - | - | $ (Wgn) | $ (Wgn.) |
| 440 CID Magnum, 4-bbl., V8 | L | 375 | 4-speed manual | - | No cost (R/T) $336 (S.B.)/$545** | No cost (R/T) | - | - |
| | | | Torqueflite automatic | - | S (R/T) $336 (S.B.) $545** | S (R/T) | $474 (ex. Wagon) | $404 (ex. Wagon) |

*340 CID V8 standard on Dart Swinger 340 and GTS.     **Except Coronet 500, Super Bee, SE, 500, Daytona or R/T.

## Major Options

| | Dart | Coronet | Charger | Polara | Monaco |
|---|---|---|---|---|---|
| Air conditioning | $361 | $358 | $358 | $395 | $395 |
| Speed control | - | $58 | $58 | $61 | $61 |
| Tinted glass | $33 | $40 | $40 | $40 | $40 |
| Power steering | $85 | $100 | $100 | $106 | $106 |
| Power brakes | $43 | $49 | $49 | $49 | $49 |
| Power driver's seat | - | $100 | $100 | $100 | $100 |
| Power windows | - | $105 | $105 | $109 | $109 |
| AM radio | $62 | $62 | $62 | $68 | $68 |
| AM/FM radio (stereo on full-size) | $135 | $135 | $135 | $184 | $184 |
| Tilt steering wheel | - | - | - | $47 | $47 |
| Chrome stamped 14" wheels | - | $86 | $48–$86 | - | - |
| Vinyl roof | $75 | $89 | $94 | $104 | $104 |

Options common to most models. (- = Not Available; S = Standard equipment.) Items may be standard equipment, optional at different pricing, or unavailable on certain models. This chart is only a guide.

## Paint Colors

| | Code |
|---|---|
| Silver Metallic | A-4 |
| Light Blue Metallic | B-3 |
| Bright Blue Metallic | B-5 |
| Medium Blue Metallic | B-7 |
| Dark Blue Metallic | B-9 |
| Cordovan Metallic | E-7 |
| Light Green Metallic | F-3 |
| Medium Green Metallic | F-5 |
| Bright Green Metallic | F-6 |
| Dark Green Metallic | F-8 |
| Beige | L-1 |
| Light Turquoise Met. | Q-4 |
| Bright Turquoise Met. | Q-5 |
| Charger Red | R-4 |
| Red | R-6 |
| Light Bronze Metallic | T-3 |
| Copper Metallic | T-5 |
| Dark Brown Metallic | T-7 |
| Hemi Orange | V-2 |
| White | W-1 |
| Black | X-9 |
| Yellow | Y-2 |
| Cream | Y-3 |
| Gold Metallic | Y-4 |
| Orange | 999 |
| Rallye Green | 999 |
| Bahama Yellow | 999 |

# Dart

*"Not only smart looking and distinctive, it's economical as well."*

**Nameplate year of origin:** 1960 (on low-end full-size models).
**Current bodystyle lifespan:** 1967 through 1976.
**Predecessor to this model:** Dart (1963 to 1966).
**Replacement for this model:** Aspen (1976 to 1980).
**Percentage of division's sales volume:** 32.49%.
**Corporate siblings:** Plymouth Valiant.
**Primary competition:** AMC Rambler American, Chevrolet Nova, and Ford Falcon.
**Notable changes:** New grille and minor trim and detail changes.
**Major standard equipment:** Cloth and vinyl front bench seat, dome light, black rubber floor mats, 2-speed windshield wipers, and 6.50 × 13 BSW tires. 270 adds: All-vinyl front bench seat (Hardtops), full carpeting, drip rail molding, deluxe instrument panel décor, cigarette lighter and wheel covers. GT adds: Vinyl front bucket seats (Hardtop), map and courtesy light (Convertible), front fender-top turn signal indicators, deluxe wheel covers and 7.00 × 13 BSW tires on convertibles. GTS adds: Bumblebee exterior striping on rear quarters, 340 CID V8 engine with dress-up kit, 4-speed manual or automatic transmission, heavy-duty suspension and handling, and E70 × 14 Wide-Oval Redline tires. Swinger 340 adds to base: 340 CID V8 engine, 4-speed manual transmission, heavy duty suspension and dual exhaust.

## Measurements

| | |
|---|---|
| Wheelbase | 111.0" |
| Length | 195.4" |
| Width | 69.6" |
| Height | 53.6" |
| Legroom — front | 41.7" |
| Legroom — rear | 35.7" |
| Headroom — front | 38.3" |
| Headroom — rear | 37.3" |
| Cargo capacity (cu. ft.) | 14.3 |
| Fuel capacity (gals.) | 18.0 |

**1969**

## Models Available

| | Style Number | Base MSRP | Change from LY | Shipping Wt. (lbs.) | Production | Change from LY |
|---|---|---|---|---|---|---|
| Dart Swinger 2-Dr. Hardtop | LL23 | $2,400 | NEW | 2711 | * | NEW |
| Dart 4-Door Sedan | LL41 | $2,413 | +2.25% | 2726 | * | * |
| Dart Custom 2-Door Hardtop | LH23 | $2,577 | +2.06% | 2711 | * | * |
| Dart Custom 4-Door Sedan | LH41 | $2,550 | +2.04% | 2726 | * | * |
| Dart GT 2-Door Hardtop | LP23 | $2,672 | +1.33% | 2716 | * | * |
| Dart GT 2-Door Convertible | LP27 | $2,865 | +1.20% | 2821 | * | * |
| Dart Swinger 340 2-Door Hardtop | LM23 | $2,836 | NEW | 3097 | * | NEW |
| Dart GTS 2-Door Hardtop | LS23 | $3,226 | +1.16% | 3105 | 6,700 | * |
| Dart GTS 2-Door Convertible | LS27 | $3,419 | +1.06% | 3210 | * | * |
| TOTALS | Avg. price | $2,773 | +2.02% | | Production 197,700 | +15.08% |

*Production by series not available. Totals are estimated.*

# Coronet

*"Dodge Coronet tempers luxury with economy."*

**Nameplate year of origin:** 1950 (hardtop models), 1953 (series).
**Current bodystyle lifespan:** 1968 through 1970.
**Predecessor to this model:** Coronet (1966 to 1967).
**Replacement for this model:** Coronet/Monaco (1971 to 1978).
**Percentage of division's sales volume:** 33.43%.
**Corporate siblings:** Plymouth Satellite.
**Primary competition:** AMC Rebel, Chevrolet Chevelle, Ford Fairlane/Torino, and Pontiac Tempest/LeMans.
**Notable changes:** New grille and taillights and minor trim and detail changes.
**Major standard equipment:** All-vinyl bench seat, glove box lock, trunk mat, color-keyed rubber floor mats, cigarette lighter, front and rear armrests, windshield wipers with washers, and 7.35 × 14 BSW tires (8.25 × 14 BSW on wagons). 440 adds: Cloth and vinyl bench seat (4-Door only), deep-pile carpeting and 3-spoke steering wheel. 500 adds: All-vinyl bucket seats (2-Doors), exterior bright trim package, and power tailgate window on 3-Seat wagon. Super Bee adds to base Coronet: All-vinyl bench seat, bumblebee striping, Rallye suspension, and floor shift transmission. R/T adds: All-vinyl bucket seats, choice of body side or bumblebee stripes, 4-speed manual or Torqueflite transmission and F70 × 14 Wide-Oval Redline tires.

## Measurements

| | Cars | Wagons |
|---|---|---|
| Wheelbase | 117.0" | 117.0" |
| Length | 206.6" | 210.0" |
| Width | 76.7" | 76.5" |
| Height | 54.7" | 55.3" |
| Legroom — front | 41.9" | 41.9" |
| Legroom — rear | 41.4" | 41.4" |
| Headroom — front | 34.6" | 34.6" |
| Headroom — rear | 37.4" | 37.4" |
| Cargo capacity (cu. ft.) | NA | NA |
| Fuel capacity (gals.) | 19.0 | 19.0 |

## Models Available

| | Style Number | Base MSRP | Change from LY | Shipping Wt. (lbs.) | Production | Change from LY |
|---|---|---|---|---|---|---|
| Coronet Deluxe 2-Door Coupe | WL21 | $2,554 | +2.69% | 2988 | * | * |
| Coronet Deluxe 4-Door Sedan | WL41 | $2,589 | +2.53% | 3018 | * | * |
| Coronet Deluxe 4-Dr., 2-S. Wagon | WL45 | $2,922 | +3.76% | 3498 | * | * |
| Coronet 440 2-Door Coupe | WH21 | $2,630 | +2.53% | 2983 | * | * |
| Coronet 440 2-Door Hardtop | WH23 | $2,692 | +2.47% | 3018 | * | * |
| Coronet 440 4-Door Sedan | WH41 | $2,670 | +2.57% | 3023 | * | * |
| Coronet 440 4-Dr., 2-S. Wagon | WH45 | $3,033 | +3.73% | 3503 | * | * |
| Coronet 440 4-Dr., 3-S. Wagon | WH46 | $3,246 | +3.38% | 3676 | * | * |
| Coronet 500 2-Door Hardtop | WP23 | $2,929 | +1.74% | 3171 | * | * |
| Coronet 500 2-Door Convertible | WP27 | $3,069 | +1.09% | 3306 | * | * |
| Coronet 500 4-Door Sedan | WP41 | $2,963 | +1.75% | 3206 | * | * |

| | Style Number | Base MSRP | Change from LY | Shipping Wt. (lbs.) | Production | Change from LY |
|---|---|---|---|---|---|---|
| Coronet 500 4-Dr., 2-S. Wgn. | WP45 | $3,280 | +2.12% | 3611 | * | * |
| Coronet 500 4-Dr., 3-S. Wgn. | WP46 | $3,392 | +2.11% | 3676 | * | * |
| Coronet Super Bee 2-Door Coupe | WM21 | $3,076 | +1.62% | 3440 | * | * |
| Coronet Super Bee 2-Door Hardtop | WM23 | $3,138 | NEW | 3470 | * | NEW |
| Coronet R/T 2-Door Hardtop | WS23 | $3,442 | +1.86% | 3601 | * | * |
| Coronet R/T 2-Door Convertible | WS27 | $3,660 | +1.30% | 3721 | * | * |
| TOTALS | Avg. price | $3,017 | +2.55% | Production | 203,400 | -8.62% |

*Production by series not available. Totals are estimated.*

# Charger

*"The most successful new car in Dodge history. One look tells why."*

**Nameplate year of origin:** 1966.
**Current bodystyle lifespan:** 1968 through 1970.
**Predecessor to this model:** Charger (1966 to 1967).
**Replacement for this model:** Charger (1971 to 1974).
**Percentage of division's sales volume:** 14.82%.
**Corporate siblings:** None.
**Primary competition:** Ford Torino SportsRoof models and Pontiac Grand Prix.
**Notable changes:** Revised trim and detail changes. New 500 and Daytona models.
**Major standard equipment:** All-vinyl front bucket seats, full carpeting, 3-spoke steering wheel, electric clock, concealed headlamps, and 7.35 × 14 BSW tires. R/T adds: Bumblebee stripes, Magnum 440 engine, automatic transmission, dual exhausts, handling package, and F70 × 14 Wide-Oval Redline tires. 500 adds to base: Flush-mounted grille with exposed headlamps, flush mounted rear window, 440 CID Magnum V8 and F70 × 14 Wide-Oval tires. Daytona adds: Fiberglass nose extension, roof-high rear spoiler, and 426 CID Hemi V8.

### Measurements*

| | |
|---|---|
| Wheelbase | 117.0" |
| Length | 207.9" |
| Width | 76.7" |
| Height | 53.2" |
| Legroom — front | 39.3" |
| Legroom — rear | 39.1" |
| Headroom — front | 38.6" |
| Headroom — rear | 36.4" |
| Cargo capacity (cu. ft.) | NA |
| Fuel capacity (gals.) | 19.0 |

*Excludes 500 and Daytona*

## Models Available

| | Style Number | Base MSRP | Change from LY | Shipping Wt. (lbs.) | Production | Change from LY |
|---|---|---|---|---|---|---|
| Charger 2-Door Hardtop | XH29 | $3,020 | -0.66% | 3103 | 69,100 | -28.10% |
| Charger R/T 2-Door Hardtop | XS29 | $3,592 | 2.45% | 3646 | 20,100 | * |
| Charger 500 2-Door Hardtop | XX29 | $3,993 | NEW | 3710 | * | NEW |
| Charger Daytona 2-Door Hardtop | NA | NA | NEW | NA | 1,000 | NEW |
| TOTALS | Avg. price | $2,938 | -9.0% | Production | 75,594 | -7.9% |

*Comparison with 1968 model unavailable. Charger 500 production unavailable.*

# Polara

*"Prestige has never been so easy to acquire."*

**Nameplate year of origin:** 1959.
**Current bodystyle lifespan:** 1969 through 1973.
**Predecessor to this model:** Polara (1967 to 1968).
**Replacement for this model:** Monaco (1974).
**Percentage of division's sales volume:** 19.25% (includes Monaco).

### Measurements

| | Cars | Wagons |
|---|---|---|
| Wheelbase | 122.0" | 122.0" |
| Length | 220.8" | 220.4" |

**Corporate siblings:** Dodge Monaco and Plymouth Fury.
**Primary competition:** AMC Ambassador, Chevrolet Full-size, Ford Galaxie 500, and Pontiac Catalina.
**Notable changes:** Completely redesigned.
**Major standard equipment:** Cloth-and-vinyl bench seat, full carpeting, 2-speed windshield wipers with washers, and 8.25 × 15 BSW tires (8.85 × 15 tires on wagons). Polara 500 adds: All-vinyl bucket seats with folding center arm rests or center floor console, wheel lip and window moldings, and wheel covers.

| | Cars | Wagons |
|---|---|---|
| Width | 79.2" | 79.2" |
| Legroom — front | 41.8" | 41.8" |
| Height | 55.7" | 57.1" |
| Legroom — rear | 39.1" | 39.1" |
| Headroom — front | 38.8" | 39.6" |
| Headroom — rear | 38.4" | 39.2" |
| Cargo capacity (cu. ft.) | 22.4 | 104.2 |
| Fuel capacity (gals.) | 24.0 | 23.0 |

## Models Available

| | Style Number | Base MSRP | Change from LY | Shipping Wt. (lbs.) | Production | Change from LY |
|---|---|---|---|---|---|---|
| Polara 2-Door Hardtop | DL23 | $3,117 | +2.97% | 3646 | * | * |
| Polara 2-Door Convertible | DL27 | $3,377 | +2.71% | 3791 | * | * |
| Polara 4-Door Sedan | DL41 | $3,095 | +3.00% | 3701 | * | * |
| Polara 4-Door Hardtop | DL43 | $3,188 | +2.84% | 3731 | * | * |
| Polara 4-Door, 2-S. Wagon | DL45 | $3,522 | +3.96% | 4161 | * | * |
| Polara 4-Door, 3-S. Wagon | DL46 | $3,629 | +5.07% | 4211 | * | * |
| Polara 500 2-Door Hardtop | DM23 | $3,314 | +2.73% | 3681 | * | * |
| Polara 500 2-Door Convertible | DM27 | $3,576 | +2.55% | 3801 | * | * |
| TOTALS | Avg. price | $3,352 | +3.23% | Production | 117,152* | +58.10% |

*Production includes Monaco. Totals are estimated.*

# Monaco

*"Except for traditional performance and dependability, Monaco is new inside and out."*

**Nameplate year of origin:** 1965.
**Current bodystyle lifespan:** 1969 through 1973.
**Predecessor to this model:** Monaco (1967 to 1968).
**Replacement for this model:** Royal Monaco (1974 to 1978).
**Percentage of division's sales volume:** Production totals included with Polara.
**Corporate siblings:** Dodge Polara and Plymouth Fury.
**Primary competition:** AMC Ambassador, Chevrolet Caprice, Ford LTD, Mercury Monterey, Oldsmobile Delta 88, and Pontiac Bonneville.
**Notable changes:** Completely redesigned.
**Major standard equipment:** Cloth-and-vinyl bench seat, full carpeting, ashtray, map and courtesy lights, 2-speed windshield wipers with washers, front fender top turn signal indicators, power tailgate window on wagons, and 8.25 × 15 BSW tires (8.85 × 15 BSW tires on wagons).

## Measurements

| | Cars | Wagons |
|---|---|---|
| Wheelbase | 122.0" | 122.0" |
| Length | 220.8" | 220.4" |
| Width | 79.2" | 79.2" |
| Height | 41.8" | 41.8" |
| Legroom — front | 55.7" | 57.1" |
| Legroom — rear | 39.1" | 39.1" |
| Headroom — front | 38.8" | 39.6" |
| Headroom — rear | 38.4" | 39.2" |
| Cargo capacity (cu. ft.) | 22.4 | 104.2 |
| Fuel capacity (gals.) | 24.0 | 23.0 |

## Models Available

| | Style Number | Base MSRP | Change from LY | Shipping Wt. (lbs.) | Production | Change from LY |
|---|---|---|---|---|---|---|
| Monaco 2-Door Hardtop | DH23 | $3,528 | +3.89% | 3811 | * | * |
| Monaco 4-Door Sedan | DH41 | $3,452 | +4.80% | 3846 | * | * |
| Monaco 4-Door Hardtop | DH43 | $3,591 | +4.63% | 3891 | * | * |
| Monaco 4-Dr., 2-S. Wgn. | DH45 | $3,917 | +5.81% | 4306 | * | * |
| Monaco 4-Dr., 3-S. Wgn. | DH46 | $4,046 | +5.50% | 4361 | * | * |
| TOTALS | Avg. price | $3,707 | +3.32% | Production | * | * |

*Production included with Polara. Totals are estimated.*

# FORD

*"It's the going thing!"*

Major styling changes were under way in the Ford line. Throughout the sixties, Ford was constantly making major revisions to at least one product line. This year it was three: completely restyled Mustang and full-size Fords, and an all-new compact Maverick. The Maverick came along on the same day the original Mustang arrived, only five years later. (Because it was sold for a substantial portion of the 1969 model year, it is included here though Ford marketed it as a 1970 model.) As with the Mustang, the Maverick was an instant success. Powerplants for the new compact were initially limited to two 6-cylinder engines, displacing 170 or 200 cubic inches. Maverick styling was part sports car with a sweeping fastback roofline and the popular long hood, short deck treatment. Intended as a replacement for the Falcon, the Maverick was initially offered in only a 2-Door Coupe style, so the Falcon was kept in the line for another year while replacement plans for the 4-Door Sedan and Wagon were worked up. The eventual replacement for the 4-Door Sedan arrived in the 1971 model year. The Wagon replacement arrived in mid-year 1970, as a Torino based Falcon Wagon. Since the Falcon and Fairlane/Torino Wagons had shared the same platform since 1966, the change was a logical one.

Mustang buyers were faced with a slightly larger and more powerful car for 1969. While only about 4 inches longer than the previous year, the styling changes made the car look more muscular. A new four-headlamp setup was used for this one season only, with the inboard lights mounted inside the grille area, and the outboard lights set outside of the grille. Other expected Mustang styling cues were still there. Two new models were added to the line, a luxury version of the coupe called Mustang Grande, and a high-performance version of the fastback, appropriately named Mach I. The Mach I featured the 351 CID V8 as standard equipment, along with beefier suspension and tires and the obligatory racing stripes. Mach I Mustangs were fierce competition to GM's newest high-performance offerings, the Camaro Z28 and the Firebird Trans Am.

Full-size Fords were completely redesigned for 1969. They now rode on the longest wheelbase in their class and could legitimately boast of having more space and a quieter ride than any of their competitors' cars. Powertrain choices were similar to last years, with the 429 CID V8 replacing the 427 CID V8 at the top end, and the new 351 VID V8 becoming a popular choice in the mid-range of the power spectrum. No model changes were made to the full-size line.

As mentioned earlier, the Falcon was nearing the end of its run, so very few changes were made for 1969. The mid-size Fairlane and Torino line was all-new in 1968, so there were few changes to that line as well. Base power derived from a newly offered 250 CID 6-cylinder as opposed to last year's 200 CID Six. A new high-performance Cobra line was added, consisting of two 2-Door models — a Hardtop and a Sports Roof fastback. All fastbacks in every line were now referred to as "Sports Roof" models. A 428 CID V8 engine powered the Cobra. Finally, the Thunderbird returned with a minor restyling to the grille, but few other changes.

Torino Cobra 2-Door Hardtop

Custom 2-Door Sedan

Fairlane 4-Door Sedan

Falcon 4-Door Sedan

Falcon 4-Door Wagon

Galaxie 500 2-Door Convertible

LTD Country Squire 4-Door Wagon

Maverick 2-Door Coupe

Mustang 2-Door Sports Roof with GT package

Mustang Mach I 2-Door Hardtop

**Model year production:** 1,937,103, up 10.53% over 1968.
**Domestic market share:** 21.76% (2nd place).
**Base price range:** $1,995 to $5,043.
**Industry average base price:** $3,386.
**Ford average base price:** $3,000.
**Introduction date:** September 1968. Maverick was introduced on April 17, 1969, as a 1970 model.
**Assembly plants:** Atlanta, GA (A); Dallas, TX (D); Chicago, IL (G); Dearborn, MI (F); Kansas City, MO (K); Lorain, OH (H); Los Angeles, CA (J); Louisville, KY (U); Mah-wah, NJ (E); Metuchen, NJ (T); Norfolk, VA (N); San Jose, CA (R); Twin Cities, MN (P); Wayne, MI (W); Wixom, MI (Y); St. Thomas, Ontario, Can. (X); Oakville, Ontario, Can. (B).
**Data plate identification:** Eleven digit code read as follows: 9 for 1969; 2nd digit is assembly plant code; 2-digit model number (see listings below); 5th digit is engine code; 100001 and up for serial number. *Example:* 9Y87N100001 is a 1969 Ford Thunderbird 2-Door Hardtop with a 429 CID V8 engine, serial number 100001, built in Wixom, MI.

## Powertrains

| Engine | Gross HP | Engine Code | Transmission Availability | Falcon & Maverick | Mustang | Fairlane & Torino | Full-size | T-Bird |
|---|---|---|---|---|---|---|---|---|
| 170 CID, 1-bbl., 6-cyl. | 105 | U | 3-speed manual | S | – | – | – | – |
| | | | Cruise-O-Matic | $175 | – | – | – | – |
| 200 CID, 1-bbl., 6-cyl. | 120 | T | 3-speed manual | $26 | S* | – | – | – |
| | | | Cruise-O-Matic | $201 | $191* | – | – | – |
| 240 CID Big Six, 1-bbl., 6-cyl. | 150 | V | 3-speed manual | – | – | – | S[2] | – |
| | | | Cruise-O-Matic | – | – | – | $222[2] | – |
| 250 CID, 1-bbl., 6-cyl. | 155 | L | 3-speed manual | – | $26* | S* | – | – |
| | | | Cruise-O-Matic | – | $217* | $201* | – | – |
| 302 CID, 2-bbl., V8 | 220 | F | 3-speed manual | $79 (Falcon) | $105* | S (GT)/$90* | S[1] $95[2] | – |
| | | | 4-speed manual | – | $310* | | | – |

| Engine | Gross HP | Engine Code | Transmission Availability | Falcon & Maverick | Mustang | Fairlane & Torino | Full-size | T-Bird |
|---|---|---|---|---|---|---|---|---|
| | | | Cruise-O-Matic | $254 (Falcon) | $306* | $222 (GT)/$312* | $222[1]/$317[2] | - |
| 351 CID, 2-bbl., V8 | 250 | H | 3-speed manual | - | S (Mach I)/$163* | $84 (GT)/$174* | - | - |
| | | | 4-speed manual | - | $205 (Mach I)/$368* | $278 (GT)/$368* | - | - |
| | | | Cruise-O-Matic | - | $201 (Mach)/$364* | $306 (GT)/$396* | $306[1]/$401[2] | - |
| 351 CID, 4-bbl., V8 | 290 | M | 3-speed manual | - | $26 (Mach) $189* | $ (GT)/$* | - | - |
| | | | 4-speed manual | - | $231 (Mach)/$394* | $ (GT)/$* | - | - |
| | | | Cruise-O-Matic | - | $227 (Mach)/$390* | $ (GT)/$* | - | - |
| 390 CID, 2-bbl., V8 | 265 | Y | 3-speed manual | - | - | - | $58[1]/$153[2] | - |
| | | | Cruise-O-Matic | - | - | - | $280[1]/$375[2] | - |
| 390 CID, 4-bbl., V8 | 320 | Y | 3-speed manual | - | $100 (Mach)/$158* | $ (GT)/$* | - | - |
| | | | 4-speed manual | - | $354 (Mach)/$412* | $ (GT)/$* | - | - |
| | | | Cruise-O-Matic | - | $322 (Mach)/$380* | $ (GT)/$* | - | - |
| 428 CID Cobra Jet, 4-bbl., V8 | 335 (320 Full-size) | Q | 4-speed manual | - | $478 (MachI)/$542* | - | - | - |
| | | | Cruise-O-Matic | - | $446 (MachI)/$510* | - | - | - |
| 428 CID Super Cobra Jet, 4-bbl., V8 | 360 | R | 4-speed manual | - | $611 (MachI)/$675 | S (Cobra)/$ (ex. Wagons) | - | - |
| | | | Cruise-O-Matic | - | $599-Mach/$663* | S (Cobra)/$ (ex. Wagons) | - | - |
| 429 CID Thunder Jet**, 2-bbl., V8 | 320 | K | Cruise-O-Matic | - | - | - | $385[1]/$480[2] | - |
| 429 CID — Thunder Jet, 4-bbl., V8 | 360 | N | 4-speed manual | - | - | $ (Cobra) | $491[1]/$586[2] | - |
| | | | Cruise-O-Matic | - | - | $ (Cobra) | $459[1]/$554[2] | S |
| 429 CID Police Interceptor**, 4-bbl., V8 | 370 | P | 4-speed manual | - | - | - | - | - |
| | | | Cruise-O-Matic | - | - | - | - | - |
| Boss 429 CID, 4-bbl., V8 | 375 | J | Cruise-O-Matic | - | $— Mach I | - | - | - |

[1]LTD and Country Squire.   [2]All but LTD and Country Squire.   *Except Mach I, Torino GT and Cobra.   **Available on a limited basis on specific models only.

## Major Options

| | Maverick | Falcon | Mustang | Fairlane/Torino | Full-size | Thunderbird |
|---|---|---|---|---|---|---|
| Select Aire air conditioning | - | - | $380 | $389 | $389 | $427 |
| Electronic cruise control | - | - | - | - | $97 | $97 |
| Tinted glass | $32 | $32 | $32 | $45 | $45 | S |
| Deck lid remote release | - | - | - | - | $ | $ |
| Power steering | $100 | $100 | $100 | $100 | $105 | S |
| Power brakes — front discs | - | - | $ | $65 | $65 — S on LTD | S |
| Power door locks | - | - | - | - | $47–$68 | $47 |
| Power drivers seat/Bench seat | - | - | - | $ | $ | $198 |
| Power windows | - | - | $ | $ | $ | $110 |
| AM radio | $59 | $59 | $59 | $61 | $61 | S |
| AM/FM stereo | - | - | $181 | $240 | $240 | $150 |
| Front seat console | - | - | $54 | $ | - | - |
| Front bucket seats | - | - | S | $ | - | - |
| Tilt steering wheel | - | - | $66 | - | $70 | $70 |
| Vinyl roof | - | $ | $84 | $95 | $105 | $ |
| White sidewall tires | $34 | $34 | $34 | $34 | $34 | $34 |
| Magnum 500 Chrome Wheels | - | - | $117 | $ | - | - |

Options common to most models. (- = Not Available; S = Standard equipment.) Items may be standard equipment, optional at different pricing, or unavailable on certain models. This chart is only a guide.

1969

## Paint Colors*

| | Code | Maverick | Mustang | Thunderbird |
|---|---|---|---|---|
| New Lime/Thanks Vermillion | 2 | | | |
| Calypso Coral | 3 | | X | |
| Silver Jade Metallic | 4 | | X | |
| Sage Bronze | 5 | | X | |
| Acapulco Blue Metallic/ | | | | |
| Hulla Blue Metallic | 6 | X | X | |
| Anti Establish Mint Metallic | 7 | | | |
| Dresden Blue | 8 | | | |
| Pastel Yellow | 9 | | X | |
| Raven Black | A | | X | T |
| Royal Maroon | B | | | T |
| Black Jade Metallic | C | | | T |
| Pastel Gray | D | | X | |
| Aztec Aqua | E | | | |
| Gulfstream Aqua Metallic | F | | | |
| Lilac Frost Metallic | G | | | T |
| Diamond Green Metallic | H | | | T |
| Lime Gold Metallic | I | X | X | T |
| Midnight Aqua Metallic | J | | | T |
| Freudian Gilt Metallic/ | | | | |
| Midnight Orchid Met. (TBird) | K | X | | T |
| Wimbledon White | M | | | T |
| Diamond Blue/Baby Blue Ice | N | | | T |
| Original Cinnamon Metallic | O | X | X | |
| Winter Blue Metallic | P | | X | |
| Brittany Blue Metallic | Q | | | T |
| Morning Gold | R | | | T |
| Champagne Gold Metallic | S | | | T |
| Candy Apple Red | T | | | T |
| Tahoe Turquoise Metallic | U | | | T |
| Copper Flame Metallic | V | | | T |
| Meadowlark Yellow | W | | | T |
| Presidential Blue Metallic | X | | | T |
| Indian Fire Metallic/ | | | | |
| Original Cinnamon Metallic | Y | | | T |
| Oxford Gray Metallic | Z | | | T |

*Most colors available on all models. Maverick and Mustang colors marked "X" available only on those models. Thunderbird available only in colors marked "T."

# Maverick

*"Wonderfully simple. Simply wonderful."*

**Nameplate year of origin:** 1969.
**Current bodystyle lifespan:** 1969 through 1977.
**Predecessor to this model:** Falcon (1966 to 1970).
**Replacement for this model:** Fairmont (1978 to 1983).
**Percentage of division's sales volume:** 6.60%.
**Corporate siblings:** None.
**Primary competition:** AMC Rambler, Chevrolet Nova, and Plymouth Valiant.
**Notable changes:** All-new model for 1969 1/2.
**Major standard equipment:** Tartan plaid cloth and vinyl interior trim, color-keyed floor mats, interior courtesy lights, flipper-type rear quarter windows, luggage compartment mat, and 6.00 × 13 BSW tires.

## Measurements

| | |
|---|---|
| Wheelbase | 103.0" |
| Length | 179.3" |
| Width | 70.6" |
| Height | 52.3" |
| Legroom — front | 41.3" |
| Legroom — rear | 31.9" |
| Headroom — front | 37.6" |
| Headroom — rear | 36.1" |
| Cargo capacity (cu. ft.) | 10.4 |
| Fuel capacity (gals.) | 16.0 |

## Models Available

| | Style Number | Base MSRP | Change from LY | Shipping Wt. (lbs.) | Production | Change from LY |
|---|---|---|---|---|---|---|
| Maverick 2-Door Sedan | 91 | $1,995 | NEW | 2427 | 127,833 | NEW |
| TOTALS | | Avg. price $1,995 | NEW | | Production 127,833 | NEW |

# Falcon

*"Seven beautiful ways to beat the high cost of buying."*

**Nameplate year of origin:** 1960.
**Current bodystyle lifespan:** 1966 through 1970.
**Predecessor to this model:** Falcon (1964 to 1965).
**Replacement for this model:** Maverick (1969 to 1977).
**Percentage of division's sales volume:** 4.91%.
**Corporate siblings:** None.
**Primary competition:** AMC Rambler, Chevrolet Nova, Dodge Dart, and Plymouth Valiant.
**Notable changes:** Virtually no changes.
**Major standard equipment:** Cloth and vinyl interior trim, front-door armrests, chrome windshield and rear window moldings, small hubcaps, and 6.95 × 14 BSW tires (7.75 × 14 on Wagons). Futura adds: Deluxe interior trim, full carpeting, rear armrests with ashtrays, side window moldings, wheel covers. Sport Coupe adds: Vinyl bucket seats, exterior bright molding, and full wheel covers.

## Measurements

| | Cars | Wagons |
|---|---|---|
| Wheelbase | 111.0" | 113.0" |
| Length | 184.3" | 199.0" |
| Width | 73.2" | 73.2" |
| Height | 54.9" | 55.5" |
| Legroom — front | 42.4" | 42.1" |
| Legroom — rear | 33.9" | 36.8" |
| Headroom — front | 38.6" | 38.7" |
| Headroom — rear | 38.8" | 37.8" |
| Cargo capacity (cu. ft.) | 12.2 | 85.2 |
| Fuel capacity (gals.) | 16.0 | 20.0 |

## Models Available

| | Style Number | Base MSRP | Change from LY | Shipping Wt. (lbs.) | Production | Change from LY |
|---|---|---|---|---|---|---|
| Falcon 2-Door Club Coupe | 10 | $2,283 | +1.38% | 2703 | 29,263 | -19.70% |
| Falcon 4-Door Sedan | 11 | $2,333 | +1.39% | 2748 | 22,719 | -22.10% |
| Falcon 4-Door Wagon | 12 | $2,660 | +1.64% | 3155 | 11,568 | -25.73% |
| Falcon Futura 2-Door Club Coupe | 20 | $2,461 | +1.90% | 2727 | 6,482 | -39.04% |
| Falcon Futura 2-Door Sports Coupe | 22 | $2,598 | +2.24% | 2749 | 5,931 | -41.14% |
| Falcon Futura 4-Door Sedan | 21 | $2,498 | +1.67% | 2764 | 11,850 | -36.74% |
| Falcon Futura 4-Door Wagon | 23 | $2,771 | +1.58% | 3191 | 7,203 | -33.06% |
| TOTALS | | Avg. price $2,515 | +1.70% | | Production 95,016 | -27.68% |

# Mustang

*"Somebody finally built a better Mustang."*

**Nameplate year of origin:** 1964 (½ (also, on a 1963 show car).
**Current bodystyle lifespan:** 1969 through 1970.
**Predecessor to this model:** Mustang (1964½ to 1968).
**Replacement for this model:** Mustang (1971 to 1973).
**Percentage of division's sales volume:** 15.45%.
**Corporate siblings:** Mercury Cougar.
**Primary competition:** AMC Javelin, Chevrolet Camaro, Plymouth Barracuda, and Pontiac Firebird.

## Measurements

| | |
|---|---|
| Wheelbase | 108.0" |
| Length | 187.4" |
| Width | 71.3" |
| Height | 51.3" |
| Legroom — front | 42.0" |
| Legroom — rear | 27.0" |
| Headroom — front | 37.4" |

1969

**Notable changes:** Completely restyled.

**Major standard equipment:** All-vinyl bucket seats, full carpeting, courtesy lights, hubcaps, and 7.35 × 14 BSW tires. SportsRoof adds: Swing-out rear quarter windows, and tinted rear glass. Convertible adds: Manually operated top, and color-keyed top boot. Grande adds to Hardtop: Cloth and vinyl interior trim, teak-toned instrument panel trim, electric clock, two-tone paint stripe, bright moldings (rocker, wheel lip, and lower back panel), dual racing-style outside mirrors, soft-ride suspension and special sound insulation package. Mach I adds to Sports Roof: High back bucket seats, teak-toned instrument panel trim, electric clock, dual racing-style outside mirrors, competition suspension, black low-gloss paint on hood, reflective dual tape stripes, special sound insulation package, and E70 × 14 Wide-Oval WSW tires.

## Measurements (cont.)

| | |
|---|---|
| Headroom — rear | 35.8" |
| Cargo capacity (cu. ft.) | 9.8 |
| Fuel capacity (gals.) | 20.0 |

## Models Available

| | Style Number | Base MSRP | Change from LY | Shipping Wt. (lbs.) | Production | Change from LY |
|---|---|---|---|---|---|---|
| Mustang 2-Door Hardtop | 1 | $2,635 | +1.27% | 2713 | 127,954 | -48.70% |
| Mustang 2-Door SportsRoof HT | 2 | $2,635 | -2.84% | 2737 | 61,980 | +46.44% |
| Mustang 2-Door Convertible | 3 | $2,849 | +1.24% | 2823 | 14,746 | -41.89% |
| Mustang Grande 2-Door Hardtop | 4 | $2,866 | NEW | 2788 | 22,182 | NEW |
| Mustang Mach I 2-Dr. SportsRoof HT | 2 | $3,122 | NEW | 3253 | 72,458 | NEW |
| TOTALS | Avg. price | $2,821 | +4.13% | Production | 299,320 | -5.62% |

# Fairlane and Torino

*"How can anything so hot look so cool?"*

**Nameplate year of origin:** 1968.
**Current bodystyle lifespan:** 1968 through 1969.
**Predecessor to this model:** Fairlane (1966 to 1967).
**Replacement for this model:** Fairlane/Torino (1970 to 1971).
**Percentage of division's sales volume:** 18.94%.
**Corporate siblings:** Mercury Montego.
**Primary competition:** AMC Rebel, Chevrolet Chevelle, Plymouth Satellite, Dodge Coronet, and Pontiac Tempest.
**Notable changes:** Revised grille and trim.
**Major standard equipment:** Cloth and vinyl bench seat, color-keyed rubber floor mats, front and rear armrests, chrome windshield molding, and 7.35 × 14 BSW tires (7.75 × 14 BSW on Wagons). 500 adds: Full carpeting, deluxe interior trim, power-operated topon Convertible, and chrome rear and side window moldings. Torino adds: Torino interior trim, accent tape stripe on Hardtop and Sedan, and full wheel covers. Torino Squire adds: Exterior wood-grain trim. Torino GT adds: All-vinyl front bench seat, styled steel wheels, hood scoop, 302 CID V8 engine, and F70 × 14 Wide-Oval WSW tires. Cobra adds: 428 CID V8 engine, 4-speed manual transmission, heavy-duty suspension, and dual exhausts.

## Measurements

| | Cars | Wagons |
|---|---|---|
| Wheelbase | 116.0" | 113.0" |
| Length | 201.1" | 203.9" |
| Width | 74.8" | 74.8" |
| Height | 55.0" | 55.5" |
| Legroom — front | 42.4" | 42.4" |
| Legroom — rear | 36.0" | 36.0" |
| Headroom — front | 38.6" | 38.6" |
| Headroom — rear | 37.4" | 37.4" |
| Cargo capacity (cu. ft.) | 16.2 | 83.5 |
| Fuel capacity (gals.) | 20.0 | 20.0 |

## Models Available

| | Style Number | Base MSRP | Change from LY | Shipping Wt. (lbs.) | Production | Change from LY |
|---|---|---|---|---|---|---|
| Fairlane 2-Door Hardtop | 30 | $2,499 | +1.75% | 3072 | 85,630 | +91.64% |
| Fairlane 4-Door Sedan | 31 | $2,488 | +0.97% | 3061 | 27,296 | +50.42% |

| | Style Number | Base MSRP | Change from LY | Shipping Wt. (lbs.) | Production | Change from LY |
|---|---|---|---|---|---|---|
| Fairlane 4-Door, 2-Seat Wagon | 32 | $2,841 | +2.56% | 3438 | 10,882 | -26.47% |
| Fairlane 500 2-Door Hardtop | 33 | $2,626 | +1.35% | 3078 | 28,179 | -15.33% |
| Fairlane 500 2-Dr. SportsRoof HT | 35 | $2,601 | +1.36% | 3120 | 29,849 | -8.02% |
| Fairlane 500 2-Door Convertible | 36 | $2,851 | +1.03% | 3280 | 2,264 | -39.80% |
| Fairlane 500 4-Door Sedan | 34 | $2,568 | +0.98% | 3067 | 40,888 | -3.54% |
| Fairlane 500 4-Dr., 2-Seat Wagon | 37 | $2,951 | +2.43% | 3458 | 12,869 | +26.29% |
| Torino 2-Door Hardtop | 40 | $2,754 | +1.62% | 3123 | 20,789 | -42.19% |
| Torino 4-Door Sedan | 41 | $2,733 | +1.67% | 3108 | 11,971 | -33.35% |
| Torino Squire 4-Dr., 2-Seat Wagon | 38 | $3,107 | +2.47% | 3473 | 14,472 | -2.04% |
| Torino GT 2-Door Hardtop | 44 | $2,865 | +3.35% | 3278 | 17,951 | -25.01% |
| Torino GT 2-Door SportsRoof HT | 42 | $2,840 | +3.39% | 3317 | 61,319 | -17.29% |
| Torino GT 2-Door Convertible | 43 | $3,090 | +2.97% | 3441 | 2,552 | -51.94% |
| Torino Cobra 2-Dr. Hardtop | 45 | $3,206 | NEW | 3546 | NA | NEW |
| Torino Cobra 2-Dr. SportsRoof HT | 46 | $3,181 | NEW | 3588 | NA | NEW |
| TOTALS | *Avg. price* | $2,825 | +3.97% | *Production* | 366,911 | -1.31% |

# Custom, Galaxie & LTD

*"This is how Ford stands in 1969. Bigger. Wider. Longer. Quieter. And alone in its class."*

**Nameplate year of origin:** 1957 (Custom), 1959 (Galaxie) and 1965 (LTD).

**Current bodystyle lifespan:** 1969 through 1970.

**Predecessor to this model:** Full-size Ford (1967 to 1968).

**Replacement for this model:** Galaxie and LTD (1971 to 1977, with several redesigns).

**Percentage of division's sales volume:** 51.56%.

**Corporate siblings:** Mercury Monterey and Marquis.

**Primary competition:** AMC Ambassador, Chevrolet Biscayne/BelAir/Impala/Caprice, Dodge Polara/Monaco, Plymouth Fury, and Pontiac Catalina.

**Notable changes:** Completely restyled.

**Major standard equipment:** All vinyl front bench seat, full carpeting, arm rests on all doors, rear window trim molding, and 7.75 × 15 BSW tires (8.55 × 15 BSW tires on Wagon). Custom 500 adds: Cloth and vinyl front bench seat, chrome windshield molding. Galaxie 500 adds: All-vinyl front bench seat on Convertible, wood-like door trim, additional interior lighting, chrome side window moldings, power-operated top and color-keyed top boot on convertible, and 8.25 × 15 BSW tires on Convertible. XL adds: All-vinyl front bench seat, lower door carpet trim and polished trim, courtesy and reading lamps, concealed headlamps, full wheel covers, and special badging. LTD adds: Padded cloth upholstery, simulated wood interior trim, additional courtesy lights, and 8.25 × 15 BSW tires.

## Measurements

| | Cars | Wagons |
|---|---|---|
| Wheelbase | 121.0" | 121.0" |
| Length | 213.9" | 216.9" |
| Width | 79.8" | 79.8" |
| Height | 54.9" | 56.8" |
| Legroom — front | 41.9" | 41.9" |
| Legroom — rear | 38.7" | 38.5" |
| Headroom — front | 38.9" | 38.9" |
| Headroom — rear | 37.8" | 38.1" |
| Cargo capacity (cu. ft.) | 18.0 | 96.2 |
| Fuel capacity (gals.) | 24.0 | 24.0 |

**1969**

## Models Available

| | Style Number | Base MSRP | Change from LY | Shipping Wt. (lbs.) | Production | Change from LY |
|---|---|---|---|---|---|---|
| Custom 2-Door Sedan | 50 | $2,649 | +2.52% | 3526 | 15,439 | -16.48% |
| Custom 4-Door Sedan | 51 | $2,691 | +1.85% | 3566 | 45,653 | -0.71% |
| Custom 4-Door Ranch Wagon | 70 | $3,091 | +3.03% | 4001 | 17,489 | -4.10% |
| Custom 500 2-Door Sedan | 52 | $2,748 | +1.82% | 3536 | 7,585 | -15.14% |
| Custom 500 4-Door Sedan | 53 | $2,790 | +1.79% | 3606 | 45,761 | -7.36% |
| Custom 500 4-Dr. Ranch Wagon | 71 | $3,155 | +3.00% | 3971 | 16,432 | -9.62% |

| | Style Number | Base MSRP | Change from LY | Shipping Wt. (lbs.) | Production | Change from LY |
|---|---|---|---|---|---|---|
| C. 500 4-Dr. Ranch Wagon w/DFRS* | 72 | $3,268 | +2.90% | 4059 | 11,563 | -13.84% |
| Galaxie 500 2-Door Hardtop | 58 | $2,982 | +2.26% | 3589 | 71,920 | -14.72% |
| Galaxie 500 2-Door SportsRoof HT | 55 | $2,930 | +1.70% | 3588 | 63,921 | -8.37% |
| Galaxie 500 2-Door Convertible | 57 | $3,159 | +1.61% | 3815 | 6,910 | -41.60% |
| Galaxie 500 4-Door Sedan | 54 | $2,914 | +1.75% | 3579 | 104,606 | -11.26% |
| Galaxie 500 4-Door Hardtop | 56 | $2,983 | +1.60% | 3650 | 64,031 | +15.45% |
| G. 500 Country Sedan 4-Dr. Wagon | 73 | $3,274 | +2.92% | 4011 | 36,287 | -7.75% |
| G. 500 Country Sedan 4-Dr. w/DFRS* | 74 | $3,389 | +2.85% | 4034 | 11,563 | -60.64% |
| XL 2-Door Hardtop | 60 | $3,069 | +2.81% | 3668 | 54,557 | +9.01% |
| XL 2-Door Convertible | 61 | $3,297 | +2.58% | 3901 | 7,402 | +22.02% |
| LTD 2-Door Hardtop | 62 | $3,152 | -0.03% | 3681 | 111,565 | +105.98% |
| LTD 4-Door Sedan | 64 | $3,110 | -0.80% | 3655 | 63,709 | +179.01% |
| LTD 4-Door Hardtop | 66 | $3,180 | -0.81% | 3725 | 113,168 | +83.25% |
| LTD Country Squire 4-Dr. Wagon | 75 | $3,661 | +3.45% | 4097 | 46,445 | +36.63% |
| LTD Cntry. Sq. 4-Dr. Wgn. w/DFRS | 76 | $3,778 | +4.39% | 4143 | 82,790 | +43.29% |
| TOTALS | | Avg. price $3,108 | +2.07% | | Production 998,796 | +15.17% |

*Dual facing rear seats

# Thunderbird

*"Unique in all the world."*

**Nameplate year of origin:** 1955.
**Current bodystyle lifespan:** 1967 through 1971 (restyled in 1970).
**Predecessor to this model:** Thunderbird (1964 to 1966).
**Replacement for this model:** Thunderbird (1972 to 1976).
**Percentage of division's sales volume:** 2.54%.
**Corporate siblings:** Lincoln Continental Mark III.
**Primary competition:** Buick Riviera and Oldsmobile Toronado.
**Notable changes:** Revised grille and taillights and minor trim and detail changes.
**Major standard equipment:** Luxury all-cloth interior with cut-pile carpeting, front bench seat, tilt away steering wheel, AM radio, "rolling lock" power door locks, power steering, power front disc brakes, sequential turn signals, full wheel covers, and 8.25 × 15 BSW tires.

## Measurements

| | 2-Doors | 4-Doors |
|---|---|---|
| Wheelbase | 114.7" | 117.2" |
| Length | 206.9" | 209.4" |
| Width | 77.3" | 77.3" |
| Height | 53.4" | 54.0" |
| Legroom — front | 42.1" | 42.1" |
| Legroom — rear | 32.2" | 34.0" |
| Headroom — front | 37.4" | 38.1" |
| Headroom — rear | 36.9" | 37.2" |
| Cargo capacity (cu. ft.) | 12.3 | 12.3 |
| Fuel capacity (gals.) | 24.1 | 24.1 |

## Models Available

| | Style Number | Base MSRP | Change from LY | Shipping Wt. (lbs.) | Production | Change from LY |
|---|---|---|---|---|---|---|
| Thunderbird 2-Door Hardtop | 83 | $4,824 | +2.29% | 4337 | 5,913 | -40.73% |
| Thunderbird 2-Dr. Landau Coupe | 84 | $4,964 | +2.46% | 4308 | 27,664 | -16.24% |
| Thunderbird 4-Door Landau Sedan | 87 | $5,043 | +2.42% | 4447 | 15,650 | -28.62% |
| TOTALS | | Avg. price $4,944 | +2.40% | | Production 49,227 | -24.19% |

# IMPERIAL

*"For the man who wants everything."*

An all-new Imperial appeared for 1969. For the first time in quite a few years, the styling and many components were shared with Chrysler models. While the Imperial was not a blatant copy of a Chrysler, there was enough similarity that one could easily mistake the identities of the two cars. At the front, Imperial models had a full-width grille with two horizontal bars over a fine, egg-crate style mesh. Headlights were of a hidden style, and the vertical parking lamps were fitted into the front fender edges. All of this was surrounded by the new "loop-style" Chrysler front bumper system. Of course, the body itself was smooth and rounded in typical "fuselage" styling. At the back, the taillights were inset into a bumper that was integrated into the body of the car. This was to be the last major styling change for the Imperial as its own brand. Powertrains remained the same as in previous years. Two model changes were made for 1969: the convertible was no longer offered, and a 2-Door Hardtop was added to the LeBaron line.

**LeBaron 2-Door Hardtop**

**Model year production:** 22,077, up 43.72% over 1968.
**Domestic market share:** 0.25% (13th place).
**Base price range:** $5,592 to $6,131.
**Industry average base price:** $3,386.
**Imperial average base price:** $5,832.
**Introduction date:** September 1968.
**Assembly plants:** Newark, NJ (F), and Detroit, MI (C).
**Data plate identification:** Thirteen digit code read as follows: four digit style number (see listings below) in which Y = Imperial, 2nd number identifies series (e.g., M is for LeBaron), 3rd and 4th digits indicate body style; 5th digit is engine code; 9 for 1969; assembly plant code; 100001 and up for serial number. *Example:* YM23T9C100001 is a 1969 Imperial LeBaron 2-Door Hardtop with a 440 CID V8 engine, serial number 100001, built in Detroit, MI.

**1969**

## Powertrains

| Engine | Engine Code | Gross HP | Transmission Availability | Imperial |
|---|---|---|---|---|
| 440 CID, 4-bbl., V8 | T | 350 | Torqueflite Automatic | S |

## Major Options

| | Crown | LeBaron |
|---|---|---|
| Air conditioning | $494 | $494 |
| Automatic speed control | $92 | $92 |
| Tinted glass | $54 | $54 |
| Rear window defogger | $27 | $27 |

## Paint Colors

| | Code |
|---|---|
| Platinum Metallic | A4 |
| Charcoal Metallic | A9 |
| Bahama Blue | B3 |
| Midnight Blue Metallic | B9 |

|  | Crown | LeBaron |
|---|---|---|
| Deck lid remote release | $31 | $31 |
| Power steering — variable-ratio | S | S |
| Power brakes | S | S |
| Power door locks | $48 (2-Dr)/$71 (4-Dr) | $48 (2-Dr)/$71 (4-Dr) |
| Power driver's seat/Bench seat | $109 | $109 |
| Power windows | S | S |
| AM radio w/power antenna | $165 | $165 |
| AM/FM radio w/power antenna | $234 | $234 |
| Tilt and telescoping steering wheel | $97 | $97 |
| Vinyl roof | $152 | S |
| Whitewall tires — standard size | $46 | $46 |

|  | Code |
|---|---|
| Dark Briar Metallic | E7 |
| Surf Green Metallic | F3 |
| Jade Green Metallic | F8 |
| Dark Emerald Metallic | F9 |
| Navaho Beige | L1 |
| Deep Plum | M9 |
| Aquamarine Metallic | Q4 |
| Bronze Mist Metallic | T3 |
| Tuscan Bronze Metallic | T7 |
| Spinnaker White | W1 |
| Formal Black | X9 |
| Champagne | Y3 |
| Classic Gold Metallic | Y4 |
| Mystic Gold Metallic | Y5 |

Options common to most models. (S = Standard equipment.) Items may be standard equipment, optional at different pricing, or unavailable on certain models. This chart is only a guide.

# Crown

*"This is the year of the Imperial revolution."*

**Nameplate year of origin:** 1957 (not the same as Crown Imperial series).
**Current bodystyle lifespan:** 1969 through 1973.
**Predecessor to this model:** Crown (1967 to 1968).
**Replacement for this model:** Chrysler Imperial (1974 to 1975).
**Percentage of division's sales volume:** 12.16%.
**Corporate siblings:** LeBaron.
**Primary competition:** Cadillac Calais and Lincoln Continental.
**Notable changes:** Completely redesigned.
**Major standard equipment:** Cloth and vinyl front bench seat, front and rear armrests (hardtops), pile carpeting, remote-control left-hand outside mirror, power windows, electric clock, trip odometer, 3-speed electric windshield wipers with washers, Torqueflite automatic transmission, power steering, power brakes, wheel covers and 9.15 × 15 BSW tires.

## Measurements

| Wheelbase | 127.0" |
|---|---|
| Length | 229.7" |
| Width | 79.1" |
| Height | 56.3" |
| Legroom — front | 41.9" |
| Legroom — rear | 41.2" |
| Headroom — front | 38.3" |
| Headroom — rear | 37.0" |
| Cargo capacity (cu. ft.) | NA |
| Fuel capacity (gals.) | 25.0 |

## Models Available

|  | Style Number | Base MSRP | Change from LY | Shipping Wt. (lbs.) | Production | Change from LY |
|---|---|---|---|---|---|---|
| Crown 2-Door Hardtop | YL23 | $5,592 | -2.27% | 4555 | 244 | -90.81% |
| Crown 4-Door Sedan | YM41 | $5,770 | +2.05% | 4620 | 1,617 | -14.31% |
| Crown 4-Door Hardtop | YL43 | $5,770 | -5.64% | 4690 | 823 | -90.31% |
| TOTALS | | Avg. price $5,711 | -4.77% | | Production 2,684 | -80.13% |

# LeBaron

*"Sculpted body, elegant refinements and incomparable new interiors."*

**Nameplate year of origin:** 1924 (as Chrysler Sedan model designation); 1926 (as series).
**Current bodystyle lifespan:** 1969 through 1973.
**Predecessor to this model:** LeBaron (1967 to 1968).
**Replacement for this model:** Chrysler Imperial (1974 to 1975).
**Percentage of division's sales volume:** 87.84%.

## Measurements

| Wheelbase | 127.0" |
|---|---|
| Length | 229.7" |
| Width | 79.1" |
| Height | 55.7" |

**Corporate siblings:** Crown.
**Primary competition:** Cadillac de Ville and Lincoln Continental.
**Notable changes:** Completely redesigned.
**Major standard equipment:** Cloth and fabric-and-leather or broadcloth split-bench front seat, pile carpeting, power seat, power windows and vent windows, electric clock, trip odometer, vinyl roof with formal carriage rear window, 3-speed electric windshield wipers with washers, Torqueflite automatic transmission, power steering, power brakes, wheel covers and 9.15 × 15 WSW tires.

## Measurements (cont.)

| | |
|---|---|
| Legroom — front | 41.9" |
| Legroom — rear | 41.2" |
| Headroom — front | 38.2" |
| Headroom — rear | 37.0" |
| Cargo capacity (cu. ft.) | NA |
| Fuel capacity (gals.) | 25.0 |

## Models Available

| | Style Number | Base MSRP | Change from LY | Shipping Wt. (lbs.) | Production | Change from LY |
|---|---|---|---|---|---|---|
| LeBaron 2-Door Hardtop | YM23 | $5,898 | NEW | 4610 | 4,572 | NEW |
| LeBaron 4-Door Hardtop | YM43 | $6,131 | -11.66% | 4710 | 14,821 | +700.27% |
| TOTALS | | *Avg. price* $6,015 | -13.33% | | *Production* 19,393 | +1047.14% |

# LINCOLN

*"America's most distinguished motorcars."*

For the first time since 1961, a completely new Lincoln design was introduced. A conceptual replacement for the 1956-1957 Mark II, the Continental Mark III was introduced in April 1968 as a 1969 model. The Mark III was a direct competitor for the Cadillac Eldorado, and was based upon the existing Thunderbird 4-Door platform. At the time of its introduction, the Mark III was one of the most fully equipped cars available on the market. A full complement of power accessories were standard equipment, with air conditioning being the only obvious item lacking from that equipment list. Within two years that too would become standard equipment. The new corporate 460 CID V8 engine was standard in the Mark III as well as the existing Continental line. The Continental models were given a new front bumper and grille design for their final year before receiving a complete redesign.

Continental 4-Door Sedan

Continental Mark III 2-Door Hardtop

**1969**

**Model year production:** 69,241, up 76.93% over 1968.
**Domestic market share:** 0.78% (12th place).
**Base price range:** $5,830 to $6,910.
**Industry average base price:** $3,386.

**Lincoln average base price:** $6,268.
**Introduction date:** September 1968. Continental Mark III introduced in April 1968.
**Assembly plants:** Wixom, MI (Y), and Allen Park, MI (S).

**Data plate identification:** Eleven digit code read as follows: 9 for 1969; 2nd digit is assembly plant code; 2-digit model number (see listings below); 5th digit is engine code; 800001 and up for serial number. *Example:* 9Y82A800001 is a 1969 Lincoln Continental 4-Door Sedan with a 460 CID V8 engine, serial number 800001, built in Wixom, MI.

## Powertrains

| Engine | Gross HP | Engine Code | Transmission Availability | Mark III & Continental |
|---|---|---|---|---|
| 460 CID, 4-bbl., V8 | 365 | A | Select-Shift Automatic | S |

## Major Options

| | Continental | Mark III |
|---|---|---|
| Air conditioning — manual | $504 | $504 |
| Automatic headlight dimmers | $51 | $51 |
| 6-way power seat | $89 | $180 |
| Power door locks | $47–$68 | $47 |
| AM-FM stereo radio w/power antenna | $302 | $302 |
| AM w/stereo 8-track w/power antenna | $297 | $297 |
| Vinyl roof | $152 | S |
| Sunroof | - | $459 |
| Tilt and telescope steering wheel | $72 | $70 |
| Leather upholstery | $164 | $164 |
| Speed control | $95 | $95 |
| Remote control trunk release | $41 | $41 |
| Stardust Metallic paint colors | $131 | $131 |

Options common to most models. (- = Not Available; S = Standard equipment.) Items may be standard equipment, optional at different pricing, or unavailable on certain models. This chart is only a guide.

## Paint Colors

| | Code |
|---|---|
| Black | A |
| Maroon | B |
| Dark Ivy Green Metallic | C |
| Medium Orchid Metallic | G |
| Light Green | H |
| Medium Lime Metallic | I |
| Dark Aqua Metallic | J |
| Dark Orchid Metallic | K |
| Light Gray Metallic | L |
| White | M |
| Platinum | N |
| Medium Green Metallic | O |
| Medium Blue Metallic | Q |
| Light Gold | R |
| Medium Gold Metallic | S |
| Red | T |
| Medium Aqua Metallic | U |
| Light Copper Metallic | V |
| Yellow | W |
| Dark Blue | X |
| Burnt Orange Metallic | Y |
| Dark Gray Metallic | Z |

# Continental

*"America's most distinguished coupe and sedan."*

**Nameplate year of origin:** 1940 (1961 as a standard sedan nameplate).
**Current bodystyle lifespan:** 1961 through 1969 (major restyles in 1964 and 1966).
**Predecessor to this model:** Premiere (1958 to 1960).
**Replacement for this model:** Continental (1970 to 1979).
**Percentage of division's sales volume:** 55.43%.
**Corporate siblings:** None.
**Primary competition:** Cadillac de Ville and Imperial LeBaron.
**Notable changes:** Minor revisions.
**Major standard equipment:** Cloth and leather front bench seat upholstery with folding center armrests front and rear, two-way power seat, trip odometer, walnut-tone instrument panel and door appliques, vanity mirror, looped-pile carpeting, variable-speed windshield wipers with washers, lined luggage compartment, power steering, power brakes, automatic transmission and 9.15 × 15 BSW tires.

## Measurements

| | |
|---|---|
| Wheelbase | 126.0" |
| Length | 224.2" |
| Width | 79.7" |
| Height | 54.2" |
| Legroom — front | 41.0" |
| Legroom — rear | 40.5" |
| Headroom — front | 39.4" |
| Headroom — rear | 38.6" |
| Luggage capacity (cu. ft.) | 18.0 |
| Fuel capacity (gals.) | 25.0 |

## Models Available

| | Style Number | Base MSRP | Change from LY | Shipping Wt. (lbs.) | Production | Change from LY |
|---|---|---|---|---|---|---|
| Continental 2-Door Hardtop | 81 | $5,830 | +1.64% | 4910 | 9,032 | -4.07% |
| Continental 4-Door Sedan | 82 | $6,063 | +1.56% | 5005 | 29,351 | -1.24% |
| TOTALS | Avg. price $5,947 | | +1.61% | Production 38,383 | | -1.92% |

# Continental Mark III

*"The most authoritatively styled, decisively
individual motor car of this generation."*

**Nameplate year of origin:** 1956 (Continental Mark II).
**Current bodystyle lifespan:** 1969 through 1971.
**Predecessor to this model:** Continental Mark II (1956 to 1957).
**Replacement for this model:** Continental Mark IV (1972 to 1976).
**Percentage of division's sales volume:** 44.57%.
**Corporate siblings:** Ford Thunderbird.
**Primary competition:** Buick Riviera, Cadillac Eldorado, and Oldsmobile Toronado.
**Notable changes:** All-new model for 1969.
**Major standard equipment:** All-leather front bench seat upholstery with folding
center armrests front and rear, full carpeting, two-way power seat, power windows,
walnut-tone instrument panel and door appliques, vanity mirror, variable-speed
windshield wipers with washers, lined luggage compartment, concealed headlamps,
power steering, power brakes, automatic transmission and 8.55 × 15 BSW tires.

## Measurements

| | |
|---|---|
| Wheelbase | 117.2" |
| Length | 216.1" |
| Width | 79.4" |
| Height | 53.0" |
| Legroom — front | 42.1" |
| Legroom — rear | 34.7" |
| Headroom — front | 37.1" |
| Headroom — rear | 36.5" |
| Luggage capacity (cu. ft.) | 13.5 |
| Fuel capacity (gals.) | NA |

## Models Available

| | Style Number | Base MSRP | Change from LY | Shipping Wt. (lbs.) | Production | Change from LY |
|---|---|---|---|---|---|---|
| Continental Mark III 2-Door Hardtop | 89 | $6,910 | NEW | 4560 | 30,858 | NEW |
| TOTALS | Avg. price $6,910 | | NEW | Production 30,858 | | NEW |

# MERCURY

*"Mercury leads the way."*

Mercury's full-size models moved toward the upper end of the mid-price class of cars for 1969. The Monterey, Marauder and Marquis were all restyled for the new year and were more substantial looking cars, looking more like a Lincoln than in recent years. In retail pricing, Mercury had moved above that of comparable Dodge and Pontiac models and into the Oldsmobile and Buick range. As if to emphasize this strategy, the Marquis was expanded from a luxury sport 2-Door Hardtop line to a full-fledged series that replaced the Park Lane. The Marquis and the new Marauder series sported Lincoln style front ends, with hidden headlights and a slightly pronounced and raised center section. At the back, each model received a variation of taillights and chrome trim set into a concave area between the rear decklid and bumper — the higher the series, the more taillights there were across the back. Powertrain choices remained similar to previous years.

Mercury took the opportunity to "clean house" with the model lines, dropping three nameplates and reviving an earlier one. The three that were gone included the aforementioned Park Lane, the mid-range Montclair, and the Commuter nameplate from the low-priced wagon line. The Commuter was moved into the base Monterey lineup. A new Monterey Custom trim level replaced the Montclair, and added its own mid-level wagon line. At the top end the Marquis nameplate replaced the Park Lane, plus a three-model Marquis Brougham series was added as an extra luxurious model, nearing the Lincoln in comfort and features. To replace the previous Marquis 2-Door Hardtop line, a new Marauder line was introduced, retaining the former car's fastback roofline and powerful engine choices, as well as a its luxurious appearances. The Marauder X-100 was given a unique matte black finished rear window and decklid paint treatment that distinguished it from lesser cars.

The sporty Cougar was substantially restyled this year while still carrying the original car's distinctive look. A new body side "swoop" was added to give a little character and slightly more aggressive look to the Cougar. Headlights continued to be hidden behind grillework, and full-width taillights were used at the rear. A new Convertible model was added to both the base and XR-7 lines, giving the Cougar a very sexy new profile. Finally, the mid-size Comet and Montego lines were given a minor facelift that included revised grille and new trim. The racing-bred Cyclone was now offered in two flavors, but from one body style. The 1968 version came in Formal Hardtop and Fastback variations. This year the Cyclone was only offered in the sleeker Fastback variety, but it came in the base Cyclone or the potent new Cyclone CJ. The "CJ," for Cobra Jet, offered all of the high performance goodies. With 335 horsepower and a 10.6 to 1 compression ratio, this car meant business.

Comet 2-Door Hardtop

Cougar 2-Door Convertible

Cougar 2-Door Hardtop

Cyclone 2-Door Hardtop

Marauder X-100 2-Door Hardtop with Interior

Marquis Brougham 4-Door Hardtop

Marquis Colony Park 4-Door Wagon

Montego MX 4-Door Wagon

Monterey 2-Door Convertible

**Model year production:** 398,510, up 11.56% over 1968.
**Domestic market share:** 4.48% (8th place).
**Base price range:** $2,644 to $4,262.
**Industry average price:** $3,386.
**Mercury average price:** $3,401.

**Introduction date:** September 1968.
**Assembly plants:** Dearborn, MI (F); Lorain, OH (H); San Jose, CA (R); Allen Park, MI (S); St. Louis, MO (Z); and Oakville, Ontario, Canada (B).
**Data plate identification:** Eleven digit code read as follows: 9

for 1969; 2nd digit is assembly plant code; 2-digit model number (see listings below) 5th digit is engine code; 500001 and up for serial number. *Example:* 9S46Y500001 is a 1969

Mercury Monterey 2-Door Hardtop with a 390 CID 2-bbl., V8 engine, serial number 500001, built in Allen Park, MI.

## Powertrains†

| Engine | Gross HP | Engine Code | Transmission Availability | Cougar | Comet/ Montego | Monterey | Marquis & Marauder |
|---|---|---|---|---|---|---|---|
| 250 CID, 1-bbl., 6-cyl. | 155 | L/3 | 3-speed manual | - | S* | - | - |
| | | | Select-Shift Automatic | - | $201 | - | - |
| 302 CID, 2-bbl., V8 | 220 | F/6 | 3-speed manual | - | S (Cyc.)/$90* | - | - |
| | | | Select-Shift Automatic | - | $201 (Cyc.)/$291* | - | - |
| 351 CID, 2-bbl., V8 | 250 | H | 3-speed manual | S | $84 (Cyc.)/$174* | - | - |
| | | | 4-speed manual | $205 | $289 (Cyc.)/$375* | - | - |
| | | | Select-Shift Automatic | $201 | $285 (Cyc.)/$371* | - | - |
| 351 CID, 4-bbl., V8 | 290 | M | 3-speed manual | $26 | $110 (Cyc.)/$200* | | - |
| | | | 4-speed manual | $231 | $315 (Cyc.)/$405* | - | - |
| | | | Select-Shift Automatic | $227 | $311 (Cyc.)/$401* | - | - |
| 390 CID, 2-bbl., V8 | 265/280 | Y/X | 3-speed manual | - | - | S | S (Marauder) |
| | | | Select-Shift Automatic | - | - | $222 | $222 (Marauder) |
| 390 CID, 4-bbl., V8 | 320 | S | 3-speed manual | $100 | $ (Cyc.)/$* | $ | $ (Marauder) |
| | | | 4-speed manual | $305 | $ (Cyc.)/$* | - | - |
| | | | Select-Shift Automatic | $301 | $ (Cyc.)/$* | $ | $ (Marauder) |
| 427 CID Cobra 390 Jet, 4-bbl., V8 | | W | 4-speed manual | - | $ (Cyclone) | - | - |
| | | | Select-Shift Automatic | - | $ (Cyclone) | - | - |
| 428 CID Cobra Jet, 4-bbl., V8 | 335 | Q | 4-speed manual | $478 | S (CJ)/$ (Cyclone) | - | - |
| | | | Select-Shift Automatic | $446 | NC (CJ)/$ (Cyclone) | $ | $ (Marauder) |
| 428 CID Cobra Jet, 4-bbl., V8 Ram Air | | R | 4-speed manual | $ | - | - | - |
| | | | Select-Shift Automatic | $ | - | - | - |
| 429 CID, 2-bbl., V8 | 320 | K | Select-Shift Automatic | - | - | - | S (Marquis) |
| 429 CID Cobra Jet, 4-bbl., V8 | 360 | N | 4-speed manual | - | $ (CJ)/$ (Cyclone) | - | - |
| | | | Select-Shift Automatic | - | $ (CJ)/$ (Cyclone) | - | S (X-100)/ $ (Marauder)/ $ (Marquis) |

†*Where 2 codes are listed, the second is premium fuel engine.*    **Except Cyclone.*

## Major Options

| | Cougar | Montego | Monterey/Marauder | Marquis |
|---|---|---|---|---|
| Air conditioning | $376 | $389 | $421 | $421 |
| Speed control | $71 | - | $64 | $64 |
| Tinted glass | $30 | $35 | $43 | $43 |
| Deck lid remote release | - | - | $14 | $14 |
| Power steering | $100 | $95 | $115 | $115 |
| Power brakes — front discs | $65 | $65 | $71 | $71 |
| Power door locks | - | - | $45–$69 | $45–$69 |
| Power driver's seat/Bench seat | - | $74 | $85 | $85 |
| Power windows | $105 | $105 | $110 | $110 |
| AM radio | $61 | $61 | $64 | $64 |
| AM/FM stereo | $213 | $213 | $240 | $240 |
| Front seat console | $57 | $57 | S (X-100) | - |
| Front bucket seats | S | $119 | S (X-100) | - |
| Tilt steering wheel | $69 | - | $45 | $45 |

1969

|  | Cougar | Montego | Monterey/Marauder | Marquis |
|---|---|---|---|---|
| Vinyl roof | $89 | $100 | $115 ($143 Wagons) | $115 ($143 Wagons) |
| Styled steel or aluminum wheels | $91–$117 | $96–$117 | $96 | $96 |

Options common to most models. (– = Not Available; S = Standard equipment.) Items may be standard equipment, optional at different pricing, or unavailable on certain models. This chart is only a guide.

## Paint Colors

| | Code | | Code |
|---|---|---|---|
| Light Ivy Yellow | 2 | Medium Lime Metallic | I |
| Competition Orange* | 3 | Dark Orchid Metallic | K |
| Medium Green Met.* | 4 | White | M |
| Bright Blue Metallic* | 6 | Medium Blue Met.* | P |
| Light Blue | 8 | Medium Blue Metallic | Q |
| Yellow | 9 | Medium Gold Metallic | S |
| Black | A | Red | T |
| Maroon | B | Yellow | W |
| Dark Ivy Green Metallic | C | Dark Blue Metallic | X |
| Pastel Gray* | D | Burnt Orange Metallic | Y |
| Dark Aqua Metallic | F | Light Ivy Yellow | Z |
| Light Green | H | | |

*Cougar or Montego only.

# Cougar

*"New Cougars on the prowl for 1969."*

**Nameplate year of origin:** 1967.
**Current bodystyle lifespan:** 1969 through 1970.
**Predecessor to this model:** Cougar (1967 to 1968).
**Replacement for this model:** Cougar (1971 to 1973).
**Percentage of division's sales volume:** 25.11%.
**Corporate siblings:** Ford Mustang.
**Primary competition:** AMC Javelin, Chevrolet Camaro, Plymouth Barracuda, and Pontiac Firebird.
**Notable changes:** Completely restyled.
**Major standard equipment:** All-vinyl front bucket seats, full carpeting, concealed headlights, sequential taillamps with wrap-around backup lights, rocker panel moldings, dual paint stripes on body side, power top on convertible, and E78 × 14 BSW tires. XR-7 adds: Leather and vinyl bucket seats, burled-walnut style interior trim, tachometer, trip odometer, electric clock, racing-style outside rear view mirror, and XR-7 specific wheel covers and emblems.

## Measurements

| | |
|---|---|
| Wheelbase | 111.0" |
| Length | 193.8" |
| Width | 75.0" |
| Height | 51.9" |
| Legroom — front | 42.7" |
| Legroom — rear | 29.9" |
| Headroom — front | 37.3" |
| Headroom — rear | 35.9" |
| Cargo capacity (cu. ft.) | 10.2 |
| Fuel capacity (gals.) | 17.0 |

## Models Available

| | Style Number | Base MSRP | Change from LY | Shipping Wt. (lbs.) | Production | Change from LY |
|---|---|---|---|---|---|---|
| Cougar 2-Door Hardtop | 91 | $3,016 | +2.83% | 3219 | 66,331 | -18.12% |
| Cougar 2-Door Convertible | 92 | $3,382 | NEW | 3343 | 5,796 | NEW |
| Cougar XR-7 2-Door HT | 93 | $3,315 | +2.57% | 3221 | 23,918 | -26.88% |
| Cougar XR-7 2-Door Conv. | 94 | $3,595 | NEW | 3343 | 4,024 | NEW |
| TOTALS | | *Avg. price* $3,327 | +7.91% | | *Production* 100,069 | -12.01% |

# Comet and Montego

*"Liveliness and luxury combined at a popular price."*

**Nameplate year of origin:** 1968.
**Current bodystyle lifespan:** 1968 through 1969.
**Predecessor to this model:** Comet (1966 to 1967).
**Replacement for this model:** Montego (1970 to 1971).
**Percentage of division's sales volume:** 29.09%.
**Corporate siblings:** Ford Torino.
**Primary competition:** Buick Skylark, Dodge Coronet/Charger, Oldsmobile Cutlass and Pontiac LeMans.
**Notable changes:** New grille and minor trim and detail changes.
**Major standard equipment:** Nylon and vinyl front bench seat, rubber floor covering, dome light, bright metal front, rear and side window trim, and 7.35 × 14 BSW tires. Montego adds: Full carpeting, deluxe interior trim, rocker moldings, and 7.75 × 14 BSW tires. Montego MX adds: Cloth and vinyl luxury interior trim (all-vinyl on convertible), deluxe steering wheel, simulated walnut interior trim, power top on convertible, and additional sound deadening materials. Cyclone adds: All vinyl bench seat, power front disc brakes, tinted rear window (fastback), specific Cyclone exterior trim, heavy duty suspension, and engine dress-up kit. Cyclone CJ adds: 428 CID CJ V8, 4-speed manual transmission, competition handling package, and dual exhausts.

## Measurements

|  | Cars | Wagons |
|---|---|---|
| Wheelbase | 116.0" | 113.0" |
| Length | 206.2" | 204.0" |
| Width | 76.0" | 76.0" |
| Height | 55.0" | 56.0" |
| Legroom — front | 42.5" | 42.0" |
| Legroom — rear | 36.0" | 34.5" |
| Headroom — front | 38.5" | 38.5" |
| Headroom — rear | 37.5" | 39.0" |
| Cargo capacity (cu. ft.) | 18.0 | 92.8 |
| Fuel capacity (gals.) | 20.0 | 20.0 |

## Models Available

|  | Style Number | Base MSRP | Change from LY | Shipping Wt. (lbs.) | Production | Change from LY |
|---|---|---|---|---|---|---|
| Comet 2-Door Hardtop | 01 | $2,554 | -1.12% | 3194 | 14,104 | -15.51% |
| Montego 2-Door Hardtop | 07 | $2,627 | -1.17% | 3181 | 17,785 | +18.55% |
| Montego 4-Door Sedan | 06 | $2,578 | -1.19% | 3167 | 21,950 | +18.70% |
| Montego MX 2-Door Hardtop | 11 | $2,758 | -0.83% | 3213 | 22,909 | -11.30% |
| Montego MX 2-Door Convertible | 12 | $3,018 | -0.72% | 3448 | 1,725 | -46.89% |
| Montego MX 4-Door Sedan | 10 | $2,740 | -0.83% | 3201 | 17,738 | +16.21% |
| Montego MX 4-Door Wagon | 08 | $3,001 | +0.67% | 3530 | 10,590 | +13.53% |
| Cyclone 2-Door Hardtop | 15 | $2,771 | +0.11% | 3273 | 5,882 | +329.97% |
| Cyclone CJ 2-Door Hardtop | 16 | $3,224 | NEW | 3634 | 3,261 | NEW |
| TOTALS | | Avg. price $2,808 | +1.30% | Production | 115,944 | +136.6% |

**1969**

# Monterey

*"Luxury within every car buyer's reach."*

**Nameplate year of origin:** 1950 (Coupe designation); 1952 (series).
**Current bodystyle lifespan:** 1969 through 1970.
**Predecessor to this model:** Monterey (1967 to 1968).
**Replacement for this model:** Monterey (1971 to 1974).
**Percentage of division's sales volume:** 15.26%.
**Corporate siblings:** Ford LTD/Galaxie 500 and Mercury Marquis.
**Primary competition:** AMC Ambassador, Buick LeSabre, Dodge Monaco, and Oldsmobile 88.
**Notable changes:** Completely restyled.
**Major standard equipment:** Cloth and vinyl front bench seat, full carpeting,

## Measurements

|  | Cars | Wagons |
|---|---|---|
| Wheelbase | 124.0" | 121.0" |
| Length | 221.8" | 218.0" |
| Width | 79.9" | 79.9" |
| Height | 56.0" | 56.8" |
| Legroom — front | 41.9" | 41.9" |
| Legroom — rear | 37.6" | 36.8" |
| Headroom — front | 38.9" | 39.0" |

wood-grain trim on instrument panel, courtesy light group, rocker panel moldings, bright exterior front and rear window trim and 8.15 × 15 BSW tires. Custom adds: Specific cloth interior trim, and bright moldings.

|  | Cars | Wagons |
|---|---|---|
| Headroom — rear | 37.7" | 40.0" |
| Cargo capacity (cu. ft.) | 20.6 | 105.3 |
| Fuel capacity (gals.) | 24.0 | 24.0 |

## Models Available

| | Style Number | Base MSRP | Change from LY | Shipping Wt. (lbs.) | Production | Change from LY |
|---|---|---|---|---|---|---|
| Monterey 2-Door Hardtop | 46 | $3,237 | +3.32% | 3970 | 9,865 | -34.86% |
| Monterey 2-Door Convertible | 45 | $3,540 | +3.03% | 4093 | 1,297 | -14.39% |
| Monterey 4-Door Sedan | 44 | $3,158 | +3.47% | 3948 | 23,009 | -25.12% |
| Monterey 4-Door Hardtop | 48 | $3,313 | +3.31% | 4008 | 6,066 | -32.05% |
| Monterey 4-Door, 2-Seat Wagon | 72 | $3,536 | +2.76% | 4277 | 2,005 | -42.67% |
| Monterey 4-Door, DFRS* Wagon | 72 | $3,628 | +1.65% | 4334 | 3,839 | -26.05% |
| Monterey Custom 2-Door Hardtop | 56 | $3,459 | +2.13% | 3998 | 2,898 | -17.13% |
| Monterey Custom 4-Door Sedan | 54 | $3,377 | +1.38% | 4013 | 7,103 | -2.10% |
| Monterey Custom 4-Door Hardtop | 58 | $3,533 | +2.14% | 4023 | 2,827 | -29.47% |
| Monterey Custom 4-Dr., 2-S. Wagon | 74 | $3,757 | NEW | 4342 | 953 | NEW |
| Monterey Custom 4-Dr., DFRS* Wgn. | 74 | $3,849 | NEW | 4432 | 967 | NEW |
| TOTALS | Avg. price | $3,490 | +5.57% | | Production 60,829 | -6.42% |

*Dual facing rear seats.

# Marauder

## "Sports car action with a luxury look."

**Nameplate year of origin:** 1963 (as hardtop model designation); 1969 (as series).
**Current bodystyle lifespan:** 1969 through 1970.
**Predecessor to this model:** None.
**Replacement for this model:** None.
**Percentage of division's sales volume:** 3.68%.
**Corporate siblings:** Ford XL.
**Primary competition:** Buick Wildcat and Chrysler 300.
**Notable changes:** All-new model for 1969.
**Major standard equipment:** Cloth and vinyl interior trim, full carpeting, tunneled rear window treatment, bright front and rear window moldings, concealed headlamps, dual pin stripes and 8.25 × 15 BSW tires. X-100 adds: Leather and vinyl front bench seat, luxury steering wheel, sports-tone matte finish on rear tunnel area, rear fender skirts, styled aluminum wheels, 429 CID V8, automatic transmission, and H70 × 15 WSW tires.

## Measurements

| Wheelbase | 121.0" |
|---|---|
| Length | 219.1" |
| Width | 79.9" |
| Height | 54.0" |
| Legroom — front | 41.9" |
| Legroom — rear | 37.6" |
| Headroom — front | 38.9" |
| Headroom — rear | 37.7" |
| Cargo capacity (cu. ft.) | 18.0 |
| Fuel capacity (gals.) | 24.0 |

## Models Available

| | Style Number | Base MSRP | Change from LY | Shipping Wt. (lbs.) | Production | Change from LY |
|---|---|---|---|---|---|---|
| Marauder 2-Door Hardtop | 60 | $3,368 | NEW | 4044 | 9,031 | NEW |
| Marauder X-100 2-Door Hardtop | 61 | $4,091 | NEW | 4191 | 5,635 | NEW |
| TOTALS | Avg. price | $3,730 | NEW | | Production 14,666 | NEW |

# Marquis

*"Never a medium priced car quite so luxurious."*

**Nameplate year of origin:** 1967.
**Current bodystyle lifespan:** 1969 through 1970.
**Predecessor to this model:** Park Lane and Marquis (1967 to 1968)
**Replacement for this model:** Marquis (1971 to 1978).
**Percentage of division's sales volume:** 26.85%.
**Corporate siblings:** Ford LTD/Galaxie 500 and Mercury Monterey.
**Primary competition:** Buick Wildcat, Chrysler Newport, Oldsmobile 88, and Pontiac Bonneville.
**Notable changes:** Completely restyled. Line expanded to replace the Park Lane.
**Major standard equipment:** Cloth and vinyl front bench seat with front seat center arm rest, full carpeting, simulated burled-walnut trim on instrument panel and doors, electric clock, courtesy light group, dual lower body accent stripes, rocker panel molding, concealed headlamps, deluxe wheel covers, and 8.55 × 15 BSW tires. Colony Park wagons adds: exterior wood-grain vinyl trim, and power tailgate window. Brougham adds: Cloth and vinyl Twin-Comfort lounge seats, vinyl roof, fender top chrome trim, and Brougham crests.

## Measurements

|  | Cars | Wagons |
|---|---|---|
| Wheelbase | 124.0" | 121.0" |
| Length | 224.3" | 220.5" |
| Width | 79.9" | 79.9" |
| Height | 56.0" | 56.8" |
| Legroom — front | 41.9" | 41.9" |
| Legroom — rear | 37.6" | 36.8" |
| Headroom — front | 38.9" | 39.0" |
| Headroom — rear | 37.7" | 40.0" |
| Cargo capacity (cu. ft.) | 20.6 | 105.3 |
| Fuel capacity (gals.) | 24.0 | 24.0 |

## Models Available

| | Style Number | Base MSRP | Change from LY | Shipping Wt. (lbs.) | Production | Change from LY |
|---|---|---|---|---|---|---|
| Marquis 2-Door Hardtop | 66 | $3,919 | +9.62% | 4192 | 18,302 | +608.28% |
| Marquis 2-Door Convertible | 65 | $4,124 | +7.90% | 4359 | 2,319 | +108.54% |
| Marquis 4-Door Sedan | 63 | $3,857 | +8.59% | 4226 | 31,388 | +347.89% |
| Marquis 4-Door Hardtop | 68 | $3,990 | +9.40% | 4237 | 29,389 | +182.86% |
| Marquis Brougham 2-Door Hardtop | 66 | $4,191 | NEW | 4215 | * | NEW |
| Marquis Brougham 4-Door Sedan | 63 | $4,129 | NEW | 4195 | * | NEW |
| Marquis Brougham 4-Door Hardtop | 68 | $4,262 | NEW | 4436 | * | NEW |
| Colony Park 4-Door, 2-Seat Wagon | 76 | $3,895 | +3.59% | 4376 | 7,601 | +33.96% |
| Colony Park 4-Door, DFRS** Wagon | 76 | $3,987 | +2.55% | 4455 | 18,003 | +16.11% |
| TOTALS | | Avg. price $3,962 | +7.52% | | Production 107,002 | +131.42% |

*Comparisons made to 1968 Park Lane models.     **Dual facing rear seats.*

# OLDSMOBILE

*"Escape from the ordinary."*

The "Youngmobile" division, as Oldsmobile called itself these days, was finding great success in catering to a younger generation of buyers. The Cutlass and F-85 models continued to find an increasing following of owners.

The traditional 88 and Ninety-Eight models, while following ever closer in Buick's footsteps, were at least styled to look sportier and more youthful. Of course, the top line Toronado also had its loyal following by now. The mid-size

**1969**

Cutlass/F-85 line was given a minor facelift for 1969. Changes to the model line were minimal, consisting of the deletion of the F-85 4-Door Town Sedan and the merging of the Cutlass and Cutlass S series into one Cutlass line. In the 88 line, the Delmont was replaced by the successful Delta nameplate, the base Delta became the Custom, and the former Custom was reduced to a single 2-Door Hardtop model christened the Royale. A new Luxury Sedan 4-Door Hardtop model was added to the Ninety-Eight line, and the Toronado continued as a one-model line.

As for styling changes, the previously mentioned facelift of the Cutlass line consisted of a new grille and revised taillight/bumper combination. Vista-Cruiser changes closely followed those of the Cutlass. Full-size models were completely restyled, yet retained the familiar Oldsmobile look — large, twin grilles divided by a hood section from the top, and a bumper section from the bottom. Changes for the unique Toronado were minimal.

4-4-2 2-Door Hardtop

Ninety-Eight 4-Door Town Sedan

Cutlass 4-Door Hardtop Holiday Sedan

Delta 88 Custom 2-Door Hardtop

Toronado 2-Door Hardtop

Vista-Cruiser 4-Door, 3-Seat Wagon

**Model year production:** 654,979, up 16.45% over 1968.
**Domestic market share:** 7.36% (6th place).
**Base price range:** $2,561 to $4,836.
**Industry average base price:** $3,386.
**Oldsmobile average base price:** $3,514.
**Introduction date:** September 1968.
**Assembly plants:** Atlanta, GA (G); Fremont, CA (Z); Lansing, MI (M); Arlington, TX (R); Fairfax, KS (X); and Linden, NJ (F).

**Data plate identification:** Thirteen digit code read as follows: 1st digit 3 = Oldsmobile; 2nd through 5th digits identify series/body style number; 9 = 1969; 7th digit is assembly plant code; 100001 and up for serial number (except Toronado is 600001). *Example:* 354399X100001 is a 1969 Oldsmobile Delta 88 4-Door Hardtop, serial number 100001, built in Fairfax, KS.

## Powertrains

| Engine | Gross HP | Transmission Availability | Cutlass/ 4-4-2 | Cut. Sup. & Vista-Cruiser | Delta 88 | 98 | Toronado |
|---|---|---|---|---|---|---|---|
| 250 CID Action-Line, 1-bbl., 6-cyl. | 155 | 3-speed manual | S* | - | - | - | - |
|  |  | Jetaway Automatic | $174* | - | - | - |  |
| 350 CID Rocket, 2-bbl., V8 | 250 | 3-speed manual | $111* | S (V.Cr.) | S (base) | - | - |
|  |  | 4-speed manual | $296* | $185 (V.Cr.) | - | - | - |
|  |  | Jetaway Automatic | $296* | - | - |  |  |
|  |  | Turbo Hydra-matic 350 | - | $227 (V.Cr.) | $227 (base) |  |  |
| 350 CID Rocket, | 310 | 3-speed manual | $158* | S (Supr.)/ |  |  |  |

| Engine | Gross HP | Transmission Availability | Cutlass/ 4-4-2 | Cut. Sup. & Vista-Cruiser | Delta 88 | 98 | Toronado |
|---|---|---|---|---|---|---|---|
| 4-bbl., V8 | | | | $47 (V.Cr.) | - | - | - |
| | | 4-speed manual* | $344* | $185 (Supr.)/ $232 (V.Cr.) | - | - | - |
| | | Jetaway Automatic | $344* | - | - | - | - |
| | | Turbo Hydra-matic 350 | $365* | $206 (Supr.)/ $274 (V.Cr.) | - | - | - |
| 400 CID Rocket, 4-bbl., V8 W31 | 350 325 w/Auto. | 3-speed manual 4-speed manual Turbo Hydra-matic 400 | S** $185** $227** | - - $348 — V.Cr. | - - - | - - - | - - - |
| 400 CID Rocket, 4-bbl., V8 W30 | 360 | 3-speed manual 4-speed manual Turbo Hydra-matic 400 | $310*/$264** $495*/$449** $537*/$491** | - - - | - - - | - - - | - - - |
| 455 CID Rocket, 2-bbl., V8 | 310 | 3-speed manual Turbo Hydra-matic 400 | - - | - - | S (ex. base)/ $63 (base) $227 (ex. base)/ $290 (base) | - - | - - |
| 455 CID Rocket, 4-bbl., V8 | 365/375 | 3-speed manual Turbo Hydra-matic 400 | - - | - - | $47 (ex. base)/ $111 (base) $274 (ex. base)/ $338 (base) | - - S | - - S |
| 455 CID Hi-Po Rocket, 4-bbl., V8 | 390; Toro. 400 | 3-speed manual Turbo Hydra-matic 400 | - - | - - | $78 (ex. base)/ $141 (base) $305 (ex. base)/ $368 (base) | - - | - $47 |

*F-85 and Cutlass only.    **4-4-2 only.

## Major Options

| | Cutlass | Vista-Cruiser | Delta 88 | Ninety-Eight | Toronado |
|---|---|---|---|---|---|
| Air conditioning | $376 | $376 | $422 | $422 | $422 |
| Electronic cruise control (V8 only) | $58 | $58 | $63 | $63 | $63 |
| Soft Ray tinted glass | $39 | $39 | $44 | $44 | $47 |
| Deck lid remote release | $14 | - | $14 | $14 | $14 |
| Tilt-Away steering wheel | $45 | $45 | $45 | $45 | $45 |
| Power steering — variable-ratio | $105 | $105 | $116 | S | S |
| Power brakes | $42 | $42 | $42 | S | S |
| Power driver's seat/Bench seat | $74 | $74 | $100 | $74–$100* | $74 |
| Power windows | $105 | $105 | $111 | S/$111* | $111 |
| AM radio | $70 | $70 | $87 | $87 | $87 |
| AM/FM stereo | $238 | $238 | $238 | $238 | $238 |
| Front seat console | $61 | - | $62 | - | $62 |
| Front bucket seats | $ | - | $ | - | $ |
| Vinyl roof | $100 | - | $121** | $137 | $126 |
| White sidewall tires (base size) | $32–$40 | $44 | $44 | $49 | $49 |
| Wheel trim covers | $21 | $21 | S | S | S |

Options common to most models. (- = Not Available; S = Standard equipment.) Items may be standard equipment, optional at different pricing, or unavailable on certain models. This chart is only a guide.

*4-Door Town Sedan only.    **Standard on Royale.

1969

## Paint Colors

| | Code | | Code |
|---|---|---|---|
| Ebony Black | 10 | Palomino Gold Metallic | 63 |
| Saffron | 40 | Topaz Metallic | 65 |
| Toronado Jade Metallic* | 46-0 | Burgundy Mist Metallic | 67 |
| Cameo White | 50 | Platinum Metallic | 69 |
| Trophy Blue Metallic | 51 | Aztec Gold Metallic | 75 |
| Crimson | 52 | Autumn Gold Metallic* | 77 |
| Nassau Blue Metallic | 53 | Powder Blue* | 80 |
| Tahitian Turquoise Met. | 55 | Flamingo Silver Metallic* | 81 |
| Glade Green Metallic | 57 | Covert Beige* | 82 |
| Meadow Green Metallic | 59 | Deauville Gray Metallic* | 83 |
| Sable Metallic | 61 | Chestnut Bronze Metallic* | 85 |

*Available only on Toronado.*

# Cutlass

*"For action! Adventure! Excitement! Join now!"*

**Nameplate year of origin:** 1962 (as F-85 model designation); 1955 (show car).

**Current bodystyle lifespan:** 1968 through 1972.

**Predecessor to this model:** F-85/Cutlass (1966 to 1967).

**Replacement for this model:** Cutlass (1973 to 1977).

**Percentage of division's sales volume:** 33.53%.

**Corporate siblings:** Buick Special/Skylark, Chevrolet Chevelle, Pontiac Tempest/LeMans.

**Primary competition:** AMC Rebel, Dodge Coronet, Ford Fairlane/Torino, Mercury Comet/Montego, Plymouth Satellite.

**Notable changes:** New grille, revised rear styling and trim and detail changes.

**Major standard equipment:** Cloth and vinyl front bench seat, aluminized exhaust system, and 7.75 × 14 BSW tires. Cutlass adds: Front and rear armrests, full carpeting, deluxe steering wheel, and exterior chrome trim moldings. Cutlass S adds: Deluxe bench seat (bucket seats on convertible) and simulated chrome hood louvers. Cutlass Supreme adds: Woodgrain interior trim, all-vinyl bench seats, and unique grille. 4-4-2 adds: All-vinyl bucket seats, floor shifter, 400 CID V8 engine, dual exhausts, heavy duty suspension, and F70 × 14 Wide-Oval Redline tires.

## Measurements

| | 2-Doors | 4-Doors | Wagon |
|---|---|---|---|
| Wheelbase | 112.0" | 116.0" | 116.0" |
| Length | 201.9" | 205.9" | 211.9" |
| Width | 76.2" | 76.8" | 76.8" |
| Height | 52.8" | 53.5" | 54.8" |
| Legroom — front | 42.8" | 42.8" | 42.8" |
| Legroom — rear | 32.5" | 35.0" | 34.6" |
| Headroom — front | 38.2" | 38.8" | 38.6" |
| Headroom — rear | 36.3" | 37.4" | 38.3" |
| Luggage capacity (cu. ft.) | 17.0 | 17.0 | 93.6 |
| Fuel capacity (gals.) | 20.0 | 20.0 | 20.0 |

## Models Available

| | Style Number | Base MSRP | Change from LY | Shipping Wt. (lbs.) | Production | Change from LY |
|---|---|---|---|---|---|---|
| F-85 2-Door Sport Coupe | 3177 | $2,561 | +1.95% | 3082 | 8,440 | -10.95% |
| Cutlass 4-Door Town Sedan | 3569 | $2,722 | +1.80% | 3155 | 34,430 | +26.12% |
| Cutlass 4-Door Hardtop | 3539 | $2,853 | +1.75% | 3212 | 7,279 | -10.18% |
| Cutlass 4-Door, 2-Seat Wagon | 3535 | $3,055 | +2.90% | 3537 | 8,739 | -9.39% |
| Cutlass S 2-Door Sports Coupe | 3577 | $2,681 | +1.86% | 3093 | 11,165 | -29.19% |
| Cutlass S 2-Door Hardtop | 3587 | $2,745 | +1.82% | 3118 | 67,061 | +9.81% |
| Cutlass S 2-Door Convertible | 3567 | $2,998 | +1.66% | 3188 | 13,732 | -2.52% |
| Cutlass Supreme 2-Door Hardtop | 4287 | $3,036 | +1.81% | 3331 | 29,163 | -12.99% |
| Cutlass Supreme 4-Dr. Town Sdn. | 4269 | $2,938 | +1.87% | 3361 | 4,522 | -18.14% |
| Cutlass Supreme 4-Door Hardtop | 4239 | $3,111 | +1.77% | 3421 | 8,714 | -42.16% |

|  | Style Number | Base MSRP | Change from LY | Shipping Wt. (lbs.) | Production | Change from LY |
|---|---|---|---|---|---|---|
| 4-4-2 2-Door Sport Coupe | 4477 | $3,141 | +1.75% | 3502 | 2,475 | -42.20% |
| 4-4-2 2-Door Hardtop | 4487 | $3,204 | +1.71% | 3512 | 19,587 | -19.01% |
| 4-4-2 2-Door Convertible | 4467 | $3,395 | +1.62% | 3580 | 4,295 | -16.47% |
| TOTALS | | Avg. price $2,957 | +2.75% | | Production 219,602 | -8.11% |

# Vista-Cruiser

*"Takes you away from it all without leaving anything behind."*

**Nameplate year of origin:** 1964.
**Current bodystyle lifespan:** 1968 through 1972.
**Predecessor to this model:** None.
**Replacement for this model:** Vista-Cruiser (1973 to 1977).
**Percentage of division's sales volume:** 5.10%.
**Corporate siblings:** Buick Sportwagon.
**Primary competition:** AMC Rebel/Ambassador, Dodge Coronet, Ford Torino, Mercury Montego, and Plymouth Satellite.
**Notable changes:** New grille and minor trim and detail changes.
**Major standard equipment:** All-vinyl front bench seats, full carpeting, Deluxe steering wheel, wood-grain exterior trim, Vista-roof windows, and 8.25 × 14 BSW tires.

## Measurements

| | |
|---|---|
| Wheelbase | 121.0" |
| Length | 217.6" |
| Width | 77.2" |
| Height | 58.6" |
| Legroom — front | 42.8" |
| Legroom — rear | 38.0" |
| Headroom — front | 38.4" |
| Headroom — rear | 40.3" |
| Luggage capacity (cu. ft.) | 108.5 |
| Fuel capacity (gals.) | 20.0 |

## Models Available

|  | Style Number | Base MSRP | Change from LY | Shipping Wt. (lbs.) | Production | Change from LY |
|---|---|---|---|---|---|---|
| Vista-Cruiser 4-Dr., 2-S. Wagon | 4855 | $3,457 | +2.67% | 3952 | 11,879 | -11.19% |
| Vista-Cruiser 4-Dr., 3-S. Wagon | 4865 | $3,600 | +2.62% | 4052 | 21,508 | -5.53% |
| TOTALS | | Avg. price $3,529 | +2.65% | | Production 33,387 | -7.63% |

# Delta 88

*"The cars with the come-closer look."*

**Nameplate year of origin:** 1965 (88 series started 1949).
**Current bodystyle lifespan:** 1969 through 1970.
**Predecessor to this model:** Delmont/Delta 88 (1967 to 1968).
**Replacement for this model:** Delta 88 (1971 to 1976).
**Percentage of division's sales volume:** 39.25%.
**Corporate siblings:** Buick LeSabre/Wildcat, Chevrolet Impala/Caprice, Pontiac Catalina/Bonneville.
**Primary competition:** Dodge Polara, Ford LTD, and Mercury Monterey.
**Notable changes:** Completely restyled.
**Major standard equipment:** Cloth and vinyl or all-vinyl bench seat, full carpeting, vinyl bodyside molding, and 8.55 × 15 BSW tires. Custom adds: Custom interior trim. Royale adds: Coarse-woven cloth upholstery, privacy rear window, chrome front fender louvers and pinstriping.

## Measurements

| | |
|---|---|
| Wheelbase | 124.0" |
| Length | 218.6" |
| Width | 80.0" |
| Height | 54.7" |
| Legroom — front | 42.5" |
| Legroom — rear | 38.5" |
| Headroom — front | 38.5" |
| Headroom — rear | 37.8" |
| Luggage capacity (cu. ft.) | 19.5 |
| Fuel capacity (gals.) | 25 |

1969

## Models Available

| | Style Number | Base MSRP | Change from LY | Shipping Wt. (lbs.) | Production | Change from LY |
|---|---|---|---|---|---|---|
| Delta 88 2-Door Hardtop | 5437 | $3,277 | +2.34% | 3812 | 46,947 | +155.27% |
| Delta 88 2-Door Convertible | 5467 | $3,590 | +2.13% | 3892 | 5,294 | +88.26% |
| Delta 88 4-Door Town Sedan | 5469 | $3,222 | +2.42% | 3859 | 49,995 | +105.19% |
| Delta 88 4-Door Hardtop | 5439 | $3,353 | +2.29% | 3901 | 42,690 | +102.75% |
| Delta 88 Custom 2-Door Hardtop | 6437 | $3,525 | +2.20% | 3927 | 22,083 | +19.36% |
| Delta 88 Custom 4-Door Town Sdn. | 6469 | $3,432 | +2.23% | 3962 | 31,013 | -7.94% |
| Delta 88 Custom 4-Door Hardtop | 6439 | $3,600 | +2.13% | 4009 | 36,502 | +21.48% |
| Delta 88 Royale 2-Door Hardtop | 6647 | $3,836 | +4.78% | 3935 | 22,564 | +136.52% |
| TOTALS | | Avg. price $3,479 | -1.81% | | Production 257,088 | +150.81% |

*Comparisons made to 1968 Delmont 88 and Delta 88 lines.*

# Ninety-Eight

*"Strong, silent, and in the classic tradition."*

**Nameplate year of origin:** 1941.
**Current bodystyle lifespan:** 1969 through 1970.
**Predecessor to this model:** Ninety-Eight (1967 to 1968).
**Replacement for this model:** Ninety-Eight (1971 to 1976).
**Percentage of division's sales volume:** 17.78%.
**Corporate siblings:** Buick Electra and Cadillac Calais/de Ville.
**Primary competition:** Chrysler New Yorker and Mercury Marquis.
**Notable changes:** Completely restyled.
**Major standard equipment:** Cloth and vinyl custom seat, fold-down front center armrest, electric clock, deluxe steering wheel, two-way power seat (except Town Sedan), power windows (except Town sedan), variable-ratio power steering, power front disc brakes, full wheel discs, and 8.85 × 15 BSW tires. LS adds: exclusive interior trim, and rear fold-down center armrest.

## Measurements

| | |
|---|---|
| Wheelbase | 127.0" |
| Length | 224.4" |
| Width | 80.0" |
| Height | 54.8" |
| Legroom — front | 41.7" |
| Legroom — rear | 37.1" |
| Headroom — front | 38.6" |
| Headroom — rear | 37.8" |
| Luggage capacity (cu. ft.) | 20.5 |
| Fuel capacity (gals.) | 25 |

## Models Available

| | Style Number | Base MSRP | Change from LY | Shipping Wt. (lbs.) | Production | Change from LY |
|---|---|---|---|---|---|---|
| Ninety-Eight 2-Door Hardtop | 8457 | $4,462 | +2.34% | 4150 | 27,041 | +76.52% |
| Ninety-Eight 2-Door Convertible | 8467 | $4,720 | +2.21% | 4223 | 4,288 | +8.78% |
| Ninety-Eight 4-Door Town Sedan | 8469 | $4,256 | +2.43% | 4150 | 11,169 | +5.53% |
| Ninety-Eight 4-Door Hardtop | 8439 | $4,524 | +2.31% | 4260 | 17,294 | -18.22% |
| Ninety-Eight Luxury 4-Door Sedan | 8669 | $4,599 | NEW | 4245 | 25,973 | NEW |
| Ninety-Eight Luxury 4-Door Hardtop | 8639 | $4,693 | +4.36% | 4288 | 30,643 | -24.81% |
| TOTALS | | Avg. price $4,542 | +2.99% | | Production 116,408 | +26.88% |

# Toronado

*"For great car lovers."*

**Nameplate year of origin:** 1966.
**Current bodystyle lifespan:** 1966 through 1970.
**Predecessor to this model:** None.

## Measurements

| | |
|---|---|
| Wheelbase | 119.0" |
| Length | 214.8" |

**Replacement for this model:** Toronado (1971 to 1978).
**Percentage of division's sales volume:** 4.35%.
**Corporate siblings:** Buick Riviera and Cadillac Eldorado.
**Primary competition:** Imperial LeBaron Coupe, Ford Thunderbird, and Lincoln Continental Mark III.
**Notable changes:** Minor trim and detail changes.
**Major standard equipment:** Cloth and vinyl Strato-Bench seat, fold-down front center armrest, electric clock, deluxe steering wheel, front wheel drive, variable-ratio power steering, power front disc brakes, and 8.85 × 15 BSW tires.

## Measurements (cont.)

| | |
|---|---|
| Width | 78.8" |
| Height | 52.8" |
| Legroom — front | 41.3" |
| Legroom — rear | 35.3" |
| Headroom — front | 37.7" |
| Headroom — rear | 36.9" |
| Luggage capacity (cu. ft.) | 14.6 |
| Fuel capacity (gals.) | 24 |

## Models Available

| | Style Number | Base MSRP | Change from LY | Shipping Wt. (lbs.) | Production | Change from LY |
|---|---|---|---|---|---|---|
| Toronado 2-Door Hardtop | 9487 | $4,836 | +1.81% | 4316 | 28,494 | +7.71% |
| TOTALS | | *Avg. price* $4,836 | +1.81% | *Production* | 28,494 | +7.71% |

# PLYMOUTH

*"Look what Plymouth's up to now."*

Nineteen sixty-nine marked a year of revitalization for Plymouth. Throughout the sixties, Pontiac had dominated the highly sought after third place in market share. Prior to 1962, Plymouth had come close several times, even reaching that position on occasion. But after a fantastic 1968 season Plymouth would attempt to attain that goal again in 1969. Unfortunately for Plymouth, Oldsmobile would have the upper hand through the seventies, and this would be the last opportunity for Plymouth as a major player in the market. In fact, this would be the last year for Plymouth to have a model (the Barracuda) that it did not share with any other Chrysler division, until the Prowler was released in 1997. Beginning in 1970, the Barracuda would share components with the new Dodge Challenger. For 1969, however, the Barracuda retained its own identity and received a light makeover, with a new grille revised interior trim, and a new optional 'Cuda 340 package. This package offered the 340 CID V8, 4-speed manual transmission, hood scoop, blacked-out grille, dual exhaust, heavy-duty brakes and suspension, and E70 × 14 Red stripe tires. The entry-level Valiant returned for 1969 with new grille and taillight treatments.

Mid-size Belvedere and Satellite models returned with similar changes. A new Road Runner Convertible and Sport Satellite 4-Door Sedan were added to the roster. The Road Runner had become successful enough to garner the attention of car magazines and enthusiasts everywhere. To honor this success, *Motor Trend* magazine picked the Road Runner as the 1969 Car of the Year.

Of course, the big news for this year would be the totally redesigned Fury line. As with all other full-size Chrysler models, the "fuselage" styling was the hot topic, and Plymouth models looked especially nice in the new sheetmetal. Like Dodge, the Plymouth had a separate front bumper and grille design for 1969, but would gain the "loop-style" bumper with inset grille for 1970. On Plymouths, the body sides wore little dress-up trim, which contributed to a cleaner look. Fender skirts continued to be offered by Chrysler on most full-size models, and on the Plymouth they made the car look exceptionally long and low. Powertrain choices remained similar to the 1968 line. The only change to the model line was the addition of a VIP 2-Door Formal Hardtop. Last year's regular 2-Door Hardtop line was now called the Formal Hardtop, while the previous Fast Top (semi-fastback) was now known as a regular 2-Door Hardtop.

**1969**

Barracuda 2-Door Convertible

Barracuda 2-Door Fastback with Cuda 340 package

Belvedere 4-Door Sedan

Fury III 2-Door Convertible and
Fury III 4-Door Sedan

Fury III 4-Door Hardtop

GTX 2-Door Hardtop

Road Runner 2-Door Convertible and
2-Door Coupe "Motor Trend" Car of the Year

Sport Suburban 4-Door Wagon

Valiant 100 2-Door Sedan

**Model year production:** 747,024, down 1.35% from 1968.
**Domestic market share:** 8.39% (4th place).
**Base price range:** $2,094 to $3,718.
**Industry average base price:** $3,386.
**Plymouth average base price:** $3,015.
**Introduction date:** September 19, 1968.
**Assembly plants:** Lynch Road, MI (A): Hamtramck, MI (B); Belvidere, IL (D); Los Angeles, CA (E); Newark DE (F); St. Louis, MO (G); and Windsor, Ontario, Canada (R).

**Data plate identification:** Thirteen digit code read as follows: four digit style number code in which first letter is series, second letter is trim level, third and fourth digits are body style; fifth digit is engine code (see chart); sixth digit 9 for 1969; seventh digit is assembly plant code; 100001 and up for serial number. *Example:* PM23C9B100001 is a 1969 Plymouth Fury III 2-Door Hardtop, with a 225 CID 6-cyl., built at Hamtramck, MI, serial number 100001.

## Powertrains

| Engine | Gross HP | Engine Code | Transmission Availability | Valiant | Barracuda | Belv./ Sat. | Sp. Sat./ R.R./GTX | Fury |
|---|---|---|---|---|---|---|---|---|
| 170 CID, 1-bbl., 6-cyl. | 125 | A | 3-speed manual | S | – | – | – | – |
| | | | Torqueflite automatic | $180 | – | – | – | – |
| 225 CID, 1-bbl., 6-cyl. | 145 | B | 3-speed manual | $49 | S | S | – | S[1] |
| | | | Torqueflite automatic | $229 | $199 | $199 | – | $199[1] |
| 273 CID, 2-bbl., V8 | 190 | D | 3-speed manual | $111 | – | – | – | – |
| | | | 4-speed manual | $299 | – | – | – | – |
| | | | Torqueflite automatic | $301 | – | – | – | – |
| 318 CID, | 230 | F | 3-speed manual | $143 | $106 | $90 | S* | S[2]/ $105[1] |

| Engine | Gross HP | Engine Code | Transmission Availability | Valiant | Barracuda | Belv./ Sat. | Sp. Sat./ R.R./GTX | Fury |
|--------|----------|-------------|---------------------------|---------|-----------|-------------|--------------------|------|
| 2-bbl., V8 | | | 4-speed manual | $331 | $294 | - | - | - |
| | | | Torqueflite automatic | $337 | $318 | $317 | $227* | $227²/$332¹ |
| 340 CID Commando, 4-bbl., V8 | 275 | P | 3-speed manual | - | $212 | - | - | - |
| | | | 4-speed manual | - | $400 | - | - | - |
| | | | Torqueflite automatic | - | $439 | - | - | - |
| 383 CID Commando, 2-bbl., V8 | 290 | G | 3-speed manual | - | - | $195 | $73* | $73²/$178¹ |
| | | | 4-speed manual | - | - | $393 | $271* | $271²/$376¹ |
| | | | Torqueflite automatic | - | - | $425 | $300* | $297²/$402¹ |
| 383 CID Super Commando, 4-bbl., V8 | 330, 335 (R.R.), 300 (Barracuda) | H | 3-speed manual | - | $334 | $266 | $144* | $144²/ $249¹ |
| | | | 4-speed manual | | $506 | $464 | S (R.R.)/ $342* | $342²/$447¹ |
| | | | Torqueflite automatic | | $545 | $493 | $39 (R.R.)/ $371* | $371²/$476¹ |
| 426 CID Street-Hemi, 4-bbl., V8 | 425 | J | 4-speed manual | - | - | - | $813 (R.R.)/ $701 (GTX) | - |
| 440 CID, 4-bbl., V8 | 350 | K | Torqueflite automatic | - | - | - | No cost (GTX) | $472 (Wgn) |
| 440 CID Super Commando, 4-bbl., V8 | 375 | L | 4-speed manual | - | - | - | No cost (GTX) | - |
| | | | Torqueflite automatic | - | - | - | S (GTX) | $508² |

*Except Road Runner and GTX.   ¹Fury I, II (ex. Custom Suburban), and III (2-Dr. HT and 4-Dr. Sedan) only. 4-speed N/A on Wagons.   ²All but Fury I, II, and III (2-Dr. HT and 4-Dr. Sedan), but including Fury II Custom Suburban.

## Major Options

| | Valiant | Barracuda | Belvedere/Satellite | Fury |
|--------|---------|-----------|---------------------|------|
| Air conditioning | $361 | $361 | $358 | $365 |
| Automatic speed control (V8s) | - | - | $58 | $61 |
| Tilt steering wheel | - | - | - | $47 |
| Tinted glass | $33 | $33 | $41 | $42 |
| Power steering | $85 | $85 | $100 | $100 |
| Power brakes | $43 | $43 | $43 | $43 |
| Front disc brakes | $49 | $49 | $49 | $49 |
| AM radio | $62 | $62 | $62 | $62 |
| AM/FM Solid-State radio | - | $140 | $140 | $140 |
| Electric clock | $16 | $16 | $16 | S/$16 (Fury I) |
| Bucket seats — vinyl (leather opt.) | - | S | S (GTX/Conv)/$100 | $102 |
| Center console | - | $53 | $54 | $54 |
| Vinyl roof | $84 | - | $96 | $106 |
| Chrome Road Wheels | - | $ | $100 | $ |

Options common to most models. (- = Not Available; S = Standard equipment.) Items may be standard equipment, optional at different pricing, or unavailable on certain models. This chart is only a guide.

1969

## Paint Colors

| | Code | | Code |
|---|---|---|---|
| Silver Metallic | A-4 | Honey Bronze Metallic | T-3 |
| Ice Blue Metallic | B-3 | Bronze Fire Metallic | T-5 |
| Blue Fire Metallic | B-5 | Saddle Bronze Metallic | T-7 |
| Jamaica Blue Metallic | B-7 | Alpine White | W-1 |
| Frost Green Metallic | F-3 | Black Velvet | X-9 |
| Limelight Metallic | F-5 | Sunfire Yellow | Y-2 |
| Ivy Green Metallic | F-8 | Yellow Gold | Y-3 |
| Vitamin "C" Orange | K-2 | Spanish Gold Metallic | Y-4 |
| Sandpebble Beige | L-1 | Citron Gold Metallic | Y-6 |
| Seafoam Turquoise Met. | Q-5 | Orange | 999 |
| Barracuda Orange | R-4 | Rallye Green | 999 |
| Scorch Red | R-6 | Bahama Yellow | 999 |

# Valiant

*"Because a compact car still makes a lot of sense to a lot of people."*

**Nameplate year of origin:** 1960.
**Current bodystyle lifespan:** 1967 through 1976.
**Predecessor to this model:** Valiant (1963 to 1966).
**Replacement for this model:** Volare (1976 to 1980).
**Percentage of division's sales volume:** 14.35%.
**Corporate siblings:** Dodge Dart.
**Primary competition:** AMC Rambler, Chevrolet Nova, and Ford Falcon.
**Notable changes:** Minor trim and detail changes.
**Major standard equipment:** Cloth and vinyl bench seat, rubber floor mat, 2-speed windshield wipers with washers, full length body side molding, and 6.50 × 13 BSW tires. Signet adds: All-vinyl bench seat, color-keyed carpeting, fender-top mounted turn signals, and interior courtesy lighting.

### Measurements

| | |
|---|---|
| Wheelbase | 108.0" |
| Length | 188.4" |
| Width | 69.6" |
| Height | 53.7" |
| Legroom — front | 41.7" |
| Legroom — rear | 34.5" |
| Headroom — front | 38.4" |
| Headroom — rear | 37.3" |
| Cargo capacity (cu. ft.) | 14.5 |
| Fuel capacity (gals.) | 18.0 |

## Models Available

| | Style Number | Base MSRP | Change from LY | Shipping Wt. (lbs.) | Production | Change from LY |
|---|---|---|---|---|---|---|
| Valiant 100 2-Door Sedan | VL21 | $2,094 | -7.10% | 2656 | 29,672 | -4.83% |
| Valiant 100 4-Door Sedan | VL41 | $2,154 | -6.39% | 2676 | 49,409 | -0.07% |
| Valiant Signet 2-Door Sedan | VH21 | $2,253 | -6.13% | 2656 | 6,645 | +6.07% |
| Valiant Signet 4-Door Sedan | VH41 | $2,313 | -5.48% | 2676 | 21,492 | -10.10% |
| TOTALS | | Avg. price $2,204 | -6.26% | Production | 107,218 | -3.23% |

# Barracuda

*"Have it your way."*

**Nameplate year of origin:** 1964.
**Current bodystyle lifespan:** 1967 through 1969.
**Predecessor to this model:** Barracuda (1964 to 1966).
**Replacement for this model:** Barracuda (1970 to 1974).
**Percentage of division's sales volume:** 4.28%.

### Measurements

| | |
|---|---|
| Wheelbase | 108.0" |
| Length | 192.8" |
| Width | 69.6" |
| Height | 52.6" |

**Corporate siblings:** None.
**Primary competition:** AMC Javelin, Chevrolet Camaro, Ford Mustang, and Pontiac Firebird.
**Notable changes:** Minor trim and detail changes.
**Major standard equipment:** All-vinyl bench seat with center arm rest (bucket seats on convertible), full carpeting, fold-down rear seat (Fastback), power top (convertible), rallye lights, full instrumentation, trip odometer and 6.95 × 14 BSW tires.

## Measurements (cont.)

| | |
|---|---|
| Legroom — front | 41.7" |
| Legroom — rear | 31.1" |
| Headroom — front | 37.2" |
| Headroom — rear | 36.5" |
| Cargo capacity (cu. ft.) | NA |
| Fuel capacity (gals.) | 18.0 |

## Models Available

| | Style Number | Base MSRP | Change from LY | Shipping Wt. (lbs.) | Production | Change from LY |
|---|---|---|---|---|---|---|
| Barracuda 2-Door Hardtop | BH23 | $2,674 | +2.65% | 2731 | 12,757 | -36.21% |
| Barracuda 2-Door Fastback HT | BH29 | $2,707 | -1.99% | 2816 | 17,788 | -21.20% |
| Barracuda 2-Door Convertible | BH27 | $2,976 | +2.37% | 2846 | 1,442 | -49.23% |
| TOTALS | *Avg. price* $2,786 | | +1.02% | *Production* 31,987 | | -29.57% |

# Belvedere/Satellite/ GTX/Road Runner

*"The name of the game this year is 'sport'."*

**Nameplate year of origin:** Belvedere: 1951 (HT model); 1954 (series). Satellite: 1965 (as a Belvedere trim level.); GTX: 1967. Road Runner: 1968.
**Current bodystyle lifespan:** 1968 through 1970.
**Predecessor to this model:** Belvedere (1966 to 1967).
**Replacement for this model:** Satellite (1971 to 1974).
**Percentage of division's sales volume:** 32.29%.
**Corporate siblings:** Dodge Coronet.
**Primary competition:** AMC Rebel, Chevrolet Chevelle, Ford Fairlane/Torino, and Pontiac Tempest/LeMans.
**Notable changes:** Revised front end, and minor trim and detail changes.
**Major standard equipment:** Cloth and vinyl front bench seat, rubber floor mats, front and rear armrests, 2-speed electric windshield wipers with washers, exterior bright trim around windows and rocker molding, hubcaps, and 7.35 × 14 BSW tires (8.25 × 14 BSW tires on wagons). Satellite adds: Full carpeting, and additional interior and exterior trim. Sport Satellite adds: All vinyl bucket seats, fender mounted turn signals, deluxe wheel covers, and additional interior lighting. Road Runner adds to Belvedere: 383 CID V8, Road Runner horn and logos, and F70 × 14 Wide-Oval tires. GTX adds to Sport Satellite: Dual hood scoops, dual exhausts, 440 CID V8, and automatic transmission.

## Measurements

| | Cars | Wagons |
|---|---|---|
| Wheelbase | 116.0" | 117.0" |
| Length | 202.7" | 207.6" |
| Width | 76.4" | 76.4" |
| Height | 54.7" | 55.4" |
| Legroom — front | 41.9" | 41.9" |
| Legroom — rear | 36.3" | 36.7" |
| Headroom — front | 38.6" | 38.7" |
| Headroom — rear | 37.4" | 38.1" |
| Cargo capacity (cu. ft.) | NA | 88.0 |
| Fuel capacity (gals.) | 19.5 | 21.0 |

**1969**

## Models Available

| | Style Number | Base MSRP | Change from LY | Shipping Wt. (lbs.) | Production | Change from LY |
|---|---|---|---|---|---|---|
| Belvedere 2-Door Coupe | RL21 | $2,509 | +2.66% | 2978 | 7,063 | -55.02% |
| Belvedere 4-Door Sedan | RL41 | $2,548 | +2.62% | 3008 | 12,914 | -24.98% |
| Belvedere 4-Door, 2-Seat Wagon | RL45 | $2,879 | +3.82% | 3488 | 7,038 | -21.64% |
| Road Runner 2-Door Coupe | RM21 | $2,945 | +1.69% | 3435 | 33,743 | +15.40% |
| Road Runner 2-Door Hardtop | RM23 | $3,083 | +1.62% | 3450 | 48,549 | +216.09% |

| | Style Number | Base MSRP | Change from LY | Shipping Wt. (lbs.) | Production | Change from LY |
|---|---|---|---|---|---|---|
| Road Runner 2-Door Convertible | RM27 | $3,313 | NEW | 3790 | 2,128 | NEW |
| Satellite 2-Door Hardtop | RH23 | $2,659 | +2.51% | 3008 | 38,323 | -17.65% |
| Satellite 2-Door Convertible | RH27 | $2,878 | +1.91% | 3123 | 1,137 | -35.80% |
| Satellite 4-Door Sedan | RH41 | $2,635 | +2.45% | 3013 | 35,296 | -16.58% |
| Satellite 4-Dr., 2-Seat Wagon | RH45 | $2,997 | +3.67% | 3493 | 5,837 | -51.75% |
| Satellite 4-Dr., 3-Seat Wagon | RH46 | $3,106 | +3.60% | 3568 | 4,730 | -56.54% |
| Sport Satellite 2-Door Hardtop | RP23 | $2,883 | +2.16% | 3156 | 15,807 | -49.03% |
| Sport Satellite 2-Door Convertible | RP27 | $3,081 | +1.48% | 3276 | 818 | -46.29% |
| Sport Satellite 4-Door Sedan | RP41 | $2,911 | NEW | 3196 | 5,836 | NEW |
| Sport Satellite 4-Dr., 2-S. Wagon | RP45 | $3,241 | +3.51% | 3596 | 3,221 | * |
| Sport Satellite 4-Dr., 3-S. Wagon | RP46 | $3,350 | +3.43% | 3666 | 3,152 | * |
| GTX 2-Door Hardtop | RS23 | $3,416 | +1.82% | 3465 | 14,902 | -16.81% |
| GTX 2-Door Convertible | RS27 | $3,635 | +1.25% | 3590 | 700 | -31.77% |
| TOTALS | | Avg. price $3,004 | +2.95% | | Production 241,194 | -4.01% |

*Comparison to 1968 models not available.*

# Fury

*"One of the few American cars that doesn't
look like a few other American cars."*

**Nameplate year of origin:** 1956.
**Current bodystyle lifespan:** 1969 through 1973.
**Predecessor to this model:** Fury (1967 to 1968).
**Replacement for this model:** Gran Fury (1974 to 1978).
**Percentage of division's sales volume:** 49.08%.
**Corporate siblings:** Dodge Polara and Monaco.
**Primary competition:** AMC Ambassador, Chevrolet Biscayne/BelAir/Impala, Ford Galaxie/LTD, and Pontiac Catalina.
**Notable changes:** Completely restyled.
**Major standard equipment:** Cloth and vinyl front bench seat, color-keyed floor covering, front and rear armrests, variable speed electric windshield wipers, bright trim around front and rear windows, and 8.25 × 14 BSW tires (8.55 × 14 BSW tire on wagon). Fury II adds: Full carpeting and full-length body side molding. Fury III adds: All-vinyl upholstery on hardtop and convertible, backup lights, and distinctive exterior trim. Sport Fury adds: All-vinyl bucket seats, floor-mounted shifter and console with compartment, and deluxe steering wheel. VIP adds: Cloth and vinyl bench seats with fold-down center armrests, reading lamps, vinyl top and specific VIP trim.

## Measurements

| | Cars | Wagons |
|---|---|---|
| Wheelbase | 120.0" | 122.0" |
| Length | 214.5" | 219.6" |
| Width | 79.8" | 79.8" |
| Height | 55.8" | 56.6" |
| Legroom — front | 41.8" | 41.8" |
| Legroom — rear | 39.1" | 39.1" |
| Headroom — front | 38.8" | 39.6" |
| Headroom — rear | 38.4" | 39.2" |
| Cargo capacity (cu. ft.) | 21.5 | 104.2 |
| Fuel capacity (gals.) | 24.0 | 23.0 |

## Models Available

| | Style Number | Base MSRP | Change from LY | Shipping Wt. (lbs.) | Production | Change from LY |
|---|---|---|---|---|---|---|
| Fury I 2-Door Sedan | PE21 | $2,701 | +3.21% | 3453 | 4,971 | -14.12% |
| Fury I 4-Door Sedan | PE41 | $2,744 | +3.16% | 3488 | 18,771 | -19.12% |
| Fury I 4-Dr., 2-S. Suburban Wagon | PL45 | $3,231 | +6.00% | 4008 | 6,424 | -4.82% |
| Fury II 2-Door Sedan | PL21 | $2,813 | +3.61% | 3458 | 3,268 | +5.01% |
| Fury II 4-Door Sedan | PL41 | $2,841 | +3.05% | 3488 | 41,047 | -16.95% |
| Fury II 4-Dr., 2-S. Cust. Sub. Wgn. | PL45 | $3,436 | +5.66% | 4103 | 15,976 | -6.45% |
| Fury II 4-Dr., 3-S. Cust. Sub. Wgn. | PL46 | $3,527 | +5.19% | 4148 | 10,216 | +2.63% |
| Fury III 2-Door Hardtop | PM23 | $3,000 | +3.02% | 3468 | 44,168 | -26.96% |

|  | Style Number | Base MSRP | Change from LY | Shipping Wt. (lbs.) | Production | Change from LY |
|---|---|---|---|---|---|---|
| Fury III 2-Door Formal Hardtop | PM29 | $3,020 | +3.00% | 3548 | 22,738 | * |
| Fury III 2-Door Convertible | PM27 | $3,324 | +2.72% | 3704 | 4,129 | -7.90% |
| Fury III 4-Door Sedan | PM41 | $2,979 | +3.08% | 3493 | 72,747 | +25.64% |
| Fury III 4-Door Hardtop | PM43 | $3,155 | +2.87% | 3643 | 68,818 | +52.43% |
| Fury III 4-Dr., 2-S. Sport Sub. Wgn. | PM45 | $3,651 | +6.07% | 4123 | 8,201 | -10.89% |
| Fury III 4-Dr., 3-S. Sport Sub. Wgn. | PM46 | $3,718 | +4.94% | 4173 | 13,502 | +2.10% |
| Sport Fury 2-Door Hardtop | PH23 | $3,283 | +2.40% | 3603 | 14,120 | +112.59% |
| Sport Fury 2-Door Formal Hardtop | PH29 | $3,303 | +2.42% | 3678 | 2,169 | -87.30% |
| Sport Fury 2-Door Convertible | PH27 | $3,502 | +2.25% | 3729 | 1,579 | -36.56% |
| VIP 2-Door Hardtop | PP23 | $3,382 | +3.74% | 3583 | 4,740 | -29.96% |
| VIP 2-Door Formal Hardtop | PP29 | $3,382 | NEW | 3668 | 1,059 | NEW |
| VIP 4-Door Hardtop | PP43 | $3,433 | +3.22% | 3663 | 7,982 | -25.71% |
| TOTALS | Avg. price | $3,221 | +3.97% | Production | 366,625 | +4.91% |

*Comparison to 1968 model not available.*

# PONTIAC

*"Break-Away ... 1969 Pontiac."*

An all-new Grand Prix was the highlight of the 1969 Pontiac season. Sales of the luxury-sport Grand Prix had been gradually declining ever since its peak during the mid-sixties. Pontiac knew that it was offering features that the public wanted, but decided that the packaging was not quite right. Pontiac chose to develop a downsized Grand Prix, built on a stretched mid-size platform. This enabled the stylist to create a unique design, while utilizing some existing components. The front end consisted of a radiator style center grille with quad headlights on each side, and parking lights set at the tips of the fenders. Side panels were somewhat slab sided, ending in a short, clean decklid and taillights set into the rear bumper. Overall, it was an elegant, yet very sporty looking package. Inside was a cockpit style driver's center with full-length console, bucket seats, and wood-grain trim everywhere. Under the long hood were various familiar, large displacement engines for plenty of power. Initially, the Grand Prix 2-Door Hardtop body design was not shared with any other GM car. That would change, but for now, the Grand Prix was set for a rebound.

Also undergoing a major redesign, full-size Pontiac models continued the familiar styling cues, but the front grille and bumper treatment was even more pronounced than in previous versions. Body sides were given sharper character lines, and the new rear styling on Bonneville fea-

tured a vinyl rub strip in the center, under the hockey stick shaped taillights. This strip was supposed to provide low speed impact protection. The potent 428 CID V8 engine made its last appearance this year in the full-size and Grand Prix lines. Model changes included the discontinuance of the 2-Door Sedan body style in the Catalina line.

Firebird models were given a restyling for their third season in the marketplace. Most noticeable was a new front end that foreshadowed the upcoming 1970 LeMans models. Front fenders were unique to the Firebird with simulated air extractors, but the rest of the body styling was shared with the Chevrolet Camaro. Interior styling was upgraded, but other features carried over from previous years. A new RPO (regular production option) was quietly slipped into the lineup during mid-year: the Trans Am, a new top line, high performance option — roughly equivalent to the GTO in the LeMans line. Power came from a 400 CID, 4-bbl. V8 in either Ram Air III or Ram Air IV versions. Either way, over 350 horsepower was available in a car that weighed just over 3,000 pounds. That provided for some amazing performance. For its first season, the Trans Am was extremely limited in production. All models were white with blue stripes. An all-new Firebird was planned for the 1970 model year, but ultimately would not be ready until mid-year. Therefore, 1969 Firebirds were carried over into early 1970. Even sales brochures for the 1969 Firebird were

**1969**

revised to eliminate any reference to the model year, so they could be sold as 1970 models. All 1969-style Firebird models are covered within this section.

Finally, mid-size Tempest, LeMans and GTO models wore revised grilles and new interior styling. There were no model line changes. However, there was a very high profile mid-year introduction: "The Judge" option package was offered on GTO models as an all-out muscle car to beat all muscle cars. Featuring a standard 366-horsepower, 400 CID, 4-bbl. Ram Air V8 engine, 60" rear spoiler, blackout grille, exposed headlamps, Rallye II wheels, Carousel Red paint and of course, Pontiac's famous Endura nose (rubber covered bumper). There was even a Ram Air IV engine available, rated at 370 horsepower, though it probably delivered much closer to 390 in reality. Horsepower ratings were often understated by the late sixties to help keep insurance rates lower.

Bonneville 2-Door Hardtop

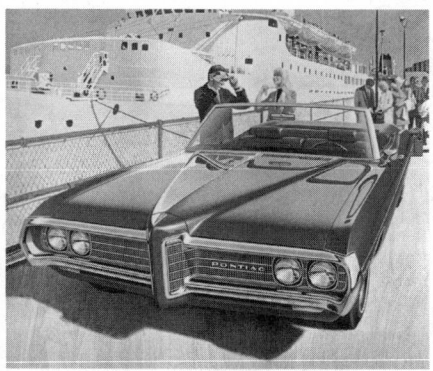
Catalina 2-Door Convertible

Executive 4-Door Sedan

Executive Safari 4-Door Wagon

Firebird 2-Door Convertible with 400 package

Grand Prix 2-Door Hardtop

GTO 2-Door Convertible

LeMans 2-Door Hardtop

Tempest Custom S 4-Door Hardtop

**Model year production:** 824,081, down 9.49% from 1968.
**Domestic market share:** 9.26% (3rd place).
**Base price range:** $2,510 to $4,104.

**Industry average base price:** $3,386.
**Pontiac average base price:** $3,242.
**Introduction date:** September 1968.

# Powertrains

| Engine | Gross HP | Transmission Availability | Firebird | LeMans/GTO | Grand Prix | Cat. & Exec. | Bonne-ville |
|---|---|---|---|---|---|---|---|
| 250 CID OHC, 1-bbl., 6-cyl. | 175 | 3-speed manual | S | S (ex. GTO) | - | - | - |
| | | 4-speed manual | $195 | - | - | - | - |
| | | 2-sp. Automatic | $174 | $174 (ex. GTO) | - | - | - |
| | | Turbo Hydra-matic | $195 | $195 (ex. GTO) | - | - | - |
| 250 CID OHC, 4-bbl., 6-cyl. | 230 | 3-speed manual | $130* | $125 (ex. GTO) | - | - | - |
| | | 4-speed manual | $325* | $310 (ex. GTO) | - | - | - |
| | | Turbo Hydra-matic | 325* | $320 (ex. GTO) | - | - | - |
| 350 CID, 2-bbl., V8 | 255 | 3-speed manual | $111 | $111 (ex. GTO) | - | - | - |
| | | 3-sp. HD man. | $195 | $195 (ex. GTO) | - | - | - |
| | | 4-speed manual | $306 | $306 (ex. GTO) | - | - | - |
| | | 2-sp. Automatic | $296 (w/o A/C) | $296 (w/o A/C) | - | - | - |
| | | Turbo Hydra-matic | $317 w/o A/C or $338 w/A/C | $317 w/o A/C or $338 w/A/C | - | - | - |
| 350 CID, 4-bbl., V8 | 325/330 | 3-speed manual | $199 | $189(ex. GTO) | - | - | - |
| | | 3-sp. HD man. | $283 | $274 (ex. GTO) | - | - | - |
| | | 4-speed manual | $394 | $384 (ex. GTO) | - | - | - |
| | | Turbo Hydra-matic | $426 | $416 (ex. GTO) | - | - | - |
| 400 CID, 2-bbl., V8 | 265 | Turbo Hydra-matic | - | No cost (GTO) | - | No cost | - |
| 400 CID, 2-bbl., V8 | 290 | 3-speed manual | - | - | - | S | - |
| | | Turbo Hydra-matic | - | - | - | $227 | - |
| 400 CID, 4-bbl., V8 | 330 (FB,LeM)/ 340 (Full-size) 350 (GP/GTO) | 3-sp. HD man. | S (w/400)** | S (GTO) | S | - | - |
| | | 4-speed manual | $195** | $185 (GTO) | $227 | - | - |
| | | Turbo Hydra-matic | $227** | $227 (GTO) | $227 | $274 | - |
| 400 CID H.O. Ram Air, 4-bbl., V8 | 335 | 4-speed manual | S (Trans Am)/$ (400) | - | - | - | - |
| | | Turbo Hydra-matic | $ (Trans Am)/$ (400) | - | - | - | - |
| 400 CID Ram Air SD, 4-bbl., V8 | 345 | 4-speed manual | $ (Trans Am) | - | - | - | - |
| | | Turbo Hydra-matic | $ (Trans Am) | - | - | - | - |
| 428 CID, 4-bbl., V8 | 360 | 3-sp. HD man. | - | - | $58 | - | S |
| | | 4-speed manual | - | - | $285 | - | - |
| | | Turbo Hydra-matic | - | - | $285 | $332 | $227 |
| 428 CID H.O., 4-bbl., V8 | 390 | 3-sp. HD man. | - | - | $177 | - | - |
| | | 4-speed manual | - | - | $404 | - | - |
| | | Turbo Hydra-matic | - | - | $404 | $482 (ex. Wgns.) | $386 (ex. Wagon) |

*Includes Sprint option package.   **Included with 400 Option package.*

## Major Options

| | Firebird | LeMans | Grand Prix | Catalina | Executive | Bonneville |
|---|---|---|---|---|---|---|
| Air conditioning (V8 only) | $376 | $376 | $421 | $421 | $421 | $421 |
| Electronic cruise control (V8 auto.) | $58 | $58 | $63 | $63 | $63 | $63 |
| Soft Ray tinted glass | $37 | $37 | $44 | $44 | $44 | $44 |
| Tilt steering wheel | $45 | $45 | $45 | $45 | $45 | $45 |
| Power steering — variable-ratio | $105 | $105 | $116 | $116 | $116 | $116 |
| Power brakes | $64 | $64 | S | $72 | $72 | $72 |
| Power driver's seat/Bench seat | $74 | $74 | $74 | $100 | $100 | $100 |
| Power windows | $105 | $105 | $111 | $111 | $111 | $111 |
| AM radio | $61 | $61 | $87 | $87 | $87 | $87 |
| AM/FM stereo | $239 | $239 | $239 | $239 | $239 | $239 |
| Front seat console | $57 | $57 | S | $57 | - | $ |
| Front bucket seats | S | $ | S | $ | - | $ |
| Vinyl roof (except Trans Am) | $85 | $100 | $142 | $116–142 | $116–142 | $116–142 |
| White stripe tires (base size) | $32 | $32 | $40 | $44–$48 | $44–$48 | $44 |
| Rally II wheels | $56 | $87 | $87 | $87 | $87 | $87 |
| Ventura package | - | - | - | $105 | - | - |
| Brougham package | - | - | - | - | - | $273–$316 |
| SJ package | - | - | $316 | - | - | - |
| Sprint package | $121 | $111–$132 | - | - | - | - |
| Firebird 350 package | $111 | - | - | - | - | - |
| Firebird H.O. package | $186 | - | - | - | - | - |
| Firebird 400 package | $275–$358 | - | - | - | - | - |
| Ram Air IV package | $832 | - | - | - | - | - |
| Trans Am package | $725 | - | - | - | - | - |

Options common to most models. (– = Not Available; S = Standard equipment.) Items may be standard equipment, optional at different pricing, or unavailable on certain models. This chart is only a guide.

## Paint Colors

| | Code | | Code |
|---|---|---|---|
| Starlight Black | 10 | Expresso Brown Metallic | 61 |
| Mayfair Maize | 40 | Champagne Metallic | 63 |
| Cameo White | 50 | Antique Gold Metallic | 65 |
| Liberty Blue Metallic | 51 | Burgundy Metallic | 67 |
| Matador Red | 52 | Palladium Silver Metallic | 69 |
| Warwick Blue Metallic | 53 | Carousel Red | 72 |
| Crystal Turquoise Metallic | 55 | Verdoro Green Metallic | 73 |
| Midnight Green Metallic | 57 | Goldenrod Yellow* | 76 |
| Limelight Green Metallic | 59 | Winward Blue Metallic* | 87 |

*Firebird only.*

# Firebird

*"Make a believer out of you? They should.
They're Firebirds. And from Pontiac."*

**Nameplate year of origin:** 1967 (used on Motorama show cars as early as 1954).
**Current bodystyle lifespan:** 1967 through 1969.
**Predecessor to this model:** None.
**Replacement for this model:** Firebird (1970 to 1981).
**Percentage of division's sales volume:** 10.64%.
**Corporate siblings:** Chevrolet Camaro.

## Measurements

| | |
|---|---|
| Wheelbase | 108.0" |
| Length | 191.1" |
| Width | 73.9" |
| Height | 50.0" |
| Legroom — front | 42.5" |

**Primary competition:** AMC Javelin, Ford Mustang, Mercury Cougar, and Plymouth Barracuda.

**Notable changes:** Major restyle and interior revisions.

**Major standard equipment:** All-vinyl front bucket seats, wood grain dash, full carpeting, 2-speed windshield wipers with washers, steering column shifter, and E70 × 14 Wide-Oval BSW tires. Sprint package adds: 4-bbl. OHC 6-cylinder, floor mounted shifter, and heavy-duty suspension. 350 adds: 350 CID V8 engine and column mounted shifter. H.O. adds: 4-bbl. carburetor and dual exhausts. 400 adds: 400 CID V8, floor mounted shifter, dual hood scoops, dual exhausts, heavy-duty suspension, and E70 × 14 Wide-Oval Redline or BSW tires.

## Measurements (cont.)

| | |
|---|---|
| Legroom — rear | 29.5" |
| Headroom — front | 37.0" |
| Headroom — rear | 36.7" |
| Cargo capacity (cu. ft.) | 9.9 |
| Fuel capacity (gals.) | 18.5 |

## Models Available

| | Style Number | Base MSRP | Change from LY | Shipping Wt. (lbs.) | Production | Change from LY |
|---|---|---|---|---|---|---|
| Firebird 2-Door Hardtop | 22337 | $2,831 | +1.80% | 3080 | 76,051 | -15.64% |
| Firebird 2-Door Convertible | 22367 | $3,045 | +1.64% | 3330 | 11,657 | -31.27% |
| TOTALS | | Avg. price $2,938 | +1.70% | | Production 87,708 | -18.12% |

# Tempest, LeMans and GTO

*"Despite all the appearances of super-expensive sportsters, they're actually priced way down."*

**Nameplate year of origin:** 1961 (as a Tempest sub-series).

**Current bodystyle lifespan:** 1968 through 1972.

**Predecessor to this model:** Tempest/LeMans (1966 to 1967).

**Replacement for this model:** LeMans (1973 to 1977).

**Percentage of division's sales volume:** 34.94%.

**Corporate siblings:** Chevrolet Chevelle, Oldsmobile Cutlass, and Buick Skylark.

**Primary competition:** Ford Torino, Mercury Montego, Plymouth Satellite, Dodge Coronet, and AMC Rebel.

**Notable changes:** New grille and minor trim and detail changes.

**Major standard equipment:** Cloth and vinyl front bench seat, vinyl floor covering, courtesy lights, 2-speed windshield wipers with washers, and 7.75 × 14 BSW tires. Custom S adds: All-vinyl front bench seats, full carpeting, and rocker panel moldings. LeMans adds: All-vinyl bucket seats or bench seat (2-Doors), Cloth and vinyl bench seats (4-Doors), and simulated walnut trim on dash. Safari adds: Exterior wood-grain paneling. GTO adds: All-vinyl bucket seats, floor shifter, dual exhausts, 400 CID V8 with engine dress-up kit, heavy duty suspension and G70 × 14 Red-line tires.

## Major Options

| | 2-Doors | 4-Doors | Wagons |
|---|---|---|---|
| Wheelbase | 112.0" | 116.0" | 116.0" |
| Length | 201.5" | 205.5" | 211.0" |
| Width | 75.8" | 75.8" | 76.3" |
| Height | 52.0" | 52.6" | 52.6" |
| Legroom — front | 42.4" | 42.4" | 42.4" |
| Legroom — rear | 32.2" | 34.8" | 34.8" |
| Headroom — front | 37.9" | 38.5" | 38.5" |
| Headroom — rear | 36.3" | 37.1" | 37.4" |
| Cargo capacity (cu. ft.) | 13.1 | 13.1 | 94.0 |
| Fuel capacity (gals.) | 21.5 | 21.5 | 21.5 |

**1969**

## Models Available

| | Style Number | Base MSRP | Change from LY | Shipping Wt. (lbs.) | Production | Change from LY |
|---|---|---|---|---|---|---|
| Tempest 2-Door Sports Coupe | 23327 | $2,510 | +1.99% | 3180 | 17,181 | -14.06% |
| Tempest 4-Door Sedan | 23369 | $2,557 | +1.91% | 3250 | 9,741 | -15.95% |
| Tempest Custom S 2-Dr. Sports Cpe. | 23527 | $2,603 | +1.92% | 3210 | 7,912 | -25.60% |
| Tempest Custom S 2-Door Hardtop | 23537 | $2,663 | +1.87% | 3220 | 46,886 | +15.56% |
| Tempest Custom S 2-Door Conv. | 23567 | $2,888 | +1.73% | 3265 | 2,379 | -32.38% |

| | Style Number | Base MSRP | Change from LY | Shipping Wt. (lbs.) | Production | Change from LY |
|---|---|---|---|---|---|---|
| Tempest Custom S 4-Door Sedan | 23569 | $2,651 | +1.88% | 3235 | 16,532 | -4.46% |
| Tempest Custom S 4-Door Hardtop | 23539 | $2,777 | +1.80% | 3315 | 3,918 | -36.26% |
| Tempest Custom S 4-Dr., 2-S. Wgn. | 23535 | $2,956 | +1.72% | 3595 | 6,963 | -15.63% |
| LeMans 2-Door Sports Coupe | 23727 | $2,773 | +1.80% | 3225 | 5,033 | -40.36% |
| LeMans 2-Door Hardtop | 23737 | $2,835 | +1.76% | 3245 | 82,817 | -24.74% |
| LeMans 2-Door Convertible | 23767 | $3,064 | +1.63% | 3290 | 5,676 | -35.65% |
| LeMans 4-Door Hardtop | 23739 | $2,965 | +1.68% | 3360 | 6,475 | -28.07% |
| LeMans Safari 4-Dr., 2-S. Wagon | 23936 | $3,198 | +2.93% | 3690 | 4,115 | -6.77% |
| GTO 2-Door Hardtop | 24237 | $3,156 | +1.77% | 3503 | 64,851 | -16.54% |
| GTO 2-Door Convertible | 24267 | $3,382 | +1.65% | 3553 | 7,436 | -25.49% |
| TOTALS | | *Avg. price* $2,865 | +1.85% | | *Production* 287,915 | -16.89% |

# Grand Prix

*"This machine was designed for one purpose — driving.*
*Personal, luxurious, spirited driving."*

**Nameplate year of origin:** 1962.
**Current bodystyle lifespan:** 1969 through 1972.
**Predecessor to this model:** Grand Prix (1967 to 1968).
**Replacement for this model:** Grand Prix (1973 to 1977).
**Percentage of division's sales volume:** 13.65%.
**Corporate siblings:** None.
**Primary competition:** Dodge Charger and Mercury Cougar.
**Notable changes:** Completely redesigned.
**Major standard equipment:** Front bucket seats, or notchback bench seat in cloth and vinyl or all-vinyl trim, loop-pile carpeting, custom cushion steering wheel, electric clock, lamp package, deluxe wheel covers, windshield radio antenna, concealed wipers, exterior bright moldings, and G78-14 BSW tires.

## Measurements

| | |
|---|---|
| Wheelbase | 118.0" |
| Length | 210.2" |
| Width | 75.7" |
| Height | 51.9" |
| Legroom — front | 42.4" |
| Legroom — rear | 31.6" |
| Headroom — front | 37.5" |
| Headroom — rear | 36.2" |
| Cargo capacity (cu. ft.) | NA |
| Fuel capacity (gals.) | 21.5 |

## Models Available

| | Style Number | Base MSRP | Change from LY | Shipping Wt. (lbs.) | Production | Change from LY |
|---|---|---|---|---|---|---|
| Grand Prix 2-Door Hardtop | 27657 | $3,866 | +4.57% | 3715 | 112,486 | 254.72% |
| TOTALS | | *Avg. price* $3,866 | +4.57% | | *Production* 112,486 | +254.72% |

# Catalina

*"We build a better car year after year,*
*and serve it up at a price that makes sense."*

**Nameplate year of origin:** 1950 on hardtop models, 1959 as series.
**Current bodystyle lifespan:** 1969 through 1970.
**Predecessor to this model:** Catalina (1967 to 1968).
**Replacement for this model:** Catalina (1971 to 1976).
**Percentage of division's sales volume:** 25.55%.
**Corporate siblings:** Chevrolet Impala/Caprice, Olds Delta 88, Buick LeSabre/Wildcat.

## Measurements

| | Cars | Wagons |
|---|---|---|
| Wheelbase | 122.0" | 122.0" |
| Length | 217.5" | 220.5" |
| Width | 79.8" | 79.8" |
| Height | 54.8" | 56.0" |

**Primary competition:** Ford LTD, Mercury Monterey, Plymouth Fury, and
   Dodge Polara.
**Notable changes:** Completely restyled.
**Major standard equipment:** Cloth and vinyl front bench seat (all-vinyl on
   convertible and wagons), full carpeting, 2-speed windshield wipers with
   washers, and 8.55 × 15 BSW tires (9.15 × 15 BSW tires on wagons). Ventura option adds: All-vinyl upholstery with specific trim.

|                           | Cars | Wagons |
| ------------------------- | ---- | ------ |
| Legroom — front           | 42.4" | 41.5" |
| Legroom — rear            | 38.1" | 38.2" |
| Headroom — front          | 39.0" | 39.2" |
| Headroom — rear           | 37.7" | 39.0" |
| Cargo capacity (cu. ft.)  | NA   | 99.9   |
| Fuel capacity (gals.)     | 26.5 | 24.0   |

## Models Available

|                                   | Style Number | Base MSRP | Change from LY | Shipping Wt. (lbs.) | Production | Change from LY |
| --------------------------------- | ------------ | --------- | -------------- | ------------------- | ---------- | -------------- |
| Catalina 2-Door Hardtop           | 25237        | $3,174    | +2.75%         | 3925                | 84,006     | -8.90%         |
| Catalina 2-Door Convertible       | 25267        | $3,476    | +2.51%         | 3985                | 5,436      | -25.93%        |
| Catalina 4-Door Sedan             | 25269        | $3,090    | +2.86%         | 3945                | 48,590     | -48.55%        |
| Catalina 4-Door Hardtop           | 25239        | $3,244    | +2.72%         | 4005                | 38,819     | -6.97%         |
| Catalina Safari 4-Dr., 2-S. Wagon | 25236        | $3,519    | +3.81%         | 4455                | 20,352     | -6.85%         |
| Catalina Safari 4-Dr., 3-S. Wagon | 25246        | $3,664    | +3.59%         | 4520                | 13,393     | +0.22%         |
| TOTALS                            | Avg. price   | $3,361    | +4.51%         | Production          | 210,596    | -23.75%        |

# Executive

*"It has decisive styling, impeccable road manners and a distinguished taste."*

**Nameplate year of origin:** 1966.
**Current bodystyle lifespan:** 1969 through 1970.
**Predecessor to this model:** Executive (1967 to 1968).
**Replacement for this model:** Bonneville (1971 to 1976).
**Percentage of division's sales volume:** 4.74%.
**Corporate siblings:** Chevrolet Impala/Caprice, Oldsmobile Delta 88,
   and Buick LeSabre/Wildcat.
**Primary competition:** Ford LTD, Mercury Marquis, Plymouth Fury,
   and Dodge Monaco.
**Notable changes:** Completely restyled.
**Major standard equipment:** Cloth and vinyl bench seat, full carpeting,
   perforated vinyl headliner, walnut grain trim on dash, electric clock,
   full length lower body molding, exterior wood grain trim on station
   wagons, full wheel covers and 8.55 × 15 BSW tires (9.15 × 15 BSW
   tires on 3-Seat Wagon).

## Measurements

|                           | Cars   | Wagons |
| ------------------------- | ------ | ------ |
| Wheelbase                 | 125.0" | 122.0" |
| Length                    | 223.5" | 220.5" |
| Width                     | 79.8"  | 79.8"  |
| Height                    | 55.0"  | 56.0"  |
| Legroom — front           | 42.4"  | 41.5"  |
| Legroom — rear            | 38.1"  | 38.2"  |
| Headroom — front          | 39.0"  | 39.2"  |
| Headroom — rear           | 37.7"  | 39.0"  |
| Cargo capacity (cu. ft.)  | NA     | 99.9   |
| Fuel capacity (gals.)     | 26.5   | 24.0   |

**1969**

## Models Available

|                                    | Style Number | Base MSRP | Change from LY | Shipping Wt. (lbs.) | Production | Change from LY |
| ---------------------------------- | ------------ | --------- | -------------- | ------------------- | ---------- | -------------- |
| Executive 2-Door Hardtop           | 25637        | $3,456    | +2.52%         | 3970                | 4,492      | -23.61%        |
| Executive 4-Door Sedan             | 25669        | $3,394    | +2.57%         | 4045                | 14,831     | -21.40%        |
| Executive 4-Door Hardtop           | 25639        | $3,525    | +2.50%         | 4065                | 6,522      | -16.90%        |
| Executive Safari 4-Dr., 2-S. Wagon | 25636        | $3,872    | +3.42%         | 4475                | 6,411      | +3.49%         |
| Executive Safari 4-Dr., 3-S. Wagon | 25646        | $4,017    | +3.26%         | 4545                | 6,805      | +16.46%        |
| TOTALS                             | Avg. price   | $3,653    | +2.87%         | Production          | 39,061     | -12.49%        |

# Bonneville

*"If you thought Bonneville could cut it before,
wait till you swing our '69 onto a piece of pike."*

**Nameplate year of origin:** 1957.
**Current bodystyle lifespan:** 1969 through 1970.
**Predecessor to this model:** Bonneville (1967 to 1968).
**Replacement for this model:** Grand Ville (1971 to 1976).
**Percentage of division's sales volume:** 10.47%.
**Corporate siblings:** Chevrolet Impala/Caprice, Oldsmobile Delta 88, and Buick LeSabre/Wildcat.
**Primary competition:** Ford LTD, Mercury Marquis, Plymouth Fury, and Dodge Monaco.
**Notable changes:** Restyled front and rear ends.
**Major standard equipment:** All-vinyl or cloth and vinyl front bench seat, full carpeting, burled elm grain dash trim, electric clock, courtesy lights, dual-speed electric windshield wipers, rear fender skirts, deluxe wheel covers and 8.55 × 15 BSW tires (9.15 × 15 BSW tires Wagon). Brougham option adds: Special upholstery trim with fold-down center armrests, and exterior badges.

## Measurements

|  | Cars | Wagons |
|---|---|---|
| Wheelbase | 125.0" | 122.0" |
| Length | 224.0" | 220.5" |
| Width | 79.8" | 79.8" |
| Height | 55.0" | 56.0" |
| Legroom — front | 42.4" | 41.5" |
| Legroom — rear | 38.1" | 38.2" |
| Headroom — front | 39.0" | 39.2" |
| Headroom — rear | 37.7" | 39.0" |
| Cargo capacity (cu. ft.) | NA | 99.9 |
| Fuel capacity (gals.) | 26.5 | 24.0 |

## Models Available

| | Style Number | Base MSRP | Change from LY | Shipping Wt. (lbs.) | Production | Change from LY |
|---|---|---|---|---|---|---|
| Bonneville 2-Door Hardtop | 26237 | $3,688 | +2.67% | 4080 | 27,773 | -6.17% |
| Bonneville 2-Door Convertible | 26267 | $3,896 | +2.53% | 4130 | 5,438 | -26.09% |
| Bonneville 4-Door Sedan | 26269 | $3,626 | +2.72% | 4180 | 4,859 | +38.87% |
| Bonneville 4-Door Hardtop | 26239 | $3,756 | +2.62% | 4180 | 40,817 | -28.46% |
| Bonneville Safari 4-Dr., 2-S. Wgn. | 26246 | $4,104 | +2.93% | 4600 | 7,428 | +7.25% |
| TOTALS | *Avg. price* $3,814 | | +2.69% | *Production* | 86,315 | -17.35% |

# 1970

It may have been the dawn of a new decade, but many car models were nearing the end of the road. The horsepower race reached its peak this year. From 1971 on, engines would be required to run on unleaded fuel, and that demand coupled with more stringent emissions requirements would reduce their output. Also, insurance rates were climbing higher on muscle cars and convertibles. These factors coupled with increasingly bad economic news combined to threaten many models that just a few years prior were at the top of the sales charts.

At American Motors, two new compact models were introduced to replace the aging Rambler. The Hornet was intended to take on the more modern Chevy Nova and Ford Maverick compacts. The Gremlin, on the other hand, was a pre-emptive move to take on the upcoming Chevy Vega and Ford Pinto. Both were successful for AMC in their missions. The remainder of the AMC line was carried into 1970 with new grilles and detail changes.

Chrysler Corporation had released all-new full-size models for 1969, so this year it was time to do some work on the compact lines. The Plymouth Valiant and Dodge Dart continued to use the same basic structure, with revised front and rear end styling. The big news was in the all-new Plymouth Valiant Duster. Sharing the Valiant 4-Door Sedan powertrain and front clip, the new Duster was all-new from the front doors back. Styling utilized the fastback profile made so popular by cars like the Dodge Charger and the Ford Mustang. One drawback of the new design was the poor rear visibility caused by the severe slant of the rear window, coupled with the large blind spot in the rear quarter. Otherwise, the car was a huge success, and far outsold the Valiant 2-Door Sedan it replaced. Dodge would get its own version for 1971.

Also new for 1970 were the Dodge Challenger and its sister car, the restyled Plymouth Barracuda. Both cars wore muscular styling and could be powered by just about any of Chrysler's powerful engines. The Barracuda rode on the Valiant wheelbase, while the Challenger was on a stretched version of the same platform. Either car could be equipped with a full complement of luxury features. Unfortunately, these new models were a little too late to be top sellers in the pony car wars, and they would be kept in the model lines just long enough to recoup development costs. By the 1974 season, rising gas prices and shrinking sales would spell the end for the Mopar twins.

Other Chrysler models for 1970 were given the usual annual styling changes. One noteworthy comment on the 1970 Imperial line is that it was the last full season for the Imperial to exist as a separate marketing line within Chrysler Corporation. More details on this can be found in the 1970 and 1971 Imperial sections.

Ford fielded all new mid-size models and heavily restyled the Thunderbird line. The new mid-size cars looked much trimmer and lighter than the 1968-1969 models, even though actual physical dimensions proved differently. The Fairlane/Torino line continued with full width grille styling, while Mercury went for an odd, extended protrusion at the grille center, unsuccessfully mimicking the Pontiac look. The Torino line was definitely the better looking of the two cars, and it went on to win the 1970 *Motor Trend* magazine Car of the Year award. A mid-year change involved pulling the plug on the compact Falcon and transferring the nameplate to a new, low price mid-sized Fairlane model. Otherwise, the model lines of both cars were changed slightly, with the Mercury version losing its Convertible body styles.

The luxurious Thunderbird also took on a frontal appearance similar to the Montego, and had about as much success carrying the look as the Montego. The roofline on 2-Door models was slightly revised, but the rear taillamp styling was left similar to previous versions. The new for '69 Maverick continued unchanged and was sold side-by-side with the Falcon for about four months into the 1970 season until the latter was dropped. The sporty Mustang

## 1970 Model Year Production by Make

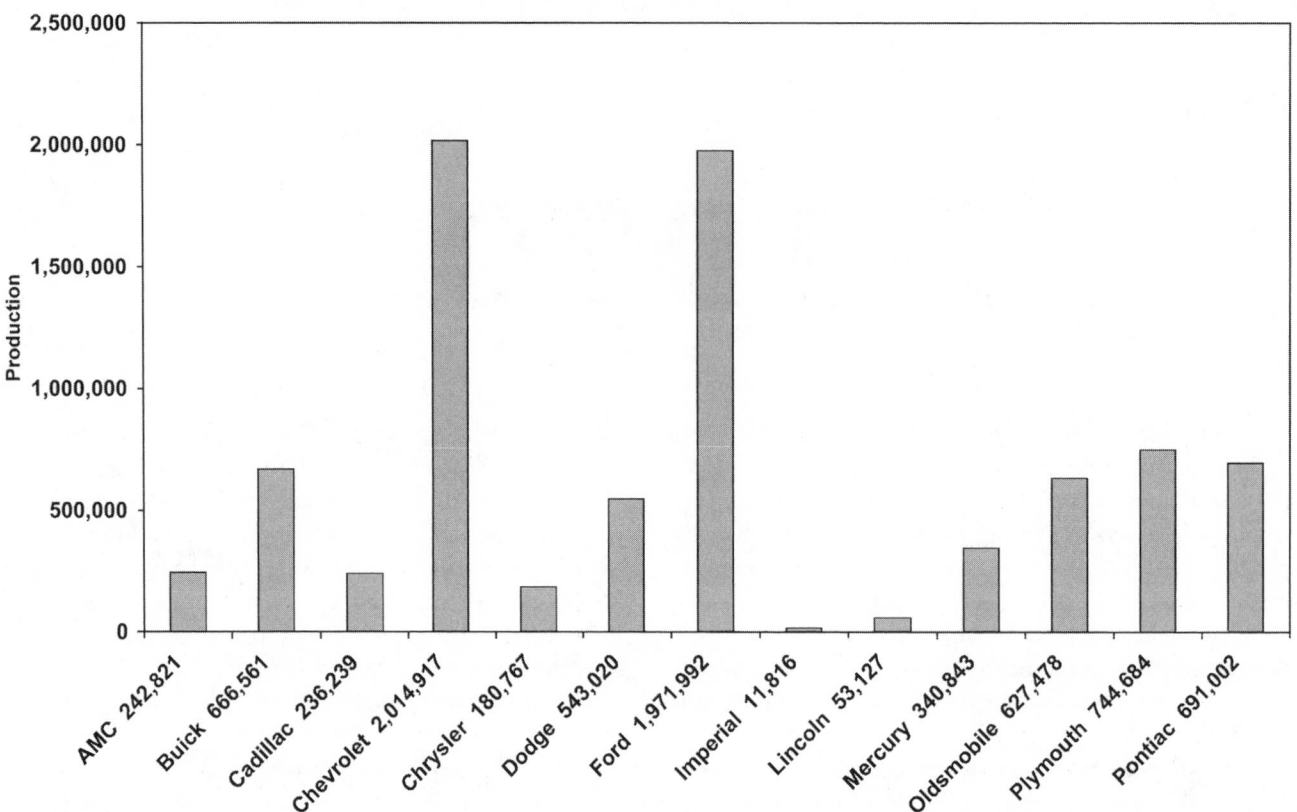

and Cougar were given minor facelifts and the full size Ford and Mercurys received only minor styling updates.

Chevrolet introduced a cousin for the Pontiac Grand Prix this season, the Monte Carlo. The new Monte Carlo took the Grand Prix concept to a lower price level, and in doing so stole many sales from the Grand Prix. The cars shared rooflines and some components underneath, but the Monte Carlo rode on the 4-Door mid size 116-inch wheelbase and used Chevrolet powertrains. A convertible model was to have joined the Monte Carlo line, but that car was axed prior to introduction.

The sporty Camaro and Firebird models started the season as carryover 1969 products. Their new replacements had been delayed and didn't arrive in showrooms until January of 1970. The new line of coupes borrowed styling influences from Ferrari and other European coupes of the day. They came off looking quite modern and were, initially, quite popular. Both lines were revamped to reflect the new choices. The Camaro came in a base model with SS, RS and Z/28 options. The Firebird dropped its model option packages, but came in 4 new variations: base coupe, luxury Esprit, sporty Formula, and high-performance Trans Am. The Chevrolet Corvette continued with few changes for this year.

Intermediate General Motors products featured an extensive facelift, with all models getting new sheetmetal for

the old bodies. They still looked like their predecessors, but the freshened styling was a welcome change, especially for the Buick Skylark and Chevrolet Chevelle lines. Oldsmobile's 4-4-2 had been given additional power in 1968 by the Hurst Corporation, creating a special model known as the Hurst/Olds. For 1970, they once again worked their magic on the 4-4-2, but this time it was to create the Indianapolis 500 pace car. The pace car Oldsmobile was painted in white with twin gold stripes that would become a Hurst trademark paint scheme. GM's entire full-size line was in a holding pattern awaiting all-new models in 1971. It would be the last season for the Buick Wildcat, Pontiac Executive and Pontiac Tempest nameplates. The very popular compact Chevy Nova soldiered on in its current form.

There were no major changes to any of the increasingly popular light truck lines for 1970. Ford and the GM twins were given new grilles and trim upgrades. The car-like Ford Ranchero was given a total makeover that followed the Torino's new styling. Similarly, the Chevy El Camino sported new styling to match the Chevelle. A new, larger Chevy Van was introduced during the year. This new design would be in production for over 25 years. It was highly popular with van conversion builders during the seventies and was the van of choice for mini-motorhome builders through the eighties.

Changes to the Checker for 1970 were minimal as usual. This would be the last year for the 327 CID V8 as a powerplant, as it would be replaced by the 350 CID Chevy V8 for 1971. The base six-cylinder continued to be the 250 CID Chevy unit that was introduced for 1969. Avanti II made no changes to the basic outward appearance for 1970.

# AMERICAN MOTORS

*"The '70's from American Motors."*

American Motors ushered in the '70s by introducing two all-new models while shedding the last vestiges of the Rambler nameplate. The first new model was the replacement for the aging but popular Rambler (American). The Hornet retained many of the key dimensions and features the Rambler was known for, but it added a stylish, modern exterior to the equation. The result was a popular, solid and reliable (and, as it turned out, long-lived) compact car. Though the new car borrowed its name from the famous race-bred Hudson Hornet of the 1950s, this was not a car to be known for its performance. This one was strictly a family-oriented economy car with a few exceptions — notably the 1971 SC/360 model. The Hornet, solidly rooted in the long-standing American Motors tradition of economy and value, would serve AMC for many years.

The other new arrival came on April 1, 1970. The subcompact Gremlin was the first of three domestic-built subcompact cars to rival the increasingly popular imported cars from Europe and Japan. Always looking to conserve monetary resources, AMC cleverly designed the Gremlin around existing Hornet components and produced a unique looking, roomy economy car, though the Gremlin would turn out to be a little too heavy to give outstanding fuel economy. That would not be a major concern for another few years. What really made the Gremlin shine was its roomy interior, powerful engine choices, variety of features available, and low base price. These were all great selling tools, especially the price! AMC was able to keep the costs of the Gremlin lower by having it share nearly all components from the doors forward with the Hornet. This left only the forward sloping rear quarter and hatchback design to tool from scratch. All in all it was a successful little car for American Motors. As for other models, the Rebel line received a restyled rear quarter section. Also the Rebel and other cars in the lineup received the requisite new grilles and trim and detail changes.

Ambassador SST 4-Door Wagon

AMX 2-Door Hardtop

Hornet 2-Door Sedan

1970

Hornet 4-Door Sedan

Javelin SST 2-Door Hardtop

Rebel SST 4-Door Sedan

**Model year production:** 242,821, down 14.14% from 1969.
**Domestic market share:** 2.92% (9th place).
**Base price range:** $1,879 to $4,122.
**Industry average base price:** $3,538.
**American Motors average base price:** $2,957.
**Introduction date:** September 25, 1969. Gremlin introduced on April 1, 1970.
**Assembly plants:** Kenosha, Wisconsin, and Brampton, Ontario, Canada.

**Data plate identification:** Thirteen digit code read as follows: A = American Motors; 0 = 1970; transmission code (see chart); car line body type series numbers (see last three digits of style number); engine code (see chart); 100001 and up for serial number (700001 and up for cars built in Ontario). *Example:* A0A797I100001 is a 1970 Torque-Command Automatic, Javelin SST 2-Door, 304 CID V8, serial number 100001 built in Kenosha.

# Powertrains

| Engine | Gross HP | Engine Code** | Transmission Availability | Trans. Code | Gremlin* & Hornet | AMX & Javelin | Rebel | Ambassador |
|---|---|---|---|---|---|---|---|---|
| 199 CID, 1-bbl., 6-cyl. | 135 | A/B | 3-speed manual | S/C | S (base)* | - | - | |
| | | | Shift-Command Automatic | A | $195 (base)* | - | - | - |
| 232 CID, 1-bbl., 6-cyl. | 145 | E/F | 3-speed manual | S | S (SST)/ $45 (base)* | S | S | - |
| | | | Shift-Command Automatic | A | $195 (SST)/ $240 (base)* | $195 | $195 | - |
| 232 CID, 2-bbl., 6-cyl. | 155 | G/Q | 3-speed manual | S | $19 (SST)/ $65 (base) | $19 | $19 | S (base) |
| | | | Shift-Command Automatic | A | $214 (SST)/ $260 (base) | $214 | $214 | $195 (base) |
| 304 CID, 2-bbl., V8 | 210 | H/I | 3-speed manual | S | $94 (SST)/ $139 (base) | $94 | $94 | $94 (base) |
| | | | Shift-Command Automatic | A | $310 (SST)/ $355 (base) | $310 | $310 | $ (base)/ S (SST/DPL) |
| 304 CID, 4-bbl., V8 | 210 | M | 3-speed manual | S | - | $110 | $110 | $110 (base) |
| | | | Shift-Command Automatic | A | - | $326 | $326 $16 (SST/ DPL) | $320 (base)/ |
| 360 CID, 2-bbl., V8 | 245 | N | 3-speed manual | S | - | $135 | $135 | - |
| | | | Shift-Command Automatic | A | - | $355 | $355 | $41 (SST/ DPL) |
| 360 CID, 4-bbl., V8 | 290 | P | 4-speed manual | F/M | - | S (AMX)/ $280 (Jav.) | - | - |
| | | | Shift-Command Automatic | A | - | $20 (AMX)/ | | |

| Engine | Gross HP | Engine Code** | Transmission Availability | Trans. Code | Gremlin* & Hornet | AMX & Javelin | Rebel | Ambassador |
|---|---|---|---|---|---|---|---|---|
| | | | | | | $300(Jav.) | $394 | $80 (SST/ DPL) |
| 390 CID, 4-bbl., V8 | 325 | S** | 4-speed manual | F/M | - | $11 (AMX) | S*** | - |
| | | | Shift-Command Automatic | A | - | $31 (AMX) | $220*** | $168 (SST/ DPL) |

*Available for Gremlin or base Hornet models.    **First code is for regular engine, second code is for low-compression engine.    ***390 CID V8 in Rebel "Machine" is code X, and rated at 340 Horsepower.*

## Major Options

| | Gremlin | Hornet | Javelin | Rebel | Ambassador |
|---|---|---|---|---|---|
| Air Conditioning | $380 | $380 | $380 | $380 | S-$380 base |
| Tilt-O-Just steering wheel | - | - | - | $45 | $45 |
| Speed control | - | - | - | $60 | $60 |
| Soft Ray tinted glass | $34 | $34 | $34 | $37 | $42 |
| Vinyl Top (excluding Wagon models) | - | - | $84 | $95 | $106 |
| Power steering— variable-ratio | $96 | $96 | $102 | $105 | $105 |
| Power brakes | $43 | $43 | $43 | $43 | $43 |
| Power windows | - | - | - | - | $105 |
| AM radio | $62 | $62 | $62 | $62 | $62 |
| AM/FM pushbutton radio | - | - | $134 | $134 | $134 |
| Custom wheel covers | $50 | $50 | $50 | $53 | $53 |
| Turbo Cast wheel covers | $74 | $74 | $74 | $74 | $74 |
| Station Wagon third seat | - | - | - | $118 | $118 |

Options common to most models. (- = Not Available.) Items may be standard equipment, optional at different pricing, or unavailable on certain models. This chart is only a guide.

## Paint Colors

| | Code |
|---|---|
| Electric Blue Met. | B6 |
| Classic Black | P1 |
| Big Bad Blue | P2 |
| Big Bad Orange | P3 |
| Big Bad Green | P4 |
| Shadow Black | P8 |
| Matador Red | P39 |
| Hialeah Yellow | P58 |
| Frost White | P72 |
| Bittersweet Orange Met. | P79 |
| Gray | P81 |
| Bayshore Blue Met. | P82 |
| Commodore Blue Met. | P84 |
| Seafoam Aqua Met. | P85 |
| Mosport Green Met. | P86 |
| Glen Green Met. | P87 |
| Golden Lime Met. | P90 |
| Tijuana Tan | P91 |
| Moroccan Brown Met. | P94 |
| Sonic Silver Met. | P95 |

*Rebel "Machine" Striping package optional for $75.*

# Gremlin

*"Our new little economy car."*

**Nameplate year of origin:** 1970.
**Current bodystyle lifespan:** 1970 through 1983 with restyle in 1979 (renamed Spirit).
**Predecessor to this model:** None.
**Replacement for this model:** Spirit (1979 to 1982) and Eagle SX/4 (1981 to 1983).
**Corporate siblings:** Hornet (shared front end components).
**Percentage of division's sales volume:** 10.42%.
**Primary competition:** None.
**Notable changes:** All-new model for 1970½
**Major standard equipment:** Vinyl bench seat, front door pockets, fold-down rear seat (4-passenger model), front seat foam cushions, front arm rests, interior lights, aluminized exhaust system, Weather-Eye heating & ventilation system, exterior pin stripes, 6.00 × 13 BSW tires.

## Measurements

| | |
|---|---|
| Wheelbase | 96.0" |
| Length | 161.2" |
| Width | 70.6" |
| Height | 51.7" |
| Legroom—front | 40.8" |
| Legroom—rear | 27.8" |
| Headroom—front | 38.1" |
| Headroom—rear | 36.4" |
| Luggage cap. (cu. ft.) | 6.0 |
| Fuel capacity (gals.) | 21.0 |

**1970**

## Models Available

| | Style Number | Base MSRP | Change from LY | Shipping Wt. (lbs.) | Production | Change from LY |
|---|---|---|---|---|---|---|
| Gremlin 2-pass., 2-Dr.Sdn | 7046-0 | $1,879 | NEW | 2497 | * | NEW |
| Gremlin 2-Door Sedan | 7046-5 | $1,959 | NEW | 2557 | 25,300 | NEW |
| TOTALS | Avg. price | $1,919 | NEW | Production* | 25,300 | NEW |

*2-passenger production included with 4-passenger total.

# Hornet

*"The little rich car."*

**Nameplate year of origin:** 1951 (used on high-performance Hudson).
**Current bodystyle lifespan:** 1970 through 1987.
**Predecessor to this model:** Rambler American (1964 to 1969).
**Replacement for this model:** Concord (1978 to 1982) and Eagle (1980 to 1987).
**Percentage of division's sales volume:** 30.72%.
**Corporate siblings:** None.
**Primary competition:** Chevrolet Nova, Dodge Dart, Ford Falcon, Ford Maverick, and Plymouth Valiant.
**Notable changes:** All-new model for 1970.
**Major standard equipment:** Cloth and vinyl front bench seat, front seat foam cushions, instrument panel package tray, front and rear armrests, interior lights, glove box lock, aluminized exhaust system, Weather-Eye heating & ventilation system, exterior pin stripes, and 6.45 × 14 BSW tires.

### Measurements

| | |
|---|---|
| Wheelbase | 108.0" |
| Length | 179.3" |
| Width | 71.1" |
| Height | 51.1" |
| Legroom — front | 40.8" |
| Legroom — rear | 36.1" |
| Headroom — front | 38.1" |
| Headroom — rear | 37.5" |
| Luggage cap. (cu. ft.) | 11.2 |
| Fuel capacity (gals.) | 16.0 |

## Models Available

| | Style Number | Base MSRP | Change from LY | Shipping Wt. (lbs.) | Production | Change from LY |
|---|---|---|---|---|---|---|
| Hornet 2-Door Sedan | 7006-0 | $1,994 | -0.20% | 2677 | 40,000 (base 6-cyl.)* | NEW |
| Hornet 4-Door Sedan | 7005-0 | $2,072 | -0.19% | 2748 | 100 (base V8's) | NEW |
| Hornet SST 2-Door Sedan | 7006-7 | $2,144 | NEW | 2705 | 29,200 (SST 6-cyl.)* | NEW |
| Hornet SST 4-Door Sedan | 7005-7 | $2,221 | 0.14% | 2765 | 5,300 (SST V8's)* | NEW |
| TOTALS | Avg. price | $2,108 | +12.9% | | Production 74,600* | -24.60%** |

*Exact Hornet production by body style is not available; estimates by series (broken down by 6 and V8 engines) are given above.   **Production total compared to 1969 Rambler American.

# AMX

*"The racy one."*

**Nameplate year of origin:** 1968.
**Current bodystyle lifespan:** 1968 through 1970.
**Predecessor to this model:** None.
**Replacement for this model:** None.
**Percentage of division's sales volume:** 1.70%.
**Corporate siblings:** Javelin (AMX created from shortened Javelin body).
**Primary competition:** Chevrolet Corvette, Chevrolet Camaro, Dodge Challenger, Ford Mustang, Plymouth Barracuda, and Pontiac Firebird.

### Measurements

| | |
|---|---|
| Wheelbase | 97.0" |
| Length | 177.2" |
| Width | 71.6" |
| Height | NA |
| Legroom — front | 42.0" |
| Legroom — rear | NA |
| Headroom — front | 39.0" |

**Notable changes:** Minor trim and detail changes.
**Major standard equipment:** Vinyl reclining front bucket seats, front seat foam cushions, front armrests, interior lights, glove box lock, dual horns, aluminized dual exhaust system, Weather-Eye heating & ventilation system, Exterior pin stripes, sports steering wheel (3-spoke), handling package, slot-style 14 × 6 wheels, space saver spare tire, E78 × 14 BSW tires.

## Measurements (cont.)

| | |
|---|---|
| Headroom — rear | NA |
| Luggage cap. (cu. ft.) | 9.6 |
| Fuel capacity (gals.) | 19.0 |

## Models Available

| | Style Number | Base MSRP | Change from LY | Shipping Wt. (lbs.) | Production | Change from LY |
|---|---|---|---|---|---|---|
| AMX 2-Door Hardtop | 7039-7 | $3,395 | +2.97% | 3126 | 4,116 | -50.37% |
| TOTALS | | Avg. price $3,395 | +2.97% | | Production 4,116 | -50.37% |

# Javelin

*"Classy, glassy, jazzy."*

**Nameplate year of origin:** 1968.
**Current bodystyle lifespan:** 1968 through 1970.
**Predecessor to this model:** Marlin (1965 to 1967).
**Replacement for this model:** Javelin (1971 to 1974).
**Percentage of division's sales volume:** 10.14%.
**Corporate siblings:** AMX (created through a shortened Javelin body).
**Primary competition:** Chevrolet Camaro, Dodge Challenger, Ford Mustang, Plymouth Barracuda, and Pontiac Firebird.
**Notable changes:** Minor trim and detail changes. New "Trans-Am" edition for SCCA racing.
**Major standard equipment:** All-vinyl front bucket seats, full carpeting, interior courtesy lights, Weather-Eye heating & ventilation system, and C78 × 14 BSW tires. SST adds: Reclining seats, wood-grain sports steering wheel and door panel trim, rocker panel moldings, wheel covers and hood-scoop moldings. Trans-Am edition adds: 390 CID V8 engine, 4-speed manual transmission and F70 × 14 tires.

## Measurements

| | |
|---|---|
| Wheelbase | 109.0" |
| Length | 189.2" |
| Width | 71.9" |
| Height | NA |
| Legroom — front | 42.0" |
| Legroom — rear | 29.8" |
| Headroom — front | 39.0" |
| Headroom — rear | 36.7" |
| Luggage cap. (cu. ft.) | 10.2 |
| Fuel capacity (gals.) | 19.0 |

## Models Available

| | Style Number | Base MSRP | Change from LY | Shipping Wt. (lbs.) | Production | Change from LY |
|---|---|---|---|---|---|---|
| Javelin 2-Door Hardtop | 70-7079-5 | $2,720 | +8.28% | 2845 | 9,580 | -44.91%* |
| Javelin SST 2-Door Hardtop | 70-7079-7 | $2,848 | +8.17% | 2863 | 20,500 | -11.96%* |
| Javelin SST 2-Door Hardtop** | 70-7079-7 | $3,995 | NEW | 3340 | 100 | NEW |
| TOTALS | | Avg. price $3,188 | +23.90% | | Production 30,180 | -25.81% |

*Estimated production.    **Special "Trans-Am" edition built to meet racing requirements.

# Rebel

*"The space car."*

**Nameplate year of origin:** 1957 (Nash Rambler model).
**Current bodystyle lifespan:** 1967 through 1978 (restyles in 1969, 1971, and 1974).
**Predecessor to this model:** Rambler Classic (1963 to 1966).
**Replacement for this model:** Matador (1971 to 1978).
**Percentage of division's sales volume:** 20.48%.
**Corporate siblings:** Ambassador (shared components from the cowl back).
**Primary competition:** Chevrolet Chevelle, Dodge Coronet, Ford Fairlane, and Plymouth Belvedere/Satellite.
**Notable changes:** Revised rear styling, new grille and trim and detail changes.
**Major standard equipment:** Cloth and vinyl front bench seat, front arm rests, rubber floor mats, hidden compartment (Wagons), Weather-Eye heating & ventilation system, roof-top travel rack (wagons) and E78 × 14 BSW tires. SST adds: Full carpeting, rear arm rests, custom steering wheel, dual horns, lock for glove box and hidden compartment on wagons and full wheel covers. "Machine" adds: All-vinyl bucket seats, power disc brakes, 390 CID V8 engine, 4-speed manual transmission, dual exhausts, and E60 × 15 white-lettered tires.

## Measurements

|  | Cars | Wagons |
|---|---|---|
| Wheelbase | 114.0" | 114.0" |
| Length | 199.0" | 198.0" |
| Width | 77.2" | 77.2" |
| Height | 54.8" | 55.4" |
| Legroom — front | 42.6" | 42.6" |
| Legroom — rear | 38.6" | 38.6" |
| Headroom — front | 39.8" | 39.8" |
| Headroom — rear | 38.0" | 38.0" |
| Luggage cap. (cu. ft.) | 18.2 | 99.1 |
| Fuel capacity (gals.) | 21.5 | 21.5 |

## Models Available

|  | Style Number | Base MSRP | Change from LY | Shipping Wt. (lbs.) | Production | Change from LY |
|---|---|---|---|---|---|---|
| Rebel 2-Door Hardtop | 10-7019-0 | $2,660 | +6.57% | 3148 | 13,000 (6-cyl.)* | * |
| Rebel 4-Door Sedan | 10-7015-0 | $2,626 | +5.72% | 3129 | 2,400 (V8)* | * |
| Rebel 4-Door Wagon | 10-7018-0 | $2,766 | -1.81% | 3356 | 7,100 (6-cyl. Wagons)* | * |
| Rebel SST 2-Door Hardtop | 10-7019-7 | $2,718 | +4.62% | 3206 | 6,300 (6-cyl. SST)* | * |
| Rebel SST 4-Door Sedan | 10-7015-7 | $2,684 | +3.87% | 3155 | 11,800 (V8 SST)* | * |
| Rebel SST 4-Door Wagon | 10-7018-7 | $3,072 | +4.24% | 3375 | 7,100 (V8 Wagons)* | * |
| Rebel "Machine" 2-Door HT | 10-7019-0 | $3,475 | NEW | 3650 | 1,900* | NEW |
| TOTALS | Avg. price $2,857 | | +7.65% | | Production 49,725 | -17.27% |

*Production by body style is not available.     **Differences in percentages due to addition of certain models.*

# Ambassador

*"The classiest."*

**Nameplate year of origin:** 1933 (from top-of-the-line Nash).
**Current bodystyle lifespan:** 1967 through 1978 (Shared basic structure with Matador).
**Predecessor to this model:** Ambassador (1963 to 1966).
**Replacement for this model:** None.
**Percentage of division's sales volume:** 24.26%.
**Corporate siblings:** Rebel (shared components from the cowl back).
**Primary competition:** Chevrolet BelAir/Impala/Caprice, Ford Galaxie/LTD, and Plymouth Fury.
**Notable changes:** Revised rear styling, new grille, and trim and detail changes.
**Major standard equipment:** Cloth and vinyl front bench seat, full carpeting, all-season air conditioning, cargo mat, and F78 × 14 BSW tires. DPL adds: Additional exterior trim, full wheel covers, roof-top travel rack (wagon), deluxe interior trim level, and H78 × 14 BSW tires on wagons. SST adds: All-vinyl reclining seats, center armrest, walnut-grain interior trim, light group, electric clock, and exterior wood grain trim.

## Measurements

|  | Cars | Wagons |
|---|---|---|
| Wheelbase | 122.0" | 122.0" |
| Length | 208.0" | 207.0" |
| Width | 77.2" | 77.2" |
| Height | 54.5" | 54.5" |
| Legroom — front | 42.6" | 42.6" |
| Legroom — rear | 38.6" | 38.6" |
| Headroom — front | 39.8" | 39.8" |
| Headroom — rear | 38.0" | 38.0" |
| Luggage cap. (cu. ft.) | 18.2 | 99.1 |
| Fuel capacity (gals.) | 21.5 | 19.0 |

## Models Available

| | Style Number | Base MSRP | Change from LY | Shipping Wt. (lbs.) | Production | Change from LY |
|---|---|---|---|---|---|---|
| Ambassador 4-Door Sedan | 80-7085-2 | $3,020 | +3.64% | 3328 | 9,600 | -34.3% |
| Ambassador DPL 2-Door Hardtop | 80-7089-5 | $3,605 | +13.29% | 3555 | 8,400 (DPL)* | * |
| Ambassador DPL 4-Door Sedan | 80-7085-5 | $3,588 | +13.36% | 3523 | * | * |
| Ambassador DPL 4-Door Wagon | 80-7088-5 | $3,946 | +12.61% | 3817 | 1,000 (6-cyl. Wagon)* | * |
| Ambassador SST 2-Door HT | 80-7089-7 | $3,739 | +3.23% | 3606 | 27,900 (SST)* | * |
| Ambassador SST 4-Door Sdn. | 80-7085-7 | $3,722 | +3.25% | 3557 | * | * |
| Ambassador SST 4-Door Wgn. | 80-7088-7 | $4,122 | +3.10% | 3852 | 13,000 (V8 Wagon)* | * |
| TOTALS | Avg. price | $3,677 | +7.30% | | Production* 58,900 | -22.69% |

*Estimated model year production shown. Breakdown by model/body style is not available.*

# BUICK

*"Now wouldn't you really rather have a 1970 Buick?"*

Mid-size Skylark models underwent a major facelift this year, bringing with it a more sporting flair. Nearly all sheetmetal was new on the 1970 models though the cars retained a traditional Buick look. The long-running sweepspear design motif was no longer used on the intermediate Buicks, and the fender-side venti-ports were removed a year earlier. It appeared that Buick wanted to change its image, at least in the mid-size market, where sport tended to sell better than luxury. The entry-level Special Deluxe model was no longer around, but the name Special would turn up again in the mid-seventies on a low-priced Century coupe. A Skylark 350 line was introduced, which was essentially the base Skylark with a 350 CID V8 engine as standard equipment. New for the mid-size GS line was a GSX option package with a 350-hp, 455 CID V8, spoilers and performance upgrades. The final model change resulted from the introduction of the full-size Estate Wagon. Prior to 1970, the SportWagon had been a stretched (121-inch wheelbase) Special Deluxe wagon with Skylark trim, sharing the Oldsmobile Vista-Cruiser glass roof treatment and larger cargo capacity. For 1970, with a big wagon in the lineup, the Sportwagon became a Skylark trimmed 116-inch wheelbase wagon, effectively replacing the former Special Deluxe model.

In the full-size Buick line, changes were minimal, with new grilles and trim arrangements. The all-new Estate Wagon became an immediate hit in the luxury wagon market. Based upon the full-size GM wagon body it carried Electra-style front end styling and interior trim and equipment. Also new this year was the LeSabre Custom 455, which replaced the base Wildcat line, perhaps signaling that the Wildcat would be discontinued soon. The new 455 model was powered by the all-new Buick 455 CID V8 engine, which was also used in the Estate Wagon, Wildcat, Electra and Riviera models. This new engine was more powerful than its predecessor. At the top of the Buick line was the sporty Riviera, which received a facelift with new exposed headlamps, set at each end of a vertical bar grille. At the back of the car was a new bumper/taillight design.

**1970**

Electra 225 Custom Limited 4-Door Hardtop

Estate Wagon 4-Door

GS 455 2-Door Convertible

LeSabre Custom 4-Door Hardtop

Riviera 2-Door Hardtop

Skylark 4-Door Sedan

Skylark Custom 2-Door Hardtop

Sportwagon 4-Door Wagon

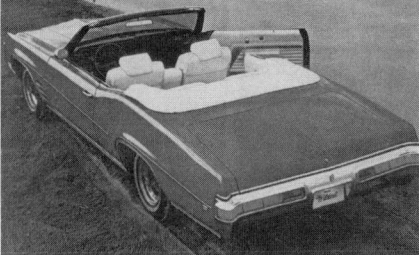

Wildcat Custom 2-Door Convertible

**Model year production:** 666,561, up 0.26% from 1969.
**Domestic market share:** 8.01% (5th place).
**Base price range:** $2,685 to $4,854.
**Industry average base price:** $3,538.
**Buick average base price:** $3,750.
**Introduction date:** September 1969.
**Assembly plants:** Southgate, CA (C); Atlanta, GA (D); Flint, MI (H); Kansas City, MO (K); Fairfax, KS (X); Wilmington, DE (Y); Fremont, CA (Z); and Oshawa, Ontario, (1).

**Data plate identification:** Thirteen digit code read as follows: five digit style number in which 4 = Buick, 2nd number identifies series (3 is Skylark, 8 is Electra, etc.), 3rd through 5th digits indicate model number; 0 = 1970; assembly plant code; 100001 and up for serial number. *Example:* 452370X100001 is a 1970 Buick LeSabre 2-Door Hardtop, serial number 100001, built in Fairfax, KS

## Powertrains

| Engine | Gross HP | Transmission Availability | Skylark | GS | LeS. & Cust. | LeS. C. 455/Wildcat/ Estate Wgn./Elec./Riv. |
|---|---|---|---|---|---|---|
| 250 CID, 2-bbl., 6-cyl. | 155 | 3-speed manual | S[1] | - | - | - |
| | | Turbo Hydra-matic | $195[1] | - | - | - |
| 350 CID, 2-bbl., V8 | 260 | 3-speed manual | $111[1]/S[2] | - | S | - |
| | | Turbo Hydra-matic | $317[1]/$206[2] | - | $206 | - |
| 350 CID, 4-bbl., V8 | 285 (315 dual exh.) | 3-speed manual | $158[1]/$47[2] | S (GS) | - | - |
| | | 4-speed manual | - | $185 (GS) | - | - |
| | | Turbo Hydra-matic | $364[1]/$253[2] | $227 (GS) | $253 | - |
| 455 CID, 4-bbl., V8 | 370 (GS 350) (Stage I 360) | 3-speed manual | - | S (GS 455) | - | S (LeS. Custom 455/ Wildcat/Estate Wagon) |
| | | 4-speed manual | - | $185 (GS 455) | - | - |
| | | Turbo Hydra-matic | - | $227 (GS 455) | - | S (Electra/Riviera)/ $227 (Others) |

[1]*Base Skylark only.*    [2]*All but base Skylark.*

## Major Options

| | Skylark | LeSabre | Wildcat | Estate Wagon | Electra 225 | Riviera |
|---|---|---|---|---|---|---|
| Air conditioning — manual | $376 | $421 | $421 | $421 | $421 | $421 |
| Air conditioning — automatic | - | $500 | $500 | $500 | $500 | $500 |
| Electronic cruise control | $58 | $63 | $63 | $63 | $63 | $63 |
| Soft Ray tinted glass | $39 | $44 | $44 | $44 | $44 | $47 |
| Deck lid remote release | $14 | $14 | $14 | - | $14 | $14 |
| Power steering — variable-ratio | $105 | $116 | $116 | $116 | S | S |
| Power brakes — front disc | $64 | $79 | $79 | $79 | S | S |
| Power door locks | $45–$70 | $45–$70 | $45–$70 | $70 | $45–$70 | $45 |
| Power driver's seat/Bench seat, 4-way | $74 (ex. 6-cyl.) | $74 | $74 | $74 | $47–$74 | $74 |
| Power windows (except on 6-cyl.) | $105 | $110 | $110 | $110 | $110* | $110 |
| AM radio | $70 | $88 | $88 | $88 | $88 | $88 |
| AM/FM stereo (not stereo in Skylark) | $134 | $239 | $239 | $239 | $239 | $239 |
| Front bucket seats | $ | - | - | - | - | $ |
| Tilt steering wheel | $45 | $45 | $45 | $45 | $45 | S |
| Vinyl roof | $102 | $123 | S | $142 | $139 | $128 |
| Wheel trim covers (deluxe on Electra) | $21 | $21 (base) | S | $21 | S | S |
| Limited package | - | - | - | - | $318 | - |
| Skylark Stage I Option and Riviera GS — performance and suspension upgrades | $200 | - | - | - | - | $132 |
| GSX package (GS models) | $1196 | - | - | - | - | - |

Options common to most models. (- = Not Available; S = Standard equipment.) Items may be standard equipment, optional at different pricing, or unavailable on certain models. This chart is only a guide.

*Standard on Convertible.*

## Paint Colors

| | Code | Skylark | LeSabre/Cent/EW/Electra | Riviera |
|---|---|---|---|---|
| Arctic White | 11 | x | x | x |
| Platinum Mist | 13 | x | x | x |
| Tealmist Gray Met. | 16 | x | x | x |
| Regal Black | 19 | x | x | |
| Cascade Blue Met. | 24 | x | x | |
| Stratomist Blue Met. | 26 | x | x | x |
| Nocturne Blue Met. | 29 | | x | x |
| Twilight Turquoise Met. | 39 | x | x | |
| Silver Fern Met. | 41 | x | x | |
| Willowmist Green | 42 | x | x | |
| Lime Mist Met. | 43 | x | x | |
| Verdemist Green Met. | 49 | | | x |
| Bamboo Cream | 50 | | x | x |
| Cortez Gold Met. | 53 | x | | |
| Cornet Gold Met. | 55 | | x | x |
| Sandpiper Beige | 61 | x | x | x |
| Bittersweet Mist Met. | 62 | x | x | x |
| Copper Mist Met. | 65 | | | x |
| Burnished Cinnamon Met. | 67 | x | x | |
| Deep Chestnut Met. | 68 | | | x |
| Pearl Beige Met. | 70 | | | x |
| Sunset Mist Met. | 73 | | | x |
| Vintage Red Met. | 74 | | | x |
| Fire Red | 75 | x | x | |
| Rosewood Met. | 78 | | x | x |

# Skylark

*"Featuring automobiles to light your fire."*

**Nameplate year of origin:** 1953 (Skylark); 1964 (Sportwagon)
**Current bodystyle lifespan:** 1968 through 1972.
**Predecessor to this model:** Special/Skylark (1964 to 1967).
**Corporate siblings:** Chevrolet Chevelle, Pontiac LeMans, Oldsmobile Cutlass.
**Replacement for this model:** Century (1973 to 1977).
**Percentage of division's sales volume:** 33.97%.
**Primary competition:** Dodge Coronet, and Mercury Montego.
**Notable changes:** Revised grille, hood and bumper designs. Also revised trim and detail changes.
**Major standard equipment:** Kimball cloth and vinyl bench seat, front ash tray, heater and defroster, Magic-Mirror finish paint, self adjusting brakes, and G78 × 14 BSW tires. Skylark 350 adds: Kirkland cloth and vinyl deluxe seats, rear ash trays, front door operated interior lighting, wheel opening moldings, dual horns, "350" emblems. Custom adds: Cloth and vinyl bench seat (all-vinyl on convertible), deluxe steering wheel, unique eggcrate-style grille. Sportwagon adds: Dual-action tailgate and H78 × 14 BSW tires. GS adds: Dual exhausts, functional hood air scoops, Heavy duty springs, shocks and stabilizer bar.

## Measurements

|  | 2-Doors | 4-Doors | Sportwagon |
|---|---|---|---|
| Wheelbase | 112.0" | 116.0" | 116.0" |
| Length | 202.2" | 206.2" | 212.6" |
| Width | 77.3" | 77.3" | 77.3" |
| Height | 53.4" | 54.1" | 57.0" |
| Legroom — front | 41.7" | 41.7" | 41.5" |
| Legroom — rear | 32.2" | 34.8" | 34.6" |
| Headroom — front | 37.5" | 38.3" | 38.4" |
| Headroom — rear | 36.3" | 37.3" | 38.3" |
| Luggage capacity (cu. ft.) | NA | NA | NA |
| Fuel capacity (gals.) | 20.0 | 20.0 | 20.0 |

## Models Available

| | Style Number | Base MSRP | Change from LY | Shipping Wt. (lbs.) | Production | Change from LY |
|---|---|---|---|---|---|---|
| Skylark 2-Door Coupe | 43327 | $2,685 | +4.80% | 3155 | 18,620 | +21.95% |
| Skylark 4-Door Sedan | 43369 | $2,736 | +4.71% | 3214 | 13,420 | +20.76% |
| Skylark 350 2-Door Hardtop | 43537 | $2,859 | +4.50% | 3180 | 70,918 | +83.45% |
| Skylark 350 4-Door Sedan | 43569 | $2,838 | +4.53% | 3223 | 30,281 | +35.49% |
| Skylark Custom 2-Door Hardtop | 44437 | $3,132 | +4.09% | 3435 | 36,367 | +2.04% |
| Skylark Custom 2-Door Convertible | 44467 | $3,275 | +3.90% | 3499 | 4,954 | -24.39% |
| Skylark Custom 4-Door Sedan | 44469 | $3,101 | +4.13% | 3499 | 7,113 | +10.74% |
| Skylark Custom 4-Door Hardtop | 44439 | $3,220 | +2.19% | 3565 | 12,411 | +29.16% |
| Sportwagon 4-Door, 2-Seat Wagon | 43435 | $3,210 | +3.82% | 3775 | 2,239 | -13.55% |
| Sportwagon 4-Door, 3-Seat Wagon | 43436 | $3,242 | +3.78% | 3898 | 10,002 | +49.80% |
| GS 2-Door Hardtop Sport Coupe | 43437 | $3,098 | +3.96% | 3434 | 9,948 | +101.66% |
| GS 455 2-Door Hardtop | 44637 | $3,283 | +3.21% | 3562 | 8,732 | +37.38% |
| GS 455 2-Door Convertible | 44667 | $3,469 | +4.33% | 3619 | 1,416 | +20.41% |
| TOTALS | | *Avg. price* $3,088 | +3.94% | | *Production* 226,421 | +35.30% |

# LeSabre

*"See those wide open spaces on a family budget."*

**Nameplate year of origin:** 1959.
**Current bodystyle lifespan:** 1969 through 1970.
**Predecessor to this model:** LeSabre (1967 to 1968).
**Corporate siblings:** Chevrolet Full-size, Pontiac Full-size, Oldsmobile Delta 88.
**Replacement for this model:** LeSabre (1971 to 1976).

## Measurements

| | |
|---|---|
| Wheelbase | 124.0" |
| Length | 220.2" |
| Width | 80.0" |
| Height | 55.3" |

Percentage of division's sales volume: 30.10%.
Primary competition: Chrysler Newport, Dodge Monaco, and Mercury Monterey.
Notable changes: Trim and detail changes.
Major standard equipment: Cloth and vinyl front bench seat, glove box light, full carpeting, front and rear armrests, Magic-Mirror finish, AccuDrive suspension, and H78 × 15 BSW tires. Custom adds: Custom interior trim (all vinyl on Convertible), deluxe steering wheel, wheel opening moldings, "Custom" nameplates, and additional exterior trim moldings.

## Measurements (cont.)

| | |
|---|---|
| Legroom — front | 42.3" |
| Legroom — rear | 37.9" |
| Headroom — front | 39.1" |
| Headroom — rear | 37.7" |
| Luggage capacity (cu. ft.) | NA |
| Fuel capacity (gals.) | 25.0 |

## Models Available

| | Style Number | Base MSRP | Change from LY | Shipping Wt. (lbs.) | Production | Change from LY |
|---|---|---|---|---|---|---|
| LeSabre 2-Door Hardtop | 45237 | $3,535 | +7.19% | 3893 | 14,163 | -12.58% |
| LeSabre 4-Door Sedan | 45269 | $3,453 | +7.37% | 3997 | 35,404 | -3.44% |
| LeSabre 4-Door Hardtop | 45239 | $3,593 | +7.06% | 4045 | 14,817 | -14.03% |
| LeSabre Custom 2-Door Hardtop | 45437 | $3,623 | +7.00% | 3948 | 35,641 | -8.35% |
| LeSabre Custom 2-Door Convertible | 45467 | $3,816 | +6.62% | 3974 | 2,487 | -31.30% |
| LeSabre Custom 4-Door Sedan | 45469 | $3,547 | +7.16% | 3977 | 36,682 | -1.22% |
| LeSabre Custom 4-Door Hardtop | 45439 | $3,687 | +6.87% | 4015 | 43,863 | -8.85% |
| LeSabre Custom 455 2-Door HT | 46437 | $3,833 | +6.59%* | 4102 | 5,469 | -55.95%* |
| LeSabre Custom 455 4-Door Sedan | 46469 | $3,757 | +7.62%* | 4153 | 5,555 | -57.68%* |
| LeSabre Custom 455 4-Door HT | 46439 | $3,897 | +6.74%* | 4179 | 6,541 | -52.62%* |
| TOTALS | Avg. price | $3,674 | +8.99% | Production | 200,622 | +1.39% |

*Comparison made to 1969 Wildcat which the LeSabre Custom 455 replaced.

# Wildcat

*"It's everything the name implies."*

Nameplate year of origin: 1962.
Current bodystyle lifespan: 1969 through 1970.
Predecessor to this model: Wildcat (1967 to 1968).
Corporate siblings: Chevrolet Full-size, Pontiac Full-size, Oldsmobile Delta 88.
Replacement for this model: Centurion (1971 to 1973).
Percentage of division's sales volume: 3.55%.
Primary competition: Chrysler 300, Dodge Monaco, and Mercury Monterey Custom.
Notable changes: Trim and detail changes.
Major standard equipment: All-vinyl front bench seat, glove box light, full carpeting, front and rear armrests, deluxe steering wheel, Magic-Mirror finish, rocker panel and wheel opening moldings, AccuDrive suspension, and H78 × 15 BSW tires.

## Measurements

| | |
|---|---|
| Wheelbase | 124.0" |
| Length | 220.2" |
| Width | 80.0" |
| Height | 55.3" |
| Legroom — front | 42.2" |
| Legroom — rear | 37.9" |
| Headroom — front | 38.9" |
| Headroom — rear | 37.7" |
| Luggage capacity (cu. ft.) | NA |
| Fuel capacity (gals.) | 25.0 |

## Models Available

| | Style Number | Base MSRP | Change from LY | Shipping Wt. (lbs.) | Production | Change from LY |
|---|---|---|---|---|---|---|
| Wildcat Custom 2-Door Hardtop | 46637 | $4,107 | +7.60% | 4135 | 9,477 | -21.91% |
| Wildcat Custom 2-Door Convertible | 46667 | $4,237 | +7.32% | 4250 | 1,244 | -47.60% |
| Wildcat Custom 4-Door Hardtop | 46639 | $4,155 | +7.48% | 4223 | 12,924 | -4.94% |
| TOTALS | Avg. price | $4,166 | +11.75% | Production | 23,645 | -64.95% |

# Estate Wagon

*"Presenting the totally-new 1970 Buick Estate Wagon."*

**Nameplate year of origin:** 1940 (as a designation for station wagon).
**Current bodystyle lifespan:** 1970.
**Predecessor to this model:** SportWagon (1968 to 1969).
**Corporate siblings:** Chevrolet Full-size, Oldsmobile Custom Cruiser, Pontiac Safari.
**Replacement for this model:** Estate Wagon (1971 to 1976).
**Percentage of division's sales volume:** 4.25%.
**Primary competition:** Chrysler Town & Country, and Mercury Colony Park.
**Notable changes:** All-new model for 1970.
**Major standard equipment:** All-vinyl bench seat, full carpeting, AccuDrive suspension system, bright rocker panel moldings, Electra-style grille, power tailgate window, and L78 × 15 BSW tires.

## Measurements

| | |
|---|---|
| Wheelbase | 124.0" |
| Length | 223.3" |
| Width | 80.0" |
| Height | 57.1" |
| Legroom — front | 41.3" |
| Legroom — rear | 38.2" |
| Headroom — front | 39.2" |
| Headroom — rear | 39.0" |
| Luggage capacity (cu. ft.) | NA |
| Fuel capacity (gals.) | 24.0 |

## Models Available

| | Style Number | Base MSRP | Change from LY | Shipping Wt. (lbs.) | Production | Change from LY |
|---|---|---|---|---|---|---|
| Estate Wagon 4-Dr., 2-S. Wagon | 46036 | $4,081 | NEW | 4727 | 11,427 | NEW |
| Estate Wagon 4-Dr., 3-S. Wagon | 46046 | $4,226 | NEW | 4815 | 16,879 | NEW |
| TOTALS | | Avg. price $4,154 | NEW | Production 28,306 | | NEW |

# Electra 225

*"If you're going to invest your money in a luxury automobile you deserve nothing less than this."*

**Nameplate year of origin:** 1959.
**Current bodystyle lifespan:** 1969 through 1970.
**Predecessor to this model:** Electra 225 (1967 to 1968).
**Corporate siblings:** Cadillac Calais/de Ville, Oldsmobile Ninety-Eight.
**Replacement for this model:** Electra (1971 to 1976).
**Percentage of division's sales volume:** 22.53%.
**Primary competition:** Chrysler New Yorker, and Mercury Marquis.
**Notable changes:** Trim and detail changes.
**Major standard equipment:** Cloth and vinyl front bench seat, deep-pile carpeting, remote control outside rear view mirror, variable ratio power steering, power front disc brakes, AccuDrive suspension system, Turbo Hydra-matic transmission, cross-hatch style grille, bright rocker panel molding and wheel opening moldings, rear fender skirts, J78 × 15 BSW tires. Custom adds: Notchback seat with front and rear center armrest. Limited package adds: Keswick cloth and vinyl upholstery, Limited script badges.

## Measurements

| | |
|---|---|
| Wheelbase | 127.0" |
| Length | 225.8" |
| Width | 80.0" |
| Height | 55.0" |
| Legroom — front | 42.2" |
| Legroom — rear | 37.8" |
| Headroom — front | 38.5" |
| Headroom — rear | 38.0" |
| Luggage capacity (cu. ft.) | NA |
| Fuel capacity (gals.) | 25.0 |

## Models Available

| | Style Number | Base MSRP | Change from LY | Shipping Wt. (lbs.) | Production | Change from LY |
|---|---|---|---|---|---|---|
| Electra 225 2-Door Hardtop | 48257 | $4,482 | +3.68% | 4214 | 12,013 | -8.49% |
| Electra 225 4-Door Sedan | 48269 | $4,461 | +3.70% | 4274 | 12,580 | -13.37% |

| | Style Number | Base MSRP | Change from LY | Shipping Wt. (lbs.) | Production | Change from LY |
|---|---|---|---|---|---|---|
| Electra 225 4-Door Hardtop | 48239 | $4,592 | +3.61% | 4296 | 14,338 | -10.29% |
| Electra 225 Custom 2-Door HT | 48457 | $4,661 | +3.53% | 4297 | 26,002 | -3.76% |
| Electra 225 Custom 2-Door Conv. | 48467 | $4,802 | +3.42% | 4341 | 6,045 | -27.12% |
| Electra 225 Custom 4-Door Sedan | 48469 | $4,677 | +3.54% | 4283 | 14,109 | -2.25% |
| Electra 225 Custom 4-Door HT | 48439 | $4,771 | +3.47% | 4385 | 65,114 | -0.19% |
| TOTALS | | *Avg. price* $4,635 | +3.55% | *Production* | 150,201 | -5.31% |

# Riviera

*"When you change a classic automobile,*
*you'd better change it for the better. We did."*

**Nameplate year of origin:** 1949 (for 2-Dr. HT); 1963 (series).
**Current bodystyle lifespan:** 1966 through 1970.
**Predecessor to this model:** Riviera (1963 to 1965).
**Corporate siblings:** Cadillac Eldorado and Oldsmobile Toronado.
**Replacement for this model:** Riviera (1971 to 1976).
**Percentage of division's sales volume:** 5.61%.
**Primary competition:** Ford Thunderbird and Lincoln Continental Mark III.
**Notable changes:** Major facelift, with new grille, bodysides and rear styling.
**Major standard equipment:** All vinyl bench seat, tilt steering wheel, vinyl body side moldings, remote control outside rear view mirror, variable ratio power steering, power front disc brakes, dual exhaust system, Turbo Hydramatic transmission, and H78 × 15 BSW tires.

## Measurements

| | |
|---|---|
| Wheelbase | 119.0" |
| Length | 215.5" |
| Width | 79.3" |
| Height | 53.6" |
| Legroom — front | 41.2" |
| Legroom — rear | 36.6" |
| Headroom — front | 37.7" |
| Headroom — rear | 37.5" |
| Luggage capacity (cu. ft.) | NA |
| Fuel capacity (gals.) | 21.0 |

## Models Available

| | Style Number | Base MSRP | Change from LY | Shipping Wt. (lbs.) | Production | Change from LY |
|---|---|---|---|---|---|---|
| Riviera 2-Door Hardtop | 49487 | $4,854 | +3.25% | 4216 | 37,366 | -29.33% |
| TOTALS | | *Avg. price* $4,854 | +3.25% | *Production* | 37,366 | -29.33% |

# CADILLAC

*"The Spirit of the Seventies."*

Outside of a new grille and a few trim changes, it was difficult to distinguish any 1970 Cadillac model from its predecessors. The main excitement was generated by the all-new 8.2 liter, 500 CID V8 engine introduced as standard equipment on the Eldorado. This huge V8 produced 400 horsepower, and 550 lb.-ft. torque. It was the largest production engine available in the world. As for other Cadillacs, some models benefited from additional standard equipment. No changes were made to the model lineup. Cadillac actually outsold Chrysler this year for the first time in five years. Despite any real improvements in the product, Cadillac managed to have a record setting run for model-year production. The lack of change was due to the fact that all-new Cadillacs, in every series, were arriving for the 1971 model year.

1970

Calais 2-Door Hardtop

de Ville 2-Door Convertible

Eldorado 2-Door Hardtop and
Sedan de Ville 4-Door Hardtop

Fleetwood Brougham 4-Door Sedan

**Model year production:** 236,239, up 7.05% from 1969.
**Domestic market share:** 2.84% (10th place).
**Base price range:** $5,637 to $11,178.
**Industry average base price:** $3,538.
**Cadillac average base price:** $7,181.
**Introduction date:** September 18, 1969.
**Assembly plants:** Detroit, MI (Q), and Linden, NJ (E).
**Data plate identification:** Thirteen digit code read as follows:

Five digit style number in which 6 = Cadillac, 2nd and 3rd digits identify series (e.g., 82 is Calais), 4th and 5th digits indicate body style number (2nd through 5th digits of VIN make up 2nd through 5th digits of body style number in listings); 0 for 1970; 7th digit is assembly plant code; 100001 and up for serial number. *Example:* 683470Q100001 is a 1970 Cadillac de Ville 2-Door Hardtop, serial number 100001, built in Detroit, MI.

## Powertrains

| Engine | Gross HP | Transmission Availability | Eldorado | All other models |
|---|---|---|---|---|
| 472 CID, 4-bbl., V8 | 375 | Turbo Hydra-matic | - | S |
| 500 CID, 4-bbl., V8 | 400 | Turbo Hydra-matic | S | - |

## Major Options

| | Eldorado | de Ville/ Calais | 60 Special | Seventy-Five |
|---|---|---|---|---|
| Automatic climate control | $516 | $516 | $516 | S |
| 6-way power seat | $90 | $90 (deV.)/ $116 (Cal.) | $90 | $90 (NA Limo) |
| Power door locks | $68 | $68 | $68 | $116 |
| AM-FM radio | $188 | $188 | $188 | $188 |
| Vinyl roof | $158 | $153 (de Ville only) | S (Brougham) | NA |
| Twilight Sentinel automatic dimmer | $37 | $37 | $37 | $37 |
| Tilt and telescope steering wheel | $95 | $95 | $95 | $95 |
| Leather upholstery | $184 | $158 (de Ville only) | $158 | - |
| Cruise control | $95 | $95 | $95 | $95 |
| Tinted glass | $53 | $53 | $53 | $53 |
| Rear window defogger | $26 | $26 ($36 convertible) | $26 | S |

## Paint Colors

| | Code |
|---|---|
| Cotillion White | 11 |
| Patina Silver Metallic | 14 |
| Phantom Gray Metallic | 18 |
| Sable Black | 19 |
| Corinthian Blue Metallic | 24 |
| Candor Blue Metallic | 29 |
| Adriatic Turquoise Metallic | 34 |
| Lanai Green Metallic | 42 |
| Glenmore Green Metallic | 49 |
| Byzantine Gold Metallic | 54 |
| Bayberry Metallic | 59 |
| Sauterne Metallic | 64 |
| Dark Walnut | 69 |
| San Mateo Red | 74 |
| Monarch Burgundy Metallic | 79 |
| Spartacus Blue Firemist Metallic* | 90 |
| Lucerne Aqua Firemist Metallic* | 93 |
| Regency Gold Firemist Metallic* | 94 |
| Cinnamon Firemist Metallic | 95 |

| | Eldorado | de Ville/ Calais | 60 Special | Seventy-Five |
|---|---|---|---|---|
| Remote control trunk release | $53 | $53 | $53 | $53 |
| Firemist paint colors | $132 | $132 | $132 | $132 |

| | Code |
|---|---|
| Nottingham Green Firemist Metallic* | 96 |
| Briarwood Firemist Metallic | 97 |
| Chateau Mauve Firemist Metallic* | 99 |

*Firemist colors available at extra cost.*

Options common to most models. (- = Not Available; S = Standard equipment.) Items may be standard equipment, optional at different pricing, or unavailable on certain models. This chart is only a guide.

# Calais

*"The most practical way to discover Cadillac luxury and distinction."*

**Nameplate year of origin:** 1965.
**Current bodystyle lifespan:** 1969 through 1970.
**Predecessor to this model:** Calais (1967 to 1968).
**Corporate siblings:** Buick Electra 225 and Oldsmobile Ninety-Eight.
**Replacement for this model:** Calais (1971 to 1976).
**Percentage of division's sales volume:** 4.20%.
**Primary competition:** Chrysler New Yorker and Lincoln Continental.
**Notable changes:** New grille and minor trim and detail changes.
**Major standard equipment:** Dorian cloth and vinyl seat upholstery, front center armrests, rear fender skirts, left side remote control outside rear view mirror, power windows, interior courtesy and warning lights, three-speed windshield wipers and washers, right side visor vanity mirrors, front cornering lamps, variable ratio power steering, power front disc brakes, Turbo Hydra-matic transmission, and L78 × 15 BSW tires.

## Measurements

| | |
|---|---|
| Wheelbase | 129.5" |
| Length | 225.0" |
| Width | 79.8" |
| Height | 54.5" |
| Legroom — front | 41.0" |
| Legroom — rear | 39.7" |
| Headroom — front | 37.8" |
| Headroom — rear | 37.2" |
| Luggage capacity (cu. ft.) | NA |
| Fuel capacity (gals.) | 26.0 |

## Models Available

| | Style Number | Base MSRP | Change from LY | Shipping Wt. (lbs.) | Production | Change from LY |
|---|---|---|---|---|---|---|
| Calais 2-Door Hardtop | 68247 | $5,637 | +2.79% | 4620 | 4,724 | -15.64% |
| Calais 4-Door Hardtop | 68249 | $5,813 | +2.70% | 4680 | 5,187 | -24.00% |
| TOTALS | | *Avg. price* $5,725 | +2.75% | | *Production* 9,911 | -20.23% |

**1970**

# de Ville

*"In all the world, de Ville stands preeminent in popularity among luxury car motorists."*

**Nameplate year of origin:** 1949 (as Hardtop designation); 1959 (series).
**Current bodystyle lifespan:** 1969 through 1970.
**Predecessor to this model:** de Ville (1967 to 1968).
**Corporate siblings:** Buick Electra 225 and Oldsmobile Ninety-Eight.

## Measurements

| | |
|---|---|
| Wheelbase | 129.5" |
| Length | 225.0" |

**Replacement for this model:** de Ville (1971 to 1976).
**Percentage of division's sales volume:** 76.92%.
**Primary competition:** Imperial LeBaron and Lincoln Continental.
**Notable changes:** New grille and minor trim and detail changes.
**Major standard equipment:** Dynasty cloth and vinyl seat upholstery (Sierra grain leather on convertible), two-way power seat adjustment, front and rear center armrests, rear fender skirts, left side remote control outside rear view mirror, power windows, interior door, courtesy and warning lights, three-speed windshield wipers and washers, right side visor vanity mirrors, front cornering lamps, variable ratio power steering, power front disc brakes, Turbo Hydra-matic transmission, and L78 × 15 BSW tires.

## Measurements (cont.)

| | |
|---|---|
| Width | 79.8" |
| Height | 54.5" |
| Legroom — front | 41.0" |
| Legroom — rear | 39.7" |
| Headroom — front | 37.8" |
| Headroom — rear | 37.2" |
| Luggage capacity (cu. ft.) | NA |
| Fuel capacity (gals.) | 26.0 |

## Models Available

| | Style Number | Base MSRP | Change from LY | Shipping Wt. (lbs.) | Production | Change from LY |
|---|---|---|---|---|---|---|
| Coupe de Ville 2-Door Hardtop | 68347 | $5,884 | +2.85% | 4650 | 76,043 | +15.65% |
| de Ville 2-Door Convertible | 68367 | $6,068 | +2.76% | 4660 | 15,172 | -7.74% |
| Sedan de Ville 4-Door Sedan | 68369 | $6,118 | +2.75% | 4690 | 7,230 | -8.37% |
| Sedan de Ville 4-Door Hardtop | 68349 | $6,118 | +2.75% | 4725 | 83,274 | +14.14% |
| TOTALS | | Avg. price $6,047 | +2.77% | | Production 194,811 | +11.45% |

# Eldorado

*"Purposefully built to be the world's finest personal car."*

**Nameplate year of origin:** 1953.
**Current bodystyle lifespan:** 1967 through 1970.
**Predecessor to this model:** Fleetwood Eldorado (1965 to 1966).
**Corporate siblings:** Buick Riviera and Oldsmobile Toronado.
**Replacement for this model:** Eldorado (1971 to 1978).
**Percentage of division's sales volume:** 10.09%.
**Primary competition:** Lincoln Continental Mark III.
**Notable changes:** New 500 CID V8 engine. New grille and minor trim and detail changes.
**Major standard equipment:** Duplex cloth and vinyl seat upholstery, two-way power seat adjustment, front center armrests, left side remote control outside rear view mirror, power windows, interior door, courtesy and warning lights, three-speed windshield wipers and washers, right side visor vanity mirrors, front cornering lamps, variable ratio power steering, power front disc brakes, Turbo Hydra-matic transmission, front wheel drive, and L78 × 15 BSW tires.

## Measurements

| | |
|---|---|
| Wheelbase | 120.0" |
| Length | 221.0" |
| Width | 79.8" |
| Height | 53.3" |
| Legroom — front | 41.1" |
| Legroom — rear | 36.2" |
| Headroom — front | 37.7" |
| Headroom — rear | 37.6" |
| Luggage capacity (cu. ft.) | NA |
| Fuel capacity (gals.) | 24.0 |

## Models Available

| | Style Number | Base MSRP | Change from LY | Shipping Wt. (lbs.) | Production | Change from LY |
|---|---|---|---|---|---|---|
| Fleetwood Eldorado 2-Door HT | 69347 | $6,903 | +2.86% | 4630 | 23,842 | +2.18% |
| TOTALS | | Avg. price $6,903 | +2.86% | | Production 23,842 | +2.18% |

# Fleetwood Brougham & Sixty-Special

*"Expressing the spirit of the seventies with eloquence and style."*

**Nameplate year of origin:** 1938.
**Current bodystyle lifespan:** 1969 through 1970.
**Predecessor to this model:** Fleetwood Sixty-Special (1967 to 1968).
**Corporate siblings:** None.
**Replacement for this model:** Fleetwood Sixty-Special (1971 to 1976).
**Percentage of division's sales volume:** 7.89%.
**Primary competition:** None.
**Notable changes:** Minor trim and detail changes.
**Major standard equipment:** Divan cloth seat upholstery, two-way power seat adjustment, front and rear center armrests, rear fender skirts, left side remote control outside rear view mirror, power windows, interior door, courtesy and warning lights, three-speed windshield wipers and washers, right side visor vanity mirrors, front cornering lamps, variable ratio power steering, power front disc brakes, Turbo Hydra-matic transmission, and L78 × 15 BSW tires. Brougham adds: Driver's side only seat adjustment, reading lights and padded vinyl top.

## Measurements

| | |
|---|---|
| Wheelbase | 133.0" |
| Length | 228.5" |
| Width | 79.8" |
| Height | 56.7" |
| Legroom — front | 42.0" |
| Legroom — rear | 44.4" |
| Headroom — front | 39.1" |
| Headroom — rear | 38.0" |
| Luggage capacity (cu. ft.) | NA |
| Fuel capacity (gals.) | 26.0 |

## Models Available

| | Style Number | Base MSRP | Change from LY | Shipping Wt. (lbs.) | Production | Change from LY |
|---|---|---|---|---|---|---|
| Fleetwood Sixty Special 4-Door Sdn. | 68069 | $6,953 | +2.57% | 4830 | 1,738 | -31.71% |
| Fleetwood Brougham 4-Door Sedan | 68169 | $7,284 | +2.45% | 4835 | 16,913 | -2.24% |
| TOTALS | | *Avg. price* $7,119 | +2.51% | | *Production* 18,651 | -6.02% |

# Fleetwood Seventy-Five

*"Splendor that is unmatched in all of motordom."*

**Nameplate year of origin:** 1927 (Fleetwood bodies), 1936 (75 series).
**Current bodystyle lifespan:** 1969 through 1970.
**Predecessor to this model:** Fleetwood 75 (1967 to 1968).
**Corporate siblings:** None.
**Replacement for this model:** Fleetwood 75 (1971 to 1976).
**Percentage of division's sales volume:** 0.90%.
**Primary competition:** None.
**Notable changes:** Minor trim and detail changes.
**Major standard equipment:** Divan cloth seat upholstery, two-way power seat adjustment, rear center armrests, automatic climate control, rear window defogger, rear fender skirts, left side remote control outside rear view mirror, power windows, interior door, courtesy and warning lights, three-speed windshield wipers and washers, right side visor vanity mirrors, front cornering lamps, fixed ratio power steering, power front disc brakes, Turbo Hydra-matic transmission, and L78 × 15 BSW tires.

## Measurements

| | |
|---|---|
| Wheelbase | 149.8" |
| Length | 245.3" |
| Width | 79.8" |
| Height | 57.0" |
| Legroom — front | 42.0" |
| Legroom — rear | NA |
| Headroom — front | 39.1" |
| Headroom — rear | NA |
| Luggage capacity (cu. ft.) | NA |
| Fuel capacity (gals.) | 26.0 |

## Models Available

| | Style Number | Base MSRP | Change from LY | Shipping Wt. (lbs.) | Production | Change from LY |
|---|---|---|---|---|---|---|
| Fleetwood Seventy-Five 4-Door Sdn. | 69723 | $11,039 | +1.83% | 5530 | 876 | -0.45% |
| Fleetwood Seventy-Five Limousine | 69733 | $11,178 | +1.81% | 5630 | 1,240 | +7.27% |
| TOTALS | | *Avg. price* $11,109 | +1.82% | | *Production* 2,116 | +3.93% |

# CHEVROLET

*"Putting you first, keeps us first."*

The nation's top-selling marque underwent a transitional year in 1970. Long a sore spot for the corporate image, the venerable Corvair was finally laid to rest during the 1969 model year with little public notice. Its replacement, the Vega, would not be available for the public until the 1971 model year. The replacement for the popular Camaro was not available at the beginning of the model year, so the 1969 version was sold as a 1970 until February, when the "real" 1970 Camaro was unveiled. The Chevelle and full-size Chevrolet models received major facelifts, while the Nova (no longer called the Chevy II) and Corvette soldiered on relatively unchanged. The 1970 Nova was the last to be offered with a 4-cylinder engine, as few were being sold.

There was, however, one totally new car. The affordable personal luxury class was virtually created by the all-new Monte Carlo. Basically the Monte Carlo took the concept of a sporty yet semi-luxurious coupe, like the Pontiac Grand Prix, Buick Riviera or earlier Ford Thunderbirds, and brought it into the low-price field. The Monte Carlo shared its roofline and some other components with the Grand Prix, but was based on the 4-Door Chevelle chassis. Most powertrain options were shared with the Chevelle as well. Sales were quite high for its initial year, and the Monte Carlo would become an icon of the seventies personal luxury car.

The other big news would not arrive until February 1970, when the new GM F-body cars debuted: the Camaro and the Pontiac Firebird. This all-new car was based upon the concepts of the original cars, but was much more modern in appearance and overall attractiveness. Its styling was so good that it would survive virtually unchanged through the 1981 model year. From the front, individual headlights were mounted at each side of the front, flanking a large, Ferrari-like grille opening. Depending on model chosen, there was either a full-width bumper or bumper-ettes that extended outward from the grille opening. Eliminating the rear quarter windows and angling the rear window down into a very short rear deck area created a sleek silhouette. At the rear were four round taillights and a slender bumper. Interiors made extensive use of plastic materials. Bench or bucket seating was offered up front, with bucket-style seating in the rear. Powertrains for the new Camaro continued to cover the spectrum, from economy sixes to high-performance V8s. The convertible Camaro was dropped, and this would turn out to be the only generation of Camaro not offered in a convertible model.

Full-size Chevrolet models received their fourth restyling in as many years. While they retained many features from the '69 models (doors, roof, glass in particular), the front and rear styling was totally new. The loop-style bumper of previous years was gone in favor of a more traditional full-width grille with headlights mounted at the extreme ends. At the rear, slot-style vertical tail lamps were inset in the bumper. For the first time since 1952, regular-line Chevrolet models sold fewer than 1 million units. Chevelle models also received a major facelift, with a new twin-grille appearance and body side highlights featuring slight bulges at the wheel openings.

Camaro 2-Door Coupe with Z28 package

Caprice 4-Door Hardtop

Chevelle 2-Door Hardtop with SS396 package

Impala 2-Door Convertible

Kingswood Estate 4-Door Wagon

Malibu 2-Door Convertible

Monte Carlo 2-Door Hardtop

Nova 2-Door Coupe

Corvette 2-Door Coupe

**Model year production:** 2,014,917, down 8.83% from 1969.
**Domestic market share:** 24.20% (1st place).
**Base price range:** $2,176 to $5,192.
**Industry average base price:** $3,538.
**Chevrolet average base price:** $3,199.
**Introduction date:** September 1969.
**Assembly plants:** Lakewood, GA (A), Atlanta, GA (D), Kansas City, MO (K), Fremont, CA (Z), Van Nuys, CA (L), Norwood, OH (N), Tarrytown, NY (T), Oshawa, Ontario, Canada (1), Baltimore, MD (B); Framingham, MA (G); Flint, MI (F); Southgate, CA (C); Arlington, TX (R); Janesville, WI (J); Wilmington, DE (Y), and St. Louis, MO (S).

**Data plate identification:** Thirteen digit code read as follows: five digit style number (see listings below) in which 1 = Chevrolet, 2nd and 3rd numbers identify series, 4th and 5th indicate body style; 0 for 1970; 7th digit is assembly plant code; 100001 and up for serial number. *Example:* 155690T100001 is a 1970 Chevrolet BelAir 4-Door Sedan, serial number 100001, built in Arlington, TX.

## Powertrains

| Engine | Gross HP | Transmission Availability | Nova | '70½ Camaro | Chevelle | Monte Carlo | †Full-size | Corvette |
|---|---|---|---|---|---|---|---|---|
| 153 CID Super-Thrift, 1-bbl., 4-cyl. | 90 | 3-speed manual / Torque-drive | S / $69 | - | - | - | - | - |
| 230 CID Turbo-Thrift, | 140 | 3-speed manual | $78 | - | - | - | - | - |

| Engine | Gross HP | Transmission Availability | Nova | '70½ Camaro | Chevelle | Monte Carlo | †Full-size | Corvette |
|---|---|---|---|---|---|---|---|---|
| 2-bbl., 4-cyl. | | Torque-drive | $147 | - | - | - | - | - |
| | | Powerglide Automatic | $226 | - | - | - | - | - |
| | | Turbo Hydra-matic | $252 | - | - | - | - | - |
| 250 CID Turbo-Thrift, 1-bbl., 6-cyl. | 155 | 3-speed manual | $104 | S | S*** | - | S* | - |
| | | 4-speed manual | - | $195 | - | - | - | - |
| | | Torque-drive | $173 | $69 | - | - | - | - |
| | | Powerglide Automatic | $252 | $164 | $164 | - | $164* | - |
| | | Turbo Hydra-matic | $278 | - | $190 | - | $190 | - |
| 307 CID Turbo-Fire, 2-bbl., V8 | 200 | 3-speed manual | $90 | $90 | S***/$90 (Others) | - | - | - |
| | | 4-speed manual | - | $285 | $185***/ $275 (Others) | - | - | - |
| | | Powerglide Automatic | $268 | $265 | $175***/ $265 (Others) | - | - | - |
| | | Turbo Hydra-matic | $280 | $291 | $201***/ $291 (Others) | - | - | - |
| 350 CID Turbo-Fire, 2-bbl., V8 | 250 | 3-speed manual | $111 | $112 | $21***/ $111 (Others) | S | $111*/S (Others) | |
| | | 4-speed manual | $296 | $307 | $206***/ $296 (Others) | $185 | - | - |
| | | Powerglide Automatic | $289 | $286 | $196***/ $286 (Others) | $174 | $285*/ $174 (Others) | - |
| | | Turbo Hydra-matic | $301 | $312 | $222***/ $312 (Others) | $201 | $312*/ $201 (Others) | - |
| 350 CID Turbo-Fire, 4-bbl., V8 | 300 | 3-speed manual | - | - | - | $47 | - | S (early) |
| | | 4-speed manual | $476 (SS) | $523 (SS)** | $275***/ $365 (Others) | $232 | - | S |
| | | Powerglide Automatic | $450 | - | $264***/ $354 (Others) | $242 | $332*/ $221 (Others) | - |
| | | Turbo Hydra-matic | $481 (SS) | $529 (SS)** | $291***/ $381 (Others) | $269 | $359*/ $242 (Others) | $222 |
| 350 CID Turbo-Jet, 4-bbl., V8 | 350/360 | 4-speed manual | - | $573 (Z28)** | - | - | - | $317 |
| | | Turbo Hydra-matic | - | - | - | - | - | $354 |
| 350 CID Turbo-Jet, 4-bbl., V8 | 370 | 4-speed manual | - | - | - | - | - | $ |
| 396 CID Turbo-Jet, 8 4-bbl., V | 350 | 4-speed manual | - | $348 | $690 (SS) | - | - | - |
| | | Turbo Hydra-matic | - | - | $727 (SS) | - | - | - |
| 396 CID Turbo-Jet, 4-bbl., V8 | 375 | 4-speed manual | - | $581 | - | - | - | - |
| 400 CID Turbo-Jet, 4-bbl., V8 | 330 | 4-speed manual | - | - | $347***/$437 (Others) | $325 | - | - |
| | | Turbo Hydra-matic | - | - | $407***/$497 (Others) | $363 | - | - |
| 400 CID Turbo-Fire, 2-bbl., V8 | 265 | Turbo Hydra-matic | - | - | - | - | $396*/$285 (Others) | - |
| 400 CID Turbo-Jet, 4-bbl., V8 | 345 | Turbo Hydra-matic | - | - | - | - | $502*/$391 (Others) | - |
| 454 CID Turbo-Jet, 4-bbl., V8 | 360 | Turbo Hydra-matic | - | - | - | $642 (SS) | - | - |

| Engine | Gross HP | Transmission Availability | Nova | '70½ Camaro | Chevelle | Monte Carlo | †Full-size | Corvette |
|---|---|---|---|---|---|---|---|---|
| 454 CID Turbo-Jet, 4-bbl., V8 | 390 | 4-speed manual | - | - | - | - | - | $406 |
| (427 CID on early Corvettes) | | Turbo Hydra-matic | - | - | - | - | $575*/$464 (Others) | $443 |
| 454 CID Turbo-Jet, 4-bbl., V8 | 450/460 | 4-speed manual | - | - | $538 (SS only)** | - | - | $622 |
| (427 CID on early Corvettes; 435 hp) | | Turbo Hydra-matic | - | - | $585 (SS only)** | - | - | $659 |

*Biscayne, BelAir, and Impala 2-Dr. HT and 4-Door Sedan only.   **Optional SS equipment packages required/included on Camaro.   ***Greenbrier and Concours 2-Seat models and all Concours Estate wagons only.   †See text for corresponding wagon models.

## Major Options

| | Nova | Camaro | Chevelle | Monte Carlo | Full-size | Corvette |
|---|---|---|---|---|---|---|
| Air conditioning | $363 | $380 | $376 | $376 | $384* | $429 |
| Soft Ray tinted glass | $33 | $33 | $43 | $42 | $42 | $17 |
| Power steering — variable-ratio | $90 | $95 | $105 | $105 | $100–$105 | $105 |
| Power brakes | $42 | $42 | $42 | S | S/$64 | $42 |
| Power door locks | - | - | - | $45 | $45–$69 | - |
| Power driver's seat/Bench seat | - | - | - | $74 | $100 (ex. Bisc.) | - |
| Power windows | - | $105 | $105 | $105 | $105 (ex. Bisc.) | $63 |
| AM radio | $61 | $61 | $61 | $61 | $61 | - |
| AM/FM stereo | $239 | $239 | $239 | $239 | $239 | $278 |
| Front seat console | $54 | $59 | $54 | $54 | - | S |
| Front bucket seats | $ | S | $ | $ | - | S |
| Tilt steering wheel | - | $45 | $45 | $45 | $45 | $84 |
| Vinyl roof | $84 | $84 | $95 | $126 | $105 | $ (Conv. w/HT) |
| Rally wheels | $79 | $36 | $36 | $36 | $21–$36 | S |
| SS package (Rally Sport also on Camaro) | $328 | $314 (RS $179) | $357–$503 | $485 | - | - |

Options common to most models. (- = Not Available; S = Standard equipment.) Items may be standard equipment, optional at different pricing, or unavailable on certain models. This chart is only a guide.

*Not available with 6-cylinder engine..

## Paint Colors

| | Code | Corvette | Other Models |
|---|---|---|---|
| Classic White | 10 | x | x |
| Cortez Silver Met. | 14 | x | x |
| Laguna Gray Metallic | 15 | x | |
| Shadow Gray Met. | 17 | | x |
| Tuxedo Black | 19 | x | x |
| Astro Blue Metallic | 25 | | x |
| Mulsanne Blue Met. | 26 | x | x |
| Bridgehampton Blue | 27 | x | |
| Fathom Blue Met. | 28 | x | x |
| Misty Turquoise Met. | 34 | | x |
| Citrus Green Metallic | 43 | | x |
| Donnybrook Green | 44 | x | |
| Green Mist Met. | 45 | | x |
| Forest Green Met. | 48 | | x |
| Gobi Beige | 50 | | x |
| Daytona Yellow | 51 | x | x |
| Sunflower Yellow | 52 | | x |
| Camaro Gold Metallic | 53 | | x |

1970

|  | Code | Corvette | Other Models |
|---|---|---|---|
| Champagne Gold Metallic | 55 |  | x |
| Autumn Gold Met. | 58 |  | x |
| Corvette Bronze Met. | 62 | x |  |
| Desert Sand Metallic | 63 |  | x |
| Hugger Orange | 65 |  | x |
| Classic Copper Met. | 67 |  | x |
| Monza Red | 72 | x |  |
| Cranberry Red | 75 |  | x |
| Marlboro Maroon Met. | 77 | x |  |
| Rosewood Metallic | 78 |  | x |

# Camaro

*"A most unusual car from the place
you'd expect: Chevrolet's Sports Department."*

**Nameplate year of origin:** 1967.
**Current bodystyle lifespan:** 1970 through 1981.
**Predecessor to this model:** Camaro (1967 to 1969).
**Corporate siblings:** Pontiac Firebird.
**Replacement for this model:** Camaro (1982 to 1992).
**Percentage of division's sales volume:** 5.84%.
**Primary competition:** AMC Javelin, Dodge Challenger, Ford Mustang, and Plymouth Barracuda.
**Notable changes:** Completely restyled and redesigned.
**Major standard equipment:** All-vinyl deep-contour front bucket seats with bucket-styled rear seats, wraparound instrumentation, deep-twist color-keyed carpeting, Astro ventilation, hubcaps, four-spoke steering wheel, front disc/rear drum brakes, and E78 × 14 BSW tires. Optional RS package adds: Unique grid pattern grille (black with argent accents) with split front bumper, parking lights next to headlights, and Rally Sport identification. SS adds: Special SS grille and identification, power brakes, heavy duty clutch, suspension and radiator, hood insulation, dual exhausts, 350 CID V8 engine, remote-control sport mirror, and F70 × 14 White-letter tires. Z28 adds: RS-style blacked-out grille, Z28 identification, Positraction rear end, remote left hand/manual right hand outside sport mirrors, special suspension components, special instrumentation, F60 × 15 white-letter tires, and trim rings.

## Measurements

| | |
|---|---|
| Wheelbase | 108.0" |
| Length | 188.0" |
| Width | 74.4" |
| Height | 49.1" |
| Legroom — front | 43.8" |
| Legroom — rear | 30.7" |
| Headroom — front | 37.4" |
| Headroom — rear | 36.1" |
| Cargo capacity (cu. ft.) | 6.4 |
| Fuel capacity (gals.) | 18.0 |

## Models Available

|  | Style Number | Base MSRP | Change from LY | Shipping Wt. (lbs.) | Production | Change from LY |
|---|---|---|---|---|---|---|
| Camaro 2-Door Sport Coupe | 12387 | $2,749 | +4.21% | 3058 | 117,604 | -45.12% |
| TOTALS |  | *Avg. price* $2,749 | +0.15% | *Production* | 117,604 | -49.04% |

*RS package: Add $188 to base V8 car (see powertrain chart); 27,136 produced. SS package: Add $290 to base V8 car (see powertrain chart); 12,476 produced. Z/28 package: Add $573 to base V8 car (see powertrain chart); 8,733 produced.*

# Nova

*"Have it your way."*

**Nameplate year of origin:** 1962.
**Current bodystyle lifespan:** 1968 through 1972.
**Predecessor to this model:** Chevy II (1966 to 1967).
**Replacement for this model:** Nova (1973 through 1979, with restyle in 1975).
**Percentage of division's sales volume:** 15.64%.
**Corporate siblings:** None.
**Primary competition:** AMC Hornet, Dodge Dart, Ford Falcon & Maverick, and Plymouth Valiant.
**Notable changes:** Refinements.
**Major standard equipment:** Cloth and vinyl bench seat, vinyl-coated rubber floor coverings, deluxe steering wheel, hubcaps, front-door vent windows, bright moldings on windshield and rear window, manual drum brakes, E78-14 BSW tires.

## Measurements

| | |
|---|---|
| Wheelbase | 111.0" |
| Length | 189.4" |
| Width | 72.4" |
| Height | 53.9" |
| Legroom — front | 41.0" |
| Legroom — rear | 32.6" |
| Headroom — front | 37.6" |
| Headroom — rear | 36.6" |
| Cargo capacity (cu. ft.) | 13.7 |
| Fuel capacity (gals.) | 18.0 |

## Models Available

| | Style Number | Base MSRP | Change from LY | Shipping Wt. (lbs.) | Production | Change from LY |
|---|---|---|---|---|---|---|
| Nova 2-Door Coupe | 11127 | $2,176 | -2.73% | 2820 | * | * |
| Nova 4-Door Sedan | 11169 | $2,205 | -2.73% | 2843 | * | * |
| TOTALS | | *Avg. price* $2,191 | -2.73% | *Production* 315,122 | | +25.10% |

*\*Production is estimated and not available by body style totals.*

# Chevelle

*"The performance starts as soon as you're seated."*

**Nameplate year of origin:** 1964.
**Current bodystyle lifespan:** 1968 through 1972.
**Predecessor to this model:** Chevelle (1966 to 1967).
**Corporate siblings:** Pontiac LeMans, Oldsmobile Cutlass, Buick Skylark.
**Replacement for this model:** Chevelle (1973 to 1977).
**Percentage of division's sales volume:** 21.85%.
**Primary competition:** AMC Rebel, Dodge Coronet, Ford Torino, and Plymouth Satellite.
**Notable changes:** All-new front and rear styling.
**Major standard equipment:** Cloth and vinyl front bench seat, color-keyed vinyl-coated rubber floor mats, small hubcaps, and D78 × 14 BSW tires, Malibu adds: Pattern cloth front bench seat (all-vinyl on convertible), color-keyed deep-twist carpeting, wheel covers, Hide-A-Way windshield wipers. Wagon models are similarly equipped with Nomad and Greenbrier same as Chevelle, and Concours same as Malibu. SS 396 package adds: All-vinyl bucket seats, console, special instrumentation, 396 CID V8 engine, SS trim and wheel covers and F70 × 14 Redline or WSW tires. SS 454 adds: 454 CID V8.

## Measurements

| | 2-Doors | 4-Doors | Wagons |
|---|---|---|---|
| Wheelbase | 112.0" | 116.0" | 116.0" |
| Length | 197.5" | 201.5" | 206.8" |
| Width | 75.4" | 75.4" | 75.4" |
| Height | 52.0" | 52.6" | 52.6" |
| Legroom — front | 42.4" | 42.4" | 42.4" |
| Legroom — rear | 32.2" | 34.8" | 34.8" |
| Headroom — front | 37.9" | 38.5" | 38.5" |
| Headroom — rear | 36.3" | 37.1" | 37.4" |
| Cargo capacity (cu. ft.) | NA | NA | 83.6 |
| Fuel capacity (gals.) | 20.0 | 20.0 | 20.0 |

**1970**

## Models Available

| | Style Number | Base MSRP | Change from LY | Shipping Wt. (lbs.) | Production | Change from LY |
|---|---|---|---|---|---|---|
| Chevelle 2-Door Coupe | 13337 | $2,572 | +4.64% | 3142 | 23,900 | * |
| Chevelle 4-Door Sedan | 13369 | $2,537 | +1.97% | 3196 | * | * |
| Chevelle Malibu 2-Door Hardtop | 13537 | $2,719 | +4.54% | 3197 | 375,800 | * |
| Chevelle Malibu 2-Dr. Convertible | 13567 | $2,919 | +4.25% | 3243 | * | * |
| Chevelle Malibu 4-Door Sedan | 13569 | $2,685 | +4.60% | 3221 | * | * |
| Chevelle Malibu 4-Door Hardtop | 13539 | $2,790 | +4.42% | 3302 | * | * |
| Nomad 4-Door, 2-Seat Wagon | 13136 | $2,865 | +7.38% | 3615 | * | * |
| Greenbrier 4-Door, 2-Seat Wagon | 13336 | $2,946 | +6.01% | 3644 | * | * |
| Greenbrier 4-Door, 3-Seat Wagon | 13446 | $3,213 | +11.10% | 3794 | * | * |
| Concours 4-Door, 2-Seat Wagon | 13536 | $3,056 | +4.26% | 3687 | 40,600 | * |
| Concours 4-Door, 3-Seat Wagon | 13646 | $3,323 | +9.17% | 3836 | * | * |
| Concours Estate 4-Dr., 2-S. Wagon | 13836 | $3,210 | +1.81% | 3794 | * | * |
| Concours Estate 4-Dr., 3-S. Wagon | 13846 | $3,455 | +5.79% | 3880 | * | * |
| TOTALS | | Avg. price $2,945 | +6.16% | | Production 440,300 | -3.23% |

*Production is estimated and not available by series, only body style totals.*

# Monte Carlo

*"Monte Carlo is a driver's car that only a handful of American-made cars have anything in common with."*

**Nameplate year of origin:** 1970.
**Current bodystyle lifespan:** 1970 through 1972.
**Predecessor to this model:** None.
**Replacement for this model:** Monte Carlo (1973 to 1977).
**Corporate siblings:** Pontiac Grand Prix.
**Percentage of division's sales volume:** 7.24%.
**Primary competition:** Dodge Charger.
**Notable changes:** All-new for 1970.
**Major standard equipment:** Cloth and vinyl front bench seat, full carpeting, wood-grained instrument panel, door-pull assist straps, full wheel covers, and G78 × 15 BSW tires.

### Measurements

| | |
|---|---|
| Wheelbase | 116.0" |
| Length | 206.5" |
| Width | 75.6" |
| Height | 52.9" |
| Legroom — front | NA |
| Legroom — rear | NA |
| Headroom — front | NA |
| Headroom — rear | NA |
| Cargo capacity (cu. ft.) | 12.9 |
| Fuel capacity (gals.) | 19.0 |

## Models Available

| | Style Number | Base MSRP | Change from LY | Shipping Wt. (lbs.) | Production | Change from LY |
|---|---|---|---|---|---|---|
| Monte Carlo 2-Door Hardtop | 13857 | $3,123 | NEW | 3460 | 145,975 | NEW |
| TOTALS | | Avg. price $3,123 | NEW | | Production 145,975 | NEW |

# Chevrolet Full-size

*"We've let other cars go their way. We're going yours."*

**Nameplate year of origin:** 1950 (BelAir); 1958 (Biscayne, Impala); 1966 (Caprice)

**Current bodystyle lifespan:** 1969 through 1970.

**Predecessor to this model:** Full-size Chevrolet (1967 to 1968).

**Corporate siblings:** Buick LeSabre/Wildcat, Olds 88, Pontiac Catalina/Bonneville.

**Replacement for this model:** Biscayne/BelAir/Impala/Caprice (1971 to 1976).

**Percentage of division's sales volume:** 48.57%.

**Primary competition:** AMC Ambassador, Dodge Polara, Ford Custom/Galaxie/LTD, and Plymouth Fury.

**Notable changes:** Restyled front and rear end.

**Major standard equipment:** Biscayne: Cloth and vinyl bench seat, full carpeting, front and rear door armrests, 2-speed electric windshield wipers with washers, and F78 × 15 BSW tires (G78 × 15 BSW tires on wagons). BelAir adds: Automatic interior lighting, bright body side molding, and power tailgate window on 3-Seat wagon models. Impala adds: Vinyl upholstery in convertible, extra-long armrests, electric clock, and G78 × 15 BSW tires on convertible and 4-Door Hardtop. Caprice adds: Specific cloth and vinyl front bench seats (with center fold-down armrest on sedan), all-vinyl upholstery in wagons, simulated walnut interior trim, deluxe wheel covers, rocker panel moldings, simulated walnut exterior trim on wagons, and special ornamentation.

## Measurements

|  | Cars | Wagons |
|---|---|---|
| Wheelbase | 119.0" | 119.0" |
| Length | 216.0" | 216.8" |
| Width | 79.8" | 79.8" |
| Height | 55.5" | 57.1" |
| Legroom — front | 42.6" | 42.6" |
| Legroom — rear | 38.5" | 38.5" |
| Headroom — front | 38.9" | 38.9" |
| Headroom — rear | 38.0" | 38.5" |
| Cargo capacity (cu. ft.) | 18.1 | 100.3 |
| Fuel capacity (gals.) | 24.0 | 24.0 |

## Models Available

| | Style Number | Base MSRP | Change from LY | Shipping Wt. (lbs.) | Production | Change from LY |
|---|---|---|---|---|---|---|
| Biscayne 4-Door Sedan | 15369 | $2,787 | +3.72% | 3600 | 35,400 | * |
| Bel Air 4-Door Sedan | 15569 | $2,887 | +3.59% | 3604 | 75,800 | * |
| Impala 2-Door Sport Coupe | 16337 | $3,038 | +3.79% | 3641 | 612,800 | * |
| Impala 2-Door Custom Coupe | 16447 | $3,266 | +5.87% | 3801 | * | * |
| Impala 2-Door Convertible | 16467 | $3,377 | +3.56% | 3843 | * | * |
| Impala 4-Door Sedan | 16369 | $3,021 | +3.78% | 3655 | * | * |
| Impala 4-Door Hardtop | 16439 | $3,203 | +3.79% | 3871 | * | * |
| Caprice 2-Door Hardtop | 16647 | $3,474 | +5.46% | 3821 | 92,000 | * |
| Caprice 4-Door Hardtop | 16639 | $3,527 | +5.41% | 3905 | * | * |
| Brookwood 4-Dr., 2-S. Wagon | 15436 | $3,294 | +7.51% | 4204 | * | * |
| Townsman 4-Dr., 2-S. Wagon | 15636 | $3,357 | +3.87% | 4208 | * | * |
| Townsman 4-Dr., 3-S. Wagon | 15646 | $3,469 | +3.71% | 4263 | * | * |
| Kingswood 4-Dr., 2-S. Wagon | 16436 | $3,477 | +3.73% | 4269 | 162,600 | * |
| Kingswood 4-Dr., 3-S. Wagon | 16446 | $3,589 | +3.58% | 4321 | * | * |
| Kingswood Estate 4-Dr., 2-S. Wgn. | 16636 | $3,753 | +5.27% | 4295 | * | * |
| Kingswood Estate 4-Dr., 3-S. Wgn. | 16646 | $3,866 | +5.11% | 4361 | * | * |
| TOTALS | Avg. price | $3,337 | +6.34% | Production | 978,600 | -20.29% |

*Production is estimated and not available by series, only body style totals.

1970

# Corvette

*"People have the idea you can tell what cars of the future will be like by looking at Chevrolet's Corvette. They're right."*

**Nameplate year of origin:** 1953 (also used on showcar of same year).
**Current bodystyle lifespan:** 1968 through 1982.
**Predecessor to this model:** Corvette (1963 to 1967).
**Replacement for this model:** Corvette (1984 to 1996).
**Percentage of division's sales volume:** 0.86%.
**Corporate siblings:** None.
**Primary competition:** None.
**Notable changes:** Trim and detail changes.
**Major standard equipment:** All-vinyl bucket seats with full-length center floor console, complete instrumentation, Astro ventilation, removable roof panels (Coupe), manually operated folding top (Convertible), wheels with bright trim ring and ribbed center hub, 4-wheel disc brakes, and F70 × 15 WSW tires.

## Measurements

| | |
|---|---|
| Wheelbase | 98.0" |
| Length | 182.5" |
| Width | 69.2" |
| Height | 47.8" |
| Legroom — front | 43.0" |
| Legroom — rear | NA |
| Headroom — front | 36.2" |
| Headroom — rear | NA |
| Cargo capacity (cu. ft.) | NA |
| Fuel capacity (gals.) | 20.0 |

## Models Available

| | Style Number | Base MSRP | Change from LY | Shipping Wt. (lbs.) | Production | Change from LY |
|---|---|---|---|---|---|---|
| Corvette 2-Door Coupe | 19437 | $5,192 | +8.60% | 3184 | 10,668 | -51.85% |
| Corvette 2-Door Convertible | 19467 | $4,849 | +9.26% | 3196 | 6,648 | -59.97% |
| TOTALS | | *Avg. price* $5,021 | +8.92% | | *Production* 17,316 | -55.33% |

# CHRYSLER

*"Your next car: 1970 Chrysler."*

Chrysler exterior styling continued its "fuselage" style bodies and loop type front bumpers, but 1970 brought new grille designs. The new-bodied Chryslers had been very successful in 1969, but constant pressure from the competition and a weakening economy meant sales for Chrysler would take a tumble this year. Under the hood, powerplant choices remained the same as previous years, with either 383 CID or 440 CID V8 engine offerings. Notably, 1970 would be the last year for a full-size Chrysler convertible, which saw sales drop 50 percent from the previous year. There were three new models to debut for the year. The first two were special-order editions of the base Newport, called Cordoba. This line consisted of a 2-Door Hardtop and 4-Door Hardtop. Features included Cordoba Gold Paint and vinyl top, special upholstery, and specific wheel covers. The other model was a limited edition 300-H 2-Door Hardtop. In this case, the "H" stood for Hurst Performance Corporation, not a part of the earlier letter series 300s. Powertrain for this big muscle car was the 440 CID "TNT" V8 engine that developed 375 horsepower. Other performance features included Torqueflite automatic transmission, heavy-duty suspension, power bulge hood with functional air scoop, hood-pin anchors, rear spoiler and styled road wheels. This high-performance, full-size coupe was an image-maker to be certain. In typical Hurst fashion, the car was painted Spinnaker White with Satin Tan accent stripes. The interior featured leather bucket seats in Saddle color only. A total of 485 300-H models were produced for the season.

300 4-Door Hardtop

Newport Custom 2-Door Hardtop

New Yorker 4-Door Hardtop

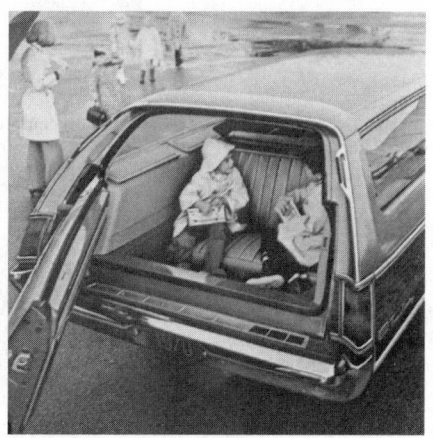
Town & Country 4-Door Wagon

**Model year production:** 180,767, down 30.68% from 1969.
**Domestic market share:** 2.17% (11th place).
**Base price range:** $3,514 to $4,824.
**Industry average base price:** $3,538.
**Chrysler average base price:** $4,186.
**Introduction date:** September 1969.
**Assembly plants:** Newark, DE (F), and Detroit, MI (C).
**Data plate identification:** Thirteen digit code read as follows:

four digit style number (see listings below) in which C = Chrysler, 2nd number identifies series (e.g., H is for New Yorker), 3rd and 4th indicate body style; 5th digit is engine code; 0 for 1970; assembly plant code; 100001 and up for serial number. *Example:* CH23T0C100001 is a 1970 Chrysler New Yorker 2-Door Hardtop with a 440 CID V8 engine, serial number 100001, built in Detroit, MI.

## Powertrains

| Engine | Engine Code | Gross HP | Transmission Availability | Newport | Town & Country | 300 & N.Y. |
|---|---|---|---|---|---|---|
| 383 CID, 2-bbl., V8 | L | 290 | 3-speed man. | S | - | - |
|  |  |  | TorqueFlite Automatic | $229 | S | - |
| 383 CID, 4-bbl., V8 | N | 335 | 3-speed man. | $68 | - | - |
|  |  |  | TorqueFlite Automatic | $297 | $68 | - |
| 440 CID, 4-bbl., V8 | T | 350 | 3-speed man. | $164 | - | - |
|  |  |  | TorqueFlite Automatic | $393 | $164 | S |
| 440 CID TNT, 4-bbl., V8 | U | 375 | TorqueFlite Automatic | $427 | $198 | $79 |

## Major Options

| | Newport | 300 | Town & Country | New Yorker |
|---|---|---|---|---|
| Air conditioning | $406 | $406 | $406 | $406 |
| Electronic cruise control | $67 | $67 | $67 | $67 |
| Soft Ray tinted glass | $45 | $45 | $45 | $45 |
| Deck lid remote release | $15 | $15 | - | $15 |
| Power steering— variable-ratio | $117 | $117 | S | S |
| Power brakes | $47 | $47 | S | S |

## Paint Colors

| | Code |
|---|---|
| Winchester Gray Metallic | A4 |
| Slate Gray | A8 |
| Glacial Blue Metallic | B2 |
| Evening Blue Metallic | B7 |
| Rallye Red | E5 |
| Burnished Red Metallic | E7 |
| Amber Sherwood Metallic | F3 |

**1970**

|  | *Newport* | *300* | *Town & Country* | *New Yorker* |  |  | *Code* |
|---|---|---|---|---|---|---|---|
| Power door locks | $46–$70 | $46–$70 | $70 | $46–$70 | Avocado Metallic | | F9 |
| Power 6-way Bench | | | | | April Green | | J4 |
| seat (bucket on 300) | $103 | $188 | $103 | $103 | Autumn Bronze Metallic | | K6 |
| Power windows | $112 | $112 | $112 | $112 | Sandalwood Beige | | L1 |
| AM radio | $92 | $92 | $92 | $92 | Aztec Gold Metallic | | L6 |
| AM/FM stereo | $187 | $187 | $187 | $187 | Coral Turquoise Metallic | | Q5 |
| Tilt & telescoping | | | | | Tahitian Walnut Metallic | | T8 |
| steering wheel | $91 | $91 | $91 | $91 | Spinnaker White | | W1 |
| Vinyl roof | $125 | $125 | $125 | $125 | Formal Black | | X9 |
| Chrome Road Wheels | $99 | $99 | - | $99 | Lemon Twist | | Y1 |
| | | | | | Crystal Dawn | | Y5 |
| | | | | | Tawny Gold Metallic | | Y9 |

Options common to most models. (- = Not Available; S = Standard equipment.) Items may be standard equipment, optional at different pricing, or unavailable on certain models. This chart is only a guide.

# Newport

*"Luxury cars should be this luxurious and this affordable."*

**Nameplate year of origin:** 1950 (as a HT model of the T & C); 1961 (as series).
**Current bodystyle lifespan:** 1969 through 1973.
**Predecessor to this model:** Newport (1965 to 1968).
**Replacement for this model:** Newport (1974 to 1978).
**Percentage of division's sales volume:** 61.01%.
**Corporate siblings:** Chrysler 300 and New Yorker.
**Primary competition:** Buick LeSabre, Mercury Monterey, and Oldsmobile Delta 88.
**Notable changes:** Minor trim and detail changes. New entry-level Royal line added.
**Major standard equipment:** Three speed manual transmission, cloth and vinyl front bench seat (all-vinyl on convertible), full carpeting, rear seat ashtrays, bright window trim moldings, wheel covers and H78 × 15 BSW tires. Custom adds: Cloth and vinyl front bench seat with fold-down arm rest, and specific exterior trim.

## Measurements

| | |
|---|---|
| Wheelbase | 124.0" |
| Length | 224.7" |
| Width | 79.1" |
| Height | 56.3" |
| Legroom — front | 41.8" |
| Legroom — rear | 42.2" |
| Headroom — front | 38.7" |
| Headroom — rear | 37.9" |
| Cargo capacity (cu. ft.) | NA |
| Fuel capacity (gals.) | 24.0 |

## Models Available

| | Style Number | Base MSRP | Change from LY | Shipping Wt. (lbs.) | Production | Change from LY |
|---|---|---|---|---|---|---|
| Newport 2-Door Hardtop | CE23 | $3,589 | +2.98% | 4030 | 21,664 | -35.60% |
| Newport 2-Door Convertible | CE27 | $3,925 | +2.67% | 4085 | 1,124 | -48.18% |
| Newport 4-Door Sedan | CE41 | $3,514 | +2.93% | 4080 | 39,285 | -28.68% |
| Newport 4-Door Hardtop | CE43 | $3,652 | +2.90% | 4110 | 16,940 | -17.80% |
| Newport Custom 2-Door Hardtop | CL23 | $3,781 | +3.53% | 4035 | 6,639 | -39.40% |
| Newport Custom 4-Door Sedan | CL41 | $3,710 | +3.63% | 4090 | 13,767 | -25.18% |
| Newport Custom 4-Door Hardtop | CL43 | $3,861 | +3.51% | 4125 | 10,873 | -31.96% |
| TOTALS | | *Avg. price* $3,719 | +3.16% | *Production* | 110,292 | -29.68% |

# 300

*"Luxury car always. A broad-stanced sports car when you turn it on."*

**Nameplate year of origin:** 1955 (letter series cars), 1962 (standard line cars).
**Current bodystyle lifespan:** 1969 through 1971.
**Predecessor to this model:** 300 (1965 to 1968).
**Replacement for this model:** None.
**Percentage of division's sales volume:** 11.62%.
**Corporate siblings:** Chrysler Newport and New Yorker.
**Primary competition:** Buick Wildcat, Mercury Marauder and Pontiac Bonneville.
**Notable changes:** Minor trim and detail changes.
**Major standard equipment:** Torqueflite automatic transmission, power steering, power front disc brakes, all-vinyl or cloth and vinyl front bucket seats, full carpeting, carpeted lower door panels, body accent stripes, dual horn, fender-top turn signal indicator lamps, full wheel covers and H78 × 15 BSW tires. 300-H adds: Leather bucket seats, heavy-duty suspension, power bulge hood with functional air scoop, hood-pin anchors, rear spoiler, special paint scheme and styled road wheels.

## Measurements

| | |
|---|---|
| Wheelbase | 124.0" |
| Length | 224.7" |
| Width | 79.1" |
| Height | 55.5" |
| Legroom — front | 41.8" |
| Legroom — rear | 42.2" |
| Headroom — front | 38.1" |
| Headroom — rear | 37.2" |
| Cargo capacity (cu. ft.) | NA |
| Fuel capacity (gals.) | 24.0 |

## Models Available

| | Style Number | Base MSRP | Change from LY | Shipping Wt. (lbs.) | Production | Change from LY |
|---|---|---|---|---|---|---|
| 300 2-Door Hardtop | CM23 | $4,234 | +3.17% | 4135 | 10,074 | -37.33% |
| 300 2-Door Convertible | CM27 | $4,580 | +2.92% | 4175 | 1,077 | -44.28% |
| 300 4-Door Hardtop | CM43 | $4,313 | +3.11% | 4220 | 9,846 | -31.93% |
| TOTALS | *Avg. price* | $4,376 | +3.06% | | *Production* 20,997 | -35.33% |

# Town & Country

*"A luxury car made into a wagon. Without compromising."*

**Nameplate year of origin:** 1941.
**Current bodystyle lifespan:** 1969 through 1973.
**Predecessor to this model:** Town & Country (1965 to 1968).
**Replacement for this model:** Town & Country (1974 to 1978).
**Percentage of division's sales volume:** 8.45%.
**Corporate siblings:** Dodge Monaco/Polara and Plymouth Fury Suburbans.
**Primary competition:** Buick Estate Wagon and Mercury Colony Park.
**Notable changes:** Revised sheetmetal and new front and rear end treatments.
**Major standard equipment:** Torqueflite automatic transmission, power steering, power front disc brakes, electric clock, lockable luggage compartment, all-vinyl front bench seat with folding center armrest, simulated walnut instrument panel trim, carpeted lower door trim and load floor, power operated tailgate window, bodyside and rear tailgate Brazilian rosewood woodgrain applique, and J78 × 15 BSW tires.

## Measurements

| | |
|---|---|
| Wheelbase | 122.0" |
| Length | 224.8" |
| Width | 79.1" |
| Height | 57.9" |
| Legroom — front | 41.8" |
| Legroom — rear | 39.4" |
| Headroom — front | 40.4" |
| Headroom — rear | 40.1" |
| Cargo capacity (cu. ft.) | 109.2 |
| Fuel capacity (gals.) | 23.0 |

**1970**

## Models Available

| | Style Number | Base MSRP | Change from LY | Shipping Wt. (lbs.) | Production | Change from LY |
|---|---|---|---|---|---|---|
| Town & Country 4-Dr., 2-S. Wagon | CP45 | $4,738 | +3.38% | 4490 | 5,686 | -43.75% |
| Town & Country 4-Dr., 3-S. Wagon | CP46 | $4,824 | +3.32% | 4555 | 9,583 | -33.49% |
| TOTALS | *Avg. price* | $4,781 | +3.35% | | *Production* 15,269 | -37.72% |

# New Yorker

*"It has always been the most luxurious Chrysler.
Now, with Torsion-Quiet Ride, it is even more so."*

**Nameplate year of origin:** 1939.
**Current bodystyle lifespan:** 1969 through 1973.
**Predecessor to this model:** New Yorker (1965 to 1968).
**Replacement for this model:** New Yorker (1974 to 1978).
**Percentage of division's sales volume:** 18.92%.
**Corporate siblings:** Chrysler Newport and 300.
**Primary competition:** Buick Electra 225, Cadillac Calais, Mercury Marquis, and Oldsmobile 98.
**Notable changes:** Minor trim and detail changes.
**Major standard equipment:** Torqueflite automatic transmission, power front disc brakes, power steering, cloth and vinyl seats with folding center armrests (front seat only on 2-Door), simulated walnut instrument panel trim, electric clock, 3-speed windshield wipers, fender-top turn signal indicator, LH remote outside rear view mirror, trunk carpeting and J78 × 15 BSW tires.

## Measurements

| | |
|---|---|
| Wheelbase | 124.0" |
| Length | 224.7" |
| Width | 79.1" |
| Height | 56.6" |
| Legroom — front | 41.8" |
| Legroom — rear | 42.2" |
| Headroom — front | 38.6" |
| Headroom — rear | 37.9" |
| Cargo capacity (cu. ft.) | NA |
| Fuel capacity (gals.) | 24.0 |

## Models Available

| | Style Number | Base MSRP | Change from LY | Shipping Wt. (lbs.) | Production | Change from LY |
|---|---|---|---|---|---|---|
| New Yorker 2-Door Hardtop | CH23 | $4,681 | +3.13% | 4235 | 4,917 | -34.76% |
| New Yorker 4-Door Sedan | CH41 | $4,630 | +3.19% | 4310 | 9,389 | -23.37% |
| New Yorker 4-Door Hardtop | CH43 | $4,761 | +3.16% | 4335 | 19,903 | -26.71% |
| TOTALS | | Avg. price $4,691 | +3.17% | | Production 34,209 | -27.13% |

# DODGE

*"If you want all the 'news' for '70 ... you could be Dodge Material."*

The big "news" from Dodge this year was its own version of a pony car—finally more than five years after the first Mustang was introduced. One would have thought the White Hat boys would have put together a pony car for the performance division of Chrysler much sooner. Apparently Chrysler had thought that with the Plymouth Barracuda already in that market, they could leave the mid-size Charger to fill the sports car role for Dodge. Unfortunately, the smaller pony car market had already peaked by 1970, but the Dodge boys did put together one very nice automobile. The Challenger was a slightly larger companion to the Barracuda. Based on a stretched Valiant/Dart platform, the new Challenger was an immediate hit, and a contender for one of the all-time best muscle cars. Using a formula similar to that developed for the Mustang and Camaro, the Challenger came in a wide array of model choices from plain jane to wild performance. What really attracted people to the Challenger over other pony cars, though, was obviously its performance capabilities. Nearly every engine that Chrysler built could be ordered for the Challenger. A luxury Special Edition model was also offered in base or R/T varieties, if you needed more luxury with your sport. The idea of a little luxury in a sporty car was just beginning to take hold, as other manufacturers offered such models as the Mustang Grande and Firebird Esprit.

Other Dodge models, excluding the Charger, received

fairly extensive facelifts. The full-size Dodge models, which were new for 1969, were given a version of the new Chrysler "loop-style" grille which fully encompassed the grille and headlights. Out back, new taillights and bumpers were used. The full-size model line was also reorganized to further differentiate the Polara and Monaco lines. For the Polara, a Special trim level was added as a base car, primarily for fleet use, but available to anyone. A Polara Custom was added to the top end as an intermediate step between the Polara and Monaco. Variations in grilles and trim distinguished the Polara from the Monaco. The mid-sized Coronet line was due to be redesigned for 1971, so it is surprising that it received such a major restyle. The front end was given the "loop-style" grille treatment also, but it was split into two halves with the hood panel coming down between

the two halves approximately six inches. The rear styling of the Coronets was also updated with new taillights and rear bumper. Dart models still were using the same body introduced in 1967, but they were also given a major facelift. At the front was a full-width grille, split in the middle with vertical bars, and underscored by a narrow, full-width bumper. At the rear end, the decklid sloped downward to a thin bumper which housed the taillights. The Dart line lost the GT and GTS models, as the Challenger filled that market position. As previously mentioned, the Charger changed very little for 1970. A loop-style grille with hidden headlights inset at each end, was the most noticeable difference. The Charger SE was not offered this year, but would return in 1971.

Challenger 2-Door Hardtop

Charger 2-Door Hardtop

Coronet 500 2-Door Hardtop

Dart Swinger 2-Door Hardtop

Monaco 4-Door Hardtop

Monaco 4-Door Wagon

Polara 2-Door Hardtop

1970

**Model year production:** 543,020, down 10.75% from 1969.
**Domestic market share:** 6.52% (7th place).
**Base price range:** $2,261 to $4,242.
**Industry average base price:** $3,538.
**Dodge average base price:** $3,228.
**Introduction date:** September 23, 1969.
**Assembly plants:** Lynch Road, MI (A); Hamtramck, MI (B); Detroit (Jefferson Ave.), MI (C); Belvidere, IL (D); Los Angeles, CA (E); Newark, DE (F); St. Louis, MO (G); New Stanton (H); Windsor, Ontario, Canada (R).

**Data plate identification:** Thirteen digit code read as follows: four digit style number (see listings below) in which 1st digit series letter (e.g., L = Dart series), 2nd number identifies trim grade (e.g., H is for Custom/Swinger trim), 3rd and 4th digits indicate body style; 5th digit is engine code; 0 for 1970; assembly plant code; 100001 and up for serial number. *Example:* LH23G0F100001 is a 1970 Dodge Dart Swinger 2-Door Hardtop with a 318 CID V8 engine, serial number 100001, built in Newark, NJ.

## Powertrains

| Engine | Engine Code | Gross HP | Transmission Availability | Dart* | Challenger | Charger | Coronet | Polara/ Monaco |
|---|---|---|---|---|---|---|---|---|
| 198 CID, 1-bbl., 6-cyl. | A | 125 | 3-speed man. | S | - | - | - | - |
| | | | Torqueflite automatic | $175 | - | - | - | - |
| 225 CID, 1-bbl., 6-cyl. | B | 145 | 3-speed man. | $46 | S (base) | S** | S** | S (Pol. Special) |
| | | | Torqueflite automatic | $221 | $199 (base) | $199** | $199** | $199 (Pol. Special) |
| 318 CID, 2-bbl., V8 | G | 230 | 3-speed man. | $111 | $102 (base) | $107** | S (500)/ $107** | S (Pol.) |
| | | | 4-speed man. | $299 | $290 (base) | - | - | - |
| | | | Torqueflite automatic | $302 | $301 (base) | $306** | $199 (500)/ $306** | $199 (Pol.) |
| 340 CID, 4-bbl., V8 | H | 275 | 3-speed man. | $ | $ (base) | - | - | - |
| | | | 4-speed man. | $ | $ (base) | - | - | - |
| | | | Torqueflite automatic | $ | $ (base) | - | - | - |
| 383 CID, 2-bbl., V8 | M | 290 | 3-speed man. | - | - | - | - | S (Mon.)/ $ (Pol.) |
| | | | Torqueflite automatic | - | $371 | $376** | $376** | $199 (Mon.)/ $ (Pol.) |
| 383 CID, 4-bbl., V8 | P | 335 | 3-speed man. | - | $138/(base) S (R/T) | $245** | S (Super Bee)/ $245** | |
| | | | 4-speed man. | - | $326(base)/ $188 (R/T) | $453** | $188 (Super Bee)/ $453** | |
| | | | Torqueflite automatic | - | $337 (base)/ $199 (R/T) | $444** | $199 (Super Bee)/ $444** | |
| 383 CID Magnum, 4-bbl., V8 | P | 350 | 4-speed man. | - | $290 (R/T) | - | $290 (Super Bee)/ $438** | |
| | | | Torqueflite automatic | - | $301 (R/T) | - | $301 (Super Bee)/ $449** | $ (Mon.)/ $ (Pol.) |
| 440 CID Magnum, 4-bbl., V8 | U | 375 | 4-speed man. | - | $329 (R/T) | No cost (R/T) | No cost (R/T)/ $336 (S.B.)/$545** | - |
| | | | Torqueflite automatic | - | $340 (R/T) | S (R/T) (S.B.)/$545** | S (R/T)/$336 $ (Mon.)/$ (Pol.) | |
| 440 CID "Six-Pack," 3 × 2-bbl., V8 | V | 390 | 4-speed man. | - | $438 (R/T) | $119 (R/T) | $119 (R/T)/ $438 (S.B.) | - |
| | | | Torqueflite automatic | - | $449 (R/T) | $119 (R/T) | $119 (R/T)/ $438 (S.B.) | |
| 426 CID Street Hemi, 2 × 4-bbl., V8 | T | 425 | 4-speed man. | - | $967 (R/T) | $648 (R/T) | $718 (R/T)/ $848 (S.B.) | |
| | | | Torqueflite automatic | - | $978 (R/T) | $648 (R/T) | $718 (R/T)/ $848 (S. B.) | - |

*340 CID V8 standard on Dart Swinger 340; 4-speed manual, $188; Torqueflite, $191.    **Except Coronet 500, Super Bee or R/T.

## Major Options

| | Dart/Demon | Challenger | Charger | Coronet | Polara | Monaco |
|---|---|---|---|---|---|---|
| Air conditioning | $380 | $380 | $380 | $380 | $423 | $423 |
| Speed control | - | - | $ | $ | $ | $ |
| Electric rear window defogger | - | - | $ | $ | $ | $ |
| Tinted glass | $36 | $36 | $40 | $40 | $40 | $40 |
| Power steering | $92 | $92 | $104 | $104 | S | S |

| | Dart/Demon | Challenger | Charger | Coronet | Polara | Monaco |
|---|---|---|---|---|---|---|
| Power brakes | $40 | $40 | - | - | - | - |
| Power brakes — front disc | $62 | $62 | $68 | $68 | $68 | S |
| Power door locks | - | - | $ | $ | $ | $ |
| Power driver's seat/Bench seat | - | - | $91 | $91 | $103 | $103 |
| Power windows | - | - | $119 | $119 | $125 | $125 |
| AM radio | $59 | $59 | $65 | $65 | $65 | $65 |
| AM/FM stereo | $125 (not stereo) | $132 | $144 | $144 | $144 | $144 |
| Tilt steering wheel | - | - | $55 | $55 | $55 | $55 |
| Sunroof | - | - | $ | - | - | - |
| Road Wheels | - | - | $28 | - | $58 | $58 |
| Vinyl Roof | $75 | $80 | $94 | $94 | $106 | $106 |
| Challenger 340 package (340 V8, performance hood, Bumble Bee stripes, rallye suspension) | - | $ | - | - | - | - |
| Monaco 500 package | - | - | - | - | - | $110 |
| Monaco Brougham pkg. | - | - | - | - | - | $220 |

Options common to most models. (- = Not Available; S = Standard equipment.) Items may be standard equipment, optional at different pricing, or unavailable on certain models. This chart is only a guide.

## Paint Colors

| | Code | | Code |
|---|---|---|---|
| Silver Metallic | A-4 | Beige | L-1 |
| Dark Gray Metallic | A-9 | Panther Pink | M-3 |
| Light Blue Metallic | B-3 | Light Turquoise Met. | Q-3 |
| Bright Blue Metallic | B-5 | Red | R-6 |
| Dark Blue Metallic | B-7 | Burgundy Metallic | R-8 |
| Plum Crazy* | C-7 | Tan Metallic | T-3 |
| Bright Red | E-5 | Dark Tan Metallic | T-6 |
| Light Green Metallic | F-4 | Hemi Orange* | V-2 |
| Bright Green Metallic | F-6 | White | W-1 |
| Dark Green Metallic | F-8 | Black | X-9 |
| Sublime | J-5 | Banana* | Y-1 |
| Green Go* | J-6 | Cream | Y-3 |
| Go Mango* | K-2 | Light Gold Metallic | Y-4 |
| Dk. Burnt Orange Met. | K-5 | Gold Metallic | Y-6 |

*Hi-impact colors available at extra cost.*

# Dart

*"For the man going compact ... a going compact."*

**1970**

**Nameplate year of origin:** 1960 (on low-end full-size models).
**Current bodystyle lifespan:** 1967 through 1976.
**Predecessor to this model:** Dart (1963 to 1966).
**Replacement for this model:** Aspen (1976 to 1980).
**Percentage of division's sales volume:** 38.69%.
**Corporate siblings:** Plymouth Valiant.
**Primary competition:** AMC Hornet, Chevrolet Nova, Ford Maverick and Ford Falcon.
**Notable changes:** Restyled front and rear end.
**Major standard equipment:** All-vinyl bench front seat, dome light, front door vent windows, 2-speed windshield wipers, and D78 × 14 BSW tires. Custom adds: Cloth and vinyl front seat (4-Door Sedan), deep-pile carpeting, 3-spoke steering wheel, drip rail molding, grille surround molding, and deluxe instrument panel decor. Swinger 340 adds: Front disc brakes, floor shifter, and E70 × 14 BSW tires.

## Measurements

| | |
|---|---|
| Wheelbase | 111.0" |
| Length | 196.2" |
| Width | 69.7" |
| Height | 54.0" |
| Legroom — front | 41.5" |
| Legroom — rear | 35.9" |
| Headroom — front | 38.6" |
| Headroom — rear | 37.3" |
| Cargo capacity (cu. ft.) | 14.3 |
| Fuel capacity (gals.) | 18 |

## Models Available

| | Style Number | Base MSRP | Change from LY | Shipping Wt. (lbs.) | Production | Change from LY |
|---|---|---|---|---|---|---|
| Dart Swinger 2-Dr. Hardtop | LL23 | $2,261 | -5.79% | 2843 | 119,883 | * |
| Dart 4-Door Sedan | LL41 | $2,308 | -4.35% | 2838 | 35,449 | * |
| Dart Custom 2-Door Hardtop | LH23 | $2,463 | -4.42% | 2833 | 17,208 | * |
| Dart Custom 4-Door Sedan | LH41 | $2,467 | -3.25% | 2843 | 23,779 | * |
| Dart Swinger 340 2-Door Hardtop | LM23 | $2,631 | -7.23% | 3179 | 13,785 | * |
| TOTALS | | Avg. price $2,426 | -12.51% | | Production 210,104 | +6.27% |

*Comparison by body style to 1969 models not available.*

# Challenger

*"The sports car with the big difference."*

## Measurements

| | |
|---|---|
| Wheelbase | 110.0" |
| Length | 191.3" |
| Width | 76.1" |
| Height | 50.9" |
| Legroom — front | 42.3" |
| Legroom — rear | 30.9" |
| Headroom — front | 37.4" |
| Headroom — rear | 35.6" |
| Cargo capacity (cu. ft.) | 8.6 |
| Fuel capacity (gals.) | 18.0 |

**Nameplate year of origin:** 1970.
**Current bodystyle lifespan:** 1970 through 1974.
**Predecessor to this model:** None.
**Replacement for this model:** None.
**Percentage of division's sales volume:** 15.29%.
**Corporate siblings:** Plymouth Barracuda.
**Primary competition:** AMC Javelin, Chevrolet Camaro, Ford Mustang, and Pontiac Firebird.
**Notable changes:** All-new model.
**Major standard equipment:** All-vinyl bucket seats, deep-pile carpeting, dome light, 3-spoke simulated walnut steering wheel, concealed 2-speed electric wipers, moldings (wheel opening, drip rail, grille, and deck lid), and E78 × 14 BSW tires. R/T adds: Longitudinal or Bumble Bee tape stripes, rallye instrument cluster, and F70 × 14 BSW tires. SE package adds: Vinyl roof with formal rear window, overhead interior consolette, and leather and vinyl bucket seats.

## Models Available

| | Style Number | Base MSRP | Change from LY | Shipping Wt. (lbs.) | Production | Change from LY |
|---|---|---|---|---|---|---|
| Challenger 2-Door Hardtop | JH23 | $2,851 | NEW | 3006 | 53,337 | NEW |
| Challenger 2-Door Convertible | JH27 | $3,120 | NEW | 3076 | 3,173 | NEW |
| Challenger 2-Door Formal Hardtop | JH29 | $3,083 | NEW | 3026 | 6,584 | NEW |
| Challenger R/T 2-Door Hardtop | JS23 | $3,266 | NEW | 3402 | 14,889 | NEW |
| Challenger R/T 2-Door Convertible | JS27 | $3,535 | NEW | 3467 | 1,070 | NEW |
| Challenger R/T 2-Door Formal HT | JS29 | $3,498 | NEW | 3437 | 3,979 | NEW |
| TOTALS | | Avg. price $3,226 | NEW | | Production 83,032 | NEW |

# Coronet

*"It still believes a low priced car ought to be low priced."*

**Nameplate year of origin:** 1950 on hardtop models, 1953 as series.
**Current bodystyle lifespan:** 1968 through 1970.
**Predecessor to this model:** Coronet (1966 to 1967).
**Corporate siblings:** Plymouth Satellite.
**Replacement for this model:** Coronet/Monaco (1971 to 1978).
**Percentage of division's sales volume:** 21.13%.
**Primary competition:** AMC Rebel, Chevrolet Chevelle, Ford Fairlane/Torino, and Pontiac Tempest/LeMans.
**Notable changes:** Revised front and rear styling.
**Major standard equipment:** All-vinyl bench seat, glove box lock, trunk mat, color-keyed rubber floor mats, cigarette lighter, front and rear armrests, windshield wipers with washers, and F78 × 14 BSW tires (G78 × 14 BSW on wagons). 440 adds: Cloth and vinyl bench seat (4-Door only), deep-pile carpeting and 3-spoke steering wheel. 500 adds: All-vinyl bucket seats (2-Doors), exterior bright trim package, and G78 × 14 tires. Super Bee adds: All-vinyl bench seat, Rallye suspension, floor shift transmission and F70 × 14 BSW tires. R/T adds: All-vinyl bucket seats and Torqueflite transmission.

## Measurements

|  | Cars | Wagons |
|---|---|---|
| Wheelbase | 117.0" | 117.0" |
| Length | 209.7" | 211.8" |
| Width | 76.7" | 76.7" |
| Height | 54.7" | 55.3" |
| Legroom — front | 41.9" | 41.9" |
| Legroom — rear | 41.4" | 41.4" |
| Headroom — front | 34.6" | 34.6" |
| Headroom — rear | 37.4" | 37.4" |
| Cargo capacity (cu. ft.) | NA | NA |
| Fuel capacity (gals.) | 19.0 | 19.0 |

## Models Available

| | Style Number | Base MSRP | Change from LY | Shipping Wt. (lbs.) | Production | Change from LY |
|---|---|---|---|---|---|---|
| Coronet Deluxe 2-Door Coupe | WL21 | $2,669 | +4.50% | 3068 | 2,978 | * |
| Coronet Deluxe 4-Door Sedan | WL41 | $2,704 | +4.44% | 3113 | 7,894 | * |
| Coronet Deluxe 4-Dr., 2-S. Wagon | WL45 | $3,048 | +4.31% | 3628 | 3,694 | * |
| Coronet 440 2-Door Coupe | WH21 | $2,743 | +4.30% | 3088 | 1,236 | * |
| Coronet 440 2-Door Hardtop | WH23 | $2,805 | +4.20% | 3108 | 24,341 | * |
| Coronet 440 4-Door Sedan | WH41 | $2,783 | +4.23% | 3108 | 33,258 | * |
| Coronet 440 4-Dr., 2-S. Wagon | WH45 | $3,156 | +4.06% | 3623 | 3,964 | * |
| Coronet 440 4-Dr., 3-S. Wagon | WH46 | $3,368 | +3.76% | 3803 | 3,772 | * |
| Coronet 500 2-Door Hardtop | WP23 | $3,048 | +4.06% | 3263 | 8,247 | * |
| Coronet 500 2-Door Convertible | WP27 | $3,188 | +3.88% | 3373 | 924 | * |
| Coronet 500 4-Door Sedan | WP41 | $3,082 | +4.02% | 3283 | 2,890 | * |
| Coronet 500 4-Dr., 2-S. Wgn. | WP45 | $3,404 | +3.78% | 3743 | 1,657 | * |
| Coronet 500 4-Dr., 3-S. Wgn. | WP46 | $3,514 | +3.60% | 3813 | 1,779 | * |
| Coronet Super Bee 2-Door Coupe | WM21 | $3,012 | -2.08% | 3528 | 3,966 | * |
| Coronet Super Bee 2-Door Hardtop | WM23 | $3,074 | -2.04% | 3563 | 11,540 | * |
| Coronet R/T 2-Door Hardtop | WS23 | $3,569 | +3.69% | 3573 | 2,319 | * |
| Coronet R/T 2-Door Convertible | WS27 | $3,785 | +3.42% | 3638 | 296 | * |
| TOTALS | *Avg. price* $3,115 | +3.25% | | *Production* 114,755 | | -43.58% |

*Comparison by body style to 1969 models not available.*

# Charger

*"Stands out with the 'in' crowd."*

**Nameplate year of origin:** 1966.
**Current bodystyle lifespan:** 1968 through 1970.
**Predecessor to this model:** Charger (1966 to 1967).
**Replacement for this model:** Charger (1971 to 1974).
**Percentage of division's sales volume:** 9.17%.
**Corporate siblings:** None.
**Primary competition:** Chevrolet Monte Carlo, Ford Torino SportsRoof models, and Pontiac Grand Prix.
**Notable changes:** Revised trim and detail changes.
**Major standard equipment:** All-vinyl front bench seat, full carpeting, 2-speed windshield wipers with washers, and F78 × 14 BSW tires. 500 adds: All-vinyl bucket seats, electric clock, and wheel lip moldings. R/T adds: Torqueflite transmission, heavy duty brakes, R/T Handling package, Bumble Bee racing stripe and F70 × 14 WSW tires. SE package adds: Leather and vinyl bucket seats, simulated walnut steering wheel and instrument panel trim, light group, and map pockets in doors.

## Measurements

| | |
|---|---|
| Wheelbase | 117.0" |
| Length | 208.5" |
| Width | 76.6" |
| Height | 53.0" |
| Legroom — front | 39.3" |
| Legroom — rear | 39.1" |
| Headroom — front | 38.6" |
| Headroom — rear | 36.4" |
| Cargo capacity (cu. ft.) | NA |
| Fuel capacity (gals.) | 19.0 |

## Models Available

| | Style Number | Base MSRP | Change from LY | Shipping Wt. (lbs.) | Production | Change from LY |
|---|---|---|---|---|---|---|
| Charger 2-Door Hardtop | XH29 | $3,001 | -0.63% | 3228 | 39,431 | -42.94% |
| Charger 500 2-Door Hardtop | XP29 | $3,139 | -21.39% | 3228 | * | * |
| Charger R/T 2-Door Hardtop | XS29 | $3,711 | +3.31% | 3638 | 10,337 | -48.57% |
| TOTALS | | Avg. price $3,284 | -7.10% | | Production 49,768 | -44.82% |

*Comparison by body style to 1969 models not available.*

# Polara

*"When bigger means better."*

**Nameplate year of origin:** 1959.
**Current bodystyle lifespan:** 1969 through 1973.
**Predecessor to this model:** Polara (1967 to 1968).
**Corporate siblings:** Plymouth Fury.
**Replacement for this model:** Monaco (1974).
**Percentage of division's sales volume:** 11.17%.
**Primary competition:** AMC Ambassador, Chevrolet Full-size, Ford Galaxie 500, and Pontiac Catalina.
**Notable changes:** New grille and bumper design. Trim and detail changes.
**Major standard equipment:** Cloth and vinyl front bench seat (vinyl in convertible and wagon), deep-pile color-keyed carpeting, 2-speed concealed windshield wipers, heater/defroster, glove box door lock, side molding with vinyl insert, roof mounted air deflector and dual-action tailgate (Wagons), and H78 × 15 BSW tires (J78 × 15 BSW on Wagons). Custom adds: Deluxe wheel covers, deluxe exterior and interior trim packages.

## Measurements

| | Cars | Wagons |
|---|---|---|
| Wheelbase | 122.0" | 122.0" |
| Length | 220.4" | 223.8" |
| Width | 79.2" | 79.2" |
| Legroom — front | 41.8" | 41.8" |
| Height | 55.7" | 57.1" |
| Legroom — rear | 39.1" | 39.1" |
| Headroom — front | 38.8" | 39.6" |
| Headroom — rear | 38.4" | 39.2" |
| Cargo capacity (cu. ft.) | 22.4 | 104.2 |
| Fuel capacity (gals.) | 24.0 | 23.0 |

## Models Available

| | Style Number | Base MSRP | Change from LY | Shipping Wt. (lbs.) | Production | Change from LY |
|---|---|---|---|---|---|---|
| Polara Special 4-Door Sedan | DE41 | $2,960 | NEW | 3745 | * | NEW |
| Polara Special 4-Dr., 2-S. Wgn. | DE45 | $3,513 | NEW | 4180 | * | NEW |
| Polara Special 4-Dr., 3-S. Wgn. | DE46 | $3,621 | NEW | 4235 | * | NEW |
| Polara 2-Door Hardtop | DL23 | $3,244 | +4.07% | 3793 | 15,243 | * |
| Polara 2-Door Convertible | DL27 | $3,527 | +4.44% | 3853 | 842 | * |
| Polara 4-Door Sedan | DL41 | $3,222 | +4.10% | 3828 | 18,740 | * |
| Polara 4-Door Hardtop | DL43 | $3,316 | +4.02% | 3873 | 19,223 | * |
| Polara 4-Door, 2-S. Wagon | DL45 | $3,670 | +4.20% | 4203 | 3,074 | * |
| Polara 4-Door, 3-S. Wagon | DL46 | $3,778 | +4.11% | 4258 | 3,546 | * |
| Polara Custom 2-Door Hardtop | DM23 | $3,458 | NEW | 3948 | * | NEW |
| Polara Custom 4-Door Sedan | DM41 | $3,426 | NEW | 3998 | * | NEW |
| Polara Custom 4-Door Hardtop | DM43 | $3,528 | NEW | 4028 | * | NEW |
| TOTALS | | Avg. price $3,439 | +2.60% | | Production 60,668 | * |

*Comparisons to 1969 models not available.

# Monaco

*"A luxury car is not measured by price alone."*

**Nameplate year of origin:** 1965.
**Current bodystyle lifespan:** 1969 through 1973.
**Predecessor to this model:** Monaco (1967 to 1968).
**Corporate siblings:** Chrysler Newport.
**Replacement for this model:** Royal Monaco (1974 to 1978).
**Percentage of division's sales volume:** 4.55%.
**Primary competition:** AMC Ambassador, Chevrolet Caprice, Ford LTD, Mercury Monterey, Oldsmobile Delta 88, and Pontiac Bonneville.
**Notable changes:** New grille and bumper design. Trim and detail changes.
**Major standard equipment:** Cloth and vinyl split back front bench seat with center armrest (4-Doors), all-vinyl seating (Wagons and 2-Doors), simulated wood-grained door inserts and instrument panel, deep-pile color-keyed carpeting, rear door automatic dome light switch, full-length exterior bright moldings, trunk light, 2-speed concealed wipers, deluxe wheel covers, and H78 × 15 BSW tires (J78 × 15 BSW on wagons).

## Measurements

| | Cars | Wagons |
|---|---|---|
| Wheelbase | 122.0" | 122.0" |
| Length | 220.4" | 225.6" |
| Width | 79.2" | 79.2" |
| Height | 55.7" | 57.1" |
| Legroom — front | 41.8" | 41.8" |
| Legroom — rear | 39.1" | 39.1" |
| Headroom — front | 38.8" | 39.6" |
| Headroom — rear | 38.4" | 39.2" |
| Cargo capacity (cu. ft.) | 22.4 | 104.2 |
| Fuel capacity (gals.) | 24.0 | 23.0 |

**1970**

## Models Available

| | Style Number | Base MSRP | Change from LY | Shipping Wt. (lbs.) | Production | Change from LY |
|---|---|---|---|---|---|---|
| Monaco 2-Door Hardtop | DH23 | $3,679 | +4.28% | 3973 | 3,522 | * |
| Monaco 4-Door Sedan | DH41 | $3,604 | +4.40% | 4033 | 4,721 | * |
| Monaco 4-Door Hardtop | DH43 | $3,743 | +4.23% | 4068 | 10,975 | * |
| Monaco 4-Dr., 2-S. Wgn. | DH45 | $4,110 | +4.93% | 4443 | 2,211 | * |
| Monaco 4-Dr., 3-S. Wgn. | DH46 | $4,242 | +4.84% | 4498 | 3,264 | * |
| TOTALS | | Avg. price $3,876 | +4.56% | | Production 24,693 | * |

*Comparisons to 1969 models not available.

# FORD

*"The 'Better Idea' Cars for 1970."*

The 1970 model year was a banner one for changes in Ford products. The Maverick, which actually debuted in April 1969, entered its first full year as a new product. The mid-size Fairlane and Torino lines were totally redesigned. The luxury Thunderbird sported new styling, and the sporty Mustang and full-size Fords offered revised frontal styling. The only car not to change, at least at the beginning of the year, was the Falcon. This was the last year for the compact Falcon, as the Maverick was its replacement in that market. The Falcon and Maverick overlapped on the sales floor for about 8 months. Part of the reason for this was that the Falcon offered 4-Door Sedan and Wagon models that were not initially offered in the Maverick line. But a Maverick 4-Door Sedan would arrive for the 1971 model year. After the compact Falcon disappeared, the name reappeared on the mid-size platform with the same three models offered: 2-Door Sedan, 4-Door Sedan and 4-Door Wagon. Mainly this move was made to offer a car in the price range of the former Falcon, while still making available a 4-Door variant. Obviously these cars were not hot sellers, and at the end of the 1970 model run, they were dropped. The new-for-1969 Maverick continued into the 1970 model year unchanged.

As previously mentioned, the mid-size line was totally revamped. Featuring slimmer, more aerodynamic lines, the Fairlane, Torino and mid-year Falcon were actually larger than the cars they replaced, but they carried it well. The model line was similar to 1969, but the names were shuffled to add a new Torino Brougham at the top of the line. The Fairlane 500 replaced the Fairlane, the Torino replaced the Fairlane 500, and the new Torino Brougham replaced the 1969 Torino line, model for model. The only models discontinued were the formal roof hardtops in the Torino GT and Cobra lines. Engine offerings remained pretty much the same. *Motor Trend* magazine was impressed enough with the new Torino to name it Car of the Year for 1970.

Also newly restyled, the Thunderbird was given a facelift unlike any other ever seen on a Ford. Gone was the flat, full-width grille look, and in its place was a full-width grille (with exposed headlights) and Pontiac-style nose that came to a point in the middle. The body lines were more rounded and lacked the previous cars sculpting. Rooflines also appeared slimmer, but underneath the cars were basically the same as earlier versions.

The perennially popular Mustang received a facelift also. The one-year-only dual headlight setup was replaced by single headlamps, set in the grille section where last year's inboard high-beam lights were located. The parking lights moved up to where the outside low-beam lights were last year. Also new for the year was the elimination of the familiar "side scoop" molding that had characterized the Mustang since its introduction. Full-size Fords were given new grilles and trim and detail changes, but powertrains remained the same. The Custom and Custom 500 lost their 2-Door Sedan models, as that body style was now gone in the full-size lines. At the top end, a LTD Brougham line was added to better compete with the Chevy Caprice and Plymouth Gran Fury lines. As for the full-size wagons, this was the last year that the Dual Facing Rear Seat (DFRS) models would be considered separate models from their 6-passenger counterparts. Beginning with 1971, the DFRS would be an option.

Fairlane 500 2-Door Hardtop

Falcon Futura 4-Door Sedan

Galaxie 500 4-Door Sedan

Maverick 2-Door Coupe

Mustang Boss 302 2-Door Fastback

LTD Brougham 4-Door Hardtop

Mustang Grande 2-Door Hardtop

Thunderbird Landau 4-Door Sedan

Ford Torino, *Motor Trend* Car of the Year

XL 2-Door Convertible

**Model year production:** 1,971,992, up 1.80% over 1969.

**Domestic market share:** 23.69% (2nd place).

**Base price range:** $1,995 to $5,182.

**Industry average base price:** $3,538.

**Ford average base price:** $3,162.

**Introduction date:** September 1969. Maverick introduced as mid-year 1969 model on April 17, 1969.

**Assembly plants:** Atlanta, GA (A); Dallas, TX (D); Chicago, IL (G); Dearborn, MI (F); Kansas City, MO (K); Lorain, OH (H); Los Angeles, CA (J); Louisville, KY (U); Mah-wah, NJ (E); Metuchen, NJ (T); Norfolk, VA (N); San Jose, CA (R); Twin Cities, MN (P); Wayne, MI (W); Wixom, MI (Y); St. Thomas, Ontario, Can. (X); Oakville, Ontario, Can. (B).

**Data plate identification:** Eleven digit code read as follows: 0 for 1970; 2nd digit is assembly plant code; 2-digit model number (see listings below); 5th digit is engine code; 100001 and up for serial number. *Example:* 0Y87N100001 is a 1970 Ford Thunderbird 2-Door Hardtop with a 429 CID V8 engine, serial number 100001, built in Wixom, MI.

## Powertrains

| Engine | Gross HP | Eng. Code | Transmission Availability | Falcon & Maverick | Mustang | 1970½ Falcon/ Fairlane/Torino | T-Bird & Full-size |
|---|---|---|---|---|---|---|---|
| 170 CID, 1-bbl., 6-cyl. | 105 | U | 3-speed manual | S (Mav.) | - | - | - |
|  |  |  | Cruise-O-Matic | $175 (Mav.) | - | - | - |
| 200 CID, 1-bbl., 6-cyl. | 120 | T | 3-speed manual | S (Fal.)/ $39 (Mav.) | S* | - | - |
|  |  |  | Cruise-O-Matic | $201 (Fal.)/ $240 (Mav.) | $201* | - | - |
| 240 CID, 1-bbl., 6-cyl. | 150 | V | 3-speed manual | - | - | - | S** |
|  |  |  | Cruise-O-Matic | - | - | - | $201** |

| Engine | Gross HP | Eng. Code | Transmission Availability | Falcon & Maverick | Mustang | 1970½ Falcon/ Fairlane/Torino | T-Bird & Full-size |
|---|---|---|---|---|---|---|---|
| 250 CID, 1-bbl., 6-cyl. | 155 | L | 3-speed manual | - | $39* | S (ex. GT/Cobra/Br.) | - |
| | | | Cruise-O-Matic | - | $240* | $201 (ex. GT/ Cobra/Br.) | - |
| 302 CID, 2-bbl., V8 | 220 | F | 3-speed manual | $90 (Falcon) | $101* | S (GT/Br.)/ $90 (Ex. Cobra) | $79** |
| | | | 4-speed manual | - | $306* | - | - |
| | | | Cruise-O-Matic | $291-Falcon | $302* | $201 (GT/Br.)/ $291 (Ex. Cobra) | $280** |
| Boss 302 CID, 4-bbl., V8 | 290 | | 4-speed manual | - | S (Boss) | - | - |
| 351 CID, 2-bbl., V8 | 250 | H | 3-speed manual | - | S (Mach I)/$146* | $45 (GT/Br.)/ $135 (Ex. Cobra) | S†/$124** |
| | | | 4-speed manual | - | $205 (Mach I)/$351* | $239 (GT/Br.)/ $329 (Ex. Cobra) | - |
| | | | Cruise-O-Matic | - | $222 (Mach I)/$368* | $246 (GT/Br.)/ $336 (ex. Cobra) | $201†/$325** |
| 351 CID, 4-bbl., V8 | 300 | M | 3-speed manual | - | $48 (Mach I)/$194* | $93 (GT/Br.)/ $183 (ex. Cobra) | - |
| | | | 4-speed manual | - | $253 (Mach I)/$399* | $287 (GT/Br.)/ $377 (ex. Cobra) | - |
| | | | Cruise-O-Matic | - | $270 (Mach I)/$416* | $294 (GT/Br.)/ $384 (ex. Cobra) | - |
| 390 CID, 2-bbl., V8 265-Full-size | 270 | Y | 3-speed manual | - | - | - | $86†/$210** |
| | | | Cruise-O-Matic | - | - | - | $287†/$411** |
| 428 CID Cobra Jet, 4-bbl., V8 320–Full-size | 335 | Q | 4-speed manual | - | $561 (Mach I)/ - | - | - |
| | | | | $707* | - | | |
| | | | Cruise-O-Matic | - | $578 (Mach I)/$724* | - | - |
| 428 CID Super Cobra Jet Ram Air, 4-bbl., V8 | 360 | R | 4-speed manual | - | $626 (Mach I)/$772* | - | - |
| | | | Cruise-O-Matic | - | $643 (Mach I)/$789* | - | - |
| 429 CID Thunder Jet***, 2-bbl., V8 | 320 | K | Cruise-O-Matic | - | - | - | $390†/$534** |
| 429 CID Cobra, 4-bbl., V8 | 360 | N | 4-speed manual | - | - | S (Cobra)/$386 (GT/Br.)/ $476 (ex. Cobra) | - |
| | | | Cruise-O-Matic | - | - | $39 (Cobra)/ $425 (GT/Br.)/ $515 (ex. Cobra) | $464†/$608**/ S (T-Bird) |
| 429 CID Police Interceptor***/Cobra-Jet, 4-bbl., V8 | 370 | P | 4-speed manual | - | - | $229 (Cobra)/ $614 (GT/Br.)/ $705 (ex. Cobra) | $*** |
| | | | Cruise-O-Matic | - | - | $268 (Cobra)/ $653 (GT/Br.)/ $744 (ex. Cobra) | $*** |
| Boss 429 CID***, 4-bbl., V8 (also Ram-Air) | 375 | J | Cruise-O-Matic | - | $ (Boss 429)*** | - | - |

*Except Boss 302 and Mach I.   **Except XL, LTD and Wagons.   ***Available on a limited basis on specific models only.   †XL, LTD and Wagons only.

# Major Options

| | Maverick | Falcon | Mustang | Fairlane/Torino | Full-size | Thunderbird |
|---|---|---|---|---|---|---|
| Select Aire air conditioning | $380 | $380 | $380 | $389 | $389 | $427 |
| Remote control decklid release | - | - | - | - | $14 | $14 |
| Tinted glass | $48 | $32 | $32 | $36 | $45 | $48 |
| Power steering | - | $95 | $95 | $100–$105 | $105 | S |
| Power brakes—front discs | - | - | $65 | $65 | $65 (S on LTD) | S |
| Power door locks | - | - | - | - | $45–$78 | $ |
| Power drivers seat/Bench seat | - | - | - | - | $84 | $99 |
| Power windows | - | - | - | $105 | $110 | $110 |
| AM radio | $61 | $61 | $61 | $61 | $61 | S |
| AM/FM stereo | - | - | $214 | $214 | $240 | $150 |
| Front seat console | - | - | $54 | $54 | - | - |
| Front bucket seats | - | - | S | $134 | $188 w/console | $78 w/console |
| Tilt steering wheel | - | - | $45 | - | $45 | $52 |
| Vinyl roof | - | $ | $84 | $95 | $105 | S (Landau) |
| White sidewall tires | $30 | $30 | $30 | $30 | $30 | $30 |

Options common to most models. (- = Not Available; S = Standard equipment.) Items may be standard equipment, optional at different pricing, or unavailable on certain models. This chart is only a guide.

# Paint Colors*

| | Code | Thunderbird |
|---|---|---|
| Calypso Coral | 1 | |
| New Lime | 2 | X |
| Medium Brown Metallic/Ginger Metallic | 5 | X |
| Acapulco Blue Metallic/Hulla Blue Metallic | 6 | |
| Anti Establish Mint Metallic | 7 | |
| Morning Gold | 8 | X |
| Pastel Yellow | 9 | X |
| Olive Fire Metallic (T-Bird) | 09 | X |
| Green Fire Metallic (T-Bird) | 19 | X |
| Burgundy Fire Met. (T-Bird) | 59 | X |
| Bronze Fire Metallic (T-Bird) | 89 | X |
| Raven Black/History Onyx | A | X |
| Dark Maroon | B | X |
| Dark Ivy Green Metallic/ Bring 'Em Back Olive Met. | C | X |
| Bright Yellow/Last Stand Custard | D | |
| Light Blue (T-Bird only) | E | X |
| Dark Bright Aqua Metallic/Young Turquoise Met. | F | X |
| Medium Lime Metallic | G | |
| Grabber Blue/Deep Blue | J | X |
| Bright Gold Metallic/Freudian Gilt Metallic | K | X |
| Light Gray (T-Bird only) | L | X |
| Wimbledon White/Knight White | M | X |
| Diamond Blue/Baby Blue Ice | N | |
| Original Cinnamon Metallic | O | X |
| Medium Ivy Green Metallic/Three Putt Green Metallic | P | X |
| Medium Blue Metallic/There She Blue Metallic | Q | X |
| Dark Brown Met. (T-Bird) | R | X |
| Champagne Gold Metallic/Good Clean Fawn Metallic | S | X |
| Candy Apple Red/Counter Revolutionary Red | T | X |
| Grabber Red | U | |
| Yellow | W | |
| Dark Blue Metallic | X | X |
| Medium Bronze Metallic | Y | X |
| Grabber Green/Dark Gray | Z | X |

*Colors available on most models except as indicated.

1970

# Maverick

*"It's a little gas."*

**Nameplate year of origin:** 1969.
**Current bodystyle lifespan:** 1969 through 1977.
**Predecessor to this model:** Falcon (1966 to 1969).
**Replacement for this model:** Fairmont (1978 to 1983).
**Percentage of division's sales volume:** 22.87%.
**Corporate siblings:** None.
**Primary competition:** AMC Hornet, Chevrolet Nova, and Plymouth Valiant.
**Notable changes:** All-new model for 1969½.
**Major standard equipment:** Tartan plaid cloth and vinyl interior trim, color-keyed floor mats, interior courtesy lights, flipper-type rear quarter windows, luggage compartment mat, and 6.00 × 13 BSW tires.

## Measurements

| | |
|---|---|
| Wheelbase | 103.0" |
| Length | 179.3" |
| Width | 70.6" |
| Height | 52.3" |
| Legroom — front | 41.3" |
| Legroom — rear | 31.9" |
| Headroom — front | 37.6" |
| Headroom — rear | 36.1" |
| Cargo capacity (cu. ft.) | 10.4 |
| Fuel capacity (gals.) | 16.0 |

## Models Available

| | Style Number | Base MSRP | Change from LY | Shipping Wt. (lbs.) | Production | Change from LY |
|---|---|---|---|---|---|---|
| Maverick 2-Door Sedan | 91 | $1,995 | 0.00% | 2427 | 451,081 | +252.87% |
| TOTALS | | *Avg. price* $1,995 | 0.00% | | *Production* 451,081 | +252.87% |

# Falcon

*"Big-car idea … small-car price."*

**Nameplate year of origin:** 1960.
**Current bodystyle lifespan:** 1966 through 1970.
**Predecessor to this model:** Falcon (1964 to 1965).
**Replacement for this model:** Maverick (1969 to 1977).
**Percentage of division's sales volume:** 0.80%.
**Corporate siblings:** None.
**Primary competition:** AMC Hornet, Chevrolet Nova, Dodge Dart, and Plymouth Valiant.
**Notable changes:** Virtually no changes.
**Major standard equipment:** Cloth and vinyl interior trim, front-door armrests, chrome windshield and rear window moldings, small hubcaps, and 6.95 × 14 BSW tires (7.75 × 14 on Wagons). Futura adds: Deluxe interior trim, full carpeting, rear armrests with ashtrays, side window moldings, wheel covers. Sport Coupe adds: Vinyl bucket seats, exterior bright molding, and full wheel covers.

## Measurements

| | Cars | Wagons |
|---|---|---|
| Wheelbase | 111.0" | 113.0" |
| Length | 184.3" | 199.0" |
| Width | 73.2" | 73.2" |
| Height | 54.9" | 55.5" |
| Legroom — front | 42.4" | 42.1" |
| Legroom — rear | 33.9" | 36.8" |
| Headroom — front | 38.6" | 38.7" |
| Headroom — rear | 38.8" | 37.8" |
| Cargo capacity (cu. ft.) | 12.2 | 85.2 |
| Fuel capacity (gals.) | 16.0 | 20.0 |

## Models Available

| | Style Number | Base MSRP | Change from LY | Shipping Wt. (lbs.) | Production | Change from LY |
|---|---|---|---|---|---|---|
| Falcon 2-Door Club Coupe | 10 | $2,390 | +4.69% | 2703 | 4,373 | -85.06% |
| Falcon 4-Door Sedan | 11 | $2,438 | +4.50% | 2748 | 5,301 | -76.67% |
| Falcon 4-Door Wagon | 12 | $2,767 | +4.02% | 3155 | 1,624 | -85.96% |
| Falcon Futura 2-Door Club Coupe | 20 | $2,542 | +3.29% | 2727 | 1,129 | -82.58% |
| Falcon Futura 4-Door Sedan | 21 | $2,579 | +3.24% | 2764 | 2,262 | -80.91% |

| | Style Number | Base MSRP | Change from LY | Shipping Wt. (lbs.) | Production | Change from LY |
|---|---|---|---|---|---|---|
| Falcon Futura 4-Door Wagon | 23 | $2,878 | +3.86% | 3191 | 1,005 | -86.05% |
| TOTALS | | Avg. price $2,599 | +3.34% | | Production 15,694 | -83.48% |

# Mustang

*"Number one on the sporty car scene."*

**Nameplate year of origin:** 1964½ (also on a 1963 show car).
**Current bodystyle lifespan:** 1969 through 1970.
**Predecessor to this model:** Mustang (1964½ to 1968).
**Replacement for this model:** Mustang (1971 to 1973).
**Percentage of division's sales volume:** 10.00%.
**Corporate siblings:** Mercury Cougar.
**Primary competition:** AMC Javelin, Chevrolet Camaro, Dodge Challenger, Plymouth Barracuda, and Pontiac Firebird.
**Notable changes:** Restyled front appearance and trim changes.
**Major standard equipment:** All-vinyl bucket seats, full carpeting, courtesy lights, hubcaps, and E78 × 14 BSW tires. SportsRoof adds: Swing-out rear quarter windows, and tinted rear glass. Convertible adds: Manually operated top, and color-keyed top boot. Grande adds to Hardtop: Cloth and vinyl interior trim, teak-toned instrument panel trim, electric clock, two-tone paint stripe, bright moldings (rocker, wheel lip, and lower back panel), dual racing-style outside mirrors, soft-ride suspension and special sound insulation package. Mach I adds to Sports Roof: High back bucket seats, teak-toned instrument panel trim, electric clock, dual racing-style outside mirrors, competition suspension, black low-gloss paint on hood, reflective dual tape stripes, special sound insulation package, and E70 × 14 Wide-Oval WSW tires. Boss 302 adds: 302 CID 4-bbl. V8, 4-speed manual transmission, rear deck spoiler, louvered rear windows, "Mag"-style wheels, and F60 × 15 Wide-Oval tires. Boss 429 adds: 429 CID V8 engine.

## Measurements

| | |
|---|---|
| Wheelbase | 108.0" |
| Length | 187.4" |
| Width | 71.7" |
| Height | 51.4" |
| Legroom — front | 42.0" |
| Legroom — rear | 27.0" |
| Headroom — front | 37.4" |
| Headroom — rear | 35.8" |
| Cargo capacity (cu. ft.) | 9.8 |
| Fuel capacity (gals.) | 20.0 |

## Models Available

| | Style Number | Base MSRP | Change from LY | Shipping Wt. (lbs.) | Production | Change from LY |
|---|---|---|---|---|---|---|
| Mustang 2-Door Hardtop | 1 | $2,721 | +3.26% | 2737 | 82,569 | -35.47% |
| Mustang 2-Door SportsRoof HT | 2 | $2,771 | +5.16% | 2704 | 45,934 | -25.89% |
| Mustang 2-Door Convertible | 3 | $3,025 | +6.18% | 2859 | 7,673 | -47.97% |
| Mustang Grande 2-Door Hardtop | 4 | $2,926 | +2.09% | 2782 | 13,581 | -38.77% |
| Mustang Mach I 2-Dr. SportsRoof HT | 5 | $3,271 | +4.77% | 3169 | 40,970 | -43.46% |
| Mustang Boss 302 2-Dr. Sptrf. HT | 2 | $3,720 | NEW | 3169 | 6,318 | NEW |
| TOTALS | | Avg. price $3,072 | +8.90% | | Production 197,045 | -34.17% |

*Boss 429 available as limited production model. Pricing not available. Production included with Boss 302.

# Torino, Fairlane and Falcon

*"Everything you could want or need in a car."*

**Nameplate year of origin:** 1968.

**Current bodystyle lifespan:** 1970 through 1971.

**Predecessor to this model:** Fairlane/Torino (1968 to 1969).

**Replacement for this model:** Torino (1972 to 1976).

**Percentage of division's sales volume:** 20.66%.

**Corporate siblings:** Mercury Montego.

**Primary competition:** AMC Rebel, Chevrolet Chevelle, Plymouth Satellite, Dodge Coronet, and Pontiac Tempest.

**Notable changes:** Completely restyled. Falcon added mid-year after Maverick was introduced and original Falcon discontinued.

**Major standard equipment:** Cloth and vinyl bench seat, color-keyed rubber floor mats, front and rear armrests, chrome windshield molding, and E78 × 14 BSW tires (G78 × 14 BSW on Wagons). Fairlane 500 adds: Full carpeting, deluxe interior trim, power-operated convertible top, and chrome rear and side window moldings. Torino adds: Torino interior trim, accent tape stripe on Hardtop and Sedan, and full wheel covers. Torino Brougham adds: Luxury interior trim, concealed headlamps, additional exterior trim, electric clock and 302 CID V8 engine. Torino Squire adds: Exterior wood-grain trim. Torino GT adds: All-vinyl front bench seat, styled steel wheels, hood scoop, and E70 × 14 Wide-Oval WSW tires (F70 × 14 on Convertible). Cobra adds: 428 CID V8 engine, 4-speed manual transmission, heavy-duty suspension, dual exhausts, and F70 × 14 Wide-Oval tires.

## Measurements

|  | Cars | Wagons |
|---|---|---|
| Wheelbase | 117.0" | 114.0" |
| Length | 206.2" | 209.0" |
| Width | 76.4" | 75.4" |
| Height | NA | NA |
| Legroom — front | 42.2" | 42.1" |
| Legroom — rear | 36.0" | 36.0" |
| Headroom — front | 38.5" | 38.6" |
| Headroom — rear | 37.3" | 37.4" |
| Cargo capacity (cu. ft.) | NA | NA |
| Fuel capacity (gals.) | 20.0 | 20.0 |

## Models Available

|  | Style Number | Base MSRP | Change from LY | Shipping Wt. (lbs.) | Production | Change from LY |
|---|---|---|---|---|---|---|
| Falcon 2-Door Sedan | 26 | $2,460 | NEW | 3096 | 26,071 | NEW |
| Falcon 4-Door Sedan | 27 | $2,500 | +0.48% | 3112 | 30,443 | +11.53% |
| Falcon 4-Door Wagon | 40 | $2,801 | -1.41% | 3468 | 10,539 | -3.15% |
| Fairlane 500 2-Door Hardtop | 29 | $2,660 | +1.29% | 3129 | 70,636 | +150.67% |
| Fairlane 500 4-Door Sedan | 28 | $2,627 | +2.30% | 3117 | 25,780 | -36.95% |
| Fairlane 500 4-Door, 2-Seat Wgn. | 41 | $2,957 | +0.20% | 3468 | 13,613 | +5.78% |
| Torino 2-Door Hardtop | 30 | $2,722 | -1.16% | 3174 | 49,826 | +139.67% |
| Torino 2-Dr. SportsRoof HT | 34 | $2,810 | NEW | 3212 | 12,490 | NEW |
| Torino 4-Door Sedan | 31 | $2,689 | -1.61% | 3159 | 30,117 | +151.58% |
| Torino 4-Door Hardtop | 32 | $2,795 | NEW | 3190 | 14,312 | NEW |
| Torino 4-Dr., 2-Seat Wagon | 42 | $3,074 | NEW | 3533 | 10,613 | NEW |
| Torino Brougham 2-Door Hardtop | 33 | $3,006 | NEW | 3276 | 16,911 | NEW |
| Torino Brougham 4-Door Hardtop | 36 | $3,078 | NEW | 3299 | 14,543 | NEW |
| Torino Squire 4-Dr., 2-Seat Wgn. | 43 | $3,379 | +8.75% | 3635 | 13,166 | -9.02% |
| Torino GT 2-Door SportsRoof HT | 35 | $3,105 | +9.33% | 3368 | 56,819 | -7.34% |
| Torino GT 2-Door Convertible | 37 | $3,212 | +3.95% | 3461 | 3,939 | +54.35% |
| Torino Cobra 2-Dr. SportsRoof HT | 38 | $3,270 | +2.80% | 3775 | 7,675 | * |
| TOTALS | *Avg. price* $2,891 | | +2.34% | *Production* 496,644 | | +52.1% |

*Comparisons made to equivalent 1969 models. See text for details.*

# Custom, Galaxie & LTD

*"Take a Quiet Break in the 1970 Ford."*

**Nameplate year of origin:** 1957 (Custom), 1959 (Galaxie) and 1965 (LTD).

**Current bodystyle lifespan:** 1969 through 1970.

**Predecessor to this model:** Full-size Ford (1967 to 1968).

**Replacement for this model:** Galaxie and LTD (1971 to 1977, with several redesigns).

**Percentage of division's sales volume:** 43.12%.

**Corporate siblings:** Mercury Monterey and Marquis.

**Primary competition:** AMC Ambassador, Chevrolet Biscayne/BelAir/Impala/Caprice, Dodge Polara/Monaco, Plymouth Fury, and Pontiac Catalina.

**Notable changes:** Revised trim and detail changes.

**Major standard equipment:** All vinyl front bench seat, full carpeting, arm rests on all doors, rear window trim molding, and F78 × 15 BSW tires (H78 × 15 BSW tires on Wagon). Custom 500 adds: Cloth and vinyl front bench seat, and chrome windshield molding. Galaxie 500 adds: All-vinyl front bench seat on convertible, wood-like door trim, additional interior lighting, chrome side window moldings, power-operated top and color-keyed top boot on convertible. XL adds: All-vinyl front bench seat, lower door carpet trim and polished trim, courtesy and reading lamps, concealed headlamps, full wheel covers, special badging, and G78 × 15 BSW tires on Convertible. LTD adds: Padded cloth upholstery, simulated wood interior trim, and additional courtesy lights. Country Squire adds: Wood grained bodyside appliques. LTD Brougham adds: Unique Brougham interior trim with bench seats, rear door courtesy lights, cut-pile carpeting, rocker panel moldings, and G78 × 15 BSW tires.

## Measurements

|  | Cars | Wagons |
|---|---|---|
| Wheelbase | 121.0" | 121.0" |
| Length | 213.9" | 216.9" |
| Width | 79.7" | 79.7" |
| Height | 54.9" | 56.8" |
| Legroom — front | 41.9" | 41.9" |
| Legroom — rear | 38.7" | 38.5" |
| Headroom — front | 38.9" | 38.9" |
| Headroom — rear | 37.8" | 38.1" |
| Cargo capacity (cu. ft.) | 18.0 | 96.2 |
| Fuel capacity (gals.) | 24.0 | 24.0 |

## Models Available

| | Style Number | Base MSRP | Change from LY | Shipping Wt. (lbs.) | Production | Change from LY |
|---|---|---|---|---|---|---|
| Custom 4-Door Sedan | 51 | $2,771 | +2.97% | 3579 | 42,849 | -6.14% |
| Custom 4-Door Ranch Wagon | 70 | $3,305 | +6.92% | 4124 | 15,086 | -13.74% |
| Custom 500 4-Door Sedan | 53 | $2,872 | +2.94% | 3582 | 41,261 | -9.83% |
| Custom 500 4-Dr. Ranch Wagon | 72 | $3,368 | +6.75% | 4125 | 15,304 | -6.86% |
| C. 500 4-Dr. Ranch Wagon w/DFRS* | 72 | $3,481 | +6.52% | 4213 | 9,943 | -14.01% |
| Galaxie 500 2-Door Hardtop | 58 | $3,094 | +3.76% | 3484 | 57,059 | -20.66% |
| Galaxie 500 2-Door SportsRoof HT | 55 | $3,043 | +3.86% | 3548 | 50,825 | -20.49% |
| Galaxie 500 4-Door Sedan | 54 | $3,026 | +3.84% | 3471 | 101,784 | -2.70% |
| Galaxie 500 4-Door Hardtop | 56 | $3,096 | +3.79% | 3541 | 53,817 | -15.95% |
| G. 500 Country Sedan 4-Dr. Wagon | 73 | $3,488 | +6.54% | 4194 | 32,209 | -11.24% |
| G. 500 Country Sedan 4-Dr. w/DFRS* | 74 | $3,600 | +6.23% | 4254 | 22,645 | +95.84% |
| XL 2-Door Hardtop | 60 | $3,293 | +7.30% | 3783 | 27,251 | -50.05% |
| XL 2-Door Convertible | 61 | $3,501 | +6.19% | 3855 | 6,348 | -14.24% |
| LTD 2-Door Hardtop | 62 | $3,356 | +6.47% | 3798 | 96,324 | -13.66% |
| LTD 4-Door Sedan | 64 | $3,307 | +6.33% | 3784 | 78,306 | +22.91% |
| LTD 4-Door Hardtop | 66 | $3,385 | +6.45% | 3831 | 90,390 | -20.13% |
| LTD Country Squire 4-Dr. Wagon | 75 | $3,832 | +4.67% | 4197 | 39,837 | -14.23% |
| LTD Cntry. Sq. 4-Dr. Wgn. w/DFRS* | 76 | $3,909 | +3.47% | 4263 | 69,077 | -16.56% |
| LTD Brougham 2-Door Hardtop | 62 | $3,537 | NEW | 3876 | ** | NEW |
| LTD Brougham 4-Door Sedan | 64 | $3,502 | NEW | 3862 | ** | NEW |
| LTD Brougham 4-Door Hardtop | 66 | $3,579 | NEW | 3909 | ** | NEW |
| TOTALS | | *Avg. price* $3,350 | +7.79% | | *Production* 850,315 | -14.87% |

*Dual facing rear seats.   **Included in LTD production.

# Thunderbird

*"The ultimate in personalized luxury."*

**Nameplate year of origin:** 1955.
**Current bodystyle lifespan:** 1967 through 1971 (restyled in 1970).
**Predecessor to this model:** Thunderbird (1964 to 1966).
**Replacement for this model:** Thunderbird (1972 to 1976).
**Percentage of division's sales volume:** 2.55%.
**Corporate siblings:** Lincoln Continental Mark III.
**Primary competition:** Buick Riviera and Oldsmobile Toronado.
**Notable changes:** Major restyle of existing platform.
**Major standard equipment:** Luxury all-cloth interior with cut-pile carpeting, front bench seat, tilt away steering wheel, AM radio, power steering, power front disc brakes, sequential turn signals, full wheel covers, and 215R15 Michelin BSW tires.

## Measurements

| | 2-Doors | 4-Doors |
|---|---|---|
| Wheelbase | 115.0" | 117.0" |
| Length | 212.5" | 215.0" |
| Width | 78.0" | 77.4" |
| Height | 53.5" | 54.2" |
| Legroom — front | 42.1" | 42.1" |
| Legroom — rear | 32.2" | 34.0" |
| Headroom — front | 37.4" | 38.1" |
| Headroom — rear | 36.9" | 37.2" |
| Cargo capacity (cu. ft.) | 12.3 | 12.3 |
| Fuel capacity (gals.) | 24.1 | 24.1 |

## Models Available

| | Style Number | Base MSRP | Change from LY | Shipping Wt. (lbs.) | Production | Change from LY |
|---|---|---|---|---|---|---|
| Thunderbird 2-Door Hardtop | 83 | $4,961 | +2.84% | 4411 | 5,116 | -13.48% |
| Thunderbird 2-Dr. Landau Coupe | 84 | $5,104 | +2.82% | 4417 | 36,847 | +33.19% |
| Thunderbird 4-Door Landau Sedan | 87 | $5,182 | +2.76% | 4521 | 8,401 | -46.32% |
| TOTALS | | *Avg. price* $5,082 | +2.79% | *Production* | 50,364 | +2.31% |

---

# IMPERIAL

*"A man is understandably proud of the things that please him most."*

---

This year's Imperial models were not vastly changed from the new-for-'69 models. A new grille was designed for the front, and a new body sill molding was added down the side, and the rear side marker lamps moved into the bumper. Otherwise, a few minor trim changes would sum up the new look for 1970. The only change in the model availability was the dropping of the Crown 4-Door Sedan.

This model year would be the last for the entire Crown series. Unfortunately sales for the model year declined approximately 50 percent this model year. This would lead to the Imperial returning to top-of-the-line Chrysler status in 1971. Since 1955, Imperial had been its own sales and marketing division within the Chrysler division.

Crown 4-Door Hardtop

LeBaron 4-Door Hardtop

**Model year production:** 11,816, down 46.48% from 1969.
**Domestic market share:** 0.14% (13th place).
**Base price range:** $5,779 to $6,328.
**Industry average base price:** $3,538.
**Imperial average base price:** $6,040.
**Introduction date:** September 23, 1969.
**Assembly plants:** Newark, NJ (F), and Detroit, MI (C).
**Data plate identification:** Thirteen digit code read as follows:

four digit style number (see listings below) in which Y = Imperial, 2nd number identifies series (e.g., M is for LeBaron), 3rd and 4th digits indicate body style; 5th digit is engine code; 0 for 1970; assembly plant code; 100001 and up for serial number. *Example:* YM23T0C100001 is a 1970 Imperial LeBaron 2-Door Hardtop with a 440 CID V8 engine, serial number 100001, built in Detroit, MI.

## Powertrains

| Engine | Engine Code | Gross HP | Transmission Availability | Imperial |
|---|---|---|---|---|
| 440 CID, 4-bbl., V8 | T | 350 | TorqueFlite Automatic | S |

## Major Options

| | Crown | LeBaron |
|---|---|---|
| Air conditioning | $475 | $475 |
| Electronic cruise control | $92 | $92 |
| Electric rear window defogger | $32 | $32 |
| Deck lid remote release | $33 | $33 |
| Power steering—variable-ratio | S | S |
| Power brakes | S | S |
| Power door locks | $49 (2-Dr)/ | $49 (2-Dr)/ |
| | $73 (4-Dr) | $73 (4-Dr) |
| Power driver's seat/Bench seat | $120 | $120 |
| Power windows | S | S |
| AM radio w/concealed antenna | $165 | $165 |
| AM/FM stereo w/concealed antenna | $234 | $234 |
| Tilt and telescoping steering wheel | $97 | $97 |
| Vinyl roof | $55 | S |
| Whitewall tires—standard size | $46 | $46 |

Options common to most models. (S = Standard equipment.) Items may be standard equipment, optional at different pricing, or unavailable on certain models. This chart is only a guide.

## Paint Colors

| | Code |
|---|---|
| Winchester Gray Metallic | A4 |
| Slate Gray | A8 |
| Charcoal Metallic | A9 |
| Glacial Blue Metallic | B2 |
| Midnight Blue Metallic | B9 |
| Burnished Red Metallic | E7 |
| Amber Sherwood Metallic | F3 |
| Avocado Metallic | F9 |
| April Green Metallic | J4 |
| Autumn Bronze Metallic | K6 |
| Sandalwood Beige | L1 |
| Aztec Gold Metallic | L6 |
| Sparkling Burgundy Metallic | M-8 |
| Coral Turquoise Metallic | Q5 |
| Tahitian Walnut Metallic | T8 |
| Spinnaker White | W1 |
| Formal Black | X9 |
| Honeydew | Y4 |
| Crystal Dawn | Y5 |
| Tawny Gold Metallic | Y9 |

**1970**

# Crown

*"We don't subscribe to the notion that the least expensive model should be the least desirable."*

**Nameplate year of origin:** 1957 (Not the same as Crown Imperial series).
**Current bodystyle lifespan:** 1969 through 1973.
**Predecessor to this model:** Crown (1967 to 1968).
**Replacement for this model:** Chrysler Imperial (1974 to 1975).
**Percentage of division's sales volume:** 13.43%.
**Corporate siblings:** LeBaron.
**Primary competition:** Cadillac Calais and Lincoln Continental.
**Notable changes:** Revised grille and trim changes.
**Major standard equipment:** Cloth and vinyl front bench seat, pile carpeting, remote-control left-hand outside mirror, power windows, electric clock, trip odometer, 3-speed electric windshield wipers with washers, Torqueflite automatic transmission, power steering, power brakes, wheel covers and L84 × 15 BSW tires.

## Measurements

| | |
|---|---|
| Wheelbase | 127.0" |
| Length | 229.7" |
| Width | 79.1" |
| Height | 55.7" |
| Legroom — front | 41.9" |
| Legroom — rear | 41.2" |
| Headroom — front | 38.3" |
| Headroom — rear | 37.0" |
| Cargo capacity (cu. ft.) | NA |
| Fuel capacity (gals.) | 25.0 |

## Models Available

| | Style Number | Base MSRP | Change from LY | Shipping Wt. (lbs.) | Production | Change from LY |
|---|---|---|---|---|---|---|
| Crown 2-Door Hardtop | YL23 | $5,779 | +3.34% | 4610 | 254 | +4.10% |
| Crown 4-Door Hardtop | YL43 | $5,956 | +3.22% | 4735 | 1,333 | +61.97% |
| TOTALS | | *Avg. price* $5,868 | +2.75% | | *Production* 1,587 | -40.87% |

# LeBaron

*"Look upon it as an unusually comfortable performance car."*

**Nameplate year of origin:** 1924 (as Chrysler Sedan model designation); 1926 (as series).
**Current bodystyle lifespan:** 1969 through 1973.
**Predecessor to this model:** LeBaron (1967 to 1968).
**Replacement for this model:** Chrysler Imperial (1974 to 1975).
**Percentage of division's sales volume:** 86.57%.
**Corporate siblings:** Crown.
**Primary competition:** Cadillac de Ville and Lincoln Continental.
**Notable changes:** Revised grille and trim changes.
**Major standard equipment:** Cloth and fabric-and-leather or broadcloth split-bench front seat, pile carpeting, rear built-in pillow and "Lavaliere" entry strap (4-Door), power seat, power windows, electric clock, trip odometer, vinyl roof with formal carriage rear window, 3-speed electric windshield wipers with washers, Torqueflite automatic transmission, power steering, power brakes, wheel covers and L84 × 15 BSW tires.

## Measurement

| | |
|---|---|
| Wheelbase | 127.0" |
| Length | 229.7" |
| Width | 79.1" |
| Height | 55.7" |
| Legroom — front | 41.9" |
| Legroom — rear | 41.2" |
| Headroom — front | 38.3" |
| Headroom — rear | 37.2" |
| Cargo capacity (cu. ft.) | NA |
| Fuel capacity (gals.) | 25.0 |

## Models Available

| | Style Number | Base MSRP | Change from LY | Shipping Wt. (lbs.) | Production | Change from LY |
|---|---|---|---|---|---|---|
| LeBaron 2-Door Hardtop | YM23 | $6,095 | +3.34% | 4660 | 1,803 | -60.56% |
| LeBaron 4-Door Hardtop | YM43 | $6,328 | +3.21% | 4805 | 8,426 | -43.15% |
| TOTALS | | *Avg. price* $6,212 | +3.28% | | *Production* 10,229 | -47.25% |

# LINCOLN

*"The finest cars built in America."*

Lincoln Continental entered the new decade with its first total revamping since 1961. The now familiar "suicide door" four-door models were gone, and the full-width grille with dual headlights at each end was replaced by a grille that protruded from the center section of the car as before, but with hidden headlights set on each side. Taillights were inset in the rear bumper, and the bodyside lines were a little more angular than before. Rear wheel opening fender skirts completed the angular styling look. Though a to-

tally new car, it was still recognizable as a Lincoln. The overall impression of the car was more formal than any Lincoln since the Thirties.

The Continental Mark III, having been new for the 1969 model year, was little changed for 1970, receiving only a few additional options and some trim and detail changes. All Lincoln models continued with the 460 CID V8 engine mated to a Select-Shift automatic transmission.

Continental 4-Door Sedan

Continental Mark III 2-Door Hardtop

**Model year production:** 53,127, down 23.27% from 1969.
**Domestic market share:** 0.64% (12th place).
**Base price range:** $5,976 to $7,281.
**Industry average base price:** $3,538.
**Lincoln average base price:** $6,489.
**Introduction date:** September 1969.
**Assembly plants:** Wixom, MI (Y), and Allen Park, MI (S).

**Data plate identification:** Eleven digit code read as follows: 0 for 1970; 2nd digit is assembly plant code; 2-digit model number (see listings below); 5th digit is engine code; 800001 and up for serial number. *Example:* 0Y82A800001 is a 1970 Lincoln Continental 4-Door Sedan with a 460 CID V8 engine, serial number 800001, built in Wixom, MI.

## Powertrains

| Engine | Gross HP | Engine Code | Transmission Availability | Mark III & Continental |
|---|---|---|---|---|
| 460 CID, 4-bbl., V8 | 365 | A | Select-Shift Automatic | S |

## Major Options

| | Continental | Mark III |
|---|---|---|
| Air condtioning — manual | $504 | $523 |
| Tinted glass | $53 | $53 |
| Automatic headlight dimmers | $51 | $51 |
| 6-way power seat | $89 | $180 |
| Power door locks | $47–$68 | $47 |

## Paint Colors

| | Code |
|---|---|
| Light Ivy Yellow | 2 |
| Medium Brown Metallic | 5 |
| Light Gold | 8 |
| Pastel Yellow | 9 |
| Olive Stardust Metallic | 09 |

**1970**

|  | Continental | Mark III |
|---|---|---|
| AM-FM stereo radio w/power antenna | $302 | $302 |
| AM w/stereo 8-track w/power antenna | $297 | $297 |
| Vinyl roof | $152 | S |
| Sunroof | - | $459 |
| Tilt and telescope steering wheel | $72 | $70 |
| Leather upholstery | $157 | $164 |
| Speed control | $95 | $95 |
| White sidewall tires | $41 | $41 |
| Stardust Metallic paint colors | $131 | $131 |

Options common to most models. (- = Not Available; S = Standard equipment.) Items may be standard equipment, optional at different pricing, or unavailable on certain models. This chart is only a guide.

|  | Code |
|---|---|
| Green Stardust Metallic | 19 |
| Red Stardust Metallic | 59 |
| Bronze Stardust Met. | 89 |
| Black | A |
| Dark Maroon | B |
| Dark Green Metallic | C |
| Light Blue | E |
| Dark Bright Aqua Metallic | F |
| Light Green | H |
| Deep Blue Metallic | J |
| Light Gray Metallic | L |
| White | M |
| Medium Green Metallic | O |
| Medium Ivy Green Metallic | P |
| Medium Blue Metallic | Q |
| Dark Brown Metallic | R |
| Medium Gold Metallic | S |
| Medium Aqua Metallic | U |
| Dark Blue | X |
| Medium Bronze Metallic | Y |
| Dark Gray Metallic | Z |

# Continental

*"As always, every inch a Continental."*

**Nameplate year of origin:** 1940 (1961 as a standard sedan nameplate).
**Current bodystyle lifespan:** 1970 through 1979 (restyle in 1974).
**Predecessor to this model:** Continental (1961 to 1969).
**Replacement for this model:** Town Car (1980 to 1991).
**Percentage of division's sales volume:** 59.66%.
**Corporate siblings:** None.
**Primary competition:** Cadillac de Ville and Imperial LeBaron.
**Notable changes:** Totally redesigned.
**Major standard equipment:** Brocade and vinyl front bench seat upholstery with folding center armrests front and rear, two-way power seat, trip odometer, walnut-tone instrument panel and door appliques, vanity mirror, looped-pile carpeting, variable-speed windshield wipers with washers, carpeted luggage compartment, rear fender skirts, power steering, power brakes, automatic transmission and 9.15 × 15 BSW tires.

## Measurements

| Wheelbase | 127.0" |
|---|---|
| Length | 225.0" |
| Width | 79.6" |
| Height | 55.7" |
| Legroom — front | 41.9" |
| Legroom — rear | 41.9" |
| Headroom — front | 38.5" |
| Headroom — rear | 37.6" |
| Luggage capacity (cu. ft.) | 18.1 |
| Fuel capacity (gals.) | 24.2 |

## Models Available

|  | Style Number | Base MSRP | Change from LY | Shipping Wt. (lbs.) | Production | Change from LY |
|---|---|---|---|---|---|---|
| Continental 2-Door Hardtop | 81 | $5,976 | +2.50% | 4669 | 3,073 | -65.98% |
| Continental 4-Door Sedan | 82 | $6,211 | +2.44% | 4719 | 28,622 | -2.48% |
| TOTALS | | Avg. price $6,094 | +2.47% | | Production 31,695 | -17.42% |

# Continental Mark III

*"Authoritatively styled, decisively individual."*

**Nameplate year of origin:** 1956 (Continental Mark II).
**Current bodystyle lifespan:** 1969 through 1971.
**Predecessor to this model:** Continental Mark II (1956 to 1957).
**Replacement for this model:** Continental Mark IV (1972 to 1976).
**Percentage of division's sales volume:** 40.34%.
**Corporate siblings:** Ford Thunderbird.
**Primary competition:** Buick Riviera, Cadillac Eldorado, and Oldsmobile Toronado.
**Notable changes:** Minor trim and detail changes.
**Major standard equipment:** Two-way power front split bench seat, automatic seat back release, walnut dashboard and steering wheel inserts, cut-pile carpeting, power windows, vinyl top, Cartier electric chronometer, spare tire cover, carpeted luggage compartment, luxury wheel covers, overhead console with warning lights, AM radio, Sure-Track brake system, and 225 × 15 Michelin WSW tires.

## Measurements

| | |
|---|---|
| Wheelbase | 117.2" |
| Length | 216.1" |
| Width | 79.4" |
| Height | 53.0" |
| Legroom — front | 42.1" |
| Legroom — rear | 34.7" |
| Headroom — front | 37.1" |
| Headroom — rear | 36.5" |
| Luggage capacity (cu. ft.) | 13.5 |
| Fuel capacity (gals.) | NA |

## Models Available

| | Style Number | Base MSRP | Change from LY | Shipping Wt. (lbs.) | Production | Change from LY |
|---|---|---|---|---|---|---|
| Continental Mark III 2-Door Hardtop | 89 | $7,281 | +5.37% | 4675 | 21,432 | -30.55% |
| TOTALS | | *Avg. price* $7,281 | +5.37% | *Production* | 21,432 | -30.55% |

# MERCURY

*"Password for action in the '70's."*

The cars at the sign of the cat were little changed visually from their predecessors, except for the mid-size Montego line. And did it make an impact! No one could mistake the front end styling for any other car on the road. The Montego used a protruding center nose section that extended as far out as the fender did at the sides, creating an exaggerated "W" or "M" effect when viewed from overhead. The Cyclone models even had what looked like a crosshair in the center section of the grille. The rest of the body shell, from the cowl back, was much more traditional and was shared with the Ford Fairlane and Torino lines. At this point in time, Mercury was still into racing, and these new cars looked intimidating and aggressive, even if they weren't very aerodynamic on the track. Powertrains were similar to previous years, but model names were shuffled. The Comet was gone, having been offered only as an entry-

level two-door hardtop for the past two years. Also gone was the Montego convertible, as Ford would only offer that body style in the Torino line this year. The Cyclone CJ was gone, but in its place were two new cars: the Cyclone GT and Cyclone Spoiler. Both of these cars offered high performance and flashy styling in a unique package. The Cyclone GT offered the smaller displacement 351 CID V8, for a more popular, price effective choice among buyers. The Spoiler was basically the CJ with a new name, but it was powered by the 429 CID V8 instead of the 428 CID V8, which Mercury only offered in the Cougar this year.

In the Cougar and full-size Mercury lines, changes were minimal. The Cougar grille was changed with the center portion of the hood dropping down to divide the grille, similar to the original Cougar. Full-size models received new grilles and revised trim also. The Monterey Custom Wagon was dropped. A new top-of-the-line Marquis Brougham was offered this year, featuring more luxurious appointments inside, a vinyl roof and distinctive exterior body moldings. Engine choices were similar to that of previous years, and 1970 would be the last year of the 390 CID V8 engine for Mercury.

Cougar XR-7 2-Door Hardtop

Cyclone Spoiler 2-Door Hardtop

Marauder 2-Door Hardtop

Marquis Brougham 4-Door Hardtop

Montego MX Brougham 4-Door Hardtop

Monterey Custom 4-Door Sedan

**Model year production:** 340,843, down 14.47% from 1969.
**Domestic market share:** 4.09% (8th place).
**Base price range:** $2,736 to $4,500.
**Industry average price:** $3,538.
**Mercury average price:** $3,596.
**Introduction date:** September 1969.
**Assembly plants:** Dearborn, MI (F); Lorain, OH (H); Kansas City, MO (K); Allen Park, MI (S); St. Louis, MO (Z); and Oakville, Ontario, Canada (B).

**Data plate identification:** Eleven digit code read as follows: 0 for 1970; 2nd digit is assembly plant code; 2-digit model number (see listings below); 5th digit is engine code; 500001 and up for serial number. *Example:* 0Z01H500001 is a 1970 Mercury Montego 2-Door Hardtop with a 351 CID V8 engine, serial number 500001, built in St. Louis, MO.

## Powertrains

| Engine | Gross HP | Engine Code | Transmission Availability | Cougar | Montego | Marauder/ Mtry/Wgns | Marquis & M. X-100 |
|---|---|---|---|---|---|---|---|
| 250 CID, 1-bbl., 6-cyl. | 155 | L | 3-speed man. | - | S** | - | - |
| | | | Select-Shift Automatic | - | $191** | - | - |
| 302 CID, 2-bbl., V8 | 220 | F | 3-speed man. | - | $105** | - | - |
| | | | Select-Shift Automatic | - | $302** | - | - |
| 302 CID, 4-bbl., V8 | 290 | F | 4-speed man. | $593* | - | - | - |
| 351 CID, 2-bbl., V8 | 250 | H | 3-speed man. | S | S (Cyclone GT)/ $150** | - | - |
| | | | 4-speed man. | $205 | $194 (Cyclone GT)/ $334** | - | - |
| | | | Select-Shift Automatic | $206 | $206 (Cyclone GT)/ $346** | - | - |
| 351 CID, 4-bbl., V8 | 300 | M | 4-speed man. | $257 | $247 (Cyclone GT)/ $397** | - | - |
| | | | Select-Shift Automatic | $259 | $280 (Cyclone GT)/ $430** | - | - |
| 390 CID, 2-bbl., V8 | 265 | S | 3-speed man. | - | - | S | - |
| | | | Select-Shift Automatic | - | - | $238 | - |

| Engine | Gross HP | Engine Code | Transmission Availability | Cougar | Montego | Marauder/ Mtry/Wgns | Marquis & M. X-100 |
|---|---|---|---|---|---|---|---|
| 428 CID Cobra Jet, 4-bbl., V8 | 335 | | 4-speed man. | $515 | - | - | - |
| | | | Select-Shift Automatic | $538 | - | - | - |
| 429 CID, 2-bbl., V8 | 320 | N | 3-speed man. | - | - | $40 | - |
| | | | Select-Shift Automatic | - | - | $278 | S (Marq.) |
| 429 CID Thunder Jet, 4-bbl., V8 | 360 | | 4-speed man. | - | S (Cyclone)/ $486** | - | - |
| | | | Select-Shift Automatic | - | $42 (Cyclone)/ $528** | $343 | S (X100)/ $65 (Marq.) |
| 429 CID Cobra Jet, 4-bbl., V8 | 370 | | 4-speed man. | - | $141 (Cyclone GT) | - | - |
| | | | Select-Shift Automatic | - | $183 (Cyclone GT) | - | - |
| 429 CID Super Cobra Jet, 4-bbl., V8 | 375 | | 4-speed man. | - | S (Cyclone Spoiler) | - | - |
| | | | Select-Shift Automatic | - | $42 (Cyclone Spoiler) | - | - |

*Available only with Eliminator package. The 351 CID, 4-bbl. V8 is standard with Eliminator package.      **Except Cyclone.

## Major Options

| | Cougar | Montego | Monterey/Marauder | Marquis |
|---|---|---|---|---|
| Air conditioning | $376 | $389 | $421 | $421 |
| Speed control | $71 | - | $64 | $64 |
| Tinted glass | $32 | $36 | $36 | $36 |
| Deck lid remote release | - | - | $14 | $14 |
| Power steering | $106 | $105 | $115 | S |
| Power brakes — front discs | $65 | $65 | $71 | S |
| Power door locks | - | - | $45–$69 | $45–$69 |
| Power driver's seat/Bench seat | - | - | $100 | $100 |
| Power windows | $105 | $105 | $110 | $110 |
| AM radio | $61 | $61 | $64 | $64 |
| AM/FM stereo | $213 | $213 | $240 | $240 |
| Front seat console | $57 | $57 | S (X-100) | - |
| Front bucket seats | S | $119 | S (X-100) | - |
| Tilt steering wheel | - | - | $45 | $45 |
| Vinyl roof | $89 | $100 | $115 ($143 Wagons) | $115 ($143 Wagons) |
| Styled steel or aluminum wheels | $91–$117 | $39–$117 | $117 | $91 |
| Wire or luxury wheel covers | $48–$75 | $42 | $47 | S |
| Option packages: | | | | |
| Eliminator package | $130 | - | - | - |

Options common to most models. (- = Not Available; S = Standard equipment.) Items may be standard equipment, optional at different pricing, or unavailable on certain models. This chart is only a guide.

## Paint Colors*

| | Code |
|---|---|
| Competition Orange | 1 |
| Light Ivy Yellow | 2 |
| Medium Brown Met. | 5 |
| Bright Blue Metallic | 6 |
| Light Gold | 8 |
| Pastel Yellow | 9 |
| Black | A |
| Dark Maroon | B |
| Dark Green Metallic | C |
| Bright Yellow | D |
| Dark Bright Aqua Met. | F |
| Medium Lime Metallic | G |
| Competition Blue | J |
| Bright Gold Met. | K |
| Light Gray Metallic | L |
| White | M |
| Pastel Blue | N |
| Medium Ivy Green Met. | P |
| Medium Blue Metallic | Q |
| Medium Gold Metallic | S |
| Red | T |
| Competition Gold | U |
| Yellow | W |
| Dark Blue | X |
| Medium Bronze Met. | Y |
| Competition Green | Z |

*All colors available on most models; some may be at additional cost.

**1970**

# Cougar

*"Still America's best equipped luxury sports car at a popular price."*

**Nameplate year of origin:** 1967.
**Current bodystyle lifespan:** 1967 through 1970.
**Predecessor to this model:** None.
**Replacement for this model:** Cougar (1971 to 1973).
**Percentage of division's sales volume:** 21.22%.
**Corporate siblings:** Ford Mustang.
**Primary competition:** AMC Javelin, Chevrolet Camaro, Dodge Challenger, Plymouth Barracuda, and Pontiac Firebird.
**Notable changes:** New grille, minor trim and detail changes.
**Major standard equipment:** All-vinyl front bucket seats, full carpeting, concealed headlights, sequential taillamps with wrap-around backup lights, dual paint stripes on body side, power top on convertible, and E78 × 14 BSW tires. XR-7 adds: Leather and vinyl bucket seats, burled-walnut style interior trim, tachometer, trip odometer, electric clock, racing-style outside rear view mirror, and XR-7 specific wheel covers and emblems.

## Measurements

| | |
|---|---|
| Wheelbase | 111.1" |
| Length | 196.1" |
| Width | 74.1" |
| Height | 51.9" |
| Legroom — front | 42.7" |
| Legroom — rear | 29.9" |
| Headroom — front | 37.3" |
| Headroom — rear | 35.9" |
| Cargo capacity (cu. ft.) | 10.2 |
| Fuel capacity (gals.) | 17.0 |

## Models Available

| | Style Number | Base MSRP | Change from LY | Shipping Wt. (lbs.) | Production | Change from LY |
|---|---|---|---|---|---|---|
| Cougar 2-Door Hardtop | 91 | $3,114 | +3.25% | 3285 | 49,479 | -25.41% |
| Cougar 2-Door Convertible | 92 | $3,480 | +2.90% | 3382 | 2,322 | -59.94% |
| Cougar XR-7 2-Door Hardtop | 93 | $3,413 | +2.96% | 3311 | 18,565 | -22.38% |
| Cougar XR-7 2-Door Convertible | 94 | $3,692 | +2.70% | 3408 | 1,977 | -50.87% |
| TOTALS | | Avg. price $3,425 | +2.95% | | Production 72,343 | -27.70% |

# Montego

*"Styling as fresh and exciting as the '70's."*

**Nameplate year of origin:** 1968.
**Current bodystyle lifespan:** 1970 through 1971.
**Predecessor to this model:** Comet and Montego (1968 to 1969).
**Replacement for this model:** Montego (1972 to 1976).
**Percentage of division's sales volume:** 35.21%.
**Corporate siblings:** Ford Torino.
**Primary competition:** Buick Skylark, Dodge Coronet/Charger, Oldsmobile Cutlass and Pontiac LeMans.
**Notable changes:** Completely restyled.
**Major standard equipment:** Nylon and vinyl front bench seat, full carpeting, dome light, bright metal front, rear and side window trim, and E78 × 14 BSW tires. Montego MX adds: Cloth and vinyl interior trim, deluxe steering wheel, simulated walnut interior trim, and F78 × 14 BSW tires. MX Brougham adds: Luxury interior trim and pedal bright moldings. Cyclone adds: All vinyl bench seat, specific Cyclone exterior trim, competition handling package, 4-speed manual transmission, 429 CID V8 engine with dress-up kit and G70 × 14 tires. Cyclone GT adds: All-vinyl high-back bucket seats, and 351 CID V8. Spoiler adds: 429 CID Ram Air Induction V8, anti-lift spoiler and full instrumentation.

## Measurements

| | Cars | Wagons |
|---|---|---|
| Wheelbase | 117.0" | 114.0" |
| Length | 209.9" | 211.8" |
| Width | 77.3" | 75.4" |
| Height | NA | NA |
| Legroom — front | 42.5" | 42.0" |
| Legroom — rear | 36.0" | 34.5" |
| Headroom — front | 38.5" | 38.5" |
| Headroom — rear | 37.5" | 39.0" |
| Cargo capacity (cu. ft.) | 16.2 | 85.2 |
| Fuel capacity (gals.) | NA | NA |

## Models Available

| | Style Number | Base MSRP | Change from LY | Shipping Wt. (lbs.) | Production | Change from LY |
|---|---|---|---|---|---|---|
| Montego 2-Door Hardtop | 01 | $2,750 | +4.68% | 3173 | 21,298 | +19.75% |
| Montego 4-Door Sedan | 02 | $2,736 | +6.13% | 3258 | 13,988 | -36.27% |
| Montego MX 2-Door Hardtop | 07 | $2,845 | +3.15% | 3278 | 31,670 | +38.24% |
| Montego MX 4-Door Sedan | 06 | $2,833 | +3.39% | 3265 | 16,708 | -5.81% |
| Montego MX 4-Door Wagon | 08 | $3,196 | +6.50% | 3703 | 5,094 | -51.90% |
| Montego MX Brougham 2-Door HT | 11 | $3,020 | NEW | 3298 | 8,074 | NEW |
| Montego MX Brougham 4-Door Sdn. | 10 | $3,001 | NEW | 3288 | 3,315 | NEW |
| Montego MX Brougham 4-Door HT | 12 | $3,142 | NEW | 3318 | 3,685 | NEW |
| Montego MX Villager 4-Dr. Wagon | 18 | $3,409 | NEW | 3718 | 2,682 | NEW |
| Cyclone 2-Door Hardtop | 15 | $3,238 | +16.85% | 3721 | 1,695 | -71.18% |
| Cyclone GT 2-Door Hardtop | 16 | $3,226 | NEW | 3462 | 10,170 | NEW |
| Cyclone Spoiler 2-Door Hardtop | 17 | $3,759 | +16.59% | 3773 | 1,631 | -49.98% |
| TOTALS | *Avg. price* $3,096 | | +7.57% | *Production* 120,010 | | +3.51% |

# Monterey

*"Password for extra value in the '70's."*

**Nameplate year of origin:** 1950 (coupe designation), 1952 (series).

**Current bodystyle lifespan:** 1969 through 1970.

**Predecessor to this model:** Monterey (1967 to 1968).

**Replacement for this model:** Monterey (1971 to 1974).

**Percentage of division's sales volume:** 16.71%.

**Corporate siblings:** Ford LTD/Galaxie 500 and Mercury Marquis.

**Primary competition:** Buick LeSabre, Dodge Polara/Monaco, Oldsmobile Delta 88 and Pontiac Catalina.

**Notable changes:** New grille, minor trim and detail changes.

**Major standard equipment:** Cloth and vinyl front bench seat, full carpeting, wood-grain trim on instrument panel, courtesy light group, rocker panel moldings, bright exterior front and rear window trim and G78 × 15 BSW tires (H78 × 15 BSW tires on wagons). Custom adds: Specific cloth and vinyl interior trim, and bright moldings (wheel lip and rear lower panels).

## Measurements

| | Cars | Wagons |
|---|---|---|
| Wheelbase | 124.0" | 121.0" |
| Length | 221.8" | 218.0" |
| Width | 79.9" | 79.9" |
| Height | 56.0" | 56.8" |
| Legroom — front | 41.9" | 41.9" |
| Legroom — rear | 37.6" | 36.8" |
| Headroom — front | 38.9" | 39.0" |
| Headroom — rear | 37.7" | 40.0" |
| Cargo capacity (cu. ft.) | 20.6 | 96.2 |
| Fuel capacity (gals.) | 24.0 | 24.0 |

**1970**

## Models Available

| | Style Number | Base MSRP | Change from LY | Shipping Wt. (lbs.) | Production | Change from LY |
|---|---|---|---|---|---|---|
| Monterey 2-Door Hardtop | 46 | $3,329 | +2.84% | 3890 | 9,359 | -5.13% |
| Monterey 2-Door Convertible | 45 | $3,668 | +3.62% | 4071 | 581 | -55.20% |
| Monterey 4-Door Sedan | 44 | $3,248 | +2.85% | 3926 | 29,432 | +27.92% |
| Monterey 4-Door Hardtop | 48 | $3,406 | +2.81% | 3961 | 5,032 | -17.05% |
| Monterey 4-Door, 2-Seat Wagon | 72 | $3,682 | +4.13% | 4235 | 1,657 | -17.36% |
| Monterey 4-Door, 3-Seat Wagon | 72 | $3,774 | +4.02% | 4327 | 3,507 | -8.65% |
| Monterey Custom 2-Door Hardtop | 56 | $3,600 | +4.08% | 3922 | 1,194 | -58.80% |
| Monterey Custom 4-Door Sedan | 54 | $3,520 | +4.23% | 3931 | 4,823 | -32.10% |
| Monterey Custom 4-Door Hardtop | 58 | $3,676 | +4.05% | 3973 | 1,357 | -52.00% |
| TOTALS | *Avg. price* $3,545 | | +1.58% | *Production* 56,942 | | -6.39% |

# Marauder

*"The look is sporty and so is the action."*

**Nameplate year of origin:** 1963 (as hardtop model designation); 1969 (as series).
**Current bodystyle lifespan:** 1969 through 1970.
**Predecessor to this model:** None.
**Replacement for this model:** None.
**Percentage of division's sales volume:** 1.77%.
**Corporate siblings:** Ford XL.
**Primary competition:** Buick Wildcat and Chrysler 300.
**Notable changes:** New grille, minor trim and detail changes.
**Major standard equipment:** Cloth and vinyl interior trim, full carpeting, tunneled rear window treatment, bright front and rear window moldings, concealed headlamps, dual pinstripes and G78 × 15 BSW tires. X-100 adds: Leather and vinyl front bench seat, luxury steering wheel, rear fender skirts, styled aluminum wheels, 429 CID V8, automatic transmission, and H70 × 15 WSW tires.

## Measurements

| | |
|---|---|
| Wheelbase | 121.0" |
| Length | 219.1" |
| Width | 79.9" |
| Height | 54.0" |
| Legroom — front | 41.9" |
| Legroom — rear | 37.6" |
| Headroom — front | 38.9" |
| Headroom — rear | 37.7" |
| Cargo capacity (cu. ft.) | 18.0 |
| Fuel capacity (gals.) | 24.0 |

## Models Available

| | Style Number | Base MSRP | Change from LY | Shipping Wt. (lbs.) | Production | Change from LY |
|---|---|---|---|---|---|---|
| Marauder 2-Door Hardtop | 60 | $3,503 | +4.01% | 3972 | 3,397 | -62.39% |
| Marauder X-100 2-Door Hardtop | 61 | $4,136 | +1.10% | 4128 | 2,646 | -53.04% |
| TOTALS | | Avg. price $3,820 | +2.41% | Production | 6,043 | -58.79% |

# Marquis

*"Luxury far beyond its medium price."*

**Nameplate year of origin:** 1967.
**Current bodystyle lifespan:** 1969 through 1970.
**Predecessor to this model:** Park Lane and Marquis (1967 to 1968)
**Replacement for this model:** Marquis (1971 to 1978).
**Percentage of division's sales volume:** 25.09%.
**Corporate siblings:** Ford LTD/Galaxie 500 and Mercury Monterey.
**Primary competition:** Buick Wildcat/Electra, Chrysler Newport, Oldsmobile Delta 88/98, and Pontiac Bonneville.
**Notable changes:** Revised grille, minor trim and detail changes.
**Major standard equipment:** Cloth and vinyl front bench seat with front seat center arm rest, full carpeting, simulated burled-walnut trim on instrument panel and doors, electric clock, courtesy light group, dual lower body accent stripes, rocker panel molding, concealed headlamps, deluxe wheel covers, and H78 × 15 BSW tires. Colony Park wagon adds: exterior wood-grain vinyl trim, and power tailgate window. Brougham adds: Cloth and vinyl Twin-Comfort lounge seats, vinyl roof, fender top chrome trim, and Brougham crests.

## Measurements

| | Cars | Wagons |
|---|---|---|
| Wheelbase | 124.0" | 121.0" |
| Length | 224.3" | 220.5" |
| Width | 79.9" | 79.9" |
| Height | 56.0" | 56.8" |
| Legroom — front | 41.9" | 41.9" |
| Legroom — rear | 37.6" | 36.8" |
| Headroom — front | 38.9" | 39.0" |
| Headroom — rear | 37.7" | 40.0" |
| Cargo capacity (cu. ft.) | 20.6 | 96.2 |
| Fuel capacity (gals.) | 24.0 | 24.0 |

## Models Available

| | Style Number | Base MSRP | Change from LY | Shipping Wt. (lbs.) | Production | Change from LY |
|---|---|---|---|---|---|---|
| Marquis 2-Door Hardtop | 66 | $4,113 | +4.95% | 4072 | 6,229 | -65.97% |
| Marquis 2-Door Convertible | 65 | $4,318 | +4.70% | 4337 | 1,233 | -46.83% |
| Marquis 4-Door Sedan | 63 | $4,052 | +5.06% | 4121 | 14,384 | -54.17% |
| Marquis 4-Door Hardtop | 68 | $4,185 | +4.89% | 4141 | 8,411 | -71.38% |
| Marquis 4-Door, 2-Seat Wagon | 74 | $3,930 | NEW | 4347 | 959 | NEW |
| Marquis 4-Door, 3-Seat Wagon | 74 | $4,022 | NEW | 4393 | 1,429 | NEW |
| Colony Park 4-Door, 2-Seat Wagon | 76 | $4,123 | +5.85% | 4442 | 4,655 | -38.76% |
| Colony Park 4-Door, 3-Seat Wagon | 76 | $4,215 | +5.72% | 4488 | 14,549 | -19.19% |
| Marquis Brougham 2-Door Hardtop | 64 | $4,428 | +5.65% | 4119 | 7,113 | * |
| Marquis Brougham 4-Door Sedan | 62 | $4,367 | +5.76% | 4166 | 14,920 | * |
| Marquis Brougham 4-Door Hardtop | 67 | $4,500 | +5.58% | 4182 | 11,623 | * |
| TOTALS | Avg. price | $4,205 | +6.13% | Production | 85,505 | -20.09% |

*Production not available for comparison with 1969 models.*

# OLDSMOBILE

*"Wouldn't it be nice to have an Escape Machine?"*

As the 1970 model year unfolded, it would have been impossible to predict that in a few short years, Oldsmobile would be the nation's number three automobile producer. But this marked the year that a key to that success was introduced. The Cutlass Supreme Holiday Coupe was introduced this year. There had been a Cutlass Supreme Hardtop prior to 1970, but it was a higher trim level of a regular Cutlass model. The new Supreme was given a more formal roofline (similar to the Monte Carlo and Grand Prix), but was based on the regular 112-inch mid-size wheelbase giving it a sportier flair. This change, coupled with the restyling received by the entire Cutlass line, produced a very appealing car at an affordable price. This new image for the Cutlass Supreme would eventually lead to the entire Cutlass line becoming the best selling car line in America. Another key to success was the performance image that the Cutlass had gained through the sixties, and which was highlighted by the Cutlass 4-4-2 being selected to pace the 1970 Indianapolis 500 race this year. This would be the first of four times during the seventies that Oldsmobiles (three of them Cutlasses) would do the honors at Indy, a testament to the popularity of Oldsmobile and the Cutlass in this period.

Changes to the remainder of the Oldsmobile line were limited to trim and detail changes. The exception was the Toronado which was given an all-new front end treatment. The leading edge of the front fenders held vertically mounted "bumpers" and rub strips. These flanked a loop-style bumper which housed the headlights and egg-crate grille. It was a rather unusual look for what had once been such a cleanly styled car. Fortunately, it was only one more year before a totally new Toronado would appear. There were no model changes of note, but 1970 would be the final year for the luxurious Ninety-Eight convertible.

1970

4-4-2 2-Door Convertible,
Indianapolis 500 Pace Car

Ninety-Eight 2-Door Convertible

Ninety-Eight LS optional interior

Cutlass Supreme 2-Door Hardtop

Delta 88 Custom 4-Door Sedan

Toronado 2-Door Hardtop

Vista-Cruiser 4-Door, 3-Seat Wagon

**Model year production:** 627,478, down 4.19% from 1969.
**Domestic market share:** 7.54% (6th place).
**Base price range:** $2,676 to $5,023.
**Industry average base price:** $3,538.
**Oldsmobile average base price:** $3,733.
**Introduction date:** September 1969.
**Assembly plants:** Fremont, CA (Z); Framingham, MA (G); Lansing, MI (M); Arlington, TX (R); Fairfax, KS (X); and Linden, NJ (F).

**Data plate identification:** Thirteen digit code read as follows: 1st digit 3 = Oldsmobile; 2nd through 5th digits identify series/body style; 0 = 1970 year; 7th digit is assembly plant code; 100001 and up for serial number (except Toronado is 600001). *Example:* 354390X100001 is a 1970 Oldsmobile Delta 88 4-Door Hardtop, serial number 100001, built in Fairfax, KS.

## Powertrains

| Engine | Gross HP | Transmission Availability | Cutlass & 4-4-2 | Supreme & Vista-Cruiser | Delta 88 | Toro. & 98 |
|---|---|---|---|---|---|---|
| 250 CID, 2-bbl., 6-cyl. | 155 | 3-speed manual | S* | - | - | - |
| | | Turbo Hydra-matic 350 | $195* | - | - | - |
| 350 CID, 2-bbl., V8 | 250 | 3-speed manual | $111* | S (V.Cr.) | S (base) | - |
| | | 4-speed manual | $296* | - | - | - |
| | | Turbo Hydra-matic 350 | $307* | $206 (V.Cr.) | $227 (base) | - |
| 350 CID, 4-bbl., V8 | 310 | 3-speed manual | $158* | S (Supreme)/ $47 (V.Cr.) | S (Cust.,Roy.)/ $121 (base) | - |
| | | 4-speed manual* | $344* | $185 (Supr.) | - | - |
| | | Turbo Hydra-matic 350 | $354* | $206 (Supr.)/ $253 (V.Cr.) | $227 (Cust.,Roy.)/ $348 (base) | - |
| 455 CID, 4-bbl., V8 | 320 | 3-speed manual | - | $107 (Supr.) | $169 | - |
| | | 4-speed manual | - | $292 (Supr.) | - | - |
| | | Turbo Hydra-matic 400 | - | $334 (Supr.) | - | - |
| 455 CID, 4-bbl., V8 | 365 | 3-speed manual | S** | $141 (Supr.) | $47 (Cust.,Roy.)/ $169 (base) | - |

| Engine | Gross HP | Transmission Availability | Cutlass & 4-4-2 | Supreme & Vista-Cruiser | Delta 88 | Toro. & 98 |
|---|---|---|---|---|---|---|
| | (375 Toro.) | 4-speed manual | $185** | $326 (Supr.) | - | - |
| | | Turbo Hydra-matic 400 | $227** | $359 (Supr.)/ $415 (V.Cr.) | $274 (Cust.,Roy.)/ $396 (base) | S |
| 455 CID, 4-bbl., V8 (400 Toro) | 390 | Turbo Hydra-matic 400 | - | - | $307 (Cust.,Roy.)/ $426 (base) | $47 (Toro.) |

*F-85 and Cutlass only.   **4-4-2 only.

## Major Options

| | Cutlass | Vista-Cruiser | Delta 88 | Ninety-Eight | Toronado |
|---|---|---|---|---|---|
| Air conditioning | $376 | $376 | $422 | $422 | $422 |
| Electronic cruise control (V8 only) | $58 | $58 | $63 | $63 | $63 |
| Soft Ray tinted glass | $39 | $39 | $44 | $44 | $47 |
| Deck lid remote release | $14 | - | $14 | $14 | $14 |
| Power steering— variable-ratio | $105 | $105 | $116 | S | S |
| Power brakes— w/front discs | $64 | $64 | $79 | S | S |
| Power driver's seat/ Bench seat | $74 | $74 | $100 | $74–$100 | $74 |
| Power windows | $105 | $105 | $111 | S/$111* | $111 |
| AM radio | $70 | $70 | $87 | $87 | $87 |
| AM/FM stereo | $238 | $238 | $238 | $238 | $238 |
| Front seat console | $61 | - | $62 | - | $62 |
| Front bucket seats | $ | - | $ | - | $ |
| Tilt-Away steering wheel | $45 | $45 | $45 | $45 | $45 |
| Vinyl roof | $102 | - | $123** | $139 | $128 |
| White sidewall tires (base size) | $28–31 | $34 | $34 | $37 | $37 |
| Wheel trim covers | $21 | $21 | S | S | S |

Options common to most models. (– = Not Available; S = Standard equipment.) Items may be standard equipment, optional at different pricing, or unavailable on certain models. This chart is only a guide.

*4-Door Town Sedan and Holiday Sedan only.   **Standard on Royale.

## Paint Colors

| | Code |
|---|---|
| Porcelain White | 10 |
| Platinum Metallic | 14 |
| Oxford Gray Metallic* | 16 |
| Ebony Black | 19 |
| Azure Blue Met. | 20 |
| Viking Blue Met.* | 26 |
| Twilight Blue Met. | 28 |
| Reef Turquoise Metallic | 34 |
| Agean Aqua Metallic | 38 |
| Aspen Green Metallic | 45 |
| Ming Jade Metallic* | 46 |
| Sherwood Green Metallic | 48 |
| Bamboo | 50 |
| Sebring Yellow | 51 |
| Nugget Gold Metallic | 53 |
| Galleon Gold Metallic | 55 |
| Burnished Gold Metallic | 58 |
| Sandalwood* | 61 |
| Copper Metallic | 63 |
| Cinnamon Bronze Met.* | 68 |
| Rallye Red | 73 |
| Grenadier Red* | 74 |
| Matador Red | 75 |
| Regency Rose Metallic* | 76 |
| Burgundy Mist Metallic | 78 |

*Available only on Toronado.

**1970**

# Cutlass

*"Break the routine. Let your hair down and swing (for) a little!"*

**Nameplate year of origin:** 1962 (as a F-85 model designation); 1955 (show car).
**Current bodystyle lifespan:** 1968 through 1972.
**Predecessor to this model:** F-85/Cutlass (1966 to 1967).
**Replacement for this model:** Cutlass (1973 to 1977).
**Percentage of division's sales volume:** 42.82%.
**Corporate siblings:** Buick Skylark, Chevrolet Chevelle, Pontiac LeMans.

## Measurements

| | 2-Doors | 4-Doors | Wagon |
|---|---|---|---|
| Wheelbase | 112.0" | 116.0" | 116.0" |
| Length | 203.2" | 207.2" | 212.9" |
| Width | 76.8" | 76.8" | 76.8" |
| Height | 52.8" | 53.5" | 54.5" |
| Legroom — front | 41.5" | 42.8" | 42.6" |

**Primary competition:** Dodge Coronet, Ford Torino, Mercury Montego, and Plymouth Satellite.

**Notable changes:** Restyle of front and rear, as well as bodyside lines.

**Major standard equipment:** Cloth or vinyl upholstery, front bench seat, left-hand outside rearview mirror, aluminized exhaust system, and F78 × 14 BSW tires. Cutlass adds: Front and rear armrests, full carpeting, deluxe steering wheel, and exterior chrome trim moldings. Cutlass S adds: Deluxe bench seat with foam cushions. Cutlass Supreme adds: Woodgrain interior trim, Strato-bucket seats, unique grille and G78 × 14 BSW tires. 4-4-2 adds: All-vinyl bucket seats, floor shifter, 455 CID V8 engine, dual exhausts, heavy duty suspension, and F70 × 14 Wide-Oval Redline tires.

| | 2-Doors | 4-Doors | Wagon |
|---|---|---|---|
| Legroom — rear | 34.1" | 35.0" | 34.6" |
| Headroom — front | 38.2" | 38.8" | 38.4" |
| Headroom — rear | 36.4" | 37.4" | 38.3" |
| Luggage capacity (cu. ft.) | 17.0 | 17.0 | 93.6 |
| Fuel capacity (gals.) | 20.0 | 20.0 | 23.0 |

## Models Available

| | Style Number | Base MSRP | Change from LY | Shipping Wt. (lbs.) | Production | Change from LY |
|---|---|---|---|---|---|---|
| F-85 2-Door Sport Coupe | 3177 | $2,676 | +4.49% | 3205 | 11,110 | +31.64% |
| Cutlass 4-Door Town Sedan | 3569 | $2,837 | +4.22% | 3287 | 36,400 | +5.72% |
| Cutlass 4-Door Hardtop | 3539 | $2,968 | +4.03% | 3340 | 9,665 | +32.78% |
| Cutlass 4-Door, 2-Seat Wagon | 3535 | $3,170 | +3.76% | 3674 | 7,765 | -11.15% |
| Cutlass S 2-Door Sports Coupe | 3577 | $2,796 | +4.29% | 3224 | 11,161 | -0.04% |
| Cutlass S 2-Door Hardtop | 3587 | $2,859 | +4.15% | 3236 | 89,307 | +33.17% |
| Cutlass Supreme 2-Door Hardtop | 4257 | $3,151 | +3.79% | 3453 | 68,309 | +134.23% |
| Cutlass Supreme 2-Door Conv. | 4267 | $3,335 | NEW | 3522 | 4,867 | NEW |
| Cutlass Supreme 4-Door Hardtop | 4239 | $3,226 | +3.70% | 3577 | 10,762 | +23.50% |
| 4-4-2 2-Door Sport Coupe | 4477 | $3,312 | +5.44% | 3667 | 1,688 | -31.80% |
| 4-4-2 2-Door Hardtop | 4487 | $3,376 | +5.37% | 3713 | 14,709 | -24.90% |
| 4-4-2 2-Door Convertible | 4467 | $3,567 | +5.07% | 3740 | 2,933 | -31.71% |
| TOTALS | Avg. price | $3,106 | +5.04% | Production | 268,676 | +22.35% |

# Vista-Cruiser

*"The one-of-a-kind wagon with a hundred-and-one wonderful uses."*

**Nameplate year of origin:** 1964.

**Current bodystyle lifespan:** 1968 through 1972.

**Predecessor to this model:** None.

**Replacement for this model:** Vista-Cruiser (1973 to 1977).

**Percentage of division's sales volume:** 5.43%.

**Corporate siblings:** None.

**Primary competition:** Dodge Coronet, Ford Torino, Mercury Montego, and Plymouth Satellite.

**Notable changes:** Restyle of front and rear end, as well as bodyside lines.

**Major standard equipment:** All-vinyl front bench seats, full carpeting, deluxe steering wheel, wood-grain exterior trim, Vista-roof windows, and H78 × 14 BSW tires.

## Measurements

| | |
|---|---|
| Wheelbase | 121.0" |
| Length | 218.2" |
| Width | 77.2" |
| Height | 58.6" |
| Legroom — front | 42.8" |
| Legroom — rear | 38.0" |
| Headroom — front | 38.4" |
| Headroom — rear | 40.3" |
| Luggage capacity (cu. ft.) | 100.5 |
| Fuel capacity (gals.) | 23.0 |

## Models Available

| | Style Number | Base MSRP | Change from LY | Shipping Wt. (lbs.) | Production | Change from LY |
|---|---|---|---|---|---|---|
| Vista-Cruiser 4-Dr., 2-S. Wagon | 4855 | $3,572 | +3.33% | 4085 | 10,758 | -9.44% |

| | Style Number | Base MSRP | Change from LY | Shipping Wt. (lbs.) | Production | Change from LY |
|---|---|---|---|---|---|---|
| Vista-Cruiser 4-Dr., 3-S. Wagon | 4865 | $3,714 | +3.17% | 4212 | 23,336 | +8.50% |
| TOTALS | Avg. price | $3,643 | +3.23% | Production | 34,094 | +2.12% |

# Delta 88

*"When you've got all the facts there's only one answer."*

**Nameplate year of origin:** 1965 (88 series started 1949).
**Current bodystyle lifespan:** 1969 through 1970.
**Predecessor to this model:** Delmont/Delta 88 (1967 to 1968).
**Replacement for this model:** Delta 88 (1971 to 1976).
**Percentage of division's sales volume:** 32.42%.
**Corporate siblings:** Buick LeSabre/Wildcat, Chevrolet Impala/Caprice, Pontiac Catalina/Bonneville.
**Primary competition:** Dodge Polara, Ford LTD, Mercury Monterey, and Plymouth Fury.
**Notable changes:** Minor trim and detail changes.
**Major standard equipment:** Cloth and vinyl or all-vinyl bench seat, full carpeting, vinyl bodyside molding, and H78 × 15 BSW tires. Custom adds: Custom interior trim. Royale adds: Coarse-woven cloth upholstery, privacy rear window, chrome front fender louvers and pinstriping.

## Measurements

| | |
|---|---|
| Wheelbase | 124.0" |
| Length | 219.1" |
| Width | 79.9" |
| Height | 54.7" |
| Legroom — front | 41.6" |
| Legroom — rear | 35.1" |
| Headroom — front | 39.1" |
| Headroom — rear | 37.8" |
| Luggage capacity (cu. ft.) | 19.5 |
| Fuel capacity (gals.) | 25.0 |

## Models Available

| | Style Number | Base MSRP | Change from LY | Shipping Wt. (lbs.) | Production | Change from LY |
|---|---|---|---|---|---|---|
| Delta 88 2-Door Hardtop | 5437 | $3,590 | +9.55% | 3967 | 33,017 | -29.67% |
| Delta 88 2-Door Convertible | 5467 | $3,903 | +8.72% | 4037 | 3,095 | -41.54% |
| Delta 88 4-Door Town Sedan | 5469 | $3,534 | +9.68% | 4110 | 47,067 | -5.86% |
| Delta 88 4-Door Hardtop | 5439 | $3,666 | +9.33% | 4019 | 37,695 | -11.70% |
| Delta 88 Custom 2-Door Hardtop | 6437 | $3,848 | +9.16% | 4060 | 16,149 | -26.87% |
| Delta 88 Custom 4-Door Town Sdn. | 6469 | $3,755 | +9.41% | 4105 | 24,727 | -20.27% |
| Delta 88 Custom 4-Door Hardtop | 6439 | $3,924 | +9.00% | 4152 | 28,432 | -22.11% |
| Delta 88 Royale 2-Door Hardtop | 6647 | $4,159 | +8.42% | 4054 | 13,249 | -41.28% |
| TOTALS | Avg. price | $3,797 | +9.14% | Production | 203,431 | -20.87% |

# Ninety-Eight

*"Your escape from the ordinary in a Grand Luxury car."*

**Nameplate year of origin:** 1941.
**Current bodystyle lifespan:** 1969 through 1970.
**Predecessor to this model:** Ninety-Eight (1967 to 1968).
**Replacement for this model:** Ninety-Eight (1971 to 1976).
**Percentage of division's sales volume:** 15.27%.
**Corporate siblings:** Buick Electra and Cadillac Calais/de Ville.
**Primary competition:** Chrysler New Yorker and Mercury Marquis Brougham.
**Notable changes:** Minor trim and detail changes.
**Major standard equipment:** Cloth and vinyl custom seat, fold-down front center armrest, electric clock, deluxe steering wheel, two-way power seat (except Town Sedan), power windows (except Town sedan), variable-ratio power steering, power

## Measurements

| | |
|---|---|
| Wheelbase | 127.0" |
| Length | 225.2" |
| Width | 80.0" |
| Height | 54.8" |
| Legroom — front | 41.7" |
| Legroom — rear | 37.1" |
| Headroom — front | 38.6" |
| Headroom — rear | 38.0" |
| Luggage capacity (cu. ft.) | 20.5 |
| Fuel capacity (gals.) | 25.0 |

front disc brakes, full wheel discs, and J78 × 15 BSW tires. LS adds: exclusive interior trim, and rear fold-down center armrest.

## Models Available

| | Style Number | Base MSRP | Change from LY | Shipping Wt. (lbs.) | Production | Change from LY |
|---|---|---|---|---|---|---|
| Ninety-Eight 2-Door Hardtop | 8457 | $4,656 | +4.35% | 4275 | 21,111 | -21.93% |
| Ninety-Eight 2-Door Convertible | 8467 | $4,914 | +4.11% | 4293 | 3,161 | -26.28% |
| Ninety-Eight 4-Door Town Sedan | 8469 | $4,451 | +4.58% | 4267 | 9,092 | -18.60% |
| Ninety-Eight 4-Door Hardtop | 8439 | $4,582 | +1.28% | 4341 | 14,098 | -18.48% |
| Ninety-Eight Luxury 4-Door Sedan | 8669 | $4,793 | +4.22% | 4344 | 29,005 | +11.67% |
| Ninety-Eight Luxury 4-Door Hardtop | 8639 | $4,888 | +4.16% | 4376 | 19,377 | -36.77% |
| TOTALS | Avg. price | $4,714 | +3.79% | Production | 95,844 | -17.67% |

# Toronado

*"The ultimate Escape Machine."*

**Nameplate year of origin:** 1966.
**Current bodystyle lifespan:** 1966 through 1970.
**Predecessor to this model:** None.
**Replacement for this model:** Toronado (1971 to 1978).
**Percentage of division's sales volume:** 4.05%.
**Corporate siblings:** Buick Riviera and Cadillac Eldorado
**Primary competition:** Imperial LeBaron Coupe, Ford Thunderbird, and Lincoln Continental Mark III.
**Notable changes:** Restyled front and rear treatments.
**Major standard equipment:** Cloth and vinyl Strato-Bench seat, fold-down front center armrest, electric clock, deluxe steering wheel, front wheel drive, variable-ratio power steering, power front disc brakes, and J78 × 15 BSW tires.

## Measurements

| | |
|---|---|
| Wheelbase | 119.0" |
| Length | 214.3" |
| Width | 78.8" |
| Height | 52.8" |
| Legroom — front | 41.3" |
| Legroom — rear | 35.5" |
| Headroom — front | 37.7" |
| Headroom — rear | 37.2" |
| Luggage capacity (cu. ft.) | 14.6 |
| Fuel capacity (gals.) | 24.0 |

## Models Available

| | Style Number | Base MSRP | Change from LY | Shipping Wt. (lbs.) | Production | Change from LY |
|---|---|---|---|---|---|---|
| Toronado 2-Door Hardtop | 9487 | $5,023 | +3.87% | 4372 | 25,433 | -10.74% |
| TOTALS | Avg. price | $5,023 | +3.87% | Production | 25,433 | -10.74% |

# PLYMOUTH

*"For 1970, if you want a car that makes it, Plymouth makes it!"*

After many years of struggle, Plymouth finally regained the third spot in the sales race. The reasons are many, but the drastic slide that Pontiac took this year helped Plymouth most. Changes for the 1970 Plymouth line mimicked those of the Dodge line, with one exception. Plymouth received an all-new body style in the Valiant line, named the Duster. The Duster was a 2-Door "fastback" style coupe, with fixed rear quarter windows and a back glass that sloped downward into a short rear deck. Rear styling was unique to the Duster, but everything from the front doors forward was pure Valiant, including powertrains. The Duster was an immediate hit as a sporty alternative to the now larger and more expensive Barracuda. Dodge would receive its own version for 1971, as the Dart Demon. The single remaining Valiant 4-Door received revised front-end styling.

The Barracuda was totally restyled for 1970, sharing its basic body shell with the all-new Dodge Challenger. This new body styling was bulky and muscular looking, and followed the "fuselage" body styling first seen on the full-size Plymouths during 1969. A thin, full-width bumper underscored the grille with single headlamps set at each end of the grille. Body sides were smooth and flowing and met the roofline where the car ended in a very short rear deck. It was a very nice looking package, and the Barracuda definitely had the power to back up the looks, with just about every powerplant Plymouth offered, available under the hood. Unfortunately sales in this segment were dwindling, and though the restyling effort sold better than the 1969 edition, this was a brief resurgence. The Gran Coupe was a new luxury/sport offering, and the 'Cuda was the new, powerful, top line image builder. The 2-Door Fastback model was no longer offered as they were falling out of favor with buyers.

As with the mid-size Dodge models, the Satellite and Belvedere lines were totally revamped at the front and rear. Meanwhile the big news for the Satellite line was the availability of a new NASCAR inspired Road Runner Super Bird 2-Door Hardtop. The "winged warrior" was similar to the 1969 Dodge Charger Daytona Hardtop. The Super Bird was essentially a stock Road Runner with aerodynamic nose (with concealed headlamps) and the large, towering wing spoiler at the rear. It was fitted with the 440 CID, 4-bbl. V8 engine. The Super Bird was built in enough quantity to qualify it for NASCAR racing, and ended up being a run of 1,920 cars. The remainder of the Belvedere/Satellite model line was unchanged, except for the dropping of the Sport Satellite and GTX convertible models. It would also be the last year for use of the Belvedere name. Fury models wore a new face, with the "loop-style" grille seen on other Chrysler products, and changes to the model line were numerous. The Fury I Suburban Wagon moved up to the Fury II line. The VIP line was integrated into an expanded Sport Fury line, that added GT and S-23 Hardtop models, but lost its convertible model. A new Gran Coupe model, based on Fury II trim level, topped off the Fury line.

'Cuda 2-Door Hardtop

Valiant Duster 340 2-Door Coupe

Fury III 4-Door Hardtop and
2-Door Hardtop

GTX 2-Door Hardtop

Sport Fury GT 2-Door Hardtop

Sport Satellite 2-Door Hardtop

Valiant 4-Door Sedan

**Model year production:** 744,684, down 0.31% from 1969.
**Domestic market share:** 8.94% (3rd place).
**Base price range:** $2,172 to $4,298.
**Industry average base price:** $3,538.
**Plymouth average base price:** $3,183.
**Introduction date:** September 23, 1969.
**Assembly plants:** Lynch Road, MI (A): Hamtramck, MI (B); Belvidere, IL (D); Newark DE (F); St. Louis, MO (G); and Windsor, Ontario, Canada (R).

**Data plate identification:** Thirteen digit code read as follows: four digit style number code in which first letter is series, second letter is trim level, third and fourth digits are body style; fifth digit is engine code (see chart); sixth digit 0 for 1970; seventh digit is assembly plant code; 100001 and up for serial number. *Example:* PM23C0B100001 is a 1970 Plymouth Fury III 2-Door Hardtop, with a 225 CID 6-cyl., built at Hamtramck, MI, serial number 100001.

## Powertrains

| Engine | Gross HP | Engine Code | Transmission Availability | Valiant Duster | Barracuda | Belv./ Sat. | Sp. Sat./ R.R./GTX | Fury |
|---|---|---|---|---|---|---|---|---|
| 198 CID, 1-bbl., 6-cyl. | 125 | B | 3-speed man. | S[1] | - | - | - | - |
| | | | Torqueflite automatic | $175[1] | - | - | - | - |
| 225 CID, 1-bbl., 6-cyl. | 145 | C | 3-speed man. | $25* | S[1] | S | - | S[2] |
| | | | Torqueflite automatic | $215[1] | $190[1] | $190 | - | $190* |
| 318 CID, 2-bbl., V8 | 230 | G | 3-speed man. | $111[1] | $101[1] | $90 | S[1] | S[3]/$105* |
| | | | 4-speed man. | - | $289[1] | - | - | - |
| | | | Torqueflite automatic | $302[1] | $292[1] | $280 | $191[1] | $191[3,4]/$294* |
| 340 CID Commando, 4-bbl., V8 | 275 | H | 3-speed man. | S (340) | - | - | - | - |
| | | | Torqueflite automatic | $191 (340) | - | - | - | - |
| 383 CID Commando, 2-bbl., V8 | 290 | L | 3-speed man. | - | $171[1] | $160 | $70[1] | $70[3,4]/$175* |
| | | | 4-speed man. | - | $368[1] | $348 | $267[1] | - |
| | | | Torqueflite automatic | - | $398[1] | $351 | $297[1] | $297[3,4]/$402* |
| 383 CID Super Commando, 4-bbl., V8 | 330 (335 'Cuda) | N | 3-speed man. | - | S ('Cuda)/$239[1] | $228 | S (Road Runner)/$138[1] | $138[3,4]/$243* |
| | | | 4-speed man. | - | $197 ('Cuda)/ $436[1] | $416 | $197 (R.R.)/ $335[1] | - |
| | | | Torqueflite automatic | - | $227 ('Cuda)/ $466[1] | $446 | $227 (R.R.)/ $365[1] | $365[3,4]/$480* |
| 426 CID Street-Hemi, 4-bbl., V8 | 425 | R | 4-speed man. | - | $1068 ('Cuda) | - | $711 (GTX) | - |
| 440 CID Super Commando, 4-bbl., V8 | 350 (375 GTX) | U | 4-speed man. | - | $328 ('Cuda) | - | S (GTX & Super Bird) | - |
| | | | Torqueflite automatic | - | $358 ('Cuda) | - | $227 (GTX & Super Bird) | S (GT)/$461[3] |
| 440 CID Super Commando Six Pack, | 390 | V | 4-speed man. | - | $447 ('Cuda) | - | $119 (GTX)/ $250 (R.R.) | - |

| Engine | Gross HP | Engine Code | Transmission Availability | Valiant Duster | Barra-cuda | Belv./ Sat. | Sp. Sat./ R.R./GTX | Fury |
|---|---|---|---|---|---|---|---|---|
| 3 × 2-bbl., V8 | | | Torqueflite automatic | - | $477 ('Cuda) | - | $149 (GTX)/ $280 (R.R.) | $119 (GT) |

¹Except Duster 340, 'Cuda, Road Runner and GTX.   ²Fury I, II (except 9-pass. Wagon), and III (2-Dr. HT and 4-Dr. Sedan) only.   ³Except Fury I, II (but includes 9-pass. Wagon) and III (2-Dr. HT and 4-Dr. Sedan)   ⁴Except GT

## Major Options

| | Duster/Valiant | Barracuda | Belvedere/Satellite | Fury |
|---|---|---|---|---|
| Air conditioning | $347 | $357 | $357 | $365 |
| Automatic speed control (V8s) | - | - | $58 | $61 |
| Tilt steering wheel | - | - | - | $53 |
| Tinted glass | $34 | $34 | $38 | $38 |
| Power steering | $85 | $90 | $105 | $105 |
| Power brakes | $43 | $43 | $43 | $43 |
| Front disc brakes | $28 | S | $28 | $28 |
| Power door locks | - | - | - | $45–$69 |
| Power windows | - | $105 | $105 (2-Drs.) | $105 |
| AM radio | $62 | $62 | $62 | $62 |
| AM/FM multiplex stereo | - | $214 | - | $214 |
| Bucket seats — vinyl (leather opt.) | - | $0–$119 | $0–$100 | $100 |
| Vinyl roof | $84 | - | $96 | $106 |
| Chrome Road Wheels | - | $50 | $67 | $34–75 |

Options common to most models. (- = Not Available; S = Standard equipment.) Items may be standard equipment, optional at different pricing, or unavailable on certain models. This chart is only a guide.

## Paint Colors

| | Code |
|---|---|
| Silver Metallic | A-4 |
| Ice Blue Metallic | B-3 |
| Blue Fire Metallic | B-5 |
| Jamaica Blue Metallic | B-7 |
| In-Violet Metallic* | C-7 |
| Rallye Red | E-5 |
| Lime Green Metallic | F-4 |
| Ivy Green Metallic | F-8 |
| Limelight Metallic | J-5 |
| Sassy-Grass Green* | J-6 |
| Vitamin "C"* | K-2 |
| Burnt Orange Metallic | K-3 |
| Deep Burnt Orange Met. | K-5 |
| Sandpebble Beige | L-1 |
| Moulin Rouge | M-3 |
| Frosted Teal Metallic | P-6 |
| Scorch Red | R-6 |
| Sahara Tan Metallic | T-3 |
| Burnt Tan Metallic | T-6 |
| Walnut Metallic | T-8 |
| Tor-Red* | V-2 |
| Alpine White | W-1 |
| Black Velvet | X-9 |
| Lemon Twist | Y-1 |
| Sunfire Yellow | Y-2 |
| Yellow Gold* | Y-3 |
| Citron Mist Metallic | Y-4 |
| Citron Gold Metallic | Y-6 |

*Hi-impact colors.

**1970**

# Valiant

*"Small enough but big enough."*

**Nameplate year of origin:** 1960 (Valiant); 1970 (Duster)
**Current bodystyle lifespan:** 1967 through 1976 (Duster 1970 through 1976).
**Predecessor to this model:** Valiant (1963 to 1966).
**Replacement for this model:** Volare (1976 to 1980).
**Corporate siblings:** Dodge Dart.
**Percentage of division's sales volume:** 35.99%.
**Primary competition:** AMC Hornet, Chevrolet Nova, Ford Maverick, and Ford Falcon.
**Notable changes:** Restyled front and rear ends. New Duster Coupe models.
**Major standard equipment:** All-vinyl bench seat, color-keyed rubber floor mat, front door vent windows, 2-speed windshield wipers, and 6.95 × 14 BSW tires. Duster adds: Dome light, ventless front windows, and swing-out side rear quarter windows. 340 adds: Flat-black grille trim, body side

## Measurements

| | Duster | Valiant |
|---|---|---|
| Wheelbase | 108.0" | 108.0" |
| Length | 188.4" | 188.4" |
| Width | 71.7" | 69.6" |
| Height | 52.5" | 54.6" |
| Legroom — front | 41.7" | 41.7" |
| Legroom — rear | 29.6" | 34.5" |
| Headroom — front | 37.2" | 38.4" |
| Headroom — rear | 36.5" | 37.3" |
| Cargo capacity (cu. ft.) | 15.0 | 14.5 |
| Fuel capacity (gals.) | 16.0 | 16.0 |

tape stripes, heavy duty suspension, rallye road wheels, front disc brakes and E70 × 14 BSW tires.

## Models Available

|  | Style Number | Base MSRP | Change from LY | Shipping Wt. (lbs.) | Production | Change from LY |
|---|---|---|---|---|---|---|
| Duster 2-Door Sport Coupe | VL29 | $2,172 | NEW | 2790 | 192,375 | NEW |
| Duster 340 2-Door Sport Coupe | VS29 | $2,547 | NEW | 3110 | 24,817 | NEW |
| Valiant 4-Door Sedan | VL41 | $2,250 | 4.46% | 2795 | 50,810 | +2.84% |
| TOTALS | | Avg. price $2,323 | +5.40% | | Production 268,002 | +149.96% |

# Barracuda

*"Only the name is the same."*

**Nameplate year of origin:** 1964.
**Current bodystyle lifespan:** 1970 through 1974.
**Predecessor to this model:** Barracuda (1967 to 1969).
**Replacement for this model:** None.
**Percentage of division's sales volume:** 7.45%.
**Corporate siblings:** Dodge Challenger.
**Primary competition:** AMC Javelin, Chevrolet Camaro, Ford Mustang, Mercury Cougar and Pontiac Firebird.
**Notable changes:** Completely restyled.
**Major standard equipment:** All-vinyl high-back bucket seats, full carpeting, 3-spoke steering wheel, concealed 2-speed electric wipers, and E78 × 14 BSW tires. Gran Coupe adds: Overhead consolette, leather bucket seats, molded headliner, and additional trim features. 'Cuda adds: Chrome moldings (wheel opening, rocker, drip rail, grille, and deck lid), heavy duty suspension and brakes, performance hood, and F70 × 14 WSW tires.

## Measurements

| | |
|---|---|
| Wheelbase | 108.0" |
| Length | 186.7" |
| Width | 75.0" |
| Height | 50.9" |
| Legroom — front | 42.3" |
| Legroom — rear | 30.9" |
| Headroom — front | 37.4" |
| Headroom — rear | 35.6" |
| Cargo capacity (cu. ft.) | 8.6 |
| Fuel capacity (gals.) | 18.0 |

## Models Available

|  | Style Number | Base MSRP | Change from LY | Shipping Wt. (lbs.) | Production | Change from LY |
|---|---|---|---|---|---|---|
| Barracuda 2-Door Hardtop | BH23 | $2,764 | +3.37% | 2970 | 25,651 | +101.07% |
| Barracuda 2-Door Convertible | BH27 | $3,034 | +1.95% | 3045 | 1,554 | +7.77% |
| Barracuda Gran Coupe 2-Dr. HT | BP23 | $2,934 | NEW | 2990 | 8,183 | NEW |
| Barracuda Gran Coupe 2-Dr. Conv. | BP27 | $3,160 | NEW | 3065 | 596 | NEW |
| Cuda 2-Door Hardtop | BS23 | $3,164 | NEW | 3395 | 18,880 | NEW |
| Cuda 2-Door Convertible | BS27 | $3,433 | NEW | 3480 | 635 | NEW |
| TOTALS | | Avg. price $3,082 | +10.62% | | Production 55,499 | +73.50% |

# Belvedere/Satellite/
# Road Runner/GTX

*"Owning your own Belvedere makes it."*

**Nameplate year of origin:** Belvedere 1951 (HT model); 1954 (series). Satellite 1965 (as a Belvedere trim level). Road Runner 1968. GTX 1967.

**Current bodystyle lifespan:** 1968 through 1970.

**Predecessor to this model:** Belvedere (1966 to 1967).

**Replacement for this model:** Satellite (1971 to 1974).

**Percentage of division's sales volume:** 21.22%.

**Corporate siblings:** Dodge Coronet.

**Primary competition:** AMC Rebel, Chevrolet Chevelle, Ford Fairlane/Torino, and Pontiac Tempest/LeMans.

**Notable changes:** Completely restyled.

**Major standard equipment:** Cloth and vinyl bench seat, trunk mat, color-keyed rubber floor covering, dome light, and F78 × 14 BSW tires (G78 × 14 BSW for wagons). Satellite adds: Deluxe upholstery, dual horns, full carpeting, and assorted bright exterior moldings. Sport Satellite adds: Leather-grain vinyl bucket seats, additional trim and moldings and full gauge instrument cluster. Road Runner adds: "Beep-beep" horn, Rallye gauges, heavy duty suspension and brakes, sway bars, performance hood, low restriction dual exhausts, and F70 × 14 WSW tires. GTX adds: Vinyl bucket seats, specific chrome moldings, low-restriction dual exhaust with chrome trumpets, and F70 × 14 White-letter tires.

## Measurements

|  | Cars | Wagons |
|---|---|---|
| Wheelbase | 116.0" | 117.0" |
| Length | 204.0" | 209.1" |
| Width | 76.4" | 76.4" |
| Height | 54.7" | 55.4" |
| Legroom — front | 41.9" | 41.9" |
| Legroom — rear | 36.3" | 36.7" |
| Headroom — front | 38.6" | 38.7" |
| Headroom — rear | 37.4" | 38.1" |
| Cargo capacity (cu. ft.) | NA | 88.0 |
| Fuel capacity (gals.) | 19.5 | 21.0 |

## Models Available

| | Style Number | Base MSRP | Change from LY | Shipping Wt. (lbs.) | Production | Change from LY |
|---|---|---|---|---|---|---|
| Belvedere 2-Door Coupe | RL21 | $2,603 | +3.75% | 3050 | 4,717 | -33.22% |
| Belvedere 4-Door Sedan | RL41 | $2,641 | +3.65% | 3085 | 13,945 | +7.98% |
| Belvedere 4-Door, 2-Seat Wagon | RL45 | $2,985 | +3.68% | 3610 | 5,584 | -20.66% |
| Road Runner 2-Door Coupe | RM21 | $2,896 | -1.66% | 3450 | 15,716 | -53.42% |
| Road Runner 2-Door Hardtop | RM23 | $3,034 | -1.59% | 3475 | 24,944 | -48.62% |
| Road Runner "Superbird" 2-Dr. HT | RM23 | $4,298 | NEW | 3785 | 1,920 | NEW |
| Road Runner 2-Door Convertible | RM27 | $3,289 | -0.72% | 3550 | 824 | -61.28% |
| Satellite 2-Door Hardtop | RH23 | $2,765 | +3.99% | 3055 | 28,200 | -26.41% |
| Satellite 2-Door Convertible | RH27 | $3,006 | +4.45% | 3175 | 701 | -38.35% |
| Satellite 4-Door Sedan | RH41 | $2,741 | +4.02% | 3075 | 30,377 | -13.94% |
| Satellite 4-Dr., 2-Seat Wagon | RH45 | $3,101 | +3.47% | 3615 | 4,204 | -27.98% |
| Satellite 4-Dr., 3-Seat Wagon | RH46 | $3,211 | +3.38% | 3685 | 3,277 | -30.72% |
| Sport Satellite 2-Door Hardtop | RP23 | $2,988 | +3.64% | 3170 | 8,749 | -44.65% |
| Sport Satellite 4-Door Sedan | RP41 | $3,017 | +3.64% | 3205 | 3,010 | -48.42% |
| Sport Satellite 4-Dr., 2-S. Wagon | RP45 | $3,345 | +3.21% | 3675 | 1,975 | -38.68% |
| Sport Satellite 4-Dr., 3-S. Wagon | RP46 | $3,455 | +3.13% | 3750 | 2,161 | -31.44% |
| GTX 2-Door Hardtop | RS23 | $3,535 | +3.48% | 3515 | 7,748 | -48.01% |
| TOTALS | | *Avg. price* $3,112 | +3.60% | | *Production* 158,052 | -34.47% |

**1970**

# Fury

*"Luxury you can afford."*

**Nameplate year of origin:** 1956.
**Current bodystyle lifespan:** 1969 through 1973.
**Predecessor to this model:** Fury (1967 to 1968).
**Replacement for this model:** Gran Fury (1974 to 1978).
**Percentage of division's sales volume:** 35.33%.
**Corporate siblings:** Dodge Polara and Monaco.
**Primary competition:** AMC Ambassador, Chevrolet Biscayne/BelAir/Impala, Ford Galaxie, and Pontiac Catalina.
**Notable changes:** Minor restyling to front and rear end.
**Major standard equipment:** All-vinyl front bench seat; floor mat; 2-speed windshield wipers with washers; temperature, ammeter and oil gauges; hubcaps; and F78 × 15 BSW tires. Fury II adds: Cloth and vinyl upholstery, color-keyed carpeting, full-length bodyside molding and J78 × 15 BSW tires on Suburban. Fury III adds: Various bright exterior moldings, acoustic insulation, and additional interior lighting. Sport Fury adds: Door pull straps, front seat center arm rest, additional interior lighting, concealed headlamps. Sport Suburban add: Wood-grain bodyside applique. S/23 and Sport Fury GT adds: Strobe stripes, HD suspension and brakes, dual exhausts, Rallye Road Wheels, and H70 × 15 white-letter tires. Gran Coupe B adds to Fury II: Luxury interior trim, additional exterior trim and 318 CID V8 engine. Gran Coupe A adds to Gran Coupe B: Air conditioning.

## Measurements

|  | Cars | Wagons |
|---|---|---|
| Wheelbase | 120.0" | 122.0" |
| Length | 214.9" | 220.1" |
| Width | 79.6" | 79.6" |
| Height | 55.8" | 57.9" |
| Legroom — front | 41.8" | 41.8" |
| Legroom — rear | 38.6" | 39.1" |
| Headroom — front | 38.8" | 39.6" |
| Headroom — rear | 38.4" | 39.2" |
| Cargo capacity (cu. ft.) | 21.5 | 104.2 |
| Fuel capacity (gals.) | 23.0 | 23.0 |

## Models Available

| | Style Number | Base MSRP | Change from LY | Shipping Wt. (lbs.) | Production | Change from LY |
|---|---|---|---|---|---|---|
| Fury I 2-Door Sedan | PE21 | $2,790 | +3.30% | 3575 | 2,353 | -52.67% |
| Fury I 4-Door Sedan | PE41 | $2,825 | +2.95% | 3625 | 14,813 | -21.09% |
| Fury II 2-Door Hardtop | PL23 | $2,903 | NEW | 3565 | 21,316 | NEW |
| Fury II 4-Door Sedan | PL41 | $2,922 | +2.85% | 3615 | 27,694 | -32.53% |
| Fury II 4-Dr., 2-S. Suburban Wagon | PL45 | $3,303 | +2.23% | 4090 | 5,300 | -17.50% |
| Fury II 4-Dr., 3-S. Suburban Wagon | PL46 | $3,518 | NEW | 4205 | 2,250 | NEW |
| Fury III 2-Door Hardtop | PM23 | $3,091 | +3.03% | 3600 | 21,373 | -51.61% |
| Fury III 2-Door Formal Hardtop | PM29 | $3,217 | +6.52% | 3615 | 12,367 | -45.61% |
| Fury III 2-Door Convertible | PM27 | $3,415 | +2.74% | 3770 | 1,952 | -52.72% |
| Fury III 4-Door Sedan | PM41 | $3,069 | +3.02% | 3625 | 50,876 | -30.06% |
| Fury III 4-Door Hardtop | PM43 | $3,246 | +2.88% | 3705 | 47,879 | -30.43% |
| Fury III 4-Dr., 2-S. Cust. Sub. Wgn. | PM45 | $3,527 | +2.65% | 4155 | 8,898 | -44.30% |
| Fury III 4-Dr., 3-S. Cust. Sub. Wgn. | PM46 | $3,603 | +2.15% | 4215 | 6,792 | -33.52% |
| Sport Fury 2-Door Hardtop | PH23 | $3,313 | +0.91% | 3630 | 8,018 | -43.22% |
| Sport Fury 2-Door Formal Hardtop | PH29 | $3,333 | +0.91% | 3645 | 5,688 | +162.24% |
| Sport Fury 4-Door Sedan | PH41 | $3,291 | NEW | 3680 | 5,135 | NEW |
| Sport Fury 4-Door Hardtop | PH43 | $3,363 | NEW | 3705 | 6,854 | NEW |
| Fury 4-Dr., 2-S. Sport Sub. Wgn. | PH45 | $3,725 | +2.03% | 4200 | 4,403 | -46.31% |
| Fury 4-Dr., 3-S. Sport Sub. Wgn. | PH46 | $3,804 | +2.31% | 4260 | 9,170 | -32.08% |
| Sport Fury S23 2-Door Hardtop | PS23 | $3,379 | NEW | 3660 | Sp. Fury HT | NEW |
| Sport Fury GT 2-Door Hardtop | PP23 | $3,898 | NEW | 3925 | Sp. Fury HT | NEW |
| Fury Gran Coupe 'A' 2-Door HT | PL21 | $4,216 | NEW | 3978 | Fury II HT | NEW |
| Fury Gran Coupe 'B' 2-Door HT | PL21 | $3,833 | NEW | 3864 | Fury II HT | NEW |
| TOTALS | | *Avg. price* $3,373 | +4.72% | | *Production* 263,131 | -28.23% |

# PONTIAC

*"We take the fun of driving seriously."*

The start of the new decade brought all-new styling to most of the Pontiac lineup. But the star of the show would be the totally redesigned Firebird, which would not appear until February 1970. In the interim, 1969 model Firebirds were produced later into the fall of '69 and sold as 1970 models. This made the new Firebird a 1970½ model. The new Firebird (like sister F-body Chevrolet Camaro) was a dramatic departure from any previous styling seen on a GM product, except for the Corvette. Undoubtedly the Corvette had greatly influenced the styling of these two cars. On the Firebird, the front end featured an Endura flexible bumper, with large twin grilles split across a traditional Pontiac nose, and single headlamps on each side. Body sides were smooth with slightly bulged wheel openings, a large driver door, and no rear quarter windows, giving the illusion of a sporty two-seat car. At the rear, a sloping rear window led into a very short decklid, and a flat vertical tail panel housed twin slotted taillights. Under the hood, engine choices were similar to prior years, but the base overhead cam 6-cylinder was replaced by a more traditional overhead valve 6-cylinder engine. The model lineup was renamed and revised slightly, but still similar to prior years. At the low-price end was a base Firebird. The next step up was a new Esprit, which took the place of the Sprint and 350 models. Next up was the Formula, which took the place of the Firebird 400. Finally there was the Trans Am, which had been a regular production option, although very few were built, in 1969. There was no longer a convertible model in any series.

Mid-size and full-size models each received extensive restyling of the front and rear treatments. Mid-size models wore a new full-width bumper, which incorporated a split grille theme. Of course, on GTO models, this bumper was made of Endura rubber-type material to deflect bumps and dings. At the back end wrap-around tail lamps were incorporated into a new bumper and decklid design. Full-size models featured a variation of this theme, but the grille was more upright and narrow, with parking lamps set into separate housings between the quad headlamps and the grille. Tail lamps on full-size Pontiacs also moved into the bumper. Model changes this year included the addition of a 2-Door Hardtop to the base Tempest line, the rebadging of the Tempest Custom as the LeMans line, and the shifting of the former LeMans line a new LeMans Sport line. The former Tempest Custom Convertible did not survive the transition to the LeMans line. No changes were made to the full-size line. The popular Grand Prix underwent minimal changes, mostly consisting of a revised grille and trim.

Bonneville 4-Door Hardtop

Catalina 2-Door Convertible

Executive 2-Door Hardtop

1970

Firebird Line (base, Esprit, Formula 400 and Trans Am

Firebird Trans Am 2-Door Coupe

GTO 2-Door Convertible

LeMans Sport 2-Door Convertible

**Model year production:** 691,002, down 16.15% from 1969.
**Domestic market share:** 8.30% (4th place).
**Base price range:** $2,623 to $4,305.
**Industry average base price:** $3,538.
**Pontiac average base price:** $3,384.
**Introduction date:** September 18, 1969. New Firebird introduced February 26, 1970.
**Assembly plants:** Atlanta, GA (A); Baltimore, MD (B); Southgate, CA (C); Linden, NJ (E); Framingham, MA (G); Kansas City, MO (K); Van Nuys, CA (L); Norwood, OH (N); Pontiac, MI (P); Arlington, TX (R); Fairfax, KS (X); Fremont, CA (Z); and Oshawa, Ontario, Canada (1).

**Data plate identification:** Thirteen digit code read as follows: 1st digit 2 = Pontiac; 2nd through 5th digits identify series/body style (see style number in listings); 0 = 1970; 7th digit is assembly plant code; 100001 and up (600001 and up on 6-cylinders) for serial number. *Example:* 252390X100001 is a 1970 Pontiac Catalina 4-Door Hardtop, serial number 100001, built in Fairfax, KS.

## Powertrains

| Engine | Gross HP | Transmission Availability | Firebird | LeMans/GTO | Grand Prix | Exec. & Catalina | Bonne-Ville |
|---|---|---|---|---|---|---|---|
| 250 CID, 1-bbl., 6-cyl. | 175 155-Firebird | 3-speed manual | S (base) | S[1] | - | - | - |
| | | 2-sp. Automatic | $165 (base) | $164[1] | - | - | - |
| | | Turbo Hydra-matic | $195 (base) | $195[1] | - | - | - |
| 350 CID, 2-bbl., V8 | 255 | 3-speed manual | $111 (base)/ S (Esprit) | $111[1] | - | S[2] | - |
| | | 3-speed HD man. | $195 (base)/ $84 (Esprit) | $195[1] | - | - | - |
| | | 4-speed manual | $296 (base)/ $185 (Esprit) | $296[1] | - | - | - |
| | | 2-sp. Automatic | $285 (base)/ $171 (Esprit) | $285[1] | - | $174[2] | - |
| | | Turbo Hydra-matic | $317 (base)/ $196 (Esprit) | $317[1] | - | $206[2] | - |
| 400 CID, 2-bbl., V8 | 265 | 3-speed manual | S (Formula)/ $53 (Esprit) | - | - | - | - |
| | | 4-speed manual | $180 (Formula)/ $259 (Esprit) | - | - | - | - |

| Engine | Gross HP | Transmission Availability | Firebird | LeMans/GTO | Grand Prix | Exec. & Catalina | Bonne-Ville |
|---|---|---|---|---|---|---|---|
| | | Turbo Hydra-matic | $227 (Formula)/$296 (Esprit) | $390[1] | - | $280[2]/$227[3] | - |
| 400 CID, 2-bbl., V8 | 290 | 3-speed manual | - | - | - | S[3]/$53[2] | - |
| | | Turbo Hydra-matic | - | $390[1] | - | $227[3]/$280[2] | - |
| 400 CID, 4-bbl., V8 | 330 (FB,LeM)/350 (Others) | 3-speed HD man. | - | S (GTO) | S | - | - |
| | | 4-speed manual | - | $185 (GTO) | $227 | - | - |
| | | Turbo Hydra-matic | - | $227 (GTO)/$438 (others) | $227 | $274[3]/$327[2] | - |
| 400 CID H.O. Ram Air, 4-bbl., V8 | 335 | 4-speed manual | S (Trans Am)/$169 (Formula) | - | - | - | - |
| | | Turbo Hydra-matic | $ | - | - | - | - |
| 400 CID Ram Air SD, 4-bbl., V8 | 345 | 4-speed manual | $ (Trans Am) | - | - | - | - |
| | | Turbo Hydra-matic | $ (Trans Am) | - | - | - | - |
| 455 CID, 4-bbl., V8 | 360 | 3-speed HD man. | - | $58 (GTO) | $58 | - | S |
| | | 4-speed manual | - | $243 (GTO) | $285 | - | - |
| | | Turbo Hydra-matic | - | $295 (GTO) | $285 | $332[3]/$396[2] | $227 |
| 455 CID H.O., 4-bbl., V8 | 370 | Turbo Hydra-matic | - | $295 (GTO) | $285 | $427[3]/$490[2] | $322 |

[1]Excluding GTO    [2]Catalina Hardtops and Sedans    [3]All but Hardtops and Sedans

## Major Options

| | Firebird | LeMans | Grand Prix | Catalina | Executive | Bonneville |
|---|---|---|---|---|---|---|
| Air conditioning (V8 only) | $376 | $376 | $421 | $421 | $421 | $421 |
| Electronic cruise control (V8 auto.) | - | $58 | $63 | $63 | $63 | $63 |
| Soft Ray tinted glass | $37 | $37 | $44 | $44 | $44 | $44 |
| Power steering—variable-ratio | $105 | $105 | $116 | $116 | $116 | $116 |
| Power brakes | $64 | $64 | S | $72 | $72 | $72 |
| Power driver's seat/Bench seat | $74 | $74 | $74 | $100 | $100 | $100 |
| Power windows | $105 | $105 | $111 | $111 | $111 | $111 |
| AM radio | $61 | $61 | $87 | $87 | $87 | $87 |
| AM/FM stereo | $239 | $239 | $239 | $239 | $239 | $239 |
| Front seat console | $57 | $59 | S | - | - | - |
| Front bucket seats | S | $ | S | - | - | - |
| Tilt steering wheel | - | $45 | $45 | $45 | $45 | $45 |
| Vinyl roof (except Trans Am) | $ | $100 | $142 | $116–142 | $116–142 | $116–142 |
| White stripe tires (base size) | $26–$28 | $28–$34 | $31 | $31–40 | $31–40 | $34–40 |
| Rally II wheels | $56 | $87 | $87 | $87 | $87 | $87 |

Options common to most models. (- = Not Available; S = Standard equipment.) Items may be standard equipment, optional at different pricing, or unavailable on certain models. This chart is only a guide.

## Paint Colors

| | Code | | Code | | Code |
|---|---|---|---|---|---|
| Polar White | 10 | Pallisade Green Metallic | 45 | Orbit Orange | 60/06 |
| Palladium Silver Metallic | 14 | Verdoro Green Metallic | 47 | Sandalwood | 61 |
| Starlight Black | 19 | Pepper Green Metallic | 48 | Palomino Copper Metallic | 63 |
| Bermuda Blue Metallic | 25 | Sierra Yellow | 50 | Carousel Red | 65 |
| Lucerne Blue Metallic* | 26 | Golden Red Yellow | 51 | Castillian Bronze Metallic* | 67 |
| Atoll Blue Metallic | 28 | Coronado Gold Metallic | 53 | Cardinal Red | 75 |
| Mint Turquoise Metallic | 34 | Baja Gold Metallic | 55 | Burgundy Metallic | 78 |
| Keylime Metallic* | 43 | Granada Gold Metallic | 58 | | |

*Firebird only.

1970

# Firebird

*"The beginning of tomorrow.
Pontiac's all-new Firebirds. New, even for Pontiac."*

**Nameplate year of origin:** 1967 (used on Motorama show cars as early as 1954).
**Current bodystyle lifespan:** 1970 through 1981.
**Predecessor to this model:** Firebird (1967 to 1969).
**Corporate siblings:** Chevrolet Camaro.
**Replacement for this model:** Firebird (1982 to 1992).
**Percentage of division's sales volume:** 7.05%.
**Primary competition:** AMC Javelin, Ford Mustang, Plymouth Barracuda, and Dodge Challenger.
**Notable changes:** Totally redesigned. Mid-year introduction.
**Major standard equipment:** All-vinyl front bucket seats, and rear bucket-type seats, loop-pile carpeting, deluxe steering wheel, Endura front bumper, hubcaps, windshield radio antenna, E78-14 BSW tires. Esprit adds: Custom cushion steering wheel, additional interior and exterior trim, dual sport mirrors, and wheel trim rings. Formula adds: 400 CID V8 engine, heavy duty suspension, and F70 × 14 tires. Trans Am adds: Formula steering wheel, power steering, power brakes Rally II wheels, and F60-15 tires.

## Measurements

| | |
|---|---|
| Wheelbase | 108.0" |
| Length | 191.6" |
| Width | 73.4" |
| Height | 50.4" |
| Legroom — front | 43.8" |
| Legroom — rear | 29.6" |
| Headroom — front | 37.4" |
| Headroom — rear | 36.1" |
| Cargo capacity (cu. ft.) | 6.4 |
| Fuel capacity (gals.) | 18.0 |

## Models Available

| | Style Number | Base MSRP | Change from LY | Shipping Wt. (lbs.) | Production | Change from LY |
|---|---|---|---|---|---|---|
| Firebird 2-Door Coupe | 22387 | $2,875 | +1.55% | 3140 | 18,874 | -75.18% |
| Firebird Esprit 2-Door Coupe | 22487 | $3,241 | NEW | 3435 | 18,961 | NEW |
| Firebird Formula 400 2-Door Coupe | 22687 | $3,370 | NEW | 3470 | 7,708 | NEW |
| Firebird Trans Am 2-Door Coupe | 22887 | $4,305 | NEW | 3550 | 3,196 | NEW |
| TOTALS | Avg. price | $3,448 | +17.36% | Production | 48,739 | -44.43% |

# LeMans

*"The kind of car you hate to put in the garage."*

**Nameplate year of origin:** 1961 (as a Tempest sub-series).
**Current bodystyle lifespan:** 1968 through 1972.
**Predecessor to this model:** Tempest/LeMans (1966 to 1967).
**Replacement for this model:** LeMans (1973 to 1977).
**Percentage of division's sales volume:** 34.54%.
**Corporate siblings:** Chevrolet Chevelle, Oldsmobile Cutlass, and Buick Skylark.
**Primary competition:** Ford Torino, Mercury Montego, Plymouth Satellite, Dodge Coronet, and AMC Rebel.
**Notable changes:** Restyled front and rear end.
**Major standard equipment:** Cloth and vinyl front bench seat, vinyl floor covering, courtesy lights, 2-speed windshield wipers with washers, and F78 × 14 BSW tires. LeMans adds: All-vinyl front bench seats, full carpeting, rocker panel moldings, and G78 BSW tires on Wagons. LeMans Sport adds: All-vinyl bucket seats or bench seat (2-Doors), cloth and vinyl bench seats (4-Doors), simulated walnut trim on dash, and H78 × 14 BSW tires. Safari adds:

## Measurements

| | 2-Doors | 4-Doors | Wagons |
|---|---|---|---|
| Wheelbase | 112.0" | 116.0" | 116.0" |
| Length | 202.5" | 206.5" | 210.5" |
| Width | 76.7" | 76.7" | 76.7" |
| Height | 52.0" | 52.6" | 54.0" |
| Legroom — front | 42.4" | 42.5" | 42.4" |
| Legroom — rear | 31.9" | 34.8" | 34.8" |
| Headroom — front | 37.7" | 38.1" | 38.5" |
| Headroom — rear | 36.3" | 36.9" | 37.4" |
| Cargo capacity (cu. ft.) | NA | NA | 83.6 |
| Fuel capacity (gals.) | 21.5 | 21.5 | 21.5 |

Exterior wood-grain paneling. GTO adds: All-vinyl bucket seats, floor shifter, dual exhausts, 400 CID V8 with engine dress-up kit, heavy duty suspension and G78 × 14 BSW tires.

## Models Available

| | Style Number | Base MSRP | Change from LY | Shipping Wt. (lbs.) | Production | Change from LY |
|---|---|---|---|---|---|---|
| Tempest 2-Door Coupe | 23327 | $2,623 | +4.50% | 3225 | 11,977 | -30.29% |
| Tempest 2-Door Hardtop | 23337 | $2,683 | NEW | 3250 | 20,883 | NEW |
| Tempest 4-Door Sedan | 23369 | $2,670 | +4.42% | 3295 | 9,187 | -5.69% |
| LeMans 2-Door Coupe | 23527 | $2,735 | +5.07% | 3240 | 5,656 | -28.51% |
| LeMans 2-Door Hardtop | 23537 | $2,795 | +4.96% | 3265 | 52,304 | +11.56% |
| LeMans 4-Door Sedan | 23569 | $2,782 | +4.94% | 3315 | 15,255 | -7.72% |
| LeMans 4-Door Hardtop | 23539 | $2,921 | +5.19% | 3385 | 3,872 | -1.17% |
| LeMans 4-Door, 2-Seat Wagon | 23535 | $3,092 | +4.60% | 3685 | 7,165 | +2.90% |
| LeMans Sport 2-Door Coupe | 23727 | $2,891 | +4.26% | 3265 | 1,673 | -66.76% |
| LeMans Sport 2-Door Hardtop | 23737 | $2,953 | +4.16% | 3290 | 58,356 | -29.54% |
| LeMans Sport 2-Door Convertible | 23767 | $3,182 | +3.85% | 3330 | 4,670 | -17.72% |
| LeMans Sport 4-Door Hardtop | 23739 | $3,083 | +3.98% | 3405 | 3,657 | -43.52% |
| LeMans Safari 4-Dr., 2-S. Wagon | 23736 | $3,328 | +4.07% | 3775 | 3,872 | -5.91% |
| GTO 2-Door Hardtop | 24237 | $3,267 | +3.52% | 3641 | 36,366 | -43.92% |
| GTO 2-Door Convertible | 24267 | $3,492 | +3.25% | 3691 | 3,783 | -49.13% |
| TOTALS | Avg. price | $2,966 | +3.53% | Production | 238,676 | -17.10% |

# Grand Prix

*"Beauty without frills. Comfort without boredom. Luxury with spirit. This is the way luxury is going to be. This is the 1970 Grand Prix."*

**Nameplate year of origin:** 1962.
**Current bodystyle lifespan:** 1969 through 1972.
**Predecessor to this model:** Grand Prix (1967 to 1968).
**Replacement for this model:** Grand Prix (1973 to 1977).
**Percentage of division's sales volume:** 9.52%.
**Corporate siblings:** Chevrolet Monte Carlo.
**Primary competition:** Mercury Cougar, Plymouth Satellite Sebring, Dodge Charger.
**Notable changes:** New grille, minor trim and detail changes.
**Major standard equipment:** Front bucket seats or notchback bench seat in cloth and vinyl or all-vinyl trim, loop-pile carpeting, custom cushion steering wheel, electric clock, lamp package, deluxe wheel covers, windshield radio antenna, concealed wipers, exterior bright moldings, and G78-14 BSW tires.

## Measurements

| | |
|---|---|
| Wheelbase | 118.0" |
| Length | 210.2" |
| Width | 75.7" |
| Height | 52.0" |
| Legroom — front | 42.4" |
| Legroom — rear | 31.6" |
| Headroom — front | 37.5" |
| Headroom — rear | 36.2" |
| Cargo capacity (cu. ft.) | NA |
| Fuel capacity (gals.) | 21.5 |

**1970**

## Models Available

| | Style Number | Base MSRP | Change from LY | Shipping Wt. (lbs.) | Production | Change from LY |
|---|---|---|---|---|---|---|
| Grand Prix 2-Door Hardtop | 27657 | $3,985 | +3.08% | 3784 | 65,750 | -41.55% |
| TOTALS | Avg. price | $3,985 | +3.08% | Production | 65,750 | -41.55% |

# Catalina

*"For the money, you could get a so-so-sized
car with hee-haw styling and a ho-hum interior."*

**Nameplate year of origin:** 1950 on hardtop models, 1959 as series.
**Current bodystyle lifespan:** 1969 through 1970.
**Predecessor to this model:** Catalina (1967 to 1968).
**Replacement for this model:** Catalina (1971 to 1976).
**Percentage of division's sales volume:** 32.33%.
**Corporate siblings:** Chevrolet Impala/Caprice, Olds Delta 88, Buick
   LeSabre/Wildcat.
**Primary competition:** Ford LTD, Mercury Monterey, Plymouth Fury,
   Dodge Polara, AMC Ambassador.
**Notable changes:** Restyled front and rear end.
**Major standard equipment:** Cloth and vinyl front bench seat (all-vinyl
   on convertible and wagons), full carpeting, 2-speed windshield wipers
   with washers, and H78 × 15 BSW tires (G78 × 15 BSW tires on Hard-
   tops, L78 × 15 BSW tires on wagons). Ventura option adds: All-vinyl
   upholstery with specific trim.

## Measurements

|                          | Cars    | Wagons  |
|--------------------------|---------|---------|
| Wheelbase                | 122.0"  | 122.0"  |
| Length                   | 217.9"  | 220.9"  |
| Width                    | 79.8"   | 79.8"   |
| Height                   | 54.8"   | 56.0"   |
| Legroom — front          | 42.4"   | 41.5"   |
| Legroom — rear           | 38.1"   | 38.2"   |
| Headroom — front         | 39.0"   | 39.2"   |
| Headroom — rear          | 37.7"   | 39.0"   |
| Cargo capacity (cu. ft.) | NA      | 99.9    |
| Fuel capacity (gals.)    | 26.5    | 24.0    |

## Models Available

|                                  | Style Number | Base MSRP | Change from LY | Shipping Wt. (lbs.) | Production | Change from LY |
|----------------------------------|--------------|-----------|----------------|---------------------|------------|----------------|
| Catalina 2-Door Hardtop          | 25257        | $3,249    | +2.36%         | 3952                | 70,350     | -16.26%        |
| Catalina 2-Door Convertible      | 25267        | $3,604    | +3.68%         | 4027                | 3,686      | -32.19%        |
| Catalina 4-Door Sedan            | 25269        | $3,164    | +2.39%         | 3997                | 84,795     | +74.51%        |
| Catalina 4-Door Hardtop          | 25239        | $3,319    | +2.31%         | 4042                | 35,155     | -9.44%         |
| Catalina Safari 4-Dr., 2-S. Wagon | 25236       | $3,646    | +3.61%         | 4517                | 16,944     | -16.75%        |
| Catalina Safari 4-Dr., 3-S. Wagon | 25246       | $3,791    | +3.47%         | 4607                | 12,450     | -7.04%         |
| TOTALS                           | *Avg. price* | $3,462    | +3.01%         | *Production*        | 223,380    | +6.07%         |

# Executive

*"Any resemblance between Pontiac's 1970 Executive
and the gray-flanneled variety is strictly intentional."*

**Nameplate year of origin:** 1966.
**Current bodystyle lifespan:** 1969 through 1970.
**Predecessor to this model:** Executive (1967 to 1968).
**Replacement for this model:** Bonneville (1971 to 1976).
**Percentage of division's sales volume:** 4.69%.
**Corporate siblings:** Chevrolet Impala/Caprice, Oldsmobile Delta 88, Buick
   LeSabre/Wildcat.
**Primary competition:** Ford LTD, Mercury Marquis, Plymouth Fury, and
   Dodge Monaco.
**Notable changes:** Restyled front and rear ends.
**Major standard equipment:** Cloth and vinyl bench seat, full carpeting, perfo-
   rated vinyl headliner, walnut grain trim on dash, electric clock, full length
   lower body molding, exterior wood grain trim on station wagons, full wheel
   covers and G78 × 15 BSW tires (L78 × 15 BSW tires on 3-Seat Wagon).

## Measurements

|                          | Cars    | Wagons  |
|--------------------------|---------|---------|
| Wheelbase                | 125.0"  | 122.0"  |
| Length                   | 223.9"  | 220.9"  |
| Width                    | 79.8"   | 79.8"   |
| Height                   | 55.0"   | 56.0"   |
| Legroom — front          | 42.4"   | 41.5"   |
| Legroom — rear           | 38.1"   | 38.2"   |
| Headroom — front         | 39.0"   | 39.2"   |
| Headroom — rear          | 37.7"   | 39.0"   |
| Cargo capacity (cu. ft.) | NA      | 99.9    |
| Fuel capacity (gals.)    | 26.5    | 24.0    |

## Models Available

|  | Style Number | Base MSRP | Change from LY | Shipping Wt. (lbs.) | Production | Change from LY |
|---|---|---|---|---|---|---|
| Executive 2-Door Hardtop | 25637 | $3,600 | +4.17% | 4042 | 3,499 | -22.11% |
| Executive 4-Door Sedan | 25669 | $3,538 | +4.24% | 4087 | 13,061 | -11.93% |
| Executive 4-Door Hardtop | 25639 | $3,669 | +4.09% | 4132 | 5,376 | -17.57% |
| Executive Safari 4-Dr., 2-S. Wagon | 25636 | $4,015 | +3.69% | 4552 | 4,861 | -24.18% |
| Executive Safari 4-Dr., 3-S. Wagon | 25646 | $4,160 | +3.56% | 4632 | 5,629 | -17.28% |
| TOTALS | | Avg. price $3,796 | +3.91% | | Production 32,426 | -16.99% |

# Bonneville

*"The most luxurious Pontiac we've ever built."*

**Nameplate year of origin:** 1957.
**Current bodystyle lifespan:** 1969 through 1970.
**Predecessor to this model:** Bonneville (1967 to 1968).
**Replacement for this model:** Grand Ville (1971 to 1976).
**Percentage of division's sales volume:** 11.87%.
**Corporate siblings:** Chevrolet Impala/Caprice, Oldsmobile Delta 88, Buick LeSabre/Wildcat.
**Primary competition:** Ford LTD, Mercury Marquis, Plymouth Fury, Dodge Monaco, AMC Ambassador.
**Notable changes:** Restyled front and rear end.
**Major standard equipment:** All-vinyl or cloth and vinyl front bench seat, full carpeting, burled elm grain dash trim, electric clock, courtesy lights, dual-speed electric windshield wipers, rear fender skirts, deluxe wheel covers and G78 × 15 BSW tires (L78 × 15 BSW tires Wagon). Brougham option adds: Special upholstery trim with fold down center armrests, and exterior badges.

## Measurements

|  | Cars | Wagons |
|---|---|---|
| Wheelbase | 125.0" | 122.0" |
| Length | 224.6" | 220.9" |
| Width | 79.8" | 79.8" |
| Height | 55.0" | 56.0" |
| Legroom — front | 42.3" | 41.5" |
| Legroom — rear | 38.1" | 38.2" |
| Headroom — front | 38.8" | 39.2" |
| Headroom — rear | 37.7" | 39.0" |
| Cargo capacity (cu. ft.) | NA | 99.9 |
| Fuel capacity (gals.) | 26.5 | 24.0 |

## Models Available

|  | Style Number | Base MSRP | Change from LY | Shipping Wt. (lbs.) | Production | Change from LY |
|---|---|---|---|---|---|---|
| Bonneville 2-Door Hardtop | 26237 | $3,832 | +3.90% | 4111 | 23,418 | -15.68% |
| Bonneville 2-Door Convertible | 26267 | $4,040 | +3.70% | 4161 | 3,537 | -34.96% |
| Bonneville 4-Door Sedan | 26269 | $3,770 | +3.97% | 4181 | 3,802 | -21.75% |
| Bonneville 4-Door Hardtop | 26239 | $3,900 | +3.83% | 4226 | 44,241 | +8.39% |
| Bonneville Safari 4-Dr., 3-S. Wgn. | 26246 | $4,247 | +3.48% | 4686 | 7,033 | -5.32% |
| TOTALS | | Avg. price $3,958 | +3.78% | | Production 82,031 | -4.96% |

# 1971

It is hard to label 1971 as a good or bad automotive sales year. On the positive side, Ford, Lincoln-Mercury, American Motors, Dodge and Plymouth all saw sales increases. Meanwhile, however, all of General Motors' divisions had large sales declines. The losses at GM were so great that they brought the overall U.S. sales down 6 percent from 1970 levels. Price increases on full-size models approaching 20 percent combined with increasing prices on other consumer products, including gasoline, were putting pressure on cars that were inefficient with fuel — something GM had a lot of. (Sales of Ford or Chrysler's large cars were not spectacular either.) GM also had many unsettled labor disputes during this era, and as a result there were many production problems. It was cars of this era that also contributed greatly to Detroit's reputation for poor quality that would greatly enhance the ability of foreign automakers to sell their automobiles in the U.S. market. Unfortunately, this legacy has carried on to the present day, even though the quality of the cars has risen significantly.

Another contributing factor to the sales decline that would continue through 1976 was the assumption on the part of manufacturers that all consumers would now buy luxury cars, or the pretense of luxury. Rising insurance rates and government pressures had led to the quick demise of the muscle car, and carmakers saw their luxury editions as a way to keep up the profits and image that had gone away with the muscle car. Even sporty makes like Pontiac fell to the temptation offering the Firebird Esprit, the Catalina Brougham, and the new luxury Grand Ville. For whatever reason, nearly every line featured a "Brougham" edition. It was suddenly one of the most over-used nomenclatures in the automotive business. Every division of every manufacturer had a Brougham, except for Buick, Chevrolet, and Lincoln. In the short term, the strategy would work. Price cuts on 1972 models would lead to stronger sales for 1972 and 1973, but the Arab oil embargoes of 1973 would curtail big car sales for the following four years. This would

give the makers of small Japanese and European cars the chance they needed for sales to grow. They had the quality, the lower prices, and the right features for the times.

As for the 1971 cars themselves, the big news came from Ford and Chevy with their new Pinto and Vega subcompact models. These new cars were designed to take on the imports head to head. Similarities in both cars could be found in their execution and in their potential marketing problems. Both cars were designed as strictly 2-Door models, but came in Sedan, Hatchback or Wagon forms (the Pinto Wagon arrived for 1972). Both cars utilized 4-cylinder powerplants, which had been little used in American cars since the early 1930s. Also, both cars were offered in very basic packaging that could be loaded up with options, which drove the price tags up greatly. That's where the downfalls came to light. European and Japanese models typically cost a few dollars more than the new American cars, but they also included more standard features. Adding options to a Pinto or Vega could easily raise the price of the car 50 percent over the base price, whereas the imported cars generally held the line on the amount of optional equipment offered. Another problem was the lack of 4-Door models in the subcompact range. Ford and Chevrolet offered compact 4-Door Sedans, but the dimensions of both the Maverick and the Nova were nearly that of a midsize model. Meanwhile, cars such as the Toyota Corolla, Datsun 510, and even "captive imports" such as the Dodge Colt and Plymouth Cricket were making inroads into the subcompact 4-Door market with no competition from Detroit. AMC, which had entered the subcompact market in 1970 with its Gremlin, was really not a contender, as the Gremlin was more of a shortened, compact Hornet with extremely poor rear seating. Plus, the Gremlin was powered by a 6-cylinder engine, which put it into a different league from the new 4-cylinder contenders.

Other potential problems for the two newcomers were their new 4-cylinder engines and the hatchback body de-

## 1971 Model Year Production by Make

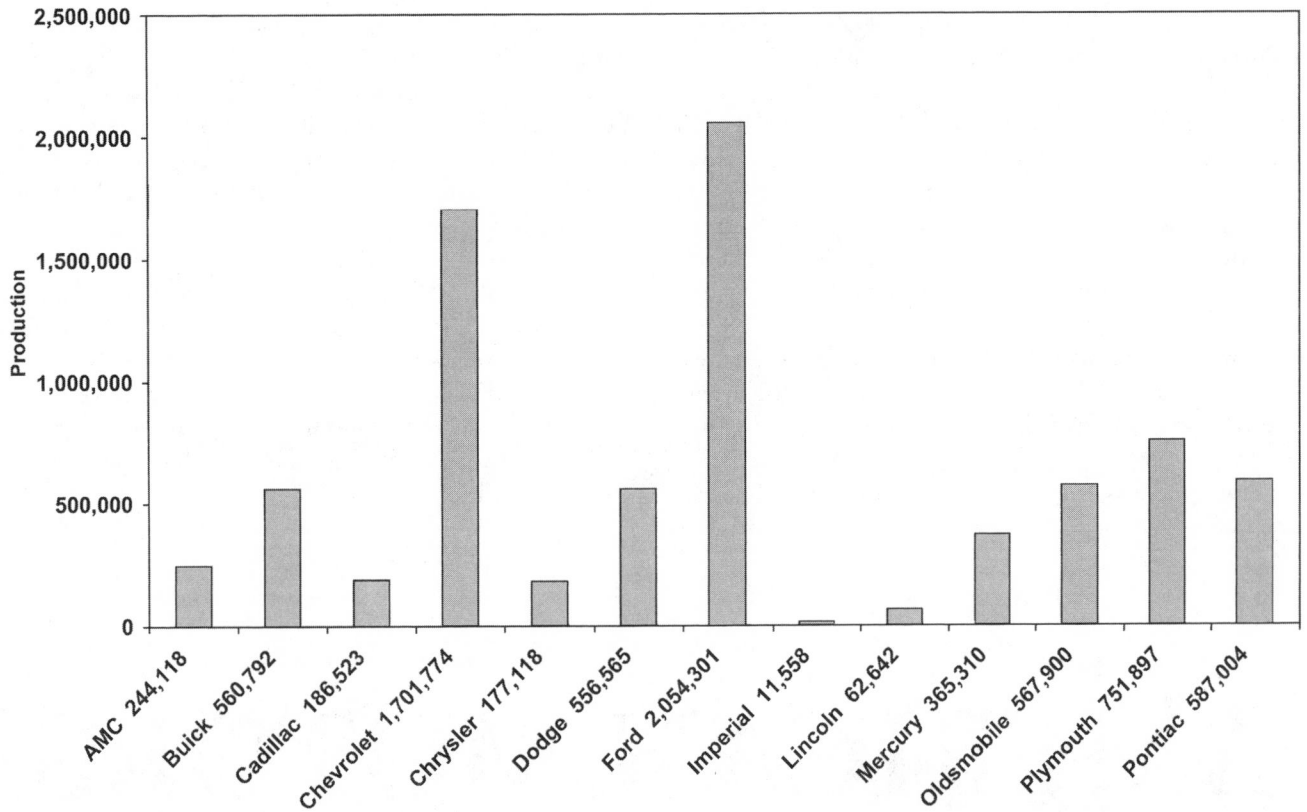

sign. Typically, American car buyers have resisted the hatchback design. Fortunately for both Ford and Chevy, their new hatchback models sold quite well initially. They would continue to do reasonably well throughout their life spans, but by the mid-seventies, Americans were showing a definite preference for coupe or sedan models. Only sporty cars seemed to sell hatchback models in quantity. As for the engines, Chevy turned out to have the real loser in the crowd. Its concept was brilliant, but its execution was another matter. Production problems plagued the early aluminum 4-cylinder engines, and puddles of coolant under a Vega were a common sight. Ford turned to its European lines to get the Pinto's 4-cylinder powerplant. As it turned out, this was a smart move, as the base British and optional German designed engines proved to be solid performers in the Pinto.

GM and Ford both offered new full-size lines. Ford went for a very traditional and conservative approach with the LTD and Monterey/Marquis lines. Rooflines were boxy, front ends were reminiscent of recent models, and the Mercury line lost its Convertible models. General Motors, on the other hand, went for new wide-bodied designs, in an effort to maximize interior space. Rooflines were somewhat rounded on Sedan and Hardtop models. Convertibles utilized an inward folding top design that widened the rear seating area to nearly a full car width. Station Wagon mod-

els were where the General really showed off its engineering prowess. Tailgates on all of the new full-size line were what was termed a "clamshell" design. The window portion raised into the roof of the car, while the door portion lowered into a space under the cargo floor. The door operation was manual on all early production cars, with power operation by key available shortly after the start of production. The window was power-operated on all models. Initially, the GM cars were not successful, but with mild restyling for 1972, sales would be regained.

Other models at GM and Ford were given facelifts ranging from mild to extensive. However, the Ford Mustang and Mercury Cougar were another set of completely new designs. It was with this new styling that the Mustang and Cougar began drifting in different market directions. The Cougar had always been the more luxurious car, but this season it began a move towards the mid-size personal/luxury market currently occupied by the Chevy Monte Carlo and Pontiac Grand Prix. The Mustang continued to be the pony car leader. Both models continued to offer 2-Door Hardtop and Convertible versions, where their GM counterparts had discontinued the convertible style at the end of the 1969 season.

At Chrysler, the Dodge Demon was introduced as a member of the Dart line. It was based upon the new for-1970 Plymouth Duster Coupe. Like the Duster, the Demon

1971

was available as a 340 model, providing good performance at a low cost. Chrysler got a jump on Ford and GM by introducing new mid-size models this season. Two-Door models were built on a shorter wheelbase than 4-Door models, and were given their own unique body shells. Dodge took the concept a step further and named all of its mid-sized 2-Door models Chargers, while all 4-Door models were in the Coronet line. Plymouth adopted a similar strategy with its 2-Doors being named Satellite Sebring, and the 4-Doors were simply Satellite models. Other Chrysler lines were given new grilles and other styling updates.

At AMC, the new Gremlin and Hornet lines were relatively unchanged, although the Hornet offered a new Sportabout Wagon model. This was the only compact station wagon model now offered by American manufacturers. Just four years prior, nearly every compact car line had a station wagon model, but the Big Three had abandoned the market for the more profitable mid-size and full-size models. The move left AMC in a great position to sell a good quantity of the little wagons, and it would have the market to itself until 1976, when Chrysler's Aspen and Volare twins were introduced with a compact wagon in the line. Other changes at AMC included the renaming of the Rebel to Matador, and a facelift for the re-christened car. The Matador would be a popular police car as well as a very nice family car.

Checker and Avanti II were generally unchanged for 1971, as usual. Light-duty truck lines were also changed very little, although GM and Dodge both introduced new versions of their van models. The Dodge B-series, Chevy Sportvan and GMC Rally Van/Vandura, were much larger than their predecessors, and were quite modern compared to the Ford Econoline design. Their basic body shells would continue until the mid–1990s.

# AMERICAN MOTORS

*"If you were to compete against G.M., Ford and Chrysler, what would you do?
See the cars that go them one better."*

The 1971 American Motors line was the final result of a brief, two-year overhaul of the company product line. It began with the dropping of the Rambler American in 1969, followed by the restyling of the Ambassador, and 1970 introductions of the Gremlin and Hornet. For the new model year, an all-new Javelin was introduced, and the Matador (the replacement for the Rebel) received a facelift. The Javelin was in the business of trying to lure Mustang and Camaro buyers to the AMC showroom. The original version had been somewhat successful in this task. Now, with the newness wearing off the Gremlin and Hornet lines, it was time to put some excitement into the other lines. The new Javelin was given a more muscular and aggressive appearance. Exaggerated bodylines curved over the wheel openings atop the fenders. Grilles were deeply inset. The fastback roofline took on a sharper appearance. Whether intentional or not, this all added up to a racy looking automobile. The Javelin was not just looking the part either, as the 1971 to 1974 models would show up in NASCAR circuits, even winning a few races along the way. The AMX was still alive, but in name only, as it was now a trim level at the top of the Javelin line. The distinct two-seat, short-wheelbase sport car was gone, and in its place was a run-of-the-mill Javelin, with four seating positions and a slightly bigger engine, although some individual AMX touches were thrown in for appearance's sake.

The newly named Matador line received a major facelift upon the old Rebel (and shared with Ambassador) body shell. The entire front clip of the Matador was freshly designed, and gave the cars a more modern appearance. Minor changes were also made to the rear of the car. Also, trim levels were upgraded slightly, as AMC tried to offer better equipped cars than its competitors, thereby offering a better value. The remainder of the 1971 AMC line was little changed.

Ambassador SST 4-Door Sedan

Gremlin 2-Passenger 2-Door Sedan

Hornet SC360 2-Door Sedan

Hornet Sportabout 4-Door Wagon

Javelin AMX 2-Door Hardtop

Javelin SST 2-Door Hardtop

Matador 2-Door Hardtop

**Model year production:** 244,118, up 0.53% over 1970.
**Domestic market share:** 3.19% (9th place).
**Base price range:** $1,899 to $4,430.
**Industry average base price:** $3,786.
**American Motors average base price:** $3,058.
**Introduction date:** October 6, 1970.
**Assembly plants:** Kenosha, Wisconsin, and Brampton, Ontario, Canada.

**Data plate identification:** Thirteen digit code read as follows: A = American Motors; 1 = 1971; transmission code (see chart); car line body type series numbers (see last three digits of style number); engine code (see chart); 100001 and up for serial number (700001 and up for cars built in Ontario). *Example:* A1A797I100001 is a 1971 Torque-Command Automatic, Javelin SST 2-Door, 304 CID V8, serial number 100001, built in Kenosha.

## Powertrains

| Engine | Gross HP | Engine Code | Transmission Availability | Trans Code | Gremlin /Hornet | Javelin | Matador | Ambdr. |
|---|---|---|---|---|---|---|---|---|
| 232 CID[3], 1-bbl., 6-cyl. | 135 | E | 3-speed manual | S/F | S | S | S | - |
|  |  |  | Shift-Command Automatic | A | $210 | $217 | $217 | - |
| 258 CID[3], 1-bbl., 6-cyl. | N/A[2] | B | 3-speed manual | S | $54 | $50 | $50 | - |
|  |  |  | Shift-Command Automatic | A | $264 | $267 | $267 | - |
| 258 CID[3], 1-bbl., 6-cyl. | 150 | A | 3-speed manual | S | $54 | $50 | $50 | S (DPL only) |
|  |  |  | Shift-Command Automatic | A | $264 | $267 | $267 | $217 (DPL only) |
| 304 CID***, 2-bbl., V8 | 210 | I | 3-speed manual | S | $101[1] | $101 | $101 | $101 (DPL only) |
|  |  |  | Shift-Command Automatic | A | $317[1] | $324 (col.)/ $380 (flr.) | $324 (col.)/ $380 (flr.) | S (SST & Brougham) |

| Engine | Gross HP | Engine Code | Transmission Availability | Trans Code | Gremlin /Hornet | Javelin | Matador | Ambdr. |
|--------|----------|-------------|---------------------------|------------|------------------|---------|---------|--------|
| | | | | | | | | $56 (Br. w/flr. shift)/ $208 (DPL) |
| 360 CID, 2-bbl., V8 | 245 | N | 3-speed manual | S | S[4] | $159[4] | $159 | - |
| | | | Shift-Command Automatic | A | S[4] | $405[4]/$461 | $405 (col.)/ $461 (flr.) | $367 (DPL)/ $48 (SST & Brougham)/ $127 (Br. w/flr. shift) |
| 360 CID, 4-bbl., V8 | 285 | P | 4-speed manual | M | - | $306[4] | - | - |
| | | | Shift-Command Automatic | A | - | $444 (col.)[4]/ $500 (flr.) | $444 (col.)/ $500 (flr.) | $435 (DPL)/ $97 (SST & Brougham)/ $176 (Br. w/flr. shift) |
| 401 CID, 4-bbl., V8 | 330 | Z | 4-speed manual | M | - | $346[4] | - | - |
| | | | Shift-Command Automatic | A | - | $550 (flr. only) | $494 (col.)/ $550 (flr.) | $170 (SST & Brougham)/ $226 (Br. w/flr. shift) |

[1]Available on Hornet only.  [2]Low-compression 258 CID listed as optional equipment, but HP rating not available.  [3]Not available in Hornet SC/360 or Javelin AMX models.  [4]Standard (with floor shifting) in Hornet SC/60 and Javelin AMX 360 (Code N). Optional 360 Code P, $49; 401 Code Z (Javelin only), $89. Shift-Command Automatic adds $246. Other equipment may affect actual pricing.

## Major Options

| | Gremlin | Hornet | Javelin | Matador | Ambassador |
|--------|---------|--------|---------|---------|------------|
| Air conditioning | $399 | $399 | $399 | $409 | S |
| Adjust-O-Tilt steering wheel | - | - | $49 | $49 | $49 |
| Speed control | - | - | - | $63 | $63 |
| Electric rear window defogger | - | - | $52 | $52 | $52 |
| Soft Ray tinted glass | $37 | $40 | $44 | $44 | $47 |
| Vinyl top (excluding Wagon models) | - | - | $ | $97 | $108 |
| Power steering—variable-ratio | $100 | $100 | $106 | $111 | $111 |
| Power brakes | $45 | $45 | $45 | $49 | S |
| Power windows | - | - | - | - | $120 |
| AM radio | $67 | $67 | $72 | $72 | $72 |
| AM/FM stereo (mono on Grem./Horn.) | $143 | $143 | $224 | $224 | $224 |
| Custom wheel covers | $50 | $50 | $50 | $53 | $53 |
| Turbo Cast wheel covers | $75 | $75 | $75 | $78 | $78 |
| Station Wagon third seat | - | - | - | $118 | $118 |

Options common to most models. (- = Not Available; S = Standard equipment.) Items may be standard equipment, optional at different pricing, or unavailable on certain models. This chart is only a guide.

Available Option packages: X package for Gremlin includes special interior options, exterior graphics: $300. "Go-Machine" package for Matador 2-Door Hardtop ($373) and Javelin AMX 2-Door Coupe ($411) includes 360 CID V8 w/4-bbl. carburetor, dual exhausts, hood decals (Javelin), Rally-Pac instrumentation (Javelin), handling package, cowl air induction system (Javelin), heavy-duty cooling, Twin-Grip differential, power disc brakes, E60 × 15 RWL tires, and styled steel wheels. The 401 CID V8 could be added for $88. Javelin Cardin bucket seat trim package (for Javelin SST only): $85.

## Paint Colors

| | Code | Gremlin/Hornet | Javelin | Matador/Ambassador |
|--------|------|----------------|---------|--------------------|
| Snow White | A1 | x | x | x |
| Canary Yellow | A2 | x | x | |
| Skyline Blue | A4 | x | x | |
| Midway Blue Metallic | A5 | x | x | x |
| Midnight Blue Metallic | A6 | | x | x |

|                        | Code | Gremlin/Hornet | Javelin | Matador/Ambassador |
|------------------------|------|----------------|---------|--------------------|
| Limelight Green Met.   | A7   | x              | x       | x                  |
| Meadow Green Met.      | A8   | x              | x       | x                  |
| Raven Green Metallic   | A9   | x              | x       | x                  |
| Burnished Brown        | B2   |                | x       | x                  |
| Quick Silver Metallic  | B3   | x              | x       | x                  |
| Charcoal Gray Met.     | B4   | x              |         | x                  |
| Deep Maroon Metallic   | B5   |                | x       | x                  |
| Electric Blue Metallic | B6   | x              | x       |                    |
| Brilliant Green Met.   | B7   | x              | x       |                    |
| Mustard Yellow         | B8   | x              | x       | x                  |
| Matador Red            | B9   | x              | x       | x                  |
| Golden Lime Metallic   | C1   | x              | x       | x                  |
| Surfside Turquoise     | C6   | x              | x       |                    |
| Baja Bronze Metallic   | D3   | x              | x       | x                  |
| Wild Plum Metallic     | D9   | x              | x       |                    |
| Classic Black          | P1   | x              | x       |                    |
| Gray                   | P81  |                |         | x                  |

# Gremlin

*"We started a small car revolution."*

**Nameplate year of origin:** 1970.
**Current bodystyle lifespan:** 1970 through 1983 — restyle in 1979 (and new name).
**Predecessor to this model:** None.
**Replacement for this model:** Spirit (1979 to 1982), and Eagle SX/4 (1981 to 1983).
**Percentage of division's sales volume:** 21.91%.
**Corporate siblings:** None.
**Primary competition:** Chevrolet Vega and Ford Pinto.
**Notable changes:** Trim and detail changes.
**Major standard equipment:** All-vinyl bench seat, front door pockets, fold-down rear seat (4-passenger model), front seat foam cushions, front arm rests, interior lights, aluminized exhaust system, Weather-Eye heating & ventilation system, exterior pinstripes, and 6.00 × 13 BSW tires.

## Measurements

| Wheelbase             | 96.0"  |
|-----------------------|--------|
| Length                | 161.2" |
| Width                 | 70.6"  |
| Height                | 51.7"  |
| Legroom — front       | 40.8"  |
| Legroom — rear        | 27.8"  |
| Headroom — front      | 38.1"  |
| Headroom — rear       | 36.4"  |
| Luggage cap. (cu. ft.)| 6.0    |
| Fuel capacity (gals.) | 21     |

## Models Available

|                             | Style Number | Base MSRP | Change from LY | Shipping Wt. (lbs.) | Production | Change from LY |
|-----------------------------|--------------|-----------|----------------|---------------------|------------|----------------|
| Gremlin 2-pass., 2-Dr.Sdn   | 40-7146-0    | $1,899    | +1.06%         | 2503                | *          | *              |
| Gremlin 2-Door Sedan        | 40-7146-5    | $1,999    | +2.04%         | 2552                | 53,480     | *              |
| TOTALS                      | *Avg. price* $1,949 |    | +1.56%         | *Production* 53,480 |            | + 111.38%      |

*2-passenger production included with 4-passenger total.*

**1971**

# Hornet

*"We build a better compact.*
*(Wouldn't you expect that from American Motors)."*

**Nameplate year of origin:** 1951 (used on high-performance Hudson).
**Current bodystyle lifespan:** 1970 through 1987.
**Predecessor to this model:** Rambler American (1964 to 1969).
**Replacement for this model:** Concord (1978 to 1982), and Eagle (1980 to 1987).
**Percentage of division's sales volume:** 30.18%.
**Corporate siblings:** None.
**Primary competition:** Chevrolet Nova, Dodge Dart, Ford Maverick, Mercury Comet, Plymouth Valiant, and Pontiac Ventura II.
**Notable changes:** Trim and detail changes.
**Major standard equipment:** Fabric-covered front bench seat, front seat foam cushions, instrument panel package tray, front and rear armrests, interior lights, glove box lock, hidden compartment lock (Sportabout), aluminized exhaust system, Weather-Eye heating & ventilation system, exterior pin stripes, 6.45 × 14 BSW tires (6.95 × 14 BSW tires on Sportabout). SC/360 adds: special exterior graphics, upgraded suspension and D70 × 14 tires.

## Measurements

|  | Cars | Sportabout |
|---|---|---|
| Wheelbase | 108.0" | 108.0" |
| Length | 179.3" | 179.3" |
| Width | 70.6" | 70.6" |
| Height | 51.1" | 53.0" |
| Legroom — front | 40.8" | 40.8" |
| Legroom — rear | 36.1" | 36.1" |
| Headroom — front | 38.1" | 38.1" |
| Headroom — rear | 37.5" | 37.5" |
| Luggage cap. (cu. ft.) | 11.2 | 61.6 |
| Fuel capacity (gals.) | 16.0 | 16.0 |

## Models Available

|  | Style Number | Base MSRP | Change from LY | Shipping Wt. (lbs.) | Production | Change from LY |
|---|---|---|---|---|---|---|
| Hornet 2-Door Sedan | 01-7106-0 | $2,174 | 9.03% | 2654 | 23,000 (base 6-cyl.)* | * |
| Hornet 4-Door Sedan | 01-7105-0 | $2,234 | 7.82% | 2731 | 500 (base V8's)* | * |
| Hornet SST 2-Door Sedan | 01-7106-7 | $2,274 | 6.06% | 2691 | 18,800 (SST 6-cyl.)* | * |
| Hornet SST 4-Door Sedan | 01-7105-7 | $2,334 | 5.09% | 2732 | 4,800 (SST V8's)* | * |
| Hornet SST 4-Door Sportabout | 01-7108-7 | $2,594 | NEW | 2827 | 25,800* | NEW |
| Hornet SC/360 2-Door Sedan | 01-7106-1 | $2,663 | NEW | 3057 | 784 | NEW |
| TOTALS | Avg. price | $2,379 | +12.9% |  | Production 73,684* | -1.22% |

*Exact Hornet production by body style is not available; however, estimates by series (broken down by 6 cyl. and V8 engines) are given above.*

# Javelin

*"Styling so hairy we even risked turning some people off."*

**Nameplate year of origin:** 1968.
**Current bodystyle lifespan:** 1971 through 1974.
**Predecessor to this model:** Javelin (1968 to 1970).
**Replacement for this model:** None.
**Percentage of division's sales volume:** 11.90%.
**Corporate siblings:** None.
**Primary competition:** Chevrolet Camaro, Dodge Challenger, Ford Mustang, Plymouth Barracuda, and Pontiac Firebird.
**Notable changes:** Totally redesigned. AMX now a 4-seat model within the Javelin line.
**Major standard equipment:** Vinyl front bucket seats, aluminized exhaust system, Weather-Eye heating & ventilation system, exterior pin stripes, and C78 × 14 BSW tires. SST adds: Custom steering wheel, upgraded interior trim, and additional exterior trim. AMX adds: Front console, 3-spoke sport steering wheel, 360 CID V8 engine, slot-style wheels, space saver spare tire, and E70 × 14 white-lettered tires.

## Measurements

|  |  |
|---|---|
| Wheelbase | 110.0" |
| Length | 191.8" |
| Width | 75.2" |
| Height | NA |
| Legroom — front | NA |
| Legroom — rear | NA |
| Headroom — front | NA |
| Headroom — rear | NA |
| Luggage cap. (cu. ft.) | 10.2 |
| Fuel capacity (gals.) | 16.0 |

## Models Available

| | Style Number | Base MSRP | Change from LY | Shipping Wt. (lbs.) | Production | Change from LY |
|---|---|---|---|---|---|---|
| Javelin 2-Door Hardtop | 70-7179-5 | $2,879 | +5.85% | 2887 | 8,000 | -16.49%* |
| Javelin SST 2-Door Hardtop | 70-7179-7 | $2,999 | +5.30% | 2890 | 19,000 | -7.32%* |
| Javelin AMX 2-Door Hardtop | 70-7179-8 | $3,432 | +1.09% | 3244 | 2,054 | -50.10% |
| TOTALS | *Avg. price* $3,103 | | -2.67% | *Production*** 29,054 | | -3.73%* |

*Estimated production.    **Compared to combined 1969 Javelin and AMX production.*

# Matador

*"We proved that a family car can be glamorous."*

**Nameplate year of origin:** 1971.

**Current bodystyle lifespan:** 1967 through 1978 (restyles in 1969, 1971, and 1974).

**Predecessor to this model:** Rebel (1968 to 1970).

**Corporate siblings:** Ambassador (shared components from the cowl back).

**Replacement for this model:** None.

**Percentage of division's sales volume:** 18.74%.

**Primary competition:** Chevrolet Chevelle, Dodge Coronet, Ford Torino, and Plymouth Satellite.

**Notable changes:** All-new front and rear styling. New nameplate (formerly Rebel).

**Major standard equipment:** Fabric-covered front bench seat, front seat foam cushions, front and rear arm rests, glove box lock, dual horns, hidden compartment lock (Wagons), aluminized exhaust system, Weather-Eye heating & ventilation system, exterior pinstripes, E78 × 14 BSW tires (Cars), G78 × 14 BSW tires (Wagons).

## Measurements

| | Cars | Wagon |
|---|---|---|
| Wheelbase | 118.0" | 118.0" |
| Length | 206.0" | 205.0" |
| Width | 77.2" | 77.2" |
| Height | 54.5" | 55.0" |
| Legroom — front | 41.0" | 41.0" |
| Legroom — rear | 37.6" | 37.6" |
| Headroom — front | 39.3" | 39.3" |
| Headroom — rear | 37.0" | 37.2" |
| Luggage cap. (cu. ft.) | 18.2 | 99.1 |
| Fuel capacity (gals.) | 19.5 | 19.5 |

## Models Available

| | Style Number | Base MSRP | Change from LY | Shipping Wt. (lbs.) | Production | Change from LY |
|---|---|---|---|---|---|---|
| Matador 2-Door Hardtop | 10-7119-7 | $2,799 | +5.23% | 3201 | 10,000 | * |
| Matador 4-Door Sedan | 10-7115-7 | $2,770 | +5.48% | 3165 | 24,750 | * |
| Matador 4-Door Wagon | 10-7118-7 | $3,163 | +14.35% | 3437 | 11,000 | * |
| TOTALS | *Avg. price* $2,911 | | +1.89% | *Production* 45,750 | | -7.99%** |

*Production by body style is not available, figures given are estimates.    **Production compared to 1970 Rebel models.*

# Ambassador

*"The only car line in America with automatic transmission and air conditioning standard."*

**Nameplate year of origin:** 1933 (from top-of-the-line Nash).

**Current bodystyle lifespan:** 1967 through 1978 (shared basic structure with Matador).

**Predecessor to this model:** Ambassador (1963 to 1966).

**Replacement for this model:** None.

## Measurements

| | Cars | Wagon |
|---|---|---|
| Wheelbase | 122.0" | 122.0" |
| Length | 211.1" | 209.7" |

**1971**

**Percentage of division's sales volume:** 17.27%.
**Corporate siblings:** Matador (shared components from the cowl back).
**Primary competition:** Chevrolet BelAir/Impala/Caprice, Ford LTD, and Plymouth Fury.
**Notable changes:** Revised grille and trim and detail changes.
**Major standard equipment:** Fabric-covered front bench seat, aluminized exhaust system, Weather-Eye heating & ventilation system, air conditioning, exterior pinstripes, power front disc brakes, bumper guards, and E78 × 14 BSW tires. SST adds: Custom steering wheel, upgraded interior trim (all-vinyl on wagon), roof rack (Wagon), additional exterior trim, and H78 × 14 BSW tires on Wagons. Brougham adds: Luxury interior trim, individual reclining front seats, and simulated wood-grain side and rear panels (Wagon).

| | Cars | Wagon |
|---|---|---|
| Width | 77.2" | 77.2" |
| Height | 54.5" | 55.0" |
| Legroom — front | 41.0" | 41.0" |
| Legroom — rear | 37.6" | 37.6" |
| Headroom — front | 39.3" | 39.3" |
| Headroom — rear | 37.0" | 37.2" |
| Luggage cap. (cu. ft.) | 18.2 | 99.1 |
| Fuel capacity (gals.) | 19.5 | 20.0 |

## Models Available

| | Style Number | Base MSRP | Change from LY | Shipping Wt. (lbs.) | Production | Change from LY |
|---|---|---|---|---|---|---|
| Ambassador DPL 4-Door Sedan | 80-7185-2 | $3,616 | +0.78% | 3315 | 7,000 | * |
| Ambassador SST 2-Door Hardtop | 80-7189-5 | $3,870 | +3.50% | 3579 | 7,400 (SST)* | * |
| Ambassador SST 4-Door Sedan | 80-7185-5 | $3,852 | +3.49% | 3537 | * | * |
| Ambassador SST 4-Door Wagon | 80-7188-5 | $4,253 | +3.18% | 3833 | 17,700 (Wagons)* | * |
| Ambassador Brougham 2-Door HT | 80-7189-7 | $3,999 | NEW | 3581 | 9,900 (Brougham)* | NEW |
| Ambassador Brougham 4-Door Sdn. | 80-7185-7 | $3,983 | NEW | 3551 | * | NEW |
| Ambassador Brougham 4-Door Wgn. | 80-7188-7 | $4,430 | NEW | 3857 | * | NEW |
| TOTALS | Avg. price | $4,000 | +8.78% | | Production* 42,150 | -28.44% |

*Estimated model year production shown. Breakdown by model/body style is not available.*

# BUICK

*"Introducing a new set of values. Wouldn't you really rather have a Buick?"*

The 1971 model year brought a new yet familiar look to the entire line of big Buicks, and subtle revisions to the Skylark line. At the top of the pricing structure, the "luxury-sport" Riviera debuted with the most radical styling ever featured on a Buick to date. At the front end was a pointed bow-type grille and hood, with dual exposed headlights set outside the grille area. Along the sides was the trademark Buick sweep-spear design (less the usual chrome trim), and arched wheel openings. At the rear was an updated take on the 1930s boattail speedster designs. A semi-fastback roofline that ended in a 2-piece glass window, bonded in the center (not divided), met with a short rear decklid that led to the center boattail section, which was flanked by horizontal taillights on each side. It was a highly distinctive design that most people either loved or hated. Sales did not seem to be helped by the redesign, though to some extent increasing sales of the Monte Carlo/Grand Prix class of cars were affecting the Riviera.

The other full-size lines were totally new automobiles too. Along with the other full-size GM cars, the Electra, LeSabre and newly named Centurion were larger, more spacious, and wore more sculpted body sides. In place of the traditional Buick sweep-spear was a sculpted line beginning at the leading edge of the hood, just inside the fender line, flowing back across the hood (through fake venti-ports on all but the Centurion), onto the leading edge of the door. Then it ran across the door through the front door handle, gently arching downward toward a point near the top edge of the rear bumper. This line gave the illusion that the cars were even longer and lower than they already were. Interiors were also larger, with the doors curved out near the center to provide more hip room. The overall effect was similar to what Chrysler had tried in 1969 with their fuselage design, but the GM cars turned out as much prettier cars, although somewhat bulkier. The new Centurion effectively replaced the Wildcat and, at least initially, sold better. With all of the station wagon models available, it is somewhat surprising that the new-for-1970 Estate wagon was so well-received. It quickly became the best seller in its class, outselling the Chrysler Town & Country, Mercury Colony Park, and Oldsmobile Custom Cruiser. The restyled 1971 model received all the new GM full-size treatments, including the infamous Glide-Away "clamshell" tailgate. The Electra and LeSabre models were similar to the Centurion in styling, with the Electra receiving the traditional four venti-ports, longer wheelbase, and plusher accommodations. LeSabre models were once again the entry-level full-size Buicks and wore three venti-ports. All full-size models utilized the GM Flo-Thru ventilation system, with louvers built into the trunk lid (or tailgate on wagons). Mid-sized models received a new front grille/bumper arrangement. A Skylark 2-Door Hardtop and GS 350 Convertible joined the lineup.

Electra 225 Custom Limited 4-Door Hardtop

Estate Wagon 4-Door

GS 455 2-Door Hardtop

LeSabre Custom 2-Door Hardtop

Riviera 2-Door Hardtop

Skylark 4-Door Sedan

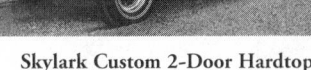

Skylark Custom 2-Door Hardtop

Sportwagon 4-Door Wagon

**Model year production:** 560,792, down 15.87% from 1970.
**Domestic market share:** 7.16% (6th place).
**Base price range:** $2,847 to $5,253.
**Industry average base price:** $3,786.
**Buick average base price:** $4,065.
**Introduction date:** September 1970.
**Assembly plants:** Southgate, CA (C); Atlanta, GA (D); Flint, MI (H); Kansas City, MO (K); Fairfax, KS (X); Wilmington, DE (Y); Fremont, CA (Z); and Oshawa, Ontario, (1).

**Data plate identification:** Thirteen digit code read as follows: five digit style number in which 4 = Buick, 2nd number identifies series (3 is Skylark, 8 is Electra, etc.), 3rd through 5th digits indicate model number; 1 = 1971; assembly plant code; 100001 and up for serial number. *Example:* 452571X100001 is a 1971 Buick LeSabre 2-Door Hardtop, serial number 100001, built in Fairfax, KS

**1971**

## Powertrains

| Engine | Gross HP | Transmission Availability | Skylark | LeSabre/Centurion Estate Wagon | Electra 225 | Riviera |
|---|---|---|---|---|---|---|
| 250 CID, 2-bbl., 6-cyl. | 145 | 3-speed manual<br>Turbo Hydra-matic | S<br>$211 | -<br>- | -<br>- | -<br>- |

| Engine | Gross HP | Transmission Availability | Skylark | LeSabre/Centurion Estate Wagon | Electra 225 | Riviera |
|--------|----------|---------------------------|---------|-------------------------------|-------------|---------|
| 350 CID, 2-bbl., V8 | 230 | 3-speed manual | $121 (base)/ S (ex. Base & GS) | S (LeSabre) | - | - |
| | | Turbo Hydra-matic | $343 (base)/ $221 (ex. Base & GS) | $221 (LeSabre) | - | - |
| 350 CID, 4-bbl., V8 | 260 | 3-speed manual | S (GS)/$169 (base)/ $47 (others) | $47 (LeSabre) | - | - |
| | | 4-speed manual | $195 (GS only) | - | | |
| | | Turbo Hydra-matic | $222 (GS)/ $390 (base)/ $268 (Others) | $269 (LeSabre) | - | - |
| 455 CID, 4-bbl., V8 | 315 | 3-speed manual | - | $217 (LeSabre) | - | - |
| | | 4-speed manual | $359 (GS) | - | - | - |
| | | Turbo Hydra-matic | $407 (GS) | S (Estate Wgn. & Centurion)/ $460 (LeSabre) | S | S |
| 455 CID (On GS Stage I), 4-bbl., V8 | 330 (GS 345) | Turbo Hydra-matic | $568 (w/Stage I option on GS) | $99 (Centurion) | - | $200 (w/ GS option) |

## Major Options

| | Skylark | LeSabre | Centurion | Electra 225 | Estate Wagon | Riviera |
|--------|---------|---------|-----------|-------------|--------------|---------|
| Air conditioning — manual | $408 | $442 | $442 | $442 | $442 | $442 |
| Air conditioning — automatic | - | $521 | $521 | $521 | $521 | $521 |
| Soft Ray tinted glass | $43 | $51 | $51 | $51 | $51 | $51 |
| Deck lid remote release | $14 | $14 | $14 | $14 | - | $14 |
| Power steering — variable-ratio | $116 | S | S | S | S | S |
| Power brakes — front disc | $70 (Std. Wgn.) | S | S | S | S | S |
| Power driver's seat/Bench seat | $79 | $105 | $105 | $105 | $105 | $79 |
| Power windows | $116 | $133 | $133 | $133 | $133 | $133 |
| AM radio | $75 | $88 | $88 | $88 | $88 | $88 |
| AM/FM stereo | $139 | $239 | $239 | $239 | $239 | $239 |
| Tilt steering wheel | $45 | $45 | $45 | $45 | $45 | S |
| Sunroof | $251 (350 2-Dr.) | - | - | - | - | $605 |
| Vinyl roof | $102 | $126 | $126 (4-Dr.) | $142 | $142 | $128 |
| Max-Trac Drive Control system | - | - | - | - | - | $ |
| Stage I Option | $ | - | - | - | - | - |
| GS Option package | - | - | - | - | - | $185 |
| GSX package | $ | - | - | - | - | - |

Options common to most models. (— = Not Available; S = Standard equipment.) Items may be standard equipment, optional at different pricing, or unavailable on certain models. This chart is only a guide.

## Paint Colors

| | Code | Skylark | LeSabre/Cent/EW/Elec. | Riviera |
|--------|------|---------|-----------------------|---------|
| Arctic White | 11 | x | x | x |
| Platinum Mist | 13 | x | x | x |
| Tealmist Gray Met. | 16 | x | x | x |
| Regal Black | 19 | | x | |
| Cascade Blue Met. | 24 | x | x | |
| Stratomist Blue Met. | 26 | x | x | x |
| Nocturne Blue Met. | 29 | | x | x |
| Twilight Turquoise Met. | 39 | x | x | |
| Silver Fern Met. | 41 | x | x | |

| | Code | Skylark | LeSabre/Cent/EW/Elec. | Riviera |
|---|---|---|---|---|
| Willowmist Green | 42 | x | x | |
| Lime Mist Met. | 43 | x | x | |
| Verdemist Green Met. | 49 | | | x |
| Bamboo Cream | 50 | | x | x |
| Cortez Gold Met. | 53 | x | | |
| Cornet Gold Met. | 55 | | x | x |
| Sandpiper Beige | 61 | x | x | x |
| Bittersweet Mist Met. | 62 | x | x | x |
| Copper Mist Met. | 65 | | | x |
| Burnished Cinnamon Met. | 67 | x | x | |
| Deep Chestnut Met. | 68 | | | x |
| Pearl Beige Met. | 70 | | | x |
| Sunset Mist Met. | 73 | | | x |
| Vintage Red Met. | 74 | | | x |
| Fire Red | 75 | x | x | |
| Rosewood Met. | 78 | | x | x |

# Skylark

*"Trim. Slim. Elegant in its styling simplicity.
A look of motion even while at rest."*

**Nameplate year of origin:** 1953.
**Current bodystyle lifespan:** 1968 through 1972.
**Predecessor to this model:** Special/Skylark (1964 to 1967).
**Replacement for this model:** Century (1973 to 1977).
**Percentage of division's sales volume:** 34.54%.
**Corporate siblings:** Chevrolet Chevelle, Pontiac LeMans, Olds Cutlass.
**Primary competition:** Dodge Coronet and Mercury Montego.
**Notable changes:** Revised grille, hood and bumper designs. Also revised trim and detail changes.
**Major standard equipment:** Front ash tray, heater and defroster, Magic-Mirror finish paint, self adjusting brakes, vinyl bench seat, G78 × 14 BSW tires. Skylark 350 adds: Cloth and vinyl deluxe seats, rear ash trays, front door operated interior lighting, wheel opening moldings, dual horns, "350" emblems. Custom adds: Deluxe steering wheel, unique eggcrate-style grille. Sportwagon adds: Dual-action tailgate. GS adds: Dual exhausts, functional hood air scoops, heavy duty springs, shocks and stabilizer bar.

## Measurements

| | 2-Doors | 4-Doors | Sportwagon |
|---|---|---|---|
| Wheelbase | 112.0" | 116.0" | 116.0" |
| Length | 203.2" | 207.2" | 212.7" |
| Width | 77.3" | 77.3" | 77.3" |
| Height | 53.5" | 54.1" | 54.8" |
| Legroom — front | 41.3" | 41.3" | 42.6" |
| Legroom — rear | 32.4" | 34.8" | 34.6" |
| Headroom — front | 37.9" | 38.6" | 38.4" |
| Headroom — rear | 36.3" | 37.3" | 38.3" |
| Luggage capacity (cu. ft.) | NA | NA | NA |
| Fuel capacity (gals.) | 20.0 | 20.0 | 20.0 |

## Models Available

| | Style Number | Base MSRP | Change from LY | Shipping Wt. (lbs.) | Production | Change from LY |
|---|---|---|---|---|---|---|
| Skylark 2-Door Coupe | 43327 | $2,847 | +6.03% | 3144 | 14,500 | -22.13% |
| Skylark 2-Door Hardtop Sport Coupe | 43337 | $2,897 | +1.33% | 3163 | 61,201 | -13.70% |
| Skylark 4-Door Sedan | 43369 | $2,918 | +2.82% | 3216 | 34,037 | +12.40% |
| Skylark Custom 2-Door Hardtop | 44437 | $3,317 | +5.91% | 3391 | 29,536 | -18.78% |
| Skylark Custom 2-Door Convertible | 44467 | $3,462 | +5.71% | 3431 | 3,993 | -19.40% |
| Skylark Custom 4-Door Sedan | 44469 | $3,288 | +6.03% | 3455 | 8,299 | +16.67% |
| Skylark Custom 4-Door Hardtop | 44439 | $3,397 | +5.50% | 3547 | 20,418 | +64.52% |
| Sportwagon 4-Door, 2-Seat Wagon | 43436 | $3,515 | +9.50% | 3928 | 12,525 | +2.32% |
| GS 2-Door Hardtop Sport Coupe | 43437 | $3,285 | +6.04% | 3461 | 8,268 | -16.89% |
| GS 2-Door Convertible | 43467 | $3,476 | NEW | 3497 | 902 | NEW |
| TOTALS | | Avg. price $3,240 | +4.92% | | Production 193,679 | -14.46% |

1971

# LeSabre

*"Step in. Stretch out. Uncommon comfort is yours."*

**Nameplate year of origin:** 1959.
**Current bodystyle lifespan:** 1971 through 1976.
**Predecessor to this model:** LeSabre (1969 to 1970).
**Replacement for this model:** LeSabre (1977 to 1985).
**Percentage of division's sales volume:** 27.43%.
**Corporate siblings:** Chevrolet Full-size, Pontiac Catalina, Oldsmobile Delta 88.
**Primary competition:** Chrysler Newport, Dodge Monaco, and Mercury Monterey.
**Notable changes:** Completely restyled.
**Major standard equipment:** Power front disc brakes, variable ratio power steering, Turbo Hydra-matic transmission, AccuDrive suspension system, Kahara cloth and Madrid-grain vinyl bench seat, bright rocker panel moldings, horizontal bar grille, and H78 × 15 BSW tires. Custom adds: Krefeld cloth and Madrid-grain vinyl bench seat (all vinyl on Convertible), wheel opening moldings, "Custom" nameplates.

## Measurements

| | |
|---|---|
| Wheelbase | 124.0" |
| Length | 220.7" |
| Width | 79.7" |
| Height | 53.8" |
| Legroom — front | 42.6" |
| Legroom — rear | 38.5" |
| Headroom — front | 38.4" |
| Headroom — rear | 37.4" |
| Luggage capacity (cu. ft.) | NA |
| Fuel capacity (gals.) | NA |

## Models Available

| | Style Number | Base MSRP | Change from LY | Shipping Wt. (lbs.) | Production | Change from LY |
|---|---|---|---|---|---|---|
| LeSabre 2-Door Hardtop | 45257 | $4,061 | +14.88% | 4049 | 13,385 | -5.49% |
| LeSabre 4-Door Sedan | 45269 | $3,992 | +15.61% | 4078 | 26,348 | -25.58% |
| LeSabre 4-Door Hardtop | 45239 | $4,119 | +14.64% | 4109 | 14,234 | -3.93% |
| LeSabre Custom 2-Door Hardtop | 45457 | $4,149 | +14.52% | 4095 | 29,944 | -15.98% |
| LeSabre Custom 2-Door Conv. | 45467 | $4,342 | +13.78% | 4086 | 1,856 | -25.37% |
| LeSabre Custom 4-Door Sedan | 45469 | $4,085 | +15.17% | 4107 | 26,970 | -26.48% |
| LeSabre Custom 4-Door Hardtop | 45439 | $4,213 | +14.27% | 4147 | 41,098 | -6.30% |
| TOTALS | *Avg. price* | $4,137 | +12.60% | *Production* | 153,835 | -23.32% |

# Centurion

*"Look. Feel. Touch. Everything is new."*

**Nameplate year of origin:** 1971.
**Current bodystyle lifespan:** 1971 through 1976.
**Predecessor to this model:** Wildcat (1969 to 1970).
**Replacement for this model:** LeSabre Luxus (1974).
**Percentage of division's sales volume:** 5.24%.
**Corporate siblings:** Chevrolet Full-size, Pontiac Full-size, Oldsmobile Delta 88.
**Primary competition:** Chrysler Newport, Dodge Monaco Brougham, and Mercury Monterey Custom.
**Notable changes:** All-new model replacing the Wildcat line.
**Major standard equipment:** Power front disc brakes, variable ratio power steering, AccuDrive suspension system, Turbo Hydra-matic transmission, bright rocker panel molding, wheel opening moldings, vertical bar grille design, and Elk-grain expanded vinyl notchback front seat, and H78 × 15 BSW tires.

## Measurements

| | |
|---|---|
| Wheelbase | 124.0" |
| Length | 220.7" |
| Width | 79.7" |
| Height | 53.8" |
| Legroom — front | 42.6" |
| Legroom — rear | 38.5" |
| Headroom — front | 38.4" |
| Headroom — rear | 37.4" |
| Luggage capacity (cu. ft.) | NA |
| Fuel capacity (gals.) | NA |

## Models Available

| | Style Number | Base MSRP | Change from LY | Shipping Wt. (lbs.) | Production | Change from LY |
|---|---|---|---|---|---|---|
| Centurion 2-Door Hardtop | 46647 | $4,678 | +13.90% | 4195 | 11,892 | +25.48% |
| Centurion 2-Door Convertible | 46667 | $4,678 | +10.41% | 4227 | 2,161 | +73.71% |
| Centurion 4-Door Hardtop | 46639 | $4,564 | +9.84% | 4307 | 15,345 | +18.73% |
| TOTALS | | Avg. price $4,640 | +11.38% | | Production 29,398 | +24.33% |

*Prices and production compared to similar 1970 Wildcat models.*

# Estate Wagon

*"Wider, more spacious. Increased load area.*
*Stretch-out comfort surrounds you."*

**Nameplate year of origin:** 1940 (as designation for station wagon).
**Current bodystyle lifespan:** 1971 through 1976.
**Predecessor to this model:** Estate Wagon (1970).
**Corporate siblings:** Chevrolet Impala/Caprice, Oldsmobile Custom Cruiser, Pontiac Safari.
**Replacement for this model:** Estate Wagon (1977 to 1989).
**Percentage of division's sales volume:** 4.29%.
**Primary competition:** Chrysler Town & Country and Mercury Colony Park.
**Notable changes:** Completely restyled.
**Major standard equipment:** Power front disc brakes, variable ratio power steering, Turbo Hydra-matic transmission, AccuDrive suspension system, Madrid-grain vinyl bench seat, bright rocker panel moldings, Electra-style cross-bar grille, Glide-Away tailgate, power tailgate window, and four-jet windshield washer, L78 × 15 BSW tires.

## Measurements

| | |
|---|---|
| Wheelbase | 127.0" |
| Length | 226.8" |
| Width | 79.7" |
| Height | 57.3" |
| Legroom — front | 42.6" |
| Legroom — rear | 39.9" |
| Headroom — front | 39.6" |
| Headroom — rear | 39.3" |
| Luggage capacity (cu. ft.) | NA |
| Fuel capacity (gals.) | NA |

## Models Available

| | Style Number | Base MSRP | Change from LY | Shipping Wt. (lbs.) | Production | Change from LY |
|---|---|---|---|---|---|---|
| Estate Wagon 4-Door, 2-Seat Wgn. | 46035 | $4,640 | +13.70% | 4906 | 8,699 | -23.87% |
| Estate Wagon 4-Door, 3-Seat Wgn. | 46045 | $4,786 | +13.25% | 4965 | 15,335 | -9.15% |
| TOTALS | | Avg. price $4,713 | +13.57% | | Production 24,034 | -15.09% |

# Electra 225

*"Sculptured beauty. Styling to excite*
*even the most discriminating taste."*

**Nameplate year of origin:** 1959.
**Current bodystyle lifespan:** 1971 through 1976.
**Predecessor to this model:** Electra 225 (1969 to 1970).
**Corporate siblings:** Cadillac Calais/de Ville, Oldsmobile Ninety-Eight.
**Replacement for this model:** Electra (1977 to 1984).
**Percentage of division's sales volume:** 22.47%.
**Primary competition:** Chrysler New Yorker and Mercury Marquis.
**Notable changes:** Completely restyled.

## Measurements

| | |
|---|---|
| Wheelbase | 127.0" |
| Length | 226.2" |
| Width | 79.7" |
| Height | 54.9" |
| Legroom — front | 42.6" |
| Legroom — rear | 40.3" |
| Headroom — front | 39.3" |

**Major standard equipment:** Kimmel cloth and Madrid-grain vinyl bench seat, variable ratio power steering, power front disc brakes, AccuDrive suspension system, Turbo Hydra-matic transmission, cross-hatch style grille, bright rocker panel molding and wheel opening moldings, rear fender skirts, remote control outside rear view mirror, and J78 × 15 BSW tires. Custom adds: Elk-grain vinyl or Keswick cloth and Madrid-grain vinyl notchback seat with front-center armrest, and Limited script badges.

## Measurements (cont.)

| | |
|---|---|
| Headroom — rear | 38.2" |
| Luggage capacity (cu. ft.) | NA |
| Fuel capacity (gals.) | NA |

## Models Available

| | Style Number | Base MSRP | Change from LY | Shipping Wt. (lbs.) | Production | Change from LY |
|---|---|---|---|---|---|---|
| Electra 225 2-Door Hardtop | 48237 | $4,801 | +7.12% | 4345 | 8,662 | -27.89% |
| Electra 225 4-Door Hardtop | 48239 | $4,915 | +7.03% | 4381 | 17,589 | +22.67% |
| Electra 225 Custom 2-Door HT | 48437 | $4,980 | +6.84% | 4359 | 26,831 | +3.19% |
| Electra 225 Custom 4-Door HT | 48439 | $5,093 | +6.75% | 4421 | 72,954 | +12.04% |
| TOTALS | Avg. price | $4,947 | +6.73% | Production | 126,036 | -16.09% |

# Riviera

*"The 1971 Riviera is motion-sculptured giving an image of movement even when standing still."*

**Nameplate year of origin:** 1949 (2-Dr. HT); 1963 (series).
**Current bodystyle lifespan:** 1971 through 1976.
**Predecessor to this model:** Riviera (1966 to 1970).
**Corporate siblings:** Cadillac Eldorado and Oldsmobile Toronado.
**Replacement for this model:** Riviera (1977 to 1978).
**Percentage of division's sales volume:** 6.03%.
**Primary competition:** Ford Thunderbird and Lincoln Continental Mark III.
**Notable changes:** Completely restyled.
**Major standard equipment:** All-vinyl bench seat, variable ratio power steering, power front disc brakes, dual exhaust system, Turbo Hydra-matic transmission, eggcrate grille design, vinyl body side moldings, remote control outside rear view mirror, tilt steering wheel, and H78 × 15 BSW tires.

## Measurements

| | |
|---|---|
| Wheelbase | 122.0" |
| Length | 217.4" |
| Width | 79.9" |
| Height | 54.0" |
| Legroom — front | 42.7" |
| Legroom — rear | 35.6" |
| Headroom — front | 37.7" |
| Headroom — rear | 37.0" |
| Luggage capacity (cu. ft.) | NA |
| Fuel capacity (gals.) | NA |

## Models Available

| | Style Number | Base MSRP | Change from LY | Shipping Wt. (lbs.) | Production | Change from LY |
|---|---|---|---|---|---|---|
| Riviera 2-Door Hardtop | 49487 | $5,253 | +8.22% | 4325 | 33,810 | -9.52% |
| TOTALS | Avg. price | $5,253 | +8.22% | Production | 33,810 | -9.52% |

# CADILLAC

*"Standard of the World."*

For 1971, every Cadillac in the model line was re-designed completely, from the base Calais to the Fleetwood Limousine and Eldorado. Historically (with rare exception), Cadillac would redesign its line over several years, usually with the Fleetwood models receiving new styling after (but sometimes before) the regular models. Being the leading manufacturer of traditional luxury cars, Cadillac made sure its new models still bore a resemblance to their predecessors, but they also displayed some of the qualities of the other new GM full-size cars — the sculpted side lines, wide-body design for more interior roominess, and thin A-pillar design. The Fleetwood Sixty-Special Brougham 4-Door had a unique roofline that would preview the Colonnade design of the 1973-77 GM intermediates. This design allows for a central B-pillar to be used for structure, while the doors use frameless glass similar to a hardtop design. It made for an attractive style on the Sixty-Special. Calais and de Ville models received rooflines similar to other B-

& C-bodied (full-size) GM cars. Changes to the model line consisted of the elimination of the base Fleetwood Sixty-Special, the de Ville Convertible and the Sedan de Ville 4-Door. There was still a Sedan de Ville, but it was the 4-Door Hardtop body style (a.k.a. Hardtop Sedan de Ville), not the previous 4-Door Sedan.

The Fleetwood Eldorado was also an all-new design. The second generation Eldorado retained the feel of the original, but with far more bodyside sculpting. Also new for 1971 was an Eldorado Convertible. As with other GM full-size convertibles this year, a new folding top mechanism was employed. This new top folded inward — the side bows folded in to allow more space for the rear seat passengers, and also to provide larger rear side windows. Another new Eldorado feature was fender skirts, which made the car look even longer. Once again, front wheel drive technology was used on the Eldorado.

Calais 4-Door Hardtop

Coupe de Ville 2-Door Hardtop

Eldorado 2-Door Convertible

Eldorado 2-Door Hardtop

**1971**

**Model year production:** 186,523, down 21.04% from 1970.
**Domestic market share:** 2.38% (11th place).
**Base price range:** $5,899 to $12,008.
**Industry average base price:** $3,786.
**Cadillac average base price:** $7,946.
**Introduction date:** September 29, 1970.
**Assembly plants:** Detroit, MI (Q), and Linden, NJ (E).
**Data plate identification:** Thirteen digit code read as follows:

five digit style number in which 6 = Cadillac, 2nd and 3rd digits identify series (e.g., 82 is Calais), 4th and 5th digits indicate body style number (2nd through 5th digits of VIN make up 2nd through 5th digits of body style number); 1 for 1971; 7th digit is assembly plant code; 100001 and up for serial number. *Example:* 683471Q100001 is a 1971 Cadillac de Ville 2-Door Hardtop, serial number 100001, built in Detroit, MI.

## Powertrains

| Engine | Engine Code | Gross HP | Transmission Availability | Eldorado | All others |
|---|---|---|---|---|---|
| 472 CID, 4-bbl., V8 | R | 375 | Turbo Hydra-matic | - | S |
| 500 CID, 4-bbl., V8 | S | 365 | Turbo Hydra-matic | S | - |

## Major Options

| | Eldorado | de Ville/Calais | 60 Special | Seventy-Five |
|---|---|---|---|---|
| Automatic climate control | $537 | $537 | $537 | S |
| 6-way power seat | $92 | $92 (deV.)/$118 (Cal.) | $92 | $92 (NA Limo) |
| Power door locks | $71 | $71 | $71 | $118 |
| AM-FM radio | $188 | $188 | $188 | $188 |
| AM-FM stereo w/8-track | $417 | $417 | $417 | $417 |
| Vinyl roof | $161 | $156 (de Ville only) | S | NA |
| Sunroof | $626 (Cpe) | $626 (de Ville only) | $626 | - |
| Tilt and telescope steering wheel | $95 | $95 | $95 | $95 |
| Leather upholstery | $185 (Cpe) | $174 (de Ville only) | $174 | - |
| Cruise control | $95 | $95 | $95 | $95 |
| Tinted glass | $59 | $59 | $59 | $59 |
| Rear window defogger | $37 (Cpe)/$63 (Conv.) | $32 | $32 | S |
| Remote control trunk release | $58 | $58 | $58 | $58 |
| Firemist paint colors | $132 | $132 | $132 | $132 |

Options common to most models. (- = Not Available; S = Standard equipment.) Items may be standard equipment, optional at different pricing, or unavailable on certain models. This chart is only a guide.

## Paint Colors

| | Code | | Code |
|---|---|---|---|
| Cotillion White | 11 | Duchess Gold Met. | 55 |
| Grenoble SilverMet. | 13 | Desert Beige Met. | 64 |
| Oxford Gray Met. | 16 | Clove Metallic | 69 |
| Sable Black | 19 | Cambridge Red Met. | 74 |
| Zodiac Blue Met. | 24 | Empire Maroon Firemist Met.* | 89 |
| Brittany Blue Met. | 29 | Bavarian Blue Firemist Met.* | 90 |
| Adriatic Turquoise Met. | 34 | Pewter Firemist Met.* | 92 |
| Lanai Green Metallic | 42 | Chalice Gold Firemist Met.* | 94 |
| Cypress Green Met. | 44 | Almond Firemist Metallic | 95 |
| Sylvan Green Met. | 49 | Sausalito Green Firemist Met.* | 96 |
| Casablanca Yellow | 50 | Primrose Firemist Met.* | 99 |

*Firemist colors available at extra cost.*

# Calais

*"Calais combines beauty with a feeling of interior spaciousness."*

**Nameplate year of origin:** 1965.
**Current bodystyle lifespan:** 1971 through 1976.
**Predecessor to this model:** Calais (1969 to 1970).
**Replacement for this model:** None.
**Percentage of division's sales volume:** 3.71%.
**Corporate siblings:** Buick Electra 225 and Oldsmobile Ninety-Eight.
**Primary competition:** Chrysler New Yorker and Lincoln Continental.

## Measurements

| | |
|---|---|
| Wheelbase | 130.0" |
| Length | 225.8" |
| Width | 79.8" |
| Height | NA |
| Legroom — front | NA |
| Legroom — rear | NA |

**Notable changes:** Totally redesigned.
**Major standard equipment:** Cloth seat upholstery, front center armrests, passenger assist straps, variable ratio power steering, power front disc brakes, Turbo Hydra-matic transmission, front cornering lights, rear fender skirts, left side remote control outside rear view mirror, power windows, interior courtesy and warning lights, 3-speed windshield wipers and washers, visor vanity mirrors, automatic parking brake release, and L78 × 15 BSW tires.

## Measurements (cont.)

| | |
|---|---|
| Headroom — front | NA |
| Headroom — rear | NA |
| Luggage capacity (cu. ft.) | NA |
| Fuel capacity (gals.) | 27.0 |

## Models Available

| | Style Number | Base MSRP | Change from LY | Shipping Wt. (lbs.) | Production | Change from LY |
|---|---|---|---|---|---|---|
| Calais 2-Door Hardtop | 68247 | $5,899 | +4.65% | 4635 | 3,360 | -28.87% |
| Calais 4-Door Hardtop | 68249 | $6,075 | +4.51% | 4710 | 3,569 | -31.19% |
| TOTALS | Avg. price | $5,987 | +4.58% | Production | 6,929 | -30.09% |

# de Ville

*"Appealing styling and spirited performance have made de Ville the most popular Cadillac model."*

**Nameplate year of origin:** 1949 (as Hardtop designation), 1959 (series).
**Current bodystyle lifespan:** 1971 through 1976.
**Predecessor to this model:** de Ville (1969 to 1970).
**Replacement for this model:** de Ville (1977 to 1984).
**Percentage of division's sales volume:** 72.61%.
**Corporate siblings:** Buick Electra 225 and Oldsmobile Ninety-Eight.
**Primary competition:** Chrysler Imperial and Lincoln Continental.
**Notable changes:** Totally redesigned; 4-Door Sedan and Convertible models dropped.
**Major standard equipment:** Cloth seat upholstery, front center armrests, passenger assist straps, variable ratio power steering, power front disc brakes, Turbo Hydra-matic transmission, front cornering lights, rear fender skirts, left side remote control outside rear view mirror, power windows, interior courtesy and warning lights, 3-speed windshield wipers and washers, visor vanity mirrors, automatic parking brake release, electric clock, power door locks, and L78 × 15 BSW tires.

## Measurements

| | |
|---|---|
| Wheelbase | 130.0" |
| Length | 225.8" |
| Width | 79.8" |
| Height | NA |
| Legroom — front | NA |
| Legroom — rear | NA |
| Headroom — front | NA |
| Headroom — rear | NA |
| Luggage capacity (cu. ft.) | NA |
| Fuel capacity (gals.) | 27.0 |

## Models Available

| | Style Number | Base MSRP | Change from LY | Shipping Wt. (lbs.) | Production | Change from LY |
|---|---|---|---|---|---|---|
| Coupe de Ville 2-Door Hardtop | 68347 | $6,264 | +6.46% | 4685 | 66,081 | -13.10% |
| Sedan de Ville 4-Door Hardtop | 68349 | $6,498 | +6.21% | 4730 | 69,345 | -16.73% |
| TOTALS | Avg. price | $6,381 | +5.52% | Production | 135,426 | -25.48% |

1971

# Eldorado

*"An outstanding personal luxury car."*

**Nameplate year of origin:** 1953.
**Current bodystyle lifespan:** 1971 through 1978.
**Predecessor to this model:** Fleetwood Eldorado (1967 to 1970).
**Replacement for this model:** Eldorado (1979 to 1985).
**Percentage of division's sales volume:** 14.67%.
**Corporate siblings:** Buick Riviera and Oldsmobile Toronado.
**Primary competition:** Lincoln Continental Mark III.
**Notable changes:** Totally redesigned; and Convertible model added.
**Major standard equipment:** Cloth seat upholstery, front center armrests, passenger assist straps, front cornering lights, rear fender skirts, left side remote control outside rear view mirror, power windows, interior courtesy and warning lights, 3-speed windshield wipers and washers, visor vanity mirrors, automatic parking brake release, electric clock, power door locks, front-wheel-drive, variable ratio power steering, power front disc brakes, Turbo Hydra-matic transmission, and L78 × 15 BSW tires.

## Measurements

| | |
|---|---|
| Wheelbase | 126.3" |
| Length | 221.6" |
| Width | 79.6" |
| Height | NA |
| Legroom — front | NA |
| Legroom — rear | NA |
| Headroom — front | NA |
| Headroom — rear | NA |
| Luggage capacity (cu. ft.) | NA |
| Fuel capacity (gals.) | 27.0 |

## Models Available

| | Style Number | Base MSRP | Change from LY | Shipping Wt. (lbs.) | Production | Change from LY |
|---|---|---|---|---|---|---|
| Fl. Eldorado 2-Door Hardtop | 69347 | $7,383 | +6.95% | 4675 | 20,568 | -13.73% |
| Fl. Eldorado 2-Door Convertible | 69367 | $7,751 | NEW | 4730 | 6,800 | NEW |
| TOTALS | | Avg. price $7,567 | +9.62% | | Production 27,368 | +14.79% |

# Fleetwood Sixty-Special

*"Distinctive in appearance, yet unmistakably Cadillac."*

**Nameplate year of origin:** 1938.
**Current bodystyle lifespan:** 1971 through 1976.
**Predecessor to this model:** Fleetwood Sixty-Special (1969 to 1970).
**Replacement for this model:** Fleetwood Brougham (1977 to 1984).
**Percentage of division's sales volume:** 8.15%.
**Corporate siblings:** None.
**Primary competition:** None.
**Notable changes:** Totally redesigned; base model dropped.
**Major standard equipment:** Cloth or leather seat upholstery, front center armrests, passenger assist straps, dual comfort front seat, rear-seat reading lights, carpeted foot rests, variable ratio power steering, power front disc brakes, Turbo Hydra-matic transmission, front cornering lights, rear fender skirts, left side remote control outside rear view mirror, power windows, interior courtesy and warning lights, 3-speed windshield wipers and washers, visor vanity mirrors, automatic parking brake release, electric clock, power door locks, automatic level control, and L78 × 15 BSW tires,

## Measurements

| | |
|---|---|
| Wheelbase | 133.0" |
| Length | 228.8" |
| Width | 79.8" |
| Height | NA |
| Legroom — front | NA |
| Legroom — rear | NA |
| Headroom — front | NA |
| Headroom — rear | NA |
| Luggage capacity (cu. ft.) | NA |
| Fuel capacity (gals.) | 27.0 |

## Models Available

| | Style Number | Base MSRP | Change from LY | Shipping Wt. (lbs.) | Production | Change from LY |
|---|---|---|---|---|---|---|
| Fl. 60 Special Brougham 4-Dr. Sdn. | 68169 | $7,763 | +6.58% | 4815 | 15,200 | -10.13% |
| TOTALS | | Avg. price $7,763 | +9.05% | Production | 15,200 | -18.50% |

# Fleetwood Seventy-Five

*"A motor car classic."*

**Nameplate year of origin:** 1927 (Fleetwood bodies), 1936 (75 series).
**Current bodystyle lifespan:** 1971 through 1976.
**Predecessor to this model:** Fleetwood 75 (1969 to 1970).
**Replacement for this model:** Fleetwood 75 (1977 to 1984).
**Percentage of division's sales volume:** 0.86%.
**Corporate siblings:** None.
**Primary competition:** None.
**Notable changes:** Totally redesigned.
**Major standard equipment:** Cloth or cloth and leather seat upholstery, front center armrests, passenger assist straps, dual comfort front seat, rear-seat reading lights, carpeted foot rests, left side remote control outside rear view mirror, power windows, interior courtesy and warning lights, 3-speed windshield wipers and washers, visor vanity mirrors, automatic parking brake release, electric clock, power door locks, dual automatic climate control, automatic level control, fixed ratio power steering, power front disc brakes, Turbo Hydra-matic transmission, front cornering lights, rear fender skirts, and L78 × 15 BSW tires.

## Measurements

| | |
|---|---|
| Wheelbase | 151.5" |
| Length | 247.3" |
| Width | 79.8" |
| Height | NA |
| Legroom — front | NA |
| Legroom — rear | NA |
| Headroom — front | NA |
| Headroom — rear | NA |
| Luggage capacity (cu. ft.) | NA |
| Fuel capacity (gals.) | 27.0 |

## Models Available

| | Style Number | Base MSRP | Change from LY | Shipping Wt. (lbs.) | Production | Change from LY |
|---|---|---|---|---|---|---|
| Fl. Seventy-Five 4-Door Sedan | 69723 | $11,869 | +7.52% | 5510 | 752 | -14.16% |
| Fl. Seventy-Five 4-Dr. Limousine | 69733 | $12,008 | +7.43% | 5570 | 848 | -31.61% |
| TOTALS | | Avg. price $11,939 | +7.47% | Production | 1,600 | -24.39% |

# CHEVROLET

*"Putting you first, keeps us first."*

The leading automobile manufacturer in the U.S.A. served up all-new vehicles at both ends of the size spectrum for 1971 but dropped out of first place in the sales race. Huge price increases on most GM products hurt sales at all divisions. As for new product, at the small end was the subcompact Vega, and at the larger end were the totally redesigned full-size Chevrolets. These two models are covered in more detail later. The remainder of the Chevrolet line received minimal changes, except for the mid-size Chevelle, which had its third facelift in as many years. The

Chevelle had a revised grille and headlight treatment that featured single headlamp units on each side with large wrap-around parking lights located at the ends of the grille on the leading edge of the fenders. The grille itself had a strong horizontal theme, compared to the eggcrate style grilles used on nearly all other Chevrolet models. At the back end, the traditional round Chevy taillights were used for the first time on a Chevelle model. In between, the same basic styling was used, and interiors were only slightly revised. As with all GM intermediates, a new model was scheduled to be introduced for the 1972 model year, but a strike during the year would change those plans, and limit the 1971 production totals for many Chevrolet lines. The compact Nova, new-for-1970 Monte Carlo and sporty Camaro and Corvette models received only minimal changes. Most of the changes involved interior/exterior trim changes, or revised grilles. Under the hoods, most cars were given lower compression ratios to help with emissions. The Nova replaced its base 4-cylinder engine with a 6-cylinder powerplant, leaving the all-new Vega as the division's economy champ.

The Vega was one of the last big gambles taken by General Motors during the 20th century. Other ambitious but seemingly "safe bet" cars, such as the X-car (Citation, et al.), J-car (Cavalier), and the down-sized full-size cars of the late 1970s were gambles only in the uncertainty of whether they would be successful and make the corporation money. Sooner or later those cars would have been produced, if for no other reason than market pressures and consumer demand for such vehicles. The Vega was a subcompact car, a safe bet in that it met the demand for small cars. The gamble came into play under the hood and in the design. The nation's economy was not as healthy as it had once been, and that state was directly translated into the well-being of larger corporations. At the same time, General Motors had reached a point of ever increasing bureaucracy that was starting to affect the design and quality of its products adversely. These factors combined would remove some of the features that the Vega was originally slated to have, and would account for some cost cutting that affected the overall quality of the car. The gamble in design was not so much in the car's styling as in the extensive use of computer-aided technology. The Vega was one of the earliest cars to be designed and built with the aid of computers on a large scale. Also, pre-introduction marketing surveys were used extensively. Finally, the powerplant used by the Vega was of an advanced aluminum construction design that would prove to be costly and troublesome for an inexpensive subcompact. But at first the car looked promising. Sales met expectations, and the press liked the car so well that *Motor Trend* magazine named the Vega its 1971 Car of the Year.

At the other end of the size scale, the full-size Chevrolets received a total makeover. The Biscayne, Bel Air, Impala, and Caprice were among the largest automobiles ever produced by Chevrolet. The wheelbase went above 120 inches, and the weight of wagon models topped 4500 pounds! As with all other full-size GM cars, these new models featured a modern wide-body design and were very well equipped automobiles, especially when compared with their counterparts of just five or six years earlier. The wider bodies allowed for increased passenger hip and shoulder room, which made the cars feel far more spacious. The increased wheelbase gave a smoother ride, which was one of Ford's big selling points during this period. Styling, especially from the front, was less like previous Chevrolets and more like Cadillac in appearance. Of course these cars were far from the stellar performance cars they had once been. The added weight, length, and features coupled with the decrease in available engine power was putting a damper on the performance image the big Chevrolet had earned during the sixties.

BelAir 4-Door Sedan

Camaro 2-Door Coupe

Caprice 2-Door Hardtop

Chevelle SS 2-Door Hardtop

Kingswood Estate 4-Door Wagon

Malibu 2-Door Hardtop

Monte Carlo 2-Door Hardtop

Nova 2-Door Coupe

Vega 2-Door Kammback Wagon

Corvette 2-Door Coupe

**Model year production:** 1,701,774, down 15.54% from 1970.
**Domestic market share:** 21.74% (2nd place).
**Base price range:** $2,090 to $5,533.
**Industry average base price:** $3,786.
**Chevrolet average base price:** $3,468.
**Introduction date:** September 29, 1970. Vega introduced September 10, 1970.
**Assembly plants:** Lakewood, GA (A), Atlanta, GA (D), Kansas City, MO (K), Fremont, CA (Z), Van Nuys, CA (L), Norwood, OH (N), Tarrytown, NY (T), Oshawa, Ontario, Canada (1), Baltimore, MD (B); Framingham, MA (G); Flint, MI (F); Southgate, CA (C); Arlington, TX (R); Janesville, WI (J); Wilmington, DE (Y), and St. Louis, MO (S).

**Data plate identification:** Thirteen digit code read as follows: four digit style number (see listings below) in which 1 = Chevrolet, 2nd number identifies series (e.g., V is for Vega), 3rd and 4th digits indicate body style; 5th digit is engine code; 1 for 1971; assembly plant code; 100001 and up for serial number. *Example:* 1V77B1T100001 is a 1971 Chevrolet Vega 2-Door Hatchback Coupe with a 140 CID 4-cyl. engine, serial number 100001, built in Tarrytown, NY.

**1971**

## Powertrains

| Engine | Gross HP | Engine Code | Transmission Availability | Vega (4) Nova (6 & 8) | Camaro | Chevelle | Monte Carlo | †Full-size | Corvette |
|---|---|---|---|---|---|---|---|---|---|
| 140 CID OHC 1-bbl., 4-cyl. (Vega only) | 90 | B | 3-speed man. | S | - | - | - | - | - |
| | | | 4-speed man. | $53 | - | - | - | - | - |
| | | | Torque-drive | $111 | - | - | - | - | - |
| | | | Powerglide Automatic | $168 | - | - | - | - | - |

| Engine | Gross HP | Engine Code | Transmission Availability | Vega (4) Nova (6 & 8) | Camaro | Chevelle | Monte Carlo | †Full-size | Corvette |
|---|---|---|---|---|---|---|---|---|---|
| 140 CID OHC 2-bbl., 4-cyl. (Vega only) | 110 | B | 3-speed man. | $42 | - | - | - | - | - |
| | | | 4-speed man. | $95 | - | - | - | - | - |
| | | | Torque-drive | $111 | - | - | - | - | - |
| | | | Powerglide Automatic | $210 | - | - | - | - | - |
| 250 CID Turbo-Thrift, 1-bbl., 6-cyl. | 145 | D | 3-speed man. | S (Nova) | S | S[4] | - | S[1] | - |
| | | | 4-speed man. | - | $206 | - | - | - | - |
| | | | Torque-drive | $115 | - | - | - | - | - |
| | | | Powerglide Automatic | $174 | $180 | $180 | - | $180[1] | - |
| 307 CID Turbo-Fire, 2-bbl., V8 | 200 | F | 3-speed man. | $95 | $95 | S[3]/$95 (Others) | - | - | - |
| | | | 4-speed man. | - | $301 | - | | | |
| | | | Powerglide Automatic | $269 | $285 | $190[3]/$285 (Others) | - | - | - |
| | | | Turbo Hydra-matic | $301 | $312 | $217[3]/$312 (Others) | - | - | - |
| 350 CID Turbo-Fire, 2-bbl., V8 | 245 | H | 3-speed man., column | $121 | - | $26[3]/$122 (Others) | S | $121[1]/S (Others) - | |
| | (270 w/dual exhaust) | | 3-speed man., floor | - | $122 | $26[3]/$122 (Others) | - | | |
| | | | 4-speed man. | - | $328 | $221[3]/$317 (Others) | - | - | |
| | | | Powerglide Automatic | - | - | - | $190 | $311[1]/$190 (Others) | - |
| | | | Turbo Hydra-matic | $327 | $338 | $243[3]/$338 (Others) | $217 | $338[1]/$217 (Others) | - |
| 350 CID Turbo-Fire, 4-bbl., V8 | 270 | J | 3-speed man. | - | $409 (SS)** | $74[3]/$169 (Others) | $47 | - | - |
| | | | 4-speed man. | $629 (SS only) | $615 (SS)** | $269[3]/$364 (Others) | $242 | - | S |
| | | | Turbo Hydra-matic | $629 (SS only) | $635 (SS)** | $290[3]/$385 (Others) | $264 | - | S |
| 350 CID Turbo-Fire, 4-bbl., V8 | 330 | K | 4-speed man. | - | $992 (Z28)** | - | - | - | $483 |
| | | | Turbo Hydra-matic | - | $1093 (Z28)** | - | - | - | $483 |
| 400 CID Turbo-Fire, 2-bbl., V8 | 255 | R | Turbo Hydra-matic | - | - | - | - | S (Capr.)/ $411[1]/$290 (Others) | - |
| 400 CID Turbo-Jet 396, 4-bbl., V8 | 300 | U | 4-speed man. | - | $618 (SS)[2] | $368 (SS)[2] | $341 | - | - |
| | | | 4-speed man.-close ratio | - | $618 (SS)[2] | $368 (SS)[2] | - | - | - |
| | | | Turbo Hydra-matic | - | $719 (SS)[2] | $410 (SS & Wagons only)[2] | $384 | $69-Capr./ $480[1]/$359 (Others) | - |
| 454 CID Turbo-Jet, 4-bbl., V8 | 365 | V | 4-speed man. | - | - | - | - | - | $295 |
| | | | Turbo Hydra-matic | - | - | $612 (SS only) | $722 (SS) | $216 (Capr.)/ $627[1]/$506 (Others) | $395 |
| 454 CID Turbo-Jet, 4-bbl., V8 | 425 | | 4-speed man. | - | - | - | - | - | $1221 |
| | | | Special 4-speed, Close-ratio | - | - | - | - | - | $1321 |
| | | | Turbo Hydra-matic | - | - | - | - | - | $1321 |

[1]Biscayne, BelAir, and Impala 2-Dr. HT and 4-Door Sedan only.   [2]Optional SS equipment packages required.   [3]Malibu Convertible & 4-Door HT, Greenbrier and Concours models only.   [4]Except Malibu Convertible and 4-Door HT, Greenbrier and Concours.   †See text for corresponding wagon models.

## Major Options

| | Vega | Nova | Camaro | Chevelle | Monte Carlo | Full-size | Corvette |
|---|---|---|---|---|---|---|---|
| Air conditioning | $360 | $392* | $408* | $408* | $408 | $416* | $465 |
| Electronic cruise control | - | - | - | $ | $ | $ | $ |
| Electric rear window defogger | $ | $ | $ | $ | $ | $ | $ |
| Soft Ray tinted glass | $37 | $40 | $40 | $43 | $46 | $51 | S |
| Deck lid remote release | - | - | - | $ | $ | $ | - |
| Power steering—variable-ratio | $95 | $103 | $116 | $116 | $116 | $116 | $116 |
| Power brakes | - | $47 | $47 | $47 | S | S | $47 |
| Power door locks | - | - | - | $ | $ | $46–$71 | $ |
| Power driver's seat/Bench seat | - | - | - | $79 | $79 | $105 (ex. Bisc.) | - |
| Power windows | - | - | $85 | $127 | $127 | $127 (ex. Bisc.) | $85 |
| AM radio | $61 | $66 | $66 | $66 | $66 | $66 | - |
| AM/FM stereo | $123 | $139 | $139 | | | | |
| | (not Stereo) | (not Stereo) | (not Stereo) | $239 | $239 | $239 | $283 |
| Front seat console | - | $ | $ | $ | $ | - | S |
| Front bucket seats | S | $ | S | $ | $ | - | S |
| Tilt steering wheel | - | - | $45 | $45 | $ | $ | $ |
| Vinyl roof | - | $84 | $90 | $95 | $126 | $109 | $63 |
| | | | | | | ($142 Wgns) | (Conv. w/HT) |
| Rally wheels | - | $ | $ | $ | $ | - | S |
| Custom interior group | - | $ | $ | - | $350 | $ | $ |
| Vega GT Package $349 | | | | | | | |
| Super Sport equipment package— | | | | | | | |
| (Rally Sport also on Camaro) | | $328 | $314 | $357 | $485 | - | - |
| | | | (RS $179) | | | | |

Options common to most models. (– = Not Available; S = Standard equipment.) Items may be standard equipment, optional at different pricing, or unavailable on certain models. This chart is only a guide.    *Not available with 6-cylinder engine.

## Paint Colors

| | Code | Vega | Full-Size | Chevelle/MC/Camaro/Nova | Corvette |
|---|---|---|---|---|---|
| Classic White | 10 | | | | x |
| Antique White | 11 | x | x | x | |
| Nevada Silver Met. | 13 | x | x | x | x |
| Silver Steel Metallic | 16 | | x | | |
| Tuxedo Black | 19 | | x | | |
| Ascot Blue Metallic | 24 | | x | x | |
| Mediterranean Blue | 25 | x | | | |
| Mulsanne Blue Met. | 26 | | | x | x |
| Bridgehampton Blue Metallic | 27 | | | | x |
| Command Blue Met. | 29 | | x | | |
| Sea Aqua Metallic | 39 | x | x | x | |
| Cottonwood Green Metallic | 42 | | x | x | |
| Lime Green Metallic | 43 | | x | x | |
| Brands Hatch Green Met. | 48 | | | | x |
| Antique Green Met. | 49 | x | x | x | |
| Sunflower Yellow | 52 | | x | x | x |
| Placer Gold Metallic | 53 | | | x | |
| Champagne Gold Metallic | 55 | x | x | | |
| Sandalwood | 61 | | x | x | |
| Burnt Orange Met./ Corvette Bronze | 62 | | x | x | x |
| Mesa Sand | 63 | | | x | |
| Hugger Orange | 65 | x | | x | |
| Classic Copper Met. | 67 | x | x | x | |
| Cranberry Red | 75 | x | x | x | |
| Mille Miglia Red | 76 | | | | x |
| Marlboro Maroon Met. | 77 | | | | x |
| Rosewood Metallic | 78 | | x | x | |
| War Bonnet Yellow Met. | 91 | | | | x |

| | Code | Vega | Full-Size | Chevelle/MC/Camaro/Nova | Corvette |
|---|---|---|---|---|---|
| Ontario Orange Firemist | 97 | | | | x |
| Steel Cities Gray Met. | 98 | | | | x |

# Vega

*"Chevy's new car is open for business."*

**Nameplate year of origin:** 1971.
**Current bodystyle lifespan:** 1971 through 1979 (under various nameplates).
**Predecessor to this model:** Corvair (1965 to 1969).
**Replacement for this model:** Cavalier (1982 to 1994).
**Percentage of division's sales volume:** 15.86%.
**Corporate siblings:** None.
**Primary competition:** Ford Pinto and AMC Gremlin.
**Notable changes:** All-new for 1971.
**Major standard equipment:** All-vinyl front bucket seats, flow-through power ventilation system, 3-point seat-belt system, padded sun visors, ashtray, self-adjusting front disc/rear drum brake system, bright-metal hubcaps, silver-finished grid-pattern grille, and A78 × 13 BSW tires.

## Measurements

| | Cars | Wagons |
|---|---|---|
| Wheelbase | 97.0" | 97.0" |
| Length | 169.7" | 169.7" |
| Width | 65.4" | 65.4" |
| Height | 51.9" | 52.0" |
| Legroom — front | 42.8" | 42.8" |
| Legroom — rear | 28.9" | 30.1" |
| Headroom — front | 38.4" | 38.5" |
| Headroom — rear | 39.4" | 38.3" |
| Cargo capacity (cu. ft.) | 8.7 | 50.2 |
| Fuel capacity (gals.) | 11.0 | 11.0 |

## Models Available

| | Style Number | Base MSRP | Change from LY | Shipping Wt. (lbs.) | Production | Change from LY |
|---|---|---|---|---|---|---|
| Vega 2-Door Sedan | 14111 | $2,090 | NEW | 2146 | 58,800 | NEW |
| Vega 2-Door Hatchback Coupe | 14177 | $2,196 | NEW | 2190 | 168,300 | NEW |
| Vega 2-Door Kammback Wagon | 14115 | $2,328 | NEW | 2230 | 42,800 | NEW |
| TOTALS | | *Avg. price* $2,205 | NEW | *Production* 269,900 | | NEW |

# Camaro

*"The closest thing to a Vette yet."*

**Nameplate year of origin:** 1967.
**Current bodystyle lifespan:** 1970 through 1981.
**Predecessor to this model:** Camaro (1967 to 1969).
**Replacement for this model:** Camaro (1982 to 1992).
**Percentage of division's sales volume:** 6.32%.
**Corporate siblings:** Pontiac Firebird.
**Primary competition:** Ford Mustang, Plymouth Barracuda, Dodge Challenger, AMC Javelin.
**Notable changes:** Trim and detail changes.
**Major standard equipment:** All-vinyl front bucket seats, full carpeting, hubcaps, four-spoke steering wheel, and E78 × 14 BSW tires. RS package adds: Grid pattern grille (black w/argent accents) w/split front bumper, parking lights next to headlights, and RS identification. SS adds: Special SS grille and badges, power brakes, heavy-duty clutch, suspension, and radiator, hood insulation, dual exhausts, 350 CID V8 engine, remote-control sport mirror, and F70 × 14 white-letter tires. Z28 adds: RS-style blacked-out grille, Z28 identification, Positraction rear end, remote left hand/manual right hand outside sport mirrors, special suspension components, special instrumentation, and F60 × 15 white-letter tires.

## Measurements

| | |
|---|---|
| Wheelbase | 108.0" |
| Length | 188.0" |
| Width | 74.4" |
| Height | 49.1" |
| Legroom — front | 43.8" |
| Legroom — rear | 30.7" |
| Headroom — front | 37.4" |
| Headroom — rear | 36.1" |
| Cargo capacity (cu. ft.) | 6.4 |
| Fuel capacity (gals.) | 18.0 |

## Models Available

| | Style Number** | Base MSRP | Change from LY | Shipping Wt. (lbs.) | Production | Change from LY |
|---|---|---|---|---|---|---|
| Camaro 2-Door Sport Coupe | 123(4)87 | $2,921 | +6.26% | 3094 | 107,496* | -8.59% |
| TOTALS | Avg. price | $2,921 | +6.26% | Production | 107,496* | -8.59% |

*RS package, 18,404 produced. SS package, 8,377 produced. Z28 package, 4,862 produced.    **Style number in parentheses is third digit for V8 powered cars.

# Nova

*"In this day of big cars and little cars where does Nova fit in? Everywhere."*

**Nameplate year of origin:** 1962.
**Current bodystyle lifespan:** 1968 through 1972.
**Predecessor to this model:** Chevy II (1966 to 1967).
**Replacement for this model:** Nova (1973 through 1979, with restyle in 1975).
**Percentage of division's sales volume:** 11.45%.
**Corporate siblings:** Pontiac Ventura II.
**Primary competition:** Ford Maverick, Mercury Comet, Plymouth Valiant, Dodge Dart, AMC Hornet.
**Notable changes:** Refinements.
**Major standard equipment:** Cloth and vinyl bench seat, vinyl-coated rubber floor coverings, deluxe steering wheel, hubcaps, front-door vent windows, bright moldings on windshield and rear window, manual drum brakes, E78-14 BSW tires.

### Measurements

| | |
|---|---|
| Wheelbase | 111.0" |
| Length | 189.4" |
| Width | 72.4" |
| Height | 53.9" |
| Legroom — front | 41.0" |
| Legroom — rear | 32.6" |
| Headroom — front | 37.6" |
| Headroom — rear | 36.6" |
| Cargo capacity (cu. ft.) | 13.7 |
| Fuel capacity (gals.) | 17.0 |

## Models Available

| | Style Number* | Base MSRP | Change from LY | Shipping Wt. (lbs.) | Production | Change from LY |
|---|---|---|---|---|---|---|
| Nova 2-Door Coupe | 113(4)27 | $2,376 | +9.19% | 2952 | ** | ** |
| Nova 4-Door Sedan | 113(4)69 | $2,405 | +9.07% | 2976 | ** | ** |
| TOTALS | Avg. price | $2,391 | +9.13% | Production | 194,878 | -38.16% |

*Style number in parentheses is third digit for V8 powered cars.    **Production is estimated and not available by body style totals. SS package, 7,015 produced.

# Chevelle

*"How do you change America's most popular mid-size car? Very carefully."*

**Nameplate year of origin:** 1964.
**Current bodystyle lifespan:** 1968 through 1972.
**Predecessor to this model:** Chevelle (1966 to 1967).
**Replacement for this model:** Chevelle (1973 to 1977).
**Percentage of division's sales volume:** 19.23%.
**Corporate siblings:** Pontiac LeMans, Oldsmobile Cutlass, and Buick Skylark.
**Primary competition:** Ford Torino, Plymouth Satellite, Dodge Coronet, and AMC Matador.
**Notable changes:** All-new front and rear styling.
**Major standard equipment:** Cloth and vinyl front bench seat,

### Measurements

| | 2-Doors | 4-Doors | Wagons |
|---|---|---|---|
| Wheelbase | 112.0" | 116.0" | 116.0" |
| Length | 197.5" | 201.5" | 206.8" |
| Width | 75.4" | 75.4" | 75.4" |
| Height | 52.0" | 52.6" | 52.6" |
| Legroom — front | 42.4" | 42.4" | 42.4" |
| Legroom — rear | 32.2" | 34.8" | 34.8" |
| Headroom — front | 37.9" | 38.5" | 38.5" |
| Headroom — rear | 36.3" | 37.1" | 37.4" |

1971

color-keyed vinyl-coated rubber floor mats, small hubcaps, and E78 × 14 BSW tires. Malibu adds: Pattern cloth front bench seat, color-keyed deep-twist carpeting, wheel covers, and Hide-A-Way windshield wipers. Wagon models are similarly equipped with Nomad and Greenbrier same as Chevelle, and Concours same as Malibu. Concours Estate adds: Woodgrain exterior trim. SS package adds: SS trim and sport wheels, left-hand remote-control sport mirror, black-out grille, domed hood with pin locks, power brakes, special suspension, and F60 × 15 white-lettered tires.

| | 2-Doors | 4-Doors | Wagons |
|---|---|---|---|
| Cargo capacity (cu. ft.) | NA | NA | 83.6 |
| Fuel capacity (gals.) | 20.0 | 20.0 | 20.0 |

## Models Available

| | Style Number* | Base MSRP | Change from LY | Shipping Wt. (lbs.) | Production | Change from LY |
|---|---|---|---|---|---|---|
| Chevelle 2-Door Hardtop | 133(4)37 | $2,712 | NEW | 3166 | ** | NEW |
| Chevelle 4-Door Sedan | 133(4)69 | $2,677 | +5.52% | 3210 | ** | ** |
| Chevelle Malibu 2-Door Hardtop | 135(6)37 | $2,885 | +6.11% | 3212 | ** | ** |
| Chevelle Malibu 2-Dr. Convertible | 13667 | $3,260 | +11.68% | 3390 | ** | ** |
| Chevelle Malibu 4-Door Sedan | 135(6)69 | $2,851 | +6.18% | 3250 | ** | ** |
| Chevelle Malibu 4-Door Hardtop | 13639 | $3,052 | +9.39% | 3450 | ** | ** |
| Nomad 4-Door, 2-Seat Wagon | 131(2)36 | $2,997 | +4.61% | 3632 | ** | ** |
| Greenbrier 4-Door, 2-Seat Wagon | 13436 | $3,228 | +9.57% | 3820 | ** | ** |
| Greenbrier 4-Door, 3-Seat Wagon | 13446 | $3,340 | +3.95% | 3882 | ** | ** |
| Concours 4-Door, 2-Seat Wagon | 13636 | $3,337 | +9.20% | 3864 | ** | ** |
| Concours 4-Door, 3-Seat Wagon | 13646 | $3,450 | +3.82% | 3908 | ** | ** |
| Concours Estate 4-Dr., 2-S. Wagon | 13836 | $3,514 | +9.47% | 3892 | ** | ** |
| Concours Estate 4-Dr., 3-S. Wagon | 13846 | $3,626 | +4.95% | 3944 | ** | ** |
| TOTALS | | Avg. price $3,148 | +6.89% | | Production 327,200** | -25.69% |

*Style number in parenthesis is third digit for V8 powered cars.    **Production is estimated and not available by body style totals.

# Monte Carlo

*"Still the only car of its kind made in the U.S.A."*

**Nameplate year of origin:** 1970.
**Current bodystyle lifespan:** 1970 through 1972.
**Predecessor to this model:** None.
**Replacement for this model:** Monte Carlo (1973 to 1977).
**Percentage of division's sales volume:** 6.62%.
**Corporate siblings:** Pontiac Grand Prix.
**Primary competition:** Mercury Cougar, Plymouth Satellite Sebring, and Dodge Charger.
**Notable changes:** Revised grille and trim and detail changes.
**Major standard equipment:** Cloth and vinyl front bench seat, full carpeting, woodgrained instrument panel, power front disc/rear drum brakes, aluminized exhaust system, full wheel covers, and G78 × 15 BSW tires.

## Measurements

| | |
|---|---|
| Wheelbase | 116.0" |
| Length | 206.5" |
| Width | 75.6" |
| Height | 52.9" |
| Legroom — front | NA |
| Legroom — rear | NA |
| Headroom — front | NA |
| Headroom — rear | NA |
| Cargo capacity (cu. ft.) | 12.9 |
| Fuel capacity (gals.) | 19.0 |

## Models Available

| | Style Number | Base MSRP | Change from LY | Shipping Wt. (lbs.) | Production | Change from LY |
|---|---|---|---|---|---|---|
| Monte Carlo 2-Door Hardtop | 13857 | $3,416 | 9.38% | 3488 | 112,599 | -22.86% |
| TOTALS | | Avg. price $3,416 | +9.38% | | Production 112,599* | -22.86% |

*SS 454 package, 1,919 produced.

# Chevrolet Full-size

*"Our apologies to people who prefer
spending big money for cars like these."*

**Nameplate year of origin:** 1950 (BelAir); 1958 (Biscayne, Impala); 1966 (Caprice)

**Current bodystyle lifespan:** 1971 through 1976.

**Predecessor to this model:** Full-size Chevrolet (1969 to 1970).

**Replacement for this model:** Impala/Caprice (1977 to 1990).

**Percentage of division's sales volume:** 39.25%.

**Corporate siblings:** Buick LeSabre/Centurion, Olds 88, Pontiac Catalina/Bonneville.

**Primary competition:** AMC Ambassador, Dodge Polara/Monaco, Ford LTD, and Plymouth Fury.

**Notable changes:** Totally redesigned.

**Major standard equipment:** Biscayne: Cloth and vinyl bench seat, full carpeting, front and rear door armrests, 2-speed electric windshield wipers with washers, rocker panel moldings, and G78 × 15 BSW tires (L78 × 15 BSW tires on wagons). BelAir adds: Automatic interior lighting and power brakes. Impala adds: Vinyl upholstery in convertible, Impala specific interior trim, and electric clock. Caprice adds: Specific cloth and vinyl front bench seats (with center fold-down armrest on sedan), all-vinyl upholstery in wagons, simulated walnut interior trim, deluxe wheel covers, rocker panel moldings, unique Caprice grille, simulated wood exterior trim on Kingswood Estate wagons, and special ornamentation.

## Measurements

|  | Cars | Wagons |
|---|---|---|
| Wheelbase | 121.5" | 125.0" |
| Length | 216.8" | 223.2" |
| Width | 79.5" | 79.5" |
| Height (Sedan only) | 53.4" | 57.1" |
| Legroom — front | 42.6" | 42.6" |
| Legroom — rear | 38.5" | 38.5" |
| Headroom — front | 38.9" | 38.9" |
| Headroom — rear | 38.0" | 38.5" |
| Cargo capacity (cu. ft.) | NA | 106.4 |
| Fuel capacity (gals.) | NA | NA |

## Models Available

| | Style Number | Base MSRP | Change from LY | Shipping Wt. (lbs.) | Production | Change from LY |
|---|---|---|---|---|---|---|
| Biscayne 4-Door Sedan | 153(4)69 | $3,096 | +11.09% | 3732 | 37,600 | 6.21% |
| Bel Air 4-Door Sedan | 155(6)69 | $3,233 | +11.98% | 3732 | 20,000 | -73.61% |
| Impala 2-Door Sport Coupe | 163(4)57 | $3,408 | +12.18% | 3742 | ** | ** |
| Impala 2-Door Custom Coupe | 16447 | $3,826 | +17.15% | 3912 | ** | ** |
| Impala 2-Door Convertible | 16467 | $4,021 | +19.07% | 3960 | ** | ** |
| Impala 4-Door Sedan | 163(4)69 | $3,391 | +12.25% | 3760 | ** | ** |
| Impala 4-Door Hardtop | 16439 | $3,813 | +19.04% | 3978 | ** | ** |
| Caprice 2-Door Hardtop | 16647 | $4,071 | +17.18% | 3964 | ** | ** |
| Caprice 4-Door Hardtop | 16639 | $4,134 | +17.21% | 4040 | ** | ** |
| Brookwood 4-Dr., 2-S. Wagon | 15435 | $3,929 | +19.28% | 4542 | ** | ** |
| Townsman 4-Dr., 2-S. Wagon | 15635 | $4,020 | +19.75% | 4544 | ** | ** |
| Townsman 4-Dr., 3-S. Wagon | 15645 | $4,135 | +19.20% | 4598 | ** | ** |
| Kingswood 4-Dr., 2-S. Wagon | 16435 | $4,112 | +18.26% | 4588 | ** | ** |
| Kingswood 4-Dr., 3-S. Wagon | 16445 | $4,227 | +17.78% | 4648 | ** | ** |
| Kingswood Estate 4-Dr., 2-S. Wgn. | 16635 | $4,384 | +16.81% | 4678 | ** | ** |
| Kingswood Estate 4-Dr., 3-S. Wgn. | 16645 | $4,498 | +16.35% | 4738 | ** | ** |
| TOTALS | *Avg. price* | $3,894 | +16.69% | *Production* | 667,900* | -31.75% |

*\*Style number in parentheses is third digit for V8 powered cars.  \*\*Production is estimated and not available by body style totals.*

1971

# Corvette

*"Eighteen years of Corvette has taught us a lot."*

**Nameplate year of origin:** 1953 (Also used on showcar of same year).
**Current bodystyle lifespan:** 1968 through 1982.
**Predecessor to this model:** Corvette (1963 to 1967).
**Replacement for this model:** Corvette (1984 to 1996).
**Percentage of division's sales volume:** 1.28%.
**Corporate siblings:** None.
**Primary competition:** None.
**Notable changes:** Trim and detail changes.
**Major standard equipment:** Complete instrumentation, Astro Ventilation, removable roof panels (Coupe), manually operated folding top (Convertible), wheels with bright trim ring and ribbed center hub, Soft-Ray tinted glass, 4-wheel disc brakes, and F70 × 15 Wide-Oval tires.

## Measurements

| | |
|---|---|
| Wheelbase | 98.0" |
| Length | 182.5" |
| Width | 69.2" |
| Height | 47.8" |
| Legroom — front | 43.0" |
| Legroom — rear | NA |
| Headroom — front | 36.2" |
| Headroom — rear | NA |
| Cargo capacity (cu. ft.) | NA |
| Fuel capacity (gals.) | 20.0 |

## Models Available

| | Style Number | Base MSRP | Change from LY | Shipping Wt. (lbs.) | Production | Change from LY |
|---|---|---|---|---|---|---|
| Corvette 2-Door Coupe | 19437 | $5,533 | +6.57% | 3202 | 14,680 | +37.61% |
| Corvette 2-Door Convertible | 19467 | $5,296 | +9.22% | 3216 | 7,121 | +7.11% |
| TOTALS | | Avg. price $5,415 | +7.85% | | Production 21,801 | +25.90% |

# CHRYSLER

*"Coming through for all the living you do."*

Imperial reached the end of an era for 1971. Chrysler Corporation made the decision to demote the Imperial from an individual sales and marketing division to a model within the Chrysler division lineup. This made the 1970 models the last "official" Imperial models. The 1971 cars were sold as Chrysler Imperials. In reality, this probably did not make much difference to the average consumer, as the Imperial was always known as a Chrysler. Making the move official saved Chrysler money and simplified the marketing campaigns. A bit of good news could be found in the sales for the 1971 Imperial, which held steady around 11,500 units, while other marques felt sharp declines. As for changes, there was a new grille design, and some minor trim and equipment changes. This was the last year air conditioning was optional equipment, as it became standard for 1972. Also, the lower-priced Crown model line was dropped, leaving only the top-line LeBaron.

Other 1971 Chrysler models were a virtual carry-over from the 1969 and 1970 models. The biggest news for the year came in the new low-priced entry, the Newport Royal. Reviving a popular entry-level nameplate originating in the forties, Chrysler hoped to attract new buyers in the lower-end mid-range market, namely Oldsmobile Delta 88 and Buick LeSabre territory. To power the new nameplate, a new engine was developed and available exclusively in the Royal for 1971, the 360 CID V8. Although the Royal sold well for a low-priced Chrysler, it was discontinued at the end of the 1972 season. In reality, a similar car continued, but for 1972 there was a shuffling of nameplates, and the Newport took over the role of entry-level Chrysler once again by 1973. Part of the reason for the nameplate shuffling was that the Imperial had rejoined the Chrysler ranks, creating duplication in product between it and the New Yorker.

The long-running 300 series would see its final year of production, perhaps a year too late. Sales of the luxury sport Chrysler had been steadily declining since the mid-sixties. Although it was always a sharp looking car, the market for large performance cars was all but gone, and the 1970 300-H by Hurst would have made a fitting finale to the performance nameplate. A Chrysler convertible was no longer offered this year. The last big Chrysler convertible came off the line during the 1970 model year, and there would not be another Chrysler convertible until the mid-sized 1982 LeBaron. This was the final year of installation of the 383 CID V8 in Chryslers, as it would be replaced by the new 400 CID V8 in 1972. The only other major news from Chrysler for the year was the announcement of an automatic transmission as standard equipment for all Chrysler models midway through the model run. At the beginning of the model year, Newport and Newport Custom models were listed as having a three-speed manual transmission as standard equipment. Prices listed on the ensuing charts are given at the beginning of the model year, and reflect cars equipped with the manual transmission.

Newport Custom 4-Door Sedan

Imperial LeBaron 4-Door Hardtop

Newport Royal 4-Door Hardtop

New Yorker 2-Door Hardtop

Town & Country 4-Door Wagon

**Model year production:** 188,676, down 2.03% from 1970.
**Domestic market share:** 2.41% (10th place).
**Base price range:** $4,078 to $6,864.
**Industry average base price:** $3,786.
**Chrysler average base price:** $4,784.
**Introduction date:** September 1970.
**Assembly plants:** Newark, DE (F), and Detroit, MI (C).
**Data plate identification:** Thirteen digit code read as follows:

four digit style number (see listings below) in which C = Chrysler, 2nd number identifies series (e.g., H is for New Yorker), 3rd and 4th indicate body style; 5th digit is engine code; 1 for 1971; assembly plant code; 100001 and up for serial number. *Example:* CH23T1C100001 is a 1971 Chrysler New Yorker 2-Door Hardtop with a 440 CID V8 engine, serial number 100001, built in Detroit, MI.

# Powertrains

| Engine | Engine Code | Gross HP | Transmission Availability | Newport Royal | Newport/ Custom | 300/N.Y./ T&C/Imp. |
|---|---|---|---|---|---|---|
| 360 CID, 2-bbl., V8 | K | 255 | 3-speed man. | S | - | - |
| | | | TorqueFlite Automatic | $241 | - | - |
| 383 CID, 2-bbl., V8 | L | 275 | 3-speed man. | $27 | S | - |
| | | | TorqueFlite Automatic | $268 | $241 | - |
| 383 CID, 4-bbl., V8 | N | 300 | TorqueFlite Automatic | $339 | $312 | - |
| 440 CID, 4-bbl., V8 | T | 335 | TorqueFlite Automatic | - | $449 | S |
| 440 CID TNT, 4-bbl., V8 | U | 370 | TorqueFlite Automatic | - | - | $83 (ex. Imperial) |

## Major Options

| | Newport | 300 | Town & Country | New Yorker | Imperial |
|---|---|---|---|---|---|
| Air conditioning | $426 | $426 | $426 | $426 | $490 |
| Electronic cruise control | $69 | $69 | $69 | $69 | $95 |
| Soft Ray tinted glass | $54 | $54 | $54 | $54 | $58 |
| Deck lid remote release | $16 | $16 | - | $16 | $33 |
| Power steering— variable-ratio | $125 | S | S | S | S |
| Power brakes | $76 | S | S | S | S |
| Power door locks | $48–$73 | $48–$73 | $73 | $48–$73 | $50–$74 |
| Power driver's seat/ Bench seat | $106 | $106 | $106 | $106 | $114–$122 |
| Power windows | $133 | $133 | $133 | $133 | S |
| AM radio | $92 | $92 | $92 | $92 | S |
| AM/FM stereo | $243 | $243 | $243 | $243 | $308 |
| Tilt & telescoping steering wheel | $91 | $91 | $91 | $91 | $97 |
| Sunroof | $598 | $598 | - | $598 | $598 |
| Vinyl roof | $128 | $128 | $145 | $128 | S |
| Chrome Road Wheels | $102 | $102 | $102 | $102 | - |

Options common to most models. (- = Not Available; S = Standard equipment.) Items may be standard equipment, optional at different pricing, or unavailable on certain models. This chart is only a guide.

## Paint Colors

| | Code |
|---|---|
| Winchester Gray Metallic | A4 |
| Slate Gray | A8 |
| Charcoal Metallic* | A9 |
| Glacial Blue Metallic | B2 |
| Evening Blue Metallic | B7 |
| Midnight Blue Metallic* | B9 |
| Rallye Red | E5 |
| Burnished Red Metallic | E7 |
| Amber Sherwood Metallic | F3 |
| Avocado Metallic | F9 |
| April Green Metallic | J4 |
| Autumn Bronze Metallic | K6 |
| Sandalwood Beige | L1 |
| Aztec Gold Metallic | L6 |
| Sparkling Burgundy Metallic* | M8 |
| Coral Turquoise Metallic | Q5 |
| Tahitian Walnut Metallic | T8 |
| Spinnaker White | W1 |
| Formal Black | X9 |
| Lemon Twist | Y1 |
| Honeydew* | Y4 |
| Crystal Dawn | Y5 |
| Tawny Gold Metallic | Y9 |

*Available only on Imperial models.

# Newport

*"It's our most affordable Chrysler. Yet it's still a Chrysler—all the way."*

**Nameplate year of origin:** 1950 (as HT model of the T & C); 1961 (as series).
**Current bodystyle lifespan:** 1969 through 1973.
**Predecessor to this model:** Newport (1965 to 1968).
**Replacement for this model:** Newport (1974 to 1978).
**Percentage of division's sales volume:** 59.11%.
**Corporate siblings:** Chrysler 300 and New Yorker.
**Primary competition:** Buick LeSabre, Mercury Monterey, and Oldsmobile Delta 88.
**Notable changes:** Minor trim and detail changes. New entry-level Royal line added.
**Major standard equipment:** Cloth and vinyl front bench seat, full carpeting, bright window trim moldings, wheel covers and H78 × 15 BSW tires. Newport adds: Additional interior and exterior bright trim. Custom adds: Cloth and vinyl front bench seat with fold-down arm rest, and specific interior trim.

## Measurements

| | |
|---|---|
| Wheelbase | 124.0" |
| Length | 224.7" |
| Width | 79.1" |
| Height | 55.2" |
| Legroom—front | 41.8" |
| Legroom—rear | 41.5" |
| Headroom—front | 38.7" |
| Headroom—rear | 37.9" |
| Cargo capacity (cu. ft.) | 21.2 |
| Fuel capacity (gals.) | 24.0 |

## Models Available

| | Style Number | Base MSRP | Change from LY | Shipping Wt. (lbs.) | Production | Change from LY |
|---|---|---|---|---|---|---|
| Newport Royal 2-Door Hardtop | CE23 | $4,153 | NEW | 4121 | 8,500 | NEW |
| Newport Royal 4-Door Sedan | CE41 | $4,078 | NEW | 4171 | 19,662 | NEW |
| Newport Royal 4-Door Hardtop | CE43 | $4,216 | NEW | 4191 | 5,188 | NEW |
| Newport 2-Door Hardtop | CE23 | $4,265 | +18.84% | 4121 | 15,549 | -28.23% |
| Newport 4-Door Sedan | CE41 | $4,190 | +19.24% | 4171 | 24,834 | -36.79% |
| Newport 4-Door Hardtop | CE43 | $4,328 | +18.51% | 4191 | 10,800 | -36.25% |
| Newport Custom 2-Door Hardtop | CL23 | $4,391 | +16.13% | 4126 | 5,527 | -16.75% |

| | Style Number | Base MSRP | Change from LY | Shipping Wt. (lbs.) | Production | Change from LY |
|---|---|---|---|---|---|---|
| Newport Custom 4-Door Sedan | CL41 | $4,319 | +16.42% | 4181 | 11,254 | -18.25% |
| Newport Custom 4-Door Hardtop | CL43 | $4,471 | +15.80% | 4211 | 10,207 | -6.13% |
| TOTALS | | Avg. price $4,268 | +14.76% | | Production 111,521 | +1.11% |

# 300

*"Proud. Distinctive. Powerful. A rare blending of elegance and extraordinary road performance."*

**Nameplate year of origin:** 1955 (letter series cars); 1962 (standard line cars).
**Current bodystyle lifespan:** 1969 through 1971.
**Predecessor to this model:** 300 (1965 to 1968).
**Replacement for this model:** None.
**Percentage of division's sales volume:** 7.39%.
**Corporate siblings:** Chrysler Newport and New Yorker.
**Primary competition:** Buick Centurion and Pontiac Grand Ville.
**Notable changes:** Minor trim and detail changes.
**Major standard equipment:** Cloth and vinyl front bench seat, full carpeting, full-width grille with concealed headlamps, full-width taillamps, automatic transmission, and H78 × 15 BSW tires.

## Measurements

| | |
|---|---|
| Wheelbase | 124.0" |
| Length | 224.7" |
| Width | 79.1" |
| Height | 55.3" |
| Legroom — front | 41.8" |
| Legroom — rear | 41.5" |
| Headroom — front | 37.7" |
| Headroom — rear | 37.2" |
| Cargo capacity (cu. ft.) | 21.2 |
| Fuel capacity (gals.) | 24.0 |

## Models Available

| | Style Number | Base MSRP | Change from LY | Shipping Wt. (lbs.) | Production | Change from LY |
|---|---|---|---|---|---|---|
| 300 2-Door Hardtop | CS23 | $4,608 | +8.83% | 4246 | 7,256 | -27.97% |
| 300 4-Door Hardtop | CS43 | $4,687 | +8.67% | 4321 | 6,683 | -32.12% |
| TOTALS | | Avg. price $4,648 | +6.22% | | Production 13,939 | -33.61% |

# Town & Country

*"The most luxurious wagon in the industry."*

**Nameplate year of origin:** 1941.
**Current bodystyle lifespan:** 1969 through 1973.
**Predecessor to this model:** Town & Country (1965 to 1968).
**Replacement for this model:** Town & Country (1974 to 1978).
**Percentage of division's sales volume:** 8.85%.
**Corporate siblings:** Dodge Monaco/Polara, and Plymouth Fury Suburbans.
**Primary competition:** Buick Estate Wagon, Mercury Colony Park, and Oldsmobile Custom Cruiser.
**Notable changes:** Revised sheetmetal, and new front and rear end treatments.
**Major standard equipment:** All-vinyl front bench seat with folding center armrest, power operated tailgate window, bodyside and rear tailgate woodgrain applique, automatic transmission, power steering, power front disc brakes, electric clock, lockable luggage compartment, and L84 × 15 BSW tires.

## Measurements

| | |
|---|---|
| Wheelbase | 122.0" |
| Length | 224.8" |
| Width | 79.1" |
| Height | 58.1" |
| Legroom — front | 41.8" |
| Legroom — rear | 39.1" |
| Headroom — front | 40.1" |
| Headroom — rear | 40.7" |
| Cargo capacity (cu. ft.) | 113.5 |
| Fuel capacity (gals.) | 23.0 |

## Models Available

| | Style Number | Base MSRP | Change from LY | Shipping Wt. (lbs.) | Production | Change from LY |
|---|---|---|---|---|---|---|
| Town & Country 4-Dr., 2-S. Wagon | CP45 | $4,951 | +4.50% | 4525 | 5,697 | +0.19% |
| Town & Country 4-Dr., 3-S. Wagon | CP46 | $5,037 | +4.42% | 4580 | 10,993 | +14.71% |
| TOTALS | | Avg. price $4,994 | +4.46% | | Production 16,690 | +9.31% |

# New Yorker

*"The New Yorker lives up to its look of quiet authority."*

**Nameplate year of origin:** 1939.
**Current bodystyle lifespan:** 1969 through 1973.
**Predecessor to this model:** New Yorker (1965 to 1968).
**Replacement for this model:** New Yorker (1974 to 1978).
**Percentage of division's sales volume:** 18.53%.
**Corporate siblings:** Chrysler Newport and 300.
**Primary competition:** Buick Electra 225, Cadillac Calais, Mercury Marquis, and Oldsmobile Ninety-Eight.
**Notable changes:** Minor trim and detail changes.
**Major standard equipment:** Cloth and vinyl seats with folding center armrests (front and rear), electric clock, additional interior lighting, LH remote outside rear view mirror, rear fender skirts, trunk light and carpeting, automatic transmission, power front disc brakes, power steering, and J78 × 15 BSW tires.

### Measurements

| | |
|---|---|
| Wheelbase | 124.0" |
| Length | 224.7" |
| Width | 79.1" |
| Height | 55.4" |
| Legroom — front | 41.8" |
| Legroom — rear | 41.5" |
| Headroom — front | 38.7" |
| Headroom — rear | 37.9" |
| Cargo capacity (cu. ft.) | 21.2 |
| Fuel capacity (gals.) | 24.0 |

## Models Available

| | Style Number | Base MSRP | Change from LY | Shipping Wt. (lbs.) | Production | Change from LY |
|---|---|---|---|---|---|---|
| New Yorker 2-Door Hardtop | CH23 | $4,961 | +5.98% | 4250 | 4,485 | -8.79% |
| New Yorker 4-Door Sedan | CH41 | $4,910 | +6.05% | 4335 | 9,850 | +4.91% |
| New Yorker 4-Door Hardtop | CH43 | $5,041 | +5.88% | 4355 | 20,633 | +3.67% |
| TOTALS | | Avg. price $4,971 | +5.97% | | Production 34,968 | +2.22% |

# Imperial LeBaron

*"Coming through in a most elegant way."*

**Nameplate year of origin:** 1924 (as Chrysler Sedan model designation); 1926 (as series).
**Current bodystyle lifespan:** 1969 through 1973.
**Predecessor to this model:** Imperial (1967 to 1968).
**Replacement for this model:** Chrysler Imperial (1974 to 1975).
**Percentage of division's sales volume:** 6.13%.
**Corporate siblings:** None.
**Primary competition:** Cadillac de Ville and Lincoln Continental.
**Notable changes:** Revised grille and trim changes.
**Major standard equipment:** Split-bench front seat with passenger-side recliner, rosewood-grain vinyl interior trim, full-luxury carpeting, power windows, air conditioning, tinted glass, interior courtesy and warning lamps, storage compartments on all doors, automatic transmission, power steering, power front disc brakes, vinyl top, formal rear window, and L84 × 15 BSW tires.

### Measurements

| | |
|---|---|
| Wheelbase | 127.0" |
| Length | 229.7" |
| Width | 79.1" |
| Height | 56.1" |
| Legroom — front | 41.8" |
| Legroom — rear | 41.5" |
| Headroom — front | 37.7" |
| Headroom — rear | 37.2" |
| Cargo capacity (cu. ft.) | NA |
| Fuel capacity (gals.) | 24.0 |

## Models Available

| | Style Number | Base MSRP | Change from LY | Shipping Wt. (lbs.) | Production | Change from LY |
|---|---|---|---|---|---|---|
| LeBaron 2-Door Hardtop | YM23 | $6,632 | +8.81% | 4800 | 1,442 | -20.02% |
| LeBaron 4-Door Hardtop | YM43 | $6,864 | +8.47% | 4950 | 10,116 | +20.06% |
| TOTALS | *Avg. price* $6,748 | | +11.72% | *Production* 11,558 | | -2.18% |

# DODGE

*"Let's look at it from your point of view."*

After introducing all-new full-size cars in 1969, and the new Challenger and restyled Dart models for 1970, it was time for all-new intermediate Dodge models. The new mid-sized Coronet and Charger models sported a toned-down variation of the full-size models' "fuselage" styling. The front end theme was dominated by a full-width grille encircled by the bumper surround. Both models had a "coke-bottle" side contour and a rear bumper with inset taillights. All models eliminated the front door side vent windows. In an effort to bring more differentiation between the models, all mid-size 2-Doors were Chargers this year, and on a 115-inch wheelbase, while Coronet models were strictly 4-Door Sedan and Wagon models on a 118-inch wheelbase. This helped create not only a visual distinction, but also a difference in road manners. The shorter 2-Door models handled better, while the longer 4-Door models had a better ride quality. Since all 2-Door models were now Chargers, Dodge was able to offer a lower-priced, lower content Charger model in place of the base Coronet models. This would detract from the Charger image, but boost the sales.

The new-for-1970 Challenger line received only minor trim changes. However, a Challenger Convertible was selected as the official Pace Car for the Indianapolis 500 race.

The Challenger Convertible for 1971 would be the last Dodge Convertible model until the early eighties. Similarly the Dart models received only minor trim and detail changes. There was a new addition to the Dart line, though: a twin to the Plymouth Duster, named Dart Demon. It was an immediate hit, as the Dart tended to have a sportier image with buyers than the Valiant-based Duster. Full-size Dodges sported revised grille and taillight treatments, as well as other detail changes. Full-size Convertible models were no longer offered. In the powertrain department, the 1971 models would be the last to feature the famous "Hemi" engines. A new 360 CID V8 engine introduced during the year offered increased power output over the 340 CID V8, but was somewhat more fuel efficient than the larger engines. Speaking of fuel efficient, the Mitsubishi-built Dodge Colt was introduced this year as Dodge's answer to the rising popularity of small imported cars and the new Gremlin, Vega and Pinto subcompacts. While not covered in this book, the Colt was approximately the same size as the Ford Pinto physically, but came in more traditional body styles — 2-Door and 4-Door Sedans, 2-Door Wagon, and a 2-Door Hardtop. Generally Colt models offered more features than their competitors.

**Challenger RT 2-Door Hardtop**

**Challenger 2-Door Convertible,
Indianapolis 500 Pace Car**

**Charger 2-Door Hardtop**

Charger RT 2-Door Hardtop

Coronet Brougham 4-Door Sedan

Dart Demon 2-Door Coupe

Monaco 2-Door Hardtop

Polara Custom 4-Door Wagon

**Model year production:** 556,565, up 2.49% over 1970.
**Domestic market share:** 7.11% (7th place).
**Base price range:** $2,343 to $4,821.
**Industry average base price:** $3,786.
**Dodge average base price:** $3,374.
**Introduction date:** September 1970.
**Assembly plants:** Lynch Road, MI (A); Hamtramck, MI (B); Detroit (Jefferson Ave.), MI (C); Belvidere, IL (D); Los Angeles, CA (E); Newark, DE (F); St. Louis, MO (G); New Stanton (H); Windsor, Ontario, Canada (R).

**Data plate identification:** Thirteen digit code read as follows: four digit style number (see listings below) in which 1st digit is series letter (e.g., L = Dart series), 2nd number identifies trim grade (e.g., H is for Custom/Swinger trim), 3rd and 4th digits indicate body style; 5th digit is engine code; 1 for 1971; assembly plant code; 100001 and up for serial number. *Example:* LH23G2F100001 is a 1971 Dodge Dart Swinger 2-Door Hardtop with a 318 CID V8 engine, serial number 100001, built in Newark, NJ.

## Powertrains

| Engine | Engine Code | Gross HP | Transmission Availability | Dart | Challenger | Charger | Coronet | Polara/ Monaco |
|---|---|---|---|---|---|---|---|---|
| 198 CID, 1-bbl., 6-cyl. | A | 125 | 3-speed man. | S | S (Coupe) | - | - | - |
| | | | Torqueflite automatic | $178 | $178 | - | - | - |
| 225 CID, 1-bbl., 6-cyl. | B | 145 | 3-speed man. | $38 | S (HT/Conv.) | S | S | - |
| | | | 4-speed man. | $223 | - | - | - | - |
| | | | Torqueflite automatic | $245 | $211 | $211 | $211 | - |
| 318 CID, 2-bbl., V8 | G | 230 | 3-speed man. | $133(Dem.)/ $150 (Dart) | $112 (S Rallye) | $107 ($ Rallye*) | $107 | S (Polara) |
| | | | 4-speed man. | $318 (Dem.)/ $335 (Dart) | $297 ($185 Rallye) | $318 ($211 Rallye*) | $211 | - |
| | | | Torqueflite automatic | $341 (Dem.)/ $358 (Dart) | $320 | | | |

| Engine | Engine Code | Gross HP | Transmission Availability | Dart | Challenger | Charger | Coronet | Polara/ Monaco |
|--------|-------------|----------|---------------------------|------|------------|---------|---------|----------------|
| | | | | | ($208 Rallye) | $347 ($240 Rallye*) | $347 | - |
| 340 CID, 4-bbl., V8 | H | 275 | 3-speed man. | S (340) | $210 ($98 Rallye) | $210 | - | - |
| | | | 4-speed man. | $185 (340) | $395 ($283 Rallye) | $411 | - | - |
| | | | Torqueflite automatic | $208 (340) | $418 ($316 Rallye) | $450 | - | - |
| 340 CID "Six-Pack," 3 × 2-bbl., V8 | H | 330 | 3-speed man. | S (340) | $210 ($98 Rallye) | $210 | - | - |
| | | | 4-speed man. | $185 (340) | $395 ($283 Rallye) | $411 | - | - |
| | | | Torqueflite automatic | $208 (340) | $418 ($316 Rallye) | $450 | - | - |
| 360 CID, 2-bbl., V8 | K | 255 | Torqueflite automatic | - | - | - | - | S (Mon.)/ $ (Polara) |
| 383 CID, 2-bbl., V8 | M | 275 | Torqueflite automatic | - | - | $ | $ | $ |
| | | | Torqueflite automatic | - | - | - | - | - |
| 383 CID Magnum, 4-bbl., V8 | P | 300 | Torqueflite automatic | - | - | $ | $ | - |
| 440 CID Magnum, 4-bbl., V8 | U | 370 | Torqueflite automatic | - | - | $ (Rallye*, SE) | - | - |
| 440 CID "Six-Pack," 3 × 2-bbl., V8 | V | 375 | Torqueflite automatic | - | - | $546 (Rallye*) | - | - |
| 440 CID Street Hemi, 2 × 4-bbl., V8 | T | 425 | Torqueflite automatic | - | $892 | $707 (R/T) /$837 (Sup. Bee) | - | - |

*Rallye model available as an option package on the base Charger.

## Major Options

| | Dart | Challenger | Charger | Coronet | Polara | Monaco |
|--------|------|------------|---------|---------|--------|--------|
| Air conditioning | $380 | $380 | $380 | $380 | $423 | $423 |
| Tinted glass | $36 | $36 | $40 | $40 | $40 | $40 |
| Power steering | $92 | $92 | $104 | $104 | $104 | $104 |
| Power brakes | $45 | $45 | - | - | - | - |
| Power brakes — front disc | $66 | $66 | $66 | $66 | $66 | $66 |
| Power driver's seat/Bench seat | - | - | $91 | $91 | $103 | $103 |
| Power windows | - | - | $119 | $119 | $125 | $125 |
| AM radio | $59 | $59 | $65 | $65 | $65 | $65 |
| AM/FM stereo | $125 | $132 | $144 | $144 | $144 | $144 |
| Tilt steering wheel | - | - | $55 | $55 | $55 | $55 |
| Road Wheels | - | - | $28 | - | $58 | $58 |
| Vinyl roof | $75 | $80 | $94 | $94 | $106 | $106 |
| Charger Rallye package | - | - | $82 | - | - | - |
| Monaco Brougham package | - | - | - | - | - | $220 |

Options common to most models. (− = Not Available.) Items may be standard equipment, optional at different pricing, or unavailable on certain models. This chart is only a guide.

1971

## Paint Colors

| | Code | Dart/Chllgr./Coronet/ Charger | Pol./Monaco |
|---|---|---|---|
| Light Gunmetal Met. | A-4 | x | |
| Gunmetal Gray Met. | A-8 | | x |
| Light Blue Metallic | B-2 | x | x |
| Brite Blue Metallic | B-5 | x | |
| Dark Blue Metallic | B-7 | | x |
| Plum Crazy* | C-7 | Opt. | |
| Indigo Metallic | C-8 | x | |
| Bright Red | E-5 | x | x |
| Burgundy Metallic | E-7 | x | x |
| Medium Green Metallic | F-3 | x | x |
| Dark Green Metallic | F-7 | x | x |
| Willow Green | J-3 | x | x |
| Lime Green Metallic | J-4 | x | |
| Green Go* | J-6 | Opt. | |
| Dark Bronze Metallic | K-6 | x | x |
| Butterscotch | L-5 | x | x |
| Turquoise Metallic | Q-5 | | x |
| Tan Metallic | T-2 | x | |
| Dark Tan Metallic | T-8 | x | x |
| Hemi Orange* | V-2 | Opt. | |
| Eggshell White | W-1 | x | x |
| Brite White | W-3 | x | |
| Black | X-9 | x | x |
| Top Banana* | Y-1 | Opt. | |
| Citron Yella* | Y-3 | Opt. | x |
| Light Gold | Y-4 | x | x |
| Heritage Gold Metallic | Y-7 | | x |
| Gold Metallic | Y-8 | x | x |
| Dark Gold Metallic | Y-9 | x | x |

*Hi-impact colors available at extra cost.*

# Dart

*"The compact that puts people, not price, first."*

**Nameplate year of origin:** 1960 (on low-end full-size models); Demon 1971.
**Current bodystyle lifespan:** 1967 through 1976.
**Predecessor to this model:** Dart (1963 to 1966).
**Replacement for this model:** Aspen (1976 to 1980).
**Percentage of division's sales volume:** 44.99%.
**Corporate siblings:** Plymouth Valiant.
**Primary competition:** AMC Hornet, Chevrolet Nova, Ford Maverick, Mercury Comet, Pontiac Ventura II.
**Notable Changes:** Revised grille and trim changes.
**Major standard equipment:** Cloth and vinyl, full-width front bench seat, dome light, simulated wood-grained finish on instrument panel, 2-speed windshield wipers, 3-spoke steering wheel, and 6.95 × 14 BSW tires. Custom and Swinger add: All-vinyl upholstery, body side moldings, drip rail molding, deluxe instrument panel decor, and full carpeting. Demon adds to base Dart: Ventless front windows and 6.45 × 14 BSW tires. Demon 340 adds: 340 CID V8 engine, cigarette lighter, exterior striping and E70 × 14 BSW tires (340 only).

## Measurements

| | Demon | Dart |
|---|---|---|
| Wheelbase | 108.0" | 111.0" |
| Length | 192.5" | 196.2" |
| Width | 71.6" | 69.7" |
| Height | 52.6" | 52.7" |
| Legroom — front | 41.5" | 41.5" |
| Legroom — rear | 30.0" | 35.9" |
| Headroom — front | 37.5" | 38.6" |
| Headroom — rear | 36.5" | 37.3" |
| Cargo capacity (cu. ft.) | 15.9 | 14.3 |
| Fuel capacity (gals.) | 16.0 | 16.0 |

## Models Available

|  | Style Number | Base MSRP | Change from LY | Shipping Wt. (lbs.) | Production | Change from LY |
|---|---|---|---|---|---|---|
| Demon 2-Door Coupe | LL29 | $2,343 | NEW | 2845 | 69,861 | NEW |
| Demon 340 2-Door Coupe | LM29 | $2,721 | NEW | 3165 | 10,098 | NEW |
| Dart Swinger Special 2-Dr. HT | LL23 | $2,402 | +6.24% | 2900 | 13,485 | -88.75% |
| Dart 4-Door Sedan | LL41 | $2,450 | +6.15% | 2900 | 32,711 | -7.72% |
| Dart Swinger 2-Door Hardtop | LH23 | $2,561 | +3.98% | 2900 | 102,480 | +495.54% |
| Dart Custom 4-Door Sedan | LH41 | $2,609 | +5.76% | 2900 | 21,785 | -8.39% |
| TOTALS | | Avg. price $2,515 | +3.67% | | Production 250,420 | +19.19% |

# Challenger

*"It earns two degrees, JPC (Just plain Challenger) and R/T."*

**Nameplate year of origin:** 1970.
**Current bodystyle lifespan:** 1970 through 1974.
**Predecessor to this model:** None.
**Replacement for this model:** None.
**Percentage of division's sales volume:** 5.37%.
**Corporate siblings:** Plymouth Barracuda.
**Primary competition:** AMC Javelin, Chevrolet Camaro, Ford Mustang, and Pontiac Firebird.
**Notable changes:** Trim and detail changes.
**Major standard equipment:** All-vinyl bucket seats, deep-pile carpeting, dome light, 3-spoke simulated walnut steering wheel, concealed 2-speed electric wipers, moldings (wheel opening, drip rail, grille, and deck lid), and 7.35 × 14 BSW tires. R/T adds: Longitudinal or Bumble Bee tape stripes, rallye instrument cluster, rallye suspension, dual exhausts, and F70 × 14 BSW tires.

### Measurements

| | |
|---|---|
| Wheelbase | 110.0" |
| Length | 191.3" |
| Width | 76.3" |
| Height | 51.0" |
| Legroom — front | 42.3" |
| Legroom — rear | 30.9" |
| Headroom — front | 37.4" |
| Headroom — rear | 35.6" |
| Cargo capacity (cu. ft.) | 8.6 |
| Fuel capacity (gals.) | 18.0 |

## Models Available

|  | Style Number | Base MSRP | Change from LY | Shipping Wt. (lbs.) | Production | Change from LY |
|---|---|---|---|---|---|---|
| Challenger 2-Door Coupe | JL23 | $2,727 | NEW | 3020 | * | NEW |
| Challenger 2-Door Hardtop | JH23 | $2,848 | -0.11% | 3065 | 23,088 | -56.71% |
| Challenger 2-Door Convertible | JH27 | $3,105 | -0.48% | 3150 | 2,165 | -31.77% |
| Challenger R/T 2-Door Hardtop | JS23 | $3,273 | +0.21% | 3495 | 4,630 | -68.90% |
| TOTALS | | Avg. price $2,988 | -7.38% | | Production 29,883 | -64.01% |

*Coupe production included with Hardtop.

# Charger

*"The tough one you can buy on looks alone ... or price alone ... or...."*

**Nameplate year of origin:** 1966.
**Current bodystyle lifespan:** 1971 through 1974.
**Predecessor to this model:** Charger (1968 to 1970).
**Corporate siblings:** Plymouth Satellite Sebring.
**Replacement for this model:** Charger SE (1975 to 1978).

### Measurements

| | |
|---|---|
| Wheelbase | 115.0" |
| Length | 205.4" |
| Width | 79.1" |
| Height | 52.2" |

Percentage of division's sales volume: 14.75%.

Primary competition: AMC Matador, Chevrolet Chevelle and Monte Carlo, Ford Torino, and Pontiac LeMans and Grand Prix.

Notable changes: Totally redesigned. Charger Coupe and Hardtop replace Coronet 2-Door models.

Major standard equipment: All-vinyl front bench seat, full carpeting (except coupe), simulated wood-grain door inserts and instrument panel trim (except coupe), 2-speed windshield wipers with washers, and E78 × 14 BSW tires. 500 adds: All-vinyl bucket seats, wheel lip moldings, and F78 × 14 BSW tires. Super Bee adds: All-vinyl bench seat, Rallye suspension, floor shift transmission, performance hood, exterior tape stripes, and F70 × 14 BSW tires. SE package adds: Cloth and vinyl split back bench seat, electric clock, light group, map pockets in doors, vinyl roof, concealed headlamps, and F78 × 14 BSW tires. R/T adds: All-vinyl bucket seats, automatic transmission, heavy duty brakes, R/T handling package, exterior tape stripe, and G70 × 14 raised white letter tires.

## Measurements (cont.)

| | |
|---|---|
| Legroom — front | 41.9" |
| Legroom — rear | 34.1" |
| Headroom — front | 37.3" |
| Headroom — rear | 36.4" |
| Cargo capacity (cu. ft.) | 14.3 |
| Fuel capacity (gals.) | 19.5 |

## Models Available

| | Style Number | Base MSRP | Change from LY | Shipping Wt. (lbs.) | Production | Change from LY |
|---|---|---|---|---|---|---|
| Charger 2-Door Coupe | WL21 | $2,707 | +1.42% | 3215 | * | * |
| Charger 2-Door Hardtop | WH23 | $2,975 | +6.06% | 3240 | 46,183 | +89.73% |
| Charger 500 2-Door Hardtop | WP23 | $3,223 | +5.74% | 3350 | 11,948 | +44.88% |
| Charger Super Bee 2-Door Hardtop | WM23 | $3,271 | +6.41% | 3640 | 5,054 | -56.20% |
| Charger Special Edition 2-Dr. HT | WP29 | $3,422 | +9.02% | 3375 | 15,811 | * |
| Charger R/T 2-Door Hardtop | WS23 | $3,777 | +5.83% | 3685 | 3,118 | +34.45% |
| TOTALS | | Avg. price $3,229* | -1.67%* | | Production 82,114* | +64.99%* |

*Production figures compared to 1970 Charger models. Pricing compared to comparable 1970 Coronet 2-Doors or Charger models. Charger Coupe production is included with the base Hardtop.

# Coronet

*"One, two, three, four — that's what doors are for."*

Nameplate year of origin: 1950 on hardtop models, 1953 as series.

Current bodystyle lifespan: 1971 through 1978.

Predecessor to this model: Coronet (1968 to 1970).

Replacement for this model: Monaco (1975 to 1978).

Percentage of division's sales volume: 13.97%.

Corporate siblings: Plymouth Satellite.

Primary competition: AMC Matador, Chevrolet Chevelle, Ford Torino, and Pontiac LeMans.

Notable changes: Totally redesigned. All 2-Door models moved to the Charger line.

Major standard equipment: All-vinyl bench seat (pleated vinyl on Custom), keyless door locking system, glove box lock, trunk mat, color-keyed carpeting (Custom only), cigarette lighter, front and rear armrests, simulated wood-grained door trim and instrument panel (Custom only), 2-speed concealed wipers, full-length body side molding (Custom only), and E78 × 14 BSW tires (H78 × 14 BSW for wagons).

## Measurements

| | Sedans | Wagons |
|---|---|---|
| Wheelbase | 118.0" | 118.0" |
| Length | 207.0" | 213.4" |
| Width | 78.6" | 79.2" |
| Height | 53.7" | 56.4" |
| Legroom — front | 41.9" | 41.9" |
| Legroom — rear | 36.7" | 36.7" |
| Headroom — front | 38.5" | 39.7" |
| Headroom — rear | 37.3" | 38.1" |
| Cargo capacity (cu. ft.) | 16.7 | 91.3 |
| Fuel capacity (gals.) | 19.5 | 21.0 |

## Models Available

| | Style Number | Base MSRP | Change from LY | Shipping Wt. (lbs.) | Production | Change from LY |
|---|---|---|---|---|---|---|
| Coronet 4-Door Sedan | WL41 | $2,777 | +2.70% | 3245 | 11,794 | +49.40% |
| Coronet 4-Door, 2-Seat Wagon | WL45 | $3,101 | +1.74% | 3745 | 5,470 | +48.08% |
| Coronet Custom 4-Door Sedan | WH41 | $2,951 | +6.04% | 3250 | 37,817 | +13.71% |
| Coronet Custom 4-Dr., 2-S. Wagon | WH45 | $3,278 | +3.87% | 3750 | 5,365 | +35.34% |
| Coronet Custom 4-Dr., 3-S. Wagon | WH46 | $3,454 | +2.55% | 3890 | 5,717 | +51.56% |
| Coronet Brougham 4-Door Sedan | WP41 | $3,232 | +4.87% | 3375 | 4,700 | +62.63% |
| Coronet Crestwood 4-Dr., 2-S. Wgn. | WP45 | $3,501 | +2.85% | 3845 | 2,884 | +74.05% |
| Coronet Crestwood 4-Dr., 3-S. Wgn. | WP46 | $3,682 | +4.78% | 3900 | 3,981 | +123.78% |
| TOTALS | | Avg. price $3,247 | +4.24%* | | Production 77,728 | -32.27%* |

*Production and pricing comparisons vary due to 2-Door models moving to Charger line.*

# Polara

*"It has the room you need — the comfort, the ride you want.
And the low price you've been looking for."*

**Nameplate year of origin:** 1959.
**Current bodystyle lifespan:** 1969 through 1973.
**Predecessor to this model:** Polara (1967 to 1968).
**Replacement for this model:** Monaco (1974).
**Percentage of division's sales volume:** 16.33%.
**Corporate siblings:** Chrysler Newport/300/New Yorker and Plymouth Fury.
**Primary competition:** Chevrolet Impala, Ford LTD, Oldsmobile Delta 88, and Pontiac Catalina.
**Notable changes:** Trim and detail changes. Convertible body style dropped.
**Major standard equipment:** Cloth and vinyl front bench seat (vinyl in wagon), deep-pile color-keyed carpeting, 2-speed concealed windshield wipers, heater/defroster, glove box door lock, side molding with vinyl insert, roof mounted air deflector and dual-action tailgate (Wagons), and G78 × 15 BSW tires (J78 × 15 BSW on Wagons). Custom adds: Split-back front bench seat, deluxe interior trim packages, and vinyl-bodyside molding. Brougham adds: Deluxe wheel covers, trunk light, Brougham trim, and H78 × 15 BSW tires.

## Measurements

| | Cars | Wagons |
|---|---|---|
| Wheelbase | 122.0" | 122.0" |
| Length | 220.2" | 223.5" |
| Width | 79.3" | 79.2" |
| Height | 54.5" | 57.1" |
| Legroom — front | 41.8" | 41.8" |
| Legroom — rear | 39.1" | 39.1" |
| Headroom — front | 38.8" | 39.6" |
| Headroom — rear | 38.4" | 39.2" |
| Cargo capacity (cu. ft.) | 22.4 | 104.2 |
| Fuel capacity (gals.) | 23.0 | 23.0 |

## Models Available

| | Style Number | Base MSRP | Change from LY | Shipping Wt. (lbs.) | Production | Change from LY |
|---|---|---|---|---|---|---|
| Polara 2-Door Hardtop | DE23 | $3,319 | +12.13% | 3715 | 11,535 | * |
| Polara 4-Door Sedan | DE41 | $3,298 | -6.12% | 3755 | 21,578 | * |
| Polara 4-Door Hardtop | DE43 | $3,497 | -3.42% | 3875 | 2,487 | * |
| Polara Custom 2-Door Hardtop | DL23 | $3,614 | +11.41% | 3805 | 9,682 | -36.48% |
| Polara Custom 4-Door Sedan | DL41 | $3,593 | +11.51% | 3835 | 13,860 | -26.04% |
| Polara Custom 4-Door Hardtop | DL43 | $3,681 | +11.01% | 3875 | 17,458 | -9.18% |
| Polara Custom 4-Dr., 2-S. Wgn. | DL45 | $3,992 | +8.77% | 4280 | 9,682 | 214.96% |
| Polara Custom 4-Dr., 3-S. Wgn. | DL46 | $4,098 | +8.47% | 4335 | * | * |
| Polara Brougham 2-Door Hardtop | DM23 | $3,818 | +10.41% | 3965 | 2,024 | * |
| Polara Brougham 4-Door Hardtop | DM43 | $3,884 | +10.09% | 4035 | 2,570 | * |
| TOTALS | | Avg. price $3,679 | +6.98%* | | Production 90,876 | +49.79% |

*Comparisons made to 1970 models with same model numbers, not same nameplates. 3-seat wagon production kept with 2-Seat models.*

# Monaco

*"No matter how much you can afford
to spend on a car, spend it wisely."*

**Nameplate year of origin:** 1965.
**Current bodystyle lifespan:** 1969 through 1973.
**Predecessor to this model:** Monaco (1967 to 1968).
**Replacement for this model:** Royal Monaco (1974 to 1978).
**Percentage of division's sales volume:** 4.59%.
**Corporate siblings:** Chrysler Newport/300/New Yorker, and Plymouth Fury.
**Primary competition:** AMC Ambassador Brougham, Chevrolet Caprice, Ford LTD, Mercury Monterey, Oldsmobile Delta 88, and Pontiac Bonneville/Grand Ville.
**Notable changes:** Trim and detail changes.
**Major standard equipment:** Cloth and vinyl split back front bench seat with center armrest (4-Doors), all-vinyl seating (Wagon), simulated wood-grained door inserts and instrument panel, deep-pile color-keyed carpeting, rear door automatic dome light switch, full-length exterior bright moldings, trunk light, 2-speed concealed wipers, power front disc brakes (wagon), deluxe wheel covers, and H78 × 15 BSW tires (J78 × 15 BSW on 2-Seat Wagon and L84 × 15 BSW tires on 3-Seat Wagon).

## Measurements

|  | Cars | Wagons |
|---|---|---|
| Wheelbase | 122.0" | 122.0" |
| Length | 220.2" | 223.5" |
| Width | 79.3" | 79.2" |
| Height | 54.5" | 57.0" |
| Legroom — front | 41.8" | 41.8" |
| Legroom — rear | 39.1" | 39.1" |
| Headroom — front | 38.8" | 39.6" |
| Headroom — rear | 38.4" | 39.2" |
| Cargo capacity (cu. ft.) | 22.4 | 104.2 |
| Fuel capacity (gals.) | 23.0 | 23.0 |

## Models Available

|  | Style Number | Base MSRP | Change from LY | Shipping Wt. (lbs.) | Production | Change from LY |
|---|---|---|---|---|---|---|
| Monaco 2-Door Hardtop | DH23 | $4,298 | +16.83% | 4000 | 3,195 | -9.28% |
| Monaco 4-Door Sedan | DH41 | $4,223 | +17.18% | 4050 | 16,900 | +257.98% |
| Monaco 4-Door Hardtop | DH43 | $4,362 | +16.54% | 4080 | * | * |
| Monaco 4-Dr., 2-S. Wgn. | DH45 | $4,689 | +14.09% | 4525 | 5,449 | +146.45% |
| Monaco 4-Dr., 3-S. Wgn. | DH46 | $4,821 | +13.65% | 4585 | * | * |
| TOTALS | Avg. price | $4,479 | +15.56% | Production | 25,544 | +3.45% |

*Production totals in 1971 for 4-Door Sedan and 4-Door Hardtop models were combined, as well as for the 2-Seat and 3-Seat Wagons.*

# FORD

*"Ford has a better idea."*

For 1971 the heat was turned up in the battle for the number one sales ranking. Ford delivered the all-new subcompact Pinto and a restyled Mustang. And like the big Chevrolets, the full-size Fords were all-new for 1971. As these were typically each division's top selling models, a lot was at stake when a company revamped these models — particularly since neither company knew what the competition had up its sleeve. At Ford, this meant taking a somewhat conservative approach in styling their new models. The look was definitely a continuation of the previous 2 or 3 years' styling. A full-width grille up front, lightly sculpted body sides, and now-traditional Ford square taillights at the back. Rooflines were more formal, giving even the base models a richer look. Interior trims also received upgrades. Full-size 2-Door SportsRoof models were dropped in the restyle, leaving only the Formal 2-Door Hardtops. Also, the sporty XL disappeared, with its convertible model moving to the LTD line.

Ford's other big news was the introduction of the Pinto. Following the successful introduction of the Maverick 18 months earlier, Ford took a more conventional approach to the Pinto than Chevy did with the Vega. From the front, the Pinto looked very much like a Maverick. The big difference in appearance was at the rear, where the Pinto featured a sloping rear glass with either a hatchback or a small trunk opening, depending on the model you chose. Ford wisely chose two existing powerplants to power the Pinto, although neither originated in the United States. The base 1.6 liter 4-cylinder was a British designed engine that was a great fuel miser, but not powerful enough for the somewhat bulky Pinto. A much stronger engine choice was the 2.0 liter, German-built 4-cylinder engine. This larger engine could also be mated with Cruise-O-Matic transmission, which was a popular choice.

Also making news this year was an all-new Mustang. Visually the new Mustang resembled its predecessors, but this was a larger, heavier, car than earlier versions. All familiar Mustang styling cues were left intact. Features added included a thinner roofline, concealed wipers, flush-mounted door handles, and a longer hood. Missing from the option list were two high-performance engine choices, the Boss 302 and the Boss 429. With demand for these muscle cars waning, it wasn't in Ford's best interest to keep them in production. The Boss 351 was a new model that took the place of the Boss 302 and 429. It was easily recognizable by the unique grille and black (or silver) hood treatment and body side stripes.

Changes for other models were mainly trim and detail revisions, although there was quite a bit of nameplate shuffling. The one other new body style was a 4-Door Sedan version of the Maverick. With a wheelbase stretched six-inches over the coupes, the new 4-Door provided additional interior space and a better ride. There was also a new sporty variant for the 2-Door called the Grabber. It was distinguished by body stripes, hood scoops, and a newly available (optional) 302 CID V8 engine. The mid-size Torino line received minor trim changes, but did a lot of model shuffling. The Torino-based 1970½ Falcon was dropped. The Fairlane 500 was renamed Torino, and the Torino line became known as the Torino 500. Finally, the top-of-the-line Thunderbird received a redesigned front bumper and other trim changes. This would be the last year for the 4-Door Thunderbird.

LTD Brougham 2-Door Hardtop

LTD Country Squire 4-Door Wagon

Maverick Grabber 2-Door Sedan

Mustang 2-Door Convertible

Pinto 2-Door Sedan

Thunderbird 2-Door Hardtop

Torino Brougham Interior and Torino Brougham 4-Door Hardtop

Torino Squire 4-Door Wagon

1971

**Model year production:** 2,054,301, up 4.17% over 1970.
**Domestic market share:** 26.24% (1st place).
**Base price range:** $1,919 to $5,516.
**Industry average base price:** $3,786.
**Ford average base price:** $3,503.
**Introduction date:** September 18, 1970. Pinto, September 11, 1970.
**Assembly plants:** Atlanta, GA (A); Chicago, IL (G); Dearborn, MI (F); Kansas City, MO (K); Lorain, OH (H); Los Angeles, CA (J); Louisville, KY (U); Mahwah, NJ (E); Metuchen, NJ (T); Norfolk, VA (N); San Jose, CA (R); Twin Cities, MN (P); Wayne, MI (W); Wixom, MI (Y); St. Thomas, Ontario, Can. (X); Oakville, Ontario, Can. (B).
**Data plate identification:** Eleven digit code read as follows: 1 for 1971; 2nd digit is assembly plant code; 2-digit model number (see listings below); 5th digit is engine code; 100001 and up for serial number. *Example:* 1Y87N100001 is a 1971 Ford Thunderbird 2-Door Hardtop with a 429 CID V8 engine, serial number 100001, built in Wixom, MI.

# Powertrains

| Engine | Gross HP | Engine Code | Transmission Availability | Pinto & Maverick | Mustang | Torino | Full-size | T-Bird |
|---|---|---|---|---|---|---|---|---|
| 98 CID (1600cc), 1-bbl., 4-cyl. | 75 | na | 4-speed manual SelectShift | S (Pinto) | - | - | - | - |
| | | | Cruise-O-Matic | - | - | - | - | - |
| 122 CID (2000cc), 2-bbl., 4-cyl. | 100 | X | 4-speed manual | $50 (Pinto) | - | - | - | - |
| | | | SelectShift Cruise-O-Matic | $225 (Pinto) | - | - | - | - |
| 170 CID, 1-bbl., 6-cyl. | 100 | U | 3-speed manual SelectShift | S | - | - | - | - |
| | | | Cruise-O-Matic | $183 | - | - | - | - |
| 200 CID, 1-bbl., 6-cyl. | 115 | T | 3-speed manual SelectShift | $39 | - | - | - | - |
| | | | Cruise-O-Matic | $222 | - | - | - | - |
| 240 CID, 1-bbl., 6-cyl. | 140 | V | 3-speed manual SelectShift | - | - | - | S*** | - |
| | | | Cruise-O-Matic | - | - | - | $217*** | - |
| 250 CID, 1-bbl., 6-cyl. | 145 | L | 3-speed manual SelectShift | $79 | S* | S (Base) | - | - |
| | | | Cruise-O-Matic | $262 | $217* | $217 (Base) | - | - |
| 302 CID, 2-bbl., V8 | 210 | F | 3-speed manual | $160 | S (Mach I)/ $95 (Other) | S (Br./GT) $95 (Base) | $75 (Custom/ 500 Sdn.) | - |
| | | | 4-speed manual | - | $216 (Mach I)/ $311 (Other) | $250 (Br./GT)/ $345 (Base) | - | - |
| | | | SelectShift Cruise-O-Matic | $343 | $217 (Mach I)/ $312 (Other) | $217 ( Br./GT)/ $312 (Base) | $292 (Custom/ 500 Sdns.) | - |
| 351 CID — Windsor, 2-bbl., V8 | 240 | H | SelectShift Cruise-O-Matic | - | $283 (Mach I)/ $382 (Other) | $262 (Br./GT)/ $357 (Base) | | - |
| 351 CID Cleveland, 2-bbl., V8 | 240 | H | 3-speed manual | - | - | $45 (Br./GT)/ $140 (Base) | S (LTD/Wgns.) $121 (G. 500) | - |
| | | | 4-speed manual | - | - | $295 (Br./GT)/ $390 (Base) | - | - |
| | | | SelectShift Cruise-O-Matic | - | - | $262 (Br./GT)/ | | |

| Engine | Gross HP | Engine Code | Transmission Availability | Pinto & Maverick | Mustang | Torino | Full-size | T-Bird |
|---|---|---|---|---|---|---|---|---|
| | | | | | | $357 (Base) | $238 (LTD/Wgns.) $359 (G. 500) | - |
| 351 CID Cleveland, 4-bbl., V8 | 285 | M | 3-speed manual | - | $93 (Mach I)/ $188 (Other) | S (Cobra)/ $93 (Br./GT) | - | - |
| | | | 4-speed manual | - | $309 (Mach I)/ $404 (Other) | $250 (Cobra)/ $343 (Br./GT) | - | - |
| | | | SelectShift Cruise-O-Matic | - | $331 (Mach I)/ $426 (Other) | $238 (Cobra)/ $331 (Br./GT) | - | - |
| Boss 351 CID, 4-bbl., V8 | 330 | Q | 4-speed manual SelectShift Cruise-O-Matic | - | S (Boss) $238 (Boss) | - | - | - |
| 390 CID, 2-bbl., V8 | 255 | Y | SelectShift Cruise-O-Matic | - | - | - | $336 (LTD/Wgns.) $457 (G. 500) | - |
| 400 CID Cleveland, 2-bbl., V8 | 260 | S | SelectShift Cruise-O-Matic | - | - | - | $336 (LTD/Wgns.) $457 (G. 500) | - |
| 429 CID Thunder Jet, 2-bbl., V8 | 320 | K | SelectShift Cruise-O-Matic | - | - | - | $406 (LTD/Wgns.) $527 (G. 500) | - |
| 429 CID Thunder Jet, 4-bbl., V8 | 360 | N | SelectShift Cruise-O-Matic | - | - | - | $506 (LTD/Wgns.) $627 (G. 500) | S |
| 429 CID Cobra Jet, 4-bbl., V8 | 370 | C | 4-speed manual | - | $588 (Mach I) | $529 (Cobra)/ $622 (Others**) | - | - |
| | | | SelectShift Cruise-O-Matic | - | $610 (Mach I) | $517 — Cobra/ $610 — Others** | - | - |
| 429 CID Super Cobra Jet, 4-bbl., V8 Ram-Air | 375 | J | | - | $ | $ | $ | - |

*Except Boss 351 and Mach I.    **Available special-order on select models only.    ***Except LTD and Wagons.

## Major Options

| | Pinto | Maverick | Mustang | Torino | Full-size | Thunderbird |
|---|---|---|---|---|---|---|
| Air conditioning | $363 | $363 | $368 | $402 | $487 | $506 |
| Electronic cruise control | - | - | - | - | $99 | $103 |
| Electric rear window defogger | - | - | $57 | $36 | $36 | $36 |
| Tinted glass | $36 | $36 | $36 | $48 | $53 | S |
| Power steering | - | $92 | $103 | $112 | S | S |
| Power brakes — front discs | - | - | $62 | $68 | $51 (S on LTD) | S |
| Power driver's seat/Bench seat | - | - | - | $102 | $102 | $101 |
| Power windows | - | - | $113 | $124 | $129 | $130 |
| AM radio | $59 | $59 | $59 | $64 | $64 | S |
| AM/FM stereo | - | - | $191 | $208 | $234 | $146 |
| Front seat console | - | - | $97 | $ | - | - |
| Front bucket seats | S | - | S | $ | - | - |
| Tilt steering wheel | - | - | $41 | - | $44 | $51 |

1971

| | Pinto | Maverick | Mustang | Torino | Full-size | Thunderbird |
|---|---|---|---|---|---|---|
| Sunroof (coupes only) | – | – | – | – | $500 | $505 |
| Vinyl roof | $75 | $74 | $80 | $93 | $110 ($148 Wagons) | $137 |
| White sidewall tires | $42 | $34 | $34 | $34 | $34 | $34 |
| Magnum 500 chrome wheels | – | – | $139 | $139 | – | – |
| Dual facing rear seats (wagons) | – | – | – | – | $114 | – |

Options common to most models. (– = Not Available; S = Standard equipment.) Items may be standard equipment, optional at different pricing, or unavailable on certain models. This chart is only a guide.

## Paint Colors*

| | Code | Thunderbird |
|---|---|---|
| Medium Bright Yellow | 2 | X |
| Bright Red, Pinto Red | 3 | |
| Medium Lime Metallic | 4 | |
| Medium Brown Metallic | 5 | X |
| Acapulco Blue Metallic | 6 | X |
| Maroon | 7 | X |
| Morning Gold | 8 | |
| Anti Establish Mint Met. (Maverick only) | 9 | |
| Walnut Fire Metallic | 39 | X |
| Raven Black/Model T Black | A | X |
| Maroon Metallic | B | X |
| Dark Green Metallic | C | |
| Burgundy Fire Metallic | C9 | X |
| Grabber Yellow/Pinto Yellow | D | |
| Blue Fire Metallic | D9 | X |
| Med. Yellow Gold/Pinto Gold | E | |
| Green Fire Metallic | E9 | X |
| Medium Blue Metallic | F | X |
| Dark Green Metallic | G | X |
| Light Green | H | X |
| Grabber Lime/Pinto Lime | I | |
| Grabber Blue/Pinto Blue | J | |
| Dark Gray Metallic | K | X |
| Wimbledon White | M | X |
| Pastel Blue | N | X |
| Light Yellow Gold | O | X |
| Medium Green Metallic | P | |
| Winter Blue Metallic | Q | X |
| Dark Brown Metallic | R | X |
| Gray Gold Metallic | S | X |
| Candy Apple Red | T | X |
| Light Pewter Metallic | V | X |
| Yellow | W | X |
| Dark Blue Metallic | X or Y | X |
| Grabber Green Metallic | Z | |

*All colors available on most models. Colors marked Grabber and Pinto are for those models only. Thunderbird available only in colors marked X.

# Pinto

*"Ford's new Pinto. The little long distance car."*

**Nameplate year of origin:** 1971.
**Current bodystyle lifespan:** 1971 through 1980.
**Predecessor to this model:** None.
**Replacement for this model:** Escort (1981 to 1985).
**Percentage of division's sales volume:** 17.15%.
**Corporate siblings:** None.
**Primary competition:** AMC Gremlin and Chevrolet Vega.
**Notable changes:** All-new model for 1971.
**Major standard equipment:** High back bucket seats with all-vinyl trim, glove box, interior dome light, rack-and-pinion steering, DirectAire ventilation system, and 6.00 × 13 BSW tires.

## Measurements

| | |
|---|---|
| Wheelbase | 94.0" |
| Length | 163.0" |
| Width | 69.4" |
| Height | 50.6" |
| Legroom — front | 40.2" |
| Legroom — rear | 30.3" |
| Headroom — front | 36.9" |
| Headroom — rear | 35.7" |
| Cargo capacity (cu. ft.) | 8.2 |
| Fuel capacity (gals.) | 13.0 |

## Models Available

| | Style Number | Base MSRP | Change from LY | Shipping Wt. (lbs.) | Production | Change from LY |
|---|---|---|---|---|---|---|
| Pinto 2-Door Sedan | 10 | $1,919 | NEW | 1949 | 288,606 | NEW |
| Pinto 3-Door Runabout | 11 | $2,062 | NEW | 1993 | 63,796 | NEW |
| TOTALS | | *Avg. price* $1,991 | NEW | *Production* | 352,402 | NEW |

# Maverick

*"No changes in the simple machine ... except for a couple of extra doors ... and a little more jazz."*

**Nameplate year of origin:** 1969.
**Current bodystyle lifespan:** 1969 through 1977.
**Predecessor to this model:** Falcon (1966 to 1970).
**Replacement for this model:** Fairmont (1978 to 1983).
**Percentage of division's sales volume:** 13.24%.
**Corporate siblings:** Mercury Comet.
**Primary competition:** AMC Hornet, Chevrolet Nova, Plymouth Valiant, and Pontiac Ventura II.
**Notable changes:** Detail changes, and 4-Door Sedan model added.
**Major standard equipment:** All-vinyl interior trim, glove box, DirectAire ventilation, interior light, and 6.45 × 14 BSW tires. Grabber adds: Dual outside color-keyed racing mirrors, Grabber stripes, Rallye road lights, wheel trim rings, and blacked-out hood and cowl treatment.

## Measurements

| | 2-Door | 4-Door |
|---|---|---|
| Wheelbase | 103.0" | 109.9" |
| Length | 179.4" | 186.4" |
| Width | 71.0" | 71.0" |
| Height | 52.3" | 53.1" |
| Legroom — front | 41.3" | 41.3" |
| Legroom — rear | 31.9" | 36.4" |
| Headroom — front | 37.6" | 37.6" |
| Headroom — rear | 36.1" | 37.1" |
| Cargo capacity (cu. ft.) | 10.4 | 10.4 |
| Fuel capacity (gals.) | 16.0 | 16.0 |

1971

## Models Available

| | Style Number | Base MSRP | Change from LY | Shipping Wt. (lbs.) | Production | Change from LY |
|---|---|---|---|---|---|---|
| Maverick 2-Door Sedan | 91 | $2,175 | +9.02% | 2508 | 159,726 | -64.59% |
| Maverick 4-Door Sedan | 92 | $2,235 | NEW | 2603 | 73,208 | NEW |
| Maverick Grabber 2-Door Sedan | 93 | $2,354 | NEW | 2563 | 38,963 | NEW |
| TOTALS | | *Avg. price* $2,255 | +13.03% | *Production* | 271,897 | -39.73% |

# Mustang

*"America's challenge to the great European road cars."*

**Nameplate year of origin:** 1964½ (also, on a 1963 show car).
**Current bodystyle lifespan:** 1971 through 1973.
**Predecessor to this model:** Mustang (1969 to 1970).
**Replacement for this model:** Mustang II (1974 to 1978).
**Percentage of division's sales volume:** 7.28%.
**Corporate siblings:** Mercury Cougar (Stretched platform).
**Primary competition:** AMC Javelin, Chevrolet Camaro, Dodge Challenger, Plymouth Barracuda, and Pontiac Firebird.
**Notable changes:** Completely redesigned.
**Major standard equipment:** High-back bucket seats, full carpeting, courtesy lights, deluxe two-spoke steering wheel, DirectAire ventilation, concealed windshield wipers, bright moldings (rocker, wheel lip, and lower back panel), dual color-keyed outside racing mirrors, wheel covers, and E78 × 14 BSW tires. SportsRoof adds: Fixed rear quarter windows and tinted rear glass. Convertible adds: Power operated top, color-keyed top boot, tinted front and rear glass, knitted vinyl seat upholstery. Grande adds: Vinyl top with script, trunk mat, Cloth and vinyl interior trim, deluxe instrument panel covering and wood-tone instrument panel applique. Mach I adds: Competition suspension, front integral spoiler, color-keyed hood and fender moldings, black grille with sports lamps, NACA-type hood (only with base engine), tape stripes and Mach I decals, wheel trim rings and E70 × 14 WSW tires. Boss 351 adds: 302 CID 4-bbl. V8, 4-speed manual transmission, rear deck spoiler, louvered rear windows, "Mag"-style wheels, and F60 × 15 Wide-Oval tires.

## Measurements

| | |
|---|---|
| Wheelbase | 109.0" |
| Length | 190.0" |
| Width | 75.0" |
| Height | NA |
| Legroom — front | NA |
| Legroom — rear | NA |
| Headroom — front | NA |
| Headroom — rear | NA |
| Cargo capacity (cu. ft.) | NA |
| Fuel capacity (gals.) | NA |

## Models Available

| | Style Number | Base MSRP | Change from LY | Shipping Wt. (lbs.) | Production | Change from LY |
|---|---|---|---|---|---|---|
| Mustang 2-Door Hardtop | 1 | $2,911 | +6.98% | 2913 | 65,696 | -20.44% |
| Mustang 2-Door SportsRoof HT | 2 | $2,973 | +7.29% | 2883 | 23,956 | -47.85% |
| Mustang 2-Door Convertible | 3 | $3,227 | +6.68% | 3035 | 6,121 | -20.23% |
| Mustang Grande 2-Door Hardtop | 4 | $3,117 | +6.53% | 2939 | 17,406 | +28.16% |
| Mustang Mach I 2-Dr. SportsRoof | 5 | $3,268 | -0.09% | 3019 | 36,449 | -11.03% |
| Mustang Boss 351 2-Dr. Sptrf. | 2 | $4,124 | NEW | 3239 | * | NEW |
| TOTALS | *Avg. price* | $3,270 | +6.45% | *Production* | 149,628 | -24.06% |

# Torino

*"The Ford that gives you better ideas ... for less."*

**Nameplate year of origin:** 1968.
**Current bodystyle lifespan:** 1970 through 1971.
**Predecessor to this model:** Fairlane/Torino (1968 to 1969).
**Replacement for this model:** Torino (1972 to 1976).
**Percentage of division's sales volume:** 15.89%.
**Corporate siblings:** Mercury Montego.
**Primary competition:** AMC Matador, Chevrolet Chevelle, Plymouth Satellite, Dodge Charger/Coronet.
**Notable changes:** Trim and detail changes.
**Major standard equipment:** Cloth and vinyl bench seat, full carpeting, deluxe interior trim, chrome rear and side window moldings, and E78 × 14 BSW tires

## Measurements

| | Cars | Wagons |
|---|---|---|
| Wheelbase | 117.0" | 114.0" |
| Length | 206.2" | 209.0" |
| Width | 76.4" | 75.4" |
| Height | NA | NA |
| Legroom — front | 42.2" | 42.1" |
| Legroom — rear | 36.0" | 36.0" |
| Headroom — front | 38.5" | 38.6" |
| Headroom — rear | 37.3" | 37.4" |

(G78 × 14 BSW on Wagons). Torino 500 adds: Deluxe interior trim, accent tape stripe on Hardtop and Sedan, and full wheel covers. Torino Brougham adds: Luxury interior trim, concealed headlamps, additional exterior trim, electric clock and 302 CID V8 engine. Torino Squire adds: Exterior wood-grain trim. Torino GT adds: All-vinyl front bench seat, styled steel wheels, hood scoop, and E70 × 14 Wide-Oval WSW tires (F70 × 14 on Convertible). Cobra adds: 351 CID V8 engine, 4-speed manual transmission, heavy-duty suspension, dual exhausts, and F70 × 14 Wide-Oval tires.

|  | Cars | Wagons |
|---|---|---|
| Cargo capacity (cu. ft.) | NA | NA |
| Fuel capacity (gals.) | 20.0 | 20.0 |

## Models Available

| | Style Number | Base MSRP | Change from LY | Shipping Wt. (lbs.) | Production | Change from LY |
|---|---|---|---|---|---|---|
| Torino 2-Door Hardtop | 25 | $2,706 | +1.73% | 3128 | 37,518 | -46.89% |
| Torino 4-Door Sedan | 27 | $2,672 | +1.71% | 3123 | 29,501 | +14.43% |
| Torino 4-Door, 2-Seat Wagon | 40 | $3,023 | +2.23% | 3474 | 21,570 | +58.45% |
| Torino 500 2-Door Hardtop | 30 | $2,887 | +6.06% | 3130 | 89,966 | +80.56% |
| Torino 500 2-Dr. SportsRoof HT | 34 | $2,943 | +4.73% | 3139 | 11,150 | -10.73% |
| Torino 500 4-Door Sedan | 31 | $2,855 | +6.17% | 3120 | 35,650 | +18.37% |
| Torino 500 4-Door Hardtop | 32 | $2,959 | +5.87% | 3156 | 12,724 | -11.10% |
| Torino 500 4-Dr., 2-Seat Wagon | 42 | $3,170 | +3.12% | 3474 | 23,270 | +119.26% |
| Torino Brougham 2-Door Hardtop | 33 | $3,175 | +5.62% | 3209 | 8,593 | -49.19% |
| Torino Brougham 4-Door Hardtop | 36 | $3,248 | +5.52% | 3256 | 4,408 | -69.69% |
| Torino Squire 4-Dr., 2-Seat Wagon | 43 | $3,560 | +5.36% | 3583 | 15,805 | +20.04% |
| Torino GT 2-Door SportsRoof HT | 35 | $3,150 | +1.45% | 3287 | 31,641 | -44.31% |
| Torino GT 2-Door Convertible | 37 | $3,408 | +6.10% | 3428 | 1,613 | -59.05% |
| Torino Cobra 2-Dr. SportsRoof HT | 38 | $3,295 | +0.76% | 3525 | 3,054 | -60.21% |
| TOTALS | Avg. price | $3,075 | +6.36% | | Production 326,463 | -19.89% |

# Custom, Galaxie & LTD

*"Only a superbly crafted car can be so quiet."*

**Nameplate year of origin:** 1957 (Custom), 1959 (Galaxie) and 1965 (LTD).
**Current bodystyle lifespan:** 1971 through 1978 (Restyles in 1973 and 1975).
**Predecessor to this model:** Full-size Ford (1969 to 1970).
**Replacement for this model:** LTD (1979 to 1991).
**Percentage of division's sales volume:** 44.68%.
**Corporate siblings:** Mercury Monterey and Marquis.
**Primary competition:** AMC Ambassador, Chevrolet Biscayne/BelAir/Impala/Caprice, Dodge Polara/Monaco, Plymouth Fury, and Pontiac Catalina.
**Notable changes:** Completely restyled.
**Major standard equipment:** All vinyl interior trim, nylon carpeting, bright front and rear window moldings, and F78 × 15 BSW tires. Custom 500 adds: Cloth and vinyl interior trim, bright moldings (wheel lip and rear lower panel), power tailgate window (Ranch Wagon) and H78 × 15 BSW tires (Ranch Wagon). Galaxie 500 adds: Upgraded interior trim, wood-grain instrument panel trim, bright moldings (wheel lip, deck lid and rocker panels). LTD adds: Luxury interior trim, electric clock, front door courtesy lights, lower bodyside trim, full wheel covers, and G78 × 15 tires. Country Squire adds: Wood grained bodyside appliques, and H78 × 15 BSW tires. LTD Brougham adds: Unique Brougham interior trim with Flight Bench seats, rear door courtesy lights, cutpile carpeting, front and rear armrests, rocker panel moldings, and G78 × 15 BSW tires.

## Measurements

| | Cars | Wagons |
|---|---|---|
| Wheelbase | 121.0" | 121.0" |
| Length | 216.2" | 219.2" |
| Width | 79.2" | 79.2" |
| Height | 53.6" | 57.0" |
| Legroom — front | NA | NA |
| Legroom — rear | NA | NA |
| Headroom — front | NA | NA |
| Headroom — rear | NA | NA |
| Cargo capacity (cu. ft.) | 18.0 | 96.2 |
| Fuel capacity (gals.) | 23.0 | 22.0 |

**1971**

## Models Available

| | Style Number | Base MSRP | Change from LY | Shipping Wt. (lbs.) | Production | Change from LY |
|---|---|---|---|---|---|---|
| Custom 4-Door Sedan | 51 | $3,288 | +18.66% | 3675 | 41,062 | -4.17% |
| Custom 4-Door Ranch Wagon | 70 | $3,890 | +17.70% | 4222 | 16,696 | +10.67% |
| Custom 500 4-Door Sedan | 53 | $3,426 | +19.29% | 3680 | 33,765 | -18.17% |
| Custom 500 4-Dr. Ranch Wagon | 72 | $3,982 | +18.23% | 4231 | 25,957 | +69.61% |
| C. 500 4-Dr. Ranch Wgn. w/DFRS* | 72 | $4,097 | +17.70% | 4281 | | |
| Galaxie 500 2-Door Hardtop | 58 | $3,628 | +17.26% | 3715 | 117,139 | +105.29% |
| Galaxie 500 4-Door Sedan | 54 | $3,594 | +18.77% | 3715 | 98,130 | -3.59% |
| Galaxie 500 4-Door Hardtop | 56 | $3,665 | +18.38% | 3770 | 46,595 | -13.42% |
| G. 500 Country Sedan 4-Dr. Wagon | 74 | $4,074 | +16.80% | 4246 | 60,487 | +87.80% |
| G. 500 Country Sdn. 4-Dr. w/DFRS* | 74 | $4,188 | +16.33% | 4296 | | |
| LTD 2-Door Hardtop | 62 | $3,923 | +19.13% | 3919 | 103,896 | +281.26% |
| LTD 2-Door Convertible | 61 | $4,094 | NEW | 4053 | 5,750 | NEW |
| LTD 4-Door Sedan | 63 | $3,931 | +18.87% | 3981 | 92,260 | +17.82% |
| LTD 4-Door Hardtop | 64 | $3,969 | +17.25% | 3976 | 48,166 | -46.71% |
| LTD Country Squire 4-Dr. Wagon | 76 | $4,380 | +14.30% | 4306 | 130,644 | +227.95% |
| LTD Cntry. Sq. 4-Dr. Wgn. w/DFRS* | 76 | $4,496 | +15.02% | 4356 | | |
| LTD Brougham 2-Door Hardtop | 68 | $4,097 | +15.83% | 3945 | 43,303 | |
| LTD Brougham 4-Door Sedan | 66 | $4,094 | +16.90% | 4111 | 26,186 | |
| LTD Brougham 4-Door Hardtop | 67 | $4,140 | +15.67% | 4006 | 27,820 | |
| TOTALS | Avg. price | $3,945 | +17.76% | | Production 917,856 | +7.94% |

*Dual facing rear seats

# Thunderbird

*"Thunderbird people have one thing in common. They're uncommon."*

**Nameplate year of origin:** 1955.
**Current bodystyle lifespan:** 1967 through 1971 (restyled in 1970).
**Predecessor to this model:** Thunderbird (1964 to 1966).
**Replacement for this model:** Thunderbird (1972 to 1976).
**Percentage of division's sales volume:** 1.76%.
**Corporate siblings:** Lincoln Continental Mark III.
**Primary competition:** Buick Riviera and Oldsmobile Toronado.
**Notable changes:** Trim and detail changes.
**Major standard equipment:** Luxury all-cloth interior with cut-pile carpeting, front bench seat, tilt away steering wheel, AM radio, power steering, power front disc brakes, sequential turn signals, full wheel covers, and 215R15 Michelin BSW tires.

## Measurements

| | 2-Door | 4-Door |
|---|---|---|
| Wheelbase | 115.0" | 117.0" |
| Length | 212.5" | 215.0" |
| Width | 78.0" | 77.4" |
| Height | 53.5" | 54.2" |
| Legroom — front | 42.1" | 42.1" |
| Legroom — rear | 32.2" | 34.0" |
| Headroom — front | 37.4" | 38.1" |
| Headroom — rear | 36.9" | 37.2" |
| Cargo capacity (cu. ft.) | 12.3 | 12.3 |
| Fuel capacity (gals.) | 24.1 | 24.1 |

## Models Available

| | Style Number | Base MSRP | Change from LY | Shipping Wt. (lbs.) | Production | Change from LY |
|---|---|---|---|---|---|---|
| Thunderbird 2-Door Hardtop | 83 | $5,295 | +6.73% | 4389 | 9,146 | +78.77% |
| Thunderbird 2-Dr. Landau Coupe | 84 | $5,438 | +6.54% | 4360 | 20,356 | -44.76% |
| Thunderbird 4-Door Landau Sedan | 87 | $5,516 | +6.45% | 4496 | 6,553 | -22.00% |
| TOTALS | Avg. price | $5,416 | +6.57% | | Production 36,055 | -28.41% |

# LINCOLN

*"The Continentals for 1971: the final step up."*

The Lincoln Motorcar Division marked its Fiftieth Anniversary this year. Unfortunately, Lincoln did not mark the occasion with any special product offerings, other than an available Anniversary Gold paint scheme. Probably the biggest news was the addition of many new standard features, albeit at a $1200 increase to the bottom line. The main addition was an Automatic Temperature Control air conditioning system. The good looking and popular Mark III was entering its final year of production. The basic styling features remained the same as on the original 1969 model. The Continental had been totally redesigned for 1970, so the new model year brought minimal changes.

Continental 4-Door Sedan

Continental Mark III 2-Door Hardtop

**Model year production:** 62,642, up 17.91% from 1970.
**Domestic market share:** 0.80% (12th place).
**Base price range:** $7,172 to $8,813.
**Industry average base price:** $3,786.
**Lincoln average base price:** $7,801.
**Introduction date:** September 18, 1970.
**Assembly plants:** Wixom, MI (Y), and Allen Park, MI (S).

**Data plate identification:** Eleven digit code read as follows: 1 for 1971; 2nd digit is assembly plant code; 2-digit model number (see listings below); 5th digit is engine code; 800001 and up for serial number. *Example:* 1Y82A800001 is a 1971 Lincoln Continental 4-Door Sedan with a 460 CID V8 engine, serial number 800001, built in Wixom, MI.

## Powertrains

| Engine | Gross HP | Engine Code | Transmission Availability | Mark III & Continental |
|---|---|---|---|---|
| 460 CID, 4-bbl., V8 | 365 | A | Select-Shift Automatic | S |

## Major Options

| | Continental | Mark III |
|---|---|---|
| Sure Track brake system | $197 | S |
| Automatic headlight dimmers | $51 | $51 |
| 6-way power seat | $92 | $184 |
| Power door locks | $106 | $50 |
| AM-FM stereo radio | $307 | $307 |
| AM w/stereo 8-track | $301 | $301 |
| Vinyl roof | $156 | S |
| Sunroof | – | $460 |
| Tilt and telescope steering wheel | $70 | $70 |
| Leather upholstery | $169 | $179 |

## Paint Colors

| | Code |
|---|---|
| Tan | 2 |
| Medium Brown Metallic | 5 |
| Bright Blue Metallic | 6 |
| Maroon | 7 |
| Ginger Bronze Moondust Met. | 39 |
| Black | A |
| Maroon | B |
| Red Moondust Metallic | C-9 |
| Blue Moondust Metallic | D-9 |
| Ivory Bronze Moondust Met. | E-9 |

1971

|  | Continental | Mark III |
|---|---|---|
| Cruise control | $92 | $92 |
| Rear window defogger | $85 | $85 |
| Remote control trunk release | $46 | $46 |
| Moondust Metallic paint colors | $128 | $128 |
| Town Car package | $447* |  |
| Town Car package with Leather | $635* |  |

| Color | Code |
|---|---|
| Bright Aqua Metallic | F |
| Dark Green | G |
| Light Green | H |
| Anniversary Gold Metallic | J-9 |
| Dark Gray Metallic | K |
| Light Gray Metallic | L |
| White | M |
| Pastel Blue | N |
| Light Yellow Gold | O |
| Medium Blue Metallic | Q |
| Dark Brown Metallic | R |
| Gray Gold Metallic | S |
| Red | T |
| Light Pewter Metallic | V |
| Yellow | W |
| Dark Blue Metallic | X or Y |

Options common to most models. (- = Not Available; S = Standard equipment.) Items may be standard equipment, optional at different pricing, or unavailable on certain models. This chart is only a guide.

*4-Door only

# Continental

*"A graceful blending of contemporary and classic."*

**Nameplate year of origin:** 1940 (1961 as a standard sedan nameplate).
**Current bodystyle lifespan:** 1970 through 1979 (restyle in 1974).
**Predecessor to this model:** Continental (1961 to 1969).
**Replacement for this model:** Town Car (1980 to 1991).
**Percentage of division's sales volume:** 56.75%.
**Corporate siblings:** None.
**Primary competition:** Cadillac de Ville and Imperial LeBaron.
**Notable changes:** Revised grille and trim and detail changes.
**Major standard equipment:** Two-way power front bench seat, front and rear seat armrests, cut-pile carpeting, automatic temperature control air conditioner, electric clock, carpeted luggage compartment, lefthand remote control outside mirror, tinted glass, visor vanity mirror, AM radio with power antenna, power windows, fender skirts, and 225-15 Michelin radial WSW tires.

## Measurements

| | |
|---|---|
| Wheelbase | 127.0" |
| Length | 225.1" |
| Width | 79.6" |
| Height | 55.5" |
| Legroom — front | 41.9" |
| Legroom — rear | 41.9" |
| Headroom — front | 38.8" |
| Headroom — rear | 38.1" |
| Luggage capacity (cu. ft.) | 18.1 |
| Fuel capacity (gals.) | 23.0 |

## Models Available

| | Style Number | Base MSRP | Change from LY | Shipping Wt. (lbs.) | Production | Change from LY |
|---|---|---|---|---|---|---|
| Continental 2-Door Hardtop | 81 | $7,172 | +20.01% | 5032 | 8,205 | +167.00% |
| Continental 4-Door Sedan | 82 | $7,419 | +19.45% | 5072 | 27,346 | -4.46% |
| TOTALS |  | *Avg. price* $7,296 | +19.72% |  | *Production* 35,551 | +12.17% |

# Continental Mark III

*"This is the single most distinctive car in America."*

**Nameplate year of origin:** 1956 (Continental Mark II).
**Current bodystyle lifespan:** 1969 through 1971.
**Predecessor to this model:** Continental Mark II (1956 to 1957).
**Replacement for this model:** Continental Mark IV (1972 to 1976).

## Measurements

| | |
|---|---|
| Wheelbase | 117.2" |
| Length | 216.1" |
| Width | 79.4" |

**Percentage of division's sales volume:** 43.25%.
**Corporate siblings:** Ford Thunderbird.
**Primary competition:** Buick Riviera, Cadillac Eldorado, and Oldsmobile Toronado.
**Notable changes:** Minor trim and detail changes.
**Major standard equipment:** Power cloth and vinyl front split bench seat, automatic seat back release, cut-pile carpeting, power windows, air conditioning, vinyl top, Sure Track power brake system, spare tire cover, carpeted luggage compartment, luxury wheel covers, Cartier electric clock, AM radio with power antenna, and 225-15 Michelin WSW tires.

### Measurements (cont.)

| | |
|---|---|
| Height | 53.0" |
| Legroom — front | 41.5" |
| Legroom — rear | 34.7" |
| Headroom — front | 37.1" |
| Headroom — rear | 36.5" |
| Luggage capacity (cu. ft.) | 13.5 |
| Fuel capacity (gals.) | 23.0 |

### Models Available

| | Style Number | Base MSRP | Change from LY | Shipping Wt. (lbs.) | Production | Change from LY |
|---|---|---|---|---|---|---|
| Continental Mark III 2-Door Hardtop | 89 | $8,813 | +21.04% | 5003 | 27,091 | +26.40% |
| TOTALS | *Avg. price* | $8,813 | +21.04% | *Production* | 27,091 | +26.40% |

# MERCURY

*"Better ideas make better cars."*

Nearly every Mercury line was revised at the sign of the cat this year. Mercury had a restyled Cougar, all-new full-size cars, and the return of the Comet nameplate. This time around, the Comet was once again returned to its status as an upscale Ford compact. In 1960, it was based on the Falcon. For 1971, it was based on the Falcon's replacement, the Maverick. "Based upon the Maverick" doesn't exactly describe the Comet however. A Maverick with a grille that had a protruding center section, and four pod taillamps, would be a more exact description. Other than those two distinguishing items, there was little difference between the two cars, save upholstery and detail items.

Full-size Mercury models were totally redesigned this year, and more like a Lincoln than ever. From the full-width wrap-around grille to the nearly full-width taillights, the big Mercury looked, drove and felt like a Lincoln.

Model choices remained the same as before with two exceptions: The sporty Marauder was gone, and all of the convertible models were dropped.

The Cougar became more of a personal-luxury car this year, adding some bulk in the process. The Cougar's physical size did not change much, but it looked larger because of more slab-sided styling and a semi-fastback roofline that blended into the rear quarter panels on 2-Door Hardtop models. Up front, the new Cougar sported a center, vertical bar grille which protruded from a recessed headlamp area. This new frontal styling foreshadowed the 1972 Montego look. Interiors were more luxurious looking this year as well. The two Cougar convertibles were the only remaining Mercury Convertibles. Mid-size Montego models were visually unchanged, other than a more subdued, eggcrate-style protruding grille.

**1971**

Comet GT 2-Door Sedan

Cougar XR-7 2-Door Hardtop

Cyclone 2-Door Hardtop

Marquis Brougham 4-Door Sedan

Monterey Custom 2-Door Hardtop

Montego MX Brougham 4-Door Hardtop

**Model year production:** 365,310, up 7.18% from 1970.
**Domestic market share:** 4.67% (8th place).
**Base price range:** $2,387 to $5,033.
**Industry average price:** $3,786.
**Mercury average price:** $3,780.
**Introduction date:** September 18, 1970.
**Assembly plants:** Dearborn, MI (F); Lorain, OH (H); Kansas City, MO (K); Allen Park, MI (S); St. Louis, MO (Z); and Oakville, Ontario, Canada (B).

**Data plate identification:** Eleven digit code read as follows: 1 for 1971; 2nd digit is assembly plant code; 2-digit model number (see listings below); 5th digit is engine code; 500001 and up for serial number. *Example:* 1Z01H500001 is a 1971 Mercury Montego 2-Door Hardtop with a 351 CID V8 engine, serial number 500001, built in St. Louis, MO.

## Powertrains

| Engine | Gross HP | Engine Code | Transmission Availability | Comet | Cougar | Montego | Marquis & Monterey |
|---|---|---|---|---|---|---|---|
| 170 CID, 1-bbl., 6-cyl. | 100 | U | 3-speed manual | S | - | - | - |
| | | | SelectShift Automatic | $183 | - | - | - |
| 200 CID, 1-bbl., 6-cyl. | 115 | T | 3-speed manual | $38 | - | - | - |
| | | | SelectShift Automatic | $221 | - | - | - |
| 200 CID, 2-bbl., 6-cyl. | 155 | T | 3-speed manual | $ | - | - | - |
| | | | SelectShift Automatic | $ | - | - | - |
| 250 CID, 1-bbl., 6-cyl. | 145 | L | 3-speed manual | - | - | S | - |
| | | | SelectShift Automatic | - | - | $218 | - |
| 302 CID, 2-bbl., V8 | 210 | F | 3-speed manual | $160 | - | $95 | - |
| | | | SelectShift Automatic | $343 | - | $312 | - |
| 351 CID, 2-bbl., V8 | 240 | H | 3-speed manual | - | S | $140 | S (Base) |
| | | | 4-speed manual | - | $250 | $390 | - |
| | | | SelectShift Automatic | - | $217 | S (Cycl. GT)/$358 (Others) | $238 (Base) |
| 351 CID, 4-bbl., V8 | 285 | M | 4-speed manual | - | $ | S (Cycl. & Spoiler) | - |
| | | | SelectShift Automatic | - | $ | $238 (Cyclone & Spoiler) | - |
| 400 CID, 2-bbl., V8 | 260 | S | SelectShift Automatic | - | - | - | S (Custom)/$336 (Base) |
| 429 CID, 2-bbl., V8 | 320 | N | SelectShift Automatic | - | - | - | S (Marquis)/$406 (Others) |
| 429 CID, 4-bbl., V8 | 360 | | SelectShift Automatic | - | - | - | $100 (Marquis)/$506 (Others) |
| 429 CID Cobra Jet, 4-bbl., V8 | 370 | | 4-speed manual | - | $ | $529 (Cycl. & Spoiler) | - |
| | | | SelectShift Automatic | - | $ | $517 (Cycl. & Spoiler) | $ (Marquis)/$ (Others) |

## Major Options

| | Comet | Cougar | Montego | Monterey | Marquis |
|---|---|---|---|---|---|
| Air conditioning | $371 | $408 | $408 | $442 | $442 |
| Electronic cruise control | - | - | - | $69 | $69 |
| Electric rear window defogger | $29 | $48 | $48 | $64 | $64 |
| Tinted glass | $37 | $16–$38 | $43 | $52 | S |
| Deck lid remote release | - | - | - | $14 | $14 |

| | Comet | Cougar | Montego | Monterey | Marquis |
|---|---|---|---|---|---|
| Power steering | $115 | $115 | $115 | $126 | S |
| Power brakes — front discs | - | $70 | $70 | $72 | S |
| Power door locks | - | - | - | $45–$69 | $45–$69 |
| Power driver's seat/Bench seat | - | $78 | $78 | $105 | $105 |
| Power windows | - | $115 | $115 | $132 | $132 |
| AM radio | $61 | $66 | $66 | $66 | $66 |
| AM/FM stereo | - | $219 | $219 | $240 | $240 |
| Front seat console | $42 | $77 | $61 | - | - |
| Front bucket seats | $72 | S | $132 | - | - |
| Third seat (DFRS*) for Wagons | - | - | $80 | $129 | $129 |
| Tilt steering wheel | - | - | - | $45 | $45 |
| Vinyl roof | $78 | $89 | $100 | $120 ($143 Wagons) | $128 |
| Styled steel wheels | - | $58 | - | - | - |
| Wire or luxury wheel covers | $24 | $84 | v$18 | $60 | S |
| Exterior Decor Groups (varied equipment) | $53 | $91 | $32 | $80 | $80 |
| Convenience Group (varied equipment) | $26 | $32–$48 | $48 | $23–$47 | $23–$47 |
| Cougar GT or Montego RamAir Super Cobra Jet 429 pkgs. | - | $130 | $65 | - | - |

Options common to most models. (- = Not Available; S = Standard equipment.) Items may be standard equipment, optional at different pricing, or unavailable on certain models. This chart is only a guide.

*Dual facing rear seats

## Paint Colors*

| | Code | | Code |
|---|---|---|---|
| Black | 1C | Light Gray Metallic | 1A |
| Blue Glamour Metallic | 3K | Light Green | 4S |
| Bright Blue Metallic | 3J | Light Pewter Metallic | 5A |
| Bright Green Gold Met. | 4B | Maroon | 2J |
| Bright Lime | 4E | Medium Blue Metallic | 3D |
| Bright Red | 2B | Medium Bright Yellow | 6E |
| Gold Glamour Metallic | 6F | Medium Brown Metallic | 5H |
| Dark Blue Metallic | 3H | Ginger Glamour Met. | 5J |
| Dark Green Metallic | 4Q | Medium Green Metallic | 4P |
| Competition Blue | 3F | Medium Lime Metallic | 4F |
| Gray Gold Metallic | 6J | Medium Yellow Gold | 6C |
| Ivy Glamour Metallic | 4C | Red | 2E |
| Light Blue | 3B | White | 9A |
| Light Goldenrod | 6B | Yellow | 6D |

*All colors available on most models. Some may be at additional cost.

# Comet

*"How do you make a better small car? Mercury's got the answer."*

**Nameplate year of origin:** 1960.
**Current bodystyle lifespan:** 1970 through 1977.
**Predecessor to this model:** Comet (1960 to 1965).
**Replacement for this model:** Zephyr (1978 to 1983).
**Percentage of division's sales volume:** 22.72%.
**Corporate siblings:** Ford Maverick.
**Primary competition:** AMC Hornet, Chevrolet Nova, Dodge Dart, and Pontiac Ventura II.
**Notable changes:** All-new model for 1971.
**Major standard equipment:** Vinyl and check cloth interior trim, full carpeting, door-operated courtesy lights, deluxe 2-spoke steering wheel,

## Measurements

| | 2-Door | 4-Door |
|---|---|---|
| Wheelbase | 103.0" | 109.9" |
| Length | 181.7" | 188.5" |
| Width | 71.0" | 71.0" |
| Height | 52.3" | 53.1" |
| Legroom — front | 41.3" | 41.3" |
| Legroom — rear | 31.9" | 36.4" |
| Headroom — front | 37.6" | 37.6" |
| Headroom — rear | 36.1" | 37.1" |

**1971**

outside rear view mirror, and 6.45 × 14 BSW tires. GT option package adds: Dual outside color-keyed racing mirrors, bodyside stripes, Power-dome hood with scoop, hubcaps with wheel trim rings, and blacked-out grille treatment.

| | 2-Door | 4-Door |
|---|---|---|
| Cargo capacity (cu. ft.) | 10.0 | 10.0 |
| Fuel capacity (gals.) | 16.0 | 16.0 |

## Models Available

| | Style Number | Base MSRP | Change from LY | Shipping Wt. (lbs.) | Production | Change from LY |
|---|---|---|---|---|---|---|
| Comet 2-Door Sedan | 31 | $2,387 | NEW | 2700 | 54,884 | NEW |
| Comet 4-Door Sedan | 30 | $2,446 | NEW | 2789 | 28,116 | NEW |
| TOTALS | | *Avg. price* $2,417 | NEW | *Production* | 83,000 | NEW |

# Cougar

*"Take the best luxury car ideas. Add the best sports car ideas.*
*And you'll have a better luxury sports car."*

**Nameplate year of origin:** 1967.
**Current bodystyle lifespan:** 1971 through 1973.
**Predecessor to this model:** Cougar (1967 to 1970).
**Replacement for this model:** Cougar (1974 to 1976).
**Percentage of division's sales volume:** 17.21%.
**Corporate siblings:** Ford Mustang.
**Primary competition:** AMC Javelin, Chevrolet Camaro, Dodge Challenger, and Pontiac Firebird.
**Notable changes:** Completely restyled.
**Major standard equipment:** All-vinyl high-back bucket seats, mini-console, sequential turn signals, dual outside rearview racing mirrors, deluxe two-spoke steering wheel, interior courtesy lights, deluxe wheel covers, and E78 × 14 BSW tires. XR-7 adds: Leather seating surfaces, unique vinyl roof, tachometer, remote-control driver's side rear view mirror, map lights, and additional interior lighting.

## Measurements

| | |
|---|---|
| Wheelbase | 112.1" |
| Length | 196.7" |
| Width | 75.8" |
| Height | NA |
| Legroom — front | NA |
| Legroom — rear | NA |
| Headroom — front | NA |
| Headroom — rear | NA |
| Cargo capacity (cu. ft.) | 10.4 |
| Fuel capacity (gals.) | NA |

## Models Available

| | Style Number | Base MSRP | Change from LY | Shipping Wt. (lbs.) | Production | Change from LY |
|---|---|---|---|---|---|---|
| Cougar 2-Door Hardtop | 91 | $3,289 | +5.62% | 3331 | 34,008 | -31.27% |
| Cougar 2-Door Convertible | 92 | $3,681 | +5.78% | 3461 | 1,723 | -25.80% |
| Cougar XR-7 2-Door Hardtop | 93 | $3,629 | +6.33% | 3360 | 25,416 | 36.90% |
| Cougar XR-7 2-Door Convertible | 94 | $3,877 | +5.01% | 3480 | 1,717 | -13.15% |
| TOTALS | | *Avg. price* $3,619 | +5.66% | *Production* | 62,864 | -13.10% |

# Montego

*"One of Mercury's better idea family cars."*

**Nameplate year of origin:** 1968.
**Current bodystyle lifespan:** 1970 through 1971.
**Predecessor to this model:** Comet and Montego (1968 to 1969).
**Replacement for this model:** Montego (1972 to 1976).
**Percentage of division's sales volume:** 15.63%.
**Corporate siblings:** Ford Torino.
**Primary competition:** Buick Skylark, Dodge Coronet/Charger, Oldsmobile Cutlass and Pontiac LeMans.
**Notable changes:** Trim and detail changes.
**Major standard equipment:** Nylon and vinyl front bench seat, full carpeting, dome light, bright metal front, rear and side window trim, and E78 × 14 BSW tires. Montego MX adds: Cloth and vinyl interior trim, deluxe steering wheel, simulated walnut interior trim, and F78 × 14 BSW tires. MX Brougham adds: Luxury interior trim and pedal bright moldings. Cyclone adds: All vinyl bench seat, specific Cyclone exterior trim, Cross-country ride package, 4-speed manual transmission, 351 CID V8 engine with dress-up kit and F70 × 14 tires. Cyclone GT adds: All-vinyl high-back bucket seats, concealed headlamps, performance hood, racing mirrors, running lights, and G78 × 14 WSW tires. Spoiler adds:, Anti-lift spoiler, Spoiler tape stripes, and full instrumentation.

## Measurements

|                        | Cars    | Wagons  |
|------------------------|---------|---------|
| Wheelbase              | 117.0"  | 114.0"  |
| Length                 | 209.9"  | 211.8"  |
| Width                  | 77.3"   | 75.4"   |
| Height                 | NA      | NA      |
| Legroom — front        | 42.5"   | 42.0"   |
| Legroom — rear         | 36.0"   | 34.5"   |
| Headroom — front       | 38.5"   | 38.5"   |
| Headroom — rear        | 37.5"   | 39.0"   |
| Cargo capacity (cu. ft.) | 16.2  | 85.2    |
| Fuel capacity (gals.)  | NA      | NA      |

## Models Available

|                                  | Style Number | Base MSRP | Change from LY | Shipping Wt. (lbs.) | Production | Change from LY |
|----------------------------------|-------------|-----------|----------------|---------------------|------------|----------------|
| Montego 2-Door Hardtop           | 01          | $2,803    | +5.20%         | 3229                | 9,623      | -54.82%        |
| Montego 4-Door Sedan             | 02          | $2,798    | +5.56%         | 3228                | 5,718      | -59.12%        |
| Montego MX 2-Door Hardtop        | 07          | $2,927    | +5.69%         | 3236                | 13,719     | -56.68%        |
| Montego MX 4-Door Sedan          | 06          | $2,904    | +5.68%         | 3235                | 13,559     | -18.85%        |
| Montego MX 4-Door Wagon          | 08          | $3,241    | +4.22%         | 3651                | 3,698      | -27.40%        |
| Montego MX Brougham 2-Door HT    | 11          | $3,111    | +5.99%         | 3275                | 2,851      | -64.69%        |
| Montego MX Brougham 4-Door Sdn.  | 10          | $3,099    | +6.26%         | 3258                | 1,565      | -52.79%        |
| Montego MX Brougham 4-Door HT    | 12          | $3,183    | +4.17%         | 3302                | 1,156      | -68.63%        |
| Montego MX Villager 4-Dr. Wagon  | 18          | $3,482    | +4.78%         | 3666                | 2,121      | -20.92%        |
| Cyclone 2-Door Hardtop           | 15          | $3,369    | +4.05%         | 3595                | 444        | -73.81%        |
| Cyclone GT 2-Door Hardtop        | 16          | $3,680    | +14.07%        | 3492                | 2,287      | -77.51%        |
| Cyclone Spoiler 2-Door Hardtop   | 17          | $3,801    | +1.12%         | 3585                | 353        | -78.36%        |
| TOTALS                           | Avg. price  | $3,267    | +5.52%         | Production          | 57,094     | -52.43%        |

# Monterey

*"If you want the extra interior spaciousness, additional luggage room and smooth, quiet ride of a full size luxury car at a lower cost, then the Monterey is Mercury's better idea for you."*

**Nameplate year of origin:** 1950 (Coupe designation), 1952 as a series.
**Current bodystyle lifespan:** 1971 through 1978 (restyled in 1973 and 1975).
**Predecessor to this model:** Monterey (1969 to 1970).
**Replacement for this model:** None.
**Percentage of division's sales volume:** 15.55%.

## Measurements

|            | Cars    | Wagons  |
|------------|---------|---------|
| Wheelbase  | 124.0"  | 121.0"  |
| Length     | 224.7"  | 221.0"  |

**Corporate siblings:** Ford LTD/Galaxie 500 and Mercury Marquis.
**Primary competition:** AMC Ambassador, Buick LeSabre, Chevrolet Impala/Caprice, Dodge Polara/Monaco, Oldsmobile Delta 88 and Pontiac Catalina/Bonneville.
**Notable changes:** Completely restyled.
**Major standard equipment:** Cloth and vinyl interior trim, full carpeting, simulated cherrywood instrument panel trim, bright front and rear window moldings, and G78 × 15 BSW tires. Monterey Custom adds: Specific cloth and vinyl interior trim and bright moldings (wheel lip and lower panels).

|  | Cars | Wagons |
|---|---|---|
| Width | NA | NA |
| Height | NA | NA |
| Legroom — front | NA | NA |
| Legroom — rear | NA | NA |
| Headroom — front | NA | NA |
| Headroom — rear | NA | NA |
| Cargo capacity (cu. ft.) | 20.4 | 96.2 |
| Fuel capacity (gals.) | NA | 22.0 |

## Models Available

|  | Style Number | Base MSRP | Change from LY | Shipping Wt. (lbs.) | Production | Change from LY |
|---|---|---|---|---|---|---|
| Monterey 2-Door Hardtop | 46 | $3,900 | +17.15% | 3959 | 9,099 | -2.78% |
| Monterey 4-Door Sedan | 44 | $3,858 | +18.78% | 4029 | 22,744 | -22.72% |
| Monterey 4-Door Hardtop | 48 | $3,968 | +16.50% | 4024 | 2,483 | -50.66% |
| Monterey 4-Door, 2-Seat Wagon | 72 | $4,283 | +16.32% | 4401 | 4,160 | +151.06% |
| Monterey Custom 2-Door Hardtop | 56 | $4,113 | +14.25% | 4074 | 4,508 | +277.55% |
| Monterey Custom 4-Door Sedan | 54 | $4,030 | +14.49% | 4144 | 12,411 | +157.33% |
| Monterey Custom 4-Door Hardtop | 58 | $4,185 | +13.85% | 4140 | 1,397 | +2.95% |
| TOTALS | | Avg. price $4,048 | +14.19% | | Production 56,802 | -0.25% |

# Marquis

*"Take the most dramatic styling in the medium price class ... add the best ride ideas and luxury features from the world's most expensive luxury cars ... and you have a better medium priced car."*

**Nameplate year of origin:** 1967.
**Current bodystyle lifespan:** 1971 through 1978 (restyled in 1973 and 1975).
**Predecessor to this model:** Marquis (1969 to 1970)
**Replacement for this model:** Marquis (1979 to 1991).
**Percentage of division's sales volume:** 28.89%.
**Corporate siblings:** Ford LTD/Galaxie 500 and Mercury Monterey.
**Primary competition:** Buick Centurion/Electra 225, Chrysler Newport/New Yorker, Oldsmobile Delta 88/Ninety-Eight, and Pontiac Grand Ville.
**Notable changes:** Completely restyled.
**Major standard equipment:** Cloth and vinyl interior with cut-pile carpeting, deluxe sound insulation, electric clock, map light, assorted courtesy lights, concealed headlamps, power steering, power front disc brakes, rear fender skirts, full wheel covers, and H78 × 15 BSW tires. Brougham adds: Cut-pile carpeting, power windows, Halo vinyl roof, carpeted luggage compartment, front door courtesy lights and other additional interior lighting, passenger-side visor vanity mirror, and color-keyed wheel covers.

## Measurements

|  | Cars | Wagons |
|---|---|---|
| Wheelbase | 124.0" | 121.0" |
| Length | 224.7" | 221.0" |
| Width | NA | NA |
| Height | NA | NA |
| Legroom — front | NA | NA |
| Legroom — rear | NA | NA |
| Headroom — front | NA | NA |
| Headroom — rear | NA | NA |
| Cargo capacity (cu. ft.) | 20.4 | 96.2 |
| Fuel capacity (gals.) | NA | 22.0 |

## Models Available

|  | Style Number | Base MSRP | Change from LY | Shipping Wt. (lbs.) | Production | Change from LY |
|---|---|---|---|---|---|---|
| Marquis 2-Door Hardtop | 66 | $4,557 | +10.80% | 4276 | 7,726 | +24.03% |
| Marquis 4-Door Sedan | 63 | $4,474 | +10.41% | 4346 | 16,030 | +11.44% |
| Marquis 4-Door Hardtop | 68 | $4,624 | +10.49% | 4341 | 5,491 | -34.72% |
| Marquis 4-Door, 2-Seat Wagon | 74 | $4,547 | +15.70% | 4451 | 2,158 | +125.03% |

| | Style Number | Base MSRP | Change from LY | Shipping Wt. (lbs.) | Production | Change from LY |
|---|---|---|---|---|---|---|
| Marquis Brougham 2-Door Hardtop | 64 | $4,963 | +12.08% | 4276 | 14,570 | +104.84% |
| Marquis Brougham 4-Door Sedan | 62 | $4,880 | +11.75% | 4346 | 25,790 | +72.86% |
| Marquis Brougham 4-Door Hardtop | 67 | $5,033 | +11.84% | 4341 | 13,781 | +18.57% |
| Colony Park 4-Door, 2-Seat Wagon | 76 | $4,806 | +16.57% | 4512 | 20,004 | +329.73% |
| TOTALS | Avg. price | $4,736 | +12.63% | Production | 105,550 | +23.44% |

# OLDSMOBILE

*"Always a step ahead."*

Like GM's four other car divisions, Oldsmobile full-size models were all-new for 1971. Leading the line with the most dramatic styling changes was the Toronado. Gone were the rounded silhouette, body lines, and arched wheel openings. In their place was a very angular body with squared off wheel openings, and a formal, upright roofline. Of course, since its introduction in 1966, the Toronado had been anything but conventional in appearance or content, and the new model was no exception. An angular front-end style with grille openings in the lower bumper area led into straight fender lines with a curve that trailed off into the mid-front door area. Just aft of the door, another vertical line made a sharp turn at the roofline and ran down the rear fender to the rear of the car where it angled down to meet the rear bumper. Under the rear window area, was the first use of what is now commonly referred to as a high-mounted stop lamp. At the time, it was primarily a novelty on the Toronado, but did provide a safety benefit. Carried over from the previous model were the front-wheel drive system and roomy interior compartment.

The luxurious Ninety-Eight and family-style Delta 88 models were also totally redesigned. While offering styling that appeared similar to previous Oldsmobiles, the cars wore the new GM "wide-body" look. Model changes to the newly styled cars included the dropping of the Ninety-Eight Convertible and Sedan models, and the con-vertible in the Delta 88 line moving from the base trim to the top-line Royale model. An all-new offering was the Custom Cruiser station wagon. This was Oldsmobile's first full-size station wagon model since the 1964 season. In the interim, the Vista-Cruiser (which was slightly larger than the Cutlass wagon had filled in as the big Oldsmobile wagon. The Custom Cruiser styling featured that of the Delta 88 at the front, while the rear featured the styling of the Ninety-Eight models, including the rear fender skirts and vertical taillights with small tailfins. As with other GM full-size wagons, the disappearing tailgate and rear window were featured.

In the mid-size Cutlass line, all models sported revised front and rear styling. While not as greatly changed in appearance as were other GM mid-size cars, the Cutlass line did feature larger grille openings, round (instead of square) parking lights in the bumper, and revised taillights at the rear. This would be the last year a 6-cylinder engine would be offered in the Oldsmobile lineup until the introduction of the Omega in 1973. Model lineup changes included the F-85 switching from a lone Coupe line to a single 4-Door Sedan model. The base Cutlass added a 2-Door Hardtop model, effectively taking the place of the 1970 F-85. Finally the 4-4-2 line dropped its 2-Door Sport Coupe model, leaving only the 2-Door Hardtop and 2-Door Convertible models.

1971

4-4-2 2-Door Hardtop

Ninety-Eight Luxury 4-Door Hardtop

Custom Cruiser 4-Door Wagon,
Vista-Cruiser 4-Door Wagon and
Cutlass Cruiser 4-Door Wagon

Cutlass 4-Door Town Sedan

Delta 88 Royale 2-Door Hardtop

Toronado 2-Door Hardtop and
Cutlass Supreme 2-Door Hardtop

**Model year production:** 567,900, down 9.49% from 1970.
**Domestic market share:** 7.26% (5th place).
**Base price range:** $2957 to $5340.
**Industry average base price:** $3,786.
**Oldsmobile average base price:** $4,026.
**Introduction date:** September 1970.
**Assembly plants:** Fremont, CA (Z); Framingham, MA (G); Lansing, MI (M); Arlington, TX (R); Fairfax, KS (X); and Linden, NJ (F).

**Data plate identification:** Thirteen digit code read as follows: 1st digit 3 = Oldsmobile; 2nd through 5th digits identify series/body style; 1 = 1971; 7th digit is assembly plant code; 100001 and up for serial number (except Toronado is 700001). *Example:* 354391X100001 is a 1971 Oldsmobile Delta 88 4-Door Hardtop with a 455 CID V8, serial number 100001, built in Fairfax, KS.

## Powertrains

| Engine | Gross HP | Engine Code | Transmission Availability | Cutlass/ 4-4-2 | Supreme & Vista-Cruiser | Delta 88 & Custom Cr. | Toro. & 98 |
|---|---|---|---|---|---|---|---|
| 250 CID, 2-bbl., 6-cyl. | 145 | Z | 3-speed manual | S** | - | - | - |
| | | | Turbo Hydra-matic 350 | $211** | - | - | - |
| 350 CID, 2-bbl., V8 | 240 | Q | 3-speed manual | $121** | S (Wagon) | S (88 base) | - |
| | | | Turbo Hydra-matic 350 | $343** | $243 (Wgn.) | $222 (88 base) | - |
| 350 CID, 4-bbl., V8 | 260 | Q | 3-speed manual | $168** | S (Ex. V.Cr.) | - | - |
| | | | 4-speed manual* | $363** | $195 (Ex. V.Cr.) | - | - |
| | | | Turbo Hydra-matic 350 | $390** | $222 (Ex. V.Cr.) | - | - |
| 455 CID, 2-bbl., V8 | 280 | U | 3-speed manual | - | $111 (V.Cr.) | $121 (base)/S (Others) | - |
| | | | Turbo Hydra-matic 400 | - | $354 (V.Cr.) | $364 (base)/$243 (Other) | - |
| 455 CID, 4-bbl., V8 | 320 | U | 3-speed manual | - | $152 (2-Drs.)/ $188 (V.Cr.) | $169 (base)/$47 (Others) | - |
| | | | 4-speed manual | - | $347 (2-Doors only) | | - |
| | | | Turbo Hydra-matic 400 | - | $395 (2-Drs.)/ $430 (V.Cr.) | $412 (base)/$290 (Other) | S (98) |
| 455 CID, 4-bbl., V8 | 340 | U | 3-speed manual | S*** | - | - | - |
| | | | 4-speed manual* | $195*** | - | - | - |
| | | | Turbo Hydra-matic 400 | $243*** | - | - | - |
| 455 CID (W30), 4-bbl., V8 | 350 | U | 4-speed manual* | $565† | - | - | - |
| | | | Turbo Hydra-matic 400 | $613† | - | - | S (Toro.) |

*Only available on certain models.*    **F-85, Cutlass and Cutlass S only.*    ***4-4-2 only.*    †*With Special Performance Package only.*

## Major Options

| | Cutlass | Vista-Cruiser | Delta 88 | Custom Cr. | Ninety-Eight | Toronado |
|---|---|---|---|---|---|---|
| Air conditioning | $408 | $408 | $442 | $442 | $442 | $442 |
| Electronic cruise control (V8 only) | $63 | $63 | $68 | $68 | $68 | $68 |
| Electric rear window defogger | $63 | - | $63 | - | $63 | $63 |
| Soft Ray tinted glass | $43 | $43 | $51 | $51 | $51 | $51 |
| Deck lid remote release | $14 | - | $14 | - | $14 | $14 |
| Power steering — variable-ratio | $116 | $116 | S | S | S | S |
| Power brakes — w/front discs | $70 | S | S | S | S | S |
| Power door locks — w/seat release | - | - | $71 | $71 | $71 | $71 |
| Power driver's seat/bench seat | $79 | $79 | $105 | $105 | $79–$105 | $105 |
| Power windows | $116 | $116 | $133 | $133 | $133 | $133 |
| AM radio | $75 | $75 | $87 | $87 | $87 | $87 |
| AM/FM stereo | $239 | $239 | $239 | $239 | $239 | $239 |
| Front seat console | $ | - | - | - | - | - |
| Front bucket seats | $ | - | - | - | - | - |
| Tilt steering wheel | $45 | $45 | $45 | $45 | $45 | $45 |
| Vinyl roof | $102 | - | $126 | $142 | $142 | $139 |
| White sidewall tires (base size) | $31-36 | $36 | $36 | $42 | $39 | $39 |
| Super Stock wheels (F85-II/88-IV) | $73 | - | $73 | - | - | - |
| Supreme Special Perf. Package | $152* | | | | | |
| 4-4-2 Special Performance Pkg. | $370* | | | | | |

Options common to most models. (- = Not Available; S = Standard equipment.) Items may be standard equipment, optional at different pricing, or unavailable on certain models. This chart is only a guide.

*Includes engine options (see powertrain chart).*

## Paint Colors

| | Code | | Code |
|---|---|---|---|
| Cameo White | 11 | Bamboo* | 50 |
| Sterling Silver Met. | 13 | Saturn Gold Met. | 53 |
| Oxford Gray Met. | 16 | Galleon Gold Met. | 55 |
| Ebony Black | 19 | Sandalwood | 61 |
| Nordic Blue Met. | 24 | Bittersweet Metallic | 62 |
| Viking Blue Met. | 26 | Kashmir Copper Met.* | 65 |
| Royal Blue Met. | 28 | Sienna Metallic | 67 |
| Monarch Blue Metallic | 29 | Sable Brown Metallic | 68 |
| Capri Aqua Met. | 39 | Doeskin Metallic* | 70 |
| Silver Mint Metallic* | 41 | Autumn Glow Metallic* | 73 |
| Palm Green Metallic | 42 | Venetian Red Metallic* | 74 |
| Lime Green Met. | 43 | Matador Red | 75 |
| Antique Jade Met. | 49 | Antique Briar Metallic | 78 |

*Available only on Toronado.*

# Cutlass

*"Owning an Olds keeps getting easier. And easier. And easier."*

**Nameplate year of origin:** 1962 (as a F-85 model designation); 1955 (show car).

**Current bodystyle lifespan:** 1968 through 1972.

**Predecessor to this model:** F-85/Cutlass (1966 to 1967).

**Replacement for this model:** Cutlass (1973 to 1977).

**Percentage of division's sales volume:** 41.21%.

**Corporate siblings:** Buick Skylark, Chevrolet Chevelle, Pontiac LeMans.

## Measurements

| | 2-Doors | 4-Doors | Wagon |
|---|---|---|---|
| Wheelbase | 112.0" | 116.0" | 116.0" |
| Length | 203.6" | 207.6" | 213.3" |
| Width | 76.8" | 76.8" | 76.8" |
| Height | 52.9" | 53.5" | 54.8" |
| Legroom — front | 41.3" | 41.5" | 41.5" |

**1971**

**Primary competition:** AMC Matador, Dodge Coronet, Ford Torino, and Mercury Montego.

**Notable changes:** Restyle of front and rear end.

**Major standard equipment:** Cloth or vinyl upholstery, front bench seat, left-hand outside rearview mirror, aluminized exhaust system, and F78 × 14 BSW tires. Cutlass adds: Front and rear armrests, full carpeting, deluxe steering wheel, and exterior chrome trim moldings. Cutlass S adds: Deluxe bench seat with foam cushions, and simulated chrome hood louvers. Cutlass Supreme adds: Woodgrain interior trim, custom sport seats, and unique grille. Cutlass Cruiser: Base Cutlass equipment, except tires are H78 × 14 BSW. 4-4-2 adds: All-vinyl bucket seats, floor shifter, 455 CID V8 engine, dual exhausts, heavy duty suspension, and F70 × 14 Wide-Oval tires.

| | 2-Doors | 4-Doors | Wagon |
|---|---|---|---|
| Legroom — rear | 32.6" | 35.0" | 34.8" |
| Headroom — front | 37.8" | 38.5" | 38.4" |
| Headroom — rear | 36.2" | 37.1" | 38.3" |
| Luggage capacity (cu. ft.) | 17.0 | 17.0 | 93.6 |
| Fuel capacity (gals.) | 20.0 | 20.0 | 20.0 |

## Models Available

| | Style Number | Base MSRP | Change from LY | Shipping Wt. (lbs.) | Production | Change from LY |
|---|---|---|---|---|---|---|
| F-85 4-Door Town Sedan | 3169 | $2,885 | NEW | 3226 | 4,419 | NEW |
| Cutlass 2-Door Hardtop | 3187 | $2,901 | NEW | 3292 | 33,623 | NEW |
| Cutlass 4-Door Town Sedan | 3569 | $2,999 | +5.71% | 3252 | 32,522 | -10.65% |
| Cutlass 4-Door, 2-Seat Wagon | 3536 | $3,454 | +8.96% | 3732 | 6,789 | -12.57% |
| Cutlass S 2-Door Sports Coupe | 3577 | $2,958 | +5.79% | 3196 | 4,452 | -60.11% |
| Cutlass S 2-Door Hardtop | 3587 | $3,021 | +5.67% | 3228 | 63,314 | -29.11% |
| Cutlass Supreme 2-Door Hardtop | 4257 | $3,323 | +5.46% | 3429 | 60,599 | -11.29% |
| Cutlass Supreme 2-Door Conv. | 4267 | $3,507 | +5.16% | 3513 | 10,255 | +110.70% |
| Cutlass Supreme 4-Door Hardtop | 4239 | $3,398 | +5.33% | 3541 | 10,458 | -2.82% |
| 4-4-2 2-Door Hardtop | 4487 | $3,552 | +5.21% | 3688 | 6,285 | -57.27% |
| 4-4-2 2-Door Convertible | 4467 | $3,743 | +4.93% | 3731 | 1,304 | -55.54% |
| TOTALS | | Avg. price $3,249 | +4.60% | Production | 234,020 | -12.90% |

# Vista-Cruiser

*"The exclusive 11-windowed wagon that's topped Olds popularity poll for years!"*

**Nameplate year of origin:** 1964.

**Current bodystyle lifespan:** 1968 through 1972.

**Predecessor to this model:** None.

**Replacement for this model:** Vista-Cruiser (1973 to 1977).

**Percentage of division's sales volume:** 4.67%.

**Corporate siblings:** None.

**Primary competition:** AMC Matador/Ambassador, Dodge Coronet, Plymouth Satellite.

**Notable changes:** Restyle of front end.

**Major standard equipment:** All-vinyl interior, foam cushion bench seats, full carpeting, deluxe steering wheel, wood-grain interior and exterior trim, drop-or-swing tailgate, Vista-roof windows, central and tailgate dome lamps, power front disc brakes, and H78 × 14 BSW tires.

## Measurements

| | |
|---|---|
| Wheelbase | 121.0" |
| Length | 218.3" |
| Width | 76.8" |
| Height | 58.6" |
| Legroom — front | 41.5" |
| Legroom — rear | 37.8" |
| Headroom — front | 38.0" |
| Headroom — rear | 40.3" |
| Luggage capacity (cu. ft.) | 105.2 |
| Fuel capacity (gals.) | 20.0 |

## Models Available

| | Style Number | Base MSRP | Change from LY | Shipping Wt. (lbs.) | Production | Change from LY |
|---|---|---|---|---|---|---|
| Vista-Cruiser 4-Dr., 2-S. Wagon | 4856 | $3,866 | +8.23% | 4163 | 5,980 | -44.41% |
| Vista-Cruiser 4-Dr., 3-S. Wagon | 4866 | $4,008 | +7.92% | 4251 | 20,566 | -11.87% |
| TOTALS | | Avg. price $3,937 | +8.07% | | Production 26,546 | -22.14% |

# Delta 88

*"Now with Oldsmobile's exclusive 'G-Ride' System."*

**Nameplate year of origin:** 1965 (88 series started 1949).
**Current bodystyle lifespan:** 1971 through 1976.
**Predecessor to this model:** Delta 88 (1969 to 1970).
**Replacement for this model:** Delta 88 (1977 to 1985).
**Percentage of division's sales volume:** 31.88%.
**Corporate siblings:** Buick LeSabre/Centurion, Chevrolet Impala/Caprice, Pontiac Catalina.
**Primary competition:** Dodge Polara, Ford LTD, and Mercury Monterey.
**Notable changes:** Completely redesigned.
**Major standard equipment:** Cloth and vinyl or all-vinyl bench seat, nylon-blend carpet, deluxe steering wheel, trunk mat, windshield radio antenna, chrome wheel covers, power steering, power front disc brakes, G78-15 BSW tires. Custom adds: 455 CID V8 engine and tires. Royale adds: Custom triple bodyside pinstriping, exclusive grille, and interior courtesy lamps.

### Measurements

| | |
|---|---|
| Wheelbase | 124.0" |
| Length | 220.2" |
| Width | 79.5" |
| Height | 53.6" |
| Legroom — front | 42.4" |
| Legroom — rear | 38.5" |
| Headroom — front | 38.3" |
| Headroom — rear | 38.0" |
| Luggage capacity (cu. ft.) | 20.1 |
| Fuel capacity (gals.) | 25.0 |

## Models Available

| | Style Number | Base MSRP | Change from LY | Shipping Wt. (lbs.) | Production | Change from LY |
|---|---|---|---|---|---|---|
| Delta 88 2-Door Hardtop | 5457 | $4,041 | +12.56% | 4122 | 27,031 | -18.13% |
| Delta 88 4-Door Town Sedan | 5469 | $3,985 | +12.76% | 4150 | 38,298 | -18.63% |
| Delta 88 4-Door Hardtop | 5439 | $4,103 | +11.92% | 4202 | 31,420 | -16.65% |
| Delta 88 Custom 2-Door Hardtop | 6457 | $4,291 | +11.51% | 4179 | 24,251 | +50.17% |
| Delta 88 Custom 4-Door Town Sedan | 6469 | $4,198 | +11.80% | 4202 | 22,209 | -10.18% |
| Delta 88 Custom 4-Door Hardtop | 6439 | $4,366 | +11.26% | 4237 | 26,593 | -6.47% |
| Delta 88 Royale 2-Door Hardtop | 6647 | $4,549 | +9.38% | 4221 | 8,397 | -36.62% |
| Delta 88 Royale 2-Door Convertible | 6667 | $4,557 | NEW | 4296 | 2,883 | NEW |
| TOTALS | | Avg. price $4,261 | +12.22% | | Production 181,082 | -10.99% |

# Custom Cruiser

*"The totally new luxury wagon with the disappearing tailgate!"*

**Nameplate year of origin:** 1971 (1940 as a designation on 90 Series cars).
**Current bodystyle lifespan:** 1971 through 1976.
**Predecessor to this model:** None.
**Replacement for this model:** Custom Cruiser (1977 to 1989).
**Percentage of division's sales volume:** 2.46%.
**Corporate siblings:** Buick Estate Wagon, Chevrolet Impala/Caprice, Pontiac Safari Wagons.

### Measurements

| | |
|---|---|
| Wheelbase | 127.0" |
| Length | 225.3" |
| Width | 79.5" |
| Height | 57.3" |
| Legroom — front | 42.4" |
| Legroom — rear | 39.0" |

**Primary competition:** Dodge Monaco, Ford LTD/Country Squire, Mercury Colony Park/Marquis.

**Notable changes:** All-new model for 1971.

**Major standard equipment:** Loop-pile carpeting, carpeted cargo area, deluxe steering wheel, Glide-away disappearing tailgate, power tailgate window, forward-facing third seat and split back second seat (3-seat models only), stowage compartment under load floor, wood-grain vinyl interior and exterior trim, central and tailgate dome lamps, rear wheel opening covers, power steering, power front disc brakes, and L78-15 BSW tires.

### Measurements (cont.)

| | |
|---|---|
| Headroom — front | 39.6" |
| Headroom — rear | 39.4" |
| Luggage capacity (cu. ft.) | 109.0 |
| Fuel capacity (gals.) | 24.0 |

## Models Available

| | Style Number | Base MSRP | Change from LY | Shipping Wt. (lbs.) | Production | Change from LY |
|---|---|---|---|---|---|---|
| Custom Cruiser 4-Dr., 2-S. Wagon | 6835 | $4,776 | NEW | 4880 | 4,049 | NEW |
| Custom Cruiser 4-Dr., 3-S. Wagon | 6845 | $4,917 | NEW | 5000 | 9,932 | NEW |
| TOTALS | | Avg. price $4,847 | NEW | | Production 13,981 | NEW |

# Ninety-Eight

*"For people who like to be surrounded by beautiful things."*

**Nameplate year of origin:** 1941.

**Current bodystyle lifespan:** 1971 through 1976.

**Predecessor to this model:** Ninety-Eight (1969 to 1970).

**Replacement for this model:** Ninety-Eight (1977 to 1984).

**Percentage of division's sales volume:** 14.67%.

**Corporate siblings:** Buick Electra 225 and Cadillac Calais/de Ville.

**Primary competition:** Chrysler New Yorker and Mercury Marquis.

**Notable changes:** Completely redesigned.

**Major standard equipment:** Cloth and vinyl bench seat, front seat center armrests, deep loop-pile carpeting and lower door panels, deluxe cushion steering wheel, remote control LH oustide mirror, electric clock, trunk lamp, trunk mat, full wheel covers, concealed windshield antenna, rear fender skirts, power steering, power front disc brakes, and H78-15 BSW tires. Luxury adds: Rear seat center armrest, rear seat clock (on certain sedans), front and rear cigar lighters, power front seat, and power windows.

### Measurements

| | |
|---|---|
| Wheelbase | 127.0" |
| Length | 226.1" |
| Width | 79.0" |
| Height | 54.6" |
| Legroom — front | 42.4" |
| Legroom — rear | 40.5" |
| Headroom — front | 39.3" |
| Headroom — rear | 38.2" |
| Luggage capacity (cu. ft.) | 20.5 |
| Fuel capacity (gals.) | 25.0 |

## Models Available

| | Style Number | Base MSRP | Change from LY | Shipping Wt. (lbs.) | Production | Change from LY |
|---|---|---|---|---|---|---|
| Ninety-Eight 2-Door Hardtop | 8437 | $4,790 | +2.88% | 4382 | 8,335 | -60.52% |
| Ninety-Eight 4-Door Hardtop | 8439 | $4,852 | +5.89% | 4467 | 15,025 | +6.58% |
| Ninety-Eight Luxury 2-Door Hardtop | 8637 | $5,065 | NEW | 4418 | 14,876 | NEW |
| Ninety-Eight Luxury 4-Door Hardtop | 8639 | $5,159 | +5.54% | 4504 | 45,055 | +132.52% |
| TOTALS | | Avg. price $4,967 | +5.37% | | Production 83,291 | -13.10% |

# Toronado

*"The Unmistakable One."*

**Nameplate year of origin:** 1966.
**Current bodystyle lifespan:** 1971 through 1978.
**Predecessor to this model:** Toronado (1966 to 1970).
**Replacement for this model:** Toronado (1979 to 1985).
**Percentage of division's sales volume:** 5.10%.
**Corporate siblings:** Buick Riviera and Cadillac Eldorado
**Primary competition:** Chrysler Imperial LeBaron Coupe, Ford Thunderbird,
    and Lincoln Continental Mark IV.
**Notable changes:** Completely redesigned.
**Major standard equipment:** Cloth and vinyl bench seat with center armrest,
    Flo-Thru ventilation, electric clock, remote-control LH outside mirror, con-
    cealed radio antenna, deluxe steering wheel, front wheel drive, power steering,
    power front disc brakes, and J78 × 15 BSW tires.

## Measurements

| | |
|---|---|
| Wheelbase | 122.3" |
| Length | 219.9" |
| Width | 79.8" |
| Height | 54.7" |
| Legroom — front | 42.4" |
| Legroom — rear | 35.8" |
| Headroom — front | 38.1" |
| Headroom — rear | 37.1" |
| Luggage capacity (cu. ft.) | 14.2 |
| Fuel capacity (gals.) | 22.0 |

## Models Available

| | Style Number | Base MSRP | Change from LY | Shipping Wt. (lbs.) | Production | Change from LY |
|---|---|---|---|---|---|---|
| Toronado Custom 2-Door Hardtop | 9657 | $5,457 | +8.64% | 4522 | 28,980 | +13.95% |
| TOTALS | *Avg. price* | $5,457 | +8.64% | *Production* | 28,980 | +13.95% |

# PLYMOUTH

*"Coming through with more for you."*

The Chrysler fuselage look expanded to the all-new intermediate Plymouths for 1971. For the first time, 2-door and 4-door models were based on different platforms, with totally different body designs. As per normal Chrysler practice, the mid-size Dodge Charger and Coronet models shared these new bodies, but there was still a great distinction, particularly amongst the new 2-Door models. The new 2-Doors (except the base coupe) were known as either Sebring or Road Runner, and sported the Mopar "loop-style" grille, fuselage "wide-body" design, and semi-fast-back rooflines. Four-door models were more traditional in appearance, with full-width grilles, ventless front door glass, and a new, longer wheelbase for improved ride. Model changes were extensive but mainly consisted of nameplate swapping. All convertible styles were dropped at the end of the 1970 run. The base Satellite now took the place of the

Belvedere line. The Satellite Sebring and Custom lines replaced the previous Satellite series. And the Sebring Plus, Satellite Brougham and Regent replaced the Sport Satellite line. The Road Runner and GTX 2-Door Hardtops remained as the sporting derivatives. Also, the famous 383 CID V8 would make its final appearance this year in the mid-size and full-size lines.

Plymouth's full-size line received a minor facelift and new rear styling while retaining its own fuselage look. There was a little model shuffling in this series also. Along with the other Mopar lines, the big convertible was now history. Also gone, was the sporty Fury S-23 Hardtop, which had been essentially an option-package equipped Sport Fury. At mid-season, Plymouth made the automatic transmission standard equipment on all Fury models, and at the same time added a Fury Custom line between Fury

1971

I and Fury II. The new Custom was essentially a Fury I with added features, and by 1972 the two series were blended together to become the Fury I.

The sporty Barracuda, which was totally redesigned for 1970, received a facelift for its second season. In an apparent move to make it look more aggressive, a new front end featuring dual headlights was employed for this one year only. The 1972 models would return to the single lamp setup used on the 1970 models. An entry-level 2-Door Coupe model was new this year, and the Gran Coupe range dropped its convertible model. The compact Valiant re-

ceived only minor trim and detail changes, but did add a nice looking Scamp 2-Door Hardtop model, based on the Dodge Dart 2-Door Hardtop. These were the only 2-Door Hardtop models available in the compact size class from 1971 through 1976, when they were discontinued. A final note: The imported Plymouth Cricket was introduced to the United States this year. The Cricket was available as a 4-Door Sedan only and was priced about $400 below a Valiant. Based on the British-built Hillman Avenger, the Cricket was not as popular as the Japanese-built Dodge Colt, and was dropped after two years on the market.

Barracuda 2-Door Convertible

Barracuda 2-Door Hardtop

Valiant Duster 2-Door Coupe

Fury Sport Suburban 4-Door Wagon

GTX 2-Door Hardtop

Satellite Sebring Plus 2-Door Hardtop

Sport Fury 4-Door Sedan

Valiant 4-Door Sedan

**Model year production:** 751,897, up 0.97% over 1970.
**Domestic market share:** 9.61% (3rd place).
**Base price range:** $2,313 to $4,146.
**Industry average base price:** $3,786.
**Plymouth average base price:** $3,299.

**Introduction date:** October 6, 1970; Valiant line introduced September 15, 1970.
**Assembly plants:** Lynch Road, MI (A): Hamtramck, MI (B); Belvidere, IL (D); Newark DE (F); St. Louis, MO (G); and Windsor, Ontario, Canada (R).

**Data plate identification:** Thirteen digit code read as follows: four digit style number code in which first letter is series, second letter is trim level, third and fourth digits are body style; fifth digit is engine code (see chart); sixth digit 1 for 1971; seventh digit is assembly plant code; 100001 and up for serial number. *Example:* VH23C1D100001 is a 1971 Plymouth Scamp 2-Door Hardtop, with a 225 CID 6-cyl., built at Belvidere, IL, serial number 100001.

## Powertrains

| Engine | Gross HP | Engine Code | Transmission Availability | Valiant Duster | Barracuda | Sat./Cust. Sat.Sebr. | S.Plus/Br./ R.R./GTX | Fury |
|---|---|---|---|---|---|---|---|---|
| 198 CID, 1-bbl., 6-cyl. | 125 | B | 3-speed man. | S | S (Coupe) | - | - | - |
| | | | Torqueflite automatic | $183 | $209 (Coupe) | - | - | - |
| 225 CID, 1-bbl., 6-cyl. | 145 | C | 3-speed man. | $39 | S (Base)/ $39 (Coupe) | S | - | S[1] |
| | | | Torqueflite automatic | $222 | $209 (Base)/ $248 (Cpe.) | $216 | - | $216 |
| 318 CID, 2-bbl., V8 | 230 | G | 3-speed man. | $124 | S (Gran)/$101 (Base)/ $126 (Cpe.) | $95 | S | $110[1]/ S (others) |
| | | | 4-speed man. | - | $198 (Gran)/$299 (Base)/$324 (Cpe.) | - | - | - |
| | | | Torqueflite automatic | $319 | $209 (Gran)/$310 (Base)/$335 (Cpe.) | $311 | $216 | $326[1]/$216 (others) |
| 340 CID, 4-bbl., V8 | 235/250 | H | 3-speed man. | - | - | - | - | $156[1]/$46 (others) |
| | | | Torqueflite automatic | - | - | - | - | $394[1]/$284 (others) |
| 340 CID[2,] 4-bbl., V8 | 275 | J | 3-speed man. | S-340 | $ | - | - | - |
| | | | 4-speed man. | $198 | $ | - | - | - |
| | | | Torqueflite automatic | $191 | $ | - | - | - |
| 360 CID, 2-bbl., V8 | 175 | K | Torqueflite automatic | - | - | - | - | $394[1]/$284 (others) |
| 383 CID, 2-bbl., V8 | 275 | L | 3-speed man. | - | $71 (Gran)/ $182 (Base) | $168 | $73 (Ex. GTX/RR) | $183[1]/$73 (others) |
| | | | 4-speed man. | - | $269 (Gran)/ $370 (Base) | $374 | $279 (Ex. GTX/ RR/Wagon) | - |
| | | | Torqueflite automatic | - | $280 (Gran)/ $381 (Base) | $406 | $311 (Ex. GTX/RR) | $421[1]/$311 (others) |
| 383 CID, 4-bbl., V8 | 300 | N | 3-speed man. | - | S ('Cuda)/$140 (Gran)/$251 (Base) | $240 | S (R.R.)/$145 (Sat./Sebr/Wgn) | $255[1]/$145 (others) |
| | | | 4-speed man. | - | $198 ('Cuda)/$338 (Gran)/$449 (Base) | $446 | $206 (R.R.) $351 (Sat./Seb.) | - |
| | | | Torqueflite automatic | - | $209 ('Cuda)/$349 (Gran)/$459 (Base) | $478 | $238 (R.R.) $383 (Sat./Seb.) | $493[1]/$384 (others) |
| 426 CID Street-Hemi, 4-bbl., V8 | 425 | R | 4-speed man. | - | $1082 ('Cuda) | - | $953 (GTX) $1090 (R.R.) | - |

1971

| Engine | Gross HP | Engine Code | Transmission Availability | Valiant Duster | Barracuda | Sat./Cust. Sat.Sebr. | S.Plus/Br./ R.R./GTX | Fury |
|---|---|---|---|---|---|---|---|---|
| 440 CID Spr. Cmdo., 4-bbl., V8 | 370 | U | 4-speed man. | - | - | - | S (GTX) | |
| | | | Torqueflite automatic | - | - | - | $238 (GTX) | S (GT)/$436 (others[3]) |
| 440 CID Six Pack, 3 × 2-bbl., V8 | 385 | V | 4-speed man. | - | $ | - | $125 (GTX) $262 (R.R.) | - |
| | | | Torqueflite automatic | - | $ | - | $343 (GTX) $500 (R.R.) | $491[3] |

[1]Fury I, II, III and Custom 2-Door HT and 4-Door Sedan models.   [2]Available on Duster 340 and Barracuda models only.   [3]Excluding Fury I, II, III and Custom 2-Door HT and 4-Door Sedan models.

## Major Options

| | Duster/Valiant | Barracuda | Satellite | Fury |
|---|---|---|---|---|
| Air conditioning | $384 | $370 | $383 | $391 |
| Remote control decklid release | - | - | - | v$16 |
| Tinted glass | $36 | $36 | $40 | $40 |
| Power steering | $100 | $97 | $111 | $111 |
| Power brakes | $40 | $40 | $40 | $40 |
| Power brakes — front disc | - | $63 | $64 | $70 |
| Power door locks | - | - | $47–$73 | $47–$73 |
| Power windows | - | $101 | $110 | $120 |
| AM radio | v$59 | $59 | $65 | $65 |
| AM/FM stereo | $125 | $125 | $209 | $71 |
| Bucket seats | $ | S | $ | $103 |
| Center console | - | $52 | $58 | $ |
| Vinyl roof | $75 | $82 | $67–$96 | $106 |

Options common to most models. (– = Not Available; S = Standard equipment.)
Items may be standard equipment, optional at different pricing, or unavailable on certain models. This chart is only a guide.

## Paint Colors

| | Code | Duster/Val./ Bar./Sat. | Fury |
|---|---|---|---|
| Winchester Gray Metallic | A-4 | x | |
| Slate Gray Metallic | A-8 | | x |
| Glacial Blue Metallic | B-2 | x | x |
| True Blue Metallic | B-5 | x | |
| Evening Blue Metallic | B-7 | | x |
| In-Violet Metallic* | C-7 | x | |
| Mood Indigo Metallic | C-8 | x | |
| Rallye Red | E-5 | x | x |
| Burnished Red Metallic | E-7 | x | x |
| Amber Sherwood Metallic | F-3 | x | x |
| Sherwood Green Metallic | F-7 | x | x |
| April Green Metallic | J-4 | | x |
| Sassy-Grass Green* | J-6 | x | |
| Autumn Bronze | K-6 | x | x |
| Sandalwood Beige | L-1 | x | x |
| Bahama Yellow | L-5 | x | x |
| Coral Turquoise Metallic | Q-5 | | x |
| Tunisian Tan Metallic | T-2 | x | |
| Tahitian Walnut Metallic | T-8 | x | x |
| Tor-Red* | V-2 | x | |
| Spinnaker White | W-1 | x | x |
| Sno-White* | W-3 | x | |
| Formal Black | X-9 | x | x |
| Curious Yellow* | Y-3 | x | x |
| Light Gold | Y-4 | x | |
| Gold Leaf Metallic | Y-8 | x | x |
| Tawny Gold Metallic | Y-9 | x | x |

*Hi-impact colors.

# Valiant

*"Coming through with traditional great economy."*

**Nameplate year of origin:** 1960 (Valiant); 1970 (Duster); 1971 (Scamp).
**Current bodystyle lifespan:** 1970 through 1976.
**Predecessor to this model:** Valiant (1963 to 1966).
**Replacement for this model:** Volare (1976 to 1980).
**Percentage of division's sales volume:** 36.89%.
**Corporate siblings:** Dodge Dart and Dart Demon.

## Measurements

| | Duster | Scamp | Valiant |
|---|---|---|---|
| Wheelbase | 108.0" | 111.0" | 108.0" |
| Length | 188.4" | 192.1" | 188.4" |
| Width | 71.6" | 69.7" | 71.1" |

**Primary competition:** AMC Hornet, Chevrolet Nova, Ford Maverick, and Pontiac Ventura II.

**Notable changes:** Revised grille and trim and detail changes.

**Major standard equipment:** All-vinyl bench seat, color-keyed rubber floor mat, front door vent windows, 2-speed windshield wipers, and 6.95 × 14 BSW tires. Duster adds: Dome light, ventless front windows, and swing-out side rear quarter windows. 340 adds: Flat-black grille trim, body side tape stripes, heavy duty suspension, Rallye road wheels, front disc brakes and E70 × 14 BSW tires.

|  | Duster | Scamp | Valiant |
|---|---|---|---|
| Height | 52.6" | 52.6" | 54.0" |
| Legroom — front | 41.6" | 41.6" | 41.6" |
| Legroom — rear | 29.6" | 31.7" | 34.6" |
| Headroom — front | 37.2" | 37.3" | 38.4" |
| Headroom — rear | 36.5" | 36.7" | 37.3" |
| Cargo capacity (cu. ft.) | 15.9 | 14.9 | 14.0 |
| Fuel capacity (gals.) | 16.0 | 16.0 | 16.0 |

## Models Available

|  | Style Number | Base MSRP | Change from LY | Shipping Wt. (lbs.) | Production | Change from LY |
|---|---|---|---|---|---|---|
| Duster 2-Door Sport Coupe | VL29 | $2,313 | +6.49% | 2825 | 173,592 | -9.76% |
| Duster 340 2-Door Sport Coupe | VS29 | $2,703 | +6.12% | 3140 | 12,886 | -48.08% |
| Scamp 2-Door Hardtop | VH23 | $2,561 | NEW | 2900 | 48,253 | NEW |
| Valiant 4-Door Sedan | VL41 | $2,392 | +6.31% | 2835 | 42,660 | -16.04% |
| TOTALS | | Avg. price $2,492 | +7.28% | | Production 277,391 | +3.50% |

# Barracuda

*"The Barracuda is knocking the stuffing out of a few old-fashioned notions about sporty cars."*

**Nameplate year of origin:** 1964.
**Current bodystyle lifespan:** 1970 through 1974.
**Predecessor to this model:** Barracuda (1967 to 1969).
**Replacement for this model:** None.
**Percentage of division's sales volume:** 2.49%.
**Corporate siblings:** Dodge Challenger.
**Primary competition:** AMC Javelin, Chevrolet Camaro, Ford Mustang, and Pontiac Firebird.
**Notable changes:** Restyled front end treatment.
**Major standard equipment:** All-vinyl bucket seats, deep-pile carpeting, dome light, concealed 2-speed electric wipers, and 7.35 × 14 BSW tires. Gran Coupe adds: Overhead consolette, leather bucket seats, molded headliner, and additional trim features. 'Cuda adds: Chrome moldings (wheel opening, rocker, drip rail, grille, deck lid), heavy duty suspension, performance hood, and F70 × 14 WSW tires.

### Measurements

| Wheelbase | 108.0" |
|---|---|
| Length | 186.6" |
| Width | 74.9" |
| Height | 50.9" |
| Legroom — front | 42.3" |
| Legroom — rear | 28.9" |
| Headroom — front | 37.4" |
| Headroom — rear | 35.7" |
| Cargo capacity (cu. ft.) | 7.1 |
| Fuel capacity (gals.) | 18.0 |

## Models Available

|  | Style Number | Base MSRP | Change from LY | Shipping Wt. (lbs.) | Production | Change from LY |
|---|---|---|---|---|---|---|
| Barracuda 2-Door Coupe | BH21 | $2,654 | NEW | 3010 | *W/HT | NEW |
| Barracuda 2-Door Hardtop | BH23 | $2,766 | +0.07% | 3035 | 9,459 | -63.12% |
| Barracuda 2-Door Convertible | BH27 | $3,023 | -0.36% | 3115 | 1,014 | -34.75% |
| Barracuda Gran Coupe 2-Dr. HT | BP23 | $3,029 | +3.24% | 3105 | 1,615 | -80.26% |
| Cuda 2-Door Hardtop | BS23 | $3,155 | -0.28% | 3475 | 6,228 | -67.01% |
| Cuda 2-Door Convertible | BS27 | $3,412 | -0.61% | 3550 | 374 | -41.10% |
| TOTALS | | Avg. price $3,007 | -2.43% | | Production 18,690 | -66.32% |

# Satellite

*"While everyone else is busy announcing new cars,
we came through with a new idea."*

**Nameplate year of origin:** 1965 (as a Belvedere trim level).
**Current bodystyle lifespan:** 1971 through 1978.
**Predecessor to this model:** Belvedere/Satellite (1968 to 1970).
**Replacement for this model:** Fury (1975 to 1978).
**Percentage of division's sales volume:** 19.45%.
**Corporate siblings:** Dodge Coronet.
**Primary competition:** AMC Matador, Chevrolet Chevelle, Ford Torino, and Pontiac LeMans.
**Notable changes:** Completely restyled.
**Major standard equipment:** All-vinyl bench seat, glove box lock, trunk mat, color-keyed rubber floor covering, dome light, hubcaps and E78 × 14 BSW tires (H78 × 14 BSW for wagons). Sebring adds: Cloth and vinyl upholstery, dual horns, full carpeting, armrests and assorted bright exterior moldings. Custom adds: Front and rear armrests, upgraded trim. Sebring Plus/Brougham/Regent adds: All-vinyl front bucket seats, deluxe wheel covers, specific bodyside moldings, and white sidewall tires (Plus/Brougham only). Road Runner adds: "Beep-beep" horn, Rallye gauges, heavy duty suspension and brakes, sway bars, performance hood, low restriction dual exhausts, and F70 × 14 WSW tires. GTX adds: Vinyl bucket seats (or bench with armrest), specific chrome moldings, low-restriction dual exhaust with chrome trumpets, and F70 × 14 white-letter tires.

## Measurements

|  | Coupes | Sedans | Wagons |
|---|---|---|---|
| Wheelbase | 115.0" | 117.0" | 117.0" |
| Length | 203.2" | 204.6" | 210.9" |
| Width | 79.1" | 78.6" | 78.6" |
| Height | 52.0" | 54.5" | 55.0" |
| Legroom — front | 41.9" | 41.9" | 41.9" |
| Legroom — rear | 36.7" | 36.7" | 36.7" |
| Headroom — front | 37.3" | 38.6" | 39.7" |
| Headroom — rear | 36.4" | 37.3" | 38.1" |
| Cargo capacity (cu. ft.) | 16.7 | 16.7 | 91.3 |
| Fuel capacity (gals.) | 19.5 | 19.5 | 21.0 |

## Models Available

|  | Style Number | Base MSRP | Change from LY | Shipping Wt. (lbs.) | Production | Change from LY |
|---|---|---|---|---|---|---|
| Satellite 2-Door Coupe | RL21 | $2,663 | +2.31% | 3185 | *W/ Sebring HT | *W/ Sebring HT |
| Satellite 4-Door Sedan | RL41 | $2,734 | +3.52% | 3249 | 11,059 | -20.70% |
| Satellite 4-Door, 2-Seat Wagon | RL45 | $3,058 | +2.45% | 3725 | 7,138 | +27.83% |
| Road Runner 2-Door Hardtop | RM23 | $3,147 | +3.72% | 3640 | 14,218 | -43.00% |
| Satellite Sebring 2-Door Hardtop | RH23 | $2,931 | +6.00% | 3210 | 46,807 | +65.98% |
| Satellite Custom 4-Door Sedan | RH41 | $2,908 | +6.09% | 3240 | 30,773 | +1.30% |
| Satellite Custom 4-Dr., 2-S. Wagon | RH45 | $3,235 | +4.32% | 3730 | 5,045 | +20.00% |
| Satellite Custom 4-Dr., 3-S. Wagon | RH46 | $3,315 | +3.24% | 3800 | 3,865 | +17.94% |
| Satellite Sebring Plus 2-Dr. HT | RP23 | $3,179 | +6.39% | 3300 | 16,253 | +85.77% |
| Satellite Brougham 4-Door Sedan | RP41 | $3,189 | +5.70% | 3330 | 3,020 | +0.33% |
| Satellite Regent 4-Dr., 2-S. Wagon | RP45 | $3,558 | +6.37% | 3815 | 2,161 | +9.42% |
| Satellite Regent 4-Dr., 3-S. Wagon | RP46 | $3,638 | +5.30% | 3885 | 2,985 | +38.13% |
| GTX 2-Door Hardtop | RS23 | $3,733 | +5.60% | 3675 | 2,942 | -62.03% |
| TOTALS | *Avg. price* $3,176 | | +2.06% | *Production* | 146,266 | -7.46% |

# Fury

*"Your invitation to the good life."*

**Nameplate year of origin:** 1956.
**Current bodystyle lifespan:** 1969 through 1973.
**Predecessor to this model:** Fury (1967 to 1968).
**Replacement for this model:** Gran Fury (1974 to 1978).
**Percentage of division's sales volume:** 41.17%.
**Corporate siblings:** Dodge Polara and Monaco.
**Primary competition:** AMC Ambassador, Chevrolet Impala, Ford LTD, and Pontiac Catalina.
**Notable changes:** Minor restyling to front and rear end.
**Major standard equipment:** All-vinyl front bench seat, floor mat, 2-speed windshield wipers with washers, left-hand outside rear view mirror, temperature, ammeter and oil gauges, hubcaps, and F78 × 15 BSW tires (J78 × 15 BSW on Suburban). Fury II adds: Color-keyed carpeting, full-length bodyside molding. Fury III adds: Cloth and vinyl upholstery, various bright exterior moldings, and additional interior lighting. Sport Fury adds: Door pull straps, front seat center arm rest, additional interior lighting, concealed headlamps. Sport Suburban adds: Wood-grain bodyside applique. Sport Fury GT adds: Hood stripes, heavy-duty suspension, dual exhausts, Rallye Road Wheels, tape striping and H70 × 15 white-letter tires.

## Measurements

|  | Cars | Wagons |
|---|---|---|
| Wheelbase | 120.0" | 122.0" |
| Length | 217.2" | 222.0" |
| Width | 79.6" | 79.6" |
| Height | 55.8" | 57.9" |
| Legroom — front | 41.8" | 41.8" |
| Legroom — rear | 39.1" | 39.1" |
| Headroom — front | 38.8" | 39.6" |
| Headroom — rear | 38.4" | 39.2" |
| Cargo capacity (cu. ft.) | 22.4 | 104.2 |
| Fuel capacity (gals.) | 23.0 | 23.0 |

## Models Available

|  | Style Number | Base MSRP | Change from LY | Shipping Wt. (lbs.) | Production | Change from LY |
|---|---|---|---|---|---|---|
| Fury I 2-Door Sedan | PE21 | $3,113 | +11.58% | 3670 | 5,152 | +118.95% |
| Fury I 4-Door Sedan | PE41 | $3,146 | +11.36% | 3705 | 16,395 | +10.68% |
| Fury Custom 2-Door Sedan | PE21 | $3,208 | NEW | 3670 | (see Fury I) | NEW |
| Fury Custom 4-Door Sedan | PE41 | $3,241 | NEW | 3705 | (see Fury I) | NEW |
| Fury II 2-Door Hardtop | PL23 | $3,283 | +13.09% | 3675 | 7,859 | -63.13% |
| Fury II 4-Door Sedan | PL41 | $3,262 | +11.64% | 3710 | 20,098 | -27.43% |
| Fury II 4-Dr., 2-S. Suburban Wagon | PL45 | $3,758 | +13.78% | 4245 | 4,877 | -7.98% |
| Fury II 4-Dr., 3-S. Suburban Wagon | PL46 | $3,869 | +9.98% | 4290 | 2,662 | +18.31% |
| Fury III 2-Door Hardtop | PM23 | $3,458 | +11.87% | 3680 | 21,319 | -0.25% |
| Fury III 2-Door Formal Hardtop | PM29 | $3,600 | +11.91% | 3750 | 24,465 | +97.82% |
| Fury III 4-Door Sedan | PM41 | $3,437 | +11.99% | 3715 | 44,244 | -13.04% |
| Fury III 4-Door Hardtop | PM43 | $3,612 | +11.28% | 3820 | 55,356 | +15.62% |
| Fury III 4-Dr., 2-S. Cust. Sub. Wgn. | PM45 | $3,854 | +9.27% | 4240 | 10,874 | +22.21% |
| Fury III 4-Dr., 3-S. Cust. Sub. Wgn. | PM46 | $3,930 | +9.08% | 4300 | 11,702 | +72.29% |
| Sport Fury 2-Door Hardtop | PH23 | $3,677 | +10.99% | 3805 | 3,912 | -51.21% |
| Sport Fury 2-Door Formal Hardtop | PH29 | $3,710 | +11.31% | 3810 | 3,957 | -30.43% |
| Sport Fury 4-Door Sedan | PH41 | $3,656 | +11.09% | 3845 | 2,823 | -45.02% |
| Sport Fury 4-Door Hardtop | PH43 | $3,724 | +10.73% | 3865 | 55,356 | +707.65% |
| Fury 4-Dr., 2-S. Sport Sub. Wgn. | PH45 | $4,071 | +9.29% | 4290 | 5,103 | +15.90% |
| Fury 4-Dr., 3-S. Sport Sub. Wgn. | PH46 | $4,146 | +8.99% | 4370 | 13,021 | +42.00% |
| Sport Fury GT 2-Door Hardtop | PP23 | $4,111 | +5.46% | 4090 | 375 | |
| TOTALS | *Avg. price* $3,613 | | +7.11% | | *Production* 309,550 | +17.64% |

**1971**

# PONTIAC

*"Pure Pontiac!"*

Pontiac entered 1971 with more visible changes to its lineup of cars than any other GM division. New nameplates were introduced at both ends of the size spectrum. Of course, at the model year introductions, the most obvious changes were the all-new full-size models featuring the new corporate body styling. The wider bodies better complemented the Wide-Track stance of the Pontiac and made for arguably better looking cars. At the front, Pontiac chose to use the "classic" style upright split-grille first popularized on the 1969 Grand Prix. On the full-size models, a small grille extension to the sides of the upright gave the front a wider look. In typical Pontiac fashion, the side sculpturing was minimal, as was the chrome trim, and at the back were slotted-style tail lamps, popularized on the Firebird models. Interior designs were upgraded to give the big Pontiac a more luxurious image. Nameplate shuffling occurred for the first time in many years. The Catalina continued as the base full-size model. The Catalina Brougham replaced the Ventura trim option. The Bonneville continued, missing the sporty convertible model, but the "sporty" Bonneville was no longer the top line car. It now filled the position formerly held by the Executive. A new "luxurious" Grand Ville line took the 1970 Bonneville position and was distinguished by a more formal roofline.

Unfortunately, this was the beginning of a downhill slide for Pontiac. If a point in time could be determined for when Pontiac lost sight of its formula for success during the sixties, 1971 would be that point. It started with the downgrading of muscle under the hood (mostly caused by government regulations), then led into trying to build a more luxurious car than Buick or Oldsmobile (i.e. Grand Ville), and wound up with corporate cars like the (1980–84) Phoenix, and (1981–86) T-1000. While there would still be great sales years to come (1973 and 1979 in particular), it

was largely downhill from this point until the Pontiac image was reborn in the mid-eighties.

In the mid-size range, the sport-luxury Grand Prix model was restyled with what Pontiac termed a "classic" theme. The front end had a more pronounced upright radiator style grille, flanked by single headlights.

The bodyside sculpturing was sharp and defined, reminiscent of the 1963 Grand Prix sculpting. At the back was a new bumper and decklid theme, with a small point at the center section. This new styling was immediately popular, and sales rebounded once more.

The LeMans series was also restyled, receiving a new front end and hood theme. The grille was slightly enlarged, and of course the Endura bumper continued on the GTO models. The T-37 line replaced the former Tempest series, and the LeMans Sport line dropped the 2-Door Coupe and Safari Wagon models.

At the bottom end of the size continuum, the big news came at mid-year, when a thinly disguised Chevrolet Nova was introduced as the Pontiac Ventura II. Matching the Nova feature for feature, the Ventura II wore a traditional Pontiac split grille and slotted taillamps. But under the hood and inside, the car was essentially a Nova. The styling differences and sportier image given to the Ventura II in advertising justified slightly higher base prices. Overall, they were popular cars that gave Pontiac the smaller car its dealers would need to survive the mid-seventies gas shortages.

Finally, the Firebird returned for 1971 with minimal changes, having been totally revamped in mid–1970. During the year, a GM strike would nearly wind up killing off the Firebird, but luckily there were a few visionaries within GM who would keep the car alive, for much greater successes.

Bonneville 2-Door Hardtop

Catalina 2-Door Convertible

Firebird Formula 455 2-Door Coupe

Grand Prix 2-Door Hardtop

GTO 2-Door Hardtop

LeMans Sport 2-Door Convertible

T-37 2-Door Hardtop

Ventura II 2-Door Coupe

**Model year production:** 587,004, down 15.05% from 1970.
**Domestic market share:** 7.50% (4th place).
**Base price range:** $2,458 to $4,790.
**Industry average base price:** $3,786.
**Pontiac average base price:** $3,700.
**Introduction date:** September 1970.
**Assembly plants:** Lakewood, GA (A); Atlanta, GA (D);
 Kansas City, MO (K); Norwood, OH (N); Fairfax, KS (X);
 Fremont, CA (Z); and Oshawa, Ontario, Canada (1).

**Data plate identification:** Thirteen digit code read as follows:
 1st digit 2 = Pontiac; 2nd through 5th digits identify se-
 ries/body style (see style number in listings); 1 = 1971; 7th
 digit is assembly plant code; 100001 and up for serial number. *Example:* 252391X100001 is a 1971 Pontiac Catalina 4-
 Door Hardtop, serial number 100001, built in Fairfax, KS.

## Powertrains

| Engine | Gross HP | Transmission Availability | Vent. II | Firebird | LeMans & GTO | Grand Prix | Catalina & Safari | Bonneville/ Gr. V./GrSaf. |
|---|---|---|---|---|---|---|---|---|
| 250 CID, 1-bbl., 6-cyl. | 145 | 3-speed man. | S | S (base) | S (ex. GTO) | – | – | – |
|  |  | 2-sp. Auto. | $180 | $180 (base) | $180 (ex. GTO) | – | – | – |

| Engine | Gross HP | Transmission Availability | Vent. II | Firebird | LeMans & GTO | Grand Prix | Catalina & Safari | Bonneville/ Gr.V./GrSaf. |
|---|---|---|---|---|---|---|---|---|
| | | Turbo Hydra-matic | – | $211 (base) | $211 (ex. GTO) | – | – | – |
| 307 CID, 8 2-bbl., V | 200 | 3-speed man. | $90 | – | – | – | – | – |
| | | 2-sp. Auto. | $270 | – | – | – | – | – |
| | | Turbo Hydra-matic | $301 | – | – | – | – | – |
| 350 CID, 2-bbl., V8 | 250 | 3-speed man. | – | $121 (base)/ S (Esprit) | $121 (ex. GTO) | – | S (ex. Br.) | – |
| | | 3-speed HD man. | – | $205 (base)/$84 (Esprit)/S (Formula) | $205 (ex. GTO) | – | – | – |
| | | 4-speed man. | – | $327 (base)/$206 (Esprit & Formula) | $316 (ex. GTO) | – | – | – |
| | | 2-sp. Auto. | – | $311 (base)/$191 (Esprit & Formula) | $311 (ex. GTO) | – | $190 (Cat.) | – |
| | | Turbo Hydra-matic | – | $343 (base)/$222 (Esprit & Formula) | $343 (ex. GTO) | – | $222 (ex. Br.) | – |
| 400 CID, 2-bbl., V8 | 265 | 3-speed man. | – | $53 (Esprit) | $174 (ex. GTO) | – | S (Br.)/ $53 (Other) | – |
| | | 4-speed man. | – | $259 (Esprit) | $369 (ex. GTO) | – | – | |
| | | Turbo Hydra-matic | – | $296 (Esprit) | $417 (ex. GTO) | – | $243 (Br.)/ $296 (Other) | |
| 400 CID, 4-bbl., V8 | 300 | 3-speed HD man. | – | $100 (Form.) | S (GTO) | S | $48 (Br.)/ $100 (Other) | – |
| | | 4-speed man. | – | $306 (Form.) | $195 (GTO) | $243 | – | – |
| | | 4-speed manual-close ratio | – | $338 (Form.) | – | – | – | – |
| | | Turbo Hydra-matic | – | $343 (Form.) | $243 (GTO) | $243 | $291 (Br.)/ $343 (Other) | – |
| 455 CID, 2-bbl., V8 | 280 | 3-speed man. | – | – | – | – | $58 (Br.)/ $111 (Other) | S (Bonn./ Gr.Saf.) |
| | | Turbo Hydra-matic | – | – | – | – | $301 (Br.)/ $354 (Other) | $243 (Bonn./ Gr.Saf.) |
| 455 CID, 4-bbl., V8 | 325 | 3-speed HD man. | – | $158 (Form.) | $279 (LeM.*)/ $58 (GTO) | $58 | – | S (Gr.V.)/$48 (Bonn./G.Saf.) |
| | | 4-speed man. | – | $396 (Form.) | $474 (LeM.*)/ $253 (GTO) | $301 | – | |
| | | Turbo Hydra-matic | – | $401 (Form.) | $522 (LeM.*)/ $301 (GTO) | $301 | $348 (Br.)/ $400 (Other) | $243 (Gr.V.) /$291 (Bonn. & G.Saf.) |
| 455 CID H.O., 4-bbl., V8 | 335 | 4-speed man. close ratio | – | S (TA)/ $475 (Form.) | $553 (LeM.**)/ $395 (GTO) | – | – | – |
| | | Turbo Hydra-matic | – | S (TA)/ $480 (Form.) | $601 (LeM.**)/ $438 (GTO) | – | – | – |

*Not available on Wagon models.    **Two-Door models only.

## Major Options

| | Vent. II | Firebird | LeMans | Grand Prix | Catalina | Bonneville | Grand Ville | Safari |
|---|---|---|---|---|---|---|---|---|
| Air conditioning (V8 only) | $390 | $408 | $408 | $442 | $442 | $442 | $442 | $442 |
| Electronic cruise control (V8 Auto.) | - | - | $63 | $68 | $68 | $68 | $68 | $68 |
| Electric rear window defogger | - | $62 | $62 | $62 | $62 | $62 | $62 | - |
| Soft Ray tinted glass | $39 | $38 | $43 | $51 | $51 | $51 | $51 | $51 |
| Power steering — variable-ratio | $116 | $116* | $116 | S | $126 | S | S | S |
| Power brakes | $46 | $70* | $70 (S Wgn) | S | S | S | S | S |
| Power driver's seat/Bench seat | - | $79 | $79 | $79 | $105 | $105 | $105 | $105 |
| Power windows | - | $116 | $116 | $133 | $133 | $133 | $133 | $133 |
| AM radio | $66 | $66 | $66 | $87 | $87 | $87 | $87 | $87 |
| AM/FM stereo | $239 | $239 | $239 | $239 | $239 | $239 | $239 | $239 |
| Front seat console | $57 | $57 | $59 | S | - | - | - | - |
| Front bucket seats | $242 | S | $ | S | - | - | - | - |
| Tilt steering wheel | - | $45 | $45 | $45 | $45 | $45 | $45 | $45 |
| Vinyl roof (except Trans Am) | $100 | $74–$90 | $100 | $142 | S | S | S | $142 |
| White stripe tires (base size) | $28–$31 | $28–$41 | $28–$31 | $33 | $33 | $36 | $36 | $42 |
| Rally II wheels | $63 | $56 | $87 | $87 | $87 | $87 | - | $87 |

Options common to most models. (- = Not Available; S = Standard equipment.) Items may be standard equipment, optional at different pricing, or unavailable on certain models. This chart is only a guide.

*Standard on TransAm

## Paint Colors

| | Code | | Code |
|---|---|---|---|
| Cameo White | 11 | Quezal Gold Metallic | 53 |
| Nordic Silver Metallic | 13 | Baja Gold Metallic | 55 |
| Bluestone Gray Metallic | 16 | Aztec Gold Metallic | 59 |
| Starlight Black | 19 | Orbit Orange | 60/06 |
| Adriatic Blue Metallic | 24 | Sandalwood | 61 |
| Lucerne Blue Metallic | 26 | Canyon Copper Metallic | 62 |
| Regency Blue Metallic | 29 | Carousel Red | 65 |
| Aquarius Green Metallic | 39 | Bronzini Gold Met. (Grand Prix) | 66 |
| Limekist Green Metallic | 42 | Castillian Bronze Metallic | 69 |
| Tropical Lime Metallic | 43 | Cardinal Red | 75 |
| Laurentian Green Metallic | 49 | Rosewood Metallic | 78 |
| Golden Red Yellow | 51 | | |

# Firebird

*"The 'basic' car, a luxurious sports car, a road car, and the ultimate sports car … pick your Firebird."*

**Nameplate year of origin:** 1967 (used on Motorama show cars as early as 1954).
**Current bodystyle lifespan:** 1970 through 1981.
**Predecessor to this model:** Firebird (1967 to 1969).
**Corporate siblings:** Chevrolet Camaro.
**Replacement for this model:** Firebird (1982 to 1992).
**Percentage of division's sales volume:** 9.05%.
**Primary competition:** Ford Mustang, Plymouth Barracuda, Dodge Challenger, and AMC Javelin.
**Notable changes:** Trim and detail changes only.
**Major standard equipment:** All-vinyl front bucket seats, and rear bucket-type seats, loop-pile carpeting, deluxe steering wheel, Endura front bumper, hubcaps, windshield radio antenna, E78-14 BSW tires. Esprit adds: Custom cushion steering

## Measurements

| | |
|---|---|
| Wheelbase | 108.0" |
| Length | 191.6" |
| Width | 73.4" |
| Height | 50.4" |
| Legroom — front | 43.8" |
| Legroom — rear | 29.6" |
| Headroom — front | 37.4" |
| Headroom — rear | 36.1" |
| Cargo capacity (cu. ft.) | 6.4 |
| Fuel capacity (gals.) | 18.0 |

1971

wheel, additional interior and exterior trim, dual sport mirrors, and wheel trim rings. Formula adds: 400 CID V8 engine, heavy duty suspension, and F70 × 14 tires. Trans Am adds: Formula steering wheel, power steering, power brakes, Rally II wheels, and F60 × 15 tires.

## Models Available

| | Style Number | Base MSRP | Change from LY | Shipping Wt. (lbs.) | Production | Change from LY |
|---|---|---|---|---|---|---|
| Firebird 2-Door Coupe | 22387 | $3,047 | +5.98% | 3164 | 23,021 | +21.97% |
| Firebird Esprit 2-Door Coupe | 22487 | $3,416 | +5.40% | 3423 | 20,185 | +6.46% |
| Firebird Formula 400 2-Door Coupe | 22687 | $3,445 | +2.23% | 3473 | 7,802 | +1.22% |
| Firebird Trans Am 2-Door Coupe | 22887 | $4,595 | +6.74% | 3578 | 2,116 | -33.79% |
| TOTALS | Avg. price | $3,626 | +5.16% | Production | 53,124 | +9.00% |

# Ventura II

*"Pontiac's small car for small-car lovers who want more."*

**Nameplate year of origin:** 1960.
**Current bodystyle lifespan:** 1971 through 1972.
**Predecessor to this model:** None.
**Replacement for this model:** Ventura (1973 through 1979, with restyle in 1975).
**Percentage of division's sales volume:** 8.26%.
**Corporate siblings:** Chevrolet Nova.
**Primary competition:** Ford Maverick, Mercury Comet, Plymouth Valiant, Dodge Dart, AMC Hornet.
**Notable changes:** All-new model for 1971.
**Major standard equipment:** Cloth and vinyl bench seat, vinyl-coated rubber floor coverings, deluxe steering wheel, hubcaps, front-door vent windows, bright moldings on windshield and rear window, manual drum brakes, E78-14 BSW tires.

## Measurements

| | |
|---|---|
| Wheelbase | 111.0" |
| Length | 194.5" |
| Width | 72.4" |
| Height | 53.9" |
| Legroom — front | 41.0" |
| Legroom — rear | 35.7" |
| Headroom — front | 38.8" |
| Headroom — rear | 37.2" |
| Cargo capacity (cu. ft.) | 13.7 |
| Fuel capacity (gals.) | 17.0 |

## Models Available

| | Style Number | Base MSRP | Change from LY | Shipping Wt. (lbs.) | Production | Change from LY |
|---|---|---|---|---|---|---|
| Ventura II 2-Door Coupe | 21327 | $2,458 | NEW | 2943 | 34,681 | NEW |
| Ventura II 4-Door Sedan | 21369 | $2,488 | NEW | 2983 | 13,803 | NEW |
| TOTALS | Avg. price | $2,473 | NEW | Production | 48,484 | NEW |

# LeMans

*"The lines are dynamic, seemingly in motion even when the car is still. Pure Pontiac!"*

**Nameplate year of origin:** 1961 (as a Tempest sub-series).
**Current bodystyle lifespan:** 1968 through 1972.
**Predecessor to this model:** Tempest/LeMans (1966 to 1967).
**Replacement for this model:** LeMans (1973 to 1977).
**Percentage of division's sales volume:** 28.27%.

## Measurements

| | 2-Doors | 4-Doors | Wagons |
|---|---|---|---|
| Wheelbase | 112.0" | 116.0" | 116.0" |
| Length | 202.8" | 206.8" | 210.9" |

**Corporate siblings:** Chevrolet Chevelle, Oldsmobile Cutlass, and Buick Skylark.

**Primary competition:** Ford Torino, Mercury Montego, Plymouth Satellite, Dodge Coronet, AMC Matador.

**Notable changes:** Restyled front and rear end.

**Major standard equipment:** Cloth and vinyl front bench seat, vinyl floor covering, courtesy lights, 2-speed windshield wipers with washers, and F78 × 14 BSW tires. LeMans adds: All-vinyl front bench seats, full carpeting, rocker panel moldings, and G78 BSW tires on Wagons. LeMans Sport adds: All-vinyl bucket seats or bench seat (2-Doors), cloth and vinyl bench seats (4-Doors), simulated walnut trim on dash, and H78 × 14 BSW tires. Safari adds: Exterior wood-grain paneling. GTO adds: All-vinyl bucket seats, floor shifter, dual exhausts, 400 CID V8 with engine dress-up kit, heavy duty suspension and G78 × 14 BSW tires.

|  | 2-Doors | 4-Doors | Wagons |
|---|---|---|---|
| Width | 76.7" | 76.7" | 76.7" |
| Height | 52.0" | 52.6" | 52.6" |
| Legroom — front | 42.4" | 42.4" | 42.4" |
| Legroom — rear | 32.2" | 34.8" | 34.8" |
| Headroom — front | 37.9" | 38.5" | 38.5" |
| Headroom — rear | 36.3" | 37.1" | 37.4" |
| Cargo capacity (cu. ft.) | NA | NA | 83.6 |
| Fuel capacity (gals.) | 21.5 | 21.5 | 21.5 |

## Models Available

|  | Style Number | Base MSRP | Change from LY | Shipping Wt. (lbs.) | Production | Change from LY |
|---|---|---|---|---|---|---|
| LeMans T-37 2-Door Coupe | 23327 | $2,747 | +4.73% | 3189 | 7,184 | -40.02% |
| LeMans T-37 2-Door Hardtop | 23337 | $2,807 | +4.62% | 3194 | 29,466 | +41.10% |
| LeMans T-37 4-Door Sedan | 23369 | $2,795 | +4.68% | 3219 | 8,336 | -9.26% |
| LeMans 2-Door Coupe | 23527 | $2,877 | +5.19% | 3199 | 2,734 | -51.66% |
| LeMans 2-Door Hardtop | 23537 | $2,938 | +5.12% | 3199 | 40,966 | -21.68% |
| LeMans 4-Door Sedan | 23569 | $2,925 | +5.14% | 3229 | 11,979 | -21.47% |
| LeMans 4-Door Hardtop | 23539 | $3,064 | +4.90% | 3314 | 3,186 | -17.72% |
| LeMans 4-Door, 2-Seat Wagon | 23536 | $3,353 | +8.44% | 3739 | 4,363 | -39.11% |
| LeMans 4-Door, 3-Seat Wagon | 23546 | $3,465 | NEW | 3789 | 6,311 | NEW |
| LeMans Sport 2-Door Hardtop | 23737 | $3,125 | +5.82% | 3199 | 34,625 | -40.67% |
| LeMans Sport 2-Door Convertible | 23767 | $3,359 | +5.56% | 3289 | 3,865 | -17.24% |
| LeMans Sport 4-Door Hardtop | 23739 | $3,255 | +5.58% | 3314 | 2,451 | -32.98% |
| GTO 2-Door Hardtop | 24237 | $3,446 | +5.48% | 3619 | 9,854 | -72.90% |
| GTO 2-Door Convertible | 24267 | $3,676 | +5.27% | 3664 | 678 | -82.08% |
| TOTALS | _Avg. price_ | $3,131 | +5.56% | _Production_ | 165,998 | -30.45% |

# Grand Prix

*"You don't tamper with a classic car. You refine it, maybe. Hone it.*
*And that's what we did to our classic luxury/sport for 1971."*

**Nameplate year of origin:** 1962.

**Current bodystyle lifespan:** 1969 through 1972.

**Predecessor to this model:** Grand Prix (1967 to 1968).

**Replacement for this model:** Grand Prix (1973 to 1977).

**Percentage of division's sales volume:** 9.94%.

**Corporate siblings:** Chevrolet Monte Carlo.

**Primary competition:** Mercury Cougar, Plymouth Satellite Sebring, Dodge Charger.

**Notable changes:** Restyled exterior, revised interior trim.

**Major standard equipment:** Front bucket seats, or notchback bench seat in cloth and vinyl or all-vinyl trim, loop-pile carpeting, custom cushion steering wheel, electric clock, lamp package, deluxe wheel covers, windshield radio antenna, concealed wipers, exterior bright moldings, power steering, power front disc brakes, G78-14 BSW tires.

## Measurements

| | |
|---|---|
| Wheelbase | 118.0" |
| Length | 213.6" |
| Width | 76.4" |
| Height | 52.0" |
| Legroom — front | 42.4" |
| Legroom — rear | 31.6" |
| Headroom — front | 37.5" |
| Headroom — rear | 36.5" |
| Cargo capacity (cu. ft.) | NA |
| Fuel capacity (gals.) | 21.5 |

**1971**

## Models Available

| | Style Number | Base MSRP | Change from LY | Shipping Wt. (lbs.) | Production | Change from LY |
|---|---|---|---|---|---|---|
| Grand Prix 2-Door Hardtop | 27657 | $4,557 | +14.35% | 3863 | 58,325 | -11.29% |
| TOTALS | | Avg. price $4,557 | +14.35% | | Production 58,325 | -11.29% |

# Catalina

*"It's hard to believe that the great features on the new 1971 Catalina don't belong to a much more expensive car."*

**Nameplate year of origin:** 1950 (hardtop models), 1959 (series).
**Current bodystyle lifespan:** 1971 through 1976.
**Predecessor to this model:** Catalina (1969 to 1970).
**Replacement for this model:** Catalina (1977 to 1981).
**Corporate siblings:** Chevrolet Impala/Caprice, Olds Delta 88, Buick LeSabre/Centurion.
**Primary competition:** Ford LTD, Mercury Monterey, Plymouth Fury, and Dodge Polara.
**Percentage of division's sales volume:** 28.44%.
**Notable changes:** Completely restyled.
**Major standard equipment:** Cloth and vinyl or all-vinyl bench seat, nylon-blend carpet, trunk mat, windshield radio antenna, power front disc brakes, and G78-15 BSW tires. Safari adds: All-vinyl interior, and L78 × 15 BSW tires. Brougham adds: Deluxe interior trim, loop-pile carpet, custom cushion steering wheel, deluxe wheel covers, and H78 × 15 BSW tires.

## Measurements

| | Cars | Safari |
|---|---|---|
| Wheelbase | 123.5" | 127.0" |
| Length | 221.4" | 227.7" |
| Width | 79.5" | 79.5" |
| Height | 53.4" | 55.0" |
| Legroom — front | 42.6" | 42.6" |
| Legroom — rear | 38.5" | 38.5" |
| Headroom — front | 38.9" | 38.9" |
| Headroom — rear | 38.0" | 38.2" |
| Cargo capacity (cu. ft.) | NA | 106 |
| Fuel capacity (gals.) | 25.0 | 25.0 |

## Models Available

| | Style Number | Base MSRP | Change from LY | Shipping Wt. (lbs.) | Production | Change from LY |
|---|---|---|---|---|---|---|
| Catalina 2-Door Hardtop | 25257 | $3,870 | +19.11% | 4042 | 46,257 | -34.25% |
| Catalina 2-Door Convertible | 25267 | $4,156 | +15.32% | 4081 | 2,036 | -44.76% |
| Catalina 4-Door Sedan | 25269 | $3,770 | +19.15% | 4077 | 59,355 | -30.00% |
| Catalina 4-Door Hardtop | 25239 | $3,939 | +18.68% | 4107 | 22,333 | -36.47% |
| Catalina Safari 4-Dr., 2-S. Wagon | 25235 | $4,315 | +18.35% | 4815 | 9,283 | -45.21% |
| Catalina Safari 4-Dr., 3-S. Wagon | 25245 | $4,462 | +17.70% | 4905 | 10,322 | -17.09% |
| Catalina Brougham 2-Door Hardtop | 25857 | $4,084 | NEW | 4119 | 8,823 | NEW |
| Catalina Brougham 4-Door Sedan | 25869 | $4,000 | NEW | 4149 | 6,069 | NEW |
| Catalina Brougham 4-Door Hardtop | 25839 | $4,154 | NEW | 4179 | 9,001 | NEW |
| TOTALS | | Avg. price $4,083 | +17.94% | | Production 173,479 | -22.34% |

# Bonneville

*"Every year we build a better Bonneville."*

# Grand Ville

*"The first true luxury car at a sensible price."*

**Nameplate year of origin:** 1957 (Bonneville); 1971 (Grand Ville).
**Current bodystyle lifespan:** 1971 through 1976.
**Predecessor to this model:** Executive and Bonneville (1969 to 1970).
**Replacement for this model:** Bonneville (1977 to 1981).
**Percentage of division's sales volume:** 14.92%.
**Corporate siblings:** Chevrolet Impala/Caprice, Oldsmobile 88, Buick LeSabre/Centurion.
**Primary competition:** Ford LTD, Mercury Marquis, Plymouth Fury, and Dodge Monaco.
**Notable changes:** Bonneville completely restyled, replacing Executive. Grand Ville an all-new model, replacing former Bonneville line.
**Major standard equipment:** Cloth and vinyl bench seat, full carpeting and on lower door panels, custom cushion steering wheel, light packages, trunk lamp, wheel covers, windshield antenna, power steering, power front disc brakes, and H78-15 BSW tires. Grand Ville adds: Deluxe cloth and vinyl front bench seat, burled elm grain dash and door trim, electric clock, additional courtesy lights, and deluxe wheel covers. Grand Safari adds: Exterior wood-grain trim, power tailgate window, and L78 × 15 BSW tires.

## Measurements

|                        | Cars    | Safari  |
|------------------------|---------|---------|
| Wheelbase              | 126.0"  | 127.0"  |
| Length                 | 226.3"  | 227.7"  |
| Width                  | 79.5"   | 79.5"   |
| Height                 | 53.7"   | 55.0"   |
| Legroom — front        | 42.6"   | 42.6"   |
| Legroom — rear         | 38.5"   | 38.5"   |
| Headroom — front       | 38.7"   | 38.9"   |
| Headroom — rear        | 37.8"   | 38.2"   |
| Cargo capacity (cu. ft.) | NA    | 106     |
| Fuel capacity (gals.)  | 25.0    | 25.0    |

## Models Available

|                                   | Style Number | Base MSRP | Change from LY | Shipping Wt. (lbs.) | Production | Change from LY |
|-----------------------------------|--------------|-----------|----------------|---------------------|------------|----------------|
| Bonneville 2-Door Hardtop         | 26257        | $4,272    | +18.67%        | 4188                | 8,778      | +150.87%       |
| Bonneville 4-Door Sedan           | 26269        | $4,210    | +18.99%        | 4213                | 6,513      | -50.13%        |
| Bonneville 4-Door Hardtop         | 26239        | $4,340    | +18.29%        | 4273                | 16,393     | +204.93%       |
| Grand Safari 4-Dr., 2-S. Wagon    | 26235        | $4,643    | +15.64%        | 4843                | 3,613      | -25.67%        |
| Grand Safari 4-Dr., 3-S. Wagon    | 26245        | $4,790    | +15.14%        | 4913                | 5,972      | +6.09%         |
| Grand Ville 2-Door Hardtop        | 26847        | $4,497    | +17.35%        | 4223                | 14,017     | -40.14%        |
| Grand Ville 2-Door Convertible    | 26867        | $4,706    | +16.49%        | 4266                | 1,784      | -49.56%        |
| Grand Ville 4-Door Hardtop        | 26849        | $4,566    | +17.08%        | 4303                | 30,524     | -31.01%        |
| TOTALS                            |              | *Avg. price* $4,500 | +16.07% |            | *Production* 87,594 | -23.47% |

1971

# 1972

The 1972 model year, while not a record-breaking year, was not entirely a bad one despite the strikes and regulations imposed throughout the year. Federal government safety regulations required seat belt warning lights and buzzers in all cars by January 1, 1972. Energy-absorbing bumper systems would be required front and rear by 1974, but some 1972 models already sported the new bumper systems. Inflation during this period had driven prices upwards at such a rate that the president declared a 90-day price freeze beginning on August 15, 1971, which stimulated sales of the '71 and '72 models. Also, strikes at various assembly plants would greatly affect 1972 car production, and in the case of GM's intermediate line, delay introduction of all-new models by a full year.

This would prove to be the year that insurance companies effectively shut down the "muscle-car" era, although it would be unfair to blame them entirely as government regulations, higher prices and lower consumer interest in these models were contributing factors. There were, however, still some muscle cars to be found for 1972, including the Buick Skylark GS350/ GS455, Ford Mustang Mach I, Chevy Camaro Z/28, Pontiac Firebird Trans Am, and Plymouth Road Runner and 'Cuda. Other names were still around in name only: AMC AMX (now a 4-passenger Javelin model), Pontiac LeMans GTO (this year returning to option package status) and Dodge Challenger. Other 1972 performance-oriented models include the Dodge Demon 340, Ford Gran Torino Sport, Mercury Montego GT (available with a Cyclone option group), Plymouth Duster 340 and several Chevrolet lines that were still offered with SS trim packages. But performance isn't everything, obviously, as compact cars and family cars made sales gains this year.

In search of something innovative, American Motors introduced its "Buyer Protection Plan" as their big selling point for the year. This plan covered everything (except tires) for 12 months or 12,000 miles at a time when some companies offered 90 days. American Motors products were carried over from 1971 with trim changes and new grille designs on most models. There were some model changes and optional equipment worth noting. The two-year old Gremlin dropped its low-line 2-passenger model and added a 304 CID V8 engine to its option list. The successful Hornet compact line was offered only in SST trim, although optional trim packages were available. These included a new "X" sport package for the 2-Door Sedan and Sportabout Wagon models, a Rallye performance and handling package on the 2-Door Sedan, and a D/L package for the Sportabout. A designer series Hornet Sportabout with Gucci package found 2,583 buyers. This car featured dark green, red and ivory interior trim and an ivory and green headliner with the Gucci double-G pattern embossed in it. The Javelin offered a Pierre Cardin designer series, of which 4,152 were produced. Also available on the Javelin was the "Go" package with the 360 CID or 401 CID V8 engine, a handling package, rally instruments, power disc brakes and a special paint and stripe treatment.

Chrysler Corporation unveiled its newly styled full-size cars for 1972, a year behind the competition. Although they looked similar to their predecessors, the sheetmetal was all-new and was most evident in the more sculpted side panels. Model availability was somewhat altered from 1971. At Chrysler the low-end Newport Royal nameplate took the place of the Newport series and also adopted its standard equipment. The top-of-the-line New Yorker took a step downmarket and replaced the 300 series, and the New Yorker Brougham nameplate took the place of New Yorker. The Dodge division dropped the Polara Brougham series but made no other model changes. Plymouth made numerous changes for 1972. Models dropped included the Fury I 2-Door Sedan, Fury Custom 2-Door and 4-Door Sedans, and Sport Fury GT 2-Door Hardtop. Also the Gran Fury series replaced the Sport Fury this year. Under the hood, a 6-cylinder engine was no longer available in Fury models. The base powertrain became a 318 CID V8 engine mated to a Torqueflite automatic transmission.

## 1972 Model Year Production by Make

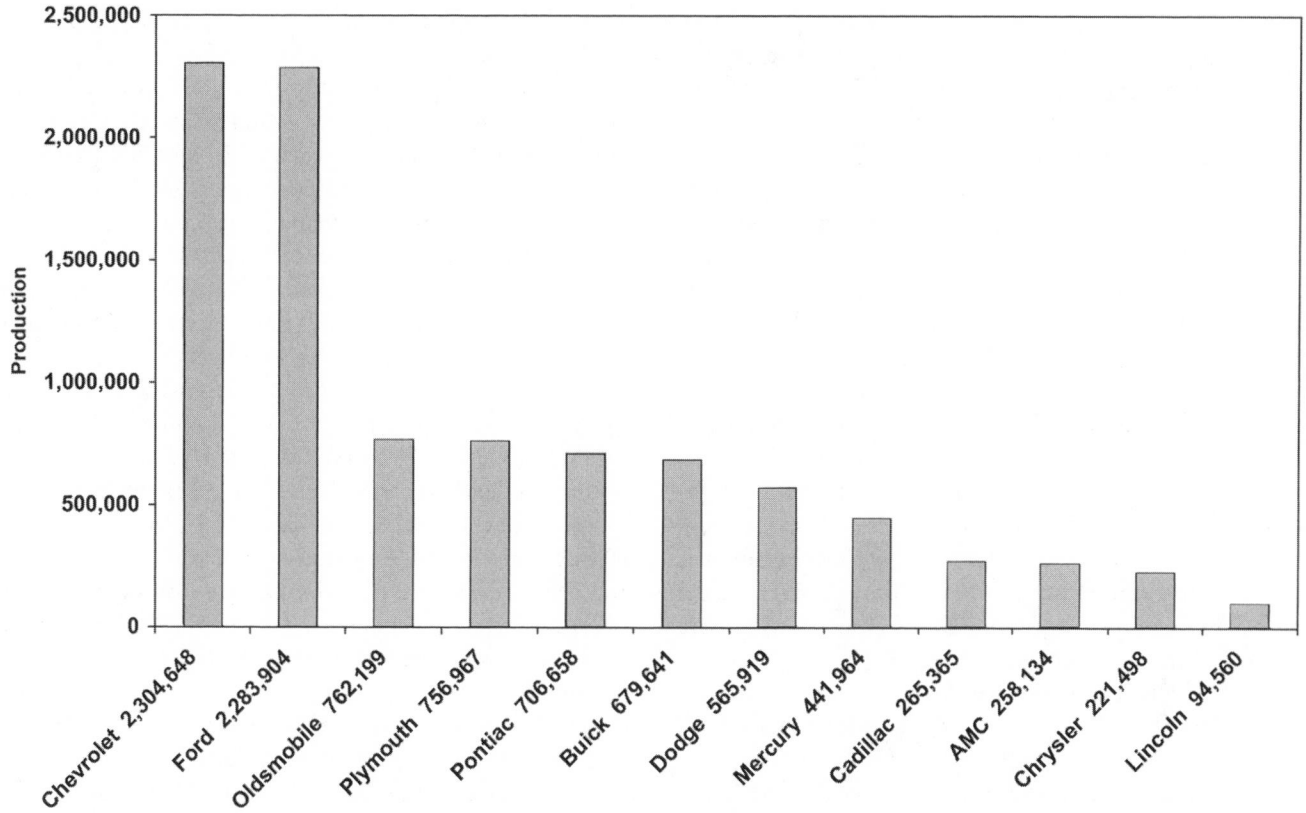

Other Chrysler Corporation lines received grille and trim changes as well as nameplate and option changes. At Dodge, the following models were dropped: Coronet Brougham 4-Door Sedan, Charger 500 2-Door, Charger Super Bee 2-Door, Charger R/T 2-Door, Challenger Convertible and Challenger R/T 2-Door Hardtop. Added to the lineup were the Challenger Rallye 2-Door Hardtop and a Rallye package for Charger models that, by the way, was the only way to get the 440 CID "Six Pack" V8 engine in a Charger. Plymouth also dropped several models including the Barracuda 2-Door Sport Sedan, Barracuda Convertible, Barracuda Gran Coupe, Hemi 'Cuda, and GTX 2-Door HT. Also worth mentioning, Chrysler replaced its 383 CID engine with a 400 CID V8 and discontinued the 426 CID Hemi V8. The Imperial LeBaron added air conditioning as standard equipment this year, which accounted for its base price increase of nearly $500 over 1971. The Dodge truck division fielded an all-new line of trucks, far more modern in appearance than Ford or Chevy. These trucks would end up serving Dodge for over 20 years, in more or less their current form. Most likely, this long stretch of production was of necessity, but during this period Ford and Chevy/GMC each ran their respective truck lines for quite a long time also. Other Dodge truck models were treated to minor restyling touches.

Full-size Ford, Mercury, and Lincoln Continental models received grille and trim changes, as did the Ford Maverick and Mustang, and Mercury Comet and Cougar models. Mid-size Ford products, however, were completely restyled, and, especially in wagon form, looked more than ever like a full-size Ford. Models dropped in the changeover included all Convertible models, the Ford Torino 500, Torino Brougham, Torino GT and Torino Cobra, and the Mercury Montego MX Brougham 4-Door Hardtop. The Ford Torino models were replaced by the Gran Torino (2-Door, 4-Door and Wagon), Gran Torino Sport (2-Door Sportsroof and 2-Door Formal Hardtop) and Gran Torino Squire Wagon. At Mercury the Montego GT 2-Door Fastback replaced the Cyclone/Cyclone GT/Cyclone Spoiler models. A Cyclone option package was offered for '72 on the GT, but was mostly for show, not go—a 302 CID 2-bbl V8 was the standard powerplant. The 429 CID V8 engine was dropped from the Mustang and Cougar option list.

The other big news at Ford Motor Company was the introduction of the new Thunderbird and Continental Mark IV luxury models. Larger and more luxurious than ever, these two models shared the same chassis and body, and both were available with the 460 CID V8 engine. The Mark IV styling followed that of the beautiful Mark III, and of course the Thunderbird had distinctive Thunderbird front and rear end treatments, but the slow-selling 4-Door

**1972**

model did not return. One other Ford model change for 1972 was the addition of a Pinto 2-Door Wagon, which became an immediate sales success, easily outselling the Chevy Vega wagon. Other than the Ranchero (whose styling changes mimicked those of the Torino), Ford trucks offered minor styling changes for 1972.

Like many other manufacturers, Buick revised most of its nameplates with new grilles and trim changes, but new designs were not to be found. Some model and powertrain changes did occur for 1972. For Skylark models, the base engine was now a 350 CID 2-bbl. V8, with a 4-bbl. version available in a Skylark 350 designation that offered deluxe interior trim as part of the package. A new "Sun Coupe" option for Skylark 350 Sport Coupes featured a folding vinyl sunroof. Also noteworthy was the passing of the Stage I option for GS models. At the top end of the line, the 1971 Limited interior trim option for Electra 225 Custom models was made standard equipment for 1972 and thus the cars name became Electra 225 Custom Limited; however, it would again be an option for the 1973 model year. The LeSabre, Centurion, Estate Wagon and Riviera continued into the new year with little change. An interesting footnote is that the new-for-'71 Centurion continued as the only full-size Buick without the traditional ventiports.

Cadillac outsold Lincoln this year nearly 3 to 1, and it was no contest with the fast-fading Chrysler Imperial which Cadillac outsold nearly 20 to 1. Changes for the year were limited to new grilles and revised trim.

"Building a better way to see the U.S.A." was Chevrolet's theme for the new model year. Most 1972 Chevys were relatively unchanged or received trim and grille changes. This carryover philosophy was continued into the entire truck line. Among the few points of interest: The SS454 option was still available for Chevelle models, while the SS option for the Monte Carlo was discontinued and the Nova SS option jumped in popularity nearly 50 percent, selling 12,309 units. Also, like other full-size GM cars, the Biscayne, BelAir, Impala and Caprice received the soon to be mandatory energy-absorbing front bumper. It should also be mentioned here that changes for GMC trucks followed those of the Chevy fleet, meaning there was relatively little change.

Styling changes at Oldsmobile were limited to the requisite new grilles and trim changes. As for model changes, the 4-4-2 returned to option package status on Cutlass S models after several years as a separate model. Also available was a Hurst/Olds package for Cutlass coupes and convertibles. A specially prepared Hurst/Olds Cutlass 4-4-2 Convertible was selected as the pace car for the 56th annual Indianapolis 500 race. Approximately 630 replicas

were built for public sale, about one-fourth of them being convertibles. In the Delta 88 line, the Custom series was dropped, but its 4-Door Sedan and 4-Door Hardtop models were moved into the Royale series.

As at the other General Motors divisions, there were no major styling changes to be found at Pontiac. An interesting limited-edition (about 500 built) option package for Ventura 4-Door Sedan models was the "SD" (Sport Deluxe, taken from the Canadian Pontiac versions of the Chevrolet Super Sport), an early attempt at a small, European-style touring sedan. The biggest model changes occurred in the mid-size LeMans line, as series names were shuffled seemingly to prepare for the new 1973 models. The Tempest T-37 series was dropped, as was the LeMans 2-Door Pillar Coupe. The LeMans Sport series was also dropped, though a LeMans Sport Convertible continued, technically a part of the base LeMans series. New for the year was a top-of-the-line Luxury LeMans, available in 2-Door or 4-Door Hardtop models and featuring a special grille, interior trim, and rear fender skirts. Available at extra cost was a LeMans Endura option that made the GTO front end treatment available for any Lemans model. Finally, the GTO option package was available on the LeMans 2-Door Hardtop or the LeMans Sport Convertible.

Independent manufacturers offered carry-over models with a few detail changes. Checker added an automatic transmission and power disc brakes to the standard equipment list and dropped the Marathon DeLuxe Limousine. As could be expected, the Avanti II was continued unchanged from previous years. As a final note, a domestic car was not selected for the *Motor Trend* magazine Car of the Year award for 1972.

The reader will note a change in the format of the chart showing model year production totals for 1972. The reason is to illustrate the huge gap separating the #1 and #2 producers, Chevy and Ford, from the rest of the industry. Although the two divisions had long enjoyed a sizeable lead over other manufacturers, the gap in 1972 was tremendous as shown below. Also included is a chart showing the sharp decline in convertible production. Compare these numbers to those shown in the chart for 1966 convertible production.

Finally, 1972 marked a change in the way horsepower was rated. The previous gross horsepower ratings (measured in ideal temperature and atmospheric conditions with optimum intake and exhaust systems, and without accessories that sapped power — including alternators) gave way to more realistic "net horsepower" figures, measured with production intake and exhaust and accessories connected. The powertrain tables for 1972 reflect the resulting low horsepower numbers.

## 1972 Convertible Production

| Convertible Models | Production | Cvt. of Market Share |
|---|---|---|
| Oldsmobile Cutlass Supreme | 11,571 | 16.07% |
| Cadillac Fleetwood Eldorado | 7,975 | 11.07% |
| Chevrolet Corvette Stingray | 6,508 | 9.04% |
| Chevrolet Impala | 6,456 | 8.97% |
| Ford Mustang | 6,401 | 8.89% |
| Chevrolet Chevelle Malibu | 4,853 | 6.74% |
| Ford LTD | 4,234 | 5.88% |
| Oldsmobile Delta 88 Royale | 3,900 | 5.42% |
| Buick Skylark Custom | 3,608 | 5.01% |
| Pontiac LeMans Sport | 3,438 | 4.77% |
| Pontiac Catalina | 2,399 | 3.33% |
| Buick Centurion | 2,396 | 3.33% |
| Pontiac Grand Ville | 2,213 | 3.07% |
| Buick LeSabre Custom | 2,037 | 2.83% |
| Mercury Cougar XR-7 | 1,929 | 2.68% |
| Mercury Cougar | 1,240 | 1.72% |
| Buick GS | 852 | 1.18% |
| Total Convertible Production | 72,010 | |

# AMERICAN MOTORS

*"American Motors introduces the buyer protection plan.
Giving American car-buyers exactly what they want."*

American Motors entered 1972 with only minor product changes. The big news for the year was the "Buyer Protection Plan," essentially a guarantee to the purchaser of a new 1972 American Motors car that it would be free from defects. The plan was promoted in all of AMC's advertising and was an apparent success. Sales for the 1972 model year were up 5.5 percent over the previous year — not an outstanding success, but a positive figure in view of the lack of new product in the showrooms and the ups and downs of AMC's sales history. All lines received only minor trim modifications, such as changed ornamentation on the Hornet and a new grille design for the Matador. The base Gremlin, Hornet, Javelin and Ambassador models were dropped for the '72 model year. This precipitated a few series names being juggled around, apparently to better suit marketing plans for future models. Also lost to history was the one-year-only Hornet SC/360.

Ambassador Brougham 2-Door Hardtop

Gremlin 2-Door Sedan with X package

Hornet SST 4-Door Sedan

1972

Javelin AMX 2-Door Hardtop

Javelin SST 2-Door Hardtop

Matador 4-Door Sedan

**Model year production:** 258,129, up 5.74% over 1971.
**Domestic market share:** 2.76% (10th place).
**Base price range:** $1,999 to $4,437.
**Industry average base price:** $3,788.
**American Motors average base price:** $3,215.
**Introduction date:** September 22, 1971.
**Assembly plants:** Kenosha, Wisconsin, and Brampton, Ontario, Canada.

**Data plate identification:** Thirteen digit code read as follows: A = American Motors; 2 = 1972; transmission code (see chart); car line-body type-series numbers (see last three digits of style number); engine code (see chart); 100001 and up for serial number (700001 and up for cars built in Ontario). *Example:* A2A797M100001 is a 1972 Torque-Command Automatic, Javelin SST 2-Door, 304 CID V8, serial number 100001, built in Kenosha.

## Powertrains

| Engine | Net HP | Engine Code | Transmission Availability | Trans Code | Hornet & Gremlin | Javelin | Matador | Ambdr. |
|---|---|---|---|---|---|---|---|---|
| 232 CID, 1-bbl., 6-cyl. | 100 | E | 3-speed manual | S/E | S | S | S | |
| | | | Torque-Command Automatic | A | $200 | $218 | $226 | - |
| 258 CID, 2-bbl., 6-cyl. | 110 | A | 3-speed manual | S | $51 | $43 | $46 | - |
| | | | Torque-Command Automatic | A | $251 | $261 | $272 | - |
| 304 CID, 2-bbl., V8 | 150 | M | 3-speed manual | S | $154 (Gr)/$138 (Hrn) | $94 | $99 | - |
| | | | Torque-Command Automatic | A | $373 (Gr)/$369 (Hrn) | $330 | $344 | S |
| 360 CID, 2-bbl., V8 | 175 | N | Torque-Command Automatic | A | $411 (Hornet) | $372 | $356 | $92 |
| 360 CID, 4-bbl., V8 | 195 | P | 4-speed manual | M | - | $273 | - | - |
| | | | Torque-Command Automatic | A | - | $378 | $376 | $112 |
| 401 CID, 4-bbl., V8 | 255 | Z | 4-speed manual | M | - | $346 | - | - |
| | | | Torque-Command Automatic | A | - | $467 | $427 | $205 |

## Major Options

| | Gremlin | Hornet | Javelin | Matador | Ambassador |
|---|---|---|---|---|---|
| Air conditioning | $377 | $377 | $377 | $377 | S |
| Adjust-O-Tilt steering wheel | $43 | $43 | $43 | $46 | $46 |
| Electric rear window defogger | - | - | $45 | $48 | $48 |
| Soft Ray tinted glass | $37 | $40 | $40 | $42 | S |
| Vinyl Top (excluding Wagon models) | - | $88 | $88 | $91 | $109 |
| Power steering—variable-ratio | $99 | $99 | $106 | $111 | $111 |
| Power brakes | $44 | $44 | $44 | $47 | S |
| Power front disc brakes | $79 | $79 | $77 | $81 | $50 |
| Power windows | - | - | - | $123 | $123 |
| AM radio | $66 | $66 | $66 | $75 | $75 |
| AM/FM stereo | $130 | $130 | $196 | $230 | $230 |
| Custom wheel covers | $50 | $50 | $50 | $53 | $53 |
| Turbo Disc wheel covers | $75 | $75 | $75 | $78 | $78 |
| Sunroof | $142 | $142* | - | - | - |

Options common to most models. (- = Not Available; S = Standard equipment.) Items may be standard equipment, optional at different pricing, or unavailable on certain models. This chart is only a guide.

*2-Door w/o vinyl top and Sportabout only.

Option packages:

• "X" package (Gremlin and Hornet) Includes special interior options, exterior graphics — $285 (Gremlin), $119 (Hornet 2-Door and Sportabout).
• "Rallye" bucket seat/performance package (Hornet): $119.
• Gucci-designed interior package with specific colors for Hornet Sportabout models: $142.
• Hornet Sportabout D/L package: $284.
• Javelin Cardin bucket seat trim package ( Javelin SST only): $85.
• Javelin AMX 360 Go-package: Includes Rally-pack, special trim, larger tires/wheels and specific powertrain upgrades — $428.
• Javelin AMX 401 Go-package: Includes Rally-pack, special trim, larger tires/wheels and specific powertrain upgrades — $505.

## Paint Colors

|  | Code | Gremlin/Hornet | Javelin | Matador/Ambassador |
|---|---|---|---|---|
| Snow White | A1 | x | x | x |
| Stardust Silver | C2 | x | x | x |
| Skyway Blue | C3 | x |  |  |
| Jetset Blue | C4 | x | x | x |
| Admiral Blue | C5 |  | x | x |
| Surfside Turquoise | C6 | x | x |  |
| Grasshopper Green | C8 | x | x | x |
| Hunter Green | C9 | x | x | x |
| Jolly Green | D1 | x | x |  |
| Yuca Tan | D2 | x | x | x |
| Baja Bronze | D3 | x | x | x |
| Cordoba Brown | D4 |  | x | x |
| Butterscotch Gold | D5 | x |  |  |
| Canary Yellow | A2 | x | x | x |
| Trans-Am Red | D7 | x | x | x |
| Sparkling Burgundy | D8 |  | x | x |
| Wild Plum | D9 | x | x |  |
| Classic Black | P1 | x | x |  |

# Gremlin

*"You'll recognize our little car anywhere."*

**Nameplate year of origin:** 1970.
**Current bodystyle lifespan:** 1970 through 1983 (restyled and renamed (in 1979).
**Predecessor to this model:** None.
**Replacement for this model:** Spirit (1979 to 1982) and Eagle SX/4 (1981 to 1983).
**Percentage of division's sales volume:** 23.91%.
**Corporate siblings:** None.
**Primary competition:** Chevrolet Vega and Ford Pinto.
**Notable changes:** Two-seat model dropped, 304 CID V8 added to option list, trim and detail changes.
**Major standard equipment:** Vinyl bench seat, front door pockets, fold-down rear seat, front seat foam cushions, front arm rests, interior lights, aluminized exhaust system, Weather-Eye heating & ventilation system, exterior pinstripes, 6.00 × 13 BSW tires.

## Measurements

| | |
|---|---|
| Wheelbase | 96.0" |
| Length | 161.2" |
| Width | 70.6" |
| Height | 51.7" |
| Legroom — front | 40.8" |
| Legroom — rear | 27.8" |
| Headroom — front | 38.1" |
| Headroom — rear | 36.4" |
| Luggage cap. (cu. ft.) | 6.0 |
| Fuel capacity (gals.) | 21.0 |

**1972**

## Models Available

| | Style Number | Base MSRP | Change from LY | Shipping Wt. (lbs.) | Production | Change from LY |
|---|---|---|---|---|---|---|
| Gremlin 2-Door Sedan | 7246-5 | $1,999 | 0.00% | 2494 | 61,717 | +15.40% |
| TOTALS | | Avg. price $1,999 | +2.65% | Production* | 61,717 | +15.40% |

*Calendar Year production shown.

# Hornet

*"Is it the best value in the compact field?"*

**Nameplate year of origin:** 1951 (used on high-performance Hudson).
**Current bodystyle lifespan:** 1970 through 1987.
**Predecessor to this model:** Rambler American (1964 to 1969).
**Replacement for this model:** Concord (1978 to 1982) and Eagle (1980 to 1987).
**Percentage of division's sales volume:** 27.53%.
**Corporate siblings:** None.
**Primary competition:** Chevy Nova, Dodge Dart, Ford Maverick, Plymouth Valiant, and Pontiac Ventura II.
**Notable Changes:** Trim and detail changes.
**Major standard equipment:** Fabric-covered front bench seat with foam cushions, instrument panel package tray, front and rear armrests, interior lights, glove box lock, aluminized exhaust system, Weather-Eye heating & ventilation system, exterior pinstripes, 6.45 × 14 BSW tires. Sportabout adds: Hidden compartment lock, and 6.95 × 14 BSW tires.

## Measurements

| | Cars | Sportabout |
|---|---|---|
| Wheelbase | 108.0" | 108.0" |
| Length | 179.3" | 179.3" |
| Width | 70.6" | 70.6" |
| Height | 51.1" | 51.3" |
| Legroom — front | 40.8" | 40.8" |
| Legroom — rear | 36.1" | 36.1" |
| Headroom — front | 38.1" | 38.1" |
| Headroom — rear | 37.5" | 37.9" |
| Luggage cap. (cu. ft.) | 11.2 | 64.6 |
| Fuel capacity (gals.) | 16.0 | 16.0 |

## Models Available

| | Style Number | Base MSRP | Change from LY | Shipping Wt. (lbs.) | Production | Change from LY |
|---|---|---|---|---|---|---|
| Hornet SST 2-Door Sedan | 7206-7 | $2,199 | -5.38% | 2627 | 34,675 (6-cylinder)* | +15.20% |
| Hornet SST 4-Door Sedan | 7205-7 | $2,265 | -15.83% | 2691 | 2276 (V8)* | +8.38% |
| Hornet SST 4-Door Sportabout | 7208-7 | $2,587 | -0.27% | 2769 | 34,100 | +32.17% |
| TOTALS | | Avg. price $2,350 | -1.14% | Production | 71,051 | -4.86%** |

*Estimated. Exact Hornet production by body style is not available.    **Differences in percentages due to discontinuance of certain models.

# Javelin

*"The calm before the storm."*

**Nameplate year of origin:** 1968.
**Current bodystyle lifespan:** 1971 through 1974.
**Predecessor to this model:** Javelin (1968 to 1970).
**Replacement for this model:** None.
**Percentage of division's sales volume:** 10.14%.
**Corporate siblings:** None.
**Primary competition:** Chevrolet Camaro, Dodge Challenger, Ford Mustang, Plymouth Barracuda, and Pontiac Firebird.

## Measurements

| | |
|---|---|
| Wheelbase | 110.0" |
| Length | 191.8" |
| Width | 75.2" |
| Height | NA |
| Legroom — front | NA |
| Legroom — rear | NA |
| Headroom — front | NA |

**Notable changes:** New Pierre Cardin special edition (4,152 built), revised grille, and detail changes.

**Major standard equipment:** Vinyl front bucket seats with foam cushions, front and rear armrests, interior lights, glove box lock, dual horns, aluminized exhaust system, Weather-Eye heating & ventilation system, exterior pinstripes, 2-spoke custom steering wheel, and C78 × 14 BSW tires. AMX adds: 304 CID V8, 3-spoke sports steering wheel, slotted 14 × 6 wheels, space saver spare tire, and E70 × 14 white-letter tires.

## Measurements (cont.)

| | |
|---|---|
| Headroom — rear | NA |
| Luggage cap. (cu. ft.) | 10.2 |
| Fuel capacity (gals.) | 16.0 |

## Models Available

| | Style Number | Base MSRP | Change from LY | Shipping Wt. (lbs.) | Production | Change from LY |
|---|---|---|---|---|---|---|
| Javelin SST 2-Door Coupe | 7279-7 | $2,807 | -6.41% | 2875 | 23,455 | +32.52% |
| Javelin AMX 2-Door Coupe | 7279-8 | $3,109 | -9.42% | 3149 | 2,729 | +32.86% |
| TOTALS | Avg. price | $2,958 | -4.68% | Production | 26,184 | -10.11%* |

*Differences in percentages due to discontinuance of certain models.*

# Matador

*"Our intermediate size car gives you most of the things you'd want in a family house."*

**Nameplate year of origin:** 1971.

**Current bodystyle lifespan:** 1967 through 1978 (restyles in 1969, 1971, and 1974).

**Predecessor to this model:** Rebel (1968 to 1970).

**Replacement for this model:** None.

**Percentage of division's sales volume:** 21.23%.

**Corporate siblings:** Ambassador (shared components from the cowl back).

**Primary competition:** Chevrolet Chevelle, Dodge Coronet, Ford Torino, and Plymouth Satellite.

**Notable changes:** Revised grille, and trim and detail changes.

**Major standard equipment:** Fabric-covered front bench seat with foam cushions, front and rear arm rests, glove box lock, dual horns, aluminized exhaust system, Weather-Eye heating & ventilation system, exterior pinstripes, and E78 × 14 BSW tires. Wagon adds: Hidden compartment with lock, and G78 × 14 BSW tires.

## Measurements

| | Cars | Wagon |
|---|---|---|
| Wheelbase | 118.0" | 118.0" |
| Length | 206.0" | 205.0" |
| Width | 77.2" | 77.2" |
| Height | 54.5" | 54.5" |
| Legroom — front | 41.0" | 41.0" |
| Legroom — rear | 37.6" | 37.6" |
| Headroom — front | 39.3" | 39.3" |
| Headroom — rear | 37.0" | 37.0" |
| Luggage cap. (cu. ft.) | 18.2 | 99.1 |
| Fuel capacity (gals.) | 19.5 | 19.5 |

## Models Available

| | Style Number | Base MSRP | Change from LY | Shipping Wt. (lbs.) | Production | Change from LY |
|---|---|---|---|---|---|---|
| Matador 2-Door Hardtop | 7219-7 | $2,818 | +0.68% | 3210 | * | * |
| Matador 4-Door Sedan | 7215-7 | $2,784 | +0.51% | 3171 | * | * |
| Matador 4-Door Wagon | 7218-7 | $3,140 | -0.73% | 3480 | * | * |
| TOTALS | Avg. price | $2,914 | +0.10% | Production | 54,813 | +19.71% |

*Production by body style is not available. **Differences in percentages due to discontinuance of certain models.*

**1972**

# Ambassador

*"We built it for the Smiths. And the Smythes."*

**Nameplate year of origin:** 1933 (from top-of-the-line Nash).
**Current bodystyle lifespan:** 1967 through 1978 (shared basic structure with Matador).
**Predecessor to this model:** Ambassador (1963 to 1966).
**Replacement for this model:** None.
**Percentage of division's sales volume:** 17.19%.
**Corporate siblings:** Matador (shared components from the cowl back).
**Primary competition:** Chevrolet BelAir/Impala/Caprice, Ford LTD, and Plymouth Fury.
**Notable changes:** Revised grille, and trim and detail changes.
**Major standard equipment:** Fabric-covered front bench seat with foam cushions, interior lights, glove box lock, dual horn, aluminized exhaust system, Weather-Eye heating & ventilation system, air conditioning, exterior pinstripes, power front disc brakes, bumper guards, 2-spoke custom steering wheel, and E78 × 14 BSW tires. Wagon adds: Roof rack and H78 × 14 BSW tires. Brougham adds: Brougham interior trim, and simulated wood-grain side and rear panels on wagon.

## Measurements

|  | Cars | Wagons |
|---|---|---|
| Wheelbase | 122.0" | 122.0" |
| Length | 211.1" | 209.7" |
| Width | 77.2" | 77.2" |
| Height | 54.5" | 54.5" |
| Legroom — front | 41.0" | 41.0" |
| Legroom — rear | 37.6" | 37.6" |
| Headroom — front | 39.3" | 39.3" |
| Headroom — rear | 37.0" | 37.0" |
| Luggage cap. (cu. ft.) | 18.2 | 99.1 |
| Fuel capacity (gals.) | 19.5 | 20.0 |

## Models Available

| | Style Number | Base MSRP | Change from LY | Shipping Wt. (lbs.) | Production | Change from LY |
|---|---|---|---|---|---|---|
| Ambassador SST 2-Door Hardtop | 7289-5 | $3,902 | +0.83% | 3579 | * | * |
| Ambassador SST 4-Door Sedan | 7285-5 | $3,885 | +0.86% | 3537 | * | * |
| Ambassador SST 4-Door Wagon | 7288-5 | $4,270 | +0.40% | 3833 | * | * |
| Ambassador Brougham 2-Door HT | 7289-7 | $4,018 | +0.48% | 3581 | * | * |
| Ambassador Brougham 4-Door Sdn. | 7285-7 | $4,002 | +0.47% | 3551 | * | * |
| Ambassador Brougham 4-Door Wgn. | 7288-7 | $4,437 | +0.16% | 3857 | * | * |
| TOTALS | *Avg. price* | $4,086 | +2.15%** | *Production** | 44,364 | +6.45% |

*Estimated model year production shown.     **Differences in percentages due to discontinuance of certain models.*

# BUICK

*"Something to believe in."*

Nineteen-seventy-two represented something of a holding pattern for Buick, as it did for almost all General Motors divisions this year. All-new intermediate models were meant to be introduced for the new model year, but a strike at GM during 1971 put those plans on hold, as the strike was a lengthy and costly one. The full-size models had been totally redesigned for 1971, and this year's models would benefit by the learning process from the mistakes of the first year models. As with other GM cars this year, a price decrease resulted from federal government intervention. This intervention was an effort to slow drastic inflationary pressures by way of a price freeze and a lifting of some of the excise taxes that had been imposed earlier.

There were few model changes for the new year. In the Skylark line, the GS was relegated to optional equipment status, and the Skylark 350 was a new designation for a base Skylark with the 350 CID 4-bbl. engine. Across the line, styling changes were minimal, and on most models consisted only of revised grilles, bumpers, etc. Also, the Full-Flow ventilation system introduced in 1971 on the full-size models was modified to eliminate the louvered deck-lid.

Centurion 2-Door Convertible

Electra 225 Limited 2-Door Hardtop

Estate Wagon 4-Door

LeSabre Custom 2-Door Convertible

Riviera 2-Door Hardtop

Skylark Custom 2-Door Convertible

Skylark Custom 4-Door Hardtop

**Production:** 679,641, up 21.23% from 1971.
**Domestic market share:** 7.28% (6th place).
**Base price range:** $2,925 to $5,149.
**Industry average base price:** $3,788.
**Buick average base price:** $3,963.
**Introduction date:** September 23, 1971.
**Assembly plants:** Southgate, CA (C); Atlanta, GA (D); Flint, MI (H); Kansas City, MO (K); Fairfax, KS (X); Wilmington, DE (Y); Fremont, CA (Z); and Oshawa, Ontario, (1).

**Data plate identification:** Thirteen digit code read as follows: five digit style number in which 4 = Buick, 2nd number identifies series (3 is Skylark, 8 is Electra, etc.), 3rd through 5th digits indicate model number; 2 = 1972 year; assembly plant code; 100001 and up for serial number. *Example:* 452572X100001 is a 1972 Buick LeSabre 2-Door Hardtop, serial number 100001, built in Fairfax, KS.

## Powertrains

| Engine | Net HP | Transmission Availability | Skylark | LeSabre/Centurion Estate Wagon | Elec. 225 | Riviera |
|---|---|---|---|---|---|---|
| 350 CID, 2-bbl., V8 | 150 | 3-speed manual | S | - | - | - |
| | | Turbo Hydra-matic | $222 | S (LeSabre) | - | - |
| 350 CID, 4-bbl., V8 | 175 | 3-speed manual | S (GS)/$48 (Others) | - | - | - |
| | | 4-speed manual | $190 (GS only) | - | | |
| | | Turbo Hydra-matic | $270 | $47 (LeSabre) | - | - |
| 455 CID, 4-bbl., V8 | 225 | 4-speed manual | $355 (GS) | - | - | - |
| | | Turbo Hydra-matic | $387 (GS) | S (Estate Wgn | | |

872

| Engine | Net HP | Transmission Availability | Skylark | LeSabre/Centurion Estate Wagon & Centurion)/ $ (LeSabre) | Elec. 225 | Riviera |
|---|---|---|---|---|---|---|
| | | | | | S | S |
| 455 CID, 4-bbl., V8 | 250 (w/ dual exh.) | Turbo Hydra-matic | $ (GS) | $99 Centurion | - | - |
| 455 CID GS, 4-bbl., V8 | 260 | Turbo Hydra-matic | - | - | - | $200 |

## Major Options

| | Skylark | LeSabre | Centurion | Electra 225 | Estate Wagon | Riviera |
|---|---|---|---|---|---|---|
| Air conditioning—manual | $408 | $442 | $442 | $442 | $442 | $442 |
| Air conditioning—automatic | - | $521 | $521 | $521 | $521 | $521 |
| Electronic cruise control | $ | $ | $ | $ | $ | $ |
| Soft Ray tinted glass | $43 | $51 | $51 | $51 | $51 | $51 |
| Deck lid remote release | $14 | $14 | $14 | $14 | - | $14 |
| Power steering—variable-ratio | $116 | S | S | S | S | S |
| Power brakes—front disc | $70/S (Spwgn.) | S | S | S | S | S |
| Power door locks | $ | $ | $ | $ | $ | $ |
| Power driver's seat/Bench seat | $79 | $105 | $105 | $105 | $105 | $79 |
| Power windows | $116 | $133 | $133 | $133 | $133 | $133 |
| AM radio | $75 | $88 | $88 | $88 | $88 | $88 |
| AM/FM stereo | $139 | $239 | $239 | $239 | $239 | $239 |
| Front bucket seats | $ (2-Dr. only) | - | - | - | - | $ |
| Tilt steering wheel | $45 | $45 | $45 | $45 | $45 | S |
| Sunroof | $251 (350 2-Dr.) | - | - | - | - | $605 |
| Vinyl roof | $102 | $126 | $126/S (2-Dr.) | $142 | $142 | $128 |
| Max Trac Drive Control System | - | $92 | $92 | $92 | $92 | $92 |
| Special trim package and performance options: | | | | | | |
| Skylark 350 Package | $135 | - | - | - | - | - |
| GS Option | - | - | - | - | - | $200 |

Options common to most models. (– = Not Available; S or STD. = Standard equipment.) Items may be standard equipment, optional at different pricing, or unavailable on certain models. This chart is only a guide.

## Paint Colors

| | Code | Skylark | LeSabre/Cent/EW/Electra | Riviera |
|---|---|---|---|---|
| Regal Black | A | | x | |
| Stratomist Blue | B | x | | |
| Arctic White | C | x | x | x |
| Crystal Blue | D | x | x | x |
| Royal Blue | E | | x | x |
| Seamist Green | F | x | x | |
| Emerald Mist | G | | | x |
| Heritage Green | H | x | | |
| Hunter Green | I | x | x | x |
| Sandalwood | J | x | x | x |
| Deep Chestnut | K | | | x |
| Sierra Tan | L | | x | x |
| Burnished Copper | M | x | | |
| Nutmeg | N | | x | x |
| Burnished Bronze | P | | | x |
| Cortez Gold | Q | x | | |
| Fire Red | R | x | x | |
| Champagne Gold | S | | x | x |
| Cascade Blue | T | x | x | |
| Antique Gold | U | x | x | x |

| | Code | Skylark | LeSabre/Cent/EW/Electra | Riviera |
|---|---|---|---|---|
| Silver Mist | V | x | x | x |
| Charcoal Mist | W | | x | x |
| Vintage Red | X | | | x |
| Sunburst Yellow | Y | x | | |
| Flame Orange | Z | x | | |

# Skylark

*"Skylark treats you very special."*

**Nameplate year of origin:** 1953.
**Current bodystyle lifespan:** 1968 through 1972.
**Predecessor to this model:** Special/Skylark (1964 to 1967).
**Replacement for this model:** Century (1973 to 1977).
**Percentage of division's sales volume:** 33.16%.
**Corporate siblings:** Chevrolet Chevelle, Pontiac LeMans, Olds Cutlass.
**Primary competition:** Dodge Coronet and Mercury Montego.
**Notable changes:** Revised grille and trim and detail changes. Skylark 350 models created from base Skylark with a 350 CID 4-bbl. V8 engine and DeLuxe trim enhancements.
**Major standard equipment:** All-vinyl front bench seat, front ash tray, self adjusting brakes, and G78 × 14 BSW tires. Skylark 350 adds: Cloth and vinyl deluxe seats, rear ash trays, front door operated interior lighting, wheel opening moldings, dual horns, and "350" emblems. Custom adds: Custom interior trim, deluxe steering wheel, and unique eggcrate-style grille. Sportwagon adds: Dual-action tailgate. GS adds: Dual exhausts, functional hood air scoops, heavy duty springs, shocks and stabilizer bar.

## Measurements

| | 2-Doors | 4-Doors | Sportwagon |
|---|---|---|---|
| Wheelbase | 112.0" | 116.0" | 116.0" |
| Length | 203.3" | 207.3" | 213.7" |
| Width | 76.8" | 76.8" | 76.8" |
| Height | 53.5" | 54.2" | 54.8" |
| Legroom — front | 41.3" | 41.7" | 42.6" |
| Legroom — rear | 32.4" | 34.8" | 34.6" |
| Headroom — front | 37.8" | 38.6" | 38.4" |
| Headroom — rear | 36.3" | 37.3" | 38.3" |
| Luggage capacity (cu. ft.) | NA | NA | NA |
| Fuel capacity (gals.) | 20.0 | 20.0 | 20.0 |

## Models Available

| | Style Number | Base MSRP | Change from LY | Shipping Wt. (lbs.) | Production | Change from LY |
|---|---|---|---|---|---|---|
| Skylark 2-Door Coupe | 43327 | $2,925 | +2.74% | 3348 | 14,552 | +0.36% |
| Skylark 2-Door Hardtop Sport Coupe | 43337 | $2,993 | +2.57% | 3403 | 84,868 | +38.67% |
| Skylark 4-Door Sedan | 43369 | $2,973 | +2.62% | 3408 | 42,206 | +24.00% |
| Skylark 350 2-Door Hardtop Sport Cpe. | 43337 | $3,124 | NEW | * | * | NEW |
| Skylark 350 4-Door Sedan | 43369 | $3,104 | NEW | * | * | NEW |
| Skylark Custom 2-Door Hardtop | 44437 | $3,255 | -1.87% | 3403 | 34,271 | +16.03% |
| Skylark Custom 2-Door Convertible | 44467 | $3,393 | -2.00% | 3476 | 3,608 | -9.64% |
| Skylark Custom 4-Door Sedan | 44469 | $3,228 | -1.82% | 3408 | 9,924 | +19.58% |
| Skylark Custom 4-Door Hardtop | 44439 | $3,331 | -1.95% | 3546 | 12,925 | -36.70% |
| Sportwagon 4-Door, 2-Seat Wagon | 43436 | $3,444 | -2.02% | 3936 | 14,417 | +15.11% |
| GS 2-Door Hardtop Sport Coupe | 43437 | $3,225 | -1.83% | 3475 | 7,723 | -6.59% |
| GS 2-Door Convertible | 43467 | $3,406 | -2.02% | 3517 | 852 | -5.54% |
| TOTALS | *Avg. price* $3,200 | | -1.23% | *Production* 225,346 | | +16.35% |

*Skylark 350 created by optional 350 CID engine. See powertrain chart.

1972

# LeSabre

*"Your 1972 LeSabre treats you like a hero."*

**Nameplate year of origin:** 1959.
**Current bodystyle lifespan:** 1971 through 1976.
**Predecessor to this model:** LeSabre (1969 to 1970).
**Corporate siblings:** Chevrolet Full-size, Pontiac Full-size, Oldsmobile Delta 88.
**Replacement for this model:** LeSabre (1977 to 1985).
**Percentage of division's sales volume:** 26.97%.
**Primary competition:** Chrysler Newport, Dodge Monaco, and Mercury Monterey.
**Notable changes:** Trim and detail changes.
**Major standard equipment:** Kalmara cloth and Madrid-grain vinyl bench seat, power front disc brakes, variable ratio power steering, Turbo Hydra-matic transmission, AccuDrive suspension system, bright rocker panel moldings, horizontal bar grille, and H78 × 15 BSW tires. Custom adds: Kasmar cloth and Madrid-grain vinyl bench seat (all-vinyl on convertible), wheel opening moldings, and "Custom" nameplates.

### Measurements

| | |
|---|---|
| Wheelbase | 124.0" |
| Length | 221.9" |
| Width | 80.0" |
| Height | 53.8" |
| Legroom — front | 42.6" |
| Legroom — rear | 38.5" |
| Headroom — front | 38.4" |
| Headroom — rear | 37.4" |
| Luggage capacity (cu. ft.) | NA |
| Fuel capacity (gals.) | NA |

## Models Available

| | Style Number | Base MSRP | Change from LY | Shipping Wt. (lbs.) | Production | Change from LY |
|---|---|---|---|---|---|---|
| LeSabre 2-Door Hardtop | 45257 | $4,024 | -0.82% | 4132 | 14,001 | +4.60% |
| LeSabre 4-Door Sedan | 45269 | $3,958 | -0.85% | 3958 | 29,505 | +11.98% |
| LeSabre 4-Door Hardtop | 45239 | $4,079 | +0.44% | 4226 | 15,160 | -61.11% |
| LeSabre Custom 2-Door Hardtop | 45457 | $4,107 | -1.01% | 4149 | 36,510 | +21.93% |
| LeSabre Custom 2-Door Conv. | 45467 | $4,291 | -1.17% | 4233 | 2,037 | +9.75% |
| LeSabre Custom 4-Door Sedan | 45469 | $4,047 | -0.94% | 4158 | 35,295 | +30.87% |
| LeSabre Custom 4-Door Hardtop | 45439 | $4,168 | -1.07% | 4238 | 50,804 | +23.62% |
| TOTALS | *Avg. price* $4,096 | | -1.00% | *Production* 183,312 | | +19.16% |

# Centurion

*"Your '72 Centurion makes you a little more aware of life."*

**Nameplate year of origin:** 1971.
**Current bodystyle lifespan:** 1971 through 1976.
**Predecessor to this model:** Wildcat (1969 to 1970).
**Replacement for this model:** LeSabre Luxus (1974).
**Percentage of division's sales volume:** 5.32%.
**Corporate siblings:** Chevrolet Full-size, Pontiac Full-size, Oldsmobile Delta 88.
**Primary competition:** Chrysler Newport, Dodge Monaco Brougham, and Mercury Monterey Custom.
**Notable changes:** Trim and detail changes.
**Major standard equipment:** Power front disc brakes, variable ratio power steering, AccuDrive suspension system, Turbo Hydra-matic transmission, H78 × 15 BSW tires, bright rocker panel molding, wheel opening moldings, vertical bar grille design, and Elk-grain expanded vinyl notchback front seat.

### Measurements

| | |
|---|---|
| Wheelbase | 124.0" |
| Length | 221.9" |
| Width | 80.0" |
| Height | 53.8" |
| Legroom — front | 42.6" |
| Legroom — rear | 38.5" |
| Headroom — front | 38.4" |
| Headroom — rear | 37.4" |
| Luggage capacity (cu. ft.) | NA |
| Fuel capacity (gals.) | NA |

## Models Available

| | Style Number | Base MSRP | Change from LY | Shipping Wt. (lbs.) | Production | Change from LY |
|---|---|---|---|---|---|---|
| Centurion 2-Door Hardtop | 46647 | $4,579 | -2.12% | 4331 | 14,187 | +19.30% |
| Centurion 2-Door Convertible | 46667 | $4,616 | -1.33% | 4233 | 2,396 | +10.87% |
| Centurion 4-Door Hardtop | 46639 | $4,508 | -1.23% | 4508 | 19,582 | +27.61% |
| TOTALS | | Avg. price $4,568 | -1.55% | | Production 36,165 | +23.02% |

# Estate Wagon

*"Aren't you glad your new Estate Wagon is so big and comfortable and secure…"*

**Nameplate year of origin:** 1940 (as designation for station wagon).
**Current bodystyle lifespan:** 1971 through 1976.
**Predecessor to this model:** Estate Wagon (1970).
**Replacement for this model:** Estate Wagon (1977 to 1989).
**Percentage of division's sales volume:** 4.26%.
**Corporate siblings:** Chevrolet Impala/Caprice, Olds Custom Cruiser, and Pontiac Safari.
**Primary competition:** Chrysler Town & Country and Mercury Colony Park.
**Notable changes:** Trim and detail changes.
**Major standard equipment:** Kalmara cloth and Madrid-grain vinyl bench seat, power front disc brakes, variable ratio power steering, Turbo Hydra-matic transmission, AccuDrive suspension system, bright rocker panel moldings, Electra-style cross-bar grille, Glide-away tailgate, power tailgate window, four-jet windshield washer, and L78 × 15 BSW tires.

### Measurements

| | |
|---|---|
| Wheelbase | 127.0" |
| Length | 228.3" |
| Width | 80.0" |
| Height | 57.3" |
| Legroom — front | 42.6" |
| Legroom — rear | 39.9" |
| Headroom — front | 39.6" |
| Headroom — rear | 39.3" |
| Luggage capacity (cu. ft.) | NA |
| Fuel capacity (gals.) | NA |

## Models Available

| | Style Number | Base MSRP | Change from LY | Shipping Wt. (lbs.) | Production | Change from LY |
|---|---|---|---|---|---|---|
| Estate Wagon 4-Door, 2-Seat Wgn. | 46035 | $4,589 | -1.10% | 4952 | 10,175 | +16.97% |
| Estate Wagon 4-Door, 3-Seat Wgn. | 46045 | $4,728 | -1.22% | 5021 | 18,793 | +22.55% |
| TOTALS | | Avg. price $4,659 | -1.15% | | Production 28,968 | +20.53% |

# Electra 225

*"Your new Electra 225 speaks softly, but definitely sets you apart."*

**Nameplate year of origin:** 1959.
**Current bodystyle lifespan:** 1971 through 1976.
**Predecessor to this model:** Electra 225 (1969 to 1970).
**Replacement for this model:** Electra (1977 to 1984).
**Percentage of division's sales volume:** 25.33%.
**Corporate siblings:** Cadillac Calais/de Ville and Oldsmobile Ninety-Eight.
**Primary competition:** Chrysler New Yorker and Mercury Marquis.
**Notable changes:** Trim and detail changes.
**Major standard equipment:** Kilton cloth and Madrid-grain vinyl bench seat, variable ratio power steering, power front disc brakes, AccuDrive suspension system, Turbo Hydra-matic transmission, cross-hatch style grille, bright rocker

### Measurements

| | |
|---|---|
| Wheelbase | 127.0" |
| Length | 227.9" |
| Width | 80.0" |
| Height | 54.9" |
| Legroom — front | 42.6" |
| Legroom — rear | 40.5" |
| Headroom — front | 39.3" |
| Headroom — rear | 38.2" |
| Luggage capacity (cu. ft.) | NA |
| Fuel capacity (gals.) | NA |

1972

panel molding and wheel opening moldings, rear fender skirts, remote control outside rear view mirror, and J78 × 15 BSW tires. Custom adds: Elk-grain vinyl or Kismet cloth and Madrid-grain vinyl notchback seat with front-center armrest, and Limited script badges.

## Models Available

|  | Style Number | Base MSRP | Change from LY | Shipping Wt. (lbs.) | Production | Change from LY |
|---|---|---|---|---|---|---|
| Electra 225 2-Door Hardtop | 48237 | $4,782 | -0.40% | 4380 | 9,961 | +15.00% |
| Electra 225 4-Door Hardtop | 48239 | $4,890 | -0.50% | 4484 | 19,433 | +10.48% |
| Electra 225 Custom Ltd. 2-Door HT | 48437 | $4,952 | -0.56% | 4411 | 37,974 | +41.53% |
| Electra 225 Custom Ltd. 4-Door HT | 48439 | $5,060 | -0.65% | 4495 | 104,754 | +43.59% |
| TOTALS | | Avg. price $4,921 | -0.53% | | Production 172,122 | +36.57% |

# Riviera

### "1972 Riviera … is this the way you look at life?"

**Nameplate year of origin:** 1949 (2-Dr. HTs); 1963 (series).
**Current bodystyle lifespan:** 1971 through 1976.
**Predecessor to this model:** Riviera (1966 to 1970).
**Replacement for this model:** Riviera (1977 to 1978).
**Percentage of division's sales volume:** 4.96%.
**Corporate siblings:** Cadillac Eldorado and Oldsmobile Toronado.
**Primary competition:** Ford Thunderbird and Lincoln Continental Mark IV.
**Notable changes:** Revised grille, trim and detail changes.
**Major standard equipment:** All-vinyl bench seat, variable ratio power steering, power front disc brakes, dual exhaust system, Turbo Hydra-matic transmission, eggcrate grille design, vinyl body side moldings, remote control outside rear view mirror, tilt steering wheel, and H78 × 15 BSW tires.

### Measurements

| | |
|---|---|
| Wheelbase | 122.0" |
| Length | 218.3" |
| Width | 80.0" |
| Height | 54.0" |
| Legroom — front | 42.7" |
| Legroom — rear | 35.6" |
| Headroom — front | 37.7" |
| Headroom — rear | 37.0" |
| Luggage capacity (cu. ft.) | NA |
| Fuel capacity (gals.) | NA |

## Models Available

|  | Style Number | Base MSRP | Change from LY | Shipping Wt. (lbs.) | Production | Change from LY |
|---|---|---|---|---|---|---|
| Riviera 2-Door Hardtop | 49487 | $5,149 | -1.98% | 4399 | 33,728 | -0.24% |
| TOTALS | | Avg. price $5,149 | -1.98% | | Production 33,728 | -0.24% |

# CADILLAC

### "Out of a Tradition of Excellence."

The seventieth anniversary of America's luxury car leader brought little new to showrooms. Cadillac, like other makes, was busy trying to keep up with stricter government regulations, and had little time to worry with updating styling. This was not a pressing concern, though, as the entire line had been revamped for 1971. The 1972 model year brought with it the requisite new grille design and minor trim changes, but otherwise the cars were little changed.

The most obvious change to the front end of the standard Cadillacs was the moving of the parking lights from the bumper to a position between the headlights.

Calais 2-Door Hardtop

Eldorado 2-Door Hardtop

Fleetwood 60 Special Brougham 4-Door Sedan

Fleetwood 75 9-passenger, 4-Door Sedan

Sedan de Ville 4-Door Hardtop

**Model year production:** 265,365, up 42.27% from 1971.
**Domestic market share:** 2.84% (9th place).
**Base price range:** $5,771 to $11,880.
**Industry average base price:** $3,788.
**Cadillac average base price:** $7,812.
**Introduction date:** September 23, 1971.
**Assembly plants:** Detroit, MI (Q), and Linden, NJ (E).
**Data plate identification:** Thirteen digit code read as follows: four digit style number in which 6 = Cadillac, 2nd digit

identifies series (e.g., C is Calais), 3rd and 4th digits indicate body style number (2nd through 4th digits of VIN make up 3rd through 5th digits of body style number in listings); 5th digit is engine code; 2 for 1972; 7th digit is assembly plant code; 100001 and up for serial number. *Example:* 6D47R2Q100001 is a 1972 Cadillac de Ville 2-Door Hardtop with a 472 CID V8 engine, serial number 100001, built in Detroit, MI.

## Powertrains

| Engine | Net HP | Engine Code | Transmission Availability | Eldorado | All other models |
|---|---|---|---|---|---|
| 472 CID, 4-bbl., V8 | 220 | R | Turbo Hydra-matic | - | S |
| 500 CID, 4-bbl., V8 | 235 | S | Turbo Hydra-matic | S | - |

**1972**

## Major Options

| | Eldorado | de Ville/Calais | 60 Sp. | Seventy-Five |
|---|---|---|---|---|
| Automatic climate control | $537 | $537 | $537 | S |
| 6-way power seat | $92 | $92 (deV.)/$118 (Cal.) | $92 | $92 (NA Limo) |
| Power door locks | $71 | $71 | $71 | $118 |
| AM-FM radio | $188 | $188 | $188 | $188 |
| AM-FM stereo w/8-track | $417 | $417 | $417 | $417 |
| Vinyl Roof | $161 | $156 (de Ville only) | S | - |
| Sunroof | $626 (Cpe) | $626 (de Ville only) | $626 | - |
| Tilt & telescope steering wheel | $95 | $95 | $95 | $95 |
| Leather upholstery | $185 (Cpe) | $174 (de Ville only) | $174 | - |
| Cruise control | $95 | $95 | $95 | $95 |
| Tinted glass | $59 | $59 | $59 | $59 |
| Rear window defogger | $37 (Cpe)/$63 (Conv.) | $32 | $32 | S |
| Remote control trunk release | $58 | $58 | $58 | $58 |
| Firemist paint colors | $132 | $132 | $132 | $132 |

Options common to most models. (- = Not Available; S = Standard equipment.) Items may be standard equipment, optional at different pricing, or unavailable on certain models. This chart is only a guide.

## Paint Colors

| | Code | | Code |
|---|---|---|---|
| Cotillion White | 11 | Tawny Beige Met. | 64 |
| Contessa Pewter Met. | 14 | Cognac Met. | 69 |
| Mayfair Gray Met. | 18 | Cambridge Red Met. | 73 |
| Zodiac Blue Met. | 24 | Coronation Red Met. | 74 |
| Brittany Blue Met. | 29 | Ice Blue Firemist Met.* | 90 |
| Adriatic Turquoise Met. | 34 | St. Moritz Blue Firemist Met.* | 92 |
| Sumatra Green Met. | 44 | Palomino Firemist Met.* | 93 |
| Brewster Green Met. | 49 | Patrician Covert Firemist Met.* | 94 |
| Willow | 50 | Balmoral Green Firemist Met.* | 96 |
| Promenade Gold Met. | 54 | Russet Firemist Met.* | 99 |
| Stratford Covert Met. | 59 | Sable Black | 19 |

*Firemist colors available at extra cost.

# Calais

*"It has to be an extraordinary investment, any way you look at it."*

**Nameplate year of origin:** 1965.
**Current bodystyle lifespan:** 1971 through 1976.
**Predecessor to this model:** Calais (1969 to 1970).
**Replacement for this model:** None.
**Percentage of division's sales volume:** 2.93%.
**Corporate siblings:** Buick Electra 225 and Oldsmobile Ninety-Eight.
**Primary competition:** Chrysler New Yorker and Lincoln Continental.
**Notable changes:** Trim and detail changes.
**Major standard equipment:** Mayfair cloth seat upholstery, front center arm-rests, and passenger assist straps, variable ratio power steering, power front disc brakes, front cornering lights, rear fender skirts, left side remote control outside rear view mirror, power windows, interior courtesy and warning lights, 3-speed windshield wipers and washers, visor vanity mirrors, automatic parking brake release, Turbo Hydra-matic transmission, and L78 × 15 BSW tires.

## Measurements

| | |
|---|---|
| Wheelbase | 130.0" |
| Length | 227.4" |
| Width | 79.8" |
| Height | NA |
| Legroom — front | NA |
| Legroom — rear | NA |
| Headroom — front | NA |
| Headroom — rear | NA |
| Luggage capacity (cu. ft.) | NA |
| Fuel capacity (gals.) | 27.0 |

## Models Available

| | Style Number | Base MSRP | Change from LY | Shipping Wt. (lbs.) | Production | Change from LY |
|---|---|---|---|---|---|---|
| Calais 2-Door Hardtop | 682C47-G | $5,771 | -2.17% | 4642 | 3,900 | +16.07% |
| Calais 4-Door Hardtop | 682C49-N | $5,938 | -2.26% | 4698 | 3,875 | +8.57% |
| TOTALS | Avg. price | $5,855 | -2.20% | Production | 7,775 | +12.21% |

# de Ville

*"This is the most popular Cadillac of them all."*

**Nameplate year of origin:** 1949 (as Hardtop designation), 1959 (series).
**Current bodystyle lifespan:** 1971 through 1976.
**Predecessor to this model:** de Ville (1969 to 1970).
**Replacement for this model:** de Ville (1977 to 1984).
**Percentage of division's sales volume:** 73.41%.
**Corporate siblings:** Buick Electra 225 and Oldsmobile Ninety-Eight.
**Primary competition:** Chrysler Imperial and Lincoln Continental.
**Notable changes:** Trim and detail changes.
**Major standard equipment:** Majesty cloth seat upholstery, front center armrests, and passenger assist straps, front cornering lights, rear fender skirts, left side remote control outside rear view mirror, power windows, interior courtesy and warning lights, 3-speed windshield wipers and washers, visor vanity mirrors, automatic parking brake release, electric clock, power door locks, variable ratio power steering, power front disc brakes, Turbo Hydra-matic transmission, and L78 × 15 BSW tires.

### Measurements

| | |
|---|---|
| Wheelbase | 130.0" |
| Length | 227.4" |
| Width | 79.8" |
| Height | NA |
| Legroom — front | NA |
| Legroom — rear | NA |
| Headroom — front | NA |
| Headroom — rear | NA |
| Luggage capacity (cu. ft.) | NA |
| Fuel capacity (gals.) | 27.0 |

## Models Available

| | Style Number | Base MSRP | Change from LY | Shipping Wt. (lbs.) | Production | Change from LY |
|---|---|---|---|---|---|---|
| Coupe de Ville 2-Door HT | 683D47-J | $6,168 | -1.53% | 4682 | 95,280 | +44.19% |
| Sedan de Ville 4-Door HT | 683D49-N | $6,390 | -1.66% | 4762 | 99,531 | +43.53% |
| TOTALS | Avg. price | $6,279 | -1.60% | Production | 194,811 | +43.85% |

# Eldorado

*"The world's most elegant personal car."*

**Nameplate year of origin:** 1953.
**Current bodystyle lifespan:** 1971 through 1978.
**Predecessor to this model:** Fleetwood Eldorado (1967 to 1970).
**Replacement for this model:** Eldorado (1979 to 1985).
**Percentage of division's sales volume:** 15.10%.
**Corporate siblings:** Buick Riviera and Oldsmobile Toronado.
**Primary competition:** Lincoln Continental Mark IV.
**Notable changes:** Trim and detail changes.
**Major standard equipment:** Majesty cloth seat upholstery, front center armrests, and passenger assist straps, front cornering lights, rear fender skirts, left side remote control outside rear view mirror, power windows, interior courtesy

### Measurements

| | |
|---|---|
| Wheelbase | 126.3" |
| Length | 223.2" |
| Width | 79.8" |
| Height | NA |
| Legroom — front | NA |
| Legroom — rear | NA |
| Headroom — front | NA |
| Headroom — rear | NA |
| Luggage capacity (cu. ft.) | NA |
| Fuel capacity (gals.) | 27.0 |

**1972**

and warning lights, 3-speed windshield wipers and washers, visor vanity mirrors, automatic parking brake release, electric clock, power door locks, front-wheel-drive, variable ratio power steering, power front disc brakes, Turbo Hydra-matic transmission, and L78 × 15 BSW tires.

## Models Available

|  | Style Number | Base MSRP | Change from LY | Shipping Wt. (lbs.) | Production | Change from LY |
|---|---|---|---|---|---|---|
| Fleetwood Eldorado 2-Door HT | 693L47-H | $7,230 | -2.08% | 4880 | 32,099 | +56.06% |
| Fltwd. Eldorado 2-Door Conv. | 693L67-E | $7,546 | -2.64% | 4966 | 7,975 | +17.28% |
| TOTALS | | Avg. price $7,388 | -2.37% | Production | 40,074 | +46.43% |

# Fleetwood Sixty-Special

*"This is Cadillac in the grand manner."*

**Nameplate year of origin:** 1938.
**Current bodystyle lifespan:** 1971 through 1976.
**Predecessor to this model:** Fleetwood Sixty-Special (1969 to 1970).
**Replacement for this model:** Fleetwood Brougham (1977 to 1984).
**Percentage of division's sales volume:** 7.82%.
**Corporate siblings:** None.
**Primary competition:** None.
**Notable changes:** Trim and detail changes.
**Major standard equipment:** Matador cloth or Sierra grain leather seat upholstery, front center armrests, passenger assist straps, dual comfort front seat, rear-seat reading lights, carpeted foot rests, front cornering lights, rear fender skirts, left side remote control outside rear view mirror, power windows, interior courtesy and warning lights, 3-speed windshield wipers and washers, visor vanity mirrors, automatic parking brake release, electric clock, power door locks, automatic level control, variable ratio power steering, power front disc brakes, Turbo Hydra-matic transmission, and L78 × 15 BSW tires.

### Measurements

| | |
|---|---|
| Wheelbase | 133.0" |
| Length | 230.4" |
| Width | 79.8" |
| Height | NA |
| Legroom — front | NA |
| Legroom — rear | NA |
| Headroom — front | NA |
| Headroom — rear | NA |
| Luggage capacity (cu. ft.) | NA |
| Fuel capacity (gals.) | 27.0 |

## Models Available

|  | Style Number | Base MSRP | Change from LY | Shipping Wt. (lbs.) | Production | Change from LY |
|---|---|---|---|---|---|---|
| Fltwd. Sixty-Sp. Brghm. 4-Dr. Sdn. | 681B69-P | $7,637 | -1.62% | 4858 | 20,750 | +36.51% |
| TOTALS | | Avg. price $7,637 | -1.62% | Production | 20,750 | +36.51% |

# Fleetwood Seventy-Five

*"Here are the most aristocratic of automobiles."*

**Nameplate year of origin:** 1927 (Fleetwood bodies), 1936 (75 series).
**Current bodystyle lifespan:** 1971 through 1976.
**Predecessor to this model:** Fleetwood 75 (1969 to 1970).
**Replacement for this model:** Fleetwood 75 (1977 to 1984).
**Percentage of division's sales volume:** 0.74%.

### Measurements

| | |
|---|---|
| Wheelbase | 151.5" |
| Length | 248.9" |
| Width | 79.8" |
| Height | NA |

**Corporate siblings:** None.
**Primary competition:** None.
**Notable changes:** Trim and detail changes.
**Major standard equipment:** Minuet cloth or Matador cloth and Sierra grain leather seat upholstery, front center armrests, passenger assist straps, dual comfort front seat, rear-seat reading lights, carpeted foot rests, front cornering lights, rear fender skirts, left side remote control outside rear view mirror, power windows, interior courtesy and warning lights, 3-speed windshield wipers and washers, visor vanity mirrors, automatic parking brake release, electric clock, power door locks, dual automatic climate control, automatic level control, fixed ratio power steering, power front disc brakes, Turbo Hydra-matic transmission, and L78 × 15 BSW tires.

## Measurements (cont.)

| | |
|---|---|
| Legroom — front | NA |
| Legroom — rear | NA |
| Headroom — front | NA |
| Headroom — rear | NA |
| Luggage capacity (cu. ft.) | NA |
| Fuel capacity (gals.) | 27.0 |

## Models Available

| | Style Number | Base MSRP | Change from LY | Shipping Wt. (lbs.) | Production | Change from LY |
|---|---|---|---|---|---|---|
| Fltwd. Seventy-Five 4-Door Sdn., 9-p. | 697F23-R | $11,748 | -1.02% | 5620 | 995 | +32.31% |
| Fltwd. Seventy-Five 4-Door Limo., 9-p. | 697F33-S | $11,880 | -1.07% | 5742 | 960 | +13.21% |
| TOTALS | *Avg. price* | $11,814 | -1.05% | *Production* | 1,955 | +22.19% |

# CHEVROLET

*"Building a better way to see the U.S.A."*

Chevrolet Motor Division had a great sales year for 1972, despite a strike at the General Motors assembly plants that wreaked havoc on many of the plans for the model year, and regained the top sales mark. The GM mid-size range of cars (including Chevy Chevelle and Monte Carlo) had been slated for a redesign for this season, but because of the strike the new models would have to wait for the 1973 season, receiving only minor trim changes this year. The Camaro (and Pontiac Firebird) would nearly die because of this strike. The reasons are complex, but basically the Camaro plant was closed for nearly six months. In this time period, new government regulations on bumpers had taken effect, resulting in the disposal of over 1,000 Camaro bodies that had been idled on the assembly line. This expensive waste, coupled with sagging sales for all muscle car/pony cars, nearly cost the Camaro its life. Luckily, some prominent Chevrolet executives managed to save the car. The Nova, which had been produced in the same facility as the Camaro, had its production transferred to other plants and survived into 1972 with spectacular sales, but only minor trim changes.

The Corvette entered the new model year with only modest changes to the powertrain lineup, although the high-powered LS-6 454 CID V8 was gone. The Vega returned virtually unchanged. Full-size Chevrolet models, which had been totally new for 1971, returned with quite a few changes. The wheelbase on all cars was up by a half inch, and overall length was up by several inches. A new grille/bumper design, new interior patterns, new decklid (sans the louvers for flo-thru ventilation), and new hood design distinguished the '72 models visually. A Caprice 4-Door Sedan was introduced in January, along with a rather historic change. Alas, by mid-year the 6-cylinder versions of the full-size Chevrolet (Biscayne, BelAir and Impala 4-Door Sedans, and the Impala Sport Coupe) were history. Poor sales of the sixes, along with weak performance resulting from conformance to government regulations, had resulted in what amounted to a repositioning of the entire full-size line. By January 1972, only about 3,900 full-size cars had been sold with a 6-cylinder engine, so at this time they were dropped, as was the Biscayne (and related Brookwood wagon), leaving the BelAir as the low-priced leader in the full-size Chevy range. This was the first time since 1928 that a 6-cylinder engine had not been available in a standard (i.e., full-size) Chevrolet. It would be a brief absence, though, as a six-cylinder would return for the 1977 model year. In the accompanying text, the prices and weights given on full-size Chevys are for V8 models. For reference, a 6-cylinder equipped car would cost approximately $334 less, and be about 188 pounds lighter.

Camaro 2-Door Coupe

Caprice 4-Door Hardtop

Chevelle Heavy Chevy 2-Door Hardtop

Chevelle Malibu 4-Door Hardtop

Impala 2-Door Convertible

Monte Carlo 2-Door Hardtop

Nova 2-Door Coupe with SS package

Vega GT 2-Door Hatchback and
Vega GT 2-Door Wagon

Corvette 2-Door Coupe

**Model year production:** 2,331,642, up 37.1% from 1971.
**Base price range:** $2,060 to $5,472.
**Domestic market share:** 24.67% (1st place).
**Industry average base price:** $3,788.
**Chevrolet average base price:** $3,461.
**Introduction date:** September 23, 1971.
**Assembly plants:** Lakewood, GA (A), Atlanta, GA (D), Kansas City, MO (K), Fremont, CA (Z), Van Nuys, CA (L), Norwood, OH (N), Tarrytown, NY (T), Oshawa, Ontario, Canada (1), Baltimore, MD (B); Framingham, MA (G); Flint, MI (F); Southgate, CA (C); Arlington, TX (R);

Janesville, WI (J); Wilmington, DE (Y), and St. Louis, MO (S).
**Data plate identification:** Thirteen digit code read as follows: four digit style number (see listings below) in which 1 = Chevrolet, 2nd number identifies series (e.g., V is for Vega), 3rd and 4th digits indicate body style; 5th digit is engine code; 2 for 1972; assembly plant code; 100001 and up for serial number. *Example:* 1V77B2T100001 is a 1972 Chevrolet Vega 2-Door Hatchback Coupe with a 140 CID 4-cyl. engine, serial number 100001, built in Tarrytown, NY.

## Powertrains

| Engine | Net HP | Engine Code | Transmission Availability | Vega/ Nova | Camaro | Chevelle | Monte Carlo | Full-size | Cor- vette |
|---|---|---|---|---|---|---|---|---|---|
| 140 CID OHC 1-bbl., 4-cyl. (Vega only) | 80 | B | 3-speed man. | S | - | - | - | - | - |
| | | | 4-speed man. | $53 | - | - | - | - | - |
| | | | Powerglide Automatic | $168 | - | - | - | - | - |
| | | | Turbo Hydra-matic | $199 | - | - | - | - | - |
| 140 CID OHC 2-bbl., 4-cyl. (Vega only) | 90 | B | 3-speed man. | $42 | - | - | - | - | - |
| | | | 4-speed man. | $95 | - | - | - | - | - |
| | | | Powerglide Automatic | $210 | - | - | - | - | - |
| | | | Turbo Hydra-matic | $241 | - | - | - | - | - |
| 250 CID Turbo-Thrift, 1-bbl., 6-cyl. | 110 | D | 3-speed man. | S | S (base only) | S | - | - | - |
| | | | Powerglide Automatic | $174 | $180 | $180 | - | S* | - |
| 307 CID Turbo-Fire, 2-bbl., V8 | 130 | F | 3-speed man. | $95 | $91 | $95/S (SS/ Heavy Chevy) | - | - | - |
| | | | Powerglide Automatic | $269 | $281 | $285 | - | - | - |
| | | | Turbo Hydra-matic | $301 | $308 | $312 | - | - | - |
| 350 CID Turbo-Fire, 2-bbl., V8 | 165 175 w/dual exhaust | H | 3-speed man. | - | - | $121/$27 (Wagons) | S | | |
| | | | 3-speed man. | - | $117 | $121 | - | - | - |
| | | | 4-speed man. | - | $343 | $316 | - | - | - |
| 350 CID Turbo-Fire, 2-bbl., V8 | 165 175 w/dual exhaust | H | Powerglide Automatic | - | - | - | $190 | - | - |
| | | | Turbo Hydra-matic | $327 | $334 | $338/$244 (Wagons) | $217 | S | - |
| 350 CID Turbo-Fire, 4-bbl., V8 | 175 | J | 3-speed man. | - | - | $168 | - | - | - |
| | | | 4-speed man. | - | - | $363 | - | - | - |
| | | | Turbo Hydra-matic | - | - | $385/$290 (Wagons) | $264 | - | - |
| 350 CID Turbo-Fire, 4-bbl., V8 | 200 | K | 4-speed man. | - | S (SS only)** | - | - | - | S |
| | | | Turbo Hydra-matic | - | $217 (SS only)** | - | - | - | S |
| 350 CID Turbo-Fire, 4-bbl., V8 | 255 | L | 4-speed man. | - | S (Z28 only)** | - | - | - | $ |
| | | | 4-speed man.(H-D) | - | $206 (Z28 only)** | - | - | - | $ |
| | | | Turbo Hydra-matic | - | $238 (Z28 only)** | - | - | - | $ |
| 400 CID Turbo-Fire, 2-bbl., V8 | 170 | R | Turbo Hydra-matic | - | - | - | - | $53/S (Caprice) | - |
| 400 CID Turbo-Jet, 4-bbl., V8 | 240 (210 Full-size) | S | 3-speed man. | - | - | $ | - | - | - |
| | | | 4-speed man. | - | - | $ | - | - | - |
| | | | Turbo Hydra-matic | - | - | $ | $291 | $144/$91 (Caprice) | - |
| 402 CID Turbo-Jet 396, 4-bbl., V8 | 240 | U | 4-speed man. | - | $206 (SS only)** | - | - | - | - |
| | | | 4-speed man.-close ratio | - | $206 (SS only)** | - | - | - | - |
| | | | Turbo Hydra-matic | - | $238 (SS only)** | - | - | - | - |
| 454 CID Turbo-Jet, 4-bbl., V8 | 270 | V | 4-speed man. | - | - | $ (SS only) | - | - | $295 |
| | | | Turbo Hydra-matic | - | - | $ (SS only) | $ | $/$ (Caprice) | $395 |

*Standard on models stated in introductory text, through mid-model year.　　**Plus cost of optional equipment packages required.

1972

## Major Options

| | Vega | Nova | Camaro | Chevelle | Monte Carlo | Full-size | Corvette |
|---|---|---|---|---|---|---|---|
| Air conditioning | $360 | $392* | $408* | $408* | $408 | $416* | $465 |
| Electronic cruise control | - | - | - | $62 | $63 | $62 | $62 |
| Electric rear window defogger | $ | $62 | $62 | $62 | $62 | $62 | $62 |
| Soft Ray tinted glass | $37 | $40 | $40 | $43 | $46 | $51 | S |
| Deck lid remote release | - | - | - | $ | $ | $ | - |
| Power steering — variable-ratio | $95 | $103 | $116 | $116 | S | S | $116 |
| Power brakes — front disc | - | $70 | $47 | $70/S (Wgn) | S | S | S |
| Power door locks | - | - | - | $ | $ | $ | $ |
| Power driver's seat/Bench seat | - | - | - | $79 | $79 | $105 (ex. Bisc) | - |
| Power windows | - | - | - | $127 | $127 | $127 (ex. Bisc) | $85 |
| AM radio | $61 | $66 | $66 | $66 | $66 | $66 | - |
| AM/FM stereo or radio | $123 | $139 | $139 | $239 | $239 | $239 | $283 |
| Front seat console | - | $ | $ | $ | $ | - | S |
| Front bucket seats | S | $ | S | $ | $ | - | S |
| Tilt steering wheel | - | - | $45 | $45 | $45 | $45 | $45 |
| Sunroof | - | $180 | - | - | $ | - | - |
| Vinyl roof | - | $82 | $87 | $126 | $126 | $109 ($142 Wagons) | $63-Conv. w/HT |
| Rally wheels | - | $ | $ | $ | $ | - | S |
| Custom interior group | - | $ | $ | - | $ | $ | $ |
| Vega GT package (special ride and handling package, GT trim, gauges, etc.) | $339 | - | - | - | - | - | - |
| Super Sport equipment package (Rally Sport also on Camaro) | | $320 | $306 (RS $118) | $350 | - | - | - |

Options common to most models. (- = Not Available; S = Standard equipment.) Items may be standard equipment, optional at different pricing, or unavailable on certain models. This chart is only a guide.

*Not available with 6-cylinder engine.

## Paint Colors

| | Code | Vega | Full-Size | Chevelle/MC | Camaro/Nova | Corvette |
|---|---|---|---|---|---|---|
| Classic White | 10 | | | | | x |
| Antique White | 11 | x | x | | x | |
| Pewter Silver Metallic | 14 | x | x | | x | x |
| Dusk Gray Metallic | 18 | | x | | | |
| Tuxedo Black | 19 | | x | | | |
| Ascot Blue Metallic | 24 | | x | | x | |
| Mediterranean Blue | 25 | x | | | | |
| Mulsanne Blue Met. | 26 | | | | x | |
| Targa Blue Metallic | 27 | | | | | x |
| Fathom Blue Met. | 28 | | x | | | |
| Spring Green Met. | 36 | | | | x | |
| Bryar Blue Metallic | 37 | | | | | x |
| Gulf Green Metallic | 43 | | x | | x | |
| Oasis Green Met. | 46 | x | | | | |
| Elkhart Green Met. | 47 | | | | | x |
| Sequoia Green Met. | 48 | x | x | | x | |
| Covert Tan | 50 | | x | | x | |
| Sunflower Yellow | 52 | | | | | x |
| Placer Gold Metallic | 53 | | | | x | |
| Desert Gold Metallic | 54 | x | x | | | |
| Cream Yellow | 56 | | | | x | |
| Golden Brown Met. | 57 | | x | | x | |
| Turin Tan | 58 | x | | | | |
| Driftwood | 62 | | x | | | |
| Mohave Gold Met. | 63 | | | | x | |

| | Code | Vega | Full-Size | Chevelle/MC | Camaro/Nova | Corvette |
|---|---|---|---|---|---|---|
| Orange Flame Met. | 65 | x | | | x | |
| Midnight Bronze Met. | 68 | x | x | | x | |
| Aegean Brown | 69 | | x | | | |
| Cranberry Red | 75 | x | x | | x | |
| Mille Miglia Red | 76 | | | | | x |
| War Bonnet Yellow Met. | 91 | | | | | x |
| Ontario Orange Firemist | 97 | | | | | x |
| Steel Cities Gray Met. | 98 | | | | | x |

# Vega

*"The little car that does everything well."*

**Nameplate year of origin:** 1971.
**Current bodystyle lifespan:** 1971 through 1979 (under various nameplates).
**Predecessor to this model:** Corvair (1965 to 1969).
**Replacement for this model:** Cavalier (1982 to 1994).
**Percentage of division's sales volume:** 16.94%.
**Corporate siblings:** None.
**Primary competition:** Ford Pinto, Plymouth Cricket (captive import), and AMC Gremlin.
**Notable changes:** Refinements.
**Major standard equipment:** Foam-filled front bucket seats with all-vinyl upholstery, flow-through power ventilation system, 3-point seat-belt system, padded sun visors, ashtray, self-adjusting front disc/rear drum brake system, bright-metal hubcaps, silver-finished grid-pattern grille, and A78 × 13 BSW tires.

## Measurements

| | Cars | Wagons |
|---|---|---|
| Wheelbase | 97.0" | 97.0" |
| Length | 170.0" | 170.0" |
| Width | 65.4" | 65.4" |
| Height | 51.9" | 52.0" |
| Legroom — front | 42.8" | 42.8" |
| Legroom — rear | 28.9" | 30.1" |
| Headroom — front | 38.4" | 38.5" |
| Headroom — rear | 39.4" | 38.3" |
| Cargo capacity (cu. ft.) | 8.7 | 50.2 |
| Fuel capacity (gals.) | 11.0 | 11.0 |

## Models Available

| | Style Number | Base MSRP | Change from LY | Shipping Wt. (lbs.) | Production | Change from LY |
|---|---|---|---|---|---|---|
| Vega 2-Door Sedan | 1V11 | $2,060 | -1.44% | 2158 | 55,839 | -5.04% |
| Vega 3-Door Hatchback Coupe | 1V77 | $2,160 | -1.64% | 2294 | 262,682 | +56.08% |
| Vega 2-Door Kammback Wgn. | 1V15 | $2,285 | -1.85% | 2333 | 71,957 | +68.12% |
| TOTALS | | *Avg. price* $2,168 | -1.68% | | *Production* 390,478 | +44.68% |

# Camaro

*"If you're looking for the closest thing to a Vette yet, you've come to the right place."*

**Nameplate year of origin:** 1967.
**Current bodystyle lifespan:** 1970 through 1981.
**Predecessor to this model:** Camaro (1967 to 1969).
**Replacement for this model:** Camaro (1982 to 1992).
**Percentage of division's sales volume:** 2.98%.
**Corporate siblings:** Pontiac Firebird.
**Primary competition:** Ford Mustang, Plymouth Barracuda, Dodge Challenger, AMC Javelin.

## Measurements

| | |
|---|---|
| Wheelbase | 108.0" |
| Length | 188.0" |
| Width | 74.4" |
| Height | 49.1" |
| Legroom — front | 43.8" |
| Legroom — rear | 30.7" |
| Headroom — front | 37.4" |

1972

**Notable changes:** Trim and detail changes.

**Major standard equipment:** Deep-contour, front bucket seats, with bucket-styled rear seats, all-vinyl upholstery, wraparound instrumentation, deep-twist color-keyed carpeting, Astro ventilation, wide-grid pattern grille, hubcaps, four-spoke steering wheel, front disc/rear drum brakes, E78 × 14 BSW tires. Optional RS package adds: Unique grid pattern grille (black with argent accents) with split front bumper, parking lights next to headlights, Rally Sport identification. SS adds: Special SS grille and identification, power brakes, heavy duty clutch, suspension, radiator, hood insulation, dual exhausts, 350 CID V8 engine, remote-control sport mirror, F70 × 14 white-letter tires. Z28 adds: RS-style blacked-out grille, Z28 identification, Positraction rear end, remote left hand/manual right hand outside sport mirrors, special suspension components, F60 × 15 white-letter tires, 15 × 7 wheels with trim rings, special instrumentation.

## Measurements (cont.)

| | |
|---|---|
| Headroom — rear | 36.1" |
| Cargo capacity (cu. ft.) | 6.4 |
| Fuel capacity (gals.) | 18.0 |

## Models Available

| | Style Number | Base MSRP | Change from LY | Shipping Wt. (lbs.) | Production | Change from LY |
|---|---|---|---|---|---|---|
| Camaro 2-Door Coupe | 1Q87 | $2,730 | -6.54% | 3121 | 68,656 | -36.12% |
| TOTALS | | Avg. price $2,730 | -6.54% | Production | 68,656 | -36.12% |

RS package: Add $118 to base V8 car (see powertrain chart); 11,364 produced. SS package: Add $306 to base V8 car (see powertrain chart); 6,562 produced. Z/28 package: Add $598 to base V8 car (see powertrain chart); 2,575 produced.

# Nova

*"How to see less of your mechanic and more of America."*

**Nameplate year of origin:** 1962.

**Current bodystyle lifespan:** 1968 through 1972.

**Predecessor to this model:** Chevy II (1966 to 1967).

**Replacement for this model:** Nova (1973 through 1979, with restyle in 1975).

**Percentage of division's sales volume:** 15.18%.

**Corporate siblings:** Pontiac Ventura II.

**Primary competition:** Ford Maverick, Mercury Comet, Plymouth Valiant, Dodge Dart, AMC Hornet.

**Notable changes:** Refinements.

**Major standard equipment:** Cloth and vinyl bench seat, vinyl-coated rubber floor coverings, deluxe steering wheel, hubcaps, front-door vent windows, bright moldings on windshield and rear window, manual drum brakes, E78-14 BSW tires.

## Measurements

| | |
|---|---|
| Wheelbase | 111.0" |
| Length | 189.4" |
| Width | 72.4" |
| Height | 53.9" |
| Legroom — front | 41.0" |
| Legroom — rear | 32.6" |
| Headroom — front | 37.6" |
| Headroom — rear | 36.6" |
| Cargo capacity (cu. ft.) | 14.6 |
| Fuel capacity (gals.) | 16.0 |

## Models Available

| | Style Number | Base MSRP | Change from LY | Shipping Wt. (lbs.) | Production | Change from LY |
|---|---|---|---|---|---|---|
| Nova 2-Door Coupe | 1X27 | $2,351 | -1.05% | 2949 | 260,215 | +81.70% |
| Nova 4-Door Sedan | 1X69 | $2,379 | -1.08% | 2982 | 89,518 | +73.32% |
| TOTALS | | Avg. price $2,365 | -0.26% | Production | 349,733 | +79.50% |

# Chevelle

*"Fits more families, more budgets, more garages."*

**Nameplate year of origin:** 1964.
**Current bodystyle lifespan:** 1968 through 1972.
**Predecessor to this model:** Chevelle (1966 to 1967).
**Replacement for this model:** Chevelle (1973 to 1977).
**Percentage of division's sales volume:** 17.08%.
**Corporate siblings:** Pontiac LeMans, Oldsmobile Cutlass, Buick Skylark.
**Primary competition:** Ford Torino, Plymouth Satellite, Dodge Coronet, AMC Matador.
**Notable changes:** Trim and detail changes.
**Major standard equipment:** Cloth and vinyl front bench seat, color-keyed vinyl-coated rubber floor mats, small hubcaps, and D78 × 14 BSW tires, Malibu adds: Pattern cloth front bench seat, color-keyed deep-twist carpeting, wheel covers, Hide-A-Way windshield wipers. Wagon models are similarly equipped with Nomad and Greenbrier same as Chevelle, and Concours same as Malibu.

## Measurements

|  | 2-Doors | 4-Doors | Wagons |
|---|---|---|---|
| Wheelbase | 112.0" | 116.0" | 116.0" |
| Length | 197.5" | 201.5" | 206.8" |
| Width | 75.4" | 75.4" | 75.4" |
| Height | 52.0" | 52.6" | 52.6" |
| Legroom — front | 42.4" | 42.4" | 42.4" |
| Legroom — rear | 32.2" | 34.8" | 34.8" |
| Headroom — front | 37.9" | 38.5" | 38.5" |
| Headroom — rear | 36.3" | 37.1" | 37.4" |
| Cargo capacity (cu. ft.) | NA | NA | 83.6 |
| Fuel capacity (gals.) | NA | NA | NA |

## Models Available

| | Style Number | Base MSRP | Change from LY | Shipping Wt. (lbs.) | Production | Change from LY |
|---|---|---|---|---|---|---|
| Chevelle 2-Door Hardtop | 1C37 | $2,669 | -1.59% | 3172 | 29,707 | +24.90% |
| Chevelle 4-Door Sedan | 1C69 | $2,636 | -1.53% | 3204 | 19,645 | +25.40% |
| Chevelle Malibu 2-Door Hardtop | 1D37 | $2,833 | -1.80% | 3194 | 212,388 | +14.00% |
| Chevelle Malibu 2-Door Conv. | 1D67 | $3,187 | -2.24% | 3379 | 4,853 | -4.60% |
| Chevelle Malibu 4-Door Sedan | 1D69 | $2,801 | -1.75% | 3240 | 48,575 | +16.70% |
| Chevelle Malibu 4-Door Hardtop | 1D39 | $2,991 | -2.00% | 3438 | 24,192 | +16.40% |
| Nomad 4-Door, 2-Seat Wagon | 1B36 | $2,926 | -2.37% | 3605 | 10,724 | +15.00% |
| Greenbrier 4-Door, 2-Seat Wagon | 1C36 | $3,140 | -2.73% | 3814 | 6,975 | +13.80% |
| Greenbrier 4-Door, 3-Seat Wagon | 1C46 | $3,247 | -2.79% | 3870 | 2,370 | +11.30% |
| Concours 4-Door, 2-Seat Wagon | 1D36 | $3,244 | -2.79% | 3857 | 17,968 | +41.30% |
| Concours 4-Door, 3-Seat Wagon | 1D46 | $3,351 | -2.87% | 3909 | 6,560 | +53.40% |
| Concours Estate 4-Dr., 2-S. Wgn. | 1H36 | $3,431 | -2.36% | 3887 | 5,331 | +18.40% |
| Concours Estate 4-Dr., 3-S. Wgn. | 1H46 | $3,588 | -1.05% | 3943 | 4,407 | +36.90% |
| TOTALS | Avg. price | $3,080 | -2.16% | Production | 393,695 | +17.30% |

# Monte Carlo

*"America's most attainable luxury car."*

**Nameplate year of origin:** 1970.
**Current bodystyle lifespan:** 1970 through 1972.
**Predecessor to this model:** None.
**Replacement for this model:** Monte Carlo (1973 to 1977).
**Percentage of division's sales volume:** 3.99%.
**Corporate siblings:** Pontiac Grand Prix.
**Primary competition:** Mercury Cougar, Plymouth Satellite Sebring, Dodge Charger.
**Notable changes:** Revised grille and trim and detail changes.
**Major standard equipment:** Cloth and vinyl front bench seat, full carpeting, wood-

## Measurements

| Wheelbase | 116.0" |
|---|---|
| Length | 206.5" |
| Width | 75.6" |
| Height | 52.9" |
| Legroom — front | NA |
| Legroom — rear | NA |
| Headroom — front | NA |
| Headroom — rear | NA |

1972

grained instrument panel, power front disc/rear drum brakes, variable-ratio power steering, aluminized exhaust system, full wheel covers, G78 × 15 BSW tires.

## Measurements (cont.)

| | |
|---|---|
| Cargo capacity (cu. ft.) | 12.9 |
| Fuel capacity (gals.) | 19.0 |

## Models Available

| | Style Number | Base MSRP | Change from LY | Shipping Wt. (lbs.) | Production | Change from LY |
|---|---|---|---|---|---|---|
| Monte Carlo 2-Door HT | 2K57 | $3,362 | -1.58% | 3506 | 91,961 | -18.33% |
| TOTALS | *Avg. price* | $3,362 | -1.58% | *Production* | 91,961 | -18.33% |

# Chevrolet Full-size

*"We want your new Chevrolet to be the best car you've ever owned."*

**Nameplate year of origin:** 1950 (BelAir); 1958 (Biscayne, Impala); 1966 (Caprice)

**Current bodystyle lifespan:** 1971 through 1976.

**Predecessor to this model:** Full-size Chevrolet (1969 to 1970).

**Replacement for this model:** Impala/Caprice (1977 to 1990).

**Percentage of division's sales volume:** 43.83%.

**Corporate siblings:** Buick LeSabre/Centurion, Olds 88, and Pontiac Catalina/Bonneville.

**Primary competition:** AMC Ambassador, Dodge Polara, Ford LTD, and Plymouth Fury.

**Notable changes:** Revised grille and trim and detail changes.

**Major standard equipment:** Cloth and vinyl bench seat, full carpeting, front and rear door armrests, 2-speed electric windshield wipers with washers, rocker panel moldings, and G78 × 15 BSW tires (L78 × 15 BSW tires on wagons). BelAir adds: Automatic interior lighting and power brakes. Impala adds: Vinyl upholstery in convertible, Impala specific interior trim, and electric clock. Caprice adds: Specific cloth and vinyl front bench seats (with center fold-down armrest on sedan), all-vinyl upholstery in wagons, simulated walnut interior trim, deluxe wheel covers, rocker panel moldings, unique Caprice grille, simulated wood exterior trim on Kingswood Estate wagons, and special ornamentation.

## Measurements

| | Cars | Wagons |
|---|---|---|
| Wheelbase | 121.5" | 125.0" |
| Length | 219.9" | 225.2" |
| Width | 79.5" | 79.5" |
| Height (Sedan only) | 53.4" | 57.1" |
| Legroom — front | 42.6" | 42.6" |
| Legroom — rear | 38.5" | 38.5" |
| Headroom — front | 38.9" | 38.9" |
| Headroom — rear | 38.0" | 38.5" |
| Cargo capacity (cu. ft.) | NA | 106.4 |
| Fuel capacity (gals.) | NA | NA |

## Models Available

| | Style Number | Base MSRP | Change from LY | Shipping Wt. (lbs.) | Production | Change from LY |
|---|---|---|---|---|---|---|
| Biscayne 4-Door Sedan | 1K69 | $3,408 | +10.08%** | 4045 | 20,538 | -7.90% |
| Brookwood 4-Door, 6-pass. Wgn. | 1K35 | $3,882 | -1.20% | 4686 | 8,150 | +53.40% |
| BelAir 4-Door Sedan | 1L69 | $3,538 | +9.43%** | 4042 | 41,888 | -0.20% |
| Townsman 4-Door, 6-pass. Wgn. | 1L35 | $3,969 | -1.27% | 4687 | 16,482 | +27.30% |
| Townsman 4-Door, 9-pass. Wgn. | 1L45 | $4,078 | -1.38% | 4769 | 8,667 | +26.20% |
| Impala 2-Door Hardtop Sport Cpe. | 1M57 | $3,720 | +9.15%** | 4049 | 52,692 | -2.20% |
| Impala 2-Door HT Custom Cpe. | 1M47 | $3,787 | -1.02% | 4053 | 183,493 | +31.60% |
| Impala 2-Door Convertible | 1M67 | $3,979 | -1.04% | 4125 | 6,456 | +41.10% |
| Impala 4-Door Sedan | 1M69 | $3,704 | +9.23%** | 4113 | 184,596 | +34.80% |
| Impala 4-Door Hardtop | 1M39 | $3,771 | -1.10% | 4150 | 170,304 | +21.40% |
| Kingswood 4-Door, 6-pass. Wgn. | 1M35 | $4,056 | -1.36% | 4734 | 43,152 | +61.20% |
| Kingswood 4-Door, 9-pass. Wgn. | 1M45 | $4,165 | -1.47% | 4817 | 40,248 | +24.60% |
| Caprice 2-Door HT Custom Cpe. | 1N47 | $4,026 | -1.35% | 4102 | 65,513 | +41.20% |

| | Style Number | Base MSRP | Change from LY | Shipping Wt. (lbs.) | Production | Change from LY |
|---|---|---|---|---|---|---|
| Caprice 4-Door Sedan | 1N69 | $4,009 | NEW | 4166 | 34,174 | NEW |
| Caprice 4-Door Hardtop | 1N39 | $4,076 | -1.40% | 4203 | 78,768 | +22.90% |
| Kingswood Estate 4-Dr, 6-p. Wgn. | 1N35 | $4,314 | -1.60% | 4798 | 20,281 | +70.20% |
| Kingswood Estate 4-Dr, 9-p. Wgn. | 1N45 | $4,423 | -1.67% | 4883 | 34,723 | +82.70% |
| TOTALS | | Avg. price $3,936 | +1.08% | | Production 1,010,125 | +32.10% |

*6-cyl. production (incl. in totals): Biscayne 1504; BelAir 868; Impala HT 289; Impala Sedan 1235.     **Price increase due to addition of V8 engine as standard equipment. See '72 Chevrolet introductory text.

# Corvette

*"America's only true production sports car."*

**Nameplate year of origin:** 1953 (also used on showcar of same year).
**Current bodystyle lifespan:** 1968 through 1982.
**Predecessor to this model:** Corvette (1963 to 1967).
**Replacement for this model:** Corvette (1984 to 1996).
**Percentage of division's sales volume:** 1.17%.
**Corporate siblings:** None.
**Primary competition:** None.
**Notable changes:** Trim and detail changes.
**Major standard equipment:** Complete instrumentation, Astro ventilation, removable roof panels (Coupe), manually operated folding top (Convertible), audio alarm system, wheels with bright trim ring and ribbed center hub, Soft-Ray tinted glass, 4-wheel disc brakes, and F70 × 15 BSW tires.

## Measurements

| | |
|---|---|
| Wheelbase | 98.0" |
| Length | 182.5" |
| Width | 69.0" |
| Height | 47.8" |
| Legroom — front | 43.0" |
| Legroom — rear | NA |
| Headroom — front | 36.2" |
| Headroom — rear | NA |
| Cargo capacity (cu. ft.) | NA |
| Fuel capacity (gals.) | 18.0 |

## Models Available

| | Style Number | Base MSRP | Change from LY | Shipping Wt. (lbs.) | Production | Change from LY |
|---|---|---|---|---|---|---|
| Corvette Stingray 2-Door Cpe. | 1Z37 | $5,472 | -1.10% | 3215 | 20,486 | +39.55% |
| Corvette Stingray 2-Door Conv. | 1Z67 | $5,246 | -0.94% | 3216 | 6,508 | -8.61% |
| TOTALS | | Avg. price $5 359 | -1.03% | | Production 26,994 | +23.82% |

# CHRYSLER

*"Coming through with luxury that lasts."*

All Chrysler models for 1972 received a major facelift. The basic "fuselage"-style bodies introduced for the 1969 model year were retained, but nearly all of the sheetmetal was redesigned. The new styling was just a little less rounded and featured what Chrysler called a loop-style grille at the front end, with taillamps set into the rear bumper on most models. This restyling effort paid off in a fairly large sales increase over the 1971 models. The slow-selling 300 series (non-letter car version) was discontinued at the end of the 1971 model run and was essentially replaced by the base New Yorker series, which itself was replaced by the New Yorker Brougham series. The Newport

1972

Royal line would be discontinued at the end of the 1972 model run, after a brief two-year run. The Royal nameplate ran previously for several years (1937 to 1950) as the low-end Chrysler, and would not reappear again. Changes for the Imperial line were similar to Chrysler's regular lines, although less obvious; they included a new grille and rear-end restyling, as well as new roofline styling on 2-Door models. The Imperial line, which had operated as its own sales division of Chrysler Corporation from 1955 through 1970, had been brought back into the Chrysler division's lineup of cars during 1971. This change had been in the process for several years. There is no mention of Imperial models being Chryslers in their 1972 literature, nor on the cars' exterior; however, Imperials were moved into the Chrysler section of the literature from this year. Previously Imperial had been recognized as its own division within Chrysler for sales reporting purposes, although it was not always considered separately as a sales or manufacturing organization within the corporation.

Imperial LeBaron 2-Door Hardtop

Newport Custom 2-Door Hardtop

New Yorker 2-Door Hardtop

Town & Country 4-Door Wagon

**Model year production:** 221,498, up 17.40% over 1971.
**Domestic market share:** 2.37% (11th place).
**Base price range:** $4,051 to $6,778.
**Industry average base price:** $3,788.
**Chrysler average base price:** $4,974.
**Introduction date:** September 28, 1971.
**Assembly plants:** Newark, DE (F), and Detroit, MI (C).
**Data plate identification:** Thirteen digit code read as follows:

four digit style number (see listings below) in which C = Chrysler, 2nd number identifies series (e.g., H is for New Yorker), 3rd and 4th digits indicate body style; 5th digit is engine code; 2 for 1972; assembly plant code; 100001 and up for serial number. *Example:* CH23T2C100001 is a 1972 Chrysler New Yorker 2-Door Hardtop with a 440 CID V8 engine, serial number 100001, built in Detroit, MI.

## Powertrains

| Engine | Net HP | Horsepower Rating—Net | Transmission Availability | Newport Royal | Newport Custom | T. & C. N.Y. | Imperial |
|---|---|---|---|---|---|---|---|
| 360 CID, 2-bbl., V8 | K | 175 | TorqueFlite Automatic | S | – | – | – |
| 400 CID, 2-bbl., V8 | M | 190 | TorqueFlite Automatic | – | S | – | – |
| 440 CID, 4-bbl., V8 | T | 225 | TorqueFlite Automatic | – | $122 | S | S |
| 440 CID, 4-bbl., V8 | T | 245 w/dual exhaust | TorqueFlite Automatic | – | $157 | $35 | $35 |

## Major Options

| | Newport | New Yorker | T. & C. | Imperial |
|---|---|---|---|---|
| Air conditioning | $416 | $416 | $416 | S/$251 (Dual) |
| Electronic cruise control | $68 | $68 | $68 | $93 |
| Electric rear window defogger | $35 | $35 | $35 | $35 |
| Soft Ray tinted glass | $42 | $42 | $42 | S |
| Deck lid remote release | $15 | $15 | - | $33 |
| Power steering/power brakes | S | S | S | S |
| Power door locks (2-Door/ 4-Door) | $47/$72 | $47/$71 | $72 | $49/$73 |
| Power driver's seat/ Bench seat | $104 | $104 | $104 | $120 |
| Power windows | $131 | $131 (S— Brghm) | $131 | S |
| AM radio | $90 | $90 | $90 | $272 (w/ 8-track) |
| AM/FM stereo | $237 | $237 | $237 | $302 |
| 60/40 front seats (Imp); 50/50 (Chry.) | $193 | $193 | $193 | $223 |
| Tilt steering wheel | $87 | $87 | - | $95 |
| Sunroof | $585 | $585 | - | $585 |
| Vinyl roof | $125 | $125 | $141 | S |
| Chrome Road Wheels | $100 | $100 | $100 | $62 |

Options common to most models. (- = Not Available; S = Standard equipment.) Items may be standard equipment, optional at different pricing, or unavailable on certain models. This chart is only a guide.

## Paint Colors

| | Code |
|---|---|
| Silver Frost Metallic | A5 |
| Charcoal Metallic | A9 |
| Blue Sky | B1 |
| True Blue Metallic | B5 |
| Evening Blue Metallic | B7 |
| Regal Blue Metallic | B9 |
| Red | E5 |
| Burnished Red Metallic | E7 |
| Mist Green | F1 |
| Amber Sherwood Metallic | F3 |
| Sherwood Green Metallic | F7 |
| Forest Green Metallic | F8 |
| Tahitian Gold Metallic | JY9 |
| Autumn Bronze Metallic | K6 |
| Sahara Beige | L4 |
| Coral Turquoise Metallic | Q5 |
| Chestnut Metallic | T8 |
| Spinnaker White | W1 |
| Sun Fire Yellow | Y2 |
| Honey Gold | Y3 |
| Honeydew | Y4 |
| Golden Haze Metallic | Y6 |
| Gold Leaf Metallic | Y8 |
| Tawney Gold Metallic | Y9 |
| Formal Black | X9 |

# Newport

*"Big is the word for Chrysler in '72."*

**Nameplate year of origin:** 1950 (as HT model of the T & C); 1961 (as series).
**Current bodystyle lifespan:** 1969 through 1973.
**Predecessor to this model:** Newport (1965 to 1968).
**Replacement for this model:** Newport (1974 to 1978).
**Percentage of division's sales volume:** 58.83%.
**Corporate siblings:** Chrysler New Yorker.
**Primary competition:** Buick LeSabre/Centurion, Mercury Monterey, and Oldsmobile Delta 88.
**Notable changes:** Revised sheetmetal and new front and rear end treatments. Base Newport and Newport Royal from '71 combined into one Newport Royal line.
**Major standard equipment:** Cloth and vinyl front bench seat, full carpeting, Torqueflite automatic transmission, power steering, power front disc brakes, electronic ignition, Torsion-Quiet ride system, and H78 × 15 BSW tires. Custom adds: Custom interior trim, and additional exterior trim.

## Measurements

| | |
|---|---|
| Wheelbase | 124.0" |
| Length | 224.1" |
| Width | 79.1" |
| Height | 55.2" |
| Legroom — front | 41.8" |
| Legroom — rear | 41.5" |
| Headroom — front | 38.7" |
| Headroom — rear | 37.9" |
| Cargo capacity (cu. ft.) | 21.2 |
| Fuel capacity (gals.) | 24.0 |

**1972**

## Models Available

| | Style Number | Base MSRP | Change from LY | Shipping Wt. (lbs.) | Production | Change from LY |
|---|---|---|---|---|---|---|
| Newport Royal 2-Door HT | HCL23 | $4,124 | -0.70% | 4132 | 22,622 | -5.93%* |
| Newport Royal 4-Door Sdn. | HCL41 | $4,051 | -0.66% | 4197 | 47,437 | +6.61%* |
| Newport Royal 4-Door HT | HCL43 | $4,186 | -0.71% | 4202 | 15,185 | -5.03%* |
| Newport Custom 2-Door HT | HCM23 | $4,357 | -0.77% | 4232 | 10,326 | +86.83% |

| | Style Number | Base MSRP | Change from LY | Shipping Wt. (lbs.) | Production | Change from LY |
|---|---|---|---|---|---|---|
| Newport Custom 4-Dr. Sdn. | HCM41 | $4,287 | -0.74% | 4287 | 19,278 | +71.30% |
| Newport Custom 4-Door HT | HCM43 | $4,435 | -0.81% | 4297 | 15,457 | +51.44% |
| TOTALS | | Avg. price $4,240 | -0.66% | Production | 130,305 | +16.84% |

*Production change from 1971 calculated by combining the production of Newport and Newport Royal models, since the 1972 Newport Royal was a replacement for both models.*

# Town & Country

*"Town & Country is the complete wagon."*

**Nameplate year of origin:** 1941.
**Current bodystyle lifespan:** 1969 through 1973.
**Predecessor to this model:** Town & Country (1965 to 1968).
**Replacement for this model:** Town & Country (1974 to 1978).
**Percentage of division's sales volume:** 9.30%.
**Corporate siblings:** Dodge Monaco/Polara and Plymouth Fury Suburbans.
**Primary competition:** Buick Estate Wagon, Mercury Colony Park, and Oldsmobile Custom Cruiser.
**Notable changes:** Revised sheetmetal and new front and rear end treatments.
**Major standard equipment:** All-vinyl front bench seat with folding center armrest, Torqueflite automatic transmission, power steering, power front disc brakes, electric clock, lockable luggage compartment, 3-way tailgate with hardtop-style window, power operated tailgate window, bodyside and rear tailgate woodgrain applique, and L84 × 15 BSW tires.

## Measurements

| | |
|---|---|
| Wheelbase | 122.0" |
| Length | 224.8" |
| Width | 79.1" |
| Height | 58.1" |
| Legroom — front | 41.8" |
| Legroom — rear | 39.1" |
| Headroom — front | 40.1" |
| Headroom — rear | 40.7" |
| Cargo capacity (cu. ft.) | 113.5 |
| Fuel capacity (gals.) | 23.0 |

## Models Available

| | Style Number | Base MSRP | Change from LY | Shipping Wt. (lbs.) | Production | Change from LY |
|---|---|---|---|---|---|---|
| Town & Country 4-Dr, 6-p. Wgn. | HCP45 | $5,055 | +2.10% | 4712 | 6,473 | +13.62% |
| Town & Country 4-Dr, 9-p. Wgn. | HCP46 | $5,139 | +2.03% | 4767 | 14,116 | +28.41% |
| TOTALS | | Avg. price $5,097 | +2.06% | Production | 20,589 | +23.36% |

# New Yorker

*"The most luxurious Chrysler."*

**Nameplate year of origin:** 1939.
**Current bodystyle lifespan:** 1969 through 1973.
**Predecessor to this model:** New Yorker (1965 to 1968).
**Replacement for this model:** New Yorker (1974 to 1978).
**Percentage of division's sales volume:** 24.75%.
**Corporate siblings:** Chrysler Newport.
**Primary competition:** Buick Electra 225, Cadillac Calais, Mercury Marquis, and Oldsmobile Ninety-Eight.
**Notable changes:** Revised sheetmetal and new front and rear end treatments. Base New Yorker filled void left from dropping the 300 Series, and new Brougham added to replace the New Yorker.
**Major standard equipment:** Cloth and vinyl seats with folding center armrests

## Measurements

| | |
|---|---|
| Wheelbase | 124.0" |
| Length | 224.1" |
| Width | 79.1" |
| Height | 55.4" |
| Legroom — front | 41.8" |
| Legroom — rear | 41.5" |
| Headroom — front | 38.7" |
| Headroom — rear | 37.9" |
| Cargo capacity (cu. ft.) | 21.2 |
| Fuel capacity (gals.) | 24.0 |

(front and rear), Torqueflite automatic transmission, power front disc brakes, power steering, electric clock, LH remote outside rear view mirror, rear fender skirts, trunk carpeting, and J78 × 15 BSW tires. Brougham adds: split bench seat, power windows, and special two-spoke steering wheel.

## Models Available

| | Style Number | Base MSRP | Change from LY | Shipping Wt. (lbs.) | Production | Change from LY |
|---|---|---|---|---|---|---|
| New Yorker 2-Door Hardtop | HCH23 | $4,915 | -0.93% | 4372 | 5,567 | +24.12% |
| New Yorker 4-Door Sedan | HCH41 | $4,865 | -0.92% | 4437 | 7,296 | -25.93% |
| New Yorker 4-Door Hardtop | HCH43 | $4,993 | -0.95% | 4467 | 10,013 | -51.47% |
| New Yorker Brougham 2-Dr. HT | HCS23 | $5,271 | NEW | 4372 | 4,635 | NEW |
| New Yorker Brougham 4-Dr Sdn. | HCS41 | $5,222 | NEW | 4437 | 6,971 | NEW |
| New Yorker Brougham 4-Dr. HT | HCS43 | $5,350 | NEW | 4469 | 20,328 | NEW |
| TOTALS | | Avg. price $5,103 | +2.66% | | Production 54,810 | +56.74% |

# Imperial

*"Imperial luxury goes far deeper than a beautiful body."*

**Nameplate year of origin:** 1924 (as Sedan model designation); 1926 (as series).
**Current bodystyle lifespan:** 1969 through 1973.
**Predecessor to this model:** Imperial (1967 to 1968).
**Replacement for this model:** Imperial (1974 to 1975).
**Percentage of division's sales volume:** 7.13%.
**Corporate siblings:** None.
**Primary competition:** Cadillac de Ville and Lincoln Continental.
**Notable changes:** Revised grille and trim changes.
**Major standard equipment:** Split-bench front seat with passenger-side recliner, full-luxury carpeting, Rosewood-grain vinyl interior trim, power windows, air conditioning, tinted glass, TorqueFlite automatic transmission, power steering, power front disc brakes, vinyl top, and L84 × 15 BSW tires.

## Measurements

| | |
|---|---|
| Wheelbase | 127.0" |
| Length | 229.5" |
| Width | 79.6" |
| Height | 56.2" |
| Legroom — front | 41.9" |
| Legroom — rear | 41.2" |
| Headroom — front | 38.3" |
| Headroom — rear | 37.0" |
| Cargo capacity (cu. ft.) | NA |
| Fuel capacity (gals.) | 24.0 |

## Models Available

| | Style Number | Base MSRP | Change from LY | Shipping Wt. (lbs.) | Production | Change from LY |
|---|---|---|---|---|---|---|
| Imperial LeBaron 2-Door HT | HYM23 | $6,550 | -1.24% | 4790 | 2,322 | +61.03% |
| Imperial LeBaron 4-Door HT | HYM43 | $6,778 | -1.25% | 4955 | 13,472 | +33.18% |
| TOTALS | | Avg. price $6,664 | -1.24% | | Production 15,794 | +36.65% |

# DODGE

*"Dodge. Depend on it."*

With the muscle car era waning, Dodge was one of the hardest hit in terms of corporate image. For Dodge (and Chrysler Corporation as a whole), 1972 would be the beginning of gloomy days, at least until the performance revival of the late eighties and early nineties. While sales would remain strong for several more years, it could not be denied that times were changing. For starters, the legendary Chrysler Hemi engine was a thing of the past. Rather than de-tune the engine to meet Federal fuel usage and emissions guidelines, Chrysler decided to retire this engine as a happy memory. Of course, the 440 Magnum engines were still around, but they were now down to a maximum of 330 net horsepower (about 375 gross), where the Hemi had 425 gross horsepower. Granted, there was plenty of power to

use, but it was a signal of things to come. Also gone this year were the Challenger Convertible and R/T models. There would not be another Dodge convertible until the early eighties. The Charger, which had been restyled in 1971 (along with the Coronet), was being marketed more towards the emerging low-end luxury coupe market. This was the market dominated by the Chevrolet Monte Carlo and Pontiac Grand Prix. Full-size Polara and Monaco models featured all-new sheetmetal this year, while retaining the previous year's overall look. The new styling was more formal looking and a little less "aerodynamic" in appearance. The entry-level Dart models returned for 1972, basically unchanged.

Challenger 2-Door Hardtop

Charger 2-Door Hardtop

Coronet Custom 4-Door Sedan

Dart Demon 2-Door Coupe

Dart Swinger 2-Door Hardtop
and Dart 4-Door Sedan

Monaco 2-Door Hardtop

Polara Custom 4-Door Wagon

**Model year production:** 577,842, up 3.82% over 1971.
**Domestic market share:** 6.06% (7th place).
**Base price range:** $2,316 to $4,756.
**Industry average base price:** $3,788.
**Dodge average base price:** $3,427.
**Introduction date:** September 28, 1971.
**Assembly plants:** Lynch Road, MI (A); Hamtramck, MI (B); Detroit (Jefferson Ave.), MI (C); Belvidere, IL (D); Los Angeles, CA (E); Newark, DE (F); St. Louis, MO (G); New Stanton (H); Windsor, Ontario, Canada (R).

**Data plate identification:** Thirteen digit code read as follows: four digit style number (see listings below) in which 1st digit is series letter (e.g., L = Dart series), 2nd number identifies trim grade (e.g., H is for Custom/Swinger trim), 3rd and 4th digits indicate body style; 5th digit is engine code; 2 for 1972; assembly plant code; 100001 and up for serial number. *Example:* LH23G2F100001 is a 1972 Dodge Dart Swinger 2-Door Hardtop with a 318 CID V8 engine, serial number 100001, built in Newark, NJ.

## Powertrains

| Engine | Engine Code | Net HP | Transmission Availability | Dart & Demon | Challenger | Charger | Coronet | Polara/ Monaco |
|---|---|---|---|---|---|---|---|---|
| 198 CID, 1-bbl., 6-cyl. | A | 100 | 3-speed man. | S | - | - | - | - |
| | | | Torqueflite automatic | $178 | - | - | - | - |
| 225 CID, 1-bbl., 6-cyl. | B | 110 | 3-speed man. | $38 | S | S | S | - |
| | | | 4-speed man. | $223 | - | - | - | - |
| | | | Torqueflite automatic | $245 | $211 | $211 | $211 | - |
| 318 CID, 2-bbl., V8 | G | 150 | 3-speed man. | $133 (Demon)/ $150 (Dart) | $112/S (Rallye) | $107/$ (Rallye)* | $107 | S (Polara) |
| | | | 4-speed man. | $318 (Demon)/ $335 (Dart) | $297/$185 (Rallye) | $318/$211 (Rallye)* | $211 | - |
| | | | Torqueflite automatic | $341 (Demon)/ $358 (Dart) | $320/$208 (Rallye) | $347/$240 (Rallye)* | $347 | - |
| 340 CID, 4-bbl., V8 | H | 240 | 3-speed man. | S (Demon 340) | $210/$98 (Rallye) | $210 | - | - |
| | | | 4-speed man. | $185 (Demon 340) | $395–$283 (Rallye) | $411 | - | - |
| | | | Torqueflite automatic | $208-Demon 340 | $418/$316 (Rallye) | $450 | - | - |
| 360 CID, 2-bbl., V8 | K | 175 | Torqueflite automatic | - | - | - | - | S (Mon.)/ $ (Polara) |
| 400 CID, 2-bbl., V8 | M | 190 | Torqueflite automatic | - | - | $ | $ | $ |
| | | | Torqueflite automatic | - | - | - | - | - |
| 400 CID Magnum, 4-bbl., V8 | P | | Torqueflite automatic | - | - | $ | $ | - |
| 440 CID, 4-bbl., V8 | T | 225 | Torqueflite automatic | - | - | - | - | $149 (Mon.)/ $193 (Polara) |
| 440 CID Magnum, 4-bbl., V8 | U | 280 | Torqueflite automatic | - | - | $ (Rallye)*, SE | - | - |
| 440 CID SixPack, Three 2-bbl., V8 | V | 330 | Torqueflite automatic | - | - | $546 (Rallye)* | - | - |

*Rallye model available as an option package on the base Charger.

**1972**

## Major Options

| | Dart/Demon | Challenger | Charger | Coronet | Polara | Monaco |
|---|---|---|---|---|---|---|
| Air conditioning | $354 | $365 | $378 | $378 | $412 | $412 |
| Speed control | - | - | $ | $ | $ | $ |
| Electric rear window defogger | - | - | $ | $ | $ | $ |
| Tinted glass | $36 | $36 | $40 | $40 | $40 | $40 |
| Power steering | $92 | $92 | $104 | $104 | S | S |
| Power brakes | $40 | $40 | - | - | - | - |
| Power brakes — front disc | $62 | $62 | $68 | $68 | $68 | S |
| Power driver's seat/Bench seat | - | - | $91 | $91 | $103 | $103 |
| Power windows | - | - | $119 | $119 | $125 | $125 |
| AM radio | $59 | $59 | $65 | $65 | $65 | $65 |
| AM/FM stereo (Dart: not stereo) | $125 | $132 | $144 | $144 | $144 | $144 |
| Tilt steering wheel | - | - | $55 | $55 | $55 | $55 |
| Road Wheels | - | - | $28 | - | $58 | $58 |
| Vinyl roof | $75 | $80 | $94 | $94 | $106 | $106 |
| Monaco Brougham package | - | - | - | - | - | $332 |
| Charger Rallye package | - | - | $82 | - | - | - |

Options common to most models. (– = Not Available; S = Standard equipment.) Items may be standard equipment, optional at different pricing, or unavailable on certain models. This chart is only a guide.

## Paint Colors

| | Code | Dart/Chllgr./ Coronet/ Charger | Pol./Monaco |
|---|---|---|---|
| Light Blue | B-1 | x | x |
| Bright Blue Metallic | B-3 | x | x |
| Red | E-5 | x | x |
| Light Green Metallic | F-1 | x | x |
| Dark Green Metallic | F-7 | x | x |
| Eggshell White | W-1 | x | x |
| Black | X-9 | x | x |
| Light Gold | L-4 | x | x |
| Gold Metallic | Y-8 | x | x |
| Dark Gold Metallic | Y-9 | x | x |
| Dark Tan Metallic | T-8 | x | x |
| Light Gunmetal Met. | A-4 | x | |
| Medium Tan Metallic | T-6 | x | |
| Super Blue | B-5 | x | |
| Hemi Orange* | V-2 | Opt. | |
| Top Banana* | Y-1 | Opt. | |
| Dark Grey Metallic | A-9 | | x |
| Dark Blue Metallic | B-7 | | x |
| Parchment | A-5 | | x |
| Turquoise Metallic | Q-5 | | x |
| Yellow | Y-2 | | x |

*Hi-impact colors available at extra cost.

# Dart

*"The compact with the split personality."*

## Measurements

|  | Demon | Dart |
|---|---|---|
| Wheelbase | 108.0" | 111.0" |
| Length | 192.5" | 196.2" |
| Width | 71.7" | 69.6" |
| Height | 53.0" | 54.0" |
| Legroom — front | 41.5" | 41.5" |
| Legroom — rear | 30.0" | 35.9" |
| Headroom — front | 37.5" | 38.6" |
| Headroom — rear | 36.5" | 37.3" |
| Cargo capacity (cu. ft.) | 15.9 | 14.3 |
| Fuel capacity (gals.) | 16.0 | 16.0 |

**Nameplate year of origin:** 1960 (on low-end full-size models); Demon 1971.
**Current bodystyle lifespan:** 1967 through 1976; Demon 1971 through 1976.
**Predecessor to this model:** Dart (1963 to 1966).
**Replacement for this model:** Aspen (1976 to 1980).
**Percentage of division's sales volume:** 46.53%.
**Corporate siblings:** Plymouth Valiant.
**Primary competition:** AMC Hornet, Chevrolet Nova, Ford Maverick, Mercury Comet, Pontiac Ventura II.
**Notable changes:** Revised grille and trim changes.
**Major standard equipment:** Cloth and vinyl full-width front bench seat (all-vinyl on Dart 4-Door Sedan), dome light, simulated wood-grained finish on instrument panel, front door vent windows, keyless door locking system, 2-speed windshield wipers, 3-spoke steering wheel, 6.95 × 14 BSW tires. Custom and Swinger add: Deluxe instrument panel decor, deep-pile carpeting, body side moldings with black painted insert, drip rail molding, and grille surround molding. Duster adds to base: Ventless front windows. Duster 340 adds: 340 CID V8 engine, cigarette lighter and E70 × 14 BSW tires.

## Models Available

|  | Style Number | Base MSRP | Change from LY | Shipping Wt. (lbs.) | Production | Change from LY |
|---|---|---|---|---|---|---|
| Dart Demon 2-Door Coupe | LL29 | $2,316 | -1.15% | 2800 | 39,880 | -42.92% |
| Dart Demon 340 2-Dr. Cpe. | LM29 | $2,759 | +1.40% | 3125 | 8,700 | -13.84% |
| Dart Swinger Special 2-Dr. HT | LL23 | $2,373 | -1.21% | 2845 | 19,210 | +42.45% |
| Dart 4-Door Sedan | LL41 | $2,420 | -1.22% | 2855 | 26,019 | -20.46% |
| Dart Swinger 2-Door Hardtop | LH23 | $2,528 | -1.29% | 2835 | 119,618 | +16.72% |
| Dart Custom 4-Door Sedan | LH41 | $2,574 | -1.34% | 2855 | 49,941 | +129.24% |
| TOTALS | | *Avg. price* $2,495 | -0.80% | | *Production* 263,368 | +5.17% |

# Challenger

*"Good looks can get you anywhere."*

## Measurements

| Wheelbase | 110.0" |
|---|---|
| Length | 191.3" |
| Width | 76.3" |
| Height | 50.9" |
| Legroom — front | 42.3" |
| Legroom — rear | 30.9" |
| Headroom — front | 37.4" |
| Headroom — rear | 35.6" |
| Cargo capacity (cu. ft.) | 8.6 |
| Fuel capacity (gals.) | 18 |

**Nameplate year of origin:** 1970.
**Current bodystyle lifespan:** 1970 through 1974.
**Predecessor to this model:** None.
**Replacement for this model:** None.
**Percentage of division's sales volume:** 4.71%.
**Corporate siblings:** Plymouth Barracuda.
**Primary competition:** AMC Javelin, Chevrolet Camaro, Ford Mustang, and Pontiac Firebird.
**Notable changes:** Minor trim and detail changes. Convertible models dropped.
**Major standard equipment:** All-vinyl bucket seats, cigarette lighter, deep-pile carpeting, dome light, simulated wood-grain door inserts, concealed 2-speed electric wipers, moldings (wheel opening, drip rail, grille, and deck lid), dual body paint stripes, and 7.35 × 14 BSW tires. Rallye adds: Body side louvers and tape stripes, performance hood with detachable scoop plates, Rallye instrument cluster, and F70 × 14 BSW tires.

## Models Available

| | Style Number | Base MSRP | Change from LY | Shipping Wt. (lbs.) | Production | Change from LY |
|---|---|---|---|---|---|---|
| Challenger 2-Door Hardtop | JH23 | $2,790 | -2.04% | 3070 | 18,535 | -19.72%* |
| Challenger Rallye 2-Door HT | JS23 | $3,082 | NEW | 3225 | 8,123 | NEW |
| TOTALS | | Avg. price $2,936 | -1.74% | | Production 26,658 | -10.79% |

*Production calculated from combined 1971 Challenger Coupe and Hardtop production, as individual body style figures were not available for 1971.

# Charger

*"The rationally priced personal luxury car."*

**Nameplate year of origin:** 1966.
**Current bodystyle lifespan:** 1971 through 1974.
**Predecessor to this model:** Charger (1968 to 1970).
**Replacement for this model:** Charger SE (1975 to 1978).
**Percentage of division's sales volume:** 13.36%.
**Corporate siblings:** Plymouth Satellite Sebring.
**Primary competition:** AMC Matador, Chevrolet Chevelle and Monte Carlo, Ford Torino, and Pontiac LeMans and Grand Prix.
**Notable changes:** Revised grille and trim and detail changes.
**Major standard equipment:** All-vinyl front bench seat, dome light, color-keyed carpeting, cigarette lighter (hardtop only), simulated wood-grained instrument panel (hardtop only), dual horns (hardtop only), 2-speed concealed wipers, body-side paint stripe (hardtop only), and E78 × 14 BSW tires. Rallye adds: Sculptured black grille, power bulge hood, rallye gauge cluster, simulated door louvers, louvered taillights, and F70 × 14 white-letter tires. SE adds over base: Pleated vinyl seats, rallye gauge cluster, formal vinyl roof, concealed headlights, chrome taillight trim, wheel-lip and drip rail moldings, and lower body side paint stripes.

### Measurements

| | |
|---|---|
| Wheelbase | 115.0" |
| Length | 205.4" |
| Width | 76.9" |
| Height | 52.1" |
| Legroom — front | 41.9" |
| Legroom — rear | 34.1" |
| Headroom — front | 37.3" |
| Headroom — rear | 36.4" |
| Cargo capacity (cu. ft.) | 14.3 |
| Fuel capacity (gals.) | 19.5 |

## Models Available

| | Style Number | Base MSRP | Change from LY | Shipping Wt. (lbs.) | Production | Change from LY |
|---|---|---|---|---|---|---|
| Charger 2-Door Coupe | WL21 | $2,652 | -2.03% | 3245 | 7,803 | +15.12%* |
| Charger 2-Door Hardtop | WL23 | $2,913 | -2.08% | 3260 | 45,361 | +15.12%* |
| Charger SE 2-Door HT | WH23 | $3,249 | NEW | 3325 | 22,430 | NEW |
| TOTALS | | Avg. price $2,938 | -9.02% | | Production 75,594 | -7.94% |

*Production of 1971 Charger Coupe and Hardtop combined, so this percentage is based on combined figures for 1972.

# Coronet

*"Yes, it is possible to get a comfortably sized, comfortably priced family car. Just ask for Dodge Coronet."*

**Nameplate year of origin:** 1950 (hardtop models), 1953 (series).
**Current bodystyle lifespan:** 1971 through 1978.
**Predecessor to this model:** Coronet (1968 to 1970).
**Replacement for this model:** Monaco (1975 to 1978).
**Percentage of division's sales volume:** 9.62%.

### Measurements

| | Sedans | Wagons |
|---|---|---|
| Wheelbase | 118.0" | 118.0" |
| Length | 207.0" | 213.4" |

**Corporate siblings:** Plymouth Satellite.
**Primary competition:** AMC Matador, Chevrolet Chevelle, Ford Torino, and Pontiac LeMans.
**Notable changes:** Revised grille and trim and detail changes. All wagons now have V8 engine as standard equipment.
**Major standard equipment:** All-vinyl bench seat, trunk mat, cigarette lighter, front and rear armrests, 2-speed concealed wipers, and E78 × 14 BSW tires (H78 × 14 BSW for wagons). Custom adds: Pleated vinyl bench seat, simulated wood-grained door trim and instrument panel, color-keyed carpeting, and full-length body side molding. Crestwood adds: Exterior wood-grain trim.

|  | Sedans | Wagons |
|---|---|---|
| Width | 77.7" | 78.7" |
| Height | 53.6" | 56.4" |
| Legroom — front | 41.9" | 41.9" |
| Legroom — rear | 36.7" | 36.7" |
| Headroom — front | 38.5" | 39.7" |
| Headroom — rear | 37.3" | 38.1" |
| Cargo capacity (cu. ft.) | 16.7 | 91.3 |
| Fuel capacity (gals.) | 19.5 | 21.0 |

## Models Available

|  | Style Number | Base MSRP | Change from LY | Shipping Wt. (lbs.) | Production | Change from LY |
|---|---|---|---|---|---|---|
| Coronet 4-Door Sedan | WL41 | $2,721 | -2.02% | 3350 | 11,293 | -4.25% |
| Coronet 4-Door, 2-Seat Wagon | WL45 | $3,209 | +3.48% | 3795 | 5452* | -67.07% |
| Coronet Custom 4-Door Sedan | WH41 | $2,891 | -2.04% | 3310 | 43,132 | +14.05% |
| Coronet Custom 4-Dr., 2-S. Wgn. | WH45 | $3,382 | +3.17% | 3800 | * | * |
| Coronet Custom 4-Dr., 3-S. Wgn. | WH46 | $3,460 | +0.17% | 3840 | * | * |
| Crnt. Crestwood 4-Dr., 2-S. Wgn. | WP45 | $3,604 | +0.08% | 3810 | 6471** | -4.63%** |
| Crnt. Crestwood 4-Dr., 3-S. Wgn. | WP46 | $3,683 | +0.03% | 3850 | ** | ** |
| TOTALS | Avg. price | $3,279 | +0.99% | | Production 66,348 | -26.99% |

*Coronet and Custom Wagon Production kept as one total.    **Coronet Crestwood 2-Seat and 3-Seat production kept as one total.

# Polara

*"The value story goes on."*

**Nameplate year of origin:** 1959.
**Current bodystyle lifespan:** 1969 through 1973.
**Predecessor to this model:** Polara (1967 to 1968).
**Replacement for this model:** Monaco (1974).
**Percentage of division's sales volume:** 19.24%.
**Corporate siblings:** Plymouth Fury.
**Primary competition:** AMC Ambassador, Chevrolet Impala, Ford LTD, Oldsmobile Delta 88, and Pontiac Catalina.
**Notable changes:** Redesigned sheetmetal, new grilles, and rooflines. Base Polara models now have a V8 engine standard.
**Major standard equipment:** Cloth and vinyl front bench seat, color-keyed carpeting, 2-speed concealed windshield wipers, automatic transmission, power steering, and F78 × 15 BSW tires (J78 × 15 BSW on 2-Seat Wagon, and L84 × 15 on 3-Seat Wagons). Custom adds: Simulated wood-grained door-trim inserts and instrument panel, and side molding with vinyl insert.

## Measurements

|  | Cars | Wagons |
|---|---|---|
| Wheelbase | 122.0" | 122.0" |
| Length | 219.4" | 222.8" |
| Width | 79.6" | 79.2" |
| Height | 55.0" | 57.1" |
| Legroom — front | 41.8" | 41.8" |
| Legroom — rear | 39.1" | 39.1" |
| Headroom — front | 38.8" | 39.6" |
| Headroom — rear | 38.4" | 39.2" |
| Cargo capacity (cu. ft.) | 22.4 | 104.2 |
| Fuel capacity (gals.) | 23.0 | 23.0 |

## Models Available

|  | Style Number | Base MSRP | Change from LY | Shipping Wt. (lbs.) | Production | Change from LY |
|---|---|---|---|---|---|---|
| Polara 2-Door Hardtop | DL23 | $3,641 | +9.70% | 3800 | 7,022 | -39.12% |
| Polara 4-Door Sedan | DL41 | $3,618 | +9.70% | 3835 | 25,187 | +16.73% |
| Polara 4-Door Hardtop | DL43 | $3,709 | +6.06% | 3875 | 8,212 | +230.20% |

**1972**

| | Style Number | Base MSRP | Change from LY | Shipping Wt. (lbs.) | Production | Change from LY |
|---|---|---|---|---|---|---|
| Polara Custom 2-Door Hardtop | DM23 | $3,830 | +5.97% | 3815 | 15,039 | +55.33% |
| Polara Custom 4-Door Sedan | DM41 | $3,808 | +5.98% | 3845 | 19,739 | +42.42% |
| Polara Custom 4-Door Hardtop | DM43 | $3,898 | +5.90% | 3890 | 22,505 | +28.91% |
| Polara Custom 4-Dr., 2-S. Wgn. | DM45 | $4,262 | +6.76% | 4320 | 3,497 | +14.20%* |
| Polara Custom 4-Dr., 3-S. Wgn. | DM46 | $4,371 | +6.66% | 4370 | 7,660 | +14.20%* |
| TOTALS | | Avg. price $3,892 | +5.79% | | Production 108,861 | +19.79% |

*Polara Custom Wagon production in 1971 was kept as a single total, therefore this increase is based off of a combined total for 1972.

# Monaco

*"Excellence without extravagance."*

**Nameplate year of origin:** 1965.
**Current bodystyle lifespan:** 1969 through 1973.
**Predecessor to this model:** Monaco (1967 to 1968).
**Replacement for this model:** Royal Monaco (1974 to 1978).
**Percentage of division's sales volume:** 6.54%.
**Corporate siblings:** Chrysler Newport.
**Primary competition:** AMC Ambassador Brougham, Chevrolet Caprice, Ford LTD, Mercury Monterey, Oldsmobile Delta 88, and Pontiac Bonneville/Grand Ville.
**Notable changes:** Redesigned sheetmetal and new, distinctive grille with hidden headlights.
**Major standard equipment:** Cloth and vinyl split back front bench seat, simulated wood-grained door inserts and instrument panel, color-keyed carpeting, combination dome and map lights, rear door automatic dome light switch, trunk light, 2-speed concealed wipers, side moldings with vinyl inserts, automatic transmission, power steering, power front disc brakes, deluxe wheel covers, and G78 × 15 BSW tires (J78 × 15 BSW on 2-seat Wagon, and L84 × 15 BSW on 3-Seat Wagon).

## Measurements

| | Cars | Wagons |
|---|---|---|
| Wheelbase | 122.0" | 122.0" |
| Length | 222.2" | 225.6" |
| Width | 79.6" | 79.2" |
| Height | 55.0" | 57.1" |
| Legroom — front | 41.8" | 41.8" |
| Legroom — rear | 39.1" | 39.1" |
| Headroom — front | 38.8" | 39.6" |
| Headroom — rear | 38.4" | 39.2" |
| Cargo capacity (cu. ft.) | 22.4 | 104.2 |
| Fuel capacity (gals.) | 23.0 | 23.0 |

## Models Available

| | Style Number | Base MSRP | Change from LY | Shipping Wt. (lbs.) | Production | Change from LY |
|---|---|---|---|---|---|---|
| Monaco 2-Door Hardtop | DP23 | $4,153 | -3.37% | 3960 | 7,786 | +143.69% |
| Monaco 4-Door Sedan | DP41 | $4,095 | -3.04% | 3980 | 6,474 | +27.30%* |
| Monaco 4-Door Hardtop | DP43 | $4,216 | -3.34% | 4030 | 15,039 | +27.30%* |
| Monaco 4-Door, 2-S. Wgn. | DP45 | $4,627 | -1.34% | 4445 | 2,569 | +41.60%* |
| Monaco 4-Door, 3-S. Wgn. | DP46 | $4,756 | -1.35% | 4490 | 5,145 | +41.60%* |
| TOTALS | | Avg. price $4,369 | -2.46% | | Production 37,013 | +44.90% |

*Production totals in 1971 for 4-Door Sedan and 4-Door Hardtop models were combined, as well as 2-Seat and 3-Seat Wagons. These figures are based on the combined totals for 1972 models.

# FORD

*"Ford gives you Better Ideas."*

Nineteen-seventy-two was a record setting sales year for Ford Motor Company. Ford dealers sold more than three million cars and trucks this year. All-new styling was seen on the Torino and Thunderbird, as all of the other lines were fine-tuned for the new year. The highly successful Pinto added a Station Wagon version during the model year, to compete with the Vega Wagon. The equally successful Maverick, which had been introduced in mid–1969, carried on for another year without styling change. However, to capitalize on its popularity, a 4-Door Sedan model was added this year as well as a sporty version of the 2-Door called the Grabber. The Mustang was relatively unchanged this year, and was in fact still available with a 351 CID V8 that put out over 300 horsepower! Mustang was one of the few muscle cars still in existence by 1972.

Ford division's mid-size line, the Torino, was completely new for 1972. After only two years with the slim and slender looking models, the Torino went the luxury route and gained weight in the process. Also gained were two Gran Torino Sport models, replacing the former Torino GTs, and there was a shuffling of model names and body styles. The new cars were larger and bulkier looking, and did not look at all like the mid-sized cars of previous years. This is not to say they were ugly, but it was more of a full-size Ford look, and less a sporty Mustang look. Full-size Fords were only given minor trim changes to differentiate them from the 1971 models. Officially the 10-passenger full-size wagons were no longer separate models in the lineup. However, one could order a 6-passenger wagon and then add the Dual Facing Rear Seat option. This would become standard Ford practice for many years. Finally, the Thunderbird completed its migration from the sport/luxury market to the luxury market with the unveiling of the 1972 model. Based on the Lincoln Continental platform, the Thunderbird now rode on a 120.4-inch wheelbase and looked every bit the Lincoln that it almost was. This new 'Bird was well received, at a time when most car buyers were leaning more towards the luxury cars. In the revamping, the 4-Door Thunderbird was lost to history.

Gran Torino 2-Door Hardtop

LTD Brougham 2-Door Hardtop

Maverick 2-Door Coupe

Mustang 2-Door Hardtop

Pinto 2-Door Sedan

Thunderbird 2-Door Hardtop

**1972**

**Model year production:** 2,283,904, up 11.18% over 1971.
**Domestic market share:** 24.45% (2nd place).
**Base price range:** $1,960 to $5,293.

**Industry average base price:** $3,788.
**Ford average base price:** $3,331.
**Introduction date:** September 24, 1971.

Assembly plants: Atlanta, GA (A); Chicago, IL (G); Dearborn, MI (F); Kansas City, MO (K); Lorain, OH (H); Los Angeles, CA (J); Louisville, KY (U); Mahwah, NJ (E); Metuchen, NJ (T); Norfolk, VA (N); San Jose, CA (R); Twin Cities, MN (P); Wayne, MI (W); Wixom, MI (Y); St. Thomas, Ontario, Can. (X); Oakville, Ontario, Can. (B).

Data plate identification: Eleven digit code read as follows: 2 for 1972; 2nd digit is assembly plant code; 2-digit model number (see listings below); 5th digit is engine code; 100001 and up for serial number. *Example:* 2Y87N100001 is a 1972 Ford Thunderbird 2-Door Hardtop with a 429 CID V8 engine, serial number 100001, built in Wixom, MI.

## Powertrains

| Engine | Net HP | Engine Code | Transmission Availability | Pinto & Maverick | Mustang | Torino | Full-size | T-Bird |
|--------|--------|-------------|---------------------------|------------------|---------|--------|-----------|--------|
| 98 CID (1600cc) 1-bbl., 4-cyl. (Pinto only) | 54 | na | 4-speed manual | S | - | - | - | - |
| | | | SelectShift Cruise-O-Matic | $170 | - | - | - | - |
| 122 CID (2000cc) 2-bbl., 4-cyl. (Pinto only) | 86 | X | 4-speed manual | $49 | - | - | - | - |
| | | | SelectShift Cruise-O-Matic | $219 | - | - | - | - |
| 170 CID, 1-bbl., 6-cyl. | 82 | U | 3-speed manual | S | - | - | - | - |
| | | | SelectShift Cruise-O-Matic | $177 | - | - | - | - |
| 200 CID, 1-bbl., 6-cyl | 84 | T | 3-speed manual | $38 | - | - | - | - |
| | | | SelectShift Cruise-O-Matic | $215 | - | - | - | - |
| 240 CID, 1-bbl., 6-cyl. | 103 | V | SelectShift Cruise-O-Matic | - | - | - | S (Fleet sales) | |
| 250 CID, 1-bbl., 6-cyl. | 98 | L | 3-speed manual | $77 | S | S | - | - |
| | | | SelectShift Cruise-O-Matic | $254 | $204 | $211 | - | - |
| 302 CID, 2-bbl., V8 | 140 | F | 3-speed manual | $160 | $87 | $90/S (Sports/Squire) | - | - |
| | | | 4-speed manual | - | $280 | - | - | - |
| | | | SelectShift Cruise-O-Matic | $337 | $291 | $301/ $211 (Sports/Squire) | - | - |
| 351 CID Windsor 2-bbl., V8 | 153 | H | SelectShift Cruise-O-Matic | - | - | - | S | - |
| 351 CID Cleveland 2-bbl., V8 | 163 | H | 3-speed manual | - | $128 | $134/$44 (Sports/Squire) | - | - |
| | | | 4-speed manual | - | $321 | - | - | - |
| | | | SelectShift Cruise-O-Matic | - | $332 | $345/$255 (Sports/Squire) | - | - |
| 351 CID Cleveland 4-bbl., V8 | 248 | M | 3-speed manual | - | $202 | $127 (Sports only) | - | - |
| | | | 4-speed manual | - | $395 | $327 (Sports only) | - | - |
| | | | SelectShift Cruise-O-Matic | - | $406 | $338 (Sports only) | - | - |
| 351 CID HO Cleveland 4-bbl., V8 | 266 | Q | 4-speed manual | - | $870 | - | - | - |
| | | | SelectShift Cruise-O-Matic | - | $870 | - | - | - |
| 400 CID Cleveland 2-bbl., V8 | 172 | S | SelectShift Cruise-O-Matic | - | - | - | $95 | - |
| 429 CID Thunder Jet 4-bbl., V8 | 205 | K | SelectShift Cruise-O-Matic | - | - | $310 | $222 | - |
| 429 CID Thunderbird 4-bbl., V8 | 212 | N | SelectShift Cruise-O-Matic | - | - | - | - | S |
| 460 CID Thunderbird 4-bbl., V8 | 224 | A | SelectShift Cruise-O-Matic | - | - | - | - | $ |

## Major Options

| | Pinto | Maverick | Mustang | Torino | Full-size | Thunderbird |
|---|---|---|---|---|---|---|
| SelectAire air conditioning | $374 | $374 | $379 | $412 | $420 | $448 |
| Electronic cruise control | - | - | - | - | $84 | $97 |
| Electric rear window defogger | - | $28*** | $44 | $48 | $53 | $84 |
| Tinted glass** | $36 | $51 | $36 | $48 | $53 | $52/S |
| Deck lid remote release | - | - | - | - | $14 | $ |
| Power steering | - | $95 | $103 | $112 | S | S |
| Power brakes—front discs | - | - | $64 | $68 | $51 (S on LTD) | S |
| Power door locks (2D/4D/Wgn— includes tailgate) | - | - | - | - | $47/$71/$80 | $61 |
| Power driver's seat/Bench seat | - | - | - | $105 | $105 | $104 |
| Power windows | - | - | $117 | $127 | $129 | $130 |
| AM radio | $61 | $61 | $61 | $64 | $64 | S |
| AM/FM stereo | - | - | $197 | $214 | $240 | $146 |
| Front seat floor console* | $42 | $26 | $70 | $60 | - | - |
| Front bucket seats | S | $101 | S | $150**** | - | - |
| Tilt steering wheel | - | - | $41 | - | $44 | $51 |
| Sunroof—N/A on wagons | - | - | - | - | $509 | $518 |
| Vinyl roof | $75 | $77 | $80 | $93 | $110 ($148 Wagons) | $137 |
| White sidewall tires | $42 | $34 | $34 | $34 | $34 | $34 |
| Magnum 500 chrome wheels | - | - | $139 | $139 | - | - |

Options common to most models. (- = Not Available; S = Standard equipment.) Items may be standard equipment, optional at different pricing, or unavailable on certain models. This chart is only a guide.

*Requires bucket seats. Pinto style is a consolette with floor shifter and electric clock. Maverick style is a consolette with column shifter and without a clock.   **Pinto Runabout, $18; Maverick Grabber, $37; Mustang Conv., $14; became standard on Thunderbird after start of model year.   ***Blower type defogger.   ****Gran Torino and Gran Torino Sport 2-Door models only.

## Paint Colors*

| | Code | Thunderbird |
|---|---|---|
| Black | 1C | x |
| Blue Fire Metallic | 3C | x |
| Blue Glow Metallic | 3K | |
| Bright Blue Metallic | 3J | |
| Bright Green Gold Metallic | 4B | x |
| Bright Lime | 4E | |
| Bright Red | 2B | |
| Bright Yellow Gold Metallic | 6F | |
| Burgundy Fire Metallic | 2G | x |
| Cinnamon Fire Metallic | 5D | x |
| Copper Fire Metallic | 5G | x |
| Creamy White | 9C | |
| Dark Blue Metallic | 3H | x |
| Dark Green Metallic | 4Q | x |
| Emerald Fire Metallic | 4U | x |
| Gold Fire Metallic | 6G | x |
| Grabber Blue | 3F | |
| Gray Gold Metallic | 6J | x |
| Green Fire Metallic | 4D | x |
| Ivy Bronze Metallic | 4C | |
| Light Blue | 3B | x |
| Light Goldenrod | 6B | |
| Light Gray Metallic | 1A | x |
| Light Green | 4S | |
| Light Pewter Metallic | 5A | |
| Lime Fire Metallic | 4G | x |
| Maroon | 2J | x |
| Medium Blue Metallic | 3D | x |
| Medium Bright Yellow | 6E | |
| Medium Brown Metallic | 5H | x |

|                          | Code | Thunderbird |
|--------------------------|------|-------------|
| Medium Coral             | 2A   |             |
| Medium Ginger Bronze Met | 5J   |             |
| Medium Green Metallic    | 4P   | x           |
| Medium Lime Metallic     | 4F   | x           |
| Medium Orange Metallic   | 5N   |             |
| Medium Yellow Gold       | 6C   | x           |
| Red                      | 2E   |             |
| Tan (Pinto only)         | 5L   |             |
| Walnut Fire Metallic     | 5C   | x           |
| White                    | 9A   | x           |
| Yellow                   | 6D   | x           |

*All colors available on most models. Thunderbird available only in colors indicated.*

# Pinto

*"The Little Carefree Car makes more sense than ever."*

**Nameplate year of origin:** 1971.
**Current bodystyle lifespan:** 1971 through 1980.
**Predecessor to this model:** None.
**Replacement for this model:** Escort (1981 to 1985).
**Percentage of division's sales volume:** 21.03%.
**Corporate siblings:** None.
**Primary competition:** AMC Gremlin and Chevrolet Vega.
**Notable changes:** Larger back window glass on Runabout. New station wagon model added.
**Major standard equipment:** High back bucket seats with all-vinyl trim, glove box, interior dome light, rack-and-pinion steering, DirectAire ventilation system, and 6.00 × 13 BSW tires.

## Measurements

|                         | Cars    | Wagons  |
|-------------------------|---------|---------|
| Wheelbase               | 94.0"   | 94.0"   |
| Length                  | 163.0"  | 163.0"  |
| Width                   | 69.4"   | 69.7"   |
| Height                  | 50.6"   | 52.1"   |
| Legroom — front         | 40.2"   | 40.2"   |
| Legroom — rear          | 30.3"   | 29.5"   |
| Headroom — front        | 36.9"   | 37.7"   |
| Headroom — rear         | 35.7"   | 38.8"   |
| Cargo capacity (cu. ft.)| 8.2     | 57.2    |
| Fuel capacity (gals.)   | 13.0    | 14.0    |

## Models Available

|                               | Style Number | Base MSRP | Change from LY | Shipping Wt. (lbs.) | Production | Change from LY |
|-------------------------------|--------------|-----------|----------------|---------------------|------------|----------------|
| Pinto 2-Door Sedan            | 62B-10       | $1,960    | +2.14%         | 1968                | 181,002    | -37.28%        |
| Pinto 3-Door Runabout HBK     | 64B-11       | $2,078    | +0.78%         | 2012                | 197,920    | +210.24%       |
| Pinto 2-Door, 4-passenger Wgn.| 73B-12       | $2,265    | NEW            | 2293                | 101,483    | NEW            |
| TOTALS                        | Avg. price   | $2,101    | +5.52%         | Production          | 480,405    | +36.32%        |

# Mustang

*"The Driving Machine."*

**Nameplate year of origin:** 1964½ (also on a 1963 show car).
**Current bodystyle lifespan:** 1971 through 1973.
**Predecessor to this model:** None.
**Corporate siblings:** Mercury Cougar (stretched platform).
**Replacement for this model:** Mustang II (1974 to 1978).
**Percentage of division's sales volume:** 5.48%.

## Measurements

|                 |         |
|-----------------|---------|
| Wheelbase       | 109.0"  |
| Length          | 190.0"  |
| Width           | 75.0"   |
| Height          | NA      |
| Legroom — front | NA      |

**Primary competition:** AMC Javelin, Chevrolet Camaro, Dodge Challenger, Plymouth Barracuda, and Pontiac Firebird.

**Notable changes:** Trim and detail changes. Boss 351 model discontinued for this year.

**Major standard equipment:** High-back bucket seats, full carpeting, mini console, courtesy lights, deluxe two-spoke steering wheel, DirectAire ventilation, concealed windshield wipers, bright moldings (rocker, wheel lip, and lower back panel), dual color-keyed outside racing mirrors, wheel covers, and E78 × 14 BSW tires. SportsRoof adds: Fixed rear quarter windows and tinted rear glass. Convertible adds: Power operated top, color-keyed top boot, tinted front and rear glass, knitted vinyl seat upholstery. Grande adds: Vinyl top with script, trunk mat, cloth and vinyl interior trim, deluxe instrument panel covering and wood-tone instrument panel applique. Mach I adds: Competition suspension, front integral spoiler, color-keyed hood and fender moldings, black grille with sports lamps, NACA-type hood (only with base engine), tape stripes and Mach I decals, wheel trim rings and E70 × 14 WSW tires.

## Measurements (cont.)

| | |
|---|---|
| Legroom — rear | NA |
| Headroom — front | NA |
| Headroom — rear | NA |
| Cargo capacity (cu. ft.) | NA |
| Fuel capacity (gals.) | NA |

## Models Available

| | Style Number | Base MSRP | Change from LY | Shipping Wt. (lbs.) | Production | Change from LY |
|---|---|---|---|---|---|---|
| Mustang 2-Door Hardtop | 65D-01 | $2,679 | -7.97% | 2941 | 57,350 | -12.71% |
| Mustang 2-Door SportsRoof | 63D-02 | $2,736 | -7.98% | 2909 | 15,622 | -34.79% |
| Mustang 2-Door Convertible | 76D-03 | $2,965 | -8.12% | 3061 | 6,401 | +4.57% |
| Mustang Grande 2-Door Hardtop | 65F-04 | $2,865 | -8.09% | 2965 | 18,045 | +3.67% |
| Mustang Mach I 2-Door SportsRoof | 63R-05 | $3,003 | -8.11% | 3046 | 27,675 | -24.07% |
| TOTALS | Avg. price | $2,850 | -12.85% | Production | 125,093 | -16.40% |

# Maverick

*"America's Favorite Compact."*

**Nameplate year of origin:** 1970.
**Current bodystyle lifespan:** 1970 through 1977.
**Predecessor to this model:** Falcon (1966 to 1969).
**Replacement for this model:** Fairmont (1978 to 1983).
**Percentage of division's sales volume:** 12.77%.
**Corporate siblings:** Mercury Comet.
**Primary competition:** AMC Hornet, Chevrolet Nova, Plymouth Valiant, and Pontiac Ventura II.
**Notable changes:** No changes.
**Major standard equipment:** All-vinyl interior trim, glove box, DirectAire ventilation, interior light, and 6.45 × 14 BSW tires. Grabber adds: Dual outside color-keyed racing mirrors, Grabber stripes, Rallye road lights, wheel trim rings, and blacked-out hood and cowl treatment.

## Measurements

| | 2-Door | 4-Door |
|---|---|---|
| Wheelbase | 103.0" | 109.9" |
| Length | 179.4" | 186.4" |
| Width | 71.0" | 71.0" |
| Height | 52.3" | 53.1" |
| Legroom — front | 41.3" | 41.3" |
| Legroom — rear | 31.9" | 36.4" |
| Headroom — front | 37.6" | 37.6" |
| Headroom — rear | 36.1" | 37.1" |
| Cargo capacity (cu. ft.) | 10.4 | 10.4 |
| Fuel capacity (gals.) | 16.0 | 16.0 |

## Models Available

| | Style Number | Base MSRP | Change from LY | Shipping Wt. (lbs.) | Production | Change from LY |
|---|---|---|---|---|---|---|
| Maverick 2-Door Coupe | 62A-91 | $2,140 | -1.61% | 2642 | 145,931 | -8.64% |
| Maverick 4-Door Sedan | 54A-92 | $2,195 | -1.79% | 2737 | 73,686 | +0.65% |
| Maverick Grabber 2-Door Cpe. | 62-93 | $2,309 | -1.91% | 2697 | 35,347 | -9.29% |
| TOTALS | Avg. price | $2,215 | -1.78% | Production | 254,964 | -6.23% |

# Torino

*"All new, quiet Mid-size cars."*

**Nameplate year of origin:** 1968.

**Current bodystyle lifespan:** 1972 through 1976.

**Predecessor to this model:** Fairlane/Torino (1970 to 1971).

**Replacement for this model:** LTD II (1977 to 1979, on same platform).

**Percentage of division's sales volume:** 21.75%.

**Corporate siblings:** Mercury Montego.

**Primary competition:** AMC Matador, Chevrolet Chevelle, Plymouth Satellite, Dodge Coronet/Charger.

**Notable changes:** Completely restyled. Series names realigned: Torino Brougham dropped, Gran Torino replaces Torino 500.

**Major standard equipment:** High-back bench seats with all-vinyl trim, floor mats, bright moldings (windshield, rear window, and guttering), hub caps with trim rings, and E78 × 14 BSW tires (F78 × 14 on 4-Door). Torino wagon adds: Three-way tailgate, power front disc brakes, and H78 × 14 BSW tires. Gran Torino adds: Cloth and vinyl interior trim, full carpeting, bright moldings (lower bodyside, wheel openings, and deck lid), dual note horn, trunk mat, deluxe steering wheel, manual front disc brakes (power on Wagons), and F78 × 14 BSW tires (H78 × 14 on Wagons). Squire wagon adds: Deluxe vinyl interior trim, full wheel covers, and exterior wood-grained trim. Sports models add: All-vinyl interior trim, hood scoops, dual color-keyed outside racing mirrors, special grille design, and E70 × 14 BSW tires (F70 × 14 on SportsRoof model).

## Measurements

|  | 2-Doors | 4-Doors | Wagons |
|---|---|---|---|
| Wheelbase | 114.0" | 118.0" | 118.0" |
| Length | 203.7" | 207.3" | 211.6" |
| Width | NA | NA | NA |
| Height | NA | NA | NA |
| Legroom — front | NA | NA | NA |
| Legroom — rear | NA | NA | NA |
| Headroom — front | NA | NA | NA |
| Headroom — rear | NA | NA | NA |
| Cargo capacity (cu. ft.) | NA | NA | 83.5 |
| Fuel capacity (gals.) | NA | NA | NA |

## Models Available

|  | Style Number | Base MSRP | Change from LY | Shipping Wt. (lbs.) | Production | Change from LY |
|---|---|---|---|---|---|---|
| Torino 2-Door Hardtop | 65B-25 | $2,673 | -1.22% | 3369 | 33,530 | -10.63% |
| Torino 4-Door Sedan | 53B-27 | $2,641 | -1.16% | 3469 | 33,486 | +13.51% |
| Torino 4-Door, 6-passenger Wagon | 71B-40 | $2,955 | -2.25% | 3879 | 22,204 | +2.94% |
| Gran Torino 2-Door Hardtop | 65D-30 | $2,878 | -0.31% | 3395 | 132,284 | +47.04% |
| Gran Torino 4-Door Sedan | 53D-31 | $2,856 | +0.04% | 3476 | 102,300 | +186.96% |
| Gran Torino 4-Door, 6-passenger Wgn. | 71D-42 | $3,096 | -2.33% | 3881 | 45,212 | +94.29% |
| Gran Torino Sport 2-Door Hardtop | 65R-38 | $3,094 | NEW | 3496 | 31,239 | NEW |
| Gran Torino Sport 2-Dr. SportsRoof HT | 63R-35 | $3,094 | -1.78% | 3474 | 60,794 | +92.14% |
| Gran Torino Squire 4-Door, 6-p. Wgn. | 71K-43 | $3,486 | -2.08% | 4042 | 35,595 | +125.21% |
| TOTALS | | *Avg. price* $2,975 | -3.25% | | *Production* 496,644 | +52.13% |

# Custom, Galaxie & LTD

*"19 models … all with quiet plus."*

**Nameplate year of origin:** 1957 (Custom), 1959 (Galaxie) and 1965 (LTD).

**Current bodystyle lifespan:** 1971 through 1978 (restyles in 1973 and 1975).

**Predecessor to this model:** Full-size Ford (1969 to 1970).

**Replacement for this model:** LTD (1979 to 1991).

**Percentage of division's sales volume:** 36.44%.

## Measurements

|  | Cars | Wagons |
|---|---|---|
| Wheelbase | 121.0" | 121.0" |
| Length | 216.2" | 219.2" |

Corporate siblings: Mercury Monterey and Marquis.
Primary competition: AMC Ambassador, Chevrolet BelAir/Impala/Caprice, Dodge Polara/Monaco, Plymouth Fury, and Pontiac Catalina.
Notable changes: Trim and detail changes.
Major standard equipment: All vinyl interior trim, nylon carpeting, power steering, bright front and rear window moldings, and F78 × 15 BSW tires. Custom 500 adds: Cloth and vinyl interior trim, bright moldings (wheel lip and rear lower panel), power tailgate window (Ranch Wagon) and H78 × 15 BSW tires (Ranch Wagon). Galaxie 500 adds: Upgraded interior trim, woodgrain instrument panel trim, bright moldings (wheel lip, deck lid and rocker panels). LTD adds: Luxury interior trim, electric clock, front door courtesy lights, rear bumper guards, power front disc brakes, and G78 × 15 tires (on convertible and 4-Door models; H78 × 15 on Country Squire). Country Squire adds: Full wheel covers and wood-grained bodyside appliques. LTD Brougham adds: Unique Brougham interior trim with Flight Bench seats, rear door courtesy lights, cut-pile carpeting, front and rear armrests, rocker panel moldings, and G78 × 15 BSW tires.

|  | Cars | Wagons |
|---|---|---|
| Width | 79.8" | 79.8" |
| Height | NA | NA |
| Legroom — front | NA | NA |
| Legroom — rear | NA | NA |
| Headroom — front | NA | NA |
| Headroom — rear | NA | NA |
| Cargo capacity (cu. ft.) | NA | 96.2 |
| Fuel capacity (gals.) | NA | NA |

## Models Available

|  | Style Number | Base MSRP | Change from LY | Shipping Wt. (lbs.) | Production | Change from LY |
|---|---|---|---|---|---|---|
| Custom 4-Door Sedan | 54B-51 | $3,246 | -1.28% | 3759 | 33,014 | -19.60% |
| Custom 4-Dr., 6-p. Ranch Wagon | 71B-70 | $3,852 | -0.98% | 4317 | 13,064 | -21.75% |
| Custom 500 4-Door Sedan | 54D-53 | $3,377 | -1.43% | 3764 | 24,870 | -26.34% |
| Custom 500 4-Dr., 6-p. Ranch Wgn. | 71D-72 | $3,941 | -1.03% | 4327 | 16,834 | -35.15% |
| Galaxie 500 2-Door Hardtop | 65F-58 | $3,572 | -1.54% | 3826 | 80,855 | -30.98% |
| Galaxie 500 4-Door Sedan | 54F-54 | $3,537 | -1.59% | 3826 | 104,167 | +6.15% |
| Galaxie 500 4-Door Hardtop | 57F-56 | $3,604 | -1.66% | 3881 | 28,939 | -37.89% |
| Gal. 500 4-Dr., 6-p. Cntry. Sdn. Wgn. | 71F-74 | $4,028 | -1.13% | 4308 | 55,238 | -8.68% |
| LTD 2-Door Hardtop | 65H-62 | $3,882 | -1.05% | 3853 | 101,048 | -2.74% |
| LTD 2-Door Convertible | 76H-61 | $4,057 | -0.90% | 4091 | 4,234 | -26.37% |
| LTD 4-Door Pillared Hardtop | 53H-63 | $3,890 | -2.00% | 3913 | 104,167 | +12.91% |
| LTD 4-Door Hardtop | 57H-64 | $3,925 | -1.11% | 3908 | 33,742 | -29.95% |
| LTD 4-Door, 6-p. Cntry. Squire Wgn. | 71H-76 | $4,318 | -1.42% | 4308 | 121,419 | -7.06% |
| LTD Brougham 2-Door Hardtop | 65K-68 | $4,034 | -1.54% | 3883 | 50,409 | +16.41% |
| LTD Brougham 4-Door Pillared HT | 53K-66 | $4,031 | -2.63% | 3949 | 36,909 | +40.95% |
| LTD Brougham 4-Door Hardtop | 57K-67 | $4,074 | -1.59% | 3944 | 23,364 | -16.02% |
| TOTALS | Avg. price | $3,836 | -2.77% | Production | 832,273 | -9.32% |

# Thunderbird

*"All-new for '72 and more Thunderbird than ever."*

Nameplate year of origin: 1955.
Current bodystyle lifespan: 1972 through 1976.
Predecessor to this model: Thunderbird (1967 to 1971; restyled in 1970).
Replacement for this model: Thunderbird (1977 to 1979).
Percentage of division's sales volume: 2.53%.
Corporate siblings: Lincoln Continental Mark IV.
Primary competition: Buick Riviera, Oldsmobile Toronado.
Notable changes: Completely redesigned. 4-Door model discontinued.
Major standard equipment: Luxury all-cloth interior with cut-pile carpeting, split bench front seat, power steering, power front disc brakes, full wheel covers, and 215R15 BSW Michelin radial tires.

## Measurements

| Wheelbase | 120.4" |
|---|---|
| Length | 214.0" |
| Width | NA |
| Height | NA |
| Legroom — front | NA |
| Legroom — rear | NA |
| Headroom — front | NA |
| Headroom — rear | NA |
| Cargo capacity (cu. ft.) | NA |
| Fuel capacity (gals.) | NA |

1972

## Models Available

| | Style Number | Base MSRP | Change from LY | Shipping Wt. (lbs.) | Production | Change from LY |
|---|---|---|---|---|---|---|
| Thunderbird 2-Door Hardtop | 65K-87 | $5,293 | -0.04% | 4420 | 57,814 | +184.01% |
| TOTALS | | Avg. price $5,293 | -2.27% | | Production 57,814 | +60.35% |

# LINCOLN

*"The finest cars built in America."*

The Lincoln Motor Car Division of Ford Motor Company, which celebrated its 50th anniversary last year, moved into 1972 announcing an all-new Continental Mark IV model. This new Mark series, while retaining the character of the 1969–71 version, was a big automobile. At 220.1", it was 4" longer than its predecessor. While not a remarkable difference, the overall impression was one of mass, not the sexy, leaner look found on the Mark III. This new Mark IV series would prove to be the most popular yet, and it would be a real sales asset for Lincoln in competing with the Cadillac Eldorado. The Lincoln Continental 2-Door and 4-Door models were mildly facelifted; having been all-new in 1970, most of the changes on these cars would pertain to upholstery and trim. Unfortunately for Ford, these cars were still selling nowhere near the quantities that GM's Cadillac was moving out the door with their ever-popular de Ville line. They were certainly nice cars, but very traditional and very "Ford" looking. Or maybe the Fords just looked too much like Lincolns. At any rate, it would be another 20 years before Lincoln would make real gains on Cadillac.

Continental 4-Door Sedan

Continental Mark IV 2-Door Hardtop

**Model year production:** 94,560, up 50.95% over 1971.
**Domestic market share:** 1.01% (12th place).
**Base price range:** $7,068 to $8,640.
**Industry average base price:** $3.788.
**Lincoln average base price:** $7,670.
**Introduction date:** September 24, 1971.
**Assembly plants:** Wixom, MI (Y), and Allen Park, MI (S).

**Data plate identification:** Eleven digit code read as follows: 2 for 1972; 2nd digit is assembly plant code; 2-digit model number (see listings below); 5th digit is engine code; 800001 and up for serial number. *Example:* 2Y82A800001 is a 1972 Lincoln Continental 4-Door Sedan with a 460 CID V8 engine, serial number 800001, built in Wixom, MI.

## Powertrains

| Engine | Net HP | Engine Code | Transmission Availability | Continental | Mark IV |
|---|---|---|---|---|---|
| 460 CID, 4-bbl., V8 | 212 | A | Select-Shift Automatic | S | - |
| 460 CID, 4-bbl., V8 | 224 | A | Select-Shift Automatic | - | S |

## Major Options

|  | Continental | Mark IV |
|---|---|---|
| Automatic headlight dimmers | $50 | $50 |
| 6-way power seat | $90 | S |
| Power door locks — inc. trunk release | $106 | $96 |
| AM-FM radio | $146 | $146 |
| AM-FM stereo w/8-track | $286 | $286 |
| Vinyl roof | $152 | S |
| Sunroof | $627 | $627 |
| Tilt and telescope steering wheel | $70 | $70 |
| Leather upholstery | $169 | $179 |
| Cruise control | $95 | $95 |
| Rear window defogger | $85 | $85 |
| Moondust Metallic paint colors | $128 | $128 |
| Town Car package — Continental 4-Door only | $394 | - |

Options common to most models. (- = Not Available; S = Standard equipment.) Items may be standard equipment, optional at different pricing, or unavailable on certain models. This chart is only a guide.

## Paint Colors

|  | Code | Continental | Mark IV |
|---|---|---|---|
| Light Gray Metallic | 1-A | x | x |
| Silver Moondust Metallic | 1-D |  | x |
| Red Moondust Metallic | 2-G | x | x |
| Maroon | 2-J | x | x |
| Light Blue | 3-B | x | x |
| Blue Moondust Metallic | 3-C | x | x |
| Medium Blue Metallic | 3-D | x | x |
| Dark Blue Metallic | 3-H | x | x |
| Black | 1-C | x | x |
| Pastel Lime | 4-A | x | x |
| Bright Green Gold Metallic | 4-B | x | x |
| Ivy Moondust Metallic | 4-D | x | x |
| Light Ivy Moondust Metallic | 4-G | x | x |
| Medium Green Metallic | 4-P | x | x |
| Dark Green Metallic | 4-Q | x | x |
| Lime Gold Moondust Met. | 4-U | x |  |
| Ginger Moondust Metallic | 5-C | x | x |
| Light Ginger Moondust Met. | 5-D | x | x |
| Dark Brown Metallic | 5-F | x | x |
| Copper Moondust Metallic | 5-G | x | x |
| Light Yellow Gold | 6-B | x | x |
| Yellow | 6-D | x | x |
| Gold Moondust Metallic | 6-G | x | x |
| Gray Gold Metallic | 6-J | x | x |
| White | 9-A | x | x |

# Continental

*"It is the quietest, smoothest riding, and most comfortable Lincoln Continental ever offered."*

**Nameplate year of origin:** 1940 (1961 as a standard sedan nameplate).
**Current bodystyle lifespan:** 1970 through 1979 (restyle in 1974).
**Predecessor to this model:** Continental (1961 to 1969).
**Replacement for this model:** Town Car (1980 to 1991).
**Percentage of division's sales volume:** 48.61%.
**Corporate siblings:** None.
**Primary competition:** Cadillac de Ville and Chrysler Imperial.
**Notable changes:** New grille and trim and detail changes.
**Major standard equipment:** Two-way power front bench seat, front and rear seat armrests, cut-pile carpeting, automatic temperature control air conditioner, electric clock, carpeted luggage compartment, left-hand remote control outside mirror, tinted glass, visor vanity mirror, AM radio with power antenna, power windows, fender skirts, and 225-15 Michelin radial WSW tires.

## Measurements

| | |
|---|---|
| Wheelbase | 127.0" |
| Length | 225.1" |
| Width | 79.8" |
| Height | 55.4" |
| Legroom — front | 42.0" |
| Legroom — rear | 42.0" |
| Headroom — front | 38.1" |
| Headroom — rear | 38.6" |
| Luggage capacity (cu. ft.) | 18.1 |
| Fuel capacity (gals.) | 24.2 |

**1972**

## Models Available

| | Style Number | Base MSRP | Change from LY | Shipping Wt. (lbs.) | Production | Change from LY |
|---|---|---|---|---|---|---|
| Continental 2-Door HT | 81 | $7,068 | -1.45% | 4906 | 10,408 | +26.85% |
| Continental 4-Door Sdn. | 82 | $7,302 | -1.58% | 4958 | 35,561 | +30.04% |
| TOTALS | | Avg. price $7,185 | -1.52% | | Production 45,969 | +29.30% |

# Continental Mark IV

*"For all of the 1970's. This will be the unique American car."*

**Nameplate year of origin:** 1956 (Continental Mark II).
**Current bodystyle lifespan:** 1972 through 1976.
**Predecessor to this model:** Continental Mark III (1969 to 1971).
**Replacement for this model:** Continental Mark V (1977 to 1979).
**Percentage of division's sales volume:** 51.39%.
**Corporate siblings:** Ford Thunderbird.
**Primary competition:** Buick Riviera, Cadillac Eldorado, and Oldsmobile Toronado.
**Notable changes:** Completely redesigned.
**Major standard equipment:** Six-way power front split bench seat, automatic seat back release, cut-pile carpeting, power windows, vinyl top, Sure Track power brake system, spare tire cover, carpeted luggage compartment, luxury wheel covers, Cartier electric clock, AM radio with power antenna, and 225-15 Michelin WSW tires.

### Measurements

| | |
|---|---|
| Wheelbase | 120.4" |
| Length | 220.1" |
| Width | 79.8" |
| Height | NA |
| Legroom — front | NA |
| Legroom — rear | NA |
| Headroom — front | NA |
| Headroom — rear | NA |
| Luggage capacity (cu. ft.) | 13.9 |
| Fuel capacity (gals.) | NA |

## Models Available

| | Style Number | Base MSRP | Change from LY | Shipping Wt. (lbs.) | Production | Change from LY |
|---|---|---|---|---|---|---|
| Continental Mark IV 2-Dr. HT | 89 | $8,640 | -1.94% | 4792 | 48,591 | +79.36% |
| TOTALS | | Avg. price $8,640 | -1.94% | | Production 48,591 | +79.36% |

# MERCURY

*"Better ideas make better cars."*

If the slogan above sounds all too familiar (cf. "Ford has a Better Idea"), so were the cars from Mercury for 1972. After 20 or more years of searching to create a divisional identity, the Mercury models were once again becoming glorified Fords or dressed-down Lincolns. All throughout the fifties, Mercury strived to differentiate itself from Ford, sometimes copying Lincoln styling cues to give it the upmarket look it needed. Then in the sixties, the mid-range division of Ford followed the lead set by GM divisions Pontiac and Oldsmobile in creating a performance image for itself. This move gave us such cars as the Comet Caliente, Cyclone, Cougar, and the Marauder. However, with the muscle-car era waning, the division was left with its more mundane cars, and consumers could only feel that they were buying a warmed-over Ford. Granted, there were differences, but sometimes they were all too subtle. For example, the Comet visually differed from the Ford Maverick only in its protruding hood and grille center section, and the four individual taillights out back. If not for the differing grille design, it would be hard to tell the totally redesigned Montego from a Torino. However, the new styling must have been viewed as a vast improvement over the 1971 models, as sales shot up over 136 percent. At least the full-size Mercury and the Cougar maintained some-

what independent identities. The Cougar carried over from the previous year with only minor trim changes. The new-for-1971 full-size models were also continued with only new grilles to distinguish them from the previous year's models. However, most people bought a Mercury for its level of luxury and comfort, so not everyone was disappointed with buying an upscale Ford, as evidenced by the strong sales that continued for 1972.

Comet 4-Door Sedan

Cougar XR-7 2-Door Hardtop

Marquis Brougham 4-Door Hardtop

Montego GT 2-Door Fastback

Montego MX Brougham 4-Door Sedan

Monterey 2-Door Hardtop

**Model year production:** 441,964, up 20.98% over 1971.
**Domestic market share:** 4.73% (8th place).
**Base price range:** $2,342 to $4,629.
**Industry average price:** $3,788.
**Mercury average price:** $3,785.
**Introduction date:** September 24, 1971.
**Assembly plants:** Dearborn, MI (F); Lorain, OH (H); Kansas City, MO (K); Allen Park, MI (S); St. Louis, MO (Z); and Oakville, Ontario, Canada (B).

**Data plate identification:** Eleven digit code read as follows: 2 for 1972; 2nd digit is assembly plant code; 2-digit model number (see listings below); 5th digit is engine code; 500001 and up for serial number. *Example:* 2Z07H500001 is a 1972 Mercury Montego 2-Door Hardtop with a 351 CID V8 engine, serial number 500001, built in St. Louis, MO.

## Powertrains

| Engine | Net HP | Engine Code | Transmission Availability | Comet | Cougar | Montego | Monterey | Marquis |
|---|---|---|---|---|---|---|---|---|
| 170 CID, 1-bbl., 6-cyl. | 82 | U | 3-speed manual | S | - | - | - | - |
| | | | SelectShift Automatic | $177 | - | - | - | - |
| 200 CID, 1-bbl., 6-cyl. | 84 | T | 3-speed manual | $38 | - | - | - | - |
| | | | SelectShift Automatic | $215 | - | - | - | - |
| 250 CID, 1-bbl., 6-cyl. | 98 | L | 3-speed manual | $77 | - | S | - | - |
| | | | SelectShift Automatic | $254 | - | $211 | - | - |
| 302 CID, 2-bbl., V8 | 140 | F | 3-speed manual | $160 | - | $90 S (GT) | - | - |
| | | | SelectShift Automatic | $337 | - | $301/$211 (GT) | - | - |
| 351 CID, 2-bbl., V8 | 163 | H | 3-speed manual | - | S | $134/$44 (GT) | - | - |
| | | | 4-speed manual | - | $ | - | - | - |
| | | | SelectShift Automatic | - | $ | $345/$255 (GT) | - | - |

**1972**

| Engine | Net HP | Engine Code | Transmission Availability | Comet | Cougar | Montego | Monterey | Marquis |
|---|---|---|---|---|---|---|---|---|
| 351 CID, 4-bbl., V8 | 262 | M | 3-speed manual | - | $ | - | - | - |
| | | | 4-speed manual | - | $ | - | - | - |
| | | | SelectShift Automatic | - | $ | - | - | - |
| 351 CID CJ, 4-bbl., V8 | 266 | Q | 4-speed manual | - | $ | $ (2-Dr. only) | - | - |
| | | | SelectShift Automatic | - | $ | $ (2-Dr. only) | - | - |
| 400 CID, 2-bbl., V8 | 172 | S | SelectShift Automatic | - | - | $ | S | - |
| 429 CID, 4-bbl., V8 | 205 | N | SelectShift Automatic | - | - | $ | $ | - |
| 460 CID, 4-bbl., V8 (Requires A/C) | 224 | A | SelectShift Automatic | - | - | - | $ | S |

## Major Options

| | Comet | Cougar | Montego | Monterey | Marquis |
|---|---|---|---|---|---|
| Whisper-Aire air conditioning | $371 | $375 | $408 | $441 | $441 |
| Electronic cruise control | - | - | - | $67 | $67 |
| Electric rear window defogger | $28* | $43 | $48 | $62 | $62 |
| Tinted glass** | $54 | $34 | $42 | $51 | S |
| Deck lid remote release | - | - | - | $14 | $14 |
| Power steering | $95 | $106 | $115 | S | S |
| Power brakes — front discs | - | $64 | $68 | S | S |
| Power door locks (2D/4D/ Wgn — includes tailgate) | - | - | - | $45/$69/ $78 | $45/$69/ $78 |
| Power driver's seat/Bench seat | - | $69 | $105 | $105 | $105 |
| Power windows | - | $103 | $115 | $132 | $132**** |
| AM radio | $61 | $61 | $66 | $66 | $66 |
| AM/FM stereo | $127 (Mono) | $201 | $219 | $240 | $240 |
| Front seat floor console*** | $42 | $70 | $61 | - | - |
| Front bucket seats — 2 doors only | $101 | S | $132 | - | - |
| Dual facing rear seats (Wagon) | - | - | $80 | $129 | $129 |
| Tilt steering wheel | - | $42 | - | $44 | $44 |
| Sunroof — N/A on wagons | - | $444 | - | $509 | $509 |
| Vinyl roof | $78 | $82/$36 (XR-7 only) | $97 | $116 ($139 Wgns.) | $125 (Halo) |
| White sidewall tires | $28 | $34 | $34 | $34 | $34 |
| Wire or luxury wheel covers | - | $75 | $18–$44 | $59 | $33 |
| Exterior Decor Groups (varied equipment) | $51 | $81 | $32 | $26–$39 | $26–$39 |
| Comet GT, Cougar GT or Montego Cyclone pkgs. | $179 | $116 | $518 (w/351 CJ)/$616 (w/429) | - | - |
| Convenience Group (varied equipment) | $26 | $43 | $26–$50 | $37–$60 | $37–$60 |

Options common to most models. (- = Not Available; S = Standard equipment.) Items may be standard equipment, optional at different pricing, or unavailable on certain models. This chart is only a guide.

*Blower type defogger. **Comet with GT package, $37; Cougar Convertible, $15. ***Requires bucket seats and includes electric clock. Comet style is a consolette with column shifter and without a clock. ****Standard on Marquis Brougham, but a delete credit option of $132 offered.

## Paint Colors*

| | Code |
|---|---|
| Black | 1C |
| Blue Glamour Metallic | 3K |
| Bright Blue Metallic | 3J |
| Bright Green Gold Met. | 4B |
| Bright Lime | 4E |
| Bright Red | 2B |
| Gold Glamour Metallic | 6F |
| Dark Blue Metallic | 3H |
| Dark Green Metallic | 4Q |
| Competition Blue | 3F |
| Gray Gold Metallic | 6J |
| Ivy Glamour Metallic | 4C |
| Light Blue | 3B |
| Light Goldenrod | 6B |
| Light Gray Metallic | 1A |
| Light Green | 4S |
| Light Pewter Metallic | 5A |
| Maroon | 2J |
| Medium Blue Metallic | 3D |
| Medium Bright Yellow | 6E |
| Medium Brown Metallic | 5H |
| Ginger Glamour Met. | 5J |
| Medium Green Metallic | 4P |
| Medium Lime Metallic | 4F |
| Medium Yellow Gold | 6C |
| Red | 2E |
| White | 9A |
| Yellow | 6D |

*All colors available on most models, some at additional cost.

# Comet

*"Comet for '72 offers everything you buy a small car for—and more."*

**Nameplate year of origin:** 1960.
**Current bodystyle lifespan:** 1970 through 1977.
**Predecessor to this model:** Comet (1960 to 1965).
**Replacement for this model:** Zephyr (1978 to 1983).
**Percentage of division's sales volume:** 18.63%.
**Corporate siblings:** Ford Maverick.
**Primary competition:** AMC Hornet, Chevrolet Nova, Dodge Dart, Plymouth Valiant, and Pontiac Ventura II.
**Notable changes:** No changes.
**Major standard equipment:** Vinyl and check cloth interior trim, color-keyed carpeting, door-operated courtesy lights, deluxe 2-spoke steering wheel, outside rear view mirror, and 6.45 × 14 BSW tires. GT option package adds: Dual outside color-keyed racing mirrors, bodyside stripes, Powerdome hood with scoop, hubcaps with wheel trim rings, and blacked-out grille treatment.

## Measurements

|  | 2-Door | 4-Door |
|---|---|---|
| Wheelbase | 103.0" | 109.9" |
| Length | 181.7" | 188.5" |
| Width | 71.0" | 71.0" |
| Height | 52.3" | 53.1" |
| Legroom—front | 41.3" | 41.3" |
| Legroom—rear | 31.9" | 36.4" |
| Headroom—front | 37.6" | 37.6" |
| Headroom—rear | 36.1" | 37.1" |
| Cargo capacity (cu. ft.) | 10.0 | 10.0 |
| Fuel capacity (gals.) | 16.0 | 16.0 |

## Models Available

|  | Style Number | Base MSRP | Change from LY | Shipping Wt. (lbs.) | Production | Change from LY |
|---|---|---|---|---|---|---|
| Comet 2-Door Coupe | 31 | $2,182 | -1.9% | 2579 | 53,267 | -2.9% |
| Comet 4-Door Sedan | 30 | $2,238 | -1.9% | 2674 | 29,092 | +3.5% |
| TOTALS |  | *Avg. price* $2,210 | -1.9% |  | *Production* 82,359 | -0.7% |

# Cougar

*"One of a kind, the best equipped luxury sports car in the country."*

**Nameplate year of origin:** 1967.
**Current bodystyle lifespan:** 1971 through 1973.
**Predecessor to this model:** Cougar (1967 to 1970).
**Replacement for this model:** Cougar (1974 to 1976).
**Percentage of division's sales volume:** 12.15%.
**Corporate siblings:** Ford Mustang.
**Primary competition:** AMC Javelin, Chevrolet Camaro, Dodge Challenger, Plymouth Barracuda, and Pontiac Firebird.
**Notable changes:** Trim and detail changes.
**Major standard equipment:** All-vinyl high-back bucket seats, mini-console, sequential turn signals, dual outside rear view racing mirrors, deluxe two-spoke steering wheel, interior courtesy lights, deluxe wheel covers, and E78 × 14 BSW tires. XR-7 adds: Leather seating surfaces, unique vinyl roof, tachometer, remote-control driver's side rear view mirror, map lights, and additional interior lighting.

## Measurements

|  |  |
|---|---|
| Wheelbase | 112.1" |
| Length | 196.7" |
| Width | 75.8" |
| Height | NA |
| Legroom—front | NA |
| Legroom—rear | NA |
| Headroom—front | NA |
| Headroom—rear | NA |
| Cargo capacity (cu. ft.) | 10.4 |
| Fuel capacity (gals.) | NA |

**1972**

## Models Available

| | Style Number | Base MSRP | Change from LY | Shipping Wt. (lbs.) | Production | Change from LY |
|---|---|---|---|---|---|---|
| Cougar 2-Door Hardtop | 91 | $3,016 | -8.30% | 3,282 | 23,731 | -30.22% |
| Cougar 2-Door Convertible | 92 | $3,370 | -8.45% | 3,412 | 1,240 | -28.02% |
| Cougar XR-7 2-Door HT | 93 | $3,323 | -8.43% | 3,298 | 26,802 | +5.45% |
| Cougar XR-7 2-Door Conv. | 94 | $3,547 | -8.51% | 3,451 | 1,929 | +12.35% |
| TOTALS | | Avg. price $3,314 | -8.43% | | Production 53,702 | -14.57% |

# Montego

*"The right-now intermediate with the big-car ride."*

**Nameplate year of origin:** 1968.

**Current bodystyle lifespan:** 1972 through 1976.

**Predecessor to this model:** Montego (1970 to 1971).

**Replacement for this model:** Cougar (1977 to 1979, on same platform).

**Percentage of division's sales volume:** 30.57%.

**Corporate siblings:** Ford Torino.

**Primary competition:** Buick Skylark, Dodge Charger/Coronet, Oldsmobile Cutlass and Pontiac LeMans.

**Notable changes:** Completely redesigned. Cyclone GT renamed Montego GT.

**Major standard equipment:** High-back bench seats with all-vinyl trim, floor mats, bright moldings (windshield, rear window, and guttering), hub caps with trim rings, front disc brakes, and E78 × 14 BSW tires (F78 × 14 on 4-Door). Montego wagon adds: Three-way tailgate, power front disc brakes, and H78 × 14 BSW tires. Montego MX adds: Cloth and vinyl interior trim, full carpeting, bright moldings (lower bodyside, and wheel openings), and F78 × 14 BSW tires (H78 × 14 on Wagons). Montego MX wagon adds: Deluxe vinyl interior trim, full wheel covers, and exterior wood-grained trim. Montego MX Brougham adds: Specific cloth and vinyl upholstery, wood-grain applique interior trim, Flight Bench front seat, and deluxe wheel covers. GT adds: All-vinyl interior trim, special black instrument panel inserts, dual hood scoops, dual color-keyed outside racing mirrors, and deluxe wheel covers.

## Measurements

| | 2-Doors | 4-Doors | Wagons |
|---|---|---|---|
| Wheelbase | 114.0" | 118.0" | 118.0" |
| Length | 208.1" | 212.1" | 215.6" |
| Width | NA | NA | NA |
| Height | NA | NA | NA |
| Legroom — front | NA | NA | NA |
| Legroom — rear | NA | NA | NA |
| Headroom — front | NA | NA | NA |
| Headroom — rear | NA | NA | NA |
| Cargo capacity (cu. ft.) | 14.8 | 14.8 | 83.5 |
| Fuel capacity (gals.) | NA | NA | NA |

## Models Available

| | Style Number | Base MSRP | Change from LY | Shipping Wt. (lbs.) | Production | Change from LY |
|---|---|---|---|---|---|---|
| Montego 2-Door Hardtop | O3 | $2,758 | -1.60% | 3390 | 9,963 | +3.53% |
| Montego 4-Door Sedan | O2 | $2,753 | -1.60% | 3454 | 8,658 | +51.42% |
| Montego MX 2-Door Hardtop | O7 | $2,881 | -1.58% | 3407 | 25,802 | +88.07% |
| Montego MX 4-Door Sedan | O4 | $2,861 | -1.48% | 3485 | 23,387 | +72.48% |
| Montego MX 4-Door, 6-p. Wgn. | O8 | $3,184 | -1.76% | 3884 | 6,268 | +69.50% |
| Montego MX Brougham 2-Dr. HT | 11 | $3,057 | -1.77% | 3433 | 28,417 | +896.74% |
| Mont. MX Brougham 4-Dr. Sdn. | 10 | $3,047 | -1.68% | 3512 | 17,540 | +1,020.77% |
| Mont. MX Villager 4-Dr, 6-p. Wgn | 18 | $3,348 | -3.85% | 3907 | 9,237 | +335.50% |
| Montego GT 2-Door Hardtop | 16 | $3,346 | -9.08% | 3517 | 5,820 | +154.48% |
| TOTALS | | Avg. price $3,023 | -4.85% | | Production 135,092 | +136.61% |

# Monterey

*"There's a new world of driving pleasure waiting for you."*

**Nameplate year of origin:** 1950 (coupe designation); 1952 (series).
**Current bodystyle lifespan:** 1971 through 1978 (restyled in 1973 and 1975).
**Predecessor to this model:** Monterey (1969 to 1970).
**Replacement for this model:** None.
**Percentage of division's sales volume:** 12.71%.
**Corporate siblings:** Ford LTD/Galaxie 500 and Mercury Marquis.
**Primary competition:** AMC Ambassador, Buick LeSabre, Chevrolet Impala/Caprice, Dodge Polara/Monaco, Oldsmobile Delta 88, and Pontiac Catalina/Bonneville.
**Notable changes:** Trim and detail changes.
**Major standard equipment:** Cloth and vinyl interior trim, full carpeting, simulated cherrywood instrument panel trim, power steering, bright window moldings, power front disc brakes, and G78 × 15 BSW tires. Monterey Custom adds: Specific cloth and vinyl interior trim, and additional bright moldings.

## Measurements

|  | Cars | Wagons |
|---|---|---|
| Wheelbase | 124.0" | 121.0" |
| Length | 224.7" | 221.0" |
| Width | NA | NA |
| Height | NA | NA |
| Legroom — front | NA | NA |
| Legroom — rear | NA | NA |
| Headroom — front | NA | NA |
| Headroom — rear | NA | NA |
| Cargo capacity (cu. ft.) | 20.4 | 96.2 |
| Fuel capacity (gals.) | NA | NA |

## Models Available

|  | Style Number | Base MSRP | Change from LY | Shipping Wt. (lbs.) | Production | Change from LY |
|---|---|---|---|---|---|---|
| Monterey 2-Door Hardtop | 46 | $3,832 | -1.74% | 4086 | 6,731 | -26.02% |
| Monterey 4-Door Pillared HT | 44 | $3,793 | -1.70% | 4136 | 19,012 | -16.41% |
| Monterey 4-Door Hardtop | 48 | $3,896 | -1.81% | 4141 | 1,416 | -42.97% |
| Monterey 4-Door, 6-pass. Wgn. | 74 | $4,445 | +3.78% | 4539 | 4,644 | +11.63% |
| Monterey Custom 2-Door HT | 56 | $4,035 | -1.90% | 4175 | 5,910 | +31.10% |
| Mont. Custom 4-Dr. Pillared HT | 54 | $3,956 | -1.83% | 4225 | 16,879 | +36.00% |
| Monterey Custom 4-Door HT | 58 | $4,103 | -1.96% | 4230 | 1,583 | +13.31% |
| TOTALS | *Avg. price* | $4,009 | -0.96% | *Production* | 56,175 | -1.10% |

# Marquis

*"The Marquis ride is a beautifully moving experience —
no matter how rough the road below."*

**Nameplate year of origin:** 1967.
**Current bodystyle lifespan:** 1971 through 1978 (restyled in 1973 and 1975).
**Predecessor to this model:** Marquis (1969 to 1970)
**Replacement for this model:** Marquis (1979 to 1991).
**Percentage of division's sales volume:** 25.94%.
**Corporate siblings:** Ford LTD/Galaxie 500 and Mercury Monterey.
**Primary competition:** Buick Centurion/Electra 225, Chrysler Newport/New Yorker, Oldsmobile Delta 88/Ninety-Eight, and Pontiac Grand Ville.
**Notable changes:** Trim and detail changes.
**Major standard equipment:** Cloth and vinyl interior with cut-pile carpeting, deluxe sound insulation, electric clock, map light, assorted courtesy lights, power steering, power front disc brakes, rear fender skirts, full wheel covers, and H78 × 15 BSW tires. Brougham adds: Cut-pile carpeting, vinyl robe cord, power windows, Halo vinyl roof, carpeted luggage compartment, front door courtesy lights and other additional interior lighting, passenger-side visor vanity mirror, and color-keyed wheel covers.

## Measurements

|  | Cars | Wagons |
|---|---|---|
| Wheelbase | 124.0" | 121.0" |
| Length | 224.8" | 221.0" |
| Width | NA | NA |
| Height | NA | NA |
| Legroom — front | NA | NA |
| Legroom — rear | NA | NA |
| Headroom — front | NA | NA |
| Headroom — rear | NA | NA |
| Cargo capacity (cu. ft.) | 20.4 | 96.2 |
| Fuel capacity (gals.) | NA | NA |

1972

## Models Available

| | Style Number | Base MSRP | Change from LY | Shipping Wt. (lbs.) | Production | Change from LY |
|---|---|---|---|---|---|---|
| Marquis 2-Door Hardtop | 66 | $4,572 | +0.33% | 4336 | 5,507 | -28.72% |
| Marquis 4-Door Pillared HT | 63 | $4,493 | +0.42% | 4386 | 14,122 | -11.91% |
| Marquis 4-Door Hardtop | 68 | $4,637 | +0.28% | 4391 | 1,583 | -71.17% |
| Marquis 4-Door, 6-pass. Wagon | 74 | $4,445 | -2.24% | 4539 | 2,085 | -3.38% |
| Marquis Brougham 2-Door HT | 64 | $4,969 | +0.12% | 4386 | 20,064 | +37.71% |
| Marquis Brougham 4-Dr. Pillared HT | 62 | $4,890 | +0.20% | 4436 | 38,242 | +48.28% |
| Marquis Brougham 4-Door HT | 67 | $5,034 | +0.01% | 4441 | 12,841 | -6.82% |
| Colony Park 4-Door, 6-p. Wagon | 76 | $4,550 | -5.33% | 4579 | 20,192 | +0.94% |
| TOTALS | Avg. price | $4,699 | -0.80% | Production | 114,636 | +8.61% |

# OLDSMOBILE

*"Always a step ahead."*

Oldsmobile was definitely ahead of the game on this model year. After many years of trailing sister divisions Buick and Pontiac in sales, Olds was about to have its turn in the industry's number three sales spot. This was due largely to the phenomenal success of its mid-size Cutlass line. For whatever reasons, Oldsmobile had finally hit upon the right marketing combination of size, performance, styling and equipment that made this line into a sales leader, particularly the Cutlass Supreme models. Also still making an impact in the waning muscle car market was the 4-4-2. A consistent performer, both on the street and in the showroom, the 4-4-2 was helped by marketing that was adapting well to the changing times. Sales were slowing, but the exposure received from events like the Indianapolis 500

pace car duty kept it in the spotlight. In fact, it is the only muscle car (not counting "pony car" types) to survive (at least in name, if not always in spirit) well into the eighties.

Changes for other Oldsmobile lines were minimal. As usual, grille and trim changes were made to differentiate model years. Since all of the large Oldsmobile models had been new for 1971, any changes made were destined to be evolutionary at best. As with other full-size GM products, adaptations were made to the Flo-Thru ventilation system. The 1971 air vents in the trunk lids were eliminated because of water problems in the trunk area. The Toronado, which had also been totally redesigned for 1971, entered the new year with minimal detail changes.

Ninety-Eight 4-Door Hardtop

Custom Cruiser 4-Door Wagon

Cutlass S 2-Door Hardtop

Delta 88 Royale 4-Door Hardtop

Toronado 2-Door Hardtop

4-4-2 2-Door Convertible,
Indianapolis 500 Pace Car

**Model year production:** 762,199, up 34.21% over 1971.
**Domestic market share:** 8.16% (3rd place).
**Base price range:** $2,957 to $5,340.
**Industry average base price:** $3,788.
**Oldsmobile average base price:** $3,867.
**Introduction date:** September 23, 1971.
**Assembly plants:** Fremont, CA (Z); Framingham, MA (G); Lansing, MI (M); Arlington, TX (R); Fairfax, KS (X); and Linden, NJ (F).

**Data plate identification:** Thirteen digit code read as follows: 1st digit 3 = Oldsmobile; 2nd through 4th digits identify series/body style; 5th digit is engine code; 2 = 1972; 7th digit is assembly plant code; 100001 and up for serial number (except Toronado is 700001). *Example:* 3L39U2X100001 is a 1972 Oldsmobile Delta 88 4-Door Hardtop with a 455 CID V8, serial number 100001, built in Fairfax, KS.

## Powertrains

| Engine | Net HP | Engine Code | Transmission Availability | Cutlass | Vista-Cruiser | Delta 88 & Custom Cr. | 98 | Toronado |
|---|---|---|---|---|---|---|---|---|
| 350 CID, 2-bbl., V8 | 160 | Q | 3-speed manual | S | S | - | - | - |
| | | | Turbo Hydra-matic | $221 | $243 | S (ex. C.C.) | - | - |
| 350 CID, 4-bbl., V8 | 180 | Q | 3-speed manual | $47 | $47 | - | - | - |
| | | | 4-speed manual* | $242 | - | - | - | - |
| | | | Turbo Hydra-matic | $268 | $290 | $47 (ex. C.C.) | - | - |
| 455 CID, 2-bbl., V8 | 185 | U | Turbo Hydra-matic | - | - | S (Custom Cr.) | - | - |
| 455 CID, 4-bbl., V8 | 225 | U | Turbo Hydra-matic | - | - | $188 (Delta)/$100 (C.C.) | S | - |
| 455 CID, 4-bbl., V8 | 250 | U | 4-speed manual* | $383 | - | - | - | - |
| | | | Turbo Hydra-matic | $409 | $431 | - | - | S |
| 455 CID W30, 4-bbl., V8 | 300 | U | 4-speed manual* | $648 | - | - | - | - |
| | | | Turbo Hydra-matic | $869 | - | - | - | - |

*Only available on select models.*

## Major Options

| | Cutlass | Vista-Cruiser | Delta 88 | Cust. Cr. | Ninety-Eight | Toronado |
|---|---|---|---|---|---|---|
| Air conditioning | $408 | $408 | $442 | $442 | $442 | $442 |
| Electronic cruise control | $64 | $64 | $64 | $64 | $64 | $64 |
| Electric rear window defogger | $63 | - | $63 | - | $63 | $63 |
| Soft Ray tinted glass | $43 | $43 | $43 | $43 | $43 | $43 |
| Deck lid remote release | $14 | - | $14 | - | $14 | $14 |
| Power steering—variable-ratio | $116 | $116 | S | S | S | S |
| Power brakes—w/front discs | $70 | S | S | S | S | S |
| Power door locks—w/Seat release | - | - | $71 | $71 | $71 | $71 |
| Power driver's seat/Bench seat | $79 | $79 | $105 | $105 | $79–$105 | $105 |
| Power windows | $116 | $116 | $133 | $133 | $133 | $133 |
| AM radio | $75 | $75 | $87 | $87 | $87 | $87 |
| AM/FM stereo | $239 | $239 | $239 | $239 | $239 | $239 |
| Front seat console | $60 | - | - | - | - | - |
| Front bucket seats | $ | - | - | - | - | - |
| Tilt steering wheel | $45 | $45 | $45 | $45 | $45 | $45 |

| | Cutlass | Vista-Cruiser | Delta 88 | Cust. Cr. | Ninety-Eight | Toronado |
|---|---|---|---|---|---|---|
| Vinyl roof | $102 | – | $126 | $142 | $142 | $139 |
| Super Stock wheels (F85-II/88-IV) | $73 | – | $73 | – | – | – |
| 4-4-2 Package | $190 | – | – | – | – | – |

Special trim package and performance options. Options common to most models. (– = Not Available; S = Standard equipment.) Items may be standard equipment, optional at different pricing, or unavailable on certain models. This chart is only a guide.

## Paint Colors

| | Code | | Code |
|---|---|---|---|
| Cameo White | 11 | Saturn Gold Met. | 53 |
| Silver Pewter Met. | 14 | Sovereign Gold Met. | 54 |
| Antique Pewter Met. | 18 | Sunfire Yellow | 56 |
| Ebony Black | 19 | Baroque Gold Met. | 57 |
| Nordic Blue Met. | 24 | Saddle Tan | 62 |
| Viking Blue Met. | 26 | Saddle Bronze Met. | 63 |
| Royal Blue Met. | 28 | Flame Orange Met. | 65 |
| Radiant Green Met. | 36 | Nutmeg Metallic | 69 |
| Pinehurst Green Met. | 43 | Matador Red | 75 |
| Sequoia Green Met. | 48 | Bamboo | 81 |
| Covert Beige | 50 | | |

# Cutlass

*"If your friends could see you now!"*

**Nameplate year of origin:** 1962 (as F-85 model designation); 1955 (show car).

**Current bodystyle lifespan:** 1968 through 1972.

**Predecessor to this model:** F-85/Cutlass (1966 to 1967).

**Replacement for this model:** Cutlass (1973 to 1977).

**Percentage of division's sales volume:** 39.71%.

**Corporate siblings:** Buick Skylark, Chevrolet Chevelle, and Pontiac LeMans.

**Primary competition:** AMC Matador, Dodge Coronet, Ford Torino, Mercury Montego, Plymouth Satellite.

**Notable changes:** Revised grille and minor trim and detail changes.

**Major standard equipment:** Cloth or vinyl upholstery, front bench seat, left-hand outside rearview mirror, aluminized exhaust system, and F78 × 14 BSW tires. Cutlass adds: Front and rear armrests, full carpeting, deluxe steering wheel, and exterior chrome trim moldings. Cutlass S adds: Deluxe bench seat with foam cushions, and simulated chrome hood louvers. Cutlass Supreme adds: Woodgrain interior trim, Strato-bucket seats, and unique grille. Cutlass Cruiser adds to base Cutlass equipment: H78 × 14 BSW tires.

## Measurements

| | 2-Doors | 4-Doors | Wagon |
|---|---|---|---|
| Wheelbase | 112.0" | 116.0" | 116.0" |
| Length | 203.6" | 207.6" | 213.3" |
| Width | 76.8" | 76.8" | 76.8" |
| Height | 53.5" | 54.2" | 54.8" |
| Legroom — front | 41.3" | 41.7" | 42.6" |
| Legroom — rear | 32.4" | 34.8" | 34.6" |
| Headroom — front | 37.8" | 38.6" | 38.4" |
| Headroom — rear | 36.3" | 37.3" | 38.3" |
| Luggage capacity (cu. ft.) | 17.0 | 17.0 | 93.6 |
| Fuel capacity (gals.) | 20.0 | 20.0 | 20.0 |

## Models Available

| | Style Number | Base MSRP | Change from LY | Shipping Wt. (lbs.) | Production | Change from LY |
|---|---|---|---|---|---|---|
| F-85 4-Door Town Sedan | D69 | $2,958 | +2.53% | 3536 | 3,792 | -14.19% |
| Cutlass 2-Door Coupe | F87 | $2,973 | +2.48% | 3509 | 37,790 | +12.39% |
| Cutlass 4-Door Town Sedan | G69 | $3,066 | +2.23% | 3549 | 38,893 | +19.59% |

| | Style Number | Base MSRP | Change from LY | Shipping Wt. (lbs.) | Production | Change from LY |
|---|---|---|---|---|---|---|
| Cutlass Cruiser 4-Dr., 2-S. Wgn. | G36 | $3,498 | -1.33% | 4049 | 7,979 | +17.53% |
| Cutlass S 2-Door Sports Coupe | G77 | $3,027 | +2.33% | 3503 | 4,141 | -6.99% |
| Cutlass S 2-Door Holiday HT | G87 | $3,087 | +2.18% | 3509 | 78,461 | +23.92% |
| Cutl. Supreme 2-Dr. Holiday HT | J57 | $3,258 | -1.96% | 3520 | 105,087 | +73.41% |
| Cutlass Supreme 2-Door Conv. | J67 | $3,433 | -2.11% | 3614 | 11,571 | +12.83% |
| Cutl. Supreme 4-Dr. Holiday HT | J39 | $3,329 | -2.03% | 3582 | 14,955 | +43.00% |
| TOTALS | Avg. price | $3,181 | -2.09% | Production | 302,669 | +29.33% |

# Vista-Cruiser

*"It's the most popular station wagon we've ever built."*

**Nameplate year of origin:** 1964.
**Current bodystyle lifespan:** 1968 through 1972.
**Predecessor to this model:** None.
**Replacement for this model:** Vista-Cruiser (1973 to 1977).
**Percentage of division's sales volume:** 4.19%.
**Corporate siblings:** None.
**Primary competition:** AMC Matador/Ambassador, Dodge Coronet, Plymouth Satellite.
**Notable changes:** Revised grille and minor trim and detail changes.
**Major standard equipment:** All-vinyl interior, foam cushion bench seats, full carpeting, deluxe steering wheel, wood-grain interior and exterior trim, drop-or-swing tailgate, Vista-roof windows, central and tailgate dome lamps, power front disc brakes, and H78 × 14 BSW tires.

## Measurements

| | |
|---|---|
| Wheelbase | 121.0" |
| Length | 218.3" |
| Width | 76.8" |
| Height | 58.6" |
| Legroom — front | 41.5" |
| Legroom — rear | 37.8" |
| Headroom — front | 38.0" |
| Headroom — rear | 40.3" |
| Luggage capacity (cu. ft.) | 105.2 |
| Fuel capacity (gals.) | 20.0 |

## Models Available

| | Style Number | Base MSRP | Change from LY | Shipping Wt. (lbs.) | Production | Change from LY |
|---|---|---|---|---|---|---|
| Vista-Cruiser 4-Dr, 2-S. Wgn | K56 | $3,734 | -3.41% | 4285 | 10,573 | +76.81% |
| Vista-Cruiser 4-Dr, 3-S. Wgn | K66 | $3,908 | -2.50% | 4373 | 21,340 | +3.76% |
| TOTALS | Avg. price | $3,821 | -2.95% | Production | 31,913 | +20.22% |

# Delta 88

*"Not just another pretty car."*

**Nameplate year of origin:** 1965 (88 series started 1949).
**Current bodystyle lifespan:** 1971 through 1976.
**Predecessor to this model:** Delta 88 (1969 to 1970).
**Replacement for this model:** Delta 88 (1977 to 1985).
**Percentage of division's sales volume:** 30.00%.
**Corporate siblings:** Buick LeSabre/Centurion, Chevrolet Impala/Caprice, Pontiac Catalina/Bonneville.
**Primary competition:** AMC Ambassador, Dodge Polara, Ford LTD, Mercury Monterey, Plymouth Fury.
**Notable changes:** Revised grille and minor trim and detail changes.
**Major standard equipment:** Cloth and vinyl or all-vinyl bench seat, nylon-blend carpet, deluxe steering wheel, trunk mat, windshield radio antenna, chrome wheel covers, power steering, power front disc brakes, G78-15 BSW tires. Royale adds: Exclusive grille and exterior trim and interior courtesy lamps.

## Measurements

| | |
|---|---|
| Wheelbase | 124.0" |
| Length | 221.5"* |
| Width | 79.5" |
| Height | 53.6" |
| Legroom — front | 42.6" |
| Legroom — rear | 38.5" |
| Headroom — front | 38.4" |
| Headroom — rear | 37.4" |
| Luggage capacity (cu. ft.) | 20.1 |
| Fuel capacity (gals.) | 25.0 |

*Royale 222.1"

**1972**

## Models Available

| | Style Number | Base MSRP | Change from LY | Shipping Wt. (lbs.) | Production | Change from LY |
|---|---|---|---|---|---|---|
| Delta 88 2-Door Holiday HT | L57 | $4,001 | -0.99% | 4296 | 32,036 | +18.52% |
| Delta 88 4-Door Town Sedan | L69 | $3,948 | -0.03% | 4324 | 46,092 | +20.35% |
| Delta 88 4-Door Holiday HT | L39 | $4,060 | -1.05% | 4375 | 35,538 | +13.11% |
| D. 88 Royale 2-Dr. Holiday HT | N57 | $4,179 | -8.13% | 4316 | 34,345 | +309.02% |
| Delta 88 Royale 2-Door Conv. | N67 | $4,387 | -3.73% | 4442 | 3,900 | +35.28% |
| D. 88 Royale 4-Dr. Town Sdn. | N69 | $4,101 | NEW | 4369 | 34,150 | NEW |
| D. 88 Royale 4-Dr. Holiday HT | N39 | $4,238 | NEW | 4404 | 42,606 | NEW |
| TOTALS | Avg. price | $4,131 | -3.05% | Production | 228,667 | +26.28% |

# Custom Cruiser

*"The station wagon that doubles as a plush sedan. And vice versa."*

**Nameplate year of origin:** 1971 (1940 as a designation on 90 Series cars).
**Current bodystyle lifespan:** 1971 through 1976.
**Predecessor to this model:** None.
**Replacement for this model:** Custom Cruiser (1977 to 1989).
**Percentage of division's sales volume:** 3.28%.
**Corporate siblings:** Buick Estate Wagon, Chevrolet Impala/Caprice, Pontiac Safari Wagons.
**Primary competition:** Dodge Monaco, Ford LTD/Country Squire, Mercury Colony Park/Marquis.
**Notable changes:** Revised grille and trim and detail changes.
**Major standard equipment:** Loop-pile carpeting, carpeted cargo area, deluxe steering wheel, Glide-away disappearing tailgate, power tailgate window, forward-facing third seat and split back second seat (3-seat models only), stowage compartment under load floor, wood-grain vinyl interior and exterior trim, central and tailgate dome lamp, rear wheel opening covers, power steering, power front disc brakes, and L78-15 BSW tires.

## Measurements

| | |
|---|---|
| Wheelbase | 127.0" |
| Length | 226.7" |
| Width | 79.6" |
| Height | 57.3" |
| Legroom — front | 42.6" |
| Legroom — rear | 39.9" |
| Headroom — front | 39.6" |
| Headroom — rear | 39.3" |
| Luggage capacity (cu. ft.) | 109.0 |
| Fuel capacity (gals.) | 24.0 |

## Models Available

| | Style Number | Base MSRP | Change from LY | Shipping Wt. (lbs.) | Production | Change from LY |
|---|---|---|---|---|---|---|
| Custom Cruiser 4-Dr, 2-S Wgn. | R35 | $4,700 | -1.59% | 5109 | 6,907 | +70.59% |
| Custom Cruiser 4-Dr, 3-S Wgn. | R45 | $4,834 | -1.69% | 5204 | 18,087 | +82.11% |
| TOTALS | Avg. price | $4,767 | -1.65% | Production | 24,994 | +78.77% |

# Ninety-Eight

*"It's quite a substantial car."*

**Nameplate year of origin:** 1941.
**Current bodystyle lifespan:** 1971 through 1976.
**Predecessor to this model:** Ninety-Eight (1969 to 1970).
**Replacement for this model:** Ninety-Eight (1977 to 1984).
**Percentage of division's sales volume:** 16.41%.

## Measurements

| | |
|---|---|
| Wheelbase | 127.0" |
| Length | 227.2" |
| Width | 79.6" |
| Height | 54.6" |

**Corporate siblings:** Buick Electra 225 and Cadillac Calais/de Ville.
**Primary competition:** Chrysler Newport/New Yorker and Mercury Marquis.
**Notable changes:** Revised grille and front bumper; minor trim and detail changes.
**Major standard equipment:** Cloth and vinyl bench seat, front seat center armrests, deep loop-pile carpeting and lower door panels, deluxe cushion steering wheel, remote control LH ouside mirror, electric clock, trunk lamp, trunk mat, full wheel covers, concealed windshield antenna, rear fender skirts, power steering, power front disc brakes, and H78-15 BSW tires. Luxury adds: Rear seat center armrest, front and rear cigar lighters, power front seat, and power windows.

## Measurements (cont.)

| | |
|---|---|
| Legroom — front | 42.4" |
| Legroom — rear | 40.5" |
| Headroom — front | 39.3" |
| Headroom — rear | 38.2" |
| Luggage capacity (cu. ft.) | 20.5 |
| Fuel capacity (gals.) | 25.0 |

## Models Available

| | Style Number | Base MSRP | Change from LY | Shipping Wt. (lbs.) | Production | Change from LY |
|---|---|---|---|---|---|---|
| Ninety-Eight 2-Dr. Holiday HT | U37 | $4,748 | -0.88% | 4537 | 13,111 | +57.30% |
| Ninety-Eight 4-Door HT | U39 | $4,807 | -0.93% | 4608 | 17,572 | +16.95% |
| Ninety-Eight Luxury 2-Dr. HT | V37 | $5,009 | -1.11% | 4549 | 24,453 | +64.38% |
| Ninety-Eight Luxury 4-Dr. HT | V39 | $5,098 | -1.19% | 4658 | 69,920 | +55.19% |
| TOTALS | | *Avg. price* $4,916 | -1.03% | | *Production* 125,056 | +50.14% |

# Toronado

*"There's nothing common about it."*

**Nameplate year of origin:** 1966.
**Current bodystyle lifespan:** 1971 through 1978.
**Predecessor to this model:** Toronado (1966 to 1970).
**Replacement for this model:** Toronado (1979 to 1985).
**Percentage of division's sales volume:** 6.42%.
**Corporate siblings:** Buick Riviera and Cadillac Eldorado
**Primary competition:** Chrysler Imperial LeBaron, Ford Thunderbird, and Lincoln Continental Mark IV.
**Notable changes:** Revised grille and trim and detail changes.
**Major standard equipment:** Cloth and vinyl bench seat with center armrest, Flo-Thru ventilation, electric clock, remote-control LH outside mirror, concealed radio antenna, deluxe steering wheel, front wheel drive, power steering, power front disc brakes, and J78 × 15 BSW tires.

## Measurements

| | |
|---|---|
| Wheelbase | 122.0" |
| Length | 220.3" |
| Width | 79.8" |
| Height | 54.0" |
| Legroom — front | 42.7" |
| Legroom — rear | 35.6" |
| Headroom — front | 37.7" |
| Headroom — rear | 37.0" |
| Luggage capacity (cu. ft.) | 14.2 |
| Fuel capacity (gals.) | 22.0 |

## Models Available

| | Style Number | Base MSRP | Change from LY | Shipping Wt. (lbs.) | Production | Change from LY |
|---|---|---|---|---|---|---|
| Toronado Custom 2-Dr. HT | Y57 | $5,341 | -2.13% | 4660 | 48,900 | +68.74% |
| TOTALS | | *Avg. price* $5,341 | -2.13% | | *Production* 48,900 | +68.74% |

**1972**

# PLYMOUTH

*"Coming through with the kind of car America wants."*

Plymouth is the Chrysler Corporation division best known for the muscle cars it has given the world, like the Road Runner and Barracuda. Now with the muscle car market drying up, it was the job of Plymouth to push its equally popular but not so exciting cars. This year there would be more Valiant models sold than any previous year, or for that matter, any year since. Also selling quite well were the restyled Fury models. The Fury lineup also underwent a juggling of series nameplates resulting in the loss of the entire Sport Fury line and an upgrading of the Fury Gran package from optional status to a full-blown series.

Satellite models, while not greatly changed for 1972, also sold well. Most likely this was at the expense of the General Motors intermediates, but the racing image and connotations that came from the Satellite and Road Runner names also deserve credit. The Satellite line lost the GTX as a model, but sales literature listed an optional 440 CID engine available as a GTX option package. The Barracuda, along with its sister car, the Dodge Challenger, lost its convertible models and most of its muscle car performance, if not the image. As with Dodge, the Hemi engines were now history, and along with them went the Hemi 'Cuda.

Barracuda 2-Door Hardtop

Gran Fury 4-Door Hardtop

Road Runner 2-Door Hardtop

Satellite Regent 4-Door Wagon

Scamp 2-Door Hardtop

**Model year production:** 756,967, up 0.67% over 1971.
**Domestic market share:** 8.10% (4th place).
**Base price range:** $2,287 to $4,466.
**Industry average base price:** $3,788.
**Plymouth average base price:** $3,427.
**Introduction date:** September 1971.
**Assembly plants:** Lynch Road, MI (A): Hamtramck, MI (B); Belvidere, IL (D); Newark DE (F); St. Louis, MO (G); and Windsor, Ontario, Canada (R).

**Data plate identification:** Thirteen digit code read as follows: four digit style number code in which first letter is series, second letter is trim level, third and fourth digits are body style; fifth digit is engine code (see chart); sixth digit 2 for 1972; seventh digit is assembly plant code; 100001 and up for serial number. *Example:* VH23C2D100001 is a 1972 Plymouth Scamp 2-Door Hardtop, with a 225 CID 6-cyl., built at Belvidere, IL, serial number 100001.

## Powertrains

| Engine | Net HP | Engine Code | Transmission Availability | Valiant/ Duster | Barracuda | Satellite | Fury |
|---|---|---|---|---|---|---|---|
| 198 CID, 1-bbl., 6-cyl. | 100 | B | 3-speed manual | S | - | - | - |
| | | | Torqueflite automatic | $178 | - | - | - |
| 225 CID, 1-bbl., 6-cyl. | 110 | C | 3-speed manual | $38 | S | S | - |
| | | | 4-speed manual | $223 | - | - | - |
| | | | Torqueflite automatic | $245 | $203 | $203 | - |
| 318 CID, 2-bbl., V8 | 150 | G | 3-speed manual | $150 (Val.)/ $133 (Duster) | $112 | S (Seb.Plus)/ $107 (Sat.) | S |
| | | | 4-speed manual | $335 (Val.)/ $318 (Duster) | $297 | - | - |
| | | | Torqueflite automatic | $358 (Val.)/ $341 (Duster) | $320 | $211 (Wgn., Seb.Plus)/ $339 (Sat.) | - |
| 340 CID, 2-bbl., V8 | 235 | | 3-speed manual | S (Duster 340) | $210/S ('Cuda) | - | - |
| | | | 4-speed manual | $185 (Duster 340) | $395/$184 ('Cuda) | - | - |
| | | | Torqueflite automatic | $208 (Duster 340) | $418/$223 ('Cuda) | - | - |
| 340 CID, 4-bbl., V8 | 250 | H | 3-speed manual | - | $277/($210 ('Cuda) | $64 (R.R.) | - |
| | | | 4-speed manual | - | $478/$411 ('Cuda) | $265 (R.R.) | - |
| | | | Torqueflite automatic | - | $500/$433 ('Cuda) | $295 (R.R.) | - |
| 360 CID, 2-bbl., V8 | 175 | K | Torqueflite automatic | - | - | - | $45 |
| 400 CID, 2-bbl., V8 | 190 | M | Torqueflite automatic | - | - | $417 (Wgn., Seb.Plus)/ (R.R.)/$423 (Sat.) | $84 |
| 440 CID, 4-bbl., V8 | 225 | T | Torqueflite automatic | - | - | $370 (R.R.)/ $525 (Sat.) | $193 |
| 440 CID GTX, 4-bbl., V8 | 280 | U | Torqueflite automatic | - | - | - | - |
| 440 CID Six Pack, 3 × 2-bbl., V8 | 290 | V | Torqueflite automatic | - | - | - | - |

*Available only with Road Runner or Sebring Plus.*

## Major Options

| | Duster/Valiant | Barracuda | Satellite | Fury |
|---|---|---|---|---|
| Air conditioning | $353 | $365 | $378 | $386 |
| Speed control | - | - | $ | $ |
| Remote control decklid release | - | - | - | $15 |
| Tinted glass | $36 | $36 | $40 | $40 |
| Power steering | $92 | $104 | $114 | S |
| Power brakes | $40 | $40 | - | - |
| Power brakes — front disc | $62 | $68 | $68 | $68 |
| Power door locks | - | - | - | $71 |
| Power driver's seat/Bench seat | - | - | - | $103 |
| Power windows | - | - | $119 4-Doors only | $125 |
| AM radio | $59 | $59 | $65 | $65 |
| AM/FM stereo | $125 | $125 | $209 | $71 |
| Bucket seats | $120 | S | $ | $103 |
| Center console | - | $52 | $ | NC — Gran Fury |
| Tilt steering wheel | - | - | $55 | $55 |

|  | Duster/Valiant | Barracuda | Satellite | Fury |
|---|---|---|---|---|
| Sunroof | $223 | $434 | $475 | - |
| Road Wheels | $58 | $81 | $58 | $58 |
| Vinyl roof | $75 | $80 | $94 | $106 |

Options common to most models. (- = Not Available; S = Standard equipment.) Items may be standard equipment, optional at different pricing, or unavailable on certain models. This chart is only a guide.

## Paint Colors

|  | Code | Duster/Val./ Bar./Sat. | Fury |
|---|---|---|---|
| Blue Sky | B-1 | x | x |
| Basin Street Blue | B-3 | x | x |
| Red | E-5 | x | x |
| Mist Green | F-1 | x | x |
| Sherwood Green Metallic | F-7 | x | x |
| Spinnaker White | W-1 | x | x |
| Formal Black | X-9 | x | x |
| Sahara Beige | L-4 | x | x |
| Gold Leaf Metallic | Y-8 | x | x |
| Amber Sherwood Metallic | F-3 | x | x |
| Forest Green Metallic | F-8 | x | x |
| Tawney Gold Metallic | Y-9 | x | x |
| Honey Gold | Y-3 | x | x |
| Chestnut Metallic | T-8 | x | x |
| Winchester Gray Metallic | A-4 | x |  |
| Mojave Tan Metallic | T-6 | x |  |
| Honeydew | Y-4 | x |  |
| True Blue Metallic | B-5 | x |  |
| Tor-Red* | V-2 | Opt. |  |
| Lemon Twist* | Y-1 | Opt. |  |
| Charcoal Metallic | A-9 |  | x |
| Evening Blue Metallic | B-7 |  | x |
| Regal Blue Metallic | B-9 |  | x |
| Silver Frost Metallic | A-5 |  | x |
| Coral Turquoise Metallic | Q-5 |  | x |
| Meadow Green | J-3 |  | x |
| Sunfire Yellow | Y-2 |  | x |

*Hi-impact colors available at extra cost.

# Valiant

*"A pacesetter in the economy field for over ten years now."*

**Nameplate year of origin:** 1960 (Valiant); 1970 (Duster); 1971 (Scamp).

**Current bodystyle lifespan:** 1967 through 1976.

**Predecessor to this model:** Valiant (1963 to 1966).

**Replacement for this model:** Volare (1976 to 1980).

**Percentage of division's sales volume:** 43.64%.

**Corporate siblings:** Dodge Dart.

**Primary competition:** AMC Hornet, Chevrolet Nova, Ford Maverick, Mercury Comet, Pontiac Ventura II.

**Notable changes:** Trim and detail changes.

**Major standard equipment:** All-vinyl bench seat, color-keyed

## Measurements

|  | Duster | Scamp | Valiant |
|---|---|---|---|
| Wheelbase | 108.0" | 111.0" | 108.0" |
| Length | 188.4" | 192.1" | 188.4" |
| Width | 71.6" | 69.7" | 71.1" |
| Height | 52.6" | 52.6" | 54.0" |
| Legroom — front | 41.6" | 41.6" | 41.6" |
| Legroom — rear | 29.6" | 31.7" | 34.6" |
| Headroom — front | 37.2" | 37.3" | 38.4" |
| Headroom — rear | 36.5" | 36.7" | 37.3" |

rubber floor mat, front door vent windows, 2-speed windshield wipers, and 6.95 × 14 BSW tires. Duster adds: Dome light, ventless front windows, and swing-out side rear quarter windows. 340 adds: Flat-black grille trim, body side tape stripes, heavy duty suspension, Rallye road wheels, front disc brakes and E70 × 14 BSW tires.

|  | Duster | Scamp | Valiant |
|---|---|---|---|
| Cargo capacity (cu. ft.) | 15.9 | 14.9 | 14.0 |
| Fuel capacity (gals.) | 16.0 | 16.0 | 16.0 |

## Models Available

|  | Style Number | Base MSRP | Change from LY | Shipping Wt. (lbs.) | Production | Change from LY |
|---|---|---|---|---|---|---|
| Duster 2-Door Sport Coupe | VL29 | $2,287 | -1.12% | 2825 | 212,311 | +22.30% |
| Duster 340 2-Door Sport Coupe | VS29 | $2,742 | +1.44% | 3140 | 15,681 | +21.69% |
| Scamp 2-Door Hardtop | VH23 | $2,528 | -1.29% | 2900 | 49,470 | +2.52% |
| Valiant 4-Door Sedan | VL41 | $2,363 | -1.23% | 2835 | 52,911 | +24.03% |
| TOTALS | | Avg. price $2,480 | -0.49% | | Production 330,373 | +19.10% |

# Barracuda

*"Two of the best-looking sporty cars made in America."*

**Nameplate year of origin:** 1964.
**Current bodystyle lifespan:** 1970 through 1974.
**Predecessor to this model:** Barracuda (1967 to 1969).
**Replacement for this model:** None.
**Percentage of division's sales volume:** 2.44%.
**Corporate siblings:** Dodge Challenger.
**Primary competition:** AMC Javelin, Chevrolet Camaro, Ford Mustang, and Pontiac Firebird.
**Notable changes:** Revised front styling, trim and detail changes.
**Major standard equipment:** All-vinyl bucket seats, cigarette lighter, deep-pile carpeting, dome light, glove box lock, heater/defroster, concealed 2-speed electric wipers, and 7.35 × 14 BSW tires. 'Cuda adds: Moldings (wheel opening, drip rail, grille, and deck lid), heavy duty suspension and brakes, performance hood, and F70 × 14 WSW tires.

## Measurements

| Wheelbase | 108.0" |
|---|---|
| Length | 191.3" |
| Width | 76.3" |
| Height | 50.9" |
| Legroom — front | 42.3" |
| Legroom — rear | 30.9" |
| Headroom — front | 37.4" |
| Headroom — rear | 35.6" |
| Cargo capacity (cu. ft.) | 8.6 |
| Fuel capacity (gals.) | 18.0 |

## Models Available

|  | Style Number | Base MSRP | Change from LY | Shipping Wt. (lbs.) | Production | Change from LY |
|---|---|---|---|---|---|---|
| Barracuda 2-Door HT | BH23 | $2,710 | | 3040 | 10,622 | +12.30% |
| 'Cuda 2-Door Hardtop | BS23 | $2,953 | | 3330 | 7,828 | +25.69% |
| TOTALS | | Avg. price $2,832 | | | Production 18,450 | -1.28% |

**1972**

# Satellite

*"Big luxury in a mid-size car."*

**Nameplate year of origin:** 1965 (as a Belvedere trim level).
**Current bodystyle lifespan:** 1971 through 1978.
**Predecessor to this model:** Belvedere/Satellite (1968 to 1970).
**Replacement for this model:** Fury (1975 to 1978).
**Corporate siblings:** Dodge Coronet.
**Percentage of division's sales volume:** 19.15%.
**Primary competition:** AMC Matador, Chevrolet Chevelle, Ford Torino, and Pontiac LeMans.
**Notable changes:** New grille and minor trim and detail changes.
**Major standard equipment:** All-vinyl bench seat, glove box lock, trunk mat, color-keyed rubber floor covering, dome light, and E78 × 14 BSW tires (H78 × 14 BSW for wagons). Sebring adds: Cloth and vinyl upholstery, dual horns, full carpeting, and assorted bright exterior moldings. Custom adds: Front and rear armrests, upgraded trim. Sebring Plus adds: All-vinyl front bucket seats, deluxe wheel covers, specific bodyside moldings. Road Runner adds: "Beep-beep" horn, Rallye gauges, heavy duty suspension and brakes, sway bars, performance hood, low restriction dual exhausts, and F70 × 14 WSW tires.

## Measurements

|  | Coupes | Sedans | Wagons |
|---|---|---|---|
| Wheelbase | 115.0" | 117.0" | 117.0" |
| Length | 203.2" | 204.6" | 210.9" |
| Width | 79.1" | 78.6" | 78.6" |
| Height | 52.0" | 54.5" | 55.0" |
| Legroom — front | 41.9" | 41.9" | 41.9" |
| Legroom — rear | 36.7" | 36.7" | 36.7" |
| Headroom — front | 38.5" | 38.5" | 39.7" |
| Headroom — rear | 37.3" | 37.3" | 38.1" |
| Cargo capacity (cu. ft.) | 16.7 | 16.7 | 91.3 |
| Fuel capacity (gals.) | 19.5 | 19.5 | 21.0 |

## Models Available

|  | Style Number | Base MSRP | Change from LY | Shipping Wt. (lbs.) | Production | Change from LY |
|---|---|---|---|---|---|---|
| Satellite 2-Door Coupe | RL21 | $2,609 | -2.03% | 3240 | 10,507 | -4.16% |
| Satellite 4-Door Sedan | RL41 | $2,678 | -2.05% | 3350 | 12,794 | +15.69% |
| Satellite 4-Door, 2-Seat Wagon | RL45 | $3,152 | +3.07% | 3785 | 7,377 | +3.35% |
| Satellite Sebring 2-Door HT | RH23 | $2,871 | -2.05% | 3250 | 34,353 | -4.16% |
| Satellite Custom 4-Door Sedan | RH41 | $2,848 | -2.07% | 3285 | 34,973 | +13.65% |
| Satellite Custom 4-Dr, 2-S Wgn | RH45 | $3,325 | +2.78% | 3780 | 5,485 | +8.72% |
| Satellite Custom 4-Dr, 3-S Wgn | RH46 | $3,403 | +2.65% | 3825 | 5,637 | +45.85% |
| Satellite Sebring Plus 2-Door HT | RP23 | $3,112 | -2.11% | 3320 | 21,399 | +31.66% |
| Road Runner 2-Door Hardtop | RM23 | $3,080 | -2.13% | 3495 | 7,628 | -46.35% |
| Satellite Regent 4-Dr, 2-S Wgn. | RP45 | $3,547 | -0.31% | 3790 | 1,893 | -12.40% |
| Satellite Regent 4-Dr, 3-S Wgn. | RP46 | $3,625 | -0.36% | 3830 | 2,907 | -2.61% |
| TOTALS | Avg. price | $3,114 | -1.95% | Production | 144,953 | -0.90% |

# Fury

*"The good life has never looked so good before."*

**Nameplate year of origin:** 1956.
**Current bodystyle lifespan:** 1969 through 1973.
**Predecessor to this model:** Fury (1967 to 1968).
**Replacement for this model:** Gran Fury (1974 to 1978).
**Percentage of division's sales volume:** 34.77%.
**Corporate siblings:** Dodge Polara and Monaco.
**Primary competition:** AMC Ambassador, Chevrolet Impala, Ford LTD, Oldsmobile Delta 88, and Pontiac Catalina.

## Measurements

|  | Cars | Wagons |
|---|---|---|
| Wheelbase | 120.0" | 122.0" |
| Length | 217.2" | 222.0" |
| Width | 79.6" | 79.6" |
| Height | 55.8" | 57.9" |
| Legroom — front | 41.8" | 41.8" |

**Notable changes:** Redesigned sheetmetal, new grille and bumper design, and trim and detail changes.

**Major standard equipment:** All-vinyl front bench seat, floor mat, 2-speed windshield wipers, automatic transmission, power steering, and F78 × 15 BSW tires (J78 × 15 BSW on Suburban). Fury II adds: Color-keyed carpeting, full-length bodyside molding. Fury III adds: Cloth and vinyl upholstery, various bright exterior moldings, and interior lighting. Gran Fury adds: Door pull straps, front seat center arm rest, additional interior lighting, concealed headlamps. Sport Suburban adds: Wood-grain bodyside applique.

|                              | Cars    | Wagons  |
|------------------------------|---------|---------|
| Legroom — rear               | 39.1"   | 39.1"   |
| Headroom — front             | 38.8"   | 39.6"   |
| Headroom — rear              | 38.4"   | 39.2"   |
| Cargo capacity (cu. ft.)     | 22.4    | 104.2   |
| Fuel capacity (gals.)        | 23.0    | 23.0    |

## Models Available

| | Style Number | Base MSRP | Change from LY | Shipping Wt. (lbs.) | Production | Change from LY |
|---|---|---|---|---|---|---|
| Fury I 4-Door Sedan | PL41 | $3,448 | +9.60% | 3840 | 14,006 | -14.57% |
| Fury II 2-Door Hardtop | PM23 | $3,589 | +9.32% | 3790 | 7,515 | -4.38% |
| Fury II 4-Door Sedan | PM41 | $3,567 | +9.35% | 3830 | 20,051 | -0.24% |
| Suburban 4-Door, 2-S. Wagon | PM45 | $3,964 | +5.48% | 4315 | 5,368 | +10.07% |
| Suburban 4-Door, 3-S. Wagon | PM46 | $4,079 | +5.43% | 4360 | 2,773 | +4.17% |
| Fury III 2-Door Hardtop | PH23 | $3,769 | +8.99% | 3790 | 21,204 | -0.54% |
| Fury III 2-Door FastTop Coupe | PH29 | $3,802 | +5.61% | 3790 | 9,036 | -63.07% |
| Fury III 4-Door Sedan | PH41 | $3,747 | +9.02% | 3830 | 46,713 | +5.58% |
| Fury III 4-Door Hardtop | PH43 | $3,813 | +5.56% | 3865 | 48,618 | -12.17% |
| Custom Suburban 4-Dr, 2-S Wgn | PH45 | $4,063 | +5.42% | 4315 | 11,067 | +1.77% |
| Custom Suburban 4-Dr, 3-S Wgn | PH46 | $4,141 | +5.37% | 4365 | 14,041 | +19.99% |
| Gran Coupe 2-Door Hardtop | PP23 | $3,925 | NEW | 3735 | 15,840 | NEW |
| Gran Coupe 2-Door FastTop Cpe | PP29 | $3,958 | NEW | 3805 | 8,509 | NEW |
| Gran Sedan 4-Door Hardtop | PP43 | $3,971 | NEW | 3865 | 17,551 | NEW |
| Sport Suburban 4-Dr, 2-S Wgn. | PP45 | $4,329 | +6.34% | 4335 | 4,971 | -2.59% |
| Sport Suburban 4-Dr, 3-S Wgn. | PP46 | $4,406 | +6.27% | 4395 | 15,928 | +22.33% |
| TOTALS | Avg. price | $3,911 | +8.25% | | Production 263,191 | -14.98% |

# PONTIAC

*"Pontiac ... a cut above!"*

**1972**

The year 1972 was not a standout one for General Motors products, although there were some notable highlights and sales were good. One bright spot was the mid–1971 introduction of the Ventura II model. Based on the Chevrolet Nova, the Ventura II was just what Pontiac needed in the way of an "economy" model. The only changes made to the Nova to present it as a Pontiac were a different front end, taillights, exterior trim, hubcaps, and interior trim. Although the differences were minor, the Ventura II was identifiably a Pontiac by virtue of its grille styling.

The strike of late 1971 had delayed the introduction of the all-new intermediate models. The LeMans body shell was now in its fifth year of production, and although styling updates were keeping the cars fresh looking, they were in need of a makeover. Unfortunately, as it would turn out, the makeover they got was a slight miscalculation, and the public would not go for the new cars in the droves that Pontiac had hoped for. Other factors hurting this lines sales were the waning interest in the GTO (and all muscle cars in general), and the great popularity of the Oldsmobile Cutlass line.

The full-size Pontiac lines were given a revised grille treatment that was more like an upright radiator-style grille, resembling that used successfully on the Grand Prix. The big Pontiac also had a revised Flo-Thru ventilation system, eliminating the trunklid louvers, and revised interior trim. The Firebird and Grand Prix received only minor styling updates. The Firebird changes consisted of revised trim and optional equipment, while the Grand Prix was treated to Turbo Hydra-matic transmission as standard equipment, and revised taillight and trim changes.

Bonneville 4-Door Hardtop

Catalina 2-Door Hardtop

Firebird Trans Am 2-Door Coupe

Firebird Esprit 2-Door Coupe and
Firebird 2-Door Coupe

Grand Prix 2-Door Hardtop

Grande Ville 4-Door Hardtop

LeMans 2-Door Coupe with GTO package

Luxury LeMans 2-Door Hardtop

Ventura II 2-Door Coupe with Sprint package

**Model year production:** 706,658, up 20.38% over 1971.
**Domestic market share:** 7.56% (5th place).
**Base price range:** $2,426 to $4,721.
**Industry average base price:** $3,788.
**Pontiac average base price:** $3,727.
**Introduction date:** September 23, 1971.
**Assembly plants:** Lakewood, GA (A); Atlanta, GA (D); Kansas City, MO (K); Norwood, OH (N); Fairfax, KS (X); Fremont, CA (Z); and Oshawa, Ontario, Canada (1).

**Data plate identification:** Thirteen digit code read as follows: 1st digit 2 = Pontiac; 2nd through 4th digits identify series/body style (see style number in listings); 5th digit is engine code; 2 = 1972; 7th digit is assembly plant code; 100001 and up for serial number. *Example:* 2L39U2X100001 is a 1972 Pontiac Catalina 4-Door Hardtop with a 455 CID V8, serial number 100001, built in Fairfax, KS.

## Powertrains

| Engine | Net HP | Engine Code | Transmission Availability | Ventura II | Firebird | LeMans | Grand Prix | Cat./ Safari | Bonn./Gr V./Gr.Saf. |
|---|---|---|---|---|---|---|---|---|---|
| 250 CID, 1-bbl., 6-cyl. | 110 | D | 3-speed man., col./flr (FB) | S | S (base) | S (LeMans) | - | - | - |
| | | | Automatic | $ | $ (base) | $ (LeMans) | - | - | - |
| | | | Turbo Hydra-matic | - | $ (base) | $ (LeMans) | - | - | - |
| 307 CID, 2-bbl., V8 | 140 | F | 3-speed man., col./flr. | $90* | - | - | - | - | - |
| | | | Automatic | $* | - | - | - | - | - |
| | | | Turbo Hydra-matic | $290* | - | - | - | - | - |
| 350 CID, 2-bbl., V8 | 160 | M | 3-speed man., column | - | - | $118/S (Lux.LeM.) | - | - | - |
| | (175 w/ dual exhaust) | N | 3-speed man., floor | - | S (Form. & Esprit)/ $118 (base) | $/S (Luxury LeMans) | - | - | - |
| | | | 3-speed HD manual, floor | - | | $ | - | - | - |
| | | | 4-speed man. | - | $ (Form.)/$ (Esprit)/$ (base) | $ | - | - | - |
| | | | Automatic | - | $ (Form.)/$ (Esprit)/$ (base) | $ | - | - | - |
| | | | Turbo Hydra-matic | $318** | $ (Form.)/$ (Esprit)/$ (base) | $ | - | - | - |
| 400 CID, 2-bbl., V8 | 175 (200 w/ dual exhaust) | R / P | Turbo Hydra-matic | - | $ (Esprit) | $ | - | S | - |
| 400 CID, 4-bbl., V8 | 200 (250 w/ dual exhaust) | S / T | 3-speed HD manual, floor | | $ (Form.) | S (GTO) | - | - | - |
| | | | 4-speed man. | - | $ (Form.) | $ (LeMans)/ $ (GTO) | - | - | - |
| | | | 4-speed manual-close ratio | - | $ (Form.) | $ (LeMans)/ $ (GTO) | - | - | - |
| | | | Turbo Hydra-matic | - | $ (Form.) | $ (LeMans)/ $ (GTO) | S | $ | - |
| 455 CID, 2-bbl., V8 | 185 (200 w/ dual exhaust) | V / U | Turbo Hydra-matic | - | - | - | - | $ | S (Bonn.) |
| 455 CID, 4-bbl., V8 | 220 (300 on GP) | W | Turbo Hydra-matic | - | - | $272 (Le-Mans)***/ $57 (GTO) | $175/S (w/ SJ option) | $ | S (Gr. V. & Gr. Saf.)/ $ (Bonn.) |
| | (250 w/ dual exhaust | Y | Turbo Hydra-matic | | | | | | |
| 455 CID H.O., 4-bbl., V8 | 300 | X | 4-speed manual-close ratio | - | S (TA)/ $ (Form.) | $349 (Le-Mans)***/ $134 (GTO) | - | - | - |
| | | | Turbo Hydra-matic | - | $ (TA)/ $ (Form.) | $ (Le-Mans)***/ $ (GTO) | - | - | - |

*Not available in California.  **Available only in California.  ***Available only on coupes and convertibles.

## Major Options

| | Ventura II | Firebird | LeMans | Grand Prix | Catalina | Bonneville | Grand Ville | Safari |
|---|---|---|---|---|---|---|---|---|
| Air conditioning | $381 | $397 | $397 | $507 | $507 | $507 | $507 | $507 |
| Electronic cruise control | - | $62 | $62 | $62 | $62 | $62 | $62 | $62 |
| Electric rear window defogger | $62 | $62 | $62 | $62 | $62 | $62 | $62 | - |
| Soft Ray tinted glass | $39 | $39 | $49 | $49 | $49 | $49 | $49 | $49 |
| Deck lid remote release | | $14 | $14 | $14 | $14 | $14 | $14 | - |
| Power steering — variable-ratio | $100 | $113/S (TA) | $113 | S | S | S | S | S |
| Power brakes | $46 | $68/S (TA) | $68 | S | S | S | S | S |
| Power door locks | - | $ | $ | $ | $ | $ | $ | $ |
| Power driver's seat/Bench seat | - | $77 | $77 | $77 | $103 | $103 | $103 | $103 |
| Power windows | - | $113 | $113 | $129 | $129 | $129 | $129 | $129 |
| AM radio | $60 | $66 | $66 | $66 | $66 | $66 | $66 | $66 |
| AM/FM stereo | $140 | $140 | $235 | $235 | $235 | $235 | $235 | $235 |
| Front seat console | $57 | $57 | $59 | S | - | - | - | - |
| Front bucket seats | $242 | S. | $ | S | - | - | - | - |
| Tilt steering wheel | - | $45 | $45 | $45 | $45 | $45 | $45 | $45 |
| Sunroof | $184 | - | - | $ | - | - | - | - |
| Vinyl roof | $82 | $87 | $97 | $138 | $138 | $138 | $138 | - |
| Honeycomb wheels | - | $123 | $123 | $62 | - | - | - | - |
| Rally II wheels | $63 | $56 | $87 | $87 | $87 | $87 | - | $87 |
| Ventura Sprint package | $190 | | | | | | | |
| LeMans GTO option (2-Dr. Cpes. only) | - | - | $344 | - | - | - | - | - |
| LeMans Ram Air option | - | - | $982–$995 | - | - | - | - | - |
| LeMans Sport option (on base 2-Dr. HT) | - | - | $164 | - | - | - | - | - |
| LeMans GT option (on Sport models only) | - | - | $23 | - | - | - | - | - |
| LeMans Endura styling option | - | - | $41 | - | - | - | - | - |

Options common to most models. (- = Not Available; S = Standard equipment.) Items may be standard equipment, optional at different pricing, or unavailable on certain models. This chart is only a guide.

## Paint Colors

| | Code | | Code |
|---|---|---|---|
| Cameo White | 11 | Quezal Gold Met. | 53 |
| Revere Silver Met. | 14 | Arizona Gold Met. | 54 |
| Antique Pewter Met. | 18 | Shadow Gold Met. | 55 |
| Starlight Black | 19 | Monarch Yellow | 56 |
| Adriatic Blue Met. | 24 | Brasilia Gold Met. | 57 |
| Lucerne Blue Met. | 26 | Spice Beige | 62 |
| Cumberland Blue Met. | 28 | Anaconda Gold Met. | 63 |
| Julep Green Met. | 36 | Sundance Orange Met. | 65 |
| Springfield Green Met. | 43 | Cinammon Bronze Met. | 69 |
| Wilderness Green Met. | 48 | Cardinal Red | 75 |
| Brittany Beige | 50 | | |

# Firebird

*"Firebird's full of innovation."*

**Nameplate year of origin:** 1967 (used on Motorama show cars as early as 1954).
**Current bodystyle lifespan:** 1970 through 1981.
**Predecessor to this model:** Firebird (1967 to 1969).
**Replacement for this model:** Firebird (1982 to 1992).
**Percentage of division's sales volume:** 4.24%.
**Corporate siblings:** Chevrolet Camaro.
**Primary competition:** Ford Mustang, Plymouth Barracuda, Dodge Challenger, AMC Javelin.
**Notable changes:** Trim and detail changes.
**Major standard equipment:** All-vinyl front bucket seats, and rear bucket-type seats, loop-pile carpeting, deluxe steering wheel, Endura front bumper, hubcaps, windshield radio antenna, E78-14 BSW tires. Esprit adds: Custom cushion steering wheel, additional interior and exterior trim, dual sport mirrors, and wheel trim rings. Formula adds: 400 CID V8 engine, heavy duty suspension, and F70 × 14 tires. Trans Am adds: Formula steering wheel, power steering, power brakes, Rally II wheels, and F60 × 15 tires.

## Measurements

| | |
|---|---|
| Wheelbase | 108.0" |
| Length | 181.6" |
| Width | 73.4" |
| Height | 50.4" |
| Legroom — front | 43.8" |
| Legroom — rear | 29.6" |
| Headroom — front | 37.4" |
| Headroom — rear | 36.1" |
| Cargo capacity (cu. ft.) | 6.4 |
| Fuel capacity (gals.) | 18.0 |

## Models Available

| | Style Number | Base MSRP | Change from LY | Shipping Wt. (lbs.) | Production | Change from LY |
|---|---|---|---|---|---|---|
| Firebird 2-Door Coupe | 2S87 | $2,838 | -6.86% | 3357 | 12,000 | -47.87% |
| Firebird Esprit 2-Door Coupe | 2T87 | $3,194 | -6.50% | 3359 | 11,415 | -43.45% |
| Firebird Formula 2-Door Cpe. | 2U87 | $3,221 | -6.50% | 3424 | 5,250 | -32.71% |
| Frbd. Trans Am 2-Door Cpe. | 2V87 | $4,256 | -7.38% | 3564 | 1,286 | -39.22% |
| TOTALS | | Avg. price $3,377 | -6.87% | | Production 29,951 | -43.62% |

# Ventura II

*"We built our 1972 Ventura II to give you more ... and make you proud."*

**Nameplate year of origin:** 1960.
**Current bodystyle lifespan:** 1971 through 1972.
**Predecessor to this model:** None.
**Replacement for this model:** Ventura (1973 through 1979, with restyle in 1975).
**Percentage of division's sales volume:** 10.30%.
**Corporate siblings:** Chevrolet Nova.
**Primary competition:** Ford Maverick, Mercury Comet, Plymouth Valiant, Dodge Dart, AMC Hornet.
**Notable changes:** Revised grille and trim and detail changes.
**Major standard equipment:** Cloth and vinyl bench seat, vinyl-coated rubber floor coverings, deluxe steering wheel, hubcaps, front-door vent windows, bright moldings on windshield and rear window, manual drum brakes, E78-14 BSW tires.

## Measurements

| | |
|---|---|
| Wheelbase | 111.0" |
| Length | 194.5" |
| Width | 72.4" |
| Height | 52.5" |
| Legroom — front | 41.0" |
| Legroom — rear | 32.6" |
| Headroom — front | 37.6" |
| Headroom — rear | 36.6" |
| Cargo capacity (cu. ft.) | 13.7 |
| Fuel capacity (gals.) | 17.0 |

**1972**

## Models Available

|  | Style Number | Base MSRP | Change from LY | Shipping Wt. (lbs.) | Production | Change from LY |
|---|---|---|---|---|---|---|
| Ventura 2-Door Coupe | 2Y27 | $2,426 | -1.30% | 2944 | 51,203 | +47.64% |
| Ventura 4-Door Sedan | 2Y69 | $2,454 | -1.37% | 2979 | 21,584 | +56.37% |
| TOTALS | Avg. price | $2,440 | -1.33% | Production | 72,787 | +50.13% |

# LeMans

*"The mid-sized Pontiac, at a manageable price."*

**Nameplate year of origin:** 1961 (as a Tempest sub-series).
**Current bodystyle lifespan:** 1968 through 1972.
**Predecessor to this model:** Tempest/LeMans (1966 to 1967).
**Replacement for this model:** LeMans (1973 to 1977).
**Percentage of division's sales volume:** 24.05%.
**Corporate siblings:** Chevrolet Chevelle, Oldsmobile Cutlass, and Buick Skylark.
**Primary competition:** Ford Torino, Mercury Montego, Plymouth Satellite, Dodge Coronet, AMC Matador.
**Notable changes:** Restyled grille and trim and detail changes.
**Major standard equipment:** Bench seat with cloth and vinyl trim (all-vinyl on Sport), loop-pile carpeting, teakwood vinyl trim on doors and instrument panel, hubcaps, bright moldings, windshield radio antenna, manual drum brakes (power on Wagons), and E78-14 BSW tires (H78-14 BSW on Wagons). Luxury LeMans adds: All-vinyl bucket seats (coupe only) or bench seat, deluxe steering wheel, deluxe hubcaps, rear fender skirts, and F78 × 14 BSW tires.

## Measurements

|  | 2-Doors | 4-Doors | Wagons |
|---|---|---|---|
| Wheelbase | 112.0" | 116.0" | 116.0" |
| Length | 202.8" | 206.8" | 210.9" |
| Width | 76.7" | 76.7" | 76.7" |
| Height | 52.0" | 52.6" | 52.6" |
| Legroom — front | 42.4" | 42.4" | 42.4" |
| Legroom — rear | 32.2" | 34.8" | 34.8" |
| Headroom — front | 37.9" | 38.5" | 38.5" |
| Headroom — rear | 36.3" | 37.1" | 37.4" |
| Cargo capacity (cu. ft.) | NA | NA | 83.6 |
| Fuel capacity (gals.) | 21.5 | 21.5 | 21.5 |

## Models Available

|  | Style Number | Base MSRP | Change from LY | Shipping Wt. (lbs.) | Production | Change from LY |
|---|---|---|---|---|---|---|
| LeMans 2-Door Coupe | 2D27 | $2,722 | -5.39% | 3294 | 6,855 | +150.73% |
| LeMans 2-Door Hardtop | 2D37 | $2,851 | -2.97% | 3234 | 80,383 | +96.22% |
| LeMans 4-Door Sedan | 2D69 | $2,814 | -4.79% | 3269 | 19,463 | +62.48% |
| LeMans 4-Door, 2-Seat Wgn. | 2D36 | $3,271 | -2.45% | 3799 | 8,332 | +32.02% |
| LeMans 4-Door, 3-Seat Wgn. | 2D46 | $3,378 | -2.51% | 3839 | 5,266 | +20.70% |
| LeMans Sport 2-Dr. Conv. | 2D67 | $3,228 | -3.90% | 3284 | 3,438 | -11.05% |
| Luxury LeMans 2-Door HT | 2G37 | $3,196 | NEW | 3488 | 8,641 | NEW |
| Luxury LeMans 4-Door HT | 2G39 | $3,319 | NEW | 3638 | 37,615 | NEW |
| TOTALS | Avg. price | $3,097 | -1.09% | Production | 169,993 | +2.41% |

# Grand Prix

*"Pontiac's luxury sports-coupe."*

**Nameplate year of origin:** 1962.
**Current bodystyle lifespan:** 1969 through 1972.
**Predecessor to this model:** Grand Prix (1967 to 1968).
**Replacement for this model:** Grand Prix (1973 to 1977).
**Primary competition:** Mercury Cougar, Plymouth Satellite Sebring, Dodge Charger.
**Corporate siblings:** Chevrolet Monte Carlo.
**Percentage of division's sales volume:** 13.01%.
**Notable changes:** Trim and detail changes.
**Major standard equipment:** Front bucket seats, or notchback bench seat in cloth and vinyl or all-vinyl trim, loop-pile carpeting, custom cushion steering wheel, electric clock, lamp package, deluxe wheel covers, windshield radio antenna, concealed wipers, exterior bright moldings, power steering, power front disc brakes, and G78-14 BSW tires.

## Measurements

| | |
|---|---|
| Wheelbase | 118.0" |
| Length | 213.6" |
| Width | 76.4" |
| Height | 52.0" |
| Legroom — front | 42.4" |
| Legroom — rear | 31.6" |
| Headroom — front | 37.5" |
| Headroom — rear | 36.5" |
| Cargo capacity (cu. ft.) | NA |
| Fuel capacity (gals.) | 21.5 |

## Models Available

| | Style Number | Base MSRP | Change from LY | Shipping Wt. (lbs.) | Production | Change from LY |
|---|---|---|---|---|---|---|
| Grand Prix 2-Door Hardtop | 2K57 | $4,472 | -1.87% | 3898 | 91,961 | +57.67% |
| TOTALS | *Avg. price* | $4,472 | -1.87% | *Production* | 91,961 | +57.67% |

# Catalina

*"Innovative styling, outstanding performance, at an easy Pontiac price."*

**Nameplate year of origin:** 1950 (hardtop models), 1959 (as series).
**Current bodystyle lifespan:** 1971 through 1976.
**Predecessor to this model:** Catalina (1969 to 1970).
**Replacement for this model:** Catalina (1977 to 1981).
**Percentage of division's sales volume:** 28.44%.
**Corporate siblings:** Chevrolet Impala/Caprice, Olds Delta 88, Buick LeSabre/Centurion.
**Primary competition:** Ford LTD, Mercury Monterey, Plymouth Fury, Dodge Polara, AMC Ambassador.
**Notable changes:** Restyled grille and trim and detail changes.
**Major standard equipment:** Cloth and vinyl or all-vinyl bench seat, nylon-blend carpet, trunk mat, windshield radio antenna, power front disc brakes, power steering, and G78 × 15 BSW tires. Brougham adds: Deluxe interior trim, custom cushion steering wheel, deluxe wheel covers, and H78 × 15 BSW tires.

## Measurements

| | |
|---|---|
| Wheelbase | 123.5" |
| Length | 222.4" |
| Width | 79.5" |
| Height | 53.4" |
| Legroom — front | 42.6" |
| Legroom — rear | 38.5" |
| Headroom — front | 38.9" |
| Headroom — rear | 38.0" |
| Cargo capacity (cu. ft.) | NA |
| Fuel capacity (gals.) | 25.0 |

**1972**

## Models Available

| | Style Number | Base MSRP | Change from LY | Shipping Wt. (lbs.) | Production | Change from LY |
|---|---|---|---|---|---|---|
| Catalina 2-Door Hardtop | 2L57 | $3,808 | -1.60% | 4129 | 60,233 | +30.21% |
| Catalina 2-Door Convertible | 2L67 | $4,080 | -1.83% | 4204 | 2,399 | +17.83% |

|  | Style Number | Base MSRP | Change from LY | Shipping Wt. (lbs.) | Production | Change from LY |
|---|---|---|---|---|---|---|
| Catalina 4-Door Sedan | 2L69 | $3,713 | -1.52% | 4154 | 83,004 | +39.84% |
| Catalina 4-Door Hardtop | 2L39 | $3,874 | -1.63% | 4179 | 28,010 | +25.42% |
| Catalina Brougham 2-Door HT | 2M57 | $3,996 | -2.16% | 4158 | 10,545 | +19.52% |
| Catalina Brougham 4-Door Sedan | 2M69 | $3,916 | -2.10% | 4188 | 8,007 | +31.93% |
| Catalina Brougham 4-Door HT | 2M39 | $4,062 | -2.11% | 4238 | 8,762 | -2.66% |
| TOTALS | Avg. price | $3,921 | -1.88% | Production | 200,960 | +30.60% |

# Bonneville

*"A big car is good for more than long stretches of straight roads. This car handles."*

# Grand Ville

*"Luxury is what Grand Ville's all about."*

**Nameplate year of origin:** 1957 (Bonneville); 1971 (Grand Ville)
**Current bodystyle lifespan:** 1971 through 1976.
**Predecessor to this model:** Executive and Bonneville (1969 to 1970).
**Replacement for this model:** Bonneville (1977 to 1981).
**Percentage of division's sales volume:** 14.08%.
**Corporate siblings:** Chevrolet Impala/Caprice, Oldsmobile 88, Buick LeSabre/Centurion.
**Primary competition:** Ford LTD, Mercury Marquis, Plymouth Fury, Dodge Monaco, AMC Ambassador.
**Notable changes:** Restyled grille and trim and detail changes.
**Major standard equipment:** Cloth and vinyl bench seat, full carpeting and on lower door panels, custom cushion steering wheel, light packages, trunk lamp, wheel covers, windshield antenna, power steering, power front disc brakes, and H78-15 BSW tires. Grand Ville adds: Deluxe cloth and vinyl front bench seat, burled elm grain dash and door trim, electric clock, additional courtesy lights, and deluxe wheel covers.

## Measurements

| | |
|---|---|
| Wheelbase | 126.0" |
| Length | 226.3" |
| Width | 79.5" |
| Height | 53.7" |
| Legroom — front | 42.6" |
| Legroom — rear | 38.5" |
| Headroom — front | 38.7" |
| Headroom — rear | 37.8" |
| Cargo capacity (cu. ft.) | NA |
| Fuel capacity (gals.) | 25.0 |

## Models Available

|  | Style Number | Base MSRP | Change from LY | Shipping Wt. (lbs.) | Production | Change from LY |
|---|---|---|---|---|---|---|
| Bonneville 2-Door Hardtop | 2N57 | $4,228 | -1.03% | 4238 | 10,568 | +20.39% |
| Bonneville 4-Door Sedan | 2N69 | $4,169 | -0.98% | 4288 | 9,704 | +48.99% |
| Bonneville 4-Door Hardtop | 2N39 | $4,293 | -1.09% | 4388 | 15,806 | -3.58% |
| Grand Ville 2-Door Hardtop | 2P47 | $4,442 | -1.22% | 4263 | 19,852 | +41.63% |
| Grand Ville 2-Door Convertible | 2P67 | $4,640 | -1.40% | 4333 | 2,213 | +24.05% |
| Grand Ville 4-Door Hardtop | 2P49 | $4,507 | -1.29% | 4378 | 41,346 | +35.45% |
| TOTALS | Avg. price | $4,380 | -1.09% | Production | 99,489 | +27.54% |

# Safaris

*"When Pontiac builds a station wagon, it has to deliver."*

**Nameplate year of origin:** 1955.

**Current bodystyle lifespan:** 1971 through 1976.

**Predecessor to this model:** Catalina, Executive and Bonneville Safari (1969 to 1970).

**Replacement for this model:** Catalina and Bonneville Safari (1977 to 1981).

**Percentage of division's sales volume:** 5.88%.

**Corporate siblings:** Chevrolet Impala/Caprice, Oldsmobile Custom Cruiser, Buick Estate Wagon.

**Primary competition:** Ford LTD/Country Squire, Mercury Villager, and Dodge Monaco.

**Notable changes:** Restyled grille and trim and detail changes.

**Major standard equipment:** All-vinyl front bench seat, loop-pile carpeting, Glide-away disappearing tailgate, power tailgate window, forward-facing third seat and split back second seat (3-seat models only), stowage compartment under load floor, power steering, power front disc brakes, and L78-15 BSW tires. Grand Safari adds: Front seat center armrest, carpeted cargo area, and custom cushion steering wheel.

## Measurements

| | |
|---|---|
| Wheelbase | 127.0" |
| Length | 227.7" |
| Width | 79.5" |
| Height | 55.0" |
| Legroom — front | 42.6" |
| Legroom — rear | 38.5" |
| Headroom — front | 38.9" |
| Headroom — rear | 38.2" |
| Cargo capacity (cu. ft.) | 106.0 |
| Fuel capacity (gals.) | 25.0 |

## Models Available

| | Style Number | Base MSRP | Change from LY | Shipping Wt. (lbs.) | Production | Change from LY |
|---|---|---|---|---|---|---|
| Catalina Safari 4-Door, 2-S. Wgn. | 2L35 | $4,232 | -1.93% | 4743 | 14,536 | +40.83% |
| Catalina Safari 4-Door, 3-S. Wgn. | 2L45 | $4,372 | -2.02% | 4818 | 12,766 | +37.52% |
| Grand Safari 4-Door, 2-S. Wgn. | 2N35 | $4,581 | -1.33% | 4918 | 5,675 | +57.07% |
| Grand Safari 4-Door, 3-S. Wgn. | 2N45 | $4,721 | -1.44% | 4938 | 8,540 | +43.00% |
| TOTALS | *Avg. price* | $4,477 | -1.67% | *Production* | 41,517 | +42.23% |

# Index

H 4/17